The Continuum Encyclopedia of

BRITISH
LITERATURE

The Continuum Encyclopedia of

BRITISH LITERATURE

STEVEN R. SERAFIN

and

VALERIE GROSVENOR MYER

Editors

continuum
NEW YORK • LONDON

2003

The Continuum International Publishing Group Inc
370 Lexington Avenue, New York, NY 10017

The Continuum International Publishing Group Ltd
The Tower Building, 11 York Road, London SE1 7NX

Printed in the United States of America

Library of Congress Cataloging-in-Publication Data

The Continuum encyclopedia of British literature /
Steven R. Serafin and Valerie Grosvenor Myer, editors.
    p. cm.
    Includes bibliographical references and index.
    ISBN 0-8264-1456-7 (hardcover)
    1. English literature—Encyclopedias.   2. English literature—
Irish authors—Encyclopedias.   3. Great Britain—Literatures—
Encyclopedias.   I. Title: Encyclopedia of British literature.
II. Serafin, Steven.   III. Myer, Valerie Grosvenor.
PR19 .C66 2003
820'.3—dc321   2002009231

Contents

Board of Advisers

Introduction

The earliest forms of literature in Britain are lost; we can only speculate as to their origin and content. We know that what evolved as charms and incantations, pagan rites, and songs of experience were meant to be recited or sung as were the later verses that survive primarily in fragments written and rewritten by numerous hands over a period of centuries. The bards and poets of the Middle Ages who composed in Early Northern English, Welsh, Old English, and Early Scots are for the most part unknown and the tale told is not the same as the tale recorded. From the time of the Roman conquest, the British literary tradition emerged through the various languages of occupation until the beginning of the sixteenth century when the English vernacular finally triumphed as the national language.

The history of British literature is one of extraordinary breadth and complexity, extending from Aneirin and the poet of *Widsith* to Cædmon and the poet of *Beowulf;* from Geoffrey of Monmouth to Geoffrey Chaucer; from the Golden Age of Scottish poetry to the completion of the English Bible; from Edmund Spenser and Sir Philip Sidney to the Elizabethan Age and Shakespeare; from Bacon and Donne to Drayton and Milton; from the Age of Dryden and the Restoration to the Age of Johnson and Gibbon; from Wordsworth and Coleridge to Sir Walter Scott and Romanticism; from sentiment to the Gothic; from modernism to postmodernism; from new age to the new millennium. It is a literature of myth and legend, kings and kingdoms, chivalry and romance; it is a literature of voyage and discovery, colonization and empire, war and retribution; it is a literature of tradition and transition, diversity and assimilation, promise and compromise.

Designed to complement the existing volume from Continuum International on American literature, *The Continuum Encyclopedia of British Literature* is envisioned as a comprehensive survey of the growth and development of literature that is by definition British in scope or origin, including the literatures written in English from the colonial to the postcolonial experience in Africa, Australia, Canada, the Caribbean, India, and New Zealand. Specific authors from the above-mentioned literatures are treated in topical articles on their respective literatures unless the author is identified by nationality as British (e.g., Ben Okri, born in Nigeria; Caryl Phillips, born in St. Kitts). Whereas Irish literature is acknowledged as distinct and separate from British literature, the unique and protracted interrelationship between the two literatures necessitated extended coverage of authors born in the Republic of Ireland and Northern Ireland.

In 1907, Rudyard Kipling became the first British author to be awarded the Nobel Prize for Literature, followed by John Galsworthy in 1932; American-born T. S. Eliot in 1948; Bertrand Russell in 1950; Winston Churchill in 1953; Austrian-born Elias Canetti in 1981, who shared dual residency in England and Switzerland; William Golding in 1983; and Trinidadian-born V. S. Naipaul in 2001. Nobel laureates born in Ireland include W. B. Yeats and Bernard Shaw in 1923 and 1925, respectively; Samuel Beckett in 1969; and Seamus Heaney in 1995. Nobel laureates writing in English from former colonial literatures include Indian author Rabindranath Tagore in 1913; Australian author Patrick White in 1973; Nigerian author Wole Soyinka in 1986; South African author Nadine Gordimer in 1991; and St. Lucian author Derek Walcott in 1992.

Incorporating entries for authors and works from Anglo-Saxon Britain to the present with a cross-section of topical articles pertaining to genre, period, ethnicity, and discipline, the present *Encyclopedia* is a collaborative scholarly effort that represents the most extensive single-volume treatment of its subject available for the general and specialized reader alike. Consisting of more than 1,200 entries, the volume serves as both guide and companion to the study and appreciation of British literature.

Bases of Selection: The selection of authors for individual entries is based primarily on assessment and evaluation of the author's literary contribution and role in relation to the growth and development of British literature. The process was designed to provide appropriate representation and balance to the volume within the constraints of length. The *Encyclopedia* includes entries for authors of international stature as well as authors noteworthy for historical, regional, or national significance. The belle-lettrist stance has been avoided: several popular authors, enjoyed by a mass readership, have been included; as have thinkers whose works, though not "literary" in the mandarin sense, have been influential. We have endeavored to be up to date without falling into faddism or triviality.

Omissions: Despite the scope of the *Encyclopedia*, it is inevitable that authors of merit have been underrepresented or omitted from the volume. Although every effort has been made for the *Encyclopedia* to be as comprehensive as possible, the limitations of a single-volume edition impacted on the selection process. Wherever possible, references to authors of merit who did not receive individual entries are incorporated into the text of the most relevant topical articles.

Entries—Organization and Data: The *Encyclopedia* consists of individual author entries, topical articles, and designated brief entries. Individual author entries are arranged in three parts: a headnote that contains vital statistics concerning birth and death; a body that incorporates brief biographical information and critical overview of the author's work and achievement; and a final section, titled "Bibliography," comprising select bibliographical material concerning the author and his or her work. A list of abbreviations used for periodicals cited is included in the front of the volume, and an index to the edition, with author dates, concludes the work. Brief entries are arranged with headnote and body. An Historical-Literary Timeline is intended to present the historic orientation of the literature.

Cross-References and Pseudonyms: Cross-references to other authors and related topics appear whenever appropriate in the texts of all entries. Where a writer with an individual entry is cited in another entry, at the first mention his or her last name appears in SMALL-CAPITAL LETTERS. Likewise, where the topic with a separate entry in the volume is cited in another entry, at the first mention the topic appears in SMALL-CAPITAL LETTERS.

Author entries are arranged alphabetically by last name. Authors known primarily by their pseudonyms are cross-referenced within the edition to the appropriate entry (e.g., under Tey, Josephine, will be found " See Mackintosh, Elizabeth").

Mechanics: For purposes of consistency, the *Encyclopedia* uses U.S. spelling of words within the text of all entries. British spelling has been maintained for original titles of works, for use in quotations, and for specific names (e.g., Labour Party, National Theatre, Centre for Contemporary Cultural Studies).

The Contributors: These have been drawn from a sphere of literary authorities from the United States, the United Kingdom, Northern Ireland, the Republic of Ireland, Canada, Australia, New Zealand, France, Spain, India, and Sweden. Each author entry and topical article in the *Encyclopedia* appears over the signature of the individual contributor or joint contributors. In general, brief entries are unsigned; in select cases, however, brief entries are signed.

ACKNOWLEDGMENTS

The editors wish to express their appreciation to the numerous individuals whose contributions have helped to make this encyclopedia a reference work of distinction, including the Board of Advisers, the contributors, the editorial and technical staff, and Evander Lomke of The Continuum International Publishing Group Inc. Hayley Horvat was the production editor and Ivy Laikwan Chong was the data-entry coordinator. Technical assistance was provided by Enercida Guererro and Stephen Sukhra. Editorial assistance was provided by Paige Bailey, Vicki Eng, Jason Berner, Colleen McCutcheon, and Michael Grosvenor Myer.

STEVEN R. SERAFIN
HUNTER COLLEGE OF THE CITY UNIVERSITY OF NEW YORK

VALERIE GROSVENOR MYER
CAMBRIDGE UNIVERSITY

Guide to Topical Articles

Abbreviations for Periodicals

A&E	Anglistik & Englischunterricht
AM	Atlantic Monthly
Ariel: A Review of English Literature	
BLJ	British Library Journal
BOMB	BOMB Magazine
Boundary 2: An International Journal of Literature and Culture	
BUSE	Boston University Studies in English
C&L	Christianity and Literature
CarQ	Carolina Quarterly
CC	Culture and Communication
CCent	Christian Century
CD	Comparative Drama
CLE	Children's Literature in Education
CLIO: A Journal of Literature, History, and the Philosophy of Literature	
CM	Cornhill Magazine
Commonweal	Commonweal Magazine
ConL	Contemporary Literature
ConP	Contemporary Poetry
CQ	Colby Quarterly
CR	Chesterton Review
Crit	Critique: Studies in Modern Fiction
CritI	Critical Inquiry
Critique: Studies in Contemporary Fiction	
CritQ	Critical Quarterly
CritR	Critical Review
CS	Creative Screenwriter
DLB	Dictionary of Literary Biography
DR	Dalhousie Review
EC	Essays in Criticism
ECent	Eighteenth Century
E-CL	Eighteenth-Century Life
E-CS	Eighteenth-Century Studies
EI	Etudes Irlandaises
EL	Essays in Literature
ELH	English Literary History
ELR	English Literary Renaissance
ELT	English Literature in Transition
English: The Journal of the English Association	
ERC	Explorations in Renaissance Culture
ERR	European Romantic Review
ES	English Studies
FemR	Feminist Review
FolkR	Folk Review
FortR	Fortnightly Review
Foundation: The Review of Science Fiction	
Gambit: International Theatre Review	
GL&L	German Life and Letters
HLQ	Huntington Library Quarterly
IowaR	Iowa Review
IUR	Irish University Review
JML	Journal of Modern Literature
JPC	Journal of Popular Culture
L&H	Literature and History
LCrit	Literary Criterion
LE&W	Literature East and West
LHR	Linen Hall Review
LitR	Literary Review
MD	Modern Drama
MFS	Modern Fiction Studies
MLR	Modern Language Review
MLS	Modern Language Studies
N&Q	Notes and Queries
NewC	New Criterion
NewR	New Republic
NewY	New Yorker
Novel: A Forum on Fiction	
NYTM	New York Times Magazine
OL	Orbis Litterarum
PAPS	Proceedings of the American Philosophical Society
PBA	Proceedings of the British Academy
PLL	Papers on Language and Literature
PMLA	Publications of the Modern Language Association
PQ	Philological Quarterly
PR	Paris Review
PRev	Powys Review
PW	Poetry Wales
RCF	Review of Contemporary Fiction
RenSt	Renaissance Studies

RES	Review of English Studies
Sagetrieb: A Journal Devoted to Poets in the Imagist/ Objectivist Tradition	
SAR	South Atlantic Review
SDR	South Dakota Review
SEL	Studies in English Literature
Shenandoah: The Washington & Lee University Review	
Signs: Journal of Women in Culture and Society	
SIR	Studies in Romanticism
SNNTS	Studies in the Novel
SoR	Southern Review
Soundings: An Interdisciplinary Journal	
SP	Studies in Philology
SPAN: Journal of the South Pacific Association for Commonwealth Literature and Language Studies	
SR	Sewanee Review
SSF	Studies in Short Fiction
SwR	Swansea Review
T&T	Time and Tide
TCL	Twentieth Century Literature
TJ	Theatre Journal
TSAR	Toronto South Asian Review
TSE	Tulane Studies in English
VP	Victorian Poetry
VS	Victorian Studies
W&Lang	Women and Language
W&P	Women and Performance
Wasafiri: Journal of Caribbean, African, Asian and Associated Literatures and Film	
WC	Wordsworth Circle
WLWE	World Literature Written in English
Women: A Cultural Review	
WRB	Women's Review of Books
WS	Women's Studies
WW	Women's Writing

ABERCROMBIE, Lascelles

b. 9 January 1881, Ashton-on-Mersey, Cheshire; d. 27 October 1938, London

A. was once considered a leader of the Georgian movement in poetry, an innovative and careful craftsman who combined interests in the dramatic and reflective elements of verse. In his poems, he created images of beauty and energy but was also capable of depicting brutal reality. He incorporated colloquial diction into works of intense and serious metaphysical speculation. Unfortunately, his work is seldom read or commented on today. In part, he suffered the fate of all the Georgian poets, who saw themselves as making the break with Victorian traditions although they did not go far enough to suit modern tastes. Because the Georgians respected and practiced older forms of versification, their work appears staid in contrast to those who were working to "make it new" in the modernist tradition. Readers may also neglect A. because he was never able to realize in practice the harmony of disparate elements of experience that he found crucial to his vision of the world. Too often his passages of realistic description clash with passages of abstract, philosophical dialogue. He frequently ignored his talents for depicting the English countryside or its people and tried to create abstract poetry in the model of Thomas HARDY's *The Dynasts*, a poem he much admired. He frequently turned to Greek mythology or the Bible for his narratives and images, creating a sense of distance between his subject matter and his audience and choosing a vehicle that was less suited to his ability than the immediacy of his poems depicting contemporary life. His poetry nonetheless remains interesting because of the intensity with which he explores passions and the complexity of his portraits of women.

A.'s first volume of verse, *Interludes and Poems* (1908), was well received by reviewers including John MASEFIELD and Edward THOMAS. In particular, the poem "Blind" was seen as a revolutionary exposition of cruelty and violence in the lower classes. This dramatic poem depicts the willfulness of a mother who would exploit her blind son to wreak vengeance on the husband who has abandoned her. While the dialogue of the mother and her supposedly half-wit son is not convincing as the speech of lower-class characters, A. uncovers great horror and passion and reveals a psychological complexity that we may not expect from the stereotypical Georgian. He also creates complex images of women in poems including "Judith" and "Mary and the Bramble"; in both cases, A. takes conventional subjects and suggests a unique perspective that may have shocked the Victorian reader but seems to have little relevance or freshness for the modern reader.

In addition to his poems of psychological complexity, A. also creates poems that attempt to take an otherworldly or more metaphysical perspective. The poems "The New God: A Miracle" or "The Fool's Adventure" include speeches from God, the Voice of the World, and the Voice from Within, illustrating an otherworldly point of view that is difficult for modern sensibilities to tolerate. In this work and in a number of poems from his second volume, *Mary and the Bramble* (1910), A. may have been trying to emulate the perspectives of the Intelligences in Hardy's dramatic EPIC *The Dynasts*, a poem that A. considered "one of the most momentous achievements of modern literature." In some poems, including *Emblems of Love* (1912) or "The Sale of St. Thomas," A. aims for a greater balance of his ideas and his narration and achieves both complex exposition and some memorable descriptive passages. People remember a vivid description of flies from "St. Thomas," but never seem to fit it into the context of the rest of the poem. There is an uneasy combination of narration and philosophy that the poet never really resolves. A. wrote his best work in the vein of the pastoral, a tradition today closely associated with the Georgians. His best poem in this tradition is "Ryton Firs," which incorporates classical models to describe the landscape but also to include the shadow of the war and the consciousness of changing time.

While there is little appreciation for the subtlety of A.'s best work, he is read and remembered today as a critic. His works, including *An Essay towards a Theory of Art* (1922), *The Theory of Poetry* (1924), *The Idea of Great Poetry* (1925), and *Romanticism* (1926), reflect A.'s interest in Hardy, especially his understanding of the inclusiveness of Hardy's diction and imagery. Both poet and critic believed that art was the result of the relationship of the parts of a whole and did not require beauty in every element. Despite interesting ideas, however, A. is so little read today in part because his execution never quite lived up to his theories, either in his criticism or his poetry. He is one of a group of writers whose work is admired without being valued by a generation trained to see allusion and the tradition in the light of MODERNISM.

BIBLIOGRAPHY: Elton, O., "L. A.," *PBA* 25 (1939): 393–421; Fisher, E. S., "L. A.: A Biographical Essay," *ELT* 25, 1 (1982): 28–49; Parker, R., *The Georgian Poets: A., Brooke, Drinkwater, Gibson, and Thomas* (1999)

CATHERINE FRANK

ABSE, Dannie
b. 22 September 1923, Cardiff, Wales

In addition to being a successful poet, A. is a medical doctor, receiving his training at King's College, London, and at Westminster Hospital. He is a member of the Royal College of Surgeons and a Licentiate of the Royal College of Physicians. This dichotomy in A.'s life—he is a man of art and a man of science—has informed a great deal of his poetic work. An exemplary poem is "The Magician," which appears in *Poems, Golders Green* (1962). This poem describes a stage illusionist who occasionally experiences "atavistic powers . . . /a raving voice he hardly thought to hear, /the ventriloquist's dummy out of hand." The image is one of a thoroughly rational man—the stage illusionist—who knows all the truth behind the supposed magic, but who has also felt something inexplicable behind the purely mechanical trappings of his craft. The parallels to the experiences of A. the surgeon are obvious.

A.'s poetic style is largely conversational. He once described his ambition as "to write poems which appear translucent." "I would have a reader enter them," he wrote, in the introduction to *Collected Poems, 1948–1976* (1977), "be deceived he could see through them like sea-water, and be puzzled when he can not quite touch the bottom." Indeed, A. largely avoids complicated imagery in favor of simple, lucid observations. Notable in this regard are poems that draw directly upon his experience as a doctor, such

as "The Stethoscope" in *Collected Poems* and "The Doctor," "A Winter Visit," and "Lunch and Afterwards," all of which appear in *Way Out in the Centre* (1981).

In *Funland and Other Poems* (1973), A. departs somewhat from this traditional style, creating a surreal world in the nine-part sequence of poems that gives the volume its title. "Funland" is inhabited by allegorical characters, such as Fat Blondie, Mr. Poet, Pythagoras, and The Superintendent, and A. experiments here with rhythms and imagery that are reminiscent of the work of T. S. ELIOT.

A. has continued to be a prolific author. More recently, his publications have included *White Coat, Purple Coat: Collected Poems, 1948–1988* (1989), *Remembrance of Crimes Past: Poems, 1986–1989* (1990), and *Be Seated Thou: Poems, 1989–1998* (1999), among others, and he has also served as the editor of *Twentieth Century Anglo-Welsh Poetry* (1997).

BIBLIOGRAPHY: Cohen, J., ed., *The Poetry of D. A.* (1983); Curtis, T., *D. A.* (1985); Hoffman, D., "D. A.," in Sherry, V. B., Jr., ed., *Poets of Great Britain and Ireland, 1945–1960, DLB* 27 (1984): 3–13

JASON BERNER

ACKLAND, Rodney
b. 18 May 1908, Westcliff-on-Sea, Essex; d. 6 December 1991, Richmond, Surrey

When first performed, A.'s plays were defiantly unfashionable and so they have remained. In a Britain whose complacency was as yet unshaken by the Suez crisis of 1956 and whose theatrical world remained safe in the drawing room before the grit of John OSBORNE's *Look Back in Anger* rebounded on the windows, his plays made uncomfortable reading. His world is usually perverse, seedy, and self-deluding; his characters, often Bohemian failures, affronted by the world's unaccountable neglect, avoid the truth by any means at their emotional and physical disposal. Yet he is championed by some of the most distinguished critics and theater directors of the very establishment from which he needed to stand back in order to reveal with uncompromising lack of flattery. When one of his plays is revived, it is received as a neglected masterpiece but never followed by further revivals, and A. remains as much outside the mainstream now as then.

In his life, A. was as chaotic and profligate as he was controlled and disciplined in his writing. He seemed to need a peripatetic, untidy existence in order to create, just as he needed to remain enraged with producers and, in particular, critics, for their perceived neglect to keep his inner fire burning. Sexually too he was protean; veering from homosexuality to marriage then back to men again with the casual bi-sexuality found in some of his characters. Furthermore, the dishevelment of his life was infectious: ordered people were drawn into the disorder of his orbit and this was one of his recurring themes—the haphazard way people affect the lives of others, often unaware of the havoc that they create around them.

As a craftsman, he was superb; the intricacy of construction, as he weaves and intertwines the lives and absurdities of his characters, dazzles. The skill with which he creates believable characters in the round, his ear for the different rhythms of language, his ability to present deep emotion without triviality or sentimentality, and best of all, the wit, scattered promiscuously, without ever a labored comic moment.

The son of a Jewish businessman, who soon went bankrupt, and a music hall singer, the major influence of his early life was Theodore Komisajevsky's production of Anton Chekhov's plays at the Barnes Theatre in London in the mid-1920s. These opened up the theater's potential for tackling social, sexual, and political challenges, and it is because A. opened up these issues that he still speaks to us.

His output was prolific. His first play, *Improper People* (perf. 1929; pub. 1930), concerning a suicide pact between two lovers who cannot afford to marry, attracted some favorable attention but was described by one critic as "nearly as boring as Chekhov." But it was his fourth play, *Strange Orchestra* (perf. 1931; pub. 1932), in which he found his dramatic world (in this case a kind-hearted Bohemian actress with an illegitimate child and a boarding house full of dispossessed lodgers) and which brought him to the West End and to the attention of Sir John Gielgud, who directed. *After October* (1936), dealing with a young playwright longing to escape his family's poverty and fecklessness, is largely autobiographical, has much charm, and was A.'s only commercial success.

The Dark River (pub. 1937; perf. 1943), considered by one critic as "perhaps the one undisputably great play of the past half-century in English," is a mood-filled state-of-the-nation play, with a schoolhouse in a quiet Thames backwater standing for England, while the characters put their heads in the sand, unaware of Europe on the brink of war. When it did appear on the stage during that war, it was too late: the audience knew what was in store. A. had more success in the world of film, where he wrote screenplays and occasionally directed.

A.'s masterpiece now appears to be *The Pink Room* (perf. 1952; rev. as *Absolute Hell*, perf. 1987; pub. 1990), set in a West End drinking club, where against the background of the 1945 general election, a diverse collection of lost souls try to keep reality at bay with drink anaesthetizing pain and dulling fears for the future. Jokes, quarrels, sex, and fantasy ward off the horrors of self-knowledge. There are as many plots as there are characters and the complexity of the play's form seems effortless. England was in the throes of postwar self-congratulation and the play infuriated. One senior theater manager called it "an insult to the British people" and the influential critic of the *Sunday Times*, Sir Harold Hobson, said it was "one of the least creditable in stage memory." This review virtually finished A. as a writer. Always touchy, he lost confidence and from then on, bitter at heart yet still endearing in manner, he did little except rewrite earlier work, greatly improving *Birthday* (1934) into *Smithereens* (1985) about a hilariously awful philistine family and rewriting *The Pink Room* into the brilliant *Absolute Hell*.

A. had a minor revival at the small Orange Tree Theatre in Richmond with *The Dark River* in 1984 and 1991 and *Absolute Hell* in 1998 and prestigious productions of the latter on BBC television in 1991 and at the Royal National Theatre in 1995 (both with Dame Judi Dench). The interest, however, does not seem to have continued. A. engages with important issues with such truth and acute wit that he makes most of his illustrious contemporaries in the theater seem pathetically frivolous.

BIBLIOGRAPHY: Ackland, R., and E. Grant, *The Celluloid Mistress* (1954); Duff, C., *The Lost Summer: The Heyday of the West End Theatre* (1995)

CHARLES DUFF

ACKROYD, Peter
b. 5 October 1949, Paddington, London

A. is among the most productive and energetic of contemporary English novelists. His sequence of London novels, blending contemporary reality and fictionalized historical events, has found a large and loyal readership. A.'s conception of London history depends on the rediscovery of significant figures, such as the ecclesiastical architect Nicholas Hawksmoor, or the Renaissance astrologer and magician John Dee. Most of A.'s biographical works are also centered on London, and his life of Charles DICKENS (1990) memorably blends fiction and nonfiction.

A. was reared in Ealing, a western suburb on the far edge of London, and—apart from brief periods spent studying at Cambridge and Yale, and living in Devon, southwest England—he has remained a Londoner. This geographical fact is crucial to the development of his literary career. As his works have consistently suggested, A. regards himself as the inheritor of other literary Londoners: Thomas MORE, John MILTON, Thomas CHATTERTON, William BLAKE, Dickens, Oscar WILDE, George GISSING, and T. S. ELIOT. Certainly, it is hard to think of any other novelist who has written more about the history of London than A.

A. began as a poet and social critic. His fragmentary modernist poems are collected in *The Diversions of Purley* (1987), and there is a significant poetic interlude in *English Music* (1992), in which A. parodies Blake's prophetic books. *Notes for a New Culture* (1976) and *Dressing Up* (1979) are both early nonfiction works, but A. later decided to suppress them.

A.'s sequence of London novels is impressive: *The Great Fire of London* (1982), *Hawksmoor* (1985), *Chatterton* (1987), *The House of Doctor Dee* (1993), *Dan Leno and the Limehouse Golem* (1994; repub. as *The Trial of Elizabeth Cree*, 1995), and *The Plato Papers* (1999). These books operate within a broad frame of magic realism: the standard plot is that the discovery of an historical object or place in the late 20th c. triggers a revenant from London's past. A.'s novels typically view history as a liquid substance, which is subject to ripples across the centuries. *The Plato Papers* is his only speculative novel to date, in which a futuristic narrator reflects on the history of the 19th and 20th cs. from the postapocalyptic viewpoint of the year 3100.

A. has written two novels about rural England, *First Light* (1989) and *English Music* (1992). The first of these is a playful rewrite of Thomas HARDY's novel, *Two on a Tower*. Critics have judged these books less successful than the London novels. There are also two fictional biographies, *The Last Testament of Oscar Wilde* (1983), written in the form of the dying Wilde's journal, and *Milton in America* (1996), a "what if" novel that imagines the Republican poet Milton fleeing England after the restoration of the monarchy, and settling among the Puritans of New England.

The extent of A.'s engagement with MODERNISM may be seen in his biographies of Ezra Pound (1980) and Eliot (1984). A.'s life of Eliot is notable because the poet's estate refused permission for A. to quote from the literary works. A. responded by writing in an artful parody of Eliot's prose style. The book was a commercial success, and it won the William Heinemann Award.

A. devoted much of his energy to BIOGRAPHY throughout the 1990s. *Dickens* is a 1,000-page biography with fictional interludes. A. reflects in a self-conscious way on his previous works when the voices of Chatterton, Eliot, and Wilde unexpectedly come together to conduct a symposium on the art of biography in the middle of the narrative. Although this book was a best-seller, the quality of the writing is very uneven, and it adds little to the preexisting fund of biographical information about Dickens.

A.'s life of Blake (1995), lavishly illustrated in its hardback editions, was well researched and warmly received. But *The Life of Thomas More* (1998) is a work fatally flawed by its own methodology because A. (as his bibliography makes clear) did not take the trouble to consult More's works in the original Latin, preferring to view this major Latinist through his translators.

London: The Biography (2000) represents the fruit of more than ten years' research. It puts forward A.'s totalizing vision of the city's history, from the earliest recorded settlements to the construction of Canary Wharf in the 1990s, although the focus of his interest is solidly on the past two hundred years. He concludes that London is a shapeless city of "broken images" that passes "beyond the natural to become metaphysical, only describable in terms of music or abstract physics." Critics are unanimous in declaring *London* to be A.'s masterpiece.

BIBLIOGRAPHY: Biswell, A., "P. A.," in Moseley, M., ed., *British Novelists since 1960,* Fourth Series, *DLB* 231 (2001): 3–14; Gibson, J., and J. Wolfreys, *P. A.* (1999); Onega Jaén, S., *Metafiction and Myth in the Novels of P. A.* (1999)

ANDREW BISWELL

ADAIR, Gilbert
b. 29 December 1944, Edinburgh, Scotland

Although A. is a prolific writer, having published several novels, a screenplay, and numerous books on the cinema, as well as newspaper and magazine articles, his claim to literary fame rests largely on the translation of Georges Perec's *La Disparition* (1969; *A Void*, 1994). The novel is ostensibly a mystery, but what makes the book—both the original and A.'s translation—remarkable is the fact that it is composed entirely without using the letter "e." A.'s willingness to undertake the translation is evidence of two of his great passions: French literature and wordplay. In addition to *A Void*, A. has published the novels *The Holy Innocents: A Romance* (1987), about the incestuous romantic triangle of three French cinephiles during the turbulent days of 1968; *Love and Death on Long Island* (1990), the story of an elderly novelist and his infatuation with a teenage actor; *The Death of the Author* (1992), a postmodern murder mystery, the protagonist of which is modeled on literary theorist Paul de Man; and *The Key of the Tower* (1997), a thriller set in France. A. has also published several books on cinema, as well as translations of books on the directors Stanley Kubrick and John Boorman.

ADCOCK, [Kareen] Fleur
b. 10 February 1934, Papakura, New Zealand

A.'s writing tends toward familiar moments and themes of daily life. Her poetry exhibits a certain attachment to place and is recognized for its juxtaposition of striking images with the common. Her childhood was divided between New Zealand and England, where her family lived during World War II. Following the war, she returned to New Zealand and earned a degree in classics from Victoria University of Wellington. Emigrating to England in 1955, she worked as a librarian in London at the Foreign and Commonwealth Office while establishing herself as a poet. In 1967, she published *Tigers*, a collection that contained new poems as well as poems from her *The Eye of the Hurricane* (1964), previously published in New Zealand. Later volumes include *High Tide in the Garden* (1971), *The Scenic Route* (1974), and *The Inner Harbour* (1979), one of her most acclaimed collections of poetry. In 1982, A. edited the *Oxford Book of Contemporary New Zealand Poetry* and in the following year published her *Selected Poems*. Returning to her classical training, A. translated medieval Latin poetry that was published as *The Virgin and the Nightingale* (1983). Afterward, she began a collaboration with composer Gillian Whitehead, a fellow New Zealander, that resulted in a ballad for music, a song cycle, and a full-length opera libretto on Eleanor of Aquitaine.

ADDISON, Joseph

b. 1 May 1672, Milston, Wiltshire; d. 17 June 1719, London

A. is of interest to the reader of 18th-c. literature as a poet, a dramatist, and, above all, as an essayist. Educated at Charterhouse School, it was with his schoolfellow Richard STEELE that he was closely associated in the production of the *Tatler* and the *Spectator*, periodicals that, often reprinted through the century, exerted a remarkable influence on the characteristic attitudes and assumptions of their age.

A.'s work as a poet need not detain us long. As a young man at Oxford, he wrote Latin verses of considerable technical accomplishment. In 1702, he published his "Letter from Italy," in which Alexander POPE took an interest, and in 1704 *The Campaign*, a rather plodding account of the battle of Blenheim, the poem achieving a degree of contemporary popularity that it is now hard to understand. Of A.'s other work in verse, the best is in his hymns, such as "The spacious firmament on high," "How are Thy servants blest! O Lord," and "The Lord my pasture shall prepare." His translations from Horace and Ovid are competent but unexciting. As a dramatist, A.'s greatest fame was achieved with *Cato* (1713), a neoclassical tragedy in blank verse. *Cato* was preceded by *Rosamond: An Opera* (1707) and succeeded by *The Drummer* (1716), a comedy. *Cato* was much lauded, as much for political as for aesthetic reasons, but since A.'s own time most have found the play very dull, its plot unexciting, and its characters decidedly lifeless.

The sheer "correctness" of its versification offers some small satisfactions. *Remarks on Several Parts of Italy* (1705) and *Dialogues on Medals* (1721) are attractive in their blend of elegance and scholarship, but it is elsewhere that we must look for the measure of A.'s importance.

In April 1709, Steele founded the *Tatler*, a periodical that appeared three times a week until January 1711. A. contributed extensively to the *Tatler*, and was directly involved with Steele in the establishment of its successor, the *Spectator*, the first issue of which appeared on March 1, 1711. The *Spectator* was published daily until December 6, 1712; in 1714, A. alone produced a further eighty issues. A. contributed some 274 numbers to the first series and twenty-four to the second. Essays by A. also appeared in a number of other periodicals, such as the *Whig Examiner* (1710) and the *Guardian* (1713). It as a periodical essayist, and most especially in his contributions to the *Spectator*, that A. found a medium perfectly suited to his talents. The *Spectator* was, in effect, a series of pamphlets, each with a single theme. The ostensible author was "Mr. Spectator," member of a club whose other members included Sir Roger de Coverley, the country-gentleman (and a kind of retired town-gallant); Will Honeycomb, wit and fop; Captain Sentry, a retired soldier; and Sir Andrew Freeport, a London merchant. Though Steele probably invented this design (perhaps in consultation with A.), A. did much to develop the characters, especially that of Sir Roger de Coverley. A.'s essays were both influential upon and responsive to the ethical and intellectual life of the upper-middle class, especially in London. In his essays, A. writes on religion and philosophy, on literature and, above all, on questions of morals and manners. A. was not perhaps an especially original thinker; but he had a genius for synthesis and popularization. He avoids extremes of opinion and his lucid prose has a subtly persuasive quality. A. offered polite instruction to his readers; instructions as to behavior and taste, instructions in political and religious loyalty (a moderate Protestantism and loyalty to the Hanoverian succession was at the core of A.'s system of values).

In his contributions to the *Spectator*, A.'s concern was not to inflame factional passions but to focus attention on questions of, in the broadest sense, civility, to persuade readers that the dilemmas of social living could be peacefully resolved if they were examined in the light of reason and good sense. The attitude involved a degree of condescension, an assumption of his own superior wisdom that can sometimes irritate; his patronizing attitude toward women is especially striking. In *Spectator* 262, he writes, "among those advantages, which the Publick may reap from this Paper, it is not the least that it draws Men's Minds off from the Bitterness of Party, and furnishes them with Subjects of Discourse that may be treated without

Warmth or Passion." That very absence of "passion" can be a limitation in A.'s work; certainly his satirical strokes are markedly lacking in the passion or poison of contemporaries such as Pope or Jonathan SWIFT. C. S. LEWIS rightly observed that A. is "above all else, comfortable." Yet, in his quiet way, A. did challenge prevailing ideas, did anticipate future developments. His essays on *Paradise Lost* made a significant contribution to criticism of John MILTON; in his enthusiasm for a ballad like "Chevy Chase," he lays, however indirectly, some of the foundations for the romantic revival of the form. His essays on "The Pleasures of Imagination" (notably *Spectator* 411) pre-echo ideas that Samuel Taylor COLERIDGE and others were to develop far more fully; elsewhere, A.'s critical opinions are essentially derived from French critics such as R. P. Le Bossu, Dominique Bouhours, and Nicolas Boileau and it is as a transitional figure between neoclassicism and ROMANTICISM that A. has a striking importance. Rather differently, his entertaining and witty papers on Sir Roger de Coverley have more than once been seen as anticipating important aspects of the later development of the novel.

A.'s achievement is perhaps to be measured not so much by the intrinsic quality of his writing (though that is often considerable) but by the extent of his influence outside the literary world. His essays were widely read long after his death; their standards of morality and taste continued to be much admired. As a writer, A. was perhaps limited by his fastidiousness of manner and by his overconscious avoidance of passionate commitment; but as the voice of an important stage in the development of English social attitudes he is of unsurpassed importance.

BIBLIOGRAPHY: Bloom, E. A., and L. D. Bloom, eds., *Addison and Steele: The Critical Heritage* (1980); Graham, W., *The Letters of J. A.* (1941); Otten, R. M., *J. A.* (1982)

GLYN PURSGLOVE

Æ. See RUSSELL, George William

ÆLFRIC
b. ca. 955, Wessex?; d. ca. 1010, Monastery of Eynsham, Oxfordshire?

Æ. has been called "the greatest prose writer of the Anglo-Saxon period." His influence was primarily insular. His work was relegated to obscurity in the 12th and 13th cs., and rediscovered in the 16th. Not much is known about Æ.'s life. He studied under the great Benedictine reformer Æthelwold. The Benedictine Reform, begun at Cluny in 910, and extended later into Britain by Dunstan, Æthelwold, and Oswald, produced a renaissance in English letters, and it is in this context that Æ. wrote. He studied first at Winchester, the intellectual heart of the reform, then moved on to

Cerne Abbas in Dorset, where he became a monk and priest, and taught at its monastic school. While there, he produced most of his works, becoming certainly the most prolific author in OLD ENGLISH. In 1005, he was appointed the first Abbot of Eynsham in present-day Oxfordshire.

Æ.'s works are all infused with a fervent desire to fulfill his role as a Christian monk and priest. Although his works form a whole, they can uncomfortably be divided into three classes. The first was directed primarily at the laity; the second at his students; and the third at his colleagues. In the first class, we find the first and second series of *Catholic Homilies* (wr. 990–92), based largely on the Carolingian works of Paul the Deacon, Smaragdus of St. Mihiel, and Haymo of Auxerre. These were written at Cerne Abbas and were to be preached to the unlearned as well as the learned. To these, we can add his English collection of saints' lives (wr. 993–98). Æ. is rightly called "the most important homilist in Anglo-Saxon England." In the second class, we find his *Grammar and Glossary*, and *Colloquy* (wr. ca. 995). The *Grammar* is, as Jonathan Wilcox notes, "the first Latin grammar in a medieval vernacular language." It is accompanied by a glossary of English and Latin terms. The *Colloquy* teaches vocabulary and syntax by dramatizing a dialogue between a teacher and his students. In the third class, we find a number of works intended to make theological, especially Augustinian, orthodoxy available in English. He translated and commented upon Genesis, translated Basil of Cæsarea's *Admonitio ad filium spirtualem*, and wrote letters to monks and bishops, and a life of Æthelwold.

Translation was the focus of Æ.'s scholarly career, and he was especially concerned that even the unlearned have access to the Christian message. He therefore wrote a simple and elegant prose in both Latin and English. He said he translated "in the clear and unambiguous words of this people's language, desiring rather to profit the listeners through straightforward expression than to be praised for the composition of an artificial style." During his translation of Genesis, Æ. developed what is termed his "rhythmical prose" style. It recollects Old English poetry, but abandons the poetry's abstruse vocabulary, repetition, and strict meter. Æ. may have been influenced by the metrical prose of his Latin sources, especially the rhythmic final clause of a sentence, called the *cursus*. Like the half-line of Old English poetry, the *cursus* has two major stressed syllables; yet Æ.'s prose has an indeterminate number of sometimes euphonic unstressed syllables (averaging fourteen per line). Æ.'s rhythmical prose syntactically connects successive but distinct four-stress phrases, themselves broken into half-lines of two major stresses each. These half-lines are usually connected by alliteration, often on semantically important words.

BIBLIOGRAPHY: Greenfield, S., and D. G. Calder, *A New Critical History of Old English Literature* (1986); Hurt, J., *Æ.* (1972); Wilcox, J., *Æ.'s Prefaces* (1994)

STEPHEN J. HARRIS

AFRICAN LITERATURE IN ENGLISH

African literature in English began in the 1950s and 1960s in West Africa with the first novels of Chinua Achebe and the plays of his fellow Nigerian Wole Soyinka, and in East Africa with the novels of the Kenyan author Ngugi wa Thiong'o. Theirs was the first generation of writers in Africa to have literary, as opposed to scholarly, polemic, or political ambitions, and the first to see themselves as creating an independent African literature. They were also the first authors to be canonized and to reach a wide readership in Africa and abroad, a success that culminated in Soyinka's Nobel Prize in 1986.

Writing in English by Africans, however, has a much longer history. Africans have been exposed to English and to English-language writing since before colonization and have been writing in English for nearly as long. The first such writing intended to prove the humanity of the writers to a British audience by displaying a mastery of the tools associated with "civilization," in particular, the English language and approved generic forms. In the 18th c., slave narratives—the most prominent of which was Olaudah Equiano's—appeared under the auspices of the abolition movement. The 19th c. saw writing by Creoles, that is, slaves and the descendants of slaves from the New World and from slave ships intercepted by the British navy who had been repatriated to Sierra Leone or Liberia. Prominent among these were Edward Wilmot Blyden, Samuel Ajayi Crowther, and James Beale Africanus Horton. Long considered the first African novel was *Ethiopia Unbound* (1911), a fictionalized autobiography by J. E. Casely Hayford. Reverend Samuel Johnson wrote a *History of the Yoruba* (1921), which had a great influence on later Yoruba and Nigerian nationalism.

These early writers were Christians: Crowther was a bishop and Johnson an Anglican minister. Their writing was usually sponsored by the mission presses that continued to play the most prominent role in publishing Africans up until independence or, in the case of Zimbabwe, until majority rule. Although they commonly had gone to mission schools, Achebe, Soyinka, and the others of the first generation of African literature all rejected the Christianity of their parents. The most prominent among them studied English at the newly established universities of Ibadan in Nigeria (Achebe, Soyinka, John Pepper Clark-Bekederemo, Christopher Okigbo, Flora Nwapa) or Makerere in Uganda (Ngugi, Grace Ogot), which offered literature

programs organized on lines very similar to those in England. Most also had some experience as students abroad, usually in Britain, where they made important contacts with Caribbean writers, but also in the U.S., where writers encountered African American models.

Unlike many West Indian writers, the first generation of African writers returned home from abroad in order to engage in the literary equivalent of nation-building. They were very conscious of the social function of literature: as Achebe put it, they saw their task as being to show that "African peoples did not hear of culture for the first time from Europeans; that their societies were not mindless but frequently had a philosophy of great depth and value and beauty, that they had poetry and, above all, they had dignity." The assertion of dignity never meant, however, just celebration of the precolonial past. Perhaps because it got under way as much as a generation after writing in French did, African writing in English has always been suspicious of the nationalist project associated with the Négritude movement whose most prominent name is the Senegalese poet Léopold Sédar Senghor.

The earliest African writing, by missionaries like Crowther or Johnson, but also by writers educated at mission schools, was inevitably influenced by the Bible and by John BUNYAN's *Pilgrim's Progress*. Models such as D. H. LAWRENCE, Joseph CONRAD, and Graham GREENE fueled the literary ambitions of the novelists. Because of their shared experience of colonialism, Africans also turned to Irish writers for inspiration: Achebe borrowed the title for his classic first novel, *Things Fall Apart* (1958), from W. B. YEATS, and James JOYCE inspired Ben OKRI and Charles Mungoshi. Of course, even as they enabled some forms of expression, British literary models imposed constraints and offered false models that had to be rejected or at least reappropriated. British literature represented both an opportunity—to do for African settings and stories what had already been done for European—and a challenge: to set the story straight. In particular, African writers wanted to "write back" to English novels set in Africa, most famously Conrad's "Heart of Darkness," but also, in Achebe's case, the portrait of Nigeria in Joyce CARY's *Mister Johnson*. Writers have also been concerned to correct the image of Africans propagated by European ethnography.

African writers have always regarded themselves as the heirs of indigenous traditions of storytelling and reciting. Two possible responses to oral tradition are illustrated by Achebe and Amos Tutuola. Whereas Tutuola wrote fantastic picaresque stories such as he knew from traditional storytelling, for example, *The Palm-Wine Drinkard* (1952), Achebe re-created in realist fiction the lives of the people who told such stories. Ngugi wa Thiong'o, who originally published under the name James Ngugi, followed Achebe's lead

and incorporated Christian imagery and Gikuyu mythology, especially the creation myths, in his first realist novels, the most prominent of which, *A Grain of
Wheat* (1967), traces the fortunes of young nationalists in the struggle for Kenya's independence.

Among African writers, Soyinka has been the most
thoroughgoing in creating and theorizing a literary
mythology of his own. In his poems and plays, Yoruba
cosmology and imagery perform the function that the
Bible or the British literary tradition performed for
the authors he had studied at school. The development
of cosmologies derived from indigenous mythology
has allowed Soyinka and his fellow Nigerian, the Igbo
Christopher Okigbo, and their successors, like the
Yoruba Niyi Osundare, to incorporate in their poetry
imagery derived from all over Africa and the world.
Soyinka attributes the particular affinity African playwrights have shown for the Greeks to the fact that
theater in Africa is particularly close to drama's origins in ritual. Soyinka has himself written a version
of *The Bacchae*; John Pepper Clark-Bekederemo has
acknowledged the influence of Euripides and Sophocles; and Ola Rotimi has rewritten *Oedipus Rex* in an
African setting.

Where English is not the first language of writer or
audience and where literacy is far from universal, the
writer faces the challenge of what register to write in.
In *Things Fall Apart*, Achebe developed a style that
maintained an international standard English but
echoed the rhythms of narrative and imagery associated with oral narrative. In particular, he incorporated
proverbs and interspersed Igbo words not just in the
speech of his characters but also in the narration. Gabriel Okara experimented with transcribing the lexis
and the syntax of his native Ijaw into English, with
highly original results, in his novel fittingly called *The
Voice* (1964). Poetry, in particular, has been inspired
by oral forms and genres. *Song of Lawino* (1966), by
Okot p'Bitek from Uganda, is a narrative poem originally written in Acholi and translated by the author.
Jack Mapanje's poems satirizing the regime of Hastings Banda in Malawi are a good example of the poetic power that derives from the imagery and ironic
tone associated with traditional riddles. While some
have been concerned with translation, other writers
have endeavored to record the English actually spoken
by Africans. Ken Saro-Wiwa, the spokesman for the
Ogoni people in the Niger delta executed by the Abacha government, wrote *Sozaboy* (Soldier Boy, 1985),
a novel in "rotten English," in which the first-person
narration expresses the idiosyncratic yet fully functional literacy of someone who has only a few years
of schooling.

The problem of language continues, however, to
haunt African literature in English. With the notable
exceptions of Swahili poetry and Soyinka's translation of *The Forest of a Thousand Daemons* (1968), a

novel in Yoruba by D. O. Fagunwa, there has been
little translation from African languages into English
or, for that matter, into other African languages. The
audiences for oral and written texts usually remain
quite separate, the distance between them one of education and of class. Since the appearance of his essay
Decolonizing the Mind (1986), Ngugi has become the
most prominent voice calling for the abandonment of
English as a medium for writing in Africa. His concern is that English traduces the African experience
because it is always the second or third language of
Africans and not the vehicle of their primary engagement with the world and because English-language
writing addresses an elite and excludes the majority
from its audience. He himself has taken to writing
novels in Gikuyu. His novel *Matigari* (1989) is a political parable designed on the lines of fable in order
to facilitate its passage from a written text to something read aloud in public venues, with the potential
to become an oral tale circulating independently of
the text.

In his desire to reach a mass audience, Ngugi has
also turned to theater. African plays commonly make
use of masks, drums, and dancing in order to blur the
distance between theater and other forms of performance. Theater has been the primary mode for development education in Africa, providing training in literacy, agricultural techniques, women's empowerment,
health, and political participation. The Kamiriithu Education and Cultural Center, led by Ngugi, mobilized
Gikuyu speakers in a critical exploration of the contemporary political scene. Ngugi was imprisoned
without trial for a year in 1977, and by 1982 the
Kenyan government had razed the center and banned
all theater activities in the area.

As a professor at the University of Nairobi, Ngugi
and others, such as Taban lo Liyong, originally from
Sudan, instigated reforms that replaced the English
department with a department of African languages
and literatures. Other university literature departments
across Africa have followed this lead and made African literature, rather than English, the center of the
curriculum. When East and West Africa acquired their
own school-examining boards, questions on African
literature quickly became a staple of school-leaving
exams. Since majority rule, Zimbabwe has also
moved in this direction. British publishers, especially
Heinemann and Longman, have been instrumental in
disseminating African texts and establishing a canon.
As a result, Achebe, for instance, has always been as
available in East and Southern Africa as in West
Africa.

The first generation of African authors, so prominent on the international stage, have almost from the
start been followed by writers who saw themselves as
successors. Among those who have written back to
Achebe and Soyinka are women who have tried to tell

the story ignored or incompletely represented by the men. Flora Nwapa and Buchi Emecheta write about Achebe's Igboland from an angle that can be described as feminist; Grace Ogot wrote the first novels and short stories by a woman in East Africa; and the Ghanaian Ama Ata Aidoo writes plays and novels with a strong political agenda.

A common distinction has it that the first generation of African writers were nationalists, conscious of the task of inventing Africa and African literature, and the second were more critical of the postindependence regimes. Perhaps a more precise distinction can be made on formal lines: the first writing tended either to REALISM, like Achebe or Ngugi, or to MODERNISM, like Soyinka or Okigbo. Since then, however, new forms have come to prominence, especially the political allegory and magic realism. While it owes something to the dictator novels of Latin America and has parallels in West Indian literature, African political allegory has developed a strong tradition of its own. Achebe (*Anthills of the Savannah*, 1987), Ngugi (*Devil on the Cross*, 1980), and Soyinka (the plays *Kongi's Harvest*, 1967; *Madmen and Specialists*, 1971) have all written political allegory later in their careers, as have younger writers, such as the Ghanaian Ayi Kwei Armah. These allegories concern themselves less with the individual than with Africa as a whole and with the structural problems associated with the nation-state in Africa. As in Latin America and the Caribbean, the realism of the pioneer novelists has recently given way to a style that imitates the modes of oral storytelling. In *The Famished Road*, published in 1991, the Nigerian Okri used as a model the fantasies of Tutuola, regarded until then with condescension. Okri's magic realism also invokes Soyinka's Yoruba cosmology, in particular, the abiku or "spirit-child." His fellow Nigerian 'Biyi Bandele-Thomas combines fantasy and satire in *The Sympathetic Undertaker and Other Dreams* (1991), while Latin American models inspire the magic realism of *The Last Harmattan of Alusine Dunbar* (1990) by Syl Cheyney-Coker from Sierra Leone.

In general, literature by black writers in Southern Africa, where majority rule was later in coming, got underway later than literature in West Africa. Zimbabwean writers, conscious of a belatedness, have produced a pessimistic literature more like Armah than Achebe. *Waiting for the Rain* (1975) by Mungoshi uses the imagery of drought to depict social decay; Dambudzo Marechera writes a bleak modernist style in *House of Hunger* (1978). Tsitsi Dangarembga's *Nervous Conditions* (1988) is a perspicacious analysis of the psychology of the colonized.

As newborn democracies gave way to military dictatorships, African writers have played active political roles as critics, activists, and prophets. A corollary is that the prison memoir (Soyinka, Ngugi, Saro-Wiwa)

and prison poetry (Soyinka, Mapanje) have became major genres, and more and more writers have been driven into exile. Soyinka fled Nigeria during the regime of Sani Abacha. Ngugi has long lived in exile in New York. Mapanje fled Malawi after suffering four years of imprisonment. During the Rhodesian regime, writers such as Mungoshi and Marechera lived in England. Paradoxically, English, as the international language, has acquired a new status in Africa as it affords writers the possibility of external witness. Nuruddin Farah from Somalia is unusual in that he writes in a language that was not the colonizer's but that he learned in exile abroad. His trilogy, *Variations on the Theme of an African Dictatorship*, portrays the tyranny of Muhammed Siad Barre. Economic conditions and the erosion of the tertiary education system have also meant that more Africans live abroad. Okri, Bandele-Thomas, and the Zanzibari Abdulrazak Gurnah live in England, the Tanzanian M. G. Vassanji in Canada, Dangarembga in Germany. Emecheta has lived much of her life in England. A whole generation of African academics now lives and teaches in Britain and the U.S. While African literature in English is flourishing and is taught at universities the world over, African writers face worsening economic and political circumstances.

BIBLIOGRAPHY: Achebe, C., *Hopes and Impediments* (1988); Appiah, K. A., *In My Father's House* (1992); Chinweizu, O. Jemie, and I. Madubuike, *Toward the Decolonization of African Literature* (1983); Gikandi, S., *Reading the African Novel* (1987); Ngugi wa Thiong'o, *Decolonising the Mind* (1988); Quayson, A., *Strategic Transformations in Nigerian Writing* (1997); Soyinka, W., *Myth, Literature, and the African World* (1976)

NEIL ten KORTENAAR

AIKIN, Lucy

b. 6 November 1781, Warrington; d. 29 January 1864, Hampstead

A. is probably best known today as the author of *Memoirs of the Court of Queen Elizabeth* (2 vols., 1818), *Memoirs of the Court of King James the First* (2 vols., 1822), and *Memoirs of the Court of King Charles the First* (2 vols., 1828), which provide a vivid depiction of over one hundred years of British history and culture. Moreover, with these books, A. became the first woman biographer to base her work on painstaking research of primary documents. In addition to these royal biographies, A. wrote a book about her father, *Memoir of John Aikin, M.D.: With a Selection of his Miscellaneous Pieces, Biographical, Moral, and Critical* (2 vols., 1823), which shows him to be something of a Renaissance man, pursuing a love of learning and literature at the same time as he practiced medicine. A. also produced a biography of the writer Joseph ADDISON (1843). In addition, she produced CHILDREN'S LITERATURE and was a prolific editor, and she remains an important early figure in the movement for women's equality.

AKENSIDE, Mark
b. 9 November 1721, Newcastle-upon-Tyne; d. 23 June 1770, London

In his own day, A. was a highly esteemed poet, and his works continued to be widely admired at least until the first half of the 19th c. Many of the major poets of the Romantic period, most notably William WORDSWORTH and Samuel Taylor COLERIDGE, acknowledged their regard for him, and many of their works show echoes of, and allusions to, his poetry. His popularity lapsed considerably at the end of the 19th c., and it was only in the 1990s that a complete edition of his poems finally appeared.

The son of a butcher in the northeast of England, A. was very much a self-made man. Precociously intelligent and talented, he was publishing poems in the *Gentleman's Magazine* before his sixteenth birthday. In 1739, a fund was set up by local Unitarians that enabled him to study for the ministry at Edinburgh University, but he abandoned theology for medicine in 1740, and graduated as a doctor of physic at Leiden in Holland in 1744. After a slow start in the provinces, his medical career flourished following a move to London: he became physician at Christ's Hospital in 1759, and physician to the queen in 1761. In addition to his major work entitled *The Pleasures of Imagination* (1744), three books—2,007 lines of blank verse, A. published a number of shorter poems including the dazzlingly erudite, classically inspired *Hymn to the Naiads* (1746) and two books of odes (1745 and 1760), many of them on political issues.

The Pleasures of Imagination, although it has its moments, is not on the whole a poem that appeals to modern tastes. Replete with 18th-c. theories of aesthetics, philosophy, and classicism, with a dash of Newtonian physics thrown in, the poem could be said to illustrate A.'s reported view that poetry "was simply true eloquence in meter." Samuel JOHNSON, in his "Life of Akenside," complained that in his poetry "the words are multiplied till the sense is hardly perceived; attention deserts the mind and settles in the ear." A careful reading of the poem, however, provides much of interest. According to A.'s analysis, the pleasures to be derived from the faculty of imagination are divided into primary (the sublime, the wonderful, and the beautiful) and secondary (the passions and sense). His concepts of imagination as a God-given faculty, of the vital inspirational role played by nature in the imaginative process, and the idea that only certain finely attuned individuals are capable of

fully appreciating the works of God in the natural world, all have obvious affinities with Romantic literary theory.

The posthumous edition of A.'s poems, edited by Jeremiah Dyson in 1772, contains a much revised version of the same poem, now entitled *The Pleasures of the Imagination*. Left incomplete at A.'s death, this poem has three books complete (1,979 lines), and a 130-line fragment of a fifth book. Book 4 is missing. The revisions were drastic, with only about ten per cent of the lines appearing unchanged, and even those often in a different sequence. Thus, the poem can almost be regarded as a new work. Overall, it is probably true to say that the verse form has become more relaxed and readable in the second version. Book 5, in particular, which shows the poet reminiscing about his solitary childhood wanderings among beautiful natural scenes, "led/In silence by some powerful hand unseen," has been much admired.

A.'s political poems, admittedly somewhat impenetrable to anyone lacking a basic working knowledge of mid-18th-c. politics, have much to offer to those with an interest in the history of ideas. Almost invariably written in immediate response to some specific occurrence, whether political or literary, these poems naturally came to appear less relevant as the events that inspired them faded in importance. The most readable is certainly *An Epistle to Curio* (1744), a vigorous satire in heroic couplets that deplores the political "apostasy" of William Pulteney: the Whig politician, initially one of A.'s heroes, had recently caused the poet deep disappointment by accepting a peerage. A slightly later poem, *Ode to the Right Honourable the Earl of Huntingdon* (1748), has lines that many have read as evidence that A. espoused highly unfashionable Republican views: in the Ode the poet looks forward with optimism to a future in which "Empire's wide-established Throne/No private Master fills." Numerous other short poems, expressing a range of views from adulatory to disapproving, are addressed to various political figures of the day. With age, A.'s views appear to have become less radical, and he was posthumously accused, probably unjustly, of becoming a Tory a few years before his death.

A.'s poetry illuminates significant aspects of various important ongoing 18th-c. debates, aesthetic and literary as well as philosophical and political. Recent indications of a reassessment of his works are welcome for what they are beginning to reveal of his contribution to the literary tradition of his day.

BIBLIOGRAPHY: Dix, R., ed., *M. A.* (2000); Houpt, C. T., *M. A.* (1944); Jump, H., "High Sentiments of Liberty: Coleridge's Unacknowledged Debt to A.," *SIR* 28 (1989): 207–24

HARRIET DEVINE JUMP

ALDINGTON, [Edward Godfree] Richard

b. 8 July 1892, Portsea, Portsmouth; d. 27 July 1962, Maison Sallé, near Sury-en-Vaux, France

As poet, novelist, and biographer, A. was closely connected with the development of MODERNISM in literature during the first half of the 20th c. He was both a versatile and a prolific writer and published over two hundred works covering a wide range of literary activity. He often seemed to invite criticism and controversy and that together with his literary facility sometimes provoked accusations of superficiality.

He began writing at an early age—adopting the name Richard in boyhood—and quickly made himself known to the rising generation of young writers. Ezra Pound introduced him to the American poet H. D. (Hilda Doolittle) whom he married in 1913, the same year that he became the literary editor of the *Egoist*. Through the influence of Pound and H. D., he became a conspicuous member of the imagist movement and both he and his wife contributed to the first imagist anthology, *Les Imagistes*, edited by Pound and published in 1914. His first book of poetry, entitled *Images 1910–15*, was published by Harold MONRO's Poetry Bookshop in 1915. The poems are, for the most part, short, skillfully executed exercises in the imagist manner, written in free verse but tightly organized around visual images juxtaposing unusual and surprising attributes. The influence of Japanese haiku is evident as is the example of Pound though A. does manage to establish his own mannerisms by the intelligent use of tone and diction. He followed this with three further volumes of poetry, *Images of War* (1919), *A Fool i' the Forest* (1925)—for which he was accused of plagiarizing T. S. ELIOT's *The Waste Land*—and *Love and the Luxembourg* (1930; repub. as *A Dream in the Luxembourg*, 1930).

In 1914, A. had acted as secretary for Ford Madox FORD, and in this capacity he copied down *The Good Soldier* from Ford's dictation. His own first novel was also centered on a good soldier. Published in 1929 and entitled *Death of a Hero*, this novel quickly established him as a best-selling author with an international following. The inspiration for the novel is drawn from his own horrifying experiences as a front line soldier in France during World War I that marked him, as it marked so many others, for life. The protagonist, named George Winterbourne, of A.'s novel is killed in action in 1918. Organized in three sections, the first part of the novel describes his being reared in the frivolous society of prewar England while the third part in violent contrast depicts his life and death in the trenches. It is a powerful indictment of war, no doubt a traumatic experience for A. who was both shell-shocked and gassed in the war, and must be counted as one of the most significant of all the antiwar novels. He quickly followed this novel with the publication of *The Colonel's Daughter* in 1931 and *All Men Are Enemies* in 1933 though he was unable to achieve the same degree of popular success.

A.'s career had always included a good deal of journalistic work, and he regularly reviewed mainly French books for the *Times Literary Supplement* and became assistant editor on the *Criterion* under Eliot's editorship. However, the writing of *Death of a Hero* perhaps encouraged by his friendship with D. H. LAWRENCE seems to have focused his disillusionment with the English literary establishment and in 1928 he moved to France. His writings became progressively more acidic as he became more openly critical. He continued to write at an impressive rate and produced a steady flow of novels, short stories, and poetry. He spent World War II in the U.S., worked as a scriptwriter in Hollywood, published his autobiography, *Life for Life's Sake* (1941), and edited a number of books of poetry and prose including *The Viking Book of Poetry of the English-Speaking World* (1941). He also began to write biographies and that of the Duke of Wellington, published in 1943 and republished in 1946, was considered distinguished enough to win the James Tait Black Memorial Prize (1947). His biographies of D. H. Lawrence (1950), Norman Douglas (1954), and T. E. Lawrence (1955) were written with a passion for truth that brought him into conflict with those who preferred more comfortable versions of their heroes. He had known both D. H. Lawrence and Douglas personally but had become impatient at the hagiographies that had grown up around Lawrence on the one hand and the refusal to discuss Douglas's homosexuality on the other. Both biographies insisted on the humanity of their subjects with all their vanities and failings. His biography of T. E. Lawrence whom he never met brought down the wrath of the establishment on his head. He always insisted that he set out to write a biography of Lawrence that would justify his place as a national idol but that during his research he had been compelled to conclude that he was both a cheat and a charlatan. No matter how inflated he considered the reputations of his three subjects had become it is difficult to resist the conclusion that A. was determined from the outset not only to demystify them but also to cut them all down to size. There is, moreover, little doubt that A. channeled his anger and his sense of neglected merit into the writing of these biographies. There is also little doubt that the antagonism he had aroused was responsible for the subsequent neglect of his work that was allowed to go out of print. Even so he continued to write and in 1956 his biography of the poet Frederic Mistral was awarded the Prix Gratitude Mistralienne in his adopted country.

In the last years of his life, A. seems to have achieved some kind of personal and professional security. His marriages had ended in failure but nonetheless he was supported by the loyalty of his old friends. Most importantly, a new generation that rejected the values of the immediate past came to appreciate his virtues of aggressively belligerent antiestablishment honesty and frankness and numbers of his works were put back into print.

BIBLIOGRAPHY: Doyle, C., *R. A.* (1989); Patmore, B., *My Friends When Young* (1968); Temple, F.-J., *R. A., an Intimate Portrait* (1965)

A. R. JONES

ALDISS, Brian W[ilson]

(pseuds.: C. C. Shackleton, Peter Pica, Arch Mendicant, John Runciman, Jael Cracken) b. 18 August 1925, Dereham, Norfolk

Although best known as one of the prime contributors to the rapid expansion of interest in SCIENCE FICTION during the 20th c., A. was involved in many other literary activities and considered himself more than just a genre writer. Educated at Framlingham College and an active member of the military during World War II, A. published his collection, *The Brightfount Diaries*—fiction about the bookselling trade, which he had practiced upon his departure from the army in 1947—in 1955. He became the literary editor for the *Oxford Mail* three years later. A. was an accomplished narrative experimenter whose explorations in the novel went widely unheralded, overshadowed by impressive achievements in his many collections of short stories and novels such as *Non-Stop* (1958; repub. as *Starship*, 1959), *Hothouse* (1962; repub. as *The Long Aftermath of Earth*, 1962), *The Dark Light Years* (1964), *Frankenstein Unbound* (1973), *Enemies of the System* (1978), and *Helliconia Spring* (1982), the initial entry in what many consider his masterwork, *The Helliconia Trilogy*. His many works of speculative fiction, whether published under his own name or pseudonymously, are characterized by intricate character development and insight over mere plot-driven space-opera constructions. Not least because of his avoidance (especially in his later work) of overusing "gee-whiz" technology in favor of constructing novels that happen to have technologically based elements, A. has often been given credit for helping to make science fiction a legitimate literary genre, rather than a derided pulp ghetto.

As the cofounder, with C. S. LEWIS, of the Oxford University Speculative Fiction Group (1960) and as the lead editor of the Penguin Science Fiction Series (1961–64), A. has been able to build bridges between the literary and popular publishing worlds. These early and unprecedented liaisons make A. a notable literary figure in at least two ways: his wordplay and his refusal of such categories as "high and low art" forms. In the former instance, his experimentations often overshadowed what some critics have seen as real weaknesses in his plot constructions and narrative structures. In the latter case (representing perhaps his greatest mark on the shifting sands of contemporary letters), he helped to eliminate the distinctions (in the minds of readers and critics alike) between "artistic" and popular texts. In this way, too, he prefigured the opening up of literary canons and the arrival of a less hierarchical literary universe.

In attempting to categorize the dizzying array of texts that A. has created over the years, critics have analyzed his oeuvre in the light of themes as varied as that of the pilgrimage or quest motif, the resurrection of classical archetypes—especially those of Prometheus, Orpheus, and Proteus—and the defamiliarization of the ordinary. His prolific publishing career makes generalization dangerous, but it is generally acknowledged that A. felt that he had pretty much done all he could do in the field of science fiction after writing a dozen or so books and innumerable short stories. One of the most satisfying mappings of his work in science fiction is, in fact, a reading of A.'s texts as cartographic explorations (by Michael Collings) of the dimensions of existence and discovery: what it means to be human in a world/culture where technology requires mini-paradigm shifts not only from generation to generation, but often intragenerationally. Inevitably, A.'s contribution to *Hell's Cartographers* (1974) lends itself to a theory that A. is attempting to reduce the unknowable world around us into smaller, mapped areas that allow for closer inspection—and the often delusional notion that we can "understand."

Of additional interest to contemporary scholars is the intertextual tendency that A. often exhibits, most notably perhaps in *The Saliva Tree* (1966), a Nebula Award winner for best novella, *Moreau's Other Island* (1980; repub. as *An Island Called Moreau,* 1981)—both homages and allusively connected to the works of H. G. WELLS. It is also easy to see this tendency in *Frankenstein Unbound* and *Dracula Unbound* (1991), with their overt connections to Mary SHELLEY and Bram STOKER, respectively. By reinvigorating classic texts—often known to his modern readers only as movies or popular culture representations rather than as novels—A. serves the purposes of POSTMODERNISM by creating intertextual works that echo their predecessors at the same time that they create a "new," more fragmented type of whole. A willful collage—or, in the language of postmodernism, a pastiche—each is more than merely the sum of its respective parts. Herein lies much of the ground for critical disagreement: although the primary definition of "pastiche" refers to a literary work comprising an assemblage of other works, a secondary connotation is more pejorative, suggesting a "hodgepodge," or a jumbled mess. For example, *A Soldier Erect* (1971), the second of A.'s *Horatio Stubbs Trilogy*, focuses upon the sexual antics of its protagonist in the midst of the chaos and banality of the British Army's involvement in India and Burma during World War II. The unsubtle, some would say prurient, erotic events, and its echoes of other, some have said better, works have made it relatively easy to dismiss this novel. In fact, it is possible to view the considerable popular success of the trilogy as a result of the overt sexuality of the work(s), and of the scandal raised by the relentlessness of the masturbation scenes in *The Hand-Reared Boy* (1970), the opening novel in the trilogy.

On the other hand, even in *A Soldier Erect* it is possible to see A.'s erudition and suggestive usage of the vast tapestry of texts about the context of Horatio Stubbs's journey through World War II as he hints at Evelyn WAUGH, James Clavell, and other fictionalizers of the war. In contrast, for example, to Waugh's occasionally misanthropic accounts in his own trilogy, Stubbs is often disingenuously indifferent to the wider scene of the war as he searches for his next prostitute. In this way, A. calls to mind not merely British chroniclers of a particular war, but also all writers who deal with the microcosmic nature of human involvement in macroscopic events. Like the protagonist of Stendhal's *The Charterhouse of Parma* (1839), who wanders unknowingly through the battle of Waterloo, Stubbs is a stand-in for each of us as we wander through history in search of ourselves. Even in this part of A.'s fictionalized autobiography, we see a final stylistic touchstone of his work: his unflagging HUMOR. Even as he presents the brutality of war and the central emptiness of middle-class existence as a whole in this "lesser" trilogy, he is able to engage in the wit and self-deprecation that make his works interesting as a whole, regardless of complaints about plot construction or the dated nature of the subjects of his speculative fiction.

BIBLIOGRAPHY: Aldiss, M., *The Work of B. W. A.* (1992); Collings, M. R., *B. A.* (1986); Henighan, T., *B. W. A.* (1999)

RICHARD E. LEE

ALFRED THE GREAT
b. 849, Wantage, Berkshire; d. 899, bur. at Old Minster, Winchester

A., king of Wessex from 871 to 899, ruled Anglo-Saxon England during a time of considerable political crisis and instability. From the 13th c. onward, he was known as "the Great" because of both his success in defending against further Viking encroachments into England and his program of literary and educational reform. A., the youngest of five sons of King Æthelwulf, assumed the throne after a complicated chain of succession among his four brothers. He spent the first seven years of his rule securing the boundaries of Wessex from Viking invasion. During the period of

relative peace that followed (879–92), A. sought to ensure political stability not only through a widespread network of military defenses, but through an intellectual investment that promoted the translation of important Latin literary works into English.

During his childhood, A. displayed a love for learning and literature. In the *Vita Alfredi* (893), his biographer Bishop Asser recounts that A.'s mother showed her sons a book of English poetry and promised it to whomever learned it the most quickly. Determined to win, A. took the book to a tutor in order to learn it. It is probable, however, that A. never achieved the level of learning he desired; Asser also reports that he himself tutored A. for seven years, and that the king still needed books in Latin to be read aloud to him by others. The effect of such exposure to, and the difficulty of, Latin literature and language presumably taught A. both the importance of learned texts and the utility of vernacular translation.

A. equated the prosperity of England with its educative status. In his preface to *Pastoral Care* (wr. ca. 890–99), A. describes the reasons behind his program of educational reform, noting that the knowledge of Latin has declined in many parts of England, and that now teachers must come from abroad if it is desired. As A. reflects on the loss of learning and books, he also observes that the written wisdom that has survived is rendered useless by the relative illiteracy of God's servants. The king also notes that, analogous to England's current dependence on foreigners for education, the country has been subject to widespread ravaging and depletion. He then recalls how in antiquity holy law was translated from Hebrew into Greek and Latin, and how other Christian nations had in turn translated important works into their own languages. A. resolves to rekindle wisdom and learning in England by translating the "books which are most needful for all men to know." To insure that the spiritual and educational worth of books such as *Pastoral Care* is understood, he orders that a copy be sent to each bishopric with a bookmark of great material value.

Though his preface to *Pastoral Care* implies that he himself interpreted the Latin source as best he could, sometimes word for word, and sometimes sense for sense, A. is not, strictly speaking, an author in the modern sense of the term. Medieval authorship was a highly collaborative and derivative process, and the line between A.'s own writing and that of the teams of translators and advisors he employed remains indistinct and at times indeterminate. During the peaceful middle period of his rule, A. was responsible for the translation of Gregory the Great's *Pastoral Care*, a set of law codes, and OLD ENGLISH translations of a set of psalms now known as the *Paris Psalter*, Boethius's *The Consolation of Philosophy*, and St. Augustine's *Soliloquies*. Though not as easily attributable to him directly, A. also likely had some connection to the *Anglo-Saxon Chronicle* (wr. ca. 890–1154), the Old English *Martyrology*, and translations of Gregory's *Dialogues*, BEDE's *Ecclesiastical History*, and Orosius's *World History*, all of which were produced during his reign.

A.'s translations were also interpretative projects, designed to make abstract theological concepts accessible through idioms, figures, and language familiar to Anglo-Saxon audiences. And though the bulk of A.'s educational writing is in prose, he also includes poetry in his writings: part of his epilogue to the translation of *Pastoral Care* survives in verse, and A. also preserves most of Boethius's intermittent meters in the *Consolation*.

Some of A.'s texts were among the first printed by early Anglo-Saxon scholars in the 16th c., while the veneration of the king as both a political and literary figure peaked in the late 19th c., culminating with a millennial celebration of his death in 1899. Recent scholarship has considered aspects of the oral and literate practices referenced in his works, and issues of textual production and reception, literacy, and cultural diversity. Most recently, it has been claimed that Asser's life of A. is a forgery that has misled scholars for centuries, though this claim has met widespread disagreement and been contested hotly.

BIBLIOGRAPHY: Asser, J., *Alfred the Great: Asser's "Life of Alfred" and Other Contemporary Sources*, trans. by S. Keynes (1983); Frantzen A. J., *King Alfred* (1986); Lerer, S., *Literacy and Power in Anglo-Saxon England* (1991); Smyth, A. P., *King Alfred the Great* (1995)

MARTIN K. FOYS

ALLDRITT, Keith
b. 10 December 1935, Wolverhampton

A.'s self-appointed literary task is to complete a twelve-volume cycle about his native West Midlands, which includes *The Good Pit Man* (1976), *The Lover Next Door* (1977), and *Elgar on the Journey to Hanley* (1979). Generally receiving favorable notice, the cycle's main accomplishment is to provide readers with an extremely well-developed sense of place through their detailed evocation of the West Midlands and its inhabitants. In addition to the West Midlands novels, A. has written critical works on George OR-WELL, *The Making of George Orwell: An Essay in Literary History* (1969); D. H. LAWRENCE, *The Visual Imagination of D. H. Lawrence* (1971), who appears to be a particular influence on A., especially in *The Good Pit Man*, with its story of a romance between a miner and a married society lady; and W. B. YEATS, *W. B. Yeats: The Man and the Milieu* (1997). A. also displays a fascination with the period of World War

II—both as a literary and historical era—in such works as *Modernism in the Second World War: The Later Poetry of Ezra Pound, T. S. Eliot, Basil Bunting, and Hugh MacDiarmid* (1989), *The Poet as Spy: The Life and Wild Times of Basil Bunting* (1998), and *The Greatest of Friends: Franklin D. Roosevelt and Winston Churchill, 1941–1945* (1995).

ALLINGHAM, Margery [Louise]
b. 20 May 1904, London; d. 30 June 1966, Colchester

A. was a popular detective novelist and short story writer, whose many books brought a literary eye to the business of Golden Age detection. A.'s work is firmly rooted in the real world, yet displays a rich streak of romance, particularly in the creation of her aristocratic and gentlemanly hero, Albert Campion, who appeared in seventeen novels and thirty stories, and matured with her writing to become one of the most successfully realized of fictional detectives. A. is inevitably compared to Agatha CHRISTIE, Dorothy L. SAYERS, and Ngaio Marsh, although her unorthodox characterization and elegant prose ally her more closely to Josephine TEY.

A.'s career began with verse plays, magazine melodramas, and an adventure novel, *Blackkerchief Dick* (1923). It was with the detective story, however, that she was to find the greatest liberation for her talent: quoted as having regarded the crime novel as "a box with four sides—a killing, a mystery, an enquiry, and a conclusion with an element of satisfaction," she published *The White Cottage Mystery* (1928), her first attempt within the genre, as a serial in the *Daily Express*. Campion made his modest debut a year later as a suspect and minor character in *The Crime at Black Dudley* (1929; repub. as *The Black Dudley Murder*, 1929). "Well-bred and a trifle absent-minded," this bespectacled, non-macho hero made an instant impact and was charmingly developed in the four high-spirited capers that followed: *Mystery Mile* (1930); *Look to the Lady* (1931; repub. as *The Gyrth Chalice Mystery*, 1931); *Police at the Funeral* (1932); and *Sweet Danger* (1933; repub. as *Kingdom of Death*, 1933), all of which are less concerned with the violent deaths that take place than with the chivalrous pursuit of sacred treasures or princely inheritances.

In the preface to *Death of a Ghost* (1934), A. distinguished between these early "picaresque" adventures and what was to follow: with the exception of *Flowers for the Judge* (1936), which shows an uncharacteristic sentimentality, the books leading up to the war—*Dancers in Mourning* (1937; repub. as *Who Killed Chloe?*, 1943), *The Case of the Late Pig* (1937), *The Fashion in Shrouds* (1938)—were assured and beautifully crafted narratives in which complex murder stories dovetailed perfectly with illuminating character studies and engaging dialogue to prove that the detective novel was not necessarily an oxymoron. Of her Scotland Yard man, Charlie Luke, she once wrote that he "talked with his whole body," and she approached her fiction in much the same way, possessing an energy and exuberance that transformed descriptions of the everyday into uniquely animated pictures of places she knew well and people whose foibles she celebrated; the gloriously exaggerated personalities surrounding Campion—the loyal valet and former cat burglar, Magersfontein Lugg, for example—are one of the great joys of her work. The theatricality of her mysteries was balanced by acute observation and precise detail: as H. R. F. Keating has noted, her REALISM extended to the invented newspaper reports and poetry that she sprinkled liberally into her work.

After completing *Black Plumes* (1940), her only non-Campion crime novel, A. returned to her popular hero but with a darker mentality that reflected the emotions of wartime and added a deep understanding of motive to the intuitive intelligence of her earlier work. Nowhere is this more evident than in the physical, mental, and moral transformation of Campion from an attractive but rather superficial Scarlet Pimpernel to the mature, omniscient commentator of *Traitor's Purse* (1941; repub. as *The Sabotage Murder Mystery*, 1943), in which he declares his "passion for his home, his soil, his blessed England"; *Coroner's Pidgin* (1945; repub. as *Pearls before Swine*, 1945); *More Work for the Undertaker* (1948); *The Tiger in the Smoke* (1952), commonly cited as A.'s finest novel; *The Beckoning Lady* (1955; repub. as *The Estate of the Beckoning Lady*, 1955), her own personal favorite; *Hide My Eyes* (1958; repub. as *Tether's End*, 1958); *The China Governess* (1962); and *The Mind Readers* (1965). Although Julian SYMONS is not alone in suggesting that these later books would have been even better without the presence of a detective who now belonged to another age, they are widely regarded as her best work; certainly, she distinguished herself from the majority of her contemporaries by treating death not as a body in the library but as a reality of which she could write with emotional depth.

A.'s final novel, *Cargo of Eagles* (1968), was unfinished at the time of her death but was completed by her husband, the artist and editor Philip Youngman Carter, according to her plans. Her canon also includes many anthologies of short stories; another straight novel, *Dance of the Years* (1943; repub. as *The Gallantrys*, 1943); novellas, published as *Deadly Duo* (1949) and *No Love Lost* (1954); two plays, *Dido and Aeneas* (WR. 1922) and *Water in a Sieve* (1925); and *The Oaken Heart* (1941), which documents the impact of war on village life.

The popularity of A.'s detective novels has endured to this day because of its controlled and powerful prose; its insightful treatment of criminal psychol-ogy and social incongruity; and the wisdom with which she writes about relationships between the sexes. Her style has been compared to P. G. WODEHOUSE; her characterization to Charles DICKENS; and her sense of adventure to Robert Louis STEVENSON; the combination, however, is completely her own.

BIBLIOGRAPHY: Pike, B. A., "M. A.," in Benstock, B., ed., *British Mystery Writers, 1920–1939*, *DLB* 77 (1992): 3–12; Rowland, S., *From Agatha Christie to Ruth Rendell: British Women Writers in Detective and Crime Fiction* (2001); Symons, J., *Bloody Murder* (1972; rev. eds., 1974, 1985)

NICOLA UPSON

ALLOTT, Kenneth

b. 29 August 1912, Glamorgan; d. 23 May 1973, Liverpool

A. was perhaps best known as a critic and scholar, holding a teaching position at Liverpool University for nearly thirty years (1946–73). During his career, he wrote or coauthored works on Jules Verne (1940), Graham GREENE (with Miriam Farris, 1951), and Matthew ARNOLD (1955); he also edited collections of the works of Arnold (1965) and Robert BROWNING (1967). With Stephen Tait, A. produced a novel, *The Rhubarb Tree* (1937), and a dramatic adaptation of E. M. FORSTER's *A Room with a View* (1951). As a poet, A. achieved a certain amount of acclaim for his first collection, *Poems* (1938), which combines a pessimistic worldview with quirky, almost surreal imagery ("The broken panes in the greenhouse like vowels missing"; "I hear the ape deafen the peninsula/ Because his hands will not invent the plough"). His second collection, *The Ventriloquist's Doll* (1943), has been criticized as overly concerned with phrasemaking at the expense of meaning. Although A. published little between 1943 and his death, the few poems that appeared were generally praised for their return to a more simple, direct style. His *Collected Poems* was published posthumously in 1975.

ALVAREZ, A[lfred]

b. 5 August 1929, London

A. is a prolific critic, literary theorist, and essayist. His early works of literary criticism, *Stewards of Excellence* (1958; repub. as *The Shaping Spirit*, 1958) and *The School of Donne* (1961), reflect his interest in the long tradition of British poetry in general and in the work of the metaphysical poet John DONNE in particular. Donne's poetry was also a great influence on A.'s own work. *The Savage God* (1971) remains one of A.'s most powerful works. A study of the suicidal tendencies of great poets, the book's most memorable segments are on the American poet Sylvia

Plath and on A.'s own attempted suicide in 1961. The strain of the artistic life and of producing literature under strenuous social conditions are also explored in *Under Pressure* (1965), a book of interviews and observations of Eastern European poets, including Zbigniew Herbert, whom A. particularly admired. A.'s other works include the novels *Hers* (1974), *Hunt* (1978), and *Days of Atonement* (1991). More recent books include *Night: Night Life, Night Language, Sleep and Dreams* (1995), a collection of essays dealing with the subject of night; the memoir *Where Did It All Go Right?* (2000); and *Poker: Bets, Bluff, and Bad Beats* (2001), a subject dear to A.'s heart—he once participated in the World Series of poker.

AMBLER, Eric

b. 28 June 1909, London; d. 22 October 1998, London

Certain writers can be considered to be the originators of the genre they practice. Their work defines its nature, how one recognizes that a work is in a genre, the rules of this genre, and the conventions that can be assumed when reading work in this genre. Such writers rarely spring from nowhere, but their precursors will not be recognized as working in the genre until the originators have enabled it to be perceived.

The detective stories of Dashiell Hammett have often been seen to have this quality, originating the notion that the detective, or investigator, will also have feelings that will affect the development of the plot, and how he will come to acknowledge the truth of the circumstances that are brought to him. A. was the originator of an adjacent genre, the thriller in which, similarly, the protagonist feels. Indeed, often, he grows until he is capable of understanding and dealing with what the villains put upon him.

Before A.—who also wrote as Eliot Reed— thrillers were mostly about hero-adventurers; for example, Baroness ORCZY's Scarlet Pimpernel or Arthur Conan DOYLE's Brigadier Gerard; otherwise, they were about military men or explorers whose dispatches from the front or from the desert were addressed to the public rather than to the War Office or the Royal Geographical Society: Erskine CHILDERS's *Riddle of the Sands* is a fine example. Essential to either tradition was that the heroes have no interior experience for the reader to identify with, although there were two works, which can be seen as precursors of A.'s tales: Rudyard KIPLING's *Kim* and W. Somerset MAUGHAM's *Ashenden* sequence; in both, one's knowledge of the interior life of the protagonists complements and strengthens the way one shares their adventures.

A. shared with Hammett a working background outside the literary world: Hammett a strike-breaking detective, A. an engineer, advertising agent, and dissatisfied (and unsuccessful) playwright. Both were, as a consequence, politically on the left. Both eschewed syntactic complexity and poetic imagery, yet succeeded in engaging the reader in the inner experiences of their protagonists. A. himself took his heroes from the socialist left, and, before 1939 was the only popular writer who required his readers to identify with socialists and communists. Usually thriller writers, if political, have been on the right, if not the fascist right. When asked, A. claimed that he chose the thriller as the least interesting genre in which a little originality would be most rewarding, financially. This illustrates his own attitude to himself, both ironic and fiercely private.

His first work was *The Dark Frontier* (1936), but it was in his second, *Uncommon Danger* (1937; repub. as *Background to Danger*, 1937), that his particular take on the thriller manifests itself. Desmond Kenton, a perfectly ordinary suburban man, finds himself in accidental possession of details of a complex pro-Nazi conspiracy threatening European stability. Two charming Russian spies, Andreas and Tamara Valeshov, try to get him to give these details to them, fascist agents of international capitalism, gloriously and viciously satirized, seek to force him to give the plot up to them. Initially, he does not know what to do; delighted by the Valeshovs' charm, he senses that it serves the same purpose as the bullying and threats of the fascists. He surprisedly finds in himself the strength to deny both sides his knowledge and finally realizes that it is for him alone to make the choice of what to do with the secrets he holds. He finds he can identify with the Valeshovs and together they defeat the conspiracy; he returns to suburban England, but not the same man. In a way, this can be seen as an anti-Romantic Bildungsroman.

Epitaph for a Spy (1938) was a more lightweight work in which a Hungarian refugee living in the south of France without proper papers is manipulated by a sûreté heavy, as he thinks, to discover which of his fellow guests is passing information to the Axis powers, but in reality to cause a distraction so that the sûreté can round up the whole gang. The refugee's self-awareness and insecurity are prescient. Also, there is a sympathetic picture of the situation of a German communist hunted by the Gestapo. *Cause for Alarm* (1938) recapitulated *Background to Danger*— indeed, the delightful Valeshovs reappear in the same role. It is interesting to compare the two; *Cause for Alarm* uses the thriller pursuits and escapes more extravagantly and more confidently.

His fifth prewar novel, *The Mask of Dimitrios* (1939; repub. as *A Coffin for Dimitrios*, 1939), is the most interesting and the richest of A.'s prewar books. Its structure is not linear but uses a character, Charles Latimer, a detective novelist, to discover, from unreliable papers and more unreliable interviewees, Demitrios's activities at various points in his career, so that episodes in his life come at one without the usual structure of temporal continuity, and so that one's attitude to Dimitrios, drug-runner, murderer, blackmailer, successful businessman, see-saws in uncertainty. Also, the author-narrator, Latimer, is unreliable and, reflexively, one begins to wonder whether the author, A., is not, himself, unreliable. This was the novel in which A. first, and most strikingly, showed that a thriller could be as deep as any other kind of novel and could receive and stand up to the same level of philosophical analysis and discussion.

In 1939, war broke out, and A. joined the army filmmaking unit, but his sixth prewar novel, *Journey into Fear* (1940), was published. An English armaments engineer is himself the target of a conspiracy; Turkish intelligence puts him, and one of their agents, on a ship to cross the Mediterranean, but the conspirators outflank them and put their agents on the ship. The other passengers are a hilarious collection of pathetic figures. A. here deeply portrays his antihero's almost justifiable paranoia. It is interesting that, perhaps because of the Nazi-Soviet nonaggression pact, the English armaments industry is no longer shown as allied with European fascism.

A. did not publish for another eleven years, during which he wrote screenplays in London and Hollywood including some strong and well-remembered films—*The Cruel Sea* (1953), *A Night to Remember* (1958); however, he felt he could only express himself successfully in novels. Incidentally, although several successful films were made from his novels, he seems never to have had a hand in their screenplays.

When he resumed, *Judgment on Deltchev* (1951) examined the people involved in Stalinist show trials, lamenting the disappearance of democracy in Eastern Europe and the chasm between private thinking and public utterance that these engendered. This novel is the only one of A.'s that expressed with approval the values of the cold war that were then at their peak. There were eleven more postwar novels to come, exploring very diverse situations and characters. A new tool to explore the interior was the creation in *The Light of Day* (1962; repub. as *Topkapi*, 1964) of comic characters, notably Arthur Abdul Simpson, the frightened little petty crook who always gets in too deep and not deep enough for his own good. He was memorably portrayed by Peter Ustinov, frantically hanging upside down in the film version, *Topkapi* (1964), but what those who know him only from the film do not realize is that in the sequel, *Dirty Story* (1967), he, as, perforce, a mercenary in decolonized states in Africa is used to exhibit the terrible way in which the arms trade and the mining industry connived with, corrupted, and were corrupted by the new leaders of the new states.

Each postwar novel explored a different environment, but the theme of the ordinary person faced with state-inspired violence almost always persisted. A.'s skill as a tale-teller increased, and increasingly he used HUMOR and SATIRE as vehicles for the portrayal of his characters, without compromising his more serious concerns. But the later novels are those of a practitioner at the top of his form exploring new fields, while his prewar novels built original ways of telling. What shines through, though, is his remarkable prescience in tackling situations less noticed then, but the source of many of today's international problems. *Dirty Story* did this for African decolonization; *The Night-Comers* (1956) portrays an engineer building a dam in a newly independent Asian country where the pragmatic army-led government is faced with a rebellion by a faction who wish Muslim values to inform their society. There is a fascinating study of a good-time girl caught up in the conflict, who knows she will have to continue to live in that society. Similarly, the protagonist of *Doctor Frigo* (1974), the son of an assassinated president who, in exile, does good as a doctor, is persuaded by French intelligence and a clutch of political conspirators to lend his name to a coup attempt that succeeds, but leaves him without any sense of helping to build better institutions for his country, it seeming dubious that the new government will be better than the old.

The Levanter (1972) deals with the Middle East as seen by a British businessman unavoidably caught up in Israel-Arab Middle Eastern conspiracies, while *The Care of Time* (1981) moved to the Gulf, where a mad ruler seeks to acquire biological weapons. This is foiled by an American ghostwriter traveling with a terrorist leader who is seeking to retire to safety with all his family. To portray, entirely credibly, such a man is a feat of imagination that is rare, especially relevant today. The terrorist's organization, traveling with him, includes another delightful and demanding girl—rare in A.'s works, these strong young women are always interesting. As well as a number of other rewarding and entertaining novels, he produced in his later years the first part of an autobiography, *Here Lies* (1985), and an autobiographically connected collection of short stories, *The Story So Far* (1993).

BIBLIOGRAPHY: DelFattore, E., "E. A.," in Benstock, B., and T. F. Staley, eds., *British Mystery Writers, 1920–1939, DLB* 77 (1989): 13–24; Hopkins, J., "An Interview with E. A.," *JPC* 9 (Fall 1975): 285–93; Lewis, P., *E. A.* (1990)

JOHN LASKI

AMIS, [Sir] Kingsley [William]
b. 16 April 1922, London; d. 22 October 1995, London

A. was one of the outstanding writers of his generation (that is, the one that came of artistic maturity in the 1950s), active for forty years and notably productive, in quantity of output, diversity of genre, and sustained quality. Though he will probably remain best known as the author of *Lucky Jim* (1954), his first novel, he wrote twenty-four novels, including a spoof mystery-thriller coauthored with Robert CONQUEST and a James Bond book published under the pseudonym of Robert Markham, three books of short fiction, four books of literary criticism, three books about drinking, anthologies of short stories, popular verse, songs, and SCIENCE FICTION; two collections of his own essays, several volumes of poetry; and his *Memoirs* (1991). If A. is, in some quarters, denied recognition as the preeminent man of letters of his generation it may be because of his lack of pomposity, his often rebarbative right-wing politics, or his persistence in writing comedy. The publication, in 2000, of his *Letters* was a major literary event, in part because it coincided with his son Martin AMIS's memoir, *Experience*, which gave new insight into the relationship between the father and son novelists.

A. began as a poet; his first book, *Bright November*, was a collection of poems published in 1947, and he published two more substantial poetry collections and his *Collected Poems, 1944–1979* (1979) as well as several anthologies, most importantly *The New Oxford Book of Light Verse* (1978). Like his best friend, Philip LARKIN, he was antimodernist in outlook and tended to write poetry that emphasized formal regularity and clarity. Suspicion of false emotion was one frequent note struck by his poetry (as by his comments on such writers as Dylan THOMAS).

His first novel, dedicated to (and in some ways inspired by) Larkin, was *Lucky Jim*. This quickly earned him a place in the supposed "school" of Angry Young Men, though A. always asserted that he was not very young or very angry and that others so defined (Iris MURDOCH, for instance) were not men. *Lucky Jim* was written while the author was still a university lecturer and it, like the later *Jake's Thing* (1978) and *The Russian Girl* (1992) was an academic novel. It was also a brilliant comedy, combining verbal wit, the triumph of the protagonist over frustration and the malignity of others, and (a point often missed, but present in much of his fiction) a serious moral dimension. At the time it attracted much attention, particularly from older readers, for its alleged Philistinism and apparently antisocial stance.

A.'s conventional novels, following *Lucky Jim*, divide into two groups, the dividing line coming somewhere in the late 1960s. Following his first book, such novels as *That Uncertain Feeling* (1955), *I Like It Here* (1958), *Take a Girl like You* (1960), and *One Fat Englishman* (1963) featured strongly spoken protagonists whose identifying characteristic was suspicion of the bogus, alienation from the society in which they found themselves, and a comically impatient way of reacting to it. *Take a Girl Like You* stands out, though, because of its female protagonist and its sympathetic treatment of her seduction by a plausible but ultimately unscrupulous man. This sympathy constitutes a partial rebuttal of the charge, increasingly laid as his career developed, of male chauvinism, misogyny, etc., and is strengthened in the sequel, showing the same two characters after marriage, *Difficulties with Girls* (1988).

Alongside these mainstream novels A. was always interested in "genre fiction," an interest that explains such nonfiction books as *New Maps of Hell: A Survey of Science Fiction* (1960) and *The James Bond Dossier* (1965), as well as his *Colonel Sun* (1968, featuring James Bond), *The Green Man* (1969, supernatural thriller), *The Riverside Villas Murder* and *The Crime of the Century* (1973 and 1989, detective fiction), and *The Alteration* and *Russian Hide-and-Seek* (1976 and 1980, both science fiction or "time romance").

I Want It Now (1968) marked a change in the tone of A.'s work. Where he had been a critic of British society from the left in his work in the 1950s, by 1968 he had shifted his political stance and, more importantly for his fiction at least, had become suspicious or even contemptuous of many of the social features that made up "The Sixties." The obsession with youth, irresponsibility and self-justification, the suggestion that values do not exist, and what he saw as the mindless pursuit of fashion: all these underlie the comedy of this novel and *Girl, 20* (1971) and, to some extent, later works like *Jake's Thing*, *The Old Devils* (1986), *The Folks That Live on the Hill* (1990), and *The Russian Girl*.

An increasing interest in the problems of old age first made itself known in his 1974 *Ending Up*, which he explained as his attempt to imagine what the people he was then living with would be like when old. It is a mordant comedy making humor of crotchety retirees, nominal aphasia and loneliness. The age and accompanying fallibilities (often including drinking problems) of the characters are important features of *Jake's Thing*, *The Old Devils*, *The Folks That Live on the Hill*, and his last completed work, *The Biographer's Moustache* (1995). A tendency to incorporate his own circumstances more fully into his fiction was also evident in the latter part of his novelistic career.

A.'s marital history was troubled. He married at Oxford and left his wife Hilly for another woman, having been routinely unfaithful to her during their marriage, in 1965; his second marriage became unbearable, starting to go wrong about 1976, and it was during this painful period that he wrote *Jake's Thing* and *Stanley and the Women* (1984) whose protagonists seem to conclude that women are insane and that men are better off without them. He later lived with Hilly and her third husband until his death. His penultimate novel, *You Can't Do Both* (1994), is essentially his autobiography.

A. was nominated three times for the Booker Prize for fiction, winning in 1986 for *The Old Devils*. He was made a Commander of the British Empire in 1981 and a knight in 1990.

BIBLIOGRAPHY: Amis, M., *Experience* (2000); Gardner, P., *K. A.* (1981); Jacobs, E., *K. A.* (1995); McDermott, J., *K. A.* (1989); Moseley, M., *Understanding K. A.* (1993)

MERRITT MOSELEY

AMIS, Martin [Louis]
b. 25 August 1949, Oxford

A. is the son of renowned English novelist, Kingsley AMIS. But A. is also generally regarded as contemporary British literature's most famous "bad boy." He has often been compared favorably with his esteemed father and has emerged as one of England's finest satirists. The London *Daily Telegraph* labeled him "the rock star of English literature." And he has also become, next to Salman RUSHDIE, the most celebrated—and wealthiest—serious writer in Britain.

Though he is primarily a writer of satirical novels, he has also written a prize-winning collection of short stories, *Einstein's Monsters* (1987), which became a best-seller in both Britain and the U.S. *The Moronic Inferno: And Other Visits to America* (1986) is a collection of articles on American topics and characters, while *Visiting Mrs. Nabokov and Other Excursions* (1993) collects his profiles on writers and celebrities and essays on nuclear weapons, chess, book fairs, and snooker. A. has served as fiction and poetry editor and reviewer for the *Observer, Times Literary Supplement*, and the *New Statesman* until 1980; he also contributed interviews and reviews to the *Sunday Times* (London) and *Esquire*. Many of his short stories have appeared in the *Atlantic Monthly* and the *New Yorker*.

A. published his first novel, *The Rachel Papers*, in 1973 to rave reviews and, as a result, won the prestigious Somerset Maugham Award for the most outstanding first novel. Critics praised the novel's sharp satiric HUMOR as well as its brilliantly witty prose. Though written as a conventional British romantic comedy, the work can also be understood as a "coming-of-age" or "rite-of-passage" memoir, with an ironic edge. Protagonist Charles Highway flaunts his narcissistic self-absorption and arrogance, making them a metaphor for modern British middle-class society's shallow permissiveness.

A.'s satire becomes even more bitter in his second novel, *Dead Babies* (1974), whose title so offended the reading public that it was changed to *Dark Secrets* for the paperback edition in 1977. Though *Dead Babies* employs the venerable British novelistic form of the "country-house novel," the characters are even more repulsively venal than the worst of *The Rachel Papers*. The self-indulgent permissiveness of the ten people at the Appleseed Rectory (an apt title for a modern-day Eden) becomes the subject matter of the novel. Drugs, alcohol, and deviant sexual behavior make all of them incapable of any kind of redemption; critics were outraged that the novel lacked any sympathetic characters at all. However, *Dead Babies* was much more loosely structured that A.'s first novel, and relied on a series of episodes built around the characters' use of alcohol, drugs, and sex as ways of distracting themselves from the emptiness of their meaningless lives.

The satiric edge of his third novel, *Success* (1978), is less offensive and generalized than *Dead Babies*, and the critics were pleased by the keener focus of the story of Terry Service and his foster brother, Gregory Riding. A.'s narrative technique is tight and presents Terry and Gregory relating their own unique perspective on the unfolding events of the novel. As the book moves along, the brothers become the antitheses of each other; Gregory's fortunes dwindle as he watches Terry's expand into greater success. Though this is ostensibly an allegorical tale, the reader gradually becomes aware that A. has constructed a complex labyrinth of ever-changing perspectives that undermines any kind of epistemological grounding of events. At the novel's conclusion, both characters are devoid of any redeeming qualities and become despicable.

Though *Success* disturbed both critics and readers alike, A.'s fourth novel, *Other People: A Mystery Story* (1981), found a more sympathetic reception. While the title of the novel is taken from a character in Jean-Paul Sartre's play *No Exit* who defines Hell as "other people," the formal technique of the novel experiments with narrative perspective in highly inventive ways. The names of the characters resonate with 19th-c. British literary classics: Mary Lamb, Amy Hide, and John Dark, to name a few. An amnesiac narrator awakens in a hospital and begins to name her world from nursery rhymes. A. seems uninterested in developing character and is content with vivid stereotypes, an approach that clears the way for him to explore the narrative possibilities of his story. By making the familiar strange—a postmodern technique—A. moves away from pure satire and into an examination of the effect of language on perception, a method that alerted some critics to the influences of Jorge Luis Borges and Vladimir Nabokov on A.'s work. And certainly, *Other People* is very much a novel about self-referentiality.

It was the publication of *Money: A Suicide Note* in 1984 that brought A. the highest praise from both British and American critics. *Money* enables A. to escape his sometimes debilitating preoccupation with formalistic matters. He admitted to an interviewer in

1995 that *Money* helped him shed certain literary constraints that, in turn, helped him to tell the truth for the first time in his fiction, in his own voice. The aptly named narcissistic protagonist, John Self, is a slave to his many obsessions: talking, drinking, working, and moving. Self's all-consuming consumerism will not allow him to reflect on what his life means; his unexamined materialism blinds him to any kind of self-assessment. Though many of the novel's characters are self-conscious caricatures with names like Spunk Davis, Butch Beausoleil, and Lorne Guyland, they seem perfectly appropriate for the fantasy world that they inhabit. Most critics agreed that since much of the story takes place in America, A. had successfully expanded his satire to the capitalistic world in general and not solely to the English middle class.

However, it was with the publication of A.'s sixth novel, *London Fields*, in 1989 that his work became intentionally futuristic and millennial. The novel takes place in 1999, an era that may turn into the apocalypse. The novel presents the narrator Samson Young (a has-been American writer who has produced nothing in twenty years) arriving in London hoping to gain a fresh perspective. The novel's structure is built on passages from narrator Samson Young's notebooks for his novel in progress alternating with passages from the finished novel itself. Out of these combined texts emerges the story of Nicola Six, a fatal woman searching for a man to murder her; and confidence man, Keith Talent, slave to sex, alcohol, money, but most especially, darts. This long and complex novel became a best-seller in both England and America and confirmed A.'s reputation for being one of Britain's most trenchant satirists.

A.'s seventh novel, *Time's Arrow; or, The Nature of the Offense* (1991), was so highly praised by the British literary establishment that it was shortlisted for the prestigious Booker Prize, A.'s first appearance on that honored venue. *Time's Arrow* is also built on the technique of defamiliarization; that is, making the familiar strange, a method he used quite successfully in *Other People*. In *Time's Arrow*, the author reverses the flow of Time itself, causing the universe to grow younger each day. The narrator, Tod Friendly, undergoes a journey back in time as the plot moves from Friendly's senility, retirement as a doctor in upstate New York, through his early years as an intern in New York City. Friendly's name changes as the story devolves and he finds himself participating in the horrors of the Holocaust in Germany, World War I, and finally back into his mother's arms as a helpless infant. Though A. was roundly criticized by some for what they saw as trivializing Holocaust atrocities, A. defended the book's ability to force its readers to reimagine history in a fresh way. Because the novel became a best-seller, A. was able to negotiate an advance of half-a-million pounds for his next novel, *The Information*.

The Information was published in 1995 and, because of the enormous publicity hype, sold well. One of the reasons it became so popular was that its main theme was literary envy. A. returned to the bitter satire of his early novels as he delineated the sordid disintegration of a friendship between two novelists when one becomes wildly successful as the other dwindles into insignificance. Novelist Richard Tull's novels are hardly selling, while Gwyn Berry's novels are generating sold-out readings in America. Berry's novel receives "The Profundity Requital" prize, an award that bears more than a passing resemblance to the Booker Prize.

There is little question that A.'s literary reputation has probably surpassed his own father's. A.'s novels have grown technically as they appeared because he has regularly forged new novelistic forms that suited the changing content of those novels in ways that his father did not. Certainly A. could be called a genuine postmodernist because of his willingness to experiment with imaginative forms and not simply be satisfied with his past work. He is also one of the most highly imitated younger novelists of his generation. His reputation has certainly been secured by three of his finest novels: *Money*, *London Fields*, and *Time's Arrow*; and his short story collection, *Einstein's Monsters*, did much to advance his reputation especially among short story readers in the U.S.

BIBLIOGRAPHY: Diedrick, J., *Understanding M. A.* (1995); Mars-Jones, A., *Venus Envy* (1990); Wilson, J., "A Very English Story," *NewY* 71 (March 6, 1995); 96–106

PATRICK MEANOR

ANCRENE WISSE [also ANCRENE RIWLE]

Ancrene Wisse, the early MIDDLE ENGLISH title usually applied to this work, means, roughly, "guide for anchoresses." *Ancrene Riwle* ("rule for anchoresses"), an alternate title concocted by 19th-c. scholars, is now seldom used.

Anchoresses were female anchorites, lay people, such as the 14th-c. visionary writer JULIAN OF NORWICH, who lived in seclusion, singly or in small groups, reading, meditating, and praying. *Ancrene Wisse*, written in the West Midlands, probably in the first third of the 13th c., is a guidebook for living this secluded life. Its anonymous male author was a counselor to three young women, sisters of noble family living as anchoresses, and he wrote the manual at their request. Other anchorites and their spiritual counselors recognized the value of the work: to meet the needs of other recluses, *Ancrene Wisse* was often copied and revised, and also translated into French and

Latin; there is evidence that the work was used as late as the early 16th c. It is now regarded as the most important prose work of the early Middle English period because of its style and its moving, imaginative expression of practical advice and spiritual counsel. *Ancrene Wisse* also merits attention as the central work in a body of important early Middle English texts, including others on women's spiritual concerns.

Scholar E. J. Dobson argued persuasively that the author of *Ancrene Wisse* was an Augustinian priest, Brian of Lingen, who was associated with Wigmore Abbey in Herefordshire, and that Brian wrote for anchoresses known to have dwelled near the abbey. But serious questions have been raised about Dobson's theory, and the author of *Ancrene Wisse* remains undetermined.

More important than the author's identity are the qualities he reveals in his writing: through *Ancrene Wisse* the reader encounters a lively and informed medieval mind. The author has extensive knowledge not only of ancient and medieval Christian works but also of secular writings, such as medical books and French romance. He translates and applies his sources freely, often elaborating upon them or allegorizing them ingeniously.

The author's knowledge of the world and the spiritual life goes beyond books. He evidently has extensive pastoral experience and the knowledge of humanity gained by such experience. He is moderate and realistic: he encourages the three sisters (whom he has apparently visited) to eat more and to be cautious in their fasting, their bloodletting, and their physical penance. His realism borders sometimes on cynicism, as when he warns the sisters that there are few priests whom they can safely trust. Adept at making his ideas memorable, he frequently uses imagery that is vivid, worldly, and even bizarre.

His metaphorical turn of mind shaped his eight-part book: the first and eighth parts give the sisters detailed instructions on what the author calls the "outer rule," the behavior suitable for anchoresses. The second through seventh parts describe the more important "inner rule," advice to the sisters on monitoring their senses and emotions, recognizing and resisting temptation, confessing sins and doing penance, and, at last, loving God more devoutly.

Writing throughout with wit, sympathy, profound emotion, and a mastery of rhetoric, the author seeks to inspire his readers' religious devotion and obedience while guiding them through the practical and spiritual problems the anchoresses would face. (The modern reader finds that he also provides fascinating details of the sisters' daily lives.) There were other guidebooks for the anchorite, but the author of *Ancrene Wisse* went beyond those in his thorough and sensitive discussion of the interior life of the recluse, the solitary heart and mind-seeking God.

The style and themes of *Ancrene Wisse* link it with two groups of early Middle English religious works, some composed specifically for anchoresses. One group, called the Wooing Group, is a collection of impassioned meditations on Christ and Mary. The other, the Katherine Group, contains several longer works: lives of the three virgin martyrs Katherine of Alexandria, Margaret of Antioch, and Juliana of Nicomedia; *Hali Meidenhad*, an argument for lifelong virginity; and *Sawles Warde,* an allegory of sin and salvation. With *Ancrene Wisse,* these works reveal that, in the 13th c., when the dominant literary languages in England were Latin and Anglo-Norman French, a sophisticated English literary culture flourished in the West Midlands. All these works are composed in a standard literary dialect, comparable to and preserving elements of West Saxon, the OLD ENGLISH literary standard, and they are composed in styles that preserve features of the Old English alliterative prose tradition of ÆLFRIC and Wulfstan.

No surviving manuscript preserves *Ancrene Wisse* in precisely its original form. To promote scholarly examination of the various versions and their interrelationships, the Early English Text Society has published all the surviving English versions of *Ancrene Wisse*, as well as the French and Latin translations.

BIBLIOGRAPHY: Dobson, E. J., *The Origins of Ancrene Wisse* (1976); Millett, B., G. B. Jack, and Y. Wada, eds., *Ancrene Wisse, the Katherine Group, and the Wooing Group* (1996); Savage, A., and N. Watson, eds., *Anchoritic Spirituality* (1991); Shepherd, G., ed., *Ancrene Wisse: Parts Six and Seven* (1959)

S. K. BREHE

ANDERSON, Robert
b. 17 July 1750, Carnath, Lanarkshire, Scotland; d. 20 February 1830, Edinburgh, Scotland

A. is best remembered for his ambitious *Complete Edition of the Poets of Great Britain* (14 vols., 1792–95, 1807), modeled in part on Samuel JOHNSON's *Lives of the English Poets.* He later expanded his biographical sketch of Johnson in the *Complete Edition* into his full-length *Life of Samuel Johnson, LL.D.* (1795; rev. ed., 1815), which borrowed freely from the work of other Johnson biographers such as John HAWKINS, James BOSWELL, and Arthur MURPHY. His numerous editions include the works of Robert BLAIR (1794), Tobias SMOLLET (6 vols., 1796), Nathaniel Cotton (1800), John Moore (7 vols., 1820), and James Grainger (2 vols., 1836), published posthumously.

ANDREWES, Lancelot
b. 1555, London; d. 25 September 1626, London

The last of a breed of bishops as famous for the piety of their private lives as for the power of their sermons,

A. was the *stella praedicantium* or "the star of preachers" at the court of JAMES I. Like his good friend Richard HOOKER, A. proved an articulate spokesperson for the Anglican church's *via media* or "middle course," defending its rejection of Roman Catholic "innovations" even while resisting the Puritans' desire to further curtail its ceremonies. Educated in Greek, Latin, and Hebrew by Richard Mulcaster at the Merchant Taylors' Grammar School, and at Cambridge University where he subsequently became Master of Pembroke Hall, A. was internationally famous in his day for his scholarship, becoming one of the translators of the Authorized or King James Version of the Bible (1611). Although as Bishop of Chichester, Ely and, finally, Winchester—and as Lord Almoner to the King, Dean of the Chapels Royal, and a Privy Councillor—he found it impossible to avoid politics entirely (he was, for example, named to the commission that granted the Countess of Essex her infamous divorce, thus allowing her to marry the king's favorite), A. was distinguished for his reluctance to seek and exercise power, and for protecting the spiritual integrity of his sees. His death within a year of King James's is seen by historians as marking the end of an era of uneasy harmony within both England and the British church, King Charles and Archbishop Laud soon launching on the extreme course that would lead to civil war and the Puritan interregnum.

A.'s prose style is often termed "metaphysical," being densely packed and containing surprising conceits that bridge the learned and the colloquial, divine language and human, the heavenly and earthly realms. It is perfectly in keeping with his theology. In a famous exchange with Cardinal Robert Bellarmine, A. said of the English church, "We do not innovate; it may be we renovate," and A.'s writing contains in its learned citation of biblical and classical texts a recovery of or "appeal to antiquity." At the same time, A.'s fascination with the theological mystery of Christ's incarnation, and with the Bible as the inspired Word of God, led him to scrutinize every word—at times every syllable—of a biblical text in order to extract every possible revelation it may hold. His mix of plain and fancy rhythms and images, of domestic and celestial images, reflects his reverence for a quotidian world in which a godhead inheres.

Just as poetic taste turned from John DONNE's famously "rough masculine force" to a smoother, more polished style of wit in the middle decades of the 17th c., so taste in sermons turned away from A.'s learned and crabbed style perhaps even before his death. Few readers other than Samuel Taylor COLERIDGE found matter to praise in A.'s SERMON style until the haunting loss of religious certainty in the early 20th c. allowed A. to be rediscovered as part of the revival of interest in Donne and the meditational practices of

17th-c. devotional writers in general. T. S. ELIOT was particularly influential in this regard. In *For Lancelot Andrewes: Essays on Style and Order* (1929), Eliot held A. up as example of the coherent world view that the modern wasteland lacks. And by including a fragment of A.'s Christmas 1625 sermon in his poem, "Journey of the Magi," Eliot inspired innumerable readers to scrutinize A.'s writing, if only to understand the nature of its appeal to Eliot.

BIBLIOGRAPHY: Lossky, N., *L. A. the Preacher* (1991); Owen, T. A., *L. A.* (1981); Reidy, M. F., *Bishop L. A., Jacobean Court Preacher* (1955)

                                    RAYMOND-JEAN FRONTAIN

ANSTEY, F.

(pseud. of Thomas Anstey Guthrie) b. 8 August 1856, London; d. 10 March 1934, London

Humorist and novelist, A. is most famous for his work in CHILDREN'S LITERATURE. His first published book, *Vice Versa; or, A Lesson to Fathers* (1882), recounts the misadventures of Mr. Bultitude after he has magically switched bodies with his son Dick. The HUMOR arises when Mr. Bultitude cannot reconcile himself to the switch, and so responds to the indignities suffered at a boys' boarding school with the reactions of a grown man. Over the next several years, A. published numerous pieces in such magazines as *Punch*, as well as short stories for children collected in such volumes as *The Black Poodle and Other Tales* (1884), *The Talking Horse and Other Tales* (1891), and *Paleface and Redskin and Other Stories for Boys and Girls* (1898). In 1900, A. published *The Brass Bottle*, the story of Horace Ventimore, who releases a "Jinnee" from a brass vase. Chaos ensues as the Jinnee attempts to express his "gratitude" to Horace. A. also wrote several novels aimed at adults, but it is his tales for children, with their moral lessons conveyed through humor and irony, for which he remains best known.

ARBUTHNOT, John

b. April 1667, Parish of Arbuthnott, Kincardineshire, Scotland; d. 27 February 1735, London

Friend of and collaborator with the leading satirists of the early 18th c., A. published on a wide range of topics: statistics, medicine, mathematics, education, and politics. Though most of his works have fallen into neglect, his creation John Bull remains the well-known symbol for England.

The History of John Bull consists of a collection of five pamphlets that appeared between March 6 and July 31, 1712. A. had met Jonathan SWIFT in 1711, and Swift had engaged A. to assist the Tory campaign to end the decade-long War of the Spanish Succession. A. adopted the metaphor of a law suit to satirize the conflict, with John Bull (England) and Nicholas Frog (Holland) suing Philip Baboon (Spain; the name puns on the House of Bourbon). Bull chooses as his lawyer Humphrey Hocus (John Churchill, Duke of Marlborough, commander of the English army). Hocus, however, carries on an affair with Bull's first wife (the pro-war Whig administration). After this wife dies, Bull finds a more faithful spouse (the Tory ministers) and abandons his suit, making peace with Philip's uncle Lewis Baboon (Louis XIV of France) at the Salutation Tavern (Utrecht, where a peace treaty was concluded).

A.'s *History* transcends simple allegory. Bull's first wife's affair with Hocus criticizes the machinations of Marlborough and the Sidney Godolphin Whig ministry, but in her attempt to justify her infidelity the first Mrs. Bull alludes to and so mocks the Whig argument that a nation may change its monarch at will. By depicting England and its government in family terms, A. was also drawing on the Tory vision of a nation as held together by ties of blood and history, as opposed to the Whig view of the state as a contractual relationship between the governors and the governed.

While focusing primarily on the War of the Spanish Succession, A.'s *History* also deals with domestic issues such as the 1707 union between England and Scotland, which A. had supported in *A Sermon Preach'd to the People at the Mercat-Cross* (1706), and the religious controversies of the period. Despite the divisiveness of these issues, A. maintains a light touch throughout, prompting Thomas Babington MA-CAULAY to call *The History of John Bull* "the most ingenious and humorous political SATIRE in our language."

A.'s other major writing appears in the unfinished *Memoirs of Martinus Scriblerus* (1741), mainly composed in 1713–14 in collaboration with Swift, Alexander POPE, John GAY, Thomas PARNELL, and Robert Harley, first Earl of Oxford. A. wrote the sections dealing with science and may be responsible for some of the other chapters as well. Pedantry, modern education, misguided pedagogical theories, affectation, foppery, the law, and prose romances are among the targets of this merry satire. A. returned to attack false learning in *Three Hours after Marriage* (with Pope and Gay, 1717), *Virgilius Restauratus* (1729) that mocks the pedantic textual scholarship of Richard Bentley and Lewis Theobald, *A Brief Account of Mr. John Ginclicutt's Treatise Concerning the Altercation or Scolding of the Ancients* (1731), and *An Essay . . . Concerning the Origin of the Sciences* (1732), this last another joint effort with Pope, Swift, and Parnell intended, in Pope's words, "to ridicule such as build general assertions upon two or three loose quotations from the ancients." In a more serious vein, A. contributed to the scientific advances of the age. Even before

taking his M.D. degree from St. Andrews University (September 1696) and being elected to membership in the Royal Society (November 24, 1704), A. published a study of probability, *Of the Laws of Chance* (1692), which the preface acknowledges as essentially "a Translation of Mons. [Christiaan] Huygens's De ratiociniis in ludo Aleae." *An Essay on the Usefulness of Mathematical Learning* (1701) serves as a foil to A.'s satires by showing how proper education applied in the correct way can benefit humanity. Although A. objected to many aspects of modern education, his 1727 Latin address to the London College of Physicians in memory of William Harvey (*Oratio Anniversaria Harvaeana*) endorses the use of the microscope, autopsies, and climatological data to advance medical knowledge. A. undertook his own studies on the influence of diet (*An Essay Concerning the Nature of Aliments*, 1731) and climate *(An Essay Concerning the Effects of Air on Human Bodies*, 1733) on health.

A. commented, "I propose no reputation," and posterity has complied. By a curious paradox, A.'s serious works have long been superseded, but his satiric jeux d'esprit retain their sparkle. They repay rereading for their HUMOR as well as for the light they shed on the intellectual and political history of the Augustan Age.

BIBLIOGRAPHY: Aitken, G. A., *The Life and Works of J. A.* (1892); Beattie, L. M., *J. A., Mathematician and Satirist* (1935); Davis, B. H., *Dr. J. A.* (1979)

JOSEPH ROSENBLUM

ARCHER, William
b. 23 September 1856, Perth, Scotland; d. 27 December 1924, London

When A. died, James JOYCE, who two years before had published *Ulysses*, is reliably reported to have remarked: "I am sorry to see that Mr. William Archer is dead, he was very kind to me at one time. I am afraid he forgot it and me." Now eighty years later, we have mostly forgotten A. but have by no means forgotten Joyce: and thus the whirligig of time brings in his revenges.

A.'s most important contributions to literature—both of them more or less lifelong—were his translating of Henrik Ibsen plays into English and his work as a theater critic in London and elsewhere. Of Ibsen's twenty-six plays, A. was the first translator into English of fourteen, published singly or in volumes containing three or four plays, between 1888 and 1905, and then in a twelve-volume *Collected Works* in 1906. Quite apart from the translation his championing of the Ibsenite cause in England also appeared in his many critical evaluations of the great Norwegian poet that A. published in British journals and magazines over a span of many years. Though Ibsen had some other distinguished British defenders during those years—Bernard SHAW, Edmund GOSSE, Elizabeth Robins, Janet Achurch, Desmond MacCarthy, for example—it is no exaggeration to claim that but for A. the introduction of Ibsen's plays to British readers and theater-goers might well have been delayed by a quarter of a century or more. A. had spent much of his childhood in Norway, spoke the language like a native, and, in his early manhood, got to know Ibsen personally. A lover of poetry himself, he greatly admired the poetic strain in Ibsen's plays and was resolute in his determination to introduce to Britain what he instantly recognized as a new and revolutionary body of work.

A.'s career as a critic began in 1879 when he became a full-time theater critic for the *London Figaro*, a twice-weekly newspaper that gave special and extensive (though not exclusive) attention to literature and the arts. He stayed with the *Figaro* for two and a half years. After a visit to Italy where he met and became friendly with Ibsen, A. returned to London and in March 1884 took up a permanent position as theater critic for the *World*, a fashionable weekly journal that had begun publication in 1874 and continued successfully until 1922. A. remained its theater critic from 1884 until 1905, at which point he was invited to join the staff of a new daily paper, the *Tribune*. Unfortunately, the new paper failed to gain a firm foothold in a highly competitive market and was compelled to cease publication in February 1908. A. moved to the *Nation* (another weekly) and remained with that paper until the end of 1910, when he finally abandoned daily and/or weekly theater criticism in order to concentrate on the more detailed critical opportunities offered by book publication.

During his thirty years as a theater critic, A. became formidably influential not only in England but all over Europe, especially on account of his championing of the serious-minded "new drama" and his advocacy of foreign plays in England. A. was the great liberal critic of his tim︿: his staunch opponent was the artistically, and socially, conservative Clement Scott. Not, of course, that A. was infallible: there were times when his enthusiasm ran away with him. Because, for instance, he was sharp enough in 1893 to notice that Arthur Wing PINERO's play *The Second Mrs. Tanqueray* was better crafted than run-of-the-mill "fallen woman" plays by which in its day it was surrounded, he naively fell into the error of supposing that it was therefore a great play. But his excuse must be that he was not alone: J. F. Nisbet of the *Times* and W. Davenport Adams of the *Globe* were equally deceived. The only critic who really got that play right on its first appearance was Shaw (writing in the *Saturday Review* as "GBS"). A. even went so far as to compare the stature of *The Second Mrs. Tanqueray* with that of some of the major Ibsen plays.

As well as his long stretch of periodical theater criticism, A. published several books of critical commentary upon drama and the theater: *English Dramatists of Today* (1882), *Masks or Faces? A Study in the Psychology of Acting* (1888), *Play-Making: A Manual of Craftsmanship* (1912), *The Old Drama and the New* (1923), and *Scheme and Estimates for a National Theatre* (1904; repub. as *A National Theatre: Scheme and Estimates*, 1907)—written in collaboration with Harley GRANVILLE BARKER. He also wrote six plays, one of which had sensationally successful first productions in both New York (1920) and London (1923). It was, clean against the pattern of the modern drama he so much admired, an old-fashioned melodrama called *The Green Goddess* (1921), which played a total of four hundred and sixteen performances, the central part being performed by George Arliss.

Several of his magazine articles, scattered over the years, were on subjects of general social and political interest—education, religious belief (he was against it), censorship, simplified spelling, and politics. In November 1923, a month before he died, he published, in a magazine called the *Guide*, an article mocking Christianity in which he exclaims: "Oh Peter, where is thy sting? Oh Paul where is thy victory?" The article that is entitled "Rehabilitating Christianity," concludes with these words: "When we consider in addition all the hideous massacres and unspeakable atrocities in which Christian zeal has, time out of mind, found expression, might we not anticipate that the first desire of reasonable men, setting out to 'construct' a new religion, would be to disclaim all kinship with a creed so redolent of brimstone and blood?"

BIBLIOGRAPHY: Archer, C., *W. A.* (1931); Archer, W., *Study and State* (1899); Robertson, J. M., ed., *W. A. as Rationalist* (1925); Schmid, H. B., *The Dramatic Criticism of W. A.* (1964)

ERIC SALMON

ARDEN, John
b. 26 October 1930, Barnsley, Yorkshire

A.'s plays are generally acknowledged by both critics and contemporaries to be "classics" within the lifetime of their author. The plays break through the confinements of REALISM with their open staging, broad poetic language, characters bordering on caricature, and complex visual imagery. Through an appropriation of traditional "popular" dramatic forms from medieval pageantry to music hall, they engage with their theatrical past while dramatizing the interactive effects of social organization and political ideals on social, personal, and political life.

Changes in form, however, necessarily signal changes in perspective and concerns. In contrast to realism's tendency toward personal identification and simple statements, A.'s plays emphasize the social context, the manipulation of language, and centralization of visual image actively engaging the audience in a complex process of meaning-making. Ironically, this process has both been lauded by critics and proved a source of their confusion.

For example, complaints that *Serjeant Musgrave's Dance* (perf. 1959; pub. 1960) does not make an overt statement about pacifism suggests a misreading of the dramatic structure. No argument is posed to polarize pacifism and war-mongering. On the contrary, the play's effects depend on the audience sharing Musgrave's desire to end war. Their mutual desire for peace and their admiration for Musgrave's commitment to order, reason, logic, and the word of God draw the audience to identify with Musgrave. When his messianic fervor and rigid logic lead to Sparky's death and Musgrave turns his guns against townsfolk and audience, these premises are discredited. The relationship between means and ends is exposed casting doubts on the unquestioned valuing of order and reason as formative qualities of human life. *Musgrave* dramatizes the process by which even the finest of intentions become corrupted by the means employed for their achievement. Although the arrival of the Dragoons saves us from Musgrave, it also signifies failure. A.'s view is essentially anarchic. The imposition of the ideals of organization and reason on everyday life distorts the improvisational inventiveness that is its very fabric. The opposition established in *Musgrave* contrasts social ideals of order, organization, and logic against the "messy scribbling" of everyday existence.

The Workhouse Donkey (perf. 1963; pub. 1964) is a boisterous music hall comedy set in a northern town. When popular ex-mayor Butterthwaite decides to run for another term, the Tories hire puritanical Inspector Feng to discredit him and his party. The premise that corruption is endemic to politics is overtly stated. The difference between the parties is not corruptibility, but the form and consequences of that corruption. Where the Labour Party drink after hours, the Tories line their own pockets from an illegal strip club. Feng's incorruptibility causes more damage than Butterthwaite's bumbling dishonesty could ever cause. Ultimately, however, both men are discredited as stealth and self-interest triumph over trust, loyalty, and human feeling.

A.'s theatrical devices, especially his frequent establishment of two main characters, serve to establish characters as active members of working societies, each based on moral precepts with both weaknesses and strengths. When one of these little worlds is confronted by another based on different assumptions, the characters find themselves in extreme situations that threaten these social preconceptions. The consequence is the dramatization of the complex relationships between the individual and society, social ideals and their practical application, means and ends. In *Live like Pigs* (perf. 1958; pub. 1964), for example, two alternative ways of living, each viable in itself, become mutually destructive in confrontation.

This process is most richly and tragically elaborated in *Armstrong's Last Goodnight* (perf. 1964; pub. 1965) in which the premises and values underlying social structure and political action are elaborated when two immutable political systems coincide. Each is represented and embodied by a significant individual: Robert Lindsey, tutor and Herald to teenage James V, seeks to facilitate James's dream of a united Scotland by convincing tribal leader Armstrong to succumb to James's integrated vision. Although both live in Scotland, Lindsay and Armstrong inhabit realities so different, they can hardly speak to each other. The way each sees and evaluates the world excludes the premises of the other. The scenes of the play are juxtaposed to emphasize misinterpretations and incompatibilities. The moral precepts that have been the strengths of each society also become their weaknesses. Armstrong's dashing individualism leads to his death. Forced to abandon personal integrity for the good of the whole, Lindsay survives, a broken man. The play offers both a double tragedy and a political polemic. Despite their opposing value systems and beliefs, both societies resort to the same exact manner of dealing with threats. Wamphrey and Armstrong are executed on the same tree, victims of the same kind of treachery. Attention is turned from the superficialities of arbitrary ideals to an exacting examination of their practical application and effects.

A. has not written for the London stage since 1979 when he and his wife Margaretta D'Arcy picketed the Royal Shakespeare Company in protest that *The Island of the Mighty* (perf. 1972; pub. 1974), his anti-imperialist treatment of the stories of King Arthur, was being performed as a glorified imperial pageant. They moved their family to Ireland where they have since collaborated on creating plays with and for their community.

The A./D'Arcy collaboration has been exceptionally successful both as a writing team and as a unique example of ideological practice. The hallmark of their collaboration lies in their active commitment to community, creating theatrical events with the community focused on issues central to that community. This commitment, exercised through a wholesale embrace of popular theater in which caricature, HUMOR, songs, and music hall asides combine pleasure with astute political analysis, has produced a startling variety of engaging dramas foregrounding a strong link between the personal and political: a Christmas play, *The Busi-*

ness of Good Government (perf. 1960; pub. 1963); a children's play *The Royal Pardon* (perf. 1966; pub. 1967). *The Ballygombeen Bequest* (perf. 1972; pub. as *The Little Gray Home in the West*, 1982) tells the story of a wealthy British businessman's unscrupulous handling of the property he has inherited in Ireland. While they are cheating the Irish of their birthright, the English are haunted by the ghosts of the dead. A boisterous energy gives the complex moral and political analysis emotional power by setting it in relief. The play improbably ends with a custard pie fight just before the disputed property is blown up by the IRA.

Radio has provided A. and D'Arcy with a vast canvas for investigating the political dynamics of private life. *In the Old Man Sleeps Alone* (perf. 1982), architecture serves as the central image monitoring the transformation of values in a changing society. *Whose Is the Kingdom* (1988) is a nine-part series deconstructing the reign of the Emperor Constantine in order to investigate the premises underlying the establishment of the Church. A. has also written two historical novels: *Silence among the Weapons* (1982, repub. as *Vox Pop*, 1982), nominated for the Booker Prize, and *Books of Bale* (1988).

BIBLIOGRAPHY: Anderson, M., *Anger and Detachment: A Study of A., Osborne, and Pinter* (1976); Hayman, R., *J. A.* (1968); Hunt, A., *A.* (1974)

ELAINE TURNER

ARLEN, Michael
(pseud. of Dikran Kouyoumdjian) b. 16 November 1895, Bulgaria; d. 23 June 1956, New York City

A. is best known as the author of the best-selling romantic novel *The Green Hat* (1924), which brought him immediate—if only short-lived—notoriety. Adapted for the stage in 1925, the play starred Tallulah Bankhead in London and Katherine Cornell in New York. The film version of the novel was released in 1928 as *A Woman of Affairs* with Greta Garbo in the title role. Later novels—none with the same fanfare as *The Green Hat*—include *Men Dislike Women* (1925), *Man's Morality* (1933), and *The Flying Dutchman* (1939). In 1941, A. left England for the U.S. where he pursued a successful career as a screenwriter in Hollywood.

ARMITAGE, Simon
b. 26 May 1963, Huddersfield, Yorkshire

The town of Marsden—where A. was reared as a child—may have been satisfied with having already produced its famous local poet, Samuel Laycock; nevertheless, A. managed to reclaim the territory in a new voice—one that married the intimate details and nu-

ances of everyday life with poetry, making the "ordinary" poetic. While studying geography at Portsmouth Polytechnic, from which he would obtain his B.A. with honors in 1984, A. yearned for the familiar West Yorkshire landscape of his childhood. If his work seems to share common grounds with poet Tony HARRISON—whose "Harrisonian quatrains" appear in some of his poetry—or local Yorkshire poet Ted HUGHES, it is likely because such nostalgia rekindled his interest in them. In his rereading of the two, A. came to an important conclusion—a tenet that was perhaps the very foundation of himself as a poet—that in order to fully participate in poetry, he would have to do more than read, he would have to write his own. A.'s engagement was realized with the publication in 1986 of his first collection of poems, *Human Geography*.

As a poet, A. has been compared to Philip LARKIN, Paul MULDOON, and Sir John BETJEMAN, the latter whose interest in place seems, as A.'s, to be contingent upon the life that inhabits it. Nevertheless, while inhabitance may also shape and define A.'s vision, his voice is singular in that its curiosity dwells particularly in the nooks and crannies of villages and towns. A. captures human experience, writing particularly about northern characters, with detail and sympathy. In many of his works, like *Xanadu* (1992), he draws upon his own experience as a probation officer in Manchester, an occupation he held after receiving his second degree, an M.A. in social work, from Victoria University of Manchester in 1988.

In A.'s work, authorial intentions, like many of his poems, seem to "hide behind themselves." Ambiguity and circumlocution are occasioned by the unexpected punchline, conventionalized in *Zoom!* (1989), his first full-length volume of poetry that launched his career as a poet. His work, as well as authorial intention, becomes more interesting and controversial in the realm of theoretical discourse, particularly poststructuralism; what may read as straightforward, honest, almost nonchalant poetry—frequently sheltered by rhyming quatrains and various formal verse schemes—actually demands a more allegorical reading, prompting some to ask: what is A. really saying?

"I Say I Say I Say," from *All Points North* (1998), is an obvious comedic cliché, a title from which the poem rolls, riotously, in comedic convention, voicing violence and brutality in outrageous, sarcastic, even unaffected tones. But there is little that appears to be humorous in the subject matter, which is, at most, darkly humorous, dealing with—as does much of the procession of work following *Zoom!*—more somber, morbid, perhaps theoretical questions of death, particularly concerning that of the author. However, the ambivalent nature of A.'s language cautions that whatever is deduced about the author may also be deduced about the reader.

Frequently marked by a northern British vernacular, A.'s colloquial diction—often full of demotic and laconic idiomatic phrases—is very much a language that belongs to the people; thus, in this sense, A. can be considered for the role of reader, while the latter is lent the credence of authorship. For this reason, A.'s practice cannot be easily disregarded, for it seems that much of what has concerned critics is this rather unusual author-reader relationship.

In *Book of Matches* (1993), as well as *CloudCuckooLand* (1997), A. is also concerned with the writing identity. There seems to be the paradoxical suggestion of both the author's presence and his absence. Poems such as "I've made out a will; I'm leaving myself" and "I thought I'd write my own obituary. Instead," both titled after their first lines, are as much indicative of the author's resurrection as they are of his death. A. writes: "I thought I'd write my own obituary. Instead/I wrote the blurb for when I'm risen from the dead." As much as resurrection is indicated, it is problematized by the rest of the poem following in third person, an unusual twist that is similarly employed in the autobiographical *All Points North*. It remains questionable as to whether A. is confirming Roland Barthes' poststructuralist "Death of the Author" thesis or opposing it. If it is the latter, it is interesting that he should employ postmodern literary devices to do so; validity and knowledge are questioned in *The Dead Sea Poems* (1995), and intertextuality is laced throughout his self-reflexive work, as classic texts are invoked. And while invocation reinforces the collectivity of the reader-writer, the authorial intentions here are still unclear. A. has been occasionally criticized as a "self-conscious" writer because of his tendency to simultaneously reveal yet conceal. However, he has quickly become a renowned poet, full of wit and HUMOR, a "front-man" for contemporary British poets; he is not only prolific and versatile but is considered a "serious" poet.

A. has written several other works, including *The Walking Horses* (1988), *Kid* (1992), and *Moon Country* (1996). In addition to his poetry, he has written a play, *Mr. Heracles* (2000), a modernized version of Euripides' *Heracles*, and his first novel, *Little Green Men* (2001). He has also edited, in collaboration with Robert Crawford, *The Penguin Book of Poetry from Britain and Ireland Since 1945* (1998). Shortlisted for the Whitbread Award in 1989, A. was commissioned to write *Killing Time* in celebration of the new millennium and in that same year was a contender for poet laureate.

COLLEEN McCUTCHEON

ARNOLD, Matthew

b. 24 December 1822, Laleham; d. 15 April 1888, Liverpool

Although great poetry should transcend the limits of time, A.'s poetry must be read in the context of his turbulent age if it is to be understood fully. He is a post-Romantic coming into full conflict with the British Empire at the height of its expansion and industrialization. The effects of this conflict comprise the themes of his poetry: spiritual stasis and enervation, humankind as an alien element in the cosmos, and the absence in the modern world of spiritual and intellectual values, values largely negated by industrial growth and materialism. A.'s poetry, however, offers no solutions, nor is it particularly articulate on the exact nature of the dilemma. Among the English poets, his mentors were William WORDSWORTH and John KEATS, both of whom influenced his style and aesthetic perspective. His best work, exemplified in poems such as "Dover Beach," "The Scholar-Gipsy," "Rugby Chapel," "Thyrsis," "The Buried Life," and "Stanzas from the Grande Chartreuse," is outwardly calm and lucid, containing the same sincerity, dignity, and restraint that characterized his Romantic predecessors. It also pursues the same elusive serenity. It is a pursuit inherently complicated by the resulting tension between the temporal or "real" world of distracting sensory phenomena and the transcendent realm of the ideal.

Specific social factors in the "real" world were largely responsible for the intellectual and spiritual division that A. felt so keenly and expressed in his poetry. Charles DARWIN's *Origin of Species* brought new, scientific knowledge that all but eclipsed the established authority of traditional beliefs; the Oxford Tractarians, following the lead of John Henry NEWMAN, sought to bring English Christianity back to a more universal, conservative view, away from the "broad church" liberalism that threatened to become a secular bulwark of British Protestantism. The Chartist reform movements of 1838 and 1848, with recurrent calls for the expansion of suffrage and broader democracy, threatened the traditional stability of government guided by aristocratic values.

To these traumatic changes, A. responded with a poetry of general lament for the divisions of modern life, and the sense of fragmentation that now pervaded the age. In "Stanzas from the Grande Chartreuse," A. describes himself as "Wandering between two worlds, one dead,/The other powerless to be born." The "dead" world of innocence and natural joy was the freely received gift of nature, a world in which emotion and intellect remained counterpoised on either side of a spiritual fulcrum. The world into which the poet is "powerless to be born" is a world of serenity characterized by unity and order. Its genesis lies in the pursuit of "culture," which A. defines in his prose essay *Culture and Anarchy* (1869) as "a study of perfection, harmonious and general perfection which consists in *becoming* something rather than *having* something." The optimistic quest for perfection is an objective with which A. deals extensively in his critical essays, but in his poetry he remains immersed in melancholy. What little hope there is for the future lies in a vaguely intuitive recognition of truth, which is hopefully stimulated by those elements of culture that awaken humankind and enrich the human condition.

In his prose, A. examines the issue of England's societal malaise in even greater detail. Having all but abandoned poetry after the 1850s, he devoted the last thirty years of his life to prose criticism. His essays addressed four general areas: education, religion, literature, and society. His writings on education dealt with contemporary issues and are of interest primarily to historians of British education in the 19th c. On religious issues, A. produced four books: *St. Paul and Protestantism* (1870), *Literature and Dogma* (1873), *God and the Bible* (1875), and *Last Essays on Church and Religion* (1877). All were written in response to religious controversy spurred in part by the ferment of the Oxford movement and the evolution theories of Darwin.

Of much greater interest to posterity than A.'s writings on education and religion have been his critical examinations of society. In *Culture and Anarchy* and *Friendship's Garland* (1871), he expresses his growing concern with the suspect values of a Victorian middle class, whom he termed "Philistines." In A.'s view, they were puritanical, inflexible, and selfishly individualistic, wholly unprepared to confront the challenges inherent in the combination of growing industrialism, expanding population and the increasingly clamorous call for widespread democracy. A. believed that to transform society, it would be necessary to eliminate the classes that divide it, an objective to be achieved through universal education that emphasized the promotion and enhancement of "culture."

The pursuit of culture is at the center of A.'s literary criticism. In "The Function of Criticism at the Present Time" (1865), he presents succinctly his critical manifesto. Criticism, as he defines it, is "a disinterested endeavor to learn and propagate the best that is known and thought in the world." It is this awareness that the critic discerns and shares with the reader who pursues culture in the process that will nourish humanity "in growth toward perfection." A.'s poetry and prose criticism are devoted to the themes of spiritual stasis, the absence of intellectual values, and the general diminution of humankind in the face of growing materialism and expanding industrialism. A. was not a social scientist and made no pretense of offering practical solutions to real problems. His responses are high-minded at best, often vague and idealistic to a fault. In a world that is fragmented and divided among many creeds and material objectives, he laments both the loss of and the failure to achieve a world of serenity characterized by unity, order, right reason, and cul-

ture. In addition to his accomplishments in poetry, A.'s remarkable achievements lie in the standards set by his literary criticism and in his perceptive analysis of England's social malaise in the latter half of the 19th c.

BIBLIOGRAPHY: Honan, P., *M. A.* (1983); McCarthy, P. J., *M. A. and the Three Classes* (1964); Trilling, L., *M. A.* (1949)

RICHARD KEENAN

ART AND LITERATURE

Art has been used to make the content of the literary artifact more understandable by rendering some aspect of the content visually, usually by illustrating a manuscript or printed book: or literature has inspired artists to make an artistic representation of some aspect of a piece of literature without necessarily directly illustrating anything of the actual content, usually as a two-dimensional picture in some form but occasionally in three dimensions as sculpture.

The roots of book illustration in the Western world, and hence the influences on later English literature, are found in the few surviving Greek rolls from the 5th c. B.C.E. illustrating scientific discourse. But there are no texts known as from their author's hand. Around the same pre-Christian era Judaism began to produce wonderful art works to illustrate its most important texts particularly the Hagadah, which not only includes expositions of biblical stories and theological works but also secular legends and FOLKLORE. The plays of Terence were part of the education of the literate and an early manuscript in the Vatican with pictures of the characters in masks as they must have appeared in performance is dated, it is believed, from the 4th or 5th c. C.E. Those few early illustrated manuscripts that are known to survive are thought to have been copied in a scriptorium from earlier texts. Constantinople, Syria, and possibly Alexandria are where most early illustrated manuscripts are believed to have originated. One such, from the late 5th or 6th c., is the Book of Genesis, in Greek, from the Cotton Collection that had 339 illustrations in the beginning and was made possibly in Alexandria in the late 5th or 6th c. Sir Robert Cotton collected manuscripts that are now held in the British Library. The Golden Cannon Tables, two leaves, from what must have been a really extravagant production of the Four Gospels produced in the 6th or 7th cs. in the eastern Mediterranean, are other examples. Book production was very important to the medieval Christian Church in which belief was founded on words; Christ and the saints were often depicted with a book in their hands and churchmen and rich nobles spent a great deal on the time and materials necessary to decorate and illustrate all kinds of religious texts pictorially.

Scriptoria were commissioned to produce illuminated Books of Hours or missals with depictions of biblical stories. Although the artists responsible for these beautiful works are usually unknown, it is known that monasteries were the usual source and during the 6th and 7th cs. scriptoria were founded in both Irish and English monasteries. Their style of painting and decoration introduced different features to the prevailing Byzantine fashion. Particularly rich ornamentation based on native Celtic art and the sometimes full page, grotesque decoration of initial letters were innovations that later extended to other European scriptoria. Certain symbolic representations, for example the depiction of the four Evangelists with the apocalyptic beasts, came to form an iconographic vocabulary. The *Lindisfarne Gospels*, probably made for Eadfrith, Bishop of Lindisfarne from 698 to 721, also from the Cotton Collection, are believed to have been made in Northumbria and show a fusion of Byzantine, Celtic, and classical styles. As time went on the artists attempted to show more realism in movement and gesture as seen in the great Bible, attributed to the Abbey of Bury St. Edmunds in 1130, which influenced many other works produced in southern England during the next century, and soon spatial perspective began to seen in the small vignettes that decorated the texts.

It is sometimes assumed that these illustrated manuscripts must have been meant for the illiterate, but this cannot have necessarily been so since the cost of the manufacture of such items could only have been borne by someone of wealth. The choice of text to be written and decorated would depend to a great extent on the taste of a patron prepared to pay for additions to his library. *The Theodore Psalter*, a manuscript of the Psalms in Greek, is known to have been written and decorated for the Abbot of the Studios Monastery in Constantinople in 1066 and a version of the Four Gospels in Slavonic was made for Czar Ivan Alexander of Bulgaria in 1355–56 with 366 illuminated miniatures illustrating Christ's life. The Bohun family were prominent in England in the 13th c., but possibly the two universities were the main buyers. Interestingly, one of the earliest manuscripts made in England, the *Luttrell Psalter* produced around 1325–35 for Sir Geoffrey Luttrell of Irnham in Lincolnshire, contains some of the earliest pictures of everyday English life rather than representations of Bible stories and characters.

Monastic books became the models for the printed book of the 15th c. At the same time, humanism influenced a taste for the classical authors of Greece and Rome and more of these were searched out and copied. They were also being illustrated; usually those with scientific content of some kind but occasionally fables and plays were illustrated and Terence was printed in Lyons in 1493 with woodcuts that again

seem to show theatrical performance. This gradually led to the appearance of books in the vernacular. Although printing was slow to become established in England and there were only five printers by 1500, William CAXTON was important because from the beginning he published in English rather than Latin, many of the books translated by himself. One of the first was his edition of *The Canterbury Tales*, published in 1484, with its well-known woodcuts of the pilgrims and of Geoffrey CHAUCER himself. Illustrations had appeared well before Caxton began work in England, the first probably in Bamberg about 1461. As well as moveable type, the printers used woodcut blocks, later often designed by an artist of note. This gave the opportunity to reproduce a picture many times and, although experiments were made with copper engraving, woodblocks remained the norm for some time as they gave a good clear impression. At first, these woodcuts were sometimes hand colored, but this seems to have stopped except for the most sumptuous and individual copies for once printing became general bookselling expanded and anyone with money was able to buy a book.

Indeed, sometime toward the end of the 15th c. itinerant dealers known as chapmen traveled with the small books called chapbooks that were cheap enough to be bought by anyone at a country market. These would contain popular tales of heroes or fables, simple Bible stories, or nursery rhymes and were illustrated by a single rather crude woodcut. They formed the major part of the reading matter of the common man, his wife, and children. John BUNYAN always maintained that he learned to read from chapbooks and their influence is seen in the many fabulous adventures in *Pilgrim's Progress*. They were exported to America from the 16th c. until that country began to publish its own. Their popularity continued into the 19th c. when periodicals and magazines became readily available and the chapbook died out. Their legacy was to CHILDREN'S LITERATURE. Books specifically for children began to appear from the beginning of the 18th c.; some were educational but others were meant to entertain. The first of these was very similar to the chapbooks in being a mixture of illustrated tales, jokes, and games. It was not until the 19th c. that well-illustrated books, *Grimms Fairy Tales* (2 vols., 1812–15), those by Hans Christian Andersen, and stories like Lewis CARROLL's *Alice in Wonderland* with pictures by Sir John Tenniel, or tales illustrated by Kate GREENAWAY, were published. Beatrix POTTER should also be remembered for her unique portrayals of anthropomorphic animals in her *The Tale of Peter Rabbit* and its companion stories. Sir J. M. BARRIE wrote the play *Peter Pan* and in 1912 commissioned the statue of Peter Pan now in Kensington Gardens.

Books of emblems consisting of several dozen illustrated mottoes began to be published during the 15th c. and were often used as subjects for embroidery. One of the earliest English ones was *Choice of Emblemes*, published in 1585. Francis QUARLES's book *Emblemes*, which had plates from Jesuit emblem books, was still well enough known to be referred to in Richard Brinsley SHERIDAN's *The Rivals* in 1775. Some maps with views of London are known from as early as 1572 when the Civitas Orbis Terrarum was published with a view of the city from the South Bank behind four figures in the costume of the time. During the 16th and early 17th cs., books were illustrated by little more than a woodcut portrait frontispiece of the author or an illustrated title page with a vignette. Christopher MARLOWE's play *Tamburlaine the Great* was published in 1590 with a woodcut of the hero and in the third edition of the play published in 1597 another woodcut of Zenocrate was added. From then on, other plays appeared in print with pictures of a prominent character or episode depicted in a woodcut, which suggests that such illustrations were popular. Although the theaters were closed from 1642 and during the Commonwealth Government, play copies were still being published and William ROWLEY's *The Witch of Edmonton* came out in 1658 with a woodcut title page showing an amalgamation of three characters and separate episodes from the play. There were of course no novels and these play copies must have satisfied a desire for exciting reading matter. Apart from these it was unusual to have illustrations except in mathematical or scientific texts until the 18th c.

William Hogarth trained as an engraver and began by making engravings to illustrate books before he established himself mainly as a print seller and painter. An edition of Samuel BUTLER's *Hudibras*, published in 1726, is possibly the best known. Although he was actually responsible for few books, he influenced the use of copper line engraving with its suitability for fine detail and from the beginning of the 18th c. its use superseded that of the woodcut. Most books now had at least an engraved frontispiece and occasionally two or three other illustrations as well. It was especially popular to illustrate verse, some by artists of note such as, for example, William Kent's title page for John GAY's *Poems*, published in 1720, or his set of four prints for James THOMSON's *The Seasons*, published in 1730, or Isaac Taylor's frontispiece for *Poems Chiefly Pastoral*, published in 1766, by John Cunningham.

William BLAKE was artist and poet combined. He designed the entire presentation of his works from the calligraphy to the illustrations to the binding of the volume. The first work in which he used his own method of what he called illuminated printing, was a colored handwritten and illustrated poem, *Songs of Innocence,* but possibly his best-known work is *Jerusalem,* published in 1804.

Samuel Palmer was very influenced by Blake. He was also a visionary painter at the beginning of his career and, although his later painting became more representational, his etchings for book illustrations retained much of the mystical qualities of his early work as in the drawings he made inspired by John MILTON's poems "L'Allegro" and "Il Penseroso." William SHAKESPEARE has also been an inspiration to many artists. In the 18th c., Hogarth was one of the first artists to paint scenes from the plays, the best known of which are those showing David GARRICK as Richard III seeing the ghosts of past kings before the battle of Bosworth, or as King Lear in the storm with the fool. Henry Fuseli chose to depict Sarah Siddons as Lady Macbeth in very atmospheric representations of her growing mental state, while Francis Hayman chose Shakespeare's *As You Like It* as the subject for a series of painting to decorate the supper rooms at Vauxhall Gardens. Among others, Jacques Philippe De Loutherbourg and Clarkson Stanfield designed scenery for the spectacular productions then fashionable from which they produced paintings to exhibit at the Royal Academy. The Pre-Raphaelite Brotherhood was formed in 1848 by seven artists and writers, among whom were Dante Gabriel ROSSETTI, Sir John Everett Millais, and Holman Hunt, in reaction against the contemporary taste for art derived from the High Renaissance principles laid down by Sir Joshua REYNOLDS. They produced narrative works that depicted some of the ills of society, from which it was a short step to illustrating episodes from Shakespeare as well as some taken from Alfred, Lord TENNYSON's *Idylls of the King* and other literary works. At the end of the 19th c., G. F. Watts painted Ellen Terry as Lady Macbeth but this was one of the last great paintings inspired by Shakespeare.

The majority of books at the beginning of the 19th c. still only had black and white engraved frontispieces, many of them produced by the Cruikshanks (Isaac, George, and Robert), a family of engravers who, like Hogarth, satirized much of contemporary society in their works. They often provided the frontispiece to the pocket editions of plays by Shakespeare and others. However, Shakespeare's works were often more formally illustrated during the 19th c. For example, John Boydell was an engraver and publisher who commissioned artists such as Fuseli, Reynolds, and George Romney to paint 162 paintings of Shakespeare's characters and then published the paintings as prints with the plays in the *Shakespeare Gallery* (9 vols., 1802) and the prints alone as a separate volume the following year.

The 19th c. brought in many changes in the production of books. Technical advances in printing and manufacture, in the use of cloth instead of leather bindings, and particularly in new and cheaper ways to provide illustrations, meant that books became less expensive with longer print runs and greater sales. In addition, the illustrated magazine came on to the market. The *Illustrated London News* appeared in 1842 with sixteen pages of text and thirty-two woodcuts and shortly afterward other such magazines appeared on the continent and later competitors appeared in London. Once photography became commonplace, around 1890, magazine and book illustration changed altogether.

Writers who could afford to might dictate how their works should be printed and/or illustrated, the choice of font, the layout, the type of paper, and even the binding of the covers. But this necessarily made for a far more expensive and exclusive product and led to the setting up of private presses and the publication of limited editions. One of the earliest was the Kelmscott Press set up by William MORRIS in the 1890s. Eric Gill was a sculptor and typographer who revived interest in book design in the early 20th c. He illustrated many books and although he had an unsavory private life his influence on printing as an art form was immeasurable. Paul Nash saw himself as a successor to Blake and like Gill was a fine book illustrator.

Literature has served as inspiration for artists all through history even before mankind became literate. But nowadays the inspiration is more toward the visual imagery of the moving pictures of film and television and many classic literary works are adapted to be seen on the large or small screen.

BIBLIOGRAHY: Diringer, D., *The Book before Printing: Ancient, Medieval, and Oriental* (1982); Martz, L. L., *From Renaissance to Baroque: Essays on Literature and Art* (1991); Myers, R., and M. Harris, eds., *A Millennium of the Book: Production, Design and Illustration in Manuscript and Print, 900–1900* (1994); Paulson, R., *Book and Painting: Shakespeare, Milton, and the Bible* (1982)

DAWN LEWCOCK

ASH, John

b. 29 June 1948, Manchester

Although A. is a British poet, his work places him more in the tradition of the American New York School poets. His innovative use of image and metaphor, his references to art and music, and his playful sense of language invite comparison to poets such as Frank O'Hara and John Ashbery. His ability to coax out connections between the most diverse of images elicits the term "surrealism" from some critics, though A. attributes such interpretations to a weakening in that term's meaning.

A.'s first book, *The Golden Hordes: International Tourism and the Pleasure Periphery* (1975), coauthored with Louis Turner, studied the cultural and economic effect of tourism on third world countries. This juxtaposition of the modern world against ancient cultures would emerge as major theme throughout A.'s poetry. Byzantine history, opera, figures from the symbolist movement, motifs from FOLKLORE—all of these topics collide in modern settings described in witty, conversational diction. A. has compared his technique to collage, stating that his use of a barrage of oddly connected images replicates the rapid accumulation of information we receive in the modern world, thus making his style a new kind of REALISM.

Casino: A Poem in Three Parts (1978) marked A.'s poetic debut. The setting, the French Riviera in winter, makes a fitting backdrop to the tone of lost innocence in exchanges between a suicide victim and several symbolists. *The Bed* (1981), A.'s first full collection, borrows imagery from other art forms in poems such as "Advanced Choreography for Beginners" and "Orchestral Manoeuvres (In the Dark)." "The Northern Symphonies" and "Accompaniment to a Film Scene" both demonstrate A.'s ability to create a fantastical setting while still maintaining a conversational tone. The following year, the poems of *The Goodbyes* continue to ask the reader to participate in connecting the diverse images of A.'s landscapes, causing critics to characterize A. as lyrically delicate and innovative, but at times elusive.

With *The Branching Stairs* in 1984, A.'s sense of ornament still draws on a kind of fin de siècle decadence, though he places his works in a modern context with questions about meaning, language, and identity. "The Saying Goes" follows a pattern of connection, dissolution, and resurgence; "The Ruins, with Phrases from the Official Guide" recalls Wallace Stevens, with its questions about the naming of objects and their actual existence, and also Marianne Moore, using excerpted material to examine more closely the nature of functional and artistic language. Throughout the volume, A. utilizes lush imagery to call up lush emotion and beauty.

Disbelief (1987) was the first volume to appear after the poet's emigration to the U.S. in 1985. The poet's same delicate linguistic constructs find more American and urban settings in this work, which drew praise from A.'s closest American influence, Ashbery. But with the publication of *The Burnt Pages* in 1991, reviewers began seeing A.'s propensity for the fantastic as whimsy rather than virtuosity, and he was faulted for a tone some perceived as self-satisfied. A.'s next work, *A Byzantine Journey* (1995), marks a return to nonfiction in a blend of historical and travel writing which examines the heritage of Byzantine Turkey, the country where the author now resides.

A.'s *Selected Poems* appeared in 1996, divided into two parts, "Before New York" and "After New York." He served as a visiting writer at the Iowa Writer's Workshop in 1988. His many awards, from both British and American institutions, include selection as the Autumn Choice of the Poetry Book Society (for *The Goodbyes*, 1982), an Ingram Merrill Grant (1985), and the Whiting Writers Award (1986).

BIBLIOGRAPHY: Guest, H., "J. A.," in Sherry, V. B., Jr., ed., *Poets of Great Britain and Ireland since 1960*, part 1, *DLB* 40 (1985): 18–22; Schmidt, M., "An Instance of Itself," in his *Lives of the Poets* (1998): 867–79

NICOLE SARROCCO

ASHLEY, Bernard
b. 2 April 1935, London

A.'s success as a writer for children enabled him to give up his job as headteacher of a London junior school. His first book, *The Trouble with Donovan Croft* (1974), is about a boy who ceases to speak. We learn that he is traumatized by his mother's return to Jamaica to nurse her father, and being delivered to foster parents by the social services when his own father can't look after him. Convinced he has been doubly betrayed, Donovan runs away. His foster-brother has to choose between protecting Donovan and enjoying himself with his own friends. A. has now written a dozen books for children, tackling problems they face in real life, including *A Kind of Wild Justice* (1978), *Linda's Lie* (1982), *High Pavement Blues* (1983), and *Running Scared* (1986). Without preaching, A.'s fictions combine clear-eyed sympathy with moral concern.

ASKEW, Anne
b. 1521, Lincolnshire; d. 16 July 1546, London

A., the second daughter of Sir William Askew, knight, was propelled into marriage with Thomas Kyme after her elder sister died. The marriage was not a success due to their religious differences (Kyme was a Roman Catholic, A. a reformer), and in 1544 A. sued unsuccessfully for divorce. At about the same time, A. moved to London and associated herself with the circle of Protestants who surrounded Queen Katherine PARR. A.'s radical Protestantism was quickly perceived as a threat to the state, and on June 13, 1545 she was arraigned under the first of the Six Articles of 1539, accused of speaking against the sacrament. She was tried for heresy in March 1546 (her "first examination"), freed from imprisonment, but subsequently arraigned a second time on June 18, 1546 (her "second examination"). Despite torture at the hands of the Lord Chancellor, Sir Thomas Wriothesley, A.

was uncooperative and was condemned to death; she was burned at the stake at Smithfield on July 16, 1546.

An eloquent autobiographical account of A.'s interrogations, trial, and conviction is given in two texts known collectively as A.'s *Examinations*. Written in plain, colloquial language, these texts are full of scriptural references and ironic applications of biblical typology. A. countered questions about her understanding of the sacrament with her own scriptural exegesis. However, her interpretation of the Bible was condemned as heretical, and she was accused of denying the Catholic doctrine of transubstantiation and the ritual of the mass. Her recourse to biblical authority only served to antagonize her interrogators since women were prohibited from engaging in theological debate, and the very fact that she spoke in her own defense defied the patriarchal convention that a virtuous woman should be silent and obedient. Her text highlights important questions concerning the Protestant attack on transubstantiation and the mass, but also contains clearly drawn gender conflict and information about the education of women.

John Bale, the Bishop of Ossery and Protestant propagandist, published versions of her interrogations: *The first examinacyon of Anne Askewe, lately martyred in Smythfelde, by the Romysh popes vpholders, with the Elucydacyon of Johan Bale* (1546), and *The lattre examinacyon of Anne Askew, lately martyred in Smythfelde, by the wycked Synagoge of Antichrist, with the Elucydacyon of Johan Bale* (1547). The title pages of each volume bear woodcuts that depict A. standing in triumph over a beast that wears the Pope's triple crown, and this representation of A. as an emblem of Christian justice is further developed through the textual apparatus that Bale added to her work. This consists of lengthy prefaces to the texts, concluding essays, and above all the numerous glosses or "elucydacyons" of A.'s words that in most cases are longer than the passages on which they offer a commentary. By these means, Bale defined A. as a saintly heroine and martyr, and though he may have edited A.'s words to some extent, his accounts of her examinations seem to be genuine; certainly in stylistic terms A.'s concise narration is markedly different from Bale's verbose commentary. When John FOXE reprinted the examinations in his *Book of Martyrs*, he took the texts to be truly A.'s own work, assuring his readers that A. had written them "with her own hande." Foxe also judiciously edited and reduced Bale's additions, in particular choosing to omit the "Ballad which Anne A. Made and Sang when she was in Newgate," a poem that is popularly anthologized but quite probably apocryphal.

BIBLIOGRAPHY: Beilin, E. V., *Redeeming Eve: Women Writers of the English Renaissance* (1987); Travitsky,

B., ed., *The Paradise of Women: Writings by English-women of the Renaissance* (1981)

MARGARET CONNOLLY

ATKINSON, Kate

b. 20 December 1951, York

A. is one of Britain's most acclaimed and popular authors. Critics and readers alike have been hard put to define her work, though it has been described as postmodern metafiction and post–magical realism. Stylistically she has been compared to James JOYCE and Margaret Atwood. Her cast of characters often includes single mothers and their daughters. A. herself reared two daughters after divorcing, and her interest in this theme figures in all of her work. Her work is frequently set in 20th-c. Britain, though, in the style of magical realism, her characters foray into past decades and centuries.

A.'s debut novel, *Behind the Scenes at the Museum* (1995), was met with great celebration. The novel won the Whitbread Award for First Novel and for Book of the Year. Narrated by Ruby Lennox, it tells the story of "The Family," from the end of the 19th c. to the present. The story begins with Ruby's conception ("I exist!" she joyfully begins), and the first forty pages are narrated from the womb. While she was being born, her father was sitting in a pub, convincing another woman that he was single. Her mother had dreams of emigrating to the U.S., and of an elegant, sophisticated lifestyle. Of course, this was not to be, and the bitterness that ensued plagued the family.

As the story unfolds, it swoops both backward and forward in time, following the destructive path of Ruby's ancestors. Although the book is ostensibly about how Ruby came to be, it offers a unique analysis of the lives of different generations of women, lives of loss, longing, and pain, and how the past affects the present; how, in fact, Ruby did come to exist as Ruby. The novel also takes an unusual view of family dysfunction. In exploring this phenomenon, A. takes the position that this dysfunction is not a result of experiences and past trauma, but that it is genetically predetermined. A. plays with language (the language of the narrative, and that of her characters) to create an uncertain world, one that the characters must navigate with caution.

The theme of family peculiarities and misfortune is one that dominates A.'s work. *Human Croquet* (1997) blends history, tragedy, and HUMOR to further explore the land of the idiosyncratic "family." Isobel Fairfax, a sixteen-year-old girl living in a North England suburb, narrates on her wildly troubled family. She also time-travels, putting an otherwise realistic novel in the realm of the magical. Although the game of croquet is never played, the analogy is clear: the characters (and the action) move back and forth, never stopping very long in one in place. As in her first novel, A.'s characters in *Human Croquet* often comment on themselves and the action to the reader, thus earning A.'s work a postmodern definition.

A.'s concerns with language and meaning, though highly touted in her first book and acclaimed by readers, did not earn consistent praise from critics. Her unique style and clever use of language were criticized as "too clever," and having a cunning that often complicated and confused.

Her third novel, *Emotionally Weird* (1999), concentrates on the power of storytelling. Effie and her mother Nora take refuge in an old mansion in Scotland and tell each other stories. Effie talks about her life at college: her boredom with her classes and her boyfriend. In turn, Nora relates stories of Effie's father, whoever he may be. Eventually, A.'s penchant for the bizarre emerges: Effie is followed, possible ghosts live among them, as well as a mysterious yellow dog. The ways the stories they are telling relate to the current action beget strange plot twists and concerns.

A.'s play *Abandonment* (2000) was produced and performed for Edinburgh's Traverse Theatre, and in 2002 she published her first collection of short stories entitled *Not the End of the World.*

MARIKA BRUSSEL

AUBIN, Penelope

b. ca. 1679, London; d. 1731, London

Poet, translator, novelist, and playwright, A. is increasingly recognized as an important early-18th-c. novelist whose tales of adventurous heroines made immediate the issues of trade that were debated in her lifetime. A.'s biography is obscure, even by 18th-c. standards. Her maiden name is unknown, as are details about her husband or family. Her excellent French and mention in Abbé Antoine François Prévost's *Le Pour et le Contre* (1734) suggest that she may have lived in France. She also appears to have been familiar with Wales and the south coast of England. The knowledge that A. preached at Charing Cross has hindered full investigation into the complexity of her work, encouraging the misguided interpretation that her writing was dully moral. A.'s novels are sensational narratives under cover of the promotion of virtue. A. claims, in her prefaces, to be writing virtuous novels, but her plots employed stock elements of scandal fiction such as lavish settings and lustful male characters. A.'s originality was in providing distinctive descriptions of the narrative settings and female characters who found more pleasure in resistance than submission.

A.'s first published writings were three long royalist poems: *The Stuarts* (1707), *The Extasy* (1708), and *The Welcome* (1708). A. did not publish again until her first novel, *The Strange Adventures of the Count de Vinevil and His Family* (1721), which was followed by *The Life of Madame de Beaumont, a French Lady* (1722). *The Noble Slaves* (1722) was succeeded by her only unsigned novel, *The Life of Charlotta du Pont, an English Lady* (1723), then *The Life and Adventures of the Lady Lucy* (1726), and *The Life and Adventures of the Young Count Albertus* (1728). A.'s are adventure tales and she is at her best when subjecting, as in *The Noble Slaves*, *Charlotta du Pont*, and *Lady Lucy*, aristocratic heroes and heroines to thrilling trials in exotic lands before reuniting them in happy marriages. A.'s royalist sympathies are always present in her novels, claiming the reign of Charles II as a standard of honor and sympathetically revealing bandits and pirates to be exiled Jacobites.

A. produced loose translations of François Pétis de la Croix's *The History of Genghizcan the Great* (1722), Robert Challes's complex novel *The Illustrious French Lovers* (1727), *The Life of the Countess de Gondez* (1729) from the novel by Marguerite de Lussan, and completed the translation of the lavishly illustrated *The Doctrine of Morality* (1721). A.'s plays were less popular than her prose, and *The Humours of the Masqueraders* (1733) was only published after her death.

A.'s synthesis of the travel narrative and the plot of virtue in distress suggests how war and international trade make victims of women. Contemporary propaganda might have attributed the growth of trade to the feminine passion for fine goods, but A.'s female characters are denied the exotic finery they encounter, and instead become traded goods themselves. In *Charlotta du Pont*, A.'s presentation of marriage between black slave and white mistress is not a fantasy solution to the problem of slavery as brutalization, but an indication that men use women to revenge themselves upon the society that excludes them.

A.'s plots reveal female characters realizing that they possess value only insofar as they are goods to be exchanged. Yet A.'s representation of the role of women in exploration is not entirely negative. The novels themselves demonstrate the possibility of feminine and compassionate experience of the masculine worlds of travel and war.

BIBLIOGRAPHY: London, A., "Placing the Female: The Metonymic Garden in Amatory and Pious Narrative 1700–1740," in Schofield, M. A., and C. Mackeski, eds., *Fetter'd or Free?: British Women Novelists 1670–1815* (1986): 101–23; Prescott, S., "P. A. and *The Doctrine of Morality*: A Reassessment of the Pious Woman Novelist," *WW* 1 (1994): 99–109; Zach, W., "Mrs. Aubin and Richardson's First Literary Manifesto (1739)," *ES* 62 (June 1981): 271–85

KATE WILLIAMS

AUBREY, John

b. 12 March 1626, Kingston, Wiltshire; d. 7 June 1697, Oxford

A.'s reputation has for three hundred years been clouded by Anthony WOOD's description of him as "a pretender to antiquities . . . a shiftless person, roving and magotie headed, and sometimes little better than crazed." This reputation is not entirely undeserved, for A.'s completely unsystematic approach to his work and his preference for social life over serious scholarship prevented him from ever finishing any of his projects or from publishing most of his research. The only work A. published in his lifetime, *Miscellanies* (1690), a collection of anecdotes concerning occult phenomena, served only to lend credence to Wood's view because A.'s observation gave him an unfair reputation for credulity. In his haphazard way, however, A. did contribute to the learning of his time.

Although A. was interested in everything, his greatest interest was in finding, collecting and preserving antiquities, the source of most of his activity and writing. In 1673, A. wrote "A Perambulation of Surrey," consisting of the natural history, antiquities, and topography of the county. He later (1685) wrote a similar work on North Wilts, *The Natural History of Wiltshire*, composed primarily of notes that A. described as "tumultuarily stitched up." Earlier, on a hunting trip near Avebury in 1649, A. realized that scattered large stones and earthworks around the village were the remains of a prehistoric temple. In addition to his discovery of the megalithic remains at Avebury, A. observed a series of slight depressions just inside the earthwork at Stonehenge, depressions that were later found to be holes used to hold timber and were named Aubrey Holes in honor of their first recorder. A.'s discoveries at Avebury and Stonehenge, along with his notes on other ancient sites and much other tangential information, was incorporated into the very long *Monumenta Britannica*, which is still in manuscript. For his work in these and other areas, A. became an early fellow of the Royal Society in 1663.

Although A.'s more important work may be the collections of antiquities, his best-known work, the *Lives of Eminent Men* or *Brief Lives*, is concerned with human nature rather than natural history. The origin of and approach to his work in BIOGRAPHY is typical. A. began these "minutes of lives" in 1669 as notes for Wood's *Athenae Oxonienses* and continued compiling information until a year before his death. Oliver Lawson Dick has described A.'s method. He quickly wrote down all that he could immediately remember of his subject, and later added any facts, dates, events, or character traits that occurred to him, sometimes in the margins of his first page, sometimes on another page, and sometimes in the middle of another life, another book or in a letter to a friend. Given these methods, it is not surprising that A.'s *Lives* are triumphs neither of organization nor of literary style. Their interest lies solely in their content, which consists of gossip, anecdote, and especially visual details tossed in, as A. said, "Tumultarily as if tumbled out of a sack." These trivial details that provoked condescending laughter in A.'s time are precisely what make these *Lives* fascinating to a modern reader, for they bring the 17th c. more dramatically to life than any other work besides Samuel PEPYS's diary.

A.'s insatiable curiosity made him among the more interesting figures of his time. A.'s work on ancient monuments give him some claim to be England's first archaeologist. His collections put him among the earliest folklorists. Most importantly, with his use of personal details and dramatic scenes that reveal personality, a form later brought to perfection by James BOSWELL and still employed by contemporary biographers, A. inadvertently became one of the first modern biographers.

BIBLIOGRAPHY: Aubrey, J., *Brief Lives*, ed. by O. L. Dick (1949); Hunter, M., *J. A. and the Realm of Learning* (1975); Powell, A., *J. A. and His Friends* (1948; rev. ed., 1988)

JOHN ROGERS

AUDEN, W[ystan] H[ugh]

b. 21 February 1907, York; d. 29 September 1973, Vienna, Austria

A.'s career is often divided into two parts, the years before his move to the U.S. in 1939 and the years after. A. himself encouraged the idea that there was a great break in his career, thoroughly revising many of his earlier poems and forbidding the republication of others, including some of the most famous. The early, or "English Auden," to use the title of the posthumous collection of his unrevised work, was the center of English literary culture in the 1930s, which one critic has christened, "The Auden Generation." While no equally cohesive group gathered around him in the U.S., A.'s influence on 20th-c. poets on both sides of the Atlantic is rivaled only by T. S. ELIOT's. His experiments in poetic forms, his mixtures of the most varied sorts of diction, and his willingness to address both public and personal issues in language that could be either elevated or conversational, made him a poet admired by his peers and much read and quoted by a larger public.

A.'s early interests were in science, and he continued to return to themes involving science or the natural world throughout his career. While still at public school, however, he realized that his true vocation was poetry, and when he went up to Christ Church, Oxford, in 1925, it was to read English. A. was not a brilliant student—he earned only a third-class de-

gree—but he became well known as a poet and oracle, someone whose opinion other students would cite to their tutors. While at Oxford, he gathered around himself the nucleus of "the Auden group," which included C. DAY-LEWIS, Louis MacNEICE, and Stephen SPENDER. Spender printed A.'s first collection of poems in 1928. After leaving Oxford, A. spent a year in Berlin, where he became fascinated by the music of the city's cabarets and by the plays of Bertolt Brecht. After returning to England, he worked as a schoolmaster for five years, and published his first books, *Poems* (1930) and *The Orators: An English Study* (1932; rev. ed., 1934). He began his lifelong practice of revising and altering his already published work by producing revised versions of both those books within three years of their first appearance. *Poems*, which includes the "charade" *Paid on Both Sides*, shows A. mixing the language and imagery of OLD ENGLISH or Icelandic literature and ideas taken from many contemporary sources, especially Freudian psychology. These early works are often striking in their imagery, but just as often quite obscure.

During the 1930s, A. became much more interested in leftist politics, and some of his work is overtly engagé. He also collaborated with Christopher ISHERWOOD on several projects, including three plays, *The Dog Beneath the Skin* (pub. 1935; perf. 1936), *The Ascent of F6* (pub. 1936; perf. 1937), and *On the Frontier* (1938), and later a travel book, *Journey to a War* (1939), which included both a prose narrative drawn from the journals both writers kept during a visit to China in 1939 and a sonnet sequence by A. He had produced a similar travel book in collaboration with MacNeice in 1937, *Letters from Iceland*, which included his *Letter to Lord Byron*, a brilliant poem in rhyme royal in which A. matches Byron in wit and technical skill and turns from the obscurity of MODERNISM to a clarity of poetic diction reminiscent of Alexander POPE and John DRYDEN.

Like many leftist writers of the 1930s, A. felt deeply about the Loyalist cause during the Spanish Civil War. His visit to Spain in 1937, however, began his disillusionment with the Left. What is more, his shock at finding how much discovering that all the churches were closed troubled him was among the events that led to his return to the Christianity of his childhood. A. wrote some of his greatest poems just as he was abandoning his leftist and Freudian views. Poems from the late 1930s and early 1940s such as "Spain," "September 1, 1939," and "In Memory of W. B. Yeats" seem to many the high point of A.'s poetic achievement, yet in the years to come he either revised them thoroughly or forbade their republication, having come to see the ideology they embodied as dishonest.

A. moved to the U.S. in 1939 and took no active part in World War II until he returned to Europe as a member of the Strategic Bombing Survey at the end of the war. His experience of bombed-out cities and displaced persons worked its way into poems like "The Shield of Achilles." A., however, no longer saw the human predicament as susceptible to political solutions. In several long poems written during the 1940s, he looks at the state of modern culture, art, and human relations from a more or less overt Christian or even Kierkegaardian perspective. In these extended pieces—*The Double Man* (1941; repub. as *New Year Letter*, 1941), the Christmas oratorio *For the Time Being* (1944) and the "commentary" on William SHAKESPEARE's *The Tempest* entitled *The Sea and the Mirror* (1944), and the Pulitzer Prize–winning *The Age of Anxiety* (1947)—A. seems to work out his religious and philosophic position. He wrote no further extended poems. Rather, he continued his well-established practice of writing poetic sequences, usually exploring several poetic forms along with several aspects of his subject—Good Friday in "Horae Canonicae" (1955), the natural world in "Bucolics" (1955), domestic life and love in "Thanksgiving for a Habitat" (1965).

From the late 1940s onward, A. was an established member of the New York intellectual scene, although he spent his summers in Europe, first in Italy and later in Austria. He thought of himself as a "man of letters," and he was a very productive one. With only a few exceptions, he wrote no more political poems, but he produced occasional verse on many other topics. Besides poems, he wrote many essays, lectures, reviews, and introductions. His critical works, including the lectures he gave as Professor of Poetry at Oxford (1956–61) are insightful and readable, and the collections *The Dyer's Hand* (1962) and *Forewords and Afterwords* (1973) are among the best critical works of their time. A. was deeply interested in music and its intersection with poetry. In the 1930s, he worked with the composer Benjamin Britten on a number of projects, including the opera *Paul Bunyan* (1941). Starting in the 1950s, he wrote or translated a number of opera libretti in collaboration with his partner Chester Kallman. The most successful was *The Rake's Progress* (1951), which was set by Igor Stravinsky.

In 1972, A. moved from New York to Oxford, where he was an honorary fellow of Christ Church. In the 1960s and 1970s, A. continued to write in a wide number of poetic forms, including varieties of light verse that made him seem less than serious in those earnest times. Yet in the best sections of his last books, *Epistle to a Godson* (1972) and *Thank You, Fog* (1974), he achieves his goal of writing in the Horatian mode: showing both mastery of his craft and a clear-eyed vision of the world.

BIBLIOGRAPHY: Carpenter, H., *W. H. A.* (1981); Hecht, A., *The Hidden Law: The Poetry of W. H. A.* (1993); Hynes, S., *The A. Generation* (1976); Johnson, W. S., *W. H. A.* (1990); Mendelson, E., *Early A.* (1981); Mendelson, E., *Later A.* (1999); Spender, S., ed., *W. H. A.* (1975)

BRIAN ABEL RAGEN

AUSTEN, Jane

b. 16 December 1775, Steventon, Hampshire; d. 18 July 1817, Winchester, Hampshire

Published within a few years of each other, in a period more often associated now with Romantic poets such as Lord BYRON and Sir Walter SCOTT, A.'s six novels quickly drew a small but influential readership that appreciated their REALISM and wit. She has long been recognized as a seminal figure in the "great tradition" of the English novel, though recent criticism has also drawn attention to her own perception of her place in relation to previous women novelists like Fanny BURNEY.

Part of the popularity of A.'s novels today is due to the superficial impression they give of a secure and confident society, but hers was in fact a period of major social change, of increasing industrialization, and of fears inspired by the French revolution and a lengthy war with France in which two of her brothers were engaged. These form the background to the lives of her characters, as indicated by references scattered throughout the novels. As her own subject matter, however, she took the lives of women of her class, lived in apparent isolation from the larger events while actually structured and constrained by them. Ian Watt in his *The Rise of the Novel* (1957) sees the novel genre as rising out of a "serious concern with the daily lives of ordinary people," and dependent on a society which values "every individual highly enough to consider him [*sic*] the proper subject of its serious literature." The most innovative but now most easily forgotten aspect of A.'s work was her implicit claim for the value and interest of the lives of ordinary women.

A. began writing at an early age for the entertainment of her family and friends. Many of the earlier juvenilia are brilliant burlesques of the sentimental novels of the day, but these gradually give way to more ambitious attempts and an increasingly sharp and satiric observation of the social world in which she lived. The original versions of *Sense and Sensibility* ("Elinor and Marianne"), *Pride and Prejudice* ("First Impressions"), and *Northanger Abbey* ("Susan") can be traced to these final stages of A.'s juvenile experiments and to her early hopes of publication. In 1797, her father offered "First Impressions" to a publisher who rejected it unseen, but A. continued revising and polishing her work for many years. In 1803, she succeeded in selling the manuscript of "Susan," but, frustratingly, it remained unpublished, and in 1809, she was enabled to buy it back again. She attempted to revise this also, changing the heroine's name to Catherine, but the lapse of time apparently proved too much of an obstacle. The novel was shelved, and appeared only posthumously, in 1818, as *Northanger Abbey*.

The title is misleading since it focuses attention on her satire on the fashion for Gothic novels, which is not A.'s principal theme. It might well have been called "a young lady's entrance into the world," like the subtitle of Burney's *Evelina*, but as A.'s opening sentence makes clear Catherine Morland, unlike Evelina, was not obviously "born to be a heroine." Neither remarkably beautiful, nor of mysterious parentage, Catherine confronts social embarrassments, makes mistakes, and has to learn to dismiss "visions of romance," and, instead, to "consult [her] own understanding" and sense of "the probable." In demonstrating an ability to learn, and in the basic good sense, integrity, and generosity that shine through her ignorance and naiveté, she shows herself A.'s kind of heroine, and is rewarded with her own romance.

Though more fully revised and polished, *Sense and Sensibility* (3 vols., 1811) and *Pride and Prejudice* (3 vols., 1813) follow a similar pattern. Marianne Dashwood is a more educated and intelligent version of Catherine, whose romantic sensibility, indulged to an extreme, causes suffering both to herself and also, as she comes to realize, to those who love her. Her judgment of her own actions as a series of "imprudence" toward herself and "want of kindness" to others, may be compared with Elizabeth Bennet's recognition that, rather than being clear-sighted and impartial, her opinions of Wickham and Darcy had been shaped by vanity. Her cry, "I have courted prepossession and ignorance, and driven reason away. . . . Till this moment, I never knew myself," is echoed by Emma Woodhouse at a key moment of *Emma* (3 vols., 1816).

By contrast, A.'s other heroines—Elinor Dashwood, Fanny Price (*Mansfield Park*, 3 vols., 1814), and Anne Elliot (*Persuasion*, 1818)—are gifted with a sensitivity to the feelings of others from the start, but reach a point where they have to show their real strength of character, and make a stand for themselves, rather than be pressured into modest docility. This may be seen more clearly in the later novels than in *Sense and Sensibility*, where the over-schematic contrast between the two sisters, a sign of the earlier origins of the book, prevents any real development in Elinor. Fanny Price has to overcome her extreme timidity, and her sense of obligation to the rich relatives who have brought her up, in order to resist their pressure to marry an eligible and charming suitor whom she believes to be without moral principle. Distressed at being accused of the major sin of ingratitude, she nevertheless maintains her stand in accordance with her own observation and judgment. Anne Elliot, also, has to assert herself against all the instincts of her training and modest nature, to give renewed encouragement to Captain Wentworth, but also to judge for herself, against all urgings, the principles upon which she bases her actions.

The moral development of the "ordinary" young women at the center of her novels is not their only subject, however. By birth and her father's profession, A. was a member of the "gentry" class, and related to several prosperous, landowning families. However, her father had no money of his own beyond his stipend, and like her heroine Elizabeth in *Pride and Prejudice*, or like Miss Bates in *Emma*, Jane must have been aware from an early age that at his death her financial, and therefore her social, status would be precarious. The period from 1801 to 1809 when, following her father's retirement and death, she was effectively without a real home, was one in which she experienced more forcibly the way in which women's lives were constricted, and attitudes toward them shaped, by their lack of legal, financial, and social independence. During this period, though unable to pursue her hopes of publication, A. was constantly engaged on revising her earlier novels, and on the unfinished "The Watsons," and the result may be seen in her satirical depiction of the attitudes taken toward young women who lack secure prospects and are therefore assumed to be on the hunt for a husband, or who, like Anne Elliot, are growing past marriageable age. Mr. Collins's proposal; Miss Bingley's hostility; the snobbery of Lady Catherine; the hearty jokes and inquisitiveness of Mrs. Jennings; and the aggressive hauteur of Mrs. Ferrars and her daughter, are all conveyed concisely but vividly through their own words, and in interchanges imagined almost like brief stage scenes. In between these episodes, A.'s authorial voice sounds directly, in neatly turned ironic summaries or rhetorically balanced comparisons, offering a critical commentary on their values and principles.

Only when settled at Chawton was A. able to conclude this work of revision, as well as begin a new phase with the three novels of her maturity. In these later works, A. also shows an interest in the way characters are shaped and influenced by their education and upbringing. Emma's faults are in part the result of romantic reading, but also of too little discipline by a father and governess with less natural intelligence and talents than herself. Her belief that she sees more clearly than others imposes itself even upon the first-time reader, who only gradually becomes aware of her delusions before Emma herself does. Emma's saving grace and final happiness are founded in her respect for the man who refuses to flatter her or concede to her arguments. In *Mansfield Park*, the effects of the different kinds of education received by Fanny, her sisters, her cousins Maria and Julia Bertram, and the city-bred Mary Crawford are all explored. Here again over indulgence, extreme severity, irresponsibility, or lack of principle on the part of parents or guardians are each shown as having damaging results, whereas Edmund's thoughtful guidance of Fanny's reading, and his "judicious" praise, help her to withstand the negative influences of her cousins and aunts. Though this novel has seldom been as popular as the others, A. herself clearly intended it as a serious contribution to the issues of her day, through its discussions of the relationship between surface manners and accomplishments, conduct and principles. Sir Thomas Bertram, though a responsible landowner and well-intentioned guardian of his children and dependents, within the limits of his own upbringing, is made aware of how he has failed to guide his family aright. In *Persuasion,* on the other hand, the irresponsible Sir Walter Elliot is convicted of failure both as father and as landowner, his ancestral home and duties sacrificed to vanity and extravagance.

This novel, with the fragmentary "Sanditon" so sadly cut short by her death*,* are the works in which A. shows most clearly her awareness of the way the society was changing. By birth and education, A. herself was part of the traditional tripartite society consisting of gentry, church, and people, each acknowledging a system of mutual responsibilities. This society, still secure in *Emma* and *Mansfield Park* but breaking down in *Persuasion,* was one to which she was emotionally committed even while aware of its failings, particularly toward women. She had little sympathy for Romantic individualism, but knew that the backlash against the revolutions of her day was suppressing many of the rationally progressive ideas which had been gathering momentum in the 18th c.

Some readers find enjoyment in A.'s vivid pictures of a bygone age, in the absurdities of her characters' words or actions, and in the earned happiness of her heroines. Others sense a sharpness in her satire which has even been described as "regulated hatred." As "a lady," but without financial or social security, A.'s view of her world was simultaneously from within and without. Her writing was kept hidden, her novels published anonymously, yet this was almost the only way allowed her of earning even a small income. The "irony" for which she is famous, that detached awareness of incongruity between actual words and actions and professed values or intents, is the means by which she brought together within one perspective the contradictions in her own observation and experience.

BIBLIOGRAPHY: Butler, M., *J. A. and the War of Ideas* (1975); Copeland, E., and J. McMaster, eds., *The Cambridge Companion to J. A.* (1997); Fergus, J., *J. A.* (1991); Harding, D. W., *Regulated Hatred and Other Essays on J. A.* (1998); Hardy, B., *A Reading of J. A.* (1975); Kaplan, D., *J. A. among Women* (1992); Lascelles, M., *J. A. and Her Art* (1939); Le Faye, D., ed., *J. A.'s Letters* (3rd ed., 1995); Southam, B. C., *J. A.* (1968); Tomalin, C., *J. A.* (1997)

JANET BOTTOMS

AUSTRALIAN LITERATURE IN ENGLISH

Just as ideas of "America" existed in the medieval world as images of the Earthly Paradise or the Isles of the Blest, so did the image of what was to become "Australia" exist for Europe as a kind of "foreglow" in the image of "The Great Southern Land." From the 4th c. B.C.E. onward, classical geographers generally concluded that, for reasons of geological symmetry, there had to be a giant land mass on the other end of the earth; from this emerged the idea of "Antipodes," places whose inhabitants had their feet opposite from where one stood, as well as the hypothetically Antarctic location of Dante's Purgatorio. Even though the real Australia, far smaller in mass if not less vivid in topography and biology, replaced the imaginary one after Captain James Cook's landing on it in 1770, Enlightenment taxonomy did not fully replace medieval fantasy. Whenever an Australian writer is published in London or New York, there is still a sense of amazement, of an almost faux-naif awe that a writer from the other side of the world could produce literature on a par with and, *mutatis mutandis,* dealing with the same issues as Northern Hemisphere metropolitan writers. Australian Aborigines would no doubt argue that today's European-dominated Australia is still a fantasy, one that must be replaced by a partially curative acknowledgment of the devastating effects of European invaders on an indigenous culture that had persisted for tens of thousands of years with little outside contact. On a more abstract level, Australian literature's place in the global system of production gives it a potentially unsettling "antipodal" effect on congealed notions of value.

Nineteenth-century Australian literature is usually seen as being provincial. The U.S.-based critics Paul Kane and Katie Trumpener have recently shown, however, that even the earliest Australian writing was, in stylistic and ideological terms, a dynamic part of the anglophone literary world-system. Australia inherits a Romantic legacy while missing out on the bounce provided by ROMANTICISM itself. Australia's brief window on the pre-Romantic 18th c. (the "First Fleet" led by Captain Arthur Phillip arrived at Botany Bay—near present-day Sydney—in 1788) may combine with the harsh, lyric-resistant Australian landscape to muffle the impact of the Romantic model, especially compared with the later-settled New Zealand whose first hundred years of English-language poetry read like a series of sequels to a Romantic original, albeit in a transplanted milieu. Compared to this, early Australian literature has much more of an energy and ambition of its own, even though models were still European (as they continue to be) and even though early New Zealand literature is, in a strictly stylistic sense, better written.

Most early Australian writers were British émigrés who had literary connections in the old country. For instance, Marcus Clarke, the author of the convict novel *His Natural Life* (1874), was a good friend of Gerard Manley HOPKINS, from whose subject matter his own could not have been more different. Other British writers such as Anthony TROLLOPE and, much later, D. H. LAWRENCE visited Australia and wrote works that are set there. In the 1850s, glimmerings of a distinctly Australian sensibility begin to emerge. Henry Kendall realizes that he is away from the flora and fauna celebrated by his inherited tradition, that he is closer to the Antarctic than to the Lake District. Though his poetry today may seem confined by the normative inversion it chronicles, Kendall's sonorous softness is a major lyric gift that is, on its own, a part of world poetry. Louisa Atkinson, in her novel *Gertrude the Emigrant* (1857), tells a story of class division and moral evolution while giving precise botanical descriptions of Australian plants, also seen in her own drawings of them. This sensory response to the Australian landscape, the attempt to render an impression of landscape as tactile in language, develops a few decades later into a full-fledged nationalism and even experimentalism. Paradoxically, the 1890s, the decade of aestheticism and "effete" artificiality in Europe, is recorded in Australian literary history as an era of domineering masculinity and nationalist excess. Henry Lawson celebrated the working class in yarns and ballads that have a more literary quality than at first appears, and his Joe Wilson stories deal in a sophisticated manner with tensions in a marriage even as "The Drover's Wife" provided an iconic portrait of ordinary Australian "battlers." But the major—albeit eccentric—voice of this era was Joseph Furphy. Writing as "Tom Collins"—also the narrative persona in his major novel, *Such Is Life* (1903)—Furphy chronicles the life of the "bullockies"—sheep-drivers who traverse the routes between civilization and the bush—of the rural Riverina region of southwest New South Wales. The novel makes asides over the heads of the characters to its readers that advertise the narrative's fictionality, while at the same time the represented reality of the novel's setting is so concrete and full of minute details that it tends to break down any successfully illusionistic sense of the narrative as constructed. Despite, or perhaps because of, these complexities, the novel vividly conveys the everyday life of rural Australia.

The situation of women writers in Australia is complicated. Australian society has historically been male-dominated, fueled by the vernacular energies of the despised convicts and unpedigreed immigrants who populated Australia's shores. Rhetorics of lower-class resistance in some ways gave license to Australian men to marginalize their female counterparts. Yet, as in most settler literatures, there is a sense that women writers are not as estranged from the canonical mainstream as even as a figure like Virginia WOOLF was for a time in British literature. Miles Franklin, for whom Australia's most prominent literary award is named, transferred the female Bildungsroman of 19th-c. writers such as Charlotte BRONTË and George ELIOT to Australian shores. Henry Handel Richardson (pseud. of Ethel Robertson) was the novelist to most seriously explore the question of Australian identity as well as most fully theorizing her relation to anterior European cultural models. "M. Barnard Eldershaw," the nom de plume of two collaborating women writers, wrote on subjects ranging from science-fictional speculations on the 24th c. to a scathing depiction of a 1930s literary conference that anticipates the later "campus novels" of writers like David LODGE. Katherine Susannah Prichard was a hard-line Communist who never regretted even the worst of Stalin's crimes. In her novel *Coonardoo* (1930), Prichard courageously explored a relationship between a white man and an Aboriginal woman. Aboriginal themes in works by white writers were succeeded by the onset of serious Aboriginal literature in English. Writers such as Mudrooroo (formerly Colin Johnson) and Archie Weller wrote novels probing into the external and internal ramifications of being an Aboriginal in a racist society; Mudrooroo also wrote poetry and cultural theory. Both writers were eventually thought by some to have betrayed the Aboriginal cause, Mudrooroo by conjectures that he was partially of black American ancestry, Weller because he began to write epic futuristic fantasy instead of realistic narratives of Aboriginal self-assertion. Future commentators may see as a crucial point in the development of Aboriginal writing the publication of Kim Scott's *Benang* (1999), winner of the 2000 Miles Franklin Award, which addresses the continuing impact of imperialist models even in 20th-c. attempts to "uplift" the Aborigines, and portrays an Aboriginal resistance manifested through imagination.

This idea of the imagination both engaging and transcending circumstances is also seen in modern Australian poetry, which ranges from the classically based A. D. Hope to the "Ern O'Malley" hoax. In the generation of poets after Kendall, Christopher Brennan and John Shaw Neilson brilliantly represented stark polarities in the practice of the lyric. Brennan saw himself as a symbolist, and corresponded with Stephane Mallarmé; his deployment of the Lilith figure from Jewish apocryphal legend and his haunted, cosmic poetic vision give the spiritual implications of his verse a vivid, palpable quality. Neilson, whose harsh, working-class life testified to the often adverse conditions affecting Australian writers, wrote simple, pure lyrics of irreducible beauty. Kenneth Slessor is the leading modern Australian poet; his "Five Bells," an elegy for a friend drowned in Sydney harbor, engages questions about linear versus cyclical time and the redemptive potential of the imagination reminiscent of the poetry of W. B. YEATS. "Beach Burial," an elegy for soldiers serving in the African theater in World War II, successfully adapts a traditional lyric mood to the anonymity of 20th-c. warfare.

While Slessor's generation was still attempting to carve out a distinctly Australian voice, that of Les Murray was freer to develop an untrammeled internationalism even while remaining resolutely rooted in local territories—in Murray's case, his "homeland" of northern New South Wales. A typical Murray poem contains wordplay, a daunting allusiveness that manages to stimulate rather than overwhelm the reader, and a firm moral perspective. Though a conscious enemy of the conspicuous cosmopolitanism so often brandished by Australian intellectuals, Murray easily achieved world standing as a poet. Murray was deployed as the concluding figure in Michael Schmidt's *Lives of the Poets* (1999), a role, combining summing up "the tradition" while at the same time incarnating its most innovative permutations, usually reserved in his generation for Seamus HEANEY.

Awarded the Nobel Prize for Literature in 1973, Patrick White was the first Australian writer to earn international stature; however, his critical reputation declined in the late 1980s and 1990s. In *Voss* (1957), White fictionalizes the experience of the 19th-c. explorer Ludwig Leichhardt. The expedition to the outback is a search for completeness, for consummation, but all the explorer Voss finds is emptiness and his own death. There is, however, redemption in the poetic ideal of the quest itself, as well as the numinous, extrasensory romance Voss has with Laura Trevelyan. *Voss*, "the great Australian novel," exemplifies the persistent Australian dilemma of seeing Australia as "the country of the future"; but finding the manifestation of that future distant or doomed to failure. *The Tree of Man* (1955) depicts a couple, Stan and Amy Parker, whose ambitions to settle a piece of land rather than explore a whole continent are less spectacular than those of Voss, but for that reason more successful. *The Vivisector* (1970) is a Kunstlerroman remarkable in being absolutely unsparing of any myths of romantic artistry; the vocation of the (in this case, visual) artist is seen as providing transcendence but at a nearly absolute cost to the artist and those around him. A later, more postmodern phase in White's work includes *A Fringe of Leaves* (1976), an historical novel concerning a 19th-c. Englishwoman whose life is changed when she is kidnapped by Aborigines, and *The Twyborn Affair* (1979), whose forays into transsexuality, Byzantine history, and the meager facade comprised by "European civilization" renders it perhaps White's most original work.

White's emergence did not really change the invisibility of Australian fiction worldwide. It was only with Peter Carey, and especially his Booker Prize–winning *Oscar and Lucinda* (1988), that Australian writers became a live commodity in London literary circles. The plot of *Oscar and Lucinda*, concerning an English clergymen who tries to transplant a glass church to the Australian countryside, is indebted to *Voss* for its theme of European fantasies being defeated by the Australian continent, but Carey brings to his material a savage HUMOR as well as an historical consciousness of not just telling the story but retelling it from a knowing, present-day stance. In *The Unusual Life of Tristan Smith* (1994), Carey goes further and, through his creation of two imaginary nations, Efica and Voorstand, shows how Australia is both beneficiary and victim of Western (American) hegemony. Carey's work spearheads a wave of novelists coming to maturity in the 1980s. David Malouf's novels are short works in which there tend to be two main characters, one having an elegiac relationship with the other; Malouf, originally a poet, was one of the finest stylists of his era in English, yet his impact was primarily political, as his work became emblematic of the movement among white Australians to "reconcile" with the Aborigines. Frank Moorhouse began as a satirist and chronicler of radical sexual mores; his League of Nations series was a more serious attempt to show the contribution Australian idealism had made to international relations. Kate Grenville and Carmel Bird, in very different idioms, expose normative national mythologies founded on the exploitation of women and children.

One of the most heartening developments in Australian fiction of the 1980s was the emergence of a quartet of writers, all older women, who started to publish only in midlife. Elizabeth Jolley's lesbians and other sidelined individuals and Thea Astley's quizzical searchers joined with Olga Masters's sufferers of hardship and Barbara Hanrahan's wondrous innocents to constitute a memorable phase in Australian literature; Hanrahan's posthumously published diaries give an unmatched portrayal of the Australian literary world in all its liveliness and malice. In the 1990s, this wave of late bloomers waned, and the writers generally promoted by publishers tended to be young (born in the late 1960s or 1970s), and often quite talented yet overly hyped. One of these was Helen Darville, who, purporting to be "Helen Demidenko," a second-generation Ukrainian migrant, wrote *The Hand That Signed the Paper* (1994), which excited controversy over its seemingly equivocal stance towards the Holocaust even before the imposture of its author was revealed. The Demidenko episode emphasizes the role of catalyzing quarrels as a way of maintaining the identity of Australian literary culture.

On a far more purely aesthetic level, Gerald Murnane explores the novel form as a medium for prose, as such, that is self-reflexive not in an attention-getting way but as part of what one might call its "mere difficulty." Murnane writes of landscapes, texts, and women that have the force of the real but are always on the verge of becoming a mirage. With a similar emphasis on the sheer power of writing, Brenda Walker writes of mysteries and quests in their most metaphysical sense as she also explores feminist concerns. Thomas Keneally won the Booker Prize with *Schindler's Ark* (1982), filmed by Steven Spielberg as the Academy Award–winning *Schindler's List* (1993), and his novel *The Playmaker* (1987) was adapted by Timberlake WERTENBAKER in the award-winning play *Our Country's Good.*

Australian drama has had the simultaneous privilege and curse of having one celebrated playwright a generation: first Louis Esson, than Ray Lawler, than David Williamson, each of whom in different ways tackled issues of Australian masculinity. Williamson's *Don's Party* (1973) is set at an election night gathering anticipating the victory of the Labor Party and the dawning of a new age of democratic socialism; Labor ends up falling short, and the partygoers lapse into a spree of sexual hijinks and ignoble behavior. Although the setting is very different from that of *Voss*, the message is the same: the redemptive dream is deferred, and nothingness (or inanition) descends in its wake. A later Williamson play *Money and Friends* (1992) seems a drawing room comedy of midlife crisis, but an interesting allusive deployment of A. S. BYATT's near-contemporaneous novel *Possession* gives the play an antiromantic bite.

Australia has produced excellent nonfiction prose, from the grave dialectical optimism of the historian Manning Clark to the venturesome genre-busting of contemporary "fictocriticism" written by Drusilla Modjeska and Stephen Muecke's delicate retracing of Aboriginal narratives.

At the turn of the 21st c., Australian literature has a higher profile worldwide than it ever has had before, and the serious student of Australian literature, while paying attention to recent trends, should read forward in all genres from the 19th c. to see what is truly at stake in this intriguing national literature.

BIBILOGRAPHY: Bennett, B., and J. Strauss, eds., *The Oxford Literary History of Australia* (1998); Edelson, P. F., *Australian Literature* (1993); Fausett, D., *Writing the New World* (1993); Jaffa, H., *Modern Australian Poetry, 1920–1970* (1979); Kane, P., A*ustralian Poetry, Romanticism and Negativity* (1996); Page, G., *A Reader's Guide to Contemporary Australian Poetry* (1995); Ross, R. L., *Australian Literary Criticism, 1945–1988* (1989); Scheckter, J., *The Australian Novel, 1830–1980* (1998); Trumpener, K., *Bardic Nationalism* (1997), Wark, M., T*he Virtual Republic: Australia's Culture Wars of the 1990s* (1997)

NICHOLAS BIRNS

AUTOBIOGRAPHY

Two strands—biographical and fictional—have dominated autobiography from the Middle Ages when Augustine wrote his famous *Confessions*. The biographical classifies a work as "autobiographical" only if it uses historical rather than fictional material. The fictional offers more amplitude, allowing writers to present themselves as they wish, even if they invent their materials. Both forms assume a knowable self or "subjectivity" and preoccupy themselves with the perennial question about the degree to which this selfhood is knowable. Given these constraints the term "self-biography" might have been more accurate over time. The word "autobiography" entered English at the very end of the 18th c., but "self-biography" as a concept had been evident since the Renaissance.

Neither version has been a precondition of autobiography; that is, autobiographers have not resorted to either feature as a necessary condition. Nor have critics leveled an edict, so to speak, requiring incorporation of one of the other, but the form has never broken out of this mold. Over time, the fictive form has overtaken the historical, to such degree that if fictional autobiography were excluded since ca. 1800 (i.e., autobiographies whose "facts" are incapable of authentication by external verification) there would be far fewer autobiographies to discuss.

Two developments have complicated this map. First, the rise of philosophical autobiography in which the biographical versus fictional quandary is secondary, if significant at all (why concern oneself whether the discovered self is historical or fictive if the discovery itself is what counts?). Secondly, the appearance of poetic or sensuous autobiography in which the autobiographer's sensations are more important than experience or reflections. These versions arose chronologically—the philosophical at the end of the Enlightenment, the sensuous among the Victorians in England—giving validity to the idea that autobiography had evolved in an almost Darwinian way. Even so, the overlap is considerable; no autobiography could be entirely devoid of these elements. It is a matter of degree and emphasis.

If autobiography evolved, so did conceptions of the "self"; therefore, some commensurability is to be expected between the notions of self held in an era and the autobiographies penned. This does not mean that eras produced identical monolithic selves, or that a type of personality could not have flourished in any period. But, to the degree that epochs manifest collective *Geists*—mentalities—they also manifested (within reason and considerable flexibility) recognizable selfhoods. History confirms the point in the major writers of European autobiography: Augustine, Benvenuto Cellini, John BUNYAN, Daniel DEFOE, Jean-Jacques Rousseau, William WORDSWORTH, John Stuart MILL (whose autobiography has been the most widely read in English), Thomas CARLYLE, W. B. YEATS, Bertrand RUSSELL, V. S. PRITCHETT, and many others. Bunyan—the self—could have been a Romantic as well as Victorian; likewise, Mill a man of the Middle Ages or Renaissance. But when we learn who they were biographically—Bunyan living in revolutionary England, Mill an early Victorian, and so forth—we expect certain types of selfhood to be represented in their autobiographies that we would not expect if they had lived three centuries earlier or later. The point seems simple but is not. If Mill, living in a secular society transformed by the European Enlightenment and French Revolution had constructed his life around the salvation of his soul, we would be surprised and think him a mystic. For Bunyan, however, alive when the soul's relation to eternity was crucial and commonplace, not to have done so would have been extraordinary.

The paradigm applies also to experimental autobiographies: i.e., works that defy the paradigm about either biographical truth or fiction. No one should curtail a writer's individuality, yet some feature must be present, even in these experimental autobiographies, which enables readers to identify them as autobiographies. It is "self" or selfhood as the primary subject or object of everything incorporated into the work: plot, setting, characters, style, all its formal and informal elements. The key word is self, for whatever else autobiography may be, it is the form par excellence that explains everything connected with, or related to, the self.

The Confessions of St. Augustine (wr. ca. 400), published before there was an English literature, has been so seminal for autobiography that it is impossible to discuss the form without starting here. Structurally, the *Confessions* are divided into three parts calculated to chronicle the state of the narrator's soul in relation to faith; in this sense the work is firmly of the first, or biographical, type of autobiography. A climax is reached at the moment of the narrator's conversion: after this, he dismisses his past life and turns his thoughts beyond historical time to a philosophical discussion of memory, the Creation, and eternity.

Yet narrator and self are not identical. Narrator is the mediator arranging and gathering Augustine's thoughts about self; deciding what goes where and when the crucial moment of conversion will occur. Self is vulnerable before narrator; lies in his power under his will. Narrator sees the entirety of self's past and present; probably knows the self's future, just as the Christian God knows the world's future. The omnipotent narrator views past events in relation to a continuum about which self knows little, existing—as it does—in ordinary temporality, while narrator lies outside, giving him a terrific advantage over his frail subject, self.

Even this cursory explication establishes what counted to the form: the writer's awareness of a division between himself as narrator and the selfhood he was constantly evaluating—the crucial importance of some type of religious, or spiritual, conversion or equivalent learning experience that changed the course of his life. It was less significant whether the narrator saw his life as forming an unbroken circle, or whether the self-knowledge gained after conversion was of one faith or experience. Paramount was the way he would present his conversion, or newly acquired self-knowledge, given this division between his narrator and selfhood.

Dante's *La vita nuova* (wr. 1292–94)—his "new life"—was written before Geoffrey CHAUCER was even born, and was also influential on later autobiographers despite its fundamental difference from Augustine. Both include conversion, but Augustine's occurs in a flash, while Dante's gradually evolves, especially in dreams and visions of the eternal life. Dantean character therefore seemed to move gradually from terrestrial to angelic life with Beatrice—his divine womanly aspiration—implying a new psychology of self comprehensible only in, and through, time. Moreover, Augustine's sudden revelation was the deity's gift; from the moment it occurred he felt compelled to renounce his former life. Dante's self is less harsh: tempered by gradual ascent, it learns the worth of comparative experience as it makes its earthly pilgrimage upward to the angelic. Here experience and action prevail over divine intervention, a view that gradually replaced the Augustinian one but which did not abandon Providential revelation. Indeed, gradual revelation in Dante constitutes the made-over refashioned man.

Many post-Dantean autobiographies, including sculptor Cellini's memoirs, begun in 1558, and those of Montaigne and Pascal, also emphasized the value of dreams and visions as guides to revelation with few whose eloquence rivaled Bunyan's in *Grace Abounding* written during the great fire of London. Here dreams are replaced by visions extending back to the narrator's sinful youth and continuing into his search for redemption. Division between good and evil is less sharply distinguished: antipodes of sin and grace, error and truth, continue to blend—indeed the nature of truth itself is less self-evident in either state. So much excitement occurs in the secular portions of Bunyan's narrative that readers have wondered whether his divine superstructure remains intact.

Nevertheless, Bunyan's dissent (he was an English Puritan) retained faith in the belief that he could chronicle the states of his soul. Neither Catholics or Anglicans of his era considered this a requisite for the religious life, nor did the Lockeans, deists, and other rationalists in the next. But Puritans like Bunyan cultivated this self-confessional mode between narrator and inner-self amounting to a daily, virtually continuous, assessment of the soul in historical time. It was detective work assessing the conscience, as well as interpreting Providence's messages (both general and particular Providence), which relied on repentance within a psychology of sin. Defoe, another dissenting writer and novelist who lived in the generation after Bunyan, also practiced it. But this variety was not the only one. In the Restoration, all sorts of distinguished personages as varied in character as Margaret Cavendish, Duchess of NEWCASTLE, Sir Simonds D'Ewes, and Richard Baxter wrote about themselves to reveal the dangers as well as the triumphs of the spiritual life. In writing out their lives, these "self-biographers" (the word BIOGRAPHY was new in the English Restoration) aimed to blend the public and private dimensions of a person. Yet as philosophies of rational and secular Enlightenment grew and skeptics arose, it became difficult to defend spiritual surveillance alone as "the truth" about the self. Other "truths" also awaited their autobiographers.

Compile the bibliography of British autobiography between 1688 (when Bunyan died) and 1788 and it is clear that *Grace Abounding* was not successfully imitated. Religious melancholics endured; some wrote spiritual memoirs. Far more engaged in the new autobiographical practices predicated on personal experience: a form emanating from the Lockean principle that we are the sum of our experiences from which we inevitably learn—even if impeded—who we are. If "truth" exists and an historical-biographical self to be discovered, it is experientially; therefore, the recollection of, and reflection upon, our experiences sifted into sequences will deliver us as proximate as we can come to the "truth" of our selfhood. Benjamin Franklin's *Autobiography* (begun in 1771 and never completed) epitomized this method: coherent in organization, constant in the knowledge that he writes a "public" autobiography rather than "personal" introspection, vigilant to the transparent persona he seeks to present. Survey dozens of contemporary autobiographers and Franklin's excels. Jonathan Edwards's *Personal Narrative* (begun in 1740) was also written by an American and was instantaneously recognizable as autobiography, even if it was not intended for publication.

These "public" autobiographies were intended for contemporary audiences, with an eye on posterity: the future was crucial insofar as the narrator claimed to want to improve mankind while instructing his contemporaries about how to get on in society and make sense of their own lives. Beholden to their fellow-men, autobiographers such as Montaigne and Pascal, claimed to care about the future of rationality (the hope of the civilized globe), and the possibility of memorializing themselves in their proper niches. This multiplicity of purpose was enhanced by an underlying Enlightenment belief in progress; it can hardly be imagined in Stoic, medieval, or Renaissance societies. Yet concurrent was an anti-Enlightenment view that only segments of the "self" were knowable: in Thomas GRAY's phrase, the lurking "stranger within" waiting to be teased out.

This Enlightenment "self" was also eminently social, and fundamentally civilized, no matter how extraordinary its peculiar experiences and recollections of them. Therefore, when Rousseau exclaimed in his *Confessions* (1764–70), "I am like no one else in the whole world," he stunned the world. His readers wondered what he could mean. Was he an anti-Platonist or anti-Cartesian? No one was sure, but he implied that his "self" exists only to the degree it "feels," and is most alive when in Nature: the field, forest, and ocean that had remained eternal consonant, he thought, since time immemorial. But emotion is subjective, therefore all truth about the self is individualistic, almost existential. Yet if the self is based exclusively on experience—secular experience—which is subjective, then the future is irrelevant. It is only to one's current "fellow men" that one wants to locate this discovered self and gain a place: not for the future but the present.

Such views as Rousseau's, generated before German Nature philosophy arose in the 1780s, were far more philosophical than historical; this despite having altered any sense of history, which is rendered less consequential than among such "self-empiricists" in the tradition from Augustine to Franklin. Why bother about history and society if selfhood is located entirely within? Romantic autobiographers diverged on this impasse. Many, like Goethe, were ambiguous; straddled a line bending in either direction. *Poetry and Truth* (2 vols., 1908), Goethe's autobiographical masterpiece, originally published in six volumes (1811–22), gave signals both ways: Goethe aims to discover his unique, almost Rousseauistic, self in Nature, but without being able to abandon "history" for very long. The English Romantics, no matter how poetic and subjective their sense of selfhood, also cultivated an empirical strain from childhood to death; avid to preserve their biographical histories over a unique metaphysical self lying outside time and history.

The philosophical debate about autobiography after the French Revolution was shaped by interstices: how could the parts of a life be understood: past self in relation to present? In *The Prelude,* Wordsworth's long philosophical poem that in time became the era's magisterial autobiography, some answers are provided. The narrator traces "the growth of a poet's mind" by recollecting the past in relation to present through "rigorous inquisition." He recalls and reflects upon his life as a child at home, as a student in Cambridge, after removing to London, traveling to France, but his "sensations" interrupt him and invade his memories. Sensory invasion, which include domestic interruptions, proves a hindrance because it "invades" memory and distracts him from the recovery of a type of pure, unfiltered memory.

Nor can the poet abandon a life of sensation, Wordsworth discovers. The sensory life disturbs his memory, may be "philosophical" in its own right, but paradoxically proves to be even more fundamentally "poetic" than memory. How can this be? Forever vigilant to the differences between philosophical and poetic recollection, Wordsworth's narrator seeks to locate a region of the imagination where the "inner self" can rest. From this "fixed point of sound humanity," his narrator sets out to discover who he is and—given his civic pride—extrapolate what the best civil societies are. Little ambivalence exists about the strands, autobiographical and fictional: Romantics, such as Wordsworth, considered these to be false dichotomies. There was no substantive divide because sensory experience was nothing to be "collected" and "analyzed" but reposefully and reflectively "recalled."

Autobiography for the Romantics was also a healing experience yielding joy because its remembered "spots of time" (Wordsworth's phrase) repaired the soul, thereby enabling continuity of selfhood. *The Prelude* may have failed as an autobiographical experiment: at least it does not resolve anything about the biographical versus fictional bind, however impossible it is to verify "the growth of a poet's imagination." But it succeeds brilliantly as a life study of the poetic way to autobiographical truth and a healing art form. Thomas DE QUINCEY, author of *Confessions of an English Opium Eater*, took up this theme philosophically and lived it—the healing art—biographically.

De Quincey's *Confessions* recount the life of an opium addict now cured of his addiction. The narrator, not the victim-subject, has kicked the habit but the victim—self—relapses; each time, the narrator engages in another round of autobiographical disclosure until light breaks and the narrator recognizes, from "knowledge unseen," that the heavenly state of addiction is as imperfect as the mundane one of commerce and trade. Apprized and converted, the narrator now aims to fuse the new knowledge with his old self in alternating states of addiction and relapse. If the human condition principally embodies suffering, the narrator concludes, then the state of addiction is no less prone to the human condition than sobriety. The subject's dreams help him amalgamate the two spheres—addiction and abstinence—dreams Freud would have reveled in.

Mill's *Autobiography* and Carlyle's *Sartor Resartus* also demonstrate the conundrums that arise when equally reflective autobiographers cast their books into different rhetorical forms. Mill's *Autobiography* is unequivocally biographical: no reader could have missed it; Carlyle's does not seem to be an autobiography on first reading, but closer examination demonstrates almost identical concerns. Carlyle's narrator, the German Teufelsdröckh, is a "Son of Time" who asks "What is this me?" but supplies no answer. Biographical scholarship has demonstrated that Teufelsdröckh's life parallels Carlyle's (he spent much time in Germany), yet the editor-narrator produces no answers about his biographee. In Rudyard KIPLING's autobiography *Something of Myself*, a fragment rather than coherent work with beginning and end, the author sketches only aspects of his life. What is to be done about such works which appear to qualify for their inclusion of abundant biographical materials?

Such an approach raises questions. What about autobiographies disguised as other forms: diaries, memoirs, novels? Or works where the studied "self" is other than human? Does the "autobiography" of a great house, a famous diamond, even a classic masterpiece viewed over time such as the *Iliad* or *Odyssey*, qualify? To return to the canon of British literature, what about James BOSWELL's landmark *Life of Johnson*, which includes his own life almost as much as Samuel JOHNSON's? Or Edward GIBBON's *Memoirs*, also published as an autobiography, which dissect his life without the overarching plan and stated intention of autobiographies of the Enlightenment? Or James HOGG's *Private Memoirs and Confessions of a Justified Sinner*, which outwardly appears to be a member of the group but is a palpably fictional GOTHIC NOVEL? Or famous novels such as *David Copperfield* where Charles DICKENS himself confirmed the thick use of biographical elements? Or Nathaniel Hawthorne's *The Scarlet Letter* (1850) or, further afield, Sigmund Freud's *Autobiographical Study* (1935), originally published in 1925, that purports to be an evaluation of the whole psychoanalytic movement but classifies itself as a member of the genre?

This inclusivity may be justified but presents problems. Extended logically it will carry a large chunk of any national literature with it on grounds it is autobiographical; or—at the least—that most of its specimens contain "autobiography." But a lack of boundaries and failure to apply the criterion about recognition discussed earlier, means that the autobiographical view of life will extend even further to include everything people do and think. Napoleon's conquest of Europe, Adolf Hitler's holocaust, even William SHAKESPEARE's plays are potentially autobiographical. This is a perilous perspective that cannot be debated here. So far as British literature is concerned, it is sufficient to claim that any scientific approach to autobiography will classify its species into types based on characteristics for recognition by readers. All the difficulty lies in defining and agreeing on the "characteristics." Yet it is little use for one reader to maintain that a play is an autobiography because it contains striking autobiographical elements if another insists it is still a play.

This vexing matter about classification will not recede through the definition of neat binary categories: biography and fiction. In one sense this dyad has always been ancillary despite the historical observation that most autobiographies have been classified on the precipice of its divide. However, it makes all the difference which side the author himself is on. This is not to equate autobiography and biography—just the opposite: to separate them by demonstrating how the latter derives from the former, how autobiography remains a rich source for biography. Biographical data are always implicit in the autobiographical act but hardly identical with it. These are the camouflaged overlaps that need to be to crossed when defining the "characteristics."

To the writer avid to discover who he really is, what difference whether the "true self" is biographical or fictive? That is, whether the discovered self really existed or not? What mattered—as illustrated by Yeats in his *Autobiographies* who found the knowledge of himself to be essentially symbolic and tragic—was anything but an empirical selfhood that he could chronicle each day. Yet the matter of fiction versus truth endured. Autobiography thus bears a crucial relation to biography. Almost all our assumptions about autobiography can withstand the test of truth and falsity because of the existence of prior knowledge of the subject without which the edifice of autobiography crumbles. Imagine that you knew nothing about Hitler and read his autobiography. You might be persuaded that it was biographically valid, not a fiction, and hence classify it as an autobiography rather than fantasy or novel.

Finally, the act of writing: autobiography without writing is a contradiction in terms. Perhaps this is why almost every major, and even minor, writer of the 20th c. wrote an autobiography—W. H. AUDEN and T. S. ELIOT were notable exceptions. The act reflected a sense of duty as well as the discovery of biographical truth. Without writing no possibility of the self-discovery of anything exists, whether true or fictive. The process of articulating versions of selfhood in words and then gathering the words into coherent thoughts permits recollection, reconsideration of events, and adequate reflection for autobiography. Autobiography in the mind alone is a contradiction in terms. We have seen that poetic autobiographers elevate the act of writing to such Parnassian heights that it (the writing) becomes the act of discovery itself. But even for those with less lofty aims—all those in history who have written out their personal histories in response to dire circumstances of war, plague, famine, geographical displacement, bereavement—the arduous process of finding the words and validating

their accuracy in sequences remains the primary autobiographical act.

Few critics will concur about these entanglements of, and reciprocities between, truth and fiction, self and its representations. Yet the lack of agreement has not deterred autobiographers from writing: more autobiographies were published in the last century than any other, so prolifically and widely that by mid century some considered it vulgar to spill out one's life to strangers despite the form's popularity. More vulgar yet if it included private disclosure about dentures, baldness, bladder failure and the like. The first strand—the biographical—prevailed, as ever increasing numbers of publishers offered generous advances to public figures if they would tell their "true story," even if a ghost writer had to write it. Every year the number of autobiographies increased; no one asked any question except the age old one about the quantum of "truth" in the story. But if biography is life without theory, autobiography has not lagged far behind.

BIBLIOGRAPHY: Anderson, L., *Autobiography* (2001); Barros, C., *Autobiography: Narrative of Transformation* (1998); Bates, E. S., *Inside Out: An Introduction to Autobiography* (1936); Bruss, E., *Autobiographical Acts: The Changing Situation of a Literary Genre* (1976); Earle, W., *The Autobiographical Consciousness* (1972); Matthews, W., *British Autobiography* (1955); Morris, J. N., *Versions of the Self: Studies in English Autobiography from John Bunyan to John Stuart Mill* (1966); Olney, J., *Metaphors of Self: The Meaning of Autobiography* (1972); Shumaker, W., *English Autobiography* (1954); Spacks, P. M., *Imagining a Self: Autcbiography and Novel in Eighteenth-Century England* (1976); Spengemann, W. C., *The Forms of Autobiography* (1980); Starr, G. A., *Defoe and Spiritual Autobiography* (1965); Stauffer, D., *The Art of Biography in Eighteenth-Century England* (1941); Weintraub, K. J., *The Value of the Individual: Self and Circumstance in Autobiography* (1978)

GEORGE ROUSSEAU

AYCKBOURN, [Sir] Alan
b. 12 April 1939, London

A. is one of the most prolific of modern dramatists and has written over fifty plays, the great majority of which have been hugely successful. Many of the earliest plays have not been published, others appear in collections after the first publication. Several of the plays have been performed on television and radio but only one, *A Chorus of Disapproval* (perf. 1984; pub. 1985), has been filmed and was released in 1989.

Superficially, the plays seem to be popular because they are domestic comedies about a narrowly circumscribed section of English society, the lower-middle-class suburban household. A. has said he does not write messages or from abstract ideas but starts from something as simple as an overheard phrase and has been compared to Anton Chekhov. Like Chekhov, he draws on common dispositions in the audience to enhance and deepen the perception and possible understanding of his plays to a greater extent than any other modern playwright except possibly Harold PINTER. One such predisposition is the cultural lore engrained in the audience by commonly held values, attitudes, and beliefs that can evoke an unconscious emotional response or reaction. These provide a group identity, define the roles within the group, and imply a common aim. He stresses the comic side and roots it, not in the ambiguity of the characters, but in their relationships with each other and the theme of the play. His audience may not consciously realize the underlying malignant pressures that are often under the comedy until after the final curtain if at all, but they will perceive the ways in which, for example, one seemingly ordinary man like Sidney in an early play, *Absurd Person Singular* (perf. 1972; pub. 1977), manipulates those around him. The whole play is redolent of children's games, but each act is set at Christmas and the games are therefore entirely in context. The audience is induced, insidiously and unconsciously, to accept the subtextual patterning while relaxing into the comic ambience it sets. The sight of the increasingly frenetic action is excruciatingly funny but underneath there is the remembrance of Sidney's earlier remark that he has thought up some "real devils," and a realization that there is something evil in his domination; a realization that the play has actually been a sadly bleak portrayal of one aspect of contemporary life and its effects on the men and women involved in it.

In Western societies, certain cultural lore is bound up in the ambience surrounding competitive games and A. uses the metaphor of competitive games playing in *Joking Apart* (perf. 1978; pub. 1979). But in this play he does not show the effect of someone consciously striving for success like Sidney but that of someone who cannot help winning at whatever they take on. Richard and Anthea are sublimely unaware that their totally self-confident success inhibits and finally shatters the lives of almost everyone with whom they come into contact. The play is set in the same garden tennis court over a span of twelve years and uses the allegory of tennis matches to show how the relationships of the characters deteriorate, how for some people one's self respect is dependent on being a winner, how always being outshone can affect one's mental and physical health as well as one's spiritual well being. The play illustrates the clichés based on a communal acceptance of certain "laws" (i.e., "let the best man win," and "the weakest must go to the wall") by which many live in contemporary society.

Not directly political, the play nonetheless demonstrates many of the ills in modern society that more radical dramatists are also trying to depict.

As he has continued writing, A.'s comedy has covered ever more disturbing and unhappy truths. *Absent Friends* (1974) explores happiness and finds it lacking in most lives. *Just Between Ourselves* (perf. 1976; pub. 1978) shows how the insensitivity of a well-meaning husband can inhibit his wife so much she becomes catatonic in a play that allegorizes Dennis's lack of understanding of Vera's situation by his incompetence with the simplest household repairs. Susan in *Woman in Mind* (perf. 1985; pub. 1986) hallucinates and her ideal family appears on stage to contrast with the reality of the relationships that are sending her insane. A. becomes more political in *A Small Family Business* (1987) in which he shows the effects on his characters of the selfish greed of Margaret Thatcher's Britain and in *Man of the Moment* (perf. 1989; pub. 1989) he explores the idea of a moral reality when the perception of who is a hero or a villain is reversed, especially as television exploits and distorts both.

A. is unique in his use of the performance space, incorporating innovative staging and juxtaposing happenings in different time frames into the substance of the plot so as to enhance the point of his theme. In *How the Other Half Loves* (perf. 1969; pub. 1971), he illustrates the complex jockeying for position between three couples whose husbands work for the same firm by placing two separate living rooms in the same stage space with simultaneous conversations taking place in each, and then sets a merged dinner party in this stage space although it is supposedly two different dinners taking place on separate evenings in each room. The hapless under manager and his wife swing on revolving chairs from one dinner to the other neatly showing both the different lifestyles of the other couples and the tensions in the business relationships between the three men and their wives. This theatrical usage becomes even more subtly complex in his later plays. *The Norman Conquests* (perf. 1973; pub. 1975) consists of three related plays that take place in different rooms of the same house and explore the same situation from different characters' viewpoints. In *Bedroom Farce* (perf. 1975; pub. 1977), none of the characters engage in sex and there is only one double entendre. The setting, of three bedrooms in different houses but side by side on the stage, is used to show how the bedroom is where a couple work out their strategies for living in the everyday routines of married life. The hilarious comedy arises as these strategies impinge on the other couples. In *Sisterly Feelings* (perf. 1978; pub. 1981), the actors/characters toss a coin at the end of scenes to determine which version of the following scene they should play which provides the plot with four variations toward the same ending. *Taking Steps* (perf. 1979; pub. 1981) is set in a three-story house in the same stage space in which simultaneous actions takes place on the ground floor, in the bedroom, and in the attic as a marriage is examined. *Way Upstream* (perf. 1981; pub. 1983) is set on a real boat as the characters cruise up river (in a tank of water) in a political metaphor to Armageddon Bridge. *The Time of My Life* (perf. 1993; pub. 1983) and *Communicating Doors* (perf. 1995; pub. 1995) both use three different time zones, the latter in a single hotel bedroom. A.'s expertise is apparent in that his staging requires little change to fit both the theater in the round in which they are usually first presented and the proscenium arch theaters to which they often transfer; both the staging and the content are as effective in one as in the other.

Almost all A.'s plays are presented first in the round at his theater in Scarborough, England, and are directed by himself, before an audience of summer holiday makers from the class in society that is depicted on stage. Dramatists demonstrate the cruelties and absurdities of life in their own idiosyncratic ways, often using new forms or structures or an intellectual code that presupposes a certain academic standard or knowledge. A.'s plays are in a conventionally comic form more accessible to, and thus popular with, the suburban middle class they usually depict. The plays then often transfer to a proscenium theater in London before a supposedly more sophisticated audience, with whom they are as successful, seeming to touch a universal chord with most "ordinary" playgoers not only in English-speaking countries but also in most others, for the plays appear in translation all over the world. While ignored for a time by the intelligentsia, his work is now being seen as relevant to today's thought even if only in demonstrating the commonplace in a comic guise, or the attitudes, behavior, aspirations, fears, and beliefs of those who live the commonplace. His use of all the possibilities of space and time to explore these facets of human life in terms of theater is acknowledged as second to none.

BIBLIOGRAPHY: Allen, P., *A. A.* (2002); Billington, M., *A. A.* (1983); Innes, C., *Modern British Drama, 1890–1990* (1992); Page, M., *File on A.* (1989); Watson, I., *Conversations with A.* (1981; rev. ed., 1988)

DAWN LEWCOCK

B

BACON, [Sir] Francis
b. 22 January 1561, London; d. 9 April 1626, London

Lord Chancellor of England, philosopher, and man of letters, B. was one of the most original thinkers of the 16th and 17th cs., and one of the first modern philosophers of science. Taking "all knowledge for my province," he proposed to reorganize natural philosophy and to found it on the experimental method. As an essayist, he is among the masters of English prose. The French encyclopedists praised his system of classification and his turn to experimental method. Enlightenment figures such as Thomas Jefferson and Immanuel Kant admired the breadth and penetration of his mind. More recent thinkers find in the Baconian project the foundations of instrumental reason and express concern over the focus on knowledge, power and the domination of nature.

B.'s life is marked by unbridled ambition, leading Alexander POPE to characterize him as "The wisest, brightest, meanest of mankind." Born among the political elite, he became a barrister and member of Parliament, seeking preferment and political advancement, serving as solicitor general and attorney general before becoming Lord Chancellor and Baron Verulam in 1618 under JAMES I. He was created Viscount St. Albans in 1621. Three months later, he fell from power over charges of bribery. In his famous essay on B., Thomas Babington MACAULAY said of him, "so much glory, so much shame."

B.'s reputation as an essayist and master of prose rests on his *Essays*. Inspired by Montaigne's *Essais* (1580), and Seneca's epistles, B.'s *Essays* went through three stages of development. The 1597 edition consisted of ten brief compositions, including *Of studie*, *Of discourse*, *Of expense*, and *Of Honour and reputation*. Each essay was essentially a list of aphorisms on the topic of the title. B. expanded these to produce a second edition, including thirty-eight essays in 1612. Finally, *Essays or Counsels, Civill and Morell* appeared in 1625, containing fifty-eight es-

says. Aimed at a general readership, B.'s style is aphoristic and provocative. Deploying balance and contrast, he constructs a series of statements confirming or refuting a thesis. Taken together, the *Essays* study human life from a sociological and psychological viewpoint.

B.'s most significant contributions to the philosophy of science are in *The Advancement of Learning* (1605), expanded to the Latin, *De augmentis* (1623), and the fragmentary *Instauration Magnae*, of which only the second book, the *Novum Organum* (1620), was largely completed.

The Advancement of Learning has two goals, the division and classification of human learning, and a critique of current systems of knowledge. B. divided learning according to the faculties of the mind. Thus history was related to memory, poetry to imagination, and philosophy to reason. More influential was B.'s attack on the authority of the ancients, especially Aristotle. Science had failed because deductive logic and scholastic systems were too narrow to interpret nature.

The *Great Instauration* was the outline of B.'s projected complete system of nature. It was to be divided into six books: *The Divisions of the Sciences*, *The New Instrument* (*Novum Organum*), *The Phenomena of the Universe*, *The Ladder of the Understanding*, *The Forerunners of the New Philosophy*, and finally, *The Second Philosophy or Active Sciences* (*Philosophia Secunda, sive scientia activa*). Second Philosophy alludes to and contrasts with Aristotle's First Philosophy (*Metaphysics*). Of this outline, *The Advancement of Learning* approximates what was probably intended for *The Divisions*. Elements of *The Phenomena of the Universe* are probably found in various other published writings such as *Historia Naturalis et Experimentalis* (1622) and *Sylva Sylvarum* (1627).

The Novum Organum alludes to the body of Aristotle's books on logic, which represented for scholastic philosophy and science, the tools of all enquiry.

B.'s new tool builds on three premises: First, men cannot know more than they can observe. Second, neither observation nor reason alone will unlock the workings of nature. Rather, they must interact together. Third, knowledge and power are inseparable. Where cause is not known, the effect cannot be produced. From these, B. develops his new method. The discovery of nature is a collective activity. No one mind has sufficient capacity, being limited by various "anticipations," hypotheses, or assumptions that color and distort our observations. B. classifies these under the four idols: idols of the tribe, those factors related to our species; idols of the cave, those related to our education; idols of the market, those related to language; and idols of the theater, those related to abstract systems. The most innovative part of B.'s logic of induction is the process of exclusion. The negative is more important in establishing an axiom than a positive, anticipating the modern principle that the laws of nature cannot be verified, but defective theories can be falsified.

The New Atlantis, published posthumously in 1627, is B.'s contribution to the literature of utopias. Indebted to Sir Thomas MORE's *Utopia* and Plato's *Republic*, B. imagines the island of Bensalem (The Good Jerusalem). Here is located Salomon House, an institution dedicated to the collective scientific enterprise envisioned in *The Novum Organum*.

BIBLIOGRAPHY: Green, A. W., *Sir F. B.* (1966); Pérez-Ramos, A., *F. B.'s Idea of Science and the Maker's Knowledge Tradition* (1988); Quinton, A., *F. B.* (1980); Vickers, B., *F. B. and Renaissance Prose* (1968)

THOMAS L. COOKSEY

BACON, Roger
b. ca. 1214; d. 1292 or after, possibly 1294, Oxford

Diversely talented and broad of interest, B.'s investigations into philosophy, logic, and mathematics, his three-volume compendium of realms of knowledge, and especially his reputation (only partially deserved) for "modern" scientific empiricism earned him the sobriquet "Doctor Mirabilis" in his time. Of little influence during the years much beyond his death, B. was rediscovered by the Elizabethans, for whom he served as a model of the "new science" espoused by Francis BACON and others.

B.'s primary work is his encyclopedia of the sciences, which meant for him the full scope of human learning. In three books written ca. 1267 (*Opus Maius* (Major Work), *Opus minus* (Minor Work), and *Opus tertium* (Third Work), B. attempted to argue the compatibility and value of scientific methods and discovery to Christian understanding. In form and general approach, the *Opera* are remarkably scholastic, but

unlike many such works of the period, B.'s volumes take critical positions on social abuses and magic, offer suggested reforms of education, and propose changes in calculation of the calendar. B.'s last major work, the *Compendium studii theologiae* (1292; Compendium on the Study of Theology), shows influence of his later experimentalism, his strong dislike of continued social disintegration, and an acquaintance with the mysticism of Joachim of Flora.

Little is known of his early years. Suggestive references in his works indicate his English origin, possibly in Somerset, where the town of Ilchester has laid claim to his birth, although no confirmation exists among remaining church records there. Apparently of good family, with sufficient fortune to help with his education, to purchase books and, later, scientific apparatus, B. studied at Oxford and the University of Paris, from which latter he received the degree of Master of Arts in 1240. B. remained in Paris, lecturing on Aristotle's natural philosophy at the university, until ca. 1247, when he returned to Oxford. There he mastered Greek and Hebrew, and continued to lecture, branching out into mathematics and logic. His works of the period show influences of Grosseteste and familiarity with Arab scholars. At this same time, B. apparently began to perform empirical experiments in earnest, optics being his primary interest.

In 1257, for whatever reason, B. joined the Franciscan Order—a decision, nonetheless, of some consequence for his future, as the Order took issue with his writings and experiments, causing B. to appeal to the future Pope Clement IV for affirmation and assistance in furthering his great project, his encyclopedia of the sciences in three volumes. This he must have received, for the *Opera* were the fruit of B.'s next years. However, again for unknown reasons (the formal charge refers to "certain suspect novelties"), B.'s project was condemned as heretical by the head of the Order in 1278, resulting in his rejection from the Franciscans, and probable imprisonment of several years' duration. It is thus possible that B.'s last work was completed under severe conditions. B. died in Oxford, as far as is known a free man.

Although B.'s experimenting contributed notably to the introduction of scientific empiricism to Western European thought, his goal of conforming science to the service of the 13th-c. church marks his effort as entirely medieval. B.'s reputation, then, as anachronistically "modern" is perhaps somewhat exaggerated, as is his involvement with the inventions (the magnifying glass, gunpowder, telescopes, microscopes, lighter-than-air flying machines) with which his name is often associated.

BIBLIOGRAPHY: Crowley, T., *R. B.* (1950); Easton, S. C., *R. B. and His Search for a Universal Science*

(1950); Lindberg, D. C., *Science in the Middle Ages* (1978)

R. F. YEAGER

BAGE, Robert

b. 29? February 1728, Darley; d. 1 September 1801, Tamworth

Owner and operator of a successful paper mill, B. in middle age turned to the writing of novels to distract himself after an iron mill in which he was a partner failed, costing him the substantial sum of £1,500. Although B. claimed that "the want of books to assist him in any other literary undertaking" drove him to write fiction, he in fact read widely and was the friend of such leading intellectuals as Erasmus DARWIN, Joseph Priestley, and William Hutton. B. shared their progressive outlook, which he embodied in his six novels. The epistolary form of the first four derives from Samuel RICHARDSON, but the comic spirit that pervades B.'s works shows his greater debt to Henry FIELDING, Tobias SMOLLETT, and Laurence STERNE.

Mount Henneth (2 vols., 1782) owes its premise to Samuel Jackson Pratt's *Shenstone-Green; or, The New Paradise Lost* (1779), which in turn was inspired by the poet William SHENSTONE's lines, "Had I a Fortune of Eight or Ten Thousand Pounds a year/I would build myself a Neighbourhood." Pratt's novel highlights the comical frustrations of Sir Benjamin Beauchamp to put Shenstone's idea into practice. B. shows the more practical James Foston's success in establishing a functioning middle-class UTOPIA in a rural setting. As he would in subsequent novels, B. in this work rejects the aristocratic values exemplified by the Stanleys and Caradocs. B. also attacks slavery, colonialism, and negative national stereotypes. A deist, B. urges toleration of all religions.

In *Barham Downs* (1784), the good-natured London lawyer William Wyman corresponds with Henry Osmond, who has retired to the countryside after being jilted by the socially ambitious Lucy Strode. B. probably based this novel on Richard GRAVES's *Columella*, in which a young man also withdraws from active life. Osmond finally rejects retirement to save Annabella Whitaker from the dissipated Lord Winterbottom. Winterbottom's pursuit of Annabella recalls Richardson's *Pamela* and *Clarissa*, but B.'s characters lack the psychological depth that Richardson provided. Instead, B. focuses on political and social issues, highlighting the corruption of the aristocracy, the evils of colonialism, and the flaws in a legal system that hangs those compelled to choose between stealing and starving.

The Fair Syrian (1787) demonstrates that good character is superior to good birth. Sir John Amington and the Marquis de St. Claur marry commoners more worthy of their love than rich or titled women. B.

praises America for its freedom and belief in self-reliance, unlike the hierarchical, overly sophisticated Old World. As B. so often does at the end of his novels, he here brings together a diverse group of people in an ideal middle-class society.

Judith Lamounde rejects Sir Anthony Havelley's marriage proposal in *James Wallace* (1788), preferring the merit of the title character to Sir Anthony's rank. Aristocrats appear as boorish or worse: Sir Everard Moreton is a rake. Like Tom Jones, Wallace learns to combine prudence with his good nature. George Paradyne in *Man as He Is* (1792) must choose between a life devoted to selfish aristocratic pleasure and one of active benevolence. In the course of a novel filled with incident, he discovers that only the latter yields happiness. B. attacks his usual targets: religious bigotry embodied in the Anglican priest Holford; dogmatic systematizers like Miss Hawbert, who becomes a convert to whatever philosopher she has read most recently; slavery; luxury. B. responds to Edmund BURKE's *Reflections on the French Revolution* with its glorification of the *ancien régime*: "The age of chivalry, heaven be praised, is gone. The age of truth and reason has commenced."

Hermsprong; or, Man as He Is Not (1796), B.'s last novel and generally regarded as his best, owes much to Voltaire's *L'Ingénu* (1767). Though Hermsprong proves to be Sir Charles Campinet rather than a Native American, he rejects the aristocratic values of the foppish Sir Philip Chestrum, the greed and political chicanery of Lord Grondale, and the religious bigotry of Dr. Blick.

Regarded by the forces of reaction of his day as radical, B. was truly revolutionary only in his emphasis on female equality. Hermsprong argues for equal education for women, and Sir George Osmond in *Barham Downs* condemns the prevailing sexual double standard. Politically, B. was more conventional. His middle-class heroes often prove to have noble blood, and they endorse the British constitution. B. shows little sympathy with striking miners in *Hermsprong*, and he never supported the redistribution of land or wealth. The conservative Sir Walter SCOTT nonetheless objected to some of B.'s views, but reprinted three of B.'s early novels (*Mount Henneth, Barham Downs,* and *James Wallace*). In his introduction to B.'s works, Scott offered the best reason for continuing to read them: "A light, gay, pleasing air, carries us agreeably through Bage's novels, and . . . we are reconciled to the author by the ease and good humor of his style."

BIBLIOGRAPHY: Faulkner, P., *R. B.* (1979); Kelly, G., *The English Jacobin Novel 1780–1805* (1976); Steeves, H. R., *Before Jane Austen* (1966); Tompkins, J. M. S., *The Popular Novel in England, 1770–1800* (1932)

JOSEPH ROSENBLUM

BAGNOLD, Enid [Algerine]
b. 27 October 1889, Rochester, Kent; d. 31 March 1981, London

Although as an author B. is now only remembered for her novel *National Velvet* (1935) and play *The Chalk Garden* (perf. 1955; pub. 1956), she has aroused interest in women's studies as one of the free-thinking "new women," whose strength of character and independence of spirit made an impact on London life just after World War I. These virtues are most evident in her work as are her faults of pretentiousness and self-satisfaction.

B.'s father was a colonel in the Royal Engineers, her education excellent in a school run by Aldous HUXLEY's mother. As a young woman, B. moved in high Bohemian circles—painting with Walter Richard Sickert and Henri Gaudier-Brzeska, being seduced by the prolific journalist and womanizer Frank HARRIS—and was also at ease in the aristocratic society of Asquiths and Bibescos, where her intelligence and spark were appreciated.

During the First World War, B. worked as a volunteer nurse and the exposé of the inhumane and incompetent hospital system in her first book, *A Diary without Dates* (1918), gave her instant fame, as her marriage to Sir Roderick Jones, proprietor, later chairman of Reuters, gave her riches and a social position that she used with aplomb.

Serena Blandish (1924) has a structure obviously inspired by Voltaire's *Candide* and concerns a penniless young girl whose eagerness to marry, with the aid of a Brazilian countess, meets with a strange result. The book's success appalled B.'s father, who thought his daughter was portraying herself as a fortune hunter of loose morals.

One of B.'s most attractive qualities was her liking for and understanding of children, happily evident in two works of the 1930s: *National Velvet* is a children's classic where the poor butcher's daughter and her horse "The Pie" win the Grand National. It is a paean to middle-class life and the film version (1944) with the young Elizabeth Taylor still gives pleasure; *The Squire* (1938; repub. as *The Door of Life*, 1938), set in an entirely female circle, centers on giving birth in graphic purple prose and describes early motherhood with a perspicacity with which many new mothers have identified.

Her first plays are not marvelous. The best is *Lottie Dundas* (1943), a psychological thriller about a dying actress who murders to play a coveted role, but in *The Chalk Garden*, B. wrote one of the most admired and successful plays of the mid-1950s. In form a conventional English drawing room drama, its intriguing theme and symbolism expressed in ornate language gives the work a universality with equal appeal in all English-speaking countries. The mysterious Miss Madrigal enters the household of Mrs. St. Maugham, once doyenne of a glittering society and her pyromaniac and mythomane granddaughter Laurel, as a breath of life, the power of salvation to the old woman whose garden will not flourish on its soil of chalk any more than Laurel will flourish in her care. Madrigal is revealed, by the unlucky accident of the judge who sentenced her coming to lunch, as a murderer but she revitalizes the lives of the small world she has entered and leaves the child liberated and Mrs. St. Maugham a hopeful pupil to Madrigal's enquiring guide. The play exerts an indefinable hold in spite of some self-conscious overwriting. It was championed by the American producer Irene Selznick, who presented it sumptuously in New York with Gladys Cooper and Siobhan McKenna with designs by Cecil Beaton and coproduced it in London with Edith Evans and Peggy Ashcroft.

None of B.'s subsequent plays were of the same stature, but *The Chinese Prime Minister* (1964) is superior to its first critical reception. An old actress—a portrait of wit and empathy—is striving to find a guide, "a Chinese Prime Minister," a wise man who, on retirement, paints and climbs mountains, to give her remaining life meaning. We meet her estranged husband and strange children. The dialogue, without quite the color or distinction of *The Chalk Garden*, is pleasingly elliptical and there is a gloriously surreal, often resurrected from death, butler called Bent.

The surreal is again found in her final play, *Call Me Jacky* (perf. 1968; pub. 1970), where an old woman "out of" but surprisingly "in touch" and surrounded by a freakish entourage deliberately chooses madness and incarceration. Much of B.'s old age was made miserable by her chronic addiction to morphine, first used as a painkiller years earlier, and her portrayal of a young junkie has accuracy and compassion. The play had more of a success rechristened *A Matter of Gravity* on Broadway in 1976, with Katharine Hepburn.

B. was a superb letter writer and in character a true original. A woman of wit and charm, especially kind to the young, she was also imperious and an interfering amateur at rehearsals. Her integrity and honesty always compensate for the overseriousness with which she took herself both in life and in her work.

BIBLIOGRAPHY: Bagnold, E., *E. B.'s Autobiography* (1969); Friedman, L., *E. B.* (1986); Sebba A., *E. B.* (1986)

                                                    CHARLES DUFF

BAILLIE, Joanna
b. 11 September 1762, Bothwell, Scotland; d. 23 February 1851, Hampstead

B. was the most respected female poet of her own age, and its most-praised playwright of either gender.

Hailed as a colleague by Sir Walter SCOTT and proclaimed by Lord BYRON to be the only woman capable of writing tragedy, she was lauded at her death as a literary celebrity. But her reputation waned quickly thereafter, and by the 20th c. she was relegated to the margins of literary history as a lesser regional poet and hack dramatist whose melodramatic creations were barely readable, let alone stageworthy. The disparity between the respect of her own era and the distaste that marked her subsequent reputation is due in part to constructions of the Romantic period that privileged the lyric over the dramatic, the individual over the communal, and the masculine over the feminine. Only today, as scholars begin to reconstruct a feminized ROMANTICISM can B. be looked at in something like the way in which her own age perceived her.

Born in 1762, B. was the daughter of a minister. Her brother was sent to school, but she and her sister received their primary education from their father before beginning boarding school in Glasgow. She did not attend college, and after her father died in 1778, the family relocated to London, where her brother took over an uncle's medical practice. B. later moved to Hampstead with her mother and her sister Agnes, who was her lifelong companion.

In London and Hampstead, the Baillie family was part of a literary circle. In 1790, B. released an anonymous volume of poems, now lost. There was thus no precedent for the release in 1798 of the first of three volumes of what is commonly called the *Plays on the Passions*. The full title is *A Series of Plays: in which it is attempted to delineate the stronger passions of the mind—each passion being the subject of a tragedy and a comedy.*

The plays caused something of a sensation in literary circles. The author—first assumed to be male—was declared the inheritor of William SHAKESPEARE. When B. acknowledged her authorship two years later with the publication of the third edition, even those who knew her expressed surprise that a woman of modest reputation could have produced not only brilliant plays, but a complete and rigorous dramatic theory as well.

The *Plays on the Passions* begin with an introduction that has often been compared to William WORDSWORTH's preface to the *Lyrical Ballads*, published the same year. Like Wordsworth, B. states her intent to help English literature regain a lost glory by dispensing with artifice and returning to a more natural language. Both see their work in highly moral terms, and both authors are fascinated by the idea of empathic identification. For Wordsworth, imitation is seen as a kind of fall from a natural state of grace. For B., however, sympathetic understanding forms the core of her moral system. Her belief in its value may have been one factor that led her to write for the stage in an era that valued drama less than any in three hundred years.

In her plays and their introductions, B. argues for a radically different notion of the self from that posited by John LOCKE and others of her own period. Rather than seeing individuals as blank slates entirely shaped by their own ability to turn experience and observation into knowledge, she argues that selves are constructed through a process of identification and relationship to others. Through the reenactment of this process, B. argues that theater can be a school for virtue, a belief that leads to her exploration of the passions and their regulation. But individual virtue is not merely personal; it is political. The well-regulated individual and the well-governed family are models for the well-managed state.

Though the *Plays* were published before they were staged, B. declares that they are not intended as closet dramas. They are written with an eye to the serious stage, honing action to its fundamental elements and avoiding distracting subplots, sparkling language, and witticisms. B. referred to her comic dramas as "characteristic comedies," plays focused on personality and the ways in which it goes awry. The tragedies have a similar focus, but end with the character's destruction instead of letting the social milieu adjust and reform him.

Volume 1 (1798) included two of the plays that would become B.'s most famous: *Count Basil*, a tragedy on love, and *De Monfort*, a tragedy on hatred. Also included was *The Tryall*, a comedy on love. *De Monfort* was staged at Drury Lane in 1800 with John Philip Kemble and Sarah Siddons in the starring roles. A revival in 1815, mounted in part through the efforts of Lord Byron, starred Edmund Kean.

Somewhat Gothic in tone, *De Monfort* traces the trajectory of the title character's hatred for a good man who once spared his life in a duel. As in most of B.'s tragedies, a passion unregulated by reason destroys its subjects and others around him. Critics have pointed out that this play influenced Byron's closet drama *Manfred*.

Volume 2 (1802) included the comic play on hatred, *The Election*, and two plays about ambition, *Ethwald*, parts 1 and 2, and *The Second Marriage*. Volume 3 (1812) included three plays on fear, one of which, *Orra*, a Gothic tragedy about a noble but superstitious maiden driven mad by a villain trying to scare her into giving in to his desire, was particularly highly regarded. A musical drama, *The Beacon*, contributed to B.'s reputation as a proficient writer of songs as well. In 1805, B. also published *Miscellaneous Plays*, which included *Rayner, The Country Inn*, and *Constantine Paleologus*, a history play.

B. developed a literary friendship with Scott in 1806, and she and Agnes visited him frequently in Scotland. With *The Family Legend* (1810), B. turned to a Scottish theme, perhaps influenced by Scott and the vogue for Scotland he had created. The play, in which stereotypical villains plot to murder the noble heroine and reinstate an age of clan warfare, was performed successfully in Edinburgh.

After the unsuccessful revival of *De Monfort* in 1815, B. turned to metrical romance. *Metrical Legends of Exalted Characters* (1821) combines narrative portraits of heroes such as William Wallace and Lady Grisell Baillie with ghost tales and ballads. B. returned to plays about passions with *Dramas* (3 vols., 1836), her last collection of plays. It included *Romiero*, a tragedy about jealousy considered one of B.'s best, and often compared to *Othello* in its day. *Henriquez*, a tragedy on remorse, was also praised, while *Witchcraft* is remarkable not only for the feminist treatment of its subject matter, but for B.'s decision to write it in prose.

After a theological tract, B. released *Fugitive Verses* (1840), a collection of poems, hymns, and Scottish folk songs, some of which were reprinted from her 1790 book. Her final new work was *Ahalya Baee* (1849), a narrative poem. She finished her life by issuing a *Complete Works* (1851). She died at home in Hampstead that same year.

B.'s reputation fell into decline soon after her death. William HAZLITT, the eminent Victorian critic, had belittled her achievement in gendered terms, calling her plays "baby-house theatricals," and the Romantic canon privileged poetry over drama. From the Victorians on, she was dropped from the canon and even the canon of women writers had little use for an earnest spinster who wrote melodramas.

Only recently has the revival of interest in Romantic drama led to increased attention for B. She is also of great interest to present-day critics who, following the lead of critic Anne Mellor, are investigating a "feminine Romantic" tradition largely elided by previous critical constructions of Romanticism. Many of B.'s key themes—the importance of balancing rationality and passion, the construction of identity through identification, the connections between the domestic and public spheres and the potential for female moral leaders—are seen as hallmarks of this tradition. In this context, B. again emerges as an influential central figure.

BIBLIOGRAPHY: Burroughs, C., *Closet Stages: J. B. and the Theater Theory of British Romantic Writers* (1997); Carhart, M. S., *The Life and Works of J. B.* (1923); Dowd, M. A., "By the Delicate Hand of a Woman: Melodramatic Mania and J. B.'s Spectacular Tragedies," *ERR* 9 (Fall 1998): 469–500; Purinton, M., *Romantic Ideology Unmasked* (1994)

GINGER STRAND

BAINBRIDGE, [Dame] Beryl
b. 21 November 1933, Liverpool

An insightful observer of the human condition, B. is one of England's most highly regarded writers of fiction. She began her career with a series of blackly humorous fictions depicting people whose mostly lower-middle-class backgrounds prepare them for disillusionment, whose romanticism serves as an escape from poverty and boredom. B.'s open-eyed approach to human frailty and irrationality almost always creates a kind of sympathy for the most despicable characters, from Adolf Hitler to a scissors-wielding maiden aunt.

B.'s stories exploit her own memories of World War II Liverpool and life in an English repertory company; they also take us from the deck of the Titanic to a Crimean War battlefield. For both ordinary people and those swept up by the events of history, life is mostly remembrance, the past the prime factor shaping us all. B.'s disparate settings and plots enjoy some common features: the frequent use of flashbacks, the use of multiple narrators, and, often, an object that serves as a kind of Proustian madeleine to unleash memory. All these devices help to structure B.'s recollection of things past.

The younger of two children, B. was reared in a fractious household, a reality reflected in B.'s fictional depictions of married couples, siblings, and family life in general. After being expelled from school, B. took to the theatrical life, acting professionally until 1972.

B.'s earliest effort, *Filthy Lucre; or, The Tragedy of Andrew Ledwhistle and Richard Soleway* (wr. 1946; pub. 1986), owes much to Charles DICKENS. B. was dissatisfied with the result because the plot was "invented;" she claims not to have invented anything since. B.'s first published novel, *Harriet Said* (1972), was rejected by publishers as "indecent" after she wrote it in 1958. Based on a news item about two girls who had murdered the mother of one of them, the novel is told by a young girl whose enthrallment by Harriet leads to the seduction of a middle-aged man and the murder of his wife. The girl experiences sex as an unromantic coupling amid a confusion of limbs and pieces of clothing. This becomes a motif in B.'s work: no matter how old the protagonists, their experience of sex comes close to being merely functional, a way of trying to fulfill some strong physical and vague emotional need. And the novel's structure, with its flashback to the awful events of the story, becomes a hallmark of B.'s style.

In *A Weekend with Claud* (1967; rev. as *A Weekend with Claude*, 1981), B. uses an old photograph to jar the memories of the four narrators. The ravenous passions of the three younger characters contrast with the lamentations of the older Shebah for what might have been—a theme pervading the lives of B.'s characters. *Another Part of the Wood* (1968; rev. ed., 1979), a response, in part, to B.'s divorce, is a painful look at several sets of couples whom love eludes.

Continuing to mine her past for inspiration, B. wrote two novels about the explosive nature of family life within a four-year period. *The Dressmaker* (1973; repub. as *The Secret Glass*, 1974) was shortlisted for England's Booker Prize. Set in 1944 Liverpool, the story shows Nellie, the seamstress of the title, imposing her own rigid standards upon her sister and niece. Her involvement in the bizarre death of a visiting Yank soldier crushes the notion that home is a place of love and acceptance. In *A Quiet Life* (1976), B. recreates her childhood in the persons of a dysfunctional quartet: teenaged Alan, his sister, and their quarrelsome parents. The story recalls Alan's angry adolescence and the spiteful words that caused his father to suffer a heart attack. Everyday family life, in B.'s worlds, inevitably erupts into violence.

Love's illusions beset the characters in the next group of B.'s novels. *The Bottle Factory Outing* (1974), which won the *Guardian* Fiction Prize, revolves around the self-effacing Brenda, who is entrapped by a needy family, and flirtatious but single Freda, who longs for love and a home. Freda's unexplained death at a company picnic and burial in an old wine barrel is a typically B. ghoulish denouement. In *Sweet William* (1975), Ann tosses aside her own life to be absorbed in that of the married William. Edward and Binny, the middle-aged couple of *Injury Time* (1977), share an odd mixture of need and sexual passion. Only a disastrous dinner party, during which the guests are taken hostage by bank robbers and Binny is raped, saves Binny from the self-delusions of Brenda and Ann. *Winter Garden*'s (1980) Ashburner, who lies to his wife so that he can spend some time in Russia with his mistress, only just manages to survive a Kafkaesque string of events in the totalitarian atmosphere of Soviet Russia.

With *Young Adolf* (1978), B. began a series of novels inspired by her reading about historical events. A biography of Hitler sparked the idea for her story about Hitler's supposed visit to Liverpool in 1910. B.'s portrait of the psychopath as a young man shows us a bumbling personality who, like many of B.'s characters, is lost and a little alone in a world whose rules cannot be figured out. The entry for John Selby Watson in the *Dictionary of National Biography*, "author and murderer," spurred B. to write *Watson's Apology* (1984). The epistolary courtship that opens the novel degenerates into murder. B. translates romantic dreams about marriage into a tragedy about a couple who are mentally and emotionally mismatched.

The title of *An Awfully Big Adventure* (1989), a Booker Prize nominee, filmed in 1994, derives from

J. M. BARRIE's Peter Pan, who thought that dying must be "an awfully big adventure." B. turned her teenage experience as a juvenile character actress into this tale of Stella and her fellow actors, whose histrionics blur the line between fantasy and real life. Like Peter's companions, they are all motherless or abandoned, "lost boys" looking for solace; but finding only that hope, like Tinkerbell's light, has been extinguished from their lives. *The Birthday Boys* (1991) is B.'s fictional reconstruction of R. F. Scott's fatal trip to the South Pole. Scott's image is refracted through his journal and the reminiscences of four members of his team on family, England, and birthdays. B. explores this last gasp of the British Empire not from a postmodern sense of irony; she resurrects for us an idealism that disappeared after the Great War. Not only were the explorers "supermen," says B.; like Peter Pan's fellows, they are also "lost boys."

B.'s novels *Every Man for Himself* (1996) and *Master Georgie* (1998) are fatalistic turns on the sinking of the Titanic and the Crimean War. In the former novel, four days upon the doomed ship convinces narrator Morgan that "it's every man for himself." *Master Georgie* repeats the devices B. has used in earlier work: multiple narrators, a photograph, and flashbacks to recollect the war and to comment on the characters' personal entanglements with fate.

B.'s move into the historical mode might appear to mark a break from her earlier, more autobiographical fiction; it does not. Instead, both forms recollect a past that cannot be washed over with nostalgia. B.'s recurrent themes—the illusory search for love and a happy family life, the ridiculousness of sex, the inevitability of a gruesome and unheroic death—run through her stories. The sadly funny events in her characters' lives provide the common thread connecting ordinary people with those caught up in the epic events of history.

BIBLIOGRAPHY: Jagodzinski, C. M., "B. B.," in Moseley, M., ed., *British Novelists since 1960*, Fourth Series, *DLB* 231 (2001): 15–30; Wennö, E., *Ironic Formula in the Novels of B. B.* (1993)

                                        CECILE M. JAGODZINSKI

BALDWIN, William
b. 1518; d. 1563?

At one time, this Protestant activist offered to present a comedy before Queen Mary's court, but B. is best known as the tireless editor and main contributor to *A Mirror for Magistrates* (1559). Originally, this book of verses—a collection of nineteen poetic tragedies that describe the fall of English princes—was suppressed under Mary Tudor's reign, but later enjoyed a wide audience and was expanded to include about one hundred tales in fourteen subsequent editions. The concept of the book is compelling. A courtly figure speaks from the grave to tell of his glory and demise. Although this collection of verses was quite popular, B.'s work as a prose writer has been virtually ignored. His lack of recognition by modern scholars is puzzling especially since he is credited with writing the first original English prose novel, *Beware the Cat* (1570), a religious satire of Catholicism. Prior to this achievement, all long prose works appearing in English were either translations or adaptations from Latin, Greek, German, or French. Even Sir Thomas ELYOT's *Image of Governance* was only partially an original work and George GASCOIGNE's *A Hundred Sundrie Flowers,* which contained the original version of *The Adventures of Master F. J.* (sometimes erroneously credited as the first English prose novel), did not appear until 1574.

A Protestant of Welsh descent, B. was a preacher, printer, poet, playwright, and prose writer. We know almost nothing about B.'s young adulthood, but what we do know is that at the age of twenty-nine, he began working for Edward Whitchurch, who published *The Book of the Common Prayer,* and, along with Richard Grafton, published one of the earliest editions of the English Bible. Shortly after B. began working, Whitchurch published B.'s *A Treatise of Moral Philosophy* (1547) and *The Canticles or Ballads of Solomon in English Meters* (1549). Although this era was a fertile period for the English printing press, the accession of the Roman Catholic Queen Mary forced many prominent Protestants including Whitchurch into hiding to avoid capture and execution. Despite his allegiance to his Protestant faith, B. was invited to perform in Mary's court and managed to present a play. Although he survived Mary's reign, his professional life prospered after ELIZABETH I's accession. He was ordained deacon in 1560 and was soon appointed vicar of Tortington. However, as the plague consumed London, B. fell victim to this illness and died in 1563.

Although B. borrowed elements of William CAXTON's *Fables of Aesop* and other works, his *Beware the Cat* is an original work. B. did not try to conceal the targets of his satire. The plot occurs in the immediate past and many of his feline characters possess contemporary names. Scholars note that at this time, most works of early English fiction were simple narratives expressed in the third person. In contrast, B.'s story occurs in the first person, but he offers a complex narrative perspective in which the narrator retells yarns that others have told him. B. composed his tale some time during the tumultuous period comprising Edward VI's death, Queen Jane's brief reign, and Mary's rise to power. Although B.'s elaborate story satirizes Catholicism, it was not published until twelve years after Elizabeth's accession, and scholars are unsure how this tale was received.

More certain was the favorable response to B.'s *A Treatise of Moral Philosophy.* Between 1554 and 1609, eight editions of this book appeared, making this collection the most popular and influential in its time second only to the English Bible. This commonplace collection of precepts, parables, and ethical maxims on Renaissance prudence and morality was influenced heavily by classical thought. Robert Hood Bowers notes that that this collection functioned as a heuristic for *imitatio*—where young men could seek and locate authoritative sayings and knowledge. Because of its popularity, this book assumed a central significance in the middle-class movement in which literacy became an important tool of middle-class ambition. Historians note that B.'s *Treatise* and other commonplace works were popular because they were used as intellectual commodities—works meant for an emerging middle-class audience that desired quick ways to improve itself. The popularity of this book may also signify, in a much more public sense, the Elizabethan desire to understand moral philosophy conveyed through stories.

BIBLIOGRAPHY: Gutierrez, N. A., "W. B.," in Richardson, D. A., ed., *Sixteenth-Century British Nondramatic Writers*, First Series, *DLB* 132 (1993): 19–26; King, J. N., *English Reformation Literature: The Tudor Origins of Protestant Tradition* (1982)

DAVID CHRISTOPHER RYAN

BALLANTYNE, R[obert] M[ichael]
b. 25 April 1825, Edinburgh, Scotland; d. 8 February 1894, Rome, Italy

Author of over one hundred books, B. led a life of adventure, going to work in Canada at sixteen, publishing his diary in 1847 under the title *Hudson Bay,* with *Snowflakes and Sunbeams; or, The Young Fur Traders* (1856), *The World of Ice* (1859), and *Ungava: A Tale of Esquimaux Land* (1857), all of which reflect his experience of the frozen north. Pre-television, his evocation of exotic locations was exciting. In search of authentic materials, he traveled widely, from Scandinavia to Africa. *Black Ivory* appeared in 1873. *Martin Rattler* (1858) is an exciting fictional account of travels in South America, whose unique fauna and flora are grippingly described. B. is remembered chiefly for *The Coral Island* (1858), a boys' adventure story in which three shipwrecked youths in the Pacific survive on breadfruit and coconuts, escape cannibals, fall into the hands of pirates, and see for themselves the changes wrought by Christian missionaries, changes presented as wholly beneficial. *The Gorilla Hunters* (1861) was a popular sequel. Narrated by Ralph Rover, the stories have as hero the resourceful Jack; the names were used by William GOLDING in his ironic reworking of *The Coral Island, Lord of the*

Flies, now better known than its original model. While B.'s tale is colonialist, didactic, and optimistic, Golding's is pessimistic, even tragic. B.'s work is unread today, being politically incorrect: his response to wild animals was to kill them. His work is interesting as a naive and blatant statement of widespread Victorian attitudes, confident of British superiority. B.'s fictions were popular until mid-20th c.

BALLARD, J[ames] G[raham]

b. 15 November 1930, Shanghai, China

Born overseas, son of a British businessman, B. spent a memorable part of his childhood as a World War II refugee in devastated Shanghai. Images of premature immersion in the shattering spectacle of war can be found in the alien landscapes and broken surfaces that permeate his work as a novelist. Other visible influences on his often clinical or technological style of writing include his previous study of medicine and his work as a pilot for the Royal Air Force. B. achieved critical acclaim with his earlier, postcatastrophic novels, and became a central figure in 1960s "New Wave" avant-garde fiction. Although his work has often received criticism for morbidity and sexual perversion, he has been praised for his insight into the flaws and ruptures of contemporary culture, and he is considered by many one of the most inventive and complex writers of the 20th c. Two of his novels, *Crash* (1973) and the semiautobiographical *Empire of the Sun* (1984), have been made into films, and his reputation as a writer of daring and innovative fiction appears now as strong as it has ever been.

B.'s early novels include *The Wind from Nowhere* (1962), *The Burning World* (1964), and *The Crystal World* (1966). The works have a repetitive theme of apocalyptic devastation overwhelming a culture. A typical hero in the B. universe, however, does not thwart the oncoming tide of destruction and save his community. Rather, B.'s heroes find their fulfillment and satisfaction in accepting and embracing their impending doom. The reigning imagery in these books is that of empty buildings, broken or open-faced machinery, and similarly abandoned spaces, with protagonists who must negotiate the eerie absences and find purpose in the face of the negativity that confronts them. Protagonists in B.'s work often find solutions to the problems in inner psychological exploration rather than outward action.

In the 1960s, B. also wrote many smaller, though no less ambitious, pieces. Much of his work came in the form of magazine publications or short story collections. *The Atrocity Exhibition* (1972; repub. as *Love and Napalm: Export U.S.A.,* 1972) reprints material from this era. *Exhibition* includes polemical, deliberately scandalous works, which B. had trouble publishing and for which he has been both criticized and praised. Experimental and fragmentary, the essays often mesh cruelty and violence with otherwise appetizing or desirable imagery. In part, the controversy is due to B.'s shocking transformations of politically idealized figures; sections include "Plan for the Assassination of Jacqueline Kennedy" and "Queen Elizabeth's Rhinoplasty." Perhaps even more controversial is the inclusion of a piece written in 1967, "Why I Want to Fuck Ronald Reagan," a prophetic look at society's tendency to fetishize and empower media figures. Despite criticisms leveled against it, *Exhibition* is one of B.'s most celebrated works, and provides an unflinching look at the disturbing side of the collective unconscious desires of American and British culture.

In the 1970s, the image of the car crash becomes a central theme for multiple works, including the novels *Crash* and *Concrete Island* (1974). A central character of *Crash* is Vaughn, the charismatic leader of a small group of crash enthusiasts, who fantasizes about dying in a collision with actress Elizabeth Taylor, and whose death from a crash is revealed in the opening paragraphs. The novel constantly blends sexual imagery with the brutal immediacy of the automobile accident. The protagonist of *Concrete Island* is an accident victim who is trapped between sections of freeway and eventually adapts to his predicament. In both works, internal fantasy or contemplation transforms the meaning of external situations.

In later years, B.'s reputation has continued to grow. One of his most popular and least controversial novels is *Empire of the Sun*, a semiautobiographical account that is his first explicit attempt to recapture the incidents of his youth as a refugee. In this account of B.'s past, readers can find the context for the shattered buildings, abandoned streets, and strange, surreal vistas that informed his previous catastrophic fiction. A more recent production, *A User's Guide to the Millennium* (1996), with essays ranging over a wide array of cultural or political topics, once again presents B.'s repetitive themes of civilization in decline, and the composition of otherwise disparate images into a unified whole. This work, like much of his previous writing, provides insight into the ways that unconscious, or private, desires interact with and influence public opinion and action.

Perhaps it is a telling irony that B.'s fictionalized novels and stories are often censured for their grotesque images of violence and fragmentation, while his depiction of real violence and historically accurate destruction in *Empire of the Sun* has received unanimous praise from critics. Today, B. is considered an imaginative and stylistic force to be reckoned with, the cornerstone of a genre of elaborate, culture-conscious writing of which he is a pioneer.

BIBLIOGRAPHY: Goddard, J., and D. Pringle, eds., *J. G. B.* (1976); Luckhurst, R., *The Angel between*

Two Walls: The Fiction of J. G. B. (1997); Stephenson, G., *Out of the Night and Into the Dream: A Thematic Study of the Fiction of J. G. B.* (1991)

STEVEN ZANI

BANKS, Iain [Menzies]

b. 16 February 1954, Fife, Scotland

B. is a cult writer with best-selling status—or indeed vice versa—and an author who, like fellow Scot Irvine WELSH some years later, is read by many people who do not usually read. B.'s debut novel, *The Wasp Factory* (1984), published in the context of the video nasty moral panic of the mid-1980s, assured him of media attention, and two less visceral follow-ups assured his champions that here was a writer of skill and depth. Then with *Consider Phlebas* (1987) he began a parallel career as a SCIENCE FICTION author, publishing under the name Iain M. Banks. These books have received the most critical attention, although even his non-science fiction has fantastical elements (*Walking on Glass*, 1985) or is set in the (near) future (*Canal Dreams*, 1989).

The Wasp Factory purports to be the story of Frank, a sadistic boy raised by his father on a Scottish island just off the mainland, whose brother Eric has just escaped from a mental asylum and is heading home. It transpires that Frank is the product of a social experiment by his father, and the whole can be read from a feminist angle. Frank's bizarre family, which deliberately defies belief, is echoed in a later family saga, *The Crow Road* (1992). The sadism, with an ironic twist, is returned to in *Complicity* (1993), a serial killer narrative in which the victims deserve to die.

B.'s most complex novel is *The Bridge* (1986), which can in part be read as the near-death delusions of a road accident victim on the Forth Bridge. The bulk of the narrative is the depiction of an apparently mentally ill patient who lives in the middle of a vast bridgelike structure, uncertain of what is at either end of the bridge, or indeed if it does have ends. The amnesiac hero's progress through the world of the bridge has echoes of Franz Kafka's *The Castle,* first published in 1926.

The other half of B.'s career is also divided: science fiction novels that are "Culture" novels, two science fiction novels that are not "Culture" novels (*Against a Dark Background*, 1993, and *Ferrsum Endjinn,* 1994) and one that may or may not be. The Culture is a galaxy-spanning UTOPIA where machines do all the hard work leaving its denizens to play games or behave as they wish. As this is a utopia that works, the narratives concentrate on people or races being recruited to the Culture, or more general dealings with other civilizations. The novels fall into the subgenre of space opera, adventure narratives that

have little regard for science and prefer to depict impossibly large spacecraft, unlikely hardware and devices, and have death-defying plot twists. While in form they hark back to science fiction of the 1930s, they have a modern, left-wing sensibility with regard to gender roles, race, and power, and are experiments in form in terms of viewpoint characters.

Consider Phlebas is the tall tale of a mercenary in the Idris-Culture war in search of a lost spaceship brain, a narrative that is barely a footnote in history. The novel takes its title from the drowned sailor of the fourth section of T. S. ELIOT's *The Waste Land* (a later volume is entitled *Look to Windward*, 2000) and it is clear that the mercenary is an analogue of that character. Other events in the novel playfully echo the poem. In *The Player of Games* (1988), a champion game-player is taken to an alien planet contacted by the Culture and is allowed to enter into the championships of the local game. The ultimate champion of the game gets to be the emperor of the planet, and his remarkable progress ends up undermining the entire structure of the society, leaving it open to assimilation by the Culture.

Use of Weapons (1990) is told in two alternating arcs, one moving forward in time, the other one backwards, and tells of the recruitment and missions of a mercenary aiding the Culture in its dealing with other races. The actions and ultimately identity of the agent call into question the utopian status of the Culture, or at the least call into question their methods of building a utopia. *Inversions* (1998) also gets told in two stories, one of a doctor, the other of a bodyguard, within a quasi-medieval empire. Both are strangers to the society they serve, and the implication is that these are Culture agents investigating a potential new partner society. This may be signaled by the capitalization of the word "Culture" in the note to the text; the link is never openly acknowledged.

This last trick has led some reviewers to wonder whether B. has become too clever a writer, and the material written in the second half of the 1990s has been less well received than in the first decade of his career. B. remains a stylist, a master technician of plotting and a questioner of social mores.

BIBLIOGRAPHY: Middleton, T., "Constructing the Contemporary Self: The Works of I. B.," in Hill, J., and W. Hughes, eds., *Contemporary Writing and National Identity* (1995): 18–28; special B. issue, *Foundation* 76 (Summer 1999)

ANDREW M. BUTLER

BANVILLE, John

b. 8 December 1945, Wexford, Ireland

Hailed by many as the best English prose stylist of the last decades of the 20th c, B.'s fascination with painting and his fierce appreciation of Samuel BECK-

ETT's aesthetics combine to shape his cunning, shadowy, and sometimes elliptical novels. His wry, discernibly Irish HUMOR is often felt but never comforting in a world of fraud, ghosts, and unease.

With Beckett-like aplomb, B. has all but disowned his first two novels, *Long Lankin* (1970) and *Nightspawn* (1971), and even *Birchwood* (1973) has an apparent immaturity in its ostentatious literariness. In his later novels, he has developed a more stylized approach—a precarious balance between detail and minimalism—in which sophistry is herald to compromise and menace. *Mefisto* (1986) is a good example of such sinister narratives: protagonist Gabriel Swan is a mathematical prodigy fallen among desperate souls in a very Faustian story.

In novels such as *Doctor Copernicus* (1976), awarded the James Tait Black Memorial Prize, *Kepler* (1981), winner of the *Guardian* Fiction Prize, and *The Newton Letter* (1982), B. explores the scientific heroes who were outsiders of their sometimes tumultuous and irrational times, and in the bargain prods at the constructive and ideological limits of BIOGRAPHY and the historical novel. In the figure of Johannes Kepler, for instance, B. explores the conflicts between nervous faith and observation, and between culture and poverty.

Among B.'s best work is his superb trilogy of novels, *The Book of Evidence* (1989), *Ghosts* (1993), and *Athena* (1995). Each of these books is centered on the obsessive attraction of art and deceit, and its female characters tend to be otherworldly and for the most part inscrutable to a persistently male gaze. Freddie Montgomery is—or simply may be—the elegant but sinister narrator of each novel, and a character to be reckoned with in any study of postmodern fiction. Rife with uncertainty, Freddie's confessions are protracted hesitations and his admiration of representation, even with the words he himself uses, is everywhere tinged with suspicion. *The Book of Evidence*, shortlisted for the Booker Prize and winner of the Guinness Peat Aviation Award, is Freddie's disarmingly suave if reluctant recounting of the bungled theft of a portrait and seemingly incidental murder of a chambermaid. *Ghosts*, with its telling title, is about haunting in every sense. Set a decade after the events of *Book*, *Ghosts* is narrated by a shifty, unnamed but Freddie-like man, at liberty from prison and serving as amanuensis to an art history professor. As Ariel to the professor's Prospero, the narrator watches as their secluded island peace is disturbed by a group of castaways who may or may not be there by chance. In *Athena*, Morrow, another incarnation of Freddie, tells of his shady dealings in stolen (and, ultimately, forged) art and his fascination with a woman named simply "A." The trilogy is perhaps most immediately comparable with Beckett's: in both, a narrator becomes more and more alienated and yet hollowly solipsistic.

B. returned to the political intrigue he had toyed with in *Nightspawn* in *The Untouchable* (1998), a remarkable roman à clef based on the affair of the Cambridge Spies. In terrain usually associated with Graham GREENE, B. ventures into the story of Victor Maskell (a recognizable version of the art historian Anthony Blunt), a man living with disgrace, cancer, and the worry that he has not truly lived. The novel is shot through with shades of betrayal and loss as Victor tries to explain and in part justify past associations and ideals.

Eclipse (2000) is narrated by an actor who can no longer bear to be observed, and retreats from both the stage and his marriage to his dilapidated childhood home. Alexander Cleave cannot so easily escape scrutiny—or the pain of existence, in B.'s play upon the notion *esse est percipi* (to be is to be perceived)—and instead finds his space and peace of mind trespassed upon by motley characters, including a silent ghost who may be either an accusation or a premonition.

In addition to his fiction, B. has forayed into theater with an original play *The Broken Jug* (1987) and an adaptation (perf. 2000) of Heinrich von Kleist's *Amphitryon*, an 1807 version of a comedy attributed to Plautus. As literary editor at the *Irish Times*, B.'s sensitive reviews have won him further respect as a critic of contemporary fiction. Narration is for B.'s characters an uncomfortable imperative, a confession not strictly called for but given, very much *faute de mieux*. The sins and crimes of B.'s characters (especially his narrators) are ever-present, the nearest thing to certainty his novels offer, but their nature and whether they can be escaped, avoided, forgotten or redeemed, remain darkly open questions.

BIBLIOGRAPHY: Imhof, R., *J. B.* (1989); McMinn, J., *J. B., a Critical Study* (1991); McMinn, J., *The Supreme Fictions of J. B.* (1999)

                                                    TIM CONLEY

BARBAULD, Anna Laetitia [Aikin]

b. 20 June 1743, Leicestershire; d. 9 March 1825, Stoke Newington

B. formed part of the Dissenting circle surrounding scientist and educator Joseph Priestley. She began experimenting with verse in the early 1760s but did not begin publishing her work until 1772, a year that culminated in the appearance of her much-praised collection *Poems*. For some time thereafter, however, B.'s published output was confined to CHILDREN'S LITERATURE and educational prose—a logical offshoot from the work she and her husband shared of managing the Palgrave School in Suffolk. Her best-known publication from this decade is *Hymns in Prose for Children*

(1781). In any event, B. published her poetry sporadically at best, despite writing verse consistently in private. Nevertheless, from at least 1769 onward, B. wrote occasional poetry that showed her to be firmly allied with radical Dissent. She kept her political opinions confined to manuscript until 1790, when she finally broke her silence with an *Address* on the government's refusal to repeal the Corporation and Test Acts. B.'s most notorious political poem, *Eighteen Hundred and Eleven* (1812), a deeply pessimistic reflection on English culture after several years of war with Napoleon, brought down a firestorm of negative criticism. A very few poems appeared in print thereafter. Several fragments and prose pieces appeared posthumously in *A Legacy for Young Ladies* (1826), edited by Lucy AIKIN.

Like many of her female contemporaries, B. eschewed the lyric experimentalism of the male Romantics. Much of her work is in the 18th-c. neoclassical tradition, written in heroic couplets with careful attention to elevated diction; some of her political and elegiac poems, such as "Corsica" (1769) and "On the Death of Princess Charlotte" (1819), however, opt for the Miltonic echoes of blank verse. Avoiding the sonnet revival pioneered by writers like Anna Seward, B. enjoyed writing epistolary poems, but she also experimented with such forms as the ode and the mock-heroic. B.'s critical revival in recent years has largely been based on *Eighteen Hundred and Eleven*, but her heroic couplets are no more than technically correct, making long poems like this rather ponderous. On the other hand, her mock-heroic poems, like "Washing-Day" (1797), still retain the power to amuse. Of the shorter poems, the most interesting remain "To Mr. S. T. Coleridge" (1799), a blank verse critique of Samuel Taylor COLERIDGE's preoccupation with the fantastic; "The Rights of Woman," a gentle but firm rejoinder to Mary WOLLSTONECRAFT; and "To a little invisible Being who is expected soon to become visible," a blessing on a child still unborn.

But B.'s most important contributions to literary history may have been made not as a poet but, instead, as an editor and biographer. Her fifty-volume *British Novelists* (1810) represents an early effort to construct a canon of British fiction, including authors such as Samuel RICHARDSON and her friend Maria EDGEWORTH. B. prefaced the collection with an introductory essay on the history and theory of novel-writing. While this essay's originality has been overstated—many of its ideas about narrative form and history had been anticipated in the work of rhetoricians like Hugh Blair—it nevertheless demonstrates how critics were attempting to position the novel within contemporary literary culture. B.'s edition of Richardson's letters (1804), accompanied by a *Life*, is still considered a landmark work in the scholarship on that author.

BIBLIOGRAPHY: McCarthy, W., and E. Kraft, eds., *The Poems of A. L. B.* (1994); Rodgers, B., *Georgian Chronicle: Mrs. Barbauld and Her Family* (1958)

MIRIAM ELIZABETH BURSTEIN

BARCLAY, Alexander

b. 1475?, Scotland?; bur. 10 June 1552, Croydon

A restless traveler, a prolific translator of Latin and French, an outspoken critic of court corruption, and a passionate advocate of the poor, B. was an accomplished man of letters and a dedicated clergyman. By most accounts, he was a man of diligence, honesty, and courage; these character traits, however, were scorned by a church that failed to find a prominent post for B. Despite this rejection, this Scottish poet managed to achieve popularity and literary prominence in England in an era of frigid relations between Scotland and England. In his writings as well as his reformist efforts, B. represents an important link between the oral culture of the underclass and the growing literate culture of the aristocracy for two reasons: first, he expressed hostility toward the vice of the ruling class and his admiration and concern for the lower class in his *Eclogues* (wr. 1513–14). Second, in his *Eclogues*, he was first to express in writing proverbial lore and commonplace idioms, characteristics often identified with the oral culture of the lower classes. Because his poetry focuses on illustrating the deep chasm among the classes and because his lyrical efforts are identified with the *literazation* of speech, his work deserves further scrutiny.

Biographical resources for B. are sketchy and irregular. Conflicting claims to his nationality and uncertainty about his education make biographical statements less than definitive. These circumstances are not unusual for early Elizabethan writers. But whether he was a Scotsman or an Englishman, whether he attended Oxford or Cambridge, or whether he was a member of the Franciscan order or a Benedictine monk have been the subject of interesting debates which rely on nebulous and ambiguous textual references as evidence. But we do know B. was a gentleman who could read and write in many languages and is best known for his translation of Sebastian Brant's widely popular allegorical poem, Sallust's *The Ship of Fools* (1509), perhaps the most popular tale in the history of Western literature. In addition to *The Ship of Fools*, B. translated *The Mirror of Good Manners* (1518?) from the Latin of the Italian monk Dominic Mancini at the request of Richard, Earl of Kent, and *The Famous Chronicle of the War which the Roman had against Jugurth* (1520?) in two editions at the request of Thomas, Duke of Norfolk.

Though he was a prolific translator and served his aristocratic patrons well, B. expressed his social and political concerns for the underclass in his *Eclogues*.

Modeled on Petrarch and Mantuan, these moral pastorals—perhaps the first eclogues to appear in English—illustrate B.'s desire to use art to improve human relations between the social classes. For instance, his first eclogue places pastoral life in sharp antithesis to court life by contrasting the shepherd's life to the courtier's, painting a portrait of England under HENRY VIII as a nation dominated by tyranny, injustice, and oppression. Furthermore, when B. was describing the anguish of the poor and the abuses of the rich, he used common language. B. adopted a distinctive poetic and stylistic identity for himself that was an outgrowth of his social and political concerns. His poetic style was simple, lucid, and familiar. Scholars contend that B.'s work was the first to express—in writing—popular and proverbial lore well before John HEYWOOD's collection of proverbs appeared in 1546. For example, B. captured expressions such as "Once out of sight and shortly out of mind," "Of two evils, choose the least," and "They rob Saint Peter therewith to clothe Saint Paul." Quite interestingly, these literary expressions of commonplace knowledge not only are meant to give a voice to the poor, the disenchanted and the disenfranchised but represent one important means by which orality influenced the development of literacy in England.

B.'s emphasis on the interaction of oral expression with literary expression is worth mentioning because his effort further illustrates a synthetic and symbiotic relationship between orality and literacy. During this period, literacy was still an evolving, developing process of expression. Although we are not sure if B.'s use of oral maxims was meant to broaden the appeal of literacy to a popular audience by giving oral expression the primacy of the written word or if he was experimenting with the growing significance of poetic language, his effort, nevertheless, illustrates the process by England adapted itself to a new technology. B.'s use of proverbial lore coupled with his clearness of expression and simplicity of vocabulary is credited with giving the underclass a sympathetic literary voice and indicates his reformist attempt at moving writing closer to speaking. In his *Eclogues*, we see B.'s reliance on the traditions of speech and writing as a vital work of poetic synthesis. Furthermore, B.'s life and work, particularly his *Eclogues*, illustrate his belief that art and politics were indivisible entities. For B., art must not only illustrate the moral divisions between the classes but must compel the classes toward social reform.

BIBLIOGRAPHY: Carlson, D. R., "A. B.," in Richardson, D. A., ed., *Sixteenth-Century British Nondramatic Writers,* First Series, *DLB* 132 (1993): 36–47; Orme, N., *Education and Society in Medieval and Renaissance England* (1989)

DAVID CHRISTOPHER RYAN

BARCLAY, John

b. 28 January 1582, Pont-à-Mousson, France; d. 15 August 1621, Rome, Italy

Despite B.'s education at a Jesuit college, his *Euphormionis Satyricon* (1603), modeled on Petronius, is a severe satire on the Jesuits, in the form of a picaresque novel. B.'s importance, however, lies in his best-known work, the *Argenis* (1621), an allegory in a contemporary setting, crucial in the development of 17th-c. ROMANCE. Printed over forty times in the original Latin, it was frequently translated, notably by Clara REEVE, published as *The Phoenix* (1772). B.'s *Icon Animorum*, translated by Thomas May as *The Mirror of Minds* (1631), is a collection of essays on national types. B.'s shorter poems, in two books, were printed in the *Delitiae Poetarum Scotorum* (1637). In the dedication to Prince Charles of England, B. refers to his earlier publication, *The Sylvae* (1606).

BARHAM, [Reverend] R[ichard] H[arris]

b. 6 December 1788, Canterbury; d. 17 June 1845, London

Clergyman and divinity lecturer, B. is noteworthy as a man of letters for his contribution to the development of English short fiction. B.'s first novel, *Baldwin; or, A Miser's Heir* (2 vols., 1820), was a failure, but success came when, under the pseudonym "Thomas Ingoldsby," B. wrote *The Ingoldsby Legends,* which first appeared in 1837 in *Bentley's Miscellany* and the *New Monthly Magazine* and were collected in 1840. They parody the period's popular preoccupation with antiquities, in which B. was himself learned. Mainly in verse, they are macabre, satirical, and witty, with surprising rhymes: the poems, in a variety of meters, are a treasure house of early-19th-c. slang and colloquialism. "The Jackdaw of Rheims" has been much anthologized: the bird steals the archbishop's ring, is cursed, falls ill but recovers when the curse is lifted, and becomes devout. Considered suitable for children, it lacks the bite of the more grotesque pieces. A short memoir, by B.'s son, was prefixed to a new edition of the *Legends* (1847) and a fuller *Life and Letters* appeared in 1870.

BARING, Maurice

b. 27 April 1874, London; d. 14 December 1945, Beauly, Scotland

B. was a multifaceted man of letters—educated at Cambridge and Oxford and fluent in several languages—who served in the Foreign Office before turning full-time to a literary career. B. held diplomatic posts in Europe and later in prerevolutionary Russia, where he immersed himself in the language and culture of the Russian people—an experience that informed works such as *A Year in Russia* (1907; rev, ed., 1917), *Landmarks in Russian Literature* (1910), and *The Russian People* (1911). He also edited *The Oxford Book of Russian Verse*, published in 1924, and translated a collection of Russian lyrics (1943). Having converted to Roman Catholicism early in the 20th c., B. was often identified with writers such as G. K. CHESTERTON and Hilaire BELLOC who infused their works with themes of religion and morality. Accomplished as a poet and short story writer, B. is best known as a novelist. His first novel, *Passing By* (1921), was followed by popular, mostly coming-of-age novels including *C* (2 vols., 1924), *Cat's Cradle* (1925), and *The Coat without Seam* (1929).

BARING-GOULD, [Reverend] Sabine
b. 28 January 1834, Exeter; d. 2 January 1924, Bovey Tracey

Best remembered as the author of the famous hymn, "Onward, Christian Soldiers," set to music by Sir Arthur Sullivan, B.-G. published dozens of works on travel, religion, history, BIOGRAPHY, mythology, FOLKLORE, and popular theology as well as some thirty novels. A Victorian "squarson" (landowner or "squire" and parson), he made an unorthodox marriage to a mill girl, the theme of his first novel, *Through Flame and Fire* (3 vols., 1868). A. C. SWINBURNE compared his best-known novel *Mehalah: A Story of the Salt Marshes* (3 vols., 1880) to Emily BRONTË's *Wuthering Heights*. Later works included *John Herring* (3 vols., 1883), *Court Royal* (3 vols., 1886), *Red Spider* (2 vols., 1887), *The Pennycomequicks* (3 vols., 1889), *Cheap Jack Zita* (3 vols., 1893), and *The Broom Squire* (1896).

B.-G. collected and often edited, bowdlerized, and "improved" folk songs from his parishioners and other country people, publishing many of them, including the famous "Uncle Tom Cobbleigh" version of the local song "Widdecombe Fair," in *Songs and Ballads of the West* (4 parts, 1888–1901) and *A Garland of County Songs* (1895), both with H. Fleetwood Sheppard. He also wrote many imitation folk songs, best known of which is "Among the New-mown Hay," set to a variant of the traditional dance tune, "Jockey to the Fair."

B.-G.'s popular contributions to the study of folklore included *Book of Werewolves* (1863), *Curious Myths of the Middle Ages* (1866), and *Curious Survivals* (1892). He produced many volumes of sermons and edited from 1871 to 1873 the *Sacristy,* a quarterly review of ecclesiastical art and literature. Published in 1923, B.-G.'s autobiographical *Early Reminiscences, 1834–1864* was followed by *My Few Last Words* (1924) and *Further Reminiscences, 1864–1894* (1925).

BIBLIOGRAPHY: Dickinson, B. H. D., *S. B.-G.* (1970); Kirk-Smith, H., *"Now the Day Is Over": The Life and Times of S. B.-G.* (1997); Purcell, W., *Onward, Christian Soldier* (1957)

BARKER, A[udrey] L[ilian]
b. 13 April 1918, Beckenham, Kent; d. 21 February 2002, Carshalton, Surrey

B. was the first recipient of the Somerset Maugham Award for her debut collection of short stories, *Innocents: Variations on a Theme* (1948). Although critics were unanimous in their approval of this collection, B.'s fiction has generally met with mixed reception. Some have found the circumstances of her characters difficult to accept while others have delighted in her use of understatement and sense of the macabre to convey the element of the absurd. In all, B. published eleven novels, including *Apology for a Hero* (1950), *The Middling: Chapters in the Life of Ellie Toms* (1967), *John Brown's Body* (1969), shortlisted for the Booker Prize, and *The Gooseboy* (1987), but she is most effective as a short story writer, as illustrated in collections such as *Lost upon the Roundabouts* (1964) *Femina Real* (1971), and *Any Excuse for a Party* (1991) where her attention to detail and authorial detachment from her characters give her work a sardonic edge.

BARKER, George [Granville]
b. 26 February 1913, Loughton, Essex; d. 31 October 1991, Itteringham

B. was recognized as a considerable and accomplished poet as soon as his first works appeared. Peaking very early indeed, he emerged into the British literary world most auspiciously, and the record shows that T. S. ELIOT was reading B. poems to Virginia WOOLF in early 1934. By 1936, at twenty-three, he was the youngest poet in *The Oxford Book of Modern Verse* (1936), edited by W. B. YEATS. B.'s poetry was published in Eliot's magazine the *Criterion*, and twenty of his books were published over many years by the firm that Eliot worked for, Faber and Faber. Eliot also provided steady and generous financial support and detailed advice on B.'s works and career (one letter from Eliot to B. patiently points out that the plural of "German" is not "Germen").

Eliot was an early admirer of the sonnet "To My Mother," one of B.'s best-loved poems: "Most near, most dear, most loved and most far,/Under the window where I often found her/Sitting as huge as Asia, seismic with laughter,/Gin and chicken helpless in her Irish hand,/Irresistible as Rabelais, but most tender for/The lame dogs and hurt birds that surround her,/She is a procession no one can follow after/But be like a little dog following a brass band./She will not glance up at the bomber or condescend/To drop her gin and scuttle to a cellar,/But lean on the mahogany table like a mountain/Whom only faith can move, and so I send/O all my faith and all my love to tell her/ That she will move from mourning into morning."

After so brilliant a beginning, however, B. seems to have fallen into a rut. It may be that his talent declined, or possibly poetry underwent a change of fashion after World War II. B.'s style hardly survived the 1930s, when his supercharged surrealist routines, yielding Joycean nuggets like "Merman Melville," had put him in the league with such contemporaries as Dylan THOMAS and W. R. Rodgers. By the time of Thomas's death, the mode in British poetry shifted away from the hyperbolic to the understated, and severe skeptics like Philip LARKIN steered the ferry of poetry away from surrealism and other extreme styles. Still, in one of the notable personal poems of the postwar period, "The True Confession of George Barker," some of the old wine stayed potent in the new containers: "Ruined empire of dissipated time,/Perverted aim, abused desire,/The monstrous amoeba cannot aspire/But sinks down into the cold slime/Of Eden as Ego. It is enough/To sink back in the primal mud/Of the first person. For what could/Equal the paradise of Self Love?"

After his formal schooling ended at Regent Street Polytechnic in 1930, B. worked at odd jobs, never prosperously; after the publication in 1933 of his novel *Alanna Autumnal* and *Thirty Preliminary Poems*, he made his living as a journalist and teacher. Between 1939 and 1974, he taught at universities in Japan, the U.S., and the U.K. He was married at least three times, and his long affair with the poet Elizabeth Smart, whom he never married, produced four children. His *Collected Poems* appeared in two volumes, published in 1957 and 1965.

BIBLIOGRAPHY: Fodaski, M., *G. B.* (1969); Gulledge, J. M., "G. B.," in Stanford, D. E., ed., *British Poets, 1914–1945, DLB* 20 (1983): 51–56

WILLIAM HARMON

BARKER, Howard
b. 28 June 1946, London

B. is without doubt a dramatist of European stature and renown whose provocative plays (over seventy in total) have challenged the mainstream critical apparatus and remolded the complexion of contemporary tragedy. Numerous collections of his work have been published, spanning three decades of prodigious activity; a volume of polemical theater-related essays is now in its third edition, and he has also published books of poetry. More recently, B. has directed productions of his own plays—revivals as well as new work—throughout Europe.

The imperatives of B.'s theater are set out in his coruscating manifesto, *Arguments for a Theatre*

(1989; rev. eds., 1993, 1997). Here, B. advocates a new kind of tragedy that aims to divide and confront the audience by destabilizing its liberal assumptions while dispensing with the impetus to reconciliation that typifies, in his view, the stultifying humanistic shibboleths of European tragic form. B.'s own antidote to the apparent banality of contemporary culture—his so-called Theatre of Catastrophe—accords a special status to the desiring subject. For B, desire is at once a will to action, an emotive dislocation of perceptions, and a profound crisis of the body that catapults his protagonists—many of them women— beyond the reassuring frameworks of moral and ideological orthodoxy to sites of exhilarating, traumatic, and indeed shameless transformation. It is often noted that actors are among B.'s most fervent admirers— due, in part, to the sheer poetical force of his dramatic language—and a group of them, led by Kenny Ireland, established the Wrestling School in 1988. This theater company, now one of Britain's most dynamic, focuses on B.'s plays and has presented over eighteen productions in thirteen countries since its inception.

B.'s early work can be contextualized as part of a tradition of political playwriting, ascendant in the 1970s, that addresses the extent and effect of Britain's postwar decline. His "State of England" plays, such as *Claw* (perf. 1975; pub. 1977) and *The Hang of the Gaol* (perf. 1978; pub. 1981), articulate a mordant despair with a parliamentary political system steeped in antiquated class traditions and endemic corruption. In the former, Noel Biledew, an illegitimate war baby turned pimp, breaks into the Establishment by procuring for Clapcott, the Home Secretary, but becomes obsessed with the politician's wife. Noel is eventually betrayed by her and deposited in a mental institution where two psychotic wardens murder him. In the latter, Jardine leads a government inquiry into the burning down of C Block in Middenhurst Gaol but the urbane Home Secretary, Stagg, orders the report to be doctored so as not to derail a forthcoming election. Such indictments of English political culture, leavened with a brittle and sardonic HUMOR, reach a theatrical apotheosis in *Crimes in Hot Countries* (perf. 1983; pub. 1984), which is set in an exotic colonial outpost: in one memorable scene, the skirt of Trellis, a prostitute, is hoisted and proclaimed as the flag of "New England." The emphasis throughout is on decayed ideals and the redemptive power of desire. A further group of plays written in the early 1980s—*The Loud Boy's Life* (perf. 1980; pub. 1982), *A Passion in Six Days* (perf. 1983; pub. 1985), and *Downchild* (1985)—share a similar thematics but focus on the Labour Party. The aspiration here is to counterpoint the tensions between ideological commitment, political expediency, and sexual passion, and the overall theatrical effect is melancholy.

It is, however, B.'s searing and frequently scatological meditations on history that have won him an enduring if controversial reputation for spellbinding theatrical innovation. *Victory* (1983), the television play *Pity in History* (perf. 1984), and *The Castle* (1985) are modern classics that combine stunning visual metaphors with a densely textured language wholly attuned to the highly developed symbolic world of each play. These, and contemporaneous works including *Scenes from an Execution* (perf. 1984), a radio play, and *The Europeans* (perf. 1987; pub. 1990), include some of the most challenging roles for women in postwar theater.

B.'s later work offers a fuller theatrical engagement with his principles of Catastrophe, and is often complex, challenging, and less frequently grounded in a recognizable historical milieu. Perhaps the most intriguing example is *The Possibilities* (1988), a sequence of ten short scenes that explore the dilemmas of logic, rationality, and consistency in scenarios of crisis.

In the past decade, B. has demonstrated an apparently inexhaustible formal versatility. His work includes plays for marionettes, *All He Fears* (1993) and *The Swing at Night* (perf. 2001); a haunting one-woman monologue, *Und* (perf. 1999); and an eight-hour millennium EPIC, *The Ecstatic Bible* (perf. 2000). The most startling of his recent works is an ambitious "annexation" of Hamlet entitled *Gertrude—The Cry* (perf. 2002), the latest in a number of B.'s typically uncompromising renegotiations of classic and canonical texts.

BIBLIOGRAPHY: Lamb, C., *H. B.'s Theatre of Seduction* (1997); Rabey, D. I., *H. B.* (1989); special B. issue, *Gambit* 11, 41 (1984)

CHRIS MEGSON

BARNES, Barnabe
b. ca. 1569, Yorkshire; d. December 1609, London

B. was the son of the Bishop of Durham; in 1598, he was charged, in the Star Chamber, with plotting to poison the Recorder of Berwick. Both his ecclesiastical background and his alleged involvement in a plot of the kind that Elizabethans thought of as characteristically Italianate are reflected in his literary output. Thomas NASHE represented the young B. as "a paltry scrivano betwixt a lawiers clerk and a poet," given to the wearing of extravagantly Italianate clothes ("with a codpisse as big as a Bolognian sawcedge"). It was out of a tension between a sensibility distinctly English and a love-hate relationship with things Italian that B.'s work was produced, work that is in some ways very individual and in others very much representative of its time.

B.'s first publication was *Parthenophil and Parthenophe: Sonnets, Madrigals, Elegies, and Odes* (1593). The collection belongs, clearly enough, in the line of Renaissance sonnet sequences, and the influence of Sir Philip SIDNEY is apparent. However, as the book's subtitle suggests, the collection is metrically and formally more diverse than is normal, and the individualized slant on tradition is also apparent in terms of tone and content. The elegies introduce a Roman influence, and there are points at which *Parthenophil and Parthenophe* resembles Ovid more than Petrarch. Certainly the conclusion to B.'s sequence is decidedly unPetrarchan. In sonnet 105 (the penultimate poem of the entire sequence), the poet-lover resolves to cease the sighs and tears he has addressed to a mistress "soft skinned, hard hearted" and to "compel" her through magic. A complexly patterned triple sestina follows, which both constitutes the promised magic spell and narrates what is, effectively, the rape of the mistress. In a poem such as this, B.'s power is real enough, if more than a little odd and disturbing. Elsewhere his determination to exploit to the full the possibilities of his conceits can seem obsessive and if the results are not always beautiful or satisfying (sometimes they are both), they are never without interest.

In *A Divine Century of Spiritual Sonnets* (1595), B. strikes a penitential posture; sonnet 1 declares "No more lewde laies of Lighter loves I sing." The repentance that characterizes the first nine of the sonnets begins an implicit narrative of spiritual progress (not without backslidings) that concludes in eloquent conviction of salvation and a triumphant "Hymne to the Glorious Honour of the Most Blessed and Indivisible Trinitie." Equally rich in biblical allusion and in a kind of poetic rhetoric that one might describe as a sacred parody of Petrarchanism, B.'s sequence belongs with other Elizabethan devotional sonnet cycles, such as those of Henry Constable and Henry Lok, but displays a distinctive fascination with formal effects of some complexity.

Foure Bookes of Offices: enabling privat persons for the speciall service of all good Princes and Policies (1606) is B.'s one prose work. It is dedicated to JAMES I and B. clearly hoped to win favor and preferment by it. In more than two hundred pages, it offers thoughts on the principles (and to some extent the practice) of civil government, divided into four books; the first is devoted to Temperance (and to the office of Treasurer), the second—the longest—is devoted to Prudence (and discusses the role of Councilors), the third to Justice (with recommendations as to the proper role of Judges and lawyers), the last to Fortitude (paying attention to the responsibilities of military men). B.'s preface expounds the relationship between these virtues through some interesting use of musical analogies, and his subsequent discussions are

enlivened by some effective use of illustrative anecdotes and examples. B.'s lucid and ostentatiously
grave pages are suitably adorned with wide-ranging
references to classical and Renaissance authorities.
More than once, B. denigrates what he calls Machiavelli's "puddle of princely policies," but one senses a
degree of fascination even in these dismissals (a copy
of *Il Principe* signed and annotated by B. survives).

In B.'s solitary surviving play, *The Devil's Charter* (1607), his interest in the "puddle" of Italianate
political intrigue receives more extended expression.
The chief historical source is Francesco Guicciardini's *Historia d'Italia*, an indebtedness registered by
the use of Guicciardini as Chorus to the play. B.'s
subject, he declares, is the "faithlesse, fearless, and
ambitious lives" of Pope Alexander VI and Cesare
Borgia, and his concern is, thus, with "Murther, foule
Incest, and Hypocrisie." The play is a rich mixture of
devils and black magic, fratricide and homosexuality,
domestic murder and ghosts, rounded off by a suitably
moral awakening in the Pope as he approaches death
(in a scene that contains many echoes of Christopher
MARLOWE's *Dr. Faustus*). Chiefly in blank verse (very
competently handled for the most part), the play has
relatively little of B.'s customary metrical inventiveness, but continues his fondness for arcane diction.
The Devil's Charter was performed before the king,
and closes with an epilogue addressed to its "heroick
and benevolent spectators" who are clearly assumed
to be of an altogether more moral cast of mind than
the Borgias who have dominated the play they have
just watched. It is presumably B.'s intention that his
audience (especially the king) should employ their
"juditious censures" not only to assess the merits of
his play but also to consider the relationship between
conscience and "policy" that his play has examined.

BIBLIOGRAPHY: Blank, P. E., Jr., *Lyric Forms in the
Sonnet Sequences of B. B.* (1974); Earl, A., "Late
Elizabethan Devotional Poetry and Calvinism: A Re-
evaluation of B. B.," *RenSt* 11, 3 (1997): 223–40;
Pogue, J. C., ed., *The Devil's Charter by B. B.: A
Critical Edition* (1980)

GLYN PURSGLOVE

BARNES, Julian [Patrick]

b. 19 January 1946, Leicester

B. has become one of England's most respected and
celebrated novelists; he is often included within a
group of younger novelists such as Martin AMIS and
Ian MCEWAN, who are also known as social critics of
modern materialism. Each of B.'s novels offers a different approach to and treatment of its subject matter
as well as a distinctive narrative voice. His prose style
is highly polished, witty, and unfailingly brilliant. He
is also not afraid to experiment with either content or

technique. Many of his novels deal with the themes of
love, jealousy, infidelity, and particularly sexual obsession. Even though his themes are dark and pessimistic, his treatment of them is often satirical and
quite humorous.

B. is also a noted journalist. He reviews novels,
television, and films for the *Sunday Times*, the *New
Statesman*, and the *Observer*. His "Letters from London" for the *New Yorker* was published in book form
with the same title in 1995. B. has also written four
books under the pseudonym of mystery writer "Dan
Kavanagh." The private detective Nick Duffy in the
novels is troubled by his bisexuality, but is extremely
ethical and even altruistic. He seems devoted to moral
and not just legal justice. *Duffy* (1980), the first novel
in the series takes place, as do several other Kavanagh
novels, in the sleazy underworld of London's Soho,
and all four are firmly grounded in the American
hard-boiled mystery tradition of Raymond Chandler
and Evan Hunter.

B.'s first novel, *Metroland* (1980), is a classic
coming-of-age work about a young man, Christopher
Lloyd, who aspires to move beyond his middle-class
suburban lifestyle, whose emptiness he detests. Instead, he celebrates and embraces French culture,
though at the novel's conclusion he finds himself buried in the London suburbs and living his parents' middle-class, bourgeois lifestyle.

B.'s next mainstream novel *Before She Met Me*
(1982) treats the obsessive jealousy of university professor Graham Hendrick toward his second wife, Ann,
a former movie actress who played the temptress in
many films. At the instigation of Barbara, his first
wife, their daughter takes her father to see some of
Ann's movies where she played unfaithful wives, and
Graham becomes disturbingly suspicious of Ann's
every move; the novel ends in violence. However, the
novel that launched B. into a major literary career was
his best-selling *Flaubert's Parrot* (1984). Clearly a
postmodern experimental work employing a variety
of discourses, including the narrator entering some
scenes, B. mixes witty satire with somber meditations
on mortality. Some commentators claimed that its formal structure moved beyond novelistic boundaries; it
appeared to be a set of variations on different forms
of discourse covering many aspects of Gustave Flaubert's life and works.

His next novel, *Staring at the Sun* (1986), departed
from the experimentation of *Flaubert's Parrot*. It
traces the phases in the life of an ordinary woman
named Jean Serjeant. B. wants to disclose to the
reader the extraordinarily courageous elements in her
everyday life, and thus, to uncover the miraculous in
a seemingly quotidian life. In *A History of the World
in 10½ Chapters* (1989), B. returns to the complex
experimentation of *Flaubert's Parrot*. The work begins with Noah's Ark while the last chapter takes

place in heaven. The chapters vary in form as well as content: art criticism, letters, court records, and dream visions, among others. B. challenges the reader to find recurring and, therefore, connecting motifs; that is, to use their imaginations to order what seems chaotic. B. suggests that truth, beauty, and even order are creations of the human imagination. *A History of the World* is one of B.'s richest philosophical novels that meditates on religion, the meaning of history, and even the meaning of life. The author also asks the reader to think about the nature of history in light of the novel's half chapter, which is love.

B.'s novel *Talking It Over* (1991) returns to the theme and setting of his first novel, *Metroland*. The novel examines sex, love, and jealousy in contemporary London. The form of the work consists of three characters addressing readers directly and inviting their participation in determining the nature of truth and its relationship to the characters' "version" of reality. *Cross Channel* (1996) is a collection of short stories grouped around relationships between the French and the English. Recurring themes concern memory, religion, the nature of the artist, sexual jealousy, and infidelity. Few modern English writers cover such a wide area of concerns and treat them in so many different forms of discourse as B.

BIBLIOGRAPHY: Amis, M., "Snooker with J. B.," in his *Visiting Mrs. Nabokov and Other Excursions* (1993): 154–58; Hulbert, A., "The Meaning of Meaning," *NewR* 196 (May 11, 1987): 37–39; Metaxas, E., "That Post-Modernism," *AM* 259 (January 1987): 36–37; Moseley, M., *Understanding J. B.* (1997)

                                    PATRICK MEANOR

BARNES, Peter

b. 10 January 1931, London

B.'s dark comedies contest Henri Bergson's contentions that comedy occurs "when something mechanical is laid on the living," that laughter "has no greater enemy than emotion" and is socially isolating, and that comedy cannot deal with matters of the spirit. In B.'s worlds, laughter is the essential humanizing influence. It breaks asunder the mechanical, isolating structures of imposed order, restoring human life to its essential anarchic spontaneity. Laughter is also a powerful socializing influence, releasing emotion, stimulating compassion and cooperation, and manifesting freedom of spirit. Through the humanizing influence of laughter, the plays make manifest the metaphysical dimension of ordinary life. Their "darkness" resides in the greed and drive for power of the few as they seek to order and control the anarchic energy of the many.

An ongoing discussion of the terms and functions of religion and the significance and responsibilities of mankind in the universe interact with political polemic. His first major play, *The Ruling Class* (perf. 1968; pub. 1969), sets the spiritual essence of Christianity against its manipulation as a means of political oppression. The Gurneys justify their wealth and position by repressing the many through literal application of Christian edict. Imagine their horror when Jack, the incumbent Earl of Gurney, proclaims himself the manifestation of Christ, the God of Love. Jack releases the democratic, joyful heart of Christian spirit, engaging all but his power-hungry family in an all singing, all dancing celebration of life. Unable to control him, the family enlist technology, engaging "The Electric Christ" to squelch his spirit. With Jack's destruction, all HUMOR ceases. Now a manageable cog in the mechanics of the organized Establishment, Jack, now Jack the Ripper, takes his "rightful" place in the festering decrepit House of Lords. B. thus reverses Bergson's premises, exposing laughter as the definitive expression of humankind. Erratic, imaginative, and chaotic, laughter breaks the imposed formulas of organization, stimulates the imagination, and engenders not only the possibility but the necessity of change. *The Ruling Class* was filmed in 1972, directed by Peter Medak and starring Peter O'Toole.

The scope and dynamics of B.'s comedies are unique. Set in historical panoramas, the action is played through as tension between life and death, opposing greed for power against the anarchic energies of ordinary life, and necessitating investigation into the limits of authority and the meaning of human life. His heroes are ordinary people, the "losers" in the onslaught of history. While the historical settings call on the audience's general assumptions, the change in focus deconstructs those assumptions, restructuring their vision to focus on ordinary people in the wake of established events and creating new meanings. Historical facts cannot be changed, but B. translates their significance from a confirmation of power to an experience of the inventiveness and spirit of human life. Though trapped in the flood of historical event, B.'s people provide a rare example of active "goodness" inspired by the anarchic spirit of humor.

In *Dreaming* (1999), four members of Richard, Duke of Gloucester's mercenary force find themselves at a loose end in the apparent peace after the battle of Tewkesbury, and agree to follow Mallory's dream of finding "home." Complex associations with their names create a resonating underlay to the action. Mallory combines the explorer with the author of *Le Morte d'Arthur*, fusing heroism, national identity, and moral ideals of chivalry. Skelton, who seeks only death, melds "skeleton" with poetic vision; Bess, who dreams of true partnership, motherliness with echoes of ELIZABETH I. Finally, there is young Davy, whose only experience is war and who can only imagine riches. When the war revives, the band refuses to fight. Richard pursues them.

What is the meaning of life in the face of death? Ostensibly, this would appear to be the business of tragedy, especially since their deaths are inevitable; but the ethos of the play is comic. Humor focuses the action on the joy of living, strengthening the bond between the characters and engaging the audience with their unity, their inventiveness, and their passions. After all, all lives are lived in the face of death, and so B.'s comedy celebrates chaos of living.

Defying Bergson, B. consistently uses the same moment of humor to create emotional content and response. Humor bonds the characters together, releases emotional response, and draws the audience to them. Mallory finds his home, wife, and child have been victims of the war, but falls in love with Susan, whose lands Richard is confiscating. Reminiscent of L. Frank Baum's *The Wizard of Oz*, each finds completion: Bess, in the preacher Jethro who dies discovering his courage; Davy gives his life for his friends; Mallory and Susan escape Richard through death, frozen in the snow, a monument transcending individual experience to express the courage and anarchy of the human spirit. Though death and the unequal forces of power may not be defeated, they can be transcended. Humor releases the anarchic spirit that makes possible the impossible and the invisible visible. B.'s plays express a profoundly democratic ethos in which even the most minor characters crave attention and exemplify the human spirit.

Red Noses (1985) is arguably B.'s masterpiece. Unique in comedy, it establishes a symbolic context through which the metaphysical content of everyday life becomes manifest. It is 15th-c. France and the plague brings chaos. The forces of order flee. Flote, a monk, asks for God's guidance, and is answered with a joke. In contrast with the flagellants, Flote concludes God wants joy and forms a band of misfits who give succor to the dying by telling jokes. The red noses they wear unite the humor of clowns with their particular relationship with God, their joy and compassion in the face of death, a series of moral values, and, ultimately, an alternative cooperative, inclusive, egalitarian social structure.

Through laughter, they bring joy and compassion to the dying and create an experience of unity in mankind. The laughter also unites the audience with Flote's hapless band and their ideals. When the plague ends and order returns, the audience's original attitude toward chaos is reversed: order signals destruction. Inevitably, the Floties are all killed, but their spirit survives. In a remarkably courageous final scene, only the red noses remain onstage. The voices of the Floties recall their exploits. Their spirit and ideals live on; the metaphysical transcends the limits of individual life; the invisible is made visible. In *Red Noses*,

the impossible is made possible, and comedy transcends the limits of the social world and manifests the world-changing spirit of mankind and its endless gift for cooperation and imaginative creation. The depth of B.'s comic vision transforms physical death from a finality to a celebration of life thus affording the audience a unique version of the comic "happy ending." His latest play, *Jubilee* (2001), commissioned by the Royal Shakespeare Company, is a satirical view of David GARRICK's Shakespeare Jubilee, and, in keeping with all of B.'s plays, a celebration of theater itself.

BIBLIOGRAPHY: Dukore, B. F., *Barnestorm: The Plays of P. B.* (1995); Woolland, B., "P. B.," in Bull, J., ed., *British and Irish Dramatists since World War II*, Second Series, *DLB* 233 (2001): 22–34

ELAINE TURNER

BARNES, William
b. 22 February 1801, Sturminster-Newton, Dorset; d. 7 October 1886, Winterborne Came, Dorset

Thomas HARDY noted that B. could claim relation to the "old unpremeditating singers in dialect" but that he was also "academic closely after; and we find him warbling his native wood-notes with a watchful eye on the predetermined score, a far remove from the popular impression of him as the naif and rude bard who sings only because he must." A number of poets including Hardy, Gerard Manley HOPKINS, Coventry PATMORE, and Alfred, Lord TENNYSON admired B.'s work both because of his depiction of a dying way of life and because of his craftsmanship, informed by his vast and eclectic study. Critics including E. M. FORSTER and Geoffrey GRIGSON have tried to revive interest in a poet who wrote "hwomely rhymes" but also used sophisticated techniques based on his understanding of over sixty languages, including Persian, Welsh, and Hebrew. It may be precisely that blend of dialect and prosodic sophistication, however, that detracts from B.'s reputation in an era where little attention is paid to the subtleties of prosody or traditional poetic forms. Readers should, however, continue to attend to his work as a philologist and as a poet who awakened his contemporaries to the possibilities of dialect as a subtle form of expression.

In addition to producing ten volumes of poetry, B. also participated in the important Victorian philological debate concerning "pure English." He published a number of volumes in which he argued for a return to "pure" Anglo-Saxon, uncorrupted by the introduction of Greek and Latin terms. In his work, he used terms like "fore-say" for "preface" or "bendsome" for "flexible" to illustrate the importance and possibility of a more robust and genuinely "English" form of expression. In works including his *Anglo-Saxon*

Delectus (1849), *A Philological Grammar, Grounded upon English, and Formed from a Comparison of More Than Sixty Languages: Being an Introduction to the Science of Grammar and a Help to Grammars of All Languages* (1854), *Tiw; or, A View of the Roots and Stems of English as a Teutonic Tongue* (1861), and *An Outline of Speech-Craft* (1878), B. maintained the importance of reviving "pure English" and theorized that languages develop according to a system of laws. Once we understand the laws of their development, he believed, we can then easily learn new tongues and can retain the vitality of individual languages. B. applied a logical, rational approach to all his studies, although many have questioned whether he was pursuing a practical end or whether even he would find it useful or natural to stick to his version of "pure English." In addition to his philological works, B. produced a number of textbooks that he used in his work as a teacher, providing materials for his students in areas he felt had been neglected or poorly covered. Further, he spent a great deal of time writing for publications like the *Gentleman's Magazine* and lecturing to working men's institutes as he became an expert on diverse areas of archaeology and history. In all of his work writing on various subjects, he brought together diverse fields in order to gain an understanding of the complex interrelationships necessary to learning. He respected tradition while aiming to keep up with the latest thinking in every field.

While scholars of Victorian philology may find much of interest in B.'s prose works, his contemporaries and his later defenders emphasize the importance of his poetry for an understanding of the possibility of depicting "homely" subjects and speakers using subtle and complex verse techniques. B. wrote some poems in what he called "national English," but both his critics and defenders concentrate on his use of dialect. Critics note that readers resist the difficulty and humorous connotations of dialect poems and dismiss B.'s work as intensely regional in its subject matter. Defenders praise volumes including *Poems of Rural Life, in the Dorset Dialect* (1844) and *Hwomely Rhymes* (1859; repub. as *Poems in the Dorset Dialect,* 1864) for their universality and immediacy, noting that dialect is not necessarily a source of HUMOR or provincialism. B. was capable of writing political poems, including his early "Eclogues," which explored the realities of rural poverty and the changes wrought by the Poor Laws or waves of 19th-c. emigration. Even in poems that present his native Blackmore Vale as an idyllic pastoral setting, B. never loses sight of the ways that change (represented by death, marriage, and moving), overturns the world of the simple folk and brings tragedy to the essentially gentle and comic cycles of rural life. Admittedly, this chronicler of Dorset life relies on a relatively limited series of images; as Alan Hertz notes, "he composes land-scapes from stereotyped elements arranged according to artistic conventions." While his subjects are conventional, it is his attention to the sounds of poetry that seem to have most intrigued his poet critics, including Hardy and Patmore. Poems like "Lindenore" or "My Orcha'd in Linden Lea" display the Welsh technique of *cynghanedd*, a pattern of consonants that creates a rich texture in the verse; while Hopkins may not have learned this technique from B., he certainly was interested in the way that his predecessor used the device to add linguistic interest to what may have struck many as a conventional celebration of country life and country women. In addition to using sound patterns from earlier Welsh and Anglo-Saxon forms, B. also created dialect poems in the forms like the Persian *ghazal* ("Green") or using devices like Hebrew psalmic parallelism ("Melhill Feast"). B. consistently displays the breadth of his study of languages and verse techniques that make him unusual as a dialect poet. Although he was a self-conscious artist, his work never has a self-conscious feeling. As Hardy wrote, "surely much English literature will be forgotten when 'Woak Hill' is still read for its intense pathos, 'Blackmore Maidens' for its blitheness, and 'In the Spring' for its Arcadian ecstasy." While B. may be a poet's poet who never found a popular audience, he wrote the kind of poetry that will continue to find readers who can appreciate both his SENTIMENT and his craft.

BIBLIOGRAPHY: Hertz, A., "The Hallowed Pleäces of W. B.," *VP* 23 (Summer 1985): 109–24; Levy, W. T., *W. B.* (1960); Parins, J. W., *W. B.* (1984); Sisson, C. H., "W. B.," in his *Art and Action* (1965): 30–46

CATHERINE FRANK

BARNFIELD, Richard
b. 13 June 1574, Norbury; d. 6 February 1620, Market Drayton

Although considered a minor poet, B. is extremely important since he was the first English poet to air publicly his homoerotic verses. When *The Affectionate Shepheard* was published in 1594, it prompted the poet to explain away his intentions one year later in the preface to a second volume of poetry, *Cynthia* (1595). In the first volume, a shepherd named Daphnis sings of his love for a boy named Ganymede, who spurns Daphnis's affections because he is in love with Guendolen. Curiously, B. identifies himself as Daphnis at the end of the book's dedication to Lady Penelope Rich, so some critics have tried to identify the historical names behind both Ganymede and Guendolen. As a successful example of pastoral, the title poem "The Affectionate Shepheard" reads nicely as a narrative piece, but its companion poem in the volume, "The Shepherds Content" seems didactic and moralistic.

The much examined preface to *Cynthia* tries to show that B.'s intention in writing the homoerotic Shepheard poems was merely to imitate Virgil's second eclogue: the author claims that he never meant to champion the love of one man for another. The volume, however, contains twenty homoerotic sonnets that are even stronger in their male-male affection than "The Affectionate Shepheard" had been. The subject of the sonnets is again identified as "Ganymede," and they represent a significant addition to the sonnet-writing craze that extended in the late Elizabethan period from Sir Philip SIDNEY to William SHAKESPEARE. The "Ode" that follows the sonnets, in the tradition of sonnet sequences, says that the author has shifted his affections from Ganymede to a lady named "Eliza," but since the lady could be the queen, the "Ode" may be considered a patent tribute to the reigning monarch rather than any proof that B. was swearing off his homoerotic love interests. "Cynthia," the title poem of the *Cynthia* volume, is not homoerotic. It is significant, however, for another reason: it is the first poem in English to use the Spenserian stanza after the publication of *The Faerie Queene*.

Following *Cynthia*, B. published only one more volume, *The Encomion of Lady Pecunia* (1598), but the book contains four sections, each with its own title page, so there is some speculation that the publisher may have intended to break the book into four parts in order to make more money off the printing. The title poem, "The Prayse of Lady Pecunia," sings of the joys of having money, and the following poem, "The Complaint of Poetrie, for the Death of Liberalitie," decries the lack of patrons willing to bankroll deserving poets. B. apparently was falling on hard times by the end of the century.

Although early biographers claimed that B. retired from his law studies in London to spend his life on the family estates in Darlston, evidence now shows that he was disinherited (twice) by his father in favor of B.'s younger brother. We now believe that B. died before his father, and the will attributed to the poet for centuries is probably the will of the poet's father. We can speculate that B.'s father either was angered by the poet's public homoerotic verses or, if B. never married (and there is no proof that he did marry), the father may have wanted the family fortune to pass to a married son. In spite of any personal setbacks, however, B. remains a singular voice in English Renaissance poetry, a brave voice for homoerotic feelings in an age that also gave us the Shakespeare homoerotic sonnets that never, apparently, raised the hue and cry that *The Affectionate Shepheard* raised because Shakespeare never authorized the printing of his own sonnets.

BIBLIOGRAPHY: Borris, K., and G. Klawitter, eds., *The Affectionate Shepherd, Celebrating R. B.* (2001); Klawitter, G., ed., *R. B., the Complete Poems* (1990); Morris, H., *R. B., Colin's Child* (1963)

GEORGE KLAWITTER

BARRIE, [Sir] J[ames] M[atthew]
b. 9 May 1860, Kirriemuir, Forfarshire, Scotland; d. 19 June 1937, London

During his lifetime, B. was held in high esteem by writers such as Robert Louis STEVENSON and Bernard SHAW and, in acting, by Mary Pickford and Ellen Terry. As early as the 1920s, however, he lost favor with critics who judged him a Victorian sentimentalist and who preferred the more robust work of Shaw, Harley GRANVILLE BARKER, and John GALSWORTHY.

B.'s earliest success was *Auld Licht Idylls* (1888). Characteristic of the late 19th c., the collection is HUMOR with considerable Scottish dialect and is based upon the author's boyhood in Kirriemuir. Most historians categorize the work with the Kailyard writers, who preferred the life and character of small town Scotland and sought to reproduce the dialect of the people. In general those tendencies further identify the work as local color. The idylls strike most readers as journalistic impressionism (B. was a newspaperman).

A number of highly popular fictions followed *Auld Licht Idylls—When a Man's Single* (1888), *A Window in Thrums* (1889), and *The Little Minister* (1891). One characteristic of all three novels is their apparent sentimentality, an excessive enjoyment of emotion for its own sake. All of the works reveal, moreover, a deep attraction to a mother figure and, for that reason, recent critics have explored the Freudian implications of B.'s texts. *The Little Minister*, for example, is a reworking of B.'s feelings regarding his deceased brother and his mother, Margaret Ogilvy, whom B. idolized.

The novels *Sentimental Tommy* (1896) and *Tommy and Grizel* (1900) chronicle the growth of a male into manhood. While Harry M. Geduld sees the *Tommy* novels as criticism of the "artistic temperament" in Tommy Sandys, Andrew Nash examines the novels as cultural responses to Thomas CARLYLE's industrialized, aggressive male society that fears the evolution of the timid, withdrawn, solipsistic and possibly masturbatory male personality.

B. was always engrossed in childhood, his own and that of his characters. Peter Pan and the myth of eternal youth were initiated in 1902 in the adult fiction *The Little White Bird*, which develops the notion that infants are birds before they are placed in the womb. However, the popular Pan legend as we know it today is based upon a six-chapter children's story *The Little White Bird*; a play for children, *Peter Pan; or, The*

Boy Who Wouldn't Grow Up (perf. 1904); and a seventeen-chapter children's story paralleling the play *Peter Pan in Kensington Gardens* (1906). The Peter Pan story is also based upon elements borrowed from CHILDREN'S LITERATURE and from a common Oedipal configuration in males. By 1950, approximately fifteen million people had seen the play. The Walt Disney film version of the legend introduced Peter Pan to millions more admirers.

The Admirable Crichton (perf. 1902; pub. 1914) has remained a popular play. Premiering in November 1902 at the Duke of York's Theatre, London, the play was developed as a silent film by Cecil B. de Mille in 1919 under the title *Male and Female*, and starred Gloria Swanson. *Crichton* is a sparkling, delightful comedy concerning English social structure and relations. The butler Crichton, a naturally superior man, becomes the leader of the aristocrats he works for when they are all shipwrecked on a deserted island. When, however, all return to London, he must revert to his place as inferior. B.'s examination of English social structure and class comes at a time when Henry JAMES and Oscar WILDE and Frances Hodgson BURNETT were making, possibly with greater poignancy, the same considerations.

B. figures significantly in English fiction and drama from the Victorian and modernist periods. His reputation has been more erratic than the reputation of some of his contemporaries. Stevenson always believed him a great writer, while Elizabeth BOWEN deprecated him. Allardyce Nicoll, for example, felt he made no appropriate condemnation of the English class system. Although *Peter Pan* and, to some extent, *The Admirable Crichton*, assure B.'s literary immortality, to recent critics his works remain flawed by his excessive, maudlin, and sometimes embarrassing sentimentality.

BIBLIOGRAPHY: Darlington, W. A., *J. M. B.* (1938); Dunbar, J., *J. M.* (1970); Geduld, H. M., *Sir J. B.* (1971); Nash, A., "'Trying To Be a Man': J. M. B. and Sentimental Masculinity," *MLS* 35 (April 1999): 113–25; Ormond, L., *J. M. B.* (1987)

GEORGE C. LONGEST

BARSTOW, Stan[ley]
b. 28 June 1928, Horbury, Yorkshire

Author of the best-selling first novel, *A Kind of Loving* (1960), B. emerged as part of a postwar group of writers from the industrial north of England that included John BRAINE, Alan SILLITOE, David STOREY, and Keith WATERHOUSE. The novel was adapted for film in 1962 by Waterhouse and in 1965 was adapted as a play by B. and Alfred Bradley. Set in the fictional West Yorkshire town of Cressley, *A Kind of Loving* introduced the central character of Vic Brown who would reap-

pear in *The Watchers on the Shore* (1966) and *The Right True End* (1976)—republished in 1981 as *The Vic Brown Trilogy*. The working-class Yorkshire milieu informed the majority of his fiction as well as his plays for radio, stage, and television—earning B. a reputation as a regional writer. His stories are collected in *The Desperadoes* (1961; rev. as *The Human Element*, 1969), *A Season with Eros* (1971), and *The Glad Eye* (1984). A latter trilogy comprising *Just You Wait and See* (1986), *Give Us This Day* (1989), and *Next of Kin* (1991) is centered around Yorkshire life during World War II.

BATES, H[erbert] E[rnest]
b. 16 May 1905, Rushden, Northamptonshire; d. 31 January 1974, Canterbury

In a career spanning more than fifty years, B. published at a rate of over a book a year, making him one of the most prolific British authors of the last century. Rather than attempting to dazzle readers with stylistic experimentation or breathless plotting, B. strove in his fiction to show, as Anthony BURGESS said, "some small human truth in rather drab and ordinary human circumstances."

B. began his literary career with the publication of a novel, *The Two Sisters* (1926). One of B.'s best-known novels is *Fair Stood the Wind for France* (1944), the story of John Franklin, a British bomber pilot trapped in occupied France, and his struggle to make it back to England; along the way, he meets and falls in love with the stoic and courageous Françoise, who assists him in his journey. In a different vein are the later comedic novels centered around the character of Pop Larkin: *The Darling Buds of May* (1958), *A Breath of French Air* (1959), *When the Green Woods Laugh* (1960; repub. as *Hark, Hark, the Lark!*, 1961), *Oh! To Be in England* (1963), and *A Little of What You Fancy* (1970). Pop is something of an entrepreneurial hedonist—the first novel, for example, tells the story of the Larkin family's efforts to entrap an unsuspecting tax collector into a marriage with the suddenly pregnant oldest daughter, Mariette—and these humorous novels are among B.'s most popular.

B.'s short stories feature a variety of plots and characters, but some central themes emerge. B. was the first writer of fiction ever commissioned by the military for the specific purpose of continuing his writing in the service of the war effort. Working for the RAF, B. assumed the pseudonym "Flying Officer X" (although the general public was aware of his true identity) and produced such works as *The Greatest People in the World and Other Stories* (1942; repub. as *There's Something in the Air*, 1943) and *How Sleep the Brave and Other Stories* (1943), two collections that, along with *Fair Stood the Wind for France*, show B.'s enduring fascination with airmen and soldiers.

What is notable about these works is that, despite being commissioned by the military, they never become pure propaganda thanks to B.'s concern with the development of believable characters.

In addition to writing about the RAF, B. wrote many stories about children. "Let's Play Soldiers" depicts a group of English children during World War II, playing at the war games that are all too real for their older countrymen. Several stories, including "The Watercress Girl," "Love in a Wych Elm," and "The Cowslip Field," describe a child's first impressions of love. On the other hand, stories such as "The Station," "The Mill," "Thelma," and "The Kimono" deal with adult sexuality—sexual relationships in these stories often lead to lack of fulfillment and despair.

B. may ultimately be best remembered for his light and humorous Larkin family novels, televised with David Jason in 1991–93. Nevertheless, he was a truly professional writer who excelled at the short story form, and whose fiction was always craftsmanlike and engaging.

BIBLIOGRAPHY: Baldwin, D. R., *H. E. B.* (1987); Eads, P., *H. E. B.* (1990); Garnett, D., *Great Friends: Portraits of Seventeen Writers* (1980): 204–9; Vannatta, D., *H. E. B.* (1983)

JASON BERNER

BAWDEN, Nina
b. Mary Mabey, 19 January 1925, London

A prolific writer whose body of work ranges from adult novels to children's books, B. has a worldwide reputation. Evacuated from London with her family during World War II, B.'s life was greatly disrupted, a concept that would be incorporated into many of her books. She always perceived herself as a writer, experiencing success as a schoolgirl by writing stories and plays. B. studied politics, philosophy, and economics at Oxford (with Margaret Thatcher as a classmate), graduated in 1946, took an M.A. in 1951, and attended the Salzburg Seminar in American Studies in 1960. She served as Justice of the Peace for the County of Surrey from 1968 through 1976.

B.'s professional writing career began with novels for adults. Three early novels are murder mysteries—*Who Calls the Tune* (1953; repub. as *Eyes of Green*, 1953), *The Odd Flamingo* (1954), and *Change Here for Babylon* (1955). *The Solitary Child* (1956) is a Gothic romance. *Devil by the Sea* (1957), a novel about a ten-year-old who identifies a child murderer, was later abridged for children in 1976. *Just like a Lady* (1960; repub. as *Glass Slippers Always Pinch*, 1960) marks the beginning of B.'s comic novels about middle-class social values with a focus on relationships. While B.'s novels contain HUMOR, they also ex-

plore the ways in which people examine their lives. *Anna Apparent* (1972) shows the adult results of childhood deprivation. *George beneath a Paper Moon* (1974) suggests possible incest. *Afternoon of a Good Woman* (1976) chronicles the decision about remaining in a marriage. In *Familiar Passions* (1979), a character finds a long-lost biological parent. *Walking Naked* (1981) is a woman's painful self-examination of her life and career. *The Ice House* (1983) is a triangle of marriage, friendship, and adultery. *Circles of Deceit* (1987) chronicles the frustrations of negotiating a personal and a professional life; it was short-listed for the Booker Prize.

Encouraged by her husband and inspired by her children's desire to have her be their storyteller, B. began writing children's books. From her own childhood, B. remembered two things: children look at the world differently from adults and they are always anxious for adventures. Her first children's book was *The Secret Passage* (1963; repub. as *The House of Secrets*, 1964), followed by *On the Run* (1964; repub. as *Three on the Run*, 1965), *The White Horse Gang* (1966), *The Witch's Daughter* (1966), and *The Runaway Summer* (1969). *Carrie's War* (1973), one of her best-known children's books, is based on a situation similar to her own evacuation in South Wales during the war. It received a Carnegie commendation in 1973 and won the Phoenix Award, presented by the Children's Literature Association in 1993. Another of B.'s most popular children's books, *The Peppermint Pig* (1975), won the *Guardian* Award in 1976. *Rebel on a Rock* (1978) returns to characters introduced in *Carrie's War*. *Kept in the Dark* (1982) was nominated for the Edgar Allan Poe Award and received a Parents' Choice citation. *The Finding* (1985) also received a Parents' Choice citation.

Many of B.'s children's books incorporate issues of childhood displacement and neglect, the effects of poverty, and children not being taken seriously by most adults. Many of her children's books will include a group of children who band together to solve a problem, an eccentric adult who does bond with the children, and a central character who is independent and curious. The books contain the complexity of childhood, exploring serious issues. The young characters are resourceful, stubborn, and emotional. Resolutions at the end of the novels do not come without an examination of the way in which characters have had to give something up to gain something else.

As B.'s career progressed, she has been able to balance writing for both adults and children, alternating between the two audiences throughout most of her career. B.'s "almost" autobiography, *In My Own Time* (1994), chronicles her growth as a writer, detailing the difficulties of her childhood, particularly displacement and poverty during the war, that later show up in so much of her children's fiction. B. was named a Commander of the Order of the British Empire in 1995 and is a Fellow of the Royal Society of Literature.

BIBLIOGRAPHY: Rees, D., *The Marble in the Water* (1980); Seaman, G., "N. B.," in Moseley, M., ed., *British Novelists since 1960*, Third Series, *DLB* 207 (1999): 25–33; Tucker, N., *The Child and the Book* (1981)

REBECCA FABER

BEAUMONT, [Sir] Francis

b. ca. 1584, Grace-Dieu, Leicestershire; d. 6 March 1616, London

The younger son of a country justice, B. was educated at Oxford and the Inner Temple before embarking on his brief but brilliant career as a playwright. B.'s first two surviving plays, both comedies—*The Woman Hater* (perf. 1606; pub. 1607) and *The Knight of the Burning Pestle* (perf. ca. 1607; pub. 1613)—were his alone or substantially so. All his subsequent dramas, with the exception of the *Masque of the Inner Temple and Gray's Inn* (perf. 1613; pub. 1613), were collaborations with John FLETCHER. The highly successful and influential partnership ended when B. married an heiress and retired to the country around 1613.

Though modern critics consider *The Knight of the Burning Pestle* a masterpiece, it failed with its first audience who, according to the play's publisher, missed "the privy mark of irony about it." Sophisticated and satirical, *The Knight* spoofs popular dramatic modes: moral plays about prodigals, romantic comedies, and stories of citizen adventurers. As B.'s metatheatrical comedy begins, an actor speaking the prologue of "The London Merchant" (a play within the play) is interrupted by a grocer and his wife (actors planted in the audience) who demand that the company rename and revise their comedy to feature their apprentice, Rafe, in "a huffing part." "The London Merchant" thus becomes "The Knight of the Burning Pestle," as Rafe's Don Quixote-like exploits are ludicrously interwoven with the plot lines of the former. Much of the comedy derives from the persistent interruptions of the grocer and wife who comment freely on the action and improvise Rafe's story to satisfy their vulgar theatrical taste. Although B.'s satirical depiction of the disruptive citizens is designed to appeal to a social elite, the satire is affectionate: George and Nell are lively, warm and good natured, and B. clearly shared their pleasure in popular theater. B. gives the last word to Nell, who generously invites the whole audience to her house for "a pottle of wine and a pipe of tobacco."

The tragicomedy *Philaster; or, Love Lies a-Bleeding* (perf. ca. 1609; pub. 1620), probably B.'s first theatrically successful collaboration with Fletcher, adapts literary romance to the stage: the eponymous hero, rightful heir to the throne of Sicily, loves Arethusa, the virtuous daughter of the usurping king. Though betrothed to a foreign prince, she remains secretly faithful to Philaster. The play's principal emotional and erotic complications emerge from Philaster's groundless jealousy of his beautiful and devoted young page, Bellario. Believing her false, Philaster attempts to execute the willing Arethusa but only wounds her in the breast before he is providentially interrupted. With exemplary loyalty, however, she conceals his guilt. The pattern of erotic punishment and loyal response is repeated when Philaster basely wounds the sleeping Bellario, who then lies to protect his master. Stricken with remorse, and wounded himself, Philaster begs to die embracing his page: "lay me gently on his neck, that there/I may weep floods and breathe forth my spirit." In the play's emotional climax, bleeding hero clings to bleeding boy, as Philaster extols Bellario's virtue and begs his forgiveness. Only in the final moments of act 5 does Bellario reveal that he is really a woman, who has disguised herself for love of Philaster. In contrast to William SHAKESPEARE's use of the female-page motif in *Twelfth Night*, B. and Fletcher conceal Bellario's "true" identity from the audience until the denouement. While Shakespeare exploits the audience's knowledge of Cesario/Viola's sex for comic effect, B. and Fletcher use the last-minute revelation of Bellario/Euphrasia's sex primarily to heighten the pathos of her position in a love-triangle that will continue indefinitely at the play's close.

In *The Maid's Tragedy* (perf. ca. 1611; pub. 1619), B. and Fletcher map a more complex network of erotic triangles in a more overtly political context. In the central triangle, the hero Amintor discovers his bride Evadne is the king's mistress: as a loyal subject he must suffer the shame of cuckoldry without seeking redress. The impasse is broken when Evadne's brother Melantius forces her at sword point to confess and repent her liaison. In the play's most sensational scene, Evadne ties the arms of the sleeping king to his bed and reproaches him with her whoredom, before stabbing him to death. The playwrights contrast the sexually corrupt Evadne with the chaste Aspatia, formerly betrothed to Amintor. Like Bellario/Euphrasia in *Philaster,* Aspatia is a figure of pathos: masochistically devoted to the hero, she too disguises herself as a man and seeks death at his hands. Inadvertently killing her, Amintor makes physical his prior emotional abuse. Her extended death scene is interrupted by the suicide of Evadne, and followed by that of Amintor. Melantius, Amintor's brother-in-law and best friend, underscores another triangle as he embraces the dying hero and weeping, vows to follow him into death.

Although *The Knight of the Burning Pestle* ensures B.'s place in the latest anthologies of Renaissance drama, his collaborations with Fletcher were widely admired and imitated in the 17th c.

BIBLIOGRAPHY: Bliss, L., *F. B.* (1987); Clark, S., *The Plays of B. and Fletcher* (1994); Finkelpearl, P., *Court and Country Politics in the Plays of B. and Fletcher* (1990)

KAREN BAMFORD

BECKETT, Samuel [Barklay]

b. 13 April 1906, Dublin, Ireland; d. 22 December 1989, Paris, France

Considered by many the most influential playwright in the mid-to-late-20th c., B. is associated with movements such as existentialism and the French *nouveau roman*, as well as with artists and intellectuals such as James JOYCE, Marcel Proust, Jean-Paul Sartre, Albert Camus, and C. G. Jung. B.'s literary efforts were varied. He was the author of novels; short stories; poetry; and scripts for radio, television, and film. In spite of his breadth as a literary figure, he is best known for his association with the mid-20th-c. French avant-garde and with what came to be known as the Theater of the Absurd. His works convey themes influenced by existentialist thinkers such as Sartre and Camus, who argued that human beings face an impenetrable mystery that cannot be rationally explained or justified. As such the world must appear darkly comic and absurd. B.'s works feature abstract a-historical plots and minimalist settings, as well as characters who react to experience with alternating degrees of wonder, bewilderment, fear, and crippling anxiety.

B.'s parents were reasonably affluent members of the Anglo-Irish professional class. Born and reared in the Stillorgan district of Dublin, B. received his early education in Stillorgan, then at Earlsfort House School in Dublin, and then at the Portora Royal School in Enniskillen, County Fermanagh, Northern Ireland. Early in his school career, B. emerged as a complicated and unpredictable individual: he was popular with classmates and excellent at athletics; but he was often brooding, aloof, and reserved, behaviors that foreshadowed the psychological traumas of his youth and early adulthood.

B. entered Trinity College, Dublin, in 1923, intending to study law with the ultimate goal of becoming a chartered accountant and joining the family firm. Perhaps because of an inherent lack of enthusiasm for business and professional life, he performed poorly in his first two years. But in his third year, he discovered modern languages, studying and performing well under the tutelage of Dr. Thomas B. Rudmose-Brown, Trinity's renowned professor of French. B.'s academic performance improved considerably, so much so that he was awarded the Foundation Scholarship in Modern Languages, which allowed him to spend a summer studying in France. He graduated first in his class from Trinity College in 1927 and prepared to serve as exchange *lecteur* at the Ecole Normale Supérieure in Paris.

From 1927 to 1935, B. alternated between Dublin, London, Paris, and Kassel. His continued study of languages and his development as a literary figure coincided during this period with serious bouts of depression and mental instability. The causes of this condition are uncertain, but they emerge from numerous factors, including B.'s introspective and contemplative nature, the expectations of his middle-class family (particularly his mother), and his sense of alienation from a father who was in temperament quite different from his precocious and inwardly directed son. B. attempted to work on his mental problems through writing and psychoanalysis. The psychoanalytical theories of Jung influenced his best-known writings. During this period, B. became associated with Joyce, a man he respected immensely and came to see as a kind of surrogate father and a model of the ideal literary artist.

Though known as a playwright, B. always considered himself a novelist, arguing that his plays were only brief and temporary diversions to channel and direct his energies when his fiction was at an impasse. His adoration of Joyce appears throughout his novels but especially in his early work, and his fiction as a whole reflects an interest in philosophy and a preoccupation with psychological issues. *Whoroscope* (1930) began as a poem but finally became a prose monologue influenced strongly by Joyce and the symbolist poets. The narrative follows the life of Descartes as written by Adrein Baillet. During this period, he also published an essay entitled *Proust* (1931); but suffering from depression and a temporary falling out with Joyce, he returned to Dublin and then moved to Kassel, Germany, to live with an aunt. Recovering slowly and considering his future, he traveled occasionally to Paris and began selling stories to magazines, many of which were gathered later in *More Pricks than Kicks* (1934). During this period, B. submitted himself to psychoanalysis and worked directly to assuage his psychological demons, supporting himself sparsely with reviews, literary journalism, and criticism, while at the same time writing poetry. The treatment was less than successful, but it was during this period that his analyst, Dr. Wilfred R. Bion, recommended that he attend Jung's Tavistock Lectures. Jung posited a theory that exerted a tremendous influence on B.'s *Murphy* (1938), arguing that the notion of a unified consciousness is an illusion, that human identity is composed of multiple and fragmentary personalities. *Murphy* deals with a common Irishman working in a mental hospital and living with a reformed prostitute, and it explores phenomenological questions and issues of identity and consciousness in an arguably modern but strangely abstracted setting. *Murphy* is followed by *Molloy* (1951; *Molloy*, 1955), *Malone meurt* (1951; *Malone Dies*, 1956), *L'Innommable* (1953; *The Unnamable*, 1958), and *Watt* (1953; *Watt*, 1968). With these novels, B. begins a practice that continued for the rest of his writing life: composing both in English and in French. Each narrative displays a dark, despairing, obsessive, and sometimes comic sensibility. His style becomes more distinctive and less marked by a Joycean influence, and there are fewer ornate constructions and a more direct minimalist technique. These works involve an overt autobiographical and psychological emphasis and the extended use of first person dramatic monologue.

B.'s plays are most commonly associated with the Theater of the Absurd, a movement in dramatic literature that emerged in Paris and became dominant after World War II. Drawing from the physical, moral, and psychological devastation of the war in Europe and from the philosophies of Sartre and Camus, absurdist dramas featured dreamlike and fantastic settings and characters groping for meaning in an environment of existential confusion. These works find their source in medieval religious dramas, particularly from the morality plays (see MYSTERIES AND MORALITY PLAYS) and allegorical works of Baroque Spain. B.'s contribution to this movement cannot be overestimated. Though his literary output in drama was comparatively prolific, arguably his most important contribution to dramatic literature in the 20th c. appears in three plays: *En attendant Godot* (1952; *Waiting for Godot*, 1954), performed in 1953, *Fin de partie, suivi de Acte sans paroles* (1957; *Endgame, Followed by Act without Words*, 1958), performed in 1957, and *Happy Days* (1962; *Oh les beaux jours*, 1963), performed in 1961.

Waiting for Godot remains B.'s most well-known play and the one work with which he is most often associated. In a simple two-act play, following the pattern established in his fiction, B. introduces two main characters, Vladimir and Estragon, mysterious figures removed from historical reference who sit for two days on a bare stage under a single tree waiting for the arrival of a man named Mr. Godot. They are told at the end of the first day (and act) that Godot will come the next day. With only slight variation, the second day repeats the first. Godot never arrives, and Vladimir and Estragon contemplate suicide but ultimately decide against it. *Waiting for Godot* involves simple but obscure verbal exchanges and has been explored by critics from a number of vantage points, among them as a demonstration of Schopenhauer's metaphysics and a veiled treatment of the role of Christian salvation. But in essence the play is an allegory of the modern existential condition, since the main characters find themselves in a world of unrealized anticipation, in a dreamlike and universalized set-

ting. They confront an essential human dilemma: the question of meaning in a universe that reveals itself almost comically as an impenetrable mystery.

Endgame and *Happy Days* follow similar formal patterns and design, involving comparatively few characters placed in abstract, historically removed settings. *Endgame* is a one-act drama of desperation and decay, dealing with blind Hamm and his attendant Clov, along with Hamm's parents who spend the play in waste-cans. Using the chess game as a presiding metaphor, *Endgame* explores issues of meaning as well as the role of self-perception as a means of self-definition. *Happy Days* deals with a character named Winnie, who is buried to her neck but is strangely attached to the contents of her handbag. The play continues the preoccupation with existential and phenomenological issues, with the relationship of perceiver and perceived, consciousness and the world of objects. B.'s other works include *Krapp's Last Tape* (perf. 1958; pub. 1959), *Come and Go* (perf. 1966; pub. 1967), and *Not I* (perf. 1972; pub. 1973), enhancing an oeuvre that earned him the Nobel Prize for Literature in 1969. Though a profoundly "philosophical" writer, whose works have been subject to countless interpretations, B. refused to acknowledge a relationship with any particular system of thought, specifically avoiding the term "existentialism." Unlike Sartre, who permits ideas and philosophical concepts to drive his narratives and the actions of his characters, B. is an artist of experience, allowing characters to demonstrate the human condition first. As a literary artist in multiple genres, B. is among the most remarkable figures in the portrayal of 20th-c. philosophical and psychological concerns.

BIBLIOGRAPHY: Andonian, C. C., *S. B.* (1989); Bair, D., *S. B.* (1978); Begam, R., *S. B. and the End of Modernity* (1996); Butler, L., St. J., ed., *Critical Essays on S. B.* (1993); Federman R., and J. Fletcher, *S. B.* (1970); Murphy, P. J., et al., *Critique of B. Criticism* (1994)

STEVEN FRYE

BECKFORD, William
b. 29 September 1760, Fonthill, Wiltshire; d. 4 May 1844, Bath

B. was rescued from near oblivion in our time, his life and works elevated to the highest standing they enjoyed until the moment just before his sexual downfall in 1784. If the Victorians viewed him as wickedly transgressive, the Edwardians cast him as tragically irresponsible, both overlooking the Regency eccentric he was. If B. was no Lord BYRON, who called him "a martyr to prejudice," he was nevertheless as aristocratic as, and much richer than, the prototypical Romantic poet (B. inherited the largest Jamaican sugar fortune in British history).

He was also bisexual, which influenced the course of his writing. But whereas Byron's escapades were conducted with adults in the name of experimental exoticism, B.'s resembled such unabashed pedophilia that he elicited no sympathy (the eleven-year-old boy, William Courtenay of Powderham Castle, who lured him to his bed and broke the back of his reputation was biographically more sinner than saint). Even so, the resuscitation of exotic 18th-c. figures after World War II, both in Europe and in the U.S., lavished new and well-deserved attention on B. and turned him into a genuine curiosity for our time.

B.'s own "life" was his main work, as important as anything he penned. On it—not merely his interior fantasies and artistic connoisseurship but his vast art collections and the palatial splendor of the buildings he inhabited—he lavished his millions. People occupied less mental space than dreams and objects, even the few young men he loved. Although he became acquainted with notables of the age (the great personalities of Enlightenment and Romantic Europe), it was his interior mind and his prize objects of art that stimulated him. This was because his temperament was composed of contradictions and extremes, none of which could annihilate the chronic melancholia he suffered.

He had a gilded boyhood in luxury's lap, intimate with friends John Robert Cozens and Philip Loutherbourg, and tarnished only by homosexual scandal. To survive, he fled; wandered almost permanently in exile, traveling through middle Europe, especially in Switzerland and Iberia. If his English parents bequeathed their millions to him, Portugal provided his solitary "lover": Gregorio Franchi, a seventeen-year-old who eventually left his wife and children and migrated to England to be constantly at B.'s side (their volumes of unpublished love letters are in the Bodleian Library in Oxford). Yet B.'s romantic agony gravitated to the sublime and supernatural in remote eastern places: the Adriatic, Levant, Arabia; so much that he was his generation's most eloquent pan-Arabic sympathizer, steeped in its lore and dedicated to its alluring temperament. It is impossible to conceptualize the rise of modern Orientalism apart from him.

B. glittered as a youth, as George Romney's portrait makes plain and as befitted England's premier millionaire playboy. Reared at Fonthill in Wiltshire, educated at home, and often alone in an era when rich boys were sent to university, he was then whisked away on the Grand Tour. At fifteen, he began to write exotic tales based on his reading; two years later, he traveled to Geneva with his tutor John Lettice. This was followed by trips to the cathedrals, monastic institutions, and country houses of Britain, on one of which (in 1779) he became intrigued by the young Courtenay, who told his parents and brought legal action. At twenty, B. witnessed the Gordon Riots in

London, and soon after crossed the Alps with Lettice, making for Naples where he accommodated with Sir William Hamilton, the English Envoy, and his cultivated wife, Catherine, who was addicted to romantic melancholics like B. and took him in as her confidante.

The 1780s—when in his twenties—were B.'s great decade. He settled into a pattern of spending winters in England, the rest of the year abroad, and keeping copious journals. In 1782, he composed *Vathek*, based on the wide reading he had made in Oriental tales, especially a 1708 English version of *Arabian Nights*. *Vathek* was the Gothic "Oriental tale" that made him famous: the story of an effeminate caliph who sells his soul to an evil jinn in exchange for the might of the pre-Adamite sultans. It was an instant success among a reading public still thirsty for Gothic fiction that embodied the acute gender tensions of its time. B. also published *Dreams, Waking Thoughts and Incidents* in 1783, an autobiographical fragment as original as Jean-Jacques Rousseau's incendiary *Reveries* (1777). But B.'s "outage" with Courtenay wrecked his political career, and by 1785 his own family exiled him to Switzerland, telling him he should never return because he was cursed on native soil.

His marriage in 1783 to his cousin, Lady Margaret Gordon, produced a daughter but nothing else, and she died, mercifully, in 1786, just weeks before *Vathek* appeared without his permission, heaping yet more disgrace on the wealthy Beckfords. Now addicted to travel, he wandered compulsively, witnessing political events (he saw the storming of the Bastille in 1789) and amassing expensive objects of art. In 1794, he visited Portugese monasteries while resident in Lisbon and Sintra about which he later wrote an account, *Recollections of an Excursion to the Monasteries of Alcobaca and Batalha* (1835). In 1807, after twenty-two years of travel, he returned to Fonthill, where he built the legendary castle he turned into a Gothic ruin. Here, he lived in seclusion until 1822, when financial circumstances forced him to sell out. Nothing he wrote after 1807 rivaled the glittering Oriental fiction of his youth, which had prognosticated entry into the pantheon of canonical writers. Instead, he quietly reveled in the collections of antiquities he had amassed with his unique connoisseur's eye and the golden memories of his youth. Who else in this exotic peacock's generation had been taught to paint by the genius Alexander Cozens and learned piano at five with the eight-year-old Mozart?

BIBLIOGRAPHY: Alexander, B., *England's Wealthiest Son: A Study of W. B.* (1962); Fothergill, B., *B. of Fonthill* (1979); Mahmoud, F. M., ed., *W. B. of Fonthill* (1960)

GEORGE ROUSSEAU

BEDDOES, Thomas Lovell

b. 20 July 1803, Clifton; d. 26 January 1849, Basel, Switzerland

B. is important as a distinguished lyric poet, a figure in the late history of English ROMANTICISM, and a poetic and dramatic genius whose full potential was never realized. B.'s talents developed at a very early age, and at Charterhouse and Oxford, where he was educated, he wrote stories and poems while still a boy, showed a remarkable knowledge of early English drama, and published in his first two years at Oxford two significant works.

B.'s first publication was a book of verse called *The Improvisatore* (1821). This consists mainly of three Gothic verse narratives that are full of demon lovers, horrific death, and wild madness. This extravagant Gothicism might be supposed to reflect a merely youthful imagination, but in fact the themes of *The Improvisatore* would remain B.'s themes throughout his life. In the year after *The Improvisatore*, B. published a much more important work, his neo-Jacobean verse drama called *The Bride's Tragedy* (1822). In this closet drama, overwhelming emotional conflict, horror, death and murder, and violent passion of every sort continue to be B.'s themes, but here there is a unity of structure, a sense of psychology, and, especially, a power of poetic expression far beyond anything in *The Improvisatore*. The richness and vitality of B.'s dramatic blank verse and his powers of lyric construction are especially remarkable anticipations of his later masterpiece, *Death's Jest-Book* (1850).

The Bride's Tragedy enjoyed a critical success, and for a time it seemed that B. was poised to become an important dramatist and poet. Indeed, between 1822 and 1825, he wrote a large number of short poems and began several verse dramas. During the same period, however, B.'s letters show increasing doubt about a literary career, and his writing during these years produced no publication.

In 1825, B. seemed to desert literature in favor of medicine. He left England to study in Germany and Switzerland, and the rest of his life was largely spent studying anatomy and medicine generally, engaging in radical European politics, and wandering from one European city to another. B.'s abandonment of literature was, however, more apparent than real. Between 1825 and 1849, B. wrote and endlessly revised the only work in which his full genius is genuinely manifest, *Death's Jest-Book*. This huge closet drama of some four thousand lines is the culmination of B.'s strange career as a writer. It shows his deep knowledge of Jacobean tragedy, his overwhelming preoccupation with death in every imaginable form, his wild power of Gothic imagination, and, best of all, his brilliant command of poetic expression in dramatic blank verse and in the many lyrics contained in the play. In these lyrics, by which B. is best known, there is a combination of formal perfection, verbal beauty, imagistic vitality, and sensuous horror that is unique to B.'s style. The plot and characters in *Death's Jest-Book* are more nightmare than drama, but the astonishing poetic power of the work marks it as one of the greatest and strangest of late Romantic poems. Among the best of the lyrics in *Death's Jest-Book* are the haunting "Sibylla's Dirge," the grotesque "Song: Squats on a Toad-Stool," and the eerie "Old Adam, the Carrion Crow."

Despite the brilliance of *Death's Jest-Book*, B. increasingly felt like a failure both as a poet and physician. In 1849, haunted by death to the end, B. was successful in his second suicide attempt and killed himself at the age of forty-five. In addition to the posthumous *Death's Jest-Book*, a volume of his dramatic fragments and unpublished poems was printed in 1851. This volume adds to B.'s stature as one of the most important late Romantic poets between 1820 and 1840.

BIBLIOGRAPHY: Bloom, H., *The Visionary Company* (1971); Donner, H. W., *T. L. B.* (1935); Heath-Stubbs, J., *The Darkling Plain* (1950); Thompson, J. R., *T. L. B.* (1985)

PHILLIP B. ANDERSON

BEDE or BEDA [Venerable]

b. ca. 673, Environs of Jarrow, Northumbria; d. 25 May 735, Monastery of Wearmouth-Jarrow, Northumbria

B. was the most influential English author of the early Middle Ages, eclipsed perhaps only by Alcuin. In Western Europe, the two centuries between 600 and 800 C.E. have been called "the Age of Bede." His published works are almost exclusively in Latin, and with the decline of Latin in this century, his influence is commonly underappreciated.

B.'s life was spent within the walls of the Benedictine monastery of Jarrow in northern England. He rarely traveled beyond its grounds, if at all, but was in correspondence with monks and priests throughout Britain. Everything B. wrote touches on his religious vocation. He is credited with dozens of works, the majority of which deal with the explication of Scripture. During his lifetime, his work gained international stature. He was ordained a priest at age thirty. In 1849, he was declared a Doctor of the Church, and was proclaimed a Catholic saint in 1935.

B.'s works divide into two major categories: the didactic and the exegetical. In the latter, one finds his commentaries on a number of books of the Old and New Testaments. In the former, one finds textbooks (*De Orthographia, De Arte Metrica, De Natura Rerum, De Temporibus*), grammars (*De Schematibus et Tropis*), geographies (*De Locis Sancties*), and histories. He is perhaps best known today for his histories, especially his *Historia Ecclesiastica Gentis Anglorum* and the *Historia Abbatum*. These are the primary sources for our knowledge of the late 7th and early 8th cs., and on their account B. is often called the "father of English history." The *Historia Ecclesiastica* has been translated into dozens of languages and commonly goes by the title of *The Ecclesiastical History of the English People*. In this work, B. describes, among other things, the poet CÆDMON's first poem; later glossators added it in various English dialects to the margins of the manuscripts. (B. is also credited with inventing the footnote, and he is responsible for the A.D./B.C. dating system.) B. also wrote Latin poems and hymns, and although he is not considered one of the great Christian poets, his poems have significant aesthetic and doctrinal merit.

B.'s Latin style is eminently clear. He avoids the complex and rarified Hiberno-Latin or "hermeneutic" style that flourished at the time, and his vocabulary is predominantly classical. B. wrote to be understood. Most of his theological works were dedicated to his bishop, Acca of Hexham, and many seem to have served to clarify difficult points of doctrine or as compilations of Patristic learning. His grammatical, orthographic, metrical, and scientific textbooks were used in Western schools for four hundred years. B. was perhaps the most learned man of his generation. He was trained in the monastic Rule, *cantus* (chanting), and in Augustinian theology by his abbots—Benedict Biscop, Ceolfrith, and Sigfrid—and by John the Archchanter and Trumbert, an Irish monk. B. worked according to the Augustinian model of literary interpretation described in Augustine's *De Doctrina Christiana*. His textual explication began with the literal and moved to the figurative and sometimes to the moral, incorporating a variety of Patristic criticism. His model of interpretation became standard when it was employed in the *Glossa Ordinaria*, a popular, multivolume work that might be described as a 12th-c. Christian version of the Talmud.

BIBLIOGRAPHY: Brown, G. H., *B. the Venerable* (1987); Hunter Blair, P., *The World of B.* (1970); Ward, B., *The Venerable B.* (1990)

                                    STEPHEN J. HARRIS

BEERBOHM, [Sir] Max [Henry Maximilian]
b. 24 August 1872, London; d. 20 May 1956, Rapallo, Italy

Widely viewed as an unsurpassed parodist, B. employed his biting technique in both prose and caricature. Since his death, more critical focus has been given to his considerable skill at caricature, but B.'s literary output is not insignificant. B. was a novelist, essayist, and critic. He also produced some verse—*Max in Verse* and *Collected Verse*, published posthumously in 1963 and 1994, respectively.

Coming of age in post-Victorian England, B. absorbed his country's shift away from strangling social mores and dove headfirst into satirical and ironical circles that included such famous wits as Oscar WILDE and Aubrey Beardsley. B.'s interest in the prevailing Aesthetic movement, which maintained that art and beauty should be the pinnacle of human endeavor, took the form of a civilized hedonism, a refined cult of pleasure. His form of parody was one in which he took his subjects to task for taking themselves too seriously. B. sought to criticize society by elevating himself above it; he rarely sought to satirize society with any idea of effecting changes. But despite B.'s reputation as a masterly parodist, his subjects were seldom, if ever, dealt with cruelly. Unkindness was against B.'s conception of art and aesthetics as needing to be at once elegant and pretty. Consequently, his parodies were without malice, and their subjects seldom had reason to feel slighted. Indeed, B. often included himself in his satirical renderings. His most celebrated parodies can be found in *A Christmas Garland* (1912), which includes parodies of, among others, Joseph CONRAD, Thomas HARDY, and Henry JAMES.

Soon after B.'s admission to Oxford, he fully incorporated all of the dandyish affectations of a typical hero of a Wilde work. The literary output that followed contained much of the flippancy, self-bemusement, and biting wit that he had incorporated into his own character. It was B.'s essay, "A Defence of Cosmetics," appearing in a new quarterly devoted to literature and art, the *Yellow Book*, which launched his literary career. "A Defence of Cosmetics" impudently suggested that English women should wear rouge to compensate for nature's deficiencies. (In Victorian England, the wearing of rouge was typically associated with prostitutes.) The essay brought out many critics, each of them missing B.'s satirical angle. Ironically, the essay's criticism made B. a known literary force. Over the years, the impertinence that defined B.'s early works, such as those appearing in the *Yellow Book*, would give way to a certain mature humorism.

After several more appearances in the *Yellow Book*, B. left Oxford to focus on a career as "some sort of writer." That generally manifested itself in essays, which would eventually be collected in five volumes: *The Works of Max Beerbohm* (1896), *More* (1899), *Yet Again* (1909), *And Even Now* (1920), and *Mainly on the Air* (1946; rev. ed., 1957). In 1898, B. became the editor of the *Saturday Review*, succeeding Bernard SHAW, who dubbed B. simply, "The Incomparable Max." It was during his tenure at the *Saturday Review* that B. honed his skills as a critic. But these works are not considered among his finest. Rarely did criticism call for the comedic or ironic tone, and thus, B. often lamented that it was not the type of writing that suited him best. B. was considered to be at his satirical (literary) best in his short stories. Of these, he wrote two fables, "The Happy Hypocrite" (1897) and "The Dreadful Dragon of Hay Hill" (1928), a tome on the immutability of man's capacity for conflict. "The Happy Hypocrite" is a good example of the B. aesthetic worldview. The fable's moral message is a simple one: act with goodness and become good. This goodness in action is an inevitable byproduct of holding and acting upon high ideals, of which love of the arts and beauty is one. The 1919 collection of short stories, *Seven Men*, is often hailed as a masterpiece. It is in *Seven Men* that B.'s most famous story, "Enoch Soames," can be found. "Enoch Soames" serves as an excellent view of the atmosphere that surrounded the *Yellow Book*. Soames is a dreadful poet, consumed with how history will view his work. When he comes to see that history has forgotten him, except as a fictional character in a B. story, he is horrified. The surrealistic nature of the fiction is the vehicle through which B. suggests the folly in taking oneself too seriously. It was this self-seriousness, of the type that plagues the fictional Soames, that B. spent his whole life mocking.

B. produced one novel, *Zuleika Dobson* (1911). The novel also plays with many of the same themes that can be found in "Enoch Soames." The title character is an irresistible woman, driving all the young men to distraction. When the Duke of Dorset fails to ensnare her love, he throws himself in the river. A parade of young men follows his example, as it becomes fashion. The obvious criticism is of the prevailing fashion of earnestness and egoism that B. rebelled against. In the end, no one comes out alive except Zuleika Dobson, who, because of her own self-importance and incapacity to enjoy the pleasures of attention, is doomed to isolation. B. ended his days in Rapallo, Italy, where, but for brief exiles during the World Wars, he spent his time mostly seeing guests and dispensing witticisms and recollections about a time that had seemed long past. The turn of the century fun had given way to grand conflicts, and B. came to be viewed as a preserved relic of more innocent times.

BIBLIOGRAPHY: Cecil, D., *Max* (1964); Lynch, B., *M. B. in Perspective* (1921); Riewald, J. G., *M. B.'s Mischievous Wit* (2000); Viscusi, R., *M. B.; or, The Dandy Dante* (1986)

E. LINDSEY BALKAN

BEHAN, Brendan

b. 9 February 1923, Dublin, Ireland; d. 20 March 1964, Dublin, Ireland

B. rose to fame in the 1950s on the back of his bawdy, exuberant, and compassionate evocations of contemporary Irish life in drama, poetry, and prose. Though B.'s reputation as a drinker has often overshadowed his standing as a writer, his best work bears enduring testament both to his tremendous talent and his humanity.

B. was reared in Dublin among a large and outgoing family, surrounded from the first by the influences that would shape his writing: religion, republican politics, and alcohol. B.'s talent as a writer first surfaced in an unpublished play, *The Landlady*, written in Mountjoy Prison during one of a series of imprisonments for his involvement in the then becalmed republican movement. Articles for various Irish periodicals followed, many of them later published as *Hold Your Hour and Have Another* (1963). In short stories such as "A Woman of No Standing" (1950) and "The Confirmation Suit" (1953), B. wrote fondly but not uncritically of the Dublin community in which he had been reared, while "After the Wake" (1950) describes homosexual seduction with a candor and understanding unusual for the time. In the serialized adventure *The Scarperer*, written in 1954 under the name Emmett Street, B. showed he could sustain a narrative to book length. All these works demonstrated a memorable turn of phrase and a penchant for the crude that would soon attract an international readership.

The short radio dramas *Moving Out* (1952), *A Garden Party* (1952), and *The Big House* (1957) were all later adapted for the stage. The first two are little more than dramatized anecdotes of Dublin life, while the last is a cartoonish tale of a landlord's robbery; none, however, entirely lack charm. More significant, the memoir *Borstal Boy* (1958) recalls the author's experience of two years of juvenile detention in England as a result of his early, and ineffectual, forays into terrorism (after which he renounced violence). Aside from its gripping opening scene, describing a seizure of explosives at the young B.'s lodgings, and the sheer assurance of its prose, by turns thoughtful and broadly comic, the book's most noteworthy feature is the curiosity and openmindedness with which B. observes his fellow inmates and captors alike.

B.'s first full-length drama, *The Quare Fellow* (perf. 1954; pub. 1956), is arguably his other great work, a prison drama of rare sensitivity and HUMOR in which the impending execution of the unseen title character overshadows the day-to-day life of both prisoners and warders. B.'s compassion for the condemned man, whose guilt he does not question, makes the play a powerful indictment of capital punishment, at that time still in use in Britain and Ireland, but it is also a vivid and humorous portrait of the prison as microcosmic society. The play was a success first in Dublin, then in London under Joan Littlewood's direction for Theatre Workshop, and finally as a film released in 1962.

The Quare Fellow was followed in 1958 by B.'s best-known work *The Hostage*, originally *An Giall* (perf. 1958; pub. 1981), a tense and touching three-act drama written in Gaelic. *An Giall* concerns Leslie, a British soldier held hostage in a Dublin brothel to prevent the execution of an IRA prisoner in Belfast, his burgeoning romance with a sympathetic Irish maid, and his untimely death by suffocation while being hidden from the police. When Littlewood asked B. to produce an expanded version in English, she found him more interested in drinking and, in consequence, a good deal of *The Hostage* as we have it today is based on improvisations by the company. Unfortunately, though the anarchic music hall jokes, outrageous comic characters, and frequent bursts of song that characterize *The Hostage* doubtless added to its contemporary appeal, they cannot be said to have aged as well as the underlying drama they augment.

By now, despite protracted periods of abstention, B.'s health was failing and his best work behind him. A series of travelogues and memoirs followed, dictated rather than written: *Brendan Behan's Ireland* (1962), *Behan's New York* (1964), and *Confessions of an Irish Rebel* (1965). These work well as permanent records of their author's skill in conversation, but suffer greatly in comparison to cohesive, considered works like *Borstal Boy* or *The Quare Fellow.*

Following B.'s death at forty-one, his colleague Alan Simpson edited some pages the author had left behind into a final two-act play, *Richard's Cork Leg* (perf. 1972; pub. 1973), its title a good indication of its inconsequentiality. The play is essentially an extended dialogue between three pairs of comic characters—two generic prostitutes, two seedy rebels, and a pious Protestant and her soon-seduced daughter—set in an Irish cemetery, linked by a plot to disrupt a fascist memorial, and incorporating many old jokes. The piece retains some of the rumbustious charm of B.'s earlier plays, though little of their dramatic structure or tension.

B. today is remembered more as a character than an artist, his spirit commemorated in the songs of Shane MacGowan and elsewhere. His best work as a writer, however, fully justifies his place in posterity on literary grounds alone.

BIBLIOGRAPHY: Gerdes, P., *The Major Works of B. B.* (1973); Littlewood, J., *Joan's Book* (1994); O'Connor, U., *B. B.* (1983); O'Sullivan, M., *B. B.* (1997)

HARRY DERBYSHIRE

BEHN, Aphra [Johnson]

b. ca. 1640, Harbledown, Kent; d. 16 April 1689, London

B. was the first woman known to have earned her living by her pen. Although she seems particularly well educated for a woman of the time, and was friends with many in and around the court, she was remarkably reticent about her birth and family. It is known from official documents that she was spying for Charles II in Antwerp from August 1666 to January 1667. There are seventeen letters from her that show an impetuous, courageous, honest woman. Nothing is known of her husband, apart from his Dutch surname. It is assumed he died in the plague of 1665 and that she had to support herself thereafter.

B. is credited with some nineteen plays between 1670 and her death, which was an amazing number for anyone let alone a woman three hundred years ago. Only John DRYDEN is known to have written more among her contemporaries. She used the possibilities of the shutters on the new scenic stage to great effect in devising disclosures and discoveries and was mainly very popular with her audiences. Yet only two or three have been performed since the 18th c. despite their theatricality, becoming thought of as disgustingly obscene, completely unworthy of serious study. Bawdy of course depends to some extent on one's point of view and most Restoration comedies have sexually explicit language and behavior. However, even in her own time there were complaints that she was writing material unsuitable for a woman, and this view that a woman should not write with as much frankness as a man has bedeviled her reputation ever since. Some critics have found an excessive number of bedroom scenes in her comedies, but it is an exaggeration to suggest that her use of bedroom scenes is pornographic. Although the dialogue leaves no doubt as to what has occurred, or is likely to happen, there is far less in the way of innuendo or double entendre than in some of the plays of contemporaries such as William WYCHERLEY or Sir George ETHEREGE.

B.'s attitude to sex is earthily realistic but retains a certain reticence in the physical manifestations on stage and in the language her characters use. Although she certainly exploited sexual relationships in her plays and made the most of the various ways in which men and women were involved together in the context of the contemporary society, its morals and attitudes, she used such themes in carefully structured stories in which the sexual muddles of the characters are an essential part, rather than a titillating enhancement added deliberately to attract the audience. The whores in her plays—Flauntit, Mrs. Driver, Jenny, and Doll—are drawn without censure but with an uncompromising eye to their squalid existence, and for a few minutes there is an uncomfortable realism on stage, as in *The Rover* (1677) when Angelica, the courtesan, acts against convention in falling in love with Willmore. B. shows that whores are people with feelings, not the romantic figures the girls suggest, when they pretend to be ladies of pleasure in *The Feign'd Curtizans* (1679), which she dedicated to actress Nell Gwyn.

Her plots illustrate many of the consequences for women in varying circumstances, and may sometimes have been based on her own experience of marriage, but there is no evidence that she meant them as any kind of feminist polemic and she was hurt that she should be reviled for writing bawdy, arguing that she had to earn her living just like the men.

Her one full-length novel, *Oroonoko* (1688), is now generally accepted as based on firsthand knowledge of the conditions in Surinam. She deals with the enslavement of the natives by the settlers in a highly charged, even romanticizing way, but with enormous sensitivity and perception. It was one of the earliest books of fiction that was not an adaptation or translation but an original written in the vernacular. It was later adapted as a play by Thomas Southerne (perf. 1695; pub. 1696).

Love-letters between a Noble-man and His Sister, published in three parts (1684, 1685, 1687), is a fictionalized account of real events, the trial of Lord Grey of Werke who absconded with his sister-in-law, Lady Henrietta Berkeley, and B. wrote several shorter novels sometimes based on true events but which she expanded to make her story more interesting or exciting. Hers was a particularly colloquial style unlike anything written before and, in the opinion of some, was the forerunner of Daniel DEFOE and Jonathan SWIFT. She published one of the earliest translations of Fontenelle's philosophical paper *The History of Oracles* (1688) and his *Discovery of New Worlds* (1688) shortly before her death.

B. wrote verse and her love lyrics appear occasionally in collections especially an ambiguous one "Love in fantastic Triumph sat" from her only tragedy entitled *Abdelazer* (perf. 1676; pub. 1677). There was a persistent, gossipy rumor into the 18th c. that she was in love with, if not the lover of, John Hoyle, an unpleasant man eventually murdered in unsavory circumstances three years after her death. Bulstrode Whitelocke called him "an aetheist, a sodomite professed, a corruptor of youth and a blasphemer of Christ." B. herself called him a "great admirer of Lucretius," and several of her more moving love poems are supposedly dedicated to him. However, it seems unlikely that she was ever any man's mistress in the sense of surrendering her financial independence. In 1683, she wrote to Jacob Tonson her publisher begging an advance on some work she was doing, and in 1685 she wrote a promissory note to a Mr. Zachary Baggs to repay £6 against the receipts of her next play.

Despite her apparent poverty toward the end of her life, B. would not compromise her own Tory principles and refused an invitation to write an ode to celebrate the arrival of William and Mary in 1688. She died soon after in poverty and pain and was buried in the cloisters at Westminster Abbey under the epitaph:

"Here lies a proof that Wit can never be/ defense enough against mortality."

BIBLIOGRAPHY: Duffy, M., *The Passionate Shepherdess: A. B., 1640–89* (1977); Todd, J., ed., *The Works of A. B.* (7 vols., 1992–96); Todd, J., *The Secret Life of A. B.* (1996); Todd, J., ed., *A. B. Studies* (1996)

DAWN LEWCOCK

BELL, Quentin [Claudian Stephen]

b. 19 August 1910, London; d. 16 December 1996, Sussex

Acknowledged as one of the reigning authorities on the BLOOMSBURY GROUP, B. was well suited for the role in that both parents were part of the inner circle—his father, Clive Bell, was a well-known critic and art historian; his mother was the artist Vanessa BELL, sister of Virginia WOOLF. His proximity to the group inspired biographies of John RUSKIN (1963) and Roger FRY (1964), a composite study entitled *Bloomsbury* (1968), and his masterly *Virginia Woolf: A Biography* (2 vols., 1972; rev. ed., 1996). In his finely crafted and sensitive portrayal of Woolf, B. vividly re-creates both the late Victorian period of the patriarchal Sir Leslie STEPHEN and the circle of literary and artistic figures identified with Bloomsbury—Fry, Duncan Grant, Lytton STRACHEY, Virginia and Leonard WOOLF, among numerous others. In addition to his literary pursuits, B. was an accomplished painter and sculptor who in 1964–65 was appointed Slade Professor of Fine Art at Oxford. Other publications include the critical study *A New and Noble School: The Pre-Raphaelites* (1982) and a novel, *The Brandon Papers* (1985). From 1977 to 1984, B. edited with his wife, Anne Olivier Bell, the five-volume *Diary of Virginia Woolf*. In 1995, he published his autobiography aptly entitled *Bloomsbury Remembered*.

BELL, Vanessa [Stephen]

b. 30 May 1879, London; d. 7 April 1961, Charleston, near Asheham, Sussex

Daughter of prominent editor and literary scholar Sir Leslie STEPHEN and sister of Virginia WOOLF, B. was part of the emerging artistic movement influenced by the European avant-garde in the early part of the 20th c. and a central figure in the so-called BLOOMSBURY GROUP. Rejecting the social as well as artistic restrictions of the period, B. enjoyed an open and independent lifestyle—characterized by her unconventional marriage to critic and art historian Clive Bell, with whom she had two children, an affair with art critic and painter Roger FRY, and her long-standing relationship with the painter Duncan Grant, with whom she had a daughter. B. was a successful artist in her own right, known primarily for her impressionistic style that included portraits of Fry, Woolf, E. M. FOR-STER, and Aldous HUXLEY, among others. B.'s *Notes on Virginia's Childhood: A Memoir* and her *Selected Letters* were published posthumously in 1974 and 1993, respectively.

BELLOC, [Joseph] Hilaire [Pierre René]

b. 27 July 1870, La Celle St. Cloud, France; d.16 July 1953, Guildford

When B. died in 1953, the obituaries were kindly and after Robert Speaight published his authorized biography in 1957 the reviews were generally favorable but, during the 1960s and 1970s, B.'s reputation declined and he was remembered almost exclusively for his light verse; his more difficult political, economic, historical, and polemical works being generally ignored. There has been no collected edition of his over one hundred books and booklets, now mostly out of print, so when A. N. WILSON wrote an irreverent study in 1984, many critics seized the chance to dismiss B.'s work as dated and didactic and to condemn a writer they had barely studied as a near-fascist bigot. Since then, despite some revision of views, his books remain unfashionable and his preoccupations alien to the modern mind.

B. was certainly a complex man and some explanation lies in his bicultural family background. He was born in France in 1870 in the midst of the Franco-Prussian war and his parents fled to England, where he was reared and educated. His father, Louis Belloc, was French, son of a successful painter; of a Catholic, yet also Republican family; he had trained for the law, but was too delicate to practice and died when young Hilaire was only two. On the other hand, his mother Elizabeth "Bessie" Parkes, a Catholic convert, was English, of Nonconformist background, daughter of the radical Birmingham member of Parliament Joseph Parkes. She did not marry until she was thirty-nine and had first a daughter, Marie (Belloc LOWNDES), herself to become a successful writer, and then B., but soon had to raise her children alone and in genteel poverty, some money she had inherited from her wealthy uncle having been lost in unwise investments.

B. proved a bright and lively child, so was offered an excellent education at the Oratory School, established by Cardinal Newman in Birmingham. Then, after completing his military service as a French citizen in the French artillery, he was accepted as a somewhat mature student into Balliol College, Oxford, where he studied history rather than classics, worked hard, and gained a first-class degree and a reputation for public speaking. Next however, he was disappointed in his application for a fellowship at All Souls and hopes for a solid academic career, so had to fall back on his writing. This financially insecure life was compounded by marriage, in June 1896, to his Irish-American sweetheart, Elodie Agnes Hogan, and con-

sequent money worries in Oxford and then London forced them, in 1906, to settle at King's Land, Sussex. They had five children, three daughters and two sons, one of whom died in World War I and one in World War II.

B.'s literary career was determined by his inheritance of these diverse traditions, from French and Irish Republican to English Radical, and his Catholic formation within a still insular Protestant society. He was moved to explore each of these tendencies in turn, searching for reconciliation and synthesis. His classical and Catholic schooling followed by academic training at Oxford, all enhanced his natural capacity for close reasoning and clarity of style, but may well have diminished his creative imagination. Yet his first literary success was *The Bad Child's Book of Beasts* (1896), featuring comic verses for children, which were well received then and still admired today. However, his more serious poetry, in *Verses and Sonnets* published the same year and later augmented, was less appreciated and has been undervalued, though a year after his death in 1953, there was a collected edition by William Roughead.

Next, to earn serious money as a freelance, B. decided to use his knowledge of France and French and even his youthful radical sympathies to research and write works on the disputed French Revolution. While in his books on *Danton* (1899) and *Robespierre* (1901), he initially defended the Jacobins, he came to appreciate the role of the early French kings and even to understand the royalist point of view, in his biography of *Marie Antoinette* (1909), his *The French Revolution* (1911), and his short profiles in *Last Days of the French Monarchy* (1916). Later he wrote *Miniatures of French History* (1925) and studies of Joan of Arc (1929), Cardinal Richelieu (1929), and Louis XIV, called *Monarchy* (1938), although after *The [Russian] Campaign of 1812* (1924), he wrote only a slight, disappointing work on Napoleon Bonaparte (1932).

He enjoyed military history and from 1911 to 1913 wrote a successful series on "Great British Battles" mostly between Britain and France over the centuries. During 1914–18, he edited the *Land and Water* review and afterward in 1919 translated *The Principles of War* and *Precepts and Judgments* by Marshal Ferdinand Foch. He knew Winston CHURCHILL, and they must have debated *The Tactics of Marlborough* (1933) and of Napoleon.

These books on France were accompanied by the exploration of B.'s English radical inheritance. He had worked out his early political and economic ideas for debates in the Oxford Union and edited a book of essays by six University men on *The Liberal Tradition* (1897) which have not weathered well. Moving to London in 1900, he next began to write some articles for the pro-Boer *Speaker* magazine, met the Chestertons, and finally secured paid work from 1906 to

1910, as literary editor of the *Morning Post*. In 1902, he became a British citizen, but his excursion into practical Liberal politics and experience as member of Parliament for Salford from 1906 to1910 proved unhappy and disillusioning and he left Parliament in 1910.

B.'s new political cynicism was expressed in his satirical novels like *Mr. Clutterbuck's Election* (1908) and *A Change in the Cabinet* (1909), which are still entertaining for those who have studied the Edwardian era and can appreciate G. K CHESTERTON's accompanying caricatures, but the characters are not memorable. His later fiction satirized more diverse evils and became rather more genial in tone.

B., like G. K. and Cecil Chesterton, has been accused of assorted now "politically incorrect" prejudices, as against the Suffragettes, Marconi men, and Jews, individuals such as Masterman, the Germans, and the Turks, but although a "prima facie" charge can be made out against him in each case, further reading reveals that he attempted to be just and modified his opinions in later works (e.g., *The Postmaster-General*, 1932).

Meanwhile, B. expressed his more serious political and economic concerns in a series of pamphlets mostly for the Catholic Truth Society, against socialism, anarchism, and also capitalism, but in favor of the ideals of Pope Leo XIII in his encyclical *Rerum Novarum*. In cooperation with Cecil Chesterton came their critical book on *The Party System* (1911), in which they attacked both main parties for merely taking turns over the spoils of office, and their founding of "The League for Clean Government" and two papers, the *Eye Witness* followed by the *New Witness*, exposing the danger of secret party funds built up by the sale of honors and policies, and the "insider trading" of the 1913 Marconi scandal.

B.'s most famous work, *The Servile State* (1912), was based on this earlier material and all his study, reflection, and practical experience of politics. Ideologically, he rejected both industrial capitalism and state socialism and advocated instead a system of well-divided property, which came to be termed distributism. However, his initial thesis was that Britain, through the early welfare measures of Churchill and David Lloyd George, was heading rather toward a fourth possibility, that of the Servile State, in which the masses would remain permanently dependent upon the few owners of land and capital. To protect the people against such a plutocracy, B. later proposed, in *The House of Commons and Monarchy* (1920), a strengthened monarchy, which would however be advised and aided by various industrial councils, not unlike those advocated by Continental Syndicalism or by G. D. H. Cole's British brand of Guild Socialism.

Although Cecil Chesterton had started out as a Fabian Socialist, rather than a Liberal like his brother, both came to share and support B.'s political beliefs. After Cecil joined up in 1916 (and died 1918), his elder brother took over as editor of the *New Witness*, which he eventually replaced by *G. K.'s Weekly* and B. supported him in occasional articles and in the formation of the Distributist League in 1926.

This now forgotten political movement did not long survive G. K. Chesterton's death in 1936, although both B. and T. S. ELIOT tried to keep it going and B. briefly edited the *Weekly Review* that had replaced *G. K.'s Weekly*, before handing over this task to his son-in-law Reginald Jebb. By this time he had also elaborated his ideas on distributism in *An Essay on the Restoration of Property* (1936).

Long before this, however, despairing of any real or immediate prospect for reform, B. decided to devote his remaining energies to the laborious and systematic rewriting of English history and BIOGRAPHY, in an attempt to promote a wholesale revisionist Catholic interpretation, in opposition to what he regarded as the false and biased Protestant Whig version. He completed four volumes of *The History of England* (1925–31), but only reached 1612, never finishing this ambitious work. Instead, he summarized his conclusions in his *Shorter History of England* (1934) and *Essay on the Nature of Contemporary England* (1937), which should be contrasted with books in the Whig tradition, G. M. Trevelyan's *History of England* (1926). Since then, both standpoints have been overtaken by later research and the growth of a consensus between Catholic and Protestant historians, e.g., over Ireland, but his corrective efforts should not be undervalued.

From 1927 to 1942, B. also wrote a series of biographies of varying merit on some leading figures in this long conflict. Notable are studies of Oliver Cromwell (1927), James II (1928), Cardinal Wolsey (1930), Thomas Cranmer (1931), William I (1933), Charles I (1933), John MILTON (1935), Charles II (1939), and ELIZABETH I (1942). But probably his best biographical work was his collection of profiles, British and foreign, entitled *Characters of the Reformation* (1936). In the course of this great effort, B. engaged in a series of bruising controversies with rival thinkers, writing short tracts, mostly again for the Catholic Truth Society, against critics such as William Ralph Inge, Dean of St. Paul's, H. G. WELLS, and G. G. Coulton, on disputes ranging from monastic achievements to Evolution. These are sometimes instructive, sometimes amusing, but most have dated and recall "battles long ago."

Assiduous readers of B. generally agree that, despite occasional aridity of style, his prose is at its best in the nonfiction work, in the short lives, essays, and even humorous digressions. The travels delight: *The Path to Rome* (1902), *Hills and the Sea* (1906), *The Cruise of the "Nona"* (1925), and *Return to the Baltic* (1938) linger in the mind. In polemics, *Survivals and*

New Arrivals (1928) and *Essays of a Catholic Layman in England* (1931) are not only eloquently argued, but remarkably prophetic. Perhaps he wrote too much and one can single out no perfect masterpiece, but the lasting impression is one of greatness.

BIBLIOGRAPHY: McCarthy, J. P., *Edwardian Radical* (1978); Pearce, J., *Wisdom and Innocence: A Life of G. K. C.* (1996); Speaight, R., *The Life of H. B.* (1957); special B. issue, *CR* 12 (May 1986); Wilson, A. N., *H. B.* (1984)

PATRICIA M. WHARTON

BENNETT, Alan
b. 9 May 1934, Leeds

Continuing an influential tradition of mild, witty social SATIRE begun in the collaboration with Jonathan Miller, Dudley Moore, and Peter Cook, *Beyond the Fringe* (perf. 1960; pub. 1963, rev. ed., 1987), B.'s career as a dramatist of skillful social commentary has continued into the new century. The *Fringe* skits gained inspiration from the works of the U.S. stand-up comedians Lenny Bruce and Mort Sahl, which combined verbal boundary-crossing with adroit social and political commentary. B.'s *Fringe* HUMOR cleverly attacked Cold War cultural tenets and subtly challenged prevailing notions of British nationalism and ethnocentrism. Later, B. would re-create well-known figures from British history to gain a critical perspective on the national character and the pervasive acceptance of middle-class culture.

B.'s interest in declining middle-class values inspired *Forty Years On* (perf. 1968; pub. 1969), which portrays the limbo of the country genteel in a dilapidated private school; *Getting On* (perf. 1971; pub. 1972), about the recommitment to life of an aging Labour member of Parliament; and *Habeas Corpus* (1973), about professional ethics and personal desire in the National Health. More recently, B. has experimented with other styles, exploiting the theatrical possibilities of London's National Theatre stage in his version of Kenneth GRAHAME's *The Wind in the Willows* (perf. 1990; pub. 1991), which received critical and popular acclaim. Also staged at the National Theatre under Richard Eyre's management was *The Madness of George III* (perf. 1991; pub. 1992), which used the lens of history to uncover the disheveled foundations of central cultural institutions. Its success produced a film version (1994), equally popular in North America and Britain. In his humor, however, B. never abandons a level of sympathy for his characters and always prefers the broad smile of reason and common sense to the merely vitriolic and snide.

By presenting the private life of George III, B. associates British national consciousness with both the ethos of colonialist expansion and the U.S. Revolutionary War. The social persona of the king resonates with the U.S. founding father and first president, another George, and in fact wears the same military uniform—blue—while his courtiers and military advisors wear traditional British red. Beyond the outward similarities, the British George seems burdened by the same celebrity dilemmas faced by, especially recent, U.S. presidents and their families. While his family members act out rivalries, hatreds, and ambitions common to most families of property or poverty, the ongoing attempt to cover over such anxious situations with an overbaked national myth of the happy and coherent nuclear family draws comparison with recent efforts of both the British royal family and the U.S. imperial presidency, which must present the first family as model of national culture. By so doing, B. allows audiences to understand their own national mythology as presented through contemporary dominant ideologies.

While B. draws short of creating an overt form of didactic drama in *Madness*—none of his plays has the sort of proclaimed message of contemporary "political playwrights" such as Naomi Wallace and Tony Kushner—parallels between 18th-c. models of national conformity and current attempts at moralistic fashioning of political figures are clearly drawn. In place of moral earnestness, B. substitutes a tone of gentle satire: sympathy for some royal family members—Queen Charlotte, George—and rejection of others—the ambitious and unappealing Prince of Wales (later George IV). While the latter and other figures, such as the politicians Charles James Fox and William Pitt, are portrayed as either overly cynical or pompous, B. never substitutes bitter indictment for his general good-natured treatment, which makes even these jaundiced personages either dramatically interesting because of their foibles or appealing because witty.

Madness's parody includes not only the medical quackery of the day but also attitudes toward celebrity that still resonate today. Thus the pompous court physician refuses to examine the royal person, instead relying on sniffing stool from silver pots brought by attendants. When Pitt and Fox conspire to have the king committed for mental incompetence in order to better control the government as a regency under the Prince of Wales, the medical profession is attacked in its self-serving treatment of mental disorders. Once again, B. prefers gentle satire to bold caricature, saving the latter only for the bumbling court physician and creating appealing, if not always congenial, characterizations of the politicians, royals, and commoners. His use of medical practice to control public opinion instances the basic knowledge-is-power tenet of postmodernist thought.

B.'s interest in the effects of disillusionment in postcolonial Britain appears throughout his work, from King George's obsession with losing the American colonies to the middle-aged ennui of the protagonists in *Me! I'm Afraid of Virginia Woolf* and *An Englishman Abroad*, televised in 1978 and 1983, respectively. His most recent plays continue to mock with gentle humor cultural institutions, such as the Church of England in *Talking Heads*—B.'s anthology of monologues published and televised in 1988 and performed in 1992—or combine the comic skit with sustained plot structure, as in *Father! Father! Burning Bright* (perf. 2000).

BIBLIOGRAPHY: Turner, D., *A. B.* (1997); Tynan, K., "The Antic Arts: A Quartet with a Touch of Brass," *Holiday* 32 (November 1962): 127–32; Wolfe, P., *Understanding A. B.* (1999)

                                    WILLIAM OVER

BENNETT, [Enoch] Arnold

b. 27 May 1867, Hanley, Staffordshire; d. 27 March 1931, London

B. was reared in the "Five Towns" of the pottery industry of Staffordshire, the subject of his best fiction. His father, a failed potter, became a pawnbroker, and during B.'s childhood spent several years becoming a solicitor, suffering under stress that perhaps contributed to the mental decay of his last years. The family showed interest in the arts, but their underlying values, like those of the community, were a grim fascination with money and a horror of financial failure. Prevailing Methodism, suspicious of nonreligious emotional expression, called for rigid morality.

At sixteen, B. went to work for his father; but after failing his legal examination, he moved to London at twenty-one as a law clerk. Soon his interest shifted to literature. In 1893, he became assistant editor of the weekly *Woman*, and its editor in 1896, a position he held until 1900. B. was extraordinarily energetic, producing a half million words a year: novels, short stories, reviews, plays, and self-help books. His first novel, *The Man from the North* (1898), was moderately successful, and *Anna of the Five Towns* (1902) enlarged his reputation. Characteristically, B. published one of his best light entertainments, *The Grand Babylon Hotel*, the same year. In 1908, when *The Old Wives' Tale* established him as a leading novelist, he published four other works and saw the production of his play *Cupid and Commonsense* (1909).

Wealthy, popular, critically respected, B. retained his position until the 1920s and then fairly well survived the attacks of younger writers. He married his secretary, Marguerite Soulié, in 1907, a year after being traumatically jilted by Eleanor Green. After years of tension, they separated in 1921. The next year, he began an affair with actress Dorothy Cheston; their daughter, Virginia, was born in 1926. During

World War I, he worked for the government, becoming Director of Propaganda in 1918.

B. combined unabashed zeal for earning money with devotion to craftsmanship. Some of his lighter works are exotic escapism, but in his serious work he emulated Gustave Flaubert, Émile Zola, and Guy de Maupassant, combining realistic subject matter with balanced form and effective diction. *The Old Wives' Tale* is a response to Maupassant's *Une Vie* (1883; *A Woman's Life*, 1885). B.'s *Anna of the Five Towns* introduces the world of the later novel. Naturally compassionate Anna Tellwright is forced into the brutal realities of business life at twenty-one when she must deal with an inherited estate. She falls in love with financially ruined William Price but never wavers in her plan to marry promising Henry Mynors whom she does not love. Sophia and Constance Baines, the two sisters whose lives B. follows in *The Old Wives' Tale*, are of the same mercantile class in Bursley, one of the Five Towns. Constance marries the family shop assistant, Samuel Povey, but Sophia elopes with salesman Gerald Scales and runs a successful Parisian boarding house after she is deserted. Her Five Towns temperament makes her impervious to French culture.

A major theme is the passage of time; the two sisters are reunited in old age, Sophia to die soon after seeing the age-shattered remains of her husband and Constance after risking illness to vote against the incorporation of Bursley into a larger unit. The once prosperous square is now dilapidated. B. deals with local values less harshly here than in the earlier novel. There is satire but no condescension, as though the author feels that the Five Towns has found a way, however unpleasant, of dealing with the world. Among his best work, the loosely autobiographical trilogy—*Clayhanger* (1910), *Hilda Lessways* (1911), and *These Twain* (1916)—also deals with Five Towns characters. He published over eighty books on varied subjects, but his Five Towns work is likely to be enduring. A fine later work, *Riceyman Steps* (1923), deals with similar preoccupations in a London slum, where miser Henry Earlforward and his wife Violet live and die sordidly.

Since the twenties, his work has paled somewhat in comparison with novels of sexuality and depth psychology, but B., perhaps sharing the repressions and conservatism of his characters, captures their world brilliantly. He was attacked by Virginia WOOLF in "Mr. Bennett and Mrs. Brown" for relying on description of character rather than genuine depiction. Ezra Pound satirized him as Nixon, the mercenary novelist in *Hugh Selwyn Mauberley* (1920), but changed his mind after reading *The Old Wives' Tale*. Today, B.'s collected works are in print, and he continues to draw the attention of scholars. He may never recapture the preeminence he once enjoyed, but he remains an important figure.

BIBLIOGRAPHY: Barker, D., *Writer by Trade: A View of A. B.* (1966); Drabble, M., *A. B.* (1974); Swinnerton, F., *A. B.* (1978)

DALTON AND MARYJEAN GROSS

BENSON, A[rthur] C[hristopher]
b. 24 April 1862, Wellington College, Berkshire; d. 17 June 1925, Cambridge

Educated at Eton and King's College, Cambridge, B. wrote the patriotic words to Edward Elgar's "Pomp and Circumstance" march, "Land of Hope and Glory," almost a second national anthem. They were originally part of the Coronation Ode for King Edward VII in 1902. Under the pseudonym "Christopher Carr," B. published a novel, *Memoirs of Arthur Hamilton* (1886) and in 1899 a two-volume life of his father, Edward White Benson, Archbishop of Canterbury. Brother of E. F. BENSON, B. was for a while a housemaster at Eton and set down his educational principles in *The Schoolmaster* (1902). Studies of Dante Gabriel ROSSETTI (1904), Edward FITZGERALD (1905), and Walter PATER (1906) were published in the English Men of Letters series. In 1907, he collaborated with Lord Esher in editing the *Correspondence of Queen Victoria* (3 vols., 1907). From 1915 to 1925, B. was master of Magdalene College, Cambridge, and in all published some fifty books.

BENSON, E[dward] F[rederick]
b. 24 July 1867, Wellington; d. 29 February 1940, London

Author of some hundred books and two hundred short stories, B. is best known for his six comic novels about Emmeline Lucas (Lucia) and Elizabeth Mapp: *Queen Lucia* (1920), *Miss Mapp* (1922), *Lucia in London* (1927), *Mapp and Lucia* (1931), *Lucia's Progress* (1935; repub. as *The Worshipful Lucia*, 1935), and *Trouble for Lucia* (1937). The genial social satire of these works captures the flavor of small-town England of the 1920s and 1930s. As absurd as B.'s characters in these novels may seem, they are based on people B. knew. The novelist Marie CORELLI, for example, served as the model for Lucia.

To keen observation, B. added an Oscar Wildean wit that delights in antithesis, paradox, and irreverence. Thus, B. writes of Dodo, the eponymous heroine of his first novel (1893) and the first of his many heartless but amusing females, "She could not bear babies. Babies had no profile, which seemed to her a very lamentable deficiency, . . . and they always howled, unless they were eating or sleeping." Major Ames (*Mrs. Ames*, 1912) "was not really an untruthful man, but many men who are not really untruthful get through a wonderful lot of misrepresentation." Florence's father in *Paying Guests* (1929) "had seri-

ously taken up the profession of invalidism instead of having no profession at all."

In addition to send-ups of London and small-town society, B. in at least a dozen novels elegiacally recalled his years at the boarding schools of Temple Grove and Marlborough as well as at Cambridge. His first book is a tribute to his school (*Marlborough Sketches*, 1888). Novels such as *David Blaize* (1916) and *David at King's* (1923; repub. as *David Blaize of King's*, 1924) capture the romantic friendships that B. enjoyed as a student. Contrasting with B.'s realistic, sometimes autobiographical fiction are his novels and stories about the supernatural. B. took ghosts seriously as a manifestation of past evil that can be exorcized only by kindness and a concern for the suffering of others.

During his lifetime, B. enjoyed the greatest praise for his nonfiction, which includes five volumes of autobiography and eight biographies. Subjects range from *The Life of Alcibiades* (1928), which reflects his education at Cambridge, where he took a first in the classical tripos, to *Queen Victoria* (1935) and *Queen Victoria's Daughters* (1938; repub. as *Daughters of Queen Victoria*, 1939).

B. wrote quickly: a novel generally required three weeks. He sought popularity rather than profundity, but he wanted to educate as well as entertain. Chief among the lessons he attempted to inculcate is the need for sympathy, which Peggy exemplifies in *Sheaves* (1907). "She had formed the excellent habit of enjoying herself quite enormously, without damage to others—an attitude toward life which is more to be desired than gold." Even when his own work lacks such charity or is marred by sentimentality, it reveals a trait for which B. praised Charlotte BRONTË in his biography of her (1932): "fine and adept English, rhythmical and dignified, with that indefinable verbal inevitability which is the hall-mark of the writer."

BIBLIOGRAPHY: Kiernan, R. F., *Frivolity Unbound: Six Masters of the Camp Novel* (1990); Masters, B., *The Life of E. F. B.* (1991)

JOSEPH ROSENBLUM

BENTHAM, Jeremy
b. 15 February 1748, Houndsditch; d. 6 June 1832, Westminster

As a philosopher and law reformer, B. has an unrivaled position in British intellectual history as a "practical idealist." John Stuart MILL called him "the great questioner of all things established," but his critiques were always accompanied by a search for rational, workable alternatives.

A precociously intelligent but lonely child, B. learned Latin from age four and French from six. His father was determined that his gifted son should succeed at the highest levels, preferably in his own profession of law, and "pushed" B. accordingly, enrolling him at public school at the age of seven, from which he matriculated at age twelve to enter Oxford University.

After university, he entered Lincoln's Inn to train as a barrister at law. His experience of legal education both here and at Oxford, where he heard the celebrated lectures of Sir William Blackstone, was one of disillusionment at the complacent pride in a system of law that was marked by anomalies, delays, obscurantism, and the self-interest of practitioners and judges. After his admission to legal practice, his first case was a suit in equity: he advised that the suit be ended and the money saved that would otherwise be wasted in the contest. Thereafter, he focused more on the analysis and reform of the law, advocating the science of legislation, and deprecating the lawyer's mastery of technicality and precedent. It was as an author of treatises and voluminous notes covering the full scope of ethics, law, and public administration that he slowly came to notice as an original and profound social theorist and activist. His first published work was the anonymous *A Fragment on Government* (1776), a devastating critique of Blackstone's authoritative *Commentaries on English Law*.

His next major work, *An Introduction to the Theory of Morals and Legislation* (1789), fully articulates the "foundation" of his lifelong attempt to secure individual and social well-being through reason and law, namely the "principle of utility." According to B.'s theory, human beings are motivated to action by basic desires to seek pleasure and to avoid pain. Moralists and legislators will achieve the goal of utility by attending to these aims in their proposals. "It is the greatest happiness of the greatest number that is the measure of right and wrong," B. insisted. His critique of tradition brought him honor in postrevolutionary France: he was made a French citizen in 1792, and invited to address the French National Convention in 1793. Once more ahead of his time, he spoke on the theme, "Emancipate Your Colonies."

In his middle years, B. strove to put his principle of utility into concrete form, first by codifying the laws of England, and secondly by promoting a new form of prison, the "panopticon." Architecturally, the latter building is circular in plan, with a surveillance tower at its center, and cells facing the inside of the circumference. The key to the design is the panoptic gaze afforded to the jailer, who can see everything inside the prison, but who remains screened from view. B. argued that through the illusion of constant inspection and an ordered routine of work, rest, and reflection, prisoners could be reclaimed from crime and vice. Although initially gaining parliamentary approval to build the panopticon, B. was opposed by influential aristocrats who owned land near the se-

lected site, and the project never came to fruition. Nonetheless, the principle of securing discipline through observation and routine dominated social planning and architecture in other areas, such as poor relief and education, and the unbuilt panopticon has come to seem the symbol of a new technology of power over the individual in the modern age.

In his *Rationale of Judicial Evidence* (1827) and in other late, unpublished writings, B. investigates language and the indispensable role of linguistic fictions in creating reality. These writings anticipate 20th-c. theories of language as constructing rather than simply picturing reality. As a writer, his own style varies between a lucid and forceful plainness in his early writings and the convoluted neologistic obscurity of his later texts. Many of his projects remained incomplete, and many of his writings were left in manuscript form, at his death. His experience of publication was initially unhappy (the ideas of the *Fragment on Government* were dismissed once his authorship was made public) and the existence of a private income made further excursions into publishing less necessary. His works became known through the editorial labors of others, such as Etienne Dumont, John Stuart Mill, and John Bowring. In 1823, he helped set up the *Westminster Review*, which became the chief journal of radical thought in England and generated reformist debate. In old age, he achieved international recognition as his ideas inspired political reformers in Spain and Portugal, Greece, and South America.

BIBLIOGRAPHY: Dinwiddy, J., *B.* (1989); Harrison, R., *B.* (1983); Ogden, C. K., *B.'s Theory of Fictions* (1932); Semple, J., *B.'s Prison* (1993)

KIERAN DOLIN

BENTLEY, E[dmund] C[lerihew]
b. 10 July 1875, London; d. 30 March 1956, London

Inventor of the popular "clerihew," a four-line verse rhyming aabb, of irregular meter, humorously summarizing or commenting on a person's life and/or character, an institution, story, etc., e.g., "Sir Christopher Wren/Went to dine with some men./He said, "If anybody calls,/Say I'm designing St. Paul's." Educated at St. Paul's School, where he became a lifelong friend of G. K. CHESTERTON, and Merton College, Oxford, B. was elected president of the Oxford Union in 1898. His *Trent's Last Case* (1913; repub. as *The Woman in Black*, 1913) is recognized as classic detective fiction. In collaboration with H. Warner Allen, he wrote *Trent's Own Case* (1936); *Trent Intervenes* (1938) was a collection of short stories, and *Elephant's Work: An Enigma* (1950) is a thriller. *Greedy Night* (1939) is a parody of Dorothy L. SAYERS. A qualified barrister, B. was also a successful journalist.

BENTLEY, Richard

b. 27 January 1662, Oulton, Yorkshire; d. 14 July
1742, Cambridge

Recognized by German scholars as the founder of historical philology, B. was the first Englishman to rank
with the great names of classical learning. In 1691, B.
earned critical recognition with the publication in
Latin of his *Epistola ad Millium*, and in the following
year delivered the first series of lectures named after
Robert Boyle at Oxford, published as *The Folly and
Unreasonableness of Atheism* (1693). Among his
scholarly projects was a comparison of the Vulgate
with the oldest Greek manuscripts, to restore the
Greek text as received at the Council of Nicea, but it
was never completed. His edition of John MILTON's
Paradise Lost, published in 1732, earned him the
scorn of Alexander POPE as "slashing Bentley," and
posterity has agreed in condemning its rash emendations and lack of poetical sensibility.

BEOWULF

Generally agreed to be the finest example of OLD EN-
GLISH literature, *Beowulf*, a poem of 3,182 lines, survives in a single manuscript, BL Cotton Vitellius
A.xv, copied approximately 1000, but dating the
poem's composition itself is a vexed matter. The narrative of *Beowulf* is organized roughly around three
fights of the eponymous hero with monsters. The first
two take place in Denmark, where the young and essentially untried Geat Warrior Beowulf travels from
his homeland in what is now southern Sweden.
Hrothgar the Danish king has been tormented for
twelve years by the huge, manlike creature Grendel
who stalks the king's hall at night, killing all who
have tried to stop him. Beowulf's own great size and
prudent speech win him permission to try his luck
against Grendel. Eschewing weapons and armor out
of fairness (Grendel does not use them), Beowulf
tears the arm off Grendel, who escapes mortally
wounded to his home at the bottom of a swamp. Great
rejoicing follows, but the next night Grendel's mother
takes revenge, attacking the sleeping warriors, killing
one. Beowulf confronts her in her underwater lair
where he is nearly slain himself, but—with the help
of a giant's sword he finds hanging on the wall—
manages in the end to kill the she-monster. Finding
Grendel's body there, he cuts off the head for proof
of his victory and returns to Hrothgar, who plies him
with treasure and advice in another, grander feast.
Beowulf sails home, where he gives his winnings to
his own lord Hygelac, only to receive yet greater
wealth and honor in return. The poem then essentially
jumps ahead to a time when Beowulf has ruled the
Geats for fifty years. An unnamed man (probably a
servant or slave) has stolen a cup from a sleeping

dragon. Enraged, the beast burns many buildings, including Beowulf's own royal hall. Bearing a special
iron shield and accompanied by eleven handpicked
warriors and the thief as guide, Beowulf braves the
dragon before its hoard. Despite the shield, the dragon's flame breath and poisonous bite mortally wound
Beowulf; nonetheless, with the help of Wiglaf, a
young warrior, Beowulf kills the dragon. The poem
concludes with Beowulf's dying words to Wiglaf, and
Beowulf's funeral, amid dire predictions of the fall
of the now-leaderless Geats to their old enemies, the
Swedes. The final lines of the poem offer a description of Beowulf intended apparently to sum up his
character: "They said that he was the most generous
of kings, the gentlest of men, the kindest to his people,
and the most eager for fame."

The history of the poem *Beowulf* remains the subject of much speculation. The single manuscript has
been shown to be a copy of a preexisting written text,
but several features of the poem itself (e.g., the description of the death of Hygelac, recorded by Gregory of Tours in his *History of the Franks* as an actual
event of the early 6th c.; or, in a different way, the
many folkloric elements) make clear that much of
Beowulf has its origins in preliterate times. The exact
degree to which *Beowulf* should be considered a product of oral singers such as those described in the
poem, and how much the work of poets with pen and
parchment, seems unlikely to be resolved. Nor will
the matter of its date: it is no longer felt among scholars that such animosity existed toward Northmen that,
after the advent of the Viking wars in the 790s, no
Anglo-Saxon could have suffered hearing celebrated
the deeds of Scandinavians, even one so admirable
as Beowulf. Hence, composition dates closer to (even
including) the copying of the manuscript itself have
been proposed, with no consensus reached. Recent
scholarship has also put into doubt traditional opinion
about the origin of the manuscript itself. The work
of two scribes ("A" and "B"), *Beowulf* was bound
together with four other Old English texts, all but one
of which have to do with "monsters": a life of St.
Christopher (in the Middle Ages thought to have been
a giant); *The Wonders of the East*, a compendium of
strange creatures; a fictional letter from Alexander the
Great to his tutor Aristotle, recounting exotic people
and beasts; and *Judith* (wr. ca. 930), a version of the
biblical book, copied by the *Beowulf* "B" scribe. Linguistic arguments, accepted for many years, placed
the copying and collecting of these works in Northumbria. These lately have been questioned, and alternative origins proposed for the manuscript in the
Midlands and the south.

Uncertainties of date, venue, and method of composition take on increased significance when an assessment of the literary and/or sociocultural meaning
of *Beowulf* is attempted. To what degree, for example,

should the poem be considered a Christian work, with a discernible Christian moral outlook and lesson, or a creation primarily of a society whose values and beliefs, despite touching up here and there by Christians, were quintessentially and visibly pagan? As with so much about the poem, there are no simple answers to these questions. Certainly its scribes were Christians, as its readers must have been (although not, perhaps, the majority of its audience, over time). Christian too is the anonymous poetic "voice" that comments occasionally on characters and events—lamenting, for example, the fate of the pagan Danes who, in their ignorance of God, pray to idols. But it is important to note as well that no biblical references other than to the Old Testament appear in *Beowulf*. No Christ, no saints, no cross: under such circumstances it is difficult to term Beowulf's evident monotheism especially Christian, or to carry forward such Christianizing allegorical analyses, as have been offered, of (for example) Beowulf as a *figura* of Christ—or contrastingly, to find in Beowulf's concern to see the dragon's treasure, or his epitaphic "eagerness for fame," evidence of damnable sins, avarice and pride. Instead of resolution, *Beowulf* seems to offer juxtaposed personae and events with little or no indication of how—or even if—they are to be connected. When Beowulf kills Grendel, Hrothgar's *scop* (poet/minstrel) sings of the legendary Germanic hero Sigemund's dragon-killing. The context suggests a similar luster for Beowulf and Sigemund, at least at that triumphant moment—but should Sigemund's victory be recalled, perhaps this time in ironic contrast, when Beowulf finally meets, and dies fighting, a real dragon?

To a large degree, this appositional style is characteristic of most Old English poetry (and, we must assume, of Anglo-Saxon outlook in general); in *Beowulf*, however, it is a refined art. Indeed, the macrostructure of the poem may be its best expression, as the defining battles of Beowulf's life—two in his youth, one in old age—are presented, with scant commentary on the fifty years between. The poem's challenge seems to be for its audience to read polyvalently, to discover connections that are rarely good or bad *simplicter*. The result is a poem at once a lament for the passing of heroes and civilizations, and a paean to the best in human nature—beneficence, intelligence, and profound courage in the face of enormous, inevitable odds.

The metrical structure of *Beowulf* adheres to the standards established for verse in Old English: that is, each line has four stressed syllables, two each on either side of a clear caesura. The first syllable of the second stressed pair alliterates with one or both of the stressed syllables in the first pair, in one of five recurrent patterns. The manuscript *Beowulf* is divided into forty-three sections, called *fitts*, each indicated by a Roman numeral, a large capital letter, or (most often)

both. The *fitts* seem for the most part to mark off important sections of the poem, and it is generally believed (despite some sharp objections) that their placement was the work of the author.

Although Beowulf the character appears in no other known literary work, he has numerous analogues, especially in Icelandic verse. The name is often etymologized as "bee-wolf" (or "enemy of bees," i.e., a bear) and ties Beowulf to a type of hero in FOLKLORE who devolves from bears. Closest perhaps to Beowulf is Bothvarr Bjarki of the Icelandic saga *Hrolfs saga kraka*; but Thorir of *Gull-Thoris saga*, Grettir of *Grettis saga*, and Samson the Fair of *Samsons saga fagra* all battle monsters resembling Grendel and his mother, and so bear resemblance also to Beowulf. In other Scandinavian sources Sigurthr (like Siegfried of the *Nibelungenlied*, and Sigemund of *Beowulf*) kills a dragon, but beyond the event itself, the similarities of these characters to Beowulf are thin.

BIBLIOGRAPHY: Bjork, R. E., and J. D. Niles, eds., *A Beowulf Handbook* (1997); Chase, C., ed., *The Dating of Beowulf* (1981); Hill, J. M., *The Cultural World of Beowulf* (1995); Robinson, F. C., *Beowulf and the Appositive Style* (1985); Tolkien, J. R. R., *Beowulf: The Monsters and the Critics* (1977)

R. F. YEAGER

BERGER, John [Peter]
b. 5 November 1926, London

If there is a unifying element in B.'s diverse body of work, it is this prolific writer's sensibility for the profound influence of period and social environment on the individual. This sensibility is evident not only in his fiction and art criticism, for which the Marxist author is best known, but also in his poetry, essays, and plays. Commanding superior skills in storytelling and character portrayal, B. has been compared with Tolstoy, T. S. ELIOT, and D. H. LAWRENCE.

His early correspondence with art critic Herbert READ is believed to have had a significant impact on B.'s interest in art. One of B.'s first jobs was as an art critic for the *New Statesman*. The subjects of B.'s art criticism have varied and include a book on Picasso and texts on the relationship between the visual and our perception of the world. His works have been influential on art theory as well as art criticism. He later began writing fiction and was awarded the Booker Prize in 1972 for his novel *G*, which established his reputation. B.'s first novel, *A Painter of Our Time* (1958), is the story of a Hungarian artist living in exile in London. The principal character, Janos Lavin, must come to terms with the politics of the art world as well as his sense of duty to promote social change in his homeland. As an outgrowth of B.'s art criticism, this novel delves into the meaning of success for the artist. According to B., success is realized when the artist has a following. The artist is in effect "gagged" without the presence of an audience. In his work, B. also pursues his belief that an artist and his art are shaped by the historical and political climate in which he lives.

B.'s next two novels, *The Foot of Clive* (1962) and *Corker's Freedom* (1964), are also set in London, but are generally considered less successful. While *The Foot of Clive* received mainly negative critical review, the response to *Corker's Freedom* was mixed. In *Corker's Freedom*, the elderly Corker is freed for the first time in his life from the constraints that his invalid sister and society have placed on him. B.'s use of monologues in this work has been called tedious; nevertheless, the work is engaging as a whole.

Published in 1972, *G* is B.'s most experimental novel. This historical fiction is set in Europe during the late 19th c. The protagonist, named G, is a latter-day Don Juan whose sexual exploits and emotional detachment are used to explore morality during a period of revolutionary change. The novel is widely praised for its inventiveness, complexity, and unusual mix of essay and fiction.

After leaving England to live in a French peasant community in the 1970s, B. began work on a trilogy that has been described as part novel, social document, and fable. Published collectively in 1992, the *Into Our Labours* trilogy, which includes *Pig Earth* (1979), *Once in Europa* (1987), and *Lilac and Flag* (1990), records the history and culture of a peasant community as well as its gradual disintegration. Through his use of stories and poems, B. paints a picture of an ancient class filled with both great beauty and intense sadness.

B.'s rich career, in addition to fiction and criticism, has also included screenplays, BIOGRAPHY, photojournalism, and poetry. The subjects of his extensive life work have most often encompassed the social issues of various ages, including recent works on homelessness and AIDS, as well as the place of immigrants and peasants in communities, and a dedicated concern for art and artists.

BIBLIOGRAPHY: Dyer, G., *Ways of Telling: The Work of J. B.* (1986); Fuller, P., *Seeing B.: A Revaluation of Ways of Seeing* (1980); Papastergiadis, N., *Modernity as Exile: The Stranger in J. B.'s Writing* (1993)

ANN O'BRIEN FULLER

BERKELEY, George

b. 12 March 1685, near Thomastown, County Kilkenny, Ireland; d. 14 January 1753, Oxford

Philosopher and mathematician, B. stands with John LOCKE and David HUME as one of the seminal figures of British Empiricism. He also helped to lay the foundation for the psychology of perception. A metaphysical idealist, he argued that all reality is the product of mind, a position that led his friend Samuel JOHNSON to kick a rock as an attempt at refutation.

B. attended Trinity College, Dublin, where he took Holy Orders, earning a B.A. in 1704, an M.A. in 1707, and becoming a junior fellow the following year. This was his most active period as a philosopher, producing *New Theory of Vision* (1709), *A Treatise Concerning the Principles of Human Knowledge* (1710), and *Three Dialogues between Hylas and Philonous* (1713). During this period, he also published *Passive Obedience* (1712), his fullest treatment of ethics, and a number of essays in Richard STEELE's *Guardian*, attacking freethinkers. From 1713 to 1714, he toured the Continent as chaplain to Lord Peterborough, probably meeting the French philosopher Nicolas Malebranche. From 1716 to 1720, he again toured the Continent, this time as tutor to George Ashe. During this period, he composed his Latin tract, *De Motu*, for the Royal Academy of Science at Paris. This was published in 1721. B. next entered into a plan to found a college on the island of Bermuda, moving to New Port, Rhode Island, in 1728, to await a government grant. During this period, he composed *Alciphron* (1732), which he published on his return to London, when the funding for the Bermuda project failed to materialize. In 1734, he was appointed Anglican Bishop of Cloyne in Ireland, earning the reputation of "the good Bishop." His later works included, *The Analyst* (1734), *The Querist* (3 parts, 1735–37), and *Siris* (1744).

B.'s place in philosophy rests on his three early works, *New Theory*, the *Treatise*, and the *Three Dialogues*. He was deeply influenced by Locke on one side, whom he termed "a Gyant [*sic*]" and the Cartesians, especially Malebranche and Pierre Bayle on the other. Ostensibly, the *Theory* looks at the optical problems related to the perception of distance and magnitude. B.'s analysis led him to conclude, however, that there is no natural geometry. Rather we learn to make judgments from various sensory cues. What we call the objects of sight are properly not images of external things, but the products of the mind.

The *Treatise* develops the philosophical assumptions underlying the *Theory*. B. concurs with both Locke and Descartes that awareness is really only awareness of ideas that are produced in our minds, and that the objects of human knowledge are built entirely on ideas. However, he attacks Locke's concept of abstract ideas. While Locke had supposed that the mind could abstract the concept of color or extension from the perception of specific things, B. contends that all ideas are based on specific perceptions. Since all knowledge is based on mental content, and all mental content derives from perception, then the act of perception creates the reality. This is summarized in the Latin tag, *esse est percipi* (to be is to be perceived). At the same time, since only mind can act on mind, the act of perception implies not the action of material bodies on the mind, but the act of another mind, which B. understands as God. All reality, in short, comes from the divine mind. The *Three Dialogues* present B.'s views in the form of a dialogue between Hylas, Greek for *earth* or *matter*, and Philonous, Greek for *lover of mind.*

Among B.'s later works, *Alciphron* and the *Analyst* remain the most interesting. *Alciphron* is an attack on skepticism and presented in the form of seven dialogues between two Christian gentlemen and two free thinkers. The latter figures echo the views of the third Earl of SHAFTESBURY and Bernard MANDEVILLE, though many contend that B. distorts them. The seventh dialogue focuses on the problem of language. Alciphron argues that words that suggest no ideas are insignificant, with the result that words like *grace* are empty. To this, B. replies that the sign aims more toward the instigation of behavior than the signification of a concept. *The Analyst* is a work in the philosophy of mathematics in which B. attacks Newton's calculus, especially the assumption of absolute space. Although the significance of B.'s contribution is still debated, he anticipates Ernst Mach and even Einstein on the relative nature of space. While often perceived as a transition between Locke and Hume, B. stands as an important thinker in his own right.

BIBLIOGRAPHY: Berman, D., *G. B.* (1994); Dancy, J., *B.* (1987); Urmson, J. O., *B.* (1982); Warnock, G. J., *B.* (1953)

THOMAS L. COOKSEY

BERKOFF, Steven
b. 3 August 1937, London

In the 1970s, B. burst onto the theater scene as an enfant terrible with a unique style of physical theater dedicated to releasing the chair-bound British theater from the tyranny of armchair discussion. In the intervening years, B. has become a major influence to both performers and playwrights. His major contribution has been the establishment of style as a meaning-making device. Reinstating the use of language as an active multifunctional theatrical device and centering the performer as the creator of the theatrical experience, B. has created a unique, identifiable style.

A self-proclaimed follower of Antonin Artaud, B. structures his work on the centralization of image, using sound, image, language, and the actor's body and voice to engage the audience's imagination in extending and completing a theatrical experience that transcends the limits of material illustration. *The Fall of the House of Usher* (perf. 1974; pub. 1977), for

example, is a series of interweaving images created entirely by three performers, supplemented by occasional dialogue reformed from Edgar Allan Poe's story. The topology of the text proposes an original and extraordinarily successful solution to the dilemma of how to present a text for performance-based work without delivering a set of mechanical instructions. On the right side of each page: the performance text, speech, and essential stage directions. On the left: a commentary elaborating the emotive content and intended effect on the audience. Even the reader becomes engaged in an active, imaginative experience.

One of B.'s trademarks is his revitalization of dramatic language through a contemporary form of blank verse that heightens speech through rhythm, vivid imagery, unexpected reference, emphasizing sound. In his East End saga *East* (perf. 1975; pub. 1977), characters speak in a form of cod Shakespeare. This contrivance creates multiple dramatic effects. The rhythm of the blank verse, itself, affects the audience on a visceral level. The sensuality of the words and the images they paint seduce an audience and enlist their imaginations, enticing them to create a world beyond the immediacy of the stage, setting the action in a developed context. But the most startling function of this linguistic construction is its social and moral effect. The association with William SHAKESPEARE implies both intelligence and a sense of beauty. The blend between Shakespearean style and East End vocabulary builds a sensation that we are hearing the way these characters would speak if they were able; the speaking of their hearts in tension with their everyday inarticulateness not only engages our sympathy with people we might normally avoid, but explicitly associates inarticulateness with social repression. *East* also presents an excellent example of B.'s ability to transform the stage through the active engagement of the audience's imagination. In dimmed light and a humming background, one actor sits aboard the other, stimulating the audience to see a man riding a Harley Davison motorcycle. B. says spectators have actually written to ask how he got such a large bike onto the stage.

Most of B.'s major plays establish present-day action on the foundation of classical works. They are not adaptations so much as dialogues in which the original work functions as both associative reference and comparative context. *Agamemnon* (perf. 1971; pub. 1977) offers a poetic consideration of Aeschylus. *West* (perf. 1983; pub. 1985) uses BEOWULF as a narrative structure exploring East End gang warfare. *Greek* (perf. 1980; pub. 1982), founded on *Oedipus Tyrannus*, is an example. The two plays are joined by the basic incidents of plot: killed his father, married his mother. However the different contexts invite comparison and create different meanings. Where Oedipus, for example, begins in the heart of society and ends up alone, Eddy begins alone and ends embracing personal and social commitment.

Greek opens with a long monologue in which Eddy draws on the audience's imagination to create the extended world of the drama. Descriptions of small-minded graft, dissatisfaction, and petty attempts to gain ground over others create not only the image of a disordered society, but also a critical perspective. Specifically, Eddy emphasizes the transformation of food into profitable merchandise: no longer tasty, satisfying, or even nourishing; profit, its only purpose. Eddy sets himself in critical distance from the world around him where pursuit of money and personal power eat away at both personal and community relationships. Sent from his Tottenham home by his father because of a shocking prophecy from a fairground fortuneteller, Eddy finds everywhere pain and destruction caused by the pursuit of individual gain, from a cheating pub owner to IRA murders. The country is disintegrating. Eddy has visions of an alternative society based on a simple moral code where benefit to others is rewarded and damage punished. An image of social integration, health in mind body and spirit. He decides to attempt to change his world.

Food is developed as a symbolic reference by which both individual health and the state of society are assessed. In a cafe, Eddy orders croissant and coffee so he might have an "integrated snack," the waitress, more interested in her own sexual experiences, brings him one item at a time. Enraged by the poor food and negligent service, Eddy kills the manager of the cafe in a uniquely theatrical fight. Eddy and the manager stand at opposite sides of the stage hurling words of violence and pain at each other. Language, and by inference thought, are overtly reinstated as effective actions with consequences. In keeping with his social ideals, Eddy takes over the cafe and marries the waitress, promising love and protection.

Ten years later, the couple extoll their love, and Eddy has transformed his world. The destruction of the social fabric through individualization and profit has been elaborated through reference to food, unhealthy food reflecting both individual and social degeneration. Now, his tasty and nourishing sandwiches have returned healthy body and spirit to both individuals and society. But dark times are ahead. His father confesses he found Eddy as a baby during the war and took him for his own, another expression of mindless individualism. Eddy's beloved wife is his mother. Eddy contemplates his choices. The implicit relationship to Oedipus now explicit, he considers in graphic detail how he might blind himself. Eddy turns his back to the audience who, stimulated by his visceral descriptions, cannot help but imagine how he will look when he turns back. Eddy turns and takes his hands from his eyes: he is unchanged. In a moment of startling theatricality, the audience experience a total regeneration.

Comparing his positive influence on his world and his mutual love with his wife with the pain, harm, and dissatisfaction around him, Eddy hurries back to his lover. The play offers a proposition: exposing the chaos and devaluation caused by the enactment of individualism, it proposes a reconsideration of conventional moral assumptions toward the aim of reconstituting a healthy, integrated society.

His innate understanding of the experiential nature of theater and its imaginative force is arguably the source of B.'s popularity and influence. The use of food as a measure in the discussion of personal and social dynamics and the use of the body as a central meaning-making device have been adopted and extended by new writers. Although it is easy to be blinded by their onslaught of imaginative spectacle, B.'s plays deserve critical consideration of their social analysis and adamant moral content.

ELAINE TURNER

BESANT, [Sir] Walter
b. 14 August 1836, Portsmouth; d. 9 June 1901, Hampstead

B. was a prolific and polemical novelist, whose most respected work evinced sympathy with the poor. After an early successful collaboration with James Rice that produced some twelve novels of uneven merit, B. earned critical recognition with *All Sorts and Conditions of Men* (3 vols., 1882), a polemical novel depicting the dismal living conditions in London's East End. Notable works that followed include *All in a Garden Fair* (3 vols., 1883), *Dorothy Forster* (3 vols., 1884), and his most acclaimed "East End" novel, *Children of Gibeon* (3 vols., 1886). Later works include *The Ivory Gate* (3 vols., 1892), *The Rebel Queen* (3 vols., 1893), and *The City of Refuge* (3 vols., 1896), among many others. B. also wrote short stories as well as biographical and critical studies, but his lasting achievement was to found the Society of Authors in 1884, serving as chairman until 1892. He was knighted in 1895. B.'s *Autobiography*, published posthumously in 1902, remains the most informative and characteristic source of his life and literary career.

BETJEMAN, [Sir] John
b. 28 August 1906, Highgate, London; d. 19 May 1984, Trebetherick, Cornwall

As a poet, B. was never likely to influence the mainstream of poetic practice in Britain. Never a disciple of MODERNISM, B. adopts the stance of entertainer on a search for faith, fighting despair, yet showing a deep love of the human comedy. He comes across in the tone of voice in his poetry that is highly observant of people and their architectural surroundings. B. chooses traditional verse forms including rhymed quatrains, blank verse, couplets and cites Alfred, Lord TENNYSON, George CRABBE, R. S. Hawker, Ernest DOWSON, Thomas HARDY, James Elroy FLECKER, Thomas MOORE, and *Hymns Ancient and Modern* as his models, choosing his meters to fit the themes at hand.

B. was educated at the Dragon School, Oxford, and Marlborough College, then at Magdalen College, Oxford, in 1925, but he left without a degree. He began his career as a schoolteacher in 1929 and after that worked in various jobs as editor, film critic, book reviewer, and columnist. His work in broadcasting in the 1950s was very successful as were the sales of his poetry, and he was able to campaign effectively on behalf of threatened architectural gems, particularly of the Victorian period. He famously saved St. Pancras station from demolition. He was awarded a long list of prizes and honorary degrees, including the Queen's Gold Medal for Poetry in 1960, the year he was knighted.

Despite B.'s incredible success with his *Collected Poems* (1958), which sold over a million copies, the academic world has frequently held him in contempt as a middle-class writer, working for a mass audience and going against the dictum that demanded that all poetry should be difficult or obscure. In short, he was rejected as a frivolous populist, refusing the serious anger of the mid-20th-c. writers or the modernist road. But Philip LARKIN championed B. for this very reason, in that B. seemed to have reestablished the link between poet and public, sweeping aside the hurdles of exegesis erected by the academic establishment. B.'s poetry remained rooted directly in what he felt and believed about life.

B.'s success is testimony to the great affection in which he continues to be held by his admirers. His first publications *Mount Zion* (1931) and *Continual Dew* (1937) already show the highly crafted qualities that B. came to perfect in his later work. The latter volume contains some poems reprinted from the former, like "Hymn." It also contains one of his most thematically characteristic poems, "The Arrest of Oscar Wilde at the Cadogan Hotel," and "Slough" with its notorious first line: "Come, friendly bombs, and fall on Slough!" The blurb inside *Continual Dew* claims that "The verse is nostalgic and designed for those who appreciate Sunday in a provincial town, the subtleties of *high*, *low* and *broad* churchmanship, gaslit London, bottle parties in the suburbs, civil servants on the hike, and half-timbered houses on the Southern Electric." This sums up the nature of B.'s poetical interests in the vanished interwar world.

Ghastly Good Taste (1933) was the first of a series of books on architecture, where B. took against both the horrors of the modern and sham antiquarianism in building trends. He followed this with a long list of publications delineating his pet interests and crusading for the issue of conservation, such as *English Cities and Small Towns* (1943), *The English Town in the Last Hundred Years* (1956), *English Churches* (1964), *Victorian and Edwardian London from Old Photographs* (1969), *London's Historical Railway Stations* (1972), and *Metroland* (1977).

From the 1940s onward, B.'s poetry began to gain that status that it still enjoys. He was moved to write poems because of what he called his "topographical predilection." *Old Lights for New Chancels* (1940) contains the extremes of HUMOR from "Pot Pourri from a Surrey Garden" to the horrific meditation upon death and decay in memory of his father "On the Portrait of a Deaf Man." This poem recalls the private fears of the poet and also shows the shocks that he can at times deliver. *New Bats in Old Belfries* (1945) contains more famous works like "A Subaltern's Love Song" and the tonally beautiful and languidly paced "Youth and Age on Beaulieu River, Hants," poetry about church bells, the strikingly Gothic "A Lincolnshire Tale," and "Parliament Hill Fields" one of his best-known poems.

B. had moved on considerably from his earlier work and was clearly inhabiting Betjeman country with supreme confidence and skill. *A Few Late Chrysanthemums* (1954) makes up the triad of publications containing classic B. including the overwhelming encounters with womanhood in "The Licorice Fields at Pontefract" and "The Olympic Girl," the anxious horror of "Devonshire Street W.1," the near-metaphysical "Late-Flowering Lust" and the satirical comedy of "Hunter Trials."

Summoned by Bells (1960) is B.'s foray into lengthy blank verse autobiography up to his teaching years, set in nine sections, where he tells us that "For myself/I knew as soon as I could read and write/That I must be a poet." Critical reactions were mixed—John WAIN loathed it, Larkin loved it, and it remains a daring venture, recalling the practice of poetic forefathers, suffering from dull patches, but remaining, as Patrick Taylor-Martin says "an interesting fragment."

B.'s poetic output continued with *High and Low* (1966) and a *Nip in the Air* (1974), which found their way into successive editions of the *Collected Poems*. But B.'s best and most enduring work had already been done. His canon has been vastly augmented and promoted by audio material, recordings which began in 1961, of his readings of poetry, the lively *Betjeman's Banana Blush* (1974) with music by Jim Parker, and video compilations such as *The Lost Betjemans* recorded between 1962 and 1964.

BIBLIOGRAPHY: Betjeman, J., *Collected Poems* (2000); Hillier, B., *Young Betjeman* (1988); Taylor-Martin, P., *J. B., His Life and Work* (1983)

CHRISTOPHER J. P. SMITH

BIOGRAPHY

Biography, or life writing, has been one of Britain's most popular and most derided genres—often at the same time. Like the novel, biography occupies a conflicted territory, regularly sharing space with such proximate forms as history, theology, and, for that matter, the novel itself. At the same time, definitions of what it means to record an individual life have shifted with the emergence of new ideas about personhood, the relationship of self to society, the presence of God, and even language. With these shifts have also come new attitudes to the very propriety of life writing, particularly what could be called a posthumous right to privacy. It is no accident that the growing emphasis on individual personality found in Enlightenment biography was matched by a growing antagonism to the biographer him- or herself.

Readers have often been frustrated by medieval biography. Devoted to saints and respected ecclesiastical figures, medieval biography shows little interest in the development of individual personality over time. Indeed, the "individual" at issue may be ascribed thoughts and actions lifted wholesale from other saints. What differentiates medieval from post-Enlightenment biography, then, is its emphasis not on a unique, interior personality, but rather on action. Saints' lives draw on the rhetorical tradition of classical biography: the saint's life is an *exemplum* designed to persuade men and women to engage in the *imitatio Christi*. The individual specificity of a given action, then, is nowhere near so important as the possibility that it might be adopted in turn by the reader or auditor. Aside from the rare exceptions like John Capgrave, hagiographers like Walter Daniel wrote in Latin prose or verse. In some cases, authors wrote the same life in prose and verse form, as BEDE did with his two lives of St. Cuthbert.

Although medieval biography's theological emphasis maintained its hold on the genre until well into the 18th c., the Tudor and Stuart periods nevertheless brought with them a subtle shift in principles. Most importantly, biographers became increasingly interested in linking the facts specific to an individual to the truth of the overall narrative. Moreover, there was a new willingness to write critical, antagonistic biographies as well as virtuous lives, offering an antiexemplary tradition to go with the exemplary one. The most notable instance of this new trend is Sir Thomas MORE's *History of King Richard III*, a vernacular assault on that monarch designed to warn future generations against repeating his political errors. Similarly, George CAVENDISH's life of Cardinal Wolsey (wr. 1557) found stern moral lessons in the Cardinal's rise and precipitous fall. The 17th c. brought with it a new interest in collections of short lives, exemplified most notably by Thomas FULLER's *The History of the Wor-*

thies of England—a work that tried to shed the connotations of tedium associated with moralizing biography. Short lives also found their place at the head of long collected works, most notably in Izaak WALTON's *Life of John Donne;* Walton's other short lives, devoted to Henry WOTTON, Richard HOOKER, George HERBERT, and Robert Sanderson, all remained popular long after their original publication. John AUBREY's *Brief Lives*, which were not published in full until 1898, are sketches rather than attempts at full biographies, but their vibrancy and sense of telling detail has given them a following that probably would have startled Aubrey himself. Another major work that went unpublished until the 19th c., Lucy Hutchinson's *Memoirs of the Life of Colonel Hutchinson* (1860), still remains an important Puritan account of the Civil War.

The 18th c. brought with it an explosion of interest in all kinds of lives—from exemplary ecclesiastics to Newgate criminals. Although hagiography, strictly speaking, was devoted to saints of whatever social origin, it was really only in the 18th c. that anyone could become a biographical subject. Writers became more interested in factual minutiae about the outer life, while demonstrating an increasing fascination with the nature of human interiority. Life writing itself, meanwhile, became an important part of the hackwriter's repertoire—which meant that the entire biographical enterprise soon found itself potentially tainted by its association with "Grub Street" commercialism and, worse, sensationalism. Nevertheless, writers seized upon the moral use-value of biography to justify their projects: theorists like Samuel JOHNSON suggested that for those who led private instead of public lives, the life of a "humble" person could have just as much exemplary force as that of a great historical figure—or even more. In addition, theorists argued, biography should not be needlessly sensational, but it also should not be uncritical hagiography. Without a doubt, James BOSWELL's *Life of Samuel Johnson* pushed the 18th-c. reader's tolerance for truth-telling to its utmost limit: his vivid portrayal of Johnson's quirks as well as his sterner characteristics enthralled some and shocked others. The *Life* also foregrounded the biographer's role to an extent that troubled many; Boswell is often on the scene, whether setting himself up as Johnson's seeming patsy or arranging situations that showcase Johnson's character traits. Despite Boswell's authorial intrusiveness, his reputation as a self-conscious narrator languished until the publication of his private journals and papers in the 20th c. Johnson himself, of course, was both one of the 18th c.'s few biographical theorists and an important practitioner in his own right. *The Life of Mr. Richard Savage* may be one of the greatest lives ever devoted to a thoroughly unsuccessful man. *The Lives of the Most Eminent English Poets* set a new standard for joining the quest for absolute truth with the desire to make serious critical judgments, and it exerted a profound influence on the practice of literary biography that persists today. Participating in the antiquarian fervor of the age, biographical encyclopedias also became increasingly significant undertakings, most famously in the case of the unfinished *Biographia Britannica*. At least one of these undertakings, George Ballard's *Memoirs of Several Ladies of Great Britain, Who Have Been Celebrated for Their Writings or Skill in the Learned Languages, Arts and Sciences* (1752) still remains of some scholarly use today.

With Boswell's *Life of Johnson* looming over them, early-19th-c. biographers found themselves directly confronted with the ethics of life writing: how much of the personal life should be exposed? Many biographies from this period came into the world accompanied by the sound of flames devouring paper. This anxiety combined with a number of emerging factors to reshape the biographical landscape. The Evangelical revival, with its insistence on religious feeling and intensive self-examination, not surprisingly generated an increasing number of works designed to exemplify such aspects of the Christian good life. Meanwhile, Johnson's *Lives of the Poets* exerted their own influence, evidenced in such undertakings as Sir Walter SCOTT's *Lives of the Novelists,* published separately in 1906, but also in collections of shorter biographical essays more generally. Romantic biography shows a genuine interest in the quotidian, an attitude partially inspired by the elevation of common life by poets like William WORDSWORTH, but also by the Christian desire to show how true moral goodness was not necessarily identical with elevated social position. Finally, the new theories of selfhood formulated by the major Romantic poets also shaped the biographer's understanding of life writing. Most importantly, biographers placed new emphasis on the idea of an organic personality emerging over time: the child as father to the man. Among literary biographies from this period, the most significant is John Gibson LOCKHART's seven-volume life of his father-in-law, Scott, which in both full and abridged versions dominated Anglo-America's understanding of that author well into the 20th c. (and continues to be an invaluable resource for scholars). Lockhart, a novelist and polemicist by vocation, also turned his narrative skills to lives of Robert BURNS and Napoleon. And the poet Robert SOUTHEY, who has long lost his place in the Romantic pantheon, contributed important, sympathetic lives of Horatio Nelson and John Wesley; the former, in particular, manifests genuine admiration tempered by equally genuine criticism.

If medieval biography has been dogged by a reputation for credulousness, Victorian biography has been dogged by a reputation for sanctimoniousness. While this reputation is not altogether unearned, as a blanket condemnation it is also markedly unfair. The rapid innovations in print technology from the 1830s onward generated an explosion of popular texts of all kinds, biographies notable among them. In terms of sheer weight, the "Life and Letters" biographical sub-genre occupies a prominent position. Often devoted to clergymen and other figures of piety, these biographies usually tried to press the boundary line between biography and AUTOBIOGRAPHY: relying on diaries and letters as much as possible, the biographer sought to reduce him- or herself to the apparently transparent "editor," leaving the subject to speak to the reader in an apparently immediate voice. Thomas CARLYLE successfully employed this technique in his six-volume life of Frederick the Great, as did A. P. Stanley in his life of the legendary educator Thomas Arnold. Carlyle's most significant contribution to biography, however, is the *Life of John Sterling* (1851), a work that supposedly belongs to the "memoirs of clergymen" school but which transcends it through Carlyle's own belief that celebrating Sterling's life is, as he put it in the conclusion, "a commission higher than the world's, the dictate of Nature itself, to do what is now done." Carlyle's personal affection for Sterling and his own acquaintance with many of Sterling's other friends and relatives enliven the narrative—as does, infamously, his devastating portrait of Samuel Taylor COLERIDGE. Another popular form was the collection of short lives, certainly continuing the Johnsonian tradition but also harking back to the medieval encomiastic biography. Like those early texts, the Victorian biography collection sought to inspire its readers to emulate virtuous behavior; moreover, the lives in question can sound suspiciously similar. Of the writers of short lives, most important was Samuel Smiles, author of such exceptionally popular works as *Self-Help* (1859), *Lives of the Engineers* (3 vols., 1861–62), and *Character* (1871). Smiles's cheerful praise for those who pulled themselves up by their bootstraps earned him a strong following, although his habit of juxtaposing men of genuinely impoverished beginnings to people like Benjamin DISRAELI can give the reader pause. Among the writers who tried to join popularity with some degree of historical seriousness, Agnes Strickland stands out; her *Lives of the Queens of England* (12 vols., 1840–48), written jointly with her sister Elizabeth, remained in print throughout the 19th c., and garnered varying degrees of respect for its original archival work.

The questions about privacy raised by Boswell's Johnson remained at a premium. Elizabeth Cleghorn GASKELL's fine life of Charlotte BRONTË, which demonstrates how novelistic technique might be put in service of biographical narrative, nevertheless raised hackles for its sometimes lurid representation of Brontë's family life. (In the 20th c., many of Gaskell's assertions about Charlotte's father Patrick, for example, have been disproven.) However, the response to Gaskell's work was nothing in comparison to the uproar greeting the historian J. A. FROUDE's life of Carlyle. Froude's revelations about Carlyle's stormy relationship with his wife, Jane, produced cries of outrage over its prurience and violation of domestic privacy; the denunciations continued until the end of the century and, indeed, beyond.

The late 19th c. produced a series of important biographical projects, many of them suggesting an underlying interest in the nature of English identity. Most monumental among them was the *Dictionary of National Biography*, under the editorship of Leslie STEPHEN and, later, Sir Sidney LEE. The goalposts for the *DNB*'s ambition to be authoritatively comprehensive have moved over time; notably, later additions have sought to repair the quantitative imbalance between "eminent" men and women in the original project. On a smaller scale, the *English Men of Letters* series, edited by John MORLEY, drew on the insights of both novelists and belles-lettrists; the contributors ranged from Anthony TROLLOPE and Margaret OLIPHANT to John Addington SYMONDS and G. K. CHESTERTON. Similarly, Macmillan's *Twelve English Statesmen* series consisted of short, often shrewd lives of English politicians, again written by authors with hands-on experience, such as Morley and Lord Rosebery.

The rejection of all things Victorian that characterizes so much of British MODERNISM found its biographical epitome in Lytton STRACHEY's *Eminent Victorians*. Strachey's slim study of Cardinal Manning, Florence Nightingale, Thomas Arnold, and General Gordon might not have killed off Victorian biographical practices, but it certainly gave the interwar generation permission to regard their progenitors and their "earnestness" with an ironic, even cynical, eye. In addition to attacking the hagiographical impulses of Victorian biography, Strachey also claimed dissatisfaction (quite unfairly) with its loose baggy monster approach, and on both counts he had company. Virginia WOOLF parodied the form in *Flush*, a life of Elizabeth Barrett BROWNING's cocker spaniel, as well as in her novel *Orlando*; however, she also did her best to write a "straight" biography with her life of Roger FRY. The quest for alternative narrative forms in biography sometimes culminated in virtual anti-biographies like A. J. A. SYMONS's *Quest for Corvo*, which is as much about the author's difficulties in writing "Corvo's" (Frederick William ROLFE's) scandalous life as it is about Corvo.

In the second half of the 20th c., biography was transformed by a number of literary and cultural factors. The rise of postmodernist criticism radically undercut notions of objectivity, individualism, and, of course, the author. The trend toward "fictionalized" biography, pioneered by the modernists, understandably gained strength from such theoretical projects.

FEMINISM opened up new avenues of investigation into the lives of women hitherto regarded as appendages to famous men, while suggesting new strategies for narrating their life courses. Similarly, changing attitudes toward sexuality allowed authors to raise new questions about the private lives of their subjects, or, in some cases, to explore those lives in detail for the first time. Michael HOLROYD's original and revised editions of his life of Strachey provide a concrete example of how the decriminalization of homosexuality in 1967 affected what a biographer could reveal. Film, too, became an important medium for fictionalized biographies of a sort, often known colloquially as "biopics." As several commentators have noted, biography in Britain tends to be a profession unto itself. In recent years, the profession has been dominated by writers like Holroyd, who, in addition to his life of Strachey, is also the author of lives of Augustus John and Bernard SHAW; Victoria Glendinning, who has written on Vita SACKVILLE-WEST, Anthony Trollope, and Jonathan SWIFT; and Richard Holmes, who has contributed important studies of Percy Bysshe SHELLEY, Coleridge, and—his most universally acclaimed work—*Dr. Johnson and Mr. Savage* (1993). More controversially, the novelist Peter ACKROYD has incorporated biography into his multinovel reflections on English history, including lives of Charles DICKENS (1990) and William BLAKE (1995).

It is important, however, not to overstate the radical trends in life writing, and to that end one might adduce the resurgence of political and historical biographies writ on a large scale. Many of these works inadvertently demonstrate that the age-old problem of balancing attention to the individual with attention to his context remains unsolved. Robert Blake's acclaimed *Disraeli* (1966) tries to resolve the problem by emphasizing the public and political man, the parliamentary "operator"; even so, Sarah Bradford's sequel of sorts, *Disraeli* (1982), shows how that picture could be significantly altered by shifting focus to Disraeli's private life. John Ehrman's herculean, three-volume *The Younger Pitt* (1969–96), meanwhile, almost entirely loses the person in the wealth of detail, and incidentally suggests that William Pitt—whose apparently inorganic life "shape" stymied earlier commentators like Coleridge and Thomas Babington MACAULAY—might benefit from some narrative experimentation.

As the success of Ehrman's work also suggests, the genre has become again tolerant of multivolume, extensively detailed, and documented works, in a way of which Strachey would not have approved. On the flip side of the coin, however, the reader finds celebrity biographies—short, sensationalized, and designed for rapid sale. Biography continues to be a genre high in demand, not only on the printed page, but also in new media: television, film, and the Internet. British television regularly airs biographical specials; biopics have long been a popular draw with audiences; and the Internet's ability to disseminate vast quantities of information and misinformation to vast quantities of people makes at least basic knowledge available with a few strokes of the keyboard. It remains to be seen if hypertext generates narrative innovation in biography; so-called blogs, on-line diaries with hypertext links to other spaces on the web, including other blogs, have certainly suggested possible directions for autobiography. Whether the Internet will also give a new terror to dying is, of course, a different question altogether.

BIBLIOGRAPHY: Altick, R., *Lives and Letters* (1965); Anderson, J. H., *Biographical Truth* (1984); Backscheider, P., *Reflections on Biography* (1999); Browning, J. D., ed., *Biography in the 18th Century* (1980); Clifford, J. L., ed., *Biography as an Art* (1962); Cockshut, A. O. J., *Truth to Life* (1974); Dunn, W. H., *English Biography* (1916); Heffernan, T., *Sacred Biography* (1988); Hoberman, R., *Modernizing Biography* (1987); Meyers, J., ed., *The Biographer's Art* (1989); Nadel, I. B., *Biography* (1984); Novarr, D., *The Lines of Life* (1986); Stauffer, D., *The Art of Biography in Eighteenth Century England* (2 vols., 1970); Stauffer, D., *English Biography before 1700* (1930)

MIRIAM ELIZABETH BURSTEIN

BISSET, Robert
b. ca. 1759, Perthshire, Scotland; d. 14 May 1805, London

B. is best known for his brief lives prefixed to his eight-volume edition of the *Spectator* (1793–94)—which included biographies of Joseph ADDISON, Richard STEELE, Thomas PARNELL, Alexander POPE, and other contributors to the renowned periodical—and for his six-volume *History of the Reign of George III* (1803). He was also the author of a full-length biography of Edmund BURKE (1798); two novels, *Douglas; or, The Highlander* (4 vols., 1800) and *Modern Literature* (3 vols., 1804); and two proslavery tracts, written in response to the bill introduced in 1804 by William Wilberforce calling for the abolition of the slave trade.

BLACKMORE, R[ichard] D[oddridge]
b. 7 June 1825, Longworth; d. 20 January 1900, Teddington

B. is best remembered for his novel *Lorna Doone: A Romance of Exmoor* (3 vols., 1869), which brought him fame and fortune and is still popular. An historical romance set in the reign of Charles II, it features a tribe of brigands called Doone who infest a valley on Exmoor. The hero falls in love with Lorna, who turns out to be Lady Lorna Dougal, kidnapped as a child, and eventually rescues and marries her. Carver Doone shoots the bride at the altar and meets a horrible death. Vivid and entertaining, the novel has been read by generations with pleasure. B.'s later fiction includes *The Maid of Sker* (3 vols., 1872), *Alice Lorraine* (3 vols., 1875), *Mary Anerley* (3 vols., 1880), and *Springhaven* (3 vols., 1887), which was included in the Everyman's Library series. B.—called the "Last Victorian" by biographer Kenneth George Budd—is often compared to Thomas HARDY for his novels of village life in the English countryside, notably *Cripps, the Carrier* (3 vols., 1876), *Christowell* (1881), and *Perlycross* (3 vols., 1894).

BLACKMORE, [Sir] Richard
b. 22 January 1654, Corsham, Wiltshire; d. 9 October 1729, Boxted, Essex

Physician and man of letters, B. was the author of *Prince Arthur: An Heroick Poem* (1695) and six other long, pious, and patriotic poems, including *Eliza* (1705), a political allegory that chronicles the defense by ELIZABETH I of Protestantism against Catholic opposition; *Creation* (1712), a versified exposition of John LOCKE's philosophy; and *Redemption* (1722), which sought, expressing an anxiety widespread in the period, to reconcile Christian faith with natural reason. Following the publication of *Alfred: An Epic Poem* (1723), B. turned his attention to historic and medical treatises as well as a religious study entitled *Natural Theology* (1728). Alexander POPE described B.'s verse as "rumbling, rough and fierce."

BLACKWOOD, Algernon [Henry]
b. 14 March 1869, Kent; d. 10 December 1951, London

Incorporating a wide variety of influences ranging from Eastern mysticism to Freudian psychoanalysis, B. was a prolific short story writer, novelist, and dramatist whose interest in the occult and the supernatural informed both his fiction and nonfiction. His first collection of short stories, *The Empty House and Other Ghost Stories*, appeared in 1906, and in 1909 he published his first fantasy novel entitled *Jimbo*. B.'s experimental novels *The Human Chord* (1910) and *The Centaur* (1911) preceded his best-known work, *Julius Le Vallon* (1916), the first of his novels about reincarnation. In 1923, he published his autobiography, *Episodes before Thirty* (1923), and later wrote several works for children before embarking on a successful career in radio and television.

BLAIR, Hugh
b. 7 April 1718, Edinburgh, Scotland; d. 27 December 1800, Edinburgh, Scotland

B.'s *Sermons* (5 vols., 1777–1801) were praised by Samuel JOHNSON and translated into most European languages. They are mentioned in Jane AUSTEN's *Mansfield Park*. B. was educated at Edinburgh University and in 1762 became Edinburgh's first Professor of Rhetoric and Belles Lettres. B. was a member of the Poker Club, a distinguished literary circle that included David HUME, Adam SMITH, Adam Ferguson, and William Robertson, among others. In 1783, he retired from his professorship and published his *Lectures on Rhetoric*, frequently reprinted. He believed in the authenticity of James MACPHERSON's *Ossian* and in 1763 published a *Dissertation* in its defense.

BLAIR, Robert

b. 1699, Edinburgh, Scotland; d. 4 February 1746, Athelstaneford, Scotland

B. was educated at Edinburgh University and in Holland and became a clergyman. His blank verse poem *The Grave*, eight hundred lines long, was influenced by Edward YOUNG's "Night Thoughts" and earned B. a reputation as a "graveyard poet." Completed by 1742, the poem was published, in quarto, in 1743 and was immediately successful. B.'s poem was illustrated in 1808 by William BLAKE, who also illustrated Young's. B.'s gloomy meditation remained popular with Dissenters for many years.

BLAKE, William

b. 28 November 1757, London; d. 12 August 1827, London

The second of five children born to a London hosier, B. began seeing visions at the age of eight or ten. When he reported seeing a tree clustered with angels, his father accused him of lying but his mother supported him. From age ten to twelve, B. attended a drawing school taught by Henry Pars. In 1769, at age twelve, he began to write poetry. He was apprenticed in 1772 to the engraver, James Basire. His twin careers as poet and artist thus began early.

To many literary critics, the visionary B. has appeared an interesting if eccentric poet, while he has been seen by art historians as a great poet but an inferior artist. The truth is that in both fields he was profoundly original and influential, while admittedly being quite separated from the prevailing Romantic poetic modes of nature poetry and instructive ballads such as William WORDSWORTH's and Samuel Taylor COLERIDGE's poems. His main sources of inspiration were the Bible (particularly the Old Testament), and John MILTON. As an artist, B. could effect delicate illustrations to children's poems, while also following James Barry in studies of the male and female nude in energetic action (at a time when prurience and the landscape painting of John Constable reigned) and drawings of monumental figures that anticipate Henry Moore's monolithic sculptures. As a poet, he was

equally master of the sublimely simple lyric line as in "The Tyger," and the characteristic long lines of his later "prophetic works" that were to influence many poets such as Walt Whitman, D. H. LAWRENCE, and Allen Ginsberg, sustaining an immense energy of held concentration.

The American War of Independence that began in 1775 awakened libertarian politics in B., as in other radicals such as Thomas Paine who wrote *The Rights of Man*. From this time on, the burden of B.'s writing and art was to be revolution—political, religious, sexual, and social. In 1779, the apprenticeship to Basire terminated and B. was accepted as a student in the Royal Academy. He seems to have had a miserable time, but managed to make friends with artists who later became famous—George Cumberland, John Flaxman, and Thomas Stothard. In 1780, B. first exhibited works at the Royal Academy. While he was a student there, the Gordon Riots in London confirmed his radical leanings that were to be cemented by the French Revolution, which broke out in June 1789, proclaiming equality and the sanctity of life and liberty. He was lucky enough to be noticed by the courageous publisher, Joseph Johnson (who published other radical writers such as William GODWIN, Mary WOLLSTONECRAFT, and Paine). Johnson commissioned engraving plates from B.

In 1782, B. married Catherine Butcher (or Boucher), his lifelong companion and collaborator (she colored many of his engravings). They remained childless. B.'s first volume destined for eventual publication, *Poetical Sketches* (1783), was printed by Flaxman and Reverend A. S. Mathew, but it was not distributed to the public.

B.'s father died in 1784, the same year that he himself began to work in partnership with James Parker in a print shop, although the affiliation was terminated in the following year. He was grief stricken in 1787 on the death of his younger brother Robert, who, B. reported, ascended "clapping his hands for joy." This event seems to have had abiding influence on his work. In that same year, B. befriended the radical painter, Henry Fuseli, also an acquaintance of the publisher Johnson. In 1788, he first used his special method of relief-etched illuminated printing, publishing *All Religions Are One* and *There Is No Natural Religion*.

In 1789, B. published *The Book of Thel* and engraved *Songs of Innocence*, his first major independent works. The latter can be read either as a much-beloved set of simple lyric poems for children or as a profound interrogation from within of the state of childly innocence which is simultaneously pure and easily exploited. "The Chimney-Sweeper" is an example. In 1790, he probably began writing *The Marriage of Heaven and Hell* (1793?), containing aphorisms like "Energy is Eternal Delight," and challenging orthodox religion.

The execution of Louis XVI in France (1793) led to a conservative backlash in Britain, which waged war against revolutionary France and increased state surveillance and political repression of freedom of speech in Britain. In the same year, B. in a defiant Prospectus advertized his work for sale, including *America a Prophecy*, which provided a radical account of the American War of Independence, characteristically coded in mythological terms. In 1794 followed the equally mythologized *Europe a Prophecy* and more "Songs" in *Songs of Innocence and of Experience.* The latter added to *Songs of Innocence* an equally gnomic and beguilingly accessible set of lyrics that further complicate and recontextualize the former. The collection as a whole includes such well-known, complementary poems as "The Tyger" and "The Lamb." In this implicitly dialectic set of poems, B. sets up a far-reaching triadic distinction between a state of innocence that is blissfully ignorant, an experience that is exploitative and destructive, and a further state of "wise experience" that painfully and sometimes satirically observes the whole spectrum. The subject matter of the poems includes child labor, religious hypocrisy, female subjection, and slavery. Underlying B.'s analysis lies his belief in "mind-forg'd manacles," what we now call "false consciousness," a state of mind inculcated by institutions persuading us that we deserve our lot, however miserable it may be. A particular target is the official church hierarchy, which is consistently seen as thwarting people's natural desires but efficient enough in its propaganda to avoid mass condemnation.

In 1795, B. engraved *The Song of Los, The Book of Ahania*, and *The Book of Los*, following them in 1796–97 with engravings for Edward YOUNG's *Night Thoughts* and illustrations and a dedicatory poem for the poems of Thomas GRAY. In 1800, the Blakes left Lambeth to live at Felpham, Sussex, as the guests of his patron, William HAYLEY, and they lived there until they returned to London in 1803. He was charged with sedition on August 12, 1803, for ordering a soldier from his garden, a charge of which he was acquitted. During this time, B. was working on *Vala,* unpublished during B.'s lifetime, *Milton* (engraved between 1804 and 1808), and *Jerusalem* (finally engraved in 1820). These are among his most difficult works, often called "prophetic" not because they prophesied the future but because the poetic stance was that of the Old Testament prophets, speaking from a bardic sense of omniscience.

In his more challenging poems, B. creates a whole personal mythology peopled by figures who lie between the allegorical and symbolic. Using the ancient Roman name for England, he creates Albion's daughters, who seek liberty from sexual restraint. Jerusalem

is the city of liberty and Beulah the realm of the subconscious, the source of inspiration. Urizen, based on Newton, stands for Reason that restrains energy, while Los personifies poetry and the creative imagination. Enitharmon is spiritual beauty, Los's female companion. Orc is the spirit of Revolution, the first-born of Los and Enitharmon. Luvah represents unrestrained love and sexual energy, while Oothoon is repressed love. The Four Zoas represent the four aspects of man: the body, reason, emotion, and imagination. They have been separated by Urizen, but their eventual reunion will lead to personal unity and the redemption of Albion.

Quite apart from the failure to sell his laboriously executed and time-consuming work, B. had other professional disappointments. The publisher Robert Hartley Cromek commissioned him to supply designs for Robert BLAIR's *The Grave* but later transferred the work to Louis Schiavonetti; and Thomas Stothard's painting of *The Canterbury Pilgrims* when exhibited in 1807 drew accusations of plagiarism from B. His own paintings, accompanied by a *Descriptive Catalogue,* were exhibited in 1809 but failed. He did, however, continue to provide engravings for the works of others: for Flaxman's designs for *Hesiod,* Milton's "L'Allegro" and "Il Penseroso," *Job* (commissioned by Thomas Butts), woodcuts for Dr. Robert John Thornton's *Virgil,* and illustrations to Dante's *Divine Comedy,* the latter commissioned by John Linnell. One of the satisfactions of his later life was a friendship with Samuel Palmer, whose group "the Ancients," provided B. with the appreciative support he had received from few others.

On April 12, 1827, B. wrote to Cumberland: "I have been very near the Gates of Death & have returned very weak & an Old Man feeble & tottering but not in Spirit & Life not in the Real Man The Imagination which Liveth for Ever." On August 12, he died, aged sixty-nine.

He had lived through revolutions, recording their social impact in his poetry, and he had charted the volcanic changes in his own mental landscape, through a detailed and vividly visualized personal mythology. It may not be an exaggeration to suggest that B. anticipated Sigmund Freud's central distinction between the ego (controlling, rational thought) and the id (subconscious imaginativeness), the central psychological dichotomy portrayed in B.'s poetry, in which the id decisively prevails. His parable of "the four Zoas" visualizes the eternal conflict between the rational mind, the body that yearns for "eternal delight," the emotions, and the imagination based on experiential unity. "Every thing that lives is holy, life delights in life" was his central credo, and freedom in all aspects of living was his watchword, although he was loyally and happily monogamous, conventional, and routined in his own style of living, building his life caringly around family and work. Despite the admiration of writers such as Northrop Frye and Kathleen RAINE, the impact of B.'s work was not fully appreciated until the 1960s. He has, however, gained recognition as the most original and unique Romantic poet and artist, in many ways comparable with his contemporary, painter J. M. W. Turner. Nowadays, his work is assured of its major status.

BIBLIOGRAPHY: Bentley, G. E., Jr., *The Stranger from Paradise* (2001); Bindman, D., *W. B.* (1982); Damon, S. F., *A B. Dictionary* (1965); Erdman, D. V., *B., Prophet against Empire* (3rd ed., 1977); Glen, H., *Vision and Disenchantment: B.'s "Songs" and Wordsworth's "Lyrical Ballads"* (1983); Mee, J., *Dangerous Enthusiasm: W. B. and the Culture of Radicalism in the 1790s* (1992); Thompson, E. P., *Witness against the Beast: W. B. and the Moral Law* (1993)

R. S. WHITE

BLOOMFIELD, Robert

b. 3 December 1766, Honington, Suffolk; d. 19 August 1823, Shefford, Bedfordshire

Aged eleven, B. was apprenticed as a laborer to a farmer, but lacked the necessary strength, so became a cobbler. Living in a garret in Bell Alley, London, he wrote the poem that made his reputation, "The Farmer's Boy." Several publishers rejected it, until Capell Lofft, a barrister and patron of the arts, arranged for its publication with woodcuts by Thomas Bewick in 1800. In two years, over 25,000 copies were sold and it was translated into various languages. *Rural Tales, Ballads and Songs* (1802), *Tales from the Farm* (1804), *Wild Flowers* (1806), and *The Banks of the Wye* (1811) followed, but B. never repeated his first success and he died in poverty.

BLOOMSBURY GROUP

The Bloomsbury group refers to a collection of writers, artists, and critics who gathered first in Bloomsbury Square in London during the first decade of the 20th c. and later at various addresses in London, Richmond, and the English countryside. The group's membership and dates, even its existence, are debated. Most, however, will agree that the group existed and included, minimally, Clive and Vanessa BELL, Virginia and Leonard WOOLF, Thoby and Adrian Stephen, Duncan Grant, Lytton STRACHEY, Desmond MacCarthy, and Saxon Sydney-Turner; most would include the economist John Maynard KEYNES, the novelist E. M. FORSTER, and the art critic Roger FRY.

Recognized as part of the intelligentsia and, perhaps, as the Bohemians of England, they saw themselves as rebels against Victorian thought and propri-

ety, although they were middle-class English men and women whose financial security was the legacy of Victorian England. They rebelled against Victorian domestic arrangements, against Victorian canons of art, against Victorian political and economic theory, and against Victorian and Edwardian literary and biographical taste. They began with their living arrangements. When Sir Leslie STEPHEN died, his sons—Thoby and Adrian and—more crucially—his daughters Vanessa and Virginia—lived without chaperon at 46 Gordon Square in Bloomsbury. This family group along with former Cambridge undergraduates—many of whom had been part of the intellectual society known as the Apostles—began socializing on Thursday evenings, with the young women entertaining various of their brothers' friends and undergraduate acquaintances. Their association was that of friends, brought together to talk—to seek truth, to abjure the hypocrisies of their "fathers," and to consider what the philosopher G. E. Moore proposed as the ethical and esthetic life in *Principia Ethica* (1903). At Cambridge, Keynes, Strachey, Thoby Stephen, and Leonard Woolf were influenced by Moore. Almost immediately, Clive Bell, another Cambridge friend, and various members of the Strachey family joined the Thursday gatherings; and later they were joined by Fry whose criticism of art became central to their esthetics and by Forster, who was—like Fry—older than most of them and already more accomplished.

When the Gordon Square home was relinquished to Vanessa and Clive Bell after their marriage in 1907, Adrian and Virginia moved to 29 Fitzroy Square, and in 1911 Adrian and Virginia, Keynes, Grant, and Leonard Woolf set up housekeeping in Brunswick Square. The latter arrangement created a stir. Their sexual relationships and their openness about homosexuality and bisexuality marked them as quite separate from the world of Sir Leslie Stephen and from the world of his stepchildren, the Duckworths.

They came first to the attention of England through the Dreadnought Hoax, dressing up as visiting dignitaries and visiting an English Man of War. While that hoax appears to be mostly high spirits, the collective interest in *épater les bourgeois* that it represents is typical: the British navy being a glorious target for young rebels. But for students of English letters, literature, and art, they are more remarkable for supporting experimentation in the arts of all kinds. In 1905, Vanessa started the Friday Club for young and new artists to discuss art and exhibit their work annually. In 1910, Clive Bell, MacCarthy, and Fry organized the first postimpressionist exhibit in London—an exhibit of contemporary French art that included Cézanne, Matisse, Gauguin, Van Gogh, Picasso, and which provoked angry and shocked responses from the establishment. Fry had already made a reputation as an art critic and connoisseur, lecturer, and writer, and had worked as European curator for the Metropolitan Art Museum in New York. Clive Bell was just beginning to establish himself. The exhibition introduced contemporary French and Continental art into England and gave rise to significant shifts in artistic taste and practice. Vanessa, a painter herself, was clearly influenced by the artists in the exhibition, as was Grant, another member of Bloomsbury.

Fry's *Vision and Design* and Clive Bell's *Art* (1914) and the later *Since Cézanne* (1922) helped move English taste away from representational art into MODERNISM. Bell's concept of "significant form" focused readers and viewers on pattern and form. These concepts had significant influence on Woolf and other modernist writers as their literary experiments moved away from the REALISM of late Victorian writing. Fry and Grant also formed the Omega Workshops (in 1913) to encourage the decorative arts in everyday life and in the publishing world.

Leonard Woolf joined the group when he returned in June 1911 from Sri Lanka (then Ceylon), disenchanted with English imperialism. Woolf's political interests continued through his life. His *Economic Imperialism* and *Imperialism and Civilization,* published in 1920 and 1928, respectively, are often neglected by literary scholars, but were important examples of Bloomsbury's resistance to the ruling ideologies of the British Empire. Bloomsbury's resident Fabian, Woolf, as well as less overtly political members of Bloomsbury—Lytton Strachey, Grant, Clive Bell— refused military service in the First World War; Grant, Bell and Strachey (conscientious objectors) worked on farm projects as alternative national service, while Leonard was declared medically unfit. While much of Bloomsbury was not always overtly political, its sentiments clearly diverged from the majority; and on the matter of the war, they agreed. Near the end of the war, Leonard Woolf helped form the 1917 Club, a haven for socialists and for artists and writers whose interest in and infatuation with Bloomsbury made the group attractive; almost simultaneously he and Virginia founded Hogarth Press. After the war, he worked with others, including Sidney and Beatrice Webb, seeking to find peaceful solutions to international conflict (as he would work, after World War II for the United Nations). Keynes, in part a member of Bloomsbury, had served with the Treasury and worked on the Versailles treaty but resigned over the reparations issue and attacked the Versailles treaty in his *Economic Consequences of the Peace.* Woolf and Keynes, each in different ways, continued to exercise political and economic influence, although of course Keynes's influence was much greater through the twenties and thirties. Keynes's economic theories did much to modernize the field.

In literature, the Bloomsbury group presents, as well, English modernism. By the end of World War I, Virginia Woolf was an accomplished novelist, having published *The Voyage Out* and finished, with some struggle, *Night and Day.* But the experimentation in narrative that marks her later books is just beginning. Her great contributions to English literature come in the 1920s and 1930s: *Jacob's Room, Mrs. Dalloway, To the Lighthouse,* and *The Waves.* In those novels, she develops her own ideas about and practice of literature that captures the life of the human consciousness, not the external life of late Victorian and Edwardian realism that she attacks in her essay "Mr. Bennett and Mrs. Brown."

Woolf was not alone in her divergence from Victorian aesthetics, nor her attack upon eminent writers of the period. Strachey both radically altered how biographies were written and lampooned well-known Victorians, starting with his *Eminent Victorians* and *Queen Victoria.* His most praised work is the later *Elizabeth and Essex.*

BIBLIOGRAPHY: Bell, Q., *Virginia Woolf* (1972); Rosenbaum, S. P., *The Bloomsbury Group: A Collection of Memoirs and Commentary* (1975); Rosenbaum, S. P., *The Early Literary History of the Bloomsbury Group* (1987); Rosenbaum, S. P., *Edwardian Bloomsbury* (1994); Stansky, P., *On or About December 1910: Early Bloomsbury and Its Intimate World* (1996)

MARGUERITE HARKNESS

BLUNDEN, Edmund [Charles]

b. 1 November 1896, London; d. 20 January 1974, Long Melford, Suffolk

B. is best known for *Undertones of War* (1928), his account of his time as a junior officer on the western front during World War I, an experience longer and more continuous than any other prominent writer's from that war. Deservedly, *Undertones* is often considered the best prose work in English on the war. It captures the nuances or "undertones" of life on the western front, where the apparently insignificant details are as important as the larger issues, and where both men and landscape participate in and endure the devastation of war. Thus, B. describes leaving a particular sector of the line: "Not the same 'we' who in the golden dusty summer tramped down in to the verdant valley, even then a haunt of every leafy spirit and the blue-eyed ephydriads, now Nature's slimy wound with spikes of blackened bone." B.'s ability to convey atmosphere through concrete image and onomatopoeia is as effective in his prose as in his poetry: "the raided bombing-post soon after appeared, trampled, pulverized, blood-stained, its edges slurred into the level of the general wilderness."

B.'s poetry was popular during his lifetime, but his adherence to what he called "the great series of metrical inventions which tradition has already evolved" and the predominance of nature as a theme in his poetry set him in opposition with experimental MODERNISM and the urban themes of poets like T. S. ELIOT, and effectively removed him from the mainstream poetic canon of the first half of the 20th c. Yet, B.'s ability to evoke rural England, its seasons, wildlife, and characters has often resulted in critics ignoring the darker elements in much of his poetry. Nature becomes the means by which he explores these darker elements of existence, as in "The Midnight Skaters" (1925), where he exhorts the young skaters to defy the death that would prey on them beneath "a crystal parapet" and "court him, elude him, reel and pass,/ And let him hate you through the glass."

The two darkest elements of B.'s own life were the lasting psychological effects of the war and the death of his first child in infancy, both experiences being addressed directly and indirectly throughout his poetry. Although much of his poetry written at the front literally, as B. himself puts it, sank in the mud, the war poetry published during and after the war is a significant contribution to war literature. Like Ivor GURNEY, whose poetry he would later edit, B. often sets the "uncreation" of war against natural beauty and the humanity of the men with whom he served; like Gurney he is also able to convey unmitigated the immediate horror and terror of sucking mud, death, mutilation and the mental agony of bombardment. In "Third Ypres" (1928), the war experience itself and the postwar inescapability of that experience become one: "All to the drabness of uncreation sunk,/And all thought dwindled to a moan, Relieve!/But who with what command can now relieve/The dead men from that chaos, or my soul?" The mental agony of his war experience pursued him throughout his life, and is more completely explored in his poetry than in the controlled understatement of *Undertones*. A birthday poem, "November 1, 1931," written at Oxford, makes this clear: "Baffled in time, fumbling each sequent date/Mistaking Magdalen for the Menin Gate."

Throughout a life of teaching in universities in Japan and Hong Kong, and at Oxford, and literary editing, most notably for the *Times Literary Supplement*, B. made important contributions to English literature in his critical essays and introductions, biographies (including one of Thomas HARDY), and in his editing collections of the poetry of John CLARE, Wilfred OWEN, and Gurney. In each case, he was first to bring the most complete collections of these poets to the public.

B. had a sustaining friendship throughout his postwar life with the poet Siegfried SASSOON that, with a brief hiatus, lasted until Sassoon's death. The two men shared a common background in their war experience and the need to impose control on it through their writing, as well as a love of cricket, the English

countryside, and a desire to retain traditional poetic forms and themes.

BIBLIOGRAPHY: Mallon, T., *E. B.* (1983); Raleigh, J. H., "E. B.," in Serafin, S., ed., *Twentieth-Century British Literary Biographers, DLB* 155 (1995): 27–39; Webb, B., *E. B.* (1990)

CAROL ACTON

BLUNT, Wilfrid Scawen
b. 17 August 1840, Petworth House, Sussex; d. 10 September 1922, Newbuildings, Devon

B. was always regarded as a minor poet. Today, he is remembered as much for his breeding of Arabian horses, his travels in the Middle East and Asia, and for having been the guest of honor at a dinner where Ezra Pound and W. B. YEATS served peacock as he is for any of his artistic talents. He does deserve recognition, however, for his development of the Victorian sonnet tradition, for his loco-descriptive verses, and for his political poems.

Most of B.'s sonnets evolved from his many passionate love affairs and display his talent for realistic description, lucid, direct language, and minor experimentation with form. In his first published volume, *The Love Sonnets of Proteus* (1881), he records many different moods of love and tells of many different affairs with women. From these early sonnets, B. developed the sequence *Esther* (1892), which focuses more specifically on the story of his involvement with the famous courtesan Catherine Walters, also known as Skittles. The work is sometimes compared to George MEREDITH's *Modern Love* (although there is some question of whether or not B. had read Meredith's poem) because of his frank treatment of the pleasures and the sordid side of love and because of his departure from the strict tradition of the fourteen-line sonnet. The poems began as blank verse, but B. experimented with his material to transform the narrative into something that would, in the best tradition of the sonnet sequence, maintain the integrity of individual poems at the same time that it would tell a story, in this case in five scenes. In addition to the sonnet sequences, B. was inspired in other poetic forms to record his loves; "Ghost of the Beautiful Past," for example, memorializes an attachment to a Lady Windsor with whom B. had one of his many affairs.

In addition to following the amorous sonnet tradition, B. published *A New Pilgrimage and Other Poems* (1889) in which he describes a tour culminating in an audience with Pope Leo XIII. In this sonnet sequence, he describes his desire to give up the sins of his past and involvement in politics in order to concentrate on his religious faith; in the end, however, he finds himself unable to leave behind his political interests. B. writes in the pilgrimage tradition and uses relaxed, modern language that creates a very different tone from the Romantic pilgrimage epitomized by Lord BYRON's *Childe Harold's Pilgrimage*. His work remains a minor and largely unread one, however, because he does little either in terms of language, verse form or ideas to distinguish his work from others in the genre or to make this a "new" form.

In addition to his love poetry, B. wrote works celebrating the English countryside and other landscapes in the tradition of the loco-descriptive poem. Poems including "Worth Forest," "Chanclebury Ring," "Gibraltar," and "Sussex Pastorals" are competent examples of the genre that are enlivened by arresting stories and images without ever rising to the level of greatness. In the genre of the social satire, *Griselda: A Society Novel in Rhymed Verse* (1893) is a surprisingly readable work in iambic pentameter couplets. The verse novel is narrated by a young man in love with an heiress who has married a man more than twice her age. The first sections of the poem are humorous as the narrator watches the young woman who does not miss passion and is reasonably content to maintain the status quo of an often hypocritical society. The narrator, however, follows her into her thirties, when she falls in love first with a Prince Belgirite (with whom her affair remains unconsummated) and then with Jerry Manton, an adventurer who proves unworthy of her love. Although it seems unlikely that a verse novel will find many modern readers, B. blends social satire and psychological insight (both into the narrator who finds himself unable to help the woman he loves and the other character types he describes) to create a notable example of this Victorian genre.

In addition to dabbling in popular poetic forms, B. transformed his political interests into poems, including *The Wind and the Whirlwind* (1883). He specifically attacked British imperialism in this volume and throughout his career. For example, B. noted with some pride that he was the only Englishman to be jailed in the cause of Irish freedom in over four hundred years, and he wrote a number of poems with Irish themes. In "The Canon of Aughrim," B. gives his opinions of English "justice" and its inequities in dealing with the Irish. In the poem *In Vinculis* (1889), B. describes his time in jail for his involvement in the Irish cause. During the Boer War, B.'s indignation at the actions of Kitchener's soldiers led to another political poem, the bleak *Satan Absolved: A Victorian Mystery* (1899), a rather grim satire in the spirit of many of Thomas HARDY's dialogues among characters of the spirit world.

In addition to his work as a poet, B. published his impressions of India in the prose works *Ideas About India* (1885) and *India under Ripon* (1909). Other political works in prose include *Atrocities of Justice under British Rule in Egypt* (1906), *Secret History of the English Occupation of Egypt* (1907), *Gordon at Khartoum* (1911), and *The Land War in Ireland* (1912). Although B. was a member of the upper classes, he never hesitated to question the status quo, and he used his writing to further the causes in which he believed.

In "To One With His Sonnets," B. wrote that his "book" was not written of dreams but "things of flesh and blood,/The past that lived and shall not live again." When the *Poetical Works* was published in 1923, B. was praised in *Poetry* magazine for his talent for writing using an "unlabored aristocracy of diction" to write about "real people of this world in actual situations and about places he had actually seen." B. may not have broken new ground politically or poetically, and readers today neglect him in part because he seems irrelevant in recording a past that will indeed not live again. For his competence and his continuing interest in finding the links between love, art, and politics, however, he was indeed worthy of the admiration of Pound and Yeats and continues to deserve attention as an exemplar of a certain aristocratic temperament of the late Victorian age.

BIBLIOGRAPHY: Going, W. I., "B.'s *Esther*: The Making of a Sonnet Sequence," *VP* 20 (Spring 1982): 63–72; Going, W. I., "A Peacock Dinner: The Homage of Pound and Yeats to W. S. B.," *JML* 1 (1971): 303–10; Longford, E., *A Pilgrimage of Passion: The Life of W. S. B.* (1980)

CATHERINE FRANK

BOLAND, Eavan
b. 24 September 1944, Dublin, Ireland

Widely considered the leading Irish female poet, B. is a writer of immense talent whose stature was enhanced with the publication of her memoir *Object Lessons: The Life of the Woman and the Poet in Our Time* (1995). B. has argued that the still-dominant Irish nationalist historical narrative has largely ignored the personal lives of women, children, and even men by privileging the story of an emergent nation above all else. B.'s most recent work that rejects the mimicry inherent in a largely invented nationalism follows on from her earlier poetry that explored the tangled relations among women's personal lives and Irish history.

B. was born the daughter of the Irish diplomat Frederick H. Boland who was president of the United Nations General Assembly in 1960. She was educated in London and New York and later did university work at Trinity College, Dublin. Married to the novelist Kevin Casey, she has two daughters and continues to split time between the Dublin suburb of Dundrum and Stanford, California, where she directs Stanford's creative writing program. B.'s suburban, liminal locale has enabled her both to escape the fierce allegiance to Dublin held by earlier Irish writers like Sean O'CASEY and to avoid the often idealized portrayals of the rural landscape by other Irish authors like W. B. YEATS. Throughout her poetry, B. registers her geographic and national ambiguity with rhetorical questions—a construction often employed by Yeats. B. has identified strongly with Yeats's cultural hybridity and even cowrote a critical study of Yeats with Micheál Mac Liammóir in 1971. B.'s poetry, almost exclusively written in free verse, often focuses upon concrete objects that lead to more expansive musings. A signature B. poetic device is her habit of inserting herself as first person into poems that began in third person in an effort to more closely identify with her subject.

Her first volume of poetry, *New Territory* (1967), contains mostly poems written at university dealing with Irish history and myth, while her second volume, *The War Horse* (1975), includes her first political work (the title poem) and other poems on Irish history and life in suburbia. In her angry third volume, *In Her Own Image* (1980), and in her more reserved, domestic volume, *Night Feed* (1982), B. explored the varying ways in which women experience their bodies, examining anorexia, breast cancer and mastectomies, and motherhood. *Outside History* (1990) focuses upon a variety of women, none more representative of her ongoing concerns with the intersection of women and nationhood than "The Achill Woman," the first poem in the sequence "Outside History." This autobiographical poem enabled B. to sense the horrible suffering of Irish women and realize the horror of the Great Famine in a way in which most public poetry written by Irish men had not.

In a Time of Violence (1994) features a series of poems on the intersection of objects with history. For example, "The Dolls Museum in Dublin" is B.'s rewriting of Yeats's "Easter, 1916." B. replaces Yeats's extended, finally elegiac descriptions of the Irish rebels with the mute dolls' witnessing of the moment immediately before the Easter Rising in Dublin. Their status as inanimate objects renders them as mute as the Irish women who had promenaded with British soldiers; their past, B. suggests, has been superseded by Irish nationalist history. Her recent volume entitled *The Lost Land* (1998) has emerged from her ongoing vexed relationship with Ireland and England. This volume is characteristically hybrid, divided into two parts, "Colony" and "The Lost Land." A number of poems in "Colony" feature images of personal and political wounds, while several poems of "The Lost Land" conflate B.'s lament for Ireland's Gaelic past with her mourning for her daughters who had recently left home.

BIBLIOGRAPHY: Maguire, S., "Dilemmas and Developments: E. B. Re-Examined," *FemR* 62 (Summer 1999): 58–66; Russell, R. R., *Yeats and Postcolonialism* (2001); special B. issue, *CQ* 35 (December 1999)

RICHARD RANKIN RUSSELL

BOLINGBROKE, Henry St. John, Viscount

b. 16 September 1678, Lydiard Tregoze, Wiltshire; d. 12 December 1751, Battersea

When Samuel JOHNSON in his *Dictionary* illustrated "irony" with the sentence, "Bolingbroke was a holy man," the lexicographer was not only expressing his dislike for B. but also turning B.'s favorite literary device against him. B.'s repeated invocation of patriotism also prompted Johnson's famous comment that patriotism was the last refuge of the scoundrel. Yet when Johnson defined "Whig" as "the name of a faction" and "Tory" as "one who adheres to the ancient constitution of the state, and the apostolic hierarchy of the church of England," he was echoing B.'s views of these two parties.

Brilliant and energetic, B. impressed his parliamentary colleagues from the moment he entered the House of Commons as member of Parliament for Wootton Bassett, a constituency traditionally represented by his family, in 1701 as a Tory backbencher. He served as secretary of war (1704–8) and then secretary of state (1710–14). With Robert Harley, B. created the *Examiner* in August 1710 to support Tory efforts to end the War of the Spanish Succession and to attack the Whig opposition. In *A Letter to the Examiner* (1710), B. wielded his potent political pen to denounce the Whigs as a "Factious Cabal" that was reducing England to "a Farm to the *Bank* [of England], a Province of *Holland*, and a Jest to the whole world."

With the death of Queen Anne (1714) and the return of the Whigs to power under George I, B.'s parliamentary career ended, though he spent the rest of his life trying to restore it. In March 1715, he fled to France just ahead of impeachment hearings that would have sent him to the Tower of London. In Paris, B. became secretary of state to "James III," Stuart pretender to the British crown, but B. was dismissed after the failure of the 1715 attempt to overthrow George I.

In 1717, in an effort to gain a royal pardon and so return to the English political scene, B. wrote the widely circulated *A Letter to Sir William Wyndham* (1753) in which he urged the remaining Jacobite Tories to abandon the Stuart line for the Hanoverians. As he would continue to do throughout his writings, he accused the Whigs of factionalism that damaged the national interest. More effective in gaining B.'s pardon was a large bribe to the king's mistress, the Duchess of Kendal, and in 1725 B. returned after a decade from France.

Barred from the seat his title should have allowed him in the House of Lords, B. used his pen to direct opposition to Sir Robert Walpole's administration. With William Pulteney, B. founded the *Craftsman* (December 5, 1726), to which B. contributed about a hundred articles over the next decade. On June 13, 1730, he began a series of twenty-four *Craftsman* letters that were collected as *Remarks on the History of England* (1743). B. presents English history as an ongoing struggle between the spirit of faction and the spirit of liberty. The letters draw parallels between George II and the corrupt Richard II and HENRY VIII. B. presents the reign of ELIZABETH I as an ideal period when national interest prevailed over factional concerns. In an unintended irony, B., the most partisan of men, here and in his subsequent writings condemned partisan politics.

From October 27, 1733 to December 21, 1734, B. published in the *Craftsman* nineteen letters that became *A Dissertation upon Parties* (1735). Once more, B. likened George II to earlier bad rulers, in this instance James I and Charles I, who had destroyed England's constitutional balance of powers and had fostered a pursuit of wealth that had corrupted the social fabric. B.'s solution was the coming to power of a national party promoting a spirit of public benevolence, i.e., the Tories.

In 1735, B. again left England for an extended stay in France. There he composed *Letters on the Study and Use of History* (wr. 1736–38; pub. 1752) in which he quotes and supports Dionysius of Halicarnassus' dictum that history is philosophy teaching by examples. In a statement that raised a storm of protests from religious readers when the work was published, B. denied the reliability of ancient historians, including the Bible, and so focused on events since 1500. B. concluded his survey of British history with a blistering attack on the current government "composed of a king without monarchical splendor, a senate of nobles without aristocratic independency, and a senate of commons without democratical freedom."

In 1736, B. wrote a *Letters on the Spirit of Patriotism* (1749), which argues against factions at the same time that it advocates a loyal opposition in Parliament. B. was not content with mere opposition, though; he wanted power. By 1739, he despaired of a parliamentary coalition's ability to replace Walpole, and so in *The Idea of a Patriot King* (wr. 1739; privately printed 1740; pub. 1749) B. placed his hopes with Frederick, Prince of Wales. Specifically rejecting Niccolò Machiavelli's remedy for a corrupt state, B. advocated virtue rather than expediency as the basis for successful rule. B. once more called for a balance of powers among king, lords, and commons and for a government by those dedicated to national rather than factional interests. B. urged the patriot king to dismiss corrupt ministers (Walpole and his supporters) and to install in their stead those dedicated to England's welfare.

Admirers and opponents alike appreciated the power of B.'s rhetoric. Alexander POPE called B. "absolutely the best writer of the age." Philip Dormer Stanhope, fourth Earl of CHESTERFIELD, who recognized B.'s flaws as a person, urged his own son to devote himself to B.'s style: "Transcribe, imitate, emulate it, if possible; . . . with that, you may justly hope to please, to persuade, to seduce, to impose." Though neither a philosopher nor historian of the first order, B. produced a series of political works that remain essential reading for the student of early-18th-c. England.

BIBLIOGRAPHY: Dickinson, H. T., *B.* (1970); Kramnick, I., *B. and His Circle* (1968); Varey, S., *H. St. J., Viscount B.* (1984)

JOSEPH ROSENBLUM

BOLT, Robert [Oxton]
b. 15 August 1924, Manchester; d. 20 February 1995, Hampshire

B. is remembered as the author of *A Man for All Seasons* (1960) perhaps the finest historical play in English since Bernard SHAW's *St. Joan* and as the greatest screenwriter of his time, whose scripts for the director Sir David Lean, *Lawrence of Arabia* (1962), *Doctor Zhivago* (1965), and *Ryan's Daughter* (1970), are among the most literate in all film.

During his earlier theatrical career, there had been much conflict in B.'s writing between his intellectual wish to write expressionist poetic plays and his natural ability that inclined toward the naturalistic. A man of conflicting opposites in his own life; intellectually attracted to communism and idealistic left-wing causes but emotionally to luxury and hedonism.

From a respectable lower-middle-class background near Manchester, B. graduated through National Service and schoolmastering to writing radio plays, twelve in six years. His first stage play, *The Critic and the Heart* (perf. 1957; rev. as *Brother and Sister*, perf. 1967), about sibling rivalry between an artist and his sister who has given up her life for him and the human havoc that can be caused around the creation of art, was performed out of London but did bring B. the services of the famous literary agent Margaret Ramsay, who shaped the first half of B.'s career.

But it was his second play that firmly placed B. in the first division of young authors. Furthermore, his plays were presented in the commercial West End of London rather than at the more ideologically fashionable Royal Court. *Flowering Cherry* (perf. 1957; pub. 1958) is about an insurance salesman whose twenty years in a soul-destroying job has been made only bearable by the dream of owning an orchard in his native Somerset. Basically, it is a play of family tensions and the relationships between sad downtrodden mother, lying husband and father, dishonest but bright son and daughter who has taken her emotional allegiance elsewhere. B. makes these conflicts, often seen before, seem new. B. himself criticized the play later for being an awkward mixture of NATURALISM and nonnaturalism but the writing, which is cerebral until the characters reach crisis point when it explodes into emotionally charged heightened prose, is superb and Jim Cherry (originally played by Sir Ralph Richardson) is a most rounded and theatrically rewarding creation.

The Tiger and the Horse (perf. 1960; pub. 1961) is a play of more intricacy and depth and also, against the author's hopes, fundamentally naturalistic. It concerns involvement: how lack of involvement with others can destroy their lives, just as how excessive involvement with the ills of the world can be self-destructive. In it the master of an Oxbridge college—an astronomer who disbelieves in cosmic order—once a brilliant scholar, now routine but respected, through lack of involvement with his daughter and wife brings misfortune to one, insanity to the other. The central public issue is a petition supporting nuclear disarmament—a cause B. was much involved with to the extent of going to prison for a short while—and whether the master will or will not sign it. This play attracted much debate and a success for the real-life father and daughter team of Sir Michael and Vanessa Redgrave.

But it is on *A Man for All Seasons* that B.'s theatrical reputation resides. B.'s real gift was for understanding history and applying it to the present rather than for contemporary social issues. In this account of the great humanist scholar and statesman Sir Thomas MORE, it is the simplicity of the writing and delineation of emotion that triumphs. Adopting a Brechtian EPIC structure and creating a character called the Common Man as link and narrator, servant, waterman, and, finally, executioner, B. draws the debate between public and private conscience with timeless clarity and presents matters of state in a simplified and personalized way. If some of the language has dated slightly, it is not because he writes a pastiche Tudor, for his idiom has an educated muscularity that sits comfortably in 16th-c. mouths speaking in the 20th but because it can occasionally sound like a 1950s red-brick university's debating society. Yet the theatrical power of the trial scene and More's defense (adapted from court records) and in particular the profoundly moving farewell between More and his family, ensure the play's everlasting attraction. More was played to great effect both on stage and in the film version (1966) by Paul Scofield.

Apart from the colorful and enjoyable children's play *The Thwarting of Baron Bolligrew* (perf. 1965; pub. 1966), B.'s theatrical career now went downhill.

Gentle Jack (perf. 1963; pub. 1964), a mish-mash of big business and folk cults, was a disaster, and *Vivat! Vivat Regina!* (perf. 1970; pub. 1971) about ELIZABETH I and Mary Queen of Scots was a pale distaff *Man for All Seasons*. Then, luckily, the cinema claimed him. His last play, *State of Revolution* (1977), about the course of the Russian revolution, had many admirers but only a short run at the National Theatre.

In 1978, B. was incapacitated following a serious stroke. Thereafter, he found speech and movement difficult. Yet his life force still blazed. He had a large personality and his Rabelaisian gusto and formidable intellectual vigor are to be found in his work. There were many from B.'s earlier theatrical life who told him and the world what a disappointment he had been for failing his great early promise. Yet B. surely had the career that was the best for him. It is far more creditable to be the author of the screenplay of *Doctor Zhivago* than to have written another *Gentle Jack* or even another *The Tiger and the Horse*.

BIBLIOGRAPHY: Chambers, C., *Peggy: The Life of Margaret Ramsay, Play Agent* (1997); Duff, C., *The Lost Summer: The Heyday of the West End Theatre* (1995); Miles, S., *Bolt from the Blue* (1996); Turner, A., *R. B.* (1998)

CHARLES DUFF

BOND, Edward
b. 18 July 1934, London

One of the most significant British playwrights of the last fifty years, B.'s consistently challenging and passionately socialist drama has earned him a formidable reputation both at home and internationally. Emerging from the social realism of the 1960s and blossoming with a series of EPIC plays in the 1970s, B. has since moved away from the mainstream, but his influence endures in the work, among others, of Caryl CHURCHILL, Howard BARKER, and Sarah KANE.

B.'s first plays, presented at London's Royal Court Theatre, only hinted at what was to come. *The Pope's Wedding* (perf. 1962; pub. 1971) explores a youth's relationship with a derelict, a theme explored by Harold PINTER and David RUDKIN, and its successor, *Saved* (perf. 1965; pub. 1966), maintains a linear, sociorealist approach. The play, which showed a baby being stoned to death in its carriage, caused much controversy and helped to hasten the end of censorship on the British stage. B.'s use of what he called "aggro-effects," and the provocative streak also evident in the surreal and sprawling *Early Morning* (1968), for some time obscured his fundamentally moral intentions.

Narrow Road to the Deep North (1968), based on an ancient Japanese story, shows a baby found in the rushes growing to be a tyrant, and was followed in

1978 by *The Bundle*, in which a similarly abandoned child leads his people to freedom. *Lear* (perf. 1971; pub. 1972), perhaps B.'s best regarded play, uses William SHAKESPEARE's characters and events to construct an epic fable of the journey out of madness, both personal and societal. In contrast, a comic light touch characterises *The Sea* (1973) a tale of fascist agitation in a rural coastal town in prewar England.

B.'s next three plays confronted the "problem of culture . . . of the burden of the past" and indeed can be called his "problem plays." In *Bingo* (perf. 1973; pub. 1974), the retired Shakespeare attempts to reconcile his artistic insights with his mercantile successes, which leads inevitably, in B.'s version, to his suicide. *The Fool* (perf. 1975; pub. 1976) tells the story of the commodification of the 19th-c. peasant poet John CLARE, while *The Woman* (1978) is set during the last days of the siege of Troy and afterward on Hecuba's and Ismene's island retreat. B. saw this play as a summation of his work up to that point, presenting history as a battle between the rational and irrational in which the latter usually, though not inevitably, triumphs.

The three plays beginning with *The Bundle* have been classed as "Answer plays": *The Worlds* (perf. 1979; pub. 1980) examining class division and industrial action, while *Restoration* (1981) explores the futility of working-class Toryism. *Summer* (1982) bears parallels to *The Tempest*, showing an older generation pursuing the struggles of the past, even while their children make the world anew. Agustina, in the Spanish Civil War drama *Human Cannon* (pub. 1985; perf. 1986) learns to become herself the ultimate weapon against fascism.

B. grew disillusioned with the major subsidized theaters following difficulties staging *Human Cannon* and his dissatisfaction with the Royal Shakespeare Company's production of his postnuclear trilogy *The War Plays* (1985), a major work as powerful as it is structurally idiosyncratic. Initially produced outside the mainstream, *Jackets Parts 1 and 2* (perf. 1989; pub. 1990), *In the Company of Men* (pub. 1990; perf. 1996), and *Coffee* (pub. 1995; perf. 1997) were described by the author as "postmodern plays" though B.'s definition of the phrase is characteristically individual. B.'s POSTMODERNISM embraces notions of indeterminacy (the precise nature of stage events is often open to question) and self-referentiality (B.'s plays commonly re-work scenes and ideas from earlier pieces by himself and others), but rejects any suggestion of the abandonment of moral responsibility. Recent plays *Have I None* (perf. 2000) and *The Crime of the Twenty-First Century* (2001) demonstrate his enduring integrity.

B. has diversified over the years, writing a number of shorter pieces for the stage, including *Passion* (perf. 1971; pub. 1974) and *Stone* (1976); translating or adapting the plays of others, notably Frank Wede-

kind; making forays into opera libretto with *We Come to the River* (1976), among others; writing two powerful television dramas, *Tuesday* and *Olly's Prison*, in 1993; and scripting his first radio drama, *Chair*, in 2000. He is a prolific (and sometimes impenetrable) essayist, and has also published volumes of his letters and poems. Of late, he has become increasingly interested in writing plays for young people such as *At the Inland Sea* (perf. 1996; pub. 1997) and *Eleven Vests* (1997), and sees Theater-in-Education as a vital project in a culture reduced by the global market to "an empty performance . . . which turns its audience into hamsters . . . *angry* hamsters." Too often ignored at home but greatly admired in continental Europe and beyond, B.'s work continues to challenge, to probe, to startle, and to enlighten.

BIBLIOGRAPHY: Lappin, L., *The Art and Politics of E. B.* (1987); Mangan, M., *E. B.* (1998); Roberts, P., ed., *B. on File* (1985); Spencer, J. S., *Dramatic Strategies in the Plays of E. B.* (1992)

HARRY DERBYSHIRE

BOORDE, Andrew
b. 1490?, Holms Dale, Sussex; d. April 1549, London

B., a physician, traveled extensively in Europe as well as North Africa and the Middle East on government business and sent a copy of his itinerary to Thomas Cromwell, who lost it. In 1542, B. wrote *The Fyrste Book of the Introduction of Knowledge* (1555?), the original Continental guidebook. He presumably in that same year published his *Dietary of Health*, which together with his *Breviary of Health* (1547) were among the first medical works composed in English for the lay reader. B.'s later career was marred by recklessness and scandal, and in 1548 he was confined to Fleet Prison, where he died in the following year.

BOSWELL, James
b. 29 October 1740, Edinburgh, Scotland; d. 19 May 1795, London

A lawyer and man of letters, B. counted among his friends the leading literary and political figures of the day, including Oliver GOLDSMITH, Edmund BURKE, John Wilkes, Sir Joshua REYNOLDS, David GARRICK, Richard Brinsley SHERIDAN, and especially Samuel JOHNSON. He was elected to the famed Literary Club in 1773. In the larger realm, he counted among his acquaintants David HUME, Voltaire, and Jean-Jacques Rousseau. B.'s *The Life of Samuel Johnson, LL.D.* (2 vols., 1791; rev. ed., 3 vols., 1793) stands as one of the greatest biographies in the English language. Since the recovery and publication of B.'s journals and private papers, he also emerged as an engaging and important diarist.

The eldest son of Alexander Boswell, Laird of Auchinleck, B. had a difficult and complex relationship with his father, who wished his son to study law and prepare for his role as Laird of Auchinleck. Chafing against his Presbyterian upbringing, B. preferred the life of a libertine in London, styling himself after the Restoration wits. Torn between the pursuit of pleasure and the desire to please his father, he eventually relented, studying law in Edinburgh, Glasgow, and Utrecht, and eventually marrying. B.'s deep friendship with Johnson represents part of a search for an approving father. Throughout his life, B. remained moody and impulsive, known for his persistent charm, but also his insecurity and indolence.

Despite the warnings of his father against a future of "mimicry, journals, and publications," B. published poetry, pamphlets, and essays throughout his life, including a series of some seventy essays in the *London Magazine* in the manner of Johnson's *Rambler*, under the signature *The Hypochondriack* (1777–83). Aside from the *Life*, his chief publications during his life were *An Account of Corsica* (1768) and *The Journal of a Tour to the Hebrides* (1785). Encouraged by Rousseau, B. took up the cause of Corsican independence, visiting the island and becoming a friend of General Pascal Paoli. His trip to Corsica and his memoir of Paoli became the basis for his *Account*. In the *Tour*, B. chronicled his 1773 trip through the Hebrides with Johnson, who had published his own account in *Journey to the Western Islands of Scotland*. B.'s *Tour* became his first attempt to capture Johnson's character.

The chance discovery of some of B.'s letters led to the search for and recovery of many of B.'s private papers—letters, diaries, and memoranda. Lieutenant Colonel Ralph Isham collected these between 1919 and 1949 and sold them to Yale University in 1949. *The Private Papers of James Boswell from Malahide Castle* (18 vols., 1928–34) were edited and privately printed by Geoffrey SCOTT and Frederick A. Pottle. From this and other discoveries, Pottle later edited the thirteen-volume Yale Edition (1950–89). This includes the *London Journal, 1762–1763* (1950), in which B. records his first meeting and early acquaintance with Johnson as well as his disastrous affair with the actress Louisa Lewis. The two volumes of *Boswell on the Grand Tour* (1953 and 1955) include his exchanges with Voltaire and Rousseau. *Boswell for the Defence* (1959) centers on his involvement with and unsuccessful defense of John Reid for sheep stealing. *Boswell, the Great Biography* (1989) presents B.'s tribulations over the composition of the *Life*. Often compared to Rousseau's *Confessions*, B.'s journals represent a history of his mind, marked by a detached and frank analysis of his motives and behavior, ranging from his enthusiasm to his despair, from his bouts of drunkenness and venereal disease to his brilliant conversations with the great figures of his age. Even as he recorded the events of his life, B. the mimic wrote in the style of Restoration and Georgian theater. The account of his affair with Lewis in *The London Journal*, for instance, echoes the manner of Sir John Brute in Sir John VANBRUGH's *Provok'd Wife*.

B. had been recording anecdotes and conversations with Johnson since 1763. His procedure was to sketch a few notes after the meeting to aid his memory. He would then work the notes into a more finished form some days later as time permitted. By 1774, his correspondence indicates that he contemplated preparing a biography. With Johnson's death in 1784, however, several rivals emerged. Hester Thrale PIOZZI published her *Anecdotes* in 1786, followed in 1788 with two volumes of the correspondence between herself and Johnson. At the same time, Sir John HAWKINS branded by Johnson as "unclubbable," but one of his executors, also took up the project, producing his *Life* in 1787. The Club and in particular Reynolds, Bishop Percy, Bennet Langton, and Edmond MALONE, favored B., providing him with materials, encouragement, and support. B. published his *Tour* in 1785 with an announcement of things to come, finally completing the *Life* in 1791.

If B. himself has often been censured for his personal weaknesses and dissipation, the *Life* stands as an enduring achievement, winning immediate success and fame. He found prototypes in the 18th-c. BIOGRAPHY, such as William MASON's *Life of Gray* or Johnson's own *Lives of the English Poets* and in the literary tradition of Table Talk. Daniel DEFOE, Samuel RICHARDSON, and the fictional tradition that grew out of letter writing and diary keeping that played on a blurring of fact and fiction also influenced him. But B.'s greatness resides in his own skills as an artist. The basic organization of the *Life* is chronological, though B. innovates the form of the biography by including material from Johnson's letters and other documents. The subject, however, is not merely a compendium of the facts and history of Johnson's life, but the evocation of his character. B. achieves this by building the *Life* around Johnson's conversations. Drawing on the accounts recorded in his journals, he constructs scenes and conversations to present Johnson dramatically in real time. The result is not an historical transcript, but the imaginative re-creation of the spirit and atmosphere of the original scene. Like Plato's Socrates, B.'s greatest achievement was the creation of an image of Johnson that transcends his history.

BIBLIOGRAPHY: Brady, F., *J. B.: The Later Years, 1769–1795* (1984); Clifford, J. L., ed., *Twentieth Century Interpretations of B.'s Life of Johnson* (1970); Lustig, I. S., ed., *B.: Citizen of the World, Man of Letters* (1995); Pottle, F. A., *J. B.: The Earlier Years,*

1740–1769 (1966); Sisman, A., *B.'s Presumptuous Task* (2001)

THOMAS L. COOKSEY

BOTTOMLEY, Gordon

b. 20 February 1874, Keighley; d. 25 August 1948, Oare, near Marlborough

Contributor to the first series of *Georgian Poetry* (1912), B. was influenced by Celtic FOLKLORE and his poetry and poetic drama reflect the influence of W. B. YEATS. Written in 1900, B.'s first play entitled *The Crier by Night* was published in 1902 but was not performed until 1916. He gained critical attention with *King Lear's Wife* (pub. 1913; perf. 1915) followed by his best-known play *Gruach* (pub. 1921; perf. 1923), which enacts the courtship of Macbeth and his lady. Later works, collected in *Lyric Plays* (1932) and *Choric Plays* (1939), include *The Bower of Wandel* and *Culbin Sands*, both performed in 1931, *Kirkconnel Lea* (perf. 1932), and *The Falconer's Lassie* (perf. 1938). Although a minor poet and dramatist, B. remains a representative literary figure of the Georgian era.

BOWEN, Elizabeth [Dorothea Cole]

b. 7 June 1899, Dublin, Ireland; d. 22 February 1973, Hythe

Anglo-Irish novelist, short story writer, critic, and autobiographer, B.'s prolific career spanned fifty years and included what many rightly regard as some of the most distinguished prose of the 20th c. Insightfully described by her biographer, Victoria Glendinning, as "what happened after Bloomsbury . . . the link that connects Virginia WOOLF with Iris MURDOCH and Muriel SPARK," she demonstrates a Jamesian attention to style throughout her work, combined with a talent for social comedy and a rare ability to bring time and place vividly to life. B. described herself in an essay as "a writer for whom places loom large," and her writing is characterized by its sensitivity to the essence of both city and countryside, yet it is her ability to people those landscapes with emotionally and psychologically convincing characters that singles her out; while most of her work deals with English middle-class life, B.'s ability to portray any behavior or age within those parameters, from the hopes and fears of naïve youth to the disappointments and regrets of old age, is quite remarkable. Such is the intensity of her language that minute observations of daily life stand shoulder to shoulder with the deepest insights into the human soul, revealing what Angus WILSON referred to as B.'s "strange and glorious manifestations of the human spirit."

B.'s upbringing as the daughter of an Irish barrister and landowner formed the basis of two nonfiction works: *Seven Winters* (1943), a short personal memoir, written through the eyes of a child, in which she candidly describes her family and Dublin childhood; and *Bowen's Court* (1942), the history of her home in County Cork from the Cromwellian settlement until she, as the last of the Bowen line, was forced to sell it in 1959; in this interesting work, written in wartime London, the personal history of the Bowens is interspersed with the turbulent history of Ireland and B.'s plea for a return to the traditions and "proper social behavior" of the past.

While Ireland inspired B.'s nonfiction, it was, she said, England that made her a novelist. Her fictional career began with the short story and her first collection, *Encounters* (1923), appeared in the year of her marriage to Alan Cameron. It was followed by more short fiction: *Ann Lee's* (1926); *Joining Charles* (1929); *The Cat Jumps* (1934); *Look at All Those Roses* (1941); and *The Demon Lover* (1945) combine reportage, social comedy, themes of war, and, occasionally, the supernatural in subtle narratives that bear out B.'s belief that the story was "a matter of vision rather than of feeling." The last collection, part of the revival of the short story in Britain at the end of the Second World War, is characterized by the fragility of style—also seen in her later novels—which was part of a widespread change in the spirit of writing and a mourning of lost prewar values.

B. traveled widely in Europe and her first novel, *The Hotel* (1927), describes the English in Italy, perfectly capturing the mood of the nation in the 1920s, freed from one war and not yet overshadowed by the next. The book is a Forster-esque comedy of manners and a satire on the social life of the middle classes, something that is prevalent in her writing and that appears again in *Friends and Relations* (1931), a fictional study of the English marriage. *The Hotel* is her lightest work, but it has hints of the psychological insight and feeling for time and place which she would develop more fully later; the same is true of *The Last September* (1929), a rare fictional interpretation of her experiences in her native land and an elegy to the destruction of one of Ireland's great country houses in the 1920 uprisings.

Themes of innocence dominate B.'s novels of the 1930s, beginning with *To the North* (1932), a story of two young women and their precarious friendship that is set in London; *The House in Paris* (1935) is a finely crafted and delicate exploration of the obscure and complex relationships between children, sex, and love; but it is *The Death of the Heart* (1938), a poignant study of the destruction of adolescent innocence and the emotional atrophy of adults, shot through with characteristically sardonic HUMOR, which is B.'s first truly great work and the earlier of the two novels for which she is best known.

The Death of the Heart is the story of Portia, a sixteen-year-old orphan who goes to live with her sophisticated half-brother and sister-in-law in London, and whose world is shattered when she falls in love with an attractive young philanderer. The novel is a startlingly original account of the clash of private desires and the disorienting nature of love; it was written after B. had spent some years in the city, and the impressionistic descriptions of London's changing seasons are one of its unique strengths. Although her male characters are well formed, it is the acute perception of the feminine in *The Death of the Heart* that shows the influence of Virginia Woolf and that has led feminist critics to adopt B. as their own; the novel's appreciation of form and structure, however, transcends any one body of criticism.

During World War II, B. worked for the government in London and brilliantly re-created the period in *The Heat of the Day* (1949), which chronicles the tragic course of the love affair between Stella Rodney and Robert Kelway after the revelation that he is a spy. The novel creates an internal drama out of a conventional thriller format, and is given a peculiar intensity by drawing directly on B.'s own experience: the impact of ever present danger and death upon a city, and the intimacy of those who face it, are palpable. With its exuberance of language, originality of thinking and sharpness of vision, *The Heat of the Day* underlined B.'s reputation as a bold and expansive novelist, ever-ready to take risks with her prose.

After the self-confessed strain of writing *The Heat of the Day*, B. completed three further novels: *A World of Love* (1955), the last of her overtly lyrical books, in which a corroding country house in Ireland is the setting for a young girl's poetic awakening to love; *The Little Girls* (1964), a humorous story, filled with mystery and half-revealed secrets, which explores a friendship between three women rekindled after fifty years; and *Eva Trout; or, Changing Scenes* (1968), a tender and imaginative tribute to the vulnerable and the dispossessed that has, at its heart, a formidable heroine with an endless capacity for making trouble.

B. was awarded the CBE in 1948. Her minor works include a play, *Castle Anna* (1945), on which she collaborated with John Perry; books on a Dublin hotel (*The Shelbourne*, 1951; repub. as *The Shelbourne Hotel*, 1951) and Rome (*A Time in Rome*, 1960); and a volume of essays (*Collected Impressions*, 1950). The posthumously published *Pictures and Conversations* (1975) amalgamates the beginnings of a final novel with a selection of criticism, most importantly "Notes on Writing a Novel," first published in 1945; in that essay, B. argues that the novelist's aim must be to create "the non-poetic statement of a poetic truth"; in the finest of her prose, she achieved that aim as undeniably as any of her contemporaries.

BIBLIOGRAPHY: Blodgett, H., *Patterns of Reality: E. B.'s Novels* (1975); Glendinning, V., *E. B.* (1977); Kenney, E., *E. B.* (1975)

NICOLA UPSON

BOWEN, John [Griffith]
b. 5 November 1924, Calcutta, India

Although he has written several novels throughout his long career, B. is best known as a dramatist, having produced an impressive body of literature for both the stage and television. B. was, in fact, one of the early champions of television's potential to bring serious drama to a mass audience. His early television plays *A Holiday Abroad* (perf. 1960), *The Essay Prize* (perf. 1960), and *The Candidate* (perf. 1961) are minor tragedies of modern life, revolving around characters who achieve self-knowledge only after suffering moments of utter disillusionment. B. later began producing more experimental dramas, such as *After the Rain* (perf. 1966; pub. 1967), a stage play he adapted from his 1958 novel of the same name. In this sociopolitical satire, a group of six people—the sole survivors of a cataclysmic flood—form a totalitarian society; B. experimented in this play with the techniques of Brechtian theater, including masks and placards. B. has also produced experimental dramatic adaptations of classic works, such as the 1965 television play *The Corsican Brothers* and *The Disorderly Women* (1969), based on *The Bacchae* of Euripides. *The Disorderly Women*, considered by many critics to be B.'s finest play, deals with many of the same themes as *After the Rain*—the quest for power, the innate human tendency for violence—but in the later play B. displays a greater maturity and achieves a more tragic grandeur. Another experimental television script, *Heil Caesar!* (perf. 1973; pub. 1974), was an attempt to "translate" William SHAKESPEARE's *Julius Caesar* into modern language to make the themes more accessible to a contemporary audience. In the 1980s, B. began to concentrate more on writing fiction; subsequent novels include *The McGuffin* (1984), *The Girls: A Story of Village Life* (1986), *Fighting Back* (1989), and *The Precious Gift* (1992). It is, however, for his contributions to dramatic literature—particularly the television play—that B. will be remembered.

BOWLES, William Lisle
b. 24 September 1762, King's Sutton, Northamptonshire; d. 7 April 1850, Salisbury

In 1789, B. published anonymously *Fourteen Sonnets, Elegiac and Descriptive, Written During a Tour*. The sonnet form had been largely neglected during the 18th c., and B.'s work influenced Samuel Taylor COLERIDGE and Robert SOUTHEY. His longer poems include *The Spirit of Discovery* (1804), which was ridiculed by Lord BYRON; *The Missionary* (1813; repub. as *The Missionary of the Andes*, 1815), *The Grave of the Last Saxon: or, The Legend of the Curfew* (1822), and *St. John in Patmos* (1833). In 1806, B. published his ten-volume edition of Alexander POPE's works with notes and an essay in which he laid down desiderata in poetry. The question as to whether Pope was a true poet had been raised in the previous century, and B. praised the "natural" style over Pope's "artificial" one. Byron defended Pope, but B. was supported by William HAZLITT and *Blackwood's Magazine*. B.'s *Poetical Works* were collected in two volumes in 1855, with a memoir, by George GILFILLAN.

BOYD, William [Andrew Murray]
b. 7 March 1952, Accra, Ghana

A popular writer whose works are informed by philosophy, B. enjoys a reputation as one of Scotland's most prominent and acclaimed literary novelists. His books have oscillated between light comedies, such as *A Good Man in Africa* (1981), *Stars and Bars* (1984), and *Armadillo* (1998), and more thoughtful works, such as *The New Confessions* (1987), *Brazzaville Beach* (1990), and *The Blue Afternoon* (1993). He has also written some twenty film and television scripts, radio plays, two volumes of short stories, and a mock-biography, *Nat Tate: An American Artist, 1928–1960* (1998). B.'s works largely reject the formal innovations of MODERNISM, and he has stated in interviews that storytelling is more important to his work than experimental narrative style. "I would rather aim for limpidity and transparence than ornament and opacity," he says.

B.'s novels are linked by a few recurring themes: the First World War; the postcolonial history of Africa; the development of powered flight; the British Public School system; the history of cinema; mathematics as metaphor; the Englishman abroad. The range of his short stories is greater than that of the novels. B. has said that he regards the short story as his "laboratory," and the two collections, *On the Yankee Station* (1981) and *The Destiny of Nathalie "X"* (1995), are central to his canon. B.'s autobiographical television plays, *Good and Bad at Games* (1983) and *Dutch Girls* (1985), are also important works. B.'s edition of these plays, *School Ties* (1985), opens with a long essay on his schooldays at Gordonstoun, in the Highlands of Scotland.

B. began as a comic novelist, but his second novel, *An Ice-Cream War* (1982), represents a turning point. Set in rural England and Nairobi during the First World War, this bitter satire against the English ruling classes and the colonial mind-set was shortlisted for the Booker Prize in 1982. *Stars and Bars*, set in the deep South of the U.S., is an outrageous comedy that owes much to Evelyn WAUGH. B. later adapted two of Waugh's novels, *Scoop* and *Sword of Honour*, for television. B.'s deep admiration for another English humorist, Anthony BURGESS, is visible in his only London novel to date, *Armadillo*, an incisive exploration of the city's eccentric criminal underworld. B. shares Burgess's interest in the varieties of spoken English, particularly the speech of London gangsters. *Armadillo* is in many ways a paradigmatic B. text: it features a double time-scheme, multiple narrative point-of-view, comic villains, games with names, and a central figure who assumes various disguises.

The New Confessions, his longest book, deals with the history of the 20th c. and the changing technologies of film and flight. The novel claims to be the memoirs of an elderly Scottish film director who has witnessed the First World War and the development of postwar cinema in Germany and the U.S. Critical opinion of this large novel is genuinely divided. Some reviewers admired it, but Francis KING has claimed that it lacks a dominating theme.

Brazzaville Beach, a complex novel about chimpanzees, mathematics, betrayal, and an African war, is thought to be one of B.'s most accomplished works. Nevertheless, the presence of equations in the text makes it a difficult book to comprehend. *The Blue Afternoon*, set in the Philippines in 1904, is an impossible detective story, with a subnarrative about the invention of powered flight. In this book B. plays games with unreliable narration that invite comparisons with the novels of Vladimir Nabokov. Repeated readings of the text fail to disclose who has committed the murder on which the plot depends.

Nat Tate: An American Artist is B.'s most controversial work. Presented as a plausible biography with photographs and reproductions of paintings, it is in fact a cunning work of fiction. B. himself painted the pictures which he attributes to Nat Tate. The story of the Tate "hoax" was widely reported by newspapers in London and New York. B. wrote a series of articles for the London *Daily Telegraph* (April 5 and 12, 1998) explaining his intentions in publishing the book. The affair confirmed his reputation as an amiable trickster.

Recently, B. has moved away from novel-writing to develop his film career. He has written screen adaptations of *A Good Man in Africa* and *Armadillo*, and directed a full-length feature, *The Trench* (1999). But he intends to return to the novel in future. He told an interviewer: "Writing fiction is absolute freedom. As an art-form it is so boundlessly generous. Novels literally have no boundaries."

BIBLIOGRAPHY: Biswell, A., "W. B.," in Moseley, M., ed., *British Novelists since 1960*, Fourth Series, *DLB* 231 (2001): 31–40; Lawson, M., "Frozen Assets," *Guardian*, February 19, 1998, section 2: 11–12

ANDREW BISWELL

BRACKENBURY, Alison
b. 20 May 1953, Gainsborough, Lincolnshire

With the publication of her sixth collection, *After Beethoven* (2000), B. remains known as a prolific poet who engages with historical and biographical themes to explore the classic issues of loss and longing, dream and myth. It is the countryside of her childhood, which had been devastated by World War II, that would inform many landscapes of her work. She was born the elder of two daughters in rural Lincolnshire, where her mother was a schoolteacher and her father was a farmworker. Her grandfather was a shepherd who drove a horse and cart until the 1960s. Her village was one of the few oases of trees, birds, and flowers. B. had been drawn to poetry since she was very young, and she cites as major influences William WORDSWORTH and Philip LARKIN. After attending the local school at Willoughton, she went to Brigg High School and took her English degree at St. Hugh's College, Oxford.

Early publications include *Journey to a Cornish Wedding* (1977) and *Two Poems* (1979). Her first collection, *Dreams of Power*, was published in 1981 by Carcanet Press and was recommended by the Poetry Book Society. *Breaking Ground* (1984) and *Christmas Roses* (1987) followed. Some poems from the earlier collections were republished alongside new ones in *Selected Poems* (1991). In 1995, B. published *1829*, her fifth collection, and the title poem was featured on Radio 3. Published to widespread literary acclaim, *After Beethoven* continues her exploration of what has been termed "the pressure of the dead on the living," among other themes.

Her title poems, usually the longest ones in her respective collections, tend to be historical epics that illustrate an emotional dialogue between the dead and the living. With each collection, she engages more directly with the dead; early poems attempt to give a voice to selected historical figures, while poems in *After Beethoven* go so far as to argue with the dead. The results are ultimately a celebration of life. The grace with which she engages each realm has become a hallmark of her writing style.

To B., the act of writing poems is compulsive, and poetry itself is necessary to keep people grounded, especially when dealing with traumatic events like the loss of a loved one. Poetry, she asserts, shares more affinities with music than with visual arts; she is reluctant to use the term "imagery" to describe the arrangements within her poems. Likewise, she often uses terms associated with musical composition when discussing her own writings and those of poets she admires.

Her poems have been widely anthologized and published in most major literary journals. They have also appeared regularly on BBC Radio 3 and 4. She has read her poems on the radio shows *Night Waves* and *Woman's Hour*. She was the recipient of the Eric Gregory Award in 1982 and the Cholmondeley Award in 1997.

BIBLIOGRAPHY: Bertram, V., "A. B. in Conversation," *PN Review* 132 (March–April 2000): 31–33; Marsack, R. L., "A. B.," in Sherry, V. B., Jr., ed., *Poets of Great Britain and Ireland since 1960*, part 1, *DLB* 40 (1985): 41–45

VICKI ENG

BRADBURY, [Sir] Malcolm [Stanley]
b. 7 September 1932, Nottingham; d. 27 November 2000, Norwich

B. was a novelist with a great comic gift, a sharp eye for the signs of social and cultural change, and a serious concern for the fate of liberal humanism in an era of extreme ideologies. He was one of the modern masters of the campus novel—the novel set in and around a university, and with university teachers as its main characters, which has proved popular well beyond the academy, and which has greatly expanded in scope with the growth of a "global campus" linked by the jet plane and the Internet. Like his near-contemporary, David LODGE, B. spent most of his adult life in universities, as a student and then a teacher of literature, and produced a considerable output of literary criticism—highlights include *Possibilities: Essays on the State of the Novel* (1973) and *The Modern American Novel* (1983; rev. ed., 1992). Both his criticism and his fiction showed a capacity to respond to new kinds of writing and to structuralism and poststructuralism. He began by producing realistic novels, but moved toward a more self-conscious kind of fiction that highlighted its technical devices while always remaining highly readable. His novels and his writing for television cross-fertilized each other; he adapted a number of works by other novelists for television, like Tom SHARPE's *Porterhouse Blue*, and created his own successful television serials, notably *The Gravy Train* (1990). He also wrote one stage play, *Inside Trading* (perf. 1996; pub. 1997).

For much of his life, B.'s energies were divided between his writing and his academic work, especially at the University of East Anglia. It was here that B. and the novelist Angus WILSON launched an M.A. in creative writing, at a time when no such courses existed in England. This proved very successful, attracting students who later became distinguished novelists in their own right, such as Ian McEWAN and Kazuo ISHIGURO. But despite academic demands, B. produced a succession of novels in which, by his own account, he tried to sum up the key attitudes and tensions of succeeding decades from the mid-1950s to the early 1990s.

His first novel, *Eating People Is Wrong* (1959), is set in a university in an English provincial town, modeled to some extent on the University of Leicester, in the English Midlands, where B. took his B.A. Its central character, Professor Henry Treece, is a characteristic B. protagonist, the beleaguered liberal humanist; the novel traces his midlife crisis as he comes under attack from one of his students, Louis Bates, and competes with Bates for the love of Emma, a postgraduate student. In B.'s second novel, *Stepping Westward* (1965), a younger man, James Walker, leaves the English provinces to take up a post as writer in residence at an American university: B. creates much comedy, and some discomfort, from the encounter between English and American codes and expectations, which becomes particularly sharp when Walker refuses to sign an American loyalty oath. *Stepping Westward* also captures a more general sense of expansion in British culture in the 1960s as it opened up to American influences that were both desired and feared.

B.'s best-known novel, *The History Man* (1975), is a vivid caricature of a left-wing sociology lecturer, Howard Kirk, presented as the epitome of the political fervor, sharp self-promotion, and facile fashionableness that, in a hostile perspective, could seem to characterize the academic radicalism of the period. Sticking to the present tense and staying close to the surface of behavior and appearance, this highly stylized novel invites allegorical interpretation: for example, Kirk's pursuit and eventual seduction of a female lecturer in English literature can be read as an allegory of the displacement of liberal-humanist literary studies by radical sociology in this period. But this stylization largely disappeared in the television adaptation of the novel.

Rates of Exchange (1983) focuses on an English academic who goes on a cultural mission to an imaginary Eastern European country called Slaka, in the days before the collapse of the Soviet Union. As in *Stepping Westward*, B. explores the comedy and disturbance produced by the clash of different cultural codes; in contrast to the earlier novel, however, *Rates of Exchange* shows a self-consciousness and a linguistic concern that indicate the influence of structuralism. It was followed up by *Why Come to Slaka?* (1986), a spoof tourist guide to B.'s imaginary country. *Cuts: A Very Short Novel* (1987) offered a critique of the monetarist economics that were dominant in England and the U.S. in the 1980s, while another short book published in the same year, *My Strange Quest for Mensonge* (1987), was an entertaining satire on the search for a fictional French professor of poststructuralism. This idea of a quest for a celebrated but suspect intellectual was developed in B.'s long novel, *Doctor Criminale* (1992), which describes a young journalist's pursuit of an enormously influential but elusive intellectual, Bazlo Criminale, who proves to

have been involved in some of the darker transactions of 20th-c. history. B.'s last novel, *To the Hermitage* (2000), was an expansive work taking in politics, philosophy, and culture, in which chapters comically portraying modern scholars who travel to St. Petersburg in 1993 to work on a "Diderot project" alternate with chapters that amusingly imagine Diderot's encounters with Catherine the Great in the same city in 1793.

To the Hermitage showed no sign of flagging energies, and B.'s premature death at the age of sixty-eight left a sense of loss among the English literary community, particularly for those writers whose careers had begun at East Anglia. His novels are likely to survive as highly entertaining, technically versatile satires of key aspects of cultural and academic life in the later 20th c. and as explorations of the liberal dilemma which strive for a higher level of seriousness, even if they do not always reach it.

BIBLIOGRAPHY: Carter, I., *Ancient Cultures of Conceit: British University Fiction in the Post-War Years* (1990); Morace, R. A., *The Dialogic Novels of M. B. and David Lodge* (1989)

NICOLAS TREDELL

BRADDON, Mary Elizabeth
b. 4 October 1835, London; d. 4 February 1915, Richmond, Surrey

B., novelist, short story writer, playwright, and poet, author of over eighty volumes, once highly popular, owes her literary survival to two things: the perennial success of *Lady Audley's Secret* (3 vols., 1862) and scholarly studies of the last twenty-five years that analyze her subtle subversion of Victorian values. The child of a solicitor who separated from B.'s mother when B. was four, she was reared in straitened circumstances that made her aware of a woman's vulnerability and gave her a lasting preoccupation with money. In 1857, she became an actress, a career she abandoned for authorship in 1860, shortly before her unpublished comedy *The Loves of Arcadia* did well on the London stage. She received financial support from Yorkshire squire John Gilby to write a poem on Giuseppe Garibaldi's Sicilian campaign (*Garibaldi*, 1861). Simultaneously, she produced her first novel, *Three Times Dead* (1860; repub. as *The Trail of the Serpent*, 1861), followed in 1862 by a second, *The Lady Lisle*.

In 1860, B. met writer and editor John Maxwell with whom she began living in 1861. Maxwell had five children and a psychotic, institutionalized wife, and until the wife's death in 1874, he and B. could not marry; they had five children. Her publication of *Lady Audley's Secret*, and her liaison with Maxwell made her both famous and notorious. This phenomenally popular novel was enjoyed by Charles DICKENS and William Makepeace THACKERAY and later by Robert Louis STEVENSON and Arnold BENNETT, but its popularity brought to a respectable readership the kind of lurid melodrama previously associated with cheap magazines and lower-class readers. Thrillers had invaded the world of the three-decker novels.

Throughout the 1860s, novels of "sensation" were attacked as corrupt, and B.'s work and personal life were favorite targets. In 1868, she broke under the pressure and could not write for a year, but she recovered. Afterward, until the last years of her life, she averaged one "sensational" novel a year and one she considered serious. She borrowed plots freely, especially from French contemporaries. One of her most ambitious, *The Doctor's Wife* (3 vols., 1864), evokes Gustave Flaubert's *Madame Bovary* (1857) in Victorian mode. She thought of this as a novel of "character" rather than incident, and was disappointed both with the work and with the critical response.

Her marriage, popularity, and wealth enabled her to move in social circles that included Oscar WILDE, Bram STOKER, Edmund GOSSE, Ellen Terry, and Henry Irving. Although she died a grande dame, her reputation faded, and it is unlikely to be revived. Robert Lee Wolff's thorough biography is convincing as a discussion of B.'s awareness of Victorian woman's plight and of the shallowness of the rich, but less convincing as an evaluation of literary quality. *Lady Audley's Secret* is the only work likely to be read for its own sake. Beautiful, ruthless Helen Talboys has been deserted by her husband George, and, as Lucy Graham, marries Sir Michael Audley. When George returns, she causes him to fall into an abandoned well. Robert Audley, Sir Michael's nephew and George's best friend, suspects her; the chilling contest between Robert and Lady Audley makes one of the best and finest of early detective works. Superficially the values are conventional, but the rhetorical moralizing Victorian readers loved sounds hollow and platitudinous to a modern. Lady Audley's bitter reflections about being poor and unprotected have a truer ring.

"Serious" novels like *The Doctor's Wife* are flawed in the same way, and in this novel of "character" B. has her heroine Isabel Gilbert's husband George die of fever just before the man she loves, Roland Landsell, dies from a beating by a forger convicted on Landsell's evidence. Landsell is recognized when he accosts the forger, who is Isabel's missing father, for seeing Isabel clandestinely. Isabel's unconsummated love for Roland is based on romance reading, not on the deeper yearnings of Madame Bovary. B. is the author of one brilliant detective work, and she is a valuable source for those interested in Victorian culture.

BIBLIOGRAPHY: Tromp, M., P. K. Gilbert, and A. Haynie, eds., *Beyond Sensation: M. E. B. in Context*

(2000); Wolff, R. L., *Sensational Victorian: The Life and Fiction of M. E. B.* (1979)

DALTON AND MARYJEAN GROSS

BRAHMS, Caryl

(pseud. of Doris Caroline Abrahams) b. 1901, Croydon, Surrey; d. 4 December 1982, London

B.'s comic novels, written mainly in collaboration with S. J. Simon, fall into three categories: spoof historical stories of greater or lesser reliability— "Warning to Scholars: this book is fundamentally unsound" reads a note appended to *No Bed for Bacon* (1941)—some of which succeed but others of which are labored and outstay their comic welcome; parodies of various genres, as the fairy tale in *Titania Has a Mother* (1944); and, probably most successful of all, backstage theatrical stories, like the account of the music hall singer and Gaiety girl *Trottie True* (1946), who starts in respectable working-class London and ends up, as did many of the Gaiety Theatre company in Edwardian days, a peeress. Distinguished among this group are two based in the Stroganoff Ballet Company (B. was herself a ballet and theater critic). *A Bullet in the Ballet* (1937), the first collaboration with Simon, is also, as the title implies, a detective novel. *Six Curtains for Stroganova* (1945) tells the company's story from its origins in Omsk in 1910 to its first postwar London appearance after World War II, taking in much convincing background of the Imperial Maryinsky Ballet and School and the great Diaghilev company's origins in St. Petersburg. After Simon's death, B. made a few attempts to write alone or with other collaborators, most notably with Ned Sherrin, but never quite recovered the freshness and wit of the best of their joint works.

MICHAEL GROSVENOR MYER

BRAINE, John [Gerard]

b. 13 April 1922, Bradford, Yorkshire; d. 28 October 1986, London

B.'s career was blighted by a wrong decision. Offered the choice of a flat fee of £5,000 or a royalty on his first novel, the young librarian chose the former. *Room at the Top* (1957), successfully filmed in the following year, made a fortune, but not for the author. Deriving distantly from Charles DICKENS's *Great Expectations,* it is a first-person story of a lower-class young man on the make, who neglects his true love, a married woman, to make an advantageous match with a rich man's daughter, whom he has made pregnant. It articulates the yearning for wealth and status of the postwar underdog, in energetic if undistinguished prose. Its strength lies in its picture of provincial life. A sequel, *Life at the Top* (1962), was comparatively forced, and nothing else B. wrote was remarkable. Later novels included *The Vodi* (1959; repub. as *From the Hand of the Hunter*, 1960), set in a sanitorium for tuberculosis, *The Crying Game* (1968), *First and Last Love* (1981), and *The Two of Us* (1984). Originally hailed as an "Angry Young Man," B. moved politically toward the right in later years.

BRATHWAIT, Richard

b. ca. 1588, Burneshead, near Kendal, Westmoreland; d. 4 May 1673, Catterick

Poet, novelist, prose writer, and satirist, B. was a significant 17th-c. man of letters. His first published work was a collection of moral and amorous verse entitled *The Golden Fleece* (1611). B.'s best-known work, *Barnabee's Journal*, appeared under the pseudonym "Corymboeus" in 1638, and tells the story of journeys to the north of England, especially the inns, in English and Latin rhyme. B. was a prolific writer in various genres, including volumes of moral verse, *A New Spring* (1619) and *Times Curtaine Drawne* (1621); a pair of courtesy books, *The English Gentleman* (1630) and *The English Gentlewoman* (1631); and political satires such as *The Honest Ghost* (1658), *The Chimneys Scuffle* (1662), and *The Captive-Captain* (1665).

BRENTON, Howard

b. 13 December 1942, Portsmouth, Hampshire

More than any other dramatist of his generation, it is B. who gives theatrical expression to the tensions and legacy of the late 1960s counterculture. B. himself has acknowledged the specific influence of the so-called Situationists on his early work with groups such as the Brighton Combination and Portable Theatre. The Situationists conceived of capitalist society as an overwhelming "spectacle" that turns citizens into consumers and prevents them from experiencing life directly. For B., the function of art is to disrupt this spectacle by provoking and confounding the audience.

B.'s prototypical Situationist-inspired plays include *Christie in Love* (perf. 1969; pub. 1970) and *Fruit* (perf. 1970). The former, consisting of eleven short scenes, subverts the lurid media coverage of the serial killer Reginald Christie. Christie's first appearance in the play is Dracula-like—he arises from beneath a "garden" of newspapers—but it transpires that ordinariness is his distinctive quality. In contrast, it is the attitude of the two caricatured policemen that establishes the violent milieu of the play: they hang Christie in defense of their sentimental ideals of love. In *Fruit*, Paul, an embittered thalidomide victim, attempts unsuccessfully to blackmail a new Tory prime minister by threatening to reveal his homosexuality. As a manhunt is launched, Paul ends up sheltering with a Leninist vagrant who teaches him how to make

a petrol bomb that is—in a memorable finale—lobbed into the audience.

The relationship between idealism and violence continues as a dominant thematic trait in B.'s major work. In *Magnificence* (1973), five youths occupy a squat but the police invade: the pregnant Mary loses her baby while Jed is jailed. In the end, the latter blows up himself and a demoted politician in a botched gesture of futility. *The Churchill Play* (1974), meanwhile, is set in a camp for political prisoners in 1984; the inmates are preparing to perform a caustic play about Sir Winston CHURCHILL for visiting dignitaries but their attempted breakout fails. *Weapons of Happiness* (1976), B.'s first play at the National Theatre, focuses on Josef Frank, a former minister in the first Czech Communist government now working in a London factory. The play documents the appropriation of his experience in the moribund context of British political struggle. The souring of ideals is also a feature of *Thirteenth Night* (1981), an urban dystopia based on William SHAKESPEARE's *Macbeth*, and *Bloody Poetry* (perf. 1984; pub. 1985), B.'s poignant excoriation of Percy Bysshe and Mary SHELLEY, Lord BYRON, and the Romantic sensibility.

B.'s most notorious play, *The Romans in Britain* (perf. 1980; pub. 1981), is divided into two parts. The first is set north of the Thames in 54 B.C.E, while part 2 alternates between Britain in 515 and Ireland in 1980. This structure enables B. to contextualize imperialism historically and to correlate the conduct of the British Army in Northern Ireland with the Roman invasion of Britain. The performance at the National Theatre generated a storm of protest: the self-styled "moral campaigner" Mary Whitehouse claimed that a scene in which a Roman soldier sodomizes a Druid priest breached a section of the Sexual Offences Act; consequently, she subjected Michael Bogdanov, the play's director, to a private prosecution. The case was eventually dropped but the debate provoked arguably the most heated controversy about theatrical representation in postwar British history.

B. has undertaken more collaborative writing than any of his peers. *Brassneck* (perf. 1973; pub. 1974) and *Pravda* (1985; rev. ed., 1986), written with David HARE, are modern classics that have formal and thematic affiliations—both focus on tycoons in order to explore the contradictions of capitalism—yet are different in style. *Brassneck* foregrounds the Bagley dynasty and local government corruption; *Pravda* wittily documents how free market imperatives have transformed the newspaper industry into a "foundry of lies."

Other collaborations have responded to the contemporary political milieu. *A Short Sharp Shock!* (with Tony Howard, 1980) interweaves two narrative elements: domestic episodes featuring the socialist-leaning Stacker family, and scenes featuring the new

Thatcher government. The play articulates a series of shocking images to signal an ideological antipathy to right-wing economic philosophy. In a sequence inspired by the film *Alien*, a dummy version of the monetarist Milton Friedman bursts from the stomach of Margaret Thatcher's ideological guru, Keith Joseph, while, in the closing moments, the Prime Minister devours the ashes of the assassinated politician Airey Neave—who is himself featured as a ghost throughout. The production at London's Theatre Royal Stratford East provoked angry exchanges in Parliament, as members of Parliment demanded the withdrawal of public subsidy from the venue. *Ugly Rumours* (with Tariq Ali, 1998) critiques and pastiches Tony Blair's ascendancy, while *Snogging Ken* (with Ali and Andy de la Tour, 2000) is a short propagandist piece staged to support Ken Livingstone's bid for the London mayoralty.

BIBLIOGRAPHY: Boon, R., *B., the Playwright* (1991); Mitchell, T., *File on B.* (1987); Wilson, A., ed., *H. B.* (1992)

CHRIS MEGSON

BRIDGES, Robert [Seymour]

b. 23 October 1844, Walmer, Kent; d. 21 April 1930, Oxford

Today, B. is remembered as the first editor of the works of Gerard Manley HOPKINS. He deserves more complete attention as the poet laureate of England from 1913 to 1930 and one of the most influential poets and critics during the time of the transition from late Victorian to early modern poetry. Even during his lifetime, he was never widely read, since his work tends to be of the gentle and agreeable sort that shuns the sentimental as well as the sensational and instead relies on a thorough understanding of craftsmanship and prosody to produce its effects. He has found a few admirers in the 20th c., and will continue to have an influence both in critical and poetic circles for his lucid discussions of the difficult subject of prosody and his intelligent experimentation in a variety of verse forms.

B. articulated his aims and interests as an artist in his critical writing and activity. He was a founder of the Society for Pure English and set for them a program of publications on issues of language and style, an important issue for Victorian philologists. He hoped that the Society would encourage the continuing "English character" of the language in the face of the introduction of foreign and classical elements. In both his correspondence and his published work, B. relied on a "simplified" spelling that was designed to be close to pronunciation, created his own system of punctuation, and was interested in issues of book design and typography. B. wrote many essays (ulti-

mately filling ten volumes), including several on famous authors, that are still important today. *Milton's Prosody* (1893)—originally published as a more limited discussion in 1889 as *Milton's Blank Verse*—explored the tension between a strict metrical reading of ten-syllable lines and the more natural rhythms of speech. Although the work is flawed, B.'s readings are still useful to students of John MILTON and of prosody and were highly regarded by Victorian scholars of poetry. Similarly, his readings in *John Keats: A Critical Study* (1895) provoked much debate about the poet's life and work. His work on William SHAKESPEARE in *The Influence of the Audience: Considerations Preliminary to the Psychological Analysis of Shakespeare's Characters* (1926) is seen as most characteristic of B.'s distaste for that which does not fulfill his image of the beautiful and agreeable. B. argued that Shakespeare included bawdy HUMOR and violent emotions and actions in his plays in order to please the tastes of his audience and that his true temper was far more refined. More interesting than this criticism of the Elizabethan audience is his exploration of character and the use of extreme emotions without motivation or explanation. B.'s criticism is both idiosyncratic and insightful, revealing as much about B.'s own methods as about the work of the authors in question.

Although B.'s critical work suggests his immersion in the artistic debates of his day, his reputation will ultimately rest on his practice as a lyric and philosophical poet. B. began his career writing fairly conventional accentual verse; he published his first collection of fifty-three poems in 1873, although he would ultimately retain only eighteen in his collected *Poetical Works* (6 vols., 1898–1905). He included poems about nature and elegies based on English tradition, alongside a number of philosophical poems and ballads. He experimented with a number of popular verse forms, including the sonnet, rondeau, and triolet. Critics noted that the work showed B.'s accomplishment in verse forms but also criticized an unfortunate emptiness of content. This assessment was to color the critical reception of B.'s work throughout his career.

In later volumes, B. continued to work in conventional forms and published in 1876 the first version of a sonnet sequence, which would grow and change over the years, *The Growth of Love*. Some critics consider the work among the best of the late Victorian sequences, while others question whether it is a sequence at all. The sonnets seem to be inspired by a woman who is valued for her intelligence, although she rarely seems very real or present. There are elements that suggest a story of courtship, but there are also discussions of different kinds of love and the growth of the poet's appreciation for the pleasures and difficulties of creation and beauty that suggest a spiritual rather than a fleshly attachment. In general, the poems lack animating details or distinctive diction and are often weighed down by self-conscious tributes to other artists. In its final form, despite its flaws, the sequence presents a good catalogue of the kinds of subjects that B. consistently addressed in his work, from loving descriptions of nature to explorations of the latest scientific discoveries.

While B. mastered standard forms like the sonnet, he began his experiments with various poetic forms early in his career and evolved a form of "stress prosody" very much like Hopkins's "sprung rhythm." Some of his most anthologized poems, including "A Passer-by," "On a Dead Child," "London Snow," and "Nightingales," all show his achievement in this vein. His version of the form is not as strained as Hopkins's and often achieves a very quiet sort of effect, especially in a poem like "London Snow." In addition to his experimentation with "stress prosody," B. attempted to use the quantitative measures of Latin and Greek poetry in the composition of English verse, although he admitted the difficulty of applying the rules of the Greek scansion system to English models. His "Wintry Delights" is a verse epistle (in the manner of Horace's verse epistles) in hexameters; the tone is easy and conversational as he argues that even without love and beauty the reason and intelligence exercised in the pursuit of science is enough of a cause for wonder and delight to justify existence and to feed our intelligence. "Johannes Milton Senex" is written in scazons; some critics consider it B.'s most successful experiment in quantitative meter, in part because of the poem's logical structure and use of repetition and balanced phrases. B. never revived the ancient systems for scanning or writing verse, but he did suggest a care in craftsmanship that certainly had its influence in an age when poets were turning away from strict verse forms to freer forms of expression.

B.'s experiments with rhythm informed all of his work. His final experiments were in "neo-Miltonic syllabics," a six-foot line with a flexible pattern of accents. His best-known example is "Noel: Christmas Eve, 1913," one of B.'s first works published as poet laureate, and a work he meant to be accessible because of its use of the rhythms of natural speech. He continued to write in conventional forms, producing end-rhymed poems in accentual syllabic verses, like "Low Barometer," fairly late in his career. It was his final poem, *The Testament of Beauty* (1929), however, that B. achieved the critical and popular success that he had sought. The long philosophical poem (four books totaling 4,000 lines) has been described as a "spiritual autobiography" that testifies to B.'s consistent tenet that our response to beauty is the most important and elevating experience available to man. The poem is full of passages cataloging the beauties of rural England. In addition to these descriptive passages, B. also addresses subjects ranging from religion to war and politics, psychology, ethics, and metaphysics. The poem was praised as the expression of a rich and noble soul exploring all of human life.

Unfortunately, B.'s achievement has been overshadowed by the achievements of the modernist movement that followed. Those who would dismiss him say that he ignored the unpleasant realities of modern life and that he experimented in styles and subjects at the expense of addressing issues of the day. As long as scholars and poets want to understand the nature of poetry and can appreciate verse that combines an attention to craft with an insistence on rational subjects, however, he will find readers.

BIBLIOGRAPHY: Guerard, A., *R. B.* (1942); Stanford, D., *In the Classic Mode: The Achievement of R. B.* (1978); Thompson, E., *R. B.* (1944)

CATHERINE FRANK

BRIDIE, James [Osborne Henry Mavor]

b. 3 January 1888, Glasgow, Scotland; d. 29 January 1951, Edinburgh, Scotland

B., distinguished and prolific Scottish playwright, was approaching middle age before he began to be recognized, both in Scotland and in England, as one of the liveliest and most important dramatists of his day. And for most of his playwriting career of twenty years or so, he continued to practice in a very active way his other profession of physician and doctor of medicine. T. C. Worsley, the theater critic and literary editor of the *New Statesman*, wrote of B. shortly after his death: "James Bridie was one of the few interesting dramatists of the thirties and forties. He was a prolific writer who worked three or four different veins but who applied to all of them his very varied gifts: a delight in story-telling above all, a boldness of handling, a witty, pungent and rhetorical style, a lively fancy with a leaning toward the fantastic and the macabre, a highly developed sense of situation in the theatrical sense, and (which was all too rare among his contemporary dramatists) a vivid awareness of the life and interests of his time. . . . From his collection of talents one—and an essential one—seemed to be lacking, namely the architectural sense which can build scene upon scene into a solid whole. B. was master of the scene, but too often the play, in the end, ran through his fingers."

Other theater critics of the time made the same point about dramatic structure: the critical commonplace in 1940s London was that B. had many of the essential gifts of the good playwright but that he did not know how to write the final act of a play. James Agate, usually regarded as the leading London theater critic of the time, in reviewing *The Last Trump* in 1938, said: "Why cannot Mr. Bridie for once, like

Matthew ARNOLD, be wholly serious? Why must he write little plays round big themes? Why does he commit the supreme mistake of keeping his best character out of his last act?" On the other hand, St. John ERVINE, himself a playwright as well as a theater critic, after seeing B.'s play *Daphne Laureola* in 1949, is reported to have said to B.: "Who told you you couldn't write a last act!" (Indeed, one of the critics had said this: it was, in fact, Ervine himself.) Other critics defended B. on other grounds. J. C. Trewin, for example, in 1947, remarked on his skill and originality in character-drawing: "B. does not borrow from stock: he creates character."

On the whole, that contemporary criticism still seems valid. Even the best of B.'s plays (and several of them still seem very good) do suffer from a slenderness of construction and a perceived lack of artistic thrust and intention. But one needs to remember the general standard of British playwriting at the time B.'s work was being done. The late 1930s and the 1940s were arguably the worst periods for new plays that the London theater has ever seen—worse even than the doldrums of 1840–80. The sharp intelligence and questing, enquiring spirit of even the lesser B. pieces stood out in sharp contrast against the general background of flat domestic NATURALISM that had, during the 1930s and 1940s, laid its clammy and debilitating hand on most of the main-line British plays of the day, with only a glimmer of imaginative hope occasionally (and then not in the theatrical mainstream) from such writers as T. S. ELIOT, W. H. AUDEN, Christopher FRY, and Stephen SPENDER. In this glum and depressing scene, B. shone like a beacon.

Clearly, he wrote too much—an average of about two full-length plays a year for some twenty years, plus a scattering of shorter pieces. The wonder is that there are some six or seven out of the whole boiling that stand out now as very fine and very substantial plays. Not, of course, great plays—which are much rarer birds (we use that word "great" far too freely and frequently)—but plays, nevertheless, with a permanent sense of life and liveliness and reality about them; plays that are a good deal better than much of what has followed; plays that, above all, are long overdue for revival. Of the long list of his forty titles the following stand out: *Tobias and the Angel* (perf. 1930; pub. 1931), *The Anatomist* (perf. 1930; pub. 1931), *A Sleeping Clergyman* (1933), *The Golden Legend of Shults* (perf. 1939; pub. 1940), *Mr. Bolfry* (perf. 1943; pub. 1944), *Daphne Laureola*, and *Mr. Gillie* (1950). And of these there is one that fairly screams for revival and reappraisal. It is *A Sleeping Clergyman*: a play that fiercely and uncompromisingly celebrates the thrust and fire of the creative spirit itself, amoral and irresistible. Appropriately, in view of B.'s other profession, the exemplification of that

spirit in the play is a young doctor's insistence upon ignoring all caution and all advice in his efforts to find a cure for a worldwide plague. The sleeping clergyman in the play is God. He sleeps comfortably throughout. He never wakes. It is left to Man, imperfect and unsteady, to make some attempt at setting the world to rights.

Never a slave to NATURALISM and realistic verisimilitude, B. wrote in a great variety of styles. Three of his plays are straightforward renderings, though in modern colloquial prose, of biblical stories; half-a-dozen of them are satirical fantasies, partly in verse; six are based on actual, well-known historical events (such as the William Burke and William Hare murder trial of 1828, or the case of Dr. Pritchard, the notorious poisoner, of the 1860s—which B. transposes to 1920); a number of the plays are set in contemporary times but written in a lightly stylized, witty, comedic dialogue that is sometimes vaguely remiscent of Bernard SHAW. In several of his major plays a constant, underlying theme is discernible, implied rather than explicitly stated and never reduced to a solemn and pretentious intellectual debate: the perennial puzzle of human good and human evil. In B.'s hands, this never becomes a simple dramatized melodrama of Good versus Evil but rather a wry and quirky implication that for the understanding of the human pattern to be complete one must needs accept that the "good" forces and the "evil" forces are both essential parts of that pattern and, while roaring condemnation or loudvoiced hallelujahs may suit the priest or the politician, the artist is best served by more subtle considerations. It is interesting to note how often the Devil puts in a personal (and very personable) appearance in B.'s plays (including one—*Mr. Bolfry*—in which, under an assumed name, he becomes the central character).

As well as some forty plays and a mass of critical articles, B. wrote two books of AUTOBIOGRAPHY— *Some Talk of Alexander* (1926) and *One Way of Living* (1939). The former gives an account of his travels in Persia, Russia, and Mesopotamia as a medical officer during World War I; the latter is a high-spirited and entertaining account of the first fifty years of his life. He was also extremely energetic and influential in many public projects, both political and cultural, among which one of the most important was the founding and nurturing of the Glasgow Citizens Theatre, in which, from 1942 until his death, B. was the prime mover. Unfortunately, there is a regrettable lack of recent critical comment on B.'s work and some of that published forty or fifty years ago is in need of challenge and qualification.

BIBLIOGRAPHY: Bannister, W., *J. B. and His Theatre* (1955); Luyben, H. L., *J. B.* (1965); Matlaw, M., *Modern World Drama* (1972); Weales, G., *Religion in Modern English Drama* (1961)

ERIC SALMON

BRIGHOUSE, Harold
b. 26 July 1882, Eccles; d. 25 July 1958, London

B. and Stanley HOUGHTON were the most distinguished writers for Annie Horniman's innovative and influential Manchester Gaiety Theatre in the first two decades of the 20th c. B.'s famous comedy *Hobson's Choice* (1915) remains an active part of the current repertoire. Its social milieu, the shopkeeping class, was new territory, like the provincial setting in Salford, a suburb of Manchester, geographically and socially far removed from London. B. reflected, with HUMOR and humanity, the realities of family life as experienced by his audience, in a moral fable. Its continuing appeal lies in the victory of a strong-willed daughter, flouting economic patriarchy, over her domineering and exploitative father. It was among the first plays performed after the long-delayed establishment of London's National Theatre in 1965, having also been filmed with Charles Laughton and John Mills in 1954. The expression "Hobson's choice" dates back to the early 17th c. when Thomas Hobson, a Cambridge carrier, leased out horses strictly in order of their availability, leaving no choice to the hirer. The saying "Hobson's choice" means no choice at all. Hobson, in the play, is defeated and thus deprived of options.

B. left the famous Manchester Grammar School at sixteen to work in the textile business, but in his spare time studied Spanish and went to the theater. Aged twenty, he moved to a London office and spent his evenings in the galleries of theaters, where the cheapest tickets entitled him to sit on coconut matting laid over concrete. In his autobiography entitled *What I Have Had* (1953), he wrote that the discomfort made him feel he was doing something for art. He saw early productions of the famous 1904–7 season at the Court Theatre in London's Sloane Square under the management of Harley GRANVILLE BARKER and J. E. Vedrenne. This season presented thirty plays by new and unheard-of authors, including Henrik Ibsen, Bernard SHAW, John GALSWORTHY, John MASEFIELD, and Granville Barker himself. From this experience, B. absorbed the principles of play construction. As the Royal Court, the same theater gave a first hearing to John OSBORNE, Arnold WESKER, N. F. SIMPSON, John ARDEN, and Samuel BECKETT, and introduced English audiences to the work of foreign dramatists such as Eugène Ionesco, Jean-Paul Sartre, Bertolt Brecht, Max Frisch, and Jean Genet.

Inspired by the success of Granville Barker at the Court, Miss Horniman, who had already worked with W. B. YEATS at the Abbey Theatre in Dublin, in 1907 funded and initiated Britain's first regional repertory companies in Dublin, Manchester, and Liverpool. She challenged the London monopoly by commissioning plays by local people about local life, tackling the new and explosive issues of class, power, and sex, paving the way for the appreciation of new writers and pointing eventually to the "kitchen sink" drama of the 1950s. The most fruitful of these enterprises was the Manchester Gaiety Theatre and its repertory company. A long-running television serial of working-class Lancashire life, *Coronation Street*, is a direct descendant of the "Manchester School" of writers.

B.'s first success was a one-act play, *Lonesome-Like* (1911), his own favorite, and always popular. In 1915, he collaborated with Houghton on *The Hillarys*. B. wrote over fifty one-act plays, many of them still performed by amateur theater companies and reprinted in collections. Notable among them was *The Price of Coal* (perf. 1909; pub. 1911), a powerful study of the impact of a pit accident on a mining community. B.'s first full-length play, *Dealing in Futures*, was presented by the Glasgow Repertory Company in 1909. From then on, B. earned his living as a writer. In the next twenty years, he wrote, in addition to his one-act plays, fifteen full-length plays and eight novels.

BIBLIOGRAPHY: Smigel, L., "H. B. (1882–1958)," in Demastes, W., and K. E. Kelly, eds., *British Playwrights, 1860–1956* (1996): 67–80; Wood, E. R., introduction to *Hobson's Choice* (1964): v–xiv

MICHAEL GROSVENOR MYER

BRITTAIN, Vera [Mary]
b. 29 December 1893, Newcastle, Staffordshire; d. 29 March 1970, London

Daughter of a wealthy manufacturer, and influenced by Olive SCHREINER, B. had to fight to go to Somerville College, Oxford, where her studies were interrupted by World War I. She became a nurse and was bereaved of her fiancé and her brother. Her autobiography *Testament of Youth* (1933) describes the nightmare of loss as one by one cousins, friends, and acquaintances were killed. *Testament of Experience* (1957) covers the years 1925–50. *Testament of Friendship* (1940) is a memorial to her college friend, novelist Winifred HOLTBY, and these books are feminist, pacifist, and socialist texts. B. also wrote poetry and several novels, including *Not without Honour* (1924), *Honourable Estate* (1936), and *Account Rendered* (1945).

BROME, Richard
b. 1590?, London?; d. 1652?, London

Once in service to Ben JONSON, B. is first mentioned by name as the playwright's "man" in the induction to Jonson's *Bartholomew Fair*. The two men apparently grew friendly and remained so even after B. left service to become a dramatist in his own right. B.

seems to have collaborated with Jonson's eldest son in the lost *A Fault of Friendship* (perf. 1623). Even in the aftermath of the disaster surrounding Jonson's *New Inn*, the old master spared B. from his general censure of the theater and went so far as to laud B.'s play *The Northern Lass* (1632). B. was universally liked by his fellows, who made many good-natured quips on his name (pronounced "Broom"). Applauded by the old guard and younger writers alike, B.'s plays display a workmanlike approach with the influence of Jonson readily ascertainable. His reputation languished after his death, and his plays even became the target of scorn in the 19th c. That reputation has improved somewhat since T. S. ELIOT's reappraisal of him. Though not a great poet, B. is a fine craftsman with an unmistakable affection for the theater. His prolific efforts record a vast knowledge of and sincere appreciation for the playhouse world of the mid-17th c. He alludes to and even spoofs many plays and playwrights, including William SHAKESPEARE, throughout his canon.

BRONTË, Anne

b. 17 January 1820, Thornton, near Bradford; d. 28 May 1849, Scarborough

The younger sister of Charlotte and Emily BRONTË, B. has usually taken a tertiary place in biographies of the famous family and analyses of their works. Both Charlotte in the 1850 "Biographical Notice" of her sisters and Elizabeth Cleghorn GASKELL in her highly influential *Life of Charlotte Brontë* were keen to depict B. as overly sensitive, fragile, and docile, and it is only recently that these views have been contested as reassessment reveals B.'s strength and the often subversive nature of her writings.

B. was the sixth child of Patrick Brontë, an Irish Church of England clergyman, and his wife Maria, and was born in the year that the family moved to the bleak township of Haworth. The following year the children's mother died, leaving B. to be reared by her elder sisters and their aunt Elizabeth Branwell. Much criticism has suggested that Miss Branwell introduced Calvinism to the parsonage with its idea of salvation only for the predestined "elect." This seems unlikely given her brother Branwell's commitment to Wesleyan Methodism, but Calvinist doctrine was nevertheless being much debated at the time and it is clear that B. was horrified by its tenets. Her fear and condemnation of predestination resonates throughout her work, both in her novels and, more overtly, in poems like "A Word to the 'Elect.'"

In 1825, B.'s two eldest sisters, Elizabeth and Maria, died as a result of the appalling conditions at the Clergy Daughters' School at Cowan Bridge, an event that bought the remaining four siblings even closer as they began to collaborate on the saga of Glass Town, a realm of political, revolutionary, and sexual intrigue. B. subsequently developed the saga of Gondal with Emily, a world that more overtly emphasized female power and that provided an impetus for their poetic and prose writings until both were in their twenties, although it clearly had more importance for Emily at this stage than it did for B. The prose framework for the saga has been lost or destroyed, but many of B.'s poems still bear Gondal references.

B.'s novels emphasize the importance of effective education for both sexes, and she herself was dedicated to making the most of educational opportunities. She read widely in the Bible, literature, history, and journals such as *Blackwood's Magazine*, and studied for nearly three years at Roe Head School, where Charlotte was a pupil-teacher. Despite a spiritual crisis during this time, B. was devoted to her studies and subsequently worked as a governess first for the Ingrams at Blake Hall (during 1839) and then the Robinsons at Thorpe Green (1840–45), resigning this post when her brother Branwell was dismissed for his infatuation with Mrs. Robinson.

B. subsequently devoted herself to developing as a professional writer. The sisters' first joint venture, *Poems by Currer, Ellis, and Acton Bell* (1846), paid for by themselves and published under the gender-ambiguous pseudonyms, was a commercial failure selling only two copies, although many of the poems were singled out for praise by reviewers. B. contributed twenty-one poems to the volume and while her poetry as a whole is not as accomplished as Emily's, it possesses a depth and strength that the simple and sparse language often belies. In terms of theme, the Gondal and the seemingly more personal poems have much in common, focusing on physical and psychological incarceration ("A Voice from the Dungeon," "The Captive's Dream," "The Captive Dove"), the power of nature as a corrective to incarceration and a means of approaching spiritual release ("The North Wind," "The Bluebell," "Lines Composed in a Wood on a Windy Day"), and marginalized, outsider figures ("An Orphan's Lament"). Like Alfred, Lord TENNYSON's *In Memoriam*, B.'s poems chart a diary of spiritual doubt and searching in works such as "Self-Communion," "A Prayer," and "O God! if this indeed be all." William COWPER is a particularly strong influence, celebrated explicitly in "To Cowper" as the "Celestial Bard" where he is cited as possible evidence of the falsity of the Calvinist doctrine still haunting B. Using lyrics, dialogues, narratives, and dramatic scenarios, B. is a poet of much greater formal range than she is often given credit for.

B.'s first novel, *Agnes Grey* (1847), fictionalizes many of her experiences as a governess, although, of course, we should be wary of reading too autobiographically. Charting the grueling and disturbing experiences of the eponymous heroine as she works in two posts in order to help support her financially weakened clerical family, the text offers a sharp critique of middle-class society's lack of concern for the governess and maps onto the governess debates of the period. Agnes is depicted as a highly independent and morally scrupulous woman, a plain heroine prefiguring Jane Eyre, and through the representation of the manipulation and violence employed by her charges and the overindulgence of their parents, B. undercuts the received Romantic notion of the child and interrogates the education and socialization of the gendered subject. As with *The Tenant of Wildfell Hall* (3 vols., 1848), B. particularly highlights the problems associated with expectations of masculine behavior in the figure of Tom Bloomfield, and the inadequacies of received notions of femininity in the figure of Rosalie Murray. Agnes herself marries the curate Weston, a relationship that emphasizes mutual respect and support and is in keeping with Agnes's hard-won independence. The novel was published as the third volume of a set with Emily's *Wuthering Heights*, a combination that was partly responsible for its neglect at the side of the other Brontë novels.

Agnes Grey opens with the assertion that "All true histories contain instruction." B.'s second and more powerful novel, *The Tenant of Wildfell Hall*, took many of the instructive messages embodied in her first novel and developed them much further, producing a text that was received by its mid-Victorian audience with a mix of shock and applause. Helen Huntingdon, the mysterious Tenant, marries a dissolute alcoholic (modeled at least in part on Branwell) who subjects her and her son to physical and psychological abuse, depicted with great REALISM. Discovering her husband's adultery, Helen departs with their child against his will—and significantly also the law—and lives in seclusion earning her own living through her art. As with *Agnes Grey*, the text tackles the potential corruptness and immorality built into received models of patriarchy, and the means by which a woman can achieve agency for herself. The novel uses a more complex structure than *Agnes Grey*, the main narrative being delivered in the form of Helen's diary that is read by the frame narrator Gilbert Markham, the man Helen eventually marries after the death of her husband and her refutation of the local gossip that she is the mistress of the man who turns out to be her brother/landlord. *Tenant* was condemned, like many of the Brontë sisters' novels, for its "coarseness," even Charlotte attempting to censure it as "an entire mistake." With this work, however, B. was following her moral and religious beliefs in exposing the family unit as a potential site of abuse and humiliation and articulating the right of women to their own independence.

The reception history of B.'s work has been characterized by marginalization and misrepresentation, but criticism is now clearly demonstrating how the youngest of the famous sisters produced sharp social critiques and protofeminist arguments with a rationality and determination that reveal her to be a powerful 19th-c. voice.

BIBLIOGRAPHY: Allott, M., ed., *The Brontës: The Critical Heritage* (1974); Barker, J., *The Brontës* (1994); Chitham, E., *A Life of A. B.* (1991); Chitham, E., ed., *The Poems of A. B.* (1979); Langland, E., *A. B.* (1989); Scott, P. J. M., *A. B.* (1983)

SIMON AVERY

BRONTË, Charlotte

b. 21 April 1816, Thornton, near Bradford; d. 31 March 1855, Haworth

B. was one of the most significant Victorian novelists, whose works had considerable influence on succeeding generations of writers and who continues to receive much critical attention. The third daughter of the Irish Reverend Patrick Brontë and his wife Maria, she was two years older than Emily and four years older than Anne. In 1820, the family moved to Haworth, an industrial township next to the West Yorkshire moors, when Patrick Brontë became perpetual curate there. From an early age, B. was ambitiously dedicated to learning but her first period of study at the Clergy Daughters' School, Cowan Bridge, was tragically terminated when her elder sisters, Maria and Elizabeth, contracted fever there and were brought home to die. B. later depicted the school as Lowood in *Jane Eyre* (3 vols., 1847) and its head, Reverend William Carus Wilson, as the tyrannical Brocklehurst (Helen Burns has also been read as an immortalization of Maria). Following on quickly from the death of her mother from cancer, the deaths of her sisters meant B. was to act as mother substitute, a role that, by all accounts, she found difficult. The figure of the female orphan was, however, to become a recurring trope in B.'s fiction.

With her sisters, B. read widely in the Bible, Homer, Virgil, William SHAKESPEARE, John MILTON, Lord BYRON, Sir Walter SCOTT, and the *Arabian Nights* as well as *Blackwood's Magazine* and the *Edinburgh Review*. During 1831–32, she attended Miss Wooler's school at Roe Head near Dewsbury, where she met her lifelong friends Mary Taylor and Ellen Nussey, and returned as pupil-teacher in 1835–38, when she was temporarily joined by Emily and then Anne. In 1842, she embarked on her most important period of education when she traveled with Emily to Brussels to study at the Pensionnat Heger. B. was dedicated to making the most of this opportunity, but Emily was less enthusiastic and when the sisters returned home following the death of their Aunt Branwell, Emily remained at Haworth while B. went back to Brussels. This second period at the pensionnat was a great trial, however, with B.'s growing isolation in a foreign Catholic environment and her increasing affection for the married M. Heger. His wife, suspecting B.'s feelings, became distant and after B.'s return to Haworth in 1844, Heger broke off all correspondence. B. used these experiences in *Villette* (3 vols., 1853) and *The Professor* (2 vols., 1857), satirizing Heger's wife in the figure of Madame Beck. During her time abroad, however, she produced some important French essays that explore key themes of her later writings: female martyrdom ("Sacrifice d'une veuve Indienne"), the nature of God ("L'Immensité de Dieu"), leadership and heroism ("Mirabeau" and "La Mort de Napoléon"), and justice ("La Justice Humaine").

Following the gift of a box of wooden soldiers to Branwell, the Brontë children had developed the saga of the imaginary Glass Town ("Verdopolis") set in remote Africa, a world of civil wars, rebellion, heroism, and sexual intrigue that B. and Branwell, working together, later modified into Angria. The male protagonists of Angria often derived from B.'s love of Byron and the literary framework she built up was to provide a crucial means of apprenticeship as she produced great quantities of prose and poetry, an "infernal world" she was to work with until her early twenties.

The sisters' first public literary venture, however, was initiated when B. discovered a manuscript of Emily's poetry and eventually persuaded her they merited publishing. The resulting *Poems by Currer, Ellis, and Acton Bell* appeared in 1846 under the gender-indeterminate pseudonyms adopted, B. records, to avoid judgment on sex alone ("Biographical Notice," 1850). B. was clearly aware of the stakes given Robert SOUTHEY's now infamous letter to her: "Literature cannot be the business of a woman's life: & it ought not to be." In general, B. is a far less accomplished poet than novelist and fails to achieve the originality of Emily's verse or the firmness of Anne's. However, some of her longer poems, including "Pilate's Wife's Dream," "The Wife's Will," "Presentiment," and "The Teacher's Monologue," are strong and deserve attention in estimates of her poetic talents.

Poems was a commercial failure, selling only two copies, but B. was by now fueled with literary ambition and urged each of the sisters to produce a novel. The results—*The Professor, Wuthering Heights,* and *Agnes Grey*—received a mixed reception, with Emily and Anne's works eventually being accepted for publication and appearing in 1847, while *The Professor* was continually rejected. This text, which B. called her "idiot child" and which was only published two years after her death, marked a change in style as B.

rejected her previous Romantically charged Angrian writing for something more "plain and homely." It is also the only B. novel to have a male narrator, a technique that feminist critics have pointed to as one of the main reasons for its relative failure. Utilizing the Bildungsroman model, B. follows her orphaned protagonist, William Crimsworth, as he leaves an insecure position in business in the North of England for a teaching post in Brussels, where he falls in love with and eventually marries the pupil-teacher Frances Henri while being pursued by Mlle Reuter. Yet this is no easy development plot, since Crimsworth continually appears to suffer great anxiety concerning his masculine self-identity that manifests itself in his attempts to overcome the threats of "feminized" inferiority and alienation by spying, conflict, and resorting to a violence that borders on sadism. Even when he marries the antiheroine Frances (thereby politically choosing the acceptable Protestant figure over the manipulative Catholic Reuter), their relationship seems grounded in power games and suffering. B.'s first novel is therefore extremely unsettling although it introduces the issues of estranged orphans, antiheroes/heroines, teacher/pupil relations, and the need for mutual understanding that would be central to her overall oeuvre.

Nevertheless, encouraged by the comments from the publishing firm of Smith, Elder in London on her rejected manuscript, B. quickly completed the novel that made her into a household name and that has continued to remain her most popular and critically successful work, *Jane Eyre*. A fictionalized autobiography whose protagonist defies convention in being "disconnected, poor and plain," *Jane Eyre* is a female Bildungsroman that combines elements of both Gothic and realist genres to portray vividly Jane's attempts to combat the patriarchal social, economic, and legal structures working against her as she seeks to claim independence and equality. The first two sections, at Gateshead and Lowood, explore the oppressive forces of gender socialization that Jane faces as a rebellious and independently spirited girl and her need to learn a degree of restraint in order to negotiate society successfully. The central sections of the text, based at the Gothic-styled Thornfield, critique the slavelike role of the governess, male sexual predatory nature as represented in the figure of the Byronic Rochester, and the marginalization of the wife. Indeed, many psychoanalytic critics have persuasively read the raging animal-like figure of Bertha Mason as Jane's alter ego of repressed desires and rage at female oppression. At the heart of the novel—and Victorian criticism of it—is Jane's fervent assertion of women's equality with men ("women feel just as men feel") and their right to autonomy and agency. Rejecting the proposal of a loveless marriage with a cousin, Jane finally returns to Rochester but only after she has secured her independence through inherited wealth and he has been semiemasculated in the fire that also kills his wife. With its representations of female rebellion and anger, bigamy, and violence, *Jane Eyre* aroused great controversy, Elizabeth Rigby calling it "anti-Christian" and suggesting it emerged from the same anarchic politics as Chartism (*Quarterly Review*, 1848). Its popularity and influence have been huge—however, B.'s third novel, *Shirley* (1849), marks a new point of departure in its wider sweep. Set in Yorkshire during the Luddite riots and the last stages of the Napoleonic Wars, it is at once a "condition of England," a feminist debate, and a ROMANCE. Critics have often suggested a problem with structural unity as a result of this broad range of issues, but as with Elizabeth Cleghorn GASKELL's novels, the oppression of both the working classes and the female protagonists can be clearly linked and the private and public histories interrelated. Writing the novel during the tragic circumstances of the successive deaths of Branwell, Emily, and Anne in 1848–49, B. put something of Emily into Shirley, a representative of freedom, nature, and individuality who adopts more "masculine" traits as Captain Keeldar, and Anne into Caroline, a more selfless figure, although not without her own questioning of received ideas. One of the key speeches concerns Shirley's reconstruction of Eve as "a woman-Titan" rather than Milton's "cook," and the text overall works to emphasize the need for opposing groups (male/female, master/workers) to reach a new understanding and empathy. Typically for B., however, the closure of the text is oddly disturbing, with a sense of Shirley being entrapped in her marriage and the loss of imaginative freedom being represented by the industrial spoiling of the Hollow.

B.'s most disturbing and arguably most mature novel, however, is *Villette,* the "heretic narrative" of Lucy Snowe's quest for self-identity in a world that brings her to the brink of psychological breakdown. The main part of the text is set in a fictionalized Brussels, making *Villette* a reworking of some of *The Professor,* but unlike that text's sometimes plodding realist and linear narrative, *Villette* is characterized by a shifting, fluid narrative in which Lucy is constantly trying to interpret events and people. Almost buried alive in Madame Beck's convent-school where surveillance and espionage are used as methods of contol, Lucy is also unable to find solace in the city that is depicted as an early version of Victorian urban Gothic, sexually and psychologically threatening. The extreme violence of the text's language marks Lucy's precarious equilibrium in a world of oppressive systems, menacing Catholicism and paranoia as she attempts to negotiate a series of alternative female models. Her autonomy is only finally achieved in the dreamlike carnival scenes where she confronts her demons in the Gothic junta of Beck, Walravens, and

Silas and returns with a new sense of determination. However, *Villette*'s notorious narrative instability reaches its climax with the most open B. ending, which continues to be much debated.

By the 1850s, B. had achieved great status and had met a range of other literary luminaries, including William Makepeace THACKERAY, Harriet Martineau, and Gaskell, who was later to write the elegant but controversial *Life of Charlotte Brontë*. In 1854, after much delay and seemingly agonizing debate, B. married her father's curate Arthur Bell Nicholls, but died the following year apparently from pregnancy complications. The opening pages of a new novel, *Emma*, were found after her death.

In 1855, Matthew ARNOLD reflected that B.'s life had been "short, but redoubled by fame." B.'s arresting representations of radical heroines and her explorations of the tensions between passion and repression, feeling and reason, mean that this fame remains strong and she continues to be recognized and read as one of the great Victorian literary innovators and thinkers.

BIBLIOGRAPHY: Allott, M., ed., *The Brontës: The Critical Heritage* (1974); Barker, J., *The Brontës* (1994); Eagleton, T., *Myths of Power* (1975); Gilbert, S. M., and S. Gubar, *The Madwoman in the Attic* (1979); Maynard, J., *C. B. and Sexuality* (1984); Showalter, E., *A Literature of Their Own* (1977); Shuttleworth, S., *C. B. and Victorian Psychology* (1996); Smith, M., ed., *The Letters of C. B.* (2 vols., 1995, 2000); Stoneman, P., *Brontë Transformations* (1996); Thormählen, M., *The Brontës and Religion* (1999)

SIMON AVERY

BRONTË, Emily [Jane]
b. 30 July 1818, Thornton, near Bradford; d. 19 December 1848, Haworth

In 1896, Clement Shorter referred to B. as "the sphinx of our modern Literature," a highly apt designation for a woman whose position as one of the great Victorian novelists and poets has continued to be fervently debated and reinterpreted from her own time until the present. Born into arguably the most famous British literary family, B. was the fifth child of the Irish-born Reverend Patrick Brontë and his wife Maria. When B. was two, her father took up the post of perpetual curate in the industrial township of Haworth, and the family moved to the parsonage backing onto the West Yorkshire moors, a topography B. later immortalized in *Wuthering Heights* (2 vols., 1847). By the age of six, however, she had witnessed the death of her mother from cancer and those of her two eldest sisters, Maria and Elizabeth, as a result of the atrocious conditions of the Clergy Daughters' School at Cowan Bridge where B. and her sister Charlotte were also pupils. This early confrontation with mortality was to suffuse B.'s writings, often interlinked with the related themes of motherlessness and the search for a secure home.

B.'s sense of dislocation and homesickness when away from Haworth is well documented, but in 1842 she and Charlotte traveled to Brussels for a nine-month period of study at the Pensionnat Heger with the aim of improving their languages so that they could open their own school on their return. What was most important for B.'s development as an innovative writer and thinker during this time, however, was her production of a series of French *devoirs* in which she began to formulate some of her challenging and icon-oclastic ideas. "Le Chat," for example, draws an anal-ogy between feline and human behavior in order to depict the hypocrisy of "civilization" supported by violence and manipulation, while the startling piece "Le Papillon" delineates a proto-Darwinian vision of the world founded on destruction and tyranny. Such key Brontëan ideas, expressed with an unswerving logic and rationalism, would recur in both the mature poetry and *Wuthering Heights*, as would the concerns with heroism and liberty explored in "Le Siège d'Oudenarde" and "Le Roi Harold." Given that so little B. material is still extant—only the poetry manu-scripts, the edited version of her novel, three letters, and four "diary papers"—these essays are an invalu-able part of her oeuvre.

Despite Charlotte's claim that her sister was an "untutored genius," B. was well read in literature, his-tory, and politics, and kept informed of current ideas through *Blackwood's Magazine* and the *Edinburgh Review*. Certainly her combined interest in politics and literature helped to fuel the young B.'s develop-ment of the imaginary world of Glass Town, with its wars, rebellions, and sexual intrigues, and a few years later the world of Gondal, which B. constructed in partnership with Anne. This more female-centered saga, focusing on the powerful Augusta Almeda rather than the patriarchs of Glass Town, became a framework for the production of extensive poetry and prose, and B. remained committed to its continuation until her late twenties, despite Anne's growing resis-tance. The saga's prose narrative has been subse-quently lost or destroyed and despite attempts at reconstruction, it remains impossible to map the origi-nal plot definitively.

In 1844, B. transcribed her existing poetry into two notebooks, one for Gondal and one for seemingly more personal poems, although a consistency in style and theme exists between the two groups. Scholarship has now recovered over 190 poems, the majority of them focusing on a dialectic of entrapment and escape as B.'s speakers strive for liberty and autonomy in "this storm-troubled sphere" ("No Coward Soul"). Imprisonment is a recurring motif and leads to the testing of strategies for achieving physical and psy-chological freedom. In "Ay, there it is now!" and the energetic "High Waving Heather," for example, en-gagement with powerful elemental nature becomes a means of escaping socially imposed identities and re-strictions, and in poems like "I see around me tomb-stones grey," this often more feminized nature is raised to the status of an alternative deity as part of B.'s explicit rejection of her father's patriarchal religion.

B.'s increasing understanding of a proto-Darwin-ian universe also meant she was aware of the more predatory role that nature could take (e.g., "The Night Wind" and "Shall earth no more inspire thee"), and therefore many of her speakers are led to search for solace internally. In line with the Romantic philoso-phies greatly influencing B.'s art, her speakers look to the powers of the imagination as a realm where "thou and I and Liberty/Have undisputed sovereignty" ("To Imagination"), and that might then permit an entrance into more mystical experiences where the boundaries of the self can be transcended and spiritual freedom acquired (e.g., "Stars" and "The Prisoner").

Throughout the poetry, therefore, there is an in-creasing emphasis on self-sufficiency, an attempt to overcome the threat of fragmentation represented in the enigmatic "Philosopher" and achieve complete unity of self. Underpinning this emphasis is a defiant, even terrifying, stoicism, which eventually leads a number of B.'s speakers to embrace death and a return to the mother earth as the ultimate celebratory release (e.g., "The linnet in the rocky dells"). B.'s most fa-mous and elliptic poem, the powerful "No Coward Soul," written while she was working on *Wuthering Heights*, is often read as a final statement of the icono-clastic rebellion she explores in her other poems since here she rejects all received belief systems in favor of union with a solipsistic "God within my breast."

It was Charlotte's discovery of one of B.'s poetry manuscripts and her conviction that this was "not at all like the poetry women generally write" that led to the sisters' first publishing venture, *Poems by Currer, Ellis and Acton Bell* (1846). Although the volume only sold a mere two copies, reviewers constantly cited the originality of B.'s contributions. Her poems have subsequently been overshadowed by the atten-tion granted to *Wuthering Heights* but in the light of recent feminist rereadings of Victorian women's poetry, the power and subversiveness of B.'s work has begun to be reassessed.

B.'s major claim to literary posterity, however, lies in her solitary novel, the masterpiece *Wuthering Heights*. Published as two volumes of a three-volume set with Anne's *Agnes Grey*, the text portrays two generations of the Earnshaw and Linton families and their violent relations with the Gothic villainlike foundling Heathcliff. The intense affinity between Heathcliff and Catherine Earnshaw, the motherless heroine, lies at the heart of the novel, with both of them "half savage, and hardy, and free" in their defiance of the various forms of patriarchal authority embodied in Catherine's father, her brother Hindley, and the religious bigot Joseph (significantly the only representative of God in a text which sharply condemns established religion). Catherine's absorption into the gentrified Thrushcross Grange results in Heathcliff's departure from the world of the text, and it not until he has somehow acquired substantial capital that he reappears in order to wreak revenge on the social and economic structures of both the Earnshaws and the Lintons following the death of Catherine in childbirth. The remainder of the novel delineates this revenge plot in detail before Heathcliff, increasingly haunted by the dead Catherine's image, seems to starve himself to death. The subversive energies thus erased, B. appears to reinstate the status quo by marrying Catherine's daughter, significantly also called Catherine, to Hindley's son, Hareton, and removing the couple from the Heights and its multifarious hauntings to the seemingly "safer" world of the Grange. In line with postmodern thinking and the notorious lack of closure in the Brontë sisters' novels, however, the ending has been much debated.

Wuthering Heights horrified many mid-Victorian reviewers who condemned it for its violence, "coarseness," and seeming amorality, while at the same time acknowledging its strange power. Charlotte, who was herself extremely shocked, attempted to make the text more acceptable after B.'s death by arguing that her sister's supposed seclusion and lack of "worldly wisdom" meant that "she did not know what she had done." The vast amount of criticism that the novel continues to generate, however, clearly defies this accusation of literary naiveté. Although F. R. LEAVIS suggested that *Wuthering Heights* was nothing more than a "kind of sport," a cul-de-sac in the development of the novel, early-20th-c. commentators were already pointing out the complexity and elegance of the text's structuring. David CECIL argued in his highly influential account in *Early Victorian Novelists* that the novel centers upon binary oppositions between the "children of storm" at the Heights and the "children of calm" at the Grange, while Charles Percy Sanger demonstrated that all the events in the text can be fully dated and that the ways in which the property and inheritance laws are worked out produces great symmetry between generations.

Many recent critics have explored the innovative narrative structures of the text where B. rejects the first-person confessional mode favored by Charlotte for layers of narrative embedded within one another, with the satirized southerner Lockwood reporting Nelly's narrative of events that itself includes conversations, letters, and other reports. No narrator has full view of all the events and Nelly's reliability is often questioned, making this an almost protomodern narrative. Similarly, attention has been paid to the generic hybridity of the text that combines elements derived from B.'s immediate Gothic inheritance with the developing Victorian discourse of REALISM in order to achieve distinctly unsettling effects in a novel that is always bizarrely unstable and slippery.

The strong image patterns of barriers and divisions have made *Wuthering Heights* particularly fruitful to psychoanalytical approaches, articulating ideas around the fragmented self and helping to suggest the destructive sexuality at the heart of the text, while more political readings by Marxist critics like Terry Eagleton have highlighted the violence associated with status and privilege in both the world of the Grange and the figure of Heathcliff in ways which significantly parallel B.'s own arguments in her French *devoirs*. Some of the most productive and innovative of recent rereadings, however, have developed out of more overtly feminist approaches, with critics focusing on the representation of the brutal processes of gender socialization in the text and the ways in which patriarchal systems such as the family, marriage, and religion work to kill Catherine, first in mind and then in body, until she can only escape her "shattered prison" through delirium, madness, and death.

B. died from consumption at the age of thirty, refusing to see a doctor in an act of defiant stoicism that has subsequently helped to fuel the B. mythology. Evidence suggests that she was negotiating a contract for a second novel but no manuscript survives. *Wuthering Heights* and the poetry, however, are clear testaments to a woman whose power and originality of thought are still startling today.

BIBLIOGRAPHY: Allott, M., ed., *The Brontës: The Critical Heritage* (1974); Barker, J., *The Brontës* (1994); Davies, S., *E. B.* (1994); Eagleton, T., *Myths of Power* (1975); Gilbert, S. M., and S. Gubar, *The Madwoman in the Attic* (1979); Homans, M., *Women Writers and Poetic Identity* (1980); Lonoff, S., ed., *The Belgian Essays* (1996); Ratchford, F. E., *Gondal's Queen* (1955); Smith, A., ed., *The Art of E. B.* (1976)

SIMON AVERY

BROOKE, Rupert [Chawner]

b. 3 August 1887, Rugby, Warwickshire; d. 23 April 1915, near Skyros, Greece

At his death, B. was a promising poet, often labeled Georgian, who is part of England's genuine lost generation of World War I. He is perhaps most famous for a sonnet, "The Soldier," written in 1915, which expresses the patriotic fervor that greeted the beginning of that war. From any year after 1916, the poem would seem ironic or sardonic or foolish; yet in its time it captured the sentiment of many Englishmen called to arms in 1914. He was educated at King's College, Cambridge, traveled widely from Germany to North America to the South Seas, before returning to England as the war started. He volunteered and was commissioned in the Royal Navy. He first saw service, briefly, in Belgium; then he was sent as part of the Dardanelle campaign (headed for Gallipoli). En route, he died of blood poisoning and was buried, not at sea, but on the island of Skyros. His obituaries often used excerpts from "The Soldier" and remarked constantly on his apollonian beauty.

His death, coming so quickly after the publication of a volume titled *1914 and Other Poems* (1915) and containing "The Soldier," has perhaps obscured much of his poetry. Used first for propaganda purposes by Sir Winston CHURCHILL, among others, the poem has been used to deride the innocence and jingoism of England in the war. Indeed, to be known as the poet who wrote, "If I should die, think only this of me:/That there's some corner of a foreign field/ That is forever England," might well after the poetry of Wilfred OWEN and Siegfried SASSOON mean that none of the other poetry would be read. Many current anthologies of modern poetry exclude his work while they include other poets like B.'s friend, Edward THOMAS, who similarly died in the war and left behind much promise, few volumes. While B. certainly sincerely believed in "an English heaven," much of the poetry even of the 1914 volume seems almost echoed by the later poets. In "IV. The Dead," B. writes of those who "had seen movement, and heard music; known/Slumber and waking; loved," of men, that is, who are now dead, "All this is ended." In another of the poems, "Safety," he imagines death as "the safest of all." To think of B. as a sentimental and wholly innocent poet is anachronistic. He had seen trench warfare, but only briefly, and writes with the clear understanding of his own mortality. He had not, however, been in France in 1916; the other war poets had. Critics may wonder what kind of poet he might have become had he reached Gallipoli and survived that doomed assault.

His earlier poems represent experimentation and skill clearly as competent as that in Thomas's or Owen's early poems. Readers can find echoes of the metaphysicals, the Victorians, especially of Robert BROWNING, and the decadents in the earlier poetry. By 1909, he had largely moved away from the poetry of Ernest DOWSON and the early W. B. YEATS. *Poems* (1911) contains ironic love poems, quite realistic poems, and satires against bourgeois life. Poems like "The Hill" (with its Hardyesque turn from conventional love poem to dissolution) and "A Channel Passage" (with its analogy between love sickness and nausea) are not merely pleasant and agreeable poems; they wish to shock their readers. By 1912, B. was

considered the quintessential Georgian poet; indeed, he and Edward Marsh edited *Georgian Poetry 1911–1912* (1913) and may have invented the term itself. It is certainly arguable that some of his poems—for instance "Fafai," "Heaven," "Tiare Tahiti," "The Great Lover"—represent a new voice, and a new form for his poetry. Two years later, he is dead.

BIBLIOGRAPHY: Delaney, P., *The Neo-Pagans: Friendship and Love in the R. B. Circle* (1987); Hassall, C., *R. B.* (1964); Keynes, G., ed., *The Poetical Works of R. B.* (1946); Laskowski, W. E., *R. B.* (1994); Lehman, J., *The Strange Destiny of R. B.* (1980); Pearsall, R. B., *R. B.* (1974)

MARGUERITE HARKNESS

BROOKE-ROSE, Christine

b. 16 January 1923, Geneva, Switzerland

B.-R. is the most boldly experimental British novelist of the postwar era. Her exploration of the possibilities of fiction in a world of competing discourses has resulted in a unique body of work. Each of her novels from *Out* (1964) to *Subscript* (1999) has challenged conventional forms of fictional representation and engaged with major themes, from racial prejudice to the omnipresence of modern electronic media. Her fiction is fertilized by her erudition: fluent in English, French, and German, and deeply versed in linguistics, literary theory, and European and American literature, B.-R. has produced a number of substantial critical studies, most notably *A Rhetoric of the Unreal: Studies in Narrative and Structure, Especially of the Fantastic* (1981).

B.-R.'s challenge to conventional perceptions and expectations begins quietly in her first two novels, *The Languages of Love* (1957) and *The Sycamore Tree* (1958). While fairly straightforward in form, both focus with sensitivity and insight on well-educated young women who, partly because of their education, do not easily fit into their society; these novels thus raise questions about dominant notions of women in the 1950s. Her third novel, *The Dear Deceit* (1960), brings issues of storytelling and truth to the fore, as the traces of a father's life are reconstructed by his son, while conventional narrative starts to fall apart in *The Middlemen* (1961), a satire on a world in which it is no longer possible to own or originate anything and all of us are intermediaries.

While recovering from a serious illness, B.-R. worked on her fifth novel, *Out* (1964)—the first of her openly experimental fictions. In complex, intriguing prose, it evokes the increasingly displaced consciousness of an unnamed protagonist in a world in which the hierarchy of racial prejudice has been turned upside down, so that the "colorless" are now on the receiving end of discrimination. Her sixth novel, *Such*

(1966), is an astonishing work in which a psychiatrist's return from apparent death to life is rendered in terms and images drawn from astrophysics, a subject of which B.-R. had acquired an impressive knowledge. *Between* (1968) explores the condition of liminality—of being on the frontier—in its evocation of a woman translator moving between different languages and discourses. Each of these novels, for all their experimentation, retain some reference to a central character; but this last vestige of conventional narration is abandoned in *Thru* (1975), B.-R.'s most deconstructionist fiction, in which fragments of fictional, philosophical, structuralist, poststructuralist, and linguistic discourse blend and clash.

Nine years passed before the appearance of B.-R.'s next novel, *Amalgamemnon* (1984), the first of "the Intercom quartet" that also includes *Xorandor* (1986), *Verbivore* (1990), and *Textermination* (1991). These novels combine linguistic and formal experimentation with a more reader-friendly approach than that of *Thru* in their exploration of the collapse of traditional culture and the triumph of digital technology. In *Amalgamemnon,* Mira Enketei, a redundant teacher of literature and history, becomes a modern Cassandra criss-crossed by a babel of voices—the texts of Herodotus, imagined conversations, radio programs, FAIRY TALES. *Xorandor* explores the difficulties of narrative and the threat of technology as two child computer wizards, Jip and Zab, try to tell the story of their discovery of a stone computer that feeds off nuclear waste but that brings forth a digital terrorist due to a programming error. In *Verbivore*, the computers that now provide the whole infrastructure of human activity rebel and stop, bringing the world to the brink of chaos. *Textermination* presents several hundred characters in search of readers, as the great personages of world literature—Homer's Odysseus, Geoffrey CHAUCER's Wife of Bath, Dante's Virgil, Jane AUSTEN's Emma Woodhouse, Gustave Flaubert's Emma Bovary, George ELIOT's Dorothea Brooke, Virginia WOOLF's Mrs. Dalloway, Salman RUSHDIE's Gibreel Farishta—gather at a San Francisco Convention to pray for the being that they can only attain if the texts in which they exist are still read.

After this imaginative sweep through key aspects of the crisis of modern culture, B.-R. turns to the autobiographical novel in *Remake* (1996)—but characteristically she challenges the genre, eschewing personal pronouns except in the account of the death of her mother, and raising questions about memory, language, and the relationship between fiction and nonfiction. This excursion into the intricacies of life writing is followed, in *Next* (1998), by a descent into the lower depths of the London homeless, whose dispossession is signified by the absence throughout the text of the verb "to have." Moving between the voices of its twenty-six characters—one for each letter of the alphabet—and pursuing the thread of a murder that stays unsolved, *Next* demonstrates how a concern with language can be combined with an exploration of contemporary social issues. *Subscript*, however, turns from the perplexed modern world to the dawn of life, providing a prehistory of humanity from one-celled organisms to early tribal culture, and relating biological evolution to the development of language. It is a remarkable imaginative vision.

B.-R. acknowledges that she has always taken the risk of alienating potential readers by her innovations; and while her reputation has been high among those interested in experimental fiction, her audience has been relatively limited. It is only now, in her late seventies, that she is starting to become a canonical author whose work features on student reading lists and attracts sustained critical attention. There is a growing recognition that B.-R. is an important modern writer who is peculiarly alert to the potential of the novel in a world dominated by science, multimedia, and digital technology.

BIBLIOGRAPHY: Birch, S., *C. B.-R. and Contemporary Fiction* (1994); Friedman, E. J., and R. Martin, eds., *Utterly Other Discourse: The Texts of C. B.-R.* (1995); Tredell, N., "C. B.-R.," in his *Conversations with Critics* (1994): 1–15

NICOLAS TREDELL

BROOKNER, Anita
b. 16 July 1928, London

An art historian and university professor, B. was led by a mid-life crisis to write her first novel at the age of fifty-three, Her characters, largely women, often consider themselves victims of idealistic and romantic illusions that are out of step with modern life, or as principled anachronisms from an earlier age who are now mysteriously out-of-date. Plot is less important than the moody, witty, and sharply intelligent narrative consciousness B. establishes in her novels—a consciousness that searches for answers to the inexplicable feelings of failure and despair that have darkened the otherwise prosperous and pleasant lives of her characters.

B.'s most important early novel is *Hotel du Lac* (1984), which won the Booker Prize in 1984, and established her reputation. Like most of her fiction, this story concerns a woman, aptly named Edith Hope, whose romantic ideals continue to inform her life choices. Having fled to a small hotel in France to escape a marriage of convenience, she is offered another by a sophisticated and successful businessman who is staying in the same hotel. Suggesting that romantic love is a canard, he offers her a practical business arrangement he suggests will suit them both. Although Edith is desperately lonely, she refuses, preferring to keep her romantic hopes alive, even if this means she will continue in a hopeless situation as the mistress of a married man back in London.

A Misalliance (1986; repub. as *The Misalliance,* 1986) also features a lonely woman whose life has mysteriously taken a wrong turn. This novel broadens B.'s themes of frustrated romantic longing through the addition of larger, philosophical issues and deeper, psychological probing, especially of her heroine's childhood. *A Misalliance* tells the story of Blanche Vernon, who has been rejected by her husband of over twenty years for a younger, more modern woman. Blanche still hopes for him to return, and in the meantime makes herself useful by helping out a young mother, Sally Beamish, and her mute, neglected daughter, Elinor, who, sadly, reminds Blanche of herself when a child. Elinor's mother, Sally, is a classic B. female character, found also in such novels as *Look at Me* (1983) and *A Private View* (1994), namely, the modern free spirit whose careless, hedonistic way of life easily shades into sociopathy. It is Sally who inspires in Blanche the theory that there are two kinds of women in the world, who are polar opposites of each other. On the one hand are the beautiful and selfish pagans who pursue pleasure without regard to scruples or conscience; on the other are the saints and martyrs like Blanche, who deny themselves while performing good works for others or practicing virtues increasingly deemed both old-fashioned and ripe for exploitation. Blanche, however, like so many B. heroines, does not remain simply a victim—the various misalliances she forms in the novel allow her to free herself from the past, and to gain a deeper understanding of herself and others.

While B. is noted for her portrayal of sensitive middle-aged heroines, she has also written books in which men are the protagonists. *Lewis Percy* (1989), for instance, is the story of a man who is appropriated by an emasculating wife and her equally difficult mother. Their cold manipulation drains his life of both meaning and vitality. Lewis's wife Tissy, an incurious and selfish narcissist, is a classic example of a type of woman who often appears in B.'s novels as a rival to her heroine, or in this case, as a subversive influence in the lives of her heroes. Lewis, however, like a number of B. heroines, eventually finds release from the sadness and inhibition of his previous life and reinvents himself as a new, younger man with new possibilities for love.

The recovery of a lost life is also a theme in *Fraud* (1992). Having spent much of her life looking after her frail mother, the gifted and undervalued Anna Durrant finds herself living a life of crushing loneliness. But to her surprise, Anna finds isolation becomes a valuable resource for her; and eventually her solitude is reconceived as a necessary stage in her reawakening. As she gradually realizes that other people

have stolen her life, expecting her to renounce her own interests in favor of theirs, her bleak soul-searching has the happy result of dismantling her false, subservient self. The emptiness in her life comes to seem filled with potential, as mysterious inner processes give her the strength to change her life dramatically, as she discovers a talent for designing inventive clothes for older women very like herself. This movement from depression and paralysis to a position of liberating, if not always cheering, insight constitutes one of the major achievements of all of B.'s novels. At times, this exhilarating sense of enlarged insight and deepened feeling leads to literal reform and release in the lives of her characters, but in any case all B.'s novels can be said, in spite of their depressive aspects, to have a good outcome if judged in terms of the journey of her narrative consciousness toward greater wisdom and insight. It is B.'s ability to draw her readers into a deep identification with the psychological journey of her protagonists that is responsible for her continued success; like her heroine Anna Durrant, B. has also found in later life that her novels spoke meaningfully to a waiting audience who recognized and understood themselves in her work.

BIBLIOGRAPHY: Sadler, L. V., *A. B.* (1990); Skinner, J., *The Fictions of A. B.: Illusions of Romance* (1992)

MARGARET BOE BIRNS

BROPHY, Brigid

b. 12 June 1929, London; d. 7 August 1995, Linconshire

B.'s father, novelist John Brophy, once wrote, "I have a daughter, ten years old, who excels me in everything, even in writing," and at an early age it seemed fated that B. should follow in her father's footsteps. She briefly attended St. Hugh's College, Oxford, but was expelled as a disciplinary action. Though the incident was a bitter one for B., it served as an indication of the future direction of her work. Positioned somewhere between a pedant and poison-tongued radical, B. was a social activist and feminist whose books tend to have a political bent constructed from a number of interrelated disciplines.

Her acclaimed first novel, *Hackenfeller's Ape* (1953), explores the issue of imprisonment through the story of a scatterbrained scientist's attempt to free the ape he is studying when he learns that the ape is slated to be used in a rocket experiment. It won the Cheltenham Literary Festival prize for a first novel in 1954, the same year that she married Michael Levey (later the director of the National Gallery). Surprisingly, marriage is one of the institutions that B. has been known to protest. This is one of the reasons that Levey thinks brought his wife into disfavor with certain critics.

Black Ship to Hell (1962), B.'s first foray into non-fiction, tries to illuminate the dynamics of hate through the use of a Freudian framework on a vast array of subjects such as the history of music and mythology. Attacked as an overly cerebral, self-indulgent work, it was touted by others as an ambitious accomplishment, and it won the *London Magazine* Prize in 1962. Published in that same year, B.'s novel *Flesh*, dedicated to Iris MURDOCH, met with a financial success that for the first time matched its critical acclaim. Not as revealing as its title would imply, the story does feel out the edges of sexual awakening through the courtship and later marital complications of two north Londoners. *The Finishing Touch* (1963), set in a girls' finishing school in the French Riviera, is filled with blackmail, scandal, and the double entendre of its title, namely masturbation. Published in 1964, *The Snow Ball* is both a study of surfaces as well as a black comedy of manners in the form of a masquerade ball in which the principal characters (dressed as Donna Anna and Don Giovanni) go through the motions of courtship and seduction.

Don't Never Forget: Collected Views and Reviews (1966) is an ensemble of B.'s journalistic works and bears witness to her many sociopolitical interests such as marriage and animal rights. It also contains pieces on B.'s opinion of opera, detective stories, and a wide range of writers as well as the transcriptions of B.'s radio talks with titles like "The Novel as a Takeover Bid." Later novels include *The Adventures of God in His Search for the Black Girl* (1973), *Pussy Owl: Superbeast* (1976), and *Palace without Chairs* (1978). Psychological studies of creative artists include *Mozart the Dramatist: A New View of Mozart, His Operas and His Age* (1964), *In Black and White: A Portrait of Aubrey Beardsley* (1968), and *Prancing Novelist* (1973), on the life of Ronald FIRBANK. Stricken with multiple sclerosis in 1981, B. continued to work on such books as *Baroque'n'Roll* (1986), a collection of essays, and *Reads* (1989).

BIBLIOGRAPHY: Newman, S. J., "B. B.," in Halio, J. L., ed., *British Novelists since 1960*, part 1, *DLB* 14 (1983): 137–47

HAYLEY HORVAT

BROUGHTON, Rhoda

b. 29 November 1840, Denbigh, Wales; d. 5 June 1920, Headington, Oxfordshire

B. in her own time was a household name, renowned for her twenty-five novels and for her personal wit and originality. By mid-20th c., her reputation had dwindled to a vague knowledge of her popular first novels, *Not Wisely but too Well* (3 vols.) and *Cometh Up as a Flower, an Autobiography* (2 vols.), both published in 1867. The superior Jane Austenish novels so full of humorous insight into human nature with its foibles, hypocrisies, and delusions that she eventually produced have been ignored, possibly because B. is deemed politically incorrect for her occasional anti-Semitic remark and anti-suffragette stand. Yet in her independence and achievement she epitomizes the feminist ideal.

Daughter of Delves Broughton, parson and squire of Broughton Hall in Staffordshire, she was steeped in English literature and well versed in classical and modern languages. She peppered her early novels with snippets from her wide reading and at times feigned a worldliness reminiscent of Rochefoucauld. The fiery passion and sexual desire crackling through these tales, however, hints of an early and deeply wounding unrequited love affair, one which she seems to have recounted in her autobiographical, posthumous novel, *A Fool in Her Folly* (1920).

Her anonymous London debut with *Not Wisely* and *Cometh Up*, novels serialized by her novelist uncle Joseph Sheridan LE FANU in his *Dublin University Magazine*, created shock waves. The demure Victorian heroine had been banished in favor of pert young girls catapulted into love and openly reveling in the embraces and kisses of their muscular guardsmen lovers. In *Not Wisely,* orphaned Kate Chester is ensnared by deceptive Dare Stamer, who re-creates the worldly protagonist of G. A. Lawrence's *Guy Livingstone* (1857). Deception also plays its role in the sunnier *Cometh Up*, narrated in the present tense (B.'s trademark) by ingenuous, lovable Nell Le Strange, whose rapture turns to misery as she is tricked out of marrying her loyal, Adonis lover, Dick M'Gregor. Both heroines suffer early deaths in the Victorian mode. Cited as forerunners of the sex novel, these impassioned but innocuous tales of doomed love, written in a fresh, bantering style with shafts of wit, won a vast readership. Critics were scathing, believing the author to be a man aping the salacious French.

Displacement of the country gentry by the nouveau riche is a favorite theme. In *Cometh Up* and *Joan* (3 vols., 1876), cultured young girls are ousted from the ancestral home, just as B. was when her father died in 1863. Already motherless B. found herself transplanted to Surbiton and then to her married sister's Welsh farmhouse near Ruthin where she dashed off *Not Wisely* in six weeks, encouraged by the example of the young novelist, Anne Thackeray [RITCHIE] and driven by frustration and the need to supplement her slender income.

B. reigned queen of the circulating library until 1890, producing ten best-sellers, including *Red as a Rose Is She* (3 vols., 1870), *Good-bye, Sweetheart!* (3 vols., 1872), *Nancy* (3 vols., 1873), *Doctor Cupid* (3 vols., 1886), and the popular ghost stories, *Tales for Christmas Eve* (1873). Never a plot maker she abandoned the multidecker format in favor of the one-volume novel more in keeping with her talent for character and situation.

Nancy with its family of riotous siblings and *Doctor Cupid*, a winsome *Sense and Sensibility* tale, have their merits, but her best work is found in her satirical one-volume novels such as *Mrs. Bligh* (1892), *A Beginner* (1894), *Scylla or Charybdis?* (1895), *Dear Faustina* (1897), *The Game and the Candle* (1899), *Foes in Law* (1900), *A Waif's Progress* (1905), and *Mamma* (1908). *Temple Bar* increased her readership by serializing many of her novels.

Though her popularity waned, critics recognized a witty chronicler in B. as she charted the changing mores and fads of her times. They urged her to take more care, one saying, "Her talent would amount to genius if she put more heart and soul into her work." But friends took precedence over writing, which financed her gowns from Worth, her sojourns in London, and her lavish hospitality.

Her capacity to charm was evident in her winning over a hostile Oxford during her residence there in the years 1878–90, making her Holywell home a preferred stop for lively talk and a warm welcome. The notorious caricature of Mark Pattison in *Belinda* (3 vols., 1883) resulted from his behavior unbecoming a friend. She enjoyed friendships with a range of eminent Victorians and particularly enduring ones with Garnet Wolseley, Commander in Chief of the Army, the Earl of Lytton, poet and Viceroy of India, and the novelist Henry JAMES. As the *Times* wrote at her death, "in her many and long and various friendships . . . she was supreme."

BIBLIOGRAPHY: Arnold, E. M., "R. B. as I Knew Her," *FortR* 114 (August 2, 1920): 262–78; Lubbock, P., *Mary Cholmondeley* (1928): 33–43; Sadleir, M., "R. B.," in his *Things Past* (1944): 84–116; Wood, M., *R. B.* (1993)

TAMIE WATTERS

BROWN, Christy

b. 5 June 1932, Dublin, Ireland; d. 6 September 1981, Parbrook, Somerset

B. is best known for his autobiography, *My Left Foot* (1954; repub. as *The Story of C. B.,* 1971), which he wrote at the age of twenty-two. The book received widespread notice through a 1989 Miramax feature film starring Daniel Day-Lewis. The story of B.'s life is one of great affliction, and the extraordinary capacity of a man to triumph in the face of overwhelming odds. B. was born with severe cerebral palsy. His disability left him with a near complete lack of control over his body, except the little toe of his left foot with which he eventually learned to write and paint. *My Left Foot* begins with B.'s birth into a large family in the Dublin slums. His mother discovers something is wrong after four months of age and the doctors, knowing little of his condition, diagnose him as mentally deficient, recommending that he be placed in an institution. His parents choose instead to care for B. at home. Although many years pass with little sign of any cognitive ability, suddenly at the age of five while propped up with pillows on the kitchen floor, B. manages to take a piece of chalk out of his sister's hand and proceeds to draw upon a slate the letter "A."

The book follows B.'s youth among a bunch of wild siblings and other neighborhood characters. It tells of his joys experiencing life alongside his brothers in a wagon he calls his "chariot," and of his many struggles including the contemplation of suicide once when loneliness overwhelmed him. A physician by the name of Robert Collis was instrumental in B.'s life, encouraging him to undergo treatment early on at the Merrion Street Clinic in Dublin for speech therapy. He was also the one who would later encourage him to take up writing, offering ongoing help with the first book. B. found that by putting his thoughts down on paper he was finally able to express himself and gain release from his tortured body and difficult emotions. The autobiography has been praised for its honesty, and called an engaging and inspiring work.

B.'s second work was the autobiographical novel, *Down All the Days* (1970). This work, which has been translated into fourteen languages, draws the reader into the poverty and despair of the working-class Dublin suburb of Kimmage where B. was reared. The novel is written with a narrator as voyeur, who observes all that goes on around him, unable to participate due to his spastic condition. B.'s style consists of many independent scenes and images of the trials of Dublin's characters, and of a general seediness. It is told in a lyrical and lively manner, noted for its rich description. *Down All the Days* became a best-seller and has been widely praised, bringing B. literary fame.

B. went on to write poetry, the first being a collection of love lyrics, *Come Softly to My Wake* (1971). It was popular with readers and sold a considerable number of copies for a volume of poetry of its time. Critics called the poetry pleasant and appreciated the imagery, yet found it lacking refinement. B.'s second novel, *A Shadow on Summer* (1974), about a crippled Irish writer named Riley McCombe who travels to New York City, was criticized for its verbosity and heavy use of clichés. *Wild Grows the Lilies* (1976) came out two years later to mixed reviews. This story of Luke Sheridan, a Dublin journalist who longs to write the great Irish novel, is lively and entertaining, full of B.'s wry sense of HUMOR. B.'s last novel, *A Promising Career* (1982), revolves around Britain's pop music scene. In it a musical duo's marital turmoil is seen against their agent's moral downfall as he forsakes his dying wife for exotic lovers.

Drawing upon the experiences of his Dublin up-bringing in much of his work, B.'s writing captures the beautiful and tragic elements of life in the city in a manner that effects the reader long after the book is finished. While the quality of B.'s writing is often found to be inconsistent, it is remarkable that a man, who lacked any formal education and faced incredible physical impediments to simply communicate, would rise to produce works that have affected and inspired many.

BIBLIOGRAPHY: Donnelly, C., "C. B.," in Halio, J. L., ed., *British Novelists since 1960*, part 1, *DLB* 14 (1982): 147–50; Rafroidi, P., *The Irish Novel in Our Time* (1976): 287–95

ANN O'BRIEN FULLER

BROWN, George Mackay

b. 17 October 1921, Stromness, Orkney; d. 13 April 1996, Stromness, Orkney

The youngest of six children, B. was born in Stromness on the main island of Orkney (a group of islands to the north of Scotland). Reared in the Presbyterian faith, he converted to Catholicism in the early 1960s, but his faith was always unorthodox. His early education at Stromness Academy stored his imagination with episodes from the history and myths of the islands and their diverse inhabitants, but he excelled only at essay-writing. A smoker from the age of twelve, he developed pulmonary tuberculosis for which, in 1941, the only treatment available was a sanatorium rest regime. He began to write poetry, and to contribute news items and book reviews to the local *Orkney Herald*, and *New Shetlander*, and was given a weekly column. In 1942, he wrote his first play, now lost. Its Viking setting marked a fascination with the Orkney past that persisted throughout B.'s writing career. In particular, the Norse *Orkneyinga Saga* inspired a number of strands in B.'s work, especially the novel *Magnus* (1973), and heroes and episodes from Viking history appear in works such as *Vinland* (1992) and *Beside the Ocean of Time* (1994).

A local bookseller gave B. his first book-publication by including several poems in the *Anthology of Orkney Verse* of 1949. A year later, the director of the local evening class that B. had joined suggested that he enter the new adult education college of Newbattle Abbey in Dalkeith, whose warden was Orkney poet Edwin MUIR. After Newbattle, B. spent four years at Edinburgh University, during which he met Stella Cartwright, who was to be muse and close friend. He sunsequently trained as a teacher at the Moray House College of Education, but his first school experience confirmed his belief that he was not meant to be a teacher. A reactivation of the tuberculosis intervened. On recovery, he began a year's research on Gerard

Manley HOPKINS under a new scholarship scheme, and once again left Orkney, for Stockbridge, near Edinburgh.

On the recommendation of Muir, Hogarth Press published a collection of poems, *Loaves and Fishes* (1959) and began a fruitful publishing relationship with the author. Although his early poetry received little attention, the nonfiction *An Orkney Tapestry* (1969) and fictional *A Time to Keep* (1969) and *Greenvoe* (1972) were immediately popular. In 1965, B. was awarded an Arts Council grant for poetry, and in 1968 the Society of Authors Travel Award, which he used to visit Ireland. *A Time to Keep* won the 1969 Scottish Arts Council Prize, and its title story the Katherine Mansfield Merton short story prize for 1971.

Many of the poems are structured as diaries or log-books, and combine the recording of the passing of time with the recording of a voyage, or the completion of an enterprise. Collections such as *The Storm* (1954), *The Year of the Whale* (1965), and *Fishermen with Ploughs: A Poem Cycle* (1971) share the major themes of the novels: faith and spirituality, the stream of time, and the cycle of rural life.

The Golden Bird (1987) was awarded the James Tait Black Memorial Prize in 1988, and *Beside the Ocean of Time* (1994) was shortlisted for the Booker Prize and judged Scottish Book of the Year by the Saltire Society. As well as the poetry and novels for which he is best known, B. also produced plays, including *A Spell for Green Corn* (1970), *The Voyage of Saint Brandon* (1984), and *The Loom of Light* (1986); nonfiction, including *Letters from Hamnavoe* (1975), *Under Brinkie's Brae* (1979), and *Portrait of Orkney* (1981). He also produced work in collaboration with others, including the composer Peter Maxwell Davies. B. was given honorary degrees from the Open University, Dundee University, and Glasgow University, in 1974 was awarded the O.B.E., and in 1977 made a fellow of the Royal Society of Literature.

BIBLIOGRAPHY: Bold, A., *G. M. B.* (1978); MacGillivray, A., *G. M. B.'s Greenvoe* (1989); Ramsey, J., *In Memory of G. M. B.* (1998); Yamada, O., H. D. Spear, and D. S. Robb, *The Contribution to Literature of Orcadian Writer G. M. B.* (1991)

SANDIE BYRNE

BROWNE, [Sir] Thomas

b. 19 October 1605, London; d. 19 October 1682, Norwich

It is safe to say that B.'s essays represent some of the most finely crafted prose of any British author. B.'s complex and often ambivalent stance toward Christianity has earned him a unique and unsettling position among critics from the start. Samuel JOHNSON in his *Life of Sir Thomas Browne* (1756) posited that

B. may have "hazarded an expression" that could be misinterpreted as blasphemous only if taken out of the overall context of his literary corpus. The real challenge and treasure of reading B.'s work is to be found in grappling with the massive breadth of learning that informed elaborate contexts of his essays and coming to terms with his often elusive tenor.

Of all the essays, the *Religio Medici* (1642) stands as the central text defining both B.'s style and worldview. In the *Religio*, B. dealt with a growing concern during the 17th c. with the physical sciences and the various mechanistic philosophies that purported purely rationalist and potentially atheistic explanations for life processes. However, B. would offer no unequivocal position here. And in the most famous section of part 2 to the *Religio* he declares: "I am above Atlas, his shoulders . . . whilst I study to finde how I am a Microcosme or little world, I finde myselfe something more than the great. There is surely a piece of divinity in us . . . Nature tells me I am the image of God as well as scripture." Besides detecting a precursor of the Whitmanesque persona, B. takes a daring stance as an individual for his time. In part 1, he offers his version of a "new religion" offering an expanded version of what Christianity ought to be wherein he considers "we being all Christians" exclusivity is a very un-Christian thing. Toward the close of the essay in speaking of Gold as the "God of the earth," B. confesses that he "is an atheist" and "for this only doe I love and honor my owne soul." B. constantly appears to be taking away with one hand the very thing given by the other.

This slippery play in B.'s text has earned him a controversial position within English literature. Stanley Fish holds the rather extreme view that B. is a "self indulgent" writer whose "words are objects frozen into rhetorical patterns which reflect on the virtuosity of the writer." It is understandable that Fish arrives at this conclusion when attempting to view B.'s work as a self-contained text. But as Stephen Greenblatt and other New Historicists have adroitly pointed out a text such as the *Religio* is born of the complex and burgeoning world of the Renaissance much of which we cannot ever hope to recapture and much less if we do not take into account impending influences such as politics, scientific trends, etc. Subsequently, B.'s work is a prime example of the decentered text wherein the organic self he presents is reflected in a dynamic prose that conveys the physician's mind in motion.

Besides his "Christian Morals," the rest of B.'s corpus holds an important place not just in terms of social and philosophical aspects but for the varied fields of inquiry he covers. His *Pseudodoxia Epidemica* (1646) is reminiscent of Robert BURTON's *Anatomy of Melancholy,* published in 1621. Although not nearly as exhaustive a study as the *Anatomy,* the

Pseudodoxia is a witty exposé of falsehoods and ill-founded beliefs. B was no empiricist and his thought ran counter to much of Sir Francis BACON's inductive approach.

Hydriotaphia: Urne-Buriall and *The Garden of Cyrus* appeared together in 1658 and are some of B.'s most idiosyncratic and fascinating essays. B. employs the discovery of some cremation urns as a figure of man's ephemeral nature in *Urne Buriall*. His knowledge of contemporary chemistry supplements his explication of decomposition or putrefaction in the alchemical sense of the transformation of decaying matter.

As in *Urne Buriall, The Garden of Cyrus* is a fluid and organic meditation initially focusing on the ancient hanging gardens of Babylon. B. holds that the quincunx or lozenge of the universe's reticulation can be found everywhere in vegetable, mineral, and animal matter. B. was assuredly a Pythagorean of the late Renaissance. In many ways, B.'s *Cyrus* is a precursor to C. G. Jung's theory of synchronicity as an a-causal or nondiachronic notion of being and existence.

B. was truly one of the last great Renaissance eclectics. He was a trained physician and chemist who had traveled extensively, and was fluent in six languages. He corresponded with Arthur Dee, a chemist and physician of note as well as the son of John DEE. B.'s contributions have been acknowledged by Samuel Taylor COLERIDGE, Herman Melville, James Russell Lowell, and many other notable authors, and there is little sign that B.'s influence has lost any momentum as a pivotal force in the art of the essay.

BIBLIOGRAPHY: Bennett, J., *Sir T. B.* (1962); Fish, S., "The Bad Physician: The Case of Sir T. B.," in his *Self Consuming Artifacts* (1985): 353–73; Huntley, F. L., *Sir T. B.* (1962); Merton, E. S., *Science and Imagination in Sir T. B.* (1949)

BOB PODGURSKI

BROWNE, William, of Tavistock

b. 1591, Tavistock, Devon; d. 1645, Dorking, Surrey

B. is the foremost member of the "Spenserian School" of English pastoral poets writing in the early 17th c. His *Britannia's Pastorals* (2 vols., 1613), a disquisitive poem of epic length and aspiration in two completed books (book 3 unfinished at B.'s death), intermittently pointed by rustic songs, celebrates the rural life and beauty of his native Devonshire countryside. John MILTON's careful reading of *Britannia's Pastorals* is apparent from echoes in "L'Allegro" and "Lycidas." B.'s influence on John KEATS is also notable.

B. entered Exeter College, Oxford, ca. 1603, and the Inner Temple in 1611. For an unknown period between 1616 and 1621, he apparently lived in France.

Appointed tutor to Robert Dormer, the future Earl of Carnarvon, in 1623, B. resided with his pupil, first at Eton and later at Exeter College, Oxford. The relationship ended by 1628, with B.'s marriage, upon which he apparently retired to Surrey to live and write. It is possible that B. benefitted from the patronage of the Herbert family, as Philip Herbert, Earl of Montgomery, was guardian to Dormer during the period of B.'s tutelage.

In addition to *Britannia's Pastorals*, B. published *Two Elegies* (1613), lamenting the death of Prince Henry, son of JAMES I, and was a major contributor to *The Shepheard's Pipe* (1614), a collection of Spenserian-style pastoral poetry that also included work by George WITHER and Sir John DAVIES. His *Inner Temple Masque*, on Circe and Ulysses, although written for a performance to have taken place in January 1615, was known only in manuscript, as was the incomplete third book of *Britannia's Pastorals*, until the appearance of a collected edition in 1772. "Sidney's sister, Pembroke's mother," once mistakenly attributed to Ben JONSON, is B.'s most famous epitaph, composed for the Countess of PEMBROKE.

While B.'s reputation is primarily as a pastoralist, his range is nonetheless wider than the genre usually suggests. His gift for song is amply demonstrated in the *Inner Temple Masque* and, although his salient influence is a backward look toward Edmund SPENSER, the work left unpublished at his death exhibits a degree of social criticism, and an autobiographical self-consciousness and erudition common to contemporary metaphysical poets.

BIBLIOGRAPHY: Doelman, J., ed., *Early Stuart Pastoral* (1999); Grundy, J., *The Spenserian Poets* (1969); Hazlett, W. C., ed., *The Whole Works of W. B.* (2 vols., 1868–69); Patterson, A., *Pastoral and Ideology: Virgil to Valery* (1987)

R. F. YEAGER

BROWNE, Wynyard [Barry]

b. 6 October 1911, London; d. 19 February 1964, Norfolk

Of all the successful middle-class English dramatists whose talents were discredited by the socially realistic Royal Court writers of the late 1950s, B. has made the least impressive return to public favor. Yet two of his plays, the quiet family drama *The Holly and the Ivy* (1950) and the comedy *The Ring of Truth* (perf. 1959; pub. 1960), might lay claim to being among the best the London commercial theater has produced since the Second World War. The truth and quality of his plays went unnoticed by the influential new wave theater critic Kenneth Tynan, whose ire was aroused by their middle-class cosiness and because they were

all produced and directed by a private patron, Frith Banbury.

B. is primarily a playwright of relationships within a specific social order who looks on his characters' lives with charity. Mood, character, and action are brought together in a sensitive and ironic whole. So he was, rather optimistically, compared with Anton Chekhov. Obviously, B. does not have Chekhov's depth and range but he does have that irony that blocks sentimentality. He is a minimalist of great charm.

B. was the son of an Irish clergyman in the Church of England and a rich banker's daughter. The diversity of his relatives was direct fodder for his work. He was educated at Marlborough—the school in *A Question of Fact* (perf. 1953; pub. 1955)—and at Christ's College, Cambridge, where he became an aesthete as well as a socialist and pacifist.

After a career as a journalist and minor novelist, at the outbreak of war, as a conscientious objector, he served most unhappily in the Non-Combatant Corps from which he was released following a nervous breakdown. During convalescence, he wrote his first play, *Dark Summer* (perf. 1947; pub. 1950), which shows the conflict of a blind boy, who loves and is loved by a morally and intellectually glorious but plain-looking Jewish refugee, when an operation restores his sight. In B.'s first three plays, plot is a pretext to observe characters written with real warmth and tolerance. Here, as later, because he never requests emotional engagement, he often receives it. Gisela, the Jewish girl, is portrayed as possessing such intelligence and humanity; and the dichotomy between the security of her belief in the freedom and worth of life and the insecurity of her belief in the worth of herself as a woman is written powerfully but never sensationally.

By far his best-known play, *The Holly and the Ivy*, became the blueprint for other family plays where Christmas, that time of year when the Lord-of-Misrule rules, traumatizes by its unexpected revelations yet clears the air by truths being told. The paterfamilias, a widowed Irish clergyman, is unable to connect to his children—in particular his alcoholic younger daughter—until harsh events open the lines of communication. Their long scene together toward the end of the play is still deeply moving and finally joyous. A period piece written with understatement, it is somehow exciting because of its truth and poetry.

With *A Question of Fact*, B. moves from poetic NATURALISM to a consideration of the power of imagination itself. The theme of its use and abuse is harnessed to a striking premise: a young schoolmaster (originally played by Paul Scofield), adopted as a baby, discovering that his real father is a murderer. How this imaginative man uses his gift constructively as an inspired teacher and destructively by incorrectly demonizing his natural father as a squalid monster, while engaging with the imagination or lack of it in the surrounding characters, is engrossing. The entrance of his birth mother (played first by Gladys Cooper) halfway through the play is superbly set up; a splendidly capable woman of insight and HUMOR, she is the exact opposite of our expectations and B. brings off the characterization with much aplomb.

His last performed play, *The Ring of Truth* (perf. 1959; pub. 1960), made little impact because the fashionable Royal Court writers, with their hero Bertolt Brecht and their champion Tynan, had dismissed successful West End playwrights like B. as outdated and middle class. A pity because it is one of the best comedies of the 1950s and in its portrayal of two stupid and brutal policemen, a precursor of Joe ORTON's black comedy. It could claim to be the last genuinely funny drawing room comedy and an antiauthoritarian one at that, although its premise of contrasting the intuitive and the rational is more conventional.

B.'s final play, *A Choice of Heroes* (wr. 1964), a radical departure from his usual genre, concerns revolutionaries in 19th-c. Russia and remains unperformed. Perhaps when B. had no more family left to pillory and understand, he was written out.

Apart from *The Holly and the Ivy*, which was also filmed (1952), none of his plays have been revived, but they are superior both in their artistry and in their knowledge of the human heart to many of those by his luckier, rediscovered contemporaries.

BIBLIOGRAPHY: Duff, C., *The Lost Summer: The Heyday of the West End Theatre* (1995); Shellard, D., ed., *British Theatre in the 1950s* (2000)

CHARLES DUFF

BROWNING, Elizabeth Barrett

b. 6 March 1806, Coxhoe Hall, Kelloe, County Durham; d. 29 June 1861, Florence, Italy

In her day, B. was considered the foremost woman poet. Her work largely faded out of fashion, with the exception of her love sonnets, until 1996, when Margaret Reynolds's critical edition of *Aurora Leigh* (1857) attracted the attention of feminist scholars. As a result of their scrutiny, B. has been regarded as a political poet rather than a lyric poet. Much modern criticism has been engaged with tracking the development of her political thinking. Her first major work, *The Battle of Marathon* (1820), published at her father's expense, reveals the influence of Whig ideas on power, leadership, and the civil rights of the individual on B.'s early writings.

Feminist poetics now tend to be seen as running parallel with politics. In an early journal, "Glimpses into My Own Life and Literary Character," written when she was fourteen, B. articulated her anxiety that

learning required a certain kind of "masculine toughness, that few women possessed," though she recognized that Mary WOLLSTONECRAFT was one example. Her other female idol was the French woman writer, George Sand (the pen name of Aurore Dudevant), to whom she dedicated two poems as well as paying homage in the choice of "Aurora" for her eponymous heroine.

B. began her career as a poet very young, writing birthday odes to every member of her large family from the age of eight. Her formative reading years fell ca. 1816–30, and she was consequently burdened with Wordsworthian concepts of the function of women in poetry as either Mother Nature who nurtures her poet-son, or as the Muse who is the silent subject of men's poetry. Margaret Homans has examined these ideas most fully in relation to B. in *Women Writers and Poetic Identity* (1980). Dorothy Mermin was the first critic to reinterpret B.'s ballads as feminist revisions of old tales.

Concomitant with a close attention to her politics is a renewed interest in the philosophical and spiritual bases of her poetry. Her early poem "An Essay on Mind" (1826), for example, is now examined in the light of Scottish "Common Sense" philosophy. Similarly, her interest in Emanuel Swedenborg is noted in critical discussions of B.'s poetic symbols in *The Seraphim and Other Poems* (1838) and "A Drama of Exile" in her *Poems* (2 vols., 1844), which could be described as an "added chapter" of John MILTON's *Paradise Lost* in which Eve is brought back into the pale of God's grace.

By the time she met Robert BROWNING in 1845, B. was an acclaimed poet, more famous than he at that time. In the face of her father's strenuous opposition, the two poets eloped and thereafter lived a life of exile in Italy, where her only child, Robert Wiedemann Barrett Browning ("Pen"), was born in 1849. During the course of their courtship, B. wrote a sonnet sequence to her lover, thereby unsettling the convention of male poet writing to his admired love object, the woman, the muse. B.'s sonnets establish Robert Browning's equal position as lover and poet with her own equal position as lover and poet, as well as to establish a woman's right to state her own desires. *Sonnets from the Portuguese* (1850) is the most popular of her volumes of poetry. Sonnet forty-three, "How do I love thee? Let me count the ways," is one of the nation's favorite poems, endlessly requoted in Valentine cards and cited at wedding ceremonies.

The Casa Guidi in Florence was the home that the Brownings rented from 1847 to 1861. In *Casa Guidi Windows* (1851), B. wrote of real political events of 1847–49 mediated by the gaze of the stationary, onlooker poet, whose vision was framed by the constraints of a twin aperture in a wall. This figures for the limitations of all political visions, although the poem is simultaneously inflected with her own personal hopes for Italian freedom and rebirth, linked to the birth of her own "Florentine" son. In *Poems before Congress* (1860), B.'s intellectual engagement with Italian politics continues; she attacks, for instance, England's refusal to assist the cause of Italian liberalism. She argues in several poems that it is a woman poet's duty to speak out. "A Curse for a Nation" is out of place in this volume as it was an attack on slavery in the southern states of the U.S., but its central sentiment: "A curse from the depths of womanhood/Is very salt, and bitter, and good" underlines her insistence on women's duty as citizens.

Critical praise for "Lady Geraldine's Courtship," whose theme was the love of a titled woman for a poor poet, inspired her ambition to write "a longer poem of a like class"—a poem comprehending the aspect and manners of modern life, and flinching at nothing of the conventional." *Aurora Leigh* is usually considered B.'s masterpiece, and is the finest exemplar of a series of 19th-c. works exploring the conundrum of what it meant to be both a woman and a poet (or artist, performer, or singer). Its form is that of a verse novel, and it is marked by a sense of doubleness; how a poet is a prophet of the times but a woman needs to find fulfillment in love. It is a meditation on how these two positions can be negotiated: "poets should exert a double vision." B. was a close observer of the world of feminist politics, especially those of the Langham Place Group. Her original choice of name for her eponymous heroine was "Vane," but in 1856 B. changed the name to "Leigh" in honor of Barbara Leigh Smith Bodichon, the feminist leader who, in 1855, had petitioned parliament to amend the Married Women's Property Laws: 26,000 women signed the petition, headed by the names of prominent writers and artists including that of B. The central theme of *Aurora Leigh* was a clarion call about exactly those things that the Langham Place group was campaigning about: that women as well as men needed to find their own "best work," their vocation, and that marriage should not be regarded as representing a profession.

BIBLIOGRAPHY: Hirsch, P., "Gender Negotiations in Nineteenth-Century Women's Authobiographical Writing," in Swindells, J., ed., *The Uses of Autobiography* (1995): 120–27; Homans, M., *Women Writers and Poetic Identity* (1980); Leighton, A., *E. B. B.* (1986); Mermin, D., *E. B. B.* (1989); Montefiore, J., *Feminism and Poetry: Language, Experience, Identity in Women's Writing* (1994); Stone, M., *E. B. B.* (1995)

PAM HIRSCH

BROWNING, Robert

b. 7 May 1812, Camberwell, London; d. 12 December 1889, Venice, Italy

During much of his early career as a poet, B.'s work was eclipsed by the reputation of his wife, the poet Elizabeth Barrett BROWNING. In the 1850s, he was commonly identified as "Mrs. Browning's husband." By the 1860s, he had developed an independent reputation. At the end of his life, he rivaled Alfred, Lord TENNYSON as the spokesman of the Victorian age, and his experiments with language and syntax had a profound influence on 20th-c. poets like Ezra Pound. His unique development of the dramatic monologue as an instrument that combined poetry and protopsychology to reveal with subtle casuistry and penetrating insight the depths of a character's doubt, anxiety, or mental aberration, is his greatest contribution to British poetry.

B. was the child of highly indulgent parents who took the greatest pleasure and satisfaction in supporting and encouraging their only son's artistic ambitions. Through the age of fourteen, he attended a number of local schools, but none of them for very long. He was a precocious child, and his education was derived largely from his father's library, where he read voraciously, and from private tutors who taught him music, French, and Italian. At sixteen, he was enrolled in the newly founded University of London, but left after a few months, unable to tolerate the strictures of formal education. He returned to the comfort and security of his father's library, and to his course of voracious albeit undisciplined reading. His interest in art, particularly the art of the Italian Renaissance, which would become a central theme of his best work, was first stimulated by his visits to the Dulwich Gallery, a brief walk from the family home in Camberwell, just across the Thames from London.

At twelve, B. had discovered the Romantic poets, and his initial enthusiasm for Lord BYRON resulted in a collection of imitative poems for which his indulgent parents attempted, unsuccessfully, to find a publisher. At fourteen, he became thoroughly absorbed in Percy Bysshe SHELLEY, who subsequently proved to be the profound influence of his creative life. Briefly, and to his parents' dismay, B. became an atheist and a vegetarian in imitation of his idol. The influence is unmistakable in his first published work, *Pauline: A Fragment of a Confession* (1833), in which Shelley is referred to by the idolatrous epithet, "Sun Treader," and appears to a lesser but quite evident degree in both *Paracelsus* (1835) and *Sordello* (1840). At the time of *Pauline,* B.'s highest aspiration was to write verse in the Shelleyan manner. Subsequent discoveries about Shelley's life lessened his enthusiasm. With maturity came the realization that he was not by inclination a poet of Romantic subjectivity given to the pursuit of metaphysical idealism, but an "objective" poet, with a keen and discerning eye for the qualities of human personality and character as they develop and manifest themselves in the temporal world. B. makes this important distinction in the "Essay on Shelley" (1852), his only prose work, and an important statement in the understanding of his development as an artist. He declared the separation to be final, but the Shelleyan influence, although far from pervasive, continued to appear sporadically in his later work.

Although *Pauline* proved to be a commercial failure in that it did not sell a single copy, it did receive some positive recognition from critics. *Paracelsus* also failed commercially, but it too was recognized by a number of influential men as the work of a poet of promise. Among these was the actor and producer William Charles Macready, who persuaded B. to write plays for the Victorian stage. B.'s attempt to become a playwright, however, ended in dismal failure. *Strafford* (1837) closed after five performances, and *A Blot in the 'Scutcheon* (1843) after three; but in his failure as a dramatist lay the key to his eventual success as a poet. Victorian audiences were accustomed to lively action and lavish spectacle. The characters in B.'s plays were by contrast introspective, given to psychological examination and character revelation presented in lengthy speeches. His emphasis, as he put it, was upon "action in character, rather than character in action." It was this realization that turned him once and for all from conventional drama to poetry, and to the "single character drama" of the dramatic monologue. The subject of a B. dramatic monologue presents a unique point of view reflecting an inner struggle to rationalize decision and action, to present to the reader his own concept of "truth" as explanation and, frequently, distorted justification for whatever action he has taken. Often the convictions they express, while condemning them from their own mouths as in the case of the Duke in "My Last Duchess" (1842) or Guido Franceschini in *The Ring and the Book* (4 vols., 1868–69), paradoxically underscore their rich but decidedly flawed humanity.

In 1846, B. eloped with the poet Elizabeth Barrett and sailed for Italy. They lived and worked together in Florence until her death in 1861, making occasional trips to Rome, Paris, and London. Their son, Robert Wiedemann Barrett Browning, was born in 1849. It was in Florence during this happy period of his life that B. produced much of his best work, most notably the two-volume collection, *Men and Women* (1855), and discovered in an open market book stall "the old yellow book," a transcript of an 18th-c. murder trial that would provide the basis for his masterpiece, a set of twelve dramatic monologues entitled *The Ring and the Book*. Two of B.'s most brilliant examples of his mastery of the dramatic monologue, "My Last Duchess" and "The Bishop Orders His Tomb at Saint Praxed's Church" (1845) had been published before he left England, but in *Men and Women* B. demonstrated in poems such as "Fra Lippo Lippi," "An Epistle of Karshish," "Cleon," "Andrea del Sarto," and "Bishop Blougram's Apology," the degree to which

he had become and would remain the most skilled practitioner of the form in English literature.

BIBLIOGRAPHY: Bristow, J., *R. B.* (1991); Hudson, G. R., *R. B.'s Literary Life* (1993); Irvine, W., and P. Honan, *The Book, the Ring, and the Poet: A Biography of R. B.* (1974)

RICHARD KEENAN

BROWNJOHN, Alan [Charles]
b. 28 July 1931, London

B. was educated at Merton College, Oxford, and taught in schools and colleges before becoming a full-time writer. His poems are taught in schools and he is widely admired, associated with Philip HOBSBAUM's "The Group." Influences include Thomas HARDY and Philip LARKIN. Described by fellow poet Peter PORTER as uniting "wit and civic responsibility," B.'s ironic stance toward contemporary life, public and domestic, is humorous rather than didactic. He stood as a Labour candidate in the 1964 parliamentary election. *Travellers Alone* (1954) was followed by *The Railings* (1961), first among several collections. *Brownjohn's Beasts* (1970) remains popular with children. B. has edited various anthologies. His *Collected Poems* appeared in 1983 (rev. ed., 1988). His novels include *The Way You Tell Them* (1990), *The Long Shadows* (1997), and *A Funny Old Year* (2001).

BRYDGES, [Sir] Samuel Egerton
b. 30 November 1767, Kent; d. 8 September 1837, Campagne, near Geneva, Switzerland

B. was a prolific man of letters—poet, novelist, biographer, and essayist—who lived for much of his later life in self-imposed exile. In 1806, he met Jane AUSTEN and described her as "fair and handsome, slight and elegant, with cheeks a little too full." His early poetry as well as his first two novels, *Arthur Fitz-Albini* (2 vols., 1798) and *Le Forester* (3 vols., 1802), met with mixed reception. In 1818, B. left England for the Continent. In Europe, B. continued to write and publish his poetry, notably *The Lake of Geneva* (2 vols., 1831), and gained increasing recognition as a prose writer. In 1834, he published in two volumes his memoirs followed in the next year by his highly regarded *Life of John Milton* (2 vols., 1835).

BRYHER
(pseud. of Annie Winifred Ellerman) b. 2 September 1894, Margate; d. 28 January 1983, Vaud, Switzerland

The introduction to a recent reissue of B.'s early autobiographical novels, *Two Novels* (2000), calls B. one of the least recognized figures in the modernist landscape. Known for years primarily as the partner of the American poet H. D., her own writing, the early autobiographical fiction, a number of historical novels written during the 1950s and 1960s, and the later memoirs, *Heart to Artemis: A Writer's Memoirs* (1962) and *The Days of Mars* (1972), remained largely neglected and long out of print. Since the mid-1990s, however, there has been a revival of interest from historians of psychoanalysis and film, and from feminist and lesbian theorists concerned with historical narrative. Although there is as yet neither a biography nor an edition, of her letters, she is increasingly recognized as an important writer, editor, and patron of MODERNISM.

Development (1920) and *Two Selves* (1923) are fictionalized accounts of B.'s own childhood and adolescence, which chart in imagist prose the growing consciousness of a woman and a writer. The heroine, Nancy, the daughter of a rich shipping merchant, has an epic childhood, full of travel and adventure, before entering an oppressive schooling in conventional femininity. *Development* offers a critique of women's education and the search for alternative models while *Two Selves*, now read as a coded lesbian romance, ends with the discovery of same-sex love. *West* (1925) completes this trilogy of autobiographical fictions, recounting a trip to the U.S. with Helga (H. D.), her new "friend" and their travels to the West Coast.

In later memoirs, this material is renarrated in relation to the question of "how external events and unconscious drives help or hinder development." In addition to her own psychoanalysis with Hanns Sachs, B. funded H. D.'s analysis with Sigmund Freud—described in H. D.'s *Tribute to Freud* (1956)—and supported a number of psychoanalytic schemes. Her commitment to psychoanalysis and modernism may be seen as her reaction to the Victorian values described in the early fiction. Her inherited wealth, and the freedom gained by a marriage of convenience to Robert McAlmon in 1921, enabled her to make a major contribution to each. She supported a number of writers and intellectuals, including James JOYCE, and in 1927, with her second husband Kenneth Macpherson, founded the avant-garde film journal *Close Up* and a film company, POOL Productions, which made the film *Borderline,* starring H. D., Paul and Eslanda Robeson. In 1935, she bought the magazine *Life and Letters Today,* publishing a number of her own short stories as well as work by Havelock ELLIS, André Gide, and Gertrude Stein. The Bauhaus home she had built above Lake Geneva was used in the later 1930s as a center to aid refugees escaping from Nazi persecution. Her antifascist activity, contributions to psychoanalysis, and pioneering role in avant-garde film have led to new readings of the previously underrated historical fiction.

Action-packed, with atmospheric detail and anachronistic dialogue, B.'s eight historical novels, read as children's fiction by her contemporaries, are set in time of war: war between Saxons and Normans in *The Fourteenth of October* (1952), World War II in *Beowulf* (1956); Greeks and Lucanians in *Gate to the Sea* (1958), or Romans and Carthaginians in *The Coin of Carthage* (1963). Although generally narrated from a male point of view, as Ruth Hoberman points out, in these and her other novels—*The Player's Boy* (1953), *Ruan* (1960), and *The January Tale* (1966)—B. reworks traditional male plotlines by creating multiple—sometimes conflicting—narrative perspectives. Undermining a single, authoritative notion of history, her narrative strategies stress the constructed nature of historical discourse and the possibility of alternative versions.

B.'s revisionist treatment of the past, like H. D.'s view of history as protean and palimpsestic, is informed in part by Jane Harrison's feminist anthropology but also draws on their experience of the psychoanalytic process—the ways in which events are selected to tell different stories about the past. Concerned with histories of the defeated rather than histories of the victors, it features the bystanders as well as the main actors of mainstream history. An identification with the conquered peoples is evident in *Roman Wall* (1954), which contrasts the enslaved feminine figures of Greeks, women, and traders with their masculine, law-ridden Roman conquerors. B. returns to the Romans in *The Coin of Carthage* and the author's foreword makes her historical aims clear: since the Romans destroyed the Carthaginian libraries, the familiar stories about Hannibal are based on Roman sources and that this is "as if England had been defeated in 1940 and we were trying to describe the last hours of London only from enemy accounts." Like Walter Benjamin, whom she tried to help escape as the Germans advanced on Paris, B.'s postwar historical fiction can be read as an attempt to articulate the connection between her own era and the conflicts of the past.

BIBLIOGRAPHY: Collecott, D., "Bryher's *Two Selves* as Lesbian Romance," in Stacey, J., and L. Pearce, eds., *Romance Revisited* (1995): 128–42; Hoberman, R., *Gendering Classicism* (1997); Winning, J., ed., *Bryher: Two Novels* (2000)

JEAN RADFORD

BUCHAN, John
b. 26 August 1875, Perth, Scotland; d. 11 February 1940, Ottawa, Canada

"I have done the state some service." Othello's words could easily have been claimed by B., although he would have been too modest to add Othello's assertive conclusion, "and they know it." B. was a director of intelligence in World War I, subsequently a member of Parliament and, ennobled as Lord Tweedsmuir, the Governor-General of Canada for the last five years of his life. The characters who figure in his most significant novels are, like their creator, public servants—even if they also happen to be adventurers.

B. began early (his first book was published when he was nineteen) and throughout a distinguished public life he also sustained a remarkably prolific and professional career in literature, producing well over a hundred works of fiction, poetry, BIOGRAPHY, history, and essays. T. E. Lawrence—Lawrence of Arabia, a real-life B. hero—characterized B.'s books as "clean-limbed, speedy, breathless," and this largely accounts for their success as well as pointing to some of the reasons for B.'s uneasy relationship with the literary establishment. He was an author of great range and set most store by his works of historical fiction and biography, but it is the thrillers for which he is remembered and still read. Critically, B. has been taken to task for traits that are, in fact, the standard reflexes of most early-20th-c. writers of "shockers" (B.'s own disparaging term): proimperialism, paternalism, a mild anti-Semitism.

In literary terms, B. bridges the gap between the Edwardian world of comparative certainty, embodied in writers such as H. Rider HAGGARD and Arthur Conan DOYLE, and the morally ambiguous sphere inhabited by Eric AMBLER and, more recently, John le CARRE. B.'s first significant fiction, the African romance *Prester John* (1910; repub. as *The Great Diamond Pipe*, 1910), is firmly in the tradition of Haggard's *King Solomon's Mines* and Doyle's *The Lost World*, imperial quests for which the rewards are treasure and renown. But in his most famous book, *The Thirty-Nine Steps* (1915), completed as World War I was beginning, there is a fusion of the dominant "thriller" modes of the 19th and 20th cs., respectively—the adventure story and the spy/conspiracy story. Richard Hannay, the central figure of *The Thirty-Nine Steps*, reappears in several other works, notably *Greenmantle* (1916) and *Mr. Standfast* (1919). With the end of the war, B. experienced the difficulty common to thriller writers of fixing on an easily identifiable enemy. Indeed, by the time of the fourth Hannay story, the relatively cerebral *The Three Hostages* (1924), the enemy is an apparently exemplary gentleman—"very English and yet not quite English"—a hunter, a politician, even a poet, hardly to be distinguished (except in his rampant egotism) from the hero. In this postwar period, the adventure may be depoliticized altogether, as in the mystic Greek romance *The Dancing Floor* (1926), or turn into psychological exploration, as in *The Gap in the Curtain* (1932), which reflects an interwar fascination with prevision and time shifts.

The majority of B.'s post-World War I novels were firmly grounded in the world of country-house weekends and high-level table talk, the world in which their creator was himself a player. Here are gathered the soldier-adventurers, magnates, and government ministers, together with a smattering of scholars—and, of course, the odd bad apple. It is not an exclusively male world, but the women who are admitted to this Homeric aristocracy are expected to endorse its values. When it comes to action, they sometimes show more stamina—and greater resolution—than the male characters.

B. probably came closest to a self-portrait in the character of Sir Edward Leithen, a lawyer and member of Parliament. Leithen, who appears in five novels, is a more versatile figure than Hannay and so better suited to the more complex conditions of the 1920s and 1930s. It is appropriate that he is the protagonist of B.'s final novel, *Sick Heart River* (1941; repub. as *Mountain Meadow*, 1941), completed only a fortnight before the author's death and published posthumously. The theme of self-sacrifice, always significant in B., reaches its apotheosis in this last work when Leithen forgoes the chance of recovering from tuberculosis so as to give heart to a physically and spiritually sick native tribe in a remote Canadian settlement. This novel, written as another "great war" was breaking across the world, provides an interesting contrast to *The Thirty-Nine Steps* in which disguise and intrigue are the required components. The later work more subtly suggests the values of stoicism, reflectiveness, and a kind of Christian acquiescence. B. had moved far beyond the boundaries of the "shocker."

B.'s strengths as a narrative writer are in his creation of place and atmosphere, and his unfailing attraction to the romantic. In his fiction the mysterious sometimes teeters on the edge of the mystic, but is always mediated through a lucid, classically influenced style. Above all, B. offers that intangible something that American writer Raymond Chandler once said that he aimed at: the feeling of "the country behind the hill."

BIBLIOGRAPHY: Green, M., *Dreams of Adventure, Deeds of Empire* (1980); Goldsworthy, V., *Inventing Ruritania: The Imperialism of the Imagination* (1998); Lownie, J., *J. B.* (1995)

PHILIP GOODEN

BUCKINGHAM, George Villiers, Second Duke of

b. 30 January 1628, London; d. 16 April 1687, Kirby Moorside, Yorkshire

Born in the year of his unpopular father's assassination, which occurred on August 23, the second Duke proved to be as unpopular as his parent had been. He became part of Charles II's inner circle, "the Cabal," and was marked out for special ridicule when John DRYDEN caricatured him as Zimri in his satire, *Absalom and Achitophel*. Later, he is to be found as a rapacious kidnapper in Sir Walter SCOTT's quasi-historical *Peveril of the Peak*. A writer of verse satires in his own right, B. is probably best remembered for his play, *The Rehearsal* (perf. 1671; pub. 1672). The play satirizes the hyperbole of heroic tragedy and pokes particular fun at Sir William DAVENANT in the guise of "Bayes" (a reference to his unofficial laureate status) and Dryden. In all likelihood, B. wrote the play in collaboration with either Samuel BUTLER, the author of *Hudibras*, who was under B.'s patronage, or Martin Clifford, who was then Master of Charterhouse.

BULWER-LYTTON, Edward George Earle Lytton [Baron Lytton]

b. 25 May 1803, London; d. 18 January 1873, Torquay, Devonshire

One can hardly count it an honor to have inspired a popular bad writing contest. Nevertheless, despite B.-L.'s magenta prose, literary historians have slowly come around to the position that he is an author worth studying. The reason is not far to seek: B.-L.'s undeniable influence on nearly all of the Victorian novel's most popular genres. At one point, he believed he had a vocation for poetry, and three collections of verse appeared between 1820 and 1826. This aspect of his career was not a success. The editor of the *New Monthly Review* from 1831 to 1833, he contributed periodical articles to the major journals; wrote several plays, one of which, the satire *Money* (1840), remains in the modern repertoire; and authored an important, Coleridgean study of English culture, *England and the English* (1834). In addition, B.-L. enjoyed a solid political career, serving as a member of Parliament from 1831 to 1841 and again from 1852 to 1866, including a stint in the cabinet as Secretary of State for the Colonies. Along the way, his politics shaded from radical into conservative. Less positively, much of B.-L.'s prodigious output was motivated by a permanent state of financial emergency, abetted by his disastrous marriage to Rosina Doyle Wheeler.

B.-L.'s eclectic artistic philosophy encompasses elements of German idealism, platonic and neoplatonic thought, Christianity, and even the occult, particularly Rosicrucianism. As many critics have noted, B.-L. was particularly influenced by Goethe and the German Bildungsroman, and many of his plots center on the intellectual and emotional education of often alienated young men. B.-L. showcased his wide reading in the German Romantics in several of his novels. *The Pilgrims of the Rhine* (1834), a love story that gently interweaves travelogue with fairy tale, intersperses its main plot with a number of inset narratives that either invent or retell German folktales and legends. B.-L. explored the more philosophical bent of his interest in all things German in the Bildungsroman, *Ernest Maltravers* (3 vols., 1837), which tracks the career of a young Englishman educated in Germany and obsessed with German thought and, indeed, educated there; his emotional education gets a harsh shove from the loss of his first love, Alice. The ending is openended, with both the reader and (apparently) the author unsure of what Ernest will do next. The next novel, *Alice; or, The Mysteries* (3 vols., 1838) completes Ernest's education and, eventually, reunites him with his lost love. In practice, B.-L. disliked REALISM, arguing that readers should contemplate things not as they are, but as they should be. He classed himself as a "metaphysical" or "philosophical" novelist, and his characters and situations should be taken as representing typical ideas or mental states—an approach that has generated some complaints about the flatness of both his narratives and his characters. Despite his antirealist position, B.-L. intended his novels to make serious contributions to social questions of the day, ranging from penal laws to the social effects of Darwinism.

B.-L.'s first two novels, *Falkland* (1827) and *Pelham* (3 vols., 1828), are "silver-fork" novels, depicting the unseemly doings among the aristocratic classes. *Falkland* fell dead from the press, but *Pelham* was another matter. Not only was the novel a huge best-seller, but it famously set the fashion for men's black evening wear. His next major successes proved scandalous: the "Newgate" criminal novels *Paul Clifford* (3 vols., 1830) and *Eugene Aram* (3 vols., 1832). The first tells the tale of a young man whose criminal tendencies were spawned by his dissolute surroundings as a child and exacerbated by punishment; the second is based on a real 18th-c. murderer. *Paul Clifford* in particular makes a radical case for penal reform that sounds remarkably similar to present-day humanitarian critiques of the prison system. In 1849, B.-L. rewrote *Eugene Aram* to make the title character innocent. He later returned to the crime genre with *Night and Morning* (3 vols., 1841), which features a young man who must overcome the legacy of his mother's unacknowledged marriage, and *Lucretia; or, The Children of Night* (3 vols., 1846), based on the career of the infamous poisoner Thomas Griffiths Wainewright. B.-L.'s attempts to analyze criminal psychology offended many critics, who felt that he was glorifying it instead. His criminal novels generated a nasty, and long-running, feud in the 1830s with *Fraser's Magazine*, carried on by William Makepeace THACKERAY and William MAGINN.

In any event, his interest shifted to historical fiction, a form he had already tried with underwhelming success in *Devereux* (3 vols., 1829). Like many of Sir

Walter scott's readers, B.-L. noted Scott's fascination with moments of transition, points when "the good old way" of life had to give before an encroaching modernity. B.-L. signals his own interest in such transitional moments by flagging "last" things: *The Last Days of Pompeii* (3 vols., 1834); *Rienzi, the Last of the Roman Tribunes* (3 vols., 1835); *The Last of the Barons* (3 vols., 1843); and *Harold, the Last of the Saxon Kings* (3 vols., 1848). The latter two novels, which examine, respectively, the clash between the Earl of Warwick and King Edward IV, and the Norman Conquest, are two of B.-L.'s most searching analyses of the nature of "Englishness." Like Scott, B.-L. often appears more sympathetic to his "losers," but he also tries to indicate how the past vitally affects the modern nation. His historical novels exemplify the aspirations of 19th-c. historical novelists toward the genre of historical writing itself, and indeed received praise from some professional historians. B.-L. took his scholarship seriously, although even a confection like *Pompeii*, for example, features antiquarian digressions that bring the narrative to a crashing halt. But in the midst of writing historical fiction, B.-L. also indulged his fascination with the occult in the Rosicrucian novel *Zanoni* (1842), which follows the encounter of an immortal man with the call of human emotion and life, climaxing in a fateful choice during the Reign of Terror.

B.-L. pursued occult and fantastic fiction throughout the rest of his career, most interestingly in the late novella *The Coming Race* (1871), a dystopian critique of Darwinism and egalitarianism. "The Haunted and the Haunters" (1857) is a ghost story that allows B.-L. to indulge his interest in mesmerism. However, of his later works, the most successful form the so-called Caxton trilogy: *The Caxtons* (3 vols., 1849), *My Novel* (4 vols., 1853), and *What Will He Do with It?* (4 vols., 1858). *The Caxtons* features a family that, in its obsession with competing visions of the past, seems to be on the verge of destroying itself; the novel's two fathers, Mr. Caxton (hard at work on "The History of Human Error") and Uncle Roland (an ex-military man), are both deeply alienated from their sons, Pisistratus and Herbert. Both children manage to redeem themselves and to find personal freedom from their fathers' deadly obsessions by temporarily emigrating to Australia; although Herbert eventually dies heroically, Pisistratus "heals" the family by marrying Blanche, Herbert's sister, and ultimately fathering Herbert's namesake. The three novels are linked not by the Caxton family's exploits, but rather in their similar storylines about the cultivation of genius and selfhood, the meaning of heroism, and the nature of England's future. Pisistratus joins all of the novels together as the "author" of both *My Novel* (with commentary from his family, who are "reading" the manuscript and quibbling with his choices) and *What*

Will He Do with It? The latter novel features one of B.-L.'s most complicated plots, involving thwarted love, political machinations, criminal misdeeds, and a man who allows himself to be punished for his son's crimes. Everyone lives happily ever after. The Caxton trilogy proved successful at a time when B.-L.'s popularity was beginning to wane. In any event, affected by his political responsibilities and recurring ill health, he wrote few other novels. *Kenelm Chillingly* (3 vols., 1873) returns to one of B.-L.'s favorite plots: the moral education of a disaffected young man. *The Parisians* (4 vols., 1873), left unfinished at B.-L.'s death, neatly embodies B.-L.'s personal political journey from radicalism to conservatism. Set during the events leading up to the Paris Commune, it turns a sardonic eye on socialist aspirations.

Although B.-L.'s work is enjoying a small-scale scholarly renaissance, it is doubtful that his reputation will undergo a mass revival. At the popular level, B.-L.'s primary appeal is now to followers of the occult; indeed, it is a press devoted to paranormal happenings and the occult that keeps his work in print. Nevertheless, B.-L. deserves considerable credit for contributing to the spread of German thought to England during the early Victorian period. His willingness to take artistic risks, as in the experimental narrative structure of *My Novel*, elevates him far above the mere hack writers of the period, and the intellectual seriousness driving much of his aesthetic philosophy influenced Victorian aspirations for making the novel a "high" art form.

BIBLIOGRAPHY: Campbell, J. L., Sr., *E. B.-L.* (1986); Christensen, A. C., *E. B.-L.* (1976); Eigner, E. M., *The Metaphysical Novel in England and America* (1978); Hollingsworth, K., *The Newgate Novel 1830–1847* (1963); Zipser, R. A., *E. B.-L. and Germany* (1974)

MIRIAM ELIZABETH BURSTEIN

BUNTING, Basil
b. 1 March 1900, Scotswood, Northumberland; d. 17 April 1985, Hexham

B.'s reputation as a poet has gradually emerged from the shadow of his slightly older and more famous associates—especially Ezra Pound. B. was chronologically a poet of the generation of the 1920s and 1930s, but his first printed collection of poems appeared in 1950. His very deliberate, even snailpaced, production, and his perfectionism (which led him constantly to edit and revise his work throughout his life) confined his reputation to a small, though enthusiastic, audience. It is seldom favorable for an ambitious poet to gain the reputation of being a "writer's writer," even worse to be considered a coterie writer (whether as part of the coterie of another writer or as the center of one's own), but while B. had great passion and commitment to his poetry, and seems to have loved to have an appreciative audience, he did not have the careerist instincts that help promote great reputations. Only late in his life—after 1960—did his name begin to gain recognition and his poetry to be cited on its own merits, rather than as the work of a disciple or associate of the Pound circle.

B. met Pound in 1919 through a connection with the editor/publisher Alfred Orage, whose publication *The New Age* had featured works by many prominent writers of the period—Wyndham LEWIS, Katherine MANSFIELD, Llewelyn POWYS, and others, including Pound. While B. remained close to Pound for many years, he did not share Pound's worldview or politics, but he did have the same conviction that poetry must be purified of 19th-c. rhetoric, and he had the same fascination with finding poets of other traditions to translate or, as B. called it, "overdraft," making not exact translations but new English poems, by B., that radically condensed and re-created the images and ideas of the other poet. Pound's "Homage to Sextus Propertius" and "Cathay" were examples for B., whose "Chomei at Toyama" performs that process for the Japanese poet, Kamo-no-Chomei. Having spent some time in Iran, B. also translated works by a number of Persian poets, as well as Latin and French poets, including Lucretius, Catullus, and Charles Baudelaire.

Where B. parted from Pound, in particular, was in his theory of the relationship between music and poetry. While Pound asserted the importance of three elements of poetry—melopoeia, phanopoeia, logopoeia—he tended to emphasize image and idea at the expense of music (despite his protests to the contrary); B. was unequivocal in his commitment to the primacy of music in, and of, poetry. He claimed to have composed his words on the page as a musician marks his score, and he repeatedly asserted the importance of reading his poems aloud. This fascination with the sound of his poetry (which led to his agreeing to record his own readings of many of his poems) set him off from the Pound group, with its fascination with the poem on the page, the printed artifact. B.'s fascination with sound and music benefited from his later association with Louis Zukofsky, an American poet who also explored the musical dimensions of his language, but where Zukofsky's verbal music was founded in the new nation, B.'s was the sound of Northumberland, with its surprising vowel music and sharp consonants.

B.'s best-known and most admired poem is *Briggflatts* (1966), a dense and condensed autobiographical poem ("Briggflatts" is the name of a hamlet where a Quaker meeting house built in 1675 is located) that alludes to some events of B.'s life, but more importantly explores and enacts his relation of poetry and the peculiar religious view that he holds. (It is difficult not to associate the poem with T. S. ELIOT's "Little Gidding," if only because of the analogous—and yet sharply different—symbolic locations at the center of the two poems.) As with many of B.'s other poems, *Briggflatts* deploys imagery of the sea, of fishing and sailing, along with pervasive images of music, of poetry, and of time. Themes of temporal change set against a sense of timelessness, especially the suspension of quotidian time to be achieved through music, link B.'s poem to major themes of other 20th-c. poets, obviously including Eliot. As is probably inevitable in a poem exploring the suspension of time, autobiographical narrative is hardly present at all, but allusions to the essential character of poetry and its relation to place create cohesiveness and visual power along with the musical effects. B.'s reputation grows and will remain secure as founded on this major poem of the 20th c.

BIBLIOGRAPHY: Caddel, R., *B. B.: The Complete Poems* (1994); Forde, V., *The Poetry of B. B.* (1991); Quartermain, P., *B. B.* (1990)

THOMAS F. DILLINGHAM

BUNYAN, John
b. 27 November 1628, Elstow, near Bedford; d. 31 August 1688, Finsbury, London

B., a tinker by trade, and one of the greatest writers of English prose, wrote over forty books including one written in jail and translated into over one hundred languages. "Bunyan is the greatest representative of the common people to find a place in English literature," says Roger Sharrock in his book *John Bunyan* (1954). And Bernard SHAW, himself a great English stylist and a keen judge and critic of style, throughout his long career frequently commented on B.'s powerful and felicitous use of the written word. In a letter of January 8, 1899 to Henry Arthur JONES, the playwright, Shaw said: "no man produces a work of art of the very first order except under the pressure of strong conviction and definite meaning as to the constitution of the world. Dante, Goethe, and Bunyan could not possibly have produced their masterpieces if they had been mere art-voluptuaries" and again, in another letter—this time to Max BEERBOHM on September 15, 1903—Shaw says "the reason Bunyan reached such a pitch of mastery in literary art (and knew it) . . . was that it was life or death with the tinker to make people understand his message and see his vision."

Twenty-eight years later, in his play *Too True to Be Good*, Shaw makes Sergeant Fielding (who always carries a copy of the Bible and *The Pilgrim's Progress* around with him) say "Look at these two books. I used to believe every word of them because they seemed to have nothing to do with real life. But war brought these old stories home quite real . . . Look at this bit here . . . 'I am for certain informed that this our city will be burned with fire from heaven . . . except some way of escape can be found whereby we may be delivered.' Well, London and Paris and Berlin and Rome and the rest of them will be burned with fire from heaven all right in the next war: that's certain. They are all Cities of Destruction . . . God's truth in the real actual world . . . This uneducated tinker tells me the way is straight before us." Ironically, *Too True to be Good* was first published in Germany and its first stage production was in the U.S., both in 1932. World War II began in 1939.

The Pilgrim's Progress was first published in two parts, *Part One* in 1678, *Part Two* in 1684. Part 1 tells the story of Christian's journey from the City of Destruction, via the Slough of Despond, the Hill of Difficulty, the Valley of the Shadow of Death, and Vanity Fair over the River of the Water of Life and on into the Celestial City; part 2 relates the story of the same journey undertaken by Christian's wife, Christiana, and her children. As an outstanding example of "quest" fiction and the "eternal wanderer" theme, *The Pilgrim's Progress* stands narratively in a long and honorable line that could be said to begin with the *Odyssey* and to contain examples as various as Apuleius's *The Golden Ass*, Rabelais's *Gargantua*, Jonathan SWIFT's *Gulliver's Travels*, and even Alain-René Lesage's *Gil Blas*. It has also become a quasi-myth in its own right. Quite apart from its immediate influence, both political and religious, in 17th-c. England, *The Pilgrim's Progress* exercised a long-term, formative, literary influence on English writing, both as to general literary style and as to the specific development of fictional narrative: it is, in fact, the first English novel, predating the one-time usual claimant, Daniel DEFOE's *Robinson Crusoe*, by forty-one years. Literary considerations apart, in terms of its content it was, along with B.'s other books (and also his activities as a religious preacher), one of the chief factors in the growth of the nonconformist (protestant dissent) movement in England, contemporary with George Fox and his Quakers, and preceding the evangelical work of John and Charles WESLEY in the 18th c.

Of B.'s other works the most important are *Some Gospel Truths Opened* (1656), a dispute with the Quaker point of view concerning personal "holiness" and the relative importance (or otherwise) of the biblical text; *Grace Abounding* (1666), an anguished account of B.'s gradually developing religious experience; *The Life and Death of Mr Badman* (1680), a kind of sequel to *The Pilgrim's Progress*, showing what was happening to the unrepentant majority of the City of Mansoul after Christian has left; and *The Holy War* (1682), describing the constant siege of the

striving soul by the powers of darkness. All these books are marked by the same imaginative allegorical treatment couched in the same plain powerful prose as is found in *The Pilgrim's Progress* and given zest and flavor by the same bold use of colloquial turn of phrase and by flashes of ironic HUMOR.

There is an interesting variation of technique between *The Pilgrim's Progress* in 1678 and *Mr. Badman* in 1680. The former is written from Christian's point of view, almost from within his head, so that the sense of doubt and of possible disaster are vividly felt from moment to moment as he himself feels them. Mr. Badman, on the other hand, is seen entirely from the outside, settled, complete, and fully identified from the start, so that the moral point is emphasised but the sense of a developing drama is lost. A remarkable feature of this book is the gritty realism of the descriptions of local and domestic detail.

It is perhaps worth noting what is going on in other branches of English literature during the thirty years or so in which B.'s works were first published: the year after *Grace Abounding* (1666) appeared saw the publication of John MILTON's *Paradise Lost* and the year after that was marked by Charles SEDLEY's *The Mulberry Garden* and John DRYDEN's *Tyrannick Love*. George ETHEREGE's *The Man of Mode* came two years before *The Pilgrim's Progress* and the Earl of ROCHESTER's "All my past life is mine no more" (set as a song to music by Henry Bowman) was published in 1677, one year before *The Pilgrim's Progress*. Thomas OTWAY's *Venice Preserv'd* appeared in the same year as B.'s *The Holy War*. B. was not an isolated oddity in an otherwise barren landscape.

BIBLIOGRAPHY: Brown, J., *J. B.* (1928); Lindsay, J., *J. B., Maker of Myths* (1937); Sharrock, R., *J. B.* (1954).

ERIC SALMON

BURGESS, Anthony
b. 25 February 1917, Manchester; d. 25 November 1993, London

One of the 20th c.'s most prolific writers, B. was at once a polyglot, voracious reader and musical composer. Though he is probably best known for *A Clockwork Orange* (1962)—in part due to Stanley Kubrick's controversial 1971 film adaptation, now something of a cult favorite—B. produced over thirty novels rich in linguistic detail, scripts for film and stage, librettos, translations of Sophocles and Edmond Rostand, language studies, books on William SHAKESPEARE, Ernest Hemingway, and James JOYCE, and two volumes of "confessions." In addition to his creative works, B. was a well-respected reviewer, notorious for actually reading the books under review. Though the quality is inconsistent, B.'s books invariably contain intelligent wordplay and scorn for the ignorant and sophomoric. At his worst, B. is a pedantic grammarian, but at his best, B.'s style, inventive wit, and ear for spoken language approach Nabokovian heights.

Born John Anthony Burgess Wilson, B. survived the influenza that killed his mother and sister. He attended Xavieran College and Manchester University. B. recalls packing *Finnegans Wake* in his bag when he began his six-year stint as a soldier during wartime, and indeed the subsequent influence of Joyce is everywhere in B.'s writing and inspired important studies such as *Here Comes Everybody* (1965) and *Joysprick* (1973). In the postwar years, he taught at Banbury Grammar School, and from 1954 to 1959 served as colonial education officer in Malaya and Brunei, which experience supplied him with matter for his early novels, *The Long Day Wanes* (also known as *The Malayan Trilogy*), made up of *Time for a Tiger* (1956), *The Enemy in the Blanket* (1958), and *Beds in the East* (1968). In 1959, B. was diagnosed with an inoperable brain tumor and given less than a year to live. The diagnosis ultimately proved false, but by then B. had established a dizzying working pace, producing several books in that "last" year, among them a medical-marital satire about a linguist with a brain tumour (*The Doctor Is Sick*, 1960) and plans for *A Clockwork Orange*.

A Clockwork Orange is the story of Alex, a gang-leading teenager with a propensity for violence and rape as well as for classical music. In this character B. dramatizes a series of moral problems, such as the conflict between social good and individual free will, differences between justice and revenge, and collusion between inhumanity and the arts. (Kubrick's film, like a corrupted American edition of the book, omits the matter of the novel's final chapter, in which Alex comes to a mature ethics of his own devising.) Alex speaks directly to his reader-audience in nadsat, a slang B. generated using Slavic roots: in the course of the novel the reader becomes familiar with the terminology, which strangely manages to be both lyrical and crude at the same time, and thus the reader undergoes a kind of "brainwashing" akin to the one Alex faces at the hands of government officials.

B.'s penchant for satire is at its fiercest in the Enderby tetralogy, comprised of *Inside Mr. Enderby* (1963), *Enderby Outside* (1968), *The Clockwork Testament; or, Enderby's End* (1974), and *Enderby's Dark Lady* (1984). F. X. Enderby is a dyspeptic, privacy-craving American poet who likes to compose while seated on the toilet, using an unused bathtub as a catch-all filing cabinet. (The first book of this series originally appeared as a work by Joseph Kell, B.'s occasional pseudonym. B. was fired from a newspaper for reviewing the book.) Enderby's writing life is beset by opportunists, plagiarists, sycophants, aca-

demics, and the general deterioration of language, while his verse won praise from no less a reader than T. S. ELIOT.

Earthly Powers (1980), probably B.'s best novel, is narrated by a sentimental novelist, Kenneth Toomey, uncertain about the integrity of his art, the sincerity of his agnosticism, and the discomfort of his homosexual desires. In eighty-two chapters, Toomey (a sympathetic sort of caricature of W. Somerset MAUGHAM) recounts his life of as many years—thus giving B. the opportunity to use as a background mural a colorful version of the 20th c.—with particular focus upon his friendship with the remarkable Carlo Campanati, a revolutionary pope under assessment for sainthood. The nature of sin and free will is a central question in this self-examination: here as elsewhere, a marked strain of Manicheism runs through the fiction.

B.'s other novels include *The Right to an Answer* (1960), *The Wanting Seed* (1962), *Honey for the Bears* (1963), *Tremor of Intent* (1966), *MF* (1971), *Napoleon Symphony* (1974), *1985* (1978), *The Pianoplayers* (1986), *Any Old Iron* (1989), and *Byrne* (1995), a novel in verse. B. enjoys weaving speculative biography of figures such as John KEATS (*ABBA ABBA*, 1977), Shakespeare (*Nothing like the Sun*, 1964), Trotsky and Freud (*The End of the World News*, 1982) as much and as often as he plays with conventions of popular genres, particularly spy thrillers and SCIENCE FICTION. In his last, posthumously published, prose novel B. returned to the subject of his university thesis, Christopher MARLOWE. *A Dead Man in Deptford* (1993) is a tale of espionage and theater, told by a boy actor (and by definition, here, the bedmate of various playwrights) in prose that simultaneously approximates and parodies Elizabethan English.

While indignant feminist dismissals of B. have abated, his reputation is, according to one astute critic, "of the sort that is bound to zoom and plunge," though the reputation itself has staying power. The B. world is a serio-comic one in which theology, sexual intrigue, music, and paronomasia coincide, and in which irrational modernity bears down upon the soul. For all of his nostalgia for MODERNISM, B. is an original and unique figure in English letters.

BIBLIOGRAPHY: Aggeler, G., *A. B.* (1979); Aggeler, G., ed., *Critical Essays on A. B.* (1986); Bloom, H., ed., *A. B.* (1987); Stinson, J. J., *A. B. Revisited* (1991)
                                                    TIM CONLEY

BURKE, Edmund

b. 12 January 1729, Dublin, Ireland; d. 9 July 1797, Beaconsfield

One of the most eloquent orators and prose stylists of the 18th c., B. took a progressive stand on many of the hotly contested issues of his day: the American Revolution, religious toleration, the abolition of slavery, the administration of India. To students of British literature, however, he is known primarily as the author of two works: *A Philosophical Enquiry into the Origin of Our Ideas of the Sublime and Beautiful* (1757; rev. ed., 1759), a treatise on aesthetics written while he was still in his twenties, and *Reflections on the Revolution in France and on the Proceedings in Certain Societies in London Relative to That Event* (1790), a scathing critique of the excesses of the French Revolution written near the end of his life.

In his first work of note, *A Vindication of Natural Society* (1756), B. parodies the deist Viscount BOLINGBROKE's arguments against religion by applying them to social institutions, imitating the style of his target so closely that some contemporaries, missing B.'s ironic tone, believed the anonymous work had come from Bolingbroke's own pen. The following year he published *A Philosophical Enquiry*, an attempt to distinguish between two aesthetic categories of increasing interest to 18th-c. readers. B. explores the psychological and physiological underpinnings of sublimity and beauty, identifying the sublime with terror, obscurity, privation, and vastness and attributing the effect of beautiful objects to their relaxing qualities. B.'s theory of the sublime was influential in Germany as well as in England, leaving its mark on the work of such thinkers as G. E. Lessing and Immanuel Kant.

The questions that occupied B. throughout most of his life, however, were not aesthetic but political. In *Thoughts on the Cause of the Present Discontents* (1770), he identifies royal patronage as a source of England's malaise and emphasizes the role of political parties in restoring the country's political health. His parliamentary speeches in the years immediately preceding the American Revolution, while opposed to American independence, urged leniency toward the colonies and supported conciliatory measures. On the domestic front, his *Speech on Economical Reform* (1780) outlined a plan to shift financial responsibility and power gradually from the Crown to Parliament. By the mid-1780s, corruption in the East India Company had spawned myriad abuses, which B. sought to expose in his *Speech on the Nawab of Arcot's Private Debts to the Europeans* (1785), a rhetorical tour de force that eventually led to the impeachment of the governor general of India, Warren Hastings.

But it was his revulsion at the course of events just across the English Channel that led B. to publish his most famous work. *Reflections on the Revolution in France* appeared at a time when many in England sympathized with the French revolutionaries. B. frames his argument as a reply to a letter from a young Frenchman, Charles Jean-François Depont, who had solicited his opinion on the situation in France at the end of 1789. B.'s attacks were aimed not only at the

French National Assembly itself but at the revolution's friends in England: men such as Thomas Paine, Joseph Priestley, and the radical preacher Richard Price. B. contests their comparison of events in France to the Glorious Revolution of 1688; the latter, he argues, effected orderly change under the constitution, whereas the former threatened to overthrow order altogether. Accused of inconsistency in his responses to the American and French revolutions, B. defended himself in *An Appeal from the New to the Old Whigs* (1791). The most memorable passage in the *Reflections*, however, is B.'s admiring portrait of Marie Antoinette, in which he laments the passing of the "age of chivalry." His effusive praise of the French queen provided ample material for contemporary caricaturists.

B.'s last writings were devoted to reaffirming his views on the French Revolution in *Thoughts on the Prospect of a Regicide Peace* (1796) and to deflecting criticism of his pension in *Letter to a Noble Lord* (1796), a passionate defense of his life as a public servant. Though neglected after the Napoleonic Wars, by the late Victorian period B.'s writings were once again greatly admired, drawing praise from Thomas Babington MACAULAY and Matthew ARNOLD.

BIBLIOGRAPHY: Boulton, J. T., *The Language of Politics in the Age of Wilkes and B.* (1963); Chapman, G. W., *E. B.* (1967); Furniss, T., *E. B.'s Aesthetic Ideology* (1993)

DENISE VULTEE

BURNET, Gilbert
b. 18 September 1643, Edinburgh, Scotland; d. 17 March 1715, Clerkenwell, London

After study at Marischal College, Aberdeen, in 1669, G. become professor of divinity at Glasgow University. He became chaplain to Charles II, but was dismissed for criticizing the king's behavior. In 1686, G. became adviser to William of Orange. G's account of the deathbed repentance of John Wilmot, Earl of ROCHESTER appeared in 1680 and his *History of the Reformation in England* (3 vols., 1679, 1681, 1715) was begun at the time of the "Popish plot," when Catholicism was seen as a national threat. G.'s best-known work, the *History of My Own Times* (2 vols., 1724–34), was published posthumously. It blends AUTOBIOGRAPHY with anecdote and history. Among other works was the *Life and Death of Sir Matthew Hale* (1682), a distinguished biography of the noted jurist.

BURNETT, Frances [Eliza] Hodgson
b. 24 November 1849, Manchester; d. 29 October 1924, "Plandome," Manhasset, New York, U.S.A.

B. generates interest in terms of her contribution to popular literature of the late 19th and early 20th cs.,

British-American REALISM, dialect and FOLKLORE, class structure and gender roles, and the shaping of CHILDREN'S LITERATURE. Much of her enduring fiction is rooted in her native Manchester, an industrialized town, which, by 1841, was known for its chasm between the rich and the poor, a social tension exemplified in her fiction.

The American Civil War devastated the Manchester economy, and B. and her mother and siblings moved to New Market (near Knoxville), Tennessee in May 1865. Two important Romantic tendencies impelled her at this point: the power of the imagination to improve upon the reality of life and her love of pastoral landscape, especially English gardens and rural Tennessee. In June 1868, B. published "Hearts and Diamonds" in *Godey's Lady's Book* under the pseudonym "THE SECOND."

Early B. fiction was popular with the editors at *Godey's*, *Scribner's*, and *Harper's*. The 1877 collection *Surly Tim and Other Stories*, for example, appealed to American readers interested in the plight of the English working class. *That Lass o' Lowrie's* (1877) was an even more popular realistic portrayal of British working-class life and employed a strong Lancashire dialect. Both B. and her mother were always interested in speech and dialect and in the implications of the two linguistic phenomena regarding class.

After B. and her physician husband settled in Washington, D.C., she began her most popular novel, *Little Lord Fauntleroy* (1886). Based on earlier serialized stories in *St. Nicholas* and, in part, on the character of her second son Vivian, the novel became a classic in children's literature selling more than one million copies. *Fauntleroy* parallels B.'s rags to riches theme in her earliest magazine work. An adorable ruffian from American streets, the little protagonist claims his title, lands, and wealth in England. The union of such an English tradition with the boy's American sense of brotherhood and egalitarianism makes an important bridge of past and present in the late 19th c.

Although it is still popular to link Fauntleroy with Vivian Burnett, in large part the reading public seems to draw its image of the boy from the sissified illustrations of the text by Reginald Birch. Read without the Birch illustrations, traditional male characteristics like bravery or running fast become more memorable to the reader, not the aesthete dress of velvet and love locks. Queer readings of the story suggest that Fauntleroy's suit is modeled after the kind of aesthete dress worn by Oscar WILDE, and that the Birch illustrations often depict the effeminate boy in close proximity to a more virile animal, his "phallic friend."

The Secret Garden (1911) was published while B. was building her villa "Plandome" in Manhasset, New York. The novel employs the three ingredients of fantasy identified in J. R. R. TOLKIEN: recovery, es-

cape, consolation. The restoration of the garden symbolizes the rebirth and rejuvenation of the protagonist Mary. As Mary learns to garden from Dickon, she moves from isolation to community. The maturation novel, moreover, owes something to both the theme and structure of the early-19th-c. English exemplum in which one who is saved then saves others.

B.'s fiction has drawn various and, in some instances, recent dramatic interpretation. *Little Lord Fauntleroy* was filmed in 1921, 1936, and 1980. *The Secret Garden* was filmed for television in 1993. The 1939 film version of *A Little Princess* (1905) included stellar performances by Shirley Temple as the little "princess" and Cesar Romero as the servant Ram Dass. Another film version in 1995 starred Liesel Matthews as Sara and Eleanor Bron as the schoolmistress, Miss Minchin.

B. is remembered primarily for the achievements in her novels for children. Her awareness of the timeless elements within children's literature and fantasy, her use of class and caste themes, maturation motifs, and her handling of dialect continue to draw readers to her work.

BIBLIOGRAPHY: Bixler, P., *The Secret Garden: Nature's Magic* (1996); McGillis, R., *A Little Princess: Gender and Empire* (1996); Thwaite, A., *Waiting for the Party: The Life of F. H. B., 1849–1924* (1974)

GEORGE C. LONGEST

BURNEY, Fanny [Frances, Madame D'Arblay]

b. 13 June 1752, Kings Lynn; d. 6 January 1840, London

Until recently, scholars have been accustomed to refer to the 18th c. as the Age of Enlightenment or the Age of Reason. Although a change in this assessment has occurred across disciplines, the careful scholarship being done in regard to B.'s novels, essays, drama, journals, and correspondence should disabuse the most ardent traditionalist of this notion. Scholars, especially feminist critics, have revealed a world where women are not only chattels, which was not an unexpected find, but they are constantly at risk if they, in any way, depart from their assigned place in this society.

The quantity of personal correspondence and diaries extant from the literate population of the period, not the least significant those of B. and her circle, reveals that B.'s first three novels, particularly, give a realistic portrait of the dearth of enlightened, rational thought or action, especially as it is directed toward women. The events and characters in these novels expose a society in turmoil, still entrenched in feudal notions of class and honor, if not in the legal institutions of feudal society. B. discloses that this holds especially true for an economically strapped nobility faced with an ever-rising middle class. In this struggle, women are caught in a vice. That issues of class and social status were a reality for B. is revealed in her own journals and letters and those of her contemporaries as they pertain to her. In one recent critical biography of B., Claire Harman quotes a letter from Samuel JOHNSON's friend and confidante, Hester Thrale PIOZZI, written in February 1779. As B. became a part of their circle after the publication of *Evelina; or, A Young Lady's Entrance into the World* (3 vols., 1778), this letter is rather telling of the duplicitous nature of this literate and educated but socially conscious group. Mrs. Thrale writes: "The Burneys are I believe a very low Race of Mortals" and B. herself is "not a Woman of Fashion."

B.'s profound contribution to the evolution of the novel is the creation of the novel of manners that would be taken up by Jane AUSTEN, and others. In her epistolary inaugural novel *Evelina*, B. stays closer to earlier models of character and situation but paints graphic images of a more revolutionary nature. The motions of stock figures like the rouged virago, the near-perfect romantic hero of noble birth, and, of course, the young and beautiful put-upon heroine, open the window to a decaying and morally decrepit society, a world far removed from polite society even when bearing the trappings of it. Money and family ties are also called into account by B.'s simultaneous adherence to and deviations from the conventions. In her other novels—*Cecilia, or, Memoirs of an Heiress* (5 vols., 1782), *Camilla; or, A Picture of Youth* (5 vols., 1796), *The Wanderer; or, Female Difficulties* (5 vols., 1814)—the stock figures fade and the grimness of the age becomes yet clearer. The most recent editors of *Cecilia* have noted that "B. is a pioneer in creating both mixed character and the mixed ending in the English novel." In this innovation, we have a character at once sympathetic and antagonistic, an ending neither tragic nor unrealistically happy or wholly resolved. In these subsequent novels, the stock figures fade and the grimness of the age becomes yet clearer. In her eight plays, *The Witlings* (wr. 1779); *Edwy and Elgiva* (wr. 1790); *Hubert de Vere* (wr. ca. 1788–91); *The Seige of Pevensey* (wr. ca. 1788–91); *Elberta* (a fragment) (wr. ca. 1788–91); *Love and Fashion* (wr. 1799); *The Woman Hater* (wr. 1800–01); and *A Busy Day* (wr. 1800–1801), B. chooses satiric comedy and verse tragedy as the format with themes, character, and subject adhering closely to those of the novels.

Through the lens of B.'s fiction and drama, her letters and journal entries, and one of the most painfully revealing writings, her letter to her sister relating her own mentally and physically painful mastectomy (1811), B. reveals the woman of her age. Woman exists to perpetuate the lineage, the wealth, and the

power of men and is always potential sport for any man's games. B.'s fictional heroines and real-life revelations show women constantly besieged by men willfully disregarding their fears and desires, their mental and physical sufferings. In B.'s society, both women and men, regardless of class, are susceptible to moral, spiritual, and physical corruption.

BIBLIOGRAPHY: Bilger, A., *Laughing Feminism: Subversive Comedy in F. B., Maria Edgeworth, and Jane Austen* (1998); Darby, B., *F. B., Dramatist: Gender, Performance, and the Late Eighteenth-Century Stage* (1997); Daugherty, T. E., *Narrative Techniques in the Novels of F. B.* (1989); Harman, C., *F. B.* (2000); Straub, K., *Divided Fictions: F. B. and Feminine Strategy* (1987)

JULIE CHAPPELL

BURNS, Robert
b. 25 January 1759, Ayrshire, Scotland; d. 21 July 1796, Dumfries, Scotland

The popular conception of B. as the plowboy poet whose poetry had sprung from nature uncorrupted by the evils of civilization and untutored by literary tradition was a prevalent myth of the second half of the 18th c., engendered at a time when Romantic idealism was in the process of displacing the long established dominance of neoclassicism. The myth was one that B. did little or nothing to dispel, and he rather enjoyed his "noble savage," poet of the primitive, image. Although largely self-educated, he was nonetheless comparatively well read, and valued deeply the established FOLKLORE and literary traditions of Scotland.

B. spent his youth behind the plow on several unproductive farms, and the strenuous exertion of 18th-c. farm life took its toll on his heart and general constitution. Their relative poverty notwithstanding, both of B.'s parents were readers, and they encouraged learning and formal schooling when work and opportunity permitted. B.'s education included mathematics, English grammar, and some Latin and French. From his mother, he learned old Scottish songs. His father died when B. was twenty-five, and he found himself the head of a family of eight. Despite the labor intensity of farm life and these new responsibilities, he somehow found time for numerous affairs with local young women, many of whom became the subjects of poems. His personal life became so complicated that at one point he considered leaving Scotland and accepted a clerkship in Jamaica. Hoping to raise the funds for his passage, he published his first volume of poetry in the summer of 1786, *Poems, Chiefly in the Scottish Dialect,* generally known as the Kilmarnock edition, for the town in which it was published. B. had hoped the book would appeal to a regional audience, but when it proved a success throughout Scotland, particularly in Edinburgh, the Scottish capital, B. abandoned his emigration plans. Instead of Jamaica, B. went to Edinburgh, then known as the "Athens of the North," where he was lionized in the town's literary circles. In 1787, a second edition of his poems was published in Edinburgh, and the income B. received enabled him to take two tours, one through the Scottish Highlands, and another through the north of England.

Eventually he tired of city life, and returned to the country. He purchased a farm near Dumfries, married Jean Armour, the "bonnie Jean" of his poems and the mother of several of his many illegitimate children, and settled into the role of devoted father and family man, albeit seasoned with periodic infidelities. He continued to write poetry through 1792, producing scores of songs, primarily lyrics set to traditional Scots tunes. Despite the fact that his farm proved a failing proposition, B. accepted no money for this work, which he did anonymously as a patriotic gesture of love for Scotland. Most of these poems and songs, along with traditional ballads he collected and edited, were published in James Johnson's anthology, *The Scots' Musical Museum* (6 vols., 1787–1803), several volumes of which were edited by B., and in George Thomson's *Select Collection of Original Scottish Airs* (5 vols., 1793–1818).

B. was a man of conflicting moods, and his poetry reflects the many facets of a seemingly simple but actually complex personality. Some of his poetry written for friends and drinking cronies reveal him to be an alcoholic seducer of women, but songs such as "Mary Morison," "Of A' the Airts," and "A Red, Red Rose" reveal the tender and romantic lover; "Holy Willie's Prayer," considered by many critics to be a brilliant satire on religious hypocrisy, shows the anticlerical side of B., but "The Cotter's Saturday Night" suggests a warm and sentimental appreciation of religious faith. For some critics, the preponderance of Scottish dialect is evidence of an insular parochialism, but few poems capture the sense of equality and international brotherhood as intensely and effectively as "A Man's a Man for A' That" (1795). Portions of his poems have become maxims, widely accepted as proverbial wisdom of the ages; the most notable although frequently misquoted examples are "The best laid schemes o' Mice and Men/ Gang aft agley" from "To A Mouse," "O wad some Pow'r the giftie gie us/ To see oursels as others see us," from "To a Louse," and the definitive anthem of every new year, "Auld Lang Syne," all of which first appeared in the Kilmarnock edition of 1786. "Tam o' Shanter" (1793) is perhaps his best and most accomplished poem, a mock-heroic, serio-comic folktale of witches and warlocks, nicely leavened by the roguish appeal of its tipsy but lovable protagonist. It was the poet's personal favorite, containing, in his view, "a force of genius and a

finishing polish that I despair of ever excelling." It was also greatly admired by William WORDSWORTH and Sir Walter SCOTT.

BIBLIOGRAPHY: Daiches, D., *R. B.* (1994); Douglas, H., *R. B.* (1996); Low, D. A., ed., *R. B.* (1974); Mackay, J. A., *A Biography of R. B.* (1992); McIntyre, I., *Dirt and Deity: A Life of R. B.* (1995)

RICHARD KEENAN

BURTON, [Sir] Richard Francis
b. 19 March 1821, Torquay; d. 20 October 1890, Trieste, Italy

Brilliant but wayward and quarrelsome traveler and linguist, B. mastered over thirty languages, including Gujurati, Marathi, Hindustani, and Persian, but was especially skilled in various dialects of Arabic. In 1853, he famously traveled to Mecca, posing as an Indian Pathan pilgrim, despite being blue-eyed. His *Personal Narrative of a Pilgrimage to El-Medinah and Meccah* (3 vols., 1855–56) is grimly humorous, keenly observant, and eccentrically opinionated. Today, his fame rests on his translations of the "Arabian Nights"—*The Thousands Nights and a Night* (16 vols., 1885–88), known also as *The Arabian Nights.* It reveals a profound knowledge of Arabian customs and vocabulary from the literary to the low. B.'s translation of the *Kama Sutra,* the Sanscrit sex manual, was published serially in 1883. B. employed native experts to find manuscript texts of this neglected ancient treatise, and to provide basic literal translations. B. polished these versions, supervised the printing, and sold copies by private subscription. Published by the imaginary "Kama Shastra Society" with imprints from fictitious locations, erotica was slily presented as scholarly research. B.'s widow, who objected to his interest in all aspects of sexuality, made a bonfire of many of his papers, including a complete translation of the Arabian *Perfumed Garden.*

BURTON, Robert
b. 8 February 1577, Lindley Hall, Leicestershire; d. 25 January 1640, Oxford

B. was educated at Brasenose College, Oxford, became a fellow at Christ Church in 1599 and remained there for the rest of his life, becoming vicar of St. Thomas's, Oxford. His only published work was *The Anatomy of Melancholy* (3 vols., 1621; rev. eds., 1624–51), a unique, rambling gallimaufry of classical and renaissance theories of depression, from which B. himself suffered, and illustrated with anecdote. His range of quotation, much of it in Latin, is astonishing, and according to one editor not amenable to checking as it came largely from B.'s capacious memory. The *Anatomy* was much loved by later writers, notably

Laurence STERNE, whose *Tristam Shandy* is full of allusion to it and by Dorothy L. SAYERS, who quotes it widely in the epigraphs to *Gaudy Night.*

BUTLER, Samuel

b. February 1613, Strensham; d. 25 September 1680, London

Under the date of December 10, 1663, Samuel PEPYS recorded in his diary that B.'s *Hudibras* (part 1, 1662; part 2, 1663; part 3, 1677; each part is dated a year later on the title page) was "now the greatest Fashion for drollery." Charles II, Andrew MARVELL, and Jonathan SWIFT memorized large portions of the work. By 1750, over eighty poems had been composed in the loose octosyllabic couplets that B. had employed in his burlesque. In his *Lives of the Poets*, Samuel JOHNSON pronounced *Hudibras* "one of those compositions of which a nation may justly boast." B.'s reputation still rests largely on his comic masterpiece, by far the longest (11,000 lines) and most successful of the eight pieces that B. is known to have published in his lifetime. However, since 1759, when Robert Thyer edited B.'s *Genuine Remains*, B.'s skill as a prose writer has been increasingly appreciated.

According to a letter that B. wrote to George Oxenden of the East India Company, the chief design of *Hudibras* "was onely to give ye world a Just Acco[un]t of ye Ridiculous folly and Knavery of ye Presbiterian & Independent Factions" that gained power during the period 1640–60. B. further claimed in that letter that the poem's main characters were based on real people, and that a central event in part 1, the arrest of the fiddler Crowdero, had actually occurred. In 1715, Roger L'Estrange published a "key" to the poem matching characters and historical figures. Some two centuries later, the usually sound Hardin Craig made a similar effort, even suggesting, though not insisting, that the bear represents Charles I.

B.'s literary debts are clearer. The fat Presbyterian justice of the peace who serves as B.'s title character takes his name from book 2 of Edmund SPENSER's *Faerie Queene*, and Hudibras's lean clerk Ralpho recalls Francis BEAUMONT's apprentice in his mock-heroic *Knight of the Burning Pestle*. The fat knight and lean squire invert Miguel de Cervantes' famous errant adventurers even as they imitate some of the incidents in *Don Quixote* (1605–15) The verse form in *Hudibras* recalls John MILTON's "L'Allegro" and "Il Penseroso," but B. loosens the form and employs many curious rhymes.

B.'s claim that his poem satirizes 17th-c. Puritans is valid. B. may have served as a royalist pamphleteer in the 1640s and 1650s. His first known publication, *Mola Asinaria* (1660), satirizes the purported author of the piece, the Puritan propagandist William Prynne. "A Ballad," first published in 1759, equates the Puritan Rump Parliament with the devil. Under the guise of sainthood, Hudibras exhibits hypocritical sensuality. He breaks oaths; he pretends to love a widow when he is attracted only to her money. The second canto of part 3 of *Hudibras* is an extended attack on the last Puritan Parliament.

B.'s targets, are not limited, however, to one sect or period. Hudibras is a figure of fun not only because he is "*Clerick* before, and *Lay* behind." He also exemplifies the misuse of learning. "[H]e by Geometrick scale/Could take the size of Pots of Ale;/Resolve by Sines and Tangents straight,/If Bread or Butter wanted weight." Among the recurring targets of B.'s criticism was the Royal Society, primarily because B. saw no practical application of their intellectual pursuits. In part 2 of *Hudibras*, the learned astronomer/astrologer Sidrophel, modeled in part on Sir Paul Neile, one of the founders of the Royal Society, mistakes a paper lantern at the end of a kite for the planet Saturn. In "The Elephant in the Moon" (1759), written in the early 1670s, a group of astronomers think that a mouse that has gotten into a telescope is a lunar pachyderm. Like Hudibras they have managed "t'incumber *Gifts* and wit,/And render both for nothing fit."

In his prose "Characters" and in his poetry, B. attacked absurdity of any kind. He maintained that "The Generall Temper of Mankind is nothing but a Mixture of Cheat and Folly." Royalists were as prone to such behavior as Puritans and so equally subject to mockery. After the Restoration in 1660, B. wrote, though he did not publish, a "Satyr upon the Licentious Age of Charles the 2nd" (1759). In his character "A Duke of Bucks," B. attacked his sometime employer George Villiers, second Duke of BUCKINGHAM. Catholics and Quakers, poets and critics, lawyers and lampooners all exercised what Johnson called B.'s "inexhaustible wit."

B. paints their follies in farfetched similes that recall metaphysical poetry, Thus, he demonstrates how an Anabaptist resembles a crocodile, a goose, and hot iron. B. loved pretentious words such as "cynarctomachy" for bear-baiting, and he drew allusions from that store of abstruse knowledge that he satirized. Unlike Hudibras or the pedant of B.'s character sketch, though, B. was applying his extensive reading to ethical ends. In bright, indeed garish, colors B. painted a world turned upside down by both Puritans and royalists. At the end of his life, B. received a pension and occasional other monetary gifts from Charles II. Yet B. remained a party of one, presenting a dark view of humanity in some of the most hilarious verses ever penned in English.

BIBLIOGRAPHY: Gibson, D., Jr., "S. B.," in Shafer, R., ed., *Seventeenth Century Studies* (1933), vol. 1: 277–

335; Veldkamp, J., *S. B.* (1923); Wasserman, G. R., *S. "Hudibras" B.* (1976; rev. ed., 1989)

JOSEPH ROSENBLUM

BUTLER, Samuel

b. 4 December 1835, Bingham, Nottinghamshire; d. 18 June 1902, London

B.'s literary reputation depends on a small number of books, but in truth he was a prolific author with an extraordinary diversity of interests and ambitions. Not that his ambitions or interests were confined to literature (however broadly defined); at various times, he was a successful sheep-breeder in New Zealand and a less successful painter and composer in London. Grandson of Bishop Samuel Butler and reared by a very stern father, B. was educated at Shrewsbury School and St. John's College, Cambridge. Product of the religious establishment, and intended for holy orders by his father, B. rebelled and later became a critic of religious belief in a series of works in various forms.

In 1865, he published *The Evidence for the Resurrection of Jesus Christ*, offering an ironic analysis of the Gospel narratives. In 1873 appeared *The Fair Haven*, in which the earlier pamphlet was incorporated as, allegedly, the work of a certain John Pickard Owen, recently dead. It is a subtle satire on the techniques of religious commentary, ironically pretending to be a work "in Defense of the Miraculous Element in Our Lord's Ministry upon Earth (both as against Rationalistic Impugners and Certain Orthodox Defenders)." In a life of the supposed author (itself written under the name William Bickersteth Owen), there are some of the seeds of B.'s greatest book, *The Way of All Flesh* (1903). In its control of tone the work is masterly and the irony of its arguments went unnoticed by some. Some of the same targets were attacked in *Erewhon* (1872; rev. eds., 1872, 1901) along with much else. Though somewhat disjointed (in part because of its genesis as a series of articles), *Erewhon* offers much to amuse and stimulate in its quietly satiric account of what B. took to be the complacencies and hypocrisies of contemporary society, with its worship of the goddess Ydgrun (i.e., Mrs. Grundy or respectability) and its Musical Banks, in which B. satirizes smug religiosity. In *Erewhon Revisited* (1901), there is more of B.'s subtle irony about the leading ideas of church and state and a slightly richer vision of human personality than in the earlier book.

Much struck by his reading of Charles DARWIN's *The Origin of Species*, B. published a series of volumes on his own biological theories; these included *Life and Habit* (1877), *Evolution, Old and New* (1879; rev. eds., 1882, 1911), *Unconscious Memory* (1880), and *Luck or Cunning?* (1886). The subject is also extensively touched upon in *God the Known and God the Unknown* (published as periodical articles in 1879 and in book form in 1909) as well as in the posthumously published *Note-Books* (1912). B.'s thinking gradually diverged from Darwin's, B. finding more intention than Darwin did in the processes of evolution, arguing for the role of "cunning" and "unconscious memory." B.'s ideas about unconscious racial memory seem to anticipate some more modern ideas about the unconscious. In the 1880s, he published two travel books, *Alps and Sanctuaries of Piedmont and the Canton Ticino* (1881) and *Ex-Voto* (1888), often very attractive in their accounts of Italian scenes and enlivened by B.'s characteristic wit. B.'s intellectual fertility, coupled one suspects with a conscious perversity that took pleasure in putting startling ideas before the public, led to publications on Homer and William SHAKESPEARE. In *The Authoress of the "Odyssey"* (1897), he argued that the Odyssey was written by a woman and proposed that the voyage of Ulysses was really the account of a circumnavigation of Sicily. B. also published lively translations, in unpretentious prose, of the *Iliad* (1898) and the *Odyssey* (1900). In 1899, B. published his *Shakespeare's Sonnets Reconsidered and in Part Rearranged*, arguing that "Mr. W. H." was a man of low social standing. One need not agree with B.'s conclusions about Homer and Shakespeare to be able to enjoy the liveliness of his manner and the value of his incidental insights.

B.'s greatest single work, *The Way of All Flesh*, was published posthumously in 1903, but was written between 1873 and 1885. The novel is essentially autobiographical, its source B.'s own mistreatment at the hands of his parents and his rebellion against this. B. himself is "represented" by two characters, the narrator Edward Overton and the "hero" Ernest Pontifex. B.'s father appears as the Reverend Theobald Pontifex, the object of furious contempt in the novel, for his egotism and moral confusions, his arrogance, and his pomposity of phrase—and much else. Christina, the wife of Theobald Pontifex, is based on B.'s mother. There are places in the novel where actual documents from the family life are incorporated; but there are also events that are entirely imaginary. Out of his own bitterness, B. constructed a novel that is not merely a matter of personal spleen. The characterization is in many respects astute and perceptive, and there is fascinating detail of daily life as well as penetrating analysis of the dynamics of a particular kind of family life. The texture of the novel is also permeated by B.'s sense that these very dynamics are the product of a kind of biological necessity, of energies larger than the individuals through which they operate. Though no work of B.'s could be entirely without irony and wit, *The Way of All Flesh* is at heart a sad book, for all that it traces the successful "escape" of Ernest Pontifex. The novel invites reading on several levels; as AUTOBIOGRAPHY; as a quasi-historical ac-

147

count of a particular period of transition in English society; as a kind of exemplary treatise in B.'s ideas on evolution. Indeed, it brings together, more completely than any other of his works, many of its author's diverse intellectual and emotional interests, making it in many ways both the key to an understanding of B. and an important work in the history of the English novel.

BIBLIOGRAPHY: Furbank, P. N., *S. B., 1835–1902* (1948); Holt, L. E., *S. B.* (1964; rev. ed., 1989); Jeffers, T. L., *S. B. Revalued* (1981); Raby, P., *S. B.* (1991)

GLYN PURSGLOVE

BYATT, [Dame] A[ntonia] S[usan]

b. 24 August 1936, Sheffield

Educated at Newnham College, Cambridge, Bryn Mawr College, and Somerville College, Oxford, B. wrote the first draft of her novel, *Shadow of the Sun* (1964; repub. as *The Shadow of a Sun*, 1993) while still an undergraduate. A critical study of Iris MURDOCH, an author B. greatly admires, entitled *Degrees of Freedom: The Novels of Iris Murdoch* (1965), was followed in 1967 by her second novel, *The Game*. In the 1970s, B. embarked on an ambitious sequence of four novels: *The Virgin in the Garden* (1978), *Still Life* (1985), *Babel Tower* (1996), and *A Whistling Woman* (2002). That the tetralogy had been carefully planned is shown by the prologue to *The Virgin in the Garden,* in which three of the main characters, Frederica Potter, Alexander Wedderburn, and Daniel Orton meet in the National Portrait Gallery in 1968, fifteen years after the events that the novel chronicles. The presence of Orton in London and Frederica's kissing a blond man mean that B. had already thought of key developments in *Still Life* and *Babel Tower.*

The Virgin in the Garden centers around the performance of Wedderburn's verse play, *Astraea,* in a north Yorkshire country house in the summer of 1953. The cast of characters is rather large, most of them highly literate and articulate, and the narrative weaves into its fabric lines and images from Edmund SPENSER, William SHAKESPEARE, John MILTON, William WORDSWORTH, and John KEATS, and alludes as well to two novelists B. particularly admires, George ELIOT and Marcel Proust. Alexander's verse play on ELIZABETH I, performed in the year of the coronation of Elizabeth II, radiates metaphorical and cultural connections. The central images in the play (blood and stone, flesh and grass, the red and the white rose) reverberate in the narrative, and when some characters watch the coronation ceremony on television, the perspective encompasses the event as it was experienced in 1953, and as it would look in later years.

The wealth of literary allusion in the novel does not mean that B. neglects the representation of things. In an article on English postwar fiction published in 1979, she spoke of the need the novelist had of "more primitive gifts of curiosity and greed, about things other than literature." In *The Virgin in the Garden*, she shows a precise eye for period details in the description of architecture, interiors, clothes, food, bodies, gardens, the northern landscape, a butcher's shop window. The main characters have strong connections to literature: Wedderburn is a teacher and playwright, Stephanie Potter read English at Cambridge, her sister Frederica is about to do the same, their father Bill Potter is a teacher of English with strong Leavisite views on the moral and communal value of literature. But two central characters are nonliterary: Orton, the curate who marries Stephanie, and Marcus Potter, Stephanie and Frederica's younger brother. The portrait of Orton is a rare triumph in modern fiction, a good man with Christian convictions. The story of Marcus's psychological and emotional difficulties and his entanglement with his deranged biology teacher probably means more to the author than to the reader, although Marcus's mental state will play a crucial role in the plot of the second novel in the sequence.

In the overall design of the tetralogy, B. had meant the second and third novels to be experimental, and the first and fourth more traditional. When she began writing *Still Life*, she had the idea that it would be a novel of "naming and accuracy," and she even tried to write without figures of speech, but had to give up. *Still Life* continues the story of the Potter sisters and Wedderburn and expands its location from Yorkshire, where Stephanie, Daniel, and their family go on living, to London, Cambridge, and southern France. If the spatial image in the title of *The Virgin in the Garden* gives way to the painterly image in *Still Life,* the focus on history explicit in Alexander's play about Elizabeth I is replaced by issues of representation in literature and painting. Alexander, who now works in London in the cultural programs of the BBC, is writing a play on Vincent Van Gogh, and the novel incorporates several extracts from the painter's correspondence with his brother. Both Frederica and Alexander spend a summer separately in Provence, and the description of the landscapes painted by Van Gogh and of the food of the region display B.'s sensuous perception of shapes, textures, and colors. B. has made use in her fiction of pictures by Samuel Palmer, Van Gogh, Henri Matisse, and Velázquez, sees in painting the opposite of literature, and is attracted by that element in the visual that completely defeats language.

Alexander's struggle with the writing of *The Yellow Chair* and Frederica's relationship at Cambridge with Raphael Faber, a brilliant teacher and poet of Central European origin, foreground issues of representation in art. Faber disdains the English traditional novel and believes that the presentation of characters, social backgrounds, and the physical life is no longer relevant in fiction. But for all her involvement with new theories of language, developments in science (especially genetics), and intertextuality, B. does not neglect the depiction of everyday life. The greatest achievement in this respect in *Still Life* is the presentation of Stephanie and Daniel Orton's married life, the birth of their two children, and Stephanie's awareness that, despite her happiness, she is losing the intellectual vocabulary that had once been part of her life first as a brilliant undergraduate at Cambridge and then as a teacher of literature.

Stephanie's death in a domestic accident and Orton's bereavement, presented with accuracy and a total lack of sentimentality, are among the most moving episodes in contemporary fiction. The chapter in which she dies ends with the bird that had provoked the fatal accident flying unobserved out of the house. This becomes more poignant if the reader remembers that the central epigraph to the novel is the well-known passage in BEDE in which human life is compared to the fleeting flight of a sparrow through a hall. It is difficult not to relate the sudden deaths in B.'s fiction, for the most part of young people, to her own loss of her eleven-year-old son in 1972.

The knowledge that life can be tragic is present through Mrs. Thone, who has lost her only son in a playground accident in *The Virgin in the Garden,* the young man who falls off the Apennines in "Precipice-Encurled" (in *Sugar and Other Stories,* 1987), the young girl and then her mother who commit suicide in "The Chinese Lobster" (in *The Matisse Stories,* 1993), and through the unnamed young man who is doomed to die of cancer in *The Biographer's Tale* (2000).

B. sees *Babel Tower* as an historical novel. The story covers the early years of the first Harold Wilson government, and B.'s antennae register the beginning of the changes in sexual mores, fashion, theories of language, and biological research that were to mark the 1960s. The intertextual connections are extremely complex and range from the echoes of Doris LESSING's experiments with fragmented narrative in *The Golden Notebook* to be found in Frederica's *Laminations,* to the influence of J. R. R. TOLKIEN and the Marquis de Sade both on some episodes of the main story, and on the embedded dystopian narrative *Babbletower.* The main characters are again Frederica (now seeking divorce and the custody of her son Leo), Alexander (whose membership of a committee looking into new and traditional ways of teaching English channels B.'s interest in developments in linguistics), and Orton (who has moved to London after Stephanie's death). Images of towers proliferate, and both titles, *Babel Tower* and *Babbletower,* allude to the issue that lies at the heart of this ambitious work: the gap between experience and the language we use to represent it.

In 1990, B. published *Possession: A Romance,* which won the Booker Prize for fiction and other awards and sold very well for a highly literary novel. The success of *Possession* has probably to do with the detective novel structure in which two contemporary scholars try to find out what happened between the fictional Victorian poets Ralph Henry Ash and Christabel LaMotte. *Possession* tells a fascinating story, and its salient technical feature is the interpolation of various poems written by Ash and LaMotte and of tales written by LaMotte. In this stylistic tour de force, B. has managed to create two distinctive poetic voices that show the influence of Robert BROWNING (Ash's) and Emily Dickinson (LaMotte's). B. displays in *Possession*—as in the two novellas that make up *Angels and Insects* (1992) and deal with two aspects of the Victorian age also present in *Possession*: Darwinism and spiritualism—her deep knowledge of Victorian culture, and the novel balances scholarship, technical virtuosity, and loving descriptions of color, texture, food, and the north Yorkshire landscape, with an absorbing plot and characters possessed by intellectual and sexual passion. B. deploys a variety of narrative forms: letters, diaries, biographical and critical accounts of the two Victorian poets, and of course the poems and FAIRY TALES they have written. She also uses a third-person narrator who, in the moving postscript and on other occasions, gives the reader information that the author has withheld from the scholars.

B.'s achievement as a novelist lies in the tetralogy and in *Possession.* She has also published several collections of short stories which range from the mostly realistic *Sugar and Other Stories,* whose title story gives an account of B.'s family background and of her father's death, to the highly original *The Matisse Stories,* her most direct engagement with the contemporary politics of gender, and the fairy stories in *The Djinn in the Nightingale's Eye* (1994). "Christ in the House of Martha and Mary," the brief last story in her collection *Elementals: Stories of Fire and Ice* (1998) sums up B.'s central concern with representation in literature and painting. When she has Velázquez, then a young painter in Seville, say that the real divide is between "those who are interested in the world and its mutiplicity of forms and forces, and those who merely subsist," she might be thinking of her own delight in words, ideas, color, and the power and pleasure of narrative.

BIBLIOGRAPHY: Alfer, A., and M. J. Noble, eds., *Essays on the Fiction of A. S. B.* (2001); Campbell. J., "The Hunger of the Imagination in A. S. B.'s *The Game,*" *Critique* 29 (Spring 1988): 147–62; Dusinberre, J., "Forms of Reality in A. S. B.'s *The Virgin in the Garden,*" *Critique* 24 (Fall 1982): 55–62; Hope,

C., *Contemporary Writers: A. S. B.* (1990); Kelly, K. C., *A. S. B.* (1996)

PILAR HIDALGO

BYRON, George Gordon [Noel, Sixth Baron Byron of Rochdale, or Lord Byron]

b. 22 January 1788, London; d. 19 April 1824, Missolonghi, Greece

As a poet and failed man of action, B.'s influence on European literature was more profound that that of any other English writer, except Sir Walter SCOTT, his friend. Those who benefited from studying him include Scott, Pushkin, Lermontov, Heine, Stendhal, and Espronceda. Only the most astute readers—first among them these six—recognized the supremacy of the facetious and far-reaching *Don Juan,* published in sixteen cantos from 1819 to 1824. The English literary establishment found little in him to admire, but *Don Juan*, once B. had left John Murray and moved to the radical downmarket publisher John Hunt, found him an audience. B.'s success in ottiva rima enabled him to speak in verse as fluently and wittily as he did in his letters. There were many sides of B. for the world to admire, vilify, model itself on, or persecute: poseur, traveler, lover, solemn poet, comic poet, revolutionary, conservative, blasphemer, admirer of Roman Catholicism, socialite, recluse, firebrand, stoic. After Napoleon, whom he admired, B. was the most famous man of his time.

B. was born with a deformity of the right calf and heel, which caused him to limp and necessitated a surgical boot, but he was a person of great beauty and charisma, much loved by both men and women. His wastrel father died soon after B.'s birth. B. was educated at Aberdeen Grammar School, where Calvinist religious instruction influenced him deeply. In 1798, B.'s uncle died and B. became a lord. In 1801, he entered Harrow and in 1805 Trinity College, Cambridge. During a vacation in 1806, he planned, for private circulation, his first book, *Fugitive Pieces*, but he considered it compromising because of the insight it gave into his love-life, so he had it destroyed (four copies survive) and replaced it with the more discreet *Poems on Various Occasions* (1807). Its success encouraged him to bring out in the same year a public volume derived from it, *Hours of Idleness,* with a second edition called *Poems Original and Translated* (1808). An offensive review of *Hours of Idleness* in the *Edinburgh Review* triggered B.'s first major work, *English Bards and Scotch Reviewers* (1809), a conservative satire in heroic couplets.

At Harrow and Cambridge, B. ran up mountainous debts and made many friends, chief among them John Cam Hobhouse. In 1809, B. and Hobhouse embarked on a Continental tour. Unable to see much of Europe because of the Napoleonic Wars, they went to Portu-

gal, Spain, Gibraltar, Sardinia, and Malta, where B. and Hobhouse were persuaded by British naval intelligence to go to the little-known country of Albania and visit the Vizir, a bisexual mass murderer called Ali Pasha, who coveted the Ionian islands. Meanwhile, the British captured the islands from the French: B.'s visit had been used as a sweetener.

In Albania, B. started *Childe Harold's Pilgrimage*, a travelogue in Spenserian stanzas based on his experience. Albania and Greece were both Turkish provinces at the time, and in Greece B. and Hobhouse were surprised to find the Turks unpopular. In Constantinople, they attended an audience with Sultan Mahmoud II. In June 1810, Hobhouse left for England and B. settled in Greece. Lord Elgin was removing the Parthenon marbles and B. wrote a disapproving poem, "The Curse of Minerva."

In 1811, B. returned to England where the first two cantos of *Childe Harold* were published in the following year, bringing instant fame. B. followed it with verse tales, using various meters, set mostly in the East: *The Giaour* (1813), *The Bride of Abydos* (1813), *The Corsair* (1814), *Lara* (1814), *The Siege of Cornith* and *Parisina*, published together in 1816. These increased his reputation by depicting exotic passion and allowing the female reader to fantasize about guilt-ridden heroes who might yet be saved by a woman's love. B. spoke three times in the House of Lords, his most celebrated speech being against the proposed death penalty for the Nottingham frame-breakers, but he rapidly became disillusioned with British politics. He also sat on the committee of the Drury Lane Theatre, which may have stimulated his ambition to be a playwright.

In 1815, B. married Annabella Milbanke, a serious error on both sides. B. was promiscuous, bisexual, and had committed incest with his half-sister; Annabella imagined she could redeem him. After thirteen months, the couple separated and public opinion turned against B. He left for Europe in 1816, never to return. He took his valet and John William Polidori, author of *The Vampyre* (1819). Riding in a customized replica of Napoleon's carriage, and taking in the field of Waterloo, about which he wrote in the third canto of *Childe Harold* (1816), B. journeyed down the Rhine to Switzerland, were he was joined by Percy Bysshe SHELLEY, Mary Godwin [SHELLEY], and Claire Clairmont. It was here that a ghost-storytelling competition led to Mary's writing *Frankenstein*. Hobhouse and B. went on an Alpine tour, which gave B. much inspiration for his most influential work, the verse-play *Manfred* (1817). By its vivid depiction of man's power to damn himself unassisted, *Manfred* established B. as the most exciting writer in Europe. His reputation had been spreading rapidly, assisted by French translations, now the Napoleonic wars were over. In Switzerland, B. wrote other fine poems, including *The Prisoner of Chillon* (1816), "The Dream," and "Darkness," an eerily accurate prediction of nuclear winter.

B. and Hobhouse went to Italy, then largely under Austrian occupation. After meeting several leading writers in Milan, they went to Venice, where B. stayed five years. Here, he found a morality different from England's and enjoyed many liaisons. He visited Florence and Rome and studied Armenian with Catholic monks. He wrote *Mazeppa* (1819), the fourth canto of *Childe Harold* (1818), and, after reading an English poem called "Whistlecraft," found a new poetic voice in the Italian measure ottava rima (six alternating rhymes concluded with an anticlimactic couplet) in *Beppo* (1818), his first satiric poem for years. B. roughed it out over two nights in 1817, rapidly mastering the form and amusingly inverting some of the themes of his earlier Eastern tales. Encouraged by its success, in 1818 he started work on the first two cantos of his great revisionist masterpiece *Don Juan*, unfinished at his death. In the poem, men are not predators on women: women are predators on men. The protagonist, instead of determinedly scouring the Mediterranean in search of his lost home like Odysseus, wanders aimlessly about Europe. As with *Beppo*, much of the enjoyment comes from B.'s digressions.

B.'s relationship with his publisher John Murray began to deteriorate: Murray was only willing to publish *Don Juan* without B.'s name on it and after the fifth canto refused to publish it at all. In November 1818, B. cleared his debts by selling his ancestral home, Newstead Abbey. One-third of his income from then on was regularly distributed among the poor. When his lawyer came to Venice with papers to be signed, B. first heard that Robert SOUTHEY, the poet laureate, had spread scandal about B. and the Shelley household. B. made his first attempt at drama along classical lines, the Venetian tragedy *Marino Faliero* (1821).

In 1819, B. met the young Countess Teresa Guiccioli and fell deeply in love. To be with her, he moved to Ravenna. Her husband was now complaisant, now ferocious, but could do nothing. Teresa's father and brother were both members of the Carbonari, a quasi-masonic organization dedicated to ridding Italy of the Austrians and to purifying the country's morals. B. was initiated, became a Capo, kept the group's records, and allowed Guiccioli's house to be used as an arsenal. The dreams of the Carbonari were shattered when a Neapolitan insurgent army fled from the Austrians on the plain of Rieti on March 1821 without firing a shot, and this was the start of B.'s disillusion with Italian politics. He was now identified as a revolutionary by both the Papal and Austrian police, who were, however, afraid to arrest him because of his na-

tionality, rank, and fame. Instead, they persecuted Teresa's father and brother, driving them from state to state, and to be near them and Teresa (separated now from her husband), B. moved to Pisa in 1821 then to Genoa in 1822. In that same year, B.'s life was darkened by the death of his illegitimate daughter Allegra and the drowning of Shelley.

While continuing with *Don Juan,* in 1821 B. wrote his finest completed poem, *The Vision of Judgement,* a depiction in ottava rima of the difficulties King George III has in trying to get into heaven, B.'s *Vision* is a travesty of Southey's turgid and offensive poem by the same title, in which George has no difficulty gaining entry. B.'s poem was partly in response to scurrilous rumours Southey had spread: Southey was B.'s worst enemy.

B. also wrote the classical plays *Sardanapalus* and *The Two Foscari,* published together in 1821 with the controversial biblical drama *Cain,* which with its alleged blasphemy and Manicheism brought him into further disrepute in England. Later, he added another play, *Werner* (1823), a political satire, *The Age of-Bronze* (1823), and a Polynesian romance, *The Island* (1823), based on the mutiny on the *Bounty*.

In 1823, tired of Italy and of Teresa, B. went to Greece, where the so-called war of independence against Turkey had started, with horrifying massacres on both sides. Staying on the British-occupied Ionian islands, he tried to work out which Greek faction to support. In January 1824, he landed at Missolonghi, hoping to see some action, but saw none. His misery was increased by the dissension and greed he found among the Greeks, and by his unrequited love for a Greek youth. Missolonghi was mosquito-ridden and early in April B. went for an ill-advised ride in the rain. He collapsed on his return. B. always loved animals and kept various pets: his death was probably caused by Mediterranean tick-fever, spread by dogs. His attendants had, according to the medical practice of the time, extracted forty-two per cent of B.'s blood, weakening him.

On hearing of B.'s death, Sir Walter Scott wrote that it was as if the sun had gone out, just as all the world's telescopes were levelled at it to examine the flaws on its surface. B.'s death, seemingly a martyrdom for liberty, sealed his reputation as a hero both in word and deed, and made him into an icon for the rest of the century.

BIBLIOGRAPHY: Barton, A., *B., "Don Juan"* (1992); Beatty, B., *B.'s "Don Juan"* (1985); Franklin, C., *B.'s Heroines* (1992); Graham, P. W., *Lord B.* (1998); Kelsall, M., *B.'s Politics* (1987); MacCarthy, F., *B.* (2002); Marchand, L. A., *B.: A Portrait* (1970); Minta, S., *On a Voiceless Shore: B. in Greece* (1997)

PETER COCHRAN

C

CÆDMON
fl. 658–80

C. is widely regarded as the first English poet, and "Cædmon's Hymn" or the "Hymn of Creation" is the earliest surviving example of Anglo-Saxon vernacular verse. Most of what is known of C. comes from the religious historian BEDE, in his *Historia Ecclesiastica Gentis Anglorum*. Bede recounts that C., an illiterate farmhand for the Northumbrian monastery of Streoneshealh (later Whitby), did not like to participate in the singing and harp playing that took place during festive occasions, and would always flee when he saw the harp being passed his way. After one such episode, C. fell asleep in a barn and was visited by a heavenly figure who commanded him to sing. When C. protested, the figure again ordered him to sing, and also provided him with a topic: "the beginning of things." Miraculously, C. began to sing verses in praise of God that he had not previously known. When C.'s ability came to the attention of Abbess Hild, he was taken into the monastery, instructed in the Scriptures, and over time produced vernacular songs for the monks on a whole range of Old and New Testament subjects, including the accounts of Genesis and Exodus, the Passion and Resurrection of Christ, the teachings of the Apostles, and eschatological events. Though the date of C.'s death is unknown, Bede records that the poet appears to have had divine foreknowledge of his end and died esteemed and revered by his monastic community.

Though Bede only provides a Latin paraphrase of the original poem C. sang for his heavenly visitor, many manuscripts of his *Historia* contain OLD ENGLISH versions of the hymn as marginalia or later additions—in all, seventeen manuscript versions of "Cædmon's Hymn" survive in a range of Anglo-Saxon dialects. The nine-line poem is also the only work that can be surely identified with C., and so allows a translation of the poet's entire known oeuvre in an encyclopedia entry: "Now shall we praise heaven's Guardian,/the Maker's might and his mindful thoughts,/the Father's wondrous work, when He of all wonders,/eternal Lord, the origin established./He first shaped for the sons of man/heaven as a roof, the holy Shaper;/then the middle-earth mankind's Guard,/eternal Lord, afterwards arranged,/the earth for men, almighty Master." In its original language, the song employs elements common to the Anglo-Saxon poetry: oral-formulaic components, alliterative verse (somewhat preserved here), half line meter, and an appositive, metaphorical style that economically fits eight descriptions of God into nine lines. Structurally, the poem first praises the Creator and His creation, and then embeds an architectural metaphor that works from the top down: roof (heaven), enclosed space (earth), inhabitants (human race), neatly encapsulating both the vertical hierarchy of divine order and the fall of man. The poem also loosely paraphrases the opening lines of the book of Genesis; fittingly, what is now known as the beginning of English poetry takes as its subject the divine beginning of all things.

In early scholarship, commentators attempted to attribute to C. other Anglo-Saxon poems with Christian content, especially the Old English adaptations of Old Testament books found in the Junius Manuscript, dating from the 10th or 11th c. Later paleographic and linguistic studies, however, have thrown a doubtful light on all such efforts. Instead, such works now are typically considered to be part of a subsequent "Cædmonian School." For "Cædmon's Hymn" and Bede's report of its composition, critics have traditionally focused on the early adaptation of the vernacular of a pagan culture for the purposes of Christian conversion and enculturation. C.'s miracle occurred only sixty or so years after St. Augustine's mission first landed in England (597), and conveniently situates the figure of unlettered farmhand *qua* monastic poet as a vernacular mouthpiece of Christianity near the beginning of a two-hundred-year-long process of conversion.

More recently, studies of C. and "Cædmon's Hymn" have explored the oral and literary aspects of the poem, itself a verbal text that only survives in written form, and its transmission and alteration through scribal practices and the evolution of literacy. In a postmodern approach, consideration has been given to the roles textual authority and the conversionary containment of resistance play in the production, reception, and dissemination of the earliest of English poems.

BIBLIOGRAPHY: Cafiero, J. L., "Cædmon and the Cædmon School," in Helterman, J., and J. Mitchell, eds., *Old and Middle English Literature, DLB* 146 (1994): 44–50; Frantzen, A. J., *Desire for Origins* (1990): 130–67; O'Keefe, K. O., *Visible Song: Transitional Literacy in Old English Verse* (1990)

MARTIN K. FOYS

CAMPBELL [LONG], Margaret Gabrielle Vere

(pseuds.: Marjorie Bowen, Joseph Shearing, George Preedy, Robert Paye, John Winch) b. 1 November 1885, Hayling Island, Hampshire; d. 23 December 1952, Kensington

Proclaimed by Hugh Walpole as the most important historical novelist of her generation, befriended and encouraged by Mark Twain, lauded by Edward Wagenknecht for her supernatural fiction, and credited by Graham GREENE with inspiring his writing career after he read her first novel when he was fourteen, C. was a prolific popular writer responsible for at least 150 books written under various pseudonyms and for numerous contributions to British and American periodicals.

Her candid *The Debate Continues: Being the Autobiography of Marjorie Bowen* (1939), written under her birth name, Margaret Campbell, delineates a horrific early life of poverty and emotional abuse that led her to withdraw to a life of the mind and turn to writing as consolation and ultimately a means of financial support. Her parents had separated when she was four. The bohemian lifestyle of her mother and sister repulsed her. Food was often scarce, and the family moved frequently to avoid paying bills. Not sent to school but taught to read and write at home, C. took advantage of libraries near her varied residences. She taught herself French, Italian, and some Latin, and developed her artistic abilities. A brief period of employment as a research assistant at the British Museum intensified her interest in historical research. As a teenager, she produced her first novel, *The Viper of Milan* (1906), which she convinced her mother to turn over to an agent. The novel's immediate success initiated a writing career that enabled her to support her family, but it also exacerbated problems in the mother-daughter relationship since her mother had vainly aspired to literary fame.

In 1912, C. married Zefferino Emilio Costanzo as an escape from life with her mother and sister. Tranquility, however, eluded her as she experienced numerous financial and emotional difficulties, including the death of her first child. She was also forced to leave her second child, a son, in England while she went to Italy to nurse her tubercular husband. Through her husband's extended illness, she continued writing to support her dependants. After his death in 1916, she returned to England to care for her son and support her mother and sister. In 1917, she married Arthur Long. They had two sons, and in this relationship she seems to have achieved the domestic stability she longed for.

Under her many pen names, C. wrote in a wide range of genres. She produced much historical fiction—a Renaissance trilogy, for example: *The Golden Roof* (1928), *Trumpets at Rome* (1936), and *The Triumphant Beast* (1937). She is known as a master of supernatural fiction with such works as *Black Magic* (1909) and *The Haunted Vintage* (1921). Under the name Joseph Shearing, she is famous for reconstructions of 19th-c. crime: the 1847 murder of the Duchesse de Praslin in *Forget-Me-Not* (1932), the 1889 Maybrick poisoning in *Airing in a Closed Carriage* (1943), and the 1876 Bravo case in *For Her to See* (1947). She also wrote novels with contemporary settings, biographies like *The Shining Woman* (1937), a life of Mary WOLLSTONECRAFT, other nonfiction (*Ethics in Modern Art,* 1939), drama often written under the name George Preedy, and CHILDREN'S LITERATURE.

C.'s output was overwhelming. In 1939, she produced three books as Bowen, three as Preedy, and an autobiography under her birth name; in 1940, she was responsible for six more books under three pseudonyms. In addition, to the Bowen, Shearing, Preedy, Paye, and John Winch pseudonyms, she may have written under the names of Evelyn Winch, Edgar Winch, W. M. Winch, and Bertha Winch. These, however, have not been confirmed. In spite of the volume of her material, she was a disciplined and professional writer. Her historical research has been commended for its painstaking detail and accuracy, especially in matters of setting and dress. A superb and fast-paced storyteller, C. emphasizes the influence of the past on the present and often focuses on women's position in society, especially women with limited options.

BIBLIOGRAPHY: DeMarr, M. J., "Joseph Shearing," in Benstock, B., ed., *British Mystery Writers, 1860–1919, DLB* 70 (1988): 269–76; Ferreira, M. A. S., "Marjorie Bowen," in Johnson, G. M., ed., *Late-Victorian and Edwardian British Novelists*, First Series, *DLB* 153 (1995): 39–50; Wagenknecht, E., "Bowen, Preedy, Shearing & Co.: A Note in Memory and a Checklist," *BUSE* 3 (1957): 181–89

FRANCES M. MALPEZZI

CAMPBELL, [Ignatius] Roy[ston Dunnachie]

b. 2 October 1901, Durban, Natal, South Africa; d. 23 April 1957, near Setúbal, Portugal

C.'s culture was cosmopolitan and he translated *Poems of St John of the Cross* (1951) and Charles Baudelaire's *Les Fleurs du mal* (1952), with a critical translation of Federico García Lorca in 1952. Aged twenty-three, he published *The Flaming Terrapin* (1924), a 1,400-line rhymed poem about the energies of nature. C. collaborated with Laurens van der Post and William Plomer on a radical magazine, *Voorslag* (1926–27; Whiplash), and wrote verse criticizing the provincialism of his native country, published as *The Wayzgoose* (1928). *The Georgiad* (1931) made him hated by literary London because it attacked current literature as exhausted. A much-anthologized epigram goes: "They praise the firm restraint with which you write./I'm with you there, of course:/You use the snaffle and the curb all right,/But where's the bloody horse?" In 1934, he published a first volume of autobiography, *Broken Record.* In the following year, he became a Roman Catholic and fought on the fascist side in Spain. Other collections of verse include *Flowering Reeds* (1933) and *Mithraic Emblems* (1936). *Flowering Rifle* (1939) still supported Franco, but C. later changed sides. He fought in Africa in World War II. *Talking Bronco* (1946) included war themes. His *Collected Poems* appeared in three volumes (1949–60). A second volume of autobiography, *Light on a Dark Horse* (1951), made him further enemies. He died in a car accident while driving to Spain from his home in Portugal.

CAMPBELL, Thomas

b. 25 July 1777, Glasgow, Scotland; d. 15 June 1844, Boulogne, France

C. was born and educated in Glasgow where he learned Greek and adopted liberal political opinions and a respect for the principles of English prosody. Although for a while he considered entering the church, he turned instead to teaching, the law, and finally literature. At the age of twenty-one, he achieved prominence by the publication of *The Pleasures of Hope* (1799), a discursive poem based on the models of Mark AKENSIDE and Samuel ROGERS that was instantly popular, owing both to its matter and its style. The brilliance of individual passages beguiled readers into overlooking its obvious structural defects. There is little or no narrative sequence and the treatment of his subject is largely literary and generalized. He draws on a broad range of literary and historical allusions, on John Byron's *Narrative* (1768), on William Falconer's *The Shipwreck* (1762; rev. ed., 1764), on Friedrich Schiller and Samuel JOHNSON. Nonetheless, the poem is charged with direct and emphatic interest and is both thoughtful and persuasive; the attractive touches of description come straight from the writer's own experience even though his experience was limited.

Throughout the poem, C. manages to maintain the resonant metrical neatness expected in the traditional heroic couplet. The striking passage on Poland marks the beginning of an enthusiasm that remained with him throughout his life. His enthusiasm for science, philosophy, and poetry, his discussion of poverty and childhood lead him to hopes of progress in uncivilized countries, attacks on the English in India and on the slave trade in addition to the subjection of the Poles. He touches on a wide variety of subjects without ever going too deeply into any of them. Consequently, the poem gives an interesting if disjointed survey of topics that give rise to hopes and disappointments though it draws what little unity it has from its style rather than from any deeply felt convictions on the part of the poet. He never again wrote with such distinction or achieved such popularity though as a poet he was ranked in his lifetime alongside Sir Walter SCOTT. A number of lines from the poem passed into language and were quoted without reference to their source: "What millions died—that Caesar might be great!"; "What though my winged hours of bliss have been, / Like angel-visits, few and far between?"—which William HAZLITT said was the best line in the poem though borrowed from Robert BLAIR's poem, *The Grave.*

In 1809, C. published *Gertrude of Wyoming*, a narrative poem describing the events surrounding the destruction in 1778 of Wyoming, a settlement in Pennsylvania, by Indians under the leadership of a Mohawk named Brandt that led to the death of Gertrude, newly married to Henry Waldegrave, and her father. Written in Spenserian stanzas, the poem was immensely popular despite the fact that although he clearly comprehends and well represents the characters and events he does so from a distance without seeming to commit himself to them. The poem lacks that bond between writer and subject without which the narrative, however interesting, lacks substance and the means to move the reader to enter into the action and lives of the characters. Despite the poem's shortcomings, its gentle pathos, its exotic narrative, and its stylistic elegance ensured its popularity. C. is now best remembered for his patriotic lyrics, particularly "Ye Mariners of England," written to the tune of "Ye Gentlemen of England," a song that he was fond of singing, "Hohenlinden," "The Irish Harper," and "The Battle of the Baltic." His strange poem "The Last Man" invites comparison with Thomas HOOD's grotesque poem of the same title.

Under C.'s editorship begun in 1821, the *New Monthly Magazine* became a powerful literary force despite his editorial timidity. He was determined to avoid all party political controversy and managed to attract numbers of excellent contributors including Mary Russell MITFORD, Horace Smith, Thomas Noon Talfourd, and Hazlitt. Nonetheless, he was otherwise ineffective as an editor though he remained until he resigned in 1830 to take up the editorship of the *Metropolitan* that he held for a year. Thereafter, he continued to make a precarious living as a professional writer working for the London publishers. His friends who did whatever they could to support him expressed concern at the deprivation of his private life. Rogers recorded in his *Table-Talk* that "Madame de Staël one day said to me, 'How sorry I am for Campbell! His poverty so unsettles his mind, that he cannot write.'" However, C. eked out a bare living by translations, biographies of Mrs. Sarah Siddons (2 vols., 1834) and Petrarch (2 vols., 1841), a travel book (*Letters from the South*, 2 vols., 1837), and a great deal of other journalistic writings. His most substantial work in this respect, *Specimens of the British Poets,* published in seven volumes, appeared in 1819. The essay on poetry, which accompanied the *Specimens*, was considered at the time to be a notable contribution to criticism; the lives of the poets though short and succinct are not always entirely reliable. His essays on John MILTON and Alexander POPE and the critical sections of the lives of Oliver GOLDSMITH and William COWPER demonstrate C.'s prose at its concise and lucid best.

Lord BYRON was a staunch admirer of C.'s poetry, and in his dedication to *Don Juan* Byron places him with Scott, Rogers, Thomas MOORE, and George CRABBE as one of those who will preserve English poetry against the corruption of contemporary taste exemplified by the poetry of Robert SOUTHEY, William WORDSWORTH, and Samuel Taylor COLERIDGE. However, his most powerful advocate, and perhaps also his most generous, was Hazlitt who in his essay "Mr. Campbell and Mr. Crabbe," published in *The Spirit of the Age*, praised C.'s poetry with uninhibited enthusiasm. He maintained that his poetry combined "glossy splendour" and "vigour and romantic interest" with "fastidious refinement" and "classical elegance." Having "produced two poems that have gone to the heart of the nation, and are gifts to the world, he may surely linger out the rest of his life in a dream of immortality." He expressed a preference for *Gertrude of Wyoming* because although it has less "brilliancy" than *Pleasures of Hope* he had nonetheless "emancipated himself from the trammels of the more artificial style of poetry, from epigram, and antithesis and hyperbole" and succeeded in "engrafting the wild and more expansive interest of the romantic school of poetry on classic elegance and precision." He also considered his songs "the happiest efforts of his Muse," citing the "Battle of Hohenlinden" of all

modern compositions as "the most lyrical in spirit and in sound."

C. published *Theodric*, a rather uneven domestic narrative, in 1824, and *The Pilgrim of Glencoe and Other Poems* in 1842. In 1825, he began to agitate for a London university, the idea of which had occurred to him while traveling in Europe. A number of liberal and dissenting politicians including Henry Brougham took up his plans. He was proud of the part he played in the founding of London University and referred to it as "the only important event in his life's little history." Owing to his popular fame as a Scots author and his interest in university education, he was elected rector of Glasgow University three times in succession between 1826 and 1829, the third time in preference to Scott. C. died in Boulogne where he had gone for his health and is buried in Westminster Abbey.

BIBLIOGRAPHY: Beattie, W., *The Life and Letters of T. C.* (3 vols., 1849); Miller, M. R., *T. C.* (1978); Redding, C., *Literary Reminiscences and Memoirs of T. C.* (2 vols., 1860)

A. R. JONES

CAMPION, Thomas
b. 12 February 1567, Witham, Essex; d. 1 March 1620, London

C.'s importance is not confined to English literature. He was one of the finest Latin poets of the English Renaissance and stands high in the ranks of English composers of song. He also wrote a treatise on counterpoint. Of more immediate relevance, he was one of the most technically assured English poets of his day. Admiration for his technical skills should not however be allowed to imply, as it has too often done, that his qualities were only ones of technique. His best poetry is equally marked by emotional and intellectual sophistication that will richly reward the attentive reader (or indeed those who perform or listen to C.'s settings of his own words). C. also made important contributions to the development of literary criticism in England, and to the history of the masque.

Most of C.'s lyrics are contained in the series of songbooks he published: *A Book of Ayres* (1601), *Two Bookes of Ayres* (ca. 1612/13), *Songs of Mourning* (1613), and *The Third and Fourth Booke of Ayres* (1617). *Songs of Mourning* is made up of an elegy and seven songs occasioned by the death of Prince Henry. C.'s other publications are more miscellaneous in character and more emotionally various. They include lyrics in a variety of stanza forms; their implied speakers (or singers) include both men and women; some of them are delicate and tender, some of them bawdy; there are love poems and devotional texts; there are paraphrases of the Psalms and imitations of Catullus, Propertius, and Tibullus.

Everywhere C.'s writing is conditioned by (but not distorted by) his desire to find verbal textures suitable for singing. His employment of patterns of amplification and repetition is subtly conceived and beautifully executed. He consistently achieves what one might call a sustained counterpoint between units of sense and units of verse structure, most notably in the elegant purposefulness with which he employs enjambment. Another particular pleasure of C.'s verse is the frequent presence, within poems essentially written in English accentual meter, of echoes of the classical quantitative rhythms with which C. was thoroughly familiar. The results are not always easy for the modern reader to "hear," but C.'s cadences are, one learns with experience, peculiarly subtle and various. However, for all his evident interest in metrical experiment, it is important to stress that C.'s lyrics are not simply technical showpieces. These are poems of emotional substance too. C.'s range includes, to take just a few examples, the classical gravitas of "The man of life upright" (an imitation of Horace) and the cheerfully innocent bawdry of "It fell on a sommers day"; the religious passion of "Never weather-beaten Saile" (which survived as a hymn into the 18th c.), the witty and emotionally sophisticated variant on the traditional *blazon* of "There is a Garden in her face," and the sheer fun of "Fire, fire." The subtitles of C.'s various collections are right to proclaim that the reader will find both "divine and morall songs" and the "light conceits of lovers." C. shows little or no sign of the influence of John DONNE and his independence of such stylistic developments has perhaps contributed to his relative neglect in modern times. Any conception of lyric that cannot find an honored place for C. is, however, seriously unbalanced.

C. was the author of four masques: *Lord Hay's Masque* (perf. January 6, 1607), *The Lords' Masque* (perf. February 14, 1613), *The Caversham Entertainment* (perf. April 27–28, 1613), and *The Somerset Masque* (perf. December 26, 1614). Mixing rhymed verse and lively prose, C.'s masques (most notably *Lord Hay's Masque* and *The Lords' Masque*) are marked by a clarity of structure that is characteristic of their author, by an alert responsiveness to the social and political demands of their various occasions, and by an apt mythological wit. In its use of the figure of Orpheus, *The Lords' Masque* raises serious questions about the social function of poetry and music, and the well-integrated use of spectacle suggests that C. collaborated very effectively with stage designer Inigo Jones in the composition of his text. Less serious and less grand was *The Caversham Entertainment*, written for performance on a visit by Queen Anne to the household of Sir William Knollys, but it offers stylish variations on familiar Renaissance themes such as the seemingly conflicting demands of the active and contemplative lives. In all of C.'s

masques, the reader will find abundant evidence of C.'s characteristic intelligence and verbal dexterity.

How seriously C. took his craft is clear from his *Observations in the Art of English Poesie* (1602), founded in his belief that "poetry . . . is the chiefe beginner and maintayner of eloquence, not only helping the eare with the acquaintance of sweet numbers, but also raysing the mind to a more high and lofty conceit." The *Observations* themselves contain both an attack on rhyme (strangely, from a master of the art), which prompted Samuel DANIEL's *Defence of Ryme*, and many interesting ideas on English prosody. His arguments for a new kind of verse, which would be without rhyme and which would employ classical feet so far as truth to the English language would allow, bore only limited fruit—though that fruit includes C.'s own beautiful lyric "Rose-cheekt *Lawra*, come," one of the many poems on which a claim can be based for C.'s status as one of the most important figures in the history of English lyrical poetry.

BIBLIOGRAPHY: Davis, W. R., *T. C.* (1987); Lindley, D., *T. C.* (1986); Lowbury, E., T. Salter, and A. Young, *T. C.* (1970); Ratcliffe, S., *C: On Song* (1981)

                                          GLYN PURSGLOVE

CANADIAN LITERATURE IN ENGLISH

Canada became an independent nation—as "The Dominion of Canada"—on July 1,1867, though it did not reach its current territorial extent until Newfoundland and Labrador joined Confederation in 1949. The first prime minister, Sir John A. Macdonald, drew the word "Dominion" from Psalm 72: "He shall have dominion from sea to sea, and from the river unto the ends of the earth." *A mari usque ad mare* ("from sea to sea") remains the national motto, but "dominion"—because the word now hints at an external imperial authority—is no longer in use.

The evolution of the society took several centuries. Numerous Native peoples (speaking over fifty-three separate languages, in at least a dozen language families) occupied the land before European arrival in the early 16th c. and settlement in the early 17th. Mistakenly called "Eskimos" and "Indians," these peoples are now respectively referred to as Inuit and Inuvialuit and as Aboriginal or First Nations peoples (among them the Haida, Cree, Ojibwa, Salish, Blackfoot, Mohawk, Mi'kmaq). Their oral cultures survived into the 19th c. and in many instances into the 21st, although the Beothuk peoples of Newfoundland were the victims of European genocide. English-language translations of the oral compositions of, for example, the Haida poets Ghandl and Skaay, were generally not available, however, until the later 20th c. By then numerous Aboriginal writers, including Jeannette Armstrong, Tomson Highway, Alootook Ipellie, Thomas

King, Lee Maracle, Monique Mojica, Daniel David Moses, and Richard Van Camp were writing drama, fiction, and poetry in English. Still other writers— among them Louise Halfe, Gregory Scofield, and Maria Campbell—claimed Métis/Métisse heritage (primarily French/Cree).

English and French are Canada's two "official" languages, though many others are or have been in use locally. As well as Inuktitut and other indigenous languages, these include Michif (the language of the Métis) and Chinook (a 19th-c. trade language on the Pacific Coast, which gave to Canadian English such words as "skookum," meaning "strong, great"). The accent of Canadian French is influenced by 17th-c. Norman practice; that of Canadian English by 18th-c. English, Scots, and Irish usage. English speech (especially in its use of diphthongs) is remarkably consistent across the country, though local speech sounds demarcate Newfoundland, Cape Breton, and the Ottawa Valley, as do borrowings from French in Quebec (e.g., *maternelle, dépanneur*). Folk literature also largely displays disparate British and French origins. By 1900, a standard spelling system, neither British nor American, had developed; so had distinctive lexical items (e.g., *riding*, to mean electoral district; *elected by acclamation*, to mean unopposed; *bluff*, in prairie usage only, to mean a grove of trees). Current idiom is strongly influenced by U.S. practice, partly because of the ready accessibility in Canada of American television, popular music, and film.

European explorers (French, English, Spanish, Russian) reached Canada as early as 1534. The journal attributed to Jacques Cartier records how Europeans constructed Canada as barren (in Cartier's words, the "land God gave to Cain"). Other French explorers (especially Samuel de Champlain) followed, as did the British, among whom were John Cabot, William Baffin, Martin Frobisher, Henry Hudson, John Franklin, James Cook, and George Vancouver, all by sea, and Henry Kelsey, Samuel Hearne, Alexander Mackenzie (the first to cross the continent, in 1793), and David Thompson, across land. These men left their names on the map, and their journals constitute vigorous records of how assumptions (about the existence of a "Northwest Passage" to China, for example) gave way to more concrete perceptions of people and land. While 18th-c. descriptions demonstrated the influence of Edmund BURKE's aesthetic theories of the sublime and the beautiful—Canada was conventionally thought more "sublime," meaning "uninhabitable," than "picturesque"—these descriptions changed after colonial European settlement expanded further west, and as "wilderness" began slowly to be valued for its own sake.

French settlement had begun on the Atlantic Coast and in Quebec as early as 1608; an early English settlement in Newfoundland in 1583 gave way to a French settlement there, only in turn to be supplanted. The history of early occupation is itself a history of trade (in fish and fur, primarily, but also in souls, with the Jesuits and the Récollet Brothers the most active: the Jesuit *Relations* evocatively tell of "martyrdom" among the Iroquois and provide details of 17th-c. daily life). This history records numerous confrontations between the English and French on Canadian territory. War came to a head in the 18th c. The Peace of Utrecht (1713) gave the Maritime colony of Acadia to the British, who forty-two years later expelled the Acadians (or "Cajuns") to Louisiana, from where many slowly returned. The Treaty of Paris (1763) led to the colony of Quebec also becoming British; in the negotiations that concluded the Seven Years' War (at a time when Voltaire, in *Candide*, was dismissing Canada as "quelques arpents de neige") France chose to keep Guadeloupe and surrender Quebec. Though the Napoleonic Code was to continue to be invoked in Quebec, British common law and British governance spread effectively at this time into the continent.

Trading into the West also pitted the English Hudson's Bay Company (established in 1670) against the Montreal-based North-West Company (established in 1783), and the expansion of trading posts across to the Pacific Coast led later still to the establishment of the British colonies of Vancouver Island and British Columbia. By this time, the continental presumptions and events that marked 18th- and early-19th-c. politics (the American Revolution, Manifest Destiny) repelled rather than attracted Canadian participation, and in the War of 1812 (as with the Fenian Raids later), francophones and anglophones alike resisted American incursions north. Abortive rebellions in 1837 in Upper and Lower Canada (now Ontario and Quebec) reinforced Canada's separateness from the U.S. and also its commitment to the parliamentary system, so that by 1867 the British colonies in Northern North America were for the most part willing to agree to "Confederation" as a tactical plan to avoid American absorption, and build a nation—a constitutional monarchy—founded on principles of "peace, order, and good government." Macdonald's "National Dream" led to British Columbia entering Confederation in 1871, reconfirming the nation's southern border; Prince Edward Island joined in 1873; the Prairie Provinces were created a few decades later after agreements had been concluded between the Hudson's Bay Company and the federal government; Nunavut was divided from the Northwest Territories in 1999.

During the years of colonial governance, British cultural influences touched Canadian society in still other ways. The first English-language newspaper appeared in Nova Scotia in 1752, and newspapers (in the hands of such powerful editors and writers as Thomas Chandler Haliburton—known for his creation of a fictional Yankee character named "Sam Slick"—

Joseph Howe, and William Lyon Mackenzie) quickly became voices of critique and dissent. The Scots "common sense" philosophy movement was to dominate English-language intellectual discussion during the 19th c. (and would have its impact on later thinkers such as George Grant), and Scots educational models (adopted by Thomas McCulloch and others) became the pattern for Canadian anglophone schools. French Catholic schools, for girls as well as boys, and for Natives as well as Europeans, had been founded in the 17th c., and francophone constructions of the history of Quebec—as that of a marginalized society, with the continuing potential of being a conservative Catholic independent state—fed a commitment to political separation well into the 20th c. While numerous later writers were to draw on their Presbyterian, Anglican, or Methodist upbringing, Irish Catholicism also exerted a cultural influence, and would continue to reverberate inside literature.

Colonial writing appeared as early as Robert Hayman's *Quodlibets* (1628), praising Newfoundland in rhyming couplets, and Donncha Ruah MacConmara's macaronic Jacobite satire of King George in the 1740s. Frances Brooke's epistolary *The History of Emily Montague* (1769), composed while she lived in the garrison community near Quebec City, was the first novel written in North America. The "Loyalist" verses of Jonathan Odell and others, following 1776, characteristically used parody to dismiss American Republican ambitions. Pastoral conventions and elevated diction also marked much poetry. Oliver Goldsmith (grandnephew of the English poet) produced in *The Rising Village* (1825) a reply to the more familiar English poem about rural decay. Captivity narratives (e.g., John Jewitt's *Adventures and Sufferings*, 1815) reconfirmed for many the "savagery" of the Native peoples, while numerous settlement and travel narratives (among the latter are those by Charles DICKENS, Anthony TROLLOPE, Walt Whitman, Rudyard KIPLING, and Henry David Thoreau) reaffirmed the "savagery" of the wilderness and the "likelihood" of American absorption. Part of the reason for these apparent misapprehensions of local reality was the fact that (until the later 19th c.) international copyright conventions were not in place and book publication happened in Britain. The U.S. English editors often rewrote fictional and autobiographical texts (such as Susanna Moodie's account of her experiences as an unprepared settler, *Roughing It in the Bush*, 1852), as they had earlier rewritten the exploration accounts of Mackenzie and others, to suit English taste and reconfirm English expectations. Moodie's tales, and those of her practical sister Catharine Parr Traill, would nevertheless become Canadian pioneer classics. About the same time as these romanticized documentaries were appearing, other writers (from John Richardson through to Gilbert Parker at the end of the cen-

tury) were shaping romance out of political history. Intended to castigate both British incompetence and French corruption, these books also celebrated Canadian virtue and manly independence; the gendering of the wilderness was already clear.

After Confederation, two influential groups began to reshape literary direction. The poets and story writers who began to write in the 1880s (among them Sir Charles G. D. Roberts, D. C. Scott, and Isabella Valancy Crawford) aimed to focus "realistically" on Canadian animals, landscapes, and people. In the same decades, the "Canada First " movement attempted to construct a uniform national identity. Espousing exclusively Protestant British models, however, proved incompatible with Canadian society. Although the movement attracted many writers (including the humorist Stephen Leacock, noted especially for his *Sunshine Sketches of a Little Town*, 1912)—just as the "Imperial Federation" movement attracted the most accomplished novelist of the period, the newspaper columnist Sara Jeannette Duncan—the First World War was effectively to bring an end to this particular aspect of cultural dependency. Women's voices had been heard from early on, but the politics of those voices had yet to be more cogently appreciated. Nellie McClung used fiction to work toward women's suffrage; Lucy Maud Montgomery, in what is still one of the most successful of children's works, *Anne of Green Gables* (1908), probed institutional limitations with irony and insight. In the early years of the 20th c., new waves of immigration (from Central and Southern Europe and from Asia) were setting in motion a series of further cultural changes. Among these people was the German writer Felix Paul Greve, who fled his name and his chequered history and reemerged in Canada as the novelist Frederick Philip Grove. After the war (Canada entered automatically as a member nation of the Empire, but signed the peace treaty separately, insisting on its independence being recognized), new literary movements developed. In some respects, Canadian writers were transferring their allegiances from Britain to the U.S.

Writers such as Morley Callaghan and John Glassco (in *Memoirs of Montparnasse*, 1970) pursued exile in Paris and the narrative experiments of *transition* and other American magazines. Canadian dramas, both satiric and expressionist, began to be performed more regularly, and the short story developed as a powerful literary genre (even more so after national radio was established in 1932). A group of young poets also emerged at McGill University in Montreal, responding to MODERNISM, the painters known as the Group of Seven, and American IMAGISM. Among them, A. J. M. Smith became an influential anthologist, F. R. Scott an influential socialist reformer and satirist, Abraham Klein a Joycean experimentalist (Montreal's Jewish community finding a literary voice in English as well as in Yiddish). E. J. Pratt, a Newfoundlander in Toronto, attempted quasi-epic reconstructions of key moments in history. Other writers, for differing periods of time, embraced Marxist causes; Dorothy Livesay, Earle Birney, Milton Acorn, and the collectives who produced agitprop theater were the most enduring. Poets Irving Layton, P. K. Page, Louis Dudek, and Ralph Gustafson continued to explore these ideas in the 1940s but later (even while criticizing cultural trends) affirmed principles of civilization they considered more enduring. Phyllis Webb's evocative poems crystallized ideas about desire and the workings of the mind. While the novel struggled to find its way toward REALISM, the leading writers of the middle decades of the century, Sinclair Ross and Hugh MacLennan, did manage to establish Canada as a legitimate literary setting in such works as *As for Me and My House* and *Barometer Rising* (both 1941). The French-language works of Gabrielle Roy and Anne Hébert were translated to great acclaim, and the gentle comedies of W. O. Mitchell attracted special attention as the literary voices of Western Canada began also to be heard. The works that at the time seemed more formally experimental or thematically daring, however, are those that subsequent criticism celebrated more: Howard O'Hagan's *Tay John* (1939), Elizabeth Smart's *By Grand Central Station I Sat Down and Wept* (1941), Malcolm LOWRY's *Under the Volcano*, Klein's *The Second Scroll* (1951), Sheila Watson's *The Double Hook* (1959), the stories of Joyce Marshall, and (from the 1950s on) the many works of Mordecai Richler.

With the 1960s, a new wave of nationalism (expressed in part through the "Quiet Revolution" in Quebec, and by the establishment of the Canada Council, the National Theatre School, and several literary magazines) coincided with a new wave of writers. Readers discovered the brilliant short stories of two of the most internationally recognized figures of the latter 20th c., Mavis Gallant (e.g., *From the Fifteenth District*, 1979) and Alice Munro (e.g., *The Moons of Jupiter*, 1982); the novels of Ethel Wilson (e.g., *Swamp Angel,* 1954) and Margaret Laurence (e.g., *The Stone Angel*, 1961); the work of Margaret Atwood (e.g., *The Handmaid's Tale*, 1985); the vernacular poetry of Al Purdy; the playful and serious myth-making of Northrop Frye in criticism, Robertson Davies in fiction, Jay Macpherson in poetry, and James Reaney in drama. Over the next decades, while immigrant writers from Ireland and Britain— including George Woodcock, Brian MOORE, and John Metcalf—came to occupy places of cultural influence, the American presence in Canadian culture dominated even more. Like Leslie McFarlane, the ghost writer of the "Hardy Boys" series in earlier decades, some Canadians in the later 20th c. entered the American pop culture scene: mystery writers such as Kenneth

and Margaret Millar, SCIENCE FICTION writers Judith Merril and William Gibson, songwriter Joni Mitchell, scriptwriters, comedians, and the coiner of the phrase "Generation X," Douglas Coupland. Other writers (Leon Rooke, Carol Shields, Keith Maillard) emigrated north from the U.S. In literary practice, the "*Tish* Group" of poets (including George Bowering and Fred Wah)—like Margaret Avison before them— embraced the Black Mountain poetics of Robert Creeley. Robin Blaser, and Robert Bringhurst won praise for their poetic enquiries into the aesthetics of cultural differences. The long poem was also reborn, with bp Nichol constructing in the multivolume *The Martyrology* (1972–90) a life in language. Among the scores of other poets, dramatists, and storytellers to emerge during the next decades are Ken Babstock, Christopher Dewdney, John Steffler, Mark Anthony Jarman, Patrick Lane, Elizabeth Hay, Steven Heighton, Jan Zwicky, Michel Tremblay, Don McKay, Dennis Lee, Ann-Marie MacDonald, George McWhirter, Harold Rhenisch, Warren Cariou, Sharon Pollock, Ray Smith, Michael Turner, and Tom Wayman.

Still other barriers were broken. Marshall McLuhan theorized communications systems into an art and an industry, while Susan Swan and Robert Kroetsch were among several who brought postmodern techniques to both fiction and poetry. Steve McCaffery and others experimented with sound poetry. Sharon Riis, Wendy Lill, Judith Thompson, Audrey Thomas (e.g., *Isobel Gunn*, 1999), Nicole Brossard, Lola Lemire Tostevin, and others made clear the multiple faces of FEMINISM. Leonard Cohen's stories, songs, and poems exuded sexuality, and turned toward Zen Buddhism. Writers such as Timothy Findley, Jane Rule, Daphne Marlatt, and John Herbert wrote the subject of homosexuality more openly into narrative and onto the stage. Urban writing increased, and so did writings that exposed issues of class and race. Austin C. Clarke, Joy Kogawa, Michael Ondaatje (e.g., *Anil's Ghost*, 2000), Rohinton Mistry (e.g., *Tales from Firozsha Baag*, 1987), Dionne Brand, Claire Harris, Sky Lee, Djanet Sears, M. G. Vassanji, Andre Alexis, Denise Chong, and others drew on non-European roots, locating their place in an increasingly multicultural Canada and a global society. Hugh Hood continued to evoke a world of Catholic sensibilities, but saw that the connection between doctrine and behaviour was changing. Antonine Maillet looked back to her Acadian heritage, David Adams Richards to the ordinary families of the Miramichi, Alistair MacLeod to Cape Breton, Wayson Choy to Vancouver's Chinatown, Rudy Wiebe to his Mennonite roots and the history of Louis Riel (the Métis visionary and rebel who had been hanged in 1885).

But the nature of "historical" writing was changing. The writers of the 1990s turned back to the past to retrieve a different understanding of their culture than that which "official" (and often "British"-biased) history had given them. Hence, among the most powerful of contemporary writers, Jack Hodgins, with *Broken Ground* (1998), recuperates a generation from World War I, examining how that war fragmented values for an entire century and so denied a people its ready access to speech. Wayne Johnston, in *Baltimore's Mansion* (1999), retrieves the history of Newfoundland's uneasy relations with Canada by remembering his father's narratives and his own place in them. Guy Vanderhaeghe, in *The Englishman's Boy* (1996), reconstructs the Cypress Hills Massacre in Saskatchewan by probing how film distorts what it represents. Anne Carson, in *Autobiography of Red* (1998), adapts a Classical Greek narrative to enquire into the impact of "difference." For all these writers, reimagining the past was a way of rethinking a culture of change. Canadian culture resists conventional definitions. In the early 21st c., a new generation of writers was already claiming both space and difference within its borders.

BIBLIOGRAPHY: Egoff, S., and J. Saltman, *The New Republic of Childhood* (1990); Heble, A., D. Palmateer Pennee, and J. R. (Tim) Struthers, eds., *New Contexts of Canadian Criticism* (1997); King, T., C. Calver, and H. Hoy, eds., *The Native in Literature* (1987); Klinck, C. F., ed., *Literary History of Canada* (2nd ed., vols. 1–3, 1976), vol. 4, ed. by W. H. New (1990); Neuman, S., and S. Kamboureli, eds., *A Mazing Space: Writing Canadian Women Writing* (1986); New, W. H., *A History of Canadian Literature* (1989); New, W. H., ed., *Encyclopedia of Literature in Canada* (2001); Verduyn, C., ed., *Literary Pluralities* (1998); Wallace, R., and C. Zimmerman, *The Work: Conversations with English-Canadian Playwrights* (1982)

W. H. NEW

CAREW, Thomas
b. June 1593 or 1594, probably at West Wickham, Kent; d. March 1640, West Park, Bedfordshire

Born into the minor gentry, C. initially attended Merton College, Oxford, graduating from Cambridge in 1612. After undertaking legal studies at the Middle Temple, he traveled to Venice as secretary to ambassador Sir Dudley Carleton, and to Paris in the entourage of Sir Edward Herbert. Charles I's accession to the throne gave C. the opportunity to advance at court, where he became a gentleman of the privy chamber, server in ordinary to the king, and the unofficial architect of the literary myth of the Golden Age of peace and prosperity that Stuart supporters believed flourished during the period of Charles's rule without Par-

liament. He suffered from, and eventually died of, syphilis contracted during his libertine years.

As poems in praise of both John DONNE and Ben JONSON demonstrate, C. was sensitive to the excellence of each of the two major poetic "schools" of the early 17th c. In "Upon a Ribband," for example, the speaker makes a ribbon of his mistress that he wears upon his arm into "an emblem of that mystic charm" by which her beauty binds his "captive soul"—a metaphysical conceit worthy of Donne, but delivered as a compliment delicate enough to be included in Jonson's "Triumph of Charis." And while many of C.'s love poems are elegant trifles—the kind of courtly tokens, light, witty, and elegant, in which the speaker affects an insouciance that make them the epitome of what would become known as Cavalier verse—they are distinguished by their emphasis upon the female's right to enjoy sexual pleasure as freely as the male. Thus, C. could write lyrics as hauntingly beautiful as "Song: Ask me no more," in addition to the sexually explicit "A Rapture" in which a male speaker exhorts his female beloved to free herself from bondage to the "goblin Honour" by fleeing with him to "Love's Elysium." "A Rapture," which enumerates in explicit detail the sexual pleasures that he would enjoy with her in this libertine retreat, is arguably the most scandalous poem of the 17th c., one contemporary complaining that C. had "reared the first bordello" on Parnassus. C.'s love poems invariably prove to be as subversive of the Caroline court's values as they do one of its greatest ornaments.

C.'s libertinism subtly informs his country house poems, "To Saxham" and "To My Friend G. N., from Wrest," as well. Portraits of country estates where social harmony flourishes because natural resources are not hoarded by the ruling family but freely shared with both neighbors and strangers, the poems argue for the same liberality in economic terms that the love poems advance in sexual. The poems' emphasis upon moderation and temperateness allows them to be read as encomia to the halcyon days of Charles's personal rule. The myth of the Stuart Golden Age is developed more explicitly in "In Answer to Aurelian Townshend," where C. argues that England has no need of a Protestant warrior king like Gustavus Adolphus of Sweden because "the blessed hand/Of our good king" ensures the "peace and plenty" of the land.

"Tourneys, masques, theatres, better become/Our halcyon days" than martial epic, C. concludes in his verse epistle to Townshend. In C.'s *Coelum Britannicum*, a masque presented at court in 1634, the Olympian gods—whose "heady riots and rapes" were so familiar to Renaissance audiences through Ovid's *Metamorphoses*—are so impressed by the exemplary lives of Charles and Henrietta Maria that they vacate the heavens, leaving members of the English court to take their places. The masque is the literary equivalent of the frescoes that Rubens painted for Charles's Banqueting House, or of the portraits of the royal family painted by Van Dyke in which the sitters' awareness of the ideal that they are portraying is the most important part of their pose. In "To My Friend G. N.," C. distinguishes between those who "act" and those who only "seem" to do so. The paradox of C.'s career is that he challenged the Stuart court to live up to the ideal that he was foremost in glorifying it as representing.

BIBLIOGRAPHY: Martz, L., *The Wit of Love* (1969); Sadler, L., *T. C.* (1979); Sharpe, K., "Cavalier Critic? The Ethics and Politics of T.C.'s Poetry," in Sharpe, K., and S. Zwicker, eds., *Politics and Discourse* (1987): 117–46

RAYMOND-JEAN FRONTAIN

CARIBBEAN LITERATURE IN ENGLISH

Exploration in the late 15th c. by European navigators led to the discovery by Christopher Columbus of the islands he christened the West Indies, and in the early decades of the 16th c. conquest and settlement of the islands was followed by economic exploitation and cultural dominance by European colonizers. Named after the Carib Indians encountered by Columbus on his second voyage to the New World, the Caribbean comprises the archipelago extending from the southern islands off the coast of Venezuela to the Bahamas in the Atlantic Ocean. The islands consist mainly of two groups: the Greater Antilles that includes Cuba, Hispaniola, Puerto Rico, and Jamaica; and the Lesser Antilles—the Leeward and Windward Islands.

Early colonization of the Caribbean was dominated by Spain, and the indigenous populations of the islands were either absorbed or decimated by their European colonizers and replaced as a work force by enslaved Africans transported to the New World. Spanish dominance was soon challenged by rival European powers—France, Great Britain, Denmark, and the Netherlands—and throughout the 16th and 17th cs. control of the islands was hotly contested until the post-Napoleonic settlement of 1815. As a result, the British Commonwealth evolved to include Jamaica, Trinidad and Tobago, Barbados, Dominica, and St. Lucia as well as smaller islands such as Grenada, Antigua, and St. Kitts. The internationalization of English during the colonial era produced in the British Caribbean a variety of English-based Creole languages used by non-Europeans that gradually replaced other indigenous and African dialects. In addition, following the abolition of slavery in the West Indies in the mid-19th c., English became the adopted language of the imported labor force drawn from various ethnicities: Chinese, Portuguese, Spanish, and East Indian. However, literatures written in English by non-Europeans were suppressed until the late 19th and early 20th cs., developing simultaneously with the emerging movements toward independence.

The first wave of West Indian writers appeared in the early decades of the 20th c. and included Jamaican-born authors Tom Redcam, Claude McKay, and H. G. de Lisser. Poet and prose writer, Redcam published his first novel, *Becka's Buckra Baby*, in 1903. McKay began writing poems as a teenager—merging the local Creole dialect and Jamaican folk tradition—and in 1912 published *Songs of Jamaica* and *Constab Ballads*. Soon afterward, McKay left Jamaica for the U.S., where he would later become a prominent member of the Harlem Renaissance—initiating a form of self-imposed exile adopted by numerous Caribbean writers in the following decades. De Lisser was a prominent Jamaican journalist and editor and in 1913 published the novel *Jane: A Story of Jamaica* (repub. as *Jane's Career*, 1914)—and later *Susan Proudleigh* (1915), *Triumphant Squalitone* (1916), and *The White Witch of Rosehall* (1929), among others—which established him as the first major West Indian novelist and an important figure in the emergence of West Indian literature.

Hindered by the events and aftermath of the First World War, the development of a distinct West Indian literature floundered until it gained momentum in the late 1920s and 1930s, fostered mainly by writers from Jamaica, Trinidad, and British Guiana (now Guyana). Born in Dominica, expatriate writer Jean RHYS published her first novel, *Quartet*, in 1928. In 1930, Jamaican writer Una Marson published her first collection of poetry, *Tropic Reveries*, and in 1933 her play entitled *At What a Price* was performed in London. Trinidadian novelist Arthur Mendes published *Pitch Lake* and *Black Fauns* in 1934 and 1935, respectively, followed in the next year by one of the most significant Caribbean novels of the decade, C. L. R. James's *Minty Alley*. In 1937, Edgar Mittelholzer—from British Guiana—published his first novel, *Creole Chips*, the beginning of a long and industrious career that produced more than twenty novels as well as other works of nonfiction and AUTOBIOGRAPHY. In the late 1930s, Louise Bennett began writing poems and reading them in public, publishing her first collection, *Jamaica Dialect Poems*, in 1942. Rooted in oral and cultural tradition, Bennett's poetry as well as her prose monologues—initially rejected as not "serious" literature—gradually earned her a prominent position in West Indian literature and recognition as a writer of international importance.

After the Second World War, European control of colonial territories began to erode throughout the Caribbean setting the stage for national independence movements and decolonization. In the West Indies, the situation coincided with two events of significant proportion: the landmark voyage of the *Empire Win-*

drush and the founding of the University of the West Indies, in 1948 and 1949, respectively. The *Empire Windrush* brought the first postwar Caribbean migrants to England—many of whom settled in Brixton, which became one of Britain's first West Indian communities—and opened the door for massive immigration in the second half of the 20th c. The founding of the university was instrumental in promoting the advancement of educational opportunities as well as a collective West Indian identity.

Postwar literary activity flourished in the Caribbean and spawned in the British Commonwealth the emergence of a West Indian intelligentsia and the creation of publishing venues that included periodicals and literary and cultural magazines—*Bim* in Barbados, *Kyk-Over-Al* in British Guiana, *Focus* and *Caribbean Quarterly* in Jamaica. This was further enhanced in Britain by Henry Swanzy's BBC radio program Caribbean Voices, initiated in 1946, which helped launch the careers of numerous writers, including Vic Reid, George Lamming, Wilson Harris, Edward Kamau Brathwaite, Sam SELVON, and Nobel laureates Derek Walcott and V. S. NAIPAUL. The publication in 1948 of Walcott's first collection of poetry followed in the next year by Jamaican-born Reid's pivotal novel *A New Day* signaled the beginning of the most significant and productive decade in the development of West Indian literature.

The 1950s and early 1960s were dominated primarily by the novel as numerous West Indian writers explored both the legacy of the colonial past and the impact of the colonial experience on the decolonized Caribbean. In 1950, Phyllis Shand Allfrey from Dominica published *Palm and Oak* followed in 1953 by *The Orchid House*. Trinidadian-born Selvon, who had emigrated to England in 1950, published his first novel, *A Brighter Sun*, in 1952 and in 1956 published *The Lonely Londoners*, one of the first examples of so-called Black British writing. In 1953, Roger Mais published his first novel of Jamaican working-class life, *The Hills Were Joyful Together*, followed by *Brother Man* (1954) and *Black Lightning* (1955). Barbadian author Lamming's first novel, *In the Castle of My Skin*, appeared in 1953 followed by *The Emigrants* (1964) and *Of Age and Innocence* (1958). Born in Canada to Jamaican parents, John Hearne lived in Jamaica until age seventeen before emigrating to England and published his first novel, *Voices under the Window*, in 1955. Later in the decade first novels appeared from Trinidadian-born Naipaul, Guyanese-born Jan Carew, and Andrew Salkey, born in Panama and reared in Jamaica.

One of the leading poets to emerge during the period was Guyanese-born Martin Carter who published *The Hill of Fire Glows Red* and *To a Dead Slave*, both in 1951, and in 1954 published *Poems of Resistance from British Guiana* (repub. as *Poems of Resistance*, 1964). Set against the political turbulence and social upheaval of the 1960s and 1970s, West Indian poetry gained increasing recognition and importance in the evolution of postcolonial literature. The publication in 1962 of *In a Green Night: Poems 1948–1960* followed by *The Castaway* (1965), *The Gulf* (1969), and the book-length autobiographical poem *Another Life* (1973) established the preeminence of Walcott as a literary figure. Likewise, Barbadian author Brathwaite assured his reputation with *Rights of Passage* (1967), *Masks*, and *Islands*, both published in 1968, which formed *The Arrivants* trilogy. Other poets to emerge included Dennis Scott, Mervyn Morris, and Andrew MacNeil from Jamaica, A. J. Seymour from Guyana, and U.S.-born Audre Lorde. Simultaneously, the postwar generation of West Indian novelists was joined by authors such as Austin C. Clarke from Barbados, Earl Lovelace, Michael Anthony, and Ismith Khan from Trinidad, Wilson Harris from Guyana, Garth St. Omer from St. Lucia, and Sylvia Wynter from Jamaica.

Decolonization in the West Indies gradually paved the way toward emancipation, and in 1959 Jamaica and Trinidad and Tobago were granted self-government and achieved full independence within the Commonwealth in 1962, setting the pattern that other islands would follow in due course. As a result, the conceptualization of West Indianness became more difficult to define and West Indian literature more difficult to categorize. Whereas the older generation of writers—including those living abroad or in exile—were for the most part identified as West Indian, the newer generation—West Indian by birth or heritage—were more likely to be treated as Caribbean or English-speaking Caribbean. In addition, writers such as Walcott and Naipaul began to distance themselves from the Caribbean—both physically and metaphorically—as their reputations gained international status. Writers continued to explore the experience of slavery and colonialism, hybridity, and exile but incorporated as well both domestic and global influences: FEMINISM, Black Consciousness, the aesthetic impact of popular culture—reggae and calypso—as well as postindependence disillusionment and nostalgia. Another significant development was the emergence of powerful new women writers: Erna Brodber, Lorna Goodison, Olive Senior, and Michelle Cliff from Jamaica; Merle Hodge and Marlene Nourbese Philip from Trinidad and Tobago; Grace Nichols and Beryl Gilroy from Guyana; Jamaica Kincaid from Antigua; and Merle Collins from Grenada.

The Caribbean diaspora in the second half of the 20th c. permanently altered the course of West Indian culture and literature and generated extensive debate extending into the new millennium on the condition of being Caribbean and its relationship to multiculturalism in other national literatures—Canadian, American, and British, among others. Many of the leading writers today identified as Caribbean are likewise identified with their adopted cultures or places of birth: Cyril Dabydeen, Dionne Brand, and Cecil Foster in Canada; Kincaid, Goodison, Paule Marshall, and Opal Adisa Palmer in the U.S.; Jean "Binta" Breeze, John Agard, Linton Kwesi JOHNSON, Caryl PHILLIPS, Fred D'AGUIAR, Andrea Levy, and Zadie SMITH in Britain. Black British writers—such as Levy and Smith—are among the new generation of authors, British by birth and identity and distinct from the immigrant voice, who represent what in effect is now an integrated and vital part of contemporary British literature.

BIBLIOGRAPHY: Chamberlain, J. E., *Come Back to Me My Language: Poetry and the West Indies* (1993); Coulthard, G. R., *Race and Colour in Caribbean Literature* (1962); Davies, C. B., and E. S. Fido, eds., *Out of the Kumbla: Caribbean Women and Literature* (1990); Ramchand, K., *The West Indian Novel and Its Background* (1970); Torres-Saillant, S., *Caribbean Poetics: Toward an Aesthetic of West Indian Literature* (1997)

STEVEN R. SERAFIN

CARLYLE, Jane [Baillie Welsh]

b. 14 July 1801, Haddington, Scotland; d. 21 April 1866, London

Often known as the "other" Carlyle, C. was a woman of tremendous wit and intelligence. Because none of her writing was published in her lifetime, she might be viewed today as a woman who sacrificed her own potential to facilitate the genius of her husband, Thomas CARLYLE, the Scottish essayist, social critic, and historian. She wrote poetry before her marriage and kept a diary, but her letters are her primary literary contribution. Some of her most interesting letters were destroyed at her own request by her friend, Geraldine Endsor Jewsbury. Approximately three thousand of C.'s letters survive and are published in the projected thirty-volume Duke-Edinburgh edition.

The only child of a doctor, C. exhibited a precocious intellectual curiosity and started school before she was five years old. By the age of nine, she was reading Virgil in Latin and had written a novel. At ten, she had a classical tutor, Edward Irving, who later introduced her to Thomas Carlyle.

The Carlyles entertained many literary and intellectual celebrities of their day at their Cheyne Row residence in Chelsea, including Thomas DE QUINCEY, John Stuart MILL, Ralph Waldo Emerson, Margaret Fuller, and Erasmus DARWIN. As a hostess, C. was celebrated for her caustic wit. Though she was content to subordinate herself publicly to her husband, her letters indirectly reveal her frustration at assuming this role. She suffered from chronic ill health and was frequently bedridden due to severe headaches, influen-

zas, and general malaise. Both Carlyles frequently suffered indisposition, insomnia, and indigestion; their biographers speculate about possible psychosomatic causes of their maladies, including the marriage itself, which was affectionate and loving but also characterized by quarrels and frequent geographical separations.

Today, C. is known for her letters and her volatile marriage to the irascible Thomas Carlyle. The letters cover her life from ages eighteen to sixty-five, including her five-year courtship with Carlyle, much of which was accomplished through letters. Her letters contain ironic character sketches and opinionated judgments. Of Elizabeth Barrett [BROWNING] and Robert BROWNING, for example, she wrote in July 1852, "he is nothing or very little but 'a fluff of feathers'! She is true and good, and the most womanly creature," but by September she had decided "I like Browning less and less—and even she does not grow on me." She proclaimed Charles KINGSLEY's anti-Chartist novel *Alton Locke* to be "not readable" and announced that one of the final installments of William Makepeace THACKERAY's *Vanity Fair* "beats Dickens out of the world." She flippantly dismissed Victorian theories of evolution: "I was no oyster, nor had any grandfather an oyster within my knowledge."

In the opinion of many of her contemporaries, perhaps most notably Lytton STRACHEY, she had the potential to become a great writer. In the era of emerging women novelists such as Charlotte BRONTË, Elizabeth Cleghorn GASKELL, and George ELIOT, C. chose instead to write in a private genre. Her letters embody the 18th- and 19th-c. tradition of female epistolary communication. The gifts of narrative composition and playful exaggeration that made her a skilled conversationalist are apparent in her letters. Characterized by wit and sarcasm, they capture the best of Victorian colloquial speech. Their content reveals the frustrations of her marriage and her mock-epic domestic struggles with servants and workmen, bedbugs and beetles. Recent critics comment on the way C. used her letters to construct a self for her husband, her friends, and for posterity.

In 1866, C. died suddenly in her carriage, apparently of heart failure or stroke. After her death, her husband's remorse for her marital unhappiness was elicited by reading her letters; as a sort of penance, Thomas Carlyle undertook the editing and selection of the *Letters and Memorials of J. W. C.*, eventually published in three volumes by his biographer, J. A. FROUDE, in 1883. Froude's four-volume biography of Thomas Carlyle (1882–84) promulgated the view that C. martyred herself to her temperamental husband. It caused scandal by repeating rumors that the marriage was never consummated because of his impotence though other biographers assume the couple were merely sexually incompatible. Thomas Carlyle survived his wife by fifteen years.

BIBLIOGRAPHY: Clarke, N., *Ambitious Heights: Writing, Friendship, Love: The Jewsbury Sisters, Felicia Hemans, and J. W. C.* (1990); Sanders, C. R., gen. ed., *The Collected Letters of Thomas and J. W. C.* (27 vols., 1970-); Surtees, V., *J. W. C.* (1986)

LYNETTE FELBER

CARLYLE, Thomas

b. 4 December 1795, Ecclefechan, Annandale, Scotland; d. 4 February 1881, London

Alternately appreciated and detested by the Victorian audience, C. remains an influential figure of the 19th c. He was a prolific writer of essays, history, and BIOGRAPHY. C. was reared in a strict Christian home and was destined for the ministry. His career path was altered at the University of Edinburgh where he was attracted to more secular ideas and soon C. found himself to be a successful writer; today, he is a seminal Victorian author.

At Edinburgh, C. studied German literature and began his writing career with series on Schiller and Goethe in the early 1820s and a four-volume anthology of German writers in 1827. In their work, he found solutions to the crises he faced in his life; for example, in translating Goethe's *Wilhelm Meister's Apprenticeship* (3 vols., 1824), C. found that Goethe had voiced what had seemed unexpressible for C.—the search for a faith, for an understanding of a universe that seemed unfriendly and cold, and for an imperative to seek knowledge. From the publication of *Sartor Resartus* in 1836, C.'s reputation continued to improve. In this work, the protagonist Teufelsdröckh seems to be loosely based on C.'s life, as he follows a difficult life-path from the terrible "Everlasting NO" and "centre of indifference" to the affirmation in the "Everlasting YEA," which marks the turning point of the book and Teufelsdröckh eventually triumphs in life. When he published his three-volume *The French Revolution* in 1837, it firmly rooted C.'s career with its fusing of several genres—essay, fiction, and poetry—to evoke a provocative view of an event that had a lasting impact on British writers from 1789 onward; C. insisted on the importance of the individual, and raised serious questions about democracy, mass persuasion, and politics. This also isolated him from the liberal and democratic tendencies of his age. Although he espoused radical ideals as a young man, he soon rejected notions of charity and humanitarianism while calling for the establishment of a government that would serve as a paternalistic entity. This attitude is reflected in later writings such as *Chartism* (1839) and *Past and Present* (1843). While he called for this new government, he also looked to the heroes of the past to identify heroic qualities as a means to improving society as he saw it. He collected his lectures on the subject and published them in 1841 as *On Heroes and Hero Worship*.

With these and other influential works, C.'s effect on the writers of the Victorian era was significant. His emphasis upon the social and political importance of literature, particularly his argument that literature was replacing religion as a source of spiritual knowledge, convinced many writers that novels and poetry were important and that the writer had the role of a prophet. His influence is clear in the works of writers such as Charles DICKENS, Alfred, Lord TENNYSON, and others whose characters suffer a series of trials during which they reject the beliefs of their upbringing, wade through a period of indifference, and finally discover themselves through an acceptance of universal beliefs. Although C.'s works are often complex and written in what became known as "Carlylese," Victorian writers embraced his notions about the significance of literature as a spiritual guide, especially as he had suffered a crisis of faith and rose above it. C. extolls the political, religious, and social importance literature has upon society, ideas that outlived him.

In 1866, C.'s wife, Jane, died unexpectedly. This sudden end to a constant yet troubled marriage affected C. greatly and his writing virtually stopped. He did produce some work before his death some fifteen years later, including the controversial "Shooting Niagara," a treatise against the Reform Act of 1867, which greatly increased the voting registers. Despite the controversy of this and other works that demonstrate C.'s shift to the right as he aged, despite the frustration many readers felt with his complex ideas, C.'s influence on British literature is solid.

BIBLIOGRAPHY: Clubbe, J., ed., *C. and His Contemporaries* (1976); Kaplan, F., *T. C.* (1983); Young, L. M., *T. C. and the Art of History* (1939)

MARCY TANTER

CARPENTER, Edward

b. 29 August 1844, Brighton; d. 28 June 1929, Guilford

Trained as a mathematician at Trinity Hall, Cambridge, C. became a fellow of the college, later taking Holy Orders. This orthodox Victorian start was followed by equally Victorian later revolt, when he worked as a university extension lecturer in the industrial Midlands, pioneering several "progressive" causes, not merely the much-mocked cults of vegetarianism and sandals, but clean air, anti-vivisection, women's rights, and socialism as taught by William MORRIS and John RUSKIN, and sexual freedom as inspired by Walt Whitman and Ancient Greece. He lived simply, practicing market gardening and handicrafts. *Towards Democracy* (1883) was a long poem on "cosmic consciousness, " republished in 1988 in the series Gay Modern Classics. *England's Ideal and Other Papers on Social Subjects* (1887) found many readers. Among C.'s other works are *Homogenic Love and Its Place in a Free Society* (1894), *Love's Coming-of-Age* (1896), *The Intermediate Sex* (1908), *Sketches from Life in Town and Country* (1908), *The Drama of Love and Death* (1912), and *My Days and Dreams* (1916), an autobiography. He was admired by both E. M. FORSTER and D. H. LAWRENCE.

CARPENTER, Humphrey [William Bouverie]

b. 29 April 1946, Oxford

C.'s fame rests on his prize-winning biographies, but he is also a writer for children, an authority on CHILDREN'S LITERATURE, and a musician. Educated at Oxford, he joined the BBC. His biography of J. R. R. TOLKIEN (1977) was followed in 1978 by a study of Tolkien's circle, called "The Inklings," which included C. S. LEWIS and Charles Williams. A biography of W. H. AUDEN appeared in 1981, and *Geniuses Together: American Writers in Paris in the 1920s* in 1987. *A Serious Character: The Life of Ezra Pound* appeared in 1988. Probably his most famous book is the exhaustive *The Brideshead Generation: Evelyn Waugh and His Friends* (1989), which exemplifies C.'s skill in dealing with interconnected groups. It was followed by *Benjamin Britten* (1992), *Robert Runcie: The Reluctant Archbishop* (1996), and *Dennis Potter: A Biography* (1998). With his wife Mari Prichard, C. edited *A Thames Companion* (1975) and *The Oxford Companion to Children's Literature* (1984).

CARROLL, Lewis

(pseud. of Charles Lutwidge Dodgson) b. 27 January 1832, Daresbury, Cheshire; d. 14 January 1898, Guildford, Surrey

With the publication in 1865 of *Alice's Adventures in Wonderland*, C. single-handedly transformed the nature of CHILDREN'S LITERATURE in England. Before *Alice*, children's books were almost entirely either primers intended to encourage the learning of reading and writing, or else (with rare exceptions such as the Nonsense Songs of Edward LEAR) ponderously didactic works, aimed at inculcating moral rectitude and spiritual piety. With *Alice in Wonderland* (as the title is invariably abbreviated), C. wrote a story that was intended purely as an entertainment. Small wonder that it was so lovingly embraced by readers and proved so liberating an influence on subsequent writers for the nursery.

The tale of the child who falls down a rabbit-hole into a topsy-turvy world now ranks—along with its sequel, *Through the Looking-Glass, and What Alice Found There* (1872)—among the most frequently quoted, often-parodied books in the English language. Many phrases and expressions from these books (such as "Curiouser and curiouser!" and "Jam to-morrow and jam yesterday—but never jam *to-day*") have passed into common currency.

C.'s characters have acquired a universal immortality alongside the best-known creations of William SHAKESPEARE and Charles DICKENS. The White Rabbit, the Cheshire Cat, the Mock Turtle, the March Hare, and the Hatter (or, as he is usually, but erroneously, named the *Mad* Hatter) occupy a folkloric status and are known and recognized even by people who have never read the books in which they appear; while those characters borrowed from other sources, such as Tweedledum and Tweedledee, now exist in our collective imaginations chiefly as C. redefined them.

Alice's two adventures are ultimately revealed as dreams that explain their hallucinatory storylines in which the heroine experiences disorientating changes in size and witnesses various bizarre metamorphoses: the Duchess's baby becoming a pig, the White Queen transforming into an old Sheep. The beings encountered by Alice are a motley collection comprising ordinary people (though in their characteristics quite extraordinary), dumb animals, talking animals, and enigmatic creatures who might pass either as animals-dressed-as-humans or as humans in animal-masks. C. also throws into the mix mythical creatures (the Gryphon), nursery rhyme characters (Humpty Dumpty), and those royal personages represented on playing cards and on the chessboard, the King, Queen, and Knave of Hearts in *Wonderland* and the Red and White Kings and Queens in *Looking-Glass*.

Of the various verses and poems that are incorporated into the stories, several parody works by popular Victorian poets and it is a curious testament to C.'s inventiveness that it is his parodies, like "You Are Old Father William," that are now remembered while the originals (in the case of "Father William," Robert SOUTHEY's poem, "The Old Man's Comforts") are now long forgotten. The adventures themselves are mostly a series of absurd confrontations that, for Alice, are constantly perplexing. Conversations turn on riddles, puns, word games, and infuriating non sequiturs and the underlying attitude of the characters toward each other and to Alice is frequently aggressive and occasionally violent.

That Alice and her fantastical dream companions were the creation of an Oxford mathematics don who was also the son of a clergyman and himself an ordained deacon of the Church of England, might seem surprising were it not for the evidence of his juvenile writings in *The Rectory Umbrella* and *Mischmasch*, posthumously published in 1932.

Within the pages of these domestic "magazines," which the young C. compiled for the amusement of his large family of brothers and sisters, are found early examples of his sharply defined and unrestrained sense of HUMOR, clear indications of his skill as a punster and comic versifier, and the earliest version of the opening stanza of what would later become one of his most famous pieces: the *Looking-Glass* poem, "Jabberwocky."

From 1851 until his death, C.'s home was Christ Church, Oxford: first as an undergraduate studying mathematics, later as a "student" (fellow). The author of a number of volumes on mathematics and logic, his fascination with numbers and logical conundrums percolated through to his humorous writing and informed much of the puzzling talk in Wonderland and the world beyond the Looking-glass. Without Oxford, there would, literally, have been no Alice. A shy, diffident man with a slight stutter, C. was most at ease in the company of the young and it was his friendship with the children of the Dean of Christ Church and, in particular, the second daughter, Alice Pleasance Liddell, that resulted in the discovery of Wonderland.

The tale had its genesis on July 4, 1862, during a much-chronicled river trip with Alice and two of her sisters during which C. extemporized the first version of Alice's exploits. At the insistent request of the real Alice, C. wrote out the story with his own illustrations and presented it to her as *Alice's Adventures Underground* (eventually published in facsimile in 1886). Encouraged by George MacDonald, C. decided to publish the story, adding various episodes (including the chapter "A Mad Tea-Party"), commissioning illustrations by the distinguished *Punch* cartoonist, John Tenniel, and changing the title, first to *Alice's Hour in Elfland* and then (more happily) to *Alice's Adventures in Wonderland*.

The book was published under the authorship of "Lewis Carroll," a pseudonym previously used on C.'s contributions to the humorous magazine, the *Train*. C. had offered several pen names to the editor, including two anagrams of his forenames, Charles Lutwidge: "Edgar Cuthwellis" and "Edgar U. C. Westhill." Luckily, the editor selected "Lewis Carroll,"

Through the Looking-Glass followed *Wonderland* seven years later and, while lacking some of the exuberant freshness of the first volume and the very particular spark of inspiration provided by his child muse, the book is more tightly structured and more satisfyingly rounded. The wit is as sharp, or sharper, the high comedy is counterpointed by a deep melancholy and a meandering thread of puzzling philosophical questions runs throughout the dream and remain unanswered even upon Alice's awakening.

In 1876, C. published his other enduring masterpiece, the epic nonsense ballad, *The Hunting of the Snark*, about a crew of misfits and oddities (led by an officious Bellman) who set sail in search of the mysterious creature of the title with disastrous results arising from the fact that "the Snark was a Boojum." Skillfully and wittily sustained across 141 stanzas (with only the occasional *longueur*), *The Snark* has a direct kinship with the *Alice* books and—since it features the Jubjub and the Bandersnatch previously encountered in "Jabberwocky"—appears to be set on an island somewhere off the shore of Looking-glass World.

Little else that C. wrote achieved the universal acclaim or the lasting appeal of the *Alice* books and *The Hunting of the Snark*. He published various political squibs on Oxford life, numerous literary games and puzzles, notably *Doublets* (1879), *A Tangled Tale* (1885), and *The Game of Logic* (1886) as well as a considerable output of verse, subsequently collected as *Phantasmagoria and other Poems* (1869); *Rhyme? and Reason?* (1883), and *Three Sunsets and Other Poems* (1898).

Following the example of Thomas HOOD, C. categorized his poems as the "grave" and the "gay." Whilet his comic verse was full of unbridled inventiveness, his serious poetry (which he personally rated far higher than it deserved), was invariably archly pious, cloyingly sentimental or (worse) took the form of anaemic homages to his poetic betters. Similar blemishes abound in C.'s sprawling, complex two-part novel *Sylvie and Bruno* (1889) and *Sylvie and Bruno Concluded* (1893). With its Sterne-like opening (seemingly in the middle of a sentence) this is a bewildering and, ultimately, frustrating work. The constantly shifting dream-states, extravagant fairy episodes, leaden passages of moral argument, unchecked sentimentality and toe-curling baby-talk, overshadow, and finally overwhelm, the occasional flashes of vintage nonsense.

Devoted students of Carrolliana may stay the course long enough to discern the fascinating autobiographical insights that lurk within the pages of *Sylvie and Bruno*, or uncover the books' hidden wells of wit and wisdom. For most readers, however, a savagely abridged version of the novels, *The Story of Sylvie and Bruno* (posthumously published in 1904), is the only remotely palatable way of savoring C.'s final foray into the realms of make-believe.

In truth, the quality of C.'s other writings matters little: it is enough that he created with his two *Alice* adventures an enduring fantasy of such startling originality that it draws us back, again and again, into those singular lands down the rabbit-hole and through the looking-glass.

BIBLIOGRAPHY: Cohen, M. N., ed., *The Letters of L. C.* (2 vols., 1979); Cohen, M. N., *L. C.* (1995); Collingwood, S. D., *The Life and Letters of L. C.* (1898);

Gardner, M., ed., *The Annotated Alice* (1960; rev. as *More Annotated Alice*, 1990); Green, R. L., ed., *The Diaries of L. C.* (2 vols., 1953); Williams, S. H., F. Maden, and D. Crutch, eds., *The L. C. Handbook* (1979)

BRIAN SIBLEY

CARTER, Angela

b. 7 May 1940, Eastbourne, Sussex; d. 16 February 1992, London

Regarded as something of a literary outsider during her lifetime, C. has become retrospectively mythologized as the "fairy godmother" of English fiction. *Nights at the Circus* (1984) controversially failed to make the shortlist for the Booker Prize, an omission many took as index of her semirespectable status. Similarly, despite her membership of the publisher Virago's advisory board from 1977 onward, she upset many feminists with her critical reappraisal of the Marquis de Sade, *The Sadeian Woman* (1979), and was accused of reinscribing pornographic stereotypes in her fiction, particularly *The Bloody Chamber and Other Stories* (1979). Her refusal to subscribe to mythic essentialism or to a form of FEMINISM that regarded women as victims also alienated her from many. However, since her early death from lung cancer, her brand of feminism has become more consonant with the times, and her work embraced by academics and popular audiences alike. This relative institutionalisation would undoubtedly have made her uneasy, as she relished her outsider role, valuing the ability of her work to unsettle and provoke.

C. had a wide range of influences, and incorporated these into her writing in a way that evades strict classification. There are elements of Gothic, magic realism, surrealism, folktale, and the picaresque in much of her work, while *Heroes and Villains* (1969) and *The Passion of New Eve* (1977) draw on SCIENCE FICTION. Her earthy HUMOR and talent for parody are displayed in novels such as *Nights at the Circus* and *Wise Children* (1991), with comic set-pieces such as the escape from a Foucauldian panopticon by its lesbian inmates in the former, and a Shakespearean musical entitled "What! You, Will?" in the latter. Dressing up in all its forms is a common theme throughout her career, from the "holiday from the persistent self" afforded by fancy dress in her early work, to the glamor of the silver screen, the circus, and the stage in her final novels. Through clothing, gender and subjectivity are shown to be socially constructed, confounding essentialism.

C. began her career as a local journalist and she was to continue writing nonfictional essays and reviews throughout her life for a variety of publications including *New Society,* the *Guardian,* and the *London Review of Books.* She read English, specializing in

medieval literature, at Bristol University from 1962 to 1965, and many of her early novels are imbued with the distinctive atmosphere of both the British provinces and the counterculture during the "Swinging Sixties." *Shadow Dance* (1966; repub. as *Honeybuzzard,* 1996), *Several Perceptions* (1968), and *Love* (1971; rev. ed., 1987), dubbed by Marc O'Day "The Bristol Trilogy"—follow "angry young men" through a decadent society littered with the detritus of the past. *Shadow Dance* and *Love* are unforgiving toward their central female characters, ending with disturbing images of their deaths. *Several Perceptions* offers a more upbeat ending, in which an anarchic "happening" in a crumbling Gothic mansion provides miraculous opportunities for renewal. Subsequent to her engagement with feminism, C. was to amend parts of *Love,* and provide a semicomical afterword (1987) in which she updated the characters' fates to fit with the times.

Other early novels describe female rites of passage and are more overtly fantastic: *The Magic Toyshop* (1967) contrasts the highly conventional adolescent fantasies of its heroine Melanie with the sinister world of her Uncle Philip's macabre toyshop. *Heroes and Villains* is set in a postapocalyptic society divided into opposed sects of Professors and Barbarians, the suggestively middle-class guardians of civilization and the counterculture-like tribespeople who threaten them. Marianne, the daughter of a Professor, is captured by the Barbarians but discovers that both communities are flawed, both operating to patriarchal systems.

As a result of winning the Somerset Maugham Award for *Several Perceptions,* C. visited Japan in 1969, eventually deciding to stay for a further two years. She dated her initiation into feminism specifically to this period, stating, "In Japan I learnt what it was to be a woman and became radicalized." Her fascination with the more sadomasochistic elements of Japanese culture is evident throughout her work from the 1970s, particularly *The Infernal Desire Machines of Dr. Hoffman* (1972; repub. as *The War of Dreams,* 1974) and *Fireworks* (1974), and her work also becomes more overtly feminist as the seventies progress. *The Passion of New Eve* is C.'s most sustained critique of mythic archetypes: its hero, Evelyn, becomes a heroine halfway through the novel, exposing gender essentialism in a speculatively apocalyptic Amerika. *The Bloody Chamber,* on the other hand, rewrote traditional FAIRY TALES with a feminist agenda. C.'s engagement with folktale also resulted in two anthologies of fairy tales, with a feminist slant, for Virago.

During the 1980s, C.'s work continued to diversify: she collaborated with Neil Jordan on the screenplay for *The Company of Wolves* (1984), based on an earlier short story; and taught creative writing at the

University of East Anglia in Britain and several locations in the U.S. *Nights at the Circus*, considered by many to be her masterpiece, appeared in 1984. Starring Fevvers, a larger-than-life Cockney trapeze artist with wings, with an expansive cast of freaks, prostitutes, and conmen, the novel is a riotous celebration of performance and artifice. Fevvers' promotional slogan, "Is she fact or is she fiction?" summarizes both C.'s magic realist style and the novel's preoccupation with cusps: fantasy and reality; 19th and 20th cs.; innocence and experience.

C.'s final novel, *Wise Children*, also celebrates performance, following the fortunes of the Hazards and the Chances, legitimate and illegitimate branches of a flamboyant theatrical family. Saturated with Shakespearean references (every play is referred to at least once), the novel deals with the Bard as national institution. The novel is a comic tour-de-force championing the outsider, through its septuagenarian narrator Nora Chance and her identical twin Dora, born in every sense on the wrong side of the tracks.

C. was in many senses a novelist ahead of her time. Both her antiessentialist views on gender and her fascination with the Gothic and grotesque accord better with a 1990s sensibility than that of the previous decades. One of the first postmodern feminists, she challenged the distinction between high and low culture, made familiar narratives strange, and insisted feminist writing could also be erotic. Above all, she maintained a lush, witty, impeccably crafted yet fiercely intelligent style that sought to continually ask questions.

BIBLIOGRAPHY: Bristow, J., and T. L. Broughton, eds., *The Infernal Desires of A. C.* (1997); Day, A., *A. C.* (1998); Easton, A., ed., *A. C.* (2000); Sage, L., *A. C.* (1994); Sage, L., ed., *Flesh and the Mirror: Essays on the Art of A. C.* (1994)

CATHERINE SPOONER

CARTER, Elizabeth
b. 16 December 1717, Deal; d. 19 February 1806, London

One of the most influential members of the Bluestocking circle that included Elizabeth Vesey, Hester CHAPONE, Francis Boscawen, Elizabeth MONTAGU, and later Hannah MORE, among others, C. was an accomplished poet, translator, and classicist. C.'s translation from the Greek of Epictetus (1758) won her a European reputation and the praise of Samuel JOHNSON, who invited her to contribute to his periodical the *Rambler*. Mistress of Latin, Hebrew, French, Italian, German, Portugese, and Arabic, she made various translations, among them Francesco Algarotti's *Newtonianismo per le Dame* as *Sir Isaac Newton's Philosophy Explain'd for the Use of the Ladies: In Six Dia-*

logues on Light and Colours (2 vols., 1739). C. published poems signed "Eliza" in the *Gentleman's Magazine*. In 1738 and 1762, she published collections entitled *Poems upon Particular Occasions* and *Poems on Several Occasions*. Her *Memoirs* appeared posthumously in 1807 followed by collections of her letters to Catherine Talbot and Vesey (2 vols., 1808) and Montagu (3 vols., 1817). Virginia WOOLF called her "valiant."

CARTWRIGHT, William
b. ca. 23 December 1611, Northway, Gloucestershire; d. 29 November 1643, Oxford

Poet and dramatist, C. was educated at Christ Church, Oxford, where he was later appointed Reader in metaphysics. C. first gained recognition as a poet and it is for his lyric poetry—a combination of metaphysical wit and Cavalier attitude—that he is best remembered. C.'s plays, all except *The Ordinary* (wr. ca. 1635), are stilted and artificial and his plots are improbable. *The Royal Slave* (1639) was performed in 1636 by C.'s students from Oxford University before King Charles I and his queen, with music by Henry LAWES (who wrote the music for John MILTON's *Comus*). Others were *The Lady Errant* (perf. ca. 1635–36) and *The Siege; or, Love's Covert*, included in C.'s *Comedies, Tragi-Comedies, with Other Poems*, published in 1651.

CARY, Elizabeth. See FALKLAND [Viscountess], Elizabeth Cary

CARY, [Arthur] Joyce [Lunel]
b. 7 December 1888, Londonderry, Ireland; d. 29 March 1957, Oxford

A trained artist and prolific writer, C. produced some twenty-eight books, ranging over fiction, poetry, art criticism, and political commentary. As with many of his heroes, his early years were marked by restlessness and wandering. He studied painting in Paris and Edinburgh (1906–7), attended Oxford with poor results (1909–12), served with the British Red Cross in the Balkans (1912–13), and finally entered the Nigerian Service in 1913, where, with the exception of a period in the West African Frontier Force in Cameroon, he served until 1920. This experience led him to fiction writing, providing material for his "African novels," and his later books, *The Case for African Freedom* (1941; rev. ed., 1944) and *Britain and West Africa* (1946; rev. ed., 1947).

Underlying his fiction is a vision of the human condition that C. termed the "comedy of freedom," echoing Honoré de Balzac's *La Comédie humaine*. His heroes, often scoundrels or tricksters, struggle to create their own realm of freedom, clashing with the boundaries of art, religion, politics, and conformity.

It was in the genre of the multiple novel that C. found the fullest expression of his artistic vision. Unlike the worlds chronicled in multiple novels such as C. P. SNOW's *Strangers and Brothers*, Anthony POWELL's *A Dance to the Music of Time*, Evelyn WAUGH's *Sword of Honour*, or Lawrence DURRELL's *Alexandria Quartet*, C.'s world is more Blakean, not so much evoking a time and place, but a moral cosmos. While not originally conceived as a multiple novel, C.'s four early "African novels" share some characters, and attempt to explore the tensions between African and British culture at all levels. These include *Aissa Saved* (1932), *An American Visitor* (1933), *The African Witch* (1936), and *Mister Johnson* (1939). During this period, he also produced his novels, *Castle Corner* (1938), *Charley Is My Darling* (1940), and *A House of Children* (1941).

C. completed his first trilogy in 1944. This included *Herself Surprised* (1941), *To Be a Pilgrim* (1942), and his masterpiece, *The Horse's Mouth* (1944). His second trilogy included *Prisoner of Grace* (1952), *Except the Lord* (1953), and *Not Honour More* (1955). Each of the trilogies is about the struggles of a woman and her relationship with two men who love and abuse her. Each component novel is narrated by one of these characters. The first trilogy is told respectively by Sara Monday, Tom Wilcher, and Gulley Jimson, while the second trilogy is by Nina Latter, Chester Nimmo, and Jim Latter. The first centers on the theme of freedom and creativity while the second centers on politics and freedom. In each case, the woman is murdered by her husband. C. planned a third trilogy, but because of declining health completed only one volume, *The Captive and the Free* (1959).

Mister Johnson is the best of the "African novels." Johnson, a young Nigerian clerk, serves Rudbeck, the district colonial officer. His energy and vision are crucial to the completion of a road project, but at the same time he is blinded by his heroic and Romantic image of himself as an equal in the white world. Anticipating C.'s greatest creation, Gulley Jimson, he is also a liar and thief, leading to his eventual downfall and death. Chinua Achebe's *Things Fall Apart* (1958) and especially *No Longer at Ease* (1960) are his reply to C. and *Mister Johnson*.

The first trilogy, and especially *The Horse's Mouth*, is C.'s most engaging and enduring work. Central to this are the figures of Sara Monday and her husband, the painter Gulley Jimson. *Herself Surprised* presents Sara's account of her youth and early experiences, building relationships in a world she does not understand. She is a sort of natural woman, standing against a bewildering social norm that constantly surprises her. *The Horse's Mouth,* the reader learns at the end, is narrated by the old Gulley Jimson, who is in a

prison hospital after suffering a stroke and after having accidentally killed Sara, trying to get back some paintings. Gulley is a confidence man and a trickster figure, juxtaposed to the natural or earth woman, Sara. His narrative recounts his numerous cons and obsessive struggles to find the means to paint his pictures. Like the archetypal trickster, he violates all norms and boundaries in the pursuit of creativity.

BIBLIOGRAPHY: Bishop, A., *Gentleman Rider: A Life of J. C.* (1988); Bloom, R., *The Indeterminate World: A Study of the Novels of J. C.* (1962); Hoffman, C. G., *J. C.* (1964); Roby, K. E., *J. C.* (1984)

THOMAS L. COOKSEY

CARY, Patrick
b. 1623?, Ireland; d. March 1657, Dublin, Ireland

Reared as a Roman Catholic, C. entered a monastery but later married and took government employment in Ireland. C.'s poems, written in 1650 and 1651, were not printed until 1771 as *Poems from a Manuscript written in the time of Oliver* Cromwell, more than a century after his death. His religious verse reflects the influence of John DONNE and Ben JONSON, but the manuscript is illustrated with emblems, in the fashion of the period, by the author. His secular work, entitled "Trivial Ballads," includes love lyrics, pastoral, and satire. First printed in 1819 as *Trivial Poems and Triolets* by Sir Walter SCOTT, the only surviving manuscript of C.'s poems is at the Scott library in Abbotsford, Scotland.

CAUSLEY, Charles
b. 24 August 1917, Launceston, Cornwall

Almost singlehandedly, C. revived the ballad in the English language during the 20th c. Although his career has spanned the fields of education, the military, and criticism, C. is best known and beloved for his poetry. While originally writing for an adult audience, C. also writes for children, with the topics for both audiences ranging from World War II, Christianity, psychological studies, and sociological commentary. His writing is unabashedly influenced by his home county of Cornwall, where he has lived virtually his entire life in the same town.

In 1951, C. published *Farewell, Aggie Weston*, his first collection of poetry. Its greatest significance lies in the fact that the poems reflect C.'s experiences in the British navy during World War II. For C., the crux came after the death of a friend who was in a convoy to Russia in 1940, while C. lasted the war on the sea. *Farewell, Aggie Weston* chronicles the difficulties endured by both C. and his peers.

Union Street, C.'s third collection of poems, included a preface by Edith SITWELL, who appreciated the unique poetry C. creates from his use of traditional poetic forms. This 1957 publication contains selections from C.'s first two books and nineteen new poems. *Union Street* displays C.'s growing maturity as a writer and clearly marks his foray into Christian poetry. Among the many war poems in the volume lies the message that it is possible to find redemption through the good and the bad of life. In this respect, C. seems to be alluding to the early Romantic poets who sought redemption from the evils of the aftermath of the French Revolution, the continuing slave trade, and the failure of the British poor laws.

Johnny Alleluia (1961) combines explicitly Christian themes with humanistic themes. With an empathetic pen, C. relates tales of grief and loss, raises questions of faith and doubt. C.'s interest in Christian themes continues throughout his oeuvre. His interest in CHILDREN'S LITERATURE surfaced soon after *Johnny Alleluia* with *Figgie Hobbin* (1970). The themes in this book mirror those of his more adult poems but his commitment to the English ballad is steadfast. C.'s *Collected Poems* in 1975 was well received in both Britain and the U.S. and helped to give C. a wider audience. In 1979, C. wrote the foreword to *Those First Affections: An Anthology of Poems Composed between the Ages of Two and Eight*, edited by Timothy Rogers. The poems were written by children and the anthology is dotted with children's art. In the foreword, C. reveals not only his respect for literature for and by children, he also discloses his own notions of what a poem is: "A poem must possess qualities both of mystery and revelation." It may tell us something of its subject, its author, of the world, and by a mysterious process of reciprocal communication "something of ourselves." C. encapsulates beautifully what his readers might deduce from reading C.'s adult work; the notion of "reciprocal communication" is evident as the themes and topics of the poems are worked into simple yet powerful ballads that invite the reader to share experiences and questions with the poet.

BIBLIOGRAPHY: Bennett, J. R., "From Patriotism to Peace: The Humanization of War Memorials," *Humanist* 58 (September-October 1998): 5–9; Gioia, D., "C. C.," in Sherry, V. B., Jr., ed., *Poets of Great Britain and Ireland, 1945–1960, DLB* 27 (1984): 40–48

MARCY TANTER

CAUTE, [John] David
b. 16 December 1936, Alexandria, Egypt

C. is a novelist, playwright, historian, and journalist who is drawn to controversy and conflict. Key topics in his work include anticolonial struggle in Africa in the 1950s and 1970s, anticapitalist agitation in the 1960s, and anti-RUSHDIE militancy in the 1990s. In both his fiction and nonfiction, C.'s chief concern is the relationship between the personal and the political: he is intrigued by the complex chemistry of individual impulses and desires that prompts or inhibits commitment in troubled historical situations.

C.'s first novel, *At Fever Pitch* (1959), drew on his experiences as a conscript in the British Army in Africa in 1955–56, but also demonstrated his desire to move beyond semiautobiographical fiction. Using a wide range of approaches, from interior monologue to pastiche African folk poetry, the novel combines the story of a troubled young officer searching for a secure identity with accounts of power struggles among African politicians. Published while C. was still an Oxford undergraduate, it won the James Tait Black Memorial Prize. *Comrade Jacob* (1961), composed when C. was a fellow of All Souls College, Oxford, goes back in time to the 17th c. in its semifictionalized account of Gerrard WINSTANLEY's attempt to establish a utopian community under Oliver Cromwell's regime. The novel succeeds in parts but reveals C.'s key problem as a realistic writer: a tendency to inadvertent caricature. *The Decline of the West* (1966), C.'s third novel, focuses, like his first, on an emergent African state, but this time its canvas and cast of characters are much wider. Its bold conception is let down, however, by its flow of inflated imagery and its increasing indulgence in caricature.

C.'s life changed in 1965, when he resigned from All Souls over a dispute about college policy, and his writing also changed, at first for the better. *The Confrontation* (1970–71) trilogy is his best work. Its first volume, a play called *The Demonstration* (1970), shows a middle-aged drama professor, Steven Bright, rehearsing a student play about a student occupation of an English university at a time when a "real" occupation is taking place in that university. *The Demonstration* constantly mixes levels of illusion and reality to dramatize its key theme: the relationship between art and political action. That theme is explored theoretically in the second volume of the trilogy, *The Illusion* (1971), which makes a lively case for a dialectical novel and theater that disrupts the fictional illusion and then recreates it at a higher level of awareness. Volume 3 of the trilogy, the novel entitled *The Occupation* (1971), charts the personal and political breakdown of a slightly different Steven Bright, a younger English novelist and historian teaching in the U.S. in the turbulent 1960s. *The Occupation* eschews florid prose and strained REALISM; it successfully combines expressionistic, realistic, fantastic, caricatural, and metafictional modes, and its disciplined prose sharpens its depiction of disintegration.

The accomplishment of *The Confrontation* seemed to promise much; but C. fell silent as a novelist for a decade, apart from two pseudonymous thrillers. His most important books in this period were two works of modern history that developed his concern with the relationship between the personal and the political: *The Fellow-Travellers: A Postscript to the Enlightenment* (1973; rev. as *The Fellow-Travllers: Intellectual Friends of Communism*, 1988) and *The Great Fear: The Anti-Communist Purge under Truman and Eisenhower* (1978). It was not until 1983 that he made a comeback as a fiction writer; his factual study of the last days of white Rhodesia, *Under the Skin* (1983), was complemented by a brisk, compelling novel, *The K-Factor* (1983). Both books deal with the identity crisis of a society undergoing fundamental and sometimes violent change: but where *Under the Skin* covers many people and events in a documentary fashion, *The K-Factor* concentrates on a small cast of characters and combines realism and symbolism to convey a profound uncertainty. C.'s longer next novel, *News from Nowhere* (1986) traces the complex story of Richard Stern's involvements with women and politics from his youthful days as a New Left lecturer at the London School of Economics to his middle age as a troubled reporter in the last days of white Rhodesia.

Veronica; or, The Two Nations (1989) comes back to 1980s Britain, dramatizing its divisions by two counterpointed narratives, one by an investigative journalist of working-class origins, the other by a Conservative cabinet minister in love with his own half-sister. Division is also the theme of *The Women's Hour* (1991), this time between two radical eras: a feminist charges an old warhorse of the Left with rape. *Dr. Orwell and Mr. Blair* (1994) explores the ways in which a writer—a partly fictionalized George ORWELL—may manipulate reality, and other people, for his own ends.

C.'s next novel proved his most controversial. *Fatima's Scarf* (1998), based on the Salman RUSHDIE affair, combines a satirical portrait of Gamal Rahman, an Egyptian writer sentenced to death for blasphemy by the Ayatollah Khomeini; a magical-realist history of modern Egypt; a realistic account of the impact of the affair on a Muslim community in a city in the North of England; and a satire on the responses of the London liberal intelligensia. C. could not find a British publisher for *Fatima's Scarf* and finally brought it out at his own expense. Responses ranged from high praise to wholesale dismissal.

Such a range of response has been characteristic of C.'s reception from *The Decline of the West* onward. There is no consensus about his standing as a novelist and little sustained critical analysis of his fiction. But his work does comprise a challenging attempt to widen the scope of the British novel to encompass key political and ideological issues and it remains worth reading for its insights and provocations, especially in *The Confrontation*.

BIBLIOGRAPHY: Tredell, N., *C.'s Confrontations: A Study of the Novels of D. C.* (1994); Tredell, N., "D. C.," in his *Conversations with Critics* (1994): 111–25

NICOLAS TREDELL

CAVENDISH, George
b. 1500?; d. 1562?, Glemsford, Sussex

C.'s biography of Cardinal Wolsey, for whom he had served as gentleman usher and confidant, is an important source for historians as well as for literary scholars. When Wolsey died in disgrace in 1530, C. was with him. The book conforms to the medieval pattern of tragedy, describing a fall from "high estate" and reflecting on "mutability" and the fickleness of fate. Written in 1557, it could not be published in the author's lifetime, though it circulated in manuscript. A garbled version was printed in 1641 as *The Negotiations of Thomas Wolsey*, and a good text was not published until 1810 as *The Life of Cardinal Wolsey*. Later editions have appeared under various titles, including *The Life and Death of Cardinal Wolsey*. Although he played a limited role as a man of letters, C. has often been called the first major English biographer.

CAVENDISH, Margaret Lucas. See NEWCASTLE, Margaret Lucas Cavendish, Duchess of

CAXTON, William
b. 1422?, Kent; d. ca. 1491, London

C. was born to prosperous parents, who apprenticed him to Robert Large, a successful silk mercer who became Lord Mayor of London. C. subsequently set up in business at Bruges, Belgium, and was employed in international negotiations. He translated books from French and in 1476 returned to London and set up a printing press. The first piece known to have been printed by him is an "indulgence" issued by Abbot Sant on December 13, discovered in the Record Office in 1928. The first dated book printed in England was a translation by Lord Rivers—revised by C.—of *The Dictes and Sayenges of the Phylosophers* (1477). C. was busy writing, translating, and printing, as a commercial enterprise, Geoffrey CHAUCER's *Canterbury Tales* (1473 and 1478?), *The Hous of Fame* (1483), *Troilus and Creseide* (1483), and the translation of Boethius (1478?), John GOWER's *Confessio Amantis,* and many poems by John LYDGATE, among others. C.'s output of translations and printed works (18,000 pages) was prodigious.

CECIL, [Lord Edward Christian] David [Gascoyne]
b. 9 April 1902, Hatfield House; d. 1 January 1986, Cranborne, Dorset

C. was educated at Eton and Christ Church, Oxford, where he graduated with a first-class honors degree in history. Apart from the seven years between 1930 and 1937 when he lived as a professional writer, he spent the remainder of his working life until his retirement in 1980 in Oxford, first as a fellow of Wadham College and then at New College where in 1949 he was appointed the first Goldsmith's Professor of English Literature.

His first publication, entitled *Cans and Can'ts* (1927), was little more than a quiz book based on a parlor game that he compiled with Cynthia Asquith and that she described as "a game-book of literary questions and answers." His first literary publication was the life of William COWPER, entitled *The Stricken Deer*, published in 1929. It was an immediate popular and critical success, and was awarded the Hawthornden Prize. The anonymous *Times Literary Supplement* reviewer set the pattern for subsequent reviews of the book. The reviewer pointed out that for one page given to the poems or the letters—"the only Cowper that matters"—he had given twenty to Cowper, "the victim of religious madness." The reviewer also objected to the fact that no sources or references were given, which often made it "difficult to distinguish in Lord David's narrative between what is known and can be related as fact and what is merely Lord David's conjectural construction of what the facts may have been where little or no direct evidence exists." Even so, despite these objections, the review does not hesitate to conclude that "As it is, he has written what is, no doubt, the best one-volume life of Cowper." Joan Haslip in the *London Mercury* pointed out that "it is the man, not the poet, in whom Lord David is primarily interested . . . unlike many biographers, he loves his hero: and makes us love that rather neglected poet." She drew attention to the style in which it is written particularly as exemplified in the now celebrated opening passages of the book which "Beautifully and fastidiously written . . . conveys to us in a few pages the whole spirit of the age." She sums up the book's achievement by saying that Cowper "has at last found a truly sympathetic biographer, one who possesses peculiar insight into the workings of the sensitive mind of a poet." However, the most telling comment of all was made by Frederick E. Pierce who writing in the *Yale Review* said that this biography held his attention as few books had held his attention in a long time. "It did not tell a great deal that was previously unknown," he said, "it had some obvious faults of detail; but it had a compelling power. Its characters lived with all the vividness of a first-class novel or drama."

His life of Cowper set a pattern for all his subsequent biographies. As the title of his short biographies of Dorothy Osborne and Thomas GRAY indicate—*Two Quiet Lives* (1948)—he was most interested in those who lived away from the mainstream and whose inner lives of sensitive contemplation were richer and more significant than their outward lives of day to day affairs. Indeed, he was often criticized for ignoring the world of passion, ugliness, and cruelty. The exception was his biography of Lord Melbourne that was published in two volumes, *The Young Melbourne and the Story of His Marriage with Caroline Lamb* (1939) and *Lord M.; or, The Later Life of Lord Melbourne* (1954). Because he was writing about a member of his mother's family, it was in that respect a work of filial piety and he was able in this biography to draw on previously unpublished private manuscript material. He gives a brilliantly illuminating picture of England during the Regency period and a convincing portrait of one of its most prominent statesmen.

In 1956, C. was invited by Max BEERBOHM's widow to write her husband's biography. After biographies of Cowper and Melbourne, the subject seems on the face of it too lightweight to warrant a full-scale biography. Yet C. presents a brilliant synthesis of memories, impressions, and anecdotes of those who knew him and creates from this mosaic a vivid portrait of an unusually gifted man presented without undue partiality but with sympathy and insight. Evelyn WAUGH who had himself experienced the difficulties facing a biographer was able to fully appreciate C.'s considerable achievement and commented that "Lord David had been content to tell it in tactfully chosen, familiar extracts from his subject's own writing. The connecting passages present a problem. Beerbohm's own literary grace was so complete that the juxtaposition of another hand must inevitably make a crude contrast. Any attempt to emulate the master's own style would have been disastrous. But Lord David has an easy, Whiggish negligence of grammar which gives the happy illusion that he is reading aloud in the drawing room and occasionally pausing to comment colloquially on the entertainment." Even allowing for the largely unfounded criticism of his grammar, Waugh well describes the tone of C.'s style—informal, conversational, and well-bred though he misses those occasions when his prose becomes rhythmic, flexible, and elegant especially when establishing social and psychological truths.

C. wrote a number of books of literary criticism and his study of *Early Victorian Novelists* (1934) was one of the first attempts to evaluate the work of Charles DICKENS, William Makepeace THACKERAY, the BRONTËS, Elizabeth Cleyhorn GASKELL, Anthony TROLLOPE, and George ELIOT. He effectively laid down the agenda for subsequent discussion of their achievements and significance. Similarly, his study entitled *Hardy, the Novelist* (1943) was largely responsible for introducing Thomas HARDY into serious, academic consideration. His critical work was always directed toward appreciation rather than analysis and he showed little or no interest in critical theory. He regarded literature as an integral art of life written by men about life and to be seen against the background of their lives and their times. Often in his critical work he adopted a predominantly biographical approach to his subject as he did in in *Visionary and Dreamer: Two Poetic Painters* (1969) where he presents the lives of Samuel Palmer and Edward Burne-Jones by relating their lives to their art while avoiding any direct examination of their painting. The outstanding work of his retirement are the two pictorial biographies of Jane AUSTEN and Charles LAMB that he published in 1978 and 1983, respectively. *A Portrait of Jane Austen* is handsomely and lavishly illustrated, and attempts to reconstruct her life and to explore its relation to her art as well as to her place in society. Like *A Portrait of Charles Lamb,* it exemplifies popular BIOGRAPHY at its best, direct and lucid and written with love and admiration for their subjects. Both books were very successful commercially.

As a writer, C. combined scholarly accuracy with elegance of style and his work achieved a wide popular appeal. He had an instinctive grasp of narrative development and always avoided the complex and the abstract keeping his work close to the story and in touch with the personalities involved so that even if they were original they were always fresh and readable.

BIBLIOGRAPHY: Cranborne, H., *D. C.* (1990); Fane, J., *Best Friends: Memoirs of Rachel and D. C., Cynthia Asquith, L. P. Hartley, and Some Others* (1990)

A. R. JONES

CHAPMAN, George

b. 1559?, Hitchin, Hertfordshire; d. 12 May 1634, London

Best known for his translation of Homer's *Iliad* (1598) and *Odyssey* (1614?), C.'s life was as exciting and multifaceted as the original poems and plays he produced. He was in fact jailed for his collaboration with Ben JONSON and John MARSTON in *Eastward Ho* (perf. ca. 1604–5; pub. 1605). Apparently, JAMES I did not take the off-hand remarks about the Scottish in this play as being humorous at all. Nonetheless, C. persevered and found a helpful patron in Robert Carr, Earl of Somerset, who provided C. with ample financial backing enabling him to complete many important poems and plays. C. stands out as one of the few Elizabethan–Jacobean playwrights who were able to make the transition from noteworthy poet to dramatist of substance.

"Ovid's Banquet of Sence" marks the pinnacle of C.'s poetry with one of the most ambitious experiments in Elizabethan verse. Consisting of 117 stanzas of nine lines, C. manages to display amazingly vast fields of inquiry as he relates the story of Ovid and Corynna. Ovid's infatuation with Corynna is broken down into five stages corresponding with each of the five senses. C. follows Marsilio Ficino's commentary on Plato's Symposium very closely on the primacy of the senses starting with vision as the most refined followed by hearing, smell, taste, and lastly touch.

Gerald Snare and several other scholars see C.'s use of highbrow conventions and references to Neoplatonism as somewhat of a distraction from the greater message of a poem that is concerned with voyeurism and eroticism. On the other hand, Frank Kermode views "Ovid's Banquet" as a reversal and perversion of the banquet of the senses. The contentions raised among various scholars over "Ovid's Banquet" are evidence of the poem's slippery decentering nature and multivalent complexity. Consequently, C.'s poetry is best approached as a mirror that reflects back to readers their own tendencies and viewpoints that are often inseparable from the text's message itself.

C.'s poetry in general introduces us to a plethora of classical allusions framed within the Renaissance mind-set. *The Shadow of Night* (1594) is a complex series of poems done in honor of Cynthia, the goddess of the moon. An elaborate legend, in fact, grew out of these poems about an alleged group of scholars, artists, and mystics referred to as the School of Night. Sir Walter RALEIGH, John DEE, C., and several others were implicated in tales of this secret school that met covertly to exchange ideas and arcane learning under the cloak of night. In the Night series, C. again forces the reader to come to terms with the wonder and shortcomings of vision and the empirical world. C. touches on similar perceptual issues in his "Andromeda Liberata," "A Coronet for his Mistress," as well as his completion of Christopher MARLOWE's unfinished "Hero and Leander." C. creates a seductive transition in and out of Marlowe's sardonic views of court and courtly love. The view C. presents is an often cruel but very telling one of Love as an implement and trope as much as an element of play in the circles of court.

One of the more difficult tasks for the serious reader of C.'s works is perceiving the relationship between his poetry and plays. C. composed several masques and plays of which approximately twelve plays survive. He is best known for his tragedies, *The Widdowes Teares* (perf. ca. 1604–5; pub. 1612) and *The Conspiracie, and Tragedie of Charles Duke of Byron* (perf. ca. 1607–8; pub. 1608), and most notably, *Bussy D'Ambois* (perf. 1604; pub. 1607). In his behind-the-scenes look at the seedier aspects of courtiership, C. paints a very dark picture of advancement and downfall in the circles of court in "Bussy." The central figure of Bussy D'Ambois is a melancholic revenger cum upstart courtier, who may have typified what C. felt about courts and their attendant etiquette as a specious and malign world where advancement means everything. In the play, Bussy works immediately to antagonize certain individuals by flirting with the Duke of Guise's wife. In his attempt to take the higher moral ground Bussy is trapped and killed for his suspected adultery with the Count of Montsurry's wife, Tamara. It is an important tale with relation to C.'s poetry because it shows his interest in people's preoccupation with appearances. While it is C.'s most successful and ambitious production, it is not without its faults as it attempts to squeeze in just about every popular convention of the Elizabethan stage including necromancy, ghosts, domestic abuse, and egregious violence.

Why C. discontinued producing poetry once he became successful as a playwright is not entirely clear. Patronage itself may have had a large role to play in this matter, and it may have been that C. could no longer devote the time to the craft necessary to create such complex and far reaching poems. And it may have been that his poetry had run its course in the terms of his ability to maintain a rarefied perspective. Nonetheless, C.'s plays are in many ways an extension of his poems as C. took his investigations of vision, and extended them to look at the ways the individual and group view and are viewed in turn.

BIBLIOGRAPHY: Beach, V. W., Jr., *G. C.* (1995); MacLure, M., *G. C.* (1966); Rees, E., *The Tragedies of G. C.* (1952); Snare, G., *The Mystification of G. C.* (1989)

BOB PODGURSKI

CHAPONE, [Mrs.] Hester
b. 27 October 1727, Twywell, Northants; d. 25 December 1801, Hadley, Middlesex

Essayist and poet, C.—who also wrote under the name Hester Mulso—was a member of the Bluestocking circle that included Elizabeth CARTER, Fanny BURNEY, and Elizabeth MONTAGU, among others. C.'s *Letters on the Improvement of the Mind* (1773) was enormously popular and influential with parents and educators. Lydia Languish, in Richard Brinsley SHERIDAN's *The Rivals*, pretends to be reading C. instead of Tobias SMOLLETT and Henry FIELDING. Lydia's preference for vital contemporary fiction is a healthy reaction, as C.'s censorious tone and repressive nagging invite rebellion. C. also published *Miscellanies in Prose and Verse* (1775) and *A Letter to a New Married Lady* (1777). Her letters to Carter and Samuel RICHARDSON were published posthumously together with a memoir in *The Works of Mrs. Chapone* (4 vols., 1807).

CHATTERTON, Thomas
b. 20 November 1752, Bristol; d. 30 August 1770, London

Any assessment of C. will seem like a struggle between the historical figure of the poet, the poetry it-self, and the overwhelming presence of the legendary Romantic archetype epitomized by the very name of William WORDSWORTH's "Marvellous Boy." The major Romantics regarded the boy poet as a luminary figure, representing the essential genius of poetry itself, and also a late companion in literary and millennial dreams. Henry Wallis's evocative painting *The Death of Chatterton* (1856) has become an integral part of the legend.

The real C. was the posthumous son of a schoolmaster father and was educated at Colston's Hospital in Bristol (1760–67) until the age of fourteen, when he became an apprentice to John Lambert, an attorney, from 1767 to 1770. He wrote, or concocted in a pseudo-medieval style, the infamous "Rowley" poems during the years 1768–69 that brought him to the attention of Horace WALPOLE, whose enthusiasm died away sharply when he suspected that C.'s work was in fact a modern forgery. C. moved to London in 1770, convinced of his own importance as a writer, in order to seek fame and reward for his work, where he died either by suicide or from a drug overdose, surrounded by the torn-up pieces of his manuscripts.

Current critical opinion seeks to show the poet seeking or inventing paternal figures or engaging in acts of filial rebellion through the medium of his poetry. His poetical experiments among a wide variety of forms and styles certainly show the presence of poetical fathers such as Geoffrey CHAUCER, William SHAKESPEARE, and major 18th-c. figures such as Alexander POPE, Charles CHURCHILL, John DRYDEN, and Jonathan SWIFT. C.'s ability in the field of imitation, and especially his precocity in lyric invention, is impressive and during his short life, he attempted hymns, fables, pastorals, verse satires, prose poetry, eclogues, and other forms. His poetry also takes note of the contemporary fashion for the antique, informed by the publication of Thomas PERCY's *Reliques* in 1765, foregrounding the ballad form.

The poet had begun to write verse while still at Colston's school, and one of his productions of that period is "Apostate Will," a satire composed in 1764, which makes moral comment upon a corrupt Bristolian religious figure in a most economically succinct way. The maturity of the poetry is immediately striking. But it was the church of St. Mary Redcliffe in Bristol that served as the place of origination for his most enduring literary productions, which supplied among other things an imaginary history of his native city. C. claimed to have had access to original medieval documents from the chests in the muniments room of the church and began to arouse local antiquarian interest in his parchments. He invented one Thomas Rowley, monk, a 15th-c. Bristolian poet, and placed him under the patronage of one (historically real) William Canynges, Bristol merchant and builder of St. Mary Redcliffe, and produced correspondence between the two men. C.'s supposedly 15th-c. Rowleyan vocabulary can be sourced from a list of originals, and this was supplemented by the poet's own coinings in what is a loose phonetic method, aping medieval spelling.

This approach is what mars the Rowley poems to some extent (as it did for Samuel Taylor COLERIDGE in the first version of his "Ancient Mariner"), forming what is at times an irritating visual barrier, underneath which poetry of real power and brilliance resides, such as in the refrain of the "Mynstrelles Songe" from *Aella: A Tragycal Interlude* (wr. 1769): "Mie love ys dedde,/Gon to hys deathe-bedde,/Al under the willow tree." Other Rowley poems might be mentioned alongside *Aella*, such as "An Excelente Balade of Charitie" (wr. 1770) and his three medieval eclogues (wr. 1769) that owe a debt to William COLLINS's work in that field. In 1770, C. also produced three African eclogues, "Heccar and Gaira. An African Eclogue," "Narva and Mored," and The Death of Nicou," which are a vivid prelude to the subject matter and taste of the first Romantics, especially William BLAKE and Robert SOUTHEY. During C.'s last two years, the poet experimented with various forms including most importantly perhaps the satirical modes that show him in 1770 trying to engage with and survive in the ethos of 18th-c. London.

BIBLIOGRAPHY: Ackroyd, P., *C.* (1987); Kelly, L., *The Marvellous Boy: The Life and Myth of T. C.* (1971); Taylor, D. S., and B. B. Hoover, eds., *The Complete Works of T. C.* (2 vols., 1971)

CHRISTOPHER J. P. SMITH

CHATWIN, Bruce [Charles]

b. 13 May 1940, Sheffield; d. 18 January 1989, Nice, France

Widely regarded as one of England's most respected travel writers, C. was also a popular journalist, novelist, and essayist. At an early age, C. became fascinated with remote and barely habitable geographical locations, an interest that took him to the Sudan, Afghanistan, and Patagonia, among many other countries. His first full-length book, *In Patagonia* (1977), was a journal of his visit to the bottom of the world. It was very favorably reviewed and placed him, according to some commentators, alongside such classic British travel writers as D. H. LAWRENCE and Evelyn WAUGH. The book won C. both the prestigious Hawthornden Prize and also the E. M. Forster Prize in 1979. His uncanny ability to amalgamate factual information with elegant fictional techniques made him a rarity among travel writers.

After a failed attempt to write a scholarly biography of a notorious 19th-c. Brazilian slave trader, Francesco de Souza, he chose to fictionalize the information he had gathered in his life-threatening journey to Benin, the new name of the ancient West African country of Dahomey, where de Souza acquired his slaves. De Souza became enormously wealthy and practiced the most sadistic forms of cruelty on the slaves that he sold to plantation owners in Brazil. C.'s novel was called *The Viceroy of Ouidah* (1980) and records the rise and fall of de Souza into well-earned disgrace.

Though C.'s reputation as one of England's finest travel writers was growing, he decided that his next book would be a novel about people who rarely left their home. *On the Black Hill* (1982) was a novel based on the lives of twin brothers in Eastern Wales whose main purpose in life was to preserve the innocence of their farm, "The Vision," from the corrupting influences of a mechanized, materialistic world. This pastoral novel was firmly grounded in the novelist tradition of Thomas HARDY and Mary WEBB. The twins, Benjamin and Lewis, exert great effort and time in combating the evils of the city and preserving the innocence of country living.

Though C.'s reputation as both an engaging travel writer and entertaining novelist grew, none of his first three books were so critically acclaimed as *The Songlines* (1987), a nonfiction travelogue based on his journey to Australia with Salman RUSHDIE. Though commentators were never sure about the actual "facts" of the trip, C. himself confessed that he created large portions of the narrative to tie everything together neatly. Nonetheless, it became C.'s first bestseller. But what drew readers to it was not so much the rather tame adventures of the characters, but the meditations and musings of the main character. The book can be read, then, as a novel of ideas about the sad fate of the helpless Aboriginals, accompanied by C.'s commentary on the fate of all nomadic communities. The Aboriginals were forced to abandon their journeys and live in enforced settlement, a condition that has done untold harm to their sacred relationship with the land.

C.'s last book was a novel *Utz* (1988), his shortest and, some would say, his finest book. He was so ill with AIDS that most of it was written in the hospital. The topic of *Utz* is the psychopathology of the compulsive collector, an area with which C. was very familiar because he had worked at Sotheby's in London for many years and observed the behavior of collectors; he himself was also a determined collector. Kaspar Utz had somehow managed to retain his million-dollar collection of rare Meissen figurines in spite of Communist rule in Prague. The novel ends with the collection's mysterious disappearance after Utz's death. Another theme surfaces as the narrator realizes the transitory nature of human life: only art conquers time's inevitability. C. was himself dead less than a year after the publication of *Utz*.

Shortly after C.'s death, a collection of his essays was published entitled *What Am I Doing Here* (1989). One of the major recurring issues throughout the essays is also the theme of virtually all of his books: the nature of human restlessness. C. called it the greatest mystery in human history. Because he had spent so much time with nomadic tribes, he began to believe remaining in one location an unnatural condition, and called it "the sins of settlement." This became for him the fall of mankind.

BIBLIOGRAPHY: Clapp, S., *With C.: Portrait of a Writer* (1997); Meanor, P., *B. C.* (1997); Murray, N., *B. C.* (1993); Shakespeare, N., *B. C.* (1999)

PATRICK MEANOR

CHAUCER, Geoffrey

b. ca. 1340, London, d. 25 October 1400, London

C. is the most varied, accessible, and remarkable of the three or four great English poets of the second half of the 14th c. He began as a courtly poet in the Age of Chivalry, in the court of the warlike Edward III, but his interests were not in combat. They could be found in the joys, sadness, and complications of love, extending to speculations about the meaning of love and death. Then his range extended through history, science (especially astronomy), several bawdy comic tales of town and village life, stories of saintly women, and finally the serious contemplations of religion. Throughout his work there is a sort of questioning, and ultimately a progress from multiplicity of interest and narrative to a final singularity of earnest conviction.

His use of the English language is notable. The literary and social dominance of the anglified French derived from the Norman Conquest had lapsed, but Continental French was the language of high culture in which much of C.'s early reading lay. English was C.'s basic language but in his writing it was blended with high-level French expressions. Though well-educated lay people could read and write English, the language of literature still had the vigor and expansiveness of the spoken word that C. fully exploited in his style. English, retaining the pure vowels and traces of grammatical inflection, which make it much harder to modernize than English only a hundred years later, had achieved a beauty of sound and wealth of vocabulary, enriched by French and Norse loan words, that C. developed with wonderful rhetorical skill. Probably C.'s earliest original poem, still heavily dependent on courtly French models, was *The Book of the Duchess* (wr. ca. 1368), an elegy that is also a eulogy of the recently dead wife of John, Duke of Lancaster, son of King Edward III. Its 1,334 octosyllabic lines in couplets comprise a courtly yet learned poem where the poet represents himself as a dreamer who hears

the lament of the noble mourner, yet in the introduction there is a touch of HUMOR. It is an entirely secular poem that marks the point of take-off of the variety and wealth of C.'s poetry and of modern English poetry as a whole. About the same time probably was written the devotional poem *An ABC*, of 184 lines in rhyming stanzas, a translation, giving us the other devotional side of C.'s work and emotional life.

By 1368, C. had served his apprenticeship to courtly life first as page and then esquire in Edward's court, having been briefly on a military foray in France (1359–60). He became a "working" courtier and the royal court is the background of all his work. The times were troubled, with plague, political turmoil, and war with France, reflected in some short personal lyrics about the badness of the times and the need for religious resignation. Only indirectly appears some sense of personal frustration in *The House of Fame*, still written in the rough octosyllabic couplets of *The Book of the Duchess* and therefore perhaps the next to be written, some time in the mid-1370s and 2,158 lines long. It is another dream poem, a bit dissatisfied, again told by the poet-narrator thus both "inside" and "outside" the poem. In one notable passage (529–660), a great golden eagle carries the poet up to the stars, lectures him, calls him "Geoffrey," complains about his plumpness making him heavy, and hears how the poet works in the Custom House all day and then reads late into the night, knowing nothing about his neighbors. Unfinished, it is a poem of questioning and deep skepticism about fame, rumor, stories, authority. Similar to *The Book of the Duchess*, it has an amazing wealth of literary reference, and in addition a delightful lightness of touch.

The touches of Italian influence in *The House of Fame*, product of C.'s Italian journeys, burst forth in the next major poem, *The Parliament of Fowls* (wr. ca. 1382), again centring on the problems and inner contradictions of chivalric love, again figuring the puzzled poet-narrator. The Italian influence is most evident in borrowings from Boccaccio and Dante, most subtle in the new longer line of ten or eleven syllables, regular stress, seven-line rhyming stanzas, making 699 lines, with rich vocabulary. A somewhat austere prelude based on a classical Latin text asks what is the "common good"? Then in a dream the poet is let into a park where first he finds another Temple of Venus featuring hot desire, then a great gathering of birds who have come to seek their mates on St. Valentine's Day under the "empress" Nature. The birds are comically characterized in groups but interest centers on three noble tercel eagles all wooing the same beautiful formel eagle. Though one is superior in rank, they all represent the nobility as do the other birds the commoners. While the common birds can readily select their mates the nobility are hopelessly frustrated, since all three have professed undying love and only one can mate the formel eagle. Some scholars see behind this a political allegory of the young King Richard II's wooing, but the intrinsic conflicts of love and the inherent contentiousness of chivalric culture seem human enough justification. Eventually, the problem of choice is not solved but postponed. Rich descriptions contrast with lively colloquial dialogue.

The hint of philosophical depth derives from C.'s interest in that most influential philosophical work of the Middle Ages and later, the *De Consolatione Philosophia* written under sentence of death by the statesman and philosopher Boethius in Latin in alternating prose and verse, tackling the problems of good and evil, fortune, true happiness, free will and destiny. So C.'s quest, or pilgrimage, for true life continues. C.'s lengthy prose translation underlies the comedy and tragedy of his major completed long poem *Troilus and Criseyde*, written in the mid-1380s, about the same time as *De Consolatione,* and like it divided into five "Books" totaling 8,239 lines of ten or eleven syllables in seven-line rhyming stanzas of great narrative fluency and variable style—at times colloquial, formal, solemn, beautifully descriptive. The essential story is simple, based on a swift lively poem in Italian by Boccaccio, *Il Filostrato,* expanded and enriched by commentary and digression, deepened and changed in characterization. The heroic young Troilus, a perfect knight, a prince of Troy that is besieged by the Greeks, falls in love with the beautiful young widow Criseyde. He wins her, helped by his older friend Pandarus, but she is sent to the Greeks and abandons Troilus's faithful love. Troilus rages desperately and is killed in battle by "the fierce Achilles." The poem then in an astonishing final turn shows him carried to a pagan afterlife from which he looks down in scorn at those who bewail his death, and on pagan gods and religion. A wholly different perspective is thrown over the reader's earlier sympathy for the admirable hero and his passionate faithful love.

Although there is no poet-narrator actually in the poem, it is told with so strong a sense of personal engagement, with such a variety of implicit attitudes, ironic, amused, sympathetic in turn that many modern critics have seen the poem as told by a dramatic narrator detached from the poet. The lovers are the first sensitively drawn characters in English literature. Pandarus, friend of Troilus, uncle of Criseyde, is fully realized as an emotional, loyal yet unprincipled go-between. Troilus is the essence of chivalric truth and youthful devotion. The stars in their courses, notably Venus, planet and goddess of love, guide the action raising questions of free will and destiny told in Boethian terms. The span of C.'s personal views, from pessimistic to light-hearted, is reflected in his lyrics, while his expert interest in astronomy is attested by the prose translation, *A Treatise on the Astrolabe.*

In full-scale poetry follows a less successful attempt to convey pathos in more stories of betrayal in love, broken off at the ninth tale, *The Legend of Good Women* (wr. ca. 1386). The whole is redeemed by the "Prologue" in which the now familiar poet-narrator presents himself in a garden, worshiping, in a teasingly exaggerated mode, the daisy newly sprung in spring, and being reproached by the god of love for defaming women. The courtly playfulness and personal touch make the lines about spring one of C.'s deservedly most famous passages. The stories, told as a penalty, vary in quality, parts flat, some extravagant, some flippant.

The Legend of Good Women was probably abandoned for the irresistible urge to retell a variety of stories. The stroke of genius was to invent different characters to tell various tales, and to gather them in the socially mixed company of a pilgrimage to Canterbury. C.'s descriptions of the pilgrims became that most famous English poem, "The General Prologue" to *The Canterbury Tales,* probably composed about 1387, in ten- or eleven-syllable rhyming couplets. The beginning, describing the coming of spring and the urge to go on pilgrimage, swoops down from the burgeoning months, the newly stirring natural growth, the fresh song of birds, to the gathering of men and women in the Tabard Inn. Then there are brief descriptions that extend from the noble Knight, through a variety of clerics, bourgeois, tradesmen to the humble Parson and his Ploughman brother, all crisply described in terms of dress and character; all England seems to be summed up there. Their origin lies in well-established social types, and the basic scheme depends on the ancient tripartite division of society into fighting men, praying men, laborers; but many fit ill into this ideal pattern and are gently or severely satirized. They agree to tell stories to liven the tedium of the journey, though the scheme was never finished. The first tale is the Knight's, based on a much longer Italian poem by Boccaccio, and indeed all the tales are, like all traditional literature, based on earlier versions, known in several languages. "The Knight's Tale" is a highly wrought chivalric romance of antiquity, telling how two young knights, Palamon and Arcite, fight for the love of the beautiful princess Emily. Being set in antiquity their respective gods are Venus, Mars, and Diana, but these have astrological powers thought to be scientifically true in the 14th c. The characters are only slightly individualized, though the middle-aged Duke Theseus, magnificent, testy, ultimately merciful with a touch of humor, is reminiscent of Edward III. The sorrows of love, the excitement of a great tournament, are adorned with mythological description and philosophical passages.

The Miller's and Reeve's tales that follow are very different "churl's tales," the Miller's a comic parallel of two young men after a girl, but they are a village barber and university clerk of Oxford, the girl a lusty eighteen-year-old married to a jealous carpenter. The highly comical plot is bawdy but not obscene. "The Reeve's Tale" set at Trumpington near Cambridge has two clerks at first tricked by a miller, who get their revenge in a romping bedroom farce involving the miller's daughter and wife. The plots of each tale are well-known European popular comic tales, adapted by C. to achieve a poetic but comic justice. The style is sinewy, direct, rich in nouns and verbs, sparing of adjectives. The village settings are realistic. The characters are stereotypes but speak with individual and comic vigor. Before these two low-class speakers tell their tales the poet pretends to apologize for their "broad speech"—he has to report what they actually say. This is a dramatic ideal new in English literature, though the degree of dramatization varies and critics differ about the extent to which in various tales the poet speaks in his own voice or as a dramatic character, ironically. "The General Prologue," "Knight's Tale," "Miller's Tale," "Reeve's Tale" with the fragmentary "Cook's Tale" make up an indisputable group. There are ten such groups within the manuscripts left at C.'s death, labeled Fragments 1–10.

In many cases, consecutive tales are connected by short passages of dramatic interplay between the pilgrims, characters in action, judging and arguing so as to almost make up a tale of their own in colloquial speech bringing the characters before us as alive to our imaginations as they were six hundred years ago. The tales that are told are different in kind, and differences are heightened by contrasts of mood in successive tales. The largest number of tales, though not the most lines, is formed by some seven popular, sometimes bawdy comic tales, of which the "Miller's Tale" and "Reeve's Tale" are examples. All are European folktales and are allotted to more or less appropriate characters. These are the tales most relished by modern taste, and for pace, incisive characterization, ludicrous events, in which the gross material aspects of life predominate over the more spiritual, they are unrivaled. The predominant tone is of detached humorous satire. But "The Wife of Bath's Prologue," a long and most original and entertaining account of her life with five husbands, almost counts as a comic tale of its own. Similar "confessional" prologues are given to the Pardoner and the Canon's Yeoman. They mark a major development in subjective dramatic expression, whereas the other tales existed, however adapted, before the characters who are supposed to tell them.

Occasionally, C. changed his mind as to the most appropriate teller. The poet-narrator Chaucer assigns to himself as pilgrim, a parody of old-fashioned English ROMANCE. Stopped because the pilgrims think it so bad, he follows with a serious prose treatise on the virtues of peace and self-restraint verging on the high

style. The serious vein in C.'s work deserves to be recognized—the grimly humorous anecdote about greed and death by the Pardoner, about honor and virginity by the Physician, the tales of holy women by the Clerk about the amazing and poignant patience of Griselda, told in a stark strong style, or by the Man of Law about the firmness of Constance, set adrift with her child on the sea, with its more obviously religious message. But all this variety is drawn together in an astonishing end to *The Canterbury Tales*, where the last tale is a treatise on penitence and the Seven Deadly Sins in prose. A final surprise comes at the very end, in which C. in his own voice "revokes" or "retracts" all his secular works as sinful and acknowledges only his overtly religious works. From variety, he has moved to a serious religious singleness of purpose. By his successors, he was revered as the "father of English poetry."

BIBLIOGRAPHY: Benson, L. D., gen. ed., *The Riverside C.* (3rd ed., 1987); Brewer, D., *A New Introduction to C.* (2nd ed., 1998); Brewer, D., *The World of C.* (2000); Brown, P., ed., *A Companion to C.* (2000); Muscatine, C., *Medieval Literature, Style, and Culture* (1999); Patterson, L., *C. and the Subject of History* (1991); Pearsall, D., *The Life of G. C.* (1992); Richmond, V. B., *G. C.* (1992); Wallace, D., *Chaucerian Polity* (1997)

DEREK BREWER

CHEKE, [Sir] John

b. 16 June 1514, Cambridge; d. 13 September 1557, London

A classical scholar in the tradition of Renaissance humanists such as John COLET, Desiderius ERASMUS, and Sir Thomas MORE, C. was educated at St. John's College, Cambridge, and later served as tutor to the future Edward VI. Appointed the first Regius Professor of Greek in 1540, C. made many translations from Greek into Latin and was influential in the development of English prose toward greater clarity. Following the death of Edward and the accession of Catholic Queen Mary, C. lost favor with the court and fled England for the Continent. Arrested by order of Philip II of Spain, C. was returned to England in 1556 and forced to publicly recant his faith. In John MILTON's Sonnet XI, the poet looks back to the "soul of Sir John Cheke" as a beacon in an age as barbarous as his own.

CHESTERFIELD, Philip Dormer Stanhope, Fourth Earl of

b. 22 September 1694, London; d. 24 March 1773, London

C.'s *Letters to His Son* were published by the son's widow in two volumes in 1774, and the book became a standard manual on how to behave in society. Samuel JOHNSON's famous condemnation that they taught "the morals of a whore and the manners of a dancing master" is unjust: C. hoped the boy (who was illegitimate) would become a diplomat and therefore urged upon him "learning, honour and virtue," graceful carriage, easy manners, and avoidance of all eccentricity. C. advises his son to adapt himself to the world as it is, which seemed to religious readers cynical. C.'s extended definition of "good breeding" amounts broadly to tact and common sense, though laughter is stigmatized as vulgar and women were "but children of a larger growth." C. criticized the then popular pronunciation "obleeged" as affected and in twenty years it had gone out of fashion. The book survives as a record of the values and manners of the Georgian gentleman.

CHESTERTON, G[ilbert] K[eith]

b. 29 May 1874, London; d. 14 June 1936, Beaconsfield

C.'s work is not generally promoted in academic circles, nor does it figure in the present narrow literary canon, but it remains popular with a wide public and is often quoted in surprising quarters; sometimes, one suspects, in an obstinate attempt to offend the tender feelings of liberal "bien pensants." His reputation has waxed and waned and sometimes seems to stand higher abroad than in his homeland.

C. was born into the very middle of the middle class, as he was to put it later. His brother Cecil was born five years later. Their father had worked as an estate agent in the family firm (which still exists) but, as a cultivated Edwardian gentleman, he had retired early to devote himself to a series of dilettante hobbies. Marie, their mother, was of both Swiss and Scottish extraction.

C. was educated at the famous London day school, St. Paul's, where he won the poetry prize and the French prize and founded the Junior Debating Society. However, instead of going to Oxford, he attended lectures at University College and a book illustration course at the Slade School of Art but did not take a final degree. Thus, he escaped some of the rigors of academic training, but kept intact his originality and imagination and the late 1880s and early 1890s saw him writing poems, stories, and three early novels.

He read widely and developed his natural skill of drawing lively caricatures. Yet it was a time of modish decadence in all the arts, rather like our own fin de siècle age, and he met some nihilistic students. This and other problems upset him and precipitated a depression. He was drawn out of this sorry state by reading poetry such as Walt Whitman's optimistic verse and leaving the rarified atmosphere of the Slade for the busy world of practical journalism. At least he was

not pressed for money, but lived at home with his generous parents and, from 1896 to 1901, earned a modest living as a book illustrator and a reader for the publishers Fisher Unwin, while he began to make a name for himself with poetry and other writings.

Like Samuel JOHNSON, C. loved London, was popular in Fleet Street, and had a wide circle of friends, and in 1901 he married Frances Blogg from the arty and fashionable garden suburb of Bedford Park. From about this time also, he began to take his Anglo-Catholic faith more seriously, although he did not become a Roman Catholic until 1922. C. and his wife lived first in a Battersea flat, south of the Thames, but from 1909 decided to make their permanent home in Beaconsfield. Sadly for them both they had no children.

In the course of a long and successful literary career, C. wrote over a hundred varied works of poetry, fiction, criticism, history, and BIOGRAPHY, with books of essays on politics, economics, and religion. However, the bulk of his prolific writing took the form of journalism, most of which is not yet collected. He began his journalistic career in 1900, by writing articles for the *Speaker*, which was a liberal paper critical of the South African War. In time, C. wrote for the *Clarion, Daily News*, the *New Era*, and *New Age*, before taking over Cecil's *New Witness* and then editing his *G. K.'s Weekly*. From 1905 until his death in 1936, he wrote regular articles for the *Daily Herald* and *Illustrated London News*.

C. wrote over six hundred poems, but although editions were published in 1915, 1927, and 1933 as well as a recent (1994) volume for the Ignatius Press, edited by Aidan Mackey, some of his best verses have still to be collected. His poetry varies from short comic verses, as collected in his early *Greybeards at Play* (1900), to long historical/religious narratives, the most important of which was *The Ballad of the White Horse* (1911), about King ALFRED's struggle with the Danes, which expresses both his love for England and his belief in her special destiny. Other serious works include *The Ballad of St. Barbara* (1922), on World War I, *The Queen of Seven Swords* (1926), and verses on *Gloria in Profundis* (1927), *Ubi Ecclesia* (1929), and *The Grave of Arthur* (1930).

Like Hilaire BELLOC, C. was attracted by the idea of the Church Militant and lacked modern qualms about celebrating crusades, or battles against assorted barbarians, politicians, financiers, Germans and Turks; "Lepanto" being a prime example. While few consider his verse the greatest poetry, it was enjoyed in his lifetime and has been appreciated since, as expressing a spirit at once humorous, optimistic and quintessentially English. He was perhaps something rarer than a great poet, a kind of modern bard.

C.'s first three novels, *Basil Howe* (wr. 1894), *The Adventurous Abbot Stephen* (wr. 1896), both published in 1996, and *The Man with Two Legs*, published in 1997, first came out in installment form. His later fiction has been analyzed by Father Ian Boyd, founder and editor of the *Chesterton Review*. C.'s most famous novel *The Napoleon of Notting Hill* (1904) expresses his belief in the values of local patriotism and self-sufficiency. A story collection *The Club of Queer Trades* (1905) followed, before, the most ingenious of all, *The Man Who Was Thursday* (1908). Then came *The Ball and the Cross* (1909), *Manalive* (1912), and *The Flying Inn* (1914). These six works were all written before the watershed of C.'s critical illness in 1914, followed by World War I. Afterward, C. published *The Man Who Knew Too Much* (1922) and *Tales of the Long Bow* (1925). *The Return of Don Quixote* (1927), though written earlier, was published as a serial in *G. K.'s Weekly*. It is his most mature novel in featuring strong women characters and best expressing his political and economic ideas. Next follow *The Poet and the Lunatics* (1929), *Four Faultless Felons* (1930), *The Well and the Shallows* (1935), and *The Paradoxes of Mr. Pond* (1937).

C. was intrigued by detective yarns and developed his own clerical sleuth in Father Brown. There were five successful volumes: *The Innocence of Father Brown* (1911), *The Wisdom of Father Brown* (1914), *The Incredulity of Father Brown* (1926), *The Secret of Father Brown* (1927), and finally *The Scandal of Father Brown* (1935). All are based on the character of the real Father (later Monsignor) John O'Connor who reciprocated with a book of his own, entitled *Father Brown on Chesterton* (1937).

C. as a child loved his toy theater and as an adult enjoyed drama. He wrote several plays himself, some for private production. These included *Magic* (1913), *The Judgement of Dr. Johnson* (1927), *The Turkey and the Turk* (1929), and *The Surprise* (1952), but he was not best known as a dramatist.

C. enjoyed history and biography, although he lacked the accurate discipline of an historian. As well as general observations on human nature in "Varied" and "Five Types," he wrote studies of the life and work of the poet Robert BROWNING (1903) and of the painter G. F. Watts (1904) and made a famous appraisal of Charles DICKENS (1906) and later prefaces to his many books. He described his friend in *George Bernard Shaw* (1909) and weighed strengths and weaknesses in *William Blake* (1910) and *Simplicity of Tolstoy* (1912). Probably his best book of criticism before the war was his *The Victorian Age in Literature* (1913). While sometimes slapdash in quoting from memory, C. as critic had the gift of penetrating below the surface of any writer or thinker and providing insights that less careful readers had often missed. After 1918, C. wrote illuminating studies of St. Francis of Assisi (1922) and St. Thomas Aquinas (1933) and also writers William COBBETT (1925), Robert Louis STEVENSON (1927), and Geoffrey CHAUCER

(1932), and he described his own early life, in an *Autobiography* (1936), published posthumously.

It was, however, in developing his philosophical and religious ideas that C. wrote his most famous books, as *Heretics* (1905) and *Orthodoxy* (1908), in which he attacked the fallacies of modern thinkers. After the war, he traveled widely to Palestine, Italy, the U.S., and Ireland and returned with fresh insights. He was moved by his visit to the Holy Land to write *The New Jerusalem* (1920) and after conversion wrote *The Everlasting Man* (1925), *The Catholic Church and Conversion* (1926), *Culture and the Coming Peril* (1927), *The Thing* (1929), and *The Resurrection of Rome* (1930).

C.'s political and economic ideas can be found in *What's Wrong with the World* (1910) and his *A Short History of England* (1917), and *The Outline of Sanity* (1926), in all of which he put forward the case for well-divided property, or distributism. His books on social policy were traditional and conservative, as we can glean from their titles, *The Superstition of Divorce* (1920), *Eugenics and Other Evils* (1922), and *Social Reform and Birth Control* (1927). He warned that the application of science could bring problems as well as benefits and recognized that scientists could be as intolerant as Puritans.

Already by far the biggest category of C.'s books comprises collections of his essays and articles. Thus, before the war he published *The Defendant* (1901), *All Things Considered* (1908), *Tremendous Trifles* (1909), *Alarms and Discursions* (1910), *A Miscellany of Men* (1912), and *Letters to an Old Garibaldian* (1915). After the war, he published *The Uses of Diversity* (1920), *Fancies Versus Fads* (1923), *The Superstitions of the Sceptic* (1925), *Generally Speaking* (1928), *Come to Think of It . . .* (1930), *All Is Grist* (1931), *All I Survey* (1933), *Avowals and Denials* (1934), and *As I Was Saying* (1936).

Some admirers think C. wrote too much for the good of his reputation. Others champion his cause and even consider that he should be declared a saint, an idea that would honestly have dismayed him. One little boy is said to have remarked on seeing the great man: "What is he for?" Although so Catholic and for the Church, he was also very English and for England, which he realized would be the very last of Britain's colonies to be freed, so he tried to speak for its people who have not spoken yet.

BIBLIOGRAPHY: Canovan, M., *G. K. C.* (1977); Coates, J., *C. and the Edwardian Cultural Crisis* (1984); Conlon, D. J., ed., *G. K. C.* (1976); Conlon, D. J., ed., *G. K. C.* (1987); Corrin, J. P., *G. K. C. and Hilaire Belloc: The Battle against Modernity* (1981); Ward, M., *G. K. C.* (1944)

PATRICIA M. WHARTON

CHETTLE, Henry
b. ca. 1560, London; d. 1607, London?

As a printer, C. published Robert GREENE's *Groats-Worth of Wit* in 1592 and later that year *Kind Heart's Dream,* in the preface to which he apologized to three people who had been attacked, one of them fairly obviously William SHAKESPEARE. In 1598, Francis MERES mentioned C. as one of the "best for comedy," and in the next five years C. wrote or collaborated in some fifty plays. His many collaborators included Thomas DEKKER, Michael DRAYTON, Ben JONSON, Thomas HEYWOOD, and perhaps John MARSTON. In 1602, his *The Tragedy of Hoffman; or, A Revenge for a Father* (1631) was performed, which is believed to be the only play of which C. was sole author. He collaborated with Anthony MUNDAY on two plays about Robin Hood, *The Death of Robert, Earl of Huntingdon* and *The Downfall of Robert, Earl of Huntingdon.* Both versions were performed in 1598 and printed in Robert DODSLEY's *Select Collection of Old Plays* (12 vols., 1744–45). The anonymous play, *Book of Sir Thomas More,* has been attributed to C. and Munday.

CHILDERS, [Robert] Erskine
b. 25 June 1870, London; d. 24 November 1922, Dublin, Ireland

Executed as an IRA gunrunner, C. famously wrote *The Riddle of the Sands: A Record of Secret Service Recently Achieved* (1903). It was written to expose the vulnerability of England to German invasion from the North Sea. C.'s deep sense of patriotism, first to England, and then to Ireland, pervades all of his work, the majority of which is nonfiction.

C.'s first published works came out of his military service in the Boer War, and include *In the Ranks of the C.I.V.* [City Imperial Volunteers] and *The H.A.C.* [Honourable Artillery Company] *in South Africa,* published in 1900 and 1903, respectively. At the war's end, C. turned to his 1897–98 experiences sailing the sand channels of the Frisian Island for his only work of fiction, *The Riddle of the Sands.* The novel is told from the point of view of Carruthers, a British civil servant. Davies, an acquaintance, invites Carruthers on a vacation to cruise the Baltic and the North Sea on his yacht, *Dulcibella;* Davies's real purpose is to investigate suspicious German military activity. In the course of uncovering the German plot to invade England using her unprotected east coast, Davies falls in love with the daughter of the villain, Dollmann, who has left the Royal Navy to spy for the German High Command.

Although *The Riddle of the Sands* is the first in the genre of English spy thrillers, its plot is, by today's standards, not terribly thrilling; it tends to bog down in excessive detail and patriotic bombast. Moreover,

as a typical Edwardian era "call-to-arms" novel, *The Riddle of the Sands* is underpinned with dated assumptions, including British imperial superiority and German deceit. Nevertheless, this novel, highly influential when first published—it spurred a national debate in Britain on the country's military preparedness—remains popular, adapted for a 1979 British film and continually reprinted. Based largely on C.'s own sailing experiences and logbooks, the novel achieves a remarkable degree of verisimilitude, bolstered by the inclusion of maps, charts, and diagrams, enhanced by C.'s ability to capture the atmosphere of this bleak northern environment. For the reader who is not an arm-chair sailor, the novel's most rewarding feature will be the development of the narrator, Carruthers, who begins as a rather fussy Edwardian gentleman and is transformed into an able and hardy seaman.

In the works immediately following his only novel, C. continued to argue for the modernization of the British military in *War and the Arme Blanche* (1910) and *German Influence in British Cavalry* (1911). But he was also becoming involved in the struggle for Irish home rule, as evidenced in *The Framework of Home Rule* (1911) and *The Form and Purpose of Home Rule* (1912). The early 1920s saw the publication of increasingly passionate propaganda for the Irish cause with *Military Rule in Ireland* (1920); *Is Ireland a Danger to England?* (1921); *Who Burnt Cork City: A Tale of Arson, Loot, and Murder* (1921); *What the Treaty Means* (1922); and *Clause by Clause: A Comparison between the "Treaty" and Document No. 2* (1922).

BIBLIOGRAPHY: Giddings, R., "Cry God for Harry, England and Lord Kitchener: A Tale of Tel-el-Kebir, Suakin, Wadi Haifa and Omdurman," in his *Literature and Imperialism* (1991): 182–219; Seed, D., "E. C. and the German Peril," *GL&L* 45, 1 (1992): 66–73

JUDITH E. FUNSTON

CHILDREN'S LITERATURE

Although substantial bodies of material specifically written for children began to be current around the cusp of the 18th and 19th cs., there is evidence in James BOSWELL that the question of children's fiction was already awake much earlier in the 18th, for Boswell, teasing Samuel JOHNSON about how, if put to it, he would address himself to the task of rearing young children, asked him if he would not tell them stories about little children like themselves. Magnificently, Johnson replies that he would, on the contrary, tell them about giants and wizards "to stretch their little minds withal." In so responding, he set up one of the great divides that have shaped children's literature ever since, that between the narrative of everyday life and that of fantasy. Every children's book may be said to fall into one or other category, though a particularly interesting group embraces both. Within fantasy, there is a further major division to be addressed later.

When Johnson gave his reply, the fairy and folktales in his mind were already being used to entertain children, but they had originally been collected for an adult audience, like other texts that were being read with pleasure by precocious young people; the metaphysical poet Abraham COWLEY recorded that he had been made a poet by stumbling over Edmund SPENSER's work among his mother's books and being "infinitely delighted" with the stories of knights, giants, and monsters he found there. By 1744, however, John Newbery had begun publication specifically for children of moral tales and pretty verses, and soon there was developed the market in improving works that ran more or less dispiritingly throughout the 19th c.

Indeed, it must be recognized that almost all children's literature, even today, has some design on improving its young readers and although Mary Martha Sherwood was mainly concerned with keeping children from a life of vice and crime, and Maria EDGEWORTH with countering greed and selfishness, while the modern writer will be more concerned with inculcating courage, tolerance, and generosity of spirit—with encouraging the positive rather than discouraging the negative qualities—the impulse to "teach the young idea how to shoot" is still strong.

However, the crude didacticism of the early days did not last long among the better writers, though a vein persisted through the century in the storybooks written to be given as Sunday school prizes, and writers like Hesba Stretton produced many narratives about angelic children who died in an odor of sanctity. But meanwhile, important writers of adult literature were delighting in working for fresh and enthusiastic readers. William Makepeace THACKERAY's *The Rose and the Ring* (1855) is a delicious comic fantasy, and Charles DICKENS's *Holiday Romance* (1868) introduces several ideas for children's writing later to be developed by other hands; even John RUSKIN produced *The King of the Golden River*. And midway through the century came the breakthrough that showed that didacticism was not inescapable: Lewis CARROLL's two Alice books (*Alice in Wonderland* and *Through the Looking-Glass*) are remarkable for their complete lack of improving qualities; Alice is a cool little girl with an only moderately nice nature who seems quite unaware of learning anything from her adventures—she simply experiences them. And this is the more remarkable in that Carroll's alter ego, the Reverend Charles Lutwidge Dodgson, was a painfully scrupulous Christian, terrified of sin, whose other children's novel, *Sylvie and Bruno*, though containing some marvellous moments, and in particular the

songs of the Mad Gardener, is ruined by the kind of preaching of which the Alice books are blessedly free.

Other good 19th-c. writers were less successful in escaping it. George MacDonald's *The Princess and the Goblins* (1872), *The Princess and Curdie* (1883), and *At the Back of the North Wind* (1871) have their share. Charles KINGSLEY's *The Water Babies*, with the two wise women, Mrs. Doasyouwouldbedoneby and Mrs. Bedonebyasyoudid, who are really two faces of the same spirit is, of course, as full of muscular Christianity as the children's stories of Charlotte M. YONGE are of Anglo-Catholicism. Nevertheless, the narrative power of Kingsley's fantasy has preserved his story for rescue by Disney and occasional transcription to television, and MacDonald's work, too, survives, an edition of his shorter FAIRY TALES being published as recently as 2000.

Toward the end of the century, other powerful writers came into the children's field: Oscar WILDE constructed new, delicately cruel fairy tales, Robert Louis STEVENSON produced the best of adventure stories in *Treasure Island* and *Kidnapped*, while Rudyard KIPLING wrote superbly for every age of young reader: for the very young, the *Just So Stories,* brilliant fables of the beginnings of things; for middling youngsters, the *Jungle Books,* horribly travestied by Disney, and the excellent collections of linked short stories, *Puck of Pook's Hill* and *Rewards and Fairies,* intensely imaginative introductions to moments of English history; and for readers of every age, *Kim,* which many Indian writers regard as the best novel ever written about India. Around this time, the use of folk tales as children's literature was revived and made literary by Andrew LANG's twelve fairy books of various colors, charmingly illustrated by fashionable artists and drawing on a remarkable range of sources, from early sagas and Norwegian folk yarns to the brothers Grimm and the French fairy writers such as Madame d'Aulnoy and Charles Perrault, with sidesteps to the Arabian Nights and Jonathan SWIFT's *Gulliver's Travels:* an enormous treasury of fancy.

It was probably from folktales, where they are often princes and princesses under enchantment, that talking animals came into children's literature. It was for Beatrix POTTER to develop the tradition of talking animals as characters in their own right, as real people dressed in fur and feathers and behaving in ways which suited their animal natures but also were proper human behaviors. As with much children's literature, it is the charm of her pictures that first captures children's attention and wins their affection, but her work's importance as arrangements of words is unarguable; as is generally recognized, to introduce a word like "soporific" in a context that makes its meaning precisely clear, in a text designed to entertain very young children, is a splendid act of education. Animals like Potter's became an important feature of

20th-c. children's fiction; writers like Alison Uttley followed her in dressing rabbits and other small creatures in ordinary clothes over their furry, feathery bodies and sending them out on small, homely adventures.

Before this, however, there had been a grander conception of talking animals, in Kenneth GRAHAME's *The Wind in the Willows*. The tentative Mole, the confident Rat whose delight in life is "messing about in boats," and above all the horrendously arrogant and absurd Toad of Toad Hall have entered the mythology of English life, perhaps because of the reflections of the English class system that have been much commented on and indeed have prompted interesting revisits to the Wild Wood and its environs from different class perspectives. More probably, however, the main force keeping this narrative fresh is the dramatization of the Toad elements of the story in the play *Toad of Toad Hall* by A. A. MILNE in 1929. Another recent dramatization by Alan BENNETT for a National Theatre Christmas production was enormously successful.

Later in the 20th c. came other kinds of talking-animal stories. Hugh Lofting's Dr. Dolittle talked to animals, including highly imagined ones like the Pushme-Pullyu, in a series of books beginning in 1920. Later still, a great success was scored by Richard Adams's *Watership Down* (1972) in which a tribe of rabbits, driven out of its home territory, sets out on a trek of biblical proportions to find a new home. Its success has bred other, lesser tales of the sort, like the *Redwall* series by Brian Jacques.

These talking animals perhaps led the way for talking toys, important throughout the 20th c., though of course the tales of Hans Christian Andersen, first translated into English in 1846, in which brave little tin soldiers and arrogant fireworks reveal human characteristics and feelings, may have played their part. The teddy bear, though it only came into existence at the beginning of the century, soon became one of the most important characters in stories that were, like the dressed animal stories, usually comedies of everyday life, with the human speech of the toys the only essential magic. Among the first and still probably the most famous and loved is Winnie the Pooh; Milne so brilliantly captures certain human characteristics in the toys who people the wood where in imagination his son Christopher Robin plays eternally (in *Winnie-the-Pooh* and *The House at Pooh Corner*) that adults recognize their counterparts in any organization or group. Almost as famous is Michael Bond's Paddington Bear, first encountered in 1958, another monument to childhood innocence, constantly causing chaos without intent. There are many other attractive bears and some other interesting talking toys, though a more intriguing offshoot, perhaps, consists of small people of other sorts, such as Mary Norton's wonderfully conceived underfloor dwellers, the Borrowers, and Terry PRACHETT's Carpet People.

Some talking animals, however, are more vitally associated with magic. One of the most influential children's writers of the early 20th c., E. NESBIT, uses such mythical creatures as the Phoenix and, her own invention, the Psammead, to launch families of children into wild adventures in the past or in distant places. Her most important contribution to children's literature was the way she succeeded in melding fantasy with the story of everyday life; the large middle-class family whose everyday exploits she describes with such comic verve in *The Story of the Treasure Seekers* and *The Wouldbegoods* forms the model for the large middle-class families who nag the Psammead for adventures in *Five Children and It* or travel on the flying carpet in *The Phoenix and the Carpet,* published in 1902 and 1904, respectively. They thus prepare the ground for one of the richest veins for the children's writer to mine, where ordinary children walk through a wardrobe or whatever and find themselves involved in quite extraordinary events, often in a vital struggle between the forces of good and evil, where their contribution is all important.

At this point, an observation should be made about another dichotomy in children's literature. As well as the split between fantasy and everyday life, there is an important split within fantasy itself. This is between what may be called the intellectual and the spiritual fantasy. The distinction between these two modes comes out most clearly toward the end, in whatever climax is reached. In the spiritual fantasy, this is a moment of epiphany, usually involving some kind of sacrifice on the part of one or more of the young protagonists; in the intellectual, it is a moment of discovery or realization, and perhaps the solution to a troubling mystery. This can be seen in the earliest days of the fantasy story, on the one hand when Tom saves his soul in *The Water Babies*, and on the other when Alice cries, "You're only a pack of cards."

The most famous example of the spiritual fantasy in the 20th c. must be the Narnia series of C. S. LEWIS, beginning with *The Lion, the Witch, and the Wardrobe*, but there are other major examples, such as Susan Cooper's the "Dark Is Rising" series, beginning with *Under Sea, Under Stone* (1965), and Alan Garner's *The Weirdstone of Brisingamen* (1960). Of intellectual fantasies, the finest examples are those by Diana Wynne Jones; when, at the end of *The Homeward Bounders* (1981) or *Archer's Goon* (1985), the reader, with the central character, realizes what has actually been going on, the revelation is a true point of growth.

One of the most encouraging developments of very recent years has been the outbreak of a broad readership for intellectual fantasy: the Harry Potter series of J. K. ROWLING, where, again, each novel provokes the realization of a new truth, has attained an astonishing popularity among adult as well as child readers, and though these novels are not as imaginatively deep as those of Wynne Jones, and have been attacked for a range of reasons by those for whom popularity is always suspect, their constant inventiveness and narrative compulsion well explain their attraction for readers who do not share E. M. FORSTER's regret that the novel tells a story. Alongside them, Philip Pullman's extraordinary antireligion trilogy, *His Dark Materials*, completed in 2001 with *The Amber Spyglass*, which is both intellectual and, in its own uncomfortable way, spiritual, provide a deeper experience; the excitement caused by the publication of both series is evidence of the present as a new golden age of children's literature.

Of course, as with all generalizing observations, it must be recognized that there is overlap; as is clear from *His Dark Materials*, some intellectual fantasies involve some sacrifice, some spiritual involve some discovery, but it is usually evident which is the overriding element. Another fairly recent overlap is that between fantasy and SCIENCE FICTION; writers like Peter Dickinson started writing science fiction for children in the 1950s; his Weathermaker series broke new ground in using the extrapolatory power of science fiction to look at not impossible futures. The other major SF effect particularly notable in children's fiction is the time travel story: *Tom's Midnight Garden* (1958) by Phillipa Pearce and *A Stitch in Time* by Penelope LIVELY are fine examples of the creative use of the idea of children visiting the past. Lively also uses the reverse notion, of people from the past disturbingly appearing in the 20th c., as in *The Ghost of Thomas Kempe*; this concept is the source of much comic writing.

In fantasy, class is often unimportant; in stories of everyday life, it may be more noticeable, and in the first half of the 20th c, with a widespread assumption that the readers of children's fiction would be middle class, so were most of the characters. In Nesbit's nonfantastic stories, like the *Treasure Seekers*, as well as in her fantasies, the children concerned are brought up by nannies in households with cooks and housemaids; they may fall on hard times, as in *The Railway Children* (1906), but they come essentially from a background of privilege, and the children in that novel learn a good deal about the problems and the pride of poverty. Subsequent writers seemed less conscious of class issues; for example, the principal family in the admirable series of stories of messing about in boats that Arthur Ransome began with *Swallows and Amazons* (1930) are the children of a senior naval officer, and the other children with whom they interact in the most friendly way are clearly of what used to be called gentle birth, in spite of their slight wildness. Ransome's stories were pioneers of a kind of story immensely popular in the years before the Second World War, in which nice children with access to boats, ponies or gipsy caravans set off, with little or no adult supervision, on gentle adventures.

Though he does not sound it, William Brown, hero of the best of all funny stories for children, is also middle class; his family household, at least in the prewar books, runs to a cook and a housemaid, paid for by his father's work in the city, to which he commutes from the Home Counties village where they live, looking down on the nouveau riche Bott family, and doubtless being looked down on in their turn by the aristocratic families who only appear occasionally, usually opening a fete. William also attends a boys' school where he is supposed to study Latin and where the masters all wear gowns. It should be remembered that the earliest of these stories by Richmal Crompton was initially published in a magazine to amuse adult readers, before it was realized what a goldmine they represented if marketed in collections to children. The parents who bought them perhaps did not realize how subversive William is—or perhaps, rather, they recognized that a subversive character in a very funny book is likely to drain off a good deal of their children's revolutionary spirit in laughter. As with the stories of Nesbit, the greater part of the HUMOR in these books arises not from William's naughtiness, but from his innocence, his misunderstandings of adult utterances and behaviors; not only adults, but many children enjoy seeing through William's mistakes, especially when they turn out successfully.

Though some of the William stories recount William's disasters at school, these are not school stories. William attends a day school; the true school story is set in a boarding school and is a descendant of Thomas HUGHES's *Tom Brown's Schooldays*. In spite of this, the boys' school story is a rarer bird than the girls'; there is no boys' school series with quite the longevity and range of Elinor Brent-Dyer's Chalet School books, which began in 1925 and are still republished, although the Greyfriars stories by Charles Hamilton writing as Frank Richards, with the immortal clown Billy Bunter, had a good run, beginning as early as 1908. At the heart of such stories are ideas about loyalty, friendship and honor which are very important to young people at a certain stage of their lives, and the scorn with which anti-Harry Potter critics have complained that these are at heart old-fashioned school stories is quite inappropriate.

Shortly before the Second World War, *The Family from One End Street* (1937), by Eve Garnett, made its mark as the first modern children's book about working-class people; its tone was somewhat patronizing, but since then, writers such as John Rowe Townsend, Leila Berg, Jan Mark, Jan Needle, Anne Fine, and Jacqueline Wilson have quite changed the picture. Realism has become an essential feature of much writing for children, and now means in children's literature much what it already meant in adult literature—a clear-sighted look at some of the bleaker and more troubling aspects of life. The one-parent family is more common in children's books than it actually is in society; few now center on a child with two parents at home, and in those cases there is still often a fear of family break-up or a problem to do with the father being out of work or involved in crime, or the mother suffering from a mental disorder.

At first, this kind of topic was confined to YOUNG ADULT FICTION; now, such topics are common in writing for children as young as eight, sometimes as central themes, sometimes as mere background. They can be made more tolerable by exaggeration, which perhaps explains the enormous popularity of the grotesque works of Roald DAHL, of which the best and most linguistically ingenious is *The BFG*, published in 1982. These darker elements also occur in fantasy fiction, where the distancing achieved by fantasy makes them even more accessible. It is also noteworthy that horror, originally a major element in young adult fiction, has slithered down into children's reading; although this trend began in American series like R. L. Stine's "Goosebumps," English writers have begun to take it up. However, there is also plenty of comfort reading available; children's love of animals is never-failing, so that series about stables, veterinary practices and animal shelters are, as a genre, the equivalent of the Mills and Boon romance for the adult reader, as well as the simple adventure, school, and talking toy stories of Enid Blyton, whose popularity never ceases to sadden adult lovers of children's literature, but is fully explained by the ease of reading them and the constant reassurance they provide. It should perhaps be noted that the popularity of the Harry Potter novels cannot be explained in the same way.

At one time, a good deal of writing for children consisted of historical novels, and a few writers, above all Rosemary Sutcliff, especially with her magnificent series of stories about the Roman settlement of Britain, Ian Seraillier and Henry Treece, following Kipling's lead, contributed important novels still reread with pleasure. In recent years, there have been fewer such visits to the past, though Berlie Doherty has written very well of the life of the working people of the north of England after the Industrial Revolution.

In the last century, there has been a substantial development in the writing of poetry for children; much used to be of poor quality, mawkish, and patronizing, but the engagement of poets with a strong adult track record, such as Brian Patten and John Agard, or a powerful comic gift, like Spike Milligan and Allan Ahlberg, or an acute understanding of children's needs, like Michael Rosen, has led to the publication of admirable collections of their verse, as well as anthologies of old and new poetry, often well edited by these and other poets. It should also be noted, though this is art rather than literature, that the work of picture book makers such as David McKee, Anthony Browne, and Brian Wildsmith enables the youngest children to discover and respond to true quality from their earliest years.

BIBLIOGRAPHY: Avery, G., *Childhood's Pattern: A Study of Heroes and Heroines in Children's Fiction, 1770–1950* (1975); Carpenter, H., and M. Prichard, *The Oxford Companion to Children's Literature* (1984); Cullinan, B. E., and D. G. Person, eds., *The Continuum Encyclopedia of Children's Literature* (2001); Hunt, P., ed., *The International Companion Encyclopedia of Children's Literature* (1996); Townsend, J. R., *Written for Children* (1965; rev. eds., 1974, 1983, 1987)

AUDREY LASKI

CHRISTIE, [Dame] Agatha

b. 15 September 1890, Torquay; d. 12 January 1976, Wallingford

One of the most translated writers in the English language, C. is the acknowledged master practitioner of the "whodunit" form of mystery as it developed after World War I. Her seventy-eight novels, 150 short stories, and nineteen plays all feature ingeniously constructed plots concerning crime and its detection, and continue to enjoy not only worldwide popularity but also increasing critical respect.

C.'s most famous creation is her detective, Hercule Poirot. In some ways a modern "antihero," the elflike Poirot is a vain, fussy, elderly Belgian who seems to have no particular abilities or expertise. Poirot's heroic first name and his high, domed forehead containing what he termed his "little gray cells," are the only clues that suggest his Herculean intelligence. The mysterious discrepancy between Poirot's generally harmless appearance and his ruthless intellect has been a source of both amusement and fascination for generations of readers.

C.'s most famous novel, *The Murder of Roger Ackroyd* (1926), features many elements typical of her work, deployed with characteristic wit and cleverness. There is a quaint English village, a number of surprising turns of plot, and most of all, a least-likely suspect. In this novel, Poirot investigates a murder with the help of the local doctor, who, like Sherlock Holmes's Dr. Watson, also narrates the story. In addition to exposing the darker realities underneath the surface of the seemingly simple village of King's Abbot, we come to realize that Dr. Sheppard, who has established himself as a trusted narrative voice, is also controlling the transmission of information. When Sheppard is eventually exposed as not so much unreliable as carefully reticent, the reader experiences a thrill of surprise that requires a complete reconsideration of what we assume has happened. The "surprise-ending" of this novel established C. as a mystery writer whose fearless imagination will leave none of her characters above suspicion.

Murder on the Orient Express (1934; repub. as *Murder in the Calais Coach,* 1934) is another important and daring novel featuring Poirot. Here, within the limits of a snowbound train, Poirot uncovers a complicated conspiracy involving a number of seemingly unrelated strangers. As is characteristic of C., many of her characters are engaged in forms of impersonation or masking that conceal identities or motives that must be kept secret. After Poirot exposes the true identities of this trainload of murderers, however, the story adds another surprise by making their crime understandable and even justifiable, while, in a twist characteristic of C., the novel's victim becomes the novel's villain.

C.'s other major literary detective is also, significantly, an elderly figure. This is Miss Jane Marple, an old maiden lady, who has spent her life virtually sequestered in the little village of St. Mary Mead, but who nevertheless acts as the ratiocinative intelligence in a number of mysteries. An unlikely detective, Miss Marple succeeds by dint of her insatiable curiosity, her extraordinary memory, and her dark view of human nature developed over years of observing life in her seemingly pleasant village. Like Poirot, Miss Marple's unremarkable exterior conceals a preternaturally sharp mind. One of the finest Miss Marple mysteries, *The Body in the Library* (1942), perfectly illustrates the charm of both her detective and her clever plots. In addition, this novel, like many Miss Marple mysteries, investigates not only crime but also the changes in English society, suggested from the start by the untoward appearance of a murdered dance-hall hostess in the library of the one of the stately homes of England. This theme of a changing society is apparent in other Miss Marple novels, notably *A Murder Is Announced* (1950), in which we see a society in the process of recovering from World War II, and *At Bertram's Hotel* (1965), which suggests that England was no longer the Edwardian society it may occasionally still like to impersonate.

C. also wrote a series of spy thrillers involving the duo of Tommy and Tuppence Beresford. They are not elderly, and enjoy normal lives with children and friends; the twist is that it is the woman, Tuppence, who is the brains of the family. But although this couple were C.'s own personal favorites, her success as a writer is strongly associated with elderly sleuths, whose gentle exteriors brilliantly disguise their steely minds. Miss Marple and Hercule Poirot can be seen as the kind of wise elders important to any healthy society, and whose function it is to serve as a mediator between the old and the new, and to ensure a safe conduct for the younger generation into a better future. In the course of solving their mysteries, Miss Marple and Hercule Poirot often enable young romantic couples to emerge into a world that has been made all the happier by the machinations of one or other of these two gimlet-eyed but benevolent elderly detectives, whose values C. increasingly felt were important to sustain and pass down to succeeding generations.

BIBLIOGRAPHY: Gill, G., *A. C., the Woman and Her Mysteries* (1990); Keating, H. R. F., ed., *A. C.* (1977); Riley, D., and P. McAllister, *The Bedside, Bathtub & Armchair Companion to A. C.* (1986); Wagoner, M. S., *A. C.* (1986)

MARGARET BOE BIRNS

CHURCHILL, Caryl
b. 3 September 1938, London

Acknowledged as one of the foremost, innovative dramatists of the contemporary British and international stages, C. is a highly influential figure in the field of feminist theater, performance, and scholarship.

C.'s early work included a significant number of radio plays, given that a radio career was one that she could combine with motherhood and family life. Her radio plays reflect a number of stylistic and thematic concerns of later work: playing with conventions of form, time, narrative, structure, language, and dialogue as well as thematizing the power structure of marital and familial relations—*The Ants* (1962), *Lovesick* (1966), *Abortive* (1971), *Henry's Past* (1972), and *Perfect Happiness* (1973); issues of identity—*Identical Twins* (1968) and *Schreber's Nervous Illness* (1972); and ecological concerns—*Not Not Not Not Not Enough Oxygen* (1971). An early television play *Turkish Delight* (1974) showed some of the gender and class issues that C. would develop in her theater, as further evidenced in *Owners,* her first professionally produced stage play performed at the Royal Court Theatre (perf. 1972; pub 1973).

During the 1970s, C. came into contact with the socialist-feminist theater company, Monstrous Regiment, with whom she staged *Vinegar Tom* (perf. 1976; pub. 1977), a play about witchcraft, and wrote her first play with Joint Stock, *Light Shining in Buckinghamshire* (perf. 1976; pub. 1977), on the English civil war in the 17th c. The Joint Stock production saw the beginning of her long association with the director Max Stafford-Clark, with *Cloud Nine* (1979), her drama of sexual politics, following as her second Joint Stock production. Working with both companies introduced C. to the experience of workshopping and marked a departure from her previous, more solitary, existence as a playwright. Her association with the Royal Court also continued through the 1970s with *Objections to Sex and Violence* (perf. 1975; pub. 1985), treating ideas of revolution and violence; a SCIENCE FICTION drama, *Moving Clocks Go Slow* (perf. 1975); and *Traps* (perf. 1977; pub. 1978), which is a further illustration of C.'s desire to experiment with dramatic form.

C.'s *Top Girls* (1982) is critically recognized as one of the major plays of the 20th c. It has been acclaimed both on account of the way C. experimented with overlapping dialogue, a technique that has influenced the playwriting of a number of contemporary British dramatists, and for its socialist-feminist critique of the "top girl," Thatcherite ethos of the 1980s. The opening dinner scene in which the invited guests include women from history, art, myth, and fiction defied stage conventions of REALISM, while C.'s dramatization of the relationship between two sisters, "top girl" Marlene and her working-class sister Joyce, offered an incisive interrogation of bourgeois feminist principles. Both *Top Girls* and *Cloud Nine* won Obie Awards and went on to be performed around the world.

Throughout the 1980s, C. pursued her socialist critique of a Britain that became more and more divided by the "us and them" she portrayed in *Top Girls*. *Fen* (1983) examined the impact of transnational capitalism on a deprived community of (mostly) East Anglian Fen women. *Soft Cops* (1984), which, in contrast to *Top Girls*, has an all-male cast, offered a dramatic representation of Michel Foucault's *Discipline and Punish* (1977; first pub. as *Surveiller et punir*), while the hugely successful *Serious Money* (1987), written in verse, satirized the world of the London stock market; the greed and corruption of the 1980s. Ironically, *Serious Money* proved particularly popular among the city speculators it set out to satirize, and made enough "serious money" to make a transfer into London's commercial West End. In the style of a road movie, *Icecream* (1989) portrayed a dark picture of transatlantic culture and identity, and C. returned to civil war and the possibility of revolution in *Mad Forest* (1990), that detailed events in Romania leading up to the fall of Nicolae Ceausescu.

The desire to experiment has involved C. in collaborations with dance-theater, most particularly in her work with the choreographer Ian Spink and the company Second Stride. C. first worked with Spink on *A Mouthful of Birds* (with David Lan, 1986), and subsequently with Second Stride on *Lives of the Great Poisoners* (1991), *The Skriker* (1994), and *Hotel* (1997). The Skriker, a mythological shape-shifting figure from a fairy underworld, is arguably C.'s most interesting theatrical figure of the 1990s, one that signifies her concern to show the dangers of a contemporary world birthing a catastrophic (socially, economically, and ecologically) future. Disaster threatens as people

are portrayed as increasingly alienated in their personal lives—*Hotel* and *Blue Heart* (perf. 1997; pub 1998), and as failing to make connections between the personal and the political—*This Is a Chair* (perf. 1997; pub. 1999). The all too real risk that all of this poses, is dramatized in C.'s first play of the 21st c., *Far Away*, in which the entire world becomes a war zone.

Like the Skriker, C.'s theater constantly shapeshifts in form, while thematically, the damage and dangers of an unequal, unjust, *man*made world are a constant preoccupation.

BIBLIOGRAPHY: Aston, E., *C. C.* (1997; rev. ed., 2001); Fitzsimmons, L., *File on C.* (1989); Kritzer, A. H., *The Plays of C. C.* (1991); Rabillard, S., ed., *Essays on C. C.* (1998)

ELAINE ASTON

CHURCHILL, Charles
b. February 1731, London; d. 4 November 1764, Boulogne

In 1761, C. published at his own expense *The Rosciad,* a satirical poem on the actors of the day, in which only David GARRICK was spared. It made C. famous. He followed it in the same year with *The Apology,* in which even Garrick was criticized. In 1762, he became assistant editor of John Wilkes's *North Briton,* filling that paper with savage satires, full of malicious portraits. In his day, he was a wealthy and notorious celebrity, but since then his reputation has sunk. His English is clear and vigorous, and his talent, especially for invective, undeniable, but appreciation depends on inwardness with 18th-c. politics, as illustrated in *The Prophecy of Famine* (1763) and the three books of *Gotham* (1764). His *Collected Poems* appeared in 1804, with a biography and letters, and a revised edition in 1892.

CHURCHILL, [Sir] Winston [Leonard Spencer]
b. 30 November 1874, Blenheim Palace, Oxfordshire; d. 25 January 1965, London

C. was a man of astounding energy and accomplishment whose political career—culminating with his legendary tenure as British prime minister during World War II—overshadows his substantial literary achievement. Even before serving as prime minister, C.'s career, which included stints as a cavalry officer, journalist, and several government positions including First Lord of the Admiralty and Minister of the Exchequer, had established him as one of the most dynamic and controversial men of the 20th c. C.'s literary energies were just as prodigious as his political efforts, and it is easy to forget that C. was also a prolific writer whose collected works comprise over thirty volumes, whose books sold in the millions, and who was awarded the Nobel Prize for Literature in 1953. Much of C.'s literary work is preoccupied with the same subjects that were the center of his public life—politics, war, great men, and the influence of these three forces on history.

Following his graduation from the Royal Military College at Sandhurst, C. began his military and journalism careers almost simultaneously. In 1895, C. received a commission as a cavalry subaltern then traveled to Cuba during his first leave, working as a paid reporter covering the Cuban rebellion against Spanish rule. In 1897, he was posted to India, and while serving there persuaded a commanding officer to permit him to accompany the Malakand Field Force in their campaign against rebellious Pathan tribesmen on the northwest frontier. This experience would form the basis of C.'s first book, *The Story of the Malakand Field Force* (1898), a lively account of the military conduct and planning of the campaign. The book was well received despite the fact that, like many of his later histories, it boldly critiqued the military strategy of officers with far more field experience than he himself possessed.

C.'s pace over the next several years was frenetic. The taste of literary success he experienced with *The Story of the Malakand Field Force* inspired him to write his first and only novel, *Savrola: A Tale of the Revolution in Laurania* (1900), an undistinguished work combining wartime adventure with moralizing about the importance of having a code of honor that will withstand adversity. In 1898, despite the objections of its commanding officer, Lord Kitchener, C. secured an assignment to the expeditionary force sent to the Sudan to subdue a revolt against British rule. After the war in the Sudan, he resigned his commission and wrote a two-volume account of the campaign, *The River War* (1899), which, like his first book, was critical of the manner in which the campaign was conducted. He then served as a special correspondent sent to cover the Boer War. C.'s remarkable adventures in Africa included capture by the Boers and escape from a prison camp in Pretoria, and were described both in his dispatches from the front and in two books, *London to Ladysmith via Pretoria* (1900) and *Ian Hamilton's March* (1900). C.'s escapades, and his vivid accounting of them, served to make him a national hero and helped him win a seat in Parliament in 1900.

Up to this point, C.'s literary efforts, with the lackluster exception of *Savrola*, had primarily been confined to lively, first-person reportage. Over the next several years, he worked on what would become his first major literary work, a two-volume BIOGRAPHY of his father, whose life and mercurial political career had both been cut short by illness. Like most bio-

graphies of the time, *Lord Randolph Churchill* (2 vols., 1906) was a public biography that emphasized Lord Randolph's political career and tells us very little about the private life or psychology of the man. Nearly twenty years later, C. would once again return to his own family's history in his four-volume biography *Marlborough: His Life and Times* (1933–38). In *Marlborough,* C. explored the life and brilliant military career of his ancestor John Churchill, the first Duke of Marlborough. As with C.'s earlier biography of his father, *Marlborough* was not so much an impartial history as the story of a hero, one whose struggles and triumphs presented an object lesson for contemporary readers.

C.'s sweeping histories of the First and Second World Wars garnered the most attention as literary works, and reflect his keen interest in war and politics, and how these influences worked to shape history. The six volumes of *The World Crisis* (1923–31) are less a comprehensive history of World War I than of C.'s own perspective on that conflict. C. had indeed held a unique vantage point from which to comment on the war, serving as First Lord of the Admiralty, and then—following the disaster at Gallipoli, for which he shouldered much of the blame—as commander of an infantry battalion on the western front. After a short period in that capacity, he was reinstated in David Lloyd George's government coalition, first as minister of munitions and then as secretary of state for war. As one political opponent sniped, *The World Crisis* was AUTOBIOGRAPHY disguised as history, but as an historical narrative of one who was there, it is an informative, fascinating work. C.'s later multivolume histories, including *The Second World War* (6 vols., 1948–53) and *A History of the English-Speaking Peoples* (4 vols., 1956–58), were enormously popular, reflecting his increased status following his inspirational wartime leadership during the Second World War.

As was the case with his political career, C.'s literary works have generated strong, often widely divergent, reactions. C.'s writing reflects a sensibility grounded in the late Victorian period, with its unquestioning support of the British Empire and the inherent superiority of British culture and traditions. His emphasis on war and politics, which often betrays a classically Machiavellian attitude toward the subject, has also drawn criticism, as has his tendency to emphasize his own perspectives and values, which have struck some commentators as dated and dualistic in their tendency to characterize opposing forces as good and evil. Although C. has drawn mixed reviews as a prose stylist, he is particularly good at constructing a clear narrative explicating complex events, particularly when it deals with things he has seen or participated in directly. Despite the varying assessments of his literary skills, there is little doubt that as an articulate, often eloquent, eyewitness and chronicler of some of the most significant events of the 20th c., C.'s literary contribution is a substantial one.

BIBLIOGRAPHY: Ashley, M., *C. as Historian* (1968); Gilbert, M., *C.* (1991); Manchester, W., *The Last Lion: W. S. C.* (1983); Weidhorn, W., *Sir W. C.* (1979); Weidhorn, W., *Sword and Pen: A Survey of the Writings of Sir W. C.* (1974)

DANIEL G. PAYNE

CHURCHYARD, Thomas
b. ca. 1520, Shrewsbury; d. 3 April 1604, London?

C.'s works, which include tracts and broadsides, are largely autobiographical, dealing with his career as a professional soldier. He wrote a verse-pageant to welcome ELIZABETH I to Bristol in 1574 and another for Norwich in 1578. In 1575, he published a collection of poems and prose called *The First Part of Churchyard's Chips,* which appeared in an enlarged edition in 1578. In that same year, he published *A Lamentable and Pitiful Description of the Woeful Wars in Flanders* followed by *Churchyard's Choice* (1579), which offended the queen, who eventually relented. C.'s contribution to *A Mirror for Magistrates* (1559) was the "Legend of Shore's Wife," considered his best work. C., who also published a translation of Ovid's *Tristia* (1578), appears as Palaemon in Edmund SPENSER's *Colin Clout.* Thomas NASHE mentions C. kindly in *Four Letters Confuted.*

CIBBER, Colley
b. 6 November 1671, London; d. 11 November 1757, London

In 1690, C. joined Thomas Betterton's company at the Drury Lane theater and in 1696 produced a play, *Love's Last Shift; or, The Fool in Fashion.* William CONGREVE said it had many things "like wit in it" and Sir John VANBRUGH wrote his brilliant *The Relapse* as a sequel. C. played Sir Novelty Fashion in his own play, and the same character, renamed Lord Foppington, in Vanbrugh's. In 1698, C. was among dramatists attacked by Jeremy Collier. In 1702, C. produced one of his best comedies, *She Wou'd and She Wou'd Not* (1703) and in 1704 *The Careless Husband* (1705), classed by Horace WALPOLE as "worthy of immortality." In 1717, C. produced the *The Non-Juror* (1718), based on Molière's *Tartuffe.* The leading character was a Roman Catholic priest who incited rebellion. This offended Jacobites and Catholics, including Alexander POPE, who in 1742 made C. chief target in the revised *Dunciad.* But C.'s Whig opinions made him poet laureate in 1730. Henry FIELDING attacked C. in *Joseph Andrews* and rebuked him for his mutila-

tion of William SHAKESPEARE in the *Historical Register for 1736,* where C. figures as Ground Ivy.

CITY AND LITERATURE, The

From the time of John GOWER, whose awareness of the London merchant class and its concerns contrasts with the broad scope of Geoffrey CHAUCER, British writers have often demonstrated an awareness of the city and its particular concerns. But the city is more than a subject for literature; it recurs as a theme and a metaphor. As Raymond WILLIAMS points out in his expansive study *The Country and the City,* much British literature has hinged on a contrast between the values represented by the country—simplicity, virtue, innocence, the natural—and those represented by the city—learning, communication, worldliness, the social. The dialectic between those values has shaped the course of British literary history.

But moving even beyond the city as metaphor, the urban landscape enters literature as an organizing principle. In many literary modes, the city appears as an analogue of form: it is episodic, instantaneous, mechanized, fragmented, oversaturated. Some forms can reflect these qualities better than others. The drama, which itself thrives in an urban environment and mirrors that environment in its communal unfolding, is perhaps the form most strongly associated with the city. But the novel also has connections to urbanism, and the rise of the novel was concurrent with the industrialization and urbanization of modern culture. More specifically, some stylistic genres have historically connected with urban life: satire, which assumes its audience shares a set of social references, often takes on an urban voice. The Bildungsroman, or coming-of-age novel, often includes an experience of the city, utilizing the country/city dialectic to parallel a progress from innocence to knowledge. And if the countryside lends itself well to meditation and rhapsody, the city is the ideal landscape for the stream of consciousness narrative: active, ever-changing, and full of stimuli.

Some literary schools are typically considered to be more urban than others. The first literary period that receives critical attention for its relationship to the city is the Jacobean drama. After the largely pastoral feel of Elizabethan comedy, in the first years of the 17th c. writers such as Thomas DEKKER and Ben JONSON turned their attention to the city, dramatizing public life in London and beginning to create the cast of city character types: merchants, gallants, lawyers, rogues, prostitutes, pimps, gamesters, widows, and fops. A new form arose: the "citizen comedy," concerned with the everyday life of "citizens," or middle-class Londoners. The "cit" became a staple dramatic type, contrasted with the wittier—and more dissolute—upper classes, as well as the eternal comic scapegoat, the country bumpkin. But even as it began the process of shaping and distinguishing these types, Jacobean comedy posed the relationship between the city and the country as one of mutual necessity: the city provided the social arena required by the country gentry to conduct the marriage market.

Following the restoration of the monarchy and the reopening of the theaters in 1660, comedy came to the foreground again, and many of the Jacobean comic themes were taken up once more. The Restoration comedies of William WYCHERLEY, George FARQUHAR, John VANBRUGH, George ETHEREGE, and William CONGREVE not only pose a multitude of complex relations between "city" and "country" types, but they often map the city's public and private places onto the plot. Scenes set in public parks, streets, and the public areas of city homes suggest the performative nature of urban public life, while scenes set in bedrooms, studies, and closets unveil the disjunctions between public and private selves.

London more than doubled in size between 1700 and 1820. The century saw the forging of modern urban social structures and the increasing centrality of London to the nation's cultural life. Concurrently, the novel began to take its place among English literary forms. With its roots in the newspaper and the broadside as much as in the prose romances that preceded it, the 18th-c. novel took shape as a distinctly urban form. The novel's realism, its focus on the individual, and its interest in the transformative power of large social forces best observed in urban environments all drew it to the city. In his influential study *The Rise of the Novel* (1957), Ian Watt argues that the novel form arose in part as a response to the individual's new relationship to society in the modern city: a series of private relationships replaces the traditional feeling of being connected to nature or society in a more organic way.

The novel thus emerged as a means of addressing the relationship between an individual and his or her environment. Novelists such as Daniel DEFOE, Samuel RICHARDSON, and Henry FIELDING often wrote of the city and its denizens, showing protagonists struggling to make their way in the urban jungle. Defoe's *Moll Flanders* and Fielding's *The Life of Mr. Jonathan Wild* are the most notable examples of novels that follow the careers of notorious criminals, in the case of Wild, from birth to gallows, detailing the various destructive forces of city life along the way.

The clubby atmosphere of Enlightenment literary London supported satire outside the novel as well. Jonathan SWIFT creates city types in "A Description of the Morning" (1709) and "A Description of a City Shower" (1710), urban parodies of the Virgilean georgic. John GAY also parodies the georgic with rich city descriptions in his *Trivia; or, The Art of Walking the Streets of London,* and he contributes to the development of city types in one of the most influential plays of the period, *The Beggar's Opera*. The 18th c.'s central literary figure, Samuel JOHNSON, also wrote a satire addressing the vices and oppressions of the city, *London*. Although he frequently criticized the dangers of urban life, Johnson led an urbane group of London literati and is said to have remarked that when one is tired of London, one is tired of life. Johnson was not alone in demonstrating a divided attitude toward the city: Enlightenment authors privileged the city as a site for learning and civic life, but excoriated it for its seamy underside.

In the late 18th c., a strong reaction against the social and rational nature of the Enlightenment began. The Romantic movement arose in part as a response to the revolutionary movements sweeping through Europe. But despite their sympathies with revolutionary politics, the Romantics' emphasis on the limits of reason and their intense focus on nature and its centrality to man limited their involvement in urban issues. Their turn toward subjects such as the supernatural, dream states, and the rustic led them away from urban realism while their emphasis on individual experience caused them to gravitate to the lyric and away from the genres typically associated with the city: drama and the novel.

Most Romantics allied the city with corruption, expressing anxiety about urbanization's effect on nature and on human relations. Percy Bysshe SHELLEY depicts London as Hell in *Peter Bell the Third*, as does Lord BYRON in *Don Juan*. William WORDSWORTH delights in its variety and its marvels, but experiences the city as a site of confusion, multiplicity, and anxiety in the seventh book of *The Prelude*, "Residence in London." William BLAKE is the exception; fascinated by the vitality, movement, and populations of urban life, he depicts London powerfully in *Songs of Innocence, Songs of Experience, Milton,* and *Jerusalem.*

With the passage of the first Reform Bill in 1832 and the accession of Queen Victoria in 1837, the transformation of Britain to a modern industrial state was well underway. Awareness of the social pressures caused by rapid industrialization naturally focused on the urban working and middle classes. Victorian writers turned to REALISM, variously defined, to represent those struggles and their work took on a distinctly urban tone. In addition, the serial publication of many Victorian novels allowed the largely urban reading public to register its response as the novel progressed, creating the potential for texts to be influenced by audiences. The novels of Charles DICKENS are the best examples of Victorian tales of the city, but William Makepeace THACKERAY, George GISSING, and to a lesser extent George ELIOT all produced urban novels. Eliot's novels and those of other women writers reflected the social conditions of women in focusing on the domestic sphere and exploring public life less than those of male contemporaries.

The drama of this period was often urban as well. Playwrights developed a taste for "realistically" presented social issues and increasingly presented exposés of urban life. Dion Boucicault helped pioneer the genre with *The Poor of New York* (1857), adapted in London as *The Poor of London*. Though these plays strike today's audiences as stilted and melodramatic, they seemed radically true-to-life to contemporary theatergoers.

With the 20th c. came MODERNISM, perhaps the literary period most associated with the city. In art, architecture, literature, and thought, modernism thrived in the period's great urban centers: Vienna, Berlin, Moscow, Prague, Paris, London, New York, Chicago. At the birth of a new, technological mass culture, cities provided not only a location but an analogue for the modernist break with tradition. Like the modern city, the modern text was given to mixing influences and voices; modernism's individual, unlike the Romantic inner self, is very often a stream of consciousness composed of thousands of impressions and encounters with an urban reality: Leopold Bloom in *Ulysses* by James JOYCE or Clarissa Dalloway in *Mrs. Dalloway* by Virginia WOOLF. The episodic nature of much modernist writing, from the monumental poem *The Waste Land* by T. S. ELIOT to the *Cantos* (1917–70) by Ezra Pound, reflects the increasingly episodic texture of life in the modern city. For the modernists, the isolation and fragmentation of urban life came to reflect the alienation of the modern self. But the interaction went both ways, for the stream of consciousness narrative voice proposed a kind of self that was constructed much like the city is: a palimpsest of fragments from the past and noisy impressions of the present, driven by anxious toiling toward the next thing.

As in so much city literature, the modernists wavered between depicting the city as a place of oppression and a place of newfound freedom. The tension has particular relevance for women and writers of color. Woolf began the process of envisioning the city as not strictly a male domain. But at the same time other modernist women like Jean RHYS saw the city as a place that reduplicated women's marginality.

As the century progressed, moral questions continued to inflect 20th-c. urban literature. Stephen SPENDER depicts the city as a place of economic oppression and despair; W. H. AUDEN presents it as confirming the individual's aloneness while simultaneously offering some hope of human connection. The plays of the "Angry Young Men," including John OSBORNE and John ARDEN, examine British social problems through the lens of teeming, multicultured urban life at midcentury.

As the 20th c. drew to a close, the association of the city with corruption and a lost, more pure way of life, continued. Several novels by Martin AMIS depict urban horrors, with city dwellers the victims of an empty contemporary life in which addictions and destructive behavior have replaced a real culture. At the same time, many women novelists carried forth the Dickensian tradition, using sharp observation and a new freedom of movement to re-see London: Margaret DRABBLE, Iris MURDOCH, Anita BROOKNER, and Doris LESSING have all engaged with the city in their fiction. The experience of immigrant writers also brings to literature a new perspective on both new and familiar urban spaces. Sam SELVON, for instance, wrote about the experience of Trinidadian immigrants in London. The works of multicultural writers such as Hanif KUREISHI, Timothy MO, Trezza Azzopardi, and Zadie SMITH continue to build on the interrelationships between literature and the city.

BIBLIOGRAPHY: Bradbury, M., and J. McFarlane, eds., *Modernism: 1890–1930* (1976); Leinwand, T. B., *The City Staged: Jacobean Comedy, 1603–1613* (1986); Pike, B., *The Image of the City in Modern Literature* (1981); Sizemore, C. W., *A Female Vision of the City* (1989); Watt, I. P., *The Rise of the Novel* (1957); Weimer, D. R., *The City as Metaphor* (1966); Williams, R., *The Country and the City* (1973)

GINGER STRAND

CLARE, John
b. 13 July 1793, Helpston; d. 20 May 1864, Northampton

C.'s first volume, *Poems Descriptive of Rural Life and Scenery* (1820), bore on its title page the designation "John Clare the Northamptonshire Peasant," a label that fixed C.'s regional and class identity and has continued to condition critical responses to his poetry. C. emphasized his social identity and experience in order to authenticate his depictions of the social marginality and destitution of the rural laboring poor at the time the English agricultural industry was undergoing the process of capitalization. C.'s first volume was remarkably successful and went through four editions in a year; however, his Evangelical patron and parts of his audience disapproved of the social criticism and "vulgar" dialect usages that characterized his distinctive style.

C.'s second volume, *The Village Minstrel and Other Poems* (2 vols., 1821), sold poorly. The response to *The Shepherd's Calendar, with Village Stories and Other Poems* (1827) was even more disappointing. In 1831, C. started to transcribe poems for a projected volume to be titled *The Midsummer Cushion*. Hoping to set himself up as a farmer, C. moved in 1832 to a cottage in Northborough that was provided by a patron. Though the cottage was only a few miles from his native village of Helpston, C. felt a profound sense of dislocation and isolation that is reflected in his verse. After numerous frustrations and setbacks trying to publish *The Midsummer Cushion,* the more modest selection *The Rural Muse* (1835) was published to some positive reviews but poor sales. In 1837, C. became a voluntary patient at an asylum for the mentally ill in High Beach, Epping Forest. C. escaped from this asylum in a delusional state in 1841, walking back eighty miles to Northborough, and was admitted months later to the Northampton General Lunatic Asylum. C. spent the remaining twenty-three years of his life in the asylum and wrote the majority of his poetry there, most of which was not published until the 20th c. C.'s introspective asylum poems, some of which are written from the assumed identity of successful contemporaries, often address his feelings of confinement and alienation with a haunting poignancy.

C.'s poetry was profoundly disturbed by the processes of parliamentary enclosure that replaced the open-field system of Helpston after 1809. Many of his poems openly resist the changes wrought to the countryside; moreover, some critics suggest that C.'s unconventional grammar, syntax, and use of dialect constitute a form of linguistic resistance to the ideology of enclosure and agricultural "improvement." This observation has led to the revaluation of C.'s editor, John Taylor, who punctuated C.'s verse and regulated its meter, cut many of his poems, and standardized much of his unfamiliar local language in order to increase his appeal. The recent Oxford English Texts (OET) edition, the first complete edition of all of C.'s surviving poetry, has generated debate in C. studies because it justifies its editorial preference for unpublished manuscript versions by characterizing Taylor's editorial work as unwarranted and intrusive. A minority of critics accuse these modern editors of "textual primitivism" comparable to the primitivism that accounted for much of C.'s initial popularity and instead stress the collaborative nature of Taylor's and C.'s editorial process. A more recent controversy in C. studies centers on Eric Robinson's—the general editor of the OET editions—claim to hold the copyright on all of C.'s 2,000 unpublished poems. Because Robinson requires anyone who publishes other readings from the manuscripts to have his approval and permission, some critics feel he is effectively delimiting the field of C. studies.

C. is one of England's best poets of place. His poetry displays his profound attachment to his native locality of Helpston as well as the pain of displacement due to the topographical and social changes brought about by enclosure. Not surprisingly, his natural descriptions clash with the conventions of the prospect tradition and the English culture of property

landscapes. C. was particularly aware of these conventions because of his reading in both poetry and natural history, his experience laboring in the fields and in landscape gardens, and his close observations of landscape art during visits to nearby estates and his four visits to London. C. memorializes the idealized open-field landscape of his youth and resists assuming the elevated perspective of conventional "picturesque" landscapes in favor of the "low" perspective of the rural laborer. He frequently decries enclosure for aesthetic reasons, arguing that fences and hedges obstruct vision at the same time as they restrict the freedom of the laborer. C.'s close observations resulted in a naturalistic style that emphasizes particularity and demonstrates his awareness of the natural cycles of his environment. Ecocritics suggest that C. felt compelled to attempt to articulate a relationship with the environment that was not based upon possession and exploitation, what C. called "a language that is ever green" in his poem "Pastoral Poesy."

BIBLIOGRAPHY: Barrell, J., *The Idea of Landscape and the Sense of Place, 1730–1840: An Approach to the Poetry of J. C.* (1972); Goodridge, J., and S. Kövesi, eds., *J. C.* (2000); Haughton, H., and G. Summerfield, eds., *J. C. in Context* (1994); Hopkins, C., *J. C.* (1991)

SEAN BURGESS

CLARENDON, Edward Hyde, First Earl

b.18 February 1609, Dinton, Wiltshire; d. 9 or 11 December 1674, Rouen, France

C. was educated at Magdalen Hall, Oxford, and later practiced law. He entered Parliament in 1640 and soon changed sides in order to support King Charles I. During the civil war between royalists and "Roundheads," C. followed the king's son, later King Charles II, into exile in the Channel Islands, where C. began his famous book, *The True Historical Narrative of the Rebellion and Civil Wars in England,* commonly known as *Clarendon's History of the Rebellion,* celebrated by John EVELYN and Thomas Babington MACAULAY for its portraits. C. fell from favor and his enemies forced him into second exile after the restoration of the monarchy, in which he played a leading role. Maintaining his dignity, he finished his *History* and his *Autobiography.* C.'s writings were first printed from a transcript by his son in three volumes in 1702–4 but a better text was edited by W. D. Macray (6 vols., 1888). C. also wrote an account of the Irish rebellion, published in 1721. His essays, political tracts, and speeches were published in 1727 as *A Collection of Several Tracts.* His critique of Thomas HOBBES, *Leviathan: A Brief View and Survey,* appeared in 1676, two years after his death. C. was for a time chancellor of Oxford University, which inherited his papers. The Clarendon Press was built on the profits from them.

CLARKE, [Sir] Arthur C[harles]
b. 16 December 1917, Minehead, Somerset

C. has had more influence on SCIENCE FICTION than any other British writer aside from H. G. WELLS and has been consistently successful on both sides of the Atlantic, from the 1960s onward being a regular appearer on the best-seller charts. His appearances on American television commentating on Moon landings, his coauthorship of the script of *2001: A Space Odyssey* (1968) with Stanley Kubrick, and his anchoring of a television series, *Arthur C. Clarke's Mysterious World*, means that he is probably the most publicly recognizable science fiction writer. It had been C. who had proposed that a satellite at a particular distance from the Earth would orbit at the same speed that the planet rotated, and therefore could be used for international communications. C.'s scientific training and interests feed into his fiction, but he has also published a series of collections of essays on science and the possibilities of science, notably *Profiles of the Future* (1962) and *Report on Planet 3 and other Speculations* (1972).

C. was of a generation of science fiction writers better known for their ideas than characterization or style, although his prose is felt to be at the least serviceable. The best known of his novels situate humanity in relation to something greater than it, either in terms of the next stage of evolution or in terms of aliens who are much more technologically advanced. A sense of the sublime, almost a religious awe, underlies these works, which some critics have seen as being at odds with C.'s scientific, rationalist outlook.

Childhood's End (1950) features an Earth saved from nuclear disaster by the intervention of benevolent aliens, known as the Overlords. In an unprecedented era of peace and tranquillity, humanity watches a new generation of children grow up and merge with the higher consciousness of the Overlords. Much of the book depicts an ongoing struggle between the forces of superstition or religion and Enlightenment scientific values, with science being given an upper hand. The aliens have been guiding humanity for generations and confused accounts of encounters with them have passed into legend, myth, and FAIRY TALES. Nevertheless, the final metamorphosis is a religious transcendence.

2001: A Space Odyssey is also a narrative of transcendence, the novel being written in tandem with the script for the movie directed by Kubrick. A lengthy prologue features early humanity's encounter with a mysterious black monolith, and its subsequent development of technology, civilization, and warfare. The action cuts to 2001 and the discovery of a monolith

on the Moon, which in turn sparks an expedition to Saturn (Jupiter in the film) to find another monolith. The final sequence of the book and film is the surviving astronaut's experience of penetrating the interior of the monolith, a stargate. Given that C. and Kubrick were attempting to depict more highly evolved intelligences, much of what he sees is incomprehensible to us, and at best ambiguous. For many years, C. refused demands for a sequel, arguing that he could not describe life so far beyond current evolution, but nevertheless several followed, *2010: Odyssey Two* (1982), filmed by Peter Hyams in 1984, *2061: Odyssey Three* (1988), and *3001: The Final Odyssey* (1996). None of these were as well received as the original novel; *2010*'s climax, the transformation of Jupiter into a sun by the monolith, in the process bringing new light and new hope to Earth, was held to be unnecessarily religious. *3001*, on the other hand, gets bogged down in trying to describe possible if unlikely scientific wonders.

Rendezvous with Rama (1973) fits into the Big Dumb Object subgenre of science fiction, and was one of several such novels written by various hands during the early 1970s. A huge alien spaceship passes through the solar system, and is brought into temporary life by the heat and light from the Sun. The novel is the account of the exploration of the vast artifact, but the origins of the ship are left clouded. A sequel was hinted at by the closing reminder that the alien Ramans did everything in threes—thus two more ships are out there—but the three sequels did not follow until 1989's *Rama II*, cowritten with, and thought to be mostly the work of, space scientist Gentry Lee.

C. remains prolific, despite steadily declining health, continuing both to collaborate and write solo works. He has endowed various good causes, within science and science fiction, notably the annual Arthur C. Clarke Award given for the best science fiction novel published in Britain.

BIBLIOGRAPHY: Hollow, J., *Against the Night, the Stars: The Science Fiction of A. C. C.* (1983); McAleer, N., *Odyssey: The Authorised Biography of A. C. C.* (1992); Reid, R. A., *A. C. C.* (1997)

ANDREW M. BUTLER

CLARKE, Gillian [Williams]
b. 8 June 1937, Cardiff, Wales

Poet, playwright, editor, and translator from Welsh whose own work has been translated into ten languages, C. has lived all her life in her native South Wales except for two years in London when she worked for the BBC after reading English literature at University College, Cardiff. She has been editor of the *Anglo-Welsh Review* (1975–84) and teaches creative writing. Her work is taught in secondary schools. C.

has always had a strong following in Wales since the publication in 1971 of her first collection, *Snow on the Mountain*, followed by *The Sundial* (1978). *Letter from a Far Country* (1982) brought her to the attention of readers outside the Principality and *Selected Poems* (1985) established her reputation. Her *Collected Poems* was published in 1997 followed by *The Animal Wall and Other Poems* (1999). The themes of her ten books are universal: nature, family life, love, death, expressed with traditional skills of versification.

CLARKE, [Victor] Lindsay
b. 14 August 1939, Halifax, Yorkshire

Since 1987, C. has published three novels and a collection of Celtic myths, but his reputation so far rests on his second novel, the Whitbread Prize–winning *The Chymical Wedding: A Romance* (1989). *The Chymical Wedding* tells two parallel stories set over one hundred years apart. One is the first-person narrative of Alex Darken, a struggling poet who has traveled to the remote town of Easterness to recuperate from a depression occasioned by the discovery of his wife's infidelity. There he meets Edward Nesbit, an older poet, and Edward's "research assistant," the apparently psychic Laura. Edward and Laura are attempting to unravel the mystery that forms the plot of the novel's second narrative strand: the story of Louisa Agnew, a 19th-c. alchemist, and Edwin Frere, the village parson with whom she has a passionate affair. Louisa writes a book revealing the secrets of the ancient alchemists but ultimately burns it, a sacrifice occasioned by the actions of Edwin, who—a representative of traditional religion and Victorian sensibility—is driven mad by his inability to reconcile his conventional beliefs with his passion for Louisa. *The Chymical Wedding* is both a compelling romance and a rich philosophical novel, developing C.'s major theme of the necessity of man's acceptance of feminine principles in order to attain a state of peace and harmony. Indeed, it is this merging of masculine and feminine that alchemy—the chymical wedding—is meant to symbolize. C.'s other novels include *Sunday Whiteman* (1987), inspired by the author's experiences as a teacher in Ghana, and *Alice's Masque* (1994), another novel dealing with male-female relationships and the need for men to accept the feminine in order to live harmonious lives.

CLELAND, John
b. September 1710, Kingston-upon-Thames; d. 23 January 1789, Westminster

While imprisoned for debt in the Fleet in 1748, the thirty-eight-year-old C. sent a manuscript to the publisher Fenton Griffiths. On November 21 of that year,

the London *General Advertiser* announced, "*This Day is Published, (Price 3s.)*/Memoirs of a Woman of Pleasure," better known as *Fanny Hill*. James BOSWELL called it "that most licentious and inflaming book," and Thomas Sherlock, Bishop of London, declared that it was "the Lewdest thing I ever saw." Although C. devoted the next forty years of his life to writing, he owes his literary reputation to this erotic classic that he wrote in jail.

In a pair of long letters Fanny Hill, the heroine of *Memoirs of a Woman of Pleasure* (2 vols., 1748–49; rev. as *Memoirs of Fanny Hill*, 1750) traces her sexual exploits from her arrival in London from Lancashire to her happy marriage to her first love, Charles. The *Memoirs* offers a realistic depiction of the mid-18th-c. London sexual underworld, with its masquerades, Covent Garden bagnios, and West End brothels. At the beginning of the book, Fanny is a sexual innocent, but sex serves as a metonymy for innocence/ignorance of various sorts. Fanny thinks that her fortune of eight guineas and seventeen shillings will last forever, and she mistakes the procuress Mrs. Brown for a fine lady. In the course of the novel, Fanny learns to become a sound economist, a good judge of character, and, in her words, a "rational pleasurist." She discovers that even in matters sexual, restraint has its uses: abstinence renders the next indulgence more delightful. The work's cleverly named "tail-piece of morality" advocating virtue is a transparent cover for the lubricity that fills the novel, but C.'s position that reason should govern passion is sincere.

Much of the charm of the *Memoirs* derives from its style. At the beginning of her second letter, Fanny acknowledges the difficulty of varying a narrative of experiences "whose bottom [is] eternally one and the same." As that phrase reveals, C. repeatedly relies on puns and euphemisms to sustain interest. He devised a seemingly endless supply of terms for sexual organs male and female, and he alters his metaphors to suit a particular situation. When Fanny makes love with a salesman, the language is drawn from business. When her partner is a sailor, she relates that he "seiz'd her for a prize" and "fell directly on board." Even the heroine's name is a pun.

Fenton Griffiths's brother and fellow publisher, Ralph, apparently paid C.'s debt. Released from prison on March 6, 1749, C. became a regular contributor to Ralph Griffiths's *Monthly Review* when it began publishing in May of that year. Over the next two and a half years, C. published twenty-four pieces in the *Monthly Review*, after which the number of his contributions declined. Most of these were reviews of belles-lettres, though C. occasionally branched out into writing about law or medicine. The latter was not totally alien to him: in 1751, C. published *Institutes of Health*, which advocated moderation in diet and sex. His review of *The Oeconomy of Human Life* (1750), variously attributed to Robert DODSLEY and

Philip Dormer Stanhope, fourth Earl of CHESTER-
FIELD, prompted C. to pen a parody, *The Oeconomy
of a Winter's Day* (1750).

For Griffiths, C. prepared an abridged and less salacious version of *Fanny Hill*, and Griffiths published
C.'s next novel, *Memoirs of a Coxcomb* (1751). The
first-person narrator, Sir William Delamor, falls in
love with the mysterious Lydia. After Lydia vanishes,
Sir William grows dissipated, indulging in the same
adventures as Fanny Hill but without providing the
reader with the graphic descriptions. At the end of the
novel, Sir William and Lydia reunite and plan to
marry. In the course of the narrative, C. satirizes gambling, wrong-headed educational practices, and other
contemporary follies.

During the 1750s, C. also turned his hand to
drama. The pieces were printed but not produced.
Titus Vespasian, based on Pietro Metastasio's *La
Clemenza di Tito* (1734), was published in 1755 with
C.'s *The Ladies' Subscription*, a satire on current dramatic conventions, and *Tombo-Chiqui; or, The American Savage* appeared in 1758. This last play contrasts
the absurd artificiality of London with the natural reason of the title character raised in the simplicity of
nature. C. returned to this theme in the epistolary
novel *The Woman of Honour* (3 vols., 1768). Clara
Maynwaring, like Fanny, goes to the metropolis from
Lancashire. Rejecting two suitors, she returns to the
countryside to marry the uncorrupted Sumners.

C. served as a hired political pen, contributing over
two hundred letters to the *Public Advertiser* between
1757 and 1787. C.'s chief concern during this period
was, however, linguistics. In 1766, he published a collection of essays on the subject, *The Way to Things,
by Words and to Words by Things*, followed by *Specimen of an Etimological Vocabulary* (1768) and *Additional Articles to the Specimen . . .* (1769). His investigation into the Celtic origins of language coincided
with renewed interest in British antiquity shared by
such figures as Thomas GRAY, Bishop Thomas PERCY,
and Evan Evans.

For all his writing, C. remains a one-book figure.
That one book, though, has never been out of print
since its first appearance, enduring not only because
of its subject but also because of its style. As Peter
QUENNELL wrote in the introduction to the 1963 Put-
nam edition, "No other book of the same kind possesses so much elegance and energy."

BIBLIOGRAPHY: Bradbury, M., "*Fanny Hill* and the
Comic Novel," *CritQ* 13 (August 1971): 263–75; Epstein, W. H., *J. C.* (1974)

                                        JOSEPH ROSENBLUM

CLEVELAND, John
b. June 1613, Yorkshire; d. 29 April 1658, London

Contemporary of John MILTON at Christ's College,
Cambridge, C. became a fellow of St. John's College,

Cambridge, but he lost his fellowship for opposing
Oliver Cromwell, suffered hardship and imprisonment. C.'s poem about their fellow-student "On the
Memory of Mr. Edward King" was included in the
same volume as Milton's "Lycidas." C.'s poems in
their day were more highly esteemed than Milton's,
despite obscurity and far-fetched "metaphysical"
conceits, giving rise to the word "Clevelandism" for
such effects, mocked by John DRYDEN. C.'s satire
"The Rebel Scot" expressed his disgust with the
Scots who surrendered King Charles I to Parliament.
"Smectymnuus" and "Rupertismus" display his invective at its most energetic.

CLIFFORD, [Lady] Anne
b. 30 January 1590, Skipton Castle, Yorkshire; d. 22
March 1676, Appleby Castle, Westmoreland

C., daughter of Margaret Russell, Countess of Cumberland, shared in the traditionally feminine acts of
literary patronage and performance during the early
modern period, but she also authored her own personal brand of texts, challenging the restricted role
of women within a patriarchal society. By writing a
memoir and diaries, by inscribing her life and that of
her family in chronicles, artworks, and monuments,
C. used writing to construct and create an independent
female self.

C.'s mother, a patroness of Samuel DANIEL, Edmund SPENSER, and others, exposed her daughter to
the literary life of the Elizabethan and Jacobean
courts. Both she and her mother were dedicatees of
verse epistles by Daniel (C.'s tutor), and formed part
of the female community idealized by Aemilia LA-
NYER in *Salve Deus Rex Judaeorum*. At court, C.
danced in Ben JONSON's masques and, later in life,
made poet and preacher John DONNE a guest in her
home. If C.'s mother was the source of C.'s lifelong
habit of reading and connection to the literary world,
then her father was the foundation for C.'s public self.
At his death in 1605, C.'s father, George Clifford,
third Earl of Cumberland, willed his lands in Yorkshire and Westmoreland to his brother and brother's
sons. Until 1646, when the last of these male relatives
died, C. struggled with her first and second husbands,
Richard Sackville and Philip Herbert, various relatives, and JAMES I himself over her right to inherit.
C.'s insistence that she was her father's true heir was
the impetus for her engagement in public life, and the
constant theme of her diaries, family chronicles—
even the inscription engraved on her father's tomb.

C. maintained diaries for a good part of her life—
the last entry was written the day before she died. Her
extant diaries cover the years 1616–17, 1619, and
1676. The period from 1650 through 1675 is covered
in the yearly chronicles of the Clifford family; these
are likely a compilation of C.'s daily diaries. C. also

wrote a memoir of the year 1603, separate lives of each of her parents, and her own life story, which begins, quite extraordinarily, not with her birth, but with her conception—a proof of the legitimacy of her hereditary claims. And, with the aid of her mother, C. compiled the "Chronicles" of the Clifford family, a detailed genealogy dating back to the 13th c. that reinforced her legal claim and preserved the family heritage for her own heirs.

C.'s diaries are of interest as a rare example of personal self-revelation and a concern with the secular, rather than the spiritual life. The mis-en-page of the extant manuscript copies (apparently similar to that of the originals) reflects C.'s conception of herself: her life and experience occupy the center of the text, while contemporaneous events are jotted in the margins. Like some massive theological work, C.'s life and writings are the canon upon which commentary can be made.

C.'s authorship, however, was not confined to the written page. In 1646, she commissioned what is now known as the "Great Picture," and appears to have been responsible for the selection of portraits, persons, literary works, and inscriptions recorded in the painting. In the center of the triptych (attributed to copyist Jan van Belcamp) are C.'s parents, deceased brothers, and portraits of her aunts. (Other male relatives are pointedly excluded.) In the left panel, a young C. is depicted with books, lute, and portraits of Daniel and her governess. The right-hand panel shows the fifty-six-year-old C., along with her books. Her two husbands are relegated to background portraits, with C. dominating this section of the painting. C., and not the artist, is clearly the genius behind the Great Picture.

Vita SACKVILLE-WEST helped revive current interest in C. with her edition of the diary (1923); Virginia WOOLF followed with her depiction of C. as one of England's first "common readers." Since then, C.'s life and works have provided feminist literary critics and historians with abundant material for examining the issues of gender and gender-based privilege in the 17th c.

BIBLIOGRAPHY: Acheson, K. O., ed., *The Diary of A. C., 1616–1619* (1995); Clifford, D. J. H., ed., *The Diaries of Lady A. C.* (1990); Lewalski, B. K., "Claiming Patrimony and Constructing a Self: A. C. and Her *Diary*," in her *Writing Women in Jacobean England* (1993): 124–51; Parry, G., "The Great Picture of Lady A. C.," in Howarth, D., ed., *Art and Patronage in the Caroline Courts* (1993): 202–19; Williamson, G. C., *Lady A. C.* (1922)

CECILE M. JAGODZINSKI

CLOUGH, Arthur Hugh

b. 1 January 1819, Liverpool; d. 13 November 1861, Florence, Italy

Two important aspects of C.'s career distinguish his place in Victorian literature. The first, his attempt to create an English version of classical hexameter, can be judged according to the success of his longer poems *The Bothie of Toper-na-fuosich* (1848; rev. as *The Bothie of Tober-na-Vuolich*, 1862) and *Amours de Voyage* (1858). C. tried to adapt the verse form from Latin to English by creating an accentual hexameter, one without a regular syllable count per line. Instead, C.'s hexameter line has a fixed number of feet—six—with each foot containing one stressed syllable and one or two unstressed, leaving the number of syllables variable in a range between twelve and seventeen.

Many critics find this adaptation, intended to accommodate the cadences of English, a clunky substitute for the original form. Some have noted that both *The Bothie* and *Amours de Voyage* read in passages like parodies of classical epics, particularly in their subject matter. The poems share a context of youthful travels and romance, *The Bothie* following a group of travelers in Scotland and their respective loves, while *Amours de Voyage* recounts in epistolary form a young man's journey through Europe half-heartedly pursuing his beloved. *The Bothie* is lighter and more pastoral while *Amours de Voyage* attempts to chronicle a young man's philosophical development as his changing environment seems to help him realize what is most important in life. The hexameter itself—over 1,700 lines in *The Bothie*—is recognized as a stylistic achievement by many, and detractors often admit a belief that true hexameter may not be possible at all in English. However, C.'s American contemporary Henry Wadsworth Longfellow did have great success with the form in his long poem, *Evangeline* (1847), and it was an American audience C. would reach with *Amours*, which was initially published serially in the *Atlantic Monthly*. Still, both C.'s hexameter works fail to deliver for most critics on the promise of C.'s linguistic gifts, stifled according to many by his position and education as a Victorian and the perceived social and moral obligations in that role. Others delight in his ironic articulation of the anxieties generated by the instability of Victorian social hierarchies.

C.'s role as a Victorian, socially as well as literarily, governs the other most important aspect of his career. According to available evidence, C. struggled with moral and philosophical issues as an individual but even more so as an artist. In his works, he questioned many accepted ideas of the day in ways that scandalized his conservative wife and family. After his untimely death, C.'s wife became her husband's editor, and many have suspected that her involvement with his work would forever alter critical perception of the poet. Much C. scholarship has been devoted to study of his papers, his manuscripts and notes as delivered to Charles Eliot Norton, his American friend and publisher who was assembling a collection of C.'s work at the time of his death. C. himself had doubts about his work and his philosophy, and these concerns resulted in contradictory instructions, reassessments and renunciations.

Dipsychus (1865), another long poem, illustrates C.'s struggles with these doubts in its style, subject, and publication history. In a series of dramatic scenes, two voices debate philosophical and religious questions. As implied by the title, the two voices at times seem to be two sides of one being. But in scene 8, these opposing natures become two separate characters involved in a Faust-like exchange, the representative of the world of action and pleasure becoming a tempting devil rather than another facet of human nature. Some have suggested that C. succumbed to societal pressures to send a more distinct moral message with his work. Others believe his wife's interpretation of C.'s intentions in his notes and manuscripts was based on her own agenda to shape her husband's image as a moral Victorian.

With a declining literacy in classical works, the hexameter never caught on as a verse form in English. C.'s reputation is still in question, though access to his manuscripts has allowed for much speculation on his talent, his intent as an artist, and the potential he might have realized with more years and a more open society. Poems such as "The Latest Decalogue" and "Say Not the Struggle Nought Availeth," from his shorter works published in *Ambarvalia* (1844) with coauthor Thomas Burbidge, keep C.'s name and his stoic Victorian SENTIMENT alive in many anthologies.

BIBLIOGRAPHY: Chorley, K., *A. H. C., the Uncommitted Mind* (1962); Greenberger, E. B., *A. H. C.* (1970); Harris, W. V., *A. H. C.* (1970)

NICOLE SARROCCO

COBBETT, William

b. 9 March 1763, Farnham, Surrey; d. 18 June 1835, Farnham, Surrey

C. played an extraordinary range of roles in his life, ranging from soldier to farmer to political journalist to member of Parliament—and in each of these roles, he wrote prolifically. Author of grammar textbooks, how-to farming manuals, conduct books, and autobiographical reflections, C. is perhaps best known today for his political writings, and in particular his *Weekly Political Register,* published almost without interruption from 1802 until his death in 1835. The *Register* not only marks C.'s gradual shift from conservative champion to radical friend of the poor; its pioneering form and lively social and political discussions allow those who read it today direct access to the daily life and controversies of early-19th-c. England.

C. began writing during his eight-year sojourn in America, from 1792 to 1800. From the fledgling country, C. wrote the autobiographical *Life and Adventures of Peter Porcupine* (1796), along with a number of conservative pamphlets in which he de-

cried the French Revolution and encouraged his English readers to support and defend their traditional social structure. C.'s pamphlets were so popular with the British government that he was offered control of a government newspaper, the *True Briton,* when he returned to England in 1800. Citing a desire for independence, C. rejected the offer and within two years started a project that was to last for the rest of his life: the *Weekly Political Register.*

The weekly newspaper was certainly not new to Britons in 1802, but C.'s *Register* differed from other weeklies in several important ways. First, C. pioneered the separation of news and opinion by offering a leading article in which he opined about the events of the week, followed by articles meant to be neutral factual reports. Second, C. often wrote this leading article as an "open letter" to a particular public figure; by taking the normally private epistolary form and making it public, C. effectively enacted the kind of individual questioning and confrontation that he encouraged his readers to undertake to expose what he saw (and personified) as "Corruption." Perhaps C.'s most important innovation with the *Register* came in 1816. Faced with Stamp Laws that would levy a heavy tax on the *Register* in its weekly news format, C. circumvented the Laws by replacing the news articles with opinion pieces and by publishing the paper as broadside. These strategies protected the *Register* from taxation and thereby secured C. a huge lower-class readership; estimates suggest that between 40,000 and 50,000 copies of the *Register* were printed each week, and that each copy would have been circulated among several readers. C.'s journalistic influence was so large in early-19th-c. England that the essayist William HAZLITT referred to him as "a kind of fourth estate in the politics of the country."

C.'s influence did not escape the watchful eyes of the British government, which in 1817 offered him a thinly veiled bribe to stop writing. C. refused the offer but feared arrest for his refusal, so he fled to the U.S., where he stayed until 1820. While there, he continued to publish the *Register* and also wrote the autobiographical *A Year's Residence in the United States of America* (3 parts, 1818–19). C.'s most enduring work from this period is a text he saw as crucial to lower-class empowerment: *A Grammar of the English Language* (1818). Written in the form of letters to his teenage son, the text offers grammatical lessons along with the claim that the newly literate, newly politicized lower classes will gain political power only if they are able to communicate in irreproachable English.

Upon returning to England in 1820, C. continued to publish the *Register*, along with a collection titled *Cobbett's Sermons* and an agricultural advice manual called *Cottage Economy* (7 parts, 1821–22). The latter work marked an important new role for C.: practical advisor to his rural lower-class readers. In the *Reg-*

ister, C. began writing a series of how-to articles about animal husbandry, crop-growing, beer-making, and other agricultural endeavors; these articles ran for nine years and were collected and republished as *Rural Rides* (1830). While critics debate whether this move toward direct address and practical advice should be read as subversive (i.e., helping readers to become self-sufficient and thus divorced from England's increasingly capitalist economic structure) or as nostalgic (i.e., fostering a false belief that retaining rural customs might allow readers to remain detached from politics), the advisory role became increasingly important to C., as is evident in the set of life lessons and advice he offers in *Advice to Young Men* (1830).

The very diversity and abundance of C.'s writings have done some damage to his reputation, causing critics to label him a superficial thinker and a careless stylist. However, C.'s critical fortunes have been waxing in the last few decades, as scholars have begun to acknowledge both the depth and the longevity of his political influence and his journalistic innovations.

BIBLIOGRAPHY: Dyck, I., *W. C. and Rural Popular Culture* (1992); Gilmartin, K., *Print Politics* (1996); Nattrass, L., *W. C.* (1995); Spater, G., *W. C.* (1982)

BONNIE J. GUNZENHAUSER

COE, Jonathan
b. 19 August 1961, Birmingham

C. jokingly characterized his breakthrough novel *What a Carve Up!* (1994; repub. as *The Winshaw Legacy*, 1995) as "a satirical novel about the [Margaret] Thatcher years, which I trustingly believed would change the face of British political fiction." In many ways, this statement offers a miniature introduction to C. himself: strikingly ambitious; committed to an explicit left-liberal political and social agenda; uncommonly aware of his work's historical and cultural location; but nonetheless ready, with that knowingness and irony so typical of the canny postmodern author, to deflate any bubbles of pomposity or complacency. C. is also typical of many contemporary writers in the range of interests and genres his work engages. In addition to his novels, he has been prolific in other media. Dissertations on Henry FIELDING and Samuel BECKETT gained him higher degrees from Warwick University (after a B.A. at Cambridge), but he chose to leave academia and pursue a writing career. He has produced a critical monograph about B. S. JOHNSON (2001), numerous introductions to other writers, and continues to review for a number of British literary magazines and newspapers. For many years the *New Statesman* film critic, he has, in addition, published appreciative biographies of Humphrey Bogart (1991) and James Stewart (1994). As a result, C.'s fiction evinces both sympathy with British literary traditions (particularly comic writing) and sensitivity to the influence of cinema, not only through multiple references and allusions, but also in the adoption and adaptation of cinematic narrative structures and devices.

Beyond this unabashed "culturally promiscuity," C.'s novels share many other features characteristic of postmodern fiction. The early works *The Accidental Woman* (1987) and *A Touch of Love* (1989) employ unreliable narrators, are intricately, even fantastically, plotted, layered with multiple ironies, and make virtuoso play with pastiche and formal innovation. In *A Touch of Love*, however, C. also begins to articulate the political concerns that so differentiate his work from that of his peers. Explicit references to the U.S. bombing of Libya foreshadow the irruption into *What a Carve Up!* of the "Arms to Iraq" scandal and Gulf War, and the Birmingham pub bombings that so reverberate through *The Rotters' Club* (2001). The satirical portrayal of Ted, a vacuous Thatcherite entrepreneur, points forward to the extraordinarily unlovely Winshaws of *What a Carve Up!*, and to the manic Doctor Dudden of *The House of Sleep* (1997), who sees sleep as the enemy of commerce and productivity; the way Britain's welfare state and justice system so signally fail the vulnerable Robin prefigures later indictments of the National Health Service (*What a Carve Up!*), and the education system (*The Rotters' Club*). This attention to contemporary mores and events, to the pattern of life in a whole society, is the hallmark of C.'s writing, and in his most recent work is achieved with rare energy and HUMOR, but also considerable pathos. The political agenda is no supplementary or gratuitous aspect in C.'s novels: it is a determinant aspect within a complex whole.

C.'s chronicling of malevolence, corruption, and ineptitude in public life finds its most potent expression in his fourth novel *What a Carve Up!*, which achieved notable commercial and critical success, its scale and power even drawing comparisons with Charles DICKENS. Shortlisted for the Whitbread Prize and the *Guardian* Fiction Prize, awarded both the John Llewyllyn Rhys Prize and the prestigious French Prix du Meilleur Livre Etranger (1995), the work represents a turning point not only its depiction of the Thatcher years, but in contemporary political and satirical writing. The novel's convoluted plotlines (this is, again, a work of exquisite formal panache) center on the unwilling biographer of the Winshaws, Michael Owen, whose record of that family's treachery, criminality, and cupidity provides an index to the sleaze of the Thatcher era. The title itself refers to the 1961 haunted-house comedy thriller from which C. borrows his principal leitmotif (a haunting, freeze-frame image of Shirley Eaton), and some of the plot structure. The film recounts the desperate goings-on in an isolated country mansion as a homicidal maniac terrorizes the weekend guests, and the climax of the novel gleefully parallels these events as one by one the repulsive Winshaws receive their just deserts. *What a Carve Up!* is at once funny, tragic, and mordantly critical, and deserving of its considerable acclaim.

The Rotters' Club confirms C.'s position at the forefront of contemporary writing. The opening volume in what promises to be a substantial account of Britain in the 1970s and 1980s, it follows a group of Birmingham schoolfriends and their families through the final years of the decade. In a finely evoked 1970s context of increased IRA activity, labor unrest, decaying public services, and political paralysis, C. once more employs a fine humor in counterpoint to righteous anger, as well as developing further the hitherto underplayed emotional and sentimental aspects of his work. Another considerable achievement in a distinctive body of work, *The Rotters' Club* suggests that C. will continue as a major figure in 21st-c.letters.

BIBLIOGHRAPHY: Biswell, A., "The Non-Literary Literary Man," *Telegraph* (London), May 30, 1997: 24; Moseley, M., "J. C.," in Moseley, M., ed., *British Novelists since 1960*, Fourth Series, *DLB* 231 (2000): 67–73

SEAN MATTHEWS

COLEGATE, Isabel
b. 10 September 1931, Lincolnshire

The author of thirteen novels written over the second half of the 20th c., C. has created and occupies a distinguished place in modern British letters. She has never reached the kind of spectacular visibility of a Margaret DRABBLE or A. S. BYATT; her novels are unsensational and can hardly be said to stretch the technical boundaries of the modern novel. And yet she has quiet power, a beautiful prose style, penetrating analysis of character, and an understanding of the historical forces underlying 20th-c. change that make her a novelist of the first rank.

She was the daughter of Sir Arthur Colegate, a member of Parliament, and Lady Colegate Worsley. After attending boarding schools, C. who said that she "never quite got the hang of being taught," left school at sixteen. By nineteen, she was working for Anthony Blond, a literary agent; when he became a publisher he brought out her first novel, *The Blackmailer* (1958). *The Blackmailer,* set in the 1950s, concerns the false reputation of Anthony Lane, a man accepted as a hero of the fighting in Korea. He was actually a coward and a traitor. The novel focuses on his widow, the blackmailer (who had served under his command), and the relations of both with Lane's upper-class family. Already C. was demonstrating her great strength, the ability to analyze exactly how the British upper

class has been weakened, compromised, and attenuated in the 20th c.

A Man of Power (1960) is a study of sexuality and class. Lady Essex Cowper, an amoral socialite, seduces a rich man away from his humble wife and eventually overplays her hand. The story is told by her shocked and fascinated daughter. *The Great Occasion* (1962) is a study of the Dodson family, all daughters, and their various accommodations to modern adult life, watched over by their impotent Lear-like father.

In 1964, in *Statues in a Garden*, C. first portrayed a period that she has made her own: that just before World War I. She has commented on her approach to this time, which has been much mythologized: "we have to guard against nostalgia, and at the same time we have to guard against oversensitivity to that charge." She succeeds in striking a fine balance. This is the story of an aristocratic family and the increasing coarseness and ambition of the younger generation, specifically a greedy young man who cuckolds his own adopted father and ruins his brother financially.

C. next turned to a trilogy of novels about Orlando King and his daughter Agatha: *Orlando King* (1968), *Orlando at the Brazen Threshold* (1971), and *Agatha* (1973). Orlando King is a flawed figure who becomes wealthy at the expense of displacing his business partner who is, unbeknownst to him, also his father; he next marries his father's widow. He favors appeasement before Munich. In the middle novel the focus shifts toward Agatha, his daughter who, in *Agatha*, is involved in public events during the British invasion at Suez and the Burgess-Maclean spy scandal.

News from the City of the Sun (1979) marks a change, though it traces social developments in the 20th c., in this case around a utopian community in rural England, seen by a middle-aged woman who was fascinated by its principles when a child. In 1980, *The Shooting Party*, another story of the period just before the Great War, was C.'s first great critical success. Set at a country house with a large and miscellaneous cast of characters, it bristles with conflict between the generations, suppressed class antagonisms, and questions about breeding versus money. Though tightly focused, it has important ramifications about the condition of England at a pivotal moment.

After *A Glimpse of Sion's Glory* (1985), three beautiful stories, she turned to her most direct investigation of the mysteries of history and BIOGRAPHY in *Deceits of Time* (1988), the story of a biographer trying to make sense of a life that was not what it seemed or, the biographer realizes, what the family has hired her to make it seem. *The Summer of the Royal Visit* (1991) is another historical novel, set a bit further back than usual: in this case in the Victorian period, in Bath. Again, social stratification is important, and finely analyzed; and there is a secret, this time a very unpleasant one, obscured by pretense, snobbery, and hypocrisy.

Winter Journey (1995) turns a seriocomic look at the decline of traditional English "quality," in this case represented by untended country property and the losses of investors in Lloyd's of London. It has the strong features that make C.'s oeuvre reliably rewarding: a finely rendered human story set in an important, and complexly understood, social milieu, delivered in pellucid prose with wit and intelligence.

BIBLIOGRAPHY: Averitt, B. T., "The Strange Clarity of Distance: History, Myth, and Imagination in the Novels of I. C.," in Hosmer, R. E., Jr., ed., *Contemporary British Women Writers: Narrative Strategies* (1993): 85–104; Moseley, M., "I. C.," in Moseley, M., ed., *British Novelists since 1960*, Fourth Series, *DLB* 231 (2001): 74–83

MERRITT MOSELEY

COLERIDGE, Hartley
b. 19 September 1796, Clevedon; d. 6 January 1849, Grasmere

C. is an important figure in English ROMANTICISM in three closely related ways. As a boy, he was the embodiment of the Romantic myth of childhood. In adulthood, his life provided a dark commentary on that myth which in its own way also became mythic. Finally, C. was a gifted minor poet, whose poems, especially his fine sonnets, express eloquently his own view of his Romantic potential and his failure to realize it.

C. was the eldest son of Samuel Taylor COLERIDGE, and William WORDSWORTH and Robert SOUTHEY were father substitutes at various times in his life. It was perhaps inevitable that C.'s childhood would be transformed into Romantic myth. In his father's "Frost at Midnight," "The Nightingale," and *Christabel* and in Wordsworth's "To H. C." and the "Ode: Intimations of Immortality," C. appears as the wonder child of Romanticism: the embodiment of purity, unspoiled genius, innocence, and oneness with nature.

Given C.'s father and his early life as Romantic symbol, it is not too surprising that C.'s adulthood was a disappointment. As he grew from childhood, C.'s erratic and eccentric behavior, his shyness, and lack of confidence became clear. He longed for love but became convinced that women had an aversion to him. At Oxford, he failed to win the annual poetry prize, and he began to drink. In 1819, he was elected a probationary fellow at Oriel College, Oxford, but the fellowship was not renewed on the grounds of intemperance. This was a blow from which neither C. nor his father ever recovered.

Following his disgrace at Oxford, C. experienced further failures as an aspiring writer and as a teacher in Ambleside. He drifted into a largely aimless life in the Lake District where he became a popular local figure, but one perhaps best known for what Wordsworth called his "pot-house wanderings." After 1822, he had no personal contact with his father, and Coleridge wrote of his anguished loss of his "magic image of the Magic Child" in his "The Pang More Sharp Than All."

C.'s own poetry grows directly from his life, both his glorious boyhood and his adult failure. He published only a single volume of verse during his lifetime, but it is a remarkable volume. His *Poems* (1833; repub. as *Poems, Songs, and Sonnets,* 1833) shows him to be a master of the sonnet. He uses the sonnet as a confessional form, and his melodious, sensitive, and wistful poems are mostly about loss and failure. Despite their prevailing sadness, however, C.'s poems have great charm. His sonnet "To a Friend" expresses how his sense of nature has been changed by his friend's absence. His "Long Time a Child and Still a Child" is a powerful expression of the contrast between his youth and the failure of his maturity. His "November" is a sensitively observed nature poem that seems to comment sadly on C.'s own life and mood. His "Night" is a mournful echo of his father's "Frost at Midnight," and his two sonnets "From Country to Town" express his love of the Lake District, his hatred of city life, and his strong sense of solitude and alienation.

C.'s *Poems* also contains memorable sonnets on Wordsworth, William SHAKESPEARE, Homer, and his father. The sonnet on Coleridge is the dedicatory poem of the collection, and it poignantly expresses his sense of his father's greatness and of his own inadequacy. Other poems in the collection demonstrate C.'s typical ambivalence. Several lyrics are dedicated to idealized women for whom C. expresses great love while making clear his own hopelessness of being loved himself. Two of his best poems, "Expertus Loquitur" and "Poietes Apoietes," express his deep love of poetry and his sense of his own inadequacy as a poet.

Although C.'s reputation as a writer is mainly based on his *Poems* of 1833, he also wrote a series of effective biographies called *Biographia Borealis* (1833) and a fine critical essay "On the Poetical Use of the Heathen Mythology" (1822). A posthumous two-volume collection of his poetry was published in 1851, and it contains several poems that make clear how real C.'s potential as a poet was.

BIBLIOGRAPHY: Griggs, E. L., *H. C.* (1929); Hartman, H., *H. C.* (1931); Holmes, R., *Coleridge: Darker Reflections* (1998)

PHILLIP B. ANDERSON

COLERIDGE, Mary [Elizabeth]
b. 23 September 1861, London; d. 25 August 1907, Harrogate

An important late Victorian literary figure, C. was admired as a novelist, essayist, and critic in her own day, and posthumously as a talented and innovative poet whose verse speaks powerfully about female oppression, gender roles, religion, art, and the divided self. Descended from an impressive literary family with Samuel Taylor COLERIDGE as her great-great-uncle and Sara Coleridge as her aunt, she regularly socialized with literary and artistic celebrities who came to her parent's London home where she lived all her life.

Largely self-educated, C. contributed articles and reviews to periodicals from the age of twenty, publishing in *Monthly Packet*, *Merry England*, the *Guardian*, and *Times Literary Supplement*. Her essays, collected in *Non Sequitur* (1900) and posthumously in *Gathered Leaves* (1910), are lively and well written and cover a range of subjects, including Elizabeth Cleghorn GASKELL, ELIZABETH I, heroism, and the nature of BIOGRAPHY. She also wrote stories, many based on her travels, and contributed some of them to *Cornhill Magazine*.

C.'s novels, for which she was most famous during her lifetime, are historical romances based on figures such as Madame de Staël, Honoré de Balzac, and Gustaf III of Sweden. The first, *The Seven Sleepers of Ephesus*, was published in 1893, and four further novels followed over the next decade: *The King with Two Faces* (1897), *The Fiery Dawn* (1901), *The Shadow on the Wall* (1904), and *The Lady on the Drawing-room Floor* (1906). Often strong and dramatic, they were well received but largely forgotten after her death.

It is primarily for her poetry that C. is now remembered, over 260 lyrics, many of which possess great power and energy. A number reflect C.'s commitment to New Woman philosophies, interrogating contemporary gender relations through fantasy and Gothic frameworks that are, in part, an inheritance from Samuel Taylor Coleridge. "The Witch," "Master and Guest," and the famously enigmatic "The Other Side of a Mirror" figure their female protagonists as outcasts, entrapped victims, or divided selves, while other poems such as "The White Women," with its depiction of powerful forest-dwelling Amazonian women living free from social restrictions, and the cutting satire "Marriage," point to sisterhood and female solidarity as a way forward. Education and intellectual liberation is also proposed in "A Clever Woman." C.'s commitment to this cause resulted in her teaching at the Working Women's College.

C.'s poems also challenge the validity of other institutions like the established church (her parents were devout Church of England followers). Her post-Darwinian spiritual questioning is evident in "Doubt," "Goodness," and "Every Man for His Own Hand," and she increasingly subscribed to a more personal religion. "O Earth, my mother!" and "Two Heavens" show her, like Emily BRONTË and Emily Dickinson, worshiping feminized nature as an alternative. The strong influence of another Victorian woman poet,

Christina ROSSETTI, can also be felt in C.'s language and concerns with isolation, betrayal, mysticism, and death.

Encouraged by Robert BRIDGES, C. published two small volumes of poetry during her lifetime: *Fancy's Following* (1896) and *Fancy's Guerdon* (1897). Unlike her prose writings, however, which were published under her own name, these volumes were published under the pseudonym "Anodos," translated as "the Wanderer," thereby suggesting the anxiety C. felt when writing in the wake of her literary ancestors. Only after her death were her poems collected and published under her own name. Like many Victorian women poets, C. was lost from view for most of the 20th c., but she is now, slowly, being reread and reassessed as a challenging and original poetic voice.

BIBLIOGRAPHY: Bridges, R., "The Poems of M. C.," *CM* (November 1907): 594–605; Halliday, J., *Eight Victorian Poets* (1993); McGowran, K., "The Restless Wanderer," in Leighton, A., ed., *Victorian Women Poets: A Critical Reader* (1996): 186–97

SIMON AVERY

COLERIDGE, Samuel Taylor

b. 21 October 1772, Ottery St. Mary, Devon; d. 25 July 1834, Highgate, London

C. is essentially a European figure in his range of interests and activities, finding intellectual inspiration in the poetry, drama, and philosophy of Germany. He admired, among many others, G. E. Lessing, A. W. Schlegel, Friedrich Schiller, and Immanuel Kant, being the chief source of German idealism as it was transmitted both to Britain and to the U.S. in the New England transcendentalist movement. He served in the wartime Mediterranean (1804–6) as acting public secretary to the civilian governor of Malta, moved at ease in intellectual circles both in Germany, where he lived for ten months (1798–99), and in Italy (1806), later making more widely known, during his 1818 lectures on European literature, the significance of writers such as Boccaccio, Petrarch, and Dante for the English poets, Geoffrey CHAUCER, Edmund SPENSER, and John MILTON.

C., the youngest of ten children, was sent, after his father's death in 1781, to Christ's Hospital School in London. Here, he showed precocious talent as a scholar and progressed to Jesus College, Cambridge, where he moved in radical circles, got into debt, temporarily enlisted in the army (under the name Silas Tomkyn Comberbache), and after university married Sara Fricker, the sister-in-law of Robert SOUTHEY, with a view to emigrating, with Southey and his wife and others, to the U.S. and there setting up a utopian community (Pantisocracy) in an attempt to realize the vision of William GODWIN's *Political Justice*. This scheme never materialized and C., settling at Nether

Stowey in the West of England with his new wife, began a life of the intellect, writing poetry, editing a radical Christian journal, the *Watchman* (1796), giving religious and political lectures, and preaching to dissenting congregations. His proposed career as a Unitarian minister was forestalled by the gift of an annuity from Tom and Josiah Wedgwood of the pottery firm, enabling him to devote his life to literature. C.'s activities in the West Country brought him into contact with William and Dorothy WORDSWORTH and through them he later met Sara Hutchinson, the sister of Wordsworth's wife, Mary. Already discovering incompatibility in what had been essentially a marriage of convenience, C. fell in love with Sara (the "Asra" of the poems), but this love was never really reciprocated and became a source of great anguish, not only to C. but also to his wife, who bore him four children, and to the Wordsworths themselves, culminating in a rift between C. and Wordsworth that was eventually patched up.

Central to C.'s formative years was the dominant figure of William Wordsworth to whose genius he always deferred. Since Milton, no man, he said, manifested himself equal to Wordsworth. In imaginative power, he stood nearest of all modern writers to William SHAKESPEARE and Milton. But Wordsworth, in turn, would himself acknowledge the "marvellous source" of C.'s own creative powers and said that his mind was distinguished by its ability to throw out grand central truths from which could be evolved the most comprehensive systems. Although their two names will always be linked through *Lyrical Ballads*, their joint production of 1798, C. was in many ways distinct both as writer and personality. Where he described Wordsworth in their early acquaintance as "at least a semi-atheist," he himself was a religious poet in the tradition of the metaphysicals, and made his intellectual quest throughout his life one of revealing man's spiritual and social being to be founded on religious truth. Late-18th-c. scholars of the revolutionary period in France were moving into the business of comparative religion, dispassionately studying the origins of myth and the emergence of pagan deities alongside the monotheistic God of the Old Testament. C., as a Unitarian, opposed the atheistical tendencies of the Revolution with a millennial blend of Christian radicalism, democratic sentiment, and patriotic fervor that can be traced most obviously in his poems "Religious Musings" (wr. 1794–96), "Reflections on Having Left a Place of Retirement" (wr. 1795), "The Destiny of Nations" (wr. 1796–97), "Fears in Solitude" (wr. 1798), and "France: an Ode" (wr. 1798). The Enlightenment had looked for evidences of religion and the 19th c. was, by turns, either divergently evangelistic or reactionary, associating moral propriety with the possession of property. C. consistently and instinctively turned from "understanding," the first

principle of a mechanized view of creation that led in his opinion to atheism, to "feeling," locating the truth of Christianity in faith, something not discoverable by reason but at the same time not opposed to it.

C. arrived at his convictions gradually, moving from the materialist and necessitarian philosophy of British empiricists such as John LOCKE, David Hartley, and Godwin, via the Unitarianism of Joseph Priestley, to the new dynamic German philosophy of Schelling and Kant. His work, in common with that of Wordsworth, becomes focused on the inner life translating action in the world of revolutionary politics to that of the imagination as the faculty most capable of producing liberal ideas and moral values in society. This tendency becomes evident in the "Conversation Poems" of the 1790s, a form of blank verse monody that C., inspired by the poetry of William COWPER, Mark AKENSIDE, and William Lisle BOWLES, made characteristically his own. Chief among these are "The Aeolian Harp" (wr. 1795), "This Lime-Tree Bower my Prison" (wr. 1797), and "Frost at Midnight" (wr. 1798), poems that take their departure from some immediate location, pastoral or domestic, proceed through a passage of intense and meditative reflection, and then return, usually in the form of a prayer that a sense of inclusive imaginative wholeness might be shared by the poet, his friends, and the entire creation in a peaceable kingdom of almost Blakean innocence. This marriage of the inner emotions with social, democratic principles found a reciprocal intelligence in Wordsworth at the time, culminating in *Lyrical Ballads* for which C. provided four poems, including "The Ancient Mariner," the longest of the collection. Here, the "Nightmare Life-in-Death" of a world deprived of imaginative commerce with creation is replaced by the Mariner's participation in a societal union of "Old men, and babes, and loving friends, And youths and maidens gay"—a conclusion reminiscent of the "Conversation Poems" themselves.

C., unlike the self-contained Wordsworth, author of "The Recluse," was by inclination sociable. Friendship was central to his principles, finding early an idealistic outlet in the youthful Pantisocracy scheme (1794). However, growing French imperialism under Napoleon Bonaparte convinced him that political notions of social liberty must be converted into concepts of the individual mind in its enfranchising relationship with the natural world. True liberty is available to every man who possesses nature by an imaginative encounter with it, and it is to C. more than anyone that the concept of the Romantic imagination owes its prominence to this day.

The fullest attempt C. makes to define it is in chapter 13 of the biographical history of his literary life and opinions, a prose version of Wordsworth's "Prelude," and published along with his collected poems, *Sibylline Leaves*, as *Biographia Literaria* (2 vols.) in

1817. Here, he distinguishes between two kinds of imagination, primary and secondary. Primary imagination, possessed by all, makes the mind active in perception and not simply passively receptive to sense impressions as it had been in the philosophy of the mechanic dogmatists, Locke and Hartley. Secondary imagination, possessed only by the artist, "dissolves, diffuses, dissipates" the world of the primary in order to create anew, to make out of this cold world of simple perception something rich and strange. C. is nearest to Shakespeare in his version of the divinity of the poet's creative faculty. Theseus's "poet's eye in a fine frenzy rolling"—the phrase used by Dorothy Wordsworth to describe C.'s aspect on first meeting him—implies the omniscience and celerity of the poet's divine glance ("from heaven to earth, from earth to heaven") as well as his God-like ability to create something out of nothing ("and gives to airy nothing a local habitation and a name," *A Midsummer Night's Dream*).

C. further distinguishes imagination from fancy. Whereas imagination is shaping ("esemplastic"), modifying, and coadunating (bringing discordant elements to a state of oneness), fancy is "aggregative," assembling all its decorative images by selecting them through a mechanical process of association. In simple terms, the poetical faculty that had previously been regarded as pleasing but, in Audrey's words, from *As You Like It*, not a "true thing," the "imaginary" or fanciful as distinct from the "imaginative," now became essentially the poet's possession as the measure of truth.

In chapter 14 of the *Biographia*, C. goes on to describe the division of labor in the creation of *Lyrical Ballads*, describing the role of imagination there as giving new life to the ordinary world of appearance and (again reminiscent of *A Midsummer Night's Dream*) using moonlight as an analogy to its function as something that idealizes without substantially changing objects. Although he would move increasingly into prose as a communicative vehicle, some of his major poems compound his thinking on the place and function of the Romantic imagination. Of these might be mentioned one of his most famous works, "Kubla Khan; or, A Vision in a Dream" (wr. 1797; pub. 1816), examining the sources of creativity and demonstrating the processes of the coadunating imagination at work, reconciling opposites, sun and ice for example, in the perfect symbolic architectural construct of the "dome." In "Dejection: An Ode" (wr. 1802; pub. 1817), written originally as an anguished verse-epistle to Sara Hutchinson, C. describes in biblical terminology the apocalyptic "new heaven" and "new earth" achievable through an imaginative "wedding nature to us." The religious dimension is central here because the distinction between imagination and fancy in C.'s literary theory carries over to

his ethical thought in the distinction he draws between understanding and higher reason. As faculties that relate to the senses and the supersensuous respectively, there is a direct line of thought in C. here from Shakespeare's distinction between "comprehension" and "apprehension" and Milton's "discursive" and "intuitive" reason. In all cases, "reason" is our means of access to truth, divine or poetical. Belief cannot be based on the senses. In any act of imaginative "knowing," be it aesthetic or religious, what C. requires is that "willing suspension of disbelief for the moment which constitutes poetic faith."

For C., poetry is something that calls the whole soul of man into activity. Instead of the product per se, he is interested in the recondite mental processes of production itself. His habitual tendency to embark on projects that remained incomplete, to ascribe to the famous "person from Porlock," for example, in his prose preface to "Kubla Khan" the reason for the poem's fragmentary form, may suggest some psychological censoring factor at work where the rational world restrains transgressive elements. One precedent would be Milton in William BLAKE's assessment of him as subconsciously preferring the "hellish" energy of Satan to the pallid orthodoxy of Christ, and Blake's "damn braces, bless relaxes" might find something comparable at work in C.'s bard, Bracy, who serves as a conscious restraint on the taboo subjects of the unfinished *Christabel* (wr. 1801; pub. 1816). The brief conclusion to part 2 that contains the line, "To dally with wrong that does no harm" implies a tension between waking constraints and dreamlike release, reflecting the nature of *Christabel* taken as a whole.

From the early years of the 19th c. until his death, C.'s health was undermined by opium addiction. But the intense and pathological self-scrutiny to which he subjected his life in his notebooks and letters is equally balanced by his active participation in the world of journalism and politics. He wrote regularly for the *Morning Post* and the *Courier*, and edited the *Friend* (1809–10), a subscription journal on politics, morals, and religion and a subsequent influence on later prominent Victorians such as John Stuart MILL, John Sterling, John RUSKIN, and F. D. Maurice. C. also lectured widely, particularly significant in this medium, and especially in the area of character criticism, being his contribution to Shakespeare scholarship. The plays must be understood as organic entities, he argued, enabling a satisfactory psychological investigation of their characters to take place. He famously identified with Hamlet, for example, the type of Romantic artist, and a figure like himself torn between obligations to the world outside and a dark inward sense of his own inadequacy to his tasks.

Throughout his career as lecturer and polemicist, however, C. consistently laid himself open to accusations of plagiarism, notably in the use he made of

Schlegel in his Shakespeare lectures and of Kant in the *Biographia*. And to some extent this has proved damaging to his reputation. In his later years, he published prose works that addressed moderate liberal opinion and that exposed him also to charges of being reactionary. Nevertheless, the need he envisaged for social change and social policies is consistent with his earliest concerns that the role of the artist is to be didactic and socially committed. In *The Statesman's Manual* (1816), he advocated a public policy on national education and the need for a concept of the spiritual in an age of science. *On the Constitution of the Church and State* (1830) argues for a national church or "Clerisy" made up of artists, writers, scientists, clergy, and teachers, who would provide a body for reconciliation synthesizing the forces of permanence (the landed interest) and progress (the manufacturing and professional classes).

In the late 20th and early 21st cs., C.'s reputation as both poet and critic of society has grown. As the unhappily married, drug-dependent, rejected lover, struggling with himself to realize his talents and to find his individual place and his happiness in the world, C. strikes a curiously modern resonance. And his "Ancient Mariner," by which he has always been popularly known, has come to speak beyond the traditional notions of Christian loss and redemption, fueling contemporary fears that if we continue to be hostile to nature, nature may, in the end, become hostile to us.

BIBLIOGRAPHY: Beer, J. B., *C. the Visionary* (1959); Beer, J. B., *C.'s Poetic Intelligence* (1977); Everest, K., *C.'s Secret Ministry* (1979); Fruman, N., *C., the Damaged Archangel* (1971); Holmes, R., *C.: Early Visions* (1989); Holmes, R., *C.: Darker Reflections* (1998); Lowes, J. L., *The Road to Xanadu* (1927); Roe, N., *Wordsworth and C.: The Radical Years* (1988)

JOHN GILROY

COLET, John
b. 1467?, London; d. 16 September 1519, London

In a December 1499 letter from Oxford, the great Dutch writer and scholar Desiderius ERASMUS wrote, "when I listen to Colet, it seems to me that I am listening to Plato himself." A mentor to both Erasmus and Sir Thomas MORE, C. was an important interpreter to Northern Europe of the intellectual trends of the Italian Renaissance. C., the son of a two-time mayor of London, studied at Oxford, in Paris, and in Italy.

After absorbing Florentine humanist thought on an extended trip to Italy in 1496, C. was ordained priest and returned to Oxford, where he gave a series of influential lectures between 1497 and 1504 on the Epistles of St. Paul. In the lectures, many of which Eras-

mus attended, C. repudiated the scholastic approach to scriptural interpretation that had prevailed in universities during the High Middle Ages. Moreover, C. passionately advocated church reform: he denounced the corruption of the bishops and the clergy, and he rejected the belief in relics and pilgrimages. Although C. anticipated Martin Luther in his emphasis upon individual enlightenment, most historians agree that C. was essentially a conservative and that he would have opposed the Protestant Reformation. C.'s circle of friends—which included such prominent humanists as More, Thomas LINACRE, William GROCYN, John Fisher, and William LILY—shared his desire for the church's internal reform. In 1504, C. became Dean of St. Paul's Cathedral, and, five years later, he established St. Paul's School with the fortune that he inherited when his father died. Under C.'s direction, the school became the center of humanist learning in London, and it served as a model for many later grammar schools. C.'s students acquired not just a basic knowledge of Latin but a thorough understanding of classical and early Christian writers. In 1509, in collaboration with Lily and Erasmus, C. wrote a Latin grammar (known as *Lily's Grammar*) that was used for over two hundred years in English schools.

In his short biography of C., Erasmus claims that his friend and mentor left no writings behind. In fact, we do have many of C.'s manuscript treatises, the most important of which are *An Exposition of St. Paul's Epistle* and *An Exposition of St. Paul's First Epistle to the Corinthians*. The commentaries, written in Latin, reflect C.'s strong dislike of scholastic works like St. Thomas Aquinas's *Summa Theologica*. In them, C. abandons the scholastic practice of interpreting scripture allegorically. Instead, he focuses on the personal character of Paul and on the apostle's historical context. C. also avoids the seemingly endless intricacies of medieval theology; indeed, he frequently asserts that it is more important to love God than to know Him. Ignoring the schoolmen, he cites Italian humanists such as Giovanni Pico della Mirandola and Marsilio Ficino. C. ends his commentaries with impassioned pleas for a return to the purity and the simplicity of the early church.

C. printed very few of his writings. Two important works that did see print are *A Rightful Fruitful Meditation* (1506) and "The Convocation Sermon of 1512" (1512). The *Meditation*, a treatise that describes the uses of piety in daily life, was reprinted twenty-two times in the next two centuries. The 1512 convocation was summoned to address the revival of Lollardry, and the Archbishop of Canterbury chose C. to give the preliminary SERMON. C. took the opportunity to attack the abuses of the bishops who sat before him. Filled with vivid descriptions of the luxury and the simony of the bishops, the sermon was published immediately in Latin and later in English.

C.'s Latin style is direct and precise. He is by no means a master stylist, but he is a highly skilled rhetorician. His writings are distinguished by his use of irony—understatement is a favorite C. device—and, above all, by his conversational style, qualities that helped make him one of the most effective exponents of Christian humanism in the early Tudor period.

BIBLIOGRAPHY: Harbison, E. H., *The Christian Scholar in the Age of Reformation* (1956); Hunt, E. W., *Dean Colet and His Theology* (1956); Miles, L., *J. C. and the Platonic Tradition* (1962)

T. D. DRAKE

COLLIER, Mary

b. 1689 or 1690, near Midhurst, Sussex; d. after 1762, Alton, Hampshire

One of the few working-class women to write and publish in the 18th c., C. was a unique figure in the history of women's writings in England. An early feminist, C. defended the work ethic of her sex against attack by the author Stephen DUCK in his poem *The Thresher's Labour*. Famous in its time, *The Thresher's Labour* described the rigorous work of male agricultural workers while at the same time disparaging the field work of women, describing female laborers as weak and lazy compared to their male counterparts. C.'s anger at this characterization spurred her on to write *The Woman's Labour* (1739). She was encouraged in this pursuit by a family with whom she was employed at the time as a nurse to a "gentlewoman in a fit of illness." Surprisingly, the ill gentlewoman's husband transcribed parts of this poem; these verses soon became, as C. notes, the "town talk"; her readers persuaded her to publish her poem for greater public consumption.

According to her own brief autobiographical preface to *The Woman's Labour*, C. was born of poor parents near Midhurst in Sussex either in the year 1689 or 1690. While her mother was alive, she received some education, learning to read and taking "great delight in it," particularly in the religious works of George Fox. She was never formally educated and after her mother's death she was "set to labour as the Country afforded." After her father's death, she worked primarily as a washerwoman and brewer, both of which she describes in some detail in *The Woman's Labour*. C. labored as a washerwoman until the age of sixty-three. Afterward, she managed a farmhouse in Alton for seven more years. She ended her life retired in a garret in Alton, where she "endeavor[ed] to pass the Relict of my days in Piety, Purity, Peace and an Old Maid." The exact date of her death is unknown.

In *The Woman's Labour*, C. is keen to emphasize women's strenuous labor in the fields, in the home, and in domestic service. As she notes in this work, women's work continues well beyond that of men. While men may work strenuously in the fields, their work is finished once they reach their home. In contrast, women's work continues in the home; in this very early work, C. describes the "second shift" that 20th-c. feminists have pointed out as the particular burden of married women with children: "[W]hen we home are come,/We find again our Work but just begun;/So many things for our attendance call,/Had we ten Hands, we could employ them all."

In this work, C. also provides a stark description of the arduous work of women in domestic service. She details the numbing drudgery of 18th-c. domestic work, writing about the unending tasks of washing, shining, and sewing that consumed the days and nights of those engaged in this work: "NOW Night comes on, from when you have Relief,/But that alas! Does but increase our Grief;/With heavy Hearts we often view the Sun,/Fearing he'll seat before our Work is done." Her poem is a sharp indictment of female wage labor in the 18th c. It also is an effective rebuttal to Duck's misogynistic discussion of women's work in *The Thresher's Labour*. Ironically, when Duck committed suicide in 1762, C. composed an empathetic elegy in his memory.

BIBLIOGRAPHY: Ferguson, M., ed., *First Feminists: British Women Writers 1588–1799* (1985): 257–65; Landry, D., "The Resignation of M. C.: Some Problems in Feminist Literary History," in Brown, L., and F. Nussbaum, eds., *The New Eighteenth Century: Theory, Politics, English Literature* (1987): 99–120

JENNIFER A. RICH

COLLINS, [William] Wilkie

b. 8 January 1824, London; d. 23 September 1889, London

Say "Wilkie Collins" to a late Victorian reader of fiction and he or she (C. appealed to both) would have fired back two words: "sensation" and "bohemian." In his lifestyle, C. was "louche." He should, probably, have been born a Parisian. In his defiance of Mrs. Grundy (Thomas MORTON's symbolic characterization of moral rigidity), he represented the kind of Victorian that Charles DICKENS would have liked to be—had he dared.

In terms of the kind of fiction he wrote, C. was seen as the pioneer of the new, high-impact, multivoiced style of narrative that was labeled "sensation fiction," "matter of fact romance," or sometimes "fiction with a purpose." The word "sensation" carries two meanings in this context. Psychologically, it implies something akin to "electric shock." This was fiction designed to keep the reader awake at night. But, as in newspapers (which, following the lifting of the last of the "taxes on knowledge" in 1850, were retailing at a penny), the word suggests "headline story." Like the new "gutter" press, the sensation novel was, inevitably, attacked by the Victorian establishment. The Archbishop of York, for example, thundered against it from his pulpit as "one of the abominations of the age." This did nothing to impair sales.

There is, of course, nothing novel in the evolution of the English novel. Another contemporary label for the "sensation" practitioners was "school of Dickens." Many of the tricks of the genre: the "curtain-line" or "cliff-hanger" at the end of a serial installment, the "make 'em laugh, make 'em cry, make 'em *wait*" suspense gimmicks, the "dead but not dead" plots, the "tremendous" scenes (dams break, houses burn, maidens face fates worse than death), the fascination with the new "science" of criminal detection and "fashionable" crimes (such as blackmail and poisoning), the "heteroglossia" (multivoiced narrative) can be traced back to one novel—Dickens's *Bleak House*.

C. was not, at birth, destined for a career in sensation fiction: or any kind of literary activity. His is one of the classic instances of a clever, aimless, young Victorian who ricocheted into writing novels. He was born the eldest son of the then eminent painter, William Collins. In addition to his father's Christian name he was given that of his father's friend, Sir David Wilkie.

C. was educated privately. He lost his virginity (as he later claimed) as a teenager to an Italian lady of mature years (sex, indulged in a most un-Victorian way, would be a topic of great interest to him in later life). His father (a Puseyite) fondly hoped his son would go into the church. But C., who inherited his father's poor health, was not up to Oxford—then in the heyday of its Newmanesque agony. Nor would he have made an orthodox clergyman. He tried, instead, the tea business. But office work did not suit. He then, fitfully, entered Lincoln's Inn and was called to the bar in 1851, but never practiced—legal training did, however, help him with his intricate plots in later life, many of which hinge on law.

In 1847, William Collins died, and C. wrote his first book, a dutiful filial biography, published in two volumes in 1848. He was also trying his hand at painting in which he discovered himself not to be talented. After some experiments with exotic South Seas fiction (arising from his experiences in the tea trade), he produced his first published novel, *Antonina; or, The Fall of Rome* (3 vols., 1850). An historical tale set in classic times it clearly owes much to Sir Walter SCOTT's late work *Count Robert of Paris* and looks forward to such works as Charles KINGSLEY's *Hypatia*. It is, for a first published work, accomplished and has such fine set pieces as the "Banquet of Famine," given by the libertine patrician Vetranio, in which the tables are laden for the starving diners not with food but inedible treasure. There is plentiful torture and sex (some of that as sadistically detailed as the mores of the age would allow). *Antonina* sold well for the publisher, but C. never wrote another historical novel. Instead, he would be a chronicler of the contemporary.

C.'s next novel, *Basil* (3 vols., 1852), marks a distinct progress in technique and points toward what would be his mature style and subject matter. A complicated "Story of Modern Life," it is consciously "dramatic"—not to say melodramatic. The genteel hero (whose surname we never know) makes an imprudent marriage with a linen draper's daughter. Terrible complications ensue. An adulterous villain has his face scraped off on a macadamized road ("modern life," don't you know). There is a terrific climax on the rocky Cornish coast (which C. had tramped along, the year before, and to which he brought a painter's eye).

In 1851, C. had formed what would be the most influential professional relationship of his life, with Dickens (then writing *Bleak House*, which C. had the privilege of hearing the Great Inimitable read). For Dickens's new magazine, *Household Words*, C. wrote his much-anthologized short thriller, "A Terribly Strange Bed" (1852). There followed two mystery novels, *Hide and Seek* (3 vols., 1854) and the more accomplished *The Dead Secret* (2 vols., 1857). Both used physical handicap in their plots (deaf-and-dumbness in the first, blindness in the second).

In 1856, C. and Dickens attended the trial of the Rugeley poisoner, William Palmer. The prosecution case depended entirely on circumstantial evidence. The younger man was struck by the way in which witnesses' testimony combined to create a kind of narrative tapestry. Dickens had just launched another weekly magazine, *All the Year Round*, in which serialized fiction was to be the lead item. In the story he was invited to write for it, *The Woman in White* (1860), as it would be, C. experimented with his new, multivoice style. The story itself, which hinges on a dastardly attempted personation (in which the heroine is falsely incarcerated in a lunatic asylum), became one of the best-sellers of the age. Contemporary readers were particularly taken with the villain of the piece, Count Fosco—a fat, sinister, mafioso. Many readers, William Makepeace THACKERAY for example, read the novel (published in three volumes in 1860) at a sitting through the night.

With the success of *The Woman in White*, C. was promoted to the ranks of the £5,000 a title novelists—second, in earning power, only to Dickens and perhaps Thackeray. Among other things, the novel gave an identity to the new school of sensationalism. Alongside C., Charles READE and Mary Elizabeth BRADDON were early recruits. C. followed up with *No Name* (3 vols., 1862), which "sensationalized" the burning issue of bastardy and the perverse English laws of inheritance. Illness ("rheumatic gout") held back his pen for a year or two. He rode back to high popularity with *Armadale* (2 vols., 1866), serialized in George Smith's monthly magazine, *Cornhill*. This novel, which has a tremendous poisoning scene at its climax, featured the most fascinating of C.'s heroine-villainesses, Lydia Gwilt.

C. returned to Dickens and *All the Year Round* with his next novel, *The Moonstone* (3 vols., 1868). Arguably his masterpiece, it is certainly the first fully fledged detective novel in English fiction (although the theft of the fabulous gem at the heart of the narrative is not solved by Sergeant Cuff of Scotland Yard, but by a scientist, Ezra Jennings). T. S. ELIOT (an admirer of C.) went so far as to salute *The Moonstone* as the best detective novel in English literature, which may be excessive. It none the less ranks high. The period from 1859 to 1869 marks the highpoint of C.'s artistic achievement. He went on to write many novels (thirty in all, by the time of his death). But chronically poor health (amanuenses were driven away by his uncontrollable screams of pain), an irregular lifestyle (he lived with two women, neither of whom he married), and an addiction to opium deteriorated his literary performance in later years (his eyes, it was said, resembled two bags of blood). And, to some extent, sensation fiction ran out of steam. It is possible, too, that with Dickens's death, in 1870, C. lost a controlling influence on his art. None the less, he remained among the most remunerated of Victorian novelists. He cleverly exploited dramatic versions of his work and, most rewardingly, cheap reprints of his novels (mainly through the publisher Chatto and Windus).

Man and Wife (3 vols., 1870) marks a significant new threshold in C.'s career. A "fiction founded on facts," it protests the British marriage laws. The governess-heroine, Anne Silvester, is seduced and victimized by the looseness of the Scottish common-law wife statute. From this point onward, C.'s fiction is principally concerned with righting wrongs. It is, in the terminology of the time, "fiction with a purpose."

Poor Miss Finch (3 vols., 1872) has another plot revolving around the author's long-standing interest in the condition of blindness. Surreally, the heroine of the title is unable to see (and therefore is not repulsed) by her husband's turning blue (whatever else, C. had a fine disregard in his fiction for the criterion of probability). *The New Magdalen* (2 vols., 1873)—protesting, as the title signifies, Victorian sexual hypocrisy—has a heroine who goes as a nurse to the recent 1870 Franco-Prussian War. Dead-but-not-dead complications (of the kind immortalized in Mrs. Henry WOOD's *East Lynne*) ensue. *The Law and the Lady* (3 vols., 1875) is, as again the title proclaims, another attack on Victorian moral hypocrisy.

C.'s hatred of Mrs. Grundy was founded in his own, unusual domestic circumstances. In the mid-

1850s, he had taken up with Caroline Graves (the original for Anne Catherick, in *The Woman in White*, it is sometimes supposed). While still cohabiting (perhaps erratically) with Caroline, in the mid-1860s he took up with a younger woman, Martha Rudd, who bore him three children, out of wedlock (an institution C. evidently despised: or perhaps there was a secret marriage elsewhere in his well-hidden past).

Toward the end of his writing career, C. wrote a number of novels that dabbled in occult themes. In *The Two Destinies* (2 vols., 1876), for example, he explores telepathy as plot device. *The Fallen Leaves* (3 vols., 1879), another novel with a moral purpose, has, as its heroine, a reformed prostitute (most of the profession are consigned to death or transportation in Victorian fiction: C. offers a more generous verdict on the "castaway"). *Jezebel's Daughter* (3 vols., 1880) is notable for some "grand guignol" scenes in a German morgue—as *The Woman in White* had concluded with a magnificent scene in the Paris morgue; C., who regularly visited these institutions, was fascinated by the sight of corpses laid out "like cod at the fishmonger's."

The Black Robe (3 vols., 1881) attacks Jesuits and *Heart and Science* (3 vols., 1883) attacks vivisectionists (C. was never at a loss for targets for his "purposive" fiction). *The Legacy of Cain* (3 vols., 1889) has two heroines, one of whom is a "bad seed" and the daughter of a murderess. But which one? C.'s last novel, *Blind Love* (3 vols., 1890), is typically up with the times. It features Fenian outrages (very topical) and insurance fraud, via photography—the villain poses as his own corpse, has his picture taken, which is then sent to the unwitting company as evidence of death.

C.'s own death overtook the composition of this last novel. He consigned his work in progress to his friend and fellow-novelist Walter BESANT with the message "tell him I would do the same for him if he were in my place." He left precise instructions as to how the novel should be completed—which Besant observed to the letter.

Blind Love is a worthy conclusion to a long and fruitful career in fiction. C.'s great achievements, however—the works, that is, which align him with Dickens, Thackeray, George ELIOT, Anthony TROLLOPE, and Thomas HARDY—are the corpus of early sensation novels which he produced from the decade 1859 to 1868.

BIBLIOGRAPHY: Ashley, R., *W. C.* (1952); Marshall, W. H., *W. C.* (1970); Page, N., ed., *W. C.* (1974); Peters, C., *The King of Inventors: A Life of W. C.* (1991)

JOHN SUTHERLAND

COLLINS, William

b. 25 December 1721, Chichester; d. 12 June 1759, Chichester

Despite his short life and small body of verse, C. is generally recognized as one of the greatest lyric poets of the 18th c. He was also one of the most prophetic 18th-c. forerunners of Romantic poetry. While still a student at Oxford, C. published his first important work, *Persian Eclogues* (1742). This collection contains four pastorals in which C. combines conventional 18th-c. pastoralism with touches of exoticism created by "Oriental" settings and imagery. In 1743, C. published his *Verses to Sir Thomas Hanmer*. This epistle in heroic couplets praises Hanmer as a Shakespearean scholar, surveys the history of European poetry, and celebrates William SHAKESPEARE as the central glory of that history.

In 1746, C. published his *Odes on Several Descriptive and Allegoric Subjects*, upon which his reputation largely rests. This volume consists of twelve odes. Roughly half of them deal with the poet's attempt to imagine and then invoke the great powers necessary to the creation of sublime poetry. Most of the other odes are also addressed to allegorical personifications, but in these the figures relate to national and political life and reflect C.'s concern with Britain after 1745, a year in which the nation was fighting France abroad and Jacobites at home.

The best known of the odes are those dealing with poetry and inspiration. The "Ode to Pity," "Ode to Fear," and "Ode to Simplicity" invoke the inspiring passions and qualities that were crucial to ancient Greek tragedy and poetry but that for C. were largely missing in the 18th c. This longing for the energy and power of true poetic inspiration is most brilliantly expressed in C.'s "Ode on the Poetical Character." In this poem, C. gives a mythic history of "Fancy" and the divine creation of poetic power and goes on to lament that that power was last seen in John MILTON and is not to be found in neoclassicism. A closely related poem is "The Passions, An Ode for Music." Here, C. not only portrays human passions with great pictorial skill, but he recalls a time in ancient Greece when music and poetry had miraculous powers which have since been lost.

Perhaps the most perfect of C.'s odes is his beautiful "Ode to Evening," in which he uses an unrhymed Miltonic quatrain to create a description of evening that is full of serenity and haunting music. Of the odes on national themes, the most memorable are the touchingly elegiac "Ode Written in the Beginning of the Year 1746" and the lofty "Ode to Liberty," which traces the history of liberty and imagines a future in which ancient British liberty will be restored along with national concord.

C.'s *Odes* of 1746 is one of the most important collections of verse published in the 18th c. It is pro-foundly imaginative and original, and C.'s lyric intensity and passionate desire for inspiration bring his allegorical personifications to brilliant life. Nevertheless, its publication was a commercial failure, and this was such a bitter blow to C. that he bought and destroyed much of the unsold edition.

C.'s last works were written amid depression and approaching madness, but his last two poems are among his best. His "Ode on the Death of Thomson" (1749) is a delicately expressed elegy for James THOMSON in which the author of *The Seasons* is treated as a modern Druid whose poetry of nature and feeling will always be sacred to the sensitive. C.'s posthumous and incomplete "Ode on the Popular Superstitions of the Highlands of Scotland" (1788) is an energetic account of supernatural Scottish legends and their potential value as sources for a genuinely magical and passionate poetry. C. died insane in his thirty-seventh year.

BIBLIOGRAPHY: Carver, P. L., *The Life of a Poet: A Biographical Sketch of W. C.* (1967); Garrod, H. W., *C.* (1928); Wendorf, R., *W. C. and Eighteenth-Century English Poetry* (1981)

PHILLIP B. ANDERSON

COLONIAL LITERATURE

Colonial literature stems directly from the historical phenomenon of colonialism, which began in the 15th c. with the domination of the New World by Spain, France, England, Portugal, and the Netherlands. Whereas today the words imperialism and colonialism are often used interchangeably, from the 19th c. up until World War II, when Britain had extensive colonies, the words were clearly distinguished. Imperialism referred to forming and maintaining an empire (a series of territories controlled by a single ruler). Colonialism, in contrast, was the establishment of colonies or settlements on territory distanced from the ruling country, ranging from the Middle and Far East to Africa, India, Australia, Ireland, and the Caribbean, indeed, anywhere that England and other colonial-imperial powers colonized. Colonial literature can, then, be defined as works written by those who have implanted colonies, mostly among non-white peoples. Closely related to colonial literature is postcolonial literature, until the 1980s sometimes known as Commonwealth literature. Postcolonial literature is most often written by formerly colonized peoples. Today, such literature includes contemporary texts by such diverse writers as Keri Hulme, Yvonne Vera, Michael Ondaatje, Vikram Seth, and Arundhati Roy as well as Nobel laureates Derek Walcott and V. S. NAIPAUL.

The term colonial literature is itself amorphous, never having been used by colonial writers themselves, although the authors today most closely identified with colonial literature, namely Rudyard KIPLING and Joseph CONRAD, would have probably acknowledged a shared ideology. For example, Kipling himself might have agreed that his *Kim* insists on a profound difference between white and non-white peoples that no amount of friendship or camaraderie can alter, while for his part Conrad might have recognized that although his work concedes that overseas domination largely consisted of self-deluding, systematic corruption, his "Heart of Darkness" never questions the basic right of the white European to rule Africans. Although works like *Kim* and "Heart of Darkness" are both generally identified as colonial literature, in other cases colonial and postcolonial critics have noted that a work does not have to be categorized as colonial in order for it to be analyzed as such. In fact, critics have found that many canonical works as diverse and separated in time as Daniel DEFOE's *Robinson Crusoe*, Jane AUSTEN's *Mansfield Park*, and Charlotte BRONTË's *Jane Eyre* all, in different ways, exhibit colonial features.

Critics have found at least three basic notions embedded in both overt and covert colonialist texts. First is the belief that colonizers occupy the center of the world; the colonized, in contrast, occupy the margins. Consequently, colonialists see themselves as living in the "metropolitan" center and therefore regard themselves as "civilized," whereas their subjects are seen as "savages" or, at least, "other." Being "other" means that these subjects are less than human, thus justifiably invaded and exploited. A second, specialized view of the colonized as "other" has been defined by the critic Edward Said as Orientalism, meaning that Western countries project all undesirable characteristics onto a fictitious "Oriental," conveniently typified as cruel, sneaky, cunning, dishonest, an invention against whom colonialists have defined themselves positively as kind, straightforward, upright, and honest. A third characteristic of colonial literature is Eurocentrism, the use of European culture as the standard to which all other cultures are negatively contrasted. Integral to the idea of European centrality is the claim that Western culture is somehow "universal," with a Eurocentric standard being used to measure the cultural values of the colonized in terms of how much they diverge from those of European culture. Dependent on the idea of European "universality" and a Eurocentric standard is political and social terminology widely used today, including the terms First World, Second World, Third World, and Fourth World, to refer to, first, Britain, Europe and the U.S., second, the white populations of Canada, Australia, New Zealand, and Southern Africa, third, the developing nations, such as India, and those of Africa, Central and South America, and Southeast Asia, and, fourth, the indigenous populations subjugated by white settlers and governed today by a ma-

jority culture, such as Native Americans and aboriginal Australians. According to postcolonial critics, such terms inform not only current colonial thinking but also underlie most, if not all, contemporary conceptual systems, which, these critics assert, ignore the existence of earlier worlds, such as those of Greece, Egypt, and Africa as well as those in China and Japan.

As to how the above-mentioned characteristics of colonial literature are demonstrated in individual works, as previously implied critics have focused specifically on *Robinson Crusoe*, *Mansfield Park* and *Jane Eyre*. They have observed how both *Robinson Crusoe* and *Mansfield Park*, for example, explicitly explore the idea of overseas expansion. *Robinson Crusoe* tells of the founding of a new world devoted to Christianity and the rule of England on a faraway, non-European island seemingly just awaiting establishment of Crusoe's fiefdom and the colonization of the black man, whom he names Friday. In *Mansfield Park*, Austen's hero, Sir Thomas Bertram, appears as the prototypical English gentleman: kind, honorable, highly moral and very rational. He presides over his home both as a patriarch and the proprietor of overseas agricultural investments that finance his family. The investments are made in Antigua, where Sir Thomas must go periodically to restore order. Equating Sir Thomas's ability to rule his own English family according to the standards he is inculcating abroad, Austen makes a strong parallel between domestic and international authority as Sir Thomas maintains control at home with the same thoroughness and severity that characterize his employment of slave labor in his Antigua plantation. Although the particular trip of Sir Thomas to Antigua described in *Mansfield Park* is peripheral to the main action of the novel, critic Said has claimed that the source of its power lies in this marginality. He states that English readers casually and unconsciously absorb the way the novel "unobtrusively opens up a broad expanse of domestic imperialist culture," educating them with all sorts of "ideas about dependent races." He adds that the imperialist venture could scarcely have been undertaken without this covert domestic acculturation.

In contrast to colonialism's peripheral treatment in *Mansfield Park*, in *Jane Eyre*, the heroine's encounter with her "Oriental" counterpart is central to the narrative, for the discovery of Bertha Mason, the West Indian wife of Edward Rochester, the man with whom Jane is in love, effectively prevents the couple's marriage. Bertha Mason herself, the descendant of white colonial settlers in Jamaica, is portrayed stereotypically in *Jane Eyre* as mad, drunken, violent, and lascivious, in other words, as the equivalent of nonwhite. Rochester shuts Mason up in a remote part of his house with the idea of protecting her and those around her. Responding to this bias, in *Wide Sargasso Sea*, Jamaican-born artist Jean RHYS "writes back" to

Brontë with a novel depicting Bertha Mason as a sane woman driven to violent behavior by Rochester's colonialist oppression. Similar counter-discourses can be found in *Foe* (1988) by South African writer J. M. Coetzee, which reveals the colonialist ideology implicit in *Robinson Crusoe*, as well as in *Things Fall Apart* (1958) by the Nigerian writer Chinua Achebe. In this novel about Ibo society in the early part of the 20th c., Achebe writes his account as a conscious attempt to counteract the distortions of the Englishman Joyce CARY's *Mister Johnson* by describing the richness and complexity of African society before the coming of the white man.

Colonial literature is thus revealed as an enormously varied body of work consisting of works that explicitly treat colonialism as part of their central theme as well as those that reveal it at their edges. Moreover, as in the case of *Robinson Crusoe*, *Jane Eyre*, and *Mister Johnson*, through the work of Coetzee, Rhys, and Achebe colonial literature itself becomes finally dependent on the postcolonial literature to which it has given birth. Certainly, the varied literatures by native peoples from different countries whose land was invaded by colonizers are those largely responsible for the richness and sophistication of discussions of the precise definition and features of colonialist literature itself as they also reshape our previous interpretations of canonical texts and rename them colonial.

BIBLIOGRAPHY: Bivona, D., *British Imperial Literature, 1870–1940* (1998); Davies, V., and R. Griffiths, *The Literature of Colonialism* (1996); Fulford, T., and P. J. Kitson, eds., *Romanticism and Colonialism* (1998); Meyers, J., *Fiction and the Colonial Experience* (1973); Said, E., *Orientalism* (1979); Said, E., *Culture and Imperialism* (1993); Scanlon, T., *Colonial Writing and the New World, 1583–1671* (1999); Sharpe, J., *Allegories of Empire: The Figure of Women in the Colonial Text* (1993)

SUSAN TETLOW HARRINGTON

COLUM, Padraic

b. 8 December 1881, Longford, Ireland; d. 12 January 1972, Enfield, Connecticut, U.S.A.

While working as a clerk, C. published poems in journals edited by Arthur Griffith, the nationalist politician whose biography C. eventually wrote (1959). A benefactor enabled C. to study at Trinity College, Dublin. Griffith encouraged C.'s first play, the anti-British *The Saxon Shillin'* (perf. 1903; pub. 1970), and C. became a founder member of the Abbey Theatre, writing *Broken Soil* (perf. 1903; rev. as *The Fiddler's House*, 1905), *The Land* (1905), and *Thomas Muskerry* (1910), attacked as gloomy. C. published several poetry collections. He left Ireland in 1914 and

lived mainly in the U.S. Commissioned to study Polynesian FOLKLORE, he published two volumes of their stories (1924–25). He continued to write poems and plays, while lecturing on comparative literature and publishing many volumes for children that retold myths and legends. With his wife Mary, he published a memoir, *Our Friend James Joyce* (1958), having met James JOYCE during a spell in Paris.

COLVIN, [Sir] Sidney

b. 18 June 1845, London; d. 11 May 1927, Kensington

Elected Slade Professor of Art at Cambridge in 1873, C. is known primarily as an art historian and curator. He was also active as a literary biographer and editor and produced monographs on Walter Savage LANDOR (1881) and John KEATS (1887), both published as part of John MORLEY's English Men of Letters series. C. was a close friend of Robert Louis STEVENSON and in 1907 edited a sizable selection of Stevenson's letters. C.'s full-length biography of Keats was published in 1917 followed by *Memories and Notes of Persons and Places, 1852–1912* (1921). In the year following C.'s death, E. V. LUCAS published *The Colvins and Their Friends* (1928), a group portrait of C. and his wife and their immediate circle that included Stevenson, Edward Burne-Jones, George ELIOT, Henry JAMES, and Joseph CONRAD, among others.

COMPTON-BURNETT, Ivy

b. 5 June 1884, Pinner, Middlesex; d. 29 August 1969, London

More comfortable in re-creating the "upstairs, downstairs" world of the late Victorian era of her youth than the modern world in which she lived, C.-B. published her first novel, *Dolores*, in 1911, which she later disclaimed as juvenilia. Her second novel, *Pastors and Masters*, published in 1925 after a fourteen-year silence, introduced the controversial themes that would inform her fiction for the next five decades—the disturbing and often sordid complexities of family life, incorporating elements of incest, violence, homosexuality, deceit, and revenge. Her reputation was solidified with the publication of the autobiographical novel *Brothers and Sisters* (1929) followed by *Men and Wives* (1931) and *More Women Than Men* (1933). Later novels include *Daughters and Sons* (1937), *Manservant and Maidservant* (1947), *Darkness and Day* (1951), and *Mother and Son* (1955), which was awarded the James Tait Black Memorial Prize. Her unfinished last novel, *The Last and the First*, was published posthumously in 1971, followed in the next year by her *Collected Works*.

CONGREVE, William

b. 24 January 1670, Bardsey, Yorkshire; d. 19 January 1729, London

C. is the playwright whose works, for many critics, epitomize Restoration comedy. Considered the greatest writer of comedies in the 17th c., he built an unassailable reputation while writing fewer plays than many of his contemporaries and retiring from the theater at age thirty. The preeminence of his masterpiece, *The Way of the World* (1700), in particular is normally attributed to C.'s witty, sparkling dialogue, but lately critics have also paid attention to the darker aspects of his work, painting a new picture of the playwright as an intelligent and incisive social critic.

C. is often considered an Irish playwright, though he was born in Yorkshire in 1670. But like so many British comic playwrights, he was reared in Ireland. His father, an officer in the British military garrison first at Youghal, then at Kilkenny, ensured that C. received a first-class education at the Kilkenny School and Trinity College in Dublin. A thriving theatrical town, Dublin fed the young student's taste for the theater.

In 1688, the family moved to London and C. enrolled in the study of law at the Middle Temple, a background that served him well in his literate comedies. The Inns of Court introduced him to an urbane group of literati who met frequently at Will's Coffeehouse, presided over by the literary lion John DRYDEN. Dryden was to become a staunch supporter of the young playwright.

C. began his writing career with a short novel, *Incognita; or, Love and Duty Reconcil'd* (1692), which he probably began while a student in Dublin. A complicated maze of intrigues, disguises, and misperceptions, the novel traces the path of two lovers who plot to marry the women they love, in spite of the usual parental obstacles. It is typically dismissed as a youthful foray that shows much of the young student's promise, but holds little interest on its own.

C. also wrote songs, Pindaric odes, and translations of classical works, receiving recognition when Dryden included one of C.'s translations of Juvenal in his complete edition of the satires of Juvenal and Persius. During this time, C. worked privately on a comedy, and in 1692 he presented *The Old Batchelour* (1693) to the playwright Thomas Southerne, who showed it to Dryden. Dryden called it the best first play he had ever seen, and he and Southerne made some edits and rearrangements before helping C. secure an opening for it at Drury Lane. The play was a success, running for an unusual fourteen days.

Following the models of popular current playwrights such as George ETHEREGE and William WYCHERLEY, *The Old Batchelour* also demonstrated C.'s thorough knowledge of classical models and the works of Ben JONSON. The characters, as in Jonson, each embody a "humour" or type, but they are psychologically believable as well, and C. proved adept in crafting vivid and specific voices for each one. The play presents a finely wrought series of tricks and dupes: the title character, a bachelor who professes to despise love, is caught mooning after a fallen woman and subjected to a sham marriage with her before being told of her reputation. The woman in truth is married off to a foolish knight, her serving woman to his lackey, and the two "heroes" of the play, Bellmour and Vainlove, manage to win their beloveds Belinda and Araminta.

C.'s first play is characteristic with its complicated contrivances and sparkling repartee. But there are darker shades as well. The humorous tricks played by the characters suggest a world in which everyone is fair game and no one is what they seem. Women are compared to hares, partridges, and melons: not only are they seen as "morsels" or game to be hunted, but Vainlove declares that only the chase makes love interesting at all. Aware of his conviction, the beloved Araminta cannot accept his marriage proposal at the end, for fear of losing his interest, and the ending is thus somewhat more inconclusive than the usual comedy conclusion. Even the central character Bellmour, whose name suggests we view him as the good lover, is a rake who seduces and abandons a number of women before and during his courtship of Belinda, and announces in one speech that his beloved's £12,000 are her best quality. In spite of the social critique lurking beneath *The Old Batchelour*, the overall tone is that of a glittering, fast-paced comedy, and the youthful couples dancing in the final scene create a theatrical impression more powerful than the bachelor's closing speech denigrating the "heat" of youth.

C.'s second play, which opened the same year as *The Old Batchelour,* turned out to be a more seriously dark play. *The Double Dealer* (perf. 1693; pub. 1694) focused on the machinations of a thoroughly evil character, Maskwell, whose villainy—far beyond the simple foolishness of most comic foils—has often been compared to that of William SHAKESPEARE's Iago. The household's matriarch, whom Maskwell pretends to love, is also more reminiscent of tragedy's vengeful furies than a comic dowager. Determined to thwart the marriage of her nephew Mellefont, whom she secretly loves, she plots to ruin him with Maskwell, who secretly loves Mellfont's intended, Cynthia. The other characters in the play are more typical comic types.

In *The Double Dealer*, C. also set himself the task—unusual in RESTORATION DRAMA—of observing the classical unities of time, place, and action. Thus the entire play unfolds in the gallery of the Touchwood's home, the time elapsed is equal to that of the production, and the play focuses tightly on Maskwell's schemes and their effects. That the play was greeted less warmly than C.'s first is clear from his somewhat crabby preface to the printed edition, in which he notes his severe observance of the unities and defends his harsh caricatures, deplored as too bitterly satiric by some detractors, as intrinsic to comedy. Dryden and others defended the play, but it was to be performed least of all of C.'s comedies.

Regardless of the angry tone of his preface, C. took the audience's tastes to heart, and his next play, *Love for Love* (1695), returned to more traditional plotting and characters. The play's hero, Valentine, is a typical Restoration type: a rake who has burned through all of his money and quarreled with his father. In love with the wealthy and intelligent Angelica, he is tormented by his father's offer of enough money to pay his debts in return for his signing a deed of disinheritance. Attempting to forestall the decision, Valentine feigns madness. The pretended insanity, part of a larger inquiry into the nature of performance and reality, has Shakespearean overtones, as does the fact that it is the heroine's wit that solves the problem and resolves the play. Feigning a desire to marry Valentine's father, Angelica convinces Valentine to sign the deed—unselfishly, out of love for her with no hope of a return. With that proof of his love, she destroys the deed and proclaims her love for Valentine.

Love for Love combined C.'s facility for dialogue and psychologically interesting characters with a popularizing moral: Valentine learns that love can be exchanged only for love. Although the play shares his other comedies' interest in disguises and deception, it offers a straightforward and easily embraced lesson. The combination worked, and *Love for Love's* success rivaled that of *The Old Batchelour*, running for thirteen days and becoming C.'s most produced comedy for the next century. Now an established playwright, C. began to have followers. At the encouragement of friends, he wrote "An Essay concerning Humour in Comedy" (1695), an outline of the different types of dramatic character in the form of a letter. Here, he grounds comic behavior in the real qualities of people, natural and individual.

C.'s next play was a tragedy. *The Mourning Bride* (1697) receives little critical attention today and is generally considered to be stilted and derivative, though with a few poetic high points. In its own day, however, C.'s one tragedy was hugely successful, performed frequently and praised by no less a critic than Samuel JOHNSON. The following year, 1698, saw the publication of one of the most famous antitheatrical tracts in English theater history, Jeremy Collier's *A Short View of the Immorality and Profaneness of the English Stage*. C., along with some of his contemporaries, was singled out for special and detailed attack: his characters were branded immoral, his allusions inappropriate, and his language profane. C. defended himself in a reply pamphlet, "Amendments to Mr. Collier's False and Imperfect Citations" (1698), and a small pamphlet war ensued, with Collier writing a counter-response and others joining the fray. C.'s defense—that comedy uses HUMOR to chastise vice, and that many of his texts were being misread—was reasonable, but not terribly convincing.

C. got further revenge in his final comedy, *The Way of the World*, where the foolish and hypocritical Lady Wishfort suggests Collier's book to entertain a friend. Generally acknowledged to be C.'s supreme achievement, *The Way of the World* centers on a single family and the struggle between two men to control it. As in the Roman comedies C. admires in his preface, the older generation is blocking the rightful ascendancy of the younger, who turn to helpful servants to help them trick their elders. C.'s hero, Mirabell, wants to marry the capriciously charming Millamant, but is blocked by Millamant's widowed aunt Lady Wishfort, who pretends an aversion to men but secretly longs to remarry. Meanwhile, Mirabell's apparent friend Fainall, who was quickly married to Mirabell's ex-mistress when she suspected she was pregnant, plots to dispose of his wife and steal Millamant's fortune for himself and his own mistress.

Like all of C.'s heroes, Mirabell is thus morally compromised, and though he triumphs in the end, it is not due to his scheming but rather because of the trust and generosity exhibited by Mrs. Fainall, an ex-mistress who, unusually, condones and helps her former lover's marriage. And true to his type for heroines, Millamant is flighty and given to hiding her true feelings behind a delightful verbal display. The scene in which Mirabell and Millamant discuss what kind of marriage they will have is both theatrically brilliant and thematically thought provoking.

Although *The Way of the World* is C.'s most polished play, its reception was not as warm as that given *The Old Batchelour* and *Love for Love*. The complicated plot was cited as a barrier to enjoyment and the originality of the play made it more difficult to assess. Tradition has it that disappointment with this reception drove C. from the theater; this is probably not true. Instead, the long-awaited attainment of a stable financial position—he was appointed commissioner of wines in 1705—the increasingly conservative tendencies of the stage and his own ill health probably combined to make him stop writing plays at age thirty. He maintained a connection to the stage, however, writing the text for the masque *The Judgement of Paris* (1701), an opera libretto *Semele*, and coauthoring an adaptation of Molière's *Monsieur de Pourceaugnac* called *Squire Trelooby* (perf. 1704). Joining with fellow playwright Sir John VANBRUGH, C. also established and helped manage a new theater in the Haymarket.

C. lived the rest of his life in a gentleman's retirement, discharging the duties of his appointments through deputies and indulging his lifelong love of good food and wine. He also took great care in the preparation of his collected *Works* (3 vols., 1710). C.'s reputation declined in the 19th c., along with that of all Restoration dramatists. His plays were rarely produced, but continued to be read. In the 20th c., a revival of interest in the plays on stage was quickly followed by a revival of critical interest.

BIBLIOGRAPHY: Hoffman, A. W., *C.'s Comedies* (1993); Love, H., *C.* (1975); Novak, M. E., *W. C.* (1971); Van Voris, W. H., *The Cultivated Stance: The Designs of C.'s Plays* (1965); Williams, A. L., *An Approach to C.* (1979); Wilson, C., *Memoirs of the Life, Writings, and Amours of W. C.* (1730); Young, D. M., *The Feminist Voices in Restoration Comedy* (1997)

GINGER STRAND

CONNOLLY, Cyril [Vernon]

b. 10 September 1903, Coventry; d. 26 November 1974, London

C. was for more than forty years a key figure in British literary life, but the nature of his contribution is now indistinct. A prodigious, influential literary journalist and essayist, he also wrote two curious, idiosyncratic works of fiction/philosophy and a highly regarded work of AUTOBIOGRAPHY, and achieved great acclaim for his stewardship of the wartime literary journal *Horizon*. The range of these achievements makes C. difficult to place, but also leaves a sense of unfulfilled potential, of a considerable talent dissipated in minor projects; his reputation also suffers from the commonplace disdain (which he largely shared) for the whole genre of literary journalism. The two recent biographies of this complex character suggest he is now remembered primarily for his personality and wit, for there have been no critical studies of his work. The biographies trace the extraordinary circle of illustrious friends and acquaintances, the epicurean lifestyle, the wealth of axioms, anecdotes, and *bons mots* ("Imprisoned in every fat man a thin one is wildly signalling to be let out"; "It is closing time in the gardens of the West and from now on an artist will be judged only by the resonance of his solitude or the quality of his despair"), but ultimately offer little insight into C.'s qualities as a writer, or his significance as a critic.

A familiar, flamboyant figure on the metropolitan scene and a prominent wit, C. was nonetheless an editor and critic of considerable influence, a defiant defender of often difficult, so-called highbrow culture, and an outspoken promoter of modernist aesthetics. He was a timely and elegant champion of such diverse figures as André Gide, James JOYCE, Thomas Mann, F. Scott Fitzgerald, Ernest Hemingway, and Henry Miller (often before they were at all well known in the U.K.), and his polemical overview, *The Modern Movement: 100 Key Books from England, France, and America, 1880–1950* (1965), remains one of the finest introductions to the field. His principal achievements were thus as an essayist and reviewer of exceptional versatility and intellectual range, first for the *New Statesman* (1927–29) and other magazines of the 1930s (*Life and Letters*; *Britain To-day*), then as founding editor of his own journal, *Horizon* (1939–49), as literary editor of the *Observer* (1942–43), and finally as principal critic for the *Sunday Times* (1951–73). His prolific and often exemplary writing, in a variety of styles and moods (autobiography, parody, pastiche, formal essay) is collected in several volumes, of which the most notable are *The Condemned Playground: Essays 1927–1944* (1945), and *Previous Convictions* (1963).

It is as editor of *Horizon* that C. made his most telling contribution to British letters. He founded the journal, with Stephen SPENDER, at the outbreak of World War II, promising "to provide readers with enjoyment and writers with opportunity, and to maintain a high literary standard during the war." Alongside cultural criticism and reviews, *Horizon* introduced, among others, the writing of Angus WILSON, Arthur Koestler, Laurie LEE, Alun LEWIS, and Patrick KAVANAGH. It provided the first platform for such masterpieces as W. H. AUDEN's "In Praise of Limestone," George ORWELL's "Boys' Weeklies" and "Politics and the English Language," and Dylan THOMAS's "Fern Hill" and "A Refusal to Mourn the Death, by Fire, of a Child in London." A measure of the journal's success is the extent to which it became identified with "Literary London," and its demise was widely mourned. Even the reviewer in *Scrutiny*, that would-be scourge of metropolitan cliques, acknowledged that the *Horizon* group "at once represent and control the taste of a very large proportion of the serious reading public."

Despite his considerable corpus of writing, and the success of *Horizon*, it is often suggested that C. failed to fulfill his potential, not least because of the stringent *mea culpa* in his most famous work, *Enemies of Promise* (1938; rev. eds., 1949, 1960). The book offers an engaging analysis of trends in 1920s and 1930s writing, but it is the account of C.'s time at Eton that most enthralls. He had been an extremely successful pupil, winning numerous prizes, the respect of his peers (he was elected to the prestigious senior boys' club, "Pop," a rare triumph for an aesthete and scholar), and finally a scholarship to Balliol College, Oxford. His contemporaries were a particularly distinguished group, including the novelists Henry GREEN, Anthony POWELL, and Orwell, as well as such characters as Brian Howard (model for Evelyn

WAUGH's Anthony Blanche in *Brideshead Revisited*), Harold ACTON (later Professor of History at Oxford), and Alan Pryce-Jones (later editor of the *Times Literary Supplement*). However, C. argues convincingly that the very intensity of this environment in some ways unfitted him for a literary career—it was one of the "enemies" that might ruin early "promise." He cites, approvingly, a friend's remark: "You've got a Balliol scholarship and you've got into Pop—you know I shouldn't be surprised if you never did anything else the rest of your life."

C. certainly did do something with the rest of his life, and the current neglect of his work is unfortunate. His essays remain models of style and acute critical intelligence, while the short works *The Rock Pool* (1936; rev. ed., 1947), and *The Unquiet Grave: A Word Cycle* (1944; rev. ed., 1945), published under the pseudonym of Palinurus, are still worth reading for their curious, elegant, struggles with conventional form. If *Enemies of Promise* is C.'s masterpiece, its narrative of failure and dissatisfaction should nonetheless be set against the strong evidence of his central role in British culture of the mid-20th c.

BIBLIOGRAPHY: Fisher, C., *C. C.* (1995); Lewis, J., *C. C.* (1997); Sheldon, M., *Friends of Promise: C. C. and the World of Horizon* (1989)

SEAN MATTHEWS

CONQUEST, [George] Robert [Acworth]
b. 15 July 1917, Malvern

C. is primarily a distinguished historian who has published seventeen books on international affairs. His major scholarly concern has been with the nature of and relations between despotic and consensual cultures, and he has been translated into more than twenty languages. Educated at Winchester, Magdalen College, Oxford, and the University of Grenoble, France, C. served in World War II, worked for the diplomatic service (1946–56), and has held senior academic posts in Britain and the U.S. He has won numerous honors and awards and is a fellow of the Royal Society of Literature, a fellow of the British Academy, an adjunct fellow of the Center for Strategic and International Studies, Washington, D.C., a research associate of Harvard University's Ukrainian Research Institute, a fellow of the British Interplanetary Society, and a member of the board of the Institute for European Defense and Strategic Studies. A one-time literary editor of the *Spectator*, he is himself a poet and anthologist, who received the American Academy of Arts and Letters 1997 award for light verse. He translated Aleksander Solzhenitsyn's EPIC poem *Prussian Nights* into English verse (1977). In 1956, C. edited the influential *New Lines*—which established the poets of "The Movement," according to

the criteria of plain language and traditional verse forms. His own verse collections include *Poems* (1955), *Between Mars and Venus* (1962), and *Arias from a Love Opera* (1969). He has written SCIENCE FICTION and collaborated with Kingsley AMIS on a spoof mystery-thriller, *The Egyptologists* (1965).

CONRAD, Joseph
b. Teodor Józef Konrad Korzeniowski, 3 December 1857, Berdyczow, Ukraine; d. 3 August 1924, Bishopsbourne, Kent

C. is the most improbable of the great English novelists. Born of parents from Poland, whose native country that had been shared out among Russia, Austria, and Prussia since 1772, he spent five years of his childhood in political detention in Russia with his parents where they had been banished for conspiring to free their dismantled homeland. Orphaned first by the death of his mother, then of his father, he was adopted by a maternal uncle in Cracow, the ancient political and cultural capital of Poland. There, despite excellent educational prospects, he persuaded his guardian to let him go to sea.

Aged seventeen, C. entered a new life in Marseilles where, during the next four years, he sailed twice to the Caribbean, developed a passion for 19th-c. French fiction, lived extravagantly, and finally attempted suicide. Following his recovery, he made another clean break, this time by joining the British Merchant Service. From 1878 to 1893, he sailed regularly to various Eastern destinations on square-rigged vessels, passing his master's examination in 1886, commanding a trading ship to and from Australia in 1888 and a Belgian craft on the Congo River in 1890. However, another still more improbable transformation was on the way, this time produced by a novel. With the success of *Almayer's Folly* in 1895, he took on a wife and a literary career. His work quickly earned the respect of the leading English-language novelists of the age, from Stephen Crane and Henry JAMES to Ford Madox FORD and John GALSWORTHY; but he had to wait until the outbreak of the First World War for financial success, achieved with the New York publication in 1913 of *Chance* and with his adoption by leading Parisian men of letters. He remained heroically productive until 1924, when his sudden death launched him into a posthumous career that, as the 20th c. unfolded, transformed him into a world novelist. This literary conquest was achieved on the basis of his third language. As the case of James demonstrates, literary achievement is the product of linguistic talent, not of an adventurous life. Yet even a selection of C.'s novels shows how much literature can gain from an abundant experience of the world.

C.'s four main sea narratives, which evoke the last decades of sail, are generally regarded as masterpieces of the genre. *Typhoon* (1902), set in the China seas, is surely beyond competition as a depiction of the power of elemental nature and of the simplicity of resolve needed to survive it; while the later novellas, "The Secret Sharer" (1910) and *The Shadow-Line* (1917), also set in the Orient, are very subtle explorations of the divisions in personal identity required for effective command. But it is the first of these, *The Nigger of the "Narcissus"* (1897), called by James "the finest and strongest picture of the sea and sea life our language possesses" that sets the standard. It evokes the voyage of a three-masted barque from Bombay via the Cape of Good Hope to the Port of London. The successive episodes—the ship drives southward before the trade winds, it nearly founders in the Southern Ocean, it is becalmed in the Atlantic doldrums, and it drives over the Northern seas until it quenches its momentum in the slushy Thames—add up to a sequence of events propelled by the impetus of the narrative art. With the completion of the voyage, we are made to feel that we are taking our farewells of the age of sail; but the novel is no exercise in nostalgia. The sea and the ship make unforgiving demands on the three officers and a crew of eighteen men drawn from all parts of the globe. The men are continuously unsteadied by a subjective individualism imported from life on land. This takes many forms, but especially that of self-pity in the form of a fear of death owed less to the sea than to the presence on board of a dying Negro; and of a philosophy of "rights" fed by the indignations of self-interest. Thus, the novel's epic grandeur is founded on a full representation of human evasiveness and self-conceit; nor does it overlook the "sordid inspiration" of the *Narcissus'* commercial voyage. But once the ship has left harbour and is alone with the sea, the challenge of collaborative survival overcomes these discontents.

C.'s Polish origins exposed him to the experience of national and personal defeat. His sea vocation may indeed have been a flight into a better life; but that his subsequent achievements did not efface his first allegiances, to which of course he owed his sense of self, is implicit in every line of his sea-fiction; and it becomes explicit in his autobiographical masterpiece, *A Personal Record* (1912; repub. as *Some Reminiscences*, 1912), which mingles family and childhood memories with evocations of his first encounter with a British merchant ship which determined his maritime career, and with memories of the defeated figure in a forgotten corner of Borneo which inspired his first novel.

The survival, even the intensification, of the sense of identity in failure is perhaps the central experience of C.'s life. For although our feelings and perceptions cannot properly belong to someone else, what one feels and perceives is governed by one's history—one's parents, class, culture, country. C.'s first novel, *Almayer's Folly*, five years in the making, already

fully exhibits this paradox. Almayer, marooned in a remote tropical Malay settlement is, in his preferences, prejudices, capacities, and ambitions, the archetypal *petit bourgeois* colonist; but the intensity of the hopes and dreams he invests in his daughter is exclusively his own—so that when the girl leaves him for a Balinese princeling allied to him, he gradually disintegrates into opium addiction and eventual death. Yet Almayer's anguish of paternity, felt by him alone, is generated by a whole complex of interactive group interests—Arab, Malay, Sulu, Chinese, British, and Dutch—which are themselves products of competitive colonialism.

Colonialism is central to the three masterpieces of early modernist fiction that follow *The Nigger of the "Narcissus."* The first of these, "Heart of Darkness" (3 parts, 1899), serialized in *Blackwood's Edinburgh Magazine,* autobiographical in origin, confronts the horror witnessed by Marlow, C.'s recurring narrator, when running a river-steamer for a Belgian company up the Congo. The exploitative brutality of the commercial "invasion" Marlow serves is capped by the near insane fantasies of the leader of a "civilizing" initiative, the omni-cultured Kurtz, who has been morally destroyed by his megalomania and who dies under Marlow's care during the return trip down river. That this appalling tale of primeval nature and civilized rapine is narrated by Marlow to a group of business friends on board a yawl anchored at the mouth of the Thames allows C. to implicate England—herself once the recipient of a Roman invasion—in 19th-c. Europe's worldwide ransacking spree.

C.'s next novel, *Lord Jim* (1900), relates, again through the narrative of a now protective Marlow, the story of the life and death of a young English mercantile marine officer who abandons a ship full of Muslim pilgrims in the mistaken belief that it is about to founder. This might appear to make it a tale of lost honor framed by redemptive friendship: yet it remains subtly colonialist in its implications. The imperialist setting of the novel—the enormous space demarcated by the phrase "East of Aden"—contains the history of colonialism since 1600, with its various cultural consequences, including the appearance of a wonderful range of international "Englishes." More directly, Jim's predicament is the result of his failure to live up to the demands of "honor"—a standard of conduct grounded in self-esteem and designed to motivate the servants of Empire. This becomes explicit in the second part of the novel, where Jim's quest for self-redemption makes him dedicate himself to the service of a remote Malay community, only to relapse into helplessness when confronted by an intruding gang of whites, with the consequent massacre of many of his supporters, and the public sacrifice of his own life.

But the grandest of these fictions is the EPIC *Nostromo* (1904), a novel concerned less with colonialism than with postcolonialism. Its subject is the secession of the Pacific province, Sulaco, of an imaginary Latin American republic, not unlike real-life Colombia, called Costaguana, racked by misrule and civil war since the expulsion of Spanish rule. The breakaway state, Sulaco, owes its eventual independence to international material interests—specifically the reopening of a silver mine by a combination of British technology and American capital. C.'s *Nostromo* is a total novel. Its history and geography, stunningly realized, include every aspect of collective life—economics, sociology, religion, architecture, communications—from the advent of the conquistadores to the formation of proletariat Marxist clubs. Yet for all these determinants, the success of Sulaco's revolution is not presented as inevitable. The novel's magnificent cast of characters enables C. to analyze secession as the outcome of an accumulation of individual projects and intentions that interact in ways unforeseen by their agents, or indeed by the national and international interests that affect them. In *Nostromo*, C.'s enactment of historical change—a shift from colonial to international formations—breaks radically new ground.

With *The Secret Agent* (1907) and *Under Western Eyes* (1911), which many regard as C.'s subtlest fictions, for the first time the location moves to Europe—respectively to London, and to St. Petersburg as seen from Geneva. *The Secret Agent* explores the story of an anarchist attempt to dynamite Greenwich Observatory. The police quickly discover the identity of the young man who has blown himself up in attempting to lay the mine. They also discover the reason for the outrage: Russia's attempt to discourage the British government from offering refuge to Continental anarchists. To be sure, C.'s pride in British liberal institutions is evident throughout the novel; but it has its limits. Drawing on the social map of the whole of London, he shows the degree to which imaginative sympathy is diluted by British individualism and especially by the anonymity of life in an enormous city. Descending deeper into the Greenwich incident, he discovers a domestic, not a political, tragedy. The dead youth is one Stevie, the feeble-minded but intensely imaginative brother of the protective Winnie who, to ensure Stevie's welfare, has married the overseer of anarchist affairs in London, Verloc—the man originally bullied by the Russian diplomat to blow up "astronomy" in order to terrify the English middle classes. Winnie's intense devotion to her brother is a response to his childlike self-identification with the innumerable instances of suffering that London provides. She therefore finds his death intolerable, and in a scene that recalls the power of William SHAKE-SPEARE's *Macbeth* she knifes her husband to death, and a few hours later is driven to drown herself. Among the very greatest of London novels, *The Secret Agent* offers a profound endorsement of a real, as

opposed to a merely principled, perception of suffering—a distinction that, elsewhere in C.'s discursive work, and notably in his essay "Autocracy and War," acquires the weight of an artistic manifesto.

Under Western Eyes develops this critique of liberal rationality as a substitute for the immediacy of felt perception. The "Western eyes" in question are those of the middle-aged, middle-class narrator—a linguist who lives in the prosperous little republican city-state of Geneva, birthplace of the "artless moralist" Jean-Jacques Rousseau, and who views all things Russian with self-satisfied incredulity. A young Russian revolutionary zealot, Haldin, assassinates the reactionary minister of the interior in a wintry street of St. Petersburg. He is betrayed to the authorities by the novel's protagonist, Razumov, and summarily executed. Thereupon Razumov is trapped into spying on Russian exiles in Geneva, including Haldin's mother and his sister Natalia. Both Razumov and the Narrator fall in love with the beautiful, high-minded Natalia, who is herself drawn to Razumov. With the removal of the one remaining witness of his association with the Russian authorities, Razumov finally achieves safety, but at the cost of his inner self, which is finally buried. However, unable to endure the solitude, he confesses first to a horrified Natalia, then to the revolutionary exiles; whereupon he is mutilated by a Russian counterespionage thug, and fastidiously repudiated by the uncomprehending narrator. The writing of this astonishing novel brought on its author a serious nervous breakdown. C. had been deeply committed by his Polish education to regarding Eastern and Western realities as polar opposites, and he was deeply disturbed by a narrative logic that forced him to destabilize that opposition. Yet it is that logic that has given the novel a prophetic power which it still retains.

The two excellent novels that followed *Under Western Eyes, Chance* (1913) and *Victory* (1915), both studies of love in protagonists suffering from acute emotional deprivation, the first in a context of the new, virtual-reality capitalism of Edwardian London, the second in relation to free-booting gangsterism in Indonesia, retain much of the sardonic richness of C.'s writing, but they do not achieve the moral-political power of their predecessors. Still less do the fictions of C.'s final phase, in which he returned to the France of his youth—although an exception must be made of his valedictory text, *The Rover* (1923), which evokes with much of the old warmth and strength of his writing the return home and the heroic death of an old independent mariner against the background of the revolutionary terror and the foreground of the Napoleonic Wars.

In 1949, George ORWELL, himself close to a premature death, was asked what he thought of C. In one of his last letters, he replied: "I regard C. as . . . one of the very few true novelists that England possesses. . . . What he did have . . . was a sort of grown-upness and political understanding which would have been almost impossible to a native English writer at that time." The half century since Orwell's death has only confirmed this verdict.

BIBLIOGRAPHY: Bennett, C. D., *J. C.* (1991); Carabine, K., ed., *J. C.: Critical Assessments* (4 vols., 1992); Ford, F. M., *J. C.* (1924); Karl, F. R., *J. C.* (1979); Meyers, J., *J. C.* (1991); Watt, I., *C. in the Nineteenth Century* (1979)

JACQUES BERTHOUD

CONSTABLE, Henry
b. 1562; d. 9 October 1613, Liège, Belgium

Educated at St. John's College, Cambridge, C. went abroad at age eighteen and remained on the Continent for much of his adult life. As a Roman Catholic, C. preferred the relative security of France to England and lived mostly in Paris, where he established himself with the French court. C.'s *Diana* (1592; rev. ed., 1594) contained twenty-three poems and was influential in the development of the English sonnet. His sixteen *Spiritual Sonnets* were unpublished until 1815. Following the death of ELIZABETH I and the accession of JAMES I, C. returned to England with renewed hope for religious tolerance but after a brief period of imprisonment went again into exile.

CONSTANTINE, David [John]
b. 4 March 1944, Salford, Lancashire

C. read modern languages at Wadham College, Oxford, and has lectured at Durham and Oxford Universities. In 1979, he published a study, *Friedrich Hölderlin,* followed by *The Significance of Locality in the Poetry of Friedrich Hölderlin* in the same year, and a first collection of poetry, *A Brightness to Cast Shadows,* in 1980. A biography of Hölderlin appeared in 1988 and a translation by C. of selected poems by the same author in 1990. C.'s translation *Hölderlin's Sophocles: Oedipus and Antigone* came out in 2001. *Early Greek Travellers and the Hellenic Ideal* (1984) displayed the erudition that informs C.'s verse, influenced by Robert GRAVES. C. has translated poems by Henri Michaux (1992), with his wife Helen Constantine, and Philippe Jaccottet (1994), with Mark Treharne. Among C.'s own verse publications are *Talitha Cumi* (with Rodney Pybus and others, 1983), *Watching for Dolphins* (1983), *Madder* (1987), and *The Pelt of Wasps* (1998). His novel entitled *Davies* appeared in 1985.

COOPER, Giles [Stannus]
b. 9 August 1918, near Dublin, Ireland; d. 2 December 1966, near Surbiton, Surrey

A prolific dramatist, C., the bulk of whose plays were written for radio and television, never achieved the sort of popular fame afforded his contemporaries who wrote primarily for the stage. Nevertheless, as an innovator of radio drama and the author of some memorable stage plays, C. was an influential figure in 20th-c. British drama. C. began to write plays in the 1950s, following an undistinguished acting career. Most of his plays could be described as dramas of ideas; that is, C. begins with a more or less off-beat concept and then allows the action to unfold with an inevitable, naturalistic, and often violent logic. One of his first stage plays, *Never Get Out* (perf. 1950), for example, tells the story of a man and a woman who attempt to create a life for themselves on an abandoned bombing range. C.'s first major stage play, *Everything in the Garden* (perf. 1962; pub. 1963), deals with a "typical" suburban couple who, in order to make ends meet, turn to prostitution and murder. *Out of the Crocodile* (perf. 1963; pub. 1964) is a more overtly comic play, telling the story of Peter Pounce and his unknowing "clients," the Hampsters. Pounce takes it upon himself to manage the Hampsters' affairs, so they may live in a state of not-so-blissful ignorance. Ultimately, complications arise when the Hampsters become aware of Pounce's efforts. C.'s finest play, *Happy Family* (perf. 1966; pub. 1967), combines his penchant for the drama of ideas with a greater dependence on character-driven action. This is the story of three siblings who retreat often to their private world of childhood rituals in order to avoid dealing with the stresses of modern life. C. died prematurely in a railway accident, but his impact on British dramaturgy lives on: in 1978, the annual Giles Cooper Awards were established to honor the best in radio drama.

COOPER, William
(pseud. of Harry Summerfield Hoff) b. 4 August 1910, Crewe; d. 5 September 2002, London

Writing as H. S. Hoff, C. published his first novel, *It Happened in PRK* (repub. as *Trina*), in 1934, followed by *Rhea* (1935), *Lisa* (1937), and *Three Marriages* (1946). In 1950 he adopted the pseudonym "William Cooper" with the publication of *Scenes from Provincial Life.* This novel and its sequels—*Scenes from Married Life* (1961), *Scenes from Metropolitan Life* (1982), *Scenes from Later Life* (1983), and *Scenes from Death and Life* (1999)—were seminal in exploring a lower-middle-class milieu, and influenced John BRAINE, Kingsley AMIS, John WAIN, Stan BARSTOW, and Alan SILLITOE, among others.

COPE, Wendy
b. 21 February 1945, Erith, Kent

C. became one of the most popular poets writing in English long after popularity became unfashionable for poets. She often works in genres that have been marginalized since serious literature became identified with the academic, including both traditional forms, such as the sonnet and the triolet, and light verse or what she calls "literary jokes." Her parodies and wry comments on pretension and romance are often very funny and irresistibly quotable. Her poems can also, however, display real emotional depth. Almost all display a metrical brilliance and a gift for rhyme that, along with her often bitter view of life and love, call to mind Dorothy Parker and A. E. HOUSMAN.

C. is the child of a solid middle-class family and talks about how the sexual frankness of her poems embarrassed her mother. She read history at St. Hilda's College, Oxford, and then studied for a diploma in education at Westminster College in Oxford. She taught in primary schools full-time for twelve years and part-time for two more, before she began to support herself by publishing poems and book reviews and reading her works in public. C. began writing poetry rather late in life, after a nervous breakdown in her mid-twenties that followed the death of her father and the end of a love affair. She spent eleven years in traditional Freudian therapy and as a result came to remember her childhood ambition to become a writer. Her earlier poems, many of which are collected in her first book, *Making Cocoa for Kingsley Amis* (1986), are both touching and satiric. The villanelle "Lonely Hearts," for example, describes the search for love of those who post personal ads in the newspaper.

Making Cocoa for Kingsley Amis was a great success for a book of poetry, selling forty thousand copies. The "literary jokes" include a version of T. S. ELIOT's *The Waste Land* in the form of five limericks as well as parodies of Ted HUGHES, Philip LARKIN, and several other prominent poets. The volume also introduces C.'s alter ego, Jason Strugnell, a pathetic male poet, more interested in beer than in the muse. His sonnets are versions of William SHAKE-SPEARE's—he writes about the expense, not of "spirit," but of spirits—and his Rubáiyát celebrates pints of lager instead of goblets of wine. C.'s parodies overlap with her love poems in works such as "My Lover," which imitates Christopher SMART's consideration of his cat. Other poems describe the intensity of love or the intensity of the disappointment it causes. A few, like "Rondeau Redoublé" with its refrain, "There are so many kinds of awful men," seem to be attacks on the whole male sex, though their wit makes them as appealing to men as to women.

In her second collection, *Serious Concerns* (1992), C. answered the objections of some critics that her worked lacked seriousness not by becoming solemn, but by mocking those who suggested that wittiness and lack of pretension could be considered a weakness in poetry. All the same, some poems, like "Some More Light Verse," do describe grim states of mind. More poems, however, are either humorous or (especially those on romance) mordantly witty. In "After the Lunch," C. uses the details of ordinary life, instead of traditional romantic trapping, to create a joyous, touching love poem. Strugnell, whose work now includes Christian poems, makes another appearance, as do poems on the inadequacies of men.

If I Don't Know (2001) disappointed many readers because it lacked some of the biting wit that marked the earlier volumes. Some ascribed the change in C.'s work to changes in her personal life: after the many failed affairs she mined for material in her earlier books, she had found in the poet Lachlan Mackinnon a congenial partner and was enjoying life with him and his children. Instead of poems about how awful Christmas is "if you're single," there is a poem about a family Christmas tree. Yet some poems, like "How to Deal with the Press," show that C. had not put her biting wit away entirely. She was, however, moving in new directions. Most notably, *If I Don't Know* includes a substantial narrative poem in loose heroic couplets, "The Teacher's Tale." C. had earlier published *The River Girl* (1991), which was composed as the narrative for a pantomime.

C. has published a book of children's verse, *Twiddling Your Thumbs* (1988), and edited several collections, including *Is That the New Moon? Poems by Women Poets* (1988) and *Heaven on Earth: Happy Poems* (2001).

BIBLIOGRAPHY: Thompson, N., "W. C.'s Struggle with Strugnell in *Making Cocoa for Kingsley Amis*," in Barreca, R., ed., *New Perspectives on Women and Comedy* (1992): 111–22

BRIAN ABEL RAGEN

COPLAND, Robert
b. ca. 1470; d. 1548, London?

Printer, editor, and bookseller, C. worked possibly for William CAXTON and certainly for his successor, Wynkyn de Worde. C. was also the author of original works of popular literature for English readers. His best-known work is *The High Way to the Spyttell House* (ca. 1536), a verse dialogue between the author and the porter of St. Bartholomew's Hospital, with much information about the vagrants who found their way there. Later works include *Jill of Brentford's Testament* (ca. 1563) and *The Seven Sorrows That Women Have When Their Husbands Be Dead* (ca.

1565). C. made various translations from the French, including works by Pierre Gringore, Pierre Garcie, and Guy de Chauliac.

COPPARD, A[lfred] E[dgar]
b. 4 January 1878, Folkestone, Kent; d. 13 January 1957, London

C.'s formal education ended at age nine, when he was apprenticed to a tailor. He did various menial jobs before moving to Oxford to become a clerk and became a full-time writer in 1919. His Oxford friends included Harold Laski and L. P. HARTLEY. C.'s first collection of short stories, *Adam and Eve and Pinch Me* (1921), was a success, which brought encouragement from Ford Madox FORD, and in 1922 C. published *Hips and Haws*, a book of poems, followed by *The Black Dog and Other Stories* (1923), *Fishmonger's Fiddle: Tales* (1925), and *The Field of Mustard* (1926). He published almost a book a year and is remembered for his pictures of country life and his sympathy for oddities and misfits. His *Selected Tales* appeared in 1946 followed by his *Collected Tales* in 1948.

CORBETT, Richard
b. 1582, Ewell, Surrey; d. 28 July 1635, Norwich

It would be wrong to make any excessive claims for C.'s verse; certainly he didn't regard his activity as a poet with high seriousness. As was often the case with poets of his social class in the 17th c., he made no attempt to publish his work during his lifetime. For him, poetry was not the creation of timeless works of art; rather it was one of the forms that social intercourse naturally took. Most of C.'s work was related to specific occasions, often written with an equally specific audience in mind.

After being educated (like so many other poets of the period) at Westminster School in London, C.'s life and career were centered on the University of Oxford. He was successively Dean of Christ Church, Oxford (1620–28), Bishop of Oxford (1628–32), and Bishop of Norwich (1632–35). Most of his verse seems to have been written during his years in Oxford, where he had a reputation as a wit, drinker, and practical joker; much of his work reflects that side of his character, but some is addressed to loftier subjects (and may often have played a part in his search for preferment). At Oxford, C. was regarded as, in the words of Anthony WOOD, "one of the most celebrated wits in the University, as his poems, jests, romantic fancies and exploits, which he made and performed *extempore*, showed." Even if we don't take literally Wood's use of the word *extempore*, it is clear that C. was not one to regard the preservation of his poetic reputation very seriously. His work circulated in manuscript; it

survives in both manuscript and printed anthologies in which attributions cannot always be trusted and are sometimes quite clearly incorrect. As a result, it is impossible, at this distance in time, to be absolutely sure of the canon of C.'s work. Still, the poems that modern scholarship has come to regard as most probably his (and we have surely lost many more) offer a picture of a more or less consistent poetic personality, and afford us an entrance to an interesting and important literary coterie in Caroline Oxford.

In some ways, C.'s most substantial piece of work, "Iter Boreale" is a kind of miniature odyssey of the ordinary; it narrates, with great good HUMOR, a journey made by a group of friends from Oxford, around the towns and countryside of the English midlands, and back to Oxford again. Its fascination with people and things, with the woman "with a leane visage, like a carved face/On a Court cupboard" or the pleasures of "a tallow-light and a dry roofe," is characteristic. Such a fascination, creatively reimagined, underlies the two nonsense poems that are probably his ("Nonsence" and "A Non Sequitur"), with their "lobster clad in logick breeches" and "blew Crocodiles." The exuberant vitality of C.'s mind, nourished by a fondness for traditional forms like the ballad, engages at every turn with the ceremonies and legends of the popular imagination. "Iter Boreale" celebrates, among others, Guy of Warwick and his defeat of Colbronde, Bevis of Hampton, and Robin Goodfellow. In the same poem, C.'s pleasure in an innkeeper "full of *Ale* and *History*" stands in antithesis to his scorn for the Puritans, with their opposition to all the traditions he so loved.

C.'s anti-Puritanism (he was a supporter of William Laud) lies behind a number of his best poems, whether in the parodic monologues of "An Exhortation To Mr. John Hammon *minister in the parish of* Bewdly, *for the battering downe of the* Vanityes *of the* Gentiles, *which are comprehended in a* May-pole; *written by a* Zealous Brother *from the* Black-fryers" and "The Distracted Puritane," or in the controlled anger of his lines "Upon Faireford Windowes." His sense of the coming changes that Puritanism might bring, of the fracturing of ancient traditions that it represented for him, gives to much of his best work an almost nostalgic, retrospective quality. This is nowhere more apparent than in "A *Proper New* Ballad intituled The Faeryes Farewell," which, with its opening line, "Farewell, Rewards & *Faeries*" (which supplied Rudyard KIPLING with the title for one of his collections of stories) has become perhaps C.'s best-known poem. Here, in memorable lines fitted to a choice of preexisting ballad tunes, is a poem that joins the distinguished company of lyric poems lamenting a lost innocence, as C. associates fairy belief and the old religion, affirming that "the *Faeries*/were of the old Profession;/Theyre Songs were *Ave Maryes,*/

Theyre Daunces were *Procession*." The poem is an eloquent lament for a rapidly disappearing world.

"The Faeryes Farewell" was perhaps the most all-embracing elegy that C. wrote. But he was also prolific in the production of elegies for named individuals. At varying length, in shifting tones and idioms, he commemorated the great and the small, most often most successfully on the less "public" occasions. Where his "*Elegie* on the late *Lord William Howard* Baron of Effingham" has a certain stiffness, there is affectionate humor in his lines "On John Dawson, Butler at Christ-Church" and tender respect in the "Elegie Upon the death of his owne Father." In most of C.'s elegies, as in all his best work, there is a directness, even forthrightness, of statement that is often engaging. Only in some rather obsequiously flattering verses addressed to those whose favor he sought does one suspect C. of being less than honest with himself and therefore with his readers. C. was not possessed of an especially subtle or profound mind, but his energy and his enjoyment of life are very attractive and his poems, though slight, have both literary and historical interest.

BIBLIOGRAPHY: Bennett, J. A. W, and H. R. Trevor-Roper, eds., *The Poems of R. C.* (1955); Bradford, M. E., "The Prescience of R. C.: Observations on 'The Faeries' Farewell,'" *SR* 81 (1973): 309–17; Brooks, C., *Historical Evidence and the Reading of Seventeenth-Century Poetry* (1991)

GLYN PURSGLOVE

CORELLI, Marie

(pseud. of Mary Mackay) b. April or May 1855, London; d. 24 April 1924, Stratford-on-Avon

C. shrouded her birth in mystery. She earned celebrity with her novel *A Romance of Two Worlds* (1886), followed by a string of best-selling romances: *Vendetta!; or, The Story of One Forgotten* (3 vols.,1886), *Thelma* (3 vols., 1887), *Ardath* (1889), *The Soul of Lilith* (3 vols., 1892), *Barabbas* (3 vols., 1893), *The Sorrows of Satan* (1895), considered to be her best work, and several others. Incorporating in much of her fiction her fascination with mysticism and occultism, C. employed a wide range of literary genres including ROMANCE, the Gothic, SCIENCE FICTION, and SATIRE. Queen Victoria was a passionate admirer, convinced C.'s work would be of lasting value. Fashion turned against C. after her death, but latterly biographers have praised C. as an early feminist and protoconservationist.

CORNWALL, Barry. See PROCTER, Bryan Waller

CORYATE, Thomas

b. 1577?, Odcombe, Somersetshire; d. December 1617, Surat, India

C. is remembered for *Coryate's Crudities* (1611), an account of his walking tour in northern Europe over five months, an entertaining period piece, prefaced by verses from celebrated contemporary poets. In the same year, C. published *Coryate's Crumb,* a further installment of his travels. In October 1612, C. began a second tour of Greece, the Middle East, and India, collecting languages on the way. In 1616, some of his letters home appeared under the title *Letters from Asmere, the Court of the Great Mogul.* On being presented, C. addressed the Mogul in Persian. Notes of his travels were later published in part in Samuel PURCHAS's *Hakluytus Postumus; or, Purchas His Pilgrimes.*

COTTON, Charles

b. 28 April 1630, Beresford, Staffordshire; d. 16 February 1687, London

C. made interesting contributions to English literature in three areas: as a poet, as a prose writer, and as a translator. In C.'s work as a poet it is perhaps his presentation of rural subjects that is most striking. These were the poems William WORDSWORTH admired, and that Samuel Taylor COLERIDGE (in his *Biographia Literaria*) described as "replete with every excellence of thought, image, and passion," while praising their naturalness of expression. The greater part of C.'s life was lived at the family home of Beresford Hall, by the River Dove. He declared himself never entirely happy save when at Beresford, and it must have given him particular pain that through the financial carelessness of his father and himself the estate was heavily laden with debt. C.'s knowledge of the countryside around Beresford was intimate, the fruit of a working life and long experience. So, in writing his "Morning Quatrains" or his "Winter Quatrains," C. moves far beyond the conventionalities of literary pastoral. The bustle of morning activity is vivaciously recorded, as "the Fore-horse gingles on the Road" and "the Field with busie People snies." Accuracy of observation is everywhere enlivened by delightful fancy, as when, in the setting sun of evening "the Shadows now so long do grow, / That Brambles like tall Cedars show,/ . . . and the Ant/Appears a monstrous Elephant."

Reared in the disturbed (and disturbing) years of the Civil War, C. valued the meditative solitude of the country life. In "The Retirement," he writes persuasively (almost rapturously, indeed) of the peace and innocence to be found among his "beloved Rocks" and rivers, where he can enjoy "Solitude, the Soul's best Friend." The pleasures of the retired country life were not, however, C.'s only poetic subject. He wrote the epistles and elegies to friends and acquaintances, celebrating births and commemorating deaths or praising poems and pictures, that those of royalist sympathies regularly exchanged among themselves, assertions of community when "bleak winds confine us home" (the bleakness being as often political as meteorological). He wrote a variety of poems on love (often influenced by French models); they include Pindaric Odes in the manner of Abraham COWLEY, some songs in the best Caroline manner, some exquisite octosyllabic sonnets, and some mildly cynical praises of promiscuity in a more obviously Restoration idiom. His drinking songs contain some rollicking praises of wine but are marked by a somewhat desperate desire to avoid troubling thoughts. A more straightforward happiness pervades the 1,500 lines of "The Wonders of the Peake," a celebration of the landscape C. loved so much, consistently engaging in manner, its couplet rhymes often highly adroit. During C.'s lifetime, little of this verse was published. Most of it had to wait for the publication of *Poems on Several Occasions* (1689) two years after the poet's death, a rather carelessly produced volume (even now there is no really satisfactory edition of C.'s work). Such contemporary reputation as C. had as a poet depended on his work as a writer of burlesques, most notably in *Scarronides* (1664; rev. ed., 1670), which presents books 1 and 4 of Virgil's *Aeneid* in bouncing hudibrastics and resolutely colloquial diction, and in *Burlesque upon burlesque, or the scoffer scofft* (1675), which its title page aptly describes as "some of Lucians dialogues newly put into English fustian."

C. has not, perhaps, been widely read and appreciated as a poet—despite being praised by Wordsworth and Coleridge. One of his prose works, however, has had a great many readers. This was the second part ("Being instructions how to angle for a Trout or Grayling in a clear Stream") that he contributed to his friend Izaak WALTON's *The Compleat Angler* on the publication of its fifth edition in 1676. C.'s continuation is everywhere filled with his love of his native landscape. He celebrates his beloved Dove, from its modest source—"a contemptible Fountain (which I can cover with my Hat)"—through its growth to navigable depth and its disappearance into the larger Trent. His affectionate respect for the much older Walton is clear, and the work's serenity of mood reflects C.'s capacity to rise above his very real difficulties. Other gentlemanly pleasures are the subject of another of C.'s most engaging prose works, *The Compleat Gamester* (1674). In it, C. is careful to warn his readers against excessive gambling, while writing entertainingly of a variety of card games, of billiards and bowls, chess and dice, as well as outdoor pursuits such as archery and riding. C.'s lively, unpretentious prose makes the whole an engaging piece of social history.

As a translator, C.'s most substantial achievement is undoubtedly his fine version of Montaigne's *Essays* (3 vols., 1685–86), which has often been reprinted. It is a generally accurate translation, though (in the manner of his day) C. feels free to add a number of interpolations of his own. Like Montaigne himself, C. has elements both stoic and epicurean in his make-up and the result is a translation in which one feels a real bond of sympathy between translator and translated. C.'s earlier translation of Corneille's *Horace* (1671) offers a similar blend of faithfulness and freedom, and his use of the heroic couplet is often subtly effective. Many of his other translations, like that of Guillaume du Vair's *Morall Philosophy of the Stoicks* (1664), are assured and lucid, C.'s prose avoiding all stylistic excesses without ever being merely bland.

C. was an English country gentleman, in whom knowledge of country life (in 1675 he published *The Planter's Manual*) was combined with wide literary knowledge. His family had long literary associations; poets such as Richard LOVELACE and Robert HERRICK, John FLETCHER, and Sir William DAVENANT were family friends. Out of his love of literature and of a particular area of England, C. wrote works, in prose and verse, that capture to perfection the ideals and attitudes of a particular phase of English society.

BIBLIOGRAPHY: Buxton, J., *A Tradition of Poetry* (1967); Grigson, G., *C. C.* (1975); Rostvig, M.-S., *The Happy Man: Studies in the Metamorphoses of a Classical Ideal, 1600–1700* (1954)

GLYN PURSGLOVE

COUNTERCULTURE AND LITERATURE

A remarkably diverse range of texts can be associated with British counterculture, to a certain extent defying categorization. They range from texts that document more or less realistically the lifestyle of a disaffected underclass or dissenting bohemia, to texts that can be identified with an indigenous tradition of the fantastic or the Gothic, generic modes conventionally situated outside the literary canon. Of course, the two strands frequently overlap, and from the 1960s onward this cross-fertilization of fantasy and REALISM can be regarded as one of the distinguishing features of British countercultural writing, embodied in writers as diverse as Angela CARTER and Irvine WELSH.

The plural term "subcultures" is perhaps more appropriate in relation to Britain than "counterculture," as it suggests the possible coexistence of a variety of underground groups rather than a straightforward dichotomy between counterculture and the mainstream. In the postwar period, Britain developed numerous home-grown "spectacular" subcultures, such as the

Teddy Boys of the 1950s, the Mods and Rockers of the 1960s, Punk in the 1970s, and Goth in the 1980s. "Swinging London" became the cultural center of the 1960s, while Manchester was nicknamed "Madchester" in the early 1990s. Counterculture was, however, often a suburban rather than urban phenomenon, with writers attempting to capture the boredom and frustration of a provincial environment. The Center for Contemporary Cultural Studies at Birmingham University, or "Birmingham School," was responsible for identifying and theorizing "subculture" in the 1970s, often focusing on what they saw as examples of working-class rebellion. However, recent theorists like Sarah Thornton have problematized this definition, suggesting that alternative culture throws conventional class divisions into question and generates its own hierarchies.

Counterculture in the sense it is now understood, as a self-conscious, articulate entity, emerged after the end of World War II, arising from the particular combination of cultural conditions in late-1940s and 1950s Britain. It is possible, however, to identify 19th-c. precedents that subsequently influenced later writers, and accrued countercultural significance through the way in which they were read by succeeding generations. The Romantic poets, particularly Samuel Taylor COLERIDGE and William BLAKE, were regarded as protopsychedelic visionaries and proponents of a countercultural lifestyle, as was Thomas DE QUINCEY. *Confessions of an English Opium-Eater* recounts De Quincey's early life living among the prostitutes and destitute of London's Oxford Street, and the ensuing illness that led to his partaking of opium for medical purposes, and ultimately, his addiction. It is the first literary evocation of the vivid hallucinations, and terrible agonies, of the opium addict. Lewis CARROLL received similar revisionary readings: *Alice's Adventures in Wonderland* and *Through the Looking-Glass* were retrospectively championed by the psychedelic generation of the 1960s and 1970s, who saw in their distorted logic and childlike sense of enhanced awareness a potent metaphor for psychedelic experience.

The Victorian period saw an increased awareness of a deprived and often criminal urban underworld, with its own fashions, slang, and customs. Midcentury, the journalist Henry MAYHEW investigated the street people of London, identifying what he called the "wandering tribes" of the city. The growing concern with the underworld of the metropolis was countered by the idealization of preindustrial Britain in the medieval revivalism of the Pre-Raphaelites. While not countercultural in the contemporary sense, the Pre-Raphaelites did demonstrate some features of later movements in the relaxed sexual attitudes and bohemian lifestyle of central figures such as Dante Gabriel ROSSETTI and A. C. SWINBURNE, and in their associ-

ates' adoption of Aesthetic Dress, a form of antifashion copied in part from medieval paintings. These two apparently contradictory worlds were brought together by Oscar WILDE in *The Picture of Dorian Gray*. The physically perfect Dorian implicitly sells his soul in order to remain eternally beautiful while his portrait decays in his stead; he subsequently flits between a world of highly charged, fashionable aestheticism and the opium dens of the East End in his spiraling descent into corruption. Coded references to a secret homosexual underworld were supposedly detected in the novel by some contemporary readers, and the novel was cited as evidence of Wilde's depravity at his trial.

In the early decades of the 20th c., Jean RHYS produced a series of novels portraying the life of women inhabiting the Parisian *demi-monde*, flitting between a succession of transient and ill-paid jobs, and roaming the streets of Paris in a problematically feminine incarnation of Charles Baudelaire's *flaneur*. *Good Morning Midnight* places its down-at-heel protagonist, Sasha Jensen, in a world of cheap hotels and sordid sexual encounters, shared by artists, immigrants, and gigolos. The first-person narrative is steeped in the rhythms of the alcoholic. A similar evocation of the alcoholic's world was created by Patrick Hamilton in *Hangover Square* (1941) and Malcolm LOWRY in *Under the Volcano*. Elsewhere, narcotics were the main focus. The notorious Aleister Crowley implicitly celebrated his own predilection for heroin and cocaine as well as black magic in *The Diary of a Drug-Fiend*, published in 1921. Aldous HUXLEY described his experiments with mescaline in the influential *The Doors of Perception*, published in 1954, which text set the trend for proclaiming Blakeian influence.

The 1950s were characterized by the emergence of the "Angry Young Man" and "kitchen sink" realism, both of which left their mark on countercultural fictions. John OSBORNE encapsulated both in his drama *Look Back in Anger*, in which the protagonist Jimmy Porter is the archetypal Angry Young Man: an articulate, jazz-playing graduate who works on a sweet-stall and rails against class, social convention, and his marriage. The gritty domestic realism of the kitchen sink drama was transferred to the novel in Alan SILLITOE's *Saturday Night and Sunday Morning*, in which the young factory-worker Arthur Seaton lives for the hedonism of the weekend, rejecting traditional moral values and fraudulent political systems. Colin WILSON provided a philosophical justification for these angry young men with *The Outsider*, suggesting that the man of genius has always been alienated from his contemporaries. It is perhaps worth noting the relative absence of Angry Young Women writing countercultural literature: presumably rebellious women of the postwar period tended to be absorbed into the burgeoning feminist movement, as countercultural texts remain a markedly male-dominated domain. In this respect at least, the counterculture appears to replicate the conditions of the mainstream culture it otherwise rejects.

The most significant countercultural writer from the 1950s is perhaps Colin MacINNES, whose London Trilogy, comprising *City of Spades*, *Absolute Beginners*, and *Mr. Love and Justice*, described the city's vibrant, multiracial underworld, composed of homosexuals, pimps, teenagers, and poets. *Absolute Beginners*, his best-known novel, describes a world of jazz, coffee shops, and sexual freedom in which teenagers possess a new economic power and a new sense of liberty from the constraints of their parents' generation. However, this freedom is soured by a backdrop of racial tension that ultimately erupts in violence. Sam SELVON covered similar ground from a black perspective in *The Lonely Londoners*, describing the difficult and often impoverished lives of West Indian immigrants in London in the period.

The 1960s saw a new wave of countercultural literature in Britain. At the beginning of the decade, Anthony BURGESS's *A Clockwork Orange* used an experimental lexicon derived largely from Russian in order to portray a gang of disaffected youths whose favoured pastimes are listening to Beethoven and practicing "ultraviolence." The novel is set in the future, but the lawless activities of Alex and his droogs reflect contemporary fears about teenage gangs and the reputed violence of the Teddy Boys. Although Alex's behavior is shown to be reprehensible, the state apparatus that attempts to brainwash him into submissiveness is portrayed as even more so, with Burgess arguing persuasively for the importance of freedom of moral choice. John FOWLES problematized the myth of the Angry Young Man in *The Collector*, in which the lower-middle-class male protagonist abducts and imprisons an upper-middle-class bohemian art student, Miranda. Countercultural activity is presented not as lower-class rebellion, but as a privilege that can only be enjoyed by those with the education and financial advantages that enable them to drop out.

As the decade progressed, Angela Carter's "Bristol Trilogy"—*Shadow Dance*, *Several Perceptions*, and *Love*—dissected the bohemian underclass of provincial Britain, incorporating both Gothic and fantastic elements. *Several Perceptions* in particular describes a kind of sixties "happening" taking place in a labyrinthine Gothic mansion, at which the sense of the fantastic is partially provided by the decor and the costumes of the guests, and partly by miraculous occurrences such as a lame girl learning to walk. *Love*, on the other hand, depicts the burnout of sixties idealism through the nervous breakdown and suicide of its heroine, Annabel. *Heroes and Villains*, which presents its Barbarians in hippy-inspired costumes and led by a Timothy Leary-like shaman, has more in common with the speculative fiction of J. G. BALLARD. Ballard characteristically extrapolates his fiction from disturbing tendencies in contemporary life: his notorious *Crash*, for example, depicts the lives of individuals who derive erotic stimulation from car accidents.

The influence of Punk in the late 1970s initiated a more nihilistic trend in countercultural literature, heralded by the release of the Sex Pistols' single "Anarchy in the UK" in November 1976. Iain BANKS caused immense controversy with the publication of *The Wasp Factory*, in many ways a traditional Gothic tale about madness and the perils of playing God, which nevertheless was received by many critics as an unremittingly sadistic and offensive text. Banks's antihero Frank enjoys getting drunk and watching Punk bands at the weekends, but his other pastimes include torturing animals, murdering his young relatives and constructing elaborate rituals from dead animal parts, bodily fluids and his arsenal of homemade weapons. However, the cause of Frank's nastiness ultimately lies with the warped hippy experimentalism of his eccentric father. Scots writers take an increasing prominence in countercultural literature from this period onward: James KELMAN caused similar controversy when he was awarded the Booker Prize for *How late it was, how late*. Critics were shocked by his harsh language and unrelenting focus on the lowest strata of society. As in previous works such as *Not Not while the Giro*, *A Chancer*, and *A Disaffection*, Kelman focused on Glasgow's dispossessed during the Thatcher era and its continuing legacy. His distinctive stream of consciousness style makes use of the indigenous rhythms of Glaswegian speech and slips in and out of realism and fantasy. Also based in Glasgow is Alasdair GRAY, whose EPIC *Lanark* juxtaposes the city with its fantastic mirror image, the surreal metropolis Unthank. Gray characteristically experiments with mixing genres and typefaces, creating fiction that is at once intensely literary and yet firmly outside the literary establishment.

Despite the confrontational nature of Banks's and Kelman's writing, which seems consonant with the iconoclastic and often deliberately offensive attitude of Punk, the scene itself seemed resistant to fictionalization. It makes a rare fictional appearance in *The Buddha of Suburbia*, in which Hanif KUREISHI charts the transition between Glam Rock and Punk through the character of Charlie, based on the Punk musician Billy Idol. The novel's protagonist, the half-Indian, half-white Karim, negotiates 1970s suburbia with more difficulty, his relationship with various subcultures problematized by his mixed-race identity. Martin Millar also demonstrates the legacy of Punk in his comic novels about South London squat culture: *Lux the Poet* (1989) and *Dreams of Sex and Stage Diving* (1994) gently parody their Punkish protagonists, exposing their selfishness and delusions of grandeur while celebrating the New Age/Crusty scene they belong to. Punk's major textual legacy, however, was perhaps the development of the fanzine. Cheap, self-published texts sporting the opinions and reviews of their editors, fanzines expanded the Punk DIY ethos from music to writing. Fanzines have continued to be responsible for the discussion and spread of subcultures, and in recent years have often transferred to the format of the webpage or Internet site.

The 1980s also witnessed the rejuvenation of the graphic novel through writers such as Alan Moore and Neil Gaiman. Moore challenged the notion that comics were for kids by dealing with adult subjects, thus inspiring a "Recommended for Mature Readers" label. This permitted comic writers not only to incorporate more explicit material but also to target a new audience appreciative of complex ideas, literary allusions and self-referential ironies. Moore's *V for Vendetta* (1982–95) and *Watchmen* (1986–87) and Gaiman's *The Sandman* cycle (1988–96) gained both critical acclaim and cult status, presenting highly literate, intertextual narratives in the comic format. Both writers showed the influence of Gothic fiction, reflecting the British Goth subculture of the 1980s. This was in itself a highly literate subculture whose adherents structured their personas around literary and cinematic reference points, particularly Bram STOKER's *Dracula* and its numerous film adaptations. Two of the principal characters in *The Sandman*, Morpheus or Dream and his elder sister, the perennially cheerful Death, take their dress sense directly from Goth subculture, while Gaiman's multilayered text reflects many of the conventions of Gothic fiction, as well as rewriting classical myth, William SHAKESPEARE, and John MILTON. Moore's writing often flirts more overtly with the occult, and *From Hell*, published in 1989, offers a historiographic metafiction based on the Jack the Ripper mystery, strongly flavored with arcane lore. In this, he closely resembles his associate Iain Sinclair, whose poetry, novels, and essays construct contemporary London as a palimpsest through which traces of a murky past are continually glimpsed. In *Lud Heat* (1975), *White Chappell, Scarlet Tracings* (1987), *Downriver* (1991), and *Lights Out for the Territory* (1997), Sinclair wanders through the city's darker corners, revealing its dirty underbelly.

The so-called Second Summer of Love of 1988, in which acid house music and the concomitant use of the drug Ecstasy swept the U.K., produced a renaissance in British countercultural writing, embodied in the so-called Repetitive Beat Generation. Although noted for their espousal of hedonism, this generation of writers was politicized by the Criminal Justice Act of 1994, which outlawed unlicensed public gatherings and amplified music with repetitive beats, in an effort to curb illicit raves.

The most prominent among these writers is Welsh, whose novel *Trainspotting* achieved massive commercial success both in its own right and in its film incarnation. The novel depicts the lives of junkies living on an Edinburgh housing estate, narrated in regional dialect. Bleak, amoral and blackly humorous, it presents the political problems underlying heroin abuse as well as the personal horrors of its victims. In *Morvern Callar* (1995), Alan Warner also makes use of Scots dialect in order to capture the idiosyncratic voice of the novel's eponymous heroine, who uses her dead boyfriend's money to escape her dead-end job in a Highlands supermarket and discover rave culture in the Mediterranean. Alternatively, Jeff Noon is based in Manchester and uses the city as a setting for chemically inspired speculative fantasy in the tradition of Ballard, with a heavy debt to cyberpunk. His novels include *Vurt* (1993), *Pollen* (1995), and *Automated Alice* (1996).

Many writers, including Warner, resist the "Repetitive Beat" label, regarding it as another kind of conformity. The question collectively raised by the Repetitive Beat Generation is that of commercialization: whether these novels with their aggressive marketing and massive mainstream success can really be called countercultural. If not, it is perhaps because the relationship between counterculture and the mainstream has shifted irrevocably in the 1990s: protest and disaffection have become marketable commodities, and the majority of the writers cited above have acquired "cult" status or become fixtures on university syllabuses. It remains to be seen whether future generations of writers will find new means of writing outside the literary and political establishment.

BIBLIOGRAPHY: Bracewell, M., *England Is Mine* (1998); Calcutt, A., and R. Shephard, *Cult Fiction: A Reader's Guide* (1998); Gelder, K., and S. Thornton, *The Subcultures Reader* (1997); Hitchcock, P., *Working-Class Fiction in Theory and Practice: A Reading of Alan Sillitoe* (1989); Plant, S., *Writing on Drugs* (1999); Redhead, S., *Repetitive Beat Generation* (1999); Sage, L., ed., *Flesh and the Mirror: Essays on the Art of Angela Carter* (1994); Thornton, S., *Club Cultures* (1995)

CATHERINE SPOONER

COVENTRY, Francis
b. 15? July 1725, Mill End, Buckinghamshire; bur. 9 January 1759, Little Stanmore

Educated at Magdalene College, Cambridge, C. was an ordained clergyman whose promising career as a man of letters was cut short by his premature death at age twenty-four. C.'s first published work was the topographical poem *Penshurst* (1750), reprinted in Robert DODSLEY's *A Collection of Poems.* C. is best known for his novel entitled *The History of Pompey the Little; or, The Life and Adventures of a Lap-Dog* (1751), narrated by a lapdog with a beady eye on his successive owners. Written in imitation of Henry FIELDING, the novel was an immediate success and remained popular for much of the early 19th c. before falling into oblivion. Despite the fragmentary structure of the novel, *Pompey the Little* offers a comic and often satiric vision of 18th-c. society.

COWARD, [Sir] Noël [Pierce]
b. 16 December 1899, Teddington, Middlesex; d. 26 March 1973, Blue Harbour, Jamaica

As playwright, composer, director, actor, despite a calculated playboy image, C. was always the hardworking professional. His versatility and prolific output militated against critical recognition. "So I made do," he said, "with the bitter palliative of commercial success." This epigrammatic reaction, turning away disappointment while summarizing a complex idea—the contrast between popular and critical esteem and the mismatch between financial and aesthetic reward—was characteristic. In two revealing scenes, from *Present Laughter* (1943) and *South Sea Bubble* (1956), a creative character puts down a bore who advises the artist on how to make his work more "significant." C.'s theatrical peers called him "the Master," without sycophancy or facetiousness. His plays continue to be revived and his reputation grows with every production.

Four of his satirical comedies, light on the surface but with a tough common sense beneath, improve on each rereading. In *Hay Fever* (1925), a family who pride themselves on their cultured insouciance are gradually exposed as egocentric pseudo-intellectuals. The audience is maneuvered from initial affection for their self-conscious charm to sympathy with their hapless guests. *Private Lives* (1930) is a cyclic, unresolved study of the pains of physical passion, the plight of the couple who can live happily neither together nor apart. The protagonist of *Blithe Spirit* (1941), an author researching spiritualism for a forthcoming novel, finds the ghost of his first wife coexisting in his house with his flesh-and-blood second, and comes to a painful recognition of the difference between youthful and middle-aged love. *Present Laughter*, which contains echoes of Molière's *Alceste*, presents in comic mode the interruptions which distract the artist from his work.

His initial great success was *The Vortex* (perf., 1924; pub. 1925), a serious drama of drug dependency with hints of sexual deviance. During the 1920s, C. produced and appeared in several revues entirely of his own composition, with words and music, songs whose titles have become proverbial: "Don't Put Your Daughter on the Stage, Mrs. Worthington"; "Poor Little Rich Girl"; "Mad About the Boy"; "I've Been to a *Marvellous* Party"; "Mad Dogs and Englishmen." C. characteristically makes skilful use of anapaestic rhythms. The song "If Love Were All," from the full-length romantic musical *Bitter-Sweet* (1929), contains the line often thought to be self-referential: "The most I've had is just a talent to amuse." *Easy Virtue* (perf. 1925; pub 1926) reflects the social changes of the 1920s, as *Relative Values* (perf. 1951) does those of the 1950s: a young nobleman wants to marry a Hollywood star who turns out to be the sister of his mother's faithful lady's maid. The satirical *Design for Living* (1933) is about a triangular relationship between a woman and her two male lovers, who are involved with each other. In 1936, C. produced the cycle of one-act plays, *Tonight at 8.30*, to be performed over three nights as a vehicle for himself and Gertrude Lawrence, with whom he had starred in *Private Lives.* He had diversified into other modes: the World War I ghost drama *Post Mortem* (1931); the patriotic family cycle *Cavalcade* (1931). *Suite in Three Keys* (1966) is a serious exploration of relationships viewed retrospectively in maturity. The trilogy is frank and moving, but it is on the exquisitely crafted comedies that C.'s reputation rests.

BIBLIOGRAPHY: Gray, F., *N. C.* (1987); Lahr, J., *C. the Playwright* (1983); Lesley, C., *The Life of N. C.* (1976; repub. as *Remembered Laughter*, 1976); Morley, S., *A Talent to Amuse* (1969)

MICHAEL GROSVENOR MYER

COWLEY, Abraham
b. 1618, London; d. 28 July 1667, Chertsey, Surrey

Fluctuations in C.'s reputation suggest the extraordinary range of his literary production. Although famous in his day as the author of love poems that, in John DRYDEN's oft-quoted description, imitate John DONNE by "affect[ing] the metaphysical," C. was better known in the post-Newtonian 18th c. as one of the founders of the Royal Society and the author of a six-book Latin EPIC on the history of plants. Having introduced the vogue in Pindaric ode writing that fostered the English interest in the sublime, C. was praised by Dryden as the reformer of English verse. But today he is best remembered as John MILTON's immediate precursor in the attempt to write a sacred epic that was also capable of commenting upon contemporary political events.

Born to the family of a prosperous London stationer, C. attended Westminster School as a king's scholar and Trinity College, Cambridge, as a "dry chorister." He was celebrated in his youth for his precocity, popularly thought to have published *Poetical*

Blossoms (1633; rev. eds., 1636, 1637) at age thirteen (he was actually fifteen); his play *The Guardian* (perf. 1642; pub. 1650) was chosen by university authorities to honor visiting Prince Charles. Ejected from his Cambridge fellowship by the Puritan faction shortly after completing his M.A., C. entered the employ of Henrietta Maria's secretary, Henry Jermyn, and accompanied the queen into exile in France, where he remained nearly ten years. His royalist loyalties color such works as *A Satire against Separatists* (1642) and *The Civil War*, a celebration of Charles I as a contemporary epic hero that C. was forced to abandon when the king's defeat at Newbury made it clear that the royalist cause could not succeed. Long thought lost, the poem was rediscovered and published in 1973.

While in the queen's service, C. wrote courtierlike love poems and witty compliments that would be collected in the highly popular *The Mistress* (1647) and *Poems* (1656). But the great product of C.'s royalist years is *Davideis*, begun around 1651 and abandoned in 1654. Subtitled "A Sacred Poem of the Troubles of David," C. uses the biblical story of David's rise to the kingship and successful defense of himself against persecution by Saul to comment upon how the divinely created order of the cosmos is disrupted by human envy and other unruly passions such as manifested themselves during the recent Civil Wars. David is the poet whose song restores order and harmony, and the friend of Jonathan and lover of Michal who, unlike Saul, is incapable of experiencing envy. The glorification of the martyred Charles in the person of beleaguered David apparently proved difficult to sustain, and C. completed only four of the projected twelve books. Returning to England in 1654, C. was arrested and imprisoned as a "malignant" (that is, an unreconstructed royalist), even while compromising himself in royalist eyes by publicly asserting that royalists needed to accept the king's defeat and subsequent execution as the will of God and go on with their lives, a statement for which he was never forgiven by the restored Charles II.

After turning to medicine, C. retired to live in the country where he concentrated on writing *Planetarum* (1662–68), a six-book Latin epic on the life of plants that reveals a providential design in the natural world, and essays in prose and verse on the Horatian ideal of fulfillment found in rustic solitude. Texts like *A Proposition for the Advancement of Learning* (1661) and poems like "To the Royal Society" expressed his interest in the new science identified with Isaac Newton and offered a practical plan for a philosophical academy such as he had first envisioned in Samuel's College in *Davideis*.

C. represents the paradox of a "poet's poet" who nonetheless enjoyed wide popularity in his lifetime. In poems like "Ode: Of Wit" and the *Davideis*, C. evidences an absorption with the nature and function of poetry, as well as a self-consciousness about how he presents himself as a poet. Significantly, Samuel JOHNSON delivered his famous criticism of metaphysical wit in his *Life of C.*, Donne (with whom the criticism is traditionally associated) not being considered important enough to merit inclusion in Johnson's *Lives of the Poets* but C. thought to be a poet of influence. His translations from Anacreon stimulated the poetic rage for the incidental that produced, most famously, most of the poems in Robert HERRICK's *Hesperides*. Milton was indebted to *Davideis* for the example of a Christian epic that spans earth, heaven, and hell, and that considers contemporary human affairs from the perspective of the divine. *Planetarum* was but the first of a long line of 18th-c. poems, like James THOMSON's *The Seasons*, that made science the subject of poetry. And C.'s Pindaric odes became the model for the most popular 18th-c. nonsatiric lyric form, inspiring such works as William COLLINS's *Odes*. Although three hundred years after his death C. is rarely read or studied, his contemporaries thought it appropriate that he be buried in Westminster Abbey between the monuments to Geoffrey CHAUCER and Edmund SPENSER.

BIBLIOGRAPHY: Hinman, R. B., *A. C.'s World of Order* (1960); Nethercot, A. H., *A. C.* (1931; rev. ed., 1967); Trotter, W. D., *The Poetry of A. C.* (1979)

RAYMOND-JEAN FRONTAIN

COWPER, William
b. 26 November 1731, Berkhamsted, Hertfordshire; d. 25 April 1800, East Dereham, Norfolk

C.'s life had more than its share of sorrow and dread, but his works show a good deal of hope and playfulness. He was one of the precursors of two of the great currents in English intellectual life during the 19th c.: the Romantic movement and the Evangelical revival. Like the Romantics, he looked past Alexander POPE to John MILTON as his poetic model, and like them he often wrote either celebrations of nature or examinations of his own sensibility. He for years found solace in the society of evangelicals, and the hymns he produced with John Newton have become a mainstay of Christian hymnody.

C. was the son of a clergyman, but from a long line of distinguished judges, and he himself trained as a lawyer. After Westminster School, he studied law at the Middle Temple, and then transferred to the Inner Temple after being admitted to the bar. His real interests, however, were already literary, and he began publishing essays. For several years his only regular work was in the post of a commissioner of bankrupts. In 1763, however, his uncle Ashley Cowper insisted that C. attempt to qualify as clerk of the journals in the House of Lords and promised that he would sanction C.'s marriage to his cousin Theodora if he was appointed the post. C., however, dreaded appearing before the bar of the house to prove his qualifications and began to suffer increasingly severe bouts of depression and anxiety. After C. made several attempts at suicide, his brother had him admitted to a lunatic asylum, where he remained almost two years.

As he recovered, C. experienced a conversion of the sort described by the growing Evangelical movement, and his experience of faith sustained him for years to come. While living in rural seclusion first at Huntingdon and then at Olney, he came under the influence of Newton, an Evangelical clergyman. Together they wrote *The Olney Hymns* (1779). He also wrote his own spiritual autobiography and later an account of his brother's deathbed conversion, which were published together as *Adelphi* in 1802.

C. underwent another mental crisis after gossip about his relationship with his friend Mary Unwin drove him into an engagement with her. He became convinced that he was inevitably damned, broke his engagement, and, although the religious element always remained present in his work, never again attended church services. He remained under Newton's influence, however, and produced first *Anti-Thelyphthora* (1781), a verse satire on a proposal to allow polygamy, and then the moral satires published in *Poems* (1782) in part to further his friend's views. C. came to use the writing of poetry, as he used his garden and his pets, as a way of keeping despair at bay. The greatest of his works, *The Task* (1785), began as such a distraction. C. complained that he had no subject for a poem in blank verse, and his friend Lady Austen assigned him "the sofa." He began describing the development of the sofa from the three-legged stool, but soon turned to other subjects, always adapting, playfully or seriously, Miltonic diction. His meditations on nature—and on his own condition—became the model for the blank verse meditations and autobiographies of Samuel Taylor COLERIDGE and William WORDSWORTH.

C. became one of the great letter-writers of his age, and sought to rival Pope as a translator of Homer. His blank-verse translation of *The Iliad* and *The Odyssey* appeared in 1791, but did not achieve the success C. hoped for. He then turned to a work on Milton, in which he would save Milton from Samuel JOHNSON, whose life of Milton he detested, as he had tried to save Homer from Pope. That project, however, was abandoned, and C.'s translations of Milton's Latin and Italian poems, together with a fragment of his commentary on *Paradise Lost*, were published only after his death.

In his last years, C. sank beneath his mental illness and the fear that God had rejected him. Nevertheless, he left in poems like "The Castaway" vivid descriptions of the pain he endured—and in his hymns and in *The Task*, evidence not just of his literary skill, but of his capacity for joy.

BIBLIOGRAPHY: Cecil, D., *The Stricken Deer; or, The Life of C.* (1929); King, J., *W. C.* (1986); Quinlan, M. J., *W. C.* (1953); Ryskamp, C., *W. C. of the Inner Temple, Esq.* (1959)

                                     BRIAN ABEL RAGEN

CRABBE, George
b. 24 December 1754, Aldeburgh, Suffolk; d. 3 February 1832, Trowbridge, Wiltshire

Lord BYRON described C. as "nature's sternest painter, yet the best" in *English Bards and Scotch Reviewers* and listed him as one of the poets who, in his opinion, were on the right track in terms of their literary style and approach. C. he thought was free of that "wrong revolutionary poetical system" that Sir Walter SCOTT, Robert SOUTHEY, William WORDSWORTH, Thomas MOORE, Thomas CAMPBELL, and Byron himself were working within. In his 1807 review of C.'s *Poems* of that year, Francis Jeffrey welcomed C.'s seemingly solid challenge to the new system, and set the trend early on for viewing C. as the embodiment of what came to be seen as the anti-Romantic. This view is largely borne out in the stance of much of C.'s poetry.

C.'s upbringing in Aldeburgh, his education in schools at Bungay and Stowmarket in Suffolk, and his apprenticeship years to a village doctor (1768–71) were fundamental in that they supplied the poet with his most central subject matter—village life. This material appears in C.'s work in the well-tried couplets of an earlier poetic school. C. in fact was a great admirer of John DRYDEN—and also of Geoffrey CHAUCER—and was not simply reiterating the practice of the Augustans. His unswerving eye for the harshness of his subjects draws comment from William HAZLITT in *The Spirit of the Age*, who thought of C. as "one of the most popular and admired of our living poets," but did not admire C.'s work as poetry. "Why not insist on the unwelcome reality in plain prose? If our author is a poet, why trouble himself with statistics? If he is a statistic writer, why set his ill news in harsh and grating verse?" C.'s status as poet is still under scrutiny from several perspectives that try to cope with the fact that C. straddles such a span of historical change and blithely runs across artificial historical periodisations.

His earliest poetry was produced around 1768 and a poem with a very moral-sounding title, *Inebriety*, was published in 1775, condemning drink. C. went to London in 1780 in a bid to seek his living as a writer and succeeded in gaining the patronage of Edmund BURKE. He was eventually introduced to such figures as Samuel JOHNSON and Sir Joshua REYNOLDS. Burke also helped him to publish a Popeian disquisition on books, *The Library* (1781), and C. was then advised to become a priest. His chaplainship at Belvoir Castle aided his literary endeavors and *The Village* (1783) was published, having been looked over by both Johnson and Burke.

This poem raised C.'s reputation and demonstrates his theoretical stance—that of the antipastoral writer, the anti-Romantic even, who uses natural detail not to decorate a landscape but to emphasize the accumulation of ills and evils that surround human endeavor as people live in that landscape. C. sought to "paint the cot/As Truth will paint it and as Bards will not." There is a direct painterly link in his work with the Dutch genre scenes of the 17th c. or with the botanist's taxonomic sketchbook (C. was a compulsive botanizer), where every detail, however stark or unpleasant, features.

C. lived at Muston in Leicestershire from 1789 to 1814, and from about 1789 to 1806 he published little until the volume of *Poems* (1807) containing "Sir Eustace Grey," "The Parish Register," "The Hall of Justice," and other earlier poems. The new works revealed C.'s abilities in narrative poetry and his facility with different types of verse form.

C.'s most famous production is the 1810 volume *The Borough: A Poem in Twenty-Four Letters*, which begins with the "General Description" of the Aldeburgh-like east coast town and which develops satirically into accounts of social events and professions in that area. His portraits of individuals though are the most striking parts of this poem. Here, we find C.'s "Blaney," "The Parish Clerk," "Benbow," and his story of "Peter Grimes" (Letter 22) and some confirmation of C.'s debt to Chaucer. Grimes himself is the haunted abuser of children who suffers torment when the ghosts of his victims return in a piece of profoundly Gothic writing. "I fix'd my eyes/On the mid stream and saw the spirits rise;/I saw my father on the water stand,/And hold a thin pale boy in either hand."

C.'s handling of couplet verse in this volume and the general pungency of his tone seemed to have sharpened considerably. C. followed this success with *Tales in Verse* (1812), twenty-one poems (with epigraphs from William SHAKESPEARE) that stand individually without narrative links, and show the destructive nature of human passions and desires. The tone can be moralizing, but not to excess, and HUMOR is also present, especially in numbers 1 and 6, "The Dumb Orators" and "The Frank Courtship."

Tales of the Hall (2 vols., 1819) is C.'s last important work, similar in structure to *Tales in Verse*, where in Jeffrey's words "Two brothers, both past middle age, meet together, for the first time since their infancy, in the Hall of their native parish . . . and the Tales are told in the after-dinner tête-à-têtes." Critics

see a decline in quality in this volume and a lack of care over the verse.

BIBLIOGRAPHY: Dalrymple-Champneys, N., and A. Pollard, eds., *G. C.: The Complete Poetical Works* (3 vols., 1988); Edgecombe, R. S., *Theme, Embodiment, and Structure in the Poetry of G. C.* (1983); Pollard, A., *C.* (1972)

CHRISTOPHER J. P. SMITH

CRACE, Jim
b. 1 March 1946, Brocket Hall, Lemsford, Herefordshire

C.'s first two novels deal with the theme of change—of modernity encroaching upon traditional societies. *Continent* (1986) is a collection of seven short stories, all set on a fictional continent, a somewhat primitive land. All the stories deal in some way with the tension between tradition and superstition on the one hand and modernity and progress on the other. Similarly, *The Gift of Stones* (1988) focuses on a tribe of stonecutters at the advent of the Bronze Age. The style of both novels, particularly *Continent*, is reminiscent of the work of Franz Kafka—deceptively simple prose and stories that verge on the allegorical.

The theme of modernity encroaching upon traditional life is renewed in *Arcadia* (1991), which focuses on the tension between the city and the countryside. *Signals of Distress* (1994) displays a bit more HUMOR than the earlier works, specifically through the buffoonish protagonist, Aymer Smith. Set in 1836, the novel tells the story of a group of sailors and passengers who are temporarily marooned in the west England port of Wherrytown. Although Aymer Smith is motivated by good intentions—for example, his intense belief in abolition leads him to free an African slave (with questionable consequences), his pedantry and self-righteousness undermine his laudable actions. Again in this novel, however, C. portrays a clash between traditional values and modernizers. *Quarantine* (1997) tells the story of a group of pilgrims, including Jesus Christ, who travel into the desert in search of spiritual renewal. Jesus is presented as the most fanatical of the pilgrims, denying himself food and water for the entire forty day period. Contrary to Scripture, however, C.'s Jesus dies in the desert. The main character of the novel is the decidedly nonspiritual Musa, an obese trader who has been stranded in the desert; he quickly surmises that the pilgrims can be exploited for financial gain and, at the novel's end, we sense that Musa will make use of his marketing gifts to exploit the story of the mystical madman Jesus.

Being Dead (1999) begins with the brutal murder of its protagonists, a middle-aged married couple, and then proceeds to unfold three separate narrative strands: one dealing with the decay and eventual discovery of the murder victims; another recounting the events of the day that culminated in the murders; and a third that goes back to the protagonists' first romantic encounter and the dark events surrounding it. In this novel, C.'s eye for detail and his journalistic skill at exposition serve him well, especially in his graphic but engaging description of the effects of death on living organisms. C.'s recent publication *The Devil's Larder* (2001) consists of a series of short sketches all dealing somehow with the subject of food. Overall, C. must be regarded as one of the most inventive and unpredictable of contemporary British authors.

BIBLIOGRAPHY: Moseley, M., "J. C.," in Moseley, M., ed., *British Novelists since 1960*, Fourth Series, *DLB* 231 (2000): 84–93

CRAIK, [Mrs.] Dinah Maria

b. 20 April 1826, Stoke-on-Trent; d. 12 October 1887, Bromley

Daughter of Thomas Mulock, an eccentric religious enthusiast of Irish extraction, C. married a publisher. Her best-selling novel, *John Halifax, Gentleman* (3 vols., 1856), was widely read until mid-20th c. A Bildungsroman, it is narrated by a sickly male friend of the hero, who rises from rags to riches, though he turns out to be of gentle blood. The character of John's blind daughter Muriel, who dies before reaching twelve, was formerly much loved. The narrator's father is a Victorian Puritan fundamentalist, who hates the arts and regards the theater as the ultimate exemplar of wickedness, and the friendship with John is liberating. A feebler example of the "condition of England" novels by Benjamin DISRAELI, Charles KINGSLEY, Charles DICKENS, and Elizabeth Cleghorn GASKELL, it glorifies the bourgeois businessman and shows the nobility as grasping and decadent. The reader is invited to share the distress of a mother whose sons both fall in love with the family governess, deceitful daughter of a French revolutionary. C.'s first novel was *The Ogilvies* (3 vols., 1849), followed by *Olive* (3 vols., 1850). *Agatha's Husband* (3 vols., 1853) is about marital misunderstandings: an orphaned heiress marries her guardian's younger brother. He knows, though she does not, that the guardian has defrauded her, but keeps silent for the honor of the family. Other novels included *A Life for a Life* (3 vols., 1859), *Christian's Mistake* (1865), *The Woman's Kingdom* (3 vols., 1869), and *Young Mrs. Jardine* (3 vols., 1879). C . also published essays and poetry.

CRASHAW, Richard

b. October? 1612, London; d. 21 August 1649, Loreto, Italy

Although C. was born into a staunchly Protestant family, he was deeply involved in the Laudian restoration at Cambridge, and when the Puritans took over the university, he fled in 1643, an action that may have helped drive him from the Anglican Church into the Roman Catholic Church. After a decade of religious tutelage at Cambridge, C. was ripe for a further spiritual journey that eventually took him to Rome in 1646 where he worked for Cardinal Palotto. But a few short years later on a pilgrimage to Loreto, he contracted a fever and died.

Most of his poetry reflects his intense spirituality. Although some early poems were penned to the usual Renaissance mistress, by the time of his first book, *Epigrammatum Sacrorum Liber* (1634), it was evident that C.'s poetry concerned mostly the supernatural and humankind's relation to it. He had a deep respect for the poetry of George HERBERT and titled his second book *Steps to the Temple* (1646) in homage to Herbert's *The Temple*, but his poetry, aside from its religious themes, has little in common stylistically with Herbert's crisp verses. He has sometimes been considered a link between Herbert and Henry VAUGHAN, but he has little more in common with the consummate mysticism of the Silurist poet than he does with the loyal Anglicanism of Herbert.

C. has often been listed among the metaphysical poets, but he does not sound or read much like John DONNE or Andrew MARVELL: his lyrics are much more readily accessible than either of those two quintessential metaphysicals. On the other hand, he has never really been considered a Cavalier poet, yet his imagery is often lush, and he in fact borrowed erotic images from Thomas CAREW's "A Rapture" for his own poem "On a prayer booke sent to Mrs. M. R." He is the only English 17th-c. poet to be called "baroque" because his poems tend to be filigreed with fancy images, sometimes to the point of absurdity. The poems on St. Teresa of Avila and Mary Magdalene are particularly suspect, those for Mary Magdalene employing endless variations on images of tears. "The Flaming Heart" was inspired by the Bernini altarpiece in which a cherub aims an arrow at Teresa's heart while she lounges backward in what has often been described as erotic bliss. Although many of his poems are meditative in nature, many have a highly dramatic flavor as well: for example, "Sospetto d'Herode" is almost a play as it follows the story of Herod and the slaughter of the Innocents. Although C. died young, his impact on the development of religious verse in England, though second to Herbert's, has never been questioned.

After his death, another volume of his poems was published under the title *Carmen Deo Nostro* (1652). Included in the book is the beautiful "Hymn in the Holy Nativity," which compares favorably to John MILTON's "Nativity Ode." "Hymn in the Glorious Epiphanie" is an attack on religious idols and ends with a meditation on the Crucifixion. The simple devotion that ripples beneath most of his poetry indicates a mind that was riveted on his own faith and demonstrates a religious tenacity that rivaled the Puritanical fanaticism that he so disliked. Yet the sensuousness of his poetry is anything but Puritan, and it is the quality of his imagery that continues to endear him to modern readers. He understood how to capture pictures in words, and if his rhetoric often seems overblown, readers delight in his obvious ability to relay feelings through poem after poem.

BIBLIOGRAPHY: Roberts, J. R., ed., *New Perspectives on the Life and Art of R. C.* (1990); Wallerstein, R. C., *R. C.* (1935); Warren, A., *R. C.* (1939)

GEORGE KLAWITTER

CROKER, John Wilson

b. 20 December 1780, Galway, Ireland; d. 10 August 1857, St. Albans Bank

Founder of and contributor to the *Quarterly Review*, C. was author of the hostile review of John KEATS's *Endymion*, which Lord BYRON and Percy Bysshe SHELLEY claimed hastened Keats's death. C.'s *Essays on the Early Period of the French Revolution* (1857) was a collection taken from the *Quarterly*. In 1831, C. also published *Military Events of the French Revolution* and in that same year edited James BOSWELL's *Life of Samuel Johnson*. Among C.'s books are *Familiar Epistles to J. F. Jones, Esquire, on the State of the Irish Stage* (1804), published anonymously, and a satire on Dublin society, *An Intercepted Letter from Canton*, published in the same year. In 1809, C. published his poem, "The Battle of Talavera," celebrating the victory over the French earlier that year. C.'s posthumously published diaries, *The Croker Papers* (2 vols., 1884), deal with C.'s political life from 1808 to 1832, when he opposed the Reform Bill, which extended the franchise and which led eventually to universal suffrage. An Anglican Christian and a Tory politician, C. is said to have been the first to use the word "Conservative." He is the original of Rigby in *Coningsby* by Benjamin DISRAELI, and is also caricatured in both Thomas Love PEACOCK's *Melincourt* and Lady MORGAN's *Florence Macarthy.*

CROSS, Victoria

(pseud. of Annie Sophie Cory) b. 1 October 1868, Punjab, India; d. 2 August 1952, Milan, Italy

Notorious in her day as the author of erotic stories of sexual identity, passion, and physical desire, C. emerged as one of the "New Woman" novelists of the 1890s that included writers such as Sarah GRAND and George EGERTON. Her notoriety was established with the publication of "Theodora: A Fragment," which appeared in the January 1895 issue of the *Yellow Book*. In that same year, John Lane published C.'s *The Woman Who Didn't* as a rejoinder to Grant Allen's *The Woman Who Did* (1895). She enhanced her reputation with *Anna Lombard* (1901), *Six Chapters in a Man's Life* (1903), *Life's Shop-Window* (1907), *Five Nights* (1908), adapted as a film in 1915, *The Eternal Fires* (1910), and *The Night of Temptation* (1912). In the early 1920s, C.'s popularity began to decline and her later fiction failed to rejuvenate her career.

CROSSLEY-HOLLAND, Kevin [John William]

b. 7 February 1941, Mursley, Buckinghamshire

The poet and translator C.-H. was educated at Bryanston School and St. Edmund Hall, Oxford (1959–62). Though he failed his first university examination in the subject, he eventually developed a passion for Anglo-Saxon literature. He has worked in publishing, for Macmillan and Victor Gollancz, and has held various academic posts in Britain and the U.S. He was Gregory Fellow in Poetry at the University of Leeds (1969–72), Fulbright Visiting Scholar at St. Olaf College, and Endowed Chair in the Humanities and Fine Arts at the University of St. Thomas. He has lectured in many countries under the auspices of the British Council, and has made a varied range of contributions to radio and television.

C.-H. has written seven collections of poetry, beginning with *The Rain-Giver* (1972), which was followed by *The Dream-House* (1976), *Time's Oriel* (1983), *Waterslain* (1986), *The Painting-Room* (1988), *The Language of Yes* (1996), and *Poems from East Anglia* (1997). He has published two selections of his poetry: *New and Selected Poems 1965–1990* (1991) and *Selected Poems* (2001), but his work has not yet been included in the standard anthologies of 20th-c. poetry. His poems show a concern to link landscape (both historical and topographical) with personal experience. In *Waterslain*, C.-H. wrote memorably of the landscape of East Anglia, and the region has subsequently become the main focus of his later poetry. In addition to this preoccupation with the physical environment, his work focuses on human relationships, especially that between father and child. Much of his poetry is richly musical, depending upon dense patterns of assonance and alliteration, and this appreciation of the sound of language probably has its roots in his extensive knowledge of medieval literature. C.-H. has translated most of the best-known Old English poems, producing modernized versions that are critically acclaimed. His principal publications in this regard are *The Battle of Maldon and Other Old English Poems* (1965) and *Beowulf* (1968), both of which were produced in collaboration with Bruce Mitchell; also *The Exeter Riddle Book* (1978; repub.

as *The Exeter Book of Riddles*, 1979) and *The Old English Elegies* (1988).

C.-H. has also written many works for children, including *The Green Children* (1966), *Green Blades Rising* (1975), and *The Labours of Herakles* (1993). Some of his children's books are inspired or informed by his knowledge of medieval literature, such as the romances *Havelock the Dane* (1964) and *King Horn* (1965), and *Storm and Other Old English Riddles* (1970). Other works such as *The Norse Myths: A Retelling* (1980) and *Tales from the Mabinogion* (1984) reveal his interest in mythology. His diversity of talents is demonstrated by the wide range of creative genres to which he can turn his hand. In addition to poetry, translation, and CHILDREN'S LITERATURE, C.-H. has coauthored (with Ivan Cutting) *The Wuffings* (1999), a play about the birth of East Anglia. He has also produced a work of travel literature, *Pieces of Land* (1972), and a history book, *The Stones Remain* (1989), the latter jointly with Andrew Rafferty. C.-H. has collaborated with a number of composers including Nicola LeFanu, with whom he has written two operas: *The Green Children* (1990) and *The Wildman* (1995). He has also edited many collections of short stories and anthologies of poetry, including *The Anglo-Saxon World* (1982) and *The Oxford Book of Travel Verse* (1986). *The Seeing Stone* (2000), a recent work of original fiction, is the first volume of a projected Arthurian trilogy, which won the *Guardian* Children's Fiction Prize.

BIBLIOGRAPHY: Tolley, A. T., "K. C. H.," in Sherry, V. B., Jr., ed., *Poets of Great Britain and Ireland since 1960*, part 1, *DLB* 40 (1985): 81–86; White, D. R., "K. C. H.," in Hunt, C. C., ed., *British Children's Writers since 1960*, First Series, *DLB* 161 (1996): 103–8

MARGARET CONNOLLY

CROWNE, John
b. April 1640, Shropshire; d. April 1712, London

At the age of seventeen, C. entered Harvard University but took no degree. He returned to England in 1660 where he probably became a gentleman usher to a noble family. His heroic romance *Pandion and Amphigeneia* (1665) was followed years later by his first play, *Juliana* (1671). In December of the same year, he achieved his first success with *Charles VIII of France* (1672). He translated or adapted works of Jean Racine and William SHAKESPEARE including *Andromache* (1674) and *Henry VI* retitled *The Misery of Civil War* (1680). His court masque *Calisto* relied on source material earlier exploited by Thomas HEYWOOD and was presented for the daughter of the Duke of York in 1675. His *City Politiques* (1683), a satire on the recent perjured attacks against Catholics, so

angered the public that C. was severely beaten by a mob. Arguably, his major success came in May 1685 with the comedy *Sir Courtly Nice*. C. retired from the stage for five years because of illness but returned in 1690 with the satire *The English Friar*. He wrote four more plays between that time and 1702, one of which, *Justice Busy* (perf. ca. 1700), went unpublished. The three others included two tragedies—*Regulus* (perf. 1692; pub. 1694) and *Caligula* (1698)—and a comedy, *The Married Beau* (1694).

CUNARD, Nancy [Clara]
b. 10 March 1896, Leicestershire; d. 16 March 1965, Paris, France

C.'s status as poet, publisher, editor, translator, journalist, and activist has been obscured by her sensationalized reputation as promiscuous and hard-drinking, a dilettante whose political campaigns were faddish and sexually motivated. Photographs by Man Ray and Cecil Beaton of her emaciated arms weighted with thick ivory bracelets are still circulated as documentation of the vogue for primitivism among the Parisian *beau-monde* in the 1920s. Fictionalized accounts of C.'s hedonism, by Michael ARLEN (*The Green Hat*) and Aldous HUXLEY, titillate and serve the myth of the "Roaring Twenties" but neglect her real achievements.

Daughter of Lady (Emerald) Cunard, hostess and patron of the arts, C.'s teenage years were spent in the company of many notable literary figures. In 1916, her poem gave the title to Edith SITWELL's anthology *Wheels*. Later, her Hours Press published the poems of modernists such as Samuel BECKETT and Ezra Pound. But as the title of her first volume *Outlaws* (1921) indicates, C.'s most successful verse was inspired by her rejection of the values of her mother's society. The concluding plea of her poem "Prayer"— "Make me symbolic'ly iconoclast/The ideal Antichrist, the Paradox"—may be read as the tenet that defined her work and life. In "Answer to a Reproof," she rejects criticism of her poetry as the miscomprehension of her radical political ideals. Though she was dismissed by contemporaries as derivative, John Lucas represents more recent critical revaluation in finding *Parallax* (1925) a "self-aware imitation of Eliot" again expressive of her desire to find a voice in the male arena and "change society."

C. continued to write poetry throughout her life contributing to anthologies and producing several collections—*Sublunary* (1923), *Poems (Two) 1925* (1930), *Psalms of the Palms and Sonnets* (unpublished), and *Rélève into Marquis* (1944)—but a move to Paris in the 1920s redirected her energies. C.'s commitment to racial equality began when she was introduced to African art by the surrealists and to black history by her African-American lover Henry

Crowder. In 1931, her polemic *Black Man and White Ladyship* denounced her mother's racism alongside slavery and imperial oppression, sabotaging her relationship with Lady Cunard and symbolically breaking with the society she represented. Like her monumental *Negro: An Anthology* (1934), this pamphlet has been dismissed as impassioned and unscholarly, but its striking juxtapositions are now recognized as collage in the manner of surrealism, inviting a consideration of the relationship between British society and the racism sanctioned by its empire. Her anthology, at over eight hundred pages, is an encyclopedia of black culture, contributed to by W. E. B. Du Bois, Langston Hughes, and Zora Neale Hurston, among many notable others. Aiming to give a voice and face to marginalized black intellectuals, C. chose only to include images of black contributors. Hugh Ford's 1970 reprint detracts attention from the multivocal nature of the text instead drawing attention to its editor by imposing her image upon it.

C. used her editing skills again to great effect in 1937 when she collected the responses of contemporary authors to the question "Are you for, or against, Franco and fascism?" in *Authors Take Sides on the Spanish War*. During World War II, she edited *Poems for France* (1944) and later *Poèmes à la France* (1949). The influence of her political beliefs upon these projects is clear, her influential role as facilitator, introducing the work of artists and intellectuals to the world and each other, is becoming more widely recognized. A prolific journalist throughout her life notably for the Associated Negro Press, Sylvia Pankhurst's *New Times,* and the *Manchester Guardian,* C.'s only autobiographical words feature in her memoirs of friends and mentors, *Grand Man: Memories of Norman Douglas* (1954) and *GM: Memories of George Moore* (1956).

BIBLIOGRAPHY: Chisholm, A., *N. C.* (1979); Fielding, D., *Emerald and Nancy: Lady Cunard and Her Daughter* (1968); Ford, H., ed., *N. C.* (1968)

TORY YOUNG

CUNNINGHAM, Alan

b. 7 December 1784, Dumfriesshire, Scotland; d. 30 October 1842, London

C. was a minor poet and novelist who is best remembered for his contribution toward the revival of Scottish literature in the early 19th c., notably his early anthologies of Scottish songs (1813) and traditional tales (2 vols., 1822) and for his biographies of Sir Walter SCOTT (1832), Robert BURNS (1836), and James THOMSON (1841). The author of the dramatic poem *Sir Marmaduke Maxwell* (1822) and three novels, *Paul Jones* (3 vols., 1826), *Sir Michael Scott* (3 vols., 1828), and *Lord Roldan* (3 vols., 1836), C. also

edited *The Works of Robert Burns* (8 vols., 1834) and *The Poems, Letters, and Land of Burns* (2 vols., 1838–40).

CYNEWULF

b. ca. 770; d. 840

C., an Anglo-Saxon poet writing sometime during the 8th-9th cs., created a unique fusion of Christian religious themes and the oral-formulaic style of OLD ENGLISH poetry in his *Fates of the Apostles, Ascension, Juliana,* and *Elene.* Unfortunately, little is known about C. save his name, which likewise would have remained unknown had he not identified himself in his four extant works with runic "signatures": in passages of all his poems, he incorporates runes representing the letters of his name into the content of the text itself. Nineteenth-century scholarship on C. focused primarily on seeking biographical information on the poet, identifying his sources, and analyzing linguistic phenomena in his poetry, while scholars of the 20th c. have examined his oral-formulaic style, his Latin rhetorical figures, the runic passages, and common themes.

Critics have been hard pressed to provide a satisfactory reading of C.'s catalogue of apostles in his 122-line *Fates of Apostles.* Rhetorical, thematic, and numerological studies of the last few decades have shown that close analysis of *Fates* reveals a highly crafted work, albeit one whose function was more religious than necessarily artistic. *Fates* portrays a devotion toward the apostles juxtaposed with a penitential concern for the poet's own fate, as manifested by his plea for prayer in the runic passage.

The Ascension (also known as *Christ II*) was previously thought to be a 426-line section of a longer work, located as it is between *Christ I* and *Christ III* in the *Codex Exoniensis,* a collection of Anglo-Saxon poetry commonly known as the *Exeter Book,* copied ca. 940. An analogue of Gregory's Ascension Day homily, *Ascension* looks back to the accomplishment of the Incarnation while simultaneously anticipating the Second Coming of Christ, nicely linking the events of *Christ I* and *Christ III.* Some debate remains as to whether this link was a conscious endeavor on the part of C. or if the compiler of the *Exeter Book* noticed the continuity of these works and is solely responsible for their arrangement.

Like *Fates,* the 731-line *Juliana* had not inspired medieval scholars on the whole before the 1970s. As hagiography, *Juliana* illustrates the Christlike paragon of faith and virtue toward which the saints should aspire; on a figural level she represents the persecution and perseverance of the Christian church. A devotee of Juliana, C. ends this poem with a plea that prayers for him be made to this saint.

Of all C.'s works, *Elene* fares best at the hands of the critics. As a 1,321-line adaptation of the *inventio crucis* legend, *Elene* depicts several encounters with the cross, most significantly Constantine's vision of the cross before battle and Elene's discovery of the cross. Each encounter sparks a spiritual revelation and produces a transformation; thus, the physical encounter with the cross both anticipates and symbolizes a spiritual encounter leading to conversion. The power of the cross to effect a spiritual transformation is again demonstrated by the resurrection of a corpse upon contact with the cross. This conversion theme runs throughout *Elene*, turning the *inventio crucis* legend into an allegory of the soul discovering Christ. The final conversion is C.'s: he recounts his own conversion experience in the concluding runic passage.

C.'s corpus as a whole is essentially typological in its emphasis on hagiography and eschatology; his poems look back to the lives of Christ and his disciples and saints as a way of looking forward to the Second Coming and the judgment of all souls, including C.'s own. C.'s runic passages at the end of each poem are especially poignant in this respect, as they reveal a keen awareness of his own impending judgment and contain entreaties for prayers to be offered on behalf of his own soul.

BIBLIOGRAPHY: Anderson, E. R., *C.* (1983); Bjork, R. E., ed., *C.* (1996); Calder, D. G., *C.* (1981); Greenfield, S. B., and D. G. Calder, *A New Critical History of Old English Literature* (1986)

ELIZABETH TRELENBERG

D

D'AGUIAR, Fred
b. 2 February 1960, London

D. is prominent among a new generation of British writers with ties to the Caribbean. Born in London to parents from British Guiana (now Guyana), D. was sent back to the Caribbean at age two to be reared by his grandmother, Mama Dot, in the village of Airy Hall. His upbringing, replete with oral traditions, rooted D.'s imagination in a Guyanese identity. He returned to England at age twelve and was politicized by the rioting of the country's inner-city black youth. Later, D. studied African and Caribbean literature at Kent University. In the years since, he has written drama, film, fiction, and poetry but is known primarily as a poet; all of his work, regardless of genre, is infused with his sense of poetic structure, voice, and metaphor.

D.'s thematic interests fall into three categories: nostalgia for the past, critique of neocolonial forces at work in the metropolis and diaspora, and exploration of slavery. D.'s celebration of childhood comes through most forcefully in his first two collections of poetry, *Mama Dot* (1985) and *Airy Hall* (1989). Each opens with a series of poems about the titled subject. The "Mama Dot" poems feature a mythic grandmother who nurtures, punishes, and heals and who, through her connection to the island's traditions, becomes a metaphor for the past; the "Airy Hall" poems offer images of place as icons of a younger identity fondly remembered.

Other D. poems, especially those contained in his collections *British Subjects* (1993) and *Bill of Rights* (1998), express the poet's preoccupation with neocolonialism. Those situated in the Caribbean call to account those politicians who have ignored the people's poverty. National corruption is also at the heart of *Dear Future* (1996), D.'s novel about a boy whose idyllic life among a family of remarkable uncles is destroyed by power struggles that destabilize the country and rob the children of a viable future. Similarly, D.'s poems about life in England, while striving to claim a sense of belonging, demonstrate the alienation that is engendered in the black population by experiences of police harassment, urban brutality, and societal indifference.

D.'s interest in slavery is central in three of his works. *The Longest Memory* (1994), a novel set on a Virginia plantation, describes a loyal slave who tries to protect his son (actually, his wife's offspring by the plantation's overseer) by reporting the boy's attempted escape. Rather than simply being disciplined, the boy is whipped to death by the overseer's son (his half-brother), and the loyal slave is haunted by guilt. *Feeding the Ghosts* (1997), another novel, is based on the actual story of an English slave ship and its captain who had 131 sick slaves thrown overboard. In the resulting court case, the captain was cleared of wrongdoing, but legislation was subsequently passed denying insurance coverage for slaves intentionally drowned. In his fictionalized version of this story, D. invents an educated female slave who tries to stop the murders by first vocalizing her objections and then staging an insurrection. Finally, *Bloodlines* (2000), a book-length poem, features a white man who falls in love with a slave and runs away with her to find a more tolerant society. After they are captured, she is reenslaved and eventually dies in childbirth. This story is told from many perspectives, including the two lovers, their lost child, and an older couple who symbolize what the lovers might have been had their relationship been allowed to flourish. D. employs a polyphonic narration in all these works to show that slavery was a system that compromised the humanity of every person affected by its many contradictions.

BIBLIOGRAPHY: Leusmann, H., "F. D.," *Wasafiri* 28 (Autumn 1998): 17–21; Madson, D. L., ed., *Postcolonial Literatures: Expanding the Canon* (1999)

RENÉE SCHATTEMAN

DAHL, Roald
b. 13 September 1916, Llandaff, Wales; d. 23 November 1990, Oxford

A prolific writer well known for his darkly humorous CHILDREN'S LITERATURE, D. presents in his work themes and ideas focused upon the belief that the good and true shall, indeed, be rewarded and the evil vanquished. Although increasingly recognizable to the general public because of film adaptations of his children's books such as *Charlie and the Chocolate Factory* (filmed as *Willie Wonka and the Chocolate Factory*, 1971), *The Witches* (1990), and *James and the Giant Peach* (1996), D. is also well known to critics and readers alike for his insightful autobiographical writings and his adult-oriented short stories. All of his works—two novels, a play, memoirs, cookbooks, screenplays, short fiction, and children's literature—display a whimsical turn of mind, highlighted by a desire to escape, by fancy and the imagination, into worlds where the cruelties of the real world are blunted and avenged.

His experiences while being reared in England, recounted in *Boy: Tales of Childhood* (1984), show him to have had an engaging family life and difficult experiences in English public schools. In a famous incident, he was caned by a future archbishop for one of his many mischievous pranks. The stern, oppressive, even vicious adults with whom he had encounters in boarding school provided him with models for his many caricatures of unfeeling and harsh grownups. D. fled the academic world as quickly as possible, hiring on with an oil company that could satisfy his desire to encounter the exotic world beyond England. His assignments in Africa and in Asia seem to have done just that. His experiences in World War II, including his service as a fighter pilot Wing Commander from 1939 to 1945, became the unlikely catapult into a writing career that would span five decades. Seriously wounded early in the war, D. was assigned to Washington, D.C., where his first published story was the result of writer C. S. FORESTER's shaping of interview notes that D. had himself taken while being interviewed by Forester. The eventual collection of his flying stories, *Over to You: Ten Stories of Flyers and Flying* (1946), established D.'s commitment to a writing life. He made a comfortable living as a mystery and suspense writer, garnering the first two of three Edgar Awards from the Mystery Writers of America before beginning to write children's books to satisfy the hungry minds of his own young children. His first major success and his second published children's book, *James and the Giant Peach* (1961), featured four unusual companions—a centipede, a ladybug, a silkworm, and a spider—aiding a boy who travels the globe in the eponymous fruit, allowing D. to revisit the Lewis CARROLL talking bestiary as well as Carroll's dry and pointed approach to life.

The quirkiness of his HUMOR, his willingness to puncture pretension, and his pointedly moralistic tone were perfectly suited to the sort of children's literature that would capture adult notice, and it is unsurprising that his critical reputation depends primarily upon that section of his oeuvre. Characterized by ironic reversal and sardonic wit, even many of his short stories, written for adults, display revenge motifs and O. Henry-esque turns of plot. In one of his best-known stories, often recycled on television and in anthologies, "Lamb to the Slaughter," anthologized in *Roald Dahl's Tales of the Unexpected* (1979), a woman clubs her husband to death with a frozen leg of lamb, then cooks the evidence and feeds it to the investigating detectives, who opine that the evidence of the crime is most likely "right under our very noses." The straightforward narrative techniques and overt calls for audience sympathy with his protagonists (even, in this case, a murderess) are combined with essentialist characterizations: readers and viewers are rarely left in doubt as to the essential nature of any character.

In *Charlie and the Chocolate Factory* (1964), for example, the unpleasant children—Veruca Salt, Augustus Gloop, Mike Teavee, and Violet Beauregard—represent cultural stereotypes as well as commentaries on the outcomes of the postwar pandering to children that D. reviled. For example, Mike Teavee is an American winner of the grand prize offered by mysterious chocolatier Willie Wonka, and joins the "bad" children and poor but good Charlie Bucket, the hero, in Wonka's fantastic factory. As a stereotypical American child, Mike Teavee relates everything he sees to pale imitations of the representations he has consumed via television. The adult companions of the monstrous children are portrayed as slaves to the children's whims, and each dyad of parent and child meets a fate appropriate to the selfishness of the children's acts—Mike is himself reduced in size by a television's beam of electrons, for example. Charlie's eventual survival of the tour as challenge results in his inheritance of the Wonka empire and the promise of only happy tomorrows: meek acceptance of one's lot in life is rewarded by ultimate happiness.

Although D. has received many awards and much kudos for his work, including the prestigious Whitbread Award in 1983 for another children's book turned movie, *The Witches*, some critics have chosen to emphasize what they see as portrayals of excessive cruelty and mean-spiritedness. In *James and the Giant Peach*, a rhinoceros eats the parents; in *The Witches*, the protagonist is orphaned by a possibly more disturbing, because more "real," car crash; and James's giant peach flattens his "horrible" aunts, Sponge and Spiker. Many more readers and critics, however, have been delighted by D.'s inventively visceral and immediate punishments. D. has publicly stated "my nastiness is never gratuitous. It's retribution. Beastly people must be punished." His critical reputation, vilifiers of his work notwithstanding, seems pegged to a sense of art as connected to the vicissitudes of being alive, to a glorification of the prosperous possibilities of overcoming adversity.

BIBLIOGRAPHY: Treglown, J., *R. D.* (1994); Warren, A., *R. D.* (1988); West, M., *R. D.* (1992)

RICHARD E. LEE

DANE, Clemence

(pseud. of Winifred Ashton) b. 21 February 1888, London; d. 28 March 1965, London

Novelist and playwright, D. was once praised by the dramatist and theater critic, St. John ERVINE, as "the most distinguished woman dramatist in the theatre." She had studied art (specializing in portraiture) at the Slade School in London and, later, in Dresden from 1904 to 1907. From 1908, she was a schoolteacher in Ireland, but she left this employment in 1913 to return to London to become an actress, using the name Diane Cortis. She played several parts in London and on tour before finally deciding in 1917 to devote herself to a writing career. She chose a nom de plume derived from the name of a London church: St. Clement Danes.

D.'s first works were novels: *Regiment of Women* (1917), *First the Blade* (1918), and *Legend* (1919). They were immediately popular and successful and were still being reprinted in the 1940s (*Legend*, for example, was reprinted by Heinemann in 1923, 1933, and 1947). From novels, she turned again to the theater in 1920–21, not this time as an actress but as a writer. She had two plays produced in London in a single year—*A Bill of Divorcement* (1921) and *Will Shakespeare* (1921)—and went on to write twenty-eight more plays between 1923 and 1959, all of which were produced in London or New York or both. During this time, she also wrote seven novels and a volume of short stories. Collaborating with Helen Simpson, she wrote three detective stories—*Enter Sir John* (1928), *Printer's Devil* (1930; repub. as *Author Unknown*, 1930), and *Re-Enter Sir John* (1932). Her memoirs, under the title *London Has a Garden*, were published in 1964.

In the theater, after a sensational start—*A Bill of Divorcement* played over four hundred performances—her plays seemed usually to be caviar to the general, their critical acclaim standing a good deal higher than their popular appeal. Rereading the texts of some of them now, one is compelled to the opinion that this is a reflection on the flippancy of the audiences of the day rather than on the quality of the plays themselves or on the faulty judgment of the major critics who were often quite remarkably unanimous in their praise. This applied particularly to *Will Shakespeare*, which still reads very well, in spite of some embarrassing moments of sentimentality and one glaring display of ignorance of the history of stage practice: the "first night" of William SHAKESPEARE's *Romeo and Juliet* is represented as being performed with two intermissions and at one point Mary Fitton,

the alleged dark lady of the sonnets, standing backstage with Shakespeare says, "There! Curtain's down! I must go." Someone called "Stage hand" calls "Last act please!" and moments later Christopher MARLOWE—yes he's there backstage, too—exclaims "Curtain's up!" So the Elizabethan stage suddenly gains not only a proscenium curtain but also the ability to fly it rather than simply drawing or opening it.

D.'s play, however, invents one attractive device that has recently been paid the compliment of being imitated by Tom STOPPARD in his film script, *Shakespeare in Love* (1999): in the course of the performance of *Romeo and Juliet*, the boy playing Juliet is injured and, to save the performance and the play (Queen ELIZABETH I is in the audience) Mary Fitton leaps into the part and triumphantly plays the last act (which she fortunately knows by heart because madly—though temporarily—in love with Shakespeare, she had been sitting at his elbow as he wrote it). D.'s play imitates Shakespeare's and is written in unrhymed iambic pentameters: pastiche, but pastiche unembarrassed and unembarrassing, much more than merely competently done and rising now and then to the point of legitimately claiming to be considered as poetry.

The slightly earlier *A Bill of Divorcement,* on the other hand, has dialogue—equally expert and equally convincing—in the straightforward naturalistic style: its first London production occurred in the same month as W. Somerset MAUGHAM's *The Circle* and only four months after the posthumous production of Harold Chapin's *The New Morality,* with both of which it can be justly compared, so far as the realism of its dialogue is concerned, without apology. It is a serious-minded, tautly constructed melodrama and its published text has an opening stage direction of particular interest: "Scene: A small house in the country. The action passes on Christmas Day 1933. The audience is asked to imagine that the recommendations of the 'Majority Report of the Royal Commission on Divorce v. Matrimonial Causes' have become the law of the land." The plot of the play concerns a woman whose husband is certified as incurably insane after suffering what in the First World War was called "shell shock." He is incarcerated in an "asylum" and she decides to remarry. Then suddenly he recovers, is discharged from the institution, and comes home just a week before the date fixed for the new marriage, to find that during his twelve-year absence his wife has divorced him on the grounds of his insanity. This would, of course, have been impossible in 1921 (the year of the play's first production) but British divorce laws were changed in 1923, making insanity a legitimate and sufficient ground for divorce. There is little doubt that this reform was at least partly inspired by D.'s play. *A Bill of Divorcement* is much her best-known play: but her best play is *Granite* (1926). It is a spare, gaunt, brilliantly plotted piece, set on the island of Lundy, off the southwest coast of England in the second decade of the 19th c. Matching the bleak terrain and the dreadful, inhospitable weather is the sense of brooding, indefinable evil that pervades the whole play and inexorably drives its plot to a powerful and disastrous conclusion.

Human bleakness, as a motif presented in an impeccable design, is one of the outstanding characteristics of D.'s work. It is there even in her first published writing, the three early novels in 1917–19. Especially remarkable is the third of these: *Legend*. The novel is a hundred and ninety pages long and consists of one evening's conversation between a group of writers and would-be writers. They talk about a young woman writer whose first two books have caused a great public sensation and who has now died in childbirth. This short novel, designed and executed with admirable classical restraint, manages to convey the sense of a whole life passionately lived; and also it conveys the overriding sense of the vital relationship between life and art. The whole book is a tour de force, a real virtuoso performance. Without any affectation or straining for effect it calls up far-reaching implications through using minimalist means. Its chief character, Madala Grey, does not appear at all: she is already dead. And the essence of the story is told by a young woman who, of all the characters, has least to say. Right at the end, the man this young woman has silently fallen in love with says to her: "Do you know—it's strange—you remind me of her. You are very like her. You are very like Madala Grey." And she replies: "Yes, I know": exquisite ellipsis.

BIBLIOGRAPHY: Ashley, L. R. N., "C. D.," in Johnson, G. M., ed., *Late Victorian and Edwardian British Novelists*, Second Series, *DLB* 197 (1999): 88–94; Trewin, J. C., *The Theatre since 1900* (1951)

ERIC SALMON

DANIEL, Samuel

b. ca. 1562, Taunton, Somerset; d. October 1619, bur. at Beckington, Somersetshire

Historian, poet, dramatist, and deviser of masques under JAMES I, D. enjoyed a certain amount of success in his career that was nevertheless punctuated by several contretemps with the Crown. He was brother-in-law to the lexicographer John Florio and a learned Italian scholar, the latter accomplishment recommending him for diplomatic missions to both Italy and France in 1586. He later became tutor to William, the third Earl of Pembroke, and afterward to Anne CLIFFORD. He began his writing career as a poet, moved to playwriting and evolved into an historian

and masque writer later. He was additionally a playhouse licenser and briefly filled the position of Master of the Revels for the upstart children's theater at Blackfriars.

After an early career in the foreign service, during which time he sent reports to Walsingham, ELIZABETH I's spymaster, from France, he earned the patronage of the Countess of PEMBROKE, and began writing. He earned his reputation after his first work, the sonnet sequence "Delia," was published in two parts in 1591 and 1592. The sequence is a well-crafted, clever homage to the then-fashionable style in imitation of Petrarch and Sir Philip SIDNEY. Delia is a conscious anagram of "ideal." During this time, he turned his hand to a closet drama, *The Tragedy of Cleopatra* (1594), inspired by his patron's play, *Octavia*. In it, D. follows the Pembroke school of Senecan construction. Under the patronage of Sir Fulke GREVILLE and Charles Blount, he wrote *Musophilus* (1599).

By the time he wrote his poem, "The History of the Civil Wars" (1595), D. was well established. Tradition holds that he succeeded Edmund SPENSER as poet laureate after Spenser's death in 1599. There was no such post, however, and the most that can be said is that D. had earned an annuity by 1601. His *Works* of that year presented to Elizabeth include the special inscription "I, who by that most blessed hand sustain'd,/In quietnes, do eate the bread of rest." D. carried on a celebrated debate with Thomas CAMPION about this time over the proper construction of English verse form. D. wrote *A Defence of Ryme* (1603) while Campion championed "numbers" or metrical weight. D. was selected as poet for the first Queen's Masque during the Christmas revels of 1603. Ben JONSON was clearly piqued by D.'s preference at court, and he can be seen to complain of D. in his *The Forest*. By 1619, Jonson allowed that D. was an honest man but no poet.

D. was prevailed upon to exercise his influence in the new court on behalf of the children's playing company at the Blackfriars Theatre. The company gained the patronage of James's queen, Anne, and a new patent was issued. In the two years of the Queen's Revels (1604–6), the syndicate and playhouse remained in nearly continuous trouble. Part of the reason for the trouble was that under the new patent of 1604 D. was named to license plays for the children's company. The syndicate paid D. an annuity of £10 for this service, but modern scholarship has taken this position to be a sinecure. The Blackfriars company was famous for skating close to the line of propriety, and that was no doubt part of its popular appeal. Because the children were technically not professional players, they did not fall under the purview of the Master of the Revels. Excluding their plays from Edmund TILNEY's and George Buc's cautious eyes, however, proved too great an incentive for abuse. Far from keeping the Children of the Queen's Revels in check, their new censor D. was the first to offend. In the same year as the new patent was issued, in fact within two weeks, on February 20, 1604, D.'s *Philotas* (perf. January 3, 1605; pub. 1607) cost the poet his position (though not his annuity). The play's resemblance to the Essex rebellion brought D. before the Privy Council to answer questions regarding the matter. He apparently acquitted himself, and the next year he is to be found writing a pastoral for Christ Church, Oxford. He returned to court and devised *Tethys' Festival* (perf. June 5, 1610; pub. 1610) for a Whitehall performance and provided the wedding pastoral *Hymen's Triumph* (perf. February 2, 1614; pub. 1615) for Jean Drummond, a lady of Queen Anne's household.

His last years were spent trying to finish his "Civil Wars" and completing his prose work *The Collection of the History of England* (1618). D.'s reputation is of a quiet poet with a subtle tone and an ear for the music of words. He consistently demonstrates a refined aesthetic appreciation and distaste for mere form over substance.

BIBLIOGRAPHY: Godshalk, W. L., "S. D.," in Logan, T. P., and D. S. Smith, eds., *The New Intellectuals* (1977): 281–301; Rees, J., *S. D.* (1964); Seronsy, C., *S. D.* (1967)

BRIAN JAY CORRIGAN

DANIELS, Sarah
b. 21 November 1957, London

D. started her career as a playwright by responding to a call in the London magazine *Time Out*. Though that initial piece was rejected, her second attempt, *Ripen Our Darkness* (perf. 1981; pub. 1986), had its premiere at the prestigious Royal Court Theatre Upstairs. D. has had a wide range of reaction to her work that focuses on feminist-based issues from the venomous as typified by critic Benedict Nightingale—"She tends to see women as victims, without the moral autonomy she pays men the unintended compliment of suggesting they possess"—to the vehement as expressed by author and photographer Jill Posener—"D. has a great skill in one-liners, an eye for the absurd and a gut level feminist anger."

Masterpieces (perf. 1983; pub. 1984), D.'s next play, tries to show a connection between pornography and violence toward women when its lead character, Rowena, pushes away a man who is harassing her in the tube station. The man inadvertently falls onto the train tracks and Rowena is charged with murder. With *Neaptide* (1986), D. was the first woman to have a play with a lesbian theme produced at the Royal National Theatre. In it, D. explores the rights of lesbians for custody of children.

The Gut Girls (perf. 1988; pub. 1989), so titled for the nickname given to women in the job of ripping

the innards from cattle, takes a look at a liberating, if unglamorous, occupation for women in Victorian England. Though the profession was seen as only slightly above prostitution, it provided a financial independence not generally enjoyed by women at that time. However, when Lady Helena, an upper-class, would-be social reformer, protests against their employers because of the unsanitary conditions, the main characters' freedom is taken away from them.

Other plays by D. include *Byrthrite* (perf. 1986; pub. 1987), *Beside Herself* (1990), *The Madness of Esme and Shaz* (1994), and *Morning Glory* (2001). Collections of her work appeared in 1991 and 1994.

BIBLIOGRAPHY: Aston, E., "Daniels in the Lion's Den: S. D. and the British Backlash," *TJ* 47 (October 1995): 393–403; Griffin, G., "Violence, Abuse, and Gender Relations in the Plays of S. D.," in Aston, E., and J. Reinelt, eds., *The Cambridge Companion to Modern British Women Playwrights* (2000): 194–211

HAYLEY HORVAT

DARLEY, George
b. 1795, Dublin, Ireland; d. 23 November 1846, London

D. contributed dramatic criticism to the *London Magazine* and art criticism to the *Athenaeum*. He was one of the first authorities to recognize the value of early Italian painting, anticipating the later work of John RUSKIN, Walter PATER, and John Addington SYMONDS. His first published poem was *The Errors of Ecstasy* (1822), and his fairy opera *Sylvia; or, The May Queen* (1827) was popular in his lifetime. Several lyrics were printed in magazines, including a 17th-c. pastiche that the anthologist Francis Turner Palgrave included in his *Golden Treasury* (1861; second series, 1897), imagining it to be genuine. D. also wrote two plays, *Thomas à Beckett* (1840) and *Ethelstan* (1841). His most admired work is the unfinished poem, *Nepenthe,* privately printed 1835, an allegory of the imagination. In 1840, D. produced his two-volume edition of the dramatic works of Sir Francis BEAUMONT and John FLETCHER.

DARWIN, Charles
b. 12 February 1809, Shrewsbury; d. 19 April 1882, Downe

A famed naturalist, best known as the man credited with devising the theory of evolution and its attendant idea of natural selection—that living things change and adapt to their environment—is principally known for two works: *On the Origin of Species by Means of Natural Selection*, first published in 1859 and revised in six editions from 1861 to 1876, and *The Descent of Man* (2 vols., 1871; rev. ed., 1874). These two works differ significantly in both tone and style from his personal letters, as can be expected in private correspondence versus very public discourse. The enthusiasm that pours out of his letters is tempered by the scientific, though not overly technical, nature of the prose found in both works. His public and private writings tend to vacillate between these two spheres, of environmental enthusiast and deliberate scientist.

D.'s scientific works, though loaded with complex ideas, are often extraordinarily straightforward and accessible, a sign that he did not attempt trying to match the exhilaration he felt in discovery with equally ecstatic language. This was a decision not so much based on the belief that the scientist must remain impartial, but because D. often felt his own power of language woefully inadequate to describe the majesty of a place such as the "inter-tropical regions." His loss of love for art, literature, and music, well documented by laments in his autobiography, *Life and Letters of Charles Darwin* (3 vols, 1887)—unexpurgated as the *Autobiography of Charles Darwin 1809–1882* in 1959—made his language very straightforward, essentially without metaphor and other expressions of speech. To D., art rendered the real world in symbols. And the hyper-real, in all its combative and unrefined glory, is what D. strove to expound. Thus, we see in his work a characteristic precision of speech. But this posed a problem in that the language of his Victorian England was fraught with theological metaphor and analogy. D.'s difficult task was to create metaphor based solely on the nature of things around him, as opposed to an unseen force. Again, this results in a refreshingly straightforward approach. Successive editions of *Origin* show a distinct minimizing of signification. This is not to suggest that D.'s language was simplistic. Indeed, much of his construction is quite long. Even so, the style is direct and clear. In complex theoretical works, like *Origin*, D. adopts a patient tone with his reader, as if he anticipates and respects potential skepticism. And though it may have been of little stylistic concern to D., his persistent use of the present tense (generally not found in his letters) endows his writing with a sense of potential discovery and excitement.

The more famed a scientist he became, the more difficult, in his estimation, it was to write lyrically. There are, however, exceptions to be found in his science writings. Though still expressed in plain language, D.'s love of botanical nature imbues a certain joyousness that can occasionally be found in his writing of it, most specifically *Insectivorous Plants* (1875) and *The Power of Movement in Plants* (1880). Additionally, a pleasantly anecdotal style dominates *The Expression of the Emotions in Man and Animals* (1872). It is in these works where we see D. engaging in decidedly literary techniques such as personifying small creatures on the grand scale of universal nature. But it is in his personal letters, *A Calendar of the Correspondence of Charles Darwin, 1821–1882 with*

Supplement (1994), that the best examples of D.'s unbridled enthusiasm reach full flowering.

His letters often betray a certain wide-eyed exuberance, where D. shows his awe and appreciation of the natural world around him. It was in this private realm that D. allowed that places like jungles were more cathedrals than hosts to never-ending battles of survival. And it is in his letters that he is at his most ebulliently free with the language. But D. was not a literary artist, not that he ever purported to be. Nevertheless, his contributions to the scientific and philosophical world had a profound effect on literature in the years after the dissemination of the notion of survival of the fittest.

To many Victorian writers, D.'s theories suggested a bleakness in human existence. Though D. focused on the beauty of man's interconnectedness with the living world, both past and present, many writers of his day treated man's evolution as a disheartening realization that humans, so recently celebrated in popular literature as the crowning achievement of a God it had given birth to, had now been rendered a mere blip in the never-ending history of the universe. Correspondingly, more and more writers took a melancholy view of humanity and its precarious position within the order of things. It can be said that the assimilation of the pessimism many ascribed to the theory of evolution became complete toward the end of the Victorian era in literature, specifically in poetics. Before the idea of survival of the fittest, nature was often presented by Victorian poets as idyllic and benevolent. But this changed dramatically with the introduction of the idea of nature as a hostile, kill or be killed force, a slight corruption of D.'s essential ideas.

D. can be viewed in literary terms in three primary ways: as a scientist—deliberate but accessible, without the creativity associated with literary masters; slightly more adventurous, with some personification, best exemplified in his less seminal science writings; and as a memoirist and letter writer, where he gives free reign to the literary skills at his disposal, without concern for retaining any scientific detachment or impartiality.

BIBLIOGRAPHY: Beer, G., *Darwin's Plots: Evolutionary Narrative in Darwin, George Eliot, and Nineteenth Century Fiction* (1983); Irvine, W., "The Influence of Darwin on Literature," *PAPS* 103 (October 1959): 616–28; Kohn, D., ed., *The Darwinian Heritage* (1985)

E. LINDSEY BALKAN

DARWIN, Erasmus

b. 12 December 1731, Elston, Nottinghamshire; d. 18 April 1802, Breadsall Priory, Derbyshire

For much of the last decade of the 18th c., D.'s poetry was regarded as the finest being written in England.

In 1797, Samuel Taylor COLERIDGE wrote that D. was "the first literary character in Europe," and his influence was felt in the early work of William WORDSWORTH, Percy Bysshe SHELLEY, and other major Romantic poets. D.'s synthesis of science and poetry was exemplary for these younger poets. After 1798, D.'s reputation was attacked on several fronts: his republicanism, imputed atheism, scientific materialism, and poetic theory and practice. Coleridge himself did much to turn public taste away from D. and toward his own Romantic ideology. Some contemporary parodies, notably "The Loves of the Triangles," published in the political magazine the *Anti-Jacobin* (1798), accelerated an exclusion of D.'s poetry from the literary canon that has persisted for two centuries. However, this loss of perhaps the most important poet of the English Enlightenment found restorers in James Venable Logan and Desmond King-Hele, among others.

D. studied classics and medicine at St. John's College, Cambridge, and the Edinburgh Medical School, being awarded his B.M. in 1755. He consistently practiced medicine thereafter, becoming, while at Lichfield and Derby, the most sought after physician of his day. D.'s interest in science and technology brought him the friendship of Benjamin Franklin. Perhaps in emulation of Franklin's American Philosophical Society, D. founded the Lunar Society of Birmingham. This group of empirical "philosophers" and manufacturers included James Watt, Joseph Priestley, and Josiah Wedgwood: seminal figures of the Industrial Revolution.

These friendships and interests fed a synthesizing, universalizing mind, rooted in strong convictions regarding the importance of a systematic approach to both the natural and human worlds. His taxonomic model was the work of Carolus Linnaeus, which D. translated into English. He promoted empiricism in his medical and agricultural prose works: *Zoonomia; or, The Laws of Organic Life* (1794) and *Phytologia; or, The Philosophy of Agriculture and Gardening* (1800), and in his sequence of EPIC poems beginning with *The Botanic Garden*, part 2, "The Loves of the Plants" (1789); part 1, "The Economy of Vegetation" (1791), and *The Temple of Nature; or, The Origin of Society* (1803). These three epic poems, written in heroic couplets, were accompanied by extensive "philosophical notes," many of them complete scientific papers. D. wished to "inlist [*sic*] Imagination under the banner of Science," and his achievement of a synthesis of the two discourses is exemplary for our own time.

D.'s classical and scientific cultural interests combine in these three epics—collected under the general title *Cosmologia* (2001)—reflecting the cosmic evolutionary scope of his scenarios. Each epic comprises four cantos that follow a progressive schema: "The Economy of Vegetation" adopts the Empedoclean elemental model of fire, earth, water, and air—thus ordered to reflect the stages in the creation of the cosmos, of Earth and its inhabitants. "The Loves of the Plants" is structured on the Linnaean taxonomy. Canto 1 exhibits floral and human sexuality; canto 2 promotes the contribution of plants to human progress in the arts and sciences; canto 3, conversely, projects a nightmare vision of human pathological behavior; and canto 4 reestablishes the prime virtues of love and sexuality. The third epic, originally entitled *The Origin of Society*, presents an evolutionary scenario. Here, D.'s headings for each canto indicate their scope: "Production of Life," "Reproduction of Life," "Progress of the Mind," and "Of Good and Evil." After hypothesizing the origin of all life from "the first specks of animated earth," D. advocates sexuality as the key mechanism of progress.

The Edenic myth and empirical science are vehicles for D.'s progressive vision, which involves material, aesthetic, and moral discourses. D.'s diction is precise in articulating mythological and scientific scenarios, while his imagery fuses the particular with the universal. Furthermore, a conscious adaptation of methodology to material occurs, within and across the boundaries of the three parts of the epic, in a shift from concrete to more abstract diction, from poetic image to empirical analogy, from substantive data to its subsumption into more systematic philosophy. This agenda is also active thematically in his conversion and subversion of Golden Age and Edenic myths into rational evolutionary scenarios. "*Cosmologia*" celebrates, in finely crafted heroic couplets, a secularized world in which the laws of nature are privileged and extended in an imaginative vision of culture and society, and a major Enlightenment epic.

BIBLIOGRAPHY: King-Hele, D., ed., *The Letters of E. D.* (1981); King-Hele, D., *E. D.* (1999); Logan, J. V., *The Poetry and Aesthetics of E. D.* (1936)

STUART HARRIS

DARYUSH, Elizabeth

b. 5 December 1887, London; d. 7 April 1977, Oxford

D. was the daughter of Robert BRIDGES, who was poet laureate for the last seventeen years of his life. Even so distinguished a pedigree might not make a great deal of difference, but in the case of D. it is significant that she lived near her parents through most of their lives and, more importantly, shared many of her father's attitudes on language and literature. In her own right, to be sure, she was a poet of originality and distinction, but she was her father's devoted daughter as well.

For the first twenty years of her life, her family lived in Berkshire; thereafter, the family moved to

Boar's Hill, near Oxford, where the elder members of the Bridges family remained. During the early years of their time at Oxford, Roger FRY painted portraits of Bridges and his daughter; at some point, Fry's sister introduced D. to a Persian government official named Ali Akbar Daryush, to whom she was married in 1923. They lived in Persia (modern Iran) for four years but returned to England in 1927 and remained.

D.'s art is so severe and spare, and she was so strict a critic of her own work, pruning poem after poem from her collections and even renouncing and suppressing entire volumes, especially the early books of poetry, that she almost qualifies as a minimalist. Several poems bear noncommittal titles like "To," and most of her books yield no more guidance than one can glean from *Verses—Verses* (1930), *Second Book* (1932), *Verses, Third Book* (1933), and so forth. Such severity of approach is matched by the subtlety of her rhythms, many of which are based, not on such percussive distinctions as long-short and strong-weak or on elaborate patterns of alliteration, but simply on a count of syllables, without regard to accent. In her general interest in the language of poetry, she resembles her father and her father's dear friend Gerard Manley HOPKINS, whose poems Bridges edited. Like the elder poets, D. was unsatisfied with the conventional technical devices of most Victorian, Edwardian, and Georgian verse. Instead of monotonously rhymed and metered accentual-syllabic poetry, she and her father experimented with syllabics. In this practice, remarkably, she closely resembles her contemporary Marianne Moore. In this and other matters, she merits comparison with Laura Riding Jackson.

A stanza from "Modern Carol" illustrates some of her principles: "when the heavens are dank,/the lands icy,/earth is on the brink/of a mystery." The rhyme between "dank" and "brink," which involves fully accented monosyllables, matches consonants only, while the vowels do not match (as would be the case with "dank" and "bank"). Between "icy" and "mystery," hardly any rhyme can be detected, but it is there in the final unaccented syllables (both represented by "y"). Most of D.'s rhymes are of the familiar sorts, just as most of her lines—like most lines in spoken English—resolve into patterns of loose iambics. But she seems to reserve the right to construct monoliths of rhyme, squarely paneled with "untrue/adieu," but to break up the uniformity with more intriguing pairings: "familiars/beguilers," "beauty/company," and "lit/spirit" (from the untitled poem beginning "Faithless familiars").

During the 1930s, one of Bridges's strongest supporters, the poet-critic Yvor Winters, also became a strong supporter of D. Subsequently, the chorus of praise was joined by Roy Fuller, Donald DAVIE, Donald E. Stanford, and many others.

BIBLIOGRAPHY: Davie, D., "The Poetry of E. D.," in D.'s *Collected Poems* (1976): 13–23; Finlay, J., "E. D.," in Stanford, D. E., ed., *British Poets, 1914–1945, DLB* 20 (1983): 109–12; Smith, L. P., *Robert Bridges: Recollections* (1931)

WILLIAM HARMON

DAVENANT, [Sir] William
b. February 1606, Oxford; d. 7 April 1668, London

Perhaps the first of the great self-promoting theater impresarios, D. claimed first to be the godson and later the illegitimate child of William SHAKESPEARE, asserting that his mother's Oxford hostelry, the Tavern Inn, often entertained the great playwright on his many trips between London and Stratford-upon-Avon. He wrote an "Ode in Remembrance of Master Shakespeare" in 1618 (pub. 1638) when he was but twelve. Nevertheless, while the King's Men, the group to which Shakespeare belonged, certainly stayed in Oxford at the Tavern Inn on October 9, 1605, D.'s claim has never been substantiated. Arthur Acheson in 1913 attempted to identify D.'s mother, Jane, with the "Dark Lady" of the sonnets with little success. His poetry, drama, services to the Crown during the Civil War, and theatrical speculation secure D.'s reputation more firmly.

Before the Interregnum, D. served Sir Fulke GREVILLE, first Baron Brooke, and distinguished himself in literary circles by creating popular comedies like *The Witts* (perf. 1634; pub. 1649), tragicomedies like *Love and Honour* (1634), and masques such as *The Temple of Love* (perf. February 10, 1635), *Britannia Triumphans* (perf. January 8, 1638), and *Luminalia* (perf. February 6, 1638) during the same period. His volume of poetry, *Madagascar*, was published in 1638. That same year, D. became poet laureate, succeeding Ben JONSON who had died the previous year, and also became a favorite of Queen Henrietta Maria. From early in the decade, he had taken to signing himself "Servant to Her Majesty." He was granted a royal patent to build a theater that was nullified by the outbreak of the Civil War.

During the war, D. served bravely. Charles I knighted him in 1643 for his efforts in running supplies across the Channel during the siege of Gloucester. In exile in Paris, D. began a chivalric verse EPIC, *Gondibert*, which remained unfinished. The 1,700 quatrains he did complete were published in 1651. D. was captured at sea while sailing to America to assist royalist forces and was confined for several years in the Tower of London. According to legend, John MILTON won his ultimate release.

Once released from prison, D. began covert attempts to undermine the Puritan ban on theater in London. Moving a company into the old Phoenix/ Cockpit theater in Drury Lane, still standing from its

Renaissance days, he set about producing disguised entertainments. In his first attempt, *The First Day's Entertainment* (perf. 1656; pub. 1659), D. sought to skirt the prohibition against stage plays by billing it as "declamations and musick." The success of this work emboldened D. to write and produce *The Siege of Rhodes* (part 1, perf. 1656; parts 1 and 2, perf. 1661; part 1, pub. 1656; parts 1 and 2, pub. 1663). *The Siege of Rhodes*, produced during the Interregnum, became the first English opera, the first play in England to import (via France) the Italian style of painted stage scenery, and the first play in England to employ a female performer. D. thereby set the style for Restoration production four years before the Restoration.

When Charles II regained the throne in 1660, D. and Thomas KILLIGREW were granted royal monopolies on theater in London. D. founded the new Duke of York's Playhouse in Lincoln's Inn Fields where he created the role of impresario, writing, producing, managing, and adapting plays. In 1667, he collaborated with John DRYDEN on his famous adaptation of Shakespeare's *The Tempest* and established the style of indoor, aristocratic production that became a feature of early RESTORATION DRAMA.

BIBLIOGRAPHY: Bordinat, P., and S. B. Blaydes, *Sir W. D.* (1981); Edmond, M., *Rare Sir W. D.* (1987)

BRIAN JAY CORRIGAN

DAVIDSON, John

b. 11 April 1857, Barrhead, Renfrewshire, Scotland; d. 23 March 1909, Penzance, Cornwall

D. studied at Edinburgh University and became a schoolteacher, leaving to become a clerk. His poetic plays *Bruce* (1886), *Smith: A Tragedy* (1888), and *Scaromouch in Naxos* (1889) were published before he moved to London. *Fleet Street Eclogues* (1893) established him as a poet. He contributed to the *Yellow Book* and knew W. B. YEATS, Max BEERBOHM, and Edmund GOSSE. D.'s most important work is in his *Ballads and Songs* (1894), *Second Series of Fleet Street Eclogues* (1896), *New Ballads* (1897), and *The Last Ballad* (1899). The ballad "Thirty Bob a Week" is best known among his verse. He authored numerous poetic dramas and published a series of sixpenny pamphlets: *Testament of a Vivisector* (1901), *The Testament of a Man Forbid* (1901), *The Testament of an Empire-Builder* (1902), *The Testament of a Prime Minister* (1904), and *The Testament of John Davidson* (1908), expressing a defiant and materialist outlook. T. S. ELIOT acknowledged his debt to D.'s "dingy urban images" and D. has been called "the first of the moderns." In 1896, D. translated François Coppée's play *Pour la Couronne* as *For the Crown*, which was performed by Sir Johnston Forbes-Robertson and

Mrs. Patrick Campbell. D.'s translations and essays were numerous, but his earnings were small. Always an unhappy man, at odds with the world—"The present is a dungeon dark/Of social problems. Break the jail!" he wrote—he drowned himself in the sea.

DAVIE, Donald [Alfred]

b. 17 July 1922, Barnsley; d. 18 September 1995, Exeter, Devon

D. is widely regarded as one of modern England's most distinguished poets, critics, translators, and editors. As a poet and literary critic, he has been associated, since the 1950s, with a group of like-minded poets called "The Movement." The group included writers such as Philip LARKIN, Thom GUNN, Kingsley AMIS, D. J. ENRIGHT, Elizabeth JENNINGS, Robert CONQUEST, and John WAIN, among others. But it was D.'s first critical book, *Purity of Diction in English Verse* (1952), that established him as the Movement's most intellectually respected spokesperson. D. and members of the Movement shared a mutual antipathy toward a kind of poetry that was built solely on symbolism and IMAGISM, had abandoned conventional poetic syntax, and whose structure was primarily musical rather than logical. They were particularly critical of the linguistic obscurity of poets such as Gerard Manley HOPKINS, T. S. ELIOT, and Ezra Pound, though D. would later revise his opinion of Pound by writing two laudatory books on him.

Another early influence on D.'s poetry and criticism was the work of American poet and critic Yvor Winters, who insisted that poetry express moral and ethical viewpoints; poetry should also reveal its message within a rational context and structure in clear and unambiguous language. D. harked back to 18th-c. poet Oliver GOLDSMITH's notion of "chaste diction" in crafting proper metaphors; D. praised William WORDSWORTH as the last poet to "purify the language of the tribe."

In D.'s next important critical work, *Articulate Energy: An Enquiry into the Syntax of English Poetry* (1955), he further develops his ideas concerning what constitutes great poetry. He finds English poetry's greatest strength in 18th-c. Augustan poetry and its elegantly balanced use of formal syntax and structure. It is these qualities that produce clear, reasoned, and readable modern verse and make it accessible to any educated reader. But D. also insists that modern poetry must always incorporate a clear ethical content.

D.'s early volumes of poetry, *Brides of Reason* (1955) and *A Winter Talent and Other Poems* (1957), contain poems of classical restraint, whose subject matter comes out of his sense of place and history, especially from his childhood in the north of England. Much of the subject matter throughout his sixteen volumes of poetry concern specific geographical locations, which some critics believe was the influence of Black Mountain poets Charles Olson and Edward Dorn, both of whom wrote about physical place. Two of D.'s most praised volumes are geographically grounded: *Essex Poems* (1969) and *The Shires* (1974) focused on specific landscapes. Indeed, *The Shires* consists of forty poems on the forty counties, or shires, of England.

Though D. had initially criticized the imagistic and symbolic obscurity of Pound's work, he eventually came to admire his work so deeply that he wrote two groundbreaking books on him. He had come to appreciate the power, depth, and comprehensiveness of Pound's imagination and memory. In both *Ezra Pound: Poet as Sculptor* (1964) and *Pound* (1975; repub. as *Ezra Pound*, 1976), D. explicates Pound's literary and historical sources from Homer, Dante, the medieval scholastics through the Latin and Greek historians, among others.

During D.'s World War II experience as a British officer, he spent several years in Arctic Russia learning Slavic languages. He became a translator of the poetry of Boris Pasternak in *The Poems of Dr. Zhivago* (1965); D.'s *The Forests of Lithuania* (1959) was his translated version of Adam Michiewicz's Polish romantic verse novel *Pan Tadeusz* (1834). Several critics noted that D.'s poetry had become metaphorically richer and more sensuous possibly due to his translations of these Slavic masterpieces.

Though D. maintained a lifelong interest in religion—he was reared a Baptist in Yorkshire—it wasn't until the late 1970s and early 1980s that he produced three important books concerning religious poetry: *A Gathered Church: The Literature of the English Dissenting Interest, 1700–1930* (1978); *The New Oxford Book of Christian Verse* (1981); and *English Hymnology in the Eighteenth Century* (1980). D. viewed religious dissent, especially from the Church of England, as a major contributing factor to the enrichment of the English language. Without dissenting voices English culture would have missed some of D.'s most admired writers: Isaac WATTS, Charles WESLEY, and especially William COWPER. He claimed that these writers were responsible for keeping the language "crisp, supple, and responsible."

D. was one of the few 20th-c. poets writing in the scholarly and pastoral traditions of Pound, Matthew ARNOLD, and Winters. He successfully combined deep learning with poetic genius, a rare occurrence in the history of modern British poetry.

BIBLIOGRAPHY: Dekker, G., ed., *D. D. and the Responsibilities of Literature* (1983); Dodsworth, M., "D. D.," *Agenda* 14 (Summer 1976): 15–32; Kermode, F., ed., *Ezra Pound/D. D.* (1976)

PATRICK MEANOR

DAVIE, Elspeth [Dryer]
b. 20 March 1919, Kilmarnock, Ayrshire, Scotland; d. 14 November 1995, Edinburgh, Scotland

Novelist and short story writer, D. is acknowledged as one of the major Scottish writers of short fiction in the second half of the 20th c. She first gained critical recognition with the publication in 1968 of *The Spark and Other Stories*, followed by what many consider her most accomplished work, *The High Tide Talker and Other Stories* (1976). Later collections include *The Funny Night of Hats and Other Stories* (1980), *A Traveller's Room* (1985), and *Death of a Doctor and Other Stories* (1992). Throughout her career, D. projected an abstract, idiosyncratic style focusing on themes of loneliness, identity, and alienation within modern society. Her novels, less successful than her short stories, include *Providings* (1965), *Creating a Scene* (1971), and *Climbers on a Stair* (1978).

DAVIES, John, of Hereford
b. 1565?, Hereford; bur. 6 July 1618, London

Of Welsh descent, D. adopted the designation of his birthplace to his name to distinguish himself from other writers with the same name, in particular, Sir John DAVIES. D.'s most well-known work is the *Microcosmus* (1603), based on Joshua SYLVESTER's influential translation in 1598 of Guillaume de Salluste Du Bartas's *La Semaine* (1578), an EPIC poem on the Creation that D. dedicated to his patrons, JAMES I and Queen Anne. D.'s *Wittes Pilgrimage* (1605?) collects sonnets and commendatory poems that share conceptual similarities with the work of John DONNE (it is thought that the two poets were acquainted with one another). Later works include *The Scourge of Folly* (1611), addressed to Donne; *The Muses Sacrifice* (1612), a volume of devotional poems; and the *Muses-Teares* (1613), written upon the death in 1612 of Henry, Prince of Wales, D.'s former student at Oxford.

DAVIES, [Sir] John
b. April 1569, Tisbury, Wiltshire; d. 8 December 1626, London

D. wrote the delightful poem *Orchestra* (1596), in praise of dancing. His translation of Ovid's *Epigrams* (1598?), printed with posthumous work by Christopher MARLOWE, was burned in 1599 by order of the Archbishop of Canterbury. D.'s *Nosce Teipsum* (1599), dedicated to Queen ELIZABETH I, is considered among the best of English philosophical poems. In quatrains, it deals with the nature and immortality of the human soul. The same year D. published *The Hymns of Astraea*, acrostics based on the words "Elisabetha Regina." With Sir Robert Cotton, D. was a founder-member of the Society of Antiquaries.

DAVIES, Thomas
b. 1712?; d. 5 May 1785, London

D. is best remembered for his biography of the actor David GARRICK (1780), but it is his own colorful life that makes for an interesting portrait of the London theater and literary scene of the late 18th c. Actor turned bookseller, D. played the original Wilmot in George LILLO's *The Fatal Curiosity* in 1736 and later edited Lillo's complete collection of plays. In 1773, D. published a two-volume edition of Samuel JOHNSON's *Miscellaneous and Fugitive Pieces*. Although it was printed without the author's permission, Johnson did not stay angry at D. long as the two remained good friends and D. is credited with introducing Johnson to James BOSWELL, whose *Life of Samuel Johnson* would become one of the most distinctive biographies in the English language. D.'s editions are marked by their fine quality, something that eventually bankrupted him. He tried to insure the prosperity of his wife by writing his *Dramatic Miscellanies* (3 vols., 1783–84), which made for insightful reading but still left his wife a pauper.

DAVIES, W[illiam] H[enry]
b. 3 July 1871, Newport, South Wales; d. 26 September 1940, Nailsworth, Gloucestershire

D.'s South-Welsh restlessness took him tramping across North America between 1893 and 1899, where he famously lost a leg as a result of jumping from a freight train in 1899. This handicap in no way circumscribed his zeal for walking and his general appetite for life, both as a hobo poet in London and as a writer in more settled environments. It was Bernard SHAW and Edward THOMAS who encouraged D. to publish these experiences in *The Autobiography of a Super-Tramp* (1908), which formed the first of a series of writings about his life. The volumes *Later Days* (1925) and the posthumous *Young Emma* (1980) might be mentioned as parts of an important triad in this vein. The latter volume, coupled with his *Selected Poems* (1985), helped prompt a revival of interest in D. and his contemporaries, most notably the group that have come to be known as the "Dymock poets," which included Robert Frost, Thomas, and others.

D.'s work has endured the change in poetical fashion and practice that characterized the first half of the 20th c. and chastened the ideas of the second half. In the early part of the century, Thomas's review of *The Soul's Destroyer and Other Poems* (1905) helped raise D.'s profile, and his work appears in all five volumes of Edward Marsh's *Georgian Poetry*. This anthology ran its course from a successful first volume,

published in December 1912, to its demise in 1922, eclipsed by the new taste for modernist productions, in a year that saw the complete versions of both James JOYCE's *Ulysses* and T. S. ELIOT's *The Waste Land*. At this point the "Georgian" audience seems to have faltered.

Ironically, it was Ezra Pound in a review of D.'s *Collected Poems* (1916) who was of the opinion that "the sound quality is . . . nearer that of the Elizabethans than of the nineteenth century." Thomas had also spotted a strong link with the traditions of Elizabethan, Jacobean, and Caroline lyrical poetry as well as a debt to William BLAKE. D. seems not to have been influenced by his contemporaries to any great extent but is a times reminiscent of William WORDSWORTH, demonstrating a vocal immediacy, a simplicity of vocabulary, rhythm, and thought. At a glance, the poetry shows a broad range of subject matter and an obvious appeal to the common reader. D.'s popularity continues to spring from this appeal, yet also paradoxically, contributes to periodical decline in interest.

D.'s belief in the "near inescapable connection between a poet's life and his writing" is at times painfully apparent as the reader moves through a literary landscape of near-visionary joys or encounters the varieties of more singular human experience, tinged by the HUMOR or grim pessimism of the poet. D.'s lyrics are often presented in four-line iambics of three, four, or five feet, and he has also used couplet rhymes, blank verse, songs, ballads, and epigrams. His poetical reputation could be said to rest upon a short canon of very well-known and well-loved poems including "Leisure" (containing the lines "What is this life if, full of care,/We have no time to stand and stare") and "The Kingfisher" ("It was the Rainbow gave thee birth"), "The Bird of Paradise," "The Beautiful," "Kitty," and "When in Praise," which cover several responses to natural life and the human condition.

BIBLIOGRAPHY: Harlow, S., *W. H. D.* (1993); Hockey, L., *W. H. D.* (1971); Stonesifer, R. J., *W. H. D.* (1963)

CHRISTOPHER J. P. SMITH

DAVIS, Dick
b. 18 April 1945, Portsmouth, Hampshire

Educated at King's College, Cambridge, D. first published his poems with Clive WILMER and Robert WELLS in the Cambridge anthology *Shade Mariners* (1970). In 1975, he published *In the Distance*, which earned him critical recognition for its technical maturity enriched by traditional poetic forms and meter. His reputation was further enhanced with later collections: *Seeing the Anvil* (1980), *Visitations* (1983), *The Covenant* (1984), *Devices and Desires* (1989), *A Kind of Love* (1991), and *Touchwood* (1996). D. is also accomplished as a literary critic, editor, and translator.

DAVYS, Mary

b. ca. 1674, Dublin, Ireland?; d. 30 June or 1 July 1732, London

Novelist, playwright, and poet, D. was the first writer to explore the dramatic possibility of including both sides of the correspondence in an epistolary novel. D. was a more inventive writer than many of her contemporaries, but her work has been largely overlooked by scholarship. Only now, with increasing interest in the subtleties of early-18th-c. literature, is her work beginning to be accorded the interest and significance that it deserves.

D. was possibly born in Ireland and probably spent the early part of her life in poverty. She married the Reverend Peter Davys, friend of Jonathan SWIFT. After his death in 1698, D. began to write for money and moved to London. D.'s first two novels, *The Amours of Alcippus and Lucippe* (1704) and *The Fugitive* (1705), were not successful. D. also wrote, but did not publish, *The False Friend; or, The Treacherous Portuguese* during 1700 to 1704. D. then moved to York, where she wrote *The Northern Heiress; or, The Humours of York*, a satire on mercenary marriages and York society. The play, staged at Lincoln's Inn and published in 1716, was a triumph. With the receipts, D. bought a coffee shop in Cambridge, which provided her with a reliable income and an audience for her work until her death.

In 1724, D. published *The Reform'd Coquet; or, Memoirs of Amoranda* with a subscription list naming Alexander POPE and John GAY. In 1725, *The Works of Mrs. Davys: Consisting of Plays, Novels, Poems and Familiar Letters* were published in two volumes by subscription. Volume 1 comprised *The Self-Rival*, an unperformed comedy; *The Northern Heiress; The Merry Wanderer*, a rewrite of *The Fugitive;* and a satirical poem "The Modern Poet." In volume 2, D. published *The Reform'd Coquet; The Lady's Tale*, a rewrite of *The Amours of Alcippus and Lucippe; The Cousins*, a revision of *The Treacherous Portuguese;* and *Familiar Letters betwixt a Gentleman and a Lady.* D. radically altered her three early novels for publication in the *Works*, infusing dramatic nuances, bawdy jokes, and philosophical ideas.

D.'s *Works* display her wit and complex plotting at their finest. *Familiar Letters betwixt a Gentleman and a Lady* is the correspondence between Berina, a sprightly town Whig, and Artander, her admirer, who has been exiled for his royalist sympathies. D.'s novel crucially rejects the monologic voice that had previously organized the epistolary novel. The presence of both sides of the correspondence undermines the sincerity of the writers' feelings, since we realize that so many of their declarations are mere point-scoring, and the prospect of their marriage is an ambiguous, rather than a happy, ending.

In *The Reform'd Coquet*, the heroine, a flighty heiress, is tamed into wifely submission by a young man disguised as her elderly guardian, Formator. D.'s tone is light, but Formator's scheme pivots on casual brutality. His program of "education" climaxes when he facilitates Amoranda's abduction and near-rape. This suggestion that cruelty and masochism underlie the male-female relationship is vital to D.'s final and most powerful novel, *The Accomplish'd Rake; or, Modern Fine Gentleman* (1727). The libertine hero, Sir John Gaillard, seduces the women of his acquaintance, before drugging and raping Miss Friendly, the daughter of his oldest friend. The novel concludes with a satire on the conventional fictional closure of a happy marriage, as Friendly marries Gaillard in order to legitimize their son.

D.'s novels make use of dramatic techniques to explore how disguise and pretense can manipulate identity, but, underneath the scene-shifting, the narratives always suggest that men's cruelty and women's attraction to the cruelty of men are ubiquitous.

BIBLIOGRAPHY: De Bruyn, F., "M. D.," in Battestin, M. C., ed., *British Novelists, 1660–1800*, part 1, *DLB* 39 (1985): 131–38; McBurney, W. H., "Mrs. M. D.: Forerunner of Fielding," *PMLA* 74 (September 1959): 348–55

KATE WILLIAMS

DAWSON, Jennifer

b. 23 January 1929, Welwyn Garden City; d. 4 October 2000, Charlbury

D. achieved instant fame with the publication of her first novel, *The Ha-Ha* (1961), which won the James Tait Black Memorial Prize. It drew on her experiences as a mental patient during her third year at St Anne's College, Oxford, which she found overwhelming, and later as a psychiatric social worker. The novel is powerful in its detail. An attack on the mental health regime of the day, it makes painful reading, and has become a standard text for trainee social and mental health workers. It was republished in 1985 and dramatized in 1962. However, although she continued to write fiction, it attracted less attention. Published in the same year as *The Ha-Ha, The Queen of Trent*, a story for children written in collaboration with Elizabeth Mitchell, was followed in 1962 with her second novel, *Fowler's Snare*. Her other books include *The Cold Country* (1965); *Strawberry Boy* (1976); *A Hospital Wedding* (1978), a collection of short stories; *A Field of Scarlet Poppies* (1979); *The Upstairs People* (1988); and *Judasland* (1989).

DAY, John

b. 1574, Cawston, Norfolk; d. 1640?, London?

D.'s fame rests on a masque, traditionally dated to 1607, though not printed until 1641, *The Parliament of Bees*. Various complaints are brought to Prorex, the Master "Bee," against the humble bee, the drone, the wasp, and others. This satirical allegory ends with a royal progress by Oberon, who distributes justice. D.'s *Isle of Gulls* (1606), performed by the Children of the Chapel at Blackfriars (Hamlet's "little eyases"), is a prose comedy based on Sir Philip SIDNEY's *Arcadia*: the jokes are now obscure, but its satire on relations between England and Scotland led to prison sentences for those involved. In 1608, D. published two comedies, *Law Tricks; or, Who Would Have Thought It* (perf. ca. 1604) and *Humour Out of Breath* (perf. ca. 1607–8). D. collaborated in writing plays for Philip Henslowe's company from 1598 onward: with Thomas DEKKER and SAMUEL ROWLEY, *The Noble Spanish Soldier* (perf. ca. 1622; pub. 1634); he also collaborated with Henry CHETTLE on *The Blind Beggar of Bethnal Green* (perf. 1600; pub. 1659), also known as *Thomas Strowd;* and with William Haughton, Richard Hathway, and Wentworth Smith. In 1607, D. wrote, with WILLIAM ROWLEY and George Wilkins, *The Travails of the Three English Brothers*.

DAY, Thomas

b. 22 June 1748, London; d. 28 September 1789, Bear Hill

D.'s infatuation with the educational theories of Jean-Jacques Rousseau led to the publication of *The History of Sandford and Merton* (3 vols., 1783–89), a didactic book for young people: Merton is rich, spoiled, and idle, while Sandford is a hardworking farmer's son, who becomes his exemplar. The book was popular with parents, though probably less so with children. Putting his theories into practice, D. adopted two orphan girls, intending to train whichever of them was most promising to be his wife. The girls were unreceptive and D. married an heiress. In 1788, D. wrote *The History of Little Jack* (repub. as *The Forsaken Infant*, 1806), another moral tale about a child suckled by goats and reared by a religious old man. Among D.'s poems were *The Dying Negro* (1773), with John Bicknell, influential in the antislavery movement, and *The Devoted Legions* (1776), which praised the spirit of American libertarianism.

DAY-LEWIS, C[ecil]

b. 27 April 1904, Ballintubber, Ireland; d. 22 May 1972, Hadley Common, Hertfordshire

Poet and later detective-novelist, D.-L. is, historically and critically, inextricably associated with that re-markable group of young poets—W. H. AUDEN, Louis MACNEICE, and Stephen SPENDER—who first met as undergraduates at Oxford in the 1920s. Inevitably, in the light of British poetic developments in the 1930s, this group of Oxford associates is now often referred to as the "Auden generation" and much critical ink has been needlessly spilled in efforts to demonstrate Auden's influence upon the others.

Of course, in a broad sense, all poets are influenced, one way or another, by other poets, dead or alive, who have written before them, but the originally influential factor at Oxford in the 1920s was not Auden but D.-L., if only because he was the oldest of the four and therefore arrived at Oxford two years before Auden and MacNeice and three years before Spender. As regards publication, D.-L. was also the first in the field: his first collection of verse, entitled *Beechen Vigil*, appeared in 1925, while he was still at Oxford; Auden's first collection entitled *Poems* was published in 1930 and MacNeice's *Blind Fireworks* in 1929. Spender has a minor collection entitled *Twenty Poems* in 1930 but his much more substantial *Poems*, which contains most of his best verse, came out in 1933. Though D.-L. was not the "leader" of the group in any formal sense, he was by no means merely a follower and was, at the time, certainly regarded publicly as an initiator and a formative influence in the 1930s.

It is noteworthy that for his second collection, *Transitional Poem* (1929), a book that firmly established his reputation as a mature and considerable poet, D.-L., in a gesture of defiance on behalf of his proletarian sympathies (and, perhaps, also as an assertion of independence) changed his family name, dropping the hyphen. It took him over twenty years of adult poetry-hood to muster the courage to reclaim it. His son, Sean Day-Lewis, in his 1980 biography of his father, comments: "The name, by the way, is Day-Lewis. It was created, with hyphen, in the Dublin of 1863 when the brothers Frank and George Day entered the business of their uncle, Fred Lewis. Cecil dropped the hyphen from his writing in 1927, as a gesture of inverted snobbery. At the end of his life, when he came to believe, wrongly, that Day had native Irish origins, and as he so disliked being addressed as Mr. Lewis, he put the hyphen back where he could."

In 1936, W. B. YEATS was invited to compile the first edition of the *Oxford Book of Modern Verse*. He fixed the limiting dates as 1892–1935. His book begins with Walter PATER's "Mona Lisa" ("She is older than the rocks among which she sits") and finishes with George BARKER's "He comes among." In between are, *inter-alia*, eight poems by D.-L., three by Auden, four by MacNeice, and two by Spender. Similar anthologies later in the century show the balance gradually changing, with Auden becoming more and more dominant and D.-L., though still recognized as a major figure, now being regarded as the lesser poet. Ironically, it was D.-L. who, on the death of John MASEFIELD in 1968, was appointed poet laureate. Both D.-L. and Auden were elected as Oxford Professor of Poetry, the former in 1951, to serve for five years, the latter in 1956 until 1961. D.-L. had also, in 1947, delivered the Clark Lectures at Cambridge and had published them in 1947 under the title *The Poetic Image.*

As well as his many collections of verse (perhaps the best of which were *From Feathers to Iron* in 1931 and *Overtures to Death* in 1938), D.-L. also published distinguished translations of Virgil—*Georgics* (1941), *The Aeneid* (1952), *The Eclogues* (1952), and, in a quite different vein, twenty novels of detective fiction, the first, *A Question of Proof*, in 1935, and the last, *The Private Wound*, in 1968: for the publication of these he adopted the pseudonym "Nicholas Blake," though there was no public mystery about this; it was a very open secret. When he was fifty-five, he wrote an autobiography called *The Buried Day* (1960).

But before all else, D.-L. was a poet. Charles CAUSLEY, a far from negligible poet himself, described D.-L. in 1958 as "the man I thought and still think the greatest lyric poet of the century, and this is including Yeats and Hardy." Of all his extensive output there are two individual poems that merit special mention. Both appear in the volume entitled *Overtures to Death:* they are "The Nabara" and the eponymous poem. Causley did not specifically cite these, but he might well have done: they perfectly bear out the opinion he expressed. "He spent his life learning to understand himself and this is what his verse is about," says Sean Day-Lewis in the preface to the biography. "The writing of poetry is a vocation, a game, a habit, and a search for truth," says D.-L. in his autobiography.

BIBLIOGRAPHY: Day-Lewis, S., *C. D.-L., An English Literary Life* (1980); Gelp, A., *Living in Time: The Poetry of C. D. L.* (1998); Scarfe, F., *Auden and After: The Liberation of Poetry, 1940–1941* (1942); Yeats, W. B., ed., *The Oxford Book of Modern Verse* (1936)

ERIC SALMON

DEE, John

b. 13 July 1527, London; d. December 1608?, London

It is difficult to asses the overall impact D. had not only on learning and the development of thought in Renaissance England but on the Western world in general. As Peter French suggested in his early study of D., it would take at least a dozen or so scholars in each subject area such as mathematics, cartography, chemistry, and hermeticism to perform an accurate assessment of D.'s scholarly acumen. In 1546, he was

awarded one of the first fellowships at Trinity College, Cambridge. And at the age of twenty-one, D. was already lecturing to full capacity audiences in Louvain on Euclidean geometry. But it was his abandonment of what are now considered the sciences for studies into the occult and magical evocation of spirits that has served to fuel many a story and play. Consequently, D. has wrongly been looked upon as England's own Dr. Faustus. But D.'s influence on Renaissance literature, albeit often an indirect one, has been substantial.

Some of D.'s more illustrious students were none other than Mary and Sir Philip SIDNEY. Chemistry and alchemy were two of D.'s specialties, so it is possible that he and Mary Sidney spent time in the laboratory exploring chemical processes. When we read Sidney's *An Apologie for Poetrie*, it is clear that hermeticism, alchemy, and a multidisciplined approach, all signature aspects of D.'s work, were ingrained in Sidney's understanding of language and the world. Sir Edward DYER was also an acquaintance of D.'s along with other attendants of ELIZABETH I's court.

D. published a fair amount of prose during his lifetime of which his *Monas Hieroglyphica* (1564) is the most important. The *Monas* is a crucial text not only about the salient role played by the emblem and figuration in the Renaissance, but it also stands as a counter-argument to the mechanistic philosophy established by Marinn Mersenne and his disciple, Descartes. D. felt that his symbol, the monas, was a theophanic figure that could explain many truths he expounded upon in the format of geometric theorems. In theorems 1 and 2, D. posits that the most basic manifestation of things occurred by means of the point, straight line, and the circle. D.'s *Monas* would have a lasting impact on figures such as Henry and Thomas VAUGHAN, various Rosicrucian sympathizers, not to mention Gottfried Wilhelm Leibniz, and entire schools of philosophy in the years to come.

Yet some of D.'s most important and intriguing texts are his magical diaries that explore the tenuous world of angelic evocation. Along with his associate and seer, Sir Edward Kelley, D. explored the spiritual planes and received an entire complex system of magic known as the Enochian calls. Based on the biblical tale of the temple that Enoch had discovered that was inscribed with the keys to the mysteries to creation, D. and Kelley received an array of incantations in the angelic or Adamic language that were said to summon the forces of creation. Many portions of these calls, in their English version, bear a strong resemblance to passages from the Book of Revelation, Isaiah, and other apocalyptic visionary texts of the Bible. In fact, D.'s angelic diaries are the only examples of their type to survive from the Renaissance.

One of D.'s greatest contributions to England's literary and bibliographical heritage was his library. It has been estimated that his entire collection was larger than Oxford's and Cambridge's combined. His holdings covered almost every conceivable important topic of the period including the occult arts. In fact, as William H. Sherman has aptly posited, because D. owned the most formidable libraries he could control the dissemination and distribution of information throughout England during the Elizabethan period.

But it has been D.'s long-standing reputation as a conjurer and alchemist that has made him the subject of many creative literary works. Although it has not been incontrovertibly proven, it is relatively clear that D. served in part as a model figure for Prospero in William SHAKESPEARE's *The Tempest*. Like D., Prospero valued his books "above all else." Prospero's subjugation of the native Caliban has been viewed in terms of early colonialism. D. himself was one of England's first colonialist ideologues evidenced in his *General and Rare Memorials Pertayning to the Perfect Arte of Navigation* (1577).

Other authors have appropriated D.'s figure in more disparaging portrayals like Samuel BUTLER's in his long poem, *Hudibras*. Butler takes a very caustic view of other-worldly inspiration and employs it to paint a sardonic picture of his conjurer, Sidrophel. And more recently, Peter ACKROYD has produced a novel of supernatural intrigue entitled *The House of Dr. Dee*.

After centuries of neglect, scholars are finally giving D.'s work some long overdue serious attention. Especially for the English mind-set, D. is a seminal figure in terms of the connection between science and the supernatural, and will continue to exert his presence upon literature in overt, and possibly unseen, ways.

BIBLIOGRAPHY: Clulee, N. H., *J. D.'s Natural Philosophy* (1988); French, P. J., *J. D.* (1972); Sherman, W. H., *J. D.* (1997); Wooley, B., *The Queen's Conjurer* (2001)

                                    BOB PODGURSKI

DEEPING, [George] Warwick
b. 28 May 1877, Southend-on-Sea, Essex; d. 20 April 1950, Weybridge, Surrey

A best-selling novelist in both Europe and the U.S. in the 1920s and 1930s, D. came to epitomize for many cultural commentators what Q. D. LEAVIS called "the faux bon." D. and Gilbert Frankau infuriated Leavis for "touching grossly on fine issues." Not only did the popularity of these middlebrow writers fuel fears of mass culture but their assumption of moral authority in attacking self-appointed guardians of the health

of English letters made such critics fear for the basis of their own cultural power.

Though all D.'s sixty-eight novels sold well, from 1903 to 1956, it was the enormous success of *Sorrell and Son* in 1925 that exposed him to the attention of writers as diverse as Graham GREENE, George ORWELL, and John Hampson. D. is still evoked by authors of higher cultural status than his own, Martin AMIS and Sebastian FAULKS for example, to characterize the shabby, twilight world of his readers whose quality of life is deplored or despised, or, in the case of John BETJEMAN's mock appreciation in "Station Syren," affectionately patronized. But for its millions of admiring readers *Sorrell and Son* had what the historian Ross McKibbin calls "talismanic status." It was translated into most European languages. Filmed twice (1927 and 1933), it was a popular television serial in 1983.

Sorrell and Son engaged anxieties, widespread at the end of World War I, about the direction of social change. Its success lay less in intricacies of plot or narrative suspense than in its fabular quality. Captain Sorrell, after honorable service in war, returns to an England where there is no guarantee of employment for a "gentleman" and no guarantee of marital fidelity from a "tigerishly" lustful and mercenary wife. She abandons both Sorrell and son. Central to the reader's emotional engagement with the hero is the sense that Sorrell is one of "thousands upon thousands of people . . . hanging on to the edge of existence." The stoic endurance of the aging hero as he takes on the menial work of a porter in a hotel is the object of sustained admiration. Despite the physical brutality of the working-class boys of the town school and the snobbish hostility of the masters at the public (private) school, the porter's son is released by academic success from social and economic anxiety to become a doctor, D.'s own profession. Controversially, this profession enables Christopher Sorrell to release his father from cancer.

In novels like *Old Wine and New* (1932), D. constructs a retrospective myth that *Sorrell and Son* was radically different from his previous novels, many having been characterized as the kind of historical "tapestry" novels written by Maurice HEWLETT. In D.'s brief and unrevealing autobiographical statements, he constantly asserts that the reality of his medical service in the trenches woke him from the "dreams" of his prewar historical fictions and enabled him to "to dip his pen in life and extract reality." In fact, D. had engaged with contemporary issues from the beginning of his career. Alcoholism, euthanasia, syphilis, pollution of the municipal water supply, ambiguity of gender identity, marital infidelity, rape, the inadequacy of sexual education, and the military machine's threat to individual autonomy were all themes before *Sorrell and Son* was written. He must be the only novelist to be compared by one reviewer to both Hewlett and Henrik Ibsen.

Despite D.'s insistence on the virility of his writing and his socially marginalized heroes, his self-justificatory fictionalizations of the middlebrow writer produce some curiously feminized images of popular authorship. *Blind Man's Year* (1937) dramatizes the popular author as a disfigured female recluse whose links with reality are maintained by the odysseys of her blinded husband on the streets of London.

D.'s embarrassed and resentful fictional assertions of his own cultural value challenge the assumption of writers as diverse as Pierre Bourdieu and Leavis that producers of popular literature are necessarily unreflective about the status and nature of their art. Modern commentators focus on D.'s snobbery, misogyny, and racism, but his anticommunitarian values are not identical with those of a notional Edwardian hegemony. His hostility to the family and his indifference to imperialist assertions of national identity suggest that his individualism is asserted as much in defiance of hegemonic values as in support of them.

BIBLIOGRAPHY: Amis, K., "Pater and Old Chap," *Observer*, October 13, 1957: 15; Johnson, G. J., "G. W. D.," in Johnson, G. J., ed., *Late-Victorian and Edwardian British Novelists*, First Series, *DLB* 153 (1995): 51–59

MARY GROVER

DEFOE, Daniel

b. 1660, London; d. 24 April 1731, Cripplegate

With over five hundred authenticated titles ranging from brief pamphlets to multivolume works of journalism to his credit, D. is one of the most prolific of the major English authors. A master of realistic prose, D. has had an enormous influence on the development of journalism and the novel; some even consider him to be England's first novelist.

D., banned from entering Oxford or Cambridge because he was a Presbyterian Nonconformist, attended Charles Morton's academy for Dissenters with the intention of becoming a minister; however, after his marriage to Mary Tuffley in 1684, D. became a merchant. Being active in politics, D. joined Monmouth's rebellion in 1685, and, in 1688, he rode with the troops of William III. In 1701, D. published *The True-Born Englishman*, a popular satirical poem that defended William III, and, in 1702, he published *The Shortest Way with the Dissenters*, a pamphlet that ironically demanded the suppression of dissent. This publication led to D.'s being fined, imprisoned, and pilloried.

Between 1703 and 1714, D. was employed by the Tory statesman Robert Harley as a government agent. D.'s assignments required him to travel throughout England and Scotland and provided him with material for his three-volume *A Tour through the Whole Island of Great Britain* (1724–27), a lively—mainly first-hand—account of the state of the country. From 1704 through 1713, D. published the *Review*, a thrice-weekly paper that greatly influenced journalism in England, especially the work of Richard STEELE and Joseph ADDISON.

However, despite these contributions to journalism, D. remains best known for his fiction, especially such novels as *The Life and Strange Surprising Adventures of Robinson Crusoe* (1719), *The Fortunes and Misfortunes of the Famous Moll Flanders* (1721), *A Journal of the Plague Year* (1722), and *Roxana* (1724). D. wrote *Robinson Crusoe*, his first novel, when he was nearly sixty, and it remains his most famous work. The novel is a turning point in fiction because, unlike most of its predecessors, it is realistic and exact in its details rather than being simply a vehicle for philosophical or anthropological observation. Against the advice of his father, the narrator, Robinson Crusoe, leaves home to seek adventure at sea. Soon Crusoe is captured by pirates and enslaved in North Africa. In fact, D. is one of the first, after Aphra BEHN, to incorporate African settings into English fiction, and D. continues to explore Africa as a setting for fiction in *Madagascar; or Robert Drury's Journal* (1729). Finally, after his escape from slavery, Crusoe is shipwrecked on an uninhabited island. For more than twenty years, Crusoe struggles against the elements and against his isolation as he builds a secure life. His routine is shattered by the arrival of Friday, a native who becomes Crusoe's slave and, later, his friend. Finally, Crusoe and Friday return to Europe where they again battle nature, in the form of a pack of wolves, as they travel from Spain to England. The major themes of *Robinson Crusoe*, which some consider the earliest adventure novel, include the conflict between people and nature, the problem of slavery, and concerns about faith, religion, and destiny.

A Journal of the Plague Year is frequently referred to as one of the first historical novels because it deals with actual events that occurred shortly after D.'s birth in 1660. H. F., a single man who has business responsibilities and who decides to stay in London rather than flee to Northamptonshire, tells the story. Indeed, H. F. is a memorable character who helps bring the past to life while using the events of the past to comment on national character. As in *Robinson Crusoe*, religion and faith are themes important to an understanding of the *Journal*.

Moll Flanders is one of the earliest social novels in English. Written in the form of a memoir, the novel is a story of sex, crime, and class struggle. Moll, one of the first fully developed women characters in the early English novel, is the daughter of a woman who has been exiled to Virginia as a punishment for theft.

The novel tells of Moll's early seduction, her marriages (including one unwitting marriage to her own brother), and her life as a successful pickpocket and thief. Moll herself is finally convicted and sent to Virginia with one of her former husbands who is also a criminal. In Virginia, Moll and her husband establish themselves as planters, and eventually, when they are nearly seventy, Moll and her gentleman return to England, resolving to do penance for their wicked lives. Throughout the novel, D. expresses an economic and social criticism of the times, and, as in several of his other works, examines the life of a character who lives on the boundaries of conventional society.

Roxana is not only D.'s last work of fiction but also the most sophisticated and elaborately constructed of his novels. Veering away from picaresque narrative, *Roxana*, like a truly modern novel, has a complex interplay of characters and a coherent sense of structure. *Roxana* presents itself to be the autobiography of Mlle. Beleau, the daughter of French Protestant refugees. Deserted by her husband, a London brewer, Roxana prospers as she passes from one man to another in England, France, and Holland. She wins the name Roxana after performing a dance she learned from a Turkish slave girl. Eventually, Roxana's past, in the form of her long-lost daughter Susan, confronts her, leading to the novel's disturbing conclusion. *Roxana* was not well received when it was first published, but, in recent decades, critics have found much to admire in the novel. To some degree, *Roxana* can be considered a feminist novel because Roxana is a complex character who seeks to survive and prosper but does not seek either a husband or a settled life.

While D.'s immortality is assured by his most popular work, *Robinson Crusoe*, his reputation also rests on his contributions to journalism and his exploration of genres (travel and adventure fiction, crime fiction, historical fiction, and feminist literature) at a time when the prose narrative was becoming the most popular mode of literature.

BIBLIOGRAPHY: Backscheider, P. R., *D. D.* (1986); Bell, I. A., *D.'s Fiction* (1985); Novak, M. E., *D. D.* (2001); Sutherland, J., *D. D.* (1971); West, R., *D. D.* (1998)

DAVE KUHNE

DEIGHTON, Len [Leonard Cyril]
b. 18 February 1929, London

Astonishingly prolific and versatile, D. writes in three distinct genres: spy thrillers, for which he is best known, the history of World War II, especially the role of the Royal Air Force, and expert books on French cuisine. He is also a skilled graphic artist. Many of his thrillers, which he likes to organize into trilogies, have been filmed and televised. *The Ipcress*

File (1962) made his name and was successfully filmed in 1965, starring Michael Caine. *Horse under Water* (1963), *Funeral in Berlin* (1964), and *The Billion Dollar Brain* (1966) all featured Harry Palmer as main character. The last two were also filmed in 1966 and 1967, respectively. *An Expensive Place to Die* (1967) was followed by *Spy Story* (1974), *Yesterday's Spy* (1975), and *Twinkle, Twinkle, Little Spy* (1976; repub. as *Catch a Falling Spy*, 1976) formed the next group. Next came a new hero, Bernard Sams, in *Berlin Game* (1983), *Mexico Set* (1985), and *London Match* (1985). In 1986, D. published the trilogy under the title *Game, Set and Match*, and wrote an elaborate introduction and prequel, *Winter* (1987). Another trilogy (*Spy Hook*, *Spy Line*, and *Spy Sinker*) came out in 1988, 1989, and 1990. Bernard Sams reappears in *Faith* (1995), *Hope* (1995), and *Charity* (1996). A series of novels set in the film industry began with *Close-Up* (1972). D. has also published short stories.

DEKKER, Thomas
b. ca. 1572, London; d. August 1632, London

Satirized by Ben JONSON in *Poetaster; or, The Arraignment* (1602) as Demetrius Fannius, the "simple . . . dresser of plays," D.'s dramatic reputation has fared little better in the ensuing centuries. He was first mentioned as a playwright by Philip Henslowe in 1598 and wrote in whole or in part over forty plays. Of his efforts only a scant half dozen survive in their original form. D. was apparently a popular collaborator. Most of his dramatic work was created in concert with such playwrights as John FORD, John WEBSTER, William ROWLEY, Thomas MIDDLETON, and Philip MASSINGER. His popularity among his collaborators might spring from a facility for rapid composition, a trait, if true, that yielded a hurried, overly rushed style that has not always stood D. well with critics. A vigorous writer with an eye to detail and colloquial speech, D. tends toward artificial plots while his tone is often moralizing.

Although D. wrote in most dramatic genres, he is thought of as mainly a writer of comedy. His solo dramatic reputation is mainly founded upon his play *The Shoemaker's Holiday* (perf. 1599; pub. 1600). This play is different from most of the genre of romantic comedy (or chronicle history) in that there are no truly wicked characters, and D. here demonstrates a preference for HUMOR through character and situation over poetic expression. The play deals with historical characters—Simon Eyre was the shoemaker who became Lord Mayor of London under the reign of Henry VI—and might, therefore, be considered a history or chronicle play in the tradition of Robert GREENE's *Friar Bacon and Friar Bungay*. However, its focus rests more upon the love relationships of Lacy and Rose and Rafe and Jane. Eyre's plot is less concerned with his historical significance than with his genial personality and upright dealings with his journeymen. It is therefore not too farfetched to consider this not a chronicle history but rather a romantic comedy. D. demonstrates here as in his other plays a spirit of gentleness toward the rascals that inhabit London's streets and a sense of humanity not unlike the better-developed sensibilities of the young Charles DICKENS of the *Sketches* and *Pickwick Papers*.

Of D.'s collaborative effort, several of his works rise to a level of modern fame if not genuine greatness. *Westward Ho* (with Webster, perf. 1604; pub. 1607), *Northward Ho* (with Webster, perf. 1605; pub. 1607), *The Roaring Girl* (with Middleton, perf. 1611; pub 1611), and *The Witch of Edmonton* (with Ford and Rowley, perf. 1621) each have claims to the second tier of RENAISSANCE DRAMA. D. is probably best remembered as one of the generals in the notorious "war of the theaters," which he and John MARSTON waged against Jonson. The various titles in the "war"—Marston's *Histriomastix; or, The Player Whipped* (perf. ca. 1598–99; pub. 1610); Jonson's *Poetaster*; D. and Marston's *Satiromastix; or, The Untrussing of the Humorous Poet* (perf. 1601)—may indicate a good-natured rivalry. D. and Jonson had collaborated under Henslowe as recently as 1599 on both *Page of Plymouth* and *The Tragedy of Robert II, King of Scots*, which are both lost. Later, in 1604, D. and Jonson collaborated on the civic devices set up in London to welcome JAMES I on his coronation entry. And Jonson answered D. and Webster's *Westward* and *Northward Ho* plays of 1604 and 1605 when he collaborated with Marston and George CHAPMAN on the superior *Eastward Ho*. Long afterward, however, in 1619, Jonson classed D. among the "rogues." The question therefore remains open regarding the true complexion of the "war."

D. took the baton from Thomas NASHE in 1609 and began writing rogue pamphlets. Nashe had been a friend of and successor to Greene in writing popular pamphlets or "discoveries" of cony catching and confidence trickery. D. continued the tradition with several popular tracts, the most important of which is *The Guls Horne-book* (1609). It is filled with wit, gentle good humor, and a sense of humanity even for villainy that must finally be regarded as the legacy of the author.

BIBLIOGRAPHY: Adler, D. R., *T. D.* (1983); Champion, L. S., *T. D. and the Tradition of English Drama* (1985); Conover, J. H., *T. D.* (1969)

BRIAN JAY CORRIGAN

DELAFIELD, E. M.

(pseud. of Edmee de la Pasture, later Elizabeth Dashwood) b. 9 June 1890, Sussex; d. 2 December 1943, Devon

D.'s pseudonym was adopted to differentiate herself from her writer mother Mrs. Henry de la Pasture. She endured a repressive upper-middle-class girlhood, only allowed to read for an hour a day. It was impressed on her that, like the heroine of her novel *Consequences* (1919), she must not "get a reputation for being *clever* . . . People do dislike that sort of thing so much in a girl!" Despite all her mother's efforts, she failed to marry and, planning to become a nun, entered a convent for a year (which she wrote about in a manuscript called "Brides of Heaven," reprinted in Violet Powell's biography of D.); after recuperating from that experience, she worked as a nurse from 1914 to 1917 and began writing in the evenings.

D.'s first novel was about a young girl eaten up with self-consciousness, who turns to Catholicism to try and find herself; her second described the strained relationships between a group of women working in a supply depot, and her third was about the close love between two sisters (she herself had one sister) and also about the effect of convent life on a young girl. The final book of this period, *Consequences*, which D. would later pick out as one of her own favorites, was a last take, as it were, on the same theme: it is a bleak and almost harrowing portrayal of a girl who is awkward in society and does not marry, becomes a nun, emerges into the world ten years later, but still cannot find herself and chooses suicide.

In 1919, D. married Paul Dashwood, a civil engineer, and went out with him to the Malay States. Slowly her style began to change, the bleak, sardonic, Catholicism-obsessed tone being tempered with HUMOR. This was in part because her husband would read what she wrote; in part because, on his return to Britain, he became a land agent in Devon and received rather a low income—it thus became a financial necessity for D. to write, and a lightly satirical tone was more salable than the intensity of the earlier novels; and in part because she was much happier after her marriage and the birth of her two children. Many novels, short stories, and articles appeared during the next twenty years, their characteristic theme being social hypocrisy and adult failure to treat children sympathetically. In 1927 came one of her very best novels, *The Way Things Are*, which is about an "ordinary" woman not unlike D. herself, who is "happily" married but falls in love with someone else; superficially the tone is light and funny but there is an undercurrent of sadness. Throughout all her novels, D. seems to be saying: life is sad and dull, but there are compensations (children, the countryside) and the only thing to do is keep cheerful and see the funny side.

Long before the advent of child psychiatry, she was making one theme very much her own: it is cruel to stifle children or to try and force them to behave in a certain fixed pattern. But her theme par excellence was exemplified by *The Diary of a Provincial Lady* (1930), reprinted many times since and still in print, which began as commissioned articles in the feminist weekly *Time and Tide* and was then published as four separate books. The circumstances of the heroine were very much like those of D. herself: she lives in Devon, a pillar of the community, has a loyal but non-communicative husband and two children, and the diary was, as she wrote, "a perfectly straightforward account of the many disconcerting facets presented by everyday life to the average woman," all described in a wonderfully funny tone that made it an instant classic. In particular, D. had an almost surreal gift for reproducing dialogue. The superficial elements may be similar to the author's own life but underneath there lurked someone much more astringent, sharper, and bleaker, a persona that became suppressed in the interests of gaining a wide reading public, making her children happy, and being a cheerful and devoted wife and friend—all of which she did to perfection. However, the 21st-c. reader might wonder whether had D. lived longer (she died when she was only fifty-three) she might have combined all the elements contained within her into one outstanding novel.

With the publication of *The Diary of a Provincial Lady*, D. became a well-known and popular author and in 1932 published the novel that is generally considered her best, *Thank Heaven Fasting* (reprinted, with an afterword by Penelope FITZGERALD, in 1988). This is on the theme of a young girl's increasingly anguished (but ultimately successful) search for a husband, and although it is an extremely funny novel, it is a fiercely feminist statement, asking why no other future is permissible for young women apart from marriage? Many of the subsequent novels are variations on this theme, such as the husband's being able to block access to the children if the wife has ever "strayed" or, in *Nothing Is Safe* (1937), the cruel effect of thoughtless divorce upon the children. D. is one of the most important women writers of the 20th c., but her humor and the apparent lightness of her style have debarred her from serious critical consideration. In addition, her charm of personality and her lack of vanity made her refuse to take herself or her work too seriously. When she wrote: "All that I have tried to do is to observe faithfully, and record accurately, the things that have come within my limited range. The fault that I have most tried to avoid is sentimentality" it is all too easy for the superficial reader to take this at face value. D. was a far more complex, subtle, and perceptive writer than this remark implies.

BIBLIOGRAPHY: McCullen, M. L., *E. M. D.* (1985); Powell, V., *The Life of a Provincial Lady: A Study of E. M. D. and Her Works* (1988)

NICOLA BEAUMAN

DE LA MARE, Walter

b. 25 April 1873, Charlton, Kent; d. 22 June 1956, Twickenham, Middlesex

Critics maintain that D. has been ignored in recent years because he was the last holdout of dreamy RO-MANTICISM in an age of densely allusive modernist verse. D. wrote ambiguous and mellifluous poems that have little appeal in a world that expects in fiction a hard edge of REALISM. He also suffers because he frequently wrote for children, leading some to assume that he took a frivolous approach to his craft. His defenders ask us to remember that even though he often adopted a child's point of view, he valued that perspective as one way to unleash the powers of the imagination and of sensitivity that he often found lacking in adult life. In his novels, short stories, and poetry, he was a careful stylist who cast a spell with his words, using suggestive diction, sound, and rhythm to make his points. Certainly his work repays attention to his craft and his ability to shed a romantic light on the world of ordinary experience.

While most critics agree that D. will be remembered primarily for his poetry, it should be noted that he was also a prolific writer of short stories and produced five novels. The settings and themes of the short stories—in collections that include *Broomsticks* (1925), *The Lord Fish* (1933), and *The Scarecrow* (1945)—are like many of the most famous of the poems, full of graveyards and haunted houses, twilight and childhood settings, waking dreams and questing figures. He experimented with various points of view, using both rather pedestrian speakers who witness fantastic events and also more uncommon figures who report their own stories and make the fantastic seem realistic. The short stories also share the symbolism of the poems, including the use of windows and mirrors and other elements that suggest states of transition and ambiguity.

Although D. wrote short stories throughout his career, he only turned sporadically to the novel. Here again, he explores the lives of characters on the fringes of adult life. He published *Henry Brocken* in 1904; in this tale, a young boy encounters characters from literature, including Lucy Gray, characters from Jonathan SWIFT's *Gulliver's Travels*, John BUNYAN's *Pilgrim's Progress*, and Charlotte BRONTË's *Jane Eyre*. Although most critics agree that Henry is not a very convincing child, defenders of the novel ask us to see in him an illustration of D.'s theory of the imagination. Henry initially approaches his journey with a sense of adventure and wonder and ultimately is forced to a more questioning and intellectual perspective that marks a loss of innocence. D.'s most famous novel is *Memoirs of a Midget* (1921), which purports to be the chronicle of one year in the life of a female midget, Midgetina or Miss M. In her adventures encountering the rather cold and aloof Fanny and the deformed but spiritual dwarf Mr. Anon, Midgetina learns the truth about herself and the limits and strengths of her imagination and heart. In this novel and throughout his prose fiction, D. explores the importance and difficulty of the human quest for self-awareness and an understanding of the truth of one's soul. While Edward Wagenknecht predicted that ultimately the novel would follow the direction implied by D.'s works, the meaning and intention of the books are obscure and the work too idiosyncratic to be widely emulated.

It is as a poet that D. is chiefly remembered, although the critics do not agree on the nature or stature of his achievement. Those critics who see D. as an escapist and outmoded Romantic admit that he was able to cast a spell with his technical facility with verse and with his command of the associative power of diction and imagery. His most often anthologized poem, "The Listeners" (1912), epitomizes the magic and the frustration of reading D. for a generation used to close explications of poems. The poem describes a Traveller knocking on "a moonlit door" and receiving no answer despite a host of "phantom listeners." Readers try to impose religious, ghostly, and artistic meaning on the poem, but D. himself claimed not to remember his intent and argued that good poems offer their reader potential meanings without having to be explicated and expounded or without having only one possible interpretation. In addition to this tantalizing indetermination, D. is fond of casting a spell over objects in the everyday world and creating in them a sense of magic. In the poem "Silver" (from the 1913 volume *Peacock Pie: A Book of Rhymes)*, for example, D. shows the way the silver light of the moon transforms a homely landscape of fruit trees, cottages, sleeping dogs, doves, fish, and mice. The poet isolates each of these images to give the poem a dreamlike intensity and uses repetition and slow-moving lines to further heighten the sense of drama. D. is above all the poet of states of transition and seems to show that the line between day and night, ordinary and extraordinary, sleep and waking, the rational and the unconscious, are frequently blurred in our awareness.

While D. creates some work in prose and in poetry of undeniable power and beauty, he suffers in part because his work can seem homogeneous, and the imagery and effects seem undistinguished. He expressed a vision of the imagination, found in the work of poets and in the minds of untainted children, that could tap resources deeper than reason or the conscious mind. It may be that his comfort with the irrational and with the nonsense of childhood will indeed appeal to the postmodern imagination. On the other hand, it may be that his use of standard musical poetic effects and his failure to change or vary his style will continue to exhaust even those readers who appreciate the beauty of individual poems and stories.

BIBLIOGRAPHY: Duffin, H. C., *W. D.* (1949); Leavis, F. R., *New Bearings in English Poetry: A Study of the Contemporary Situation* (1932; rev. ed., 1950); Reid, F., *W. D.* (1929)

CATHERINE FRANK

DELANEY, Shelagh
b. 25 November 1939, Salford, Lancashire

D.'s major claim to fame is her play *A Taste of Honey* (perf. 1958; pub. 1959). At the center of this play is Jo who, along with her slatternly mother Helen, has taken up residence in a squalid Manchester flat. Helen abandons Jo to run off with her latest love interest, and Jo soon seeks comfort in the arms of a black sailor. By the second act, Jo is pregnant with the sailor's child, and the maternal role of the absent Helen is now being filled by Jo's new roommate, Geoff, a homosexual art student. Ultimately, Helen returns and chases Geoff away. The play, though somewhat bleak, nevertheless contains a great deal of HUMOR, and its development of the two central female characters has been justly praised by critics and audiences alike; *A Taste of Honey* won several awards, including the New York Drama Critics' Circle Award for best foreign play. *A Taste of Honey* was filmed in 1961 with Dora Bryan, Rita Tushingham, and Murray Melvin. D.'s later work was never to achieve the success of her first play. Her other works include *The Lion in Love* (perf. 1960; pub. 1961), another play centering on lower-class family dynamics; *The House That Jack Built* (1977), a television serial; the screenplay for *Dance with a Stranger* (1985), for which she won an award at the Cannes Film Festival; and *Sweetly Sings the Donkey* (1963), a collection of semiautobiographical fiction.

DE MORGAN, William [Frend]
b. 16 November 1839, London; d. 15 January 1917, London

After a brilliant career as a stained-glass artist, an expert potter, and tile maker in the William MORRIS circle, D. began a successful career as a novelist at the age of sixty-five. His wife, the artist Evelyn de Morgan, rescued fragments of an unfinished novel, which appeared in 1906 as *Joseph Vance*. This was followed in the next year by the publication of *Alice-for-Short*, in which D. admitted to putting much of himself into the character of Charles Heath. Eight more novels followed, the last two completed by Evelyn, *The Old Madhouse* (1919) and *The Old Man's Youth and the Young Man's Old Age* (1921). In the Dickensian manner, they recall the London of their authors' youth. D. and his wife were the subjects of a dual biography by A. M. W. Stirling, published in 1922.

DENHAM, [Sir] John
b. 1615, Dublin, Ireland; d. ca. 19 March 1669, London

Samuel JOHNSON in his *Lives of the Poets* described D. as "one of the fathers of English poetry." Indeed,

D. may very well be remembered as being the father of city poetry in the more modern tradition of combining the CITY AND LITERATURE. D. began his literary career with a tragedy, *The Sophy* (1642), set in the Turkish court, but is chiefly remembered for his pastoral poem *Cooper's Hill* (1642; rev. ed., 1655). John H. Johnston in his critical study *The Poet and the City* (1984) cites D. as one of the primary English poets to incorporate the Virgilian elements of the topographical poem, namely man's relation to the earth, and apply it to the narrator's relation to the cityscape. Alexander POPE writes of D.'s "strength and [Edmund] Waller's sweetness" in the *Essay on Criticism* and pays tribute to *Cooper's Hill* in *Windsor-Forest*.

DE QUINCEY, Thomas
b. 15 August 1785, Manchester; d. 8 December 1859, Edinburgh, Scotland

Essayist and critic, D. stands with Charles LAMB and William HAZLITT as the leading writer of nonfictional prose in the Romantic period. At its best, his writing can be described as prose poetry. He was a friend of William WORDSWORTH and Samuel Taylor COLERIDGE and an early advocate of the *Lyrical Ballads*, becoming part of the larger circle around the Lake District. His published accounts of the Lake Poets are an important, if subjective, source of information on them. His literary criticism is regarded for its psychological insight. He is most famous, however, for his largely autobiographical *Confessions of an English Opium Eater* (1822), which influenced writers such as Edgar Allan Poe and Charles Baudelaire as well as offering the inspiration for Berlioz's *Symphonie fantastique*, and remains a gripping account of the effects of opium addiction and the role of the subconscious on the construction of dreams.

Brilliant but restless, the young D. was in and out of various grammar schools. Running away in 1802 from the Manchester Grammar School to Wales, then London, he was befriended and saved from starvation by the sixteen-year-old prostitute, Ann, whom he recalled with deep affection in *Confessions* and who became the haunting image in one of his opium dreams. In 1803, he began taking opium (laudanum) for rheumatism and by 1813, was completely addicted, remaining under its influence for the rest of his life. In 1808, he left Oxford without a degree, taking up residence in the Lake District. Earning the confidence of Wordsworth, he helped to supervise the printing of Wordsworth's pamphlet, *The Convention of Cintra*. He was also one of the few people to read Wordsworth's *The Prelude* in manuscript. In 1816, Margaret Simpson, Wordsworth's serving girl, bore D. a son. They were married the following year. Thereafter, between bouts of narcosis and activity, he supported himself and his growing family as an editor and journalist for the rest of his life.

D. was a prolific writer, publishing articles on a wide variety of topics in periodicals such as the *London Magazine*, *Blackwood's Magazine*, the *Edinburgh Literary Gazette*, and *Tait's Edinburgh Magazine*. The topics ranged over German metaphysics, political economy, "Recollections of the Lake Poets" (1834–39), the American Gold Rush, and literary criticism. In his lifetime, he produced only three books: *Confessions; Klosterheim; or, The Masque* (1832), a Gothic romance set in the Thirty Years' War, and dismissed by D. as hackwork; and *The Logic of Political Economy* (1844), a defense of David Ricardo against the criticism of Thomas Robert MALTHUS. Essays such as "On Murder Considered as One of the Fine Arts" and "On the Knocking at the Gate in Macbeth" show D. at his best, with a sustained mixture of dark irony and psychological penetration. In these he develops his theory on the primacy of imagination over the faculty of understanding.

Confessions of an English Opium-Eater is universally recognized as D.'s masterpiece. It was first serialized in the *London Magazine* (1821), and then published in book form the following year. This was followed by a sort of sequel, *Suspiria de Profoundis* with "Savannah-la-Mar," serialized in *Blackwood's* in 1845 and "The English Mail-Coach" with "Dream-Fugue" in 1849. Both works are autobiographical accounts of his experiences and the effects of opium on his dreams. He writes in a style at once stately, self-ironic, and occasionally facetious, yet at the same time carefully observant and deeply humane. In the section "Preliminary Confessions," he describes his early experiences wandering the streets of London with Ann and how she saved his life. In "The Pleasures of Opium," he offers a treatise on opium, describing its properties and effects. Contrasting it with wine, he suggests that opium orders and intensifies the mind while wine disorders it. He also recalled an anecdote about a visit to him by a Malaysian sailor while he was living in Grasmere. The third part, "The Pains of Opium" recounts a series of vivid opium dreams. He explained how his mind and imagination would involuntarily summon and combine images from his memory, distorting time and space. Thus, the memory of the Malay brought forth a cascade of scenes by association. The effect is both a powerful prose poem and a careful analysis of all of the supposedly forgotten memories that construct the dream. Anticipating Sigmund Freud, the *Confessions* lays out a case history of the facts of D.'s life that become the raw material of his dreams.

BIBLIOGRAPHY: Baxter, E., *D.'s Art of Autobiography* (1990); Burwick, F., *T. D.* (2001); Russett, M., *D.'s Romanticism* (1997); Sackville-West, E., *T. D.* (1936)

THOMAS L. COOKSEY

DETECTIVE FICTION BEFORE 1945

"A murder occurs; many are suspected; all but one suspect, who is the murderer, are eliminated; the murderer is arrested or dies." So W. H. AUDEN summed up the plot of a typical detective novel or short story as it flourished in its classic form, particularly during the so-called Golden Age between the two world wars. Detective fiction was rigorously preoccupied with mystery, and usually took a crime—almost always a murder—as its starting point. The investigations of a detective determined the shape of its narrative, and its ending was supplied by the discovery and revelation of the truth. Detective fiction thus appealed to several long-standing interests that had already spawned their own literary traditions. Mystery had featured in riddles and puzzle tales since the Bible. Crime, always a staple of world literature, had been a particular object of fascination in Europe since the Renaissance; literature usually catered to it with the fictional confessions of notorious criminals, nominally offered in warning to potential victims or offenders but really appealing to more salacious tastes. For these disparate interests to coalesce into detective fiction required, first, the development of organized police forces in their modern form and, secondly, the rise of scientific methodology as the basis for the detective's procedure.

Arguably Britain led the world in both these areas during the 19th c. Yet in developing the distinctive characteristics of detective fiction, British writers received considerable help from abroad: notably from the U.S., in the "tales of ratiocination" about the Chevalier Dupin that Edgar Allan Poe published in the 1840s, and from France, in Émile Gaboriau's *L'Affaire Lerouge* (1865) and the host of other popular *romans policiers* with which he followed it. In Britain, the first great landmark was established by the work of Wilkie COLLINS, particularly *The Moonstone*. The novel differs from its successors in its considerable length (later detective fiction would often find its most congenial home in the short story) and in its concentration not on murder but on theft (of the ill-starred diamond of the title). At the same time, however, it set a major precedent. It showed how an entire narrative may be dictated, in a deliciously teasing manner, by the unraveling of a mystery. And, in the character of Sergeant Cuff, it presented a detective whose enigmatic character could prove almost as intriguing to the reader as the mystery itself.

Charles DICKENS, who had already included his own police detective, Inspector Bucket, in the ample framework of *Bleak House*, plainly set out to rival *The Moonstone* in his last, unfinished novel, *The Mystery of Edwin Drood*. Other writers, however, were content merely to add detectives and detection to the melodramatic brew—villainous intrigues, long-lost wills, and stirring chases—characterizing what the Victorians usually called "sensation fiction." The next major development in detective fiction per se was left to Sir Arthur Conan DOYLE. He introduced Sherlock Holmes in *A Study in Scarlet*, which first appeared in *Beeton's Christmas Annual* for 1887, and *The Sign of Four*. Neither novel attracted much attention. The popularity of Sherlock Holmes began with two series of short stories published in the *Strand Magazine* and collected as *The Adventures of Sherlock Holmes* and *The Memoirs of Sherlock Holmes*. By the time he wrote the last of these stories, "The Final Problem," Doyle had sufficiently tired of his own creation to kill him off. He went on to publish adventure stories, SCIENCE FICTION, historical novels, and, increasingly, works defending the cause of spiritualism, all of which he considered more worthy than his detective fiction. Yet the reading public, as well as magazine editors and publishers, would not allow him to forget his detective, and he was persuaded to revive Sherlock Holmes for two more novels, *The Hound of the Baskervilles* and *The Valley of Fear*, and a number of short stories, collected as *The Return of Sherlock Holmes*, *His Last Bow*, and *The Case-Book of Sherlock Holmes*.

Conan Doyle never welcomed the prospect of being remembered simply as the creator of Sherlock Holmes. Yet today that title remains as proud as any that detective fiction can boast, and Conan Doyle's achievement has proved the most influential in the entire history of the genre. In essence, he began with a formula both simple and directly indebted to the brief hints that Poe had provided in his stories about Dupin. The detective himself is brilliant to the point of infallibility, eccentric in his personal habits yet systematic in his approach to mystery. He might live in an atmosphere of tobacco and cocaine, and alternate between moods of peevish boredom and nervous energy, but his reasoning is always grounded in the most immaculate and precise logic. His cases are usually brought to him by distressed clients, arriving at his lodgings at 221B Baker Street with puzzling tales that have baffled or misled the police authorities. Usually these stories contain some apparently trivial detail—a league of red-headed men, a dog that did nothing in the night—which is yet extraordinary enough to engage his attention. By turns a chivalrous knight errant, a hero of the scientific method, and a master of the melodramatic surprise, Sherlock Holmes is always an expert in the bizarre lurking not far beneath the apparently conventional surface of Victorian and Edwardian middle-class life.

In Poe's stories about Dupin, the atmosphere is distinctly Gothic, and in "The Murders in the Rue Morgue" the details of the crime are conspicuously bloodthirsty. Such elements recur in the Sherlock Holmes stories, but the least expected—as well as the happiest—of Conan Doyle's innovations was to establish a prevailing note of comedy. A good deal of it comes from the presence of Dr. Watson. Poe had taken care to equip the otherwise solitary Dupin with a friend to narrate the story, and in borrowing the device Conan Doyle showed himself alert to its advantages. An observant yet comparatively unintelligent companion, noting the clues and what the detective has to say about them without understanding the significance of what he sees and hears, provides detective fiction with an ideal viewpoint. Yet Conan Doyle went far beyond Poe's shadowy and anonymous narrator to create, in Dr. Watson, a fully rounded character. He is bluff, sentimental, studiously conventional in his tastes and opinions—in short, the very opposite of Holmes himself. The comedy of manners resulting from the contrast between the two men is, in no small degree, responsible for the enduring charm of the stories.

Other writers were busy emulating Conan Doyle long before Sherlock Holmes's fictional career had ended, concentrating on the salient features he had made so widely popular: a rigorously presented puzzle, an eccentric but brilliant detective, and a loyal companion to tell the story. Many of these imitators are now all but forgotten: few people bother to read Matthew Phipps Shiels's *Prince Zaleski* (1895) or William Hope HODGSON's *Carnacki, the Ghost-Finder* (1913), let alone Israel ZANGWILL's *The Big Bow Mystery* (1892) or Hal Meredith's tales of Sexton Blake (started in 1893). Arthur Morrison's *Martin Hewitt, Investigator* (1894), Baroness ORCZY's *The Old Man in the Corner*, and Ernest Bramah's *Max Carrados* (1914) are still sometimes remembered. Of the few works to have earned a permanent reputation, the most important are R. Austin Freeman's stories of Dr. Thorndyke, introduced in *The Red Thumb Mark* (1907), which delve far more deeply into the details of science than Conan Doyle ever did; and G. K. CHESTERTON's stories of Father Brown, introduced in *The Innocence of Father Brown*, which ingeniously combine mystery with metaphysical parable.

Together with E. C. BENTLEY's sly and witty *Trent's Last Case,* the work of Freeman and Chesterton marks the transition from the era of Sherlock Holmes to the era that historians of detective fiction like to call its Golden Age. There was no sudden break, but rather an attempt to exploit the possibilities of the form that Conan Doyle had demonstrated, particularly in an increasingly rigorous concentration on how the mystery and its solution were presented. Writers came to treat detective fiction as a game between the author and the reader, played according to strict rules of fair play, and to make themselves expert in particular types of puzzle; locked-room mysteries, timetable mysteries, and least-likely person mysteries all had their specialist practitioners. The best-known

writer was Agatha CHRISTIE, who introduced her Belgian detective Hercule Poirot in *The Mysterious Affair at Styles* and her village spinster Miss Marple in *Murder at the Vicarage*, published in 1920 and 1930, respectively. Many critics regard *The Murder of Roger Ackroyd* as the masterpiece of the Golden Age. Almost equal in reputation was Dorothy L. SAYERS, who introduced Lord Peter Wimsey in *Whose Body?*, published in 1923, and his companion and sparring partner Harriet Vane in *Strong Poison*. These two names stand at the head of a list that also includes H. C. BAILEY, Freeman Wills Crofts, Philip MacDonald, Anthony Berkeley (Anthony Berkeley Cox, who also wrote as Francis Iles), John Rhode (Cecil John Street, who also wrote as Miles Burton), Ronald Knox, Patricia Wentworth, Margery ALLINGHAM, Josephine Tey (Elizabeth MACKINTOSH, who also wrote plays as Gordon Daviot), John Dickson Carr (an American-born resident in Britain, who also wrote as Carter Dickson), Ngaio Marsh (a New Zealander who usually set her work in Britain), Michael Innes (otherwise the Oxford don J. I. M. Stewart), Nicholas Blake (the poet C. DAY-LEWIS), Cyril HARE (A. A. Gordon Clark), and, at the very end of the Golden Age, Edmund Crispin (the composer Bruce Montgomery) and Michael Gilbert.

In addition to the features they derived from Conan Doyle, these writers are united by the characteristics marking a distinct literary school. They all show a preference for milieus that, though not necessarily aristocratic, are resolutely middle- and upper-middle class. Their favorite settings are not just country houses but Oxbridge colleges, London clubs, cruise liners, or villages where the population consists mainly of the leisured, the modestly affluent, and the retired. All these, of course, are closed environments that offer the detective and reader a conveniently limited list of suspects. Yet so do prisons, lunatic asylums, and army barracks, which do not appear in the fiction of the Golden Age and could not easily have done without violating the note it sought to strike.

This note is determinedly removed from the ordinary realities in which crimes usually occur. Nor does the arrival of the detective bring those realities any closer. The detective may be a policeman (such as Marsh's Roderick Alleyn or Innes's John Appleby) or a private investigator (like Christie's Hercule Poirot), but he is more usually an unpaid amateur (such as Sayers's Lord Peter Wimsey or Allingham's Albert Campion or Blake's Nigel Strangeways). Whichever is the case, he almost always belongs to the same class as the victim and the suspects. He bears about him some evidence of his sophistication—connoisseurship in wine, or art, or old books—which sets him apart from the common ruck of policemen who follow perspiringly in the wake of his investigation. Sherlock Holmes had also been in the habit of showing himself knowledgeable in the most unlikely subjects, but he wore his learning severely, rising occasionally to dry wit. The detectives of the 1920s and 1930s are, by contrast, light-hearted and facetious in their manner, given to slangy speech and breezy chatter. Brilliant and penetrating they might be in their private reflections on the mystery, but outwardly they often wear the mask of silly asses. Bailey's Reggie Fortune, like Lord Peter Wimsey and Albert Campion, are particularly close cousins of the heroes of interwar comedies. And, despite the presence of crime and murder, the world in which they operate is every bit as innocent as the world created by P. G. WODEHOUSE.

Writers themselves, let alone the critics and historians of detective fiction who were already setting to work, took particular pride in the intellectual refinement to which the form had been wrought by the eve of World War II. Detective fiction, they loved to point out, had become the favorite light reading of prime ministers and High Court judges. It might still belong to the relatively humble category of popular fiction, but it had purged itself of the vulgarities marring thrillers or adventures stories, dealing in violent action, and romances, dealing in tear-drenched sentimentality. Concentration on the puzzle and observance of the rules of fair play (famously formulated as "Ten Commandments" by Ronald Knox) assured that it had achieved the abstract severity of the mathematical formula, the cryptogram, or the crossword puzzle. Perhaps, Jacques Barzun was not the only commentator to hint, it upheld the principles of truly classical art in rebuke to the undisciplined outpourings of MODERNISM.

Such claims contrast sharply with the judgments of the Golden Age passed by later generations of readers and critics. To them its intellectual refinement often seemed like an increasingly strained ingenuity, forever seeking to ring new changes on a form that in fact offered only a limited number of variants. By the same token, the milieu it evoked could easily look narrowly elitist, if not downright snobbish. From whatever vantage point it was regarded after 1945, detective fiction of the Golden Age belonged as completely as spats and monocles, manservants and housemaids, to a world that was rapidly passing away. Some discontent with the form, even at the point it was proclaiming its peak of perfection, had already been apparent among the writers of the Golden Age themselves. Sayers had tried to embrace serious preoccupations in her last novels about Wimsey and Vane, *Gaudy Night* and *Busman's Honeymoon*, published in 1935 and 1937, respectively. Rather more successfully, Berkeley had injected a sharper and more realistic note into detective fiction when he adopted the pseudonym Francis Iles for *Malice Afore-thought* (1931) and *Before the Fact* (1932).

Moreover, serious challenges to the assumptions and the practice of the Golden Age were coming from abroad. In France, where writers had once sought to write country-house murder mysteries, Simenon had already begun his downbeat, reflective novels about Maigret. In the U.S., where S. S. Van Dine and Ellery Queen had modeled their work on the British example, Dashiell Hammett, Raymond Chandler, and other writers for *Black Mask* had established the "hard-boiled" school. All these factors guaranteed that— even for many of the writers from the Golden Age whose careers continued after the war—detective fiction in Britain would undergo radical change. The English murder, as George ORWELL was already announcing in 1946, would never be quite the same again.

BIBLIOGRAPHY: Barzun, J., and W. H. Taylor, *A Catalogue of Crime* (1971); Henderson, L., ed., *Twentieth-Century Crime and Mystery Writers* (3rd ed., 1991); Hubin, A. J., *Crime Fiction, 1749–1980: A Comprehensive Bibliography* (1984; and supplement, 1988); Messac, R., *Le "Detective Novel" et l'influence de la pensée scientifique* (1929); Murch, A. E., *The Development of the Detective Novel* (1958; rev. ed., 1968); Ousby, I., *Bloodhounds of Heaven: The Detective in English Fiction from Godwin to Doyle* (1976); Ousby, I., *The Crime and Mystery Book* (1997; repub. as *Guilty Parties*, 1997); Symons, J., *Mortal Consequences* (1972; repub. as *Bloody Murder*, 1985); Watson, C., *Snobbery with Violence* (1971)

IAN OUSBY

DETECTIVE FICTION SINCE 1945

Julian SYMONS, in his preface to the second edition (1985) of *Bloody Murder: From Detective Story to the Crime Novel*, says: "I hope it will convince a new generation of readers that the best crime stories are not simply entertainments but also literature." It is an interesting question and a moot point, well worth a debate. Obviously, if the item in question is, say, Fyodor Dostoevsky's *Crime and Punishment*, first published in 1866, then there isn't likely to be much argument; but what if the specimen under investigation is *Murder on the Orient Express* by Agatha CHRISTIE? In England in the late 1930s and early 1940s, there wasn't much doubt about the matter: the two categories were quite distinct and easily recognized until, that is, the novels of Nicholas Blake and Michael Innes, both of whom published their first detective fiction in 1935. Blake's was called *A Question of Proof* and Innes's was *Death at the President's Lodging*.

The sudden incursion of "literature" into detective yarns is, in these two cases at any rate, easily accounted for: "Nicholas Blake" was the pseudonym of the distinguished poet (and future poet laureate) C. DAY-LEWIS; and "Michael Innes" the pseudonym of the literary critic and fellow of Christ Church, Oxford, J. I. M. Stewart. Both of them, of course, published extensively in the purely "literary" field but that does not concern us here: in the category that we can loosely label "detective fiction," each of them contributed some twenty or so novels between 1945 and 1970. They are elegant, distinguished works, and they represent a bridge, stylistically speaking, between the earlier "Golden Age" of Margery ALLINGHAM, Ngaio Marsh, and Dorothy L. SAYERS and late-20th-c. writers such as P. D. JAMES and Ruth RENDELL. A further example of the "interim" literary-detective novel, gripping though not entirely typical of its genre, is Roy Fuller's *The Second Curtain* (1953). Fuller's main output was poetry, beginning with his *Poems* and continuing through twelve other collections between 1939 and 1980. *New and Collected Poems* appeared in 1985, and he held the position of Professor of Poetry at Oxford from 1968 to 1973, publishing his lectures under the title *Owls and Artificers* in 1974. He is, therefore, a minor—though not a negligible—figure in the annals of detective fiction. One of his three crime novels, though, *The Second Curtain*, was worth its publication, if only for a single short sentence early in the book: "He had reached the age when the importance of endowment policies outweighed the uncertainty of history." The book is also remarkable for the fact that Fuller on several occasions uses his central character, who is also a novelist, as an instrument by which to discuss the development of the detective novel in England and the way that the figure of "outsider," rebel against society, gradually moved from being the fugitive criminal to being the "private detective" and then, sometimes, to being a disaffected member of the police authority itself. Along the way, there are frequent and quite telling passages of social commentary that add depth and insight to the book but, some would say, run the risk of taking the work out of the "detective fiction" and "light entertainment" categories altogether.

Social comment apart, there have been considerable changes in the regular and easily recognizable "detective-fiction" genre itself since 1945. W. H. AUDEN (who incidentally was used by his friend Day-Lewis, in his alter ego of Nicholas Blake, as a model for his detective-hero, Strangeways) in an essay on popular fiction gives a definition of the detective story as follows: "The basic formula is this: a murder occurs; many are suspected; all but one suspect, who is the murderer, are eliminated; the murderer is arrested or dies." At the time Auden wrote this it was true—more or less—of a great majority of detective fiction. The death, and even the body itself, are the merest tokens and are not meant to be taken seriously. The reader is not meant to agonize over the suffering of the particular victim or the general question of man's inhumanity to man. Nor is the reader meant to ponder on the psychological or pathological disorders of the murderer. The core of the book, the essential, central matter, is not psychology or human personality but the intriguing challenge of the chase: the ingenuity of the puzzle and unexpectedness of the solution. Reading it is essentially a game. The subject matter is trivial but the design, the aesthetic, is classical. There is about it a sense of intellectual gaiety, a quality of jeu d'esprit. Even the titles sometimes invite this kind of response—Marsh's *Died in the Wool* (1945), for example; or Sayers's *Clouds of Witness* (1926; rep. as *Clouds of Witnesses*, 1927).

Gradually, during the 1950s and 1960s, the tone changed. The elegance of writing disappeared and solemnity set in. One of the writers who started this new trend was Edgar Lustgarten, his best book being *A Case to Answer* (1947), which abandons the excitement of watching the detection puzzle gradually unravel and instead follows the trial of the criminal in great detail, examining the evidence given by witnesses for the prosecution and defense in a manner that reminds one of Émile Zola. It is, indeed, a thorough-going example of NATURALISM, with any threatened intrusion of imagination or wit held firmly at bay. Another kind of variation is evidenced by *The Daughter of Time* by Josephine TEY, in which a detective-inspector, marooned in hospital for a lengthy period, passes the weary hours by ferreting out the truth about the murder of "the princes in the Tower" in 1483. He arrives at the conclusion that the murderer was not Richard III (popularly speaking, the usual suspect) but Henry VII.

Lord Clanmorris, writing under his family name of John Bingham, introduces a change of a more radical and subversive kind. Whereas the earlier kind of detective story took as a sine qua non the clarity and infallibility of justice (and, usually though not quite always, the agents of justice—police, lawyers, courts, etc.) increasingly in the 1950s and 1960s they are portrayed as variable, questionable, unreliable. Bingham's books are excellent examples of this new trend. The first, *My Name Is Michael Sibley* (1952), is particularly challenging. Its central character is accused of a murder that he, clearly, did not commit. His innocence is indubitable. Yet he lies to the police about a whole series of minor matters. Throughout the book, the possibility of an innocent man's being convicted of a murder he did not commit is kept vividly before the reader. Sibley is imprisoned and is constantly interrogated. The sense that innocence is sure to prevail is implicitly denied by the whole tone of the book. Sibley's trial examines the evidence in great and fascinating detail and Sibley is finally released not because he is innocent (though the reader knows that he is) but because the court fails to prove him guilty. The mystery of the murder is left unsolved. Obviously, we have here left far behind the high spirits and intellectual games of Michael Innes or Nicholas Blake and have ventured into the more somber world of social observation.

A quick backward glance at an interesting hybrid may be permissible and instructive: six years before Bingham's first book the composer, Bruce Montgomery, writing under his pseudonym of Edmund Crispin, published a whodunit called *The Moving Toyshop* (1946), the title being taken from Alexander POPE's *The Rape of the Lock:* "With varying vanities, from every part,/They shift the moving toyshop of their heart." Three-quarters of the book is written (quite brilliantly) in the old, high gamesome style. There are two or three violent deaths (one easily forgets exactly how many, since they matter so little and the book doesn't seem to care). The only one that does evoke a slight pang of sorrow in the reader is the shooting of a Dalmatian puppy called Danny who dies simply as a result of his being happy and friendly. That sounds suspiciously like an intrusion of Real Life into the novel's intellectual tennis match: it seems so unfair— why should innocence be wantonly punished in this way? However, the intriguing detecting yarn quickly recovers its stride and momentum and continues on its merry way until about twenty pages from the end when, once again, the tone momentarily darkens as if the book's social conscience stirs and its native resolution is sicklied over with the pale cast of thought. But by the time we come to Bingham, such dangerous dichotomies disappear: all is serious and silken dalliance in the wardrobe lies. Bingham can, at his best, write a tale that grips the reader and maintains the suspense to the very end. Unfortunately, he is not always at his best: he tends, indeed, to be very variable from book to book but critics are generally agreed about the consistently high quality and the genuine originality of his first book, *My Name Is Michael Sibley.*

Another of the neorealist school of British detective fiction is Nicholas Freeling. He is an Englishman who has chosen to live on the Continent, first in France and then in Holland. All his books are set in one or other of these countries. His detective, Van der Valk, is a character drawn with a good deal of sympathy and is, in turn, a man who has himself a good deal of sympathy for and understanding of the criminal mind. His investigations become not exciting, clue-driven paper chases but subtle explorations of psychological states and half-hidden fears. There is some critical controversy as to which is the best, but perhaps one could, without too much risk, nominate either his first book, *Love in Amsterdam* (1962), or *Criminal Conversation* (1965).

Julian Symons was described by the *Times Literary Supplement* as "the leading exponent and advocate" of the crime novel, and the book he published that year, entitled *The Progress of a Crime*, received an excellent notice from the *Spectator*, which said it was "one of the truest and most compellingly readable English crime novels for years." T. J. Binyon, in the *Sunday Times*, spoke of Symons as "incontestably the doyen of British crime writers." The *Irish Times* joined in his praises: "The leading exponent of the crime novel. Power and harshness and an uninhibited appreciation of the strength of the sexual motive are the hallmarks of his work." Between 1950 and his death, Symons wrote some thirty "crime novels." Most of them display considerable ingenuity of plot construction and a good deal more interest in the characters' psychology and motivations than in the excitement of the chase. Several of them betray, in passing, signs of the author's other literary interests: for example, in *The Blackheath Poisonings* and in *Bland Beginning*, published in 1949, the deceptions and mysteries and solutions depend to a large extent upon the interpretations of some half-forgotten (and, in fact, fictitious) Victorian poems—the same device, indeed, as that used in a very different kind of book by A. S. BYATT in *Possession*. Symons's first literary work was as editor of *Twentieth-Century Verse* in the late 1930s.

The canvas of the last two decades of the 20th c. is crowded with interesting figures but two of them stand out as quite obviously of particular importance. They are, of course, James and Rendell. In their books, perhaps more than any others, the changing character of the genre can be seen. Their books are certainly about crime and the effects of crime but only marginally about the process of detecting crime: and they are, on the whole, far too serious-minded about crime to want to turn it into an excuse for a gentlemanly game. *Innocent Blood* by James is a case in point. Here, the author dispenses with the services of her celebrated detective, Adam Dalgleish (who has appeared in many of her books), and concentrates on the effects of a sudden and unpremeditated savage murder on a closely observed, disparate group of people. The victim is a child of eight, killed in a moment of passionate fear and frustration by a woman who is vainly trying to shield her husband. After serving ten years of a life sentence, she is released from prison. (Her husband, also imprisoned, has died in jail.) The two people awaiting her release are her daughter, who is now eighteen, and the widowed father of the murdered child. There are detective elements of a sort in the story in that the daughter has been adopted by a university professor and his wife and does not know, until a few days before the prisoner's release, who her mother is and why she was imprisoned. And the murdered child's father, who is a meek and ineffectual clerical worker, has promised his wife, just before her death, that he will avenge their child's murder by tracking down and killing her murderer. The search and pursuit scenes, all over London, are excitingly done but the real concentration is on the portrayal of the central figures—the murderess, the daughter, the professor with his very inadequate wife, and the father of the murdered child. All are drawn in great detail and with considerable sympathy. Any sort of exaggerated or meretricious melodrama is avoided. There are no heroics. The qualities that bind the five together are inadequacy and that kind of self-wisdom that always comes too late. Clearly, the "crime novel" has come a long way since both Wilkie COLLINS's *The Woman in White* and Sayers's *Busman's Honeymoon*, published in 1937. And this is evident from several other of James's books—say, *A Taste for Death*—the title is a quotation from A. E. HOUSMAN—or *The Children of Men*. The same is true of the extraordinarily prolific Rendell: though she has shown herself adept at the plot-puzzle detection story, with her favorite detective, Chief Inspector Wexford, her most interesting books from a literary point of view are those that depend on the psychological analysis of the warped minds of murderers: books such as *A Demon in My View*, *A Judgment in Stone*, and *The Bridesmaid,* published in 1989.

Out of a host of successful writers of recent years a few may particularly be mentioned. Antonia Fraser, whose main output is BIOGRAPHY and books of history-popularization, has nevertheless produced two or three "mystery thrillers" based on cases investigated by a female detective called Jemima Shore: the best one, perhaps, is a novel with a Wordsworthian title, *Quiet as a Nun* (1977). H. R. F. Keating is also distinguished by one particular work: *The Perfect Murder* (1964), which won the Crime Writers" Association Award for 1964. David Williams, an actor and theater director who later turned to novel-writing, is noteworthy for his easy and elegant literary style in such books as *Murder in Advent* (1985) and *Holy Treasure!* (1988). Simon Brett, in sharp contrast, for example, to Rendell and James, represents something of a return to the lighter comic treatment of potentially somber themes in *A Shock to the System* (1984) and *A Series of Murders* (1988). Mention should also be made of Michael Dibdin for a sudden spurt of quite remarkable writing: *Vendetta* (1990), *Dirty Tricks* (1991), *Cabal* (1992), *The Dying of the Light* (1993), *Dead Lagoon* (1994), *Dark Spectre* (1995), *Cosi Fan Tutti* (1996), and *A Long Finish* (1998). And another younger writer who has done a whole series (twelve up to the present date) of books about the cases investigated by the same detective, is the Scotsman, Ian Rankin: his invented detective is Detective Inspector John Rebus. The writing, as such, is not especially distinguished but the intellectually teasing crime puzzles are intriguing and ingenious: one of the best of them is *The Falls* (2001). It has a touch of fetishism about it (seventeen tiny coffins, six inches long, each with a wooden doll in it and each associated with a recent murder) and macabre echoes of the 19th-c. "body snatchers," William Burke and William Hare.

Recent writing of this kind is fairly obviously conceived with more than half an eye on the possibility of adaptation to television and there is by now a healthy handful of entirely fictional crime investigators who to the general public have more vivid and more instantly recognizable personal characteristics than any actual, mundane, "real" person could possibly pretend to: Inspector Morse (Colin Dexter); Dalziel and Pascoe (Reginald Hill); Adam Dalgleish (James); Chief Inspector Wexford (Rendell), and so on. Is this massive inflation, one wonders, altogether a healthy thing from the literary point of view? One must not make the mistake of supposing that "detective fiction" and "crime fiction" are automatically entitled to be called literature just because they get published in hardback or make much-heralded and fanfare-greeted appearances on television (indeed, this latter accolade often calls their artistic standing seriously into question) but the fact remains that in some cases (a minority, but a quite sturdy minority, nevertheless) books of these genres can and do transcend their populist origins and become works of genuine artistic merit with something wise and illuminating to say about the grotesque times in which we live and, especially, about modern humanity's lunatic fixation on violence both personal and official, both individual and government-sponsored. And aside from all of that, at its more modest levels, a good whodunit is still a very entertaining read and will well serve, on the idle occasion, to while away the long age of three hours between our after-supper and bedtime.

BIBLIOGRAPHY: Reilly, J. M., *Twentieth-Century Mystery and Crime Writers* (1980); Routley, E., *The Puritan Pleasures of the Detective Story* (1972); Symons, J., *Bloody Murder: From Detective Story to Crime Novel* (1972; rev. eds., 1985, 1992)

ERIC SALMON

DICKENS, Charles [John Huffam]

b. 7 February 1812, Portsea (now Portsmouth); d. 9 June 1870, Gad's Hill Place, near Rochester, Kent

Immensely popular throughout his career, D. remains the most famous novelist in English, and perhaps world, literature: certain characters, scenes, and expressions in his fiction are familiar to many who have never read any of his books. So, too, is the scarifying ordeal in the writer's own boyhood, which he fictionalized in *David Copperfield* (20 parts, 1849–50) but the autobiographical basis of which was not revealed until two years after his death by his first biographer and close friend, John FORSTER. Having been reared to regard himself a young gentleman, with great expectations of becoming "a learned and distinguished man," D. was sent out to work in a blacking warehouse at the age of twelve, as his father languished in the Marshalsea debtors' prison. Elevated to mythical status in a class-based society, this experience has been widely recognized as a key to the writer's intense sympathy with (especially young) victims of injustice and privation, and to his imaginative identification on occasions with the socially transgressive. D.'s sense of having been saved from perdition by Providence alone may well have driven, as Forster suggested, the spectacularly successful launch of his literary career in his mid-twenties, when steely ambition made him a sometimes ruthless negotiator with publishers and helped him produce five best-selling, critically acclaimed novels (and a substantial miscellany of other writings) in as many years.

His first novel, *The Posthumous Papers of the Pickwick Club* (20 parts, 1836–37), mainly on the strength of its buoyant and resourceful comedy of situation, character, and style, gained a large appreciative audience with a social range almost matching that of his fictional world. It also initiated a flood of translations and adaptations of his work that has scarcely ever abated. D.'s name—and/or his youthful nom de plume "Boz"—had become a household word on both sides of the Atlantic long before the family magazine *Household Words*, with the heading "Conducted by Charles Dickens" on every page, was launched in 1850. Soon after that date, critical opinion started to turn against his work, but the novelist's popular audience remained as loyal as he did to it. This special relationship was sustained by his fidelity to serial forms of publication (in weekly and/or monthly installments) for all fifteen of his novels over a period of three-and-a-half decades. It acquired a further dimension in the grueling public reading tours that sapped even D.'s remarkable energies in his later years.

Those semistaged performances have since been reenacted by a string of notable imitators, while fully dramatized adaptations confined to the theater in the 19th c. have subsequently proliferated in film and broadcasting media. Moreover, the original works now engage critical enthusiasm on some of the very grounds accounting for their depreciation during the second half of D.'s career and for several decades after his death. In our postmodernist age, which has seen a dismantling of traditional cultural hierarchies and a mixing of high and popular art forms, the tonal and stylistic discontinuities characterizing D.'s "polyphonic" novels seem less problematic than they once did. With the genres of Gothic and melodrama back in fashion, there is renewed interest in his fiction's formal affinities and wealth of allusion to popular theater, balladry, and fairy tale. The same is true, given the current critical preoccupation with the human body, of D. theatrical reliance on physical features

and mannerisms in the presentation of character, and his extraordinary techniques of effigiation—the deanimated body of, for example, Mrs. Clennam in *Little Dorrit* (20 parts, 1855–57) implying a death of the soul—and synechdoche—in which one bodily part, like Jenny Wren's golden hair in *Our Mutual Friend* (20 parts, 1864–65), stands for the whole being. Through a long-established organic metaphor, there is a correlation between the body and the city. D.'s atmospheric evocations of London have always been acknowledged as supreme in English fiction and as a feature of integral importance in all his novels except *Hard Times* (1854), where a different kind of urban landscape is similarly prominent.

Most of D.'s earliest years were spent in Chatham, Kent, where his father was employed as a naval pay clerk. The family moved to London in 1822, and D. retained a vivid and odoriferous memory of the damp coach-journey he took alone to join them there. Despite this symbolic disenchantment, the capital city and especially its slum areas made a potent, glamorous appeal to the new young resident's imagination. Ten years later, he started contributing to newspapers and magazines the pieces soon to be collected in his first book, *Sketches by Boz* (2 vols., 1836; second series, 1837). Many already display authoritative knowledge and acuteness of observation with regard to London scenes, one of several ways in which the collection foreshadows D.'s later work. In addition to those frankly presented as fiction under the sectional heading of "Tales," many of the sketches are partly cast in narrative form and contain a blend of documentary and imaginative writing, an intimation that the young journalist is poised to stake his claim as novelist. In truth, of course, D. never abandoned journalism, and his journalistic career was to run in close harness with that of novelist to the end.

The Pickwick Papers, indeed, was initially undertaken as a piece of journalistic improvisation, D. having been invited to supply accompanying text for a monthly series of engravings depicting Cockney sporting life. However, he straightaway assumed the primary role in the project, "thought of Mr Pickwick," and launched this retired businessman, an incarnation of innocence and benignity, on a quixotic coaching tour of the southern counties, in a road narrative heavily indebted to Tobias SMOLLETT and Henry FIELDING. Pickwick's identity as a latterday Quixote more clearly emerged with the introduction of his Sancho Panza, Sam Weller, in the fourth number. The initially low sales figures rapidly rose (eventually to a sensational forty thousand per number) following the appearance of this resourceful, streetwise character, with an endless stream of witty Cockney patter but a proper sense of his subordinate place as unflinchingly loyal manservant. The novel's motif of embarrassment is made more than episodic by the development of plot in respect of Mrs. Bardell's suit against Pickwick for breach of promise, leading eventually to his imprisonment in the Fleet Prison. Comic entertainment is then tempered by pursuit of themes of social injustice, but the book ends as it began in symbolic sunshine.

Yet nearly a year before that conclusion was written or read, D. had plunged his contemporary audience into the much darker worlds of workhouse and criminal rookery in *Oliver Twist* (3 vols., 1838). The darkness appears all the more intense in that it encompasses the life of an innocent child, and even when the melodramatic principle of fluctuating fortune allows Oliver interludes of (and eventually more permanent release into) bourgeois comfort and pastoral tranquillity, their mood tends to be elegiac rather than exuberantly comic. Most of the comedy in *Oliver Twist* is satiric, targeting inhumanity and abuses of power in poor-law administration and the magistracy. Among the novel's many dualities is a tonal tension between satire and elegy, identified by Hippolyte Taine as a hallmark of D.'s fiction: "He contrasts the souls which nature creates with those which society deforms." Taine's observation is partly borne out by the long series of ill-treated or neglected children in D., a line of Oliver's followers extending all the way to Pip in *Great Expectations* (3 vols., 1861). Pip, though, is a complex character, emotionally and psychologically, handled without a shred of the sentimentality marring the treatment of previous unfortunates. Internalizing a condition of shame and guilt as a prelude to the selfish embrace of unearned wealth and status, Pip illustrates the ultimate inadequacy of Taine's striking formulation: he is a typical figure in D.'s mature vision in being a soul both created by nature and deformed by society.

One testament to the scale of D.'s achievement is that he never merely repeated a successful formula. *Oliver Twist* was followed by (and written partly simultaneously with) *The Life and Adventures of Nicholas Nickleby* (20 parts, 1838–39), for the most part a rollicking theatrical comedy, this by his most allegorical, fairy tale-like novel, *The Old Curiosity Shop* (2 vols., 1841), and that by *Barnaby Rudge* (1841), an historical novel about the Gordon Riots of 1780 in the very different vein of Sir Walter SCOTT, though with Carlylean and Victorian-Gothic embellishments. Thus concluded the first, frenetically productive, phase of D.'s career. During the following decade, he wrote "only" three full-length novels, widening his horizons in spells of foreign travel and residence and in new journalistic ventures, including the short-lived editorship of a daily newspaper. However, this second phase also yielded two travel books, *American Notes* (2 vols., 1842) and *Pictures from Italy* (1846), and a series of Christmas books, of which the first, *A Christmas Carol* (1843), an instantly huge success, has con-

tinued to be regarded as the quintessentially Dickensian work. Moreover, the two novels completed in the 1840s, *Martin Chuzzlewit* (20 parts, 1842–44) and *Dombey and Son* (20 parts, 1846–48), represent a significant development in artistic design, the narrative of each being consciously organized round a single moral theme—selfishness and pride, respectively—with a representative social currency. In these novels, D. brings middle-class sins into sharper critical focus than he had before, satirizing the dominant values of commercial society. They thus herald the darkening social vision of D.'s fiction in the mid-1850s, following the autobiographical interlude of *David Copperfield*. That novel, the favorite of many Victorians, contains some marvelously vivid writing, but in the light of D.'s later work (and especially the antidotal *Great Expectations*), now seems close to self-indulgent romance.

It was followed by *Bleak House* (20 parts, 1852–53), a novel of strikingly different tonality and of structural originality. Its narrative responsibilities are divided almost equally between an impersonal narrator of sweeping vision and enormous rhetorical power (in the present tense) and Esther Summerson, an insistently modest voice and character with a more conventional narrative style (in the past tense). This formal dichotomy is arguably expressive of ideological and temperamental contradictions within D. himself. The optimism that he never lost, especially with respect to providentially rescued individuals, sustains Esther's retrospective account of personal progress through adversity to eventual happiness. The present tense of the impersonal narration bespeaks a public world in which there is no discernible progress, a world brilliantly symbolized by the tactile mud and fog of the opening paragraphs. The Court of Chancery "at the very heart of the fog" typifies the institutionalized stranglehold of reactionary and secretive power, enriching its agents by destroying its clients to the end. Yet the intermeshing of the two narratives defies schematic bifurcation. The tragic division between Lady Dedlock's secret past and her emotionally frozen present demonstrates the continuum between private and public life, with secret documents a major motif in the private plot of Esther's parentage as well as in the public one of the Jarndyce and Jarndyce legal suit.

After *Bleak House* came *Hard Times* (1854), a dark, compressed satire on contemporary excesses of mechanism and materialism, especially in the industrial and educational spheres. In *Little Dorrit*, D. returned to the panoramic scale of *Bleak House* and further developed some of that novel's patterns and social ideas. Here, too, a stifling, obstructive secrecy characterizes both private histories (especially the past deeds and relations of the Clennams and the Dorrits) and the operation of public institutions (expressively represented by the Circumlocution Office). The leading female character again embodies selfless duty in a generally irresponsible world, but the overall mood in *Little Dorrit* is more somber, partly because of its ubiquitous prison imagery. Not only does the Marshalsea prison foster a culture of false appearances and relations, primarily signified in the condescendingly paternal role assumed by the longest-serving inmate William Dorrit, but many other characters inhabit social and psychological prisons that are equally inescapable. Neither is there anything escapist about the concluding affirmation of liberating love shared by hero and heroine as they go "down into the roaring streets," a blessed couple engulfed by the unredeemed urban crowd that "fretted and chafed."

No one fretted and chafed more than D. himself in the later 1850s. Already socially and politically discontented, he was increasingly prey to a personal restlessness as well as to severe health problems. A keen participant in amateur theatricals over many years, in 1857 he played Richard Wardour in Wilkie COLLINS's *The Frozen Deep*, a role upon which he drew for the character of Sidney Carton in his next novel. When the play was staged in Manchester, a seventeen-year-old professional actress, Ellen Ternan, performed alongside him; the couple soon formed a close relationship. In 1858, D. embarked on his first professional reading tour, pursued a very public separation from his wife, and severed relations with his publishers of long standing as well. *Household Words* ceased publication, to be succeeded by *All the Year Round*, which D. owned as well as edited for the remainder of his life. Aptly enough in these circumstances, the first novel to be serialized therein, *A Tale of Two Cities* (1859), was a story of revolution in which, as in D.'s only other historical novel *Barnaby Rudge*, a prison popularly symbolizing oppression is stormed by a wild mob. One can only marvel that amid emotional disturbances and practical distractions on this scale, he did all the preliminary research (Thomas CARLYLE's *The French Revolution* was a major but by no means the only source), planned, and wrote this tightly patterned novel within a single year.

D.'s productivity rates did decline in the 1860s. Following publication of *Great Expectations*, he completed only one more novel in the remaining nine years of his life, leaving another tantalizingly half-finished. *Our Mutual Friend* is a successor to *Bleak House* and *Little Dorrit* in its broad social sweep, its linkages between social extremes, its satirical attacks on society and the current mania for "Shares," and its investment of symbolic power in the physical landmarks of river and dust-heaps. There is, though, a more marked turning-away from the public world and the possibilities of social renovation to matters of personal identity and private relationship, of psychology and passion. Idle gentlemen toying with the affections of vulnerable young women are generally cast as villains in earlier D.; here, Eugene Wrayburn survives a murderous attack by the obsessively jealous schoolmaster, Bradley Headstone, to become a worthy husband for Lizzie Hexam, self-improved daughter of an illiterate river-scavenger. The dark places of psychology and passion were evidently to be further probed in D.'s final novel, *The Mystery of Edwin Drood* (1870). John Jasper, the respectable choirmaster at Cloisterham Cathedral, is the last in a series of dualistic characters in D. A drug-taker himself, he drugs and mesmerizes others, including his nephew Edwin Drood. When the latter disappears, Jasper leads a murder hunt, but meanwhile declares his love for Rosa, Edwin's ex-fiancée. D. died before the story confirmed Edward to be dead and Jasper to be the murderer, as most commentators have assumed it would. There are several Oriental and colonial aspects to the narrative, and it is likely that the mystery to be unfolded would have had an exotic Eastern connection. D.'s capacity to break new ground to the last is also displayed in the novel's dramatic opening in an East End opium den: with Jasper emerging from a drug-induced stupor, the opening paragraph is a prototype of modernist stream of consciousness writing.

BIBLIOGRAPHY: Andrews, M., *D. and the Grown-Up Child* (1994); Butt, J., and K. Tillotson, *D. at Work* (1957); Collins, P., *D.* (1971); Forster, J., *The Life of C. D.* (3 vols., 1872–74); Murray, B., *C. D.* (1994); Schad, J., *D. Refigured: Bodies, Desires and Other Histories* (1996); Schlicke, P., *D. and Popular Entertainment* (1985); Slater, M., *D. and Women* (1983); Stewart, G., *D. and the Trials of Imagination* (1974); Wilson, E., "D.: The Two Scrooges," in his *The Wound and the Bow* (1941): 1–104

RICK ALLEN

DICKENS, Monica [Enid]

b. 10 May 1915, London; d. 25 December 1992, Reading

Great-granddaughter of Charles DICKENS, D. was a talented and versatile journalist, children's writer, and novelist, who wrote vividly about her own varied experiences. Educated at the prestigious St. Paul's School for Girls, she trained as an actress, was presented at court in 1935 and worked as a cook and general servant. *One Pair of Hands* (1939) was a fictionalized account of her life below stairs. During World War II, she was a hospital nurse and wrote *One Pair of Feet* (1942). A stint as a junior reporter resulted in *My Turn to Make the Tea* (1951). Among her many novels the most memorable is also semiautobiographical: *No More Meadows* (1953; repub. as *The Nightingales Are* Singing, 1953) tells the story of an English girl's dislocation and culture shock when she marries an American, as D. did herself. *The Listeners* (1970) is a novel about the work of the Samaritans. D founded the Boston branch of Samaritans in 1974. Her moving novel *The Winds of Heaven* (1955) is a reworking of William SHAKESPEARE's *King Lear.*

DISCOVERY AND EXPLORATION ACCOUNTS

The writings of discoverers and explorers are often to be distinguished from those of travelers by their outlook and attitude as much as by their antecedence. Britain has spawned a rich library of such writing, largely because of the nation's long seafaring traditions and (in known preserved and published form) it stretches back to the early 16th c.

Early written accounts were by-products of the urge to explore and were often sporadically kept as well as fanciful in their style. Sir Walter RALEIGH on a visit to the northeastern coast of South America in 1596 wrote of "men in Guina [Guiana] with eyes in their shoulders and mouths in their chests," the line between reality and fantasy evidently being somewhat blurred. Epic tales of endurance in challenging circumstances also shine through and this characteristic, as well as exotic tales of "otherness," commended these writings to a wider public as printing and the advent of literacy became more widespread.

As the Age of Discovery progressed, explorers became more keen to make a scientific record of their adventures and kept daily logs in which maps and charts were compiled and in which astronomical observations and supposed navigational positions were faithfully recorded. The accuracy of such material is open to doubt, however, particularly in the period before reliable chronometers were carried on expeditions. Dava Sobel's book *Longitude* (1995) has brilliantly revealed the importance and significance of John Harrison's mid-18th-c. invention in this respect.

Frequently added to this material were colorful accounts of encounters with unfamiliar environments and peoples, in which apparently unproblematic records of heroism and triumphant discovery were prominent. Viewed from an Anglo-centric position, other cultures were usually shown to surrender their secrets and their treasures before the powerful gaze of "civilized men" and of reason. The application of reason and a supposed advantage in culture did not, however, prevent imagination sometimes gaining a powerful hand in these accounts.

In the writings of early explorers there was also a rhetoric of acquisition in which the cataloguing of commodities and trading exchanges frequently prevailed over description and aesthetic appreciation. Nevertheless, with careful reading, such accounts do provide information and insight about early encounters between Britons and "new worlds." Of equal sig-

nificance is the way in which original accounts were reworked and distilled in subsequent tellings in order to be popularized and made more widely available. Such accounts often also had ulterior political and colonial motives influencing their emphasis. Thus, some of those best known for British discovery and exploration writing are not the explorers themselves but compilers and editors who labored to standardize and complete fragmented accounts, and in doing so sometimes unwittingly "smoothed out" or falsified aspects of the original experience.

One of the most famous of these writers is Richard HAKLUYT, an English geographer and cleric, who was educated at Westminster School and who went on to lecture in geography at Christ Church, Oxford. He published *Divers Voyages Touching the Discovery of America* in 1582, partly as an account of the voyages of Raleigh and others but also as an advocacy of North American as a base for exploration of the East, via the Northwest Passage. Though never venturing further than the chaplaincy of the English embassy in Paris, he wrote *Discourse concerning Western discoveries* and then returned to England to gather material for his major work *Principal Navigations, Voyages, Traffiques, and Discoveries of the English Nation.* This three-volume work on the history of exploration was a consummate piece of anthologizing of firsthand accounts in many languages. Samuel PURCHAS, who studied at St. John's College, Cambridge, was ordained and then became successively Vicar of Eastwood, Nottinghamshire, and of St. Martin's Ludgate, assisted Hakluyt in his later years. His own greatest works were *Purchas His Pilgrimage; or, Relations of the World and Religions Observed in All Ages*, and the four-volume *Hakluytus Posthumis; or, Purchas His Pilgrimes*, the latter based on the papers of Hakluyt and the archives of the East India Company.

Some combined practical exploration with authorship. One such was William Dampier, a hydrographer who took part in many voyages in both Atlantic and Pacific in the late 17 c. Some of these tales were recounted in his *Voyage round the world* (1697) after which he made further visits to the South Seas, full of adventure. On his way home, he and his crew were wrecked off Ascension Island and lived on turtles and goats for five weeks until they were rescued. His supposed cruelty to his lieutenant led to his subsequent court-martial. These events were recorded in *Vindication* (1707) which, as its title indicates, was intended as something more than a record of his adventures, though it did little to restore his reputation.

The improvement of maps and navigational aids in the 18th c. ensured more accurate locational records but does not diminish the need for a thorough examination and deconstruction of exploration and discovery accounts. For instance, the eventual published record of Captain James Cook's third voyage (1776–79) is a composite account. The original day-to-day entries in the ship's log, were supplemented by entries in Cook's own personal journal. These two sources were edited by James Douglas into a third account before an official version emanated from the Admiralty. Into this fourth account were also incorporated such points as seemed relevant from the journals of Cook's officers. Thus, by the time the account of the voyage reached publication, its veracity had been somewhat compromised. It is also worth noting that Cook was accompanied by draftsmen-cartographers and by artists who also recorded their experiences; the written accounts need to be read in conjunction with the material produced in these other forms, which itself also, of course, carried subjective overtones.

Though early explorers were mainly motivated by political and trading imperatives (and directly funded by governments and monarchies as a result), a greater range of motives became apparent from the mid-17th c. onward. The desire for greater scientific knowledge through exploration reached its apogee in the voyages of HMS *Beagle*, leading to Charles DARWIN's seminal writings on the evolution of species. There were also many 19th-c. British explorers (e.g., David Livingstone in Africa, Charles M. DOUGHTY in Arabia) who set out with Christian evangelistic motives, usually allied to a wish to improve medical and educational conditions in the lands that they explored, and whose writings reflect this outlook.

Writing about discovery could also be shaped to become advocacy and evidence. The partnership and later rivalry between Richard BURTON and J. H. Speke and the dispute over who had found the true source of the Nile is to be measured in the differing accounts which these two explorers provided of their exploits. Burton went on to equal his exploratory adventures with his literary ones in authoring unexpurgated translations of *The Kama Sutra* and *The Arabian Nights.*

By the time the end of the 19th c. was reached, the literary output of explorers was as significant as their adventures. This is illustrated well by the literature that surrounds the race to the South Pole in 1911. The daily journals of R. F. Scott and Roald Amundsen provide firsthand graphic accounts of the heroism and privations of this competitive adventure, but our understanding of what went on is supplemented by "literary" work such as E. R. G. Evans's *South with Scott* (1921), Apsley Cherry-Garrard's *The Worst Journey in the World* (1922), and the diaries and poetry of E. A. Wilson, one of those who died with Scott. Later, the episode would be further investigated, analyzed, represented, and revaluated by Roland Huntford's biography *Scott and Amundsen* (1979), which is critical of Scott and explains his rise to a subsequent iconic status in Britain as being because "he was the better writer," by film (Ealing Studios' *Scott of the Antarc-*

tic, 1948), and by a play (*Terra Nova* by Ted Tally, 1981).

It is a short step from the shaped reminiscence of exploring experience to the form of the adventure novel. One of the earliest was Daniel DEFOE's *Robinson Crusoe*, based on the experiences of Alexander Selkirk, marooned by Dampier on the island of Juan Fernandez off the coast of Chile 1704–8. This was one of several novels of this kind that Defoe wrote. Another was *Captain Singleton*, published in 1720, in which the hero makes a crossing of Africa from east to west. It is significant that Defoe was also a traveler and travel writer. Though not strictly accounts of discovery in the traditional sense, the insights of such temporarily expatriate British writers as Rudyard KIPLING and E. M. FORSTER (in India), of D. H. LAWRENCE (in Mexico and Australia), of Evelyn WAUGH (in East Africa), and of Graham GREENE (in Central America) have made more recent notable "explorations" of other cultures through novels with a substantial basis of documentary fact and experience at their heart.

As blank spaces on the map became fewer in the late 19th and early 20th cs., the ascent of mountains replaced the discovery of new lands as the prime form of new exploration. The culminating climbing feat of reaching the summit of Mount Everest was recounted comprehensively in John Hunt's *The Ascent of Everest* (1953) and more personally in Edmund Hillary's *High Adventure* (1955) and has given rise to many other graphic accounts of climbs since. The modern situation is exemplified in the life and work of Christian Bonington, a distinguished contemporary mountaineer who makes his living and finances his climbs by writing and lecturing about the journeys and expeditions which he makes.

In recent years, subcategories of discovery and exploration writing include those which recount the reaching or traversing of particular locations by particular modes of transport for the first time, e.g, flying to new destinations and over uncharted regions (a particular enthusiasm and media eye-catching activity in the 1920s and 1930s), circumnavigations of the globe by various kinds of sailing vessel and two recent exploits: paddling round Britain by canoe and cycling across the Himalayas.

There are also those who seek to simulate the journeys of early explorers by re-creating their conditions of travel and their craft (e.g., Tim Severin's voyages across the Atlantic in the steps of St. Brendan, from Muscat to China, replicating the seven voyages of Sinbad) and in the wake of Jason and Odysseus, and the EPIC *Kon-Tiki* and *Ra* expeditions of Thor Heyerdahl and writing about their experience. There is now a substantial business in which the writing and marketing of a subsequent book rather than the attaining of the geographical location or the journey itself may be construed as the major objective: from this point, "discovery" and "exploration" accounts shade into the more general category of travel writing.

Further subgenres include the accounts of those who have searched for lost explorers or followed in their footsteps, most famously Sir Henry M. Stanley, looking for Livingstone in Africa, and those who have set out to write amusing or picaresque accounts of their adventures. Peter Fleming's *Brazilian Adventure* (1933) notably combined both these genres in its account of an expedition to seek the missing Colonel Percy Harrison Fawcett in the Mato Grosso.

A greater multicultural consciousness in the late 20th c. has also produced a number of exhibitions and associated volumes that have attempted to contextualize and evaluate the deeds and writings of early British discoverers and explorers.

BIBLIOGRAPHY: Baker, J. N. L., *The History of Geography* (1963); Duncan, J., and D. Gregory, eds., *Writes of Passage: Reading Travel Writing* (1999); Hanbury-Tenison, R., ed., *The Oxford Book of Exploration* (1993); Keay, J., ed., *The Royal Geographical Society History of World Exploration* (1991); Jeal, T., et al., *David Livingstone and the Victorian Encounter with Africa* (1996); Stefansson, V., ed., *Great Adventures and Explorations* (1947)

REX WALFORD

DISRAELI, Benjamin, First Earl of Beaconsfield

b. 4 December 1804, London; d. 19 April 1881, London

D. was the only British prime minister who was also a successful novelist (cf. Winston CHURCHILL). Analyzing his own dreams of power, D. invented the political novel; his fictions deal with political issues, whereas Anthony TROLLOPE's concentrate on the social background. However, D.'s plots are sometimes less gripping than his discussion and his solution to social problems is reactionary, a benevolent feudalism.

D.'s first novel, *Vivian Grey* (5 vols., 1826–27), a Bildungsroman about an unscrupulous young man on the make, offers lively dialogue and betrays a precocious obsession with politics. The original edition is franker and more playful than the 1853 version, edited by the author. As Sir Leslie STEPHEN said, D. hovers between the ironical and the serious. D.'s work is concerned with a conflict between the life of the artist and that of action. His semiautobiographical *Contarini Fleming* (4 vols., 1832) shows a cultivated intellect actively engaging with history as the hero travels in Europe; the first-person narrator is in search of identity and fiercely ambitious. In *The Wondrous Tale of Alroy* (3 vols., 1833), an historical romance, D. ex-

pressed his dislike of utilitarianism. Alroy is a medieval Jewish prince who conquers much of Asia but compromises his integrity and loses both his kingdom and his life. D. described these early works, all published anonymously, in his diary as "the secret history of my feelings."

Henrietta Temple (3 vols., 1837) is less original and less personal, but once more about life choices: in a plot explicitly echoing Samuel RICHARDSON's *Sir Charles Grandison,* the well-born Ferdinand Armine finds himself engaged to two women simultaneously, the first for money, the second for love. It is a "silver fork" or high society novel, with witty dialogue. It ends happily with Ferdinand's election to Parliament, thanks to the Catholic Emancipation Bill of 1828. In 1832, D. had stood unsuccessfully for Parliament as a Radical. *Venetia* (3 vols., 1837) disappoints insofar as it features poets loosely based on Lord BYRON and Percy Bysshe SHELLEY, while "Lady Monteagle" represents Lady Holland, the great Whig hostess, none with much conviction. But when the poets talk to each other, their conversation is brilliant. Lady Annabel's embargo on discussion with her daughter about the husband and father who deserted them is psychologically truthful. The vulgar Mrs. Cadurcis is a study in possessive and self-defeating motherhood. D. portrayed the pain and alienation of these women with understanding and originality.

In 1837, Queen Victoria came to the throne, which meant an election, and D. at last entered Parliament as a Tory. The next three novels explore the values of conservatism, which D. dreamed of revitalizing. *Coningsby* (3 vols., 1844) opens with the passing of the Reform Bill of 1832, which abolished "rotten" and "pocket" electoral boroughs and led indirectly, as D. prophesied it would, to universal suffrage almost a century later. The eponymous hero is the grandson of Lord Monmouth. Like William Makepeace THACKERAY's Lord Steyne in *Vanity Fair*, Monmouth is a portrait of the notoriously debauched Lord Hertford, and represents aristocratic decadence. Young Coningsby travels to Manchester and D., like Thomas CARLYLE, Charles DICKENS and Elizabeth Cleghorn GASKELL in their "condition of England" writings, recognizes the growing power of the manufacturing classes, despite the resistance of the hereditary aristocracy. In the marriage of Coningsby and the aptly named Miss Millbank, the warring classes are symbolically united to give the responsible leadership the self-indulgent nobility will not. The real power in D.'s fictional world, however, is the mysterious Jew Sidonia, richer than Rothschild, who regards the English nobility as *parvenu*. Sidonia is an outsider, proud of his race, the looker-on who sees most of the game.

Although a talented social satirist, the young D. had a romantic admiration for old English families and aristocratic tradition, especially recusant Roman Catholicism, combined with indignation at the plight of the poor and exploited; D.'s best book, *Sybil; or, The Two Nations* (3 vols., 1845) memorably exposes industrial abuses. D. approved of Robert Owen's experiment in social welfare; Owen appears as "Mr Trafford." Equality is to be achieved "not by levelling the Few, but, by elevating the Many." *Sybil* has echoes of Carlyle's *Chartism* and *Past and Present*, and Chartism, with its "five points" and social unrest, is crucial in the plot, which offers a cross-section of English life from 1832 onward. For D., Chartism was not a reasonable demand, but anarchy, evidence of a failure in government. D.'s propertied classes are under an obligation to provide for the people, dispossessed by industrial capitalism, as the monasteries did before the dissolution.

In the third volume of the trilogy, *Tancred* (3 vols., 1847), Sidonia reappears, revealed as an international negotiator. Tancred, Lord Montacute, a thoughtful young man, retraces the journey made by his Crusader ancestors to Jerusalem, to find the roots of his own Christianity. There he becomes the unwitting pawn in political machinations, is kidnapped for ransom, discovers a community who still worship the old Greek gods, and falls in love with Eva, daughter of a Jewish financier. Eva, an acute theologian, lectures the fascinated Tancred on the history of Mediterranean civilization, ripe when "flat-nosed Franks" were mere savages. In the final pages, Tancred declares his love for Eva, but she refuses him and when his anxious parents arrive from England to claim him he can only swoon. The book embodies special pleading for the value of Jewish culture, despite the disclaimer that Christianity is the "perfection" of Judaism. However, like D. himself, Tancred is a 19th-c. Christian who cannot embrace Judaism, however deep the author's nostalgia.

Lothair (3 vols., 1870) pursues the theme of religious conflict. Lothair, a rich young nobleman, is an Anglican like his guardian, a vicar. The guardian, based on John Henry NEWMAN, is converted to Rome and becomes a Cardinal. Lothair is tempted to follow him, but is saved by two good women. D.'s viewpoint has shifted. The Roman faith is treated here as an insidious trap, involving pious fraud. The smooth-talking Cardinal is excellently drawn. But despite dealing with Fenianism and with Garibaldi, much of the tale is lifeless. *Endymion*, in which the eponymous hero becomes prime minister, was published in 1880. D. also left nine chapters of an unfinished novel, *Falconet*.

BIBLIOGRAPHY: Braun, T., *D. the Novelist* (1981); Richmond, C., and P. Smith, eds., *The Self-Fashioning of D., 1818–1851* (1998); Schwartz, D. R., *D.'s Fiction* (1979)

VALERIE GROSVENOR MYER

D'ISRAELI, Isaac

b. 11 May 1766, Enfield; d. 19 January 1848, Bradenham

D.'s first book, *A Defence of Poetry* (1790), was a statement justifying his chosen career as a writer, although his father wanted him to go into commerce. He intended to succeed as a creative writer, but is best known for his discursive *Curiosities of Literature* (1791; rev. eds., 1793, 1817, 1834, 1838), comprising historical and literary anecdotes. He also wrote *Miscellanies; or, Literary Recreations* (1796), *Calamities of Authors* (2 vols., 1812–13), and *Quarrels of Authors* (1814). *Amenities of Literature* (1841) formed the first three volumes of an unfinished history of English letters. His *Essay on the Manners and Genius of Literary Character* (1795) contains further anecdotes, and sets out to chart the temperamental make-up of writers. He supported Lord BYRON and Thomas CAMPBELL in defending Alexander POPE's poetry against William Lisle BOWLES and William HAZLITT in the *Quarterly Review* (July 1820). In 1797, D. published a novel: *Mejnoun and Leila*, said to be the first Oriental romance in English. His novel *Despotism* (2 vols., 1811) was unsuccessful. In 1833, he published a short history of the growth of the Talmud called the *Genius of Judaism*. He was author of two historical studies: a defense of King JAMES I of England (King James VI of Scotland), (1816), and a learned *Commentary on the Life and Reign of King Charles I* (5 vols., 1828–31), narrative poems and fictions. A brief memoir by his son Benjamin DISRAELI appeared in the 1849 edition of *Curiosities of Literature*.

DIXON, Richard Watson

b. 5 May 1833, Islington; d. 23 January 1900, Warkworth

As a student at Pembroke College, Oxford, D. and others, notably Edward Burne-Jones and William MORRIS, came under the influence of Dante Gabriel ROSSETTI, who inspired in D. a passion for aesthetic pursuit. After a promising start as a poet, D. established himself instead as an historian and from 1878 to 1902 published his six-volume *History of the Church of England from the Abolition of the Roman Jurisdiction*. Encouraged later in his career by Gerard Manley HOPKINS, whom D. had taught at Highgate School, London, D. returned to writing poetry and in 1883 published his long narrative poem entitled *Mano, a Political History of the Close of the Tenth Century*. In 1909, D.'s *Poems* appeared posthumously, edited with a memoir by Robert BRIDGES.

DOBELL, Sydney [Thompson]

b. 5 April 1824, Cranbrook, Kent; d. 22 August 1874, Gloucester

D. was educated privately, never going to school or university. An enthusiastic Liberal, D. wrote poems advocating political reform. *The Roman* appeared in 1850, under the pseudonym "Sydney Yendys." His second long poem, *Balder*, appeared in 1854. It features a young poet who has taken his bride and baby daughter to a "tower gloomy and ruinous": the baby dies, the wife goes mad, and the husband kills her as an act of mercy. Balder's cry "Ah!" (repeated twelve times), attracted the mockery of William Aytoun who stigmatized it as belonging to the "spasmodic school" (the epithet originally applied by Thomas CARLYLE to Lord BYRON's works). The school included George GILFILLAN and Alexander SMITH and was characterized by a mood of discontent, by unrewarded struggle, skeptical unrest, and an uneasy straining after the unattainable, thus exemplifying aspects of 19th-c. thought. In 1855, with Smith, D. published sonnets on the Crimean war and a volume called *England in Time of War* (1856) that includes the ballad containing the refrain "O Keith of Ravelston, the sorrows of thy line," which was admired by Dante Gabriel ROSSETTI. D.'s essays, *Thoughts on Art, Philosophy, and Religion*, appeared posthumously in 1876.

DOBSON, [Henry] Austin

b. 18 January 1840, Plymouth; d. 2 September 1921, Ealing

In March 1883, the artist Edwin A. Abbey created a bookplate for D. The design shows an 18th-c. man reading a journal. Above his head hangs a William Hogarth print from the series *The Harlot's Progress*. These images capture D.'s enthusiasms, which the author described in his characteristic verses: "You love, my Friend, with me, I think,/That Age of Lustre and of Link;/Of Chelsea China and long 's'-es,/Of Bagwigs and of flowered Dresses;/That Age of Folly and of Cards,/Of Hackney Chairs and Hackney Bards." D. loved old books, old china, old friends, old times, which he celebrated in society verse and charming familiar essays.

D.'s first poem, "A City Flower," appeared in the December 1864 *Temple Bar*. Shortly afterward, William Cosmo Monkhouse, a colleague at the Board of Trade (where D. worked from 1856 to 1901), introduced D. to the editor of the *Englishwoman's Domestic Magazine*, to which D. submitted poetry and four early essays later collected as *Four Frenchwomen* (1890). After Anthony TROLLOPE founded *St. Paul's Magazine* in October 1867, D. published verses there as well, and D. dedicated his first volume of poetry, *Vignettes in Rhyme* (1873) to Trollope. These early poems show some Pre-Raphaelite influence. *Proverbs in Porcelain* (1877), D.'s next book, is more indebted to Théodore de Banville's discussion of medieval French verse forms in *Petite traité de poésie française* (1872), though D. also encountered these in his reading of such authors as François Villon, Charles d'Or-

léans, Vincent Voiture, Pierre de Ronsard, and Clément Marot. About a third of D.'s poetry consists of ballades, triolets, pantuns, rondeaux, rondels, and villanelles.

D. produced most of his poetry before 1887, though about a quarter of his collected poems were composed after that date. As his poetic output declined, his prose productions proliferated. In 1879, he published the first version of his life of Hogarth (rev. eds., 1891, 1898, 1902, 1907), followed by biographies of Henry FIELDING (1883; rev. ed., 1907), Thomas Bewick (1884), Richard STEELE (1886), Oliver GOLDSMITH (1888), Horace WALPOLE (1890), Samuel RICHARDSON (1902), and Fanny BURNEY (1903). He also published eleven volumes of essays on 18th-c. subjects, generally exploring by-ways of the era. He made this period so much his own that some fifty books published in the late 1880s and early 1900s dealing with the 18th c. carried introductions by D.

In verse and prose, D. courted the muses of elegance and propriety. Though he loved the Augustan Age, he wrote about it from the perspective of a Victorian. His friend Sir Edmund GOSSE commented that to open a book by D. is to enter "a rose-coloured world, suffused with a transparent radiance of ideality, and founded, no doubt, more on an illusion as to what things should be than on observations of what they were." D.'s biographies have been superseded; the SENTIMENT and nostalgia in his poetry and essays are out of fashion. Still, like a lavender sachet or an old-fashioned rose, they retain a charm and sweetness undiminished by time.

BIBLIOGRAPHY: Dobson, A., *A. D.* (1928); Ellis, S. M., "A. D.," in his *Mainly Victorian* (1925): 211–21; Weygandt, C., "A. D., Augustan," in his *Tuesdays at Ten* (1928): 232–39

JOSEPH ROSENBLUM

DODSLEY, Robert

b. 13 February 1703, Mansfield; d. 23 September 1764, London

Footman turned man of letters, D.—through a combination of talent, wit, and good fortune—elevated himself from servitude to become one of the most important British publishers of the 18th c. as well as a literary editor, bookseller, and dramatist. His plays include *The Toy-Shop* (1735), *The King and the Miller of Mansfield* (1737), *The Triumph of Peace* (1749), and the highly successful *Cleone* (1758). He published the work of numerous authors, including Edward YOUNG, Joseph and Thomas WHARTON, Samuel JOHNSON, Daniel DEFOE, Thomas GRAY, Edmund BURKE, and Laurence STERNE, and from 1748 to 1758 edited in six volumes the influential miscellany *A Collection of Poems*.

DONNE, John

b. 1572, London; d. 31 March 1631, London

Best known in his lifetime as a brilliant and captivating preacher, D. is one of the most original and most influential poets in the history of English literature. Born to a wealthy Roman Catholic family, D. studied for a time both at Cambridge and at Oxford, but because of his religion, he could not take a degree. In 1610, D. recounted how, while studying law at Lincoln's Inn in the early 1590s, he experienced a religious crisis that prompted him to undertake a thorough examination of Christian theology. Some time later, D. abandoned Roman Catholicism and became, at least nominally, a member of the Church of England.

During the mid to late 1590s—the years that D. later called his "Jack Donne" period—he enjoyed the life of a court gallant; in London, he was known as "a great visitor of ladies, a great frequenter of plays, a great writer of conceited verses." After serving the Earl of Essex on his Spanish expeditions in 1596 and 1597, he won the prestigious post of secretary to Sir Thomas Egerton, Lord Keeper of the Great Seal, in 1598. His career as a public servant, however, was cut short in 1601 when he secretly married Egerton's niece Anne More. D. was dismissed and temporarily imprisoned; he spent the next fourteen years struggling to support his growing family. By 1607, he was writing pamphlets against the Roman Catholic Church. In 1610, D. published *Pseudo-Martyr*, a tract exhorting English Catholics to take the oath of allegiance. *Ignatius His Conclave*, a prose satire against the Jesuits, followed a year later. JAMES I admired these works and, believing D. would be an excellent preacher, encouraged him to take holy orders; when D. expressed reluctance, the king barred him from secular preferment at court. In 1615, D. put aside his doubts and was ordained as a priest of the Church of England, thus inaugurating the phase of his life that he would call the "Dr. Donne" period (D. received an honorary doctorate from Cambridge shortly after his ordination). D. soon became a royal chaplain and, in 1621, he was made Dean of St. Paul's Cathedral in London, a position that he held until his death.

D.'s poems are notoriously difficult to date. In the first edition of D.'s works, published posthumously in 1633, the order of the poems seems arbitrary; in the second edition (1635), the poems are arranged according to genre. Scholars now generally agree that the *Elegies* and the *Satires* constitute the earliest of D.'s important works. D.'s twenty elegies, probably written in the mid-1590s, are erotic poems modeled on Ovid's *Amores*. Five *Elegies*—including the two most famous, "On His Mistress" and "To His Mistress Going to Bed"—are so sexually frank that they were censored from the first edition of his poetry. Taking

the savage writings of Juvenal and Persius as his models, D. wrote his five *Satires* sometime between 1593 and 1598. "Satire 3," which deals with D.'s own dilemma of choosing between competing Christian sects, is an early masterpiece. In the best of the elegies and satires, the chief characteristics of D.'s unique style are fully articulated for the first time. D. throws out many of the central conventions of Elizabethan poetry. His poems are marked by colloquial language, intricate and varied stanzaic patterns, irregular meter, and elliptical syntax. Perhaps the most distinctive feature of his poems are his witty and frequently shocking conceits (later called "Metaphysical conceits"), extended metaphors that develop complex images as far as D. can logically take them. Careful to avoid the clichés of earlier poetry, which he ruthlessly mocks, D. intellectualizes his conceits by drawing the vehicles for his figures from such diverse areas of knowledge as theology, philosophy, law, mathematics, cartography, alchemy, and astrology. Irony, paradox, and pun are other favorite D. devices. The poems often begin abruptly and present a dramatic situation. The speakers—who are *dramatis personae* distinct from the poet—are direct, sometimes harsh and coarse.

D.'s poetic reputation rests largely on the love lyrics comprising the *Songs and Sonnets* section of his collected poems. Although the majority of the *Songs* were likely written in the late 1590s, D. was apparently working on some of them as late as 1617. Taken as a whole, *Songs and Sonnets* is distinctly anti-Petrarchan. More often than not, the man and woman in a D. poem have already consummated their relationship; a few of the lyrics (i.e., "The Blossom" and "The Relic") profess a Neoplatonic view of love, but many more, including "The Canonization" and "Love's Infiniteness," reject it. In a further break with Petrarchan traditions, D. refrains from describing the women addressed in the poems. The collection is justly celebrated for its variety. Some of the speakers that D. presents in the *Songs* are pure cynics, while others are passionate idealists who believe in companionate love. "The Flea" and many other of the *Songs* are wickedly funny. On the other hand, few poems are as deeply moving as "A Nocturnal upon St. Lucy's Day, Being the Shortest Day," which deals with the grief of a bereaved lover. Throughout the *Songs*, D. demonstrates the verbal ingenuity for which he is famous: to take one example, in "A Valediction: Forbidding Mourning," D. memorably compares separated lovers to the legs of a compass.

Many of the religious poems that he wrote in later life rank among his greatest literary achievements. D. wrote "An Anatomy of the World (The First Anniversary)" in 1611 on the first anniversary of the death of Elizabeth Drury, the daughter of a patron; he wrote a companion piece, "Of the Progress of the Soul (the

Second Anniversary)," in 1612. The difficult, lengthy *Anniversary* poems are highly philosophical works notable for D.'s reflections on the scientific advances that were occurring in the early 17th c. D.'s finest devotional poems are his nineteen "Holy Sonnets," which were likely written between 1609 and 1617. Whereas in the *Songs*, D. describes erotic love in religious terms, in this collection, he consistently describes religious experience in erotic terms. The sonnets—as well as the remarkable "Good Friday 1613, Riding Westward"—record in vivid detail D.'s struggles with his faith. The paralyzing doubt expressed in the sonnets is for the most part absent from D.'s three great hymns, "A Hymn to Christ, at the Author's last going into Germany" (1617), "Hymn to God my God, in my Sickness," and "A Hymn to God the Father" (both 1623).

As a writer of prose, D. has few equals in the early modern period. D. was perhaps the most famous English preacher of the 17th c., and 145 of his sermons were published posthumously between 1640 and 1660. His sermons, like his poetry, are at once extremely passionate and highly intellectual. Replete with stunning metaphors, they are perhaps the most linguistically rich sermons ever written. For the most part, he avoids the controversial issues dividing Protestants and Catholics, instead focusing on God's mercy, on repentance, and, above all, on death and dying. D.'s brush with death during a lengthy illness in 1623 inspired his prose masterpiece, *Devotions upon Emergent Occasions* (1624), a series of twenty-three meditations. In the work, D. describes the phases of his illness in order to make larger points about the frailty of humanity and the need for God's grace. D.'s prose brilliantly combines the Ciceronian and Senecan styles, making for intensely dramatic writings.

With the exception of *The First and Second Anniversaries* (1611, 1612), "The Elegy on Prince Henry" (1613), and five short lyrics, none of D.'s poetry was published before 1633. It did, however, circulate at the court and at the universities in manuscript form. His readers included aspiring poets. It is perhaps too much to say that he inspired his own poetic school, but it is clear that early 17th-c. poets such as George HERBERT, Richard CRASHAW, Henry VAUGHAN, Henry KING, Thomas CAREW, Andrew MARVELL, and Abraham COWLEY drew extensively upon his work. D.'s style went out of fashion in the latter half of the 17th c. John DRYDEN, the most important poet of the Restoration, castigated D. for lacking decorum, and, in the 18th c., Samuel JOHNSON did not include D. among his *Lives of the Poets*, but in his "Life of Cowley" writes of the "metaphysical poets" that "the most heterogeneous ideas are yoked by violence together." Although D.'s sermons were widely admired, his poetry was for the most part ignored by readers in the

18th and 19th cs. The early 20th c. saw an extraordinary resurgence of interest in D. the poet. D.'s poetry strongly influenced Rupert BROOKE, T. S. ELIOT, W. B. YEATS, W. H. AUDEN, John Crowe Ransom, Theodore Roethke, and many other modernists. Eliot found in D.'s work a union of thought and emotion that he believed had largely disappeared from English poetry after the early 17th c. Writers, scholars, and general readers came to view D. as the most "modern" of the Renaissance poets. After spending over two centuries on the periphery of the English canon, D. is now one of its central authors.

BIBLIOGRAPHY: Bald, R. C., *J. D.* (1970); Carey, J., *J. D.* (1990); Gardner, H., ed., *Twentieth-Century Views: J. D.* (1962); Legouis, P., *D. the Craftsman* (1938); Lewalski, B. K., *D.'s "Anniversaries" and the Poetry of Praise* (1973); Sanders, W., *J. D.'s Poetry* (1971); Sherwood, T. G., *Fulfilling the Circle: A Study of J. D.'s Thought* (1984); Webber, J., *Contrary Music: The Prose Style of J. D.* (1963)

T. D. DRAKE

DOUGHTY, Charles M[ontagu]
b. 19 August 1843, Suffolk; d. 20 January 1926, Sissinghurst, Kent

Like his contemporary Thomas HARDY, D. was a polymath who wrote prose in the 19th c. and poetry in the 20th. Unlike Hardy (of whom D. had never heard until a reviewer compared their long poems), D. was very little celebrated in his lifetime and very little remembered in the decades since his death. The only mention of him in any popular medium came in 1962 in the movie *Lawrence of Arabia*, when Prince Feisal (played by Alec Guinness) tells Lawrence (Peter O'Toole), "I think you are another of these desert-loving Englishmen, Doughty, Stanhope, Gordon of Khartoum." For many readers, D.'s association with Lawrence, who was a most influential advocate, is their chief reason to pay any attention to D. at all.

D. was a researcher into foundations, and he favored settings that smack of origins: dawn, desert, glacier. He could now and then write about submarines and airplanes, but his best artistry was devoted to much older things. To study geology and geography, he had to travel; to travel, he had to learn languages, so that he became a geologist or paleontologist of words themselves, and his innovations in style remain after the truth or error of his science has evaporated.

From his twenty-one months of traveling in the Arabian desert (1876–78), he fashioned *Travels in Arabia Deserta* (2 vols., 1888), a work that continues to find thousands of readers. Very few Europeans had traveled among the Bedouin and other tribal peoples of the desert, and even fewer had left reliable written records; D.'s rather unorganized book was the first and best accounting of many details of terrain, manners, and speech in Arabia.

The style of that book is a striking mixture of archaic English vocabulary and syntax given further strangeness by Arabic words and idioms, some of them spelled according to discredited habits of transcription, and all punctuated idiosyncratically. In 1920, in the preface to the second edition of the book that had appeared almost a third of a century earlier, D. produced a sentence that showed his style had changed little: "A re-print has been called for; and is reproduced thus, at the suggestion chiefly of my distinguished friend, Colonel T. E. Lawrence, leader with Feysal, Meccan Prince, of the nomad tribesmen; whom they, as might none other at that time, marching from Jidda, the port of Mecca, were able, (composing, as they went, the tribes' long-standing blood feuds and old enmities), to unite with them in victorious arms, against the corrupt Turkish sovereignty in those parts: and who greatly thus serving his Country's cause and her Allies, from the Eastward, amidst the Great War; has in that imperishable enterprise, traversed the same wide region of Desert Arabia."

When *Travels in Arabia Deserta* first appeared, Robert BRIDGES wrote to share his enthusiasm with his friend Gerard Manley HOPKINS, but the latter was not impressed enough to read beyond a few extracts printed in reviews. "You say it is free from the taint of Victorian English. H'm. Is it free from the taint of Elizabethan English? Does it not stink of that? for the sweetest flesh turns to corruption."

While still in his early twenties, D. formed the ambition to write an EPIC poem about early Britain, under the provisional title "The Utmost Isle." This poem appeared in 1906 with the title *The Dawn in Britain*; its twenty-four books were printed in six volumes. In 1943, D.'s centennial, the poem appeared in one volume. Various other books of poetry appeared in the succeeding years, but none matches *The Dawn in Britain* in scope or novelty. The poem is written in what can be understood as blank verse, but the vocabulary and syntax are even more exotic than the prose of *Travels in Arabia Deserta*.

It is on record that Ezra Pound tried to read *The Dawn in Britain* to W. B. YEATS around 1913. Almost a century later, D. continues to attract admirers and adherents. In the 1930s, Hugh MACDIARMID wrote an impassioned article called "Charles Doughty and the Need for Heroic Poetry." The American writer Frederick Manfred was an advocate, but no one's advocacy was stronger than that of Laura Riding Jackson and her husband Schuyler Jackson, who considered D. a forerunner of literary MODERNISM.

BIBLIOGRAPHY: Corwin, J., "C. M. D.," in Thesing, W. B., ed., *Victorian Prose Writers after 1867, DLB*
57 (1987): 71–78; Fairley, B., *C. M. D.* (1927); Tabachnick. S. E., *C. D.* (1981)

WILLIAM HARMON

DOUGLAS, Gavin [or Gawin]

b. ca. 1474, Tantallon Castle, East Lothian; d. September 1522, London

The first translator of Virgil's *Aeneid* into Scots-English (*Eneados*, 1513), author of the protohumanist poem *The Palice of Honour* (wr. 1501), and possibly a short poem entitled "Conscience," on church corruption (wr. ca. 1514), D. is one of the important writers bridging the late Middle Ages and the Renaissance in the British Isles.

Third son of Archibald, fifth Earl of Angus, D. was reared for a career in the church, and educated at St. Andrews; he may also have studied in Paris. Between 1501 and 1514, he was in Edinburgh, either as dean or provost of the Church of St. Giles. But D. was born into turbulent times. Following the death at Flodden of James IV of Scotland (1513), D.'s nephew the sixth Earl of Angus married the widowed queen, Margaret Tudor. Through her influence, D. was named Bishop of Dunkeld in 1515—an appointment much objected to by his enemies who, to prevent his consecration, engineered his imprisonment for more than a year on the obscure charge of "receiving bulls from the pope." D. received installation at Dunkeld late in 1516, serving until 1521, when his nephew the sixth Earl of Angus fell from power. Again beset by enemies, D. sought help from HENRY VIII, but caught the plague in London, where he died in 1522.

D.'s reputation rests on his two major poems, *The Palice of Honour* and the *Eneados*. Both reflect his ambition as a courtier and man of letters of the new mode, who for preferment put to the service of his pen a wide-ranging erudition encompassing English, Scots, and Continental vernacular literatures, as well as the classics and contemporary Italian humanists. *The Palice* reflects its earlier date, in that it is a courtly allegory, polished and freshened by D.'s new learning, but nonetheless backward-looking in conception to established medieval style. Its conceit is the life of a man, who seeks to earn "honor" through chaste and faithful love. Noteworthy are its "aureate" vocabulary, and the role accorded to poetry in this quest, to a degree and in a manner subsequently given fuller voice by Elizabethan writers.

It is however for the *Eneados* that D. is most remembered, and rightly. A truly ambitious project, the translation in heroic couplets of the greatest Latin poet for the first time into English—a language not yet accepted as suitable for the sublime verses of Virgil—marks D. as a writer of courage as well as capacity. Nor is the *Eneados* a "mere" translation: D. clearly viewed himself as a conduit for medieval and

Renaissance Latin commentary and poetics, the full range of which he attempted to lay before his Scottish, and English, readership. To this end, D. added significant prologues of his own making to each book of the *Aeneid* and, following the example of contemporary Virgilian manuscripts and black-letter editions, attached as well prose commentaries and verse summaries throughout. The prologues offer a variety of verse forms, from heroic couplets to alliterative stanzas to rime royal and others; and these, along with the many expansions D. adds to Virgil, drawing on his own enthusiasms for battles, hunting, ships and the outdoors to "rise" to Virgil's standard, show D. at his best. The commentaries are also important, in that there D. invokes his humanist scholarship to soften Virgil's paganism with Christian and scientific explanation. The translation itself is accurate and skilled, making up in vigor (especially in descriptions of action, and emotional scenes) what it lacks of Virgil's genius at nuance.

The Palice of Honour exists in three 16th-c. printed editions, but no manuscript survives; the *Eneados*, in manuscript only, but in a number of copies, the best being MS Trinity College, Cambridge 1184.

BIBLIOGRAPHY: Bawcutt, P. J., *G. D.* (1976); Blyth, C. R., *"The Knychtlyke Stile": A Study of G. D.'s Aeneid* (1987); Coldwell, D. F. C., ed., *Virgil's "Aeneid" Translated into Scottish Verse by G. D., Bishop of Dunkeld* (4 vols., 1957–64)

R. F. YEAGER

DOUGLAS, Keith [Castellain]

b. 24 January 1920, Tunbridge Wells, Kent; d. 9 June 1944, near St. Pierre, Normandy, France

D. is generally regarded as the finest British poet of the Second World War. He developed from his First World War predecessors, a poetry that is antiheroic and in the voice of the active combatant. His prose account of his experience as a tank commander in the desert, *Alamein to Zem Zem* (1947; rev. eds., 1966, 1979), published with his own expressive ink and color illustrations, is established as the true successor to the classic narratives of the British soldier poets of 1914–18. D. has also been repeatedly championed by the generation of poets following his own, as one of the century's major poets, despite his short career. To Charles TOMLINSON, Ted HUGHES, Geoffrey HILL, and many others, D.'s work showed the direction British poetry should have taken from the fifties on. Locally recognized from the first, through vagaries of publication it was only in the 1960s that D. gained widespread recognition.

At boarding school from the age of six, through difficult family circumstances and divorce, D. wrote, drew, painted, rode, swam, and filled his life with activity to combat loneliness and dark moods. His father had won the Military Cross in the First War and remained for D. very much an emblem of the military. His mother's background was French and D. was able to read, speak, and translate poetry from that language by the time he left school, as well as competently translating from German, Latin, and Greek. Christ's Hospital was a boarding school that valued intellect as well as toughness and boasted a proud literary past: Samuel Taylor COLERIDGE, Charles LAMB, and Edmund BLUNDEN were former pupils. Nearly expelled at one point, D. left school in 1938 with a scholarship to read English at Oxford despite sitting the entrance exams in history.

D. had already published in the prestigious *New Verse* while at school, a poem "Dejection" that he had written as a conscious imitation of W. H. AUDEN in the certainty that it would please the editor. Such an act was typical of both the skepticism and humour with which he faced any authority and the distinctly low opinion he had of any literary world. Nonetheless, in his teens he was widely read in his fashionable contemporaries, looking down on them as facile and taking from them whatever he wanted. "On Leaving School," written at eighteen, combines the sophisticated and the poignant with perfect timing; "Villanelle of Gorizia" shows an enviable mastery of form at seventeen; and "Famous Men," at fifteen, already has the detached ironic voice he was later to use to such effect.

During two years at Merton College, with Blunden for tutor, D. developed a more elaborate, lyrical style, giving voice to the moods of his generation faced with oncoming war and active service. The intensification of the love under these pressures is shown through many fine love poems, most notably in "Canoe," his valedictory poem to the girlfriend of his first year Yingcheng and to Oxford. Editor of the *Cherwell*, coeditor of an antimilitaristic literary miscellany, *Augury*, D. acted as something of a spokesman for his university generation, betrayed into war by their elders. His work was to be included in *Eight Oxford Poets* in 1942 and a three poet *Selected Poets* set up by J. C. Hall in 1943. In army training, D. developed a more metaphysical style with such poems as "The Prisoner" (addressed to Yingcheng), "Time Eating," and "The Marvel." Once in the Middle East he added sharply focused poems of place and displacement such as "Syria," "Egypt," and "Jerusalem."

It is the poems written shortly after his direct experience of battle in the desert on which his reputation now most firmly rests. "How to Kill" and "Vergissmeinnicht" look steadily at the battlefield from the view of the soldier as killer; several poems meditate on the transformed postures and appearances of the dead: "Dead Men," "Landscape with Figures," and "Cairo Jag"; and in "Desert Flowers," D. directly invokes the spirit of his poetic ancestors, addressing Isaac ROSENBERG. D.'s now famous letter of August 10, 1943 defines his new battlefield poetry, made up of reportage, lacking in hope but not hopeless, close to the spoken voice, unsentimental and anti-lyrical. As he himself recognized, he was where other European poets, rather than his English contemporaries, had reached.

Before taking part in the Normandy Landings of 1944, D. completed his narrative of the desert campaign—swift, vivid, and memorably outspoken, it was first published posthumously in 1947. Three days after landing he was killed. Obituaries appeared in *Personal Landscape*, the magazine from exiles in Egypt, and in *Poetry London*, whose editor, Meary James Tambimuttu, had discovered D. and contracted to publish a collection. It finally appeared in 1951; *Keith Douglas: A Prose Miscellany* followed in 1984 and *Keith Douglas: The Letters* in 2000.

BIBLIOGRAPHY: Hughes, T., "The Poetry of K. D.," *CritQ* 5 (Spring 1963): 43–48; Graham, D. K., *D. 1920–1944: A Biography* (1974); Scammel, W. S., *D.* (1988)

DESMOND GRAHAM

DOUGLAS, [George] Norman
b. 8 December 1868, Thuringen, Austria; d. 9 February 1952, Capri, Italy

Novelist, travel writer, and memoirist, D. achieved modest success with the popular novel *South Wind* (1917) but is best remembered for the erudite and entertaining quality of his picturesque travelogues. After a short-lived career in the Foreign Office and a brief marriage that ended in divorce, D. left England for Europe where he traveled extensively and turned to writing as a means to support his extravagant and—at times—perverse lifestyle. In 1916, he published his first travel book, *Siren Land*, followed in the next year by *Fountains in the Sand: Rambles among the Oases of Tunisia*. Later travelogues collect his experiences in Italy, *Old Calabria* (1915) and *Alone* (1921), in his native Vorarlberg, *Together* (1923), and Greece, *One Day* (1929). In 1930, he published his authoritative *Capri: Materials for a Description of the Island*. Based in London during the Second World War, D. became increasingly bitter toward the end of his life and after returning to the Continent spent his final years in Capri.

DOWDEN, Edward
b. 13 May 1843, Cork, Ireland; d. 3 April 1913, Dublin, Ireland

Scholar, critic, and poet, D. was educated in Queen's College, Cork, and at Trinity College, Dublin, where he won the Wray Prize in metaphysical studies, the vice chancellor's prize in English, and graduated with a first-class moderatorship in logic and ethics. He was appointed to the newly founded chair of English literature in 1867, four years after he graduated, and held the post until his death.

He is chiefly remembered as a great Shakespearean scholar and his first book, *Shakespeare: A Critical Study of His Mind and Art* (1875), is still, perhaps, his most important work. Thereafter, he was linked with A. C. SWINBURNE and A. C. Bradley as one of the three major Shakespearean scholars of the Victorian era. His book was an immediate success and quickly went through sixteen English editions. He was the first to attempt to establish William SHAKESPEARE's personality from a study of his plays and poems and presents a Shakespeare, a man of the people and for the people, accommodating powerful passions to the demands of practicality. His approach to Shakespeare was powerfully influential on subsequent critics from Bernard SHAW to George Wilson Knight. He followed up this work by publishing in 1877 his primer, *Shakespeare*, which was aimed at a general, nonacademic audience and that achieved wide popularity though its oversimplified treatment of Shakespeare's career tended to detract from his critical standing.

D.'s most ambitious work was his two-volume biography of Percy Bysshe SHELLEY, published in 1886. Though he showed remarkably little sympathy for his subject and was compelled in his research to juggle the opposing interests of Shelley's two families by his wives Harriet Westbrook and Mary Godwin [SHELLEY], D.'s Shelley is, in the words of a recent critic, a work of "impressive scholarship, dignity and magnitude." Moreover, it dominated Shelley studies for half a century until superseded by Newman Ivey White's *Shelley* (1947). D.'s work on the impact of the French Revolution on English literature (based on lectures he gave at Princeton in 1896) and his short biographies of Robert SOUTHEY, Robert BROWNING, Edmund SPENSER, and Montaigne though dated somewhat in their scholarship still repay readers' efforts. *The French Revolution and English Literature*, published in 1897, a forceful beginning to the serious study of the relationship between France and the pre-Romantics, is lively in its characterizations and rich in biographical detail. His criticism of Browning is impressively sensible and his remarks on the relation of his poetry to the English novel are especially pertinent.

D.'s scholarly and critical work commands respect and attention and is remarkable for both its range and critical depth. His output in these areas was enormous. His editions of Edward John TRELAWNY's *Recollections of the Last Days of Shelley and Byron* and Thomas Jefferson Hogg's *Life of Percy Bysshe Shelley*, both published in 1906, were both standard until recently. He collected in five volumes his essays and lectures on transcendentalism, the relationship between science and literature, and numerous literary figures. In addition, he published book-length studies of Montaigne, Southey, and Spenser. His editions of writers' works are really too numerous to list; W. J. Craig's edition of Shakespeare's *Works*, containing D.'s introductory studies of the plays, was republished by Oxford University Press as recently as 1962.

D. showed early promise as a poet of some distinction. He published a volume of his poetry, entitled *Poems*, in 1876 and a second edition was called for within the year. Another volume of his poetry, entitled *A Woman's Reliquary*, was published posthumously in 1913 (both volumes of his poetry were republished as edited by his widow in 1914). Nonetheless, D.'s early promise as a poet failed to develop and mature. He never really found his own voice in poetry that continues to echo other poets. Whatever passions and events motivated his desire to compose, his feelings were always so tightly reined in that what in other, more successful, poets might have been considered as control or classical equilibrium between emotion and expression emerged in D.'s poetry as placidity. However, in his case as in others, there can be little doubt that the corruption of the poet was the generation of the critic. He worked hard to bring stature and respectability to the discipline of English literature that previously had been given to classics, divinity, and mathematics. He applied himself to it with the same spirit and some of the same tools of more traditional studies, including careful editing and the scrupulous handling of materials. His work is characterized by immense industry and a graceful writing style. He was never quite comfortable with traditional religious forms. He was from early life a transcendentalist: ethical concerns were important to him, as was manifest in his earliest choices of writers to study and as a transcendentalist he sought in his examination of literature to discover some single principle dominating the temperament of the writers—an aim inspired, possibly, by Ralph Waldo Emerson's *Representative Men* (1850) and Thomas CARLYLE's *Heroes and Hero-Worship*. Though much of D.'s work is dated and some simply no longer fashionable, at least ten of his books have been reprinted in the last twenty years, while *Shakespeare: His Mind and Art* has influenced Shakespearean studies longer than the work of anybody except Bradley.

BIBLIOGRAPHY: Dowden, E. D., and H. M. Dowden, eds., *Letters of E. D. and His Correspondents* (1914); Ludwigson, K. R., *E. D.* (1973)

A. R. JONES

DOWSON, Ernest [Christopher]
b. 2 August 1867, Lee, Kent (now in Lewisham); d. 23 February 1900, Catford

D.'s literary reputation rests almost entirely on one volume of poems called *Verses* (1896), which secured his place as a poet and called attention to his personal life. A creature of the night from London's gaslit era, D. was a small, tubercular, chain-smoking, and alcoholic womanizer whose self-destructive ways were so pronounced that they remained legendary a full century after he died breathless, broke, and toothless in a London suburb. He is permanently associated with that group of artists descended intellectually from Walter PATER, whose love of "art for art's sake" culminated in the 1890s in the Decadence period—also known as the Yellow Nineties and the Mauve Decade.

Reared partly in France and in Italy, to which his family traveled in search of relief for his father's consumption, D. learned largely on his own and began writing poetry well before he enrolled at Queen's College, Oxford, in 1886. There he studied the classics, practiced his verse forms, and published his first poem, "Sonnet—To a Little Girl." The sonnet introduced themes that D. would focus on for the remainder of his brief life: a love of beauty and innocence (often in young girls), the sad inevitability of maturity and disillusionment, and a fascination with death. It also reflected his lifelong habit of expressing himself in challenging verse forms.

Following his departure from Oxford without a degree in 1888, D. worked at his father's unprosperous London dock, wrote and published poems and short stories, drafted a novel, and wrote reviews for the *Critic*. He was also active in the Rhymers' Club with W. B. YEATS and Lionel JOHNSON, among others, and a member of a drinking society calling itself "The Bingers," in whose company he completed his addiction to absinthe.

In 1891, D. published in *The Century Guild Hobby Horse* his most enduring poem, "Non Sum Qualis Eram Bonae Sub Regno Cynarae"—known to the world simply as "Cynara." Its Alexandrine lines tell of a man waking up next to a prostitute with whom he has spent the night, only to be tortured by memory of the unattainable woman he really loves: "I have forgot much, Cynara! gone with the wind,/Flung roses, roses riotously with the throng,/Dancing, to put thy pale, lost lilies out of mind;/But I was desolate and sick of an old passion,/Yea, all the time, because the dance was long:/I have been faithful to thee, Cynara! in my fashion."

Written at a tavern table with the help of absinthe, the poem became D.'s masterpiece, and in only two dozen lines captured the essence of an era. Fascinated by the beautiful (but attracted to the lurid), the decadents' midnight world of illicit vices and conflicting emotions nowhere found superior expression. Like fellow decadents Oscar WILDE, Aubrey Beardsley, and others, D. knew that his lifestyle would catch up with him but did nothing to change it, thus living the life he chose and recording it in his art, to which he was "faithful"—in his fashion.

In the early 1890s, D. began a several years' emotional entanglement with a girl who was only eleven at the start of their relation. As time went by, she showed a declining interest in him, his parents committed suicide within a few months of each other, and D., depressed, wandered off to Europe, carousing and writing. During these years, he earned a poor living by translating and by publishing poems and stories, some of which he collected in *Decorations in Verse and Prose* (1899). The volume did little to help either his literary reputation or his finances, a failure shared by his verse play, *The Pierrot of the Minute* (1897).

D. died at age thirty-two, along with the decade he had helped define, his untidy life neatly encapsulated in one of his own lines: "They are not long," he had observed in *Verses*, "the days of wine and roses."

BIBLIOGRAPHY: Adams, J., *Madder Music, Stronger Wine: The Life of E. D., Poet and Decadent* (2000); Swann, T. B., *E. D.* (1964)

HERBERT K. RUSSELL

DOYLE, [Sir] Arthur Conan

b. 22 May 1859, Edinburgh, Scotland; d. 7 July 1930, Crowborough

A genuine polymath, D. published at least seventy books in a prolific writing career. Although best known as the creator of the world's most famous fictional detective, Sherlock Holmes, D. also wrote a number of historical romances and essays on spiritualism. Throughout his life, D. managed to reconcile his fictional emphasis on rational deduction with his increasingly public and private interest in the spiritual world. Born into the confident Victorian era, D. was raised as part of a Roman Catholic family and attended Jesuit schools in England. As a young man, he was an ardent athlete and somewhat surprisingly, given his average academic record, chose to study medicine at the University of Edinburgh beginning in 1877. Before he had even finished his degree, D. signed on as a ship's surgeon on an Arctic whaler, and he accepted a similar post on a ship bound for Africa shortly after finishing his degree. These early sea voyages give some indication of D.'s penchant for the exotic that recurs with some frequency in his fiction, notably in *The Sign of Four* (1890) and *The Lost World* (1912).

During his medical studies, D. met and was fascinated by Joseph Bell, surgeon at the Edinburgh Infirmary, who stressed observation and rational deduction in his instruction of his medical students. Bell inspired D. to create a detective of superior observational powers, obsessively dedicated to scientific and forensic inquiry. Written while D. was a general doctor in practice at Portsmouth in 1886, *A Study in Scarlet* was his novelistic introduction to this detective,

Sherlock Holmes, and his friend and narrator, Dr. Watson. After being turned down by several publishers, the novel appeared in *Beeton's Christmas Annual* in December 1887 and was eventually published in book form in 1888. Although D. soon wrote two historical novels, *Micah Clarke* (1889) and *The White Company* (3 vols., 1891), the publication of his second Holmes novel, *The Sign of Four*, brought him a wide public following. In 1891 *The Strand Magazine* published "A Scandal in Bohemia," featuring Holmes and Watson, and over the next thirty-five years, D. would serially publish in that magazine over fifty stories and two novels concerning the adventures of his two most famous characters. Early in 1891, D. gave up his medical career and became a full-time writer.

The popularity of D.'s Holmes and Watson stories were greatly enhanced by the deft illustrations of Sidney Paget. Additionally, the reading public was attracted to the contrast of Watson's warmth, ordinariness, and professional knowledge with Holmes's aloofness, exoticism, and arcane knowledge. Watson as trusted narrator provided a safe entry for D.'s Victorian readers to a strange fictional world populated with twisted criminals on the margins of society.

D. borrowed heavily from the two great earlier masters of the detective genre, Edgar Allan Poe and Emile Gaboriau, in writing his detective fiction. The character of Holmes is indebted to Poe's amateur detective, Auguste Dupin, and Gaboriau's police detective, Lecoq. T. J. Binyon has brilliantly pointed out that Holmes, as a "consulting detective," constitutes a third type of detective, halfway between the amateur detective epitomized by Dupin and the professional detective exemplified by Lecoq: the "professional amateur." Additionally, Holmes's eccentricities and amazing ratiocinative abilities are directly adapted from Poe's Dupin, while the narrative structure of three of the four Holmes novels (the exception is *The Hound of the Baskervilles*, 1902) is undoubtedly borrowed from Gaboriau's predilection for narrating the discovery of the crime and the detective's activities in the first half of his novels, then describing the events leading up to the crimes in the second portion. D.'s short stories of Holmes and Watson were collected in *The Adventures of Sherlock Holmes* (1892), *The Memoirs of Sherlock Holmes* (1894), *The Return of Sherlock Holmes* (1905), *His Last Bow* (1917), and *The Case-Book of Sherlock Holmes* (1927).

Eventually tiring of his detective stories, D. famously killed off Holmes in "The Final Problem," (1893) but finally wrote a Holmes adventure set in the early 1880s, *The Hound of the Baskervilles*, published serially in the *Strand* in 1901–2, after a furious public cried for his return. In 1903, D. resurrected Holmes in "The Empty House," which inaugurated the last three series of Holmes stories. A final Holmes novel, *The Valley of Fear*, appeared in 1915.

D., ever the patriot, volunteered as a forty-year-old for service as a medical officer in the Boer War, and wrote a massive history and analysis of the conflict, *The Great Boer War* (1900), and a shorter book defending it, *The War in South Africa, Its Cause and Conduct* (1902). For these efforts, he was knighted by King Edward VII in 1902. Always interested in the occult, after the death of his son from wounds suffered in World War I, D. sought solace in spiritualism, vigorously dedicating himself to promoting it in print and through lecture tours in England and the U.S.

BIBLIOGRAPHY: Booth, M., *The Doctor, the Detective and A. C. D.* (1997); Lellenberg, J. L., *The Quest for Sir A. C. D.* (1987); Nordon, P., *Conan Doyle* (1966); Orel, H., ed., *Critical Essays on Sir A. C. D.* (1992)

RICHARD RANKIN RUSSELL

DOYLE, Roddy
b. 8 May 1958, Dublin, Ireland

D. is a popular and critically acclaimed Irish novelist, who has also written a number of screenplays and books for children. D.'s early work made an immediate impact through its animated dialogue and appealing optimism, and through its original combination of comedy with a profound exploration of the human heart. After winning the Booker Prize with his fourth novel, D. changed direction, moving toward a darker fiction, a fiction less assured of human goodness but that nevertheless displays a moving faith in the characters that people its pages. It is a testament to his versatility and storytelling powers that his latest and most ambitious novel, an intimate evocation of one of the darkest periods of Irish history, has been as warmly received as his more accessible early work.

Originally a teacher at his old school, D. took the students there as the inspiration for his self-published first novel, *The Commitments* (1987). Made into a successful film by Alan Parker in 1991, this charming and truthful comedy of the everyday possesses an imaginative command of language that is rare in a fictional debut. It was followed by *The Snapper* (1990), the story of an out-of-wedlock pregnancy, and *The Van* (1991), set in a Dublin suburb during the 1990 World Cup and shortlisted for the Booker Prize. All three novels, which were subsequently published together as *The Barrytown Trilogy* (1992), share an intuitive understanding of family life, with its triumphs and humiliations; a perfect ear for dialogue; and a HUMOR that has led critics to compare D. to Flann O'BRIEN. *The Van*'s honest investigation of the male psyche through the character of Jimmy Rabbitte, who struggles to maintain his dignity while coping with the degradation of unemployment, is particularly impressive.

Paddy Clarke Ha Ha Ha (1993) flouted the anti-populist snobbery that so often surrounds the Booker Prize by selling more copies than any previous winner. Set in 1968, when its eponymous hero is just ten, it pays homage to James JOYCE's *Portrait of the Artist as a Young Man* and brilliantly evokes the speech, peculiar logic, and wonder of childhood. D.'s work has darkened over the years and, although *Paddy Clarke* still possesses the characteristic D. humor, there is a deep sadness in Paddy's story, as he witnesses his parents' marriage breakdown, which contrasts sharply with the poignant optimism and comic survivalism of *The Barrytown Trilogy*.

Even bleaker is *The Woman Who Walked into Doors* (1996), in which D. uses a first-person narrator for the first time—an alcoholic, abused woman called Paula whom he had first created for a television drama, *Family*. D.'s ability to write himself under the skin of a woman is quite remarkable: Paula's narrative is both shocking and moving, an inspired monologue in which the author becomes invisible and which haunts the reader by its refusal to overdramatize or understate the damaged consciousness that has resulted from the "jumble of violence" that constituted her marriage.

With his next book, D. entered completely new territory, moving from the domestic to the EPIC in a retelling of recent history. *A Star Called Henry* (1999) is the first novel in *The Last Roundup*, a planned trilogy about Ireland's bloody 20th c. It views the Irish Revolution of 1916–21 from the viewpoint of Henry Smart, a teenager of the Dublin slums who becomes a docker, joins the socialist Citizens' army and the Fenian movement, fights in the 1916 Rising at the age of fourteen, trains freedom fighters and becomes a Republican legend, one of Michael Collins's boys. The book, which is well grounded in historical sources, combines a driving narrative with unforced dialogue, and is both a subversive exploration of Irish Republicanism and a passionate love story; a sense of destiny runs through Henry's story, represented, as in Joyce's *Finnegans Wake*, by the water that runs through Dublin.

In addition to his novels, D. has written two plays: *Brownbread* (perf. 1987; pub. 1992), in which a bishop is kidnapped; and *War* (1989), which revolves around a pub quiz; and an original film script, *When Brendan Met Trudy* (2001), the warmth and humor of which pay unashamed homage to the traditions of romantic comedy.

BIBLIOGRAPHY: Abel, M., "R. D.," in Moseley, M., ed., *British Novelists since 1960, DLB* 194 (1998): 107–12; White, C., *Reading R. D.* (2001)

NICOLA UPSON

DRABBLE, Margaret
b. 5 June 1939, Sheffield

D. was born into an upwardly mobile middle-class family; her father became a judge, her mother took a degree in English at Cambridge. The couple had four children, of whom D. is the second. The first born, now A. S. BYATT, is, like D., a celebrated novelist.

After studies at a Quaker boarding school, D. went to Newnham College, Cambridge, as her mother and elder sister had done before her. D. also chose the same subject, English. This college is well known as a nursery for writers and other distinguished women; apart from D. and Byatt, the alumnae include Jane Harrison, an influential scholar in the field of early Greek religion. Published writers of fiction include Hilary Bailey, Elaine FEINSTEIN, Valerie Grosvenor Myer, Audrey LASKI, Sue Limb, Jessica Mann, Salley Vickers, and playwright Michelene Wandor. Iris MURDOCH and Sylvia Plath did graduate work at Newnham. D.'s undergraduate career was brilliant: she got a Double First with distinction, the best result possible.

During a spell as an actress, D. wrote her first and rather immature novel, *A Summer Bird-Cage* (1963), which is partly based on her experiences as a recent Cambridge graduate, but also provides glimpses from the world of acting. This book was followed by the more carefully crafted *The Garrick Year* (1964), drawing on a frustrating year that D. spent as a housewife and mother of young children at Stratford-upon-Avon, where her first husband, the actor Clive Swift, worked with the Royal Shakespeare Company.

By and large, D.'s first five novels use much autobiographical material, and their heroines mostly seem to represent aspects of herself at various periods. However, Louise in *A Summer Bird-Cage* is clearly a not very flattering portrait of Byatt, and, according to D., *Jerusalem the Golden* (1967) dramatizes her mother's struggle against her oppressive, puritanical background. In spite of this, it is easy to discern in Clara, the protagonist, some of D.'s own, similar conflicts.

Almost all her major characters could be regarded as modern puritans in some sense. While the religious superstructure of puritanism has normally, if not always, been dismantled, in her novels as in society, the anxious scrutiny of one's daily life remains, as does the sense of responsibility to one's conscience. This may involve acute feelings of guilt and a tendency to expect some kind of retribution. Critics have often stressed the psychologically and sociologically interesting material in D. Her own concerns are basically moral and metaphysical, however. She has stated that her novels are about "salvation"—although obviously in a nontraditional sense.

These early books have sometimes been conveniently lumped together, and said to be chiefly about young women in Britain, an oversimplification. Another tag for the majority of her first nine novels, including *The Waterfall* (1969), *The Needle's Eye* (1972), *The Realms of Gold* (1975), and *The Middle Ground* (1980), has been that they present "graduate wives" as something of a literary novelty. Only two of the heroines of these books are both graduates and wives, however, and of these women, one leaves her husband, while the other has been left by hers.

One of D.'s major themes is that of privilege and its opposite, the lack of privilege. This theme exemplifies her emphasis on morality, as the distribution of privileges is always regarded as unfair. A privilege implies, by definition, that its own negation exists elsewhere. And the status of any privilege is ambiguous: it is non-morally good, but morally bad. D.'s treatment of her privilege theme has successively widened. In early works, obvious advantages tend to be highlighted, such as money, a university education, and good looks. Later, the concept of privilege grows more inclusive and sophisticated, occasionally slightly absurd. A happy love life (*The Waterfall*), to live in a state of grace (*The Needle's Eye*), biological existence, as distinct from physical death (*The Realms of Gold*), and being born to the English language (*The Middle Ground*) are all seen as privileges, and therefore enviable.

Also the "bearers of privilege" is a category that has gradually expanded, from pretty, Oxford educated girls in *A Summer Bird-Cage* to the human species, compared to other animals, in *The Witch of Exmoor* (1996). As in much other British fiction, class distinctions may assume paramount importance in D. A global approach to the problem of privilege is first glimpsed in *The Millstone* (1965), where the heroine's parents, for a mixture of moral and political reasons, go off to work, first in some unspecified African country, then in India. Characteristically, D.'s international focus was to widen, so that in *The Realms of Gold* she sets a fictitious African state called Adra against Britain and, by implication, the whole Western civilization (privileged) against the developing world (non-privileged). In *The Garrick Year*, D. presents man as the privileged sex, but her FEMINISM is normally less explicit. She has stated that it is only "part of a whole." There are other exceptions from this rule, though, notably in *The Realms of Gold* and *The Peppered Moth* (2000). The latter tells the story of Marie Bloor, D.'s mother, and her frustrations as a highly educated woman in prewar Britain.

D. has often presented privileges, in many senses, as static. For this reason, her privilege theme is intertwined with a profound concern with fate and fatalism, chance and determinism. In her novels, it is possible to gain or lose advantages, however. There are many ambitious social climbers in them, but also characters who, like Rose, the protagonist of *The Nee-*

dle's Eye, choose to sink in society. To become privileged at the expense of others is always morally wrong in D. Flagrant instances, like the career of the ruthless property developer Anthony in *The Ice Age* (1977), usually get authorially punished in the end. Conversely, freely to refrain from privileged status may be rewarded.

D. is, basically and deliberately, a traditionally realistic novelist whose moral earnestness may recall that of many Victorian writers. Her awareness of being part of literary history is especially obvious in her first few novels, which frequently allude to works by other authors. George ELIOT, Gustave Flaubert, and William Makepeace THACKERAY are three examples. Several of D.'s characters in these books have surnames apparently borrowed from certain well-known writers: Arnold BENNETT, Sir John DENHAM, Oliver GOLDSMITH, Thomas GRAY, D. H. LAWRENCE, and W. Somerset MAUGHAM.

These multiple frames of reference make D.'s *A Writer's Britain* (1979), a work of nonfiction, solid and satisfying. She has also written a critical study of William WORDSWORTH, and biographies of Bennett and Angus WILSON. And she has edited a collection of essays on Thomas HARDY, as well as juvenile and unfinished texts by Jane AUSTEN. D.'s supreme achievement as an editor, however, is *The Oxford Companion to English Literature* (1985; rev. ed., 2000).

D.'s realism and her commitment to social and ethical issues have given her a reputation as chronicler of developments in contemporary Britain. The structure and narrative method of her fiction are mostly traditional, but they admit of some variations. D. moves closest to an experimental mode of writing in *The Waterfall*, where in every second section, she refers to her heroine in the third person, but otherwise in the first. The effect is that of a dialectic movement between "objective" and "subjective" narrative, the protagonist's self as discovered and as created. In *The Radiant Way* (1987) and *A Natural Curiosity* (1989), there are attempts at a cinematic technique, with rapidly changing brief scenes.

While D.'s imagery in her first novels may feel poorly integrated with their plots, she has in many works offered beautifully created images, sometimes as leitmotifs. Many are of traditional kinds: light, darkness, water, vegetation. *Jerusalem the Golden* abounds with light, glitter, and gold; *The Waterfall* is full of liquids, such as water, ink, blood, and milk. More startling is the use of bones and teeth, but also of the four elements, in *The Realms of Gold*; dust, garbage, sewers, insects, and infectious diseases in *The Middle Ground*; and severed heads in *A Natural Curiosity*.

During the years when D. edited *The Oxford Companion to English Literature*, no novel of hers was published. After this seven-year silence as a creative writer, she came back with *The Radiant Way*. Some critics feel that she has lost energy and enthusiasm since *The Middle Ground*, despite interesting details from FOLKLORE, painting, and other fields, in her later books. These also tend to have a broader canvas in sociological and geographic terms. D. received an honorary doctorate from Sheffield University in 1976, as well as a CBE (Commander of the British Empire) in 1980.

BIBLIOGRAPHY: Creighton, J. V., *M. D.* (1985); Grosvenor Myer, V., *Puritanism and Permissiveness* (1974); Grosvenor Myer, V., *M. D.* (1991); Roxman, S., *Guilt and Glory* (1984); Stovel, N. F., *M. D.* (1989); Wojcik-Andrews, I., *M. D.'s Female Bildungsromane* (1995)

SUSANNA ROXMAN

DRAMA SINCE 1956

Britain's decline, and the end of its pretensions to superpower status, was confirmed by the Suez debacle of 1956. A country that had won a war but lost an empire was shown to be very much the junior partner of its wartime ally, the U.S., which stepped in to call time on Britain's gunboat diplomacy. Not coincidentally, 1956 is widely regarded as the year British drama changed, Jimmy Porter's trumpet blast in John OSBORNE's *Look Back in Anger* reverberating through the theater and beyond, signaling a widespread dissatisfaction with the continuation of prewar life, conditions, and expectations by the same means. A decade after the end of "the people's war" the promise of "homes fit for heroes" rang hollow, and in *The Entertainer* Osborne's portrayal of an exhausted and disillusioned comic personified not only the country's bankruptcy but the theater's. The year 1956 marks a turning point, the beginning of a shift away from comfortable, bourgeois, drawing room drama. But if Osborne is the first of a "new wave" of dramatists conscious of the need for theater to register the changing world, and Britain's place in it, and *Look Back in Anger* the first success of the most important postwar theater organization, the English Stage Company at the Royal Court under George Devine, in the longer term there were to be other, more significant influences. Looking back over half a century, two momentous events stand out: the London premiere of Samuel BECKETT's *Waiting for Godot* in 1955, and the visit of Bertolt Brecht's Berliner Ensemble the following year.

For almost a decade after the end of World War II, dramatists played it safe, as the resurgence of interest in the poetic drama of T. S. ELIOT and Christopher FRY suggests. By the end of the 1950s, however, a new generation of playwrights had emerged, frustrated by the theater's failure to address urgent social and political issues. Mostly, though not exclusively, working class and self-educated, Ann JELLICOE, John ARDEN, Arnold WESKER, N. F. SIMPSON, Harold PINTER, and Shelagh DELANEY adopted strategies designed to discomfort audiences. Using sparse, Brechtian staging (Arden), or broadly naturalistic scenery (Wesker), and ranging from absurdist situations (Simpson, Pinter) to dramatizations of localized social conflict (Jellicoe, Wesker, Delaney), their plays were a far cry from the drawing room fare of their predecessors. "Kitchen sink" drama, as it became known, brought the off-stage on—literally. Wesker's *The Kitchen* rather than taking the dining area of a restaurant as its focus—the classic bourgeois setting—explores work behind the scenes. Not only does the play pursue a socialist agenda in showing who does the work—and for whom—but it articulates, in quasi-Marxist fashion, how economics and politics determine social relations. While the writers who emerged in the late 1950s can hardly be said to belong to a coherent political or theatrical "school," they believed that drama can and should be relevant to the postwar world and its various alienated constituents.

At the forefront of this shift was the Royal Court, which actively encouraged its young writers, Osborne, Arden, and Edward BOND, and later Christopher HAMPTON, David STOREY, David HARE, Howard BARKER, and Howard BRENTON, followed by Caryl CHURCHILL and Timberlake WERTENBAKER. The Court provided support playwrights today can only dream of, but there were other theaters, such as the Belgrade in Coventry, as well as organizations that clearly had much in common with Brecht's Ensemble model, notably Joan Littlewood's Theatre Workshop, which had relocated from Manchester in 1953 to the Theatre Royal in Stratford East, London. Indeed, it is indicative of a broader cultural shift that just two weeks after *Look Back in Anger* opened the Theatre Workshop staged Brendan BEHAN's *The Quare Fellow*. In the space of a decade British theater was radically transformed through both London-based companies and provincial theaters. But if the history of British drama in the second half of the 20th c. "begins" with a radical realignment which signals a break with the past, this opposition is necessarily parallel to other traditions that in turn make these distinctions and departures possible.

Drama after 1956 is marked by breadth and diversity. If it is convenient to begin with *Look Back in Anger,* the influence of Brecht and Beckett established the political and theatrical coordinates for a generation of playwrights. While absurdist and Brechtian drama have since fallen from favor, postwar British playwrights are indebted to the possibilities they offered. Various absurdist and Brechtian techniques fitted a range of responses to the world situation,

depending on whether an "existentialist" or "materialist" approach was favored. Whereas writers on the left were drawn to Brecht, notably Arden, whose *Serjeant Musgrave's Dance* is perhaps the clearest example, others, such as Simpson, Pinter (to a degree), and Tom STOPPARD owe much to Beckett. This set the pattern for the next decade. Playwrights like Bond, whose early plays *The Pope's Wedding* and *Saved* share with Wesker's trilogy *Chicken Soup with Barley, Roots,* and *I'm Talking About Jerusalem* a broadly naturalistic aesthetic, adapted Brechtian strategies to suit their own purposes, as did the post-1968 generation of Brenton, Barker, and David EDGAR. It is not their adherence to Brechtian theory, however, but their shared investment in promoting political theater that distinguishes them from their contemporaries.

While the term "political theater" is invariably—and correctly—qualified by the rejoinder "all theater is political," clearly some of these playwrights were (and are) more political than others. Few would claim that Alan AYCKBOURN, whose *Absurd Person Singular, The Norman Conquests,* and *Bedroom Farce* are sharply observed middle-class comedies, is a political writer. Acclaimed by critics and audiences alike, Stoppard, whose first and phenomenally successful play *Rosencrantz and Guildenstern Are Dead* draws so heavily on *Waiting for Godot,* has explored both metatheatrical (*The Real Inspector Hound*) and intellectual (*Arcadia*) territory. *Arcadia,* which exploits the vogue for Chaos Theory, epitomizes the philosophical and playful nature of Stoppard's plays. Michael FRAYN's examination of the Nazis' atomic bomb program, *Copenhagen,* intentionally leaves many questions unanswered. These writers exemplify the shift away from political commitment to a more uncertain, postmodern position. Yasmina Reza's *Art* (1996), translated by Hampton, one of the most successful plays in the West End, taps into the apolitical intellectualism of this trend in its discussion of the meaning and value of art.

If it is the case that plays produced in Britain today are less politically driven than those of the Cold War period, one constant factor is their interest in history. In response to stage violence critics used the term "new Jacobeans," comparing contemporary theater with the "excesses" of the Jacobean stage. The label was apposite, for of the many pasts to which these writers have returned Jacobean theater features prominently. In addition to adaptations of Thomas MIDDLETON and John WEBSTER, Bond "rewrote" *Lear* and in *Bingo* portrayed a William SHAKESPEARE who commits suicide, unable to accept the contradictions of his society; similarly, Wesker's *The Merchant,* a reworking of *The Merchant of Venice,* and Barker's "collaboration" with Middleton on an updated *Women Beware Women* (1986), make explicit connections between the early modern and 20th-c. worlds. More importantly perhaps, they demand that literature is political, and *Bingo* in particular anticipates the ideological battles in Shakespeare studies in the 1980s and 1990s. British playwrights have also turned to the Greeks, Bond, Barker, Wertenbaker, Churchill, Tony HARRISON, and Steven BERKOFF representing classics for the contemporary audience—not in homage to a great canonical past but to emphasize their contemporary relevance.

The treatment of history varies in tone, ranging from Robert BOLT's *A Man For All Seasons* to Littlewood's *Oh, What a Lovely War!* (1963), both of which draw in different ways on Brecht, to Stoppard's *Travesties*, which irreverently sends up history and its players. The range of approaches may be illustrated by a comparison between Brenton's *The Romans in Britain*, which juxtaposes the Roman invasion with the British army in Northern Ireland, and Alan BENNETT's *A Question of Attribution* (perf. 1988; pub. 1989) and *The Madness of George III,* both of which seamlessly bridge the gap between middle-class sensibilities and (potentially) significant political questions. In common with Irish playwrights who take Anglo-Irish history as their subject, such as Brian FRIEL (*Translations*), Frank McGuinness (*Observe the Sons of Ulster Marching Towards the Somme*, 1985), and Sebastian Barry (*The Steward of Christendom*, 1995), Brenton offers an uncompromising, uncomfortable diagnosis; Bennett's plays are characterized chiefly by their playfulness, and a gentle, unthreatening HUMOR for which he is renowned. For left-wing or oppositional playwrights, however, what's past is prologue. In Churchill's treatment of attitudes to witchcraft in the 17th c., *Light Shining in Buckinghamshire* and *Vinegar Tom*, and her analysis of British imperialism in *Cloud Nine*, history is deployed not only to illustrate class divisions, but to explore past and present from a feminist perspective.

In two plays in particular Churchill captures the mood of Margaret Thatcher's Britain. *Top Girls* asks what price women's economic success, and concludes bleakly that in the dog-eat-dog 1980s there is no "trickle down" benefit for the poor: successful women literally have no time for sisterhood, and the price of independence is a high one. *Serious Money* depicts the get-rich-quick world of the stock market and attacks the money ethos that so dehumanizes, though the Jacobean satire it offers was compromised when it was found that it was a popular play among stockbrokers. Brenton and Hare's *Pravda* attacks the power of press barons, while Berkoff's *Sink the Belgrano!* (perf. 1986; pub. 1987) parodies Shakespeare's *Henry V* and attacks Britain's jingoistic enthusiasm for the war against Argentina over the Falklands in 1982. The 1980s saw a resurgence of politically committed drama, largely in response to Thatcher's divisive social policy, that threatened to

dismantle the postwar consensus on public health provision and access to education. It is precisely these issues which underpinned the Labour government's program when it came to power in 1945; ironically, in the 1980s radical theater was given a shot in the arm by the very forces it opposed.

Radical theater has not only been staged in mainstream, "establishment" theaters, but also promoted by companies such as Joint Stock (and later Out of Joint), John Godber's Hull Truck, Wesker's Centre 42, established in 1961, and John MCGRATH's 7:84 (Scotland and England), named after a report which revealed that 7 percent of the population owned 84 percent of the wealth. 7:84 was set up in the early 1970s in England and Scotland (funding in England being withdrawn for political reasons in 1984). Staging plays by McGrath, Arden, and Edgar, it was an attempt to break free of the bourgeois hold on theater by targeting working-class audiences. This raises key questions about political theater: whether it is best served by playing to middle-class audiences or to socialism's "natural" constituency, the working class. Theatre in Education (TIE), originating in the Belgrade Theatre, Coventry, offers another avenue, and writers such as Jellicoe, Bond, and Edgar have written specifically for community and children's groups. With the decline of the National Theatre, and the tourist-dominated West End commissioning money-spinning musicals, writers have deplored the state of British theater, comparing it unfavorably with the blossoming and nurturing of talent in the 1950s and 1960s. However, in the last few years there have been some grounds for optimism, and reports of drama's downfall may have been exaggerated.

A measure of the theater's cultural significance since 1956 is its relationship with the state, and one sign of health is a recent controversy that recalled the heady days of the 1960s, when plays were subject to censorship by the Lord Chamberlain. In 1965, the Lord Chamberlain demanded that *Saved* be cut; Bond refused, and the Royal Court was prosecuted. It was clear to most observers that these powers of censorship were inappropriate, and the practice was ended—though ironically the last play to be challenged was Bond's next, *Early Morning* (1968). However, the theater was still vulnerable to determined opponents, and in 1980 *The Romans in Britain* was subjected to legal proceedings on the grounds of sexual indecency. More recently, Sarah KANE's *Blasted* was attacked by critics and the tabloid press for its violence, which for many offered comparisons with *Saved*. If this demonstrated that despite "the new Jacobean" plays of the 1960s critics are still disturbed by scenes of violence and torture, it was also a reminder that theater can unsettle and discomfort an audience, shocking it out of its complacency—a complacency to which much post-1956 theater has contributed.

280

Osborne did not provide a political or theatrical lead: later plays, such as *Inadmissible Evidence* and *West of Suez,* are nostalgic laments for an England long gone. Of the group of playwrights who flourished under the aegis of the Royal Court, Arden has withdrawn from mainstream theater to write proto-Marxist plays for nonprofessional groups; Wesker has found it increasingly difficult to get his plays staged, though a recent revival of *The Kitchen* proved successful; Pinter became more politically conscious in the 1980s, and his plays are frequently revived in Britain and abroad; while Bond, immensely successful in France, Germany, Italy, and Spain, refuses to allow his plays to be performed in Britain. The playwrights who followed, in the 1970s, have produced work that has been broadly more acceptable to a theater environment far removed from the Royal Court of the 1960s. The success of Hare's trilogy on the church, the judiciary, and the Labour Party—*Racing Demon, Murmuring Judges,* and *The Absence of War*—may be taken as an indication of the extent to which British theater remains a forum for middle-class entertainment and—sometimes—debate. Barker's *Scenes from an Execution* brilliantly captures the predicament of the revolutionary artist whose work is appropriated by the state to serve its own purposes: it is a pessimistic vision, but one that aptly summarizes the current situation.

Today, with few exceptions, writers are acquiescing. There are few oppositional voices, and critics who look to emerging dramatists like Conor MCPHERSON, whose *The Weir* and *Dublin Carol* enjoyed considerable success, will be disappointed. The vibrant theater of the late 1950s and 1960s appears a long way off at present, but Kane's plays, and Mark RAVENHILL's plays like *Shopping and Fucking* offer hope for a theater in need of rejuvenation. In terms of the Beckett/Brecht dichotomy it is clear that the intellectual escapism of the former has prevailed over the political commitment of the latter—for now.

BIBLIOGRAPHY: Barnes, P., *A Companion to Postwar British Theatre* (1986); Bigsby, C. W. E., *Contemporary English Drama* (1981); Rebellato, D., *1956 and All That* (1999); Shank, T., *Contemporary British Theatre* (1994); Shellard, D., *British Theatre since the War* (1999); Taylor, J. R., *Anger and After: A Guide to the New British Drama* (1962; rev. ed. 1969)

MARK HUTCHINGS

DRAYTON, Michael

b. 1563, Hartshill, Warwickshire; d. December 1631, London

D. might reasonably be called the quintessentially Elizabethan poet. He displays the characteristically Elizabethan blend of conservatism and innovation. He wrote in most of the genres typical of his age, such as the pastoral and the love sonnet, historical poetry and religious verse, topographical poetry and verse drama, mythological narrative and satire. His earliest appearance in print was with *The Harmonie of the Church* (1591), unexciting versifications of biblical passages. Poetically speaking, the volume was something of a false start. In 1593, there appeared *Idea, the Shepheards Garland,* which displays the influence of one of D.'s enduring models, Edmund SPENSER. His conception of pastoral, however, is rather less grand than Spenser's; D. confines his subject matter to poetry and love (and a certain amount of diplomatic panegyric), where Spenser had engaged with great matters of politics and religion. D., who took the craft and vocation of poetry very seriously, produced a second, extensively revised, edition of his pastorals in 1606 (as part of *Poemes Lyrick and Pastorall*), the habit of revision characterizing most of his later career. He made his contribution to another popular genre with his publication, in 1594, of *Peirs Gaveston,* the first of a series of historical narratives that later included *Matilda* (1594), *The Tragicall Legend of Robert, Duke of Normandy* (1596, pub. with revised versions of its two predecessors), and *The Legend of Great Cromwel* (1607). All have moments of beauty and interest, though such moments are almost overwhelmed by longer stretches of clotted verse weighed down by the load of information it has to carry.

Most modern readers are likely to find the sonnets of *Ideas Mirrour* (1594) more immediately attractive. D.'s sonnets proved very popular (it was issued a further eleven times during the poet's lifetime); characteristically, he continued to revise the poems long after their first publication. New sonnets were added, old ones omitted, the order changed, minor (and sometimes quite major) changes made to the text of individual poems. The best of D.'s sonnets (e.g. "Since there's no help, come let us kiss and part," "How many paltry, foolish, painted things") are striking and individual; elsewhere, D. can seem all too responsive to the influence of authors such as Samuel DANIEL, Sir Philip SIDNEY, and William SHAKESPEARE.

In 1595, D. published *Endimion and Phoebe,* his exquisite contribution to the Elizabethan genre of mythological narrative that included such poems as Christopher MARLOWE's *Hero and Leander* and Shakespeare's *Venus and Adonis.* Shot through with Neoplatonism, the poem is also richly descriptive, not least in its presentation of the lavish landscape of Mount Latmus. There is a subtlety and delicate exactness to much of the writing in *Endimion and Phoebe* that isn't always to be encountered in D.'s historical poems. His handling of the heroic couplet is impressive. After its publication, D. seems largely to have concentrated on the composition of further historical poems. In 1596, appeared *Mortimeriados*, a narrative, in rhyme royal, of the wars between Edward II and the barons. This was, typically, rewritten and published as *The Barrons Wars* in 1603; now the poem was in an eight-line stanza (the reasons for the change being explained in an interesting preface). In 1597, he published what is perhaps the most interesting of his historical works, *Englands Heroicall Epistles*. With Ovid's *Heroides* providing his obvious model, D. offers the reader a series of pairs of imaginary letters supposedly exchanged between famous historical lovers—Henry II and Rosamond, Edward IV and Jane Shore, the Earl of SURREY and "Geraldine." In the reprintings and revisions (characteristically) that the work underwent, some twelve such couples were treated. At their best, these are assured pieces of psychology, and show an attractive lightness of touch in the delineation of circumstances There is, too, a sureness in the handling of couplets that anticipates later developments in English versification.

The accession of JAMES I seems to have prompted in D. a certain disillusionment and sense of exclusion. Such a mood is reflected in *The Owle* (1604) and *The Man in the Moone* (1606), two relatively uninteresting satires. Altogether more important were his *Odes*, published as part of *Poemes Lyrick and Pastorall*. In these, D. has some claims to be one of the English pioneers of a form later to become very important. D. himself shows an awareness of classical, French, and (interestingly) Welsh models, and the resulting poems, which are short-lined and strongly rhythmical, are interestingly various in subject. They include some of D.'s most successful lyrics, such as "The Heart," "To the Virginian Voyage," "To His Coy Love," and "To The Cambro-Britans, and their Harpe, his Ballad of Agincourt." The range of tones is considerable too, and these poems represent a new and distinctive achievement in the English lyric.

Between 1612 and 1622, D.'s massive *Poly-Olbion* was published. A topographical and historical account of the wonders of Britain, a patriotic and frequently nostalgic undertaking the composition of which must have occupied many years of D.'s life, but which met with little success on its publication. Its title page describes it as "A *Chorographicall* Description of *Tracts, Rivers, Mountaines, Forests*, and other Parts of this renowned *Isle of Great Britaine*, with intermixture of the most Remarquable *Stories, Antiquities, Wonders, Rarityes, Pleasures, and Commodities* of the same" and the work is every bit as various as this implies (though the poem discusses only England and Wales, not Scotland). As one might expect from his other works, D. is often at his best in dealing with Britain's history, and the work is underpinned by a vision, both historical and geographical, of genuine coherence. Unsurprisingly, there are some dull stretches in *Poly-Olbion*; but its rhymed twelve-syllable

lines are generally readable and sometimes memorable. D.'s attitudes and sensibilities are conservative, and essentially rural; in a time of increasing confusion and doubt, D. clearly believed that it was in the knowledge and understanding (in his antiquarian terms) of the past that some kind of security could be found. D.'s responsiveness to the myths of his nation's past is a source of real, if intermittent, creativity.

In 1627 (in *The Battaile of Agincourt*) and 1630 (*The Muses Elizium*), D. published his last two substantial collections. Among the poems included in *The Battaile of Agincourt* was "Nimphidia," a delightful mock-heroic poem on a fairy theme—the effect of which might be described as an intermingling of Geoffrey CHAUCER's "Sir Thopas" and Shakespeare's *A Midsummer Night's Dream*. It was perhaps the last English poem to find effective means of making poetry out of the fairy-lore that was rapidly being swept aside. Alongside "Nimphidia" were published two of D.'s finest pastorals, "The Quest of Cynthia" and "The Shepeards Sirena." D.'s renewed interest in the pastoral also found expression in "The Muses Elizium," which gave its title to the poet's final book. Throughout these belated pastorals, D.'s versification is often at its finest and most musical, his imagination at its liveliest.

D. was an enormously prolific poet. The standard modern edition of his work occupies some two thousand pages; there are many aspects of his work that it has been impossible to discuss, however briefly, in this short account. No one would want to read D. from cover to cover, certainly. But, just as certainly, no one who wants to understand and appreciate the Elizabethan achievement in poetry can afford to ignore the best of D.'s short poems or the most striking of his historical and narrative pieces. D. was little read or discussed for some 150 years after his death. Romantics such as Charles LAMB and Samuel Taylor COLERIDGE, however, recognized him as a real poet. He has never become widely popular and perhaps he never will; but for the last two centuries his centrality to the history of English poetry has generally been acknowledged.

BIBLIOGRAPHY: Berthelot, J. A., *M. D.* (1967); Hardin, R. F., *M. D. and the Passing of Elizabethan England* (1973); Newdigate, B. H., *M. D. and His Circle* (1941; rev. ed., 1961); Westling, L. H., *The Evolution of M. D.'s "Idea"* (1974)

GLYN PURSGLOVE

DRINKWATER, John

b. 1 June 1882, Leytonstone, Essex; d. 25 March 1937, Kilburn, London

D. was educated in London and then at the City of Oxford High School and aged fifteen joined the

Northern Assurance Company in Nottingham as the first in a series of jobs as well as pursuing his career on the stage. D. demonstrated skills as an actor, dramatist, critic, and manager. His long list of critical work includes studies of William MORRIS (1912), A. C. SWINBURNE (1913), Oliver Cromwell (1921), Robert BURNS (1925), Samuel PEPYS (1930), and William SHAKESPEARE (1933), essays, and histories. He tried his hand at an autobiography *Inheritance* (1931) and *Discovery* (1932), which remains unfinished. D. was also a prolific poet with an output covering the period 1903 to 1933. He was essentially a townie who loved the countryside and this quality comes across in many of his poems.

Early in the 20th c., there arose the provincial repertory movement and D. founded the amateur Birmingham company the Pilgrim Players (1907–13) with Barry Jackson that mainly focused on English poetic drama, and later became the Birmingham Repertory Theatre. Their first significant production in 1907 was the 16th-c. *Interlude of Youth*. Jackson's Birmingham New Street Theatre opened on February 15, 1913, when D. played Malvolio in Shakespeare's *Twelfth Night*. To celebrate the event D. had composed *Lines for the Opening of the Birmingham Repertory Theatre*, and the following extract gives a clue to how he viewed his trade: "We stand with one consent/To plead anew a holy argument—/For art is holy." He lists the players and playwrights of the past and sees himself in that traditional line.

Overall, D. played forty parts and directed sixty productions, spending the period of World War I in the theater. In 1918, his play *Abraham Lincoln* was a success and was transferred for a year's run to the Lyric Theatre, Hammersmith, in London. D. then took the play to America to the Cort Theater, New York. His *Bird in Hand*, a comedy, took a similar route in 1927, moving from Birmingham to New York. He also enjoyed successes in Paris and recognition from the Italian government for his theater writing.

D.'s poetry, which he began publishing from 1903, has never achieved the status and acclaim of his fellows, but there has been recent revival of interest in the work, some of which has been set to music. Much of this interest relies upon the fact that D. was heavily involved with poets of a higher caliber, such as Rupert BROOKE and the so-called Dymock poets, in whose circle he enjoyed the country pleasures that feature in his verse. The artist William Rothenstein, from whom the poet rented a cottage, said of D. "the poet incarnate, generous, high-minded, enthusiastic over the work of other poets, delighting in the countryside, in his little garden, in playing host to friends in his cottage." Alongside Brooke, Wilfrid Wilson GIBSON, and Lascelles ABERCROMBIE, D. contributed verse to *New Numbers* that had two hundred subscribers by December 1913, and ran to four volumes. D. also contributed

to all five volumes of Edward Marsh's *Georgian Poetry*, which began its run with a successful first volume, published in December 1912, to its demise in 1922.

In 1916, S. P. B. Mais called D. "a poet of a very brilliant calibre," but now critics perceive him as showing allegiance to the typical values of the Georgian school, where the post-Romantic quest for the timeless in nature coupled with a determination to show the rural tradition still unbroken and in continuity, lends a forced quality to the sense of the work. His poem "The Midlands" is a typical example in this vein, where rurality and history imbue the Gloucestershire landscape with a rather contrived visionary loftiness. D.'s poetry has been selected for anthologies by such diverse editors as Abercrombie, W. H. DAVIES, W. B. YEATS, and Philip LARKIN. The poems that characterize his most favored style are as follows: "The Carver in Stone," "The Town Window," and "Of Greatham" from *Swords and Ploughshares* (1915); "Birthright" and "Olton Pools" from *Olton Pools* (1916); "For a Guest Room," "The Midlands," and "Moonlit Apples" from *Tides* (1917).

BIBLIOGRAPHY: Pearce, M., *J. D.* (1977); Ross. R. H., *The Georgian Revolt 1910–1922: Rise and Fall of a Poetic Ideal* (1965)

CHRISTOPHER J. P. SMITH

DRUMMOND, William, of Hawthornden

b. 13 December 1585, Hawthornden, near Edinburgh, Scotland; d. 4 December 1649, Hawthornden

W. D. of Hawthornden has a place in the history of English literature both as a poet and as a writer of miscellaneous prose texts. His father was gentleman-usher to JAMES I, and the poet's own attitudes were much shaped by his loyalty to the Crown. In 1610, the poet (who had previously studied in Edinburgh and Paris) succeeded his father as laird of Hawthornden, with its country house in a beautiful wooded glen. D. spent most of his life on his estate, and his literary output was, in effect, the chief product of a life of aristocratic retirement (along with a number of mechanical inventions, such as a battering ram and an anemometer, which he patented). D. was a widely read man (his library was donated to Edinburgh University on his death), with interests in classical literature and the modern literatures of Italy, Spain, and France. There is much, indeed, that is "bookish" in his work, and his poetry provides many fascinating studies in influence, imitation, and translation. But at its best it has more than such merely scholarly pleasures to offer.

It is perhaps as a writer of sonnets that D. the poet has his greatest importance. In 1616, D. published *Poems: Amorous, Funerall, Divine, Pastorall, in Son-*

nets, Songs, Sextains, Madrigals, a volume whose range of themes and forms is well indicated by its lengthy subtitle. Central to the collection is a sequence in praise of his lady's beauty and goodness, and in lamentation upon her early death. But in offering a sequence shaped thus, and made up both of sonnets and of interspersed poems in other lyrical forms, D. was not merely imitating Petrarch's *Rime*, though the influence of that model is very evident in D.'s work. D. was betrothed to a Miss Cunningham of Barns who sadly died immediately before their wedding was due to take place in 1615. The pattern of Petrarch's great sequence, in which the first half deals with the poet's wooing of Laura and the second half concerns itself with the lady's death and the poet's reaction to it, naturally suggested itself to D. as one that bore directly on his own experience. His sonnets, interwoven as they are with his madrigals, songs, and sestains, are permeated by a melancholy that finds expression in verse of sweet musicality. The resulting poems are narrow in range of mood and effect, but often exquisitely perfect in their workmanship. Many of his individual poems are more obviously indebted to poets later than Petrarch, such as Torquato Tasso and Giambattista Marino; but the poems he chooses to imitate seem to be ones that help him to articulate his own distinctive sensibility. Almost all of D.'s work is marked by his sense of earthly mutability, his strongly developed awareness of the transience and frailty of all that is merely human or worldly. Such a sense informs most of his best poems, notably "A Daedal of my death" or "This life which seems so fair," among his madrigals, "Sith gone is my delight and only pleasure," among the sestains, and "My lute, be as thou wast when thou didst grow" or "Dear Wood, and you sweet solitary place" among his sonnets.

In "Urania" and *Flowres of Sion* (1623), a closely related response lies at the heart of much of D.'s best religious verse. *Flowres of Sion* is, again, a sequence made up of both sonnets and poems in other lyrical forms. The indirect narrative this time, however, is concerned, not with human love and death, but with the chief events in the life of Christ. The sequence begins, characteristically, with a sonnet on "The Instabilitie of Mortall Glorie" and goes on to celebrate the life of Christ as that which enables man to transcend what one poem calls "The Miserable Estate of the World before the Incarnation of God." D.'s sonnet "For the Baptist" (beginning "The last and greatest herald of Heaven's king") has been much admired, but there are other fine poems here worthy of note, such as the beautiful "Hymn of the Resurrection" and the impressive couplets of "An Hymn on the Fairest Fair."

D.'s occasional verse, such as his *Teares on the Death of Moeliades* (1613), one of the many elegies

for Prince Henry, *Forth Feasting* (1617), a panegyric on James I's return to Edinburgh, and *The Entertainment* (written in 1633 when Charles I visited Edinburgh), are competent but not especially distinctive. Much the same might be said of the bulk of D.'s prose, such as his *History of Scotland, from the Year 1423 until the Year 1542* (1655). There are two major exceptions to this generalization. The first is the meditative essay *A Cypress Grove* (published with *Flowres of Sion* in 1623), one of the masterpieces of English prose in the period. D.'s reflections on death and the afterlife of the soul are grand without emptiness, formal, even mannered in their expression, but always lucid and often memorable. The Christianized Platonism of these fifty or so pages is a crystallization of much of what mattered most to their author. Altogether different, but every bit as valuable, is D.'s record (in note form) of his *Conversations* with Ben JONSON, published posthumously. A friend and correspondent of Michael DRAYTON and other poets, D. received Jonson as a visitor in 1618. Jonson spent two weeks with D., and it is clear that D.'s evident respect for the older poet's work did not entirely outweigh his fastidious dislike of much in Jonson's manner and habits. For all that, D.'s record of Jonson's aphorisms and stories, prejudices and perceptions, is one of the most valuable informal documents that students of the period have at their disposal.

BIBLIOGRAPHY: Fogle, F. R., *A Critical Study of W. D. of Hawthornden* (1952); MacDonald, R. H., ed., *The Library of D. of Hawthornden* (1972); Masson, D., *D. of Hawthornden* (1873)

GLYN PURSGLOVE

DRYDEN, John
b. 9 August 1631, Aldwincle, Northamptonshire; d. 1 May 1700, London

D. is the preeminent figure in English literature of the second half of the 17th c. Authoring plays, poetry, translations, collections, satires, and criticism, he led the era's predominant literary circle and supported younger talents who went on to become literary giants themselves. He helped usher in a new, more modern literary language, easy, natural and focused on understanding and sense rather than artifice and ornamentation. While his work touched on all the key social and political issues of the day, he was highly aware of his predecessors, building on their achievements in poetry and drama while working in his criticism to establish a native literary tradition and place himself within it. Since Alexander POPE's acknowledgment of a tremendous debt to D., the years between 1660 and 1700 have often been called "The Age of Dryden." Unfortunately, D.'s reputation suffers today because of modern readers' rejection of rhymed couplets, and his style is often anachronistically considered stilted and overwrought.

The son of non-radical Puritans, D. was given a country gentleman's upbringing and education. After getting a solid background in the classics at the respected Westminster School in London, where Ben JONSON, Christopher Wren, and John LOCKE had also gone, he entered Trinity College, Cambridge, in 1650. Graduating third in his class, he moved to London and got a government clerkship through family connections. His first important literary effort was a political poem: *Heroic Stanzas* (1659) eulogized the Lord Protector Oliver Cromwell. This does not indicate that D. was antiroyalist; immediately following the restoration of the monarchy he published *Astraea Redux* (1660) and *To His Sacred Majesty* (1661), both lauding the restored monarch Charles II. This apparent change of heart is in keeping not only with D.'s inherent conservatism but also with the general sentiment in a nation exhausted by civil strife. He did, however, draw upon himself charges of political expediency, as he would do throughout his career.

The return of the monarchy brought the reopening of the theaters, closed by Puritans during the Interregnum. New companies needed new plays, and D. applied himself to providing them. His first play, *The Wild Gallant* (perf. 1663; pub. 1669), was a lightweight comedy. Over the next thirty years, he wrote or collaborated on twenty-seven more plays. Many are largely insignificant comedies, relying heavily on farce, double meanings and bawdy jokes, including *The Rival Ladies* (perf. 1663; pub. 1664), *Secret Love* (perf. 1667; pub. 1668), *Sir Martin Mar-All* with William Cavendish, Duke of Newcastle (perf. 1667; pub. 1668), and *The Assignation; or Love in a Nunnery* (perf. 1672; pub. 1673).

Success came, however, when the young playwright turned to pioneering a new form: the heroic drama. Written in heroic couplets, the popular genre featured music, dancing, exotic locales and splendid costumes. The protagonist is always an almost impossibly noble hero, beset by intrigues spawned by ambitious villains, pretenders or evilly licentious women. The plots serve to test the hero's virtues rather than advance his character; after passing with flying colors he either dies or is united with the virtuous woman he loves. The formulaic quality of these plays was noted by critics and hilariously spoofed by George Villiers, second Duke of BUCKINGHAM, in his satiric play *The Rehearsal*, in which D. appears as a bombastic and laughable playwright named John Bayes. Nevertheless, audiences loved the spectacle and SENTIMENT of heroic dramas, and their period of vogue lasted more than ten years.

The first heroic drama to win D. praise was *The Indian Queen* (perf. 1664), which was quickly followed by a sequel, *The Indian Emperour* (perf. 1665;

pub. 1672). Using the conquest of South America as a setting, these plays follow the example of 16th-c. French essayist Michel de Montaigne in playing out a conflict between art and nature as a clash of Spanish and Indian cultures.

The Conquest of Granada by the Spaniards (perf. 1670; pub. 1672), a drama in two parts, is sometimes cited as D.'s best effort in heroic drama. The play uses the romantic elements of his previous heroic dramas, but shows D. moving toward a form he held sacred: the EPIC. Some critics argue that he successfully draws together these modes, along with political commentary, but others find it nearly as bombastic as the earlier heroic dramas. However, this is really to blame D. for the palates of his audiences, which D. spent much of his career consciously trying to please.

The early heroic dramas built D.'s reputation as a playwright sufficient to generate interest in his own dramatic theories. His first—and in many ways best—piece of criticism was *An Essay in Dramatick Poesie* (1667). Written in debate form, the *Essay* explores a series of opposing arguments about the theater: ancient theater versus modern, French playwrights versus English, blank verse versus rhyme. D. expounds his opinions through his mouthpiece, Neander.

Although D.'s pronouncements have the intended consequence of justifying his own dramatic practices, the *Essay* accomplished several important goals. It began the process of designating a native English dramatic canon, and the playwrights D. here and later elevates—William SHAKESPEARE, John FLETCHER, Jonson, William WYCHERLEY, William CONGREVE—still constitute the canon today. D. dispensed with the idea of classical dramatic rules, including Aristotle's overcited three unities, as a yardstick for all drama. D. not only points out that Shakespeare and even the classical authors themselves often ignore such rules, but he upholds a pragmatic standard, arguing that drama is best judged by what works on stage. The *Essay* was not only a breakthrough piece of criticism in its own day: it is still usefully read today.

D. clarified and expanded on his dramatic theories in subsequent prefaces, responding to critiques and theatrical developments. In all essays, his ultimate criterion of quality was dramatic efficacy. Give the audience what it wants, his theories proclaimed, and he spent most of his career following that law himself. But D. was always as much a man of letters as of the theater. His *Annus Mirabilis* (1667), a long poem praising the leadership of Charles II in the events of 1666, including the Great Fire and the English victory over the Dutch, struck a strong blow against critics who blamed the court for that year's disasters. The publication of the poem had positive consequences for D.: in the following year, he was named poet laureate, and in 1670 he became historiographer royal as well. Both appointments carried substantial financial rewards as well as prestige.

As an established literary authority, D. wrote what critics consider his best comedy, *Marriage à la Mode* (perf. 1671; pub. 1673). Like many plays of the age, the comedy has a double plot; uncharacteristically, the two plots rarely intermingle, because one is romantic heroic, involving lofty, high-born characters speaking rhymed couplets, and the other is a pure comedy of manners concerning the scurrilous escapades of free-wheeling courtiers who utilize prose. Much of the criticism on this play has focused on finding the connections between these two plots. There are thematic connections, contrasting the nobles' lofty attitudes toward love and marriage with the licentiousness of the courtiers. But the relationship is also one of formal juxtaposition: D. was taking his own literary advice in creating a capacious dramatic text that, like Shakespeare's, expanded to include multiple social groups and linguistic modes.

D.'s last straight heroic drama was *Aureng-Zebe* (perf. 1675; pub. 1676), and many critics agree with the playwright in naming it his best. Although it depicts the struggle of an emperor's noble son to defend his honor and loyalty against assaults from his evil brothers and stepmother, the play is less overwrought and extravagant than his previous heroic dramas. In the prologue, D. suggests that he may be making an even more serious change, announcing his intention of abandoning rhyme in future plays.

After *Aureng-Zebe*, D. wrote a dramatic adaptation of John MILTON's *Paradise Lost*, called *The State of Innocence and the Fall of Man* (1677), meant to be read rather than performed. His adaptation of Shakespeare's *Antony and Cleopatra*, entitled *All for Love; or, The World Well Lost* (1678), applied the dispensable unities to S.'s unwieldy plot, achieving a psychological intensity admired by many critics and utilizing an eloquence that has been called Miltonic. Again with this play, modern sensibilities stand in the way of appreciation for D.'s work: most modern audiences are uninterested in adaptations of Shakespeare. But *All for Love* displaced Shakespeare's original from the English stage for nearly a century. D. also adapted Sophocles in *Oedipus* (perf. 1678; pub. 1679), collaborating with Nathaniel Lee, and tackled Shakespeare again in *Troilus and Cressida* (1679). But this period saw D. moving away from the theater more and more. His first poetic satire, *Mac Flecknoe* (1682) was a mock-heroic poem written in 1676 and published in a pirated edition after the tremendous public success of his most famous satirical poem, *Absalom and Achitophel* (1681).

Absalom and Achitophel takes on the Exclusion Crisis of 1681, in which forces in Parliament attempted to exclude the Catholic James, Duke of York, as heir to the British throne. Utilizing the scriptural story of the revolt against the Hebrew King David by his illegitimate son Absolom, aided and abetted by the bad councilor Achitophel, D. writes contemporary history as scriptural allegory. James Scott, Duke of Monmouth and the illegitimate son of Charles II, appears as Absalom. Anthony Ashley Cooper, first Earl of Shaftesbury, leader of the Parliamentarians, who attempted to force Charles to name Monmouth his successor, appears as Achitophel. In finely wrought rhymed couplets, D. argues that Parliament's attempt to meddle with the laws of succession was tantamount to a Satanic revolt against God. The poem is remarkable not only for its powerful verse, but for the facility with which it makes a vehement argument in highly rational terms. The poem has been hailed as the best satiric poem in the English language. It was not, however, effective, and Shaftesbury was not only exonerated but given a medal by his supporters, prompting D.'s sequel satire, *The Medall* (1682).

D. returned to the drama with *The Duke of Guise* (1682), a political allegory that served the same propagandistic purposes as *Absalom and Achitophel* and *The Medall*. But he was largely focused on poetry and translations. He published miscellanies of classical works in 1684 and 1685, including his own translations as well as those he selected by others. His long poem *Religio Laici* (1682) upheld his devout Anglican faith. However, in 1685 Charles II converted to Catholicism on his deathbed and the Catholic James II ascended the throne. Around this time, D. himself converted, explaining and justifying his surprising choice in *The Hind and the Panther* (1687), his longest original poem. Although he was again accused of political expediency, he upheld his Catholic faith for the rest of his life, even after the Glorious Revolution of 1688 caused him to lose his court positions and status.

With the assumption of William of Orange and the loss of his court income, D. was forced to return to the theater to support his family. *Don Sebastian, King of Portugal* (perf. 1689; pub. 1690), another play interweaving two plots, one comic-erotic and one heroic-romantic, effectively addresses many of the political and social themes D.'s work had raised to this point. The play is a study of the complexity of loyalty, particularly when it conflicts with self-interest. *Amphitryon* (1690), with songs set by Henry Purcell, returns to the comic modes, but adds political satire to its bawdy and farcical plot. D. again collaborated with Purcell on *King Arthur*, an underappreciated semi-opera that substantially revises the traditional Arthurian legend.

D. proclaimed his retirement from the theater with *Love Triumphant* (1694), a comedy that returns to many of his earlier themes and methods. He turned instead to translations, translating sections of Ovid, Homer, Boccaccio, Virgil, and Geoffrey CHAUCER. But his major triumph in translation was his *Aeneid* (1697), a translation of Virgil's epic that stands to this day of an example of a translation's ability to preserve the spirit of the original while adapting it to a contemporary and native poetic idiom. Rarely read today because modern readers find the heroic couplets annoying, the work is surely one of D.'s great poetic achievements. It proved a success, bringing him financial stability and increased renown.

While generally accepted to be important to literary history, D. is infrequently read today. His plays, considered to be too much of his own age to be enjoyed by moderns, are rarely produced, and read far less frequently than those of his contemporaries. His poetry is far less central to the canon that that of his great satiric successor, Pope. His translations have been replaced by more modern ones and his criticism, mostly appearing in prefaces and prologues and never quite adding up to a unified, coherent theory, is marginalized in both literary and dramatic theory. Nonetheless, his legacy is far-reaching. Having established a new way of using the English language and a new way of thinking about the English literary tradition, his influence was not only upon the generation immediately succeeding him, but extends all the way to our own age.

BIBLIOGRAPHY: Aden, J. M., ed., *The Critical Opinions of J. D.* (1963); Bloom, H., ed., *J. D.* (1987); Bywaters, D., *D. in Revolutionary England* (1991); Hammond, P., *J. D.* (1991); Hughes, D., *D.'s Heroic Plays* (1981); McFadden, G., *D., the Public Writer, 1660–1685* (1978); Schilling, B. N., ed., *D.* (1963); Ward, C. E., *The Life of J. D.* (1961); Winn, J. A., *J. D. and His World* (1987)

GINGER STRAND

DUCK, Stephen
b. 1705, Wiltshire; d. 31 March 1756, Reading

An agricultural worker who educated himself by reading John MILTON, but afraid to emulate Milton's lofty blank verse, D. wrote *The Thresher's Labour* from his own experience in heroic couplets, and doggerel ballads, which earned him the nickname of "the thresher poet." D.'s best-known poem appeared in pirated editions of his *Poems on Several Subjects* from 1730 to 1733 and in an authorized edition in 1736. Given a pension by Queen Caroline, he was considered for the post of poet laureate, but his poetry had become lifeless and conventional. Later works include *The Vision* (1737), a poetic elegy to the queen, and *Caesar's Camp; or St. George's Hill* (1755), a patriotic poem on national spirit. D. later became a popular preacher, but apparently ended his own life by drowning himself.

DUFFY, Carol Ann
b. 23 December 1955, Glasgow, Scotland

Marked by dramatic monologues and multiple perspectives, D.'s poetry is largely evocative of themes concerning love, loss, nostalgia, and the construction of reality through language—themes that resonate throughout her work, recurring in the various voices of unique personae. It is the latter theme that is central in understanding D.'s work, not only because her poetry largely circles around the philosophy of language, but also in that her questioning of language is perhaps reinforced by the "simplistic," rhymed, short-lined verse for which she has been criticized. Simplicity of language may seem inadequate for the breadth of reference in D.'s work, but makes it accessible.

Poet and playwright D. began her career at an early age. Reared in Staffordshire, she attended St. Joseph's Convent and Stafford High School for girls. She studied the works of Geoffrey CHAUCER, John KEATS, and Rudyard KIPLING, but was also introduced to the so-called Liverpool Poets—Roger MCGOUGH, Brian Patten, and Adrian Henri, with whom she became involved at the age of sixteen. At eighteen, she published her first work, *Fleashweathercock* (1973), a pamphlet of poems, and in the following year moved to Liverpool.

In 1977, D. graduated with an honors degree in philosophy from Liverpool University. In her studies, she was particularly influenced by the writings of Ludwig Wittgenstein, whose notion about the inability of language to say anything recurs throughout her work. The focus on the construction of reality through language is particularly evident in *Standing Female Nude* (1985) and *Selling Manhattan* (1987). In both of these collections, the fictionality of reality is exposed. This theme is again of concern in her later work, *Mean Time* (1993). In "Nostalgia," D. addresses the gap between emotion and words, as the speaker claims that "Some would never fall in love had they not heard of love." Here, not only language is thrown into question, but reality—that reality constructed through language. Language proves to be unreliable and inadequate for many of the speakers in D.'s poems; the idea that the meaning of words can never be fixed, that language is unable to say anything—notions reminiscent of Wittgenstein and Jacques Derrida—also appear in *The Other Country* (1990).

The straightforward language of D.'s poetry is, nevertheless, not without fresh voice. Her playful, often humorous verse, along with her deliberate use of clichés, teases reality, frequently probing at gender stereotypes. Her language has a sharpness that seeks to overthrow the conventional. Classical form is used with razor-sharp technique; D. juxtaposes realist and fantastic elements to question normality, reality, and the dimension, she seems to claim, that they do not necessarily share.

The World's Wife (1999) presents an unexplored world of subverted histories and myths, those traditional narratives unwoven and reinterpreted in a witty, contemporary feminist voice. It was perhaps this same will to overhaul the traditional—complicated by D.'s homosexuality—that, in 1999, saw both the nomination and rejection of D. as England's new poet laureate, the position instead falling to the less controversial Andrew MOTION. The pending appointment of laureate had at once turned D. into a public figure. The young lesbian poet came to represent a generational change and the voice of a modern, more democratic, and "cool Britannia." But D.'s outspokenness, her sexuality, and unwillingness to write for the royal family were all elements that perhaps counted against her.

In addition to her many published collections of poetry, including *The Fifth Last Song* (1982) and *I Wouldn't Thank You For A Valentine* (1992), D. has written two plays that were performed at the Liverpool Playhouse, *Take My Husband* (perf. 1984) and *Cavern Dreams* (perf. 1986). She has received several prizes for her poetry, including the Whitbread Award in 1993. As a poet, D. has triumphed not only in her ability to make known, but also successful, a language that, ironically, so often fails. It may be said that D.'s work, subtly powerful in the complexity that underlies its simplicity—is, in fact, as "sly as a rumour."

BIBLIOGRAPHY: Rees-Jones, D., *C. A. D.* (1999); Wojcik-Leese, E., " 'Her Language Is Simple': The Poetry of C. A. D.," in Klein, H., and S. Coelsch-Fisher, eds., *Poetry Now: Contemporary British and Irish Poetry in the Making* (1999): 307–15

COLLEEN McCUTCHEON

DUFFY, Maureen [Patricia]

b. 21 October 1933, Worthing, Sussex

Novelist, dramatist, historian, and poet, D. incorporates the political, social, and sexual struggle of the human (often on the social fringes) in her writing in each of these genres. Her novels in particular are noted for their strong characterization and vivid descriptive detail, and while her writing has not always garnered her the critical praise or the wider reading audience deserved, it has secured and consolidated her position as one of the major novelists of postwar Britain.

After graduating from King's College, London, in 1956, D. taught in various state schools. She published her first novel, *That's How It Was*, in 1962. It is a semiautobiographical account of D.'s childhood dealing with poverty and the war. The emotions expressed in the novel are unsentimental, and the drama of daily life genuine. It was critically well received as "one of the few authentic accounts in British fiction of a working-class childhood and . . . one of the most

successful." Her third novel, *The Microcosm* (1966), focuses on the underground lesbian scene in London.

The Paradox Players (1967) reaffirmed D.'s ability to shape characters intricately and artistically. In a self-imposed exile the main character, Sym, chooses to "drop out" of society and live among a colony of social misfits in houseboats moored on a small island in the Thames. The characters are "impeccably drawn and treated with thorough understanding." *Housespy* (1978) and *Gor Saga* (1981) both garnered enthusiastic criticism on publication. In them, "her fiction takes on a richer, darker coloring, and its structure becomes more intricate and complex." *Housespy* is a twisted espionage thriller with complex plot twists spinning around characters that, in turn, carry their own identity tricks. In *Gor Saga*, D. presents a fable that revolves around the main character, Gor, an engineered "humanoid," part gorilla, part human.

D.'s fiction often plays with sexual ambiguity among its characters as in *Love Child* (1971), whose central character's sex and age are unknown. She combines this sexual ambiguity with stylistic experimentation in *The Microcosm* as well as *Wounds* (1969), a series of vignettes of characters fragmented by the conversation of two nameless lovers as they meet and make love. D. invokes history's muse in her later works, *Capital* (1976), *Illuminations* (1991), *Occam's Razor* (1993), and *Restitution* (1998). The first three books "move back and forth along a historical timeline" incorporating politically and socially pertinent issues such as terrorism and "post–Cold War flux." *Restitution* (1998) deals with the "political minefield" of genetic predisposition, "nature versus nurture" and identity.

While D. is more widely known for her fiction, she has also received recognition for her poetry and work as a playwright. In 1962, she received the City of London Festival Playwright's award for *The Lay-Off* (perf. 1961). In addition, she has written several works of nonfiction including *The Erotic World of Faery* (1972). She has written two biographies: *The Passionate Shepherdess: Aphra Behn* (1977) and *Henry Purcell* (1994). Recently, D. has addressed the myth of England and national identity in *England: The Making of the Myth from Stonehenge to Albert Square* (2001).

BIBLIOGRAPHY: Bode, C., "M. D.: A Polyphonic Sub-Version of Realism," *A&E* 60 (1997): 41–54; Werson, G., "M. D.," in Halio, J. L., ed., *British Novelists since 1960*, part 1, *DLB 14* (1982)

PAIGE BAILEY

DU MAURIER, [Dame] Daphne [Lady Browning]

b. 13 May 1907, London; d. 19 April 1989, Par, Cornwall

Daughter of famous actor Gerald Du Maurier and granddaughter of novelist George DU MAURIER, D.

was predestined to have a successful life. A celebrated author by the time she was twenty-five, D. later saw three of her works brought to the screen by Alfred Hitchcock. Renowned for stories that often entwined Gothic and horror elements, D. is mostly remembered as a popular novelist.

D. began publishing romantic stories at the age of twenty-one. Her first two novels, *The Loving Spirit* and *I'll Never be Young Again,* were published in 1931 and 1932 respectively. *The Loving Spirit* was a touchstone for many of D.'s later novels. It was based on events in the lives of the Slade family, who lived in D.'s county of Cornwall. D. set the majority of her works in Cornwall as a tribute to its beauty and history. Her fondness for history is evident in the novel she wrote chronicling her French ancestors, *The Glass-Blowers* (1963). The historical backgrounds of her novels were well received by her readers. Her third novel, *Jamaica Inn* (1936), was inspired by a coaching house on Bodmin Moor that had been the stomping ground of highwaymen and smugglers for over four hundred years. The romantic story of a young girl and her pirate lover was well received. The less popular film version was Hitchcock's last British film, produced in 1938. D. was not happy with the film as it softened the violence she tried to depict accurately in the book.

As the film version of *Jamaica Inn* was in production, D. was working on the novel that became her benchmark: the Gothic romance *Rebecca* (1938). The famous first line of the novel, "Last night I dreamt I went to Manderley again," sets up the mysterious setting and plot in which the narrator is never named and the title character, Rebecca de Winter, is never seen. The narrator marries Rebecca's widower, Maxim, and is brought home to Manderley, his family estate presided over by the housekeeper, Mrs. Danvers. Mrs. Danvers's fierce loyalty to her dead mistress results in attempts to destroy the current Mrs. de Winter, who ultimately discovers that Rebecca's death was not an accident and that things are not always what they seem. An instant success, the novel was eventually translated into at least twenty languages and was one of the best selling novels of D.'s lifetime. Hitchcock's 1940 production of the film won the Academy Award for Best Picture. However, both movie and later stage adaptations fudge the subversiveness of D.'s text.

During World War II, D. wrote inspirational short stories meant to inspire her fellow countrymen and women. The *Edinburgh Evening News* published a short series of "comforting words" by D., which were picked up by provincial papers around the country. Ten of the stories were collected and sold in book form, with all proceeds going to the Red Cross. D. saw this as her war effort and was gratified to see almost 600,000 copies sold in three months.

The success of *Rebecca* and later novels like *The King's General* (1946) ensured D.'s place in British literary history, but her short stories continued to enthrall her readers as the popularity of the horror and mystery genres increased dramatically after the war. Still a popular author even after her death, D. is honored by her fans with a literary festival in Cornwall every spring.

BIBLIOGRAPHY: Cook, J., *D.: A Portrait of D. du M.* (1991); Du Maurier, D., *Growing Pains* (1977; repub. as *Myself When Young,* 1977); Forster, M., *D. du M.* (1993)

MARCY TANTER

DU MAURIER, George
b. 6 March 1834, Paris, France; d. 8 October 1896, London

Intent on becoming an artist, D. studied painting in Paris and for more than two decades was a popular cartoonist for *Punch* as well as a leading book illustrator. Late in his career, D. was encouraged by Henry JAMES to try his hand at writing fiction, and in 1891 at the age of fifty-five he published *Peter Ibbetson*, noteworthy for exploring the nature of the unconscious mind and the psychological implications of dual personality. His second novel, the highly sensational and compelling *Trilby* (3 vols., 1894), became one of the best-selling books of the 19th c. and gave its name to a men's hat popular in the first half of the 20th c.—the foot fetishism featured in the novel even led a U.S. manufacturer to produce a lady's high-heeled shoe called "the Trilby." Published in 1897, D.'s third novel, *The Martian*, incorporates elements of the supernatural with fantasy to further probe the depth of human psychology.

DUNBAR, William
b. ca. 1460–65, Scotland; d. before 1530

Noted for his aureate style, verbal energy, and poetic virtuosity, D. stands with Robert Henryson and Gavin DOUGLAS as a leading poet of the Scottish golden age. Sometimes known as a Scots Chaucerian, he stands at the end of a poetic tradition that includes the MIDDLE ENGLISH poets Geoffrey CHAUCER, John GOWER, and John LYDGATE.

What little is known about D.'s life derives largely from the accounts of the Treasurer of Scotland that record various pensions and benefices, and what may be inferred from D.'s poetry. He is identified with the William Dunbar who was awarded a bachelor's degree from St. Andrew's University in 1477 and a master's degree in 1479. He was a Franciscan novice, probably traveled to England and France in the king's service, and took priestly orders in 1504. He is also assumed to be the "Rhymer of Scotland" referred to in the 1501 and 1502 records of Henry VII's Privy Purse, for the role he played in arranging a treaty of marriage between Henry's daughter, Margaret Tudor, and the Scottish king, James IV. In honor of this marriage, D. wrote "The Thrissil and the Rois," an allegorical dream sequence. D.'s poetic career is entirely linked with the court of James IV, and official references to him cease after the king was killed in the battle of Flodden in September 1513. David LYNDSAY's *Testament of the Papyngo* (wr. ca. 1530; pub. 1538) includes D. among the dead poets of Scotland.

D. often refers to himself in his poetry. In "Of a Dance in the Quenis Chalmer," he describes himself as a lively dancer ("nane frackar"). In the famous insult contest presented in "The Flyting of Dunbar and Kennedie," D. has his poetic rival, Walter Kennedy, describe him as small in stature, with wild hair and a beak nose. Kennedy also describes him as the spawn of the devil and a she-bear. On the other hand, D. speaks of Kennedy with affection in "Lament for the Makaris [makers, poets]." The figure that emerges in D.'s poems, like Chaucer's persona in *The Canterbury Tales*, should probably be taken more as a pose than an autobiographical portrait.

D. by his own designation is a makar, suggesting that his poems were probably read or even sung in public performances before the court. The eighty-five or so poems attributed to him with certainty are written in Middle Scots, which derives from a northern dialect of Middle English, and is distinct from both the dialect of the English court, and the Highland Scottish Gaelic. John Barbour's *The Bruce* (wr. 1376) is also composed in this dialect.

Because of his virtuosity and variety, it is difficult to identify what is characteristic of D.'s poetry. He is a master of a wide variety of poetic types, including narrative, love, comic, bawdy, laudatory, panegyric, invective, religious, and petitions. In turn, he deploys a large range of stanzaic patterns, rhythms, meters, and alliteration. He is also known for his highly eloquent and ornamental "aureate" style, and his wild, exuberant, and grotesque "eldritch" style. In all cases he is a skillful craftsman, calculating every effect.

Among D.'s best work is the debate poem, "The Merle and the Nychtingall," an exchange on sacred and profane love between a blackbird and a nightingale. Another is "The Goldyn Targe," a dream vision and an allegorical psychomachia between Venus and reason. It is also intertwined with D.'s views on poetry. His most ambitious piece is "The Tretis of Tua Mariit Wemen and the Wedo," in the form of three speeches between three women dressed in green overheard in an arbor on Midsummer's Eve. They offer frank and often satirical looks at love and sexuality, and are often compared with Chaucer's Wife of Bath and La Vieille (wr. ca. 1275) from Jean de Meun's

Roman de la Rose (wr. ca. 1275). Though contemporary with John SKELTON and François Villon, D.'s art is marked less by innovation than by his mastery of the traditional forms and styles of medieval poetry.

BIBLIOGRAPHY: Bawcutt, P., *D. the Makar* (1992); Lewis, C. S., *English Literature in the Sixteenth Century* (1954); Reiss, E., *W. D.* (1979); Wood, H. H., *Two Scots Chaucerians, Robert Henryson, W. D.* (1967)

THOMAS L. COOKSEY

DUNCAN, Ronald [Frederick Henry]

b. 6 August 1914, Salisbury, Rhodesia; d. 3 June 1982, London

Without any doubt one of the chief formative influences on D.—poet, playwright, and novelist—was the circumstance of his own birth and early life. D.'s parents were married in 1913 and almost immediately left England for Rhodesia—as the British colony was then called: on its liberation in 1980, it was renamed Zambia (Northern Rhodesia) and Zimbabwe (Southern Rhodesia). His father's intention had been to study farming in Rhodesia but in 1914, on the outbreak of war, he was interned because of his German name (Dunkelsbühler). (In point of fact, he was a British subject, though born in Germany of German parents: they had moved to England when D.'s father was a small child and the boy had been reared in England, had attended Cambridge University, and spoke no German.) Just before his internment, guessing what was coming, D.'s father sent his wife and their baby son back to England. He himself remained in internment for the whole of the war and, on his release in 1918, volunteered his help with fighting an influenza epidemic among local black residents, caught the disease himself, and died. D.'s mother never saw her husband again after the first year of her marriage and D. himself never knew his father, There runs through all D.'s work a streak of pain, loss, bitterness, and, on occasion, downright paranoia.

While still at Downing College, Cambridge (he graduated in 1936), D. began to write plays and film scripts and in 1940 he published a play called *The Dull Ass's Hoof*. It was never performed. In 1945, however, he had his first public success with a masque called *This Way to the Tomb* (perf. 1945; pub. 1946), which ran for nearly a year in E. Martin Browne's "plays by poets" series at the tiny Mercury Theatre in Notting Hill Gate, London. It deals with the temptations of St. Antony on the island of Zante and is based, in its dramaturgical design, on the masques of Ben JONSON. D. equips it with a satirical antimasque that enables him to parallel the ancient story with a commentary in jazz and light verse on the problems of faith and temptation in modern times (though his

1946 "modern times" seem a bit quaint now). However, the variations in tone and texture of the verse between masque and antimasque constitute a virtuoso performance that has not lost its élan in the passage of fifty years.

His next play was *Stratton* (perf. 1949; pub. 1950). Written in a mixture of verse and prose but prose that frequently rises to the heightened sensitivities of poetry, it is an exploration of the nature of love and the intimate connection between love and hate. It uses a melodramatic plot but sedulously avoids the temptation to descend into the banalities of melodrama. A fashionable barrister who has always insisted upon taking only cases for the defense, never for the prosecution, and has consistently turned down invitations to ascend the bench as a judge, on the grounds that no man is worthy enough to judge another, suddenly changes his mind and accepts the judiciary appointment. The play examines the psychological processes which precipitate this volte-face and reveals his corroding jealousy and envy which underlie what he had taken to be his love for his son and heir, and the intense sexual desire he feels, underneath all the conventional, civilized niceties for his daughter-in-law. "And every brat born—/Saint, sinner, judge or jailer—/Is with the most commendable equality/Each imprisoned in his own personality/To drag a chain of trivial dreams/Round and round his narrow cell;/And our jailer is our pride."

Lesser plays followed in 1950 and 1951—*Nothing Up My Sleeve*, also called *St. Spiv* (perf. 1950; pub. 1971), and *Our Lady's Tumbler* (1951). The former of these was turned into a novel called *St. Spiv* and published in 1961. Much more substantial; are the two plays based on the Spanish legendary figure: *Don Juan* (perf. 1953; pub. 1954) and *The Death of Satan* (perf. 1954; pub.1955). Mordantly witty, deeply serious, and very funny, both are written in verse—perhaps the most accomplished of all D.'s dramatic verse—and portray the Don not as a commonplace lecher but as a frustrated idealist in search of truth, reality, and an escape from triviality. The gist of the argument in both plays turns on the nature of Hell. Herein, its debt to act 3 of Bernard SHAW's *Man and Superman* is obvious ("Hell is full of musical amateurs: music is the brandy of the damned" says Shaw's Devil); and, indeed, Shaw himself turns up as one of the characters in *The Death of Satan* (along with Oscar WILDE and Lord BYRON) now resident in Hell, who idle away their time playing cards, discussing their respective reputations (two out of the three had written about Don Juan) and commenting generally on the place of Hell in man's mythology. If faith is allowed to atrophy, then Hell (as a place of punishment) has no meaning: it is as casual, comfortable, and accidental as Earth. Without faith, there can be no purpose; and without purpose, there can be no fail-

ure and therefore no Hell. Satan is appalled by such reasoning, for it puts him out of work. "What of my mission?" he asks. He also asks "Why don't people suffer in Hell any more?" and Don Juan replies: "Because they no longer love as I have loved./Because they no longer believe as she believed." The faith that Don Juan (and D.) here talk about is not conventional religious faith (and certainly not the milk-and-water stuff of modern pre-packaged Christianity) but faith in a human reality and nobility which, by definition, cannot be known but that can nevertheless, because of humanity's sense of the nature of life and of his own place in it, be intuited. (One needs to remember that when Job—and Handel—say "I *know* that my redeemer liveth" they are acknowledging that no one can possible know such a thing but that one's intuition of it is so strong as to feel like actual knowledge. That is the very nature of faith and belief. Handel gets it peculiarly, exactly and triumphantly right when he gives that word "know" the advantage of a soaring soprano note—"I KNOW . . ." and this special kind of knowing is the essence—albeit in a minor key—of D.'s poetry in the two Juan plays.)

D. also wrote the libretto for Benjamin Britten's opera *The Rape of Lucretia*, first performed at the Glyndebourne Opera House in 1946. The libretto was published in 1953. It met with a mixed reception at the time but the more discerning critics recognised and gave unqualified approbation to the revolution that it represented. The Earl of Harewood in his introduction to the published libretto said: "Now that English music has started to re-acquire what amounts to confidence in its ability to seize an audience's attention and hold it, there is every reason to hope that poets will once again be anxious to collaborate with musicians, knowing that their combined work will be equal to something bigger than the sum of the two . . . This libretto is an example of such collaboration; one must hope that it is an indication that poets and musicians as well as audiences are beginning to see the point of Purcell's remark that the proper combination of music and poetry was like finding 'wit and beauty in the same person'— no less admirable, and no less rare." D., at present more or less forgotten, and poetry and music (in any serious sense) at present much neglected in the theater, may yet, in the long vistas of artistic appreciation, be seen to stand out with a new importance.

The Catalyst (perf. 1958; pub. 1964) is a two-act comedy written entirely in prose. It is deftly plotted and is very sound theatrically. Because of its subject matter, it was, almost as a matter of course, banned by the Lord Chamberlain, acting under the ludicrous theater censorship laws: the play deals with a ménage à trois (husband-wife-secretary) but there is an additional complication in that, during the course of the play, the wife discovers that the secretary, an attractive young woman of twenty-five, is in love with her and that she herself (the wife) finds that she is strongly attracted, sexually, by the younger woman. Finally, they all agree to accept the truth of the individual relationships and to renounce the whole notion of monogamy: love, they decide, need not lead to an exclusive possessiveness. They settle permanently into a single and singular, though not unsatisfactory household. Tolerance and truth are more valuable than the crudities of "owning" another person. Even the Lord Chamberlain's sense of tolerance increased with the impending annulment of the antiquated censorship laws. In 1963, he granted a public performance licence to D.'s play that was then duly presented at the Lyric Theatre in London, under a new title: it was called *Ménage-à-Trois* and it ran for thirty-eight performances. The Theatres Act of 1843, which had contained the censorship clauses, was finally annulled in 1968.

D.'s final group of plays include *Abelard and Heloise* (perf. 1960; pub. 1961), *The Rabbit Race* (perf. 1963), *The Seven Deadly Virtues* (perf. 1968; pub. 1971), and *The Gift* (perf. 1968; pub. 1971). They are lesser works and do not add anything of great significance to the general pattern of his work. He also published seven volumes of verse, the first in 1940 and the last in 1969. His *Collected Plays* appeared in 1971. There are four volumes of autobiography, an edition of some of the writings of Gandhi, and a miscellaneous collection of other books with titles as various as *Journal of a Husbandman* (1950), *Tobacco Growing in England* (1956), *All Men Are Islands* (1964), and *The Perfect Mistress and other Stories* (1969). As well as his writing, he was interested and influential in promoting the growth of serious theater (and especially verse plays) in London and elsewhere in England and among his ventures in this field was the initiation of the movement, in 1956, that led to the creation, under George Devine's direction, of the extremely important English Stage Company at the Royal Court Theatre in Sloane Square, London: the company is still there and is still one of the leading producers of new, modern plays in London.

BIBLIOGRAPHY: Findlater, R., *At the Royal Court* (1981); Haueter, M. W., *R. D.* (1969); Wahl, W. B., *A Lone Wolf Howling: The Thematic Content of D.'s Plays* (1973)

ERIC SALMON

DUNN, Douglas [Eaglesham]

b. 23 October 1942, Renfrewshire, Scotland

D. is a Scottish poet, short story writer, and literary critic whose prolific and distinguished output has received significant critical acclaim and many awards, including the Hawthornden Prize, the Somerset

Maugham Award, and the Whitbread Award. D. has said that most of his writing is a "conflict between reality and imagination"; whether delivering searing attacks on callous governmental policies or composing tender poems of love and remembrance, he is an eloquent and compassionate writer who, since the early 1970s, has been widely regarded as a major figure in British poetry.

Although much of D.'s work is drawn from an obsession with and love of Lowland Scotland and its people, his first volume, *Terry Street* (1969), was written during a seventeen-year period of self-exile in England. *Terry Street* is a collection of vignettes that evoke life in a deprived working-class suburb of Hull, and its publication inevitably drew comparisons with Philip LARKIN, who, with W. H. AUDEN, was a strong influence on D.'s early work. With titles such as "Incident in the Shop" or "Death in Terry Street," the poetry is characterized by its dour REALISM, detailed observation, and black HUMOR, occasionally relieved by a confidently subtle use of unexpected imagery. In 1972, Anthony THWAITE named the collection, which has a much wider relevance than its name suggests, as one of the four best collections of poetry by a living British writer to have appeared in the previous ten years.

Terry Street was followed by two minor publications, *Backwaters* (1971) and *Night* (1971), and then by *The Happier Life* (1972), which introduced rhyme and meter and a much broader subject matter. More enthusiastically received, however, was *Love or Nothing* (1974), a volume full of energy and fun that was influenced by a period spent in France. Moving away from urban realism, D. showed himself to be a poet of great versatility, capable of switching from the prosaic and minimalist to the deeply fanciful with equal skill.

His status was underlined with the publication of *Barbarians* (1979), which is both elegant and technically superb, and *St. Kilda's Parliament* (1981), a volume of verse dominated by his homeland, in which a more mature vision of love, art, and modern politics is accompanied by a tighter rhythmic structure. In *Europa's Lover* (1982), a brave extended poem only seventy lines shorter than T. S. ELIOT's *The Waste Land*, D. creates a visionary piece from European history and aesthetics; at once serious and whimsical, it is a respectful celebration of Europe which nevertheless recognizes its mistakes and terrors, and ends in a commemoration of the victims of concentration camps.

Elegies (1985), an unflinching collection of poems written after the death of his wife from cancer at thirty-seven, is perhaps D.'s most widely known work. From the diagnosis of the illness, through harrowing grief and an aching sense of loss, to a redemptive celebration of their relationship, *Elegies* is an assured collection from a poet working at the height of his powers and from the depths of his emotions; it is a consummate embodiment of Kierkegaard's belief that while art may begin with a scream, it must translate that scream into music.

After *Northlight* (1988), which is set in Scotland, Italy, Australia, and France, D. published his most self-consciously experimental collection, *Dante's Drum-Kit* (1993); drum kit is D.'s name for "terza rima," the form that supplies him with the structure for "Disenchantments," a meditation on the afterlife. While the book occasionally lapses into linguistic playfulness for its own sake, it is a dazzling display of technical adroitness that still has room for moving poems on the plight of the underdog.

Two volumes appeared in 2000: *The Year's Afternoon* and *The Donkey's Ears*; the latter, which relates the story of the Russian Baltic fleet that set sail from St. Petersburg in 1905 and voyaged halfway round the world, only to be crushed by the Japanese Imperial Navy, is clever, lyrical, and enlightening. Told through verse letters, secretly written by the flag engineer on board one of the ships to his wife, the narrative catalogues the squalor and frustrations of life aboard ship in a skillful portrait of a man caught in the destinies of progress, history, and geography.

D. has written two volumes of short stories, *Secret Villages* (1985) and *Boyfriends and Girlfriends* (1995), both of which show a sharp and tolerant eye for human foibles and a beautifully controlled balance of dialogue and description. He is the author of many screenplays, and the editor of *The Faber Book of Twentieth Century Scottish Verse* (1992) and *The Oxford Book of Scottish Short Stories* (1995); his translation of Jean Racine's *Andromaque* appeared in 1990.

BIBLIOGRAPHY: Crawford, R., and D. Kinloch, eds., *Reading D. D.* (1992); Warner, V., "D. D.," in Sherry, V. B., Jr., *Poets of Great Britain and Ireland since 1960*, part 1, *DLB* 40 (1985): 103–9

NICOLA UPSON

DUNN, Nell [Mary]

b. 4 June 1936, London

D. contributed to several notable developments in British culture in the post-World War II period, particularly the focus on inner-city working-class lives and the innovation of television documentary-drama. One of the few women involved in advance of the Women's Movement, she pioneered the open representation of active female sensuality. While remaining true to her idiosyncratic feminist vision, she has worked collaboratively with male creative artists such as the television and film director, Ken Loach, and the poet, Adrian Henri. Her career as an author has traversed a variety of popular forms, from the episodic novel to children's fiction like *The Incurable* (1971), from plays to collections of interviews like *Talking to Women* (1965). This may be why her work has not gained due scholarly recognition. An exception is the feminist critical debate over her stage play, *Steaming* (1981). Her writing tackles issues of serious social concern with simple sincerity. Unpretentious and frequently bleak, it is marked by startling moments of sensuous joy. As Margaret DRABBLE noted, these have a "bodily source" that suggests amenability to analysis as *écriture féminine*.

In 1982, D. took part in Anthony Clare's radio series, *In the Psychiatrist's Chair*. The interview elicited connections between her literary aesthetic and her family background, especially her traumatic early childhood. She talked there of "the idea of deep contact between people being ultimate bliss, being whatever is known as heaven to me" and she makes her writing a plea for such contact, for people to recognize that "we're all in this together, let's share our experience." Born into a wealthy, upper-class family, with a working-class nanny, D. was evacuated to the U.S. with only her sister during World War II while still a toddler. She eventually received psychiatric help for the shock. Reared a Catholic and convent educated, she left school at fourteen and was married by twenty-one. In 1959, searching for warmth and spontaneity, she crossed the River Thames from Chelsea to Battersea with her first child and became a member of the local female community, working in a factory. It was her vignettes of life there, some originally published in *New Statesman*, which became *Up the Junction* in 1963. This *succès de scandale* detailed not only closely observed coarse dialogue but also gleeful sexual freedom and a resultant abortion, without moralizing. Loach adapted the book for television, an early example of his documentary approach; it was filmed by Peter Collinson in 1967. That same year, D. followed this success with the novel *Poor Cow*, which Loach helped her to script for a cinema film. The heroine, pointedly called Joy, is a working single mother who, despite economic hardship, freely enjoys her sensuality and emotional relationships, particularly with her baby. Both books were republished in 1988 as Virago Modern Classics. A sequel to *Poor Cow*, *My Silver Shoes*, appeared in 1996. Another, similar "Joy" figures in D.'s nonfictional reportage, *Grandmothers* (1991).

Steaming was first performed in 1981 at Joan Littlewood's Theatre Royal in the working-class East End of London, with Brenda Blethyn as Dawn. The play has an all-female cast portraying eight women who meet regularly on women's day at a local municipal baths. In this safe, intimate space they gradually reveal their lives to each other, growing in self-confidence. Although they lose the public fight to save the baths from being redeveloped by the council, they gain each other's esteem and a mutual sense of self-worth. The play in effect shows a women's consciousness-raising group in process, tackling taboo issues such as wife beating, child abuse, and sex for gain. What was particularly revolutionary was that the group is also shown breaking down barriers of class and age to win their personal battles. The audience is invited to share in one special moment of bliss when Dawn, a working-class girl who has been drugged and silenced since being abused as a child, finally takes off all her clothes; she paints her body and triumphantly gallops around the stage in delighted self-abandon, to the admiration of the others.

The influential feminist theater critic, Helene Keyssar, instanced the play as an example of work produced in commercial theaters and heralded as feminist by "mainstream critics and spectators," but that was "not authentically feminist." The play was too reminiscent of conventional drama by men, with "familiar female types." She has grudgingly admitted that, in its final image, *Steaming* captures women's power from mutual support and praised the play for its focus on mature women. However, she found that the later West End and Broadway productions of the play titillated members of the audience, turning them into "voyeurs of women's secret worlds rather than participant-observers." Trevor R. Griffiths echoed this judgment: *Steaming* presented "the acceptable face of female dramatic creativity" open to recuperation by "reactionary perspectives" in commercial theaters. Agreeing that the play turned the audience into eavesdroppers and voyeurs, he judged it "sentimental" and criticized it for leaving the characters trapped in male control. Elaine Aston claimed that the play achieves "no radical transformation of women's lives," fails to subvert the male gaze, and is typical of bourgeois FEMINISM for its inability to engage with radical critiques of class and gender. Yet Joseph Losey's 1985 film version demonstrates that commercially successful productions of the play need not encourage voyeurism.

The major feminist champion of the play has remained Michelene Wandor. She has praised the play's "basic radical feminist dynamic" that celebrates the variety of women's lives, while criticizing its "secondary dynamic" as "feminine" for leaving women dependent on male authority and reinforcing voyeurism. Despite the play's "profound contradiction" between women's solidarity in resistance and their dependent vulnerability, she acclaims *Steaming* for asserting women's right to self-chosen sexuality. Theater audiences are, of course, gendered. Like all eavesdroppers, men may hear little good of themselves; women, on the other hand, may be encouraged by the risks taken on stage. Henri rightly pinpoints such "psychic risk-taking" as central to D.'s work. Her oeuvre is unified by her documentary approach to the fundamental women's issue of reconciling the rearing of children with women's need for sexual ful-

filment and personal development that might, as she says, result in "singing the private joys of life."

BIBLIOGRAPHY: Clare, A., *In the Psychiatrist's Chair* (1984); Drabble, M., introduction to D.'s *Poor Cow* (1988): xi-xviii; Wandor, M., *Post-War British Drama: Looking Back in Gender* (2001)

CLAIRE M. TYLEE

DUNNETT, Dorothy [Halliday]

25 August 1923, Dunfermline, Fife, Scotland; d. 9 November 2001, Edinburgh, Scotland

One of the most popular writers of historical fiction in the second half of the 20th c., D. turned to writing after a successful career as a portrait painter. She published her first novel, *The Game of Kings* (1961), at age thirty-eight and remained productive for nearly four decades. *The Game of Kings* initiated the six-volume "Lymond Saga," set in 16th-c. Scotland, which included *Queens' Play* (1964), *The Disorderly Knights* (1966), *Pawn in Frankincense* (1969), *The Ringed Castle* (1971), and *Checkmate* (1975). Simultaneously, D. began a series of suspense novels, published in Britain under the name Dorothy Halliday. In 1986, D. published *Niccolo Rising*, the first novel in the eight-volume "House of Niccolo" series, which ended with the publication in 2000 of *Gemini*. In 1992, D. was made an Officer of the British Empire for services to literature.

DUNSANY, [Edward John Moreton Drax Plunkett] Lord

b. 24 July 1878, London; d. 5 October 1957, Dublin, Ireland

Although D. 's career parallels the Irish literary renaissance, his connections with it are ambiguous. Known today as a writer of fantasy fiction, D. was an outspoken unionist, conservative in both literature and politics. He was the eighteenth baron, whose castle in County Meath had been in the family with one short intermission since 1190. D. spent most of his childhood in Kent, went to Eton and Sandhurst, joined the Coldstream Guards in 1899, and served in the Boer War. Indifferent to formal education, he was fond of cricket, hunting, and chess. Following the war, D.—who had succeeded to the title in 1899—settled in Meath, where he hunted extensively and organized cricket matches. Eventually, he hunted big game in Africa and in 1938 played a close but losing match with Alexander Alekhine, the world chess champion. In 1904, he married Lady Beatrice Child-Villiers, and their son, Randal was born in 1906. He served in the army throughout World War I, partly in France, partly in the War Office, and partly in Ireland, where he was wounded and captured fighting against the rebels of

1916. During World War II, he served in the Home Guard. D. believed poetry should deal with elevated, inspiring, and heroic subjects, and in the 1950s he and Stanton A. Coblentz were part of a small, ineffectual minority attacking modern poetry as mundane, sordid, defeatist, and obscure.

Although he published six volumes of poetry and a translation of the odes of Horace, he owes his reputation to fantasy fiction and plays. His first collection of fantasy stories, *The Gods of Pegana*, appeared in 1905, and his play, *The Glittering Gate*, written at the instigation of W. B. YEATS, was produced successfully at the Abbey Theatre in 1909, followed in 1911 by the equally successful *King Argimenes and His Unknown Warrior*. Both these plays were collected in *Five Plays* (1914); both were published separately in 1917. He had written four additional collections of fantasy tales when *Selections from the Writings of Lord Dunsany* (1912), with a Yeats introduction, was published by the Cuala Press. For reasons never adequately explained, he became estranged from Yeats and Lady GREGORY, but remained on good terms with George William RUSSELL, James STEPHENS, and Oliver St. John GOGARTY. Later plays, *A Night at an Inn* (1916) and *The Queen's Enemies* (perf. 1916; pub. 1923), were received enthusiastically in the U.S. but tepidly in the British Isles.

Forty of D.'s more than fifty volumes are fantasy. There is a progression from short tales about invented gods to stories about humans and to the longer structures of the novel in the 1920s, although the story remained his favorite form. Until the 1930s, his works were set in imaginary places or places having nothing in common but their names with real ones. Later works such as *Up in the Hills* (1935) and *The Story of Mona Sheehy* (1939) were set in Ireland and others in actual but exotic locations. The moderate reception of his work was enhanced by *My Ireland* (1937) a popular travel book. In *The Travel Tales of Mr. Joseph Yorkens* (1931), he invented the drunken club-man who spun tales through four later volumes. As D. himself remarked, *Patches of Sunlight* (1938), *While the Sirens Slept* (1944), and *The Sirens Wake* (1945), his three volumes of autobiography, are limited as self-revelation.

D. is known as a founder of fantasy fiction whose techniques are still imitated. He invented gods and heroes with names that felt classical, and he developed an archaic style, given to heavy use of parallelism and coordination, with descriptions that seemed wistfully otherworldly. Fantasy and SCIENCE FICTION writers such as H. P. Lovecraft, L. Sprague de Camp, and Arthur C. CLARKE honor him as a predecessor. His works are marked by paradox and irony rather than profundity. In his recurrently popular *The King of Elfland's Daughter* (1924), for example, citizens of Erl ask for magical rulers, only to have their kingdom overrun by magic. Though D.'s work had been nearly forgotten, recent attempts at revival have proved successful. Fourteen of his titles are currently in print.

BIBLIOGRAPHY: Amory, M., *Biography of Lord D.* (1972); Joshi, S. T., *Lord D.* (1995); Littlefield, H., *Lord D.* (1959)

DALTON AND MARYJEAN GROSS

D'URFEY [or DURFEY], Thomas
b. 1653, Devon; d. 26 February 1723, London

Songwriter, satirist, and playwright, D. was famous for his scandalous and scurrilous life and works. A celebrity, he counted both kings Charles II and James II among his circle. His comedies are mainly of a contemporary interest, being in large measure clever commentaries on current events. For example, his *Campaigners* (1698) was written in reaction to Jeremy Collier's *Short View of the Immorality and Profaneness of the English Stage* (1698), published that same year. Spurred by Collier's pamphlet, D. was prosecuted, but the effects of Collier's objections were not long lived. Alexander POPE wrote a foreword to D.'s *Modern Prophets* (1709). A prolific songwriter, D. wrote over five hundred songs, some of his lyrics being set to music by Henry Purcell, notably "The Yorkshire Feast Song." It has been claimed for D. that he paved the way for the style of sentimental comedy that followed. D.'s *Wit and Mirth, or, Pills to Purge Melancholy* (6 vols., 1719–20) remains a significant collection of popular song of the late 17th and early 18th cs.

DURRELL, Lawrence
b. 27 February 1912, Julundur, India; d. 7 November 1990, Sommieres, France

Eldest child of an English engineer working in India, and an Irishwoman, D. as an adult identified a tension between "English" and "Irish" in his own personality. The former stood for sober responsibility, but also dullness and emotional repression. The latter was linked with poetry and music, the imagination and feelings. He styled himself "A child, a poet, a drunken Irishman," and it has been asserted that Ireland was to him more a state of mind than an actual country. It is obvious that he saw his creative writing as a manifestation of "Irishness." Other but similar antitheses run through D.'s work. He pits Christianity against Taoist philosophy (*A Smile in the Mind's Eye*, 1980), or classical mythology. Against death, spiritual or physical, D. asserts the possibility of rebirth (*Clea*, 1960). He describes the "English death," a gloomy attitude that flourishes in England (*The Black Book*, 1938), while rebirth is typically depicted in a Mediterranean setting. These conflicts between various opposites proved extremely fertile, and one could not properly understand D.'s oeuvre without an awareness of his attempts to reconcile them.

D. was sent to an English public school, St. Edmund's. Although he was not unhappy there, he rebelled against conventional Christian practices by constructing small altars, one to Aphrodite, goddess of love, another to Apollo, god of poetry (among other things). When D.'s father died prematurely, the surviving family members went to England. D.'s mother gave him a regular allowance as long as she was able. But she also had to support herself and three younger children. A mixture of economic reasons and precocious literary ambitions precluded D.'s attending university.

He became a published author very early: his first offering, *Quaint Fragment*, a chapbook of poetry, appeared in 1931, when he was only nineteen. *Pied Piper of Lovers*, his first novel, was published in 1935, *Prospero's Cell*, his first work of nonfiction, in 1945.

D.'s relatively slow rise to fame may have been due to the fact that he seldom lived in Britain, and therefore was regarded as an outsider in British literary circles. But he also rushed several rather immature books into print, something he was to regret. Later, he seemed reluctant even to mention some of his earliest poetry collections, and to this day there is some disagreement among scholars as to how many of these there actually were. He also referred to *Pied Piper of Lovers* as "the shit novel." Artistically and commercially, it turned out to be a flop: his second work of fiction, *Panic Spring* (1937), was published under the pseudonym Charles Norden, as his reputation at that time was felt to be tarnished. However, this was D.'s first book brought out by Faber, London, which became his regular publisher.

In 1934, D. persuaded his mother and siblings to move with him to Corfu. He was never to reside permanently in Britain again. Instead, he chose to live in Greece, Egypt, the south of France (Provence), and elsewhere. His long stay in Corfu (until 1940) was documented in *Prospero's Cell*.

D. started corresponding with American author Henry Miller, who became something of a mentor and father figure to him. *The Black Book*, his first important novel, is clearly inspired by the American author's frank treatment of sex. But D. could not be pigeonholed as a Miller disciple: D. was much more interested in literary form and style, and his fiction is considerably less marred by sexism. While T. S. ELIOT praised *The Black Book*, this was chiefly on stylistic grounds. Its first English edition appeared in Paris because of British censorship. Not until 1973 was an unexpurgated edition published in Britain.

After the outbreak of World War II, D. fled from Greece to Egypt, where he worked as a press attaché and a columnist, among other occupations. He would claim that he had spent his happiest years in Rhodes; he found employment there as a newspaper editor after the war. In Cyprus, he taught English and served as a British government official during the Enosis struggle in the 1950's. His "island trilogy"— *Prospero's Cell, Reflections on a Marine Venus* (1953), and *Bitter Lemons* (1957)—is set in Corfu, Rhodes, and Cyprus, respectively. His more substantial, award-winning *The Greek Islands* appeared only in 1978.

D.'s talent, even in his works of prose, always had a marked lyrical slant. He gained recognition as a poet with several Faber collections: *A Private Country* (1943), *Cities, Plains and People* (1946), *On Seeming to Presume* (1948), *The Tree of Idleness* (1955), *Selected Poems* (1956). Although these are basically avant-garde in style, D., with George BARKER, Louis MACNEICE, and others, ironically found himself representing mainstream British poetry.

In 1957, D. moved to Provence because he thought it resembled Greece. This year has been called his literary annus mirabilis: *Justine*, a novel, was published as the first volume of the *Alexandria Quartet*, soon to make him world famous. Also *Bitter Lemons* was brought out to general acclaim; it won the Duff Cooper Memorial Prize. *Balthazar* (1958), *Mountolive* (1958), and *Clea* completed the *Quartet*. *Justine* won D. the French Prix du Meilleur Livre Etranger.

It is almost a cliché in D. scholarship to point out the emphasis on place in his work. One of D.'s special skills was the description of landscape; as a novelist, he relied on atmosphere rather than plot. His characters in the *Quartet* are presented as mere functions or "exemplars" of that city. One poem by D. is, characteristically, called "Deus Loci" ("God of the place"), and a collection of his travel writings bears the title *Spirit of Place* (1969), edited by Alan G. Thomas.

D. came too late to be part of the first generation of anglophone modernists, such as Eliot, James JOYCE, and Virginia WOOLF. However, in another sense D. was too early. The relativity of truth is a major theme in the *Quartet*. Different versions of the same characters, scenes, and events are juxtaposed, and D. leaves key questions unanswered in order to make a metaphysical statement. If the *Quartet* had appeared twenty-five years later, most such devices would no doubt have been categorized as postmodernist.

The first three novels of D.'s *Quartet* treat of time past, but not chronologically. Only in *Clea* does he permit his narrative to unfold into the fictitious future. D. stated that he intended the *Quartet* to illustrate Albert Einstein's four dimensions, with *Clea* standing for that of time. He also wrote short stories, mostly humorous, in the spirit of P. G. WODEHOUSE, but based on his own experiences as a diplomat. Several collections of these hilarious stories appeared; the earliest one is *Esprit de Corps* (1957).

D. composed three verse plays during a period when the genre had become fashionable, largely thanks to the example set by Eliot. D.'s *An Irish Faustus* (pub. 1963; perf. 1966) is a strikingly original version of the well-known legend. His Faustus finds salvation by retiring to the mountains and becoming a kind of Taoist sage. Margaret, corresponding to Goethe's Margareta (Gretchen), is Faustus's disciple and successor, rather than an innocent girl exposed to the conventional trauma of seduction and betrayal. And Mephistopheles never personifies absolute evil—an example of D.'s hostility to Western antithetical ways of thinking.

The heroine of *Sappho* (pub. 1950; perf. 1959) appears to have little in common with her historical namesake. Quite improbably in psychological terms, D.'s Sappho eventually turns into a ruthless warlord. Although *Acte* (perf. 1961; pub. 1965), set in imperial Rome, feels uninspired and slackly written, all three plays proved very popular in Germany. *Sappho* has also been successfully produced in Edinburgh (1961) and Evanston, Illinois (1964).

An often overlooked aspect of D.'s work is his commitment to Eastern philosophy and what may be loosely characterized as esoteric wisdom. Faustus is not the only Durrellian character to become a sage similar to those in Taoist tradition. Fangbrand in a poem of the same name and Ruth in an early novel, *The Dark Labyrinth* (1958; first pub. as *Cefalû*, 1947), are two other cases in point. Gnosticism serves as a leitmotif in D.'s *Avignon Quintet* (1975–85).

Tunc (1968) and *Nunquam* (1970), known together as the "Revolt of Aphrodite," were the first novels D. wrote after his resounding success with the *Alexandria Quartet*. Almost inevitably, they disappointed many of his admirers. He complained, with some justification, that his "double-decker" had been misunderstood. Often seen as apolitical, modernist, and "difficult," D. moves in *Tunc* and *Nunquam* startlingly close to a left-wing position. Both novels convey and imply some devastating criticism of global capitalism, particularly the arts market.

In his *Avignon Quintet*, D. similarly, but on a larger scale, criticizes Western civilization. Mingling Marxist and Freudian theories, he regards the industrialized world as stuck at a neurotic "anal" stage. Profits equal excrement, and it is as unhealthy to get enthusiastic about the former as the latter. Structurally, D. uses a Chinese box technique in the *Quintet*: there are narratives within narratives, and mind-boggling encounters between a novelist and one of his fictional characters, another novelist—both, of course, created by D., a third novelist.

To sum up, his favorite themes include place/landscape, love, art, time, death, rebirth, and wisdom. In addition, he had a predilection for Gothic motifs, such as gloomy castles, hidden treasure, madness, and

vampires. However, he normally treats them ironically and playfully. Motifs from classical mythology are also prevalent: Aphrodite, in various (dis)guises, haunts his imaginary worlds. D.'s style is so lush as to have been called baroque, and occasionally dismissed as not really "British." Perhaps for this reason, he has been more admired in Canada, France, Germany, and the U.S. than in Britain. As a poet, he has been compared to W. H. AUDEN, but D. possessed a keener eye, and a better ear for musical qualities. He was the most versatile and prolific of authors, and it is possible that these characteristics, too, clashed with British preferences. There is hardly a literary genre that D. never tried.

Sometime in the 1970s, D.'s reputation began to suffer a long eclipse from which it has not yet wholly recovered. This might be connected with the fact that his fame reached its zenith during a period when novelists and playwrights of different persuasions were emerging in Britain—the "angry young men," followed by several, more or less left-wing writers. Unlike D., they tended to accept the conventions of literary REALISM. But certain straws in the wind—notably two extensive D. biographies published in the second half of the 1990s—seem to indicate a renewed interest in D.'s work.

BIBLIOGRAPHY: Bowker, G., *Through the Dark Labyrinth: A Biography of L. D.* (1996); Fraser, G. S., *L. D.* (1968); Friedman, A. W., *L. D. and the Alexandria Quartet* (1970); Moore, H., ed., *The World of L. D.* (1962); Raper, J. W., et al., eds., *L. D.* (1995); Roxman, S., "The Making of a Goddess," in Johausson, G., ed., *The Making of a Goddess* (2001)

SUSANNA ROXMAN

DYER, [Sir] Edward

b. October 1543, Weston Zoyland; d. May 1607, London

A courtier, venture capitalist, Protestant nationalist, and intimate friend of Sir Philip SIDNEY, D. was, by all accounts, a gentleman of good taste and, for a period of time, a court favorite and benefactor of Queen ELIZABETH I. As one of the earliest English lyricists, D. earned high praise from Thomas NASHE as a writer and singer of his poetry. Despite his courtly popularity, most of D.'s work was little known outside the royal court. However, his best-known ballad, "My Mind to Me a Kingdom Is" (1575), which originally appeared in William Byrde's collection, *Psalmes, Sonnets, and Songs* (1588), struck the fancy of the people, becoming one of England's most popular songs for twenty years—though few knew who composed this popular lyric. Unfortunately, the majority of D.'s material has failed to survive, and his surviving work has been obscured by critical neglect.

In Elizabeth's era, the royal court was a place of high energy, drama, and intrigue. Historians point out that after the medieval baronial houses declined in dominance and before parliament ascended to full prominence, Elizabeth and her ministers ruled England. Consequently, England's most gifted and affluent convened at the court to compete for her attention and to serve at her discretion as part of her sovereign audience. Although the Queen supported and funded courtly entertainment, court life was not a place for mere idle play. Elizabeth made great efforts to consolidate autocratic power by developing relationships with her courtiers and by choosing her most trusted courtiers to fill her professional and diplomatic staffs. D. probably entered Elizabeth's court in 1565–66 as an apprentice through the influence of Robert Dudley, Earl of Leicester. Soon thereafter, D. spent most of his literary efforts as a courtier writing and performing his verses, often presenting them as gifts to his friends and to the queen. D. well understood that the lyrical arts were not just about creating pleasant entertainment. The lyrical arts were a political and social necessity. Courtiers understood that their good fortune was contingent on forming alliances with other noblemen and developing good relations with the queen. Great demonstration of wit, eloquence, and intellect were necessary characteristics of a favorable courtly ethos. Because of his loyal service, D. at the age of twenty-six won from the queen the stewardship of the manor and property of Woodstock, a palatial estate built by Henry I. However, the precariousness of court life and the fickleness of the queen plunged D. out of royal favor for a period of time—although why is unknown. In this time, he wrote "The Song in the Oak" specifically for the queen. When Elizabeth visited Woodstock on a retreat, he presented this lyrical poem and won back her favor. Soon thereafter, he regained some political status and received an exclusive license as a tanner of leather in 1576.

In his literary life, D. acquired a reputation as a benefactor of letters, but he spent the majority of his leisure time writing and reading poetry. Quite often, D., Sidney and Sir Fulke GREVILLE read and sang their works together and composed companion pieces for each other's works. This poetic fellowship grew to include Samuel DANIEL, Abraham Fraunce, Mary Herbert, Countess of PEMBROKE, Nicholas Breton, and a young Edmund SPENSER. Even though gentlemen were expected to have skills in dance, music, and verse, the aesthetic value of courtly lyrics was quite fleeting in the earlier part of Elizabeth's reign. Although courtly lyrics had their social and political uses beyond entertaining a select audience, they were often treated as transitory treats, lyrics for the moment, lyrics offered for a dance or in praise of a guest—lyrics to beautify a courtly society. Though D.

probably kept a notebook of his songs or wrote his verses in his commonplace book, he made no apparent attempt to preserve or publish his writing. As a result, many of his works are obscured or have been lost. Literary scholars note that D.'s lyrical efforts achieved a serviceable poetic convention: D. preferred the iambic foot; he composed normally in six lines and favored ballads and hymns. His rhetorically influenced lyrics made for easy memorization and recitation because his poetic style was suited for song and dance. Although D. had the talent to achieve poetic simplification and clarity, his style was also meant to reflect the modes and manners of address preferred by his aristocratic audience. Unfortunately, there is great difficulty in cataloging how many songs he wrote due to any number of works wrongly ascribed to him. Scholars have ascribed thirteen compositions to D. "The Song in the Oak" and "My Mind to Me a Kingdom Is" are his best known, but D.'s "Elegy on the Death of Sidney" (1593), a poem attributed to D. long after his death, is his most touching.

Critics have noted that poems of this era were stiff, lacked vigor, and resisted experimentation. Although these critical observations may be valid when compared to later Elizabethan poems, most of D.'s formulaic lyrics—which favored certain rhetorical tropes and schemes—were suited for memorization and singing. Lyrics from Elizabeth's early era often suffer from critical neglect because modern critics have a tendency to treat these lyrics as textual objects. D.'s lyrics—as with most songs—follow the psychodynamics of oral transmission. For instance, his fluid words and rhythmic patterns were meant to be carried from voice to ear—not from script to eye. The true value of D.'s work is found in its aural presence combined with the physical performance of his work. Courtly lyrics enlisted the aid of the senses to achieve their intended effects as an instrument of ethos. We can only imagine how D. performed his verses in the presence of his audience. Unfortunately, all that we have are his words. D. used poetic structure and language suited for a 16th c. listening audience, but his allegiance to the economies of the lyrical and rhetorical arts makes his songs congenial to a modern audience.

BIBLIOGRAPHY: May, S. W., *The Elizabethan Courtier Poets* (1991); Sargent, R. M., *At the Court of Queen Elizabeth: The Life and Lyrics of Sir E. D.* (1935)

DAVID CHRISTOPHER RYAN

DYER, John
b. August? 1699, Aberglasney, Wales; bur. 15 December 1757, Coningsby

D.'s topographical poem "Grongar Hill" (1727) celebrates the River Towy in D.'s native Wales and is considered a forerunner of the Romantic attitude to landscape. An earlier version had appeared in a miscellany published by the poet Richard SAVAGE in 1726. In 1740, D. published *The Ruins of Rome*, a six-hundred-line poem in the Miltonic manner. D.'s poem *The Fleece* (1757) describes in four books the care of sheep, shearing and preparation of wool, weaving and the manufacture of woolen goods. It has occasioned some mockery, but has its defenders, among them such diverse authors as William WORDSWORTH and Margaret DRABBLE.

EARLE [or EARLES], John
b. ca. 1601, York; d. 17 November 1665, Oxford

Fellow of Merton College, Oxford, later to become Bishop of Worcester in 1662 and Bishop of Salisbury in 1663, E. wrote the witty work entitled *Micro-cosmographie; or, A Peece of the World Discovered in Essayes and Characters* (1628; rev. eds., 1628, 1629, 1633), which ran to ten editions in E.'s lifetime. It analyzed varied social and moral types, ranging from the countryman to the poet. The most complete edition (1633) consists of seventy-eight characters—only two of which are women—beginning with "The Child" and ending with "A Suspicious or Jealous Man." E. was praised by Izaak WALTON who compared him to Richard HOOKER for his "innocent wisdom" and his "peaceable, primitive temper."

EDGAR, David
b. 26 February 1948, Birmingham, Warwickshire

"I'm realizing this as I speak: if I have a 'grand subject' it's not so much about socialism as socialists." E.'s comment, in an unpublished interview, signals the interlinking of personal and political, private and public concerns that animates his dramatic writing over the past three decades. E. is typically described as the chronicler of the mixed fortunes of the left in the tumultuous post-1956 period, and he is best known for large-scale plays on "public" themes. While such observations indicate his abiding interest in ideology—the "grand narratives" of modern European political history, they overlook the distinctive qualities of his theater: that is, formal diversity—a preoccupation with the impact of large-scale structures of power on individual personality, and, latterly, a sympathetic engagement with the travails of the former Soviet bloc.

E.'s early plays, written for socialist touring companies such as Bradford University's Drama Group and the influential General Will, are agitational and propagandist, responsive to topical issues such as the industrial militancy of the early 1970s. They link contemporary subject matter with established popular forms, and deploy comic techniques of ironic reversal and cartoon parody to provoke as well as entertain. *Tedderella* (perf. 1971) is a camp mock-pantomime critiquing Britain's entry into the Common Market; it features Edward Heath as the unlikely heroine whose Ugly Sisters—played, in the original production, by drag queens impersonating prominent Labour members of Parliament—try to prevent her from attending the Common Market Ball. *Rent; or, Caught in the Act* (perf. 1972) pastiches the form of Victorian melodrama to bemoan the deleterious effects of the Housing Finance Act on the beleaguered Harddoneby family. Among the most theatrically inventive of E.'s many plays from this period is *Dick Deterred* (1974), a subversion of *Richard III* in which President Richard Nixon is cast as the conniving monarch.

E.'s studied rejection of agitprop in the mid-seventies coincided with a changing political climate in Britain and a related desire, on E.'s part, to embrace complexity in his work. His first play for the Royal Shakespeare Company, *Destiny* (1976), inherits its episodic structure from agit-prop but embraces the documentary aspiration of social realism. *Destiny* controversially accounts for the structure of feeling that gives rise to fascism and contextualizes this in terms of the contemporary British experience (the play focuses on a by-election in the fictional town of Taddley). British imperial decline is established as a key issue—the opening scene is set during Independence Day in India, 1947—but strict chronology is avoided: scenes jump backward and forward in time to properly illuminate the social forces and situations that produce the range of attitudes espoused by the four central characters. *Destiny* is notorious for setting out the social conditions in which fascism flourishes, and for its refusal to demonize those who join the far-right "Nation Forward" party in the play. *Maydays* (1983; rev. ed., 1984), in contrast, critiques the ideological left. The play is panoramic in historical scope—spanning twenty-five years—and counterpoints the experience of three generations of socialist defectors within the wider framework of revolutionary activity and, ultimately, disillusionment. Both of these plays are landmarks in postwar British theater.

The imperatives of social realism surface again in two of E.'s adaptations from the seventies: *The Jail Diary of Albie Sachs* (1978) and *Mary Barnes* (perf. 1978; pub. 1979). Both identify, as E. puts it, "paradigmatic figures" within representative social contexts and trace the contours of isolation brought on by solitary confinement and madness, respectively. Arguably, E.'s most famous play is his adaptation of a Charles DICKENS novel, *The Life and Adventures of Nicholas Nickleby* (perf. 1980; pub., 2 vols., 1982). Staged to enormous acclaim by the RSC, it deploys processes of theatrical distancing and alters Dickens's finale to levy a potent critique of Thatcherite social exclusion. His other successful adaptations include *The Strange Case of Dr. Jekyll and Mr. Hyde* (perf. 1991; pub. 1992; rev. ed., 1996), E.'s reworking of Robert Louis STEVENSON's novel, and *Albert Speer* (2000), inspired by Gitta Sereny's biography of the same name.

A triptych of E.'s plays meditates on the formation of the "New Europe," triggered by the collapse of the Berlin Wall in 1989 and the subsequent meltdown of the Soviet empire. *The Shape of the Table* (1990) is set in "a baroque palace in an Eastern European country." In the play, politicians negotiate the revolutionary changes affecting their country while the diplomatic table itself becomes a motif for the possible configurations that may transpire. *Pentecost* (1994) begins as a cultural "whodunit," with a curator and art historian discussing a fresco inside an ancient church in southeastern Europe. It is suggested that this masterpiece, demonstrating advanced techniques of perspective, could revolutionize understanding of Western art history. Prior to the ending of act 1, however, the church itself is invaded by a motley collection of armed refugees who take the other characters hostage. This startling structural upheaval refocuses audience attention on issues of narrative, language, and cultural exchange in Europe, and the problematic nature of "freedom" in the hegemonic West. E.'s recent work, *The Prisoner's Dilemma* (2001), takes place in the fictional ex-Soviet republic of Khavkhazia that is now rife with escalating internecine conflict. The series of labyrinthine negotiations staged in the play illuminate the frustrations of diplomatic and humanitarian work in which the West itself is culpable.

E. is cofounder of the Theatre Writers Union (1975); a former literary adviser (1984–88) and, later, honorary associate (1988) of the RSC, and is responsible for establishing and teaching the first postgradu-ate playwriting course in the United Kingdom (at the University of Birmingham, 1989; he was appointed Britain's first Professor of Playwriting in 1995). E. is also a respected essayist and commentator on the politics of culture (a lively collection of his work is published in *The Second Time as Farce*, 1988).

BIBLIOGRAPHY: Page, M., and S. Trussler, eds., *File on E.* (1991); Painter, S., *E. the Playwright* (1996); Swain, E., *D. E., Playwright and Politician* (1986)

                                        CHRIS MEGSON

EDGEWORTH, Maria

b. 1 January 1768, Blackbourton, Oxfordshire; d. 22 May 1849, Edgeworthstown, Ireland

As much educational theorist as prolific writer of children's books and adult novels, praised and at times imitated by Sir Walter SCOTT, Jane AUSTEN, and William Makepeace THACKERAY, E. is remembered as the author who reintroduced believable children into literature, as an experimenter with stream of consciousness, and the first regional novelist in British literature. E. and her father, Richard Lovell Edgeworth, whom she assisted in teaching her twenty siblings, have been compared to Johann Heinrich Pestalozzi. Her earliest stories were written to entertain, amuse, and inform her brothers and sisters.

E. produced nine children's books, many of them running to two or three volumes. Besides this body of writing, she produced voluminous fictional writing, which began with *Letters for Literary Ladies* (1795) and her novel most read by contemporary audiences, *Castle Rackrent* (1800), the first serious fictional treatment of Irish peasants and among the earliest family-history novels tracing the development of a family through several generations.

Living on her father's estate in Edgeworthstown, County Longford, Ireland, from her fifteenth year, 1782, until her death in 1849, and helping to manage these properties, she became keenly aware of Irish peasantry. Her Irish fiction, for which she is best known, is centered in *Castle Rackrent* and three other novels, *Ennui* (1809) and *The Absentee* (1812), both published as part of E.'s *Tales of Fashionable Life* (6 vols.,1809–12) and *Ormond* (1817), published with *Harrington, a Tale* (1817) in three volumes.

E.'s Irish fiction had a profound effect upon the development of the novel in Britain. Although she was technically not the equal of Austen, E. was a more influential novelist. Critics acknowledge that the social novel originated by Fanny BURNEY in the 18th c. became a permanent literary form because of E., who modeled her *Belinda* (3 vols., 1801) on Burney's *Evelina* and who explored and expanded in her writing the themes that enticed 18th-c. novelists.

E.'s feminist ideas were radical for her day. She scorned the upper-class female herd instinct that expects women to conform to the social views of the men who dominate them. Ever using her novels as a means of teaching moral lessons rather than merely as entertainment, E. called for women to receive an education of the heart that would cultivate their emotions and moods. These qualities are emphasized in such novels as *Belinda, Leonora* (2 vols., 1806), and *Helen* (3 vols., 1834). E.'s heroines are not bent on finding husbands, as were most of the fictional heroines of her day, but were devoted instead to achieving self-fulfillment through knowledge.

Her concern with the status of women did not divert E. from considering the roles of men in society. *Vivian* (1812), *Patronage* (4 vols., 1814), and *Harrington*, focus on such matters as the civic duties and responsibilities that are the lot of males. In *The Absentee*, she strays into a controversial area by highlighting how absentee landlords shamelessly exploit the peasants maintaining their properties.

A close observer of the people around her, E. was superb in shaping believable and memorable characters. Among her unforgettable women are Lady Delacour in *Belinda* and Lady Davenant in *Helen*, who make indelible impressions upon readers. E. also demonstrated a marked ability to communicate with children by reducing complex ideas to lucid, understandable information. As an older sibling in a family of twenty-one children, she gained infinite practical experience communicating with young people.

Following her father's death in 1817, E. was faced with huge responsibilities. She managed her father's properties and was involved in the lives of her siblings. Immediately after Richard's death, she turned to the task of completing his memoirs, which appeared in two volumes as *Memoirs of Richard Lovell Edgeworth, Esq.; Begun by Himself and Concluded by His Daughter, Maria Edgeworth* (2 vols., 1820*)*.

Throughout her life, E. was an innovator. She established the social novel as an enduring literary genre. She made a social impact both for her feminist views and for her penetrating social and economic perspectives. She was versatile in her use of language, writing easily for children but demonstrating equal ease with sophisticated adult audiences. She captured authentically the vernacular speech of Irish peasants in her Irish novels and stories. Her contributions to literature, applauded by literary figures during her lifetime, have had a lasting impact.

BIBLIOGRAPHY: Butler, M., *M. E.* (1972); Harden, E., *M. E.* (1984); Kowaleski-Wallace, E., *Their Fathers' Daughters: Hannah More, M. E., and Patriarchal Complicity* (1991)

R. BAIRD SHUMAN

EDWARDS, Richard
b. ca. 1523, Somersetshire; d. 31 October 1566, Oxford

Playwright and musician, E. was a scholar of Corpus Christi College, Oxford. Appointed as master of the children of the Chapel Royal, he entered Lincoln's Inn in 1564, where at Christmas he produced a play acted by his choirboys. On September 3, 1566, E.'s now-lost play, *Palamon and Arcite*, was performed before Queen ELIZABETH I in the hall of Christ Church, Oxford. His play *Damon and Pythias* (perf. 1564) appeared posthumously in 1571. Tragic in theme, it contained farcical scenes. Sir John HAWKINS credited E. with the part song "In going to my Lonely Bed" and the fine poem "The Soul's Knell" is said to have been written by E. when dying.

EGAN, Pierce
b. 1772, London; d. 3 August 1849, London

Best remembered for *Life in London*, published serially in 1820 and in book form in 1821, which describes the day and night adventures of "Corinthian Tom," a young man about town, his country cousin Jerry Hawthorn, and their Oxonian friend Bob Logic. The young men frolic through society from a royal palace to the lowest dives. Discursive, allusive, and entertaining, the book is remarkable as a record of Regency life and the slang of the day, some annotated. E. contributed to the 1823 edition of Francis GROSE's *Classical Dictionary of the Vulgar Tongue*. With illustrations by George Cruikshank, *Life in London* became so popular that the artists who hand-colored the prints could not satisfy the demand. It was so successful it spawned numerous forgeries and plagiarisms. In 1822, the printer James Catnach published a broadside called "Life in London or the Sprees of Tom and Jerry" showing a dozen episodes from the story, each with a verse and crude black and white copies of the exquisite original pictures. Catnatch shamelessly claimed copyright. Dramatized versions played to packed houses in Britain and in the U.S. As well as attending cockfights and dogfights and a racecourse, Tom and Jerry go for lessons in boxing to the famous John ("Gentleman") Jackson, among whose real-life pupils was Lord BYRON.

In 1818 came *Boxiana*, an expert account of all the notable pugilists and their matches. E.'s weekly newspaper, *Life in London and Sporting Guide*, first appeared in 1824. In 1814, E. wrote, set, and printed with his own hands a book of 144 pages entitled *The Mistress of Royalty: or, The Loves of Florizel and Perdita,* about the Prince Regent (later King George IV) and the actress Mary ROBINSON. Despite this satire, the Prince accepted the dedication of *Life in London* and E. was presented at court.

William Makepeace THACKERAY recalled E.'s book with affection in his paper on Cruikshank in the *Westminster Review* (June 1840), noting that Tom and Jerry had been as popular in the 1820s as "Mr. Pickwick and Sam Weller now are." The humorous writer Jerome K. JEROME at the end of the century described the student prank of stealing a hansom cab as "the acme of Tom and Jerryism." "Tom and Jerry" became a stock phrase, surviving as the name of punch made from hot rum and eggs, and of the popular animated cartoon series.

BIBLIOGRAPHY: Sales, R., "P. E. and the Representation of London," in Martin, P. W., and R. Jarvis, eds., *Reviewing Romanticism* (1992): 154–69; Schlicke, P., "The Pilgrimage of P. E.," *JPC* 21 (Summer 1987): 1–9

VALERIE GROSVENOR MYER

EGERTON, George

(pseud. of Mary Chavelita Dunne) b. 1859, Melbourne, Australia; d. July 1945, Ifield Park, Crawley, Sussex

Taking as pseudonym the name of her first husband, George Egerton Clairmonte, E.'s first volume of short stories, *Keynotes* (1893), with a jacket by Aubrey Beardsley, attracted attention, and a second, *Discords* (1894), brought an invitation to contribute to the *Yellow Book*. Two more collections of short stories followed, *Symphonies* (1897) and *Fantasies* (1898), and two novels, *The Wheel of God* (1898) and *Rosa Amorosa: The Love Letters of a Woman* (1901), in which E. looks forward to a bright future for the "New Woman." Influenced by Henrik Ibsen and August Strindberg, she translated the novel *Hunger* by Knut Hamsun in 1920 from Norwegian.

ELIOT, George

(pseud. of Mary Ann, later Marian, Evans) b. 22 November 1819, Arbury, near Nuneaton, Warwickshire; d. 22 December 1880, London

E. is now indubitably the most highly regarded 19th-c. woman writer. Her work was highly acclaimed in her own lifetime, but went out of fashion toward the end of the Victorian period and only commenced on the road to critical recovery with the publication in 1948 of F. R. LEAVIS's highly influential *The Great Tradition*, which placed E. in a tradition of novelists whose concerns are to eschew "complacent confusions of judgement" but whose texts are "distinguished by a vital capacity for experience, a kind of reverent openness for life, and a marked moral intensity." Gordon S. Haight's publication of nine volumes of E.'s letters (1954–78) formed the indispensable base of modern critical scholarship. Barbara Hardy's

critical work *The Novels of George Eliot: A Study in Form* (1959) rescued E. from the criticism that she was not a great formal artist that had previously undermined her reputation by demonstrating that her novels gratified "the formal pleasure in balance and opposition and unity, and at the same time present its intellectual and moral analysis of men and societies." From this point, the E. critical industry has shown no signs of abating; whatever new fashion in literary theory arises, the richness of her texts never fails to offer opportunities for new readings.

Although reared in an Anglican and Tory voting home, E.'s desire for friendship led her to engage with a group of Coventry intellectuals, centered around Charles Bray's house, Rosehill. They were radical in politics and dissenters or free-thinkers in religious terms. One of them, Charles Hennell, had written *An Enquiry into the Origins of Christianity* (1838), which contributed to the undermining of her religious faith. By 1841, she no longer regarded Christianity as a divinely revealed religion, but accepted Hennell's view of Jesus as a Jewish philosopher, human not divine. The Unitarians, in particular, were committed to promoting German "Higher" criticism as part of a political campaign against the Anglican establishment. Her first major assignment as a professional writer was to translate the German theologian David Friedrich Strauss's *Das Leben Jesu* into *The Life of Jesus, Critically Examined* (3 vols., 1846). Her second foray in this field was her translation of Ludwig Feuerbach's *Das Wesen Christenthums* as *The Essence of Christianity* (1854). Feuerbach's philosophy influenced both her personal morality and her narrative methodology: as she wrote to a friend "speculative truth begins to appear but a shadow of individual minds, and we turn to the truth of feeling as the only universal bond of union." In her practice as the writer of fiction, she was to insist that the full complexities of individual human experience must be taken into account; empirical philosophies that left individual subjectivities out of their accounts she regarded as inadequate models. She disliked any philosophy that appeared "to consider the disregard of individuals as a lofty condition of mind."

In June 1846, E. started writing a series of articles for Bray's radical periodical, the *Coventry Herald*. She adopted the persona of an elderly eccentric man (a persona she was to take up once more in her last published work, *Impressions of Theophrastus Such*, 1879). This brought her into contact with John Chapman who bought the *Westminster Review* in 1851 and appointed E. as its (anonymous) editor while he remained the public face of the periodical. Founded by James Mill and Jeremy BENTHAM in 1824 as a Radical review, it was an intellectually heavyweight quarterly committed to parliamentary reform and addressed issues such as education and women's rights. The magazine suited her interests and talents, and increased her range of friends, including her long-term partner, George Henry LEWES. In addition to editing numerous issues, she contributed a number of very fine essays and reviews. These, along with other journalistic writings, were collected in a useful edition by Thomas Pinney in 1963.

Although we may now tend to see E.'s translations and journalistic work as the apprenticeship for her career as a novelist, these polemical writings are interesting in themselves as well as the opportunity for identifying themes that would appear in her novels. Considerations of the history of religion, a condemnation of the intolerance of evangelicalism, and an enquiry of how women should write are obvious examples. She herself was anxious not to swell the ranks of ladies producing "silly novels," yet neither did she assume that a woman could become a great writer by simply imitating male writers, a procedure she sardonically symbolizes by reference to "the old story of La Fontaine's ass, who put his nose to the flute, and, finding that he elicits some sound, exclaims, '*Moi, aussi, je joue de la flute.*'"

Lewes, himself a writer and editor, was the perfect partner; throughout his life, he acted as her literary agent and negotiated all contracts with publishers. The fly in the ointment, however, was that he was unable to obtain a divorce from his wife under contemporary divorce laws, even though she had borne two children fathered by his friend. The first published fiction were three tales that appeared anonymously, as was usual in periodicals in the first half of the 19th c., in *Blackwood's Magazine*; even John Blackwood himself was in ignorance of the identity of the author. When they were later reprinted as *Scenes of Clerical Life* (2 vols., 1858), however, a signature needed be attached, and together E. and Lewes chose the now famous pseudonym so that her work might receive a fair critical hearing. The choice of "George" was homage to the woman writer she most admired, George Sand (the pen name of Baronne Dudevant), and indicated a commitment to write about ordinary, often rural people, without condescension, but to engage with their moral problems in an entirely serious way.

Scenes of Clerical Life was well received and encouraged her to write her first full-length novel, which also drew closely on her memories of her early life in Warwickshire. *Adam Bede* (3 vols., 1859), set at the time of the Methodist revival, was sensationally popular with library readers, although its success brought with it an unexpected problem, in that authorship was attributed to a certain Joseph Liggins, who chose not to deny authorship. The consequence was that George Eliot was "outed," and her work attracted, as a consequence, some hostile reviews. *The Lifted Veil* (1859), a tale of clairvoyance—unusually for her, told autobiographically—may fictively express some of her horror at the predicament of perceiving the animus against her.

The Mill on the Floss (3 vols., 1860) was published to great acclaim and confirmed E.'s standing as a novelist of the first rank; the skill with which she had analyzed "the interior of the mind" meant her work was compared favorably to that of Emily BRONTË and Jane AUSTEN. The portrayal of an intense and painful brother-sister relationship was much admired, although there were some critical objections to the near seduction of Maggie Tulliver by Stephen Guest in the third volume. E. herself, as she was "living in sin," was not socially accepted by respectable women, although her closest woman friend, Barbara Leigh Smith Bodichon, the leader of the organized women's movement usually called the Langham Place Group, continued to encourage her personally and was a major influence on E.'s thinking on the woman question.

Silas Marner: The Weaver of Raveloe (1861) is the closest she comes to one of Sand's *bergeries* and its deceptively simple form (like Sand's) belies its radicalism. E.'s sympathy is with the people who have "done the rough work of the world"; as she said: "in this world there are so many of these common coarse people, who have not picturesque sentimental wretchedness! Therefore let Art remind us of them . . . your common labourer, who gets his own bread, and eats it vulgarly but creditably with his own pocket-knife." Many critics have dismissed *Silas Marner* as merely a fairy tale, or charming divertissement. There is, as Q. D. LEAVIS has expressed it, a "multiple typicality about Silas Marner"; E. described him as a member of "a disinherited race," disinherited both by the effects of the industrial revolution and by fundamental evangelicalism.

E.'s next major project was a story of 15th-c. Florence, *Romola* (3 vols., 1863), and can perhaps best be described as a fairly honorable defeat, despite the fact that it earned her more money than any other novel as Lewes negotiated an unprecedented offer of £10,000, which included serializing it in George Smith's *Cornhill Magazine*. Despite E.'s intensive research, the characters never come to life as she cannot realistically "translate" her excellent ear for the patterns of English speech into mock-Italian dialects. Nevertheless, its interest lies in her fictive examination of the democratic experiment inspired by Savonarola's preaching, which continued beyond his martyrdom, as much in the cause of liberty and as in that of religion.

Not surprisingly, her next major novel, *Felix Holt, the Radical* (3 vols., 1866), examines the political situation in England at the time of the 1832 Reform Bill reconstructed in the light of the second Reform Bill of 1866. As usual, E. uses "dissent" in its religious and political incarnations to enable her to question the old order. The Tory aristocracy is clearly represented as incapable of evolutionary change and therefore doomed to extinction. Gillian Beer's *Darwin's Plots* (1985) is a key critical text in unpacking the significance of Darwinian theory to the imagination of 19th-c. novelists, including E. The limits of E.'s political radicalism are, however, often indicated by the closure of her narratives, when the need for change becomes incompatible with the need for continuity.

Middlemarch: A Study of Provincial Life (8 parts, 1871–72), a panoramic fictional account of the life of the English provinces before the Reform Bill, has always been considered E.'s masterpiece. It was recognized as such immediately. R. H. Hutton's review in the *Spectator* (February 12, 1876) drew attention to the central role in this novel of E.'s aspirations for women: "She cannot bear to treat them with indifference. If they are not what she approves, she makes it painfully, emphatically evident. If they are, she dwells upon their earnestness and aspirations with an almost Puritanical intensity that shows how eagerly she muses on her ideal of a woman's life." The centrality of the woman question to this novel, however, was not to be taken up again until the mid-1970s, when feminist critics started to reread her texts, discussing the limitations (or otherwise) of her FEMINISM. It is considered her masterpiece because here, most successfully, she re-created a recognizable community in fiction, which created a community of feeling in her readers. Suzanne Graver's critical work *George Eliot and Community: A Study in Social Theory and Fictional Form* (1984) maps how E.'s developing aesthetic, always predicated on social concerns, reaches its apogee in *Middlemarch*.

E.'s last novel, *Daniel Deronda* (8 parts, 1876), the only novel not set back in time, has met with an obstinate critical resistance to recognizing her deliberate doubling of the social oppression of women and Jews, despite her desperate protest: "I meant everything in the book to be related to everything else." Both of her protagonists have to come to an identification with their own community by means of an understanding of gender politics and their relation to political history. F. R. Leavis argued that "there is no equivalent of Zionism for Gwendolen"; yet clearly there is, and that is her identification with other women, which is the first stage in the development of feminist theory and practice.

E. published only two volumes of verse in her lifetime, *The Spanish Gypsy* in 1868 and *The Legend of Jubal and Other Poems, Old and New* in 1874, although many of the epigraphs that serve as chapter headings in her novels *Felix Holt, the Radical, Middlemarch*, and *Daniel Deronda* are by E. herself. In her poetic works, E. seems often to grapple with emotional difficulties and conundrums not fully resolved in her fiction, as though the poetry functions as a par-

allel text to the novels. One such anxiety was that her own ambition, which she described as "a desire insatiable for the esteem of my fellow creatures," might be a selfish rejection of the ordinary lot of women. Her poem "Armgart" (1871) dramatizes the case of a famous opera singer, who in the triumph of her exceptional talent has despised the common fate of her gender, and is punished for it. This poem crystallizes anxieties about female ambition circling around singers (Caterina, Rosamond, Gwendolen) and performers (Mirah, Alcharisi) who figure in her novels. *The Spanish Gypsy*, an EPIC narrative set in 15th-c. Spain, rehearses arguments about political identity, leadership, and the role of women, which she goes on to work out more thoroughly in *Daniel Deronda*.

E.'s last published work, *Impressions of Theophrastus Such*, was an experimental departure from the genre of the novel that has been largely ignored by 20th- c. criticism. It is neither a novel nor a short story, yet it is still a fictional work. Still less is it a collection of essays in E.'s voice. It consists of eighteen chapters supposedly narrated by a 19th-c. English bachelor. E. adopts the persona of an irascible middle-aged man who is, unlike herself, a failed author (perhaps a discreet dig at the unfortunate Liggins). The only link between the chapters is that each continues a debate on the relationship between community and its individual members. Its last and longest chapter, "The Modern Hep! Hep! Hep!," was preoccupied with Jewish culture and deplores English Christian prejudice against Jews and other peoples. Arguably, her last and certainly most experimental work is the least examined and the most unpopular.

BIBLIOGRAPHY: Beer, G., *Darwin's Plots: Evolutionary Narrative in Darwin, G. E., and Nineteenth-Century Fiction* (1985); Graver, S., *G. E. and Community: A Study in Social Theory and Fictional Form* (1984); Haight, G. S., ed., *The G. E. Letters* (9 vols., 1954–78); Hardy, B., *The Novels of G. E.* (1959); Hirsch, P., *Barbara Leigh Smith Bodichon, 1827–1891: Feminist, Artist and Rebel* (1998); Jenkins, L., ed., *Collected Poems: G. E.* (1989); Pinney, T., ed., *Essays of G. E.* (1963); Rignall, J., ed., *The Oxford Reader's Companion to G. E.* (2000)

PAM HIRSCH

ELIOT, T[homas] S[tearns]

b. 26 September 1888, St. Louis, Missouri, U.S.A.; d. 4 January 1965, London

Critic, poet, and playwright, E. has earned a unique position of authority among 20th-c. writers. Beginning in 1920, he directed the course of literary criticism for approximately two decades. Although his poetic output was relatively modest, *The Waste Land* (1922) is regarded as the century's most influential poem, and *Four Quartets* (1943) is discussed as the century's equivalent to John MILTON's *Paradise Lost*. His five plays have been cited as landmark attempts to revive the tradition of verse drama. During his lifetime, E. was awarded the Nobel Prize for Literature, the Dante and Goethe medals, the Order of Merit, the French Legion of Honor, and the United States Medal of Freedom. American poet Karl Shapiro once commented, "Eliot is untouchable; he is Modern Literature incarnate and an institution unto himself."

E. was born into an established family that judged itself by its accomplishments. In 1834, his great grandfather graduated from Harvard Divinity School and moved to St. Louis where he later founded the city's first Unitarian church and Washington University. E.'s father became a prominent St. Louis businessman as president of the Hydraulic-Press Brick Company, and his mother, devoted to social service, helped reform the Missouri juvenile court system. E. entered Harvard in 1906 and completed his undergraduate degree in three years. He studied ancient classics, read Dante and John DONNE, became friends with Conrad Aiken, and edited the *Harvard Advocate*. In 1908, he came upon Arthur SYMONS's book *The Symbolist Movement in Literature*, which he said changed the course of his life. Influenced by the works of Charles Baudelaire and Jules Laforgue, E. discovered that the squalid aspects of industrialism could serve as raw material for his poetry.

Before finishing his master's degree in English literature, E. enrolled in Irving Babbitt's course on French literary criticism of the 19th c. Babbitt, a conservative thinker, preached classicism in art and encouraged E. to study Eastern philosophy and religion. E. traveled abroad in October 1910 and immersed himself in Parisian intellectual life: he was tutored by Alain-Fournier at the Sorbonne, attended lectures by Henri Bergson at the University of Paris, and was drawn to the social theories of Charles Maurras. After Paris, he visited London and Munich before entering the Harvard Graduate School. E.'s time abroad had been useful, for by November 1911 he had completed the best poems to be included in his first volume, *Prufrock and Other Observations* (1917). For his doctorate, E. pursued a degree in philosophy, and Josiah Royce, William James, George Santayana, and Bertrand RUSSELL influenced him considerably during his graduate school years. Awarded a Sheldon Traveling Fellowship, E. planned to spend 1914–15 in Marburg, Germany. When World War I broke out, he went to England and became a member of Merton College, Oxford.

E. married in 1915, and after teaching school for two years, he became assistant editor for the *Egoist*, of which Ezra Pound was the literary advisor. That same year he also accepted a position in the Colonial and Foreign Department of Lloyd's Bank in London.

Through his close friendship with Pound, E. came to know many prominent literary figures including W. B. YEATS, James JOYCE, Virginia WOOLF, and Wyndham LEWIS. After establishing himself as a contributor to the *Athenaeum* and the *Times Literary Supplement*, he was appointed London correspondent for the *Dial*. E. founded his own quarterly in 1922, and for the next seventeen years, he aimed for the *Criterion* to be "a living embodiment of the mind of Europe." E. joined the publishing firm of Faber and Gwyer (now Faber & Faber) in 1925, and two years later, he became a British citizen and a member of the Anglican Church. When he died, "the Age of Eliot" seemingly drew to a close.

E. established himself as a literary critic in his first two collections, *The Sacred Wood* (1920) and *Homage to John Dryden* (1924). "Tradition and the Individual Talent" (1919), E.'s most famous essay, centers upon the relationship between the modern writer and his precursors. E. argues that individual works of art are important only in relation to great works in the past and present and that tradition, thus, is ever evolving. A serious writer must, he contends, develop an historical sense that will permit composition "with a feeling that the whole of literature of Europe" is in his bones. With respect to individual talent, E. rejects direct expression of emotion and favors an "impersonal theory of art" whereby the writer continually escapes from personality to engage with the work to be done. Written at the same time as "Tradition and the Individual Talent," in "Hamlet and His Problems" (1919), E. sets out to adjust the ranking of William SHAKESPEARE's plays by describing *Hamlet* as an "artistic failure." He criticizes Shakespeare for being unable to present an "objective correlative," that is "a set of objects, a situation, or a chain of events," that will serve as the "formula" for Hamlet's tangled emotions. Making a brash claim, E. stresses that emotion must exist within a work of art and cannot be inferred by speculating about what the artist, in this case Shakespeare, might have been feeling. In "The Metaphysical Poets" (1921), E. furthers his view of tradition by claiming that the metaphysical poets were more in the "direct current" of English poetry than previous critics had credited them for being. Moreover, he finds in Donne, Andrew MARVELL, and George HERBERT a "direct sensuous apprehension of thought" that elevates them above subsequent writers who have been burdened by a "dissociation of sensibility." In his later collections, *The Use of Poetry and the Use of Criticism* (1933), *After Strange Gods* (1934), *The Idea of a Christian Society* (1939), and *Notes towards the Definition of Culture* (1949), E. presses forward Christian orthodoxy as a means toward achieving a "higher" culture.

E.'s poetry can be divided into three periods: the first coinciding with his years at Harvard and culminating in *Prufrock and Other Observations*; the second coinciding with his personal exhaustion and culminating in *The Waste Land*; and the third coinciding with his religious conversion and culminating in *Four Quartets*. As the title of E.'s first volume indicates, several of his early poems are meant as impersonal "observations" of people and city scenes. The speaker in "Portrait of a Lady," for instance, tells of his encounters with an older woman during the course of a year, his attendant moods being carefully marked by the changing of seasons. In truth, E. offers two objective portraits for study. The first being that of an aging woman hoping to entangle a younger man in a web of greater intimacy, and the second being that of an egotist depicting himself as a victim of coldhearted banality. The polite drawing room game between the two will do neither lasting harm, for the world provides many distractions—Chopin's music, the latest events, lilacs in bloom—from insincerity. "The Love Song of J. Alfred Prufrock," E.'s most important early poem, mixes historical and cultural allusions with tawdry images of urban life to accentuate themes of modern malaise. Presented as a dramatic monologue, "Prufrock" compares an evening social gathering to a descent into Dante's eighth circle of hell, a chasm where false counselors are seared by their fraudulent words and deeds. A well-dressed specimen of upper class society, Prufrock fears being misunderstood by those who are indifferent to any emotion beyond the placid surface of things. Although he disdains superficially, he "murders and creates" himself for the occasion, playing the part others have assigned to him. Being too weak to act against those circumstances—sexual or otherwise—that humiliate him, Prufrock is self-critical to a fault and has come to symbolize emotional paralysis.

Following *Prufrock*, E. published *Poems* (1920) in the U.S. and *Ara Vos Prec* (1920) in England, their contents being nearly identical. *Ara Vos Prec* includes E.'s quatrain poems and "Gerontion," the latter being a dramatic monologue that he once considered including as a prelude to *The Waste Land*. Written between 1917 and 1919, E.'s quatrain poems reflect both his reading of Théophile Gautier's *Emaux et Camées* and his conviction that *vers libre* had run its experimental course. E. employs a structured form in these poems, the octosyllabic quatrain being one of the great traditions of 17th-c. English verse, yet his personae continue to be detached recorders of contemporary scenes ranging from sexual corruption, as in "Burbank with a Baedeker: Bleistein with a Cigar," to murderous intrigue, as in "Sweeney Among the Nightingales."

E. was busy in the years leading to *The Waste Land*. Between 1917 and 1920, he published two collections of critical essays and three collections of verse. In addition to his literary pursuits, Lloyd's had put him in charge of settling all pre-World War I debts with its German clients. And on a more personal level,

his wife gave in to severe depression after learning that her father had fallen ill. Near exhaustion, E. was forced to take a three-month leave of absence from his bank duties. While recuperating in Lausanne, Switzerland, he completed the final sections of a new long poem, various segments of which he had already passed along to Pound. In the months that followed, E. deferred to Pound's editorial suggestions, and *The Waste Land* was first published in the October 1922 issue of the *Criterion* and then in the November 1922 issue of the *Dial*. E. described *The Waste Land* as "the relief of a personal and wholly insignificant grouse against life," but it quickly became the most talked about poem of its day. E.'s far-reaching symbols and allusions added a throng of knowledge about literature, anthropology, philosophy, and religion that seemingly had to be decoded for one to find the poem's meaning. Some critics were impatient, others were not. While Louis Untermeyer flatly declared *The Waste Land* "a pompous parade of erudition," Pound, prejudicially, hailed it as "one of the most important 19 pages in English." Despite decades of contradictory opinions about the poem as a unified work of art, critics agree that on its most fundamental level *The Waste Land* is about human longing and the quest for meaning in a world disconnected from any divine purpose. The poem's five sections comprise a plurality of voices, yet those voices express a unified perspective about modern life: Western civilization is disintegrating into a sterile land of deadening routine. In his "notes" appended to the book editions of the poem, E. acknowledged his indebtedness to *The Golden Bough* by Sir James FRAZER and *From Ritual to Romance* (1920) by Jessie L. Weston for providing him with a "mythic method" through which he could structure a journey toward spiritual regeneration.

E. was received into the Anglican Church in 1927, and from that time forward, his poetry changed from depicting the despair of contemporary life to depicting a personal journey toward faith. As a poet who never repeated himself, E. composed *Four Quartets* between the ages of forty-seven and fifty-four, and he considered them his major poetic achievement. The book's title points to its evocative musical form, each Quartet being comprised of five sections or "movements" that are carefully modulated to express repeated themes, a pattern that critics suggest E. derived from Beethoven. And just as surely as Beethoven strove to get to a place beyond music, E. strives in *Four Quartets* to get to a place beyond poetry. Given that the poem-cycle explores the intersection of time and eternity, each Quartet is titled after a place where E. had experienced some profound moment of illumination. "Burnt Norton" (1935) refers to a deserted English manor house and garden near the market town of Chipping Camden where E. stayed as a visitor in the summer of 1934, and while there, he glimpsed a divine moment of love's transforming power. "East Coker" (1940) refers to the Somerset village from which his ancestor Andrew Eliot, seeking religious freedom, emigrated to America in 1699. "Dry Salvages" (1941) refers to a group of rocks off the northeast coast of Cape Ann, Massachusetts, where E. went sailing as a young boy. It remained in memory for him a place where sea (endless time) and land (historical time) impinged upon one another. "Little Gidding" (1942) refers to the Huntingdonshire village where in 1625 Nicholas Ferrar established an Anglican religious community based on rules of personal faith. The village's church was partially destroyed by fire during the English Civil War, and E., mindful of this fact, conceived of "Little Gidding" while he was taking his turn as a nighttime fire watch during the bombings of London in World War II. E. has stated that each of the *Quartets* bears relation "to one of the four elements and the four seasons." In sequence, these elements appear first as air and spring, second as earth and summer, third as water and autumn, and fourth as fire and mid-winter. After divesting himself of all that he has been, E. arrives at a place of spiritual insight where the Word is made Incarnate. For him, faith, love, and wisdom emanate from and return to God as beginning and end.

E.'s interest in classical and liturgical drama had long been simmering before 1934 when E. Martin Browne invited him to collaborate on a religious pageant play to be produced on behalf of the Forty-Five Churches Fund of the Diocese of London. To this end, E. joined a Greek chorus to the pageant play, contributing verse passages wherein the chorus links various scenes depicting the literal and spiritual difficulties of building a church in the secular world. Although E. was discontent with the conditions under which he wrote the choruses for *The Rock*, conditions that he articulates in "The Three Voices of Poetry" (1953), the experience impelled him forward to more satisfying achievements in verse drama. In 1935, Browne commissioned him to write a religious play for the Canterbury Festival, and *Murder in the Cathedral* (1935), E.'s best play, was staged that year in the Chapter House where Thomas à Becket had been killed in 1170. E. presents Becket as a devout man who triumphs over temptation and avoids doing "the right deed for the wrong reason,"—becoming a martyr, that is, to secure eternal glory. By submitting his own will to God's will, Becket stands forth as a figure of divine incarnation.

Modeled upon Aeschylus's *Oresteia*, E.'s *The Family Reunion* (1939) was considerably less successful than his previous full-length play. Set on his estate in Northern England, Lord Monchensey (Harry) returns home after an eight-year hiatus abroad and tells his gathered relatives that he killed his wife during a voyage. Although Harry's chauffeur insists that her drowning was accidental, Harry believes he is being pursued by mythical Furies who seek to punish him for wishing her dead. During a psychological about face, he later conceives of these supernatural beings as friendly guides who might rescue him from a family curse. So he surrenders his estate in order to follow these "bright angels," his Eumenides, wherever they might lead. Neither tragedy nor comedy, *Family Reunion* is often criticized for failing to offer an explanation for Lord Monchensey's reparation.

Ten years elapsed before E. again turned to playwriting. In *The Cocktail Party* (perf. 1949; pub. 1950), religion infiltrates the world of drawing room comedy when a gin-drinking psychiatrist named Sir Henry Harcourt-Reilly conspires with two associates (collectively they are referred to as the Guardians) to help Edward and Lavinia Chamberlayne rejuvenate their failing marriage. Reilly fulfills his spiritual role by encouraging the Chamberlaynes to peel away the illusions they have of one another and "work out their salvation" to the best of their abilities. Reilly also interviews Celia Copleston, Edward's mistress, but he is unable to break through to her. Disillusioned with Edward and herself, Celia decides to become a nun, and while serving her calling on a tropical island, she is crucified and attains martyrdom. Whereas Celia chooses a destructive means for atoning for her sins, the Chamberlaynes choose a constructive means by seeking to rekindle, without illusions, their love for one another. *The Cocktail Party* enjoyed long runs in New York and London, becoming something of a milestone in the revival of poetic drama.

In *The Confidential Clerk* (perf. 1953; pub. 1954), E. draws on Euripides' *Ion* to weave an elaborate farce involving hidden paternity. Some twenty-five years before the present action begins, Sir Claude and Lady Elizabeth Mulhammer have each had an illegitimate child. Complications ensue when Sir Claude invites Colby Simpkins into his home as a replacement for his retiring confidential clerk, Mr. Eggerson. Predictably, Sir Claude and Lady Elizabeth each lay claim to Simpkins, who, in fact, is the son of a deceased musician named Herbert Guzzard. Under the protection of Mr. Eggerson, Simpkins escapes from the Mulhanners and pursues his dream of becoming a church organist, thus resolving all issues of inheritance and identity.

As a source for his last play, *The Elder Statesman* (perf. 1958; pub. 1959), E. drew upon Sophocles' *Oedipus at Colonus* to stress once again that redemption can be achieved by confronting the past. After a lifetime of imposing his will upon others, Lord Calverton, a retired but terminally ill business tycoon, finds sanctuary in a nursing home until two people whom he previously has wronged set out to blackmail him. A man of many sham identities, Calverton finally breaks free of self-deception, expresses love for his children, and goes serenely to his death. Without being dogmatic, E.'s plays throw light on the relevance of religion in contemporary human affairs. Although *The Cocktail Party* made him fashionable, *Murder in the Cathedral* has retained the most lasting interest of all of E.'s plays.

E. said of his favorite writer, Dante Alighieri: "He is a poet to whom one grows up over a lifetime." The same, of course, might be said of E., whose importance to modern literature cannot be overstated. Appropriately, two lines from "Little Gidding" are inscribed on E.'s memorial in Westminster Abbey: "The communication of the dead is tongued with fire beyond the language of the living."

BIBLIOGRAPHY: Bergonzi, B., *T. S. E.* (1972); Gardner, H., *The Art of T. S. E.* (1949); Gish, N. K., *The Waste Land: A Poem of Memory and Desire* (1988); Gordon, L., *E.'s New Life* (1988); Headings, P. R., *T. S. E.* (1964; rev. ed., 1982); Jones, D. E., *The Plays of T. S. E.* (1960); Kenner, H., *The Invisible Poet: T. S. E.* (1959); Margolis, J. D., *T. S. E.'s Intellectual Development, 1922–1939* (1972); Mathiessen, F. O., *The Achievement of T. S. E.* (1935; rev. ed., 1947); Raffel, B., *T. S. E.* (1982); Smith, G., *T. S. E.'s Poetry and Plays* (1956); Spender, S., *T. S. E.* (1976)

JOE NORDGREN

ELIZABETH I

b. 7 September 1533, Greenwich; d. 24 March 1603, Richmond

E. was the daughter of HENRY VIII and Anne Boleyn. She acceded to the throne in 1558 on the death of her elder sister, Mary Tudor. E. was educated by the eminent scholar and humanist Roger Ascham and his pupil William Grindal, and their tuition ensured that she was well-informed in matters of history, classical literature, and modern languages. Evidence of her linguistic facility may be perceived in her literary endeavors, both in terms of her original writing and her works of translation.

In 1544, as a child of about eleven years of age, E. translated the 13th Psalm into tetrameters. She also made a prose translation of Marguerite de Navarre's *Le Miroir de L'Âme Pécheresse* (*The Mirror of the Sinful Soul*), which she presented to her stepmother, Katherine PARR, as a New Year's gift. This work was printed in 1548 as *The Godly Medytacyon*. Another early translation, this time into verse, was of ninety lines from Petrarch's "Trionfo dell' Eternita," which is probably her most accomplished piece. Much later in life she translated Boethius's *De Consolatione Philosophiae* (1593), and Horace's "Ars Poetica" (1598). Boethius's work was the longest translation that E. attempted. Her version makes frequent use of alliteration, retains much of the Latinate word order of the original, and also contains numerous instances of mis-

translation; critics have attempted to excuse the latter by referring to the prodigious speed at which E. apparently worked (a point noted by her contemporaries).

E.'s original works include a collection of private prayers, *A Book of Devotions*, perhaps compiled in the 1570s. These most personal of her writings again demonstrate her linguistic dexterity as they are written in five languages: English, French, Italian, Latin, and Greek. E. also wrote original poems, though only six of those that have commonly been ascribed to her are now definitely thought to be genuine. The poems are short: all are under twenty lines in length, and three are merely brief epigrams. The poems known to be hers deal with actual events in her life, both political and personal. "The doubt of future foes" concerns her cousin, Mary Queen of Scots, and "On Monsieur's Departure" may refer to the breaking off of marriage negotiations with the Duke of Anjou in 1582 (though an alternative view is that the poem refers to an association with the Earl of Essex, E.'s favorite). Both these poems are characterized by frequent alliteration and rough meter, and are typical examples of mid-16th-c. lyrics. "When I was fair and young," a disquisition on the familiar carpe diem theme, is somewhat more fashionable in style; its sentiments, though commonplace, can be easily linked to E.'s refusal to marry.

Many of E.'s letters and about a dozen of her speeches also survive. The latter include her speech to the troops at Tilbury in 1588 as the Spanish Armada approached, and the "Golden" speech made to the last parliament of her reign in 1601. These two most famous speeches are particularly dramatic and direct; the rest more typically refer to her people's goodwill and security, and rely upon rhetorical features and a comparatively complex prose style. Her speeches were printed throughout the 17th c. and were widely distributed.

BIBLIOGRAPHY: Bassnett, S., *Elizabeth I* (1988); Bradner, L., ed., *The Poems of Queen Elizabeth I* (1964); Neale, J. E., *Queen Elizabeth I* (1934); Travitsky, B., ed., *The Paradise of Women: Writings by Englishwomen of the Renaissance* (1989)

MARGARET CONNOLLY

ELIZABETHAN LITERATURE

The principal characteristics of Elizabethan literature are its diversity and inventiveness, which were spread across not only the already traditional forms of poetry and drama, but the less securely established one of prose fiction. The building of the first theater—simply titled "The Theatre"—in 1576, rapidly followed by others like the Rose, the Swan, and, most famously, the Globe in 1599, led to an explosion of dramatic writing, with the relatively crude and relentlessly scatological Tudor interludes and short plays like Nicholas Udall's *Ralph Roister Doister* (perf. 1553; pub. ca. 1566) giving place to rapid increases in scope, length, and sophistication. The Jesuit priest Jasper Heywood, son of the Henrician playwright John HEYWOOD, published a number of translations of Seneca in the earliest years of ELIZABETH I's reign (1558–1603) and launched a vogue for bloodthirsty, ghost-haunted tragedy that was further fueled by *Gorboduc*, a collaboration by Thomas NORTON and Thomas SACKVILLE, which showed the dangers of civil war and was intended to convince the queen that she must marry. Thomas KYD's immensely successful *The Spanish Tragedy*, performed ca. 1585–90, featuring onstage ghosts, a feisty heroine, and a complicated play-within-the-play, inaugurated the genre of revenge tragedy, and though unsubstantiated Kyd may also have been responsible for an early version of *Hamlet*.

Kyd's lead was followed in plays such as Henry CHETTLE's *The Tragedy of Hoffman* and the anonymous *Locrine* (perf. ca. 1591; pub. 1595). These two plays together exemplify the two major tendencies of serious dramas in the period: either to set plays abroad, in increasingly exotic settings that can be seen as related to the growing importance of trade and adventuring—illustrated too by Richard HAKLUYT's *The Principal Navigations, Voyages, Traffiques and Discoveries of the English Nation*—or to channel material into history plays, such as those written by the young William SHAKESPEARE, which tended to draw either on material from GEOFFREY OF MONMOUTH or the MATTER OF BRITAIN or reigns of English kings as recorded in the chronicle of Edward HALL and the later *Chronicles* of Raphael HOLINSHED. Wherever the setting, though, all such plays turn a sharply anatomizing lens on contemporary society, as is indicated by the growing strictness with which they were policed and censored. The only non-royal story to receive prominent coverage in Holinshed's *Chronicles*, the murder of Master Arden of Feversham by his wife Alice, was also turned into an early, anonymous play, part of the lively but often ephemeral genre of domestic tragedy, the Elizabethan equivalent of the true-crime story—except that in Elizabethan terms, Alice's crime of husband-murder was "petty treason," a term that clearly signals the conception of the private household as a commonwealth in miniature that gave the doings of individual households a wide political and social resonance.

Perhaps the most famous of all the plays set abroad was Christopher MARLOWE's *Tamburlaine the Great*, performed in 1587. This also whetted still more the appetite for violence and bombast, and among writers eager to cater to this was Robert GREENE, whose *Alphonsus, King of Aragon* (perf. ca. 1588) and *Selimus* (perf. ca. 1591) both aspire (not altogether successfully) to the braggadocio of a Tamburlaine. Greene, however, did not confine himself to this vein alone; he wrote in a wide variety of styles and genres, not least because he always needed the money. He died young, impoverished, and in a mood of bitterness that he recorded in his *Greene's Groats-Worth of Wit*, published after his death by his friend Chettle, in which he expresses resentment against the success of Shakespeare, which he alleges to be due to the latter's pillaging of others' works. He wrote romantic comedies, histories, poetry, prose romances, of which the most famous, *Pandosto*, was used by Shakespeare as the source for *The Winter's Tale*, and, in the last year of his life, popular pamphlets that promised to reveal the truth about the highly active Elizabethan underworld. A similar versatility was shown by George PEELE, who wrote mythological plays, masques, pageants, poetry, biblical plays, the Tamburlaine-influenced tragedy *The Battle of Alcazar*, the history play *King Edward the First*, and the fantasy-comedy *The Old Wives Tale*. Chettle too was named as an excellent writer of comedies in Francis MERES's listing of contemporary authors in *Palladis Tamia*, but none survive.

Greene was much influenced by John LYLY, who wrote plays based on classical stories but is most famous for two works, *Euphues: The Anatomy of Wit* and *Euphues and His England*. The astonishingly elaborate style of these makes them difficult to read today, but in their day they had the distinction of making people take prose writing seriously, and the effects of this can be seen in works as diverse as Thomas LODGE's romance *Rosalynde: Euphues Golden Legacie*, written on a privateering ship to the Americas and a principal source for Shakespeare's *As You Like It;* Thomas NASHE's *The Unfortunate Traveller*, which has some claim to be seen as the first English novel; and Richard HOOKER's *Of the Laws of Ecclesiastical Polity*, of which the first book appeared in 1593. George GASCOIGNE's *The Adventures of Master F. J.*, printed in two versions (1573, 1575), is another early piece of prose fiction illustrative of the diversity of approach in the period, and the reign also saw the publication of the earliest of Francis BACON's *Essays* and a growth in interest in translation, principally but not exclusively of classical texts and of the Bible; George CHAPMAN published his famed translation of Homer in 1598. This was also an area that appealed to women, perhaps because it avoided the stigma sometimes attached to individual creation; Elizabeth I translated Boethius's *The Consolation of Philosophy* and Marguerite of Navarre's *The Mirror of the Sinful Soul*, and the Countess of PEMBROKE, sister of Sir Philip SIDNEY, translated Robert Garnier's *Antonie* and the Psalms.

The masterpiece of Elizabethan prose fiction is undoubtedly Sir Philip Sidney's own ambitious, popular, and hugely influential *The Countess of Pembroke's Arcadia* (1591), a complex and sophisticated romance that exists in two versions, the original *Old Arcadia* and the extensively revised new version that Sidney left uncompleted at his untimely death in 1587. Its apparently simple pastoral story of the love of Prince Pyrocles, who is disguised as the Amazon Zelmane, for the Arcadian Princess Philoclea, and that of his cousin Prince Musidorus, disguised as the shepherd Dorus, for her sister the Princess Pamela, is complicated by the many inset narratives, and by the richly ironic voice in which they are relayed. It was a favorite work of the period, and Charles I on the eve of his execution recited Pamela's prayer.

Sidney's achievement was by no means only in prose, however. His *Apologie for Poetrie,* which argues for a distinction between history—bound to facts and therefore inevitably uninspiring—and poetry—able to soar imaginatively and thus offer cultivated aspiration—remains a key theoretical tool for the understanding of Elizabethan and Jacobean literature, and the sonnet sequence *Astrophel and Stella*, together with the numerous inset poems in the *Arcadia*, make him one of the major poets of an age distinguished for the abundance and inventiveness of its poetry.

Sonnets had originated in Italy with Petrarch, and rapidly crossed Europe to arrive in England in the reign of HENRY VIII with the translations of Petrarch by Henry Howard, Earl of SURREY, and Sir Thomas WYATT. Both were prominent courtiers much involved in the tumult of Henrician politics; Surrey was a cousin of Anne Boleyn, and Wyatt had hoped to marry her. For them, as for the poets of the remainder of the century, poetry was not a private, ethereal activity but an essential part of the equipment and public image of a gentleman. Though both Elizabeth I and the Pléiade-trained Mary Queen of Scots also wrote verse, not until the next century would women of lesser rank, particularly Sidney's niece Lady Mary WROTH, produce a significant output. Sonneteering became a vogue, and the proliferation of sonnet-sequences by Sidney, Edmund SPENSER, Samuel DANIEL, Michael DRAYTON, and Shakespeare led to highly crafted poems in which small variations of meter or image assumed big significance; Sidney's Astrophel opens *Astrophel and Stella* by lamenting the popularity of the genre and the resulting difficulty of sounding fresh and authentic. The tightness of the form and its inherent restriction on the number of words available also led to much resort to ambiguity and wordplay, by means of which two (or more) meanings could be packed into one line or phrase, with the result that the typical sonnet richly repays detailed analysis.

The development and increasing popularity of entire sequences of sonnets also allowed for a rich vein of character development and psychological exploration, with the best of the sequences combining the expressive aid of meter with the pleasures and excitements of both narrative and drama. This exploitation of the potential for drama, together with the conscious artificiality of the form and the social pressures to produce it, mean that the sonnet enjoys the richly ambiguous position of being a poem ostensibly about emotions which is probably best read as very much the product of the head rather than the heart. Sidney's *Astrophel and Stella* may have been prompted by his own doomed love for Penelope Rich, sister of his friend the Earl of Essex, Elizabeth's last favorite, but it holds its protagonist at a comic distance, and Shakespeare is surely creating rather than confessing in the complex emotional delineations and verbal wizardry of his own sonnet sequence, with his famed negative capability at least as much in evidence there as anywhere in his plays.

The sonnet was not the only poetic form popular and widely used in the period. Lyric was also popular, appearing either as an integral part of a prose romance, as it does in the *Arcadia*, or in collections and miscellanies like Richard TOTTEL's of 1557, and few who have ever heard them are likely to forget Nashe's "Brightness falls from the air" or Marlowe's haunting "Come live with me and be my love." Pastoral, a richly resonant mode to Elizabethan minds because it was both Edenic and Arcadian, opening the doors to both a prelapsarian world and the lost ideal landscapes of that most culturally prestigious of art forms, classical literature, was a particularly popular source of inspiration. The highly flourishing state of Elizabethan music, with the prominence of several composers of genius, further stimulated the development of lyric.

The other major poetic genre practiced was the EPIC and its derivatives. The history of virtually all major European countries in the Renaissance is littered with translations into the vernacular of the classical epics, and unfinished or never-begun attempts to write new national ones. Spenser's *The Faerie Queene*, published in two installments in 1590 and 1596, was originally intended to reach the appropriate epic length of twelve books, but Spenser managed no more than six and a fragment before dying, allegedly of hunger because an ungrateful Elizabeth would not reward him for it. It is little read today because of the intensely complex nature of its allegorical representations of the queen and her policies, its numerous topical allusions, and its wild paranoia about the Irish (even more clearly exemplified in the prose dialogue *A View of the Present State of Ireland*, not published until after Spenser's death), but its imaginative scope and formal innovation, together with its deployment of Spenser's invention of the Spenserian stanza, make it one of the most notable achievements of its age. Less daunting in length, and therefore more widely attempted, was the epyllion, a short, erotic mini-epic, of which the most notable instances are Marlowe's *Hero and Leander,* published in 1598, and Shakespeare's *Venus and Adonis*. The epyllion combines lightly worn classical learning with exuberant vernacular verbal inventiveness and a mastery of tone and emotional range, and is thus perhaps the ultimate illustration of the distinctiveness and flexibility of narrative voice that allows so much of Elizabethan literature still to speak so clearly today.

BIBLIOGRAPHY: Braden, G., *Renaissance Tragedy and the Senecan Tradition* (1985); Comensoli, V., *Household Business: Domestic Plays of Early Modern England* (1996); Hamilton, A. C., et al., eds., *The Spenser Encyclopedia* (1990); Lever, J. W., *The Elizabethan Love Sonnet* (1966); MacQueen, J., *Allegory* (1970); Marinelli, P., *Pastoral* (1971); Pincombe, M., *The Plays of John Lyly: Eros and Eliza* (1996); Spiller, M., *The Development of the Sonnet* (1992); Waller, G., *English Poetry of the Sixteenth Century* (1986)

LISA HOPKINS

ELLIS, Alice Thomas
(pseud. of Anna Margaret Haycraft) b. 9 September 1932, Liverpool

E.'s works cover a wide range, including two cookbooks under Anna Haycraft *Darling, You Shouldn't Have Gone to So Much Trouble* (with Caroline BLACKWOOD, 1980) and *Natural Baby Food* (1985); two studies of the psychology of delinquency, coauthored with Tom Pitt-Aikens, *Secrets of Strangers* (1986) and *Loss of the Good Authority* (1989); as well as two volumes of essays critical of the post-Vatican II Catholic Church, based on her columns for *The Catholic Herald* during the 1990s: *Serpent on the Rock: A Personal View of Christianity* (1994) and *Cat among the Pigeons* (1994). During the late 1980s, she wrote a weekly column, "Home Life," for the *Spectator*; these personal sketches, which describe the seemingly unremarkable occurrences of family life in rural Wales but which also display E.'s acerbic wit, have been collected into four volumes: *Home Life* (1986), *More Home Life* (1987), *Home Life Three* (1988), and *Home Life Four* (1989). She has also contributed regular columns to *The Universe* (1989–1991) and most recently to *The Oldie* (1996 to present). E.'s memoir, *A Welsh Childhood* (1990), complemented by the black-and-white photography of Patrick Sutherland, weaves together anecdotes from the author's early life on the coast of North Wales with profiles of eccentric characters and the lore of the region.

E.'s most widely known work, however, is her fiction, which includes eight novels, a collection of short stories, *The Evening of Adam* (1994), and a trilogy of novellas, *The Clothes in the Wardrobe* (1987), *The Skeleton in the Cupboard* (1988), and *The Fly in the Ointment* (1989), published together as *The Summer-*

house Trilogy (1991) and which was adapted to film (*The Summer House*) in 1993. The trilogy documents the weeks leading up to the impending marriage of Margaret and Syl; each novella is narrated by one of the significant women: Margaret, Margaret's mother-in-law-to be, and Margaret's scandalous Aunt Lili. Highly comic with a strong moral undercurrent, the trilogy highlights the best qualities of E.'s fiction, including an economic rendering of character and dry, witty dialogue.

E., the fiction editor for the Duckworth publishing house in 1970, was a member of what came to be known as "The Duckworth Gang," which included Blackwood, Beryl BAINBRIDGE, and Patrice Chaplin. Their novels typically focus on contemporary British women at odds with their domestic milieux. For the most part, E.'s novels exemplify the "Duckworth style," but her work also contains strongly traditional Catholic and moral components. *The Sin Eater* (1977), given the Welsh Arts Council Award, chronicles the final days of a man whose family gathers around him. *The Birds of the Air* (1981), also given the Welsh Arts Council Award, explores the nature of grief and at the same time critiques the silliness of the English Christmas. *The Twenty-Seventh Kingdom* (1982), shortlisted for the Booker Prize, focuses on the deceptiveness of appearances, while *The Other Side of the Fire* (1983), is a study of unrequited love. *Unexplained Laughter* (1985), honored as the *Yorkshire Post* Novel of the Year, chronicles the adventures, both worldly and spiritual, of a woman who has come to Wales to recuperate from a failed love affair.

E.'s 1990 novel, *The Inn at the Edge of the World* (1990), which won the Writers' Guild Award for Best Fiction in 1991, describes five people who go to a remote Scottish inn to escape Christmas. *Pillars of Gold* (1992) shows the impact of a woman's disappearance on her neighborhood. E.'s recent novel *Fairy Tale* (1996) blends the real and the fabulous in a social comedy set in a remote Wales valley. A smart couple retreats there to escape urban life, to be confronted by strange and mysterious occurrences. E.'s novels are typically "short, edged comedies of human failure in the face of some ultimate good"; blending eccentricity with the transcendent, they explore the retreat from the quotidian and the confrontation with the mystical.

BIBLIOGRAPHY: Burgass, C., "A. T. E.," in Moseley, M., ed., *British Novelists since 1960*, Second Series, *DLB* 194 (1998): 113–19; Waugh, A., "A Modern Emma Woodhouse," *Spectator* 255 (August 31, 1985): 24–25

JUDITH E. FUNSTON

ELLIS, [Henry] Havelock
b. 2 February 1859, Croydon, Surrey; d. 8 July 1939, Hintlesham

Medically qualified, E. soon gave up general practice for literary and scientific work. *Sexual Inversion*

(1897; rev. ed., 1915), *Studies in the Psychology of Sex* (7 vols., 1900–1928), *The Erotic Rights of Women* (1918), and *Marriage Today and Tomorrow* (1929) made him notorious until his work, especially on dreams, was overshadowed by that of Sigmund Freud. E. edited the unexpurgated Mermaid edition of the Elizabethan dramatists and translated Émile Zola's *Germinal* from the original French and was an elegant essayist and popularizer of science. He was a friend of Olive SCHREINER, Edward CARPENTER, Arthur SYMONS, and Margaret Sanger, the pioneering advocate of birth control. His autobiography, *My Life*, appeared in 1939. Today, he is considered to have been a liberating influence, though his scientific accuracy has been questioned.

ELTON, Ben[jamin Charles]
b. 3 May 1959, London

E. has made a broad impact on contemporary culture, including standup comedy on stage and television, playing Verges in Kenneth Branagh's film adaptation in 1993 of William SHAKESPEARE's *Much Ado About Nothing*, and writing and co-writing award-winning television sitcoms (*Blackadder; The Thin Blue Line*), several stage plays—including, *Silly Cow* (perf. 1991; pub. 1998), and *Gasping* (perf. 1992; pub. 1998), the book of an Andrew Lloyd Webber musical about football and the Northern Ireland "Troubles" *The Beautiful Game* (perf. 2000), and half a dozen novels.

His most distinguished work of fiction is *Popcorn* (1996), a Hollywood novel that climaxes in a nationally televised confrontation between an Academy Award–winning director of homicidal satires and a pair of psychotic serial killers who attempt to make him accept the blame for their crimes. The earlier *Stark* (1989) and *This Other Eden* (1993) are in satirical sci-fi mode, while *Gridlock* (1991) is an ingenious dystopic fantasy predicated on the irrecoverable breakdown and jamming up of London's entire traffic system. *Blast from the Past* (1998) deals with the problem of stalking, together with the political implications of Anglo-American Coldwar cooperation, while *Inconceivable* (1999) is a semiautobiographical account of a young couple's difficulty in attaining parenthood combined with a satire on the world of television and film. Similarly, in *Dead Famous* (2001) the structure of a traditionally ingenious whodunit, set in a "reality-television" closed community where everyone is under multivideo surveillance 24/7, is used as a vehicle for cogent satire on the dynamics of group living, the values of the multimedia, and the effect in 21st-c. civilization of the overwhelming hunger for fame. E. has adapted two of his novels for other media, but has lost narrative and dramatic impetus in the process. The film version of *Inconceivable* entitled *Maybe Baby* (2000), which he both wrote and

directed, lacked the bite and drive of the original, as did his stage version of *Popcorn* (perf. 1997; pub. 1998).

MICHAEL GROSVENOR MYER

ELYOT, [Sir] Thomas
b. 1490?, Wiltshire; d. 20 March 1546, Carlton, Cambridgeshire

One of the finest classicists of the 16th c., E. is best known as the author of *The Boke Named the Governour* (1531), a highly influential treatise on the training of young gentlemen. By writing the *Governour* and the rest of his works in English, E. made the ideas of the Renaissance accessible to literate English men and women who had no knowledge of ancient languages. E. drew his insights on statecraft not only from classical texts but also from his own experiences in government service. After learning Latin and Greek at an early age from his father, a judge, E. completed his education at the Middle Temple in London and at Oxford University. During his time at Oxford, he befriended Sir Thomas MORE and studied medicine and Greek literature under Thomas LINACRE. In 1523, Cardinal Wolsey made him Clerk of the Privy Council, a post he held until 1529, when Wolsey fell from power. In 1531, through the influence of Thomas Cromwell, E. became the ambassador to the court of Charles V. HENRY VIII sent E. to the Netherlands with the important task of gaining the emperor's assent to Henry's divorce from Catherine of Aragon. Henry soon became dissatisfied with E. and recalled him in 1532. E. spent the rest of his life in Cambridgeshire, serving at various points as a member of Parliament and as sheriff.

Shortly before E. took up his ambassadorship, E. composed the *Governour*. In the first part of book 1, E. famously invokes the Great Chain of Being, arguing that hierarchy is necessary and that the best form of government is absolute monarchy; the monarch, he continues, requires members of the aristocracy to act as his subordinates, and it is crucial that these men be properly educated. The rest of the *Governour* lays out in exhaustive detail E.'s humanistic curriculum for educating future state servants. In E.'s system, instruction in Greek and Latin begins at age seven. E. stipulates that students should be praised and rewarded, not threatened and punished. Recreation is also part of E.'s program: in order to produce complete gentlemen, E. recommends that young men practice music, sculpture, and painting and that they take part in hunting, archery, and dancing. E. is particularly enthusiastic about the moral value of allegorized dancing, to which he dedicates seven of the *Governour*'s sixty-eight chapters. The final two books have generated considerably less critical discussion than the first.

Book 2 focuses on the characteristics of the just ruler: here, E. stresses the importance of mercy, liberality, benevolence, and friendship. Book 3 presents a rather commonplace discussion on the cardinal virtues. To clarify and reinforce the arguments he sets out in the *Governour*, E. uses anecdotes and exempla from an astonishing variety of classical, biblical, and early modern humanist texts. E.'s prose is clear, concise, and rhythmical, even when he is dealing with very abstruse concepts. His attempt to enrich English by borrowing words from other languages was scorned by many of his fellow humanists. Nevertheless, modern scholars generally agree that the *Governour* constitutes a significant advance in the development of English prose. The treatise enjoyed great popularity in the 16th c.: it went through eight editions before 1600, and, as E. had hoped, gentlemen and tutors made use of it in the education of the young.

E. wrote a number of important works during his final years in Cambridgeshire. Between 1533–36, he translated Isocrates, Plutarch, and Pico della Mirandola. The Lucianic dialogue *Pasquil the Playne*, published anonymously in 1533, considers good and bad counselors. Pasquil, a statue come to life who is the only counselor in the work to offer honest advice instead of flattery, has, like E., lost favor with his master. Through Pasquil, E. avers that Henry has been ill counseled and that lust has prompted the king to seek a divorce. In 1534, E. published his immensely popular medical treatise *The Castel of Helth*, a collection of prescriptions and remedies based on Galenic physiology. Four years later, he completed *The Dictionary of Syr Thomas Elyot, knyght* (better known by its later title *Bibliotheca Eliotae*), the first Latin-English dictionary for students of classical Latin. His final work, *A Preservative agaynste Deth* (1545), harshly criticizes Protestant theology.

BIBLIOGRAPHY: Baker, D. W., *Divulging Utopia: Radical Humanism in Sixteenth Century England* (1999); Lehmberg, S., *Sir T. E.* (1960); Major, J. M., *Sir T. E. and Renaissance Humanism* (1964); Wilson, K. J., *Incomplete Fictions: The Formation of English Renaissance Dialogue* (1985)

T. D. DRAKE

EMPSON, [Sir] William

b. 27 September 1906, Howden, England; d. 15 April 1984, London

An influential critic for over forty years, E. is probably best known for the publication early in his career of *Seven Types of Ambiguity* (1930), a seminal text in what was to be called the "New Criticism" by John Crowe Ransom in the 1940s. Unfortunately, this labeling elides the fact that E. refused to consider the central tenets of New Criticism, especially what has come to be called "the intentional fallacy"—the insistence that the biography and the "intent" of the author

need to be ignored in the service of correct reading—as unassailable. His wide range of critical writings reveal him to be one of the 20th c.'s more enigmatic critics, one who tended to look askance at prevailing literary critical tendencies in favor of a heretical stance that might have been occasioned by his long sojourns at seats of learning outside mainstream Anglo-America. This heretical tendency has meant that, in many ways, E. still "matters" to those who engage in philosophies of literature while many—if not most—of his peers have become ancient windmills against whom one need no longer tilt.

Supervised by I. A. Richards during his fourth year at Cambridge (the only year he studied English as his major subject), E. tied for the highest marks possible when tested. More important, it was during Richards's tutelage of E. that *Seven Types of Ambiguity* took shape, and it was during this period that he began writing the estimable poetry—lyrical, imagistic, and abstract—that is too often ignored in favor of his critical writings. In 1931, E. took a post as the chair of English literature at the Tokyo University of Literature and Science—the first of several positions in Asia that would include over nine years as a professor of English in Beijing. The period between 1931 and 1952 (when E. began a twenty-year affiliation with Sheffield University in England), which was largely spent overseas or in thrall to the war effort as an editor for the BBC, saw the publication of the major works of E.'s career. He published two important works of literary criticism, *Some Versions of Pastoral* (1935; repub. as *English Pastoral Poetry*, 1938) and *The Structure of Complex Words* (1951), and the first edition of his collected poems appeared in print (1949). Although he would edit and write criticism until his death in 1984, including *Milton's God* (1961; rev. ed., 1965) and the posthumous publication of *Faustus and the Censors* (1986), he had essentially stopped writing poetry by the start of World War II, and the trilogy of works beginning with *Seven Types of Ambiguity* would frame E.'s interests in literature as consonant with the sweeping revolutions in literary theory that would arise during the last four decades of the 20th c.

If the *sine qua non* of poorly practiced New Criticism in American classrooms—which held sway for some thirty years—consisted of a relentless search for the "right" meaning of a poem without regard to authorial intention or any didactic or delightful effect that poem might have on a reader, then it is ironic that *Seven Types* became a founding text in support of this text-centered methodology. As E. defined it, an ambiguity is "any verbal nuance, however slight, which gives room for alternative reactions to the same piece of literature." The resolution of ambiguities (and paradoxes and the tensions of opposites in poetry) allowed a close reader to find the unifying center of a poem. Thus did New Critics fix meaning in the text alone, without recourse to author or audience. Yet E. was adamant about the possibility of seeing authorial psychology in action and was equally adamant that literature's purpose—its value, perhaps—was that it provided a ground for evaluation in a murky world. Readers must learn and be affected by texts lest they lose a yardstick for life's missed opportunities.

Some Versions of Pastoral continues, in broader form, the focus of *Seven Types*, but it also looks forward to socially oriented approaches to literature— such as Marxist analysis—by virtue of its concern with finding pastoral forms in strikingly unlikely places: Alice's romp through Wonderland or in *The Beggar's Opera*, for example. Like so many others during this period, E. was also quite taken with Freudian analysis as a novelty and his adoption of a psychoanalytic literary method can be seen as a precursor to the wave of theorists who now take their cues from Jacques Lacan and others. *The Structure of Complex Words* is overall concerned with locating the etymological and historical contexts of words and trying to shift a concern with "meaning" back to his interests in the ambiguities of words' meanings. Moreover, E. began here to fight the good fight against the missionary impulse that lay beneath much of New Criticism smug insistence—inherited from Matthew Arnold— that literature could replace the missing spiritual strut in civilization. The heretical E. refused the religious impulse that would make priests out of professors, preferring a more modest role for art in the way of the world.

What is too often overlooked in this singular man's life is the strength and vitality of his poetry. Although several of his poems are occasionally anthologized— including "This Last Pain" and "Aubade"—his critical reputation and his many enthusiastic defenses of his cherished apostasy have overshadowed this portion of his oeuvre. No less a light than W. H. AUDEN dedicated a poem to E. on the occasion of his retirement from Sheffield in 1971, saying that "Good Voices are rare, still rarer singers with perfect pitch . . . Our verbal games are separate, thank heaven, but Time twins us."

BIBLIOGRAPHY: Gill, R., ed., *W. E.* (1974); Norris, C., *W. E. and the Philosophy of Literary Criticism* (1978); Willis, J. H., Jr., *W. E.* (1969)

RICHARD E. LEE

ENGLISH VERSE FORMS

Apart from certain nursery rhymes whose origins are obscure, the earliest known poems in English are religious in context of which CÆDMON's "Hymn of Creation," written ca. 600, is one of the best-known examples. It is written in OLD ENGLISH as are the more secular *The Seafarer* and *The Wife's Lament* although both have Christian connotations. These were found in a collection copied in 975 and given to Exeter Cathedral by Bishop Leofric. The manuscript of the EPIC poem of *BEOWULF*, the earliest known European poem in the vernacular, is also dated from the 10th c. although it is thought to have been composed between 700 and 750. All these show that early English verse was meant to be sung or at least told orally to an illiterate audience.

Geoffrey CHAUCER is the first known to have written his verse to be read rather than recited; the invention of printing was only decades in the future and the more literate society on which its success was to depend was coming into being. However, although he is spoken of as the father of English literature and wrote in MIDDLE ENGLISH, he lived in a multilingual society where French was more often spoken and better understood by the literate classes and was seen as the cultural language, using French forms and styles still in use today. Although English was beginning to be seen and used as a language in its own right for parliamentary or legal business, English culture was marginalized, native literary tradition flourishing only in regional dialects remote from capital, court, and universities. Chaucer therefore adapted French precedents and since his time English poetry has often fed from Continental sources.

The rhythms and patterns that structure English verse are based on a pattern of sound in which the poet sets the stress on a syllable in those words he wishes to give prominence in the line. Unlike many other languages, in English the syllable stress can depend on the context of the word. Old English verse was based on accentual meter where a line of verse had only four stressed syllables in each line but could have any number of unstressed syllables and links were made by alliteration. The usual form of English verse, which began to develop from the 16th c., is in accentual-syllabic meter in which both the stressed and unstressed syllables are counted. This combined unit of stress is known as a foot. The commonest unit or foot in English verse is the combination of one unstressed syllable followed by one stressed syllable, called the iambic foot. This is the unit of most English verse and is found in Chaucer, in the old ballads, in blank verse, in heroic couplets, and in sonnets as well as other verse. If the iambic foot is reversed or inverted to give a stressed syllable followed by an unstressed syllable, it is called the trochaic foot. This is usually used to add variety or emphasis to iambic verse as in John MILTON's "L'Allegro" lines 25–29 and rarely for a whole poem although Henry Wadsworth Longfellow's *Hiawatha* and Robert BROWNING's "Soliloquy in a Spanish Cloister" are exceptions.

In English verse, the length of a stanza can vary from a couplet of two lines to fourteen lines in a sonnet, and poets sometimes use two or three different stanza forms in one poem. A quatrain, or four-line stanza, rhymed or unrhymed, is the most common English form. But other lengths appear. There is the three-line stanza, or terza rima after Dante, when a tercet has one unrhymed line or a triplet has all the three lines rhyming. The rhyme scheme can often dictate the length of the stanza. The seven-line rhyme royal was first used by Chaucer in *Troilus and Criseide* and is in iambic pentameter rhyming *ababbcc*. The Spenserian nine line stanza has eight lines of iambic pentameter followed by a single iambic hexameter (known as an Alexandrine) rhyming *ababbcbcc* as in Edmund SPENSER's *Faerie Queene*. Blank verse is not divided into stanzas but is based on unrhymed lines of iambic pentameter, although certain feet may be in another meter. Some poets have experimented with shape poems that try to illustrate the content visually in the shape of the poem's stanza on the page, as illustrated in George HERBERT's "The Altar" or his "Easter Wings."

The chosen rhyme scheme can both structure the verse and interlock with the meaning of the content of a poem. Rhyme is usually seen in the final syllables of line endings; when it is the penultimate syllables that rhyme, it is known as a feminine rhyme; this often occurs with words ending in "ing." There can also be internal rhymes, words within a line rhyming with other words in that line or another line, and assonance where the vowels are the same but the final consonant is changed. Occasionally, there is eye rhyme or printer's rhyme where the words look the same but are pronounced differently, although in the poet's day this might have been a full rhyme.

The simplest form of structure is the ballad, which can be found in at least two forms. The first is the traditional folk ballad in which traces of the oral tradition are still found, which has come down by word of mouth, and is often anonymous, for example, "Sir Patrick Spens" and "Barbara Allen." These are in common meter where there are eight syllables in the first line, six in the second, eight in the third line, and six in the fourth to give a stanza of four lines, a quatrain. The second line usually rhymes with the fourth line. It is noteworthy that some verse may be called a ballad without being in common meter like the anonymous "Lord Randall." The second form is the literary style, when certain later poets deliberately choose to use common meter to enhance their theme when they have something to say that seems to fit the simplicity of the style, for example, Thomas HARDY's "The Darkling Thrush." In *The Rime of the Ancient Mariner*, Samuel Taylor COLERIDGE uses common meter but makes many variations, adding a line to a stanza to make a five line pentain, using triple rhyme, internal rhymes and assonance. He also uses many examples of the poet's other tool, rhetorical tropes and schemas. A trope here means a semantic change or transfer of a word's meaning as in metaphor, allegory, or hyper-

bole. A schema or figure is concerned with the shape and structure of the language, the place of words in a syntactical pattern. For example, anaphora repeats a word at the beginning of a sequence of clauses or sentences, epistrophe repeats a word to end a sequence. These are derived from classical usage and their use was learned in school.

Education across Europe until the end of the 19th c. was based on learning, translating, and understanding the Latin authors, and to a lesser extent those in Greek. Latin was therefore considered the pinnacle of correct language usage. This type of education, in which certain formalities were inculcated, made for a cultural and social background in which educated people understood and would appreciate the many schemas and figures of rhetoric that poets of the past were educated in using, although few are known today. The trends from abroad that set English verse on its way began with attempts to adapt classical meter into English. Spenser called Chaucer the English Virgil, and he shows in *The Shepheardes Calender* how far classical influences and figures of speech colored his own work although he deliberately uses expressions as well, which he suggests are obsolete ones from earlier English.

Seventeenth-century poets in particular tried to adapt into English the standard classical structure of certain poems like the ode and the elegy that they knew from Latin authors. The ode is a dignified, long poem written to celebrate or praise something or someone in elevated language. There were four main classical forms deriving from Pindar, Horace, Sappho, and Alcaeus. Ben JONSON used the structure of a Pindaric ode in his "To the Immortal Memory and Friendship of that Noble Pair, Sir Lucius Carey and Sir Henry Morison." This has three stanzas of the specified form, a strophe and antistrophe metrically identical with each other plus an epode metrically and formally distinct from them. Jonson called these the turn, the counter turn, and the stand, but their function was the same. His "Ode to Himself" is in the looser style of an Horatian ode as are Andrew MARVELL's "Upon Cromwell's Return from Ireland" and John KEATS's "To Autumn." Isaac WATTS attempted an English Sapphic ode, "The Day of Judgement," in largely dactylic meter that gives a very uneven rhythm and is not often used. In "Intimations of Immortality," William WORDSWORTH developed what became accepted as the English ode form made up of various combinations of iambic lines of varying length.

The elegy is also a formal long poem but more intimate than the ode and with less restrictive structures; it is often in memory of someone dead or is at least in a reflective mood. Thomas GRAY's "Elegy Written in a Country Churchyard" gives its name to the elegiac meter of iambic pentameter in quatrains with alternate rhymes: there is little enjambment and the regularity of beat gives it a plodding feel. Other poets use more varied meters. Milton's "Lycidas" consists of eleven stanzas of differing lengths and rhyme patterns. Alfred, Lord TENNYSON's *In Memoriam* is in quatrains but in tetrameters with an arching rhyme, abba, which both closes the thought and looks back as one does in memory of someone who has died. It is called the Tennysonian stanza. Percy Bysshe SHELLEY uses the Spenserian stanza in his elegy on the death of Keats, *Adonais.*

Other influences came from the formal Italian rules, as seen in the structure of Dante's works, and from the more flowing French ballade styles. A particularly important transition was by Sir Thomas WYATT who adapted the sonnet form from Petrarch in the early 16th c. This formal structure of fourteen lines in pentameter stayed basically the same as the source, differing only in the rhyme schemes adopted by certain poets which affects the way in which the argument is carried forward, for sonnets usually present an argument. In the petrarchan form, the fourteen lines divide into an octave, rhyming *abbaabba,* followed by a sestet, rhyming *cdecde* or similar. This allows for a statement or observation to be followed by a counter statement or an expansion of the theme. Keats's "On First Looking into Chapman's Homer" follows this pattern. Spenser uses an interlocking rhyme scheme of *ababbcbccdcdee* in his sonnet sequence *Amoretti.* The Shakespearean sonnet has three quatrains and a concluding couplet, in a rhyme scheme of *abab, cdcd, efef, gg,* which allows for an argument to be developed and then concluded. Milton, John DONNE, and later Wordsworth and Elizabeth Barrett BROWNING were the primary users of the sonnet form rarely used by 20th-c. poets although Gerard Manley HOPKINS called several of his poems "curtal" sonnets as they were shorter than the norm.

Like Hopkins, other poets in the 20th c. have used the formal "rules" to create their own accent. For example, T. S. ELIOT uses older styles in new ways. In *The Waste Land,* he alludes to, or quotes from, Dante, Spenser, Marvell, Milton, and William SHAKESPEARE, among other previous authors. Others who have broken or adapted those "rules" to provide their own individual voice include Wilfred OWEN who uses pararhyme in "Strange Meeting" and Ted HUGHES who uses unrhymed free verse in "Walt," both poems exploring men at war. Free verse is verse that makes little use of the traditional structures and can occasionally seem to stray into prose but that has an underlying poetic rhythm and often uses internal or pararhymes. "After the Funeral" by Dylan THOMAS is an example, which, like most free verse, may need reciting aloud to be fully appreciated as poetry.

Not that free verse is the only style enhanced by recitation. Most verse repays silent study but full understanding comes more easily when it is read aloud.

Paradise Lost with its unusual syntax is particularly difficult to grasp, but when Milton's epic poem is read aloud the linked meanings underlying the references and the phraseology are understood more easily. In essence, English verse depends so much on oral patterns that reciting it to oneself or to others is still usually the best way to find the rhythms of the stress patterns, hear the echoes of the rhymes, and thus perceive both the obvious meaning and its context of underlying allusions. English verse came from an oral tradition and still depends upon the aural rather than the visual image for full appreciation.

BIBLIOGRAPHY: Grierson, H. J. C., and J. C. Smith, *A Critical History of English Poetry* (1944); Lennard, J., *The Poetry Handbook: A Guide to Reading Poetry for Pleasure and Practical Criticism* (1996)

DAWN LEWCOCK

ENRIGHT, D[ennis] J[oseph]

b. 11 March 1920, Leamington, Warwickshire; d. 31 December 2002, London

Most so-called members of "The Movement," a group of nine British poets loosely united in a rejection of ornament and poetic pretension in favor of a frank, spare tone, denied knowledge of any organized movement at all. While no principles were formally agreed upon, the designated poets did share some characteristics: they were middle class, retained comfortable academic positions, and were socially and politically conservative. E. fit few of these criteria; nonetheless, he remains, after Philip LARKIN, the best known and most influential of the group. His mixture of gravity and ironic wit exemplified Movement poetics, honesty over design, conversational rhythm over the musical.

E.'s early academic promise brought a scholarship to Cambridge and deliverance from the Midlands working class. As a result of his beginnings, E. wrote from the perspective of the outsider. His poetry counters the formal, decorative verse of the previous generation, particularly that of Dylan THOMAS. One of E.'s notable volumes, *The Terrible Shears* (1973), can be seen as a direct contrast to the kind of pastoral nostalgia Thomas evoked of his childhood Wales; E. instead portrays the hardships of poverty and ignorance in direct, often brutal poems. "Two Bad Things in Infant School," "Anglo Irish," and "A Bookish Boy" all depict humiliation and rebellion under the constriction of rules and organizations. "A Bookish Boy" in particular tells the story of a romantic child attempting to create for himself a replica of mythic dignity, though the episode ends inevitably with misunderstanding and embarrassment.

The appearance of the pamphlet *Season Ticket* in 1948 began E.'s prolific career. Concurrent with these poems, E. was a visiting lecturer at the University of Alexandria, the setting for his first novel, *Academic*

Year (1955). Each successive lectureship took E. to new territory both literally and figuratively: *Heaven Knows Where* (1957) follows a character from *Academic Year* to the fictional, utopian island of Velo; *Insufficient Poppy* (1960) and *Figures of Speech* (1965) draw descriptive details from the author's time in Bangkok and Kobe, Japan, respectively. E.'s experiences as a visitor in a foreign environment developed the perspective he had already established, that of the cultural outsider. Physical descriptions of geography and native tradition have the care and attention of a naive eye, though the sentiment of the narration carries the bitter knowledge of one who understands the nature of humanity, the cruelties of institutions that exist in all cultures. E.'s protagonists are often at the mercy of authority and custom, victims of bureaucracy rather than fate.

Books of poems appeared at regular intervals following *The Laughing Hyena and Other Poems* in 1953. Poems such as "The Egyptian Cat" from *The Laughing Hyena,* "Tea Ceremony" from *Bread Rather than Blossoms* (1956), and "Entrance Visa" from *Some Men Are Brothers* (1960) demonstrate the influence of the foreign landscape on E. Later poems become more personal, the speaker interacting more directly with subjects, as in "Dreaming in the Shanghai Restaurant" in *Addictions* (1962) and "Meeting the Minister for Culture" in *The Old Adam* (1965). Even the earliest poems of this period display the E. style: conversational, flowing lines eschewing decoration in favor of wry HUMOR and apt observation. "Sometimes I ask myself: Do I live in foreign countries/Because they cannot corrupt me," the poet asks in "Reflections on Foreign Literature" (*Addictions*), a poem in which he later defines the exotic as "a rest from meaning." It is with this exotic, alien element that E. most often identifies.

Unlawful Assembly (1968) and *Daughters of Earth* (1972) show both increased authority in E.'s poetic voice and increased outrage at mindless bureaucracy. By this point in his career, E. had suffered misunderstandings both with academic institutions and foreign governments, confirming his mistrust of institutions. Poems like "The Mysterious Incident at the Admiral's Party" attack the inadequacy of manners and social rules, while "Board of Selection" portrays the often-romanticized realm of academia as petty and small minded. *The Terrible Shears* and *Sad Ires and Others* (1975) address issues of empire and of economy in poems such as "Hands off, Foreign Devil" and "Oyster Lament."

Without leaving behind the social and political awareness of his earlier work, E. ventured into mythic territory in the late 1970s with *Paradise Illustrated* (1978), an often humorous account of Adam and Eve in the Garden of Eden, and *A Faust Book* (1979), a modernization of the Faust tale utilizing dramatic scenes, prose, and poetry. Around the same time, E.'s fanciful trio of novels for children also appeared: *The Joke Shop* (1976), *Wild Ghost Chase* (1978), and *Beyond Land's End* (1979). The books follow the adventures of three literate and clever children in the Shadow Land, an imaginative realm.

E.'s many prose works include cultural studies like *The World of Dew* (1955), concerning Japanese life and collections of literary essays such as *Conspirators and Poets* (1966) and *A Mania for Sentences* (1983). *Fields of Vision: Essays on Literature, Language and Television* in 1988 demonstrated E.'s ability to continue making relevant, timely observations on contemporary culture. His diversity of interest is shown by his editorship of the Oxford Books of Contemporary Verse, Friendship, Death and the Supernatural, as well as the works of Proust and Ben JONSON. *Fair of Speech: Uses of Euphemism* (1985) explores language and manners, two subjects often explored in his poems.

An edition of *Selected Poems* was published in 1968; E.'s *Collected Poems* appeared in 1981, with a revised and enlarged edition in 1987. Even so, his career has continued with *Under the Circumstances: Poems and Proses* (1991) and *Old Men and Comets* (1993). A fellow of the Royal Society of Literature, E.'s other awards include the Cholmondeley Award for Poetry from the British Society of Authors (1974), the Queen's Gold Medal for Poetry (1981), honorary degrees from the University of Warwick (1982) and the University of Surrey (1985), and the Order of the British Empire (1991). His autobiography, *Memoirs of a Mendicant Professor* (1969), recounts his personal, academic, and literary history with characteristic candor and wit.

BIBLIOGRAPHY: Bradley, J., *The Movement: British Poets of the 1950s* (1993); Simms, J., ed., *Life by Other Means: Essays on D. J. E.* (1990); Walsh, W., *D. J. E.* (1974)

NICOLE SARROCCO

EPIC

In his essay "Epic and Novel" (1941), Mikhail Bakhtin defined epic as a genre formally oriented toward the distant past, a world of beginnings and peak times in a nation's history, a world of fathers and founders, of firsts and bests. Bakhtin describes epic in this way so as to set the scene for the emergence of a new and very different genre, one that newly represents events on the same time-and-value plane as the author and reader or listener. Thus, Bakhtin represents the shift from epic to novelistic worldview. In reaction to the polemical bias of this essay, some critics have rejected Bakhtin's views outright, while others attempt to reverse his terms or cite exceptions to his rule. But the serious implications of his analysis are sometimes too easily overlooked. The point, for Bakhtin, is not that epics deal with past subject matter (though many do), but that they project everything of value into the past. Thus, it is the past that contains a society's truths, its ethical systems, its modes of evaluating itself and the world. From this complete and finalized world, the contemporary listener and poet are forever cut off, the only appropriate attitude to the past being one of humble reverence. In Bakhtin's essay, the term "epic" becomes synonymous with unificatory, hierarchized discourse, which is then negatively contrasted with the joyous, democratic, polyphonic discourses of the novel. It is not surprising that critics have taken umbrage at this polarization of genres, even if elsewhere Bakhtin analyzes epic poetry in more nuanced terms.

There are several aspects of Bakhtin's description in "Epic and Novel" that are fundamental to the study of epic, particularly European Renaissance epic. First, Bakhtin places the listener (or reader) and the poet on the same plane of experience. So if epic poetry deals with elevated subjects, with first causes of evil, and grand narratives of history, the epic poet himself is not morally elevated above his audience; he is "a man speaking about a past that is to him inaccessible." This immediately introduces a dynamic and unstable element to the relation between the epic narrator and his material. It explains why the narrator so frequently voices anxiety about whether he is equal to the task at hand (e.g., the epic narrator in John MILTON's *Paradise Lost*). So we can agree that the epic story is sacred, monologic, and unified. But, modifying Bakhtin's emphasis, we might say the epic text is necessarily dialogic because it is uttered by a narrator who inhabits the "post-fall," contemporary world of his audience.

Secondly, the "one who utters the epic word" (in most cases, this means the text's narrator) adopts the point of view of a descendant toward his subject matter. So epic provides the narrator and his audience with an extended time frame; epic situates the human subject in "great time" rather than in the immediacy of the present tense. This elongated temporal perspective need not work in only one direction, as Bakhtin suggests, but may require the narrator, hero, or reader to picture himself as an ancestor as well as a descendant. In fact, a reader's temporal engagement with epic is more closely related to the way s/he reads a novel, than other genres of poetry, simply by virtue of the novel's and epic's comparable length. But even considering the formal constitution of time in epic, without reference to the reader's experience, what we find are not finalized certainties about a Golden Age, but shifting, sliding perspectives on historical process.

Finally, epic represents "the environment of a man speaking about a past": a man, rather than a woman

(unless we redefine the boundaries of epic to include prose romances, such as Mary WROTH's *Urania* or the Countess of PEMBROKE's continuation of Sir Philip SIDNEY's *Arcadia*). This "man" who speaks of the "world of fathers and founders of families" nevertheless addresses himself to women and men in his contemporary world. Edmund SPENSER dedicated his *Faerie Queene* to ELIZABETH I, and even if she was regarded as an exceptional case, Spenser still faced the task of translating his contemporary, female-centered, court, into a masculine, epic worldview. Thus, the representation of women plays a crucial part in the fashioning of a mythic world of fathers and founders.

When we turn to Renaissance theories of epic (or as they also termed it, heroic verse), we will find many similarities with Bakhtin's view. Although of course the Renaissance theorists meant it in a positive sense, they too stressed epic's "firstness," its elevated subject matter, its capacity to instruct the present age in the higher virtues of the ancient past. Poetry in general was defended on the grounds that it could teach virtue more effectively than theology, history or philosophy, because its method, imitation of real life, was more pleasurable than unmediated instruction (e.g., Sidney's *An Apologie for Poetrie,* which echoes the standard line from Horace's *Ars Poetica*). But because epic poetry imitated only the most noble and heroic actions from the past, its virtuousness (rather than its virtuosity) was the most easily defended of all the literary genres. Thus, Sidney argues that while poetry in general teaches the truth, and more importantly persuades people to act on it, epic poetry teaches and "moves to the highest, and most excellent truth." Sir John HARINGTON likewise argues that people will digest the highest matters in epic narrative, while they would find such things indigestible when served up as philosophy.

We move closer to the Bakhtinian concept of unificatory, hierarchized discourse, when we hear that epic poetry aims to educate only the highest classes of society, and that this education consists of learning how to be a good prince (male or female) or a good courtier. Thus, Aristotle's observation that epic is directed to noble audiences, and tragedy to the lower classes, is cited often and approvingly by Renaissance critics (less often do they note that Aristotle nevertheless ranked tragedy as the higher genre). Spenser chooses epic narrative to fashion a gentleman or person in virtuous and gentle discipline, his declared aim in the letter prefacing *The Faerie Queene* ("A Letter of the Authors Expounding the Whole Intention . . ."). Renaissance theorists accepted without much reservation the classical view that poetry could be ranked high (epic), middle (georgic), and low (pastoral); Torquato Tasso, for example, approvingly borrows and amplifies this three-tiered classification from Cicero. Moreover, Renaissance editions of Virgil's *Aeneid* were commonly prefaced with four lines referring to the poet's progression from pastoral to georgic to epic verse. These lines were adopted as the *cursus honorum*, or career path, appropriate to the serious poet. Spenser thus signals that he has reached the highest rung of the ladder, when he renounces pastoral's "oaten reeds" in the Virgilian opening lines of the *Faerie Queene*.

But when we recall Bakhtin's observation that the epic poet stands on the same plane as his audience, a lower plane with respect to his elevated subject matter, we will discover a much less monologic, less harmonious relationship amongst the three constituent parts of epic narration: the poet, the text, and his audience. In the first place, the poet may intend an ironic contrast between the ideal heroes of his epic and the real-life courtiers to whom his text is addressed. Thus, when Spenser declares that in the Faerie Queene, he means particularly to represent Elizabeth I, this can be taken either as flattery or as a warning to his royal audience not to fall below the heroic ideal. Even the heroes within Renaissance epic rarely embody the perfected ideals to which they aspire. Both Tasso and Spenser represent their knights acquiring heroic virtue painfully and laboriously; the knight provides a model for the reader, in that both must strive for a perfection that seems beyond mortal reach.

Moreover, while the epic poet may aim his poem at an elevated audience, he has no guarantee that this audience of powerful, influential people will actually listen to him. In *Epic Romance* (1967), Colin Burrow has shown that the decline of regal patronage under Charles I drastically changed both the substance and the function of epic poetry. While Spenser, Edward Fairfax, and Harington all dedicated their volumes to the queen, the later epicists, Giles and Phineas FLETCHER, and Sir Arthur Gorges, all lacked powerful patrons. Rather than continue the fiction that the personal has direct application to political life, they chose to invert Spenser, and appropriated government as a metaphor for self-regulation. Epic turns away from its elevated audience, when that audience ceases to hear.

Furthermore, the epic poet is as far below the heroic ideal as his audience is. Like them, he approaches the high truths of heroic poetry indirectly, via the pleasures of the text. Thus, Spenser does not offer us gentle discipline in plain style, but rather, cloudily wrapped in allegory. This is perhaps why, although theoretically epic stood above the other poetic genres, in practice it tended to embrace all other genres within itself. In order to fashion the heroic ideal, epic continues to make use of the "lower," more devious, strategies of pastoral and georgic, not to mention the dramatic genres, and most contentiously of all, the conventions of romance. To a modern reader, Renaissance epic may appear to speak with the voice of unchallenged, regal authority. But when we turn to the

poems themselves, we find that the heroic ideal takes shape in the midst of bitter and polemical argument with contemporaries, by means of narrative strategies that call into question the very efficacy of epic poems as vehicles for heroic virtue.

The dynamic interplay between the idealized image of epic and its concrete realization is especially evident in Renaissance translations, or better, emulations of classical epic. George CHAPMAN prefaces the 1611 edition of his *Homer's Iliads* with a letter to the reader which claims that Homer is the first and best of all writers. Chapman elevates Homer's work high above his own poetic endeavors, but curiously this reverence for an ancient author empowers Chapman to lash out freely and vindictively at his own contemporary rivals and critics in the preface to his translation. Moreover, he feels no obligation to be slavishly faithful to Homer, his task being rather to interpret Homer for his own age.

While hostile to contemporary detractors, Chapman preserves a marvelous flexibility and open-mindedness toward the Greek text. The 1611 edition announces that the first two books of Chapman's original edition (*Seven Books of the Iliades*, 1598) have been systematically revised, while due to lack of time, the other five have been reproduced without further revision. Books 3 through 6 and 12 are reproduced from the 1608 edition, and the whole second half of the *Iliad*, books 13 through 24, have been newly translated for the 1611 edition. Such a gradual evolution is not unusual in the history of translation; what is unusual is how Chapman himself lays bare the inconsistencies among the various parts of the work. If we want to see him at his best, his least "paraphrastical" and most Greek, Chapman tells us, we should read the last books of the translation. With such frank and extensive notation about the text's genesis, it is impossible to read Chapman's Homer monologically; we are always aware of the varying degrees of license, of estrangement from the Greek worldview in the unrevised books or estrangement from English idiom in the first two and final twelve books.

Much might be said about the relation of the poet to his audience and his text, but surely, it might be argued, the text itself depicts idealized, heroic characters far removed from the context of its early-17th-c. readers? But the extraordinary aspect of Chapman's Homer is that it manages to be both archaic and contemporary at once. Thus, for example, the argument between Achilles and Agamemnon, over the slave-girl Briseis, acquires pointed resonance against the context of the Earl of Essex's rebellion against Queen Elizabeth in 1601. Chapman's *Seven Books* were dedicated to the Earl of Essex, in 1598 (the year in which Elizabeth "insulted" Essex); the complete *Iliads* (1611) were dedicated to Prince Henry. One might expect that in the later edition, Chapman was dissociating himself from the disgraced Essex, and from the theme of "injured merit," which the rebellion came to represent. But as Burrow has shown, Chapman actually underlines Achilles' resentment, lengthening and sharpening his speeches in the 1611 edition. Under the veil of translation, Chapman was able to develop a much sharper criticism of ungrateful royalty than epicists such as Samuel DANIEL and Michael DRAYTON, poets writing directly in English.

If Renaissance epic translations were dialogic in their relation to the original classical texts, other epics were dialogic in their embrace of contestant genres, most notably, the chivalric romance. Chivalric romances typically depicted the wandering of a knight-hero, whose journey was shaped by chance, rather than destiny. Romances were structured episodically, with several plot lines interleaved in one text, in contrast to the teleological (end-directed), linear narrative of epic, which typically followed the fate of a single, national hero. Accommodating an endless variety of "marvelous" incidents, romances aimed to inspire their readers with wonder, rather than (perhaps) nationalistic duty. But epic often stretched to incorporate romance elements (just as romance aspired to the comprehensiveness and aesthetic coherence of epic). The *Odyssey*, cited as the founding romance text by Renaissance critics, follows the fate of a single hero, epic-style. And the *Iliad,* epic par excellence, celebrates the lives and deaths of many different heroes, in true romance style. In *Poetics,* Aristotle states that the distinctive characteristic of epic is that it accommodates the irrational, which is exactly the distinguishing characteristic of romance in Renaissance criticism.

The event that seems to have sparked the major critical debate about epic and its relation to romance in the Renaissance period was the publication of Ariosto's *Orlando Furioso* in 1516. Interlacing the adventures of Orlando and Angelica (a Carolingian knight and an Eastern princess) with those of Ruggiero and Bradamante (legendary ancestors of the Ferraran house of Este, the poet's patrons), Ariosto created a new kind of work that threatened to upstage the more traditionally defined epic narrative. Significantly, the *Furioso* came out several decades before the first Italian commentaries on Aristotle's *Poetics*, and it may be that Ariosto would have broken fewer epic rules if he had been aware of what was at stake. But coming after him, Tasso worked painstakingly to contain the energies Ariosto had unleashed, redefining the principles of post-Ariostan epic in his *Discorsi* (1587), and reforging romance as epic in his own ground-breaking poem, *Gerusalemma Liberata* (1575). In the *Discorsi*, he argues that all poetry should profit and delight, but that epic poetry should do it by moving the reader to wonder. Not content to invoke Aristotle as the last word, Tasso admits in his

Discorsi that this "new genre," represented by *Orlando Furioso*, can produce more marvels, more variety, more surprise, than traditional epic, and consequently is preferred by the modern, 16th-c. reader. But Tasso draws the line at multiplicity (rather than unity) of action. *Variety* is acceptable, even laudable up to a point, but a true epic poem must serve a unified purpose; its moral and aesthetic objectives should be clear. Thus romance enters epic as moral and aesthetic errancy; it is allowed in to delight the reader, but in the end its centrifugal energies must be reined in to serve the teleological aims of epic. In 20th-c. criticism, the history of epic as a genre self-riven by its interjection of the marvelous, has been told with a bewildering number of permutations. According to some, Ariosto is as seriously epic as Tasso; according to others, Tasso is as romance-torn as Ariosto. In some of these literary histories, Virgil is said to have founded the tradition of "imperial" epic, in the process discrediting Homer by reconfiguring both the *Iliad* and the *Odyssey* as romance. In other histories, Virgil figures as the romancer whose tragically limited hero finds fulfillment within the moral framework of subsequent, Christian epic. Spenserian critics commonly cite the Tasso-like (linear epic) structure of the second book of the *Faerie Queene* as opposed to the Ariostan (multiplotted) structure of the central books, three and four. But again there is disagreement about how (or whether) Spenser resolved these conflicting narrative drives.

When Spenser turns directly to Elizabeth I, in the Ariostan center of his work, to address her as the Queen of love and Prince of peace, he is clearly attempting, not so much to turn romance into imperial epic, as to deflect desire into love and honor. Or as Burrow argues, he is trying to persuade the queen to follow the law, rather than persuading the people to trust in a monarch's clemency. For English writers of the 1590s, it might be said that the discourses of power were too romance-infected; English epic had to express, not the will of the monarch, but the merit of the courtier. Similarly, when Chapman sides with Achilles over King Agamemnon in his *Iliads* of 1611, he is expressing his view that monarchs should recognize merit and reward it. In the hands of Chapman, Spenser, and others, epic poetry is made to criticize present government even as it reveres the mythic past.

BIBLIOGRAPHY: Bakhtin, M., "Epic and Novel" and "Forms of Time and of the Chronotope in the Novel," in Holquist, M., ed., *The Dialogic Imagination: Four Essays by M. M. Bakhtin* (1981): 3–40, 84–258; Burrow, C., *Epic Romance: Homer to Milton* (1993); Cook, P. J., *Milton, Spenser and the Epic Tradition* (1996); Falconer, R., "Bakhtin and the Epic Chronotope," in Adlam, C., et al., eds., *Face to Face: Bakhtin in Russia and the West* (1997): 254–72; Fichter, A.,

Poets Historical: Dynastic Epic in the Renaissance (1982): 327–38; Gregerson, L., *The Reformation of the Subject: Spenser, Milton, and the English Protestant Epic* (1995); Hainsworth, J. B., *The Idea of Epic* (1991); Lewalski, B. K., *Paradise Lost and the Rhetoric of Literary Forms* (1985); Martindale, C., *John Milton and the Transformation of Ancient Epic* (1986); Murrin, M., *History and Warfare in Renaissance Epic* (1994); Quint, D., *Epic and Empire* (1993); Tasso, T., *Discourses on the Heroic Poem* (1973); Watkins, J., *The Specter of Dido: Spenser and Virgilian Epic* (1995); Webber, J. M., *Milton and His Epic Tradition* (1979)

RACHEL FALCONER

ERASMUS, Desiderius

b. 27 October 1469, Rotterdam, The Netherlands; 12 July 1536, Basel, Switzerland

The foremost humanist and scholar of the northern Renaissance, E. was a pioneering editor of the New Testament and Church fathers as well as of a number of classical authors. His many writings, including *The Antibarbari*, *The Adages*, *The Education of a Christian Prince*, *The Enchiridion*, *The Colloquies*, and *In Praise of Folly*, in addition to a wide correspondence, made him an influential man of letters. He was a friend of theologian John COLET and Sir Thomas MORE, and an opponent and rival of Martin Luther. Calling for spiritual renewal and seeking a Christian community based on the consensus of the devout, E. was a voice of moderation in the Reformation, earning the opprobrium of both Protestants and Catholics.

E.'s initial reputation as a scholar rested on his *Adages*, a collection of Greek and Latin sayings and proverbs. It became an important source for writers as diverse as William SHAKESPEARE and Martin Luther. The first version, *Adagiorum collectanea*, appeared in Paris in 1500, and included 818 adages. In 1515–18, he published an expanded version, *Adagiorum Chiliades* with 3,260 entries. The 1536 Froben edition had 4,151 entries. Each entry includes the proverb in Latin and Greek where relevant, followed by a commentary that explains its literal and figurative meaning, traces its classical sources, and glosses any historical, mythical, or geographical allusions. Many of these commentaries expand into personal observations and fully developed personal essays, anticipating Montaigne's *Essais*. "The Sileni of Alcibiades," for instance, offers an important commentary on Plato's *Symposium* that subsequently influenced Rabelais. "War is sweet to those who do not know it," is probably the most famous, and includes an essay on the importance of peace.

In his own day, the *Enchiridon*, or *Handbook of the Christian Soldier*, was E.'s most influential book, summarizing both his educational and spiritual philosophy as a Christian humanist. First published in 1501, it soon saw its way into eleven modern languages and many editions. Influenced by the Franciscan spiritualism of Jean Vitrier and Origen's homilies and commentary on Paul's Epistle to the Romans, E. proposed to lay out a practical guide for the conduct of life, in which the individual is equipped to be his own spiritual guide. Concerned with the spirit rather than the letter of Christianity, he suggested that the Christian had two weapons: prayer and knowledge. The latter included the pagan classics, which he took as part of the foundation on which Christ built.

The Novum Instrumentum is E.'s most important work. First published in 1516, this was the first printed edition of the Greek New Testament, though not a critical edition in the modern sense. In many ways more significant was the accompanying revised Latin version with annotations and extended commentary on the Vulgate of Jerome. Influenced by Colet's lectures on the Epistles of Paul, E. was concerned with establishing the basis for theological reflection based on the direct reading of scripture and the Church Fathers without the mediation of scholastic philosophy.

E.'s most popular work is *In Praise of Folly*, a Lucianeque satire in the form of a speech delivered by Folly (Stulticia). The title, *Encomium Moriae*, is a multilingual pun, implying in Greek a speech of praise *by* Folly (Moria), and in Latin a speech in praise *of* (Thomas) More. E. began composing the work on a stay with More in 1509. It was published in 1511 and went through thirty-six editions by 1536. Folly explains how she makes life possible. Only fools, for instance, would marry. Only fools would endure life with all its sorrows. At times, the focus and tone of the satire are not always consistent. When Folly praises prelates and monarchs as fools, the intention is clearly satirical. When she praises the folly of the Cross, E. is profoundly serious. Playing on the semantic field of the word *ecstasy*, which can signify drunkenness, insanity, or rapture, according to context, E. develops a humanist vision of a Christianity based on intuition and divine grace rather than reason and scholastic philosophy. Were Christianity based on entirely on reason, it would little differ from ancient Stoicism. It is only as Christian "fools" that we can love our neighbor, ignore self-interest, or hope for salvation.

BIBLIOGRAPHY: Faludy, G., *E. of Rotterdam* (1970); Halkin, L.-E., *E.* (1993); Jardine, L., *E., Man of Letters* (1994); Screech, M. A., *E.* (1980)

THOMAS L. COOKSEY

ERVINE, St. John [Greer]

b. 28 December 1883, Ballymacarrett, Belfast, Ireland; d. 24 January 1971, Sussex

Playwright, theater critic, novelist, and biographer, E. evinced an early love of the theater. He began by writing plays and was at first generally regarded as a part of the turn-of-the-century revival of Irish theater of which W. B. YEATS, John Millington SYNGE, and Lady GREGORY were the leaders. Between 1911 and 1920, E. had six plays presented at the Abbey Theatre in Dublin (though for the whole of that time he was living in London). But neither by temperament nor by virtue of his writing style was he naturally a part of the Celtic-Romantic-poetic movement and his outspoken and sometimes irascible approach often set him at odds with the Abbey hierarchy. The title of his 1920 play at the Abbey is cunningly and ironically significant: *The Island of Saints and How to Get out of It.*

E. became to all intents and purposes a London dramatist, increasingly well known and respected though he did have two further plays whose first productions were at the Abbey—*Mary, Mary, Quite Contrary* (1923) and *William John Mawhinney* (1940). In all, he wrote twenty-seven plays (of which several are still quite important and eminently playable). In parallel with his playwriting, he practiced as the resident London drama critic for leading newspapers—the *Observer* (1919–23 and 1928–29), the *Morning Post* (1924–28)—and as guest critic for the *New York World* (1928–29). His critical sense was acute and well informed, his opinions illuminating, but his critical manner was often unnecessarily bellicose. Something of the same sort could justifiably be said of his six novels; what the eminent literary critic, Frank SWINNERTON, described as E.'s "shouting and clouting"—though Swinnerton, in fact, admired E. and described him as "a serious and extraordinarily able novelist." And in addition to plays, drama criticism, and novels, E. also wrote biographies of Charles Stewart Parnell (1925), Edward Carson (1929), "General" William Booth (1934)—founder of the Salvation Army—Percy Bysshe SHELLEY (1942), Oscar WILDE (1951), and Bernard SHAW (1956).

Much of this prodigious output still makes interesting reading but the fact remains that E. should be remembered chiefly as a playwright. His plays are of very variable and uneven quality but the best of them are—just short of greatness—very good indeed. The American critic Ludwig Lewisohn, writing in the *Nation* in 1922, said of *Jane Clegg* (perf. 1913; pub. 1914): "It allows no sense of artificial transition from mood to mood to awaken in us, and it preserves inviolable its seamless illusion of life. Thus the spectator need never become aware of it as of something consciously done, but can yield himself to the power of the embodied play as to an undivided artistic and spiritual experience." Lewisohn's admiration for E.'s *John Ferguson* (1915) is only slightly less than his total commitment to *Jane Clegg*, his one reservation being expressed: "In *John Ferguson* the people are real enough . . . But these people are involved in a

coil of circumstance which smacks strongly of the melodramatic theater." Myron Matlaw, on the other hand, writing fifty years later in his *Modern World Drama* (1972), confidently describes *John Ferguson* as "E.'s masterpiece" and says "*Jane Clegg* and *John Ferguson* established him as a major Irish dramatist, though he was never again to equal such accomplishments."

Jane Clegg and *John Ferguson* are written in a strictly and uncompromisingly naturalistic style (anticipating Sean O'CASEY's early work for the Abbey, but without O'Casey's flair and flourish). They deal realistically and soberly with social issues of the working class, rather similar in kind to the sort of play favored by the new, so-called repertory theaters in the big industrial cities of northern England at that time, such plays as Stanley HOUGHTON's *Hindle Wakes* and Harold BRIGHOUSE's *Hobson's Choice*—both written for Annie Horniman's Gaiety Theatre in Manchester. E.'s plays in this mode are distinguished—as are Houghton's and Brighouse's—by excellently taut construction and vividly accurate, meticulously detailed characterization. After becoming settled and successful in London, E. changed his style, adopting for his rather brittle—and now faded—comedies that now followed, a lighter, more artificial tone. It is tempting, and perhaps justifiable, to argue that this came about because of the influence, in the London theater of the 1920s, of the plays of two authors in particular—W. Somerset MAUGHAM and Noël COWARD: Maugham's *The Circle* was first produced in 1921; Coward's *Fallen Angels* came in 1924 and his *Easy Virtue* in 1925. E.'s *Mary, Mary, Quite Contrary* was first seen in London in 1925 (the same year as Coward's *Hay Fever*). The first production of Maugham's *The Constant Wife* was in 1926, and E.'s *The First Mrs. Fraser* followed in 1929. It ran for two years, overlapping with the opening of Coward's *Private Lives* in 1930. E. was for a while keeping very good company indeed. His *Anthony and Anna*, first produced in 1926 at the Liverpool Playhouse, was especially revised by him for its opening in London in 1935, where it, also, ran for two years.

One of E.'s plays of the 1920s was of a different stamp. It has been unjustly neglected by critics and producers alike but ought not to be allowed to slip into oblivion. Written in 1923, it was published (in that same year) before being staged. It was eventually produced in London in 1927. It is a satirical sequel to William SHAKESPEARE's *The Merchant of Venice*, set "exactly ten years after the date of Antonio's trial" and called *The Lady of Belmont*. Bassanio is making love to Jessica behind Portia's back; Gratiano is making love to everyone within striking distance; Nerissa has become a shrew and a scold. The only character who shows any generosity of human feeling is Shylock and even he is marred by bouts of self-pity. The play is written (sensibly) in modern prose: no pastiche iambics or quaint Elizabethan oaths. Its relationship to its great original is an honest and humble one; but a true one and one that is not without value. It could be splendidly revived in the theater of the 21st c. without any apology or patronizing condescension.

Among other of E.'s plays are *Boyd's Shop* (1936), *Robert's Wife* (perf. 1937; pub. 1938), *Friends and Relations* (perf. 1941; pub. 1947), and *The Christies* (perf. 1947; pub. 1948). By the time he came to these, he had abandoned the drawing room comedy and was writing what one might call "plays of social and moral responsibility," though concerned now not with the "working class" but with the professional middle classes.

BIBLIOGRAPHY: Lewisohn, L., *The Drama and the Stage* (1922); Matlaw, M., *Modern World Drama* (1972); Swinnerton, F., *The Georgian Literary Scene* (1935); Trewin, J. C., *The Theatre since 1900* (1951)

ERIC SALMON

ETHEREGE, [Sir] George
b. 1634?, Maidenhead, Berkshire?; d. ca. 10 May 1692, possibly in France

Creator of the so-called comedy of manners, E. is also credited with inspiring both the heroic tragedy of John DRYDEN and the comic realism of William CONGREVE, Oliver GOLDSMITH, and Richard Brinsley SHERIDAN. E.'s own literary output is relatively modest. His play, *The Comical Revenge; or, Love in a Tub* (1664) is often said to have influenced the next two generations of playwrights. Its serious main plot was written in heroic couplets while the comic subplot reveled in a free-spirited prose style that would not be equaled again until the mature works of Congreve. His significant writing beyond this play is limited to his two masterly comedies, *She Would If She Could* (1668) and *The Man of Mode; or, Sir Fopling Flutter* (1676). Both of these later works demonstrate E.'s skill at mannered comedy and social satire while maintaining his characteristic élan and ease of style.

EVELYN, John
b. 31 October 1620, Wotton House, Surrey; d. 27 February 1706, London

In 1657, the physician William Rand dedicated to E. *The Mirrour of True Nobility & Gentility. Being the Life of the Renowned Nicolaus Claudius Fabricius Lord of Peiresk* because like Rand's subject E. possessed a "sprightful curiosity [that] left nothing unsearcht into, in the vast and all-comprehending Dominions of Nature and Art." In nearly all of the some 4,000 books that E. collected, he wrote his motto, "Omnia Explorate, Meliora Retinete," which he translated as "Proove All things, Retaine the Best." This library provides one measure of E.'s eclectic intellect. E.'s 1687 catalogue lists 782 theological works, 518 volumes of poetry, 231 dealing with law, another 204 on philosophy, 189 about medicine, 148 on philology.

E.'s fifty publications, beginning in 1649 and continuing for half a century, are equally wide-ranging. E. translated the first book of Lucretius' Latin *De rerum natura* (1656). In 1659, he translated from the Greek *The Golden Book of St. John Chrysostom, Concerning the Education of Children*. E.'s *Character of England* appeared that same year, offering a satiric portrait of the Interregnum. His 1661 *Fumifugium* addressed London's air pollution, proposing that industry be removed from the city and a green belt of fragrant trees, shrubs, and flowers be planted around the metropolis. Other of his writings include the first history of engraving in England (*Sculptura*, 1662), studies of architecture, medicine, and painting, and a book on the collecting of medals (*Numismatica*, 1697).

E.'s greatest love was, however, plants. At his home at Sayes Court, Kent, he created a model garden, and he published repeatedly on the subject, beginning with *The French Gardiner* (1658), a translation of Nicolas de Bonnefons's *Le Jardinier François* (1651) and continuing with *The English Vineyard* (1666), *The Compleat Gard'ner* (1693), which is largely a translation of Jean de la Quintyne's *Instruction pour les Jardins Fruitiers et Potagers* (1690), and E.'s *Acetaria* (1699), a charming disquisition on salads.

In his own day, E. was best known for *Sylva; or, A Discourse of Forest Trees* (1664). When in 1689 Sir Godfrey Kneller painted E.'s portrait for E.'s friend Samuel PEPYS, E. posed with a copy of *Sylva* in his right hand. England had been suffering from deforestation, and the Royal Navy needed trees. On October 15, 1662, E. presented a "Discourse Concerning Forest-Trees" to the Royal Society, which E. had joined at its inception. The Royal Society ordered the work printed, and Charles II thanked E. in person. The 1664 edition included *Pomona*, a short piece on growing fruit trees for cider, and *Kalendarium Hortense*, a month-by-month guide for gardeners.

The work for which E. is remembered, however, is not one that he published or even intended for publication, his *Diary*, part of which first appeared in print in 1818. Combining memoir and daily jottings, the diary begins with E.'s birth and ends on February 3, 1706. Unlike the diary of E.'s contemporary Pepys, E.'s rarely expresses emotion. It mentions his engagement to Mary Browne in a parenthetical aside and devotes more space to describing a ring-tailed lemur than to recounting the birth of his son George.

E. was a keen observer, though, so the *Diary* serves as an indispensable record of public and private life in 17th-c. England. E. takes the reader to the funeral of Oliver Cromwell, which E., a royalist, called "the joyfullest funeral that ever I saw" (November 22, 1658). With E., one sees the return of Charles II to England in 1660 and his coronation the next year. E. vividly records of the Great Fire of London: "all the skie were of a fiery aspect, like the top of a burning Oven, and the light seene above 40 miles round about for many nights" (September 2, 1666). With E., one watches the royal mistress Nell Gwyn lean over a garden wall to talk to her lover, and one visits the fair on the Thames when the river froze so thickly in winter of 1683–84 that "whole streetes of boothes" were erected on the ice, "so as it seem'd to be a bacchanalia, Triumph or Carnoval on the Water" (January 9 and 24, 1684). In "Rambling Round Evelyn" (1920), Virginia WOOLF notes that E. never in his diary exposed "the secrets of his heart." Still, from these pages a world emerges, as does E., despite himself. Here is a man cautious, conservative, perhaps a bit smug, but always curious, always watching, and, happily for posterity, always writing.

BIBLIOGRAPHY: Hiscock, W. G., *J. E. and His Family Circle* (1955); Keynes, G., *J. E.* (2nd ed., 1968); Welcher, J. K., *J. E.* (1972); Willy, N., *English Diarists: E. and Pepys* (1963)

JOSEPH ROSENBLUM

EWART, Gavin [Buchanan]

b. 4 February 1916, London; d. 23 October 1995, London

Following the domestic, conversational, ironically witty but emotionally distant poems of Philip LARKIN and other Movement poets, E.'s bawdy but elegantly formal verse reanimated British poetics. E. showed early promise with the publication of *Poems and Songs* in 1939, but his military service delayed his literary career for nearly three decades. Returning from active duty during World War II, E. spent most of the 1950s and 1960s as an advertising copywriter. His second book of poems did not appear until 1964. *Londoners* and the following volume, *Pleasures of the Flesh* (1966) both retained some of the sad but comic tone of "The Movement" while expressing a much more frank sexuality. Adding the influence of John BETJEMAN to earlier affinities with T. S. ELIOT and W. H. AUDEN, E. also returned to structure and form, paying closer attention to stanza and language than the poets of the 1950s.

The Deceptive Grin of the Gravel Porters (1968) showed the development of E.'s individual voice with more autobiographical poems, a sense of punning and playful language, and even fragmentary structures reminiscent of advertising copy. "Daddyo" addresses one of the same subjects as Larkin's "High Windows," age observing and coveting the folly of youth. "Now it is my turn/to be the red-faced fool," the speaker laments, distancing himself enough to assess his own absurdity in the eyes of the "sneering miniskirts," girls so remote and unapproachable they are reduced to a metonym. In 1971, E. embraced popularity with the title *The Gavin Ewart Show*, in which poems such as "People Will Say We're In Love" and "& Son" burlesque middle-class desires and mock the implied stability there. *An Imaginary Love Affair* (1974) uses the title scenario as the setting for a series of comic, romantic verses with titles such as "The Lover Complains," "The Lover Writes a One-Word Poem," and "The Lover Reflects." The self-deprecating HUMOR of the speaker creates an atmosphere of honesty and intimacy. The closeness is reinforced by tight forms and regular rhythms.

Another of E.'s strengths is parody. His revisions of other poets' poems not only amuse but often reassert the importance of the earlier work. As early as *Pleasures of the Flesh*, familiar titles like "To the Virgins, to Make the Most of Time" appeared, and with *Be My Guest* (1975), "The Larkin Automatic Car Wash" both celebrates and tweaks the work of the most well-known British contemporary poet. "The Larkin Automatic Car Wash" borrows Larkin's stanza form from "The Whitsun Weddings," as well as many of the major themes of his works. In it, the speaker visits a car wash with a car full of teenagers, precipitating a comic epiphany for all. The excitement of the mechanized device provides "an exit from our boring life," and during the process they find "a notable peak where all is flat." "Cars too grow old and dirty," muses the speaker, finding his philosophy personified in the workings of his middle-class world. "Found!" in the same volume is a series of advertising slogans culled from a women's magazine, the poet again finding higher meaning embedded in the everyday.

No Fool like an Old Fool (1976) continues the E. pattern of humor, wisdom, and sexual themes in carefully wrought forms: Anglo-Saxon verse, sonnet, Venus and Adonis stanza. *Or When a Young Penguin Lies Screaming* (1977) presents more lust-minded speakers in "A Passionate Woman" and "What It Is." In 1980 came *The Collected Ewart, 1933–1980*, along with *All My Little Ones*, a collection of shorter forms, most notably the clerihew, a favorite of E.'s; he even edited the complete works of E. C. BENTLEY, originator of the form. Another *Collected Poems* extends to 1990; a later *Selected Poems* was published in 1996. E. edited several anthologies on a variety of topics: school songs, children's verse, light verse. Among his honors were the Chomondeley Award (1971) and the Michael Brande Award for Light Verse from the American Academy (1991).

BIBLIOGRAPHY: Reading, P., "G. E.," in Sherry, V. B., Jr., ed., *Poets of Great Britain and Ireland since 1960*, part 1, *DLB* 40 (1988): 110–16

NICOLE SARROCCO

EXPATRIATES

In the present age of globalization, characterized by the rapid transit of both people and data, it is ironic that the basic attitudes toward travel are still those described in the 12th c. by a Saxon monk, Hugo of St. Victor. Hugo writes: "The man who finds his homeland sweet is still a tender beginner; he to whom every soil is as his native one is already strong; but he is perfect to whom the entire world is as a foreign land. The tender soul has fixed his love on one spot in the world; the strong man has extended his love to all places; the perfect man has extinguished his." Clearly there is an athletic quality to Hugo's hierarchy. It is a virtue, he notes, "for the practised mind to learn, bit by bit, first to change about individual and transitory things, so that afterwards it may be able to leave them behind altogether." Through striving, in other words, the "tender" person with limited sensibilities can become a "strong" one with broader tastes and perhaps even a "perfect" being who floats above the world, detached from the mundane.

While Hugo is describing a quest for spiritual perfection, his basic terms may be applied to aesthetic stances as well. An example of a "strong" writer is W. H. AUDEN, who was born English, became a U.S. citizen in 1946, returned to England in 1956, and seemed equally comfortable throughout his adult life in England, the U.S., and Austria, where he died; his work reflects an attachment to these and other cultures, including Iceland, China, and Spain, all subjects of his writing. And a "perfect" writer would be Joseph CONRAD, who spent twenty years at sea; who wrote in his third language (Polish and French were the first two); and whose best-known tale, "Heart of Darkness," is set in Africa. Another example of the "perfect" writer is James JOYCE, the great chronicler of Irish life who left Ireland for good as a young man.

The examples of Conrad and Joyce recall Terry Eagleton's startling but irrefutable assertion that "the seven most significant writers of 20th-c. English literature have been a Pole, three Americans, two Irishmen, and an Englishman. . . . With the exception of D. H. LAWRENCE, the heights of modern English literature have been dominated by foreigners and émigrés: Conrad, James, Eliot, Pound, Yeats, Joyce." Virginia WOOLF is the egregious exception to Eagleton's list of important authors, but his general point is unassailable. According to Eagleton, this dominance by non-English poets and novelists "points to certain central flaws and impoverishments in conventional English culture itself," a culture unable to encourage great lit-

erary production among the native born. Yet Henry JAMES, Ezra Pound, and T. S. ELIOT all stated explicitly that, whereas they found American air thin and stifling, thus making the same argument about their native land as Eagleton makes about England, they flourished in what was to them a rich and heady transatlantic atmosphere. It seems somewhat parochial to argue that one country rather than another is more or less likely to produce great literary art. The larger point is that all writers participate in a complex transaction between self and society; some engage best with their native settings, while others seek engagement on foreign soil. Eagleton points to William BLAKE, William WORDSWORTH, Charles DICKENS, and George ELIOT as examples of the former, while this essay will concentrate on three representative examples of the latter group, those who found expatriate life not only desirable but necessary.

Born Teodor Josef Konrad Korzeniowski, the writer who came to be known as Joseph Conrad is in many ways the quintessential expatriate writer. Born of Polish parents, he went to sea on a French vessel as a teenager and became a British subject in 1886; after twenty years at sea, he settled in England and began to write in English, his third language. Alienation is a constant in Conrad's work, and it shows nowhere better than in his two best-known works, *Lord Jim* and the short story "Heart of Darkness." In the novel, Jim is the chief mate of a ship that appears to be in danger of sinking; in an incomprehensible moment, Jim jumps to safety, but when the ship stays afloat, his cowardice becomes a matter of public record. Guilt-stricken and morally confused, Jim wanders the earth, finally ending in a remote East Asian village where he takes advantage of his chance to start over again and becomes a community leader, though in the end, he literally lays down his life when he is unable to save the village from massacre. Like *Lord Jim*, "Heart of Darkness" is set far from the English comfort in which Conrad composed it. It is the story of Mr. Kurtz, who, like Jim, loses his moral bearings once he penetrates the wilderness. Kurtz is a phenomenally successful ivory trader, but he has also become the murderous dictator of the African village he rules, a crime he himself recognizes as he dies muttering "The horror! The horror!" Interestingly, the events of both novel and story are seen through the eyes of a thoughtful observer named Marlow, a character with a journalist's love of detail and a philosopher's flair for moral distinctions: in other words, a person, albeit fictional, much like Conrad himself.

Like Conrad, Rudyard KIPLING wrote of the dangers of empire-building and its corollary departure from home virtues, though his stances on the subject are less ambiguous and therefore more controversial. Born in India, Kipling came to England as a child but returned to the country of his birth to work as a journalist. While in India, he wrote many of the poems and stories that would make him famous; he scrutinized the British presence in India with a hard-boiled cynicism but was generally supportive of England's attempts to "civilize" the natives. Wildly popular during the Empire's heyday, Kipling's work became a subject of contention when the public's mood turned less jingoistic. When he referred to "the white man's burden" in his poem of the same title (1899), he mixed praise of empire-building with somber warnings of the inevitable price of domination.

It would be hard to imagine a less Kiplingesque figure than the ultra-aesthete Joyce. Born and educated in Ireland, Joyce lived in Paris for a year, returned to Dublin briefly, then left his native country more or less permanently, living in Trieste and Geneva before settling in Paris. What makes Joyce an especially interesting case of expatriatism is that, unlike Kipling, Joyce recognized exile as both an interior as well as an exterior condition. Indeed, his famous self-description in the semiautobiographical *A Portrait of the Artist as a Young Man* is of a character who appropriates "silence, exile, cunning" and ultimately has to go abroad if he is to face "the reality of experience and to forge in the smithy of my soul the uncreated conscience of my race." Set in Dublin during a single day, his novel *Ulysses* is place-bound on the surface, but the parallels between its principal character Leopold Bloom and Homer's Ulysses, who wanders the Aegean Sea encountering marvels and terrors, cleverly illustrates that no one is ever truly at home and is perhaps most abroad when he is treading the familiar. From the straightforward early prose of *A Portrait* to the complex and allusive style of *Ulysses*, Joyce deliberately makes himself all but unreadable in *Finnegans Wake*, a fall-and-resurrection cycle written in a prose that is poetic to the point of obscurity. A joy for specialists and the bane of students everywhere, *Finnegans Wake* is a work that dramatizes what Joyce evidently saw as a fundamental human condition of alienation by isolating readers and exiling them from that which is closest, i. e., their own language.

The examples of Conrad, Kipling, and Joyce illustrate that the permutations of ideas and feelings about expatriate life and its many corollary topics are both complex and infinite in number. Those interested in other notable writers who lived and wrote abroad might consider the writings of W. Somerset MAUGHAM, Lawrence, Jean RHYS, George ORWELL, and Graham GREENE. As different as they are from each other, all of the writers mentioned in this essay assumed voluntarily the personal inconvenience that comes with life in another country as well as the damage to relationships, the loss of a familiar culture, the expense. So why all this fuss? Is every expatriate a misfit or a snob, and is life abroad their only option? To look at the lives and work of the artists discussed here is to understand the particular nature of the bargain the expatriate author has made, a pact in which a price is paid for a priceless commodity and much is sacrificed so that much more is gained. Anyone who has done no more than leave town for a few days will understand critic Adam Gopnik's statement that "the loneliness of the expatriate is of an odd and complicated kind, for it is inseparable from the feeling of being free, of having escaped."

With so much still to be said on this rich subject, one could do worse than conclude with two summary statements by Paul THEROUX, an acclaimed novelist but also the author of such travel books as *The Old Patagonian Express*, *The Great Railway Bazaar*, *Riding the Iron Rooster*, and *The Happy Isles of Oceania*. According to Theroux, "Travel, which is nearly always regarded as an attempt to escape from the ego, is in my opinion the opposite: nothing induces concentration or stimulates memory like an alien landscape or a foreign culture." And "when people ask me what they should do to become a writer . . . I say, 'You want to be a writer? First leave home.'"

BIBLIOGRAPHY: Broe, M. L., and A. Ingram, eds., *Women's Writing in Exile* (1989); Eagleton, T., *Exiles and Emigrés* (1970); Gopnik, A., *Paris to the Moon* (2000); Lagos-Pope, M.-I., ed., *Exile in Literature* (1988); Said, E. W., *Reflections on Exile and Other Essays* (2000); Seidel, M., *Exile and the Narrative Imagination* (1986); Theroux, P., *Fresh Air Fiend: Travel Writings, 1985–2000* (2000); Tucker, M., ed., *Literary Exile in the Twentieth Century* (1991)

DAVID KIRBY

FAIRBAIRNS, Zoë [Ann]
b. 20 December 1948, England

F. studied history at St. Andrews University and in the U.S. at the College of William and Mary in Williamsburg, Virginia. A freelance writer, she has been poetry editor of *Spare Rib* magazine, tutor in creative writing, and writer in residence at various London schools, Deakin University in Geelong, Australia, and at Sunderland Polytechnic. She has also been involved in running the Women's Research and Resources Centre, a feminist library in London. She campaigns against nuclear weapons and historical insight shapes her fiction. In 1978, she published her feminist short stories in the anthology *Tales I Tell My Mother*, followed in 1988 by a supplemental volume, *More Tales I Tell My Mother*. F.'s best-known work is her first novel, *Benefits* (1979), a dark, dystopic vision of the future in which women are disempowered by successive governments. Her irony and wit are original and challenging. Her novel *Stand We at Last* (1983) tells the story of five generations of women over 120 years. The narrative moves from England to Australia to America to India, reflecting the battle for the vote, the devastation of war, the growth of sexual freedom along with birth control and the rise of the women's movement. Among her other works are *Here Today* (1984), *Closing* (1988), *Daddy's Girls* (1991), and *Other Names* (1999).

FAIRY TALES

Fairy tales are a part of the world's vast common stock of stories, literally folktales. Fairy tales have, however, their own special quality and not all folktales are fairy tales. The essence of a fairy tale is a story of growing up, maturation, usually with a strong element of wish-fulfillment by way of fantasy, and normally with a happy ending. The element of fantasy gave rise, in French, to the idea that a fairy tale was necessarily a "story about fairies," but it is a misnomer for there are few fairies at least as we think of them in the tales, though there are persons with magic properties. Fantasy and daydreaming used to be taken as a reason for contempt or hostility to "fairy tales" but that view is now rare. Fairy tales control fantasy by demonstrating the need for the young protagonist, female or male, to suffer and strive, be clever, brave, kind, at first in adversity. The reward is usually to meet someone of similar age and opposite sex, often of superior social status ("prince" or "princess"). The two fall in love and the fairy tale usually but not always ends in marriage. It represents the passage from youth to adulthood, where the youth, male or female, has been tested by adversity, become an adult individual, and can then join the adult community. To this extent, the underlying structure is common to most cultures and protagonists of either gender. Although since the 18th c. the ostensible audience has been children, any person of any age can easily identify with the protagonist. It is a process all adults recognize and are usually ready to reimagine, for it is never complete until we die. The tests vary according to social and historical circumstance and whether the protagonist is male or female. The elements of fairy tale are very ancient, evidence often surviving incidentally in references by other written, later, printed forms, for the earliest stories existed in oral form, told and retold through generations. The fundamental setting is thus the family, mother, father, protagonist, siblings, and eventually one another, the Outsider, the marriageable one, for exogamy is the rule. This central passage of every surviving human life, from adolescence to youthful maturity, is of continuing interest to young and old, and only since the 18th c. in Western Europe have fairy tales been regarded as specifically for children. Even so, adults continue to enjoy them either as they tell them to children or when disguised as the underlying structure of perhaps most novels for adults. In some rural communities even late in the 20th c., fairy tales were part of the body of common tales told in social gatherings of family and friends.

Typical fairy tales in the Western tradition, too well known to need summarizing, are *Cinderella* (though with ultimate origin apparently in 9th-c. China); *Beauty and the Beast; Little Red Riding Hood; Snow White and the Seven Dwarfs; Sleeping Beauty;* these all with heroines. Typical tales with male protagonists are *Puss in Boots; The Golden Goose; The Magic Table, the Golden Donkey and the Club in the Sack; Jack and the Beanstalk* (though unusually the hero goes back to mother after killing the giant he has robbed); *The Brave Little Tailor; The Tinder Box;* though there are more female than male protagonists among the fairy tales. What is listed here is only a tiny fragment of examples and there are many others. Hero or heroine must find a mate outside the family. It is usual for the protagonist to suffer some sort of disadvantage or discontent, called a "lack," which may be of many different kinds. Adversity and adventure of various kinds follow. Quite often the protagonist commits some apparent fault, infringement of some rule or command, at first to her or his disadvantage but eventually, since overcome by ingenuity, bravery, industry, or cunning, usually, though not always, leading to success. The circumstances of the fairy tales are preindustrial as well as fundamentally domestic, though the outside world is there as the wild wood, and journeys on foot, horse, or carriage, are undertaken often with danger.

The patterns and potential complications of the basic "family drama" are as varied as the potential tensions any person or family may experience when growing up but are not the only driving forces. Hunger in various sometimes symbolic forms is not unusual. The classic fairy tale of hunger is *Hansel and Gretel*, small children abandoned by their parents for lack of food in the forest, found by a witch who lives in a gingerbread house and who wants to fatten Hansel to be eaten. They only just escape. The desire for wealth and beauty are further natural driving motifs.

The social scale ranges from talking animals, little old men, robbers, poor woodcutters, merchants, to princes, princesses, and kings, though the "kings" may well be of the kind that open their own front doors. Almost all old women (Cinderella's Fairy Godmother excepted) are sinister. The far fewer old men may be helpful, like the little old man who helps the hero to the magic golden goose, as a reward for sharing the miserly crust that his mean-spirited mother has given him, in contrast to the excellent lunches his mother gives to his selfish elder brothers, where resentment at parents and siblings is shown.

The progress of the story depends at one or more stages on special luck, disadvantage or advantage, some fantasy, which is the absolute fundamental nature of the fairy tale, its value as an imaginative escape from a life that promises to be constrained or dull, and the reason why some serious-minded persons at all times have condemned it as "mere" escapist daydreaming. Serious modern psychology has plenty of evidence that the imaginative strength that comes from daydreaming benefits the developing personality and can refresh the imagination at any age. This is part of the importance of all literature and art, and the fairy tale makes its own particular contribution, with its conscious element of fantasy or magic. Although there is some similarity with medieval romances, the fairy tale is always short. It is not to be confused with longer fictional forms, especially the modern novel as developed since the 18th c., nor the modern short story nor the longer fantasy fictions, or magic realism, for example L. Frank Baum's *The Wizard of Oz* (1900), Kenneth GRAHAME's *The Wind in the Willows*, J. R. R. TOLKIEN's *The Hobbit*, or the series of Harry Potter stories by J. K. ROWLING at the beginning of the 21st c.

Fairy tales retain many verbal and social characteristics from their rural origin: characters are simple, hierarchical social structures ranging from peasants to kings. Above all, fairy tales have fantasy and daydreaming at heart, enriching the imagination with strange events, talking animals, magic tricks, princes, heroines, sturdy tricksters, some witches and villains, but also supernatural helpers. Daydreaming and wish-fulfillment are basic to fairy tale, and generally the outcome is successful for the protagonist, whether female or male, who is trying to grow up. The stories nourish the imagination by being entertaining, before teaching or warning, though they may do both. They feed our hunger for experience in a special way, through evoking forces that particularly as children we know but are hardly aware of. We imaginatively experience threats and hopes. The fairy tale encourages a basic self-esteem and confidence. It conveys the idea that if we persist, if we keep our nerve and our wits about us, are kind to the apparently weak and unfortunate, we shall win through, shall grow up. This is why fairy tales appeal to children, as a kind of prophecy, but as grown-ups we still need encouragement and hope as we confront the recurring tests of life. That is why much literature of a highly complex and sophisticated kind, engaging more directly the adult problems of life and death on a more realistic scale, relies on an underlying fairy-tale structure, even if a tragic end ensues. Examples are some medieval romances with their magic plots and tests, such as *Sir Gawain and the Green Knight*, William SHAKESPEARE's *A Midsummer Night's Dream*, and even *King Lear* (a variant of *Cinderella* with a tragic end, the central figure displaced from the heroine to her father); Jane AUSTEN's and Charles DICKENS's novels; these are only outstanding examples. In the late 20th c., sophisticated feminist socialist writers resented the patriarchal gender-stereotyping of the original tales. Angela CARTER is the most famous and able in, for example, *The Bloody Chamber and Other Stories,* where the wolf in *Little Red Riding Hood* is portrayed as a genial and welcome seducer of girls. But such inversions and perversions are necessarily parasitical, depending on the strong base of the earlier tradition. This earlier tradition portrays a hierarchical society that is strongly gender-typed, which is why the modern politically correct attempt to change it. There is nothing unusual in the change in itself. Fairy tales change according to time, place, teller, audience. The elements are age-old, recognizable even in modern postindustrial Western society, but it seems likely that the type of fairy tale we now recognize began to be consolidated from about the 14th c. Though so variable in detail, the main lines are clear—the rural and family setting, the striving, the element of fantasy and luck.

Originally oral, fairy tales naturally found their way into print when relatively cheap small books became available and from then on there is a constant exchange between printed and oral versions, as parents of small children know. The first collection, *Le Piacevoli notti* (Delightful Nights) appeared in Italy about 1550–53. Other collections followed. A great boost was given in the royal court of France at the end of the 17th c. Various fashionable ladies held salons where for a little while sessions of telling fairy tales among adults became common. Some of these stories were published by Charles Perrault in 1697, first translated into English by Robert Samber in 1729. These give essentially the modern form but that there were earlier fairy tales in England is shown by traces in Geoffrey CHAUCER, Shakespeare (*A Midsummer Night's Dream*), and especially by George PEELE's strange jumble of a play *The Old Wives Tale.* Probably a combination of Puritanism, combined with the 17th-c. idea that words should be as close as possible to things, as Thomas HOBBES urged—both forces working against fantasy and daydreaming—together with early industrialization, broke up rural continuities and helped to destroy the native English rural tradition of folktale and thus fairy tale. As soon as similar stories came back in cheap and easily available printed form in the 18th c., they were eagerly seized upon. From the late 18th c., ROMANTICISM with the cult of the child and the German cult of "the folk" gave new impetus that was given new force by the work of German scholars, the brothers Grimm, who collected folktales and whose publication of them, somewhat edited, first appeared in 1812. It was added to progressively in the 19th c., the tales sometimes being rewritten, as is common with folktale and fairy tale. *The Household Tales* of the brothers Grimm were first translated into English in 1823 and have now been translated and appreciated all over the world. The ti-

tles given here to various fairy tales have been taken from the latest translation of Grimm's fairy tales by Jack Zipes (1992). The 19th c. saw many collections, the most notable being the twelve "color" books of fairy tales edited by Andrew LANG from 1889, but Celtic oral sources provided another rich field when collected and printed. Hans Christian Andersen remarkably invented many fairy tale-like stories, not quite true fairy tales but related in style and theme, like "The Ugly Duckling" (1845), and enormously successful. But the greatest success of all was achieved by Walt Disney whose cartoons based on fairy tales have enjoyed huge success worldwide, despite, or perhaps because of, their sentimentality and banality, and the occasional menacing cartoon images that deliciously terrify small children.

The latter part of the 20th c. saw an immense increase in scholarly studies and very considerable controversy has arisen both on what constitutes a fairy tale (should oral sources only qualify or may printed editions be counted?) and on how should fairy tales be interpreted. The best modern collection in English of manageable size is *The Classic Fairy Tales,* compiled by Iona and Peter OPIE. The basic study is by Bengt Holbek, *Interpretation of Fairy Tales* (1987), somewhat neglected because of its vast extent. A very penetrating psychoanalytical study of perhaps excessively Freudian nature is Bruno Bettelheim's *The Uses of Enchantment* (1976). Marina Warner in *From the Beast to the Blonde* (1995) discusses especially the contribution of the French in the 17th and 18th cs. The Russian scholar V. Propp deduced an unchanging deep structure of folktale and hence fairy tales that has been very influential. Derek Brewer discusses "the family drama" in fairy tales and its uses and variations in mostly later English literature. Many other scholars have written well, and though the association with CHILDREN'S LITERATURE is now very strong the former hostility or contempt for fairy tale both by adults generally and scholars seems to have disappeared. Something of their true value is now appreciated.

BIBLIOGRAPHY: Bettelheim, B., *The Uses of Enchantment: The Meaning and Importance of Fairy Tales* (1976); Brewer, D., *Symbolic Stories* (1980); Holbeck, B., *Interpretation of Fairy Tales: Danish Folklore in a European Perspective* (1987); Lüthi, M., *The Fairytale as Art Form and Portrait of Man,* trans. by J. Erickson (1984); Opie, I., and P. Opie, eds., *The Classic Fairy Tales* (1974); Perrault, C., *Histoires ou Contes du temps passé* (1697; *Histories or Tales of Past Times,* 1729); Propp, V., *The Morphology of the Folktale,* trans. by L. Scott (1958; rev. ed., 1968); Singer, J. L., *Daydreaming and Fantasy* (1976); Warner, M., *From the Beast to the Blonde: On Fairy Tales and Their Tellers* (1995); Zipes, J., *Breaking the*

Magic Spell: Radical Theories of Folk and Fairy Tales (1979); Zipes, J., ed., *The Oxford Companion to Fairy Tales* (2000)

DEREK BREWER

FALKLAND [Viscountess], Elizabeth Cary

b. ca. 1585, Burford, Oxfordshire; d. October 1639, London

One of the most widely studied Renaissance woman writers, F. is the first known Englishwoman to write both a tragedy and a full-length historical narrative. She had, however, only mixed success in her own time. Initially a greatly respected writer and an influential enough literary patron to be placed in the same category as Mary Herbert, Countess of PEMBROKE, and Lucy Russell, Countess of Bedford, F.'s fame in her own time turned to notoriety when she converted to Roman Catholicism around 1626.

F.'s best-known work, the Senecan closet drama *The Tragedie of Mariam, the Fairie Queene of Jewry*, was most likely written between 1603 and 1604 and published in 1613; it was, however, performed for the first time only in 1994 at the Bradford Alhambra Studio, U.K. *The Tragedy of Mariam*, often compared to William SHAKESPEARE's *Othello*, deals explicitly with the difficulty of presenting oneself accurately through language, particularly for women; the nature of male tyranny and women's possible responses to it; and the paradoxical and enigmatic nature of feminine virtue. The parallels between the innocent but doomed protagonist Mariam and her vicious, Iago-like foil, Salome, have been much discussed and are seen as integral to F.'s harsh questioning of the Renaissance's exclusive equation of female virtue with chastity, silence, and obedience.

The equally intriguing parallels F. makes between Mariam and her jealous and murderous husband Herod, however, have received little critical exploration. These similarities do not necessarily undermine the currently predominant protofeminist reading of the text; rather, they may be seen as part of F.'s attempt to destabilize Renaissance notions of both female virtue specifically and the belief in an implicit connection between gender and identity generally, the latter of which is seen in Salome's musings of divorce.

The other surviving work attributed to F. is the long, stylistically unusual history of Edward II. There are two surviving versions of the text; both claim to have been written in 1627 but were not published until 1680 during the Exclusion Crisis. Scholars have yet to concur either on whether F. was the author of the texts or on how exactly the two texts are related. The longer text, *The History of the Life, Reign, and Death of Edward II, King of England, and Lord of Ireland. With the Rise and Fall of his great Favourites, Gaves-*

ton and the Spencers, is the text universally subjected to critical study. An unusual combination of prose, blank verse, and dramatic dialogue, *The History* deals with many of the same issues worked out in *The Tragedy of Mariam*, particularly the disjoint between the spoken word and reality. The narrator harshly criticizes Edward's personal and magisterial failings yet ultimately places more blame on those that depose him; similarly, F.'s portrayal of Queen Isabel is hardly as straightforwardly sympathetic as critics have tended to assert. Though she is portrayed initially as a modest, innocent, abused wife, and later as a brave woman engaging on a romantic quest that leads to her claiming the English throne on behalf of her young son, Isabel is ultimately constructed as the stereotypical shrew, somehow both dangerous and incompetent.

According to her eldest daughter's biography entitled *The Lady Falkland: Her Life* (wr. 1643–49; pub. 1861), F. wrote many more works that did not survive. Among the lost texts are a childhood translation of Abraham Ortelius's *Le Miroir du Monde*; some hymns and poems dedicated to the Virgin Mary; saints' lives of Mary Magdalene, Agnes the Martyr, and Elizabeth of Portugal; an epitaph on George Villiers, first Duke of Buckingham (wr. ca. 1628); and a translation of *The Reply of the Most Illustrious Cardinall of Perron* (1630).

BIBLIOGRAPHY: Chedgzoy, K., et al., eds., *Voicing Women: Gender and Sexuality in Early Modern Writing* (1996); Lewalski, B. K., *Writing Women in Jacobean England* (1993); Purkiss, D., ed., *Renaissance Women: The Plays of E. C.; The Poems of Aemilia Lanyer* (1994)

COLLEEN SHEA

FALKNER, John Meade

b. 8 May 1858, Wiltshire; d. 22 July 1932, Durham

F. is an interesting case as a writer. He produced three novels, a small quantity of poetry, and handbooks to Oxfordshire, Berkshire, and Bath. He enjoyed a range of scholarly pursuits, eventually becoming librarian to Durham Cathedral and honorary reader in paleography at Durham University. The way in which F.'s fiction went hand in hand with his academic interest in ecclesiastical architecture or heraldry or church music is reminiscent of how the ghost stories of his contemporary M. R. JAMES grew out of the latter's cloistered existence at King's College, Cambridge.

Yet there was another, substantial dimension to F.'s public life. After Oxford, he was taken on as tutor to the family of Sir Andrew Noble of the armaments firm of Armstrong in Newcastle-upon-Tyne. The Noble connection largely determined the next four decades of F.'s life. He became secretary to the company (by then Armstrong Whitworth), later a director, and was eventually elected chairman in 1915. That F. was appointed to head a major armament concern in the middle of a world war is testament to rather more than simple business acumen. Yet even during this period F. continued to write poetry and shorter fiction.

F. was not therefore a "professional" writer in the usual sense. He was not dependent on writing for an income nor was he a member of any literary set (although he was a friend of Thomas HARDY, whom he greatly admired). His work, though small in quantity, is disparate and does not quite add up to an oeuvre. Yet each "piece," while having affinities with particular genres or models, has a unique quality. His first novel, *The Lost Stradivarius* (1896), is a ghost story. The 18th-c. settings—an Oxford college, country estates, a Neapolitan villa—are standard enough, but there is a bleak and unresolved aspect to the narrative that indicates that F.'s interest goes beyond the traditional frisson provided by James or Joseph Sheridan LE FANU. In particular, in *The Lost Stradivarius* F. begins to explore a theme that haunts his other two fictions, the malign overshadowing of the present by the past.

This theme is more fully developed in F.'s best-known work, *Moonfleet* (1898). Rightly described as a classic, this narrative—a tale of smugglers on the Dorset coast, cliff-top chases, and hairbreadth escapes—also provides an unobtrusive parable on the corrupting effects of greed and obsession, as the narrator John Trenchard goes in pursuit of a legendary diamond "as big as a pigeon's egg." It is characteristically Victorian that at the end of the novel redemption can be gained only through sacrifice and restitution. The strengths of *Moonfleet* are its evocation of place (particularly of weather) and the straightforward sympathy of its characterization. Like *The Lost Stradivarius, Moonfleet* is set in the 18th c. and F. displays an unshowy grasp of the idiom of a slightly earlier age than his own. Above all—and this is what has kept *Moonfleet* in print ever since—it is a determined, forward-driving narrative, a page-turner.

For his third and most complex fiction, *The Nebuly Coat* (1903), F. moved into the late 19th c. The setting, an imagined Dorset estuary town that seems to be an amalgam of Dorchester and Chichester, owes something to Hardy. It may be significant that one of the principal figures is a young architect come to superintend the restoration of the minster church in Cullerne, where he meets Anastasia Joliffe, F.'s most fully realized heroine. This strand of the story is reminiscent of the real-life account of Hardy's meeting with his first wife on an architectural commission in Cornwall. Other aspects of *The Nebuly Coat* recall Anthony TROLLOPE's Barchester novels—Cullerne is comically depicted as a place of petty gossip and ecclesiastical snobbery—and Wilkie COLLINS's *The Woman in White*, since key elements in the plot turn on the question of legitimacy and the frantic hunt for documents. Yet the novel does not stand in the shadow of any other work and, like its author, refuses to be pigeonholed.

F. is an author who is at the moment appreciated rather than properly assessed. His following is narrow but enthusiastic, the 1932 obituary in the *Times* referring to *The Nebuly Coat* as "one of the test novels, appreciation of which establishes a curious link of sympathy between its admirers." There is something oddly self-effacing about this author, variously chairman of a major armaments firm, cathedral librarian and scholar, antiquarian, poet and novelist. For all the accomplishments, even the minor mastery of his novels, it is hard to discern his footprints in them. If F. remains in the literary margins, one feels that that is his preferred place.

BIBLIOGRAPHY: Daly, N., "Somewhere There's Music: J. M. F.'s *The Lost Stradivarius*," in St. John, M., ed., *Romancing Decay* (1999): 95–106; Warren, J. M., *J. M. F., 1858–1932* (1995)

PHILIP GOODEN

FANSHAWE, [Sir] Richard

b. June 1608, Hertfordshire; d. 26 June 1666, Madrid, Spain

In 1647, F. translated from Italian Battista Guarini's *Il Pastor Fido* (1590; *The Faithful Shepherd*)—the most important Renaissance pastoral drama—and in 1655 from the Portuguese the national EPIC by Luis de Camões's *Os Lusíados* (1572; *The Lusiad*). From Spanish, he translated Antonio Hurtado de Mendoza's *Querer por Solo Querer* (1623; *To Love Only for Love Sake*) and *Fiestas de Aranjuez* (1623; *Festivals at Aranwhez*), published together in 1670. F. also translated from Latin *Selected Parts of Horace* (1652) book 4 of Virgil's *Aeneid* in Spenserian stanzas. He wrote verse in English. His widow, Lady Anne Fanshawe, wrote a memoir, published in 1829, which includes a selection of F.'s letters.

FANTHORPE, U[rsula] A[skham]

b. 22 July 1929, London

Having studied at St. Anne's College, Oxford, and then at the University of London Institute of Education, F. obtained a teaching diploma. Following many years of pedagogy, she later became the head of the English department at Cheltenham Ladies College in Gloucestershire, a position she resigned from in 1972 to take a job at Bristol Hospital as an admissions clerk. Her experience at the latter had doubtlessly lent itself as much of the subject matter for her first collection of poems, *Side Effects* (1978), published when she was nearly fifty years old.

Although graceful and often times humorous, F.'s poetry is not always comfortable; such inquietude is, in no small part, the result of unusual subject matter, both fascinating and disturbing in intimate examination of human dysfunction. Whether a wise, almost omniscient narrator or reflective first person, the speakers involved in F.'s work are frequently in the position of the outsider, removed, and thus, somewhat safe, yet powerless, in the realm of her subject matter. Readers are offered a unique menagerie of human types through which the world may be experienced.

Despite the nature of her poetry and a tendency to call attention to injustice—both of which may evoke a sense of vulnerability, F.'s work triumphs in its remarkable ability to be subtle in assertion and humble in conviction—characteristics of how meaning thrives on careful craft. Memorable lines and, perhaps more importantly, the reiterative technique of crucial line breaks are critical in making successful her interpretative lyricism—in heightening solidarity and effectivity, especially in that she does not strictly adhere to formal verse schemes.

The titles of F.'s work—witty and of thoughtful design—often inform the work to which they refer. *Side Effects* is no exception. In "The List," the speaker has created an orderly list of names and numbers for "tomorrow," pointing out that "orderly, equal, right/on the edge of tomorrow, they pause." Here, the "list" is that boundary or edge that marks seemingly inconsequential moments as turning points, similar to the way in which insignificant action can determine unexpected consequences—a theme of repeated concern in F.'s work. There is an anxiety in the reality that awaits the speaker's vision of order. Nonetheless, being an observer and wise beyond the attempt to rectify inevitable disorder, the speaker's awareness and almost stoic acceptance of such helplessness are reinforced in the not uncommon laconic ending, in which the speaker confesses "I am the artist; the typist/I did my best for them."

If F.'s poetry seems suggestive, even foretelling of consequence, it is perhaps most significantly the case in *Standing To* (1982), where the resurrection of history and classic themes are particularly evident. F. claims that "nothing happens in isolation from the past," and the tones underlying her work are at times foreboding—her resurrected ghosts perhaps as much indicative of the future as they are the past. F.'s anxious concern with consequence and its link to the past surfaces again in *Voices Off* (1984), as she writes in "Tomorrow and" of how "*was* and *will be* are both uneasy ground."

F. has written several other works, including *Four Dogs* (1980), *A Watching Brief* (1987), *Neck-Verse* (1992), *Safe as Houses* (1995), and *Consequences*

(2001). Her culmination of published work also includes *Selected Poems* (1989), a collection compiled from *Side Effects*, *Standing To*, and *Voices Off*. Since her mature entrance into the literary world, she has quickly proven herself a poet of great importance, emerging unexpectedly as a leading contender for poet laureate in 1999, and prior to this, in 1994, as the first nominated female for the post of Professor of Poetry at Oxford. In addition, F. was made a fellow of the Royal Society of Literature in 2001. Her success and recognition are no small consequence of extraordinary compassion and craftsmanship.

BIBLIOGRAPHY: Delany, P., "Hearing the Other: Voices in U. A. F.'s Poetry," *C&L* 46 (Spring-Summer 1997): 319–40; McCully, C. B., "'Laboratories of the Spirit': Recent Poetry," *CritQ* 29 (1987): 106–12

COLLEEN McCUTCHEON

FARJEON, Eleanor
b. 13 February 1881, London; d. 5 June 1965, London

F. is remembered for three things: as a poet of distinguished lyric poetry, including the words of the hymn "Morning Has Broken" (set during the 1920s to a traditional Welsh melody), given renewed life in a recorded performance by the artist known at the time as Cat Stevens (later Yusuf Islam); as a writer of stories and adaptations for children; and as a friend of many personages, including the Dymock Poets (who included Robert Frost and Edward THOMAS) and Walter DE la MARE.

She was the daughter of Benjamin Leopold Farjeon, a popular novelist, and the granddaughter of the celebrated American actor Joseph Jefferson. Two of her brothers, Joseph and Herbert, were also writers. With such a literary background, it was natural for F. to pursue a career as a writer. She wrote light and serious verse as well as prose fiction and nonfiction for magazines, including *Punch* and *Time and Tide,* and in 1911 she published *Dream Songs for the Beloved.* Lady Sybil Myra Caroline Primrose Grant, who was two years older than F., published a book called *Dream Songs:* the works by Grant and F. came years before "dream songs" by T. S. ELIOT and American poet John Berryman. She published *Martin Pippin in the Apple Orchard* in 1921. Like several other works intended for adults, it was construed as a children's book, and for several years after its appearance she produced poems, stories, plays, and books of retellings (from Geoffrey CHAUCER and Herodotus) that were indeed for children. Her best-known plays are *The Glass Slipper* (perf. 1944; pub. 1946) and *The Silver Curlew* (perf. 1949; pub. 1953).

For several years prior to 1917, F. was closely associated with Thomas and his wife. It is possible that

F. introduced Thomas to Frost, who soon persuaded Thomas, who had been known as a prose writer, to become a poet, so that, for three or four years before his wartime death, Thomas wrote poems of enduring originality and distinction.

F. remained single throughout her life, but she had a relationship with the popular writer Stacy Aumonier, who, like Thomas, was a married man. She eventually wrote two sets of sonnets called *First and Second Love*, published in 1947. In her later life, she found a loyal friend in the actor Denys Blakelock.

BIBLIOGRAPHY: Blakelock, D., *Eleanor: Portrait of a Farjeon* (1966); Colwell, E. H., *E. F.* (1961); Walsh, J. E., *Into My Own: The English Years of Robert Frost, 1912–1915* (1988)

WILLIAM HARMON

FARQUHAR, George

b. ca. 1677, Londonderry, Ireland; bur. 23 May 1707, London

A late Restoration dramatist, F. is often seen as a transitional figure whose more realist approach to comic plots and characters helped move plays from the glittering verbal artifice of the Restoration to the middle-class concerns and melodramatic tone of 18th-c. sentimental comedy. One of the most popular playwrights at the end of the 17th c., F. is still one of the most frequently performed Restoration dramatists, a fact critics often attribute to the vivacious believability of his characters and the freshness of his largely original plots.

Born in 1677 or 1678 in Londonderry, F. showed early promise in literary arts and entered Trinity College, Dublin, in 1694 as a sizar—a work-study student. Through he received a scholarship in his second year, he did not finish college, dropping out to become an actor at Dublin's Smock Alley Theatre. After an incident in which he accidentally wounded another actor on stage, he took the advice of a friend and quit acting for playwriting, leaving Dublin for London.

In 1698, F.'s first play opened at Drury Lane. *Love and a Bottle* (1699) was a very typical Restoration comedy, with two sets of lovers, disguises and mistaken identities, clever servants, strategies for duping lovers into marriage, and a cast of familiar stock characters. But F. also showed early signs of his penchant for comic realism, giving the main character an Irish immigrant history that matched his own.

A few weeks after *Love and a Bottle* opened, a novella entitled *The Adventures of Covent Garden* appeared anonymously. Critics have reliably attributed the novella to F., but its predictable plot and standard treatment have garnered little interest other than as source material for other works by F.

F.'s next play, *The Constant Couple* (perf. 1699; pub. 1700), was a tremendous success and made F. one of London's hottest playwrights. It also helped Drury Lane compete with the upstart competition at Lincoln's Inn Fields. The play's popularity centered on its rakish central character, Sir Harry Wildair, engagingly played by F.'s actor friend Robert Wilks. Although the plot built around this appealing character was a typical Restoration plot, F. had added a strong note of originality by setting the play in London during the spring and summer of that very year, when an act of Parliament had disbanded most of the army.

In Sir Harry Wildair, F. had created a character who is charming and affable in his rakishness, and avoids much of the cynical world-weariness of many Restoration protagonists. Though he is verbally deft, his wit is not on display for its own sake, and he comes across as a good person. Audiences loved him, and it is no surprise that F.'s next play was a sequel entitled *Sir Harry Wildair* (1701).

Sir Harry Wildair was not nearly as successful as *The Constant Couple*; it has the feel of a hastily written sequel for which the playwright had little heart. But F.'s reputation was made. Though the embittered members of the rival company attacked him as a lightweight in prefaces and prologues, his status as one of London's most popular theatrical figures is evident from the number of prologues and prefaces he himself was asked to write. He was also included in collections of letters on various subjects, and in 1702 published *Love and Business*, a miscellany comprising letters, poems, and a discourse on comedy, including items written previously and specially for the volume.

F.'s next project was *The Stage-Coach* (perf. 1702; pub. 1704), a translation of a French farce done with Peter Anthony Motteaux. He followed this quickly with a semiadaptation of John FLETCHER's *The Wilde Goose Chase* called *The Inconstant* (1702). Though F. revised Fletcher's play substantially, he was accused of plagiarizing it, and some subsequent critics have argued that his revision is inferior to the original. His addition of a moral that stresses familial obligation at the end, however, shows that he was already heading in a new direction.

With *The Twin-Rivals* (perf. 1702; pub. 1703), F. took a serious step toward the new sentimental comedy. Switching gears from the lighthearted wittiness of earlier comedy, *The Twin-Rivals* focuses on the heart-wrenching plight of a young man whose wicked twin is attempting to steal his inheritance. The tricks and contrivances in this play—the evil twin's plotting with lowlifes to back his claims, an old bawd's arrangements for a convenient rape—are perpetrated by serious villains and have the potential for real consequences. In stark contrast to the Restoration comedy tradition, a seducer attempting to get rid of his pregnant mistress is forced to marry her. Actions in plays,

F. seems to be suggesting, ought to have moral consequences, a view upheld by Jeremy Collier in his famous 1699 polemic *A Short View of the Immorality and Profaneness of the English Stage.*

In spite of his new play's moralistic tone, F. was criticized even for dealing with such bold-faced evil in a comedy. He disappeared from the theater for three years, during which time he married and took up an army commission. His time spent garrisoned in Ireland provided him the material for his next and most successful play yet, *The Recruiting Officer* (1706).

The Recruiting Officer places the typical comic grouping of two symmetrical pairs of thwarted lovers into the thoroughly contemporary setting of a recruiting officer's work. The combination plays to F.'s strengths: the creation of believable, likable characters and fresh, easy dialogue. The play was a huge success and remained so throughout the 18th c. Critics again pointed out that F. was no classical dramatist, but he had proved once more that he had irresistible audience appeal.

Tradition has it that F. wrote his final masterpiece, *The Beaux Stratagem* (1707), in six weeks, while gravely ill and financially ruined. True or not, the play proved to be the best legacy he could leave his two daughters, who continued to receive money from benefit performances of the play for forty years. Utilizing a common plot device—two friends search the countryside for rich wives while posing as a gentleman and his valet—*The Beaux Stratagem* takes up a hot contemporary issue: divorce. In the end, when one of the love objects is freed from an oppressive and miserable marriage by mutual consent in order to marry the hero's friend, the play takes a powerful stand for divorce. The events of the play are somewhat contrived. The main character, Aimwell, gains access to his love interest Dorinda through a ruse, pretending to be his older brother; the convenient death of this brother is announced in the final scene so that Aimwell inherits his estate and can marry Dorinda. But before this he has confessed all to the woman he loves. Counterbalanced with the strong attraction between his friend Archer and the unhappily married Mrs. Sullen, the play argues that marriage for love is more socially stabilizing than marriage for other reasons.

F. died just over two months after the Queens Theatre premier of *The Beaux Stratagem*, in May 1707. His plays stayed in the popular repertory much longer and more consistently than those by many Restoration dramatists. His language was natural and untortured, his wit clever without being overpowering, and his plays sentimental while avoiding the sententious. Most importantly, perhaps, he began bringing the real world into comedy, a move that had reverberations beyond the London stage, particularly influencing

18th-c. German drama, and through it, the 20th-c. innovations of Bertolt Brecht.

BIBLIOGRAPHY: Bull, J., *Vanbrugh and F.* (1998); Farmer, A. J., *G. F.* (1966); James, E. N., *The Development of G. F. as a Comic Dramatist* (1972); Rothstein, E., *G. F.* (1967)

GINGER STRAND

FAULKS, Sebastian
b. 20 April 1953, Newbury

F. has gained recognition in England through novels about the two world wars, usually in combination with romantic love. While his books have brought F. popular success, critics do not agree on the literary merit of his work: on the one hand, his novels have been judged masterpieces of their genre, and on the other they have been called melodramatic accounts with too-easy happy endings. Critics do agree, however, that F. writes with accuracy and deep compassion about ordinary people placed under extraordinary duress.

Marking out his literary direction quite early, in 1989 F. published *The Girl at the Lion d'Or*. Set in a small town in 1930s France, the novel explores the effects of World War I, which still haunts the inhabitants of the town. The female protagonist, Anne Louvet, works at the hotel Lion d'Or and falls in love with a middle-aged lawyer, Charles Hartmann, who has lost the ability to care about himself or anybody else. Hartmann lives in a rambling, dilapidated house. Since in all F.'s works both setting and character reflect historical realities, Hartmann's house and ennui are metaphors for a general malaise afflicting France, including guilt at its ready capitulation to the Germans.

Like *The Girl at the Lion d'Or,* F.'s second important novel, *Birdsong* (1993), also depicts World War I, this time exploring an English perspective. Like the poetry of Siegfried SASSOON, *Birdsong* records setting with relentless accuracy, from the lice and filthy food to the aroma of rotting corpses in the trenches. F.'s point is that war is not heroic, only horrible, and that this horror must be experienced to be understood. Suffering emotional trauma at having been deserted by his French lover, the hero, Stephen Wraysford, has the reputation among other soldiers of being cold-hearted and frigid. Like Hartmann in *The Girl at the Lion d'Or*, though, who finally undergoes a metamorphosis, Wraysford finds himself influenced by the stoical attitude of a fellow English comrade and survives being wounded and left for dead in a tunnel behind enemy lines.

In *Charlotte Gray* (1998), the third volume of his war trilogy, F. once again examines the way war insidiously affects ordinary lives. Dealing with World War

II, the book reveals insight into the power relationship between Britain and France as it tracks the effect on England of France's belief that Germany would win World War II. Mirroring France's loss of faith in itself is a young Scotswoman, Charlotte Gray, who feels she can only reconnect her own future to her past happiness if France can regain its fatal loss of direction. Gray decides to join the French resistance, a movement that the British keep firmly under its control. As soon as it becomes obvious that Germany will lose the war, F. shows how England's effort to become the most powerful country in post–World War II Europe leads it to willingly sabotage French resistance efforts and to sacrifice spies like Gray herself.

In 1999, F. edited with Jorg Hensgen *The Vintage Book of War Stories*. The forty writers in this anthology of works of fiction set in the wars of the 20th c. include familiar names such as Ernest Hemingway and Erich Maria Remarque as well as unfamiliar ones such as Bao Ninh and Shusaku Endo. Because it makes available F.'s vast historical knowledge and circumvents the melodramatic excess some critics have found in his novels, many regard this postmodern compilation as highly successful, perhaps even his best work. This was followed with the publication in 2001 of *On Green Dolphin Street*, a novel set within the turbulence of the U.S. in the late 1950s and early 1960s.

BIBLIOGRAPHY: Allen, B., "Illustrations of Inertia and Compromise," *NewC* 17 (April 1999): 60; Moseley, M., "S. F.," in Moseley, M., ed., *British Novelists since 1960*, Third Series, *DLB* 201 (1999): 87–93

SUSAN TETLOW HARRINGTON

FEINSTEIN, Elaine
b. 24 October 1930, Bootle

F. graduated in English literature from Newnham College, Cambridge, then read for the bar. Her work as poet and novelist has been translated into fourteen languages. Her themes include Jewish life, before and after the Holocaust, and the inevitable ambivalences in human relationships. Her first novel, *The Circle,* appeared in 1970; *Lady Chatterley's Confession* (1996) was a sequel to D. H. LAWRENCE's *Lady Chatterley's Lover;* and *Dark Inheritance* (2001) was a thriller. She has published thirteen volumes of poetry and *Daylight* (1997) was a Poetry Book Society Recommendation. Her translations of the Russian poet Marina Tsvetaeva have remained in print since their first appearance in 1970, and were a *New York Times* Book of the Year. Her biography of Tsvetaeva appeared in 1987: other biographies are of Bessie Smith (1986), Lawrence (1993), Alexander Pushkin (1998), and Ted HUGHES (2001). She has written short stories and many plays for television and radio. In 1981, she

was made a fellow of the Royal Society of Literature, and in 1990 she received the Cholmondeley Award and was made an honorary doctor of letters at Leicester University.

FELLTHAM [or FELTHAM], Owen
b. 1602 or 1609, Suffolk; d. 23 February 1688, Great Billing

F. in his day was as popular a moralist as Francis QUARLES. Starting at eighteen, F. wrote a collection of essays called *Resolves*, later adding forty poems. Eleven editions appeared before 1700. F. attacked Ben JONSON shortly before Jonson's death, but contributed an encomium to the *Jonsonus Virbius*, a memorial tribute. His only other printed work was an anti-Dutch tract entitled *A Brief Character of the Low Countries under the States*, which existed in manuscript form during the tense political situation of the 1640s until a pirated edition appeared in 1648. The work was republished in an authorized edition in 1652 when war broke out between England and Holland

FEMINISM

Feminism is a social, historical movement grounded in the advocacy of equality of rights for women; feminist literary criticism and theory incorporate these same ideas to explore and expose patriarchal ideologies of sex, gender, power, and politics in literary texts.

In Britain, feminism finds its beginnings in the mid-1600s when a political voice of and for women began to be heard. As early as the 1790s, the first recognizable feminist polemics, *Thoughts on the Education of Daughters* and the more famous *A Vindication of the Rights of Woman*, were written in England by Mary WOLLSTONECRAFT to express her dissatisfaction with the role of women in the home and in society. Wollstonecraft demanded an end to the double standards of male and female behavior; additionally, she advocated women's right to independent work, education for women, freedom from "domestic tyranny," and voice in civil and political life in order to free woman from the role of subordinate to man. While these ideas might seem self-evident in the 21st c., even forty years after her manifesto for change the British Reform Bill of 1832 carefully excluded women from the franchise with the carefully worded phrase, "male person." Within a few years, there came a further demand for female suffrage when the Chartist Petition of 1838 withdrew the promised clause on the vote for women in fear that the issue of working men's rights would be obscured.

At the midpoint of the 19th c., women were still rigidly excluded from the professions and from higher education; economically and socially, a woman was expected to confine herself to the private sphere and provide for herself by making an advantageous marriage. It was not until the official campaign for Women's Universal Suffrage began in 1866 that the first committee on women's rights and freedoms (consisting of Emily Davies, Barbara Bodichon, and Helen Taylor) presented a petition formally requesting female enfranchisement for parliamentary consideration to John Stuart MILL, who went on to author *The Subjection of Women*. In 1867, Mill supported the committee's request and moved an amendment to the Reform Act; it was defeated. Outraged by this denial of woman's rightful place in social and political life, many organizations across the country began to join forces to form the National Union of Women's Suffrage Societies (NUWSS).

During this period of British history and literature, there is the development of what is called the "Woman Question"—the escalating debate over the nature and role of women. Debates on suffrage, sexual emancipation, and economic rights pervade the era; in addition, demands for financial security and responsibility resulted in the important Married Women's Property Acts of 1870 and 1882 that allowed women to retain the ownership of their own properties and inheritances after marriage. The Industrial Revolution and the expansion of the British Empire had already created an army of working women: mill-girls, domestic servants, milliners, seamstresses, and governesses who were no longer inclined to languish in a patriarchal household. While in previous decades and centuries women had been confined to the home or in domestic service, the factory girls began to work together free from parental oversight and held their own wages. As the pressure increased for women to have a say in their own futures, an ideological split developed between those supporters who believed the vote for women was the most important cause and those who believed that an improvement in female education and employment opportunities were of primary importance. Female workers began to agitate for reform with the eventual support of many members of Parliament voting in favor of women's suffrage bills only to have them blocked by the government. The campaign became more militant with the founding of the Women's Social and Political Union (WSPU) in 1903 by Mrs. Emmeline Pankhurst, her daughter, Christabel, and their suffragette followers. The WSPU tactics were designed to make the government take women's demands seriously; the women of the NUWSS, led by Millicent Garrett Fawcett, became known as suffragists. By 1912, the Pankhursts began to advocate the destruction of abandoned property to gain the attention of the public, but the First World War brought the campaign to an end. The increased role of women in the war effort and their patriotism forced Parliament finally to grant women's suffrage in 1918, but only to those women over thirty years of age. Every man could vote at age twenty-one. It was not until 1929 that universal suffrage allowed women to vote at the same age as men.

Many women writers supported the emerging feminist movement; in 1908, the Women Writers Suffrage League was founded by journalists Cicely Hamilton and Bessie Hatton. Elizabeth ROBINS was its president, while other supporters included Olive SCHREINER, Mary SINCLAIR, Alice MEYNELL, Sarah GRAND, and Violet Hunt. Suffragettes, suffragists, and the so-called New Women were widely portrayed in the literature of the period, both in fiction and in fact, as well as in accounts of the movement that were found in periodicals such as *Women's Suffrage Journal* and the *Common Cause*. From this early alignment of women's causes with women writers, there evolved a mode of reading literary texts which was woman-centered.

While there is no single, unified theory of feminism or feminist literary criticism and/or theory, this multiplicity is, in fact, its strength. The resistance to an "authorized" reading or ready-made response to texts makes reading as a feminist adaptable to different contexts with few assumptions about the political or textual outcomes that it pursues. It is fair to say that reading as a feminist posits an ongoing series of interventions in reading practices under the assumption that the way one reads can make a difference to one's experience of the world. There are several common interests in any feminist critique of a text and/or literary theory. First, a feminist reading of a text assumes that there is a direct correlation between the words that create the fictional world, characters, etc. and the real world. Texts are a result of the reality from which they arise in that the text reflects, creates, and offers alternatives to the real world; therefore, every text is seen to be a product of historical context, i.e., its time, place, and mode of production. Second, the relationships found between texts and the world are necessarily political because they deal, at least in part, with relations of power. Androcentric ideology pervades the writings that have traditionally been considered as the canon of great literature; only recently have texts more often been written by women and for women with a focus on female protagonists. Previously, the lack of strong female role models leaves the woman reader feeling marginalized in the process by the assumption that she should identify with the male protagonist's position, an identification made impossible by the nature of her lived experience. These texts, sometimes called coercive texts, attempt to define constructions of "proper" behaviors and beliefs as defined by society; alternatively, subversive texts might attack such conventions of propriety as oppressive to women. In addition, traditional aesthetic criteria for analysis of literature (although represented as universal and objective) are infused with masculine assumptions and are, therefore, unmasked as gender biased.

Feminist theory tries to reconstitute the ways we evaluate literature to include women's multiple points of view, concerns, and values. The act of reading with an eye to understanding the political implications of a narrative, and a will to political agency in one's own reading—to be a resisting reader—are at the core of feminist literary theory. Third, all feminist theories of literature, whether combined with Marxism, psychoanalysis, poststructuralist, or postmodernist theories, focus on women and images of women. There are a multitude of possibilities to this focus just as the types and needs of women are full of differences; however, at the core is the belief that women are oppressed by various social, physiological, cultural, and psychological structures found in the home, state, church, and law that create a patriarchy (rule of the father) where power relations subordinate women's interests to the interests of men. In fact, women are defined in relation to, and as a lack of, masculinity; women have been the "object" while men have retained the position of power as the "subject." Historically, women have internalized the conscious and unconscious presuppositions about male superiority and have become complicit in their own subordination. On the whole, texts were written by and for men, and the stereotypes of women found in those texts fall into the basic categories of the idealized "Angel" (Madonna, Muse) who is beautiful, passive, and virginal, or the "Whore" (Femme Fatale, Witch, Castrating Mother) who is independent, dangerous, and sexual. Real women are not reflected in these images; rather, male writers were responsible for inaccurate images of women. This began a revolution in understanding that would then lead to women as regular consumers and producers of texts. Feminism desires to make explicit and effect change to such pervasive structures of inequality both in life and in literary representation.

In the 20th c., feminist literary theory underwent several transitions in approach, the beginnings of which were in the examination of images of women in literary texts by women readers. In *A Room of One's Own*, Virginia WOOLF creates a series of reflections on what she believes has caused the silence of women in the literary canon before Jane AUSTEN; through a patchwork of various kinds of writing—reflection, BIOGRAPHY, anecdote, story, questions—Woolf uses the feminine style to discuss the construction of women by their personal circumstance and the circumstances of history. Simone de Beauvoir's *The Second Sex* (1953; first published in French as *Le Deuxième Sexe,* 1949), looks at literary images of women and posits famously that "One is not born, but rather becomes, a woman," which revolutionizes the idea of gender as construction versus sexual biology.

By mid-20th c. in Britain, these early texts lead to a feminist critique (woman as reader) of male culture and a female aesthetic (women's writing as a distinct female consciousness) of celebrating women's culture. The retroactive naming of feminist criticism by Woolf and de Beauvoir, among others, is replaced with a distinct identity in the late 1960s and 1970s in England and the U.S. with the publication of such works as Mary Ellmann's *Thinking about Women* (1968), Eva FIGES's *Patriarchal Attitudes*, Ellen Moers's *Literary Women* (1976) as well as Susan Gubar and Sandra M. Gilbert's *The Madwoman in the Attic* (1978) that are, for the most part, feminist readings of women's writings unlike the French feminist theories that rely heavily on the theories of linguistics, language, and psychoanalysis, in addition to the central concepts of *écriture feminine* and *jouissance.* Anglo-American critics are wary of a feminism that is not seemingly directly linked to a politics of social change.

The impetus of these critical texts are, perhaps, most easily exemplified by Elaine Showalter's description in *A Literature of Their Own* (1977) of the female literary tradition in the English novel from the BRONTË sisters to the present day; Showalter demonstrates a female subculture in writing that is unified by values, conventions, experiences, and behaviors. Showalter identifies her work as gynocriticism, that is, studying writing by women and problems associated with female creativity and language. In her very useful exposition, there are three historically distinct phases of women's writing: the "feminine" period is from the appearance of the male pseudonym in the 1840s to the death of George ELIOT in 1880; the "feminist" period spans from 1880 to 1920, or the winning of the vote; and the "female" period is from 1920 to the present, but enters a new age of self-awareness about 1960. For "feminine" writers, Showalter sees the male pseudonym as a loss of innocence while indicating a will to write as a vocation that directly conflicts with their status as women. While the social novels of the 1840s and 1850s, into the problem novels of the 1860s and 1870s, were pushing boundaries, the novels of the "feminist" phase directly confront male society that created Victorian sexual stereotypes into a cult, denounce self-sacrifice, attack patriarchy, and construct a theoretical model of female oppression. The "female" phase then becomes psychologically focused. These new insights into the reading of texts highlight, with the aid of a new awareness or "raised consciousness," the stereotypes of men and women, women's economic situation as authors, the supposed prejudice of male critics and publishers as well as the relationship between writing and gender. The first feminist publishing houses are established in the late 1970s with Virago and the Women's Press. Much of feminist criticism and theory is associated with the reclamation and republication of works by women writers of the past, as it is with reconsiderations of those writers and the evaluation of new feminist creative and scholarly writing.

In the 1980s and 1990s, feminist enquiry starts to engage with its own inherent essentialism by revisiting the question: what is a woman? Theorists such as Diana Fuss in *Essentially Speaking* (1989) and Judith Butler in *Gender Trouble* (1990) argue that sex as much as gender is a cultural construction while sexual identity is a kind of masquerade or performance. This implies that the reading of any text is, in itself, a performance that calls into question the authenticity of readers and writers who are, at least in part, always performing multiple identities. Other critics now speak of postfeminism, some have moved to womanism as a term, and some dispute the notion of woman as a category at all and want to speak only of the construction of gender. Women now often come to feminist criticism and/or theory without having been part of a context of active feminism, from theory rather than from protest, through psychoanalysis and deconstruction rather than from demonstrations. Feminism, whether political or literary, raises key questions regarding assumptions of gender, sexuality, race, class, practice, and value in society and literature.

BIBLIOGRAPHY: Bolt, J. C., *Women's Movements in the United States and Britain 1790–1920* (1993); Butler, J., and J. Scott, eds., *Feminists Theorize the Political* (1992); Caine, B., *English Feminism 1780–1980* (1997); Donovan, J., *Feminist Theory* (2000); Kent, S., *Sex and Suffrage in Great Britain* (1987); Lovell, T., *British Feminist Thought* (1990); Moi, T., *Sexual/Textual Politics* (1985); Todd, J., *Feminist Literary History* (1988); Warhol, R., and D. Herndl, eds., *Feminisms* (1997)

SARAH E. MAIER

FENTON, [Sir] Geoffrey
b. ca. 1539, Fenton, Nottinghamshire; d. 19 October 1608, Dublin, Ireland

While living in Paris in 1567, F. wrote *Certaine Tragicall Discourses written oute of Frenche and Latin,* a free translation of François de Belleforest's and Pierre Boaistuau's French rendering of Matteo Bandello's Italian novellas. F.'s version is loaded with rhetorical devices, maxims, and proverbs. Other works include *Monophylo* (1572), from Etienne Pasquier, *Golden Epistles* (1575), from Antonio de Guevara, *The Historie of Guicciardini, Conteining the Warres of Italy* (1579), and a number of Protestant tracts.

FENTON, James
b. 25 April 1949, Lincoln

F., erstwhile Oxford Professor of Poetry, regular reviewer with the *New York Review of Books,* former political correspondent, has established a justifiable reputation as one of Britain's finest living poets. F.'s poetic career developed at an early age when in 1968 he won the Newdigate Prize at Oxford for his poem, "Our Western Furniture." The Newdigate Prize is given for the best poem by an undergraduate on a set theme. F. wrote with remarkable control and finesse on Admiral Perry and the forcible opening of Japan. The poem written during his first year as an undergraduate displays his later sympathy for cultures and peoples under siege and on the periphery.

F.'s mature reputation was established with the publication of *The Memory of War* (1982), reissued with a later collection, *Children in Exile* (1983), on both sides of the Atlantic as *Children in Exile: Poems 1968–1984* (1984). The latter collection contains a remarkable range of poems, from the political and committed to the quotidian and whimsical. F.'s political poems are marked by clarity and passion combined with a nonpolemical attitude and aesthetic. The politics of the poems do not degenerate into propagandist or prophetic ranting (as they often do in stateside antiwar poetry during the Vietnam War); instead, politics and poetry are finely fused into an aesthetic of concern. "A German Requiem," a series of nine short poems on the Holocaust and the trauma of survival, embodies this balance. At one level, it is a pounding indictment of Nazism, at another it enacts memories that have been repressed: "It is what you have forgotten, what you must forget." The selective re-creation of the past is a classic trauma survivor tactic but the poet will not allow for forgetfulness. Survivor guilt predicates certain strategies for coping: "And it seems there is no limit to the resourcefulness of recollection." "The resourcefulness of recollection" refers also to cynical rewritings of history and the poem resists revisionism. In this and other poems, there is an overarching concern about the ways in which history is remembered and occasionally distorted. F.'s poems are political not only because of their subject but also because of their aesthetic and ideological resistance to the dismemberment of often painful memories.

F. traveled to Vietnam and Cambodia as a freelance reporter and his hands-on experience is reflected in his prose writings (*All the Wrong Places: Adrift in the Politics of Asia*, 1988) and poetry. "Cambodia" conveys the pointlessness of war through an economy of outrage and expression: "A million men to one./ And still they die. And still the war goes on." "Children in Exile" is about a group of Cambodian refugee children in northern Italy living with their American sponsors. F. displays acute insight and sympathy for a country seemingly condemned to eternal violence: "And save us too from that fatal geography/Where vengeance is impossible to halt./And save Cambodia from threatened extinction./Let not its history be made its fault." The "fatal geography" is not only a physical but also a psychological landscape as the children are burdened by their memories of terror and grief: "Caught in the tight security of grief." The plight of these children F. contrasts with the easy "hybridity" (a fashionable phrase in postcolonial studies) of the globalization myth: "And it is we who travel, they who flee,/We who may choose exile, they who are forced out." The Western reporter or observer has the luxury of democratic protest and choice, for these children exile is a brutal necessity. It is this perception of alterities that allows F. to transcend easy oppositional clichés between East and West, democracy and dictatorship, tyranny and freedom. The pain of exile is at least somewhat ameliorated by the promise of America: "Let them dream/Of Jesus, America, maths, Lego, music and dance."

F.'s poems about everyday life are often markedly different in tone and intention from his political poems. "The Skip" is a philosophical, jocular, and almost chatty disquisition on the worth (or otherwise) of his life that he has tipped into a skip. "Letter to John Fuller" combines wit with verbal dexterity (a quality available in more serious poems): "Hardy and Hopkins hacked off their honkers./Auden took laudanum in Yonkers./Yeats ate a fatal plate of conkers./On Margate sands/Eliot was found stark staring bonkers/Slashing his hands." "Exempla" attempts to disprove Erasmus DARWIN's theory that poetry is not precise. The set of poems is occasionally amusing but otherwise more of an exercise than "felt" poetry.

Partingtime Hall (1987), a collection written in collaboration with John Fuller, exhibits similar limitations. The poems are clever and witty, sometimes a trifle too clever without much substance. The HUMOR is almost laddish and the ubiquitous references to sex do not add either depth or meaning to the poems. There is also programmatic verse, very unsubtle and propagandist. With *Out of Danger* (1993), F. reestablished his stature as a poet rather than merely a dextrous juggler that *Partingtime Hall* reduced him to. A series of love poems is followed by a clutch of excellent political poems. It is the quality of felt emotion distilled into precisely appropriate lines, the fusion of the personal and the universal, that makes these poems so moving and memorable.

The political poems range over conflict and bigotry in the Middle East, Iran, China, and Cambodia. In "Out of the East," F. returns to the horrors of war in Cambodia and its mind-numbing futility. "Jerusalem" is a ten-stanza poem where F. is scathing about the perpetual history of conflict in that region. Religious fanaticism motivates all sides and F. refuses to be partisan: he will not condone ideologies of hate. The concluding stanza encapsulates the divide wrought by religion and politics and the inevitable human, individual cost: "Stone cries to stone,/Heart to heart, heart to stone./These are the warrior archae-

ologists./This is us and that is them./This is Jerusalem./These are the dying men with tattooed wrists./Do this and I'll destroy your home./I have destroyed your home. You have destroyed my home."

In "The Ballad of the Imam and the Shah" and "Tiananmen," F.'s distaste for all kinds of tyranny, political hypocrisy, and doctrinaire hatred is made apparent. Similar to his earlier poems, these too are marked by the ability to provide a genuine aesthetic and deeply personal sense of the political. Tiananmen, Cambodia, or Jerusalem are not poetic subjects or locales chosen for making appropriate poetic noises. Like his mentor W. H. AUDEN (although in very different contexts), F. is able to coalesce seemingly disparate elements of subject and concern into moving poetic tapestries of our times. He is a poet of distinction and quality with a rare ability to translate the quotidian, the farcical, the political, and the horrible into forms of luminous poetry.

BIBLIOGRAPHY: Gioia, D., "J. F.," in Sherry, V. B., Jr., ed., *Poets of Great Britain and Ireland since 1960*, part 1, *DLB* 40 (1985): 122–29

SUBARNO CHATTARJI

FERGUSSON, Robert

b. 5 September 1750, Edinburgh, Scotland; d. 17 October 1774, Edinburgh, Scotland

A poet whose reputation until recently rested on the poetic influence he is known to have had on Robert BURNS, F. is now recognized in his own right as an important 18th-c. urban poet and satirist, an accomplished stylist in both English and Scots idiom, and a metrical experimentalist of great virtuosity. At the high schools of Edinburgh and Dundee and the University of St. Andrews, he received a more extensive formal education, classical and modern, than either Alexander POPE or Burns, and embarked on ambitious poetic projects including an abandoned "national tragedy" of Scotland, and at least one important comic poem in Scots in the traditional "Standard Habbie" stanza form (probably composed at the age of fourteen), an "Elegy on the Death of Mr. David Gregory, late Professor of Mathematics in the University of St. Andrews." As a student and later as a clerk in the Commissary Office in Edinburgh, F. wrote daily, subjecting himself to the rigorous traditional poetic training for a great classical poet: progressive exercises in pastoral, SATIRE, translation, and EPIC. His first published poems, "Three Pastorals," which appeared in Walter Ruddiman's *Weekly Magazine* in 1771, have been dismissed as vapid exercises in style; they reveal not only a sophisticated understanding of the conventions of the genre, but impressive control of rhythm and tonal modulation.

Notwithstanding his dedication to a poetic vocation, F.'s horizons were not merely scholarly; a great lover of music and skillful singer, he regularly attended theater and opera, becoming a friend of the celebrated Italian tenor Giusto Ferdinando Tenducci, who introduced three of F.'s lyrics into his performance of Thomas Arne's *Artaxerxes*. He participated actively, too, in Edinburgh's exuberant midcentury homosocial club culture. Elected to the Cape Club in 1772, he took the soubriquet "Sir Precentor" on account of his good musical ear and singing voice. Fellow members included the ballad collector David Herd, the artist Henry Raeburn, and the later notorious housebreaker Deacon William Brodie. A series of F.'s poems published by Ruddiman the same year displayed a confidence in idiomatic Scots that won F. local popularity, prompting comparison with Allan RAMSAY.

F.'s poetic matter was now firmly urban, rooted in locality ("The King's birth-Day in Edinburgh," "Caller Oysters," "To the Tron Kirk Bell") but far from parochial in its range of poetic reference. Combining an older tradition of Scoto-Latin humanist writing with a post-Union Scottish national feeling and an allegiance to the sophisticated satiric diction of English Augustanism, these poems stand comparison with the works of William DUNBAR, and the urban pastorals of John GAY and Jonathan SWIFT in English tradition. The moderate success of F.'s first collected volume in 1773 was followed in that same year by publication of his longest and most ambitious poem, *Auld Reikie*, which was probably intended as the first canto of a mock-epic celebration of Edinburgh life. F.'s poetic virtuosity is displayed to full effect in this poem, whose pace, metrical flexibility, and sharpness of social satire are unmatched in midcentury verse. The poem was never continued; ill health forced his resignation from the Commissary Office, and penury compounded physical and mental distress. Scholars have recently disputed the moralistic story told by earlier biographers of dissipation, syphilis, and madness; toward the end of his life, F.'s earlier conviviality gave way to debility and bouts of religious melancholy.

In life, F. was the friend of actors and himself a master of disguise and mimicry; his poetic voices too command a range of idiom from broad demotic Scots through a macaronic comic doggerel to refined neoclassical English. In thirty-three Scots poems and about fifty in English, his tone reaches from the broad comedy of the monologue "To my Auld Breeks" to the chilling satiric dialogue "The Ghaists," and the dignity of "Job, Chap. III, Paraphrased," composed a few weeks before his early death following a fall, in the Edinburgh madhouse. The poetry of Burns, who declared F. "by far my elder brother in the Muse," is suffused with his influence. Robert Louis STEVENSON too announced his sense of affinity with F.'s riotous and stricken Edinburgh oeuvre; more recently, Robert Garioch has written distinguished tributes to his neglected poetic forebear.

BIBLIOGRAPHY: Daiches, D., *R. F.* (1982); Freeman, F. W., *R. F. and the Scots Humanist Compromise* (1984); McDiarmid, M. P., ed., *The Poems of R. F.* (2 vols., 1954–56); Smith, S. G., ed., *R. F., 1750–1774* (1952)

SUSAN MANNING

FERRIER, Susan [Edmonstone]
b. 17 September 1782, Edinburgh, Scotland; d. 5 November 1854, Edinburgh, Scotland

The Edinburgh society into which F. was born and the circles in which she moved provided ample material for her three novels, *Marriage* (3 vols., 1818), *The Inheritance* (3 vols., 1824), and *Destiny; or, The Chief's Daughter* (3 vols., 1831). Her keen wit and sharp eye for characterization and satire are qualities that mark her fiction, yet she herself saw instruction as the main purpose of her writing.

Marriage was intended as a joint project between F. and her friend and confidante, Charlotte Clavering. In the end, Clavering contributed only the opening section of the novel, but their early plans, discussed in lively correspondence, show F.'s insistence that the book must have a moral. She wrote, "as the only good purpose of a book is to inculcate morality, and convey some lesson of instruction as well as delight, I do not see that what is called a good moral can be dispensed with in a work of fiction." Although, as her letters demonstrate, she was far from being a stuffy spinster—she was able to poke fun at herself as well as others—and while she was not a member of any established, conventional church, F. nevertheless adhered to a strict Christian outlook, one that was based on rationality not sentimentality. Her heroines, therefore, represent enlightened Christian womanhood. Their marriages, for such are the rewards of the novels, are based on the equality of two rational minds. Mary Douglas, the heroine of *Marriage*, is the cast-off, sickly twin daughter of the spoiled and selfish Lady Juliana and is raised in Scotland by her aunt, Mrs. Douglas. While her mother and sister live lives of genteel frivolity in London, Mary is given an education aimed at inspiring a reasonable, independent mind. When the three are reunited, the stage is set for a contrast of characters designed to show the best and the worst qualities of female human nature. The heroine of *The Inheritance*, Gertrude St. Clair, is first seen as a coquette and she must learn in the course of the novel to think and act without the haze of fancy or imagination. In short, she must learn to reason and her quest for marriage becomes a quest for enlightenment.

The most self-effacing of F.'s three heroines is Edith Malcolm of *Destiny* and her overwhelming virtue and piety correspond to the overt didacticism of F.'s last novel. Highly charged, melodramatic incidents are designed to elicit pity and to instruct the reader in appropriate ways of feeling.

Critics have lamented the ever-increasing moralizing in F.'s novels, but they have praised the comedic characters that fill each text. Lady Maclaughlan and the aunts of Glenfern in *Marriage*, Miss Pratt and Lord Rossville in *The Inheritance*, and M'Dow in *Destiny*, are examples of F.'s comic skill. Her use of Scots dialect while sometimes employed as parody is also a showcase for a vigorous language, often labeled as mere provincial or uneducated speech. Among all the ideals of high-minded romantic love, there is in F.'s novels an underlying questioning of the social constraints and a tension between rebellion and conformity. Embedded within the religious and moral teaching are quite radical ideas about women's education and the need for marriages based on equal partnerships. F. even has a word or two to say about spinsterhood, its virtues as well as its bonds.

A close friend of Sir Walter SCOTT and a gifted storyteller, F. has been compared to Jane AUSTEN, Fanny BURNEY, and Maria EDGEWORTH. Her novels provide a rich store of material with which to examine a particular view of upper- and middle-class life in Scotland in the first half of the 19th c.

BIBLIOGRAPHY: Doyle, J. A., *Memoir and Correspondence of S. F.* (1898); Latané, D. E., "S. F.," in Mudge, B. K., ed., *British Romantic Novelists, 1789–1832, DLB* 116 (1992): 95–103

JANE POTTER

FICTION SINCE 1945

In England "the situation of the novel"—as the critic Bernard Bergonzi once memorably termed it—has long been the subject of keen public concern. Indeed, in Britain, even more than in the U.S., critics and journalists are forever assessing the health of the novel— and almost always with gloomy results. In 1980, for example, Bill Buford, the editor of *Granta*—that decade's most influential literary magazine—suggested that the English novel was dying, or at least rotting, owing largely to the "inert and backward-looking" nature of the nation's publishing industry. "Today's British book trade," Buford wrote, "is sweet, old-fashioned, and self-protected," and therefore unwilling to offer "experimentation in the real sense, exploiting traditions and not being wasted by them." Buford cited the common charge that, in Britain, "there were only 'middle-class novels for middle-class readers with middle-class problems.'"

D. J. Taylor similarly argued that too many of Britain's leading novelists had remained too detached from "the mess of our contemporary reality." These "mastodons of modern English literature," wrote Taylor in 1988, "fail to perceive, or do not wish to perceive, the powerful forces at work in society," including "America, television, international finance, and especially language, the constantly revivified, endlessly self-renewing language of transatlantic and transcontinental culture." Compared to their peers in North and South America, British novelists can often seem narrower, more patrician, less ambitious in their aims. And yet, when considered within the wider context of forty or fifty years, the record of British fiction is clearly more vibrant than stagnant. Many writers have, in varying ways, and in every decade, broadened the range of the novel to reflect more completely the massive social and cultural changes that are at work throughout Europe and in much of the world.

Immediately after World War II, Britain's leading novelists—including C. P. SNOW and Angus WILSON—continued to work within a realist tradition that dated back to the Victorian era. Wilson's literary heroes included both Charles DICKENS and Émile Zola, and his best novels—*Anglo-Saxon Attitudes* and *Late Call*—evoke 19th-c. models with their multitude of characters and multilayered plots. Because they wrote at midcentury, many postwar British writers also show an interest in examining social structures and cultural attitudes that, during the first decades of the 20th c., produced such dire consequences. Joyce CARY's *Mister Johnson*, set in Nigeria, explores the troubled legacy of colonialism. Published in 1956, Sybille Bedford's *A Legacy*, set in Germany at the turn of the 20th c., wryly examines the unanticipated consequences of German unification, including the rise of Prussianism and two world wars.

A more expansive note in British fiction is already evident in the 1950s, a decade of accelerating social change. Britain after the war was bombed, broke, and faced with the vast task of dismantling an untenable foreign empire. From the late 1940s and until the 1960s, political energy came mainly from the left as Labour Party initiatives on health, employment, and education came to the fore. In this climate, novelists who addressed social and political issues attracted wide attention.

Alan SILLITOE, David STOREY, and John BRAINE were among the most prominent of these writers, enduringly dubbed "Angry Young Men" in the British press. These writers shared roots in the working or lower middle class, and their books focus on the persistent effects of a social system that, in key respects, had scarcely changed since the 19th c. To the dismay of many critics, these "angry" novelists were not politely or conventionally "literary"; they employed direct, colloquial language and created protagonists at odds with the conventions of respectable middle-class society. Sillitoe's *Saturday Night and Sunday Morning* and Storey's *This Sporting Life* are both compelling—and grim. But other writers of the era, including Kingsley AMIS, Bernard Kops, and Keith WATERHOUSE, faced similar issues with the more explicit use of comedy and farce. Amis's *Lucky Jim* is widely hailed as an unusually funny satire of cultural pretentiousness and academic life. But it also assumes that class-based prejudices pervade and distort every aspect of British society. Waterhouse's *Billy Liar* is an amusing portrayal of an ineffectual dreamer, but it also offers an affecting critique of stifling conformity and low social expectations.

In fact, comedy is a persistent, if often unappreciated force in modern British fiction—perhaps because it is often subtle and dark. During the 1950s, elements of HUMOR and mordant wit can be found in the fiction of Walter Allen, P. H. Newby, Pamela Hansford JOHNSON, and Anthony POWELL, among many others; Powell earned particular acclaim for a continuing series of linked novels, *A Dance to the Music of Time*.

Iris MURDOCH is also a complexly comic writer, as such novels as *Under the Net* and *A Severed Head*, published in 1954 and 1961, respectively, reveal. But Murdoch was trained as a philosopher, and as her novels explore values and ideals, they also reveal an array of intellectual influences, including Plato, Wittgenstein, and G. E. Moore. The novels of Muriel SPARK and Graham GREENE are also often darkly comic—but also seriously concerned with intellectual and moral issues; both writers, significantly, converted to Roman Catholicism as adults.

William GOLDING is less directly political than Greene, but no less concerned with the dark side of human nature. Golding, who saw combat as a naval lieutenant during the Second World War, is best known for *The Lord of the Flies* and as the 1983 winner of the Nobel Prize for Literature. In several novels—including *The Inheritors* and *Pincher Martin*—Golding took intriguing artistic risks, mixing elements of allegory, symbolism, and myth. Golding's critical and popular reputation probably peaked in 1960s, when—against the larger backdrop of social turmoil and unprecedented economic prosperity—many novelists experimented more overtly with language and form. Thus, B. S. JOHNSON published *The Unfortunates* in loose, transposable sections in order to better convey both the arbitrariness of conventional narratives and the randomness of life.

Experimental impulses also influence works by Andrew SINCLAIR, J. G. BALLARD, and Angela CARTER, among others. To varying degrees, these writers broke with conventional modes of novel writing, often by rejecting REALISM in favor of more extravagant characters and nonlinear storytelling techniques. Ballard, for example, turned to SCIENCE FICTION for inspiration in works like *Crash*; in *Gog* and *Magog*, Sinclair combined Rabelaisian comedy and myth. Carter described her novels and stories as drawing from, among other things, "Gothic tales, cruel tales, tales of wonder, tales of terror, fabulous narratives that deal directly with the imagery of the unconscious."

Anthony BURGESS and John FOWLES also emerged during the 1960s and 1970s as two of England's more innovative and ambitious writers whose works reflect a keen interest in a wide range of literary, aesthetic, and linguistic matters. For example, Fowles's *The French Lieutenant's Woman* is, among other things, an assured parody of the Victorian novel; his *Daniel Martin* breaks with standard narrative structure through the use of shifting points of view. With *A Clockwork Orange*, Burgess experimented memorably with language in a dark telling of generational conflict and social decay.

Burgess was hardly alone in his bleak assessment of late-20th-c. life; as Malcolm BRADBURY noted, throughout the 1970s and 1980s, "many of our novelists, good and bad, have inherited the 'English' view of the novel as a record of our moral, social, and political condition. And the story they tell seems to be one of progressive decline in all departments; of characters who no longer bestride the world, of a world no longer worth bestriding." *The Ice Age* by Margaret DRABBLE is an especially notable example of this tendency. *The Ice Age* is a realist novel imbued with images of financial ruin, moral decline, and social collapse.

Margaret Thatcher's 1979 election as prime minister marked a major turn in contemporary British history. For more than a decade, Thatcher's advocacy of laissez-faire economics brought controversial and continuing changes to every aspect of English life. Throughout the Thatcher era, many novelists, including Bradbury and David LODGE, took note of these transformations, often satirically. Martin AMIS's *Money: A Suicide Note* is perhaps the most wholly memorable novel of the 1980s, an unsettling, darkly comic account of one man's self-destruction in a time of raging vulgarity and greed.

Amis became the most visible and quotable writer to emerge during the Thatcher years. But, by any measure, the 1980s was a particularly good decade for British fiction. Many other writers—including Jeannette WINTERSON, Julian BARNES, Graham SWIFT, and William BOYD also established productive careers. Winterson's *Sexing the Cherry* and Barnes's *A History of the World in 10½ Chapters* were described as "postmodern" novels—a term widely if loosely applied to much literary fiction published during the final decades of the 20th c. Variations abound, but much postmodern fiction is both ironic and playful, in a knowing way; it assumes that truth is relative and identity unstable, "constructed." It also assumes that attempts to re-create Victorian fiction are inevitably doomed. As Bradbury puts it, contemporary novelists "know they live in an age of dissolving moral community, of depleted human substance, in a denuded, polyglot social and cultural order in a time of profound historical uncertainty."

This recent and continuing revival of the British novel in all of its forms can be traced to several cultural and economic factors. After 1945, educational opportunities in Britain expanded steadily, creating new pools of readers—and writers. The market for paperback books, which grew rapidly during the 1950s and 1960s, exploded once more, aided by the rapid growth of chain bookstores and the aggressive application of more sophisticated marketing and packaging techniques. As sales increased, the gap between serious and popular, "highbrow" and "lowbrow," inevitably narrowed. For the first time since the 1950s, the era of "angry young men," literary novelists found themselves the subjects of wide interest in the public and the press.

Growing media interest in national literary prizes also helped boost literary fiction as the 20th c. came to a close. The Booker Prize, for example, continues to prompt wide speculation and debate, becoming—as Ian MCEWAN puts it—"one of those huge, totally British institutions, like the Oxford-Cambridge boat race." Since the 1970s, the list of Booker Prize winners and nominees has included, among many others, McEwan, Michael FRAYN, Alan HOLLINGHURST, Kazuo ISHIGURO, Beryl BAINBRIDGE, Salman RUSHDIE, and V. S. NAIPUAL—the 2001 Nobel Laureate.

The particularly visible careers of Rushdie and Naipaul underscore the growing internationalism of British fiction. As Britain has become increasingly multiracial, British fiction has become increasingly cosmopolitan and pluralistic in view. Many writers have dealt directly with the immigrant experience, and the assorted tensions that inevitably accompany the assimilation of the "foreigner" into a postimperial society. Best-selling novels such as *The Buddha of Suburbia* by Hanif KUREISHI and *White Teeth* by Zadie SMITH are two more recent examples of this trend.

An interest in historical fiction has also become increasingly evident, as novels by Peter ACKROYD, Rose TREMAIN, Robert NYE, and Penelope FITZGERALD attest. Historical research has also inspired novels by Pat Barker, Lawrence Norfolk, author of *Lempriere's Dictionary* (1991) and *The Pope's Rhinoceros* (1996), and—perhaps most notably—A. S. BYATT, whose *Possession* was commercially successful and critically acclaimed. In a spirited collection of essays, *On Histories and Stories*, published in 2001, Byatt hailed "the sudden flowering of the historical novel in Britain, the variety of its forms and subjects, the literary energy and real inventiveness that has gone into it."

But as the 1990s came to a close, commentators were again noting that, by focusing on the past, British novelists were practicing a form of literary escapism and failing "to chart contemporary themes." They praised instead such novels as *Trainspotting* by Irvine WELSH and *How late it was, how late* by James KELMAN. Both writers dealt with contemporary Scottish life in a style described as "gritty urban realism"; both employed language in a graphic, highly colloquial manner. Another well-publicized reaction to the historical novel came in the form of the "New Puritans," a loose group of rising young writers (including Candida Clark, Alex Garland, and Toby Litt) whose published works revealed a shared disdain for the kind of "middle-class" fiction that Buford had similarly dismissed two decades before. In a 2000 manifesto, Nicholas Blincoe and Matt Thorne, the movement's founders, denounced literary fiction that displayed too much artifice and "poetic licence in all its forms"; instead, they advocated work that was plot-driven, grammatically simple, free of all authorial intrusions, cinematic in style, and focused on the here and now.

BIBLIOGRAPHY: Bergonzi, B., *The Situation of the Novel* (1970); Blincoe, N., and M. Thorne, eds., *All Hail the New Puritans* (2000); Bradbury, M., *Possibilities: Essays on the State of the Novel* (1973); McHale, B., *Postmodernist Fiction* (1987); Taylor, D. J., *After the War: The Novel and English Society since 1945* (1993)

BRIAN MURRAY

FIELD, Nathan [Nathaniel]
bap. 17 October 1587, London; d. ca. 1619–20, London

Educated at St. Paul's School, F. was a child actor with the Chapel Royal company, and worked later with the Lady Elizabeth's Players. He performed in several pieces by Ben JONSON and played the lead in George CHAPMAN's *Bussy D'Ambois*. F. left in 1615 to join the King's Men. He authored *A Woman Is a Weathercock* (perf. 1609; pub. 1612) and *Amends for Ladies* (perf. 1611; pub. 1618) and possibly collaborated with Francis BEAUMONT and John FLETCHER and with Philip MASSINGER. He is listed as a player in the First Folio of William SHAKESPEARE's plays, edited by John Heminge and Henry Condell (1623).

FIELDING, Henry
b. 22 April 1707, Sharpham Park, Somerset; d. 8 October 1754, Lisbon, Portugal

The self-proclaimed founder of a "new Province of Writing," F. attained wide popularity as a manly novelist, the antithesis of his sentimental contemporary, Samuel RICHARDSON. Eclipsed after the late 1980s by

Richardson, F. now enjoys a resurgence of critical attention for his theory of the novel.

F. first made himself known as a playwright. From 1728 to 1737, he wrote twenty-eight comedies and became the most renowned playwright in London. His five-act social satires offered average heroes subjected to the corruptions of the city and overcoming them with Christian values. Incorporating contemporary events, his comedies such as *Love in Several Masques* (1728), *The Letter-Writers* (1731), *The Modern Husband* (1732), and *The Universal Gallant* (1735) encouraged audiences to strive not for perfection but for moral goodness. But it was F.'s burlesques and political satires that gained him popular success.

The Author's Farce (1730; rev. ed., 1750), the first of his "irregular" comedies, presents Harry Luckless (a version of F. himself) who is advised to write only nonsense if he wants reward. His puppet show, set in Hades, features representatives of all the empty popular entertainments: Signior Opera, Mrs. Novel, Don Tragedio, Sir Farcical Comic, Dr. Orator, and Monsieur Pantomime. F.'s SATIRE of frivolous and inferior art continued in *Tom Thumb* (1730), revised into *The Tragedy of Tragedies; or, The Life and Death of Tom Thumb the Great* (1731) with annotations by "H. Scriblerus Secundus." Here, F. parodied contemporary drama and criticism. The diminutive Tom is loved by Queen Dollalolla, the giantess Glumdalca, and the princess Huncamunca. Lord Grizzle attempts a rebellion, Tom is eaten by a cow, and seven murders close the play. It is highly entertaining and thoroughly ridiculous. In *The Historical Register for the Year 1736* (1737), a rehearsal-format play, Medley brings the events of a whole year to the stage. Major theatrical and political figures are satirized as F. demonstrates the corruption in the world theater. It was the most explicit of F.'s satires of Sir Robert Walpole, after *Pasquin* (1736), and in part led to the 1737 Licensing Act that effectively prohibited F. from the stage.

F. changed his genre, but not his targets. In *An Apology for the Life of Mrs. Shamela Andrews* (1741), F. parodied Richardson's *Pamela*, presenting her as a prostitute who tricks Mr. Booby into marriage through her "vartue." *Shamela* hilariously showed how the moral vocabulary was prostituted by the arts and politics, and manifested F.'s concern about the irresponsible use of words for deception.

The History and Adventures of Joseph Andrews, and his Friend Mr. Abraham Adams (2 vols., 1742) began as another parody. Joseph, Pamela's chaste brother, is sexually accosted by Lady Booby, Mrs. Slipslop, and Betty the chambermaid. He defends his purity with physical force and puritanical speeches. F.'s lesson is that virtue is composed of much more than virginity. The introduction of Parson Abraham Adams, a simple man who believes in active charity, transforms the book. Adams is a good man with

human flaws. Expecting to find all men as honest as himself, he is surprised by hypocrisy but is prepared to use his cudgel to defend innocence against villainy. Together, Joseph and Adams, self-control and active benevolence, embody the Christian virtues. *Joseph Andrews* continues F.'s critique of irresponsible writing by initiating a new kind of writing, the "comic Epic-Poem in Prose." He deliberately draws attention to the work's own artificiality through the ironic narrator, mock-epic similes, and epistles that just happened to be memorized. In this way, F. introduces his own conception of the purpose of the novel: to encourage readers to become critics of literature and life.

In *The History of Tom Jones, a Foundling* (6 vols., 1749), the meaning is inseparable from its form. The Author governs the world of the novel just as a benevolent God presides over His creation. The Author is such a congenial character, it has been debated whether he is a persona or F. himself. The essays that begin each of the eighteen books offer a distancing from the plot as the Author teaches the art of writing. He states that Genius, Learning, Conversation with all men, and a good heart are necessary to be a good historian, but they are also helpful in life. Only at the novel's end do we realize the whole architecture of the work; the careful use of coincidence and trivial events; the hints and ironies that are only clear after Tom's parentage is disclosed. The subject of *Tom Jones* is Human Nature, "the History of the World in general." Tom, through his travels from Paradise Hall to London and back, learns Prudence and becomes worthy of his love, Sophia (wisdom) Western. Tom encounters the spectrum of 18th-c. society and morals, from the Squire Allworthy, tutor Thwackum, hypocritical Blifil, earthy Molly Seagrim, mercenary Lady Bellaston, innkeepers, Jacobites, soldiers, and Methodists. It captures the spirit and variety of the age and defines F.'s philosophy of charity and good nature.

After the celebration of life that was *Tom Jones*, F.'s last novel, *Amelia* (4 vols., 1751), was dark and pessimistic. The action centers on a married couple, Billy and Amelia Booth, and the corrupt institutions and moral weaknesses that threaten their happiness. F. exposes vice in the law courts, the army, and in the upper classes. The central images of the prison and the masquerade convey the deception and disguise that are rampant. The wife's pandering of Trent and Colonel James, Mrs. Bennet's rape, the seduction of Booth by Miss Mathews, the backstabbing and blackmail are some of the vices the Booths must strive against. The narrator states that the novel can teach the art of life if we attend to the minute causes that lead to the catastrophes. But the reassuring author of *Tom Jones* is absent, and the fate of the characters is uncertain. Allusions to *Othello* underscore the potential tragedy; and the REALISM and social satire make the novel claustrophobic. The comic conclusion rings false but emphasizes F.'s theme that we know goodness is not always rewarded in this corrupt world.

F. also authored the *Miscellanies* (3 vols., 1743), a collection of earlier poetry, essays, prose pieces, and plays. The last volume included *The Life of Mr. Jonathan Wild*, an extended ironic satire of Walpole. F. wrote for the Opposition for a time, and during the Jacobite crisis started the weekly periodicals, the *True Patriot* (1745–46) and the *Jacobite's Journal* (1747–48). He produced the *Covent-Garden Journal* (1752) satirizing manners and morals. *The Journal of a Voyage to Lisbon* (1755), F.'s last work, described his ill-fated trip to Portugal. Despite failed health and constant pain, F.'s HUMOR, satire, and indomitable lust for life still shine.

BIBLIOGRAPHY: Battestin, M. C., with R. R. Battestin, *H. F.* (1989); Cross, W. L., *The History of H. F.* (3 vols., 1918); Hume, R. D., *H. F. and the London Theatre, 1728–1737* (1988); Smallwood, A. J., *F. and the Woman Question* (1989); Thomas, D., *H. F.* (1991); Wilputte, E., "'Women buried': H. F. and Feminine Absence," *MLR* 95, 2 (2000): 324–36

EARLA WILPUTTE

FIELDING, Sarah

b. 8 November 1710, East Stour, Dorset; d. 9 April 1768, Bath

Popular in her own time for delving into the labyrinths of the heart, F. was later eclipsed by her brother Henry FIELDING and friend, Samuel RICHARDSON. Rediscovered by feminist scholars in the 20th c., F. is lauded for her prose fiction experiments, use of irony, allegory, and sentimentalism, and explorations of gender.

F. began her career with Leonora's letter in Henry Fielding's *Joseph Andrews* and the Anna Boleyn narrative in his *Journey from this World to the Next*, published in 1743. Her first novel, *The Adventures of David Simple* (2 vols., 1744), was initially mistaken for Henry's because of its picaresque structure and irony. The innocent David's travels to find a friend explored the value of benevolence in a corrupt world. Through the feminized hero, and Cynthia, a witty woman, F. destabilized sexual opposition to satirize socially prescribed behaviors. *Familiar Letters between the Principal Characters in David Simple* (2 vols., 1747) led readers to expect a sequel to her first novel; however, it disappointed by offering an epistolary miscellany on moral subjects. In *Volume the Last* (1753), David, his friends Valentine and Cynthia, and wife Camilla suffer through the hypocrisy, greed, and verbal manipulations of people such as Mrs. Orgueil and Mr. Ratcliff. David's little community of love is destroyed and only the satirical Cynthia and David's daughter Camilla live to the novel's end. In both

David Simple and *Volume the Last*, F. demonstrates the untrustworthiness of language as her characters come to depend on nonverbal communication to express emotions. To correct her style in *David Simple*, Henry Fielding edited out hundreds of F.'s dashes that she used for emotional REALISM. In the rest of her works, F. addressed feminine language and its suppression in patriarchal society.

F.'s third book, *The Governess* (1749), was written specifically for girls. Mrs. Teachum's academy for nine girls is primarily concerned with moral lessons. The plot consists of the eldest girl, Jenny Peace, under the guidance of Mrs. Teachum, reading stories to the others who comment on them and tell their own histories. By the end, the girls have improved themselves and achieved personal peace through reason and restraint of passion. F.'s inclusion of FAIRY TALES, a genre frowned upon in the 18th c., was controversial. Mrs. Teachum points to their lessons of feminine patience and prudence; however, their subtexts (not commented upon by Jenny or her mentor) teach female courage, endurance, and a happy life without marriage.

In *The Cry: A New Dramatic Fable* (1754), coauthored with Jane Collier, F. continued to experiment. Structured like a five-part play, it presents an apparent trial of the heroine, Portia, before Una (Truth) and "The Cry," an assembly of negative, antagonistic voices. It has a loose romance plot. A fascinating and challenging piece that investigates society's malignant contortion of words, it deserved a better recognition. In *The Lives of Cleopatra and Octavia* (1757), the eponymous ghosts narrate their own histories. Cleopatra tells how she played upon Antony's expectations of feminine vulnerability to control him; while Octavia describes how his prejudices prevented him from recognizing her virtues and ability to help him. Demonstrating the sexes at odds with one another, F.'s text subtly suggests that both must work toward an understanding in order to change.

The Countess of Dellwyn (1759) and *The History of Ophelia* (1760) are more conventional in form but still continue her study of human behavior. They are also significant in that they react against Henry Fielding's *Amelia* and Richardson's *Pamela*, respectively, demonstrating that F. was not blindly governed by these influential authors. Charlotte's devolution into the adulterous wife of Count Dellwyn is counterbalanced by the subplot's Mrs. Bilson who takes on moral and business responsibilities to create an ideal community, foreshadowing Sarah SCOTT's *A Description of Millenium Hall*. Ophelia Lenox's abduction from Wales to London by Lord Dorchester allows F. to pose pertinent questions about relationships between the sexes and society's use of insincere language. *Ophelia* offers a virtuous heroine who is more forthright with the man she loves than was Pamela. F.

also authored *Remarks on Clarissa* (1749), a pamphlet defending Richardson's novel. The only work F. published under her own name was her translation from the Greek, Xenophon's *Memoirs of Socrates* (1762).

No longer simply Henry Fielding's sister or a member of Richardson's coterie, F. is appreciated for her witty and analytical presentations of virtue, female intelligence, sexual double standards, and the hypocrisy of socially employed language.

BIBLIOGRAPHY: Barchas, J., "S. F.'s Dashing Style and Eighteenth-Century Print Culture," *ELH* 63, 3 (1996): 633–56; Battestin, M. C., and C. T. Probyn, *Correspondence of Henry and S. F.* (1993); Bree, L., *S. F.* (1996); Paul, N., "Is Sex Necessary? Criminal Conversation and Complicity in S. F.'s *Ophelia*," *Lumen* 16 (1997): 113–29

EARLA WILPUTTE

FIGES, Eva
b. 15 April 1932, Berlin, Germany

F. is known as an experimental novelist and an author of nonfiction, as well as a translator and children's book and script writer. She emigrated to England in 1939, from Germany, which accounts for many of the themes in her writing. Her work for adults tends to focus on alienation, female identity, and the exploration of the inner self. The latter has caused a comparison between F. and Virginia WOOLF. Her novels are technically experimental, psychological, and often fragmented in structure. In her fiction, her narrators are likely to be "unreliable." These narrators tend to twist or bend reality according to their perceptions. F.'s novels reject the realist tradition and move instead toward postmodern experimentation.

Her first novel, *Equinox* (1966), delves into the mind of a woman in her thirties who is unhappy in her marriage. The narrative was not met well critically, though her next novels, for the most part, were. *Winter Journey* (1967), which won the *Guardian* Fiction Prize, is narrated by an old, bitter, deaf man, Janus, who is living out his last days. The novel closely follows Janus's state of mind: a path that is difficult. Although the novel is relatively short, the pages are tightly packed, with stream of consciousness passages that show an ignorant, fearful man stripped to his bare essentials.

Konek Landing (1969) is the novel that F. considers her most important. Critics generally found it unnecessarily difficult and self-important. *Konek Landing* is a political novel, a story of victims and executioners. Konek, the novel's central character, mirrors F.'s own sense of alienation. Konek is a homeless refugee looking for an identity. It is in this novel that F. begins to explore her German-Jewish roots.

The experimental nature of the book, and the language F. uses, full of innovative sentence constructions, pronouns, and articles, at times obscures the actual narrative.

With subsequent novels, F. constructs moods and thought processes through complex narrative motifs. In *B* (1972), a writer and a character he has created become interwoven. Many other of F.'s novels also deal with confused identity: the narrator of *Days* (1974) is actually a composite of three women of different generations; and *Nelly's Version* (1977) is told by an amnesiac. In *Waking* (1981), the novel is structured around seven waking moments. *Patriarchal Attitudes* (1970) is a feminist text that looks at the history of male dominated society. In this nonfiction study, F.'s structure is more conventional than her fictional work. It is perhaps for this reason that this text has been more widely embraced by critics and scholars. In *Little Eden: A Child at War* (1978), F. again looks at alienation and the refugee experience, though in this case the subject is herself. F.'s experiences as a German-Jewish refugee in England during World War II are described in this autobiographical work.

F.'s other novels include *Light* (1983), *The Seven Ages* (1986), *Ghosts* (1988), and *The Tenancy* (1993). In addition, she has edited *Women's Letters in Wartime: 1450–1945* (1993) and translated numerous books and articles. Her other nonfiction books include *Tragedy and Social Evolution* (1976) and *Sex and Subterfuge: Women Writers to 1850* (1982).

BIBLIOGRAPHY: Conradi, P., "E. F.," in Halio, J. L., ed., *British Novelists since 1960, DLB* 14 (1982): 298–302; Stuby, A. M., "'A Piece of Shrapnel Lodges in My Flesh, and When It Moves, I Write': The Fiction of E. F.," *A&E* 60 (1997): 113–27

MARIKA BRUSSEL

FILM AND LITERATURE

While film theory usually considers film as a kind of text, the relationship between film and literature has often been somewhat vexed. In the early days of film, filmmakers borrowed freely from literature, and film was seen as a more realistic way to tell a story. As the studio system evolved, filmmakers used the cultural capital of literature to lend their studios a highbrow tone. But as film began to develop as an art form in its own right, other critics and theorists aimed to differentiate film from literature. While film's storytelling capacity proved to be its most profitable side, film artists and theorists called for more exploration into the particular capacities of the medium.

From literature's side, the lines were also drawn. As film's capacity for REALISM quickly outstripped that of either the novel or drama, those forms moved away from realism. At the same time, film became one of the 20th c.'s defining technologies and literature began to borrow from it, first as a way of envisioning the world, then as a way of capturing human consciousness.

At the end of the 19th c., short, silent films arose as a powerful new mass medium simultaneously in Europe, Russia, and the U.S. Originally more of a novelty than an art form, these early films had little relationship to the literary arts, and were seen by many as a debased form of popular entertainment. As the technology improved rapidly, there were calls for the development of a true cinematic art. One response came from a group of British craftsmen who came to be known as the Brighton School, after their city of origin. They began to develop a cinematographic language, showing that filmic devices such as cross-cutting, montage, reverse shot editing, and elliptical editing could be used to make narrative sense in film, even without sound. While they never found financial success, the Brighton School had a profound influence on cinema's first great director, D. W. Griffith. Griffith used their techniques to make hundreds of films, and as transition from short novelty films to novelistic narratives. Griffith proclaimed that his models were literary, at one point defending cross-cutting on the grounds that Charles DICKENS had done it. Indeed, there were many similarities between Griffith's style and that of Dickens, as noted by Russian director Sergei Eisenstein, who was very much influenced by Griffith.

Griffith marks the beginning of film's strong association with realist narrative. What is known as the "classical Hollywood cinema" uses a plot that, like the 19th-c. novel, is driven by individual characters as agents. Psychological motives are the most common narrative engine, and cause and effect are highlighted in the film's unfolding. Most often, the story is told from a relatively "objective" point of view, although the audience's access to information may, as in novels, be limited by the character's perspective. Classical Hollywood thus allied itself with the 19th-c. realist novel.

As film outpaced them in the depiction of real life, both the novel and the dramatic form moved away from realism. The modernist novels of the early 20th c. were in part a reaction against film, even as they were powerfully influenced by it. Novels such as James JOYCE's *Ulysses* and Virginia WOOLF's *To the Lighthouse* dispensed with realist narrative in favor of an impressionistic stream of consciousness. Even as it rejected realism, however, the lush, observant, visually oriented voice of these novels reflected the position of the camera-eye, and the shifts in perspective, temporal distortions, changing points of view, and juxtaposition of images created a literary analogue for film's montage.

World War I solidified the leadership position of the American film industry, and the rise of the studio system guaranteed its dominance. Committed more to good business than great art, the American studio system reinforced film's alliance with a novelistic narrative. Hollywood frequently turned to literary adaptations, utilizing the talents of novelists and playwrights to create a popular product. Some authors lent themselves to film better than others. Griffith himself had adapted Robert BROWNING's poem "Pippa passes" (1909). As to be expected, 19th-c. novelists fared well on film. Dickens was perhaps the most successful. David Lean's *Great Expectations* (1947) is generally considered one of the greatest films ever made. No fewer than five versions of *Oliver Twist* have been made, with Lean's *Oliver Twist* (1948) and Carol Reed's musical version *Oliver!* (1968) topping the list. *David Copperfield* (1935), *A Tale of Two Cities* (1935), and *Nicholas Nickleby* (1947) were also succeeded onscreen.

Other notable screen adaptations of 19th-c. novels include William Wyler's film version of Emily BRONTË's *Wuthering Heights* (1939) with Merle Oberon and Laurence Olivier; Robert Stevenson's version of Charlotte BRONTË's *Jane Eyre* (1944) starring Orson Welles and Joan Fontaine; John Schlesinger's *Far from the Madding Crowd* (1967) from the Thomas HARDY novel; Stanley Kubrick's *Barry Lyndon* (1975), an adaptation of William Makepeace THACKERAY; *The Man Who Would Be King* (1975), John Huston's adaptation of Rudyard KIPLING's novella; and *Portrait of a Lady* (1999), Jane Campion's adaptation of Henry JAMES. Some filmmakers were more adventurous in adaptation, moving beyond the novel. Italian filmmaker Pier Paolo Pasolini, for instance, often used literary sources, and made a film version of Geoffrey CHAUCER's *The Canterbury Tales* (1972).

Early films were often simply filmed versions of plays, and countless successful plays were made into films. However, the relationship between the theater and film has been surprisingly undynamic. Hollywood hired many American playwrights and some British ones to write screenplays, but playwrights had little incentive to become screenwriters, who are valued less than directors in the film industry. Furthermore, the transposition of stage plays to film was often difficult, and there have been many disappointing results. Oscar WILDE's comic masterpiece *The Importance of Being Earnest*, for instance, was only filmed once before the 21 c., in 1952, and the unexceptional result was a British production rather than a Hollywood one. Bernard SHAW's many plays were not filmed nearly as often as one might expect, and the most famous film version of a Shaw play is the musical *My Fair Lady* (1964), based on his play *Pygmalion*. Noël COWARD is one British playwright who moved between film and drama: he wrote original screenplays and saw his plays adapted. Several of his plays were made into films in 1933, the most successful of which was *Design for Living* (1933). *Blithe Spirit* (1945) and *Brief Encounter* (1946) were also successes. *Easy Virtue* (1927) was directed by Alfred Hitchcock.

William SHAKESPEARE, however, has held perennial interest for filmmakers. In England, Olivier directed and starred in what critics still consider some of the best film versions of Shakespeare plays: *Henry V* (1944), *Hamlet* (1948), and *Richard III* (1955). Orson Welles tackled Shakespeare in *Macbeth* (1948), *Othello* (1952), and *Chimes at Midnight* (1967), a compilation of five history plays. Roman Polanski also made a well-received *Macbeth* (1971). Italian director Franco Zeffirelli made the most acclaimed film version of *Romeo and Juliet* (1968), and Kenneth Branagh received accolades for his *Henry V* (1989) and *Hamlet* (1996).

As the studio system generated fierce rivalries, Louis B. Mayer and Irving Thalberg, as general manager and supervisor of production at Metro Goldwyn Mayer (MGM), began a campaign to promote the new mega-studio as purveyors of "classy" entertainment. Thalberg oversaw the production of many English literary properties, including *Private Lives* (1931), based on a play by Coward, *The Barretts of Wimpole Street* (1934), a drama about the romance between Elizabeth Barrett BROWNING and Robert Browning, Jack Conway's Dickens adaptation *A Tale of Two Cities* (1935), George Cukor's *David Copperfield* (1935) and *Romeo and Juliet* (1936), and Robert Z. Leonard's version of Jane AUSTEN's *Pride and Prejudice* (1940). With elaborate sets and lavish costumes, MGM strove to advance their own claims to highbrow status through association with distinctly literary content. The MGM approach continued in the late 20th c. in the lush, romanticized films of James Ivory and Ismail Merchant. *The Europeans* (1979) and *The Bostonians* (1984)—from the novels of Henry James—*Howard's End* (1992), *A Room with a View* (1996), and *Maurice* (1997)—from the novels of E. M. FORSTER—all have impeccable literary pedigrees, and are filmed with gorgeous costumes and decor.

For filmmakers less concerned with creating a highbrow aura, genre fiction, like suspense stories, translated well to the screen. Hitchcock, who began his career adapting plays and novels, took up Joseph CONRAD's *The Secret Agent* for his film *Sabotage* (1936). Horror and SCIENCE FICTION are also genres where the film versions can transcend the often-clumsy texts. Film's ability to depict the imaginative or the macabre has resulted in many horror and science fiction films becoming better known and more influential than texts on which they are based. The Universal Studios versions of *Frankenstein* (1931) and *Dracula* (1931) may not be as complex as the novels by Mary SHELLEY and Bram STOKER, but visualized they became enduring cultural icons, spawning hosts of sequels. H. G. WELLS's novels were less influential, but still found success onscreen, especially *The Invisible Man* (1933), *Things to Come* (1936), and *The Time Machine* (1960).

While scholars and the general public have often focused on measuring an adaptation's "truth" to the original, some of the most compelling film adaptations have adhered only loosely to the original, or utilized a literary text to create an entirely new vision. Perhaps the most famous of these is Robert Wise's *West Side Story* (1961), a musical reimagining of Shakespeare's *Romeo and Juliet* set in New York's Hell's Kitchen in the 1950s. Another famous transposition is Francis Ford Coppola's *Apocalypse Now* (1975), which begins with Conrad's story "Heart of Darkness," but layers onto it a contemporary tale about the horrors of the Vietnam War. The result is often considered the best depiction of Vietnam on film, and one of the most acclaimed films ever made. Similarly, Japanese director Akira Kurosawa reset Shakespeare's *King Lear* in Japan to create his magnificent EPIC *Ran* (1985). Some adaptations work to deconstruct literary texts: Peter Greenaway used Shakespeare's *The Tempest* as a starting point for *Prospero's Books* (1991), a wandering, nonnarrative sensual film. Other treatments are less serious in tone: Amy Heckerling set the plot of Austen's *Emma* among spoiled teens in Southern California to make the ironic and hilarious *Clueless* (1995).

Beyond adaptations, film and literature interact when artists travel between the two. In general, Great Britain has proved friendlier to crossovers between literature and film than the U.S. Authors such as Coward and Graham GREENE not only saw their works made into films, but worked in the film industry as well. Greene worked as a film critic at the *Spectator* in the 1930s. His stories and novels provided the basis for many films including *This Gun for Hire* (1942), *Confidential Agent* (1945), and *The Quiet American* (1958). In addition, he wrote many screenplays, some original and some adaptations of his own work. *The Third Man* (1949) is perhaps the most famous.

More recently, Harold PINTER has established himself as a presence in both the worlds of drama and of film. Pinter has scripted adaptations of his own plays, including *The Homecoming* (1973) and *Betrayal* (1983). But he has also written many screenplays adapted from other authors' work, including *The Last Tycoon* (1976), *The Handmaid's Tale* (1990), and *The French Lieutenant's Woman* (1981), for which he won an Academy Award.

Britain's Channel 4, established in 1980, has also provided a space for fruitful collaboration between the film and literary worlds. The New British Cinema has garnered international attention with films made for

Channel 4 like *My Beautiful Laundrette* (1985), written by playwright Hanif KUREISHI and directed by theater director Stephen Frears. Kureishi and Frears have both gone on to have successful careers both on and off screen.

The relationship between film and literature seems to have been marked by mutual envy: film has craved literature's cultural value while literature has envied film's technological capacities for visualization. Critics denigrate film adaptations of literature as superficial and film theorists argue for the independence of the film text from literary precursors. There is some hope that, in a world of multimedia, interactions between literature and film will increase, and the relationship will grow in complexity and value. And while there have been failures, there have been enough successes that it's fair to say that the relations between literature and film have already changed the course of both literary and film history.

BIBLIOGRAPHY: Beja, M., *Film and Literature* (1979); Boynum, J. G., *Theater and Film* (1979); Costello, T., ed., *International Guide to Literature on Film* (1994); Davidson, P., ed., *Film and Literature* (1997); Davies, A., and S. Wells, eds., *Shakespeare and the Moving Image* (1994); Tibbets, J. C., and J. M. Walsh, *Novels into Film* (1999); Zambrano, A., *Dickens and Film* (1976)

GINGER STRAND

FILMER, [Sir] Robert
b. ca. 1586, East Sutton, Kent; d. 30 May 1653, East Sutton Park

F.'s chief work, *Patriarcha; or, The Natural Power of Kings*, was not published until 1680, twenty years after the monarchy had been restored. Defender of absolute monarchy and its biblical origins, F. began writing his political treatises in the mid-1640s, notably *The Necessity of the Absolute Power of All Government* (1648), as Jean Bodin, and the anonymous *Observations concerning the Original of Government* (1652). A staunch royalist, F. suffered in the Civil War, but continued to argue for the "divine right" of kings: God gave authority to Adam, who passed it to Noah, who gave it to his three sons. From these patriarchs, kings and governors inherited absolute authority: the king was independent of human control. F.'s political position generated widespread opposition but none more effective than that of John LOCKE in his *Two Treatises of Government*.

FINCH, Anne. See WINCHILSEA, Anne Finch, Countess of

FINLAY, Ian Hamilton
b. 28 October 1925, Nassau, Bahamas

Sent to a Scottish boarding school, F. at the outbreak of war was evacuated to the Orkney Islands, and his formal education ended at thirteen, apart from a short spell at art school in Glasgow. F. joined the army in 1942 and after the war worked as a shepherd, studied philosophy, and began to write short stories and plays, some sold to the BBC. He is a sculptor and "concrete poet" and has created a unique garden, "Little Sparta," at his home at Stonypath, near Edinburgh, which he never leaves, despite his international reputation. In concrete poetry, the arrangement of words on the page (as in George HERBERT's "Easter Wings") contributes to meaning. This art led naturally to the arrangement of words on stone, wood, and other materials, incorporating poetry with garden design. F.'s use of lettering is beautiful. His postmodern vision is founded on classicism: "Adorno's Hut" is a steel construction modern on one side with classical pillars on the other. The primitive hut was made of tree branches, and the work links the primitive, the classical, and the modern. F. laments the fall of Roman civilization with a cracked wall with the word "World" in Roman lettering. He believes that the modern world lacks true culture and that we have lost true power, wisdom, virtue, and tradition. Attacked as "sentimental" and "whimsical" by David Black and Hugh MACDIARMID, F. riposted "The best a writer writes is Beautiful./He should ignore the Mad and Dutiful."

FIRBANK, Ronald
b. 17 January 1886, London; d. 21 May 1926, Rome, Italy

When F. arrived at Trinity College, Cambridge, he knew he was gay and he had already published his first book. Critics are now beginning to attend to this writer whose work was so unappreciated in his lifetime that he had to finance the publication of eight out of ten of his books.

Most often, F.'s world features members of the upper class, whether royalty, cardinals, or titled gentry. With a sensibility known as "Camp," which emphasizes artifice and exaggeration at the expense of naturalness, F. presents heroes and heroines who cultivate detachment, disdain, ennui, and good taste. His works include early masterpieces such as *Vainglory* (1915), a satire of London social life, *Valmouth* (1919), an exposé of the goings-on at a spa, as well as his most controversial novel, *The Flower beneath the Foot*. Published in 1923, this at once attacks the Roman Catholic Church (to which F. had converted while he was at Cambridge) and mounts a passionate indictment of an arranged royal marriage. In this novel, F. also describes the suffering of the frustrated heroine, Laura de Naziani, who, like other F. characters, tries to find solace in good works and enters a monastery. In other words, happy, fulfilled love is a rarity in F.'s novels.

Technically, F. is highly innovative. He developed a unique way of compressing his novels, which, since his time, has become "part of the economy of fiction." Moving from scene to scene cinematically, with narrative quite incidental, the works exist primarily through dialogue, which in F. evolves to a high art. Perhaps his most noteworthy means of reproducing the exact tones of real speech remains his tape recorder method: the reader is placed in the position of eavesdropping at a party, hearing snatches of talk from several separate conversations. Other writers, such as Osbert and Sacheverell SITWELL, as well as the sculptor Jacob Epstein, soon recognized the man's genius and sought F. out.

Prancing Nigger (1924; repub. as *Sorrow in Sunlight*, 1924) is F.'s most widely known book and was particularly successful in the U.S. Although F. depicts with a combination of amusement and dismay the social gaffes of a West Indian family who move from a country home to a capital city, the novel has a serious theme: racial discrimination. *Concerning the Eccentricities of Cardinal Pirelli*, published in 1926, remains F.'s most daring undertaking. Plot is at a minimum and structure reduced to a set of conversation pieces, many of them explicitly bawdy. In this work that refuses to have a story, the book opens with Cardinal Pirelli administering the sacrament to a puppy, a young police dog called Crack, and ends when the naked cardinal falls dead chasing a boy around a cathedral. F.'s American publisher would not print the manuscript, fearing that it would alienate its audience. The book remained unpublished until after F.'s death, which occurred four months before his fortieth birthday.

Most critics find F. a hard writer to assess. Some find him too self-conscious and lacking in seriousness; others are beguiled by his unique vision as an outsider and his playfulness. Still others object to his morality, which they find limited to "naughtiness," noting that in contrast, say, to Fyodor Dostoevsky, F. depicts no great sinners. Nevertheless, in achieving in his books the shimmering surface, purity, and dewy freshness of a Jean-Antoine Watteau or a Mozart, critics agree that F. produced books whose message is that life, like F.'s work itself, should be enjoyed for its own sake.

BIBLIOGRAPHY: Benkovitz, M. J., *R. F.* (1969); Brooke, J., *R. F. and John Betjeman* (1962); Brophy, B., *Prancing Novelist* (1973); Horder, M., ed., *R. F.* (1977)

SUSAN TETLOW HARRINGTON

FISCHER, Tibor

b. 15 November 1959, Stockport

F. achieved prominence at thirty-three with *Under the Frog: A Black Comedy* (1992), a type of Bildungsro-

man centered on Gyuri Fischer, Pataki, and the Locomotive basketball team. The novel is a brilliant, sardonic portrait of the alternating horror and boredom of living in communist Hungary. As the narrator muses: "That was one of the worst things: the boredom. Dictatorship of the proletariat, apart from the abrasive and brutal nature of its despotism, was terribly dull." The narrative is loaded with this sense of dreadful and seemingly eternal ennui, which forms a stifling barrier to freedom of thought and the "outside" world. The paranoia instilled by a totalitarian government forms a serious subtext, or rather Gyuri and other characters devise modes of pretending that totalitarianism is a subtext. Gyuri resists the colonization of the self by communist totalitarianism through HUMOR and hope. The Locomotive basketball team perfectly satirizes the cult of the physical and also provides narrative movement. Schoolboy pranks combine with the dead seriousness of getting arrested by the secret police and informing on one's mates. Pataki, Gyuri's idol, encompasses both poles. Farce serves as a means of coping with the claustrophobia and the suppressed rage that dictatorship engenders. F.'s writing masterfully interweaves the bizarre, outlandish, the comic, and the serious. The eating contest between Ladanyi, a Jesuit village hero, and Farago, former Nazi collaborator and Party Secretary; Wu, a Chinese basketball player who farts out the Internationale are just two instances of the absurd as a political strategy to counter straitjacketed dogma.

Understatement, wit, and irony are concomitants of humor deployed with devastating effect. Hungary's history of defeat is aptly summed up by Gyuri's teacher: "Fischer, Fischer, this is deplorable. You can't let a little war interfere with serious scholarship. You know our history. As a Hungarian you should be prepared for the odd cataclysm." Gyuri's ambiguous political status arises from his bourgeois background, the fact that his father, Elek, is a failed businessman. Elek's reaction to utter ruin and destitution is a type of philosophical calm: "Destitute at the age of sixty, even allowing for the common denominator of a world war and vast industries of suffering and misery, you would have expected some cursing and shrieking. A gnawing of fists. A denouncing of higher powers. But Elek didn't issue any unseemly lamentations. He simply sat in the armchair, at ease, as if enjoying a day off."

Perhaps this calm represents resistance or perhaps it is just hopelessness. Gyuri is sustained by his fantasy of being a street sweeper anywhere outside Hungary where "you wouldn't need an examination in Marxism-Leninism, you wouldn't have to look at pictures of [Mátyás] Rákosi or whoever had superbriganded their way to the top lately." Sexual escapades, food, and drink are modes of coping with the interim imprisonment. Gyuri's final attainment of freedom is profoundly moving and encompasses the sorrow and liberation that exile brings. His escape seems emblematic of other such experiments with liberation and is valuable even in a post–iron curtain world where the memory of survival remains. Histories of survival are central to this book and Miklós, an incidental character who survived Dachau and was then imprisoned in Hungary, embodies a vast tragedy involving millions. With its dextrous writing, acute observations on history, memory, and tyranny, its often wild humor, *Under the Frog* is a profound and brilliant novel.

F.'s next novel, *The Thought Gang* (1994), belies this early promise. If *Under the Frog* is in the tradition of Czech author Milan Kundera, *The Thought Gang* is partly in the tradition of academic satires like Kingsley AMIS's *Lucky Jim*. It is also reminiscent of J. P. Donleavy's sagas of the drunk, angst-ridden loner often caught in bizarre situations. Professor Coffin, failed philosophy don at Cambridge turned bank robber, is arrested in the nude in a flat with child pornography magazines and no recollection of how he came there. The narrative that follows is a series of capers where Coffin robs banks with his one-eyed, one-armed, one-legged comrade Hubert. The deal is that Hubert will teach Coffin the art of bank robbery and Coffin will initiate Hubert into philosophy. The pair pull off sensationally successful robberies and become the center of media and police attention and are dubbed the thought gang. The narrative structure mirrors the chaotic drunken forays of the pair and is largely sustained by humor and witticisms as well as the idea that both philosophy and robberies are cons. Verbal dexterity—"Boxed in the gonad's monad"—combines with moving meditations on old age, mortality, and memory. There is sadness underlying the endless mayhem. At the same time, however, there is a thinness, a lack of genuine pathos found in the first novel, and finally a sense of overt cleverness with little substance.

The Collector Collector (1997) confirms this decline despite the original idea of an ancient bowl as narrator. As in *The Thought Gang*, a convoluted plot and quixotic humor dominate, but the subject matter is even flimsier. Rosa's search for an ideal partner with its innocent desire is in obvious contrast to the thieving, lying nymphomaniac, Nikki, and her sexual manipulation of people. Critics have variously interpreted the gratuitous sex that courses through the narrative. It could signify a search for happiness, boredom, or manipulation. It certainly objectifies women as abused, lost, or dead. Just as the bowl as narrator is object of lust and covetousness so too are the women and Nikki turns her potential victimhood into a weapon of control.

In *Under the Frog*, farce is a kind of existential mode of coping for underlying that is a deep-seated,

personal, and political seriousness. Perhaps the imprint of his parents' migration from Hungary informs the novel with gravitas. In the later novels, farce dominates at the expense of political and ideological insights. This seems to be a sad decline: while the writing remains pointed and occasionally brilliant, its object and consequently the substance of the later novels seem sadly depleted.

BIBLIOGRAPHY: Matthews, S., "T. F.," in Moseley, M., ed., *British Novelists since 1960*, Fourth Series, *DLB* 231 (2001): 112–17

SUBARNO CHATTARJI

FISHER, Roy
b. 11 June 1930, Handsworth, Birmingham

Now that the critical consensus on the benefits of the so-called Movement's aesthetic counterrevolution is fracturing, the few poets such as Basil BUNTING, Christopher MIDDLETON, and F. who kept English MODERNISM alive after 1945 are finally getting their due, although it almost seemed to take a stroke for F.'s solid merit to be recognized with a collection of essays and festschrift.

The ambiguous nature of F.'s writing makes him a difficult poet to categorize. Born into a long-settled, working-class family in Birmingham, he was acutely aware that the city's workers were scarcely visible in English literature since only middle-class authors—W. H. AUDEN, Louis MACNEICE, Henry GREEN, Walter Allen—had written memorably about their town. He would make his people perceptible by voicing the ways they inhabited their environment; yet so obliquely has F. pursued this project early critics either missed it, calling him an aesthete, or misinterpreted it, finding right-wing authoritarianism in work that is, in fact, implicitly anarchist in its revolt against any repressive system, whether it be capitalism, Christianity, or closed poetic form.

The strength of F.'s imaginative engagement with Birmingham can be gauged by the fact that—apart from a couple of years in Devon—he hardly left his hometown until he reached his forties and that many of his most substantial works—*City* (1961), "Handsworth Liberties (1–16)" (1978), "Wonders of Obligation" (1979), *A Furnace* (1986), and *Birmingham River* (1994)—have confronted that native city and the surrounding "Black Country." Since 1972, he has merely changed his base within the Midlands twice. Yet his fixedness does not necessarily denote devotion to locality: travel phobia rather than a Mercian affinity kept him in the region and although his poetry does find beauty in the utilitarian, it is often quietly menaced or depressed by the area's infernal aspects. Though minutely attentive to townscape, F. has largely avoided place names. By forgoing documentary realism, he makes location representative: the unspecified Birmingham of *City* stands for any British industrial town, whose postwar redevelopment replaced Victorian "slums" with high-rise buildings.

Despite this distrust of documentation, F. claims to be a realist, believing in an autonomous material world, which his senses can contact and poetry fix ("The Memorial Fountain"). This explains his lifelong allegiance to the imagist-objectivist tradition and preference for metonym over metaphor; yet his empiricism is qualified by a skeptical temper, conscious how much of "reality" is constructed by society's dominant ideologies and the individual's conceptual models and temperamental filters. His struggle to free himself from these impositions has manifested itself in a Blakean suspicion of system, a tentative, scrupulous investigation of the mechanics and validity of perception, and an imaginative remaking of the world in all its strangeness by defamiliarizing common objects and habitual actions. This remaking often takes the form of metamorphosing what initially seemed objective notation into expressionist or surrealist mindscape, or, latterly, urban sublime (*A Furnace* pays ambiguous homage to Wordsworthian transcendentalism by having gasholders and public conveniences stir the observer to epiphany). F. rearranges renovated shapes and colors into poem-paintings without ever permitting his fictiveness to lose touch with life's moral demands. An awareness of perception's relativity also leads him to organize work around several views or instances of the same subject.

This sober, low-key poetry of perception can appear unemotional and—with its repudiation of the self's empathetic tales—far removed from confessional verse: the "I" ostensibly enters the poems only as a sensory apparatus with processing facilities. In fact, however, buried narrative fragments do give his work deep resonance. Thus, the fact that his father, whose lifespan coincided with Birmingham's confident late Victorian expansion and post-1945 diminishment, was dying as *City* was born lends tremendous pathos to its descriptions of buildings flattened by wartime bombing or postwar redevelopment and almost psychotic tension to its dream visions. Far from being a dry, cold poet, F. has a robust sense of HUMOR, which finds expression in splendidly direct satires.

"A Modern Story," lampooning Arts Council patronage, reflects his aggrieved sense that English poetry's public school-Oxbridge-London axis marginalizes provincial writers like himself. He was initially consigned to small, "underground," non-metropolitan presses (1961–79); yet when he joined the establishment Oxford University Press, which gathered his disparate writings in *Poems 1955–1980* (1980) and *Poems 1955–1987* (1988), he rather passed up the opportunity these collected editions offered by omitting the highly experimental, virtually unobtainable *The Cut Pages* (1971), as he has also done in *The Dow Low Drop: New and Selected Poems* (1996).

F.'s modernist texts can be roughly divided into assemblages, which gather poetry and prose material from years of notebooks and juxtapose it in cubist collages (*City, A Furnace*) or rearrange collections of magazine images and cinematic stills into Eisensteinian montages ("Stopped Frames and Set-Pieces," "Interiors with Various Figures"), and into improvisations, which lay down literary riffs and proceed wherever the variations take them (*The Ship's Orchestra, The Cut Pages*). This latter technique, F.'s subtle, hesitant free-verse cadences and the title poem of *The Thing about Joe Sullivan* (1978) are among the few instances where this eminently visual poet reminds us of his alternative career as a jazz pianist.

F.'s status as a modernist is unambiguous. What is unclear is whether his aesthetic derives predominantly from the U.S. (no ideas, but in things; projectivist indeterminacy) or Europe (Russian formalism; cubist collage; Vorticist dynamism; and Franz Kafka, Paul Klee, and Oskar Kokoschka's visionary cities); whether he retains unbroken contact with high modernism as a retromodernist or neomodernist or whether a postmodernist mode separates him from it; and whether recent works renounce modernism in favor of a neo-Romantic pursuit of myth and the numinous in nature. What, finally, remains debatable is whether the variously experimental *City, The Cut Pages*, or *A Furnace* is his masterpiece.

BIBLIOGRAPHY: Fraser, T., ed., *R. F.: Interviews through Time, and Selected Prose* (1999); Kerrigan, J., and P. Robinson, eds., *The Thing about R. F.* (2000); Robinson, P., and R. Sheppard, eds., *News for the Ear: A Homage to R. F.* (2000)

DAVID FULTON

FITZGERALD, Edward

b. 31 March 1809, Bredfield, Suffolk; d. 14 June 1883, Merton, Norfolk

F.'s reputation as a poet rests on his brilliant "translation" called the *Rubáiyát of Omar Khayyám* (1859). Drawing from hundreds of short poems written by the 12th-c. Persian poet Omar Khayyám, F. forged an English masterpiece that is sensuously musical in style, exotically colorful in imagery, and daringly skeptical in its largely epicurean and nihilistic outlook. Upon its first appearance in 1859, the *Rubáiyát* went almost totally unnoticed. By 1900, it was widely recognized as a unique and fundamentally original contribution to English poetry, and it has come to be one of the most popular and widely known poems in the English language.

F.'s first significant publication was *Euphranor* (1851; rev. ed., 1855), a prose dialogue on education and chivalry influenced by Plato's symposia. Neither this nor his next work, a collection of aphorisms called *Polonius* (1852), was notably successful. His highly distinctive career as a translator began with his *Six Dramas of Calderón* (1853) and was continued through his *Salámán and Absál* (1856), *Agamemnon* (1865), and *The Downfall and Death of King Oedipus* (2 vols., 1880). In all of these works, F. demonstrates his very personal approach to translation. He treats his Greek, Spanish, or Persian texts less as originals than as sources. He emphasizes what interests him, deletes what does not, and imparts to all of the works under his hand his own distinctively sensuous, musical, and graceful style. The result in each case is an essentially original production in the guise of a translation.

F.'s abilities, especially his artistic command of the English language, are evident in all of his published work, but F.'s real place in English literature is, of course, based on the *Rubáiyát*. In the early 20th c., there was much debate about the "faithfulness" of F. to Omar Khayyám. More recent critics have realized that this debate is largely beside the point. Fewer than half of F.'s 101 stanzas represent paraphrases of actual individual poems by Omar; the rest are based on combinations of Omar's poems or do not derive from him at all. Moreover, F.'s *Rubáiyát* has a unity of structure, theme, imagery, and tone that is nowhere to be found in Omar. Also, whatever may be the poetic merit of Omar's original poems, the diction, prosody, music, and cadences of F.'s poem belong to the English language and to F. himself.

F.'s special stylistic magic in the *Rubáiyát* is largely the result of his exotic and sensuous imagery and his characteristic diction, which is both resonant and simple, haunting and direct. F.'s verse form is, in addition, a very successful and original contribution to English prosody. His stanza, now usually called "the *Rubáiyát* stanza," is an iambic pentameter quatrain rhyming *aaba*. In terms of themes and vision, F.'s *Rubáiyát* is a powerful meditation on life, death, and the cosmos. From a notably skeptical point of view, it celebrates sensuous and immediate experience while rejecting worldly glory and religious doctrine. The poem's treatment of conventional views of God is questioning, sardonic, and even satiric, and the epicureanism and nihilism of the poem shocked and fascinated Victorian readers.

Modern critics see in the *Rubáiyát* a great English poem that is only nominally a translation. Those critics have also begun to see in F.'s roughly four thousand letters one of the great literary correspondences in English.

BIBLIOGRAPHY: Alexander, D., *Creating Literature Out of Life: The Making of Four Masterpieces* (1996); Martin, R. B., *With Friends Possessed: A Life of E. F.* (1985); Terhune, A. M., *The Life of E. F.* (1947)

PHILLIP B. ANDERSON

FITZGERALD, Penelope

b. 17 December 1916, Lincoln; d. 28 July 2000, London

F. did not start publishing novels until she was in her late fifties, but in spite of a late start, she managed to produce nine novels and three biographies. The mother of three children, she also worked at a variety of jobs including bookshop clerk, a producer for the BBC, a teacher, and a contributing journalist for the *London Review of Books* and the *New York Times Book Review*. Her first published work was a biography of the English neo–Romantic painter Edward Burne-Jones in 1975.

After the death of her husband in 1976, she published another biography, but this one documents the lives of her father, the editor of *Punch*, and his three brothers: *The Knox Brothers* (1977). Out of the four characters, the most famous was the Reverend Ronald Knox, a novelist, biographer, and translator of the New Testament, who was a convert to Roman Catholicism and an intimate of other converts such as G. K. CHESTERTON, Graham GREENE, and Evelyn WAUGH. In the same year, F. published her first novel, *The Golden Child*, a book that gently satirizes the lives of bureaucrats involved in potential scandal in a London museum. However, it was her next novel, *The Bookshop* (1978), for which she received her first Booker Prize nomination. Set in the East Anglian village of Hardborough in the 1950s, the plot centers on the life of idealistic Florence Green who opens a bookshop in an historic old building in the center of town. She, like many of F.'s protagonists, is an innocent and is deeply disturbed when the local politicians try to take over the shop and transform it into a museum.

Her third novel, *Offshore* (1979), won the prestigious Booker Prize the year it was published. The novel is a study of economic and social class that evolved in a community of seeming outcasts, a group of barge dwellers living on the Thames near Battersea Bridge. The community consists of a wide range of humanity, including petty criminals, assorted drunks, a homosexual prostitute, and an investment counselor. *At Freddie's* (1982) explores F.'s interest in educational communities; Freddie's is the name of a school that trains children specifically for working in the plays of William SHAKESPEARE and other English classical dramatists. Freddie's actual name is Frieda Wentworth who supervises the school and hires the tutors, but whose main purpose is to save the school from financial ruin. The school sits in the middle of London's theater district.

The setting for her 1986 novel *Innocence* is Florence, Italy, rather than England. It concerns the fortunes of two historically distant families: the aristocratic Ridolphis of the 16th c. and a working-class 1920s family, the Rossis. However, both families suffer from the lethal effects of their naive innocence, which blinds them to political realities. *The Beginning of Spring* (1988) was also shortlisted for the Booker Prize and, like *Innocence*, is not set in England. Though the major character is an expatriate Englishman, he has moved to Moscow. After his wife leaves him, he suffers a breakdown but begins to recover because of the courageous examples of his three children and the return of spring in Moscow.

F.'s eighth novel, *The Gate of Angels* (1990), was again shortlisted for the Booker Prize. The novel is set in Cambridge, England, at the fictional college of St. Angelicus, founded by an anti-pope, Benedict XIII. Both a love story and a philosophical study of atheistic empiricism, F. ingeniously intermixes personal and spiritual issues but leaves their solutions open for the reader to find.

Perhaps F.'s finest novel is *The Blue Flower*, published in 1995. Unlike anything she had ever written, the novel is her longest and most thoroughly researched. It is historically grounded on the life of German Romantic poet Friedrich von Hardenberg, who took the name Novalis. Fritz—F.'s name for von Hardenberg—is being pressured by his father to become a salt merchant, but instead, he falls hopelessly in love with a young rather dull girl named Sophie von Kuhn. Fritz idealizes her into the "mystical rose," but as she lies dying of tuberculosis he renames her "The Blue Flower." After her death, she becomes Fritz's muse. He then renames himself Novalis and becomes one of Germany's greatest Romantic-mystical poets.

F.'s reputation has grown enormously since her death. One of her greatest honors was to be chosen, at the age of eighty-one, to be a judge on the Booker Prize panel.

BIBLIOGRAPHY: Bawer, B., "A Still, Small Voice: The Novels of P. F.," *NewC* 10, 7 (1992): 33–42; Sudrann, J., "Magic or Miracles: The Fallen World of P. F.'s Novels," in Hosmer, R. E., Jr., ed., *Contemporary British Women Writers* (1993): 105–27

PATRICK MEANOR

FLECKER, James Elroy

b. 5 November 1884, London; d. 3 January 1915, Davos, Switzerland

While F. enjoyed some posthumous success with his drama *Hassan* (pub. 1922; perf. 1923), even his greatest supporters admit that his short life has caused him to remain a relatively minor literary figure. The few

commentators dispute whether he was simply a dilettante and a dreamer or whether, in T. E. Lawrence's words, he was an exacting craftsman who had made "a wide, exact, skilful study of how other men had written." Lawrence in fact mourned that, with F.'s death, England had lost "the sweetest singer of the war generation." F.'s critical works reveal that he aspired to write according to the ideals of the aesthetes and Parnassians and believed that the artist should display an "enthusiasm for the world in every detail." He rejected the idea that a poet should convey a religious or political message and argued that it "is not the poet's business to save man's soul but to make it worth saving." While he never produced a polished work or a great volume of poetry, he did strive to create work that could address the complexity and beauty of human life.

While F. wished to be remembered as a poet, he did produce a body of prose works, including a novel, short stories, an Italian grammar, a treatise on education, and a body of literary criticism. F. began his novel, *The King of Alsander*, in 1906. Because of his own changes in the plan for the novel and the request of publishers for repeated revisions, it was not published until 1914. The work borrows heavily from a number of sources and has a picaresque structure that loosely parallels the popular *Prisoner of Zenda* by Anthony HOPE. A common grocer, Norman, ends up as ruler in the land of Alsander and finds himself able to unleash much of the untapped beauty and wealth of the country. At the same time, he must fight enemies and lovers as he comes to understand his own worth. While critics note the use of themes of love, beauty, cruelty, and art that dominate F.'s other work, they disagree about the worth of the novel. Those who see F. as a dilettante view the work as a rather undisciplined piece that shows the author's facility with language and interest in certain themes but gives little evidence of mature talent. Those who defend the work note that the wild mixture of tones in the piece is in fact a fitting way to depict Norman's growth through his trials. F. admitted that he only intended a "light and fantastic piece of writing."

While his short fiction also leans heavily on fantasy, F. maintained the importance of the artist's understanding of the reality of his times and produced a body of essays, literary criticism, and works on education that fulfill this function. He wrote appreciative essays about contemporary authors, including Arthur SYMONS and A. E. HOUSMAN. He stated some of his own principles as a poet in "The Public as Art Critic" and in his preface to his volume of poetry *The Golden Journey to Samarkand* (1913). While his criticism is for the most part unremarkable, it is judicious and well reasoned. He most consistently maintained the importance of creating art that shows a delight in all phases of human existence and argued that artist and critic alike must have an understanding of the technical aspects of composition. He declared his allegiance to the "art for art's sake" movement and proposed the French Parnassians for a model but emphasized that this did not require that one ignore the real world. It is in this practical spirit that he created *The Scholars' Italian Book* (1912) to help students with some understanding of classical and Romance languages to be able to learn the great literature of Italy. He also created a Platonic dialogue entitled *The Grecians* (1910) to propose a system of education that would produce the sense of a cultural heritage that F. felt could create leaders for England.

During his time, F. may have been best known for his play *Hassan*. This was not his first play; he had written a version of *Don Juan*, although it was not performed until 1926. Even his staunchest defenders can only call it a "near masterpiece." *Hassan*, on the other hand, is acknowledged as F.'s single most important work. Based in part on a group of Turkish farces, F. set out to write a farce himself, but ended up with a much more complex work. Admittedly, the transition of the work from farce to tragedy was awkward, and the play lacks form and coherence. Although *Hassan* was initially popular as a spectacle with a fantastic oriental setting, critics have since come to appreciate the way that F. explores the question of the relation between life and art and the importance of the artist's continuing attention to humanity.

F. most consistently devoted his talents throughout his career to his poetry, and it is most likely that he will be remembered for a few poems, including "The Old Ships," a poem that epitomizes his love of the Middle East and of classical literature. This work incorporates a love of exotic, sensual imagery, and a firm sense of structure. F. creates patterns of contrasts between dark and light, fire and flowers, violence and peace, many of which suggest the influence of Charles Baudelaire and *Les Fleurs du mal* (1857). Images of sleep ("swans asleep" and "drowsy ship") alternate with images of violent action (the "hell-raked" ship attacked by pirates) and images of the past alternate with images of the present. F. structures the poem around certain rhetorical patterns such as alliteration, repetition, echoing images, and rhyme, but none of these patterns intrudes on the dreamlike flow of images. The poem ends on a note of disappointment, as the speaker waits "in vain" for the kind of animation and revitalization implied by a ship bursting into bloom. In addition to the exotic imagery of his most anthologized poem, F. was also capable of expressing his love of his native England (in a poem like "Oak and Olive") and of creating order and beauty in his descriptions of the pain that marred the end of his life (in a poem like "In Hospital").

F. was an accomplished craftsman capable of creating works of great beauty. He engaged his talents in some of the most important poetic debates of his time, including the place of the artist in a world of increasing brutality. Finally, however, his work lacks the kind of individuality that would make him a major writer rather than a minor craftsman of passing interest.

BIBLIOGRAPHY: Davis, M. B., *J. E. F.* (1977); Munro, J. M., *J. E. F.* (1976); Sherwood, J., *No Golden Journey: A Biography of J. E. F.* (1973)

CATHERINE FRANK

FLEMING, Ian
b. 28 May 1908, London; d. 12 August 1964, Canterbury

F.'s own fame as a novelist has been eclipsed by that of his character, British spy James Bond, who lives on in the long-running series of stunt-filled films. The blend of designer fetishism, sadism, and initiatives in Cold War imperialism is as much F.'s trademark as Bond's "licence to kill" and "shaken, not stirred" martini are his, and the formula of thrillers such as *Casino Royale* (1953; repub. as *You Asked for It*, 1955), *From Russia, with Love* (1957), and *Goldfinger* (1959) has been repeatedly and variously imitated and parodied. Inheritors of the genre, from John LE CARRÉ to Len DEIGHTON, cannot escape comparison with his work.

The death of his father, an affluent and respected member of Parliament, occurred just before F.'s ninth birthday, and left him in the hands of his mother, a woman whose great wealth depended upon the provision she never remarry. Thus, F. was quickly introduced to a world of luxury bound up with death, of competition for favor and glory, and of impossible standards. He was educated at Eton and Sandhurst military academy and went on to a stint as a journalist with Reuters, followed by a career as a banker and stockbroker. His work with British Naval Intelligence during World War II involved the plotting of operations, some of which were themselves stranger than fiction. After the war, he settled in Jamaica, married, and began to write.

Casino Royale was the world's introduction to agent 007. The book's detail-driven account of high-stakes card games, secret codes, and other exotica met with great success. F. once claimed that "James Bond" was the most innocuous name he could think of for his hero, an elite double-0 agent of MI6, a hedonist who fears nothing save the chance of becoming bored. Bond oscillates between refinement and brutality, displaying elegant tastes in his peccadilloes though able to break a neck with only slightly less ease than that with which he beds girls (never women). The Bond villain, by contrast, bears an outlandish name (Dr. No, Auric Goldfinger, or the arch-foe Ernst Stavro Blofeld), unusual pedigree, wealth, and, if he or she is not simply a Russian agent, membership in a secret society of terrorists. Typically ugly, deformed, or physically handicapped, the villain often displays a sexuality clearly marked as perverse (for example, in *From Russia, with Love*, Rosa Klebb's lesbianism is revolting: "She looked like the oldest and ugliest whore in the world") and a proclivity for torture. The villain's nobility is a sham undone by Bond's willpower, nationality, and unfading aura of good fortune. Similarly, the Bond girl is ultimately unable to resist these forces, though she may be fiercely self-preserving, like Honey Ryder, or even criminally lesbian, like Pussy Galore ("I never met a man before").

F. wrote a total of fourteen Bond books, though after his death the banner was taken up by other authors, including Kingsley AMIS and John E. Gardner. Less well known are F.'s nonfiction books such as *The Diamond Smugglers* (1957) and *Thrilling Cities* (1963), and his books for children, the *Chitty-Chitty-Bang-Bang* adventures (3 vols., 1964–65). Besides the more obvious avenues of anti-imperialist criticism, semiotic studies have enjoyed using F.'s work as a springboard for consideration of narrative structures and codes, though the greatest devotion continues to come from diehard and not infrequently cultish fans.

BIBLIOGRAPHY: Bennett, T., and J. Woollacott, *Bond and Beyond: The Political Career of a Popular Hero* (1987); Black, J., *The Politics of James Bond* (2001); Lycett, A., *I. F.* (1995)

TIM CONLEY

FLETCHER, Giles, the elder

bap. 26 November 1548, Cranbrook, Kent; bur. 11 March 1611, London

Father of the poets Giles and Phineas FLETCHER and uncle of John FLETCHER, F. was educated at Eton and King's College, Cambridge, where after graduating M.A. he lectured on Greek. He became a member of Parliament in 1584. He was sent as a diplomat to Russia and recorded his impressions in *Of the Russe Commonwealth* (1591). He also published *Licia* (1593), a collection of sonnets that also contains an ode, a dialogue, some elegies, and a monologue representing Richard III's reflections on his rise to power. The Earl of Essex was F.'s patron and F. was briefly imprisoned as contaminated by association with the rebel earl, who was executed.

FLETCHER, Giles, the younger

b. ca. 1584, London; d. 1623, Alderton, Suffolk?

F. was educated at Westminster School and Trinity College, Cambridge. He was a parson and poet much

influenced by Edmund SPENSER. F.'s principal work was the allegorical *Christs Victorie and Triumph in Heaven and Earth* (1610). The devotion, the lyricism, and the vision of paradise are very much F.'s own and may have influenced John MILTON. F. contributed to *Epicedium Cantabrigiense* (1612), a collection of poems commemorating the death of Prince Henry, and F.'s *The Reward of the Faithfull*, a book of devotional prose, appeared in 1623. F. is considered a better poet than his brother Phineas FLETCHER.

FLETCHER, John

b. December 1579, Rye, Sussex; d. August 1625, London

One of the most prolific and admired playwrights of his time, F. wrote or contributed to at least sixty-nine plays. Although best known for his several early collaborations with Francis BEAUMONT, including the tragicomic *Philaster; or, Love Lies a-Bleeding* (perf. ca. 1609; pub. 1620) and the sensational *The Maid's Tragedy* (perf. ca. 1611; pub. 1619), F. worked with William SHAKESPEARE on the lost play *Cardenio* (perf. 1612), *Henry VIII* (perf. 1613; pub. 1623), and *The Two Noble Kinsmen* (perf. 1613; pub. 1634). By 1614, F. had succeeded Shakespeare as principal playwright for the King's Men, and had begun to collaborate frequently with the younger Philip MASSINGER, and occasionally with Nathan FIELD and William ROWLEY. Nevertheless, the folio publication (1647) of many of F.'s later plays, attributed indiscriminately to both Beaumont and F., helped to perpetuate the hybrid "Beaumont-and-Fletcher." Their joint reputation, higher than Shakespeare's during the Restoration, declined after the 18th c. Recent critical interest in the representation of sexuality, gender, and politics has, however, brought renewed attention to F.'s extensive theatrical oeuvre.

F.'s first independent play, *The Faithful Shepherdess* (perf. ca. 1608; pub. ca. 1609), a "pastoral Tragiecomedy," initially failed in the theater; F.'s defensive preface to the first edition blamed an ignorant audience. A revival at court in 1633, however, and subsequent successful performances at the Blackfriars, a private theater, vindicated F.'s sophisticated adaptation of Italian models. The play, which schematically examines aspects of love through contrasting figures, signaled F.'s characteristic interest in sexual aggression and punishment. The active desire of the shepherdess Amarillis is punished with attempted murder and rape, while the innocent Amoret is mistakenly stabbed by her beloved when he believes she has expressed her desire for him ("Death is the best reward that's due to lust"). F. idealizes the safely virginal sexuality of Clorin, the faithful shepherdess, who is dedicated to celibacy in memory of her dead lover.

357

Bonduca (perf. ca. 1612; pub. 1647), one of two tragedies F. wrote independently, dramatizes the story of the ancient British queen, Boadicea. Although he might plausibly have made the warrior queen a heroic figure, F. depicts her as a dangerous virago who unnaturally usurps masculine authority, and whose final incompetence in the masculine sphere of war dooms the British rebellion to failure and the royal succession to extinction. F. also demonizes the queen's daughters. Raped by Romans before the play begins, they are obsessed with exacting revenge, and twice basely attempt to torture Roman captives. F. emphasizes the monstrosity of the women through contrast with the nobility of the play's hero, the British general Caratach. Dedicated to honorable combat, Caratach describes its pleasure in homoerotic terms: "I love an enemy. I was born a souldier;/And he that in the head on's Troop defies me,/Bending my manly body with his sword,/I make a Mistris." F. depicts the homosocial world of the Roman camp with sympathy, and the suicide of the Roman general Penys with admiration. In this play, virtue is understood primarily in martial terms, and the bond between soldiers is the strongest affective force. Nationality is less significant than gender: noble Roman soldiers pay homage to Caratach, and Caratach pays tribute to them. The play ends with the Roman commander embracing him and ordering that "through the Camp in every tongue,/The Vertues of great *Caratach* be sung."

The figure of the noble Roman soldier is at the center of F.'s other independent tragedy, *Valentinian* (perf. ca. 1612; pub. 1647). Set in the late Roman Empire, the play depicts the fall of the eponymous emperor, whose sexual crimes provoke a palace revolt. Raped by Valentinian, the virtuous matron Lucina dies of shame. F.'s handling of the death highlights her husband's interest in it: Maximus urges Lucina to die to prove the crime was rape, not adultery. An ideal wife, Lucina complies, leaving her husband to debate the propriety of wreaking vengeance on the emperor. This debate, and the conflict it provokes between Maximus and his best friend, the loyal general Aecius, are F.'s chief interests in the story. Torn between his love for Aecius, who refuses to support his revenge, and his adherence to a masculine code of honor, which demands it, Maximus finally sacrifices his friend: his need to be perceived as virile by other men outweighs his love for one particular man, and pushes him to treachery, violence, and self-aggrandizement. Maximus's heterosexual connection thus alienates him from Aecius—"that pretious life I love most"— and his community. As in *Bonduca*, the ideal implicit in F.'s treatment of gender relations seems to be the exclusively male world of the army (the context of the friendship between Aecius and Maximus). The play's emotional climax is Aecius's spectacular and prolonged suicide in a scene of intense male bonding.

Here, as in *Bonduca*, the wounded male body is the site of virtue and the focus of erotic pleasure.

BIBLIOGRAPHY: Clark, S., *The Plays of Beaumont and F.* (1994); Finkelpearl, P., *Court and Country Politics in the Plays of Beaumont and F.* (1990); McMullan, G., *The Politics of Unease in the Plays of J. F.* (1994); Pearse, N. C., *J. F.'s Chastity Plays* (1973)

KAREN BAMFORD

FLETCHER, Phineas

bap. 8 April 1582, Cranbrook, Kent; d. before 13 December 1650, Hilgay, Norfolk

Elder son of Giles FLETCHER the elder, F. was educated at Eton and King's College, Cambridge. Like his brother, he was an Anglican priest. In 1627, he published *Locustae, vel Pietas Jesuitica, The Locusts or Apollyonists,* two parallel poems attacking the Jesuits, one in Latin, the other in English. He is remembered for *The Purple Island; or, The Isle of Man* (1633), a poem in twelve cantos describing in cumbrous allegory the physiological structure of the human body and the mind of man. It is written in the Spenserian manner and its chief charm lies in its descriptions of rural scenery. Some critics believe it to have influenced John BUNYAN.

FLINT, F[rank] S[tuart]

b. 19 December 1885, London; d. 28 February 1960, Berkshire

F., poet and translator, became a prominent member of the imagist movement and at their best his poems reflect the disciplined economy of that school. He was the son of a commercial traveler whose early life was passed in squalid poverty. He left school at the age of thirteen and he worked at a variety of jobs. At the age of seventeen, his reading of poetry, particularly the poetry of John KEATS, excited his enthusiasm for literature. Two years later, he entered the civil service as a typist. At the same time, he enrolled at a workingman's night school where he studied French and Latin. He became more or less bilingual in French and English and within a decade or so was contributing to *Mercure de France.* He wrote extensively on French literature in the *Chapbook*, the *Egoist*, the *Poetry Review*, the *Times Literary Supplement,* and elsewhere. An accomplished linguist, he taught himself ten languages and was fluent in French, Italian, Spanish, German, and Russian.

He published his first volume of poetry, *In the Net of the Stars,* in 1909. His stylistic innovations in these poems fell a good way short of his claim in the preface that "I have . . . not rimed where there is no need . . . I have followed my ear and my heart, which may be false. I hope not." In fact, the poems are largely a collection of conventional love lyrics in which the influence of the Romantic poets is clearly evident. However, although youthful, they give clear hints of an emerging poetic talent.

By February 1909, the Poets' Club had established its reputation as the center of fresh poetic life and had become prominent enough for F. to attack in the *New Age:* "I think of this club and its after dinner ratiocinations, its tea-parties in suave South Audley Street," he wrote, "and then of Verlaine at the Hôtel de Ville, with his hat on the peg , as proof of his presence, but he himself in a café hard by with other poets, conning feverishly and excitedly the mysteries of their craft— and I laugh. These discussions in obscure cafés regenerated, remade French poetry; but the Poets' Club—! . . . the Poets' Club is death." As secretary of the Poets' Club, T. E. HULME replied to F.'s attack on behalf of the club. He pointed out that there was not necessarily any correlation between obscure cafés and good poetry. F.'s nostalgia for French poetry and his assumption that the life of the poet must be bohemian gave Hulme his excuse for attacking him as a "belated romantic." This clash between them led to a firm friendship. Hulme came, probably owing to F., to regard the Poets' Club as dilettante and formed his own group that though never formalized held regular weekly meetings in the Eiffel Tower, a Soho restaurant. F.'s knowledge of the work of the French symbolist poets brought Hulme and later Ezra Pound into contact with contemporary French poetry.

In 1915, F. wrote a history of the club and the birth of IMAGISM in the *Egoist.* He said that, "what brought the real nucleus of the group together was a dissatisfaction with English poetry as it was then (and still is alas!) being written. We proposed at various times to replace it by pure *vers libre*; by the Japanese tanka and haiku. In all this, Hulme was ringleader. He insisted too on absolutely accurate presentation and no verbiage. "There was a lot of talk and practice among us of what we called the Image." F. contributed poetry to the second volume of *The Book of the Poets' Club,* published in 1909. Also, there is good reason to believe that he contributed heavily to the translations of work by Henri Bergson and Georges Sorel that were published by Hulme. Pound's anthology, *Des Imagistes* (1914), contains five of F.'s mature poems.

His friendship with Hulme and Pound helped him to develop his own distinctive poetic style and *Cadences* (1915) and *Otherworld* (1920), vastly different from his early poetry, established him as a leading member of the imagists. Much of the poetry in these volumes is written in what he called "unrimed cadence" and displays an intense sense of pathos, profound humanity, and an impressive philosophic range. He included several poems translated from the French, and the influence of the French symbolist poets as well as the influence of imagism is clearly

apparent. In a poem like "Eau-Forte," for example, he combines exact, visual imagery based on sharp observation with a tone that derives from contemporary French poetry. In his poetic practice, he articulated the three propositions that he says in his preface he kept before in mind: that "poetry is a quality of all artistic writing"; that "rhyme and meter are artificial and external additions to poetry"; and that the "artistic form of the future is prose, with cadence—a more accentuated variety of prose in the oldest English tradition—for lyrical expression."

After the death of his first wife in 1920, F. suddenly stopped writing poetry. According to his friend J. G. Fletcher, F. was always conscious of his Cockney forebears and his growing sense of inferiority made him a "tragically ineffectual figure." He became chief of the Overseas Section, Statistics Division of the Ministry of Labour and an expert on international relations. He was awarded the Imperial Service Order. He did, however, continue to produce translations, mostly of French works including Marguerite Audoux's *Marie Claire's Workshop* (1920) and André de Hevesy's *Beethoven, the Man* (1927).

BIBLIOGRAPHY: Gates, N. T., "Richard Aldington and F. S. F.: Poets' Dialogue," *PLL* 8 (Winter 1972): 62–69; Pondrom, C. N., *The Road from Paris: French Influence or English Poetry* (1974)

A. R. JONES

FOLKLORE

The term "folklore," with its derivatives folk song, folk dance, folktale, and so on, is not of great antiquity: it is generally attributed to a coinage by W. J. Thoms in 1846. Before that, scholars and collectors found other terms for what would nowadays be called the folk arts: the Grimm brothers called their celebrated collections of what to us would be folktales *Children's and House Tales* (1812) and *German Mythology* (1835); John Brand's *Observations on Popular Antiquities* (1777) was a collection of what would now be called folk customs; Bishop Thomas PERCY called his mid-18th-c. ballad collections *Reliques of Ancient English Poetry.* Even after the useful term caught on, some authorities preferred to avoid it: Professor F. J. Child of Harvard called his definitive collection in five volumes of 1882–98 *The English and Scottish Popular Ballads*, and in 1882 J. Collingwood Bruce and John Stokoe published their "Collection of the ballads, melodies, and small-pipe tunes of Northumbria" under the title *Northumbrian Minstrelsy.*

But if the nomenclature, and concomitant scholarly interest, are recent, the phenomenon of traditional, orally transmitted literature and music, with their multiplicity of versions, is of incalculable antiquity. Although "The Ballads" (a ballad being a particular type of narrative folk song) constitute a topic often recommended for study in the medieval sections of university English courses, most of the ballads, folk songs, and tales exist nowadays in versions no earlier than the 17th c., when the voracious broadside press took to publishing (often debased) versions of ballads and country songs as part of its diet of popular songs, amazing tales, true confessions, and the "last good-nights" of executed criminals. With the growth of scholarly interest in the 18th and 19th cs. among authors like Sir Walter SCOTT and antiquarians like Allan RAMSAY, folk artifacts reached a more bourgeois audience, with an obvious tendency to try and fix the form of what is, by definition, a floating multiversional art. When Scott published his *Minstrelsy of the Scottish Border* in 1802–3, the peasant mother of his friend James HOGG complained that "There was never ane o' my songs prentit till ye prentit them yourself, and ye hae spoilt them a'togither. They were made for singin' and no for readin', but ye hae broken the charm now, and they'll never be sung mair." Her words have been called prophetic, but the resultant decline in living folklore was probably a factor of the same influences that led to the folkloric researches of Scott and others in the first place—awareness that urbanization and the spread of easily accessible forms of popular entertainment (pleasure gardens, music hall; later, radio, cinema, television) were undermining those popular roots on which the uninhibited spread of living folklore depends, and a consequent desire to preserve what could be saved before it vanished entirely. Although the folk forms have turned out tougher than this pessimistic view suggested, it is true that, from the invention of printing onward, every technological and popular artistic development had tended to fix the form. Mrs. Hogg, alas, was too late.

All was far from lost, though. Variant versions were preserved by the fact that different collectors and anthologists preferred different renderings. Oral collection from source singers, from the 1880s, led to the discovery of previously unknown variants thought to be extinct, together with increased scholarly accuracy in their preservation. When Cecil J. Sharp collected folk songs of English origin in the Appalachian Mountains in the early 20th c., he found over one hundred versions of the ballad "Barbara Allen" (which Samuel PEPYS recorded hearing sung by a London actress 250 years earlier) in Virginia alone, every one of which he noted and preserved. Sharp's original interest was in folk dance, but he was alerted to the riches of English song by hearing a gardener in Somerset with the uncannily appropriate name of John England singing at his work. The London headquarters of the English Folk Dance and Song Society is named after Cecil J. Sharp.

Early in the 20th c., the composer Percy Grainger used recording cylinders in the interests of even greater authenticity. H. E. D. and Robert Hammond and George B. Gardiner were collecting in southern and southwest England, as were Alfred Williams in the Upper Thames Valley, Frank Kidson in Yorkshire, and Gavin Greig in Scotland. The great composer Ralph Vaughan Williams was also an active folk song collector, as was Sabine BARING-GOULD, author of the hymn "Onward, Christian Soldiers." Joseph Jacobs, and Katharine M. Briggs with Ruth L. Tongue, published pioneering and definitive collections of folktales.

For all the pessimism that affected scholarly devotees for more than a century, folklore did not stop happening. New forms emerged: the industrial folk songs sedulously studied by A. L. Lloyd and Ewan MacColl, songs of colliers, railwaymen, weavers, keelmen, lead miners, from the tin mines of Cornwall to the whale fisheries of Peterhead in Aberdeenshire. Of particular interest was the well-known sea-shanty, the sailors' work-song at capstan and bunt that grew up in the late days of sail: Stan Hugill, the last man known to have signed on as a specialist "shantyman," died in 1992. His *Shanties from the Seven Seas* (1961) is the definitive collection. Shanties are a peculiarly international form of folklore: the crews of clippers, sealers, whalers, Blackballers and Lowlanders were cosmopolitan, as any reader of Herman Melville's *Moby-Dick* (1851) or Henry Richard Dana Jr.'s *Two Years before the Mast* (1840) knows; and many a shanty contains discrete elements of English, Scottish, Irish, Welsh; American and Caribbean; Polish, Dutch, German, Scandinavian, Italian; Lascar and Chinese; Australasian and Polynesian, reflective of the crews of the ships on which it was used, as it spread throughout the fleets plying from Liverpool and Bristol to Baltimore and Halifax, Shanghai or Sydney to Valparaiso or San Francisco or Tumbes.

At home, the fashion for folkloric exploration affected 19th-c. letters. Poets from Scott and Samuel Taylor COLERIDGE to R. H. BARHAM, Lewis CARROLL, and W. S. GILBERT imitated folk forms, especially, but not exclusively, the ballad. William WORDSWORTH's "The Solitary Reaper" relates how the poet heard a young Scottish Highland woman singing at her work in the field and speculated on the meaning of the Gaelic words of her song. In "Dejection, An Ode," Coleridge refers to "The grand old ballad of Sir Patrick Spence" (recalling Sir Philip SIDNEY's reference three centuries earlier to his love for "the old song of Percy and Douglas"—the ballad generally known as "Chevy Chase" or "The Hunting of the Cheviot"). The refined novelist Jane AUSTEN has, in *Emma,* an incident where a shepherd's son is brought into the parlor to sing to a lady guest; in *Northanger Abbey,* a young man urges his suit by referring to an "old song" about one wedding bringing on another.

At the other end of the century, the country-set novels of Thomas HARDY abound in references to folk song, often to point a theme. Hardy was himself a church and country-dance musician, and had a collection of local songs and airs. *Under the Greenwood Tree* has as a main theme the effect of new forms of hymnody and organ music on the traditional church choir; while in *The Return of the Native,* the mummers' play provides a cover for the heroine's adulterous plans. Other leading novelists used folk music: in *Adam Bede,* George ELIOT makes the squire patronizing toward a parish clerk's dance to the fiddle; in "Mr Gilfil's Love Story," second of her *Scenes of Clerical Life,* a butler is noted below stairs for his Scotch singing. A song called "The Red Rovier" [*sic*], mentioned in *Silas Marner,* has not been identified. Emily BRONTË's *Wuthering Heights* mentions several ballads. In *Dombey and Son,* Charles DICKENS's Captain Cuttle sings a shanty called "Cheer'ly" and quotes the traditional song of a girl's love for the sailor "whose tarry trousers shine to me like diamonds bright." In *Great Expectations,* the song sung by the blacksmith Joe Gargery at his forge is given in full. Elizabeth Cleghorn GASKELL has the leader of a naval press-gang cite "William Taylor," a widespread song of a sailor pressed to sea, in *Sylvia's Lovers,* and in *Mary Barton* quotes entire the Lancashire lament of "The Poor Cotton Weaver." The folkloric element in Bram STOKER's *Dracula* is self-evident, influencing 20th-c. writers like Angela CARTER.

Narrative forms of folklore are international. Child points out many Danish analogues in his ballad collection (possibly because the Danes had been actively at work on their ballad tradition in the mid- to late 19th c.). Most folktales exist in most languages. Literary knowledge of the tales in England has been largely based on translations: of Grimm in Germany and Charles Perrault's 17th-c. reworkings of French stories, *Les Contes de Ma Mère l'Oie* (*Tales of My Mother the Goose*—a traditional French phrase; it is a charming but untenable piece of American folklore about folklore, retold by Burl Ives and others, that the name Mother Goose comes from a Mrs. Elizabeth Goose of Boston who told stories from the Old Country to her grandchildren in colonial days). The traditional English folktale derives largely from the great international pool of such tales: there is a useful index, *The Types of the Folktale,* compiled by the Finnish scholar Antti Aarne in 1910, translated into English and enlarged by Stith Thompson (1961); a fairly strong school of thought traces all known folktales back to Arab sources. But of course the English versions in the collections of Jacobs, Briggs and Tongue, and others, display expected national characteristics, and a few, like the well-known "Chicken Licken," do not appear to be more widespread, though in this case related to the standard tales of cun-

ning animals. The folktale persists in two modern forms: the joke, which emerges none knows whence and blankets the earth (and did so even before the invention of radio and the Web); and the "urban myth," the experience that invariably happened to "the friend of a friend"—or FOAF in English folklorist Rodney Dale's useful acronym—such widespread tales as the car stolen with grandma rolled in a carpet on the roof and never seen again, and the man who passed out at a party and came to himself minus a kidney. Many such have been documented by Dale and by the American folklorist Jan Harold Brunvand.

The mid-20th c. and onward has brought a new development into folklore with the so-called folk revival. This is predominantly a left-wing movement, started by Marxist-oriented singers and folklorists such as Lloyd and MacColl in Great Britain, and simultaneously by Woody Guthrie, Pete Seeger, and others in the U.S., who saw popularization of folklore, and especially of folk song, as a means of politicizing the working class through involvement in its own traditional artifacts. The revival attracted bourgeois intellectuals and so failed in its main political agenda. But it has led to much study and research, to the foundation in Britain of a national network of folk clubs meeting in pubs and hotels, to a thriving folk record industry on such labels as Topic (originally a branch of the Workers' Musical Association affiliated in its turn to the Communist Party of Great Britain, but long independent) and Leader. Aesthetic appreciation of folk song spread across the political and social spectrum. Performance took equal pride of place with scholarship. The bowdlerization of love songs that the *zeitgeist* and their use in schools had forced upon early collectors and editors was despised and songs were restored. Many singers steeped in traditional song, such as MacColl, Cyril Tawney, Peter Bellamy, Bob Pegg, and Peter Coe, succeeded in creating new songs in the traditional idiom that the revival had brought to a wider audience. Simultaneously, other musical forms, especially electric rock, were folk-influenced, leading to the work of such respected folk-rock groups as Steeleye Span and Mr. Fox. Though the original impetus may have weakened a little, the club and folk festival movement remains active, and the tradition continues.

BIBLIOGRAPHY: Briggs, K. M., and R. L. Tongue, *Folktales of England* (1965); De Vries, L., *'Orrible Murder* (1971); Gerould, G. H., *The Ballad of Tradition* (1932); Harker, D., *Fakesong* (1985); Hodgart, M. J. C., *The Ballads* (1950); Jackson-Houlston, C. M., *Ballads, Songs, and Snatches* (1999); Kidson, F., *Traditional Tunes* (1891); Lloyd, A. L., *Folk Song in England* (1967); Logan, W. H., *The Pedlar's Pack* (1869); Myer, M. G., "Folksong in Thomas Hardy," *FolkR* (December 1972): 6–7; Opie, I., and P. Opie,

The Lore and Language of Schoolchildren (1960); Palmer, R., *A Touch on the Times* (1974); Purslow, F., ed., *Marrow Bones* (1965); Reeves, J., ed., *The Idiom of the People* (1958); Sharp, C. J., *English Folk Song, Some Conclusions* (1907)

MICHAEL GROSVENOR MYER

FORD, Ford Madox

b. Ford Hermann Hueffer, 17 December 1873, Merton, Surrey; d. 26 June 1939, Deauville, France

F. was the son of the German music critic Francis Hueffer and Catherine Brown, the daughter of Ford Madox Brown, one of the foremost Pre-Raphaelite painters. His mother's sister was married to William Michael ROSSETTI. His childhood was spent in cultured, Pre-Raphaelite circles and he was strongly affected by his upbringing. He was educated at a Folkestone private school and at University College School, London. Because of anti-German feeling and his wish to identify with the English landed classes, he changed his name by deed poll in 1919.

He was a prolific author and published more than eighty books of fiction and nonfiction. During his long career as a writer, he produced many kinds of writing—novels, poetry, BIOGRAPHY, travel books, belles lettres—and while his work is never less than competent, much is not particularly distinguished. He published his first book, a "fairy story" entitled *The Brown Owl*, in 1892 and followed this by publishing biographies of Ford Madox Brown (1896) and Dante Gabriel ROSSETTI (1902). For several years from 1898 onward, he collaborated with Joseph CONRAD in the writing of various works including *The Inheritors* (1901) and *Romance* (1903). Both authors were intensely interest in technique and studied the French novel, particularly the work of Gustave Flaubert, and both were intent on establishing the novel as a work of art. Afterward, F. published a vivid, dramatically written trilogy of historical novels, *The Fifth Queen* (1906), *Privy Seal* (1907), and *The Fifth Queen Crowned* (1908), that centered on the fate of HENRY VIII's wife, Catherine Howard.

Between 1908 and 1910, F. edited the remarkable *English Review,* where he first demonstrated his ability to recognize and encourage the talent of young, emerging writers. He was the first to publish work by D. H. LAWRENCE and Wyndham LEWIS. At the same time, he also published some of the best work of more traditional and established writers such as Thomas HARDY, Henry JAMES, H. G. WELLS, and John GALSWORTHY. In the early 1920s, he showed the same editorial skills when he moved to France and between 1924 and 1925 edited the expatriate magazine *transatlantic review* and published work by Gertude Stein, James JOYCE, E. E. Cummings, and Ernest Hemingway.

Begun in 1913, *The Good Soldier* (1915) is a remarkable achievement, a highly lucid, composed, and taut psychological novel of sexual relationships. Despite its title, it has nothing to do with war; in fact, "The Saddest Story" was F.'s original title. It is a highly organized, very intricate story about the adulterous relationship between two rich families, the Ashburnhams and the Dowells, in their successive meetings in a German spa town during the 1900s. The subject is perhaps conventional enough but the whole quality of the work resides is in its intricate form and style of narrative. The essence of the novel is in its passionate revelation of the human condition; bewilderment and misery are successively revealed in the intricately plotted movements of the central figures. The truth of the relationships is revealed only gradually and piecemeal through the successive discoveries made by the deceived narrator, John Dowell. The novel has been described as "a masterpiece of modern English fiction," and certainly it has attracted a great deal of critical attention in recent years. In the same year as the publication of *The Good Soldier*, F. enlisted and was commissioned in the Welch Regiment. He served with distinction on the western front where he was gassed and shell-shocked and was invalided out from France in 1917.

His other major work of fiction—in addition to *The Good Soldier*—are the four novels, often referred to as the "Tietjens" tetralogy after the name of the central character, collectively titled *Parade's End*, which comprises *Some Do Not . . .* (1924), *No More Parades* (1925), *A Man Could Stand Up* (1926), and *The Last Post* (1928; repub. as *Last Post*, 1928). It gives an expansive and inclusive picture of society in the prewar period leading up to the outbreak of war and is thus an historical panorama and psychological landscape both of Tietjens and the society of which he is a part. He brings together in himself a number of forces that he comes to represent: he is a representative of the old feudal line, an 18th-c. gentleman keeping alive as best he can the old ways and values. As a member of the ruling classes, he combines both the public world and the private, as the last of a line he and all he represents face extinction. He sustains an empty marriage with an unfaithful wife and serves in a war in which bureaucracy and political intrigue are in many ways more hostile than the enemy he is fighting. The war kills all he and his ancestors once held in trust for future generations and he endures in a new world without values where the aristocrat has given way to the bureaucrat. The death of old England, lovingly depicted by F., and the birth of the modern world is dramatized through the experiences of Tietjens and also by a vivid realization of the society in which he finds himself and from which he, eventually disillusioned, withdraws. There is a certain romanticizing of the old English virtues, a nostalgia for a vanished past, and yet at the same time he makes plain the decay inherent in Victorian society that led inevitably to the war and the breakdown of social values that followed it. It is a novel in the tradition of Victorian realistic fiction, with its psychological and social analysis, its fully developed characters, and the brilliance of what F. liked to call an impressionist prose that fills historical events with a sense of actuality. It is a remarkable and on the whole a rather neglected achievement.

F. spent his later years in the U.S. as a lecturer at Olivet College, Michigan, and in France. He published several volumes of somewhat unreliable autobiography and memoirs, including *Return to Yesterday* (1931) and *It Was the Nightingale* (1933), and an ambitious volume of criticism, *The March of Literature* (1938). He is also celebrated for his generosity toward two generations of young writers and his ability to detect and encourage the talent of others.

BIBLIOGRAPHY: Goldring, D., *The Last Pre-Raphaelite: A Record of the Life and Writings of F. M. F.* (1948); MacShane, F., *The Life and Work of F. M. F.* (1965); Mizener, A., *The Saddest Story: A Biography of F. M. F.* (1971); Smith, G., *F. M. F.* (1972)

A. R. JONES

FORD, John

b. 1586, Ilsington, Devon; d. after 1638, possibly in Devonshire

Chronologically speaking, F. is a Caroline author, but in tone and subject matter he is so close to the early Jacobean dramatists that it is sometimes suggested that his plays were written then, though none was published before the late 1620s. He is primarily remembered for the daring theme and sensational violence of *'Tis Pity She's a Whore* (perf. ca. 1630–33; pub. 1633), and both here and in *Love's Sacrifice* (perf. ca. 1632–33; pub. 1633) he comes close to the savagery, bloodthirstiness, and dark moral tangles of Jacobean revenge tragedy. What is less frequently noticed, though, is that he also has equally strong affiliations with William SHAKESPEARE. His last play, *The Lady's Trial* (perf. 1638; pub. 1639), echoes *Othello* but allows its heroine to convince her husband of her innocence even though there is no actual proof, and his first to be published, *The Lover's Melancholy* (1629), mixes elements of both *King Lear* and *Twelfth Night* with Burtonian theorizing on the mind to offer a sustained reflection on madness and melancholia, with passages of great lyricism and beauty.

The Chronicle Historie of Perkin Warbeck (1634), a very late revival of the long-dead history play, revisits the genre with which Shakespeare opened and closed his career. It begins with a close paraphrase of the opening of *Henry IV,* part 1, and fills the gap between *Richard III* and *Henry VIII,* though F.'s failure to include any definitive statement that Warbeck is not who he says he is makes this a very different affair from Shakespeare's tendency to adhere to the Tudor and Stuart party line. Its inclusion of reference to all four corners of the British Isles, including Ireland, also makes it a telling intervention in discussion of the "British problem," and it seems no coincidence that it was probably first performed in the year of Charles I's Scottish coronation and includes reference to a topical controversy about the royal Stuart ancestry.

F.'s major interest, though, is the relationship between the sexual and the social self, and his characters are riven by irreconcilable tensions between the two. In *Love's Sacrifice*, Biancha loves Fernando but is married to the Duke; in *The Broken Heart* (perf. ca. 1630–33; pub. 1633), Penthea complains of a forced divorce between her body and her soul. The incestuous brother and sister of *'Tis Pity She's a Whore*, Giovanni and Annabella, live in Parma, a city then governed by a scion of the Habsburgs, a family that had virtually institutionalized inbreeding as a way of preventing fragmentation of its possessions; Giovanni also makes reference to Jove and Juno, who were both brother and sister and husband and wife, reminding us that almost all myths of origin and of founding families have incest at their heart. Giovanni and Annabella, however, belong, as Hippolyta scornfully observes, merely to the merchant class, and are thus denied the privileges of gods and kings: for those of their status, exogamy is a social necessity.

Similarly, in both *The Broken Heart*, unpublished until 1653, and *The Queen*, a play of uncertain authorship but probably written by F., royal women find the demands of their hearts at odds with those of their realm; the nameless queen eventually reconciles the two, but Calantha in *The Broken Heart* dies in a richly emblematic scene that reminds us that F.'s baroquely bizarre stagings of violence are not merely sensational but have richly symbolic meanings. It is likely that F. was sympathetic to Catholicism, but whether or not this was the case he certainly makes rich use of iconography with Catholic associations, particularly in his obsessive use of the words heart, blood, sweat, and tears. Giovanni's horrific cutting out of Annabella's heart has been preceded by some fifty uses in the play of the word "heart," an accumulation that forces us to examine its meanings and associations.

Indeed, much of the immense emotional power of F.'s plays surely lies in the sharply delineated contrast between the extravagance of the violence and suffering and the restraint and limitation of the spare, elegiac language and mournful verse cadences. F.'s characters typically adhere to an aesthetic of silence and distrust of mere words, though that this has its own dangers is abundantly illustrated in *The Fancies Chaste and Noble* (perf. ca. 1635–36; pub. 1638) where the most interesting character, Flavia, has infuriatingly little to say, and her story, as too often in F., gets swamped in a seriously unfunny comic subplot. F. need not, as is often (but without evidence) assumed, have died immediately after writing his final plays, he might simply have found his own aesthetic of reticence incompatible with further dramaturgy.

BIBLIOGRAPHY: Hopkins, L., *J. F.'s Political Theatre* (1994); Lomax, M., *Stage Images and Traditions: Shakespeare to F.* (1987); Neill, M., ed., *J. F.* (1988); Wymer, R., *Webster and F.* (1995)

LISA HOPKINS

FORESTER, C[ecil] S[cott]

(pseud. of Cecil Lewis Troughton Smith) b. 27 August 1899, Cairo, Egypt; d. 2 April 1996, Fullerton, California, U.S.A.

F. is best remembered as the author of the novel on which the famous Academy Award–winning film *The African Queen* was based, and for his long sequence of novels and stories featuring the Napoleonic Wars Royal Navy officer Horatio Hornblower—admired and acknowledged precursor to Patrick O'BRIAN's later much respected series featuring Captain Jack Aubrey and Dr. Maturin. Largely an historical novelist, his works were set as far apart as the Spanish conquistadors—the ironically named *The Earthly Paradise* (1940), which features a horrible incident of the burning for heresy of a group of innocent natives who have naively embraced the blandishments of Catholicism and then ingenuously decided that they had been better off as they were—and World War II: *The Ship* (1943), to write which F. actually sailed in action with one of His Majesty's warships. His special interest was in the study of people under strain, like the ill-assorted protagonists of *The African Queen* (1935), English missionary spinster and drunken American riverside bum thrown together in the eponymous small boat and forced to navigate upriver in dangerous wartime conditions. The highly successful film version appeared in 1951, directed by John Huston, with a screenplay by James Agee.

In particular, F. excelled in studies of what made the fighting man tick. His heroes were of all ranks, from the Penisular War Rifleman Dodd in *Death to the French* (1932) fighting his way through enemy lines to rejoin his lost unit, to Great War Lieutenant-General Sir Herbert Curzon, KCMG, CB, DSO, *The General* (1936); from Leading-Seaman Brown single-handedly defending his island in *Brown on Resolution* (repub. as *Single-Handed,* 1929) to the celebrated Admiral Lord Hornblower of the best-known works.

Supposedly based on the personality of Admiral Lord (Horatio) Nelson (with whom, significantly, he shares his Christian name), Hornblower is a complex

personality. The reader is constantly reminded of his tone-deafness, and of the sort of *deformation professionelle* that convinces him that *The Rime of the Ancient Mariner* would have been infinitely better if Alexander POPE had dealt with the theme, assisted by someone who knew more about navigation and seamanship than "this Coleridge fellow." He is introspective and lacking in confidence, constantly spurred to action but prevented by an overactive conscience from ever enjoying his triumphs. He cannot avoid distress at his crews' sufferings, or even those of conquered enemies such as the mad and sadistic Nicaraguan dictator El Supremo; but he hates and despises such weaknesses in himself.

Though F. can re-create the spectacle of battle and storm as well as any, he is just as concerned with the more mundane aspects of naval life: the logistical slog that goes into organizing a ceremonial state occasion like Nelson's funeral; the technicalities of calculating the length of fuse-hose required for breaching a wreck at seventeen fathoms; the exasperation of the captain compelled to victual his own ship in a hurry because his first lieutenant, though well-meaning, turns out to be a broken reed. He provides a convincing account of how the Royal Navy, despite the iniquities of impressment, near-starvation, harsh and brutal discipline, fought the Napoleonic Wars with the cheerful devotion and acceptance of adversity without which no fighting force can function efficiently.

BIBLIOGRAPHY: Parkinson, C. N., *The Life and Times of Horatio Hornblower* (1971); Sternlicht, S., *C. S. F.* (1981)

MICHAEL GROSVENOR MYER

FORSTER, E[dward] M[organ]

b. 1 January 1879, London; d. 8 June 1970, Coventry, Warwickshire

During his long lifetime—ninety-one years, of which only three decades served to produce the fiction for which he was particularly admired—F. was sometimes described as an "all too reticent" novelist whose work was "elusive" and even "evasive." Since his death in 1970 and the posthumous publication in the next year of his homosexual Bildungsroman *Maurice*, F. has in some quarters been enlisted among "gay" novelists. But that anachronistic term ("gay" meant the same to F. as it had to William WORDSWORTH) does not at one stroke solve the mystery of the former adjectives. The homosexual F. was also the liberal-humanist he appeared to be to readers in his lifetime; and if his liberal beliefs were undermined by a decreasing sense of the primacy of human relationships, this process had as much to do with a perception of some spiritual dimension beyond them as with his personal dissatisfaction with a social system that left part of his nature without a public voice.

F. was born in central London to middle-class parents. His father died before he was two, and from four to fourteen he was reared by his mother, who never remarried, in the Hertfordshire countryside, in a house that he immortalized in his fourth novel, *Howards End* (1910). A substantial legacy from his paternal great-aunt, who died in 1887, provided him with the independent means useful to a young writer, and, before that, the education and early travels that contributed so much to the pool of experience on which F.'s writings drew. His pre-college education, at private schools in Eastbourne and Tonbridge, was comparatively uncongenial; he discovered himself, the world of the mind, and a degree of personal freedom at the University of Cambridge from 1897 to 1901, as an undergraduate member of King's College, architecturally splendid, liberal-minded, and intellectually challenging. There, F. read classics, then history, and met Hugh Meredith, the first man with whom he fell in love, who became the dedicatee of his novel *A Room with a View* (begun in 1901) and who was the origin of Clive Durham in *Maurice*, completed in its earliest form in 1914. On graduating from Cambridge, F. spent much of his time until 1903 traveling in Italy, Sicily, and finally Greece—countries that deepened his feeling for the reality and vitality of the past, but which also offered, to someone irked by the bourgeois suburban respectabilities of Victorian and Edwardian England, a liberating sunlight and a sense of magic casements opening in the present.

F.'s earliest published writings were essays, written from his university days onward, and short stories, the first two or them ("The Story of a Panic" and "The Road to Colonus") stimulated by his visits to Italy and Greece, respectively. These stories, and ten others written before World War I, were collected together in two small and widely separated volumes, *The Celestial Omnibus* (1911) and *The Eternal Moment* (1928). They are lively, often fantastic, occasionally enigmatic, and frequently involve a character's experiencing a sudden emancipating moment of vision. Another group of mostly later short stories, unpublished in F.'s lifetime because of their frankly homosexual content, appeared in 1972 in a collection entitled *The Life to Come*: of particular note for their power and poignancy are the title story and two others, "Arthur Snatchfold" and "The Other Boat," the latter not finished until F. was nearly eighty.

The republication, in a collection, of F.'s earliest short stories in 1911 was the result of the fame he had gained by then as the author of four novels; his second collection (of stories that had originally appeared between 1905 and 1920) was partly a spin-off from, and partly a publisher's substitute for a successor to, his enormously successful last novel, *A Passage to India*

(1924). It is on his achievement as a novelist that F.'s reputation has been generally taken to rest; though that reputation was, in the latter part of his life, solidly buttressed by his energy and productivity as an essayist and reviewer. His two collections of essays published in late middle and old age, *Abinger Harvest* (1936) and *Two Cheers for Democracy* (1951), contain over 120 pieces, but this is only a fraction of what he actually published in England, World War I Egypt, and the U.S., gaining in the process almost the status of a sage, and certainly that of a defender of individual and political freedoms of many kinds. F.'s essays lack, naturally enough, the imaginative reach and suggestiveness of his novels: clarity is what they aim for, and splendidly achieve. But the essays share with the novels an easy air of knowledge and command. F. "speaks with authority, and not as one of the scribes," to such an extent that his work may almost be said to transcend categorizing terms such as "novel," "short story," and "essay."

F.'s first novel, *Where Angels Fear to Tread*, appeared in 1905, and was the rapid result of three converging elements: his impatience with the narrowness of English suburban life (which from 1904 to 1925 he experienced in Weybridge, southeast of London); the great pleasure he had felt in Italy, particularly in the many-towered Tuscan hill town of San Gimignano (the "Monteriano" of his novel); and a story he had heard while in Italy of a visiting English woman marrying an Italian. Out of all this, he spun a plot adequate to convey, not crudely but with touches sometimes of opera and melodrama, the clash between bourgeois bigotry, both English and Italian, and the pressure toward self-realization and love, the last two, considered in terms of the main English characters, Philip Herriton and Caroline Abbott, more attainable in Italy than at home. A similar sense of contrast between values, and places embodying them, is conveyed by F.'s third novel, *A Room with a View*, started earlier than *Where Angels Fear to Tread* but slower to grow and not published until 1908. *A Room with a View* is denser and more detailed in its observation and character presentation, but simpler in its construction—a section in Italy where Lucy Honeychurch and George Emerson accidentally share experiences that draw them together, a section in England where the obstacles between them are explored and removed, a brief coda showing them married (unlike Philip and Caroline) and back in the Florence *pensione* where everything began. In both novels, Italy is liberating, but in *A Room with a View* English attitudes, displayed in an area of Surrey made congenial to F. by relatives and friends, are given a more positive aspect than is exhibited by "Sawston" and its dangerous fools in *Where Angels Fear to Tread*.

Between F.'s two Italian novels came an entirely English one, *The Longest Journey* (1907). It was F.'s own favorite—its central character, Rickie Elliott, represents important aspects of himself; and it contains, particularly in its scenes set in Wiltshire, some of his most lyrical writing. In it, three worlds are contrasted: intellectual undergraduate Cambridge, where F. had become a member of the elite discussion society known as the Apostles (and through it, later on, of the BLOOMSBURY GROUP); the much narrower ethos of the English public school (called "Sawston" here, and clearly based on F.'s Tonbridge); and the high, bare downland of south England near Salisbury, an area steeped in early human history and the mystical spirit of the earth itself. *The Longest Journey*'s powerful, but not always clear, three-sided shifting battle between intellect, convention, and instinctive decency is simplified—solidified perhaps—in F.'s fourth novel, *Howards End*, in which central male characters (two half-brothers, one illegitimate) are replaced by central female ones, the cultured sisters Margaret and Helen Schlegel. Their differing temperaments—reasonable, impetuous—lead to the establishment of connections ("Only connect . . ." is the novel's epigraph) with the Philistine, business world of the Wilcox family males, with the ailing, intuitive Ruth Wilcox, whose small country house Howards End eventually becomes the sisters' home, and with the aspiring and ill-starred clerk Leonard Bast, whose illegitimate son by Helen looks set to inherit the pastoral and spiritual England that F. valued. What would happen to the "imperialist" England he disliked, in which London and the birthrate were unstoppably enlarging, he left ominously open—the novel was published in the death year of Edward VII. It received a degree of critical and public acclaim that signalized F.'s arrival, at thirty-one, as a major English novelist.

In old age, F. described *Howards End* as "my best novel, and approaching a good novel"; but it left him cold, and its success with a large audience left him suddenly uncertain of his direction, partly because his awareness of his sexual orientation made him impatient with the standard novel format, dependent as that seemed to be on heterosexual relationships and a worldview based on them. In 1911, he started but could not complete a novel entitled *Arctic Summer*, and late in 1912 he made a six-month trip to India, where he began, but could not continue, the novel that became *A Passage to India*. His writer's block was broken a year later by a visit to the courageous homosexual thinker and writer Edward CARPENTER, which prompted the completion within nine months of his only novel to deal with the development and self-realization of an avowed homosexual. Entitled *Maurice*, it dealt frankly and movingly, but not sensationally, with the emergence, frustration, and eventual satisfaction through a working-class partner, of desires that were essentially F.'s own, though distance was carefully maintained by a sympathetic yet bleak au-

thorial voice. For F., there was no question of publication at that time, and delay led to considerable revision and expansion, over some forty years, of a novel completed in its first version just before the start of World War I.

F. spent most of World War I in Alexandria, Egypt, working for the Red Cross. He also wrote a substantial *History and Guide* to the city, published there in 1922. In 1921, F. revisited India, and for six months acted as private secretary to the Maharajah of a Native State near Bombay. This experience provided F. with much of the material for part 3 ("Temple") of his most famous novel; but it was not until he returned to England that he took up what he had set aside in 1912, and it was with considerable difficulty that he continued and finished it. *A Passage to India* was published in 1924 and reconfirmed F.'s very high reputation among contemporary novelists: from then until his death, the yoking together of F. with James JOYCE, D. H. LAWRENCE, and Virginia WOOLF as an indication of where he stood became a critical commonplace, and *A Passage to India,* entirely set in that country except for several scenes showing passages from it, has generally been treated as his masterpiece. F. once described India as "the great opportunity of my life," and his novel about it offers his most penetrating and disturbing vision of the difficulties, as well as the rewards, of communication with fellow humans and with the world that lies beyond them. Rich in incident and symbolism, *A Passage to India* is among F.'s novels the one with the most satisfying structure, and though its presentation of the English ruling classes abroad has struck some as caricature, the portraits of Adela Quested and Mrs. Moore are searching and impressive, and the Indian characters, Dr. Aziz especially, are rendered with great verve, sensitivity, and—as corroborated by Indian critics—verisimilitude. *A Passage to India* owes part of its success to the impersonal distance of its authorial voice, not always a characteristic of F.'s earlier novels, into which he sometimes enters to comment, explain, and judge. A more external reason for its interest in 1924 was the topicality, after the Amritsar Massacre of 1919, of India as a subject: F.'s characters seemed involved in larger and more public issues than hitherto.

After *A Passage to India*, F. produced no more novels, but he did not cease to write, and voluminously, with a directness, simplicity, elegance, and charm that drew the reader powerfully and easily in. In 1927, he gave the Clark Lectures at Cambridge, published as *Aspects of the Novel*, and until late in his life was active not only as an essayist and reviewer but also as a broadcaster with a rare gift for intelligent simplification. Between 1925 and 1945, he lived with his mother in a house designed by his father near Dorking in Surrey, and twice wrote the "book of words" for local pageant plays, the music for which was supplied by his neighbor Ralph Vaughan Williams. F. was also an active member of English PEN, and twice (in 1934 and 1942) president of the National Council for Civil Liberties.

After 1945 and the death of his mother, F. was offered, very unusually, a resident honorary fellowship at his Cambridge college, King's. Here, accessible to friends old and new, and to generations of undergraduates, he lived in a set of rooms until just before his death, which occurred in the Coventry home of Bob and May Buckingham, close friends since the 1920s. While at King's, he published recollections and letters related to his visits to India (*The Hill of Devi*, 1953), and a biography of the great-aunt whose legacy in 1887 had meant so much to him (*Marianne Thornton*, 1956). He also finished his revisions to *Maurice* and wrote his very last story, "Little Imber" (1961), a homosexual fantasy set in a bleak future when the number of humans, and especially of males, has been much reduced. In about 1950, F. was offered a knighthood, which he declined; but in 1953 he accepted appointment as a Companion of Honor, and in 1968 he was made a member of the Order of Merit, the highest honor personally awarded by the monarch.

BIBLIOGRAPHY: Furbank, P. N., *E. M. F.* (2 vols., 1977–78); Gardner, P., *E. M. F.* (1977); King, F., *E. M. F. and His World* (1978); Lago, M., and P. N. Furbank, eds., *Selected Letters of E. M. F.* (2 vols., 1983–85); McDowell, F. P. W., *E. M. F.* (1969; rev. ed., 1982); Stone, W., *The Cave and the Mountain: A Study of E. M. F.* (1966); Trilling, L., *E. M. F.* (1943)

PHILIP GARDNER

FORSTER, John

b. 2 April 1812, Newcastle; d. 2 February 1876, London

One of the most prominent Victorian men of letters, F. is often acknowledged as the first professional biographer in the history of English literature. He first gained critical attention with the publication of his *Lives of Eminent British Statesmen* (5 vols., 1836–39) and continued the practice of life writing for the remainder of his career. F.'s biography of his close friend Charles DICKENS (3 vols., 1872–74) is still required reading. F. was editor of, literary and dramatic critic for, various newspapers, and biographer of, among others, Oliver GOLDSMITH (4 vols., 1848), Sir John Eliot (2 vols., 1864), Walter Savage LANDOR (2 vols., 1868), and Jonathan SWIFT (1875, uncompleted), together with books on politics and history.

FORSYTH, Frederick

b. 25 August 1938, Ashford, Kent

One of the foremost writers of the political thriller, F. established his reputation in the 1970s with three nov-

els, *The Day of the Jackal* (1971), *The Odessa File* (1972), and *The Dogs of War* (1974). He had written a work of nonfiction, *The Biafra Story* (1969), and has written six works (including a collection of short stories) since but none of them quite match up to the early "classics." Like all thrillers that are popular and sell (more than thirty million copies have been sold), F.'s books follow a well-conceived and constructed formula. The central character is a loner working against a system or government. Of course, there are variations within this bald framework. The Jackal plans to assassinate Charles de Gaulle in keeping with right-wing colonist (Algerian) politics, and therefore represents a threat to the status quo. Peter Miller in *The Odessa File* uncovers and tracks down a former SS concentration camp commandant and in the process comes up against the ruthless Odessa who protect former Nazis. Cat Shannon is a mercenary who works for a corporation that wishes to engineer a coup in an African state. The protagonist is well organized, has an excellent knowledge of varied fields, and is a thorough professional. This specialized expertise is often reflected in technical narrative that is steeped in detail such as the construction of a special rifle or gunrunning. Detail, whether technical, political, or organizational, creates the illusion of verisimilitude, an authentication of often bizarre plots and contrived endings. F.'s emphasis on detail is reminiscent of Ian FLEMING's similar obsession with the "solidity of specification." It is a characteristic common to the thriller and F.'s phenomenal success is testimony to his ability to write a riveting tale.

The Day of the Jackal encapsulates the best of F.'s writing: meticulously plotted and building up to a thrilling climax as Commissioner Claude Lebel thwarts the Jackal's plan. There is an air of truth apparent about the whole narrative and this is heightened by the contrast between the professional and the amateur. F. contrasts the professional assassin with an OAS terrorist, the professional detective with political appointees. This dichotomy is common to the narrative and ideological construction of the thriller and has numerous parallels in Fleming. Thus, only Lebel, a professional, can catch a fellow professional and revalidate the power of the state by saving de Gaulle. *The Day of the Jackal* is F.'s best-known book and was made into a successful film in 1973 with Edward Fox as the Jackal.

The Dogs of War is Forsythian in its attention to detail and careful plotting. The fictional state of Zangaro with its huge platinum deposits becomes the focus of corporate desire. Sir James Manson, a corporate tycoon, hires Cat Shannon, a mercenary, to engineer a coup and place a pliable ruler amenable to the exploitation of Zangaro's resources. At one level, the book is a representation and critique of multinational corporations and their vast greed. Sir James declares

"Knocking off a bank or an armored truck is merely crude. Knocking off an entire republic has, I feel, a certain style." Shannon, the narrative indicates, is not the only mercenary for Sir James, and his henchmen Simon Endean and Martin Thorpe are equally men without moral scruples. Simultaneously, the book elides certain problems regarding mercenaries and tends to make them heroes. This could be related to F.'s experiences as a journalist in Biafra and his support for a coup in Equatorial Guinea in the 1970s. What is more disturbing is the representation of Africa and its inhabitants. Africa is like an addiction: "For Africa bites like a tsetse fly, and once the drug is in the blood it can never be wholly exorcised." In many ways, Cat prefers the harsh simplicity of Africa to the urbane hypocrisies of Europe (but like a good Westerner he is at home in both worlds). Yet Cat's observations on arrival in Zangaro are stereotypical and racialized: "Long ago in the Congo he had seen the same attitude, the blank eyed sense of menace conveyed by an African of almost primeval cultural level, armed with a weapon, in a state of power, wholly unpredictable, with reactions to a situation that were utterly illogical, ticking away like a moving time bomb." Prior to this scene, we are told that the Consul is illiterate and corrupt. The Africans in this book (such as they are) have no voice and the subtext of the representation is that although the country is mesmerizing it has not progressed much beyond an original state of barbarism.

The amateur-professional divide is present here in a specifically gendered context. Sir James's daughter, Julie, sleeps with and falls in love with Shannon. As in the earlier novels, F. presents women in subordinate and sexualized roles. The specifically male orientation of the mercenary and the narrative is evident: "There would be, Shannon knew, no other woman in his arms. Just a gun, the cool comforting caress of the blue steel against his chest in the night." Shannon is at least gentler than the Jackal who kills the woman he has sex with before he sets out to kill de Gaulle. F.'s subsequent novels, *The Shepherd* (1975), *The Devil's Alternative* (1979), *The Fourth Protocol* (1984), *The Negotiator* (1989), and *Icon* (1996), all display trademark plotting, the seamless combination of fact and fiction, conflict between an individual and an organization, the amateur-professional divide, and ability to tell a good tale. These qualities are also evident in *No Comebacks* (1982), a collection of ten short stories. The collection offers sharp, delightful stories with occasional glitches. "There Are No Snakes in Ireland" has an Indian medical student in Ireland as its protagonist and displays an uncharacteristic lack of research on F.'s part. He exoticizes India (in keeping with a long tradition of British fiction) and basic factual errors are overlooked. This is sur-

prising for an author who prides himself on the accuracy of his "factions."

Icon is testimony to F.'s prolific output and ability to update himself. The plot centers on the theft of the Black Manifesto, a neo-Nazi document written by Igor Komarov, the president-in-waiting in chaotic, mafia-ridden Russia. While Komarov plots and kills to regain the Manifesto, Western powers set about thwarting him. Jason Monk, ex-CIA operative, returns to Russia to fight Komarov with the aid of Nigel Irvine (ex-master British spy runner) and a Chechen ganglord whose life he had saved years ago in Aden. *Icon* is comparable to John LE CARRÉ's *Russia House* although it lacks the complex insights of the latter. The end of history rhetoric and triumphalism are particularly jarring but do not overly impinge on the sheer pleasure of reading a well-crafted, well-paced thriller. In the final analysis, F. is the master craftsman of political thrillers and his phenomenal sales and longevity are testimony to his continuing popularity.

BIBLIOGRAPHY: Macdonald, A. F., "F. F.," in Benstock, B., ed., *British Mystery and Thriller Writers since 1940*, First Series, *DLB* 87 (1989): 125–35

SUBARNO CHATTARJI

FOWLES, John
b. 31 March 1926, Leigh-on-Sea, Essex

Widely recognized as one of England's most distinguished novelists, F. is also a respected existential thinker and writer of naturalistic essays. He has also published a volume of poetry and a collection of short stories. In spite of the sometimes considerable intellectual challenge of his complex narratives, his novels have consistently brought him popular commercial success and the acclaim of some of England's and America's most discriminating literary critics. His work has always attracted both a mass audience and intellectuals. Three of his novels have been made into successful motion pictures, earning him financial security and enabling him to devote himself to writing on a full-time basis.

His studies at New College, Oxford, included serious research in philosophy, particularly the emerging French existentialists such as Albert Camus and Jean-Paul Sartre. Their influence can be detected in virtually all of F.'s fiction and nonfiction, particularly in F.'s preoccupation with problems of human freedom and choice. F.'s early French studies also led him to the study of Celtic lore and its influence on the medieval French tales of courtly love and the chivalric quest tradition. F. believes that that material became the origin of much of modern European fiction.

His first novel, *The Collector*, published in 1963, became an immediate best-seller, and was made into a critically acclaimed motion picture starring Terence

Stamp and Samantha Eggar. The financial rewards of both the book and the movie enabled F. to retire from teaching in boarding schools and to live independently. The subject matter of *The Collector* is the kidnapping of a beautiful affluent young woman by an introverted young man, Clegg, from the lower classes. He had become a devoted collector of butterflies and, after becoming obsessed with her beauty and freedom, decided to add her to his collection. After winning a fortune on a football pool, Clegg built a luxurious basement prison for her. His motivation stemmed from his desire not to use her sexually, but to "own" her and her seeming freedom. The theme of the novel is both a moral and social one. The novel criticizes a modern industrial society's obsession with "owning" not only objects but also people. Though Clegg now "owns" the helpless young lady, he finds himself, ironically, imprisoned by his transgressive act, a condition that F. attributes to the greed of an exclusively materialistic society.

Although F.'s next published novel was the controversial *The Magus* (1965; rev. ed., 1977), he had actually begun writing it as early as 1952, during his time as a teacher at a private boarding school on the Greek island of Spetsai. Unlike the moral message of *The Collector*, *The Magus* deals with the more complex theme of illusion versus reality, and how time and experience can change the very ground of perception. Englishman Nicholas Urfe takes a job teaching on the Edenlike island of Phraxos, a place dominated by magus Maurice Conchis, who has created a world of psychodrama by manipulating a series of mythic masks that reduces Nicholas to a condition of utter mystery and loss of identity. F. introduces a new theme into his literary cosmos: the empowering energy of mystery to drive human beings into seeking their own answers. In *The Magus*, all so-called facts are built on the ever-shifting sands of individual perceptions, which change constantly. Though *The Magus* became a huge popular success among university students, F. was so unhappy with it that he completely revised it in 1977.

F.'s third novel, *The French Lieutenant's Woman* (1969), introduced new technical elements into the way F. crafted his narratives. Adhering to his longheld existential doubts concerning any kind of epistemological truth, F. rejects the writer's omniscient authority throughout the novel. Though the work starts out as a conventional Victorian novel, by page eighty, F. dramatically exposes its fictive scaffolding, thereby transforming it into a parody of the classic Victorian novel, making it an experimental work. Harold PINTER wrote the prize-winning screenplay that made stars of both Jeremy Irons and Meryl Streep.

F.'s fourth novel, *Daniel Martin*, was published in 1977 and borrowed very little from any of his earlier ones. F. called both *The Collector* and *The Magus* fa-

bles; he considered *The French Lieutenant's Woman* an exercise in literary technique. *Daniel Martin*, while autobiographical in some ways, is about a playwright becoming a screenwriter. There is little doubt that F. was utilizing the time he spent in Hollywood in 1969 when he first experienced the existential emptiness of actual Hollywood movie sets. The character Daniel Martin's two-pronged journey is both to redeem the past and, simultaneously, to create the future by the power of the imagination in its quest for spiritual and aesthetic wholeness.

F.'s last two novels, *Mantissa* (1982) and *A Maggot* (1985), were considerably shorter than his earlier ones. *Mantissa* is a consciously mythic fantasy on the themes of freedom, art, and sex, with characters named Dr. Delfie (the oracle of Delphi) and Nurse Cory (Kore or Persephone). *A Maggot* is his most bizarre novel. Though it is set in the 18th c., it is a fictionalized version of the life of the mother of Ann Lee, founder of the Shakers.

F. suffered a stroke in 1988 that seemed to limit his writing to travel pieces and favorite authors. His capacity for writing novels seems to have disappeared. F.'s novels will be remembered not only for their highly imaginative content but also because each of them was written in a different narrative form that embodied his persistent philosophical enquiries into the way literature can accurately represent the complexities of the human condition.

BIBLIOGRAPHY: Foster, T. C., *Understanding J. F.* (1994); Huffaker, R., *J. F.* (1980); Pifer, E., ed., *Critical Essays on J. F.* (1986); Tarbox, K., *The Art of J. F.* (1988)

PATRICK MEANOR

FOXE, John

b. 1517, Boston, Lincolnshire; d. 18 April 1587, London

F. was educated at Braesnose College, Oxford, and became a fellow of Magdalen, but his Puritan convictions led him to resign his fellowship in 1545. A committed reformer, F. went into exile at the beginning of Mary Tudor's reign in 1553, traveling to Frankfurt and later to Strasbourg.

His early works demonstrate religious tolerance: *De non plectendis morte adulteris* (1548) is a plea for mercy, and *Christus Triumphans* (1557) is an appeal for tolerance on the part of the English nobility. However, his most famous work, best known as *Foxe's Book of Martyrs*, can only be described as anti-Catholic. Published in Strasbourg, this work first appeared in Latin as the *Commentarii rerum in ecclesia gestarum* (1554). At this stage, the martyrology was concerned mostly with persecutions suffered by early reformers such as John Wycliffe and Jan Hus. It was quickly enlarged to include victims of the Marian persecution, and published in Basle as *Rerum in ecclesia gestarum . . . digesti . . . commentarii* (1559). After the accession of ELIZABETH I in 1558, F. returned to England and produced a further enlarged version of his book, this time translated into English and published by John Day, under the title *The Actes and Monuments of these Latter and Perilous Days, touching matters of the church, wherein are comprehended and described the great persecution and horrible troubles that have been wrought and practiced by the Romish prelates from the year of Our Lord a thousand to the time now present* (1563). A revised text, with additions and omissions, appeared under the title *The Ecclesiastical History* in 1570; at the directive of the government, this second edition was placed in churches throughout England. F. also edited *The Whole Works of William Tyndale, John Frith, and Doctor Barnes*, three authors who had been burned alive under HENRY VIII. His edition of their works, published by John Day in 1573 as a companion to *The Book of Martyrs*, quickly became the most important collection of Tudor religious prose.

The Book of Martyrs was issued in four editions during F.'s lifetime, and its popularity was outstripped in the 16th c. only by the Bible. It was the best illustrated book of its age, and was also extremely large: its final version, printed in 1583, ran to more than six thousand folio pages, and contained four million words. F. had noted the longstanding popularity of medieval hagiographical texts and attempted to supplant these, giving pride of place to the writings ("monuments") of his Protestant martyrs, whereas the earlier genre had concentrated on the miracles performed by Catholic saints. *The Book of Martyrs* was the most powerful work of Protestant propaganda for its period; its impact lay in its reliance on eyewitness accounts and in the prominence given to descriptions of torture. It contains numerous highly charged polemical accounts of the suffering of Christians who had maintained faith with the "true" church of Christ, as opposed to the false church of Rome. Some of its best-known narratives are those that describe the deaths of John Rogers, Thomas Cranmer, Nicholas Ridley, and Hugh LATIMER. Many of its narratives concern female spirituality and are by women or designed for a female audience; both low-born women and aristocratic figures such as Katherine PARR and Lady Jane Grey are featured, and the book concludes with a narrative account of Princess Elizabeth's imprisonment, idealizing Elizabeth I as a Protestant heroine who eluded martyrdom.

The Book of Martyrs was central to Reformation English culture. It contains such a diverse array of literary genres that it resembles a veritable encyclopedia of popular literature. In addition to increasing anti-Catholic sentiment, *The Book of Martyrs* also encour-

aged nationalist pride, since it portrayed England as the land of the new chosen people. F. was attacked during his own lifetime by Roman Catholics, but among Protestants he was regarded as a quasi-scriptural authority. His reputation suffered during the 19th c. when he was widely regarded as an unscrupulous lie-peddling propagandist; since then, he has been somewhat rehabilitated as an historian.

BIBLIOGRAPHY: Haller, W., *Foxe's Book of Martyrs and the Elect Nation* (1963); Olson, V. N., *J. F. and the Elizabethan Church* (1973); Wooden, W. W., *J. F.* (1983)

MARGARET CONNOLLY

FRANCIS, Dick [Richard Stanley]
b. 31 October 1920, Tenby, Wales

After aging and repeated injuries ended F.'s successful career as a steeplechase jockey in 1957, he began writing a racing column for the London *Sunday Express* and published his autobiography, *The Sport of Queens* (rev. eds., 1968, 1974). With the publication of *Dead Cert* in 1962, he turned from nonfiction to fiction, and he has since published a new novel almost every year. Even though all of F.'s novels portray crime and detection, he prefers to call them adventure stories rather than mysteries. The novels are bestsellers but also receive critical acclaim for their skillful exploration of such issues as emotional healing, maturation, and tangled family relationships.

Most of the novels (especially the earlier ones) deal with horse training and racing in Great Britain, but F. moves beyond this realm to create convincing protagonists from different professions whose work takes them to many countries. Thus, one of the delights in reading a F. novel is becoming immersed in a new world. For example, Edward Link in *Smokescreen* (1972) is a movie actor assisting a friend in South Africa, Charles Todd in *In the Frame* (1976) is an artist who travels to Australia, Andrew Douglas in *The Danger* (1983) is a security expert working in Italy and the U.S., and Perry Stuart in *Second Wind* (1999) is a meteorologist who risks a hurricane in the Caribbean. F. was a Royal Air Force pilot during World War II, and he uses his prior knowledge of aviation in novels such as *Flying Finish* (1966) and *Rat Race* (1970). More often, though, he pursues meticulous research to reveal an unfamiliar realm to readers.

F.'s protagonists are seldom professional detectives, and he rarely uses the same hero in more than one novel. A significant exception in *Odds Against* (1965), *Whip Hand* (1979), and *Come to Grief* (1995) is Sid Halley—a former jockey whose hand injury forces him to become an investigator. Nevertheless, F. readily admits that all his protagonists share certain important traits. All are idealists who exhibit considerable grace under pressure. Just as they are strict in their pursuit of high professional standards, they also display moral rigor (though they may bend the law to achieve a higher end). Hardly superheroes, they may feel intense fear and experience dramatic failures before an ultimate triumph.

Like Sid Halley, whose deformed hand parallels injuries to his spirit, many of F.'s protagonists suffer psychic wounds. Depression and suicidal tendencies haunt Gene Hawkins in the early chapters of *Blood Sport* (1967). James Tyrone in *Forfeit* (1969) must confront guilt with regard to his paralyzed wife. While these older protagonists grow through their pain, some younger heroes (frequently orphaned or estranged from their blood fathers) acquire fatherlike mentors who guide them through the process of maturation. For example, the youthful wine merchant Tony Beach in *Proof* (1984) teams up with the more mature Gerard McGregor to defeat both brutal criminals and Tony's debilitating grief over the recent death of his wife. Typically, while the protagonist pursues a physical foe, he also explores dark recesses of his own soul. Daniel Roke in *For Kicks* (1965) assumes the role of a dishonest stable lad to investigate the doping of horses. In this disguise, he begins to learn his true identity. Philip Nore, a jockey and part-time photographer in *Reflex* (1981), untangles a complex blackmail scheme and simultaneously discovers unpleasant family secrets and a lost sister. In many of F.'s works, then, solving the external mystery parallels achieving greater personal insight, and the crime novel frequently becomes a story of psychological growth.

BIBLIOGRAPHY: Barnes, M., *D. F.* (1986); Davis, J. M., *D. F.* (1989); Knepper, M. S., "D. F.," in Bargainnier, E. F., ed., *Twelve Englishmen of Mystery* (1984): 222–48; Wilhelm, A., "Fathers and Sons in D. F.'s *Proof*," *Critique* 32 (Spring 1991): 169–178

ALBERT WILHELM

FRASER, George MacDonald

b. 25 April 1925, Carlisle

F.'s considerable output ranges from Scottish history in *The Steel Bonnets: The Story of the Anglo-Scottish Border Reivers* (1971) to critical film study in *The Hollywood History of the World* (1988). His historical novels deal with border feuds (*The Candlemass Road*, 1993), bare-knuckle boxing in the time of the Regency (*Black Ajax,* 1997), and Edwardian England through the eyes of an expatriate American (*Mr. American,* 1980). Three volumes of short stories derive from his war service as junior officer in a highland regiment: *The General Danced at Dawn* (1970), *McAuslan in the Rough* (1974), and *The Sheikh and the Dustbin* (1988). A volume of war memoirs, *Quartered Safe Out Here* (1992), deals with his active ser-

vice as an infantryman fighting the Japanese in the Burmese jungle.

F.'s main project has been the dozen novels known collectively as *The Flashman Papers.* Flashman was the bully in Thomas HUGHES's *Tom Brown's Schooldays.* Inventing Flashman's military career after his expulsion from Rugby School, F. creates a memorable antihero, a handsome, womanizing coward with the knack of evading danger and emerging from his many adventures with undeserved glory.

From the publication in 1969 of *Flashman* onward, Flashman has served in the Afghan wars, the Crimea, the Indian Mutiny, the American Civil War, the Chinese "Opium" conflict, the Sikh wars (from which he emerges carrying the Koh-i-Noor diamond), in addition to running slaves from West Africa to the U.S., captaining a wagon train of prostitutes from a New Orleans brothel to the Californian gold fields, and serving as military chief of staff to the mad Queen of Madagascar. F. demonstrates great ingenuity in setting up the various situations and in inventing plausible escapes. During his undeserved rise from ensign to brigadier-general, Flashman meets Victoria and Albert, presidents Abraham Lincoln and Ulysses S. Grant, Rajah Brook of Sarawak, "Iron Chancellor" Bismarck, the famous Victorian cricketers Pilch, Mynn, and Felix (all of whom he manages to bowl out at Lord's cricket ground), Sherlock Holmes and Dr. Watson. He is witness to important events such as the charge of the Light Brigade, the relief of Lucknow, and John Brown's attack on Harpers Ferry, casting a fascinating and carefully researched sidelight on 19th-c. military, political, and social history.

BIBLIOGRAPHY: Bargainnier, E. F., "The Flashman Papers: Picaresque and Satiric Pastiche," *Crit* 18, 2 (1976): 109–20; Voorhees R. J., "Flashman and Richard Hannay," *DR* 53 (1973): 113–20

MICHAEL GROSVENOR MYER

FRASER, G[eorge] S[utherland]

b. 8 November 1915, Glasgow, Scotland; d. 3 January 1980, Leicester

Educated at the Glasgow Academy and at Aberdeen Grammar School, F. was awarded a bursary at St. Andrews University where he won a competition for a one-act play about the death of Christopher MARLOWE, *At the Mermaid,* and edited the university magazine. He graduated in 1937 with a degree in English and history and worked on Aberdeen papers as a trainee journalist. In 1939, he volunteered for military service and was enlisted in the Black Watch. He was transferred to the Royal Army Service Corps in 1940 and embarked for Egypt in 1941 where he worked on army publications. In Cairo, he made many literary friends including Lawrence DURRELL, Bernard Spencer, and Terence Tiller who were members of the group of exiles who contributed to the magazine *Personal Landscape*. In 1943, *Poetry London* published a pamphlet of his poems entitled *The Fatal Landscape* and in 1944 also published *Home Town Elegy*. His autobiography, *A Stranger and Afraid: Autobiography of an Intellectual*, was written in 1949 though not published until 1983. It gives a vivid picture of his upbringing in Aberdeen and how his lack of confidence in his social self was compensated by the confidence and determination of his literary self and concludes after his experiences in Cairo with the emergence of the promising man of letters.

F. returned to London in 1945 and for the next thirteen years he lived as a freelance literary journalist contributing to journals such as the *New Statesman*, *Encounter*, and *London Magazine*. He acted as poetry editor for the *Times Literary Supplement*, worked for the British Council, did broadcasts and edited a poetry program for the BBC as well as lecturing and translating. He also held open evenings at his Chelsea home to which young poets came and read their work, and numbers of poets have testified to the influence these gatherings exerted on the development of their poetry. In 1947, he made a lengthy visit to South America and from 1950 to 1951 he was cultural advisor to the United Kingdom Liaison Mission in Japan. In January 1958, he was appointed lecturer in English at Leicester University where he stayed until he retired in 1979 as Reader in Poetry. In *A Short History of English Poetry* (1979), he summarized his career by stating that, "Poetry is my gift. But to earn a living I became first a literary journalist, then a university teacher, and now teaching, especially the teaching of poetry, has become as true a vocation as writing."

His impressive strengths as a critic are exemplified in the quality and range of his sympathies in *The Modern Writer and His World* (1953), the incisive essays on modern poetry contained in *Vision and Rhetoric* 1959), and his pioneering study of Durrell (1968).

The Modern Writer and His World, which has gone through a number of revisions and impressions in hardback and in paperback, was initially planned and written in Tokyo as a lecture course for Japanese students of English literature though the published work goes well beyond its original brief. He expresses severe reservations about what he believes to be the "cul-de-sac of symbolism," is notably understanding of James JOYCE's *Ulysses*, especially the character of Bloom, reminds his readers of Sean O'CASEY's genius, and gives a sensitive appraisal of the poetry of Robert GRAVES and William EMPSON. Above all, he makes a staunch and finely judged assessment of the greatness of W. B. YEATS's poetry. Though he covers the entire range of modern writing and he neglects very little, his treatment of Joseph CONRAD is, perhaps, rather meager and his failure to give D. H. LAWRENCE more

than faint praise looks like an unexpected blindspot. Otherwise, he varies his approach from exercises in close analysis to chatty reminiscences about the literary life. In the section on criticism, he makes clear that he admires a good many modern critics including F. R. LEAVIS. Throughout the study, the most prominent feature is the breadth and generosity of his judgments. Indeed, the book has been criticized on the grounds that he speaks so kindly and indulgently of so many people.

The essays that comprise *Vision and Rhetoric* are notable for their clarity, concision, and cogency. He shows the same breadth of reading and critical approach as he had demonstrated in *The Modern Writer and His World* and the same determination to understand the poems and the poet. He discusses a series of poets from Yeats to Dylan THOMAS, Ezra Pound to Louis MACNEICE. He argues that T. S. ELIOT and Pound were not a "breakaway from the romantic tradition but a continuation and completion of it." His most impressive essays are those in which he discusses individual poets, particularly MacNeice, Thomas, and Graves. He cannot entirely disguise his aversion for W. H. AUDEN and his most impressive essays are those on Yeats.

As a poet, his wartime pamphlet *A Fatal Landscape* grew into a full volume in *Home Town Elegy* a year later and together with *The Traveller Has Regrets* (1948) completes his most productive decade. He himself considered the poems as being typical of the young poets writing just before, during, and after the war and said that they showed a response to the contemporary crisis, the impact of foreign places, and the theme of loneliness and exile. They show a concern for exact visual description and deploy a conversational diction. They are partly reflective, partly descriptive, and show the influence of Yeats. One theme that runs through them is the regret at being separated from his youth in spite of whatever gains there may be. His last published volume of poetry, *Conditions* (1969), records the increasing cynicism of middle age with a disarming honesty. Its main achievement is possibly the narrative poem "Barrington in 1798." Based on an 18th-c. memoir, it is evocative of a life that is authentic and rough. The poems he wrote from 1970 that are published in his *Poems of G. S. F.* (1982), including those he addressed to his wife and daughter, are consistently impressive. There is a sense of impending departure, intimation of an ending confronted with love and HUMOR.

A memorial gathering of friends of all ages was held on June 6, 1980, at Leicester University when tributes were paid to him by, among others, Empson. He was described as "a man of high standards yet kindly sympathies, a large shambling convivial body with a thin tough acute literary character lurking inside." His work adds distinction to the craft of criticism and the art of poetry.

BIBLIOGRAPHY: Alexander, M., "The Poems of G. S. F.," *Agenda* 19/20 (Winter-Spring 1982): 115–17; Fletcher, I., and J. Lucas, eds., *The Poems of G. S. F.* (1982)

A. R. JONES

FRAYN, Michael
b. 8 September 1933, London

Originally a journalist, F. became a novelist, but found greater success as a playwright before returning, successfully, to fiction. Both his plays and novels are admired for their wit, but they also explore weighty philosophical issues such as perception and reality, the nature of certainty, and the human quest for order. And while less overtly political than many of his contemporaries, F.'s work is attentive to the political and cultural realities that shape his characters' worlds.

Born in London, F. trained as a Russian interpreter during his compulsory military service, a skill that he later used to translate a number of Anton Chekhov's plays. After military service, he attended the University of Cambridge, graduating with a degree in the "moral sciences." His interest in philosophy is manifested in a philosophic bent to his literary work, as well as a book of philosophy, *Constructions* (1974).

After university, F. worked as a journalist and published several collections of essays, then turned to the novel. *The Tin Men* (1965), *The Russian Interpreter* (1966), and *A Very Private Life* (1968) all drew on F.'s experiences as journalist and interpreter, although with his characteristic comic/philosophic spin. *The Tin Men*, for instance, follows the careers of a group of programmers who create programs to write incomprehensible yet soothing newspaper stories.

In 1970, after having some plays rejected by a producer, F. self-produced his own evening of one-acts, *The Two of Us*. Focused on one of F.'s major themes, the ever-changing relations between couples, the one-acts were disliked by critics. Undaunted, F. went on to write a full-length play, *The Sandboy* (perf. 1971), which again centers on a couple's relationship, this time exploring the theme of happiness and its dependence of the existence of unhappiness.

F.'s first critical success on stage came with *Alphabetical Order* (perf. 1975; pub. 1976). Drawing on his own newspaper experience, the play focuses on the denizens of a chaotic library for a provincial newspaper. Positing the interdependence of order and chaos in a witty and enjoyable way, the play won the *Evening Standard* Award for Best Comedy of the Year.

F. continued to focus on writing plays, and *Clouds* (perf. 1976; pub. 1977), *Donkeys' Years* (perf. 1976; pub. 1977), *Make and Break* (1980), and *Balmoral*

(1987) were all successes, with *Make or Break* winning another *Evening Standard* Award. But *Noises Off* (1982) would prove to be his greatest commercial success. The play is a farce about a farce, depicting a group of second-string actors producing a mediocre farce called "Nothing On." The first act of "Nothing On" is performed three times in the course of the play; the audience of *Noises Off* sees it twice from the perspective of the audience and once from backstage. As the lives of the actors become increasingly muddled, the play is disrupted in turn, eventually producing a farce that is hilariously perfect in its complete departure from the script. Ironically, even as it parodied the popular British "sex farce" genre, *Noises Off* joined that tradition. Translated into thirty-six languages and breaking the Savoy Theatre's record for running length, the play's popularity made its author financially independent. A second play about the theater, *Look Look* (1990), was less successful.

Benefactors (1984) was a departure for the playwright. Returning to the theme of relationships and betrayal, F. contrasted the lives of two couples, friends with similar middle-class lives and liberal social convictions. While the human search for order and meaning still provides comic potential, *Benefactors* is much darker and more political than F.'s previous plays.

F. returned to fiction successfully with *The Trick of It* (1989), a novel about an academic who marries the novelist he specializes in, then turns to writing novels himself. *A Landing on the Sun* (1991) and *Now You Know* (1992) both feature characters embarked on investigations inside the civil service that become not only journeys of self-discovery, but inquiries into the nature of identity. Both are written with stream of consciousness narration that highlights the author's facility with voice and dialect.

Returning to the theater, F. had an international success with *Copenhagen* (1998), an imagined version of an actual 1941 conversation between the Danish physicist Niels Bohr and his former student Werner Heisenberg, then head of the Nazi nuclear fission program. The play became somewhat controversial when some scientists accused F. of whitewashing Heisenberg's reputation, although the play maintains a scrupulous ambivalence about all its characters. Like *Benefactors*, *Copenhagen* moves freely between past and present, and F. seizes upon Heisenberg's "Uncertainty Principle" as a metaphor for the difficulty of understanding human motivation. The play won another *Evening Standard* Award for F., as well as a Tony Award for Best Play in the U.S. and Best New Play at France's prestigious Nuit des Molières.

F.'s fiction was honored at a level similar to his stage work with the publication of *Headlong* (1999), a novel about a philosopher who becomes convinced that his neighbor unknowingly owns a lost masterpiece by Bruegel. Again using stream of consciousness to follow a narrator's progress from intellectual investigation to self-examination, *Headlong* follows the pattern of many of F.'s plays and novels, playing a game of cat-and-mouse with the reader and remaining ambivalent about the status of the painting. The novel was nominated for the Booker Prize.

F. has been likened to fellow playwrights Alan AYCKBOURN and Alan BENNETT, both well-known comic playwrights, but he is perhaps more similar to Tom STOPPARD. Like Stoppard's, his plays and novels usually begin with an intellectual proposition, and then go on to explore the human impulses and emotions that surround it. Like Stoppard, he is drawn to academic debates and literary or historical puzzles. Increasingly recognized as one of Britain's leading living playwrights, F.'s reputation has grown steadily, and his later work takes up the themes of his earlier work in popularly successful ways.

BIBLIOGRAPHY: DiGaetani, J. L., *A Search for Postmodern Theater: Interviews with Contemporary Playwrights* (1991); Page, M., ed., *File on F.* (1994); Worth, K., "Farce and M. F.," *MD* 26 (March 1983): 47–53

GINGER STRAND

FRAZER, [Sir] James [George]
b. 1 January 1854, Glasgow, Scotland; d. 7 May 1941, Cambridge

F. was educated at Glasgow University and Trinity College, Cambridge, where in 1879 he was elected a fellow, being called to the bar in the same year. He is famous for *The Golden Bough*, published in two volumes in 1890, reissued in twelve volumes under seven titles between 1907 and 1915, issued under the original title in an abridged edition 1922. In 1936, he published *Aftermath: A Supplement to the Golden Bough*. In 1926, F. issued the first of two volumes of *The Worship of Nature*, dealing with the worship of sky and earth. Among his many other publications are *Totemism* (1887); *Adonis, Attis, Osiris: Studies in the History of Oriental Religion* (1906; rev. eds., 1907, 1914), *Totemism and Exogamy* (1910), and *Folklore of the Old Testament* (3 vols., 1918). In 1907, he was appointed the first Professor of Social Anthropology at Liverpool University.

Stylistically seductive, F.'s work gave currency to the themes of fertility ritual, the sacrificial murder of kings, and the scapegoat. It suggested that Christianity was not a unique revelation but merely one among many regeneration myths: this view, apparently backed by science, chimed with 19th-c. skepticism and belief in human progress. F. assumed that there were three stages of intellectual development: magical, religious, and scientific. This naively ethnocentric

model was for a while influential, but was increasingly challenged during the second half of the 20th c. Mary Douglas in 1966 described F.'s legacy as "baneful." F. is today respected more as classical scholar than as anthropologist: his commentary on *Pausanias* (1898) and his edition of Ovid's *Fasti* (1929) survive. F.'s imagery influenced T. S. ELIOT and D. H. LAWRENCE.

FREUD, Esther
b. 2 May 1963, London

Many novelists take cues from their own lives, and F. is no exception. She consistently draws inspiration from her own life. Her work explores the realms of unconventional childhood and contemporary domestic life. The arenas F. chooses to work in are filled with mid- to late-20th-c. angst and confusion about alienation, family, and conforming to society. F.'s work also presents unusual aspects of growing up during the 1960s and 1970s, a time when the dynamic between parents and children was often reversed.

F.'s first novel, *Hideous Kinky* (1992), which was shortlisted for the John Llewellyn Rhys Prize, is based on the author's own childhood experiences. The story is a fictionalized account of F.'s few childhood years in the 1960s that were spent traveling with her mother and sister in Morocco. The narrator of *Hideous Kinky* is a five-year-old child. She, her bohemian mother, and sister travel through Marrakech in the late 1960s. On the surface, the novel appears to be about a frivolous adventure, a few years spent exploring an exotic country with no worries that cannot be fixed. On a deeper level, however, F.'s first novel delves into the themes that persist throughout her work: family, unconventionality, and the embarrassment that occurs when the two meet. The novel was made into a film of the same title in 1998.

Peerless Flats (1993), F.'s second novel, has shades of AUTOBIOGRAPHY as well. The story takes place in modern-day London where sixteen-year-old Lisa has been accepted into an acting course. F. herself was trained as an actress in London before she began her writing career. Lisa, along with her mother and brother, moves to London, and because they are poverty-stricken, they move into a temporary housing project called Peerless Flats. The environment is permeated with drugs, sex, and general discontent and malaise. Before long, Lisa starts to spend time with her heroin addict sister, Ruby. Ruby is in and out of drug rehabs, steals money to support her habit, and takes the boy Lisa likes. Their mother allows Lisa total freedom, although Lisa doesn't know what to do with her independence. Throughout all this, she tries to attend her method acting classes, and make sense of her world as it changes. Although the novel is fraught with tensions, F. writes it without sentimentality and with good HUMOR and care for her characters. *Peerless Flats* further illuminates F.'s interest in children's lack of control of their worlds, and what they do to compensate.

F.'s third novel is more ambitious than her first two. *Summer at Gaglow* (originally entitled *Gaglow*, 1997) is really two stories, separated by seven decades, that intertwine and eventually come completely together. The first story, loosely based on F.'s ancestors, takes place in Germany just before and during World War I. The second story is about Sarah, a modern-day young London woman who is pregnant. Her father, an artist, begins painting her, and as he does, tells her about his family in Germany who spent summers their estate, Gaglow. Sarah attempts to elicit more of the story from him, and as he does she becomes more and more intrigued. The two stories are interesting counterpoints: Sarah's difficulties and concerns with single motherhood, and the trials her ancestors faced in the Kaiser's Germany.

The Wild (2000) looks again at family, and in particular, the child's view of the family. Tess, the novel's nine-year-old protagonist, wants badly to have a father and a happy family. She, her brother, and mother move into a converted bakery along with a single father and his children. F. focuses on the making of stepfamilies and on their falling apart.

MARIKA BRUSSEL

FRIEL, Brian
b. 9 January 1929, Killyclogher, near Omagh, County Tyrone, Northern Ireland

In a century of Irish dramatic genius extraordinary in number and reputation of playwrights and breadth of theatrical animus and style, F.'s career is pantheon-class. F.'s work is Irish in the most traditional, definitive way, in its preoccupation with history. Protagonists in his drama include major historical figures (St. Columba, in *The Enemy Within*, perf. 1962, pub. 1975; Hugh O'Neill, in *Making History*, 1988); dramatic situations include major historical episodes (the "Flight of the Earls," in *Making History*; the British Ordnance Survey, in *Translations*, perf. 1980, pub. 1981), or refer to them in general (emigration, in several plays, most notably *Philadelphia, Here I Come*, 1965) or indirectly (Bloody Sunday, in *Freedom of the City*, perf. 1973, pub. 1974). The stage imagery he employs (an ancestral great house, in *Aristocrats*, perf. 1979, pub. 1980; an archaeological dig in a city center, a literal unearthing of layers of local history, in *Volunteers*, perf. 1975, pub. 1979) bears historical import. F.'s creation of Ballybeg—from baile beag, Irish for "small town"—as the setting for a number of his plays, conflates the local and the national, as centuries of politics and cultural change play out in a common community.

If his central theme is identifiably Irish, his handling of that theme, in its vigorous, often eloquent, ambivalence, is, too. He examines, with a cold eye but a generous nature, the personal history of history makers, from tribal chieftains and churchmen to politicians and schoolmasters to parents and children, detailing the crushing dialectics of ideology and personality that hobble truth, of public and private that deconstruct text, of desire and defeat that compromise memory. The recording and reckoning of event are relative, as in *The Faith Healer* (perf. 1979, pub. 1980), which presents four monologues by three characters, from which the audience must cull and accumulate the narrative, implicating the listener in the act of storytelling. There are at least two sides to every story, because, as *Philadelphia, Here I Come* dramatizes, there are two sides to every storyteller. So the personal conflates with the national, as the border that characterizes almost a hundred years of Irish politics, and that symbolizes the last thousand years of Irish history, is recognized, analogically, structurally, in the dualistic psychological and political struggles of F.'s characters.

Born in County Tyrone, living in Donegal, F. is himself a man of the borderland. As a founding member of the Field Day Theatre Company (*Translations* was their first production), F. is committed to political engagement in his drama. Yet his own translation of Anton Chekhov's *Three Sisters* (1981) into an Irish-inflected English demonstrates his equally serious and sustained commitment to the history of drama, his engagement with theatrical voices beyond national borders, as also demonstrated by his early work with Tyrone Guthrie in the development of *Philadelphia, Here I Come*. When he turned from a writer of predominately prose fiction (two volumes of short stories, *A Saucer of Larks*, 1962, and *The Gold in the Sea*, 1966) to become a full-time playwright, he found his art. Over the course of his career, he has tried his dramatist's hand at almost every permutation and innovation of theatrical form available, from the play-within-the-play (in *Crystal and Fox*, perf. 1968, pub. 1970), to the dual representation of a single character (in *Philadelphia, Here I Come*, with two actors portraying the protagonist and his inner self; in *Dancing at Lughnasa*, 1990, with a single actor playing the adult narrator and himself as a child within the narrative), to direct address to the audience (in the monologues of *The Faith Healer*; in the narration of *Living Quarters*, perf. 1977, pub. 1978, and *Dancing at Lughnasa*). No aspect of theatricality goes unexplored in the service of the complex and compromised stories and the difficult but enduring characters of F.'s drama.

And no aspect of language. From soliloquizing to stuttering to silence, speech reveals—indeed, constitutes—not only character, but the heart of the historical matter, what happened, how it is remembered, what it means. And when, in *Tranlsations*, names separate lovers, they are drained of meaning, and language is, for a moment, free. And when, in *Dancing at Lughnasa,* the failed lives of the Mundy sisters fray into near nonexistence, and words are no solace or support, they dance and make rhythmic music, they reach deep, back, to the preverbal, prehistoric impulse of ritual drama, and find community. The tribal Irish W. B. YEATS sought to re-create in a revival of Celtic mythology are dancing in a cottage in Ballybeg, as the emblematic figures of Irish history are striding the stage, as the troubled children of "the Troubles" in the North argue among and with themselves, as the lonely, isolated Irish émigrés and locals live their lives, or at least try to tell their tales, in the life's work of Ireland's leading living playwright, F. Recent plays include *Wonderful Tennessee* (1993) and *Give Me Your Answer, Do!* (1997).

BIBLIOGRAPHY: Dantanus, U., *B. F.* (1988); O'Brien, G., *B. F.* (1990); Pine, R., *B. F. and Ireland's Drama* (1990)

DENNIS PAOLI

FROUDE, J[ames] A[nthony]

b. 23 April 1818, Dartington, Devonshire; d. 20 October 1894, Salcome, Devonshire

Historian, biographer, and proponent of imperialism, F. remains one of the most controversial figures of the Victorian period. Best known for his biography of Thomas CARLYLE, F. rose to prominence on the basis of his historical revaluation of the Tudor monarchy in his *History of England from the Fall of Wolsey to the Defeat of the Spanish Armada* (12 vols., 1856–70). He was a follower of Carlyle in propounding the value of social change, and his ideologically invested interpretation of the Elizabethan period raised questions about historical objectivity. Similarly, his *Thomas Carlyle: A History of the First Forty Years of His Life* (2 vols., 1882) and *Thomas Carlyle: A History of His Life in London* (2 vols., 1884) spawned lasting controversy about biographical control. Always contentious in its combination of skepticism and orthodoxy, F.'s work remains an important articulation of both positive and negative aspects of Victorian social theory.

Ordained and an Oxford fellow in 1845, F. was initially influenced by the Anglo-Catholic Oxford movement, led by John Henry NEWMAN and in which F.'s older brother, Hurrell, had been prominent. However, F. became increasingly disillusioned with Newman's Catholic tendencies and voiced his growing doubts about the institutionalization of religion in *The Nemesis of Faith* (1849). Spawning immediate religious controversy, the book was publicly burned in lecture halls and F.'s contentious literary career had

begun. Forced to leave Oxford, F. embarked on his twelve-volume *History of England* that vindicated the Tudors' religious and political choices, and argued for a return to heroic leadership ideals in Victorian politics. Offering a compelling description of Tudor England as a model for Carlyle's theories of hero worship and orderly social change, F.'s historical interpretation was praised for its brilliant style and insightful, if subjective, approach. He returned to this period in two subsequent works: *The Divorce of Catharine of Aragon* (1891) and *English Seamen in the Sixteenth Century* (1895).

Pursuing the idea of a revitalized English society, F. became a vocal supporter of imperialism. His second major historical work, *The English in Ireland in the Eighteenth Century* (3 vols., 1872–74), argued against Irish self-rule on the basis of English social and racial supremacy. In addition to visiting Ireland and the U.S., F. traveled to South Africa, the West Indies, Australia, and New Zealand during the 1870s and 1880s, collecting material for a series of lectures and historical observations on colonial government. F.'s *Oceana; or, England and Her Colonies* (1886) and *The English in the West Indies* (1888) argued for stronger English presence and greater economic development in the colonies. While F.'s colonial texts are fraught with problematic racialist assumptions, his work remains significant in representing the social theory behind Victorian imperialism.

F. had also established his reputation as a biographer of great men, publishing the lives of Julius Caesar (1879), John BUNYAN (1880), Benjamin DISRAELI (1890), and *Life and Letters of Erasmus* (1894), as well as short studies on Martin Luther (1883) and St. Thomas Becket (1878). F.'s sometimes opinionated approach in these, as well as in his historical works, had for years provoked accusations of factual inaccuracy from conservative scholars like Edward A. Freeman. After Carlyle's death in 1881, however, F.'s four-volume biography (ostensibly based on Carlyle's own papers) became the center of a heated controversy over what constituted historical fact and the limits of biographical license. F. was criticized for his portrayal of the Carlyles' private lives and suspected of malicious personal motivation. The controversy over F.'s biographical representation continues among scholars to this day and may be significant more for questioning the generic conventions of history and BIOGRAPHY than for any of its specific details.

Appointed Regius Professor of Modern History at Oxford in 1892 and immensely popular despite public criticism, F. combined Victorian moral concerns with a persistent questioning of received knowledge. His eloquent style and compelling historical and biographical observations express the vitality as well as insecurities of his age.

BIBLIOGRAPHY: Broughton, T. L., *Men of Letters, Writing Lives* (1999); Dunn, W. H., *J. A. F.* (1963); Goetzman, R., *J. A. F.* (1977)

                                        JORDAN STOUCK

FRY, Christopher

b. Christopher Harris, 18 December 1907, Bristol

Starting his professional theater career as an actor and, a little later, as a director ("producer" they called it in England at that time) of the Tunbridge Wells Repertory Players and then at the Oxford Playhouse, he began to write plays in the late 1930s and early 1940s. The early ones, all on Christian–religious subjects, were in style strongly reminiscent of the plays of T. S. ELIOT. Most of them—*The Boy with a Cart* (perf. 1938; pub. 1939), *The Firstborn* (perf. 1946; pub. 1948), and *Thor with Angels* (1948), for example—were written in response to commissions from various religious festivals. Then, in 1947, he suddenly found a voice and a style of his own. The play, a brilliant half-length piece for three players, was *A Phoenix Too Frequent* (1946). It is a breathless and ecstatic celebration of *joie de vivre,* giddy with its awareness of its own self-confidence. With it, F. leapt into prominence and then, a year later, into downright fame with *The Lady's Not for Burning* (perf. 1948; pub 1949).

In 1950, F. had four plays running concurrently in London. All of them were written in lightly handled, iridescent verse, full (perhaps too full) of every kind of verbal trick, pun, and wordplay. They were blessedly free from the kind of pompous, ponderous, self-regarding solemnity that marred much 19th-c. verse drama and they were often genuinely funny: no more "sitting as at a solemn musick." To counter any tendency toward a cheap and obvious sentimentality, F. frequently makes use, at the end of phrases, sentences, or speeches, of a delicious bathos, designed to anchor ecstasy to reality. A great chorus of critics hailed him as the savior of poetry in the theater and saw him as the pinnacle, the apogee toward which the curve of modern dramatic verse had been struggling through the work, since the beginning of the 20th c., of Gordon BOTTOMLEY, Lascelles ABERCROMBIE, John DRINKWATER, John MASEFIELD, Eliot, W. H. AUDEN, Stephen SPENDER, and others. Of course, a sunburst—by very definition—does not last. F.'s moment of glory lasted some twelve years or so and his heady adventure of new verse on the great public stages of the world began to be compared, unjustly, with that earlier sunburst of Stephen PHILLIPS in the first decade of the 20th c. But F.'s work, slight as some of it seems in retrospect, is a deal better than Phillips's: more original, much less derivative, at its best more genuinely poetic—and much more entertaining.

F. is a genuine poet, though a minor one: Phillips is a poetaster, a solemn versifier. F.'s great weakness is his Christianity, which gets in his light and blurs his artist's vision. Ironically, the play in which this is least in evidence is the one that is set in a Christian church—*A Sleep of Prisoners* (1951). It was written in response to a commission to provide a new play for the Festival of Britain in 1951. Written to be performed in a Christian church, its first production, directed by Michael Macowan, was at the University Church of St. Mary the Virgin, Oxford, England. One must not pretend that this is a play that faces and faces down the ultimate horror of human living six years after Hiroshima—F. is no Samuel BECKETT, nor yet a John Millington SYNGE; but, nevertheless, it is a play that is aware of its time: in its final scene one of the prisoner-of-war characters says: "The human heart can go to the lengths of God./Dark and cold we may be, but this/Is no winter now. The frozen misery/Of centuries cracks, begins to move,/The thunder is the thunder of the floes,/The thaw, the flood, the upstart Spring./Thank God our time is now when wrong/ Comes up to meet us everywhere."

But this was 1951. Perhaps his optimism and naiveté can be forgiven. F.'s next play was *The Dark Is Light Enough* (1954): set in 1848, the year of revolutions when "France sneezed and all Europe caught cold," the play's particular revolution is that of the Hungarians against their Austrian Hapsburg masters. The central figure is the Countess Ostenburg whose sympathies embrace Austrians and Hungarians alike and whose bravery, obstinacy, and compassion succeed, in spite of the fact that she knows herself to be dying, in rescuing her nihilist son-in-law from his own misanthropy. The play is altogether darker than any of its predecessors and the verse, though fluent, is less effervescent, has fewer flourishes. Cast in a comic mode, though with moments of high seriousness, the play as a whole is a most civilized piece of writing. F. has, after that, only one more work of consequence— *Curtmantle* (pub. 1961; perf. 1962). "Curtmantle" was Henry II's nickname, because of the plain, short cloak he chose to wear. So this is yet another Becket-Henry story to add to the procession (Alfred, Lord TENNYSON, Eliot, Jean Anouilh) but this one concentrates not on heroics and martyrdom but on the contribution made to the general human pattern by three remarkable people—St. Thomas Becket, Henry, and Eleanor of Aquitaine. In a very finely written three-cornered confontation, Eleanor says: "Let me say this to the man who makes the world—/And also to the man who makes himself the Church:/Consider complexity, delight in difference./Fear, for God's sake, your exact words./Do you think you can draw lines on the living water?" And a little later, when the two men have gone: "When the glorious battle turns into the vendetta/The great issues, no longer controlled by men,/Themselves take over command. You may yet

                                              377

see/Your signs in the heavens. The private feud/May be written across the sky."

But Henry is unpersuaded of his own virtue and his own usefulness and, when he is dying in despair at the end of the play, his bastard son says to him, in an effort to comfort him: "Sir, believe what you've accomplished./Your laws are fixed on England: grumbled at/Like the weather, but, like the weather, accepted/As a source of strength. The people have become/Their own law, in the twelve men representing them:/Unparalleled in Christendom, this new nature of the island."

The consistent neglect of *Curtmantle* since it was first performed is curious. It is, for example, no more demanding theatrically or financially then the other large-scale "historical" piece of the early 1960s, Robert BOLT's *A Man for All Seasons,* and is arguably the better and more profound play of the two, yet the former is forgotten while the latter is lauded.

In all, F. has published some dozen or so plays. Several of them are still quite lively and would still play very well. They would not much suit those moderns who go to the theater only to confirm their political and/or sociological prejudices, but there is (or ought to be) another audience than this. For the sake of that other audience—and in common honesty—some of F.'s plays ought to be more often revived in the theater than they are. As a body of work, they are not the world-shaking event they were initially claimed to be but—though now neglected—they are far from negligible. They are not pretentious, nor pompous, nor portentous and, at their best, they aptly illustrate F.'s own definition of poetry: "the language in which man explores his own amazement." He has also published distinguished translations of plays by Anouilh and Jean Giraudoux, an English verse version of Henrik Ibsen's *Peer Gynt* (based on a literal translation by Johan Fillinger), and a volume of criticism called *An Experience of Critics* (1963).

BIBLIOGRAPHY: Roy, E., *C. F.* (1969); Salmon, E., *Is the Theatre Still Dying?* (1985); Stanford, D., *C. F.* (1951); Whiting, J., *On Theatre* (1966)

ERIC SALMON

FRY, Roger [Eliot]

b. 14 December 1866, London; d. 13 September 1934, London

F. is known primarily as the impresario of the two postimpressionist exhibitions held at the Grafton Gallery, London, in 1910 and 1912, which introduced modern French painting (Cézanne, Gauguin, Van Gogh, Matisse) to the English public. It would be difficult to overestimate the significance of these for visual culture and MODERNISM in the early 20th c. F.'s important role as organizer, curator, and acquisitions

director in New York and London is also well recognized—as is his involvement with the circle of painters and writers known as the BLOOMSBURY GROUP. His own work, as a painter and critic concerned with the function and meaning of art, was comparatively neglected until a recent exhibition at the Courtauld Gallery, London (October 1999–January 2000).

F. came from a distinguished Quaker family that included the 19th-c. philanthropist Elizabeth Fry. At Cambridge reading natural sciences, he first became seriously interested in the history and philosophy of painting. Friendships with Goldsworthy Lowes Dickinson and John McTaggart, the neo-Hegelian philosopher, were formative influences and while Dickinson became interested in the application of dialectics to history and politics, F. early decided that he was concerned with the phenomenal world, with the Hegelian "Absolute" only as it manifested itself in "Appearances." Painting was the art of appearances and it was to this art that he devoted the rest of his life.

He became an indefatigable traveler, visiting the major galleries and museums across Europe, writing regularly on classical and Renaissance art, publishing a monograph on Giovanni Bellini (1899), helping to establish the *Burlington Magazine* in 1903, and discovering modern French painting through the work of Cézanne in 1906. Organizing the exhibition "Manet and the Post-Impressionists" (1910) brought him into contact with Clive and Vanessa BELL, Leonard and Virginia WOOLF, Lytton STRACHEY, and Duncan Grant, among others. He weathered public hostility to the postimpressionist exhibitions and went on to found, with Grant and Vanessa Bell, the Omega Workshops (1913–19). These workshops produced furniture, furnishings, and objects for everyday use, designed by contemporary artists—which included at one time Wyndham LEWIS, Henri Gaudier-Brzeska, and Nina Hamnett. Although short-lived, the Omega was important in introducing modernist design to a wider public and F. went on to become an enormously popular lecturer, attracting audiences of thousands.

His essays, lectures, and critical reviews appeared after World War I in two main anthologies: *Vision and Design* (1920) and *Transformations* (1926). *Vision and Design* became a standard reference work for the interwar years and was one of the first books to be published by Penguin in 1937. Containing some twenty-four essays, written between 1901 and 1919 (with a Retrospect written by F.), it is itself a modernist bricolage. As Virginia Woolf commented in her biography of F., the collection has something of the enthrallment of a novel and the excitement of a detective story.

The opening essays entitled "Art and Life," "An Essay in Aesthetics," "The Artist's Vision," and "Art and Science" set forth F.'s claims for the importance of art as distinct from those of science or economics.

In life, he argues, the field of vision is organized around action; we learn to see only what is necessary for living. Art, the art of painting, on the other hand, is "pure vision abstracted from necessity"; it allows us to see objects and the world not for their human uses and functions but as a set of phenomena. Thus, painting exposes the conventional nature of "seeing" and teaches the spectator to "look" again, at the objects represented and at the emotions called into being. He rejects both John RUSKIN's demand for a moral evaluation of art and the claims of REALISM. While F.'s emphasis on form and "design" links him with formalists like Clive Bell (for which he was attacked by I. A. RICHARDS), his theory of "vision" anticipates some of the points later made by Maurice Merleau-Ponty and other phenomenologists.

The group of mainly prewar essays on African sculpture, ancient American art, bushman art, and Mohammedan art, make a case against the eurocentricity of Victorian art history. Arguing against the assumption that "Greece was the only source of culture," F. identifies qualities of "significant form" (plasticity, vitality) across different periods and cultures. Despite his anti-imperialist views, like other modernists, F.'s appreciation of "primitivism" contains a number of evolutionary assumptions as later critics have pointed out. Other essays in the collection, like those in *Transformations*, which follow, display a continuing tension between formalism and F.'s historical awareness. Despite, or because of, these unresolved theoretical points, F. remains a key figure in 20th-c. debates on the nature of art.

BIBLIOGRAPHY: Green, C., ed., *Art Made Modern: R. F.'s Vision of Art* (2000); Reed, C., *A R. F. Reader* (1996); Spalding, F., *R. F.* (1980); Woolf, V., *R. F.* (1940)

JEAN RADFORD

FRY, Stephen
b. 24 August 1957, London

Actor, comedian, novelist, poet, playwright, and screenwriter, F. has achieved nothing less than celebrity status in Britain and is best known in the U.S. for his starring role in the film *Wilde* (1998), based on the life of Oscar WILDE, and for his performance in *Gosford Park* (2001), directed by Robert Altman. He was educated at Queen's College, Cambridge, where he met his future comedy partner Hugh Laurie—together they would later appear in popular television shows such as *Jeeves and Wooster* and *A Little Bit of Fry and Laurie*. F.'s first play, *Latin!; or, Tobacco and Boys*, was awarded a Fringe First at the 1980 Edinburgh Festival, and in the next decade he became a familiar performer on British radio and television. His first novel, *The Liar*—which provides a cynical and

satiric portrait of London society viewed through the character of his defiantly unconventional protagonist—was published in 1991 followed in the next year by *Paperweight*, a collection of articles, stories, and essays. Other novels include *The Hippopotamus* (1994) and *Making History* (1996), and in 1998 he published the autobiographical *Moab Is My Washpot*.

FULLER, Thomas
b. June 1608, Aldwincle, Northamptonshire; d. 16 August 1661, London

Wit, sometime poet, preacher, devotional writer, ecclesiastical historian, and biographer of England's "worthies," F. was an unflagging royalist whose moderate views, while failing to endear him to, also did not alienate him from, any faction during the Civil War. The nephew of two bishops, F. married into a prominent royalist family and did not lack for church preferment; his allegiance to the throne and reputation for learning made him one of the party chosen to escort Charles II home from France for the Restoration. In January 1643, however, F. had been one of six delegated by the House of Lords to present to Charles I the compromise crafted in the Westminster Petition, and in *The Holy State* (1642) he emphasized that "whatsoever the Theories of absolute Monarchy be," the true king "willingly orders his actions by the Laws of his realm." F.'s good nature and ready wit allowed him to maintain friendships with prominent parliamentarians both during and after the Interregnum, despite his known royalist loyalties. Ironically, while he survived the Interregnum with his livings intact, he was deprived of a probable bishopric under Charles II by his sudden death from fever.

F. was best known in his day as a moralist and devotional writer. *The Holy State*, which includes a corresponding section titled *The Profane State*, drew upon the Theophrastan character tradition to offer maxims concerning virtue and vice, with examples of each drawn from history. The trilogy *Good Thoughts in Bad Times* (1645), *Good Thoughts in Worse Times* (1647), and *Mixed Contemplations in Better Times* (1660)—like *The Cause and Cure of a Wounded Conscience* (1647)—accomplished what the subtitle of *Andronicus* (1646) promised: "Shewing, Sin: Slowly Punished. Right, Surely Rescued." The appeal of F.'s moral tracts lies in their mix of learned scriptural meditations with historical examples, their observations delivered in pithy wit.

Of greater interest to the modern reader, however, are F.'s ecclesiastical histories and the deft comments that he made through them upon current events. The pattern of his operation is evident in *David's Hainous Sinne, Heartie Repentance, Heavie Punishment* (1631), his first published work. Drawing upon the medieval devotional tradition that applied the seven so-called Penitential Psalms to the narrative of David's adultery with Bathsheba and consequent murder of her husband Uriah, as recorded in 2 Samuel, F. makes his narrative a delicate comment upon Charles I's intransigence and the king's need to scrutinize his behavior more closely. Similarly, F.'s *Historie of the Holy Warre* (1639) takes up Judeo-Christian history from where Flavius Josephus's 1st-c. narrative left off, concentrating upon the Crusaders' attempt to retake Jerusalem. But, published on the eve of the Civil War, its analysis of the economic and social ruin created in the Holy Land seems a prescient warning to antiroyalist factions of what their own "holy war" will bring. And, as Florence Sandler has shown, *A Pisgah-Sight of Palestine* (1650), while surveying the geography of the Holy Land, deftly challenges misguided millenarian attempts to turn England into a New Jerusalem.

But F. will probably be best remembered for the posthumously published *History of the Worthies of England* (1662). A biographical survey of all the "worthies" produced by each region in England, the text is a celebration of the English national character and created a conciliatory nationalist myth at the close of the most troubled period of English history; it is the advance guard of the movement that would culminate in the late 18th c.'s canonizing William SHAKESPEARE as the national genius. His piquant observations regarding character made F. beloved by such influential readers as Samuel PEPYS, Samuel Taylor COLERIDGE, Charles LAMB, and Robert SOUTHEY.

BIBLIOGRAPHY: Houghton, W. E., *The Formation of T. F.'s Holy and Profane States* (1938); Lyman, D., *The Great Tom Fuller* (1935); Sandler, F., "T. F.'s *Pisgah-Sight of Palestine* as a Comment on the Politics of Its Time," *HLQ* 41 (August 1978): 317–43

RAYMOND-JEAN FRONTAIN

G

GALLOWAY, Janice
b. 2 December 1956, Ayrshire, Scotland

After attending Jack's Road Primary School, G. went to Ardrossan Academy, where she developed an interest in music. It was her music teacher who convinced her to go to university, though he cautioned her against limiting her attention to music. She studied music and English at Glasgow University, dropped out briefly to become a welfare rights activist for a year, and returned to finish her degree. She worked as a teacher until 1989, when she resolved to pursue a writing career.

Her first novel, *The Trick Is to Keep Breathing*, was published in 1989 by Polygon Press and received widespread critical acclaim. The novel, a chronicle of a woman's recovery after a nervous breakdown, is notable for its experiments with form; she employs a range of discourses—first-person narrative, stream of consciousness, and deliberately fractured text—to simulate the experience of the protagonist. It won a Scottish Arts Council Book Award, the MIND/Allen Lane Book Award, and was shortlisted for the Whitbread First Novel Award and the Scottish First Book of the Year. A short story collection, *Blood*, followed in 1991. The stories explore feminist themes of repression and identity-creation. As the title suggests, the collection is bound by the visceral landscapes of the body and mind. Her second novel, *Foreign Parts*, was published in 1994. Centering on the experiences of two women on a driving holiday through France, the novel is a statement about the complex nature of female friendship. It won the 1994 McVitie Prize. The same year, G. received the E. M. Forster Award. Her next short story collection, *Where You Find It*, was published in 1996. She has been translated into seven languages.

Having recognized limitations of the written word, she has collaborated extensively with artists of different disciplines. Her recent book, *Pipelines* (2000), is a collaborative work of mixed media. Other works include three song cycles, one play, an opera libretto, and a wide variety of anthologized stories and collaborative texts. Several of her works have been adapted for the stage, and she has given much of her work and attention to various artistic forums. Much of her appeal lies in the way she defies societal and literary conventions. She pokes fun at the myriad of social rituals that work at once to define one's identity and limit it. Indeed, she conveys that sense of defiance by manipulating the texts with her choice of subject matter and her use of graphics and space. She plays with margins, breaks up text, and isolates significant words or phrases.

Some critics read her textual play as a commentary on the way women have to disconnect themselves from their experience; through these experiments, she constructs the mechanisms that oppress and contain women. Connotations of life and death are rampant in her imagery and themes, but it is her honest and unflinching portrayal of the momentary pleasures of everyday experience that illuminate her work. She imbues her characters with the resilience to transcend the bleak circumstances that haunt them; ultimately, it is the appreciation of those extraordinary, often overlooked moments that define her characters. A Scottish sensibility grounds her stories in REALISM and accounts for some of her recognition. Contemporaries of hers include Alasdair GRAY and James KELMAN. However, it is her engagement with the complex inner lives of her characters that distinguishes her work.

BIBLIOGRAPHY: Metztein, M., "Of Myths and Men: Aspects of Gender in the Fiction of J. G.," in Wallace G., and R. Stevenson, eds., *The Scottish Novel since the Seventies* (1993): 136–46; Norquay, G., "The Fiction of J. G.: Weaving a Rout Through Chaos," in Norquay G., and G. Smyth, eds., *Space and Place: The Geographies of Literature* (1997): 323–30

VICKI ENG

GALSWORTHY, John

b. 14 August 1867, Kingston Hill, Surrey; d. 31 January 1933, Grove Lodge, Hampstead

G. received the Nobel Prize for Literature in 1932, but his reputation as a novelist and playwright had already begun to decline at the time. He was often identified by modernists like Virginia WOOLF with the sort of old-fashioned novelists whose pattern they were rejecting. Nevertheless, G.'s achievement as a dramatist and, more importantly, as a novelist is a substantial one. He attempted to use the realistic novel and the "well-made play" as vehicles for the examination of social problems, especially those social problems that stem from the institutions of property and law.

G. was the son of a prosperous solicitor and was educated at Harrow and New College, Oxford. He prepared for a career as a barrister and was called to the bar in 1890. Before he settled down to practice, he took a world tour whose purpose was, according to various sources, to allow him to inspect mining operations in Canada in which his father held an interest, to help him forget an unhappy love affair, or to fit him for a specialty in maritime law. In the course of his voyage, he made the acquaintance of Joseph CONRAD, then the mate of a merchant vessel. Conrad was another man whose first career did not perfectly suit him, and they became close friends as each embarked on the career of the writer.

G.'s first books, including the Kiplingesque stories *From the Four Winds* (1897) and the novel *Jocelyn* (1898), were published under the pseudonym John Sinjohn. G. did not truly find his voice or begin his frank explorations of the intersections of sexuality, property, and law in English life until after his father's death in 1904. At that point, G. became financially independent, but, more importantly, he became free to take the steps in his personal life that he had delayed for fear of distressing his father. In 1905, he married Ada Pearson, the divorced wife of G.'s first cousin. At the time of their marriage, G. had been involved with Ada for ten years. Starting with *The Island Pharisees* (1904), he began publishing under his own name and basing his works on modern social problems, but his first great success came in 1906, when he published the first of his works describing the Forsyte family, *The Man of Property.*

That first installment of what would become *The Forsyte Saga* shows that G.'s training in law was not wasted, for its central theme is how law warps human relationships and can be used by the powerful to force others to submit to their will. Soames's rape of his wife Irene (a version of Ada) shows G. addressing the issue of spousal rape and the law's attitude toward it many decades before judges and legislators would tackle the question. During the same period in which he was writing his first important novels, G. also

began his career as a playwright. His plays also often involve the law, and several, starting with *The Silver Box* (1906), include courtroom scenes. In later plays, such as *Strife* (1909), which depicts a mining strike, *Justice* (1910), a tragedy that prompted calls for prison reform, and *Loyalties* (1922), an exploration of anti-Semitism, G. addressed social problems and demanded social change with all the intensity of Bernard SHAW, but without his sparkling dialogue and tolerance for ambiguity.

During World War I, G. attempted to enlist in the army, but was deemed unfit because of his poor eyesight. He instead first worked with the Red Cross, serving at a hospital in France and aiding Belgian refugees, and then wrote, mostly about the needs of disabled soldiers, for the Office of War Propaganda. Despite the antiestablishment thrust of his work, G. was offered a knighthood in 1918, which he refused. (G. accepted the Order of Merit in 1929, as well as many academic honors.) After the war, G. returned to his major work, which was the continuation of the story of the Forsytes in one of the great roman-fleuves of the 20th c. *In Chancery* (1920) and *To Let* (1921) trace the divorce of Soames and Irene, their second marriages, and the romantic involvements of their children. Two short stories were added as interludes when the three novels appeared as *The Forsyte Saga* in 1922.

While G. continued the story of the Forsytes, he also wrote fiction outside the series, as well as more plays and many essays. He was active in several reform movements and agitated for the rights of authors. He was one of the founders of PEN, the international writer's organization, and donated the monetary portion of his Nobel Prize award to it. The next Forsyte novels, *The White Monkey* (1924), *The Silver Spoon* (1926), and *Swan Song* (1928), were collected as *A Modern Comedy* in 1929, and a book of short stories, *On Forsyte Change* appeared the following year. They reveal a change in attitude that had already begun to appear in the last books of the *Saga.* G.'s vision of the Forsytes, and of his own family, on which they are partially based, become more sympathetic. Rather than appearing as imperfectly cultured people obsessed with their rights of property, they become more attractive figures who embody some of the good values of England. Even Soames wins some of the reader's sympathy.

While G.'s works continued to attract readers after his death, his reputation did not begin to revive significantly until *The Forsyte Saga* was produced as a television serial by the BBC in 1967. That production was hugely popular across the world, and since it appeared, readers have never forgotten the involving soap opera qualities of G.'s fiction, even as scholars have begun to recognize them as serious and skillful explorations of moral questions involving law and society.

BIBLIOGRAPHY: Barker, D., *The Man of Principle: A View of J. G.* (1963); Dupré, C., *J. G.* (1976); Gindin, J., *J. G.'s Life and Art* (1987); Holloway, D., *J. G.* (1969)

BRIAN ABEL RAGEN

GARDAM, Jane

b. Jean Mary Pearson, 11 July 1928, Coatham, North Yorkshire

G. started writing fairly late in life, at the age of thirty-nine, but she has since produced an impressive body of work. Many of her novels deal with children and adolescents, and, indeed, it is often difficult to tell whether the primary audience is intended to be adults or children. Her first novel, *A Few Fair Days* (1971), recounts a series of episodes in the life of its young protagonist; the book begins when Lucy is five and follows her up to the age of eleven. Jessica Vye, the main character of *A Long Way from Verona* (1971), is an aspiring writer. What makes these first two books noteworthy is their use of young narrators who are able to speak convincingly to both child and adult readers. Another recurring element in G.'s fiction, which is apparent in *A Long Way from Verona,* is the presence of characters who revel in the art of story-telling. The Whitbread Award–winning novel *The Queen of the Tambourine* (1991), for example, is about an eccentric woman who creates an elaborate fantasy life in her letters, and the children's story collection *Through the Dolls' House Door* (1987) features a group of dolls who tell each other stories to pass the time. After *A Long Way from Verona,* G. produced two coming-of-age novels, *The Summer after the Funeral* (1973) and *Bilgewater* (1976), both of which feature beautiful protagonists making the transition to adulthood. G. can truly be considered a "writer's writer": Many of her works refer directly or obliquely to classic works of literature. *The Summer after the Funeral* borrows much of its atmosphere from Emily BRONTË's *Wuthering Heights*; the title story of the collection *The Sidmouth Letters* (1980) features a novelist who seeks to protect the reputation of Jane AUSTEN from a character assassin; and *Crusoe's Daughter* (1985) features a young protagonist who comes to identify with the isolated hero of Daniel DEFOE's novel. While literary, however, G. is highly accessible, and whether she is writing for children or adults, she has proven herself an engaging and craftsmanlike writer.

GARFIELD, Leon

b. 14 July 1921, Brighton, Sussex; d. 2 June 1996, London

G. went to art college before serving in the Medical Corps during World War II. He became a full-time writer in 1966. His fictions, set in the 18th c. and featuring stage coaches, dark streets, and candlelit rooms, are quality reading for young adults. His plots are exciting: they deal with prison escapes, missing heirs, stolen wills, pickpockets (*Smith,* 1967), highwaymen (*Black Jack,* 1968), but usually involve moral choices. *The Strange Affair of Adelaide Harris* (1971) is a comic, fast-moving farce set in Regency Brighton and *The Apprentices* (1978; repub. as *Garfield's Apprentices,* 4 vols., 1979) are short stories. With Edward Blishen, G. produced two volumes of re-created Greek myths, *The God beneath the Sea* (1970) and *The Golden Shadow* (1973), and in 1980 G. earned some measure of literary notoriety by completing Charles DICKENS's *The Mystery of Edwin Drood.*

GARNETT, David

b. 9 March 1892, Brighton, East Sussex; d. 17 February 1981, Le Verger Charry, France

Although G. wrote and edited many volumes, perhaps none are as compelling as *The Golden Echo* (1953), *Flowers of the Forest* (1955), and *The Familiar Faces* (1962), which together form a three-volume autobiography and one of the best accounts written about life in the BLOOMSBURY GROUP. A fourth volume, *Great Friends: Portraits of Seventeen Writers* (1980), is also autobiographical, presenting candid accounts of his literary friendships. G.'s novels received less attention from critics and the public, although two satirical fantasies—*Lady into Fox* (1922) and *A Man in the Zoo* (1924)—were admired for their unusual plots. In *Lady into Fox,* a man's wife quite suddenly, as the title suggests, changes into a fox. *A Man in the Zoo* is also explained by the title: it is the story of a one-man homo sapiens exhibit in the London Zoo. G. also edited *The Letters of T. E. Lawrence* (1938) and *Carrington: Letters and Extracts from Her Diaries* (1970). His other novels include *Aspects of Love* (1955), *Two by Two* (1963), and *A Clean Slate* (1971).

The son of translator Constance Garnett, G. studied at the Royal College of Science, Kensington, before his connections with Bloomsbury diverted his career path to literature. As Robert Skidelsky mentions in his biography of John Maynard KEYNES, G. was remarkable in his Bloomsbury social circle because he was neither a Stephen nor a Strachey nor a member of the Cambridge intellectual society known as the Apostles. "Bunny," as his Bloomsbury friends called him, was, however, a handsome young man and was sought out, perhaps for that reason, by Bloomsbury figures Adrian Stephen, Rupert BROOKE, and James and Lytton STRACHEY. His four autobiographical volumes are noteworthy foremost for their candor, a candor suggested even in the illustrations, which include a nude photograph of himself. G. admits his reputation as a womanizer was deserved but does not shy away from his homosexual liaisons, including those with Bloomsbury figures Duncan Grant and Francis Birrell.

It was to G. that D. H. LAWRENCE made his now-famous remark about black beetles. G. had taken Birrell with him for an overnight stay at Lawrence's home. Afterward, Lawrence wrote to G. describing how unbearable it was for him to think about "men loving men." He continued, "Never bring B. to see me any more. There is something nasty about him, like black-beetles. He is horrible and unclean. . . . Go away, David, and try to love a woman." Instead of taking the advice, G. ended his visits with Lawrence instead. "Lawrence's letter upset me, frightened me and made me angry," he writes in *Great Friends*. "I was frightened because my friends were homosexuals, and I thought that if Lawrence went on talking like that, it might lead to prosecution, or do their reputations harm. But Lawrence's letter made me angry for his daring to tell me that I had always known the wrong people . . . I decided that my friendship with Lawrence was over." G. notes that later, when *The Rainbow* was seized by authorities on obscenity charges, "It was the loathsome black-beetles who rallied in defence of Lawrence."

One of the more notable romantic episodes described in G.'s autobiographies is his cohabitation with Grant and Vanessa BELL. All three were lovers at one time or another, and when Grant and Bell had a daughter, G. said he would marry her when she was older—which, in fact (and much to the dismay of her parents), he did.

Like Brooke, G.'s literary importance is eclipsed to a large degree by his own life and personality. Fortunately, life and art merge in his four engaging autobiographical volumes.

BIBLIOGRAPHY: Edel, L., *Bloomsbury: A House of Lions* (1979); Roche, P., *With Duncan Grant in Southern Turkey* (1982); Skidelsky, R., *John Maynard Keynes*, vol. 1 (1983)

KEITH HALE

GARRICK, David

b. 19 February 1717, Hereford; d. 20 January 1779, London

After attending the grammar school at Lichfield, G. at nineteen went to the academy opened in summer 1736 by Samuel JOHNSON, seven years older. On 2 March 1737 Johnson and G. left Lichfield for London. G.'s first play, *Lethe, or Aesop in the Shades*, was perf. at Drury Lane on 15 April 1740, and in March 1741 he performed in pantomime, replacing a sick actor. He was an immediate success, and was soon praised by Alexander POPE. G. adapted numerous plays and was joint author with George Colman the Elder of *The*

Clandestine Marriage (1766). Among G.'s farces and afterpieces are *The Lying Valet* (1741), *Miss in Her Teens* (1747), *A Peep Behind the Curtain* (1767), *The Irish Widow* (1772) and *Bon Ton or High Life above Stairs* (1775). He was also responsible for several ill-judged adaptations of William SHAKESPEARE, and a new version of William WYCHERLEY's *The Country Wife,* retitled *The Country Girl.* He bequeathed his valuable collection of old plays to the British Museum.

GASCOIGNE, George

b. ca. 1539, Cardington, Bedfordshire; d. 7 October 1577, Stamford

Among the first great dramatic innovators of the Elizabethan Age, G. created, translated, or suggested plots and dramatic forms that would inform and influence the works of many playwrights to follow him, including William SHAKESPEARE. An adventurer and riotous liver, G.'s life is marked by incident. Shipwrecked, held in a Spanish prison, prevented from taking a seat in Parliament because according to the petition he was "defamed . . . for manslaughter . . . a common Rymer . . . a notorious Ruffian . . . a Spie . . . [and] an Atheist and Godles personne." G. nevertheless ingratiated himself with the mighty of his time and counted among his patrons, sympathizers, and friends William of Orange, Sir Humphrey Gilbert, the Earl of Leicester, and ELIZABETH I herself.

Of noble birth, G. was educated at Trinity College, Cambridge, and Gray's Inn. He spent his early career as a hanger-on in the court as protégé of Arthur, Lord Grey of Wilton, among others. During this time, he earned a reputation as a poet. He married in 1566 and became stepfather to the poet Nicholas Breton. In that same year, he wrote two of his most influential works. Both *Jocasta* (with Francis Kinwelmershe, perf. 1566) and *The Supposes* (perf. 1566) were created as intramural entertainments for the gentlemen of Gray's Inn and Elizabeth's court.

Jocasta continued the tradition begun in Thomas SACKVILLE and Thomas NORTON's *Gorboduc* of rendering English drama in blank verse. It also adhered to the Senecan notions of play construction. G. thereby helped to establish the precedents established by *Gorboduc* that would be followed throughout the period. *Jocasta* also represents the first known English adaptation of a Greek play. Although the play is now generally accepted to be a translation from Lodovico Dolce's Italian play, *Giocasta*, the title page (pub. 1573) claims it is "A Tragedie written in Greke by Euripides, translated." The play traces its roots through *Giocasta* to Euripides' *Phoenissae* and thereby sets a new English standard of play craft by authorizing the importation of Continental and ancient texts onto the English stage.

The Supposes represents the first prose comedy written in the English language. It also introduced the use of the prose prologue onto the English stage. Based directly on Lodovico Ariosto's play, *I Supposi-ti* (1509), *The Supposes* demonstrates a clear link between the Italian school, with its roots imbedded deeply in commedia dell'arte, and early English comedy. In *The Supposes*, G. reinvents and develops the New Comedy tradition for the English stage and consequently comes closest to neoclassic comedy of any of the pre-Jonsonian plays. Much of Ben JONSON is anticipated here. The play strictly observes the neo-Aristotelian unities of time, place, and action. The play takes place in the street before the houses of the main characters Erostrato and Damon. Only a few hours pass in the play: from before dinnertime to just after dinnertime, and the action flows in an undisturbed, linear manner. Despite these restrictions, the comedy develops in an unforced, character-driven manner that would become the hallmark of the best of the comedy to follow. So well developed was the comedy in *The Supposes* that it was transplanted a generation later to become the Bianca subplot for Shakespeare's *The Taming of the Shrew*.

G. had another possible influence upon the later period of play development. As a masque writer, G. devised *The Montague Mask* (1572), *The Woodstock Entertainment* (1575), and *The Kenilworth Entertainment* (1575, again with Kinwelmershe). Although it is probably too much to suggest that G. anticipated or influenced the Jonsonian masque, he certainly helped to keep the masque form fresh and in favor. Several commentators have additionally suggested that the eleven-year-old Shakespeare could have been witness to the *Kenilworth Entertainment* and recalled it in Oberon's "fair vestal" speech from *A Midsummer Night's Dream*. Although G.'s dramatic production was small, it had a strong influence upon the developing drama.

BIBLIOGRAPHY: Johnson, R. C., *G. G.* (1972); Prouty, C. T., *G. G.* (1942); Tannenbaum, S. A., *G. G.* (1942)
                                    BRIAN JAY CORRIGAN

GASCOYNE, David [Emery]
b. 10 October 1916, Harrow; d. 25 November 2001, Isle of Wight

G. is the most famous English surrealist poet. Educated at Salisbury Cathedral Choir School and the Regent Street Polytechnic in London, he published his first book, *Roman Balcony and Other Poems* (1932), at age sixteen and a novel, *Opening Day,* in 1933. Soon he mixed in literary and artistic circles in London and in Paris, translating many modern French works. *A Short Survey of Surrealism* (1935) established him as an authority. His surrealist poems,

Man's Life Is This Meat (1936), coincided with the first international surrealist exhibition in London, which he helped organize. He became a friend of Salvador Dali, Max Ernst, André Breton, Paul Eluard, and Pierre Jean Jouve. *Hölderlin's Madness* (1938), *Poems 1937–1942* (1943), illustrated by Graham Sutherland, and *Night Thoughts* (1956), a long poem commissioned by Douglas Cleverdon for the BBC, are his most important works. G. became internationally celebrated as poet and translator. His *Collected Poems* (1965) were reprinted six times and revised 1970 and 1978. G.'s work often deliberately frustrates the reader's expectations of meaning and coherence. In 1996, G. was made a Chevalier dans l'Ordre des Arts et Lettres by the French Ministry of Culture for his lifelong services to French literature.

GASKELL, Elizabeth Cleghorn
b. 29 September 1810, London; d. 12 November 1865, Holybourne, Hampshire

One of the 19th c.'s most accomplished novelists, short story writers, and biographers, G. was the daughter of William and Elizabeth Stevenson, both of whom were strongly committed to Unitarianism, an extremely tolerant version of nonconformist Protestantism that stresses reason and freedom of thought and argues that God exists only in one person, thereby denying the divinity of Christ. Unitarianism was to be one of the greatest influences on G.'s life, thought, and works and is seen in particular in the panaceas she offers for the social ills explored in her novels.

A year after her birth, G.'s mother died (the importance of mothering and nurturing resonates throughout her writings) and G. was subsequently reared by an aunt in Knutsford, Cheshire, a town later fictionalized firstly as Cranford and then as Hollingford in *Wives and Daughters* (2 vols., 1866). While later living with a cousin in Newcastle-upon-Tyne, G. met her husband William, a Unitarian parson and professor of English history and literature at Manchester New College. From the time of their marriage, the couple lived and worked in the north of England, and despite the death in infancy of two of their six children, G. successfully combined her competing roles as wife, mother, and writer.

G. began her professional career writing stories for the radical *Howitt's Journal* and continued to produce skillful, innovative stories throughout her life, with some nearing a novella in length. They often demonstrate acute psychological insight and emphasize that need for tolerance that is fundamental to her work as a whole. "Lizzie Leigh" (1850) records a mother's harrowing search for her lost daughter with poignancy and depth, while the startling "Old Nurse's Story" (1852) has remained one of the most frequently anthologized Victorian ghost stories. Indeed, many of

G.'s stories are heavily influenced by Gothic elements, "The Crooked Branch," first published as "The Ghost in the Garden Room" (1859), being a narrative of the return of the dead and "Lois the Witch" (1859) depicting the hysteria of the Salem witch trials. The longer story *My Lady Ludlow* (1858; repub. as *Round the Sofa*, 1858) reworks the anxieties concerning social change embedded in many of G.'s novels.

G.'s first novel, *Mary Barton*, was published in two volumes in 1848 at the end of the decade known as the "hungry 40s." Belonging to the "condition of England" genre, it vividly depicts the horrific working and living conditions experienced by Manchester industrial laborers, whom G. had been able to observe firsthand through her philanthropic work. The novel delineates the growing agitation of the Chartist movement as a group of workers decide to kill Henry Carson, their employer's son and the potential suitor of the eponymous heroine, as a warning that their class will no longer tolerate such treatment. John Barton, Mary's father and an otherwise upstanding man, is elected to perform the murder and the remainder of the text details the various attempts to work through the resulting personal and political consequences.

In the preface, G. wrote that she knew "nothing of Political Economy or theories of trade," but nevertheless the work received great acclaim from other writers and social commentators, including Charles DICKENS (who subsequently asked her to write for *Household Words* and *All the Year Round*), Thomas CARLYLE, and Charles KINGSLEY, and was reprinted three times in two years. Factory owners were, unsurprisingly, less impressed by the revelations of exploitation and class antagonism, but G. returned to interrogate further industrialization and laissez faire economics in her third novel, *North and South* (2 vols., 1855). This text opposes the industrial north with the rural south, "masculine" aggression and more "female" empathy, and as with *Mary Barton*, it takes a strong, confident heroine, Margaret Hale, to bring about a reconciliation between these opposites. Margaret initially detests the politics of industrialism in Milton-Northern, supporting the mill workers in their grievances, but when the mill owner, Thornton, is attacked by a mob, she protects him. Through a subsequent series of romantic misunderstandings set within this wider political context, Margaret helps Thornton to realize the need for a more humanitarian attitude toward his workers. Central to both *Mary Barton* and *North and South*, then, is the call for greater communication and understanding between employer and worker, achievable, G. suggests, through adherence to Christian principles (at the close of *Mary Barton*, for example, the dying John Barton is forgiven by Carson's father).

The controversy surrounding the industrial novels was mirrored by the controversy surrounding G.'s second novel, *Ruth* (3 vols., 1853), which like a number of key women's texts written during the 1850s (for example, Elizabeth Barrett BROWNING's *Aurora Leigh*), deals with the issue of the unmarried mother. Seduced and abandoned by a country gentleman, the young seamstress Ruth Hilton is placed center stage by G. in order to give the "fallen woman" a new dignity while exposing the double standard that automatically condemns the woman and the illegitimate child, and exploring how she can be "redeemed" back into society through religion, maternal love, and philanthropic work. Despite the fact that G. seemed to conform to literary expectation by having Ruth die at the close (an ending Charlotte BRONTË particularly disliked), the engagement with some of Victorian society's major taboos meant that *Ruth* was widely condemned, although it was to have a great influence on subsequent women writers and social reformers like Josephine Butler.

That same year saw the publication in volume form of a very different text, *Cranford*, which had been running in *Household Words* since December 1851. Focusing on a community of women who are mildly satirized, *Cranford* became G.'s most popular work after her death when critics attempted to downplay the harder-edged controversial writer. Recent rereadings, however, have drawn attention to the (somewhat ambivalent) proto-feminist elements, the antilinear narrative, and the social anxieties lying behind its apparently conservative plot.

In 1850, G. had met and become firm friends with Charlotte Brontë, and after Brontë's death in 1855, her father asked G. to be her biographer. The result was the monumental *Life of Charlotte Brontë* (2 vols., 1857), one of the major 19th-c. literary biographies, but G. again faced controversy on its publication with threats of libel over the representation of the Clergy Daughter's School at Cowan Bridge and the affair between Branwell and his employer Lydia Robinson (later Lady Scott), and she was therefore forced to remove passages after the second edition. As later biographers have demonstrated, the *Life* is particularly problematic in its insistence on making Charlotte into a Christlike figure of stoicism and duty, facing hardship at every turn, while omitting almost any consideration of Charlotte the highly successful author. Certainly the work was responsible for initiating many aspects of the mythologization that has dogged Brontë criticism ever since, but its overall power and attention to detail mean it remains a great testament of respect for one woman writer by another.

In 1863, G. returned to fiction with *Sylvia's Lovers* (3 vols.), an historical romance set in 18th-c. Monkhaven (Whitby) that focuses on Sylvia's complex interrelations with two men, her cousin Philip who tricks her into a loveless marriage, and Charley Kinraid, the man she loves but who she thinks is drowned. Played out against scenes of the contemporary whaling industry and the cruel realities of pressganging, *Sylvia's Lovers*, like all of G.'s fictions, clearly demonstrates how personal and political histories are intertwined, not least in the mirroring of the pressgang victims' entrapment with Sylvia's own private entrapment. The novel is a complex and accomplished work, but to date it has received relatively little critical attention in comparison with the industrial and social problem fictions.

G.'s final novel, *Wives and Daughters*, remained unfinished at her sudden death from heart failure in 1865, although it had been published in installments in *Cornhill Magazine* since August 1864 and was clearly near completion. More in the style of Jane AUSTEN than G.'s previous works, *Wives and Daughters* is another historical novel but this time a domestic social comedy which draws in large part on post-Darwinian thought. Indeed, Roger Hamley is in many ways a reflection of Charles DARWIN, G.'s own cousin. The novel charts the development of Molly Gibson into a confident young woman, while interrogating issues around successful motherhood (Molly is another Victorian motherless heroine), the place of money and status in marriage choice, and the new Darwinian sense of change and adaptation.

G.'s oeuvre is wide-ranging in setting and style and is currently witnessing a resurgence in interest from feminist and new historicist critics. Her agendas and arguments are often complex but at the heart of all her work lies a call for tolerance and understanding and the need to grant a voice to those groups traditionally silenced in literary discourse.

BIBLIOGRAPHY: D'Albertis, D., *Dissembling Fictions* (1997); Hughes, L. K., and M. Lund, *Victorian Publishing and Mrs. Gaskell's Work* (1999); Nestor, P., *Female Friendships and Communities* (1985); Schor, H. M., *Scheherazade in the Marketplace* (1992); Spencer, J., *E. G.* (1993); Stoneman, P., *E. G.* (1987); Uglow, J., *E. G.* (1993)

SIMON AVERY

GAWAIN-POET, The

A small and undistinguished manuscript written toward the end of the 14th c. in the northwest Midlands of England, with a dozen clumsy illustrations, holds four of the best poems written in English about 1375, equal in quality to the contemporary poetry of Geoffrey CHAUCER and William LANGLAND, but very different in style and attitude. The manuscript, numbered Cotton Nero A.x. in the British Library, was unknown until a limited edition of one of them, *Sir Gawain and the Green Knight*, was printed in 1839. The other three, now called *Cleanness* (sometimes *Purity*), *Pearl*, and *Patience*, were first edited by Richard Morris for the Early English Text Society in 1864, as was *Sir Gawain*. After that, neglect again, until after World War II a slow start was followed by the current flood of editions, translations, and critical books and articles. The bulk of modern response testifies to the poems' unified complexity of medieval courtliness, chivalric romance, devout expository biblical narrative, wide reading, profound religious conviction, occasional comedy, and ironic commentary. These unusual poems could possibly be by different authors living very closely together, but almost all scholars believe them to be by the same poet. Another poem, *St. Erkenwald*, with some slight resemblances, occasionally attributed to him is not by him.

We shall never know his name, nor for what courtly provincial audience he wrote. Although his writing has a strong personal stamp, and he appears to address an audience directly, he does not place himself in his poetry as a "real" locatable person, like so many 14th-c. European and English poets (e.g., Chaucer and even Langland) though in *Pearl* he represents himself as a father mourning the death of his not quite two-year-old daughter. His personality is in a sense his narrative, whose sources are biblical stories, French secular Arthurian romance, and scriptural commentary. Compared with Chaucer, he is old-fashioned in the best sense, and has a genius for courtly description (disdained by Chaucer), for rough landscapes, wintry weather, stormy sea unknown in Chaucer's work. The joy of feasting combines with the anguish of parenthood and sense of the wrath of God. Suffering is taken as inevitable—his art is to overcome it. His style of mind, of verse, as of his dialect, is toward the north rather than the south of 14th-c. England, whether he were cleric or lay, traveled or not. Probably, he was a member of some baronial household. In no other medieval English author is the life of the nobility so idealized into Christian form. With him the center of the Christian life is moved from the monastery or abbey to the baronial or even royal court. He is no Christian leveler or puritan for whom the poor bulk large, like Langland.

This richly paradoxical author, whose poems combine oral with literate elements also combined his albeit slightly old-fashioned European sources with the traditional English alliterative style of verse derived from OLD ENGLISH but looser in syntax and structure, different from the new metrical regularity of verse and rhyme derived from modern French sources as developed by Chaucer. It is also different from Langland's alliterative verse whose vocabulary was easily understood in the London area. Our poet's style is an elaborate yet forceful mixture of words of more northern currency, some from Old Norse, but also with French words; a poetic diction, where alliteration demands many synonyms and variants. This differs greatly from that East Midland dialect in which Chaucer wrote and is the ancestor of modern standard English.

The *Gawain*-poet (so called for convenience, or *Pearl*-poet) after his two greatest poems thus at first makes heavy demands on a modern reader, amply repaid however when met.

Concern with courtesy both secular and spiritual, honor, truth in its widest sense (*trawthe*), and purity runs through all four poems with varied emphasis. The order in which they were composed is not discernible. In the manuscript, they appear in the order *Pearl* (1,212 lines, a dream vision that is also an elegy and theological argument); *Cleanness* (1,812 lines, based on biblical accounts of disasters caused by impurity); *Patience* (531 lines, telling Jonah's need for patience); *Sir Gawain and the Green Knight* (1,530 lines, a chivalric adventure showing the saving power of chastity). All titles are editorial.

Sir Gawain opens with the Christmas and New Year's festival at the young King Arthur's court. On New Year's Day, before the feast begins there bursts rudely into the hall a huge knight on horseback, green in clothing and complexion, carrying a holly branch and great axe. He challenges the court to a Beheading Game—cut off his head, then if he survives, he to cut off the head of his opponent in a year's time. The young Gawain (a different character here from the gallant womanizing hero of French romance) volunteers. Headless, the Green Knight hurtles out. Gawain has only to ask to find out where he lives for the return blow. Gawain sets off next All Saints' Day (November 1) and after skirting North Wales crosses the Wirral to the less specifically named rough hill country (probably where the poet lived), a harsh journey in bad weather. On Christmas Eve, he comes to a splendid castle where he is courteously and lavishly entertained. After Christian worship and games, he is anxious to resume his search but his burly, genial middle-aged host tells him that the Green Chapel where the Knight resides is only two miles away. On December 29, 30, and 31, the host goes hunting while Gawain luxuriates in bed. On each morning, the beautiful young wife of the host comes to his bedroom and by suggestive witty remarks, countered with equal courtesy and wit by Gawain, tries to seduce him. He will only accept on the first morning one kiss, the second two, the third three. He has made a jesting pact with his host that each shall give to the other what he has "won" that day—the Exchange of Winnings. Gawain gives kisses in exchange for the host's quarry whose hunting has been done in parallel with Gawain's evasions. (Kissing between men was a normal greeting in medieval times.) But at her last attempt the lady persuades Gawain to accept the gift of her silk belt that she claims will magically preserve his life. This he conceals from his host. On New Year's Day, Gawain faithful to his promise (and uncertain of the belt's value) goes to the Green Chapel (probably an ancient burial mound) in a valley by a stream and

a cliff (cf., the Manifold Valley in Derbyshire). The Green Knight frighteningly appears. Gawain kneels in the snow, bare headed. After two feints, the Knight inflicts only a slight flesh wound on Gawain. The feints match his resistance to seduction, the slight wound his partial failure in accepting and concealing the lady's belt, which has no power at all. But Gawain's chastity has saved his life, for the Green Knight is no other than his host, who has tried to trap Gawain through the wiles of his wife, but appears quite cheerful about failure, names himself as Bertilak, and praises Gawain's truth. Gawain is mortified by even partial failure, but on his return to Arthur's court is praised by all. The folkloric type of plot is masterfully handled to cover some curious gaps in logic interspersed with vivid descriptions of people, festival, armor, wintry weather, and rich in implicit and symbolic meanings. The style is rich, written in blocks of four-stress alliterative lines varying from fifteen to twenty-seven lines long, each block accompanied by a single stress phrase (the "bob") and concluded with a rhyming stanza of four lines each with three stresses. The 101 stanzas is a symbolic number, and the last line echoes the first (as with *Pearl* and *Patience*). This is the best medieval romance in English.

Very different, and even more highly wrought, is *Pearl*. It opens with the poet, sometime in August (probably the 15th, the festival of the Assumption of the B.V.M.) in an "arbor" praising a most precious pearl, which he has lost there. Sick at heart he falls asleep in that flowery spot, whence his spirit springs to a landscape of jewels, with a stream. On the other side appears a young and beautiful lady, gracious in royal array, to his awe. They greet each other and she gently reproves his mourning. He defends himself—she is both his greatest joy and sorrow, and now she is in bliss, although not two years old when he lost her. It becomes clear that she is the soul of his beloved dead daughter. But how can she who died so young be now exalted in heaven, a queen no less? She expounds the parable of the laborers in the vineyard (Matthew 20:1–16), justifies their unequal payment, applies the parable more widely. Some critics find this a barren stretch in an otherwise deeply moving poem but it is the intellectual backbone of the whole. All comes through God's grace, which is his courtesy. The poet represents himself as a father slow to understand, inclined to correct his daughter. It is she who instructs him for she is a queen in heaven where all are both equal yet in hierarchy, a spiritualized medieval court. Finally the poet sees her in procession as one of the 144,000 virgins, brides of Christ (as in Revelation, 14), in the jeweled city, New Jerusalem. Overcome with longing he flings himself across the stream to join her, only to wake from his vision, and learn to bear his sorrow sustained by love of God. The depth of feeling is conveyed by the most elaborate skill in verse, as of the "jeweller" he calls himself who makes a rich setting for his Pearl. The poem has 101 stanzas of twelve lines each with rhyme and some alliteration, in groups of five except for one of six, the groups linked by repeated lines ("concatenation"). There are thus 1,212 lines, and 12 × 12 = 144. These are all significant numbers, and an ancient way of creating effect as in parts of the Bible, especially Revelation (in the Latin Vulgate called Apocalypse). Number symbolism balances theological exposition but all rests on a tender paternal anguish.

Cleanness also seems to have number symbolism marked by manuscript divisions based on the golden section. The poem invokes many concepts of "cleanness"—physical, metaphorical, spiritual. Like *Pearl* and *Patience*, it opens with the clarion call of the key word. "Clannesse," the theme of this poem, then refers to God's wrath at the uncleanness in so many ways of the world. The poet moves rapidly into the parable of the Wedding Feast to which the invited guests refused to come. The point is that one of the pressed guests came in dirty clothes and was punished accordingly (and to modern notions unjustly, but we are in the realm of didactic folktale, not novelistic probability and the dirty clothes signify sin). God is likened to some 14th-c. feudal lord. We then move to an account of the iniquities committed that the Flood was sent to punish, and there is a moving and surprisingly sympathetic account of the suffering of the drowned. The story of the visit of angels to Abraham and the destruction of Sodom and Gomorrah for their sexual uncleanliness ends in a striking description of their desolation. We then turn to Balshazzar who in his feast pollutes the holy vessels from the temple of the Jews. The poet describes the glories of the feast with real relish, as concrete if somewhat heightened a description of a joyous medieval royal or high ecclesiastical feast as we can find in English. Here, the poet who normally places courtly life in a spiritual and aesthetic mold, for a change visits terrible punishment by enemies on the land because of the defilement of the sacred vessels. Other biblical episodes support the main stories. God is seen in a highly personal way as a rather testy feudal king with a passion for "cleanness." The poem is rich in imagery of flood and feast, fire and disaster, yet in its vigor and positive feeling it avoids a depressing negativity. It praises what is good, most notably and surprisingly sexual pleasure, though sodomy brings disaster. Again the vigorous alliterative style is rich in energy and beauty, and like *Patience* without stanzaic pattern.

The hero of *Patience* is Jonah, not the usual Job, and Jonah is forced against his will to be patient, as, says the poet in a rare personal aside, is he himself in his poverty. (One of the poet's constant themes is the need to do what we do not want to do, or it will be the worse for us. Except in *Cleanness* the lesson is accepted.) In *Patience*, a spare biblical narrative of folkloric nature is as usual filled out with illustration, motive, and exposition in a lively style. Jonah is called on by God to preach to the sinful Ninevites. He is angry and disobedient, afraid for his safety, absurd in thinking he can escape God's all-seeing eye. He is a great arguer with God. To escape Jonah takes ship. The mechanics of embarkation are vividly described and even more the storm that God sends and causes the sailors to throw Jonah overboard, bringing immediate calm. God sends a whale to swallow him, both saving and punishing him further in the whale's stinking stomach. God orders the whale to spew the repentant Jonah up on the shore of Nineveh itself after he has spent three days in the whale's belly (traditionally a "type" or forecast of Jesus's resurrection). Jonah cleans his clothes, a metaphor for cleaning himself of sin (an image also in *Cleanness*), and prophesies God's vengeance on Nineveh to such effect that the inhabitants repent and avoid disaster. But Jonah is annoyed and accuses God for being so courteous as to let them off. Jonah goes off to sulk in an "arbor," where God sends a woodbine first to shelter him, then wither in heat, and Jonah again reproaches God and wishes he himself were dead. God justifies his exercise of mercy and tells Jonah, and perhaps the poet, not to be so angry but endure suffering patiently. This lively poem is in the same four-stress alliterative line as *Cleanness*. The vigorous dialogue between God and Jonah is based on the Bible but more personal, and with an ironically humorous undertone. Action, speech, description, are vivid, and exposition is livened by human feeling. This shortest and least elaborate of the four poems shows doctrine as entertaining and God more merciful than *Cleanness*.

BIBLIOGRAPHY: Andrew, M., and R. Waldron, *The Poems of the Pearl Manuscript* (1978; rev. eds., 1987, 1996); Brewer, D., and J. Gibson, eds., *A Companion to the Gawain-Poet* (1997); McColly, W., "The *Gawain*-Poet," in Helterman, J., and J. Mitchell, eds., *Old and Middle English Literature, DLB* 146 (1994): 156–71

DEREK BREWER

GAY, John

b. 30 June 1685, Barnstaple, Devon; d. 4 December 1732, London

Though somewhat ignored by critics and scholars of the 19th and 20th cs., poet and dramatist G. resided at the center of the lively culture of early-18th-c. England. His sustained personal and literary association with Alexander POPE and Jonathan SWIFT, and his membership in the Scriblerus Club placed him in the heart of the literary establishment and evinces his contemporaries' high regard for his work. The ironic and satiric voice that characterizes much of his best work (often directed toward the Whig ministry) is also what, ultimately, limited his political advancement in the world of patronage and court favors. His most successful and frequently studied text, *The Beggar's Opera* (1728), introduced the dramatic form that anticipated the modern musical comedy. In all his works, he displayed a keen concern with issues of class and social relationships, experimented with genre, and maintained a self-consciously reflexive tone that provides his texts with a distinctly "modern" sensibility.

In his life as in his writing, G. had a familiarity with a diversity of classes and cultural milieus. Born in the port town of Barnstaple, his classmates included Aaron Hill, author, publisher, and center of his own literary circle (that included Richard SAVAGE) of the 1720s. G. went briefly into the silk trade, but went to London in 1706 where he worked for Hill who helped launch his writing career. His early poems like "Rural Sports" (1713) possess a hybridity and, like much of his work, simultaneously embrace and parody classical conventions such as the georgic and the pastoral. This approach anticipates the more sophisticated nature of *The Sheperd's Week in Six Pastorals* (1714), which provides a picture of shepherds and milkmaids in a realistic rather than idealized way. While imitating the pastoral, G. also infused it with contemporaneous references making it distinctly modern and political. Similarly, *Trivia; or, The Art of Walking the Streets of London* (1716) details a walk through London by day and by night. By focusing on the wide range of individuals encountered, the poem becomes a meditation on class, and urban and social topography.

His early dramatic works are similarly suggestive. *The What D'Ye Call It* (1715), a one-act farce used as an afterpiece, positions itself parodically between "high" and "low" art; its subtitle, *A Tragi-Comi-Pastoral Farce*, suggests its experimental form. A play-within-a-play acted by the tenants of Sir Roger, it addresses such serious issues as the treatment of common soldiers and the predicament of pregnant servants. Similarly, *Three Hours after Marriage* (1717), in which Pope and Swift had a hand, satirizes dramatic conventions and subverts established audience expectations. The old Dr. Fossile has just married the young Susannah Townley, but has yet to consummate the union. Her other lovers plot to gain access to her through unusual disguises and, in the end, Townley is revealed to be already married. The absurd plots of these pieces suggest G.'s consistent generic experimentation as well as his preoccupation with complicating social and literary hierarchies.

His best theatrical piece is *The Beggar's Opera*, arguably the most influential drama of the century. A satire on Italian opera, class relationships, and the Whig ministry of Robert Walpole, it played almost continuously throughout the 18th c., and has been widely produced and adapted. *The Beggar's Opera* is a ballad opera, a hybrid genre that uses well-known popular tunes as the basis for its music. Focusing on the criminal underworld, the play compares the activities and attitudes of the upper classes with those of the poor—all act in a predatory and duplicitous manner. As "Newgate pastoral," the play focuses on the romantic and financial relationships between Mr. Peachum, who earns his living by receiving stolen goods and informing against his clients, his daughter Polly, and Macheath, the dashing highwayman who she marries. Their union is complicated by Macheath's arrest and the fact he has also impregnated Lucy Lockit, whose father runs Newgate prison. This play had a notable influence on Bertolt Brecht. The sequel, *Polly* (1729) transports Polly and Macheath to the West Indies, but its production was banned. Contemporaneous with these plays, G. also published *Fables* (1727), which were tremendously popular and published throughout the 19th c.

BIBLIOGRAPHY: Dugaw, D., *Deep Play: J. G. and the Invention of Modernity* (2001); Nokes, D., *J. G., a Profession of Friendship* (1995); Winton, C., *J. G. and the London Theatre* (1993)

CATHERINE INGRASSIA

GAY MALE LITERATURE

Even if no coherent "tradition" of gay male literature has existed from the Middle Ages to the present, certain continuities have endured. These include the idea that desire reaches its natural fulfillment in sexual acts, that friendship is a type of love in which love and sex are intrinsically related (indeed that they often lead to each other), and that a life bereft of sex—not merely sexual acts but sex broadly construed to include friendship and camaraderie—is greatly impoverished. The resonance of each idea varies from age to age, century to century, as do its moral consequences and types of expression. But the ideas themselves endure, like hills and mountains in set landscapes.

The difficulty has resided in fixing the limits, let alone deciding what is, or is not, gay. If physical bodily touch is removed, then the territory of both love and sex greatly expands. Provided that genital contact is not a necessary precondition, and deep emotional attachment is sufficient, then the domain of the male homosexual—or gay male—becomes so much enlarged that some term such as "queer" is needed to denote the expanded area. Conversely, labels such as homoerotic and homosocial will be necessary to describe the degrees of attachment: the former connoting almost any same-sex attachments, the latter these attachments viewed in their social contexts and settings. But we must not become obsessed with the definitions, or consumed by the metaphysical problems involved; it is just that some conceptual framework is necessary to understand how a British tradition of gay male literature developed.

Three main ideas were already present in the Renaissance, enhancing the likelihood of these continuities. Despite their having been transformed over time by social and political circumstances, it makes sense to consider that a significant part of body of British literature, or a queering of English literature, has endured as one of its mainstays. The sheer number of major writers who have, in one way or another, been homosocial, homosexual, or—more recently—openly gay is remarkable. The further fact that "gay" is a recent word, coined in the 20th c. to describe groups of people partaking of same-sex relations without the pathological stigma of the medical "homosexual" is less important for our purposes. Friendship, love, desire, sex, and sexuality are the mainstays of the tradition. Therefore, we need not become vexed that this recent coinage ("gay") is being unwisely applied. It would be another matter if we were historians concerned here with a tradition of British homosexuality that had suddenly become "gay" in the 20th c.

The Renaissance displays all three themes in its literature, especially its drama. Christopher MARLOWE's *Edward II* is a play containing many major themes, like court politics, but it equally highlights the intense friendship, leading to sex, of its king and his favorite, Gaveston. The king, who claims that his love for the young man leads him naturally to physical desire, has no intention of denying himself the pleasure. Marlowe's plays provide so many examples that whole books have been written about them. But in Marlowe the need for the expansion just discussed requiring new words makes itself felt: it is not merely the themes that are embodied in characters but the idea of desire itself which is enlarged; so much that William SHAKESPEARE's plays can be divided into groups based according to their degree of same-sex attachment: homosocial for those like, homoerotic for those that, homosexual for those who actually seem to penetrate each other, and perhaps even "gay" for those plays and characters where some element appears to resemble the modern condition, as it so often does in Shakespeare.

Shakespeare's sonnets, however, pose another type of problem. They have been the source of debate about the identity of the dedicatee, "W. H.," who may or may not have been male. Those favoring a male, argue that the youth is proof of Shakespeare's own desire and orientation (the fact that a man married in Elizabethan England did not preclude homosexual activity), and use this biographical material as evi-

dence of pervasive same-sex attachments throughout his oeuvre. But whether or not male, the sonnets themselves are rich in same-sex desire. Several are explicit, suggesting that—whatever his orientation—Shakespeare was profoundly practiced in the arts of masculine love and masterful in describing its attachments.

Renaissance pastoral elegists, imitating the Greek bucolic poets, also rhapsodized about their same-sex lovers, especially when mourning them. Some, like Edmund SPENSER, descanted widely, listing male friends in *The Faerie Queene*, as well as in his elegy for Sir Philip SIDNEY. The death of the friend was felt so poignantly that poetry alone could be the balm to its wound. This is the image John MILTON incorporates in "Lycidas," his famous pastoral elegy written for his late dead friend Edmund King. This Greek elegiac tradition continued to be imitated by British poets: Thomas GRAY cultivated it in the "Ode for the Death of Richard West" and the "Elegy Written in a Country Churchyard," as did, later on, Percy Bysshe SHELLEY for John KEATS in *Adonais* and Alfred, Lord TENNYSON, for Arthur Henry Hallam in *In Memoriam*. The form fused elegy (lament) and pastoral (nature and the countryside) to adumbrate loss; its constant jeremiad is that loss of the beloved resembles deprivation of nature, or even the death of nature itself.

During the English Restoration commencing in 1660, the drama incorporated some of these themes. Unlike the lament-mode of pastoral elegy, its concern was the psychological effect of the friend, or beloved, on others, especially on those courting or married couples. Nathaniel LEE was a dedicated dramatist who wrote eleven tragedies, mostly based on Greek and Roman historical figures and always dealing with impassioned friendships and loves. Not even his eventual dementia and declared insanity, however, could disguise the homosexual element of his works. In almost all his tragedies, especially *Sophonisba* and *The Rival Queens*, his male-male friendships are erotically charged and teeter toward the sexually illicit en route to their tragic ending. No wonder that many were banned or censored. Comedy also conveyed these themes but in other keys. William WYCHERLEY's *The Country Wife* seems to be a play about cuckoldry but abounds with male characters unusually absorbed in each other: Pinchwife (jealous), Sparkish (foppish), Horner (described as "bad as an eunuch" who pretends to be impotent), Harcourt (ambiguous). Horner may be castrated but is actually more heavily invested in all-male bonds of homosocial connection than in female romance. No wonder the play ends in his sending Margery Pinchwife back to her husband. These gender arrangements, often farcical but immensely clever, continued in other of Wycherley's plays, especially *The Plain Dealer* and *Love in a Wood*.

Restoration and Augustan poetry was more diverse in its treatment of the three overarching themes. If the Earl of ROCHESTER's scabrous verse often refers to bisexual urges and outright homosexual actions, he hardly does so in a persecutory sense but to flaunt creative possibility. Persecution was rare, so a literature of libertinism arose: Charles II, the king, promoted the hedonism of his day and may have indulged himself while encouraging his courtiers and writers to display their best erotic imagination. Even a poetic-playwright as staunchly conservative as John DRYDEN (in the sense that he followed the neoclassical forms and returned to historical themes) constructed same-sex couples hewn out of the timber of intimate friendship. The "Club of Scriblerians" (composed of authors Jonathan SWIFT, John ARBUTHNOT, Alexander POPE, John GAY, Thomas PARNELL, and several others who dined in London after Queen Anne's death to exchange literary ideas) were themselves rather homosocial, yet could be scathing to others. Pope's *Epistle to Dr. Arbuthnot* contains the most vehement homosexual attack of the era against Lord Hervey: "Sporus, that curd of Asses milk" who had eight children but who was nevertheless—according to Pope—an "Amphibious Thing! that acting either Part,/The trifling Head, or the corrupted Heart!/Fop at the Toilet, Flatt'rer at the Board,/Now Trips a Lady and now struts a Lord." Pope's rhetoric is dazzling, his motives complex, and he may even have been pointing a finger at himself; either way, they demonstrate how themes of male love and friendship could be inverted and used against public figures.

London, the capital where most of these writers were based, was being transformed by "molly-clubs" (sexually transgressive establishments where older men met younger men, often called them by female names, and routinely paid for their versions of sexual pleasure) and new underground gay networks ruled by money and rank. It is therefore hardly surprising that the earliest British novelists felt some compulsion to include the London homosexual underworld in their social commentary: the difference is that their treatment is less nuanced than the poets'. Daniel DEFOE's "catamites" (a passive sodomite: a vast new vocabulary arose by ca. 1700 providing code words to heap disdain on same-sex arrangements) are as stereotyped as those in "Ned" Ward's molly-houses. When Henry FIELDING refers in *Tom Jones* to "a bunch of h—-s" he means "hermaphrodites" and hurls opprobrium. Tobias SMOLLETT's "pathics" in his early poetry and the array of gay characters in *The Adventures of Roderick Random* are entirely repulsive. None more so than "Captain Whiffle" who dresses in the "French manner" and dabs himself with French perfume. Smollett's men are among the first to have somewhat rounded personalities, and there may be biographical reasons why he was so ho-

mophobic. Poet Charles CHURCHILL's night-tour in *The Rosciad,* first published in 1761, a satire on London, also presents arrays of gay figures, stereotyping them as viciously his contemporaries did.

Why then are there are no sympathetic representations in these early novels and satires? Horace WALPOLE and his "Quadruple Alliance" of schoolboy friends, which included Gray, typified these school romances based on all-male friendship whose subtle dynamics may now be lost to time. When the group traveled together to Europe on the Grand Tour, they fell in and out of love as ardently as any romantics, but not one would identify "The love that dare not speak its name." Gray came closest in his Latin odes and English elegies (the genre that flourished in the Renaissance). All four sustained impassioned correspondences lasting into adulthood when back in England, as did Lord BYRON and his school chums, but when Walpole took to writing "Gothic fiction" he disguised and transformed same-sex elements so no one could tell. It has taken Freudian critics of the 20th c. to decode its meanings. So too Matthew "Monk" LEWIS in his Gothic writings, where the varieties of disguise are as transformative through character, place, and atmosphere. If Walpole had disguised Manfred's only son in *The Castle of Otranto* as a woman, his readers might have succumbed. Lewis actually disguised the promiscuous "Matilda" as a boy, but the ruse notwithstanding his readers considered the book largely unreadable rather than primarily indecent. Marcel Proust was not yet born: another century was needed before this strategy of gender disguise would be used. Walpole's weird play *The Mysterious Mother* in hindsight almost seems a homosexual tragedy in pre-Freudian Gothic disguise. William BECKFORD, the author of *Vathek,* was also of this cast but his imagination was more Oriental than Gothic; exotic in its dreamy, almost surrealistic, landscapes. His imagination was fired by young swarthy men raised south of the Alps and, preferably, to the east.

English ROMANTICISM bred its own versions, especially through literary collaborations and networks of writers. Precedent had existed, but the character assassination evident in Pope's Sporus-invective was losing its force as secular life in the capital cities—London and Edinburgh—expanded its notions of sexuality. The young Samuel Taylor COLERIDGE and William WORDSWORTH collaborated for years, were not homosexual in any sense, but a case can be made that they were homosocial in the intensity of their shared intellectual agendas. Yet by the Regency period it was becoming evident that some terms like "third sex" (bisexual outside of plant classification was not coined until the 1890s) was needed. If the key to Romanticism is the self's discovery of its interior soul, then this inner self was, as several early-19th-c. commentators noted, essentially androgynous: neither male or female but partaking of each and compassionate to the desires of the other.

As the British Empire continued to expand and extend its sway around the globe, and the T. E. Lawrences conquered the Arabian continent, dreams of the Other, the non-European, became entrenched as objects of sexual desire. Victorianism was diverse, including even many sexual perspectives that are broadly reflected in Victorian literature; it was also a body of codes and laws that gave permission or withheld it. English society now tightened its grip. Despite Jeremy Bentham's prior claims for reform of the buggery laws it touted Christian morals, legislating what could, or could not, be sexually licit. Paradoxically some brands of literature idealized this colonial Other (different racially, religiously, ethnically, every way) while other types turned inward, almost monastically, to an idealized ascetic self located in Roman Catholicism. If Rudyard KIPLING's verse romanticizes subcontinent Indians and Ganges-worshipping raj princes, Gerard Manley HOPKINS's celebrates the naked body of Christ. Hopkins's "Lantern out of Doors" resurrects Christ's erotic physique and the carnal nature of spirituality. But the Aesthetes, in contradistinction, were more nostalgic, glancing back to an Italian Renaissance when human activities were governed—so the line went—by the beautiful and sublime. Walter PATER's study of Johann Joachim Winckelmann, a German aesthete devoted to all things Italian (half in love with men, he was stabbed in a Venice bar), located the erotic within the aesthetic. His *Studies of the History of the Renaissance* was as erotically charged.

The "Wilde phenomenon" changed this landscape. Oscar WILDE had studied with John RUSKIN at Oxford and read Pater's influential works; he was very young and impressionable when he met Walt Whitman, a transformative moment of his life. His affinities with Whitman were numerous; he saw a new side of gay masculinity, a world of possibility opening up he had not imagined in hierarchical, class-riddled England. Wilde was brazenly homosexual and sufficiently courageous to defend his sexuality in the "name of art" when taken to court by the father of Lord Alfred Douglas ("Bosie"), Lord Queensberry, for "posing as a Somdomite [sic]." Some of this penchant derived from his innate theatricality: his life and works—especially the repartee in his plays and *The Picture of Dorian Gray*—fused ideas of "art-for-art's-sake" with articulation of this "love" that "dared not speak its name." Wilde lost his legal case in the fin de siècle but has triumphed over time: no other gay icon of the last century rivals him. So far as Victorian social and legal reform is concerned, it is unthinkable to ponder homosexual pathways without him, just as it is impossible to imagine his literature—plays, poetry, his erotic dramatic fantasy *Salome*, his prison justification to Bosie called *De Profundis*—

apart from the liberal spirit of his sexuality. In this sense his "life" was his greatest art, as he himself once quipped, forever demonstrating by example what the limits of art could be for a sexual iconoclast.

Other Victorian authors—John Addington SYMONDS (an Italophile who wrote a daring homosexual biography of Michelangelo), Edward CARPENTER and Havelock ELLIS—contributed their fair share of reform, but society had to understand what same-sex love was before it could take an informed stand. In the aftermath of Darwinian evolution, sexologists claimed that homosexuals were "uranians" or "urnings:" new evolving "species" selected out by the laws of survival of the fittest. For a generation after the 1870s, these theories were suspect.

The ideas were too theoretical for most writers who preferred case histories, especially live ones: for example, E. M. FORSTER visited Carpenter in 1913, who sympathetically popularized the "intermediate sex" in his books. Forster went to visit him in the Midlands and watched him and his lover cooking and doing housework. One darned socks, the other wore an apron. Forster was struck, returned to Cambridge that night before the outbreak of war, and began to write *Maurice*, his only explicit same-sex love story. As he wrote, he discovered that it was not an "evolving third sex" that mattered but attraction based on age, physique, smile, and social class. His story ends unhappily, yielding to the temptation that same-sex love enacts tragic experience. Published posthumously in 1971, *Maurice* contained a candid preface by Forster explaining the delay and his sense of the insurmountable homosexual predicament.

As war clouds gathered, D. H. LAWRENCE became preoccupied by the new theories of sex and published a highly eroticized account in 1913 of *The Prussian Officer* who becomes fatally attracted to his orderly. The setting and characters were timely. Soldiers and life in the trenches were destined to fix public attention for the next four years, many of these writers, like Rupert BROOKE, expounding on male bonding under life-or-death circumstances. This war genre was in stark contrast to the cheerful boarding-school fiction of the Edwardians, an adolescent genre gurgling over with robust energy. Most of these writers conveyed an underlying pessimism: if not entirely tragic in their vision of same-sex relations, they were nevertheless fatalists about the difficulty of transforming their infatuation to enduring love.

By the turn of the 20th c., Wilde dying in 1900, it was clear he had been a martyr to the homosexual cause, placing his life on the line for beliefs he thought would eventually prevail. Twenty years later, in the aftermath of World War I it was less clear: the law had not been reformed since 1885; no new improvements were legislated. Life for gays in Britain was stifling, forcing them into exile, as reflected in their literature. If school and university afforded some freedom of desire, as in Alec WAUGH's *The Loom of Youth*, adulthood proved constraining even for aristocrats. This was the world into which "Christopher and his kind" (Isherwood's phrase)—Christopher ISHERWOOD, W. H. AUDEN, Ronald FIRBANK, Stephen SPENDER—were born. They fled to postwar cabaret Berlin and wrote autobiographical works such as (Isherwood's) the appropriately titled *A Single Man* (1964), *Goodbye to Berlin* (1939), and *Christopher and his Kind* (1976), retrospects of the Twenties' and Thirties' hedonistic exile they now nostalgically remembered.

Other English writers moved abroad in self-imposed exile—Norman DOUGLAS went to Italy where he wrote his novels, W. Somerset MAUGHAM to the French Riviera—to escape the England which inhibited their homosexual proclivity. They especially worried that their creative urge would dry up if their sexuality was stifled. Auden had a particularly oblique attitude to his sexual bind: impressed with the neo-classical wit of the Augustan poets, he nevertheless sought to remove BIOGRAPHY from poetry and discovered a technique of allusion in his early verse behind which to conceal his living experience. It worked: only recently have critics decoded it. Many writers, like the Isherwood circle, had met at Oxford or Cambridge, places they idealized as a prelapsarian Arcadia they were some day destined to lose, even if none could have predicted that global cataclysm after 1939 would again deter their free movement. Evelyn WAUGH resurrected this romance about dreaming spires in *Brideshead Revisited*, ripe in romantic homosexual infatuation among a privileged upper class. But Auden migrated across the ocean to start a new life with his young American lover Chester Kallman, never to return, and Isherwood followed later and became a naturalized American citizen.

Each generation seemed to produce its martyrs to the cause followed by backlashes and devastation: Wilde among the Victorians, a bevy of Edwardian war poets, Isherwood and his kind in the interregnum of two wars, and now—in 1939—yet another catastrophe. No one could augur (although they may have suspected) that the Germans would murder thousands of "pink triangles" as part of their European holocaust. While millions were being gassed in concentration camps, and others at home billeted and starving, writers did not stand aside. They wrote, even from the camps, their private memoirs and accounts. Yet the faces of public sexuality also became inexorably altered in a world of heterosexual dictatorship. After the Germans retreated and cities ceased smoldering, postwar writing courted the gay as a type waiting to be discovered. Some, like George ORWELL in *Nineteen Eighty-Four,* located him in a dystopian landscape lorded over by Big Brother, where he seemed not to belong, even four decades into future time. Other writers were more domestic and familiar, anticipating that peace would bring emancipation and new freedoms. All implied that a literature as sensitive to social conditions as "gay lit" had to be guided by political swings.

It was therefore predictable that writing in the aftermath of the Nazi debacle would be different. More domestic and local, less frenetic and political, it sought to explore gay character more than anything else. It was as if its writers took a deep sigh: they had been waiting for this chance, now they had it. Angus WILSON wrote *Hemlock and After*, a social anatomy that character Bernard Sands presides over; even so he cannot reconcile the sexual antipathies of different types of "queens" despite the new postwar sexual fluidity. *The Middle Age of Mrs. Elliot* is altogether different, arguing through its plot for the legitimacy of the stable and caring gay couple, David and Gordon. Compare these with Terrence RATTIGAN's plays *Deep Blue Sea* or *Separate Tables* in the same period and it becomes clear how diversely the homosexual in society was being configured.

No equivalent of 1950s Macarthyism swept Britain; if anything, the tide looked as if it was going out to sea in an opposite direction liberating the homosexual. In the 1960s, gay writers openly established themselves in Britain, such as James Purdy whose *Eustace Chisholm and the Works* (1967) explores the brute violence inherent in all forms of masculinity. The Wolfenden Act of 1967 decriminalized homosexuality in private (in return for making it part of the Lewd Persons Act in public); for the first time permitting gay persons like Quentin Crisp to come out publicly with impunity.

This was easier in theory than practice. Joe ORTON, for example, was one of the most promising young playwrights of that decade, the author of *Loot* and many other plays. His comedies are dark, well constructed, and imbued with autobiographical content about the ardor of his homosexual life, as are *Loot* characters Hal and Dennis. Partnered up with another writer who was jealous of his career, Orton had his brains beaten out at thirty-three with a hammer. Biographical reconstructions have demonstrated how much is revelatory of himself, especially the domestic poverty, professional discouragement, but—most of all—his explorations of the kinship of death and eros, and the near impossibility of forging successful homosexual partnerships. Here was a uniquely gifted playwright, already established, in search of a surrogate family, which was not to be. Families, real and imagined, seem to have been the nub of the matter. Was Bruce CHATWIN's unrelenting travel, for instance, a substitute for families, a theme suggested in his novel *On the Black Hill* and also evident in his travel journal *In Patagonia*? Chatwin's "travels" hardly reproduce the Enlightenment Grand Tour and 20th-c. "Erotic Tour," but authenticate places in their own right while sustaining the renewed 20th-c. obsession with self-imposed exile. If writers in the century from Wilde to Chatwin, had to leave England to nurture their rightfully reclaimed sexualities, they learned that a home away from home can often be a better mother land.

The 1970s, with their feel of gay emancipation and the blossoming, finally, of "gay lib" felt less turbulent, but with the 1980s new perils arose through disease and backlash. HIV and AIDS—the gay plague of that decade—targeted homosexuals primarily and a parallel homophobia arose in response. This was part of a more generalized homoerotophobia or fear of all things gay. It was the view that gayness was contagious and that no one was immune; just breathe the same air and you could succumb. Much AIDS literature presented these themes, usually in disgust and weariness. Yet committed gay novelists continued to publish domestic novels about ordinary gay life and its vicissitudes, as in the novels of Francis KING.

If AIDS memoirs swept the U.S. in the decade after the first diagnosed cases in 1981, a smaller number were written in Britain. Less hysteria prevailed there, as did the temperature of shock in its same-sex literature. Whitman may have been prophetic for America, but he lived only a century ago, whereas sexually impassioned friendships had been known in England since Edward II's day. Besides, America had never had its own brand of Wilde: it took AIDS to provide the illusion that America had now caught up. If James Baldwin had discovered his sexuality in post-war Paris, where he "came out" and wrote *Giovanni's Room* (1956), gay Americans in the 1980s were still going abroad to find themselves. But most gay British writers stayed at home, exploring themselves in the big metropolis.

The interior journey to the center of the "gay self" has been so layered it is hard to describe it. Derek Jarman, for example, wrote *Modern Nature* (1991), as a factual *aide mémoire* of his medical struggle; one of dozens of similar poignant AIDS narratives on both sides of the Atlantic spurred by the terror of death. Entirely different, however, were Alan HOLLING-HURST's bitingly comic and—alternatively—lyrical plots, capturing what it is experientially to be "gay": the phenomenon itself. His *Swimming Pool Library* is somewhat inescapably nostalgic; set in central London in the 1970s—the heyday of promiscuity—it captures episodic states of the free-and-fancy-loose. *The Folding Star*, in contrast, scrupulously charts Edward Manner's sojourn as a visiting teacher in Belgium, but without the protagonist ever being able to remove his

eyes from the bulging bodies of his attractive male students. Hollinghurst's novels justify their overwritten style by the verbal virtuosity required to pinpoint these different ways of living. These contrasts—Jarman and Hollinghurst—may form the basis for an aesthetics; they also demonstrate, in brief, the remarkably diversity of gay literature of the 1970s and 1980s.

An entry of this type can only hope to present a few of the main lines of this body of literature: a sense of the tradition (to the limited extent that it was a coherent current unified by the themes announced at the start), discussion of its historical and political contexts in the belief that most literature is written in response to these developments, and a sense of the difference with the American scene. Both literatures, British and American, cultivated many of the same themes, but it would be wrong to think they evolved similarly or simultaneously or that pressing matters in one era in one country mirrored those in the other; and just as wrong as to claim that (for example) the curve of American gay fiction was similar to British in the 19th c. The differences were more pronounced, then and now.

BIBLIOGRAPHY: Bray, A., *Homosexuality in Renaissance England* (1982); Bremmer, J., *From Sappho to de Sade: Moments in the History of Sexuality* (1989); Clum, J. M., *Acting Gay* (1992; rev. ed., 2000); Cohen, E., *Talk on the Wilde Side* (1993); Coote, S., ed., *Penguin Book of Homosexual Verse* (1983); Crompton, L., *Byron and Greek Love: Homophobia in 19th-Century England* (1985); Dowling, L., *Hellenism and Homosexuality in Victorian Oxford* (1994); Duberman, M. B., et al., eds., *Hidden from History: Reclaiming the Gay and Lesbian Past* (1989); Goldberg, J., *Sodometries* (1992); Greenberg, D. F., *The Construction Of Homosexuality* (1988); Haggerty, G. E., *Men in Love* (1999); Hyde, H. M., *The Love that Dared Not Speak Its Name* (1970); Mason, M., *The Making of Victoran Sexual Attitudes* (1994); Meyers, J., *Homosexuality and Literature, 1890–1930* (1977); Rousseau, G. S., *Perilous Enlightenment* (1991); Rowse, A. L., *Homosexuals in History* (1977); Sedgwick, E. K., *Between Men: English Literature and Male Homosocial Desire* (1985); Sedgwick, E. K., *Epistemology of the Closet* (1990); Sinfield, A., *The Wilde Century* (1994); Smith, B. R., *Homosexual Desire in Shakespeare's England* (1991); Weeks, J., *Sex, Politics, and Society* (1981); Woods, G., *A History of Gay Literature* (1998)

GEORGE ROUSSEAU

GEMS, [Iris] Pam[ela]
b. 1 August 1925, Bransgrove, Hampshire

G. is best known for her dramatic treatment of biographical subjects and in particular for her revisionist feminist slant on biographical "greats." Although her writing career did not begin until G. was in her forties—like so many women in the 1950s she gave up work to raise a family (of four children)—she has achieved a prolific output of some twenty plays and several adaptations of European classics. Reflected in G.'s work is her experience of a time before the Second Women's Liberation Movement when women had far less reproductive control over their bodies and far fewer opportunities, especially if, like G., they were working- rather than middle-class women.

Following a move to London in the 1970s that brought her into contact with fringe theater and the Women's Liberation movement, G. began to write for theater. Early plays include *Betty's Wonderful Christmas* (perf. 1972), *The Amiable Courtship of Miz Venus and Wild Bill* (perf. 1973), *My Warren* and *After Birthday* (perf. 1973), and *Go West, Young Woman* (perf. 1974). It was against the backdrop of 1970s FEMINISM that G. wrote *Dusa, Fish, Stas and Vi* (perf. 1976; pub. 1977), a dramatization of an all-female community of four very different women who find common ground in their struggle to survive in a "man-made" world. Although criticized at the time by some feminists for the suicide of its central protagonist Fish (signaled in the original title of the play, *Dead Fish*), the play has since been widely accepted as a feminist classic.

The sometimes irreconcilable demands for women between their political and personal lives (the reason for Fish committing suicide), is an issue to which G. returned in her dramatization of *Queen Christina*, the first play by a woman to be staged by the Royal Shakespeare Company in Stratford (perf. 1977; pub. 1982). Epic in form and content, *Queen Christina* takes an historical subject as a vehicle for contemporary feminist issues: women at "war" with their reproductive bodies and doing "battle" in a world where power is invested in all things masculine. G.'s dramatic portrayal of the cross-dressed queen was also designed to engage deconstructively with Greta Garbo's rather more glamorous cinematic portrait (1933).

By contrast, *Piaf* (perf. 1978; pub. 1979), G.'s second production for the RSC and arguably her most successful and best-known play, focused on a working-class, rather than royal, subject. Despite differences in class, however, Christina and Piaf have a lot in common: as women who are insecure about their physical appearance in a world where women are judged by their looks, and as women who are desperate to secure loving relationships in which they are loved for themselves, rather than for what they represent, or can be used for. The Brechtian style of *Piaf* constantly serves to point to the "gap" between desire and reality; between the legend of the singer who has "no regrets" and the painful reality of Piaf's desire

to be loved, her drug addiction, illnesses, and early death.

Demythologization is also a strategy in G.'s *Camille* (perf. 1984; pub. 1985), her rewrite of Alexandre Dumas's *The Lady of the Camellias* that desentimentalizes the representation of the 19th-c. courtesan Marguerite Gautier. In *The Danton Affair* (1986) and later in *The Snow Palace* (1998), G. engages with the work of another writer: the Polish woman playwright Stanislawa Przybyszewska and her dramatization of the French revolution.

G. acknowledges the influence of movie stars on her generation—a generation who grew up with the cinema, rather than television. She has a particular interest in Marlene Dietrich, which is detectable in *The Blue Angel* (1991), G.'s version of Heinrich Mann's *Professor Unrat* (1905), and central to *Marlene* (1996). Written in two parts, the first set backstage where an elderly Dietrich reflects on her career, and the second that re-creates a Dietrich concert, *Marlene* served as a star vehicle for actress Siân Phillips.

Given the woman-centered direction of G.'s theater, her biographical portrait of the 20th-c. painter Stanley Spencer, which opened at the Royal National Theatre in 1996, may seem rather surprising. For G., however, the connection between *Stanley* and some of her other biographical subjects is class rather than gender. G. likens Spencer to Piaf "both little squits but both geniuses." While *Stanley* was G.'s first authored stage play at the National, it was certainly not the first time she had explored masculinity: *Franz into April* (perf. 1977) looked at the pioneer Gestalt therapist Fritz Perls; *Aunt Mary* (perf. 1982; pub. 1982) explored gender through the lives and relationships of two male transvestites; and *The Project* (perf. 1976), subsequently revised as *Loving Women* (perf. 1984; pub. 1985), examined the triangular relationship of one man and two women.

G. has always argued that writing is a difficult career choice for men and women, but especially for women given the unequal opportunities of the theater profession. The inequalities of a male-dominated world are a constant feature of her stage plays that show, through her biting, hard-edged, socialist realism, the enduring difficulties for women in both their private and public lives. What interests G. the most are those women whom she describes as "pathfinders," who attempt, not always successfully, to carve out different paths for themselves and for other women.

BIBLIOGRAPHY: Aston, E., "P. G.: Body Politics and Biography," in Aston E., and J. Reinelt, eds., *The Cambridge Companion to Modern British Women Playwrights* (2000): 157–73; Reinelt, J., "The Politics of Form: Realism, Melodrama, and P. G.'s *Camille*," *W&P* 4, 2 (1989): 96–103; Stephenson H., and N.

Langridge, *Rage and Reason: Women Playwrights on Playwriting* (1997): 88–97

ELAINE ASTON

GEOFFREY OF MONMOUTH
b. ca. 1100, Monmouth?; d. 1154 or 1155, Llandaff, Glamorgan, Wales?

Twelfth-century chronicler and a central figure in Arthurian tradition, G. was probably born in Monmouth, South Wales. The historical sources show G.'s principal association for much of his life to have been with Oxford where he appears to have been active as a teacher and to have been associated with the Augustinian secular college of St. George. His three extant works, all Arthurian in subject matter, were produced between 1129 and 1151. The most famous, the *Historia Regum Britanniae* (wr. ca. 1136) is one of the central texts of the Middle Ages and the *locus classicus* for the Arthurian story as received by later medieval tradition.

A patriotic impulse underlies the work that responds to a need for the indigenous British and Norman settlers alike to articulate a national identity and myth of origin. G.'s *Historia* details a lineage of British kings from the establishment and settlement of Britain by Brutus, descendant of Aeneas of Troy, onward. The reigns of kings Cymbeline, Gorboduc, Lear, and Vortigern are thus documented but the *Historia* gives its most animated and embellished regal portrait in treating the life, betrayal, and death of King Arthur.

G.'s narrative establishes the key framework of the Arthurian story as it would endure throughout the English Middle Ages (with the notable exception that Sir Lancelot is not yet numbered among the king's retainers). Upon his accession, Arthur repels Saxon invaders and suppresses northern rebellions, his skill as warrior enhanced by his sword Caliburn—a brand forged in the Isle of Avalon. The great British king takes a wife, Queen Guinevere, and establishes a period of peace during which his court is looked to as an exemplar of noble accomplishment. Later, he and his knights embark upon campaigns in Europe, subduing the forces of the Roman Emperor Lucius in Gaul and advancing into Burgundy. At this point of highest achievement, Arthur is betrayed by his nephew Mordred to whom he has entrusted the stewardship of the realm. The traitor usurps the Crown, pursues an affair with Queen Guinevere, and sponsors a Saxon invasion. Returning to face the traitor, Arthur makes his final stand at the battle of Camblam. He suppresses the rebellion but is grievously wounded; the king is carried away to the Isle of Avalon for healing. G.'s account does not invoke the possibility, cherished in folk tradition, of Arthur's future return—but it does not dispel it.

Aside from furnishing this amplified biography of the king in historical guise, G. effectively invents the figure of the wizard and prophet Merlin. A composite character drawn from a range of sources, Merlin is afforded a central role in the *Historia* while G.'s other compositions develop the figure still further. The *Prophetiae Merlini*, initially an independent text but later incorporated by G. into the *Historia*, records the prophet's foretelling of the overthrow of the Saxons and the resurgence of the Celts. The verse *Vita Merlini* (wr. ca. 1150–51) embodies legends of Merlin's madness and prophetic faculties.

Much attention has been paid to G.'s claim that his *Historia* is translated in turn from a certain Welsh book given to him by Walter, Archdeacon of Oxford. If such a source indeed existed, no trace of it can be discovered. The chronicler's identifiable sources are the 6th-c *De Excidio et Conquestu Britanniae* of Gildas, the 8th-c. *Historia Ecclesiastica Gentis Anglorum* of BEDE, and the 9th-c. *Historia Britonum* attributed to NENNIUS. Much translated, adapted, and paraphrased, G.'s text exerted a sustained influence into the late Middle Ages and well beyond, furnishing material for Sir Thomas MALORY's *Le Morte d'Arthur*; Edward SPENSER's *Faerie Queene*, and William SHAKESPEARE's *King Lear* and *Cymbeline*.

BIBLIOGRAPHY: Fletcher, R. A., *The Arthurian Material in the Chronicles* (1906); Parry, J. J., and R. A. Caldwell, "G. of Monmouth," in Loomis, R. S., ed., *Arthurian Literature in the Middle Ages* (1959): 72–93; Wright, N., ed., *The Historia Regum Britanniae of G. of Monmouth* (1985)

ROGER DALRYMPLE

GERHARDIE, William [Alexander]
b. 21 November 1895, St. Petersburg, Russia; d. 15 July 1977, London

Early in his career, G. befriended Katherine MANSFIELD and John Middleton MURRY who encouraged his development as a writer and helped to arrange for publication of his first novel, *Futility* (1922), based in part on his experience as a military attaché during the Russian Revolution. His other novels include *The Polygots* (1925), the experimental *Resurrection* (1934), and *Of Mortal Love* (1936). Following the publication in 1939 of his biographical study *The Romanovs*, G. became increasingly reclusive and his projected tetralogy called "This Present Breath" was left incomplete at the time of his death. Several chapters of the work were anthologized in *The Wind and the Rain*, published in 1962.

GIBBON, Edward
b. 8 May 1737, Putney; d. 16 January 1794, London

Like John MILTON, like John BUNYAN, and like James BOSWELL, when we speak of G. we speak of a particular book. Published in six volumes, *The History of the Decline and Fall of the Roman Empire* (1776–88) is conventionally regarded as the finest achievement of English historiography, a monument of the European Enlightenment, and a prose EPIC of outstanding literary quality. While its sheer length has sometimes deterred the audience it deserves, each generation of readers has discovered amid its multifaceted surfaces qualities that appeal to its own sensibility and circumstances. Thus, among more recent enthusiasts have been the practitioners of the magic realist school of South American fiction, far removed from either 18th-c. rationalism or the Augustan turn of G.'s pen. Writers such as Jorge Luis Borges and Gabriel García Márquez have expressed admiration, seduced perhaps by the labyrinthine yet sublimely moth-eaten grandeur G. imparts.

It is unusual, in modern times, for an historian to travel so widely. Even Thucydides, Xenophon, and Tacitus, once the staple of a liberal education, have become the preserve of academe. Too much contemporary history is written either from a narrow nationalist point of view or from an equally narrow concern for scholastic reputation, or from a shallow infatuation with "current affairs." All three pitfalls tempted G. Before he alighted upon Rome he considered, among other topics, writing a life of Sir Walter RALEIGH; his erudition, based partly on the labors of contemporaneous antiquarians, was such that his professional successors still struggle to fault him in his detail; and his truculent conservatism, in sympathy with "mankind," but never more than superficially exercised by the plights of "common man," is manifest in such phrases as "the tyranny of Democracy." For him, the revolutionaries who established the American republic or threatened the despotic French monarchy were simply representative of a new, fanatical barbarism. But, in his masterwork at least, if not in his much-loved but overly opinionated *Memoirs* (1796), G. set aside his parochial loyalties to produce a narrative of compellingly cosmopolitan reach.

G. belonged to the monied upper-gentry, and, but for his father's profligacy, would have continued so until his death. Aged fifteen, he enrolled at Magdalen College, Oxford. He fell foul of the authorities however by embracing Catholicism, at a time when English Protestantism still dominated English institutions. Expelled, he was sent by his father to study with Daniel Pavillard, a Calvinist minister in Lausanne. There he became fluent in French and acquired a solid grounding in the Latin classics. Back in England, he served as an officer in the Hampshire militia, and represented Liskeard as a member of Parliament during Lord North's ministry. His family's increasingly shaky finances were offset by his appointment as Commissioner of Trade and Plantations, but when North's administration fell in 1782 G. lost both his

seat and his position. Unable to sustain the style his birth had accustomed him to in London, he returned to Lausanne, lodging with his friend Georges Deyverdun while he completed his magnum opus. Because of his familiarity with Swiss and French intellectuals, G. could justly boast a Continental provenance. Of those authors who nourished his style and thought, Cicero, Pierre Bayle, and Montesquieu sit alongside Joseph ADDISON, Jonathan SWIFT, and Alexander POPE. He was also influenced by the "Scottish Enlightenment," notably David HUME, Adam SMITH, and the historian William Robertson. It took G. time however to settle on his eventual subject matter, initially suggested to him while visiting Rome during a "Grand Tour" undertaken in 1763–64.

In all, G. spent twenty years writing the *Decline and Fall*, which spans thirteen centuries, from the 2nd c. C.E. to the fall of Constantinople in 1453, in seventy-one chapters of which some may be read as self-contained essays. In addition, G. supplied some eight thousand footnotes. While these are often omitted in part or altogether from modern editions, among scholars and bibliophiles they have gained a lasting reputation, both for their acuity and their savage wit.

It is, though, the history proper that commands the greater respect. Taking the Rome of Marcus Aurelius and Antoninus Pius as the high point of civilization anywhere, G. traces the transformation of Europe into an assemblage of mainly bickering states in the wake of Rome's protracted demise. He does not attribute decline to any one cause. Rather he allows his net to spread wherever it is tugged, so that along the way the reader is greeted with generous accounts of such outlanders as the Slavs, Arabs, Turks, and Mongols.

Decline and Fall then is not simply the narrative of the struggles of a hard-pressed and usually corrupt court to maintain continuity, first in the west, then in Byzantium: rather it is big-picture history, sustained by G.'s unique capacity to enter into ironic intimacy with his chosen terrain. His set pieces, describing either individuals or events, whether the peculiarly licentious Empress Theodora, or the final hours of Constantinople itself, are models of dramatic description. Yet throughout his odyssey G. is equally equipped to draw out the ideas and preoccupations of each succeeding era, so that his is also an intellectual history, at the heart of which lies the evolution of Christianity.

About Christianity, G. entertains ambiguous views. On the one hand, he says that the slow disintegration of the Roman Empire is what enabled the spread of Christian practice. On the other, he says that the same practice, with its emphasis on the individual rather than the common good, hastened disintegration. Relentlessly, he satirizes the theological disputes and schisms that shaped the early church. Conversely, his treatment of Islam is sympathetic, and he entertains a guarded welcome for the uncorrupted lifestyles of some at least of the barbarian hordes who cumulatively unsettled the empire's frontiers.

Such unorthodox notions aroused the fury of church leaders. Nor did it help that G. frequently engages in felicitous exhumations of the manifold vices, sexual as well as political, of the figures who promiscuously crowd his pages. Yet what his own beliefs were remains obscure. His assault on Christianity is as a divisively institutionalized religion, not as a faith in itself.

In places, G.'s gift for irony borders on the facetious. History for him is serious, and sad, but also a measured riot. Where in retrospect he may be said to stumble is in his reluctance to concede that Byzantium as a civilisation in its own right was more than the detritus of what had gone before; or to allow that the competitive pluralism of post-Roman Europe was already prompting new strengths, among them the sort of philosophic free thinking that underpins his own project.

BIBLIOGRAPHY: Burrow, J. W., *G.* (1985); Low, D. M., *E. G., 1737–1794* (1937); Norton, J. E., ed., *The Letters of E. G.* (3 vols., 1956); Porter, R., *E. G.* (1988)

                                                    JUSTIN WINTLE

GIBSON, Wilfrid Wilson

b. 2 October 1878, Hexham, Northumberland; d. 26 May 1962, Surrey

G. is one of the purest examples of the Georgian poet, typified in the anthologies compiled by Edward Marsh; he was both writing in conventional verse forms and reacting against the neglect of modern themes in contemporary poetry. G. wrote poetry in the manner of William WORDSWORTH and Thomas HARDY and also showed a keen understanding of the lives of the working men and women of his time, beginning with studies of the rural poor and expanding to include office workers and industrial laborers. While he may not have had the academic, technical understanding of verse forms cultivated by his predecessors, in his best work he was skillful in his manipulation of form and texture, of imagery and language. Many of his best works are in dramatic form (although he always anticipated that his audience would encounter his work on the page rather than on the stage) because he had an ear for dialogue and the speech of the north of England. Whether in descriptions of rural life, his dramatic works or his war poetry, he had a simple, direct style that allowed him to empathize with a variety of people and to capture the essence of lives with an economy of language and imagery. Unfortunately, the poetry that seemed new and fresh at the turn of the century and in the face of Victorian decoration and fin de siècle decadence seemed outdated after the advent of the war and the

rising fame of the modernists. Most critics feel that G. simply outlived his time. He never adapted to new styles and subjects of poetry, although the psychological acuity of his best poems certainly matches the work of Robert Frost and others who worked in more traditional and conventional styles and managed to remain in the mainstream of poetic debate despite changing times.

G. began his career writing Tennysonian imitations, with volumes titled *The Queen's Vigil* (1902), *Urlyn the Harper* (1902), and *The Golden Helm* (1903). Although there are those who argue that G. always had an understanding of the lives of the poor, others argue that he made an abrupt shift in subject matter with the publication of *The Stonefolds* (1907) and *Daily Bread* (3 vols., 1910). In these volumes, G. anticipated the Georgian attention to the lives of the working poor in the north of England and displayed an unsentimental attitude to common people. The poems "Devil's Edge" and "The Hare" from the 1912 three-volume *Fires* exemplify his use of folk materials. "Devil's Edge" is a dramatic monologue. The speaker tells of a magical outdoor landscape "Between the sky and sea" where his sense of "starry peace" and holiness is disturbed by a mysterious "wild song." He hears first what he assumes to be the mournful song of a wife who has lost her husband; he later hears the song transformed to a lullaby for a sleeping child. It is this use of mystery that recalls folk ballads, although it is characteristic of G. to turn the mystery and tragedy of the story to a happy domestic resolution. "The Hare" is another dramatic monologue in which a young wanderer tells of releasing a hare and then being haunted by its presence. This story, where the hunter and the hunted become confused, is attached to the story of the speaker's encounter with a gypsy girl who is being threatened with marriage to a brutal man with the rather unfortunate moniker "Long Dick." The girl runs away with the smitten young hunter to avoid the unpleasant match. The two seem to live happily, but the young man continues to see the "hunted hare" in the girl's eyes. Ultimately, he realizes that the look is replaced with the contentment of motherhood and once again the hunter and the hunted seem to exchange roles.

Although some middle-class late Victorian critics found the work of G. brutal and vulgar, for the most part it seems rather gentle by today's standards. By all accounts, G. did not suffer or enjoy the life of wandering or the struggle to earn a livelihood often described in his poems; he did work for a while as a social worker in Glasgow, and his experiences may have aroused his liberal conscience. Poems about his own life tend not to describe hardship but to be tales of domestic bliss, such as "Roses" and "For G." from *Friends* (1916) or "The Stair" and "The Empty Cottage" from *Home* (1920). Indeed, many note the capacity for "negative capability" as one of G.'s signal talents, one best exemplified in his volume of war poems titled *Battle* (1915). The poem "Breakfast," for example, takes us to the front lines as the men eat on their backs and talk about football until one of them is killed when he raises his head to make a point. "Back" convincingly describes the soldier's inability to make sense of his experiences in battle in the context of his everyday life. Such moments are captured without sentiment in very matter-of-fact language that is all the more amazing because G. was never actually in battle. He also wrote poems in which his speakers exercise their own ability to transport themselves to altered states. One of his most famous poems, "The Ice Cart" (from *Friends*), describes a moment when a bored city office worker transports himself from the "grey and grimy heat" of the city to the beauty of an "everlasting Polar night" and imagines himself gamboling with seals and being transported "fathoms deep into a cold slumber" until the sound of a carter's whip startles him back to his present mundane reality. The poem exemplifies G.'s ability to transport himself in his imagination and to convey scenes with concise and sensual details.

Students of G. and the Georgians admit that the search for simplicity can create banal poetry. At his best, G. created poetry that followed Wordsworth's attempt to "choose incidents and situations from common life, and to relate or describe them, throughout, as far as was possible in a selection of language really used by men." In poems like "The Hare" or "Bloodybush Edge," he conveys his tales with a sense of detachment that combines a sense of the pathos of lives on the margins of society with a wry HUMOR. In other poems like "Solway Ford" or "The Blind Rower," he tends to mere pathos. He reached the height of his critical reputation in 1925 and after that time tended to repeat himself. While he remains a minor rather than an influential figure, his work certainly repays a closer reading for his dramatic and descriptive abilities.

BIBLIOGRAPHY: Dilla, G. P., "The Development of W. G.'s Poetic Art," *SR* 30 (January 1922): 39–56; Parker, R., *The Georgian Poets: Abercrombie, Brooke, Drinkwater, G., and Thomas* (1999); Ross, R. H., *The Georgian Revolt 1910–1922: Rise and Fall of a Poetic Ideal* (1965)

CATHERINE FRANK

GILBERT, W[illiam] S[chwenk]

b. 18 November 1836, London; d. 29 May 1911, Harrow Weald, Middesex

There is a small chance that G. without Sir Arthur Sullivan might be remembered a century after G.'s death. Anthologies still contain some of his comic verses, such as the tale of cannibalism at sea, "The Yarn of the *Nancy Bell*." A few adherents read his plays, serious as well as comic, but the overwhelming likelihood is that G. has gained immortality at the price of being forever joined to Sullivan. A few of G.'s verses appear from time to time, but none of his plays are produced; on the other hand, versions of several of the fourteen G. and Sullivan "Savoy Operas" are running somewhere in the world at any time; the greatest—*H. M. S. Pinafore* (1878), *The Pirates of Penzance* (perf. 1879; pub. 1880), *Patience* (1881), *Iolanthe* (1882), and *The Mikado* (1885)—will endure as long as there are theaters.

An early verse, published in the magazine *Fun* in 1870, foresaw G.'s destiny: "I dreamt that somehow I had come/To dwell in Topsy-Turveydom!" Then, more than a century later, in 1999, the prediction came true in Mike Leigh's respected film, *Topsy-Turvy*, in which Jim Broadbent portrayed G. most convincingly. The son of a naval surgeon (also a novelist), G. received military and legal training, practicing law for four years before risking everything on a career in the theater. His early background stayed with him, however, and some of his most vivid comedy satirizes the professions that he knew best: navy, army, law, journalism, and politics. In much of his writing, the principle of Topsy-Turveydom rules: young and old switch places, as do rich and poor, mythical and mundane, wise and foolish.

As a writer and director, G. was an important force in the modernization and professionalization of the theater. He was among the first to write for a theater with electric lighting, and he was notorious for his high standards of rehearsal and performance. He was a notable satirist of excess in the arts and made fun of many contemporary figures, including the venerable poet laureate, Alfred, Lord TENNYSON. G. and Sullivan's *Princess Ida* (1884) adapts an earlier G. play called *The Princess*, which makes fun of Tennyson's *The Princess* in a take-off that G. called a "respectful per-version of Mr. Tennyson's poem." More broadly, *Patience* ridicules the pretensions of decadent artists, ribbing Oscar WILDE, A. C. SWINBURNE, and James McNeill Whistler. The words and the music of *Iolanthe* mimic Wagner's *Ring of the Nibelung*. Making fun of writers, painters, and musicians will entertain some; but many more will remember G.'s words, especially in the great patter songs, which have never been excelled for ingenuity or difficulty. *The Pirates of Penzance* features these lines: "I am the very model of a modern Major-General/I've information vegetable, animal, and mineral/I know the kings of England, and I quote the fights historical/From Marathon to Waterloo, in order categorical." Somewhat darker, a number from *Iolanthe* has earned the nickname "The Nightmare Song": "When you're lying awake with a dismal headache, and repose is taboo'd by anxiety, I conceive you may use any language you choose to indulge in, without impropriety." Within fifteen years of G.'s death, T. S. ELIOT included a mimetic tribute in *Sweeney Agonistes*: "When you're alone in the middle of the night and you wake in a sweat and a hell of a fright."

G. wrote a comic sketch called *Rosencrantz and Guildenstern* in 1874; one cannot be sure of any detailed connection with Tom STOPPARD's *Rosencrantz and Guildenstern Are Dead*, but the possibilities are amusing. Similarly, G.'s popular *Pygmalion and Galatea* (1871) could have prepared an audience for Bernard SHAW's *Pygmalion*, although Shaw brilliantly applied the mythological title to a modern story of education and deception (which in time produced *My Fair Lady*). G. and Sullivan are among the characters in Anthony BURGESS's *The Devil's Mode*. The credits of *Topsy-Turvy* include "Anthony Burgess: Special thanks."

BIBLIOGRAPHY: Ayre, L., *The G. and Sullivan Companion* (1972); Baily, L., *G. and Sullivan and Their World* (1973); Crowther, A., *Contradiction Contradicted: The Plays of W. S. G.* (2000); Eden, D., *G. and Sullivan: The Creative Conflict* (1987)

WILLIAM HARMON

GILCHRIST, Alexander

b. 25 April 1828, London; d. 30 November 1861, London

Author of the first full-length biography of William BLAKE, G. is credited with reviving interest in Blake that restored his critical reputation in the second half of the 19th c. Although flawed as an academic BIOGRAPHY, G.'s *Life of William Blake, "Pictor Ignotus"* (2 vols., 1863) provided a reassessment of Blake as one of the major figures of the Romantic movement. Married to Anne Burrows [GILCHRIST], G. had previously published a biography of the painter William Etty (2 vols., 1858). Turning his attention to Blake, G. had printed the first eight chapters of the *Life* before to his untimely death at age thirty-three. Additional parts were completed by his wife and other collaborators including Dante Gabriel and William Michael ROSSETTI.

GILCHRIST, Anne Burrows

b. 25 February 1828, London; d. 29 November 1885, Hampstead

Only in the last two decades of the 20th c. has G. been perceived as the essayist, critic, and biographer she decidedly was. For many years, she existed obscurely in the shadows of two distinguished men. If acknowledged at all, she was identified either as the widow of Englishman Alexander GILCHRIST, who wrote bio-

graphies of painter William Etty and poet William BLAKE, or as the would-be wife of the American Walt Whitman, who authored the revolutionary poems of *Leaves of Grass*. G., however, was an individual in her own right, a woman possessing an advanced education, intellectual curiosity, and literary aspiration. In England, she moved in circles that included Thomas CARLYLE, the ROSSETTIS (William Michael, Dante Gabriel, and Christina), and Alfred, Lord TENNYSON, In the U.S., to which she traveled in the late 1870s, she became acquainted with John Burroughs, Ralph Waldo Emerson, and, of course, Whitman. Among her accomplishments as a writer were essays published in popular magazines, the substantial work required to complete her husband's biography of Blake, a landmark article entitled "A Woman's Estimate of Walt Whitman," and a biography of Mary LAMB, the sister of essayist Charles LAMB.

Despite the demands made on her as wife and mother, G. proceeded during the 1850s to write a series of articles on various scientific subjects, for example, electricity, the gorilla, and human evolution, and the changelessness of atoms. Though these pieces appeared in journals with broad appeal, they were nevertheless well researched, reliable, and, at times, scholarly. When, in November 1861, at age thirty-three, Alexander Gilchrist died from scarlet fever, G. was left with four young children and his unfinished manuscript on the life of Blake. Undaunted by her difficult situation, G. met the challenge of completing the *Life of William Blake*. She plunged into the tasks of researching, copying, checking, indexing, and writing and, with the assistance of several friends, especially the Rossetti brothers, managed to publish the two-volume biography in 1863. Years later, in 1880, she would write a memoir of her husband and include it in a second edition of his biography. She would also write the entry on Blake for the *Dictionary of National Biography*.

In 1869, G. was introduced to Whitman's *Leaves of Grass* and promptly fell passionately in love with its author. Her various attempts to articulate her reactions to the poet's striking style and powerful thought eventually resulted in her most famous work—"A Woman's Estimate of Walt Whitman," a lengthy essay published in 1870 in the Boston *Radical*. Although some critics have disparaged "Estimate," seeing it less as literary commentary than as a romantic effusion, others have ranked it among the finest (and timeliest) examples of criticism Whitman had received since 1855, when he first published *Leaves*. In "Estimate," G. defends Whitman against the charges of indecency and formlessness, analyzes his poetic techniques, and endorses his ideas on science, death, and, in particular, sex.

G.'s most important work is *Mary Lamb* (1883), a biography issued in London by David Bogue for its

Famous Women Series. Objectively and yet compassionately, G. reveals how Lamb often struggled with mental illness (how, indeed, in a fit of madness she killed her mother), but nevertheless managed to collaborate with her brother Charles in writing books for children, including *Tales from Shakespeare* (1807) and *Mrs. Leicester's School* (1809). Although focusing on Mary, the biography also offers insights into Charles and fascinating glances at Samuel Taylor COLERIDGE, William WORDSWORTH, and William HAZLITT.

Two other works deserving mention are "Three Glimpses of a New England Village" (1884), a travel sketch notable for its remarks on the plight of single women, and "A Confession of Faith" (1885), another stalwart defense of Whitman and his poetry. These and earlier publications, many of which express G.'s advanced views on women's education and women's sexuality, reveal a writer whose true merit has yet to be measured.

BIBLIOGRAPHY: Alcaro, M. W., *Walt Whitman's Mrs. G: A Biography of A. G.* (1991); Ferlazzo, P. J., "A. G., Critic of Walt Whitman," *SDR* 10 (Winter 1972–73): 63–79; Gilchrist, H. H., ed., *A. G.* (1887); Harned, T. B., ed., *The Letters of A. G. and Walt Whitman* (1918)

DONALD D. KUMMINGS

GILFILLAN, George

b. 30 January 1813, Comrie, Perthshire; d. 13 August 1878, Dundee

G. was, for a relatively brief period, one of the most influential voices in the formation of literary taste in Britain. He edited a series of editions of British poets (both major and minor) that was attractively produced and widely read; he wrote popular biographies of Robert BURNS and Sir Walter SCOTT. He published a series of essays, under the collective title of *Literary Portraits*, which exerted a considerable influence on middle-class taste. It was largely under his critical patronage that two poets, Alexander SMITH and Sydney DOBELL, became, for a while at least, immensely fashionable. In retrospect, it is clear that much in G.'s work was superficial; that behind the stylistically lavish rhapsodies to which he was prone there was often little real thought. Yet if the praise he initially received was excessive, so to has been some of the denigration to which he has since been subject.

Toward the end of the 1830s, G., a Presbyterian minister, began to contribute essays on a variety of literary topics to a newspaper called the *Dumfriesshire and Galloway Herald*. These attracted a good deal of interest and a collection of the essays was published in 1845 as *A Gallery of Literary Portraits*. This Edinburgh edition was followed, in the next year, by

an American edition, now entitled *Sketches of Modern Literature*. The vivacity of G.'s manner perhaps explains the popularity of this initial collection; it was succeeded by a second in 1850 and a third in 1854. The more than eighty essays gathered in these collections included colorful studies of Romantics such as Robert SOUTHEY, Percy Bysshe SHELLEY, Samuel Taylor COLERIDGE, and William WORDSWORTH; Victorians such as Thomas Babington MACAULAY and Thomas CARLYLE, as well as figures from much earlier periods, such as Aeschylus and William SHAKESPEARE. In the years in which these collections were printed (and reprinted), G. was in much demand as a preacher and lecturer, a reviewer, and a critic. In 1849, for example, he published the texts of two lectures: *The Christian Bearings of Astronomy* and *The Connection between Science, Literature and Religion*. In 1851, there appeared an anthology, *The Book of British Poesy*; a SERMON, *The Apocalypse of Jesus Christ*; and a collection of essays, *The Bards of the Bible*, a lively study of Hebrew poetry that was to become one of his most popular works. Indeed, G.'s output was far too voluminous and various for more than a few of his publications to be noted here. *The History of a Man*, published in 1856, is part fiction and part AUTOBIOGRAPHY, of interest for its accounts of some of G.'s friends and acquaintances, such as John WILSON ("Christopher North") and Thomas CAMPBELL. G.'s most substantial poetic work is *Night: A Poem* (1867), a lengthy moralistic poem unlikely to interest many readers now or in the future.

Alongside the studies in the various *Galleries of Literary Portraits*, it is as an editor and a biographer that G. makes such claims as he can on our attention. He was editor of the Library Edition of the British Poets, published between 1853 and 1860 and made up of forty-eight volumes. There were several thousand subscribers to the series, as well as many more purchasers of individual volumes. The frequency of publication meant that G.'s contributions had, generally, to be written in some haste; his introductions are generally spirited and readable. G.'s tastes in poetry centered on the rapturous and the ardent; verse of passionate yearning was likely to win his greatest praise. His own enthusiasm often bubbles up in the form of personal reminiscence and digression; lengthy passages of generalization, in themselves often quite entertaining, often look suspiciously like padding. Often G.'s religious prejudices (as in his essay on John DRYDEN) get in the way of genuinely literary judgment. Even so, G.'s editions of the British Poets remain of interest, both as documents in the history of taste and as being "a great thing for an armchair reader" (they were described thus by Dante Gabriel ROSSETTI).

G.'s *Life of Sir Walter Scott, Baronet* (1870) is an altogether more substantial affair than these introductions, though even here G.'s work is essentially that of a popularizer. G.'s book, well-timed for the 1871 centenary of Scott's birth, is firmly based on John Gibson LOCKHART's biography, adding little to it factually, digesting some of Lockhart's more complex material into a form more readily accessible to the general reader. The result is a lucid account—G.'s prose style was by this time less mannered than in his youth—with some honest and interesting literary judgments offered (albeit briefly). In 1878, G. contributed what was described as "an Original Life" to a four-volume edition of the works of Burns, *The National Burns*. G. values Burns's natural vitality, calling him "the most intensely living man modern times have produced." He is careful to do justice to Burns the "painstaking ploughman . . . devoted father . . . kind husband" as well as Burns the poet. The picture he paints is an attractive one and though it has naturally been superseded in many respects by later biographies, G.'s account of Burns's psychological instability ("He was at the mercy of innumerable moods, as diverse from each other as heaven from hell") carries a certain conviction.

In his "Life of Burns," G. comes closest, perhaps, to freedom from his besetting vices. There is less empty rhetoric and less that is dubiously relevant. Here, as elsewhere, G. was a persuasive enthusiast, a successful popularizer who introduced the lives and works of many poets to nonspecialist audiences. It is perhaps the inevitable fate of such popularizers that their work will appear very dated once the audience for which they wrote has disappeared. That has been G.'s fate; but it should not blind us to his importance in his own day.

BIBLIOGRAPHY: Macrae, D., *G. G.* (1891); Watson, R. A., and E. S. Watson, eds., *G. G.: Letters and Journals, with Memoir* (1892)

GLYN PURSGLOVE

GISSING, George

b. 22 November 1857, Wakefield, Yorkshire; d. 28 December 1903, Ispoure, Saint-Jean-Pied-de-Port, France

Although he lived to be only forty-six years old and went through many difficult periods when he would begin works that he could not finish, G. produced over twenty novels and one hundred short stories, an influential work of criticism, and an intriguing travel book. During his lifetime, he enjoyed moderate success, although he was often considered too dour, writing about realistic subjects such as poverty and the difficulties of marriage that were unacceptable to the tastes of the sheltered middle-class girls who made up the clientele of the Mudie's Lending Libraries. During the 20th c., he has still not found a place alongside the other late great late Victorian novelists, in part because his technique is not polished. He loads

his novels with subplots that are not well integrated and indulges in long narrative passages where he hashes out the issues of the novel rather than trusting the reader to draw his own conclusions.

A number of critics have felt that G. writes to express a "grudge" against the vulgarity and shallowness of his times rather than as a means of artistic expression; even those who appreciate the work feel that G. lacks the objectivity necessary to create lasting art. While he did draw heavily on his own experiences (and in fact felt that an author should not seek to give a photographic portrait of life but rather an image of life as he saw it), his reputation has suffered from biographical criticism. Critics too often analyze his marriages to an alcoholic prostitute, a difficult girl of the working class, and his final mock marriage to an intellectual equal (who nonetheless failed to give him the care that he wanted in his final illness) and neglect more objective evaluations of his work. Since the 1960s, however, G.'s work has been gaining attention, especially from feminists who have been intrigued by his complex understandings of the damage caused by treating women as social inferiors. While his novels are imperfect, his images of poor and middle-class life in times of increasing industrialization and democracy, his understanding of the difficulties of those who would cross barriers imposed by class, education, and gender, and his keen attention to the details of daily life repay the attention of readers interested in G.'s times and in our ongoing struggles with these problems.

G.'s most powerful and polished novel about the realities of urban poverty is *Thyrza* (3 vols., 1887), the story of Thyrza Trent's struggle to cultivate her talent and taste in the face of grinding poverty and her ultimate difficulty in rising out of the circumstances imposed by class. In the novel, she is torn between the affections of Gilbert Grail, a working man who seeks solace in books, and Walter Egremont, a wealthy idealist who hopes to enlighten factory workers by providing them with lectures on the arts. Although Thyrza herself is presented in sentimental terms, the image of Grail as the "proletarian intellectual" who cannot find a position that fits his talents and his means, presents a new type to English literature that has never been more skillfully portrayed. In addition to these complex characterizations, G. sympathetically portrays the shallow pastimes of the music halls and low HUMOR of the streets as triumphs over circumstances and thus creates sympathy for the poor that even he rarely achieved in his other work.

While *Thyrza* depicts poverty realistically, critics acknowledge *New Grub Street* (3 vols., 1891) as G.'s masterpiece. G. exposes the ways that the literary marketplace corrupts those who aspire to write work of lasting merit and argues that competition and modern commercial life have infected society as a whole so that men lead shallow and vulgar lives. While many English novels include writers as characters, few explore in such detail the mechanics and difficulties of filling blank pages. Critics attribute the success of the novel to G.'s familiarity with the literary profession and to his ability in this instance to manage a variety of subplots. Unfortunately, even critics who admire the novel have too often reduced its plot to a simple contrast between the pragmatic Jasper Milvain and the idealistic Edward Reardon as each tries to succeed in the harsh environment of the London literary scene. G. in fact creates complex characters who must operate in a world that requires a mechanical output to meet the demands of the age, where literature is not art but a commodity. While he admires idealists like Reardon, he also sympathizes with the practical approach of men like Milvain who survive and maintain their humanity even as they compromise the highest standards.

Marian Yule is one of the most admirable characters in *New Grub Street*. She toils as a researcher in the British Museum to aid her father, the insensitive hack writer Alfred Yule, but manages to maintain her intelligence, sensitivity, strength, and endurance. She lacks conventional beauty and wealth but remains attractive to even the most hardened characters in the novel. It is G.'s depiction of such women that has attracted feminists to revaluate his work, particularly his novel *The Odd Women* (3 vols., 1893). In this story of the Madden sisters, G. captures the fate of women who have no place in society because they have no husbands and no training to earn a living. He exposes the absurd idea that such women were expected to cling to middle-class respectability without the appropriate means. While the Madden sisters see unhappy marriage or escape through alcohol as the only possible alternatives to a life of isolated subsistence, the "new woman," Rhoda Nunn, takes a more constructive approach. She runs a school to train women for professions so that their talents are not wasted. She proposes work as a way out of the despair of the isolation of "odd women" like the Madden sisters. The novel also introduces the themes of marriage and the relations between the sexes into a tale that focuses on the "new woman question." The tortured Edmund Widdowson, the possessive husband of the youngest Madden sister Monica, and the callous, wealthy Everard Barfoot, who resists all gainful employment, as a suitor for Rhoda Nunn, add complexity to the story and keep the novel from being simply a didactic treatise or a miserable naturalistic tale.

In his lifetime, G.'s most popular work was the curious and unclassifiable *The Private Papers of Henry Ryecroft* (1903), a series of essays in the style of Charles LAMB. G. presents the papers as the work of a struggling writer who has been able to retire to the country on a small inheritance. Although G. was only in his forties and his narrator is only fifty-three, the tone is that of an old man near death, surveying his life and expressing his opinions in a leisurely way. Critics at the turn of the century tended to see the book as a recantation of G.'s pessimistic image of life. This critical commonplace sells short a work where the quest for identity, Ryecroft's inability to choose between retirement and the writing life, continue many of the themes of G.'s greatest works. G. certainly deserves attention not only for his presentation of social problems and the details of Victorian life but for what he can show us about the creation of fiction and the writer's life. Critics should be careful to seek a more subtle interpretation of the work of this complex if imperfect chronicler of late Victorian life.

BIBLIOGRAPHY: Allen, W., *The English Novel: A Short Critical History* (1958); Coustillas, P., and C. Partridge, eds., *G.* (1972); Korg, J., *G. G.* (1963); Poole, A., *G. in Context* (1975)

CATHERINE FRANK

GLANVILLE, Brian [Lester]
b. 24 September 1931, London

G. is famous among the general public as a journalist and writer of numerous books on sport, especially football (soccer), but he is also a perceptive and accomplished mainstream novelist, who has authored fifteen novels and four collections of short stories. His areas of interest are, naturally, the lives of athletes (*The Olympian*, 1969, and *Goalkeepers Are Different*, 1971), Jewish culture (*The Bankrupts*, 1958), and life in show business (*A Second Home,* 1965, and *The Comic*, 1974). His *Footballers Don't Cry: Selected Writings* appeared in 2000.

GLYN, Elinor
b. 17 October 1864, Jersey; d. 23 September 1943, London

Known primarily for her scandalous romance novel *Three Weeks* (1907), G. was a prolific author who in the first decades of the 20th c. enjoyed celebrity status in both in England and the U.S. In the 1920s, G.'s faltering career was rejuvenated when she was lured to Hollywood to work as a screenwriter. She was most successful collaborating on adaptations of her novels, including *The Great Moment* (1921), *His Hour* (1924), *Three Weeks* (1924), *It* (1927), *The Man and the Moment* (1929), and *Such Men Are Dangerous* (1930). However, G. achieved some measure of motion picture notoriety when her scripts brought fame to Clara Bow, the "It" girl and symbol of the "new" woman.

GODOLPHIN, Sidney

b. January 1610, Godolphin Hall, Cornwall; d. 9 February 1643, Chagford, Devon

The epitome of the young poet of promise cut off before his time, G. left just enough verse to justify the high opinion held of him by discerning literary contemporaries. A handful of his poems survives, few having circulated during his lifetime, either in print or in manuscript collections. Of these the foremost is *The Passion of Dido for Aeneas*, a verse translation from the *Aeneid* on which G. was at work at the time of his death. Completed by Edmund WALLER, a friend and admirer of G., *The Passion of Dido* saw print in 1658.

A committed royalist, G. was member of Parliament for Helston from 1628, and accompanied the Earl of Leicester on the Continent in 1632. He was one of the last to leave the House of Commons when the king withdrew his supporters. Immediately he joined Sir Ralph Hopton, with whose force he fought at Chagford, Devonshire, falling in battle.

In addition to Waller, G. counted among his friends Ben JONSON and (despite differences over the impeachment of Thomas Wentworth, first Earl of Strafford, G. being strongly opposed) Edward Hyde (later first Earl of CLARENDON), and Thomas HOBBES. Both Clarendon (in his *History of the Rebellion and the Civil Wars in England*) and Hobbes (in *Leviathan*) wrote tributes to G.

The Passion of Dido for Aeneas demonstrates a knowledgeable approach to Virgil, and a capacity for capturing powerful emotion. G.'s couplets are skillful, often turning with a surprising delicacy; technically, he has been cited as having anticipated Alfred, Lord TENNYSON's meter in *In Memoriam*.

BIBLIOGRAPHY: Dighton, W., ed., *The Poems of S. G.* (1931); Roebuck, G., "S. G.," in Hester, M. T., ed., *Seventeenth-Century British Nondramatic Poets, DLB* 126 (1993): 122–32

R. F. YEAGER

GODWIN, Mary. See SHELLEY, Mary Wollstonecraft

GODWIN, William

b. 3 March 1756, Wisbech; d. 7 April 1836, London

While G. is perhaps best known today as the husband of the early English feminist Mary WOLLSTONECRAFT and as the father of novelist Mary SHELLEY, he was one of the most famous, and often infamous, radical philosophers and theologians of his time. The publication of his work *An Enquiry Concerning Political Justice, and Its Influence on General Virtue and Happiness* (2 vols., 1793), a treatise on political and

philosophical anarchism, catapulted him into instant literary and political fame and notoriety. G. enjoyed moderate success with prolific writings during his life, although the only text besides *Political Justice* to generate immediate, as well as scandalous, attention was his *Memoirs of the Author of a Vindication of the Rights of Woman* (1798), a biography of Wollstonecraft. Despite his notoriety, however, and despite relative poverty through the years, G. outlasted many of his contemporaries, and with shifting political fortunes, was eventually vindicated with an appointed government position in 1833, and when he died in 1836 he held the respect afforded an influential political writer, novelist, and humanitarian.

G. was born into inauspicious circumstances. His early educational trials heavily influenced his work—work that would exemplify the religious controversy and political turmoil that swept through England at the time. The austere Calvinism of his father was challenged and modified by his tutor, Samuel Newton, who taught the religious doctrine of Sandemanianism, the effects of which can be seen even in G.'s later works. After the death of his father, G. enrolled in the Dissenting Academy at Hoxton, where he came into contact with radical thinkers of his day, and further began to question his religious and political upbringing. With these influences in his background, G. eventually became known as one of the best writers of radical political thought in an era known for controversy and revolution.

His first book, *The History of the Life of William Pitt, Earl of Chatham* (1783), was published anonymously and contains some of the seeds of his future attitudes about mankind, primarily the idea that the goal of culture and education is to lead man toward the perfection of his nature. While the biography was not financially successful, G. was not discouraged by the setback, and continued to write and develop his political ideology. With the publication of *Political Justice*, he became instantly celebrated as a preeminent radical thinker. The book argues for the possibility of the perfection of mankind, and argues for the dissolution of the present political structures that restrict human growth. While G. himself escaped persecution for his political arguments, the turmoil of the recent French Revolution made the English government react strongly to potential threats to their authority. Several other radical writers suffered exile, and G.'s writings of the time often defended free speech and argued against the apparent tyranny of the current government.

G.'s most distinguished novel is *Things As They Are; or, The Adventures of Caleb Williams* (3 vols., 1794), a work that intended to duplicate the ideals of *Political Justice*. The book was well received, although it also gathered criticism from a number of G.'s political opponents. *Caleb Williams* addresses the complicated political system of the time and describes the problems of the individual aligned against outmoded social institutions. While the work was not a strong influence on the tradition of the English novel, it is often considered representative of the period, and has been praised as an early precursor to the detective novel.

In 1795, G. began a relationship with Wollstonecraft, already well known for her own political writing. She died a few days after giving birth to their daughter, Mary, only six months after their marriage in 1797. The publication of his *Memoirs* of Wollstonecraft again catapulted him to notoriety. G. believed in intellectual and literal honesty, and his revelations of their intimate relationship outside of wedlock were far too much for the audience of his day. The immediate reaction to the work was that Wollstonecraft's texts were shunned, then and later, by feminists, eager to distance themselves from the suggestion that FEMINISM and depravity were concomitant, although later critics have found the *Memoirs* a compelling and useful biography.

When G. died in 1836, it was after publishing several further novels and essays, continuing his social criticism and further literary development. While not entirely unsuccessful, his later works—including various biographies and histories published under pseudonym—did not achieve acclaim, nor are they considered particularly noteworthy today. Although his reputation rests primarily on *Political Justice*, contemporary critics from the 1950s onward have had increasing regard for his other works, and he is seen today as a central figure of the Romantic era.

BIBLIOGRAPHY: Smith, E. E., and E. G. Smith, *W. G.* (1965); St. Clair, W., *The Godwins and the Shelleys* (1989); Wardle, R. M., ed., *Godwin and Mary: The Letters of W. G. and Mary Wollstonecraft* (1977)

STEVEN ZANI

GOGARTY, Oliver St. John

b. 17 August 1878, Dublin, Ireland; d. 22 September 1957, New York City

It is G.'s misfortune to be best remembered as the model for Buck Mulligan, the rakish medical student of James JOYCE's *Ulysses*—witty, but thoughtless and heartless, the author of obscene and blasphemous doggerel. But G. was much more than this. An accomplished surgeon, a member of the Irish senate, G. was also a poet, a playwright, a novelist, an essayist, and a writer of memoirs. Although his poetry was acclaimed by such friends as W. B. YEATS and George RUSSELL, it has never been widely accepted. G.'s forms are traditional, his subject matter often conventional, and his rhymes often predictable. His poetical works include *Hyperthuleana* (1916), *An Offering of*

Swans (1923; rev. ed., 1924), *Wild Apples* (1928), *Selected Poems* (1935; rev. as *Others to Adorn*, 1938), and *Collected Poems* (1951).

His plays are social satires, written under pseudonyms to protect his medical practice. *Blight* (1917), presented as the work of Alpha and Omega, ridicules the stupidities and corruption of exploiters of Dublin slums. *The Enchanted Trousers* (1919) and *A Serious Thing* (1920) both presented as the work of Gideon Ouseley, satirize the English occupation. In the former an Irishman is tutored to appear sufficiently stupid and English to win a lucrative sinecure. In the latter, markedly English Roman soldiers ponder how to cope with the resurrection of Lazarus. All three plays were highly successful at the Abbey Theatre, and are funny but dated.

G.'s most enduring work is *As I Was Going Down Sackville Street* (1937), a memoir of the great days of the Irish literary renaissance, with anecdotal reminiscences of Yeats, Russell, and George MOORE. G. often praises extravagantly, only then to make his subjects look ridiculous, satirizing numerous friends and acquaintances, some named, others easily identifiable.

But there is no satire in his depiction of the struggle for Irish independence. A member of Sinn Fein, G. was a close friend of Arthur Griffith, the Sinn Fein leader who later became president of the Irish Free State, and of Michael Collins, military leader during the struggle for independence and later military commander in the new government. G., himself bullied by the Black and Tan English troops, saw friends arbitrarily imprisoned.

During the civil war between the Irish government and the Republicans who refused to accept the treaty with England, G. gave medical advice to Griffith, who was dying of a stroke brought on by tension, and had the hospital room changed to elude assassins. He shared his home with Collins, who shifted residences to avoid hit squads. G. later removed his latch key from the body of the murdered Collins. G., like other members of the Irish Senate, was placed under police protection, and his country house, like many houses, was burned. This memoir, like most of G.'s later work, is colored by his contempt for the Republicans and their leader Eamonn de Valera, and by his distaste for the governments under de Valera's sway. He saved the full depiction of his most harrowing experience for *It Isn't This Time of Year at All!: An Unpremeditated Autobiography* (1954). He was kidnapped by Republican gunmen and escaped by diving into the Liffey. With few exceptions, however, G.'s richest material appears in his earlier memoir.

Tumbling in the Hay (1939), a thinly fictionalized version of his experiences as a medical student, was well received but is no longer read. G. moved to the U.S. in 1939 as a professional writer and lecturer. In *Going Native* (1940), an Irishman, addressed as

"Ouseley," is told by Yeats that the only good conversation is now in England; when he has at last adjusted to the eccentricities and complacencies of English society, he becomes homesick. Later works include two historical novels, *Mad Grandeur* (1943) and *Mr. Petunia* (1945), and an account of a return trip to Ireland, *Rolling Down the Lea* (1949) that reiterates his distaste for de Valera's influence, but G.'s first memoir remains his finest work.

BIBLIOGRAPHY: Carens, J. F., *Surpassing Wit: O. St. J. G., His Poetry and His Prose* (1979); O'Connor, U., *The Times I've Seen: O. St. J. G.* (1963)

DALTON AND MARYJEAN GROSS

GOLDING, William
b. 19 September 1911, St. Columb Minor, Cornwall;
d. 19 June 1993, Perranarworthal

The predominate concern of G.'s novels is an examination of human evil. This curiosity was no doubt provoked by his experiences in the violence of World War II as the commander of a rocket launching ship. He once observed that what his generation had discovered was that there was more evil in man "than could be accounted for simply by social pressure."

G. possessed an early interest in literature and graduated from Oxford University in 1935 with a degree in English literature. Even before the war, his interest in writing had led him to publish an anthology of poetry in 1934. After the war, G. returned to his interest in writing and published *Lord of the Flies* in 1954. The book was popular with college students during the 1960s obtaining almost a cult following. It has since been translated into over twenty languages and two movies have been made based upon it. G.'s subsequent works have not enjoyed the success of *Lord of the Flies*, and in spite of the Nobel Prize for Literature he received in 1983, he is mainly known for his first novel. As a writer, G. takes an innovative approach to story telling employing unusual narrative perspectives, fragmented timelines, and sudden shifts of viewpoint. Most critical attention centers around his first five novels.

Lord of the Flies is set in the future during a nuclear war. Several English schoolboys are stranded on an island in the South Pacific without adult supervision. Some critics have noted the similarity in the setting and the names of the major characters to R. M. BALLANTYNE's *The Coral Island*. G., however, rejects Ballantyne's idealistic view of human nature believing that evil can emerge even in innocent children in an idyllic setting.

At first, the boys work together to build a primitive society and to maintain a signal fire. Later, rumors emerge of a dangerous beast that is also living on the island. These rumors seem to be confirmed when a strange object is sighted. This knowledge causes the society to break down and the worst tendencies of the adult world to emerge in the boys' behavior. The boys form rival tribes, and in the novel's final episode a hunting party is attempting to capture the leader of the rival party to offer as a sacrifice to the beast.

G.'s point is largely conveyed through Simon, who doubts that the strange object seen by the others is really a dangerous beast. He climbs the island's mountain and discovers that the object mistaken for the beast is a dead parachutist. Simon realizes that the real beast on the island is not some external thing but rather something inherent within the boys themselves. In a scene filled with symbolism, Simon comes down from the mountain with the knowledge that will set the boys free from their fears, but in the darkness they mistake him for the beast and kill him.

G.'s second novel, *The Inheritors* (1955), examines the issue of evil in primitive man. The novel is presented from the viewpoint of a Neanderthal family, which makes reading it particularly challenging. In some respects it is a rebuttal to H. G. WELLS's comments concerning Neanderthals in his *Outline of History*. G.'s creatures are far from being the cannibalistic ogres that Wells suggests. Lok and his family express love and concern for one another. Men, however, are depicted as drunken, violent, and unfaithful creatures. They destroy the Neanderthal family while kidnapping the Neanderthal's child to serve as a pet for the chief's indolent and trouble making wife.

In *Pincher Martin* (1956; repub. as *The Two Deaths of Christopher Martin*, 1957), G.'s focus shifts from looking at evil within groups to examining evil within the individual. The story is an hallucination of a man stranded on a rock in the middle of the ocean desperately trying to cling to life. Through a series of flashbacks, Martin is presented as a winner in the battle of the survival of the fittest. He respects no law and takes what he wants without regard for others. Now he fears the judgment of God, and his hallucination ends when he is confronted with that reality.

In *Free Fall* (1959), G. looks at both the issues of sin and redemption. In it Samuel Mountjoy, a prisoner in a German POW camp, is being psychologically tortured to obtain information about a possible escape attempt. Mountjoy realizes that he has lost his "freedom," the ability to choose between good and evil, and fears he will not withstand his ordeal. He searches through his mind reflecting upon his individual sins attempting to find that moment when his fall occurred. The story's timeline is fragmented; some chapters are flashbacks to the past while others appear to be almost hallucinations of the future. Mountjoy realizes that his seduction and subsequent rejection of Beatrice Ifor is his free fall. In the darkness of the torture chamber, however, he understands and faces the consequences

407

of his sin thus obtaining a type of religious transcendence. The novel's problem is in actually understanding this religious experience. Redemption is surely an idea within the novel, but how it is acquired remains a mystery.

G.'s *The Spire* (1964) is also concerned with human sin. The situation is unique in that the sin is committed by Jocelin, the dean of a cathedral. His obsession with what he believes is a heavenly call, to erect a tall spire on the cathedral whose foundation cannot possibly support the structure, is the cause of great harm. The construction closes the church for years thus denying its spiritual function. It also leads to acts of adultery and murder as it destroys the lives of those most closely connected with the construction. Jocelin realizes the folly of his obsession at his death as he utters: "It's just like the apple tree." That is for him the spire was the object of temptation over which he stumbled.

G.'s most significant later works include *Darkness Visible* (1979), the story of an orphan boy, Matty Windrove, horribly scarred in the Blitz, and his novel *Rites of Passage* (1980), written in a journal form by Edmund Talbert, a rather imperceptive and conceited narrator. It concerns a voyage on board a British ship to the West Indies in the early 19th c.

G. has also written a play, *The Brass Butterfly* (1958), and several works of nonfiction including *The Hot Gates* (1965) and *An Egyptian Journal* (1985). These works, however, have enjoyed only limited success.

BIBLIOGRAPHY: Babb, H. S., *The Novels of W. G.* (1970); Johnston, A., *Of Earth and Darkness: The Novels of W. G.* (1980); Kinkead-Weekes, M., and I. Gregor, *W. G.* (1968); Tiger, V., *W. G.* (1974)

MAX LOGES

GOLDSMITH, Oliver

b. 10 November 1730?, probably at Pallas, County Westmeath, Ireland; d. 4 April 1774, London

G.'s literary talent was so marked, as T. S. ELIOT noted, that he could excel in any form. His weakness was lack of originality, compensated by the deftness and breadth of his intellect. It was an ironic disparity noted by many in his era. Samuel JOHNSON, the most influential literary critic of the time, held him in the highest esteem—perhaps too high in view of Johnson's doubts about *The Vicar of Wakefield* (2 vols., 1766)—but Johnson's pronouncement did not endure into the next generation despite the statistical fact that two of G.'s poems (discussed below) and *The Vicar* continued to be among the most frequently read works of the 19th c.

His great works are easily identified: two plays— *The Good Natured Man* (1768) and *She Stoops to Conquer* (1773); two poems—*The Traveller* (1764) and *The Deserted Village* (1770); dozens of reviews in Tobias SMOLLETT's *Critical Review* and numerous London newspapers and periodicals; the "Chinese Letters" collected and published as *The Citizen of the World* (2 vols., 1762); his famous essay "A Comparison between Laughing and Sentimental Comedy" (1773) that argues for the moral value of laughter over empty tears; biographies of Richard Nash (1762), Thomas PARNELL (1770), and others; histories of the earth and nature's wide kingdom, as well as histories of Rome (2 vols., 1769), England (4 vols., 1771), and Greece (2 vols., 1774); large compendiums of philosophy and BIOGRAPHY: these would have earned anyone else in the 18th c. a place at the top of the Republic of Letters.

Certainly, G.'s prolific hack writing for Francis Newbery did, but G. also had drawbacks. His poetry's formal cast and rhetorical mold superficially appears regressive but its themes—socioeconomic, geographic, national—are up to the minute: the idea that the countryside is tragically depopulating and folding up; the notion that commerce and luxury are wrecking manners and morals; that countries vastly differ in customs despite the belief that only wise people— "philosophers"—are genuine "citizens of the world" (G.'s phrase that he later used as the title for a book, see below); the traveler-wanderer's exhilaration when "pushing ahead" over land and on the high seas at the prospect of discovery; the value of simplicity in an epoch growing increasingly complex. Equally topical were G.'s essays. These, like Joseph ADDISON's and Richard STEELE's in the *Spectator* and Johnson's in the *Rambler* and *Idler* before his, spoke to the Georgians as did few others. G.'s ranged over diverse topics from the development of cities and the breadth of human emotions to comparative university education in Britain and abroad and the value of reading highbrow literature. G. commented on these subjects by assuming the persona of a wise oriental sage, "Lien Chi Altangi," who travels from China to England to impart the fruits of his wisdom. It was, of course, an age when few Britons had been to the Orient and, more locally, when journalism began to approach the heights it would reach over the next two centuries. Elsewhere in his literary output, if G.'s poems are nearly perfect in their conception and execution, and his comic plays delightful to the audiences who watched them—only Richard Brinsley SHERIDAN in the 18th c. rivaled them—it is nevertheless his journalism that has decided his second-class niche. They are masterly essays, but ever since the Edwardians found them too rational, they have been undervalued and even now they remain largely unread.

The Vicar is a curious piece of fiction, altogether different from the novels of G.'s contemporaries, Samuel RICHARDSON and Henry FIELDING, Smollett and Fanny BURNEY. Although shorter, less experimental, and stylistically less ambitious, it provoked negative criticism in its time. Indeed, it seems anachronistic in its decade of the 1760s: a throwback to an earlier 18th c. when character could be presented as simpler—less psychologically complex—and morality less riveted by the new industrial crime and violence. Mr. Primrose and his family suffer every form of distress and ensuing pain. But just when their misery appears guaranteed, their woes vanish and they live happily ever after. Somehow (and it is not entirely clear what the agency of change is), simplicity of head and heart have prevailed. Simplicity had always been one of G.'s favorite themes. But here the moral seems to be that the distresses of the virtuous (i.e., the Primroses) evoke resignation and fortitude among their viewers. For the rest of the 18th c., *The Vicar* found a permanent niche among readers unable to cope with the dazzling stylistic ingenuity of *Tristram Shandy* or the brave new world of Gothic fiction. Yet some critics thought G.'s imagination too steeped in nostalgia for a sentimental world that had been lost. Small wonder then that G. never wrote another novel.

Doubt about G.'s achievement has also been created by the tension between his unhappy, bachelor life and stunning writing. Biographically, he lacked the polish of his glittering Georgian era and was unable to construct an attractive public persona: solitary, homely, physically frail, and often unwell (Mr. Primrose is autobiographical in more ways than one), he was routinely bailed out by friends (the anecdote about Johnson ascending to his garret when he was broke and ill and asked him if he had any writing to sell, to which G. replied that he had the *Vicar*, is probably true). Although a fixture in Johnson's dining club of which he was a founding member, he was incapable of successful networking and even appeared to be pathetic in part as the result of his bachelordom. Nevertheless, the members of Johnson's "club" of painters, politicians, historians, and writers all acknowledged that G., however flawed, possessed unique ability.

Any definitive summary of his literary achievement is necessarily problematic because he cannot be placed in a single school or tradition of writing. Labels fail because his oeuvre is so diverse, and popular terms such as primitivism, sentimentalism, and sensibility—successfully applied to contemporaries—are too limited to describe him. Simultaneously he also cultivated simplicity, the grotesque, sublime, Oriental; furthermore, the classification omits the range of topics in his journalism. It is easier to rank his writing according to quality; here it is uniformly high. One can demonstrate, for example, that the development of English comedy from the Restoration dramatists to the Victorians and Edwardians would have been different without him. If summary must be made perhaps he is best viewed not merely as an Enlightenment figure, which he was, despite his breadth of interests in a era when the value of learning still counted for much, but as the perfect embodiment of his own sentimental edicts. Johnson may have said the last word when he asked, on hearing of G.'s death, "Was ever poet so trusted before?"

BIBLIOGRAPHY: Bloom, H., ed., *O. G.* (1987); Lonsdale, R., ed., *The Poems of Thomas Gray, William Collins, O. G.* (1969); Rousseau G. S., *G.* (1974); Wardle, R. M., *O. G.* (1957)

GEORGE ROUSSEAU

GOOGE, Barnabe

b. 11 June 1540, Alvingham, Lincolnshire; d. February 1594, Cockering, Lincolnshire

G., a poet, minor courtier, and an eclectic translator of works on moral instruction, farming, and Protestant religious polemic, is best known for his *Eclogues, Epitaphs and Sonnets* (1563). Falling between Sir Thomas WYATT and Henry Howard, Earl of SURREY, and the advent of Edmund SPENSER, G.'s work exhibits the experimentation and interests of this transitional period. At once influenced by contemporary taste for Petrarch (e.g., "Cupido Conquered") and the classics, G. nonetheless echoes native English poetics with a heavy reliance on alliteration. His frequent use of "poulter's measure," or the "fourteener" (a seven-foot iambic line), seems borrowed from Surrey. Of special importance are the eight eclogues that, along with those of Alexander BARCLAY (wr. ca. 1514), are the earliest examples of the form in English.

Born into a Lincolnshire family of gentleman-farmers, G. attended both Oxford and Cambridge Universities, apparently breaking off his studies to travel on the Continent and taking a degree from neither. Through his familial connection with Sir William Cecil, Lord Burghley, who employed him in various capacities in Ireland between 1574 and 1585, G. established a presence at court, sufficient ultimately to be appointed gentleman-pensioner by ELIZABETH I.

As well as poetry, G. published translations, beginning with *The Zodiac of Life* (1565), a Calvinist work by Marcello Palingenio (P. A. Manzoli), condemned by the Inquisition in 1536. G.'s most important translation is Heresbachius's *Four Books of Husbandry* (1577), in which G.'s Lincolnshire roots and grounding in classical pastoral tradition are in evidence. In addition, G. translated *The Popish Kingdom*, an extensive polemic by "Thomas Naogeorgos" (Thomas Kirchmeyer), in 1570.

BIBLIOGRAPHY: Alsop, J. D., "B. G.'s Birthdate," *N& Q* 38 (1991): 24; Kennedy, J. M., "B. G.," in Richardson, D. A., ed., *Sixteenth-Century British Nondramatic Writers*, First Series, *DLB* 132 (1993): 141–48

R. F. YEAGER

GORDON, Giles [Alexander Esmé]

b. 23 May 1940, Edinburgh, Scotland

G. is best known today as one of Britain's leading literary agents. He has, however, written several novels and some short stories and poems. Although he has not published a novel in the last two decades, G. was, in retrospect, one of the most innovative writers of the 1970s, and his novels and short stories presage some of the developments that we have now come to see as characteristic of POSTMODERNISM.

The key features of his fiction emerged early with his first collection of short "fictions," *Pictures from an Exhibition* (1970), which experimented with narrative and self-consciously explored fictional representation. He continued to show an interest in the aesthetics of fiction, especially in relation to questions of typography. However, his novels are also preoccupied with the detailed analysis of domestic life and, in particular, of marriage and adultery. It is the experimental and self-reflexive nature of his work that prevented him from achieving popular acclaim. Critical reviewers, while appreciating that G.'s project included an investigation of literary aesthetics, felt that he was only partially successful. While often intentionally frustrating the reader's expectations of narrative progression, G.'s work can often seem like a series of experiments in writing and can therefore make for a rather dry reading experience. For the most part, G.'s characters are educated members of the British middle classes, and for this reason, they are rarely extraordinary. He concerns himself with the details of their daily life, both in the home and at the office. This fascination with the banal can also contribute to the inaccessibility of the work.

G. has had a very distinguished career in the world of letters. He has held a number of academic posts, and has been a journalist and publisher. As a literary agent, he has represented some of the most significant novelists of the late 20th c., including Vikram Seth, Barry UNSWORTH, and Fay WELDON. His experience and knowledge of the literary world is nicely reflected in *Aren't We Due a Royalty Statement?: A Stern Account of Literary, Publishing, and Theatrical Folk* (1993). Rather in the manner of a witty 18th-c. memoir, this portrait of the London literary world contains innumerable amusing anecdotes, often accompanied by a telling moral. It is less an AUTOBIOGRAPHY than a history of his encounters and relationships with prominent members of the literary, publishing, and theatrical worlds. Indeed, although he has published a number of poetry collections with personal subjects, including *Two and Two Make One* (1966), *Two Ele-*

gies (1968), *Eight Poems for Gareth* (1970), *One Man, Two Women* (1974), and *The Oban Poems* (1977), G.'s writing career may be said to have grown out of his life in publishing and journalism. Many of the pieces in *Pictures from an Exhibition* and his other short story collections, *Farewell, Fond Dreams* (1975) and *The Illusionist and Other Fictions* (1978), had already been published in a variety of newspapers and magazines.

In his first novel, *The Umbrella Man* (1971), G. uses three narrative perspectives: the first-person voices of Felix and Delia, and a third-person narrator. The three often conflicting perspectives frustrate any attempts to establish a clear version of events. *Girl with Red Hair* (1974) was influenced by the French nouveau roman, as represented by Alain Robbe-Grillet, and characterized by the lack of character and plot description, which challenged readers' assumptions of what constitutes coherence of character and action in literature. G.'s adoption of nouveau roman techniques prompted Valentine Cunningham to say of him that he was "one of few serious anglicizers of French modes." G.'s most critically and commercially successful novels were *About a Marriage* (1972) and *100 Scenes from Married Life* (1976). The first, which G. has called his only fully autobiographical novel, focuses on the everyday domestic life of a married couple, Edward and Ann, and is based on his own marriage to his first wife. Through a series of reflections, Edward overcomes marital difficulties and refreshes his marriage. The second of these novels is structurally more fragmentary and features the same couple a few years later. *Enemies: A Novel about Friendship* (1978) continues G.'s rather cynical interest in marriage and adultery, and uses some nouveau roman techniques to enter into the characters' thoughts. In a change of subject, his last novel, *Ambrose's Vision: Sketches towards the Creation of a Cathedral* (1980), explores the nature of creative genius.

Throughout his career, G. has published editions of short stories by contemporary writers. He published *Factions* in 1974, with Alex Hamilton, an anthology of stories that intermingle fact and fiction, and other collections, including *A Book of Contemporary Nightmares* (1977), *Modern Scottish Short Stories* (1982), with Fred URQUHART, and *Shakespeare Stories* (1982).

BIBLIOGRAPHY: Stevenson, R., "G. G.," in Moseley, M., ed., *British Novelists since 1960*, Third Series, *DLB* 207 (1999): 131–37

LANA ASFOUR

GORE, Catherine [Grace Frances]

b. 1800, London; d. 29 January 1861, Lyndhurst, Hampshire

Born Catherine Moody, G. was a novelist of the "silver fork school": her fictions were peopled by aristocrats and wealthy people, offering glimpses of high life to those excluded in reality. G.'s work was parodied as "Lords and Liveries" by William Makepeace THACKERAY in *Mr. Punch's Prize Novelists* (1847). Between 1824 and 1862, G. published some seventy novels, including *Mothers and Daughters* (3 vols., 1831), *Women as They Are; or, Manners of the Day* (3 vols., 1830), *Mrs. Armytage; or, Female Domination* (3 vols., 1836), *Cecil; or, The Adventures of a Coxcomb* (3 vols., 1841), and *The Banker's Wife; or, Court and City* (3 vols., 1843). G. also wrote plays and short stories and composed music.

GOSSE, [Sir] Edmund
b. 21 September 1849, Hackney (London); d. 16 May 1928, London

Known today primarily as the author of *Father and Son* (1907), a book describing his early struggles to free himself from the Calvinist views of his father (eminent zoologist Philip H. Gosse), G. made significant contributions in the areas of literary history, criticism, and BIOGRAPHY. He also wrote poetry, three verse dramas, and fiction. He was largely educated at home.

G. became assistant cataloguer at the British Museum in 1867, where he met the likes of Alfred, Lord TENNYSON, Coventry PATMORE, John Payne, and to the extreme discomfort of his father, A. C. SWINBURNE. Under the influence of the Pre-Raphaelites, he began writing and publishing poetry at this time, but he still maintained the appearance of his father's creed. In 1875, he accepted a position as translator to the Board of Trade, a position he held for twenty-nine years. From 1885 to 1889, he was the successor to Sir Leslie STEPHEN as Clark Lecturer in English Literature at Cambridge. He also served as librarian to the House of Lords (1904–14), literary writer for the *Daily Chronicle*, and literary essayist for the *Sunday Times*. He was knighted in 1925.

An important incident in G.'s life was his competition with John Churton Collins for the Clark Lectureship in English Literature at Trinity College, Cambridge. Collins read G.'s work *English Literature from Shakespeare to Pope* (1885), on the strength of which G. had defeated Collins for the appointment, and found it riddled with errors, which he detailed in a long review. G. was warned to stay away from Collins ("He who wrasseleth with a turd will be beshite"), but he responded to the charges nevertheless. Fortunately for G., Collins's infamy (Tennyson called him a "louse on the locks of literature") allowed him to escape the imbroglio with his reputation intact.

G. was an authority on northern languages and early in his career published *Studies in the Literature of Northern Europe* (1879), which included essays on Danish, Swedish, Norwegian, and Dutch poetry. His work on Henrik Ibsen and other Scandinavian writers in the early 1870s introduced them to England. In addition, G. wrote several other important critical histories: *Seventeenth Century Studies* (1883); *Eighteenth Century Literature* (1889); *Questions at Issue* (1893), an examination of the literature of his contemporaries; *The Jacobean Poets* (1894); and *A Short History of Modern English Literature* (1898).

G.'s work as a biographer pioneered the so-called scientific biography, though he also employed psychological speculation. G. wrote distinguished lives of Thomas GRAY (1882), Sir Walter RALEIGH (1886), William CONGREVE (1888), John DONNE (1899), Robert BROWNING (1890), Jeremy TAYLOR (1904), Patmore (1905), Sir Thomas BROWNE (1905), and Swinburne (1917). He also wrote a biography of his father (1890) that anticipates *Father and Son*. In addition to these longer works of criticism and biography, G. was adept at the short critical portrait of contemporary writers.

In writing *Father and Son*, G. benefited from his previous experience as critical historian and biographer. The work functions as both biography (of his father) and AUTOBIOGRAPHY. He details his own early life, especially his efforts to comply with his father's radical Protestant faith while maintaining "a hard nut of individuality." The difficulty for the young G. was not discovering his true beliefs, but hiding them from his father, who took his son's spiritual salvation as his primary duty because of a promise he made to his first wife on her deathbed when Edmund was seven years old. *Father and Son* is an affectionate, if conflicted, portrait of his father, whose obsession with keeping his son within the fold actually had the effect of catapulting him out of it and into the world of letters. G. tells the story in a lively and informal style infused with HUMOR, detailing many incidents to illustrate the child's growing awareness of the strangeness of his upbringing. Especially moving is G.'s telling of his father's bitter disappointment when his book *Omphalos* (1857), a study of creation intended to reconcile the evolution-embracing scientific world with fundamentalist Christianity, met with nearly universal ridicule. "But, alas! Atheists and Christians alike looked at it and laughed and threw it away."

G.'s contributions to the world of poetry and fiction are by any standard, minor. He also published three plays, and some fiction, including a novel, *The Secret of Narcisse* (1892), a gloomy story, set in the mid-16th c. about an artist's struggle in a world unsympathetic to his aesthetic nature. This work's main interest lies in its prefiguring of some themes found in *Father and Son*.

BIBLIOGRAPHY: Allen, P., "E. G. and his Modern Readers," *ELH* 55 (Summer 1988): 487–503;

Thwaite, A., *E. G.* (1984); Woolf, J. D., *Sir E. G.* (1972)

PAUL H. SCHMIDT

GOTHIC NOVEL, The

In the prologue to his play *The Castle Spectre,* published in 1791, M. G. LEWIS imagined Romance as an enchantress living in a dark rural retreat in locations such as churchyards, forests, dungeons, ecclesiastical and fortified ruins, exulting when storms disturbed moonlit nights. Such venues had gained a popularity when depicted in the 17th-c. paintings of Gaspard Poussin, Claude Lorraine, and Salvator Rosa, dictating by the 18th-c. places to be visited by the traveler: thus, the Lake District, ruins such as Netley Abbey, and even country churchyards exerted a fascination. There was a constancy about these locations; in the course of the 18th c., they cropped up not only in paintings, novels, poems, and plays but were also imitated on a small scale in the gardens of landed gentry: Gothic ruins, a cascade, a grotto, and a forest prospect were all to be found in the Hon. Charles Hamilton's estate at Painshill in Surrey. However, it would be a mistake to think of this as a movement with a philosophical underpinning; not even the Gothic apparatus was itemized. Rather this was a sweeping spirit that guided from within and, possibly in consequence, imitation was rife. Gardening in the hands of a scholar like William Kent became a literary exercise; for example at Stowe, Buckinghamshire, he created the Elysian Fields within which the journey of Aeneas could be traced.

Horace WALPOLE is often credited with creating the seminal Gothic work in his novel *The Castle of Otranto,* published in 1764, but this view neglects the earlier writing of the Reverend John Home, a Church of Scotland minister, whose drama *Douglas* (1756) was as well known "in the closet" of private reading as on the stages of Edinburgh and London. The woodland setting around the castle formed a suitable context for the mourning heroine, Lady Randolph. Principal thematic devices were the social position of the titled solitary, her mysterious attachment to Young Norval, the pivot of the long-lost-child subplot, and her forced marriage to Randolph, the ingredients for future use in the Gothic novel. Response to the plot on a private reading was muted but in the theater one discovered the emotions engendered: the weeping of the spectators at the heroine's pitiable state, the applause as she asked the question about her missing son, "Was he alive?" and finally the shout from the gallery, "What think you of Wully Shakespeare now?"

Walpole leased a cottage in Twickenham, Middlesex, from 1749. Beginning with the addition of a Gothic staircase, Walpole enlarged the building, turning it into a late-medieval castle. *The Castle of Otranto* immediately put readers in mind of this but the fictional setting was on a much larger scale as the court of Trinity College, Cambridge, was the model for the central jousting area. Nevertheless, the castle was the true hero of the book. Fearful for the novel's reception, Walpole published the work as if it were a translation from a Renaissance Italian manuscript. In a letter to the Reverend William Cole, he described the conception of the work: "I waked one morning in the beginning of last June from a dream . . . that I thought myself in an ancient castle (a very natural dream for a head filled like mine with Gothic story) and that on the uppermost banister of a great staircase I saw a gigantic head in armor (March 9, 1765)." Later that headpiece falls and kills Conrad, heir to the estate. Antiquity played a significant role in Walpole's daydreaming; for him a Gothic work was set in the Middle Ages, however vaguely. He claimed the events of *Otranto* took place between the first and second Crusades, a spread of one hundred years. Walpole suffered imitators. One was Clara REEVE who wrote in a similar vein *The Old English Baron: A Gothic Story*, set in Oxfordshire's Minster Lovell. She differed from Walpole in as much as she attempted to neutralize the supernatural element, creating rationalizations which aroused Walpole's ire.

In the year of the publication of *The Castle of Otranto*, Ann RADCLIFFE was born. Her novels, published in the 1790s, brought a different tone to the Gothic narrative. Radcliffe was a strict Protestant who shared Reeve's habit of rationalizing; the "thrill" of mystery was merely an expedient to maintain suspense. The simple plot of *The Mysteries of Udolpho* is soon outlined: Emily St. Aubert is carried away by her uncle, the villainous Montoni, and removed to a remote castle in the Apennines; there her life is threatened by strange powers; the progression is completed by Emily's escape and return flight to France. Closely linked with the emotions of the heroine is the scenery through which she travels—or sees from her chamber windows—and the changing light of day. Not a tourist until late middle-age, Radcliffe pored over engravings of the landscapes of the popular 17th-c. masters and re-created from them the settings for this novel, filling in from a variety of guide books. The influence of William Gilpin and the Picturesque movement—reaching its apogee in this decade—was not limited to the British traveler but extended to all readers of romances. Poetic quotations, principally from James THOMSON, John MILTON, and William SHAKESPEARE, used either as chapter headings or incidentally within the body of the text, help also to convey the sensations the heroine feels, for this is as much an internal novel as a description of activity.

The year before the publication in 1797 of *The Italian* Radcliffe had read Lewis's horror story *The Monk*, and it is evident that his Ambrosio had an influence on her monastic hero Schedoni. While digni-fied, the latter is a proud and melancholy solitary and in the fashion of many 18th-c. novels his physical background, a sparsely furnished austere cell, speaks of his character. He commands the first half of the book after which the persecuted maiden, Ellena, ap-pears, as much the society heroine in flight (this work could be shelved as a "pursuit novel") as the Gothic ingénue. Little bothering with historical details of Schedoni's monastic life, Radcliffe's interest lay with the Gothic heroine, the heir of Samuel RICHARDSON's Clarissa. American critic Leslie A. Fiedler compared the two women in his pithy equation: "The sentimen-tal heroine confronts the dangers of the present, that is, of life as recorded in the newspaper; the Gothic heroine evades the perils of the past, that is, of life as recorded in history." Whereas in *Udolpho* the narra-tive was often taken up wholly with visually descrip-tive elements, in *The Italian* Radcliffe's interests have widened: a complexity of sounds—a cluster such as monastic bells, choral singing and the organ's rever-beration was added to the occasional architectural glimpse and there were also reminders of the leisured reader's travels, thus making the novel interactive.

Radcliffe treated the rigors of monastic life in *The Italian* with delicacy. Not so Lewis in *The Monk,* giv-ing his readers—as noted by Samuel Taylor COLE-RIDGE—a "poison for youth and a provocative for the debauchés." The plot hangs on Ambrosio, the popular ascetic preacher and superior of the Capuchin friars at Madrid, a chink in whose protective armor leaves the way open to lust. In pushing the work further than a tale of terror, Lewis created a horror story that many of the original readers found shameless with its vi-gnettes of sadism, sexuality, and human decay, so much so that Lewis expunged many passages in the second edition (1796) of the novel. However, the sub-jects of transvestism and transsexuality remained in Rosario's change from novice-monk to mistress. With the eventual interrogation of Ambrosio by the Inquisi-tion one meets an institution that fascinated the late Georgian reading and theater-going public. Radcliffe had inserted it into *The Italian* and found difficulty in conveying its excesses of torture and injustice; unlike her, Lewis revels in the sadism. Horror is piled high when the friar is seized by a demon and dragged to the wilds of the Sierra Morena during which he learns that Elvira, whom he slew when pursuing her daugh-ter, was his mother and the subsequently raped An-tonia, his sister. The grossness of these extravagances point to the distance Lewis stood from Radcliffe whom he professed to admire: the tenor of their writ-ing, their interests, the contrast of frenzied pace with leisurely appreciation of the setting, their moral and religious upbringing, Radcliffe's fondness for reading and Lewis's instinctive approach, all emphasize their differences.

Published in 1818, Jane AUSTEN's *Northanger Abbey* is a novel about novels. Austen was herself an omnivorous reader who had studied the works of both Lewis and Radcliffe, those of Charlotte SMITH—a popular "Gothicist" of the 1790s—as well as the ear-lier works of people as vicious and shocking, in Sam-uel JOHNSON's judgment, as the Reverend Laurence STERNE. Catherine Morland is the virtuous heroine, guided by Henry Tilney, in her reading, her under-standing of aesthetics and her travels. As the couple sit on Beechen Cliff, Henry instructs Catherine on the nature of landscape: his lesson is based on a Gilpines-que approach, in which the city of Bath nestling below is viewed as a painting with its frame, fore-ground and foils. A visit to the Tilney family home, Northanger Abbey, brings her into closer contact with Henry's father, General Tilney, a man who poses problems for Catherine. Small points suggest to the girl's excited mind that he has the qualities of a Mon-toni, Radcliffe's villain. In the leisurely style of Rad-cliffe, Catherine eventually discovers that all is well and she and the general form a pact of mutual accep-tance. What is unfortunate about the romance is not the plot but the impression that the work is an exercise in the practice of a literary genre with the truly Gothic material introduced almost as a superfluity.

Perhaps Thomas Love PEACOCK is on safer ground in *Nightmare Abbey,* published in 1818. A gathering of acquaintances, some obviously based on contem-porary writers, discuss literary trends of the day. One of the book's aims was to attempt to "let in a little daylight on [the] atrabilarious complexion" of current literature, including Austen's novel published in the same year. By the second decade of the 19th c., the Gothic apparatus had rusted and to some extent be-come obsolescent, but Peacock takes the reader past often-used set pieces: Glowry speaks of classical ruins with their one legged Venus or buried Jupiter; Alexander POPE's reference to the "Genius of the Place" is fused with the *tutela* of Nightmare Abbey, a figure reminiscent of Lewis's Romance, who throws the veil of melancholy over Marionetta, for whom Skythrop has fallen; and there is talk of decay, given a tangible image in the "south-western tower, which was ruinous and full of owls [and] might, with equal propriety have been called the aviary."

In *Nightmare Abbey,* the passage of ideas predomi-nates; the insubstantial plot is no more than a peg from which they hang. On the other hand, *Franken-stein; or, The Modern Prometheus* contains a remark-ably strong narrative line, while allowing its author, Mary SHELLEY, to bring to the fore myriad ideas about the nature of man as a social being. Dr. Frankenstein's principal interest is in the nature of life yet in order to find the scrap humanity from which it is to be con-structed, he searches graveyards and charnel houses. This morbidity is in turn fastened on to the creature, which brings death to Elizabeth, the creator's wife. With a sudden transition from the Geneva cemetery to the plains of Russia, Shelley introduces scenery filled with immensity, the kind to which Edmund BURKE referred in his essay on the sublime, *A Philosophical Enquiry into the Origins of Our Ideas of the Sublime and Beautiful.* Shelley's *Frankenstein* is told in three concentric layers. A series of letters from a sea-captain who has picked up Frankenstein on the Arctic ice frames a narrative by Frankenstein to the writer, and embeds the monster's own story as told to Frankenstein.

Although the Georgian Gothic romance finds a natural termination point here, the genre continues to the present day through such works as Bram STOKER's *Dracula,* Iris MURDOCH's *The Bell,* published in 1958, and the novels of Susan HOWATCH, among others. The cinema has been responsible for ensuring the continuance of terror and suspense as products of contemporary Gothic. Alfred Hitchcock's *Psycho* (1960) has many of the elements of its 18th-c. counterpart: the dilapidated dwelling; the cascade reappears as the shower, which is the setting for the murder; the murderous psychopath whose knowledge of the territory makes him its overlord; and the heroine, sister of the victim, running on the tramlines of virtue and danger through the plot. Looking back over this survey, one may legitimately inquire, "Why were the Gothic novels termed 'Gothic?'" Contemporaries of Walpole accepted that the plots of the romances took place in an undefined "mediaeval period" and that selected appurtenances, such as castles, dungeons, villainous overlord, and a supernatural world of specters, would feature. This spirit of antiquarianism in part gave way to contemporary aesthetic movements like the Picturesque (leaving the way open for descriptions of wild landscapes) and the apprehension of the sublime, earlier codified as an aesthetic theory. Alongside this, there was a tendency for writers to dampen the impact of the supernatural and to clarify through rationalization, a practice that led to the intensification of suspense in the novel. Further changes in taste opened the way for parodies of the Gothic romance. It was left to Mary Shelley, in a novel difficult to categorize, to utilize the theories and artifacts of the Gothic that had preceded her writing as well as contemporary scientific interests in the nature and creation of "artificial" life.

BIBLIOGRAPHY: Birkhead, E., *The Tale of Terror: A Study of the Gothic Romance* (1921); Hussey, C., *The Picturesque* (1967); Jarrett, D., *The Gothic Form in Fiction and Its Relation to History* (1980); Manwaring, E. W., *Italian Landscape in Eighteenth-Century England* (1925); Punter, D., *The Literature of Terror* (1980); Ranger, P. V., *"Terror and Pity Reign in Every Breast": Gothic Drama in the London Patent Theatres, 1750–1820* (1991); Sage, V., *Horror Fiction in the Protestant Tradition* (1988); Varma, D. P., *The Gothic Flame* (1957)

PAUL RANGER

GOWER, John

b. 1330?, probably in Kent; d. 1408, Southwark

G., a contemporary of Geoffrey CHAUCER, with whom he shared a friendship and exchanged work, was until the mid-18th c. commonly paired with Chaucer as the cofounder of English poetry. The author of some 80,000 lines of verse in Latin, French, and MIDDLE ENGLISH, G. was truly a trilingual poet—a unique achievement among English literary figures to this day. His reputation then as now rests primarily on the popularity of his major poem in English, the *Confessio Amantis* (wr. ca. 1390–92), or "Lover's Confession," and perhaps to a lesser degree on "To King Henry IV, In Praise of Peace," a poem also in English; but in fact the bulk of G.'s known writings are in Anglo-Norman French (*Mirour de l'Omme,* or *Speculum Meditantis,* and two ballade sequences, *Traitie pour les amantz marietz* and *Cinkante Balades*) and in Latin (*Vox Clamantis, Cronica Tripertita,* and various shorter poems). That G. took pride in his ability to compose in all three of the salient languages of his time is clear from his tomb in St. Saviour's Church, Southwark, where the head of his near-life-size effigy is supported by three large tomes clearly labeled "Speculum Meditantis," "Vox Clamantis," "Confessio Amantis."

Little definite is known of his early life, although Kent is generally accepted as G.'s birthplace. He perhaps had some formal legal training, possibly at the Inns of Court; if so, he would have acquired knowledge useful in land dealings recorded ca. 1365–82 for properties in Norfolk, Suffolk, and Kent. Perhaps because of G.'s legal acumen (or merely because of his evident probity), Chaucer gave G. his power of attorney when the former traveled to Italy in 1378. Sometime after 1377, G. took formal residence in the priory of St. Mary Overeys in Southwark, apparently as a lay brother. On January 23, 1398, G. obtained a license to marry one Agnes Groundolf, thought to have been his nurse, on the priory grounds. G.'s will, dated August 15, 1408, leaves substantial property to his wife and several religious houses, but makes no provision for children. A social and religious conservative, G. evidently understood the role of poet to be that of moral legislator, and in all his works fiercely criticized corruption at every level of church and state—an aspect of his friend's character Chaucer must have had in mind when he dedicated his *Troilus and Crisyede* to "moral G." Politically, G. shifted his support from Richard II to Henry IV, perhaps as early as 1387, but in any case well before Richard's deposition in

1399, a prescient loyalty Henry rewarded with a collar of silver "SS" links. This may be seen in replica around the neck of G.'s tomb effigy. Further testimony to the significance of G.'s association with the House of Lancaster are the translations into Portuguese and Castillian of the *Confessio Amantis*, copies of which undoubtedly the daughters of John of Gaunt carried with them when they married Iberian kings. G. is thus the first known English poet to have poetry translated into other languages.

The primary concern of all G.'s works is the moral reformation of society. His general method is to describe, often in vivid detail, the vices and corruption peculiar to each of the social classes, followed by a call for repentance and change. G. is fearless and uncompromising in his criticism, sparing no group from the papacy and higher clergy, and kings and nobles, to the lowest peasantry. In the *Mirour de l'Omme* (wr. ca. 1376–79), thought by some to be G.'s earliest extant work, the subject is the complete moral life of Man. (The *Mirour* exists today in a single manuscript of 28,603 lines arranged in twelve-line stanzas of octosyllabic verse, rhyming *a a b, a a b, b b a, b b a*.) The poem is in three parts, apparently of equal importance but of unequal length. The first section, comprising about two-thirds of the poem, presents the allegory of the Devil's coupling with Sin, his own daughter, to beget Death; the subsequent incest of Sin and Death begetting seven daughters (the so-called Deadly Sins); the marriage of the World to the Seven Sins; their mutual assault on Man; the prayer of Conscience and Reason to God for assistance, and God's answering that with the marriage of the Seven Virtues to Reason; descriptions of the offspring of the Virtues and Reason, and their pairing off against the Sins and their children. In the second part, the battle between good and evil is waged in the world. The Three Estates—clergy, knights and lords, and peasants—are subdivided and examined: all, from pope to parish priest, emperor to laborer, are found corrupt and in need of divine grace. The third and final section offers that grace in the form of the Virgin Mary, whose life, joys and sorrows are related in detail. The last lines of the *Mirour* as we have them (it is likely the manuscript has lost a dozen leaves from front and back) are a prayer to the Virgin for mercy and grace.

G. follows a similar pattern in the *Vox Clamantis* (wr. ca. 1377–81; from "vox clamantis in deserto, voice crying in the wilderness," John 1:23), a poem of some 10,265 unrhymed elegiac lines, and G.'s most important Latin work. The *Vox* consists of seven books, the first of which (sometimes called the "Visio") is a lightly veiled allegory of the Peasants' Revolt of 1381, presented as a horrific dream, in which "New Troy" (London) is destroyed by anthropomorphic animals. The Dreamer flees, at first running, then later on a ship, itself becoming subject to storms and attacks by monsters of the deep. Eventually the ship makes land again, in the kingdom of "Brute," where the dream began. Book 2 describes the many miseries of humanity, condemns Fortune (but points out her ultimate powerlessness) and ends with a powerful reaffirmation of the Christian faith. In the following three books the degeneracies of the Three Estates are detailed and examined, beginning with the clergy (books 3 and 4), then the knights and peasants (book 5). Book 6 is reserved exclusively for "ministers of law," including not only the legal profession but also those who enforce the laws; a lengthy address to the king as guardian of the nation ends the book. In the final book, the statue of Nebuchadnezzar's dream (Dan. 2) is used to focus discussion on human wickednesses and precarious mortality. G. brings the book and poem to a close with a strong appeal to the English to heed the lesson of the statue and reform both themselves and their country.

By far G.s best-known poem is the *Confessio Amantis*, of some 33,000 lines in tetrameter couplets separated into eight books of roughly equal length. The *Confessio* departs in format, if not altogether in subject, from G.'s practice described above. Although it too contains much social satire, and is reformist in intention both of the individual and of society, in the *Confessio* G. borrows many of the conventions of courtly love (the spring morning, the sleepless lover walking the woods and finding a vision) and adapts them to create a "lover's confession" of the main character, Amans, to Genius, priest of Venus. Each Book is thus devoted to one of the seven "sins" of love, and related sub-sins, with the exception of book 7, which offers advice to rulers built around "five points of policy" (Truth, Largesse, Justice, Pity, and Chastity). As Genius examines Amans, he relates stories of varying length and complexity by way of illustration. Several of these Chaucer also narrates, notably in the *Canterbury Tales*: G.'s "Tale of Constance," for example, apparently helped shape the "Man of Law's Tale"; his "Tale of Florent" the "Wife of Bath's Tale"; "Phebus and Cornide" the tale of the Manciple. G.'s style and craftsmanship, although significantly different from Chaucer's, are at their best in the *Confessio Amantis*, and reveal G. to have merited the high esteem in which his poetry was held by his now-more-famous friend. G. closes the *Confessio Amantis* by returning to the courtly landscape, where Amans (revealed to be too old to be a proper lover) is cured of his passion by Venus, who presents him with a set of beads and the instruction to "Pray for the peace."

G.'s reputation has changed over the years, being highest through the beginning of the 17th c., his work variously praised and plundered by the likes of Hoccleve, John LYDGATE, William DUNBAR, Robert Henryson, Edmund SPENSER, William SHAKESPEARE (whose *Pericles* adapts the "Apollonius of Tyre" story from *Confessio Amantis* book 8, and brings "Ancient G." onto the stage as a chorus), and John MILTON (who may have borrowed from the *Mirour de l'Omme* for parts of *Paradise Lost*). Recently G.'s direct, straightforward narratorial style—especially in the Confessio Amantis—has attracted renewed attention, as have the independence of his literary theories, and the strength of his convictions regarding the role of poetry in shaping a good society.

BIBLIOGRAPHY: Bullon-Fernandez, M., *Fathers and Daughters in G.'s Confessio Amantis: Authority, Family, State, and Writing* (2000); Fisher, J. H., *J. G.* (1964); Minnis, A. J., ed., *G.'s Confessio Amantis* (1983); Olsson, K., *J. G. and the Structures of Conversion* (1992); Yeager, R. F., *J. G.'s Poetic: The Search for a New Arion* (1990)

R. F. YEAGER

GRAHAM, W[illiam] S[ydney]

b. 19 November 1918, Greenock, Scotland; d. 9 January 1986, Madron, Cornwall

G. left school at age fourteen and trained as an engineer then attended Newbattle Abbey Adult Residential College near Edinburgh. *Cage without Grievance,* G.'s first collection of poems, appeared in 1942, published by the philanthropist David Archer, facilitating friendships with artist John Minton and poet Dylan THOMAS in London. G. shared Thomas's taste for drink and the Bohemian lifestyle. G.'s early work showed the influence of Rimbaud and Hart Crane. *The White Threshold* (1949) reflected the seascapes of G.'s own youth. G.'s principal publisher was Faber and Faber, of which T. S. ELIOT was a director. Eliot admired G.'s poetry but said it was difficult and would sell slowly because people did not like to think. G. achieved enough recognition, however, to perform in Britain and abroad. Residence in Cornwall brought him into contact with many artists and his poems for and about them helped to define the community. Best known is his collection *The Nightfishing* (1955). *Malcolm Mooney's Land* (1970) and *Implements in Their Places* (1977) were both Poetry Book Society choices. His later work evinced philosophical interests and a native Scottish HUMOR.

GRAHAM, Winston [Mawdsley]

b. 30 June 1910, Victoria Park, Manchester

G.'s novels fall into three main groups. Among his contemporary studies of criminal psychology, the most celebrated, through having been filmed, with the setting changed to the U.S., by Alfred Hitchcock is *Marnie* (1961). Others in this genre to be filmed are *Take My Life* (1947) and *The Walking Stick* (1967), and others worthy of note are *The Sleeping Partner*

(1956), *Angell, Pearl and Little God* (1970), *Woman in the Mirror* (1975), and *The Green Flash* (1986). Of his historical novels the best known are the sequence set in late-18th-c. Cornwall concerning the Poldark family, starting with *Ross Poldark* (1945; repub. as *The Renegade*, 1951): early novels in the saga became a popular and highly regarded British television series in the 1970s. G.'s books about character-forming experiences in exotic settings include *Greek Fire* (1957) and *Tremor* (1995).

GRAHAME, Kenneth

b. 8 March 1859, Edinburgh, Scotland; 6 July 1932, Pangbourne

G. is best known for *The Wind in the Willows*, published in 1908, a work often ranked with Lewis CARROLL's *Alice's Adventures in Wonderland* and Mark Twain's *Tom Sawyer*. Other of his tales, such as *The Reluctant Dragon* (1938), also continue to enjoy popularity. G. described himself as a "stream," not a "pump"—his literary output was small, but enjoyed fans as diverse as Theodore Roosevelt, the German Kaiser, and the poet A. C. SWINBURNE.

G.'s life has been described as "complex." Born in Edinburgh, the death of his mother and the abandonment of the nine-year-old G. and his siblings by their alcoholic father to a maternal grandmother set a pattern of sadness and disappointment. Although showing a scholarly aptitude, he was sent to London, entering the Bank of England in 1879 where he worked until his retirement in 1908. His marriage was disappointing, and his son, for whom the adventures of Toad, Rat, and Mole began as bedtime stories, was killed while walking along the railroad, a possible suicide. It is not surprising, then, that much of G.'s writings are marked by nostalgia for a lost childhood, a retreat into genteel retirement, and the pleasures of convivial bachelorhood.

F. J. Furnivall first nourished G.'s literary career. At twenty-one, he became honorary secretary of the Shakespeare Society, and *St. James' Gazette* published his first attributed essay, "By a Northern Furrow." Encouraged by W. E. HENLEY, G. began publishing essays in Henley's *National Observer*, which also included among its contributors W. B. YEATS, Joseph CONRAD, Hart Crane, and H. G. WELLS. G. based his first book, *Pagan Papers* (1894), on eighteen of the twenty-one pieces published by Henley. Typical was "The Rural Pan," which imagines the god Mercury traveling up and down the Thames in a rented steam launch, Apollo lounging at the Guard's Club, and Pan enjoying the solitude of some backwater, dabbling with music on his pipes, pointing both to G.'s playfulness and to the recurrent theme of retirement. Frequently compared to the essays of Robert Louis STEVENSON, *Pagan Papers* is often linked with the late Romantic movement called neo-Paganism.

The Golden Age (1895) represents a move from the personal essay to fiction. The work consists of eighteen stories, narrated by an unnamed child about the adventures of himself and his orphan siblings under the care of elderly aunts and uncles identified as the "Olympians." The stories hint at G.'s own childhood experiences under the care of his dutiful, but distant relatives. The stories are noted for their empathetic but unsentimental appreciation of the child's world, laying the groundwork for E. NESBIT.

Dream Days (1898) collected eight stories, including "The Reluctant Dragon," later republished separately, and "The Headswoman." The latter, which had appeared in the *Yellow Book* in 1894, was G.'s only purely adult story. It is a mildly antifeminist satire in the tone of Voltaire's *Candide* about a young woman named Jeanne, who wishes to inherit her father's post as town executioner. "The Reluctant Dragon" is G.'s first animal story, and marks the first work in literature ever to treat a dragon as a comic character and not some medieval monster. The three main characters dramatize the tensions in G. himself, with the boy embodying the vital child, Saint George, Victorian duty, and the Dragon, the leisurely, poetic lifestyle.

All of G.'s themes come together in his masterpiece, *The Wind in the Willows*. The book is broadly patterned around the adventures of Odysseus. Mole, Rat, and Toad present a world of genteel and convivial bachelorhood, an escape from the pressures of the modern world that does not upset the status quo. As in the "Reluctant Dragon," they negotiate the tensions between duty and pleasure, responsibility and adventure. The equanimity of their Arcadian serenity is threatened only by the intrusion of modern technology, such as Toad's automobile, or by the invasion of the lower classes, as when the stoats and weasels seize Toad Hall.

Encouraged by friends to expand the bedtime stories, G. found publishers at first reluctant to publish the completed work because of uncertainty about animal fantasy. While the initial response was muted, *Wind in the Willows* won champions such as A. A. MILNE, whose Christopher Robin stories were influenced by G. It has also influenced works such as J. R. R. TOLKIEN's *The Hobbit*. Enjoying increasing popularity and influence, it has now taken its place among the classics of CHILDREN'S LITERATURE.

BIBLIOGRAPHY: Green, P., *K. G., 1859–1932* (1959); Kuznets, L. R., *K. G.* (1987); Prince, A., *K. G.* (1994)

THOMAS L. COOKSEY

GRAND, Sarah

(psued. of Frances Elizabeth Bellenden Clarke) b. 10 June 1854, Donaghadee, County Down, Ireland; d. 12 May 1943, Calne, Wiltshire

G. was a feminist whose 1894 article "The New Aspect of the Woman Question" coined the phrase "New Woman" to describe the feminist activists in the late 19th c. who fought for women's social and political rights. From 1873 until 1922, G. published thirteen books, as well as many short stories and essays, the most popular of which were *The Heavenly Twins* (3 vols., 1893) and *The Beth Book* (1897). Both of these novels were best-sellers in the U.S. and Britain, and thanks to the recent rediscovery of G.'s work by feminist scholars, are once again in print.

The New Woman novel, as described by journalist W. T. Stead in 1894, "is not merely a novel written by a woman, or a novel written about women, but a novel written by a woman about women from the standpoint of Woman." These novels restructured the marriage plot, considered controversial issues such as the Contagious Diseases Acts and vivisection, lobbied for women to be properly educated, and asked that men live up to the same moral standards as those set for women. G.'s characters are upper-middle-class British women who have the financial freedom required for their political activities and younger women with promise, caught in stifling marriages to unappreciative men. G.'s style is logical, even scientific. She appears to be dissecting gender relationships by looking closely at the arguments given by men to support their beliefs in women's inferiority and exposing their inconsistencies. This style twists the common marriage plot by thwarting the romantic appearance of gender relations to examine the dissatisfaction that lies beneath. Her novels are deeply psychological in that much of importance occurs within the female characters' evolution or in discussions that illustrate women's logic and intelligence. *The Heavenly Twins*, a novel that explored the lives of several women, was more popular than *The Beth Book*, which followed Beth's personal growth, because it was less internally focused and its plot more varied.

G.'s fiction is still relevant in many of the issues it raises, and though ideological dialogue can at times be too strongly present (especially in her less popular novels like *Ideala*, 1888), the characters and their situations are realistic and appealing. *The Heavenly Twins* provides an interesting narrative style, with the five different books told from the perspectives of several characters. According to Sally Mitchell, this unusual narrative structure helps to further distort the marriage plot, already disrupted by unconventional thinking by the female characters. Angelica (one of the two heavenly twins, the other being her brother Diavolo) proposes to her husband, an older male friend whom she calls "Daddy," when she realizes the limitations placed on her future because of her gender: "Marry me, *and let me do as I like*." Evadne refuses to have sexual relations with her husband once she learns he is not a virgin, and Edith dies from contracting syphilis from her military husband.

G.'s work was controversial because of explicit references made to subjects such as venereal disease and the immoral and oftentimes degrading behavior of men toward their wives. Yet she does not place all the blame on men. Evadne tells her women friends that as long as they forgive men their sins, "men will do anything." G. considered her role to be that of educator, and felt that her literature could change lives. Her desire was that women teach men to accept them as equals and thus improve the lives of both. Her popularity among recent scholars illustrates the contemporary nature of her work.

BIBLIOGRAPHY: Broomfield, A., and S. Mitchell, eds., *Prose by Victorian Women* (1996); Kersley, G., *Darling Madame; S. G. and Devoted Friend* (1983); Magnum, T., *Married, Middlebrow, and Militant: S. G. and the New Woman Novel* (1998)

LYNNE CROCKETT

GRANVILLE BARKER [or GRANVILLE-BARKER], Harley

b. 25 November 1877, London; d. 31 August 1946, Paris, France

G. B. was a polymath: London actor by the time he was twenty-two; "inventor" of the position of director in the theater by the age of thirty; leading playwright; Shakespearean scholar. Had he done no practical theater work at all he would be reckoned a major figure for his literary work alone, comprising as it did several outstanding plays, a considerable body of critical theory and some of the liveliest and most profound commentary on William SHAKESPEARE of the 20th c. His fourteen plays (not counting translations and adaptations) are remarkable for their quick growth to maturity and artistic complexity, beginning with the imitative and jejune *A Comedy of Fools* and *The Family of the Oldroyds* written in collaboration with Berte Thomas in 1895–96 when G. B. was eighteen and progressing to the high originality and sensitivity of *The Madras House* in 1910 and of *The Secret Life* in 1923.

G. B. himself said, early in his playwriting career, that the two major influences on his playwriting were Henrik Ibsen and Maurice Maeterlinck. This, at first glance, seems a curious and contradictory combination but an examination of his plays does support his theory in this. In *The Voysey Inheritance* (perf. 1905; pub. 1906) and *Waste* (perf. 1907; pub. 1909) the Ibsen influence is paramount though one needs to remember that Ibsen was primarily a poet, not a mere social reformer. In The *Marrying of Ann Leete* (perf. 1902; pub. 1909) and *The Secret Life*, the traces of the transmuted Maeterlinckian strain are clear. It seems a hopeless oversimplification to try to jam him, as so many critics and commentators have attempted to do, into a category called "Edwardian social realism" (itself a tired and only half-true cliché) and Margery

Morgan is, surely, mistaken to regard English governmental politics as the essential center of his work.

His best play, *The Madras House* (perf. 1910; pub. 1910), whose aesthetic brilliance and poetic profundity are only now beginning to be fully realized, is an excellent example of the mature artist in whom the various influences which he has absorbed have by now coalesced and have formed a unified style which is recognizably and uniquely his own. Only one theater critic of G. B.'s own time immediately realized the quality and stature of this play. This was Ludwig Lewisohn who, in reviewing in the New York magazine the *Nation* (November 16, 1921), the first American production of *The Madras House* said: "An infinite number of plays have been written on the relations of the sexes, but none except *The Madras House* has called attention to the pervasive and voluntary sexuality of the whole of Western civilization. Such is the intellectual content of *The Madras House*. But I am acquainted with few modern plays in which that content is more skillfully or unobtrusively handled or is more firmly and delicately woven into the texture of those human lives which make the play." This same kind of stylistic perfection is clearly visible in G. B.'s exquisite little one-act play, "Farewell to the Theatre" (pub. 1917; never performed in G. B.'s lifetime).

G. B.'s most striking—and still challenging—book of theater criticism is *The Exemplary Theatre* (1922) in which he describes in fascinating detail the fruits of his own experience. His description of the intrinsic and essential relationship between director, actor, and text is at least as important as Stanislavsky's work on the same subject—and was published some twelve years earlier. He also has four books of textual criticism: *On Dramatic Method* (1931), *The Study of Drama* (1934), *On Poetry in the Drama* (1937), and *The Use of the Drama* (1945).

Apart from his plays (some, indeed, would say including his plays) his best-known and most enduring literary works are his *Prefaces to Shakespeare* (5 series, 1927–47). They were begun in 1927 in response to an invitation from Ernest Benn Ltd., the London publisher, who was planning a special edition of Shakespeare—one play per volume, handmade paper, illustrations by Charles Ricketts, Norman Wilkinson, and other famous stage designers, and a preface by G. B. for each play. After only three volumes had appeared, the project collapsed commercially under its own weight, but by then G. B. had the bit firmly between his teeth and went on writing prefaces for nonexistent editions. He had, in effect, devised an entirely new method of Shakespeare criticism: he examines each text slowly and carefully, word by word, but he does so always from the point of view of what it will sound like in the theater, what interpretational problems it will give the actors, and what imaginative, creative opportunities it creates for them. Most of all, he tries to envisage what the overall gesture of the whole play will appear to be to the audience. In a word, he writes an introduction to the play as seen by a director—albeit, in this instance, a director of much more than average intelligence and poetic sensibility. Between 1927 and 1946, he completed ten of these masterly pieces, the last one, *Coriolanus*, being finished only just before he died. Over the years, they have been published in Britain and the U.S. by three or four different publishers, and they have never been allowed to go out of print.

His literary career, complete, distinguished, and important in itself, is nevertheless only half the story. His "season" at the Court Theatre from 1904 to 1907 changed the face of British theater and, incidentally, created the position of "director" (not that the term was ever used by or of G. B.) as a permanent and essential functionary in the artistic structure of the new theater. And his three revolutionary productions of Shakespeare—*The Winter's Tale* (1912), *Twelfth Night* (1912), *A Midsummer Night's Dream* (1914)— in which he whole-heartedly embraced the visionary ideas of William Poel and dealt a massive and mortal blow to the superficial and meretricious pseudo-Shakespeare of Sir Henry Irving and Sir Herbert Beerbohm Tree, initiated an approach to Shakespearean production whose influence can clearly be traced (though it was not always followed) through the whole of the 20th c.

BIBLIOGRAPHY: Kennedy, D., *G. B. and the Dream of Theatre* (1985); Morgan, M. M., *A Drama of Political Man: A Study in the Plays of H. G. B.* (1961); Salmon, E., *G. B.* (1983)

ERIC SALMON

GRAVES, Richard

b. 4 May 1715, Mickleton; d. 23 November 1804, Claverton

Soon after G. became rector of the village of Claverton, near Bath, a journeyman shoemaker turned itinerant Methodist preacher invaded the parish. The intruder quickly vanished, but he was immortalized as Geoffry Wildgoose, the protagonist of G.'s best and best-known comic novel, *The Spiritual Quixote* (3 vols., 1773).

The Spiritual Quixote draws heavily on Miguel de Cervantes' original as well as such English derivatives as Henry FIELDING's *Joseph Andrews*. Many of the incidents, however, derive from life. G.'s brother Charles Caspar actually took to the road as a Methodist preacher, and G. used material from the published journals of the Wesleys and George Whitefield. Book 6, which recounts the history of Mr. Rivers and Charlotte Woodville, is a thinly disguised narrative of G.'s

love affair with and marriage to Lucy Bartholomew. Despite his loyalty to the Church of England, G. treats Methodism and its adherents gently, though he presents Whitefield as a humbug. The novel reveals G.'s love of the English countryside through which he leads Wildgoose. Translated into German, the novel was sold as a guide to tourists.

This celebration of the rural also characterizes G.'s third and fourth novels: *Eugenius* (2 vols., 1785) and *Plexippus* (2 vols., 1790). *Columella* (2 vols., 1779), G.'s second work of prose fiction, shows the dangers of rustication. Based on the life of G.'s long-time friend, the poet William SHENSTONE, it argues that an active life is essential to happiness.

Shenstone prompted other literary efforts from G. Shenstone sent the publisher Robert DODSLEY to G. when Dodsley needed an epilogue to his tragedy *Cleone* (1758). As Shenstone's literary executor, G. edited his friend's poems, prose works, and letters (3 vols.,1764–65). When Samuel JOHNSON's "Life of Shenstone" appeared in 1781, G. took exception to some observations there and responded with *Recollections of Some Particulars in the Life of the Late William Shenstone, Esq.* (1788).

An admirer of the poets of the early 18th c., G. imitated their forms and, at times, their satiric bent. Increasingly, though, he turned to panegyric, writing the praises of such friends as Dodsley and Ralph Allen. For some years, he read poems at the Thursday morning salons of Lady Anna Miller of Bath Easton; these verses were collected in *Euphrosyne* (2 vols., 1776–80).

To supplement his income G. kept a school at Claverton (1750–90), which Thomas Robert MALTHUS attended. G.'s translation of the Greek historian Herodianus' life of Commodus (*The Heir Apparent*, 1789) may have been prompted by G.'s teaching that work. Among G.'s other translations was the *Meditations* of Marcus Aurelius (1792). This work appealed to G. because he shared its concern for proper social behavior. Whether advising his son against the teachings of Joseph Priestley (*A Letter from a Father to His Son at the University*, 1787), taking a Burkean stand against the excesses of the French Revolution, or warning against solitude, G. urged and exemplified moderation, conformity, and, above all, good HUMOR.

BIBLIOGRAPHY: Hill, C. J., *The Literary Career of R. G.* (1935); Tracy, C., *A Portrait of R. G.* (1987)

JOSEPH ROSENBLUM

GRAVES, Robert [von Ranke]

b. 24 July 1895, London; d. 7 December 1985, Deyá, Majorca, Spain

G. regarded himself as a poet mainly, and, as poet, he has a devoted and discerning following. He is, though, better remembered for his prose works, particularly *Good-Bye to All That* (1929; rev. ed., 1957), *I, Claudius* (1934), and *Claudius the God* (1934). He wrote prolifically, and wrote nothing dull. He was a fine classical scholar who produced excellent translations of Apuleius's *The Golden Ass* (1950) and Suetonius's *The Twelve Caesars* (1956), as well as a guide to Greek mythology, *The Greek Myths* (2 vols., 1955). Little else of his often eccentric contribution to mythography is now read, with the exception of the *The White Goddess* (1948; rev. eds., 1952, 1961), a fascinating introduction to his theory of poetic inspiration. His literary criticism is of little repute in a theoretical age of byzantine complexity. *A Survey of Modernist Poetry* (1927), written with Laura Riding, defines his relationship to literary MODERNISM.

Good-Bye to All That is AUTOBIOGRAPHY. Perhaps the finest memoir to emerge from the First World War (G. was an officer in the Royal Welch Fusiliers), *Good-Bye to All That* provides a clear-eyed, unsentimentally understated account of the cruelty and degradation of trench warfare. The coolly devastating analysis of civilian incomprehension and political betrayal of the army is shot through with grimly ironic comedy. G. changed the narrative of war for the rest of his century. Many comment on the influence of this work on Evelyn WAUGH and American author Joseph Heller, for example. "All That" is the flawed civilization that condemned him and his generation to the trenches. Writing the book was to be his farewell to "all that." Although the proceeds allowed him to leave England forever, the psychic wounds never healed properly. In great old age, he was haunted by the thought of the Germans he might have killed.

The powerful evocation of the experience of war overshadows the many virtues of the earlier part of the book. G. attended Charterhouse School and leaves an affectionately ironic and gently unsentimental insight into public-school life in the last few years before the Great War. Equally moving is the melancholy that tinges his account of childhood holidays spent with his German relatives, some of whom would later occupy the trenches opposite his own on the western front.

I, Claudius and *Claudius the God* were written to make money. They did that and much more. The television production in the 1970s introduced G. at his best to a huge and appreciative audience. G. understands and feels early imperial Rome as intimately as he does the world of *Good-Bye to All That*. In Claudius's lifetime, the imperial family turns Rome into a chamber of horrors. Morally deformed by their attempts to control an explosive world, the Julio-Claudians increasingly resort to public and private ferocity and depravity. Claudius survives this Roman version of "all that" and comes to uneasy terms with what he cannot finally control. Like the modern world, imperial Rome feasted upon terror and crippling insecurity. G. does not force the analogy between then and now. His acute sense of the quotidian in Roman history makes it appear frighteningly familiar. Readers usually fail to notice the extent of G.'s scholarship, a tribute to his narrative genius. His knowledge of how ordinary things were done in ancient Rome produces a density of texture rare in historical novels. G. is distinguished from contemporary purveyors of historical fiction in his respect for the historical autonomy of his characters and for the integrity of historical fact. In short, he is the model of how to do it. The writing of the finest historical novels of the 20th c. is sufficient to secure G.'s reputation.

G., however, would have preferred to be remembered as a poet. W. H. AUDEN admired his poetry, but G. is rarely mentioned in the same breath as poets such as T. S. ELIOT, Ezra Pound, W. B. YEATS, or Auden himself. He stood apart from his modernist contemporaries. His poetry is more inward, less public than theirs. The poetry produced after the Great War seeks to come to personal terms with that experience. He is, perhaps, most successful as a love poet. His lyricism recalls the Georgian poets, and brings the English Romantic tradition into the 20th c. His theory of poetry is the focus of *The White Goddess*, *The Crowning Privilege* (1955), and *Oxford Addresses on Poetry* (1962). These polemical works distinguish between "Muse poets" and "Apollonian poets." Apollonian poets have deserted the Muse for Apollo, the rational god of the patriarchy. *The Crowning Privilege* gives a scathing account of most of his contemporaries, all of whom have betrayed the muse. Of Eliot he says: "what I like about Eliot is that though one of his two hearts, the poetic one, has died . . . he continues to visit the grave wistfully and lay flowers on it." The muse is mother, bride, and layer-out of the dead. The poet is to be the servant and lover of the muse in her many manifestations. Much of his poetry turns on his complex relations with women, and with women as muses.

However, G. is a modern poet. His ROMANTICISM is not nostalgic. He combines it with elegance, a fine irony, and a deep moral awareness. His verse is technically superb. His response to the "godawfulness" of "all that" is to turn away from it, to turn toward the pre-Apollonian muse of *The White Goddess*. Much of his poetry gives form to his search for the goddess/muse, betrayed by the civilization that gave us the Great War. G.'s voluntary exile in Majorca was not flight but exploration. His *Collected Poems* (1975) are testimony to the richness of the endeavor.

BIBLIOGRAPHY: Bryant, H. B., *R. G.* (1986); Graves, R. P., *R. G.: The Assault Heroic, 1895–1940* (1986);

Graves, *R. P.*, *R. G.: The Years with Laura, 1926–1940* (1990); Graves, R. P., *R. G. and the White Goddess, 1940–1985* (1995); Seymour-Smith, M., *R. G.* (1982; rev. ed., 1995)

ANGUS SOMERVILLE

GRAY, Alasdair [James]

b. 28 December 1934, Glasgow, Scotland

Artist and writer, G. trained at the Glasgow School of Art and worked as an art teacher and scriptwriter for radio and television before earning critical recognition as a novelist with the publication of *Lanark: A Life in Four Books* (1981). Similar in part to George ORWELL's *Nineteen Eighty-Four*, the novel is a complex, intricate work merging the life and death of a Glasgow art student and writer, who closely resembles G. himself, with the reincarnated title character trapped in a futuristic dystopia. The acclaimed novel established G. with other experimental writers such as Liz Lochhead, Agnes Owens, James KELMAN, and Irvine WELSH as part of a new wave of contemporary Scottish fiction. His reputation was further enhanced with the publication of *Unlikely Stories, Mostly* (1983), a collection of short stories, and his second novel, *1982 Janine* (1984). Later works include *Something Leather* (1990), *Poor Things: Episodes from the Early Life of Archibald McCandless M.D., Scottish Public Health Officer* (1992), a postmodern revision of the Frankenstein story, *A History Maker* (1994; rev. ed., 1996), and *Working Legs: A Play for People without Them* (1997).

GRAY, Simon [James Holliday]

b. 21 October 1936, Hayling Island, Hampshire

Influenced by Joe ORTON and Harold PINTER, G. emerged in the late 1960s as a writer of black comedy before earning critical recognition for his plays that dissect the milieu of contemporary middle-class academic and intellectual life. Often compared with playwrights Tom STOPPARD and Christopher HAMPTON, G. is known for his use of clever, often biting, dialogue as a means to expose the complexities of emotional detachment and resignation. Well acquainted with the world of academia, G. taught at the University of British Columbia, Trinity College, Cambridge, and from 1966 to 1986 was lecturer in English at Queen Mary College, London.

Evacuated to Canada during World War II, G. returned in 1954 and received his B.A. with honors in English from Dalhousie University. Afterward, he taught in France before earning a second degree in English from Cambridge University. In 1963, he published his first novel, *Colmain*, followed by *Simple People* and *Little Portia*, in 1965 and 1967, respectively. Simultaneously, he also began writing for British radio and television. His first stage play, *Wise Child* (perf. 1967; pub. 1968), was written originally as a teleplay, but the subject matter—incorporating themes of verbal abuse, sexual ambiguity, and violence—was considered too controversial to be shown on television. Reviews of the play were generally mixed, and G.'s second play, *Dutch Uncle* (1969), was panned, but in 1971 he returned to the West End with the critically acclaimed *Butley*, which established his reputation as a serious dramatist. The first of several of his works directed by Pinter and with Alan Bates in the title role, the play was a major success in both Britain and in the U.S. and was adapted for film in 1974.

Butley is a searing, uncompromising portrait of a toxic, tormented college professor locked in a downward spiral of depression and self-destruction. Abusive and manipulative, he uses his intellectual gifts as weapons in a war of words waged against the outside world. Similar themes of denial and dissolution inform G.'s next play, *Otherwise Engaged* (perf. 1975; pub. 1976), which like *Butley* enjoyed successful runs on the West End and on Broadway. Less successful were *Dog Days* (perf. 1976; pub. 1977) and *Molly* (perf. 1977; pub. 1978) followed by *The Rear Column* (1978), an historical play exploring the dark interior of British colonialism. Afterward, G. returned to the more familiar milieu of academia and publishing with *Close of Play* (1979), *Quartermaine's Terms* (1981), and *The Common Pursuit* (1984) followed by *Melon* (1987), revised as *The Holy Terror* (pub. 1990; perf. 1991). His later plays include *Simply Disconnected* (1996), *Life Support* (1997), which reunited G. with Pinter and Bates, *Just the Three of Us* (1999), *The Late Middle Classes* (1999), and *Japes* (pub. 2000; perf. 2001).

The author of more than thirty plays for stage and television, G. periodically ventures into other genres. In 1997, he published a novella entitled *Breaking Hearts* and works of nonfiction include *An Unnatural Pursuit and Other Pieces* (1985), *How's That for Telling 'em, Fat Lady: A Short Life in the American Theatre* (1988), and *Fat Chance* (1995), a wry, entertaining account of the disastrous production of *Cell Mates* in which actor Stephen FRY mysteriously disappeared after receiving negative reviews and for a time was thought to have committed suicide before resurfacing in Europe—something of a play-within-a-play that one might expect from G. himself. The autobiographical *Enter a Fox: Further Adventures of a Paranoid* appeared in 2001.

BIBLIOGRAPHY: Burkman, K. H., ed., *S. G.* (1992); Stephenson, A., "S. G.," in Weintraub, S., ed., *British Dramatists since World War II*, part 1, *DLB* 13

(1982): 199–208; Taylor, J. R., *The Second Wave: British Drama for the Seventies* (1971)

STEVEN R. SERAFIN

GRAY, Thomas

b. 26 December 1716, London, d. 30 July 1771, Cambridge

Scholarly efforts continue on the quest to place G. somewhere between the Augustan Age and the first stirrings of ROMANTICISM in English poetry. He is characteristically portrayed as a transitional figure with a foot in both camps, displaying the splendid polish of neoclassicism and straying willfully into subject areas and linguistic areas that were to become the predilections of the Romantic poets. G. therefore will it seems remain a hybrid-poet, from a period of fundamental hybridization, and enjoying the status of being the best-known living poet of his time.

G. was born in Cornhill, London, educated at Eton College, Berkshire (1727–34), and was associated with Peterhouse, Cambridge, from 1734. He also studied law in London in 1741. He traveled with Horace WALPOLE through France and Italy between 1739 and 1741 and famously quarreled in Florence with his companion on the same trip. G. immersed himself in the historic cultures through which he passed, reveling in the moods of landscape around him. He returned to England to teach at Peterhouse between 1742 and 1756 and then in Pembroke Hall between 1756 and 1771, declining the laureateship in 1757 on the death of Colley CIBBER. His travels abroad gave him time to think about the nature of his poetry and to begin to flesh out something akin to a manifesto. His most important and most often-quoted remark came in a letter to Richard West on April 8, 1742, where he claimed that "The language of the age is never the language of poetry."

This statement sets him somewhat at odds with the new practice of poetry that William WORDSWORTH came to promote, but not entirely, as scholars claim that G.'s "Elegy Written in a Country Churchyard" (1751) contains both a self-consciously distinct poetic diction and other more intensely personal passages. Certainly G.'s allusiveness, his displays of erudition, his personifications, in this and his other poetry, show an Augustan practice but coupled with his involvement with the sublime, lead in other directions. He is thought of as either G. the scholar or G. the man of common feelings, with the common touch.

It is surely the mark of a great writer that his or her words are incorporated into the language. G.'s enduringly famous "Elegy" is a groundbreaking poem in its focus upon the largely undocumented lives of ordinary folk. The empathy and introspection displayed in the poem look forward obliquely to the philanthropic concerns of the revolutionary period and

foreground the possibility of social change for the lower classes. The melancholy musing voice in the "Elegy" is caught within a four-line stanza in iambic pentameter, with alternate rhymes, sometimes called the heroic stanza, lending a steady rhythm to the poetry, apposite to the subject matter. G. makes a new personalizing twist to the neoclassical framework when the poet-persona appears in the final stanzas.

There are many popular and memorable lines in the poem, so popular in fact that modern criticism sometimes sees this as a problem. In his *Lives of the English Poets*, Samuel JOHNSON approved of the poem and claimed that "The 'Churchyard' abounds with images which find a mirror in every mind and with sentiments to which every bosom returns an echo." Johnson found these aspects of G.'s work in tune with his own generalizing tendencies in writing and really Johnson's criticism set the trend for later critical appraisals in that poetry such as the "Elegy" was understandable by all and therefore acceptable, but the "Odes" were hung with ungraceful ornaments and riven with harsh language showing a poet retreating into a world of poetic artifice.

If G.'s "Elegy" provided the later 18th-c. poets with a fund of images to imitate as they learned their craft, then his Pindaric odes set the tone of imitation in another sense. In "The Progress of Poesy" (1757), G. describes the various forms of poetry in a progress from Greece to Italy to Britain, poetry's primitive origins and varying powers and poetry's connections with political liberty. He pays homage to William SHAKESPEARE, John MILTON, and John DRYDEN and concludes that no one can equal them.

"The Bard" (1757) is based on a tradition that Edward I ordered the violent suppression of the Welsh bards. The poem opens with the surviving Bard cursing the English army of Edward returning from Snowdon in 1283 and, as he laments his murdered comrades, their ghosts prophesy the fate of the Plantagenets. The Bard before suicide foretells the return of the house of Tudor, and G.'s summary of history here shows ironically how the Welsh house accedes to the English throne. The poet's own antiquarian studies in history and mythology surfaced in poems where pseudoclassical form meets nonclassical, subject matter. G. also became very interested in the new discoveries in Old Norse and Welsh poetry. His imitations include "The Fatal Sisters" and "The Descent of Odin" (1768).

Other poems of note in G.'s small but varied canon include the "Sonnet [on the Death of Mr. Richard West]" (wr. 1742, not published in G.'s lifetime), the "Ode on a Distant Prospect of Eton College" (wr. 1747), and the "Ode on the Death of a Favourite Cat Drowned in a Tub of Gold Fishes" (wr. 1748) from Robert DODSLEY's *Collection of Poems*. This last work gives us a glimpse of the poet working in a much lighter, wittier, vein and shows the debt to Alexander

POPE. G.'s later years were devoted to the pursuit of botany and the quest for the picturesque.

BIBLIOGRAPHY: Hutchings, W. B., and W. Ruddick, eds., *T. G.* (1993); Ketton-Cremer, R. W., *T. G.* (1955); Lonsdale. R., ed., *The Poems of T. G., William Collins, and Oliver Goldsmith* (1969); Toynbee, P., and L. Whibley, eds., *The Correspondence of T. G.* (3 vols., 1935)

CHRISTOPHER J. P. SMITH

GREEN, Henry

(pseud. of Henry Yorke) b. 29 October 1905, Forthampton Court, Gloucestershire; d. 15 December 1973, London

Henry Green was the name under which Henry Yorke wrote his nine novels, a memoir, and some twenty short stories. Many critics have claimed him as a major experimental novelist, and his novels were held in high regard by other writers during his lifetime. However, his posthumous reputation has been curious. There have been several excellent critical studies and a recent biography, as well as a number of reprintings of his novels (though they tend not to stay in print). Nevertheless, he has not established the secure place among either the reading public or academic readers of contemporaries such as Evelyn WAUGH or Anthony POWELL. His novels are remarkable for combining modernist experiment, an idiosyncratic and highly poetic style, and often an allegorical or mythic aura with a traditional novelistic interest in complex plots and full casts of well-realized characters.

"I was born a mouth-breather with a silver spoon in 1905," starts G.'s characteristically odd memoir, *Pack My Bag* (1940). His father was an industrialist, to whose company, Pontifex, G. eventually succeeded as director. G. went to Eton, to Oxford for a period, worked on the shop-floor at his father's Birmingham factory, and then went into the business as a manager. During World War II, he served in the Auxiliary Fire Service in London. Thereafter, he worked at Pontifex until his retirement in 1959. Nearly all his novels are based closely on these experiences.

His first novel, *Blindness* (1926), about how a schoolboy who goes blind perceives the world, received favorable notice in the *Times Literary Supplement*. His second, *Living* (1929), had mixed responses. Some reviewers were puzzled by the novel's disconcerting style and disregard for whether the reader could decode or follow all of the details. Others, particularly Waugh, argued that the novel was an outstanding and original achievement. It is set in a factory and concerns the lives of both the owners and a whole range of its workers and their families. If in one way it is socially responsible in a "proletarian fiction" mode, it is also highly experimental, inter-

ested in the aesthetic evocation of the textures, particularly visual, of ordinary urban life. The style is notable for its omission of the definite article, particularly in descriptions of the working-class characters: "She met Bert in corner." This is partly, but not wholly, explainable as a way of rendering dialect.

G.'s next novel, *Party Going* (1939), is similarly of the 1930s in its sustained hints of class division and coming revolution, but it also is comic and ambiguous, and leaves many issues unresolved. A party of "bright young things" setting off on holiday are trapped in a railway hotel by dense fog. Outside, the less fortunate classes make the best of it in the damp station. Despite the rich party's dark fears about the "masses," it is actually those out in the cold who seem to have the better time of it and to behave better. A servant trapped outside with the crowds says, "it's fellow feeling, that's what I like about it." The reader is left to make his or her own connections, but it is notable that those inside the hotel are made uncomfortable by a mysterious middle aged woman called Miss Fellowes who is carrying a dead pigeon around with her.

G.'s other novels—*Caught* (1943), *Loving* (1945), *Back* (1946), *Concluding* (1948), *Nothing* (1950), *Doting* (1952)—are similar in general texture, though each is very much eccentric in its own way. Each manages to combine what are usually contradictory veins in the novel form: an ability to represent and evoke the detail and specificity of ordinary experience, and an interest in prose as an autonomous artistic order that is allusive, irrational and not responsible in any way to the familiar modes of ordinary life. G.'s novels are still very much, as Waugh said of *Living* in 1930, "neglected masterpieces."

BIBLIOGRAPHY: Mengham, R., *The Idiom of the Time: The Writings of H. G.* (1982); Russell, J. D., *H. G.* (1960); Stokes, E., *The Novels of H. G.* (1959); Treglown, J., *Romancing: The Life and Work of H. G.* (2000)

CHRIS HOPKINS

GREENAWAY, Kate [Catherine]

b. 17 March 1846, London; d. 6 November 1901, London

During her visits to relatives in Rolleston, Nottinghamshire, the Victorian children's poet and artist G. saw farm workers in blue smocks, women in frilly lace and poke bonnets, fields filled with flowers. These inspired her pictures of a rural, preindustrial world. As her long-time friend John RUSKIN observed in "Fairy Land: Mrs. Allingham and Kate Greenaway," she shows "no railway . . . to carry the child away . . . no tunnel or pit mouth . . . no league-long viaducts . . . no blinkered iron bridges." Though she occasionally illustrated her own verses, she is best known for the water colors she executed to accompany texts by others. Perhaps better than any other artist, she captured the pre-Freudian Victorian view of childhood innocence. As the *Spectator* (December 1879) said of her first book, *Under the Windows* (1879), she offered "a better land, where strawberries are larger, cakes plummier and sweeter, and children prettier and more engaging than in this work-a-day world."

GREENE, Graham [Henry]

b. 2 October 1904, Berkhamsted Hertfordshire; d. 3 April 1991, Vevey, Switzerland

G. produced a staggering volume of reviews, essays, short stories, travel books, plays, screenplays, autobiographies, entertainments, and novels. By the end of the 1930s, he was one of the most widely read English writers of his generation; by the end of the 1940s, he had earned an international reputation; and by the end of the1950s, he had become a major figure in 20th-c. literature. G. turned away from the high MODERNISM of his day and chose instead to write seriously for a mass audience.

G.'s unhappy childhood and adolescence have been well documented, including his occasional attempts at suicide to escape from boredom, which became a lifelong fear. He completed a B.A. degree in modern history at Balliol College, Oxford, in 1925, and after meeting his future wife, he was formally received into the Roman Catholic Church in 1926. While employed as a subeditor for the *Times* in London, G. published *The Man Within* (1929) and earned a three-book contract from the Heinemann publishing firm. Unfortunately, his next two efforts, *The Name of the Action* (1930) and *Rumour at Nightfall* (1931), were dismal failures. Needing money, G. went to work on a "pot-boiler" that would lend itself to the motion pictures. *Stamboul Train* (1932; repub. as *Orient Express*, 1933) rescued his career, and for the next fifty years, G. wrote nearly always at the top of his form.

Between 1932 and 1958, G. labeled his books as entertainments or novels, distinguishing for readers between works of action and works of characterization. The action-filled plots of his entertainments often turn on political intrigues, duplicitous sexual affairs, mercenary financial ventures, grotesque murders, and breathtaking escapes. In *Stamboul Train, A Gun for Sale* (1936; repub. as *This Gun for Hire*, 1936), *The Confidential Agent* (1939), *The Ministry of Fear* (1943), and *The Third Man* (1950), G. displays his consummate skills as storyteller while portraying contemporary history in terms of the Manichean struggle between good and evil. For instance, in *The Third Man*, Rollo Martins travels to Vienna after World War II in order to visit his idol of twenty-five years, Harry Lime. While searching for a secretive "third man" who may know about his friend's murder, Martins, in fact, is pursuing the nefarious Lime, who has faked his own death to avoid being arrested for selling contaminated penicillin on the black market. Whereas G.'s heroes are often sympathetic victims of betrayal, in this case Martins betrays Lime to achieve social justice.

Brighton Rock (1938) marked a turning point in G.'s career in that a seventeen-year-old gangster becomes the unlikely figure through whom he first inquires into "the appalling strangeness of the mercy of God," a topic that critics isolate as his "grand theme" in *The Power and the Glory* (1940), *The Heart of the Matter* (1948), and *The End of the Affair* (1951). *The Power and the Glory*, G.'s finest religious novel, evolved from a trip he made through Tabasco and Chiapas in 1938, when Mexico's churches were ordered closed and its priests were to be either exiled or murdered. Patterned like a thriller, a Red Shirt police lieutenant hunts down a nameless whiskey priest who tries to meet his religious obligations despite being on the run. Although a sinner, the whiskey priest exemplifies the human spirit in service to the power and the glory of God, bringing him to the level of sainthood. Set in British West Africa during World War II, *The Heart of the Matter* presents G.'s most challenging character, a middle-aged police officer irrevocably corrupted by pity. Feeling responsible for the happiness of others, Major Scobie lies, commits adultery, succumbs to blackmail, implicates himself in murder, receives Communion while in a state of mortal sin, and commits suicide to save God from suffering over judgment of his soul.

G.'s religious novels were so popular that laymen and clergy alike sought his advice on matters of church doctrine. The unwanted notoriety exhausted him, and in response to being claimed as the Catholic novelist of his time, G. said he was simply a novelist who happened to be a Catholic. Against this backdrop, G. drew out M. Querry in *A Burnt-Out Case* (1961). Querry, a retired Catholic architect, abandons Europe and seeks for anonymity at a leprosarium in the Belgian Congo. He professes to be so spiritually mutilated that he is no longer of use to anyone. This does not, however, keep others from making scandalous use of him, particularly Marie Rycker who lies about being pregnant with Querry's child in order to get away from her loveless Catholic husband. Ironically, Querry's reentry in human affairs leads to his death.

G. took up the political novel in the 1950s, and it became a habit for him to visit "troubled places" in order to gather material for his books. From 1951 to 1955, he spent his winters in Vietnam reporting on the French Wars for the *Sunday Times*, which led to his scathing critique of democratic idealism in *The Quiet American* (1955). Based on his visits to Haiti in the late 1950s, *The Comedians* (1966) evolved into a dark comedy about survival under a despicably corrupt government like that being run by François "Papa Doc" Duvalier. G. returned to familiar soil in *The Human Factor* (1978), an espionage novel based on the defection of his friend Kim Philby to the Soviet Union. Conflicts ensue for Maurice Castle, a sixty-two-year-old double agent, when someone in his square (department) leaks information to the Communists about a secret plan between England and the U.S. to control various gold and uranium assets in South Africa. Castle's loyalty to Britain is complicated by the fact that he is married to a black South African woman whom he had once used as an agent when he was in the field. Moreover, Castle owes his present happiness to a Communist agent who years earlier had helped Sarah escape from an apartheid prison. Although Castle deeply loves Sarah and Sam, his stepson, he is forever separated from them when he crosses frontiers only to learn that the Russians have used him as a pawn for passing back false information to the British. Finally, G.'s interests in religion and politics converge in *Monsignor Quixote* (1982), a light-hearted picaresque that equals his previous comic revelry in *Our Man in Havana* (1958) and *Travels with My Aunt* (1969). G.'s homage to Cervantes is the story of a humble parish priest and a communist ex-mayor who embark on a journey across Spain. During their hours alone, Father Quixote and Henrique (Sancho) Zancas spend their time debating Christianity and Marxism, each trying to sway the other to his point of view.

G. passed through several stages during his lengthy career as an entertainer and novelist. In doing so, he perfected a spare yet highly charged style, he raised the formula thriller to literary respectability, and he affirmed that human actions still account for something. Proclaiming the virtue of disloyalty, G. once said: "It is a writer's duty to make trouble for any dominant power, to force complacent authorities and submissive followers to confront difficult questions." For his achievements, G.'s popular and critical staying-power seems guaranteed.

BIBLIOGRAPHY: DeVitis, A. A., *G. G.* (1964; rev. ed., 1986); Kelly, R., *G. G.* (1984); Sharrock, R., *Saints, Sinners, and Comedians: The Novels of G. G.* (1984); Shelden, M., *G. G.* (1994); Sherry, N., *The Life of G. G.* (2 vols., 1989–94); Spurling, J., *G. G.* (1983); Wolfe, P., *G. G.* (1972)

JOE NORDGREN

GREENE, Robert

b. 9? July 1558, Norwich; d. 3 September 1592, London

G. is best known today through his *Greenes Groats-Worth of Wit* (1592), a deathbed repentance in which he makes the first supposed references to William SHAKESPEARE as a playwright. He was in his own day variously known as a libertine, moralistic pamphleteer, and author of a number of romances and comical-historical dramas. He received a B.A. from Cambridge (St. John's) and master's degrees from both Cambridge and Oxford. He described himself as *Academiae Utriusque Magister in Artibus* (Master of Arts of each Academy). After university, G. led a dissolute life on the Continent before returning to England where he lived the life of a self-professed malcontent. His first work, *Mamillia*, was entered in the Stationers' Register on October 30, 1580.

G. wrote several autobiographical works including *Greenes Neuer Too Late* (1590), *The Repentance of R. G.* (1592), and *Greenes Groats-Worth of Wit*. It is through these works that we learn of G.'s early career. They are moralities mostly with long passages of repentance interspersed with righteous indignation through which G. paints a picture of a sensualist, a rioter, and a wicked amoralist. He married and had a daughter, but soon left his family when his wife tried to reform him. He moved to London and lived a dissolute life with the sister of a notorious criminal, one Cutting Ball who was eventually hanged at Tyburn. He had a son by his mistress and named him Fortunatus. Fortunatus died in 1593, a year after his father.

G. followed the fashion of writing euphuistic romances at first. But he reports that he fell into the company of actors who persuaded him to write for the stage. His first plays met with success, and according to his own account he was much sought after by the playing companies. His work for the stage brought him into a rivalry with fellow "university wit" Christopher MARLOWE. G., never one to withhold an opinion in print, alludes to Marlowe in both his *Perimedes the Blacke-Smith* (1588) and *Menaphon Camillas Alarum to Slumbering Euphues* (1589), referring to him variously as one of "two mad men," "scoffing poets," a "Cobler's eldest son," and the teller of "a Canterbury [e.g., lewd or worthless] tale." G. refers to Marlowe's work as well, enviously noting that it has become more popular than his own drama and criticizing Marlowe's blank verse as "the humor of the novice."

G. wrote a number of moralizing pamphlets including *Greenes Mourning Garment* (1590) and *Greenes Farewell to Folly* (1591). G. also made use of his contacts in the underworld to produce exposés of confidence trickery. His "cony-catching" pamphlets reveal the world of "cross-biters" and their tricks. They are apparently G.'s effort to repent of the life he has fallen into. He was not, however, above confidence trickery himself and sold his play, *The History of Orlando Furioso* (perf. ca. 1589–91) to the Queen's Men for twenty "nobles" (about £15) and when they went on tour into the country sold it again to the Admiral's Men for a like amount. When they complained of his sharp dealing, G. reportedly replied that because players were false fellows there was no obligation to hold faith with them.

G.'s dramatic reputation is founded upon his romantic chronicle history *Friar Bacon and Friar Bungay* (perf. ca. 1589–91), *Orlando Furioso, The Scottish History of James IV* (perf. ca. 1592), and (possibly by G.) *George a Green, the Pinner of Wakefield* (perf. ca. 1593). His plays display the sensibilities of his prose works, often tending toward love-romance and themes of depravity either scourged or redeemed. He made friends with Thomas Nashe, who picked up the mantle from G. and wrote moral prose tracts and "discoveries." G. died in desperate circumstances apparently of food poisoning after surfeiting upon pickled herring and wine. Gabriel Harvey, the Cambridge academic, was at his deathbed and reported that his only visitor was his mistress, who came demanding that G. officially recognize their bastard son. G. died after sending instructions to his estranged wife to settle his account of £10 with the landlord. As a final humiliation, his romance, *Pandosto* (perf. ca. 1589) supplied the plot for *The Winter's Tale* by Shakespeare, the "upstart crow" G. bitterly resented.

BIBLIOGRAPHY: Crupi, C. W., *R. G.* (1986); Dean, J. S., *R. G.* (1984); Jordan, J. C., *R. G.* (1965)

BRIAN JAY CORRIGAN

GREENWOOD, Walter

b. 17 December 1903, Salford, Lancashire; d. 13 September 1974, Isle of Man

G. left school early and held ill-paid jobs, with spells of unemployment. His famous first novel, *Love on the Dole: A Tale of the Two Cities* (1933), came from bitter experience and highlighted the hardships of the British working classes in the recession of the 1930s. The book was a popular success, dramatized (with Ronald Gow) in 1934 and filmed in 1941. G. wrote other novels including *His Worship the Mayor* (1934), adapted for the stage as *Give Us This Day* (perf. 1940), *Standing Room Only* (1936), and *The Secret Kingdom* (1938), but he is remembered for just one poignant book. His autobiography, *There Was a Time,* appeared in 1967.

GREER, Germaine

b. 29 January 1939, Melbourne, Australia

In 1971, in a new decade of a regenerating feminist movement—and in the collective spirit of such earlier 20th-c historical figures as Emma Goldman, the compelling advocate of women's economic autonomy, and Ellen Key, the voice of women's sexual freedom—G. stepped into the feminist arena in England and the U.S. with her critically and popularly acclaimed book *The Female Eunuch* (1970)—which became a best-seller in both countries. *The Female Eunuch*, noted at the time as insightful, erudite, erotic, and artful, catapulted G. out of the halls of Cambridge, where she had written her doctoral dissertation on love and marriage in William SHAKESPEARE's early comedies, and into the international feminist platform, from which she quickly became a chosen person by the media.

G. was a confident, charismatic, sexy, trendy, and publicity friendly scholar and feminist. She was also, at that time, an answer to a man-hating feminist rhetoric. She was as academically and emotionally ardent about the condition of women around the world as she was sensually charged. Straight away, G. was championed by men—even the then antifeminist Norman Mailer was on her side of the ring—who appreciated this brilliant writer and feminist who took pleasure in sex and took blame off them. G. turned instead to women themselves as being responsible for their passive condition, yet she also adamantly made clear the gender practices that cultural history perniciously enforced and reinforced in women's lives. *The Female Eunuch* doesn't offer revelations, but it does artfully disclose G.'s thinking about women and men, particularly in her attention to the urgent redirection of women's energy, a remapping that would unbind women, releasing their sexuality and subsequently their capability in all sectors of their lives.

G. was reared in Melbourne, went to strict Roman Catholic schools, and had an ambivalent relationship with her mother and her neglectful father. After receiving her B.A. in 1959 from the University of Melbourne and her M.A. in 1961 from the University of Sydney, G. received a scholarship to study at Newnham College, Cambridge, and so gladly left her homeland to pursue doctoral work in England. She earned her Ph.D. in 1967. Christine Wallace's biography of G., published in 1998, tells of her earlier sexual experiences: she was licentious and had abortions and gynecological difficulties, and then yearned to bear children but could not. Disturbingly, these experiences appear to have lent themselves to her more current thinking on such important issues as contraception—she now asserts that modern birth control methods are to be avoided, the pill included, because they are akin to abortion and are part of a male conspiracy against women. By 1984, G. had also withdrawn her advocacy of women's sexual promiscuity and denounced it as a degradation of women. This was indeed a turn around by a feminist who had appeared naked in *Screw* magazine, proudly worn the title of "super-whore," championed pornography, and publicized her sexual encounters with rock stars.

G. is not fighting for an easy solution to women's exclusion in the academy and professions, and she has attested that carelessly dropping women into the basket of the Western canon could mean lowering standards in the cause of inclusion. But G. is, surprisingly, suspicious of including such poets as Christina ROSSETTI and Elizabeth Barrett BROWNING—in *Slip-Shod Sibyls: Recognition, Rejection, and the Woman Poet* (1995)—into what she deems as the worthy version of the canon. G., thus, slips into a quagmire comparable to that of the English theorists such as F. R. LEAVIS and I. A. RICHARDS, who were antielitist but in turn created their own system of selectiveness, thus placing herself into a paradoxical position: she wants the academy to repossess women's work, but she also wants the academy to uphold an exclusionary process, which, by its defining nature, foils the very act of reclamation.

However, there is strength in G.'s subject matter, and in *The Madwoman's Underclothes: Essays and Occasional Writings* (1986), she journeys into the needs of women not from middle-class enclaves, and in this work she does achieve a global look at how women, the poor, the uneducated, live their lives and endure. In *The Change: Women, Aging, and the Menopause* (1991), G. entered into a more personally felt concern of Western women, who as they grow older, feel their invisibility in a Western world that no longer sees them as sexual beings and, since the extended family is no longer a reality, hardly viable. In *Daddy, We Hardly Knew You* (1989), G. became more intimate in her writing as she sought to understand and possibly reconnect her feelings to her absentee father, who had died in 1983. Her desire was not however sated as the more she did find out about him, the less she came to like him, particularly his outright lying about his working-class roots.

G. has more recently come to provoke her critical audience with a stirring but sometimes duplicitous rhetoric, in *The Whole Woman* (1999), which has not been enthusiastically received by critics because of the book's lack of coherency and its defensive stance. Critics have repeatedly questioned why the book became a best-seller in England. In it, G. defends the act of female genital mutilation in non-Western cultures while she condemns breast augmentation in the Western world; she champions women's sexuality while she rails against modern contraceptive measures; she lauds the female body while she rants against the medical testing procedures to protect it, such as pap smears and ultrasounds for pregnant women; and she quietly appropriates American feminist writers' ideas, without giving due credit, while she loudly disowns these same writers, asserting that this American version of FEMINISM has contaminated the global cause of feminism.

G. began her work bravely, artfully, and with wit. However, a writer and thinker who was quick to glare at others' work—she disparaged Betty Friedan and Kate Millet—needs to rise above her own piercing scrutiny. G. had vowed that she would never return to Australia until the government formally made reconciliation with the Aboriginal population, which as of this writing still hasn't happened. Yet it has been reported that she has just purchased land in Queensland and is moving back home. One only hopes that G. will take her anger and put it to use where it is sorely needed.

BIBLIOGRAPHY: Kaplan, G., *The Meagre Harvest: The Australian Women's Movement 1950s-1990s* (1996); Plante, D., *Difficult Women: The Memoir of Three* (1983); Wallace, C., *G. G., Untamed Shrew* (1998)

LISA TOLHURST

GREGORY, [Isabella] Augusta, [Lady]

b. 15 March 1852, Roxborough, Galway, Ireland; d. 22 May 1932, Coole, Galway, Ireland

An unlikely figure for a central role in the Irish literary renaissance, G. combined the movement's focal interests in the Irish language, the rich tradition of folk expression found particularly in western Ireland, and drama. Born Isabella Augusta Persse into a Protestant landlord family in County Galway and widowed after a twelve-year marriage to Sir William Gregory, former governor of Ceylon and member of Parliament, she began her literary career by completing two of her husband's projects: an edition of his autobiography and a collection of the correspondence of one of his ancestors.

Her turn toward her own creative work arose from several influences. The environment where she had grown up was the land of what W. B. YEATS would call the "Celtic Twilight"—the remnants of a culture that had once dominated most of Europe. The fairy beliefs and folktales that G. encountered as a child derived, she and others believed, from that rich past. The publication of this FOLKLORE had begun with T. Crofton Croker's *Fairy Legends and Traditions of the South of Ireland* in 1825. G. knew that book and others which followed it, but she also knew oral tradition first-hand from the tenants on her family's estate and through her charitable work at the workhouse near her home.

Unlike most members of her class, G. was drawn to the Irish language, and she had tried to learn Irish since childhood, inspired by the work of Standish O'Grady, a kinsman whose translations of Gaelic manuscripts and oral traditions were published as *Silva Gadelica* in 1892. After her marriage, she studied the language with her husband's gardener, and she finally mastered it by reading an Irish translation of the Bible. Though never a linguistic scholar, G. could read and converse fluently.

In addition to her personal background and her language interests, she was drawn to folklore by two books. Yeats's *The Celtic Twilight* reinforced G.'s recognition of the literary potential of traditional culture. Douglas Hyde's *Love Songs of Connacht* (1893), which presents Gaelic lyrics with annotated translations, alerted her to the scholarly side of folklore study. Her interests first bore fruit in a translation from manuscripts of the Ulster cycle of legends. *Cuchulain of Muirthemne* (1902) presents the exploits of the demigod who served King Conchubar in his quest for the Brown Bull of Cualgne. Instead of rendering the Irish into standard English, G. used the syntax and vocabulary of the English dialect spoken in western Ireland. This first important literary use of Irish peasant English—what she called the "Kiltartan" dialect after the fictional village where many of her plays are set—led to two more volumes of similar translations: *Gods and Fighting Men* (1904), which presents the Fenian cycle of legends, and *A Book of Saints and Wonders* (1907), a collection of Christian hagiography and miracle stories. G. also published several volumes based on her own folklore collecting, the most significant being *The Kiltartan History Book* (1909), which includes oral narratives covering Irish history from the times of Finn to the reign of Queen Victoria, and *Visions and Beliefs in the West of Ireland* (1920), a two-volume collection of supernatural legends.

G.'s interest in drama represents another facet of her contribution to the Irish renaissance. With Yeats and Edward Martyn, she founded the Irish Literary Theatre, which gave its first performance in 1899. Her involvement, at first primarily administrative, led to more creative activity as she contributed dialogue in Irish peasant English to some of Yeats's early plays. The first of her plays to see production—under the auspices of the Irish National Theatre Society, which succeeded the Irish Literary Theatre in 1902—was a one-act comedy called *Twenty-Five* (perf. 1903). Though she regarded it dismissively, it as well as her other plays was more popular with audiences than the plays of Yeats or those of John Millington SYNGE, whose material often generated controversy.

G.'s role in supporting plays that nationalists and religious leaders in Ireland regarded as anti-Irish or blasphemous began with *The Countess Cathleen*, written by Yeats and produced by the Irish Literary Theatre at its initial performances. She was the principal defender of Synge's *The Playboy of the Western World*, which generated extreme reactions when in opened at the Abbey Theatre in 1907. G. also superintended that play through an American tour in 1911 and faced down hostile crowds of Irish-Americans in several east coast cities.

Though most of her own plays have not stood the test of time, she was the most prolific playwright in the movement. Her work consists largely of one-act pieces: comedies that hinge upon misunderstandings, tragedies that reflect the fatalism that she believed to characterize the peasant mentality, history plays that retell events of the Irish past from a folk perspective, and translations of Molière's comedies into Irish peasant English. Characterized by good-humored sympathy for human foibles, G.'s dramatic work is marred by its sameness and topicality. Her use of dialect redeems the material somewhat as does her familiarity with the folk culture upon which she drew for most of her creative work.

BIBLIOGRAPHY: Adams, H., *Lady G.* (1973); Coxhead, E., *Lady G.: A Literary Portrait* (1966); Saddlemyer, A., *In Defence of Lady G., Playwright* (1966)

WILLIAM M. CLEMENTS

GREVILLE, Charles Cavendish Fulke
b. 2 April 1794, Wilbury; d. 18 January 1865, London

Of aristocratic family and in royal service, G. was well placed to observe current affairs, which he recorded in his eloquent, waspish, and entertaining diary. Educated at Eton and Christ Church, Oxford, he was a page to King George III and served as clerk to the Council in Ordinary under George IV, William IV, and Victoria. G. gave his papers to his friend Henry Reeve with instructions to publish. Journals covering 1820 to 1837 appeared in 3 volumes in 1875. Five large editions sold quickly and the demand in the U.S. equaled that in England. G. knew everybody important and records not so much public events as the private causes that led up to them, with a sharp, censorious eye for scandal. Some passages gave great offense and were suppressed in later editions. Further diaries were published in 1885 (3 vols.) and 1887 (2 vols.). Perhaps no English memoir-writer has left behind him a more valuable contribution to the history of the 19th c.

GREVILLE, Fulke [First Lord Brooke]
b. 3 October 1554, Beauchamp Court, Warwickshire; d. 30 September 1628, Warwick

G. is significant for his friendship with Sir Philip SIDNEY whom he honored with a celebrated biography. They met as schoolmates at Shrewsbury and stayed friends until Sidney's death at the battle of Zutphen in 1586. The biography was written ca.1610, but it was not published until 1633 in *Certaine Learned and Elegant Workes*. Almost all of G.'s writings were printed posthumously. The biography lionized Sidney as a hero for generations of the English and fixed forever the famous anecdote about the fatally wounded

Sidney who gave his water bottle to a common soldier on the Netherlands battlefield and said, "Thy necessity is greater than mine."

Were it not for Sidney, G. would be remembered for his poetry, particularly *Caelica*, a cycle written over a period of years to celebrate the lady "Caelica," whom no one has ever been able to trace to an individual woman. Many of the 109 poems are sonnets, but many are not, so although the collection has been often catalogued as a "sonnet sequence," it is better described as a miscellany of verses. The collection begins in the Petrarchan style, G. focusing attention on a woman who does not apparently return his affections. In the early poems, G.'s style is "golden," and the verses are noteworthy for their elegance and smoothness. No doubt G. was influenced by Sidney's *Astrophel and Stella*, although *Caelica* has never received the attention nor recognition afforded Sidney's poetry. G. may have aspired to his friend's poetic excellence, but he never attracted the audience that Sidney has enjoyed. The final third of *Caelica* changes tone rather dramatically, the narrator showing more pious devotion than he had in earlier romping lyrics.

The other poetic works for which G. is best remembered are all didactic and philosophical treatises in verse. G. called them "Treaties." In *A Treatie of Humane Learning* (1633), G. counsels readers not to rely on human learning but to put their stock in divine revelation. In this regard, he both mirrors his contemporary religious writers and anticipates the resurgence of interest in intuition that would come with the earliest of the existentialist writers in the 19th c. Science should grow from observation of nature, he maintains, not from studying books, and thus G. reflects the method of Sir Francis BACON. Art should also come from practice, not from study. *An Inquisition upon Fame and Honour* (1633) counsels readers to place their trust in God and not in the passing fame afforded them by fellow human beings. *A Treatie of Warres* claims that military battles bring only horror and confusion, a sentiment one expects from a writer who had lost his best friend in war and who lived in a time of English peace. The reaction to war would, of course, be challenged by the next generation, which had to live through the British Civil War when pro-war sentiment would be more evident, for example, in works like Sir William DAVENANT's *Gondibert*.

As a statesman, G. was a member of Parliament for Warwickshire and was Secretary of the Principality of Wales. Knighted by ELIZABETH I in 1597, he served as Treasurer of the Navy for fifteen years and Chancellor of the Exchequer for nine years. JAMES I named him the first Lord Brooke in 1621 and gave him the estate of Warwick Castle, which remains one of the finest Renaissance residences still standing.

BIBLIOGRAPHY: Rebholz, R. A., *The Life of F. G., First Lord Brooke* (1971); Rees, J., *F. G., Lord Brooke, 1554–1628* (1971); Waswo, R., *The Fatal Mirror: Themes and Techniques in the Poetry of F. G.* (1972)

GEORGE KLAWITTER

GRIFFITH, Elizabeth

b. 11 October 1727, Dublin, Ireland; d. 5 January 1793, Naas, Country Kildare, Ireland

Actress, playwright, poet, translator, critic, and editor, G. was the daughter of a Dublin actor and theater manager, Thomas Griffith. G.'s father was ambitious for his daughter, but in 1746, she fell in love with Richard Griffith (no relation), a noted libertine. The pair finally married in 1751, and moved to London, where G. acted in minor roles at Covent Garden. It was partly to rehabilitate her reputation after the protracted and dubious courtship with Richard and partly to support their growing family, that she published their courtship correspondence by subscription as *A Series of Genuine Letters between Henry and Frances* (6 vols., 1757–70). The *Genuine Letters* were a sentimental triumph and London society feted the Griffiths as the model of the fashionable "polite marriage."

G. sustained a constant flow of novels, plays, poetry, essays, and translations until a son returned wealthy from India a few years before her death. Richard spent much of their married life in Ireland while G. lived in Bloomsbury, London. Their separation occasioned additional letters, and G. published their correspondence in two further volumes of letters in 1767 and 1770. These were moderately successful, but it was as a playwright that G. most effectively capitalized on the sentimental triumph of the *Genuine Letters*. Between 1765 and 1779, five of her plays were performed at major London theaters and she wrote up to eight further plays. G.'s first London play, *Amena*, was published by subscription in 1764. In 1765, she tried satire, but the witty and cunning heroine of *The Platonic Wife* was not well received and the play was condemned. The fashion was for less independent heroines and G.'s plays were more successful when she assumed a dramatic persona of female moralist and exposer of female frailties. The admired *The Double Mistake* (1766) exposed the learned female as foolish and rewarded the heroine fond of needlework. Other popular plays were *The School for Rakes* (1769), *A Wife in the Right* (1772), and *The Times* (perf. 1779; pub. 1780).

G.'s three epistolary novels drew on sentimental perceptions of female feeling, rather than comic types, and were more sympathetic representations of women's position in public life. The heroines of *The Delicate Distress* (1769), *The History of Lady Barton* (3 vols., 1771), and *The Story of Lady Juliana Harley* (2 vols., 1776) are drawn with much psychological insight. In these novels, G. develops the model of the unassailably virtuous wife married to the unworthy husband. G.'s novels show her familiarity with the French fictional tradition, exemplified in Madame de La Fayette's *La Princesse de Clèves* (1678), translated by G. in 1777, in which the heroine's ostensibly self-denying behavior can also function self-interestedly.

After the publication of *Juliana Harley*, G. increasingly rejected fiction for compilations, essays and translations. *The Morality of Shakespeare's Drama Illustrated*, a succession of critical commentaries on extracts from the plays, appeared in 1775. In 1777, she published a three-volume collection of novels written by women, including *La Princesse de Clèves*, with critical introductions to the works. She translated widely, including, probably, Voltaire's *The Spirit of Nations,* which was published in 1779–81. *Novelettes*, a collection of her own fiction that included stories previously published in the *Westminster Magazine*, was published in 1780. G.'s *Essays, Addressed to Young Married Women* (1782), which instructed wives not to complain, lest they alienate their husbands further, was the final work of a long and productive literary career.

G.'s literary reputation has suffered from critical inattention to 18th-c. sentimental comedy and her advertisement of a passive moral code for women. A critical reconsideration of her extensive oeuvre, which simultaneously resists and reworks sentimental conventions, is long overdue.

BIBLIOGRAPHY: Eshleman, D. H., *E. G.* (1949); Napier, E. R., "E. G.," in Battestin, M. C., ed., *British Novelists, 1660–1800*, part 1, *DLB* 39 (1985): 247–51; Tompkins, J. M. S., *The Polite Marriage* (1938)

KATE WILLIAMS

GRIFFITHS, Trevor
b. 4 April 1935, Manchester

A highly gifted dramatist and committed socialist, G. has divided his talents between the stage and television, with excursions into cinema. His work combines a belief that successful art does not preclude concentrated thought, a rare ability to put contrary arguments simultaneously into play, and a warm and constant humanism.

G.'s first drama, *The Wages of Thin* (perf. 1969), was not written until he was thirty-four, his career as playwright following stints of teaching and journalism. Two short plays, *Apricots* and *Thermidor* (perf. 1971; pub. 1978), provide an early indication of his range, the former being an intimate examination of the disintegration of a couple's sex life, the latter an examination of the rise of Stalinism in 1930s Russia. His first major work, *Occupations* (perf. 1970; pub. 1972), dramatizes exchanges in the 1920s between the

Italian workers' leader Antonio Gramsci and the Communist envoy Kabac, exploring the conflict between the idealism that motivates revolutions and the ruthlessness necessary for their success. In 1972, G. produced his first work for television, contributing episodes to the BBC's dramatization of the life of Adam SMITH under the name Ben Rae.

Sam, Sam (perf. 1972; pub. 1978) followed, a stage play concerning two brothers negotiating their class background in different ways, and *Gun* was produced in Edinburgh in 1973. The following year saw major work in both media. On television, *All Good Men* (perf. 1974; pub. 1977), set during the British General Strike of 1926, was given added topicality by its broadcast during the three-day week caused by miners' action; and "Absolute Beginners" depicted Lenin as charismatic and unscrupulous in part of the BBC series *Fall of Eagles*. On the stage, *The Party* (perf. 1973; pub. 1974), set in 1968 at a late night meeting of British socialists of various stripes, achieved success in two important productions: one at the National Theatre, featuring Laurence Olivier in his last stage role, the other a touring production by fellow playwright David HARE. Both demonstrated G.'s unrivaled talent for the presentation of ideological debate as gripping drama.

Widely considered to be G.'s masterpiece is *Comedians* (perf. 1975; pub. 1976), in which six aspiring comics in the North of England attempt to reconcile their integrity and their ambition: most are prepared to make compromises; one is not. During this period, however, the dramatist's energies were mainly focused upon television, reflecting his desire to reach as large an audience as possible. His best remembered television work is probably the series *Bill Brand* (perf. 1976), which concerned the dilemmas encountered by an idealistic Labour politician in his first year of office, but his reputation is also built upon a series of single episode dramas. *Through the Night* (perf. 1975; pub. 1977) made the deepest impression, a highly personal story of a sufferer from breast cancer that helped to broach what was at that time a highly taboo subject. An intricate and thoughtful political drama, *Country* (1981), described the decline of the British ruling class with objectivity if not sympathy, while *Oi for England* (1982) was a more urgent piece, confronting the problem of racism in the heated climate of early 1980s Britain. In 1981, G. also adapted Anton Chekhov's *The Cherry Orchard* and D. H. LAWRENCE's *Sons and Lovers* for television, and worked with Warren Beatty on the screenplay for *Reds*. A major historical series, *The Last Place on Earth* (perf. 1985; pub. as *Judgement Over the Dead*, 1986), concerned the race to the South Pole, G. giving the tale his own slant by questioning the British Captain R. F. Scott's moral victory over his competitor Roald Amundsen. His screenplay for *Fatherland*, concerning a singer expelled from Soviet East Germany and exploited in the West, was filmed by Ken Loach in 1987.

Since the 1980s, the conditions of writing for television having become more circumscribed, G. has returned to the stage as "the only relatively free space left." *Real Dreams* (perf. 1984; pub. 1987), adapted from a short story by Jeremy Pikser and again set in 1968, explores the aspirations of, and difficulties faced by, a group of student revolutionaries in Cleveland, Ohio, in the U.S. *Piano* (1990) draws upon the film *Unfinished Piece for a Mechanical Piano* and several works by Chekhov to paint a picture of the pre-revolutionary Russia's upper classes as less deserving of sympathy than of overthrow.

Since the fall of Russian Communism, G.'s emphasis has necessarily shifted from the possibility of a socialist society to the evils of a capitalist one, specifically U.S. foreign policy and British social schism. *The Gulf between Us* (1992) strongly questioned the West's actual or moral victory in the Gulf War, while *Thatcher's Children* (perf. 1993; pub. 1994) cast a compassionate eye over the legacy of that prime minister's divisive period in office. Both met with criticism from the national press in Britain, confirming G. in his preference for regional productions. Happily, a treatment of the last days of the French revolutionary leader Danton, televised as *Hope in the Year Two* (1994) and staged as *Who Shall Be Happy . . . ?* (perf. 1996; pub. 1997), found greater favor, its combination of idealism, REALISM, and emotional truth bearing testament once more to G.'s unique capabilities.

BIBLIOGRAPHY: Bull, J., *New British Political Dramatists* (1984); Garner, S. B., *T. G.* (1999); Kerensky, O., *The New British Drama* (1977); Poole, M., and J. Wyver, *Powerplays: T. G. in Television* (1984)

HARRY DERBYSHIRE

GRIGSON, Geoffrey [Edward Harvey]

b. 2 March 1905, Pelynt, Cornwall; d. 28 November 1985, Broad Town Farm, Wiltshire

Poet, anthologist, editor, and controversialist, G. attacked reputations he considered inflated, including that of Edith SITWELL, who was deeply wounded, and promoted writers previously underrated, notably John CLARE and William BARNES. Educated at St. Edmund Hall, Oxford, he became a journalist. G. founded and edited the influential modernist periodical *New Verse* (1933–39). Much of his work celebrates his native Cornwall. His first collection of poems, *Several Observations* (1939), was followed by many others, including *Under the Cliff* (1943), *The Isles of Scilly* (1946), *A Skull in Salop* (1967), *Ingestion of Ice-Cream* (1969), *Discoveries of Bones and Stones* (1971), *Angles and Circles* (1974), *History of Him*

(1980), *Montaigne's Tower*, and *Persephone's Flowers* (1986). G.'s autobiography, *The Crest on the Silver*, appeared in 1950, and editions of his *Collected Poems* were published in 1963 and 1982. G. also wrote many books on nature, literature, and art.

GRIMALD, Nicholas

b. ca. 1519; Huntingdonshire; d. 1562

According to John Bale's *Index Britanniae Scriptorum*, G. was the author of thirty-nine works, mostly in Latin. Educated at Cambridge University where he distinguished himself in languages and classical literature, G. composed *Christus Redivivus, Comoedia Tragica, sacra et nova* (perf. 1541; pub. 1543). This tragicomedy of Christ's triumph over death blends classical and Christian conventions to include elements not found in the scriptures: a large cast of characters including a Chorus and Roman soldiers who brag about their courage; an emotionally distraught Mary Magdalene who finally recognizes the risen Christ; and passages taken directly from the *Aeneid*. G. advances the ideas and beliefs of a conservative Protestant theology in language appealing not only to scholars and churchmen but to students and citizens alike.

Five years later, he published *Archiprophetae* (1548), a tragedy in the classical form based on the life of John the Baptist. His varied meter adapts to different stage settings and enhances the dramatic soliloquies. Expansive scenes involve banquets, singing, and dancing, which anticipate William SHAKESPEARE's comedies. The emergence of the wise fool echoes Desiderius ERASMUS's *Moriae encomium*, translated as *The Praise of Folly*, and precedes Shakespeare's extraordinary development of this figure.

In 1551, G. published *Congratulatorium Carmen*, an encomia of 155 poems that celebrates the life of Edward Seymour, Duke of Somerset, Lord Protector of Edward VI, on his release from the Tower where he had been imprisoned for allegedly attempting to seize the throne. Soon after, in 1552, G. was appointed chaplain to Nicolas Ridley, the reformist Bishop of London, and began preaching at St. Paul's Cathedral. A few years later, when the Catholic Mary Tudor ascended the throne, G. was forced to recant his evangelical Protestant views in Oxford's Bocardo prison; there is little evidence, however, that his confession betrayed Ridley, Thomas Cranmer, and Hugh LATIMER, who were shortly burned at the stake. His translation of Cicero's *De officiis* as *Thre Bokes of Duties* (1556) enjoyed many reprints in the Elizabethan period.

On June 5, 1557, Richard TOTTEL published *Songes and Sonettes*, a compilation of 271 poems, forty of which by G. followed those by Henry Howard, the Earl of SURREY and Sir Thomas WYATT, and preceded a large section by "Uncertain Auctours." In the second edition published eight weeks later, July 31, 1557, G.'s poems, reduced to ten in number, were given the privileged position of closing the enlarged compilation of 280 poems. His omitted poems are translations of classical epigrams, *encomia* to the ladies of the Seymour or Audley houses, and epigraphs on G.'s personal acquaintances. The remaining poems, mostly translations of the Continental reformist Theodore Beza expand and develop cultural and political issues explored in the structural and thematic trajectories of each of the preceding authorial sections of Tottel's compilation.

The final poems by G. in the revised *Songes and Sonettes* describe the executions of Zoroaster and Cicero and thus continue his interest in the theme of martyrology apparent in his earlier Oxford dramas and in the lost *Protomartyr*, assumed to dramatize the life of St. Stephen, the first Christian martyr. G. therefore contributes to the prevalence of the theme in the mid Tudor period: for example, in John Bale's theatrical account of the Church's martyrs in his *Brief Chronicle Concerning . . . Sir John Oldcastle* (1544) and in the *Examination of Anne Askewe* (1547), and later in John FOXE's *Actes and Monuments of These Latter and Perillous Dayes*. G.'s final epigram in *Songes and Sonettes*, however, does not end in despair but in a reaffirmation of the importance of the poet as a witness to the violence of political betrayal in the community: "Tullie lives, and styll shall bee." We are assured of the educative power of poetry to immortalize those who sacrifice themselves rather than compromise their integrity. G.'s work thus anticipates the position of numerous authors of cultural and political criticism in the Elizabethan period.

BIBLIOGRAPHY: Byrom, H. J., "The Case for N. G. as Editor of *Tottel's Miscellany*," *MLR* 27 (April 1932): 125–43; Merrill, L. R., *The Life and Poems of N. G.* (1925); Rollins, H. E., ed., *Tottel's Miscellany (1557–1587)* (2 vols., 1928–29; rev. ed., 1996)

PAUL A. MARQUIS

GROCYN, William

b. 1446?, Colerne, Wiltshire; d. 1519, London

The scholar and teacher G. was educated at Winchester College and Oxford. He was admitted to Winchester as a scholar in September 1463, and to New College, Oxford, in 1465, becoming a full fellow of New College in 1467. While at New College, G. acted as tutor to William Warham, later Archbishop of Canterbury. After 1481, G. held the office of Divinity Reader at Magdalen College. Much of his career until the end of the 15th c. was spent in Oxford, though he also held various ecclesiastical preferments. By the beginning of the 16th c., he was resident in London,

where he often preached at St. Paul's Cathedral. He held the rectorship of St. Lawrence Jewry and, simultaneously, the mastership of the collegiate church of All Hallows, Maidstone.

G.'s most important scholarly discovery was that the writings attributed to the Areopagite Dionysius were not really by him. He lectured on Pseudo-Dionysius at Oxford, initially believing him to have been the convert of St. Paul, but eventually becoming convinced that the *Celestial Hierarchy* belonged to a later period. His thinking in this regard was influential, particularly on John COLET, to whom G. introduced the writings of Dionysius. However, G.'s prime importance lies in the fact that he was among the first to teach Greek at Oxford. He may have obtained tuition in Greek literature from the Italian Cornelio Vitelli, a visitor to Oxford who was also a Greek scholar. In 1488, G. visited Italy himself and studied in Florence under Politian and Chalcondyles. He also made the acquaintance of the Venetian printer Aldus Manutius and assisted him in producing a text of Aristotle's works.

G. was the oldest of a group of humanist scholars who have long been regarded as the fathers of the revival of learning in England. In Oxford and London, G. was closely associated with such eminent figures as Colet, Thomas MORE, Thomas LINACRE, William LILY, and the Dutchman Desiderius ERASMUS who described G. in 1514 as "the patron and preceptor of us all." G. preferred to teach and to hand on his knowledge to younger scholars, and his influence was imparted in this way rather than by the more traditional method of the printed word. Indeed, he tended to spend his time and energies in private study and tuition, rather than in writing. Despite various reports of G.'s learned epistles, no writings by him are known except two small items. The first of these is a letter that G. wrote to the printer Aldus Manutius and that the latter included as a preface to his 1499 edition of Linacre's *Procli Sphæra*. In the letter, G. congratulates Aldus on preparing an edition of Aristotle, whom G. preferred to Plato. G. had retained his affection for the medieval schoolmen in spite of his extensive Greek learning and his influence on Greek studies in the English Renaissance. The other text attributed to him is even more ephemeral, consisting of an epigram on a lady who threw a snowball at him.

BIBLIOGRAPHY: Lewis, C. S., *English Literature in the Sixteenth Century* (1944); Mackie, J. D., *The Earlier Tudors, 1485–1558* (1952; rev. ed., 1957); Roston, M., *Sixteenth-Century English Literature* (1982)

MARGARET CONNOLLY

GRONOW, [Captain] R[ees] H[owell]

b. 7 May 1794, Glamorganshire, Wales; d. mid-November 1865, Paris, France

Of ancient family, G. was educated at Eton, where he befriended the eccentric and unpopular Percy Bysshe

SHELLEY. His life was eventful and his fame rests on his *Recollections and Reminiscences* (4 parts, 1862–66). Knowing everybody, he provided valuable source materials for historians and entertainment for the general reader. Duelist, dandy, raconteur, and student of manners, he fought at Waterloo and left a sharp-eyed and crisply written account of his era as the reigns of Georges III and IV were succeeded by that of Victoria. G.'s descriptions of the costume and behavior of the Regency dandies, led by "Beau" Brummell, lounging insolently in the window of White's, the most exclusive of London clubs, hating and verbally abusing everybody, are often quoted.

GROSE, Francis

b. 1731?; d. 12 June 1791, Dublin, Ireland

Nicknamed "the antiquarian Falstaff," G. was a graphic artist of wide and eclectic interests, an expert on heraldry, and remembered for his pioneering work in superstitions, FOLKLORE, and slang. *Antiquities of England and Wales* came out from 1773 to 1787. G. published *A Classical Dictionary of the Vulgar Tongue* in 1785, reissued posthumously in 1811 as *Lexicon Balatronicum, A Dictionary of Buckish Slang, University Wit and Pickpocket Eloquence.* In 1823, this book was edited and augmented by Pierce EGAN. The 1811 edition was reissued in facsimile in 1984. Its value lies in that it is a record of Cockney dialect and underground vocabulary of the 18th and early 19th c., otherwise ignored and even avoided by the polite, but with a coarse vitality of its own. Robert BURNS wrote two songs about him, one commenting that G. was always "taking notes."

GROSSMITH, George

b. 9 December 1847, London; d. 1 March 1912, Folkestone

GROSSMITH, [Walter] Weedon

b. 9 June 1854, London; d. 14 June 1919, London

G. and W. G. were brothers and joint authors of *The Diary of a Nobody,* which W.G. also illustrated. Originally appearing in parts in *Punch* magazine, and appearing, with some alterations, in book form in 1892, the *Diary* chronicles the everyday life of the unreliable narrator, Charles Pooter, a city clerk. The HUMOR derives from the socially and physically accident-prone Pooter's unconsciousness of how ridiculous he makes himself by his petty snobberies, and from his invariably unsuccessful wrangles with his rebellious son Lupin. Nevertheless, a character of respectability and integrity emerges, so that the reader rejoices in the eventual rise in the fortunes of Pooter and his faithful, though frequently irritated, wife Carrie. The then-current fashion for spiritualist seances is exemplified by the activities of Mrs. James, that for bicy-

cling by the dignified but dull friend Cummings, and for imitations of the adulated actor Sir Henry Irving by Lupin's fiery friend Fosselton. Memorable among the other characters are the hearty, facetious Gowing and his vulgar friend Padge, "who appeared to be all moustache." W. G. also wrote a novel, *A Woman with a History* (1896), and G. G. published *Reminiscences of a Clown* (1888) and *Piano and I* (1910), memoirs about his time as a comic actor and creator of the "buffo" roles in the Savoy operas by W. S. GILBERT and Sir Arthur Sullivan.

MICHAEL GROSVENOR MYER

GUILPIN [or GILPIN], Everard [or Edward]

b. ca. 1572; d. ca. 1608, London?

Little is known of G., except that he had studied at Emmanuel College, Cambridge, and Gray's Inn. He is believed to be the author of the anonymously published *Skialetheia; or, A Shadowe of Truth, in certaine Epigrams and Satyres* (1598), a collection of seventy epigrams and seven formal verse satires modeled after Martial and Juvenal. John Whitgift, the Archbishop of Canterbury, considered the work socially disruptive and ordered the book burned in June 1599. G. is also acknowledged as the author of *The Whipper of the Satyre His Pennance in a White Sheete*, published anonymously in 1601.

GUNN, Thom[son William]

b. 29 August 1929, Gravesend, Kent

Noted for his adroit use of spare, powerful language, G.'s career has spanned half a century. Moving to San Francisco in 1954, G.'s oeuvre includes numerous volumes of poetry, a collection of essays, and edited collections. His poetry typically creates a dialectic between conflicting values. Pitting style against subject matter, G. often uses traditional controlled poetic forms in dealing with less traditional subjects, such as LSD, homosexuality, and AIDS, and, inversely, uses open forms to discuss the traditional.

Published in 1954, *Fighting Terms: A Selection*, marked G.'s first published collection of poetry. Written while G. was a student at Cambridge, the poems demonstrate a certain sophistication of style while presenting an unflinching realism. G. focuses on soldiers, themes of will and choice, and metamorphosis, anticipating his more mature works. *Fighting Terms* associated G. with "The Movement," a short-lived literary movement of the 1950s, generally defined by the rejection of neo-Romanticism and concentration on practicality, regularity, and solid middle-class values. Indicative of youthful writing, the collection now seems somewhat affected and overly clever.

In *The Sense of Movement* (1957), G. also uses more formal construction, focusing on a Sartrean existentialist viewpoint of living in a world without value. G. adopts a stance whereby the individual can only create meaning through deliberate action. Drawing on contemporary subject matter, G. incorporates elements of pop culture such as motorcycle gangs, Elvis Presley, jukeboxes, and leather fashions.

A transitory work, *My Sad Captains* (1961) is deliberately divided into two parts. Mirroring G.'s earlier works, the volume is, in the first part, characterized by the combination of formal control with a focus on freedom of choice and action. The second part marks a definitive shift in G.'s writing in which he adopts freer verse forms and syllabics, centering not on the metaphysical, but the physical, natural world. Softening his previous pugnacious stance, he now embraces emotional human contact, adding a quality of tenderness previously unseen.

Touch (1967) appeared as a series of seventeen sequential poems. The central character of this volume is the seemingly sole survivor of a global war, finding, much to his surprise, a group of some forty other survivors. Little exposition as to circumstance is supplied, with G. focusing primarily on first and last things. Problematic with this volume, however, is the fact that any questioning or philosophizing that G. does engage in takes place in a void.

Indebted to his involvement with San Francisco's radical counterculture and LSD use in the 1960s, the poems of *Moly* (1971) deal with LSD experiences, whether directly or indirectly. In this instance, moly serves as a stand-in for LSD and its liberating powers. Throughout the volume, G. explores this freedom while embracing the connection between humankind and the natural world, allowing the two to coexist harmoniously in a communal vision.

The poems included in *Jack Straw's Castle* (1976) represent a definite shift for G. His voice becomes darker and more determined throughout the course of the volume, and, by the final poems he experiences a nightmarish angst, freely mixing metered and rhymed verse with fragmented free verse. It is G.'s vulnerability in this volume that allows him to explore change and renewal. Unlike *Moly*, the liberation G. experiences in this volume is a result of his exploration of a painful and terrifying surrender.

The Passages of Joy (1982), the title of which was drawn from Samuel JOHNSON, contains what some critics consider G.'s most revealing poems. For the first time, G. speaks frankly about his homosexuality, the work described as plainer and more direct than previous ones. Some critics focused on the homosexuality issue, criticizing the work's forced SENTIMENT and use of clichés; however, G. also included poems which deal with heterosexual relationships, albeit unhappy ones. In this volume, G. avoids metaphor, symbol and allegory, relying, instead, on casual observation and realistic language.

Praised for his honesty in *The Man with the Night Sweats* (1992), G. deals in an unsentimental way with a world ravaged by the AIDS epidemic. Using meter and rhyme, Gunn combines the lyrical with a sense of restraint, creating a gap between tone and subject matter. Because of the implicit difficulty of the topic, this gap is what ultimately makes the work so successful; it effectively creates the sense of detachment necessary for the poetry to fully impact the reader's consciousness. Although the volume grows progressively darker throughout, G. manages to end with a profound sense of hope.

Serving as a set of variations, *Boss Cupid* (2000) tackles the subject of wanton human desire. Through his deft handling of meter and rhyme, G. creates a freedom of expression, exhibiting a paradoxical fusion of lightness and weight. Throughout his long career, G. has gradually moved from the existential and intellectual to the corporeal and tangible, exploring and questioning the joys and terrors of being human.

BIBLIOGRAPHY: Bold, A., *T. G. and Ted Hughes* (1976); Gunn, T., and J. Campbell, *T. G. in Conversation with James Campbell* (2000); Hagstrom, J. W. C., and G. Bixby, *T. G.* (1979); Powell, N., "The Abstract Joy: T. G.'s Early Poetry," *CritQ* 13 (Autumn 1971): 219–27

SAMUEL GAUSTAD

GURNEY, Ivor [Bertie]

b. 28 August 1890, Gloucester; d. 26 December 1937, Dartford, Kent

A musician and a poet, G.'s literary reputation is now firmly established as one of the finest British poets of the 20th c. and one of the best of those who wrote poetry from experience as a soldier in the First World War. He has long been cherished as a poet of his beloved Gloucester and its surrounding country. Recognition came slow and late partly because of the limits these accurate identifications were made to impose: he was pigeonholed as musician rather than poet, as a regional (i.e., limited) writer. Finally, through the stay of fifteen years in a mental asylum, from 1922 until his death, he was seen as a "mad" poet. G. was not without supporters: Marion Scott kept manuscripts and papers; selections of his poems appeared, with a memoir from Edmund BLUNDEN in 1954 and 1973; a biography by Michael Hurd, emphasizing the composer, appeared in 1978. It was only with the *Collected Poems* edited by P. J. KAVANAGH in 1982 that all this changed. G.'s work now found a new and welcoming public that was sustained with R. K. R. Thornton's editions of G.'s *Collected Letters* (1991) and recent scholarly editions, including *Best Poems* (1995), from Thornton and George Walter. As composer, G.'s song settings have not been out of performers' repertoires since Oxford published the first two volumes of its edition in 1938 and they are frequently recorded.

G. comes from that Edwardian/Georgian and distinctly English background that made the music of his teacher Ralph Vaughan Williams and an outstanding generation of English composers. In literary terms, this meant that when he turned to poetry as a soldier serving with the 2nd/5th Glosters, he turned to a lyric style derived from Ben JONSON and 17th-c. poetry, to William WORDSWORTH and the Romantics and to his contemporary Georgian poets. He wrote of the locations he loved, the trees, hills, and rivers of home, the city of Gloucester and its cathedral where he had been in the choir school before studying at the Royal College of Music (1911–14). In two collections made from poems he wrote during the war, *Severn and Somme* (1917) and *War's Embers* (1919), that love of place and home was increasingly embattled. A longing for a future, for release from war became the theme. There were a few trench scenes but these were set out of battle or behind the lines. One poem, still his best known piece, stands out, "To His Love." Here, a fine lyric movement is constantly disturbed by line-endings bringing syntactical ambiguity. This plainly written, damaged lyricism G. now brought more often into his writing, particularly through the influence of the work of Edward THOMAS. Further influenced by Gerard Manley HOPKINS and, above all, by Walt Whitman, G. developed his own distinctive verse line: often in couplets, with long, digressing sentences, strange disjunctures and disturbances within a colloquially narrative voice. Equally at this time, his thoughts turned back to the comradeship and manly life of the trenches in contrast to a current England that had betrayed the returning soldier's hopes.

Once confined to an asylum, in 1922, G. looks back on the war and its pains and hardships as a provisional world of simple things and resourcefulness, wonderfully constructed by the soldiers to protect themselves against terror and fear of failure. Courage, honor, and comradeship become his theme but as qualities won against the odds, never invulnerable and always expressed through small things. We read of the songs of the Welsh that sustained them in "First Time In"; the lovely chatter of a Bucks accent lost with the soldier on the wires in "The Silent One." G. praises unmilitary misfits in "The Bohemians" and individualists, in "Signallers." He writes wonderfully of tobacco and cups of tea and vin rouge and vin blanc. He does write of deaths and of killing but through small details and unexpected quirks of character. His are the poems of the common soldier trying to do a job in impossible conditions and with the certainty of death or heartbreak. Within and alongside these poems of the war remembered, G. also built a whole geography of the New World, above all Manhattan: the place of democracy, where somehow the history of the Romans in the Cotswolds and the greatness of Gloucester men would be honored. He continued to write lyrics, many of them heart rending. Masses of material remain as yet unedited and unpublished in the archive in Gloucester. What we have already establishes his great individuality and importance.

BIBLIOGRAPHY: Hurd, M., *The Ordeal of I. G.* (1978); Hill, G., "G.'s Hobby," *EC* 34 (April 1984): 97–128; Waterman, A., "The Poetic Achievement of I. G.," *CritQ* 25 (Winter 1983): 3–19

DESMOND GRAHAM

HABINGTON, William

b. 4 November 1605, Hendlip Hall, Worcestershire; d. 30 December 1654, Worcestershire

A Roman Catholic whose father was implicated in the Gunpowder plot, H. was educated at St. Omer, northern France, and Paris. H.'s *Castara* (1634) was a set of love poems to his wife, published anonymously. The following year came a second edition enlarged by three prose characters, fourteen new lyrics, and eight touching elegies to his friend and kinsman, George Talbot. The third edition (1640) contains a third part consisting of a prose character of "A Holy Man" and twenty-two devotional poems. H. also wrote (possibly with his father, Thomas) *The Historie of Edward the Fourth* (1640; repub. as *Praeces Principum; or, The President of Illustrious Princes*, 1659), *The Queene of Arragon* (1640), a tragicomedy revived at the Restoration, and *Observations upon History* (1641).

HAGGARD, [Sir] H[enry] Rider

b. 22 June 1856, Norfolk; d. 14 May 1925, London

Distinguished for his mastery of Victorian adventure fiction, H. produced more than forty novels. Inspired by his own exploits in colonial service, H. intertwined fantastic and mystical themes with the natural and societal landscapes of the Empire. H.'s work is continuously valued for its literary, as well as historic, appeal.

Unable to enter the military as a young man, H. entered colonial service as an assistant to the governor of Natal and later with the High Court in the Transvaal. He was profoundly inspired by the vastness and mystery of the land and native people of South Africa and his experiences inspired him to write a series of adventure novels that he produced throughout the late Victorian era. Employing the backdrop of colonial Zululand for its themes and characters, H.'s convention is never far from that of Rudyard KIPLING with whom he clearly shared an imperialistic disposition. Critics readily observe, however, that H.'s paradoxi-

cal celebration of the Zulu society and persona implies a significant personal departure from contemporary paternalist ideologies.

In his first and best-known novel, *King Solomon's Mines* (1885), H. conceives an adventure plot in which a quest for hidden treasure leads his characters into the darkest unexplored corner of Africa where they encounter mystical forces and figures. The novel's rousing appeal prompted *She: A History of Adventure* (1887) in which his African explorers discover a lost tribe led by the mysteriously alluring Ayesha, the female ruler who C. G. Jung would later observe to be the embodiment of the anima concept. The resounding success of the two novels enmeshed to inspire not only an African adventure formula that H. employed to frame many of his later works but also a host of vital characters. In his quest narrative, *Allan Quatermain* (1887), he revives the figure of the white hunter hero from *King Solomon's Mines* who embodies the Victorian ethos but does not subscribe to the racist principles of the Empire. Allan Quatermain would serve as H.'s most enduring character.

A commonly noted feature of H.'s adventure novels is his seemingly ironic embrace of both British colonial policy and the values of primitive culture. Although H.'s stories were often premised on the fantastic, each possessed a reality of tribal culture that was animated by his strong personal understanding of tribal Zulu history and humanity. The bravery, wit, and strength of the Zulu characters that featured so prominently in *King Solomon's Mines, Allan Quatermain,* and *Nada the Lily* (1892) demonstrate an affinity seldom observed in contemporary portrayals. Despite his imperialist underpinnings, H. maintained a discernible sense of regret for Western encroachment on native societies. This sensitivity was evidenced by his Zulu trilogy, *Marie* (1912), *Child of the Storm* (1913), and *Finished* (1917), as well as *Montezuma's Daughter* (1893), which observed the conquest of native Mexico.

Although H. produced a number of successful fictional works, his rural discourses were among his most significant nonfiction literary contributions. An experienced farmer himself, H. maintained an acute interest and expertise in the agricultural and social condition of England and went on to study these dynamics in depth as a member of the Dominions Royal Commission. His regional observations of Britain were incorporated in *Rural England* (1902) and *The Poor and the Land* (1905) and his insights on the methods of cultivation offered in *A Farmer's Year* (1899) remain of permanent value. For his service to the commissions and contributions of his written work, H. was knighted in 1912. Though H. continued to write extensively for the rest of his life, producing dozens of additional adventure volumes of various fantastical themes, none would achieve the renown of his earliest works. His autobiography, *The Days of My Life* (1926), was published posthumously.

BIBLIOGRAPHY: Cohen, M., *R. H.* (1960); Katz, W. R., *R. H. and the Fiction of Empire* (1987); Stiebel, L., *Imagining Africa: Landscape in H. R. H.'s African Romances* (2001)

JACK BRODERICK

HAKLUYT, Richard
b. ca. 1552, London; d. 23 November 1616, London

English geographer, editor of exploration narratives, and advocate of English colonialism, H. was born into a family of practical geographers and was profoundly influenced by his cousin, the elder Richard Hakluyt, lawyer and merchants' consultant. In his dedication to the second edition of *Principal Navigations* (3 vols., 1598–1600), H. writes that as a boy he saw a world map in his cousin's chamber and resolved "by God's assistance" to pursue the study of geography and exploration. H. carried this interest from Westminster School to Christ Church, Oxford, and took B.A. and M.A. degrees in 1574 and 1577. After taking holy orders, H. served for five years as chaplain to the English ambassador in France. This is as far from England as he ever traveled. H. returned to increasingly gainful church livings in England, where, through his writing and editing, he promoted a program of expanding his nation's borders.

H.'s modern reputation rests chiefly on his essay, *A Discourse of Western Planting* (wr. 1584), and on his collections of exploration narratives: *Diverse Voyages Touching the Discovery of America* (1582); *The Principal Navigations, Voyages, and Discoveries of the English Nation* (1589); and a second, much expanded edition, *Principal Navigations, Voyages, Traffiques, and Discoveries of the English Nation*. After H.'s death, Samuel PURCHAS acquired his unpublished collection, which Purchas used as the basis of *Hakluytus Postumus; or, Purchas His Pilgrimes*.

Discourse of Western Planting was not written for publication but presented to Queen ELIZABETH I in support of efforts to colonize North America. This document, divided into twenty-one chapters, gives modern readers a glimpse into the scramble among European nations for the Americas in the years following 1492. H. argues that England should immediately "plant" (create settlements) along the American coast, from Florida to the arctic. While H. begins with the familiar Elizabethan-era argument for colonization, to Christianize the native "idolaters," in general he sees colonizing as a way to achieve economic advantage over other European powers, especially Spain. H. argues that colonies would provide duty-free trading partners for England; yield staple commodities, such as wood, pitch and tar, grains, grapes, and metals, to supply virtually all England's needs; establish a base from which to launch expeditions seeking the Northwest Passage; and encourage, through contact with colonists, the native population to rise against Spain and the pope and declare allegiance to the queen. Moreover, H. describes social benefits of establishing colonies: the idle, dissolute, and criminal could be transported across the Atlantic.

Principal Navigations, especially its three-volume second edition, is a huge and varied collection of travel narratives and associated documents. Critics disagree over the degree of unity in the work. H. organized the collection chronologically within three great divisions: voyages north and northeast of England (vol. 1), south and southeast of England (vol. 2), and west to America and the West Indies (vol. 3). H. discusses his editorial aims in some detail in dedicatory epistles and prefaces to the three volumes. His primary goal is two-fold: to save these "memorable exploits" from the "devouring jaws of oblivion," and to inspire and inform future adventurers. With the English seafarer in mind, he included logs, lists, instructions, weather data, technical details, official papers, recent maps, and "secrets" gathered from captured Spanish ships—to "avail us or annoy them." Recent critics have remarked on H.'s preference for first-hand accounts over the writings of traditional authorities. Some familiar narratives are those of the Cabots' voyages to North America, Martin Frobisher's search for the Northwest Passage, Francis Drake's circumnavigation, and Sir Walter RALEIGH's voyage to Guiana.

Perhaps it was H.'s reliance on the voices of nobles and commoners alike that led J. A. FROUDE to call *Principal Navigations* the "prose EPIC of the modern English nation." Froude, writing in 1854, admired the work's celebration of empire and the feats of those—of every social station—who inaugurated a "new era"; postcolonial critics argue that *Principal*

437

Navigations helped to fashion a self-defining narrative for the incipient British Empire.

BIBLIOGRAPHY: Helfers, J. P., "The Explorer or the Pilgrim?," *SP* 94 (Spring 1997): 160–86; Taylor, E. G. R., ed., *The Original Writings and Correspondence of the Two Richard Hakluyts* (2 vols., 1935)

PATRICK McHENRY

HALDANE, J[ohn] B[urdon] S[anderson]

b. 5 November 1892, Oxford; d. 1 December 1964, Bhuhaneswar, India

Author of *The Marxist Philosophy and the Sciences* (1938), H. was a geneticist and popularizer of science. After serving in the First World War, he worked on improving the design of gas masks. In 1933, he became professor of genetics at University College, London, and later of biometry, having published *Enzymes* (1930) and *The Causes of Evolution* (1932). *Possible Worlds* (1927) influenced Aldous HUXLEY's novel *Brave New World.* H. appears in Huxley's *Antic Hay* as Shearwater, a biologist with an unreliable wife. *Science and Everyday Life* (1939) brought H. to the attention of the general public. *Everything Has a History* (1951) was in similar vein. H. also wrote a collection of stories for children, *My Friend Mr. Leakey* (1937). During the Spanish Civil War, H. joined the Communist Party and from 1940 to 1949 was chairman of the *Daily Worker* editorial board. In 1950, he left the party because of Stalin's interference with science. Eventually, he became a citizen of India, where he established a genetics and biometry laboratory.

HALES, John

b. 19 April 1584, Bath; d. 19 May 1656, Eton

Praised by Andrew MARVELL and Lord CLARENDON, H. was a Greek scholar and Protestant Christian priest, who argued in his most famous work, *A Tract Concerning Schism and Schismatics*, written ca. 1636 and published anonymously in 1642, that each person should be guided by the authority of Scripture, avoiding alike the extremes of Roman Catholicism and Calvinism. H. was part of a literary circle that included Lucius Cary, Sidney GODOLPHIN, and Edmund WALLER. His sermons and tracts were collected in 1659 as *Golden Remains* (rev. ed., 1673).

HALL, Edward

b. 1497, London; d. April 1547, London

H. shaped Tudor historical thought and indirectly poetry, as the first English chronicle writer to demonstrate the new moralizing of history that came in with the waning of the Middle Ages. His great work, *The Union of the Two Noble and Illustre Families of Lan-caster and York,* known familiarly as *Hall's Chronicle,* is one of the prime sources both for the later chronicler Raphael HOLINSHED and for the history plays of William SHAKESPEARE. The early part is condensed, but the *Chronicle* is an important source for the reign of HENRY VIII, describing his court and the famous Field of the Cloth of Gold. The first edition is so rare that no complete copy is believed to exist; an unfinished second edition appeared in 1548; Richard Grafton completed the work in 1550. Henry's daughter, Catholic Queen Mary, banned the *Chronicle* because it enshrined what has been called "the Tudor myth," in which a state of prosperity is broken by a great crime and only recovered after a terrible chain of criminal disasters; providence worked out a pattern of justice through the English kings, culminating in the triumphant reign of Henry VIII and his Protestant Reformation. Because Holinshed drew on H., it is not always clear which source Shakespeare was using, but details suggest direct transmission. As one of the leading historical writers of the early 16th c., H. was largely responsible for creating the intellectual climate of the 1550s that produced the influential compilation, *A Mirror for Magistrates* (1559).

HALL, Joseph

b. 1 July 1574, Bristow Park, Leicestershire; d. 8 September 1656, Higham, Norfolk

Cleric and man of letters, H. was influential on a number of literary fronts. One of the earliest practitioners of railing satire, H. helped popularize the Theophrastan character, inaugurated the genre of the imaginary voyage, and was the author of influential meditations. His life followed a trajectory opposite to that of John MILTON, his great adversary in the pamphlet war over episcopacy. Whereas Milton, disappointed not to be able to pursue a career in the church, initially lived a quiet and studious life, only to enter the circle of power as Latin secretary under the Protectorate, and live the remainder of his years under a monarchy that he was disappointed to see restored, H.—after receiving his B.A. and M.A. from Emmanuel College, Cambridge—achieved early notoriety as the self-proclaimed first English satirist and took orders only after the condemnation of his most secular poems. Achieving a Doctor of Divinity degree, he rose in the church hierarchy as chaplain to Prince Henry (1608), Dean of Worcester (1616), King JAMES I's emissary to the Synod of Sort (1618), and Bishop of Exeter (1627). His 1641 translation to the wealthier see of Norwich, however, was preempted by his arrest and five-month imprisonment by parliamentary forces. Released to find his episcopal revenues impounded, H. lived out the remainder of his years in the village of Higham, where he died four years before he could be reinstated by Charles II.

Thus, if Milton felt himself to have been "Churchouted by the Prelates" (as he famously put it in *Reason of Church Government*), H. was locked out of his cathedral by the Puritans. Ironically, the man whose satires were condemned by the government at the outset of his career spent his middle age and last years as the great defender of orthodoxy. Capitalizing upon the new fashion for "strong lines," the six books of H.'s *Virgidemiarum* (1597; rev. ed., 1598; A Harvest of Rods) appropriate both the "toothless" satiric mode of Horace and "biting" style of Juvenal to whip the proud and greedy denizens of London back onto the virtuous path. H.'s boast that his satires are "hard of conceipt [understanding], and harsh of style" placed him among the young malcontents of the day who rejected the golden or aureate style that flourished in the 1590s in favor of a more direct and aphoristic style, as well as a more frank and sincere society.

The products of H.'s humanist education, his *Characters of Virtues and Vices* (1608) adapted the Theophrastan character to the analysis of contemporary moral psychology, while his three "Parnassus" plays (acted as part of the Christmas festivities at St. John's College, Cambridge, beginning in 1598) were aimed at the reform of certain academic and literary abuses. *Mundus Alter et Idem* (1605; *The Discovery of A New World*, 1609?) used the device of travel to imaginary lands to expose the weakness of English behavior, religious practice, and government. But like that of his friend John DONNE (in praise of whose *Anniversaries* H. wrote insightful commendatory poems), H.'s early satiric spirit reflected a dissatisfaction with the social status quo that found more powerful expression in his subsequent devotional writing.

The Art of Divine Meditation (1606) attempted systematically to teach the reader how to "bend . . . the mind upon some spiritual object, through diverse forms of discourse, until our thoughts come to an issue." Distinguishing between "occasional" and "deliberate" meditations, H. exhorted the Christian to "read" more exactly the revelations contained in the Book of Nature, the Holy Scriptures, and the reader's own conscience, thus perfecting his/her moral life. H. applied his meditational techniques to passages from the Bible in eight volumes of *Contemplations* (1612–26).

H.'s reformist spirit led him to write as well in defense of the established Church, where his gifts as a satirist failed him. His *Episcopacy by Divine Right* (1640) involved him in an increasingly bitter pamphlet war with a group of Puritan divines who wrote collectively under the pseudonym "Smectymnuus," and eventually with Milton. One of the great voices of moderation in a heated and divisive age, H. is now unfortunately best remembered as the object of Milton's most scurrilous ad hominem attacks.

BIBLIOGRAPHY: Huntley, F. L., *Bishop J. H. 1574–1656* (1979); Martz, L., *The Poetry of Meditation* (1962); McCabe, R., *J. H.* (1982); Tourney, L. D., *J. H.* (1979)

RAYMOND-JEAN FRONTAIN

HALL, Radclyffe

b. Marguerite Antonia Radclyffe-Hall, 12 August 1880, Bournemouth; d. 6 October 1943, London

H., called "John" by her friends, is known primarily for her controversial *The Well of Loneliness* (1928), generally considered the first English novel to openly describe lesbian relationships. The novel narrates the story of a young woman's discovery that she is an "invert," a term adopted from Havelock ELLIS, an early sexologist who argued that sexual preference is inborn, who also contributed a preface to the novel. While the amount of scholarship devoted to H. has grown in recent years with the advent of queer studies, she still occupies a rather marginalized space in the new canon of female modernists.

H.'s posthumous reputation probably has suffered because, though a contemporary of modernists Virginia WOOLF and Gertrude Stein, her novelistic technique remained fairly traditional, characterized by chronological and omniscient narration. Few critics have noted H.'s innovation of embedding the controversial subject matter of lesbian love into the form of a Victorian Bildungsroman. *The Well of Loneliness* follows the childhood and youth of Stephen Gordon, an upper-class woman who gradually discovers the significance of her physically masculine traits. The novel ends pessimistically as the protagonist feigns an affair with the notorious lesbian Valérie Seymour to free her lover, Mary Llewellyn, for a more conventional, and thus socially gratifying, marriage to Martin Hallam, her own former suitor.

The subject of a censorship trial in November 1928, *The Well of Loneliness* was prosecuted by the British Home Office under the Obscene Publications Act of 1857. During the trial, H. received support from fellow writers including Woolf, Bernard SHAW, Rebecca WEST, Arnold BENNETT, and E. M. FORSTER, although some of them expressed reservations about the literary merit of the novel. The novel contains no explicit sex other than kisses. However, it clearly suggests sexual consummation through a scene in which the protagonist and her female lover spend their first night together and "are not divided." H. lost the case and the novel was banned in England.

Banned in her homeland, the novel was nevertheless sold in Paris and smuggled back into Great Britain. Though disappointed at the result of the trial, H. was gratified to receive hundreds of letters and telegrams of support. The novel was generally positively reviewed, although some readers were critical of its polemic call for toleration of homosexuals: "Give us also the right to our existence!" Judged as obscene in the U.S., *The*

Well of Loneliness sold 100,000 copies and had earned its author $60,000 in royalties by 1930 after the American decision was reversed. Upon H.'s death from cancer in 1943, the novel, still banned in Britain, was selling 100,000 copies a year internationally.

Before the controversy surrounding *The Well of Loneliness* made her an international cause célèbre, H. had already established a reputation as a poet and novelist. Her career began in 1906 with publication of a first volume of poetry, *'Twixt Earth and Stars*. The *Well of Loneliness* was not her only novel to deal with lesbianism. H.'s first novel, *The Unlit Lamp* (1924), used the Victorian convention of romantic friendship to disguise a lesbian relationship between Joan Ogden and her governess, Elizabeth Rodney. Her somewhat autobiographical novel *The Forge* (1924) uses a couple coded as heterosexual, Hilary and Susan Brent, to represent, in comic form, some of the experiences of the author and her long-term lover, Una Troubridge. In addition to this twenty-eight-year relationship, H. had a prior eight-year relationship with "Ladye," Mabel Veronica Batten. After Ladye's sudden death in 1916, H. and Troubridge sought the help of a medium to communicate with Ladye and became active participants in spiritualist research. The two were also involved in antivivisection movements and the Animal Protection Society .

H.'s novel about a waiter who becomes disgusted with food and nearly starves, *Adam's Breed* (1926), was well reviewed and won the Prix Femina and the James Tait Black Memorial Prize. Like this novel, H.'s favorite novel, *The Master of the House* (1932), and her final novel, *The Sixth Beatitude* (1936), explore religious and spiritual themes. The title story from the collection *Miss Ogilvy Finds Herself* (1934) is often anthologized and is notable for its suggestion of transsexuality and for its depiction of women ambulance drivers in World War I. H.'s novels frequently depict alienation and isolation, the effects of childhood on the adult, the struggle of the female artist, as well as sacrifice and martyrdom. H. deserves a significant place in literary history not only for writing the first lesbian novel but also for writing highly readable though relatively unexperimental novels—like those of Rebecca West and Vita SACKVILLE-WEST—fiction that made notable a contribution to British MODERNISM.

BIBLIOGRAPHY: Baker, M., *Our Three Selves: The Life of R. H.* (1985); Cline, S., *R. H.: A Woman Called John* (1998); Franks, C. S., *Beyond the Well of Loneliness* (1982); Newton, E., "The Mythic Mannish Lesbian: R. H. and the New Woman," *Signs* 9 (Summer 1984): 557–75

LYNETTE FELBER

HAMBURGER, Michael [Peter Leopold]
b. 22 March 1924, Berlin, Germany

H.'s German family emigrated to Edinburgh and later to London in 1933. He was educated at St. Paul's School and Oxford University. Poet and translator, H. draws on the European tradition. He is the distinguished translator of Hugo von Hofmannsthal (1961), Gunter Grass (1966), Hölderlin (1966), Peter Bichsel (1968), and Paul Celan (1972 and 1980). G.'s own collections of poetry include *Flowering Cactus* (1950), *Weather and Season* (1963), and *Ownerless Earth: New and Selected Poems* (1973). Editions of his *Collected Poems* appeared in 1984 and 1995. His critical book *The Truth of Poetry* (1969) is a useful introduction to the themes of modern poetry from Charles Baudelaire to the 1960s.

HAMILTON, [Robert] Ian
b. 24 March 1938, King's Lynn, Norfolk; d. 27 December 2001, London

Poet, editor, critic, and biographer, H. read English at Keble College, Oxford, where he earned his B.A. in 1962. In that same year, he founded the Oxford-based *Review* (1962–72), a literary journal that attracted poets such as David HARSENT, Hugo WILLIAMS, and Colin Falck. From 1965 to 1973, H. served as poetry and fiction editor for the *Times Literary Supplement* and in 1970 published *The Visit*, a collection of thirty-three poems. His biography of American poet Robert Lowell appeared in 1982, but soon thereafter H. found himself at the center of controversy when the publication of his biography of writer J. D. Salinger was suppressed by the court. The legal confrontation between author and subject prevented H. from releasing the biography and instead he produced a compromised version entitled *In Search of J. D. Salinger* (1988). H. was most accomplished as an editor, and his numerous editions include *The Modern Poet* (1968), *The New Review Anthology* (1985), and *The Oxford Companion to Twentieth-Century Poetry in English* (1994).

HAMPTON, Christopher [James]
b. 26 January 1946, Faial, Azores

H. burst onto the theatrical scene in 1966 with his first play, *When Did You Last See My Mother?* (1967). This is the story of a love triangle between two young men, Ian and Jimmy, who have had a relationship in the past, and Jimmy's mother, who has an affair with Ian. Despite touches of melodrama—the mother dies in a car crash after a fight with Ian—this play was hailed as an impressive theatrical debut. This work also explores themes of sexuality that feature prominently in H.'s later works. His next full-length play, for example, *Total Eclipse* (perf. 1968; pub. 1969), is an historical drama about the homosexual relationship between the French poets Arthur Rimbaud and Paul Verlaine.

The Philanthropist (1970) was conceived by H. as a sort of answer to Molière's *Le Misanthrope*. In this play, the well-meaning Phillip is constitutionally incapable of finding fault with other people. This is a black comedy dealing with the contrast between action and contemplation—most of the "action" of the play, however, is violent and destructive, whereas the contemplative life represented by Phillip is shown to be ultimately ineffective. The play was well received, winning the *Evening Standard* Drama Award for best comedy and being named best new play by a group of London theater critics.

H. is a prolific adaptor of the works of other playwrights, including Anton Chekhov's *Uncle Vanya* (perf. 1970; pub. 1971); Henrik Ibsen's *Hedda Gabler* (perf. 1970; pub. 1972), *A Doll's House* (perf. 1971; pub. 1972), *Ghosts* (perf. 1978; pub. 1983), *The Wild Duck* (perf. 1979; pub. 1980), and *An Enemy of the People* (perf. 1997); Molière's *Don Juan* (perf. 1972; pub. 1974) and *Tartuffe; or, The Impostor* (perf. 1983; pub. 1984); Ödön von Horvath's *Tales from the Vienna Woods* (1977), *Don Juan Comes Back from the War* (1978), and *Faith, Hope, and Charity* (1989), among others. His most popular play to date, however, is an adaptation of Choderlos de Laclos's 1782 epistolary novel *Les Liaisons Dangereuses* (1985).

Set in pre-revolutionary France, this intricately plotted drama tells the story of the aristocratic hedonists Vicomte de Valmont and the Marquise de Merteuil. Valmont, a Lothario of epic proportions, is dispatched by the Marquise to seduce Cecile, the young fiancée of the Marquise's former lover. At the same time, Valmont is planning his great triumph, the seduction of one Madame de Tourvel, known throughout France for her purity and fidelity. When Valmont finds himself having true feelings for Madame de Tourvel, he is effectively ordered by the Marquise to discard her, which he does. The drama of the play arises from the fact that Valmont and the Marquise are in love with one another, yet unable to overcome the nihilistic impulses that drive them to destroy others and, ultimately, themselves. Despite its historical setting, the play's modern focus on sexual politics, as well as its scintillating, highly literate dialogue made it a tremendous success both in its stage and film version (*Dangerous Liaisons*, 1989), for which H. also wrote the screenplay. He also wrote and directed the film *Carrington* (1995).

H. also adapted George Steiner's novel *The Portage to San Cristobal of A. H.* (perf. 1982; pub. 1983) and translated Yasmina Reza's highly acclaimed *Art* (1996) and *The Unexpected Man* (1998). Although the bulk of H.'s work has consisted of adaptations of

others' writings, he remains a highly talented dramatist. His sense of stagecraft and ability to create intelligent and compelling dialogue make him a major figure in contemporary theater.

BIBLIOGRAPHY: Francis, B., *C. H.* (1996); Gross, R., ed., *C. H.* (1990); Tyson, B. F., "C. H.," in Weintraub, S., ed., *British Dramatists since World War II*, part 1, *DLB* 13 (1985): 226–34

                                                    JASON BERNER

HANKIN, [Edward Charles] St. John [Emile Clavering]

b. 25 September 1869, Southampton, England; d. 15 June 1909, Llandrindod Wells, Wales

J. C. Trewin, the theater historian and drama critic, in *The Theatre since 1900* (1951), says: "St. John Hankin . . . is apparently quite dead. So at least we are told in 1950—this although *The Return of the Prodigal* had a revival at the Globe Theatre in the winter of 1948, and the Birmingham Repertory Theatre, during 1949 produced *The Cassilis Engagement*. The Return of the Prodigal met with the testiest annoyance: I gathered from some of my colleagues that the occasion was the disinterment of a mummy whose tomb was to be sealed at once and forgotten: John Gielgud was to be admonished soundly for assisting at the rites. I could not agree. H. straddles the theaters of entertainment and ideas. *The Return of the Prodigal*, done in 1905, is still a well-proportioned comedy with several recognizably human personages, many quivers of a wit that is both theatrical and civilized, one excellent serious scene for a stay-at-home sister whom life is passing by and always an unwavering sense of style."

The Return of the Prodigal (perf. 1905; pub. 1907) was H.'s second play and was always the one that attracted the most controversy. Even now, another fifty years on, it still reads very well and Trewin's commendation of it still seems justified. On any absolute scale of critical approbation/disapprobation (if there were such a thing), H.'s *The Return of the Prodigal* would surely rate among the treasures to be preserved—a minor treasure, admittedly, but not something to be cast thoughtlessly into oblivion. (Both music and painting take greater care of their minor masterpieces than does the theater, which submits everything, willy-nilly, to the fickle and precarious judgment of the barbarous multitude.)

H. wrote nine plays in all (two of them in collaboration with other writers): all of them produced in London theaters between 1893 and 1913. Max BEERBOHM, reviewing the first production of the first of these, *The Two Mr. Wetherbys* (1907), by the Stage Society in 1903, described it as: "quite the best-written comedy vouchsafed to us in recent years." In

1905, reviewing the first production, at the Court Theatre, of H.'s second play *The Return of the Prodigal*, he said: "Mr. Hankin has been much likened by the critics to Mr. Bernard Shaw. It is quite true that Mr. Hankin has come—what young playwright, nowadays, could fail to come?—somewhat under Mr. Shaw's influence. But the likeness of Mr. Hankin's play to what Mr. Shaw would have made of it is a merely technical and superficial likeness. Mr. Hankin does not set out to prove anything or to probe anything. He merely observes what is going on in the world and is moved to communicate to us his good-natured amusement." William ARCHER, though he praised H.'s play for its technical fluency and "lifelike" qualities, regretted its lack of sociological seriousness.

This dichotomy of critical views continued throughout the remainder of H.'s regrettably short career, other well-known and respected theater critics, like Desmond MacCarthy, also becoming involved. *The Charity That Began at Home* (1906), *The Cassilis Engagement* (1907), and *The Last of the De Mullins* (perf. 1908; pub. 1909) all attracted critical comment from both sides of this critical divide. It was generally agreed, however, that H. was a playwright of unusual promise, with an assured technical gift, a quick ear for realistic dialogue, and a mordant though ultimately good-humored cynicism in his view of human nature. "He was not forced to write for money," says John DRINKWATER in his introduction to the three-volume *Dramatic Works of St. John Hankin* (1912): "and he neither expected nor wished his plays to be readily accepted by the general public. He was deliberately in the camp of the pioneers and did not look for the rewards of conformity." Rereading these three volumes afresh after a gap of many years, one is struck all over again by the freshness, liveliness, and modernity of this little handful of plays and also by the originality and uniqueness of H.'s tone. He was not like Bernard SHAW; he was not like Harley GRANVILLE BARKER: he was like himself. More than that one cannot say of any genuine artist.

Though now largely forgotten and overlooked and fairly difficult to find, his work as a critic is equally distinguished. The best of these essays appeared in the *Fortnightly Review* from 1906 to 1908. Particularly commendable are the ones entitled "Mr. Bernard Shaw as Critic" and "The Collected Plays of Oscar Wilde." Both have striking and challenging things still to say to us. For example, in these days of the early 21st c. when it is the almost universal practice to exaggerate grossly Oscar WILDE's genius as a playwright, it is refreshing to read: "The difficulty about Wilde as a playwright was that he never quite got through the imitative phase. *The Importance of Being Earnest* is the nearest approach to absolute originality that he attained. In that play, he seemed to be tearing

himself away from tradition and to be evolving a dramatic form of his own. Unhappily, it was the last play he was to write and so the promise in it was never fulfilled." H. wrote this in May 1908. In June 1909, fearing that he may have inherited syphilis from his father, he committed suicide, leaving his own rich promise as a playwright unfulfilled.

BIBLIOGRAPHY: Beerbohm, M., *More Theatres* (1969); Beerbohm, M., *Last Theatres* (1970); Drinkwater, J., ed., *Dramatic Works of St. J. H.* (3 vols., 1912); Trewin, J. C., *The Theatre since 1900* (1951)

ERIC SALMON

HARDY, Thomas
b. 2 June 1840, Higher Bockhampton, Dorset; d. 11 January 1928, Dorchester, Dorset

H. is the only English author, except perhaps D. H. LAWRENCE, who left a substantial number of major novels and also major poems. Indeed, he had two careers, first as a Victorian novelist and short story writer and then as a 20th-c. poet.

His life, outwardly quiet, was racked by contradictions. He was born in a remote and old-fashioned part of Dorset (he called the region "Wessex"), but spent his twenties in London, working as an architect, and was very aware of contemporary currents of thought. Like most of his characters, he belonged to an "intermediate class," which is always striving to better itself but has many links with the working poor and can easily topple over the edge. He was the first professional man in his family, but did not get into university. The struggles of the self-educated are a theme of the stark story "A Tragedy of Two Ambitions" (1894) and *Jude the Obscure* (1895). Like Tess Durbeyfield, he sometimes felt that he was talking two languages, one to his family and friends in Dorset, and one to educated strangers.

Two traumatic events colored his worldview. One was the execution of a woman in 1856, which he witnessed; the other the suicide in 1873 of his friend Horace Moule. He would always be interested in self-destructive behavior and conscious that there was no Providence that protected the innocent; this was why the Victorians sometimes found his work intolerably depressing. He himself insisted that he was not a pessimist but a "meliorist," believing that if human life was to be improved its darker aspects must be honestly faced.

The changes in H.'s England could be symbolized, physically by the railways that opened up communities like his own, culturally by the rise of agnosticism. He knew the Bible thoroughly, and it is an influence on his work, but he lost his religion early although he continued to believe in Christian ethics. John Stuart MILL's *On Liberty* and Charles DARWIN's *Origin of*

Species were also powerful influences, as were William SHAKESPEARE and the Greek tragedies.

As a young man he wrote several poems that did not find a publisher, and decided to concentrate on fiction. The title of his first, lost work *The Poor Man and the Lady*, is highly significant. He was aware that men and women were constantly marrying people "above" or "below" them and that this affected their careers. His own marriage in 1874 to Emma Gifford, who was a "lady," would eventually fail.

He was able to give up architecture and become a self-supporting novelist, publishing *Desperate Remedies* (3 vols., 1871), *Under the Greenwood Tree* (2 vols., 1872), and *A Pair of Blue Eyes* (3 vols., 1873). But it was *Far from the Madding Crowd* (2 vols., 1874) that made his name. Readers to whom Dorset was another world were delighted by his story of a woman farmer and her three suitors, and his detailed and loving descriptions of the rhythms of the country year. It is not an entirely cheerful novel; it contains a murder and an unmarried mother who dies. But it does have a basically happy atmosphere, and as each later novel appeared critics would complain that it was darker than *Far from the Madding Crowd*.

H.'s next book, *The Hand of Ethelberta* (2 vols., 1876), particularly disappointed them. Yet it has an interesting theme that echoes his own situation; a successful writer conceals from her smart London audiences the fact that she comes from a family of servants.

The seven "Novels of Character and Environment"—*Under the Greenwood Tree, Far from the Madding Crowd, The Return of the Native* (3 vols., 1878), *The Mayor of Casterbridge* (2 vols., 1886), *The Woodlanders* (3 vols., 1887), *Tess of the D'Urbervilles* (3 vols., 1891), and *Jude the Obscure*—are as a group far superior to the seven others that he wrote over a quarter of a century. The characteristic H. novel takes place in a small town or village, often in the past, in a partly real, partly dream-landscape vividly described, and among people from the "metamorphic" class, neither farmers nor laborers, into which he himself had been born. Their customs are picturesque and old-fashioned (to the Victorians, they were delightful and refreshing), but we are aware that the world is changing fast and that only those who can adapt to change will survive. Such a novel will also tell an absorbing story; H. believed that a novelist had no right to bore his audience and did not at first have much trouble writing serials for magazines. There is a certain amount of melodrama, due to the need to keep the reader in suspense, and coincidences are frequent, because his characters live in a very small world.

The Return of the Native, set on the heath around H.'s birthplace, introduces a new theme; a man who has done what his mother wanted and "got on" begins to doubt the value of his work. Clym Yeobright re-

fuses to be a diamond merchant, dreams of educating the heath workers' children, and ends up as an unconventional traveling preacher, and celibate. The other great theme in this novel is marriage, and this would become increasingly important to H. His characters fall in love with, and sometimes marry, an incompatible person, ignoring their genuine other half or not meeting them until it is too late. "To be yearning for the difficult, to be weary of that offered; to care for the remote, to dislike the near," is the nature of Wildeve in *The Return*. H. was aware of this tendency in himself and satirized it in *The Well-Beloved* (1897). The fatal attraction, the chance that will not come again, the present which is not valued until it has become the past, are the great subjects of his poetry and fiction.

He went on to write three minor novels; *The Trumpet-Major* (3 vols., 1880), set during the Napoleonic Wars; *A Laodicean* (1881), and *Two on a Tower* (3 vols., 1882), in which the theme of class differences between lovers is particularly pronounced. After moving back permanently to Dorchester, he published one of his most impressive works, *The Mayor of Casterbridge*, set in his hometown. There is a love interest, and the characters make the wrong choices as usual, but H.'s real concern is with the rise and fall of a passionate man who cannot fit into a competitive, and changing, society. It is subversive, because it hints that the successful man is not necessarily the one who deserves most sympathy, and because Henchard grows to love a girl who is not his daughter but another man's illegitimate child. H. would become steadily more at odds with Victorian conventions.

The Woodlanders is still darker, suggesting that the struggle for existence has nothing to do with morality. Nature in this novel is particularly lush and inviting, but not innocent. It is a Darwinian world where trees fight for space, animals prey on one another and the best characters die or fail to thrive while the amoral Fitzpiers does quite well. In his last two great novels, H. would challenge orthodox Christianity head on.

His best short stories were written in the 1880s and 1890s—"Fellow-Townsmen," "The Three Strangers," "The Withered Arm," "The Melancholy Hussar," "A Tragedy of Two Ambitions," the notorious "Barbara of the House of Grebe," "The Son's Veto," and "The Fiddler of the Reels." Their themes are the familiar ones; class, religion, a wrong marriage choice, brutality to women and often, in the background, an execution, which would form the climax of *Tess of the D'Urbervilles*.

He had always caused offense to some readers, but he now felt it was impossible for him to write what he wished while being serialized in a family magazine. *Tess* was a great success for the wrong reasons, causing scandal because H. described his heroine, who had been seduced and ended up committing murder, as "a pure woman." Tess is the archetypal woman betrayed, a victim of the double standard, but she has also been identified with the "English peasantry," the vanishing "better-informed class," and animals and birds which are ruthlessly hunted down. H. said that his books were "one plea against 'man's inhumanity to man'—to woman—and to the lower animals," and his sympathy for victims, whether they are slaughtered pheasants or the rural poor, was intense.

His last novel, *Jude the Obscure*, is untypical, and feels much more "modern" than the rest, because the hero leaves his village very early and the traditional culture of that village has gone. Jude is a self-educated scholar who is kept out of Oxford University and wanders restlessly from town to town by train, supporting himself and his unconventional family by work that is not the kind he would have chosen. The natural world, often kindly in the earlier works, has become bleak and threatening. The novel is a tragic one and its attacks on the Church and the marriage laws provoked several hostile reviews.

Partly as a result, H. decided to renounce fiction and return, as he had always wished, to poetry. He felt, correctly, that it was easier to say in verse things which conventional readers did not wish to know. His first collection, *Wessex Poems* (1898), which contained both old and recent work, surprised everyone, and was attacked as "slovenly, slipshod, uncouth." This perception would change over a generation as he went on to publish seven more volumes of poetry, the last posthumously in 1928.

The uncouthness cannot be wholly denied. He deliberately avoids the "jewelled line" of Alfred, Lord TENNYSON or A. C. SWINBURNE and uses many puzzling and unexpected words or compounds—"hap," "unhope," "ruers," "unweeting," "sense-sealed," "foot-folk"—which show the influence of the Dorset poet William BARNES. He also shuns "poetic" imagery, instead looking at his own wrinkled face in a mirror and, in "The Darkling Thrush," which invites comparison with the great odes of John KEATS and Percy Bysshe SHELLEY, painting the bird that makes wonderful music as unglamorous. So he is anti-Romantic in a sense, but he is not a modernist either; he disliked "rhymeless, rhythmless poets" and wrote in 1918 that the "fashion for obscurity" would drive readers away. His work is, despite some eccentric phrases, thoroughly accessible. He uses a great variety of forms; the themes, though, are much the same as in his fiction. Many of them tell stories, about love and disillusionment. Others are to do with nature, religious doubt, and the ravages of time, and he occasionally wrote magnificent poems about public events. They include a group on the Boer War ("Drummer Hodge," "A Christmas Ghost Story," "The Souls of the Slain") and "The Convergence of the Twain," written after the sinking of the *Titanic*.

Over nine hundred short poems survive. Not all can be dated, and it is difficult to say in what sense his poetry "developed." The earliest are obviously Victorian yet include the striking "Neutral Tones" (1867); sixty years later, in 1927, he was still capable of writing a marvelous piece like "Lying Awake." But the numbers of good poems increased as he was able to give more time to them, and many of the best were written in his seventies.

Before that, there was a diversion. In the early years of the 20th c., H. was preoccupied with *The Dynasts* (3 parts, 1904–8), a huge drama, not intended to be performed and written mostly in blank verse, about the Napoleonic Wars. He had always been fascinated by this period; the Boer War reawakened his interest in conflict and he wove the unrecorded history of ordinary Wessex people into the history of "dynasts" and statesmen. It is not much read today, although younger poets who had been through the First World War greatly admired it. But it is interesting to see how the Spirit of the Pities and Spirits Sinister and Ironic who comment on the action reflect his own attitudes to human folly. The blank verse is not very impressive and the characters are one-dimensional, but it contains some fine lyrics.

H. and his wife had been semi-estranged for years when, in 1912, she suddenly died. During her lifetime, he had written wistful love poetry to other women, including Florence Dugdale who eventually became his second wife. But, characteristically, once Emma had gone for good his original feelings returned and inspired the "Poems of 1912–13," which are among the greatest poems in the language about bereavement. The fact that there had been a "deep division" and "dark undying pain" adds to their intensity. Other poems written in old age, "In Time of 'The Breaking of Nations'" and "Afterwards" are profound meditations on time and death.

During and after his lifetime, H. triumphantly faced down all criticism. His novels have always been popular and are now more popular than ever, constantly being filmed, adapted for television and radio, and set as academic texts. Up to about 1960, he was not much discussed in the universities, but there now exist literally thousands of books and articles on various aspects of his work. Marxists are interested in his treatment of class, feminists in his treatment of women, and he has attracted the attention of poststructuralist critics too. His poetry took longer to make its way and it was argued, for a time, that he had written only a handful of good lyrics, but he is now recognized as one of the great figures of the early 20th c. and an influence on each generation which came after.

BIBLIOGRAPHY: Bailey, J. O., *The Poetry of T. H.* (1970); Brady, K., *The Short Stories of T. H.* (1982); Gibson, J., *T. H.* (1996); Hardy, F. E., *The Life of*

T. H. (1962); Millgate, M., T. H. (1982); Morgan, R., Women and Sexuality in the Novels of T. H. (1988); Page, N., ed., Oxford Reader's Companion to H. (2000); Sumner, R., T. H. (1981); Taylor, R. H., The Neglected H. (1982); Widdowson, P., T. H. (1996); Williams, M., Preface to H. (1993)

MERRYN WILLIAMS

HARE, Cyril

(pseud. of Alfred Alexander Gordon Clark) b. 4 September 1900, Mickleham, Surrey; d. 25 August 1958, Surrey

Classical detective novelist, who wrote within the traditions of the legal thriller, H. was called to the bar in 1924, and practiced in civil and criminal courts; he was a legal assistant in the Director of Public Prosecutions Department during the Second World War and a County Court judge in Surrey for the last eight years of his life. His career gave him a uniquely informed perspective on crime and justice that he transferred to his fiction, blending it with a superb sense of comedy and an instinct for the dramatic. H. was the creator of two popular series characters: the Scotland Yard detective, Inspector Mallett; and the ageing lawyer, Francis Pettigrew. His work was critically applauded during his lifetime, but fell into neglect after his death: recent years have seen a welcome reevaluation of his erudite and elegant contribution to the genre.

H.'s favorite novel, and the one generally recognized as his masterpiece, is *Tragedy at Law* (1942). Set in wartime and deeply rooted in his own experiences as judge's marshal, it follows the trials and tribulations of Mr. Justice Barber who, while on circuit, injures a pedestrian while driving his car when drunk. *Tragedy at Law* is somewhat unorthodox in that no murder occurs until very near the end, and most of the book's puzzle element is concerned with sabotage, hoaxes, and threats of violence, and with the judge's increasingly desperate attempts to avoid scandal and prosecution. The atmosphere of fawning reverence, rivalry, petty jealousies, and rigid bureaucracy is quite brilliantly observed, and the book is notable, too, for its acute characterization: H. breathes glorious life into a full cast of stock characters—the judge, who knows only too well the cost of his mistake; his beautiful, ambitious, and clever wife; an unpleasant butler; a young romantic; and Francis Pettigrew himself, who makes his first appearance as a jobbing defense barrister, plagued with cynicism and disillusionment and haunted by the circumstances that have stifled a once-promising career. Cited by many lawyers as a classic fictional representation of the wheels of justice, *Tragedy at Law* received excellent reviews on publication and has stood the test of time, remaining one of the finest legally based detective novels ever written.

Until 1942, H.'s work had failed to make much impact and consisted of three competent crime novels, typical of the decade in which they were published: Inspector Mallett makes his debut in *Tenant for Death* (1937), unraveling a complex case involving the death of a financier; in *Death Is No Sportsman* (1938), murder disrupts a pastoral setting and a fishing syndicate of four businessmen; and *Suicide Excepted* (1939), another entertaining but unremarkable novel in which Inspector Mallett investigates a suspicious suicide. The novels written after *Tragedy at Law*, however, emulated its success: similarly distinguished by their wit, unexpected plot twists, and refreshingly unclichéd characterization, they placed H. at the forefront of his craft.

H. continued to allow his personal experience and interests to inform his fiction: *With a Bare Bodkin* (1946), in which the Blitz forces the evacuation of government offices to a seaside resort, draws heavily on his service in the Ministry of Economic Warfare; and *When the Wind Blows* (1949; repub. as *The Wind Blows Death*, 1950) sets the murder of a top violinist, strangled with a silk stocking, against a knowledgeable and vividly sketched musical backdrop. The latter vies with *Tragedy at Law* as the pinnacle of H.'s achievements but, for sheer popularity, *An English Murder* (1951; repub. as *The Christmas Murder*, 1953) is also a contender: this textbook country house murder and fair play, Christie-esque whodunit is a consummate example of how to show respect for tradition while extending its boundaries.

H.'s last two novels were not quite of the same caliber. *That Yew Tree's Shade* (1954; repub. as *Death Walks the Woods*, 1954) recalls Pettigrew from retirement to solve another Markshire murder; and *He Should Have Died Hereafter* (1958; repub. as *Untimely Death*, 1958) is a short and rather episodic narrative that unites Mallett and Pettigrew in Exmoor, the latter now happily married to a much younger woman.

Careful plotting and a certain detachment from the world that he described evocatively yet economically made H. a skilled practitioner of the short story; much of his short fiction was published in *Punch* and Ellery Queen's *Mystery Magazine* and the volume, *Best Detective Stories*, edited by his friend and colleague Michael Gilbert, appeared in the year following his death, prefaced by an informative and respectful essay on his work. H. also published a juvenile work, *The Magic Bottle* (1946), and contributed to legal works and a guide to music in his home county. A play, *The House of Warbeck*, was produced in 1955.

H. has been compared to Freeman Wills Crofts and Nicholas Blake, among others, but his style is utterly his own and has won the admiration of contemporaries such as Elizabeth BOWEN and modern writers of crime fiction, such as Francis Fyfield and P. D. JAMES, who filled the gap that his death left in Faber's publishing output. Meticulous detail, lively dialogue, and a warm compassion for human nature and its foibles make his a delightful legacy.

BIBLIOGRAPHY: Steiner, T. R., "C. H.," in Benstock, B., ed., *British Mystery Writers, 1920–1939*, DLB 77 (1989): 153–56

NICOLA UPSON

HARE, [Sir] David
b. 5 June 1947, Bexhill, Sussex

H.'s distinctive achievement as a playwright is his theatrical articulation of the impact on the individual of social change in Britain since the end of the Second World War. His plays are characterized by an ethical as well as political force that derives from, respectively, his insistent correlation of public and private aspects of experience; his exploration of the personal conflicts wrought by duty and responsibility, and his foregrounding and questioning of the status of individual conscience and moral commitment in a secular society. The meaning of H.'s plays is often grounded in terms of the experience of his women characters.

After graduating from Cambridge University in 1968, H. founded Portable Theatre with Tony Bicât. With H. working mainly as director, Portable toured the country for three years, developing a reputation for experimental and confrontational productions. H. subsequently wrote two landmark plays with his former colleague from Portable, Howard BRENTON: *Brassneck* (perf. 1973; pub. 1974), a panoramic saga about corruption in local government, and *Pravda* (1985), a satirical morality tale focusing on the degradation of popular journalism.

Slag (perf. 1970; pub. 1971), H.'s first play, is set in Brackenhurst girls' boarding school where three female teachers open the play by pledging to abstain from sex. *Slag* establishes H.'s aptitude for pithy dialogue and a robust engagement with contemporary issues. Another early (and under-rated) work, *Knuckle* (1974), subverts the thriller format to deliver a stinging critique of British capitalism and provincial decay; it also presages the ascendancy of Thatcherite economic ideology.

H.'s first major work is *Fanshen* (perf. 1975; pub. 1976), adapted from William Hinton's book on the Chinese Revolution. The play was written for Joint Stock, a company that developed collaborative approaches to theater, and examines the process and effects of revolution in the Chinese village of Long Bow during the land reforms of the 1940s. H. deploys techniques of theatrical distancing inherited from Bertolt Brecht in order to illuminate the contradictions that irrupt within the revolutionary moment.

The protagonist of *Plenty* (1978), Susan Traherne, has become an iconic figure in postwar drama; the play itself exemplifies H.'s technique of projecting a broad political and historical canvas in terms of the personal experience of one individual. *Plenty* begins with Susan leaving her dissipated diplomat husband, Brock, in 1962; the next scene takes place in France, 1943, where Susan is working undercover for the Special Operations Executive. The final moments in the play deploy a similar technique: in 1962, Susan is reunited with the agent who featured in scene two; they embark on a fumbled liaison in a seedy hotel bedroom in Blackpool, but this scene dissolves into a glorious vision of the French countryside—it is August 1944, the time of Liberation, and Susan rhapsodizes to a French onlooker that "there will be days and days and days like this." The structure of the play enforces the ironic contrast between the nostalgia-idealism associated with the past, and the grim reality of the present; H. politicizes this opposition in order to critique the stultifying, suffocating nature of British institutional structures. The chronological scenes that form the substance of the play trace Susan's experiences against a backdrop of symbolic episodes in British postwar history.

A recurring feature of H.'s playwriting is his use of political scenarios to identify the tensions between public and private responsibilities. *The Great Exhibition* (1972), an idiosyncratic early play, documents the political disillusionment and bizarre private life of Hammett, a disgruntled Labour member of Parliament. *The Secret Rapture* (perf. 1988; pub. 1989) and the screenplay *Paris by Night* (1988), both feature women Conservative politicians whose personal and professional priorities are brought into stark confrontation. This enables H. to negotiate broad ethical questions, not least the viability of "goodness" and liberal-humanistic values in the context of Margaret Thatcher's Britain.

The David Hare Trilogy (1990–93) is H.'s most accomplished achievement to date, in respect of its monumental scale, theatrical ambition, and contemporary resonance. The performance of all three plays in repertory at the National Theatre, in 1993, was one of the major theater events of the decade. *Racing Demon* (1990) explores the profound identity crisis that divides the Church of England. Structurally, the plot unfolds in an orthodox linear fashion with short, interspersed scenes advancing each strand of the narrative. A more interesting feature of the play is the attitude it builds toward the various clerics, from the evangelistic Tony to the liberal Lionel, whose views and doubts establish the terms for an impassioned debate about the nature of faith in the contemporary world. *Racing Demon*, through its careful appropriation of a particular form of monologue—the prayer—manages to convey the human dimension of a debilitating theological schism.

Murmuring Judges (1991) focuses on the British legal, judicial, and penal systems. At first, the play promises to be a courtroom thriller about a miscarriage of justice: the presence of two women who are committed to righting the wrongs of the legal system—Irina, a firebrand lawyer, and Sandra, a police officer—intimates that Gerard, the youth whose conviction is the dramatic focus, may be freed at the end. Yet *Murmuring Judges* is not a generic courtroom drama and Gerard's plight is barely alleviated. Instead, H. illuminates the set of institutional pressures that produce such an injustice, from the inflated pretensions of Edgecombe QC, to the crazed bureaucracy that drives Barry, the bullish detective, off the rails. Since the facts surrounding Gerard's conviction emerge gradually, it is the legal process itself that is seen to be prejudiced and corrupted.

The final play of the trilogy, *The Absence of War* (1993), accounts for the Labour Party's defeat in the 1992 General Election and, in so doing, identifies the damaging consequences of the media manipulation of political charisma. It is tempting to see the play as a dramatic reconstruction of Neil Kinnock's defeat in 1992. Much of the initial criticism of the play—including from Labour politicians—was that H. betrayed the trust placed in him by the Kinnock leadership that granted him unprecedented access to Labour's deliberations throughout the 1992 contest. H. himself counters that modern politicians have embarked on a "Faustian pact with respectability," suppressing their actual convictions to win media approval: the play interweaves scenes that counterpoint the discrepancies between private feelings and public actions, most notably during and after the keynote rally speech. In this way, the audience ascertains the extent to which George Jones, the Labour leader in the play, can never "be himself" in public. The sense of institutional stagnation and lost opportunity that permeates the play, and indeed the whole trilogy, is symbolized by the haunting commemoration scenes at the Cenotaph which book-end the dramatic action. H.'s *Asking Around* (1993), a published collation of his research for the trilogy, provides a searing testament to the effect of Thatcherism on Britain's beleaguered institutions.

H.'s recent playwriting—indicatively, *Skylight* (1995) and *Amy's View* (1997)—is marked by its formal conservatism, a domestic focus and an unusual intimacy. *My Zinc Bed* (2000) operates within this framework but dispenses with naturalistic detail: the effect is to intensify the focus on the highly charged relationship between Paul, a recovering alcoholic who is also the play's narrator, and Elsa, the flirtatious wife of an elderly internet tycoon. In contrast, *Via Dolorosa* (1998) marks a bold new departure for H.: it is a combative monologue that reports his experience of visiting the Middle East. H. himself performed the play in London and on Broadway, and his recollections are published in *Acting Up: A Diary* (1999).

H. has worked as resident dramatist of the Royal Court Theatre (1970–71) and Nottingham Playhouse (1973), but it is his long-term relationship with the National Theatre, especially under Richard Eyre's stewardship, that represents one of the great creative partnerships in postwar theater. H. has also worked as director, librettist, and screenwriter (he founded Greenpoint films in 1982 whose productions include H.'s renowned *Wetherby*, 1985). He was knighted in 1998.

BIBLIOGRAPHY: Fraser, S., *A Politic Theatre: The Drama of D. H.* (1996); Haill, L., ed., *Asking Around: Background to the D. H. Trilogy* (1993); Homden, C., *The Plays of D. H.* (1995); Pattie, D., "The Common Good: The H. Trilogy," *MD* 42 (Fall 1999): 362–74; Su, J. J., "Nostalgic Rapture: Interpreting Moral Commitments in D. H.'s Drama," *MD* 40 (Spring 1997): 23–37

CHRIS MEGSON

HARINGTON [or HARRINGTON], [Sir] John

b. 1561, Kelston, near Bath; d. 20 November 1612, Kelston

H. is best known as translator of Lodovico Ariosto's *Orlando Furioso* into English retaining the original *ottava rima* pattern (1591) and promoter of the water closet (*The Metamorphosis of Ajax,* 1596). Educated at Eton and Christ's College, Cambridge, H. was godson to Queen ELIZABETH I. His *Epigrams* were printed in a collection entitled *Alcilia* in 1613 and separately in 1615. His works include *The Englishman's Doctor; or, The School of Salerne* (1607) and *Nugae Antiquae*, miscellaneous papers collected by Henry Harington in two volumes (1769–75; rev. ed., 3 vols., 1779).

HARRADEN, Beatrice

b. 24 January 1864, Hampstead; d. 5 May 1936, Barton-on-Sea, Hampshire

Suffragette and novelist, H. had a cosmopolitan education in Dresden, Cheltenham Ladies College, Queen's College, London, and Bedford College, London University, graduating in 1883. An ardent feminist, she traveled extensively in Europe and the U.S., selling newspapers and making speeches. In 1930, she was awarded a Civil List pension for her services to literature. H. contributed many short stories to *Blackwood's Magazine* before publishing her novel *Ships That Pass in the Night* (1893), which sold over a million copies. Set in a winter resort for consumptives, the story features a fragile heroine who dies in a street accident. *In Varying Moods* (1894) was a collection of short stories written in Sussex and the South of

France. Other titles included *Hilda Strafford and the Remittance Man* (1897), *The Fowler* (1899), *Katharine Frensham* (1903), *Interplay* (1908), *Youth Calling* (1924), and *Search Will Find It Out* (1928).

HARRIOT [or HARIOT], Thomas
b. 1560, Oxford; d. 2 July 1621, London

H. was mathematical tutor to Sir Walter RALEIGH and in 1585 accompanied Sir Richard Grenville on Raleigh's expedition to Virginia, where H. made an unprecedentedly sophisticated statistical and economic survey. H.'s account of this expedition was published 1588 as *A Brief and True Report of the New Found Land of Virginia* and was later reprinted in Richard HAKLUYT's *The Principal Navigations, Voyages and Discoveries of the English Nation.* H. improved algebraical notation, introducing symbols still in use. He was also an astronomer and meteorologist, preparing a treatise on the rainbow and colors. He was described as "the universal philosopher," indicating his scientific versatility.

HARRIS, [James Thomas] Frank
b. 14 February 1856, Galway, Ireland; d. 26 August 1931, Nice, France

Editor, biographer, autobiographer, playwright, novelist, journalist, and writer of short stories, H. at the zenith of his career was a leading figure in the London literary and social world. As editor of the prestigious *Fortnightly Review* (1886–94) and the *Saturday Review* (1894–98), H. knew many of the greatest late Victorian writers and political figures—among them H. G. WELLS, Arnold BENNETT, Bernard SHAW, George MEREDITH, and Randolph Churchill. This milieu eventually provided the material for his best work. Son of a customs ship official, H. ran away from school at fifteen and traveled to the U.S. where he worked as a sand hog in New York and a hotel clerk in Chicago before forming a partnership with his brother in a butcher's shop in Lawrence, Kansas. He was inspired by classics professor Byron Caldwell Smith to study at the University of Kansas in Lawrence and to pass the bar. He traveled to Paris where he mastered enough French to teach it at Brighton College in 1877. Here, in 1878, he married Florence Ruth Adams, who died the following year. With an inheritance from his wife, he traveled to Europe and by 1882 was writing for London papers.

In 1883, he became editor of a small, failing conservative paper, the *Evening News.* Fired in 1886, he assumed the editorship of the *Fortnightly Review.* In 1887, he married Emily Clayton, a forty-eight-year-old wealthy widow, with the understanding that he would enter politics. In 1890, H. ruined his chance for a parliamentary seat by defending Charles Stewart Parnell during the latter's adultery scandal. Separated from his wife in 1894 and fired from the *Fortnightly Review,* H. bought the *Saturday Review* to which Wells and Shaw became regular contributors. In 1895, his first collection of short stories, *Elder Conklin,* aroused controversy because of its erotic content. In 1899, his play *Mr. and Mrs. Daventry,* based on an Oscar WILDE scenario, had a successful run. It was not published until 1956. Another collection of short stories, *Montes the Matador,* followed in 1901, and in 1909 H. published *The Man Shakespeare,* an attempt to reconstruct William SHAKESPEARE's life from his work.

After selling the *Saturday Review,* H. edited relatively minor publications sporadically while he indulged in speculation: stocks, real estate, and casinos. In 1898, he began his liaison with Nellie, whom he could not marry until his wife's death in 1927. With bankruptcy pending, H. left England in 1914 and went again to the U.S., where he owned *Pearson's* from 1916 until 1922. Most of his friends and acquaintances were alienated by his pro-German *England or Germany?* (1915), an alienation furthered by the publication of *Oscar Wilde: His Life and Confessions* (2 vols., 1916). Already suspected of shady business dealings, he was now accused of lying pornographically about Wilde. Between 1915 and 1922, he produced four volumes of *Contemporary Portraits* in which H. claims many prominent people owe their success to him. H. spent the rest of his life in Nice hounded by financial difficulties and writing *My Life and Loves,* which for censorship reasons did not see full publication until 1964. The last of the five volumes was compiled from notes by Alexander Trocchi.

H.'s fiction no longer draws attention, and he has left no mark in Shakespearean scholarship, but two of his works, the Wilde biography and *My Life and Loves,* remain fresh and vital. H.'s account of conversations with Wilde are unconvincing, but the factual structure is not. H. L. Mencken, Upton Sinclair, John Middleton MURRY, and Shaw praised the book. (Shaw knew Wilde personally.) *My Life and Loves* is unreliable and monomaniacally obsessed with sex, but it is also a rich panorama of late-19th-c. England, filled with quickly and deftly drawn portraits. It is hardly likely that John RUSKIN discussed his sex life with H. or that Thomas CARLYLE and his wife's doctor discussed Carlyle's with H. And perhaps H.'s mentor Smith did not suffer from health-destroying wet dreams in memory of a passionate love affair. But *My Life and Loves* remains a valuable, readable book.

BIBLIOGRAPHY: Brome, V., *F. H.* (1959); Pearsall, R. B., *F. H.* (1970); Pullar, P., *F. H.* (1975)

DALTON AND MARYJEAN GROSS

HARRISON, Tony
b. 30 April 1937, Beeston, Leeds, Yorkshire

H. was born into a working-class district of Leeds and was educated at a local primary school where he won a scholarship to the prestigious Leeds Grammar School. After reading classics at Leeds University, he embarked on postgraduate research into translations of the *Aeneid*, but abandoned academic life in order to devote himself to poetry. He has lived and worked in Africa, Prague, Cuba, the U.S., and Greece, but has made Newcastle-upon-Tyne in the north of England his base for many years. Early poems appeared in student magazines such as *Poetry and Audience*, and were later taken by periodicals such as *London Magazine* and *Stand*. His first pamphlet-length publication (as "T. W. Harrison") was *Earthworks* (1964), which was followed by a pamphlet publication of his long poem *Newcastle Is Peru* (1969), but his first book proper was *The Loiners* (i.e., residents of Leeds), published in 1970, which won the Geoffrey Faber Memorial Prize in 1972. Subsequent poetry collections include *From "The School of Eloquence"* (1978), *Continuous* (1981), *v.* (1985; rev. ed., 1989), *A Cold Coming* (1991), *The Gaze of the Gorgon* (1992), which won the Whitbread Poetry Prize in 1992, and *Laureate's Block* (2000). The poetry takes many forms: more conventional lyrical, elegiac and narrative poems; humorous and scurrilous pieces; journalistic poems written in response to current events, and published in newspapers; verse plays, original and adapted; verse-films for television; verse scripts for cinematic films; but the verse is always integrated with the images; never subordinate to or merely descriptive of them.

A number of H.'s plays and adaptations have been performed at the London National Theatre as well as in particular spaces for which they were written, such as Salt's Mill, Saltire, in Yorkshire, and the theater in Delphi, Greece. The theater work includes *The Oresteia* (perf. 1981; pub. 1985), which won the European Poetry Translation Prize in 1982, *The Mysteries* (1985), *The Trackers of Oxyrhyncus* (perf. 1988; pub. 1990), *Square Rounds* (1992), *A Common Chorus* (1992), *Poetry or Bust* (1993), *The Kaisers of Carnuntum* (perf. 1995; pub. 1996), *The Labourers of Herakles* (perf. 1995; pub. 1996), and *The Prince's Play* (1996). The poem-films for television and cinema include *The Blasphemers' Banquet* (1989), *v.* (1989), winner of the Royal Television Society Award, *Black Daisies for the Bride* (1993), winner of the 1994 Prix Italia, *A Maybe Day in Kazakhstan* (1994), *The Shadow of Hiroshima* (1995), and *Prometheus*, which H. directed (1999). He has worked with a number of leading producers and directors, including George Cukor, Peter Hall, and Richard Eyre.

H. lists among his poetic influences his "household gods" of John MILTON and John KEATS, but also cites music hall artists Max Miller and "Professor" Leon Cortez. Embracing both "high" and "low" culture, and insisting that neither should be the exclusive province of any sector of society, H. combines in his work elements from classical literature and myth, canonical poetry of many cultures, and popular song and jokes. The language he employs to convey this eclectic mix is highly flexible, incorporating dialectal and standard English, non-English languages, profanity, and specialized registers. A master of form, he uses strict metrical and rhyme-schemes, but breaks up his forms on the page and includes typographical devices (i.e., italic and bold type, Gothic script, small caps) in order to represent the division and fragmentation which are important themes in his work.

The poems abound in ambiguities, inconsistencies, and paradoxes, as does H.'s public persona. By English standards he is a popular poet (one of the very few to make a living from poetry), yet his writing is not populist. Though he often seems to be writing from the margins and pushing at boundaries, many of his forms and themes are rooted in the traditions of English poetry. He is the subject of study in colleges and schools, and of much critical, but (relatively) little academic attention. He seems to typify modern urban man, yet produced some of his most admired poetry while living in rural Florida. He is cosmopolitan and wide-ranging, yet inalienably Yorkshire. He has been president of the Classical Association, a champion of high culture, but depicts education as a process of rote-learning, ritual humiliation, and cultural kidnap. His language is usually accessible and often demotic, but many of his references and allusions are erudite or obscure. Notoriously pessimistic and skeptical, he writes love poetry of calm security. He demands a radical voice for poetry, but imagines peace and unity achieved through personal relations.

BIBLIOGRAPHY: Byrne, S., *H, v., & O: The Poetry of T. H.* (1998); Byrne, S., ed., *T. H.* (1997); Kelleher, J., *T. H.* (1996); Rowland, A., *T. H. and the Holocaust* (2001); Spencer, L., *The Poetry of T. H.* (1994)

SANDIE BYRNE

HARSENT, David
b. 9 December 1942, Devonshire

H. emerged as an innovative voice in contemporary British poetry in the late 1960s and early 1970s as part of a group of writers associated with the literary magazine *Review*, edited by Ian HAMILTON. With other *Review* poets such as Colin Falck, Peter Dale, and Hugo WILLIAMS, H. became identified with a sparing, precise use of language both praised and criticized as poetic "minimalism." H. gained critical recognition with the publication in 1968 of his first collection of poetry, *Tonight's Lover*, followed in the next year by *A Violent Country*. Other collections include *After Dark* (1973), *Dreams of the Dead* (1977), and *From an Inland Sea* (1985). As a poet, H. combines lyricism with a heightened sense of emotion as a means to confront both the disparity and the dislocation of contemporary existence. H.'s *Selected Poems* appeared in 1989, followed by *Storybook Hero* (1992), *New from the Front* (1993), and *A Bird's Idea of Flight* (1998). H. also writes mystery thrillers under the name Jack Curtis and for both radio and television. H. wrote the libretto of *When She Died . . . Death of a Princess,* an opera with music by Jonathan Dove about public reaction to the death of Diana, Princess of Wales. Original and powerful, the piece deals with misfits who appropriate the image of Diana in self-serving ways. Specifically written for television, it was screened in August 2002, five years after her death.

HARTLEY, L[eslie] P[oles]

b. 30 December 1895, Whittlesey, Cambridgeshire; d. 13 December 1972, Bathford, Avon

The major theme of the novels and short stories of H. is the conflict between desire and inhibition. The protagonists of his best-known works—Eustace Cherrington in the *Eustace and Hilda* trilogy (1944–47), Leo Colston in *The Go-Between* (1953)—want to take part in life, but their sensitivities and scruples paralyze them and leave them vulnerable to the less diffident. This theme links H. with Henry JAMES, while his use of symbolism shows an affinity to Nathaniel Hawthorne; but H. also displays a post-Freudian awareness of libidinal drives and sexual symbolism. Like James, H. at his best entices the reader into a web of intrigue; in contrast to James, his style is always accessible.

Throughout his life, H. was firmly ensconced in the English upper middle class; born into a wealthy brickmaking family, he went to one of England's most prestigious public [private] schools, Harrow, and to Balliol College, Oxford; he served in the Norfolk Regiment in World War I, and afterward lived in England and Venice supported by a private income. This social position shows in his work; most of his major characters are socially and economically privileged. But he is also fascinated by figures from the lower orders who seem to incarnate frank masculinity: the tenant farmer Ted Burgess in *The Go-Between*, the chauffeurs in *The Hireling* (1957), and *The Harness Room* (1971).

H. first won a reputation as a short story writer with the kind of compelling tales, often with supernatural resonances, collected in *Night Fears* (1924) and *The Killing Bottle* (1932). His novella *Simonetta Per-*

kins (1925) introduced his favorite theme of desire and inhibition: a young American woman on holiday in Venice fails to consummate her relationship with a gondolier. But this theme was not developed in a full-length novel until *The Shrimp and the Anemone* (1944; repub. as *The West Window*, 1945), which, together with *The Sixth Heaven* (1946) and *Eustace and Hilda* (1947), comprises the *Eustace and Hilda* trilogy. This traces Eustace Cherrington's life from boyhood to Oxford to Venice, focusing in particular on his relationship—that of a vulnerable "shrimp"—to his elder sister Hilda, the devouring "anemone." Eustace is the quintessential H. protagonist: deeply sensitive, ineffectual, and doomed, but highly valued for his aesthetic and moral responsiveness.

H. followed up the trilogy with *The Boat* (1949), a novel that centers around Timothy Casson, an unmarried writer living in a village in wartime England who finds his greatest satisfaction on the river, sailing his boat—a symbol of sensuous and spiritual fulfillment. When local residents try to stop his excursions, he determines to thwart them, with results that are fatal to others. *The Boat* is a fascinating but disorderly novel; it tries to encompass too wide a range of topics and characters. By contrast, H.'s next novel, *My Fellow Devils* (1951), focusing on a woman who marries a corrupt film star and eventually becomes a Roman Catholic, is too rigidly structured, and lacks symbolic resonance.

His sixth novel, however, combined structural control, symbolic concentration, and moral complexity: *The Go-Between*. The narrator, Leo Colston, now old and withered, recalls in intense detail the summer he spent at a country house as a pubescent boy, when he became the unwitting go-between for the daughter of the house, Marian, and her lover, Ted Burgess. Leo's growing awareness of the truth about their relationship culminates in a climactic scene when Marian's mother forces him to witness their lovemaking. Shamed, Burgess shoots himself; shattered, Leo will never achieve an adult relationship. *The Go-Between*'s powerful account of the impact of premature exposure to sexual experience is deepened by its insight into the extent to which Leo is complicit with those who abuse his innocence. It became H.'s best-known book, and, in 1971, a notable film, scripted by Harold PINTER and directed by Joseph Losey.

H.'s subsequent novels vary in quality. *A Perfect Woman* (1955), for example, concerns an accountant's wife, Isabel Eastwood, who becomes involved with a middle-aged author, Alec Goodrich, but eventually settles down again with her husband in a marriage in which each party has supposedly achieved an independent sense of self. Suburban adultery was not quite H.'s forte, however. *The Hireling* is much more successful. Its protagonist, Stephen Leadbitter, becomes the confidante of an upper-class widow, Lady Franklin, but his sexual advances are rejected, unleashing a compelling chain of events that mount up to a shattering climax.

H.'s first novel of the 1960s, *Facial Justice* (1960*)*, was a surprisingly successful voyage into an imaginary future. Like Aldous HUXLEY's *Brave New World* and George ORWELL's *Nineteen Eighty-Four*, this is a SCIENCE FICTION dystopia, a picture of an apparently ideal future world that turns out to be deeply flawed. In his next novel, however, H. returns to the traumas of the past: in *The Brickfield* (1964), Richard Mardick, an ageing bachelor writer, reveals to Denys Aspin, his young secretary, the long-concealed secret of his life: his adolescent love for Lucy Soames and her death by drowning, perhaps because she mistakenly thought she was pregnant. This poignant, evocative novel is H.'s last substantial achievement. Its sequel, *The Betrayal* (1966), explores the emotional consequences for Richard of Denys's treachery, but it is a less successful work, and H.'s remaining novels were slighter, though *The Love-Adept* (1969) is an entertaining excursion into metafiction—fiction about the making of fiction—while *The Harness Room* is notable for its frank treatment of homosexuality.

Current awareness of H. is largely confined to *The Go-Between*. But this impressive novel should not overshadow the rest of H.'s work, which has been unduly neglected in recent years. While an invaluable biography by Adrian Wright came out in 1996, no book length critical study has appeared since 1978. It seems that H. is now confined to what *The Go-Between* famously called the "foreign country" of the past; it is time that he found a new readership and received a full critical revaluation.

BIBLIOGRAPHY: Bien, P., *L. P. H.* (1963); Bloomfield, P., *L. P. H.* (1962; rev. ed., 1970); Jones, E. T., *L. P. H.* (1978); Wright, A., *Foreign Country: The Life of L. P. H.* (1996)

NICOLAS TREDELL

HARWOOD, [Travers Rafe] Lee
b. 6 June 1939, Leicester

Since the mid-1960s, H. has written a distinctive poetry, which typically deploys the use of juxtaposed fragments of descriptive imagery, apparently random citation, and nominative statements to evoke a multifaceted, almost mosaic-like, sense of place and sensation. A singular voice in British poetry, he is one of the generation of postwar British poets, like Barry MacSweeney, whose work has been relatively neglected during the 1980s, as a general public audience for poetry receded, and whose subsequent writing has depended upon small press publication. Sometimes described as a "painterly" poet in the New York tradition of James Schuyler and John Ashbery (a long-time champion of his work), it would be more accurate to

state that he shares with them an interest in European surrealist techniques of montage and association, in a tradition of Apollinaire, André Breton, and Pierre Reverdy. H., who has translated Tristan Tzara and edited a journal of contemporary surrealism *Tzarad*, draws away from the irrational violence of original surrealist imagery in favor of a calmer and patient exploration of various tones, distinguished by its understatement, its lucidity, and an attention to landscape.

H. has supported his writing with a variety of jobs in the U.K. and the U.S. before settling in Brighton on the English South Coast, a recurrent subject of his poems. His first substantial collections—*The White Room* (1968), *Landscapes* (1969), and *The Sinking Colony* (1970)—established his subsequent techniques: the evocation of place or conscious states through apparently unrelated particulars and rumination upon such acts of artifice. H.'s avoidance of figurative excess or otiose metaphor, along with a recitation of commonplace speech, can risk sounding prosaic to a readership expecting self-conscious displays of virtuosity. A typical H. poem will instead invite a consideration of the play of sequences to its whole. In the early work "Plato was Right Though," a schematic digestion evokes a luxuriant and fictitious realm, which the poem subsequently unravels in a languid contemplation of artistic limitation: "Plato was right to banish/poets from the Republic. Once they try to go beyond the colours and shapes, they only ever fail, miserably—/some more gracefully than others." H. attempts to evoke sense not through recasting empirical experience through metaphor but in the compilation of localized visual detail.

This content can be supplemented by the use of apparently historical or otherwise fictional narratives that remain inconclusive: for example, "The Sinking Colony" invents apparent diary material to evoke an uncertain sense of imperial decline. This technique lends itself to a topographical poetry where the competition of personal and public discourses can be staged together, such as the study of London's politics in "Cable Street" and, especially, the long meditation on the quotidian routine of Brighton life in *Boston-Brighton* (1977). The poem "Dreams of Armenia" from *Morning Light* (1998) provides an archive of historical data alongside more delicate observations to evoke historical trauma of the region. The lack of cynicism and refusal to don an ironic persona in his poems places him outside mainstream poetry fashion, and the surrealism is arguably also a continued neo-Romanticism. H. is generally a poet of everyday experience transfixed by sensation, sudden wonder at the natural world and the persistent bonds of sociability, whereby "in a well-loved landscape/this coast and the hills behind/we find 'the daily' amazing."

BIBLIOGRAPHY: Caddel, R., "L. H.," in Sherry, V. B., Jr., ed., *Poets of Great Britain and Ireland since 1960*, part 1, *DLB* 40 (1985): 173–78; Sheppard, R., "L. H. and the Poetics of the Open Work," in Hampson, R., and P. Barry, eds., *New British Poetries* (1993): 216–33

J. M. TINK

HARWOOD, Ronald

b. Ronald Horwitz, 9 November 1934, Cape Town, South Africa

Although he has produced work in a variety of genres, H. has achieved his greatest fame as a dramatist. His best-known work is the play, *The Dresser* (1980), an affectionate and touching backstage portrait of a London theater company during World War II. Norman, the dresser of the title, has devoted himself to the service of a great Shakespearean actor, identified only as "Sir." Sir is by turns charming and infuriating; however, as the action of the play progresses, it becomes clear that he is perhaps the last true example of the great tradition of theatrical actor-managers. Based at least partially on H.'s own experiences as the dresser for the actor Sir Donald Wolfit, *The Dresser* provides audiences with an intimate look at the backstage side of theater. H.'s other dramatic efforts have met with limited success. These include *Country Matters* (perf. 1969); *The Good Companions* (perf. 1974), a musical based on a novel by J. B. PRIESTLEY; *The Ordeal of Gilbert Pinfold* (perf. 1977), based on Evelyn WAUGH's autobiographical novel; *A Family* (perf. 1978), about a patriarch's attempts to impose a strict code of loyalty on his family, and the ultimately destructive results of this code; and *Taking Sides* (pub. 1995; perf. 1996), which deals with the theme of artistic responsibility, as German composer Wilhelm Furtwangler—a favorite of Hitler—is interrogated by an American soldier in the days after World War II. In addition to plays, H. has produced novels, including his first published work, *All the Same Shadows* (1961; repub. as *George Washington September, Sir!*, 1961), which was inspired by the shooting of a young black man in H.'s native South Africa. He has also written or edited several books about the London stage, including a biography of Wolfit (1971), and books about the great English actors John Gielgud (1984) and Alec Guinness (1989).

HASTINGS, Michael [Gerald]

b. 2 September 1938, London

Trained as an actor, H. established himself as a playwright with early plays such as *Don't Destroy Me* (perf. 1956), *Yes, and After* (perf. 1957), and *The World's Baby* (perf. 1965), published together in 1966. He earned critical attention with *The Silence of Lee Harvey Oswald* (1966), followed by *For the West (Uganda)* (perf. 1977), *Gloo Joo* (perf. 1978; also

perf. as *Two Fish in the Sky*, 1982), and *Full Frontal* (1979), published together in 1980. His major success is *Tom and Viv* (perf. 1984; pub. 1985; rev. ed., 1992), based on the marriage between T. S. ELIOT and Vivienne Haigh-Wood, which was adapted for film in 1994. H. is also accomplished as a novelist, poet, biographer, and screenwriter.

HAWES, Stephen

b. ca. 1470, Suffolk; d. ca. 1529, London?

The early Tudor humanist and courtier, H. was born in Suffolk and was educated at Oxford. He traveled in France, and was familiar with French and Italian poets; he was also well versed in the classics, as is evident from his writing, though it is not clear whether he knew Greek. In 1502, he was appointed as Groom of the Chamber to Henry VII, but was dismissed from this position on the accession of HENRY VIII.

H. seems to have written his chief work, *The Pastime of Pleasure; or, The Historie of Graunde Amoure and La Belle Pucel*, in 1505 or 1506. This allegorical romance in verse was dedicated to Henry VII and reveals H.'s debt to the medieval authors he emulated, namely Geoffrey CHAUCER, John GOWER, and above all John LYDGATE whom he cites as his master. *The Pastime of Pleasure* begins with a dream or vision, and then becomes an allegorical journey. The hero, the knight Graund Amour, must acquire all the accomplishments of a perfect knight in order to win the love of La Belle Pucel. The knight's successful overcoming of a long series of trials of courage and patience is typical of chivalric romance; the *Pastime*'s most original feature lies in its blending of the winning of a fair lady of higher degree with the pursuit of a course of training in the seven liberal arts. In fact, the text contains a multiplicity of elements: scholastic and classical learning, philosophy, religion, mythology, chivalry, romantic love, and fantastic adventures. H. also combined a variety of stylistic and metrical elements within the poem, employing both the seven-line rhyme royal stanza (rhyming *ababbcc*) and rhyming couplets couched in iambic pentameter; as a result, there is considerable variation in the length of lines.

The Pastime of Pleasure was printed four times in the 16th c., appearing in small quarto, black-letter editions. It was first printed in 1509 and again in 1517 by Wynkyn de Worde, who was responsible for printing all of H.'s works. The text was subsequently printed under the title *The Historie of Graunde Amoure* by John Waylande in 1554 and by Richard TOTTELL in 1555. H.'s other best-known work is *The Example of Virtue* (1512). Its full title, *A Compendyous Story . . . called the Exemple of Vertu in whiche ye shall finde many goodly Storys and naturall Dysputacyons bytween four ladyes named Hardynes, Sa-*

pyence, Fortune, and Nature, indicates the work's allegorical import; this time the poem details a life spent in pursuit of purity, but in other respects the work is similar to the *Pastime*, though it is set in rhyme royal throughout and so is less metrically mixed. As a court poet, H. was expected to turn out verse to mark special events such as royal occasions; an example of his work in this regard is his *A Joyfull Medytacion to all Englonde of the Coronacyon of our moost naturall soveryne lorde kynge Henry the eight* (1509). Lesser known works are *The Convercyon of Swerers* (1509) and *The Conforte of Louers* (1515), in which H. presented himself as a courtly lover and tried to win the favor and patronage of Henry VIII's sister.

H. was popular in the 16th c., but has been regarded as little more than a dull versifier ever since. C. S. LEWIS condemned him as a "bad poet," but recently H.'s role in the transition between medieval and Renaissance writing has begun to receive renewed appreciation, largely because he was one of the first poets to write exclusively for print and has thus attracted the attention of New Historicist scholars of printing and 16th-c. court culture.

BIBLIOGRAPHY: Edwards, A. S. G., *S. H.* (1983); Gluck, F. W., and A. B. Morgan, eds., *S. H.* (1974); Mead, W. E., ed., *S. H.* (1928)

MARGARET CONNOLLY

HAWKESWORTH, John
b. October 1720, London; d. 17 November 1773, London

Versatile 18th-c man of letters, H. was a prominent editor, dramatist, and essayist. From 1744 to 1752, he edited the *Gentleman's Magazine* and then the *Adventurer* (1752–54). Drawn to the theater, H. began adapting plays by Restoration dramatists, including John DRYDEN's *Amphitryon; or, The Two Sosias* (perf. 1756) and Thomas Southerne's *Oroonoko* (perf. 1759). His original play *Zimri* was performed in 1760 followed by *Edgar and Emmeline* (1761) and *The Fall of Egypt* (perf. 1774). Intended for the stage, *Almoran and Hamet* was rewritten as a novel and published anonymously in two volumes in 1761. H. was also the editor of the *Works of Jonathan Swift* (16 vols., 1754–65) and the best-selling though controversial *Account of the Voyages, by Captain James Cook and Others* (3 vols., 1773).

HAWKINS, [Sir] John
b. 29 March 1719, London; d. 21 May 1789, London

For inspiring a memorable neologism by Samuel JOHNSON, H. has gone down in literary history as the "unclubable" man. Indeed, H. withdrew from Johnson's Literary Club after an argument with Edmund BURKE, an act that typified his contentious personal relationships. Trained as an attorney, H. was appointed a magistrate in 1760 and knighted in 1772. A keen amateur musician, H. joined the Academy of Ancient Music and in 1776 published, in five volumes, *A General History of the Science and Practice of Music*. The work was the first of its kind in English and the scope of H.'s research astonished contemporaries. However, a similar work by Charles Burney, better written and more clearly organized, soon supplanted the *General History*. Today, its merits may be found in H.'s insider's knowledge of the London musical scene early in the 18th-c. and in his discussion of 16th- and 17th-c. composers, a group undervalued by Burney.

H.'s friendship with Johnson apparently began in the 1730s, when both were contributors to the *Gentleman's Magazine*. After Johnson's death, as one of the executors H. was asked by a consortium of booksellers to write Johnson's biography and edit his works. *The Life of Samuel Johnson, LL.D.* appeared in 1787 and, after an initially brisk sale and a second edition, was severely damned by reviewers, until it became a universal object of parody and ridicule. The narrative, critics argued, had been rendered absurd by legalisms and swelled to twice its length by digressions, while the characterization of Johnson was malevolent and inaccurate. The *European Magazine*, for example, charged that H., "with all the humanity and very little of the dexterity of a Clare-Market butcher, has raised his blunt axe to deface the image of his friend."

In 1791, James BOSWELL attacked what he called H.'s "farrago," pointing to its "dark uncharitable cast, by which the most unfavorable construction is put upon almost every circumstance in the character and conduct of my illustrious friend." His own biography, Boswell asserted, would "vindicate" the lexicographer from this "injurious representation." H.'s *Life of Samuel Johnson* could not survive such reviews and the formidable competition of Boswell. It sank into obscurity, not to be reprinted until 1961, in an abridgement by Bertram H. Davis; in 1897, George Birkbeck Hill had included excerpts in the *Johnsonian Miscellanies*. The biography was, however, consulted by generations of scholars, who cited it in footnotes to Boswell's *Life* or used it to prepare their own biographies of Johnson. If H.'s account is less palatable than Boswell's, it frequently is more emotionally honest. H.'s prose lacks both the esprit that Hester Thrale PIOZZI brought to her *Anecdotes* and the narrative genius of Boswell, but in items such as his unsparing portrait of Johnson's marriage or his magisterial judgments of Johnson's character, he provides a valuable supplement and even corrective to the more popular work of his biographical rivals.

BIBLIOGRAPHY: Davis, B. H., *Proof of Eminence: The Life of Sir J. H.* (1973); Scholes, P. A., *The Life and Activities of Sir J. H.* (1953)

LISA BERGLUND

HAYDON, Benjamin Robert

b. 26 January 1786, Plymouth; d. 22 June 1846, London

Now best known for his posthumously published *Autobiography and Journals* (3 vols., 1853), a treasure-trove of anecdote about his famous contemporaries, H. was an English painter of historical subjects, friend of John KEATS, William WORDSWORTH, Leigh HUNT, William HAZLITT (all portrayed in H.'s painting *Christ's Entry into Jerusalem*), Mary Russell MITFORD, and Elizabeth Barrett BROWNING. He was instrumental in the purchase of the Elgin marbles for the British Museum. H. advocated art education and lectured widely to working-class audiences, but the vehemence of his expression made enemies, especially when he attacked the Royal Academy, and his thirst for fame became an obsession. After he shot himself, the coroner's jury declared him to have been insane. Charles DICKENS was fascinated by H. and, perhaps unfairly, combined his personality with that of Hunt to create the character of the self-centered and irresponsible Harold Skimpole in *Bleak House.* Aldous HUXLEY, who wrote a new introduction to the *Autobiography* in 1926, portrayed H. as Casimir Lypiatt in *Antic Hay*, and Huxley's long short story "The Tillotson Banquet" also draws on H.'s personality.

HAYLEY, William

b. 29 October 1745, Chichester; d. 12 November 1820, Earlham

Friend and patron of William BLAKE, H. was a prominent man of letters who named himself "the poet of Earlham"—the family estate where H. associated himself with a wide circle of artists and writers, including George Romney, Joseph Wright, Edward GIBBON, Charlotte SMITH, and William COWPER. One of the most popular poets of the late 18th c., H. was also accomplished as a dramatist, novelist, and philosophical and historical essayist. His plays included *The Two Connoisseurs* (1784), *Eudora* (perf. 1790; pub. 1811), and *Zelma; or, The Will O' Th' Wisp* (perf 1792). In 1796, H. published his revisionist biography of John MILTON and later produced lives of Cowper (3 vols., 1803–4) and Romney (1809). Notable among H.'s publications are *Little Tom the Sailor* (1800) and *A Series of Ballads* (1802), both of which are illustrated with engravings by Blake.

HAYS, Mary

b. 1760, London; d. February 1843, London

Radical novelist, poet, essayist, and historian, H. was a member of the London circle of eminent radicals that included the scientist Joseph Priestley, the philosopher William GODWIN, and the publisher Joseph Johnson. She learned her FEMINISM from a contemporary whom she ardently admired, the radical feminist writer Mary WOLLSTONECRAFT, whose disciple she became after reading Wollstonecraft's *Vindication of the Rights of Woman*. She never married, but managed to support herself for most of her long life by writing, occasionally supplemented by schoolteaching.

Born into a middle-class Dissenting family in Southwark, London, H. lost her father at an early age. In her late teens, she fell in love with a young neighbor, John Eccles, with whom she carried on an intense correspondence by letter. They planned to marry despite the opposition of both their families, but Eccles's death in 1780 prevented this outcome. H. then concentrated on her own self-education, attending lectures at the Dissenting Academy in Hackney. Her first writings were short stories and poems, followed in 1792 by *Cursory Remarks*, a pamphlet in defense of public worship addressed to the nonconformist scholar Gilbert Wakefield. This was followed a year later by *Letters and Essays, Moral and Miscellaneous*, in which she was encouraged by Wollstonecraft. At about this time, she began a correspondence with Godwin in whom she confided her unrequited love for the Unitarian philosopher William Frend. Her letters, and Godwin's replies, were incorporated more or less verbatim in her radical novel *Memoirs of Emma Courtney* (2 vols., 1796). A second novel, *The Victim of Prejudice* (2 vols.), followed in 1799. The revolutionary principles expressed in both these works led to attacks on H. in the conservative journals of the day. In addition, she was caricatured as Brigetina Botherim, an unattractive man-chasing female philosopher, in Elizabeth Hamilton's satirical novel, *Memoirs of Modern Philosophers* (1800). H. later moderated her radical feminism to some extent, probably as a result of the antifeminist backlash that followed Wollstonecraft's death in 1797. Her six-volume *Female Biography* (1803) celebrates historical women of achievement but is notable for its exclusion of Wollstonecraft. Historical works for children and collections of "moral tales" appeared at intervals over the next twenty years, and H.'s last major work was *Memoirs of Queens, Illustrious and Celebrated* (1821). Her last years were spent in London, where she had become friends with Mary and Charles LAMB, Robert SOUTHEY, and Hannah MORE.

H. is probably best remembered today for her *Memoirs of Emma Courtney*, a work that brought her much notoriety, not only because of its scandalous mingling of fiction with AUTOBIOGRAPHY but also for its heroine's offer to live unmarried with her lover. Emma has had a faulty education and has read too many novels, including Jean-Jacques Rousseau's notorious love story *La Nouvelle Heloise* (1761), and as a result has developed an excessive sensibility, which manifests in a passionate attachment to Augustus Harley. She writes to him confessing her feelings and offering herself to him, but he rejects her. Initially, she believes this to be on the grounds of her "advanced principles," but later discovers he is married to another. She then immerses herself in a philosophical correspondence with Mr. Francis, in which she argues that women's miserable condition results from society's demands that they repress their natural sexual desires. She attempts, unsuccessfully, to follow his advice that the passions should be controlled by means of reason. She enters into an unsuccessful marriage, but discovers when she nurses Harley on his deathbed that he has always loved her. She then devotes herself to inculcating in his young son the need to avoid "the tyranny of the passions."

Undeterred by the outrage occasioned by this novel, H. published the equally radical *Victim of Prejudice* three years later. In this work, the central characters are a mother and daughter, and the issues confronted are those of seduction, illegitimacy, and rape. Society, rather then sensibility, is to blame here: a combination of the despotic and vicious nature of "man," and backward-looking social prejudice, which condemns women for acts committed against their wills.

H. is often assumed to have been the author of an anonymous polemical text, *An Appeal to the Men of Great Britain in Behalf of Women* (1798). If so, this work, which argues for the intellectual equality of the sexes and deplores women's subjection to a patriarchal society, may have been written in collaboration with her sister Eliza.

In her *Female Biography*, H. celebrated the achievements of women from all walks of life: scholars, queens, writers, and philosophers. Although H. had by this time moderated her feminism, she had not abandoned it entirely, and a recurring theme in this work is that women can easily become victims, led into errors that their faulty moral and intellectual training has not equipped them to overcome. These arguments reappear in her late work, *Memoirs of Queens*. H.'s determination and persistence in the face of the extreme unpopularity of her feminist beliefs make her an interesting subject of study, and her writings are important documents in the history of ideas of her day.

BIBLIOGRAPHY: Kelly, G., *Women, Writing, and Revolution 1790–1827* (1993); Spencer, J., *The Rise of the Woman Novelist* (1986); Wedd, A. F., ed., *The Love-Letters of M. H. (1779–1780)* (1925)

HARRIET DEVINE JUMP

HAYWOOD, Eliza Fowler

b. 1693?, London; d. 25 February 1756, Westminster

Author of some seventy-two works, H. was the most prolific woman writer of her time. H.'s sex, the eroticism of her texts, and her creation of a discourse of desire for women resulted in her exclusion from the literary canon for more than two centuries. Today, H. is again immensely popular. Her amatory and her moral works combine to articulate feminine passion and critique the dominant political discourses of her era.

H. refashioned herself many times during her career to fit the changing literary market. She wrote fiction, drama, poetry, periodicals, translations, and conduct books. Her first novel, *Love in Excess* (3 vols., 1719–20), was a phenomenal success. Tracing the sexual adventures of Count D'Elmont, its real interest lies in the subjectivity of its many female characters. Its spectrum of female desire manifests the dangers for women in giving way to passion. H.'s novels punish aberrant females like *Love in Excess*'s sexually aggressive Alovisa and foreign seductress Ciamara, and the sexual predator Baroness de Tortillée in *The Injur'd Husband* (1723), even while they revel in their agency and sympathize with their desires. Heroines such as the eponymous Idalia (1723), Lasselia (1723), and *The City Jilt*'s Glicera (1726) are presented with ambivalence: they suffer for acting on their love as H. insisted on adhering to society's rules even while she resented them.

Critics accuse H. of being formulaic in her plots and settings; but fainting and dreaming allowed her virgins to be passionate and virtuous, repressing and expressing emotion at the same time. The garden, that liminal space between the domestic and the public worlds, represents the female body—natural, lovely, and controlled by the male gardener.

In masquerade novels like *Fantomina* (1725), H. showed how women must constantly reconstruct themselves for men, while the gender-reversing behaviors of Montamour (*The Injur'd Husband*), Alathia (*The Double Marriage*, 1726), Annilia (*The Distress'd Orphan*, 1726), and Placentia (*Philidore and Placentia*, 1727) showed that men and women share essential qualities. Therefore, one sex should not dominate relationships.

H.'s two scandal novels, *Memoirs of a Certain Island Adjacent to the Kingdom of Utopia* (2 vols., 1725) and *The Secret History of the Present Intrigues of the Court of Caramania* (1727), expose the politics of sexual relationships. These works resulted in H. being cast as a licentious woman in book 2 of Alexander POPE's *Dunciad*. Soon, H. joined sex with politics: in her tragedy *Frederick, Duke of Brunswick-Lunenburgh* (1729), she depicted the Prince of Wales's namesake as untrustworthy in love and leadership; and in *Adventures of Eovaai* (1736) she suggested that Sir Robert Walpole's government was a Bacchanalian debauch pandering to the minister's desire to dominate. H.'s engagement with politics culminated in her arrest for her pro-Jacobite pamphlet *A Letter from H—— G——g, Esq.* (1749).

In response to Samuel RICHARDSON's *Pamela*, H. wrote *Anti-Pamela* (1741) that described the adventures of Syrena Tricksy and showed how women use male constructions of femininity against men. H. then modified her writing style and plots. *The Fortunate Foundlings* (1744) marks what critics have called H.'s moral conversion. It tells the story of twins Louisa and Horatio to "encourage Virtue in both Sexes"; however, there are mixed political themes with the inclusion of the Old Pretender and Charles XII of Sweden as characters.

H.'s theme of moderation is paramount in her monthly periodical the *Female Spectator* (1744–46). The wise, middle-aged persona Mira offered women advice, letters and tales on everything from marriage and masquerades, to the dangers of tea and the wonders of the microscope.

H.'s most popular moral novel, *Miss Betsy Thoughtless* (4 vols., 1751) was a female Bildungsroman. Betsy is a spirited, independent girl who enjoys the power of courtship but her flirtatious behavior loses her Mr. Trueworth. Married off to Munden, an obsequious lover who becomes a tyrannical husband, Betsy must learn humility and prudence the hard way. In her long-awaited marriage to Trueworth, it seems as though Betsy has been broken rather than rewarded. H. continued her consideration of the seriousness of marriage in *Jemmy and Jenny Jessamy* (3 vols., 1753) as Jenny puts off her wedding until she can learn more of the world; and in her conduct books *The Wife* and *The Husband*, both published in 1756, she advised that marriage is a mutual partnership.

Once regarded as the crudest of moral melodrama, H.'s works are now seen as presenting a sophisticated critique of patriarchal systems and discourses. Although H.'s style changed from the 1720s ecstatic transports of passion, with dashes and exclamation marks, to the sober tone of her later work, she never altered her message about the sexual, moral and social dangers passion posed for women.

BIBLIOGRAPHY: Ballaster, R., *Seductive Forms* (1989); Merritt, J., *Beyond Spectacle* (2002); Pettit, A., ed., *Selected Works of E. H.* (3 vols., 2000); Saxton, K., and R. Bocchicchio, eds., *The Passionate Fictions of E. H.* (2000); Whicher, G. F., *The Life and Romances of Mrs. E. H.* (1915)

EARLA WILPUTTE

HAZLITT, William

b. 10 April 1778, Maidstone, Kent; d. 18 September 1830, London

H. has the distinction of being the finest writer in prose of his age and someone who preserved, against all odds, his belief in radical politics, shown in his adoration of Napoleon Bonaparte, when famous contemporaries had long ago turned their backs upon the ideals of the French Revolution. Critical attention is currently turning strongly in the direction of H. in the fashionable reassessment of the varieties of the Romantic canon.

H.'s father was a Unitarian minister who took the family to the U.S. in 1783 but returned four years later having failed to establish himself. H. inherited his father's liberal views and this grounding fed his beliefs and colored his work, which was spread across a career in journalism, parliamentary reporting, lectures and critical essays upon politics, art, literature, and drama—and upon the people involved in these various spheres.

Initially, H. began to train for the ministry at the Unitarian New College, Hackney, London, but he left this route and then over the next few years, faced the choice between becoming a painter or a writer. H. profoundly admired Edmund BURKE's prose style, and felt early on the power in writing after reading *A Letter to a Noble Lord*. But his famous meeting with Samuel Taylor COLERIDGE, who was preaching in January 1798, decided him upon the latter course, especially as this event was reinforced by his also being brought into contact with the Wordsworths at Alfoxden and reading *Lyrical Ballads* in manuscript. His love of art, especially of the Italian masters, and his hopes of training to be a painter lingered for some time, taking him to the Louvre in Paris in 1802 during the Peace of Amiens, but eventually H. chose to be an art critic, rather than an artist, and the knowledge he had acquired helped his choice considerably.

H.'s first book was published in 1805, *An Essay on the Principles of Human Action*, in which he writes rather stiffly in favor of human altruism and against the mechanistic philosophies of the period. In 1807, he published *A Reply to the Essay on Population, by the Rev. T. R. Malthus* and other work focusing on the characters of contemporary politicians, including Burke and William Pitt. Further developments in his career began in the year 1812, the year of his *Lectures on English Philosophy*, when he joined the *Morning Chronicle* as a reporter and contributed work to periodicals like the *Edinburgh Review*. Here, H. began to flourish as an essayist and as a literary critic, while maintaining his strong political interests.

But his *Examiner* essay "Observations on Mr. Wordsworth's Poem The Excursion," (1814) was his real beginning in prose composition, his first triumph, where his characteristically provocative daring surfaces in such statements as: "Vanity and luxury are the civilisers of the world, and sweetness of human life." H.'s uncompromising metropolitan attitudes strongly cut across the locus of William WORDSWORTH's poetry.

H.'s literary critical output now flourished as he surveyed the *Characters of Shakespeare's Plays* (1817) and the figures of English drama, and in 1818 published *Lectures on the English Poets* covering the period from Geoffrey CHAUCER onward, including fine essays "On Poetry in General" and the striking "On the Living Poets."

It is certainly true that H.'s most superior and accessible work is in this vein, where his lectures and essays are published as collections, sometimes thematically coherent, sometimes apparently serendipitously broad in focus. *Lectures on the English Poets* at times affects the rehabilitation of figures, some of whom were unjustly neglected at that time. His *Lectures on the English Comic Writers* (1819) brings together H.'s contributions to the *Monthly* and *New Monthly* magazines and foregrounds such figures as Ben JONSON, Abraham COWLEY, Samuel BUTLER, Sir John SUCKLING, William WYCHERLEY, William Hogarth, and others in a richly appealing volume. These works coupled with *Lectures, Chiefly on the Dramatic Literature of the Age of Elizabeth* (1820) established H. solidly as both literary critic and literary historian.

Earlier in 1818, H. had received the adverse attentions of *Blackwood's Magazine* and the Tory *Quarterly Review*, and absurd abuse from John WILSON and John Gibson LOCKHART, who infamously tried to show H. as a member of the "Cockney School" along with John KEATS and Leigh HUNT. But H.'s *Political Essays* (1819) marked his withdrawal from political journalism in favor of a concentration upon art, literature, character sketches, travel writing, and a four-volume biography of Napoleon Bonaparte (1823–30) that has never been critically esteemed.

In 1820, H. was employed by John Scott of the *London Magazine* to make contributions to "Table Talk" and comment upon drama. Here, H. entered his last and finest decade, producing *Table-Talk; or, Original Essays* (2 vols., 1821–22) and *The Spirit of the Age* (1825). With the latter volume, H. covers the figures of his age, his contemporaries, some of whom he knew personally, including politicians and the Lake Poets, with a flowing, journalistic hand.

BIBLIOGRAPHY: Howe. P. P., ed., *The Complete Works of W. H.* (21 vols., 1930–34); Jones, S., *H.* (1989); O'Neill. M., ed., *Literature of the Romantic Period* (1998); Sikes. H. M., ed., *The Letters of W. H.* (1978)

CHRISTOPHER J. P. SMITH

HEANEY, Seamus [Justin]
b. 13 April 1939, "Mossbawn," County Derry, Northern Ireland

In "Befast," an autobiographical essay in *Preoccupations* (1980), H. says that the secret of being a poet "lies in the summoning of the energies of words," and from his first poems onward it was clear that H. was a poet utterly attuned to the energies that sound brings to poetry. In "Digging," the now-famous poem that opened H.'s first book, *Death of a Naturalist* (1966), the alliteration and assonance suggest to the ear the turf-cutting being described: "the squelch and slap/Of soggy peat, the curt cuts of an edge/ Through living roots awaken in my head." Also clear in these early poems was that the poet had claimed for poetry the rural Ulster farms and people he had grown up among. The wells and pumps of the farmyard, he writes in one poem, were his personal Helicon. In "Feeling into Words," an essay also in *Preoccupations*, he writes that learning the craft of poetry is like turning a windlass at a well, the breakthrough being when the bucket dips into the waters and the rope pulls tight. With great psychological and metaphorical accuracy, H. says that at that moment, you will have "broken the skin on the pool of yourself." That too was one of the energies hidden within words.

In that same essay, H. tells us also that "Digging" was the first poem in which he thought his own stance toward reality had found its way into language. That stance can be seen in the somewhat reassuring analogy made between the spade and the pen that sits in the poet's hand. By recalling his forebears, those men who could really wield a spade, the poet has placed his artistry in a tradition of hard but meaningful physical labor. Given the fact that H. was reared and educated in the minority Catholic community of the North, the poem also launches H.'s career with an ominous note, for as the poet says, the squat pen sits in his hand, "snug as a gun." By the end of the poem, the gun has disappeared, as if the poet wants to show that words can be more lasting than violence, but this simile has already announced that H. has come of age in what would continue to be a nightmare of sectarian violence, anti-Catholic discrimination, internments, bombings, and assassinations. H. writes that "words as bearers of history and mystery" had begun to beckon him, but their invitations required that he pick up some of the weight of Irish history. H. tells us that in the summer of 1969, when British troops were deployed in Belfast and Derry, "the problems of poetry moved from being simply a matter of achieving a satisfactory verbal icon to being a search for images and symbols adequate to our predicament."

In that same year, H. read P. V. Glob's *The Bog People*, translated from the Danish, a book about the retrieval of well-preserved Iron Age corpses from the peat bogs of Jutland. Photographs of these victims of ritual sacrifice connected in H.'s mind with photographs of the victims of sectarian violence in his own time, and to H. this suggested the presence of an archetypal pattern. The analogy prompted a number of poems in H.'s next two books, *Wintering Out* (1972) and *North* (1975). In "The Tollund Man," "The Grauballe Man," and "Punishment," H. envisions these "bog people" in such a way that the overlay of contemporary violence is unmistakable. Some critics mistakenly thought the parallels suggested H. was sanctioning the violence by citing historical precedent, but the real thrust of these poems emerged from H.'s longing to name the problem at its core. Written in what came to be known as H.'s signature "artesian" stanzas—short-lined, unrhymed quatrains—they fundamentally express a soul-distress at the barbaric attitudes underlying all forms of violence, whether communal or private, ritualized or random, Catholic or Protestant.

In 1972, after having taught in St. Joseph's College of Education and Queen's University in Belfast (both of which he had attended as a student), H. had with his wife and children moved to Glanmore, in the Republic of Ireland. H. said that the move was an effort to place poetry at the center of his life, and devote himself full time to his writing. But it was also in response to the increased violence in Belfast. Throughout the next decade's work, H. questioned the rightness distancing of himself from the problems in the North. As much as he had felt a need to cast those clarifying images of the "bog people," so too he increasingly felt an even deeper, inchoate need: that of the artist's freedom to think and write as he himself determined or wished. One can hear this note in the title poem of *North*. The poem opens with H. imagining the raiding Vikings who settled in various places of medieval Ireland, including Dublin. But the poem shifts, and H. imagines the dragon's head on a Viking ship speaking to him, the carved tongue telling him to "lie down in the word hoard" and "trust the feel of what nubbed treasure/your hands have known."

There were other sources of similar advice during this decade. H. now began his first attempts at translating *Buile Suibhne*, a medieval Irish work in which an Irish king is cursed by a priest and transformed into a bird. H. later says in his introduction to his translation (*Sweeney Astray*, 1984) "it is possible to read the work as an aspect of the quarrel between free creative imagination and the constraints of religious, political, and domestic obligation." Devoting himself full time to his writing while living in the relative safety of Glanmore, H. felt he was kin to Sweeney astray in the woods. H. also said in "Exposure" (in *North*) that in Glanmore, he had become an "inner émigré, grown long-haired/And thoughtful; a wood-kerne/Escaped from the massacre."

H.'s next two books are as a result haunted by the dead. "The Strand at Lough Beg," "A Postcard from North Antrim," and "Casualty" (*Field Work*, 1979) are elegies for acquaintances or relatives killed in the sectarian conflicts. H.'s next book, *Station Island* (1984), pivots on a long sequence of poems in which the poet goes on a pilgrimage to an island in Lough Dergh in Donegal, where in a series of meditations several revenants appear to him, some of whom were also killed in the political violence. The poet thus confronts his own conflicted sense of responsibility. The final ghost is that of James JOYCE, and in the imagined voice of the novelist, H. gives himself the advice he most needs. "The main thing," says Joyce, "is to write for the joy of it." He also counsels that "You lose more of yourself than you redeem/doing the decent thing," and that now "it's time to swim/out on your own and fill the element /with signatures on your own frequency."

In 1982, H. began teaching one term each year at Harvard University, where in 1984 he was appointed Boylston Professor of Rhetoric and Oratory. In 1988, H. was elected to a five-year term as Professor of Poetry at Oxford, the position requiring him to give three lectures each year. In the same year, H. published his second collection of essays, *The Government of the Tongue*. This richly ambiguous title contains within it the fundamental questions H. had been pondering. One kind of governing of the tongue is the harnessing of it, and making it serve or be silent or at least polite. Another sort of government of the tongue is an idea of poetry as "its own vindicating force." It is a faith that poetry is its own domain of being, with its own authority, its own unique, irreplaceable forms of wisdom. "Poetry is its own reality," writes H., "and no matter how much a poet may concede to the corrective pressures of social, moral, political, and historical reality, the ultimate fidelity must be to the demands and promise of the artistic event."

In his poetry, almost as a sign of this fidelity, H. experiments with quasi-allegory in poems such as "From the Frontier of Writing" and "From the Republic of Conscience," both in *The Haw Lantern* (1987). In "Fosterling," from *Seeing Things* (1991), H. notes with amazement that he was nearly fifty before he could credit marvels. That faith in the intuitive is what governs also the lectures H. gave at Oxford, collected as *The Redress of Poetry* (1995), where H. argues that poetry's manner of witness to history is to offer a counterweight, a countervailing image that casts the real into a light one could not have had access to any other way. In 1995, H. was awarded the Nobel Prize for Literature, and in his acceptance speech he "credited poetry" for "making possible a fluid and restorative relationship between the mind's center and its circumference." H.'s 1999 verse translation of *BEOWULF* is also part of his clear affirmation of the worth of poetry as poetry. Not only does that story celebrate the pre-Christian, Anglo-Saxon warrior ethos. In the hands of the anonymous and Christian *Beowulf* poet, it is also an imaginative critique of the limits of that ethos, especially the waste inherent in revenge killing, a theme so deeply embedded in H.'s own writing.

No living poet writing in English has been more alert to or more articulate about the idea of poetry as a vocation. From his first book to the recent *Electric Light* (2001), H. has centered his work on exploring the often conflicting meanings, both personal and social, of his calling. As it has evolved, his work has thus become the most substantive and important defense of poetry in our time.

BIBLIOGRAPHY: Andrews, E., ed., *The Poetry of S. H.* (1998); Burris, S., *The Poetry of Resistance: S. H. and the Pastoral Tradition* (1990); Corcoran, N., *The Poetry of S. H.* (1998); Curtis, T., ed., *The Art of S. H.* (1982; rev. ed., 1994); Hart, H., *S. H.* (1992); Haviaras, S., ed., *S. H.* (1996); Morrison. B., *S. H.* (1982); Murphy, A., *S. H.* (1996); Vendler, H., *S. H.* (1998)

FRED MARCHANT

HEATH-STUBBS, John

b. 9 July 1918, London

H.-S. is a major (if never especially fashionable) figure in English poetry of the 20th c. He first made his poetic reputation as one of a loose group of brilliant young poets at the University of Oxford in the early 1940s. His contemporaries included Drummond Allison and Sidney Keyes (with whom H.-S. was especially associated), Keith DOUGLAS, David Wright, and William Bell. His work appeared in *Eight Oxford Poets*, edited by Keyes and Michael Meyer, and published by Routledge, with the enthusiastic support of their poetry editor, Herbert READ, as were H.-S.'s first three books, beginning with *Wounded Thammuz* in 1942. H.-S. has remained vigorously productive since these early publications. A substantial *Collected Poems* appeared in 1988 and has been followed by several later collections.

H.-S. is a learned poet, but his learning is never used defensively or ostentatiously, never operates to exclude the reader. On the contrary, most of his best poems are familiar in their address, lucid in their idiom. H.-S.'s learning is both basis and function of a coherent sense of culture. H.-S. is one of relatively few living English poets whose work convinces the reader that it belongs in, and grows out of, a living tradition of some antiquity. He is a poet of history and mythology, Christianity and the arts. But he is not only a poet of the man-made world; he has written wittily and beautifully of a whole range of animals and birds. In an interview published in issue 4 of the

magazine *Acumen*, he describes it as the poet's duty "to show the world the value of the world and of creation which are in danger of being destroyed." It is a duty H.-S. has preeminently fulfilled.

H.-S.'s poetry is rewardingly various in both subject and form. At one extreme, it includes the lengthy mock-heroic satire *The Triumph of the Muse* (1958) and the remarkable EPIC *Artorius* (1972); at the other end, it includes epigrams on "Goldfinches," witty lines on cats famously associated with poets ("Foss," "Jeoffrey," etc.), and charms for modern contingencies (e.g., "To Inhibit the Breeding of Maggots in a Cheese," "For Unblocking the Sink"). H.-S.'s work as a translator (sometimes as a co-translator) has included volumes from Giacamo Leopardi, Omar Khayyám, Shams ud-din Muhammad Hāfiz, and others. His work has often been inspired by that of his great predecessors. It is important (and fascinating), for example, to read H.-S.'s "Quatrains" ("The Dog Star now, negating all desires") in the light of Edward FITZGERALD's *Rubáiyát of Omar Khayyám*; the same presence informs H.-S.'s work elsewhere, such as the "Three Poems Written for Dinners of the Omar Khayyám Society" (included in the *Collected Poems*), "The Toast of the Omar Khayyám Society" (*Sweetapple Earth*,1993), "The Nightingale and the Rose" and "For the Centenary Dinner of the Omar Khayyám Society" (both in *Galileo's Salad*, 1996), "Villanelle, On a theme from the Rubáiyát" (*The Game of Love and Death*, 1990), and "Fitz and the Mouse" and "Sonnet for the Spring Dinner of The Omar Khayyám Club, 1996," both in *The Sound of Light* (1999).

The assurance and intelligence with which H.-S. conducts a creative dialogue with such past masters of his art is one of the hallmarks of his own achievement. The easy familiarity of his knowledge of a very considerable body of poetry (for the list above might readily be replaced by many other "conversations" with other poets), and the good judgment evident in his handling of his knowledge, also characterizes his work as a critic. *The Darkling Plain* (1950) is a very individual and enduringly useful study of ROMANTICISM in the later 19th c.; his three short books on poetic genres—*The Verse Satire*, *The Ode*, and *The Pastoral*—all published in 1969, are models of their kind. *The Literary Essays*, published in 1998, that displays a variousness of knowledge that would be beyond the competence of most scholars nowadays, in this day of specialization, and which is informed by a richly experienced poet's alertness to matters of phrase and rhythm, tone, and form.

There is much delightful HUMOR in H.-S.'s work, whether in some of his self-deprecating presentations of himself (e.g., "Epitaph" and "Epitaph Revisited"), in some of his celebrations of the diversity of the earth's creatures (e.g., "Hurrah for Pachyderms"), or in delightful squibs like "A Ballad of the Piltdown

Man." But he is also capable of dignified and moving elegy (e.g., "Icarus, In memory of Adam Johnson 1965–1993" and "For Vernon Watkins 1906–1967"), of attractive poems of friendship (e.g., "Letter to David Wright"), and love poems of considerable power (not least the twenty-one Italian sonnets that make up the sequence "The Heart's Forest"). Whether writing poems about William SHAKESPEARE (e.g., "Winter in Illyria"), poetry (e.g., "Ars Poetica"), music (e.g., "Mozart," "Couperin at the Keyboard"), or episodes of myth or history (e.g., "Tiberius on Capri" and "The Cave of the Nymphs"), H.-S.'s brief poems manage a perception and suggestiveness often absent from weighty volumes on their subjects. He is the master of the occasional poem, a celebrant of birthdays and anniversaries whose historical vision enables him to find the universally significant in the superficially ephemeral. That sense of historical and cultural continuity informs poems like "The Timeless Nightingale," which has both a formal beauty and a wisdom rare in the poetry of its time. In a poet as prolific as H.-S., it is hardly surprising that his output should include a certain amount that is trivial or flat; what is surprising, and impressive, is that so much of his work should be accomplished and assured.

BIBLIOGRAPHY: "J. H.-S. Talks to Glyn Pursglove," *SwR* 16 (1996): 16–23; special H.-S. issue, *Aquarius* 10 (1978); Van Domelen, J. E., *The Haunted Heart* (1993)

GLYN PURSGLOVE

HEMANS, Felicia

b. Felicia Dorothea Browne, 25 September 1793, Liverpool; d. 16 May 1835, Dublin, Ireland

Until recently largely forgotten, or remembered only as the author of the much parodied poem "Casabianca" ("The boy stood on the burning deck . . ."), H. was almost as successful in her own day as her most popular male contemporary Lord BYRON. She began publishing at the age of fourteen (*Poems*, 1808), and produced a new collection almost every year until her death at the age of forty-one. Her poems were much admired, and she had many imitators. She earned substantial sums of money from publication not only in volume collections but also in annuals and periodicals, and her work remained in print well into the early years of the 20th c.

The daughter of a Liverpool merchant who moved to Wales when his daughter was seven, H. was precociously intelligent. A voracious reader, she supplemented her mother's home education with studies of her own, became proficient in Spanish, French, Italian, Portuguese, and German, and had private tuition in Latin from a local vicar. At the age of twenty, she

married Captain Alfred Hemans, who was some years her senior, but her husband departed for Italy six years later, when H. was pregnant with her fifth son, and never returned. Thereafter, she lived with her mother, and supported the whole family by means of her writing. Following her mother's death in 1827, she moved back to Liverpool and began making some literary visits: she stayed with Sir Walter SCOTT in 1829 and with William WORDSWORTH, who became a friend, in 1830. The following year, she moved to Dublin where, a few years later, she died from complications following an attack of scarlet fever.

In her early works, H. gravitated toward historical or classical subject matter. Byron considered her long poem *The Restoration of the Works of Art to Italy* (1816) to be "a good poem—very," and her *Tales and Historic Scenes in Verse* (1819) was a critical and financial success. But in the 1820s she turned increasingly to shorter, more personal lyric poetry and it was then that she produced what is generally regarded as her best work. H.'s contemporary readers tended to conflate the poetry with what they saw as the fundamental nature of the poet herself: "essentially womanly—fervent, trustful, unquestioning," as an early biographer put it. Although H. undoubtedly did construct herself, through her work, as the supreme poet of the domestic realm, more recent commentators have noted a profound ambivalence in those of her poems that deal with women's lives and expectations. This is most clearly marked in one of her most successful and popular volumes, *Records of Woman: with Other Poems* (1828), a collection into which, as she wrote to a friend, she had "put her heart and individual feelings . . . more than in any thing else I have written." Undoubtedly colored both by her private feelings about her husband's departure some years earlier and by the loss of her mother the previous year, the poems in the volume, while ostensibly celebrating the courage and nobility of women's lives, actually show the domestic sphere to be fraught with tragedy and suffering. The men who appear in the poems are sometimes faithless, often absent and frequently dying or dead, generally as a result of violence: in "Edith: A Tale of the Woods," the heroine sits "pale and silent on the bloody ground" following her husband's murder; "Gertrude" is forced to witness her husband's slow and painful death; in "Imelda," the heroine discovers her murdered lover's body in the woods; and in "The Bride of the Greek Isle," the heroine's husband is massacred at the wedding feast. Women in these poems suffer, but not always passively: some take violent revenge, others embrace death themselves.

Another theme that recurs in H.'s poetry is the conflict faced by women who engage in public endeavors. In her poem "Woman and Fame," she eschews the heady pleasures of the "charmed cup" of

Fame in favor of "[s]weet waters from affection's spring," an attitude which has been seen by many as disingenuous, since H. herself worked tirelessly and ambitiously in pursuit of public success. Her ambivalence on the subject is most noticeable in "Properzia Rossi," one of the most interesting poems in *Records of Woman*. Based on the true history of Rossi, a celebrated female artist in Renaissance Italy, the poem exemplifies an inner conflict that, H. suggests, is an inescapable problem for women who engage in creative activity. Rossi, a famous and celebrated sculptor, is capable of losing herself momentarily in the profound satisfactions of her own creativity and knows that her art will guarantee her a kind of immortality. But her genius and fame have not won her the love of the one man whose opinion she cares for, and she believes that her art has suffered from her loveless solitude and isolation. The poem shows Rossi going to a death which she welcomes as a release from suffering, and leaving her last work to her beloved in the hope that after her death he may come to appreciate her art, as he had failed to do while she was alive. The same problem is viewed from another angle in the poem "Joan of Arc, in Rheims." In this poem, Joan longs to return to the idyllic, peaceful existence of her "happy infancy," but realizes that the "paradise of home" can never again be hers, since she has gained "too much of fame." For H., it seems, domestic contentment cannot coexist with public success.

The recent revival of interest in women's writing has undoubtedly benefited H.'s reputation, and her works are increasingly being included in anthologies of the Romantic period of literature. Her poetry provides an interesting demonstration of the conflicts that faced successful and talented female artists of her day.

BIBLIOGRAPHY: Clarke, N., *Ambitious Heights: Writing, Friendship, Love: The Jewsbury Sisters, F. H., and Jane Welsh Carlyle* (1990); Trinder, P. W., *Mrs. Hemans* (1984)

HARRIET DEVINE JUMP

HENDERSON, Hamish
b. 11 November 1919, Blairgowrie, Perthshire, Scotland; d. 8 March 2002, Edinburgh, Scotland

Founder of the School of Scottish Studies, Edinburgh University, H. had always an uneasy relationship with the cultural establishment of which he became a dissenting pillar. BBC Scotland largely ignored him. Offered honors, H. refused them. Orphaned early, H. won scholarships to Dulwich College and Downing College, Cambridge, where he read French and German. He fought with distinction in World War II, serving in Italy. After the war, H. wrote *Elegies for the Dead in Cyrenaica* (1948), which won the 1949 Somerset Maugham Award for poetry. His edition of *Bal-*

lads of World War II: A Collection of Songs in Five Languages (1947) made famous the bitter soldiers' song, "We are the D-Day Dodgers," sung to the tune of "Lilli Marlene." He translated Dante and the prison letters of Antonio Gramsci, which led to adulation from Italian communists, but got him deported from postwar Italy as an undesirable alien. With a portable tape recorder, he collected traditional folk songs from previously "undiscovered" Scottish singers. In 1951, he was one of the instigators of what became the Edinburgh Festival Fringe. He also quarreled publicly with Hugh MacDIARMID and others. He continued to write verse and translated poetry from Gaelic, French, German, Latin, and Greek. With his former student, Timothy Neat, H. made several films, including *The Tree of Liberty: The Songs of Robert Burns*, which won the prize for best documentary at the 1987 Celtic international festival of film and television. In *Play Me Something*, a feature film about storytelling, H. starred alongside John BERGER and Tilda Swinton; it won the Europa Prize for best film at the 1989 Barcelona Film Festival. His *Collected Poems and Songs* appeared in 2000.

HENLEY, W[illiam] E[rnest]
b. 23 August 1849, Gloucester; d. 12 July 1903, Woking

On July 11, 1907, during ceremonies at St. Paul's Cathedral, a bronze bust of H. by Auguste Rodin was unveiled to honor the life and work of a courageous force in late-19th-c. British culture. The bust carries the words: "W. E. Henley, Poet, 1849–1903." His contemporaries, however, knew him as much more than that: he was editor, art critic, literary critic, playwright, as well as poet. His career and his temperament were akin to those of Samuel JOHNSON—both were famed conversationalists who did not hesitate to speak authoritatively about life as well as literature; both played major roles in defining the spirit of their times. Now, H.'s position is greatly eclipsed by those of numerous contemporaries whose talent he recognized and promoted: Robert Louis STEVENSON, Joseph CONRAD, Rudyard KIPLING, Thomas HARDY, and W. B. YEATS—not to mention Rodin and James McNeill Whistler from the world of visual arts. But one poem by H. takes its place among the most famous of his century: "Invictus." Easy to mock in the academy, the poem has been a source of inspiration to many. It was written when H. was a young man unwilling to accept the medical verdict that tubercular arthritis necessitated amputation of his remaining leg. Instead, H. sought out Joseph Lister at Edinburgh infirmary, where he remained for almost two years and where Lister's treatment proved successful. H.'s resolve and courage would help shape him for the role of antagonist to the aesthetes of the 1890s. H. embodied a joyous and energetic acceptance of life and bold action. Stevenson portrayed him in fiction as John Silver in *Treasure Island* and as Burly in *Talk and Talkers*.

Following his release from the hospital in 1875, H. struggled to make his way in the world of letters. He soon left Edinburgh for London, where he began to make his reputation as an editor. From *London* (1877–79) and *Pen* (1880), he moved to editing three major periodicals: *Magazine of Art* (1881–86), *Scots Review* (1888–94; later called the *National Review*), and the *New Review* (1894–97).

Departing from the moralizing bias of Victorianism, H. helped to remake art criticism, most notably in his energetic championing of Rodin. H.'s art criticism was gathered in 1902 as volume 2 of *Views and Reviews: Essays in Appreciation*. Volume 1 carried his assessments of a great number of writers, mainly 19th-c. British, but also a generous sampling of 17th and 18th-c. appreciations and a scattering of authors from other nations, chiefly France. H.'s most sustained and valuable literary criticism lies in his essays for editions of the work of Robert BURNS, Henry FIELDING, William HAZLITT, Tobias SMOLLETT, and Lord BYRON—now gathered in two volumes of his collected works. H.'s criticism is characterized by the gusto of the confident arbiter of taste. He mocks the sentimental and prizes a masculine vigor as he protests the squeamishness of Victorian sexual attitudes.

H., who had worked as a drama critic, exercised his penchant for action in literature through a collaboration with Stevenson on four plays: *Deacon Brodie* (1880; rev. ed., 1888), *Beau Austin* (1884), *Admiral Guinea* (1884), and *Macaire* (1885). Romantic and melodramatic, the plays looked backward rather than to the future. Although the plays were performed, none met with enthusiastic reception. *Deacon Brodie* holds special interest because it anticipates *Dr. Jekyll and Mr. Hyde* and *Admiral Guinea* because of its affinities with *Treasure Island*—but also because it was pivotal in leading to a quarrel between H. and Stevenson that could not be mended. *Macaire*, the most even of the plays, was rushed through before the breach was definitive. *Mephisto*, H.'s one attempt at a play on his own, failed in 1887 and was never published.

As poet, however, H. continues to receive attention as a force in 19th-c. British letters. *In Hospital* (1875), a sequence of twenty-eight poems and an envoy, helped turn poetry in the direction of a new REALISM as it described his lengthy hospital experience in a variety of poetic forms, most frequently the sonnet. The sequence has held special import for medical personnel and continues to have immediacy for many. His sense of mortality heightened by his hospital experience, H. made death a frequent topic for poems, even as a young man. As he had in the hospital sequence, he later used the sonnet form to provide realistic portraits of London types.

In Poem XXIX from *Echoes* (1876), dedicated to Stevenson, the poet finds metaphor for his philosophy of an eager acceptance of life followed by welcoming death: "A child/Curious and innocent,/Slips from his Nurse, and rejoicing/Loses himself in the Fair." At the poem's end, man, "tired of experience" finally "turns/To the friendly and comforting breast/Of the old nurse, Death." In the lyric "Madame Life's a Piece in Bloom," the pace is quick and comic as Death dogs the Madame. Although he did not embrace any conventional religion, H. never feared death. Sometimes his theme recalls the American poet Walt Whitman, as in "The Ways of Death are Soothing and Serene" and in the early, moving "A Late Lark Twitters."

The majority of H.'s poems are short and—especially the late poems—occasional, mainly memorial poems such as those for his boyhood teacher the poet T. E. Brown and for Queen Victoria. His chief categories for his poems—indicating their scope—are "Bric-à-Brac," "Echoes," and "Hawthorn and Lavender." But he did not have the spirit of the experimenter in him, as *In Hospital* gave notice, and in "London Voluntaries" he aimed for the power of an organ solo. As he neared the end of his life, H. celebrated the new century in "A Song of Speed," which in 322 free-verse lines (all short) took a Mercedes automobile as vibrant symbol for the future, an outlook strikingly different from the somber one Hardy expressed in his poem greeting the new century, "The Darkling Thrush." Like Kipling, H. was a strong advocate of nation and empire and supported the Boer War. His jingoism is famously expressed in "England, My England."

BIBLIOGRAPHY: Buckley, J. H., *W. E. H.: A Study in the "Counter-Decadence" of the 'Nineties* (1945); Cohen, E., *The H.-Stevenson Quarrel* (1974); Flora, J., *W. E. H.* (1970); Robertson, J. H. [Connell, J.], *W. E. H.* (1949)

JOSEPH M. FLORA

HENRY VIII OF ENGLAND
b. 28 June 1491, Greenwich; d. 28 January 1547, London

Henry Tudor came to the throne of England in 1509 as the first king in more than a century whose right to the throne was unquestioned and without the taint of real or alleged usurpation. His father, Henry VII, heir to the house of Lancaster's claim to the throne, married Elizabeth, daughter of Edward IV of the house of York, thus bringing to a close the fierce contention between the two houses known as the Wars of the Roses. Soon after his accession, H. married the Spanish princess Catherine of Aragon, the widow of his brother Arthur. It was an impetuous and unfortunate union, based on personal infatuation rather than the careful and practical considerations that generally characterize a royal union.

By 1527, H. had determined to divorce his queen, ostensibly because she had been unable to give him a male heir to the house of Tudor. Their union had produced only one surviving child, a daughter, Mary, ironically a future sovereign of England. The issue of a male heir was indeed a vital concern for H., but his infatuation with Anne Boleyn, one of Catharine's ladies in waiting, was perhaps the more compelling factor in the decisive actions that were subsequently taken. H. charged Thomas Cardinal Wolsey, his first great minister for church and state affairs, with the responsibility of negotiating with the Pope to secure a divorce from Catherine so that he might marry Anne. Wolsey was ultimately unsuccessful. Although such divorces were not uncommon when royal succession was an issue, this one was complicated by the fact that Catherine's nephew was Charles V, the Holy Roman Emperor, whose pressure upon and influence in Rome far exceeded H.'s. Wolsey's successor, Thomas Cromwell, fared no better with Rome. Instead, Cromwell initiated a policy by which H. renounced the Pope's authority and established a national Church of England with the king as the supreme head of both state and church. The king's archbishop, Thomas Cranmer, then divorced H. from Catherine, clearing the way for H.'s marriage to Anne Boleyn. Five years of this second marriage, however, produced only a daughter, the future Queen ELIZABETH I.

The king's impetuous nature and mercurial temperament were clearly evident in these actions which rather abruptly brought the Protestant Reformation to England. For H., it was a complete reversal of his personal views and established policy on religion. When Martin Luther had so publicly broken with the Roman Catholic Church in 1517, H. was in the forefront of the opposition to Luther, whom he despised. In 1521, H. produced his major contribution to the literature of England, albeit it was written in Latin. He wrote a book entitled *Assertio septem sacramentorum adversus Martinum Lutherum* ("Declaration of the Seven Sacraments against Martin Luther") refuting Luther step by step on matters of church doctrine. For his efforts in support of the papacy, H. was awarded the title of *Fidei Defensor* ("Defender of the Faith") by Pope Leo X. Thus H., staunchly opposed to any form of religious reform, had ironically become the factor that established Luther's reformation in England. His title of *Fidei Defensor* was taken from him by Leo X.'s successor, Pope Paul III. The English Parliament, however, restored the designation in 1544, and it has been used by all of his successors. In the years following his break with Rome and the establishment of the Anglican Church, H.'s marital troubles continued. He had his second wife executed in 1536 on questionable

charges of adultery, although the real reason may have been his frustration at her inability to produce a male heir. His third wife, Jane Seymour, did produce a male successor, Edward VI. Edward, however, was sickly, and died at sixteen after a reign of six years. H.'s marriage to his fourth wife, Anne of Cleves, was politically arranged. Neither found the other sufficiently appealing, and the union was quickly nullified on grounds of incompatibility. With his fifth wife, H. again followed his heart, but fared no better. Catherine Howard was executed in 1542 for adultery, an action taken on more substantive charges than those brought against Anne Boleyn. H.'s sixth wife, Catherine PARR, proved a gentle and tolerant companion for an aging king, and was with Anne of Cleves unique among his six wives in that she outlived him.

His excesses and his cruelty notwithstanding, H. proved a formidable ruler who inspired great affection among his people. His great concern was the perpetuating of his dynasty, and it is ironic that the House of Tudor is most remembered for the daughter, rather than the much desired son. She came to the throne in 1558 and ruled as one of the most politically astute sovereigns to ascend to the British throne. The terms "Tudor" and "Elizabeth" identify the age of England's greatest contribution to both the Renaissance and all of world literature.

BIBLIOGRAPHY: Bernard, G. W., *Power and Politics in Tudor England* (2000); Guy, J., ed., *The Tudor Monarchy* (1997); Newcombe, D. G., *H. VIII and the English Reformation* (1995); Plowden, A., *The House of Tudor* (1976)

RICHARD KEENAN

HERBERT, [Sir] A[lan] P[atrick]

b. 24 September 1890, Ashstead, Surrey; d. 11 November 1971, London

H. was educated at Winchester and New College, Oxford, where he studied law. Versatile author and polemicist, he was preeminently a wit, and joined the staff of *Punch*. H. was in his lifetime very famous, but is now chiefly remembered for his *Misleading Cases in the Common Law* (1927), which ridiculed absurdities in court procedure, and for his amusing but cogent attacks on bad written English. He fought in World War I and his novel *The Secret Battle* (1919) is a critique of its horrors, together with two volumes of verse (1916 and 1918). His most popular novel, *The Water Gipsies* (1930) reflected his love of the English canals. He was also a playwright. As Independent member of Parliament for Oxford University (1935–50), he campaigned for divorce reform. He wrote the libretti for a number of successful stage musicals and was knighted in 1945. His autobiography, *A.P.H.: His Life and Times,* appeared in 1970.

HERBERT, Edward [First Lord Herbert of Cherbury]

b. 3 March 1582, Eyton-on Severn, Shropshire; d. 1 August 1648, London

H. was the son of John DONNE's friend, Lady Magdalen Herbert, and eldest brother of the poet George HERBERT. In philosophy, he has long been recognized as a founder of deism, which permeates his works, and his history *The Life and Raigne of King Henry the Eighth* (1649) is highly regarded. As a poet, H. is usually considered to belong to the "metaphysical school" that centers on Donne, but often his lyricism and his distinctive use of Platonic and Neoplatonic ideas are stressed. His autobiography, *The Life of Edward, First Lord Herbert of Cherbury* (1764), written in the last years of his life and left unfinished, has "enduring charm," according to J. M. Shuttleworth, the editor of a modern edition of it.

Within the last thirty years, critics have revaluated much of H.'s work. They have found his portrayal of HENRY VIII more complex than had once been thought. They suspect that some passages in his autobiography may parody traditional religious writings and concepts; for example, conscious of his deism and views on revelation, readers may not know whether to take H. seriously or consider him mocking when he reports that a "gentle noise" came from the Heavens—a positive indication—when he prayed for guidance on whether or not to publish *De Veritate* (1624), the major philosophical work setting forth his theory of knowledge.

In his autobiography, H. sought to present passages in his life that would "best declare me," but would also be useful to his posterity. Early on, he sets forth what he has found to be the five "catholic and universal" common notions of religion, which are also discussed in *De Veritate* and which form the basis of his deism; he also presents his plan for educating children. An interesting passage narrates events surrounding his being made Knight of the Bath by King JAMES I. For the most part, the rest of the autobiography recounts his duels and near-duels, his Continental adventures, particularly his service as ambassador to France under James I, and the mutual attraction between himself and a number of beautiful women. H. comes through as honest and honorable (which may account for his lack of political success later in life), virtuous according to the standards of his class and time, rather vain, and choleric at times, but usually reasonable.

H. wrote poems from 1608 to at least 1645, but most were not published until 1665. One highly regarded poem is "An Ode upon a Question moved, Whether Love should continue for ever?," a question Celinda raises in a beautiful pastoral setting and that her lover, Melander, answers with a clear Neoplatonic argument that their souls descended from the stars, acquired "virtuous habits," and "love and knowledge here," and upon death will be refined so that earthly imperfections will disappear and they and their love will be perfect and immortal. H. anticipates Alfred, Lord TENNYSON's "In Memoriam" stanza, which distinguishes steps in the argument but simultaneously provides continuity. Compared to Donne, H. uses few metaphysical conceits, and the reader seldom finds the metaphysical poets' tension. Many of his poems embody his philosophy in an interesting way, and a few are movingly lyrical.

BIBLIOGRAPHY: Hill, E. D., *Edward, Lord Herbert of Cherbury* (1987); Hoey, J., "A Study of Lord Herbert of Cherbury's Poetry," *RMS* 14 (1970): 69–89

KENNETH A. ROBB

HERBERT, George

b. 3 April 1593, Montgomery Castle, Wales; d. 1 March 1633, Bemerton, Wiltshire

H. vies only with John DONNE for the title of the greatest of the metaphysical poets. His works lack Donne's metrical roughness and his celebrations of earthly, as well as divine, love, but they match them in wit and surpass almost all other devotional poems in their blend of spiritual sweetness, doctrinal rigor, and technical skill.

H. came from a family that was both extremely literary and known for distinguished soldiers and politicians. His elder brother, who became the first Lord HERBERT of Cherbury, is an important secular metaphysical poet and his mother was a patron of poets, one to whom both her son and Donne addressed poems. After the early death of H.'s father, she managed his education. H. attended Westminster School, and entered Trinity College, Cambridge, in 1609. His career there was distinguished, and after receiving his degrees and being appointed to fellowships, he gained the prestigious position of university orator. In that office, he was the university's voice, not just on internal questions, but also on public affairs. The orator's post often led to careers at court, and H. was politically well connected, both through his family and through friends such as Francis BACON. He was elected to Parliament in 1624.

While at Cambridge, H. was already writing poetry as well as letters and orations for the university. As early as 1610, he had made religion the central subject of his verse. He probably wrote the long poems that begin and end *The Temple: Sacred Poems and Private Ejaculations* (1633), "The Church Porch" and "The Church Militant," at Cambridge, as well as many poems in Latin. (The only works H. published during his lifetime were the Latin and Greek poems he wrote after his mother's death, which appeared as *Memoriae Matris Sacrum* in 1627.) In the mid-1620s, many of H.'s political connections had either died or lost their positions, and that may have influenced his decision to make the church his profession, but he had been struggling with the issue of his true vocation for some time, and he made that struggle the subject of a number of his poems. He was ordained a deacon by 1626, married in 1629, and became a priest in 1630. He served as rector of the small parish of Bemerton until his death, and it was there that he wrote many of his greatest poems.

H. did not live entirely in rural seclusion, since his parish was near enough to Salisbury to allow him to take part in the life of a cathedral city and also not far from the religious community founded by his friend Nicholas Ferrar at Little Gidding. H., however, did the work of a rural parson diligently. At Bemerton, he also assembled, from old and new poems, the work on which his reputation rests, *The Temple*. The poems in the central section of this collection, "The Church," show an amazing variety of forms. They include the best-known concrete or "pattern" poems in English, "Easter Wings" and "The Altar," and many poems, like "The Wreath," in which H. uses words alone to create visual images. Some of the poems are on parts of the church building, some on church rituals, and some on abstract concepts, such as Love, but almost all deal with the struggle of the unworthy believer to serve God. They are full of the verbal wit that characterizes metaphysical poetry, though the imagery is more often homely than farfetched. In "Love (III)," for example, Christ is presented as an innkeeper. H. left *The Temple* in manuscript at the time of his death, leaving to Ferrar the decision whether to publish or destroy it. While at Bemerton, H. also composed a description of the ideal country parson, *A Priest to the Temple*, as well as a collection of proverbs, published together in 1652.

H.'s poems were read with admiration even in the years when the metaphysical school was out of fashion, and his life became almost as important as an element in English culture as his work. His first three biographers, Ferrar, Barnabas Oley, and, most importantly, Izaak WALTON, painted an idealized portrait of a poet who, after much struggle, chose to devote all his gifts, including his talent, to God rather than to worldly advancement.

BIBLIOGRAPHY: Bloch, C., *Spelling the World: G. H. and the Bible* (1985); Charles, A. M., *A Life of G. H.* (1977); Stewart, S., *G. H.* (1986); Tuve, R., *A Reading of G. H.* (1952)

BRIAN ABEL RAGEN

HERBERT, Mary. See PEMBROKE, Mary, Countess of

HERRICK, Robert

b. August 1591, London; d. 15 October 1674, Dean Prior, Devon

Almost all of H.'s poetry was published in *Hesperides* in 1648. Its full title is *Hesperides; or, The Works both Humane and Divine* and certainly the poet designed the collection to represent the range of his achievement. To publish so complete a collection, one that shows signs of the careful designing of contexts for individual poems, was an unusual thing to do, in an age when most poets of H.'s tastes and social class were content to allow their work to be "published" only in manuscript. H.'s decision may be taken to reflect that high regard, almost reverence, for poetry and its traditions that is more than once evident in H.'s work. Whatever the reason, it is certainly the case that to a degree unusual among his contemporaries *Hesperides* "represents" H.'s achievement in much the way the "Collected Poems" of a modern poet does.

H. provides his collection with a fourteen-line "Argument" that hints at the collection's broad design, moving, as he surveys its contents, from "Blossomes, Birds, and Bowers" via the seasons and their appropriate festivals, through the erotic and "Times transhifting" to an affirmation (in the face of Puritan onslaughts) of the enduring significance of native fairy-lore and a final movement to closure in the Christian afterlife. This "Argument" moves unmistakably from the earthly to the heavenly. The 1,130 poems of *Hesperides* do not trace such a movement in quite such simple terms, though such a shape can, perhaps, be discerned behind the rich detail of its surface. It is such a sense that shapes and deepens the full significance of individual poems as they are read in the context of the collection as a whole.

At his best, H. was a poetic craftsman of exquisite skill and sensibility, often seen at his finest in miniature. Many of his finest poems are, very properly, represented in all the standard anthologies of English verse. They include "Delight in Disorder," a poem that reflects on the art of its maker as much as on its ostensible subject and "To the Virgins, To Make Much of Time" one of the finest of all English *carpe diem* poems. "To Daffadills" is one of H.'s many eloquent meditations on human transience and "Upon Julia's Clothes" is a startling piece of implicit eroticism. The pleasures the reader may—and should—take in such poems are likely, however, to be enhanced if they are read in the larger context of *Hesperides* itself. The sensuousness of much of H.'s best writing, its celebratory attentiveness to textures of skin and cloth, of the effects of "Moone-light tinselling the streames," of "Purple Grapes" (and of

"Canarie Sack"), is fascinating and rewarding both in itself and in the role it plays in H.'s serious (but never solemn) attempt to place his delight in the earthly within a proper context of religious understanding.

Relatedly, the problematical power of art to immortalize the natural is a question to which he returns with great frequency. H. is a master craftsman and an intensely self-conscious artist; he frequently pays tribute to the predecessors he admires, whether classical, such as Ovid and Tibullus, Catullus and Virgil, or modern, like Ben JONSON. In one poem, indeed ("His Prayer to Ben Jonson"), he petitions "Saint Ben" for his poetic aid, promising him candles "and a new altar," and the playfulness of the lines does not entirely disguise the ways in which H. sees poetry as having religious dimensions. H.'s employment of a range of verse forms accommodates lines of considerable rhythmical subtlety and his indebtedness to the tradition of the epigram sometimes encourages a striking brevity of expression. H., indeed, might well be regarded as the greatest English master of the two-line poem, as in "The Definition of Beauty": "Beauty, no other thing is, then a Beame/Flashed out between the Middle and Extreame." H. is not, however, only a miniaturist. In poems such as "A Nuptiall Song, or Epithalamie, on Sir Clipseby Crew and his Lady" or "Oberons Palace," H. displays a talent for design on a larger scale and a capacity to sustain structures of thought and image in rewarding fashion.

The second part of *Hesperides*, containing almost three hundred poems, is given its own title page introducing "His Noble Numbers: or, his Pious Pieces, Wherein (among other things) he sings the Birth of his Christ: and sighes for his Saviours suffering on the Crosse." Many have found H.'s religious poems "childish" or "tepid." While it would be wrong to deny that as a Christian poet H. falls short of his greatest contemporaries, such as John DONNE and John MILTON, George HERBERT and Henry VAUGHAN, *Noble Numbers* surely has much to reward the attentive reader. H.'s Laudian sense of the importance of ritual is striking, as his repeated affirmation of the final unknowability of God, "To seek of God more then we well can find,/Argues a strong distemper of the mind." Formally, the poems are quite various; there are epigrammatic couplets; there are poems in the kind of subtly heterometric stanzas of which H. was always such a master; there is one quite effective pattern poem; there are carols and prayers; there is a versified creed. The poetry employs a fair variety of voices, too. One poem is "The dirge of Jephthah's Daughter: sung by the Virgins"; another takes on the persona of "The Bell-Man"; several poems adopt the voices of children. The simplicity of such poems, stands at the opposite stylistic extreme to the baroque conceits of "Good Friday: Rex Tragicus, or Christ going to His Crosse." *Noble Numbers* has some mo-

ments of striking beauty, as in "The white Island: or place of the Blest," contrasting, as it does, "this world" where men "sit by sorrowes streames" and "that *whiter Island*, where/Things are evermore sincere." In the greatest age of English religious poetry, *Noble Numbers* has been overshadowed; its achievements may be modest by comparison, but they are real enough. Taken together, the two parts of *Hesperides* offer us a fascinating picture of one of the most distinctive personalities in the history of the English lyric.

BIBLIOGRAPHY: Coiro, A. B., *R. H.'s "Hesperides" and the Epigram Book Tradition* (1988); Rollin, R. B., *R. H.* (1966; rev. ed., 1992); Rollin, R. B., and J. M. Patrick, eds., *"Trust to Good Verses": H. Tercentenary Essays* (1978)

GLYN PURSGLOVE

HERVEY, John [Baron Hervey of Ickworth]
b. 16 October 1696, London; d. 5 August 1743, Ickworth, Suffolk

H., educated at Westminster School and Clare Hall, Cambridge, wrote detailed and brutally frank memoirs of the court of King George II, published in two volumes in 1848, where H. served as a courtier from 1727 to 1737. H. gave an unflattering account of the quarrels between the king and his son the Prince of Wales, though he had respect and affection for the queen and her daughter. H.'s manuscript was preserved in the family and published in 1848 under the editorship of John Wilson CROKER, who softened some acerbities of the original. H. was the object of Alexander POPE's unforgettable satire *Epistle to Dr. Arbuthnot* as Sporus.

HEWITT, John [Harold]
b. 28 October 1907, Belfast, Ireland; d. 27 June 1987, Belfast, Northern Ireland

H. has only slowly been accorded the critical respect he deserves for his poetry; his influence on the generation of Northern Irish poets who began publishing in the 1960s, however, has long been recognized. H. established himself as the primary promoter of Northern Irish culture and literature through his emphasis on regionalism. H. was influenced early on by his socialist father, Robert Telford Hewitt, and attended various lectures by leading contemporary socialists in Belfast in the 1920s and 1930s. H. worked at the Belfast Museum and Art Gallery from 1930 to 1957 and directed the Herbert Art Gallery in Coventry, England, from 1957 to 1972. H.'s first major publication was *Collected Poems 1932–1967* (1968), which gathered together his earlier, mostly privately printed work. The majority of his poetry was written in an intense period of poetic activity between 1972 and 1987 after his return to Belfast.

Frank Ormsby credits the war-time travel restrictions beginning in 1939 to H.'s increasing geographic explorations of the province; H. also lectured on art, Marxism and other subjects at army camps all over the province during World War II. H. and his wife spent many holidays in the Glens of Antrim, an isolated, heavily Protestant area in the northeastern corner of Northern Ireland. His immersion in this area enabled him to begin articulating his concepts of political and literary regionalism in the 1940s.

H. argued that the province of Northern Ireland, established in 1922, provided a sense of regional community for all of its disparate people groups across national and religious affiliations. Regionalism, for H., provided a permanent entry for Ulster Protestants into the history and contemporary culture of the province while ideally also transcending sectarian differences. H.'s most famous poem "The Colony," for example, details his poetic efforts to write Northern Protestants into the landscape and establishes a parallel between a Roman colony and plantation Ireland. At the same time, his regionalist conception of Ulster largely excluded Catholics, since it only included the part most heavily populated with Protestants: the province's northeast corner along with Belfast and parts of County Armagh.

It took several decades for H. and his coterie of Sam Hanna Bell, John Boyd, Roy McFadden and other writers to consciously define the parameters of Northern Irish literature. As Gillian McIntosh has shown, the forums of the BBC and PEN enabled these Northern writers to formally and informally begin articulating their view of Northern Irish literature at least as early as the late 1940s. The publication of the collection of essays entitled *The Arts in Ulster* (1951), edited by H., Bell, and Nesca A. Robb, was the quasi-academic apogee of this initial Northern Irish cultural movement.

H. criticized both the lack of references to the province in books written on Ireland and what he saw as the disengagement of writers in the province from daily life there. He recognized regional literary developments in Scotland and Wales and sought analogies in Ulster regionalism, while acknowledging the particular intractability of his province to a vibrant literary culture. H. sought to make Northern Irish literary regionalism paradoxically both local and cosmopolitan, arguing that the Ulster writer "must carry the native tang of his idiom like the native dust on his sleeve," but also pointing out what he perceived as correspondences to Ulster's anomalous political situation with similar ones worldwide such as French Quebec's position within Canada.

H.'s poetry demonstrates his independent cast of mind and belief in rationalism across a range of rhymed and free verse. Despite his deep and abiding interest in the rural northeastern part of the province, his urban socialism creates a pervasive unease in his sympathetic nature poetry.

BIBLIOGRAPHY: Clyde, T., ed., *Ancestral Voices: The Selected Prose of J. H.* (1987); McIntosh, G., *The Force of Culture: Unionist Identities in Twentieth-Century Ireland* (1999); Ormsby, F., ed., *The Collected Poems of J. H.* (1991)

RICHARD RANKIN RUSSELL

HEWLETT, Maurice [Henry]
b. 22 January 1861, Kent; d. 15 June 1923, Broad-Chalke

H. published in 1895 two books on Italy, *Earthwork Out of Tuscany* and *The Masque of Dead Florentines* (in verse). *Songs and Meditations* followed in 1896, and in 1898 he made his reputation with *The Forest Lovers*, a medieval romance. His pastoral play *Pan and the Young Shepherd* (pub. 1898; perf. 1906) was followed by *Little Novels of Italy* (1899), a collection of short stories, which showed a close knowledge of medieval Italy. *The Life and Death of Richard Yea-and-Nay* (1900), on King Richard I, and *The Queen's Quair* (1904) on Mary Queen of Scots, showed historical insight, but he returned to Italian subjects with *The Road in Tuscany* (2 vols., 1904), and others. Later, his main interest was in verse: *The Song of the Plow* (1916) is a narrative poem describing the life of the English farm laborer over the centuries.

HEYER, Georgette
b. 16 August 1902, London; d. 5 July 1974, London

When H. slipped into the mantle of Jeffrey Farnol in 1921 with *The Black Moth*, it did not seem likely that what had, in his hands, been a vapidly pretty, sentimental and melodramatic form of period pleasantry could ever become anything more worthy of notice, but with *These Old Shades* (1926) she began to show, and in *Devil's Cub* (1932) thoroughly established that the Regency romance could, given a writer with a precise ear and a turn for sprightly comedy, become a minor literary genre worthy of affectionate respect.

The precise ear is the most essential quality here, as is oddly illuminated by H.'s relative failure in another genre. In *Why Shoot a Butler?* (1933) and others, she attempted several detective stories set in the 1920s and 1930s, when the mode of speech of the "Bright Young Things" with which she peopled them was so jejune that even Nöel COWARD was hard pressed to make it sparkle. She reproduces it faithfully, and these novels are very disappointing, though some critics of the detective story have judged them well crafted, because the talk is so thin. In the Regency romances, she reproduces, not merely faithfully, but exuberantly, the extraordinary range of tongues—thieves' cant, dandies' patois, society's high diction—in which the late 18th and early 19th c. was rich, slipping from one to another as suited her characters with an enviable elegance and ease, and these stories can be read with pleasure for this linguistic richness if for nothing else.

There are, however, other pleasures, one of which is the observation of how many variations an inventive mind can run on the same basic plot, or on the same character type. She has perhaps six fundamental stories, but a constantly refreshed and refreshing series of mutations to perform on them. Among the basic forms, as might be expected, are some FAIRY TALES, the most frequently recurring being "Cinderella," occasionally intertwined with "Rumplestiltskin." These, as some of the titles suggest, are stories of apparent marriages of convenience, where the Cinderella heroine is already in love with the hero while he often believes himself to be in love with someone else: this is the case in both one of the relatively earliest and best, *Friday's Child* (1944) and one of the relatively latest and best, *A Civil Contract* (1961). In both, the hero must marry for financial reasons, though, in the former, Lord Sheringham is a callow young egoist who needs the sentimental education of his marriage to Hero Wantage to make him fit for her, while, in the latter, Viscount Linton is a sensitive, courteous gentleman whose feelings are lacerated by the crude generosity of his wealthy father-in-law, and who never comes to feel more than a grateful tenderness for plain, everyday Jenny.

The egotistic young charmer and the quiet gentleman are two of her standard hero types; another, rarer but delightful, is the young dandy who is believed by everyone, especially his father, to be completely empty-headed, but whose quiet considerateness actually leads him to display surprising ingenuity; the star of this type is Freddy in *Cotillion* (1953) who organizes a convenient engagement to himself for his cousin Kitty to enable her to have a London season and probably to marry their cousin Jack, though he dearly wants her himself; he seems at first almost half-witted—and H. includes a genuinely half-witted character to show the difference—but gradually comes out as a man with head as well as heart, certainly not an intellectual, but with wit enough to resolve his friends' difficulties as well as his own. Greatly different from any of these heroes is the kind necessarily central to the other principal fairy tale model H. uses: Beauty and the Beast. These are stories where an established rake with an appalling reputation is reclaimed by a loving woman, either a complete innocent, or, as in *Venetia* (1958), a young woman past her early bloom and with the intelligence to see through the mask of cynicism; in this novel, the twist

that provides the happy ending is a particularly neat one, the heroine using the fact that her own mother has disgraced herself to prove that she is not too good for the Byronic Lord Damerel. It will be noted that all these heroes are members of the high and usually wealthy aristocracy; the dream of wealth and power accompanying sexual attraction is, of course, as important in these romances as in the sexually explicit novels of the late 20th c.

Apart from the fairy tale form, H.'s other main narrative device is the one that she also attempted in modern dress, the detective story or thriller. In a novel like *The Quiet Gentleman* (1951) or *The Toll-Gate* (1954), there is a mystery, perhaps even a murder mystery, to be solved, and the hero has to be a detective as well as the fulfillment of a young woman's dream. The typical, though not obligatory, hero of this story type is a large man, newly retired from the army, and able to pretend, at need, to be stupid and uneducated. One of the best examples is Hugo in *The Talisman Ring* (1936), who takes on this role in self-defense when he realizes that the family he has never met before believes his grandfather to have been a weaving hand rather than a wealthy mill-owner; his performance as a simpleton enables him to rescue his young cousin from a disastrous career as a smugglers' leader.

Such large heroes often, though again not regularly, and indeed not in *The Talisman Ring,* are matched with large heroines, magnificent Junoesque women in such novels as *Bath Tangle* (1955), where Lady Serena is furious to find her newly dead father has appointed the immense Corinthian he wanted her to marry as her guardian, or *The Grand Sophy* (1950) where Sophy is indeed grand in stature as well as in the splendid confidence with which she manages her acquaintances' lives. The virtues of these women are generosity of spirit and ingenuity of mind; their faults, pride and willfulness; these qualities are invaluable for generating variations in plot. In *Faro's Daughter* (1941), for example, the heroine presides over a gaming house and the plot depends on the large hero's determination to rescue, as he sees it, a young and foolish relative from her clutches; her indignation is all that is needed to produce a series of events, some similar to those in other of her novels, some quite unusual, before the eventual realization of the two substantial protagonists that they belong to each other.

Other heroines are quite different from these magnificent women: some naive, very young innocents like Hero Wantage or the enchantingly direct Horatia Winwood in *The Convenient Marriage* (1934)—it is intriguing to observe the initial correspondence of these names; some mature, poised ladies, governesses or companions, or young women who have been kept at home by selfish or overprotective parents until they believe themselves to be settled spinsters, such as An-cilla Trent in *The Nonesuch* (1962), the eponymous Venetia, or Elinor Rochdale, in *The Reluctant Widow* (1946), who, setting out for a painful but apparently inevitable career as a governess, finds herself instead married to a dying rake so that another masterful hero can avoid inheriting his estate; needless to say—and it is, of course, the weakness of all such romances that it is needless to say—he does acquire it in the end by marrying her himself.

Though Elinor finds herself bending to Lord Carlyon's will, willfulness is a major characteristic of many of H.'s heroines; in *An Infamous Army* (1937) she brings together the formerly headstrong Judith from *Regency Buck* (1935) and a deplorably behaved granddaughter of the central characters of *Devil's Cub* in what might have been a highly enjoyable conflict of sisters; unfortunately, this is one of the novels in which H. tried to combine her romance writing with a serious historical novel, and this fails because of the incompatibility of the frivolity of the love interest with the desperate realism of her account of the battle of Waterloo. Here, and in *The Spanish Bride* (1940), her ambition is damaging: the very excellence of her two modes of work, the thoroughly documented and intelligently structured account of Wellington's war and the passionate but ultimately trivial account of the taming of Lady Barbara, make them sit awkwardly with each other. The romance in *The Spanish Bride*, based as it is, like the account of the Peninsular War, in actual documents, is less intrusive, but there is still a sense of conflicting modes which do not work together.

And yet there was something more. As early in her career as 1931, with *The Conqueror,* she had experimented with addressing a much earlier period than the Regency. Her last work, unfinished at her death, was an historical novel that is almost more of a BIOGRAPHY. *My Lord John* (1975), if completed, would have been an enormous work on the life of John, Duke of Bedford, the younger brother of Henry V, and at the point she had reached, a thick volume already written, there was absolutely no romance involved; John's emotional life is shown as centered entirely in his family feeling, and chiefly his devotion to his older brother, his sexual life merely hinted at in the suggestion that the four brothers visited the stews as part of the wild behavior with which they relieve their nerves. Starting, delightfully, when John was only about four and the brothers were in constant mischief, she was working her way steadily through a life devoted to war and administration, and making it fascinating. Had it been completed, it would surely have required some upward revaluation of her reputation.

BIBLIOGRAPHY: Chris, T., *G. H.'s Regency England* (1989); Hodge, J. A., *The Private World of G. H.* (1984); Fahnestock-Thomas, M., *G. H.* (2001)

AUDREY LASKI

HEYWOOD, John

b. 1497?, London; d. ca. 1580, Louvain, Belgium

H., courtly musician, playwright, and writer of epigrams, is often considered to be the figure who marks the beginning of RENAISSANCE DRAMA. Attached to four Tudor courts, he maintained his position through his merry wit, and was best known in his own time for his collections of epigrams.

H. entered the court of HENRY VIII in 1519, the same year as Sir Thomas MORE, leading scholars to speculate that he was already a follower of More. It is certain that afterward he became part of More's humanist circle, later marrying More's niece. But H.'s pro-Catholic sympathies nearly cost him his pension at several points in newly Protestant England, and the high status he was accorded in the Catholic Mary Tudor's retinue was short lived. Though he managed to join the court of Mary's successor, ELIZABETH I, he soon fled England for the Spanish Netherlands, dying a penniless exile.

His plays, or interludes, have typically been divided into debates and farces. The first four plays securely attributed to H. were printed by his brother-in-law, William Rastell, in 1533. *The Pardoner and the Frere* is the simplest. The two titular characters each sermonize a congregation in an attempt to raise alms for their respective causes. Fiercely competitive, they make their speeches simultaneously, eventually entering a verbal altercation that quickly becomes physical. When the parish priest separates them and threatens them with the stocks, the two escape together. *A Play of Love* may have been performed in 1527 or 1528 at the Inns of Court. Here, two pairs of characters debate their relative misery or happiness: Lover Not Loved asserts that his pain is worse than that of Beloved Not Loving, while Lover Loved argues that his happiness surmounts that of Neither Lover Nor Loved. The debaters judge one another's cases, and both disputes end in a tie.

The Play of the Wether takes as its conceit Jupiter's decision to hear complaints about the weather. A variety of characters present complaints driven by selfish desires, making the argument that a strong ruler is necessary to mediate among the competing interests of a nation. The anonymous *Johan Johan the Husbande, Tyb His Wyfe & Syr Jhan the Preest* (1533) is widely ascribed to H. A close translation of a French farce, it has H.'s lighthearted tone and treatment of language without his typical moral. H. has also been attributed with *Witty and Witless* (wr. ca. 1533; pub. 1846 abridged), a simple debate play in which two characters debate whether it is better to be a fool or a wise man.

A more important play, *The Playe Called the Foure PP* (1544?), brings together four realistic characters: a Palmer (pilgrim), a Pardoner, a Pothecary, and a Pedlar. The first three resolve to enter into a lying contest with the Pedlar as judge. Much of the amusing dialogue is centered on diatribes against women, and when in response to the Pardoner's long tale the Pothecary claims he has never known "any woman out of patience," the Pedlar instantly awards him the prize for biggest lie.

H. surely wrote many other interludes and masques, but none has survived. His most popular nondramatic work was *A Dialogue Conteinying the Number in Effect of All the Proverbs in the Englishe Tongue, Compacte in a Matter Concernying Two Maner of Mariages* (1546; enl. ed., 1550). In this narrative poem, an older, married man gives a young man advice on whether he should marry for love or for money: rather than answer the question directly, the older man narrates stories demonstrating the problematics of each, leaving the young man—and the reader—to decide for himself.

H. was perhaps best known in his own lifetime for his epigrams. A short poem that concludes with a clever turn of thought, the epigram was very popular in 16th-c. England. H. may have been the first author to write epigrams in English, and his epigrams show originality and a great linguistic wit. Their popularity is evidenced by the number he produced: *An Hundred Epigrams* (1550) was followed by *Two Hundred Epigrams upon Two Hundred Proverbs, With a Third Hundred Newly Added* (1555) and *A Fourth Hundred of Epigrams, Newly Invented* (1560).

H. seems to have become attached to Mary Tudor's retinue at some time before her accession, and he wrote poems in honor of her accession and her unpopular marriage to Philip II of Spain. In 1556, he printed a poem he had worked on for some time, called *The Spider and the Flie: A Parable*. A complicated allegory concerned with social developments in England, the poem presents as a maid who mediates between the Spiders and the Flies, interpreted as either the nobility and the commons or the Protestants and Catholics. More straightforward was an occasional poem called "A breef balet touching the traytorous takyinge of Scarborow Castell" (1557), which though it predictably restates the importance of obeying God and monarch, is generally considered to be better written than his other state poems. No writings exist from the time H. spent in Elizabeth's court, and in 1564 he left England in self-imposed exile.

H.'s influence on later Tudor drama has become a point of some contention. H. utilized true-to-life characters, comic subplots, colloquial language and Continental models—all hallmarks of English high Renaissance comedy. But no direct influences can be traced, and though he seems to have been widely read even after his death—his complete works were reprinted four times before 1600—he seems to have been appreciated largely for his wit and mirth. Nevertheless, he experimented with the English language, bending

it to both serious intent and musical gaiety that found their fullest expression, fifty years later, in the works of William SHAKESPEARE.

BIBLIOGRAPHY: Altman, J. B., *The Tudor Play of the Mind* (1978); Bolwell, R. W., *The Life and Works of J. H.* (1921); Hudson, H. H., *The Epigram in the English Renaissance* (1947); Johnson, R. C., *J. H.* (1970); Kolin, P. C., "Recent Studies in J. H.," *ELR* 13 (Winter 1983): 113–23

GINGER STRAND

HEYWOOD, Thomas

b. 1573 or 1574, Rothwell, or Ashby, Lincolnshire; d. August 1641, London

Educated briefly at Cambridge, H. began his literary and theatrical career in London in the mid-1590s. By 1601–2, he had joined the Earl of Worcester's company (known as Queen Anne's after 1603), with whom he served for many years as actor, playwright, and leading member. In his preface to *The English Traveller* (perf. ca. 1627?; pub. 1633), H. plausibly claimed to have had "either an entire hand, or at the least a maine finger" in 220 plays, most of which are no longer extant. The two dozen that survive range widely in matter and genre, including sentimental comedy, like *The Wise Woman of Hogsdon* (perf. ca. 1604; pub. 1638); patriotic history, like the two-part *If You Know Not Me, You Know Nobody* (perf. ca. 1603; pub.1605), a celebratory account of Queen ELIZABETH I; and topical satire, like *The Late Lancashire Witches* (1634), coauthored with Richard BROME. In addition to his prodigious dramatic output, H. wrote many translations, miscellanies, and pamphlets, including his *Apology for Actors* (1612), a lively defense of the stage against Puritan attacks.

H. is best known for his domestic tragedy, *A Woman Killed with Kindness* (perf. 1603; pub. 1607). Like *The English Traveller*, it focuses on female chastity. In the tragic main plot a wife yields to sexual temptation, while in the tragicomic subplot a virgin resists it. Both women move within a network of male bonds: Anne Frankford's adultery destroys her husband's relationship with his best friend and disrupts his home; by contrast Susan Mountford's exemplary preservation of her chastity allows a reconciliation between her brother and his bitter enemy, Sir Francis Acton. Although murder was neither a socially nor legally permissible response to adultery in early modern England, H. represents John Frankford as heroic in his self-restraint (he refrains from killing the guilty couple), and as noble in his subsequent treatment of his erring wife (he merely banishes her from home and family). Shamed before her children and servants, Anne functions as an exemplary adulteress, directly addressing the wives in the theater audience: "O, women, women, you that have yet kept/Your holy matrimonial vow unstained,/ Make me your instance." Anne's extended penitence and self-punishment, as she starves herself to death, are clearly calculated to elicit tears from her audience, onstage and off. Her suffering expiates her sin and earns her husband's forgiveness: she dies happily in his arms ("Pardoned on earth, soul, thou in Heaven art free;/Once more thy wife dies thus embracing thee.") In the subplot, the virtuous Susan is rewarded with marriage to the man who has tried to seduce her and ruin her brother. Recent critics have been fascinated by the play's punitive treatment of the female body, its celebration of male homosocial bonds, and the anxiety it betrays about domestic relations.

H.'s *The Rape of Lucrece* (perf. ca. 1608; pub. 1608) demonstrates his success in writing for a broadly popular market. Revived both at court (1612) and in the public playhouses, it was presumably still in demand in 1638 when the fifth printing appeared. Based on Livy's *History*, the play dramatizes the overthrow of the monarchy and birth of the Roman republic. H. contrasts his titular heroine with her opposite, Tullia, the old king's daughter: while the latter intrudes into public affairs, wickedly usurping patriarchal authority, goading her husband into rebellion and killing her father, the former manifests the domestic virtues of prudent housewife and decorous spouse. H. underscores the political consequences of both feminine vice and virtue: figuratively Tullia's corrupt sexuality breeds a diseased body politic that must be redeemed by the sacrifice of the "soule-chast" Lucrece. H.'s chief interest, however, is not in Lucrece's rape and consequent suicide, but in the renewed male heroism these generate. Departing widely from his source, H. scripts a climactic battle between Sextus Tarquin, the rapist, and Brutus, the leader of the Romans. The combatants praise each other ecstatically before dying, locked in a homoerotic embrace. The play apparently drew its contemporary appeal not only from the martial excitement of the final scenes, but from the many songs, variously bawdy, comic, and satirical, which punctuate the action. Most notable of these, for the modern reader, is the three-part "catch" sung shortly after the rape, *"Did he take faire Lucrece by the toe man?"* The song titillates the audience by successively naming the parts of Lucrece's body from toe to thigh; in effect, reenacting the rape in a jocular context.

BIBLIOGRAPHY: Baines, B., *T. H.* (1984); Clark, A. M., *T. H.* (1931); McLuskie, K., *Dekker and Heywood: Professional Dramatists* (1994)

KAREN BAMFORD

HILL, Geoffrey

b. 18 June 1932, Bromsgrove, Worcestershire

As a poet, H. commands immense respect from the literary establishment where his relatively few collec-

tions of verse are eagerly anticipated and widely reviewed. His academic career is also exemplary. He was educated at the County High School, Bromsgrove, and then at Keble College, Oxford, where he received a B.A. in 1953. He became professor of English literature at the University of Leeds between 1976 and 1980 and fellow of Emmanuel College Cambridge between 1981 and 1988. He is now a professor of literature and religion at Boston University and has served as visiting lecturer in several other establishments.

Since receiving a Gregory Award in 1961, H.'s work has attracted a long list of prizes including the Geoffrey Faber Memorial Award (1970), the Duff Cooper Memorial Prize (1979), the American Academy Russell Loines Award (1983), and the Ingram Merrill Foundation Award (1983). H. has achieved a certain positive recognition for his poetry and has drawn comment from academics like Harold Bloom who claims that "Strong poetry is always difficult, and Geoffrey Hill is the strongest British poet now active, though his reputation in the English-speaking world is somewhat less advanced than that of several of his contemporaries."

Perhaps the reason for this is that H.'s work is genuinely resistant to easy immediate readings. He has produced verse, a play *Brand* (1978; rev. ed., 1981) after Henrik Ibsen and a volume of critical writings. H.'s work remains allusive, erudite, and difficult with overtones that are seated in the most rigorous moral foundations. H.'s poetry is also layered with private thought and allusion that can at times seem impenetrable or surprisingly personal. Peter Robinson feels that at "the heart of Geoffrey Hill's poetry is a meditation upon the relationships between authority and suffering." It is certainly true that H. is always keen to examine the violence and the pain that humans like to inflict upon one another, and he effectively applies what is a modernist allusiveness to his chosen themes, therefore ensuring a readerly interest, but also endlessly courting inevitable misreadings.

H.'s early poetry set the tone for much that was to follow. He remains an objective writer, avoiding subjectivity or confessional writing and incorporating historical or religious episodes or themes, mythology, discussions of power that represent for good or ill the known world in its manifest and characteristic cultural and social forms. Indeed, the formal but accessible *For the Unfallen* (1959) displays elegies, battles, and in "Genesis" the divine fascination with "flesh/and blood and the blood's pain." The poem "Requiem for the Plantagenet Kings" is also of note here, characteristically melding history, power, religion, and elegy.

H. moves closer to finding his trademark voice in *King Log* (1968) focusing upon the fate of poets, poetry, and history, but retaining a fascination in "Ovid in the Third Reich" with "ancient troughs of blood." With *Mercian Hymns* (1971), one feels that

H. achieves a balance among the presence of history, personal history, themes of power and brutality, and the relief of HUMOR. H. places himself covertly among the recorded events of his own birthplace but erects around this sense of place an appealing mélange of ancient and modern lexis. Offa here is both "King of the perennial holly-groves" and "overlord of the M5." H. revels in the choice and placement of his sounds: "Coiled entrenched England: brickwork and paintwork/stalwart above hacked marl. The clashing prim-/ary colours—'Ethandune,' 'Catraeth,' 'Maldon,'/'Pengwern.' Steel against yew and privet. Fresh/dynasties of smiths."

In *Tenebrae* (1978), H. builds upon his previous work, extending the reference to overtly religious ceremonial, especially in relation to figures like Robert SOUTHWELL in the epigraph to "Lachrimae." He also produces T. S. ELIOT-like passages in "Tenebrae" itself demonstrating strong links with MODERNISM: "this is the ash-pit of the lily-fire."

Canaan (1996) largely explores British social and political life in such poems as "To the High Court of Parliament, 1994" and "Churchill's Funeral." Whilst these poems show a profound understanding of the subject matter, other shorter examples in the volume, like "To John Constable: In Absentia," demonstrate a profound joy in the craft and use of words. *The Mystery of the Charity of Charles Péguy* (1983) once again blends history, politics, and religion, and shows H.'s capacity for the sustained long poem. The poet seems to have gradually come to terms with the sense of absurdity in the divine and history the "supreme clown, dire tragedian." H.'s erudition both impresses and oppresses in the free verse flow of *The Triumph of Love* (1999) where church corruption, the Holocaust, public and private lives, the horrors of war are set down as a crushing indictment of the last century. The verdict upon poetry itself is less than positive.

H.'s recent *Speech! Speech!* (2000) contemplates the last century and modernity, where history interacts on the page with the realist operators of contemporary technology and a global overview of political life. H.'s poetry and his prose work present the reader with a difficult allusive facade, but also with the clear objective voice of the poet, almost leading us to believe in his work as one whole work, a constant stream into which we, as readers, are tapping.

BIBLIOGRAPHY: Bloom, H., ed., *G. H.* (1986); Hill, G., *The Lords of Limit: Essays on Literature and Ideas* (1984); Robinson, P., ed., *G. H.: Essays on His Work* (1985)

CHRISTOPHER J. P. SMITH

HILL, [Sir] John

b. 17 November 1714, near Peterborough; d. 2 November 1775, Golden Square, London

H., called "The Inspector" for editorial columns signed that way at the pinnacle of his career every Tuesday and Friday in the *Daily Advertiser and Gazetteer* (1751–52), was a household name in his time. A self-proclaimed "universal man," he also wrote on every topic and practiced all trades and professions. Yet his enduring achievement is rarely noted: a European best-seller translated into many languages that played a role in the print trail of the French Revolution. This was a short prose SATIRE entitled *Lucine sine concubitu* (1750), the story of Lucine who conceives without male intervention.

H. constructed his fantastic story out of (what we would call) genetic technology, for Lucine not only procreates sans a man but uses a machine that captures *animalcula* carried by the west wind. William Wollaston, a philosopher contemporaneous with John LOCKE and George BERKELEY, claimed that these *animalcula* were "the seeds of all future generations" dispersed by the wind throughout the world. Men inhale them, distill them in bodily digestion, and transfer them to women during sexual intercourse. Building on Wollaston's unlikely theory, H. facetiously claimed he had invented an electrical machine (it was not true, of course) "electrified to the nicest Law of Electricity," which captured these *animalcula* in flight. Once caught in the instrument, the "little seeds" were inhaled by women, bypassing men, then incubated in the female womb, thereby eliminating the age-old moral dilemmas associated with copulation, such as venereal disease, guilt over fornication, and even the need for marriage.

H.'s reviewers savaged *Lucine*, not least because he removed the pleasure from sexual intercourse and fatally separated sexuality and procreation. The Royal Society, H.'s primary target, had banned H. from membership; the appearance of *Lucine* guaranteed he would never be elected. The Anglican and Catholic Churches responded as negatively, although it is hard to understand their logic that H.'s book would encourage women to dress and live as men so they could inhale the powerful atoms. The satire was reissued during the French Revolution, in expanded forms and interpreted allegorically, Lucine now symbolizing France, a country currently breeding monstrous new political forms of government without a male (France sans her partner allies). By the 1790s, *Lucine* had been translated into several European languages, including Russian. Within one generation, H.'s reputation as a sexual and political devil sank to the bottom of the pit.

Given this remarkable, if somewhat nefarious, career it is curious that H. has never been the subject of a full-length biography. For he was one of the most colorful coffee house figures of an age when galleries of geniuses and eccentrics—the [James] Boswells and [Samuel] Johnsons of Georgian England—captured popular imagination, even defined the spirit of the age. His contemporaries were amazed at the speed with which "Proteus H.," refashioned himself as actor, apothecary, botanist, chemist, composer (he wrote an opera called *Orpheus*), doctor, gardener, journalist, publisher, tradesman—and, not least, lover: the lover of actresses, celebrities, and aristocrats, one of whom he eventually married. He published dozens of books in all these fields. As self-centered as the members of Samuel JOHNSON's Literary Club, H. became a household name whose fame was based on a brazen personality so self-absorbed that it continuously promoted itself. In most of these activities, he lacked authority, and his lack of university education owing to humble circumstances made him the constant butt of jokes. Yet it was his fame as a journalist in the early 1750s, when he was probably England's highest paid hack, which solidified his reputation. Scholars now refer to his didactic tracts on subjects ranging from acting and child rearing to marriage and medicine; but then, his serial refashioning and self-puffery rendered him a constant figure of fun.

H.'s 252 "Inspector" essays published every Tuesday and Friday in the *London Daily Advertiser* in 1751–52 touch on contemporary moral, social, and cultural topics; viewed as a compendium, they form one of the best guides to the collective mind-set of mid-18th-c. England. If less polished than Joseph ADDISON's and Richard STEELE's *Spectator* or, later on, Johnson's and Oliver GOLDSMITH's in (respectively) the *Rambler* and the *Citizen of the World*, they are equally shrewd and insightful. Nowhere else in his oeuvre do H.'s moral and didactic positions lie in such contrast to his eccentric, unpredictable behavior in public.

H. was also a principal player in the history of "PR"—"puffing" was then the term. Puffery—the art of promoting oneself in the public sector—was still in its infancy in an epoch when patronage counted for more than puffery and when public readership decided which authors deserved to enter the Republic of Letters. H.'s tactic was to print a work, then swiftly attack the publication anonymously—thereby precipitating a fracas—and finally reply to the attack in his own name. Literary scuffle ensued, the public was mystified, H.'s name became a household word. This self-puffery accounts for the dozens of works written about him, like poet Christopher SMART's hilarious mock-epic poem *The Hilliad*. No wonder one contemporary caricaturist drew him as a grotesque under the caption "Lusus naturae," wonder of nature.

BIBLIOGRAPHY: Gross, J., *The Rise and Fall of the Man of Letters* (1969); Lemay, J. A. L., and G. S. Rousseau, *The Renaissance Man in the Eighteenth Century* (1978); Rousseau, G. S., ed., *The Letters and Papers of Sir J. H.* (1982); Rogers, P., *Grub Street: Studies in a Subculture* (1972)

GEORGE ROUSSEAU

HILL, Susan [Elizabeth]
b. 5 February 1942, Scarborough

H. was educated at King's College, London, and is novelist, short story writer, children's writer, and author of plays for radio and television. Loneliness is a persistent theme. *In the Springtime of the Year* (1974) is about bereavement, while *A Change for the Better* (1969) is about a hotel that serves as a refuge for unhappy, isolated people. In 1972, H. won the Whitbread Award for the highly acclaimed *The Bird of Night*. *I'm the King of the Castle* (1970), her novel about childhood brutality, was for a while studied in British schools. *The Woman in Black* (1983) is a ghost story, which has been successfully dramatized and frequently revived. Later works include *The Mist in the Mirror* (1992), *Mrs. DeWinter* (1993), and *Listening to the Orchestra: Four Stories* (1996).

HISTORY AND LITERATURE

It was Aristotle who first posited the proposition that there was something interesting and challenging to be said about the difference between what a poet writes and what an historian writes. But although he insists that their works are of different essences, he equally firmly insists that there is an intrinsic relationship between the two. "The poet and the historian differ," says Aristotle in *Poetics*, "not by writing in verse or prose. The work of Herodotus might be put into verse and it would still be a species of history, with meter no less than without it. The true difference is that one relates what has happened, the other what may happen. Poetry, therefore, is a more philosophical and a higher thing than history: for poetry tends to express the universal, history the particular. By the universal I mean how a person of a certain type will on occasion speak or act, according to the law of probability or necessity; and it is this *universality* at which poetry aims in the names she attaches to the personages. The *particular* is—for example—what Alcibiades did or suffered in actuality."

The translation quoted above is that of S. H. Butcher, first published in 1894: it is still one of the most exact, but no serious-minded person seeking to summon Aristotle to support an argument would rely on one translator only. Other translations to consider in relation to this particular passage are John Warrington's, first published in 1963, and Kenneth McLeish's, published in 1998. Warrington, like Butcher, refers to the "other" kind of writing as "poetry" and calls the writer of it a "poet." McLeish calls the thing written "drama or epic" and the writer "an author of drama or epic." Warrington, in a footnote, acutely points out that the Greeks had no general word for what we in the 21st c. call "literature," but it seems clear from the context that by "poetry" Aristotle means something far broader and deeper than simply "written in verse": he seems, indeed, to mean any writing, whether in verse or prose, that seeks to explore and reflect something of the profundity and ambiguity of universal human experience: in a word, he means "literature," even though he had no word for it. He himself observes (and here we are back with Butcher's translation again): "There is another art which imitates by language alone, [that is to say, as well as the arts of music and dance] and that either in prose or verse . . . but this has hitherto been without a name." So, to go one better than Aristotle, we will here and now boldly call it "literature"—but we will try to use the term with discretion. Aristotle himself acidly remarks that not everything written in verse turns out to be poetry. We could well add that not everything written in prose is literature. George ELIOT's *Middlemarch* is written wholly in prose and can be, with some confidence, declared to be literature. *The Way of an Eagle* (1912)—by Ethel M. Dell—is also written wholly in prose and can be, with equal confidence but with less chance of universal agreement, declared to be not literature (along with, say, the "novels" by Barbara Cartland and the thousands of paperback "romances" published by Mills and Boon and Harlequin.)

So can we accept Aristotle's guidance in distinguishing these two different forms of writing—poetry (literature) and history—or have societies, cultures, and civilizations changed so much in the more than two millennia since he wrote that his thinking, though perhaps still academically interesting, is no longer relevant in any practical way? In particular, can we accept that history speaks only of what has happened, while "poetry" (literature) speaks of aspirations and what may happen? And even if this distinction is valid, does this, in fact, demonstrate that the imaginative writing of the poet is somehow more elevated, more profound, ultimately more commendable and more important, than the writing of history? This is an ancient battlefield, much trodden and trampled. It derives, ultimately, from Plato's famous, infamous, and now largely ignored comment on pathos (in the Ancient Greek sense, which has little or nothing to do with our modern "pathos" or "pathetic"): "the ancient quarrel between poetry and philosophy."

Certainly the attitude of historians and the style of writing history changed radically during the 20th c., and many historians would now maintain that history at its best contains a good deal of poetic sensibility. Consider, for example, a book like Hayden White's *Metahistory: The Historical Imagination* (1973). There is, in fact, an organic relationship between "history" and "literature" that justifies both and makes both culturally necessary if anything like the truth is ever to be told and is ever to be honored, or even recognized. We need to read both history and literature (that is, imaginative, serious writing of at least some poetic sensibility) and draw our sense of truth from the chemistry of their intermingling. Can one really fully understand and be moved by Anton Chekhov or Ivan Turgenev without having first read something of the history of 19th-c. Russia? Or appreciate the cataclysmic and apocalyptic vision of W. B. YEATS's "Easter 1916"—and those other poems that cluster around it: "Sixteen Dead Men," "The Rose Tree," and "On a Political Prisoner"— without knowing something of the historical facts of that troubled island? And aren't there perfidious English ears that still cringe under the lash of Yeats's lines? "What is it but nightfall?/No, no, not night but death;/Was it needless death after all?/For England may keep faith." But you do need to know, as you read, about the passing and the subsequent suspension of the Irish Home Rule bill by the English parliament in 1913. "And what if excess of love/Bewildered them till they died?/I write it out in a verse—/MacDonagh and MacBride/And Connolly and Pearse/Now and in time to be,/Wherever green is worn,/Are changed, changed utterly:/A terrible beauty is born."

This does not mean that all poetry and all fiction should be based on known and famous historical events and it certainly does not give any special cachet to, say, the novelettes of Georgette HEYER. Mervyn PEAKE's *Gormenghast* and Thomas Love PEACOCK's *Nightmare Abbey* are both indisputably great literary works and, though rooted in a firm understanding of literary and cultural history, neither of them makes any attempt to relay narratives of actual historical occurrences: both are honored for their imaginative, poetical (though neither is written in verse), philosophical qualities—in a word, for their sense of truth. Or look at the question from the other end, so to speak: take a random sampling of some of our best-reputed historians—say, Thomas Babington MACAULAY, G. M. Trevelyan, A. J. P. Taylor. One of the foremost qualities for which all three are (rightly) praised is the literary nature of their writing. Trevelyan, speaking of literature, once said "it is joy, joy in our inmost heart." And Macaulay, whose greatest work is universally acknowledged to be the monumental *History of England*, while still a student at Cambridge twice won the Chancellor's Medal for Poetry, began his writing career by publishing extremely favorably reviewed essays on John MILTON and Robert SOUTHEY, and sealed his permanent claim to literary fame in 1842 with *Lays of Ancient Rome* ("Now who will stand on either hand/And keep the bridge with me? . . . And even the ranks of Tuscany/Could scarce forbear to cheer"). Any self-respecting modern critic would now dismiss that last item as a populist jingle and not a poem at all, but at least, in 1842, it was attempting to be poetry. So what was a reputed historian—and a very self-confident one at that—doing writing poetry?

While writing history is certainly not always literature (though it is sometimes), all literature is, in a certain sense, always history. Art's function, whether consciously so or not, in all ages is to reflect those underlying universals that belong to all times and all peoples, so the literature of one period becomes a part of the history of the next, not less important than the social, political, or military history. Percy Bysshe SHELLEY was right: "Poets are . . . the gigantic shadows which futurity casts upon the present . . . the trumpets that sing to battle . . . the unacknowledged legislators of the world."

In practice, the "historical novel" in Great Britain has been, since its inception by Sir Walter SCOTT in the early 19th c., one of the staple forms of fiction. Its quality has, of course, varied very widely: occasionally silly, often mediocre, but, at its best, very fine indeed—as, for example in William Makepeace THACKERAY's *Vanity Fair* and Charles DICKENS's *A Tale of Two Cities*. Scott himself wrote twenty-six novels based either on known historical incidents or on popular legends about alleged incidents or characters, starting with *Waverley* and continuing until *Castle Dangerous*, published in 1831—twenty-six novels in seventeen years. Other distinguished examples are *Parade's End* by Ford Madox FORD, in which the second and third (out of four) volumes consist of a fairly detailed account of the central character's experiences during World War I, a conflict that spawned a great deal of imaginative and anguished fictional writing from all over Europe. One thinks of Richard ALDINGTON's bitterly satirical novel *Death of a Hero*, Wilfred OWEN's poetry, R. C. SHERRIFF's play *Journey's End*—its title taken from the song "O Mistress mine," in *Twelfth Night*—and, from the Continent, Erich Maria Remarque's *All Quiet on the Western Front* (1929), André Obey's play *La Bataille de la Marne* (perf. 1931; pub. 1932; Battle of the Marne), Mikhail Bulgakov's play *Beg* (wr. 1928; pub. 1957; *Flight*, 1972). An earlier trilogy by Ford is an even better example of a modern book on a long-ago historical incident: *The Fifth Queen* has as its central character Catherine Howard, the nineteen-year-old wife of HENRY VIII. In more recent years, Paul SCOTT has contributed his *Raj Quartet*, four novels set in India during World War II and in the years leading up to Indian Independence: the well-known historical incidents are made to have a profound influence upon the lives of the main characters, who are fictitious.

If one turns from novels to plays, one notices that many more works are (not surprisingly) actually centered not on a group of fictitious characters placed against a background of "real" events but on actual historical figures who are given living personalities and powerful dialogue (not always readily recogniz-

able to an historian). The example of William SHAKESPEARE is so obvious as to require no comment, except to remark that his portraits of English kings are not, and are not meant to be, factual and documentary reports of scrupulous practical accuracy: they are poems about the perils of ambition, the realities of public responsibility and public conscience, the loneliness of a leader's position ("uneasy lies the head that wears a crown"). What Shakespeare does is what Aristotle prophesied he would do: he takes an interesting-sounding man like Richard II whose motives are muddled, mysterious and hard to guess at and suggests what those motives might have been. In all honesty, can we ever hope to know *more* than that, whether we are considering a king or a penurious professor? Other Elizabethan and Jacobean dramatists often employed the same techniques: Christopher MARLOWE (*Edward II*); Ben JONSON (*Sejanus, His Fall*, perf. ca. 1603–4, pub. 1605; *Catiline*, 1611); John FORD (*Perkin Warbeck*), and several others.

In modern times Bernard SHAW is a good example, in such plays as *The Man of Destiny* (perf. 1897; pub. 1898)—Napoleon; *The Devil's Disciple*—General "Johnny" Burgoyne; *Caesar and Cleopatra*; *The Dark Lady of the Sonnets* (perf. 1910; pub. 1914)—Shakespeare and Queen ELIZABETH I; *Androcles and the Lion*; *Saint Joan*; *In Good King Charles's Golden Days* (perf. 1939; pub. 1946)—Charles II, James, Duke of York, George Fox, Nell Gwynn, Isaac Newton. Incidentally, the first part of Shaw's preface to this play is a perfect example of the application of Aristotle's principle: "For instance (says Shaw) Charles might have met that human prodigy Isaac Newton. And Newton might have met that prodigy of another sort, George Fox, the founder of the morally mighty Society of Friends, vulgarly called the Quakers. Better again, all three might have met." There are, of course, more recent examples than Shaw that could be quoted: Robert BOLT's *A Man for All Seasons*, Alan BENNETT's *The Madness of George III*, Michael FRAYN's *Copenhagen*, and many others.

That form of literature which expresses itself in verse yields a plethora of examples of poets looking back at human actions, sometimes of hundreds or even thousands of years ago, and seeing imaginative detail that the mundane historical record missed: John KEATS, imagining himself as "stout Cortez" and imagining Cortez's thoughts as he gazed, for the first time, at the Pacific "silent upon a peak in Darien," or Robert BROWNING, imagining himself at a recital in the 18th c., given by Baldassaro Galuppi, and imagining the fashionable audience's thoughts and comments as they also listened to the music—"Those commiserating sevenths—'Life might last! We can but try'"—or Alfred, Lord TENNYSON, remembering the sinking of the Revenge ("At Flores in the Azores Sir Richard Grenville lay").

In a good play or novel or poem, this device of half-imagining the past against a background of known facts is often used as a way of drawing attention to a present trouble or social problem (as American dramatist Arthur Miller did, for instance, in *The Crucible* (1953), turning 17th-c. hypocrisy, prejudice, and violence into savage symbols of 20th-c. governmental injustice). But in a great work this is too slight a target: the device now becomes a way of reflecting some sense of the permanent, unchangeable nature of humanity as it was then, is now and ever shall be. And in the achieving of this objective, art and factual report, literature and history, poetry and philosophy, go hand in hand and begin, indeed, to reflect each other.

BIBLIOGRAPHY: Cohen, R., and M. Krieger, *Literature and History* (1974); Gould, T., *The Ancient Quarrel between Poetry and Philosophy* (1990); Macaulay, T. B., *The History of England from the Accession of James II* (5 vols., 1848–61); White, H. V., *Metahistory: The Historical Imagination in Nineteenth-Century Europe* (1973)

ERIC SALMON

HOBBES, Thomas

b. 5 April 1588, Westport; d. 4 December 1679, Hardwick Hall

With justifiable exaggeration, H. described himself as the founder of political science. Michael Oakeshott called *Leviathan* (1651) "the greatest, perhaps the sole masterpiece of political philosophy written in the English language." While H.'s reputation rests securely on this work, H. also published on optics, mathematics, history, ethics, psychology, philosophy, and law.

On the eve of his departure for Oxford in 1603, H. presented his teacher, Robert Latimer, with a Latin translation of *Medea*. H. remained a lover of the classics throughout his life, translating Thucydides (1629) and Homer (*Odyssey*, 2 vols., 1673–75; *Iliad*, 1676). H. later claimed that Thucydides taught him to distrust democracy, though it would be more accurate to say that the classical writer who most influenced H. was Euclid. According to H.'s friend and first biographer, John AUBREY, H. first encountered Euclid's work about 1628. As a mathematician, H. left something to be desired, but H. became a convert to geometry to the extent that he maintained, "They that study natural philosophy, study in vain, except they begin at geometry." H. regarded geometry as the science of motion, and for H. motion explains all human behavior. H. was writing when motion was a popular subject. William Harvey had just discovered the circulation of the blood (*De motu cordis*, 1628), and Galileo was examining the movement of the planets. H. knew

both men. H. was also seeking a scientific basis for understanding human action, and geometry seemed to him to offer such a foundation. Already in *A Short Treatise on First Principles,* written between 1630 and 1638, H. argued that sensation and behavior result from motion.

H. proposed a universal system of philosophy. *De corpore* (1655) would deal with the physics and psychology of individual bodies. *De homine* (1658) would explain how feelings, thoughts, and desires were the products of internal motions of one human body in contact with other bodies, and *De cive* (1642) would show that the state is the result of bodies moving toward or away from each other.

Political unrest in England prompted H. to turn his attention to this last subject first. In both *De cive* and his better known *Leviathan,* he argued that in a state of nature life is "solitary, poor, nasty, brutish, and short." For self-preservation, individuals accept a social compact in which they relinquish sovereignty in exchange for safety. Sovereignty can reside in a monarch, aristocracy, or democracy, but H. deemed a monarchy the most satisfactory form of government. Fearing that his views would anger the Puritan Parliament, H. fled England in 1640. For the next decade, he moved in French intellectual circles and published on optics (*Opticae liber septimus,* 1644; *A Minute on the First Draught of the Optiques,* 1646), served as mathematics tutor to the Prince of Wales, and wrote a treatise denying free will as inconsistent with H.'s mechanistic views (*Of Libertie and Necessitie,* 1654).

H. denied the right of rebellion, but he maintained that when a sovereign no longer could protect his subjects, allegiance ceased. Hence, in 1651 H. returned to England and reconciled himself with Oliver Cromwell. When Charles II returned to the throne in 1660, he awarded his former tutor a pension of a hundred pounds a year (not always promptly paid) but barred him from publishing on politics and history. During the Protectorate, H. had begun a publication war with Seth Ward, Savilian Professor of Astronomy at Oxford, and John Wallis, Savilian Professor of Mathematics. H. claimed that he had discovered the formula for squaring the circle, and he blamed the universities for fomenting revolution and for promulgating antiquated teachings. These debates continued after the Restoration. H. also attacked Robert Boyle and the Royal Society (*Dialogus Physicus,* 1661). Although barred from publishing about politics, H. wrote a history of the English Civil War, which appeared without license the year of H.'s death (1679), and in 1681 appeared his *Dialogue between a Philosopher and a Student of the Common Laws of England* reaffirming his view that the sovereign is the sole arbiter of legality.

Though most of H.'s work is no longer read, his *Leviathan* continues to prompt debate. H. has been called an atheist and a deist, a Marxist and a monarchist, a radical and a reactionary. Such ongoing argument attests to the vitality of his masterpiece.

BIBLIOGRAPHY: Martinich, A. P., *H.: A Biography* (1999); Rogow, A. A., *T. H.: Radical in the Service of Reaction* (1986); Sorrel, T., ed., *The Cambridge Companion to H.* (1996)

                                    JOSEPH ROSENBLUM

HOBSBAUM, Philip
b. 29 June 1932, London

H. earned a B.A. and M.A. from Cambridge in 1955 and 1961 respectively, and a Ph.D. from Sheffield in 1968. At Cambridge, he studied under the noted critic F. R. LEAVIS and at Sheffield, he was supervised by William EMPSON. He was part-time lecturer and teacher from 1955 to 1959 and lectured in English at Queen's University in Belfast, Northern Ireland, from 1962 to 1966. H. moved to Glasgow, Scotland in 1966 and was lecturer in English, then professor of English at the University of Glasgow. Recently retired from Glasgow, he continues to publish criticism. Although a poet in his own right, H. has developed an extraordinary ability for discovering and fostering the poetic talent of others—most notably the Irish Nobel Prize–winner Seamus HEANEY—through creative writing groups in London, Belfast, and Glasgow. His criticism includes books on Charles DICKENS (1972), D. H. LAWRENCE (1981), Robert Lowell (1988), and several outstanding studies of poetry in English. His study of prosody, *Metre, Rhythm and Verse Form* (1996) is exemplary for its nuanced, jargon-free approach to the technical aspects of poetry.

In 1955, H. founded a creative writing movement in London known as "The Group." From 1955 to 1959, he was chairman at the poetry readings, which were followed by discussions between the poets and the audience. Members of this group included Christopher HAMPTON, Edward LUCIE-SMITH, George MACBETH, Peter PORTER, and Peter REDGROVE, all of whom would become well-known English authors.

H. formed his creative writing group at Queen's University in Belfast in 1963 and it ran under his direction from October of that year until March 1966. He was nervous about attracting a diverse group of writers in Belfast, given the sectarian conditions that prevailed there. H.'s courage in putting together this group in the heart of such a divided city is striking, even given his opportunity to recruit from a broader range of students because of the educational acts of the 1940s in the province.

The Group writers in Belfast met each week, eight times a term, at Queen's. Contributions were distributed in advance so that feedback at a given evening's reading would be thoughtful and informed. Criticism was intensely text-based and specific, and although fiction writers and dramatists participated, the emphasis was always on poetry. The Group aesthetic, promulgated by H., abhorred rhetoric and disdained rhyme. Heaney was clearly H.'s star and his early poetry featured prominently in many meetings.

In 1965, a series of poetry pamphlets featuring poetry by members of H.'s group appeared from *Festival Publications* and garnered a great deal of critical interest. With the publication of poetry by Group members Stewart Parker, Heaney, Michael LONGLEY, and Derek MAHON over the next several years Northern Irish poetry became something of a literary phenomenon that has continued to generate critical and popular accord to this day.

The Belfast Group also prefigured a new, more ecumenical society in Northern Ireland, as Dillon Johnston has pointed out in *Irish Poetry after Joyce*: "the friendship of Catholic poets . . . and Protestant poets serves also as a political model for a new integrated society." Additionally, as Edna Longley has noted, H. "helped to create a recognizable and recognized focus for poetry in the North: a prototype for subsequent literary devolution in the British Isles." Group members in Belfast began to think of themselves as writing from a political, cultural, religious background that was curiously unique to Northern Ireland, just as later group members in Glasgow would begin to conceive of themselves as writing out of a milieu unique to Scotland.

During the early 1970s, H. coordinated a creative writing group in Glasgow that was attended by the now well-known writers Alasdair GRAY, James KELMAN, Tom Leonard, Agnes Owens, and Liz Lochhead. As in the other groups, creative work would be photocopied and distributed in advance for the group to discuss and criticize. Ironically, it has taken an Englishman to promote the literary devolution in Northern Ireland and Scotland that has produced most of the best new "British" literature over the last several decades.

BIBLIOGRAPHY: Heaney, S., "Belfast," in his *Preoccupations: Selected Prose, 1968–1978* (1980): 28–37; Longley, M., "The Empty Holes of Spring: Remembering Trinity and The Group," in his *Tuppenny Stung: Autobiographical Chapters* (1994): 33–42; Longley, E., *The Living Stream: Literature and Revisionism in Ireland* (1994)

                            RICHARD RANKIN RUSSELL

HOBY, [Sir] Thomas
b. 1530, Leonminster, Herefordshire; d. 13 July 1566, Paris, France

H. translated Baldassare Castiglione's *Il Cortegiano* as *The Book of the Courtier* in 1561. Samuel JOHN-

SON, two centuries later, called it "the best book that ever was written upon good breeding." The first edition contained a letter from Sir John CHEKE, dated July 16, 1557. The original, published in Venice in 1528, was in the tradition of the medieval "courtesy book" or manual of good manners. Enormously influential, Castiglione's book became a standard work throughout Europe for that humanistic preoccupation, the education of a gentleman. It gives revealing sidelights on social life, ethics, politics, HUMOR, sports, and relations between the sexes. Its immediate influence was on Sir Thomas ELYOT's *The Book Named the Governor* and Roger Ascham's posthumous *The Schoolmaster* (1570). Among others influenced were Edmund SPENSER, Ben JONSON, and William SHAKE-SPEARE. Lord CHESTERFIELD's *Letters* to his son are in the courtesy book tradition. H.'s translation was edited in 1900 by Walter Raleigh for the "Tudor Translations" series.

HODGSON, William Hope

b. 15 November 1877, Essex; d. 19 April 1918, near Ypres, Belgium

H. was an early-20th-c. author who wrote in a variety of genres—adventure, mystery, fantasy, horror, and SCIENCE FICTION. At age thirteen, H. ran away from boarding school for a life at sea—and his experience as a cabin boy and seaman would later inform much of his fiction as well as his poetry. He published his first novel, *The Boats of the "Glen Carrig,"* in 1907, followed in the next year by the highly praised science fiction allegory *The House on the Borderland.* H.'s vivid imagination and sense of the macabre are best illustrated in the novel *The Night Land*, published in 1912. Commissioned as an officer during World War I, H. was killed in action. Two collections of his poetry appeared posthumously, *The Calling of the Sea* (1920) and *The Voice of the Ocean* (1921).

HOGG, James

b. 25 January 1770, Selkirk, Scotland; d. 21 November 1835, Altrive, Scotland

"The Ettrick Shepherd," as H. was styled, merited "An Extempore Effusion" from William WORDS-WORTH at his death—not a full-blown elegy, but a lament over the death not only of H., but of Wordsworth's other poet friends, recognizing H.'s humble but favored position among them. This may not have been a purposeful demotion by the poet laureate, but a recognition of the special character of this unusual poet who wished to be a popular voice of the people, and who maintained as a point of particular pride that he came from humble beginnings and was entirely self-educated. H. was convinced that since he claimed to share his birthday with Robert BURNS (and may

have manipulated or simply fabricated his birth records in order to sustain that claim), he could succeed as Burns had succeeded, singing in the voices of his countrymen, celebrating their history and their Scots heritage. While he achieved wide popularity and respect during his lifetime, his publications seldom sold as well as he hoped (and needed), and in subsequent generations he suffered first a decline into obscurity and then an ironic restoration to fame for a novel, about a man who may have lived his life under the power and influence of the devil, that was not among his prouder achievements.

H. aspired to be a popular poet; he wrote songs, pastorals and light lyrics, many of which he would perform in public, with or without musical accompaniment; he was primarily a narrative poet, however, writing ballads and narratives in other forms. An early success was his collection of lyrics framed with a narrative and published as *The Queen's Wake* (1813) that includes his most famous poem, "Kilmeny," which portrays the beauty of life in a "faery" world, separate from the sadness of earth. H. enjoyed writing about supernatural and unearthly phenomena, and his popularity seems to have been tied to these "mystical" tales. Later book-length narrative poems included *Mador of the Moor* (1816) and *Queen Hynde* (1825), and he collected a set of parodies of his famous Romantic contemporaries in *The Poetic Mirror* (1817).

H. began life in extreme poverty, gained some financial security from his writing at some periods of his life, but frequent reversals left him dependent on the financial support of admirer and friends. In an effort to secure himself financially, H. began an active career in periodical publication, contributing to *Blackwood's Magazine,* the influential Edinburgh literary journal; he also published numerous prose tales, later collected in *The Brownie of Bodsbech and Other Tales* (1818) and *Winter Evening Tales* (1820). Unfortunately, these did not rescue him from his financial distresses, nor did his novels.

In recent times, H. is best known for his satirical and supernatural novel, *The Private Memoirs and Confessions of a Justified Sinner* (1824). This complicated narrative, told from several points of view, using letters and diary entries, as well as direct narrative (comparable in its "framing" tactics to Mary SHELLEY's *Frankenstein*), satirizes religious fanaticism while exploiting the possibilities of the horror story as it recounts the increasingly evil and destructive behavior of its central character, Robert Wringhim, who is convinced by his "double," Gil-Martin, that he is one of the elect and therefore predestined to go to heaven because he will not be punished and cannot be damned, no matter what he does during his life. Some have seen the influence of the stories of E. T. A. Hoffmann on H.'s narrative (especially *Die Elixir des Teufels,* which was published in English translation in

1824, not long before H. published his work), but the distinctive Scots ambience and the portrayal of Scottish manners is clearly native to H. and more than enough to assure his essential ownership of the narrative.

H. offers many pleasures to the modern reader; his evocation of the life and customs of the Scottish borderlands, his nostalgic recapitulation of beliefs and values tied to the rural areas of 18th-c. Scotland, are comparable to the works of Burns and Sir Walter SCOTT, but H. projects a distinct personality and a different perspective on the materials he has in common with his more famous compatriots. H. is a deft, if not elegant, versifier, and he has a fine eye for the details of his neighbors' lives that make his poems and tales worth rereading.

BIBLIOGRAPHY: Batho, E. C., *The Ettrick Shepherd* (1927); Simpson, L., *J. H.* (1962); Smith, N. C., *J. H.* (1980)

THOMAS F. DILLINGHAM

HOGGART, Richard
b. 24 September 1918, Leeds

One of the most influential figures in the development of media and cultural studies in 20-th c. Britain, H. is best known as the author of the highly acclaimed critical study *The Uses of Literacy* (1957). Educated at the University of Leeds, H. held academic appointments at the University of Hull (1946–59), the University of Leicester (1959–62), and the University of Birmingham (1962–73). In addition, he was the director of the Centre for Contemporary Cultural Studies from 1964 to 1973. Emerging in the late 1950s as an advocate for educational equity and reform, H. sought throughout his career to explore the interrelationship between literature and society as well as the political and commercial structure of contemporary culture. His reputation was further enhanced with the publication of *On Culture and Communication* (1972), *The Way We Live Now* (1995; repub. as *The Tyranny of Relativism*, 1998), and *First and Last Things* (1999). In 1988, H. published the first of three volumes of autobiography, *A Local Habitation*, followed by *A Sort of Clowning* (1990) and *An Imagined Life* (1992).

HOLINSHED [or HOLINGSHED], Raphael
fl. 1560–78; d. ca. 1580, possibly at Bramcote

Probably member of a Cheshire family, H. may have been the man of that surname who graduated from Christ's College, Cambridge, in 1544. About 1560, H. came to London and was employed as a translator on a project for a universal history, which dwindled into the *Chronicles of England, Scotland and Ireland* (2 vols., 1577). William SHAKESPEARE apparently used the 1581 edition, which offended Queen ELIZABETH

I, as source for most of the history plays, and also for *Macbeth, King Lear*, and part of *Cymbeline*.

HOLLINGHURST, Alan
b. 26 May 1954, Stroud

As a poet and novelist, H.'s reputation was firmly established with the publication of his first critically acclaimed novel, *The Swimming Pool Library*, in 1988. The novel was one of the first modern British novels by a mainstream press that dealt with an exclusively homosexual world. Though some critics complained that its subject matter limited its appeal, few could deny the stunningly elegant style with which the book was written.

H. earned both a B.A. and a M.Litt. at Oxford, and remained to teach there from 1977 through 1981; he began teaching at the University of London in 1982, while also assuming a position as a deputy editor at the *Times Literary Supplement* where he remained for eight years. His first publication was a volume of verse entitled *Confidential Chats with Boys* (1982), and the book was so well received by the literary establishment that Faber and Faber offered him a contract for another book of poetry. What he gave them instead was the novel called *The Swimming Pool Library*; his verse translation of the French dramatist Jean Racine's play *Bajazet* was published by Chatto and Windus in 1991.

The plot of *The Swimming Pool Library* traces, quite vividly, the sexual adventures of the handsome young protagonist, William Beckwith, but a secondary story emerges after Beckwith saves the life of the eighty-year-old Lord Nantwich in a public men's room. The two become friends and Lord Nantwich asks young Beckwith to write his biography, an assignment he accepts. But in the course of reading Nantwich's memoirs he realizes the problems of being a homosexual at the beginning of the 20th c. He further discovers that his grandfather had been one of the principal prosecutors of gay men during Nantwich's youth and was responsible for sending him to prison. H. juxtaposes the enormous differences in the fearful lifestyles of older gay men with the relative comfort of his own gay generation's freedom. Sympathetic critics praised the book for its honest and unapologetic celebration of gay sexuality; gay novelist Edmund White found it a worthy successor to Jean Genet's *Notre Dame des fleurs* (1944; *Our Lady of the Flowers*, 1949) and Vladimir Nabokov's *Lolita* (1955).

H.'s next novel, *The Folding Star* (1994), was also acclaimed by most commentators and was shortlisted for the Booker Prize in 1994. It won the prestigious James Tait Memorial Book Prize for fiction; the Lambda Award for gay men's fiction, and the American Library Association Gay, Lesbian, and Bisexual

Book Award. *The Folding Star* concerns the life of a homosexual British tutor, Edward Manners, and his infatuation with one of his students, Luc Altidore, a seventeen-year-old Flemish tempter who may remind readers of a less innocent version of Thomas Mann's "Tadziu" from *Death of Venice*. The relationship with his students becomes even more complex when Manners discovers that the father of another student had an affair with a German soldier in World War II.

H.'s third novel, *The Spell* (1998), departs in some ways from his two earlier novels. H. has pared down his usual brilliantly detailed prose style into a more austere one, and the plot and action became much more structured than the series of random sexual encounters that made up his first two works. Missing are the usual witty, sophisticated Oxfordian banter between beautiful young gay men. The story concerns the lives of four middle-class gay men in London during the 1990s. Several of them are heavily involved in the drug ecstasy, but all of them are alternately sexually desperate or bored even as they experiment with different couplings among themselves. The "spell" of the title alludes to their use of ecstasy in vivifying their dull lives and in transforming their sexual escapades into visionary revelations that they hope will become a permanent form of consciousness.

BIBLIOGRAPHY: Bradley, J. R., "Disciples of St. Narcissus: In Praise of A. H.," *CritR* 36 (1996): 3–18; Hopes, D., "A. H.," in Moseley, M., ed., *British Novelists since 1960*, Third Series, *DLB* 207 (1999): 138–43

PATRICK MEANOR

HOLROYD, Michael [de Courcy Fraser]
b. 27 August 1935, London

After his parents divorced, H. was reared by his elderly paternal grandparents. His family background is fully investigated and described in his recent autobiographical memoir, *Basil Street Blues* (1999). Since his father did not wish him to go to University, after leaving Eton College, H. worked as an articled clerk in a solicitor's office for two years before joining the army. He left the army in 1958 and from then on concentrated on a career as a professional writer.

While in the army, H. came across the works of William GERHARDIE and read most of them and an introduction to the author led to a long and fruitful friendship. Not only did Gerhardie introduce him into literary London but he also encouraged him to write the first critical biography of his friend Hugh KINGSMILL, the novelist, biographer, and literary critic. H. described himself as having "read English literature at Maidenhead Public Library," which is where he read the works written by Kingsmill and did much of the research for his biography. *Hugh Kingsmill: A*

Critical Biography was published in 1964 and was respectfully, though not widely, reviewed. Gerhardie published an over-enthusiastic review in the *Spectator* in which he described the biography as "authoritative" as well as "entrancing and singularly profound." A more sober reviewer in the *Times Literary Supplement* described it as "an admirable study of an original, complex and enigmatic personality."

On the strength of this biography, he was commissioned to write a revaluation of the work of Lytton STRACHEY, but when Strachey's brother James allowed him access to his papers he decided to write a comprehensive biography that would "provide a selection of the best of Lytton's letters . . . attempt a completely original reappraisal of his work . . . [and] present a panorama of the social and intellectual environment of a remarkable generation." He was also determined to give his subject's love life the same prominence in his book as it had in his life and career. The two-volume edition of *Lytton Strachey: A Critical Biography* was published in 1967–68. It was widely reviewed and generally acclaimed. A good deal of discussion centered on the manner in which H. dealt with Strachey's homosexuality and he was charged with being too reticent by some and too blatant by others. Noel Annan in a more balanced assessment described the biography as "a remarkable achievement. He is the first to begin to make a map of Bloomsbury and to establish the identity of the minor as well as the major characters." Annan was not alone in noticing H.'s lack of critical intelligence though recognizing that the writing of BIOGRAPHY demands other virtues. The work was outstandingly successful and established H.'s reputation as a biographer. It was also commercially successful and quickly published in a paperback version. H.'s biography demonstrates a remarkable ability to master a wealth of heterogeneous materials and to deal with events in detail without losing touch with the narrative framework or losing his readers' interest. The character of Strachey in all its contradictions emerges convincingly as the biography progresses while the other characters surrounding Strachey are not only authentic in their own right but also authenticate the character of Strachey. At the end of the biography with the death of its subject and the suicide of Dora Carrington, H. achieves a rare pathos without seeming to manipulate either the reader's response or the actuality of the events. The biography carries conviction not only because of H.'s mastery in marshaling the multiplicity of facts but also because the narrative sweep of Strachey's life is brought to a satisfactory conclusion, a moving death followed by a coda that seems to confirm its significance.

H. followed his biography of Strachey by writing the biography of the artist Augustus John (2 vols., 1974–75; rev. ed., 1996), widely criticized for its length. Kenneth Clark voiced a general complaint when he commented "The book has only one fault: it is too long." Denys Sutton emphasized the point: "His book might have gained in quality if he had used the blue pencil." Nonetheless, it was also widely agreed that the biography combined scholarship with an absorbing story. H. took particular pleasure in describing John's many love affairs and the women with whom he was involved. Yet central to the design of the book—and the design of John's life—are his wife, Dorelia John, who is presented as both beautiful and enigmatic, and his sister Gwen, a remote and haunting presence, and perhaps in the end the more gifted artist.

H. was invited by the Shaw Trustees to write the official biography of Bernard SHAW, the first volume of which, entitled *The Search for Love,* was published in 1988. This was followed by two further volumes, *The Pursuit of Power* (1989) and *The Lure of Fantasy* (1991). He succeeded in his aim of capturing the interest of the general reader by presenting Shaw as immediately as possible without the distractions of references, sources, or footnotes, which he published separately. He concentrated on the narrative of Shaw's life. As James Sutherland said for H. "the tale is all . . . Shaw sought for love, and never found it . . . pursues power and never possesses it" and the lure of fantasy similarly disappoints. He concludes that the biography is a masterpiece of narrative efficiency. The reviewers were generally agreed that the biography is first and foremost readable with as Richard Holmes says "the swift, complex life of a novel of manners . . . If he does not make us like Shaw, he makes us understand him." H. published a fourth volume of his biography outlining Shaw's "posthumous" life, which was well described by E. S. Turner as a "lively and witty, if a shade emaciated, postscript to his three-volume biography. It offers an engaging rundown on those who, in the past forty years, defied or defended the playwright's wishes, or those who used him to give lift-off or fulfillment to their careers." A fifth volume, entitled *The Shaw Companion,* giving source notes, acknowledgments, and cumulative index, was published in 1992.

H. followed his biographies by editing selections of his subjects' work. The results were *The Best of Hugh Kingsmill* (1970); *Lytton Strachey by Himself: A Self-Portrait* (1971); *The Shorter Strachey* (1980), with Paul Levy; *The Art of Augustus John* (1974), with Malcolm Easton; and Shaw's *Major Critical Essays* (1986). In 1973, he republished a selection of his articles and reviews under the title *Unreceived Opinions.* His only novel, *A Dog's Life,* was published in the U.S. in 1969 but was never republished or published in Britain because, he said, his father threatened to sue him for libel. Presumably, he found his son's portrait of the family too close to personal experience for comfort thus confirming that his one attempt at fiction turned out to be biography after all.

BIBLIOGRAPHY: Jones, A. R., "M. H.," in Serafin, S., ed., *Twentieth-Century British Literary Biography, DLB* 155 (1995): 167–79

A. R. JONES

HOLTBY, Winifred

b. 23 June 1898, Rudstone, Yorkshire; d. 29 September 1935, London

Feminist and pacifist, H. interrupted her studies at Somerville College, Oxford, during World War I to serve with the Women's Auxiliary Army Corps in France, and later lectured widely on political issues. H.'s most famous work is the novel *South Riding* (1936), set in an imaginary region of Yorkshire and dealing with a community. Its originality lies in its framework of local government. In her dedication to H.'s mother, Alderman Alice Holtby, H. explains that the novel deals with the way "apparently academic and impersonal resolutions passed in a county council were daily revolutionizing the lives of those men and women whom they affected. The complex tangle of motives prompting public decisions, the unforeseen consequences of their enactment on private lives appeared to me as part of the unseen pattern of the English landscape." Other novels include *Anderby Wold* (1923), *The Crowded Street* (1924), *The Land of Green Ginger* (1927), *Poor Caroline* (1931), and *Mandoa, Mandoa!*(1933), which satirizes European influence in Africa. H. also authored a critical study of Virginia WOOLF (1932) and two books of short stories, *Truth Is Not Sober* (1934) and *Pavements at Anderby*, published posthumously in 1937.

HOOD, Thomas

b. 23 May 1799, London; d. 3 May 1845, London

H. is best known for his single volume of Romantic poetry, his large body of comic verse, and two poems of social protest written late in life. H.'s literary career began with the publication of *Odes and Addresses to Great People* (1825), coauthored with John Hamilton REYNOLDS, and *Whims and Oddities* (1826). These early volumes reveal H.'s comic powers and his exploitation of narrative verse, outrageous plays on words, and a curious combination of the absurd and the grotesque. Among the most memorable of his early poems are the punning "Faithless Nelly Gray" (1826) and the grotesquely apocalyptic *The Last Man* (1826).

In 1827, H. showed a completely different side of his genius when he published *The Plea of the Midsummer Fairies.* This volume is obviously H.'s attempt to establish himself as a serious Romantic poet, and it is a very impressive collection. The ambitious title poem is essentially a defense of ROMANTICISM. Two other long poems, *Lycus the Centaur* and *Hero and Leander,* deal with Romantic love that in H.'s rather dark poems fails to be redemptive. All three of these poems are remarkable for their technical finish, their Keatsian lushness, and their seriousness of theme.

The shorter poems in *Midsummer Fairies* are among H.'s best. His "Ode: Autumn" is indebted to John KEATS but has its own power; "The Sea of Death" is a haunting expression of Romantic melancholy; "Silence" is a sonnet of extraordinary beauty, and "I Remember, I Remember" is a classic expression of Romantic longing for lost innocence.

Despite its manifest quality, *Midsummer Fairies* was commercially unsuccessful, and H. had little choice but to return to more popular modes. H. soon produced two annuals, the *Gem* (1829) and the *Comic Annual* (1830), for which he wrote popular light verse, but in the *Gem* he also showed a gift for melodramatic horror in *The Dream of Eugene Aram* (1831). This poem is a grim narrative dealing rather crudely but effectively with the psychology of a murderer. The compelling if unsubtle power of *Eugene Aram* looks forward to some of H.'s later serious verse.

Ill health and poverty began to afflict H. in the late 1830s, but he nevertheless continued his flow of mainly comic verse. "Domestic Asides" (1839) and "Sally Simpkin's Lament" (1839) are typical of this period. Also, between 1841 and 1843 H. published *Miss Kilmansegg*, a long and energetic SATIRE on Victorian materialism. In his last years, H. produced two remarkable protest poems: "The Song of the Shirt" (1843) and "The Bridge of Sighs" (1844).

Generally speaking, H.'s short comic poems of his last period are marked by the qualities that first made him a famous comic poet: facetiousness, extravagant puns, inventive versification, ballad narratives, and comedy often based on violence, death, and the macabre. In *Miss Kilmansegg* and other late satiric verse, there is a social realism, moral seriousness, and HUMOR that link these poems with the early Victorian novel. H.'s poems of social protest also belong to the early Victorian period, in which they were tremendously popular. The "Song of the Shirt" is indeed an unforgettable protest against dehumanizing working conditions, and "The Bridge of Sighs" is similarly forceful in its attack on Victorian moral smugness.

Critics have debated whether H. was a talented Romantic poet who was forced into comedy and melodrama or a comic genius who outgrew an early Romantic phase. Perhaps the best view is that H. was a gifted poet whose variety should not be held against him. He was both an important late Romantic poet and a writer whose gifts for comedy and melodrama

helped create the early Victorian literary world. His achievement as a whole deserves wider appreciation.

BIBLIOGRAPHY: Clubbe, J., *Victorian Forerunner: The Later Career of T. H.* (1968); Heath-Stubbs, J., *The Darkling Plain* (1950); Jerrold, W., *T. H.* (1907); Reid, J. C., *T. H.* (1953)

PHILLIP B. ANDERSON

HOOKER, Richard

b. March 1554, Heavitree, Exeter; d. 2 November 1600, Bishopsbourne

One of Protestantism's greatest theologians, H. is the author of the most important 16th-c. defense of the Church of England, *Of the Laws of Ecclesiastical Polity* (1593, 1597, 1648, 1662). A key early influence on H.'s thought was Bishop John Jewel, an ardent supporter of the Elizabethan religious settlement. In 1568, through Jewel's patronage, H. entered Oxford, where he received a humanistic education. After taking orders in 1581 and serving for a time as a minister in Buchinghamshire, H. became master of London's Temple Church in 1585. Theological controversy soon erupted between H. and the Temple's afternoon lecturer, the well-known Presbyterian Walter Travers. Travers and his fellow Presbyterians contended that the Bible should serve as the sole guide for all human action. Thus they called for the abolition of the hierarchical organization of the English Church because they found no scriptural basis for it. For the same reason, they rejected many of the Church's ceremonies. In 1591, H. requested a country benefice so that he could focus on producing a comprehensive response to the positions advanced by the Presbyterians.

Of the Laws of the Ecclesiastical Polity, one of the most intellectually demanding English religious texts of the 16th c., presents the case for the Church of England over the course of eight lengthy books. The first four books were published in 1593, the fifth in 1597, the sixth and eighth in 1648, and the seventh in 1662. Book 1 introduces the most important concept in H.'s philosophical system, the law of nature, which he defines as the embodiment of God's infinite reason. H. posits an essentially rational universe governed by natural law; even after the Fall, he argues, human beings can discern natural law through the use of reason. In book 2, H. takes on the Presbyterians' Scripturalism. H. asserts that natural law, which supplements, clarifies, and affirms Scripture, is also a valid guide for human action. H. goes on to argue that "the laws of nature and of God" are the basis for all laws in a Christian society. After showing that Scripture does not prescribe a form of church government, H. concludes in book 3 that, through "discourse of reason aided with the influence of divine grace," the lawful authorities of England have formulated the appropriate ordinances for governing the church. In the next four books, H. attempts to demonstrate the reasonableness of the various elements of the Church of England that the Presbyterians had attacked. Books 4 and 5 focus on the ceremonies of the English Church, book 6 church discipline, and book 7 the episcopacy. In recent years, scholars have paid particular attention to book 8, which deals with the powers of the magistrate. In the book, H. presents a view of governance that is in sharp contrast to the divine right ideology espoused by the Tudors. H. asserts that the English monarch's power is strictly limited by law; for H., public acceptance is the basis of the monarch's authority. In composing the *Polity*, H. drew upon an extraordinary range of authorities. Unlike most other Protestant theologians, H. made extensive use of the philosophical system of St. Thomas Aquinas; indeed, many historians regard H. as an early modern Thomist.

H. is generally considered to be one of the finest writers of the early modern period. Clarity and control are the chief characteristics of H.'s style. His prose is thoroughly Ciceronian: his sentences are marked by the inversion of word order, the employment of parallelism, subordination, and pleonasm, and the suspension of the sense. Few English prose writers use repetition more effectively—anaphora, epistrophe, ploche, and anadiplosis are favorite H. devices. He never uses a rhetorical figure for its own sake, but always to clarify and to intensify his meaning. In his own day, H. was justifiably praised for avoiding affected language. H. also avoids the inflammatory religious rhetoric that was so prevalent in the 16th and 17th cs. Although he is occasionally caustic, he is for the most part eloquent and calm.

BIBLIOGRAPHY: Davies, E. T., *The Political Ideas of R. H.* (1946); Faulkner, R. K., *R. H. and the Politics of a Christian England* (1981); Hill, W. S., ed., *Studies in R. H.* (1972); Sisson, C. J., *The Judicious Marriage of Mr. Hooker and the Birth of "The Laws of the Ecclesiastical Polity"* (1940)

T. D. DRAKE

HOPE, Anthony

(pseud. of Sir Anthony Hope Hawkins) b. 9 February 1863, London; d. 8 July 1933, Walton-on-the-Hill, Surrey

H. added an indispensable term to the language: "Ruritania," described in *Chambers Dictionary* as "a fictitious land of historical romance (in S.E. Europe) discovered by A. H." Noël COWARD described his own play *The Queen Was in the Parlour* (1926) as "my one and only expedition into Ruritania," acknowledging his debt to H. and admitting that his play would be old-fashioned long before H.'s *The Prisoner of Zenda* (1894) and its sequel *Rupert of Hentzau*

(1898). George MacDonald FRASER likewise acknowledges H.'s influence: he attributes the similarity of plot in *Royal Flash* to *The Prisoner of Zenda* to General Flashman having drunkenly revealed to "young Hawkins, the lawyer" the secret of his involvement with Bismarck in a royal imposture at the time of the Schleswig-Holstein conflict.

H. had published three now forgotten novels in the intervals of his successful law practice before 1894, but the success of *Zenda*, followed in the same year by *The Dolly Dialogues* (sketches contributed to the *Westminster Gazette*, reprinted in one volume), led H. to embrace full-time authorship. The *Dialogues* are tales about a flirtatious countess with a past and her circle, told by one of her old admirers. These tales, with hints of adulteries in high life, probably struck contemporaries as daring. They were amusing enough to be reprinted several times up to the late 1960s. H. published several more novels of the "Ruritanian" type, but none has lasted so well as *Zenda,* which has remained constantly in print.

The stage adaptation of *Rupert of Hentzau* opened at the Lyceum Theater in New York in 1898 and in London at the St. James Theatre in 1900. *The Prisoner of Zenda* had three silent film versions, the best-known made in 1922, directed by Rex Ingram, with Lewis Stone (who played a supporting role in the sound version of 1952) in the lead dual role, and Ramon Navarro as Rupert of Hentzau. Sound versions appeared in 1937, directed by John Cromwell, W. S. Van Dyke, and George Cukor, with Ronald Colman, Douglas Fairbanks, Jr., Madeleine Carroll, David Niven, C. Aubrey Smith, Mary Astor, Raymond Massey; in 1952, directed by Richard Thorpe, with Stewart Granger, James Mason, Deborah Kerr, Louis Calhern; and an unsuccessful spoof version in 1979, with Peter Sellers and Lynne Frederick, directed by Richard Quine, scripted by Dick Clement and Ian La Frenais. *Royal Flash* was filmed in 1975, directed by Richard Lester, scripted by Fraser from his own novel, starring Malcolm McDowell, Alan Bates, Britt Ekland, and Oliver Reed.

BIBLIOGRAPHY: Holmes, J. R., "A. H.," in Naufflus, W. F., ed., *British Short-Fiction Writers, 1880–1914: The Romantic Tradition, DLB* 156 (1996): 162–69; Mallet, C., *A. H. and His Books* (1935)

MICHAEL GROSVENOR MYER

HOPKINS, Gerard Manley

b. 28 July 1844, London; d. 8 June 1889, Dublin, Ireland

Parallel to the practices of the Roman Catholic Church, to which he converted from Anglicanism in 1866 and within which he subsequently became a Jesuit priest, the canonization of H.'s poetry occurred posthumously. Largely unpublished and unread during his lifetime, H. has since the publication of his *Poems* in 1918 become one of the most respected and popular of Victorian poets. While it was H.'s old friend the poet Robert BRIDGES who arranged for his poems to be published, it was mainly the younger generation with its modernist taste for literary experiment that first championed his work. His reputation was further enhanced with the publication in the 1930s of most of his extant letters, and some of the early diaries, journals, early essays and notes, and religious writings. The formal innovations of the poetry that resonated so strongly with the modernists are still central to criticism of the poet, as are his religious beliefs and ideas, which were brought to the fore by his early Roman Catholic critics. Recent criticism has, however, related such considerations to the ways in which H. engages passionately with the intellectual, social and cultural life of his day.

H. was born into comfortable middle-class circumstances in Hampstead, London, and was among the first generation of middle-class young men to go to Oxford, where from 1863 to 1867 he studied classics and philosophy. The influences of John KEATS in particular, but also Christina ROSSETTI, John Henry NEWMAN, and Coventry PATMORE can be discerned in poetry from this time. Upon deciding to enter the Society of Jesus in May 1868, he renounced poetry composition and allowed himself to write no further poems until 1875, when at the suggestion of a superior he wrote *The Wreck of the Deutschland*. This, his longest poem, establishes a radical new poetic that he practices for the rest of his life in the so-called mature poetry for which he is best known.

The distinctiveness of H.'s poetry after 1875 can be traced not so much to the poetry of his youth as to his early notes and speculations on language, nature and philosophy in the early diaries, journals and undergraduate essays. All of this work culminates in the doctrine of "instress" and "inscape" he formulates in early 1868, in some notes on the pre-Socratic philosopher Parmenides. H. draws upon classical and modern metaphysics and contemporary concepts of energy in his conception of ubiquitous and dynamic being, which he terms "stress." God is the source and upholder of all being or stress, which is accordingly regarded by H. as a form of grace. H.'s coinage "instress" refers to instances of such stress or being, the pattern of energy that sustains and defines an individual being. "Inscape" describes the complete principle of the form of such a being, the way in which the pattern of energy is manifest in matter, which we perceive in its "scapes" or appearances. These distinctive coinages also explain and describe how we can know the truth or form of such being. Through our shared being or "stress" we can ourselves "instress" the being of another, and "inscape" its definitive form.

H.'s principle of instress is meant to describe every instance of determinate being, every coherent thing, including that peculiar pattern of stresses, the poem. H. emphasizes the importance of reading poetry, especially his poetry, aloud so that we give the matter of words breath, rather as in the Bible God breathed life into the clay of Adam. The emphasis required in declaiming instances of metrical stress demands a greater and more rapid expiration of breath: "Is out with it! Oh,/We lash with the best or worst/Word last!" H. sees his poetry to not only testify to being, but to participate in it, and more than this to accentuate and intensify it. He accordingly makes stressed syllables the focus of his prosody. His system of "Sprung Rhythm" makes a single stress the measure of each foot, which may accordingly consist of an isolated stress or a stress with up to three (and sometimes more) "slack" or unstressed syllables. H. describes poetry as the inscape of ordinary speech and sees sprung rhythm to intensify it, make it more "stressy" and "lustrous." The formal flexibility and experimentalism of H.'s verse extends to modifications of the sonnet form, to which he adds extra codas and longer lines (or "outriders"), as in for example, "That Nature is a Heraclitean Fire and of the comfort of the Resurrection" (wr. 1888).

H.'s sprung rhythm places stress, the energy of emphasis, at the heart of poetry, where it functions along with other formal accentuations of the physicality and musicality of poetry, such as alliteration and assonance, to express a dynamic world of nature: "Nothing is so beautiful as Spring—/When weeds, in wheels, shoot long and lovely and lush." The poem "Spring" from which this extract is taken, and the others he also wrote in 1877 during his happy period at St. Beuno's College, Wales (1874–77), such as "The Windhover," "Pied Beauty," and "God's Grandeur," highlight his use of poetry to celebrate nature as Creation, as assurance of God's ubiquitous and benign presence in the world. Subsequent poems such as "The Leaden Echo and the Golden Echo" (wr. 1880–82) and "Spelt from Sybil's Leaves" (wr. 1884), are distinguished by their lyrical compression, often to the point of words being piled upon each other in apparent disconnection: "Earnest, earthless, equal, attuneable, vaulty, voluminous, . . . stupendous/ Earth strains to be tíme's vást, womb-of-all, home-of-all, hearse-of-all night" ("Spelt from Sybil's Leaves"). The pessimistic tone of this description of the world after sunset, densely packed with syllables and heavy stresses, belongs to 1884, the start of H.'s unhappy period in Dublin, in which he wrote the so-called terrible sonnets or sonnets of desolation. Such poems as "No worst, there is none" and "To seem the stranger lies my lot" (wr. ca. 1885) hark back to the expressions of religious doubt and confusion and personal loneliness in many of the early poems, but with all the intensity that the formal achievements of the later poetry enabled him to convey.

BIBLIOGRAPHY: Gardner, W. H., *G. M. H.* (2 vols., 1944, 1949); Lawler, J. G., *H. Re-Constructed* (1998); Miller, J. H., "H.," in his *The Linguistic Moment* (1985): 229–66; White, N., *H.* (1992)

                                        DANIEL BROWN

HOPKINS, John. See under STERNHOLD, Thomas

HORNBY, Nick
b. 17 April 1957, London

H. occupies the privileged position of a best-selling author who is also much respected by reviewers. His work offers a witty, affectionately critical portrait of contemporary masculinity, desire, communication (especially between men and women), and British pop culture. Stylistically, he is sometimes compared to Martin AMIS and Irvine WELSH, but he also shares Helen Fielding's sense of late-20th-c. isolation amid chaos. His characters are frequently self-destructive but generally loveable and his universe—north London—is largely white and middle-class.

H.'s first book, *Fever Pitch* (1992), offers a sustained and brilliant analysis not of football (soccer), but of "the consumption of football." His analysis of fandom and the culture surrounding the game incorporates precise and often hilarious observations about the British class system, 1970s suburbia, contemporary masculinity, and the nature of obsession. *Fever Pitch* defies generic categorization, melding memoir and confessional journalism with sociological perspective and the fierce passion of a thoroughly besotted—but self-conscious—football fan. The book stands alone in contemporary sports writing for its alternately indulgent participation in and stringent scrutiny of fan behavior and its sharp description of "the hatred and anger of fandom"; entertainment as pain. The forceful intelligence and highly engaging tone of *Fever Pitch* earned it high critical acclaim, bestseller status and the William Hill Sports Book of the Year Award in 1992. H. later wrote the screenplay for the 1997 film version of the book, also called *Fever Pitch*.

High Fidelity (1995), H.'s debut novel, also met with both critical and popular approval. Here, H. continues his robustly comic analysis of masculinity, obsession, maturity, and 1970s suburban England, but his vision is rather darker. His narrator and protagonist, Rob, struggles with the unattractive paradox of being a thirty-five-year-old adolescent who is apparently still scarred by "that terrible war-torn interregnum between the first pubic hair and the first soiled Trojan." Rob's reflections on desire, fear, death and control reflect the same willful inconsistencies that are delightful in the context of *Fever Pitch*, but appear menacing once the focus of this obsession shifts from a football team to a single woman, Laura. The novel's title puns on Rob's obsession with his record collection and devout musical snobbery as well as his struggle to build a balanced adult love relationship.

Although the novel is ostensibly about Rob's relationship with Laura, it focuses most intensely on Rob's solipsism. H.'s success is such that readers are both charmed by Rob's slacker appeal and dismayed by his lazy cruelty, both of which emerge through Rob's frank narcissism. The novel was also made into a film of the same title (1999).

H.'s second novel, *About a Boy* (1998), continues this analysis of the man-child paradox and the pain of growing up, this time through the twin perspectives of Marcus, an oddly adult twelve year old, and Will, another thirty-something slacker who refuses to grow up. H.'s first attempt at an omniscient third-person narrator seems stilted at times. The rich, vigorous demotic of *Fever Pitch* and *High Fidelity* gives way to simple declarative sentences that mimic more childish speech. This shift is somewhat confusing, since only half the story is told from Marcus' perspective; although Will is in many ways a shallower, more complacent Rob (from *High Fidelity*), he is not as naive as the language of the narrative seems to imply. And while H. is still eloquent on the subject of male sexual desire and meandering thought processes, Will's and Marcus' eventual conversions to acting more their age are less than convincing.

The first-person narrator of *How to Be Good* (2001) is Katie, a smugly respectable doctor living in north London. Katie's self-congratulatory "goodness" receives a rude shock when her husband, David ("The Angriest Man in Holloway"), undergoes a moral transformation at the hands of a spiritual healer called GoodNews. Cynical, snarky David promptly quits his job, invites GoodNews to move in, and begins ministering to the poor, ill, and unlovable. Katie's narrative focuses on her quest to salvage some certainties, her confession that she is "heartily sick of liberalism," and her attempts to justify her now apparent selfish heartlessness. The genial comedy of H.'s first two novels gives way here to a darker examination of love, hypocrisy, and ethical certainties. Some critics find David's conversion (GoodNews's healing powers are never explained) a clumsy device that overbalances the rest of the novel. Even more troublesome, however, is Katie's ultimate regeneration and her closing optimism that, given books, music, and the time to enjoy them, she may find her way back to some form of redefined goodness.

H. is also the editor of *My Favorite Year: A Collection of Football Writing* (1993), *The Picador Book of*

Sportswriting (1996), with Nick Coleman, and *Speaking with the Angel* (2001), a collection of short fiction.

BIBLIOGRAPHY: Moseley, M., "N. H.," in Moseley, M., ed., *British Novelists since 1960*, Third Series, *DLB* 207 (1999): 144–48

YING S. LEE

HOROVITZ, Michael
b. 4 April 1935, Frankfurt, Germany

Poet, editor, performer (with jazzman Stan Tracey), H. emigrated to England in 1937 and was educated at Brasenose College, Oxford. He edited *Children of Albion: Poetry of the "Underground" in Britain* (1969) and is publisher of the magazine *New Departures,* described as the most substantial avant-garde magazine in Great Britain. His books include *The Wolverhampton Wanderer* (1971), *Growing Up: Selected Poems and Pictures, 1951–1979* (1979), and *Wordsounds and Sightlines: New and Selected Poems* (1994).

HOUGHTON, [William] Stanley
b. 22 February 1881, Ashton-upon-Mersey; d. 11 December 1913, Manchester

Like Harold BRIGHOUSE, H. was a product of Annie Horniman's Manchester Gaiety Theatre, where most of his plays were first produced. A prolific writer, he is now best remembered for *Hindle Wakes* (1912), a pioneer "new woman" play in which H.'s preoccupation with the generation gap is illustrated: Fanny Hawthorn, a mill-girl, has a weekend affair with the boss's son and then confounds expectation by refusing to compromise her happiness by marriage for the sake of appearances to someone she doesn't love. An early post-Ibsen liberated female, she sees no reason why she should "make an honest man of him" at the cost of her own freedom. The refusal to marry was courageous indeed at the time, when sexual relations outside marriage could ruin a woman's reputation, blighting her prospects of marriage to anybody else; as dramatic material it was daring (turned down by the Liverpool Repertory Theatre as too outspoken). Until the 1950s, outward respectability was essential and hypocrisy widespread. Fanny's clearsightedness and sense of self-worth are inspiring. Here is the first working-class heroine in British drama, brave and independent, and few plays previously had been set in the industrial north of England. H.'s plays celebrate youthful rebellion, erosion of class barriers and a new, more honest, morality. The play has no villains: the young man's father, the girl's parents, and the young man all behave impeccably; the mill owner's determination that his son shall do right even at the cost of an advantageous marriage is thwarted by the girl's own principled refusal to be done right by. The *Dictionary of National Biography* describes *Hindle Wakes* as perhaps the greatest play of its time. The 1928 silent film version was successfully revived in 2000 at London's National Film Theatre with a new musical score.

H.'s success was linked with a remarkable development in the English theater. Annie Horniman moved from Dublin, where she had worked with W. B. YEATS at the Abbey Theatre, to northwest England. From 1904 to 1907, the Court Theatre in London had presented thirty new plays, a theater of NATURALISM and of ideas. This was a challenge to what has been described as the stale declamatory syrup of the mainstream London theater. Miss Horniman's project was to energize the provinces by drawing on local writers and local life. In 1907, she founded the first regional repertory company at the Midland Theatre, Manchester. Within six months, she had acquired the Gaiety Theatre and appealed to local writers to provide plays of interest to Lancashire people. Manchester was the world center of the cotton-spinning industry, yet apart from Elizabeth Cleghorn GASKELL's novels *Mary Barton* and *North and South* almost nothing had been written about the workers in the mills. H. worked in his father's cotton business, mixing with shipping merchants, cloth barons, financiers, shop assistants, clerks, and customers. Most of his work deals, with sympathy and insight, with ordinary people. H. gave a voice to the new feminist consciousness. He was an enthusiastic amateur actor and director.

Some of H.'s one-act comedies are occasionally performed, notably another play about generational conflict, *The Dear Departed* (perf. 1908; pub. 1910), which, like John Millington SYNGE's *The Shadow of the Glen,* concerns a patriarch erroneously believed by his family to be dead; a social comedy, *Marriages in the Making* (perf. 1909), about minor society in Cheshire; *The Perfect Cure* (perf. 1913); *The Fifth Commandment* (1913); *Fancy Free* (perf. 1911; pub. 1912). Another comedy, *The Younger Generation* (1910), a study of middle-class life in Lancashire, whose theme is implicit in its title, is also still occasionally revived. Like his friend and colleague Brighouse, H. worked as unpaid drama critic and book reviewer for the *Manchester Guardian*. H. and Brighouse also collaborated on a play, *The Hillarys* (1915).

BIBLIOGRAPHY: Bain, J., "W. S. H. (1881–1913)," in Demastes, W., and K. E. Kelly, eds., *British Playwrights, 1860–1956* (1996): 213–24; Brighouse, H., ed., *The Works of S. H.* (3 vols., 1914); Mortimer, P., "W. S. H.: An Introduction and Bibliography," *MD* 28 (September 1985): 474–89

MICHAEL GROSVENOR MYER

HOUSMAN, A[lfred] E[dward]
b. 26 March 1859, Fockbury, Worcestershire; d. 30 April 1936, Cambridge

H. published only two books of poetry during his lifetime, but they included some of the most moving and popular poems of his time. He himself recognized "the narrow measure" of his work, but he was also right in saying that it captured, "tears of eternity and sorrow, not mine, but man's." H. has been brilliantly parodied and sometimes dismissed as a poet for adolescents, but his admirers have included both the foremost practitioners of formal verse, such as W. H. AUDEN and Wendy COPE, and eminent artists in other forms, including Ralph Vaughan Williams and George Butterworth, who set his works to music, and Tom STOPPARD, who wrote a play about him.

H.'s childhood was not a happy one. His beloved mother died when he was twelve, and he had little in common with his father, a solicitor who fancied himself a country squire. Nevertheless, he was an excellent student at Bromsgrove School and won a scholarship to St. John's College, Oxford. At Oxford, he at first excelled in his studies in classics, making Propertius his specialty, and received first-class honors on his first public examination. He also developed friendships that would shape the rest of his life. The most important of these friendships was with Moses Jackson, whose subject was science and whose orientation was heterosexual. H. fell in love with him, and the emotional crisis he experienced after Jackson failed to return his affection may have caused his disastrous performance on his final examinations in 1881, in which he failed to earn even a pass degree, much less honors. He may also have simply neglected the parts of the curriculum that did not interest him. While he received a pass degree the following year, his hopes for an academic career were dashed, and he spent more than a year at his father's home preparing for the civil service examination.

In 1882, H. received a position as a clerk in the patent office, and shared rooms in London with Jackson and Jackson's brother Adalbert. He did not, however, give up the classics and spent his free time at the British Museum preparing studies of the texts of Latin and Greek authors. He published a series of scholarly articles and by 1892 had achieved such a reputation as a classicist that he was appointed Professor of Greek and Latin at University College, London. H.'s new-found financial security, the departure of Moses Jackson, who took a faculty post overseas and then married, and the death in 1892 of Adalbert, of whom H. was also very fond, opened a period of great poetic activity for H., one that was interrupted and then intensified by the death of H.'s father in 1895. H. filled notebooks with poems influenced by the *Greek Anthology*, Heinrich Heine, and many English poets, but all unmistakably his own. He speaks in the voices of common country people—private soldiers, farmers, condemned convicts—but always with a great lucidity and purity of diction. While some elements of the poems, such as their forthright patriotism, seem Victorian, in more ways they seem, like Thomas HARDY's novels, out of keeping with their era. H.'s view of the

world is pessimistic, he hopes for no afterlife, and his characters seem the playthings of fate. Every sort of pleasure or love is poignantly transitory. The very sadness of his vision is what attracted readers to *A Shropshire Lad* (1896), which became more and more popular as the years went by.

H.'s scholarship, which eventually included editions of Juvenal and Lucan and the definitive edition of the minor Roman poet Manilius, won him appointment as Kennedy Professor of Latin at Cambridge in 1911. His slashing comments on lesser scholars made him feared in the world of classics but attracted some readers beyond his narrow specialization, and his critical prose, like "The Name and Nature of Poetry" (1933) is still stimulating. In 1922, H. published *Last Poems*, which included lyrics equal to those in his earlier book, but did not show him extending his range or breaking new ground. H. left a number of poems unpublished at his death, including a few alluding to subjects his reticence would not allow him to publish during his life time, which appeared in collections beginning with *More Poems* (1936).

BIBLIOGRAPHY: Gardner, P., ed., *A. E. H.* (1992); Graves, R. P., *A. E. H.* (1979); Legget, B. J., *The Poetic Art of A. E. Housman* (1978); Page, N., *A. E. H.* (1983)

                                      BRIAN ABEL RAGEN

HOUSMAN, Laurence
b. 18 July 1865, Bromsgrove, Hereford; d. 20 February 1959, Glastonbury

H.'s *Times* obituary describes him as a "born radical under a conservative skin . . . the belligerent suffragist, the pugnacious pacifist, the intellectual nihilist, the dubious socialist, the lover of cats, the romantic moralist, the English anti-nationalist, the all but Christian critic of institutional Christianity . . . [the] uneasy cuckoo in the nest" who "nevertheless regarded himself, as indeed he was, a 'Victorian.'" H.'s prolific career included work as a dramatist, novelist, essayist, poet, and illustrator, though his brother, A. E. HOUSMAN, remains the more immediately recognizable of the family. H. is most often remembered as an illustrator for authors including Christina ROSSETTI (*Goblin Market*, 1893) and Percy Bysshe SHELLEY (*The Sensitive Plant*, 1898) and as a dramatist.

H. was the sixth child in a family of seven. In 1883, he and his sister Clemence left their childhood home in Bromsgrove in order to study art in London. He remained a bachelor all his life and spent most of his adult life living with Clemence, to whom he was devoted. H. discovered himself to be a gifted illustrator, and had several successes illustrating both his own manuscripts and those of other writers. Why he ceased working as an artist remains somewhat unclear; some scholars maintain that he turned to writing to support himself when he could not find enough work as an artist, while others assert that it was only his failing eyesight that drove him from drawing to writing.

H.'s first publication was composed primarily of archetypal tales (myths, legends, FAIRY TALES) and poems. His 1901 anonymous publication of *An Englishwoman's Love Letters* gained him considerable popular success, though the text was falsely attributed to numerous possible authors, among them Queen Victoria, before he revealed himself as the writer.

At one point in his dramatic career, H. held the record for the most plays banned by the Lord Chamberlain's Office—thirty-two at once. His first conflict with censorship occurred with his Nativity play *Bethlehem* (1902), for works depicting sacred Christian figures were not allowed to be performed publicly. The play was privately produced in 1902 and then later revived in 1923 with no textual alterations. But his greatest critical and commercial success was *Victoria Regina* (1935). Though criticized for episodic structure and character development depending on dialogue rather than action, H. received praise for his portrayal of Victoria, particularly for the play's representation of the monarch as queen, mother, wife, and woman. Present-day critics find *Victoria Regina* emblematic of early-20th-c. history plays that seek to stage the past without added political or social commentary on present day society.

H.'s dramatic works include closet dramas (none of which were ever staged or read publicly), classical dramas (*The Death of Orpheus*, 1921; *The Death of Socrates*, 1923), pageant plays, adaptations, and religious works. His adaptations included three dramas: first was *The Vicar of Wakefield* (1906), based on the novel by Oliver GOLDSMITH; second, a modernized rendering of Aristophanes' *Lysistrata* (perf. 1910; pub. 1911); and lastly, *Alice in Ganderland* (1911), an adaptation of Lewis CARROLL's *Alice in Wonderland* written (as was *Lysistrata*) in support of the suffrage movement. H. often used his writing to support political and social causes.

H.'s religious plays served to make the religious drama a popular form again, primarily through its importance to amateur theater groups. Some critics charge that a dismissal of H.'s religious works as trite and unimaginative is premature. Closer readings of the plays reveal not a naïve treatment of a complex subject, but instead a link to H.'s personal views on organized religion—that a deeper spirituality could be reached through individual communion with God.

Scholars credit H. with the invention of the play cycle, a series of short dramas that all focus on a single figure, the structure that H. used most effectively in *Victoria Regina*. Though play cycles are rare today, critics feel that the dramatic structure H. developed in the cycle directly influenced episodic television dramas and situation comedies. Additionally the current emphasis on words rather than action to develop characters in modern drama can also be traced to H.'s dramatic contributions.

BIBLIOGRAPHY: Engen, R. K., *L. H.* (1983); Housman, L., *The Unexpected Years* (1937); Kemp, I., *L. H., 1865–1959* (1967)

MONICA SMITH

HOWATCH, Susan
b. 14 July 1940, Leatherhead, Surrey

H. was at first seen as a writer of conventional bestsellers, but later became known as one of the leading Christian novelists of her era and perhaps the novelist to give the fullest portrait of the practice and beliefs of the Church of England.

H.'s early novels resemble the family sagas of a writer like R. F. Delderfield, but with an interesting conceptual difference. H. uses famous plots from history and drama and redeploys them in contemporary times. Thus, *Penmarric* (1971) tells the story of the dynastic intrigues surrounding Henry II of England, but displaced to a wealthy family in modern Cornwall, while *The Rich Are Different* (1977) retells the story of Julius Caesar and Cleopatra in a milieu of swanky modernity. *Cashelmara* (1974), based on the story of King Edward I and his son and grandson displaced to 19th-c. rural Ireland, has a gripping plot, is psychologically acute, and interestingly argues that Ireland under the Protestant Ascendancy was comparable to medieval England under Norman rule. Though H. is well known for inventive and suspenseful plots, there is always an abstract template behind her narratives. The early books also contain plural narrators, an H. trademark.

The six-novel Starbridge series marked a notable departure for H. Not only is this sextet linked not in a straightforwardly consecutive sequence but, through complex narratilogical and intertextual techniques, it also takes up serious theological themes. Though Anglicanism is more central to English culture than is Roman Catholicism, discussions of "literature and theology" in the modern British novel are often restricted to Catholic writers such as Evelyn WAUGH, G. K. CHESTERTON, and Graham GREENE. The Starbridge series can serve as an introduction to the strands of belief and the prominent personalities in the Church of England during the 20th c.

H. opens the sextet with *Glittering Images* (1987), concerning the personal formation of Charles Ashworth, a young Anglo-Catholic priest, who makes inquiry into the suspect personal life of a prominent bishop. The book thus becomes a "mystery," with conscious allusion made to the work of Agatha CHRISTIE. The "mystery" is doubled by Ashworth's own,

Oedipus-like investigation into his parentage as a corollary to his external inquiry, bringing on a personal crisis healed by the benign mystical monk Jonathan Darrow. Darrow himself is the focus of *Glamorous Powers* (1988), in which he steps down from his monastic role to marry a younger woman. *Ultimate Prizes* (1989) takes up the story of Stephen (later Neville) Aysgarth, a Broad Church Anglican minister whose theological stance of optimism is deepened when he comes to terms with the mistakes he has made in his own life. In *Scandalous Risks* (1990), the story is narrated from the perspective of an aristocratic laywoman, Venetia Flaxton, who embarks on a dangerous flirtation with Aysgarth. *Mystical Paths* (1992) concerns Jonathan Darrow's son, Nicholas, as he comes to recognize the potential corruption of his spiritual gifts.

Published in 1994, *Absolute Truths* returns to an older (now Bishop) Ashworth as he grapples with an unexpected crisis in his own life. Influenced by Jungian concepts of participation in common archetypes as well as by the expression of Christian doctrine by diverse narrative means in the four canonical Gospels, H. implies that Darrow, Aysgarth, and Ashworth are different versions of the same character, a similarity underscored by recurring motifs (e.g., all three men outlive at least one of their wives). Ashworth and Aysgarth, as high and low churchman, respectively, are theologically opposed, and are in many respects rivals. Though H. shows a preference for Ashworth's theology, she does not present the opposition melodramatically. Indeed, excessive similarity, rather than difference, may be the danger in the relationship, as seen when Aysgarth makes a pass at Ashworth's wife, Lyle, only to remember that he loathes her, as if he was in danger of slipping into Ashworth's emotional space. It is no accident that the two men have such similar names; the unusual nature of the name "Aysgarth" is H.'s way of calling the reader's attention to this similarity. This is but one indicator of the outstanding quality of H.'s work, her ability to use decidedly sophisticated techniques within an undisguisedly popular format.

H. formally ended the Starbridge sextet with *Absolute Truths*, but continued to delve into the lives of some of its characters in later works. In *The Wonder-Worker* (1997) and *The High Flyer* (2000), H. increasingly focuses on the role of women within the Church and the succor a profound immersion in Christian practice can bring to the lives of women at a crossroads who do not feel entirely satisfied with the expectations secular society has projected onto them.

BIBLIOGRAPHY: Bush, T., "Adventures of Faith with S.H.," *CCent* 115 (April 22–29, 1998): 443–45; Harris, J. A., "A Dangerous Gift," *The World and I* 13, 2 (1998): 248–57; Virtue, D. W., "A Novelist Looks at Faith and Fiction," *Touchstone* 12 (March–April 2000): 40–44

NICHOLAS BIRNS

HOWELL, James

b. ca. 1594, Abernant, Carmarthenshire, Wales; d. 3 November 1666, Holborn

From 1616, H. traveled abroad on business, on behalf of Sir Robert Mansell's glass making company; in four years' travel, he visited the Low Countries, France, Spain, and Italy. Later travels, in a minor diplomatic capacity, took him to many of these countries again, as well as to Denmark. In 1627, he entered Parliament. Between 1632–42, he seems largely to have worked as a spy for the Earl of Strafford and Charles I and from 1642 to 1650 he was imprisoned. This wealth and variety of experience underlies his extensive literary output.

H.'s extensive literary activity seems effectively to have begun with his imprisonment, though his much admired *Dendrologia: Dodona's Grove; or, The Vocall Forrest*, a pro-royalist political allegory in prose, was one work that predated his imprisonment, being first published in 1640. In a second, revised edition of 1644, two further pieces were added to it "Parables, reflecting upon the Times" and "England's Teares for the present Warres." He went on to publish more than forty books. They included his polyglot dictionary *Lexicon Tetraglotton* (1660); works discussing many topics in history, politics, and lexicography; he made vigorous contributions to contemporary political and religious controversy. He was a considerable linguist and published translations from several European languages, including Alessandro Giraffi's important *An Exact Historie of the Revolution in Naples* (1663). His most famous work, *Epistolae Ho-Elianae; or, Familiar Letters*, was published in successive volumes in 1645, 1647, 1650, and 1655 and is a collection of letters, ostensibly written at various times and places in Britain and abroad, but probably written (for the most part) during his imprisonment, perhaps based on notes he had taken while traveling and often incorporating extensive borrowings from other authors.

The letters offer H.'s analyses of political events, and brief historical studies, as well as lively reportage and observation on such diverse topics as the Overbury trial, Ben JONSON at supper, or the wines and languages of the world. H. cannot always be trusted so far as the accuracy of his facts is concerned (such as his story of the woman who gave birth to 365 children at once!), but the general liveliness of his manner, his sharp eye for a good story (including that of the Pied Piper of Hamelin), and the fascination of some of the information he puts before the reader make for very entertaining reading. The book has had important admirers, such as William Makepeace

THACKERAY, who declared that "Montaigne and How-ell's *Letters* are my bedside books," and it is perhaps as a development of the Renaissance essay that we should think of the book. It is both unfortunate and extraordinary that it should have been out of print for almost a hundred years.

H.'s *Instructions for Foreign Travel* (1642) has claims to be regarded as the earliest guide book to Europe in English, designed to guide the young Englishman through France, Spain, and Italy and then back home. As a document in the history of British attitudes to Europe, it is of considerable importance and its observations of men and manners are consistently interesting. *Londinopolis: An Historical Discourse or Perlustration of the City of London* (1657) is a lively and informative guidebook to London; comparing it with other great cities, H. has no doubts as to London's superiority. H.'s historical and political writings on Italy, such as his *S.P.Q.V. A Survay of the Signorie of Venice* (1651) and his *Parthenopoeia; or, The History of Naples* (1654), the latter translated and adapted from a number of Italian texts, display a good deal of prescience and a more secure understanding than is to be found in many of his contemporaries. *A German Diet; or, The Ballance of Europe* (1653) is a well-written and perceptive dialogue on a range of political and cultural themes. H.'s output also included a multilingual collection of proverbs, attacks on the Dutch, as in *A Brief Character of the Low Countries* (1660), *A New English Grammar for Forreners to Learn English* (1662), and much else.

H. contributed an elegy to *Jonsonus Virbius* (1638) on the death of Jonson, elsewhere described by H. as "the Poet of His Time" and "his Honoured Friend and Father." H.'s own poetry is mixed in quality and various in subject; the greater part of it was collected in *Poems On several Choice and Various Subjects* (1663). Among many occasional poems and commendatory verses contributed to the works of friends and associates are some pleasant love poems, such as "Upon Black Eyes, and Becoming Frowns," and some quietly impressive divine poems, such as his beautiful tercets "Upon the Nativity of our Saviour, Christmas-Day."

BIBLIOGRAPHY: Hale, J. R., *England and the Italian Renaissance* (1954); Vann, W. H., *Notes on the Writings of J. H.* (1924)

GLYN PURSGLOVE

HUGHES, Richard [Arthur Warren]

b. 19 April 1900, Weybridge, Surrey; d. 28 April 1976, near Talsarnau, Wales

H. began his writing career while an Oxford undergraduate. His early work included children's stories, short stories, and poetry, but H.'s first real success was as a dramatist. Three of H.'s plays had West End productions in the early 1920s, and *Danger*, commissioned by the BBC in 1924, was apparently the first play written especially for radio. Despite his interest and success in the theater, however, H. is best known for his four novels that appeared at increasingly long intervals between 1928 and 1972.

H.'s first novel, *The Innocent Voyage* (1928; repub. as *A High Wind in Jamaica*, 1929), though in form an historical adventure story, is startlingly original in its view of childhood. The ironic narrator tells us that babies are "of course not human—they are animals" and that children's minds are "not just different and stupider than ours, but differ in kind of thinking (are mad, in fact)." H. dramatizes this iconoclastic view in his story of the Bas-Thornton children, who after a hurricane in Jamaica are sent to England for school and safety, are inadvertently kidnapped by pirates, have a series of comic and tragic adventures aboard the pirate ship, and ultimately arrive safely in England to the sympathy and admiration of their elders. A familiar plot, but the characters and themes are original and disturbing. As soon as the constraints of civilization are removed, the children start to act like untamed animals, to the dismay of the sentimental, child-worshipping pirates, who only gradually discover "what diabolic yeast had been introduced into their lump." The central character, ten-year-old Emily Thornton, progresses from an overly civilized and innocent child to one who feverishly and brutally murders a Dutch sea captain and, on arrival in England, by telling another woman her version of what happened brings about the hanging of the pirate Captain Jonsen, whom she loves. These actions seem at first to change Emily, as even her father realizes he is now afraid of her, but when she arrives at school the narrator remarks that only God could have picked Emily out from the other innocent young girls, leaving the reader to agree with Emily that "the universe soon became a very unstable place indeed."

H.'s second novel, *In Hazard* (1938), again uses a shipboard setting, this time the cargo ship *Archimedes*, to tell an allegorical story of men against the sea. In part 1 of the novel, H. provides a lovingly detailed description of the mechanisms and internal workings of the ship; presents the crew as a kind of microcosm of the English class system, with English, Scottish, and Chinese sailors roughly corresponding to the upper, middle, and lower classes; slyly acknowledges his source by stating "The days of Conrad's 'Typhoon' are passed; the days when hurricanes pounced on shipping as unexpectedly as a cat on a mouse"; then shows us the *Archimedes* confronted by just such a hurricane. Part 2 deepens the story by showing the ship's crew confronting not only the hurricane but also their own pasts and inner demons in their individual responses to the storm. Captain Edwardes, deciding that a storm of this ferocity amounts to a conflict between himself and God, becomes "like an artist in a bout of inspiration." The rest of the crew perform heroically, exemplifying what H. terms "Virtue, in the Roman sense." H. further deepens the story's meaning with two seeming digressions, lengthy descriptions of the past experiences of the two youngest characters, the English Dick Watchett and the Chinese Ao Ling, that explain their profound devotion to a belief, Watchett's in God, Ao Ling's in Mao's communist revolution.

H. published no more fiction until *The Fox in the Attic* (1961) and *The Wooden Shepherdess* (1973). These works were conceived not as self-contained novels but as the opening installments of a planned multivolume series, *The Human Predicament*, in which H. planned to blend historical events with the stories of two upper-class families, the Welsh Penry-Herberts and their German cousins the Von Kessens, during the interwar years to explain some of the historical and personal factors leading to World War II. H. bases his narrative on a series of conflicts: the political and cultural conflicts between Britain and Germany; the generational conflict between those born just too late to serve in World War I and their elders; class conflicts in both countries; conflicts between the individual characters and their societies; and internal conflicts within most of the major characters. These conflicts are firmly embodied in characters representing vastly different cultures, characters whose interactions are marked by misunderstandings often verging on incomprehensibility. The primary strength of these two works is in H.'s depiction of the historical characters, particularly that of the young Adolf Hitler, and his utterly convincing descriptions of such historical events as the Beer Hall Putsch and the Night of the Long Knives. The weakness of the work as H. left it is that several of the characters, including the central character of Augustine Penry-Herbert, are not fully developed and sometimes verge on the stereotypical, while the significance of some of the fictional incidents, particularly in *The Wooden Shepherdess*, is obscure. These faults are perhaps inherent in an unfinished work and would almost certainly have been corrected had H. finished the series, but he had completed only a few chapters of the third volume at the time of his death in 1976.

BIBLIOGRAPHY: Graves, R. P., *R. H.* (1994); Morgan, P., *The Art of R. H.* (1993); Poole, R., *R. H.* (1986); Thomas, P., *R. H.* (1973)

JOHN ROGERS

HUGHES, Ted [Edward James]

b. 17 August 1930, Mytholmroyd, Yorkshire; d. 28 October 1998, London

In *Poetry in the Making* (1967), H. recalls that during his childhood in Yorkshire he spent most of his time capturing animals, and that when his enthusiasm for this waned, he started to write poems. He goes on to say that capturing animals and writing poems have much in common. Poems "have their own life, like animals, by which I mean they seem quite separate from any one person . . . and they have a certain wisdom. They know something special . . . something perhaps which we are very curious to learn." These words reflect the way in which H. conceived of his art as a way of imagining and dramatizing the profound otherness of the natural world. Identifying and exploring the wisdom to be found in the nonhuman was a fundamental dimension of his lifelong poetic project.

A literary legatee of William BLAKE, Samuel Taylor COLERIDGE, and William WORDSWORTH, H. was reared in a rural setting scarred by mills and smokestacks; he also dwelt for many years on or near a functioning farm in Devon. He brought to his experience a capacity for intense observation, an almost Lawrentian eye for the details of blood and sinew. He also brought the devoted belief that somehow the things one might typically flinch from in the natural world are not only sources of wisdom but precisely the wisdom most desperately needed. In his earliest published work, it was obvious that H. had reacted against the prevailing mode of British lyric poetry in the 1950s, namely the well-structured, urbane, and understated poems of writers such as Donald DAVIE, John WAIN, and Philip LARKIN. In both content and form, H. sought a poetry that would be stranger, rougher, and less tame. It is remarkable how many poems in his first three books—*The Hawk in the Rain* (1957), *Lupercal* (1960), and *Wodwo* (1967)—center on an encounter with wildness. In these ten years, there is also a deepening intimacy and an intensification of energies in response. The more the speakers of poems such as "The Thought-Fox" and "Pike" attend to what they see and hear, the more these animals in effect enter into consciousness and thereby alter the soul.

H.'s nature poetry, both early and later in his career, is more than the result of rural loyalties, and even more than just a seeking out of intimacy with the authentic, elemental dimensions of existence. His motive is also more than a response to the ongoing ecological crisis of the modern era, though this too is embedded in H.'s poetry. Above all, H. is responding to the broader crises of meaning and belief in the second half of the 20th c. In effect, H.'s poetic goal is the resacralizing of existence. It is an effort at remythologizing and re-creating deities and spirits, while at the same time an effort at dramatizing our own human and anxiety-laden relations with them. These spirits are not necessarily tender or loving, and they are surely remote from Judeo-Christian notions of Providence and Salvation. Yet the speakers in his poems are drawn ineluctably to them, as if in recognition of a most profound and heretofore hidden connection.

The least tender-hearted spirit in H.'s work is *Crow* (1970). This bird, however, is no creature that ever quite appeared in nature. In fact, this is not nature poetry as much as it is mythic creation. As H. remarked in a later essay (in *Winter Pollen*, 1995), the Crow poems constitute a song-legend, and the figure Crow should be understood as kin to the "Trickster" in folk and anthropological literature. For H., the Trickster is a playful yet savage spirit of survival, a figure of "biological optimism" beyond all suffering. It is, as H. presents it, greater than death, literally conversant with God, and in these poems, far more interesting than both. The landscape of Crow is postapocalyptic, and this reflects the origins of these poems in the World Wars, genocides, and nuclear terrors of the 20th c. Neither simply human nor simply a bird, neither as wicked as demons nor as decent as angels, but some amalgam of all of these, Crow ultimately offers a sardonic laugh at the ultimate questions, all the while "flying the black flag of himself."

One source of the H.'s interest in a survivor's energy is the sorrow related to H.'s marriage to Sylvia Plath in 1957, and her subsequent suicide in early 1963. H. met the young American poet while both were studying at Cambridge. After their marriage, the couple lived in the U.S., London, and Devon. The dissolution of their marriage, her suicide, and H.'s later work as executor of Plath's literary estate marked the rest of his life, forever entwining the two poets. For over thirty years after her death, H. tried to maintain an almost complete silence on the matter of their relationship, and specifically on the extent he felt his infidelities had contributed to Plath's suicide. His silence was perhaps largely in response to the way in which Plath had become an icon of feminist struggle, while he was sometimes virulently denounced as a male chauvinist. Nonetheless, he continued a prolific output of work that was widely recognized as some of the best British poetry in the latter half of the century, a recognition that led to his appointment in 1984 as poet laureate.

In 1998, the year before his death, H. published *Birthday Letters,* a collection of eighty-eight poems addressed to Plath. In this sequence, H. evoked and explored their courtship, marriage, children, separation, and above all their partnership as young poets together. Underneath the reminiscence is the painful specter of Plath's suicide. Many of the poems had been written at various times in the years since Plath's death, but throughout a vivid tenderness is present in the sequence. *Birthday Letters* may have been in part an effort to tell his side of the story. H. offers the idea that her suicide was foreordained by Plath's unresolved childhood attachment to her dead father. But he also portrays Plath as devoted to her art, and in

the process of discovering her voice, she had conjured dangerous psychic energies that ultimately overwhelmed her. To H., it was in effect a story of a terrible and tragic metamorphosis facilitated by a very great poetic gift. Only a year earlier, H. had published his *Tales from Ovid.* In his introduction to these translations from the *Metamorphoses,* H. wrote that Ovid was above all interested in what it feels like to be possessed by a passion. Not just ordinary passion, wrote H., "but human passion in extremis—passion where it combusts, or levitates, or mutates into an experience of the supernatural." H. says that for Ovid the metamorphic moment operates as a guarantee "that the passion has become mythic, has achieved the unendurable intensity that lifts the whole episode onto the supernatural or divine plane." It is a moment, he says, when the "all-too-human victim stumbles out into the mythic arena, and is transformed." *Birthday Letters* and *Tales from Ovid* are thus companion pieces, stories of metamorphosis that indirectly reflect and comment on one another.

H.'s thoughts on Ovid apply also to his own lifelong work as well. In approximately fifty books, including a dozen major poetry collections, a thick volume of literary criticism, and several children's books, as well as several works of translation, H. steadily sought out and focused on those moments of human feeling so intense that there would or could be some revelation of what he might have called the divine. This would not be divinity in any ordinary sense, but something more primeval, more like a pagan sense of multiple divinities inhabiting a natural world we think we know but do not actually see. In our desacralized, postindustrial world, H.'s fundamental achievement was to create an art that could reclaim and restore a sense of awe at the facts of our own existence.

BIBLIOGRAPHY: Bentley, P., *The Poetry of T. H.* (1998); Feinstein, E., *T. H.* (2001); Gammage, N., ed., *The Epic Poise: A Celebration of T. H.* (1999); Robinson, C., *T. H. as Shepherd of Being* (1989); Sagar, K., *The Laughter of Foxes: A Study of T. H.* (2000); Scigaj, L., *T. H.* (1991)

FRED MARCHANT

HUGHES, Thomas

b. 20 October 1822, Uffington; d. 22 March 1896, Brighton

The original novel of boarding school life, which spawned a genre, *Tom Brown's Schooldays* (1857) retains its popularity after almost a century and a half and is often reprinted, despite its unfashionable doctrine that to become "a gentleman and a Christian" is a more important outcome than academic excellence. Its importance lies in its lively portrait of Rugby, H.'s own school, under Dr. Thomas Arnold, who made it into a moral powerhouse, sending out into the world young men with finely tuned consciences and high seriousness. A polemic against bullying, the book was influential in the gradual reform of the public (private) school system. H.'s bully, Flashman, has an extended life in the admirable fictions of George MacDonald FRASER. H.'s sequel, *Tom Brown at Oxford* (1861), was less successful and his numerous other works are forgotten.

HULME, T[homas] E[rnest]

b. 16 September 1883, Endon, Staffordshire; d. 16 September 1917, Flanders, Belgium

Educated at the High School, Newcastle-under-Lyme, H. was elected to an Exhibition in mathematics at St. John's College, Cambridge, where he was admitted in 1902. He was sent down from Cambridge in 1904 and after spending eight months in Canada in 1904 followed by a period in Brussels perfecting his French and German he returned to London in 1908 and rapidly established himself at the center of a small but influential group of poets, writers, and artists. In January 1909, he published two of his best-known poems, "A City Sunset" and "Autumn," in *For Christmas MDCCCCVIII*, which was printed under the auspices of the Poets' Club of which he was the secretary. In that same year, he became a regular contributor to the *New Age* writing on a large variety of subjects ranging from Henri Bergson to domestic politics.

Thereafter, he created his own informal group whom he persuaded to free poetry from what he saw as the restrictions of 19th-c. Romantic tradition advocating *vers libre*, aiming for accurate, precise, and definite presentation with no verbiage and the creation of the "hard, dry image." When Ezra Pound joined the group in 1909, he built on H.'s principles to establish IMAGISM and recruited other poets, in particular Richard ALDINGTON and H. D. (Hilda Doolittle) to the cause. In January 1912, H. published five poems in the *New Age* under the title "The Complete Poetical Works of T. E. Hulme" that were republished by Pound as an appendix to *Ripostes* (1912). T. S. ELIOT maintained that he had written "two or three of the most beautiful short poems in the language."

In his essay "Romanticism and Classicism," H. predicted that "after a hundred years of romanticism, we are in for a classical revival" and that the new poetry would be "cheerful, dry and sophisticated." He defines ROMANTICISM as being characterized by a belief in the infinite perfectibility of man. Classicism on the contrary is the religious attitude, the acceptance of man's limitations characterized by a belief in Original Sin. The Romantic attitude regards man as a reservoir full of possibilities whereas the classical regards him as a very finite and fixed creature. He

regards religion as a basic human need "parallel to appetite and the instinct of sex," thus if man ceases to believe in God, he begins to believe that man is a god. The Romantics' belief in the infinite possibilities of human nature is in his view the religious impulse manifesting itself in a perverted form, what he called " spilt religion." He criticizes Romantic poetry for its vagueness and for the Romantic poet's feeling that poetry must lead to a beyond of some kind. The classical poem is bathed in the light of ordinary day whereas in the Romantic poem it is "the light that never was on sea or land." H. argues that other contrasts in ethics, politics, and metaphysics follow from this Romantic/classical opposition. In politics, for example, while right-wing thinkers consider politics to be the art of the possible, left-wing thinkers believe themselves to be building some future UTOPIA; no longer believing in a religious heaven, they envisage the possibility of a heaven on earth.

These oppositions are developed further in his essay "Humanism and the Religious Attitude," where he maintains that there is "an absolute, and not a relative, between humanism . . . and the religious spirit." The two worlds that are entirely distinct have been "muddled" together so that, for example, art like Romantic poetry confuses both human and divine things, by not clearly separating them. It is precisely this confusion that he deals with in his essay "Modern Art and Its Philosophy" in which he argues that at the Renaissance at the time when Copernicus demonstrated that man was not the center of the universe, the artists for the first time depicted man as if he was. There was a decisive shift away from abstract representation toward a naturalistic representation of man and his world, from a religious toward a humanistic attitude. In the art of his contemporaries, H. noted a movement back toward elements of the geometric art he had seen in the Byzantine mosaics at Ravenna. He therefore interpreted this change in modern art as a precursor of a fundamental change from the humanism that had prevailed since the Renaissance. Thus, he believes, man's sense of alienation from the universe in which he lives finds expression in a change of sensibility that results in abstract art rather than naturalistic. With this in mind, H. encouraged his friends, particularly Jacob Epstein, Henri Gaudier-Brzeska, and Wyndham LEWIS, to produce the kind of sculptures that his theories demanded.

H. was an enthusiastic advocate of Bergson's philosophy that he welcomed as an alternative to 19th-c. rationalism and as an answer to the evolutionary determinism of post-Darwinian biology. He translated Bergson's essay *An Introduction to Metaphysics* (1913). He also translated Georges Sorel's *Reflections on Violence* (1916) and associated himself with a reactionary Toryism. In 1916, he contributed a series of short articles that he signed North Staffs to the *Cam-*

bridge Review defending the war as being as necessary as repairing sea walls in order that what has been achieved may be preserved. He countered the argument of those pacifists such as Bertrand RUSSELL who believe that force settles nothing by claiming that force "does settle things, does create facts, which you have henceforth to deal with." Having served in France in the front line since December 1914, he experienced the horrors of war but was nevertheless convinced of its necessity. H. was killed in action near Nieuwpoort in Flanders.

When a selection of his papers, edited by Herbert READ, were published in 1924 under the title *Speculations*, his ideas became widely influential. Eliot commented that "in this volume he appears as the forerunner of a new attitude of mind, which should be the 20th-c. mind, if the 20th c. is to have a mind of its own. H. is classical, reactionary and revolutionary: he is the antipodes of the eclectic, tolerant and democratic mind of the last century. And his writing, his fragmentary notes and his outlines, is the writing of an individual who wished to satisfy himself before he cared to enchant a cultivated public."

BIBLIOGRAPHY: Jones, A. R., *The Life and Opinions of T. E. H.* (1960); Roberts, M., *T. E. H.* (1938)

A. R. JONES

HUME, David
b. 26 April 1711, Ninewells, Berwick-upon-Tweed, Scotland; d. 25 August 1776, Edinburgh, Scotland

The foremost philosopher of the 18th-c. Scottish Enlightenment, H. is also celebrated as an historian, economist, and essayist on political science. His major contribution to philosophy, *A Treatise of Human Nature* (3 vols., 1739–40) was published following his return to Britain after an intensive period of study amongst the Jesuits at La Flèche, Anjou, when its author was still in his twenties. This revolutionary work applied the empirical inductive method of Sir Isaac Newton and John LOCKE to the study of mind; instead of asking (as had Locke's *Essay Concerning Human Understanding*) how and what we know of the external world, H. turned the investigation inward to inquire how and what we know of the human mind. His conclusions were unorthodox and—understood in the full starkness of their implications—deeply unsettling.

Employing strictly empirical principles, the *Treatise* addressed the origin of ideas, our sense of space and time, causality, the testimony of the senses, and human identity, to arrive at the interim position that all we can know of ourselves is a "heap, or bundle of impressions" without demonstrable continuity or identity, and that the connection between these perceptions and anything existing beyond them in an ex-

ternal world cannot be demonstrated. These conclusions about human understanding are quickly arrived at before the end of the first book of the *Treatise*, which ends with a bravura conclusion dramatizing the effect of such skeptical thoughts on the mind that admits them. Logically, the narrator points out, empirical inquiry leads inescapably to this point; humanly, however, its consequences are recognized immediately to be untenable. Whatever their actual status (forever unknowable), personal identity, extension, time, and space are necessary fictions, upon which the conduct of human life depends. On these principles, but without abating the philosophical skepticism that underlies their pursuit, book 2 of the *Treatise* investigates the psychology of the passions, to demonstrate that reason is always, and must always be, subordinate to the rule of passion in human affairs. The third, final book pursues this thought into the domain of ethics, to describe moral goodness not in terms of divine sanction or innate ideas, but as the product of feelings of approval or disapproval experienced by an individual, based on observing agreeable or disagreeable consequences of behavior.

Although the *Treatise* did not achieve immediate celebrity on its publication (H. later described it, quoting Alexander POPE, as having fallen "dead-born from the Press"), its influence spread gradually through subsequent epistemology (which, in the "Moral Sense" or "Common Sense" school of H.'s Scottish opponents, was largely devoted to refuting the *Treatise*'s premises, on the ground of a universal—common—innate sense of identity and externality in human nature), and moral philosophy. Attempting to find an audience for his ideas, H. recast some of the conclusions of his skeptical treatise as a series of *Essays, Moral and Political* (2 vols., 1741–42), designed to appeal to a broad "polite" audience, male and female. These highly readable short pieces are models of urbanity, employing a deceptively accessible Addisonian style that masks potentially unpalatable or inflammatory implications. They achieved a measure of popular success, but did not prevent H.'s enemies in the ecclesiastical Establishment from thwarting his candidature for the Chair of Moral Philosophy in Edinburgh in 1745 on grounds of heresy and infidelity.

Disappointed of both professional preferment and financial gain from his writing, H. took temporary employment first as a private tutor and then as secretary to General James St. Clair, in which capacity he briefly experienced military action in Brittany. In 1748, he published *Three Essays, Moral and Political*, and a suaver, more circumspect, rewriting of the first book of the *Treatise* as *Philosophical Essays Concerning Human Understanding* (rev. in 1758 as *An Enquiry Concerning Human Understanding*, the title by which the work subsequently became known). This work develops the logic of H.'s earlier view that the causal relation assumed between two events or facts cannot be demonstrated to have any inherent necessity, but reduces always to an observation of constant conjunction that leads the mind to form a habitual association between the two occurrences. The *Philosophical Essays* also contains an important addition, the notorious essay "On Miracles," written to refute the argument that miracles could be accommodated within the evidential basis of Natural Religion. The complex ironic stance of this essay made it a favorite source for later charges of atheism against H., although in fact the carefully poised tone allows equally for it to be read as an exposition of the mystery of faith. It is consistent with his philosophical position that belief, in every sphere, cannot strictly be demonstrated either from empirical inquiry or by reasoning, but appears to derive from some necessary propensity of human nature.

H.'s next important publication, *An Enquiry Concerning the Principles of Morals* (1751), derived from book 3 of the *Treatise*, to develop an ethics of sympathy which revised and extended the "Moral Sense" philosophy of H.'s mentor Francis Hutcheson; it would become central to Scottish Enlightenment emphasis on sociability. On this basis, H.'s friend Adam SMITH's *Theory of Moral Sentiments* elaborated the fully developed and highly influential ethic based on the "fellow feeling" of an observer that underlies 18th-c. sentimental fiction. H.'s attempt to succeed Smith in the Chair of Logic at Glasgow foundered, once again, on his enemies' imputation of atheism; his appointment in 1752 as Keeper of the Advocates's Library in Edinburgh gave him at once economic security to pursue his ideas and access to a collection of 30,000 volumes. In this near-sinecure, he published, between 1754 and 1762, six volumes of a *History of England*, extending from the Roman Conquest until the "Glorious Revolution" of 1688–89. This work, a masterpiece of philosophical or "conjectural" history broadly along the lines of his fellow Scots historiographers William Robertson and Tobias SMOLLETT, demonstrated an inevitable and by-and-large laudable sequence of Britain's progress from a state of near-savagery through internecine war to the stability and refinement of Civil Society. H.'s *History*, like his compatriots', was an important ideological document in establishing the assimilation of Scotland and England as a unified Britain following the Union of Parliaments in 1707.

A series of *Political Discourses* (1752) whose speculations on wealth, exchange, and commodities influenced the formation of the "Classical Economics" of Smith and others later in the century, *Four Dissertations* (1757) and further important works on religion, also belong to the period of H.'s librarianship. In 1763, he traveled to Paris as secretary and later *chargé d'affaires* to the British Embassy, where,

as "le bon David," he became an idol of the French salons and befriended Jean-Jacques Rousseau, who later unjustly accused him of betrayal. Returning to Edinburgh in 1769, H. revised his *History*, collected his *Essays* (1777), and prepared a further masterpiece, the *Dialogues Concerning Natural Religion* (1779), whose skeptical (though not atheistic) conclusions led friends to advise its reservation for posthumous publication. His serenity in facing death without belief in an afterlife produced admiration in some, consternation in others, including James BOSWELL, who recorded his own reactions following a specially staged "deathbed interview" that would become notorious. H.'s carefully honed conversational style, his skillful melding of individuals and events into a narrative of the development of a unified and constitutional Britain, and his political and economic insights into the nature of Civil Society, were celebrated during his life, while his daring philosophical and religious speculations made him a notorious and feared enemy of Established views. His most important successor in epistemology was Immanuel Kant, who declared that H.'s work had "roused him from his philosophical slumber"; in reaction Kant developed an immensely influential theory of Idealism. H.'s philosophical influence extends also in the development of Comtean positivism and the utilitarianism of John Stuart MILL, while his contributions to political philosophy and the implications of his work for subsequent literary history have more recently been recognized.

BIBLIOGRAPHY: Forbes, D., *H.'s Philosophical Politics* (1975); Grieg, J. Y. T., ed., *The Letters of D. H.* (2 vols., 1932); Klibansky, R., and E. C. Mossner, eds., *New Letters of D. H.* (1954); Mossner, E. C., *The Life of D. H.* (1954; rev. ed., 1980); Norton, D. F., *D. H., Common-Sense Moralist, Sceptical Metaphysician* (1982); Phillipson, N., *H.* (1989); Smith, N. K., *The Philosophy of D. H.* (1941)

                                          SUSAN MANNING

HUMOR

Humor includes comedy (the literary form characterized by a happy ending like marriage), wit, satire, irony, farce, nonsense, black humor, burlesque, parody, farce: in essence, anything likely to provoke laughter or quiet amusement. Other terms used to analyze English literary humor are humor of character, situation, attitude, and language.

Britain has produced no great theorist of humor. Thomas HOBBES wrote in *Leviathan* that "*Sudden Glory*, is the passion which maketh those *Grimaces* called LAUGHTER; and is caused either by some sudden act of their own, that pleaseth them; or by the apprehension of some deformed thing in another, by comparison whereof they suddenly applaud themselves," and in this he rewords classical theory that humor depends on a stance of superiority. This theory is didactic and corrective, and humor establishes a norm. William Makepeace THACKERAY is anecdotal and chatty, giving examples of humor rather than analyzing it. The same can be said of William HAZLITT and George MEREDITH, although Meredith provides a useful category of "thoughtful laughter" and defines humor as peculiarly feminine: "The higher the comedy, the more prominent the part [women] enjoy in it."

For analysis and theory, we must cross the Channel to Europe. Henri Bergson says humor is a response to rigid, mechanical, or dehumanized gestures, again establishing laughter as holding a superior and normative stance, but Sigmund Freud sees humor as expressing some kind of vulnerability. It can either be an expression of nostalgia as we find a safe way to return to the sense of well-being of childhood, or as a socially sanctioned way of releasing inhibitions and taboos about "tendentious" matters such as sex, race, and gender. Mikhail Bakhtin counters these conservative positions, seeing humor as "carnival," liberating, and politically radical, its roots in social rituals lending it a rebellious and antiauthoritarian streak. Some stress the collaborative, therapeutic, and renewing capacities of humor, while others have stressed its divisive, potentially offensive, and conservative tendencies. All these paradoxical facets of humor are manifested from time to time by English practitioners.

Historical and cultural relativity dates verbal humor; in general, humor that turns on attitudes to race, class, and gender is nowadays regarded generally as unfunny. Nonetheless, they are undoubtedly a part of the history of British humor, dishonorable relics of imperial and patriarchal superiority. They can still evoke nostalgia in those who hark back to the days when Britain ruled the waves, aristocrats were born to rule, and men assumed a God-given superiority over women. Such humor can be seen to conform to both Bergson's and Freud's theories.

Anglo-Saxon literature usually expresses resignation in the face of adversity, and yields no belly laughs. This is no surprise because the Benedictine Rule governing scribes' lives forbade indecorous laughter or humor. There are occasional examples of overweening gestural laughs (e.g., Bhyrtnoth's in the OLD ENGLISH poem *The Battle of Maldon*, wr. ca. 1000), as well as moments of wry amusement in the *Riddles*, and even in heroic literature and saints' lives. But to us the Old English are an alien society, and they are not known for humor as we know it.

Geoffrey CHAUCER, writing in the later 14th c., is the first to use modes of humor that can still be recaptured and appreciated. His comic range in *The Canterbury Tales* is considerable, spanning the scatological in "The Miller's Tale" and comedy of relations between the sexes in "The Wife of Bath's Tale" and

"The Nun's Priest's Tale" to the more subtle, ironic effects in "The Knight's Tale." The volume as a whole is the first great work of sustained humor in the English language.

William SHAKESPEARE exemplifies the broadest range of humorous effects of any writer in any language. His drama draws on the spectrum from wordplay through to the literary form that he perfected, romantic comedy, the humor derived from observing the behavior of lovers whose eventual "journey's end" is almost always marriage. *A Midsummer Night's Dream, Twelfth Night,* and *As You Like It* are perfect vehicles for humorous observation of people in love. The history or chronicle plays give us the most archetypal comic character in the English language, Sir John Falstaff, who is both a coward and an indomitable comic hero. Shakespeare also wrote "problem comedies" such as *Measure for Measure* and *All's Well That Ends Well*, which push laughter to an edge of danger and even death. His last plays, such as *The Winter's Tale* and *The Tempest*, are sometimes called "tragi-comedies" (or romances) because they represent a genuinely mixed mode, which enact benevolent cycles like the movement from winter to spring and summer. Even his tragedies contain moments of "comic relief" such as the Porter's intrusion in *Macbeth* or the speeches of Osric and Polonius, not to mention those of the hero himself, in *Hamlet*, as well as amusing grotesquerie.

Shakespeare's contemporary Ben JONSON drew on contemporary medical roots of the word when he wrote his "comedy of humours," a physiological explanation for different dispositions of people, depending on whether they are governed by the blood (sanguine), choler (choleric), phlegm (phlegmatic), or black bile (melancholic). On stage, Jonson's humor in plays such as *Volpone, The Alchemist,* and *Bartholomew Fair* transcends its historical specificity and still raises laughter in audiences, through genuinely funny, if obsessively one-noted, characters representing particular facets of human vices and foibles in situations of satiric intrigue. Thomas MIDDLETON in, for example *A Chaste Maid in Cheapside* with its ironic title, and *A Mad World My Masters*, developed "citizen comedy," turning on commercial expedience. A Restoration comedy like William CONGREVE's *The Way of the World* exaggerated the pretensions of fops, and later Richard Brinsley SHERIDAN in *The School for Scandal* exploited the literary fashion for "the good natured man" and the class system.

Thackeray's *The English Humorists*, published in 1853, gives us a retrospective map of the field in the 18th c. He includes essays on writers who use humor as satirical weapon: Jonathan SWIFT (Irish, but by inclination English), John GAY, Alexander POPE, William Hogarth, and Matthew PRIOR; as urbanity— Congreve, Joseph ADDISON, and Richard STEELE;

sentimentality—Tobias SMOLLETT, Henry FIELDING, and Oliver GOLDSMITH; and sublime eccentricity in Laurence STERNE (also Irish). Most of these expose contradictions and hypocrisies in court, society, and class relations. The poet Pope stands out as the most cutting, and the novelists Fielding and Goldsmith as creating a mode of sentimental humor that, in kindly but magistratelike fashion, punctures affectation by appealing social and poetic justice. These self-consciously neoclassical writers employ humor in a socially corrective and politically conservative way, ridiculing as antisocial the eccentric, the low-born, and the wicked. Sterne's novel *Tristram Shandy* is the strangest and most individual work of comic genius in the English language, satirizing the fledgling form of the novel itself as well as creating pseudo-biographical "Shandyean" characters. Samuel JOHNSON's mordant brand of humor punctures "the vanity of human wishes," and the Scottish poet, Robert BURNS writes with affectionate wryness of peasant folk.

In the Romantic period, Jane AUSTEN aims her witty barbs at middle-class pretensions, English provincial life, and the institution of marriage. *Pride and Prejudice* and *Emma* are her most assured works of humor. Thomas Love PEACOCK satirizes Romantic poets, and Lord BYRON in *Don Juan* pokes fun at human foibles in general.

The mid-19th c. produced two great novelists of humor. Thackeray's *Vanity Fair* is panoramic of all social classes, and its resourceful heroine, Becky Sharp, exposes hypocrisy in English society by exploiting those around her. Thackeray also sustained the influential and long-lasting *Punch*, an English illustrated periodical (1841–1992), famous for its satiric humor, caricatures, and cartoons. Humbug was its chief target, and it spared no classes from its savage treatment.

Charles DICKENS joined Rabelais, Cervantes' *Don Quixote*, Shakespeare (alongside his creation, Falstaff), and Sterne's *Shandy* in giving to the English language a new phrase, "Dickensian humor," at its most obvious in the good-humored *The Pickwick Papers* and used more sparingly and to more serious and even dark effect in later works like *David Copperfield*. It draws on a shrewd insight into incongruity in human motivation, and is essentially created by a sardonic narratorial stance, comedy of character, and mastery of language. When he died, the *Spectator* anointed Dickens as "the greatest humorist whom England ever produced—Shakespeare himself certainly not excepted."

Among comic poets, Robert BROWNING's dramatic monologues allow villainous speakers to condemn themselves from their own mouths. Edward LEAR is a kind of forerunner to Spike Milligan in his zany and sometimes dark nonsense poetry. Of the later writers,

Lewis CARROLL uses his *Alice* books to play wittily with words and logic, while Oscar WILDE's comedies of manners, like *The Importance of Being Earnest*, disguise very serious issues of social morality by creating paradoxes reversing conventional virtue and vice. W. S. GILBERT, one half of the famous "Gilbert and Sullivan," created lyrics that rollick in the mind through their musical accompaniments.

Among 20th-c. humorists, Bernard SHAW, an Anglo-Irishman, is a rare example of one who uses a sprightly wit of logic in the service of radical, socialist politics rather than conservatism, with a refreshing iconoclasm. By contrast, G. K. CHESTERTON, John BETJEMAN, and P. G. WODEHOUSE have dated badly because their humor is that of class-bound "little England." Compton MACKENZIE is a Scottish humorist who observes fondly small local communities whose dotty customs and characters anticipate the television comedy *Ballykissangel*. Hilaire BELLOC contributes to the line of nonsense initiated by Lear, as does the mock Gothic *Titus Groan* trilogy by Mervyn PEAKE in the 1940s. In the 1930s, Evelyn WAUGH wrote novels of vitriolic intensity about class snobbery and anglophobia, and Aldous HUXLEY lightly satirizes the technological future. George ORWELL's *Animal Farm* provides a fable that ridicules totalitarian states.

Samuel BECKETT, an Irish dramatist and novelist who lived in Paris, produced a very influential and powerful kind of "black humor," drawing on fashionable existentialism by laughing at vulnerability of pathetic human beings in a meaningless void. His most famous play is the "absurd" *Waiting for Godot*. Harold PINTER also produced dark humor of a more localized, English petty-bourgeois kind. Tom STOPPARD, an émigré from Czechoslovakia, wrote plays that amusingly reverse audience expectations—cerebral comedies of situation and ideas rather than character. *Rosencrantz and Guildenstern Are Dead* reinvents the canonical tragedy, *Hamlet*, by cleverly observing the action from the point of view of minor characters, and his script for the film *Shakespeare in Love* generates humor by overlaying fiction and fact.

After the 1950s, we find humorists mainly not among novelists, playwrights, or poets, but scriptwriters for the relatively new media, film, radio, and television. Films from the Ealing Studios in the 1950s, such as *The Lavender Hill Mob*, are exquisitely scripted comedies of character, while the *Carry On* films provide broad and bawdy farce. Radio series like *The Goon Show*, individual stars like the lugubrious Tony Hancock, and television series such as *Monty Python, Steptoe and Son, Absolutely Fabulous*, and *Fawlty Towers* all develop traditions of British humor ranging from the absurd to comedy of character, class, and social manners, usually ridiculing pretensions and insularity of the British themselves

There are also writers of specific niche or professional humor, such as John MORTIMER's *Rumpole of the Bailey* stories about the law, Richard Gordon's *Doctor in the House* (1953), and David LODGE's novels on academic life. So far none has emerged writing humorously about dentists.

BIBLIOGRAPHY: Bakhtin, M., *Rabelais and His World*, trans. by H. Iswolsky (1968); Bremmer, J., and H. Roodenburg, eds., *A Cultural History of Humour from Antiquity to the Present Day* (1997); Freud, S., *Jokes and Their Relation to the Unconscious* (1905); Ganz, M., *Humor, Irony, and the Realm of Madness* (1990); Hazlitt, W., *Lectures on English Comic Writers* (1818); Meredith, G., *On the Idea of the Comic and the Uses of the Comic Spirit in Literature* (1897); Muecke, D. C., *Irony and the Ironic* (1982); Nilsen, D. L. F., *Humor in Eighteenth- and Nineteenth-Century British Literature* (1998); Nilsen, D. L. F., *Humor in Twentieth-Century British Literature* (2000); Thackeray, W. M., *The English Humorists of the Eighteenth Century* (1851); Wilcox, J., *Humor in Anglo-Saxon Literature* (2000)

R. S. WHITE

HUNT, [James Henry] Leigh
b. 19 October 1784, Southgate, Middlesex; d. 28 August 1859, Putney

H. wrote narrative and lyric poetry, personal and political essays, drama and literary criticism, Christian philosophy, a play, biographies, and an autobiography, most justly unremembered, yet he was one of the most important and influential men of letters of the first half of the 19th c. He edited several magazines of historic importance, providing forums public and private for the great geniuses of the second generation of Romantic writers.

His loyalist family fled America, and he was born in Southgate, Middlesex. Sickly and poor, he was educated at Christ's Hospital, where the authoritarian masters and bullying bluecoat boys drove him to escape into poetry. His own *Juvenilia* (1801) achieved two editions, and though decidedly juvenile, confirmed his career choice.

When twenty years old, he went to work as the theater critic for the *News*, published by his brother John. He is credited, by himself among others, with initiating a new, independent, disinterested spirit of serious drama criticism. But it was his political writing in another Hunt brothers publication, the *Examiner*, that made his name. He became a liberal spokesman and an enemy of the Crown, serving a two-year prison sentence for a libelous attack on the Prince Regent. During his imprisonment, he was visited by Lord BYRON, William HAZLITT, Charles LAMB,

Thomas MOORE, Maria EDGEWORTH, Jeremy BENTHAM, James MILL, and other radicals and writers.

H. edited magazines and compilations for most of his life, their pages filled with the early works of Hazlitt, Lamb, Percy Bysshe SHELLEY, and John KEATS, the major voices of later English ROMANTICISM. The friendly competitions he hosted among young writers are now literary legend, and when "the Cockney School" was attacked in established journals, the *Quarterly Review* and *Blackwood's Magazine*, H. editorialized vigorously in their defense.

H. considered himself a poet; however, of his voluminous life's work, including the long romance *The Story of Rimini* (1816), only two lyrics, often anthologized, are left standing on their merit. They memorialize aspects of his character. "Jenny Kissed Me," written wishfully about Thomas CARLYLE's wife, records his flirtatious nature, enduring despite a long marriage and eleven children. An accomplished and delightful piece, it also serves as evidence of his shallow Romanticism. He rarely reached insights beyond SENTIMENT, though he could recognize the deeper strain in others' works and reward it with publication and apt praise; his biographical sketch of Keats is built around one of the better contemporary appreciations of the poetry. H.'s epitaph, "write me as one who loved his fellow man," is taken from "Abou Ben Adhem," perhaps his best poem, that with the potent simplicity of earlier Romantic ballads, expresses his philosophy of "Christianism," a humanistic, nondogmatic faith that, again, did not run deep, but which he applied tirelessly in his efforts, later in life, to reconstruct his great friend Shelley's reputation and pave the way for the Victorian reappraisal of the atheist radical activist as a sensitive, benign, ethereal spirit.

His biography of Byron, *Lord Byron and Some of His Contemporaries* (1828), is unfriendly and unfair, but it depicts its subject so vividly that all subsequent biographies must account for its portrait. His own *Autobiography* (1850) cannibalizes much of his earlier biographical and critical prose but is cheerfully achieved and became a popular success, so popular that H., one of the few surviving Romantics at the time of its appearance, entertained a fantasy of becoming poet laureate. Yoke that fond wish with the scathing caricature of H. as Harold Skimpole in his friend's Charles DICKENS's *Bleak House* and you span the contradictions of H.'s character in the context of the extraordinary talents with which he will ever be associated.

BIBLIOGRAPHY: Blainey, A., *Immortal Boy: A Portrait of Leigh Hunt*; Blunden, E., *L. H.* (1930); Russell, R., *L. H. and Some of His Contemporaries* (1984)

DENNIS PAOLI

HUNTER, Jim
b. 24 June 1939, Stafford

Born of Quaker parentage, H. was educated at Ackworth, a Quaker boarding school, and read English at

Cambridge, where he took a double first-class honors degree. He has combined a long career in education as schoolmaster, headmaster, and university lecturer with a writing career that includes seven novels, nine anthologies of both short stories and contemporary verse, and critical works on Gerard Manley HOPKINS, the "metaphysical" poets, and two studies of the plays of Tom STOPPARD.

The Sun in the Morning (1961), written when he was only twenty-one, won the Authors' Club First Novel award, and was reprinted (unaltered) in 1975. In it, H. presents the lives of six youngsters growing up in a northern industrial town and charts their parallel experiences of family, education, dawning sexuality, and leaving home. This sympathetic study of adolescents in all "their awkwardness, their goodness, and their need" introduces a key preoccupation throughout his fiction. In *Sally Cray* (1963), he tackles the development of a teenage girl trying to come to terms with both her social awareness and her sexuality in the contrasting settings of Britain and the U.S., but with less success. Throughout *Earth and Stone* (1963; repub. as *A Place of Stone*, 1964) and *Kinship* (1973), the myth and the reality of the middle-class family are subjected to intense scrutiny. Conflict typically emerges from the relation between a flawed father and his adolescent son, and from the marital disillusion of husband and wife. Much of the action depends on a series of arguments between two characters, which can begin to resemble debates, sometimes to the detriment of characterization. Protagonists remain committed to the idea of the family, however uneasy the equilibrium established at the close. Some of H.'s most vividly realized scenes occur in *Kinship*, where the breakdown of the wife, Alison, has enormous dramatic conviction.

H. shows considerable prescience in reading the signs of the times. He anticipates the popularity of the cross-cultural campus novel so effectively exploited by David LODGE and Malcolm BRADBURY among others, but his concern is with social realism and not comedy. *The Flame* (1965) traces the career of a conservative religious movement aimed at wiping out the moral decadence which its idealistic founder, Douglas Cameron, finds endemic in the Britain of the 1960s. Cameron's cause is compromised by the alliances he naively forms with a press baron and a politician, Blenkiron, whose inflammatory speeches lead to an attack on immigrant children. Fact caught up with fiction when, four years later, a Conservative member of Parliament, Enoch Powell, launched a crusade to stem the tide of immigration and keep Britain white. *The Flame* similarly anticipated the call of the Thatcher government of the 1980s for a return to Victorian values, particularly in the areas of family life and morality.

Lyrical writing of a high order marks H.'s two novellas, *Walking in the Painted Sunshine* (1970) and *Percival and the Presence of God* (1978). In the former, two teenage lovers and their mentor (always a key figure with H.), the enigmatic Allen, spend a brief holiday in a remote Scottish cottage. The story consists largely of the business of everyday living in this superbly realized landscape. However, this is no idyllic retreat from the problems of the world. As the three relive and exchange experiences, past, present, and future come into relationship. The narrative modulates into a profound meditation on the themes of identity, time, and the reality of suffering. In *Percival*, H. employs a terse yet poetic style to overcome the notorious problem of historical dialogue. Action, theme, and characterization work together in this haunting existential version of the quest for the Holy Grail. Restriction to the first-person point of view encloses the reader within the 20th-c. consciousness of the young knight. Although Christian and pagan elements figure prominently, this is a book about agnosticism, about a youthful idealist learning to live in doubt in a world where God, if He exists, preserves a "grey neutrality." The marriage between outer scene and inner awareness is successful throughout, rising to a climax when Percival, having failed to ask the key question of the Fisher King at the Grail ceremony, awakens to find the castle deserted and the air palpably silent.

H.'s most extensive influence has been as teacher and critic. One of his textbooks, *Modern Short Stories* (1964), has been continuously in print for forty years. He has always sought to be an intermediary between text and reader and to avoid the excesses of critical theory. Although he continues to write fiction, the market place has changed. Literary taste has moved away from his individual synthesis of liberal ideology, gritty realism, and objective reportage. His women characters have tended to be secondary, sometimes shadowy figures, unmarked by FEMINISM, a disadvantage in a contemporary novelist, although the bulk of his fiction was produced before the women's liberation movement really gathered momentum. In his representation of landscape, weather, and sense impression he is exceptionally vivid. In particular, *Percival*, which was republished in 1997 as the first volume of Raymond H. Thompson's series "Modern Arthurian Literature," is a work of enduring quality.

BIBLIOGRAPHY: Matthews, S., "J. H.," in Halio, J. L., ed., *British Novelists since 1960*, part 2, *DLB* 14 (1983): 420–26

MARGARET HAMER

HUNTER, N[orman] C[harles]

b. 18 September 1908, Derbyshire; d. 19 April 1971, North Wales

In England, H.'s name still exemplifies the slightly bloodless but elegantly written well-made drawing room drama of the 1950s—sumptuously mounted and starrily cast—which the English Stage Company at the Royal Court happily swept away with contempt. Indeed his plays always represent civilized values expressed in a literate, if not particularly distinguished, manner; and, because they provide good roles for the middle-aged, they were staple fare for amateur dramatic societies on both sides of the Atlantic, although they never made a professional impression in the U.S.

H. was born into an upper-middle-class army family (his father a colonel) and was trained at Sandhurst Military Academy. That he was both well educated and a gentleman is obvious from his work. Before the Second World War, he wrote several novels and six plays, only one of which *All Rights Reserved* (1935) had any success. During the war, serving with the Dragoon Guards, he found what he believed to be his purpose in life. In his backpack, throughout the conflict, he carried the complete works of Anton Chekhov. H. fell in love with Chekhov so deeply, he became a man possessed and his great ambition was to write plays in the shadow of his master. On demobilization, H. and his devoted Belgian wife went to live in North Wales, where he supported his writing by being a schoolmaster. Living so far from any theatrical center, he was always quite uninfluenced by fashionable trends. Then in 1950, he had a startling reversal of fortune. His play *Waters of the Moon* (1951) was selected as the official contribution by H. M. Tennent (the most famous theatrical management in London) to the Festival of Britain, with a cast led by the great actresses Dame Edith Evans and Dame Sybil Thorndike (the only time they were to work together).

The cornerstone of this rather synthetic piece of faux-Chekhov is humiliation: for the once prosperous family who run the West-country hotel and for their permanent guests living in reduced circumstances. Into this group's shabby but ordered lives come the Lancasters (car stuck in a snow-filled ditch), a family of rich cosmopolitans, who shake up the routine, give variously hopes and fears, and disappear when the snow has thawed, leaving behind the same circumstances but altered perceptions.

If the echoes of Chekhov in *Waters of the Moon* are loud, in *A Day by the Sea* (perf. 1953; pub. 1954) they are thunderous. This, H.'s feeblest successful play, had one of the most distinguished casts the postwar British theater ever assembled: Dame Sybil Thorndike, as the matriarch Laura Anson, Sir John Gielgud (who also directed) as her frustrated diplomat son Julian, Sir Ralph Richardson, Sir Lewis Casson, and Irene Worth. H.'s marked "Englishness" dilutes the mood to Chekhov and water and although his affection for and understanding of the characters are obvious, he has little irony and no natural wit or poetry. When he uses heightened language he becomes self-conscious.

A Touch of the Sun (1958) is an immeasurably better play because—briefly—H. found his own voice: he had assimilated the lesson of Chekhov rather than copying the teacher. He does not strain to conjure up poetic atmosphere and his more naturalistic approach is a relief. Here, the family split by riches and poverty and the loss of confidence and self-esteem that poor relations feel in the orbit of their richer counterparts is truthfully and expressively handled. He treats all his characters fairly and, most important, is using his own experience: Philip, the ascetic stick-in-the-mud schoolmaster, has elements of H. himself; and his wife Mary, who has known a smarter world on the Riviera, shares certain qualities with H.'s wife Germaine. H. then floundered about trying to find a new style. Of his later plays, only *The Tulip Tree* (perf. 1962; pub. 1963) has much merit.

H. was outstandingly successful in his day and *Waters of the Moon* has had major revivals on stage (1977) and television (1982) possibly because it provides in the volatile and sympathetic Helen Lancaster a vividly effective vehicle for a mature actress. *A Day by the Sea* had an acclaimed radio production in 1991. H. writes a pure, literate English. Separated from city life, he seldom uses contemporary jargon and slang, so his prose has dated little. For all his limitations, actors liked to speak his lines and some of the most famous of the time were eager to appear in his plays.

BIBLIOGRAPHY: Duff, C., *The Lost Summer: The Heyday of the West End Theatre* (1995); Salmon, E., "N. C. H.," in Weintraub, S., ed., *Modern British Dramatists, 1900–1945*, part 1, *DLB* 10 (1982): 242–47

CHARLES DUFF

HUXLEY, Aldous [Leonard]

b. 26 July 1894, Godalming, Surrey; d. 22 November 1963, Hollywood, California, U.S.A.

H. descended from two prominent Victorian families. His paternal grandfather, T. H. HUXLEY, championed science during a time of intellectual turmoil, and his mother, Julia Arnold Huxley, was a niece of the poet and critic Matthew ARNOLD. Undaunted both by his ancestry and by his partial blindness, H. attempted nearly every literary form, and his published works surpassed fifty volumes during a career that spanned four decades.

After graduating from Balliol College with first-class honors in English literature, H. was working as a journalist when he completed the first of his eleven novels, *Crome Yellow* (1921), for which he achieved celebrity status as a liberating force for the younger generation in Great Britain. H.'s literary ascent was shaken in the mid-1930s when he unexpectedly turned toward mysticism, a philosophical shift that closely coincided with his decision to settle permanently in southern California. Since then, critics have debated his place in the English canon. H. scholars typically enlist in one of three camps: those who contend that he was a two book author whose accomplishments reside in *Point Counter Point* (1928) and *Brave New World* (1932); those who contend that he ranks with Evelyn WAUGH as a modern satirist of the highest order; and those who contend that he advanced the novel of ideas further than any other writer of his generation.

Throughout the 1920s, H. used satire as his weapon of choice to censure human shortcomings and outdated social mores. *Crome Yellow, Antic Hay* (1923), *Those Barren Leaves* (1925), and *Point Counter Point* are therefore populated by egotists and eccentrics who are victimized by their own foibles. As an example of root stupidity, Theodore Gumbril in *Antic Hay* conspires with a hardnosed entrepreneur to market trousers with pneumatic seats, a real godsend, he claims, for humankind. Whereas H. described *Those Barren Leaves* as a "gigantic [Thomas Love] PEACOCK gathering of oddities in an Italian scene," in *Point Counter Point* he creatively merges classical music techniques with narration by juxtaposing an assortment of characters who express discordant views about life, love, and dying. Like individual instruments in a collective orchestra, they achieve rare moments of communal harmony, but soon break apart, each unable to hear the other. Throughout the novel, H. displays his fascination with "the human fugue" and its infinite number of subjective responses to reality.

Four years after *Point Counter Point*, H. completed his famous antiutopian or dystopian novel, *Brave New World*, which has been in print ever since its initial publication. Set in the future in the year A. F. 632 (After [Henry] Ford or After Freud for psychological matters), H. explores the dehumanizing effects of advances in science and technology, including assembly line genetic engineering and neo-Pavlovian behavioral conditioning. The action shifts from utopian London to a pueblo reservation in New Mexico and then back to London, where John, the Savage refugee, and Mustapha Mond, the Resident Controller of Western Europe, debate happiness and freedom. Dismayed by all he has experienced since coming to the "brave new world," John claims "the right to be unhappy" and eventually hangs himself from the ceiling of an abandoned lighthouse. In a 1946 foreword written for the novel, H. regretted forcing John to choose between an absurd life in UTOPIA or a primitive life on a reservation, wishing instead that he had given him a chance to live in a sane community where "Science and technology would be used as though, like the Sabbath, they had been made for man, not as though man were to be adapted and enslaved to them."

H. wrote two other marginally successful novels based on the utopian theme, *Ape and Essence* (1948)

and *Island* (1962). *Ape and Essence* begins on the day of Mohandas Gandhi's assassination and signals the defeat of nonviolence in the postatomic era. The pretext for the novel is a discovered Hollywood film script about a mutant society that springs up in southern California after a nuclear third world war. In the fictitious realm of Belial in the 22nd c., humankind has abandoned its rational essence for the hatred of the "ape-mind." Conversely, when the hero of *Island,* Will Farnaby, wrecks his boat on the shores of Pala, he discovers an idyllic civilization born of an unlikely union between the technological West and the enlightened East. Given that the Palanese have devised pragmatic solutions for problems ranging from child-rearing to mystical self-transcendence, critics point out that the book reads more like a philosophical tract than it does a novel.

The autobiographical *Eyeless in Gaza* (1936) is the most important of H.'s other "mystical" narratives, which include *After Many a Summer* (1939; repub. as *After Many a Summer Dies the Swan*, 1939), *Time Must Have a Stop* (1944), and *The Genius and the Goddess* (1955). *Eyeless in Gaza* begins on August 30, 1933, and ends on February 23, 1935, during which Anthony Beavis works out his relationship with his lover of several years, Helen Ledwidge. The intervening fifty-two narrative units, however, jump forward and backward in time, detailing the important segments leading to Beavis's conversion to pacifism in middle age. Dating from his school days, Beavis has been faithless to himself and to his friends, but during a journey to Mexico in 1933, he meets the Scottish doctor James Miller and is challenged to put his intellect to better use. By expanding his self-awareness, Beavis achieves personal enlightenment via a commitment to goodness, love, and compassion.

During the last ten yeas of his life, H. lectured at a number of universities throughout the U.S. In 1959, he was honored by the American Academy of Arts and Letters, and in 1962 he was elected a Companion by the British Royal Society of Literature. Although critics most recently have focused on the internal cohesion between H.'s early satires and his later mystical responses to the problems inherent in the 20th c., he remains best known for his efforts to bridge the gulf between science and literature.

BIBLIOGRAPHY: Atkins, J., *A. H.* (1956; rev. ed., 1967); Bedford, S., *A. H.* (2 vols., 1973–74); Brander, L., *A. H.* (1970); Firchow, P., *A. H.* (1972); May, K. M., *A. H.* (1972); Nance, G. A., *A. H.* (1988); Thody, P., *H.* (1973); Watts, H. H., *A. H.* (1969)

                                        JOE NORDGREN

HUXLEY, Elspeth
b. 23 July 1907, London; d. 10 January 1997, Gloucestershire

H. has been described as a witty and energetic writer with an eclectic output. As a "popular" writer with more than thirty books to her credit, including novels, travel books, mysteries, BIOGRAPHY, and AUTOBIOGRAPHY, H. is a colonial author, meaning that she wrote about the colonies for a white, middle-class or upper-middle-class audience.

Married to Gervas Huxley, a cousin of the British author Aldous HUXLEY, H. set many of her works in Kenya, where she spent her childhood. Her most important early work is *Red Strangers* (1939). In contrast to most colonial writing, it is written from the point of view of the native Kikuyu and depicts life in Kenya before the coming of the white man. The Macmillan publishing company was interested in the work, but Harold Macmillan demanded that a section on female circumcision be cut on the grounds that "the whole idea is unfamiliar and abhorrent." Retorting that "the whole of native life is unfamiliar to European readers" and that it is inadvisable "merely to present those aspects of native life which are pleasant and acceptable to the European mind," H. refused to make the desired changes and the book came out under the aegis of a different publisher. Nine years later, H. produced *The Walled City* (1948), describing the lives of a colonial official and his wife in a work that acknowledged the futility of attempts to graft one culture onto another. *A Thing to Love*, published in 1954, followed this same theme. Examining Mau Mau, the revolutionary movement that preceded Kenyan independence, to some critics H. revealed a procolonialist bias in her depiction of African revolutionaries as preternaturally cruel figures.

In the late 1950s, H. shifted her focus to her childhood in Kenya. Like other popular colonial works, such as Isak Dinesen's *Out of Africa* (1937) and Beryl Markham's *West with the Night* (1942), H.'s autobiographical memoir *The Flame Trees of Thika* (1957) was written for Britishers nostalgic for the days of Empire when Africa was empty and unexplored. On the one hand, these authors present a world in which self-discovery and self-discipline are made possible by life in Africa, for example, through attempts to grow crops and make gardens out of wilderness. On the other, they evoke an Africa capable of generating intense physical and psychological sensation, especially through sexual freedom. That is, in a confluence

of subject, audience and author, these women, all of whom were themselves members of a privileged class, discussed the goings-on among the Europeans who occupied the Rift Valley in Kenya, as they created virtual Camelots out of these white highlands. In contrast to Dinesen who filters out hard work and Markham who offers Africa as a landscape charged with eroticism, H. is credited with presenting a realistic account: her childish directness creates a perspective where living out the imperial mission becomes itself an anachronistic fantasy. Like Dinesen and Markham, however, H. does portray a feudal society in which Africans are distinctly "other" and take on the role of servants. That is, like pioneers in the western U.S., these writers all celebrate the imposition of power on a people unable to resist.

After independence came to Kenya in 1963, though, H. wrote empathetically about the challenges facing the many new African countries. *Out in the Midday Sun* (1985), for example, includes favorable portrayal of Jomo Kenyatta, Kenya's first president under majority rule. In addition, H.'s wide-ranging anthology of Kenyan literature, *Nine Faces of Kenya* (1990), begins with quotations from Pliny, moves through anthropology and ethnography, and ends with the modern poetry of Kenya. Nevertheless, critics found the work lacking in African perspective, both through its omission of key Kenyan authors as well as any mention of numerous historical mechanisms, like restrictive registration cards, intended to keep the African in his place.

On the whole, H. is at once resistant to and ruled by conventions that presume colonialism benefited Africans. Ultimately, she emerges as less critical of colonialism than she was capable of being. Nonetheless, as one who challenged and negotiated this ideology, H. is assured an important position in the colonial genre.

BIBLIOGRAPHY: Cross, R., and M. Perkin, *E. H.* (1996); Githao-Mugo, M., *Visions of Africa* (1978); Knipp, T. R., "Kenya's Literary Ladies and the Mythologizing of the White Highlands," *SAR* 55 (January 1990): 1–16

SUSAN TETLOW HARRINGTON

I

IMAGISM

The interest in free verse that gained momentum prior to World War I was strengthened by the appearance of imagist poetry, a type of free verse derived in part from the ideas of young British philosopher T. E. HULME and developed as a poetic movement by a small group of English and American poets from 1912 through 1917. Although imagism did not present a consistent poetic style, its ideology was explained often in print and its premises were highly influential. By creating a widespread audience for the "new poetic," imagism helped establish literary MODERNISM and launched the careers of many major poets. It is most closely associated with Ezra Pound and Hilda Doolittle, who published under the initials H.D. Exemplary imagist poems include H.D.'s "Hermes of the Ways" (1913), "Oread" (1915), and "Sea Rose" (1916), and Pound's "The Return" (1912) and "In a Station of the Metro" (1913).

The imagist movement originated in London from the discussions of the Poets' Club, which met in 1908 and included Hulme, F. S. FLINT and Edward Storer. Under the influence of work by metaphysical thinker Henri Bergson, Hulme discussed the importance of fresh language that communicated a clear impression of experience. This idea attracted Pound as early as 1909, when Pound joined Hulme's subsequent discussion group in London. Pound was also interested by the aesthetic pronouncements of Ford Madox Hueffer, later Ford Madox FORD, an influential literary critic and author. In the *Poetry Review* for February 1912, Pound published a "Prologomena" [*sic*] in which he mused about tradition and contemporary poetics. This piece offers early evidence of Pound's thinking about an "absolute rhythm" in poetry that exactly corresponded to emotion, about the use of natural objects as adequate "symbols," and about developing a poetic technique that would avoid conventions in favor of a "harder" modern language that was "austere, direct, [and] free from emotional slither."

Pound began using the imagist rubric in 1912. He printed five of Hulme's poems at the back of his own book *Ripostes* (1912) with a hint about an obscure "school of images" connected with Hulme. The definitive imagist movement coalesced in late 1912, when Pound, in response to some poems by H.D., declared them to be "imagiste" (the final "e" in early versions of the title reflected French influence). Three of H.D.'s poems sent in by Pound appeared in Chicago's *Poetry* magazine in January 1913, followed by comments about the imagists in Pound's letter "Status Rerum" in the same issue. At that point, Pound considered the imagists to include H. D., the young English poet Richard ALDINGTON, and himself; shortly thereafter, Flint was added. In March 1913, *Poetry* printed Flint's "Imagisme" (probably written by Pound) and Pound's "A Few Don'ts by an Imagiste," prose statements that outlined the predominant principles followed by imagists: direct treatment of the "thing" whether subjective or objective; to use absolutely no word that does not contribute to the presentation; as regarding rhythm: to compose in the sequence of the musical phrase, not like a metronome.

While Flint only hinted at an unwritten "doctrine of the image," in "A Few Don'ts" Pound characterized the dynamic nature of the image as "that which presents an intellectual and emotional complex in an instant of time" and carries the liberating emotional charge "of the greatest works of art." The essential thrust of these two short articles was that poetic vision and language were in the process of being reinvented by the imagists, who vigorously rejected the tired traditions of literary ROMANTICISM and drew energy from fresh and unexpected sources—particularly French symbolism and impressionism, ancient Greek lyrics, and Japanese syllabic verse.

Imagism appeared at an auspicious moment as one of the heralds of a "poetry renaissance" already underway in American and English letters. England was experiencing the popular Georgian revival, carried on in five anthologies published from 1912 to 1922 by

Edward Marsh. The Poetry Bookshop was launched by Harold MONRO at the end of 1912; his journal *Poetry and Drama* in March 1913. In the U.S., William Stanley Braithwaite of the *Boston Evening Transcript* had begun publishing his annotated *Anthologies of Magazine Verse* in 1913, which, like *Poetry* magazine, elicited fresh appreciation for poetry, while Carl Sandburg's "Chicago Poems," Edgar Lee Masters's *Spoon River Anthology*, and Robert Frost's *North of Boston* were shortly to make their sensational debuts in 1914. The innovative poetry published under the imagist mantle was accompanied by doctrinal articles explaining this new mode, which brought imagism critical and public attention as a legitimate, if seemingly minor, development at the time.

The basic tenets of imagism presented by Flint and Pound in 1913 gave sharper definition to the intuitive poetics that had earlier been proposed by Hulme. Imagism was intended to provide hard, clear pictures of particular objects through the use of precise language, creating visual impressions analogous to sculpture. Although sheer description was never imagism's aim, its emphasis on the emotional power of vivid depiction remained one of imagism's most appealing elements. As a type of free verse, developed in part from the work of the French symbolists, imagist poetry was intended to convey an intrinsic rhythm that arose organically from the poet's response to experience rather than from any strict metrical pattern. Flint's extensive knowledge about French poetry was a significant factor in the development of imagism and free verse in English, while Aldington and H. D.'s deep interest in Greek lyric added another strain, and Pound's response to Walt Whitman and to medieval Provençal lyrics yet another. Since the poem and the reader's response both depended on emotions evoked through a complex interplay of language, sound, and image, imagist poetry could not be adequately appreciated through traditional prosodic or formal analyses, and as such it provoked great interest and scandalized criticism on both sides of the Atlantic.

Even for its practitioners, imagism proved to be a flexible, perhaps imprecise, designation. Scattered publications of poems and articles were followed in 1914 by *Des Imagistes*, an anthology anonymously edited by Pound. Its eleven contributors showed a considerable degree of variation from the imagist tenets that had appeared in 1913, and the volume lacked a preface that might have explained what was particularly "imagist" about the contents, which included poems by Aldington, H. D., Flint, Hueffer, Pound, Skipwith Cannell, Amy Lowell, William Carlos Williams, James JOYCE, Allen UPWARD, and John Cournos. The movement began to lose impetus late in 1913. Impatient at what he viewed as a dilution of imagism, Pound by mid-1914 shifted his attention to another aesthetic, vorticism, which displayed generally the same principles as imagism.

Imagism received its next important push when Lowell, on a visit to England in summer 1914, offered to sponsor a series of imagist anthologies. Lowell invited D. H. LAWRENCE and the American poet John Gould Fletcher to participate in the volumes, along with Lowell, H. D., Aldington, and Flint; Pound declined. The split between the two strong personalities of Pound and Lowell has been variously interpreted. Pound accused Lowell of taking over the imagist movement, although he had already turned to vorticism. Lowell, on her part, had already investigated taking over a literary review in order to have a place to promote new poetry regularly. For the serial anthologies, Lowell proposed a democratic editorial process in which each poet critiqued the others' submissions and helped make collaborative decisions about which poems to use.

The series *Some Imagist Poets* (1915, 1916, 1917) put imagism permanently on the literary map, saving the movement from the disruptions caused by the war. As with *Des Imagistes*, there was considerable stylistic variation among the volumes' contents. The editions for 1915 and 1916 included prose introductions that expanded on the principles Flint and Pound had outlined in 1913. The regular appearance of *Some Imagist Poets* was supported by Lowell's extensive schedule of lectures and by a special imagist issue in 1915 of the fortnightly paper the *Egoist*. In America, numerous magazines printed discussions about imagism and free verse, which expanded the movement's impact. *Some Imagist Poets* sold fairly well, providing income and exposure for the poets in wartime England (although, due to an error, the 1917 volume was not issued by the English publisher, Constable). By the end of the war, the six poets who had participated in *Some Imagist Poets* had drifted apart temperamentally, and imagism as a movement effectively ceased, although Aldington helped compile an imagist anthology that appeared in 1930.

It proved to be important that those who developed imagism were also its early historians and apologists. The radical changes in aesthetic understanding brought about by imagism required explanations, which proved successful and appealing. Imagism's brief span of activity nevertheless exerted an immediate and enduring influence over the development of modern poetry. The premises of imagism appeared simple enough to induce many poets to try it, although many poets and critics misread imagism's ingenious subjectivity. Imagism provided the impetus that allowed free verse to flourish after the First World War, and the long-term achievements of many of the poets associated with imagism suggest the lasting influence of imagism's doctrines of vivid, economical language and sharp visual effects used to elicit particular emotional responses. No less a critic than T. S. ELIOT stated that imagism was central to the history of modern poetics, and the revolutionary impulses of the imagists can still be sensed in poetry today.

BIBLIOGRAPHY: Coffman, S. K., *Imagism* (1951); De Chasca, E. S., *John Gould Fletcher and Imagism* (1978); Gage, J. T., *In the Arresting Eye: The Rhetoric of Imagism* (1981); Gould, J., *Amy: The World of Amy Lowell and the Imagist Movement* (1975); Harmer, J. B., *Victory in Limbo: Imagism 1908–1917* (1975); Jones, P., ed., *Imagist Poetry* (1972); Pondrom, C. N., "H. D. and the Origins of Imagism," *Sagetrieb* 4 (Spring 1985): 73–100; Pratt, W., *The Imagist Poem* (1963; rev. ed., 2001)

JAYNE E. MAREK

INCHBALD, Elizabeth

b. Elizabeth Simpson, 15 October 1753, Stanning-field, Suffolk; d. 1 August 1821, Kensington

I. was one of the first women to live by her pen in the theater. A writer mainly of genteel sentimental comedies, she did not demonstrate the freewheeling bawdiness of her predecessors Aphra BEHN and Susanna Centlivre. Rather, she was a pragmatist, wrenching a livelihood from the theater in an era that frowned on ribald drama. She had an instinct for what worked onstage, and her two novels were successful as well. With feminists prompting revaluation of marginalized female dramatists, I. is now the subject of debate over her cultural significance. Though a professed liberal—she was a friend of William GODWIN—she is often accused of developing a conservative style that employs pathos with little political purpose. But her works addressed issues of patriarchal control and feminine standards of virtue, and it seems likely that I. can be seen as a stepping stone in the development, one century later, of the problem drama.

I. was born not only to parents of modest means, but a woman, a combination that guaranteed her none of the formal schooling her genteel and masculine contemporaries enjoyed. Instead, she learned her trade by immersing herself in it, marrying actor Joseph Inchbald at the age of nineteen and touring with an acting company. It was not an easy life, and I.'s husband died in 1779. Although country appearances had brought her some fame, her London stage debut in 1780 was not well received. Accounts relate that an occasional stutter spoiled her delivery. In need of money, she turned to writing and produced a group of farces, now lost, which were rejected by theaters.

Her first known success was *A Mogul Tale* (perf. 1784; pub. 1788), a farce that took advantage of the public interest in India and in ballooning. In it, a cobbler and his wife take a balloon ride with a quack balloon doctor, ending up in the garden of India's Great Mogul, where hilarious confusions occur.

Like I.'s other two known early farces, *Appearance Is against Them* (1785) and *The Widow's Vow* (1786), *A Mogul Tale* based some of its HUMOR on bawdy double entendre. I. was to find greater success, and the grounds for her reputation, in the sentimental comedies popular at the time. *I'll Tell You What!* (perf. 1785; pub. 1786) neatly blends comedy and pathos in the tale of a destitute wife whose father-in-law comes to her rescue. *Such Things Are* (perf. 1787; pub. 1788) followed in this comic/pathetic vein, adding an exotic locale, referred to both as Sumatra and India. Following the tradition of Thomas Southerne and earlier Restoration playwrights, I. interwove two plots, one comic and one dramatic. The comic plot involves mistaken identities, but the dramatic plot made reference to the contemporary prison reform movement in its portrayal of the Sumatran tyrant's dungeons.

Her next play, *All on a Summer's Day* (perf. 1787) was performed only once: criticized for her female protagonist's inappropriate behavior, I. withdrew it after opening night. She then embarked on a series of adaptations of French genteel comedies, a task that allowed her to find easy success on stage while refining her own style. Of these, *The Midnight Hour* (1787), *Animal Magnetism* (1788), and *The Child of Nature* (1788) were solid successes. I. also utilized the plays of the liberal French dramatist Louis Sébastían Mercier for another series of plays interweaving comic plots with pathetic tales of woe. *Next Door Neighbors* (1791) and *The Massacre* (1792) touch on the politics of revolution that infuse their sources, but are careful not to offend genteel audiences.

In 1789, I. retired as an actress and turned to completing her first novel, *A Simple Story* (1791). Contradicting its title, this work has often been criticized for its puzzling disunity: Volumes 1 and 2 focus on the courtship and marriage of a spirited flirt who becomes Lady Elmwood. Volumes 3 and 4 begin seventeen years after the end of volume 2, and are centered on Lady Elmwood's daughter Matilda, who is banished from her father's presence because of Lady Elmwood's adulterous affair. Whereas the first two volumes lead up to the marriage of the heroine, the second two revolve around the reconciliation of the stern father and the virtuously suffering daughter. Modern critics have generally praised the first half of the novel and disparaged the second. The feminist reappraisal of I., however, has provided an alternative view, in which the author radically utilizes the disunity to reflect cultural restrictions on women's behavior and writing.

A Simple Story was well received in I.'s day and made a name for its author as a novelist. But though she would soon release a second novel, *Nature and Art* (1796), I. returned to the theater, telling confidants that it was economically far more efficient to write plays. Whether because of her experience as a novelist or her years of working with French texts, her next group of plays were not only immediate successes, but became stock pieces for the next hundred years.

Every One Has His Fault (1793) introduced the stage to a newly delightful character: Mr. Harmony, a philanthropist who goes to great lengths to unite parties at odds. Playing to the tastes of the time, the play combined just the right amount of comic plotting and pathos. Similar in construct was *Wives as They Were and Maids as They Are* (1797), which utilized a conceit I. had used in *A Simple Story:* the disguised father who spies on his daughter. But the play's Miss Dorillon is a female rake, though an appealing one. The play has been of particular interest to feminist critics for its debates about the correct behavior of wives, and for its implicit critique of the culture's use of the threat of sexual violence to control women. Critics have argued that I. connects issues of intellectual property and physical sovereignty, particularly interesting as I. herself was recounted to have resisted an attempted rape on the part of her theatrical manager. I. is perhaps best known today for her adaptation of German dramatist August Friedrich von Kotzebue's *Das Kind der Liebe* as *Lover's Vows* (1798). Adding just enough comic lightness to the German playwright's heavy melodrama, I. created one of the era's biggest moneymakers. Its popularity is reflected in Jane AUSTEN's use of *Lover's Vows* as the play the young people scandalously get up in *Mansfield Park*.

After another Kotzebue adaptation, *The Wise Man of the East* (1799), and an attempt at Gothic drama, *A Case of Conscience* (wr. ca. 1801–2; pub. 1833), that was never performed, I. wrote her final comedy, *To Marry, or Not to Marry* (1805). Like William CONGREVE's *The Old Batchelour* and many less-famous plays, *To Marry, or Not to Marry* finds fun in the situation of a bachelor determined not to marry. The play is polished and elegant and delighted audiences for many years.

In 1805, I.'s publishers, Longman, Hurst, Rees, and Orne, persuaded her to write "remarks," or introductions, to a series of plays they were issuing under the name *The British Theatre*. I. agreed—reluctantly, it seems—and went on to become the English drama's first female critic of note. Beginning with William SHAKESPEARE, the plays were issued weekly over two years, and the final collected edition, published in 1808, comprised 125 plays. They became the theater's standard acting edition for years.

I.'s comments were intelligent, and, as could be expected, attuned to the realities of performance. She does not hesitate to moralize, though she argues that characters should be allowed a realistic mix of virtue and vice. She criticizes male playwrights and critics, even while expressing herself with an extreme feminine humility—when attacked for her opinions, she generally responded by claiming that she was, after all, "only a woman." Critics have read her statements of modesty both as disappointingly conformist and as radically duplicitous. It seems likely that here, as throughout her career, I. was acting as a pragmatist.

After *The British Theatre*, I. lived in increasing retirement, emerging once to defend the theater in a "Letter on the Present State of our Drama," which was signed "A CHRISTIAN, but no FANATICK." She died in 1821, when her plays were still being regularly performed. Though her own plays were included in *The British Theatre*, after the mid-19th c. she was forgotten, and it is only recently that she has been considered part of the canon of English drama, or more than a footnote to the development of the English novel.

BIBLIOGRAPHY: Littlewood, S. R., *E. I. and Her Circle* (1921); Lott, A., "Sexual Politics in E. I.," *SEL* 34 (Summer 1994): 635–48; Manvell, R., *E. I.* (1987); Rogers, K. M., "Britain's First Woman Drama Critic: E. I.," in Schofield, M. A., and C. Macheski, eds., *Curtain Calls: British and American Women and the Theater, 1660–1820* (1991): 277–90

GINGER STRAND

INDIAN LITERATURE IN ENGLISH

Historically and psychologically, the history of Indian literature in English is situated in two interrelated fantasies: the fantasy of the British colonial governance of India that got dissolved with the independence of the country; and later the reinstituted fantasy of the new sovereign nation state. Undoubtedly, these two fantasies represent two phases of Indian writing in English. The history of the colonial governance in India is in one sense the history of confrontation between tradition and modernity and yet in another intriguing and more comprehensive sense it defines the ethics of the imperial center. It is commonly acknowledged that the battle of Plassey (1757) marks a sudden and dramatic changeover of the East India Company to a colonial power and the firmer establishment of British colonial India as a part of the British Empire.

Among the numerous sociohistorical developments that have directly impacted the growth of Indian literature in English are the colonial administration's policies on education and indigenous culture, languages and literatures, political governance and industrial progress. In modern assessments of India's struggle for freedom, the Mill-Macaulay line of thinking generally stands discredited as does the British progressive liberalism. Although India as a crown colony became a laboratory of Utilitarianism, the general character of the British colonial administration remained repressive and authoritarian. In the midst of the Anglicist-Orientalist controversy, one finds that the famous Minutes on Law and Education of Thomas Babington MACAULAY and the attitudes of James and John Stuart MILL were basically rooted in a bold contempt for indigenous languages, literatures, cultures, and religions and a spasmodic desire for the modernization (Europeanization) of India. Thus, it is safe to assume that the Macaulalyan system of education, the conflict between tradition and modernity, and the rise of Indian nationalism are the three most important influences that have historically shaped Indian writing in English. It is a strange irony of history that although the minds of the educated and Westernized Indians were nurtured by the European intellectual traditions—ideas at the heart of the French Revolution and the English Romantic movement—their hearts remained Indian. While they had rejected colonialism and imperialism uncompromisingly and vociferously, they continued a genuine search for East-West synthesis and a cross-fertilization of languages and literatures.

Raja Rammohan Roy, the founder of the Brahmo Smaj who led the struggle for reformation even before Macaulay's Minute, is known to have become one of the first important writers of English prose. Of the three early practitioners of English verse, Henry Derozio, Michael Madhusudan Dutt, and Kashiprasad Ghose, it was certainly Dutt whose creative genius flowered. Derozio, a poet and teacher who died young like John KEATS, wrote under the influence of the younger English Romantic poets. Dutt who like Derozio was also influenced by the Romantic poets and who had embraced Christianity was a gifted writer of English prose, verse, and drama. In the writing of the Dutt sisters, Toru and Aru, there is ample evidence to show an earnest effort to achieve a synthesis of East and West. Since they were educated in France, their knowledge of French and English was instrumental in the production of *A Sheaf Gleaned in French Fields* (1876), which is primarily a work of Toru. Her ardent desire to learn Sanskrit took her to the study of Indian classics, notably the *Ramayana*, the *Mahabharata*, Kalidasa's *Sakuntala*, and to the putative volume of another sheaf, but this one gleaned in "Sanskrit Fields," which appeared posthumously as *Ancient Ballads and Legends of Hindustan* in 1882 with an introduction by Edmund GOSSE. Romesh Chander Dutt, a cousin of Toru Dutt and a retired ICS officer, understood the task of translating the classical Indian epics, the *Ramayana* and the *Mahabharata*, into English verse. But it is Manmohan Ghose, the older brother of Sri Aurobindo, whose unalloyed achievements as a poet have been well recognized. Educated at Christ Church, Oxford, he became a lifelong friend of Laurence Binyon. In a review of *Primavera* (1890), a collaborative work of Ghose, Binyon, Arthur Shearly Cripps, and Stephen Phillips, Oscar WILDE praised Ghose's poetic ability, hoping for the close-

ness of "the bond of union that may some day bind India to us by other methods than those of commerce and military strength." His *Love Songs and Elegies* had appeared in 1898, but the most admired work *Songs of Life and Death* was published posthumously in 1926 with an introduction by Binyon.

In considering the Bengali renaissance, especially the Bengali novel, one must consider the contributions of Bankim Chandra Chatterjee, the doyen of the Bengali novel, Sarat Chandra Chatterjee, the pioneer of REALISM in the Indian novel and Rabindranath Tagore, the Nobel Prize–winning poet, novelist, and dramatist. While Bankim's first published novel, *Rajmohan's Wife* (1864), was written in English, several of his Bengali novels were translated in English. Sarat Chandra Chatterjee's contribution must be considered in terms of his unswerving commitment to realism, especially the misery and suffering of the common man. Significantly, the early Tagore was influenced by Bankim, although the later Tagore achieved his own stature as an outstanding novelist and poet. Undoubtedly, Tagore eminently belongs both to Bengali literature and Indo-Anglian literature. His vision as a poet and a thinker has encompassed all of humanity. As a humanist, he is essentially a universalist and cosmopolitan. Although a nationalist at heart, he stood for progress and for a healthy synthesis of East and West. As an educator, he founded Visvabharati, an international university, where all cultures, Eastern and Western, were to be brought together in a broader understanding of unity and harmony. His religion, he says, is the religion of Man. Tagore wrote mostly in Bengali, but later he started translating his own works into English. The poem *Gitanjli*, a collection of his own Bengali lyrics that he had translated into English, was published in 1912. Written after the Indian tradition of *bhakti* poetry, it carried a spirited introduction by W. B. YEATS and in 1913 earned him the Nobel Prize for Literature. The poem was admired by William Rothenstein and Ezra Pound and was also warmly received in England and the U.S. Of the three major novels that appeared in English versions, *The Home and the World* (1919), *The Wreck* (1921), and *Gora* (1923), it is undoubtedly *Gora* that enjoys the reputation of being a greater work, although *The Home and the World* with a strong political theme is the dramatization of the "complexity and tragic dimensions of Tagore's own times, and ours." In assessing Tagore as a poet, one can hardly ignore Tagore's achievements as a musician and a painter.

Although Tagore and Aurobindo belong to the early phase of Indian literature in English, they still occupy an enviable position in history. Aurobindo, one of the greatest geniuses of the 20th c., wears several hats—the radical politician, the mahayogi, the philosopher, the poet, the critic, and the interpreter of Indian thought. Educated at St. Paul's, London, and

King's College, Cambridge, Aurobindo was deeply immersed in European intellectual thought and English and classical literatures. His greatest achievement as a philosopher is *The Life Divine* (2 vols., 1939–40) and indeed his greatest poetical work is the EPIC poem *Savitri* (1950). It is generally recognized that the poem *Savitri* is a companion piece to *The Life Divine*. In a review of his earlier work, *Collected Poems and Plays* (1942), the *Times Literary Supplement* reviewer has warmly noted several characteristics of Aurobindo's poetic genius and vision, comparing him to Samuel Taylor COLERIDGE and Heinrich Heine. Aurobindo, notes the reviewer, "is a new kind of thinker, one who combines in his vision the alacrity of the West and the illumination of the East." Indeed, his greatest contribution to philosophical thought is his theory of evolutionary progress. In the formulation of his social and political thought, Aurobindo, as is evident from *The Human Cycle* (wr. ca. 1916–18; pub. 1949) and *The Ideal of Human Unity* (1919), redefines nationalism and the ideas of freedom, equality, and brotherhood as three godheads of the human soul. But his poetic vision of human progress is much more inclusive and comprehensive. If Satyavan in the poem is suffering and dead humanity, Savitri is the symbolic representation of the idea of *shakti*, the regenerative power of Stayavan. In a recent revaluation, the modern Indian poets have designated him as their John MILTON. Aurobindo's critical genius is evident in *The Future Poetry* (wr. ca. 1917–20; pub. 1953) where he boldly proposes the application of classical Indian aesthetic to the progressive development of English poetry.

There is hardly any doubt that in the history of Indian writing in English, the novel has shown startling progress. Starting with K. S. Venkataramani's *Murugan the Tiller* (1927), we encounter the famous trio, Mulk Raj Anand, Raja Rao, and R. K. Narayan, the early experimentalists who have closely observed both the colonial and postcolonial eras. While Anand and the early Rao have been concerned with sociopolitical and sociohistorical realities, Narayan has successfully shut off all possible incursions of Western history and discourse. Like Sarat Chandra Chatterjee, Anand is a stark realist. His realism, especially his blatant and direct descent into the lowest depths of human life somewhat resembling the tradition of "dirty realism," derives its moral strength from his humanism. Anand returned to India after twenty-five years as a well-established novelist. Anand, the first Indian novelist to have received wide recognition, used the biographical form and models from the English and Continental novel to represent the truth of Indian life in its most naked and raw form. E. M. FORSTER's preface to Anand's first novel *Untouchable* (1935; rev. ed., 1970) can only be read as a significant statement on the literary merits of the novel and on

Anand's originality, objectivity, and directness. The two characters, the untouchable Bakha in *Untouchable* and the coolie Munoo in *Coolie* (1936), are sociohistoric metaphors of human enslavement, subjugation, and servitude. In the four novels created thus far in *The Seven Ages of Man* (1951–84) series, Anand's greatest triumph is the creation of the biographical figure of Krishan Chandar. Although *Morning Face* (1968) won Anand the prestigious Sahitya Akademi Award, *The Bubble* (1984) with its different genres and narratological techniques remains Anand's most ambitious work. This philosophical maturity of looking at history is reflected in *Conversations in Bloomsbury* (1981), a fictional biography and a dialogical discourse on coloniality. While Anand's fame as a novelist has risen over the years, it is important to take into account his outstanding work as a critic and as an editor of *Marg,* a prestigious art journal.

It is important to remember that both Anand and Rao have come to literature from philosophy. The latter's reputation as a novelist is based on his four novels, *Kanthapura* (1938), *The Cow and the Barricades* (1947), *The Serpent and the Rope* (1960), and *The Cat and Shakespeare* (1965). While *Kanthapura* is admittedly an epic of Gandhian philosophy*, The Serpent and the Rope* is a larger epic, "a magnificent guide to India." *The Cat and Shakespeare* is a "metaphysical comedy," consisting of a witty mixture of narrative, philosophical discourse, dialogue, and reflective commentary. Apparently, Rao has moved from the historical to the inner and meditative concerns of the mind affirming that art is *tapasya* or *sadhana* and that India is not history but "an idea, a metaphysic." His novel *Comrade Kirillov* (1976) is an intriguing work on the conflict between Indian values and other traditions. But the case of Narayan is distinctly different from that of Anand or Rao. Following the publication of his first novel *Swami and Friends* (1935), there appeared *The Bachelor of Arts* (1936) and *The Dark Room* (1938). After an interval of seven years, Narayan published four novels—*The English Teacher* (1945; repub. as *Grateful to Life and Death*, 1953), *Mr. Sampath* (1949; repub. as *The Printer of Malgudi*, 1957), *The Financial Expert* (1952), and *Waiting for the Mahatma* (1955). But it is the famous *The Guide* (1958) that earned Narayan the Sahitya Akademi Award in 1960. The creation of fictional Malgudi, a universal and mythic structure, is one of Narayan's unique and original achievements. His novel *The Painter of Signs* (1976) takes us again to the heart of Malgudi in an attempt to trace the impact of modernity on the Malgudi culture.

Two distinct movements appear to be at the center of the Indian novel. Although the nationalist struggle was finished, most Indian novelists such as Bhabani Bhattacharya, Manohar Malgonkar, and Khushwant

Singh have continued the historical tradition, very much in the tradition of Paul SCOTT, portraying events of the colonial and postcolonial periods. At the same time, there has also developed a genuine interest in the art of the novel. Malgonkar's *A Bend in the Ganges* (1964) is essentially an historical narrative, dealing with British colonialism, India's nationalistic struggle, and the impact of World War II. While Singh's *Train to Pakistan* (1956) deals with India's division, Balachandra Rajan's *The Dark Dancer* (1958), modeled after the *Mahabharata,* is focused on social, political, and moral issues, especially the East-West relationship.

Arun Joshi's second novel, *The Strange Case of Billy Biswas* (1971), has given him the well-deserved recognition of a successful novelist, but it is *The Last Labyrinth* (1981) that portrays the tragedy of modern man and the metaphysics of social and moral evil. G. V. Desani's trend setter *All about H. Hatterr* (1948), republished with an introduction by Anthony BURGESS, is a Joycean experiment that drew T. S. ELIOT's praise. Although one clearly sees the extension of Desani's literary artistry in Salman RUSHDIE's *Midnight's Children*, the writer who bears a close resemblance to Desani is Sudhin N. Ghose who has experimented with the fusion of myth, FOLKLORE, and history. Among the relatively younger group of novelists who have received wide recognition are Rushdie, Vikram Seth, and Amitav Ghosh.

The distinct achievements of such writers as Ruth Prawer JHABVALA, Kamala Markandaya, Anita Desai, Nayantara Sahgal, and Attia Hosain show the distinct quality of a female writer's perception of sociohistorical reality and progress. Jhabvala's novels *A New Dominion* and *Heat and Dust* are written from the perspective of an outsider. Her shifting identities have often created confusion about her perception of India; she looks at India not as an independent and detached observer but as a European looking at the preindependence India as an exotic place. Desai's *In Custody* (1984) and *Baumgartner's Bombay* (1989) are representations of history. In *Baumgartner's Bombay,* however, Desai combines the histories of British colonial India and Europe, thus providing a broader and more universal view of human indignities. Her novel *Fire on the Mountain* (1977) won her the Sahitya Akademi Award. Markandaya's first novel *Nectar in the Sieve* (1954), a portrayal of Indian peasantry, is essentially a conflict between tradition and modernity, a theme she has developed with more dexterity and maturity in *The Coffer Dams* (1969). Sahgal's novels mostly deal with the social and political realities of the upper-class Indians.

It is debatable whether the greatest achievement of Indian literature in English in the postindependence era is in the area of the novel or poetry and whether such cultural developments and aestheticizations are in any significant sense related either to postcolonial consciousness or to psychohistorical fantasy of the new nation-state or even to postmodernist skepticism. While both the novel and poetry have made significant strides, the achievement in the field of drama is admittedly very scanty. Indeed, the evolution of English prose is an important area of interest in the examination of Indian literature in English. Whatever the judgment in the years ahead, the emergence of the "new" poets such as Nissim Ezekiel, Dom Moraes, A. K. Ramanujan, Kamala Das, R. Parthasarathy, P. Lal, Jayanta Mahapatra, Pritish Nandy, and Adil Jussawalla simply shows that poetry has made some noticeable gains. Of the five volumes of poetry written by Ezekiel, *The Unfinished Man* (1960), admittedly a Yeatsian effort, remains his best work. Moraes, also a widely published poet like Ezekiel, has been influenced by the English modernist poets. Ramanujan's *The Striders* (1966) had basically established his reputation as a poet. While *Relations: Poems* (1972) reminisces childhood memories, *Selected Poems* (1976) dramatizes the diasporic hybridity and the conflict between Ramanujan's Indian background and the culture of his adopted home. But whereas the achievements of such novelists as Salman Rushdie, Anita Desai, Vikram Seth, and Amitav Ghosh have been well recognized, the work of the "new" poets continues to be the subject of critical scrutiny.

BIBLIOGRAPHY: McCutchion, D., *Indian Writing in English* (1969); Mukherjee, M., *The Twice Born Fiction: Themes and Techniques of the Indian Novel in English* (1971); Narasimhaiah, C. D., *The Swan and the Eagle* (1969); Srinivasa Iyengar, K. R., *Indian Writing in English* (1962; rev. eds., 1973, 1983); Stokes, E., *The English Utilitarians and India* (1959); Verma, K. D., *The Indian Imagination* (2000); Williams, H. M., *Indo-Anglian Literature, 1800–1970* (1976)

K. D. VERMA

IRISH LITERATURE

By any definition, by any measure, the Irish are arguably the most significant colonial or postcolonial literary culture. Along critical axes of invention, influence, and intransigent nationalism, Irish literature is remarkable, and often unique, in its endurance, adaptation, and the quality and quantity of its genius.

In large part, of course, the extraordinary reach and assurance of English imperialism created the conditions by and against which Irish identity, including Irish literary identity, would define itself. An island at England's back, inhabited by a different dominant culture, which later would adhere for its life to a rival religion, Ireland was a strategic threat to English imperial ambition. When Norman knights claimed Ireland for Henry II in 1169, the native Celtic tribes surrendered, but it was the capitulation of a people who had for several centuries absorbed and warred with Viking invaders before finally repelling them. The Norman-English "conquest" of Ireland would be a centuries-long, almost ceaseless war of cultural attrition.

By the 14th c., the feudal government complained that the settlers, including titled lords, had become "Hibernis Hiberniores"—more Irish than the Irish themselves. By the 16th and 17th cs., though, when European nationalist economic policies of expansion and exploitation created colonialism, and market share was determined by religious alliance, Ireland became a laboratory for pacification strategies, like plantation, and a killing field for Catholics who rallied behind tribal chieftains and English Pretenders in failed uprising after failed uprising. When the smoke cleared upon a century, the 18th, of punishing penal laws, the Irish had lost the power of public speech in their native idiom: business, legal proceedings, national and local governance, official communication of any kind, public debate, theatrical performance, book and periodical publishing were all conducted in English. By the British Ordnance Survey of the 1830s, which remapped the island and anglicized place names (and was the subject of Brian FRIEL's play *Translations*), Irish was a living language, literary or vernacular, in a few villages and corners of counties mostly in the far west, the *Gaeltacht*. On the battlefield of language, the English, it seemed, had won the culture war.

Imperial power controls the economic and educational systems, creating the market for literature and the language in which business is done. The imperial culture has more exchange value than the native culture, drawing talent to its wealth and forming talent in its image. At the beginning of the 19th c., Thomas MOORE's romantic, elegiac, internationally popular ballads took as their subject the passing of Celtic culture, specifically the waning of political idealism (after the institution of an Anglo-Irish parliament and the republican rising of 1798 failed to establish democratic self-government) and the collapse of the bardic tradition, and signaled the beginning of a century-long "Celtic twilight," as W. B. YEATS would call it. It need hardly be noted that Moore's verse was in English. Irish literature, that is, literature in Irish, from ancient sagas and satires to ballads exhorting the followers of the Stuart Pretender, was available for translation by scholarly antiquarians and romantic nationalists, Protestants and Catholics, Samuel Ferguson and James Clarence Mangan, but was otherwise fallow, exhausted.

At the century's end, Lady [Augusta] GREGORY would popularize the tribal warrior tales, as Yeats would intellectualize them, under the banner of the Anglo-Irish Literary Revival, claiming EPIC status for them and mustering the literary troops, writers and readers, to "revive" the expiring tradition with new editions, new translations, and salon conversation—and in the process demonstrating the final, irrevocable nightfall on the culture that had created the tales. In the next generation, when a Catholic schoolboy decided to reinvent literature, English literature was the obvious, the only choice for James JOYCE. And in the generation after, when a County Monaghan farmer gave up the soil for poetry, he would write in English, would Patrick KAVANAGH. Long work by the Gaelic League, an organization contemporaneous with the Literary Revival, and by Irish governments helped restore Irish as a widespread spoken language, but the native language of literature in Ireland had become English.

English had always been the native language of a minority population who, for two hundred years before the Literary Revival, had created a tradition of Irish genius published and performed in English. This Anglo-Irish subculture was a sturdy transplant of English settlers, Scots Presbyterian planters, and anglicized Celts, primarily. After the Reformation, the Anglo-Irish became a Protestant aristocratic "Ascendancy" (except for middle-class Nonconformists, who, surrounded by Catholics, remained loyal, local allies) joined by, among others, Huguenot refugees and apostate Catholics seeking to claim a crest and save title to family estates. They and their descendants were usually educated at Trinity College, Dublin, and, if they had talent and ambition, rode the market forces to England, usually London, where the exchange rate for genius was at a comparative premium. From Richard STEELE and Jonathan SWIFT to Richard Brinsley SHERIDAN to Edmund BURKE to Dion Boucicault to Oscar WILDE and Bernard SHAW to Elizabeth BOWEN and Iris MURDOCH, the exodus was relentless and draining. Dublin, though at times recognized as the second city of the empire, was throughout its imperial history a cultural backwater. The theme of exile that recurs in Irish culture in tales of saintly hermitage, songs of banished heroes, and autobiographical portraits of artists' self-imposed expatriation, reverses itself in the case of Swift, who returned home to Dublin as Dean of St. Patrick's, recognized the assignment as an exile from the literary-political life of his time.

Such antipodal vectors along cultural axes are common in colonial studies but are arguably more complex and powerful in Irish/Anglo-Irish literature. Consider language again, along the axis of influence. As Irish wasted as a literary, even a spoken, language, its effect on Anglo-Irish (and English) literature became more robust. The narrator of Maria EDGEWORTH's *Castle Rackrent*, which influenced Sir Walter SCOTT and the 19th-c.'s first wave of novelists, is a retainer whose peasant English is so Irish-inflected and colloquial that the author (or her collaborator father) appended a glossary of Irishisms to the text. A little more than a hundred years later, John Millington SYNGE poeticized the speech of his groundbreaking drama's peasant characters by listening closely to the talk of marginalized Irish men and women and adopting the peculiar rhythms and idioms of their oral culture in his highly literary prose. And roughly mid-19th c., William Carleton, a peasant himself, wrote stories and novels of local color in vigorous English.

And then there is Yeats. His unquestioned genius and importance aside, his poetry often betrays the identity crisis implicit in the hyphenation of "Anglo-Irish." The lists of forbears, familial and intellectual, and of fellows, in causes and like-mind (and across genders), that give spine to many of his signature poems—"To Ireland in the Coming Times," "Pardon, old fathers," "In Memory of Major Robert Gregory," "Easter 1916," "The Tower," "Beautiful Lofty Things"—claim an Anglo-Irish cultural identity by contextualization and an Irish nationalist credential by association. But the sheer number of lists and variety of the listed belie the authority, if not the authenticity, of the claims, until in "The Circus Animals Desertion" he takes account of his characters and finds himself among them, a creation of an imagination, his own, pulled by discordant desires toward antithetical denominations.

Postcolonial Ireland, like many postcolonial cultures, has suffered trauma and posttraumatic stress simultaneously. Birth by civil war followed by decades of poverty and censorship stunted the growth of the nation. It attained independence piecemeal, desultorily, and at the cost of partition, an Anglo-Irish border with Britain-bound Northern Ireland cartographically representing the persistence of the national/cultural identity question and keeping the wound fresh. Literature, however, had achieved a perceived historical privilege as a memorial, a consolation, an engine of the process of nation-making, and governments' commitment to education (following from the principles of Padraic Pearse, a leader of the Easter Rising, who was a poet, translator, and founder of a bilingual school) assured a readership, a bilingual readership, since instruction in Irish was institutionalized in state schools.

In the 20th c., Ireland would produce two of the monumental figures of MODERNISM, Yeats and Joyce, and four Nobel Prize winners for literature, Yeats, Shaw, Samuel BECKETT, and Seamus HEANEY. Extraordinary genius was supported by extraordinary talent, fiction writers such as Edna O'BRIEN and Booker Prize winner Roddy DOYLE, poets such as Austin Clarke and John MONTAGUE, playwrights such as John B. Keane and Hugh LEONARD. In the stress of cultural redefinition, traditional issues take postcolonial twists, and what was an applicable cartographic

representation of Irish literary history becomes a topological curiosity, opening into and out from itself like a Klein bottle or a passage from Joyce's *Ulysses*, some postmodern pretzel of a problem. Language: Beckett, who joined Joyce in European exile, wrote works, great works, in French. Are they Irish literature? Identity: track the names of Beckett's novels, specifically *Murphy*, *Molloy*, *Malone Dies*, *The Unnamable*. Is Irish identity lost in the question of identity, the loss of language? Language and identity: Brian O'Nolan, a.k.a. Flann O'BRIEN, whose novels *At Swim-Two-Birds* and *The Third Policeman* discover the postmodern in the postcolonial, also a.k.a. Myles na gCopaleen, who wrote a regular humorous newspaper column in Irish—did different languages demand different identities? (He went on to write alternate columns in Irish and English, fragmenting further within a single identity. Or is that alternation evidence of a synthetic identity developing from the dialectic?) Exile and identity: Martin MCDONAGH, one of the most praised and produced of contemporary Irish playwrights, was born and lives in London. Is London-Irish the reverse image of Anglo-Irish? Did emigration thematically subsume exile?

And some traditions have kept a relatively steady course. Translation: contemporary poet Thomas KINSELLA has translated, in prose and poetry, the *Táin Bó Cuailnge* (*The Tain*), the central myth of Irish Celtic warrior culture, and *An Duanaire, 1600–1900: Poems of the Dispossessed* (1981), a collection of verse by tribal poets, poor scholars, priests, and itinerant laborers in the age of their culture and language's decline. The success of the revival of Irish as a literary language in a thriving bilingual literary culture is apparent, to point to a single example among a possible many, in Paul MULDOON's translations of the Gaelic poems of Nuala Ní Dhomhnaill. Invention: from Yeats and Lady Gregory's creation of the Abbey Theatre as a national stage, to the innovative Gate Theatre (where Orson Welles cut his theatrical teeth), to the growing regional theater scene today, Irish drama has tended toward the cutting edge and the controversial. Irish dramatists have found their voices, as often as not, in the dissonance of disparate forms and styles, as in Synge's peasant tragedy and serious comedy, in Sean O'CASEY's early tragicomedies and later experiments in expressionism, in Beckett's world-class absurdism, in Brendan BEHAN's music hall modernism (in Joan Littlewood's London production of Behan's naturalistic script for *The Hostage*, originally written in Irish as *An Giall*), and currently in Friel's explorations of theatricality in an oeuvre dramatizing numerous major events of Irish history.

And like Yeats, a critic can argue and imagine the greatness, in every sense, of Irish literature in lists (partial), of poets: Mad Sweeney, Brian Merriman, Blind Raftery, Oliver GOLDSMITH, Speranza (Lady

Wilde, Oscar's mother), Katharine TYNAN, Æ (George RUSSELL), Louis MacNEICE, Denis Devlin, Richard MURPHY, Brendan Kennelly, Michael Hartnett, Michael LONGLEY; playwrights: William CONGREVE, Thomas Southerne, George FARQUHAR, Goldsmith, Lennox ROBINSON, Padraic COLUM, Tom Murphy, Frank McGuinness, Sebastian Barry, Marina Carr, Conor McPHERSON, Mark O'Rowe; of men and women of letters: Lady Gregory, Standish O'Grady, Daniel Corkery, Terence deVere White, Conor Cruise O'Brien, (Irish-American) Thomas Flanagan, Seamus Deane; of storytellers, especially of storytellers, in fiction, short and long and written for the screen, and in memoir: Laurence STERNE, Goldsmith (again), Lady MORGAN, Charles Robert MATURIN, Gerald Griffin, Joseph Sheridan LE FANU, Edith Somerville and Violet Martin (SOMERVILLE AND ROSS), Bram STOKER, Lord DUNSANY, George MOORE, Oliver St. John GOGARTY, Erskine CHILDERS, James Plunkett, James STEPHENS, Francis Stuart, Frank O'CONNOR, Liam O'FLAHERTY, Sean O'FAOLAIN, Peig Sayers, Mary Lavin, William TREVOR, Benedict Kiely, Brian MOORE, (American born) J. P. Donleavy, John McGahern, Maeve Binchy, John BANVILLE, Neil Jordan, Patrick McCABE, Anne Enright, Nuala O'Faolain, Mary Morrissy, et. al.

BIBLIOGRAPHY: Bradley, A., ed., *Contemporary Irish Poetry* (1988); Brown, T., *Ireland: A Social and Cultural History 1880–1980* (1985); Deane, S., ed., *The Field Day Anthology of Irish Writing* (3 vols., 1991); Flanagan, T., *The Irish Novelists, 1800–1850* (1959); Kenner, H., *A Colder Eye: The Modern Irish Writers* (1983); Kenny, H., *Literary Dublin* (1974); Mahony, C. H., *Contemporary Irish Literature* (1998)

DENNIS PAOLI

ISHERWOOD, Christopher

b. 26 August 1904, Cheshire; d. 4 January 1986, Santa Monica, California

I. is best remembered for his two novels about Berlin in the 1930s: *Mr. Norris Changes Trains* (1935; repub. as *The Last of Mr. Norris,* 1935) and *Goodbye to Berlin* (1939). These are certainly important achievements, which register both his engagement with the dominant aesthetics of the time and a degree of individual dissent. However, he also produced some interesting work before his Berlin years and in his postwar life in the U.S.

His first novel, *All the Conspirators* (1928), was autobiographical in some respects. The central figure, Philip Lindsay, comes from a slightly impoverished upper-middle-class family. His father is dead (I.'s father was killed in 1915), and he lives with his mother, who is a suffocating presence. The central theme is Philip's desire to break away from his family

and the kind of society it represents by becoming a painter and writer. After failing as an artist, Philip is forced to play a conventional "manly" role by setting off to take up a job in Kenya. However, he has a breakdown and at the end of the novel is left still under the power of his mother, but allowed, as an invalid, to pursue his fantasies of artistic success.

I. later said that the novel was burdened by the all too obvious influence of E. M. FORSTER, Virginia WOOLF, and James JOYCE. However, it showed considerable command of technique, using (or overusing) many of the resources of the modernist novel. It developed interests that remained central to I.'s novels: conflict between generations, between allegedly "purposeful" and allegedly "escapist" ways of living, and a complex irony toward its characters. I.'s much more accomplished work *Lions and Shadows: An Education in the Twenties* (1938) revisits this material. It is a more-or-less autobiographical text, but the foreword advises the reader to "read it as a novel." I.'s friends of the time—including W. H AUDEN, Edward Upward, and Sir Stephen SPENDER—are portrayed in the novel, but given fictitious names to emphasize that this is not in the ordinary sense "autobiography," is not, in the words of I.'s foreword "even entirely true." This fictionalized autobiographical mode is variously used again in *Goodbye to Berlin,* in *Prater Violet* (1945), and in his later account of his parents and himself in *Kathleen and Frank: the Autobiography of a Family* (1971).

His next novel, *The Memorial: Portrait of a Family* (1932), again concerned the rebellion of a son against a mother, the conflict between prewar and postwar generations. Like *All the Conspirators,* this has strong Forsterian resonances, as suggested by its subtitle. However, it was also a novel very much of the late twenties/early thirties in its aggressive attack on the older generation who had led England to war. Nevertheless, both older and younger generations are seen in complex and ironic ways: there is no longer any simply natural way of behaving, precisely because all live in the shadow of that European trauma, the Great War.

In the period from 1935 to 1939, I. produced his major works, while also collaborating on some significant pieces with Auden. The collaborations consist of three verse dramas and a travelogue: *The Dog beneath the Skin* (1935)*, The Ascent of F6* (1936)*, On the Frontier* (1938), and *Journey to a War* (1939). The individual works are *Mr. Norris Changes Trains* and *Goodbye to Berlin.* These are based on I.'s experience of living in Berlin at the end of the Weimar and beginning of the Nazi periods. Both apply lessons learned from his earlier fiction writing to this central crisis of European culture. Thus, both draw on the authority of first-person/autobiographical testimony, yet also show through complex narrative strategies and complex ironies that witnesses do not always at all understand what is going on in front of them. If the earlier novels tried to show cultural battle lines clearly drawn, these two novels show that appalling political shifts happen while—and because—the ordinary, and in one way or another bankrupt, people of Germany are distracted by their own modes of escape and survival. Similar themes of escapism, fantasy, and fictionalized autobiography are used to serious ends in the postwar novel, *Prater Violet*. Set in the 1930s, the novel concerns "Christopher's" work with an Austrian film director, Friedrich Bergmann. His opposition to fascism and his seriousness as an artist are exposed to the "charade" of entertainment filmmaking. Nevertheless, Bergmann's commitment to art is sustained.

Having moved to the U.S. in 1940, I. became committed to belief in Vedanta. He published a number of books about Vedanta, and all his later fictional works explore its values. *Down There on a Visit* (1962) revisits the twenties and thirties and examines them in the light of Vedanta, and its attitudes toward commitment and sexuality. This postwar writing was able to deal more openly with homosexuality. I.'s writing retains a considerable reputation; Gore Vidal describing him as "the best prose writer in English."

BIBLIOGRAPHY: Berg, J. J., and C. Freeman, eds., *The I. Century* (2000); Finney, B., *C. I.* (1979); Summers, C. J., *C. I.* (1980); Wade, S., *C. I.* (1991)

CHRIS HOPKINS

ISHIGURO, Kazuo

b. 8 November 1954, Nagasaki, Japan

An immigrant to Britain at age five, I.'s absorption of British culture formed a critical awareness of difference, dislocation, and polite delusions that forms the fabric of his fiction. Educated at the Universities of Kent at Canterbury and of East Anglia, I. is the author of five highly acclaimed novels, among them *The Remains of the Day* (1989), upon which a well-received Merchant and Ivory film was based. Each of I.'s novels offers an incisive, mannered study of delayed recognitions, both personal and social. I.'s representation of an individual consciousness is inevitably parallel to one of a nation or culture: primarily it is instances of shame, as well as the strategies by which such instances are sublimated, that they share.

The historical settings of I.'s fictions are chosen for their crises and consequent moral complexities, and the narrators for their misplaced faith. *A Pale View of Hills* (1982), which won the Winifred Holtby Prize of the Royal Society of Literature, is the first book in a pattern of first-person narratives in which a past life is at times diffidently examined. Etsuko, a middle-aged Japanese widow living in England, at-

tempts to talk about her life (particularly her relationships with a friend and her daughter) without directly acknowledging the bombing of Hiroshima. In *An Artist of the Floating World* (1986), winner of the Whitbread Book of the Year Award, Masuji Ono is a man vaguely out of step with the modern world of postwar Japan. As his youngest daughter's marriage is being cautiously arranged, Ono is barely able to perceive how troubled he himself is by his past as a craftsman of imperialist, pro-war propaganda. I.'s title refers to the kind of artist Ono ultimately failed to be: one of a self-sustaining purity. Ono's narration is filled with hesitation, qualification, and doubt as he meanders between memories of teachers and friends he has almost unwittingly betrayed and exchanges with the remains of his family. A new economic and cultural fascination with America is warily observed by Ono, who watches his grandson play at being a cowboy and wonders about the direction of youthful enthusiasm.

Like *Artist*, the Booker Prize–winning *The Remains of the Day* is a psychological portrait more significant for its gaps and slight omissions than for the details most conspicuously provided. Stevens, like his father before him, is a butler who cherishes the mix of decorum and humility that is his job and social position. The novel moves between a trip Stevens takes to England's west country in 1956 and his recollections of his years of service before the war. The purpose of the journey seems clear—Stevens is to track down his former coworker at Darlington Hall, the exemplary housekeeper Miss Kenton, to reengage her services—but it is not, even, sadly, for Stevens. Disillusionment comes uneasily to the devoted professional, who is reluctant to realize that his idolized Lord Darlington was a political tool of the Nazis, that his own relationship with his father was a depersonalized sham, and that he loved and lost Miss Kenton. I. uses conventions of melodrama to present a pathetically failed romance featuring members of a class unlikely to feature in such a genre. Stevens's life is one devoid of personal action or commitment, and he is readily absorbed into the Hall's new household under an American plutocrat, as any self-deceiving citizen transfers allegiance from one empire to another.

The largest and most oneiric of I.'s novels, *The Unconsoled* (1995), winner of the Cheltenham Prize, is a fascinating puzzle. In an unnamed European city, a narrator named only Ryder arrives to give a piano concert. From this vague starting point the story descends into the completely nebulous, as Ryder apparently discovers startling but elementary things about himself—that he has a family, for example—at the same time that the matter of his concert becomes gradually more indeterminate. With its surreal HUMOR, the novel unfolds like a grand anxiety dream, and the reader eventually pieces together a man deeply in need of assurance: I.'s definition, perhaps, of an artist.

When We Were Orphans (2000) adds to I.'s customary ironic examination of dutiful detachment a marked parody of the literary genre most associated with such a quality: the British mystery. Christopher Banks, illustrious detective, can solve any mystery but the one surrounding his own identity. As he searches for his lost parents in Shanghai, Banks's narrow vision is upset by the inconvenient realities of the Sino-Japanese war.

I. owes much to the impressionism of writers like Ford Madox FORD, but the political critique underwriting his fallible narrators puts him in contemporary comparison with authors such as Salman RUSHDIE and John BANVILLE. I. continually addresses the ways in which we compromise and forget ourselves in submission to systems, traditions, and formalized hypocrisies.

BIBLIOGRAPHY: Petry, M., *Narratives of Memory and Identity: The Novels* of *K. I.* (1999); Rose, J., *States of Fantasy* (1996); Shaffer, B. W., *Understanding K. I.* (1998)

TIM CONLEY

J

JACOB, Naomi [Ellington]

b. 1 July 1884, Ripon, Yorkshire; d. 27 August 1964, Sirmione, Lake Garda, Italy

Her first novel, *Jacob Ussher* (1926), based on a play by H. V. Esmond, was followed by numerous others, including possibly her best, *Four Generations* (1934), *The Loaded Stick* (1934), a biography of music hall star Marie Lloyd (1936), novels *Straws in Amber* (1938), *The Cap of Youth* (1941), *The Morning Will Come* (1953), and several volumes of autobiography. J.'s Jewish heritage inspired a series of novels published from 1930 to 1958 and reissued as *The Gollantz Saga* (7 vols., 1973–74). Her lesbianism has led to a revival of interest in her life and work.

JACOBS, W[illiam] W[ymark]

b. 8 September 1863, London; d. 1 September 1943, London

J.'s early short stories, published in the *Strand Magazine* in the 1890s, were characteristically set among the coastal workers, barge crews, and night watchmen he grew up among. In 1896, he published *Many Cargoes,* the first of eight collections and gave up his day job. Author of eight collections of short stories and four novels, *The Skipper's Wooing* (1897), *At Sunwich Port* (1902), *Dialstone Lane* (1904), and *Salthaven* (1908), he was popular chiefly for his short stories, which were about either sailors and the sea, or country people. He remains famous for his much-anthologized short story, "The Monkey's Paw" (1902), in which wishes come true but with unforeseen and disastrous results. It was successfully dramatized for the stage and adapted for film.

JACOBSON, Dan

b. 7 March 1929, Johannesburg, South Africa

Son of Eastern European Jewish immigrants, J. graduated from the University of Witwatersrand in 1949, and worked in public relations and the family cattle feed business before a spell on a kibbutz in Israel. He moved to Britain in 1958. His novels deal with minds under stress beneath calm social surfaces. *The Trap* (1955), *A Dance in the Sun* (1955), and *The Price of Diamonds* (1957) are all set in South Africa. In *Evidence of Love* (1960), love crosses racial boundaries. They were followed by *The Beginners* (1966), about conflicting loyalties, and by an apparent change of material in *The Rape of Tamar* (1970), based on an Old Testament story of treachery. *The Wonder-Worker* (1973) is about schizophrenia and *The Confessions of Joseph Baisz* (1977) also deals with mental disturbance. J. has published several volumes of short stories and an autobiography, *Time and Time Again* (1985).

JAMES I OF ENGLAND. See JAMES VI OF SCOTLAND

JAMES I OF SCOTLAND

b. July 1394, Dunfermline, Scotland; d. 21 February 1437, Perth, Scotland

J., the younger son of Robert III and Annabella Drummond, became King of Scots in 1406, but spent the first eighteen years of his reign as an English prisoner. Between 1420 and 1422, he campaigned in France with Henry V of England. J.'s release was negotiated in 1423–24, and as part of the terms of this he married Joan Beaufort, the daughter of the Earl of Somerset and a cousin of Henry VI, in February 1424. He returned to Scotland determined to increase the authority and resources of the Crown. To achieve this, he used forceful, even violent methods, and as a consequence was brutally murdered; the events leading up to his death, and the execution of the murderers, are described in *The Dethe of the Kynge of Scotis* by John SHIRLEY.

J. is attributed with the authorship of the poem known as *The Kingis Quair*. This work survives in a single manuscript (Oxford, Bodleian Library, Arch. Selden. B.24), a collection of English and Scottish verse that dates from the late 15th or early 16th c. The poem's title and colophon in the manuscript suggest that J. was the author, as does the work's autobiographical content. In addition, J. enjoyed a contemporary reputation as a man of culture, as Walter Bower, the Abbot of Incholm, records, and the early-16th-c. historian John Major also states that J. wrote a poem about his queen.

The Kingis Quair consists of 197 stanzas in rhyme royal (seven-line stanzas rhyming *ababbcc*). The language of the poem is Northern or Scots English with a mixture of Midland sounds and forms. In literary terms, the poem is clearly influenced by the writing of Geoffrey CHAUCER and John GOWER, whom J. names as his "maisteris dere" in the final stanza, and John LYDGATE. J.'s indebtedness to Chaucer can be seen in meter, vocabulary, and narrative setting, though the central section also seems to draw on Lydgate's *Temple of Glass*. In addition, the influence of Boethian philosophy on the poem's action and thought is palpable. The poem begins with a sleepless narrator (a prince) who reads Boethius's *Consolation of Philosophy* and realizes that he is as subject to Fortune as any of his servants. He decides to write his own story and tells how, while traveling to France, he was captured by the English and spent eighteen years in exile as a prisoner. His prison cell affords him a view of a garden, and he falls in love with a woman that he sees there. In a dream vision, he goes to the House of Venus and is instructed by Minerva (Divine Reason). He then goes to an earthly paradise and steps onto Fortune's wheel, which is turning upward. After this, he awakes to find love and freedom together (that is marriage and release from prison). The poem thus charts a circular course of experience and learning, and C. S. LEWIS praised its originality as a real-life application of the allegory of love.

A few other poems have been attributed to J., including "The Ballad of Good Counsel," "Christis Kirk on the Green," and "Peblis to the Play"; the first may be his, but the latter two are probably later in date. Walter W. Skeat claimed that J. was responsible for part of the MIDDLE ENGLISH translation of the *Romaunt of the Rose*, but this is now generally disputed.

BIBLIOGRAPHY: Brown, M., *James I* (1994; rev. ed., 2000); Boffey, J., et al., *The Works of Geoffrey Chaucer and "The Kingis Quair"* (1997); McDiarmid, M. P., ed., *The Kingis Quair of James Stewart* (1973)

MARGARET CONNOLLY

JAMES VI OF SCOTLAND [later James I of England]

b. 19 June 1566, Edinburgh, Scotland; d. 27 March 1625, Hertfordshire

J. was crowned King of Scotland in 1567, at just one year of age, following the forced abdication of his mother Mary Queen of Scots. He became King of England after the death of Queen ELIZABETH I, from 1603 to 1625. The majority of J.'s writings were produced during his Scottish reign and early in his English reign.

While J. was young, Scotland was ruled by a series of regents, and the king was tutored by George Buchanan, one of the best-known scholars in the period. This early education helped to shape J. as a scholar, and he gladly took on the role of philosopher-king in both his reigns. When J. was eighteen, he began his personal reign of the kingdom, at the same time publishing a collection of poetry entitled *Essayes of a Prentise in the Divine Art of Poesie* (1584). This official, formal, and lengthy publication served as an introduction to the king, and created a court of which the monarch was the political and cultural center. The *Essayes* includes a treatise on Scottish poetry, outlining a series of poetic rules, and marks the renaissance of Scottish court literature. The collection reveals J.'s poetic capabilities in a diverse range of styles; it includes a number of sonnets, translations of Guillaume de Salluste Du Bartas's *Uranie* and of Lucan, and a long allegorical poem on the disappearance of one of J.'s court favorites, Esmé Stuart. J.'s early foray into poetry and his patronage of a number of poets helped to develop a vibrant literary culture at court.

J.'s second publication, *His Maiesties Poeticall Exercises at vacant houres*, appeared in 1591. As the title indicates, the king had little time to spend on literary creativity amid the demands of ruling a kingdom. This collection consists of two poems, a translation of Du Bartas's *Furies*, and J.'s own heroic *Lepanto*, a poem outlining the victory of the Catholic league against the Turks in the naval war of 1571. *Lepanto* was one of J.'s most popular poems; in addition to a French translation by Du Bartas, there were translations into Latin, Dutch, and German. The poem was also republished in London in 1603. J. also wrote a third collection of poetry that was never published, perhaps because of the more personal and casual nature of some of the poems. This collection comprises poetry in a variety of verse styles, including love poetry and dedications to authors and historical figures. During his English reign, J. wrote occasional verses on individuals such as Queen Anne and the Duke of Buckingham, and a political rebuke entitled "The Answere to the Libell called the Comons teares" (1622).

J. wrote two prose treatises on kingship. The first, *The True Law of Free Monarchies* (1598), was a public justification of the divine right of kings, and an explanation of the relationship between monarch and subject. The second, *Basilikon Doron* (1599) or "the king's gift," was ostensibly meant as a guide on kingship for his son Henry and initially had a limited publication run of seven copies. The text found its way into other hands, however, and so *Basilikon Doron* was revised and republished in both Edinburgh and London in 1603; it quickly became internationally famous.

J.'s literary and scholarly writings were wide ranging. He was a serious student of the Bible, two of his better known biblical exegeses being "A Paraphrase upon the Revelation of the Apostle S. John" and "A Meditation upon the Lords Prayer." He also wrote a number of metrical versions of the Psalms. In 1611, he endorsed a new translation of the Bible, known as the Authorized King James Version. J. was also a believer in witchcraft, and wrote a treatise on the subject, *Dæmonologie* (1597). Early in his English reign, J. wrote an anti-tobacco treatise entitled *Counterblaste to Tobacco* (1604), in which he deftly uses medical arguments to attack the generally held belief in the therapeutic properties of tobacco, as well as moral, national, and political arguments to outline the dangers of social smoking and addiction.

The varied, wide-ranging writings of J. are slowly becoming the focus of more critical analysis; the political and religious compositions have been studied rather more than the poetical output. However, J. has always been well known as a patron of the arts. He established a court circle of poets in Scotland and, shortly after his arrival in England, was patron to the King's Men, the dramatic troupe that included William SHAKESPEARE. J. and his wife Anne's patronage of court entertainments also helped to develop the genre of the court masque. J.'s connection to scholarship and literature made his roles as monarch and as poet inseparable. As English poet Ben JONSON's welcoming verse of 1603 states, "How, best of kings, dost thou a sceptre bear! / How, best of poets, dost thou laurel wear!"

BIBLIOGRAPHY: Goldberg, J., *James I and the Politics of Literature* (1983); Peck, L. L., ed., *The Mental World of the Jacobean Court* (1991); Shire, H. M., *Song, Dance and Poetry of the Court of Scotland under King James VI* (1969); Wormald, J., "James VI and I: Two Kings or One," *History* 68 (1983): 187–209

SANDRA BELL

JAMES, G[eorge] P[ayne] R[ainsford]
b. 9 August 1799, London; d. 9 June 1860, Venice, Italy

Privately educated in London and in France, J. composed his first stories while in his teens, publishing them later as *The String of Pearls* (2 vols., 1832). Like Alexandre Dumas in France, J. in England built upon the legacy of Sir Walter SCOTT to satisfy the public's taste for historical novels, and over thirty years published more than one hundred books, comprising novels, history, BIOGRAPHY, and verse narratives. In 1850,

he went to America as British Consul for Massachusetts. Among his best works are *Richelieu* (3 vols., 1829), *Darnley* (3 vols., 1830), *Philip Augustus* (3 vols., 1831), *Mary of Burgundy* (3 vols., 1833), and *The Smuggler* (3 vols., 1845). He was parodied by William Makepeace THACKERAY in *Mr. Punch's Prize Novelists.*

JAMES, Henry
b. 15 April 1843, New York City; d. 28 February 1916, London

J.'s influential writing career spanned over fifty years. His twenty-two novels and one hundred and fourteen short stories reflect a literary transition from 19th-c. REALISM to early-20th-c. MODERNISM; his criticism represents some of the earliest articulations of the theory of fiction. In addition he wrote seven books of travel writing, two biographies, three volumes of AUTOBIOGRAPHY, fifteen plays, and some ten thousand extant letters.

J.'s father was Henry James Sr., a theologian and social reformer, and his mother, Mary Walsh James. He had four siblings: William James, Garth Wilkinson James, Robertson James, and Alice James. William, a teacher, philosopher, and psychologist, was one of the preeminent American intellectuals of the early 20th c. Garth Wilkinson and Robertson fought in the Union Army in the American Civil War, later establishing a short-lived cotton plantation in Florida. Alice was a lifelong invalid and neurasthenic. Her revealing diary (unpublished until 1934) documents her illness.

J.'s earliest years were spent crossing the Atlantic. The family lived in England and France from 1843 until 1845, and he later claimed that his first memory, during his second year, was of the Place Vendôme in Paris with its Napoleonic column. For the next decade, the Jameses lived in Albany and New York City, where J.'s education was rarely formal. During this period, he was taught by a succession of private tutors. He was also introduced to art and theater, and started to compose and illustrate his own dramatic scenes. Between 1855 and 1858, the family traveled again around Europe—Geneva, London, Paris, and finally to Boulogne. A brief return to America in 1858–59 saw the Jameses settled in Newport, Rhode Island, where J. met the young painter John La Farge who introduced him to the work of the French literary elite in the journal *Revue des Deux Mondes*. However, James Sr.'s continued dissatisfaction with American educational practices resulted in yet another trip to Geneva in October 1859. Initially enrolled in an institution specializing in engineering (he would later comment on his parents' "flattering misconception of my aptitudes"), J. quickly focused all his studies on French, German, and Latin. The peripatetic lifestyle continued with a return to Newport in the summer of 1860, where William studied painting with William Morris Hunt. J. turned his attention to translating French literature.

The American Civil War broke out in April 1861. In October, J. was injured while serving as a volunteer fireman; his "obscure hurt," as he later described it in his autobiography, enabled him to avoid enlistment. Instead, he enrolled at Harvard Law School, becoming a keen admirer of James Russell Lowell, Professor of European Literature. In 1863, J. withdrew from university to concentrate on his writing. His first unsigned tale, "A Tragedy of Error," was published in the *Continental Monthly* in February 1864, and in October that year his first review appeared in the *North American Review*, under the editorship of Charles Eliot Norton (with whom J. would maintain a lifelong friendship). J.'s first signed tale, "The Story of a Year," was published in the *Atlantic Monthly*, a magazine with which he would have a long association, in March 1865. Reviews continued to be written, including notices of work by Walt Whitman, Charles DICKENS, and George Sand.

In February 1869, J. embarked on his first solo tour of Europe. In London, he soon met Sir Leslie STEPHEN, John RUSKIN, Dante Gabriel ROSSETTI, William MORRIS, Charles DARWIN, and George ELIOT (in whose "vast ugliness resides a most powerful beauty," he reported in a letter to his father). Returning to America in May 1870, J. maintained a regular output of book reviews, travel sketches, and short stories. The following year saw the serial publication in the *Atlantic Monthly* of his first novel (although later disowned), *Watch and Ward*, and his first substantial piece of short fiction, "A Passionate Pilgrim," an early example of the so-called international theme that J. was to make his own. Another trip to Europe in 1872 enabled more literary friendships to be cemented. J.'s old lecturer at Harvard, James Russell Lowell, became a regular companion, as did the actress Fanny Kemble. He found a ready-made artistic salon in Rome at the home of the sculptor William Wetmore Story.

J. returned to New York in the summer of 1874. His first book, *A Passionate Pilgrim and Other Tales*, was published in January of the following year. In 1875, J. also oversaw the serialization in the *Atlantic Monthly* of what he regarded as his first proper novel, *Roderick Hudson* (1876; rev. ed., 1879). It describes the relationship between Rowland Mallet, a wealthy New England art connoisseur, and Roderick Hudson, a talented but wayward sculptor whose career in Rome Mallet patronizes. J.'s book presents an analysis of the artistic sensibility and the moral dangers to it of the European environment. The work also demonstrates an early example of his favored technique of establishing a "center of consciousness" within his

narrative, a participant who is also the primary observer of events. J. found living in New York too expensive and decided to move to Europe, arriving in Paris in November 1875. There he met Ivan Turgenev and became a regular member of Gustave Flaubert's Sunday parties, where he was introduced to Edmond de Goncourt, Émile Zola, Guy de Maupassant, and Alphonse Daudet. Moving to London in December 1876, J. quickly joined a literary scene that included Robert BROWNING, Anthony TROLLOPE, J. A. FROUDE, Alfred, Lord TENNYSON, and George DU MAURIER. In June of that year, the *Atlantic Monthly* had started serial publication of his novel *The American* (it appeared in book form in 1877). Describing the attempts of a virtuous young American, Christopher Newman, to marry into a sinister aristocratic French family, the book is an at times unstable combination of Balzacian realism and high Gothic. J. later came to regard it as excessively melodramatic, thoroughly revising it for publication as part of his New York Edition.

Two works published in 1878 were more carefully controlled. *The Europeans* reverses the journey of the previous book by exploring the New World encounter between two Europeanized Americans, the bohemian Felix Young and his sister Eugenia Münster, and their Massachusetts relatives. Unlike the stylistic extremes of *The American*, here J. created a gently comic narrative that managed to direct its mild satire at both New England rigidities and European pretensions. "Daisy Miller: A Study" proved a popular success and remains one of J.'s most pleasing and sophisticated stories. His eponymous heroine is an example of the American new woman, assertive and independent, who fails to realize the very different moral and cultural codes operating in Europe. J. set himself the challenge of having his "center of consciousness" in this story lie with Frederick Winterbourne, a shallow and unperceptive character who mediates Daisy's story for the reader and whose prejudices cloud the account of her exploits and early death. The tale is an early meditation on the narrative problem of point of view, a topic to which J. would return on numerous occasions. *Hawthorne* (1879) marked the appearance of J.'s most important critical piece to date, in which he sought to distinguish himself from his illustrious American predecessor whose overreliance on allegory and symbolism J. found limiting and provincial. Of the two novels by J. published in 1881, *Washington Square* and *The Portrait of a Lady* (3 vols.), the latter book is generally considered to be the author's first masterpiece. Isabel Archer, an idealistic, newly wealthy American woman, marries Gilbert Osmond, an attractive but ultimately selfish American dilettante living in Italy. The novel is an examination of emotional ownership, commodification, and the difficulties of interpretation; Isabel's sense of her own independence and individualism is put to the test in the history-saturated playground of Europe. Readings of the book have continued to disagree about its delicately ambiguous ending—Isabel's apparent return to Gilbert and a loveless marriage.

J.'s parents both died in 1882. His productivity during this period was remarkably high. Two novels began appearing serially in 1885. *The Bostonians* (3 vols., 1886) is a satire on post–Civil War regional identity in the shape of Olive Chancellor, a New England advocate of women's rights, and Basil Ransom, her unreconstructed Southern cousin, who both fight for possession of a young woman, Verena Tarrant. *The Princess Casamassima* (3 vols., 1886), set in the world of underground revolution in London, examines the tension in the central character Hyacinth Robinson between political activism and aesthetic pleasure. Both books are J.'s most explicitly social texts, revealing his continued appreciation of the narrative realism of Balzac and Dickens. The previous year J. had written his important essay "The Art of Fiction," in which he advocated the primacy of artistic freedom in the face of restrictive narrative and moral conventions. It asserts a commitment to the aesthetics of realism, with its "solidity of specification." Of J.'s other work during this period, *The Aspern Papers* (2 vols., 1888) is a masterful novella about the pursuit of biographical knowledge and the possessive curiosity of modern culture. The story's manipulative narrator, an American editor, travels to Venice in search of letters written by Jeffrey Aspern, a Romantic poet, to his mistress "Juliana." Unwilling to marry "Juliana's" spinsterish niece as a means of gaining access to the correspondence, he discovers at the end that the letters have been burnt. Two other tales deserve a mention: "The Author of Beltraffio" (1884) is a fictional meditation on one of the elements of J.'s "Art of Fiction" essay that year, the tension between the creative freedom of art and the imprisoning values of life; and "The Lesson of the Master" (1888) examines the competing demands on the author of artistic integrity and commercial success.

The Tragic Muse (2 vols., 1890) anticipates J.'s involvement in theater in the first half of the 1890s. The novel looks at the nature of aesthetic commitment—to art and drama—and the sacrifices that such commitment requires. The following year J.'s dramatization of his novel *The American* opened in Southport, England, moving to London where it ran for only seventy performances to moderate-sized audiences. Undeterred, J. continued writing plays, inspired by his admiration of Henrik Ibsen, but his work went unproduced until *Guy Domville* in 1895. J.'s appearance at a curtain call on the opening night provoked both loud applause and vehement howls of derision. Shocked by the outburst, he denounced the theater as "an abyss of vulgarity" and abandoned any ambitions he might have had in that quarter. J. returned to fic-

tion. Between 1895 and 1899, he wrote four novels and fourteen short stories, many of which anticipate the modernism of his late phase. "The Figure in the Carpet" (1896) is a resolutely ambiguous tale that dramatizes the relationship between the act of creation and the critic's inevitable failure to achieve comprehensive interpretation. "The Turn of the Screw" (1898), although dismissed by J. as "a shameless potboiler," remains one of his most critically analyzed works. Belonging to the ghost story genre, its labyrinthine structure and multiple narrators anticipate a modernist concern with narrative fragmentation and interpretive indeterminacy. The governess-narrator becomes convinced that the two children in her charge, Miles and his sister Flora, can see the ghosts of two former employees of their uncle, and that in the past the relationship between the four of them had been an unhealthy one (there is the implication of sexual impropriety, but typically J. is never explicit). Readings of the story have continued to debate the legitimacy of the governess's claims: perhaps the apparitions are a figment of her overactive imagination. J.'s story cleverly invites such speculation at the same time as it refuses to endorse any theory the reader may care to propose. His focus on children and their moral development was again the subject of two novels from the period: *What Maisie Knew* (1897) describes the growing maturity of a young girl as she is shuttled between divorced parents and their new lovers; and *The Awkward Age* (1899), an experimental story told almost entirely in dialogue form (evidence of J.'s earlier brush with the theater), concerns the "coming-out" of Nanda Brookenham into her mother's permissive circle of friends. Both novels are preoccupied with the hypocrisy of Victorian morality and the dangers of exposure to inappropriate kinds of knowledge.

J. moved to Lamb House in Rye, Sussex, in 1899, where his neighbors included H. G. WELLS and Stephen Crane. His first novel of the 20th c., *The Sacred Fount* (1902), amplifies the narrative issues of limited perspective explored in "The Turn of the Screw." An unnamed first-person narrator, invited to a weekend house party and observing the other guests, invents the theory that in a relationship one person drains strength and vitality from the "fount" of another. The narrator inflexibly pursues this premise as he tries to detect signs of adulterous liaisons. Firmly held within this narrow perspective, the reader's ability to evaluate and interpret events is radically challenged.

Over the next three years, J. published the trilogy of novels that has come to define the style of his late phase, *The Wings of the Dove* (2 vols., 1902), *The Ambassadors* (1903), and *The Golden Bowl* (1904). Their prose is characterized by the increased length and complexity of sentences; multiple clauses serve to incessantly pursue and refine meaning, such that facts remain tentative, intentions fluid, and conclusions evanescent. Each novel focuses on questions of moral responsibility and returns the reader to the "international theme" of much of J.'s earlier work. In *The Wings of the Dove*, an engaged British couple, Merton Densher and Kate Croy, plot to acquire the fortune of Milly Theale, a wealthy American woman suffering from a mysterious illness. Kate encourages Merton to pursue Milly, in the hope that they will marry and that he will subsequently become a rich widower. Milly learns of the scheme and, in J.'s moving phrase, "turns her face to the wall." Merton is left enough money by Milly in her will to marry Kate, but he will only do so if she agrees not to accept his new wealth. The novel is a highly textured, sophisticated analysis of power relations and competing moral values, written in a style that embodies the rhythm of the way the mind moves. J. regarded *The Ambassadors* as his favorite work. It describes the arrival in Paris of Lambert Strether, an American, dispatched on a mission to discover why Chad Newsome refuses to return to his New England home. Strether attempts to discover whether or not Chad's relationship with the beautiful Marie de Vionnet constitutes a "virtuous attachment." The novel enacts the growing into cosmopolitan awareness, with all its attendant bewilderment, of a middle-aged man suddenly confronted with life's complexities. *The Golden Bowl* is perhaps the most formally flawless of J.'s novels. Adam Verver, a wealthy American art collector, marries Charlotte Stant, the mistress of his daughter Maggie's new husband, Prince Amerigo. The bowl of the title is one bought by Charlotte for Amerigo; it contains a crack, an imperfection that is emblematic of the moral deceit that the novel explores. J. constructs his story using two "centers of consciousness"—Amerigo's in the first book and Maggie's in the second—ensuring a plurality of viewpoint and heightened ambiguity, as the ramifications of the adulterous relationship are played out.

J. visited the U.S. between August 1904 and July 1905, traveling as far afield as the Midwest and California. The journey resulted in the composition of *The American Scene* (1907), a remarkable account of the "restless analyst's" observations of a country he had not visited for over twenty years. J.'s reaction to the modernity of New York—including its expanding immigrant population—caused him profound discomfort. *The American Scene* has become a key text in discussions of J.'s response to issues of race and ethnicity; it demonstrates its author struggling to come to terms with and represent the unfamiliar. J.'s next major project was the creation of the New York Edition of his works (24 volumes published between 1907 and 1909), for which he undertook a project of wholesale revision of much of his writing. He also composed a series of eighteen prefaces for the edition, elaborating both on his own creative procedures and

on issues of narratology more generally. Taken together, the prefaces constitute a major contribution to the developing theory of fiction.

J. last complete novel, *The Outcry*, an adaptation of one of his plays, appeared in 1911. In August of that year, he returned with his brother William to America. William died shortly thereafter and J. spent the winter in New England. Returning to England in July 1911, J. moved to London and began work on *A Small Boy and Others* (1913), the first volume of his autobiography. His last major piece of criticism, "The Novel in *The Ring and the Book*," was delivered as a lecture to the Royal Society of Literature marking the centenary of Browning's birth. It was both a tribute to the poet and an astute account of how J. would have rewritten Browning's great poem as a novel. *Notes of a Son and Brother*, J.'s second autobiographical work, was published in 1914. Horrified at the outbreak of the First World War—"a nightmare from which there is no waking"—the seventy-one-year-old novelist visited the wounded in hospital and accepted the chairmanship of the American Volunteer Motor Ambulance Corps in France. In July 1916, he was granted British citizenship, a final symbolic identification with the country in which he had lived for so long. Afflicted by strokes at the end of the year, J. developed pneumonia. In a state of delirium, he began dictating a series of notes and letters imagining himself as Napoleon. J. received the Order of Merit from King George V on New Year's Day 1916, and died on February 28. His body was cremated and the ashes were buried in the family plot in Cambridge, Massachusetts. At the time of his death, a number of works remained unfinished. Three of these were published in 1917: *The Middle Years*, a third volume of autobiography, and two incomplete novels, *The Ivory Tower* and *The Sense of the Past*.

J. sought to elevate the practice and criticism of fiction to a new level of seriousness and sophistication. His substantial corpus reflects his own changing tastes and preoccupations, both formal and thematic. But his prose continually grapples with problems of representation; the insistent rhythm of his late style is the culmination of a desire to express the incessant workings of the sensitive and inquiring minds of his characters. Combined with a formal attentiveness, J. required that fiction reveal rather than proclaim moral values. For J., conclusions were always tentative, never final. He brought to his craft a self-consciousness that previously had been lacking; and his position as an expatriated American allowed him to reflect on both the culture that had formed him and the one he adopted.

BIBLIOGRAPHY: Bell, I. F. A., *H. J. and the Past* (1991); Bell, M., *Meaning in H. J.* (1991); Bradbury, N., *H. J.* (1979); Edel, L., *H. J.* (5 vols., 1953–72);

Freedman, J., *Professions of Taste: H. J., British Aestheticism and Commodity Culture* (1990); Horne, P., *H. J. and Revision: The New York Edition* (1990); Posnock, R., *The Trial of Curiosity: H. J., William James, and the Challenge of Modernity* (1991); Rowe, J. C., *The Theoretical Dimensions of H. J.* (1984); Salmon, R., *H. J. and the Culture of Publicity* (1997); Wagenknecht, E., *The Novels of H. J.* (1983); Wagenknecht, E., *The Tales of H. J.* (1984)

ANDREW TAYLOR

JAMES, M[ontague] R[hodes]

b. 1 August 1862, Goodnestone, Kent; d. 12 June 1936, Eton

J. was a scholar and writer of ghost stories who, at an early age, developed the passionate interest in medieval books and antiquities that was to remain his most constant companion. J.'s life was, in fact, devoted to studying the past: he applied his knowledge and ready command of archaic language and detail to his fiction, seamlessly placing years of accumulated tradition within a familiar, modern setting, while paying deference to "the rules of FOLKLORE." The resulting body of work includes supernatural mysteries that still stand as some of the most exquisitely crafted, psychologically acute, and hauntingly memorable short stories ever written.

J.'s precocious reverence for the past was nurtured by being educated—and by spending most of his life—at Eton and King's College, Cambridge, where he took a double first in classics and became assistant in classical archaeology at the Fitzwilliam Museum. He was elected a fellow of King's in 1887, lecturing in divinity, and, in the course of a distinguished career, became provost in 1905, served as director of the Fitzwilliam from 1893 to 1908, as vice chancellor of the university from 1913 to 1915, and as provost of Eton from 1918. He was a brilliant linguist and biblical scholar, who wrote many pioneering studies and edited and translated the *Apocryphal New Testament* (1924); an expert on the art and literature of the Middle Ages, who gave advice on the restoration of the stained glass in King's College Chapel; and he wrote a large number of distinguished reviews, monographs, articles, and works on bibliography, paleography, and antiquarian issues, often editing volumes for specialized societies. His academic career ran parallel with his more populist publishing, and remains inseparable from it, littered as his stories are with erudite references and sharply drawn vignettes of university life. He published his memoirs, *Eton and King's*, in 1926.

Imagination and curiosity played a significant role in J.'s brilliance as a scholar, and his mind was as open to the question of the supernatural as it was to more academic concerns: "I am prepared to consider evidence and accept it if it satisfies me," he declared in the preface to his *Collected Ghost Stories* (1931), and confessed happily to looking into the dark corners of his room before retiring, "with a sort of pleasurable uncertainty as to whether there might not be a saucer-eyed skeleton or a skinny-chested ghost in hiding somewhere." Delving also into the dark corners of his mind, J. translated that compelling blend of fear and excitement into the volumes for which he is now best remembered: *Ghost Stories of an Antiquary* (1904); *More Ghost Stories of an Antiquary* (1911); *A Thin Ghost, and Others* (1919); *The Five Jars* (1922); *A Warning to the Curious and Other Ghost Stories* (1925); and the collected edition of his works.

Although J. was an admirer of Irish mystery-writer Joseph Sheridan LE FANU, whose stories he edited, his fiction was in no way derivative and his tales of the supernatural were written according to rules he invented for himself and laid out in the preface to one of his collections: ghosts should be "malevolent or odious" rather than benign, as fear is the desired effect; their victims must be "introduced in a placid way, undisturbed by forebodings"; and the technicalities of "occultism" or "pseudo-science" should be avoided. As the horror writer H. P. Lovecraft noted, J. was "gifted with an almost diabolic power of calling horror by gentle steps from the midst of prosaic daily life": many of his stories begin with an almost casual recollection, which is developed with scholarly control and a conversational tone until the accumulation of detail produces a chilling sense of quiet terror in the reader; often, as in the brilliant "The Haunted Dolls' House," J. employs a layered narrative that has, at its heart, what he called "the malice of inanimate objects." In a departure from the Gothic tradition of pale apparitions, the typical J. ghost is, Lovecraft continues, "dwarfish and hairy—a sluggish, hellish night-abomination midway betwixt beast and man—and usually *touched* before it is *seen*."

The superlative quality of J.'s contribution to the genre, however, lies in the recognition, expressed in his introduction to the anthology *Ghosts and Marvels* (1924), that the ghost story was "only a particular sort of short story" and demanded the same literary qualities as any piece of short fiction. His mastery of fear was his mastery of form and structure, and a degree of psychological insight that allowed him to create, in a series of short scenes, the conviction that the vulnerability of the character is at once the vulnerability of the reader. His economic style, tendency toward understatement, and teasing allusions leave much to the imagination, and the malevolent force is hardly ever completely revealed; occasionally, the absence of a clear climax and a reliance on intellectual rather than emotional fear are disappointing, but very few stories could be described as weak, and all are distinctive in style and method. There is significant argument as to which stories represent J.'s best work, but "Oh, Whistle, and I'll Come to You, My Lad," which appears in many anthologies of the supernatural, "Casting the Runes," and "The Stalls of Barchester Cathedral" are generally recognized as masterpieces of the genre.

J.'s research often took him abroad; many of his stories are based on real places—be it a cathedral, a library, or a seaside town—and have an affinity for Europe or, more specifically, for East Anglia; most were written in King's College, and first read to friends there each Christmas. His supernatural fiction is still appreciated today, and his style and ideas have served as inspiration for many modern authors in a genre that has enjoyed several generations of revival; in some senses, J. is a writer's writer—his circle of admirers can be expanded from Lovecraft to authors as diverse as Sir John BETJEMAN, Penelope FITZGERALD, and P. D. JAMES—and his style is seen by some as too antiquated and elusive for an age that prefers its horror more crudely visualised on stage and screen; nevertheless, at his best, he never fails to satisfy what Virginia WOOLF referred to as "the strange human craving for the pleasure of being afraid."

BIBLIOGRAPHY: Cox, M., *M. R. J.* (1983); Lubbock, S. G., *A Memoir of M. R. J.* (1939); Pfaff, R. W., *M. R. J.* (1980)

NICOLA UPSON

JAMES, P[hyllis] D[orothy], Baroness James of Holland Park

b. 3 August 1920, Oxford

In an overpopulated genre, the crime novels of J. are distinguished by their interplay of classical discipline, contemporary morality, and remarkable evocation of place. Writing, for the most part, within the conventions of the detective story, J. has proved its constraints to be a liberating force for the creative imagination, extending its boundaries and conferring upon the crime novel a literary credibility. Without exception, her works explore the psychological and social implications of death and, unlike their Golden Age predecessors, they offer no comforting restoration of Eden. A versatile and extremely modern writer, J. continues to be held in high critical regard for her powerful REALISM, eclectic cultural references, and masterly command of the English language.

J. made her debut with *Cover Her Face* (1962), a traditional country house murder that introduces her series detective, Adam Dalgliesh. A Chief Inspector attached to Scotland Yard and an established poet, Dalgliesh is an unorthodox, solitary figure who has lost his wife and child in childbirth; at once romantic and detached, he remains J.'s embodiment of the triumph of individual endeavor over evil. *Cover Her Face* is more derivative than anything J. has subsequently produced (with the exception, perhaps, of *Unnatural Causes*, 1967), but it foreshadows themes that were to be developed in more sophisticated detail in later works: the contaminating effects of murder; the lasting spread of sin over time; and a careful attention to psychology, combined with a profound understanding of human relationships. In addition, it highlights her fascination with malice domestic, or what she refers to as "a woman's interest in the small change of life"; a definite sense of female strength, whether for good or for evil, underpins much of J.'s writing.

Throughout the 1960s and 1970s, J. worked first as a hospital administrator and then for the Home Office, where her areas of responsibility included the Forensic Science Service and the Criminal Policy Division. Her knowledge of hospital procedures, forensic investigations, and institutional life have contributed much to the strong factual basis that her novels always possess, particular in four Dalgliesh novels from this period: *A Mind to Murder* (1963), which deals with the brutal murder of an administrative officer in a psychiatric clinic; *Shroud for a Nightingale* (1971), in which a teaching hospital is the backdrop to a particularly gruesome death through intragastric feeding; *The Black Tower* (1975), where Dalgliesh becomes involved in a murder at a private home for the disabled; and *Death of an Expert Witness* (1977), which is set in an East Anglian forensic science laboratory.

In many ways, *Shroud for a Nightingale* is J.'s coming-of-age novel and her re-creation of the oppressive atmosphere in a nurses' training college—with its lack of privacy, petty jealousies, and stifling, destructive female friendships—is particularly striking. It is the first novel in which a building becomes a character in its own right: J. effortlessly fuses past and present, linking modern-day horrors with the story of a tortured 19th-c. maidservant through the tangible power of bricks and mortar. *Shroud for a Nightingale* is also notable for its emphasis on deepseated personal motivation, not just for murder but for other everyday acts of love and hate. For J., there are no absolute heroes or villains, and evil can reside in any heart; no amount of detection can redeem the essential darkness of the human psyche.

In the same year, J. published *The Maul and the Pear Tree* (1971), which she coauthored with the assistant secretary of the Police Department, T. A. Critchley. The book is an investigation into the Ratcliffe Highway Murders—a series of notorious killings that took place in Wapping in 1811—and concludes that John Williams, a young sailor arrested for the crimes, was an innocent victim. A departure in the sense that it is a work of nonfiction, *The Maul and the Pear Tree* nevertheless relies on the same evocations of place and character that color J.'s fiction.

When she returned to the novel, it was with an entirely different protagonist, one who, as a woman and an amateur, is the antithesis of Dalgliesh. *An Unsuitable Job for a Woman* (1972), which contrasts an appalling murder with the beauty of Cambridge in high summer, introduces Cordelia Gray, a pioneer in the development of the independent female private eye who was earlier and more convincingly fallible than her many English and American counterparts. Gray makes a second appearance ten years later in *The Skull beneath the Skin* (1982), one of J.'s most original and perhaps most misunderstood novels. In its setting of Gothic melodrama, deliberate use of cliché, and air of playful excess, *The Skull beneath the Skin* demonstrates J.'s consciousness of the form within which she is working, and her ability to use it either to serious or ironic ends.

With *Innocent Blood* (1980) and *The Children of Men* (1992), J. chose to write outside the mystery genre but continued to put death at the center of her narrative. The former is a psychological novel that deals with the effects of crime on an adopted young woman, who discovers that her real parents were imprisoned for the murder of a child. As the book chronicles the growth of love between the girl and her mother, as well as the suffering of the murdered child's father, it touches upon J.'s most persistent concern as a novelist: the way in which murder, Orwell's unique crime for which no one can make reparation, temporarily removes the support of law and religion, and faces people with the truth about themselves. *The Children of Men* is a futuristic novel, set in 2021 and dominated by universal disillusionment in a world where no children have been born for twenty-five years. One of J.'s strengths in her crime novels—the specifics of time and place—is never more important than in this deeply serious departure from the genre, which provides a fictional basis for her to examine the place of faith, science, and love in society.

J.'s novels invariably originate from her response to a place. In one of her finest, *A Taste for Death* (1986), the violent murders of a Conservative minister and a local tramp are given a heightened resonance by having occurred in a London church, the site of man's aspirations toward holiness; *Devices and Desires* (1989) takes place on a sinister stretch of coast, overshadowed by Sizewell Power Station; she chose to set *Original Sin* (1994) on the Thames, which runs through the story, linking character and events; *A Certain Justice* (1997) places murder at the heart of another bastion of order, the Middle Temple; and *Death in Holy Orders* (2001) returns to the Suffolk coast to investigate suspicious death in a theological training college. It is the power and the contrast of the settings in which her series characters find themselves that keeps the novels fresh.

In 1999, J. published a "fragment" of autobiography, *Time to Be in Earnest*. The record of a year, between her seventy-seventh and seventy-eighth birthdays, the book is a beautifully crafted reflection of its time and a unique insight into the craft that she has made her own.

BIBLIOGRAPHY: Joyner, N. C., "P. D. J.," in Bargainnier, E. F., ed., *Ten Women of Mystery* (1981): 108–23; Morton, M., *A Mind to Murder*, BBC Radio 2 (1998)

NICOLA UPSON

JAMESON, Anna Brownell
b. Anna Brownell Murphy, 19 May 1794, Dublin, Ireland; d. 17 March 1860, London

J.'s writing career spanned thirty years in all and she proved a popular writer of nonfiction works on a variety of topics. She was probably the first professional woman art critic and historian in the Victorian era and her popular series, the five-volume *Sacred and Legendary Art* (1845–64) continued to be published well into the 1920s. The final volume, *The History of our Lord*, was completed by Lady Eastlake after J.'s death. While her focus was the Italian Renaissance, she also produced a Crystal Palace guide (1854) on modern British sculpture suggesting the extent to which she was cognizant of modern trends in the art world.

J.'s working life was a constant battle against poverty. She supported her parents, and her unmarried sisters. She separated from her husband, Robert Jameson, after his appointment to Upper Canada as attorney general, and the occasion of her trip to Canada was designed to formalize the separation and obtain an annuity. She was a valued friend of the BROWNINGS and of Ottilie von Goethe. J. was often in debt to her publishers, selling her copyrights when hard-pressed financially. In 1851, she was granted a pension of £100 from Her Majesty's Pension List and after her husband's death in 1854 her friends raised a subscription that resulted in an annuity of £100.

J.'s writing was not confined to art criticism. Other important publications included *Characteristics of Women, Moral, Poetical and Historical* (2 vols., 1832), a work about women based on female characters from William SHAKESPEARE's plays. Gerard Manley HOPKINS ranked her as a Shakespearean critic of genius, along with Schlegel, Samuel Taylor COLERIDGE, and Charles LAMB. As a travel writer, she produced popular books about Italy, *Diary of an Ennuyée* (1826); Germany, *Visits and Sketches at Home and Abroad* (4 vols., 1834), and Canada, *Winter Studies and Summer Rambles in Canada* (1838), this last still in print today. She also published historical and biographical studies, including *Memoirs of Celebrated*

Female Sovereigns (2 vols., 1831). Her publications consistently received lengthy reviews in the important periodicals of the day (i.e., *Edinburgh Review, Quarterly Review*), and reviewers included noted contemporaries Mary SHELLEY, Charles KINGSLEY, Christopher NORTH, and Geraldine Jewsbury. She wrote for periodicals herself publishing articles and reviews in the *Athenaeum* and the *Art Journal*, among others. By the time of her death, her publications on art were considered to be "standard" works.

J.'s publications focused on women and she always claimed to write specifically for women readers. As a professional woman of letters, J.'s work was significant. While she cannot be regarded as a feminist per se, she developed a distinct feminist polemic across her thirty-year career. In the last five years of her life, J. became involved with the feminists of Langham Place as a mentor to women such as Barbara Bodichon and Bessie Rayner Parkes. The latter, as editor of the *English Woman's Journal*, consulted J. regularly about articles for the journal. When this group initiated the Married Women's Property Petition, J.'s name headed the list of signatories. Her last two publications, *Sisters of Charity, Catholic and Protestant, at Home and Abroad* (1855) and *The Communion of Labour* (1856), were based on public lectures designed specifically to address the issue of professional work for women.

John RUSKIN notoriously denigrated J.'s ability as an art critic in his private letters and in *Praeterita* (1886). She was more generous to him. While refusing the role of acolyte, she pays due deference to Ruskin's popularity as a writer in *A Commonplace Book of Thoughts, Memories, and Fancies* (1854), but at the same time claims for herself an equal place as a critic on art with him. Both Henry JAMES in *The American* and Virginia WOOLF in *Orlando*, acknowledge the extent of J.'s reputation by making comic reference to "Mrs. Jameson." James's character Mr. Babcock takes J.'s books with him to Italy. The very nature of James's joke relies for its impact upon J.'s enormous popularity and credibility as a guide to sacred art. George ELIOT refers to J. implicitly in *The Mill on the Floss*, as "my private hagiographer" and felt no need to explicate the reference to her reading public. In 1860, the year *The Mill on the Floss* was published, and the year of J.'s death, no one with any literary pretensions would have been puzzled by the reference.

BIBLIOGRAPHY: Johnston, J., *A. J.* (1997); Thomas, C., *Love and Work Enough: The Life of A. J.* (1967)

JUDITH JOHNSTON

JAMESON, [Margaret] Storm

b. 8 January 1891, Yorkshire; d. 30 September 1986, Cambridge

Writing her own mock obituary in her AUTOBIOGRAPHY, J. presents herself as "bedevilled" by contrary impulses: "The ambition, a blind hunger to become a figure, and to use her brain and exceptional energy, which drove her to write and brought her a measure of success, was undermined by a certain weakness of character and by a paradoxical lack of respect for money and honours, and her hatred of a settled life." Yet this somewhat self-deprecating definition omits her achievement as a writer and intellectual who published thirty-seven novels as well as several volumes of autobiography and critical essays.

Her early writing—she began publishing novels in 1919—and the later fictional autobiography *The Journal of Mary Hervey Russell* (1945) are concerned with the position of women of her generation both during and in the immediate aftermath of World War I. J.'s preoccupation with the war, which killed her younger brother, and her fear of another war, identify her with contemporaries who were writing during the war and in the 1920s and 1930s, such as Enid BAGNOLD, Vera BRITTAIN, and Irene Rathbone, although J.'s work does not deal with women's experience in war service, but with their struggle to survive and carve out independent lives for themselves in spite of hardship and poverty. In particular, she depicts the psychological and economic burden carried by the woman who wants both independent work and to bring up her children. The emotional pain of leaving her young son behind in Yorkshire while she worked in London is revisited almost compulsively in her novels and in her autobiography, *Journey from the North* (2 vols., 1969–70). In spite of her sensitivity to this dilemma, her writing is not a feminist polemic, but a sharply perceptive detailing of everyday existence that captures both the emotional and physical lives of her characters. Her novels of the twenties and her autobiography continually evoke the mood of an almost unbearable loss in the aftermath of the war; the absent young men who had been her companions as an undergraduate at the University of Leeds are paradoxically ever-present, as are the lost prewar selves of those who survived. Her *Mirror in Darkness* trilogy—*Company Parade* (1934), *Love in Winter* (1935), and *None Turn Back* (1936)—shows an acute awareness of the psychological tensions between the men who returned from the war and the women who loved them.

Her novels of the 1930s are increasingly preoccupied by the conditions in Europe and the rise of fascism. *In the Second Year* (1936) foresees another war. Her writing of this period is necessarily informed by her involvement with European politics on an intellectual and practical level that led to her presidency of the British chapter of International PEN from 1938 to 1945. During World War II, she worked indefatigably to rescue Jewish intellectuals and other writers, providing practical aid in the form of food and shelter and writing thousands of letters to governments and other agencies in Britain and Europe. Her efforts saved thousands of lives and yet she felt the terrible frustration of her task: "For one person we got out, ten, fifty, five hundred sank." J. still managed to publish twelve novels during the war. In its immediate aftermath, she traveled to devastated areas of Europe, such as Warsaw and Cracow, endeavoring to make contact with writers and commenting on the conditions in her autobiography, essays, and in novels like *The Black Laurel* (1947)

A certain perversity toward writing as a profession is revealed in a vitriolic attack on a female novelist in the novella "Delicate monster" in *Women against Men* (1933). "The novelist hardened by his profession," J. wrote, "will take notes—of his feelings, exclamations and so on—at his child's deathbed." J. was too concerned with writing novels that carried intellectual weight to embrace experimental forms of MODERNISM. However, her ability to convey the psychology of her characters owes something to stream of consciousness writing, and at her best she succeeds in convincing her reader of the connection between the private inner world of the individual and the larger movements of history.

BIBLIOGRAPHY: Labon, J., "Tracing S. J.," *Women* 8, 1 (1997): 33–47; McDowell, M. B., "S. J.," in Staley, J. F., ed., *British Novelists, 1890–1929: Modernists, DLB* 36 (1985): 70–79

CAROL ACTON

JEFFERIES, [John] Richard
b. 6 November 1848, Coate Farm, near Swindon; d. 14 August 1887, Goring

J. was reared in rural Wiltshire; his experiences there underlie all of his best writing. While working as a journalist in Swindon, he began a series of articles about the agricultural world, seeking, in his words, to show "some of the lights and shades of the labourer's daily life impartially presented." These early pieces reveal a class-consciousness that favors the landowner but accurately portray the hard life of farm workers. A weekly series on rural life begun in late 1877 for the *Pall Mall Gazette* became *The Gamekeeper at Home* (1878), which Edward THOMAS described as "perhaps the first thoroughly rustic book in English, by a countryman and about the country, with no alien savours whatever." Other collections of J.'s essays about rural England followed: *Wild Life in a Southern County* (1879; repub. as *An English Village*, 1903), *The Amateur Poacher* (1879), *Round about a Great Estate* (1880), *Hodge and His Masters* (2 vols., 1880), and *Nature Near London* (1883). Two books for children that J. wrote at this time, *Wood Magic* (2 vols., 1881) and *Bevis* (3 vols., 1882), cast a nostalgic look back at J.'s own rustic childhood, and *The Story of My Heart*

(1883) continues this autobiographical theme. J.'s later essays, gathered in such volumes as *The Life of the Fields* (1884), *The Open Air* (1885), and the posthumously published *Field and Hedgerow* (1889) unite the closely observed detail with an impressionistic and a quasi-mystical response to nature.

JOSEPH ROSENBLUM

JELLICOE, [Patricia] Ann
b. 15 July 1927, Middlesbrough, Yorkshire

J.'s most memorable theatrical works are notable for their willingness to experiment with form and narrative. J. described her first play, *The Sport of My Mad Mother* (1958), as an "anti-intellectual" piece. In this nonlinear work, J. uses dialogue that often contradicts the action onstage. She also uses the rhythm of language and percussive instruments to heighten the emotional effect on an audience. J. used similar techniques in her most popular play, *The Knack* (perf. 1961; pub. 1962), a comedy about a group of roommates and their relative success with members of the opposite sex (to which the title refers). J.'s other plays include *Shelley; or, The Idealist* (perf. 1965; pub. 1966), an experimental drama about the life of the poet Percy Bysshe SHELLEY; *The Giveaway* (perf. 1969; pub. 1970), a farce about a woman who wins a ten-year supply of corn flakes, but who then has to constantly pretend to be a fourteen-year-old girl; and *The Reckoning* (perf. 1978), *The Western Women* (perf. 1984), and *Changing Places* (perf. 1992), which deal with people and events from English history. J.'s theatrical works for children include *You'll Never Guess* (perf. 1973), *Clever Elsie, Smiling John, Silent Peter* (perf. 1974), and *A Good Thing or a Bad Thing* (perf. 1974), published together in 1975. J. has also written adaptations of plays by Henrik Ibsen and Anton Chekhov, and she has achieved acclaim as a director of her own and others' works.

JENKINS, [John] Robin
b. 11 September 1912, Flemington, Scotland

J. became an English teacher after studying at Hamilton Academy and Glasgow University. A conscientious objector to World War II, he worked in forestry, the background of his best-known novel, *The Cone-Gatherers* (1955). His novels are permeated with class-consciousness and form a running critique of Scottish Calvinism. Other targets are racial prejudice and the substitution of football (soccer) for religion. Later novels include *A Very Scotch Affair* (1968), *A Toast to the Lord* (1972), *A Would-Be Saint* (1978), and *Fergus Lamont* (1979). J.'s short stories were collected in *A Far Cry from Bowmore* (1973).

JENNINGS, Elizabeth [Joan]

b. 18 July 1926, Boston, Lincolnshire; d. 26 October 2001, Oxford

J. attended Oxford High School and then continued on to St. Anne's College, Oxford, where she graduated in 1949. It was there that she met a group of poets, later to become "The Movement," who gathered regularly to discuss and critique one another's poetry. In 1953, J. published her first book of poetry, *Poems*. It was critically well received and won the Arts Council Prize for a first book of poems. Her second book, *A Way of Looking* (1955), did not enjoy the critical praise of her first, but won the Somerset Maugham Award. Unlike other members of the group that included Kingsley AMIS, Robert CONQUEST, and Philip LARKIN, J. often incorporated religious feeling into her poetry. Her poetry also investigates human relationships through simple moments using a quiet, contemplative voice. The majority of J.'s poetry is lyric; however, she did use different poetic forms in later collections such as *Moments of Grace* (1980), *Times and Seasons* (1993), and *Familiar Spirits* (1995). She does not rely heavily on imagery, but rather examines the moment, meditating on its significance. J. continued to live in Oxford throughout her life. In addition to over twenty volumes of poetry, she also wrote several volumes of children's verse.

JEROME, Jerome K[lapka]

b. 2 May 1859, Walsall, Staffordshire; d. 14 June 1927, Northampton, Northamptonshire

During his lifetime, J. was an actor, a writer of essays, a humorist and lecturer, an editor of popular journals, a playwright, and a novelist. Today his reputation rests almost solely with his autobiographical comic work *Three Men in a Boat (To Say Nothing of the Dog)*, published in 1889, and some of his essays written as "the Idler." J. enjoyed great popular success in many different genres, but the critics tended to dismiss an author they labeled a "new humorist." They mistrusted his easy, colloquial style, and his very popularity caused many middle-class writers to disdain as vulgar the man *Punch* dubbed "'Arry K. 'Arry." Today, his gentle and discursive style of HUMOR is not as popular, and his novels and plays are difficult to find in print.

J. wrote for the popular press and then collected his work in volumes. His collections about his life in the theater, *On the Stage—and Off: The Brief Career of a Would-Be Actor* (1885) and *Stage-land: Curious Habits and Customs of Its Inhabitants* (1889), take a humorous, if sometimes harsh, look at life in the theater dominated by stock characters and predictable productions. Part of the appeal of these collections lies in the voice of the narrator, who never removes himself too far from the imperfection of the world he describes. The works are still interesting for their humor and for the way they chronicle this important era in theatrical history.

J.'s essays *The Idle Thoughts of an Idle Fellow* (1886) seem to have been perfectly suited to the reading audience that enjoyed his easy style and familiar observations. In his preface, he promises not to "improve, instruct, or elevate" his reader, and in his ruminations on topics like "Being Hard Up," he provided a mix of humor and philosophy that his readers found realistic. The critics, on the other hand, consistently berated J. for his "vulgarity." The colloquial language and low humor were dismissed as an affront to the middle-class values that magazines like *Punch* were meant to uphold.

J. also had popular success and critical failure as a playwright. The texts of his plays suggest that he was able to create popular entertainment not by creating well-made plays but because he had a good eye for stage business. Unfortunately, even his most popular and long-running play, *The Passing of the Third Floor Back* (1908), seems rather melodramatic and heavy-handed to a modern audience. The play tells the story of the encounter of a group of rather unpleasant stage types with a mysterious and anonymous stranger. By allowing the characters to confront their own pettiness and limitations, the stranger reforms them all, suggesting that there is good in all men waiting to be uncovered. While the critical reception was mixed, the public loved *The Passing of the Third Floor Back* because it both entertained and taught. The play had long runs in New York and London and was successful with touring companies in the U.S. and Canada.

There were those who were reluctant to produce *The Passing of the Third Floor Back* because they felt that audiences would be disappointed that it did not live up to J.'s reputation for comedy created by his prose work *Three Men in a Boat*. This work tells the story of three city men on a rowing trip on the Thames and is based on J.'s own experience. The narrator "J" describes his adventures with his companions as they find themselves dealing with the realities rather than the romance of camping and "roughing it" outside the comfort and familiarity of the city. Critics have noted the influence of humorists like Mark Twain and the use of exaggeration, understatement, and digression in the work. J. had a keen ear for dialogue and was a careful student of behavior so that his images of people are at once funny and truthful. Critics at the time berated the work because they felt the humor was based on the American style rather than the wit of Oscar WILDE and Max BEERBOHM, but the book has never been out of print.

Although he has never had a critical following, J.'s blend and balance of humor and a keen observation of human foibles (including his own) appealed to his late Victorian readers. The few critics who have attended to his work agree that for these very reasons the autobiographical novel *Paul Kelver* (1902) deserves a larger readership. The book has self-conscious overtones of Charles DICKENS's *David Copperfield* (and some critics have suggested Samuel BUTLER's *The Way of All Flesh* and Edmund GOSSE's *Father and Son*) and is based on J.'s difficult upbringing, first as a child of Nonconformists and then as an orphan after the age of fourteen. In addition to this autobiographical work, J. wrote a number of other novels, including an account of the growth of a popular periodical (*Tommy and Co.*, 1904), a humorous account of a family's move to the country (*They and I*, 1909), and two more serious novels that explored the issue of religious doubt and the problem of poverty, *All Roads Lead to Calvary* (1919) and *Anthony John* (1923).

J. captured the imagination of readers and audiences of his time by presenting them with realistic and funny images of their lives. It may be that humor simply does not lend itself to analysis, and it is the rare comic author like Twain who is seriously studied and continues to be read. Nonetheless, J. deserves the attention of those who would understand the nature of popular taste as England emerged from the Victorian to the modern era.

BIBLIOGRAPHY: Connolly, J., *J. K. J.* (1982); Faurot, R. M., *J. K. J.* (1974); Faurot, R. M., "J. K. J.," in Stanley, T. F., ed., *British Novelists, 1890–1929, DLB* 34 (1984): 204–8

CATHERINE FRANK

JHABVALA, Ruth Prawer
b. 7 May 1927, Cologne, Germany

Some critics have compared J.'s work to earlier Anglo-Indian authors such as Rudyard KIPLING, E. M. FORSTER, and Paul SCOTT; others have claimed that she has far more in common with Indo-Anglian writers such as R. K. Narayan and Anita Desai. This divergence of opinion gives some indication of the distinctive place that J. holds among writers who have chosen to write about India— that of an "outsider with unusual insight," to use Ramlal G. Agarwal's apt description. In a sense, as a Jewish refugee who was forced to flee Nazi Germany in 1939, J. has always been a cultural outsider, and this has given her a unique perspective on her three adopted homelands, England, India, and the U.S.

After leaving Germany, J.'s family settled in England, where she was naturalized as a British citizen in 1948, and received a master's degree in English literature from London University in 1951. Later that year, she married Cyrus Jhabvala, an Indian architect, and moved to New Delhi. J.'s first two novels, *To*

Whom She Will (1955; repub. as *Amrita*, 1956) and *The Nature of Passion* (1956), reflect her newcomer's enthusiasm for India, with their romanticized depictions of family life in India. *To Whom She Will* revolves around a young woman's desire to marry for love rather than submit to an arranged marriage and this tension between freedom and familial duty is a theme J. frequently explores in her fiction. Marriage and family life are also central to *The Nature of Passion*, but the overriding passion of the central character, Lalaji, is for making money. The portrayal of Lalaji's sometimes questionable business ethics and his avarice is softened, however, redeemed by his loving generosity toward his family. While some of the issues raised in these two works are important, such as the generational tensions raised by the question of family obligations as opposed to personal desire, there is little sense of the harsher realities of life for India's poor.

Beginning with her third novel, *Esmond in India* (1958), and continuing with her next two novels, *The Householder* (1960) and *Get Ready for Battle* (1962), J.'s view of India became more ambivalent and complex. As in J.'s first two novels, all three of these novels are set in Delhi and are centered around one or two middle-class families. Marriage and family life are still important themes, but for the first time J. moves beyond the confines of middle-class life in Delhi, both geographically and culturally. Esmond Stillwood is J.'s first major European character, and in *Esmond in India*, J. describes the three stages that she believes a Westerner experiences in India: everything Indian is marvelous; everything Indian is not so marvelous; everything Indian is abominable. By the time Esmond reaches the third stage, he is so overwhelmed by his revulsion to India that he has to leave the country for the reassuring comfort of England. In *The Householder*, J. returned to the domestic themes of her earlier novels, albeit at a different social level, as the story is primarily told from the perspective of Prem, a young husband and schoolteacher, struggling to adjust to his responsibilities as a householder, the second of the four stages of personal development in Hindu tradition.

In J.'s later Indian novels, *A Backward Place* (1965), *A New Dominion* (1972; repub. as *Travelers*, 1973), and *Heat and Dust* (1975), she focuses less on Indian domestic life and more on the experiences of Europeans in India. The lure of India's religious traditions for Westerners seeking spiritual meaning, which becomes a major theme in J.'s later fiction, is explored in depth for the first time by J. in *A New Dominion*. In a reversal of colonial roles, the master-servant relationship leads to abuse and violence when Lee, a young woman who comes to India in order to find herself, is raped in the ashram by her guru. The colonial past is explored further in *Heat and Dust*, the novel for which J. won the Booker Prize in 1975. *Heat and Dust* alternates between the first-person narration of a woman who comes to India on a quest to learn more about herself, and the story of her grandmother, Olivia, who had come to India during the raj as the wife of a British colonial officer. Olivia becomes pregnant, probably as a result of an affair with an Indian prince, and although the pregnancy is terminated, she eventually rejects her life as a colonial wife. The parallels between the narrator and Olivia are carefully developed, and become so closely tied that by the end of the narrative they seem almost to merge into one unified voice.

In 1975, J. moved to New York City, a shift in geography that is reflected in her fiction, which no longer focuses primarily on India although she continues to explore the theme of exile and the search for "home," either in a physical or spiritual sense. *In Search of Love and Beauty* (1983), a novel that depicts three generations of German-Jewish émigrés in New York, is at once a departure for J., whose move to New York brought about a reawakening of her childhood in Europe, and a reexamination of many of the themes she had explored in her Indian novels. In both this novel and her next, *Three Continents* (1987), fraudulent gurus—a "psycho-spiritual" therapist named Leo Kellerman in *In Search of Love and Beauty* and a bogus Eastern mystic in *Three Continents*—prey on gullible seekers looking for spiritual meaning in their lives. J.'s novel *Shards of Memory* (1995) ties together many of the themes present in her later fiction as she constructs a narrative based on four generations of a single family with ties to England, India, and New York, and who are all linked to a spiritual figure known only as the Master.

In addition to her work as a novelist, J. has written six collections of short stories, many of which focus on the themes of marriage and domestic life, alienation, and spiritual longing developed at length in her novels. Her work as a writer of short stories, including her recent collection, *East into Upper East: Plain Tales from New York and New Delhi* (1998), has been compared to such masters of the form as Anton Chekhov and Henry JAMES. Starting with her adaptation of her novel *The Householder* for Merchant-Ivory productions in 1963, J. has also written or cowritten numerous screenplays, including *A Room with A View* (1985), *Mr. And Mrs. Bridge* (1990), *Howard's End* (1992), *The Remains of the Day* (1993), and *Surviving Picasso* (1996).

The reaction of Indian critics to J.'s work is split between those who see novels like *Heat and Dust* as culturally biased, negative portraits of India and those who see her as a culturally sensitive observer whose view of India is perceptive and even-handed. Western appraisals of her work have been overwhelmingly favorable, and her novels, short stories, and screenplays

have all won critical praise as well as a number of prestigious fellowships, honors like the Booker Prize for *Heat and Dust*, and a MacArthur Foundation Award in 1986. Her body of work in any one of these genres would be considered impressive; her mastery of all three forms is little short of remarkable.

BIBLIOGRAPHY: Agarwal, R. G., *R. P. J.* (1990); Crane, R. J., *R. P. J.* (1992); Gooneratne, Y., *Silence, Exile, and Cunning: The Fiction of R. P. J.* (1983); Shahane, V. A., *R. P. J.* (1976)

DANIEL G. PAYNE

JOHNSON, B[ryan] S[tanley]

b. 5 February 1933, London; d. 13 November 1973, London

In his fiction and his polemics, J. vigorously challenged what he saw as the constraints of the traditional realistic novel. This challenge took two forms: the further development of modernist techniques to achieve a more faithful rendering of reality, and the deployment of savagely exuberant modes of caricature and black comedy. These seemingly diverse approaches converged in J.'s underlying vision of existence: the roads to reality and caricature both led, in the end, to a confrontation with a dark chaos that had to be painfully witnessed but that might be at least slightly mitigated by lacerating laughter.

In terms of theme and tone, J.'s first novel, *Travelling People* (1963), seems typical of British first novels of the period; it is a largely comic tale of the misadventures of a young man, fresh out of university, who finds a summer job and a girl at a high-class club in Wales. It breaks with mainstream fiction, however, in the variety of techniques that it employs, including interior monologue, a scene in the form of a film script, staggered print intended to mimic the movements of the eye across advertisements as an escalator descends, and grey and black pages that stand, respectively, for unconsciousness and death. This technical virtuosity continued into J.'s second novel, *Albert Angelo* (1964), which includes devices such as a special type-character to draw attention to descriptions of faces, and double-column pages that counterpoint the protagonist's silent thoughts with the words he speaks and hears. But the subject matter of *Albert Angelo* seems familiar enough; it is a portrait of the artist—or in Albert's case, the architect—as a young man, struggling to pursue his vocation while having to eke out a living by other work—Albert is a supply teacher at tough London schools. As the novel nears its end, however, an urbane authorial voice explodes in frustration "OH FUCK ALL THIS LYING," and goes on to offer what it claims to be the "truth" that the previous fiction has disguised and distorted. It sums up its quarrel with fiction in an axiom: "telling stories is telling lies."

J. therefore pursued "one hundred per cent truth" in his next novel, *Trawl* (1966), though he did not want to call it an AUTOBIOGRAPHY. *Trawl* combines the narrator's experiences as a passenger on a fishing trawler with his recollections of key experiences in his past, such as his boyhood evacuation from London during World War II. The novel is somber in tone, reasonably straightforward in structure, and relatively subdued in style, though J. cannot wholly resist wordplay and verbal exuberance. The somber tone and subdued style continue and deepen in *The Unfortunates* (1969), a pained witnessing of the slow death from cancer of J.'s friend, Tony. But such sobriety is not maintained in the physical form of the novel, which spectacularly breaks away from the standard format and offers instead a box containing twenty-seven loose sections, all of which, apart from the first and the last, can be read in any order the reader wishes. The result is that a different version of the novel emerges each time the sections are rearranged and reread. Every version, however, reinforces J.'s fundamental vision: death is implacable.

This truth is driven home in *House Mother Normal* (1971), set in a nursing home for the elderly. Eight interior monologues convey the thoughts and feelings—and sometimes, through textual breaks and blanks, the absence of thoughts and feelings—of eight people on the edge of life; the novel combines these moving, unsparing representations of the traumas of old age with a grotesque portrait of the sadistic manipulations and sexual exhibitionism of the House Mother. A similar sort of dark grotesquerie is evident in *Christie Malry's Own Double-Entry* (1973), a concise and chilling black comedy in which the protagonist decides to apply the system of double entry bookkeeping to life; his urge to balance the books whenever he feels that a slight or injustice has been done leads him from fairly harmless gestures to putting cyanide in a reservoir and killing 20,479 West Londoners.

While J.'s main energies went into his novels, he also wrote poems, play scripts, and short stories, and the publication of a selection of these stories in *Aren't You Rather Young to Be Writing Your Memoirs?* (1973) provided him with a platform to state his views on modern fiction: his introduction to the volume stands as his most sustained credo. Ironically, the year in which it appeared was also the year of his death. His last novel came out two years later. *See the Old Lady Decently* (1975) had been meant to inaugurate a trilogy that would pursue three themes: the death of J.'s mother from cancer; the decay of the "mother country" of the British Empire; and the renewing power of motherhood. The first volume is a promising start, employing a variety of techniques from concrete

poetry to transcribed oral history, and encompassing a range of J.'s characteristic tones and topics. But J. never got beyond the first volume: in a state of deep depression, he killed himself at the age of forty.

Over a quarter of a century has now elapsed since J.'s suicide, but he has remained a point of reference and a subject of debate in discussions of English fiction, and his influence has spread further afield—the extraordinary novel *Drift* (1994), by the Asian Australian writer Brian Castro, provides a postcolonial completion and revision of J.'s projected trilogy. An attempt to produce a J. revival in 1983 foundered, but another one may be gathering pace: *The Unfortunates* and *Christie Malry's Own Double-Entry* have recently been reissued. J.'s work is likely to remain of interest because of its energetic exploration of the possibilities of the novel form and its unflinching engagement with the pain and pathos of mortality.

BIBLIOGRAPHY: Levitt, M. P., "The Novels of B. S. J.: Against the War against Joyce," *MFS* 27 (1981–82): 571–86; Parrinder, P., "Pilgrim's Progress: The Novels of B. S. J.," *CritQ* 19 (1977): 45–59; special J. issue, *RCF* 5 (Summer 1995); Tredell, N., *Fighting Fictions* (2000)

NICOLAS TREDELL

JOHNSON, Linton Kwesi
b. 24 August 1952, Chapelton, Jamaica

J. invokes the oral poetry tradition and transforms it into spoken word activism. His racially charged poetry has been significant in expanding the parameters of contemporary British literature to include issues of the black British experience. Internationally recognized as one of the first "reggae" poets, he constructs his verses in Jamaican patois and infuses them with reggae, dub, and Rastafarian rhythms.

J. moved from Jamaica to London in 1963. The move was traumatic; the racism and hostility he encountered as a black teenager would set the themes of his future work. After attending Tulse Hill Secondary School, he studied sociology at Goldsmith's College, University of London. While in school, he joined the Black Panthers and learned about black history and culture. It was during this time of his life that he began to construct his politics and express them through art. The work of such writers as W. E. B. Du Bois inspired him to write poetry. He organized a poetry workshop and performed with Rasta Love, a group of poets and drummers. He also helped found Creation for Liberation, one of the first organizations dedicated to promoting exhibitions for black artists.

His first collection of poetry, *Voices of the Living and the Dead,* was published in 1974. His second collection, *Dread Beat an' Blood,* was published in 1975 and recorded as an LP in 1978. The work illuminates a black experience marked by oppression, violence, and disenfranchisement. It was received with so much acclaim that in 1978 a documentary film on J. was released and also called *Dread Beat an' Blood*. His third collection, *Inglan Is a Bitch* (1980), with its optimistic tone, marked a new direction for J., as it advocated a celebration of life in the face of death and struggle. His fourth collection, *Tings an' Times*, was published in 1991. A father and grandfather at the time of this collection's publication, he cited as his inspiration the generation of black children who were reared removed from the issues that provoked their parents to action. His concern for the ability of these children to challenge the effects of colonial oppression informs his mission of what he calls "institution-building." In this collection, he advocates a form of social consciousness and political awareness that would reach beyond the goal of establishing ethnic pride. Pride, he maintains, is only a starting point from which people must work toward the elimination of oppression in any form.

J.'s poetry is interwoven with his careers as a musician and live performer. He has released more than twelve albums, and has been nominated for an American Grammy Award. He has received numerous awards in Italy for his poetry and music. In 1981, he launched his own record label that continues to promote and distribute socially conscious black artists.

His accomplishments extend beyond his creative contribution to contemporary British literature and music; he has also established himself as a respected journalist and academic. In the 1980s, he worked with the Brixton-based Race Today collective. His ten-part radio series on Jamaican popular music was aired in 1982 and repeated in 1983. From 1985 to 1988, he was a reporter for Channel Four's race relations series, "The Bandung File." In 1977, he was awarded a C. Day Lewis Fellowship, becoming the writer in residence for the London borough of Lambeth for that year. He did work in the Library Resources and Education Offices at the Keskidee Centre, the first home of black theater and art. In 1985, he was made an associate fellow of Warwick University, and in 1987 an honorary fellow of Wolverhamton Polytechnic.

The articulation of his poetry to music makes his message more accessible and may account for much of his international popularity. By exploring the racial discrimination, violence, and optimism of the black British experience, his work has served as a compass of politics and social conscience.

BIBLIOGRAPHY: D'Aguiar, F., "L. K. J.," in Lindfors, B., and R. Sander, eds., *Twentieth-Century Caribbean and Black African Writers*, DLB 157 (1996): 123–30; Hitchcock, P., "It Dread Inna Inglan: L. K. J., Dread, and Dub Identity," in Potash, C., ed., *Reggae, Rasta,* *Revolution: Jamaican Music from Ska to Dub* (1997): 163–67

VICKI ENG

JOHNSON, Lionel [Pigot]

b. 15 March 1867, Broadstairs, Kent; d. 4 October 1902, London

Poet and critic, J. was educated at Winchester and New College, Oxford. He reviewed for the *Academy, Pall Mall Gazette*, and other journals. His conversion to Roman Catholicism in 1891 permeated his later verse. His first collection of poems appeared 1895, which included his most anthologized poems, "The Dark Angel," "By the Statue of King Charles in Charing Cross," "Mystic and Cavalier," and "The Church of a Dream." His second volume, *Ireland with Other Poems* (1897), reflected his growing interest in his Irish ancestry and he became a friend of W. B. YEATS. His *Complete Poems* appeared in 1953.

JOHNSON, Pamela Hansford

b. 29 May 1912, London; d. 18 June 1981, London

J.'s first novel, *This Bed Thy Centre* (1935), was followed by several others, which displayed her gift for light SATIRE. She is best known for her Helena trilogy, comprising *Too Dear for My Possessing* (1940), *An Avenue of Stone* (1947), and *A Summer to Decide* (1948), and for *An Impossible Marriage* and *The Last Resort* (repub. as *The Sea and the Wedding*, 1957), both published in 1954. *The Unspeakable Skipton* (1959) was her greatest success: it is an amusing tale of an unscrupulous writer on his uppers in Bruges. J. wrote one play, *Corinth House* (perf. 1948; pub. 1954). As critic, she published studies of Thomas Wolfe (1947), Ivy COMPTON-BURNETT (1951), and Marcel Proust (1958).

JOHNSON, Samuel

b. 18 September 1709, Lichfield; d. 13 December 1784, London

A popular image of "Doctor Johnson" is "Conversation Johnson," the argumentative and dominating character represented in one of the most entertaining of biographies, James BOSWELL's *The Life of Samuel Johnson, LL.D.,* published in 1791. It is a masterly presentation of a privileged society in 18th-c. London and delights by presenting the encounters of Johnson with notable figures of his day, such as John Wilkes, Joshua REYNOLDS, Hannah MORE, Elizabeth MONTAGU, David GARRICK, and Oliver GOLDSMITH as well as with lesser known intimates, such as Hester Thrale [PIOZZI], Topham Beauclerk, Bennet Langton, and Boswell himself. So powerful is the book that it has dominated the view of J., making him a reactionary to William WORDSWORTH and a hero to Thomas CARLYLE. Often this is to the exclusion of his writing, providing an ironic twist to his own witticism on William CONGREVE's novel *Incognita* that "I would rather praise it than read it." In addition, Boswell's artful presentation of J. as an archconservative father-figure, presiding over "The Club," is based mainly on his own encounters with him, which totalled only 425 days in the last twenty-one years of J.'s life. John HAWKINS, who knew J. from the 1730s, in his own biography gave a different account of The Club, remarking that "disputation was not, as in so many associations of this kind, the purpose of our meeting" and that J. contributed much wit and a fund of excellent stories, giving the lie to the idea "that he could only reason and discuss, dictate and control."

J. was the son of an elderly bookseller of Lichfield, Staffordshire. He studied at Pembroke College, Oxford, for only a year before poverty forced him to discontinue. For a short time, he ran a school, near Lichfield, and then, accompanied by Garrick, a former student (who was to become a famous Shakespearean actor), he sought his fortune as a hack journalist in London (translating lives and writing accounts of parliamentary debates). Often he wandered at night with his friend, the minor poet, Richard SAVAGE, in conditions that he subsequently described in his *Life of Richard Savage* (1744), "sleeping on benches or the ashes of a glasshouse." A huge man, afflicted with the scrofula that adversely affected his hearing and the sight of one eye, he had obsessive tics of behavior and suffered from a deeply oppressive melancholia that made him fear that he would become mad. His experience of hardship and disability may have fuelled the vigorous rationality of his writing and his determination to succeed in London society, where he became one of the most celebrated writers and personalities of the latter part of the 18th c.

The strong moral tendency of his writings was shown in his early imitations of satires of Juvenal, the book-length poems *London* (1738) and *The Vanity of Human Wishes* (1749). The latter provided contemporary examples, such as the Duke of Marlborough, Charles XII of Sweden, and Jonathan SWIFT, showing how man is betrayed by hope and fear to misery and ruin: "Yet hope not life from grief or danger free,/ Nor think the doom of man reversed for thee." The gravity of the sentiments and the sober stoicism with its stately inevitability caught the imagination of the public and J.'s fame was established, leading him to publish a series of periodical essays on moral subjects: a twice-weekly sheet called the *Rambler* (1750–52), essays in the *Adventurer* (1753), and the *Idler* essays (1758–60) in the *Universal Chronicle*. These show J.'s gift for compressing in a few lines a memorable statement that has the ring of truth. But frequently, once he had expressed and had printed one view, a

contrary or modifying position would occur to him in equally compelling language that he would print subsequently. Using the device of multiple imagined correspondents, he entertained his readers with an ongoing debate on such matters as the value of the public's appreciation of literature, the function of the moralist, the limitations of empirical science in relation to religion, and the interconnection of vice and virtue. The debate seems to arise not according to a plan but as the pressure of writing to the clock prompted his mind to reflect on his previous arguments.

While J.'s morality is within the tradition of Anglican Christianity, he refused an easy optimism. His awareness of contrarieties and his paradoxical turn of mind enabled him to write within seven days his masterly fable, *The Prince of Abyssinia* (2 vols., 1759; repub. as *The History of Rasselas, Prince of Abyssinia*, 1768), an episodic narrative in the convention of an Eastern tale in which the high-born characters set out on a search for the secret of how best to live and dispute the meaning of life with vigor and conviction, often with unintended effects, optimistic and pessimistic by turns. The HUMOR of the tale is tender, compassionate, and robust. Memorable pithy remarks abound: "Marriage has many pains, but celibacy has no pleasures"; "Be not too hasty to trust, or to admire, the teachers of morality: they discourse like angels, but they live like men." And it is filled with shrewd observations of human behavior, such as the assembly of academics whose "manners were somewhat coarse, but their conversation was instructive, and their disputations acute though sometimes too violent, and often continued till neither controvertist remembers upon what question they began." J.'s wit so elegantly turns situations inside out to endorse contrary positions that it is inevitable that the tale ends in a "conclusion where nothing is concluded."

Two years earlier, J. had energetically attacked conclusions that overlook the complication of life. Soame Jenyns had proposed that all is for the best in this world in his *A Free Inquiry into the Nature and Origin of Evil* (1757). It was possible, Jenyns believed, that our misfortunes contribute to happiness of higher beings elsewhere in the cosmos. J. developed the idea in his *Review* (1757): "Many a merry bout have these frolic beings at the vicissitudes of an ague, and good sport it is to see a man tumble with an epilepsy, and revive and tumble again, and all he knows not why." A deep compassion for the misery of man provoked J.'s indignation, just as it could also modulate into the understanding wisdom of his sympathetic letter to Dr. Lawrence who had lost his wife. J. saw a loved wife as the only companion with whom a man "could set his mind at liberty, to retrace the past or anticipate the future" and the loss as a laceration of the "continuity of being" (1780).

At the same time as J. was writing the periodical essays, he was preparing his great *A Dictionary of the English Language* (2 vols., 1755) and intermittently from 1756 his edition of *The Plays of William Shakespeare* (1765). All three activities cross-fertilize. The *Dictionary* for its illustrative quotations capitalizes on his excellent memory of wide reading (commencing as autodidact in his father's bookshop) to provide a work of literary and scientific fascination, fulfilling his wish to "afford light to the repositories of science, and add celebrity to *Bacon*, to *Hooker*, to *Milton*, and to *Boyle*." The collective force of quotations for many entries often provides a running commentary on the definition and a sense of J.'s choice encouraging the reader to reflect, sometimes skeptically or with amusement, on the ideas that arise. The scientific definitions often gave rise to his reflective essays in the periodicals and the Shakespearean quotations assisted the notes of his edition of the plays.

As a literary critic, J. was flexible and diverse. His aim was to produce an edition of William SHAKESPEARE where the student could "read Shakespeare on the wing" not detained by academic paraphernalia. He satirized the "art of writing notes" that were customarily excessively long and self-congratulatory and he set a standard of suggestive writing, showing "so much as may enable the candidate of criticism to discover the rest." Despite his sharing the contemporary neoclassical liking for genre and poetic justice, he was enthusiastic for "the mingled drama" of Shakespeare as representing the complexity of life and for the "progress of the fable," the overall movement of the play as a crucial element of its significance rather than the final apportioning of rewards and punishments. In the later *Lives of the English Poets* (10 vols., 1777–81), J. exhibits the same robust personal engagement with the authors. (These were fifty-two poets from the time of Abraham COWLEY, chosen mostly by the booksellers, who asked J. to provide prefaces to the poems they published in a series of volumes.) J. revels in the tension between largeness of spirit in the "excentric violence" of John DRYDEN and the polished correctness of Alexander POPE (nevertheless "an imagination perpetually on the wing"). These lives were composed at opposite ends of the period of writing the sequence in order to enable his mind to move from one polarity to the other. As before, the reader is aware of a personality distinctive and challenging operating on the materials. J. relied on his reflective capacity combined with a fertile mind well stored with learning to make his judgements. On occasion, as in the "Life of Swift," a merely personal distaste for elements that he feared in himself raises matters to contest but even where he is less in sympathy, as here and on the metaphysical poets, in the "Life of Cowley," many of his judgments encapsulate perceptive characterizations. The stimulation of original

thinking is the mark of most of J.'s writing. His last work, *A Journey to the Western Islands of Scotland* (1775), is not a journal of his travels but "deals more in notions than in facts." Based on the very long letters he wrote to his friend, Hester Thrale, who kept open house for him, the *Journey* is a reflective re-creation that focuses on the misery of the depopulation of Scotland and the sturdiness of surviving communities, such as that of the Isle of Coll.

BIBLIOGRAPHY: Bate, W. J., *S. J.* (1977); Boswell, J., *Life of Johnson*, ed. by R. W. Chapman (1953); Bronson, B. H., *J. Agonistes and Other Essays* (1965); Greene, D., *S. J.* (1970; rev. ed., 1989); Grundy, I., *S. J. and the Scale of Greatness* (1986); Redford, B., ed., *The Letters of S. J.* (5 vols., 1992–94); Tomarken, E., *A History of the Commentary on Selected Writings of S. J.* (1994); Wimsatt, W. K., *Philosophic Words: A Study of Style and Meaning in the Rambler and Dictionary of S. J.* (1948)

KEITH CROOK

JOHNSTONE, Charles
b. ca. 1719, Carrigogunnel County, Limerick, Ireland; d. ca. 1800, Calcutta, India

One of the many writers of London's Grub Street whose literary endeavors are now all but forgotten, J. was popular in his day as the author of *Chrysal; or, The Adventures of a Guinea* (4 vols., 1760–65). The so-called adventures—narrated by the "spirit of gold" within the guinea possessed with the power to reveal both the past and the future—unfold as the coin is passed from owner to owner. Later works, none of which would match the success of *Chrysal*, include *The History of Arsaces Prince of Betlis* (2 vols., 1774), *The Pilgrim; or, A Picture of Life in a Series of Letters* (2 vols., 1775), and *The History of John Juniper Esq., Alias Juniper Jack* (3 vols., 1781).

JONES, David [Michael]
b. 1 November 1895, Brockley, Kent; d. 28 October 1974, Harrow, London

The son of a printer, J. attended Camberwell School of Art from 1910 to 1914 and enlisted in the Welch Fusiliers in 1915. He served as a private soldier in a London unit of David Lloyd George's "Welsh Army" and served in France until December 1918, an experience that powerfully influenced his life and work. In 1921, he was received into the Catholic Church and worked under Eric Gill, first at Ditchling in Sussex and later at Capel-y-ffin in Powys. In 1928, he was elected to the Seven and Five Society and exhibited his work with artists such as Henry Moore, Christopher Wood, Barbara Hepworth, and John Piper.

J. had established a reputation particularly as a visionary water colorist, calligrapher, and engraver, before he began writing. His first book, *In Parenthesis,* for which he was awarded the Hawthornden Prize, was published in 1937. T. S. ELIOT described it as "a work of genius . . . A work of literary art which uses language in a new way or for a new purpose . . . a book about the experiences of one soldier in the War of 1914–18. It is also a book about War, and about many other things also, such as Roman Britain, the Arthurian Legend, and divers matters which are given association by the mind of the writer." The narrative structure of the poem begins, as J. says in his preface, "early in December 1915 and ends early July 1916. The first date corresponds to my going to France." Written in cadenced prose and free verse, the story of Private John Ball's experiences of war on the western front are interwoven with the history of war and rooted in Welsh history and legend. It is a highly allusive work: the intense experiences of trench warfare expressed by the soldiers themselves are interpenetrated with voices from the past. There is an attempt to dramatize their lives through the speech of the common soldiers and to depict their sufferings from their point of view and at the same time to place their experience within the perspective of history. The book is a poignant statement of J.'s own experience of war while at the same time realizing a monumental sense of impersonality as a statement about war itself. The poem reinforces a powerful sense of continuity with the past.

This was followed in 1952 by the publication of *The Anathemata,* described by W. H. AUDEN as "very probably the finest long poem written in English in this century" It is sub-titled "fragments of an attempted writing" and is written as a series of fragments, epic in scope, about the origins and material of our civilization and sensibility. As in *In Parenthesis,* Welsh and Latin phrases, past and present, are juxtaposed, poetry in the grand manner is juxtaposed with the colloquial cockney speech of the London soldiers. Despite its complexity and the looseness of its structure, this long poem nonetheless achieves an imaginative abundance that carries conviction. David Blamires in his study of the poetry writes that *The Anathemata* "shares the qualities of chronicle, EPIC, drama, incantation and lyric and is at the same time none of these and more than all put together. . . . The poet himself defected in his own description of it as 'fragments of an attempted writing,' and yet this does contain a necessary truth . . . He is right to call it an attempt—an attempt at a vision of Britain . . . And the fragments are inevitable, since the knowledge of one man must be fragmentary, though he may possess a perception of essentials and the things that will stand for others and be the light shining in darkness."

In 1959, J. published a book of his collected essays entitled *Epoch and Artist* in which he discusses much of the materials he draws on in his poetry. He writes about Wales, about the MATTER OF BRITAIN, about art and sacrament, about the Arthurian legend and Roman Britain. He also includes individual essays on abstract art, Eric Gill, Bernard Berenson, Christopher SMART, and James JOYCE's Dublin. In 1974, he published *The Sleeping Lord* that consists of several complete sections of a work he projected on Roman soldiers in Palestine at the time of Christ and is centered on the crucifixion. The unfinished *The Kensington Mass* was published in 1975 and a further collection of his essays, *The Dying Gaul,* in 1978. A selection of material he left in manuscript was published in 1981 under the title *The Roman Quarry.*

He was made a Commander of the Order of the British Empire in 1955 and a Companion of Honour in 1974. He was awarded an honorary D.Litt. by the University of Wales. Retrospective exhibitions of his work were mounted at the National Library of Wales and the Tate Gallery in 1954–55 and again posthumously in 1981. He had a remarkable range of interests and was widely read in archaeology, mythology, anthropology as well as theology and had a gift for friendship. He was a prolific and generous letter writer and his letters to René Hague were published in *Dai Great-coat* in 1980. He corresponded with a wide circle of friends and admirers including Saunders Lewis, Vernon WATKINS, and Aneirin Talfan Davies, and his letters to them have also been published. Because of its originality and its visionary quality, his art has often been associated with the tradition that goes back to William BLAKE and Samuel Palmer. As a poet, his use of long disconnected narratives and his profound sense of myth and history connects him to the main current of MODERNISM, the tradition of Joyce, Eliot, and Ezra Pound.

BIBLIOGRAPHY: Blamires, D., *D. J.* (1971); Hague, R., *D. J.* (1975); Hooker, J., *D. J.* (1975); Ward, E., *D. J., Mythmaker* (1983)

A. R. JONES

JONES, [Morgan] Glyn
b. 28 February 1905, Merthyr Tydfil, Wales; d. 10 April 1995, Cardiff, Wales

Poet, short story writer, and novelist, J. was born, he said, "into a Welsh-speaking family, so that my first language was Welsh." He attended Cyfarthfa Castle Grammar School and trained as a teacher at St. Paul's College, Cheltenham. He worked as a schoolmaster in Cardiff where he was appalled by the poverty of some of the children he taught. He chose to write in English because, as he explained, his early feeling for the power of words and the potency of the imagination had been in English. "While using cheerfully enough the English language," he said, "I have never written a word in it about any country other than Wales or any people other than Welsh people." He read widely in modern literature though he said, "My literary hero then was D. H. LAWRENCE."

Publication in 1937 of *The Blue Bed,* a collection of nine short stories, first brought him to the attention of the reading public. The volume was widely and well reviewed. Edwin MUIR described it as "the work of a very remarkable writer," and Edward Garnett wrote that "Glyn Jones is a genius." The stories combine the tragic with the humorous in a manner that is wholly distinctive. In style, he seems to have been influenced by the luxuriant and rhythmical prose of Dylan THOMAS on the one hand and by the sparse economy of Caradoc Evans on the other. His affinity with Lawrence with whom he shared a similar background is also apparent. In 1944, he published a further volume of short stories, *The Water Music,* a series of twelve stories about childhood. Influenced by Thomas's stories of his childhood, J. recalls his own childhood though his memories are transformed by his imagination in stories that are both stylistically and thematically more uniform than those in *The Blue Bed.*

In 1956, he published his first novel, *The Valley, the City, the Village.* Structured in three sections as indicated by its title, the novel builds on his success as a short story writer. The narrative traces the development of Trystan from his youth in the valley, through his student days in the city, to his maturity in the village where his dreams find a kind of fulfillment. He draws on his own life in Merthyr Tydfil, Cardiff, and Llansteffan in each of the stages of his Trystan's growing-up and the novel is notable for its impressionistic portrayal of authentic incidents, acutely observed characters, and evocative landscapes. *The Learning Lark* (1960) has a more coherent structure and a more uniform style. The novel sets out to expose the way in which headmasters are appointed in South Wales though J.'s criticisms of the chicanery involved are probably too good-natured to be effective. *The Island of Apples* (1965) is a poetic novel that combines REALISM and fantasy novel. It is based on the legend of Affallon, one of the Celtic "Isles of the Blest," to which Arthur was carried after his death. The theme, the departure of youth's dreams, is translated into despairing action and marvelous natural imagery that embody the sense of loss and the boy's torment when he is compelled to face reality. This is probably J.'s finest achievement as a novelist.

Though his output is small, J. thought of himself primarily as a poet and his short stories and novels are notable for their poetic qualities. His first collection, *Poems,* published in 1939 reflect the early influence of Lawrence though later after he had been exposed

to the poetry of Thomas and Gerard Manley HOPKINS, the texture and rhythms of his poems become more complex and resonant. He published *The Dream of Jake Hopkins* in 1954 followed in 1975 by *Selected Poems* that included a number of new poems. As he matured as a poet, he seems to have become more aware of the practice and example of Welsh poetry. He translated the poetry of Dafydd ap Gwilym and, with T. J. Morgan, *The Saga of Llywarch the Old* (1955). Later, he published two selections of harp stanzas, *When the Rose Bush Brings Forth Apples* (1981) and *Honeydew on the Wormwood* (1984). His poems demonstrate his strong sense of place and his sensuous appreciation of NATURE AND LANDSCAPE. He insisted that, "A poem for me is a structure," and many of his poems are written in complex verse forms and depend on sharply and exactly observed scenes and precise descriptions. He is always aware of reality of death and loss and of man's imperfections that he embraces with compassion for individual and for communal man. His later poetry, in which he celebrates his own past and those he has known who have passed away, is characterized by a simple, elegiac directness that is deeply affecting.

In his autobiography, *The Dragon Has Two Tongues* (1968), which he subtitled *Essays on Anglo-Welsh Writers and Writing,* in a warm yet confident way he relates his own background and links it to the situation of Anglo-Welsh writing in general. In doing so, he discusses the work of three prose writers, Caradoc Evans, Jack Jones, and Gwyn THOMAS, all of whom he had known personally, and three Anglo-Welsh poets, Huw Menai [Huw Owen Williams], Idris Davies, and Thomas. He knew his material intimately and while producing an authentic memoir of his subjects he also recorded a period in Anglo-Welsh literature through which he had lived and does so in a relaxed, urbane, and kindly manner. As in his many reviews he shows himself to be a clear-sighted, well-informed critic deeply engaged with literature. In collaboration with John Rowlands, he published a books of essays, *Profiles: A Visitors' Guide to Writing in Twentieth Century Wales* (1980), devoted to some of the more important Welsh and Anglo-Welsh writers. He wrote the libretto for the opera *The Beach of Falesá* based on a short story by Robert Louis STEVENSON with music by Alun Hoddinott that was performed by the Welsh National Opera Company in 1974.

J. was the first chairman and then president of the English language section of Yr Academi Gymreig, and in 1988 he was inducted into Gorsedd Beirdd Ynys Prydain. J. is buried in Llansteffan where his gravestone is inscribed simply "Llenor," Man of Letters.

BIBLIOGRAPHY: Brown, T., ed., *The Collected Stories of G. J.* (1999); Norris, L., *G. J.* (1973); Stephens, M., ed., *The Collected Poems of G. J.* (1996)

A. R. JONES

JONES, Gwyn

b. 24 May 1907, Blackwood, Monmouthshire; d. 6 December 1999, Aberystwyth, Dyfed

The son of a miner, J.—scholar, novelist, short story writer, and editor—was possibly the preeminent man of Anglo-Welsh letters in the 20th c. He was educated at the County School, Tredegar, and at the University of Wales, Cardiff. In 1927, he was awarded a first-class degree in English. In 1929, he submitted a thesis on "Legal Procedures and the Conduct of a Feud in the Icelandic Sagas" for the degree of M.A. After working as a schoolmaster in Wigan Grammar School and Manchester Central High School, he was appointed to a lectureship in the University of Wales, Cardiff, in 1935 and in 1940 he was appointed to the chair of English Language and Literature in the University of Wales, Aberystwyth.

In 1935, Princeton University Press published his translations of *Four Icelandic Sagas* for the American-Icelandic Foundation. He then wrote four very different kinds of novels in four years. In 1935, he published his historical novel, *Richard Savage*, which was widely reviewed and highly acclaimed. The portrait of Savage was described as being brilliantly sharp while the historical background was sketched in with assurance and conviction. The narrative holds the reader's imagination and as well as accurately capturing the period. He followed this by *Times like These* (1936), a novel set before and after the 1926 general strike that demonstrates a deep animosity toward the coal owners though at the same time notable for its restraint, balance, and HUMOR. *The Nine Days' Wonder* (1937) is set near Manchester but although the atmosphere is well established, the characters are unsympathetic and the background seedy. *Garland of Bays* (1938) is an historical novel based on the life and times of Robert GREENE, the Elizabethan dramatist and pamphleteer. The novel achieves an impressive narrative momentum and successfully re-creates the man and his time.

J. did not write another novel until *The Flowers beneath the Scythe*, published in 1952. Set in Wales during the period between 1930 and 1940, it describes the passing of the generations and the sense of loss this entails. *The Walk Home* (1962), his last novel, an historical novel set in the industrial landscape of South Wales in the early 19th c. is a somewhat dark story of the lives of the working people. He also published three collections of his short stories, *The Buttercup Field* (1945), *The Still Waters* (1948), and *Shepherd's Hey* (1953). In his short stories, he shows

himself to be an acute observer of the Welsh rural scene that he views with sympathy, exasperation, and aversion. His attitude toward his characters and toward the natural landscape in which they live is by no means sentimentalized, and in several of his stories the past impinges on the present in a terrifying and grotesque way so that time itself becomes an instrument of revenge. Many of his stories draw on the past in such a way as to lend many of them the attributes of folktales.

In February 1939, J. founded the influential monthly magazine, *Welsh Review*, for English-speaking Welshmen, and edited ten numbers in which he published works by, among others, Glyn JONES, Geraint Goodwin, Margiad Evans, Alun LEWIS, Lynette Roberts, and a number of writers who were unknown until published by him. In 1948, in collaboration with Thomas Jones, he published his translation of *The Mabinogion* (subsequently published in Everyman's Library) that made available to English readers in a style both appropriate and graceful these astonishing Welsh tales. This translation also initiated his association with the Golden Cockerel Press for which he produced a number of books including *Salmacis and Hermaphroditus* (1951), *Sir Gawain and the Green Knight* (1952), and *The Poems and Sonnets of William Shakespeare* (1960). The Golden Cockerel Press specialized in finely printed, beautifully illustrated, and splendidly bound books that are now recognized as among the outstanding productions of the time.

J. maintained his interest in Old Icelandic sagas and in 1942 published his translation of *The Vatnsdalers' Saga*. Between 1960 and 1965, he published translations of ten sagas, including *Egil's Saga* (1960) and *Eirik the Red* (1961). His publication of *The Norse Atlantic Saga* (1964) and *A History of the Vikings* (1968) established his reputation as one of the foremost Icelandic scholars of his time. In 1963, he was awarded the Knight's Cross, and in 1987 the Commander's Cross, Order of the Falcon by the President of Iceland for services to scholarship. In 1972, he was awarded the Christian Gauss Award for *Kings, Beasts and Heroes* (1972) in which he examined the story content and the storytelling in BEOWULF, *Culhwch and Olwen*, and *King Hrolf's Saga*.

He was a preeminent figure in Anglo-Welsh literature that he promoted in editorials, numerous scholarly articles, lectures, and broadcasts. He edited a number of anthologies of Anglo-Welsh literature including *Welsh Short Stories* (1941 and 1956) and *The Oxford Book of Welsh Verse in English* (1977), in which he included "The Blue Day Journey," one of his own poems. He retold old legends with warmth and enthusiasm in *Welsh Legends and Folk-Tales* (1955) and *Scandinavian Legends and Folk-Tales* (1956). His love for Wales, its landscape and its history, was tempered by his realization that the Anglo-

Welsh are not willingly allowed an inheritance. As he points out, "the majority of the Anglo-Welsh have been quite painfully modest and deferential in face of native Welsh criticism: we should no more talk back to a proper Cymro than we would cheek our mother." J. was awarded the honorary degree of D.Litt. by the Universities of Nottingham, Southampton and Wales, and received the Cymmrodorian Medal in 1991. In 1965, he was made a Commander of the Order of the British Empire.

BIBLIOGRAPHY: Price, C., *G. J.* (1976); Riley, E. P., "G. J.," in Baldwin, D., ed., *British Short-Fiction Writers, 1945–1980,* DLB 139 (1994): 137–48

A. R. JONES

JONES, Henry Arthur

b. 20 September 1851, Grandborough, Buckinghamshire; d. 7 January 1929, London

There is an irony inherent in any retrospective consideration of the writings of J.: in essays, lectures, articles, books, and even in his will, he proclaimed that the English theater could never recover its lost stature and lost dignity until "the drama" was taken seriously as literature—yet now, in the 21st c., rereading his once-famous plays such as *The Dancing Girl* (perf. 1891; pub. 1907) or *Michael and His Lost Angel* (pub. 1895; perf. 1896) or *The Case of Rebellious Susan* (1894) one has the greatest of difficulty in taking these solemn, melodramatic pontifications seriously in any literary sense. Yet his intentions were wholly serious and sincere and for a while were taken seriously by critical opinion of the day (William ARCHER, for instance).

J. was, in his own day, often compared with Arthur Wing PINERO and that comparison is still frequently cited. A more cogent comparison, however, might be made with his French contemporary, the incorrigibly didactic Eugene Brieux—whom Bernard SHAW, in an excess of social reform enthusiasm, once referred to as (incredibly) "incomparably the greatest writer France has produced since Molière." It is true that some great literature is unjustly neglected and ignored by future generations; but in some cases, the neglect and the ignoring reflect sound critical thinking. Some things thought to be literature turn out not to be. In English 19th-c. writing, a good example of this would be Edward BULWER-LYTTON: another would be J., whose desperation shows most poignantly, perhaps, in his preface to his play *The Divine Gift* (1913). This preface takes the form of an open letter to Gilbert MURRAY, thanking him, as a great scholar and literary figure, for taking live theater performances seriously as art.

Between 1879 and 1928, J. wrote fifty-six plays, many of which were presented at leading London and New York theaters and some of which ran for two years or more. His commercial success and popularity are, therefore, not in question. Artistic and literary success is, however, a different matter entirely. Some of the better known titles are *The Silver King* (1882), *Judah* (1890), *The Dancing Girl, The Case of Rebellious Susan, Michael and His Lost Angel, The Liars* (1897), *Mrs. Danes's Defence* (1900), *The Hypocrites* (1906), and *The Lie* (perf. 1914; pub. 1915). Of all of these, it is fair to say that in them J. shows considerable ability in the deftness of their dramatic structure and their sureness of theatrical touch. He has on occasion (though not lately) also been praised for his perception of and acute rendering of realistic character portraits but a rereading of the plays now scarcely supports this claim. From a literary standpoint, his characters seem simple, flat, two-dimensional caricatures cut to a very conventional model; and this becomes very obvious in the literary context of the time.

At the time when J. was writing *The Liars*, for instance, Thomas HARDY was writing *Jude the Obscure,* Joseph CONRAD was writing *The Nigger of the "Narcissus,"* and Henry JAMES was busy with *The Spoils of Poynton.* Alongside these, J.'s details of in-depth character portrayal look more than a bit thin. Despite J.'s fervent pleas for more "serious," elevated, literary drama, the truth is that J., Pinero, and Oscar WILDE were all (with the single outstanding exception of Wilde's marvelously original *The Importance of Being Earnest*) writing formula plays of no consequence, designed only to meet the current popular trivial taste, none of them of the slightest literary significance (again excepting that one Wilde play). The cardboard figures that inhabit Wilde's *Lady Windermere's Fan,* Pinero's *The Second Mrs. Tanqueray,* and J.'s *The Liars,* for instance, could perfectly well be interchanged with each other without doing any violence to any of the plays; and the perennial, pervading presence of the "Fallen Woman" had become, in a great many plays of the period, a universally accepted icon that requires no distinguishing individual features at all: you can buy her by the yard in any cheap theatrical store. J.'s plays are no worse than those of his contemporaries in this regard—and no better. He was not a writer of any great originality.

The playwriting of J., in spite of these strictures, does possess other, humbler, qualities that can be greeted with unfeigned and unqualified admiration. The first of these is industry: he labored unremittingly to improve his craft. The second is ingenuity, both in choice of subject and in handling it: his plays were neat. The third is his untiring and tenacious seizing of all the leading social issues of the day: he had a journalist's instinct for homing in on attitudes and people that could be relied upon to become talking points and centers of interest—at least for a little while. Not that he was cynical about such things: on the contrary, he was sincere to the point of a smothering solemnity, moral to the point of asphyxiation. And his moral code, intuitive rather than rational, was already old-fashioned and out-of-date even in his own day. His plays, even the comedies, are full of moral anguish, of one sort or another, rendered in bold, melodramatic-theatrical terms with a canny eye to strong curtain lines and startling climactic moments: and heart-felt confessions galore, as in, for example, *Michael and His Lost Angel* where the vicar has forced a young girl to make public confession of her "sin" only to be overtaken by his own passionate feeling for Audrie Lesden, a sexually seductive married woman living apart from her husband. Inevitably, act 3 ends with his public confession, staged with some splendor in front of the entire congregation, and act 4 ends in an Italian monastery where Audrie, who has searched all over Europe for him, finally finds him and dies in his arms. What the Victorians referred to as "sexual sin" was one of J.'s leitmotifs; the other was hypocrisy in various forms: consider the titles of some of his plays—*The Masqueraders* (1894), *The Liars*, *The Hypocrites* (1906), *The Lie*. Lying and adultery were J.'s stock-in-trade.

Though J.'s plays do not really possess any great literary quality, they nevertheless do (or, at least, did) possess great theatrical qualities. Given the taste of the town at the time, they were spellbinders. They were rather like high-quality crossword puzzles (with sumptuous scenic effects): the clues are intriguingly teasing but lead eventually to the right conclusion, the always-anticipated solution; and the completed solution is flattering to the solver's vanity.

BIBLIOGRAPHY: Cordell, R. A., *H. A. J. and the Modern Drama* (1932); Griffin, P., *Arthur Wing Pinero and H. A. J.* (1991); Jones, D. A., *The Life and Letters of H. A. J.* (1930); Matlaw, M., *Modern World Drama* (1972)

ERIC SALMON

JONES, [Sir] William
b. 28 September 1746, London; d. 27 April 1794, Calcutta, India

Lawyer and Orientalist, J. taught himself Arabic and Hebrew while a schoolboy at Harrow, and at University College, Oxford, studied Oriental literatures, including Persian and Chinese, as well as European languages. He was called to the bar in 1774, becoming a High Court judge in Calcutta. A pioneer of Sanskrit studies and founder of the Asiatic Society, he made the culture of the ancient Hindus accessible to Occidental scholarship and is remembered for his translations. J. is best known for his rendering from the Persian of "A Persian Song of Hagiz," published in his *Poems, Consisting Chiefly of Translations from the Asiatick Languages* (1772). His influence persisted in the Oriental themes of Lord BYRON, Robert SOUTHEY, and Thomas MOORE.

JONSON, Ben
b. 11 June 1573?, London; d. 6 August 1637, Westminster

J. is a true subversive—a creator of grand carnivals, giant belches, Latin tags, and mighty verse—so it is not unsurprising that he has difficulty finding a place in the present-day theater devoted to the small and the transitory. As a dramatist, J. wrote speeches to be acted. His seeming failures of characterization are not failures when his words are spoken and his characters given flesh by actors. His characters come on in midflight, there is no pausing, all is forward movement, and every second is packed. Stage directions are built into the speeches so an actor cannot say certain lines without moving. To criticize J. from the text alone is like criticizing an opera from the libretto without hearing the music. To do this dramatist justice, you always have to hear the music.

In Elizabethan times, no one thought writing was a career for a gentleman; J., thank goodness, was no gentleman, but an apprentice bricklayer, who had the good fortune not to go to university and be corrupted by literature. For though he was saturated in the classics, he never sacrificed theatrical qualities to them. Most dramatic dialogue is ineffective, degenerating into mere gossip. But for J., it has a dark depth even if the light around shines brightly. He is also the master of invective, one of the marks of a good playwright. When J.'s characters quarrel most violently, they reveal themselves most fully. In his plays, he uses bad temper like other playwrights use alcohol to loosen up his characters; for when social restraints are momentarily dropped and we "forget ourselves," it is then we show our real faces. With J., character revelations are always shown in dynamic action, not in static introspection. His characters do not sit around talking, they are up and doing.

J. is best known for his comedies of "humour"—*Every Man in His Humour* (perf. 1598; pub. 1601), *Every Man Out of His Humour* (perf. 1599; pub. 1600), *Volpone* (perf. 1606; pub. 1607), *Epicoene; or, The Silent Woman* (perf. 1609; pub. 1620), *The Alchemist* (perf. 1610; pub. 1612), *Bartholomew Fair* (perf. 1614; pub. 1631), *The Devil Is an Ass* (perf. 1616; pub. 1631)—imaginative and boisterous plays that come to life with theatrical brilliance, unfolding like beautiful Japanese paper flowers in water. It is a wonder and a mystery, but it works in the theater. Unlike his contemporary William SHAKESPEARE, J. did not give his nobles verse to speak and common folk prose. There are, thankfully, few, if any, nobles in J. In fact, *The Alchemist*, a tale of three crooks taking over an empty London house in the middle of a plague and swindling everyone that comes to the door, is in verse. *Bartholomew Fair*, a great fresco of buying and selling, work and leisure, is in prose. This division is probably because *The Alchemist* is about people's dreams and *Bartholomew Fair* is about how they live. *Volpone* is in magisterial verse, because Volpone himself could be considered the noblest of rogues who deserves verse for the magnificence of his dreams.

In the comic masterpiece *The Devil Is an Ass*, an incompetent apprentice devil, Pug, is sent down to earth for a day to prove himself. Once on earth, Pug encounters a classic bone-headed "straight-man," Master Fitsdotterel, walking along, muttering to himself, and decides immediately to become the man's servant. Interestingly, Fitzdotterel is on his way to see a new play called *The Devil Is an Ass*, by Ben Jonson. What sets J. apart is that his HUMOR never degenerates into a complacent sneer at other people, but embraces all humanity, including himself. Some of his bitterest thrusts are aimed at his own vanity as a man and artist. J. saw that many are pleased to live by luck and lies, and get the means of commanding the labor of others, without contributing anything of value to society: we dig and never plant. His world has become a vast lottery, and mankind scrambles for pennies. The specific target in the play is the monopoly abuses of the time, but the topic is timeless, proving the more profoundly a work is embedded in its own time, the greater its chance of surviving.

J. was able to bring to the stage a unique mix of high and low, merging ethereal beauty and brute nature, as illustrated in a speech from *The Devil Is an Ass* where a young gallant, Wittipol, is trying to seduce a married woman. He does so with some of the most beautiful verse in the English language: "That since love hath the honor to approach/These sister-swelling breasts, and touch this soft/And rosey hands; he hath the skill to draw/Their nectar forth, with kissing; and could make/More wanton salts from this brave promontory,/Down to this valley, then the nimble roe/ . . . Could play the hopping sparrow 'bout these nets,/And sporting squirrel in these crisped groves." The true Jonsonian shock comes with the crudity of the physical action and the loveliness of the verse. It is a potent mix of high, flying poetry, and gutter prose.

J. will always be our contemporary because his perennial theme is greed. His heroes have their eyes fixed on the main chance. When they take their eyes off it, they go under. His comedies demonstrate the social impossibility of good behavior and integrity. They show that anyone who is not a crook has it in his heart to become one. The greatest cheater in a nest of cheaters in *The Alchemist* is the "honest" house-owner who comes back at the end to "clean up" after

everyone else has done the hard, dirty work. *Volpone* sings of the heroism of greed; *The Alchemist* and *Bartholomew Fair*, the joy of greed; and *The Devil Is an Ass*, the pettiness of greed. He never writes about kings and queens or indeed of any of that moth-eaten hierarchy of privilege and incompetence, but about people who have to work for a living. He is always a Republican, not a royalist. His brilliant original comic plots range from *The Silent Woman* (perf. ca. 1609–10; pub. 1620)—where a man who hates noise marries a woman who he thinks can't speak but who turns out to be someone who never stops, and then is revealed as a young man in drag—to *The Staple of News* (perf. 1626; pub. 1631), where some prototype amoral journalists corner the market in news, gain a monopoly of the stuff, and sell it at so much an item.

Critics often complain about J.'s brutality, but overlook his endings, which are far from depressing or cruel. Two of the crooks in *The Alchemist* have to make a quick exit over the garden fence and the third goes back to his old job. They have gained nothing, but they are no worse off than when they started. The villains, Volpone and Mosca, go down gloriously with the ship, and *Bartholomew Fair* ends on a wonderful note of reconciliation and peace, when, after a day out at the fair, full of tumult and drama and fun, Justice Overdo gives up any idea of rooting out vice and instead invites everyone to dinner.

That J. was also a masterly poet and charming writer of song lyrics (e.g., "Drink to me only with thine eyes") only adds to his towering stature. Even his late plays, so long dismissed as "dotage," are at last coming into their own. *The Magnetic Lady* (perf. 1632; pub. 1640) is a magical mix, part fairy tale, Shavian "talk-fest," deconstructive fable, and encyclopedia of dirty jokes. Typically audacious for J., the play begins with two theater enthusiasts, Probee and Damplay, who go into a shop to buy a new play. The boy in charge recommends Ben Jonson's latest *The Magnetic Lady*, but Probee and Damplay have heard the author is old, sick, and long past his prime. So the shop people stage *The Magnetic Lady* for them and we get critical comments from the two men after each act; what we have is a running commentary on the piece as it is being performed. Fittingly, *The Magnetic Lady* was J.'s last play. The cutting edge and magnificent hate and scorn of his great comedies have mellowed into a tolerant amusement, a resigned wistfulness at the mess we make of our lives.

BIBLIOGRAPHY: Beaurline, L. A., *J. and Elizabethan Comedy* (1978); Bryant, J. A., Jr., *The Compassionate Satirist: B. J. and His Imperfect World* (1972); Parfitt, G., *B. J.* (1976)

PETER BARNES

JOYCE, James [Augustine Aloysius]

b. 2 February 1882, Dublin, Ireland; d. 13 January 1941, Zurich, Switzerland

J. is recognized as a crucial innovator in fiction and central to any study of MODERNISM or 20th-c. literature in general. He was born in Ireland, educated in Jesuit schools and at University College, Dublin. In 1904, he left Ireland permanently, returning only for brief visits. His travels took him to Paris, Rome, and then to Trieste where he completed both *Dubliners* (1914) and most of *A Portrait of the Artist as a Young Man* (1916). He left Trieste for Zurich to escape World War I; after the war, he settled in Paris, where he finished *Ulysses* (1922) and *Finnegans Wake* (1939). With the beginning of World War II, J. returned to Zurich where he died.

His reputation rests on four volumes: *Dubliners, A Portrait of the Artist, Ulysses,* and *Finnegans Wake.* Additional volumes are *Chamber Music* (1907), *Pomes Penyeach* (1927), and *Exiles* (1918). An early publication, "A Portrait of the Artist" (1909), announced some of his major themes, that the past is "a fluid succession of presents," that character is a "rhythm," a motion, representing the "curve of emotion," and that the artist is necessarily at odds with his culture. In many of these ideas, J. is an inheritor of Walter PATER and the Aesthetic movement. But even so early in his career, he views this artist figure with some irony, an attitude absent in much of aestheticism. And his earliest stories resemble not aestheticism, but rather the beginning of a melding of symbolism and REALISM.

The gritty surface realism of *Dubliners* is paired with experiments in point of view and novelistic form. The text is both a collection of short stories and a diachronically organized novel, whose unity stems from repeated motifs and images, conflicts and resolutions rather than from shared character or plot. The first story, "The Sisters," announces the three central images of the whole: paralysis, simony, and gnomon. Each describes the work's Dubliners so that the collection or the novel dramatizes what J. called a "chapter of the moral history of my country."

J. ordered his stories chronologically. The first three "The Sisters," "An Encounter," and "Araby" center on childhood, while the second cluster— "Eveline," "After the Race," "Two Gallants"— centers on adolescence, the third on maturity, "The Boarding House," "A Little Cloud," "Counterparts," "Clay," the fourth on public life, "A Painful Case," "Ivy Day in the Committee Room," "A Mother," "Grace," and finally a long story or novella, "The Dead," which recalls the earlier stories and comments obliquely on them. It serves as a coda to the whole. In this collection/novel, J. developed what Hugh Kenner called the Uncle Charles Principle, a narrative tech-

nique that adopts the point of view and language of a character. Thus "The Dead" opens with "Lily, the caretaker's daughter" being "literally run off her feet," a phrase the working-class Lily would use and, of course, literally not be true. This narrative feature complicates how we read J.'s epiphanies. Each story ends with an epiphany. But do the characters in fact suddenly perceive some truth? Or does their very language betray their inability to see outside the prison of that language? In "Araby," for instance, a young man discovers that his crush on the sister of a classmate is inappropriately aggrandized (he has thought of her as his "chalice . . . [carried] safely through a throng of foes"); yet the language of his realization— that he is "a creature driven and derided by vanity"— suggests that his self-aggrandizing continues. The reader is left to wonder whether he has experienced an epiphany, or simply exchanged one charade for another. Many readers of J. conclude that characters are caught in their prison of language and field of reference and hence cannot experience sudden revelations.

For J., the culture of Dublin and Ireland more generally stultified the artistic, suffocating rebels and reinforcing the strictures of propriety against those of passion. In "The Dead," the final scene contrasts the passions of a dead Michael Furey with the careful precision of Gabriel who foresees his own death as a dwindling into nothingness.

This double interest—in realistically portraying Dublin and its constraining influence and in capturing human consciousness—informs the second major work, *A Portrait of the Artist,* as well. J. uses significant events and settings from his childhood and his brother's to construct the development of the modernist artist. That young artist is isolated from community, aware of his differences from others, focused on the rightness of art against all claims of language, religion, and country, the nets that Stephen Dedalus escapes when he flies from Ireland to Paris, as indeed J. left Ireland for Paris at approximately the same age. But Stephen is not J.; Stephen is a prototype of the artist. He uses, with or without attribution, ideas about art from W. B. YEATS, from Pater, from Gustave Flaubert, from Oscar WILDE, from a vast array of contemporary writers. These allusions firmly establish Stephen's inheritance from the Aesthetic movement and suggest that J. intends his artist to be "the" artist as a young man.

J.'s second fiction, *A Portrait of the Artist,* like his first, encountered difficulties getting published and conflicting reviews when it was. Ezra Pound recommended it to the *Egoist,* which published it in serial form first; then Huesch published the entire novel in the U.S. While some reviewers found the novel scandalous and obscene, more astute readers concurred with later evaluations: here was the first overtly modernist text. Pound was enthusiastic; and Virginia

WOOLF preferred J.'s sincere effort to "reveal the flickerings of that innermost flame which flashes its messages through the brain," to the traditional realism of Arnold BENNETT and John GALSWORTHY. It was, and still is, experimental fiction; subsequent criticism of the novel discovered in it New Criticism, Jungian or Freudian insights, FEMINISM, Lacanian analysis, deconstruction, postcolonial discourse—in short whatever individual critics brought or bring to the text themselves. It is an open novel, with overt gaps and fissures, and with a structure and narrative point of view that create what Phillip F. Herring called an uncertainty principle.

Each of the five chapters sets a conflict within Stephen, resolves that conflict with some sense of triumph, and leads into the next chapter, the opening of which deflates the previous triumph. This structure opens the text to a variety of readings. The final triumphant conclusion of the novel, because of the structural pattern, may be just another temporary triumph for Stephen. It has led to a variety of interpretations about whether Stephen is an artist, or whether he is a success as an artist. The limited third-person point of view does not assist readers seeking a single, determined, certain answer. We are privy only to Stephen's understandings of the world—and how to evaluate or judge those understandings is problematized by stylistics, by the responses of other characters, by the very structure of the text. The gaps in the plot of the text, sometimes marked by asterisks, encourage readers to supply transition or causality, rewriting the text each time they read. The text, then, dramatizes a modernist obsession with epistemology—how do we know what we know? Is there a reality separate from our perception of it? Who controls the meaning of a text?

J.'s obsessions with Ireland, with novelistic form, with truth, possibility, and linguistics (or stylistics) continue into his third novel, *Ulysses*, in which he constructs the world of Dublin on June 16, 1904, through the experiences of two protagonists—Stephen Dedalus, the artist returned from Paris, and Leopold Bloom, the advertising agent, cuckolded husband of Molly Bloom, wandering Jew, and modern Ulysses of the title. J. regularly referred to chapters of the novel by their parallel chapters in Homer's EPIC (e.g., Hades, Circe, Lestrygonians), although those titles were not used on publication. Like Homer's Ulysses, J.'s Bloom moves through the various trials seeking always the return to his Penelope, the unfaithful Molly Bloom. Like Homer's Telemachus, Stephen Dedalus is adrift in the world, seeking his own (spiritual) father. Dedalus and Bloom move through Dublin, meeting in the play scene/Circe and separating again at Bloom's home/Ithaca. J. was meticulous in the realistic detail of his novel, checking train schedules, the tide on the Liffey on June 16th, the advertising of the day, the race on which various characters bet, etc. At the same time, the novel is heavily allusive and symbolic, with a variety of points of view, narrative modes, and stylistic experiments.

The first three chapters provide "male monologue," a continuation of the Uncle Charles Principle of *Dubliners* and a further development of the point of view employed in *A Portrait*. Other chapters, however, present narratives appropriate to the action of the chapter, or the chapter presents action appropriate to the narration and style of the chapter. In Nausicaa, Gerty McDowell's sentimental, cheap romance language begins the chapter as she sees Leopold and imagines a dark, swarthy man with a secret sorrow passionately falling in love with her. Suddenly, the narrative and the language swing to Leopold Bloom, who masturbates as he watches Gerty display herself. The contrast of the style forms substance in the chapter. Multiple points of view and multiple styles thus become part of the overt meaning of the text. The novel ends with a long female monologue to balance, J. thought, the male monologues of the beginning. Here, Molly Bloom's interior monologue, as she drifts off to sleep, takes the form of eight sentences (and thirty-six pages), presaging the night world of J.'s last novel.

Ulysses is both about the characters and their lives on June 16, 1904, and about all of Western civilization. The present itself is a succession of past presents; the past and the present existing simultaneously in the consciousness of characters and cultures. J. was interested in portraying human consciousness: the day world. In *Finnegans Wake*, his last novel, he moved from the world of the day to the world of the night, more interested in dream and nightmare than in waking consciousness. The most overt development from *Ulysses* to *Finnegans Wake* centers on language. While J. created portmanteau words in the former, in the latter he developed a polyglot vocabulary that combines multiple languages and references within the same word—or orthographically indicated unit. The novel begins "riverrun, past Eve and Adams, from swerve of shore to bend of bay, brings us by a commodius vicus of recirculation back to Howth Castle and Environs." And it ends, "A way a lone a last a loved a long the": a non-sentence that leads us back to "riverrun." While J. could not have his novel bound in a spiral, he could indicate the cyclical nature of his universe linguistically: the last sentence runs, like the river, back into the first sentence again. Life is fluid; life is episodic; life is universal, no matter how bound to the concrete realities of Ireland. The central male figure Humphry Clinker Earwicker is also "Here Comes Everybody," and a host of other HCEs. Past and present again collide, diverge, meld in the text that both asserts and denies linearity and asserts and denies idiosyncratic individualism. Jostling against each other are allusions of all sorts—to philosophers, physicians, artists, writers, advertisers, and popular song. The title itself is taken from a Dublin street ballad celebrating the Finnegan who rises from the dead at his own wake.

J. began publishing *Finnegans Wake* in serial form as *Work in Progress* (1928–37). The full volume appeared in 1939 and was followed shortly thereafter by Joseph Campbell and Henry Morton Robinson's *A Skeleton Key to Finnegans Wake* (1944), a study of the structure and the mythic patterns of the novel. J. remains one of a handful of figures central to modernism, recognized by his contemporaries and future generations as a crucial innovator in fiction.

BIBLIOGRAPHY: Attridge, D., *J. Effects: On Language, Theory, and History* (2000); Blamires, H., *The New Bloomsday Book: A Guide through Ulysses* (3rd ed., 1996); Bowen, Z., and J. F. Carens, eds., *A Companion to J. Studies* (1984); Ellmann, R., *J. J.* (1959; rev. ed., 1982); Henke, S. A., *J. J. and the Politics of Desire* (1990); Herring, P. F., *J.'s Uncertainty Principle* (1987); Kenner, H., *Dublin's J.* (1955); McHugh, R., *Annotations to Finnegans Wake* (1980; rev. ed., 1991)

MARGUERITE HARKNESS

JULIAN OF NORWICH [also Juliana or Dame Julian of Norwich]
b. 1342?; d. after 1429

J. was an anchoress to the church of St. Julian at Norwich, and her only book, *Revelations of Divine Love* (wr. ca. 1393), is composed (possibly by a scribe) in a mixture of East Anglian and northern dialect. Existing in two versions of differing lengths, the book describes visions of Christ experienced when J. was thought to be on her deathbed. Her contribution to Christian thought is her emphasis on the "motherhood" of God. Quoted by T. S. ELIOT in "Little Gidding," the last of his *Four Quartets*, her reassurance has become famous: "Sin is behovely (i.e., inevitable); but all shall be well and all shall be well and all manner of thing [*sic*] shall be well."

KANE, Sarah

b. 3 February 1971, Essex; d. 20 February 1999, London

At age twenty-eight, K. committed suicide, depriving her friends of a much-loved companion and the theater of an original talent. Early critical responses to K.'s work were shocked and angry, a reaction, arguably, not only to content but to form for the organizing process of her plays is unique. Focusing on emotional logic, K. develops a style in which the individual functions as a microcosm of the social dynamic, not only offering a social critique, but also reinstating in overt, existential terms, the essential metaphoric, propositional nature of theater itself.

Her first play, *Blasted* (perf. 1995; pub. 1996), is set in a Leeds hotel room to which Ian, a journalist, brings Cate, a vulnerable young woman, for sex. Despite her protestations, he rapes her. Suddenly, without any narrative explanation, there is an explosion and the hotel becomes part of a war zone. A soldier enters, rapes and blinds Ian, and kills himself. Cate enters from the streets with a dying baby. When she leaves to find food, the starving Ian eats the baby. Cate returns and comforts the dying Ian now buried to the neck in rubble. The apparent incongruity between the opening scene and subsequent violence follows an emotional logic. The rape of an individual woman escalates into wholesale war and destruction. Individual violence sets the premises and possibilities, if not the inevitability, of social violence.

Phaedra's Love (1996), based on Seneca, continues this process of experiential logic. The narrative charts the progress between two powerful images that open and close the play. The play opens on an unmistakable crystalization of modern life: Prince Hippolytus alone in his room playing with a video game, watching a violent film on television and masturbating into a sock. The room is strewn with the detritus of instant gratification: electronic toys, empty pizza boxes, video games. The play closes on total destruction. The false accusation of rape by his stepmother

Phaedra who subsequently commits suicide and his unwillingness to refute the charge have led to Hippolytus' public execution. Emasculated, burned, and ripped apart, Hippolytus' desecrated body lies alongside those of his suicidal father and his stepsister whom his father has "accidentally" raped and murdered during a riot. Hippolytus "manages a smile" and says, "If there could have been more moments like this." The interrelationship of these images deconstructs the social dynamics of the action. The chaste Hippolytus of Seneca and Euripides has turned into his shadow. However, he is equally isolated, unreachable and insensible. Moreoever, he is the very impersonation of contemporary living. The riches of consumerism create isolation, weaving the individual into a web of virtual experience resulting in numb dissatisfaction.

In the extremity of his physical destruction, Hippolytus achieves genuine experience. He has moved from insulated arbitrariness and depression to public and thus social engagement. He has become a martyr; his senses, revived through pain; his self-enclosed irrelevance, transformed into public significance. The juxtaposition of these two images exposes an analysis of contemporary society. Instant gratification creates violence. The more plentiful and accessible the means of instant gratification, the more "virtual" experience becomes, the stronger the craving for genuine experience, and the more extreme and violent the means necessary for the individual to achieve a sense of genuine reality and significance—consequently, the more violent the society. The shocking extremity of the action is integral to the discussion, which takes place not through linear narrative and explanation but in experiential terms. Shock at the extremity of the action is integral to the effect of the drama that aims to engage the spectator in genuine experience.

Cleansed (1998) focuses on a collection of individuals incarcerated in a university campus presided over by the sadistic Tinker. Actually nothing in the text but the stage directions suggests this is a university. In the opening scene, Graham persuades Tinker to inject him with heroin. The following scenes show Tinker's sadistic manipulation of the inmates. The lack of linear narrative presents distinct interpretive problems. The original production chose Grace, Graham's sister, as central character, a problematic decision as only Tinker appears in every scene. It is also possible to read the action as Graham's drug dream. However, considering K.'s use of the individual to reflect society, it is more revealing to approach the play as the external manifestation of Tinker's thoughts and fantasies. As such, each action presents Tinker's nightmarish attempt to deconstruct human relationships in order to destroy emotions he cannot feel. Even in his most grotesque fantasies, however, Tinker is unable to eliminate the need to love. Despite his excessive cruelties and attempts to erase individual identities, the characters persist in reaching toward each other. All make sacrifices for their loved ones. At the end of the play, Grace and the mutilated Carl watch the sun rise together. Instead of exterminating the drive to love, Tinker's dissections have proved love the essence of human nature. Little wonder K. saw *Cleansed* as her most optimistic play.

In *Crave* (1998) and *4:48 Psychosis* (2000), K. extends the theatrical experience to a poetic and entirely experiential level. In *Crave,* four adults (two men and two women) relate glimpses of stories, moments of disappointment, abuse, cravings for attachments, and feelings, creating the experience of an entire society misused, longing—craving.

4:48 was first performed after K.'s death. It is tempting to see it as autobiographical, as it is ostensibly a conversation between a patient and a psychiatrist with the patient's monologues. Character is unassigned. It was first performed by three actors. Although based on personal experience, the play transcends personal history. It reads like an extended poem, the use of rhythm and changing dynamics creating dramatic content. Lacking the safety nets of narrative, context and character, the play discomforts its audience, but through rhythm, image and associations externalizes an internal state, making it immediate and confrontational. The greatest shock is that this remarkable work is K.'s last.

BIBLIOGRAPHY: Dromgoole, D., *The Full Room* (2000); Sierz, A., *In-Yer-Face Theatre: British Drama Today* (2001); Stephenson, H., and N. Langridge, *Rage and Reason: Women Playwrights on Playwriting* (1997)

ELAINE TURNER

KAVANAGH, Patrick [Joseph]

b. 21 October 1904, Inniskeen Parish, County Monaghan, Ireland; d. 30 November 1967, Dublin, Ireland

The author of one novel (*Tarry Flynn*, 1948), an autobiography (*The Green Fool*, 1938), and large amounts

of criticism, K. is best known for his poetry. He is justly famed as Ireland's greatest poet of the peasantry, though this title can distort the breadth of K.'s work. Seamus HEANEY has said that K.'s great rural poetry represents only the first half of his achievement. This part of his work evokes the landscape of County Monaghan with extraordinary freshness; examples include the very early lyric "Ploughman," (1936) and K.'s masterpiece, the long poem *The Great Hunger* (1942). Heaney describes the poetry of the second half of K.'s career as one that transcends rootedness in a single place; it is a more meditative and transcendental poetry that K. wrote in the 1950s and 1960s. Increasingly, K. is being recognized as one of Ireland's greatest religious poets.

The poetry of both the earlier and later periods has a powerful religious element. K. himself spoke of poetry as both a mystical and a dangerous thing. He was a master of traditional poetic forms, skilled in the use of many types of rhyme and traditional genres; his Canal Bank sonnets, for example, are widely admired. The popularity of "On Ragland Road," which has been frequently recorded by folk musicians, is due in part to its haunting rhythms and mastery of internal rhyme, as well as the stunning images that evoke both the real world and the ephemeral world of the demon lover.

For all his religious imagery, K. could also be an angry and satirical poet. He often lamented his feeling that his poetry, at least in his lifetime, was not widely appreciated by scholars, and he portrayed literary critics as a brood of vipers. The lyric "Who Killed James JOYCE" is a prime example of this satirical bent. K. regarded his own poverty as a sign of his rejection as a poet: his brief "Author's Note" to his *Collected Poems* (1964) reflects his anger in such statements as "Poetry made me a sort of outcast," and "On many occasions I literally starved in Dublin." Since his death, however, K.'s reputation has grown, and he is highly regarded by an audience both inside and outside Ireland.

The Great Hunger demonstrates the full range of K.'s poetic talents. Its opening line ("Clay is the word and clay is the flesh") reflects K.'s ability to unite the earthly and the sacramental. K. returns to this image of the clay throughout the poem. He portrays the peasant farmer, Patrick Maguire, sympathetically while resisting sentimentality. Maguire is both pathetic and larger than life. On the one hand, he is portrayed as a powerful figure within the landscape of rural Monaghan; on the other, K. emphasizes Maguire's bachelorhood, his emasculation by his mother (who does not die until Maguire is sixty-five), and his frustrations over repressed sexual desire. Remarkably, K. rescues his character from bathos and makes him a symbol of an undervalued, though overly romanticized, way of Irish life. Maguire is, in the final analysis, both a type and an individual. K. delicately manipulates reader response to his protagonist by invoking the motif of a theater; he begins and ends the poem with the symbol of the curtain, first rising and then falling on the final act.

K. celebrated the use of local scenery in his poetry. However, his work transcends local color in its narrowest sense. His evocation of his birthplace, Inniskeen, invites comparisons to William WORDSWORTH and Heaney. K. is an especially important figure in the evolution of contemporary Irish poetry; many of the younger Irish poets of the late 20th c. have regarded K. as a major inspiration.

BIBLIOGRAPHY: Heaney, S., *The Government of the Tongue: Selected Prose, 1978–1987* (1988); Kavanagh, P., ed., *P. K.* (1987); Nemo, J., *P. K.* (1979); O'Brien, D., *P. K.* (1975)

DAN ROSS

KAVANAGH, P[atrick] J[oseph Gregory]
b. 6 January 1931, Worthing, Sussex

Educated in Switzerland and Paris and Merton College, Oxford, K. worked for the BBC and the British Council before becoming a full-time writer in 1970. Traditional in form, his verse shows the influence of William WORDSWORTH, W. B. YEATS, and Edward THOMAS. His first wife died young and his early poems are preoccupied with love and death, themes pursued in his autobiography, *The Perfect Stranger* (1967). Collections include *One and One* (1959), *On the Way to the Depot* (1967), *About Time* (1970), *Edward Thomas in Heaven* (1974), and *Life before Death* (1979). He has also worked as anthologist and editor. His *Collected Poems* appeared in 1992, followed by *Voices in Ireland: A Traveller's Literary Companion* (1994).

KAYE-SMITH, Sheila
b. 4 February 1887, St. Leonards-on-Sea, near Hastings, Sussex; d. 14 January 1956, Northiam, Sussex

Spanning a literary career of nearly half a century, K.-S. produced more than forty works of poetry, fiction, and nonfiction. Designated by critics as the "novelist of Sussex," K.-S. published her first novel, *The Tramping Methodist*, in 1908, and earned critical recognition with the publication in 1916 of *Sussex Gorse*. As a novelist, K.-S. was known for her realistic and unsentimental portrayal of local Sussex men and women struggling to survive against hardship and human frailty. Later novels include *Tamarisk Town* (1919), *Joanna Godden* (1921), *The End of the House of Alard* (1923), and *Superstition Corner* (1934). She frequently collaborated with her friend G. B. STERN, most memorably in *Talking of Jane Austen* (1943; repub. as *Speaking of Jane Austen*, 1944) and *More*

About Jane Austen (1949; repub. as *More Talk of Jane Austen*, 1950).

KEATS, John
b. 31 October 1795, London; d. 23 February 1821, Rome, Italy

K.'s achievement puts him among the greatest poets in English literature. His talents were early described as comparable with those of John MILTON and William SHAKESPEARE, which is remarkable given that his career as a poet occupied little more than seven years. K. was the eldest of five children. When he was only nine, his father died in an accident and his mother left her children and swiftly remarried. The Keats children were then taken to live with their maternal grandparents. Their inheritance from their grandfather, who died in 1805, was tied up in Chancery causing them lifelong financial difficulties. K.'s legal guardian, Richard Abbey, was grudging and difficult when it came to negotiating money, and consequently K. was to some extent always dependent on the good will and assistance of friends and acquaintances. Among his most happy and trouble-free years (setting aside the death of his mother in 1810) were 1803–11 when he attended John Clarke's school at Enfield. Clarke, a dissenting minister, provided enlightened and kindly methods of education and his son, Charles Cowden Clarke, introduced K. to literatures ancient and modern equally fitting him for the description Samuel Taylor COLERIDGE used of himself a generation earlier— "a library cormorant."

In need of a profession, K. took an apprenticeship as apothecary surgeon with Thomas Hammond in 1811, entering Guy's Hospital, London, in 1815 and graduating as a licensed apothecary in July 1816. However, he then abandoned medicine for the profession of poetry, pursuing it with an intense devotion until his death from tuberculosis in Rome, to which he had gone for his health, at the age of twenty-six.

K.'s stature has never been questioned and his influence can be traced widely in the 19th c. in the work of major Victorian writers such as Alfred, Lord TENNYSON, Robert BROWNING, Matthew ARNOLD, and Gerard Manley HOPKINS, and in poets and artists of the Pre-Raphaelite movement. Throughout the 20th c., he has influenced important poets from Wilfred OWEN and T. S ELIOT, to Thomas HARDY, W. B. YEATS, and Tony HARRISON. Modern scholarship has continued to enhance and consolidate K.'s reputation, concentrating less on the aesthetics of his poetry and philosophy that, since his death, had been the focus of critical debate, and investigating rather his part in the radical cultural climate of his early manhood which made him a congenial associate of prominent political activists such as Leigh HUNT and Percy Bysshe SHELLEY.

It was Hunt in his weekly periodical, the *Examiner,* who first published one of K.'s poems, "On Solitude" (May 1816), and who welcomed him into the "new school of poetry" in his "Young Poets" article for the *Examiner* in December of that year. K.'s association with Hunt and his circle made anything he was likely to produce objectionable to the conservative literary establishment on two counts. On political grounds, Hunt was regarded as a dangerous radical, having been sentenced to two years imprisonment in 1813 for slandering the Prince Regent. On a literary level, Hunt's own poetry combined political subversiveness with a variety of stylistic innovations perceived as "low" culture by established contemporary arbiters of taste. In fact, the two were inseparable and most of the attacks leveled at K. as one of Hunt's "Cockney School" of poets in *Blackwood's Magazine* and the *Quarterly Review*, among others, were politically motivated.

K.'s early years produced a mixture of decorative and derivative verse in the style of Hunt, himself, and in that of the poets he was avidly reading and assimilating, like Edmund SPENSER. One of his sonnets from this period, "On First Looking into Chapman's Homer" (wr. 1816), is usually taken as representing the potential strength of his own voice in poetry, and two longer pieces, "I stood tiptoe" and "Sleep and Poetry" (wr. 1816), all of which were published in K.'s *Poems* (1817), contain between them all the hallmarks carried by his mature work, a subtle weaving together of myth and art, and a sensuous apprehension and penetrating observation of the natural world. "Sleep and Poetry" also contains K.'s poignant imprecation for "ten years" only in which to "overwhelm (himself) in poesy," an attack on what he saw as the stultifying and mechanical verse form of the school of Alexander POPE (a temerity for which he was himself attacked), and an early assertion that his status as poet would depend on his leaving behind the self-indulgence of romantic "joys" to engage with "the agonies, the strife of human hearts"—the subject of a later sonnet, "On Sitting Down to Read *King Lear* Once Again" (wr. 1818), unpublished until 1848.

"I stood tiptoe" was an abandoned introduction to his early attempt at an EPIC poem, *Endymion: A Poetic Romance* (1818), and it was to the literary provenance of epic that K. was drawn from the outset. *Endymion* is over four thousand lines in length and, although an uneven performance, owing much to Shelley's *Alastor* and not itself highly regarded by K., it nevertheless contains some of his best-known lines, from the opening "A thing of beauty is a joy forever" to the "Hymn to Pan," described by William WORDSWORTH as "a pretty piece of paganism" after K. read it aloud to him in London in December 1817. This well-known remark, reported by the artist friend of K.,

Benjamin Robert HAYDON, points to a crucial distinction between the older poet and the young Romantic school. Although himself very influenced by Wordsworth's poetry and especially by book 4 of *The Excursion* in which Wordsworth traces the origins of religion to classical nature-worship, for K. "paganism" represented warm, freeing, imaginative, and life-giving ideas as opposed to those of the ideologically conservative Wordsworth who attributed such animism to "the unenlightened swains of pagan Greece." K.'s poetry, like that of Shelley and Lord BYRON, is full of gods and goddesses reflecting his generation's interest in all religions: solar, pantheistic, dualistic, and their often "materialist" deities (e.g., Pan, Bacchus, Ceres). In one of the great odes of 1819, "Ode to Psyche," published in 1820, K. celebrates the hedonism and sexuality of Cupid's and Psyche's relationship and implies that Psyche herself, in being "too late" in the canon of deities to have been worshiped with the ancient fervor rightfully hers, has at least escaped the restrictive, orthodox Christian rituals with their "altars," "virgin" choirs, "chain-swung" censers, and "pale-mouthed" prophets. At the same time, however, K. acknowledges that poets who once celebrated such deities and their animistic world with "fond believing lyre" have been supplanted by post-Enlightenment Romantic poets like himself who, in writing now about such things, may stand accused of foolishly believing lies ("fond believing *liar*").

This conflict between an ideal and mythopoetic past and a demythologized present lies at the heart of *Lamia* (wr. 1819; pub. 1820) and many of K.'s greatest poems. The present, seen in "Ode to Psyche" as a "wide vacancy" where the poet can do no more than "dress" a "rosy sanctuary," has become a time when "Pan is no longer sought" ("To Leigh Hunt, Esq.," 1817), and to animate an intractable scientific world increasingly requires effort. Thus, the "thoughtless" opening of the ode, somewhere between dream and waking, is replaced by "shadowy thought" and the "wreathed trellis of a working brain," pointing to the difficulty of the poet's task in an unromantic age. This transference in "Ode to Psyche" away from the actual world to the individual's reinvention or free interpretation of mythology is perfectly imaged in K.'s friend Joseph SEVERN's painting of Shelley writing "Prometheus Unbound" in the ruins of the Baths of Caracalla in Rome (1845). Here, the relaxed and hatless figure of Shelley, sitting atop the fragments of a collapsed antique civilization, reflects such uninhibited and creative encounters of the poets of his age with the texts of classical antiquity.

K. turned again to the subject of epic in 1818, producing this time an extended fragment in three books entitled *Hyperion*. In the guise of mythic narrative, it addresses modern themes of evolution, the development of consciousness, and particularly, in the figure of Apollo, poetic consciousness and "the progress of poesy." K.'s genius, however, was clearly for lyrical rather than for epic verse as the opening lines of book 3 with their reference to the weakness of his muse to engage with the "tumults dire" of such narratives make clear, while the "lonely grief" and "solitary sorrow" of his muse point up a peculiar characteristic of his gods that is not their heroic triumphalism but instead their capacity to suffer. In his revised version of this poem, a fragment entitled *The Fall of Hyperion* (wr. 1819–20), published in 1856, K. makes himself the subject. In a nightmarish encounter with him, Moneta, the mother of the Muses, distinguishes his role from that of mere "dreamer" by allowing him, as true poet, to take on the full knowledge of human suffering by revealing to him its delineations etched upon her face. In this way, a particular focus on the mind of the poet overwhelms the machinery of historical epic and K., making excuses for its overindebtedness to Milton, abandoned the poem a second time. In so doing, however, he established its credentials as a new kind of work more akin in content, as it turns out, to the subject of Wordsworth's *The Prelude* than to the epic narrative of tradition.

The poems of K.'s final creative phase, 1818–19, include verse tales and some of the supreme lyrical poems in the language. They are subtly dialectical in the Shakespearean sense, representing oppositions and tensions that K. allows to play one against the other with little or no authorial intervention to guide his reader's response. In *Isabella* (wr. 1818; pub. 1820), the intensity of personal experience comes into conflict with wider social visions of destruction. In *The Eve of St Agnes* (wr. 1819; pub. 1820), the satisfied love between Porphyro and Madeline is the obverse of the destructive love of the eponymous *Lamia*. The odes—"To Autumn," "Ode on Melancholy," "Ode to a Nightingale," and "Ode on a Grecian Urn"—explore variously the commerce between joy and pain, between temporality and eternity, and the tension between art and life that would become one of the central themes of 19th-c. literature.

K. transmitted from medicine to poetry his "idea of doing some good for the world." He saw his role as poet, no less than physician, as that of one who "pours out a balm upon the world" (*The Fall of Hyperion*), so that for him the practice of poetry and medicine become in a sense coterminous. For K., the highest ideal for an artist, and a characteristic of Shakespeare he particularly admired, was disinterestedness, or a capacity to lose one's personal identity in the existence of others. K.'s own identity, moreover, unlike that which he himself described as preeminently Wordsworth's, that "egotistical sublime . . . a thing per se (that) stands alone," emerges from within the sociable context of the extensive and illuminating correspondence he conducted with his wide circle of friends. The distinctness of that identity is nowhere better assured than in the eloquent simplicity of the poet John Hamilton REYNOLDS and the epitaph for his own tombstone—THE FRIEND OF KEATS.

BIBLIOGRAPHY: Aske, M., *K. and Hellenism* (1985); Coote, S., *J. K.* (1995); Gittings, R., *J. K.* (1968); Jack, I., *K. and the Mirror of Art* (1967); Jones, J., *J. K.'s Dream of Truth* (1969); Motion, A., *K.* (1997); Ricks, C., *K. and Embarrassment* (1974); Roe, N., *J. K. and the Culture of Dissent* (1997)

JOHN GILROY

KELMAN, James
b. 9 June 1946, Glasgow, Scotland

With authors such as Irvine WELSH, Janice GALLOWAY, and Jeff TORRINGTON, K. is part of a new vogue in Scottish fiction characterized by urban disaffection, blunt language rendered in Glaswegian dialect, rough-and-tumble HUMOR, and a spirit of perseverance. Novelist, dramatist, and short story writer, outspoken essayist and pamphleteer, K. has received surprisingly muted critical reception despite (or, as one commentator has remarked, perhaps because of) his winning the Booker Prize for *How late it was, how late* (1994).

K.'s formal education was at the University of Strathclyde, but it is the working streets of Glasgow that have been his real school. His various experiences as a semiskilled laborer and a socialist alertness together inform his appreciation of members of the working class. K.'s aims to represent in fiction and onstage characters (usually Scottish) of this class are fueled by an opposition to the sentimentality and stereotypes too often employed in the exercise. Balanced between the comic and the sorely pathetic, the lives of characters such as the multiethnic workers of the story "Renee" (included in *Greyhound for Breakfast*, 1987) are ones of mean subsistence, a struggle for survival between hostel beds and something akin to wage slavery.

The prominence of the vernacular in all of K.'s work, cursing included, is an act of cultural self-assertion, a resistance to standardized and imperial "English." K.'s most effective narratological device is a special form of indirect discourse. Whereas in a book like *A Chancer* (1985) K.'s relation of events is more or less dissociated from the participants, in *The Busconductor Hines* (1984) and *A Disaffection* (1989), winner of the James Tait Black Memorial Prize, narrative outlook shifts between external reportage and interior monologue. Patrick Doyle, the hero of the latter novel, feels displaced, culturally removed as he is from his working-class routes by his profession as a teacher, and unavailingly attracted to a colleague in the bargain. As is often the case in K.'s male protagonists, a certain self-loathing struggles against a compulsive dignity, and alcohol proves a poor salve. Here, as in other works, K. diagnoses a frustrated inertia in his entities, removed as they are from political-economic power and their own identity.

The awarding of the Booker Prize to *How late it was, how late* was so controversial that one of the judges refused to be involved. Sammy completes a weekend bender with a skirmish with the police, leaving him blind, aching, and unable to remember anything of Saturday. The world of difficulties and discomforts opened up by his new disability only add to his concerns, one of which is his future with Helen, the woman who has threatened to leave him and indeed may have. Yet throughout his stumbling misadventures Sammy elects to "plough on": amid pain, inconvenience, and loneliness he clings to snatches of country music and a fierce sense of self-reliance. K. presents, on the one hand, a cool critique of a state more bent on policing than welfare, and on the other, a potential for community in the casual sympathies unknown and even unseen characters extend to one another. In his drive to be treated as a human being, Sammy reflects the author's own resolve: "One of these days he was gony write his own song, that would show the bastards."

K.'s collections of short stories include *An Old Pub Near the Angel* (1973), *Not Not while the Giro* (1983), *Greyhound for Breakfast, The Burn* (1991), and *The Good Times* (1998). Some of his stories are very short, in some instances no longer than a single page. Part thumbnail portraits, part jesting anecdote, pieces such as "Cute Chick!" and "The small bird and the young person" are both quirky and pitiful, owing as much to pub talk as to Samuel BECKETT's *Fizzles*. K.'s plays include *The Busker* (perf. 1985; pub. 1991), *In the Night* (perf. 1987; pub. 1991), and the historical drama, *Hardie and Baird: The Last Days* (perf. 1990; pub. 1991).

For the economy of his stories, K. has been compared to James JOYCE, and to Franz Kafka for his portraits of torment and listlessness. Always funny, K.'s ironic wit is a respite from quotidian tedium, which is also reflected in K.'s work by the nature of its sometimes criticized repetitiveness. With his unflinching eye always upon its tenacious if downtrodden souls, K. has made his mark upon Glasgow as much as it has placed its upon him.

BIBLIOGRAPHY: Craig, C., "Resisting Arrest: J. K.," in Wallace, G., and R. Stevenson, eds., *The Scottish Novel since the Seventies* (1993): 99–114; Kirk, J., "Class, Community and 'Structures of Feeling' in Working-Class Writing from the 1980s," *L&H* 8 (Autumn 1999): 44–63

TIM CONLEY

KEMPE, Margery
b. ca. 1373, Norfolk; d. ca. 1439

Daughter of John Brunham, sometime mayor of King's Lynn, Norfolk, K. married John Kempe ca. 1393 at the age of twenty. She gave up pride, worldliness, and married life to devote herself to religion, dressed in white, wept copiously, saw visions, and traveled on pilgrimages to Jerusalem, Rome, Compostella and Wilsnack in Poland. Illiterate, she dictated her autobiography, *The Book of Margery Kempe* (wr. ca. 1436–38), in which she records a visit to JULIAN OF NORWICH. Modern readers might see her experience as a struggle for female independence: K. offered advice to her contemporaries, claiming divine inspiration, and was accused of heresy, charlatanry, and hypocrisy.

KEMPINSKI, Tom
b. 24 March 1938, London

The work of prolific playwright K. has enjoyed a mixed reception by critics and audience. At times genuinely moving, his characters have also been seen as melodramatic. While his writings are in some instances political, such as *Dreyfus* (perf. 1982) and *Self-Inflicted Wounds* (perf. 1985), in others morbidly and overdrawnly funny, like *Sex Please, We're Italian* (perf. 1991), K.'s strengths are in the intense drama of small-cast plays. At the heart of his works lie the challenges of interpersonal relationships, many of which go horribly wrong in the face of personal limitations and the difficult situations K. creates for his characters. Several of his plays, such as *Duet for One* (perf. 1980; pub. 1981) and *Separation* (perf. 1987; pub. 1989), continue to be produced in England and have made their way to the screen, although the writer's strength predominantly lies in the territory of the more personal fringe theater.

In *Duet for One*, K. presents a violinist, Stephanie Anderson, who has been struck with multiple sclerosis and, in sessions with her therapist, sets out to first suffer the breakdown K. himself describes as "predictable and inevitable," only to forge ahead through this despair into a deeper realm of elementary fears. While the original play was staged to limit the characters to the violinist and her therapist, his screenplay, with Jeremy Lipp and director Andrei Konchalovsky, of the same title (1987), with Julie Andrews in the role of the afflicted musician, extends the list of characters to include Stephanie Anderson's husband, her manager, her old accompanist, and others, creating a visually more satisfying and interesting experience at the expense of the tight emotional focus and framework of the original concept.

Another one of his plays that focuses on disease as a metaphor is *Separation*, an autobiographically informed work that matches Joe Green, a depressed, overweight British playwright whose affliction with severe agoraphobia has left him trapped in his apartment in London, with Sarah Wise, an actress in New York City, who in turn suffers from a paralyzing disease but hopes Green's play will restart her career. The friendship progresses over the phone, and eventually the two meet in London. *Separation* was produced as a film starring Rosanna Arquette and David Suchet and opened to a mixed reception, due to what critics dismissed as a contrived dramatic situation. But in the center of *Separation* as much as in *Duet for One*, believable flawed and damaged individuals reach out for unlikely connections, and watching them succeed is sufficiently uplifting to make up for the contrivances.

One of his later plays, titled *Family* (perf. 2001), revisits the theme of Pierre Corneille's *Le Cid* (1637), a story about family obligations and doomed love, in a modern Mafia milieu. Maria and Sergio, offspring of Mafia families, are hoping to become engaged, when an insult passed between the two fathers presents Sergio with the choices to either avenge his father's honor or continue his courtship of the enemy's daughter. The melodrama of the situation is offset by K.'s wit and his willingness to roll with clichés rather than resist them, and while theater reviewers have classified *Family* as entertainment rather than art, it is clearly K.'s intention to both amuse and question as he once again sets up his characters for the impossible.

While the situations K. devises for his characters seem at times overdrawn and the juxtapositions of their individual weaknesses and phobias contrived, the process that results from the characters' attempts to resolve these impossible situations carries their efforts out of the realm of the strange and into a larger arena of human struggle toward interpersonal connection, if ever so elusive. K. claims his intentions to be the search for the sources and limits for the strengths embodied in his protagonists, and his plays tend to plumb the depths of human resources.

JULIA F. KLIMEK

KENNEDY, Margaret [Moore]

b. 23 April 1896, London; d. 31 July 1967, Adderbury, Oxfordshire

K. went to Cheltenham Ladies' College and Somerville College, Oxford. Her first book was a history, *The Century of Revolution, 1789–1920* (1922). Her first novel, *The Ladies of Lyndon* (1923), was successful, but her next was *The Constant Nymph* (1924), which became a world best-seller, filmed three times (in 1928 with Ivor Novello and Mabel Poulton, in 1933 with Brian Aherne and Victoria Hopper, and in 1943 with Charles Boyer and Joan Fontaine). It is re-

markable less for its story of doomed love than for its coolly shocking picture of neglect in a Bohemian family of spirited girls. None of K.'s other novels is remembered, although *Troy Chimneys* (1952) won the James Tait Black Memorial Prize in 1953. K. also wrote for the theater. A critical biography of Jane AUSTEN appeared in 1950 and *The Outlaws on Parnassus* (1958) was a study of the art of fiction.

KEYNES, John Maynard

b. 5 June 1883, Cambridge; d. 21 April 1946, Firle, Sussex

"In the long run, we are all dead." K.'s most famous quotation goes a long way to understanding what a radical break his thinking posed for the field of economics. K.'s contemporaries, and, indeed, generations before him, had preached an economic gospel of laissez faire. Operating under the imprimatur of Adam SMITH, economists before K. tended to advise governments to refrain from intervening in times of economic crisis; Smith's theories made it clear that the business world was subject to rising tides of prosperity just as much as falling tides of hardship. Conventional wisdom encouraged envisioning the long run.

In his *Treatise on Money* (1930), K. focused on the relationship between investor savings and business investment as crucial to understanding the ebb and flow of the economy. Businesses don't normally pay for expansions with money saved from their revenue; those funds are usually insufficient. To expand they must utilize the capital markets, or, in other words, borrow from investors. And those investors get their money from their savings. Conventional wisdom held that whenever businesses did not see a way to turn an additional profit through new projects—for whatever reason—and refrained from expansion, the reduced demand on investors' savings would cause the rates those investors charged for the use of their money to drop. Eventually, the rates would get so cheap that businesses would be enticed into investing again. Therefore, no matter how slow the economy became, at some point businesses would restart the growth by utilizing investors' savings to expand. Thus, a depression could not continue indefinitely.

When K. traveled to Washington to consult with President Franklin Roosevelt in 1934, the U.S. had been mired in a depression so troubling that it threatened to collapse political order. Clearly conventional economic wisdom was wrong about the temporary nature of an economic slowdown. Roosevelt had already started government intervention via the New Deal, but K. arrived to provide the theoretical basis for government intervention in an economic crisis. Yet he had some shocking conclusions to deliver as well.

As K. would later outline in his most significant work, *The General Theory of Employment, Interest, and Money* (1936), there was no predetermined end to an economic depression. Despite the standard interpretation of the savings and investment cycle, a downturn left untended could be prolonged indefinitely. K. pointed out that during a slowdown, when businesses were not expanding, and therefore not borrowing investors' savings, the rates for borrowing those savings wouldn't decline because fewer people would be in a position to save. The money market would dry up because during hard times people and businesses don't have surplus income to loan out to investors as they did during flush years.

K. stated that therefore the government must, as Roosevelt phrased it, "prime the pump." Government investment in public works could create jobs and increase worker income so that there would be more income to save for investing. Unlike his predecessors, K. argued that government intervention was the only way out of a depression. And in arguing for an active role of government in the economy, he reshaped the role of economists generally, adding to their value as advisors to the government on behalf of the public good. It was the beginning of the Keynesian era for economics.

There are, of course, several other works in addition to the masterpiece *General Theory* and its precursor *A Treatise on Money*. These include his *Indian Currency and Finance* (1913), his *Economic Consequences of the Peace* (1919), a protest against the unforgiving nature of the Versailles Treaty, his *Treatise on Probability* (1921), and his *Tract on Monetary Reform* (1923; repub. as *Montetary Reform*, 1924). But his contributions to the 20th c. go well beyond the economic sphere. Never one to be caught with only one project at a time, K. was a member of the intellectual coterie known as the BLOOMSBURY GROUP. What might at first seem to be an odd association for an economist actually is in keeping with both the liberal breadth of K.'s ideas and his independent thinking, which biographer Robert Skidelsky characterizes as K.'s "ability to think orthogonally—at right angles from existing ideas."

BIBLIOGRAPHY: Crabtree, D., and A. P. Thirlwall, eds., *K. and the Bloomsbury Group* (1980); Skidelsky, R., *J. M. K.* (3 vols., 1983–2000); Wood, J. C., ed., *J. M. K.* (8 vols., 1994)

ROBERT E. CUMMINGS

KILLIGREW, Thomas, the elder

b. 7 February 1612, London; d. 19 March 1683, London

KILLIGREW, Thomas, the younger

b. February 1657, London; bur. 21 July 1719, London

Page to King Charles I, in 1647 T. K. the elder followed the king's son, later King Charles II, into exile in France. When the monarchy was restored in 1660, K. worked for the king and Queen Catherine. According to Samuel PEPYS, K. was the court jester, with cap and bells, and could be as rude as he liked. He was famous for his wit. With Sir William DAVENANT, K. was granted a patent to build a new playhouse, and K. formed a new company called the King's Servants. Eventually, they performed at the original Theatre Royal in Drury Lane, built for them in 1663. In 1664, K.'s plays were published as *Comedies and Tragedies*, comprising *Claracilla, The Princess; or, Love at First Sight, The Parson's Wedding, The Pilgrim, Cicillia and Clorinda; or, Love in Arms, Thomaso; or, The Wanderer,* and *Bellamira, Her Dream; or, Love of Shadows.* William CONGREVE borrowed some of the jokes from *The Parson's Wedding.* T. K. the younger, the son of T. K. the elder, authored a successful play called *Chit-Chat,* played at Drury Lane in 1719, with the celebrated Mrs. Oldfield as Florinda. He followed his father into royal service as gentleman of the bedchamber to King George II while George was Prince of Wales.

KILLIGREW, [Sir] William

b. May 1606, Hanworth, Middlesex; d. 17 October 1695, London

Dramatist and brother of Thomas KILLIGREW the elder, K. was the author of *Pandora,* a comedy published in 1664 and republished in the next year with *Selindra* and *Ormades; or, Love and Friendship,* both tragicomedies. He also published miscellaneous works of prose and verse as well as the successful *The Siege of Urbin* (1666). Knighted in 1626, K. was a member of Parliament (1628–29) and later a gentleman-usher to Charles I. Following the Restoration, K. was appointed by Charles II as vice-chamberlain to Queen Catherine.

KILVERT, [Robert] Francis

b. 3 December 1840, Hardenhuish, Wiltshire; d. 23 September 1879, Bredwardine, Herefordshire

Discovered and edited by William PLOMER, K.'s *Diary* (3 vols., 1938–40) records the quiet, but not dull, life of a mid-Victorian country parson on the Welsh borders in the 19th c. K., who walked everywhere, had a keen ear for dialect and an appreciative eye for weather, scenery, and the beauty of girls. Educated at Wadham College, Oxford, he was the son of a clergyman. The diary, in twenty-two notebooks, covers from January 1870 to March 1879, but two sections (September 1875-March 1876 and June 1876-December 1877) were destroyed by K.'s widow.

KING, Francis [Henry]

b. 4 March 1923, Adelboden, Switzerland

K.'s later childhood was spent in India, the setting for his murder mystery, *Acts of Darkness* (1983), distantly based on a real case. He wrote three novels while still an undergraduate at Balliol College, Oxford. He worked for the British Council in five countries until 1964 when he became a full-time writer. K.'s work is distinguished and powerful in its psychological penetration, often into warped minds. Novels include *To the Dark Tower* (1946), *The Dividing Stream* (1951), *The Widow* (1957), *The Custom House* (1961), *Flights* (1973), and *The Action* (1979). He has published several collections of short stories, a biography of E. M. FORSTER (1978), and edited the writings of Osbert SITWELL (1974), J. R. Ackerley (1982), and Lafcadio Hearn (1984).

KING, Henry

b. 16 January 1592, Worminghall, Buckinghamshire;
d. 30 September 1669, Chichester

A distinguished and historically important churchman, Bishop of Chichester before and after the Civil War, K. is of literary importance both as a poet and as the author of some striking sermons. K.'s *The Psalmes of David, from the New Translation of the Bible Turned into Metre* was published in 1651 and in an enlarged edition in 1654. In it, K. seeks to balance the demands of faithful translation and aesthetic form in ways that are only inconsistently successful. The meters and rhyme schemes he chooses seem often to trap him into awkwardness and banality. A few decided successes—such as Psalm CVII—suggest possibilities that went largely unfulfilled.

The collection of *Poems, Elegies, Paradoxes, and Sonnets* (1657) forms—along with several manuscript collections that have survived—the basis for any judgment of other aspects of K.'s achievement as a poet. K.'s work is hardly ever less than competent; a lover of music, his own ear for rhythm and meter is generally sure. Of his intelligence, the reader is not left in doubt, though the poems are rarely marked by any great intellectual complexity. There is, though, a good deal that is rather slight among K.'s poems. His subjects are often public and private occasions to which, one feels, K.'s response is essentially no more than an expression of what he felt to be his duty. When he writes "An Elegy Upon Mrs. Kirk unfortunately drowned in Thames" or addresses lines "To the Queen at Oxford," it is difficult to find in the poems anything that transcends their occasion, however well they might have exercised an appropriate social function in the eyes of that occasion's contemporaries.

Some of K.'s elegies, notably those on fellow poets such as John DONNE ("Upon the Death of my ever Desired Friend Dr Donne Deane of Paules") and Ben JONSON ("To my Dead Friend Ben: Johnson") are likely to have a greater interest for most modern readers. The elegy for Donne was first published in 1632 with Donne's famous SERMON, *Death's Duell*,

and then reprinted in the first publication of Donne's poems in the following year. It is an eloquent poem whose eloquence is paradoxically built upon the assertion that all eloquence has died with Donne, those who would write in his honor having to rely on newly "Widdow'd Invention." It movingly recalls Donne's preaching of *Death's Duell* and the weight of K.'s emotions is clear throughout. (K. was one of Donne's two executors after his death). The elegy for Jonson is less grand in manner, but no less impressive in its tribute to a writer K. deems to have "taught'st the ruder age/To speak by Grammar, and Reformd'st the Stage." The influence of both Donne and Jonson is discernible in K.'s work. In poems like "Sonnet. The Double Rock," K. writes in an idiom that has something of Donne's conceited wit and aggressive verbal energy in a stanza form made up of long and short lines (the bulk of K.'s work is in rhyming couplets); K.'s "Madame Gabrina" is very obviously indebted to Donne's "The Anagram" (though it has other sources too).

Elsewhere—and more often—one encounters a terseness more characteristic of Jonson. K.'s Jonsonian manner is well displayed in poems such as "To my honourd friend Mr. George Sandys" or "To my Noble and Judicious Friend Mr Henry Blount upon his Voyage." There is something of Jonson's manner in K.'s love poems too, such as "Tell mee no more how faire shee is" and "Upon a Braid of Haire in a Heart sent by Mrs. E. H," just as another aspect of Jonson's art is reflected in some of K.'s witty trifles and epigrams. None of this is meant to suggest that K. was damagingly derivative; merely that he was no great innovator and that he naturally registered the influence of the two primary exemplars that English poetry offered a poet of his generation. Certainly K.'s most famous, and his finest, poem is not to be explained in terms of such influences alone. This is "An Exequy. To his Matchlesse never to be forgotten Friend," written on the death of the poet's wife Anne in 1624. Structured around an imaginary approach to the grave, the poem effects a complex mixture of moods and impulses, as love and loss, grief and consolation, simplicity and wit, perfectly poised in a poetic idiom that contrives simultaneously to achieve a sense both of quasi-ritual dignity and conversational intimacy.

K.'s sermons were much admired in his own day, but have since been largely overlooked until recently. They would certainly repay greater attention than they have hitherto received. Twenty-one sermons survive, eleven of them originally published in 1628 as *An Exposition upon the Lords Prayer*. Other sermons date from as early as 1621 and as late as 1664. In prose that avoids excessive artifice, but is often attractive in its balancing of clauses, and its counterpointing of long and short sentences, K.'s sermons are unostentatiously allusive and often invigorated by colloquialisms. In his extended meditations on his texts K. avoids both stylistic and doctrinal extremism. These are by no means the most immediately striking glories of 17th-c. preaching, but they are rewardingly readable to a degree not always found in some more famous sermons.

BIBLIOGRAPHY: Berman, R., *H. K. and the Seventeenth Century* (1964); Crum, M., ed., *The Poems of H. K.* (1965); Hobbs, M., ed., *The Sermons of H. K.* (1992)

GLYN PURSGLOVE

KINGSLEY, Charles
b. 12 June 1819, Devon; d. 23 January 1875, Eversley

K.'s first novel, *Yeast* (1851), criticized the gentry for neglecting the rural poor, whose misery it vividly evoked, and was considered offensively radical. K. is associated with a modified socialism, influenced by Thomas CARLYLE and later by F. D. Maurice. K. was an Anglican clergyman who stood for "muscular Christianity." His timid enthusiasm for reform is in tension with his insistence that heaven cannot be reached in this world, and thus Alton Locke, eponymous hero of K.'s next novel, published in 1850, dies on his way to the South Seas in a doomed search for health. Carlyle appears in the book as "Sandy Mackay," and cures Alton of his Chartist opinions.

Like other authors of "condition of England" novels, K. enjoined patience on the unenfranchized lower classes. He had more faith in plumbing as a force for good than in political change. *Two Years Ago* (3 vols., 1857) is about a cholera epidemic. K. is associated with Carlyle's "gospel of work" and the cult of moral earnestness. His paradoxical attraction to violence was dissipated on political and religious controversy. Passionately patriotic and passionately Protestant, he admitted that *Westward Ho!* (3 vols., 1855) set in Elizabethan England, was "bloodthirsty." K. was widely read for generations, but is now best remembered for *The Water-Babies* (1863), a rambling, idiosyncratic fable about redemption and evolution, which has never been out of print. His novel *Hypatia* (1853), about conflict in the early Church, is now hard to find, but supplied motifs later adopted by Charles DICKENS and George ELIOT, and still has admirers. *The Heroes* (1856), K.'s retelling of the Greek myths, is still read. *Hereward the Wake* (2 vols., 1865) is a romance about the last Saxon chieftain to surrender to the Normans. K. was also a vigorous popular poet in a variety of meters.

K. was Professor of Modern History at Cambridge and his review of J. A. FROUDE's anti-Catholic *History of England from the Fall of Wolsey to the Defeat of the Spanish Armada* in 1864 provoked John Henry

NEWMAN into writing his religious autobiography, *Apologia Pro Vita Sua.* K.'s output of pamphlets, polemics, poems, and fictions was prodigious and overwork led to frequent nervous breakdowns. K.'s widow edited a memoir and letters, published in two volumes in 1876.

BIBLIOGRAPHY: Chitty, S., *The Beast and the Monk: A Life of C. K.* (1974); Colloms, B., *C. K.* (1975); Myer, V. G., "C. K.'s *Hypatia:* A Seminal Novel," *N&Q* 39 (June 1992): 179–80; Sharma, S. K., *C. K. and the Victorian Compromise* (1989)

VALERIE GROSVENOR MYER

KINSELLA, Thomas
b. 4 May 1928, Dublin, Ireland

K. enjoys a critical esteem that outstrips the popular knowledge of his work. A minority of critics recognize him as the most important Irish poet of his generation, but K. has retained an aura of solitude befitting an audience-conscious poet who insists that poems engage the reader in private conversation. Often intertextual, broadly allusive and searching, K.'s poems are charged with longing for "recovered order," as he phrased his great preoccupation early on in "A Lady of Quality," published in *Poems* (1956).

K. began his career as a civil servant while exploring his considerable talents in poetic avocation. His first volume, *Poems*, was followed by *Another September* (1958), which garnered a Guinness Poetry Award. Along with *Downstream* (1962), these early works show K. searching for his own poetic voice. Wary of the long shadow cast by W. B. YEATS, K. favored lyrical poetry in his melodic early style, relying on traditional rhyme schemes and universal subjects (death, time, love, creativity).

During this early phase, K. helped found Dolmen Press. With recognition by appreciative audiences in Ireland and abroad, K. secured an appointment as writer in residence at Southern Illinois University and devoted himself to literature entirely. He commented on the enormous inheritance as well as the lost patrimony of Irish literature in an influential address entitled "The Irish Writer" (1966), subsequently adopted as a virtual manifesto for a generation of Irish writers. K. coined the phrase "the divided mind" to describe the Irish world-view brought about by the coexistence of Irish and English cultures and tongues. *Wormwood* was published the same year, a dark meditation on the limits of love and human relationships, a work inspired in part by his wife's chronic illness.

Nightwalker and Other Poems (1968) marked a turning point for K. as he delved into poetry more experiential than literary. The title poem jettisons the

551

end rhymes of earlier work, adhering to the free verse and fragmentation instead that are hallmarks of K.'s mature work. Some of the well-known companion poems also reveal new directions: "Ritual of Departure" abounds with imagery from rural Irish life, while "Phoenix Park" offers a street-level view both temporally and spatially located in K.'s Dublin. The *Nightwalker* collection is freighted with weighty corporeality and sensuality, foreshadowing what critics have identified as K.'s attempt to reach a stripped-down Jungian self. The book also raises favorite themes that characterize much of K.'s later work: a sense of dislocation and loss counterpoised with love and artistic creation.

In the years that followed, K. approached issues of political fealty and national identity. He returned to his homeland and finished an ongoing labor of love, a painstaking resurrection of the ancient Irish EPIC *Táin Bó Cuailnge*. His singularly vivid translation, *The Tain* (1969), revitalized the epic for a new generation while honoring the verbal inventiveness of the epic's oral tradition, much as Lady GREGORY's work had done for an earlier set.

When thirteen protesters were shot down in Derry on the infamous Bloody Sunday, K. plied his outraged pen to *Butcher's Dozen* (1972), a widely known poem that draws on the venerable *aisling* genre of political vision poetry. The critically divisive poem was published by his homespun Peppercanister Press (colloquially named for a Dublin church). Peppercanister has brought out new K. poetry pamphlets since its inception, including such works as *The Good Fight* (1973), a reflection on the tenth anniversary of John F. Kennedy's death. *Songs of the Psyche* (1985) and *Personal Places* (1990) are much remarked.

Notes from the Land of the Dead (1972) remains a watershed volume that arguably sacrificed K.'s broad readership for the sake of artistic integrity. Sometimes arcane, sometimes spare, the innovative collection generated a good deal of critical confusion. Important later works include *An Duanaire: Poems of the Dispossessed* (1981), an influential and popular anthology. K. edited and translated the poems in *The New Oxford Book of Irish Verse* (1986), a fitting successor to Yeats and Donagh MacDonagh's collections. Poetry volumes of this late period include *Her Vertical Smile* (1985) and *Poems from Centre City* (1990). K. retired from teaching in 1990 but has remained active, bringing his critical view of Irish literature to fruition in *The Dual Tradition* (1995), and printing new poetry through Peppercanister (*Godhead* and *The Familiar*, both published in 1999).

K.'s contribution to literature can be most accurately sketched by a series of maturations. As a teenager, he resented mandatory Irish language instruction and went on to carry out some of the best Irish translations ever rendered into English. K. described his

early translations from old Irish as "offerings to the past," but the path of his career was a faithful reclamation of that past. Writing as a young poet, he disclaimed interest in "Irish" subjects, but his mature work reflects a writer deeply concerned with rehabilitating Irish life, politics, and language.

Like great poets before him, he has labored to both create and exhume a literary tradition in his own language. As a skillful poet, translator, and critic, K. has done much to diagnose and heal the "divided mind" of a country that has nearly lost its language.

BIBLIOGRAPHY: Badin, D. A., *T. K.* (1996); Harmon, M., *The Poetry of T. K.* (1974); John, B., *Reading the Ground: The Poetry of T. K.* (1996); Johnston, D., *Irish Poetry after Joyce* (1985)

BRYAN A. GIEMZA

KIPLING, [Joseph] Rudyard
b. 30 December 1865, Mumbai [Bombay], India; d. 18 January 1936, London

K., aged five, was sent to England to board for six years with a Mrs. Holloway, who instilled in him a sense of irredeemable sinfulness and sharpened his faculty for lying and concealment. The episode (fictionalized in the 1889 "Baa Baa Black Sheep") nurtured his love of mystification, his suspicion of, yet dependence on, women, his sympathy with outcasts, and his power of depicting underworlds and infernos. It probably seeded, too, one of the keystones of his creed: that duty and self-discipline also require licensed opportunities for disobedience and fooling around.

This creed was reinforced at his unconventional school, the model for *Stalky and Co* (1899). K. returned to India (1882) to become a journalist who moved freely between barracks, ballrooms, bazaars, and byres. He joined a Freemason's lodge, which satisfied his need for ritual, brotherly community, and secrecy. (Masonic references are embedded as "private marks" sporadically in his tales, and exemplify his lifelong tendency to write for an "Inner Ring.") He began writing short tales for his newspaper, and learned, like Ernest Hemingway after him, that a story gathers power from cutting out: readers feel the effect of what is absent.

Plain Tales from the Hills (1888) was his first collection, followed by titles in the Indian Railway Library, later collected as *Soldiers Three* and *Wee Willie Winkie*, both published in 1890. Success prompted K. to seek more fame in England. He was hailed as a blast of fresh air, revivifying an effete literary scene. It was the hey-day of the magazine tale, and K.'s gifts were perfectly adapted to the medium. Not since Charles DICKENS had there been such a *succès fou*; "Kipling's India"—a world of common soldiers, Pathan tribesmen, uncanny happenings, blushing subalterns, machinating memsahibs, seductive Eurasians, Martini-Henri rifles, heat, dust, blood, fighting, riding, adultery—was as vivid a creation as "Dickens's London." K. had given a voice to British Tommies, Indian grooms, and toiling civil servants. He had made Britain's Empire real to the folks back home. The Kiplingesque narrator— a compound of knowing insider, spy, and Scheherezade—added a catch-phrase to the language: "But *that* is another story."

K.'s first attempt at full-length fiction, *The Light That Failed* (1890), drew on his first, unhappy, love affair. Its misogyny is unpleasant, but it captures poignantly the vulnerable pride of youth. *Life's Handicap* (1891) and *Many Inventions* (1893) collected some of his best tales, including the tender, tragic "Without Benefit of Clergy." In 1892, he married the sister of the American publisher Wolcott Balestier, and settled in Vermont. He turned toward children's fiction. The result was the much-loved *Jungle Books* (2 vols., 1894–95) and *Just So Stories for Little Children* (1902). K. used reports of feral boys reared by wolves to rewrite the Eden myth. Mowgli is Primal Boy, a new Adam amid the animals, who teach him survival arts and instil the Law of the Jungle. K.'s Eden is not a state of lost perfection, but a place of wonder and danger, freedom and control, where we learn the truth of William BLAKE's dictum that "Man was made for joy and woe." The *Just So Stories* are delightful myths of origin, written for the story-telling voice, and enlivened by K.'s illustrations. Curiosity is presented not as the cause of the Fall of Man, but as the means of getting wisdom. Central to the volume is the cave girl Taffy, her father's boon companion and co-inventor of the alphabet, a character based on K.'s sassy daughter Josephine, who was to die aged six.

The Vermont years began buoyantly. *"Captains Courageous": A Story of the Grand Banks* (1899) and two tales in *The Day's Work* (1898), where K.'s fascination with technology strongly emerges, have North American settings. But a combination of domestic and public events alienated K. from the U.S., and in 1897 he returned to England. For the next five years, he was unsettled, belonging properly nowhere. He was by now the world's most famous writer, and, to liberals and "Little Englanders," the herald of a militaristic imperialism. He aligned himself with Cecil Rhodes's expansionist African vision and did propaganda work during the South African War (1899–1902). Yet it was during this period that he published his acknowledged masterpiece, a farewell to India, the "nakedly picaresque" *Kim* (1901). Kim, a streetwise "Little Friend of all the World," racially European, culturally Indian, seeks for his identity. Containing some of K.'s most vivid writing, this Bildungsroman also captures a cultural moment—India under the British Raj.

In 1902, K. threw in his lot with England and bought an estate. *Traffics and Discoveries* (1904), a collection showing him in transition, contains "Mrs. Bathurst," which still maddens readers who try to work out what actually happens. Themes of respect for the land, responsible stewardship, the House Beautiful, and national heritage now come to the fore, both in *Actions and Reactions* (1909) and his children's collections (*Puck of Pook's Hill*, 1906; *Rewards and Fairies*, 1910). There is an underlying regret for lost, freewheeling youth, and a dark note of foreboding as shades of World War I gather.

K. saw the war (in which his own son was killed) in apocalyptic terms, as Armageddon, with the forces of good confronting Absolute Evil, the Hun. *A Diversity of Creatures* (1917) contains the brilliant, notorious "Mary Postgate," in which a sexually repressed English spinster takes an orgasmic pleasure in watching the death-throes of a German airman. That the airman could be a hallucination is a Kiplingesque twist. After the war, K.'s prejudices and political views hardened and became uglier. Although he never lost his worldwide following, to a new generation of writers he was a dinosaur.

Yet it is from this period, and especially from the collection *Debits and Credits* (1926) that some of his finest late stories derive, formerly—as noted by Edmund Wilson—the "Kipling that Nobody Read," now esteemed by a later generation. Densely written, multilayered, enigmatic, they constitute the best case for regarding K. as a modernist in spite of himself. These include "The Eye of Allah," "The Wish House," and "The Gardener." This last, a humane tale of women mourning dead sons and lovers, grew out of K.'s work with the Imperial War Graves Commission, and affirms his trust in the healing power of ritual, truth, and love. "Dayspring Mishandled," the story of a faked manuscript and a life wasted by revenge (*Limits and Renewals*, 1932), is a late, dark, masterpiece. K. left a beautifully written final message to posterity, *Something of Myself* (1937), reticent yet self-revealing, containing his last reflections on his art.

In addition to his enormous contribution to the art of the short story, K. was a travel writer and a poet whose verses are still learned by heart for pleasure. T. S. ELIOT (an admirer) called him a "great verse writer" while George ORWELL settled for his being a "good bad poet." K. loved marches, music hall songs, and rousing hymns, but to label him a demotic poet or balladeer is only partly true: he also wrote haunting lyrics like "The Way through the Woods" and experimented skillfully with a huge variety of metrical forms in the high style. From *Traffics and Discoveries* onward, his collections alternate verse with prose. The verse relates to the prose in intricate ways. The inter-lacings are part of K.'s experiments with the form of the short story *collection* (comparable to James JOYCE's later *Dubliners*).

K. was an omnivorous reader and consummate *pasticheur* who could imitate almost anyone. A list of the most important influences upon form and style would have to include Robert BROWNING, Geoffrey CHAUCER, Dante, Joel Chandler Harris, Mark Twain, Edgar Allan Poe, and John RUSKIN, but that is only a fraction of the tally. He was a verbal magician with, for better or worse, a journalist's flair for coining memorable phrases ("White man's burden" "East of Suez" "Lest we forget") and graphic, unexpected, sometimes horrific similes (a polo pony wheeling round "like a cockchafer on a pin"). His writing is intensely visual, even painterly. His scenes often re-semble the symbolic Pre-Raphaelitism of his favorite uncle, the artist Edward Burne-Jones. This painterli-ness is bound up with his predilection for emblem, allegory, and fable and with his success in the short story, which carried with it a corresponding failure to colonize the novel. His longer fictions are episodic, a series of linked short stories rather than what he called a "built book."

Work, art, and play, are his major themes. So are the breaking strain, overwork, male hysteria and its antidotes: laughter, fellowship and exorcism. The overwrought, hallucinating masculine subject who drops into an existential black hole appears at the cen-ter of his fiction years before the shellshocked genera-tion of World War I. A peculiarity of his writing is its tendency to elicit totally contrary interpretations. This goes beyond what is normally understood by diversity of response. "The Village that Voted the Earth was Flat" has left some in helpless stitches of mirth, while others have read it as an apocalyptic Dance of Death. The same story is read as straight REALISM and as an uncanny tale, the same character as a rescuer and a destroyer. One way to accommodate such polariza-tions is to recognize K. as a fantastic writer, in Tzvetan Todorov's sense: the reader is unsettlingly obliged to hesitate between a naturalistic and a super-natural explanation of the facts of a story. Another is to see him as consciously exploiting the ability of the same word to mean its opposite, operating at Brow-ning's "dangerous edge of things," where extremes meet and laughter and horror become interchange-able.

K.'s influence on 20th-c. writers, from Hemingway to Salman RUSHDIE, is immense, and is visible in au-thors whose ideological alignments were totally op-posed to his. His power to outrage and offend re-mains, and cannot be easily uncoupled from his artistry, even when the concept of "two Kiplings" is invoked. Self-contradiction, or, as he put it, "Separate sides to my head" is his essence. A highbrow pretend-ing to be a lowbrow, a hard-nosed craftsman subject to a mystical Daemon of inspiration, a relisher of re-venge fantasies who writes movingly of forgiveness, a womanish masculinist, a white man in a brown mask, he might have said with Walt Whitman (another of his unacknowledged influences), "Very well then I contradict myself,/ (I am large. I contain multitudes.)"

BIBLIOGRAPHY: Crook, N., *K.'s Myths of Love and Death* (1989); Gilbert, E. L., *K. and the Critics* (1965); Keating, P., *K. the Poet* (1994); Kemp, S., *K.'s Hidden Narratives* (1988); Lycett, A., *R. K.* (1999); Mason, P., *K.* (1975); Orel, H., *K., Interviews and Recollections* (2 vols., 1983); Page, N., *A K. Compan-ion* (1984); Tompkins, J. M. S., *The Art of R. K.* (1959)

NORA CROOK

KIRKUP, James
b. 23 April 1923, South Shields, Durham

K. published his first book in 1942; he has written and published with extraordinary abundance ever since. The abundance is the measure of a remarkable open-ness to life and a matching facility (the word is used without pejorative overtones) for the articulation of experience in poetic form. K.'s subject matter is as-tonishing in its variety. He writes of other poets and of jazz; of football and sex; of travel and death; of potholing and surgery; of Hiroshima and Nagasaki; of science and SCIENCE FICTION; of mythology and the sea; and much else. In the range of poetic forms he employs, he is equally various. He is an acknowl-edged English expert on and master of such brief Jap-anese forms as the haiku and the tanka; he is also the author of *Pikadon* (1997), which carries the subtitle "An Epic Poem," and of *An Extended Breath* (1996), which collects together his "Longer Poems and Se-quences."

K.'s very earliest work was perhaps rather over-written, prone to a kind of luxuriating in opulent lan-guage that promised rather more than it actually yielded. But in volumes such as *The Submerged Vil-lage* (1951), *A Correct Compassion* (1952), *A Spring Journey* (1954), and *The Prodigal Son* (1959), K. de-veloped an altogether less fanciful idiom. "A Correct Compassion," an account of a heart operation, has rightly been much admired (and anthologized), for the exactness of its observation and its language, both of statement and of metaphor. But the poem is not, of course, mere reportage (however accomplished); as a meditation on art, on its "correct compassion," it is sophisticated and assured; as a kind of "defense of poetry" it is persuasive and moving. It would be a shame, however, if proper admiration of "A Correct Compassion" were to lead readers to overlook much else that is admirable in K.'s work of the 1950s, whether in his moving lines "On a Dead Child," in the metaphysical wit of "Stars Compared to Worms," in the disturbingly atmospheric "A House in Summer."

K.'s later work has perhaps not always been so concerned with exactness of form as his poetry of the 1950s was. Occasionally, it can seem casual. It may be that he has not written many individual poems as perfectly finished as his best work of the 1950s. But no attentive reader, surely, could fail to find much to enjoy and admire in the poems of more recent years. Since 1959, much of K.'s time has been spent in Japan and his work has naturally been much marked by this experience. He has written many poems on Japanese and other oriental subjects; his *Zen Contemplations* (1978) includes two remarkable sequences "The Tao of Water" and "Ten Ox-Herding Pictures," which were composed during meditation and then written down almost without later correction; *Tanka Tales* (1997) employs the ancient Japanese form of thirty-one syllables in five lines (5,7,5,7,7) on a range of subjects, including tales from the brothers Grimm and the pottery of Bernard Leach. *Pikadon*—the title comes from a word invented by the children of Hiroshima and Nagasaki to describe the flash and explosion of the atomic bomb—is a book-length poem that combines detailed focus on individuals with larger historical analysis, its lyrical passages often moving, its anger intelligent and exact.

In *A Certain State of Mind* (1995), K. gathers together many of his translations of Japanese haiku, alongside some of his own haiku and essays on the form. *A Book of Tanka* (1996) is a substantial selection of K.'s translations of tanka from all periods of Japanese literature and of his own poems in the form. *Modern Japanese Poetry* was first published in 1978 and reissued in an enlarged edition as *Burning Giraffes* in 1996. It contains many poems of which no other English versions are available, and poem after poem in its pages "works" as an English poem to a degree one has come not always to expect from translations from Oriental languages. K.'s own work as a translator has extended far beyond Japanese, however. He has published translations from Polish, Romanian, German, and French; from Malayan and Vietnamese. His versions from Jean Cocteau, Jean Genet ("A Song of Love"), and Raoul Ponchon ("The Shepherd's Tale") are masterly. His 1970 translation of Paul Valéry's *La Jeune Raoul Parque* (*The Eternal Virgin*) captures much of its original's elusive quality. His fourteen versions from Paul Celan's *Fadensonnen*, included in *Strange Attractors* (1995), are distinctive, even strange, in their idiom (appropriately) and benefit from their presentation alongside the original poems by K. included in the same volume, written out of the aspiration to compose "poems that exist in their own right, without the need of meaning or interpreta-

tion." Influenced by Georges Perec and the Oulipo group, these are remarkable poems, evidence of K.'s refusal ever simply to repeat himself and his constant, seemingly effortless self-transformation as a poet.

K. is also a dramatist of some distinction, working both for the theater and for radio and television. Both his original plays, such as *The True Mistery of the Nativity* (1956) and *An Actor's Revenge* (1978), and his many adaptations and translations—including works by Friedrich Dürrenmatt, Henrik Ibsen, and Heinrich von Kleist—display a strong sense of theatricality and a characteristic vigor of language. In several volumes of autobiography, K. often writes very memorably (especially of his childhood); his travel writings are full of acute observation of both people and places. The range and quality of K.'s work is, in short, remarkable. While he has attracted a certain amount of attention as a "gay" poet, full recognition of his achievement is yet to come (perhaps, in part, because he has lived, for so long, so far away from the literary establishment in London).

BIBLIOGRAPHY: Hogg, J., ed., *Diversions: A Celebration for J. K.* (1998); Sadler, A. W., "J. K. as Haiku Poet," *LE&W* 9 (1965): 238–45

GLYN PURSGLOVE

KNOX, John

b. ca. 1514, Haddington, East Lothian, Scotland; d. 24 November 1572, Edinburgh, Scotland

K. was educated at Haddington School and Glasgow University. He was converted to the reformed religion by the militant Lutheran, George Wishart, and began to preach the reformist cause in 1547. He was subsequently appointed chaplain to Edward VI, but fled abroad after the accession of Mary Tudor. In Geneva, K. encountered Jean Calvin who would prove to be a major influence on his thinking. K. returned permanently to Scotland in 1559, and eventually became the leader of the Scottish Reformation.

K. was a pastor and theologian, a rhetorician, pamphleteer and historian. He wrote extensively on the theme of resistance to political authority, viewing himself as a propagandist rather than a writer. His overriding concern was to ensure the triumph of reformation doctrine, and this objective permeates all his writings. In general, his works were hastily written and undertaken in response to rapidly changing circumstances. Several were written and published on the continent, predominantly in Geneva.

Early works, such as *A Godly Letter of Warning* and *A Faithful Admonition*, both published in 1554, were written in Frankfurt and addressed to K.'s former English congregations. With *The Letter to the Re-*

gent of Scotland (1556), K. aimed higher, addressing his work to Mary of Guise who held the regency of Scotland during her daughter Mary's infancy. The best known and also the most embarrassing of all K.'s works, and one that gained notoriety even in his own lifetime, is *The First Blast of the Trumpet against the Monstrous Regiment of Women*, published in Geneva in 1558. K. was primarily concerned to appeal to the people of England to rebel against their queen (Mary Tudor), and accordingly vilified feminine government in his text in order to encourage insurrection. At this time, it was widely believed that for women to rule over men was contrary to natural and divine law, and K.'s views were very much in line with those of the most influential 16th-c. thinkers. The timing of his work, however, was unfortunate, and it gave grave offense to ELIZABETH I, undoubtedly contributing to her hostility to Calvin and developing her distaste for the more extreme forms of evangelical piety. *The Appellation to the Scottish Nobility and Estates*, also published in 1558, is possibly the most important of K.'s writings and at the same time the most easily misconstrued. It constitutes both an appeal against persecution and (in the long run) an appeal for counterpersecution. K. addressed similar sentiments to the lower sections of Scottish society in *The Letter to the Commonalty of Scotland* (1558).

Among K.'s numerous other works are *The First Book of Discipline* (1559), which promoted national education; the *Scottish Confession* (1560), which comprised the confession of faith of the Reformed Church, and which stated that attendance at mass should incur the death penalty; and the *Treatise on Predestination* (1560), in which K., following Calvin, articulated his belief that only the Elect would attain salvation. K.'s other best-known work is the *Historie of the Reformation of Religioun within the Realme of Scotland* (1587). The work is divided into five books, only four of which were completed in K.'s lifetime; he had drafted considerable parts of the fifth book, but it was finished by an unknown author. The *Historie* narrates events following a chronological structure, and cites sources and documents, but despite its thin historical veneer is explicitly a partisan statement, dealing only with religious affairs, and not with civil polity.

BIBLIOGRAPHY: Mason, R. A., *J. K. and the British Reformations* (1998); Reid, W. S., *Trumpeter of God: A Biography of J. K.* (1974); Shaw, D., ed., *J. K.* (1975)

MARGARET CONNOLLY

KUREISHI, Hanif

b. 5 December 1954, Bromley, Kent

K. emerged in the late 1970s as part of London's fringe theater and in 1981 became writer in residence at the Royal Court Theatre. His early plays staged at the Royal Court include *Borderline* (1981), *Cinders* (perf. 1981), adapted from a play by Janusz Glowacki, and *Tomorrow—Today!* (1983). K.—the son of a Pakistani father and English mother—first gained broad critical recognition with his screenplay for *My Beautiful Laundrette* (1986), directed by Stephen Frears, for which he received an Academy Award nomination. Like his earlier plays and in much of his later fiction, the film explores themes of racial tension, sexual identity, and the subculture of contemporary British society. K. also collaborated with Frears on the film *Sammy and Rosie Get Laid* (1987) and wrote and directed the film *London Kills Me* (1991). K.'s highly acclaimed first novel, *The Buddha of Suburbia* (1990), received the Whitbread Award and was adapted by K. in 1993 as a miniseries for the BBC. His second novel, *The Black Album* (1995), was followed by a collection of short stories, *Love in the Blue Time* (1997), which included "My Son, the Fanatic," adapted as a film under the same title. K.'s third novel, *Intimacy* (1998), also adapted for film, was followed by *Midnight All Day* (1999), a collection of short stories, and *Gabriel's Gift* (2001).

KYD, Thomas

b. November 1558, London; d. August 1594, London

Little is known about K.'s life and considerable disagreement exists about what he wrote, although he was indisputably the author of *The Spanish Tragedy* [or *Tragedie*] (perf. ca. 1585–90; pub. 1592), of a translation of Torquato Tasso's *Il Padre di Famiglia* that he called *The Householder's Philosophie* (1588), and of a translation of Robert Garnier's *Cornelie* that he called *Cornelia* (1594). Another work sometimes attributed to K. is *Arden of Feversham* (perf. ca. 1587–92; pub. 1592), although a number of people who have studied the play closely, comparing its style of composition with writing categorically known to be K.'s, challenge this attribution.

Some scholars think that K. wrote a Hamlet play in the Senecan tradition, termed the *Ur-Hamlet* (ca. 1588), before William SHAKESPEARE wrote his *Hamlet*, which was probably based on K.'s version. The Hamlet story, it must be remembered, had existed in various forms since early Germanic times and was recorded by Saxo Grammaticus as early as the 12th c. The extant *Ur-Hamlet* is a revenge play, the genre for which K. is best known. Shakespeare, with his accustomed genius, turned the play into one that focuses more on the complexity of Hamlet's nature than revenge. The impenetrability of Hamlet's character as Shakespeare presents it is as beguiling as the mysterious smile of Leonardo da Vinci's *Mona Lisa*.

The play for which K. is best remembered is *The Spanish Tragedy*, also known in its day as *Hieronimo* or *Jeronimo*, the name of its protagonist. Revenge tragedy is drama in which revenge is exacted for an injury, real or imagined. Hieronimo, a Spaniard, grieves over the death of his son, Andrea, who, in the tradition of Senecan drama, appears as a ghost. Hieronimo, consumed by grief and not always rational, discovers his son's murderers and plots a diabolical way of assuaging his grievous loss. He carries out his plan to stage a play involving the murderers, then he kills them before killing himself. Like most revenge tragedies of the Elizabethan and Jacobean periods, *The Spanish Tragedy* is a violent and bloody drama. Elements of this play, including the ghost and the play within a play, are apparent in Shakespeare's *Hamlet*. In most revenge tragedies, both the avenger and the victim die. Other plays that *The Spanish Tragedy* probably influenced are Shakespeare's *Titus Andronicus*, John MARSTON's *Antonio's Revenge*, Henry CHETTLE's *Tragedy of Hoffman*, Cyril TOURNEUR's *Revenger's Tragedy*, and George CHAPMAN's *Revenge of Bussy D'Ambois* (perf. ca. 1610–11; pub. 1613).

K. apparently attended the Merchant Taylors' School in London. Its headmaster, Richard Mulcaster, emphasized reading and writing in English rather than in Latin. He also placed great emphasis on drama, training his students to give presentations at court. K. probably did not continue his education beyond the secondary school level. He is thought to have shared quarters with playwright Christopher MARLOWE. In 1593, K. was imprisoned, charged with public libels against foreigners. When his rooms were searched, the authorities uncovered heretical and atheistic literature. Subjected to torture, K. claimed these to be Marlowe's property. Finally, all charges against him were dropped, but the disgrace of having been imprisoned caused K.'s patron to abandon him.

Just as there is uncertainty about when K. was born, although a baptismal record for a Thomas Kyd, son of Francis Kyd, is dated November 16, 1558, so is there confusion about when he died. A record at the church of St. Mary Colchurch in London indicates that a "Thomas Kydd" was buried there on August 15, 1594. K.'s mother, Anna Kyd, is known to have renounced her right to administer her dead son's estate on December 30, 1594, presumably because K. was so deeply in debt at the time of his death that there was no estate to administer.

Despite his thin output, K. made an inestimable contribution to English drama by popularizing the revenge tragedy in Britain. He also demonstrated that Senecan drama was a medium that could be used effectively in revenge dramas. His influence on future English playwrights was considerable.

BIBLIOGRAPHY: Barber, C. L., *Creating Elizabethan Tragedy: The Theatre of Marlowe and K.* (1988); Freeman, A., *T. K.: Facts and Problems* (1967); Murray, P., *T. K.* (1969)

R. BAIRD SHUMAN

L

LAMB, Charles

b. 10 February 1775, Inner Temple, London; d. 27 December 1834, Edmonton, Middlesex

L. was born a Londoner and staunchly remained so for all his life with a few forays outside the city. He told William WORDSWORTH in 1801 that "I often shed tears in the motley Strand from fullness of joy at so much life . . . My attachments are all local, purely local—I have no passion . . . to groves and valleys." This condition, the love of the bustle and variety of city life, fed the essential basis of L.'s literary abilities, which were attracted to human diversity, to personal history and places rather than to Romantic landscapes.

L. was educated at Christ's Hospital, London, where he initiated his relationship with the young Samuel Taylor COLERIDGE. He wrote movingly about this period of his life, notably in "Christ's Hospital Five-And-Thirty Years Ago" and "Recollections of Christ's Hospital," included in L.'s "Elia" essays, written mostly for the *London Magazine* from 1820 to 1826. He took employment at the South Sea House, and then as a clerk at the East India House, where he stayed for thirty years until his retirement in 1825. The dull nature of his employment (which he complained of in his writing) was compensated for by an affectionate circle of friends, which included such prestigious figures as Wordsworth, Coleridge, John KEATS, William HAZLITT, Thomas DE QUINCEY, Leigh HUNT, Thomas HOOD, and Robert SOUTHEY.

His literary output includes poetry, drama, essays, sketches, a novel, writing for children—and his letters that show his lively and mischievous nature. Critical opinion does not favor L.'s poetry as his strongest work, nor does it seem to be the most appropriate outlet for his character. He published four sonnets in Coleridge's *Poems on Various Subjects* at a time when the sonnet was undergoing considerable fashionable revival. In 1798 (that great year of collaboration in English poetry), he collaborated with Charles Lloyd

in a volume called *Blank Verse*, which contains the much-anthologized "The Old Familiar Faces" and "Hester" in imitation of Southey's and Wordsworth's ballad experiments. He had a penchant for subjects of sensibility and an elegizing tone, which comes across in the fine poem "On an Infant dying as soon as born" (1827).

In 1798, he also produced a novel, *A Tale of Rosamund Gray and Old Blind Margaret*, which has never been highly regarded and is full of fashionable sentimental and melodramatic writing, where Rosamund is "polluted and disgraced . . . an abandoned thing" who "might have given a lesson to the grave philosopher in death."

L.'s interest in the antique drew him to the Elizabethan and Jacobean period and was a move that gained success for his talents. But he was tempted into trying to write in imitation of the Jacobeans in *John Woodvil: A Tragedy* (1802) and his *Mr. H—; or, Beware a Bad Name* (1813), which was a failure in 1806 at Drury Lane. Other drama by L. appeared in *Blackwood's Magazine* between 1828 and 1830. Along with his sister Mary (for whom L. acted as guardian because of her delicate mental condition), he collaborated in *Tales from Shakespeare: Designed for the Use of Young Persons* (2 vols., 1807), which remains globally popular. Various other publications designed for children such as *The Adventures of Ulysses* (1808) and *Mrs. Leicester's School; or, The History of Several Young Ladies Related by Themselves* (with Mary LAMB, 1809) followed with indifferent success.

L.'s selections from Elizabethan and Jacobean dramatists proved to be a better vehicle for his real abilities. He edited the volume *Specimens of the English Dramatic Poets Who Lived about the Time of Shakespeare* (1808), which coupled with his other writings on William SHAKESPEARE for Hunt's *Examiner* (from 1808) and the *Reflector* (1810–11), helped considerably in the rehabilitation of much neglected but key figures in the history of English drama. Among other things, L. enjoyed drawing out the differences in manners of the relative periods (e.g., "On the Representation of Poverty on the Stage," 1808) or making comment upon the inadequacy of the stage in "On the Tragedies of Shakespeare, considered with reference to their fitness for Stage Representation" (1811), where he claims that "Lear is essentially impossible to be represented on a stage." L.'s sense of criticism stems directly from common sense empathies and elicits comments that tend to the general but strike at the heart of his subject, like the essay "On Some of the Old Actors" (1823), where he discusses Robert Bensley's Malvolio. L. avoids making theoretical pronouncements in favor of engaging the reader in the more welcoming method of speaking from his own experience and impressions and implicitly appealing to the reader to follow suit.

In 1818, *The Works of Charles Lamb* appeared, collecting together his prose and verse in a miscellany of two volumes. This publication seems to have signaled success in terms of L.'s reputation, even though it did not make him wealthy. But the aforementioned Elia essays and the *Last Essays of Elia* (1833) remain the pinnacle of L.'s achievement, touching a literary tradition that embraces Montaigne and Jean-Jacques Rousseau. L. writes under the pseudonym of an Italian clerk from the South Sea House, and writes of himself on occasion in the third person. L. seems to have had a predilection for the pseudonymic disguise, and ironic play, perhaps out of a sense of sorrow for the tragedies in his family life and the need for humorous escape from official daily grind. But he told Wordsworth in 1822 that "Thirty years I have served the Philistines, and my neck is not subdued to the yoke." L.'s penchant for "solemn mockery" shines through the Elian essays like "The South Sea House" and the essential chattiness of his style is what the reader continues to value. Readers feel as if Elia is speaking directly and personally to them and involving them in reminiscence, as in "Dream Children," where L.'s sense of the past and the brightness of the imagination is striking, or in the obvious love of nonsense in "A Dissertation upon Roast Pig."

BIBLIOGRAPHY: Bate, J., ed., *Elia; and, The Last Essays of Elia* (1987); Lucas, E. V., ed., *The Works of Charles and Mary Lamb* (7 vols., 1903–5); Lucas, E. V., *The Life of C. L.* (2 vols., 1905); Marrs, E. W., Jr., ed., *Letters of Charles and Mary Anne Lamb* (3 vols., 1975–78)

CHRISTOPHER J. P. SMITH

LAMB, Mary [Ann or Anne]

b. 3 December 1764, London; d. 20 May 1847, London

L. collaborated with her brother Charles LAMB on *Tales from Shakespeare: Designed for the Use of Young People* (2 vols., 1807), prose summaries for children of William SHAKESPEARE's plots, with some direct quotation of dialogue. L. wrote the items relating to comedy, while her brother dealt with the tragedies. These essays valuably relied on the original texts, not on 18th-c. adaptations and travesties that had proved popular on the stage. The siblings also shared the authorship of *Poetry for Children* (2 vols., 1809). She wrote most of *Mrs. Leicester's School; or, The History of Several Young Ladies Related by Themselves* (1809), a book of children's stories. Her life was blighted with bipolar illness and, after she stabbed her mother, whom she was nursing, to death in 1796, Charles was appointed his sister's keeper except during the periods when she was hospitalized. His was a life of devoted self-sacrifice and his essays have undertones of bitterness.

LANDON, Letitia Elizabeth

b. 14 August 1802, London; d. 15 October 1838, Cape Coast Castle, West Africa

One of the most successful poets of her era, L., known to her adoring public by her initials ("L. E. L."), was hailed as a "female Byron." Intensely hardworking, often at the expense of her own health and peace of mind, she published prolifically, producing five volumes of poetry between 1821 and 1828 alone. A recent estimate of her output of poetry suggests a corpus of over eleven hundred poems, many of which have not been republished since her death. Her private life was, however, dogged by scandal, and the dramatic circumstances of her early death have been the subject of much speculation.

Born in London, the daughter of an army agent, L. was educated in Chelsea. When she was about thirteen, her family moved to Brompton, then a suburb of London. It was here that she came to know William Jerdan, the editor of the *Literary Gazette,* to whom her mother showed some of L.'s poems. Impressed by her precocious talent, Jerdan began publishing her work: her poem "Rome" appeared in the gazette in 1818 when she was not yet sixteen. Three years later, he commissioned her to write a series of "Poetical Sketches" that appeared in each issue for the next three years. By the time she was in her early twenties, she was producing a prodigious amount of work including poetry, reviews, and short stories for various magazines and journals. Following her father's death in 1824, her writing activities enabled her to support a separate household for her mother, to pay for her brother's university education and to buy him a clerical living. By the 1830s, she had taken on the editorship of several of the newly popular annuals and gift books, and she also wrote three novels in this decade. Attractive, lively, and independent, her name was linked at various times in her life with those of several men: Jerdan, William MAGINN, the editor of *Fraser's Magazine,* and the novelist Edward BULWER-LYTTON, among others. L.'s friends stoutly denied the truth of the rumors, but it has recently emerged she did in fact give birth to three of Jerdan's children between 1822 and 1829, the unlucky consequences of an affair that lasted for fifteen years. In 1838, she married the rather disagreeable George Maclean, governor of Cape Coast, West Africa. This was certainly a bid for respectability, but it had an unfortunate outcome: L. was found dead in her room in Africa only months later, a bottle of prussic acid in her hand. Accident, murder, and suicide have all been put forward as possible causes.

L.'s early poetry frequently plays on the image of the lovelorn heroine, suffering for "hopes betrayed, [and] hearts forsaken" ("Different Thoughts," 1823). Guilty or forbidden love, and the fear of betrayal and ruin, surface repeatedly in her work: "loving you—/ Oh God! I dare not think to what that leads;/I dare not think on all I have been told/Of all man's cruelty to woman—how/He will soothe, flatter, vow, till he has won/And then repay her confidence with ruin/Leaving her trusting heart a desolate place." Like her contemporary Felicia HEMANS, she foregrounds the dangers and difficulties attendant on female creativity: her second volume, *The Improvisatrice* (1824), for example, shows the poetess as heroic but doomed. Unlike Hemans, however, she offers no comforting domestic alternative: the heroine of "The History of the Lyre" (1829), having fed too much on "the lotos fruits/ Imagination yields," has made her heart "too like a temple for a home," and death is her only recourse.

Several recent critics have detected a darkening, and a growth of skepticism, in L.'s more mature poetry. The "Fragments" that she used as epigraphs in her novel *Ethel Churchill* (3 vols., 1837) in particular seem to speak of disillusionment with social pressures ("Life is made up of vanities . . ."), with the need for concealment ("Life has dark secrets . . ."), and with her own poetic practice: "What worthless hours! to what use have I turned/The golden gifts which are my hope and pride!/My power of song, unto how base a use/ Has it been put!" Her social conscience is evident in poems like "The Factory" (1835), which exposes the cruelties of child labor.

It is in her prose writings, however, that L. shows most clearly the more cynical literary persona that she developed in the 1830s. Readers of her first novel, *Romance and Reality* (1831), were somewhat disconcerted to find that "L. E. L." the sweet and melancholy poetess was capable of such lively wit and sparkling dialogue. Many of the short stories that she wrote for various of the annuals during this decade show her at her witty and ironic best: her "Sefton Church" (*Fishers Drawing-Room Scrapbook for 1834,* 1833), for example, offers a skeptical, humor-ous, and intelligent critique of sentimental expectations of marriage.

Several collected editions of L.'s works appeared between her death and the end of the 19th c. Her tragic end, and the known hardships of a life devoted to producing work to order, quickly resulted in her becoming something of an icon for later female poets. Elizabeth Barrett BROWNING paid tribute to her in "L. E. L.'s Last Question" (1844), and Christina ROSSETTI played on what she saw as the dichotomy between L.'s public face ("I laugh and sport and jest with all") and her private griefs: "My heart is breaking for a little love" ("L. E. L.," 1863). Largely neglected throughout most of the 20th c., L.'s work is increasingly being accorded well-deserved recognition.

BIBLIOGRAPHY: Blain, V., "L. E. L., Eliza Mary Hamilton, and the Genealogy of the Victorian Poetess," *VP* 33 (Spring 1995): 31–52; Stephenson, G., *Letitia Landon: The Woman Behind L. E. L.* (1996)

                                        HARRIET DEVINE JUMP

LANDOR, Walter Savage
b. 30 January 1775, Warwick; d. 17 September 1864, Florence, Italy

L. was a classical writer in a Romantic age. In all of his writings, L. celebrated and exemplified the classical virtues of precision, formal perfection, and clarity of outline. Speaking of his own poetry in contrast to that of his contemporaries, L. wrote in 1859: "Poetry, in our day, is oftener prismatic than diaphanous: this is not so: they who look into it may see through." L.'s classical severity did not court popularity, and he has never been a widely popular writer. His best works, however, including his *Imaginary Conversations* (1824 and later) and the numerous distinguished lyrics scattered through his works, have always found readers and admirers.

The young L. was a precocious student of Greek and Latin, and his first important publication, the short EPIC *Gebir* (1798), shows his mastery of a classically austere blank verse and his deep understanding of Homer, Virgil, and Ovid. In 1806, he published a collection of short poems called *Simonidea* that demonstrated L.'s special talent for the graceful, brief, and often elegiac lyric. *Simonidea* contains one of L.'s most famous lyrics, "Rose Alymer," and it also contains several of the "Ianthe" poems, a series of restrained love poems that L. wrote for Jane Sophia Swift.

In 1812, L. published *Count Julian,* a verse tragedy based on Spanish history. L. later wrote other verse tragedies such as *Giovanna of Naples* (1839) and *Fra Rupert* (1840), but despite occasional beauties, these closet plays do not rank among his very best works.

In 1824, however, L. found a form in which his interest in the dramatic could be given more effective expression.

This form, the "imaginary conversation," is a prose dialogue between two historical figures in which the conversation itself is fictional. L.'s emphasis in these works is on ideas and principles in literature, philosophy, and politics and, secondarily, on human character conceived in classically clear terms. In such "imaginary conversations" as "Lord Brooke and Sir Philip Sidney," "Southey and Porson," "Henry VIII and Anne Boleyn," and "Marcellus and Hannibal," L. develops his views on the importance of literature, the evils of tyranny and religious prejudice, the greatness of the classical heroic past, the value of stoic and epicurean approaches to life, and the great distance between heroism and meanness in human affairs. L.'s *Imaginary Conversations* of 1824 was followed by additional collections in 1828, 1829, 1853, and 1856. Artistically, the greatest achievement of these works is L.'s prose style. This style is dignified, grand, marmoreal, and perfectly controlled; it is also delicate, precise, and beautifully nuanced.

Although after 1825 L. was increasingly a writer of prose, he continued throughout his long life to produce significant poetry. Perhaps the most important of his later poems are the idylls based on classical subjects that he published in *The Works of Walter Savage Landor* (1846) and *The Hellenics* of 1847 and 1856. These poems, inspired by the narrative poems of Ovid and the idylls of Theocritus, are sometimes narrative and sometimes dramatic. In chiseled blank verse, they explore tragic and amatory themes using Greek figures and myths.

Of L.'s other major works, the best are his *Pericles and Aspasia* (1836) and *The Pentameron and Pentalogia* (1837). *Pericles and Aspasia* uses fictional prose letters and interpolated lyrics to paint an idealized portrait of Periclean Athens, while *The Pentameron and Pentalogia* is largely an extended series of imaginary conversations between Petrarch and Boccaccio in which they discuss literature.

L.'s classical defiance of the Romantic period has made him a controversial figure. His critical supporters see him as carrying on noble literary values in the midst of modern confusion and chaos; those less enthusiastic often view him as a master of form who had nothing important to say about his age. It should be finally noted, however, that contemporaries as diverse as William WORDSWORTH, Percy Bysshe SHELLEY, Robert SOUTHEY, Robert BROWNING, and A. C. SWINBURNE admired both him and his work.

BIBLIOGRAPHY: Bush, D., *Mythology and the Romantic Tradition in English Poetry* (1937); Elwin, M., *L.* (1958); Pinsky, R., *L.'s Poetry*, 1968; Super, R. H., *W. S. L.* (1954)

PHILLIP B. ANDERSON

LANG, Andrew
b. 31 March 1844, Selkirk, Scotland; d. 20 July 1912, London

The quintessential Victorian man of letters, L. wrote, edited, or translated almost three hundred books and some five thousand articles treating varied subjects. The diversity of those concerns is reflected in the range of titles for the articles he contributed to the ninth edition of the *Encyclopædia Britannica* (1875–99): "Apparitions," "Ballads," "The Casket Letters," "Crystal-gazing," "Fairy," "Family," "Edmund Gurney," "Hauntings," "La Cloche," "Molière," "Mythology," "Name," "Poltergeist," "Prometheus," "Psychical Research," "Scotland," "Second Sight," "Tale," and "Totemism." The unifying focus in these pieces and generally of L.'s witty journalism, eclectic scholarship, fiction, and poetry was love of romantic adventure.

That love is particularly evident in the colorful series of twelve fairy tale anthologies—beginning with *The Blue Fairy Book* in 1889 and concluding with *The Lilac Fairy Book* in 1910—which L. edited. Aimed at children, each volume contains retold stories—frequently translated by L.'s wife, Leonora, who was an accomplished linguist—from both oral and literary tradition. The contents of the first volume in the series gives a sense of the books' scope: thirty-seven narratives taken from Charles Perrault, the Grimm brothers, and the *Arabian Nights,* the work of French fairy tale writers, the oral tradition of Scandinavia, *Gulliver's Travels* (a retelling of the voyage to Lilliput), and classical mythology (the story of Perseus). As the series progressed, the Langs included material from outside the European heritage, especially Japan and Africa. The books were immensely popular and are credited with reviving fantasy in CHILDREN'S LITERATURE. Though not as successful, L. also wrote five original fairy tale books for children.

L.'s devotion to romantic adventure had been nurtured by his early reading, especially the novels of Sir Walter SCOTT, and he championed authors such as Robert Louis STEVENSON and H. Rider HAGGARD in the literary criticism that he contributed to various periodicals. He and Haggard collaborated on a novel, *The World's Desire* (1890), which continued the action of *The Odyssey* by having Odysseus journey to Egypt in search of Helen. L., who had studied under the noted classical authority Benjamin Jowett at Oxford, attained some notice as a Homeric scholar, producing three books that championed the single-author theory. He was also cotranslator of a prose version of *The Odyssey,* which remained standard throughout the late 19th c. His version of *The Iliad,* though competent, did not achieve the same canonical status.

L.'s scholarship extended to Scottish history, which he approached with a detachment that offended some Scottish patriots and seemed at odds with his own devotion to his homeland. He produced a multivolume overview of Scottish history as well as books treating specific topics such as the role of John KNOX in the Reformation. He wrote several book-length biographies, including Scott and Joan of Arc among his subjects. L. was also an avid folklorist and cultural anthropologist who championed the theory of unilinear cultural evolution that dominated anthropological thought into the early 20th c.

This view of the development of culture held that societies everywhere progressed along similar lines, though at a particular point in time they might be at different stages in that progression. Thus, Australian Aborigines (at an earlier stage in the evolutionary process) lived life as the ancestors of Victorian Englishmen had eons previously. Aborigines could expect that eventually their culture would evolve in much the same way taken by that of the primitive Britons as their descendants moved toward the pinnacle of human attainment, Victorianism. Though ethnocentric, this theory represented an enlightened rejection of scientific racism, since it recognized the intellectual compatibility of all humankind and the potential for so-called savages (or their descendants) to become the cultural equals of late-19th-c. northern Europeans. Perhaps the most accessible presentation of this theory, whose major proponent was anthropologist E. B. Tylor, appeared in L.'s essay "Mythology and Fairy Tales" (1873).

Drawn to folkloristic and anthropological topics by his interest in romantic adventure and by a fascination with psychic phenomena, L. treated these subjects and his myriad other concerns in the regular columns he wrote for *Longman's Magazine* called "Under the Sign of the Ship." The essays for *Longman's*, like his other writing, were marked by clarity of expression that made them accessible to a variety of readers. In fact, L. wrote primarily for a popular audience. Not afraid of controversy—which he sometimes courted—he nevertheless presented his arguments with a wit that drew readers to his cause even when they might not fully understand the terms of the dispute. For example, his espousal of unilinear cultural evolution put him at odds with the philological theories by which Oxford don Max Muller explained the occurrence of similar myths in disparate cultural settings. L.'s clever and simplistic dismissal of Muller's ideas as "solar mythology" allowed him to triumph without fully engaging the philologist's point.

While he was reflecting current opinion when he wrote on such anthropological matters, L.'s literary interests did not extend to the NATURALISM and REALISM that many of his contemporaries were espousing. His facility in presenting his ideas and the sheer volume of his output helped make L. a central figure in late Victorian literature, though, and while his influence waned as the 20th c. progressed, he did pave the way for the continued popularity of romantic fantasy for both children and adult readers.

BIBLIOGRAPHY: Dorson, R. M., *The British Folklorists: A History* (1968); Green, R. L., *A. L.* (1946); Langstaff, E. D., *A. L.* (1978)

                                    WILLIAM M. CLEMENTS

LANGLAND, William

b. ca. 1330, Worcestershire?; d. ca. 1400, London?

Little direct information exists about L., although he is known to have been roughly contemporary with Geoffrey CHAUCER. From internal evidence gleaned by associating him with Dreamer Will in his only notable contribution to MIDDLE ENGLISH literature, *Piers Plowman*, and from a 15th-c. annotation to one manuscript of that poem, it is surmised that L. was born in the Malvern hills in Worcestershire around 1330. He is thought to have been the son of Stacy de Rokayle, a member of the gentry who had substantial land holdings at Shipton-under-Wychwood. Further internal evidence suggests that he may have attended the Benedictine school at Great Malvern, that he was familiar with London and Westminster, and that he may have been a cleric or have had some other formal association with the Roman Catholic Church.

Piers Plowman cannot be dated precisely. This long poem, running in some versions to over six thousand lines, exists in three versions, called the A-text, B-text, and C-text, each quite different from the others. The A-text, usually dated around 1360, is clearly unfinished. The B-text, best known of the three and the first to be printed, contains material that places its completion sometime after the coronation of King Richard II in 1377. It appeared in print in London around 1550, nearly two hundred years after its composition. Certainly, the poem was well known by 1381. It served as a rallying cry for the Peasants' Revolt in that year. The C-text is such a major revision of the B-text that some scholars question whether it was the work of L. or was done by another hand. At present, however, the scholarly consensus is that L. was indeed the author of all three versions.

Despite his deeply conservative religious outlook, L. was committed fully to social reform. His conservatism made him disdainful of many of the practices he observed in the church of his day. He felt keenly that drastic reform was necessary, so his conservatism helped turn him into the social reformer he finally became.

In the poem, Dreamer Will, a simple tiller of the earth, becomes an embodiment both of Christ and a kind of Everyman. The B-text, by far the best known version, begins with a prologue followed by seven divisions—L. called each division a *passus*—that comment on avarice, the presence of the Seven Deadly Sins in contemporary life, and the hard lives of average peasants. This portion is followed by thirteen divisions that present the lives of Do-wel, Do-bet, and Do-best, allegorical characters who grow in grace, charity, and wisdom as the poem advances. Each of these characters represents a manifestation of Christ but also presents contrasting views of active and contemplative religious lives (Do-wel and Do-bet) and of the amalgamation of the two (Do-best).

L. admired the asceticism of St. Bernard of Clairvaux and scorned some of the religious practices and abuses rampant in the church of his time. Will's dream visions present an overview of society and religion in a 14th-c. England poised to move toward a renaissance followed by the Reformation, during which *Piers Plowman* became a document that stirred those who sought reform.

Through such allegorical characters in the poem as Thought, Wit, Dame Study, Hawkin, the fat friar, and Lady Meed, as well as such biblical figures as Abraham and Moses, L. transports his readers to both Will's inner mind and the outer world that surrounds him. His often biting criticism of the church is ultimately the product of his conservatism in the face of a church in many ways running amok.

BIBLIOGRAPHY: Bowers, J., *The Crisis of Will in Piers Plowman* (1986); Justice, S., and K. Kerby-Fulton, eds., *Written Work: L., Labor, and Authorship* (1997); Kirk, E., and J. Anderson, eds., *Will's Vision of Piers Plowman* (1990)

R. BAIRD SHUMAN

LANYER, Aemilia

bap. 27 January 1569, London; bur. 3 April 1645, London

The daughter of a court musician, L. published only one book in her rather long life, but the book contains two very significant poems, each important for a different reason. *Salve Deus Rex Judaeorum* (1611) goes out of its way to champion women and question the superiority of men. It thus belongs to the long tradition of works that debate the issue of female inferiority. The book begins with nine poems dedicated to various noble women. Not a single dedicatory poem is addressed to a man. L. does not hide her belief that rich women are of more significance to her than rich men. In one sense, she was beginning a small revolution in Jacobean England. The first poem praises the virtues of the dead Queen ELIZABETH I who still had, half a dozen years after her death, a strong presence in England. Even more interesting is the poem written to Mary SIDNEY, sister of Sir Philip SIDNEY, because L. writes that Mary is greater than her brother. Philip had begun a translation of the Psalms, but Mary com-

pleted them after his death, and according to L. Mary showed more virtue and learning than he did. Critics today recognize that Mary's translations are superior to her brother's, but Sidney was such an icon in Renaissance England that no one, outside of L., ever dared question either his virtue or his learning. At the end of the dedicatory poems, L. includes a prose preface in which she attacks not only men who speak against women but also women who speak against women. Men she compares to vipers who crucified Christ. Women, she counsels, should remember their courageous forebears in the Bible: Deborah, Jael, Esther, Judith, and Susanna.

Although the dedicatory poems were written in various meters, the poem "Salve Deus Rex Judaeorum" is written in ottava rima. A long poem of 1,840 lines, the subject matter is basically Christ's Passion and death. The nine scenes covered are: Christ in the Garden of Olives, Christ before Caiaphas, Christ before Pilate, Christ before Herod, a second scene with Pilate, the Via Dolorosa, the Crucifixion on Calvary, the deposition, and the Resurrection. L. arranges each scene as a kind of meditation with a focus on details (e.g., Christ's meeting with his mother on the Via Dolorosa) that lead to analysis, application, and prayer.

There are two digressions in the poem, and the first is the most revolutionary: "Eve's Apology." Sandwiched into Portia's appeal to her husband Pilate are nine stanzas that show Adam to be more at fault than Eve in the loss of Eden: he was stronger, he was not deceived by Satan, she sinned only by having too much love. Not only are the ideas theologically curious, the language gives no indication that L. has any doubt about what women should believe in regard to Eve's being made a scapegoat for the fall. This segment of *Salve Deus* is often chosen to represent L. at her finest moment. Along with the prose preface, it is the most vigorously feminist of her writings. The second digression in the poem consists of fourteen stanzas in praise of Christ's mother, for whom most Renaissance Protestants had little devotion, and thus L. shows herself again unusual as a Renaissance figure.

The only other poem in L.'s volume is "The Description of Cooke-ham," two hundred and ten lines on the estate where the Countess of Cumberland lived. Although Ben JONSON's "To Penshurst" has been considered the first English poem to anatomize an estate, we now realize that L. beat him to the "country-house poem" by half a decade.

BIBLIOGRAPHY: Grossman, M., ed., *A. L.: Gender, Genre, and the Canon* (1998); Lewalski, B. K., *Writing Women in Jacobean England* (1993); Woods, S., ed., *The Poems of A. L.* (1993)

GEORGE KLAWITTER

LARKIN, Philip [Arthur]

b. 9 August 1922, Coventry; d. 2 December 1985, Hull

The most durable and accomplished English poet of the second half of the 20th c., L. wrote as the ordinary man living an ordinary life. But he wrote with a sensibility and a craft that marked him as extraordinary. He produced just three short collections of any significance but many of his lines have lodged in the public mind. The same could be said for very few poets of his generation. His first collection of verse, *The North Ship* (1945), shows verbal facility and at times felicity and suggests some of his later themes, but it is dominated by the influence of other poets, most notably W. B. YEATS. L. also flirted in a purely literary sense with W. H. AUDEN.

As a young man, L. hoped to become a novelist, and two novels—*Jill* and *A Girl in Winter*—were published in 1946 and 1947, respectively. Neither would probably be remembered had L. not risen to fame as a poet, but both show his eye for mundane provincial detail, and *A Girl in Winter* in particular has the air of bleak melancholy that permeates much of his verse. However, it was when his first mature collection of poetry, *The Less Deceived,* was published in 1955 that L. came to the attention of the literary world, and, increasingly, the general public. The title, an ironic reference to Ophelia's "I was the more deceived," is as neat a summary of his poetic stance as any critic has managed—for L.'s poetry is a process of peeling away deception, of testing and self-interrogation in search of some nugget of irreducible truth on which he can rely, or thinks that he can rely. His poetry suggests that one can hardly hope to be undeceived in this life but the less deceived one can manage to be, the better.

His is very much the poetry of postwar disillusion. He is considered a member of "The Movement," a group that included his lifelong friend Kingsley AMIS and that was regarded as the new voice of English poetry in the 1950s, but the Movement is not a useful term. These poets issued no manifesto of poetic intention or aesthetic belief, and they had little in common beyond the deflationary postwar zeitgeist. They are also sometimes referred to as the New Lines poets, after Robert CONQUEST's publication of the same name in 1956, but overall there is little to be gained from seeing them collectively.

From *The Less Deceived,* one poem received more critical attention than any other. The magisterial "Church Going" towers over any other poem of the period. Its ironic self-mockery—"Hatless, I take off/ my cycle clips in awkward reverence"; its sense of the decay of a former England and its quest for some explanation of the value that a church "this accoutred frowsty barn"—may have for human society and the human mind, make it a landmark poem of an agnostic generation. The conclusion that L. reaches is typically minimal and grim but it has been whittled down by a process of clear and honest thought. In this and many of his poems the grand notions, the sweeping ideals of faith and love are dismantled and replaced with a horror of mortality and a general sense of dissatisfaction but also with a quiet, modest, and invaluable honesty. Here is the authoritative voice of hesitance, the exquisite expression of intelligent doubt, the understated reserve of English provincialism.

The publication in 1964 of *The Whitsun Weddings* confirmed L.'s reputation. The most successful poems in this collection match the magnificence of "Church Going" and there is not a single failure. In 1974, his last collection emerged, *High Windows,* which contains his bleakest verse. A few late poems went uncollected, including the remarkable "Aubade," but overall his reputation rests on fewer than a hundred poems. Publishers cashed in on his success. His critical writings on jazz—a lifelong passion that he shared with Amis—were collected under the title *All What Jazz* (1970), a book that makes fine and accessible reading even for the nonmusical, and his prose on various subjects was collected in *Required Writing* (1983). But though L. achieved considerable fame, he shunned publicity. He was by nature shy and he also felt an old-fashioned and admirable reluctance to discuss his work, preferring to let it speak for itself.

Born in the Midlands, L. spent almost all his life in England and the great majority of it in the deeply unliterary fastness of Hull where he became University librarian. This reinforced his status as an ordinary man in ordinary employment, bedeviled like all employees with a sense of frittering life away to no purpose while being afraid to let go of the lifeline that is work. The poems "Toads" and "Toads Revisited" ironically consider that dependence while "Poetry of Departures" considers the flip side of work. It dissects the fantasy of the buccaneer life, the escape from responsibility, the great stride into freedom and finds it more false than the alternative. Thus, he voices a debate enacted in a million minds a million times a day and it is precisely because his poetry deals with such common concerns that it is revered.

L. is seen as the poet of the suburbs. Many of his poems pin down in remorseless detail the recognizable truths of ordinary suburban lives. He writes of parks, playgrounds and hospitals, of ambulances, posters, and trains, the public furniture of an industrial postwar world. His skill at capturing their essence makes an immediate bridge to the reader who feels he shares a world in common with the poet. But the poet expresses it uncommonly well. In distinction to his suburban preoccupations, L. was a nature poet of an unusual sort. He juxtaposed his images of human affairs with stunning images of an uncaring, godless but invaluable natural world—unpeopled places where "silence stands like heat," beaches and seascapes and land covered in snow that represent "unfenced existence." "Such attics cleared of me," he calls them with typical irony. He takes pains to avoid any hint of the pathetic fallacy. The natural world just is—we may see it as beautiful but it is morally neutral. It acts as a touchstone to secular human life. Both are mortal worlds without purpose. The only distinction is that the natural world lacks consciousness.

In this theme, L. echoes Thomas HARDY whom he considered to be among the greatest of English poets. And, like Hardy, L. was an original and brilliant technician. His unemphatically regular verse forms are generally his own. His rhyme schemes are often masked by enjambment. The effect is a superficial sense of a prosaic speaking voice, in keeping with the modest and insistently anti-Romantic themes of the poetry. At the same time, the form establishes an unobtrusive melody of which the reader may not be conscious but which grants a sense of disciplined control, of formal unity, and of significant utterance. Never does L. seem bardic; but neither does he seem loose. Always he comes across as a craftsman, a man sculpting his words into a shape that pleases and thus reinforcing another of his themes, the consolation of art as something that preserves by enduring in a fleeting world.

On the occasions when L. uses emphatic, end-stopped rhymes or clearly repetitive rhythmical patterns, he is normally using them ironically, as in "Naturally the Foundation will Bear Your Expenses" or "Annus Mirabilis." His poetry is also remarkably funny remarkably often. He was a master of the figurative image. Typically memorable is his image of the ship of death, "a black-/sailed unfamiliar, towing at her back/a huge and birdless silence" or his bitter descriptions of the elderly in "Old Fools" crouching under "extinction's alp." Ever wary of pomposity or grandiosity, L. frequently descends into coarse colloquial language especially on the subject of sex. The line of his that is perhaps most commonly quoted is "They fuck you up, your mum and dad." Even though, as here, there is often an irony in his slang it nevertheless has the effect of grounding him ever more firmly in the reality of the everyday.

Some critics, most notably A. ALVAREZ, have dismissed L. as a mere and dreary social realist. They miss the point. While being very much the voice of his age L. continues a tradition of quietly accessible English poets that includes Hardy and Edward THOMAS, poets who are lyrical, wistful, impelled first by emotion but tempered by intelligence. And the secular age in which L. lived, an age in which doubt grew, faith faltered, and the old certainties crumbled, the first age of television in which the importance of

literature in general, and poetry in particular, declined, responded by embracing L. as its spokesman.

BIBLIOGRAPHY: Alvarez, A., *The New Poetry* (1962; rev. ed., 1966); Davie, D., *Thomas Hardy and British Poetry* (1972); Motion, A., *P. L.* (1982); Salwak, D., *P. L.: The Man and His Work* (1989); Thwaite A., ed., *Selected Letters of P. L., 1940–1985* (1992)

JOE BENNETT

LASKI, Audrey [Louise]

b. 12 March 1931, London; d. 18 January 2003, London

Poised and ironic, L.'s novels reflect the mores and speech of the 1950s and 1960s and satisfy on multiple levels. L. makes telling use of interior monologue and apt literary allusion; she writes for an educated readership. Her running themes are identity, cultural differences, group dynamics, and self-deception. In *Venus in Transit* (1964), a liberated young woman, taking serial lovers, hitchhikes round Europe in search of a role, using her art training in various jobs. At the time, such a lifestyle was just becoming possible. An agricultural development project in southern Italy is distorted by the discovery of cave paintings and the threat of tourism. The word "neon" is used by this intelligent heroine to signify cultural degradation, the cheap and flashy. The ending is deliberately inconclusive. L.'s tone is compassionate but unsentimental.

In *A Very Kind Undertaking* (1965), a childless intellectual couple take an interest in a working-class schoolgirl who wants to be a hairdresser. She intends to drop out of school and start work as soon as possible; with the best of intentions and a self-regarding admiration for formal qualifications, they put pressure on her to take a beautician's training course, with disastrous results. The social shibboleths of an English provincial town are wittily deconstructed. Carrying her learning lightly, L. set *Seven Other Years* (1967) in Cambridge University, where a Hungarian refugee comes to do literary research after the 1956 uprising. The novel deals subtly with an outsider's linguistic and social interactions with an English family living in Cambridge, the growth and development of an imaginative girl, and a crisis of conscience. The denouement comes as a shock.

The Keeper (1968) is a novel of ideas. A failed academic goes to investigate a reclusive community of fundamentalist Puritans and of course changes it in the process, which reveals to him his true nature and powers of leadership he never knew he possessed. *The Dominant Fifth* (1969) explores questions of identity, ethnicity, and dissolution in metaphors of harmony, imaged by a string quartet with one mortally ill member, whose replacement does not fit in, though technically a better musician. As always, character and milieu are convincing and fresh. Her next novel, *Night Music* (1974), arguably the best, foregrounds Ivor, the leader of the quartet, a self-confessed "closet queen," who has a troubled relationship with his conventional mother. A chance encounter reveals an appalling darkness in his own soul. In fastidious yet sturdy prose, painful truths are explored with sympathy and bittersweet HUMOR, generous wisdom as well as wit.

VALERIE GROSVENOR MYER

LASKI, Marghanita

b. 24 October 1915, London; d. 8 February 1988, London

Novelist, critic, journalist, broadcaster, and lexicographer, L.'s varied creative work spanned the period from the 1940s to the 1980s. Her six novels were written in the ten years following the Second World War, and she is now remembered principally for her journalism and as a broadcaster, in which capacity she appeared regularly on such programs as *The Brains Trust, Any Questions,* and *The Critics.* As a member of the Arts Council (1979–86), she attempted to put into practice her general principle of making high art (according to her own eclectic definition) available to everyone. A passionate champion of the English language and its vocabulary, she contributed a prodigious number of illustrative quotations to the Oxford English Dictionary.

Born to a family of Jewish intellectuals—her grandfather was Moses Gaster, scholar and chief rabbi of Sephardic Jews in England, and her uncle was Harold J. Laski, the socialist thinker—she was reared and educated first in Manchester and then in London. Her first training on leaving school was as a dress designer, and her delight in clothes, and style in general, provided a counterpoint to the left-wing sympathies with which she is often associated. She then went to Oxford, where she met her husband and future publisher, John Howard. She lived mostly in London, but also spent time in the English countryside, and in France, which she loved, and each of her novels draws on her knowledge of life in a particular place and milieu.

L.'s novels seem almost to represent an extension of her journalism. None of them is long, and each one is quite different, like a sort of exercise in a type of novel. A preoccupation that runs through them all is with the subtleties of the English class system. Her own background and experience—as a Jewish atheist with a profound interest in religion, and as an intellectual married into an English upper-middle-class family—gave her a peculiarly detached position for surveying English social life. She was a fascinated and penetrating observer of the changing manners of her time, and of the distinctions and motives of her characters.

Love on the Supertax (1944), *To Bed with Grand Music* (1946), written under the pseudonym Sarah Russell, and *Tory Heaven* (1944; repub. as *Toasted Heaven,* 1944) are satires on life on the home front during and immediately after the Second World War. *Love on the Supertax* is a world-turned-upside-down fable, rooted in the transformation that English society was undergoing, with the aristocracy and old rich finding themselves unemployed rather than independently at leisure, and the socialist movement enjoying rising success. Clarissa, the daughter of an impoverished duke, imagines that her dreams of a better life may be within her grasp when she falls in love with Sid, a worker and communist, but their romance is fraught with Clarissa's gaffes, which include wearing a couture silk dress decorated with tiny hammers and sickles to a Party event. *To Bed with Grand Music* depicts a hedonistic mode of London life during the war, and the temptations that ensnare a young woman when her husband is posted abroad. The book's real strength lies in the way it exposes Deborah's hypocritical self-justification of her behavior, which leads her through a seemingly endless succession of men, from whom she accepts ever more lavish gifts. The thoroughly unpleasant Deborah prefigures the more complicated characters of the later novels. In the social science fiction of *Tory Heaven,* a nostalgic fantasy of "the good old days" is enforced by an institutionalized class system. With characteristic wit, L. illustrates at once the English predilection for putting each person in his place, and the danger of compartmenting individuals.

Little Boy Lost (1949), in many ways L.'s most successful novel, charts an Englishman's search for the child he had never known, who had been lost in Paris during the war. The novel gives a heart-breaking evocation of a devastated France, plagued by corruption, as it is seen by the francophile Hilary. This is reflected in the bleakness felt by Hilary at the death of his wife, which has left him resistant to the love of which he now feels himself to be incapable. He is therefore cruelly ambivalent toward the appealing child he finds in an orphanage, who may or may not be his son. Of all L.'s novels, *The Village* (1952) was the one most concerned with English life as many people at the time knew it. The village of the title contains in microcosm the full range of English social life. The novel, which centers on a sweet story of love across the class divide, contains brilliant but agonizing depictions of the collision of the classes, effected by the war and changing social climate. *The Victorian Chaise-Longue* (1953) is a ghost story, in which Melanie, a happy young mother recovering from tuberculosis, falls asleep on a sofa and wakes up in the body of Milly, its incumbent of a hundred years earlier, who is not recovering, but dying, of the same disease. Like Melanie, Milly has just had a baby, but hers was illegitimate, and the details of her story, with their parallels in Melanie's own life, are gradually revealed through the hints of sinister visitors to the dark, stuffy sickroom that had been Milly's and is now Melanie's prison. Melanie falls asleep in a state of ecstasy, and her transportation is effected through a conceit that in such a state, time can be reentered at a different point from that at which it was left. L. subsequently made a scholarly study entitled *Ecstasy in Secular and Religious Experiences* (1961), in which she hoped to show that what are generally recognized as religious experiences are basically identical in kind with experiences known to people who would not interpret them in religious contexts. *Everyday Ecstasy* (1980) concentrated on the effects of ecstatic experiences in daily secular life.

L. was a great admirer of Rudyard KIPLING, whose work she felt was underappreciated. Her popular radio series "Kipling's English History," which related a history of England illustrated by Kipling's poems, attempted to rekindle enthusiasm for his poetry, as well as suggesting an accessible approach to history, and to poetry in general. She was also the author of biographical and critical works on Jane AUSTEN (1969), and George ELIOT (1973); and was a founder of the Charlotte Yonge Society. Among her other publications were anthologies of Victorian children's stories, and *The Offshore Island* (1959), a play about nuclear war. A poetry anthology, *Common Ground*, which was intended to help make beautiful and useful poems accessible, was published posthumously in 1989.

BIBLIOGRAPHY: Lassner, P., "'Between the Gaps': Sex, Class and Anarchy in the British Comic Novel of World War II," in Finney, G., ed., *Look Who's Laughing: Gender and Comedy* (1994): 205–19; Schmitt, N. C., "Ecstasy and Peak-Experience: W. B. Yeats, M. L., and Abraham Maslow," *CD* 28 (Summer 1994): 167–81

ESTHER GODFREY

LATIMER, Hugh

b. ca. 1492, Thurcaston, Leicestershire; d. 16 October 1555, Oxford

L. is better known as an ecclesiastical figure of the first half of the 16th c. than as a literary figure. His surviving writing consists exclusively of about forty-five sermons. A committed, doctrinaire Roman Catholic, L. attended Cambridge University through the master's degree and was ordained to the priesthood on July 15, 1515. He remained at Cambridge reading theology toward a divinity degree, granted in 1524, and for several years afterward. Although the Roman Catholic Church was being assailed from many quarters, L. remained zealously Catholic. The "New Life," resulting from a renaissance in Britain, swept

through university circles, but L. railed against those who veered from religious orthodoxy, sometimes interrupting sermons and lectures questioning Roman Catholic doctrine.

In 1524, delivering the public disputation required for the B.D., L. attacked famed German theologian, Philip Melancthon. Afterward, Thomas Bilney, a brilliant reformer, visited L., who said that through Bilney's visit, he learned more than he had in the many years of his previous education. He soon became zealous for ecclesiastical reform, calling for an authorized English Bible, denial of transubstantiation, deemphasizing of saints, and an end to selling indulgences.

By 1528, L.'s sermons demanded these reforms. In 1529, he preached his legendary "Sermons on the Card," the earliest of his surviving sermons. In these sermons, he addressed theological questions by using playing cards. His first such SERMON evoked a rebuttal from Robert Buckenham, prior of the Dominican House at Cambridge, called a "Sermon on the Dice." L. retaliated with his second "Sermon on the Card," reducing Buckenham to a laughingstock.

L. attracted King HENRY VIII's attention as a result of this second "Sermon of the Card." The following year, he gained the king's favor by spearheading the movement for Cambridge University's approval of the annulment of the king's marriage to Catherine of Aragon.

L. filled any church in which he preached. Part of the magic he brought to his preaching was his keen awareness of audience, employing simple terms for the humble servants at Grimsthorpe but quickly reversing course when he preached to more sophisticated audiences. In his surviving sermons, the progression of ideas is disorderly, the organization weak. This is because L., cognizant of his audiences, was not bound by his manuscript but was comfortable meandering extemporaneously when a word or phrase suggested something to him as he spoke. This sort of flexibility captivated audiences. L. imbued his sermons with HUMOR, a quite unheard-of innovation. He was a master at producing the ready phrase, such as "strawberry preachers" who come but once a year, and do not tarry long.

L. lost the king's favor as his sermons became increasingly controversial, but, although he received warnings from Henry VIII and was placed under arrest, his life was safe while Henry lived. On Henry's death in 1547, the Protestant boy king, Edward VI, ascended. L. retained some favor, although he retired officially in 1550. When, upon Edward's death in 1553, Mary Tudor ascended, the Catholic queen had L. imprisoned along with Thomas Cranmer and Nicholas Ridley.

L. was tried and found guilty of heresy in 1555. He was burned at the stake on October 16, 1555, along with Ridley. His last words to Ridley as the flames inched toward them were, "we shall this day light such a candle, by God's grace, in England as I trust shall never be put out."

BIBLIOGRAPHY: Chester, A., *H. L.* (1954); Chester, A., ed., *Selected Sermons of H. L.* (1968); Darby, H. S., *H. L.* (1953)

R. BAIRD SHUMAN

LAW AND LITERATURE

Although law and literature now appear to be separate, if not antithetical, fields, they have historically enjoyed a close and symbiotic relationship. The great legal historian F. W. Maitland declared in 1898 that, "English law and English literature grew up together in the court of Henry II." His comment alerts us to a common intellectual and cultural environment and to shared ideological functions. More fundamentally, law and literature have a common origin in rhetoric, in the self-conscious use of an authoritative language that commands assent to particular representations of reality.

Henry's initiative of sending itinerant justices throughout his realm to administer a common law in the king's courts laid the foundations for a distinctive English legal system, in which written law was increasingly to take the place of oral customary law. The success of this new system was underpinned by a belief that law was the ordering principle of the universe: the ultimate reality was the divine law of God, from which stemmed certain fundamental principles of right and wrong; these principles formed "natural law," which could be accessed by all humans through their reason; and which should be consulted by all rulers in promulgating laws for their realms. Thus, the rule of law became an important ideology in Anglo-Norman and later society, and its cultural significance is seen in the prevalence of legal diction and trial scenes in literary works. One such trial occurs in the courtly love setting of Marie de France's *lai,* "Lanval" (wr. ca. 1189). The same culture of legality informs ideas of proprietary rights to land in romances, such as *King Horn* (wr. ca. 1225) and *Havelok the Dane* (wr. ca. 1280–1300). This idealized view of justice through law is pitted against corrupt power and violence throughout MIDDLE ENGLISH literature, reflecting popular anger at historical abuses of the law. William LANGLAND's *Piers Plowman* uses the device of the vision to present a savage critique of the greed of lawyers and the corruptibility of legal officials. Similar concerns led others to mythologize the outlaw in ballads about Robin Hood. Geoffrey CHAUCER too is cautiously critical of the Sergeant-at-Law in *The Canterbury Tales;* however, his stories of crime and trial indicate an abiding faith in law.

From the 16th to the 18th c., the intertwining of English law and literature was furthered within the Inns of Court in London. In addition to being the home of legal education, the Inns were also an important site of cultural activity and political education for young gentlemen. Students wrote and performed their own plays here, and also hosted professional companies. Performances included William SHAKESPEARE's *Comedy of Errors* and *Twelfth Night.* Many writers studied in this legal milieu, whether or not they went on to become lawyers, including Sir Philip SIDNEY, Sir Walter RALEIGH, John DONNE, and John MARSTON. The early modern period was a highly litigious one, and legal concepts were embedded in everyday life. Legal language is employed even in the seemingly enclosed and private space of the sonnet. The period's major work of literary theory, Sidney's *Apologie for Poetrie,* published in 1595, follows the pattern of a legal defense, and proposes an analogy between law and literature as two systems of world creation. As a result of the economic and intellectual changes taking place, equity, a flexible system of remedies, was developed to relieve injustices in cases where the form-bound common law proved inadequate. The competing claims of these two rival systems of law are dramatized in the trial of Shylock in Shakespeare's *The Merchant of Venice.* The close relationship between law and literature was not only positive; censorship flourished, and eventually drew forth the first great defense of freedom of expression, John MILTON's *Areopagitica,* published in 1644. Two notable writers held the highest judicial and political offices, Sir Thomas MORE and Francis BACON. As a philosopher of science, Bacon advocated the superiority of a new form of scientific knowledge, based on observation and experiment, rather than ancient authorities. Henceforth, law and literature were increasingly to be governed by scientific notions of truth and probability.

REALISM defined the first new form of the modern world, the novel. Its narrative method, whether using a first-person narrator speaking of personal experience, or an impersonal third-person narrator assembling a comprehensive network of facts, drew heavily on contemporary developments in the law of evidence. Legal concepts supplied many of the novelists' preferred norms, and thus there was an ideological continuity in the work of the magistrate and novelist, Henry FIELDING. Early in the 18th c., legal education had degenerated into formulaic repetition, providing fertile ground for legal SATIRE. The abuse of law in colonized Ireland prompted Jonathan SWIFT to the acerbic denunciations of English law in *Gulliver's Travels.* Against this background, Sir William Blackstone's *Commentaries on the Laws of England* (4 vols., 1765–69), a laudatory account of the entire English common law, was published. Blackstone's grandiloquent prose mythologized the law as a heritage of freedom, continuing the entrenchment of the rule of law as a dominant ideology. While the Inns of Court were in decline, lawyers in Edinburgh were engaging in dialogue with philosophers and historians to make a systematic study of how law developed in relation to other social, economic, and philosophical forces. This broad grounding provided Sir Walter SCOTT with the intellectual framework to explore questions of legality and violence in his historical novels.

The French Revolution inspired British radicals to thorough-going critiques of the traditional social order. William BLAKE in his lyrics and visions attacked the "mind-forged manacles" of oppression, and demonstrated the power of poetry to imagine alternative worlds. The prison figures everywhere in Gothic poetry and fiction. Mary WOLLSTONECRAFT argued compellingly against a gender-specific understanding of the rights of man in *A Vindication of the Rights of Woman*. William GODWIN's novel, *The Adventures of Caleb Williams,* identifies how class power can thwart the rule of law. Blackstone's paean to the common law was rigorously critiqued by Jeremy BENTHAM, and a new theory of law as the will of the sovereign became dominant. In this context, literature came to seem a space of possibility rather than orthodoxy, and was enlisted in a politics of hope in which poets are, in Percy Bysshe SHELLEY's words, "unacknowledged legislators of mankind" (*Defence of Poetry*). This Romantic conception of the author as original creator was in turn enshrined in a new copyright law declaring works to be the property of their authors by the case of *Donaldson v. Beckett* (1774) and by the Copyright Act of 1842.

To ameliorate the oppressive conditions that led to revolution, British governments adopted a policy of managed reform, using parliamentary statutes as instruments of social change. Charles DICKENS, Elizabeth Cleghorn GASKELL, and other Victorian writers fostered this climate of reform through the "social problem novel." Matrimonial law is one of the targets of Dickens's *Hard Times*. Caroline Norton, a late Romantic poet who suffered under these laws, turned herself into an effective pamphleteer, and achieved improved laws for women. Dickens's *Bleak House* makes the Court of Chancery a remarkable symbol of law as an ever-expanding vortex and of a nation held in thrall to the forms of the past. Industrial society required new means of social control, and the modern police force was a key invention, the cultural influence of which is seen in the rise of the detective as hero. The form of the legal trial is closely imitated in the evidentiary form of Wilkie COLLINS's *The Woman in White* and Robert BROWNING's *The Ring and the Book,* but both texts also criticize law and lawyers. In *Adam Bede,* George ELIOT proposes an analogy between the narrator of a realist novel and a witness giving evidence under oath. Late in the century, this cooperative project of law and literature constructing a modern community through gradual change was put under pressure by free thought, aestheticism, and the New Woman. Law's repressive response is indicated by the trial and imprisonment of Oscar WILDE.

In the early 20th c., the modernist movement positioned literature in the avant-garde of social change. Male and female sexuality became a topic of frank representation, and brought literature into conflict with law. James JOYCE's *Ulysses,* Radclyffe HALL's *The Well of Loneliness,* and D. H. LAWRENCE's *Lady Chatterley's Lover* were all banned. Appropriately enough, Joyce had travestied this conflict in the "Circe" episode of *Ulysses*. Illicit sexuality brought forth some of the law's harshest sentences, particularly against women. F. Tennyson Jesse's novel *A Pin to See the Peepshow* (1934) fashions the case of the executed Edith Thompson into a powerful story of desire versus law. The desire for political freedom and the ill effects of imperial power are shown in the trial scene in E. M. FORSTER's *A Passage to India*. Realist drama engaged productively with the law: John GALSWORTHY's *Justice* so moved Sir Winston CHURCHILL with its portrayal of imprisonment that he reformed the law governing prisons. Terence RATTIGAN's *The Winslow Boy* revisited the Archer-Shee case of 1912, in which a boy wrongly accused of stealing five shillings was expelled from Naval College and his parents embarked on a long but finally successful legal battle against the British government, turning it into a powerful dramatic defense of the ideology of the rule of law. With the relaxation of censorship in the 1960s, law and literature seemed properly separate domains, meeting only in the double lives of exceptional individuals like the barrister-writer John MORTIMER or the solicitor and poet Roy Fuller.

The trial remains a significant element in recent fiction, holding out the twin promise of judgment and justice, but often in this era registering failure, as in John FOWLES's *A Maggot*. Such epistemological doubts were fortified by a series of miscarriages of justice in British courts. Ideological bias and unjust police practices against the Irish were exposed by the wrongful conviction of the Guildford Four and the Birmingham Six from 1989. This crisis in the criminal law was radically represented in the theater, with Caryl CHURCHILL's *The Judge's Wife* (perf. 1972; pub. 1990) and David HARE's *Murmuring Judges* and in the television series *Blind Justice* (1990), devised by Helena Kennedy QC and Peter Flannery. Their political critique, along with POSTMODERNISM's insistence that reality is always mediated by language, reawakened interest in Sidney's insight that poet and lawyer are both verbal "makers," imaginers of the real, prompting new investigations of storytelling in and about the law, and of the mutually constructive relationship between law and literature.

BIBLIOGRAPHY: Crane, S., *Insular Romance: Politics, Faith, and Culture in Anglo-Norman and Middle English Literature* (1986); Dolin, K., *Fiction and the Law* (1999); Schramm, J.-M., *Testimony and Advocacy in Victorian Law, Literature, and Theology* (2000); White, R. S., *Natural Law in English Renaissance Literature* (1996); Ziolkowski, T., *The Mirror of Justice* (1997); Zomchick, J., *Family and the Law in Eighteenth-Century Fiction* (1993)

KIERAN DOLIN

LAWES, Henry

b. 5 January 1596, Dinton, Wiltshire; d. 21 October 1662, London

Though not himself a poet, L. deserves a place of some prominence in any history of English poetry. He was the most important songwriter of the Caroline period and the Interregnum. This was a period when much of the finest lyrical poetry was designed for musical setting and among the poets of this period there seems to have been a widely shared agreement that it was L. who could be relied upon to do fullest justice to their work, in ways that would respect both their art and his. He himself declared (in the preface to his 1655 collection of *Ayres*) that "the way of *Composition* I chiefly profess . . . is to shape *Notes* to the *Words* and *Sense*." For John MILTON ("To My Friend, Mr. Henry Lawes, on His Airs"), it was L. "whose tunefull and well measur'd song/First taught our English Music how to span/Words with just note and accent." Edmund WALLER praised the way L.'s setting of words fully respected, and indeed enhanced, the poet's own craft: "others with Division hide/The Light of Sense, the Poets Pride,/But you alone may truly boast/That not a syllable is lost/The Writer's and the Setter's skill/At once the ravish't Eare do fill." Another poet, John Cobb, went so far as to suggest that L.'s settings sometimes actually clarified the poet's meaning in ways that a written text alone could not do: "No pointing Comma, Colon, half so well/Renders the breath of Sense; they cannot tell/The just Proportions how each word should go,/To rise and fall, run swiftly or march slow;/Thou shew'st 'tis Music only must do this,/Which as thou handlest it can never miss."

L. set texts by most of the finest lyrical poets of his time. They include John DONNE, Milton, Thomas CAREW, Richard LOVELACE, Robert HERRICK, William CARTWRIGHT, Waller, James SHIRLEY, George HERBERT, Sir John SUCKLING, William STRODE, and many others. As the praise he received from poets might suggest, L. was careful in his use of texts. Unlike some of his musical contemporaries, L. largely resisted the temptation to "improve" the texts he set, or to change them to make his own compositional tasks easier at the cost of poetic complexity. Evidence of

the care L. took is plentiful in the fascinating holograph manuscript, a large folio volume, in which L. wrote his settings of more than three hundred songs. Such, indeed, was L.'s respect for his texts that there are many instances—they include some examples in the work of Herrick and Carew—where L.'s setting of a poem provides important textual evidence. Others, it seems, turned to him for information and assistance in such matters. The editor of the Countess of PEMBROKE's *Poems*, published in 1660, explained that "In the collecting of these Poems . . . I was fain first to send to Mr. *Henry Laws,* who furnishing me with some, directed me for the rest."

Milton's *Masque Presented at Ludlow Castle* (more commonly known as *Comus*) benefited from music composed for it by L., who also played the role of the Attendant Spirit. From 1631, L. held the title of "Musician for Lutes and Voices" in the King's Musicke; that he was a fine player of the lute is attested by a poem of Herrick's (*"To M.* Henry Lawes, *the excellent Composer of his Lyricks"*). No doubt he was much involved in the court masques of the 1630s, perhaps as both composer and performer. His name is associated with *Coelum Britannicum* (1634), a masque written by Carew, but none of the music survives. His name appears in connection with some other entertainments. Strode's play *The Floating Island,* which was presented to Charles I at Oxford in 1636, carries on its title page (1655) the information that "The *Aires* and *Songs* [were] set by Mr. HENRY LAWES, servant to his late Majesty in his publick and private Musick." Late in his life, L. wrote at least some of the music for Sir William DAVENANT's *The Siege of Rhodes* (1656), which has often been described (with doubtful accuracy) as the first English opera.

It is, however, in his songs that L.'s greatest importance resides, some 430 of which survive. In 1638 and again in 1648, he published settings of the Psalms. In the 1650s, many of his finest songs appeared in a series of three collections: *Ayres and Dialogues, for One, Two, and Three Voyces* (1653), *The Second Book of Ayres, and Dialogues* (1655), and *Ayres and Dialogues for One, Two, and Three Voices: The Third Booke* (1658). No other composer of the period displayed so consistent an alertness to questions of poetic structure and tone. For a poem or poet to have been set by L. seems to have constituted a kind of recognition of quality; clearly it was thought to recommend poems to potential readers to be able to say, either on title pages (as in collections by, for example, Carew, Waller, and Suckling) or in giving the titles of individual poems (as with Lovelace) that they had been set by L. Given the range of his contacts and the quality of his work, L. is of central importance to any student of the English lyric in the 17th c. He, more than any other figure, helps us to understand the role of music in the poetry of the period; he provides or confirms texts of important poems; he preserves some valuable poems that we would otherwise have lost.

BIBLIOGRAPHY: Evans, W. M., *H. L.* (1941); Spink, I., *H. L.* (2000); Willetts, P. J., *The H. L. Manuscript* (1969)

GLYN PURSGLOVE

LAWRENCE, D[avid] H[erbert]
b. 11 September 1885, Eastwood, Nottinghamshire; d. 2 March 1930, Vence, France

In the decades since his death, L. has been seen as the best and the worst of writers. The court action in 1960 that eventually resulted in the first British publication of his 1928 novel *Lady Chatterley's Lover* is often seen as the symbolic start of sexual liberation and the 1960s. For the Cambridge-based critic F. R. LEAVIS, L. was simply the most important modern writer in the language, and the culmination of "The Great Tradition" of novel writing. Others argued that L. was the first significant writer to come from the industrial working class, representing women in new ways that at last acknowledged and celebrated their sexuality, and continuing a line of British writers (which includes William BLAKE, Thomas CARLYLE, John RUSKIN, and William MORRIS) who exposed the damaging effects of economic change on individuals and society. In the 1970s and 1980s, however, the pendulum swung against L. For Kate Millet, the representation of women in L.'s texts showed a strong belief in male dominance, and an effort to script women's experience from a male perspective. Racist and colonialist stereotypes abounded in the writing on non-Western peoples and cultures. FEMINISM, postcolonial studies, and literary theory—as initially taught in English studies—found other modernist writers, such as James JOYCE and Virginia WOOLF, more congenial. However, work on L. did not come to an end. The Cambridge University Press edition of L.'s works and letters and a three-volume critical biography (1991–98) have revealed a L. who constantly used his life in his writing, exploring possible new directions he could take. In recent scholarship, there has been a strong effort to look at L.'s relationship to philosophical writing on language and the individual's engagement with the world, in particular the writings of Heidegger and Wittgenstein. Recent work, viewing L. in his historical context, has extended the debates on class, gender, sexuality, and race in the writing. L.'s interest in man's relationship to the natural world, and opposition to the effects of modernization on landscape, community, and selfhood, has attracted those pursuing environmental criticism.

L. was born in the single-industry mining town of Eastwood. His father worked down the pits, and was at home in this community. His mother came from a poorer background, but with her middle-class aspirations she was determined that her children would not have to work in the mines. Despite initial promise, and a scholarship to Nottingham High School, at sixteen L. was working as a clerk in a surgical appliances factory in the city. An illness forced him to give up this job, and he went back into education, in time attending Nottingham University College to train as a teacher. L. read widely, and he began to write poems, short stories, and his first novel, eventually published after much redrafting as *The White Peacock* (1911). L. left Eastwood to teach in Croydon, a satellite suburb of London, in 1908. The following year saw his literary breakthrough, when some of his poems were published in the *English Review,* then edited by Ford Hermann Hueffer (later Ford Madox FORD). Following his mother's death from cancer in late 1910, L. suffered another breakdown of health, and gave up being a schoolmaster. He tried to deal with the issues of class, family structure, and early relationships that had been so important to him in these early years in his third novel, *Sons and Lovers* (1913).

In 1912, L. eloped to the Continent with Frieda Weekley, the wife of his former modern languages professor. After her divorce, L. and Frieda were married in 1913. His new relationship led him to explore further what he saw as the transformative potential of heterosexual marriage. How such a relationship could be formed by a modern woman became the spur to his next novel. Finding that he needed to give a sense of how the modern crisis in relationships had been produced, the project split into two texts, *The Rainbow* (1915) and *Women in Love* (1920). The years of World War I were difficult for L. The downturn in the publishing industry brought by the war, combined with heightened censorship, affected his income. *The Rainbow* was banned due to sexual content soon after publication, and he could not find a publisher for *Women in Love.* Opposed to the war and married to a German, he was expelled from Cornwall in 1917 on suspicion of spying.

From that year, L.'s interest shifted from heterosexual relationships toward how a whole self could be produced, and to alternative societies. He believed that European culture had been exhausted by the war. After recovering from a further breakdown of his health, L. left England in November 1919, going south, and spending much time in Sicily. His output had been somewhat reduced in the last years of the war, but many L. texts were published in the years immediately after, including *The Lost Girl* (1920) and *Aaron's Rod* (1922), and he began to find that he could sell his books in the U.S. The feeling that Europe was damaged beyond repair led L. to want to travel in search of better ways of living. After six weeks in Ceylon, he spent a month and a half in Australia. He wrote most of a novel, *Kangaroo* (1923), while there and later coauthored with M. L. Skinner another Australian novel, *The Boy in the Bush* (1924). His time in New Mexico deeply impressed him, and he wrote about it in powerful essays and short stories, including "The Woman Who Rode Away" and in one of his short novels, *St. Mawr* (1925). He also went south to Mexico, writing a novel about a society that reasserted Indian belief systems in the face of Spanish settler culture, entitled *The Plumed Serpent* (1926).

After experiencing what was probably a tubercular hemorrhage at his ranch in Taos, New Mexico, in 1924, L. was dangerously ill in Mexico in 1925. He went back to Europe later that year, and the rest of his life was a search for health. Continuing to write, but increasingly eschewing fiction, he now looked for better forms of society in the past of the Continent. His last novel, though, was to be a restatement of his views on sexuality and modern living, now with a more direct language for sex. *Lady Chatterley's Lover* was privately printed in Florence in 1928. Nearly two years later, he finally succumbed to tuberculosis. His late poetry movingly addressed his approaching death, which came after an extraordinarily productive and event-filled life of just forty-four years.

Modern L. criticism has been interested in looking at the whole body of L.'s writing, and anxious to avoid the distorting effect of picking out a small number of the novels just because that form has had the most cultural capital. Many have claimed anyway that the control exercised in the short stories and short novels make them his most successful works. L. was one of the great letter writers in the language because, while careful to consider his correspondent, he found a way of moving from the particular to the wider issues for life raised by a particular situation. The early plays, in particular, are significant—in a period of conventional and moribund writing for the theater, L.'s dialect plays, *A Collier's Friday Night* (wr. 1909; pub. 1934), *The Daughter-in-Law* (wr. 1913; pub. 1988), and *The Widowing of Mrs. Holroyd* (1914), show how working-class experience could be represented on stage. L. published many poems: some would argue that if he had revised and selected his work more carefully his reputation as a poet would be higher. However, this would perhaps be to accept modernist notions of the honed and revised body of work too easily. Though the rhyming poems from early in the career seem awkward and overly indebted to late-19th-c. poetry, the breakthrough came with the poems written in response to his relationship with Frieda, in the volume *Look! We Have Come Through!* (1917). His engagement with nature during his travels is captured in the volume *Birds, Beasts and Flowers* (1923); while in the late volumes, *Pansies* (1929), the poems are barbed *pensées* (thoughts) on events. The nonfiction began to receive sustained attention from

the 1980s on; high points include literary criticism (particularly the groundbreaking work, *Studies in Classic American Literature*, 1923), travel books including *Sea and Sardinia* (1921) and *Sketches of Etruscan Places* (wr. 1927; pub. as *Etruscan Places*, 1932), and the *Memoir of Maurice Magnus* (1924). As this suggests, a full critical response to L. needs to be able to think about each individual work as part of the large body of his writing.

For all this stress on the dangers of trying to read L. through the "big four" novels, it remains likely that these will remain an early port of call for many readers. *Sons and Lovers* is an intense depiction of family, class, and early sexual relationships. The close relationship between L.'s early life and the experiences of the main protagonist Paul Morel has led to discussions of the need to treat it as a novel, rather than AUTOBIOGRAPHY, though without losing what L.'s adaption of the material from life tells us about the workings of his creative process and ideas. The experience of Paul's brother, William, provides an example of excessive mother-love leaving the adult unable to handle sexual relationships: William dies young. Paul avoids repeating his brother's experience, though this looks to be a possible outcome of his first relationship, with Miriam: eventually, though, he finds a rounded (if short-lived) relationship with Clara. It is his mother who dies, seeing her son moving away from her. As this schematic account suggests, psychoanalytic critics have found much of interest in *Sons and Lovers*. However, though the text presents the strong feeling for the mother powerfully, perhaps its major achievement is that it keeps conflicting interpretations in suspension. That quality is also seen in the novel's attitude toward Paul's father; though generally condemnatory, and taking Mrs. Morel's side in the account of their unhappy marriage, it provides enough evidence for a counterposition, that here is a man at home in his work and community. Other major themes in the novel include the representation of the working-class life of miners and its description of dawning sexuality for both sexes. However, it has also been noted that the novel rejects the working-class world of the father and that there are problems with the novel's attitudes toward gender, particularly in "The Test on Miriam" chapter, which is disturbing in its account of Paul's ruthless efforts to assess Miriam's sexual compatibility.

L.'s two novels based on the Brangwen family, *The Rainbow* and *Women in Love,* are perhaps his most successful. They are an effort to think about how a good modern relationship could be formed—with, behind them, the contention that such relationships were the very building blocks of a newly reborn society. L. felt that first it was necessary to go back to discuss how the then current state of society came into being. To do this, he depicts what some critics have identified as a myth of an organic, preindustrial rural community around the Brangwen farm. The coming of the canals and railways in the mid-19th c. starts to write itself on the landscape and on the subjectivities of the inhabitants. *The Rainbow* offers the comparison between three generations of marriages. That between Tom Brangwen and Lydia Lensky shows how economic change, the possibilities of travel, and the new European politics (her first husband was a Polish nationalist) alter the supposedly age-old order of relationships between the sexes. Though not unhappy, a level of distance persists between the partners. The relationship between Lydia's daughter from her first marriage, Anna, and Will Brangwen, Tom's nephew, shows the extent of the damage industrialization has wreaked on sexual relationships. The novel charts the ebb and flow of feeling in relationships, and offers ways of comparing the different generations, by using symbolic scenes that attempt to capture the underlying situation. The last part of the novel addresses the maturation of Will and Anna's daughter, Ursula, and her first, failed, relationship with the soldier Anton Skrebensky. Other themes in the book, as well as this attentiveness to modernization, sexuality, and gender include religious faith (the very language of the text echoes that of the Authorized Version of the Bible), childhood, teaching, and education.

The Rainbow leaves Ursula, after the end of her relationship with Skrebensky and a breakdown, on the edge of realizing a more successful relationship. The school inspector Birkin is introduced in *Women in Love,* and she eventually marries him. The relationship of Ursula's sister, Gudrun, and the son of the local mine owner, Gerald, provides the comparison. Though *Women in Love* can be seen as a sequel to *The Rainbow,* it is written in a very different way, with short, hard-edged chapters. Many have seen it as the most formally modernist text L. produced. With the chapters based in London and through the character of Loerke, it comments on art and the artist life as part of its narrative. The novel uses a language of dissolution and decay, which it sees as characteristic of the modern world and as a necessary precursor to renewal into a new and active life. Birkin and Ursula move toward a better future, but Gerald's journey is toward death, effectively realized in the icy conditions of the Alps in the novel's closing chapter.

L.'s last novel, *Lady Chatterley's Lover,* sees him returning to the English Midlands. It deals with a period of renewal in the lives of Mellors and Connie Chatterley. Mellors's previous relationships and life experience have left him embittered and isolated, working as a gamekeeper to the Chatterleys. Connie experiences an escape from her dead marriage and a sexual awakening with her husband's servant. The text had begun as a shorter text about cross-class relationships (two earlier versions of the novel survive

and have been published), but the opportunity to print and distribute the work privately from Florence meant that L. could develop a direct and frank language for describing the sexual encounters. The success of the sex scenes in the novel, with their use of a direct, Anglo-Saxon vocabulary, has been much debated by critics interested in issues in sexuality and gender. Some argue that it broke new ground and that it is not L.'s fault that he has been badly imitated. Others feel that it reasserts male attitudes toward sexual relationships. The novel's harsh treatment of the new generation of miners has also provoked criticism, as has the depiction of Clifford Chatterley's disability, which is used to represent masculine weakness and modern sterility. Through Clifford, L. attacks new forms of mechanization, attitudes to the arts (when Clifford becomes a successful popular writer) and new media, in particular the deadening effects of radio.

But the main point needs to be restated: while looking individually at the "big four" novels of L. offers many rewards, modern L. criticism has received a new lease on life from historically aware work that sees his texts—in all genres—as a remarkable series of responses to the world around him.

BIBLIOGRAPHY: Bell, M., *D. H. L.: Language and Being* (1992); Clarke, C., *River of Dissolution: D. H. L. and English Romanticism* (1969); Draper, R. P., ed., *D. H. L.: The Critical Heritage* (1970); Ellis, D., *D. H. L.: Dying Game, 1922–1930* (1998); Fernihough, A., *D. H. L.: Aesthetics and Ideology* (1993); Holderness, G., *D. H. L.: History, Ideology, and Fiction* (1982); Kinkead-Weekes, M., *D. H. L.: Triumph to Exile, 1912–22* (1996); Leavis, F. R., *D. H. L.: Novelist* (1955); Macleod, S., *Lawrence's Men and Women* (1985); Pinkney, T., *D. H. L.* (1990); Worthen, J., *D. H. L.: The Early Years, 1885–1912* (1991)

HOWARD J. BOOTH

LAYAMON [also Laȝmon or Lawman]
fl. late 12th to early or mid-13th c.

A priest in the village of Ernley, now Areley Kings, in Worcestershire, L. composed one known work, a legendary history of Britain now known as L.'s *Brut* (wr. ca. 1205), an alliterative poem of 16,095 lines. The preeminent work of the early MIDDLE ENGLISH period, the *Brut* is the first major narrative poem in Middle English literature and best known as the first account of King Arthur in the English language.

L. begins his history narrating the travels of Brutus and his followers, Trojans who escaped the fall of Troy. Far from home, they eventually arrive at an island unknown to humankind, take possession by defeating the giants dwelling there, and declare Brutus the ruler of their new nation, Brutland (Britain). There follow the stories of all the succeeding rulers, including Lear and Cymbeline (whose stories L. also records in English for the first time), Vortigern, Uther, and Arthur, through the death of Cadwallader in 689, the last of the British kings, and the conversion of the now-triumphant Anglo-Saxons to Christianity. L. appears to have structured this long poem into episodes, each short enough for an evening's reading.

In writing the *Brut,* L. freely translated and significantly altered his main source, Robert Wace's Anglo-Norman French poem, *Roman de Brut* (or *Geste des Bretons*), completed in 1155, which in turn translates and expands upon GEOFFREY OF MONMOUTH's influential Latin prose chronicle *Historia Regum Brittaniae.* In his many deletions from and additions to Wace, L. significantly changes the tone and nature of this traditional narrative, making it more closely resemble fiction. He omits, for example, courtly elements and military terminology. L. adds many dramatic speeches and entire scenes to Wace's narrative, illuminating events with figurative language and revealing detail, all in energetic, sonorous language. He makes creative use of the traditional phrases of alliterative poetry, employing them (for example) figuratively or ironically. He gives particular attention to scenes of pathos, betrayal, and individual heroism, to the magical and miraculous, transforming the story of the ancient Britons into a stern but wondrous moral chronicle that reveals the working of God and the Devil in history.

L. composed his poem using a remarkably free variety of the English alliterative line, quite different from the two better known alliterative meters, the OLD ENGLISH verse used in *BEOWULF* and the later Middle English alliterative verse used in *Sir Gawain and the Green Knight.* As in those other meters, L.'s basic metrical unit is the half-line, and these half-lines are typically linked by alliteration on the stressed syllables. But L. uses alliteration in every possible pattern, including many not permitted in the other meters. In this respect and others, L.'s verse more closely resembles the rhythmic, alliterative prose ÆLFRIC used in his Old English sermons. But in L.'s meter, rhyme appears frequently in the final syllables of the two half-lines and is also used to unite the line, in addition to or instead of alliteration.

The *Brut* is preserved in two manuscripts, Caligula A. IX and Otho C. XIII, made in the mid-13th c. and later part of the famous manuscript collection of the 17th-c. antiquarian Robert Cotton. Both are now in the British Library. Scholars usually refer to the version in the Caligula manuscript, which is complete and reproduces the original text more accurately. The Otho manuscript, which contains an extensively revised abridgement of the poem, was seriously damaged by fire in 1731.

All we know about L.'s life we learn from his preface to the *Brut,* and the two manuscripts give us different versions of his career. While Caligula indicates that he was a village priest, Otho says that he lived with (and therefore served) a knight in the village, perhaps as a household chaplain. It is not known which of these statements is accurate or whether L. held both positions, successively or simultaneously. Nor can we date the poem precisely: evidence within the work indicates only that L. composed it in the last years of the 12th c. at the earliest, or sometime during the first half of the 13th c. The antique language of the Caligula version misled scholars in early attempts to estimate the poem's date of composition; some scholars now believe that L. deliberately composed his history in an archaic style. This theory raises questions—for example, what readers would have recognized and appreciated such a style?—that have not yet been fully answered.

In the Caligula manuscript, the author's name is spelled Laʒamon, using the now discarded letter *yogh.* Today, his name is best known in the U.S. by the inaccurate modernization Layamon; Lawman is the more correct modern spelling.

BIBLIOGRAPHY: Allen, R., ed. and trans., *Lawman: Brut* (1992); Barron, W. R. J., and S. C. Weinberg, eds. and trans., *Layamon: Brut* (1995); Donahue, D. P., *L.'s Brut, an Early Arthurian Poem: A Study of Middle English Formulaic Composition* (1991); Le Saux, F. H. M., *L.'s Brut: The Poem and Its Sources* (1989)

S. K. BREHE

LEAR, Edward
b. 12 May 1812, London; d. 29 January 1888, San Remo, Italy

L. was a painter and a poet. Most of his poems, of which a few snatches, if not whole poems, are still known by heart by a great many people, are to the unimaginative what is usually called "nonsense." But it is not the sort of dangerous and pernicious nonsense uttered daily by presidents and prime ministers; rather, it is a kind of divine "non-sense" that reaches beneath and beyond conventional cliché and reflects the essential illogic of all human experience. Reviewing a recent new edition of L.'s poems—*The Complete Verse and Other Nonsense* (2001), edited by Vivien Noakes—Christopher REID says in the *Times Literary Supplement* (December 21, 2001): "The rules of nonsense writing are severe, in that they demand the finest negotiation between readability and mysteriousness. L.'s mastery resides in his being at the same time, and in equal measure, charming and unknowable."

L.'s drawings reflect the same nonsense-logic as his writing and are so at one with the poems as to make themselves part of the poems: neither should ever be printed without the other; they are artistically inseparable. On the other hand, one must remember that L. was also, in another department of his artistry, so to speak, a gifted and accomplished landscape painter in a more conventional "no-nonsense" style, as well as an expert draughtsman producing, throughout his long career, exquisite drawings of plants, flowers, and birds (especially parrots) in a no-nonsense mode, as well as a few flowering plants in a very distinctly nonsense mode (such as the *Tigerlillia Terribilis* and the *Nasticreechia Krorluppia*).

L.'s first "nonsense" publication was *A Book of Nonsense* (1845), which he had written, originally, for the entertainment of the grandchildren of the Earl of Derby. It consisted of a hundred and seven examples of that five-lined verse that we now call the "limerick" (though L. did not know it by that name). L. did not invent this rhythmic form: the first known examples of it appear in the anonymous *The History of Sixteen Wonderful Old Women* (1820); but L., with his ingenious use of it and his wittily melancholic drawings, was certainly the author who popularized the limerick and put it on the literary map. (The origin of the name "limerick" is, incidentally, unknown. There have been several ingenious guesses, but no certainty: the name, for example, cannot be shown to connect with the Irish town of Limerick.)

A Book of Nonsense went through several editions in the 1860s and was then followed in 1870 by *Nonsense Songs, Stories, Botany and Alphabets*. This one contained no limericks, but a lot of other delicious nonsense, including the immortal "The Owl and the Pussycat" and the Jumblies. In 1872 came *More Nonsense Pictures, Rhymes, Botany, Etc.*, which has one hundred more limericks, each one—as before—with a splendidly witty colored drawing: "There was an Old Person of Ware/Who rode on the back of a bear;/ When they asked 'Does it trot?'/He said 'Certainly not!'/He's a Moppsikon Floppsikon bear!" The expression on the face of the bear is a little work of art in itself: and note the logic absolute of his reply to the question from "they," that sinister, omniscient, ubiquitous, lurking "they" who appear in so many of L.'s limericks, always intent, in their mean insinuating way, upon demonstrating the superiority of the literal, the mediocre, the average, to the eccentric, the individual, the nonconformist.

L.'s two final books of nonsense, *Laughable Lyrics: A Fourth Book of Nonsense Poems, Songs, Botany, Music, Etc.* (1877) and *Nonsense Songs and Stories* (1895), contain no further limericks but do contain some of his greatest poems and his finest imaginative creations: here are the Dong with the Luminous Nose, the Yonghy-Bonghy-Bo, the Pobble (who had no toes), the Akond of Swat, and Aged Uncle Arly (sitting on a heap of barley).

The names of L.'s far, romantic places are fascinating: they hover, as is proper for poetry, between factual, actual geography and the magic countries of the mind (as also do, for instance, W. B. YEATS's Byzantium and James Elroy FLECKER's Samarkand). The Coast of Coromandel (where the early pumpkins blow) is, as we say, "real"—though one still needs to enquire whether it is the one in southern India or the one in New Zealand. But the Great Gromboolian Plain and the Chankly Bore—the haunts of the Dong—are not "real": they exist only in the landscape of fantasy. But in the persuasive rhythms and locutions of L.'s poems, Coromandel and Chankly Bore and Gromboolian Plain are all equally believable and equally authentic: they seem to be perfectly natural companions. L.'s poems, in fact, though based on acute observation of the phenomena of natural objects around him (remember that he was a great traveler, especially in the Near and Middle East), come ultimately from the poet's sense of the inner nature of life, the nature that is ongoing, permanent, underlying all human responses, the product of a process that William SHAKESPEARE has the Duke Theseus describe in act 5 of *A Midsummer Night's Dream*: "And as imagination bodies forth/The forms of things unknown, the poet's pen/Turns them to shapes and gives to airy nothing/A local habitation and a name."

L.'s "shapes" are deliciously, vividly unusual, quite out of the ordinary, and all the more captivating for that. This, from a man who, though he had many distinguished friends, spent much of his time alone, a solitary: perhaps he was thinking at least partly of himself when he began one of his limericks: "There was an Old Person of Bow/Whom nobody happened to know."

BIBLIOGRAPHY: Davidson, A., ed., *E. L., Landscape Painter and Nonsense Poet* (1938); Levi, P., *E. L.* (1995); Noakes, V., *E. L.* (1968); Noakes, V., ed., *E. L.: Selected Letters* (1988)

ERIC SALMON

LEAVIS, F[rank] R[aymond]

b. 14 July 1895, Cambridge; d. 14 April 1978, Cambridge

L. served during World War I on ambulance trains in France. He later said that the early poems of T. S. ELIOT helped him keep going: they were personal, intimate, un-Victorian or Edwardian, sensitive to "the subtleties of living speech." Eliot's poetry subsequently became his touchstone for authenticity in writing, as against rhetoric. L. became reader-as-propagator, promoting his "lifeline" authors by explication and analysis, and detecting the creative possibilities they opened up. He moved, when Cambridge student and teacher, from being appreciator to critic, a discriminator of what was growing in the present and what was modern in the past, which he believed had in the 1920s to be reviewed with post-Eliot spectacles. "If Eliot is our author," he said by implication, "how do Pope, Keats or Tennyson fare now?"

The young L. had something piratical about him (as did the older one). It is ironical that he was so frequently called "Dr. Leavis," as if he were a scholarly authoritarian. Actually, he cared little for the academic deferences, the respect for "field" and "work done." But there were three ways in which L. truly belonged to the university, even if it was the idea of one, the university in his head, lovingly described in *Education and the University* (1943) with hopes for postwar reform.

First, L. was initially educated at Cambridge as an historian. He became fascinated with the interlocking elements that made up a total culture. He was one of the first British commentators who related literature to its cultural conditions, and did so qualitatively, believing that some cultural conditions were inimical to liveliness of thought and experience. He was therefore an enemy of liberalism, especially that of the BLOOMS-BURY GROUP, which said that the best would find it. L. thought the best was stifled by cultural mass production. He defined a field of study that became an academic discipline.

Secondly, L. was very much the teacher. Even if he was sometimes more of a performer (criticism has to be performed) than listener, he did have earnest concern for the individual experience of the student, his or her capacity for response (rather than applied conceptualizing), and for the conditions under which students studied—for instance, the lack of time for the huge subject of literature, a shortage that meant they should have been and wanted to be trained in prioritizing, some cynically for cynical reasons, but many idealistically because they wanted to know what really mattered. L. liked to quote Robert GRAVES's account of being reproved by an Oxford tutor: "It seems, Mr. Graves, that you prefer some books to others."

Thirdly, L. was, indeed, a special "Doctor." He took one of the first English literature doctorates by thesis in the Cambridge system. It had been thought odd for a literary academic to have a scientific-sounding degree. But L. was one of the new professionals. He believed that something like "scientific" research was just what was needed in studies of literature and society, the studies that (he never hesitated to say polemically) belonged to the modern age and had to replace the genteel aestheticism, the belle-lettrism, first of Edwardian culture and later Bloomsbury sensibility. This approach was attractive to young literary intellectuals in the 1920s and 1930s, not least those who went to Cambridge from overseas (Sri Lanka, New Zealand) and wanted models of analysis of culture and society in their home environments. There was as

yet no Raymond WILLIAMS (and when he came, he could not match the vivacity of L.'s taste).

However, one way in which L. was not attuned to the university was his love of journalism—strange to say, it may seem, in view of his famous contempt for the "Metropolitan Literary World," for mutually amiable reviewing that he sardonically dismissed as "log rolling." But L.'s medium of preference was the essay rather than the book (paradoxically like the belle-lettrist) and especially the review rather than the "study." The journal is the natural home of the review. L.'s *Scrutiny: A Quarterly Review* ran from 1932 to 1953 and virtually all L.'s best work to the terminal year appeared in it, as did much good (and some obsequious) work from allies and pupils. Scrutiny of what?—not only English literature and not only "scrutiny" as close reading, called then "practical criticism." L. believed that English was a crossroads subject, a point at which multiple concerns intersected, so he wanted a wide-ranging journal. Some of the time he got it, and overall the results were exhilarating, rewarded by popularity (especially in war time, when people wanted to know what was worth reading) and such tributes as Eric Bentley's American selection from its contents, *The Importance of Scrutiny* (1948), and, posthumously, the publication of the total run of issues by Cambridge University Press in 1963. The pace of production was grueling, but quarterly publication suited the temperament of one for whom spontaneity of response was paramount, who relished immediacy of connection between text and reader, without the intervention of explanatory soft furnishings. Every three months, it suited L. to be direct—or, they said, "aggressive." Many of L.'s *Scrutiny* essays and reviews were collected in *The Common Pursuit* (1952).

For one temperamentally tuned to the spontaneous, poetry was an important medium and poetry or poetics was actually his central subject—another paradox considering his interest in the qualitative analysis of culture and society. It is sometimes assumed that his concern was primarily with the novel, with "concrete realism" and "moral seriousness." Both concepts mattered to L., and both were idiosyncratically interpreted: for him, moral seriousness did not mean ethical dogma, but a commitment to emotional observation and discrimination; he believed, following Henry JAMES, that "moral sense" in artistic practice depended on "the amount of 'felt life' concerned in producing it." And REALISM for him was not photographic, but a prose alert to presence, a prose that edges toward poetry. So the group of books that seemed to be about prose fiction was really about a species of poetry. *The Great Tradition: George Eliot, Henry James, Joseph Conrad* (1948) and *D. H. Lawrence, Novelist* (1955) were made out of essays originally published under the head "The Novel as Dramatic Poem" and *Dickens the Novelist* (1970) found wiry affinities between Charles DICKENS and William BLAKE. It was written jointly with Q. D. LEAVIS, who also wrote significantly in *Scrutiny* on Jane AUSTEN, the other member of the "great tradition." L. would admire novels for "Shakespearean" qualities, as analyzed in his essays on *Measure for Measure, Othello,* in passing on *Macbeth,* and the late plays.

So L.'s writing on fiction was not the departure it appeared. The concepts of "Shakespeare" and "dramatic poem" were carried forward from *New Bearings in English Poetry* (1932), which showed the contemporary constellation irradiated by Eliot, and *Revaluation: Tradition and Development in English Poetry* (1936), which reviewed the English traditions in poetry with modernist reprioritizing—Percy Bysshe SHELLEY, for instance, was relegated, as was Alexander POPE in elegant vein, while the metaphysical Pope was critically fortified.

In the 1960s, L. continued to write and lecture, often polemically (on C. P. SNOW), and more philosophically ambitious than hitherto. He never let up his desire to meditate in print on D. H. LAWRENCE and Eliot. He became preoccupied with some non-British authors (Eugenio Montale and Leo Tolstoy). His prime, his time of political effect on the humanities agenda was long: say, from 1930 to 1960.

In his time, L. was valued because he promoted self-reliant reading, which excited educators (including self-educators). His scope and firmness of judgment were appreciated in the U.S. by such diverse scholars and critics as Donald Greene, Lionel Trilling, and Marius Bewley. But his decisiveness fell out of favor in Britain. He was perceived to be restrictive, establishing an honor roll of writers, a "canon." The *Critical Quarterly* complained that he "blamed Snowdon for not being Everest." In the 1970s, Continental structuralism arrived in the British academy, as did fresh concerns for the politics of race, gender, and colonialism, both trends overriding L.'s desire to analyze and judge texts on their own terms and in relation to modern poetics. The evaluative close reading fell out of fashion. The very phrase "literary criticism" became academically tainted as journalistic or subjective, and literary theory held sway, especially when the concept of the "death of the author" gained ascendancy, contesting the Leavisian focus on individual writers. After the expansion of higher education in the 1960s, the universities gained: there were more English departments, more academics, more specialisms, and therefore a pluralism that contradicted the intensity of L.'s belief in discrimination. The post-L. world was not one of sensibility, nor of hierarchies of value that came to be understood to be constructed rather than created. L. had never been happy with the avant-garde (the James JOYCE not the Lawrence tradition). The Leavisian oeuvre seemed out of touch in an

academy in which the concept of oeuvre had evaporated.

However, from the start L. sowed seeds that rooted miles from their source. The bibliographer D. F. McKenzie confessed that he became interested in textual detail by means of L.'s analyses, especially his widely circulated analysis study sheets. The theater director Peter Hall believed "he had more influence on the contemporary theater than any other critic." The film critic Robin Wood said he could not have written without L. Teaching method always interested L.: he despised what he called "stand-and-deliver" examinations (the three-hour examinations), favoring assessment of student work by essay or dissertation. This practice became common. L. had always admired "Life, Literature, and Thought" courses on the Cambridge model that enabled literature to be studied as one among many cultural artifacts (paradoxically at odds with L.'s passion for the specific text). That such courses became standard practice in the late-20th-c. British humanities curriculum owes something to L.

L. said in *The Great Tradition* that the best way to promote profitable discussion is "to be as clear with oneself about what one sees and judges, to try and establish the essential discriminations in any given field of interest and state them as clearly as one can (for disagreement, if necessary)." He did this in a style both responsive to nuance and mordantly clear. And the sheer cheek of his asides is still oxygenating ("It is tempting to retort there is only one Brontë."). The persistence of reference to L., sometimes ruefully, in the early 21st c. shows the longevity of his passionate individualism. There were attempts at revaluation of his work in the 1990s, notably by Gary Day. There continue to be literary critics, such as Terry Eagleton and Christopher Ricks, who respect L.: though ostensibly different, their concerns for the aesthetic, their possession of a pragmatically wide range of concern and their distaste for relativism, echo his work.

BIBLIOGRAPHY: Bell, M., *F. R. L.* (1988); Day, G., *Re-Reading L.: Culture and Literary Criticism* (1996); MacKillop, I., *F. R. L.* (1995); Samson, A., *F. R. L.* (1992); Singh, G., *F. R. L.* (1995)

IAN MacKILLOP

LEAVIS, Q[ueenie] D[orothy]

b. 7 December 1906, London; d. 17 March 1981, Cambridge

In his lifetime, F. R. LEAVIS was often known as "Dr. Leavis," the title supposedly highlighting his austerity. His wife and long-term aide was also, of course, "Dr. Leavis," like him one of the early bearers of the title from the Cambridge English faculty, and herself a dynamic literary critic.

L. was born into a Jewish London family, proceeding to brilliant achievements at Cambridge where her marriage to the gentile Leavis in 1929 alienated her from her family. He encouraged her doctoral work, on the sociology of the novel, a highly original investigation, pioneering the use of questionnaires in the new field of literary cultural studies. (One was completed by Edgar Rice Burroughs, creator of "Tarzan.") Her thesis was assessed by E. M FORSTER and published to acclaim as *Fiction and the Reading Public* (1932). Its thesis subtitle had been "A Study in Social Anthropology," appropriately because L. used popular and classic fiction as data to analyze successive English cultures after the Elizabethan period, inspired by the historical sociology of H. M. Chadwick's "Early Literature and History" course at Cambridge in which the artifacts of ancient societies were used to detail pictures of cultural identity. L. did not shrink from evaluating her data, believing that methods of mass publication leveled down the taste of the English reading public in the modern era. Her subsequent publications were fiercely critical of the second-rate. In 1932, her husband became editor of *Scrutiny,* published quarterly until 1953. L. worked indefatigably at editorial business, but also made nearly fifty contributions, on fiction and the sociology of the literary world, or the "literary racket"—as she once called it.

Her taste was eclectic, with a love for the classics as well as the best in popular writing: she read Damon Runyon to her children and repeatedly sent secondhand copies of Randall Jarrell's *Pictures from an Institution* (1954) to friends and pupils. She disliked the BLOOMSBURY GROUP and Virginia WOOLF's belief that a woman must have "a room of one's own." L. thought the management of a busy household was not inherently decreative, a belief that restricted her own career as an academic, as did the scant employment opportunities in Cambridge, her commitment to *Scrutiny* and her husband's work, her role as a mother (she had three children), and her frequent illnesses. Her decisive, scholarly, and vivid writing gained in reputation, especially her wartime essays on Jane AUSTEN. When her husband delineated a definitive line of English novelists in *The Great Tradition,* he considered that his wife's work made it unnecessary to include a chapter on Austen. In the 1960s, she taught English literature at several Cambridge colleges. She visited Harvard with her husband, which resulted in an important essay on Emily BRONTË in their joint book *Lectures in America* (1969). Another collaboration, *Dickens the Novelist* (1970), followed.

Her husband died in 1978. As a widow, L. began work on a memoir of her husband, and lectured widely in schools and universities on novelists in the English and other traditions. Her last lecture, for the Cheltenham Festival of 1980, was on "The Englishness of the English Novel." She knew well the work of Alexsander Solzhenitsyn, on whom she was preparing in her last weeks to lecture. L. was an important critic of the novel, English, American, and European, on which three posthumous volumes of essays were published. Personally, she was vivacious, even domineering. She had a strong visual sense, for clothes, house decoration, and book illustration.

BIBLIOGRAPHY: Kinch, M. B., *Q. D. L., 1906–1981* (1982); Robertson, P. J. M., *The Leavises on Fiction* (1981); Thompson, D., ed., *The Leavises: Recollections and Impressions* (1984)

IAN MacKILLOP

LE CARRÉ, John
(pseud. of David John Moore Cornwell) b. 19 October 1931, Poole, Dorset

The most respected British spy novelist of the 20th c., L. uses espionage as a metaphor to examine themes of widespread betrayal and corruption in contemporary life. L. has called the spy novel "the collective couch where the subconscious of each nation is confessed," and raised the status of the genre, pitting his gritty authenticity against what he saw as unrealistic glamor and caricature used by writers like Ian FLEMING. While he enjoys popular success, L.'s complexity has also been compared favorably to that of Joseph CONRAD. Writing under the pseudonym John le Carré because of the necessity, as a Foreign Office employee, to disguise his spy-novelist identity, L. became the foremost British novelist of the Cold War, promoting obsessive awareness of double agents, or "moles" (a term he popularized). Hallmarks of L.'s style are colorful dialogue and minute analysis of intelligence casework. The actual aims of espionage operations are often vague or secondary; primary are bonds between characters and attention to investigative detail.

L.'s father, a charming but manipulative con artist who fronted dozens of nonexistent businesses, provided the model for one of L.'s most memorable characters, Rick Pym in *A Perfect Spy* (1986). L.'s mother left the family; he did not meet her again until he was an adult. Family is a source of pain in nearly all of L.'s novels. Mothers are distant and marriage usually disastrous. Like Magnus Pym in *A Perfect Spy,* L. went to Europe in his teens, studied languages at the University of Berne, and did army intelligence work in postwar Vienna. In the 1950s, he took a first in modern languages at Oxford. In the early 1960s, he joined the Foreign Office, serving in Bonn. The extent to which the Foreign Office provided cover for intelligence work has been much debated, but L. has admitted to some spying.

His first two novels, *Call for the Dead* (1961; repub. as *The Deadly Affair*, 1964) and *A Murder of Quality* (1962), were murder mysteries rather than espionage thrillers. They do introduce L.'s most famous spy, George Smiley, who appears in eight novels. Smiley's character is completely realized on the first page of *Call for the Dead:* he is short, fat, shy, and repeatedly compared to a toad. Described as "breathtakingly ordinary" by his incongruous wife, the beautiful Lady Ann, Smiley stands in opposition to the heroic stereotype of the spy. Like his creator, Smiley is a first-rate linguist with a particular interest in German culture and literature.

Smiley has a minor role in *The Spy Who Came In from the Cold* (1963), L.'s first secret service story and most influential novel. Alec Leamas, a British agent, is sent on one last mission before retiring, or "coming in from the cold." Control, head of the Circus (L.'s name for the British Intelligence Service), uses Leamas as a mock defector to East Germany. Leamas is unaware that Control's actual aim is to protect a double agent, the brutal Mundt, highly placed in the East German spy service. Leamas and his lover are shot at the symbolic Berlin Wall, site of several of L.'s most vivid scenes, while Smiley looks on helplessly.

Although bleak and labyrinthine, *The Spy Who Came In from the Cold* was an enormous critical and popular success and L. left the Foreign Office to write full time. The two spy novels that follow, *The Looking-Glass War* (1965) and *A Small Town in Germany* (1968), display an increasing pessimism about both political and personal ethics. They were less successful, and in 1971 L. published an experimental novel about an unorthodox romantic triangle, *The Naive and Sentimental Lover,* leaving the thriller genre and showing instead the influence of James JOYCE. Much of the response was negative, and his next book returned to the character of George Smiley.

The ambitious style of *The Naive and Sentimental Lover* did influence the books that followed. The three novels in *The Quest for Karla* trilogy are leisurely and expansive, and *Tinker, Tailor, Soldier, Spy* (1974) and *Smiley's People* (1980) are considered among L.'s best. In *Tinker, Tailor, Soldier, Spy*, Smiley traces a mole at the Circus's highest level who has been passing information to Moscow Center, the Soviet Union spy service. Working against elements in the British establishment that would rather not reveal the depth of the treachery, Smiley unmasks the Circus's second-in-command, charismatic aristocrat Bill Haydon. Haydon's treachery is at two levels: he seduces Smiley's wife, the chronically unfaithful Ann, at the same time as he destroys government faith in the Circus's entire network. The reputation of the trilogy's middle book, *The Honourable Schoolboy* (1977), has not fared well. It was one of L.'s first novels set outside Europe and seems too thoroughly researched; details about southeast Asian war zones become overwhelming. In the last two books of the trilogy, Smiley's compassion diminishes as he determines to bring down a Moscow Center chief known only as Karla. A doppelganger for Smiley, Karla obsesses him as Kurtz haunts Marlow in Conrad's "Heart of Darkness."

The Little Drummer Girl (1983) is L.'s first novel with a female protagonist and its focus is the Middle East. Charlie, an English actress, is used by the Israelis to infiltrate a Palestinian guerilla group. In one of L.'s most acute examinations of double loyalties, Charlie is encouraged by her Israeli controllers to use her immense capacity for affection to bind her to both sides in the conflict. The scrutiny of doubleness is most intense in *A Perfect Spy*. Magnus Pym spies both for the British and the Czechs and dreads discovery of the self-loathing and emptiness at his core. As the son of a confidence trickster, Pym assumes that any lie is acceptable in his quest to charm and please others. *A Perfect Spy* contains some of L.'s most effective comic writing. Its memorable, eccentric characters suggest the influence of Charles DICKENS.

The Russia House (1989) and *The Secret Pilgrim* (1991) finish the cycle of Circus novels. The former offers a relatively friendly look at post–Cold War Russia, its military capabilities a shambles. The latter is Smiley's farewell, offering anecdotes about past cases. With *The Night Manager* (1993), L. entered a new arena. His novels from this time concentrate less on politics than on destructive economic power. The villain in *The Night Manager* is a British businessman who deals arms and drugs. In *Our Game* (1995), former British spies enlist in the Quixotic effort to help a tiny Islamic nation in the Caucasus trampled underfoot by the great powers. *The Tailor of Panama* (1996) is a parodic spy story about corrupt or deluded men fabricating intelligence for personal gain.

"The mere fact that communism doesn't work doesn't mean that capitalism does," L. said in the 1990s, and he now reserves special reproach for "bent Brits." *Single and Single* (1999) returns to the theme of dishonest father and damaged son. The father is Tiger Single, head of an immoral British bank laundering money for international criminals. *The Constant Gardener* (2001) is a stinging indictment of Western indolence in the face of third world suffering. L., who has said that a "sense of colonial guilt" lingers over his writing, targets a pharmaceutical industry greedy for profits and careless of human life. The novel's hero, Tessa Quayle, is L.'s first convincing feminist character. The novels after the cathartic *A Perfect Spy* are less ambiguous, less cynical about women, love, and family, and correspondingly exacting in their censure of what L. has called "crimes of unbridled capitalism" in the public sphere.

BIBLIOGRAPHY: Barley, T., *Taking Sides: The Fiction of J. L.* (1986); Beene, L., *J. L.* (1992); Bloom, H., ed., *J. L.* (1987); Cobbs, J. L., *Understanding J. L.* (1998); Lewis, P., *J. L.* (1985); Monaghan, D., *The Novels of J. L.* (1985)

SUE SORENSEN

LEE, Laurie

b. 26 June 1914, Stroud, Gloucestershire; d. 13 or 14 May 1997, Slad, Gloucestershire

L. is best remembered for his country-childhood memoir *Cider with Rosie* (1959; repub. as *The Edge of Day*, 1960): less a straightforward AUTOBIOGRAPHY than a series of essays on the author's upbringing and early memories in a Cotswold village in the 1920s; "that generation which saw, by chance, the end of a thousand years' life." Observably the work of a poet (L. had previously published three collections of sensuous poems of the natural world in the 1940s and 1950s), the book has a few otiose purple patches; but these tend to be forgotten among the wealth of fascinating atmosphere and reminiscence of life in his oddly extended family—his loving but scatterbrained mother, whose recollections of being in service in great houses in the late 19th c. were among L.'s most formative influences, had been deserted by L.'s father and left to rear her own children along with those of his first marriage; so that L. was reared by a group of half-sisters. In retrospect, it is the anecdotes and memories of village life, and of L.'s first sexual experience, seduced under a harvest cart by a village hoyden with a jug of the beverage that gives the book its title, which stay in the memory.

The successor volume, *As I Walked Out One Midsummer Morning* (1969), a title redolent of traditional English love songs indicating the attitude of quest and adventure with which L. left home to roam, deals equally effectively with his late 1930s wanderings, carrying little but his violin, to London and then around Spain. In 1983, L. published his *Selected Poems* followed in 1991 with *A Moment of War: A Memoir of the Spanish Civil War*.

Late in life, L. put the fame gained by his recollections to use by returning to Slad, the village of his childhood, to become a noted local figure and to campaign vigorously against attempts to alter the local environment that he had loved, and recorded, so well.

BIBLIOGRAPHY: Shires, L. M., "L. L.," in Sherry, V. B., Jr., ed., *Poets of Great Britain and Ireland, 1945–1960, DLB* 27 (1984): 206–9; Tolley, A. T., *The Poetry of the Thirties* (1975)

MICHAEL GROSVENOR MYER

LEE, Nathaniel

b. ca. 1645–52, Hatfield, Hertfordshire, Middlesex, or Walthamstow, Essex; d. 6 May 1692, London

Educated at Charterhouse and Trinity College, Cambridge, L. performed the role of Duncan in Sir Wil-

liam DAVENANT's version of William SHAKESPEARE's *Macbeth* (1673) before beginning his career as playwright. His contract with the King's Players kept him writing for the Drury Lane theater during his early career. His early plays include *The Tragedy of Nero* (perf. 1674; pub. 1975), *Sophonisba* (perf. 1675; pub. 1676), *Gloriana* (1676), and *The Rival Queens* (1677). His friendship with John DRYDEN began in 1677 with his poem "To Mr. Dryden," and Dryden wrote the epilogue for L.'s next play *Mithridates* (1678). That same year, he broke his contract with the King's Players to collaborate with Dryden on *Oedipus* (perf. 1678; pub. 1679), which was played by the Duke's Men at Dorset Garden. This remained the state of affairs during the next four years during which time he wrote *Theodosius* (1680). The two companies merged by 1682 when L. and Dryden wrote *The Duke of Guise* (1683), which was played at Drury Lane, as was his *Constantine the Great* (perf. 1683; pub. 1684) for which Dryden supplied the prologue.

LEE, [Sir] Sidney

b. Solomon Lazarus Lee, 5 December 1859, London; d. 3 March 1926, Kensington

Historian and literary scholar, L. earned a prominent and lasting place in English letters as the editor of the *Dictionary of National Biography* (63 vols., 1885–1901), one of the most ambitious and exacting literary achievements of the late 19th and early 20th cs. Initially hired as an assistant to Sir Leslie STEPHEN and later a coeditor, L. assumed full editorship in 1891 when Stephen's declining health forced his withdrawal from the project. After completing the original edition and the three-volume *Supplement,* L. published a *Second Supplement* (3 vols., 1913) and a concise edition (1920). In addition to his responsibilities with the *DNB,* L. maintained a scholarly interest in William SHAKESPEARE and ELIZABETHAN LITERATURE, publishing numerous critical editions of Shakespeare including his *Complete Works* (20 vols., 1906–8). L. revised several of his own entries that first appeared in the *DNB* into full-length biographies, including lives of Shakespeare (1898; rev. eds., 1904, 1909, 1915), Queen Victoria (1902; rev. eds., 1903, 1904), and King Edward VII (2 vols., 1925–27).

LEE, Sophia

b. 1750, London; d. 13 March 1824, Bristol

A successful dramatist, poet, and novelist, L.'s reputation now rests on *The Recess; or, A Tale of Other Times* (3 vols., 1783–85), a pioneer work hailed as the first fully developed GOTHIC NOVEL and one of the first historical novels in English. A probable influence upon Ann RADCLIFFE and Sir Walter SCOTT, it caused a stir among the contemporary reading public and went through four editions in the 1790s, as well as several translations.

Written for atmosphere rather than historical accuracy, *The Recess* is the story of Matilda and Ellinor, the illegitimate daughters of Mary Queen of Scots. Concealed and reared in the Recess, a subterranean cavern buried under the ruins of St. Vincent's Abbey, they eventually emerge into the world only to form relationships fated to disaster with two of the best-known characters of the Elizabethan era—the Earl of Leicester and the Earl of Essex. When Matilda's identity is discovered after their secret marriage, she and Leicester flee to the Continent, but are caught and Leicester is murdered at midnight before his wife's eyes. Separated from Essex, imprisoned and forced into marriage with Lord Arlington, Ellinor slowly loses her reason. The sisters are reunited after years apart, but their lives end in tragedy and obscurity.

A novel of intense, sustained suspense, the complex plot of *The Recess* is a sequence of rapid, dream-like events, underlined by an atmosphere of continual anxiety and danger. The disorientation is heightened by an innovative modified epistolary technique in which the events are recounted in turn by the sisters, who turn out to have quite different narratives, perspectives and voices.

L.'s sophisticated themes and use of Gothic machinery opened new possibilities for the Gothic RO-MANCE. The novel offers an ambivalent comment on the female quest for identity and experience in a patriarchal world. The womblike space of the Recess represents both safe retreat and nightmare burial. Matilda and Ellinor are indoctrinated to appreciate their retirement, encouraged to remain in "woman's sphere," yet criticized for their narrow understanding. The sisters long for escape but regret it when they do, as they come to understand their vulnerability in an exhilarating but dangerous world.

Also significant is L.'s delving beneath the accepted facts to represent Elizabethan history from a female point of view. While the male characters can choose to bury their sorrows in activities for which they are commemorated, the sisters' lives are a nightmare of passive suffering, as Ellinor slips into insanity and Matilda is continuously imprisoned. Their inevitable disappearance from the pages of history is part of the strange realism of the book.

As a novelist, L. also had limited success with *Warbeck: A Pathetic Tale* (1786), based on Baculard d'Arnaud's *Warbeck* (1774), and *The Life of a Lover* (6 vols., 1804), an autobiographical epistolary narrative that follows Cecilia Rivers's struggle to maintain herself as a governess. L. also contributed three tales to *The Canterbury Tales* (5 vols., 1797–1805), principally authored by her sister, Harriet.

The daughter of actor John Lee, a distinguished member of David GARRICK's company, L. also tried her hand as a playwright. *The Chapter of Accidents* (1780) was a popular and frequently staged comedy, the profits of which enabled L. to establish and head a school for young ladies in Bath. L.'s blank verse tragedy, *Almeyda, Queen of Grenada* (1796), was produced with Charles Kemble as Alonzo and Mrs. Sarah Siddons in the title role. L. also published *A Hermit's Tale* (1787), a tragic ballad set in the time of the crusades.

BIBLIOGRAPHY: Doody, M. A., "Deserts, Ruins and Troubled Waters: Female Dreams in Fiction and the Development of the Gothic Novel," *Genre* 10 (Winter 1977): 529–72; Rogers, K., *Feminism in Eighteenth Century England* (1982)

REBECCA MORGAN

LEE, Vernon

(pseud. of Violet Paget) b. 14 October 1856, Boulogne-sur-Mer, France; d. 13 February 1935, San Gervasio, Italy

Although born an English citizen, L. spent most of her life in Italy, the focus of the majority of her work. A prolific writer whose circle of friends included Henry JAMES and Edith Wharton, L. is best remembered for her essays on Italian culture and her travel sketches, though she wrote novels, a play, numerous tales, BIOGRAPHY, and social commentary.

L.'s first book-length publication, *Studies of the Eighteenth Century in Italy* (1880), drew critical attention for its analysis and appreciation of a previously neglected period in music and literary history. The writings of Walter PATER shaped L.'s aesthetic philosophy; her *Euphorion: Being Studies of the Antique and the Medieval in the Renaissance* (2 vols., 1884) was written at the peak of Pater's influence. *Renaissance Fancies and Studies: Being A Sequel to "Euphorion"* (1895) and *Limbo and Other Essays* (1897) continue L.'s "Pateresque" strain, but she animates his ideas with her ability to bring to life the figures within the art works she describes, as exemplified in "The Love of the Saints" in *Renaissance Fancies and Studies*.

However, the reader will find L. at her most typical and best in her travel sketches on Germany, Italy, France, and Switzerland. Self-educated, L. read widely in geology, geography, zoology, botany, climatology, biology, language, history, magic, comparative religion, and philosophy; the travel sketch, a favorite genre of this period, was the perfect venue for L. to weave her wide but undisciplined knowledge into an imaginative tapestry. A central purpose of her travel writing is to evoke the *genius loci* or spirit of the place, so that L.'s impressionistic travel sketches re-create the mysterious essence of an area, imbuing its physical locale with its past, often embellished by magical or spiritual elements, as in "Holy Week in Tuscany" from *Genius Loci: Notes on Places* (1899).

By contrasting the ornate splendor of the Tuscan churches with the somber solemnity of their peasant congregations, L. captures the atmosphere and the spirit of the season. The best of L.'s sketches are found in *Genius Loci, The Enchanted Woods and Other Essays on the Genius of Places* (1905) and *The Sentimental Traveller: Notes on Places* (1908).

L.'s aesthetic interests never existed in a vacuum; she was deeply engaged in the social issues of her day, including the status of women, economics, politics, psychology, and international relations. These issues dominate her later volumes, including *Peace with Honour: Controversial Notes on the Settlement* (1915), *The Handling of Words and Other Studies in Literary Psychology* (1923), and *Music and Its Lovers, An Empirical Study of Emotional and Imaginative Responses to Music* (1932). However, because she was an amateur lacking formal training, the impact of L.'s nonfiction diminished as the influence of the university-trained expert increased.

L.'s fiction, in contrast, was much more influential during her lifetime as a vehicle for her social philosophy and critiques. Today, her ghost stories, collected by I. Cooper Willis in *Supernatural Tales: Excursions into Fantasy* (1987), will be of most interest to the reader because of the "undercurrents of inherited fears and ecstacies" L. captures beneath the surface. Much of her fiction grew out of her extensive knowledge of Italian culture; in her first novel, *Ottilie: An Eighteenth-Century Idyl* (1883), L. re-creates an historical period and peoples it with believable men and women. When L. turned to contemporary society, as she did in *Miss Brown* (1884), she was unable to sustain the satire she proposed to create; this roman à clef has been described as "a very bad novel." L.'s fiction, on the whole, is not strong; ironically, it is her nonfiction that remains most successful because she employs the techniques of fiction to animate and shape her extensive knowledge.

BIBLIOGRAPHY: Gregory, H., "The Romantic Inventions of V. L.," in his *Spirit of Time and Place* (1973): 100–12; Gunn, P., *Vernon Lee: Violet Paget, 1856–1935* (1964)

JUDITH E. FUNSTON

LE FANU, Joseph Sheridan

b. 28 August 1814, Dublin, Ireland; d. 7 February 1873, Dublin, Ireland

L., the son of a Protestant clergyman in predominantly Roman Catholic Ireland, was distantly related by marriage to the literary Sheridan family. Like many writers, he trained for the bar but opted for the pen instead. His first short story was published by the *Dublin University Magazine* in 1838; this was followed by an eclectic series of tales supposedly told to

an Irish priest, "Father Purcell," and collected in 1880 as *The Purcell Papers,* published in three volumes. Some of the tales introduced themes characteristic of his later work, such as a fascination with decrepit aristocratic clans and, of course, the supernatural; indeed, two of them would later be reworked into novels. From 1840 to 1842, L. occupied himself with journalism as writer, newspaper editor, and proprietor. In 1845, however, L. made his first attempt at novel-writing with *The Cock and Anchor,* an historical novel published in three volumes featuring one of his "aristocratic decline-and-fall" plots—here, through the heir's gambling. This was followed two years later by *The Fortunes of Colonel Torlogh O'Brien,* another historical novel set during the battle of the Boyne. Both books showed a strong interest in the state of Roman Catholic-Protestant relations—understandable given L.'s youthful experiences with sectarianism. Such politically tense religious questions would give way in most of L.'s later fiction to a related but less loaded issue, namely, the hypocrisy of "nominal" Christians. However, L.'s career as a novelist stalled for several years after the unenthusiastic reception accorded to the two novels.

The death of L.'s wife in 1858 (along with the spiritual torments that preceded it) seems partly responsible for L.'s growing interest in "dark" tales of mystery and the supernatural. He purchased the *Dublin University Magazine* in 1861 and, over the next several years, used it as a venue for serializing his own fiction. *The House by the Churchyard* (3 vols., 1863), an historical novel set in a village on the outskirts of Dublin, centers on a murderer's attempt to maintain his new identity after being recognized and blackmailed—a plot L. would recycle later on in *Checkmate* (3 vols., 1871). This was followed by L.'s most indisputably successful novel, *Uncle Silas* (1864), which L. developed from "Passage in the Secret History of an Irish Countess," one of the *Purcell* stories. The plot, constructed with what for L. is unusual tautness, follows the designs of the eponymous Silas Ruthyn on the fortune of his innocent ward and niece, Maud. Far more Gothic than L.'s earlier work, this suspenseful novel also introduces another of L.'s favorite plot devices, the woman confined against her will. Told in the first person, the novel convincingly represents the terrors of a naive young woman harshly brought into contact with passions previously outside of her ken.

Unfortunately, L.'s other novels never repeat his achievement in *Uncle Silas.* The problem is generally one of plot: L. has a habit of multiplying subplots and misplacing the central problems. *Wylder's Hand* (3 vols., 1864) revolves around the mysterious disappearance of Mark Wylder and its consequences for both his fiancée and his immediate relatives. The female characters are strong, the villains unpleasant, and the mystery fairly well kept-up. L. also experiments with narrative form here, alternating back and forth between first- and third-person narrators; that being said, the device feels clumsy and does little to propel the story along. *Guy Deverell* (3 vols., 1865) is a tale of would-be vengeance, stolen deeds, and illicit passion, with the central mystery revolving around a supposedly haunted—and architecturally bizarre— "green room." The characterizations are adequate, especially the sharp-tongued Lady Alice, but the plot decompresses at the end. *The Wyvern Mystery* (3 vols., 1869) comes with some intricate literary-historical baggage. It was expanded from another of the *Purcell* stories, "A Chapter in the History of a Tyrone Family," which had possibly inspired Charlotte BRONTË's *Jane Eyre*. In turn, L. tips his hat to Brontë by offering not only a bigamy plot but also a big, smallpox-scarred, blind "other woman" named Bertha. The lecherous yet somehow kind Squire Harry is one of L.'s better mixed villains. *The Rose and the Key* (3 vols., 1873) features two of L.'s strong female characters: the conflicted villain of the piece, Lady Barbara Vernon, and her daughter Maud. Lady Vernon's seemingly inexplicable passion for a much younger man and her loathing for her daughter drive the narrative, which meanders for the first half of the novel but picks up steam notably in the second. The plot twists are striking, if not always convincingly explained, and L. finds time to work in a bit of social commentary on treatment of the insane. L.'s other novels include *All in the Dark* (2 vols., 1866), *The Tenants of Malory* (3 vols., 1867), *Haunted Lives* (3 vols., 1868), *A Lost Name* (3 vols., 1868), and *Willing to Die* (3 vols., 1873), his last published work.

Not surprisingly, given L.'s difficulties with extended plots, he is at his best when forced to strip down his tales. Many of his best supernatural stories were collected in *In a Glass Darkly* (3 vols., 1872). Like the *Purcell Papers*, the stories in *In a Glass Darkly* are linked by a single narrator; here, it is the German scientist Doctor Hesselius, a student of the supernatural who practices "metaphysical medicine"; the good doctor's pretensions to expertise, however, are treated with some dramatic irony. Appropriately, given the narrator's profession, the stories take on the shape of case studies. "Green Tea," one of the most famous of the group, details a clergyman's increasingly terrifying haunting by a spectral monkey; the haunted man's psychological torments are convincingly delineated, and the story glances at the problem of shaken religious faith. "Mr. Justice Harbottle" touches on a popular subject in supernatural fiction: the "hanging judge" who receives his comeuppance. "Carmilla" is a classic of vampire literature, with oft-noted overtones of lesbian eroticism. L. uses the supernatural here to explore the relationship between sex and death; as the narrator suggests

near the end, the vampire's desire for a particular victim "resembl[es] the passion of love." Both the title character and the eroticism owe much to Samuel Taylor COLERIDGE's unfinished poem on the same subject, *Christabel*.

Although L.'s difficulties with plot construction and the slightness of his later novels place him in the second rank of Victorian writers, he is nevertheless a key figure in the history of Gothic and mystery fiction. His best female characters, like Lady Barbara Vernon, are well individualized and memorable, and he is capable of slyly ironic touches—like the excessively gooey love-talk between the lovers in *The Wyvern Mystery*. And his best supernatural stories pass the strictest test of all: they leave the reader foolhardy enough to read them after dark wishing for the safety of broad daylight.

BIBLIOGRAPHY: Begnal, M. H., *J. S. L.* (1971); McCormack, W. J., *S. L. and Victorian Ireland* (1980); Melada, I., *S. L.* (1987)

MIRIAM ELIZABETH BURSTEIN

LEHMANN, John

b. 2 June 1907, Fieldhead; d. 7 April 1987, London

L. transformed the shape of contemporary English writing almost single-handed when, in the 1930s and 1940s, he published the New Writing series of literary journals. Although his first aim had been to achieve success as a poet, and he was closely linked with many of the thirties poets by friendship and shared outlook, as time went on he came to recognize that it was in his role as editor and publisher that his true creativity lay. He came from a gifted and privileged literary family, brother of Rosamond LEHMANN and of the actress Beatrix Lehmann, and developed his commitment to poetry and his ideas of its future at Cambridge through friendships with Julian Bell and Christopher ISHERWOOD. However, the deciding event of his career was the invitation from Leonard and Virginia WOOLF to become their manager at the Hogarth Press in 1931. There he learned the detail of printing and publishing, and introduced the work of the thirties generation, securing Michael Roberts's pioneering New Signatures collection of poems for the press.

This early and brief association was crucial for L.'s future. In 1936, with encouragement from Isherwood and Ralph Fox, he launched *New Writing*. This was to be a forum for writing that was antifascist (in keeping with L.'s politics of the time) but without *Left Review*'s sectarian agenda, to find space for the long short story and the novella, and to include writers from working-class backgrounds as well as those from abroad. The formula was an instant success, and the early issues of *New Writing* already foreshadowed its future development. Alongside Isherwood's "The Nowaks," V. S. PRITCHETT's "Sense of Humour," W. H. AUDEN's "Lay your sleeping head," and John Cornford's poems from Spain are stories by B. L. Coombes and Ralph Bates, works by Boris Pasternak, Ignazio Silone, André Chamson, and Anna Seghers.

New Writing was soon widely admired for its freshness, commitment, and inclusiveness, but its audience was restricted and it was relatively expensive, running on a tight budget. Through L.'s persistence, it continued to appear with the same high standard until the outbreak of war. The real breakthrough, however, was a quite unexpected one: in 1940, with Allen Lane's encouragement (and a generous paper allowance), L. relaunched the journal, renamed *Penguin New Writing,* as a low-priced paperback. With no concessions in content, and with the same inclusive formula, *Penguin New Writing* reached a mass audience as no English journal of modern literature has done before or since. At its peak, in 1946, its circulation was around 100,000 and, as buyers were encouraged to leave their copies in the Post Office for servicemen to read, its readership was probably much more. From 1946 on, L. added to this success by starting his own publishing imprint, introducing many of his favored writers (William PLOMER, Laurie LEE, Saul Bellow, Jean-Paul Sartre, Nikos Kazantzakis) to English readers, and illustrating his books with the work of rising graphic artists—Elizabeth David's *Mediterranean Food* (1950) with John Minton's illustrations is an enduringly popular example. By the end of the 1940s, *Penguin New Writing*'s circulation was falling, and it ceased publication in 1950. The *London Magazine,* L.'s attempt at a replacement, was always more elitist and never achieved its earlier success.

Although he now had unquestioned status at the center of the English literary world, his own writings rarely gained recognition. His poems, some of which are still anthologized in thirties collections ("We Remember," "The Summer Story"), were often belittled in review even by his friends who found them cut off from experience, tending to rely on an old-fashioned appeal to nature and dynasty. His commitment to poetry continued all his life, finding most interesting expression in the pagan sexual prose-poem "Christ the Hunter" (1964), intended for the radio. At the same time, he wrote and rewrote his autobiography, whose first installment *The Whispering Gallery* (1955) is lucid and evocative, as well as being an important source for the story of thirties writing; a late attempt to retell the story with more sexual explicitness as a novel, *In the Purely Pagan Sense* (1976), was judged a failure both as novel and as confession.

A better appreciation for L.'s gifts as a writer may have to await the publication of the intimate diaries and letters to which he confided his ideas on writing and poetry, his dreams, and his many often unhappy

homosexual passions. Given his current low standing, this may take some time. Yet the seriousness, generosity, and commitment that he brought to the *New Writing* venture, albeit coupled with a naturally autocratic and egocentric disposition, made it possible for a mass audience to share his vision of a literature that transcended class and national boundaries. Fortunate in his moment, he seized his opportunity and created a literary phenomenon.

BIBLIOGRAPHY: Stewart, R., "J. L.," in Beum, R., ed., *Modern British Essayists*, Second Series, *DLB* 100 (1990): 150–59; Tolley, A. T., *J. L.* (1987); Wright, A., *J. L.* (1998)

JEAN RADFORD

LEHMANN, Rosamond [Nina]

b. 3 February 1901, Bourne End, Buckinghamshire; d. 12 March 1990, London

Born into a privileged family, L., for the first eighteen years of her life, had little exposure to the world outside the family estate, Fieldhead, built by her father Rudolph Chambers Lehmann, a writer and for thirty years editor of *Punch*. Rudolph had a school constructed on his property for the exclusive use of his children and a handful of carefully selected other children from good families. Here, L. received her pre-university education. In 1919, she went to Girton College, Cambridge, to which she won a scholarship to study English literature.

L.'s novels so closely follow events in her life that it is difficult in them to separate fact from fiction. In *Dusty Answer* (1927), her first novel, she recounts the exhilaration and newly found independence she experienced in university life, where she first had to face the joys and disappointments of romance. Her next novel, *A Note in Music* (1930), is intensely personal. It details the tribulations and disenchantment of a passionless marriage, much as her marriage to Wogan Philipps was thought to be.

In *Invitation to the Waltz* (1932), as she had done in *Dusty Answer* and later did in *The Ballad and the Source* (1944), L. examines relationships from an adolescent viewpoint. She characterizes her quirky brother John (James in the novel) masterfully, as she does her relationship with her two sisters. She ably presents her material from an adolescent point of view, consistently maintaining an authentic and convincing tone. In many of her novels, L. emphasizes the dynamics of family relationships, their strains, tensions, and rewards.

The last novel of L.'s early period, the years from 1927 until 1936, during which she produced four novels, was *The Weather in the Streets* (1936) in which her protagonist, Olivia Curtis, separated from her husband, is between twenty-five and thirty. The book examines her eight-month affair with a married man, her pregnancy and abortion, and the end of the relationship that leaves Olivia disillusioned and, like Grace Fairfax and Norah MacKay in *A Note in Music,* disenchanted.

L.'s next novel did not appear until 1944, when *The Ballad and the Source* was published, followed two years later by a collection of her stories, *The Gipsy's Baby and Other Stories* (1946). Her play, *No More Music*, produced in 1938, was published the following year. It was not until nine years after *The Ballad and the Source* that L.'s next novel, *The Echoing Grove* (1953), appeared to great acclaim and influenced the subsequent generation of women novelists. Her autobiography, *The Swan in the Evening*, was published in 1967 followed in 1976 by her final novel, *A Sea-Grape Tree.*

A considerable lapse in L.'s productivity occurred following the sudden death from polio of her daughter, Sally, in 1958 at the age of twenty-four, although she produced mystically oriented works of nonfiction during this period. She collaborated with Wellesley Tudor Pole on *A Man Seen Afar* (1965) and with Cynthia Hill Sandys on *Letters from Our Daughters* (1972). She and Sandys also edited *The Awakening Letters* (1978).

All of L.'s writing has a distinctly feminine slant, which in some circles has caused her to be dismissed as a "feminine novelist," with an implication that she is inferior. As recent critical theory has advanced, however, and as feminist readings of works like L.'s have demonstrated how cogent their sometimes veiled social criticism is, writers like L. have been viewed with a renewed interest and understanding.

In her autobiography, L. acknowledges that her mother imbued in her quite early stern puritanical principles that often were at war with the pleasure-loving aspects of her personality. Through creating tensions between control and license, as she did in all of her fiction, L. deals intelligently with the individual's responsibility to his or her world.

BIBLIOGRAPHY: LeStourgeon, D., *R. L.* (1965); Siegel, R., *R. L.* (1989); Simons, J., *R. L.* (1992)

R. BAIRD SHUMAN

LELAND, John
b. 1506, London; d. 18 April 1552, London

Appointed "King's Antiquary" in 1533—a position created solely for him—L. traveled throughout England during the succeeding nine years "on the King's business," visiting cathedral and monastic libraries in search of manuscripts of historical significance. The journals he kept during these itinerant years became the basis for his best-known work, *The Laboryouse Journey and Serche of J. Leylande for En-* *glandes Antiquities, Given of hym as a Newe Yeares Gyfte to Kinge Henry the VIII* (or simply "A Newe Yeares Gyfte," as it is often called), which he presented to the king in 1545. The work was edited by L.'s friend and fellow antiquarian John Bale, to appear in print in 1549. *A Newe Yeares Gyfte* contains as well L.'s detailed proposal to HENRY VIII to describe the British Isles and contiguous islands topographically, to identify and provide biographical histories of the nobility, and information on all palaces and castles, throughout the realm—a plan cut short by L.'s growing mental instability, and unexpected death in 1552 at age forty-six. Less well known, but probably more influential as a resource turned to by Elizabethan and Jacobean scholars, is L.'s work of literary historical criticism, *Commentarii de Scriptoribus Britannicis* (2 vols., 1709).

Born in London, educated there at St. Paul's School under William LILYE, L. took a degree at Christ's College, Cambridge, and continued his studies at All Souls, Oxford, and the University of Paris. After taking holy orders, L. was by 1530 chaplain and librarian to Henry VIII, who made him the first "King's Antiquary" and gave L. his charge to seek out what L. described as "a whole worlde of thinges very memorable" in the ancient religious houses of England. For his efforts, and for his solid support of Henry's church policies, L. was duly rewarded with preferments, receiving the rectories of Peuplingues (Calais) and Haseley (Oxfordshire), a canonry at what is now Christ Church (then King's) College, Oxford, and a prebend at Salisbury. In the manner of the day, it is likely L. never officially took up the duties of any, but rather paid assistants to carry on with a portion of the salary, while he resided in London. In March 1550, L. was certified insane, a condition from which he failed to recover before his death two years later.

Although very little of the grand plan proposed in *A Newe Yeares Gyfte* was realized, L.'s contribution to English letters was nonetheless substantial. The manuscripts he gathered throughout the realm and secured for the king in a single collection housed in London, where they could be drawn upon by many, arguably anchored the heritage of British writing. Before their ultimate deposition in the Bodleian Library at Oxford in 1632, L.'s manuscripts are known to have been seen and used by prominent humanists, antiquarians and historians, including Bale, William Camden, William Harrison, Raphael HOLINSHED, and Sir William Dugdale, whose views on their nation's history helped shape generations of Englishmen. Thomas Hearne edited the travel history (in nine volumes, as *The Itinerary of John L. the Antiquary*) in 1710–12, and the major manuscripts in 1715, in six volumes, as *Collectanea*.

BIBLIOGRAPHY: Burton, E., *The Life of J. L.* (1896); Carleys, J. P., "J. L.," in Richardson, D. A., ed., *Six-*

teenth-Century British Nondramatic Writers, Second Series, DLB 136 (1994): 224–29; Chandler, J., ed., J. L.'s Itinerary: Travels in Tudor England (1993)

R. F. YEAGER

LENNOX, Charlotte

b. ca. 1730, possibly in Gibraltar; d. 4 January 1804, London

One of the earliest professional women writers, L. was the author of both a sizeable and diverse literary oeuvre. Her circle of friends and supporters included many notable literary men of the age, such as Samuel JOHNSON, Samuel RICHARDSON, Henry FIELDING, Oliver GOLDSMITH, and David GARRICK. She was less popular with the Bluestocking circle, though, and Fanny BURNEY's Diary reports, "Mrs. Thrale says that though Mrs. L.'s books are generally approved, nobody likes her." Based on widespread belief that she was American by birth, L. has been named the first American novelist, and though it now seems clear she only lived there a few years, her use of the New York colony as a setting for her first and last novels shows some familiarity with the colony and its inhabitants. After returning to England, she published her passable Poems on Several Occasions (1747) and briefly attempted a stage career (1748–50), before publishing her first novel, The Life of Harriot Stuart (2 vols., 1750). This semiepistolary novel demonstrates L.'s early taste for picaresque narrative in the improbable adventures of Harriot, a lively self-confessed coquette. Upon its publication, Johnson hosted a celebratory party, where he reportedly crowned L. with a laurel wreath.

L.'s most popular and enduring work, The Female Quixote; or, The Adventures of Arabella (2 vols., 1752), is one of the finest of several works modeled on Cervantes' Don Quixote (1605, 1615). L.'s novel was praised by Fielding as superior to its model, and, a favorite of Jane AUSTEN, it may have influenced her Northanger Abbey. By inverting the sex of the quixotic protagonist, L.'s burlesque adds an element of gender-reversal to the Cervantean prototype. Reared in complete seclusion on a diet of 17th-c. French romances by Scudéry, La Calprenède, and others, Arabella develops a quixoticism characterized by her desire for adventures denied to women by contemporary societal norms. Despite the farcical results of Arabella's delusions, she wields an extraordinary degree of control over the men in the novel: rival suitors Mr. Glanville and Sir George Bellmour scramble to accommodate her folly and eventually duel for her favors; generic distinctions blur as REALISM begins to resemble ROMANCE. The penultimate chapter, in which Arabella is cured of her quixoticism through scholarly discourse with a learned divine, almost disappoints, as Arabella accepts the danger of her ideals

and submits to prosaic domestic felicity with Mr. Glanville. The authorship of this chapter has confounded critics since 1843, when Reverend John Mitford first noted its marked Johnsonian style. While there is no critical consensus on the issue, internal evidence does suggest either L. and Johnson collaborated in writing Arabella's cure, or L. herself assumed Johnson's style in that chapter; in either case, the cure and its author pose an intriguing puzzle.

Chronic financial distress led L. to undertake hack writing and a series of translations later in her career. Her Shakespeare Illustrated (3 vols., 1753–54) was one of the first studies to trace and evaluate William SHAKESPEARE's use of his sources, but it is not always distinguished by good scholarship and her critical commentary attracted much censure, possibly resulting in the poor reception of her play, The Sister (1769). Garrick refused to stage her dramatic pastoral Philander (1758), and L. went on to publish a third novel, Henrietta (2 vols., 1758), modeled on Pierre Carlet de Chamblain Marivaux's La Vie de Marianne (11 parts, 1731–41). From 1760 to 1761, she edited the Lady's Museum, a periodical containing several contributions from herself and her friends. L.'s most didactic novel, The History of Harriot and Sophia, serialized in the Lady's Museum and later published separately as Sophia (2 vols., 1762), is symptomatic of the increasingly moral tone and probable hasty gestation of L.'s later work. Her play, The Sister, a comedy adapted from Henrietta with an epilogue by Goldsmith, was hissed off the stage after its first performance at Covent Garden, though her Old City Manners (1775), an adaptation of George CHAPMAN, Ben JONSON, and John MARSTON's Eastward Ho, enjoyed success at Drury Lane. L.'s final novel, Euphemia (4 vols., 1790), returns to the epistolary style and American setting of Harriot Stuart, and seems to recycle much of that novel's material, save that the protagonist, Euphemia Neville, is not a rambunctious coquette, but a mature and unhappily married woman who reluctantly undertakes adventure in America at her husband's behest. Despite this sizeable literary output, L. died in penury, barely supported by the Royal Literary Fund.

BIBLIOGRAPHY: Doody, M. A., "Shakespeare's Novels: C. L. Illustrated," SNNTS 19 (Fall 1987): 296–310; Langbauer, L., Women and Romance (1990); Ross, D., "Mirror, Mirror: The Didactic Dilemma of The Female Quixote," SEL 27 (1987): 455–73; Small, M. R., C. R. L. (1935)

TANYA BUTLER

LEONARD, Hugh

(pseud. of John [Keyes] Byrne) b. 9 November 1926, Dublin, Ireland

L. is one of the most successful Irish dramatists of the late 20th c., perhaps second only to Brian FRIEL in international acclaim. Adopted shortly after his birth by a working-class family, L. chose as his nom de plume the name of a character from an early, unsuccessful play, *The Italian Road* (perf. 1954). Ironically, the first play he submitted under his pseudonym, *The Big Birthday* (perf. 1956), was accepted by the Abbey Theatre, Dublin, which had rejected the earlier work

L.'s earliest successes came with adaptations of other authors' novels and plays. *The Passion of Peter Ginty* (perf. 1961) is an "Irish" version of Henrik Ibsen's *Peer Gynt*. L. adapted Irish authors in *When the Saints Go Cycling In* (perf. 1965), based on Flann O'BRIEN's *The Dalkey Archive*, and *Stephen D.* (perf. 1962; pub. 1964) and *Dublin One* (perf. 1963), both based on the works of James JOYCE. *Stephen D.* earned L. high praise, which was somewhat ironic since, as L. himself admitted, it contained very little of L.'s own writing: The play consisted almost completely of Joyce's own words from *A Portrait of the Artist as a Young Man* and its earlier draft, *Stephen Hero*. Nevertheless, L.'s stagecraft was apparent and the play garnered international acclaim.

L.'s first major original play was *The Poker Session* (perf. 1963; pub. 1964), a psychological drama revolving around the Beavis family, who are playing a game of poker to celebrate the release of Billy Beavis from an asylum. The plot is reminiscent of American dramatist Eugene O'Neill's *The Iceman Cometh* (1946), as, through the action of the play, Billy strips away his relatives' illusions of their own sanity and civility, until, at the end, we discover that Billy himself is not as sane or as self-aware as he may have considered himself to be. *The Au Pair Man* (perf. 1968; pub. 1974) has been compared to the works of Harold PINTER. This drama deals with the relationship between the aristocratic Mrs. Rogers and her companion, Eugene. Eugene eventually manages to break away from Mrs. Rogers only to find that the object of his affections is his former employer's niece, thus trapping him all over again. *The Patrick Pearse Motel* (1971) is a farcical satire about the incongruity between the Irish desire to maintain illusions of a noble and heroic past while coveting the materialistic trappings of modern life.

Da (perf. 1973; pub. 1975), for which L. received both the New York Drama Critics' Circle Award and the Antoinette Perry Award (1978), remains his most successful play. It is also one of the most overtly autobiographical dramas of modern theater. The play deals with the return to Dublin from London of a successful writer, who has come back to Ireland to sort out the affairs of his recently deceased father. Alone in his room, the son is visited by Da, and the two of them reenact the scenes and memories of the author's childhood. Along with the prose autobiographies *Home before Night* (1979) and *Out after Dark* (1989),

Da provides a compelling picture of L.'s youth in northern Ireland.

L. has written extensively for television and has authored several screenplays, including his adaptation of *Da* (1988) and *Widow's Peak* (1994). Other plays include *A Life* (perf. 1979; pub. 1980), *Moving* (1994), and *Love in the Title* (2000). His novel entitled *A Wild People* was published in 2001.

BIBLIOGRAPHY: Kosok, H., "H. L.," in Weintraub, S., ed., *British Dramatists since World War II*, part 1, *DLB* 13 (1982): 284–91

JASON BERNER

LESBIAN LITERATURE

The category "lesbian literature"—like *lesbianism* and *lesbians*—is often overlooked in academic circles. This lesbian invisibility is hardly surprising, given the comforting assumption until well into the 20th c. that virtuous, or "normal," women did not experience sexual arousal or satisfaction. Even in the 1970s, 1980s, and 1990s, lesbians have suffered as well as benefiting from frequent elision with gay men as "queer" or with heterosexual feminists. "Lesbian literature," then, needs explicit definition. This article defines lesbian literature by its content rather than by the gender or sexuality of its author; it is concerned with same-sex desire between women, with or without the added complexities of male gender identification or gender ambiguity. Both lesbian sexuality and gender ambivalence have often been disguised or "cross-written" by women in works about gay men, heterosexual women, or even animals; censorship, whether by legal or social pressure, continues to be a very real issue for writers about homosexuality and lesbianism in Britain.

Until the 20th c., almost all British lesbian literature (indeed, most published literature of any kind) was written by men. Their representation of lesbian eroticism was usually titillating but negative, as in Samuel Taylor COLERIDGE's *Christabel*, A. C. SWINBURNE's *Poems and Ballads*, and Charles DICKENS's characterization of Miss Wade in *Little Dorrit*. The theme of gender ambiguity, in contrast, was treated with greater tolerance, especially in Elizabethan and Jacobean drama, as is evident in the romantic friendship between Rosalind and Celia in William SHAKESPEARE's *As You Like It* and in Thomas MIDDLETON and Thomas DEKKER's *The Roaring Girl*. The latter centers on the real-life feminist transvestite Molly Frith or "Moll Cutpurse," an urban, female Robin Hood who defended women against male violence but championed any "honest" love. Even in the more repressive Victorian era, Swinburne's Lesbia, in his 1860s fragment *Lesbia Brandon*, published in 1952, is an attractively Byronic figure.

Lesbian literature by women writers of the 17th, 18th, and 19th cs. focuses mainly on romantic friendship, as in Mary WOLLSTONECRAFT's *Mary, a Fiction* (1788). This theme occupies women poets, too, from Katherine PHILIPS ("the matchless Orinda") through Anna Seward, a friend of the Ladies of Llangollen, Eleanor Butler and Sarah Ponsonby, to Michael Field, the pseudonym of Katherine Bradley and Edith Cooper, aunt and niece as well as lovers, friends of Oscar WILDE and other late Victorian aesthetes. Lesbian eroticism is explicit and unashamed, however, in the love poems of Aphra BEHN and is clearly perceptible two hundred years later through the symbol of goblin fruit in Christina ROSSETTI's *Goblin Market*. "New Women" at the end of the 19th c., such as the poet Amy LEVY and Vernon LEE, were more sexually self-aware than Rossetti. As early as the 1890s, Lee's open sexual independence of men could enable her to challenge their intellectual hegemony; she lived on until 1935, providing a model of sexually dissident courage and self-confidence for the new generation of lesbian writers after the First World War.

There is evidence that Rose Allatini, Virginia WOOLF, and Sylvia Townsend WARNER all read Lee's bitter satire of patriarchal politics and war in *The Ballet of the Nations* and *Satan the Waster*, published in 1915 and 1920, respectively. All three writers deal with left politics in conjunction with "deviant" sexuality, often crosswriting about gay men instead of or as well as lesbians. Allatini's only explicit representation of lesbianism occurs in *Despised and Rejected*, published in 1918, a novel banned under the Defense of the Realm Act because of its sympathetic portrayal of conscientious objectors. Its protagonists are a gay man in the process of coming out of the closet and a young woman for whom lesbianism offers so shadowy a future that she abandons it. The man acknowledges and consummates his gay romance, but the initially lively and attractive lesbian becomes a mere onlooker, doomed to celibate invisibility. This neglected novel is an essential document of lesbian literary history.

Woolf's sexual ambivalence in the 1920s is reflected by her use of crosswriting in her understated, elegiac representations of war: depicting homoerotic loss, she distances both grief and desire. The most intense sexual desire in *Jacob's Room* is between men; Clara, Florinda, Laurette, and Fanny Elmer do not enter the room—or closet—where photographs of the Greeks preside over the visits of a succession of male friends; only on the novel's last page does Jacob's mother burst in, to find Bonamy, "who couldn't love a woman," mourning for her son. Septimus Warren Smith in *Mrs. Dalloway* cannot grieve for Evans because he has suppressed his homosexual desire; in *To the Lighthouse*, Mr. Carmichael expresses his grief for Andrew Ramsay, blown up by a shell in France,

by bringing out a volume of poems. But most of these novels also have explicitly lesbian themes: Lily Briscoe's love for Mrs. Ramsay propels the narrative of *To the Lighthouse*, while *Mrs. Dalloway* can be read as a survey of suppressed lesbianism whose motive force was Woolf's growing interest in Vita SACKVILLE-WEST. With her sharp eye for class difference, Woolf delineates the socially acceptable ways by which the rich lesbians distract themselves from their sexual frustration. The poor women, on the other hand—Doris Kilman and Milly Brush—must endure the pain of repression, be it raging or resigned. And at the novel's heart, Clarissa Dalloway stands rigid and solitary beside her narrow bed, re-creating her memories of lost lesbian desire. In *Orlando*, however, Woolf replaces grief with sheer delight in the absurdities of the sex/gender system. Her narrator is at once insistently male and "enjoy[s] the immunity of all biographers and historians from any sex whatever." Woolf appears to be crosswriting as long as her narrative concerns Orlando as a man, but in places he is a very girlish boy; her biographer crosswrites when he portrays Orlando as a woman, but then Orlando delights in deconstructing her gender by crossdressing and indulging in intimate friendships with prostitutes. When she dresses most clearly as a woman, she and her husband seem most uncertain about one another's gender. *Orlando* is not crosswritten: it is about crosswriting. Woolf was correcting—and prudently cutting—the proofs of *Orlando* during the scandal preceding the censorship trial of Radclyffe HALL's *The Well of Loneliness*.

This brave but sentimental, snobbish, and racist lesbian Bildungsroman incurred the wrath of the governing class because its form and style were so conventional that its sympathetic portrayal of female inversion was all too immediately recognizable. Woolf ridiculed in her next book, *A Room of One's Own*, three of the men of law and politics who banned *The Well of Loneliness*, but she eliminated overt references to lesbianism from her published text. There is evidence that she also cut lesbian material from drafts of her next two novels, *The Waves* and *The Years*, although Miss La Trobe, the lesbian in the posthumously published *Between the Acts*, remains unmistakable. For more than thirty years, few novelists risked depicting lesbianism positively. Even Warner, whose three 1920s fantasies, *Lolly Willowes, Mr. Fortune's Maggot,* and *The True Heart,* gleefully depict Satanism, pederasty, and the quest of an orphaned maid-of-all-work for her middle-class, "idiot" lover, protected her Marxist lesbian romance by setting it in Paris during the 1848 revolution.

In *Summer Will Show,* Sophia Willoughby, an Englishwoman as privileged as Hall's Stephen Gordon, learns her lesbian love and revolutionary politics from a Jewish storyteller, Minna Lemuel. At the novel's end, the revolution has failed: Minna has died defending the barricades, and Sophia is devastated by grief, but on the last page she is completely absorbed in reading *The Communist Manifesto*. The implication is that her life is far from over although she may never love again. Whereas Stephen Gordon dedicates her doomed, lonely future to writing novels that will make inversion acceptable, Sophia will fight the injustices of capitalism together with her communist comrades; she has transformed from an unhappily heterosexual upper-class bigot into a revolutionary. Warner's joint publication with her lover, Valentine Ackland, of a volume of poetry, *Whether a Dove or Seagull*, was an "experiment in the presentation of poetry and a protest," a political act aimed at both compulsory heterosexuality and the literary canon: although both poets names are on the title page, the volume does not attribute individual poems to either author. Some of Ackland's love poems, in particular, evince a lesboeroticism reminiscent of the love poetry of Charlotte MEW. Warner continued to write poems, novels, and short stories about women's desire into the 1960s and 1970s.

Most women novelists depicting lesbianism between 1928 and 1965 made sure that their lesbians were either thoroughly distanced by comedy, as in Ivy COMPTON-BURNETT's *More Women than Men* and Molly Keane's *Devoted Ladies* (1934) or doomed to a heterosexual or otherwise unhappy ending, as in Mary RENAULT's *The Friendly Young Ladies* and Dorothy Strachey's *Olivia* (1949). Olivia, however, is less homophobic than most representations of lesbian romance in schools, from D. H. LAWRENCE's *The Rainbow* and Clemence DANE's *Regiment of Women* to Muriel SPARK's *The Prime of Miss Jean Brodie* and Elizabeth BOWEN's *The Little Girls* and *Eva Trout; or, Changing Scenes*. Even Brigid BROPHY, whose later novels contain explicit representations of unashamed lesbians, represents lesbian panic between schoolgirls in *The King of a Rainy Country*, published in 1956. Only Rosemary Manning, revisiting her adolescence in *The Chinese Garden*, succeeds in redressing the balance. Her novel represents the suppression of lesbian desire in 1928 at the boarding school, Bampfield. Its main theme is lesbian silence: the silence of suppression on the part of the teenage protagonist and of betrayal on the part of crossdressing teachers who hypocritically expel students who have been found naked together in bed (and in possession of that "filthy" book, *The Well of Loneliness*). The teachers who founded the school served, like Stephen Gordon, in an ambulance unit in the war; at Bampfield, discipline is spartan, living conditions are crude, and the landscape resembles that of the Somme. The novel's form is a double narrative; parts of the adolescent's story are told in the third person, though always from her limited point of view, while others are remembered and reflected upon by the now adult narrator. The tone of *The Chinese Garden* is both lyrical and melancholy; it is a memorable novel.

The Chinese Garden was published three years after the 1959 Obscene Publications Act replaced that of 1857, under which both *The Well of Loneliness* and *The Rainbow* had been banned. In 1968, the Lord Chamberlain's censorship of the theater was finally abolished, permitting, for a brief twenty years, the free development of lesbian-feminist fringe theater projects by such groups as the Siren Theater Company, the Women's Theater Group, and Monstrous Regiment. Playwrights such as Michelene Wandor, Bryony Lavery, Sue Frumin, Penny Casdagli, and Caroline Griffin addressed issues of class and/or race as well as gender and sexuality. But funding became progressively harder to obtain after the inclusion of Section 28 in the 1988 Local Government Act; it prohibited local authorities from "intentionally promot[ing] homosexuality." Without local funding to supplement intermittent grants from the Arts Council, even the Gay Sweatshop, an initially male but later mixed group that lasted for twenty years, eventually had to shut down. It had commissioned and/or produced many plays by lesbians, including Jill Posener and Jackie Kay. The only widely known black lesbian British writer, Kay has also published, in addition to her plays, two volumes of poetry, a biography of Bessie Smith, and a novel, *Trumpet* (1998).

Contemporary lesbian novels range from the courageous, lugubrious portrayal of life in the closet and a lesbian bar in Maureen DUFFY's *The Microcosm* through the numerous upbeat, popular, lesbian romances of the 1970s and 1980s to the ironic lesbian-feminist REALISM of Anna Wilson's *Cactus* (1980) and *Altogether Elsewhere* (1985). Jeanette WINTERSON's *Oranges Are Not the Only Fruit*, whose protagonist is reared as a missionary until her sexuality is discovered by her evangelical community, is perhaps the most original and witty lesbian coming-out story yet published. *The Passion*, set in France, Russia, and Venice during and after the Napoleonic Wars, is the first and most engaging of Winterson's series of progressively more obscure explorations of adulterous bisexual triangles. Among the most recent generation of lesbian novelists, Sarah Waters and Kay are the most promising. Waters has written three historical novels, *Tipping the Velvet* (1998), a picaresque turn-of-the-century coming-out story with a feminist ending, *Affinity* (2000), which represents lesbian seduction and betrayal in the context of Victorian spiritualism, and *Fingersmith* (2002). Waters's presentation of class difference is especially complex and astute. Kay's *Trumpet* centers on the exposure after his death of a transgender black jazz musician who has passed as a man to everyone except his wife for more than fifty years. Narrated from the conflicting points of view of his surviving relatives, colleagues, friends, and all the officers of death—the doctor, the registrar, the mortician, the journalist—this is a complicated, lyrical, surprisingly unsensational novel.

The work of both these writers, along with the beautifully crafted, resonant, explicit poetry of Carol Ann DUFFY, indicates that contemporary lesbian literature is becoming increasingly subtle, mainstream, and diverse. While British lesbians have never lived in as much legal danger as gay men, their literature suffered aesthetically for many generations from lesbian invisibility: it is hard to represent women with active sexual desire if most of the readership does not believe that such desire can exist. Hence the modernist literary devices of crosswriting about gay men or setting one's work in a more sexually tolerant time or place than the present. It is sadly ironic, however, that writing lesbian literature became legally risky immediately it was made visible to the patriarchy before and during the trial of *The Well of Loneliness*, so that little literary development took place between 1936 and and the 1960s. But it seems that we may now be witnessing a new trend toward courageous literary experimentation, similar to that which occurred after the First World War. The writing of Carol Ann Duffy, Kay, and Waters is certainly comparable in subtlety and power to that of Woolf and Warner at their best.

BIBLIOGRAPHY: Castle, T., *The Apparitional Lesbian: Female Homosexuality and Modern Culture* (1993); De Lauretis, T., *The Practice of Love: Lesbian Sexuality and Perverse Desire* (1994); Duncker, P., *Sisters and Strangers: An Introduction to Contemporary Feminist Fiction* (1992); Marcus, J., *Virginia Woolf and the Languages of Patriarchy* (1987); Mulford, W., *This Narrow Place: Sylvia Townsend Warner and Valentine Ackland* (1988); Palmer, P., *Contemporary Lesbian Writing* (1993); Smith, P. J., *Lesbian Panic: Homoeroticism in Modern British Women's Fiction* (1997); Wachman, G., *Lesbian Empire: Radical Crosswriting in the Twenties* (2001); Weeks, J., *Sex, Politics, and Society* (1989)

GAY WACHMAN

LESSING, Doris

b. Doris May Tayler, 22 October 1919, Kermanshah, Persia

Over the past five decades, L.'s consequential and prolific literary life has rendered her one of the most significant 20th-c. writers of fiction, alongside other celebrated authors such as D. H. LAWRENCE, T. S. ELIOT, and Iris MURDOCH. L. is allied with, but never categorized by, a diversity of literary perspectives, including 19th-c. REALISM, mysticism, and SCIENCE FICTION. Iconoclastic in her approach to narrative and genre, and always a formidable champion of the un-

derdog, L. has led generations of followers into stories that carry a transposition of psychological, political, and social conflicts. Regardless of whether her characters' struggles are situated within the family or the state, within a familiarly landscaped realism or apocalyptic future, her recurring theme brings readers to the idea of individual freedom and moral accountability.

Colonialism, apartheid, communism, the fracture of the self, woman's position in society, global catastrophe, and higher forms of consciousness are some of the issues underpinning L.'s fiction. Her preoccupation with these matters reflects her own meditations, which have broadly ranged from her associations with Marxist thought—in her early years; C. G. Jung's and R. D. Laing's psychoanalytical theories; and, in her mystical association, Sufi spiritualism. However, L. has made clear that she has no patience for those who type her work according to purpose or ideology: she snarls at FEMINISM, for example, and is offended that *The Golden Notebook* (1962) is considered to be one of the movement's early "bibles." Critics, who don't view L.'s body of work within the context of 19th-c. realism, have suggested that this refusal on her part to be defined correlates to what they see as her game with fiction, in the making of metafiction: an intentional self consciousness of language and its alleged rendering of reality and truth. In the end though, it doesn't really matter whether L. is pushed into realism, science fiction, or metafiction: what the reader experiences is an enlightened individual who examines ambivalence within an individual's psyche, and the polarity between singular principles and the collective good.

Born to British parents living in Kermanshah, Persia, L. immigrated with her family in 1924 to Southern Rhodesia, where they had bought a thousand or so acreage of land in the secluded area of Banket, one hundred miles west of Mozambique. They came to the bush seeking financial gain as maize farmers and better opportunities for their children's education, but their dream of wealth was never realized. L.'s mother, however, refused to allow her daughter to forego what she believed to be a traditional British upbringing, and in these aims, she sent L. to an austere convent school and later to a government school for girls. By the age of thirteen, L. had abandoned her conventional education, instead opting to educate herself through reading and writing.

L. has commented that her childhood was largely an unhappy one, except for such pleasures of the land that she and her younger brother experienced—as vividly recounted in her autobiography, *Under My Skin* (1995)—as well as her passion for literature, which was made possible by the many books sent over from London. It didn't take long for L. to escape her mother's overbearing eye and their abysmal living conditions in Banket. At the age of fifteen, L. took a position as a nursemaid and during the next three years, she wrote two drafts for novels as well as, by age eighteen, selling two stories to South African magazines. In that same period, L. met and married Frank Wisdom, an older man with whom she had two children. However, L.'s unhappiness in that marriage and her need to escape the limitations of wife and mother—which she had seen her own mother and other women of that generation fall prey to—beckoned her to leave both her husband and her children four years later. L. then found respite from racism as well as her intellectual life in the Communist Left Book Club, where she met her second husband, Gottfried Lessing, one of its most active members. For the next ten years, L. was committed to the Communist Party, but she and her son Peter moved to London in 1949, where she has remained, after her marriage had been dissolved.

L. is known for her autobiographical approach to fiction, and the intensely drawn protagonists of her earlier works, including Mary Turner in *The Grass Is Singing* (1950), who comes to an impoverished farm in an alienated area of Rhodesia to marry a man she does not love; the protagonist in *Martha Quest* (1952) whose journey of consciousness is traced throughout the five volumes in the "Children of Violence" series; and Anna Freeman Wulf in *The Golden Notebook*, regarded by many as L.'s masterwork, who seeks wholeness in a fragmented life—do carry parts of L.'s inner life as well as, in many respects, her life's circumstances. However, such a classification of oeuvre would undermine L.'s astute and striking capacity to observe and to imagine.

When *The Grass Is Singing* was published, L. was critically applauded for her ground breaking exposé of apartheid. In this story of Mary Turner, L. lays bare the wastage of such human possibilities as autonomy, morality, and self-respect that cannot be realized for those who have been living under the weight of unjust social laws. Mary is an outgrowth of this conditioning, and as such she is driven by sadistic and masochistic impulses that eventually lead to her brutal treatment of the natives, on the isolated and impoverished farm to which she comes at age thirty to marry Dick Turner. Her subsequent fixation on Moses, her black houseboy, uncovers the web of fear, resentment, and hatred that resides in them both and his consequent power over her reverses the master/slave relationship but does not break their ties. Mary is killed by Moses, and he accepts his punishment.

In L.'s next novel, *Martha Quest*, which over the next seventeen years she developed into a five-novel series, she created a Bildingsroman with a heroine to whom she admits having given many autobiographical features, including a close portrait of her father. The series—which, after *Martha Quest*, includes *A Proper Marriage* (1954), *A Ripple from the Storm*

(1958), *Landlocked* (1965), and *The Four-Gated City* (1969)—chronicles the life of Martha Quest from the beginning of her journey when, at the age of fifteen, she is eager to leave her restrictive family life until her middle-aged years when she is living in a postwar apocalyptic England. What binds the volumes, during that time when L.'s writing would evolve into more pioneering forms, is Martha's drive toward nonconformity and individualism.

While L. began the "Children of Violence" series with her roots in realism, during the next ten years or so she would advance toward a more radical approach to writing fiction, and *The Golden Notebook* is a powerful deliverance of her exploration of narrative. This novel is valued as a masterpiece, and it has long been considered one of the most important early examples of contemporary feminist literature. In it, L. introduces Anna Freeman Wulf, whose series of profound notebooks are interwoven within the novel, the form of which is a combination of nonlinear sequenced short stories and novellas that offer differing perspectives of Anna's identity: a writer who, freed from the confines of marriage and from her involvement with communism, seeks a difficult journey toward autonomy. The work spoke strongly to women of that generation, and has continued to do so, as L. dismantled feminine myths and gave to her character the freedom to live independently and to refuse the proscriptions of what a woman should do and feel, and what she should accept. In *A Man and Two Women* (1963), a collection of nineteen stories, including "To Room Nineteen," composed while L. was writing *The Golden Notebook*, L. investigates the emotional conflicts within male and female intimacy as well as the private emotional struggles within each individual. "To Room Nineteen" is a prelude to *The Summer before the Dark* (1973) in its depiction of a woman's psychological undoing as she confronts the emptiness of her domestic life.

By the end of *The Golden Notebook*, Anna Wulf experiences mystical insights, which reflect L.'s own engagement, beginning in the 1960s and continuing until now, with Sufi mysticism. It was at this time that L. began writing what she has called "inner-space fiction," an explicit turning away from the historical realism that had in many respects determined the first ten years of her writing. Within this context, L. offers differing versions of reality itself, and in, for example, *Briefing for a Descent into Hell* (1971), she questions what individuals take for granted as their truths, creating two synchronous realities. L. was also influenced by the psychologist Laing, whose theories called upon a rethinking of the notion of fixed identity as well as society's perception of normal and abnormal behavior.

L.'s vision of the future is a bleak one, which makes sense given that when she writes of the contemporary world, she refuses to turn a blind eye to the political and personal assaults of which humans are so capable. The means toward survival after hardship or even nightmarish world endings is often her subject matter, and in *Memoirs of a Survivor* (1974), it is psychic awareness and intuition that replace rationalism as a necessary tool of existing. In this novel, L. continued to draw upon the prospect of alternative parallel realms and their relationship to the shifting parts of the self. Her unnamed speaker enters other forms of reality as she journeys beyond vanishing walls in retreat from an ominous environment. Science fiction became, in the late 1970s, the arena for L.'s philosophy and in the five-novel series *Canopus in Argos: Archives* (1979–83), she became a phantasmal visionary. L. did not write the series to be read sequentially although the novels share the premise of the fictive galactic empire, Canopus. In this series, her attendance upon the beliefs of Sufism was more directly infused into the novels' thematic bearing, which communicates the collective obligation all people have toward the good of the universe rather than the singular fulfillment of individual needs. *Mara and Dann* (1999)—like the *Canopus* series—is set in the future. The story opens with the predicament of a young brother and sister, who are taken from their home as protection against their enemies. Their journey, which spans more than four hundred pages, takes them through past and present, and still violent, civilizations.

From the 1970s to the 1990s, there have been exceptions to L.'s work within the quasi-mystical genre, including her well-known novel *The Summer before the Dark*, which, although containing a sequence of dreamscapes, depends upon an everyday understanding of domestic, suburban life and of a middle-aged wife and mother who no longer can depend upon her role in the home as a means toward self-realization. In *The Diary of a Good Neighbor* (1983) and *If the Old Could* (1984), L. played a game on publishers and critics by assuming the pen name of Jane Somers, the purpose of which was to show how difficult it was for new writers to get their work in print. And she did have trouble finding a publisher. In both novels, L. continues to probe the social conditions of women in society, and in *Love Again* (1996), L. explores an older woman's reconnection to love, in its varying forms.

The idea of antisocial behavior within middle-class suburban life is realized in several of L.'s novels. *The Good Terrorist* (1985) introduces a bourgeois woman, who becomes a leader of a terrorist group, and in *The Fifth Child* (1988), L.'s thirty-fifth book, considered to be a "minor" classic, readers meet the freakish Ben, a social misfit born into a once happy and secure family. L.'s calls this work "a classic horror story," and its sequel, *Ben, in the World* (2000), continues with the mature aged Ben and his discord with society and his family.

L. has produced two volumes of AUTOBIOGRAPHY, mainly out of the need to speak for herself rather than have biographers misrepresent her life. *Under My Skin* received the James Tait Black Memorial Prize, and in it L. journeys to her past in Southern Rhodesia, her two failed marriages, and her early political beliefs. *Walking in the Shade* (1997) begins in the year 1949 when L. had just relocated to London and takes up political and social issues of the time, including the sexual revolution. Over the years, L. has written a significant number of essays and articles, looking into such issues as the evils of sloganism and political correctness and the disintegrating attention span of people all over the world, who "are not interested in ideas." She has written a number of nonfiction texts, including her trek to Afghanistan: *The Wind Blows Away Our Words: And Other Documents Relating to the Afghan Resistance* (1988); her return to her homeland: *African Laughter: Four Visits to Zimbabwe* (1992); and her portrait of London: *The Real Thing: Stories and Sketches* (1992). L. has also written a large number of celebrated short stories, plays, and poetry. In 1997, she worked for the second time with Philip Glass, furnishing the libretto for the opera *The Marriages between Zones Three, Four and Five*. In 2000, *The Old Age of El Magnifico* was published; it is a recognition of L.'s love of cats, specifically her relationship with a stray she had picked up and lived with for eighteen years. Her passion for cats was also revealed in an earlier work, *Particularly Cats* (1967), and *Rufus the Survivor* (1979).

L. has had received many awards for her work, including an appointment in 1999 as Companion of Honour by Queen Elizabeth II. She has always been an individual who mines the depths of the soul, also inviting her readership to, by her very subject matter, become aware of the individual's responsibility to the world and to the self. Always humble, mysterious, self-styled, and controversial, L. has declined offers to teach full-time because she perceived her "own academic background somewhat meager"; given much of her money away to philanthropic causes; pursued spiritual development; and argued against social and political hypocrisy. It is difficult to sum up this author, who has journeyed into such different literary genres and ideas, except to say, as Joyce Carol Oates states about L.: "I think it is true of our greatest writers that their effect on us is delayed, that it may take years for us to understand what they have done to us. L. possesses a unique sensitivity, writing out of her own intense experience, her own subjectivity, but at the same time writing out of the spirit of the times. This is a gift that cannot be analyzed; it must only be honored."

BIBLIOGRAPHY: Galin, M., *Sufism in the Novels of D. L.* (1997); Greene, G., *The Poetics of Change* (1995); Lessing, D., and E. G. Engersoll, *Putting Questions Differently: Interviews with D. L. 1964–1994* (1996); Oates, J. C., "A Visit with D. L.," *SoR* 9 (October 1973): 873–82; Rowe, M. R., *D. L.* (1994); Sprague, C., *In Pursuit of D. L.* (1990)

LISA TOLHURST

LEVERSON, Ada [Esther]

b. 10 October 1862, London, d. 30 August 1933, London

L., who was born into a cultured Jewish milieu, was at the center of the *Yellow Book* circle in the 1890s, and particularly close to Oscar WILDE, to whom she gave crucial support both between his two trials and after his release from Reading Gaol. Between 1907 and 1916, she wrote six novels that have, since their republication in the 1960s, been admired by a select group, while in the 1920s she was an early patron of MODERNISM, and of the SITWELLS in particular.

In the 1890s, L. was admired by the *Yellow Book* group as a witty writer of short stories, sketches, and parodies of her friends' work. (Max BEERBOHM was an admirer, and Wilde, who nicknamed her "the Sphinx," a particular devotee.) Wilde's personal tragedy and the difficult break-up of her marriage to Ernest Leverson led both to a darker view of life and to a need to supplement her income by writing, and the novels that she produced for Grant Richards were successful enough to make this possible. The typical L. plot, which recurs with variations through all six novels, hinges on a marriage that is endangered but saved at the last minute. The implication in the text is always that the danger is real, the marriage not necessarily worth saving, and the act of salvage precarious.

This scheme is most visible in *Tenterhooks* (1912), the second of L.'s three novels centered on the Ottleys—the intelligent and sensitive Edith and the obtuse and boorish husband Bruce whom she manipulates successfully. Here, Edith finds herself drawn to a friend, Aylmer Ross, who is the complete antithesis of Bruce. Bruce providentially leaves her for an art student with whom he sets sail for Australia; but rather than seizing the opportunity, Edith conceals his disappearance, refuses to release him, and waits for him to return to her, which he does. The Ottleys are reunited, and Aylmer leaves in understandable disappointment. The surface writing, as in the earlier short pieces, is in the brilliant epigrammatic tradition of the 1890s. However, the often lively satirical depiction of Edwardian society is weakened by L.'s overidentification with her heroine—since neither Edith nor Aylmer is allowed any weaknesses and their positive qualities are described at length, the effect is dangerously close to conventional romance.

The distance is better preserved in the first Ottley novel, *Love's Shadow* (1908), where the HUMOR is broader; although most critics agree that the structure is flawed. Here, while the main interest for the reader (and the main entertainment) is provided by the Ottleys' ongoing domestic drama, the plot of marriage-rescue centers on another figure, Edith's best friend Hyacinth, and is treated in a more perfunctory way—so that at times the effect is of two novels, a SATIRE and a ROMANCE, having been interleaved. However, the division works better for the character of Edith, who is freed from the role of romantic heroine, and the treatment of Hyacinth is lighter than that of Edith in the later novels.

L.'s last novel was written in 1915, although she continued to write occasional short pieces, particularly promoting the cause of her friends the Sitwells and of modernism in general; like most of her contemporaries she was accordingly satirized by Wyndham LEWIS in *The Apes of God*. She also edited her correspondence with Wilde in 1930. After forty years of relative neglect, the Ottley trilogy was republished in 1962 with a glowing commendation from Colin MacINNES; and L.'s reputation as a writer in her own account, rather than as a muse-figure for Wilde and Osbert SITWELL, is now securely established. In her concerns far removed from FEMINISM and "New Woman" writing, she nonetheless created a quite individual voice—domestic drama in a register that recalls Wilde and foreshadows Ronald FIRBANK.

BIBLIOGRAPHY: Burkhart, C., *A. L.* (1973); Speedie, J., *Wonderful Sphinx: The Biography of A. L.* (1993); Wyndham, V., *The Sphinx and Her Circle* (1963)

JEAN RADFORD

LEVI, Peter [Chad Tigar]

b. 6 May 1931, Ruislip, Middlesex; d. 1 February 2000, Frampton on Severn

Formerly a Roman Catholic priest, L. was educated at Beaumont and Oxford, and trained as a Jesuit. His range of accomplishment is astonishing. He taught classics at Campion Hall, Oxford, and worked as an archaeologist in Greece. His translation of Pausanias's *Guide to Greece* was published in 1971. L. became a fellow of St. Catherine's College, Oxford, in 1977 and was elected Professor of Poetry at Oxford in 1984. Since his first volume of poetry, *The Gravel Ponds*, appeared in 1960, L.'s reputation has risen steadily among his peers. Poetry collections include *Water, Rock and Sand* (1962), *The Shearwaters* (1965), *Fresh Water, Sea Water* (1966), and *The Echoing Green* (1983), the year in which L. published his autobiography, *The Flutes of Autumn. The Noise Made by Poems* (1977) was a volume of criticism.

L. also published travel books, translations of Eastern European poets, and detective novels.

LEVY, Amy
b.10 November 1861, London; d. 10 September 1889, London

After long neglect, L. has been rediscovered. The first Jewish student at Newnham College, Cambridge, she was a feminist, cosmopolitan in her learning, questioning the norms of society, which at the time meant chaperonage of young women. Her essay "Middle Class Jewish Women of Today" (1886) bitterly reflects what she saw as her plight. L. was a regular contributor to the *Jewish Chronicle* and other journals, and an accomplished poet and novelist. L.'s irony plays constantly with that agonized concern over the tidemark of gentility that activated Victorian society and her ambivalences are uncomfortable, even disturbing.

In her novel *The Romance of a Shop* (1888), a family of impoverished sisters set up a fairly successful photography business, shocking their well-heeled friends. But one sister dies and the others find husbands, solving the economic problem. In *Reuben Sachs* (1888), Reuben and Judith love each other, but as a poor relation Judith is ineligible as a wife for a rising barrister. She is maneuvered into a grotesquely inappropriate (and unconvincing) marriage of convenience. Nineteenth-century London Jewry, in its minute social gradations, is anatomized. The portrait is harsh (Jewish men are "ugly") and while the ostensible object of L.'s satire is the marriage market, the book gave offense within L.'s community. The concern with minorities and outsiders reappears in *Miss Meredith* (1889). The narrator goes as a governess to an aristocratic Italian family and overcomes their opposition to her cross-cultural marriage with the heir. The Italians are well observed, without the cruelty of *Reuben Sachs.* L.'s other fictions reflect a healthy pleasure in clothes, dancing, and flirtation. Her literary criticism is distinguished and she was an accomplished poet, illustrated in *Xantippe and Other Verses* (1881), *A Minor Poet and Other Verse* (1884), and *A London Plane-Tree and Other Verse*, published posthumously in 1989.

In the poem entitled "Xantippe," the widow of Socrates reflects on her initial physical repulsion and her eventual resentment that "he kept his love/For this Athenian city and her sons," whom elsewhere she describes as "the gay group," with how strong an undertone we can only speculate. At other times, L. assumes a male persona. In "Run to Death," a gypsy and her baby are hunted with dogs by perfumed nobles. The poems and some of her stories are preoccupied with suffering and suicide. The short story "Cohen of Trinity" (1889) expresses her worst fears.

A scholarship student at Cambridge, Cohen is a misfit, ambitious and conceited, who fails academically and socially, suffers a breakdown, and eventually shoots himself, despite having published a distinguished book. Notwithstanding her brilliance and wit, L. felt herself to be "a creature maimed and marred." Shortly after completing her third collection of poetry, L. committed suicide aged twenty-seven.

BIBLIOGRAPHY: Beckman, L. H., *A. L.: Her Life and Letters* (2000); New, M., ed., *The Complete Novels and Selected Writings of A. L., 1861–1889* (1993); Wagenknecht, E., "A. L.," in his *Daughters of the Covenant: Portraits of Six Jewish Women* (1983): 55–93

VALERIE GROSVENOR MYER

LEWES, G[eorge] H[enry]
b. 18 April 1817, London; d. 30 November 1878, The Priory, St. John's Wood

L. is remembered primarily as the man who lived with George ELIOT for the last twenty-four years of his life and encouraged her development as a novelist. But this is only one aspect of his many-faceted career. He was critic, actor, novelist, biographer, scientist, and philosopher. His friends and acquaintances comprised a cross section of mid-Victorian intellectual life. His associates included Leigh HUNT, Charles DICKENS, Charlotte BRONTË, Anthony TROLLOPE, William Makepeace THACKERAY, John Stuart MILL, Charles DARWIN, T. H. Huxley, and Herbert SPENCER. In 1837, he became a member of Hunt's radical circle while working on an abortive biography of Percy Bysshe SHELLEY. After traveling on the Continent in search of material, he returned to London in 1840 where he wrote articles for the *Monthly Chronicle* and *Westminster Review* and in 1841 married Agnes Jervis with whom he had five children. He wrote articles on subjects as varied as French criticism, Spinoza, George Sand, and Goethe. In 1845, he published the first two volumes of his highly popular *Biographical History of Philosophy*, following with the last two volumes in 1846, and with later editions in 1857, 1867, 1871, and 1880. In 1847, he acted with Dickens's amateur company and published an unsuccessful novel, *Ranthorpe*, which was followed by another failed three-volume novel, *Rose, Blanche and Violet*, the next year. His *The Life of Maximilien Robespierre* appeared in 1849, and in 1850 his moderately successful tragedy, *The Noble Heart*, was produced and published; it was later revived in the U.S.

L., who believed in free love rather than the constraints of marriage, ended his own, de facto, in 1849; when his wife became pregnant by his close friend, Thornton Leigh Hunt, L. accepted legal responsibility only to have his wife again become pregnant by Hunt.

L. spent the rest of his life supporting the growing family of his wife and Hunt. This was his position when he met Eliot in 1852 and shocked Victorian England by living with her publicly in 1854.

In 1853, he published *Comte's Philosophy of the Sciences* and in 1855 his two-volume *Life and Works of Goethe*, but increasingly his interests shifted to science with *Sea-Side Studies* (1858), *The Physiology of Common Life* (2 vols., 1859), and "Studies in Animal Life" in *Cornhill Magazine* (1860). His last work, the five-volume *Problems of the Life and Mind*, a physiological approach to psychology, was published between 1874 and 1879, the last two volumes appearing posthumously. This work met with a tepid reception.

Most of L.'s work is colored by the empiricism of Auguste Comte. His *Biographical History of Philosophy* owed its popularity not only to its clear, vigorous style, but also to its dismissal of theology and metaphysics as earlier stages of development superseded by empiricism. As a critic, he judged works individually rather than as parts of movements. Although he favored REALISM, he did not insist on it. Usually his judgments in literature and science were perceptive. An early admirer of Dickens, he was one of few contemporaries to appreciate Herman Melville's *Moby-Dick* (3 vols., 1851), and he concurred essentially with Darwin's *Origin of Species* shortly before Huxley debated with Bishop Samuel Wilberforce. His still valuable biography praised Goethe for what he considered the grasp of reality in his poetry, and treated his life with a directness rare in Victorian England.

But L.'s most important contribution to literature remains his encouragement of Marian Evans, a woman given to self-doubt and depression. At the time L. and Eliot began living together she was a minor essayist; he persuaded her to try fiction—which proved immediately successful—and she became one of the most highly respected novelists of the century. L. was certainly supportive, and quite possibly he was a necessary catalyst.

BIBLIOGRAPHY: Ashton, R., *G. H. L.* (1991); Haight, G. S., *The G. L. Letters* (9 vols., 1954–78); Williams, D., *Mr. George Eliot: A Biography of G. H. L.* (1983)

DALTON AND MARYJEAN GROSS

LEWIS, Alun

b. 1 July 1915, Aberdare, South Wales; d. 5 March 1944, Burma

Educated at Cowbridge Grammar School, Glamorgan, and the University of Wales, Aberystwyth, L. began writing while at school and published a poem and six short stories in the *Dragon*, the university magazine. In 1935, he gained a first-class degree in history and went on to Manchester University to do a two-year postgraduate course in medieval history. He returned to Aberystwyth in 1937 to take a teacher-training course and in 1938 took up a teaching post in Lewis Boys' School, Pengam. He enlisted in the Royal Engineers in the spring of 1940 but then applied for a commission in the infantry and his first posting as an officer was with the South Wales Borderers.

He had begun to publish his poetry in national newspapers and journals in 1937 and had already established a reputation as a poet when his first volume of poems, *Raiders' Dawn*, was published in March 1942 and was well received by the public and by the critics. The *Listener* welcomed him as "the most assured and direct poet of his generation" while the *New English Weekly* praised him for looking at life steadily and "without romantic subterfuge." By August, three impressions had been printed and sold. The volume contained forty-seven poems practically all of which he says in a note "have been written since September, 1939; two-thirds of them have been written on active service." The first section of the volume, entitled "Poems in Khaki," introduced a new war poet for a new war even though he had not at that time been engaged in the fighting. They were concerned with the life of soldiers in wartime rather than with war itself. The poems were praised for their lyricism, for their tragic vision, and for their unswerving honesty in confronting the vicissitudes of personal experience intensified by separation from the comforts of home, family, and familiar life. The second section is headed "Poems in Love" and consists of six poems inspired by his relationship with his wife Gweno and are personal, passionate, and lyrical celebrations of love. Perhaps, however, the most affecting of his love lyrics is "Post-script: for Gweno" that he placed as the last poem in "Poems in Khaki" since it encompasses death and their final separation. He considered the poem he wrote to celebrate his marriage, "War Wedding," to be the most important poem in the volume. The other sections, headed "Songs," "On Old Themes," and "And Other Poems," consist largely of short lyrics on a variety of themes including five fine "Poems from the Chinese." The poem "All day it has rained . . ." with its reference to Edward THOMAS together with his poem "To Edward Thomas" demonstrate the meditative, largely rural tradition of personal poetry within which L. placed himself.

His first collection of short stories, *The Last Inspection*, was published in June 1942. Although the volume included stories he had written before the war, as he mentions in his "Author's Note," eighteen of the twenty-three stories are concerned with the army in England during the two years since Dunkirk. The "main motif is the rootless life of soldiers having no enemy, and always, somehow under a shadow." For the most part, the stories are concerned with the happiness and desolation of ordinary soldiers. Out of the common materials of day-to-day life, L. creates with authenticity and compassion the fear, confusion, and isolation of the serving soldier. As with his poems, he shows an intense concern for the deprived and for the victims of cruelty and oppression. His sympathy for the common people, his love of children, and his identification with ordinary soldiers impelled him to write out of personal experience about the lives of those among whom he lived and worked. They are, he said, "rather personal observations than detached compositions." They are also the stories told by a poet who seizes the inner meaning of an incident or a series of incidents in images and language that carry immediate conviction. The volume also includes "They Came," a much-anthologized story that was first published in *English Story* and for which in 1941 he was awarded the Edward J. O'Brien Prize.

In 1942, L. was posted with his battalion to India and then in 1944 to Chittagong, Burma, where he was killed. *Ha! Ha! Among the Trumpets: Poems in Transit,* a title taken, he said sarcastically, from the Book of Job, was published posthumously in 1945. The poems were arranged in three sections, those written in England, those written on embarkation, and the third and largest section of twenty-nine poems, those written in India. Poems such as "On Embarkation" and "The Departure" dealing with his parting from his wife and the more personal poems he wrote to her on the voyage and from India are most notable for their direct lyric beauty. "In Hospital: Poona (1)," for instance, in which he unites, at least for a brief time, the valleys and the mountains of Wales with his present experience of India and thus bridges their separation is a moving expression of longing and love. The poems in which he discusses his experiences of India, particularly "Village Funeral," "Holi," "The Mahratta Ghats," "The Peasants," and "Karanje Village," demonstrate his understanding of and admiration for the integrity of their simple, uncluttered lives in contrast to his own life filled with anxiety and complexity. His *Letters from India* was published in 1946 and a second volume of six stories, entitled *In the Green Tree,* was published in 1948. This included one of his best-known stories, "Ward '0'3(b)" based on the time he spent in hospital after having broken his jaw playing football and that is said in Lieutenant Weston to include a self-portrait. A miscellany of his writings including further uncollected poems and prose, edited by John Pikoulis, was published in 1982.

He was twenty-eight when he died but despite the fact that he had published so little and had not been given the time for his abilities to mature fully, his reputation was nonetheless secured. As a writer of compassion and sensitivity, of intense lyricism and imaginative power, he developed his own quiet voice of true feeling.

BIBLIOGRAPHY: John, A., *A. L.* (1970); Pikoulis, J., *A. L.* (1984); special L. issue, *PW* (1982)

A. R. JONES

LEWIS, C[live] S[taples]

b. 29 November 1898, Belfast, Northern Ireland; d. 22 November 1963, Cambridge

During a career that spanned nearly four decades, L. established himself as a literary scholar, poet, novelist, devotional writer, essayist, and children's writer. Educated at Oxford, he was a fellow of Magdalen College from 1925 to 1954 when he became professor of medieval and Renaissance literature at Magdalene College, Cambridge.

His earliest publications included two volumes of poetry, *Spirits in Bondage: A Cycle of Lyrics* and *Dymer*, writing as Clive Hamilton, in 1919 and 1926, respectively. Following the publication in 1933 of *The Pilgrim's Regress: An Allegorical Apology for Christianity, Reason and Romanticism*, an autobiographical account of his conversion to Christianity, L. was commissioned to write *The Problem of Pain* (1940). The success of the book, in which L. explored the complexities of moral and ethical issues for a general readership, led to a series of popular broadcasts for the BBC in the 1940s—later collected and published as *Mere Christianity* (1952).

After the publication in 1936 of his critical study *The Allegory of Love: A Study in Medieval Tradition*, L. turned to fiction and—highly unusual for an Oxford don—ventured into the world of SCIENCE FICTION with the publication of *Out of the Silent Planet* (1938), the first volume in a "space trilogy" that included *Perelandra* (1943) and *That Hideous Strength* (1945). Simultaneously, he also published two works of religious fiction, *The Screwtape Letters* (1942) and *The Great Divorce* (1945).

L.'s next literary venture would be the most intriguing of his career and the one for which he is perhaps best known: writing stories for children. In 1950, L. published *The Lion, the Witch and the Wardrobe*, the first of the seven-volume "Chronicles of Narnia" that included *Prince Caspian: The Return to Narnia* (1951), *The Voyage of the Dawn Treader* (1952), *The Silver Chair* (1953), *The Horse and His Boy* (1954), *The Magician's Nephew* (1955), and *The Last Battle* (1956). Merging allegory with adventure and fantasy, the "Chronicles" established L. as a best-selling author and have remained popular in both Britain and the U.S.

With the success of the "Chronicles," L. continued to write in a wide variety of genres—stories, essays, literary criticism—and numerous editions of his work appeared posthumously throughout the last decades of the 20th c. In 1955, L. published the autobiographical *Surprised by Joy: The Shape of My Early*

Life followed in 1961 with the publication of *A Grief Observed.*

BIBLIOGRAPHY: Carpenter, H., *The Inklings: C. S. L., J. R. R. Tolkien, Charles Williams, and Their Friends* (1978); Green, R. L., and W. Hooper, *C. S. L.* (1974; rev. ed., 1994); Wilson, A. N., *C. S. L.* (1990)

LEWIS, M[atthew] G[regory]
b. 9 July 1775, London; d. 16 May 1818, at sea en route from Jamaica to England

The novelist and dramatist L. is chiefly remembered for one work: his GOTHIC NOVEL, *The Monk* (3 vols., 1796), which was written when he was just nineteen and which earned him his nickname of "Monk Lewis." To the conventional Gothic influences of William SHAKESPEARE and Jacobean drama, L. added an eclectic blend of German ROMANTICISM, ballads and FOLKLORE, the writings of the Marquis de Sade and Samuel RICHARDSON's *Clarissa*. He was the most skillful of Ann RADCLIFFE's many imitators, who flourished at the end of the 18th and beginning of the 19th cs. during the public fascination with horror and the grotesque.

What L. did not share with Mrs. Radcliffe was her sense of restraint. *The Monk* is a violent tale of ambition, murder, and incest set in the monastery of the Capuchins in Madrid. A struggle between maintaining monastic vows and the fulfillment of personal ambitions leads its protagonist, Ambrosio, to temptation, sin, sexual obsession, and rape, and then to murder to conceal his guilt. He is discovered and tortured by the Inquisition, and sentenced to death; finally, he makes a pact with the Devil, only to be hurled to damnation at the end of the novel.

This sensational mixture of the supernatural and the carnal, so daring in its treatment of sexual fantasy and violence, was immensely popular on publication, but regarded by many as obscene: L. was, in fact, forced to withdraw and expurgate the third edition. For all its excesses, though, it is a powerfully written novel with profound insights into criminal psychology and erotic neuroses, all of which is quite brilliantly set in monastic cells, burial vaults, and underground passages that mirror the depths of Ambrosio's depravity. *The Monk* draws energetically on all the conventions of horror and the Gothic tradition, and subverts them by ridicule and parody; ultimately, the extremities that appear at first to be so dangerously radical are placed safely in the realms of fantasy.

L. wrote many verses, of which "Alonzo the Brave and the Fair Imogene" is the most famous because of its appearance in *The Monk*. He has been both praised and lambasted by the reading public, but he remains, above all, an entertainer.

BIBLIOGRAPHY: Howells, C. A., *Love, Mystery, and Misery: Feeling in Gothic Fiction* (1978); Peck, L. F., *A Life of M. G. L.* (1961); Van Luchene, S. R., *Essays in Gothic Fiction: From Horace Walpole to Mary Shelley* (1980); Varma, D. P., *The Gothic Flame* (1957)

NICOLA UPSON

LEWIS, [Percy] Wyndham
b. 18 November 1882, aboard a yacht off Amherst, Nova Scotia, Canada; d. 7 March 1957, London

Writer and artist, L. was the son of an American father and a British mother of Scots and Irish descent. His parents separated in 1893, and his mother brought him to London where they lived in genteel poverty. He was educated at Rugby and at the age of sixteen he won a scholarship to London's Slade School of Art but leaving three years later without completing his course, he traveled to Germany, visited Spain and Holland, and went to Paris where he painted and attended lectures at the Sorbonne. He returned to England in 1909 and began to write and to exhibit his paintings. He had three stories printed by Ford Madox FORD in the *English Review*. He became the director of the Rebel Art Centre, described as the seat of the Great London Vortex and in June 1914 and July 1915 he published the only two issues of *Blast,* a Vorticist review, much of which he wrote himself. *Blast* showed the influence of IMAGISM while the designs by L. and others in their theatrical and uncompromising shapes showed the influence of futurism that made speed and machinery a central preoccupation.

L. enlisted in March 1916 and served during World War I with great distinction in France, first as an artillery officer and later as an official war artist. *Tarr*, his first novel, that is partly autobiographical, was published in 1918. Set in Paris, it is concerned with the lives of a set of rather unsympathetic, impecunious artists. The self-destructive German Kreisler, driven by demons of uncontrollable violence, rapes Tarr's mistress Bertha, kills his opponent after the duel is finished, and finally kills himself. All the characters are presented as mechanical constructions without an inner life. None is presented as a human being and since the author's attitude toward them is completely lacking in sympathy, they remain unsympathetic figures so far as the reader is concerned. L. is not interested in the emotional lives of his characters but stands aside from them callously mocking their absurdity. They seem to be in the novel only in order to illustrate L.'s belief in man's essential uselessness and repulsiveness. He is engaged in creating a Bergsonian farce in which we are invited to laugh at people, to regard people as inanimate objects that closely resemble people, interacting like things. His SATIRE is directed not against the follies and vices of man but against mankind itself and this set the pattern for his subsequent fictions.

Between the wars, L. held a number of exhibitions, published some twenty books and a number of articles and edited two issues of the *Tyro* (1921–22) and three book-length issues of the *Enemy* (1927–29). His novels included *The Apes of God* (1930), a satire on Bloomsbury and literary London; *The Revenge for Love* (1937); and *Self Condemned* (1954), which draws on the experiences of his three-year stay in Canada. His projected four-part work titled *The Human Age*—including *The Childermass* (1928), *Monstre Gai* (1956), and *Malign Fiesta* (1956)—remained unfinished. It has been described as "his greatest imaginative work—too confusing in its intention—partly supernatural SCIENCE FICTION, partly allegorical satire, partly intellectual debate—to rank as a coherent work." He perfected an angular, harsh prose style in his novels that seems to emulate the relentless, mechanical world that his fictional figures inhabit. In 1955, T. S. ELIOT described him as "the most distinguished living novelist" though few other critics have agreed with this opinion. His work never achieved popularity and in recent years has been almost entirely neglected by readers and the critics. It is hard to escape G. S. FRASER's conclusion that, "The most damaging general criticism that can be made of Lewis is that he is too exclusively the virtuoso of negative emotions."

He was a writer of forceful, original, and often intemperate opinions. He wrote numbers of essays and books of criticism including *Time and Western Man* (1927), *The Lion and the Fox* (1927), *Men without Art* (1934), and *The Writer and the Absolute* (1952). In addition, he wrote two autobiographies, *Blasting and Bombardiering* (1937) dealing with the early part of his life and *Rude Assignment* (1950) with later events. His polemical writings are often brilliant and occasionally profound though they are also sometimes argumentative and quarrelsome. Too often his views are an expression only of his injured egotism and his opinions become prejudices, unsupported by evidence. As in all his writings, his critical writings while containing some of his most powerful and attractive prose are too often flawed by a lack of discipline.

In the early 1930s, his admiration of Adolf Hitler as a man of peace and the Nazis as an aristocracy of intellect brought him into disrepute. Despite the fact that he fully repudiated these views in 1939, the hostility he had aroused never entirely left him. He and his wife spent the war in the U.S. and Canada where he had gone in the hope of a lecture tour and portrait commissions.

When he returned to England in 1945, he reestablished his reputation to a large extent. In 1949, he was give a retrospective exhibition at the Redfern Gallery followed in 1951 by a major retrospective exhibition at the Tate Gallery. He was awarded a Civil List pension and from 1946 to 1951, when his eyesight deteriorated so badly that he could no longer see the pictures, he was art critic for the *Listener* where he used his influence to further the work and reputation of young artists including Michael Ayrton and Francis Bacon. He is best remembered now as an artist and an outstanding draughtsman. Many of his paintings are in national collections including the Tate, the Victoria and Albert, the British Museum, and the Imperial War Museum. His portraits particularly those of Eliot, Ezra Pound, and Edith SITWELL are still some of the most famous icons of our time.

BIBLIOGRAPHY: Kenner, H., *W. L.* (1954); O' Keeffe, P., *Some Sort of Genius: A Life of W. L.* (2000); Wagner, G., *W. L.* (1957)

A. R. JONES

LILYE [or LILY], William
b. ca. 1486, Odiham, Hampshire; d. 10 December 1522, London

Having traveled to the Middle East, Italy, and Greece, L. settled in London where his circle included such notable scholars as John COLET, Desiderius ERASMUS, Thomas LINACRE, and Thomas MORE. L. pioneered the teaching of Greek at St. Paul's School and was part-author of the Latin grammar in use at Eton as late as the 19th c. L.'s grammar first appeared as *Rudimenta grammatices* (wr. ca. 1509) and was later revised by Erasmus and published anonymously in 1513. L. is regarded as Tudor England's most important grammarian.

LINACRE [or LYNAKER], Thomas
b. ca. 1460, Canterbury; d. 20 October 1524, London

Associated with a circle of Oxford scholars that included William GROCYN, Hugh LATIMER, and John COLET, L. was physician to King HENRY VIII and translator of Galen, the Greek physician, into Latin, then the lingua franca of educated Europeans. Latin translations were studied in medical schools until the start of the 19th c. Galen was the founder of experimental physiology. His theory of the "humours," and an ascending triad of "spirits" derived from Aristotle, was influential in the Renaissance and was thought to unite body and soul. References appear in, for example, William SHAKESPEARE and John DONNE ("that subtle knot that makes us man").

LITERARY AWARDS AND PRIZES

Great Britain's thriving literary culture is reflected in the number of literary prizes given out and the amount of fanfare given their distribution. British writers not only frequently receive very prestigious international prizes, but many of the specifically British literary prizes garner international acclaim for their winners. The best-known prizes involve heavy publicity, and are avidly followed not only by the literary community, but by the British general public who "vote" for their favorites in regular newspaper and online polls and even place substantial bets on the top prizes. Professional bookmakers read the shortlisted books and place odds on their chance of winning, and the announcements of prizes are often much-anticipated events. The fanfare, in fact, points up the fact that while literary prizes are established as a way of rewarding literary achievement, they have increasingly gained attention as an ever-more valuable marketing tool. The imprimatur conferred by a major prize not only makes critics sit up and take notice; it can make the difference between an unprofitable book and a best-seller.

Many of Britain's literary prizes are administered by the Book Trust, an organization dedicated to promoting literature and reading, including what is perhaps the best known of British prizes: the Booker Prize (now the Man Booker Prize). Supported by Booker PLC, a food retailing and wholesaling company, the prize was established in 1969 to choose the year's best contemporary novel. Judges selected from the U.K.'s leading writers, critics, and academics read a long list of nominees submitted by publishers. Previous winners and shortlisted authors are automatically entered as well, causing the prize to tend slightly toward more established authors. The first winner was P. H. Newby for *Something to Answer For* (1969).

The Man Booker Prize award is £50,000, but the prize is worth far more to authors and publishers. The announcement of the Booker Prize shortlist causes an instant upswing in sales for the six authors chosen, and the winner often becomes a best-seller. In 1999, for instance, prizewinner J. M. Coetzee's *Disgrace* moved from its position at 1,431 on the London *Times* best-seller list to sixth after the award was announced. Sales increased almost 1,800 percent in five days. Critics have pointed out that the stamp of approval a prize like the Booker confers makes an even greater difference to little-known authors, who might otherwise be ignored by consumers at the bookstore. Other recent winners of the Booker Prize include Indian author Arundhati Roy (1997), Ian MCEWAN (1998), Canadian authors Margaret Atwood (2000) and Yann Martel (2002), and Australian author Peter Carey (2001).

The Book Trust administers several other prizes as well. The Commonwealth Writer's Prize is awarded to the best book and best first book in four regions of the British Commonwealth: Africa, Eurasia, Canada and the Caribbean, and Southeast Asia and the South Pacific. The Nestlé Smarties Book Prize issues awards for best children's book in three age categories, the Kurt Maschler Award is given for both text and illustration of a children's book, and the Sainsbury's Baby Book Award is given to the best book aimed at children under one year old. The John Llewellyn Rhys Prize, established in 1942 and now sponsored by the *Mail on Sunday,* is awarded to the best literary book by a writer under the age of thirty-five.

The Book Trust also administers England's largest annual award for a single work of fiction, the Orange Prize. Launched in 1996, the prize is given for the best novel published in English by a woman of any nationality. It was the brainchild of a group of senior women in publishing who got together to ask why so few women were winning the major literary prizes. The prize of £30,000 is awarded at a festival, and the Orange Prize, like the Booker Prize, is quickly becoming a major marketing opportunity. Winners have included Helen Dunmore (1996), Anne Michaels (1997), Carol Shields (1998), Suzanne Berne (1999), Linda Grant (2000), and Kate Grenville (2001).

In its informational material, the Book Trust lists more than 150 other prizes besides its own available to writers in English. The International IMPAC Dublin Literary Award is the world's largest prize for a single work of fiction, awarding IR£100,000 annually. Established in 1994 by a Dublin City Civic Charter, the Irish prize was first awarded in 1996 to Australian novelist David Malouf. The IMPAC Dublin Award is unique in that nominees are submitted by more than one hundred public libraries worldwide, and any works of fiction published in English are eligible, regardless of whether they were originally written in English or published in translation. Award winners have thus included international authors such as Javier Marias (1997) and Herta Müller (1998).

The Whitbread Award, established in 1971 and sponsored by Whitbread PLC, is also very prestigious. Two awards are given, one for Best Book of the Year and one for Best Children's Book of the Year. The children's book shortlist is selected by five judges, two of whom are young people. The best book shortlist is composed of one work each from four categories: poetry, BIOGRAPHY, novel, and first novel. Recent winners of the £30,000 prize for best book have included Ted HUGHES (1998) and Seamus HEANEY (1999) with poetry and Kate ATKINSON (1995) with a first novel. David Almond (1998) and J. K. ROWLING (1999) are recent winners of the best children's book prize.

The oldest of the famous literary prizes is the Hawthornden Prize, founded in 1919 and awarded to the year's best work of imaginative literature, a category that can include nonfiction. There are no submissions for this prize; rather a panel of judges determines the shortlist and the winner. The Booksellers'

Association also issues a series of annual prizes, the British Book Awards, given out at a festive ceremony. Chosen by representatives from all areas of the book trade, the British Book Awards include not only Author of the Year and Book of the Year awards, but also awards for the year's best publisher, illustrator, newcomer, and children's book.

There are numerous smaller prizes for every genre of literature, including the *Guardian* First Book Prize, the Thomas Cook/*Daily Telegraph* Travel Book Award, and the Arthur C. Clarke Award honoring the best SCIENCE FICTION novel first published in the U.K. The Somerset Maugham Awards are given to a writer under the age of thirty-five for a variety of genres. In poetry, the Forward Prizes honor the best collection, best first collection, and best single poem annually. The T. S. Eliot Prize is given for the best new book of poetry. Nonfiction is honored with a number of prestigious prizes, including the Samuel Johnson Prize for a work of history. The Heinemann Award for a work of "literary distinction" is usually awarded to a nonfiction book.

A few prizes depart from the tradition of using illustrious panels of judges to nominate and select books. The David Cohen British Literature Prize, administered by the Arts Council of England, is given to one book each year selected from a shortlist nominated by members of the public. Recent winners include V. S. NAIPAUL (1996), Harold PINTER (1997), Murial SPARK (1998), William TREVOR (1999), and Doris LESSING (2000). The W. H. Smith Book Awards, sponsored by the chain bookseller, include nine awards, eight of which are chosen by public voting. Winners for the year 2000 included Maeve Binchy for fiction, Zadie SMITH for new talent, and Simon Schama for general knowledge. Other categories are biography/AUTOBIOGRAPHY, travel, children's, and home and leisure.

Prizes for plays are mostly given as part of awards for theatrical achievement, including acting, directing, and production. The most prestigious theatrical honors in the U.K. are the Olivier Awards, established in 1976 and presented by the Society of London Theatre. The Olivier Awards include prizes for Best New Play, Best New Comedy, and Best New Musical. Recent winners have included Richard Nelson (2000), Joe Penhall (2001), and Marie Jones (2001). Other high profile theatrical awards are the Critics' Circle Theatre Awards, founded in 1913 and selected by a group of theater critics from newspapers and other journals, and the *Evening Standard* Theatre Awards, which provide prizes for Best Play and Best Musical Event.

British authors have also won some of the world's most prestigious international prizes. Perhaps the most prestigious, the Nobel Prize for Literature, is awarded annually for an author's entire body of work, rather than a single book. Worth approximately one million U.S. dollars, the Nobel laureate in literature is announced each year in October. British and Irish Nobel laureates include Rudyard KIPLING (1907), W. B. YEATS (1923), Bernard SHAW (1925), John GALSWORTHY (1932), T. S. ELIOT (1948), Bertrand RUSSELL (1950), Winston CHURCHILL (1953), Samuel BECKETT (1969), William GOLDING (1983), Seamus Heaney (1995), and V. S. Naipaul (2001). In 1956, English author Eleanor FARJEON won the first Hans Christian Anderson Award for writing CHILDREN'S LITERATURE. These awards, given biannually by the International Board on Books for Young People to an author and illustrator for a body of work, have become the world's most prestigious award for children's literature.

BIBLIOGRAPHY: Clapp, J., *International Dictionary of Literary Awards* (1963); Pribic, R., *Nobel Laureates in Literature* (1990); Strachan, A., *Prizewinning Literature: U.K. Literary Award Winners* (1989); Todd, R., *Consuming Fictions: The Booker Prize and Fiction in Britain Today* (1996)

GINGER STRAND

LITERARY CRITICISM BEFORE 1945

A recognizable English literary criticism began to emerge in the Elizabethan era. Its chief concerns were to define and promote poetry, to vindicate writing in English rather than in Latin or Greek, and to provide precepts, based partly on classical rhetoric, for the writing of poetry and prose. The most enduring work of Elizabethan literary criticism is Sir Philip SIDNEY's *An Apologie for Poetrie*, written ca. 1580–81 and published in 1595, also known as *A Defence of Poetry*, which aims to restore the status of an art that, in Sidney's view, had sunk into low esteem. His crucial argument concerns poetry's relationship to nature. Poetry is an art of imitation or mimesis, but not in the sense that it merely mimics nature; indeed, poetry, unlike philosophy, science, jurisprudence, medicine, grammar, and rhetoric, is unique because it is not subject to nature but creates a second nature that improves on or exceeds the original by bringing forth forms that never existed in nature. This creation is not an end in itself, however, but the process by which poetry achieves its two chief aims: to teach and delight.

In the 17th c., the focus of critical debate shifted from poetry to drama, and centered on the attempt to reconcile a just appreciation of William SHAKESPEARE's achievement with the neoclassical criteria of decorum and proportion that began to become dominant after the restoration of the monarchy in 1660. The key critical text in this period is John DRYDEN's *Essay in Dramatick Poesie*. It takes the form of a dialogue about a range of literary topics, especially the relative merits of the ancient and modern dramatists and of French and English playwrights. To the claim that French drama, which largely observes the three classical unities of time, place, and action, is superior to English drama, a figure called Neander—representing Dryden himself—responds by defending the liveliness and variety of English drama, especially in Shakespeare's work.

The dominance of neoclassical critical criteria continued into the early to mid-18th c., when writers promoted the idea that they were living in an "Augustan age" of cultural excellence that rivaled that of the Roman Emperor Augustus. The work that summarizes the Augustan critical position most vividly is Alexander POPE's witty poem, the *Essay on Criticism*. Pope provides a set of criteria for the critic of poetry: for example, good poetry follows both nature and the rules that the ancients derived from nature, though master poets can sometimes successfully break the rules; it can succeed as a whole even if some parts are flawed; it subdues elaborate invention to the effective expression of the commonplace; it subordinates style and pleasing sound to sense. Pope's criteria were echoed in the journals that began to emerge as an important forum of critical and cultural debate in this era, especially the *Spectator* (1711–12) under the editorship of Richard STEELE and Joseph ADDISON.

In the later 18th c., Samuel JOHNSON came to assume an unprecedented critical authority for his forceful and memorably phrased critical judgments, especially in his *Lives of the English Poets*. Combining sometimes dubious biographical anecdote with close attention to poetic detail, Johnson offers many critical appraisals that still seem judicious, for example of Dryden and Pope. Other critical judgments now appear more questionable, however, such as his condemnation, in his "Life of Cowley," of what he saw as the excesses of the metaphysical poetry that was to become central to the critical revaluations proposed by T. S. ELIOT and F. R. LEAVIS in the early 20th c.

As the 18th c. drew to a close, neoclassicism crumbled under the impact of revolution, industrialization, and ROMANTICISM. The crucial critical statements of the earlier Romantic era were made by two of its major poets, William WORDSWORTH and Samuel Taylor COLERIDGE. In his preface to the second edition of their *Lyrical Ballads* (1802), Wordsworth argued for a kind of poetry that broke away from neoclassical diction and decorum and used the real language of men to trace, in the incidents of common life, the primary laws of human nature. Coleridge in his *Biographia Literaria*, provided a definition of the poet as one possessed of the synthetic and magical power of the imagination that can bring all the human faculties into play. "Imagination" is not only possessed by poets, however; what Coleridge calls the primary imagination is the vital force of all human perception,

which repeats the divine act of creation and self-affirmation; the secondary imagination is its echo that coexists with the will and operates in a more conscious way. Fancy, by contrast, simply works by the law of association, putting together fixed tokens without any vital shaping spirit.

The idea of the imagination, in various forms, was crucial to Romantic aesthetics. It also features significantly in Percy Bysshe SHELLEY's *A Defence of Poetry*. Like Coleridge, Shelley sees the imagination as a synthesizing faculty, and he contrasts it with the analytical faculty of reason. But for Shelley, the imagination has a more explicitly moral and indeed socially progressive function than for Coleridge, because it liberates us from our own egos and enables us to identify with the beautiful as it exists in thoughts, actions, or people. Poetry is justified because it is the means of strengthening the faculty of the imagination on which moral awareness and action, and social and political change, depend. It is in this sense that poets are, as Shelley declares in his famous conclusion, the unacknowledged legislators of the world.

Shelley's sense of the ethical and social importance of poetry persisted into the mid-Victorian criticism of Matthew ARNOLD, though in a much more politically conservative mode. In his essay "The Study of Poetry," Arnold, a significant Victorian poet himself as well as a major critic and cultural commentator of the period, defined poetry as a "criticism of life" that would largely replace religion and philosophy and provide the necessary complement of science. Arnold's redefinition of poetry as a kind of criticism related to his sense of the importance of criticism itself: in "The Function of Criticism at the Present Time," he offered a definition of criticism as a disinterested effort to grasp and disseminate the best that has been known and thought in the world.

Victorian criticism was also marked by an increasingly intense debate over the most dominant literary form of the era—the novel. The English novel had taken off in the 18th c. and risen to prominence in the 19th c. with relatively little theoretical baggage. But by the later Victorian era, this insouciance no longer seemed acceptable. The classic statement of the changing attitude to the novel in England was Henry JAMES's essay "The Art of Fiction." James satirized the mid-Victorian attitude to the novel as one of bluff common sense, in which a novel was a novel as a pudding was a pudding. Now, he felt, the novel in England was starting to be taken seriously as an art form, as had already happened in France. The truth of James's comment was borne out by the revaluations of established reputations that began to appear in the periodicals that formed such an important part of Victorian cultural life: the novelist who came above all to stand for the flaws of English fiction was Charles DICKENS, whom George ELIOT's partner G. H. LEWES ruthlessly attacked, in his essay "Dickens in Relation to Criticism" (1872) in the *Fortnightly Review*, as an unthinking, almost unhinged writer. By the end of the century, the idea of the novel as a highly wrought art form with profound moral implications was poised to dominate English literary criticism.

The first years of the 20th c. seemed to confirm the exhaustion of Romantic poetry and saw the start of the new developments in poetic theory and practice that later came to be called modernist. In poetry, the quintessential critical manifesto of early MODERNISM was "A Few Don'ts by an Imagiste," which appeared in the magazine *Poetry* in 1913. It was largely the work of the poet Ezra Pound, who like T. S. Eliot, was then living in London. Practicing in prose the economy that he advocated in poetry, Pound produced a set of terse maxims that slashed through the veils of Victorian verse: the poet should eschew abstractions and superfluous adjectives and aim to convey complex intellectual and emotional meanings in as concrete and concentrated a way as possible. These notions were developed by Eliot, in his advocacy of the metaphysical poets whose apparent oddities had been rejected by Johnson. In "The Metaphysical Poets," Eliot proposed a literary and cultural history that was to prove enormously influential, arguing that, for a metaphysical poet like John DONNE, thought and experience were fused; later in the 17th c., however, a dissociation of sensibility severed thought and experience and the split has never been healed. Only the mind of the poet could still create unity: while the experience of the ordinary person consisted of fragments, the poet's mind was constantly forming those fragments into new wholes. But in the chaos of the modern world those new wholes could not be easily accessible: modern poetry must be difficult.

The difficulty of modern poetry, not least Eliot's own, required trained readers; and it increasingly seemed that the place to train them was the university. It was in the later 1920s that the transfer of critical power from the literary journal to the academy accelerated. Cambridge University was the key site for this, though its major critics—I. A. RICHARDS, William EMPSON, and Leavis—characteristically had an uncertain or fraught relationship to the institution. The historical specter that stalked the development of Cambridge criticism was World War I, a devastating demonstration of the cultural debacle for which literary studies might be able to provide a remedy by teaching people to distinguish between vital and inert uses of language.

Despite this intense sense of mission, Richards's own involvement with Cambridge English began, by his own account, in a comically ad hoc way. He went to ask Mansfield Forbes, who was then forming the Cambridge English School, to help him to get work as a guide on the Isle of Skye; they started to talk about Wordsworth and two hours later Forbes took him on as a lecturer in English. But it was still unclear what "English studies" entailed. Richards's primary contribution to clarifying this was the famous experiment he describes in *Practical Criticism;* this involved giving poems, with authors and dates omitted, to a group of volunteers and asking them to write comments on them. Their responses revealed a remarkable capacity for misinterpretation. It was clear that it could not be taken for granted that even conventionally well-educated people would have the skills required to read and interpret poems correctly. From this research, both a purpose and a method for literary studies emerged. Its purpose was to teach people how to read literature; its method would come to be called "close reading"—a careful attention to the language of a text, to its general and local meanings, to its nuances and implications. Richards's assumption that it was possible, by close reading, to identify the correct meaning of a text was, however, implicitly challenged by one of his students, Empson, whose *Seven Types of Ambiguity* was seminal in its demonstration of a range of ways in which a piece of literary language may mean two or more different things.

Empson, Richards, and Eliot made vital contributions to modern English literary criticism; but it was F. R. Leavis, combining elements from Empson and Richards and Eliot with his own distinctive insights, whose contribution would be the most significant. Leavis had a clear sense of the mission of criticism: its task was to keep alive the insights into human life that only great literature could provide, in an era when the threat of mass culture was greater than ever before. A major influence on Leavis's sense of cultural menace was *Fiction and the Reading Public*, by his wife, Q. D. LEAVIS. This traced an increasing division between a cultivated minority of readers and a mass audience avid for low quality fiction. In 1932, Leavis began the quarterly magazine *Scrutiny*, which was to last until 1953 and in which he and important collaborators like L. C. Knights were to publish a range of key essays that would later be collected in such books as Leavis's *The Common Pursuit* and Knights's *Explorations* (1946). Leavis also published two important studies of poetry: *New Bearings in English Poetry*, which endorsed Gerard Manley HOPKINS, Pound's *Mauberley* (1920), and above all Eliot; and *Revaluation*, which contrasted poets such as Ben JONSON, Donne, Pope, Wordsworth, and John KEATS, whose work fused thought and emotion and the strengths of popular and educated speech, with poets in whom sound was divorced from sense, such as Shelley, Alfred, Lord TENNYSON, and A. C. SWINBURNE.

In the 1930s, Leavis and other *Scrutiny* contributors saw off three aspects of literary criticism that would not enjoy a revival in Britain until the 1980s:

Marxism, FEMINISM, and theory. The political crises of the 1930s had produced a significant strand of English Marxist criticism, represented above all by Christopher Caudwell, a poet and detective story writer who was killed in the Spanish Civil War and whose posthumously published *Illusion and Reality* (1937) aimed to develop a Marxist history of poetry. Leavis, however, in "Under Which King, Bezonian?" had rejected what he saw as the Marxist dogma of the priority of economic conditions, and in "Retrospect of a Decade" he characterized *Scrutiny*'s position in the 1930s as one that acknowledged the pressure of material circumstances but also insisted on the recognition of an element of human autonomy. Feminism, for *Scrutiny*, was represented above all by Virginia WOOLF's *Three Guineas*, which Q. D. Leavis, in "Caterpillars of the Commonwealth Unite!" castigated for what she saw as its self-indulgent hostility to men and its patronizing attitude to ordinary women. The claims of theory were advanced by René Wellek, who, reviewing Leavis's *Revaluation* in *Scrutiny* in March 1937, urged him to provide a theoretical defense of his critical position. In "Literary Criticism and Philosophy," Leavis replied that a concern with theory would detract from that close attention to the text that was crucial to the proper understanding and evaluation of literature.

By the 1940s, it looked as though Leavis had won. Both Marxist criticism and feminism had run into the sands; theory had made no headway. While the Second World War seemed to radicalize the English politically, leading to the landslide election victory in 1945 of a Labour government with an emphatically left-wing manifesto, its effects upon literary culture were more conservative. In the aftermath of war, there appeared to be little desire to revive and develop Marxist or feminist critical perspectives or to pursue theory. The publication in 1948 of Leavis's *The Great Tradition*, which constructed a narrow canon of English novelists that led from Jane AUSTEN, through George Eliot, James, and Joseph CONRAD, to D. H. LAWRENCE, consolidated his critical approach. For some time to come, critical debate in England, whatever questions it might try to raise, would largely be conducted in Leavis's terms.

BIBLIOGRAPHY: Baldick, C., *The Social Mission of English Criticism, 1848–1932* (1983); Blamires, H., *A History of Literary Criticism* (1991); Brown, B., *The Cambridge History of Literary Criticism: Romanticism*, vol. 5 (2000); Litz, A. W., L. Menand, and L. Rainey, eds., *The Cambridge History of Literary Criticism: Modernism and the New Criticism*, vol. 7 (2000); Mulhern, F., *The Moment of "Scrutiny"* (1979); Nisbet, H. B., and C. J. Rawson, eds., *The Cambridge History of Literary Criticism: The Eighteenth Century*, vol. 4 (1997); Norton, G. P., ed., *Cambridge History of Literary Criticism: The Renaissance*, vol. 3 (1999)

NICOLAS TREDELL

LITERARY CRITICISM SINCE 1945

Three dominant features of British criticism since World War II distinguish this phase of its history from the preceding period of energetic "modernist" controversy led by Ezra Pound, T. S. ELIOT, and Virginia WOOLF in the 1920s and 1930s. These may be labeled as academic incorporation, cultural demotion, and international reorientation. In the first place, criticism's institutional base shifted away from the Soho restaurants in which avant-garde poets had debated their aesthetics in the early decades of the century, and into the seminar rooms of the universities, especially after the modest but significant expansion of higher education in the mid-1960s. Before the war, most leading critics were poets, novelists, or freelance essayists writing in "little magazines" or more popular periodicals; and the notable exceptions to this rule at Cambridge, I. A. RICHARDS, F. R. LEAVIS, and William EMPSON, were marginal to the academic establishment. After the war, there are no significant poet-critics or novelist-critics of the stature of Eliot or Woolf, and most critical writing was produced by professional academics. This professionalization of literary criticism was widely lamented, as it tended toward predictable routines of "interpretation," and a growth of obscure jargon, leaving behind the qualities of creative engagement, risk, and iconoclasm that had made the period 1914–40 so fertile in critical debate.

The second major feature of the post-1945 dispensation, related to the first, is a decline in the public standing, cultural prestige, and self-confidence of literary criticism. This loss of conviction did not set in at once; indeed, it was preceded and perhaps precipitated by a hubristic phase of excessive self-importance. The account offered below of criticism since 1945 is accordingly divided into two periods, the first (roughly 1945–68) marked by a relatively assured cultural authority, the second (since about 1968) by fractious self-doubt. In the first phase, criticism enjoyed the continuing prestige of its prewar achievements, identified with Eliot, Leavis, Empson, and their American counterparts the "New Critics," now consolidated into a powerful orthodoxy. Furthermore, it addressed a large educated public of "common readers," through such journals as *Encounter*, the *New Statesman*, and the BBC magazine the *Listener*, in the shared confidence that literary criticism was, as Leavis insisted, the "central" intellectual activity of any living culture. Nonacademic readers were prepared to accord critics an authority more extensive than those of historians or philosophers, to assess matters of meaning and value that stretched from psychology to sociology: the concept of the "dissociation of sensibility," for example, proposed by Eliot and developed by Leavis, embraced problems both of mental equilibrium ("poised maturity," in Leavis's phraseology) and of social cohesion ("the organic community"). After the cultural turbulence of the 1960s, however, the centrality of criticism could no longer be assumed so confidently; the predominance of academic professionals increasingly divorced criticism both from creative practice and from the public arena, leaving only a slender connection in the shapes of the literary "media don" and the surviving public journals of intellectual debate—notably the *London Review of Books* (founded 1979). In this second phase, criticism still harbors "imperial" ambitions to annex neighboring intellectual territories, but its victories here—mostly Pyrrhic—take place within the academy, under the headings of Cultural Studies (in which literary methods intrude upon sociology) and Literary Theory (in which critics treat psychology, history, and philosophy as "text").

The third salient feature of the postwar critical scene is more positive, if at first destabilizing: the opening of British critical debate to a wide range of international influences. Prewar critical discussion had not been conducted in an insular vacuum, and American connections, through Henry JAMES, Eliot, and Pound, had often been strong, but usually the British critic had been more attentive to the indigenous tradition of Samuel JOHNSON, Samuel Taylor COLERIDGE , and Matthew ARNOLD than to contemporary European voices. This all changed quite suddenly in the 1970s with the influx of successive theoretical models from France, followed by academic refinements of them developed in the U.S. By the 1980s, the centrality once assumed by Cambridge or Bloomsbury had clearly been ceded: the most influential critical ideas were emerging instead from Paris or from the top-flight U.S. campuses—Yale, Harvard, Chicago, Duke, Cornell, Princeton, Johns Hopkins, or Berkeley. British criticism struggled to domesticate and synthesize a bewildering array of international critical schools and movements, as it did to adjust itself to second-rank status.

In this and in other respects, the fortunes of criticism follow larger changes in British society and culture in this period. The end of Empire and subordination to the economic and cultural supremacy of the U.S. are reflected in the deflation of English critical "centrality." Similarly, the dissolution of social hierarchy and deference in favor of a more multicultural and socially liberal polity finds its echo in a contemporary critical scene that is pluralistic and no longer concerned to defend literary sensibility against the imagined menace of mass entertainment.

The first phase of this period, from the immediate postwar years until the late sixties, is one in which the influence of Leavis and his collaborators reaches its zenith, while encountering a new range of dissenting alternatives. The Leavisite journal *Scrutiny*, founded in 1932, suffered the usual insolvency of literary periodicals in 1952, but its twenty volumes were soon reprinted in 1963. Meanwhile, a predominantly Leavisite survey, *The Pelican Guide to English Literature* (7 vols., 1954–61), edited by Boris Ford, was establishing itself as the standard account of literary history used by students and teachers. The Leavis group won many converts in the educational system to its curious blend of antiestablishment vigilance and nostalgic social conservatism, using its conception of literary value as a weapon against the alleged moral bankruptcy both of cultural elites (the BBC, the London literary press) and of the utilitarian ("technologico-Benthamite") assumptions of modern British politics.

Leavis himself had shifted his position since the 1930s in some important ways: abandoning his early discipleship to Eliot's "classicism," he had become an implacable romantic, defending the work of William BLAKE, D. H. LAWRENCE, and eventually the Charles DICKENS of *Hard Times* as vital resources of the antiutilitarian imagination, while scorning the modernist work of James JOYCE, Woolf, and Eliot as sterile aestheticism. He still insisted on close engagement with the linguistic texture of literary works, but the moral urgency of his critical approach led him increasingly to divide writers into those who were "for life" and those who were "against life," on grounds that were more instinctive than rationally argued. One result was a severely restricted canon of truly admirable writers. Leavis's book *The Great Tradition* notoriously dismissed all but a handful (Jane AUSTEN, George ELIOT, James, Joseph CONRAD) of novelists in English as lacking in moral seriousness or reverence for "life"; Dickens was later to be rehabilitated as a "great" novelist after all, and Lawrence was acclaimed as the modern heir of this tradition in *D. H. Lawrence, Novelist*. It is worth noting that whereas before the war Leavis's books had been devoted mainly to traditions of English poetry, after it they concentrated on prose fiction. This is one important instance of a general trend, away from the prewar "New-Critical" emphasis on short lyric poems, and toward a fresh interest in narrative, especially in the novel.

Coherent alternatives both to the Leavisite camp and to the tenuously allied tradition of prewar modernist criticism became more visible in the late fifties, and converged into a significant "counter-modernist" backlash. This development can be linked with a similar kind of skepticism found among the contemporaneous "Movement" writers such as Philip LARKIN and Kingsley AMIS; and its basis can be found in the changed political context of postwar austerity and welfare-state social democracy. Intellectuals who had recently lived through a war against fascist powers, in which Pound had made broadcasts in support of Mussolini, were no longer willing to accept the critical authority of such modernist writers without a fundamental reassessment of their writings and their political implications. Eliot, W. B. YEATS, and Pound were all to some degree tainted by their fascist sympathies, and even Leavis's hero Lawrence had espoused violent authoritarianism. In the new postwar era of social responsibility, the formal experimentalism and linguistic obscurity of these writers now looked sinister, and their iconoclastic critical principles were unpicked by a new generation of critics associated with the Oxford journal *Essays in Criticism* (founded 1951).

Donald DAVIE, in *Purity of Diction in English Verse* and *Articulate Energy*, led a reaction against the imagistic cult of concreteness in the Pound-Eliot-Leavis critical tradition, arguing for a return to the older virtues of discursive lucidity that he associated with William WORDSWORTH and 18th-c. verse. For Davie, the arrogant abandonment by the modernists of syntactical connection and of an assumed contract with the common reader was equivalent to fascist contempt for civilized consensus. Echoing some of these views, Graham Hough in his *Image and Experience* (1960) condemned the modernist phase of revolt against accepted linguistic norms as a dead-end, disconnecting poetry from ordinary discourse. Two other important critics emerged in the fifties as contributors to *Essays in Criticism*, and they too played their part in the dismantling of the Eliot-Leavis orthodoxies: Frank Kermode's book *Romantic Image* (1957) traced the Romantic irrationalist origins of modernist poetics, and in doing so undermined Eliot's concept of the "dissociation of sensibility." Kermode's more ambitious work, *The Sense of an Ending* (1967), is devoted in part to replacing the modernist conception of "myth," which he sees as potentially regressive, with a more skeptical and exploratory model of "fiction" as the means by which we may shape our sense of time and value. Raymond WILLIAMS offered in *Culture and Society, 1780–1950* an historical investigation of the meanings of "culture" in Britain, pitted against the conservatism of Eliot's *Notes towards the Definition of Culture*, and conducted with the aim of fostering a "common culture" conceived in socialist terms. Williams's early work has been seen as a left-wing variant of Leavisite approaches, but his unfolding career revealed an ever bolder rejection of Leavis, culminating in *The Country and the City*, which assaults the myth of the rural "organic community."

At the height of its influence, the Leavisite conception of literature and criticism was increasingly contested in the sixties, and on several fronts. George STEINER in his *Language and Silence*, for example, accused it of insular provincialism for its lack of inter-est in European literature. Meanwhile, other junior critics more sympathetic to Leavis regretted his disdain for living writers; their new journal *Critical Quarterly* (founded 1959) set out to reconnect criticism with contemporary writing. The postwar generation of critics was, on the whole, seeking new stimulation both from contemporary culture and from the international circulation of ideas. Kermode, for example, was absorbing and critically resisting the impact of the Canadian literary theorist Northrop Frye, and he moved on to encounter French structuralist theories; Steiner ranged freely among modern linguists and philosophers; and the novelist-critic David LODGE also began to explore linguistic theory and Continental structuralist concepts. The new universities at Sussex, York, Warwick, Essex, and elsewhere fostered "interdisciplinary" encounters between literary study and philosophy, sociology, psychology, and linguistics, that opened the rather narrow sphere of criticism to multiple intellectual cross-currents in the 1970s.

The stage was set, then, for the arrival in the seventies and eighties of what became known simply as "Theory," a mixed body of ideas derived from Russian formalism, Western Marxism, Czech and French structuralism, American FEMINISM, psychoanalysis, and the broader European modernist tradition, including eventually the Parisian poststructuralist thought of Roland Barthes and others, provisionally bundled together by the political radicalism of 1968, which fired younger intellectuals with deep suspicion of the liberal academy as (in Louis Althusser's influential term) an "ideological state apparatus." The encounters of established British academic critics with structuralist and related ideas, in, for example, Lodge's *The Modes of Modern Writing* or Kermode's *The Classic* (1975) are notable for their cautious, critically selective responses. A new wave of more politically radical critics was emerging, though, with a more thorough commitment to the theories of the Parisian masters: Colin MacCabe's *James Joyce and the Revolution of the Word* (1978) and Catherine Belsey's *Critical Practice* (1980), for example, both follow Barthes and other poststructuralist theorists in seeking a "subversive" (in effect, modernistic) alternative to the allegedly regressive dominance of bourgeois literary REALISM. Terry Eagleton in *Criticism and Ideology* (1976) sought to renew the hitherto feeble tradition of British Marxist criticism by employing concepts of "ideology" derived from Althusser. The most impressive individual talent to have emerged from this phase of British criticism, Eagleton quickly moved on to a more relaxed and eclectic orchestration of ideas drawn from poststructuralism, feminism, and psychoanalysis as well as from Western Marxist sources, in *Walter Benjamin* (1981), *William Shakespeare* (1986), and his popular survey *Literary Theory: An Introduction* (1983). His readiness to mix and match from an international palette of theoretical styles is in important ways characteristic of the British reception of "Theory."

By the mid-1980s, when the dust had settled from recent controversies, certain features of the British critical forum emerged that distinguished it from its North American counterpart. In the first place, the connection between criticism and historical study remained strong and almost instinctive, never having been severed as radically as it had across the Atlantic by the New Critics and by Frye: the emergence of a Californian "New Historicism" in the 1980s was met with some puzzlement by British critics who had never relinquished the older versions. Although ahistorical "textualist" kinds of theory such as deconstruction or Lacanian psychoanalysis have had their impact, they have usually been absorbed into the dominant "contextualist" approaches influenced by Marxism, feminism, or traditional literary history. British feminist criticism has been notably more committed to historical investigation than its American or French counterparts. In the second place, the local culture of criticism, generally consensual and skeptical in temper, has been less marked by any fragmentation into distinct schools of interpretation led by "star" theorists.

British culture in the eighties and nineties also went mostly unravaged by the American "Culture Wars," by the claims of identity-politics and the attendant disputes over the literary canon. British criticism has adopted, partly from such American debates, a new sensitivity to the significances of gender, race, nationality, and sexual orientation, while retaining a long-standing awareness of social class; but it has done so almost en bloc, in line with educated opinion at large, and without lasting internal divisions. Having come through the crisis of "Theory," it is in many respects sadder but wiser than it was before: more self-conscious, more ecumenical, more modest in its goals, less inclined to interpret a poem than to trace its antecedents and study its reception within a larger cultural history. The most noticeable transformation since the heyday of Leavis has been a leftward swing in political assumptions, such that a Leavisite critic of the 1950s who sought in a poem or novel its "poised maturity" has been replaced by a poststructuralist critic who might praise the same work for its "transgressive subversion" of gender categories. In this sense, the deforming pressures of academic fashion have proved stronger than any particular critical position.

BIBLIOGRAPHY: Baldick, C., *Criticism and Literary Theory, 1890 to the Present* (1996); Bergonzi, B., *Exploding English: Criticism, Theory, Culture* (1990); Borklund, E., *Contemporary Literary Critics* (2nd ed., 1982); Day, G., ed., *The British Critical Tradition* (1993); Parrinder, P., *Authors and Authority: English and American Criticism 1750–1990* (1991)

CHRIS BALDICK

LIVELY, Penelope

b. Penelope Margaret Green, 17 March 1933, Cairo, Egypt

One of the most prolific contemporary British novelists, L. began her literary career as critically acclaimed author of children's books; she wrote eleven in all. She began writing adult novels in 1977 with the prize-winning *The Road to Lichfield*. She was born in Egypt and lived there until she was twelve. Her 1994 memoir, *Oleander, Jacaranda: A Childhood Perceived*, not only records in vivid detail the facts of her childhood but also explores the nature and formulation of a child's perception of that world. Her removal from the Edenlike Egypt was a traumatic separation from her beloved nanny, Lucy, who taught her virtually everything; she never attended any school in Cairo. From the time she moved to England and began attending boarding school, L. experienced deep feelings of alienation; she said she felt like an exile for years, which may explain why so many of her characters also feel like exiles. Indeed, one of the reasons that her fictional children become so involved in history and reading is to assuage their feelings of isolation.

Using her fascination with the dual aspects of her Egyptian and English experiences and background, L. decided to take a degree in modern history at St. Anne's College, Oxford, in 1954. Since her first children's novel, *Astercote* (1970), she has published over forty books. Many of her adult and children's books deal in some way with variations on the themes of time, memory, and history, and how they interconnect. Her narratives frequently investigate the intersection of people with natural and fabricated geographical landscapes. An almost permanent subtheme in many of her historically oriented novels is how place helps construct identity and generate relationships. L.'s favorite metaphor illustrating the dynamics of these complex relationships is a palimpsest; that is, a parchment manuscript that has been written over but that still reveals an earlier text dimly visible.

Her novels are often built on layers of memory and physical data out of which characters can understand themselves and their world better. In *The Ghost of Thomas Kempe* (1973), her best-known children's novel, a 17th-c. sorcerer haunts his former house, now inhabited by a ten-year-old boy named James, who discovers that the only way to exorcise Kempe is by using the diaries of an earlier inhabitant of the house. In *A Stitch in Time* (1976), the eleven-year-old protagonist, Maria, makes contact with a former inhabitant of her Victorian house named Harriet, who was also obsessed with the identical fossils that Maria is. And fossils are clearly a kind of geological palimpsest. But it was with *The Road to Lichfield* that L. entered the world of adult fiction. The Lichfield Road is not only a geographical path to her dying father but also a metaphorical connection to the narrator's father's earlier scandalous life. Fifteen novels after *The Road to Lichfield*, L. published the adult novel that won her the prestigious Booker Prize, *Moon Tiger* (1987), a novel that also made her world famous. Composed of highly crafted multifaceted narrative fragments, L. interweaves memories of her dying protagonist, Claudia Hampton, into a vividly revealing tapestry illustrating the way history, time, and circumstance constructed her life. L.'s brilliant use of the metaphor of a Moon Tiger—that is, a mosquito coil that gradually burns away during the night leaving only a skeletal trace of ash behind— became an objective correlative for the way Claudia's life and the historical past merge and remain in the present.

L. enlarged the use of the metaphorical palimpsest from personal history to her highly praised portrait of a metropolis with *City of the Mind* (1991). Protagonist Matthew Halland is a devoted father and architect who is ideally suited to explore the many-layered configurations of modern-day London. He travels throughout the city looking for potential building projects and serendipitously uncovers the glory and the horror of London's past. He also begins to understand how the collective past is composed of innumerable private pasts and how personal, social, and historical memory coalesce.

One of L.'s most recent novels, *Heat Wave* (1996) combines her interest in the family life of two generations. Pauline, her daughter Teresa, and Teresa's husband, Maurice, all live together. Pauline is editing a novel about romantic love, a story that comes uncomfortably close to her troubled relationship with her philandering ex-husband and also to her son-in-law's suspected adulteries. Pauline begins to see her life and the life of her family as hopelessly trapped in tragic circumstances over which she has no control.

There is little doubt that L. has become one of Britain's major novelists. Her highly polished and sophisticated style is able to combine compelling narratives with a deep sense of historical accuracy, with memory, time, and landscape as common denominators.

BIBLIOGRAPHY: Moran, M. H., *P. L.* (1993); Raschke, D., "P. L.'s *Moon Tiger*: Re-Envisioning a 'History of the World,'" *Ariel* 26 (October 1995): 115–32; Townson, J. R., "P. L.," in his *A Sounding of Storytellers: New and Revised Essays on Contemporary Writers for Children* (1979): 125–38

PATRICK MEANOR

LIVINGS, Henry

b. 20 September 1929, Prestwick, Lancashire; d. 20 February 1998, London

Although relatively unknown now, L. was one of the many noteworthy British dramatists of the 1960s. Generally speaking, his plays may be described as farcical. One of his earliest works, *Stop It, Whoever You Are* (perf. 1961; pub. 1962), consists of five interconnected, somewhat absurdist skits centered around the character of Warbeck, a factory janitor. His most successful work, *Eh?* (perf. 1964; pub. 1965), shares many similarities with the previous play. In *Eh?*, a boiler-room attendant struggles with the machines he is supposed to be managing. With this play, L. achieved his greatest critical success, winning the prestigious Obie Award in 1967. Despite achieving some popular success with his farcical comedies, L. was notably less successful when he tried to write more conventional plays. *Kelly's Eye* (1963), for example, tells the relatively straightforward story of a fugitive and a young woman with whom he runs off. Despite winning an award from the *Encyclopaedia Britannica* (1965), the play was not overly well received. L. did not have any other major productions after the early 1970s, but his early work was a noteworthy example of contemporary British dramaturgy.

LLEWELLYN, Richard

(pseud. of Richard Dafydd Vivian Llewellyn Lloyd)
b. 8 December 1907, St. David's, Pembrokeshire, Wales; d. 30 November 1983, Dublin, Ireland

Aged sixteen, L. went to Italy to study hotel management and in his spare time studied painting and sculpture. In 1926, he became a regular soldier. During the 1930s, he worked as a film director in England, served in the Welsh Guards in World War II, and afterward lived abroad, spending many years in Patagonia tracing the Welsh connection. His own wandering, polyglot life was a far cry from that of the tightly knit mining community invoked in his celebrated novel *How Green Was My Valley* (1939). Less a novel than a series of episodes, told in the first person, it is about a family in Wales where the only work available is below ground and the narrator's family scatters in search of a better life. It has HUMOR, tenderness, and authenticity and has acquired added piquancy now that the Welsh coal industry is dead. It was filmed in 1941, directed by John Ford, with Roddy McDowall, Maureen O'Hara, and Walter Pidgeon. Other novels included *None But the Lonely Heart* (1943) and *A Few Flowers for Shiner* (1950), both set in London, and a sequence of spy stories. *A Night of Bright Stars* (1979), about a Brazilian pioneer aviator, was set in late-19th-c. Paris.

LOCKE, John

b. 29 August 1632, Wrington, Somerset; d. 28 October 1704, Oats, Essex

Philosopher, political thinker, and physician, L., along with George BERKELEY and David HUME, stands among the seminal figures of British empiricism. Laying the groundwork for the epistemological foundation of science, L. was the first major figure of Anglo-American philosophy. Thomas Jefferson rated him, along with Francis BACON, the greatest man of all time.

Educated at Westminster School, and Christ Church, Oxford, L. earned a bachelor's degree in 1656, a master's degree in 1658, and became a tutor in Greek, rhetoric, and philosophy. Although not taking the degree, he also studied and practiced medicine. He joined the household of the statesman Anthony Ashley Cooper, first Earl of Shaftesbury, in 1667, as secretary, advisor, and physician. L.'s life and career were closely linked to Shaftesbury's political fortunes. From 1675 to 1679, he lived in France, studying science, engineering, and philosophy. Shaftesbury's fall and the accession of James II sent L. into exile in Holland. He returned to England after the "Glorious Revolution" and the accession of William and Mary. The last of L.'s life was devoted to writing, publishing, and responding to critics of his philosophical and political doctrines. His major works include *A Letter Concerning Toleration* (1689), *Two Treatises on Government* (1690), *Essay Concerning Human Understanding* (1690), *Thoughts Concerning Education* (1693), *Reasonableness of Christianity* (1695), *The Conduct of the Understanding* (1706), and *Miracles* (1716). It is upon the *Two Treatises*, and the *Essay* that his fame and influence rest.

The *Two Treatises* reflect a combination of L.'s Protestant heritage, his observation of Louis XIV's revocation of the Edict of Nantes, and his own experiences in Shaftesbury's circle. Developing the theories of natural law found in Richard HOOKER, Grotius, and Pufendorf, the *Treatises* begin as a refutation of Robert FILMER's argument that government is a biblically based patriarchalism. Filmer argued that the ruler, as the descendant of Adam, is the inheritor of Adam's property and the corresponding power and sovereignty over the earth. L., on the other hand, argued that a state of nature is prior to personal property. Property arises in the state of nature from the act of appropriation open to all as part of the natural need to survive. The deer killed by an Indian, L. remarks, belongs to that Indian. In other words, each has a right to the labor of his person in accord with reason. Thus, in the state of nature, each individual has a natural right to life, liberty, and property. Civil society forms to protect these rights. The obligations of law to protect the rights of others are a natural extension of the right to protect one's own rights. A government that fails to protect those rights, such as those of Charles II and James II, has betrayed its trust, and the governed are justified in replacing it. Much of L.'s thinking, and even his phrasing, inform Jefferson's *Declaration of Independence*.

The *Essay* was the product of over twenty years of rumination, and enters as part of a larger debate between the scientific theories of Descartes, and the Platonic-Augustinians on one side, and those of Thomas HOBBES and Pierre Gassendi on the other. The fundamental problem revolves around how to account for the mental content that is the basis of knowledge and how to establish trustworthy knowledge. The Cartesians had argued that mental content is innate, appealing to universal assent. L. points out that universal assent is neither obtainable, nor even adequate, to explain innate ideas. Drawing on his medical background, he argues for a model of mental activity that comes close to anticipating modern theories of brain and neural activity. Consciousness begins as a blank surface, the tabula rasa. Mental content derives from sensation (external sense perception) and reflection (internal perception). Qualities in the object stimulate the production of a corresponding mental object, the idea. Combinations of ideas, or ideas of combinations of ideas (complex ideas), produce the mental content. Much of the *Essay* uses this model to distinguish legitimate knowledge from false. Thus, for instance, religious revelation is meaningful only if it can be explained in terms of empirically verifiable sense perception. He also offers an original contribution on the concept of personal identity. Instead of focusing on the material continuity of the person through time, he focuses on the continuity of consciousness, passed along through memory. L.'s use of epistemology to analyze and dissolve metaphysical problems anticipates much in modern analytic philosophy, and his discussion of identity remains the starting point for modern examinations of the problem.

BIBLIOGRAPHY: Bennett, J., *L., Berkeley, Hume* (1971); Cranston, M. W., *J. L.* (1957); Jolley, N., *L., His Philosophical Thought* (1999); Woolhouse, R. S., *L.* (1983)

THOMAS L. COOKSEY

LOCKHART, John Gibson

b. 14? July 1794, Cambusnethan, Scotland; d. 25 November 1854, Abbotsford, Scotland

Recognized today chiefly as the first biographer of his father-in-law Sir Walter SCOTT, L. was known during his lifetime not just for BIOGRAPHY, but also for his translations, his novels, and his caustic but trenchant literary criticism (first with *Blackwood's Magazine* and later as editor of the *Quarterly Review*). In all of these genres, L. repeatedly insists that the writer's primary duty is to awaken and preserve individual and national self-consciousness; in fact, this consistency of purpose unifies what might otherwise seem a disparate body of work.

L. came to public attention in 1816, when he joined the editorial staff of *Blackwood's* in Edinburgh. The magazine's writers worked pseudonymously, creating multiple personae and exchanging those personae in the pieces they wrote for the magazine. But L.'s voice is frequently distinctive, because his acerbic style and nationalistic focus emerge even in these first literary efforts. For example, L.—who dubbed himself "the Scorpion" in an 1817 issue of *Blackwood's*—defended his version of what should count as "British literature" in a particularly virulent 1818 attack on John KEATS. Condemning Keats and the other members of the so-called Cockney school of poetry, L. argued that poetry like Keats's *Endymion,* filled with "absurd affectations and superficial conceits" drawn from classical Greek literature, was a national disgrace. Deeply read in contemporary German literature and literary theory, L. praised the Germans' rejection of classicism and development of a native literary tradition. So taken was L. with German ideas that he produced the first English translation of August Wilhelm von Schlegel's *Geschichte der alten und neuen Literatur* (*Lectures on the History of Literature, Ancient and Modern*) in two volumes in 1818. Interested in national literary traditions throughout his career, L. also translated a collection of Spanish manuscripts that he published as *Ancient Spanish Ballads* in 1823.

L.'s marriage in 1820 to Scott's daughter Sophia marked a turning point in his career. Under the influence of Scott, whom L. respected deeply, L. turned his attention away from criticism and translation and toward novel writing. He produced four novels in as many years: *Valerius* (3 vols., 1821), *Some Passages in the Life of Adam Blair* (1822), *Reginald Dalton* (3 vols., 1823), and *The History of Matthew Wald* (1824). With the exception of *Valerius,* an historical novel set in ancient Rome, L. used the genre to explore the reciprocal effects of personality and environment. The picaresque *Matthew Wald,* for instance, shows how its eponymous Scottish protagonist behaves and develops when confronted with a broad sweep of British cultural life, from Highland clan meetings to the machinations of parliamentary debate. The restrictive rural Scottish parish in which L. sets *Some Passages in the Life of Adam Blair* proves equally important in shaping the personality of that novel's hero. In all of the novels, L.'s debt to German literary theory resurfaces in his thoroughly explored, clearly articulated connections between national and individual identity.

It is not entirely surprising that L.'s preoccupations with literary nationalism and character development would lead him to focus his most mature literary efforts on writing the biographies of Scottish literary heroes. Although L. moved to London and assumed the chief editorial post of the *Quarterly Review* in 1825, his ties to his Scottish homeland remained strong. Fascinated by the Scottish folk hero-poet Robert BURNS since childhood, L. compiled his collected manuscripts and anecdotes into a *Life of Robert Burns,* which was published in 1828 to mixed reviews. Critics of the biography leveled charges of fabrication and conjecture against L., insisting that he could not document many of the episodes he recounted in the *Life.* L. was almost certainly guilty of the charge. He was also unapologetic. Advocating a kind of biography in which the available documentary evidence formed not the limits but the basis for a narrative of character development, L. argued that the biographer and the novelist need many of the same skills, including a keen eye for personal and cultural detail and the imaginative capacity to explain how those details combine to form a fully coherent character.

L. claimed to use a different authorial strategy in his best-known biography, *Memoirs of the Life of Sir Walter Scott* (7 vols., 1837–38). In the *Life,* L. drew heavily upon Scott's letters and diaries so that the novelist's character would, as he put it, "develop itself." However, critics have noted that L. exercises considerably more poetic license than he claims. Dates, characterizations, and even some episodes in the *Life* have clearly been rearranged or even invented to enrich L.'s portrait of Scott as an ideal national literary figure. Despite these embellishments, L.'s life has served as the definitive Scott biography for nearly two hundred years.

BIBLIOGRAPHY: Hart, F. R., *L. as Romantic Biographer* (1971); Hildyard, M. C., *L.'s Literary Criticism* (1931); Lang, A., *The Life and Letters of J. G. L.* (2 vols., 1897); Lochhead, M., *J. G. L.* (1954)

BONNIE J. GUNZENHAUSER

LODGE, David [John]

b. 28 January 1935, Dulwich, South London

L. has created an outstanding career as a novelist-critic, or professor-novelist combination unusual in Britain, particularly before the rise of L. and his friend and collaborator, Malcolm BRADBURY. In his use of literary theory, in his relationship with his audience, and in his fictional subjects (his first novel was about movies, his most recent about information theory), L. has continued to change and evolve.

L. was the only child of William Frederick Lodge, a musician, and Rosalie Murphy Lodge, in whose Roman Catholicism he was reared. He attended St.

Joseph's Academy, a Catholic grammar school in London, then University College London, where he received his B.A. (Honors) in 1955. After two years in the army, he returned to UCL and completed an M.A. in 1959; he taught English in London for a year, then accepted an appointment in the English Department at the University of Birmingham, where he remained (aside from visiting appointments elsewhere) until his retirement in 1987.

His first publication was a short book called *About Catholic Authors* (1957). Among his other critical works are two others on Roman Catholic authors, *Graham Greene* (1966) and *Evelyn Waugh* (1971). One of his most important nonfiction works was *Language of Fiction* (1966), which focused on the centrality, in reading and criticizing fiction, of the linguistic function. Never overly dogmatic, L. has incorporated the insights of new currents of literary theory, especially structuralist and poststructuralist, into succeeding volumes of criticism: *The Novelist at the Crossroads* (1971), *The Modes of Modern Writing* (1977), *Working with Structuralism* (1981), and *After Bakhtin* (1990). *Write On: Occasional Essays '65-'85* (1986) included more informal and personal essays, as did *The Practice of Writing* (1996), which also analyzed his new work in playwriting. *The Art of Fiction* (1992) is a practicing novelist's guide to fiction, arranged in short chapters on subjects such as naming characters and the unreliable narrator, that began life as a weekly column in a Sunday newspaper.

Beginning in 1963, when he collaborated with Bradbury and James Duckett on a revue, *Between These Four Walls,* performed in Birmingham, L. has had a secondary, or tertiary, career in writing for the theater; there was another revue, *Slap in the Middle,* in 1965, and he has written two further plays, *The Writing Game: A Comedy* (1991) about a creative writing school and the intellectual and sexual interplay of its students and staff, which was performed in Birmingham in 1990, and adapted by the author for television in 1996, and *Home Truths*, a dark farce about writing, publishing, and interviewing, performed in 1998, after which the author adapted it as a novella, published in 1999. He has also done some adapting for television, including *Martin Chuzzlewit* (5 parts, 1994), as well as his own *Nice Work* (4 parts, 1989).

Despite all this activity in diverse realms (he is also a frequent periodical reviewer and essayist), it is as a novelist that he has made his greatest impact. He began in a contemporary realist vein partly indebted to the "Angry Young Men" of the 1950s, in his first novel, *The Picturegoers* (1960), a study of a large, lower-middle-class Roman Catholic family living in South London (based, he later said, on his wife's family). His second novel, *Ginger, You're Barmy* (1962), was partly autobiographical, set at Catterick camp,

where he did his army training, and demonstrating the culture shock of national service to a sensitive intellectual.

In 1965, partly as a result of his work on comic revues, he wrote his first comic novel, *The British Museum Is Falling Down*. This was also his first venture into academic fiction, a genre he was to make very much his own. *The British Museum Is Falling Down* tells the story of a day in the life of Adam Appleby, an unfortunate postgraduate student beset with troubles academic (inability to progress on his thesis), financial, and marital (fear of another pregnancy added to his poorly supported family). The novel is in part a tribute to James JOYCE's *Ulysses*, including as it does pastiches of a number of 20th-c. literary styles. *Out of the Shelter* (1970) returned to the realistic style of the earlier books in a Bildungsroman about a young boy growing up in World War II.

Changing Places: A Tale of Two Campuses (1975) was a return to the comic treatment of academic life. It brilliantly counterposed two academics—British Philip Swallow and American Morris Zapp—who exchange their teaching posts at, respectively, Rummidge University and Euphoria State University. There are incisive observations about love and sex as well as academic life and the excitements of the 1960s. Swallow and Zapp reappeared in *Small World: An Academic Romance* (1984) and *Nice Work* (1988). The first is an ambitious, brilliantly patterned, work that combines the structure of the medieval romance with the world of academic conferences. *Nice Work* is grimmer, set in an academic world under threat; it shows how the pairing arrangement between a young literary theorist and academic and an aging industrialist changes them both.

How Far Can You Go? (1980; repub. as *Souls and Bodies*, 1982) was another work that experimented with form, particularly with self-referentiality, while tracing the lives of a group of Roman Catholics in a changing Britain from February 1952 to 1980. *Paradise News* (1991) and *Therapy* (1995) were both about midlife crisis and midlife love; the first takes a confused Rummidge citizen to Hawai'i; the second a television writer on a pilgrimage to Santiago de Compostella and the errors of his past life. L.'s recent novel, *Thinks . . .* (2001) returns to the campus, though not to the English departments; instead it features the director of a Centre for Cognitive Science who has an affair with a novelist.

L.'s imagination works best in a binary way (U.K. versus U.S.; academics versus business; souls versus bodies) and *Thinks . . .* provides another example of his thoughtful and humane ability to inhabit and animate both parties to an antithesis and to balance the intellection with the traditional arts of the artist to produce a novel of ideas in which the ideas do not swamp the novel.

BIBLIOGRAPHY: Bergonzi, B., *D. L.* (1995); Martin, B., *D. L.* (1999); Morace, R., *The Dialogic Novels of Malcolm Bradbury and D. L.* (1989); Moseley, M., *D. L.* (1991)

MERRITT MOSELEY

LODGE, Thomas

b. 1557 or 1558, West Ham; d. September 1625, London

L. is best known as the author of the prose ROMANCE *Rosalynde* (1590), William SHAKESPEARE's primary source for *As You Like It*. Four other romances, *Robert, Second Duke of Normandy* (1591), *Euphues Shadow* (1592), *William Longbeard* (1593), and *A Margarite of America* (1596), followed, none achieving the success of his first effort. Evidently energetic, L. turned his hand to most of the miscellaneous contemporary genres. A pamphleteer in the vituperative manner of the day, L. carried on a vigorous exchange with Stephen Gosson, begun in 1579 and concluding with *An Alarum against Usurers* (1584), and produced of note as well *Catharos* (1591), *The Divil Conjured* (1596), *Wits Miserie and the Worlds Madnesse* (1596), and *Prosopopeia* (1596). His poetic efforts include *The Lamentable Complaint of Truth Over England*, appended to *An Alarum*; *Scillaes Metamorphosis* (1589); *Phillis* (sonnets and other poems, 1593); *A Fig for Momus* (eclogues, satires, and epistles, 1595). L. also wrote two plays, *The Wounds of Civil War* (perf. ca. 1586–87; pub. 1594) and, in collaboration with Robert GREENE, *A Looking Glasse for London and England* (perf. ca. 1591; pub. 1594), as well as a medical work, *A History of the Plague* (1603). In his later years, he produced mainly translations: of Luis de Granada (selections, 1601), Josephus (1602), Seneca (prose works, 1614), and a French commentary on Guillaume de Salluste Du Bartas (1621).

A son of Sir Thomas Lodge, elected Lord Mayor of London in 1562, L. attended the Merchant Taylors' School (1571–73), Trinity College, Oxford, from which he graduated in 1577, and Lincoln's Inn, beginning in 1578, to study for the law. High spirited and (apparently) gregarious (Gosson described L. as "little better than a vagrant, looser than liberty, lighter than vanity itself," an opinion upheld by L.'s mother's will [1579], which notes L.'s untrustworthiness with money), L. took part in two freebooting expeditions, to the Canary Islands (ca. 1588) and South America (1591), the latter the calamitous last voyage of Thomas Cavendish, which nonetheless provided L. with material for *A Margarite of America*.

The activity of L.'s pen, like his nautical adventurism, was undoubtedly driven by poverty, which perhaps to avoid he studied medicine at Avignon (1598–1600). There he also became a Catholic. In 1603, L.

was incorporated M.D. at Oxford; his practice was from time to time in the Netherlands, which offered him safety as a recusant, and in London, until his death there in 1625.

While a good measure of L.'s writings may be dismissed as hackwork-for-hire, he nonetheless envisioned himself a serious writer, and produced several works variously of note. The romance is L.'s best genre: *Rosalynde* can stand on its own, and *A Margarite of America* (which L. claimed he took from "a historie in the Spanish tong" plundered from a Jesuit library in Santos, Brazil, while sailing with Cavendish) is nearly as good, drawing in an original way from Euphuism, Seneca, and Arcadian motifs. L.'s integration of verse and prose in the romances was ingenious and influential. Of the plays, the less said the better (L. had no ear for drama); but two pamphlets (*Wits Miserie* and *An Alarum*) are readable, pungent, and offer vignettes of contemporary London lowlife in the manner of Thomas NASHE.

BIBLIOGRAPHY: Gosse, E. W., ed., *The Complete Works of T. L.* (1883); Kinney, A. F., *Humanist Poetics: Thought, Rhetoric, and Fiction in Sixteenth-Century England* (1986); Sisson, C. J., ed., *T. L. and Other Elizabethans* (1933)

R. F. YEAGER

LOGUE, Christopher

b. 23 November 1926, Portsmouth, Hampshire

L. attended Portsmouth Grammar School and in 1943 became a commando, serving in the Middle East. Poet, playwright, scriptwriter, and actor, he moved to Paris in 1951, where he published his first books, *Wand and Quadrant* (1953), influenced by Ezra Pound, *Seven Sonnets* (1954), and *Devil, Maggot and Son* (1956). *Songs* (1959) revealed his conversion to radical socialism. When he returned to London in 1956, the theatrical "revolution" was happening at the Royal Court Theatre, London, and among L.'s plays produced there were *The Trial of Cob and Leach* (perf. 1959), cowritten with Harry Cookson, *The Lily White Boys* (perf. 1960), and *Antigone* (perf. 1960), which showed L.'s debt to Bertolt Brecht. Partnered by Adrian MITCHELL, L. gave poetry readings. During the 1960s, L. published translations from Homer for which he received a Bollingen Foundation grant and numerous volumes of poetry that include *The Arrival of the Poet in the City* (1963), *Logue's ABC* (1966), and *New Numbers* (1969). He wrote screenplays for *The End of Arthur's Marriage* (1968), directed by Ken Loach, and *Savage Messiah* (1972), directed by Ken Russell. L. has appeared in several films as an actor and has also written several children's books. He is best known for his magnificent *War Music* (1981), a cumulative translation of Homer's *Iliad*, praised by

P. J. KAVANAGH and George STEINER. *War Music* was produced as a show with music by Donald Fraser in 1977.

LONGLEY, Michael
b. 27 July 1939, Belfast, Northern Ireland

L. is widely recognized as one of the world's leading love poets. He has also written a series of outstanding poems on the fragility of human life set amid the conflict in Northern Ireland that are in a dialectic with his rural poems featuring delicate natural objects set in the western Irish counties of Clare and Mayo. L. is starting to receive long-overdue critical acclaim, winning the Queen's Gold Medal for Poetry in 2001 and both the Hawthornden Prize and the T. S. Eliot Prize for his volume *The Weather in Japan* (2000).

Reared in a middle-class Protestant family in Belfast, L. attended a local elementary school composed mainly of lower-class Catholics. He took a degree in classics from Trinity College, Dublin, and returned to Belfast in the early 1960s. L. emerged from Philip HOBSBAUM's creative writing group at Queen's University during this time and published his first poetry pamphlet in 1965. "The Group" provided a needed critical and cultural context for writing poetry. L. fostered local Northern Irish artistic talent by initiating programs for literature, arts-in-education, and the traditional arts in his role as Combined Arts Director of the Arts Council of Northern Ireland. He is also a founding member of the Cultural Traditions Group, which aims to encourage acceptance and understanding of diversity in the province.

L. published four full volumes of poetry between 1969 and 1979. He took early retirement from the Arts Council in 1991, after working there twenty years. Not coincidentally, his first book of completely new poetry in twelve years, *Gorse Fires,* was published that same year and won the Whitbread Award. Later volumes include *The Ghost Orchid* (1995) and *Selected Poems* (1999). Every Northern Irish poet writing in the last three decades has had to come to terms with conflict in the province; only a few, including L., have done so thoughtfully and imaginatively. Some of L.'s early poetry registers the shock from the violence in the late 1960s and 1970s. For example, "Wounds" recognizes the contribution of Ulster Protestants in World War I, but also acknowledges the victims of contemporary violence on both sides in the province. Other poems about the conflict include "Wreaths," "The Butchers," "The Ice Cream Man," and "Ceasefire." This last poem and L.'s other poems about the conflict in Ulster continually suggest the very real potential of imaginative literature in the North for opening the "cultural corridor" between nationalists and unionists about which the critic (and L.'s wife) Edna Longley has written so perceptively.

The major reason L. has transcended the sectarian politics of his province is his dual literary inheritance. Heavily influenced by the English poet Philip LARKIN and Northern Irish Protestant poets John HEWITT and Louis MacNEICE, L. was also impressed by the work of the Irish W. B. YEATS and Irish Catholic Patrick KAVANAGH. Larkin's preference for rhyme influenced L. to employ rhyme in his own early poetry. Larkin's stylistic influence on L. has lessened over the years and, beginning with *Gorse Fires,* L. has experimented with free verse forms. L.'s poetry is marked by an intense concern with the local and often features skillfully integrated lists of objects from urban or natural landscapes.

Many of L.'s poems arose from the outlook he developed while working in the Northern Irish Arts Council and later in the Cultural Traditions Group. They demonstrate how literature has been an effective, nondidactic tool for cultural communication in Northern Ireland. L.'s work ultimately suggests the real and potential success for reconciliation effected through the coalescence of imaginative literature and Christian forgiveness.

L.'s staggering range of allusions also suggests a universal voice. Influences include classical and contemporary poets, Sibelius, jazz, Greek literature and mythology, and Asian culture. L.'s kaleidoscopic interests are rendered in a poetic style that is structured, lyrical, and achingly beautiful. His most recent poems are strikingly concise, resulting from his interest in *karumi*, the Japanese art of economy in form.

BIBLIOGRAPHY: Longley, M., *Tuppenny Stung: Autobiographical Chapters* (1994); McDonald, P., "M. L.'s Homes," in his *Mistaken Identities: Poetry and Northern Ireland* (1997): 110–44; Russell, R. R., "Of Flowers and Fighting: M. L.'s *Selected Poems*," *CarQ* 52 (Spring 2000): 74–79

RICHARD RANKIN RUSSELL

LONSDALE, Frederick
(pseud. of Lionel Frederick Leonard) b. 5 February 1881, St. Helier, Jersey; d. 4 April 1954, London

L. began his career as writer of libretti for musical comedies, including *The Maid of the Mountains* (perf. 1917) and *Madame Pompadour* (perf. 1923). Worldly, epigrammatic, and light-hearted, his drawing room comedies were commercially successful and at the time compared to the work of W. Somerset MAUGHAM and Noël COWARD. The best of L.'s eleven plays is *The Last of Mrs. Cheyney* (1925), in which the maid who has been involved in burgling the employer class gives up her criminal ways to marry into the aristocracy. His other plays include *Aren't We All?* (perf. 1923; pub. 1924), *On Approval* (perf. 1926; pub.

1927), *The High Road* (1927), and *Canaries Sometimes Sing* (1929).

LOVELACE, Richard

b. 1618, London (or possibly Holland); d. 1657?, London

The poems of L. were published in two 17th-c. collections, *Lucasta: Epodes, Odes, Sonnets, Songs, etc, to which is Added Aramantha: A Pastoral* (1649) and *Lucasta: Posthume Poems* (1659 or 1660). His work belongs securely within the idioms of Cavalier verse but, seen whole, establishes a distinct identity.

Though the body of L.'s work is not great, his poems are strikingly various, both in kind and in level of achievement. Some of his poems are beautifully made, polished, and lucid, elegantly turned in phrase and rhythm; others seem slapdash and careless. He famously affirms the ideals of honor and fidelity in "To Lucasta, Going to the Warres," when he must leave "the nunnery" of his lady's "chaste breast," and celebrates his relationship with his lady as one in which "Above the highest sphere we meet/Unseen, unknown, and greet as angels greet" ("To Lucasta. Going Beyond the Seas"); yet he also dismisses honor as "the fool's giant," preferring, he tells us, "love and sherry" to the pursuit of glory (in his remarkable poem "A Loose Saraband") and makes clear the pleasure he takes as a "huntsman" of fine female flesh ("La Bella Bona Roba"). L.'s "The Vintage to the Dungeon" (which was set to music by William Lawes) is a drinking song that insists upon the power of wine to liberate the imprisoned soul; in a more famous prison-poem, "To Althea. From Prison" (another song to be set to music, this time by John Wilson), love is joined with wine to ensure that "Stone walls do not a prison make,/Nor iron bars a cage."

L. was an active supporter of Charles I before and during the Civil War. He appears to have ruined his estate by his expenditure in support of his king and to have had direct experience of several disastrous military defeats. He was imprisoned more than once. One response to the painful overthrow of all that he held most dear was the cultivation, in his poetry, of a kind of disengaged superiority to mere events. Even when imprisoned he can, he says, sing of the goodness of his king and in doing so experience supreme liberty. In "The Grasshopper," developed from a Greek original among the Anacreontea, L. creates what one might call a philosophical drinking song, recommending withdrawal and privacy (almost a voluntary self-imprisonment) in the face of a harsh world. Probably written after the execution of Charles I, it imagines a small world in which "the best of men and friends" (women are noticeably absent) "will create/A genuine Summer in each other's breast" in "spite of this cold

time and frozen fate." The claim is a dignified one, but can seem dangerously close to mere escapism.

A different kind of escapism, less interesting and less intelligent, characterizes L.'s *Aramantha*, an excessively artificial pastoral, charming but slight, seemingly altogether detached from any kind of reality. There is, indeed, an oddly disengaged quality to much of L.'s work. In the best poems, it takes the form of a kind of openness to conflicting attitudes and tones that are successfully held in tension, shaped by an assured art and purpose. "To Aramantha. That She Would Dishevel Her Hair" begins with excited responsiveness to a natural world itself charged with an eroticism in which lover and beloved can participate but moves to a sense of the transience of all joys, of how briefly human happiness can "deceive" the underlying sorrows of human existence. On one level, the poem charts the movement from erotic anticipation to postcoital sadness, but it also speaks of a more universal truth about human experience and it does so because of the way L. is able to speak with equal conviction about its joys and its despairs in stanzas that have a logic and concision that owe much to the example of Ben JONSON. In some weaker poems, like "Night. To Lucasta," some of L.'s characteristic motifs, such as images of imprisonment, of man as a microcosm of the natural world, are rehearsed but left largely undigested, the language of the poem achieving neither clarity nor purposeful shape, the syntax decidedly knotty and the tone confused.

For a cultured gentleman-poet like L., it was natural that his work should register his awareness of Continental poetry. His translations include a number of assured versions of Latin and French epigrams, as well as a selection of poems by Catullus accurately and attractively translated. His "Dialogue. A Mock Charon" contributes to a vogue begun by the French poet Olivier de Magny, and a number of other poems show clearly his familiarity with European traditions. Nor does he fail to celebrate the arts so valued at the court of Charles I, as in his lively "Peinture. A Panegyrick to the best Picture of Friendship Mr. Pet. Lilly" (the Dutch painter Sir Peter Lely who made his reputation at the English court) and "Princesse Loysa drawing," as well as his several poems on music and dancing, such as "Gratiana dauncing and singing" and "A Dialogue. Lute and Voice." The number of L.'s lyrics set by contemporary composers suggests that the poet worked in collaboration with some of the best musicians of his time.

L.'s range is greater than this brief account has been able to suggest. His life and work—and the relationship between them—present problems that scholarship and criticism have yet to solve. L. has suffered from the overfamiliarity of one or two of his poems, which have presented an over-simple picture of a

613

complex man and (at his inconsistent best) an accomplished poet.

BIBLIOGRAPHY: Allen, D. C., *Image and Meaning* (1960); Hartmann, C. H., *The Cavalier Spirit and Its Influence on the Life and Work of R. L. (1618–1658)* (1925); Weidhorn, M., *R. L.* (1970)

GLYN PURSGLOVE

LOWNDES, Marie [Adelaide] Belloc
b. 5 August 1868, London; d. 14 November 1947, Eversley Cross, Hampshire

The daughter of Bessie Rayner Parkes and sister of Hilaire BELLOC, L. was a prolific writer with novels, biographies, volumes of AUTOBIOGRAPHY, and innumerable articles, reviews, and short stories to her name. Yet it is *The Lodger* (1913), her fictionalized account of the unsolved crimes of Jack the Ripper, for which she is now best known. It sold over one million copies, was admired by Gertrude Stein and Ernest Hemingway and was filmed in 1926 by Alfred Hitchcock. Marked by L.'s flair for psychological suspense and her ability to create a claustrophobic atmosphere, the novel is infused with tension, anxiety, and fear.

The Buntings, former domestic servants, run a lodging house on the Marylebone Road. Having fallen on hard times and on the verge of destitution, they joyously welcome the arrival of a new lodger, Mr. Sleuth. The Buntings accept his nervous demeanor, odd habits, and propensity for quoting from the Bible because he is so obviously a "gentleman." Meanwhile, a serial murderer has been butchering down-and-out women in the East End and Mrs. Bunting gradually begins to suspect that her lodger is "The Avenger." It is her increasing hysteria caused by sleepless nights and her efforts to conceal Mr. Sleuth's true identity that create the most tense moments in the novel. She decides she will not alert the police, not out of monetary concerns but because "in the long history of crime it has very, very seldom happened that a woman has betrayed one who has taken refuge with her." Despite the horrible crimes she knows he has committed, she feels a sense of pity for the man and a queer identification with him as an outsider. The novel has been called "a peerless index to the Edwardian state of mind" for the ways in which it highlights issues of class and of gender, concerns about the degeneration of society, and the struggle by those on the verge of poverty to maintain a "respectable" facade. *The Lodger* also touches on issues that are as relevant in the early 21st c. as they were in the early 20th, including the hysteria whipped up by the press and the morbid curiosity of the public that attends gruesome crimes (the inquest scene, in particular, is a masterful depiction of the courtroom as entertainment).

The Lodger is indicative of L.'s penchant for turning the details of true crime into the subjects of her own fiction. *What Really Happened* (1926) and *Lizzie Borden: A Study in Conjecture* (1939) are two further such examples. She also favored the intertwining of mystery and love story, for running alongside the narrative of suspense in *The Lodger* is the blossoming romance of Mr. Bunting's daughter, Daisy, and Joe Chandler, a family friend and police detective working the Avenger case. Other novels like *Good Old Anna* (1915) in which the German housekeeper of an English woman is unwittingly caught up in a Great War spy network, also follow this two-pronged storyline. Yet the "happy endings" generated by the working-out of the romances do not eradicate the unease left by the denouements of the mysteries. For however much she adheres to the norms of romantic fiction, L.'s nevertheless succeeds in raising questions about human character that are not easily answered. L.'s achievement as a writer, therefore, rests not only with her vivid and intense tales of psychological suspense but her studies of the moral dilemmas that face us all.

BIBLIOGRAPHY: DeMarr, M. J., "M. B. L.," in Benstock, B., ed., *British Mystery Writers, 1860–1919,* DLB 70 (1988): 199–204; Kester, J. A., *The Edwardian Detective: 1901–1915* (2000); Lowndes, S., ed., *The Diaries and Letters of M. B. L., 1911–1947* (1971)

JANE POTTER

LOWRY, [Clarence] Malcolm
b. 28 July 1909, Liscard, Cheshire; d. 27 June 1957, Ripe

Whereas writing gave purpose to L.'s troubled life, drinking led to his death at the age of forty-seven. He remained a half-forgotten author until the 1960s and the posthumous publication of several of his edited works-in-progress to fill in his oeuvre: *Hear Us O Lord from Heaven Thy Dwelling Place* (1961), *Dark as the Grave Wherein My Friend Is Laid* (1968), *Lunar Caustic* (1968), and *October Ferry to Gabriola* (1970). Although L.'s standing has since advanced, his legacy will always be defined by *Under the Volcano* (1947), one of the great tragic novels of the 20th c.

Inspired by his readings of Jack London, Herman Melville, and Joseph CONRAD, L. signed on for six months in 1927 as a deckhand aboard a steamer bound for the Orient. The following summer he persuaded Conrad Aiken to become his literary mentor at a time when the mania for introspection was brooding over the contemporary scene. After three months under Aiken's tutelage, he returned to England with plans for a "modern novel" of a young man's initiation into life at sea. Five years later, Jonathan Cape brought out *Ultramarine* (1933; rev. ed., 1962), one of only two novels that L. published during his lifetime. The plot line deals with two days in the life of nineteen-year-old Dana Hilliot on board the *Oedipus Tyrannus*, a tramp steamer returning from the Far East with a cargo of circus animals destined for the Dublin Zoo. Douglas Day aptly describes the narrative as a "*Kunstlerroman* in reverse," given that Hilliot abandons his quest to become a novelist when he discovers that the desire to write is like a childish disease. Critics who make a case for the book generally praise its surrealistic elements and its counterpointing of dialogue and interior monologue. L., however, considered it an adolescent work of plagiarism—Aiken's *Blue Voyage* and Nordahl Grieg's *The Ship Sails On* were both published in 1927—by which he remained embarrassed.

L. seemingly had to suffer through events in order to raise them to the level of fiction. *Under the Volcano*, in part, is based on his failed first marriage and descent into alcoholism while he and his wife were living in Mexico from 1936 to 1938. After that experience, he worked for nearly ten years to transform a brief story about a murdered peon into a monumental novel about an alcoholic ex-consul, Geoffrey Firmin, grappling with unimaginable powers of darkness. *Under the Volcano* has been described as "the best account of a drunk in fiction," but it also is a deeply serious work of art. Its twelve chapters equate to the labors of Hercules, the twelve hours of action enclosed within a single day, and the twelve months enclosed within a year. Its cinematic techniques are drawn from German Expressionist films whereby emotional states are conveyed through visual juxtaposition. Its setting is at once paradisal and infernal; allegorically, humankind has been evicted from the Garden of Eden. Geoffrey Firmin is compared to Oedipus, Prometheus, Adam, Judas, Christ, Hamlet, Faustus, and Maximilian. Symbols abound, and in addition to literary sources ranging form Dante to Jean Cocteau, L. drew on his knowledge of Greek tragedy, Aztec mythology, biblical numerology, and arcane mysticism to insure the novel would have depths.

The story begins at sunset on November 2, 1939, when Jacques Laurelle embarks on a final walk through the small town of Quauhnahuac, during which he reflects upon the deaths of Geoffrey and Yvonne Firmin. Their ghosts impress upon him that it is not possible to live without loving. At the close of chapter 1, the narrative clock revolves backward precisely twelve months to the day. Chapters 2–12 then detail events that begin at 7:00 a.m. and end at 7:00 p.m. on the Day of the Dead in 1938. The four principal characters are in Quauhnahuac for quite different reasons. Geoffrey Firmin has served there as His Majesty's Consul until the spring of 1938 when England cut its diplomatic ties with Mexico. Drinking

has ruined his career and marriage. For the past eleven months, Yvonne has been in the U.S. trying to obtain a divorce. She returns unexpectedly to reunite with her former husband. Hugh, the consul's younger half-brother and a journalist for the *London Globe*, is in town investigating local anti-Semitic activity. Laurelle came to Mexico in 1935 in order to make a film about the Faustus legend with Leon Trotsky as its protagonist. At different times in the past, Yvonne has had adulterous affairs with Hugh and Laurelle. Her return, thus, is the catalyst for a narrative about laboring under the psychological weight of the past. The plot's crisis occurs at the close of a horrendous day when Geoffrey accuses Yvonne and Hugh of reviving their relationship under the guise of safeguarding him from drinking. Claiming to love hell, Geoffrey runs to Parian, a village that is the sanctuary for his despair. Thereafter, Yvonne is trampled to death by a panic-stricken horse, and the consul is murdered by fascist policemen who roll his body, along with that of a dead dog, down a ravine.

The many one-dimensional background characters in *Under the Volcano* attest to the sadness of Mexico—its abject poverty and political violence. Conversely, L. employs stream of consciousness techniques to develop Geoffrey, Yvonne, Hugh, and Laurelle as fully individuated characters. All of the novel's themes derive from some facet of betrayal: lust supersedes fidelity, murder supersedes compassion, and despair supersedes hope. Within L.'s "dense forest of symbols," the Tree of Life has been turned upside down, leading to darkness.

Under the Volcano was planned as part of a seven-novel sequence entitled "The Voyage That Never Ends," which as a whole would trace "the battering the human sprit takes in its ascent towards its true purpose." After 1946, he turned to his own brand of autobiographical metafiction, drafting novels and stories about writers haunted by their previous works and personal failures. Nothing L. wrote either before or after *Under the Volcano* equals the novel's technical experimentation or agony of consciousness. Although no single sentence can adequately summarize either L.'s life or his achievement, he embodied José Ortega y Gasset's supposition that "every life is like a work of fiction" and "every man is a sort of novelist of himself."

BIBLIOGRAPHY: Bareham, T., *M. L.* (1989); Binns, R., *M. L.* (1984); Bowker, G., *Pursued by Furies: A Life of M. L.* (1995); Bradbrook, M. C., *M. L.* (1974); Breit, H., and M. B. Lowry, eds., *Selected Letters of M. L.* (1965); Costa, R. H., *M. L.* (1972); Day, D., *M. L.* (1973); Smith, A., ed., *The Art of M. L.* (1978)

JOE NORDGREN

LUBBOCK, Percy
b. 4 June 1879, London; d. 2 August 1965, Lerici, Italy

While L.'s two novels, *Roman Pictures* (1923) and *The Region Cloud* (1925), were critical failures, L.'s most enduring work was as editor, critic, and biographer. L. was the first and perhaps the most influential interpreter of Henry JAMES.

L.'s earliest book-length work, *Elizabeth Barrett Browning in Her Letters* (1906), broke ground as a BIOGRAPHY, in that L. drew heavily on Elizabeth Barrett BROWNING's letters to create a dramatic narrative and established L. as a graceful prose stylist. *Samuel Pepys* (1909) followed, to critical acclaim; but L. perfected the memoir in which he evokes a living portrait of his subject. His memoirs include *George Calderon: A Sketch from Memory* (1921) and *Mary Cholmondeley: A Sketch from Memory* (1928), but his most notable and controversial memoir is his *Portrait of Edith Wharton* (1947). As the first biography of Wharton, *Portrait* was the main source for information on Wharton until the appearance in the mid-1970s of biographies based on her papers. L.'s *Portrait* offers a lively though problematic view of Wharton, since it is highly colored by L.'s own relationship with the novelist. L. became one of Wharton's closest friends beginning in 1906, and for many years they spent much time together. However, L.'s 1926 marriage to Lady Sybil Scott (whom Wharton intensely disliked) prompted Wharton to cut him entirely from her circle of friends. Thus, L.'s *Portrait* is colored by this rift; while L.'s book is filled with lively anecdotes enabling the reader to get a sense of the real woman, it also—as noted by Wharton biographer R. W. B. Lewis—"subtly denigrat[es]" Wharton as woman and writer.

Wharton first met L. as one of James's friends, and L.'s most enduring influence is as the first editor and interpreter of James. L. edited and wrote prefaces for the final two volumes of the New York Edition, *The Ivory Tower* (1917) and *The Sense of the Past* (1917); he also edited the thirty-five-volume *The Novels and Stories of Henry James* (1921–23), the final volume of James's autobiography *The Middle Years* (1917), as well as the two-volume *The Letters of Henry James* (1920), which would be the only published access to James's letters until Leon Edel's four-volume *Letters* (1974–84).

L.'s most important work, however, is *The Craft of Fiction* (1921). Discussing the work of Leo Tolstoy, Gustave Flaubert, Samuel Makepeace THACKERAY, and Honoré de Balzac, but concentrating on that of James, L. argues that "form, design, composition, are to be sought in a novel, as in any other work of art." While this seems obvious and even simplistic today, L. was one of the first critics to argue for an "art" of

fiction; according to Mark Schorer, he framed not just the terminology to discuss how novels are made but also the questions that need to be raised. L. based his views of fiction heavily on those of James, as discussed in the New York Edition prefaces; thus he places the highest value on a story dramatized through a character's consciousness rather than directly narrated.

BIBLIOGRAPHY: Auchincloss, L., "'My Dear Blest Percy,'" *NewC* 3 (May 1985): 83–85; Goodman, S., *Edith Wharton's Inner Circle* (1994)

JUDITH E. FUNSTON

LUCAS, E[dward] V[errall]
b. 11 June 1868, Eltham; d. 26 June 1938, London

In a career spanning five decades, L. published over a hundred books. His essays ranged over a wide variety of subjects, from cricket (one of his great passions) to custard, from artist Jean-Baptiste-Camille Corot to matches. Arthur St. John Adcock commented that L. could "write a delightfully quaint, witty or wise essay on nothing at all." L.'s thirteen novels possess these same qualities as his essays. Indeed, most are little more than collections of essays, couched in the guise of a narrative, commenting on the manners of the day. *Over Bemerton's* (1908), the best of the lot, paints London in the early 20th c. *The Vermilion Box* (1916) shows the same world at war, and *Verena in the Midst* (1920) depicts the immediate postwar era, with its jazz, short hair, and short skirts. L.'s most enduring legacy lies in his work on Charles LAMB. His biography (2 vols., 1905; rev. ed., 1921) and edition of the works of Charles and Mary Lamb (7 vols., 1903) remain standard a century after they first appeared. In his life of Lamb as well as in those of Lamb's friends Bernard Barton (1893) and the Lloyds (1898), 18th-c. Lichfield poet Anna Seward (1907), and Sir Sidney COLVIN and Lady Colvin (1928), L. allows the subjects largely to speak for themselves. He quotes copiously from their correspondence, limiting himself to supplying a connecting narrative rather than analysis. Never profound, he nonetheless treats every subject with a pleasant gentility that cannot fail to entertain.

LUCIE-SMITH, [John] Edward
b. 27 February 1933, Kingston, Jamaica

L., a central figure in British poetry of the 1960s, has gone on to distinguish himself as an internationally known art critic. He has authored over sixty books on modern art, as well as working as an editor, translator, biographer, novelist, and photographer.

He was a founding member of "The Group," a British movement in poetry characterized by an emphasis on the spoken voice and Robert BROWNING-inspired monologues; its members included Geoffrey HILL, Alan BROWNJOHN, George MACBETH, and Anthony THWAITE. L. chaired the Group meetings at his flat in Chelsea for some six years. Philip HOBSBAUM, active with the Group, encouraged L. to publish his first collection of poetry, *A Tropical Childhood* (1961), which earned him the John Llewellyn Rhys Prize. This first collection had clarity and a tighter form that reflected more on the style of another poetry development of this time known as "The Movement" rather than that of the Group. However, in his second published collection, *Confessions and Histories* (1964), the influence of the Group is apparent with L.'s use of dramatic monologues and a more imaginative style. His interest in art and artists is also manifested in this second work. L. resigned from the Group in 1965 due in large part to the growing amount of work involved in managing the gatherings, but also likely due to an interest in newer styles. He was increasingly drawn to the simplicity of form and language of the Black Mountain and Beat movements. His third book of poetry, *Towards Silence* (1968), reflects this shift in style.

During this period, L. began using his growing influence and his writing to champion the avant-garde. Roger Garfitt has written on L.'s associations with the Liverpool pop artists after he became acquainted with Adrian Henri, a Liverpool artist and pop poet. L. edited the *Liverpool Scene* (1967), documenting this movement, which prompted feelings of betrayal from other members of the Group who disagreed with the Liverpool developments in poetry. He went on to edit a *Primer of Experimental Poetry 1870–1922*, published in 1971. In addition, his first edition of *British Poetry since 1945* (1970; rev. ed., 1985) was highly inclusive covering the varied representations in the British poetry scene during this period. When the second edition came out in 1985, much had changed in this regard and conservatism was in again. In his *The Well-Wishers* (1974) volume, his poetry is written largely with an artist audience in mind. This volume featured some of his last published poetry, as he later became primarily concerned with writing about art and art history.

L.'s art criticism has contributed a great deal to our understanding of modern art. His books cover British, American, French, and Latin American art and have tackled many of the art movements and periods of 20th c. L.'s work is noted for being informative and sophisticated while also quite accessible to the average reader. A number of his works are now used as standard texts in universities and colleges, including his *Movements of Art since 1945* (1969; rev. eds., 1984, 2001), *Art Today* (1977; rev. ed., 1983), *The Dictionary of Art Terms* (1984), and *Visual Arts in the 20th Century* (1996). His books consistently feature large numbers of high quality color illustrations, which is so important for understanding the work of a particular artist and yet something that is all too often neglected in more academic works. His deep interest and understanding of his subjects is evident in his choice of illustrations as well as in his text. The illustrations used are rarely the ones often featured in other art books but rather draw upon less familiar artwork.

L.'s active involvement in the art world has no doubt influenced his informed commentary. He has lectured widely on issues of art and has curated over half a dozen art exhibitions. Most recently his passion for art has brought him recognition as a practicing photographer with work held by the National Portrait Gallery in London and in exhibitions throughout Europe.

BIBLIOGRAPHY: Garfitt, R., "E. L.-S.," in Sherry, V. B., Jr., ed., *Poets of Great Britain and Ireland since 1960, DLB* 40 (1985): 315–21; Lucie-Smith, E., *The Burnt Child: An Autobiography* (1975)

ANN O'BRIEN FULLER

LYDGATE, John
b. ca. 1373, Lydgate, near Newmarket; d. ca. 1450, Bury St. Edmunds

L. was educated at the Benedictine abbey at Bury St. Edmunds and priested in 1397. His *Fall of Princes* (wr. 1431–39) comprises 7,000 stanzas, and his authentic writings amount to more than 140,000. A friend of Geoffrey CHAUCER's son Thomas, L. shows the influence of the older poet, especially in the allegorical poems *The Complaint of the Black Knight* and *The Temple of Glas* (wr. ca. 1403), and was founder of the school that obtained between Chaucer and Edmund SPENSER. He is medieval in his pessimism, his Mariolatry, and his horror of death, and has been criticized for prolixity and platitudes. He was, though, versatile enough to turn out as well as elaborate epics popular poems such as the *Mumming at Hertford, A Ditty of Women's Horns*, and *London Lickpenny*.

LYLY, John
b. 1552?, Kent; d. November 1606, probably London

L. was a contemporary of William SHAKESPEARE and one of the "University Wits," the name given a group of Elizabethan authors who utilized an academic style based on principles of debate and rhetoric. L. is best known for his prose romance, *Euphues, the Anatomy of Wit* (1578), a hugely popular book that gave rise to a host of imitators of the style that became known as "euphuistic." However, euphuism lost currency quickly, and L. turned to writing elegant court comedies that came to be seen as minor predecessors to Shakespeare's festive comedies. Frustrated in his attempts to find patronage, L. lived his own transition from literary phenomenon to minor figure, a position he holds today.

L.'s academic background is essential to his style. His grandfather, William Lily, coauthored a widely used Latin grammar. L. began his training in rhetoric in grammar school in Canterbury, and then attended Magdalen College, Oxford, graduating with a B.A. in 1573. Like other "University Wits," L. would have attended the Latin lectures of Dr. John Rainolds, an influential teacher and orator. Accounts differ as to whether L. was a studious scholar or a rambunctious carouser, but his academic experience clearly shaped his work throughout his life.

Upon finishing university, L. went to London and began the lifelong process of trying to secure an academic position or a patron. Partially to this end, he published *Euphues, the Anatomy of Wit*. The book was an immediate success. The thin plot tells the story of Euphues, a young man with more promise than wisdom, who sets out to learn of the world in spite of advice from his elders.

Euphues partakes of the Elizabethan vogue for prodigal son stories, in which the son's return symbolizes the importance of submission to patriarchs. The narrative is frequently interrupted so that the author can interpose moral lessons. Nevertheless, the romance was tremendously popular, and went through thirteen editions by 1613, with imitators writing additional euphuistic romances. L. published the sequel, *Euphues and His England*, in 1580.

The euphuistic style has been called "monstrous," "eccentric," "immoderate," and "over prodigal." Based on the dialectical style of debate, the style depends upon antithesis. Building on both structural and thematic oppositions, it creates a pastiche of rhetorical devices including syntactical conceits like parallelism and balance, sound effects such as alliteration, assonance and rhyme, and descriptive embellishments such as elaborate imagery, similes from natural or "unnatural" history, and mythological and classical allusion. Initially imitated, the style was soon parodied and then decried as overelaborate and obstructive to sense.

In spite of the style's difficulty, L. demonstrated that one could bring style to English prose. But the two *Euphues* books did not secure him an academic position and he became attached, perhaps as secretary, to Edward de Vere, Earl of Oxford. Given access to a boy actor troupe under the earl's patronage, L. began writing a series of comedies for court entertainments and private audiences at the Blackfriars Theatre. The charming and decorative style of these comedies has often obscured their importance to the development of English comic drama.

The comedies share many similarities. The first, *Campaspe*, was performed for ELIZABETH I in 1583. A portrait of Alexander the Great largely taken from Plutarch, *Campaspe* is less a narrative than an investigation of what makes a good ruler, in particular focusing on the relationship between a prince and his councilors. *Sapho and Phao* (perf. 1583/84; pub. 1584), also involves a ruler who renounces love, paying obvious tribute to England's virgin queen.

Elizabethan literature is influenced by a long tradition of medieval syncretism: the weaving together of seeming disparate worldviews. Thus, L.'s comedies combine multiple elements: philosophical investigations, erotic love plots, pastoral settings, contemporary references, Christian allegory and classical allusions. With *Galatea* (perf. ca. 1585), L. integrates the different elements with success, creating an engaging story about two maidens whose fathers disguise them as boys to avoid the chance that they be sacrificed in an annual virgin sacrifice to Neptune. As in Shakespeare, writing plays for a boy actor troupe gave L. the intellectual freedom to create forceful, witty, opinionated female characters.

In 1588, L. seems to have lost the Earl of Oxford's patronage. However, he continued to write plays presented by the Children of St. Paul's at court, aiming for court appointment to the position of Master of the Revels. The first play of this period, *Endimion* (perf. 1588; pub. 1591), offers its title character as one of many frustrated lovers, each of whom eventually wins the love of their object through devotion. *Midas* (perf. ca. 1589; pub. 1592) interweaves two Ovidian Midas stories with contemporary references, creating a political allegory that cast King Phillip II of Spain as a foolish ruler making unwise choices. Like *Galatea*, *Love's Metamorphosis* (perf. ca. 1588; pub. 1601) expresses L.'s interest in mutability and transformation while moving to a more emblematic dramatic style. *Mother Bombie* (perf. ca. 1588; pub. 1594) is unique, a comedy based on the Roman New Comedy mode used by Terence but applying L.'s characteristic parallelisms.

In 1589, L. was asked to contribute a pamphlet for the Marprelate controversy, in which Puritan authors were attacking the church under the pseudonym Martin Marprelate. L.'s pamphlet, *Pap with a Hatchet, Alias, a Fig for my Godson* is considered by critics to be an awkward, somewhat tasteless contribution written without much spirit for the task. In the following year, the Children of St. Paul's were suppressed. It is not known for which company L. wrote his last play, *The Woman in the Moon* (perf. ca. 1591). This play, a retelling of the Pandora story, again takes change as its theme. The play was probably presented at court, where L. was still hoping to be appointed Master of the Revels. He was disappointed, and though he was elected to Parliament four times, he continued to hope for something better; his last known literary works are letters to the queen begging for preferment of some kind, whether "lands, goods, fines or forfeitures."

A collection of L.'s plays, *Six Court Comedies*, was published in 1632. Thereafter, his work, both drama and prose, was mostly neglected. In the 19th and 20th cs. a revival of interest occurred when studies of the festive aspects of Shakespeare's comedy caused a revaluation of other Elizabethan comic dramas. Euphuism has enjoyed a resurgence of interest with poststructuralists. L.'s literary reputation is perhaps as strong as it has ever been.

BIBLIOGRAPHY: Barish, J. A., "The Prose Style of J. L.," *ELH* 23 (March 1956): 14–35; Bates, C., "'A Large Occasion of Discourse': J. L. and the Art of Civil Conversation," *RES* 42 (November 1991): 469–86; Houppert, J. W., *J. L.* (1975); Hunter, G. K., *J. L.* (1962); Steinberg, T. L., "The Anatomy of *Euphues*," *SEL* 17 (Winter 1977): 27–38

GINGER STRAND

LYNDSAY [or LINDSAY], [Sir] David

b. ca. 1490, Fife or Lothian, Scotland; d. ca. April 1555, Scotland

Diplomat and courtier to King James V of Scotland, L. gave voice in his poetry to the first expression of the Renaissance in Scotland. Last of the Makars, he used the forms of Geoffrey CHAUCER but belongs in spirit to the Reformation. In 1529, he wrote the *Complaynte to the King,* in octosyllabic couplets, commenting on the improved social conditions of the country, except those relating to the church, lamenting that others had been preferred before him at court and asking the king for money. A satirist, he chastized his royal master and all other classes of society, expatiating on Scotland's woes. His didacticism was exercised in the over 6,000-line *Dialog* (also known as the *Monarchie*), a universal history in the medieval mode, in which the falls of corrupt princes supply an object lesson to the unreformed church. The *Satyre of the Thrie Estatis* (wr. ca. 1540) attacks ecclesiastical abuse more directly, and is the only surviving example of a complete Scottish morality. It was performed before the king and court. L.'s *Descriptioun of Pedder Coffeis* (pedlars) is an early example of the studies of lowlife that became common in later Scottish literature. L.'s works were printed in Edinburgh in 1568. A complete edition was published in three volumes in 1879.

MACAULAY, [Dame] [Emilie] Rose

b. 1 August 1881, Rugby; d. 30 October 1958, London

In the fifty years of her writing life, M. produced twenty-three novels, scores of articles, including autobiographical essays, critical essays on authors such as John MILTON and E. M. FORSTER, travel essays and historical pieces, and several poems. Despite her eclectic writing tastes, M. remains best known as a novelist. Born into a family of some means, M. had the opportunity for education and experience and used such to a great degree in her writing, beginning with her first novel, *Abbots Verney* (1906). This first novel tells the story of Verney Ruth and his coming of age. The novel delves into family issues, including the protagonist's struggle to decide where exactly he fits in to the family. This novel is considered a reaction by M. to her own life experiences, as are many of her works. She is also known for reacting to social and political events of her time, often using elements of SATIRE and wit and engaging principles of modern-day FEMINISM along the way. Such can be seen very particularly in *Potterism* (1920) and in *Dangerous Ages* (1921).

Potterism reveals the story of twins Jane and Johnny Potter, both talented and both seeking literary success. In a classic study of gender differences in the eyes of society, M. illustrates the many social disadvantages for women through the character Jane. While Johnny is producing his first book, Jane is producing her first child and facing the frustrations of social double standards. M. delves into gender issues of sexual freedoms or lack thereof as well. *Potterism* was enthusiastically received by both popular audiences and critics upon its publication; *Dangerous Ages* found the same warm reception the following year.

Dangerous Ages, which won the 1922 Femina-Vie Heureuse Prize, is another social satire. This novel focuses on four specific women: Mrs. Hilary; her daughters Neville and Nan; and Neville's daughter Gerda. In this novel, M. treats generational differences along with the challenges and problems of individual life stages. Women's interactions with one another, women's choices in life, women's desires and constraints, marriage tribulations, relationships between men and women, lesbianism, and androgyny are important themes in the novel, making it a work far ahead of its time. *Dangerous Ages* is an important part of M.'s canon, as it reveals en masse a group of literary themes that remain consistently important to her overall body of work.

M.'s last novel, *The Towers of Trebizond*, was published in 1956 and won the James Tait Black Memorial Prize. This novel continues to explore M.'s famous themes of gender differences and sexuality, pairing the cousins Laurie and Vere in an adulterous relationship that also explores ambiguities between and blurring of gender lines. M. additionally deals with gender issues in the Catholic Church in this novel. Anglo-Catholic herself, M. brings a strong sense of feminist theology to this novel, exploring gender restrictions and rules in the church and supplying brilliant arguments against such restrictions and rules. Because of the author's treatment of theology and other issues in the novel, *The Towers of Trebizond* is considered to be a work with autobiographical elements. This final novel was well received in M.'s own time. M.'s contemporaries declared it her finest work; current critics continue to hold this view.

While M.'s literary output was remarkable and while her work received consistently positive reviews throughout her lifetime, M.'s work has been largely ignored since her death. Those scholars and critics who have studied M. and worked to revive her writings have been enthusiastic about M.'s forward-thinking themes and about the fascinating study of human nature present in M.'s work.

BIBLIOGRAPHY: Bensen, A. R., *R. M.* (1969); Emery, J., *R. M.* (1991); Passty, J. N., *Eros and Androgyny: The Legacy of R. M.* (1988)

TERRY D. NOVAK

MACAULAY, Thomas Babington [Lord Macaulay]

b. 25 October 1800, Leicestershire; d. 28 December 1859, Holly Lodge, Camden

It was M. who coined the much (and often ironically) quoted formulation, "Every schoolboy knows . . . ." For generations, every British schoolboy (and girl) knew M.'s poem "Horatius," first of the four ballads that constitute the *Lays of Ancient Rome* (1842). The story, taken from Livy and others, tells how the eponymous "captain of the gate," with two companions, patricians like himself, saved Rome from the Tuscan armies by defending the only bridge across the flooded Tiber, until the citizens had hewed it down, thus denying the attackers access. It was used to teach love of country, heroism, and respect for brave enemies: when Horatius, the bridge being down, swims for his life, "Even the ranks of Tuscany could scarce forbear to cheer." Some of the same characters appear in "The battle of Lake Regillus."

The third poem, "Virginia," tells of the desire of a tyrannical patrician for the daughter of the honorable plebeian Virginius. He plots to obtain her by making a deceitful dependant claim her as a stolen slave, and a corrupt patrician court gives judgment in his favor, but the plot is thwarted when the girl's father, to save her from "taunts and blows, the portion of the slave," and even more from the "nameless evil that passeth taunt and blow, Foul outrage which thou knowest not, which thou shalt never know," publicly stabs his daughter to death; whereupon the downtrodden mob is inspired to rebellion and the long-suspended tribunes are restored. The final poem, "Capys," relates the eponymous seer's prophecies to Romulus and Remus of the future glories of Rome.

Poignant narrative, stirring rhythms, and memorable phrases that have passed into general currency earned the poems their widespread popularity. Reflecting M.'s main preoccupation as Whig historian and historical and literary essayist, they are more subtle than they have been given credit for. M.'s main motive was an attempt at scholarly reconstruction. Convinced that the early period of Rome's history, as related by Livy, Dionysius, and others, was based on traditional oral, rather than reliable written, sources, M. imagined the ballads, on which the four stories, variously treated by different historians, might have been founded. He cites as analogues variant versions of the same event in British history in ballads from Thomas PERCY's *Reliques of Ancient English Poetry* and David HUME's having relied, in his *History of England,* on William of Malmesbury's 12th-c. chronicle, without citing William's acknowledged use of what he admitted to be historically unreliable traditional balladry. M. admits to some irony in his reconstructions at the expense of "good old times which never existed" and is selective as to which Roman virtues were worthy of emulation.

In 1830, M. entered Parliament as an active reformer, writing articles for the *Edinburgh Review.* His *The History of England from the Accession of James II* (5 vols., 1848–61) was a best-seller, translated into a dozen languages. Writing of the rise of Whig principles in the later 17th c., he identfied with the cause and has been accused of bias and exaggeration, but he is always cogent and readable. The Whig belief in the inevitability of progress was much criticized in the 20th c. and M. went out of fashion. His recommendation that Indians under the Raj should be taught to think like Englishmen has become notorious.

BIBLIOGRAPHY: Cruikshank, M., *T. B. M.* (1978); Stephen, L., "M.," in his *Hours in a Library* (vol. 3, 1879): 279–324; Trevelyan, G., *The Life and Letters of Lord M.* (2 vols., 1876)

MICHAEL GROSVENOR MYER

MacBETH, George [Mann]

b. 19 January 1932, Shotts, Scotland; d. 17 February 1992, Tuam, County Galway, Ireland

As a producer for the BBC, M. was influential in forming literary taste. He was educated at Sheffield and at New College, Oxford. During the 1950s, he was a member of "The Group," an informal association of writers set up by Philip HOBSBAUM in 1955. From 1955 to 1976, M. worked for the BBC on arts and poetry programs. He was part of the movement for public poetry readings. His early work was experimental, at times macabre, but later collections show (in his own words), fewer "comic and performance and experimental elements." His works include *A Form of Words* (1954), *The Broken Places* (1963), *The Colour of Blood* (1967), *Shrapnel* (1973), *Poems from Oby* (1982), and *The Long Darkness* (1983). In 1973, M. published the autobiographical *My Scotland: Fragments of a State of Mind.* His *Collected Poems, 1958–1982* appeared in 1989.

MacCAIG, Norman [Alexander]

b. 14 November 1910, Edinburgh, Scotland; d. 23 January 1996, Edinburgh, Scotland

M.'s maternal relatives were Gaelic speakers. Highly regarded as a poet, M. was educated at the Royal High School, Edinburgh, and read classics at Edinburgh University. He was creative writing fellow at the university from 1967 to 1969, becoming lecturer in English and eventually Reader in Poetry at Stirling University until 1977. He published fifteen volumes of poetry, including *The Inward Eye* (1946), *Riding Lights* (1955), *Surroundings* (1966), and *The White*

Bird (1973). His *Collected Poems* appeared in 1985 and in an enlarged edition in 1990. Close friend of Hugh MacDIARMID and Sydney Goodsir SMITH, he was deeply affected by their deaths. M. has earned numerous awards, including the Queen's Gold Medal for Poetry (1986). A recording of M. reading his own poems was made in 1971, entitled *As I Say It*.

MacDIARMID, Hugh

b. Christopher Murray Grieve, 11 August 1892, Langholm, Scotland; d. 9 September 1978, Edinburgh, Scotland

Identity, in all of its manifestations, was ever M.'s central concern, and the adoption in 1925 of his Celtic nom de plume represents a public, political act by which he declared himself the poetic voice of Scotland. Although he spent much of his life in penury, he was an amazingly prolific poet and journalist. M.'s unabashed egotism (his home was filled with pictures of himself) is a driving force of his poetry, which rejects lofty disinterest in favor of a distinct voice with strong feelings, opinions, and history. M.'s fascination with language, the primary source of his proclaimed kinship with James JOYCE, led to his adoption "that is to say, fabrication" of "Lallans" (Lowland Scots) dialect. For complex works such as *A Drunk Man Looks at the Thistle* (1926) and *In Memoriam James Joyce* (1955), M. has been acknowledged as being among the greatest poets of European MODERNISM and, with his predecessor Robert BURNS, Scotland's preeminent man of letters.

The son of a republican postman, M. was educated at Langholm Academy and the University of Edinburgh and taught at the Broughton Junior Student Centre. At an early age, he became a voracious reader, and would later in life boast that he often encountered professionals and specialists of diverse subjects about which he had read and knew considerably more than they. He turned his hand to journalism before and after the First World War, during which he served in the medical corps. The atrophy of the poetic tradition in his country roused M. to edit and publish a series of poetry anthologies called *Northern Numbers* in the early 1920s and his own books, *Annals of the Five Senses* and *Sangschaw* in 1923 and 1925, respectively. In addition to the legacy of Burns, the influences of Walt Whitman, Ezra Pound, and various Russian writers quickly took hold of him.

M.'s own most famous contribution to modernist poetry is *A Drunk Man Looks at the Thistle*. The long poem is, as its title suggests, an often ironic exercise in defamiliarizing the idea and the fact of Scotland. The Scotland heralded by the thistle (which ecstatically "rises and forever will!") is not the parochial, sentimental picture of a colony gladly oppressed, but a site of fierce self-examination and mythological depth. M. thus writes as much against his nation as he does for it, all the while announcing his fraternity with international authors and thinkers like Dostoevsky, Marx, and Nietzsche as well as with medieval Scottish poets (makars) Robert Henryson and William DUNBAR. M. is also deep in conversation with himself in the poem on the direction of his poetics. *A Drunk Man* is written in "synthetic Scots," neither the rejected Queen's English nor a standardized subspeech of an inferior people.

In his vast *In Memoriam James Joyce*, which runs more than six thousand lines, M. argues, very much in the spirit of *Finnegans Wake*, that "The universal *is* the particular." M. plunders vocabularies of disparate languages and specialized disciplines, matching the sciences to history and philosophy, in his unabated quest for names and ideas. The alliance with Joyce is an optimistic one against the Anglicization of the world.

His socialist ideals led M. to join the Communist Party in 1934, but the party expelled him in 1938 for his Scottish nationalism: he was a founding member of the Scottish National Party, from which he was also expelled. After the Second World War, M. moved with his wife, Valda, to Brownsbank, where he continued to write in quantity until his death. One would be hard-pressed to find a more self-aggrandizing literary AUTOBIOGRAPHY than M.'s *Lucky Poet* (1943; rev. ed., 1972). Name-dropping and flourishing quotations at every turn, M. crowns himself poet supreme and sneers at the critics (his one-time friend Edwin MUIR, for example) for being too obtuse and too devoted to English studies dogma to recognize his innovations. A lifelong champion of the Scottish Renaissance, M. became president of the Poetry Society in 1976.

Critical studies of M. have begun to mushroom in recent years, in part because of debates about his anti-imperialist, socialist declarations in the light of instances of racism and elitism in his writing. Furthermore, M.'s liberal use of modernist pastiche has spawned serious plagiarism controversies, since he rarely offers citations, and textual scholarship is troubled by the composition of *In Memoriam*, which M. continuously revised and published in segments over the years. These controversies notwithstanding, the range, originality, and industriousness of his mind insure that M.'s reputation will only increase. The two volumes of his *Complete Poems* (1994) belong on the shelf of anyone interested in modern verse.

BIBLIOGRAPHY: Bold, A., ed., *The Letters of H. M.* (1984); Gish, N., ed., *H. M* (1992); Kerrigan, C., *Whaur Extremes Meet: The Poetry of H. M. 1920–1934* (1983); Scott, P. H., and A. C. Davis, eds., *The Age of M.* (1980)

TIM CONLEY

MACHEN, Arthur Llewellyn [Jones]

b. 3 March 1863, Caerleon-on-Usk, Wales; d. 15 December 1947, Amersham

Recognized as one of the seminal figures in the development of the weird tale, M. was responsible for a wide range of essays and translations that moved beyond his stereotyped role in Western literature. He produced many critical essays and an array of social commentaries on religion, politics, and morals. Even though M. felt his grasp of French was weak, he managed translations of demanding works such as *The Heptameron* (1886) of Marguerite of Navarre, and the twelve-volume set of *The Memoirs of Jacques Casanova* (1894). M. also worked as a reporter producing a vast number of articles for various London based papers including the *Sunday Times*. Chiefly, M. made his greatest contributions to English literature through his highly stylized weave of supernatural and occult influences in his fiction.

M.'s nonfictional works are not without merit even though his style is often discursive and diction baroque. Surprisingly, M. considered writing a vocation and not a primary pursuit. As a result, he broached a wide range of subjects. His rather Edwardian and stuffy *Anatomy of Tobacco* (1884) along with *Dog and Duck* (1924) and *Dreads and Drolls* (1926) are almost forgotten nowadays. Nonetheless, M.'s *Hieroglyphics: A Note upon Ecstacy in Literature* (1902) is a refreshing icon in criticism. In the *Hieroglyphics*, M. expressed his admiration for Rabelais iterated by an often elaborate invective and sharp sardonic wit that surfaces constantly in M.'s essays and fiction. Most importantly for M., "the language of the soul transcends the language of the understanding" and through certain literature that can arouse an ecstatic response we may learn of the divine. The most fascinating aspect of M.'s work is that he felt that all transcendent literature pointed toward a mystical type of Catholicism. M. was close friends with the noted occultist, Arthur Edward Waite, and had ties with the hermetic order of the Golden Dawn. Furthermore, M. felt that in order to convey this ecstasy the writer is essentially in a state of possession where conscious reasoning is no longer at the helm. And throughout his life, M. labored tirelessly to convey and depict this transcendence in his fiction.

M. chose to explore the effects of terror or the dark side as it were of ecstasy in his fiction. As a result, his most subtle and penetrating novel is *The Hill of Dreams* (1907), in which the main character, Lucian Taylor, closely parallels M. Lucian was reared in rural Wales as was M., and took up the craft of writing at the expense of all else. And like M., Lucian eventually moved to London to pursue his literary career. Lucian's obsession with the dream world eventually led him to the ecstasy and horror that took complete possession of his soul and caused his early demise. Clearly, M. played with his notion of possession as a necessary ingredient in the passionate artist's life and carried it beyond the brink through his fictional counterpart.

Hill of Dreams stands as M.'s only substantial novel with his remaining noteworthy fiction appearing in short story form. *The Three Impostors; or, The Transmutations* (1895) is an important and innovative project but it is actually more of a vignette than an actual novel. The two men and their female accomplice are the implied impostors, who tell a series of weird tales to a Mr. Dyson and a Mr. Phillips. It appears that these three accomplices are responsible for the death of a mysterious "spectacled man" whose story is one of the last to be told. Mr. Dyson and Mr. Phillips are interesting figures as they embody M.'s dichotomy of the intuitive, and the overly rational "scientistic" mind-set he felt a great antipathy toward.

M.'s respective autobiographies, *Far off Things* (1922) and *Things Far and Near* (1923), offer great insights into his growth as a writer and into the psychology of many of his characters. Among his many professions, M. even tried his hand at acting and his involvement with theater helped to reinforce his love of ornate and dramatic use of language. His fascination with the dark and mysterious side of nature, antiquarian studies, mystical Catholicism, and the Welsh countryside are richly described in his autobiographies and make for as good a read as any of his fiction.

M.'s idiosyncratic oeuvre is not easy to appreciate as a whole because his work is often demanding and voluminous. Frequently whimsical and bitterly sarcastic, M.'s voice represents a particular flavor of a turn-of-the-century English man of letters who attempted to stay firmly rooted in a Blakean Albion, one where the poetic and unfettered mind could still roam freely through the land of fairy and living myth.

BIBLIOGRAPHY: Michael, D. P. M., *A. M.* (1971); Reynolds, A., and W. Charlton, *A. M.* (1963); Sweetser, W. D., *A. M.* (1964)

                                    BOB PODGURSKI

MacINNES, Colin

b. 20 August 1914, London; d. 23 April 1976, Hythe, Kent

The novelist and journalist M. is best known for three lively novels that explored hitherto neglected London subcultures of the 1950s: that of black immigrants in *City of Spades* (1957), of teenagers in *Absolute Beginners* (1959), and of prostitutes and ponces in *Mr. Love and Justice* (1960). M.'s sympathy with those on the social margins related to his rebellion against his own privileged family; his relatives included prominent figures in English political and cultural life, such as the painter Edward Burne-Jones, the writer Rudyard KIPLING, and the Conservative prime minister Stanley Baldwin, and his mother was the popular novelist Angela THIRKELL, from whom he became bitterly estranged. He was also set apart from English life because he had lived in Australia from the ages of six to sixteen, and because he was a gay man at a time when homosexuality was illegal in England and could lead to imprisonment and social disgrace. All these elements contributed to the distinctive, "half English" perspective that his fiction and journalism provided.

For M., fiction, journalism, and personal experience were always closely intertwined, and his first novel, *To the Victor the Spoils* (1950), drew, in a semidocumentary fashion, on his wartime involvement in the Normandy landings, and in the pursuit of Nazi spies and sympathizers. The novel also demonstrated M.'s capacity to question received versions of events, through its controversial portrayal of British soldiers looting in the wake of victory. His next, very different, novel may also have ruffled some feathers. Set in rural Australia in the 1920s, *June in Her Spring* (1952) portrayed, in terms close to those of D. H. LAWRENCE, a passionate love affair between a sixteen-year-old girl, June, and a seventeen-year-old youth, Benny, that runs into trouble because of a history of insanity in June's family and homosexuality in Benny's. While the novel received some praise, it became, M. believed, the object of a spontaneous boycott by British critics and public libraries because of its homosexual aspect, and its sales were relatively low. But it remained his own favorite among his novels.

The novels the public and critics liked best, however, came out between 1957 and 1960. The initial appeal of *City of Spades*, *Absolute Beginners*, and *Mr. Love and Justice* was partly a documentary one, akin to that of the articles by M. collected in *England, Half English* (1961). While their documentary interest remains, it is more suspect today; the representations of London immigrant life in *City of Spades*, for example, should also be compared with those in two slightly earlier novels by writers of West Indian provenance, George Lamming's *The Emigrants* (1954) and Samuel SELVON's *The Lonely Londoners*. For the 21st-c. reader, the three novels of the London trilogy seem not so much slices of life as well-crafted and rather romanticized fictions. In a tradition that goes back to Ben JONSON's dramas of London life, like *Bartholomew Fair*, the characters are vivid types, illustrations of forms of behavior, rather than psychologically rounded figures. As in drama, they are brought to life mainly by dialogue and monologue, which takes on a distinctive flavor through M.'s use of actual and invented slang. The trilogy also departs from documentary because of its ethical and philosophical resonances, which become particularly evident in the last, most austere novel, *Mr. Love and Justice*. Tracing the collusion between a ponce and a vice squad policeman, this novel raises complex questions about the complicity between law and crime.

M.'s sixth novel, like his first, was set in Australia in the 1920s: based on a radio play he had written in 1947 but had failed to get produced, *All Day Saturday* (1985) achieves a classical concentration, confining its action within a single day and focusing on an openair party that releases a range of disturbing desires. Two historical novels followed: *Westward to Laughter* (1969), a vigorous yarn that satirizes Robert Louis STEVENSON's *Treasure Island*, and *Three Years to Play* (1970), an inventive intrigue set in the Elizabethan era and including William SHAKESPEARE and his mysterious "Dark Lady" among its cast of characters. These are both entertaining novels that effectively pastiche the language of the periods in which they are set, but neither achieves the immediacy or insight of the London trilogy. M.'s last novel, *Out of the Garden* (1974), returns to the troubled Britain of the 1970s: it tells the story of a retired army officer, Captain Rattler, who takes over a stately home called Otranto Towers and tries to turn it into a profitable enterprise, while also running guns to Northern Ireland and plotting a military coup in England. The novel was felt to be too allegorical—Otranto Towers and its garden are intended to symbolize postimperial Britain in decline—but it remains an interesting attempt to produce a "condition of England" novel for the 1970s.

M.'s London trilogy and his journalism will stand as his surest achievements, however. His journalism, in its observations and analyses of popular culture, continues the work of George ORWELL into the postwar world, complements and implicitly challenges Richard HOGGART's *Uses of Literacy* and remains a key point of reference in modern cultural studies. His trilogy captures for posterity the excitement of a moment in which the somewhat drab and repressed English society of the 1950s was starting to open up as previously ignored forces impinged upon it; it also merits a minor place in that rich tradition of literary visions of London that includes, at its higher levels, Jonson, William BLAKE, and Charles DICKENS.

BIBLIOGRAPHY: Bergonzi, B., *Wartime and Aftermath: English Literature and Its Background, 1939–1960* (1993); Gould, T., *Inside Outsider: The Life and Times of C. M.* (1983)

NICOLAS TREDELL

MACKAY, Shena
b. 6 June 1944, Edinburgh, Scotland

From the outset of her career, M. has proven herself adept at the art of black HUMOR. Her first published fiction consisted of a pair of novellas, *Dust Falls on Eugene Schlumburger and Toddler on the Run* (1964), filled with absurd episodes, including the accidental interment of a deceased nun in a well and a manic search party conducted in wheelchairs. *Music Upstairs* (1965) paints a somewhat dark picture of bohemian life in 1960s London. *Old Crow* (1967) is a grim, thoroughly unromantic look at English village life, and *An Advent Calendar* (1971) recounts in an episodic manner the absurd misadventures of a highly unfortunate working-class family during one dreary December. After a hiatus, M. resumed her novelistic career with the publication of *A Bowl of Cherries* (1984). This novel displays a more mature writing style, as it recounts the story of two brothers—twins—Rex and Stanley Beaumont, the former a successful writer and the latter essentially a failure. Nevertheless, it is Stanley who provides the novel's moral center, caring for Rex's children and forgiving his brother for taking credit for a novel that he, Stanley, actually wrote. *Redhill Rococo* (1986), the story of Luke Ribbons, an ex-convict, and Pearl Slattery, his landlady and eventual lover, has been praised as one of M.'s finest novels, filled with keen observation and humor. Spanning eighty years and thousands of miles, M.'s next novel, *Dunedin* (1992), tells the story of a profligate minister in turn-of-the-century New Zealand and his descendants in London, who must deal with personal crises and the indignities visited upon the poor in Thatcherite England. *The Orchard on Fire* (1996) is one of M.'s darkest novels, dealing with child abuse; however, it also provides a touching portrait of the friendship between two lonely girls. In addition to novels, M. is also a successful editor and the author of several collections of short stories.

MACKENZIE, [Sir] [Edward Montague] Compton

b. 17 January 1883, West Hartlepool, Durham; d. 30 November 1972, Edinburgh, Scotland

A prolific writer, who produced BIOGRAPHY, essays, poems, travel books, and journalism, as well as the novels for which he is remembered, M. was educated at St. Paul's School, London, and Magdalen College, Oxford. He studied law, but his *Poems* (1907) and early novels, *The Passionate Elopement* (1911) and *Carnival* (1912), attracted attention. Among his best work is *Sinister Street* (2 vols., 1913–14), televised in 1969, *Guy and Pauline* (1915; repub. as *Plashers Mead*, 1915), *The Early Life and Adventures of Sylvia Scarlett* (1918), *Extraordinary Women* (1928), *Our Street* (1931), *The Four Winds of Love* (6 vols., 1937–45), and the well-known Scottish novels, *The Monarch of the Glen* (1941) and *Whisky Galore* (1947; repub. as *Tight Little Island*, 1947), filmed in 1948 with an all-star cast, including the author. M. drew on

his experience of serving in the Dardanelles in World War I for *Gallipoli Memories* (1929), *First Athenian Memories* (1931), and *Greek Memories* (1932). M. published ten volumes of AUTOBIOGRAPHY, *My Life and Times* (1963–71).

MACKENZIE, Henry

b. 6 August 1745, Edinburgh, Scotland; d. 14 January 1831, Edinburgh, Scotland

Novelist, dramatist, and essayist, M. is now remembered primarily for his first novel, *The Man of Feeling* (1771), yet M. profoundly affected Scottish letters both through his merits as a writer and through his promotion of Robert BURNS, James MACPHERSON, and Sir Walter SCOTT.

In 1765, while studying law in London, M. began sketching tales of an idealistic young man who leaves his rural home for the city to seek the lease of some lands adjoining his family estate. M. developed these episodes into a loosely structured novel, yet had difficulty finding a publisher until 1771. Upon its publication, *The Man of Feeling* became the most popular British novel of its decade. Readers and critics alike recognized its debt to Laurence STERNE's *A Sentimental Journey* (which M. denied having read). In a time in which young men imitated Sterne's protagonist by exchanging snuff boxes and young women judged each other's emotional worth by how many tears they shed, M.'s novel found a ready audience.

Harley, the protagonist of *The Man of Feeling*, possesses an excessive amount of sensibility; governed solely by his emotions, he offers tears and charity to relieve the many people whom he meets during his brief life. While such altruism was applauded by M.'s audience, M.'s novel implies a darker view of Harley's sensibility. His trusting nature leaves him an ideal target for London sharpers; he is defeated in his suit for the lease by a self-serving scoundrel; and finally, his self-effacing nature keeps him from declaring his love for Miss Walton, a neighboring gentlewoman, until he is on his deathbed suffering from a fever caught while nursing his aged servant. While modern readers catalog the tears shed by the novel's protagonist, many overlook the implication that behaving only according to one's better feelings leads to failure. In addition to beginning M.'s exploration of the power of human feelings, this novel begins his experiment with narrative form. The narrator "discovers" the remains of Harley's biography while hunting with a curate who has been using the manuscript as wadding for his powder; the story thus unfolds as a series of fragments.

In M.'s second novel, *The Man of the World* (1773), the central character, Sindall, serves as an antithesis to Harley. Sindall, who behaves solely from self-interest, devotes his life to creating misfortunes for three generations of the overly sensitive Annelsly family. This novel, while resembling M.'s first in its sentimental vignettes and its narrative experimentation, is flawed by a cumbersome plot and by the uncertain development of Sindall's character. M.'s last novel, *Julia De Roubigné* (1777), again explores the disasters resulting from self-sacrifice. Another creature of excessive sensibility, Julia feels obligated for her parents' sake to marry their benefactor Montauban. Her childhood sweetheart, whom she thought was married, returns from the colonies and requests an interview; Montauban discovers their meeting, assumes that his wife has been unfaithful, and poisons her. This novel is M.'s most carefully wrought work of fiction; he uses the epistolary form effectively to explore each of his central characters. Examining M.'s novels in sequence, one senses M.'s design of presenting sensibility as a viable alternative to Hobbesian self-interest, yet only when tempered by common sense and a devotion to self-preservation. Harley, the Annelslys, and Julia all fail through placing others' needs before their own.

M.'s dramas experienced little success. His *Prince of Tunis* (perf. 1773; pub. 1808) enjoyed a run of seven nights at the Theatre Royal in Edinburgh; *The Shipwreck* (perf. 1784), adapted from George Lillo's *Fatal Curiosity* (perf. 1736; pub. 1737), and *The Force of Fashion* (perf. 1789) managed only one night apiece in Covent Garden. As an essayist, M. founded and was the major contributor to two influential Scottish periodicals, the *Mirror* (January 1779-May 1780) and the *Lounger* (February 1785-January 1787). In addition to M.'s critical assessment of the characters of Hamlet and Falstaff, his contributions to the former journal include two experiments with short fiction: "The Story of La Roche" (June 1779), the central character of which is based on M.'s friend David HUME; and "Louisa Venoni" (May 1780), another study of the pitfalls occasioned by relying only on one's sensibility. M.'s contributions to the latter journal include another short story, "The Story of Father Nicholas" (August 1786) and his enthusiastic review of Burns's poetry. After 1799, when M. accepted the post of Comptroller of Taxes for Scotland, his literary efforts waned, with two notable exceptions: in 1805, he chaired the Committee of the Highland Society of Scotland in its investigation of the Ossian poems; in 1822, he published his biography of John Home, author of the tragedy *Douglas* (perf. 1756; pub. 1757).

To remember M. solely for his brief, sentimental novel is to undervalue a leading literary figure of the Scottish Enlightenment whose influence spanned at least two generations. He was an original member of the Royal Society of Edinburgh, a friend of Adam SMITH, and the whist partner of Hume. When the prospective publishers of *Waverley* were uncertain as to whether or not to print the novel, they called upon M.

for his critical opinion. His unhesitant recommendation resulted in its publication in 1814. Scott dedicated his novel to M., whom he called the "Scottish Addison."

BIBLIOGRAPHY: Barker, G. A., *H. M.* (1975); Duckworth, A. M., "H. M.," in Battestin, M. C., ed., *British Novelists, 1660–1800*, part 2, *DLB* 39 (1985): 329–42; Thompson, H. W., *A Scottish Man of Feeling* (1931)

JIM OWEN

MACKINTOSH, Elizabeth

(pseuds.: Gordon Daviot, Josephine Tey) b. 25 June 1896, Inverness, Scotland; d. 13 February 1952, London

M. was the creator of two remarkable literary figures: Gordon Daviot, one of the most popular playwrights of her age; and Josephine Tey, whose ingenious crime novels remain highly regarded among readers of detective fiction on both sides of the Atlantic. A writer of great originality, who used a diverse body of work as a vehicle for exploring human behavior, M. is frequently allied to Dorothy SAYERS, Margery ALLINGHAM, Ngaio Marsh, and Agatha CHRISTIE, but is arguably more significant: her truthful characterization, evocative descriptions, and fluent dialogue, sharpened by writing for the stage, are not only notable in DETECTIVE FICTION but belong to the mainstream of the novel.

M. wrote a number of non-crime books under the Daviot name, and all were moderately successful in their day. Having contributed verse and short stories to the *Westminster Gazette*, *Westminster Review*, *Glasgow Herald*, and *Literary Review*, she published her first novel, *Kif: An Unvarnished History*, in 1929. The story of a young boy's suffering after World War I, *Kif* is important mainly as an early example of M.'s idiosyncratic style; it was followed by *The Expensive Halo* (1931), a sentimental comedy about life in 1920s London, and *The Privateer* (1952), a fictionalized life of the pirate Henry Morgan. *Claverhouse* (1937), M.'s only work of nonfiction, is a passionate vindication of Viscount Dundee and a vigorous assault on the Kirk.

But the name Gordon Daviot achieved celebrity primarily as a dramatist. *Richard of Bordeaux* (1933), which was directed by and starred a young John Gielgud, ran for a year in the West End. With its timely investigation of war versus culture, its brilliant design by Motley, and its heavy streak of romanticism, the play gained a phenomenal popularity but has proved too much of its age to warrant revival. Its success was never matched by M.'s many subsequent works for the stage, although *The Laughing Woman* (1934) and *Queen of Scots* (1934) were both critically acclaimed.

A three-volume edition of her later plays, with a fore-word by Gielgud, was published in 1953–54.

M.'s first crime novel, *The Man in the Queue,* appeared in 1929. Written in an uncharacteristically stilted style and conforming to the "rules" of Golden Age detective fiction, it is nevertheless significant for its introduction of Inspector Alan Grant, one of the earliest fictional detectives to be both a gentleman and a credible, fallible professional. Grant appeared in many of M.'s subsequent novels including *A Shilling for Candles* (1936), her first book published as by Josephine Tey, which was later filmed by Alfred Hitchcock as *Young and Innocent* (1937).

M.'s own Golden Age, though, was undoubtedly just after World War II, when she published six sophisticated and innovative crime novels: *Miss Pym Disposes* (1946)*, The Franchise Affair* (1948), *Brat Farrar* (1949; repub. as *Come and Kill Me,* 1951)*, To Love and Be Wise* (1950), *The Daughter of Time* (1951), and *The Singing Sands* (1952). Although these are all, in a sense, written within the conventions of the classical detective story, the books, like their characters, are far from stereotypical and are distinguished by M.'s ability to use her own experience effectively; by her originality in creating a mystery that did not always center around a murder; by her powerful narrative thrust; and, most importantly, by her skill in evoking a strong sense of place, a realistic setting against which abstract considerations of good and evil could be convincingly played out.

Moreover, M.'s interest in the aftermath of criminal activity rather than the violent confrontation between killer and victim was very much ahead of its time. Unlike her more orthodox contemporaries, M. does not always restore order at the end of her novels and offers no protection against the poisoning influence of crime: the innocent often suffer; the evil sometimes escape unscathed. Many of her books represent a definite challenge to the reader, particularly in their distinctions between justice and the legal system, and her sensitivity to the limitations of human justice gives a modern edge to her work, even in the 21st c.

Her premature death from cancer cut M.'s career regrettably short and means that her reputation rests on a very small output. While her Daviot work failed to outlive her, M.'s contribution to the crime genre has been lasting, and one to which writers as diverse as Raymond Chandler and P. D. JAMES have paid tribute.

BIBLIOGRAPHY: Morris, V. B., "Josephine Tey," *DLB* 77 (1989): 284–96; Roy, S., *Josephine Tey* (1980); Talburt, N. E., "Josephine Tey," in Bargainnier, E. F., ed., *Ten Women of Mystery* (1981): 42–76

NICOLA UPSON

MacNEICE, [Frederick] Louis
b. 12 September 1907, Belfast, Northern Ireland; d. 2 September 1963, London

M., whose father was a rector, and later a bishop, and whose mother died young, showed early signs of being hypersensitive, for good and bad: "When I was five the black dreams came;/Nothing after was quite the same." He always retained a sense of nostalgia for his childhood, however, especially its experiences of wonder, and the freshness of a child's perception and ideas—clearly, at least in his own case, involving synesthesia: "words were coloured/(Harlot and murder were dark purple)," from "When We Were Children." It could be argued that this rather Romantic sympathy and empathy for his child-self became the mainspring of M.'s lyrical art.

Also intellectually precocious, M. was sent to school and university in England, where he would spend most of his relatively short life. He wrote as an adult that he relished his Irish origin—but partly for the ignoble and funny reason that it gave him "a hold on the sentimental English" (*Autumn Journal,* 1939). In a similar vein, he claims that he wishes to honor western Ireland "In doggerel and stout" ("Western Landscape").

M. studied classics and philosophy at Oxford University. An exceptionally bright student, he took a B.A. (honors), then accepted positions as a lecturer in classics at Birmingham University, and later in Greek at Bedford College, London. In his poetry, he treats his own elite education in an off-hand and ironic manner: "having once been to the University of Oxford/ You can never really again/Believe anything that anyone says and that of course is an asset/In a world like ours;/Why bother to water a garden/That is planted with paper flowers?"

Befriending W. H. AUDEN at Oxford, M. has often been regarded as one of certain more or less left-wing students with literary ambitions who, in the 1930s, supposedly "gathered around" the former. Apart from M. and Auden, this constellation included C. DAY-LEWIS and Stephen SPENDER. As a matter of fact, the group proved both brittle and brief; also its socialism has mostly been exaggerated. M. was in any case the least politically committed of these writers.

His early poetry shows some elements similar to that by Auden—notably the emphasis on contemporary life and the use of colloquialisms—but it would be both impossible and pointless to try to determine which of the poets influenced which. The notion that Auden dominated the "Oxford group" (as distinct from a "Cambridge group" consisting of William EMPSON, Kathleen RAINE, and others) is a little misleading. It has contributed to M.'s reputation still being somewhat overshadowed by that of Auden. However, today there is a tendency to emphasize M.'s

Irishness as a quality that distinguishes him from most of his contemporaries. This slant has helped to establish him as an important poet in his own right, rather than as second best of the Oxford poets.

M.'s first poetry collection, *Blind Fireworks* (1929), was brought out by Gollancz, but many of his subsequent ones were published by Faber, London. Like Auden and Lawrence DURRELL, M. could be pigeonholed as one of T. S. ELIOT's "discoveries." Eliot, employed by Faber for decades, was instrumental in compiling the distinguished poetry list of that publisher.

M. found his lyrical voice unusually early. To begin with, his poetry was regarded as harsh, bleak, and "modern." But M., with Auden, Day-Lewis, and Spender, should be seen against a background of rather bland and idyllizing verse, popular in Britain before and during the 1920s. To 21st-c. readers, M.'s approach to his various themes and topics must be called gentle, even wistful, and at times humorous, while his style is musical, and seldom abrasive or drastic. His imagery, though, occasionally verges on surrealism: "Tonight is so coarse with chocolate" ("Ode"); "From the chandeliers the snow begins to fall" ("The Brandy Glass"). It is a matter of opinion and emphasis whether M. should be labeled a modernist or not.

With Auden, M. wrote *Letters from Iceland* (1937), an eccentric mixture of prose and poetry. The writers were soon to drift apart, for two or three reasons. Auden settled in the U.S., and the ambitions of both men may have been turning their relationship into a less pleasant one, marked by a competitive spirit. But also M.'s heterosexuality may have played some part. The homosexual Auden preferred to move in other circles.

M.'s long masterpiece, *Autumn Journal,* making up a volume of its own, presents most convincingly the period—particularly its atmosphere—immediately before the Second World War. Also Spain, on the eve of its civil war, figures in this work. Political and personal concerns are skillfully interwoven. The form is rhapsodic, the diction looks relaxed, often colloquial; as a matter of fact, it is tautly constructed and perfectly controlled. One may not notice at first that every second line rhymes. M.'s images sparkle or startle: the speaker's future glints with a beloved woman's "presence/Like moon on a slate roof," and Spain, just before the fall of Barcelona, "At Easter [is] ripe as an egg for revolt and ruin." Despite the fear and occasional despair conveyed by this work, it ends on an optimistic note, with metaphors that one forgives, in their context, for being mixed: "there will be sunlight later/And the equation will come out at last."

This sunshine, on the contrary, "Hardens and grows cold" in one of M.'s most exquisite short poems, "The Sunlight on the Garden." As distinct from *Autumn Journal*, it must be classified as stylistically almost wholly traditional. Similar in mood—caused perhaps by similar world events—it could be interpreted as depicting the loss, not merely of prewar Europe, but of grace, innocence, childhood, the Garden of Eden.

M.'s supposed socialism could easily be reduced to a fairly sentimental attitude to the working classes, as well as an insistence on the uniqueness and equality of individuals, independent of class. The fullest statement of this individualism is a fascinating, rather long account, in free verse, "The Kingdom." It is not the Kingdom of Heaven that interests M., but, explicitly, that "of Earth." Some religious connotations appear to linger, however, as when he asserts that children (literal or figurative) belong to "the Kingdom." Several "case studies" describe people of both sexes and various age groups, who are wholly themselves, unable to run with the pack, but "loyal to a different/ Order." Each person has his or her preoccupations, and special imagery. A young woman with strong feelings and an independent mind becomes a river goddess carrying "a pitcher/Of ice-cold wild emotions." Unexpectedly, a town drunk is one of these chosen: even more surprisingly, he seems to be alone among the characters in knowing that he does not belong to society in any normal sense, but to "the Kingdom." A priest in the same poem, who is "dead in daffodil time," and styled both a child and "A generous puritan," may be a portrait of M.'s father. M.'s celebrated, much anthologized short poem "Snow" has a theme analogous to that of "The Kingdom": the diversity and contradictoriness of this world, as a source of joy.

Critics generally agree that his poetry at some point—roughly, between the mid-1940s and the mid-1950s—became less satisfying and more superficial. It is possible that the fact that he wrote radio journalism regularly during these years had a negative effect on his creative writing. M.'s last new collections, though, *Solstices* (1961) and *The Burning Perch* (1963), belong to his finest books.

M. also authored plays, radio plays, books of criticism, and, as Louis Malone, one novel, *Roundabout Way* (1932). He was a careful translator who rendered Aeschylus' *Agamemnon* (1936) and an abbreviated version of Goethe's *Faust* (1951) into English. His unfinished autobiography *The Strings Are False* was published posthumously in 1966.

For many years, M. worked as a producer and feature writer at the BBC in London. He spent two periods in the U.S., as visiting lecturer at Cornell University and Sarah Lawrence College, respectively. In 1950–51, he was director of the British Council/British Institute, Athens, Greece.

In Muriel SPARK's autobiographical *Curriculum Vitae* (1992), M. puts in a cameo appearance, in his absence, as "the Professor." The young Spark much admired his successful professionalism; he was the first established writer she almost met.

BIBLIOGRAPHY: Devine, K., and A. J., Peacock, eds., *L. M. and His Influence* (1998); Hynes, S., *The Auden Generation* (1976); McDonald, P., *L. M.* (1991); McKinnon, W. T., *Apollo's Blended Dream: A Study of the Poetry of L. M.* (1971)

SUSANNA ROXMAN

MACPHERSON, James

b. 27 October 1736, Ruthven, Inverness, Scotland; d. 17 February 1796, Belville, Inverness, Scotland

The writer at the center of one of the great literary causes célèbres of the 18th c. was a Scottish Highland schoolmaster whose early experience included witnessing family members suffer the brutal consequences of Hanoverian military oppression after the Jacobite defeat at Culloden (1746). As a young man, M. studied at Aberdeen University under leading rhetoricians of the Scottish Enlightenment who combined strong classical affiliations with commitment to forging a polite "British" style and poetics to consolidate the process of unification of Scotland and England following the political Act of Union of 1707.

Like many of his peers, M. became under their influence an amateur antiquarian and poet, collecting and translating Gaelic manuscripts, and publishing a first book of EPIC poetry in stilted Anglo-Scots idiom, *The Highlander* (1758). This ambitious work invokes the heroic, nostalgic attitude toward a passing race for which M. would later become famous, but its verbose style and mannerism made little critical or popular impression. However, M.'s Gaelic translations and renditions of the oral poetry of the Highlands attracted the attention of the poet John Home, who introduced him to the influential Professor of Rhetoric and Belles Lettres Hugh BLAIR and other figures of literary Edinburgh. To them, M.'s rendition of translated fragments of oral Gaelic poetry indicated a surviving native tradition of primitive poetry of great virtue and antiquity. Excited by the possibility of a recoverable Scottish epic on a Homeric or Virgilian scale, Blair and others commissioned M. to travel further in the Highlands in search of further material. The results of his research appeared in 1760 as a slender volume, *Fragments of Ancient Poetry, Collected in the Highlands of Scotland, and Translated from the Galic* [sic] *or Erse Language*, with a brief preface composed by Blair indicating their antiquity, their authenticity and their relation to an epic cycle composed by the Bard Oscian or Ossian and telling of the exploits of Fingal.

The fifteen "Fragments" created an immediate sensation. Reviewers and readers heralded their heroic matter, their muted diction and dignified style, as the authentic voice of a vanished age; the prose poems seemed to offer a return to primitive simplicity as an alternative to attenuated Augustan poetic modes. Enthusiasm in Scotland was unanimous, and often uncritical, with leading figures such as David HUME and Adam Ferguson joining in on grounds that were as much nationalistic as aesthetic. The possibility that the *Fragments* were the tip of a Celtic epic, the source of a unified Scottish mythology independent of and prior to the existence of English nationhood, was irresistible; funds were readily procured to send M. on a more extensive mission to gather further evidence. Response in English literary circles was more qualified: here too there was interest and excitement at the possible recovery of a primitive poetic voice from the national past, but also skepticism, as figures like Samuel JOHNSON doubted the authenticity of "translations" that had no tangible "originals." In the absence of Gaelic manuscripts, which M. declared to exist but repeatedly failed to supply for scrutiny, hostile critics began to denounce the *Fragments* as fakes or forgeries. Controversy intensified when M.'s new field work produced exactly what he had been commissioned to discover: *Fingal, an Ancient Epic Poem*, in 1762, rapidly followed the following year by *Temora, an Ancient Epic Poem in Eight Books. Together with several Other Poems composed by Ossian, the Son of Fingal*. In 1765, the two volumes were published together, with extensive historical, critical, and editorial material by M. and Blair, as *The Works of Ossian* (repub. as *The Poems of Ossian*, 2 vols., 1773). The fame of the reconstructed epics spread throughout Europe, and exerted extraordinary influence not only on Herder and other writers seeking inspiration for a revival of German national feeling, but on Napoleon, who found his military ideal in them. Their emphasis on natural imagery, on evocative setting and melancholy mood, as well as the revolutionary implications of their implied resistance to reigning poetic and political Establishments, inspired a younger generation of poets and prose writers, and may be regarded as initiating the Romantic movement.

On the crest of his success, M. moved to London, where patronage secured him a position as secretary to the Governor of Florida in 1764. Returning to England in 1766, he became a political writer in the pay of the government, and produced a propagandist and Unionist interpretation of the *History of Great Britain from the Restoration to the Accession of the House of Hanover* (2 vols., 1775). Investing in the East India Company, he became rich enough to purchase an estate near his birthplace in the Highlands, and on his death received the ultimate accolade of a resting place in Poet's Corner in Westminster Abbey. It was an equivocal honor for one who had spent much of his career defending his position as merely the humble collector and translator of great poetry composed by long-dead national heroes. The "Ossianic Controversy" rumbled on well beyond the initial acrimonious and personal accusations of forgery that provided a focus for national animosities between Scots and English, to a more decorous phase of scholarly investigation that included the appointment of a Highland Society Committee to inquire into "the Nature and Authenticity of the Poems of Ossian." Under the chairmanship of Henry MACKENZIE, and having received reports from correspondents throughout the Highlands, it concluded in 1805 that M. had adapted, augmented, and in some cases drawn very loosely upon genuine Gaelic poetry of great but unspecified antiquity that continued to circulate orally in the Highlands. The ferocity of the authenticity debate had abated, but it generated a complex debate that helped to define several characteristic discourses of ROMANTICISM: the relationship between tradition and inspiration, the nature of creativity and originality and inspiration, and a new interest in editorial procedures and the principles of translation.

BIBLIOGRAPHY: Gaskill, H., ed., *Ossian Revisited* (1991); Gaskill, H., ed., *The Poems of Ossian and Related Works* (1996); Stafford, F., *The Sublime Savage: A Study of J. M. and the Poems of Ossian* (1988)

SUSAN MANNING

MacSWEENEY, Barry

b. 17 July 1948, Newcastle-upon-Tyne; d. 9 May 2000, Newcastle-upon-Tyne

Poet and professional journalist by trade, M. produced a consistently provocative and restless body of work from his teens, when as a young school leaver and admirer of French symbolism he corresponded with Basil BUNTING and J. H. PRYNNE. He won early recognition as a precocious "pop" poet with *The Boy from the Green Cabaret Tells of His Mother* (1968), the reputation of which was arguably detrimental to subsequent recognition of his mature verse. M. cultivated an energetic, sometimes caustic, lyric poetry attracted to the mythology of the rebel and outsider, be that Thomas CHATTERTON or Jim Morrison, as exemplified by the declamatory "The Last Bud" (1969) and the *Odes* (1978). This spirit also inspired the more explicitly political tribute to the mining community *Black Torch* (1978). A committed yet nonprofessional poet, M. suffered from the neglect of his collection *Ranter* (1985), inspired by the English Civil War, and of selected poems, *Tempers of Hazard* (pulped by its publishers in 1993) containing the extraordinary new work "Jury Vet." Recognition was forthcoming for *Pearl* (1995), a haunting elegy of language and child-

hood inspired by a friend and *The Book Of Demons* (1997), an acknowledgment of the author's ill health and alcoholism. M.'s lyric agility and rhetorical force, along with the swaggering invective of his adopted personae, is impressive.

MAGINN, William

b. 10 July 1794, Cork, Ireland; d. 21 August 1842, Walton-on-Thames

M.'s literary work has been almost completely obscured by his reputation as a "character," and he is now little more than a footnote in British literary history. In his own day, however, M.'s writings, which included verse, essays, short stories, and political and literary polemics, made him one of the most successful if controversial of 19th-c. journalists.

M. began his writing career by sending pseudonymous contributions from Cork to the *Literary Gazette* and, more importantly, to *Blackwood's Magazine*. His most important contribution was his suggestion for *Noctes Ambrosianae*, or "Nights at Ambrose's Tavern," a series of imaginary conversations between a group of friends who discuss the topical issues of the day. M. wrote the first and, under his favorite pseudonym of Sir Morgan O'Doherty, Adjutant, several of the early dialogues, some of which became such savage personal attacks that William Blackwood had to caution M. that "it really will not do to run a-muck in this kind of way."

Based on the success of this early work, in 1823 M. decided to leave Cork for London, where he soon became and for the next two decades remained a highly successful journalist, but one whose success was constantly undermined by his alcoholism and irresponsibility. His career began promisingly when John Murray asked M. to write Lord BYRON's life, although Murray became so unhappy with M.'s plan to show Byron "in his true and natural colours" that he burned Byron's memoirs and hired Thomas MORE to write a more flattering portrait of the poet. Murray then sent M. to Paris as representative of the Tory daily the *Representative*; here M. started but did not complete a serious novel, but he also fell so deeply into debt and drunkenness that Murray brought him back to London to edit the "lighter side" of the paper. In 1827, M. published, anonymously and possibly in collaboration with John Wilson CROKER, *Whitehall; or, The Days of George IV,* a sometimes vicious but more often humorous parody of then popular historical novels.

In 1829, M. left *Blackwood's* to establish, with his friend Hugh Fraser, a new magazine, *Fraser's Magazine for Town and Country*, his most important and influential venture as writer and journalist and his most significant contribution to British letters. Although he was never officially listed as its editor, from the first issue in 1830 the content and style of *Fraser's* were primarily M.'s work. Although a family magazine that published reviews, light fiction and verse, and diverse articles to appeal to all readers, *Fraser's* emphasis on politics and literature made it the most interesting periodical of the 1830s. Under M.'s influence, *Fraser's* writers turned almost all of their subjects into Tory polemics, particularly against Whig laissez-faire policies that M. felt were uncharitable and led to poverty, the source of all crime. The magazine's other favorite targets were the fashionable novels of the time, especially those of Edward BULWER-LYTTON, a writer M. and William Makepeace THACKERAY attacked unrelentingly for years. M.'s most important contribution to *Fraser's*, however, was the "Gallery of Illustrious Literary Characters" (1830–38). With illustrations by Daniel Maclise, M.'s brief, satiric, and sometimes overly personal one paragraph biographies of the leading writers of the day became the magazine's most popular feature, as the *Noctes Ambrosianae* he initiated were the most popular feature of *Blackwood's*. During this period, M. also published his two best short stories, both in *Blackwood's* in 1834. "The Story without a Tail" concerns a group of Irishmen who attempt, far into the evening and into the bottle, and with absolutely no success, to remember Humpy Harlowe's "Tale of wondrous length" but get no further than the first words "Humphries told me." The other tale, "Bob Burke's Duel with Ensign Brady of the 48th," concerning the rivalry between two lovers who become very reluctant duelists, is M.'s comic masterpiece.

These two tales, with his essays on William SHAKESPEARE and his "Homeric Ballads," are the only works of M. that have survived his era. The topical content and often careless writing characteristic of his work make it of little literary value, although M. himself remains an important figure in the history of British journalism.

BIBLIOGRAPHY: Latané, D. E., Jr., "W. M.," in Greenfield, J. R., ed., *British Short-Fiction Writers, 1800–1880, DLB* 159 (1996): 204–10; Thrall, M. M. H., *Rebellious Fraser's: Nol Yorke's Magazine in the Days of M., Thackeray, and Carlyle* (1934)

JOHN ROGERS

MAHON, Derek
b. 23 November 1941, Belfast, Northern Ireland

M.'s poetry is elegant, restrained, and carefully crafted. His concerns are centered on individuals and society, particularly the "outsider" or those on the margins of groups, who stand aside from the crowd. Reared as an only child in a Protestant family in Northern Ireland, he felt an outsider himself, a solitary, sometimes lonely, individual who preferred reading to sports at school; this perspective is maintained throughout his work. As a young adult, he and his contemporaries felt that the "Irish Question" was not his problem, resisting the draw of division and sectarianism.

In his first volume, *Night Crossing* (1968), M. faces his sense of resistance to his native ground, feeling out of touch with the area that is necessarily part of him. "Home" is presented as a difficult concept; the difficulty and distress are nevertheless carefully and precisely contained within the masterful rhymes and cadences of his formal structures. Anthropological interests are explored in *Lives* (1972); the title poem reflects on a variety of different manifestations of life as artifact, implement, natural resource, and human being—past, present, and future.

A sense of doom and apocalypse is developed in many of M.'s collections, fostered by his shock at the realization of violence destroying the fabric of his homeland, to which he returned after five years of traveling. The tone of many poems is of despairing resignation and a questioning of the poet's role, distanced from the actualities of everyday life in his academic circle. To counteract this, M. celebrates the everyday joys and mundane trivialities that can lift the spirits despite the wider reverberations of disaster.

In the title poem of *The Snow Party* (1975), M. presents the civilized rituals of social intercourse as a counterbalance to the distortion and disruption of political unrest. Throughout the poetry, the carefully measured lines, ordered rhyme schemes, and balanced phrasing reflect the poet's desire to impose order on chaos, to relish the craft and skill of poetic practice. M. also recognizes other artistic representations of life, extending the concern for pattern and discipline to painting. Many poems reflect the world glimpsed in a picture, the poetry expands that insight with telling evocation of mood and atmosphere. A number of such poems are collected in M.'s *The Hunt by Night* (1982). In the title poem, color and form are keenly and clearly related to the psychological development of human maturity, which nevertheless still retains connections with primitive tribal consciousness.

The evolution of Western social and political consciousness is charted in M.'s work, together with an ironic and satirical sense of the mismanagement of ecological resources, the mass consumerism of contemporary society that M. derides. In relation to this sense of waste, in his poetic structures he resists the use of free verse, implying its very freedom could turn to excess and formlessness. Thus, in *Antarctica* (1985), there is a range of tightly constructed, beautifully composed pieces, such as the title villanelle, a meditation on the fate of the solitary climber who leaves the security of the camp. The containment of verse reflects his containment of self, his valuing of the solitary over the communal.

The Hudson Letter (1995) develops a longer verse form of connected sequences, which still maintains the careful rhyming pattern of M.'s more usual, shorter lyrics. The context of this volume is America rather than Europe, New York rather than Belfast or Dublin; the theme, that of homelessness, links with the continuous concern in the poetry as a whole, for those on the "outside." The detailed attention to minutiae of the environment and thoughtful observation of sights, sounds, tastes, smells, create a cumulative cityscape in eighteen sections of couplets, triplets, and alternate rhyming lines.

The Yellow Book (1997) returns to Europe and specifically to Dublin, contrasting its present with its past and M.'s own relationship to the city at different times, with a more jaded and satirical tone. Wider resonances relate to a sense of "end of the age" and the poet's anxiety about the decadent lifestyle of 20th-c. humankind. Once again, the ecological and anthropological perspective is explored, shown in his *Collected Poems* of 1999 to be an evolving and absorbing consideration throughout his work, developing in maturity and gravity, but containing flashes of wit and HUMOR, typical of this urbane and yet humane poet.

BIBLIOGRAPHY: O'Neill, M., "Holding Nature Up to Art: The Poetry of D. M.," in Klein, H., et al., eds., *Poetry Now: Contemporary British and Irish Poetry in the Making* (1999): 215–23; special M. issue, *IUR* 24 (Spring-Summer 1994)

ROSE ATFIELD

MALET, Lucas

(pseud. of Mary St. Leger Kingsley Harrison) b. 4 June 1852, Eversley, Hampshire; d. 27 October 1931, Tenby, Wales

Author of the best-selling novel *The Wages of Sin* (3 vols., 1891), M. was one of the most popular writers of the late 19th c., but by the early 20th c. her reputation had rapidly declined and her works are now largely forgotten. The daughter of writer Charles KINGSLEY, she published her first novel in 1882, the two-volume *Mrs. Lorimer, a Sketch in Black and White*, followed by the successful *Colonial Enderby's Wife* (3 vols., 1885), but she is best known for *The Wages of Sin*, the frank portrayal of a struggling artist involved in an illicit sexual relationship with his model, and *The History of Sir Richard Calmady* (1901). Although productive throughout her career, M.'s later novels failed to match the sensationalism and popularity of her earlier fiction.

MALONE, Edmond

b. 4 October 1741, Dublin, Ireland; d. 25 April 1812, London

The son of Irish landowners, M. studied law but applied his interest in evidence and argument to editorial scholarship. Projects associated with fellow members of the Literary Club include an edition of the poems and plays of Oliver GOLDSMITH (2 vols., 1777) and a memoir of Sir Joshua REYNOLDS (2 vols., 1797). More important was the assistance M. provided James BOSWELL in editing his *Journal of a Tour of the Hebrides with Dr. Samuel Johnson* and in writing his *Life* of Samuel JOHNSON; M. also edited the posthumous third through sixth editions (1799–1811). Both M.'s editorial skill and his moral guidance bore fruit in the *Life;* he helped to shape a massive collection of Johnsoniana into a coherent narrative, while softening Boswell's intemperate attacks on rival biographers. Drawing on his antiquarian learning, M. also decisively exposed as fabrications the Shakespearean documents "found" by William Henry Ireland, and he was a prominent critic of the Thomas CHATTERTON forgeries. But it is as an editor of William SHAKESPEARE that M. made his most lasting contribution. The conclusions of his "An Attempt to Ascertain the Order in Which the Plays Attributed to Shakespeare Were Written" (1778) dominate modern thinking about Shakespeare's oeuvre. M.'s own edition of Shakespeare (10 vols., 1790) broke new ground: it discriminated fact from legend in Shakespeare's biography, offered a systematic chronology of the plays, identified a canon, systematically argued the First Folio's superiority to the second, and supplied scholarly apparatus and notes for the sonnets. By privileging a demonstrable standard for editorial intervention, M. changed the profession of the scholarly editor; after M., Shakespeare scholars did not require the poetic reputation of an Alexander POPE or a Samuel Johnson. Indeed, despite the fame of these earlier editors, it is to M. that we trace the lineage of modern Shakespearean studies.

LISA BERGLUND

MALORY, [Sir] Thomas

b. probably ca. 1410, Warwickshire; d. ca. 1471, London

The legend of King Arthur remains alive in English literature today largely because of the work of M., who shaped it into what is sometimes seen as the first novel in English, published by William CAXTON in 1485 as *Le Morte d'Arthur* (wr. ca. 1470). Before then, ironically, this MATTER OF BRITAIN—the huge conglomeration of tales more or less revolving around Arthur, had developed mostly in French, after the departure of Britons fleeing England for France when Rome withdrew its troops from Britain. With the enormous influx into England of all things French in the centuries following the Norman Conquest came the return and gradual repatriation of Arthur. In the 15th c., M. took the whole mishmash of French tales, poems, overlapping themes, undeveloped ideas, characters, mythical lessons, and mystical quests, together with some similar material in English, and composed the story as we have it today. In a nutshell, he Anglicized Arthur. In France, the legends had become highly romantic, almost completely divorced from everyday characters and verisimilitude; M. reduced the supernatural elements and introduced a certain hominess to Arthur and his knights. The archetypal appeal, combined with M.'s matter-of-fact English realism, has made a powerful, lasting work of art. Its influence on literature, drama, and the pictorial arts is immeasurable.

Yet, important though his work has proved, nobody knows for sure who this M. was. After years of argument for this or that candidate, the question seemed to have been answered satisfactorily in 1897 by George Lyman Kittredge, who identified the author as a knight of Newbold Revel in Warwickshire. In Caxton's edition, our author says that he is writing as a prisoner; Kittredge's candidate was in and out of prison, charged at various times with robbery, extortion, vandalism, rape, assault, and attempted murder. However, in 1966 William Matthews argued convincingly in favor of another Thomas Malory, from Hutton and Studley, Yorkshire, an upstanding citizen who may have been a political prisoner. Matthews offered new evidence, suggested by a remarkable discovery in 1934. In that year, W. F. Oakeshott, rummaging through the library at Winchester College in search of interesting things to put into a display case to impress visitors, found a 15th-c. manuscript of M.'s work. This script not only gave clues to the author's identity; it also raised a serious critical question concerning the work, which has been under discussion ever since: How much of Caxton's 1485 edition is Caxton's work, rather than M.'s? The printer had published the material as a single long story, very much like a novel, and called it *Le Morte d'Arthur*. The Winchester manuscript, believed to be closer in time and intention to M.'s own, although not in his own hand, is a collection of separate stories. Oakeshott turned it over to Eugene Vinaver, who was working on an edition of the Caxton *Morte*; Vinaver abandoned that project and produced instead, in 1947, the edited Winchester manuscript, calling it *The Works of Sir Thomas Malory.*

So, the questions continue to tease critics: Who is Thomas Malory? And what did he really write, "of this vast assemblage of stories one story and one book," as George Saintsbury claimed, or a series of "works"? Meanwhile, Arthur and Guinevere, Lancelot and Gawain, the Round Table united by human nobility and broken by human frailty, Merlin and Mordred, and the Holy Grail continue to claim their place in the imagination of each new generation, remarkably easy to recognize as the characters and themes of the knight-prisoner, Thomas Malory.

BIBLIOGRAPHY: Bennett, J. A. W., ed., *Essays on M.* (1963); Kittredge, G. L., *Sir T. M.* (1897); Matthews, W., *The Ill-Framed Knight* (1966); Vinaver, E., *M.* (1970)

CECELIA LAMPP LINTON

MALTHUS, Thomas Robert

b. 13 February 1766, near Guildford, Surrey; d. 23 December 1834, Haileybury

M. studied mathematics at Jesus College, Cambridge, and was elected to a fellowship, later being ordained. His father believed, with William GODWIN, that society could be perfected and M.'s arguments to the contrary so impressed the father that he suggested his son should write them down. In 1798, M. published the first edition of his great work, *An Essay on the Principle of Population as It Affects the Future Improvement of Society, with Remarks on the Speculations of Mr. Godwin, Mr. Condorcet, and Other Writers*. M. warned that population tends to outrun food supplies because population grows geometrically whereas food increases arithmetically: poverty and disease were necessary checks on population. This shocked readers, because it seemed to deny God's providence, but sank deep into 19th-c. thought. Charles DARWIN read in M. of "the struggle for existence" and acknowledged M.'s influence on his own *Origin of Species*. M. published several revised editions of his chief work, and his later writings were on economics, notably *An Investigation of the Cause of the Present High Price of Provisions* (1800), *Observations on the Effect of the Corn Laws* (1814), and *The Principles of Political Economy* (1820). He was a friend and correspondent of David Ricardo and is said to have been the first to formulate the law of diminishing returns as applied to agriculture.

MANDEVILLE, Bernard [de]

b. ca. November 1670, Rotterdam, Holland; d. 21 January 1733, Hackney

After studying philosophy and medicine at the University of Leyden and practicing briefly in Holland, M. traveled to England to learn the language. By 1699, he had married an English woman, settled in London, and specialized in nervous and gastric disorders. M. published a medical text entitled *A Treatise of the Hypochondriack and Hysterick Passions* (1711), several fables, and occasional verse, but his major publications were prose commentaries on individual and social morality.

M.'s most significant literary work, *The Fable of the Bees*, expanded and changed form with each new edition. As early as 1703, M. wrote several short fables in the style of La Fontaine. In 1705, he published the long poem *The Grumbling Hive; or, Knaves*

Turn'd Honest, which he described as "a story told in doggerel." This pamphlet publication was popular enough to be pirated, but the poem received much more attention in 1714 when it reappeared as part of *The Fable of the Bees; or, Private Vices, Publick Benefits*. Along with the poem, this volume contained twenty prose "remarks" (extensive commentaries on individual lines) and the essay "An Enquiry into the Origin of Moral Virtue." A subsequent edition (1723) offered still more "remarks" and two additional essays—"An Essay on Charity and Charity-Schools" and "A Search into the Nature of Society." A further accretion, published as part 2 of *The Fable of the Bees* (1729), included six dialogues between Horatio and Cleomenes. The later character speaks for M. and defends the ideas in *The Fable*.

The ambiguous subtitle of *The Fable* merely identifies two qualities—vices and benefits. This juxtaposition introduces M.'s major topic throughout the evolving work but does not specify his moral position. The initial story of the grumbling hive obviously portrays humans in the guise of bees. Here, in clear opposition to the benevolence of Lord SHAFTESBURY, selfish passions govern all actions. Individual bees display envy, vanity, and lust, but the entire hive is a paradise. For example, vanity stimulates desires for luxury items, such desires promote industry and trade, and the flourishing economy produces a happy and prosperous society. When Jove responds to hypocritical complaints by turning the hive honest, many desires wane, the economy fails, and the society reverts to a more primitive state. Thus, M.'s fable does not declare that individual vices are equal to public benefits. It apparently suggests that clever political leaders can use moral flaws to increase public good. Indeed, the extended title of the 1714 edition states that "Human Frailties" may "be turn'd to the Advantage of the Civil Society" and thereby "made to supply the place of Moral Virtues."

Even though M. was a physician, his primary aim was to diagnose the ills of society and not to suggest cures. One significant departure from this stance was his *A Modest Defence of Publick Stews* (1724). After the Middlesex County Grand Jury declared *The Fable* a public nuisance (for allegedly supporting whoring), M. presented a detailed plan for public management of prostitution. This piece (with its title recalling Jonathan SWIFT's *A Modest Proposal*) may be at least partly ironic. Because of such irony throughout M.'s works, many of his statements are subject to divergent interpretations. Some regard him as a pious moralist who attacks hypocrisy by pointing out ignoble motives behind apparently beneficent acts. Others see him as a cynic who argues that virtue simply does not exist, or even a libertine who actually sanctions vice. Although M.'s values may be hard to pin down, his works clearly anticipate later concepts in psychology

(like Freud's notion of the id) and applications of modern political theory (like "sin taxes").

BIBLIOGRAPHY: Chiasson, E. J., "B. M.: A Reappraisal," *PQ* 49 (October 1970): 489–519; Cook, R. I., *B. M.* (1974); Harth, P., "The Satiric Purpose of *The Fable of the Bees*," *E-CS* 2 (1969): 321–40; Munro, H., *The Ambivalence of B. M.* (1975)

ALBERT WILHELM

MANLEY, [Mary] Delarivier [or Delarivière]
b. 6 or 7 April 1663, Jersey; d. 11 July 1724, London

Novelist, memoirist, poet, playwright, editor, critic, and satirist, M. has become notorious as a scandalous writer, but received greater renown in her lifetime as a political satirist for the Tory party. M.'s novels, most famously *The Secret History of Queen Zarah and the Zarazians* (2 vols., 1705) and *Secret Memoirs and Manners of Several Persons of Quality of Both Sexes from the New Atalantis* (2 vols., 1709), demonstrate how love and sex have been corrupted into political tools of the court. M.'s other major prose work, *The Adventures of Rivella* (1714), was autobiographical in tone and argued that men are celebrated for passion, whereas desiring women are condemned.

On the death of her father, Lieutenant Governor of Jersey, M. became the ward of her cousin, John Manley. In 1688, John and she were married and a son was born three years later. In *New Atalantis* and *Rivella*, M. implied that she had been unaware that John had a living wife, but her involvement in a bigamous marriage seriously damaged her reputation. When John finally deserted her, M. stayed with friends in the south of England and her travels inspired her first foray into print, *Letters Written by Mrs. Manley* (1696). In the same year, M. settled in London and began to make her name as a playwright. Her first play, *The Lost Lover; or, The Jealous Husband* (1696), was not successful, but her second in the same year, *The Royal Mischief*, was a hit.

In 1705, when political controversy in London was running high, *The Secret History of Queen Zarah and the Zarazians* appeared in print and was an immediate success. The novel was a thinly veiled satiric portrait of Sarah, Duchess of Marlborough, notable Whig and favorite of Queen Anne, that exposed the duchess as sexually and politically depraved. Although there are doubts over the authorship of *Queen Zarah*, scholars generally judge the work to be M.'s. In 1706, M.'s play, *Alymna*, was performed and in 1707, she published her correspondence with Richard STEELE and letters concerning her love affair with John Tilly as *The Lady's Paquet Broke Open*.

In May 1709, the first volume of the *New Atalantis* was published. The novel described the return of the goddess Justice to earth in search of information about mortal conduct for the prince whom she is training to be king. Justice, guided by Intelligence around Atalantis, is shocked to find only scenes of vice and depravity. The *New Atalantis* satirized the Whig aristocracy and nine days after the publication of the second volume, in October 1709, M., her publisher, and her printer were arrested for libel. M. was tried and discharged in February 1710. The controversy only increased the popularity of the *New Atalantis*, which had gone through at least seven editions by 1736, and M. remained dedicated to the cause of Tory propaganda. In 1710, M. published another political satire in two volumes, *Memoirs of Europe, towards the Close of the Eighth Century.*

With the death of Anne in 1714, and restoration of Whig supremacy, M. turned away from politics. She wrote the autobiographical *Rivella*, according to the scurrilous publisher Edmund Curll, to prevent Charles Gildon from distributing his defamatory biography of her. In *Rivella*, M., rather than endorsing herself against conventional morality as in *Atalantis*, declares that her irregular life has supplied her with the experience necessary to be a successful writer. In 1717, M.'s last play, *Lucius*, was performed and her final collection of fiction, *The Power of Love, in Seven Novels,* appeared in 1720. M.'s wit, skillful narration, and lively dialogue, when not validating her personal choices, was directed toward proving that England should be governed by the Tories, so it is fitting that she died when the Whigs' hold over the country was, seemingly, unassailable.

BIBLIOGRAPHY: Ballaster, R., *Seductive Forms* (1992); Köster, P., "D. M. and the DNB: A Cautionary Tale About Following Black Sheep with a Challenge to the Cataloguers," *E-CL* 3 (1977): 106–11; Todd, J., "Life after Sex: The Fictional Autobiography of D. M.," *WS* 15, 1 (1988): 43–55

                                    KATE WILLIAMS

MANNING, Olivia

b. 1915, Portsmouth; d. 23 July 1980, Isle of Wight

M. was considered one of the more talented writers of her era, but her commercial success was never enormous. She had a respectable following in England, yet was virtually unknown in the U.S. Born in Portsmouth to an Irish mother and a father who was a commander in the Royal Navy, M. spent much of her youth in Northern Ireland. She entered art school and trained as a painter, then decided she was better suited to the pen than the brush. In 1939, she married a British Council lecturer in Bucharest, and moved abroad. They were forced to flee to Greece and the Middle East just before the German invasion, and it is in these circumstances and locations that M. found her greatest source of material. M. published nearly twenty

works of fiction and several works of nonfiction. In addition, she regularly contributed to journals and newspapers, including the *Observer* and the *Times* (London). However, it is her two trilogies based around World War II that gained her the most notoriety. The first, *The Balkan Trilogy*, focuses on the upcoming war and the early years of it, and includes *The Great Fortune* (1960), *The Spoilt City* (1962), and *Friends and Heroes* (1965). *The Levant Trilogy* comprises *The Danger Tree* (1977), *The Battle Lost and Won* (1978), and *The Sum of Things* (1980). The theme of the two trilogies is consistently referred to as "uncertainty," and both are known for their juxtaposition of monumental historical events with the trifles of the everyday, creating a true sense of place and situation. During her life, she felt neglected, but the televising of *The Balkan Trilogy* with Emma Thompson and Kenneth Branagh brought her posthumous fame.

MANSFIELD, Katherine

b. Kathleen Mansfield Beauchamp, 14 October 1888, Wellington, New Zealand; d. 9 January 1923, Fontainebleau, France

M. is best known among the general reading public for her five collections of short stories, published between 1911 and 1923. Since their appearance in a single volume in 1945, they have never been out of print. After her death, John Middleton MURRY, her second husband and literary executor, also edited and published her *Journal*, her letters, some poetry, a novella *The Aloe*, published in 1930, and her literary reviews. These have all since been further researched and reprinted in more scholarly editions. Together this oeuvre established M. among the foremost writers of her generation, both her creative practice and critical theory having helped to construct literary MODERNISM. A general reassessment of her work took place in the 1980s based partly on two biographical studies by Antony Alpers (1980) and Claire TOMALIN (1987). This was affirmed by M.'s inclusion in Bonnie Kime Scott's *The Gender of Modernism* in 1990. There Clare Hanson argued for the value of M.'s "distinctive 'female aesthetic'" as defined in her letters, journals, and reviews, not least because of her influence on other writers like Virginia WOOLF.

Born to a wealthy bourgeois family in New Zealand, M. was determined to escape its restrictive norms, perhaps inspired by the example of her aunt, the novelist Elizabeth von Arnim. Her own life was adventurous. She traveled to Europe and explored sexual freedoms that included, beside a lifelong, same-sex relationship, two marriages, miscarriages, and various extramarital affairs. Even though it probably led to her early death from gonorrhea and tuberculosis, such adventurousness fueled her writing. Frequently in the stories, crucial changes in insight are provoked by journeys and, for many of her characters, these insights concern the limitations of bourgeois values, especially on women. Whatever vindictiveness she may have felt concerning such values seems to have been exorcized by her first collection of stories, *In a German Pension* (1911), somewhat limited caricatures of the Bavarian bourgeoisie. Her perceptions were certainly deepened by the events of World War I, above all the death of her brother. As she said in a letter in 1919, now "we see death in life"; although not explicitly, "deserts of vast eternity . . . *must* be there." In her later collections, she honed a powerfully suggestive, symbolic method that has much in common with the imagist poetry of her period and with James JOYCE's stories in *Dubliners*.

The title story of her second collection to be published, *Bliss and Other Stories* (1920), is generally reckoned one of her most interesting. It is open to feminist psychoanalytic interpretation and indicates female homosexual attraction of the kind described by her friend of twenty years, Ida Baker, in *Katherine Mansfield: The Memories of L. M.* (1971). Murry gathered work written between those first two collections, together with four early tales dating from before 1911, and published it as *Something Childish and Other Stories* (1924). This includes her lengthy First World War story, "An Indiscreet Journey." M.'s masterpiece is her third planned collection, *The Garden Party and Other Stories* (1922), with the important stories "At the Bay," "The Garden Party," "Daughters of the Late Colonel," and "Life of Ma Parker." At her death, her proposed fourth collection remained incomplete, but Murry assembled what she had left as *The Doves' Nest and Other Stories* (1923). He included some unfinished work as well as what are probably the three most frequently anthologized of her stories: "The Doll's House," "The Fly," and "The Canary." The last of these bears comparison with Susan Glaspell's *Trifles* (1916).

Although M. kept a journal from at least 1909, she destroyed most of what she called the "huge complaining diaries" from before the First World War, and started again in earnest after her brother was killed in action in 1915. The *Journal* was constructed by Murry (first in 1927 and then in a fuller edition in 1954) out of her writer's workbooks that she used to maintain her resolve: "I have a duty to perform to the lovely time when we were both alive." It is a compilation from her irregular diaries of 1915, 1920, and 1922, thirty exercise books of notes, and odd sheets of jottings and memoranda. Some pages record her physical and mental suffering, as for instance when she first coughed up blood. Other pages express her merriment, as with her mock-epitaph for Lloyd George in 1917: "In the heart of England's most imminent peril he grasped his Niblick and struck out for the Open

Course." There are comments on authors she was reading: Colette, Henry JAMES, Dostoevsky, William SHAKESPEARE, Anton Chekhov, and famously on E. M. FORSTER who "never gets further than warming the pot." Inserted among these entries are extracts from letters and plans for her short story collections. Above all, she squirreled away there descriptions of events and miniature portraits of people (like the emotionally demanding woman in white depicted as a gull screaming, "Feed me!"), and accounts of what she called "glimpses," those moments of spiritual suspension for which she devised a "special prose." The reader can delight in such treasures that frequently concern the sea, seen at times as "like a mass of half-set jelly" and at other times "like liquid metal."

Read alongside the four volumes of her *Letters* and the reviews she wrote for the *Athenaeum* (1919–20), published as *Novels and Novelists* (1930), the *Journal* provides a critical insight into the craft of the writer. This is partly because she demonstrates there how she honed her prose by rewriting, It is also because of the understanding she displays into the experiments of other female modernist writers such as Gertrude Stein, Woolf, Dorothy RICHARDSON, and May SINCLAIR. In letter-writing, keeping a journal, reviewing, creating short stories, she was contributing to important female traditions in English literature. Her critical reviews stand alongside those of Woolf, Rebecca WEST, and Angela CARTER; her diaries take their place in a line including Fanny BURNEY's, Dorothy WORDSWORTH's and Woolf's. There she explored the inconsistencies between the public mask and the evanescent feelings of the multiple private self. There, too, she pinned down the apparently trivial details and fragments that actually reveal an overall pattern to a life.

BIBLIOGRAPHY: Alpers, A., *The Life of K. M.* (1980); Hanson, C., "K. M.," in Scott B. K., ed., *The Gender of Modernism* (1996): 298–315; O'Sullivan, V., introduction to M.'s *The Aloe* (1985): v–xviii

CLAIRE M. TYLEE

MANTEL, Hilary [Mary]
b. 6 July 1952, Derbyshire

M. studied at the London School of Economics and the University of Sheffield. She has lived in Botswana (1977–82) and in Saudi Arabia (1983–86), experience she has drawn on in two distinguished novels, *Eight Months on Ghazza Street* (1988) and *A Change of Climate* (1994). She analyzes wryly the psychology and sociology of expatriates and abjures political correctness: she is unfashionably honest about the fact that it is possible to live in a foreign culture with the best of intentions and yet to realize after a while that one has good reason to hate it. A powerful stylist, M. is strong on the political and business backgrounds to her plotting. She is a mistress of black HUMOR and, reared as a Roman Catholic, she combines searching treatment of religious and political themes with suspense, though her present attitude to the church seems ambivalent. M. is aware of evil as a force in the world but offers no easy answers. Unobtrusively learned, she can be playful, in a manner reminiscent of Muriel SPARK—as in M.'s *Fludd* (1990). M.'s narrative can be oblique and suggestive rather than explicit, but is always enthralling and satisfying. Her other novels are *Every Day Is Mother's Day* (1985), *Vacant Posession* (1986), *A Place of Greater Safety* (1992), *An Experiment in Love* (1995), and *The Giant, O'Brien* (1998). Her achievement has been recognized by the Shiva Naipaul Memorial Prize (1987), the Winifred Holtby Award (1990), and the Hawthornden Prize (1996).

MARCUS, Frank

b. 30 June 1928, Breslau, Germany; d. 5 August 1996, London

The first play by M. to be produced on London's West End was a highly conceptual work, *The Formation Dancers* (perf. 1964). The play, which incorporates multiple possible endings, has been produced with a revolving stage, the final position of which determines the ending of the play. The following year saw the premiere of M.'s best-known play, *The Killing of Sister George* (1965). In this black comedy, the "killing" of the title refers to the decision by a broadcaster to kill off a soap-opera character in pursuit of higher ratings. The play is an ironic commentary on the futility of individuals battling against major corporations, as the protagonist, June Buckridge (who plays the character of Sister George in the soap opera), suffers both personal and professional humiliation through the actions of the broadcaster. *The Killing of Sister George* was highly acclaimed, winning best play awards from *Evening Standard*, *Plays and Players*, and *London Critics' Variety*, as well as a Tony nomination. In addition to writing original plays, M. produced noteworthy adaptations of the works of other playwrights, including Ferenc Molnár, Arthur Schnitzler, and Gerhart Hauptmann. M. also directed numerous productions of his own and others' works, and wrote theater reviews for such publications as *Sunday Telegraph*, *London Magazine*, and *Dramatists' Guild Quarterly*.

MARLOWE, Christopher

b. February 1564, Canterbury; d. 20 May 1593, Deptford

M.'s innovations and unique dramatic skills are frequently overshadowed by his being murdered and by his exact contemporary, William SHAKESPEARE. Unique to M. is his focus on language as a central dramatic device: a form of action, image-maker, and manifestation of thought.

M.'s attitude toward language contrasts significantly with his former roommate Thomas KYD whose *The Spanish Tragedy* protests the failure of language as an effective means of action, culminating in the unforgettable but apt conclusion when Hieronimo bites off his own tongue. M.'s plays passionately argue not only the effectiveness of language but the necessity of its acknowledgment both as the manifestation of thought and the creator of significance and effect.

M.'s " mighty line" functions more actively than Shakespeare's ordered, simile-based dramatic poetry. Its insistent sweeping movement, gathering associations and metaphors in its wake until its force is abruptly capped by a few forceful words is integral to the dramatic experience of his plays. Form and rhythm create an experience of passion and insistence intensifying the action. This majestic form also allows M. to pursue one of his more formidable dramatic devices: to people the stage through language by engaging the audience's imagination in manifesting personages from MYTH AND LEGEND.

Arguably, one of M.'s most profound contributions to the new dramatic age is his centralization of language and thought as viable fields of action in *Dr. Faustus* (perf. 1594; pub. 1604). The prologue orientates the action of the play and its concerns in relation to current works. Faustus is not a great warrior, a hero of legend, or a great lover, says M. Faustus is exceptional in only one way: his scholarship. He is a thinker. In a manipulation of the medieval morality form, M. sets the action in Faustus's mind. The action of the play is the externalization of his thoughts. Through this process, M. establishes "thought" as a viable field of action.

Thought is action. Faustus is a man whose imagination is limited and rendered self-defeating by his inability to couch his desires in language that will lead to its achievement. The play opens with Dr. Faustus trying to decide what profession he will follow (thus putting paid to the assumption he is an old man). He perceives the major obstruction to success in any profession is that "man must die" and embraces magic in order to transcend the limits of mortality. Thus, it is particularly shocking that when given the opportunity to choose any boon in exchange for his soul, he asks for twenty-four years of life. Although he craves a new and exceptional relationship to the processes of life, he avoids the one choice that would ensure it: everlasting life. The ironic center of the play is Faustus's self-condemnation. His imagination is circumscribed by his language and the terms by which he makes meaning of his world. Although fired by the insight that he might see himself as the center of meaning rather than a part of a larger whole, he lacks the language and imagery to inspire his action to success. From the start, he condemns himself and prescribes the punishment: damnation.

In Mephistopheles, Faustus constructs an alter ego who consistently confirms all that he purports to deny. Though Faustus eschews the existence of the soul, he insists on signing it away in a contract written in blood. Each choice Faustus faces pits immediate gratification against lasting spiritual value. In each case, he chooses material reward. Even in his final attempt to repent, his thoughts turn to self-condemnation. His cry "Ah! Mephistopheles" is arguably not fear, as frequently assumed, but recognition. The finale he expected from the beginning has finally come to pass.

In his choice of the immediate and material against lasting spiritual/moral values, Faustus can be seen as the first "modern hero," the archetype for "selling out," his story an ironic confirmation of the value system he sought to transcend, but had not the language or imagery to manifest and validate its alternative. Failure in creating a new structure of values, however, is not inevitable. M.'s Tamburlaine is more successful in manifesting a personal vision. *Tamburlaine the Great* (2 parts, perf. 1587–88; pub. 1590) is deceptive to the modern reader. On the surface, it appears to be a conventional narrative elaborating the process of a central character. The problem lies in the fact that the character of Tamburlaine does not progress. Although he is the initiator of all the action, Tamburlaine remains the same while everyone and everything—even the shape of the world—changes around him. Tamburlaine is the catalyst for change and the criteria by which change is monitored. Whereas *Faustus* exposes the implicit structure of meaning by elaborating Faustus's inability to muster the language and imagery necessary to manifest a new worldview and value system, Tamburlaine's success in reconstituting meaning elaborates this process and the inherent difficulties in an individualized perspective. Tamburlaine's "tragedy" lies not in his failure but in his success.

M. is one of the first Elizabethans to question the "divine right" of rulership and propose merit as a term of assessment. Cosroe challenges his brother Mycetes' right to rule because of his lack of wit and inability to express himself, bringing the warrior Tamburlaine to assist his bid for the throne. Once successful, Tamburlaine uses the same terms to assess his superiority over Cosroe and launches his own campaign against Cosroe and the kings of the East who form an uneasy alliance against him. The significance of the contest lies in the confrontation between an integrated worldview justified by hierarchy and tradition represented by the kings, and Tamburlaine's individualist vision. The kings' predictable inability to acknowledge Tamburlaine as a viable opponent (after all, he is only a shepherd from insignificant Scythia) renders them incapable of mustering a defense. The established hierarchy that proposes the whole as greater than the sum of its parts proves unexpectedly vulnerable to Tamburlaine's personal skills, and he sets about establishing a value system based on individual merit. Tamburlaine even rewards his men "in accordance with their worth."

Misreadings in terms of conventional expectations have led to the assumption that M. lacks the skills of structuring a dramatic narrative. However, considered in terms of the fundamental issue—the drive to create and possess meaning as a necessity of power—Tamburlaine is startlingly well structured. The central debate is a struggle over the possession of language and meaning. Just as Mycetes' poverty of language is the source of his failure, so Tamburlaine's success lies not merely in his abilities as warrior but in his skill as a poet. Tamburlaine's poetic nature engenders both a language and images by which to justify, create meaning, and communicate his individualist vision and give it significance. He wins the love of Princess Zenocrate, whose father he has murdered with words. Through Zenocrate, Tamburlaine is transformed from a barbarian rebel to the criterion by which value and worth are assessed.

By the end of part 1, Tamburlaine has changed not only the map of the world but its meaning. Instead of speaking of a collection of hierarchical nations valued by their relative power, the world now speaks of Tamburlaine. All meaning is assessed through relationship to him. Words spoken in part 1, confirming hierarchical world order, in part 2, speak of Tamburlaine. Tamburlaine's success lies not in his military might, but in his ability to create language and images that express, make meaningful, and validate the social/political structure he creates. The inherent weakness of an individualist vision, however, lies exactly in the fact that it is the vision of a single individual. Tamburlaine now faces more indomitable opponents: Time and Death.

Part 2 delineates the process by which Tamburlaine struggles to consolidate his personal vision. In part 2, Tamburlaine embarks on the difficult task of establishing his personal vision as a permanent structure. When Zenocrate dies, for example, he burns the town down as a "monument." On his deathbed, even as he instructs his incompetent sons how to sustain his world, Tamburlaine perceives its inevitable disintegration. When he dies, his world dies with him. Misreading of M.'s structure has also led to puzzlement over *The Jew of Malta* (perf. ca. 1590; pub. 1633). Barabas's deeds are presented not as the scurrilous acts of an arbitrary Machiavelli but as specific responses to political deceit and corruption. Although called "Machiavell" in the prologue, Barabas lacks both the skills and position to exercise diplomacy. Systematically marginalized and impoverished by the state and those close to him, Barabas becomes increasingly maddened, obsessively bent on violent revenge. Among other issues, the play exposes the process whereby materialism and the abuse of power marginalize the individual and promote self-interest resulting in the violent dissolution of the social fabric.

Edward II (perf. ca. 1592–93; pub. 1594) constructs a materialistic world in which the bloated demands for power engendered by Mortimer and the queen are pitted against the connivances of low-born Gaveston and Edward's love for him, highlighting a tension between social role and personal desire. For the desired effect, Gaveston must be as attractive to the audience as he is to Edward, confronting the audience with an insoluble choice—a sympathy with Edward's emotional attachment, itself problematic since Gaveston is not only a conniving commoner but a man—against the demands of his role as king.

M. was both an initiator and an inspiring influence for playwrights who followed. The exceptional range of his subjects, intensity of his dramas, and power of his language are equalled by his prophetic initiation of issues that were to become central in the modern age.

BIBLIOGRAPHY: Bartels, E. C., ed., *Critical Essays on C. M.* (1997); Grantley, D., and P. Roberts, eds., *C. M. and English Renaissance Culture* (1996); Hopkins, L., *C. M.* (2000); Nicholl, C., *The Reckoning: The Murder of C. M.* (1992); Steane, J. B., *M.* (1964)

ELAINE TURNER

MARRYAT, [Captain] Frederick

b. 10 July 1792, London; d. 9 August 1848, Langham, Norfolk

The first sailor to become a novelist, M. joined the navy at fourteen and was promoted commander at age twenty-three. M.'s first semiautobiographical novel, *The Naval Officer* (3 vols., 1829), was so popular that M. retired from the sea to become equerry to the Duke of Sussex the following year, and soon became a full-time author, traveling widely in the U.S., Canada, and Europe. He published fifteen more novels, mostly stirring adventure tales, as well as journalism. M.'s best book, *Peter Simple* (3 vols., 1833–34), is a firsthand account of life at sea, interspersed with entertaining yarns. His story of a foundling, *Japhet in Search of a Father* (4 vols., 1835–36), was followed by *Mr. Midshipman Easy* (3 vols., 1836), a good-humored SATIRE on the opinions of Thomas Paine and William GODWIN, and surprisingly on the pseudo-science of phrenology. In 1837 came *Snarleyyow*, about a fiendish dog, followed by *The Phantom Ship* (3 vols., 1839) and in 1840 *Poor Jack*. M.'s children's books continued to be read until mid-20th c. M. insisted that fiction for children should have a basis in truth, and he was careful to get details right. *Masterman Ready* (3 vols., 1841–42), a story of resourcefulness after shipwreck,

influenced by Daniel DEFOE's *Robinson Crusoe,* was to influence R. M. BALLANTYNE's *The Coral Island. The Children of the New Forest* (2 vols., 1847) was set in the English Civil War of the early 17th c. A royalist family of children learn how to live off the land until the Restoration in 1660, when they can claim their inheritance. Read to and by schoolchildren, its ideology became iconic, forming attitudes to the conflict. *The Little Savage* (2 vols., 1848–49) was published after M.'s death, and he left an incomplete novel, *Valerie.* M.'s work, humorous and readable, forms an important link between Tobias SMOLLETT and Henry FIELDING, and Charles DICKENS. M.'s novelist daughter, Florence Marryat, published his two-volume *Life and Letters* in 1872.

MARS-JONES, Adam

b. 26 October 1954, London

Since his first appearance in print in 1980, M.-J. quickly became known for his skillful, concise style of writing, particularly his adroit handling of language. As a novelist, short story writer, and essayist, he consistently imbues his characters with a strong sense of REALISM, creating profound, yet accessible, fiction. M.-J., a gay writer who specializes in AIDS fiction, has dealt with the AIDS epidemic in a sensitive, yet humorous, fashion while avoiding a sentimental and manipulative emotionalism. In both character and plot structure, M.-J. combines the comic and tragic and focuses on everyday human concerns, giving his work a universal appeal.

"Lantern Lecture," published in *Quarto* magazine in 1980, marked M.-J.'s debut as a published writer. Editor Robert McCrum of Faber and Faber was quite taken with the story and signed M.-J. immediately. *Lantern Lecture*, a collection of three long stories, was the resulting 1981 publication. The volume includes "Lantern Lecture," which focuses on Philip Yorke, an English eccentric; "Hoosh-Mi," which creates a world in which the Queen of England contracts rabies from one of her dogs; and "Bathpool Park," which deals with Dennis Nilson, the Black Panther who kidnapped and murdered Lesley Whittle. *Fabrications* was the subsequent American edition of the stories, with "Lantern Lecture" omitted. Both editions were critically well received.

M.-J. next served as editor for *Mae West Is Dead*, a collection of contemporary gay and lesbian fiction published in 1983. In the introduction to this volume, M.-J. discusses the contribution of America "in the shaping of gay attitudes in Britain," as well as its importance in the development of a gay subculture.

First published in 1987, *Darker Proof: Stories from a Crisis* marks M.-J.'s emergence as a writer of AIDS fiction. This volume was a series of seven stories written in collaboration with Edmund White, noted gay American author. M.-J. contributed four of the stories, with White contributing three. Receiving mixed reviews, these stories examine the effect of AIDS on the lives of gay men and their families.

The overall theme of *Monopolies of Loss*, published in 1992, was once again AIDS. *Monopolies of Loss* is a collection of nine short stories, eight of which concern gay men with AIDS; four of the stories appeared earlier in *Darker Proof: Stories from a Crisis*. M.-J. deals with the epidemic from as many viewpoints as possible, whether intimately or peripherally. Although the characters inhabiting these stories are fictional, M.-J. creates a feeling of verisimilitude through his particular attention to detail; the characters are all recognizable and apprehensible. Adhering consistently to the first-person voice, M.-J. deftly presents the devastating effects of AIDS in ways that are dark, funny, articulate, and courageous, but avoids the sentimental. Many of these stories end without a clear sense of resolution, mirroring the ongoing effects of AIDS.

The Waters of Thirst, published in 1993, was M.-J.'s first novel. Created as a stream of consciousness monologue, *The Waters of Thirst* avoids the traditional division into chapters. Even in this form, M.-J. maintains the intensity and HUMOR of his previous short stories. William, the narrator, is a failed actor who has found work doing voice-overs for television commercials. He and his lover, Terry, an airline employee, have been living together in London in a monogamous relationship for fourteen years. They chose monogamy before it was imposed by the AIDS crisis. Although M.-J. draws inspiration from the AIDS epidemic, he deals with the topic circuitously. The lovers are threatened not by AIDS, but by William's chronic renal failure. Having suffered from a kidney disease for many years, he is waiting for a kidney transplant. Ironically, *The Waters of Thirst* finds William in an AIDS ward, not because he is infected with the disease, but because of a transplant that did not go well. Because of M.-J.'s human and humane treatment of his protagonist, critics have described William as a type of homosexual everyman. Interweaving the tragic and the comic, M.-J. deals with ordinary moments of everyday lives, revealing profound insights about the human condition.

BIBLIOGRAPHY: Wood, M., "The Contemporary Novel," in Richetti, J., ed., *The Columbia History of the British Novel* (1994): 969–70, 985–86; Woods, G., *A History of Gay Literature: The Male Tradition* (1998)

SAMUEL GAUSTAD

MARSTON, John

b. 1576, Wardington, Oxfordshire; d. 25 June 1634, London

M. wrote in his preface to *Parasitaster; or, The Fawne* [or *Fawn*] (perf. 1604; pub. 1606): "Comedies are writ to be spoken not read: remember the life of these things consists in action." These are the words of a born dramatist, and M. is the most vividly theatrical of all Jacobean playwrights. Everything is pushed to extremes. His violent language, stabbing similes, headlong tirades, jet-fueled action, and bug-eyed characters lurching toward the abyss, work marvelously in theatrical terms. Aptly illustrated in *The Dutch Courtesan* (1605), the character of Cocledemony, a rich young man who will literally kill for a laugh, is prepared to send an innocent man to the gallows as a practical joke. In essence, Cocledemony is driven mad by the insane compulsion to be funny.

The Dutch Courtesan neither preaches nor deals with the problems of prostitution or the plight of the whore who wants to reform but is prevented by the very men who condemn her trade. Franceschina, the beautiful Dutch courtesan whose savage and treacherous nature is concealed by charming songs and dances, is not explained: she simply "is." In the theater, explanations only deepen mysteries while making characters shallower. As in life, they should exist in a cloud of unknowing. Analysis, Freudian or otherwise, merely dilutes the drama. All we know is that Franceschina has been driven to become "La Dame Sans Merci."

M. was always able to write great parts for women. In *The Dutch Courtesan*, besides Franceschina there is Crispinella, a bright, sophisticated young woman who tells us: "O i' faith, 'tis a fair thing to be married and a necessary to hear this word 'must'; if our husbands be proud we must bear his contempt, if nawsome we must bear with the goat under his armholes." The part of the dazzling Rossaline from *Antonio and Mellida* (perf. 1600; pub. 1602) is worthy of American screwball comediennes of the 1930s. When asked when she will marry, she replies, "Faith, kind uncle, when men abandon jealousy, forsake taking of tobacco and cease to wear their beards so rudely long. O, to hear a husband with a mouth continually smoking."

Despite the dark power of *The Malcontent* (perf. ca. 1602-3; pub. 1604) and the strangeness of *The Dutch Courtesan*, M.'s most original achievement is the dangerous comedy *Antonio and Mellida* and its sequel, *Antonio's Revenge* (perf. 1600; pub. 1602), a black, blood-boltered farce. The *Antonio* plays are full of theatrical delights; the Brechtian prologue with the leading actors discussing the play and moaning about their parts (nothing changes); a scene between Antonio and Mellida conducted entirely in Italian; Antonio appearing in drag in the opening scenes, disguised as a distraught Amazon; the tyrant Piero having his tongue cut out so he can only give inarticulate grunts and cries before dying.

Though a comedy and a revenge drama, the two *Antonio* plays are made all of a piece by M. annihilating cynicism. Like Jonathan SWIFT, he has no positive values. He does not need to have any to be successful. His pessimism is beyond the tragic. It is so extreme it becomes funny. He is even cynical about cynicism. The Malcontent urges Jacomo to despise a dukedom: "Come, be not confounded, th' art but in danger to lose a dukedom, think this: this earth is the only grave and Golgotha wherein all things that live must rot." But he doesn't believe what he is saying. For even as he says it, he is scheming to get back the dukedom for himself.

M. collaborated with Ben JONSON and George CHAPMAN on the wild and delightful city comedy, *Eastward Ho* (perf. ca. 1604-5; pub. 1605), about London crooks, scoundrels, and scallywags. They are being booted out of England to make their fortunes in America where Captain Seagull says, "Why man, all their dripping pans and their chamber-pots are pure gold; and all their chains with which they chain up their streets are massy gold; all prisoners they take are fettered in gold." One need hardly add that when Captain Seagull sails for France he ends up in the Isle of Dogs. *Eastward Ho* was censored by JAMES I for a joke about Scotsmen. No one knows which of the three authors actually wrote it, but they all ended up in prison for the offense.

The only way to prove M. is the most blazingly theatrical of Jacobean playwrights is in the theater. His unique talent can only truly come alive in performance, in front of a live audience. The rest is a pale shadow. The printed page is (like a film script) only a blueprint. Unfortunately, M.'s plays are rarely performed, so contemporary audiences have little exposure to his extraordinary and masterful talent.

BIBLIOGRAPHY: Caputi, A., *J. M., Satirist* (1961); Ellis-Fermor, U., "J. M.," in her *The Jacobean Drama: An Interpretation* (1953; rev. ed., 1958): 77–97; Lyons, B. G., *Voices of Melancholy* (1971)

PETER BARNES

MARTYN, Edward [Joseph]

b. 30 January 1859, Tulira, Ardrahan, County Galway, Ireland; d. 5 December 1923, Tulira, Ardrahan, County Galway, Ireland

Irish but Oxford educated, M. was one the founders with Lady [Augusta] GREGORY, W. B. YEATS, and George MOORE of the Irish Literary Theatre, the forerunner of Dublin's Abbey Theatre. Among its earliest productions were his plays *The Heather Field* (1899) and *Maeve* (pub. 1899; perf. 1900). Fiercely nationalistic, he quarreled with Yeats and satirized him in two further plays, *Romulus and Remus* (1907) and *The Dream Physician* (1914), the year M. founded the Irish Theatre to produce plays in Gaelic. Influenced by Henrik Ibsen, M. attempted in his plays to apply the techniques of Ibsenism to Irish subject matter.

MARVELL, Andrew

b. 31 March 1621, Winestead-in-Holderness, Yorkshire; d. 16 August 1678, London

M. is a poet whose work reflects the tension between his quiet private life and his turbulent times. Although readers associate him with other metaphysical poets, like John DONNE, he led a much more political life than other metaphysicals. He was an enigmatic man—which was perhaps the saving grace for one who successfully navigated the treacherous political ebbs and flows of the Caroline Age, the Interregnum, and the Restoration—and this enigmatic quality is reflected in his poetry.

No doubt M.'s most famous poem is the oft-anthologized "To His Coy Mistress," collected in his *Miscellaneous Poems* (1681). It is the epitome of the carpe diem style of poetry. The speaker makes his argument to his mistress that if time were of no consequence, he would not dare seek the fulfillment of his passions in physical union with his mistress. Rather, he would dedicate himself to praising the beauty of her body, spending "An age at least to every part/And the last age should show your heart:/For, Lady, you deserve this state;/Nor would I love at a lower rate." Of course they do not have "world enough, and time" their physical beauty is quite temporary. Thus, the speaker reasons, it would be a waste for them to allow time to carry away their beauty; as he states it, "The grave's a fine and private place,/but none, I think, do there embrace." The best tribute to her beauty is to enjoy it now, for the only alternative is to squander it. And yet, for all of the speaker's energy for his mistress, there is a pointed absence of devotion. Instead, the speaker casts a dim and anxiety-ridden view of the world to frighten his mistress into bed. Even in the act of making love, this is a voice that remains aloof and refuses to reveal too much of itself; the speaker's unacknowledged fear of intimacy threatens to overshadow his heralded fear of time's ravages. Again, it is this quality—the ability to lure his reader into sympathy with him while remaining distant—that haunts the love poetry of M. and undergirds it with rich complexity.

"The Definition of Love" is a similar poem in that the speaker is thwarted from the realization of his love by an unstoppable force. Yet this poem reveals more clearly M.'s metaphysical identity, as he employs a memorable conceit. Here, the two lovers are likened to parallel geometric lines, always within view of one another, yet fated never to intersect. Similar to the drafting compass of Donne's "Valediction: Forbidding Mourning" in that both conceits rely upon the idealization of the geometric plane, here the lovers' souls form an eternal stasis rather than a dynamic union. Again the forces that hold the speaker back from achieving union with the beloved fuel his passion, so much so that the reader wonders whether or not the speaker prefers to celebrate the hunt.

Although we mainly celebrate M.'s love poetry, he also leaves a complicated political legacy as reflected in substantial prose writings, praise poetry, and satirical poetry. "An Horatian Ode upon Cromwell's Return from Ireland" would purport to offer praise for its subject, yet the reader is left to interpret conflicting signals as to the poet's exact stance. Much of the dramatic action of that poem focuses not on the arrival of Oliver Cromwell, but the final departure of the king. Similarly, M. penned "Upon Appleton House" as a tribute to Lord Fairfax and his principled retirement from political life, but yet again the nuances of that poem make it clear that the poet has reservations about Fairfax's decision. To secure public recognition for a tribute to a leader seems to have one value for M., yet he cannot resist undercutting that stance with calculated ambiguities in the event he might later wish to distance himself from the original position. Such enigmatic dexterity may have been a political asset, but the reader is left to wonder whether or not M.'s degree of felicity is entirely demanded by his environment, or whether it reflects his natural inclinations.

Readers who enjoy teasing out the many possible inferences of M.'s oblique poetical statements, both in politics and love, champion his work. T. S. ELIOT, who is largely responsible for revitalizing M.'s critical reputation in the 20th c., ranked him ahead of canonical giants such as John KEATS, William WORDSWORTH, Robert BROWNING, and Alfred, Lord TENNYSON—although he later tempered this enthusiasm. M.'s poems are at once idiosyncratic and personal; they defy categorization, they resist grouping, just as they always reveal a great wit and penetrating insight.

BIBLIOGRAPHY: Eliot, T. S., "A. M.," in his *Selected Essays* (1950): 251–63; Kermode, F., and K. Walker, eds., *A. M.* (1990); Murray, N., *World Enough and Time: The Life of A. M.* (2000)

ROBERT E. CUMMINGS

MASEFIELD, John [Edward]

b. 1 June 1878, Ledbury, Herefordshire; d. 12 May 1967, Clifton Hampden, Oxfordshire

M. was a prodigiously prolific writer, greatly admired—even revered—during his long career, whose fame and reputation fell away rather sharply after his death. There are signs, though, of a revival of interest and admiration in recent years, especially in relation to certain specific works (some of the lyric poems, in particular). In all, he published over fifty books: sev-

eral volumes of verse; single, long poems—such as *The Everlasting Mercy* (1911), *Dauber* (1913), and *Reynard the Fox* (1919); twenty-one novels; two long children's stories; seventeen plays; two volumes of AUTOBIOGRAPHY; and a number of miscellaneous prose items. He was appointed poet laureate in 1930, in succession to Robert BRIDGES.

M.'s literary career began in 1902 with the publication of *Salt Water Ballads:* several of its poems reflected directly his own experiences during the three or four adolescent years he spent as a crew member on the sailing ships ("and all I ask is a tall ship and a star to steer her by") plying—even as late as the 1890s—between England and the Americas. A year later, he published a second volume of verse, called *Ballads*.

Then, suddenly (partly under the influence of Harley GRANVILLE BARKER), he turned from poetry to playwriting. His first play was *The Campden Wonder* (perf. 1907; pub. 1909), followed closely by *The Tragedy of Nan* (perf. 1908; pub. 1909): both were, for their first productions, directed by Granville Barker. And then another change of emphasis—in 1908 he published his first novel *Captain Margaret: A Romance*. Then poetry returned with *Ballads and Poems* (1910)—containing among other things the once famous but now faded "Cargoes" ("Quinquireme of Nineveh from distant Ophir . . .") and, in 1911, the long narrative poem *The Everlasting Mercy*, which aroused considerable controversy and finally established M. as a major figure. Throughout the late teens and the 1920s his publications continued; never a year without one or two new books—plays, novels, volumes of verse. To this period belongs *Reynard the Fox,* surely the best and most moving of his long narrative poems, of which Muriel SPARK, in her book *John Masefield* (1953), said, "I am prompted to define first and analyze afterward; what kind of poem is it? And the first answer that occurs to me is that it is a classic narrative of events. I mean 'classic' in the sense that it is a finished, consummate work of its kind; and I use 'narrative of events' to mean that the important thing about the story is the balanced sequence of events. The opening is no less important than the outcome; the characters are no more important than the location; the verse is no less important than the conception of the poem."

To the 1920s (one of his most active periods) belong three particularly striking works—the strangely haunting play *Melloney Holtspur* (pub. 1922; perf. 1923) with its streak of mysticism, and the two linked novels *Sard Harker* (1924) and *Odtaa* (1926), which are set in an imaginary South American country—a fact that might tempt one to suppose that the curious title of the second represented the name of some esoteric Indian tribal god or a magical evil ritual: but it doesn't; M. assures us that it is merely a string of initials that stand for One Damn Thing After Another. These novels were tremendously popular in their day and sold thousands of copies, as also did the *Collected Poems* (1923). The curious mixture of a homely kind of HUMOR with adventure-yarns that owe something to H. Rider HAGGARD (minus the Haggard pretentiousness) and with poetry that reflects a melancholy that is sometimes—especially in the nature poems—reminiscent of Thomas HARDY and with a toughly unsentimental tragic sense that is uniquely M.'s own, speaks of a literary talent of considerable stature and amplitude.

Ironically, by the time of his elevation to the laureateship in 1930 his most important work was over, though he went on writing industriously to within a year of his death. Though his poetry often caught the travail of the times and belongs indisputably to the 20th c., its prosody remained unremittingly "traditional." It was completely untouched by the revolution in form, vocabulary, and meter caused by Ezra Pound, T. S. ELIOT, W. H. AUDEN, and the later works of W. B. YEATS.

BIBLIOGRAPHY: Binding, P., *An Endless Quiet Valley* (1998); Smith, C. B., *J. M.* (1978); Spark, M., *J. M.* (1953)

ERIC SALMON

MASON, William

b. 12 February 1725, Hull; d. 7 April 1797, Aston

Educated at St John's College, Cambridge, M. took Holy Orders and obtained preferment in the Church of England. In 1744, he wrote *Musaeus*, a poetic lament for Alexander POPE in imitation of John MILTON's "Lycidas" and became a friend of the poet Thomas GRAY. In 1749, he published *Isis*, a poem attacking Jacobite tendencies at Oxford University. M. wrote two plays in pseudo-classical style, *Elfrida* (pub. 1752; perf. 1772) and *Caractacus* (pub. 1759; perf. 1776). Gray said he read *Caractacus*, the true story of a native British warrior who resisted the Roman invaders, "not with pleasure only, but with emotion." Horace WALPOLE, however, described it as "laboured, uninteresting, and no more resembling the manners of Britons than of Japanese." Gray made M. his literary executor, and in 1775 M. prepared an edition of Gray's poems with a memoir, helped considerably by Walpole, until they quarreled about politics. M.'s poems were collected in 1764 and 1774.

MASSINGER, Philip

b. 21? November 1583, Salisbury; d. 18 March 1638, London

The son of Arthur Massinger, who was confidential secretary to Henry Herbert, second Earl of Pembroke,

M. attended Oxford but left without obtaining a degree. His conversion to Roman Catholicism alienated him from the Herberts for decades. His career as playwright probably began as an apprenticeship, collaborating with other, better-established, writers. Although he may have had a hand in *Henry VIII* and *The Two Noble Kinsmen*, written chiefly by John FLETCHER and William SHAKESPEARE, the evidence is slight. From 1616, he certainly collaborated with Fletcher, Thomas DEKKER, and Nathan FIELD, finally beginning his solo career around 1621 with the tragedy of the *Duke of Milan*. His work is largely nostalgic for the Tudor era, which often leads to thinly veiled attacks on modern Stuart policies, in particular the foreign policy of Buckingham, and outright pilfering from earlier playwrights, particularly from Thomas MIDDLETON.

M.'s early collaborations date from as early as 1616 and the more certain ascriptions include: with Fletcher, *Thierry and Theodoret* (perf. ca. 1615), *Sir John van Olden Barnavelt* (perf. 1619), *The Custom of the Country* (perf. ca. 1619), *The False One* (perf. ca. 1619), *The Double Marriage* (perf. ca. 1621), *The Little French Lawyer* (perf. ca. 1623); with Field, *The Fatal Dowry* (perf. ca. 1617–19); with Fletcher and Field, *The Jeweller of Amsterdam* (perf. ca. 1617), *The Knight of Malta* (perf. ca. 1618); with Middleton and William ROWLEY *The Old Law* (perf. ca. 1618); and with Dekker, *The Virgin Martyr* (perf. 1620). These plays run the gamut from tragedy to comedy, tragicomedy to classical history, and suggest that M. was receiving a full apprenticeship in the popular forms. M.'s hand in the collaborations is not always easy to identify. He has a chameleon quality in his writing that allows him to adapt to the styling and approach of his senior partners. Unlike Rowley, whose collaborative work maintains a rich if not always happy individuality, M. appears to have learned chiefly through imitation.

M.'s individually written plays are marked by consistency if not excellence, and his work generally treats of the bourgeoisie. An early success, *A New Way to Pay Old Debts* (perf. 1625), enjoys a lively popularity in the Renaissance canon today. It is a straightforward reworking of Middleton's *A Trick to Catch the Old-One*, and depicts Wellborn, a young man cheated of his property by a wily older man, Overreach, who succeeds through cunning in wresting away his lands. It explores the same dynamic that Middleton employed between his young Witgood and Uncle Lucre, the titular "old-one." Unlike Middleton's ending, however, M. crafts an untidy, open-ended conclusion that requires his stained hero to march forth and regain his honor before he can hope to regain his property. Despite the original ending, M.'s play harks back to the intrigue comedies of the early Stuart period. Delighting in the stock types popular a generation earlier, M. peoples his world with characters named Greedy, Marall, Allworth, Wellborn, and Overreach, and allows the name to carry the characterization. As is true of M.'s style throughout his career, he is better at creating complexity of situation than depth of character.

M.'s life was marked by poverty and the ostracism brought on by his conversion to Roman Catholicism. It is therefore not surprising that his other two most notable works, *The Roman Actor* (perf. 1626), a tragedy from the middle of his solo career, and *The City Madam* (perf. 1632), a comedy from his latter period, like *A New Way to Pay Old Debts,* should depict a variety of viciousness characteristic of M.'s work. William HAZLITT has noted that his characters behave "like drunkards or madmen" and their conduct is both "extreme and outrageous." M. creates characters that fail to win sympathy even in sympathetic situations and tend perhaps to hint at a creator unsympathetic to the human condition. M.'s underworld characters, for example, unlike the riotously funny bawds in Middleton and Ben JONSON, do nothing endearing nor make any pithy commentary about their profession, but merely scrape their victims for whatever they can. Even the titular character of *The City Madam*, Lady Frugal, fails to deserve the distinction of nominal heroine in the plot. She represents only a secondary plot, subordinate to Luke's avaricious intrigues. She is rather foolish and detestable as the proud city matron who wishes to be a fine lady. Her forced conversion and deep contrition at the end, therefore, are difficult to accept. We would like to continue thinking of her as a laughable character, but after her sincere conversion we cannot, and are instead left in a quandary familiar in much of M.'s characterizations.

M. died mysteriously; he went to bed "well and was dead before morning." Actors escorted his body to St. Saviour's churchyard where, according to tradition, he was buried in the same plot where Fletcher had been inhumed in 1625. The record of his burial at the church is a final testament to the perpetual outsider. It reads: "1638 March 18th. Philip Massinger, stranger, in the church—2*l.*"

BIBLIOGRAPHY: Adler, D. R., *M.* (1987); Garrett, M., ed., *M.* (1991); Howard, D., ed., *P. M.* (1985)

BRIAN JAY CORRIGAN

MASSON, David [Mather]

b. 2 December 1822, Aberdeen, Scotland; d. 6 October 1907, Edinburgh, Scotland

One of the most prominent literary scholars of the Victorian era, M. was Professor of Rhetoric and English Literature at the University of Edinburgh from 1865 until his retirement in 1898. In 1859, M. published the first volume of his monumental *Life of John Milton* (7 vols., 1859–80), which evolved as his most significant and lasting achievement as an author. He also wrote lives of William DRUMMOND of Hawthornden (1873), Thomas CHATTERTON (1874; rev. ed., 1899), Thomas DE QUINCY (1878), Thomas CARLYLE (1891), and William SHAKESPEARE (1914). His numerous editions included *The Poetical Works of John Milton* (3 vols., 1864*), The Miscellaneous Works of Oliver Goldsmith* (1869), and *The Collected Writings of Thomas De Quincy* (14 vols., 1889–90).

MATHIAS, Roland

b. 4 September 1915, Glyn Collwn, Talybont-on-Usk, Wales

Poet, short story writer, critic, editor, scholar, educator, son of a Welsh-speaking army chaplain and puritanical mother, M. was educated at a British military school in Germany, Caterham School, Surrey, and Jesus College, Oxford, where he was awarded a first-class honors degree in history. He undertook research on "The Economic Policy of the Board of Trade, 1696–1714" for which he was awarded a B.Litt. After holding several teaching posts in English schools, in 1948 he was appointed headmaster of Pembroke Dock Grammar School. During the Second World War, his application to be registered as a conscientious objector was rejected and he spent three months in jail for refusing to attend a medical examination.

His first volume of poetry, *Days Enduring*, was published in 1942 and consists of sixty-one poems written between 1935 and 1942. Since the poems are arranged chronologically, it is possible to chart the development of his poetic talent and the emergence of a hardening attitude from the early romantic poems influenced strongly by John KEATS and Alfred, Lord TENNYSON. Also, although his formative years were spent largely in England, there is also a growing awareness of his Welsh roots. One of his poems, "Balloon over the Rhondda," was reprinted in Keidrych Rhys's influential anthology *Modern Welsh Poetry* (1944) where it appeared alongside poems by other young Anglo-Welsh poets such as Alun LEWIS, David JONES, R. S. THOMAS, and Dylan THOMAS. Thereafter, his poems were frequently published in the *Listener, Poetry London, Outposts,* and the *Welsh Review*. His second volume of poems, *Break in Harvest* (1946), is concerned largely with themes of love, family, and Wales. As an historian, his poems often link landscape and history. He has a strong sense of place and of time, and the descriptions of the Welsh countryside are often linked with his father's family. However, his poetry comes to maturity in his third volume, *The Roses of Tretower* (1952). Most of these poems have their genesis in Wales and in them M. found his own distinctive voice, poised, melancholic, and witty even though he also writes dramatically through the voices of his personae. The influence of the metaphysical poets is evident, particularly John DONNE and Henry VAUGHAN, and he emerges as a Christian, deeply religious, poet with a dark sense of the human predicament.

Of the thirty-three poems published in *The Flooded Valley* (1960), twenty-five had already been published in *The Roses of Tretower*, only eight representing the years between 1952 and 1960. But unlike his earlier volumes, this volume was widely reviewed and highly praised. In the Welsh topographical poems, the influence of Gerard Manley HOPKINS was now evident and reviewers noticed the exact imagistic portrayal of Welsh town and country scenes, the odd and often upsetting landscapes and the poet's taciturn, rather stoically unhappy references to himself. The poems of *Absalom in the Tree* (1971) are remarkable for the ways in which he faces man's, and his own, mortality. Death figures large in most of the poems, which represent the complex contrast between the past and the present. The volume was awarded the Welsh Arts Council's prize for poetry in 1972. The poems of *Snipe's Castle* (1979) demonstrate his concern with the history, origins, and culture of Wales. The natural world that M. observes and describes so precisely is both physical and emblematic, both real and symbolic. A selection of his poems published between 1944 and 1979 was published under the title *Burning Bramble* in 1983.

In 1956, M. published a volume of short stories, *The Eleven Men of Eppynt and Other Stories,* containing fourteen stories most of which are based on his personal experience and his interest in history. His collected short stories, edited by Sam Adams, were published in 2001. His continuing scholarly interest in history resulted in the publication of the monograph *Whitsun Riot* (1963) in which he examines the documentary evidence surrounding the uprising among Catholics at Archenfield, Herefordshire, in 1605.

In 1949, M. was one of the founders of the magazine *Dock Leaves* that later became the *Anglo-Welsh Review* and was editor between 1961 and 1976. He was a consistent contributor to the magazine for which he wrote extensive editorials, articles, and reviews as well as contributing poems. His reviews are notable for their thoughtfulness, their range of interest, and because they made clear his belief that criticism should be guided by precise standards of morality. Thus, for instance, he praises the poetry of Vernon WATKINS while criticizing him for sterility and he detects the influence of the metropolis in Dylan Thomas whose achievement he believes to be impressive though lacking in spiritual development. A collection of his essays, *A Ride through the Wood,* appeared in 1985 and established him as one of the most perceptive of Anglo-Welsh critics. It contains essays on Lewis whom he regards as the tragically lost leader

of Anglo-Welsh literature, as well as essays on Dylan Thomas, R. S. Thomas, and Watkins. Together with Raymond Garlick, he edited *Anglo-Welsh Poetry 1480–1980* (1984), which has become a standard anthology. With Adams, he edited a book of short stories by Anglo-Welsh writers, *The Shining Pyramid* (1970), and the collected stories of Geraint Goodwin. In addition, he has written a critical biography of Watkins (1974) in the Writers of Wales series and a study of the poetry of John Cowper POWYS, *The Hollowed-Out Elder Stalk* (1979).

Having moved from Pembroke Dock to Herbert Strutt School in Belper, Derbyshire, and then to King Edward VI grammar school in Birmingham in 1968, he retired from teaching to live in Brecon near to his mother. In the same year, he was honored by the Welsh Arts Council for services to writing in Wales.

BIBLIOGRAPHY: Adams, S., *R. M.* (1995); Hooker, J., "The Poetry of R. M.," *PW* 7 (Summer 1971): 6–13

A. R. JONES

MATTER OF BRITAIN, The

The term widely taken to denote the principal subject matter of a large number of medieval English romances was established in the late 12th c. by the French poet Jean Bodel who opined that three great themes or *matières* alone were worthy of literary treatment in French ROMANCE at that time. These were the Matter of Rome (comprising tales of antiquity); the Matter of France (embracing legends of Charlemagne); and the Matter of Britain (centered upon Celtic British identity, achievement, and adventure as epitomized in tales of King Arthur and his knights). Intrinsic to the Matter of Britain is the tradition popularized in GEOFFREY OF MONMOUTH's *Historia Regum Britanniae* that the lineage of the Britons may be traced to Brutus, great-grandson of Aeneas of Troy and founding father of the British nation to which he gives his name. The Matter of Britain thus embodies a politically resonant myth of origin.

Adopted with some reservation by modern scholars, Bodel's category has proved restrictive in the classification of many medieval English works: treatments of the Matter of Britain in medieval romance vary significantly. Some texts depict the Celtic world as a mere backdrop to adventures while others explore and mythologize the dynastic heritage of the Britons, their historic resistance to the invasions of the Saxons, and, in defeat, their expectation of future political resurgence under King Arthur—"the once and future king." This political dimension fueled the growth of Matter of Britain literature under the early Norman kings who found an expedient in aligning themselves with the hero of the Britons and in perpetuating his memory, thereby articulating a shared national identity and myth of origin for the mixed races of the British isles.

In many Matter of Britain romances, King Arthur serves as a peripheral figure, his court simply providing the setting for a narrative centered upon a knight of the Round Table who goes on an individual quest, returning for reward or celebration at the quest's successful conclusion. This pattern is evident in such texts as *Sir Perceval of Galles* (wr. ca. 1300–1340), *Ywain and Gawain* (wr. ca. 1300–1350), *Sir Gawain and the Green Knight* (wr. ca. 1375–1400), and *The Wedding of Sir Gawain and Dame Ragnell* (wr. ca. 1450). Closer attention is given to the figure of King Arthur himself in those Matter of Britain romances most closely derived from the chronicle tradition inaugurated by Geoffrey of Monmouth's *Historia*. LAYAMON's *Brut*, an alliterative English poem based upon Robert "Maistre" Wace's Anglo-Norman translation of Geoffrey, presents Arthur as belligerent warrior-king, fiercely resisting the pagan Saxon invaders and rallying the Britons with his patriotic and stirring battle cries. The alliterative *Morte Arthure* (wr. ca. 1360) restates the grand theme of Arthur's Continental wars against the Roman Emperor Lucius, his betrayal by Mordred, and his death, while the Stanzaic *Morte Arthur* (wr. ca. 1400) moves away from this tradition in diminishing the focus upon Arthur to elevate the love-tragedy of Lancelot and Guinevere. The grand culmination of the tradition is evident in Sir Thomas MALORY's prose *Le Morte d'Arthur* that draws upon the alliterative and stanzaic English poems together with the great body of French Arthurian material known as the Vulgate cycle.

While some recent surveys and studies of the development of MIDDLE ENGLISH romance point out the limited value of employing the Matter of Britain category as a descriptive term, it retains currency on account of the theme's strong resonance in the genre.

BIBLIOGRAPHY: Barron, W. R. J., *English Medieval Romance* (1987); Mehl, D., *The Middle English Romances of the Thirteenth and Fourteenth Centuries* (1968)

ROGER DALRYMPLE

MATURIN, Charles Robert
b. 25 September 1782, Dublin, Ireland; d. 30 October 1824, Dublin, Ireland

Remembered chiefly for his novel *Melmoth the Wanderer* (4 vols., 1820), which supplied Oscar WILDE with the pseudonym "Sebastian Melmoth" after his disgrace and imprisonment, M. was educated at Trinity College, Dublin, and became curate of St. Peter's, Dublin. His first novels, *Fatal Revenge* (3 vols., 1807), *The Wild Irish Boy* (3 vols., 1808), and *The Milesian Chief* (4 vols., 1812), earned only ridicule,

except from Sir Walter SCOTT, who recommended M. to Lord BYRON. Thanks to their influence, M.'s tragedy of *Bertram* was performed at Drury Lane Theatre in 1816, starring Edmund Kean, and a French version was staged in Paris. Honoré de Balzac wrote a sequel to *Melmoth* called *Melmoth réconcilié à l'église* (Melmoth Reconciled to the Church) in 1835. M.'s other novels were *Women* (3 vols., 1818) and *The Albigenses* (4 vols., 1824). M.'s tragedies *Manuel* (1817) and *Fredolfo* (1819) were unsuccessful, as was his poem *The Universe* (1821).

MAUGHAM, W[illiam] Somerset
b. 25 January 1874, Paris, France; d. 16 December 1965, Nice, France

His novels, plays, and short stories, which are marked by an honest yet cynical portrayal of human nature, brought M. widespread celebrity and literary recognition. It was through the plays that M. first won acclaim. Running throughout the first three decades of the 20th c., they were witty and light-hearted, capitalizing on the drawing room style comedies that were the preference of the day. *Lady Frederick* (perf. 1907; pub. 1912) is a play about a high society woman and the young suitor who determinedly pursues her. It became an overnight hit. In 1908, M. had four plays running concurrently in London's West End theaters. His plays brought him financial freedom and made him renowned in Britain's social circles. When taste in drama changed in the 1930s away from the Edwardian style that he worked so well, M.'s plays lost their appeal, and most have never recovered. His brilliant play *The Circle* (1921), about a young wife who meets and falls in love with a rubber planter, is one of the few plays that continues to draw attention.

He is best known for his autobiographical novel, *Of Human Bondage* (1915), which portrays the psychological and emotional development and struggles of Philip Carey, the novel's main character. Orphaned at a young age, the clubfooted Philip is sent to live with his aunt and uncle who show little interest or concern for the boy. This treatment from his uncle, a vicar, has the effect of turning Philip against religion. At boarding school, the boy's difficult childhood continues as he is shunned by the other children and becomes an outcast and a loner. The novel follows his life and his relationships with women and men, most notably a despicable young waitress named Mildred with whom he becomes obsessed. The story and the relationships impart a belief that morality is pointless and human existence ultimately meaningless. While some critics find fault with the depressing nature of the novel and the length, said to be some 90,000 words, it has more often been admired for its unflinchingly honest portrayal of a journey of self-discovery and understanding in a cold and harsh world.

The general critical response to the work has been mixed although it is widely considered to be his best work.

M. acknowledged the autobiographical basis of *Human Bondage*. Like the young Philip of the novel, M. was orphaned, losing both mother and father by the age of ten. After the death of his parents, he went to live with his aunt and uncle in Kent. Instead of Philip's clubfoot, the young M. was plagued with a stammer throughout his childhood, making him fearful of talking. As a result of these hardships, M. was shy and withdrawn as a child. He went on to graduate from medical school but never practiced medicine, choosing the life of a writer instead. He felt compelled to write *Of Human Bondage* as a way of coming to terms with and moving beyond the memories and disturbing emotions of his youth.

Other important works by M. include *The Moon and Sixpence* (1919) based on the life of the artist Paul Gauguin, just one of many M. novels drawn from his travels in the South Pacific, which have mythological and Christian symbolism representing the dichotomy between the simplicity and purity of primitive civilizations and the dogmatic and judgmental Christian missionaries. *The Razor's Edge* (1944) is a popular M. novel about the spiritual struggles and relationships of a young veteran of World War I.

M.'s SATIRE of the commercialism of the literary establishment in *Cakes and Ale* (1930) is believed to be based on the life of the writer Thomas HARDY and includes among its host of characters other noted literary personalities of the day like novelist Hugh Walpole. The story involves a biography that is to be written about a revered author, and details the dissension among the book's main characters on the issue of how truthfully the author's life should be depicted. While highly controversial in its time for offending Hardy fans soon after the author's death, it is one of the works most often prized by critics. M.'s characters were often drawn to varying degrees from people whom he knew. The practice often brought M. trouble from friends and acquaintances who became irate upon finding personal elements of their lives reflected in M.'s stories. Nevertheless, this reliance on those he knew may be the secret of the credibility and depth of characterization for which M. was known.

The subjects of M.'s essays, which were published in collections such as *The Vagrant Mood* (1952) and *Points of View* (1958), run the gamut from history and art to travel and literary figures of the day. M.'s talent for writing about the art of fiction in his essays has often been commended by critics. It is M.'s short story writing, however, that has been said to be the genre for which he was best suited. He wrote over a hundred stories, one of the strongest of which was "Rain," about an American prostitute and a Scottish missionary in Samoa with interesting twists of plot,

published in *The Trembling of a Leaf* (1921; repub. as *Sadie Thompson and Other Stories of the South Sea Islands*, 1928).

Critics often referred to M. as a professional writer, playing down any greater importance that might be attributed to his work. Not known for dramatic plots and criticized for his propensity for using clichés, he was nevertheless praised for his craftsmanship, his ability as a storyteller to hold the reader's attention, and the sheer honesty of his work. M.'s work continues to be prominent today, having prompted over forty film and television adaptations.

BIBLIOGRAPHY: Archer, S. W., *S. M.* (1993); Calder, R. L., *W. S. M. and the Quest for Freedom* (1973); Curtis, A., *S. M.* (1977); Maugham, W. S., *The Summing Up* (1938); Morgan, T., *M.* (1979); Raphael, F., *S. M.* (1977; rev. ed., 1989)

ANN O'BRIEN FULLER

MAY, Thomas
b. 1595, Mayfield, Sussex; d. 13 November 1650, London

His father having lost his fortune, M. became a writer after three years at Sidney Sussex College, Cambridge. His comedy *The Heir* was produced in 1620. He also wrote tragedies about classical figures such as Antigone, Cleopatra, and Agrippina. More important was his translation in heroic couplets of Lucan's *Pharsalia* (1626), praised by Ben JONSON and so successful that M. wrote a continuation, published in the following year. King Charles I, ever a friend to the arts, became M.'s patron and commissioned him to write metrical histories of Henry II and Edward III, completed in 1635. By 1646, M. was working for the parliamentary side and in 1650 published *A Breviary of the History of the Parliament of England* in Latin and English.

MAYHEW, Henry
b. 25 November 1812, London; d. 25 July 1887, London

The son of a London lawyer, M. was educated at Westminster School and then worked with his father for three years. However, it was a stormy relationship, and in 1831 M. abandoned law for journalism. For the next eight years, he worked for the journals, *Figaro in London* and the *Thief*. M. also wrote plays such as *The Wandering Minstrel* (1834) and *But However* (1838).

In 1841, M. joined with Mark Lemon, a fellow journalist and playwright, to start a a new journal, *Punch* magazine. The two men were initially joint editors and recruited a group of talented writers and illustrators to join the venture, including Douglas Jerrold, Shirley Brooks, Angus Reach, John Leech, and Richard Doyle. In the early years, *Punch* sold about six thousand copies a week. However, sales of ten thousand were needed to cover the costs of the venture. In December 1842, it was decided to sell the magazine to Bradbury & Evans. Lemon was reappointed as editor and M. was given the role of "suggester-in-chief." M. wrote his last article for *Punch* in February 1845 and launched *Iron Times*, a railway magazine that lost him so much money that in 1846 he ended up in the Court of Bankruptcy.

The summer of 1849 saw a serious outbreak of cholera. Within three months, an estimated thirteen thousand people in London died from the disease. On September 24, M. wrote an article on the impact of cholera on the working-class district of Bermondsey. Soon afterward, M. suggested to the editor of the *Morning Chronicle*, John Douglas Cook, that the newspaper should carry out an investigation into the condition of the laboring classes in England and Wales. Cook agreed and recruited Brooks, Reach, and Charles Mackay to help M. collect the material. The first article appeared on October 18, 1849. M. concentrated on London, and the rest of the team were assigned other parts of England and Wales to investigate. An article appeared every day for the rest of the year and for most of 1850. M. wrote two of these a week and the rest were written by Brooks, Reach, Mackay, and some unnamed provincial journalists.

The articles in the *Morning Chronicle* received considerable attention. The *Economist* attacked the publication of such material that it believed was "unthinkingly increasing the enormous funds already profusely destined to charitable purposes, adding to the number of virtual paupers, and encouraging a reliance on public sympathy for help instead on self-exertion." Christian Socialists, such as Charles KINGSLEY, Thomas HUGHES, and F. D. Maurice praised M. and the *Morning Chronicle*. Radicals also approved and newspapers such as the *Northern Star* and the *Red Republican* published substantial extracts from these reports. M.'s collected articles on poverty were eventually published as *London Labour and London Poor* (3 vols., 1851–52). M.'s investigation into the plight of the poor revealed the impact that unemployment, starvation, and disease were having on the working class.

In 1856, M. started a new series of articles for the *Morning Chronicle* entitled "The Great World of London." The articles appeared monthly and those dealing with crime and punishment were collected together and published as a book called *The Criminal Prisons of London* (1862). Another book based on newspaper articles he had written was published as *London Characters* (1874). M. wrote books on a wide variety of different subjects including novels, *The*

Good Genius That Turned Everything into Gold (1847) and *Whom to Marry and How to Get Married* (1848), and historical works such as *The Boyhood of Martin Luther* (1863) and *German Life and Manners in Saxony* (2 vols., 1864). In 1949, Peter QUENNELL edited *M.'s London*, followed by *London's Underworld* (1950) and *M.'s Characters* (1951).

BIBLIOGRAPHY: Humphreys, A., *H. M.* (1984); MacKay, L., "H. M.," in Kelly, G., ed., *British Reform Writers, 1932–1914, DLB* 190 (1998): 180–88

WILLIAM HARMON

MAYOR, Flora Macdonald

b. 20 October 1872, Kingston Hill, Surrey; d. 28 January 1932, Hampstead, London

M. was forgotten for many years because her subject, Victorian spinsters who survive unhappily into the 20th c., was far from fashionable. But some contemporaries praised her highly, placing her in the tradition of Jane AUSTEN, Elizabeth Cleghorn GASKELL, and the BRONTËS, and her novels have come back into print.

Almost her entire life was spent with her birth family, although she graduated from Cambridge and tried, disastrously, to become an actress. She was briefly engaged, but her fiancé died. Her novels *The Third Miss Symons* (1913) and *The Rector's Daughter* (1924) are about women like herself, who do not marry or have jobs and who feel that they are unloved, even by their closest relatives, and their talents not used. Each book ends with the death of a middle-aged woman, after an apparently dull and empty life; this, and the fact that each has missed her one chance of marriage, suggests that they belong to a breed that cannot survive.

Around a quarter of Englishwomen, in M.'s time, remained spinsters, and her novels are a thoughtful weighing-up of the options open to them. She belonged to the Anglican and conservative class that regretted the decline of traditional values; an inferior novel, *The Squire's Daughter* (1929), suggests that England went to pieces morally after World War I. But, prewar, she sympathized with the suffrage movement and understood that women could not be satisfied with being a "daughter at home." Her two good novels show two different paths that an unmarried woman may take.

The Third Miss Symons, which is very short and apparently simple, traces Henrietta's life from birth to death and shows how she is trapped in a vicious circle, knowing she is unattractive and therefore behaving unattractively. "Cursed with her tidy little income," she need not work and fills her days with trivia. Only at the end is it hinted that her life had a certain value, because she was at least capable of feeling love.

In the much more complex *Rector's Daughter*, Mary has to watch, like Anne Elliot in Austen's *Persuasion*, while the man she loves pairs off with a younger, more attractive, woman. Her life, spent caring for her aged father and his parishioners, conceals an intense, unconsummated love that neither Victorians nor moderns can understand. We are made to feel the selfishness of the older generation, who expect an unmarried daughter to devote her entire life to others, but there is also a critical picture of some young literati, rather like the BLOOMSBURY GROUP, who form "light elastic unions" and are incapable of deep feelings. Mary, like her creator, is a writer, but her work is lost and she never gets a husband or children.

The novel is remarkably nonjudgmental, for although it is Mary we feel for we also realize that the man who, in a sense, loves her, is happy with his more commonplace wife. Mary eventually sees that she was right not to interfere in the marriage and that her rival is a vulnerable human being with her own good qualities. Both women in this novel are very convincing, although the author is less skilled at dealing with men.

M. differs from the older women writers who influenced her in that she is not afraid of the tragic ending. It was almost compulsory for a 19th-c. heroine to get married; genuine spinsters appear only on the margins of novels like Austen's *Emma* or Charlotte BRONTË's *Shirley*. M.'s work, as one admirer wrote, "is like a bitter *Cranford*." The focus is firmly on the women who are social and sexual failures; this author knew all about rejection, humiliation, and the tensions within families. She is therefore able to say many things that the Victorians were afraid to admit. But although "nothing in this life goes by deserts," M.'s work is implicitly Christian and stresses that there may be another life in which the unhappiness is cancelled out.

So she is the one writer to have put a despised and neglected group in the center of her canvas. She refuses to generalize; many of her spinsters are not frustrated and do valuable work. But she feels that they are shut out from the best kind of happiness and her tone is often bleak. Her unique contribution is to look back to the generation of women before her own and describe their lives through a modern sensibility.

BIBLIOGRAPHY: Oldfield, S., *Spinsters of This Parish: The Life and Times of F. M. M. and Mary Sheepshanks* (1984); Williams, M., *Six Women Novelists* (1987)

MERRYN WILLIAMS

McCABE, Patrick
b. 27 March 1955, Clones, County Monaghan, Ireland

Novelist M. is noted for portrayals of madness, misfortune, and violence; for dark depictions of contemporary Irish life and its connections to the past; for outrageous characters who commit despicable acts but retain reader sympathy; for allusions to popular culture; and for the distinctive voices of his narrators.

M. took the title of his first novel from a Leonard Cohen song. In *Music on Clinton Street* (1986), M. uses what will become a familiar technique—two intertwined, contrasting storylines. Des is a rebellious schoolboy whose conflict with Phillip, a dean at Des's school, illustrates the bewildering pace and the violence of change in Ireland during an eighty-year period.

M. deals with a shorter time frame and won critical attention with his second novel, *Carn* (1989). Set in a desolate small town on the border between the Irish Republic and Northern Ireland, not unlike the town where M. was reared, the novel weaves three individual stories with the harsh realities of national and international forces beyond the characters' control or understanding. Critics praised M.'s abilities to create vital characters and to portray the complexity of contemporary life and its connections to the past.

M.'s third novel, *The Butcher Boy* (1992), won a Booker Prize nomination. The success of *The Butcher Boy* is due to the voice of Francie Brady, a madman stuck in a preadolescent twilight zone. All of the stereotypes of the abused child are here—poverty, drunken father, ineffectual mother, sexual abuse by a priest, small-minded townspeople. The themes of the book are not especially original—betrayal is common; Ireland isn't caring for its outsiders; through the lenses of insanity, the so-called real world looks crazy. But M. presents them unsentimentally, and he finds symbols that tie together parts of the narrative—a goldfish that Francie's beloved friend Joe accepts from their common enemy, Philip Nugent, echoes earlier scenes when Francie and Joe played by the river and comes to symbolize betrayal. M. creates another dual narrative: the Nugent family represents the growing middle class with its new values and possessions; the Brady family represents a stagnant Ireland stuck in the past. Critics praised the rushing rhythm with which Francie pours out his story and the depiction of a person who commits an unforgivable act of brutality but is never an unsympathetic character. M. wrote the script for Neil Jordan's successful 1997 film of the novel.

M. says that the 136 short sections of his next novel, *The Dead School* (1995), are meant to compete with the attraction and speed of videos for younger readers. M. again uses a double narrative, the stories of Raphael Bell (born 1913), who holds on to a glorified Irish past, and Malachy Dudgeon (born 1956), who lives only for the present. Both characters come from homes where the father dies early; both become teachers; both go mad. Again the narrator's brutally mocking voice, this time in the third person, creates an energy that provides delightful reading of dark stories. M.'s theme is that happiness, love, and tradition exist as illusions, no more lasting than a television show or drug experience. Not as original or searing as *The Butcher Boy*, *The Dead School* is nevertheless an effective novel.

M. received a second Booker Prize nomination for *Breakfast on Pluto* (1998), in which he returns to a wisecracking first-person narrator—the transvestite prostitute Patrick "Pussy" Braden. In fifty-six short titled chapters, Pussy tells the story of being reared in a foster home, escaping to London, and enjoying long-term and short-term affairs with men and women. Pussy's mocking, sarcastic voice is not as frenetic as Francie's but is occasionally childish and silly; occasionally brave and romantic. Pussy also experiences mania, but he is oddly heroic and refuses to give up his individuality. He ends up living as a woman in a housing complex where people seem to accept him.

M. continues to experiment with narrative in *Mondo Desperado: A Serial Novel* (1999). Phildy Hackball has sent to an "editor" a manuscript of ten short stories set in Barntrosna, another Irish border town. The reader is not as involved by these characters—such as the would-be priest who is tortured by running water through a hose into his anus, the nephew and uncle who are forced to perform in pornographic movies, or the woman who leaves town to become a nurse but becomes a mugger instead. Though outrageous and often funny, M.'s stories lack the uniting symbols and integrated narratives of earlier novels.

Another series of related stories, *Emerald Germs of Ireland* (2000) centers on one character—Pat McNab, a merciless forty-five-year-old mass murderer who buries bodies (the "germs") in his garden. Among the victims are certainly his mother, possibly his father, and fifty other people who made him angry. M. introduces each story with song lyrics that Pat sometimes sings to his victims. His mother appears in hallucinations to sympathize with, harangue, and direct Pat, somehow forgetting that he murdered her for being a shrew. One story, "The Little Drummer Boy," is genuinely moving, as the adult Pat finds a toy soldier that his father threw out the window decades before to teach Pat to be tough and unattached. The boy kills the father, and the mother weeps but forgives her son. So begin the secrets that Pat spends a lifetime trying to keep buried. M. means Pat's stories to create some understanding about why he kills, but insinuating that a victim might know something about Pat or treats Pat like a servant are flimsy excuses for the repetitive and cold-blooded brutality.

M. has carved out his own place in contemporary Irish fiction. Without condoning anything, he turns a critical but sympathetic and humorous eye upon the harsh conditions that help create humanity's defects.

BIBLIOGRAPHY: Harte, L., and M. Parker, eds., *Contemporary Irish Fiction* (2000); Imhof, R., "The Fiction of P. M.," *LHR* 9 (1992): 9–10; Mahoney, C. H., *Contemporary Irish Literature* (1998)

STEVE FEREBEE

McDONAGH, Martin
b. 1970, London

A high school dropout with no formal training in playwriting, M. captured critical and popular attention during the 1990s as a reviver of the well-made plot structure through shocking reversals and devastating character confrontations. His rural Irish characters generally reflect the harshness of life and lament lost opportunities but also reveal the poignancy of deferred hopes and human striving within an unforgiving world. Although M. lives in South London, his family background is Irish, and his plays take place on the western coast of Ireland near Galway. M. honed his skills as a writer of radio dramas, which were intended for production at the BBC. His first play, *The Beauty Queen of Leenane* (perf. 1995; pub. 1996), was presented by the Druid Theatre Company in Galway and in 1996 at the Theatre Upstairs of the Royal Court Theatre in London. It also received critical and popular acclaim at the Off-Broadway New York premier by the Atlantic Theater Company in 1998. Together with *The Lonesome West* (1997) and *A Skull in Connemara* (1997), *Beauty Queen* comprises *The Leenane Trilogy*. M.'s *The Cripple of Inishmaan* (1997), part of a proposed second trilogy, opened later in 1996 at London's Royal National Theatre, where M. became a writer in residence.

All of M.'s original trilogy take place in the town of Connemara and fall within the tradition of Sean O'CASEY and John Millington SYNGE in their sharp depiction of Irish characters with cutting dialogue, but the playwright claims affinity with such recent, non-Irish dramatists as Harold PINTER and David Mamet. These latter have in common a strong sense of irony and underlying menace, which M.'s plays possess. In addition, his characters at times elicit a level of pathos often juxtaposed with unthinking cruelty, a feature unlike the Theater of Cruelty only in its lack of sustained violence and threat. Instead, his characters exhibit sudden cruel actions or thoughts that just as suddenly dissipate into apathy or even warmth.

Beauty Queen, the first play of M.'s first trilogy, is striking in its sudden tone shifts and unexpected reversals, which depend upon shifting character moods. Although the characters often respond reactively in an extroverted manner, their actions are purposeful rather than capricious, motivated by primal passions and a basic kind of justice outside accepted laws and conventions. Mag is an elderly woman cared for by her daughter Maureen, who tries to work her private life around her mother's constant needs and demands. When Maureen dates Pato, a local man, Mag becomes increasingly concerned about her abandonment. After the couple sleep together, Maureen is open about their newfound love; she walks around the house in a slip and bra, a gesture that incites Mad and embarrasses Pato. Challenging Pato to defy the town's narrow moral standards that demand the denial of sexual feeling, Maureen disdains Pato's reticence and the couple separate. Pato leaves for a job in America and sends a letter confessing his love to Maureen and his wish that she follow him, but his brother Ray allows Mag to obtain the letter. She reads and destroys it, hoping that Maureen will forget Pato and continue to care for her. When Maureen learns of the contents of the letter, she pours hot kitchen oil over Mag in a "lazy motion" as she speaks dreamily of going to America with Pato. When she rushes out to meet the train, Mag in quiet agony calls out, "But who'll look after me, so?"

In the next scene Mag is motionless in her chair, which rocks slowly, while Maureen speaks earnestly of meeting Pato in Boston. Only when Mag falls onto the floor does the audience realize she has been killed by Maureen's poker. In the final scene, Maureen speaks longingly with Ray about her last-minute meeting with Pato at the railway station, but the audience learns that Pato left the town by taxi, not by train. Maureen is left in the rocking chair, taking the place of her mother, speaking dreamily of her love for Pato.

The power of the play lies in its unique juxtapositions, of extreme horror and romantic passion, cruelty and compassion, hopefulness and fatalism. M. presents social issues indirectly, interwoven throughout the plot and dialogue, rather than as direct statements. Allusions to the narrow morality affecting personal relationships in Ireland, to the issues of parental care, family ties, underemployment, the diaspora, and the role of women in rural and small-town society are presented at times with sarcastic dialogue, more often through character interaction and storyline. M.'s affinity with Pinter, Mamet, Sam Shepard, and other contemporary playwrights appears in the pervasive sense of menace and irony that lies just below a good-natured surface that seems at first to depict typical Irish wit.

While critics have praised *Beauty Queen*, they have generally looked less favorably on M.'s subsequent plays, finding that the delicate balance of genuine pathos and cruelty in the first play has not been sustained. The exception is *The Lonesome West,* which is more tightly constructed than *Beauty Queen*, with more developed character motivations. This judgment remains provisional, however, since the playwright is young and only beginning his career.

BIBLIOGRAPHY: Brustein, R., "The Rebirth of Irish Drama," *NewR* 216 (April 7, 1997): 28–30; Feeney, J. J., "Where Pain and Laughter Meet: The Irish Plays of M. M.," *America* 117 (November 22, 1997): 20; Lyman, R., "Most Promising (and Grating) Playwrights," *NYTM* (January 25, 1998): 16–19

WILLIAM OVER

McEWAN, Ian

b. 21 June 1948, Aldershot, Hampshire

M. is one of the finest writers of his generation, and among the most controversial. He has achieved unbroken popular and critical success since, on graduating from Malcolm BRADBURY's creative writing program, he won the Somerset Maugham Prize for his collection of short stories, *First Love, Last Rites* (1975). Nominated three times for Britain's most prestigious literary award, the Booker Prize, he finally secured the honor with *Amsterdam* (1998), confirming his position with Graham SWIFT, Julian BARNES, and Martin AMIS, at the forefront of contemporary British writing. Although primarily a novelist and short story writer, M. has also written three television plays, collected in *The Imitation Game* (1981), a children's book, a libretto (*Or Shall We Die?* 1983), a film script (*The Ploughman's Lunch,* 1983), and a successful film adaptation of Timothy MO's novel *Sour Sweet.* Across these many forms his writing nonetheless retains a distinctive character, perhaps best summed up in Kiernan Ryan's phrase "the art of unease."

M.'s early pieces were notorious for their dark themes and perverse, even Gothic, material. Controversy surrounding the extreme subject matter of the first four works, which are concerned with pedophilia, murder, incest, and violence, was exacerbated by their troubling narrative framework, the way in which conventional moral perspectives are disrupted or overturned, the reader frequently drawn into prurient involvement with the characters. M.'s perpetrator-narrators draw us into complicity with their crimes, while his victims seem strangely collusive in their own exploitation and destruction. The three tales in *First Love, Last Rites* recount episodes of child sexual abuse: an adolescent boy's rape of his younger sister; a man's molestation and murder of his neighbor's nine-year-old daughter; and a schoolboy's submission to his aunt's transvestite fantasies. *In Between the Sheets* (1978) offers further exploration of sadomasochistic, vicious, and exploitative sexual relations, extending the range (in "Psychopolis") into a troubling examination of the moral contradictions within so-called consenting relationships. M.'s first novel, *The Cement Garden* (1978), is the story of siblings who bury their mother in the cellar rather than acknowledge her death, then slowly revert to a feral state, avoiding the outside world until, in a powerful conclusion, the authorities simultaneously discover the body, and the elder children locked in incestuous climax.

M. evokes a disquieting sense of inevitability in the unfolding of these events, generating an odd suspension of standard moral and narrative expectations. In the final work of this period, the exquisite short novel *The Comfort of Strangers* (1981), M. also crafts an eerily convincing tale from bizarre materials. A haunting account of the murder of an English couple during their holiday in Venice, it is striking for its portrayal of the victims' dreamlike collusion with their charismatic assassin.

Although M.'s subsequent writing has moved away from the more disquieting of these themes, he continues to explore the impact on ordinary people of unusual or extreme situations, as they face sudden, shocking violence, or slip into acute psychological states. At the same time, his writing has begun to address broader themes, examining how social and political issues determine our personal lives. In *The Child in Time* (1987), which centers on the abduction of the narrator's own child, a further subplot explores the psyche of a (fictitious) senior politician, and a repulsive Margaret Thatcher figure makes a memorable appearance. *The Innocent* (1990) and *Black Dogs* (1992), both set in Berlin, probe the impact of the Cold War, the former (set at the outset of the division of Europe) representing M.'s unique approach to the spy thriller genre; the latter following the story of a man struggling to compile his memoirs as the Wall comes down. M. has also focused increasingly on issues of sexual politics, most prominently in the television plays published as *The Imitation Game*, which specifically addresses the position of women in contemporary society. This aspect of his work has generated some disapproval: Adam MARS-JONES, for instance, teasingly described M. as "one of the few successful literary examples of the New Man." In fact, such comments ignore the consistency of M.'s writing. In these texts, his preoccupation with unexceptional protagonists wrenched from their conventional sense of reality or self is reiterated, even magnified, as the claustrophobic settings of the early pieces are extended into the familiar but dislocated contexts of modern life.

Despite its success, *Amsterdam* occupies a curious place in M.'s oeuvre. Finely if rather predictably plotted, it functions almost as a pastiche of those common themes: two lifelong friends/rivals conspire to murder each other, each convinced that he is in fact fulfilling the other's real desire. The novel is readable, even entertaining, but lacks the moral menace and disconcerting mood of the previous tales. Its flavor is a sort of "McEwan-Lite": the approval of the Booker jury seemed, in effect, to signal the domestication of the artist formerly known as "Ian MacAbre," the integration of a radical presence into the comfortable contemporary mainstream.

M.'s recent novel, *Atonement* (2001), however, is an altogether more challenging and ambitious work. Hugely acclaimed, this is writing on a new scale, recognizably M. in the well-wrought prose and fine articulation of character, the cool precision of moral nuance, the adept and surprising effects of plot, but also a revelation in the new and powerful sense of history, of the pattern of individual lives and actions within the sweep of great events—in this case, the Second World War. The narrative voice itself is an astonishing achievement: we read the words of an elderly novelist, in 1990, writing the perspective of her own younger self in first 1935, then 1940. Her story hinges on a crucial error of perception, which may have been an act of malice, with which she effectively destroys the harmony of her childhood home. The atonement to which the title refers becomes the goal of her life, and her text, as she struggles somehow to make amends for the irrevocable damage she has caused. The dark, closing ambiguities of the book call into question the very possibility of achieving such grace, and expess a troubled awareness of the complexities of responsibility and agency—in writing as in life. Few British novelists have matched the seriousness and sustained force of *Atonement:* it is the work of a unique imaginative voice demanding our attention and respect.

BIBLIOGRAPHY: Byrnes, C., *Sex and Sexuality in I. M.'s Work* (1995); Ryan, K., *I. M.* (1994); Ryan, K., "Sex, Violence and Complicity: Martin Amis and I. M.," in Mengham, R., ed., *An Introduction to Contemporary Fiction* (1999): 203–18

SEAN MATTHEWS

McGOUGH, Roger
b. 9 November 1937, Liverpool

A popular poet in every sense, M. commands respect from fellow poets such as Charles CAUSLEY and Carol Ann DUFFY. M. graduated from Hull University and in 1973 was elected fellow of poetry at the University of Loughborough. He first became famous as a writer and singer with the pop group, The Scaffold, and later with Brian Patten and Adrian Henri, as one of the so-called Liverpool poets; he is now a freeman of the City of Liverpool and Officer of the Order of the British Empire. His poetry is witty and original and he is a skilled performer. Among his thirty-odd books are *Summer with Monika* (1967; rev. ed., 1978), *After the Merrymaking* (1971), *Out of Sequence* (1972), *Gig* (1973), *Sporting Relations* (1974), and *Waving at Trains* (1982). M. is also accomplished as a playwright, editor, and children's writer. He has recorded verses on the following albums: *Fresh Liver* (1972), *Grimms* (1973), and *Sold Out* (1974).

McGRATH, John [Peter]
b. 1 June 1935, Birkenhead; d. 22 January 2002, London

M., best known for his work with the left-wing theater company 7:84, is a highly prolific playwright whose contribution to British and particularly Scottish theater is considerable and unique. His best-known play, *The Cheviot, the Stag and the Black, Black Oil* (perf. 1973; pub. 1974), demonstrates the possibility of making effective political theater that is genuinely popular.

Educated at Oxford, M. began his writing career conventionally enough with teleplays for popular series such as *Z Cars* and naturalistic plays like *Events While Guarding the Bofors Gun* (1966). Soon, however, he was moving toward a bolder kind of socialist theater, seeking to reach a working-class audience by drawing on popular forms and performance styles. *Random Happenings in the Hebrides* (perf. 1970; pub. 1972) signaled a looser, more epic, approach to playwriting, but it was during his time at the Liverpool Everyman Theatre in the early 1970s that M.'s style really evolved. There he blended elements of theater and music hall with popular music to address local issues in plays such as *Soft or a Girl* (perf. 1971) and *Fish in the Sea* (perf. 1972; pub. 1975), which broke the theater's box office records. The year 1971 also saw the formation of 7.84 Theatre Company, a touring group whose name derived from the contemporary concentration of 84% of the country's wealth in the hands of 7% of its population. In 1972, 7:84 toured with *Trees in the Wind*, *Plugged into History*, and *Underneath*, all by M., as well as Trevor GRIFFITHS's *Occupations*.

In 1973, 7:84 divided into two companies, one to tour England and the other to work primarily in Scotland. While writing for both, M. worked more closely with the latter, and the first production of the new offshoot was to be its most significant. Devised to tour the Highlands and islands of Scotland, *The Cheviot, the Stag and the Black, Black Oil* was written by M. in collaboration with the company and traced the history of exploitation of the people and natural resources of the Highlands from the land clearances of 1745 to the oil drilling operations of the 1970s. The form of the piece was based on the traditional Gaelic evening of songs and stories the *céilidh*, an inspired decision that not only allowed the exploration of a range of issues in a variety of styles, but obliged the company to form a rock group to provide the audience with dancing after the show. The play drew a warm response from most local audiences, toured the Scottish Highlands and islands twice, and was televised by the BBC. The piece remains an exemplar of entertaining, politically committed theater that successfully engaged with a community more commonly excluded by the art form.

7:84 (Scotland) continued its work with subsequent touring productions such as *Boom* (1974), again concerning oil production in Scotland, and *Little Red Hen* (perf. 1975; pub. 1977), which examined the failure of nationalist and socialist activists to achieve social change at the time of the "Red Clyde" in the 1920s. *Swings and Roundabouts* (perf. 1980; pub. 1981) attempted to expose the continuing influence of class in contemporary Britain. Other pieces included *Out of Our Heads* (1976) and *Blood Red Roses* (perf. 1980; pub. 1981). All employed the distinctive mix of theater and popular music that characterized M.'s work with the company.

M.'s writing for 7:84 (England) continued until 1986 when the company's funding was withdrawn by an Arts Council wary of accusations of left-wing bias—the most tangible effect for the company of the changing political climate of the 1980s in which the socialist society for which it campaigned grew increasingly distant. The company's final production, *All the Fun of the Fair* (1986), was formally innovative in its transformation of the auditorium into a funfair, but its satire of the British Conservative government was judged heavy-handed. The passion of his beliefs at times led M. to overinsistence, as he admitted: "if the politics of [my] plays sometimes appears a little strident . . . please forgive, for what lies under and behind is an ignited sense of reality."

M. continued to write for audiences both in England and Scotland, later pieces including *Border Warfare* (1989), which examined the history of the two countries' relationship, and *Watching for Dolphins* (perf. 1991), in which a former socialist activist considers her transformation into a bed-and-breakfast proprietress with rueful HUMOR. M. was also the author of three penetrating volumes of essays, *A Good Night Out* (1981), *The Bone Won't Break* (1990), and *Naked Thoughts That Rove About* (1996), in which he argued compellingly for the popular, socialist theater that his best work exemplified.

BIBLIOGRAPHY: Bold, A., *Modern Scottish Literature* (1983); Hayman, R., *British Theatre since 1955* (1979); Itzin, C., *Stages in the Revolution* (1980)

                                    HARRY DERBYSHIRE

McPHERSON, Conor
b. 1971, Dublin, Ireland

M.'s plays are, so far, so idiosyncratic in their insistence on drama as monologue that they brave marginalization. They are so sure in their faith, however, and so assured in conception and performance, that the playwright's courage is rewarded. His work has been embraced by the London and Broadway theatrical establishments and, in its success, organizes a whole tradition around itself, from Brian FRIEL's *Faith*

Healer to the *Talking Heads* of Alan BENNETT, to Mark O'Rowe's *Howie the Rookie* (1999). These are not the riffs of monologist performance artists; M.'s monologues focus on the character, not the characterization, even when they explore the supernatural or reach low for a joke. As in the work of American playwright David Mamet, whom M. has praised in interviews, the choice of title may seem obscure and events may unfold enigmatically, but the voices are clear and credible, whether the characters are young men finding their way (*This Lime Tree Bower*, perf. 1994; pub. 1996), a middle-aged critic losing his way (*St. Nicholas*, perf. 1996; pub. 1997), or male locals in a country pub entertaining a city woman (*The Weir*, 1997). M. helped found the company that presented his first work (*Rum and Vodka*, perf. 1992; pub. 1996, and *The Good Thief*, perf. 1994; pub. 1996) and later plays include *Dublin Carol* (perf. 1999; pub. 2000) and *Port Authority* (perf. 2000; pub. 2001). While *The Weir*, for example, has dialogue, the play proceeds in stretches of single voices revealing their singularity, but M.'s script for the film *I Went Down* (1998) offered dialogue and a buddy-film (but think Samuel BECKETT, whose work M. has directed) structure that brought Hollywood calling.

DENNIS PAOLI

MERCER, David

b. 27 June 1928, Wakefield, Yorkshire; d. 8 August 1980, Haifa, Israel

M. was reared in a "respectable" working-class family with a socialist, engine-driving father and an apolitical Lawrencian mother. While his brother went to grammar school and became a scientist, M. left school at fourteen and took a job as a laboratory technician. A sensitive teenager, he was made more introspective by having to attend autopsies in a civilian hospital and encountering badly mutilated servicemen in a military hospital. These imperfectly repressed traumas were reactivated in his late twenties by a painful separation from his Czech wife, which led to a nervous breakdown and prolonged analysis at the Tavistock Clinic.

M. first gained recognition as part of the northern working-class renaissance of the late 1950s and early 1960s, yet always remained apart. Although his earliest plays presented a committed view of northern proletarian experience in an insular realist mode, he soon moved into formal experiments sensitive to European practice and the pursuit of politics by other—comic and existential—means. In this sense, he resembles David STOREY, who like M. began as a painter—unsuccessfully in M.'s case—before concentrating on the novel and drama. However, M. is rendered more unusual by the fact he entered public consciousness not through traditional literary forms, but the relatively new democratic medium of television drama. It

is indeed as a television rather than theater dramatist that he will chiefly be remembered. His television plays are not only more than twice as numerous, but more ambitious in scope and adventurous in technique. They include two trilogies—*The Generations: Where the Difference Begins* (1961), *A Climate of Fear* (1962), *The Birth of a Private Man* (1963); and *On the Eve of Publication* (1968), *The Cellar and the Almond Tree* (1970), *Emma's Time* (1970)—and their settings range from Yorkshire mining villages, bohemian London and the London of activist flats, police vans and prisons to the Eastern bloc and Berlin Wall in an effort to articulate the nation's acutest concerns. Their technical experiments sprang from M.'s collaboration with three cinematic *auteurs*—Ken Loach directed both his television play *In Two Minds* (1967) and its film version, *Family Life* (1972), Joseph Losey shot his adaptation of Henrik Ibsen's *Doll's House* (1973), and Alain Resnais filmed his script, *Providence* (1977)—which made him realize television drama was essentially a cinematic rather than theatrical genre. This insight led to a distinctive style of brisk intercutting between short scenes, opposed in terms of theme or protagonist, but linked by recurring image or phrase. Too stark a binary structure was avoided by recourse to memory sections, involving flashback, or dream sections, exploring surreal discontinuity.

M.'s work progressed from the public sphere of collective action to the private one of personal impasse. In *The Generations*, for instance, two grammar school educated sons move geographically and intellectually away from their Yorkshire working-class father and his heroic, but simple-minded socialism, one becoming a conservative nuclear scientist, the other a failed artist, politically immobilized by his awareness of how Stalinism has perverted Bolshevik ideals; the grandson with his antinuclear civil disobedience seems to be reoccupying his grandfather's position, but begins to experience such alienation from activism and notions of working-class solidarity that he goes mad.

This narrowing of political focus characterizes M.'s later drama. Since England would rather pursue the romance of consumerism than consider it is minutes away from nuclear annihilation and since working-class commitment is undermined by patriarchal, racist prejudices, a serious theater of collective action must be replaced by one that represents the politics of personal existence comically. Individual madness and eccentricity become ways of subverting bourgeois norms by playfully rejecting adult responsibilities and genital sexuality in favor of infantile bonding with animals. R. D. Laing, who acted as consultant on *In Two Minds*, shaped M.'s conception of these misfits as anarchistic wise fools or victims of familial and societal repression.

A concern with personal politics also finds expression in metadramas about aging, hard-drinking novelists, filmmakers or actors, whose dissatisfaction often stems from the sense that artistic commitment is being tested not in the affluent West, but among the Eastern bloc's privations. Aesthetic debilitation is matched by a bodily one, yet these sacred monsters are still able to maintain bullying relationships with considerably younger women.

His plays' persistent acknowledgment of how badly men treat women and admiration for politicized women, intent on shaping their own lives, reflect M.'s sympathy for the nascent feminist movement. However, his progressive approach to the politics of sexuality does not extend to gays, who are repeatedly seen as symptoms of society's decadence.

BIBLIOGRAPHY: Deeken, M., "D. M.," in Weintraub, S., ed., *British Dramatists since World War II*, part 2, *DLB* 13 (1982): 334–41; Jarman, F., ed., *The Quality of M.* (1974)

DAVID FULTON

MEREDITH, George
b. 12 February 1828, Portsmouth; d. 18 May 1909, Box Hill, Surrey

The son of a tailor who managed all his life to separate himself from "trade" (though he used his autobiographical beginnings in two novels), M. at one time was compared with Henry JAMES as a master of style and psychological REALISM. Today, he is in the ambivalent position of having lost all popularity among readers of 19th-c. novels but of having received attention from feminist critics for at least some of his work, most notably *Diana of the Crossways* (3 vols., 1885), a novel about a woman, separated from her husband, who succeeds as a journalist, and for a while as a friend—an equal—of a rising politician.

M.'s disastrous marriage to Mary Ellen Nicolls, widowed daughter of Thomas Love PEACOCK, ended when Mary abandoned M. and their five-year-old son, Arthur, to live abroad with her lover, Henry Wallis, a Pre-Raphaelite painter. M. turned his own painful trials into two of his best-known works, the novel entitled *The Ordeal of Richard Feverel* (3 vols., 1859) and the narrative sequence of fifty sonnets, *Modern Love* (1862).

In *Richard Feverel*, Sir Austin Feverel, a baronet deserted by his wife (who has left him for a poet), sets out to rear Richard in accordance with a "System" that, among other things, prohibits falling in love until Richard is mature enough for marriage and, most importantly, until Sir Austin has found the right bride for him. Blinded by egotism, and by the fact that the real motive for the "System" is the wound his wife inflicted on him, he does not see that Lucy Des-

borough, with whom Richard has fallen in love, meets all his own requirements—sees only that she is a farmer's niece and, worse, was not chosen by Sir Austin himself. When they marry despite him, he does all he can to keep husband and wife separated, with disastrous consequences. A son has been born to Lucy, while Richard is in Germany. Awakened as it were by the sign and voice of nature—a storm and its clearing—Richard returns to Lucy. He learns that while he was away Lord Mountfalcon has tried (unsuccessfully) to seduce Lucy. Against her pleas, Richard tears himself away from her to fight a duel with Mountfalcon. Richard is wounded but recovers. Lucy, however, is destroyed by all she has had to endure; she loses her mind and then dies. *Richard Feverel* is the first of M.'s works to assert his lifelong theme: that nature, in this case human nature, cannot be perverted or suppressed without tragic consequences.

In *Modern Love,* a series of sixteen-line poems, a narrator tells of a marriage that began in passionate love and ended in discord, and finally tragedy, as the wife ("Madam") takes a lover, and the husband reciprocates with his own ("The Lady"). In the end, his wife gives him his release by committing suicide.

Three main themes can be discerned in M.'s novels and poems. Nature in its various manifestations—human and landscape—is the problem and solution. Nature violated leads to tragedy. Nature followed leads to happiness—a kinship with natural creatures who inspire a lyricism at which M. is very good, as in the poem "The Lark Ascending."

Second, and of more interest today, is gender, or more specifically, M.'s creating a group of female protagonists who are independent in so many different ways that they are witness to his most creative powers. Diana (of the Crossways) has been mentioned. But deserving membership in the sisterhood M. creates are the women in *The Egoist* (3 vols., 1879), one of whom defies her father's wishes by refusing to marry the insufferable Sir Willoughby Patterne, the epitome of self-centeredness; while another, who has worshiped him for years, accepts his proposal, made in desperation after the first has refused him, but on her own terms. *Vittoria* (3 vols., 1867), a novel that is a sequel to an earlier one, *Emilia in England* (3 vols., 1864; repub. as *Sandra Belloni*, 1886), has as its female protagonist an opera singer who at the Milan opera house gives the signal for revolt in the 1848–49 uprising by northern Italy against Austria. And Carinthia of *The Amazing Marriage* (2 vols., 1895)—unformed and untamed by urban notions of civilization—is a woman whose will is stronger than that of her husband, Lord Fleetwood, who first refuses to live with her and then tries, unsuccessfully, to win her back.

Well deserving mention, too, are M.'s politically oriented novels, *Beauchamp's Career* (3 vols., 1876) and *The Tragic Comedians* (2 vols., 1880). Nevil Beauchamp, a young naval officer whose political tutor is the fiery Dr. Shrapnel, stands for Parliament as a Radical, when "radical" meant the left wing of the Liberal Party, denounces exploitation of the working class in terms that echo John RUSKIN and anticipate late-19th-c. socialism. Nevil dies in an attempt to rescue a working-class child from drowning. In *The Tragic Comedians*, Alvan is based entirely on the socialist Ferdinand Lasalle. M. is sympathetic to Lasalle's socialism and writes the literal tragedy of Lasalle's life, his falling in love with the aristocrat Helen von Donniges, and his death in a duel, fought, as it were, for love rather than politics. What is noticeable about M.'s historical-political novels (and *Vittoria* could be included in this group as well) is that the events on which they are based took place in the recent past and the political issues at their heart were still very much alive when the novels were written.

Finally, and in the same vein, M.'s *Odes in Contribution to the Song of French History* (published together in 1898 but written over a period of twenty years) begin by locating the start of modern French history in the French Revolution and end with a warning that France will destroy its own cultural gift to the world if she provokes war with Germany in an attempt to recover Alsace-Lorraine. Given the growing desire in France to do just that, the final ode, titled "Alsace-Lorraine," is as contemporary as newspaper accounts at the time.

The novels have intertwined themes. Nature, the enemy of sentimentalism, causes tragedy for political figures who, like Beauchamp and Alvan, are sentimentalists. In each of the novels in which nature governs the shaping of a politically active male protagonist, an independent woman is associated with him. And not to be forgotten is the way comedy casts a shadow upon each of M.'s novels or lights it up. All the tragedies are comic tragedies, and all the protagonists have character traits that cause them to be punished by the "comic spirit," itself the theme of M.'s *An Essay on Comedy,* first published in book form in 1897 and still regarded as background reading or a reference for many theorists of comedy today.

The main reason M. is no longer widely read is that all his work has been swept up in a generalization applicable only to his later novels. His prose in these is strained, marked by forced attempts at wit. But a few of his novels are lucid experiments in style and deserve to be rediscovered. These are *The Ordeal of Richard Feverel, The Egoist, Beauchamp's Career,* and *Diana of the Crossways.* And worth rereading as well are one long poetic work and several individual lyrics: *Modern Love* and the first version of "Love in the Valley," both initially published in *Poems* (1851); and "The Lark Ascending" and "Lucifer by Starlight" in *Poems and Lyrics of the Joy of Earth* (1883).

BIBLIOGRAPHY: Beer, G., *M.: A Change of Masks* (1970); Kelvin, N., *A Troubled Eden: Nature and Society in the Works of G. M.* (1961); Roberts, N., *M. and the Novel* (1997); Shaheen, M., *G. M.* (1981); Wilt, J., *The Readable People of G. M.* (1975)

NORMAN KELVIN

MERES, Francis

b. 1565, Kirton, Lincolnshire; d. 29 January 1647, Wing, Rutland

Educated at Pembroke College, Cambridge, M. arrived in London sometime after 1593 and published *Gods Arithmeticke* in 1597. M. rendered immense service to the history of Elizabethan literature, by publishing his *Palladis Tamia, Wits Treasury* (1598), which enumerates the English poets from Geoffrey CHAUCER until his own day, and enables us to date William SHAKESPEARE's early plays. M. praises Shakespeare's "sugred sonnets." In an age that produced little record of English artistic activity, M. emerged as an invaluable source to historians of literature, art, and music.

MEW, Charlotte [Mary]

b. 15 November 1869, London; d. 24 March 1928, London

M. was either one of the last poets of the Victorian era or one of the first modernist authors, depending upon which critic is consulted. She has been uncomfortably and disquietingly situated between the two literary periods, and many contemporary literary scholars, both those specializing in literature of the Victorian era and those dedicated to study of the fin de siècle, seek to label her. M.'s works, however, especially her poetry, complicate the notions of what makes a work belong to either age. Feminist scholars in particular have heralded M.'s work as challenging the masculine, male-centered notion of MODERNISM that has evolved from a critical and scholastic dedication to bourgeois, male-authored manifestos of modernist purpose and thought.

M.'s life was riddled with tragedy. One of seven children, she was the oldest to survive. Steadfastly dedicated to her family, especially her mother and her sister Ann, M. was heartbroken by the loss of three brothers to childhood maladies and two other siblings (one brother and one sister) to madness and institutionalization in their twenties. After the deaths of her mother and Ann, M. began suffering from delusions. Both she and those close to her feared insanity, and M. moved to a nursing home. After only a brief period there, she committed suicide by drinking a bottle of cleaning fluid.

Themes of madness, depression, loneliness, sexual frustration, fear, disillusionment, and unrequited love permeate M.'s works, particularly her poetry. Additionally, critics trace some of the tension in her works to her own struggle with her sexuality and the unreturned feelings she had for other women. A profound love and respect for her sex resounds in her verse and short stories. M.'s story "Elinor"—unpublished until 1981—is generally considered to be a fictional representation of Emily BRONTË. A passionate and devoted fan of Brontë, M. praised her as the finest writer of the three Brontë sisters. Running throughout "Elinor" is the rejection, even renunciation, of all love, and the subsequent transmutation of that dismissal into another, deeper kind of passion.

M. submitted the short story "The China Bowl" to the *Yellow Book*, a modernist artistic journal published by John Lane and Elkin Mathews. Since she had published in the journal before, she was surprised and disheartened to learn that managing editor Henry Harland would not publish it. Thus, a discouraged M. did not resubmit or review her story for a full three years. The story revolves around a Cornish fisherman named David Parris, a man locked in a tug-of-war between his mother and wife. "The China Bowl" ends tragically, with Parris's wife leaving him and his death at sea. This particular story was one of M.'s personal favorites, and she seems to have studied the Cornwall dialect closely and attempted to craft it accurately. But the characters have been criticized as hyperstylized, stiff, unwieldy, noble and good to excess, and rebellious to a fault. After Harland's rejection of "The China Bowl," M. never contributed to the *Yellow Book* again, partly because of his refusal but also because of the later scandal attached to the journal after the arrest of Oscar WILDE in 1895. M. retained a strong fear, even loathing, of controversy, and could not bring herself to remain part of that artistic circle.

The year 1916 brought M.'s first collection of verse, *The Farmer's Bride* (rev. as *Saturday Market*, 1921), titled after a poem of the same name. Published during a time of fierce public debate surrounding the proper duties of both husband and wife in marriage, "The Farmer's Bride" struck a chord with readers and later critics alike. Critical analyses of the poem vary from investigation into M.'s work with and adaptation of the dramatic monologue to readings of the last stanza as the depiction of marital rape.

Another critically popular work is "The Fête" (1914), which shifts the traditional origin/locus of evil from female to male sexuality. In the verse, an adolescent boy discovers sex, and though it is unclear what exactly happens to the speaker, he is nonetheless left feeling alienated and traumatized.

Sexual themes become tangled with issues of nationality and religion in M.'s short story "A White Night" (1903). Characterized by critics as one of the darkest, most disturbing stories of the fin de siècle, it revolves around a male protagonist, his sister, and his brother-in-law. All three become trapped in a Spanish monastery and unwillingly witness the ritualized live burial of a young woman. The male speaker finds himself simultaneously frightened, frozen, and titillated by the scene, while his sister is reduced to hysteria and left with recurring thoughts of terror.

The Rambling Sailor, M.'s last collected volume of poetry, was published posthumously in 1929, despite the instructions she left in her will to have all her manuscripts destroyed.

BIBLIOGRAPHY: Davidow, M. C., *C. M.* (1960); Fitzgerald, P., *C. M. and Her Friends* (1984); Mew, C., *Collected Poems and Prose*, ed. by V. Warner (1981)

MONICA SMITH

MEYNELL, Alice [Christiana Gertrude]

b. 11 October 1847, Barnes, Surrey; d. 27 November 1922, London

Before her marriage to journalist and poet Wilfrid Meynell in 1877, Alice Thompson had published a book of poems called *Preludes* (1875). Her family had influential friends, including Charles DICKENS, and her poems were praised by George ELIOT, John RUSKIN, and Dante Gabriel ROSSETTI, and brought her a husband. M. bore him eight children and campaigned for women's emancipation and other worthy causes. She had become a Roman Catholic in 1868. She wrote for the *Scots Observer* and the *National Observer* under the editorship of W. E. HENLEY and later had a column in the *Pall Mall Gazette*. George MEREDITH sought her friendship, praising her "grace of manner and sanity of thought." Coventry PATMORE proposed her for the laureateship when Alfred, Lord TENNYSON died. Francis THOMPSON, whom she and her husband rescued from destitution, wrote poems to her, and G. K. CHESTERTON predicted that her "fullest fame" was "yet to come," a prophecy unfulfilled. Her essays were collected under various titles, including *The Rhythm of Life* (1893), *The Colour of Life* (1896), and *The Spirit of Place* (1898). Her several volumes of verse include *Poems* (1893), *Later Poems* (1902), and the posthumous *Last Poems* (1923). A centennial volume of *Poetry and Prose* (1947) was introduced by Vita SACKVILLE-WEST.

MIDDLE ENGLISH

The Middle English period is generally acknowledged to have begun in 1066, the year of the Norman Conquest, and to have ended in 1476, the year in which William CAXTON established the first printing press in England. For practical purposes, the dates of the Middle English period are generally given as about 1100 to about 1500, although a minority of scholars consider the period to have continued until as late as 1550.

Certainly a distinct period in both language and literature developed when the OLD ENGLISH period, which began with the Germanic invasions of Britain starting in 449, was replaced both culturally and linguistically following the Norman Conquest, after which the Norman variety of French, Anglo-French, was imposed upon parts of Britain and was the language of the court. Celtic languages continued to be spoken by the Scots, Irish, Cornish, and Welsh. Viking immigrants clung to various Scandinavian languages. Jews wrote their most important documents in Hebrew. The educated, including many members of the clergy, could read and write Latin, the language of many significant medieval documents.

The Middle English period is divided into Early Middle English, extending from the Norman Conquest until about 1350, and Later Middle English, which extends from 1350, when a revolution in language and literature began in England, to the beginning of the 16th c. The Renaissance, with its Greco-Roman emphasis, had begun almost three centuries earlier on the Continent but did not make significant inroads in England until the first half of the 16th c.

Caxton's printing press had, for the first time in England's history, made books available to a general population, bringing about increased popular education and creating a more informed public than previously existed. Prior to the invention of the printing press, books were copied laboriously, and sometimes inaccurately, by hand. Little ephemeral literature, which undoubtedly existed in oral form, was preserved in writing. Because the scribes who copied books were primarily monks, much of the literature that was committed to writing had strong religious and didactic overtones.

Most Old English poetry used alliteration, the repetition of initial consonant sounds, rather than rhyme as its major auditory device. Toward the end of the Old English period, however, rhyme was found in some poetry. The use of alliteration carried over into early Middle English poetry such as "Durham," a poem about the famed cathedral, and "Instructions for Christians," a didactic religious poem, both dating to the early 12th c. These poems used the eight-syllable, four-stress line that characterized Old English and Norman poetry. Another poem of this period, "The Grave," uses rhyme in some of its lines, while a poem about the death of William the Conqueror found in the *Anglo-Saxon Chronicle* (wr. ca. 890–1154) employs rhyme more than alliteration.

The Owl and the Nightingale (wr. ca. 1200) takes the form of a debate between an owl, representing the gloomy aspects of life, and the nightingale, representing the wonders and joys of life. The two debate such issues as marriage, worship, personal hygiene, and ap-

pearance, presenting their arguments to a wise man, Nicholas of Guildford. Using metrically regular eight-syllable lines, it suggests Norman influences in both its meter and vocabulary. Debate poetry was a favorite genre of Middle English writers.

The *Brut* of LAYAMON intermixes rhyme and alliteration. It employs an Anglo-Saxon vocabulary. This poem is based on the *Roman de Brut* (wr. ca. 1155) of Robert "Maistre" Wace, a Norman, whose poem is based on GEOFFREY OF MONMOUTH's *Historia Regum Britanniae*. Through these works, the heroic Arthurian legend and the story of the knights of the Round Table, culminating in Sir Thomas MALORY's *Le Morte d'Arthur,* written ca. 1470, became popular in England. Two versions of Layamon's *Brut* exist, the first dating to about 1200, the other, much revised, dating to about 1250. Comparing the two versions reveals the changes in language and literary conventions that occurred during that half century. *The Proverbs of Alfred*, which predate Layamon's *Brut*, mixes rhymed couplets with alliteration, as does the *Bestiary* (wr. ca. 1225), which uses alliteration mixed with three- and four-stress couplets and occasional seven-syllable lines, possibly reflecting the meter of the poet's Latin model.

The *Ormulum*, written by Orm in the 13th c., consists of twenty thousand unrhymed lines arranged in pairs. It reflects Orm's attempt to regularize English spelling. At this time, at least five Middle English dialects existed, each sufficiently different from the others that, unlike Anglo-Norman and Latin, they were not easily intelligible outside their immediate geographical limits. This diversity of dialects impeded the development of writing in English.

In the preface to his translation of the French *Eneydos*, printed in 1490, Caxton called for and, in his subsequent publications, established a more standardized English than that of previous works in English. The language began to be regularized, although English spelling remained variable for three more centuries.

Along with such didactic works as the *South English Legendary* and Robert Mannyng's *Handlyng Synne* in the early 14th c., verse romance was gaining popularity, particularly such Arthurian romances as *Ywain and Gawain* and *Of Arthur and Merlin* in the early 1300s. People also liked ancient tales recorded in such works as *The Seege of Troye* and *King Alisaunder*. Fables such as *The Fox and the Wolf*, adapted from the French *Roman de Renart*, began to appear in the 13th c. *The Land of Cockayne* is a utopian work from the same period. It depicts a place in which rivers of oil, milk, honey, and wine flow freely. The flying geese are already cooked. Monks engage in falconry and dance with nuns. These romances and many surviving lyrics, probably meant to be sung rather than recited, clearly demonstrate that much poetry of the early Middle English period was not courtly but rather was written from a working-class perspective. Among the lyrics best known to present-day readers are "Sumer is icumen in" and "Mirie it is while sumer ilast," both from the early 13th c., and such love lyrics as "Alysoun" and "Blow, Northerne Wynd," both from the early 14th c.

The *Anglo-Saxon Chronicle*, begun in the Old English period but continued for nearly a century after the Norman Conquest, typifies the prose writing of the period. Its *Peterborough Chronicle* continues through 1154. Sermons exist from the late 12th c., but prose was more often written in Anglo-Norman, the variety of French used at court, and in Latin, which literate speakers of both French and English could read. In the 13th c., much vernacular writing was produced for those who understood only English. Most of this audience was female.

Among prose writing that has survived are several pieces of the so-called Katherine Group that focus largely on the lives of women saints. Another valuable work of this period is the ANCRENE WISSE, or *Rule for Anchoresses*, probably written in the 13th c., which exists in at least twelve versions, some in English, others in French and Latin. It suggests guidelines for female religious recluses. The best prose of the 14th c. is in *The Commandment, Meditations on the Passion*, and *The Form of Perfect Living* by Richard ROLLE of Hampole, a reclusive mystic, all models of strong and excellent prose style. Especially memorable is Rolle's definition of love as "a yearning burning."

English drama had its beginnings during this early period. Initially, clerics performed scenes from the Bible for their parishioners. These eventually grew into lengthy plays that fell into two categories, mystery plays, emphasizing events from the Bible, and miracle plays, depicting the lives of saints. By the 13th c., morality plays (see MYSTERIES AND MORALITY PLAYS), whose characters represented such qualities as good and evil or selfishness and generosity, were being widely performed.

Significant literary activity marked the later Middle English period, beginning around 1350. A lengthy alliterative poem that exists in three versions, William LANGLAND's *Piers Plowman*, appeared in its earliest and shortest form around 1360. A major revision and enlargement of the poem was completed in the late 1370s. It comments critically on England's social and religious problems. The spiritual and political coexist in this version, whose religious sentiments are at times sublime but whose satire is at times stinging and scatological, especially when aimed at baseness among the friars, whom Langland reveled in attacking. The third version, produced in the 1380s, emphasized the poem's social and political issues more clearly than the other versions had. The second version is literarily the most interesting. In it Langland

loosened the structured meter and eliminated much of the lofty language of the earlier version, making the poem accessible to a broad public. *Piers Plowman* generated other poems that focused on the same problems as those Langland reacted to in his writing. Notable among these are the anonymous *Pierce the Ploughman's Creed* (wr. ca. 1395) and *Mum and the Sothsegger* (wr. ca. 1400).

The greatest change during the later Middle English era was that English began to replace Anglo-French as the preferred language at court. Vernacular authors gained the favor of noble and royal patrons, who valued their love poems, which reflected strong human sentiments. They departed from the didacticism of earlier poets, often favoring heart over soul in their lyrics.

Geoffrey CHAUCER, born in London around 1340 to a mercantile family, is the undisputed literary giant of later Middle English literature. Best known for his collection, *The Canterbury Tales,* narrated by a group of travelers on a pilgrimage to and from the shrine of St. Thomas Becket at Canterbury, Chaucer in this work stood aside and let his characters tell their stories. Among the pilgrims were a cleric, a man of law, a miller, a prioress, a pardoner, a knight, a shipman, a bawdy housewife, and others. Through this varied array of characters, Chaucer could comment on virtually every facet of life, which he did with extraordinary wit, biting satire, and stylistic mastery.

Before *The Canterbury Tales,* Chaucer, who served variously as a functionary at court, as a diplomat, and in government posts, had produced two volumes of poetry, which, significantly, he wrote in English rather than French. Despite this decision, the poems in both the *Book of the Duchess*, a commemoration of the death of John of Gaunt's wife in 1369, and *The House of Fame* were influenced by the popular French love poetry of that era and reflected the metrical conventions of French poetry, notably the eight-syllable, four-stress line, which Chaucer later abandoned in favor of iambic pentameter, a five-stress line, that characterizes much of his later work and that served as a model for future writers, including William SHAKESPEARE. In both the *Parlement of Fowls* and *Troilus and Criseyde*, he successfully employs iambic pentameter in the seven-line stanzas called rhyme royal. The *Legend of Good Women*, begun in 1385 but never completed, was written in ten-syllable iambic couplets, as was a major portion of *The Canterbury Tales.*

Chaucer translated the *Roman de la Rose* from the French and, judging from his poetry, gleaned a great deal from its representations of courtly love, many elements of which are reflected in his own work. He was also acquainted with the writings of Dante Alighieri, Boccaccio, and Petrarch, from whom he borrowed for "The Clerk's Tale." "The Knight's Tale" was based on Boccaccio's *Teseida* and *Troilus and Criseyde* on his *Filostrato*, both completed in the late 1330s. *Troilus and Criseyde* also reflects the influence of Boethius, whose *De consolatione philosophiae* (wr. ca. 524) Chaucer translated.

Contemporary with Chaucer was John GOWER, best remembered for his *Confessio Amantis*, a poem of thirty-three thousand lines of eight-syllable couplets. The tales in this long poem are in the form of a lover's confession to his priest. This poem is didactic whereas Chaucer's poems of the same period left open many of the moral questions upon which they might have commented. Gower knew classical literature well, reflecting considerable classical mythology in his poetry. His writing reveals the influence Ovid's *Metamorphoses* had upon him.

Both Chaucer and Gower attracted noble and royal patronage, which was now more forthcoming for vernacular writers in England than ever before. Spurred by the desire to attract such patronage, a number of writers became imitators of both of these poets. Thomas Hoccleve claimed an affinity to Chaucer, hoping to attract potential patrons. He dedicated his *Regiment of Princes* (wr. 1411–12) to the future king, Henry V, obviously hoping for patronage. His work, however, never approached Chaucer's level, although some of it provides interesting insights into Hoccleve's era and its society. Hoccleve's writing was soon eclipsed by that of John LYDGATE, a monk who produced several books, including *Troy Book* (wr. ca. 1412–20), *The Siege of Thebes* (wr. ca. 1420–22), and *Fall of Princes* (wr. ca. 1431–39) based on Boccaccio's *De casibus virorum illustrium* (wr. 1355–60). Compared with Chaucer, Lydgate, who was remarkably prolific, wrote crudely and with a verbosity that detracted substantially from his literary style.

As the invention of printing made printed books available, the English language stabilized and learning increased, especially in the classics of Greek and Rome. The waves of change that had been cresting on the continent as the Renaissance advanced from its 13th c. beginnings in Italy began to reach England during the reign of King HENRY VIII, who ruled from 1509 to 1547. A renaissance was taking place in Britain. The Middle English period was winding down and giving way to what was referred to as "The New Life."

BIBLIOGRAPHY: Baugh, A. C., *A History of the English Language* (2nd ed., 1957); Baugh, A. C., ed., *A Literary History of England* (2nd ed., 1967); Bennett, J. A. W., and G. V. Smithers, eds., *Early Middle English Verse and Prose* (2nd ed., 1968); Conlee, J. W., ed., *Middle English Debate Poetry* (1991); Diller, H.-J., *Middle English Mystery Play* (1992); Dunn, C., and E. Byrnes, eds., *Middle English Literature* (1990); Gibbs, A., ed., *Middle English Romances* (1966); Helterman, J., and J. Mitchell, *Old and Middle English Literature* (1994); Laing, M., *Middle English Dialectology* (1989)

R. BAIRD SHUMAN

MIDDLETON, [John] Christopher
b. 10 June 1926, Truro, Cornwall

Poet, translator, and critic, M. studied at Oxford and has taught at universities in Zurich, London, and Austin, Texas. A versatile and erudite writer, M. has avoided the path of his contemporaries in the so-called Movement in favor of a more cerebral poetry influenced by European MODERNISM and has belied those who would deny a contemporary English modernist tradition. He is also been a prolific and lauded translator of German literature into English. Poems in *Torse 3* (1962) and *Our Flowers and Nice Bones* (1969) such as "Child at the Piano" and "Shoreham Walk" were exacting evocations of particular experiences deploying a sparse syntax to great effect, while other poems included meditations on historical trauma and personages. Other collections include *The Lonely Suppers of W. V. Ballon* (1975), *Carminalenia* (1980), and *The Word Pavillion* (2000). M.'s willingness to experiment with form and wordplay has led to a diverse, and often entertaining, body of work that is committed to the serious vocation of poetry to apprehend the world anew through language, such as the poems "Wild Horse" and "The Prose of Walking Back to China" (both 1980). The influence of German philosopher Martin Heidegger can be discerned in the essay "Reflections on a Viking Prow" in the prose work *The Pursuit of the Kingfisher* (1983). He remains an experimental but accessible poet outside the British mainstream.

MIDDLETON, Stanley
b. 1 August 1919, Bulwell, Nottinghamshire

A one-time Nottingham schoolmaster, M. is a regional novelist. His material is the crises of everyday suburban life in the provinces, and the action takes place in his native region. M. is a prolific author of some thirty-five novels and for much of his career he produced a novel a year. His best-known novels include *Holiday* (1974), joint winner of the Booker Prize with South African writer Nadine Gordimer's *The Conservationist*, *Distractions* (1975), and *Two Brothers* (1978). His later novels include *Beginning to End* (1991), *A Place to Stand* (1992), *Married Past Redemption* (1993), *Toward the Sea* (1995), *Live and Learn* (1996), and *Small Change* (2000).

MIDDLETON, Thomas
b. 18? April 1580, London; bur. 4 July 1627, Newington Butts

M. is the third major playwright of the Jacobean period after William SHAKESPEARE and Ben JONSON. He wrote innumerable civic pageants, poems, and pamphlets and some thirty-odd plays, even the most problematic of which contain scenes of unrivaled theatrical power. Some were written with a motley collection of collaborators, including William ROWLEY, Thomas DEKKER, and Philip MASSINGER.

M. wrote tragic-comedies or comic-tragedies; academic terms that are practically meaningless. Four of them are undisputed masterpieces: *A Trick to Catch the Old-One* (perf. ca. 1605; pub. 1608); *A Chaste Maid in Cheapside* (perf. ca. 1613; pub. 1630); *Women Beware Women* (perf. ca. 1621; pub. 1657); and *The Changeling* (perf. 1622; pub. 1653), coauthored with Rowley. Six plays are merely extraordinary: the sprightly *Blurt, Master Constable* (wr. 1601–2), often attributed to Dekker; *Your Five Gallants* (perf. ca. 1605; pub. 1608); *A Mad World, My Masters* (perf. ca. 1606; pub. 1608); *Michaelmas Term* (perf. ca. 1606; pub. 1607), where the audience has to switch sympathies halfway through; *The Old Law* (perf. ca. 1618), despite its weak ending; and *More Dissemblers Besides Women* (perf. ca. 1619). Among his less successful plays but intriguing nonetheless are *The Roaring Girl* (perf. 1611), *Hengist, King of Kent* (perf. ca. 1618), and *Anything for a Quiet Life* (perf. ca. 1621; pub. 1662). This does not include the most famous political allegory of its time, *A Game at Chess* (perf. 1624; pub. 1625) or his lost plays like *The Viper and Her Brood* (perf. 1606). If nothing else, this list shows the author's unerring eye for a great title.

M. is the most modern of all Jacobean dramatists for his clashing style where farce merges into tragedy, tragedy into comedy, comedy into SATIRE. What begins in laughter ends in horror. M.'s most contemporary trait is his all-pervasive use of irony. *A Chaste Maid in Cheapside* is built on it, layer upon layer, starting with the title—"Moll" is the chaste maid, but the women chased in Cheapside were prostitutes. In this merciless satire of lust and money, Sir Walter Whorehound's mistress is Allwit's wife who has given birth to seven bastards, brought up at Sir Walter's expense. When Sir Walter is ruined, Allwit turns on him after years of complacent cuckoldom with sublime hypocrisy: "I must tell you, sir/You have been somewhat bolder in my house/Than I could well like of: I suffered you/Till it struck here at my heart. I tell you truly/I thought you had been familiar with my wife once." The "once" is a masterstroke, considering seven of Sir Walter's bastards are frolicking around at the time. M. depicts a world where money rules, overwhelming love, lust, honor, and mercy.

A Trick to Catch the Old-One concerns the mutual hatred of two rich old men, Hoard and Lucre. They only live to cheat, rob, and betray each other. As always, M. mixes styles. Within the high comedy of cross and double-cross, there are the tragic-comic scenes between a maid, Audrey, and Dampit, an alcoholic lawyer who is drinking himself to death. Filled with self-loathing, and a vile temper, he greets Audrey with violent abuse whenever she tries to help. On his deathbed, Dampit still rages against the dark, unforgiven and unforgiving, while his creditors gather round to jeer. Only at the very last, Audrey gently rocks the old man as if he were a child, murmuring "Sleep in my bosom, sleep." The dialogue is plain, caustic, and sharp-edged. Its power does not come from rich similes and marvelous metaphors. The poetic flights of Shakespeare and Jonson are deliberately repressed. Nothing gets in the way of the dramatic situation—not even language.

M. doesn't "judge" as a playwright, he "shows." His prostitutes are simply women earning a living, no better, no worse, than anyone else. *Your Five Gallants* are, in fact, a pimp, a prostitute, a gambler, a pickpocket, and a con-man. They cheat everyone, including each other. When a highwayman robs a young man, he finds his booty consists of a purse and chain he had just given to his mistress: "he keeps me and I keep her, she keeps him: it runs like quicksilver from one to another." His unstable characters and wild plots mirror the disorder around him, holding up a mirror to distorting nature. There is no place for sunny comedy or unrelieved tragedy for neither is true to life. Even the virtues have false bottoms. Overwhelming generosity in the character of Sir Bounteous Progress in *A Mad World, My Masters* is looked on as another destructive obsession. Sir Bounteous in his megalomania would be utterly incapable of letting anyone else pick up a check in a restaurant. *No Wit, No Help like a Woman's* (perf. ca. 1611) even suggests that happy endings are deeply unnatural.

In *The Changeling*, even the traditional Jacobean revenge drama is turned in on itself where a beautiful woman, Beatrice, hires a disfigured hit man, De Flores, to eliminate her fiancé, so she can marry her lover, but finds herself blackmailed by the hired assassin. The subplot is a brutal farce about madness that reflects the insane world Beatrice and De Flores inhabit. This is the beauty and the beast fable in reverse, where beauty turns into a beast; and the beast, De Flores, at first invokes scorn, which at the end dissolves into a grudging respect for his horrific grandeur.

M. is a republican author like Jonson, not a royalist like Shakespeare. His characters, despite their monstrosities (perhaps even because of them), are like us. They live in the real, working world. If they are nobles, they are mercilessly attacked by M. for being lazy parasites, twisted mutants. M.'s world center is not some royal court, but a lawyer's office, or a merchant bank. Nothing and no one stays the same. As in life, there is no consistency of character. We change as circumstances change, we play the chameleon to protect ourselves. Andrugio is the only consistent character in *More Dissemblers Besides Women*, but his very consistency marks him out as pathetic and stupid.

In the play *Women Beware Women*, Leantino changes from a foolish, jealous young man into a sour, would-be murderer of his unfaithful wife. (This is *Romeo and Juliet* where the young lovers do not die. The play shows what might have happened to them if they had lived.) Leantino's love and idealism wither in the winter air of having to earn a living, while worrying about money and adultery—in that order: "Young gentlemen that only love for beauty,/ They love not wisely; such a marriage rather/Proves the destruction of affection."

The only thing you can be sure of in M.'s universe is that nothing is what it seems. *Anything for a Quiet Life* ends in a series of amazing reconciliations. These are, however, presided over and blessed by the hypocritical and debauched Lord Beauford, a man who taints everything he touches. M.'s roller coaster world of hairpin turns and vertiginous falls is clearly revealed in his little-known black comedy, *The Old Law*, where a Prince brings back an old law that condemns to death all men reaching the age of seventy and all women reaching the age of sixty for no longer being of any value to the state. Almost all the young people are delighted and hurry their aged and infirm parents to their deaths. Simonides explains his attitude simply: "I am a young man with an old father." Gotho urges his wife to commit suicide and not wait, so he can marry a younger woman: "Ay, so if thou woulds't go away quickly." Sex and death ride together. Diocles, an old husband, goes to his grave "as weeping brides receive their joys of night/With trembling, yet with patience." This fable is a prophetically twisted image of our own corruption, where we laugh at characters who are not laughable, for we instantly recognize ourselves as we hurry to bury our old ones in homes instead of under an executioner's axe.

M.'s genius is comic, even his so-called tragedies, for they violate every major element of the tragic form—no heroes of stature, no reversal of suffering, no recognition and purification. Instead, he shows the real world where tragedy and comedy mingle, where the division between the tragic and the comic, sacred and profane, serious and trivial, do not exist. Expect no neatness here, only the mess of living. Like all Jacobean playwrights, M.'s greatness can only truly be seen in performance. But their plays are rarely performed, and so for many M.'s genius still lies hidden compared to such luminaries of the period as Jonson and Shakespeare.

BIBLIOGRAPHY: Barker, R. H., *T. M.* (1958); Holmes, D. H., *The Art of T. M.* (1970); Schoenbaum, S., *M.'s Tragedies: A Critical Study* (1955)

PETER BARNES

MILL, James

b. 6 April 1773, Logie-Pert, Scotland; d. 23 June 1836, London

After attending the Montrose Academy, M. distinguished himself as a Greek scholar at Edinburgh University. Although licensed as a preacher, he pursued historical and philosophical studies and occasionally taught. In 1802, he went to London and became a journalist. In 1808, M. became a disciple of Jeremy BENTHAM, opposing all tendencies to ROMANTICISM. M. was a regular contributor to the *Anti-Jacobin Review*, the *British Review*, the *Electric Review*, and the *Edinburgh Review*. In 1811, he worked with William Allen, a Quaker chemist, on a periodical called the *Philanthropist*. M.'s topics were education, freedom of the press, and prison discipline. M. promoted Bentham's "panopticon," whereby prisoners would be under constant and universal surveillance. In 1817, he published his three-volume *History of British India*, which had taken him twelve years to write. It is his greatest literary monument. Although it criticized British rule, M. was appointed to India House. His *Elements of Political Economy* appeared in 1821 (rev. ed., 1826). This summarized the views of the philosophic radicals. M. maintained that increase of population must be restrained, as capital does not increase with it, and that the value of a thing depends entirely on the labor put into it. M. influenced Karl Marx. From 1824 to 1826, he contributed to the *Westminster Review*, attacking the ecclesiastical establishment, and the *Edinburgh* and *Quarterly Reviews*. His two-volume *Analysis of the Phenomena of the Human Mind* appeared in 1829, developing the psychological side of Benthamism. M.'s psychology was fiercely opposed by Samuel Taylor COLERIDGE.

MILL, John Stuart

b. 20 May 1806, London; d. 6 May 1873, Avignon, France

M. was born to James Mill, known for the development of Utilitarianism with Jeremy BENTHAM. His father insisted that he should argue through every idea he was offered, a habit he would continue. The junior M., after a breathtaking acquisition of knowledge under his father's tutelage, ended his formal education at the age of fourteen. In 1822, he began a thirty-five-year career with the British East India Company at the age of sixteen. During this period with the East India Company, he had a simultaneous and remarkably productive career as writer and editor, contributing to and editing *Westminster Review*, *London Review*, and *London and Westminster Review*. He also published two books, *System of Logic* (2 vols., 1843; rev. eds., 1846–72), his most substantial philosophical treatise, and *Principles of Political Economy* (2 vols., 1848; rev. eds., 1849–72), his economic treatise. In 1865, he entered Parliament for one three-year term. Although he may have ultimately been a more effective author than politician, he was also a vociferous statesman for the liberal cause, arguing during his tenure for land reform, liberalizing relations with Ireland, and a woman's right to vote.

Reared in the shadow of formidable philosophical thinkers like his father and Bentham, M.'s intellect matured rapidly, but his emotional development was stunted. Until his early twenties, M. diligently followed the Benthamite tradition he was reared with, which insisted that one compelling idea should lie at the heart of all social policy: that government should choose a course that leads to the greatest good for the greatest number of people. This remained M.'s guiding light until that fateful day in his twentieth year when, as he records in his *Autobiography* (1873), he asked himself, what if all the "objects in life were realized; that all the changes in institutions and opinions which you are looking forward to, could be completely effected at this very instant: would this be a great joy and happiness to you?" The answer was no. The resulting crisis led M. into a prolonged depression, which was turned around by an honest literary conversion. M. discovered for himself the necessity of an aesthetic consciousness primarily by reading William WORDSWORTH's poetry. As economist Robert Heilbroner phrases it, "while other youths had to discover that there could be beauty in intellectual activity, poor Mill had to find out that there could be beauty in beauty." A transformed man, he was then able to clearly see the shortcomings of his own philosophical traditions and their inability to address the whole consciousness.

M. wrestled with the social and political issues that defined Victorian Britain, and his thinking had a profound effect upon others that rippled outward. The 19th c. saw Britain in a time of tremendous social, religious, political, and economic upheaval that affected all stations of society. Politically, Britain made substantial changes to establish religious freedoms and political rights through the Catholic Emancipation Act of 1829 and the Reform Bill of 1832. M. consistently championed the rights of the individual during this time, realizing that a free society depended upon the consent of the governed for its power: at the core of his writing is the desire to fully explore the balance between the individual and the majority, acknowledging their mutual dependence. In his essay "The Spirit of the Age"(1831), M. asks unnerving questions about the vaunted and sacrosanct majority whose collective will supposedly lends legitimacy to government: if we rest authority in a free society upon the consent of the majority, what is the source of moral authority? Of intellectual authority? Certainly

the majority errs often. Knowing that, how do we challenge it, and preserve its power?

M. further explores the relationship between the majority and the individual in his most influential work, *On Liberty* (1859). He starts by stating that his purpose is to defend the principle that the only case in which the majority (or government, through the consent of the majority) may interfere with the rights of the individual is in self-protection. Conversely, he insists upon not only the absolute freedom of written and verbal expression for individuals, but upon the exercise of that freedom. M. held that truth is found through the conflict of ideas; therefore, we can hold opinions honestly only if those ideas are free to be challenged. Exploring the rights of perhaps the most widely oppressed individuals in his society, M. published *The Subjection of Women* in 1869, his defense of the rights of women in marriage, the workplace, and the polling booth. When M. died, Britain lost an economist, philosopher, activist, politician, and suffragist, and, rarer still, a writer who could address all of those audiences.

BIBLIOGRAPHY: Berger, F. R., *Happiness, Justice, and Freedom: The Moral and Political Philosophy of J. S. M.* (1984); Carlisle, J., *J. S. M. and the Writing of Character* (1991); Heilbroner, R. L., *The Worldly Philosophers: The Lives, Times, and Ideas of Great Economic Thinkers* (7th ed., 1999); Ryan, A., *J. S. M.* (1970)

ROBERT E. CUMMINGS

MILMAN, Henry Hart

b. 10 February 1791, London; d. 24 September 1868, Sunninghill, Ascot

M.'s literary output seems incongruous to the modern reader. During the earliest phase of his career, M.—who had won the Newdigate Prize for poetry at Oxford—concentrated on verse dramas. Only the first of them, the Italian tragedy *Fazio* (1815), was actually produced for the stage; it enjoyed a considerable success at Covent Garden. It was followed thereafter by the EPIC *Samor, Lord of the Bright City* (1818), *The Fall of Jerusalem* (1820), *The Martyr of Antioch* (1822), *Belshazzar* (1822), and *Anne Boleyn* (1826). Of this latter group, *The Fall of Jerusalem* and *The Martyr of Antioch* were ultimately the most successful; the first, a biblical drama, details Rome's sacking of the city; the second draws on the conversion and death of Saint Margaret. *The Martyr*'s critique of religious fanaticism prefigures M.'s reasoned approach to ecclesiastical history. M.'s success led to his appointment as Professor of Poetry at Oxford (1821–31). Although his long poems have long fallen out of favor, several of M.'s hymns have remained popular within the Church of England, including "Ride on! Ride on in Majesty," "When Our Heads Are Bowed with Woe," "Oh Help Us, Lord, Each Hour of Need," and "Christ Crucified." He collected them as *A Selection of Psalms and Hymns* (1837).

As M.'s clerical career progressed and the popularity of his long poems declined, his attention turned to more historical issues. M. began contributing to the *Quarterly Review* in 1820 and was invited to deliver the prestigious Bampton Lectures. Shortly thereafter, the publisher John Murray commissioned a history of the Jewish people for his "Murray's Family Library" series. The result, *The History of the Jews* (3 vols., 1829), proved scandalous. For some time, the British had been frightened by the threat the new German biblical criticism posed to older ideas about inspiration and scriptural truth. M. refused to read the events of the Old Testament literally: instead, he sought for scientific, poetic, or rational explanations of supposedly miraculous events. Contemporaries saw German influence at work—although, like many other scholars of his time, M. seems to have had little acquaintance with German scholarship. The scandal notwithstanding, M.'s career in the church continued to advance. He established himself as the leading ecclesiastical historian of his era with the publication of his *History of Christianity* (3 vols., 1840) and his *History of Latin Christianity* (6 vols., 1854–55), both marked by the eminently reasonable Anglicanism of the *History of the Jews*. As a historian of Christianity, M. was well known for his even-handedness and scrupulosity, as well as his perhaps rather arid take on Christian spirituality.

M. was appointed Dean of St. Paul's in 1849, and remained there for the remainder of his career. His scholarly contributions extended beyond ecclesiastical history, however. He undertook to rehabilitate Edward GIBBON, first by editing an important edition of the *Decline and Fall* (12 vols., 1838–39), and then by writing Gibbon's biography (1839). He also returned to his earlier interests in poetry and drama—not as author, but as the editor and translator of Horace (1849) as well as Aeschylus and Euripides (1864). Such classical interests were hardly unusual for a Victorian clergyman, but M. also grew interested in Sanskrit, publishing translations of parts of the *Mahabharata* (1863). His final original publication, however, was devoted to St. Paul's itself; the *Annals of St. Paul's Cathedral* appeared in the year of his death.

Later readers have not been able to work up much enthusiasm for M.'s historical work, and—the hymns aside—none at all for his poetry. He was not a great stylist like Thomas Babington MACAULAY; nor did he wield a sharp ideological axe like J. A. FROUDE. And M.'s ecclesiastical history has lost most of its authority. Nevertheless, M.'s attempt to historicize the writing of the Old Testament marks a significant moment

in the 19th-c. encounter between historiography and theology.

BIBLIOGRAPHY: Clements, R. E., "The Intellectual Background of H. H. M.'s *The History of the Jews* (1829) and its Impact on English Biblical Scholarship," in Reventlow, H. G., and W. Framer, eds., *Biblical Studies and the Shifting of Paradigms, 1850–1914* (1995): 246–71; Milman, A., *H. H. M., D.D., Dean of St. Paul's* (1900); Smyth, C., *Dean Milman (1791–1868)* (1949)

MIRIAM ELIZABETH BURSTEIN

MILNE, A[lan] A[lexander]

b. 18 January 1882, London; d. 31 January 1956, London

A poet, a playwright, and a satirist as well as an author of children's stories, M. is almost exclusively known as the latter, his fame resting on two works: *Winnie-the-Pooh* (1926), and the sequel *The House at Pooh Corner* (1928). M.'s son Christopher Robin, born in 1920, is credited as the inspiration and catalyst for the stories. Indeed, Christopher Robin is the name of the little boy who frolics with the animal characters Winnie-the-Pooh, Rabbit, Piglet, Eeyore, Kanga, Roo, and Tigger in the tales. The animal characters personify various types of human beings, and the character Christopher Robin takes on the role of wise leader among these characters. Winnie-the-Pooh cannot control his appetite and suffers from dullness as a result. Rabbit practices perfectionism to a fault. Piglet lives with many fears, real and imagined. Eeyore lacks self-confidence and harbors an air of despondency. Tigger acts without thinking, concerned only with his own happiness at the moment. It is up to young Christopher Robin to be the mediator, the father figure. Only the mother Kanga and her youngster Roo are able to function without primary input from Christopher Robin. The characters combine to offer valuable lessons and insights to the children reading or hearing the tales.

Both Pooh works were published from the beginning in England and the U.S. and have continued in their popularity into the new century. Much critical attention has been given to these stories, especially in later years as the field of CHILDREN'S LITERATURE has been given more scholarly attention. Earlier critics were concerned that M. ignored the social and political problems of his day, particularly World War I, as well as the concerns of modern life. More recent critics have noted that fantasy was the norm for early-20th-c. children's literature and that that norm is useful in the genre. Others have been critical of the idealistic nature of the Pooh stories; such criticisms have been countered by those who see important messages on character and human nature in the stories.

Many have been critical of the commercialization of the Pooh stories, noting that many more products than actual books have been sold over the years. Works such as Benjamin Hoff's *The Tao of Pooh* (1983) have been criticized as taking away from the true Pooh. In any case, the legend of Pooh has continued to live on vibrantly through the years, which is much more than can be said for M.'s other works.

It has been reported that M. was unhappy that Pooh overshadowed his other works, especially his plays and other adult writings. M. became assistant editor of the periodical *Punch* at age twenty-four and contributed many pieces of SATIRE, in the form of poetry and essays, to the magazine. In 1921, M. published the play *Mr. Pim Passes By*. Another play, *Toad of Toad Hall*, an adaptation of Kenneth GRAHAME's *The Wind in the Willows*, was produced in 1929 to high critical acclaim. In addition, M. published two successful books of children's poetry, *When We Were Very Young* (1924) and *Now We Are Six* (1927). As were the Pooh stories, these two collections were conceived from M.'s experiences with his young son. In 1952, M. published a collection of his essays, *Year In, Year Out*. Yet M.'s reputation today continues to rest predominantly on his Pooh stories.

Regardless of M.'s uneasiness with his perceived place in literary history, his place does indeed remain secure. Perhaps unfairly, the plays and essays he left behind remain interesting and important to but a smattering of critics while his Winnie-the-Pooh stories continue to be passed along from one generation to the next. There is security of fame in that phenomenon, however, and, to the astute reader, there is a certain fascination in reading Pooh with the art of the satirist in the back of one's mind.

BIBLIOGRAPHY: Connolly, P. T., *Winnie-the-Pooh and The House at Pooh Corner* (1994); Milne, C., *The Enchanted Places* (1974); Thwaite, A., *A. A. M.* (1990)

TERRY D. NOVAK

MILTON, John

b. 9 December 1608, London; d. 8 November 1674, Chalfont St. Giles

After William SHAKESPEARE, M. is considered the greatest poet of the English language. He began his education at home, with his mother devoting herself to his religious training. He later went to St. Paul's School, and then to Christ's College, Cambridge, with the intention of becoming a clergyman. At the university, M. took to his studies with an intense seriousness. In his personal demeanor, he was highly reserved, and not altogether at home with his fellow students, who often proved too docile in their approach to education. He also objected to much in the

curriculum and established routine, and took particular exception to his tutor. The result of the friction between the two was M.'s suspension for a term at the beginning of his second year. He returned to Cambridge in the following term and was assigned another tutor, with whom he had no difficulty. He soon won the esteem and respect of the other students, as much, perhaps, for his skill at fencing as for his intellectual eminence. He received his B.A. degree in 1629, and in the same year composed his ode, "On the Morning of Christ's Nativity," the most important of his early poems. He continued his studies at Cambridge for the M.A. degree, which he received in 1632. During this time, he wrote two of his most charming and widely anthologized poems, "L'Allegro" and "Il Penseroso." When he left Cambridge, he had given up any plans to join the church, largely because of what he considered the corrupt practices of the bishops and the clergy. He subsequently retired to his father's house at Horton, about twenty miles from London, where for five years he devoted himself to intense preparation for becoming a poet, which he had come to consider a sacred vocation.

The ripening of his poetic genius is shown in his chief compositions of this period: *Comus* (perf. 1634; pub. 1637) and "Lycidas" (1638). *Comus*, a masque written at the request of Henry LAWES, master of the king's music, and supplied with musical settings by Lawes, reveals M.'s passion for music and his kinship with the lyric poets of the Elizabethan period. It also combines Renaissance grace and artistry with Puritan seriousness. The death of Edward King, a young poet and college classmate of M.'s who was drowned off the coast of Wales, furnished the occasion for "Lycidas," a pastoral elegy of exceptional beauty. Although King was not a close friend, the death of a contemporary who shared his ambition gave M. the opportunity to lament the transience and uncertainty of life, to question the value of long preparation for a career that might be cut short just as it was beginning. Along with this doubt and uncertainty is the stern voice of M.'s Puritanism in his attack on the corruption of the clergy and the perceived threat to English spiritual life posed by Roman Catholicism, "the grim wolf with privy paw." At the conclusion of the poem, M. indicates both the need and resolution to move on to "fresh woods and pastures new." In the following year, 1638, M. left his idyllic country retreat at Horton to undertake a grand tour of the European continent.

M.'s later life was filled with much sadness, but his time as a young man in Italy was a period of considerable, albeit short-lived, happiness. As a charming and cultivated young Englishman, he was welcomed by men distinguished in letters, politics, and science, among them Galileo, the controversial astronomer. After about a year, his travels were cut short by news of impending civil strife in England, and by the sad news of the death of Charles Diodati, a close friend from his days at St. Paul's whose family he had recently visited in Lucca. He expressed his grief for the loss of Diodati in a Latin elegy, *Epitaphium Damonis* (1640), in which he bade farewell to his youth and his Latin verse, as well as to his friend. Back in London, M. became a teacher, numbering among his small group of pupils his nephews, John and Edward Phillips.

His plans to write great poetry were now subordinated to his preoccupation with what he saw as his civic duty in the cause of liberty. He began writing pamphlets, an occupation that would consume his intellectual energies for the next twenty years. In later years, in his *Defensio Secunda,* published in 1654, he summarized the prose works of his middle years as efforts on behalf of "three species of liberty which are essential to the happiness of social life—religious, domestic, and civil." In defense of what he considered religious liberty, he wrote five pamphlets in 1641 and 1642 attacking the system of episcopacy and the alliance between church and state in the Church of England, and argued for the rule of conscience in spiritual affairs.

In 1642, when he was thirty-four, M. married Mary Powell, the seventeen-year-old daughter of a Cavalier family, who found the scholarly and sedate household of M. uncongenial, and left him within the year. The separation proved a great shock to M., who had highly idealized the state of marriage. They were reconciled three years later, and his wife bore him three daughters and a son before her death in 1652. The circumstances of the separation turned M.'s attention to the divorce laws of the country and he produced between 1643 and 1645 four treatises on divorce, arguing for dissolution of marriage when husband and wife are spiritually and temperamentally incompatible. The divorce pamphlets were punctuated by two other treatises on other phases of "domestic liberty." The first was a little tractate *Of Education* (1644), which contains an outline for an extensive course of study and a noble statement of its objective: "I call therefore a complete and generous education that which fits a man to perform justly, skillfully, and magnanimously all the offices, both private and public, of peace and war." Later in the same year came the most famous of his prose works, *Areopagitica*, his eloquent plea for freedom of the press. In 1645 appeared his first volume of collected poems, containing verse in three languages—English, Latin, and Italian.

At this time, the dissension between the king and Puritan Parliament was coming to a head, and M. entered into the struggle to champion the cause of "civil liberty." The first of his political treatises, *The Tenure of Kings and Magistrates,* appeared within a few weeks of the execution of King Charles I in 1649. In recognition of his services to the new Commonwealth

government, M. was appointed secretary for the Foreign Tongues to the Council of State. For the next eleven years, he threw himself energetically into his work, giving not only his energy and talent, but what remained of his failing eyesight. His political fortunes were reversed, however, with the Restoration of Charles II, son of the executed king, in 1660. He was arrested, but through the intervention of friends in high places, including the poet Andrew MARVELL, he was released after the payment of fees and was ultimately pardoned. The preceding ten years had brought great sorrow and domestic upheaval to M.'s life. By 1652, he was totally blind; in that same year, his wife and infant son also died. His second wife, Katherine Woodcock, whom he married in 1656, died in 1658, along with a baby daughter.

Despite these adverse circumstances, M. had begun writing the EPIC poem that would ultimately be recognized as his masterpiece, *Paradise Lost*, in 1658. In 1663, he married for a third time and he and his wife, Elizabeth Minshull, retired to a small cottage outside London where once again he concentrated his remaining energies on poetry, completing, along with *Paradise Lost, Paradise Regained* and *Samson Agonistes* (1671).

Paradise Lost was published in ten books in 1667, and republished in twelve books in 1674. M.'s first choice for the epic poem he had decided to write by the time he was nineteen was the story of King Arthur. He eventually abandoned the topic and decided on some aspect of the fall of man. The elements of *Paradise Lost* are drawn from all of M.'s experience and all his reading and thinking. The Christian material is a composite of modern and medieval, and the Hebraic elements are integrated with it and further shaped by M.'s thorough knowledge of the Greek and Latin classics. The purpose of the poem is to "justify the ways of God to men," and in every real sense the hero of the poem is Man, created, preserved, counseled, tempted, betrayed, punished, and ultimately banned from Paradise. All of this comes about through the machinations of Satan, the villain of the poem. M.'s Satan, from the viewpoint of dramatic interest, is the author's most brilliant creation, a point recognized and celebrated by the Romantic movement of the 19th c., particularly in the works of William BLAKE, Lord BYRON, and Percy Bysshe SHELLEY. M. is unique among English poets; no other poet dedicated himself so early and so completely to the vocation of poetry, gave his prime years to his perceived duty as a citizen and patriot, or produced his greatest work in the closing years of his life. *Paradise Lost* is one of the world's greatest poetical compositions. In theme, scope, and execution it has no equal in English, nor perhaps in any other language.

BIBLIOGRAPHY: Evans, J. M., *Paradise Lost and the Genesis Tradition* (1968); Milner, A., *J. M. and the*

English Revolution (1981); Parker, W. R., *M.* (2 vols., 1968); Potter, L., *A Preface to M.* (1971; rev. ed., 1986); Webber, J. M., *M. and His Epic Tradition* (1979)

RICHARD KEENAN

MINGHELLA, Anthony

b. 6 January 1954, Ryde, Isle of Wight

Together with Jane Campion, Laura Jones, and Alan Parker, M. is regarded as one of the most important late-20th- and early-21st-c. screenwriters. Like these filmmakers, M. is known for classy, richly textured screen adaptations of famous novels and combines a literary background with a fascination for cinema. Born off the south coast of England on the Isle of Wight to Italian immigrants who lived adjacent to the local movie theater, as a youngster M. attended the traditional Saturday morning movies with his peers and also made frequent visits to the theater projection booth, thanks to the projectionist who befriended him. During his adolescence, he became mesmerized by the films of Federico Fellini, Woody Allen, Eric Rohmer, Akira Kurasawa, and Krzysztof Kieślowski, also with the work of the movie actor Robert De Niro. Later, after spending ten years at Hull University studying and teaching and, above all, reading, he started out his career as a dramatist for theater, radio, and television—including writing for Jim Henson's *The Storyteller* (perf. 1987–88; pub. 1991) and several episodes for *Inspector Morse* (1994). In 1991, M. made his film debut with *Truly, Madly, Deeply*, a whimsical ghost story and comedy about bereavement, which he both wrote and directed. Some critics found the film both sentimental and derivative.

In terms of popular appeal, M.'s most important work so far has been his 1996 screenplay and direction of *The English Patient* (1992) by the Canadian novelist, Michael Ondaatje, for which M. received an Academy Award. Telling of a Hungarian pilot shot down and burned with his English lover in the Sahara Desert at the beginning of World War II, the Ondaatje novel combines this love story with an affair between a Canadian nurse and an Indian sapper. In the novel, events are presented by several narrators in separate, threaded narratives. Although the novel's magical realist style contains brilliant, almost cinematic, imagery, M. judged that sticking faithfully to the novel would be impossible. Instead, he reproduces a response to the book rather than an adaptation, by foregrounding the love affair between the pilot Almasy and the Englishwoman Catherine, and cutting political elements included in the book such as the Indian sapper's outrage at the dropping of the atomic bomb on an Asian country. Elsewhere, M. justifies such

omissions by citing not only a book's complexity as compared to a movie but also the limited time in which the audience views a movie. For example, he claims that in contrast to the written word, which is often "implicit," film is limited because it is "very prosaic and explicit." For M., it must contain the "necessary dramatisation of the implicit" through visual detail: "something specific that you shove in front of the camera." Whereas deconstructive and feminist critics found fault with *The English Patient* because it replaced elements of race, gender, and class with a sensational plot line and extravagant setting, popular critics acclaimed the grandeur of the story's passions and the film's panoramic sense of the vastness of the desert and its orchestration of the exotic Cairo setting.

M. followed *The English Patient* with the screenplay of *The Talented Mr. Ripley* (1999), based on a suspense story about a clever social climber who assumes the identity of a wealthy American in the Italy of the 1950s. According to M., the film reveals the extent to which we are convinced by others that we are inadequate and unworthy and thus thrust into adopting the personality of another.

M.'s career is still in process. His upcoming films include *Play* (2000), based on a 1963 drama by Samuel BECKETT. It consists quite literally of talking heads: each member of a love triangle fulfills a punishment to confess his or her sins ad infinitum to a prompter in front of a camera whose whirring, clicks, and zooms intrude on the action. Destroying dramatic space and interrogating the author-character relation, *Play* represents M.'s most radical work to date.

BIBLIOGRAPHY: Argent, D., "The Talented Mister: An Interview with A. M.," *CS* 7 (January-February 2000): 63–67; Urban, A. L., *Urban Cinefile* (1999)

SUSAN TETLOW HARRINGTON

MITCHELL, Adrian

(pseud.: Gerald Stimpson) b. 24 October 1932, London

Privately educated, M. went to Christ Church, Oxford. His poetry has always been politically left of center, apocalyptic, and implicitly utopian, a stance punningly exemplified in the title *Heart on the Left: Poems, 1953–1984* (1997). His wit is used for polemic against bad government and the threat of nuclear war, imaged by *Love Songs of World War Three* (1988) and his poem beginning, "I'm standing on the Beach at Cambridge." The town is some seventy miles from the actual coast. *On the Beach at Cambridge* (1984) was an admired collection. Earlier poems appeared in two successful anthologies, Michael HOROVITZ's *Children of Albion* and Alan Bold's *The Penguin Book of Socialist Verse* (1970). *For*

Beauty Douglas (1982) brings together poems from earlier volumes, including *Out Loud* (1968) and *The Apeman Cometh* (1975). *Blue Coffee: Poems, 1985–1996* appeared in 1996 and *All Shook Up: Poems 1997–2000* in 2000. M.'s novels include *If You See Me Comin'* (1962) and *The Bodyguard* (1970). He has adapted and translated works by Pedro Calderón de la Barca and Nikolai Gogol for the stage and written libretti for opera. Other dramatic work is collected in *Plays with Songs* (1996), which includes *Tyger Two, Man Friday, Satie Day/Night,* and *In the Unlikely Event of an Emergency.* His adaptation for the stage of Peter Weiss's *Marat/Sade* (perf. 1964; pub. 1965) is celebrated. Often in partnership with Christopher LOGUE, M. has given dramatic public performances, and he has also written books for children.

MITCHELL, [Charles] Julian [Humphrey]
b. 1 May 1935, Epping

M. began his career as a novelist but later wrote for the stage. Educated at Winchester College and Wadham College, Oxford, M. is most famous for his play *Another Country* (perf. 1981; pub. 1982), filmed in 1984 with Rupert Everett as the homosexual defector to Russia who reflects on the pressures at his elite public (private) school that have molded him. M.'s other stage work includes *Half-Life* (1977), about an aging archaeologist, *The Enemy Within* (perf. 1980), and *Francis* (perf. 1983; pub. 1984). He has adapted several novels by Ivy COMPTON-BURNETT. M.'s own novels include *Imaginary Toys* (1961), *A Disturbing Influence* (1962), *As Far As You Can Go* (1963), *The White Father* (1964), set in Africa, *A Circle of Friends* (1966), and *The Undiscovered Country* (1968), an experimental fiction that features a novel within the novel.

MITCHISON, Naomi [Mary Margaret]
b. 1 November 1897, Edinburgh, Scotland; d. 11 January 1999, Mull of Kintyre, Scotland

M. was the daughter of the physiologist J. S. Haldane and sister of biologist J. B. S. Haldane. She published some seventy books, among them novels and stories that appeared in the 1920s and 1930s, set in classical Greece and Rome: *The Conquered* (1923), *When the Bough Breaks and Other Stories* (1924), *Cloud Cuckoo Land* (1925), *Barbarian Stories* (1929), *Black Sparta: Greek Stories* (1928), *The Corn King and the Spring Queen* (1931), and *The Delicate Fire and Other Stories* (1933). *The Blood of the Martyrs* (1939) is a novel about the early Christians in Rome. *The Big House,* a novel, appeared in 1950. Married to the barrister and socialist politician G. R. Mitchison, M.

supported progressive causes and in 1985 was named Commander of the Order of the British Empire.

MITFORD, Mary Russell
b. 16 December 1787, Alresford, Hampshire; d. 10 January 1855, Swallowfield, near Reading

M. is best remembered as the author of *Our Village* (5 vols., 1824–32), fresh and humorous sketches of country life. M.'s friend Elizabeth Barrett BROWNING said M.'s conversation was even more amusing than her books. M. wrote poetry: *Miscellaneous Verses* (1810), reviewed by Sir Walter SCOTT in the *Quarterly; Christine* (1811), a metrical tale; *Blanche* (1813). Several plays were successfully performed, notably *Julian* (1823), *The Foscari* (1826), *Rienzi* (1828), and *Charles I* (1834). *Belford Regis,* a novel idealizing the town of Reading, was published in three volumes in 1835. M. was battened on by a parasitic father who, having spent his wife's fortune and his daughter's lottery winnings, squandered her earnings. In 1837, she received a Civil List pension and five years later her father died. M.'s *Life and Letters* (5 vols.) appeared in 1870 and 1872.

MITFORD, Nancy [Freeman]
b. 28 November 1904, London; d. 30 June 1973, Versailles, France

Formerly dismissed as a brittle entertainer, M. is increasingly recognized as recorder of a vanished era: she writes, a self-elected spokesperson for the peerage, with the authentic voice of a time and class. Her values were courage, gaiety, and a determination never to be a bore. As a novelist and biographer, M. worked long and hard to present an appearance of effortless frivolity, turning into comedy her painful upbringing by eccentric parents who had a large family and not enough money.

Educated cheaply at home, so that all she learned was French and horsemanship, M. taught herself about art, history, and literature. Her novels are studded with allusion. Her books are a critique of the then custom of rearing daughters with no preparation for life apart from marriage. *The Pursuit of Love* (1945) hilariously depicts her relatives, especially her father, Lord Redesdale, who, as "Uncle Matthew," is given to violent prejudices and rages. He notoriously believes that "abroad is bloody," and that "foreigners are fiends." In the novel, Matthew's daughter, Linda, after two disastrous marriages, finds true love with a cultured French duke, Fabrice, who makes her his mistress, but Linda dies in childbirth and Fabrice is shot by the Gestapo. Alan BENNETT has described the book as touching and profound. The irresistible Frenchman reappears in *The Blessing* (1951), a comedy of manners. Charles-Edouard marries Protestant

English Grace, but only in a register office, which to a Catholic "does not count," leaving a loophole. M. analyzes the cultural differences between English aristocrats and French ones.

Love in a Cold Climate (1949) makes comedy out of decadence. Lady Montdore's lover, Boy Dougdale, discreetly "arouses the sexual instincts of little girls" and Lady Montdore's daughter Polly falls in love with him. Boy's wife dies and Polly insists on marrying him, despite being disinherited. Meanwhile, Lord Montdore's heir, flamboyant, effeminate Cedric, becomes Lady Montdore's platonic lover and adviser on extravagant beauty treatments, one of which kills her. Polly is disillusioned with Boy and soured by poverty, but inherits from another relative and runs off with a duke, while Boy and Cedric settle down together. *Don't Tell Alfred* (1960) was prophetic. The narrator is wife to an Oxford don who gets a diplomatic posting to Paris. Their sons, both brilliant Oxford graduates, refuse to follow traditional careers and become "Teddy boys," obsessed with pop music. Early entrepreneurs, they make a fortune. At the time of writing, this denouement seemed improbable, yet events have proved that M. had spotted a trend.

M.'s prose style is crisp, economical, and elegant and her jokes stand the test of time. After World War II, during which she worked in a bookshop, she settled in Paris and translated French literature. Her insightful biographies, based on her reading of history in French, were best-sellers. Her friend Harold Acton wrote of her, "The same narrative skill was diverted to Mme. de Pompadour, Voltaire and Louis XIV, hence plodding academic historians have sneered at her brilliant achievements in their field." However, M.'s biographer Selina Hastings accuses her of romanticizing France and the French, and glamorizing a repressive class system. Perhaps, but M.'s family had been short of money, and in the postwar period of austerity French cuisine and French couture were objects of longing to British readers, few of whom had traveled abroad, and who liked to read about style and luxury beyond their reach.

It was M. who chiefly popularized an article by Alan Ross on differences in idiom between the upper classes and the middling sort (the U and non-U controversy) that made many people adopt a different vocabulary. She claimed to be a socialist, yet cleverly commercialized her own social advantages, editing two volumes of family letters, *The Ladies of Alderly* (1938) and *The Stanleys of Alderly* (1939).

BIBLIOGRAPHY: Acton, H., *N. M.* (1975); Hastings, S., *N. M.* (1985); Mosley, C., ed., *Love from Nancy: The Letters of N. M.* (1993)

VALERIE GROSVENOR MYER

MO, Timothy
b. 30 December 1950, Hong Kong

M.'s novels often explore the struggles of intercultural relations. In them, the reader finds a dark comic side that is a part of everyday life. M. handles these themes using wit and a skill with language and its idiosyncrasies. Born in Hong Kong to a Cantonese father and an English mother, M. moved to England with his mother at age ten. He attended St. John's College, Oxford, reading history. In addition to his novels, M. contributes to various periodicals, including the *New Statesman* and *Boxing News*.

M.'s first two novels, *The Monkey King* (1978) and *Sour Sweet* (1982), "hold a mirror up to the life of the family, which is at the very center of the Chinese universe." In both, there is also a certain humanistic preoccupation with exile. *The Monkey King* is centered around Wallace Nolasco. A typical outsider for M.'s novels, Wallace is a Chinese-Portuguese from Macao exiled to Hong Kong to marry the daughter of his father's business partner, Mr. Poon. Here, Wallace's difficulties begin, as he is shown very little regard within the family and in return has little regard for the Hong Kong Chinese. Further exiled to mainland China, Wallace comes to terms with the Chinese culture, while he and his wife, May-Ling, begin to settle into a more comfortable partnership. With his successes from the mainland, Wallace returns to Hong Kong at the bidding of the dying Poon and is given control of the family dynasty, triumphant, yet still in a sort of exile. In *Sour Sweet*, M.'s first novel to be shortlisted for the Booker Prize, Chen and his wife, Lilly, having moved from mainland China to London, subsequently open a "take-away" restaurant in the suburbs. There they are forced out of the cultural safety of the Chinese quarter of London, and wrestle with the Westernization of their son, Man Kee, and the odd and wonderful metamorphosis of Lilly's sister, Mui, from recluse to the intermediary between the family and their customers. Both novels show a keen insight into society and a deft handling of the irony and HUMOR of family life.

M.'s third novel, *Insular Possession* (1987), was again shortlisted for the Booker Prize, but received mixed reviews by critics. It mixes traditional dialogue with journalism, painting, and minute details from engineering to the practices of a Chinese barber. These aim to surround the reader in the world as it was during the first Opium War. M. is lauded for his research, ambition, and rich attention to detail. *The Redundancy of Courage* (1991), a fictionalized account of Indonesia's occupation of East Timor in 1975, was also shortlisted for the Booker Prize. Due to a dispute with his publisher, M. established Paddleless Press and published his fifth book, *Brownout on Breadfruit Boulevard* (1995), himself. M.'s break with his publisher received more press than the book did; however, his recent novel *Renegade or Halo²* (1999) was awarded the James Tait Black Memorial Prize. Again, the reader finds a cultural outcast at the center of the story. Rey Archimedes Blondel Castro, the child of a black American serviceman and a Malaysian barmaid, is an "underclass hero of epic stature." His origins place him in a cultural gulf; he fits in nowhere. It is a picaresque novel that takes Rey from the Philippines to Cuba to London and various stops in between. His "life is an allegory of the postcolonial world," a product of mixed race, mixed culture, and the speed of the modern world, a relevant hero of the moment. M.'s insightful treatment of the clash of cultures and the plight of the outsider, as well as his own struggle with the giants of the publishing world, have combined to make him a relevant literary hero of the moment.

BIBLIOGRAPHY: Ho, E. Y. L., *T. M.* (2000); Lim, S. G., "Race, National Identity, and the Subject in the Novels of T. M.," in Stummer, P., and C. Balme, eds., *Fusion of Cultures?* (1996): 91–101

PAIGE BAILEY

MODERNISM

Modernism remains one of the most widely used terms in contemporary literary criticism; and yet, like ROMANTICISM, it contains multitudes and is not easily defined. Modernist values and attitudes pervade much of the literature produced in Europe and the U.S. between the end of the 19th c. and the start of World War II. Modernism is synonymous with artistic innovation, but there is no group manifesto of modernism, no self-regulating modernist "school." Moreover, one increasingly finds the term loosely applied to nearly all serious writing published during the first half of the 20th c. But academic criticism has tended to reserve the term more strictly to works published between 1900 and 1930, when modernist values and attitudes can be found in all literary genres, but particularly in fiction and poetry. Strictly defined, modernism was never the dominant force in English literature, where more expected aesthetic assumptions prevailed, in all genres, until after World War II.

As Malcolm BRADBURY has noted, what unites modernist writers of varying styles and temperaments is "a prevailing sense of dislocation from the past, and a commitment to the active remaking of art." Modernism, in other words, began as a reaction against aesthetic beliefs and practices that were dominant during the 19th c. The modernist novelist, for example, was far more likely than his Victorian predecessors to experiment radically with language, style, and narrative structure. Thus, James JOYCE's *Ulysses*, a principal modernist text, is imbued with allusiveness and irony; it discards plot, as conventionally understood; it employs shifting narrative voices, and, most notably, a stream of consciousness interior monologue technique meant to convey more convincingly the odd and changeable flow of human thought.

In poetry, Ezra Pound also experimented with language, imagery, and cadence, and dismissed as an "old lie" the belief that poetry "is meant to entertain." In such essays as "The Serious Artist" (1913) and "How to Read" (1929), Pound expresses key modernist beliefs, insisting on the inviolability of the artist's vision, and the vital importance of art. The arts, Pound asserts, "are a science, just as chemistry is a science." Literature and poetry, he stresses, "give us a great percentage of the lasting and unassailable data regarding the nature of man, of immaterial man, of man considered as a thinking and sentient creature."

Both Pound and Joyce, quintessential modernists, aimed to strengthen and refresh English writing not only through the use of narrative and linguistic experimentation, but by infusing it with other, older literary traditions. Thus, *Ulysses* draws explicitly from the works of Homer and Dante, among numerous other non-English traditions, and embeds Greek and Italian phrases directly into its text. Like Joyce, Pound was a polyglot, and much of his work is informed by various non-English sources and languages, including Chinese. "Great literature," Pound wrote, "is simply language charged with meaning to the utmost possible degree"—a notion that informs not only Pound's *Cantos*, begun in 1917 and completed in fragmentary form in 1969, but Joyce's *Finnegans Wake*, perhaps the consummate modernist text.

Of note, however, Joyce was Irish and Pound an American; the novelist Joseph CONRAD, another important modernist figure, was born a Pole. During the 1920s and 1930s, their work was widely admired and discussed among British artists and intellectuals; and yet, in England, more conventional aesthetic assumptions continued to hold sway. Indeed, prominent British novelists of the era such as John GALSWORTHY, H. G. WELLS, Arnold BENNETT, and even Ford Madox FORD—a notable supporter of literary experimentation—wrote novels that, at least in terms of structure or language, would not have startled Victorian readers to any great degree. To be sure, these writers dealt more frankly with social and sexual questions than any of their British predecessors. But, broadly and essentially, they continued to work within the same tradition of literary REALISM as Charles DICKENS, George ELIOT, and Thomas HARDY.

Pound famously called on poets to "Make it new!" And some—like Richard ALDINGTON and F. S. FLINT—heeded the call. So did T. S. ELIOT, whose polylingual poem, *The Waste Land*, makes complex use of symbol and myth and has long been studied as a key modernist text. But Eliot, born an American, did not become a British citizen until 1927, when his literary career was well under way. Still, one can point to several British-born novelists who have long been placed in the modernist camp. Between 1915 and 1945, Dorothy RICHARDSON wrote and published *Pilgrimage*, a novel in twelve volumes that chronicles the evolving consciousness of a single highly autobiographical character, Miriam Henderson. In order to convey more realistically the nature of Miriam's sensibility, and the pattern of her thoughts, Richardson employs an extensive stream of consciousness technique similar to the one used by Joyce in *Ulysses*.

Virginia WOOLF employs a similar method in her novels *Mrs. Dalloway*, *To the Lighthouse*, and *The Waves*. Woolf, indeed, was an open proponent of fictional innovation, and several of her essays display modernist views that, in their own way, parallel Pound's. In "Modern Fiction," published in 1925, for example, Woolf attacks Bennett, Galsworthy, and Wells for their superficial, predictable, "materialist" vision of art. Simultaneously, she praises *Ulysses*. Joyce, writes Woolf, understood that if artists seek to reveal the truth about human nature, they must be willing to enter into "the dark places of psychology." Joyce, she writes, aims "to reveal the flickerings of that innermost flame which flashes its messages through the brain." And in doing so, he "disregards with complete courage whatever seems to him adventitious, whether it be probability, or coherence, or any other of these signposts that for generations have served to support the imagination of a reader when called upon to imagine what he can neither touch nor see."

Woolf insisted that the novelist of integrity must repeatedly examine and question prevailing assumptions about art's limitations; he must "contrive means of being free to set down what he chooses." The phrase certainly applies to D. H. LAWRENCE, one of the 20th c.'s most influential artistic figures. After Lawrence, the English novel becomes more overtly symbolic, political, and autobiographical. Highly controversial in their day, Lawrence's *The Rainbow* and *Women in Love* particularly broke new ground. These novels have been aptly described as "symbolic and dramatic poems in prose."

Lawrence's political views contain clear fascistic tendencies and have been widely questioned and condemned. Indeed, in recent decades, modernist writers have been frequently criticized by critics and scholars for espousing, at least implicitly, disturbingly antidemocratic views. Of course, not all modernist writers were politically motivated. But one does find an animating disdain for mass culture, in all of its ramifications, in much modernist work. John Carey's *The Intellectuals and the Masses* (1992) is a notable example of what might be termed "antimodernist" critical writing. Carey takes for granted that such writers as Pound, Woolf, and Lawrence made significant contributions to poetry and fiction and influenced the shape and direction of 20th-c. art. But like other contemporary critics, Carey also finds their work morally marred by elements of snobbism, elitism, and misanthropy.

BIBLIOGRAPHY: Bloom, H., ed., *British Modernist Fiction, 1920–1945* (1987); Carey, J., *The Intellectuals and the Masses* (1992); Gilbert, S. M., and S. Gubar, eds., *The Female Imagination and the Modernist Aesthetic* (1986); Jameson, F., *Modernism and Imperialism* (1988); Kenner, H., *The Pound Era* (1971); Levenson, M., ed., *The Cambridge Companion to Modernism* (1999); Sherry, V., *Ezra Pound, Wyndham Lewis, and Radical Modernism* (1993); Weir, D., *Decadence and the Making of Modernism* (1995)

BRIAN MURRAY

MOLESWORTH, [Mrs.] Mary Louisa

b. Mary Louisa Stewart, 29 May 1839, Rotterdam, Holland; d. 20 July 1921, London

One of the most popular children's writers of her time, M.—or "Mrs. Molesworth" as she was known to her readers—was the author of more than one hundred books. Her early novels, from *Lover and Husband* (3 vols., 1870) to *Cicely* (3 vols., 1874), and her first two children's books, *Tell Me a Story* (1875) and *"Carrots": Just a Little Boy* (1876), were published under the pseudonym "Ennis Graham." *"Carrots"* was republished in 1879 under the name Mary Louisa Molesworth, which she would continue to use for the remainder of her career. Her numerous works include *The Cuckoo Clock* (1877), *The Tapestry Room* (1879), *Two Little Waifs* (1883), and *That Girl in Black* (1889). Her stories took on added charm when illustrated by Walter Crane.

MONRO, Harold [Edward]

b. 14 March 1879, St. Gilles, Brussels; d. 16 March 1932, Broadstairs, Kent

T. S. ELIOT said in his introduction to M.'s *Collected Poems* (1933) that they were "more nearly the real right thing than any of the poetry of a somewhat older generation than mine except Mr. [W. B.] YEATS's." M. was a poet of "the ceaseless question and answer of the tortured mind, or the unspoken question and answer between two human beings." M.'s subject matter was actually rather wider than that: some of his poems are passionately concerned with large social and environmental issues, while others are carefully observed portrayals of animals and other living things. His work as a poet and friend of poets spans the first thirty years of the 20th c., the period in which "modern" poetry developed out of the remains of

Victorianism. No one was more closely involved in that development or did more to bring it about.

As a young man, influenced by H. G. WELLS, Edward CARPENTER, and others, and by living in utopian communes abroad, M. was fervently optimistic, believing humanity was approaching a great evolutionary advance. His first significant book of poems, *Before Dawn* (1911), prophesies a world free from religion, sexual taboos, and social injustice. In 1912, he founded a new periodical, the *Poetry Review*, in association with the Poetry Society, hoping to discover and unite the poets of "the great wonderful future," the men and women who would lead the way to the new order. As editor of the *Review* throughout 1912, he presided over an extraordinary revival of English poetry. He succeeded in finding many young writers, and in making their work known, but instead of the hoped-for unity a rift opened up between the two groupings soon to be known as Georgians, led by Rupert BROOKE, and imagists, led by Ezra Pound. M. himself remained neutral, helping both factions. Some of the poems in his next book, *Children of Love* (1914), are influenced by the modernist ideas of Pound and T. E. HULME, while others are more nearly Georgian.

At the end of 1912, M. founded his famous Poetry Bookshop in Bloomsbury, London. The Bookshop not only sold poetry but also published it, in due course producing over fifty books, among them the celebrated anthologies *Georgian Poetry* (5 vols., 1912–22) and *Des Imagistes* (1914). Regular poetry readings were given, bedrooms were available for poets and artists (lodgers included Hulme, Wilfrid Wilson GIBSON, and Jacob Epstein), and M. held frequent parties for writers. When the Poetry Society fired him as editor of the *Review*, considering him far too modern, he started his own quarterly, *Poetry and Drama* (1913–14). In 1914, he became one of the first poets to write about World War I from the point of view of the ordinary soldier; his "Youth in Arms" quartet influenced Wilfred OWEN, who stayed at the Bookshop in 1916. *Poetry and Drama* soon had to be suspended, and in the spare time thus gained M. wrote some of his most characteristic poems, including "Lament in 1915," a moving elegy for a friend killed in action; "Trees," a mystical exploration of the relationship between trees and humans; the sonnet-sequence, "Week-End"; and "Strange Meetings," a series of William BLAKE-like "oracles of paradise." These and other poems were collected in *Strange Meetings*, published in 1917.

Home service in the army (1916–19) damaged M.'s health and hopes. Hostile reviews of the 1919 series of *Georgian Poetry* confirmed his growing loss of faith in the Georgians, and his survey, *Some Contemporary Poets* (1920), is useful but sadly disillusioned. He launched another periodical, the *Chapbook*

(1919–25), which ran for forty numbers until financial troubles forced him to abandon it. He befriended the new generation, including Eliot and the SITWELLS, the Bookshop eventually becoming the principal meeting place for Eliot's circle of advisers, the *Criterion* club. The poems in M.'s *Real Property* (1922) are meditations on heredity, memory, and the subconscious, with a separate section of lyrics he ruefully admitted to be more "Georgian" than he would have liked—some critics said they were the best things in the book. By the time of his last collection, *The Earth for Sale* (1928), he was deeply unhappy, feeling forgotten by the many poets he had helped. His gloomy predictions of solitude, death, and environmental disaster are far from the optimism of *Before Dawn;* similarly, the modernist style of his last poems is very unlike the tired ROMANTICISM of his earliest work. M.'s poetry stands as a remarkable achievement, highly original yet reflecting the changing concerns and styles of its period; and his labors for his fellow-poets deserve to be gratefully remembered.

BIBLIOGRAPHY: Grant, J., *H. M. and the Poetry Bookshop* (1967); Hibberd, D., *H. M.* (2001)

DOMINIC HIBBERD

MONSARRAT, Nicholas [John Turney]
b. 22 March 1910, Liverpool; d. 8 August 1979, London

M.'s lasting reputation rests largely on *The Cruel Sea* (1951), the best fictional portrait of the battle of the North Atlantic during World War II and one of the finest novels about any aspect of the war. In it, he makes vivid the efforts and sufferings of the mostly amateur sailors who shepherded the convoys that sustained Britain during the worst days of the U-boat blockade. M.'s association with the sea, which continued through several more novels, may have cost him a larger reputation, but it has gained him an enduring place in the salty yet romantic subgenre created by such naval writers as Frederick MARRYAT, C. S. FORESTER, and Patrick O'BRIAN.

M. was reared in Liverpool, but the highlights of his youth were summers spent in Wales, where he took up sailing at an early age. After unhappy years at Winchester School, he read law at Trinity College, Cambridge. He then spent two years working in a solicitor's office, but he soon left the law to devote himself to writing. He was a prolific author from the beginning, publishing his first novel in 1934. He later came to think that of his early work, only *This Is the Schoolroom* (1939) had any merit. During the 1930s, M.'s politics were leftist and pacifist, but after the war began, he joined the Royal Navy.

M. served in the small ships known as corvettes. Even while at sea, he continued writing, producing three slightly fictionalized books about his experiences afloat: *H. M. Corvette* (1942), *East Coast Corvette* (1943), and *Corvette Command* (1944), later collected as *Three Corvettes* (1945). The books remain thoroughly readable and present an interesting snapshot of one man's war, but they also show the restraint of an officer avoiding anything that might demoralize the public. M. himself later called them the notebooks from which he would create a very different book, *The Cruel Sea*. That large work, which followed two slighter novels about the war, was written while M. served as the British government's information officer in South Africa. It received the Heinemann Foundation Prize for literature in 1951 and was a best-seller in both Britain and the U.S. Its account of the battle of the Atlantic remains powerful. Though M. never probes his characters very deeply, the account of life aboard a small ship fighting the sea as much as the enemy is gripping.

M. continued work as a civil servant for several more years, serving as British information officer in Canada. His next novel, *The Story of Esther Costello* (1953), described how what began as charity could be transformed into something thoroughly selfish. Drawing on his experiences in Africa, M. wrote two novels set in a mythical British colony, *The Tribe That Lost Its Head* (1956) and *Richer Than All His Tribe* (1968), which essentially argued that the African colonies were not ready for independence and needed the continued guidance of Britain. Now a full-time writer, M. remained prolific, producing historical fictions (*The White Rajah*, 1961), several more books involving the sea, and a book describing the siege of Malta during the Second World War (*The Kappillan of Malta*, 1973). M. made Malta his home for the last decades of his life.

In his later years, M. worked on two very large projects. One was an AUTOBIOGRAPHY, *Life Is a Four-Letter Word*, published in two volumes in 1966 and 1970, and in a condensed version as *Breaking In, Breaking Out* in 1971. The book is thoroughly readable, but omits large portions of M.'s life, including much information about his three marriages. The other was his last sea novel, which was to cover the whole sweep of England's maritime experience from the time of Sir Francis Drake to the postwar decay of Britain's empire and the shipping industry that had helped create it. *The Master Mariner* (1978) follows a single sailor, cursed to sail for centuries after an act of cowardice before the Spanish Armada, through the whole story. The first volume, taking the story up to the death of Admiral Nelson, was published in 1978 as *Running Proud*. M. died before finishing the second volume, but his notes and a completed section on the slave trade appeared in 1980 as *Darken Ship*.

BIBLIOGRAPHY: Jaffe, J., "N. M.," in Oldsey, B., ed., *British Novelists, 1930–1959*, part 2, *DLB* 15 (1983): 369–75

                                    BRIAN ABEL RAGEN

MONTAGU, Elizabeth

b. Elizabeth Robinson, 2 October 1720, York; d. 25 August 1800, London

M., "Queen of the Blues," as Samuel JOHNSON named her, is known less for her literary and critical contributions than for her founding of the fashionable English salon in the mid-18th c. known as the Bluestocking circle. Unlike other social gatherings where the discussion of trivialities and gossiping were the order of the day, M.'s social conversations were reserved for the consideration of literary topics. Born to an upper-middle-class educated family in York, M. received an impressive education in classics and literature for a young woman in 18th-c. England. This unusual education may be attributed to her close association with her maternal grandmother who was married to Conyers Middleton, librarian of Cambridge University. Although M. was never formally educated, upon her marriage to a Cambridge-educated man twenty-nine years her senior, Edward Montagu, Middleton reflected that Cambridge could "claim a share" in both Edward and Elizabeth's education.

M.'s conversation circles were not originally her own creation. Rather she continued the tradition of conversation circles begun by Mrs. Vesey, wife of the Irish parliamentarian, Agmondesham Vesey. Like M., Vesey abhorred the stifling conversation of conventional circles and wished to engage in more substantive discussions of literature, thus uniting the disparate social and literary circles in which she traveled. Considered within the context of the later campaign for women's education waged by feminists such as Mary WOLLSTONECRAFT and others, Vesey and M.'s organized discussions may be seen as important precursors to the later push for women's formal education. Tired of "overhearing" men debating issues of social and literary importance while frustratingly confined to topics considered appropriate to ladies, Vesey and M.'s conversations were a concerted attempt to participate in the kinds of intellectual debate usually the province of men. In a radical departure from the social conventions of her day, M. issued invitations regardless of social degree, remarking that only "idiots" were to be excluded from the discussions.

Regulars in M. and Vesey's salons came to be known as "bluestockings." The term has an uncertain origin. While it later became a term of derision, referring to ladies of pedantic literary tastes, it was said to originate with one particularly impecunious participant—Benjamin Stillingfeet—who, unable to afford evening dress, attended these gatherings in his every-day "blue" stockings.

M. left behind several works: her correspondence; a dramatic collaboration with Lord Lyttelton, *Dialogues of the Dead* (1760); and her best-known work, her essay on William SHAKESPEARE published in 1769. M.'s letters are specimens of great wit; in a famous letter to the Reverend Dr. Shaw, about to be married for the third time, she equivocates on the nature of marriage, writing: "matrimony . . . brings with it all the advantages of reproof and the great profit of remonstrances."

M.'s collaboration with Lord Lyttelton was not well received by her contemporaries. Johnson called the *Dialogues* "nugatory performances" while Horace WALPOLE saw them as the "dead dialogues." M. is said to have penned the last three dialogues. They are primarily critiques of the social and literary tastes of the day structured as dialogues between figures of ancient Rome and Greece and contemporary fine ladies and booksellers. The dialogue between Mercury and Mrs. Modish is a fine example of 18th-c. polite sarcasm; it satirizes the social obsessions of the fashionable—modish—ladies of her day.

M.'s essay on Shakespeare is perhaps her best-known work. It is a concerted defense of Shakespeare against the criticism of Voltaire as well as a consideration of several plays, such as *Henry IV,* part 1, and *Julius Caesar.* In her introduction to her readings of Shakespeare and Pierre Corneille, M. inveighs against what she sees as Voltaire's flawed translation of Shakespeare's *Julius Caesar* as well as his general disparagement of the bard. While she acknowledges Shakespeare's faultiness at points—in particular his disregard for Aristotle's dramatic "laws"—she nevertheless affirms that "nature and SENTIMENT will pronounce our Shakespeare a mighty genius." While somewhat parochial in its approach, her essay reveals a well-founded knowledge of the dramatic context of Shakespeare's plays. For the most part, her essay was applauded in England, especially by members of her own circle. It was said to be read aloud by Voltaire in the French salons he frequented, much to the delight and mirth of his audience.

BIBLIOGRPAHY: Johnson, R., ed., *Bluestocking Letters* (1926); Myers, S. H., *The Bluestocking Circle* (1990)

JENNIFER A. RICH

MONTAGU, [Lady] Mary Wortley
b. 26 May 1689, London; d. 21 August 1762, London

Both admired and reviled in her day, read, gossiped about, adored, and later attacked by Alexander POPE, among others, M. was a bright social and literary light in the court circles of George I. Today, she is best known for the lively letters she wrote during her husband's brief posting as ambassador to Constantinople, making some of the best travel literature ever published. However, along with such literary friends and acquaintances as Pope, Joseph ADDISON and Richard STEELE, John GAY and William CONGREVE, and later Mary Astell, M. also wrote much else, including satirical poems, essays, and criticism. Some of her work was published (anonymously) during her life; most of it was circulated in manuscript among acquaintances. Of her poems, the most familiar today include "Epistle of Mrs. Charlotte Yonge to Her Husband," a proto-feminist poem attacking the double standard inherent in the divorce laws of the time (not published in M.'s lifetime), and "The Reasons," a bawdy response to Jonathan SWIFT's poem "Lady's Dressing Room."

M. was born Mary Pierrepont, the eldest of the future Lord Dorchester's four children. She began reading voraciously and writing as a very young girl, filling albums with her juvenilia of poems and prose. She also undertook, at thirteen, to teach herself Latin in order to read ancient classics in the original language. To escape a forced marriage, she eloped with Edward Wortley Montagu in 1712. Then in 1714, Montagu was offered an appointment at the court of George I, and later won a parliamentary seat in Westminster. These events brought M. into a prominent position at court, where she cultivated a number of literary friendships and circulated her own writing. During 1715–16, inspired by Pope and Gay, M. wrote a series of "town eclogues," poems in imitation of Virgil's pastorals, which recorded and satirized the rivalries and concerns of the fashionable London society. Of these, perhaps the most poignant is "Eclog V," in which "Flavia" laments the loss of her beauty because of smallpox. M., whose only brother had died of smallpox in 1713, fell victim herself in December 1715, and was left permanently scarred.

In 1716, Edward Wortley Montagu was appointed ambassador to Constantinople. M., unusually for her time, chose to accompany him, excited by the prospect of distant travel. Her letters from Turkey to friends and family have become the writing for which M. is most famous. Open-minded and interested in everything she saw, M. wrote letters describing, often approvingly, Turkish life and customs. She overturned prevailing bias by suggesting that Turkish women actually had more freedom than did Western women. Observing in a letter to one correspondent that "common voyager-writers . . . are very fond of speaking of what they don't know," M. set out to present the reality of what she saw, including such titillating subjects (for Westerners) as the Turkish women's bagnio, or bath, and the harem. Sadly, M.'s frankness on such subjects would later be used by her enemies to smear her reputation. While in Turkey, M. also observed, wrote about, and later championed in England, the Turkish practice of inoculation against smallpox.

M.'s letters are lively, humorous, and filled with description. She continually punctures the myths and prejudices of her English readers, writing at one point that "[t]hese people [the Turks] are not so unpolished as we represent them." M. herself recognized the importance of her letters and expressed a desire to have them published after her death. Today, they are considered a classic of travel writing.

After M. returned home, she continued to write poetry, most of which circulated, as usual, privately and anonymously. During the 1720s, Pope's admiration for her changed, for uncertain reasons, into enmity, which he expressed in violent literary attacks (and which she and her supporters answered in kind).

Eventually separated from her husband, M. spent the last twenty years of her life in Italy, returning to London only a short time before her death. By then, a new standard of female decorum had made M. something of an embarrassment to her family. Indeed, the posthumous publication of the "Turkish Letters" horrified them. Today, however, M. is appreciated as an early, robust female voice among the male literati of her time.

BIBLIOGRAPHY: Epstein, J., "Wise, Foolish, Enchanting Lady Mary," *NewC* 13 (January 1995): 8–18; Grundy, I., *Lady M. W. M.* (1999); Pick, C., ed., *Embassy to Constantinople: The Travels of Lady M. W. M.* (1988)

LYNN McDONIE

MONTAGUE, John [Patrick]
b. 28 February 1929, New York City

Although born in the U.S., M. was reared in County Tyrone, Northern Ireland, and much of his poetry is concerned with rural Ireland. Other poems reminisce about time spent in France and the U.S. and rehearse family history. Collections are *Forms of Exile* (1958), *Poisoned Lands* (1961; rev. ed., 1977), *A Chosen Light* (1967), *Tides* (1970), *A Slow Dance* (1975), *The Great Cloak* (1978), *The Dead Kingdom* (1984), and *Time in Armagh* (1993). His *Collected Poems* appeared in 1996. Educated at St. Patrick's College, University College, Dublin, and the University of Iowa, he taught widely in the U.S. and Canada and returned from Paris in 1974 to teach at University College, Cork. In addition to his poetry, M. has published collections of essays and short stories and has edited various anthologies of Irish literature, including *The Faber Book of Irish Verse* (1974; repub. as *The Book of Irish* Verse, 1976).

MOORCOCK, [John] Michael
b. 18 December 1939, Mitcham, Surrey

Throughout his career, M.'s prolific output has been matched only by his ability and willingness to experi-

ment with literary genres and other avenues of expression. Early in his career, M. was a founding member of the 1960s "New Wave" of SCIENCE FICTION writers. He has since written novels, short stories, screenplays, pamphlets, and has composed songs for his own band, as well as the bands Hawkwind and Blue Oyster Cult. His characters have even appeared in a diverse collection of comic books and role-playing games, and several of his fictional creations have achieved a near-cult status among his readers. While some of M.'s work has been categorized as merely representative pulp science fiction and fantasy, he also has a reputation for imaginative experimentation and uncompromising attitudes about writing. While still known for mainstream fantasy and science fiction work, in more recent years he has received particular critical success for nonscientific fiction, and his iconoclastic opinions and the variety of his work continue to earn him the status of a noteworthy contemporary author.

In the 1960s, after leaving behind an editorial/writing position producing pulp-work for the magazine *Tarzan Adventures*, M. produced a number of traditional, commercially successful fantasy novels. He also published more diverse kinds of science fiction (occasionally under various pseudonyms), and eventually took over as editor of the New Wave magazine *New Worlds*. In 1961, M. created what would become one of his more popular creations, Elric, an albino, philosophical, introverted, fantasy swordsman who can only live by stealing the life energy of people whom he kills with his sword. The morally ambiguous hero confronts a universe where the forces of "Law" and "Chaos" leave little room for freedom or individual happiness. Often, M.'s works blend and intertwine, with the stories of Elric becoming linked over several narratives to M.'s other fictional worlds and heroes. While Elric has remained one of M.'s most enduring and popular figures, the 1960s would also see the creation of another of M.'s enduring and critically acclaimed characters, Jerry Cornelius, a character subsequently used by numerous other writers in their own stories. While Elric appeals to a collection of sword-and-fantasy aficionados, Cornelius was a scientific-oriented secret agent, and his adventures appeal to readers interested in SATIRE, or intricate and subversive critiques of contemporary culture and politics.

M. himself has shown public distaste for his own earlier work, which is perhaps one reason he has sometimes rewritten sections of his work in subsequent publications. Perhaps the clearest sign of his dislike for his earlier fiction is his willingness, particularly in the past few decades, to produce radically different works from those that made him originally well known as an author. *Gloriana; or, The Unfulfill'd Queen* (1978) is one such attempt to reestablish a standard for British writing, a tradition M. has proclaimed tarnished by what he considers overly sentimental and conformist authors such as J. R. R. TOLKIEN or C. S. LEWIS. Taking its subject matter from Edmund SPENSER's *Faerie Queene*, *Gloriana* is psychological in nature, with dark sexual subject matter, and with multiple ironic and enigmatic turns showing as much influence from POSTMODERNISM as it does from traditional readings of Spenser.

If *Gloriana* shows just how far from conventional fantasy M. has traveled, in the past several years he has been praised most for leaving it behind altogether. His most proclaimed recent work is *Mother London* (1988), an optimistic account of life, or intertwining lives, in the city, accounts given by people exchanging stories for psychotherapy. At times personal and individual, the novel is also historical and geographical in nature, mapping out the spaces and territories of London, including M.'s own memories of the shattered remnants of the city after World War II. The strength of the novel, according to critics and M. himself, lies in its attitude toward the possibilities and miracles of urban life.

Political, outspoken, and both immensely prolific and creative, M. continues to produce original and complex works at this point in his career. Though it is difficult to predict what he is likely to produce in the future, his current works alone are enough to grant him a place in 20th-c. British literature as the rare example of an author whose works have met acclaim from both critics and readers of popular fiction.

BIBLIOGRAPHY: Davey, J., *M. M.* (1991); Greenland, C., *The Entropy Exhibition: M. M. and the "New Wave" in British Science Fiction* (1983); Moorcock, M., and M. Foreman, *Letters from Hollywood* (1986)

                                    STEVEN ZANI

MOORE, Brian

b. 25 August 1921, Belfast, Northern Ireland; d. 11 January 1999, Malibu, California, U.S.A.

During a writing career that spanned almost half a century, M. was variously described as a Canadian writer, as an American writer, and sometimes, even, as an Irish writer. He was, in fact, an Irishman, born into a well-to-do Belfast Catholic family in the year that saw Ireland partitioned by the recent treaty with Britain into two separate political jurisdictions, the new Irish Free State and the smaller Northern Ireland in the northeast of the island. His father was an eminent Belfast physician, a senior surgeon at Belfast's Mater Infirmorum Hospital, later a member of the senate of the Queen's University as well as a lecturer and examiner. M. did not follow his father and older brother into the medical field and was soon to turn his back on his family's religious and political views. He

grew to young manhood just as World War II broke out in 1939. He joined the Air Raid Precautions Unit and witnessed the bombing of Belfast by the Germans in 1941. His experiences at this time were to provide memorably horrific scenes as the climax to his most autobiographical novel, *The Emperor of Ice Cream* (1966). In 1943, M. left Belfast to work as a civil servant with the British Ministry of War Transport in Algiers and toward the end of the war he worked with the United Nations Relief and Rehabilitation Administration in this capacity in Warsaw, Poland. He emigrated to Canada in 1948. Having failed to find work as a journalist in Toronto, he moved to Montreal where he got a job with the *Gazette*, first as a proofreader and later as a reporter. His experiences at this time would inform his novel *The Luck of Ginger Coffey* (1960).

About six years would pass before M. embarked on the writing of serious fiction. In this interim period in Montreal, in addition to his journalistic work, he wrote a number of crime novels under various pseudonyms. The fact that he chose to conceal his real identity, writing this kind of fiction as "Bernard Mara" or "Michael Bryan," suggests that M. was consciously serving a kind of necessary apprenticeship before embarking on his main career as novelist in 1955 with the publication of his first serious novel, *Judith Hearne*. Determined not to produce yet another Joycean Bildungsroman in the style of *A Portrait of the Artist as a Young Man,* M. chose as his first serious fictional protagonist not an arrogantly aspiring youth but a frustrated, middle-aged spinster, Judith Hearne, in whom he embodied his detestation of his native Belfast, with its provincial prudery and endemic sectarianism. This was the book in which he began to exorcise his youthful demons and to articulate fictional concerns that would continue to animate his subsequent novels for many years. He said of *Judith Hearne:* "In that first novel I discovered a subject which was, over the years, to become central to most of my writing. It is loneliness. It is, in particular, that desperation which invades people who discover their lives have no meaning."

Believing that failure is a more interesting condition than success and that women are more honest than men, M. would return again and again to the depiction of vulnerable female characters. Titles such as *I Am Mary Dunne* (1968), *The Doctor's Wife* (1976), *The Temptation of Eileen Hughes* (1981) echo this preoccupation and his last novel, *The Magician's Wife* (1997), gives it a final emphasis. The character of Judith Hearne, his seminal female figure, was based on a family friend, Mary Judith Keogh, who used to visit the Moore home in Belfast. M. traces Judith's decline from middle-class respectability to drunken despair with clinical skill. One by one, he removes the props on which her life in an unlovely city depends. Friends fail her, she loses the man who has come to represent her last hope of marriage, she seeks solace in religion and loses her faith in God, until in the end she lapses into alcoholic escapism and final despair. Her characterization establishes M. as the precise analyst of a particular kind of Irish-Catholic despondency that derives from an unlooked-for loss of a previously sustaining faith. He was to continue the exploration of such figures in *The Feast of Lupercal* (1957), *The Luck of Ginger Coffey*, and *Fergus* (1970). He would also extend his surgical explorations of despair into the area of the creative artist in such novels as *An Answer from Limbo* (1962) and *The Great Victorian Collection* (1975).

M. retained Canadian citizenship even after he left Canada for the U.S. and was to become what he himself dubbed "a chameleon novelist," a literary citizen of the world who achieved with striking success what is for many Irish writers the most difficult of transitions, the internationalization of his craft, setting stories not only in Belfast but also in Montreal, New York, Paris, London, California, Poland, and Haiti. One of his best novels, *Black Robe* (1985) is a superb evocation of the Canada of the 17th c. His determination not to repeat himself and to continue to find new plots in new places may well have cost him a settled audience. He essayed successfully genres as varied as the novella (*Catholics*, 1972); documentary (*The Revolution Script,* 1971); the Bildungsroman (*The Emperor of Ice Cream*); religious fantasy (*Cold Heaven*, 1985); the political thriller (*The Colour of Blood*, 1987); historical fiction (*Black Robe*), as well as the grim urban realism of the early Belfast novels. It is hardly surprising that Graham GREENE, that other great literary "entertainer," named M. as his personal favorite among modern novelists.

BIBLIOGRAPHY: Dahlie, H., *B. M.* (1981); Flood, J., *B. M.* (1974); Sampson, D., *B. M.* (1998)

JOHN CRONIN

MOORE, George [Augustus]

b. 24 February 1852, Moore Hall, County Mayo, Ireland; d. 22 January 1933, London

Ford Madox FORD once described M. in the *Atlantic Monthly* as "the most skilful man of letters of his day—the most skilful in the whole world"—no small feat for a man who came to writing as a painter manqué. Nearly every major artistic figure of his time encountered M. in one way or another, and he is credited (along with Henry JAMES) as one of the first writers to treat the novel as an art form in its own right. Oscar WILDE famously opined that M. conducted his education in public, but it was precisely his willingness to experiment with various styles that ultimately earned him a deserved reputation as an artistic visionary. The

Irish-born M. was advantaged by his unique position at the center of two important artistic movements of his day: the impressionist movement in Paris, and later, the Irish literary revival in Dublin. He proved a canny observer of and participant in both.

After abandoning painting (and befriending Degas and Manet, who advised him to "be ashamed of nothing but to be ashamed"), M. immersed himself in French literature. He aimed to bring French NATURALISM to Victorian England, to be "a ricochet of Zola in London." The stamp of the Flaubert art novel is clearly seen in his early efforts and he showed an early facility in *A Modern Lover* (1883). *A Mummer's Wife* (1885) delivered an unsentimental, naturalistic telling of a seamstress who abandons her husband for a Bohemian actor, including her gradual dissipation and death through alcoholism. The novel was followed by a harsh look at the peasant's miserable lot in *A Drama in Muslin* (1886). Anglo-Irish M. was a born aristocrat, if rather self-consciously so, and his book was regarded as traitorous by the upper class. The anonymously published *Parnell and His Island* (1887) irritated both landed and indentured classes alike. Next came *Confessions of a Young Man* (1888), the scandalous, ironically inflected recollections of an aesthete. *Esther Waters* (1894), which achieves a blend of unsentimental detachment and sympathy, has been widely hailed as M.'s "classic" novel. Lavishly praised by Katherine MANSFIELD, the book would today be recognized as the story of a struggling single mother and its feminist undertones are unmistakable.

In the frustrated lives of *Celibates* (1895) and the Wagner-spirited *Evelyn Innes* (1898), M. continued his trailblazing in the nascent sphere of English psychological literature, adapting the interior monologue technique from his friend Edouard Dujardin. Around that time, he scented the potential for a cultural renaissance in Ireland and decamped to Dublin where he joined the inner circle of Lady GREGORY's Coole Park intelligentsia. His collaboration with W. B. YEATS on the play *Diarmuid and Grania* (1901) brought about a rift (curiously exacerbated by M.'s insistence on the phrase "singing in the breasts") that was never repaired. M. would later tell all (to the embarrassment of family and acquaintances alike) in his masterly wry memoir, *Hail and Farewell* (1911).

M. distanced himself from the Irish revival after a few years but continued to write about Irish subjects. An outstanding volume of short stories entitled *The Untilled Field* (1903) resulted, followed by the poetic, religiously searching novel *The Lake* (1905). Clearly influenced by M.'s reading of Ivan Turgenev, some of the stories in *The Untilled Field* hold up favorably to the best Russian writing of the day. The collection probably influenced James JOYCE, who occasionally aped M. in print and harbored a lifelong admiration for him. Indeed, critic Ben Forkner marks the birth of the modern Irish short story with *The Untilled Field* for its definitively potent blend of native literary revival themes and Continental REALISM.

M. returned to London in 1911 and commenced work on *The Brook Kerith* (1916), an innately heretical prose EPIC about Jesus (the man) of Nazareth. His projects turned to the past: he essayed historical fiction again in *Héloïse and Abélard* (1921), rendered into English *The Pastoral Lives of Daphnis and Chloë* (1924), and enthused about ancient aesthetics in *Aphrodite in Aulis* (1930). The posthumously published *A Communication to my Friends* (1933) was M.'s parting shot.

M. is most often remembered for his novels, but he was also a trenchant art critic, a poetic dabbler, and playwright. He was a declared enemy of the censorship that hounded his career. A chronic but disciplined provocateur, astoundingly prolific and scrupulously faithful in his dedication to art, M. was a literary adept whose influence is still being apprehended. His grave marker states that "he deserted his family and friends for his art," but for all that, he was reclaimed.

BIBLIOGRAPHY: Brown, M., *G. M.* (1955); Frazier, A., *G. M., 1852–1933* (2000); Grubgeld, E., *G. M. and the Autogenous Self* (1994); Hone, J., *The Life of G. M.* (1936)

BRYAN A. GIEMZA

MOORE, Thomas
b. 28 May 1779, Dublin, Ireland; d. 25 February 1852, Sloperton Cottage, Wiltshire

M. wrote the words of several world-famous songs, among them: "The Last Rose of Summer," "The Minstrel Boy," "The Harp That Once through Tara's Halls," and "Believe Me, If All Those Endearing Young Charms," becoming a national bard of Ireland. A Roman Catholic, he went to Trinity College, Dublin, registering himself as a Protestant. At college, he made friends with Robert Emmet and became involved in nationalist politics. Emmet was executed in 1803 and M.'s poem "O Breathe Not His Name," published in *Irish Melodies* (1808), commemorates him. In 1798, M. moved to the Middle Temple, London, to study law, and became a social success, living beyond his means.

M. published anonymously *The Poetical Works of the Late Thomas Little, Esq.* (1801), referred to by Lord BYRON, in *English Bards and Scotch Reviewers*, and *Epistles, Odes and Other Poems* (1806). In 1803, M. was made registrar of the admiralty prize court in Bermuda, which established the value of captured enemy shipping and how the prize money should be distributed. M. tired of this employment and appointed a deputy. He produced two more books of

SATIRE, although the heroic couplet did not suit his talents. He returned to Dublin, but his songs were so popular that he had to keep returning to London to sing them to grand people. For twenty-five years, he wrote words to traditional Irish tunes and earned a regular income. Between 1812 and 1835, he published various political satires. In 1814, he was commissioned for three thousand guineas to supply a metrical romance on a Far Eastern subject, but was forestalled by Byron's *The Giaour* and *The Bride of Abydos*. However, when *Lalla Rookh* appeared in 1817, it was an immediate success and M. moved to Wiltshire. But his deputy in Bermuda had embezzled £6000, which M. was responsible for, so M. fled to mainland Europe, visiting Byron, who gave him the manuscript of his *Memoirs,* in Italy. M. was not able to return to England until 1822. During his exile, he had written another Oriental poem, *The Loves of the Angels* (1823), almost as popular as *Lalla Rookh*. *The Memoirs of Captain Rock* (1824) describes English misgovernment in Ireland, fueled by a tour with Lord Lansdowne. His *Memoirs of the Life of Sheridan* appeared in 1825. A prose tale, *The Epicurean*, appeared in 1827, *Legendary Ballads* in 1828, and the *Life and Death of Lord Edward Fitzgerald* in 1831.

Byron died in 1824. M. had sold the *Memoirs* to John Murray, Byron's publisher, but, after some dispute, Byron's irreplaceable manuscript was burned. M. wrote instead for Murray the *Letters and Journals of Lord Byron, with Notices of his Life* (1850). M. left an enormous number of books, among them *Travels of an Irish Gentleman in Search of a Religion* (2 vols., 1833), and his collected letters filled eight volumes (1853–56). M. was frequently mentioned in contemporary writing, especially by Byron.

BIBLIOGRAPHY: DeFord, M. A., *T. M.* (1967); Hoover, H. H., *Bolt Upright: The Life of T. M.* (2 vols., 1975); Strong, L. A. G., *The Minstrel Boy: A Portrait of T. M.* (1937)

MOORE, T[homas] Sturge
b. 4 March 1870, Hastings; d. 18 July 1944, Windsor

M. did not enjoy popular success during his lifetime, and there has been little scholarly attention paid to his work since. He remains a figure for discussion, however, because he seems to have been a "poet's poet," earning the respect of W. B. YEATS, Ezra Pound, Yvor Winters, and Douglas Bush. M. uses traditional materials and maintains a style of high philosophical seriousness that earned respect from fellow practitioners but also tended to make his work inaccessible. He used classical literature and the Bible as the sources of his inspiration, arguing that the use of old materials allows the poet the "distance that enchants, and a marriage of old associations with new insight without which it remains raw and indigestible." He thus rejected the ethic of the Georgians who sought contemporary REALISM and distinguished himself from the modernists who sought to make new the materials of the literature of the past with arresting new styles or the juxtaposition of the old and the new. Unfortunately, he did not found a movement or fit in with other like-minded poets, so he never connected with a large audience. Over a fairly long career, M. wrote criticism, verse dramas, and an impressive body of both short and longer poems. His work reminds us of the many possibilities of modern poetry as it entered the 20th c.

M. had studied art as well as poetry and produced, on commission, three works of art criticism: *Altdorfer* (1900), *Albert Dürer* (1905), and *Correggio* (1906). M. found these artists attractive because they devoted themselves to their craft and because they celebrated classical themes and the representation of physical beauty in the light of Christian teachings. In addition to works on specific visual artists, M. wrote essays on Matthew ARNOLD, Yeats, and the soldier poets of World War I. He provided useful notes in volumes of his own poems to elucidate his critical perceptions of the nature of poetry. He also carried on a correspondence with Yeats for over thirty-five years; the surviving letters show very different approaches to the use of the past and of contemporary materials. In addition to these scattered works and remarks, M.'s most extensive critical work appeared in *Art and Life* (1910), *The Powers of the Air* (1920), and *Armour for Aphrodite* (1929). *Art and Life* is a study of Gustave Flaubert and William BLAKE, both artists who dedicated themselves wholly to the pursuit of their work and who pursued intellectual as well as physical beauty in their art. As he surveys the work of these very different artists, M. discusses art and style as forces running counter to natural tendencies to chaos. This approach leads to a view of the artist as one who brings order as he draws upon the past to create something that has universal and objective appeal rather than the fleeting meaning of a given historical moment. *The Powers of the Air* takes the form of a Platonic dialogue in which the interlocutors debate the question of beauty and the function of art in society. Finally, in *Armour for Aphrodite*, M. looks at the relation between beauty, truth, and goodness. He argues for the importance of using old themes and images to represent universal truth and of the necessity of art for the continuation of society. Although none of these works contains any particularly original thought, they all suggest the mind of an artist struggling with the big questions of art both in his time and as a universal principle.

Although his criticism is largely ignored, Winters ranked M.'s verse dramas alongside the work of the Renaissance masters. In his plays, M. turned to the biblical and classical past for his materials, although

he also wrote one play based on Norse legend (*Tyrfing*, 1920) and two using Spanish materials, including *Roderigo of Bivar* (1925), using stories from the EPIC *El Cid*. The three biblical dramas *Absalom* (1903), *Judith* (1911), and *Mariamne* (1911) explore the relations between love, beauty, and trust as they are played out in M.'s dramatization of the moral choices that define the characters of his protagonists. While M.'s defenders see what is "new" or at least what is universal in these stories, the often complex and tangled language dilutes the dramatic impact that the works have either in performance or on the page. Several critics nevertheless defend *Daimonassa* (1930), which Winters called "M.'s greatest work and one of the greatest works in English." The play recounts the story of King Kyrkaeus of ancient Greece. The ruler seeks revenge against his brother Orcan by persuading his two daughters to marry Orcan's two sons and then to kill them on their wedding night so that Orcan's only heirs will be Kyrkaeus's grandchildren. The play centers on the moral choices and guilt that face Daimonassa as she must decide between her loyalty to her father's need for revenge and her loyalty to a husband she loves. Although readers may be impressed with the complexity and passion of the drama, many will find the final triumph and tragedy of Daimonassa hard to fathom. As Bush has noted, we do not feel the "moving reality" of a story full of "violent and improbable incidents," characters who are little more than "silhouettes" and a rather "unsympathetic" heroine who nonetheless triumphs in the end at the expense of her humanity.

While M.'s defenders tout his importance as a philosopher of art and a verse dramatist, his work remains most accessible in his short lyric poetry. He wrote a number of longer poems based on classical and biblical themes and characters, including *Danäe* (1903), *The Rout of the Amazons* (1903), and *Medea* (1904). One of the most interesting, and according to some critics "ambitious," of these poems is *Judas* (1924), which is notable because M. takes an objective attitude to the character of Judas, the archetypal betrayer. Here again, some critics have been impressed by M.'s ability to sustain a long poem that addresses important concerns of universal importance (in contrast to the poems of realistic detail or personal confession that seemed to dominate the poetry of M.'s day and indeed of our own). These critics argue that M. was indeed finding a way to suit his individual talent to the tradition. On the other hand, it is often hard to see exactly how these high-minded verses constitute something "new." Indeed, even the most familiar of M.'s shorter poems like "Silence" or the "picture poem" entitled "From Titian's 'Bacchanal' in the Prado at Madrid," with their cool and complex treatment of artistic themes, may strike the modern reader as somehow effete, as too detached from the complexity of human experience to have the universal appeal that M. sought.

In a 1932 review, the poet J. V. Cunningham ranked M. alongside Thomas HARDY, Robert BRIDGES, and Yeats as a "major poet" because of his attention to "the central moral temptation of our time: That spiritual pride which would overreach natural limits." Certainly questions of morality and choice are perennial concerns that should continue to command our attention. M. unfortunately failed to create a sense of the urgency for his artistic concerns that may have relegated him to the status of a minor poet whose work no longer has the currency of Hardy and Yeats. Even his defenders note the faults of his rather cluttered and complex style and his tendency to suggest rather than make his ideas explicit. Defenders never seem to feel that they have understood the work; some complain of an unfinished quality, although they express the hope that the work of a mind of such "purity" and "seriousness" will not be lost or neglected. It is as a poet to be tackled rather than enjoyed that M. will endure.

BIBLIOGRAPHY: Bush, D., *Mythology and the Romantic Tradition in English Poetry* (1932; rev. ed., 1963); Cunningham, J. V., "Moral Poetry," *Commonweal* 16 (July 27, 1932): 335; Winters, Y., "The Poetry of T. S. M.," *SoR* 2 (1966): 1–16

CATHERINE FRANK

MORE, Hannah

b. 2 February 1745, Stapleton; d. 7 September 1833, Clifton

M. has long been widely dismissed as an earnest, limited moralist, and a dull writer. For much of her life, M. certainly saw it as her mission to reform the morals of both the upper and lower classes. However, unusually for her time, M. also advocated education for girls and for the rural poor. In the service of both aims, she was a prolific writer, publishing five plays, numerous poems, religious tracts (for which she is best known today), a novel, and, in her old age, four works distilling her religious thoughts and principles.

M. was strongly influenced by her father, Jacob More, a teacher and headmaster of a school near Bristol, who believed in the power of education for girls as well as boys. He taught the five More sisters at home; unlike nearly all of their female contemporaries, the Mores studied such traditionally masculine subjects as Latin and a limited amount of mathematics. In 1758, when M. was only thirteen, the More sisters established a boarding school in Bristol for young ladies, offering a curriculum that was more rigorous than the usual superficial accomplishments taught at fashionable boarding schools.

It was at this period that the teenaged M., who had been writing since she was three, first began to write her plays, four of which were eventually produced on the public stage. The first play, *The Search after Happiness* (1773), a morally edifying play written for the pupils of her school to perform, was designed to be as free from morally suspect "wit" as possible. Though it was dull theater, *The Search after Happiness* became popular with teachers and parents, selling thousands of copies by 1787. While the play's moral—happiness cannot be found through worldly pursuits—is a conventionally pious one, M. also seemed, at least in this play, to advocate the fairly radical idea that women must obey God rather than man. This challenged the prevailing notion that women must look to husbands and fathers for moral and intellectual guidance. It was a stand, however, that M. regularly seemed to undercut in her numerous later works. All of M.'s writings, in any case, reflect her generally conservative moral and social concerns: the need for the moral and religious reform of all classes of society; the importance of educating women and the poor; and (sometimes paradoxically) the importance of maintaining the traditional social and sexual hierarchies. This was achieved by refusing to teach village children to write and by limiting their training to such "coarse work" as might fit them for servants.

An annuity left to M. in 1772 allowed her to leave the Bristol school and move in London intellectual circles. She went on to write and stage another four plays, and, with the help and advice of the actor David GARRICK, learned to write livelier characters and better dramatic action, while still teaching a Christian message. She also began writing and publishing poetry—didactic, like her plays—attracting enthusiastic audiences in London, including Samuel JOHNSON. M.'s intensely moral poetry shows her facility with the rhymed couplet, the popular verse form among the wits and satirists of the time.

After Garrick's death in 1779, M. wrote no more for the London stage, instead undergoing a conversion to Evangelicalism. M. and her sisters then turned to founding rural Sunday schools in the villages of Somerset, while she continued to write poetry, stories, tracts, and biblical dramas for the moral edification of both the upper and lower classes. M. also became involved in, and wrote for, the antislavery movement.

In 1792, M. published *Village Politics*, a pamphlet for the common people that argued against the dangerous ideas of "liberty and equality" that had begun to migrate from France during the Revolution. This pamphlet, in turn, led in 1795 to the work with which M.'s literary reputation is most associated today. For three years, she wrote as well as edited the collection of ballads, allegories, and short stories that would become the Cheap Repository Tracts (3 vols., 1795–98), intended to reform the habits and morals of the middle and lower estates of British society. Deeply conservative, even reactionary, the work reflected widespread alarm at the excesses of the French Revolution. Illustrating a firm belief in a class-based hierarchy, the stories in Cheap Repository supported the doctrine of "paternalism," which held that those in authority were obliged to "comfort and control" dependents to ensure social stability. The fifty stories and ballads that M. contributed, addressed to both the lower and "Middle Ranks" of society, confer rewards on the religious and virtuous characters—including the "deserving" poor—who defend the status quo; their discontented or irreligious antagonists suffer various dreadful punishments. Other characters, like Jack Brown in "The Two Shoemakers," are morally flawed but likable characters who eventually convert and change their sinful ways. Heavy-handed and unsubtle as they are, today M.'s stories are also recognized as contributing to the development of the short story.

When M. was sixty-three, she published her only novel, *Coelebs in Search of a Wife* (1808), in which she again outlined her theories on female education, while also dramatizing her ideas of the qualities necessary for a perfect marriage. Reviews were mixed, but the book, which also insisted on separate spheres for the sexes, was hugely popular. However, as Madame de Staël (who loved the novel) seems to have been aware, the serious female education that M. urged was more likely to blur separate spheres for men and women than to reinforce them.

Near the end of her life, M. published her four major religious works, including a study of the life of St. Paul. Today, as was often the case in her own day, M.'s writing is generally dismissed as numbingly didactic; her social views are regarded as rigidly static, defending the class system and the inherent right of the upper classes to authority over the lower classes; her views on women's roles appear conflicting and contradictory. Often overlooked, however, is her belief (shared, ironically, by the radical Mary WOLLSTONECRAFT) in rigorous, rather than frivolous, education for well-off girls as well as for their brothers; her championing of schools (and thus literacy) for the poor; and her example of an active, engaged life, at a time when women were generally consigned to the domestic sphere.

BIBLIOGRAPHY: Demers, P., *The World of H. M.* (1996); Ford, C. H., *H. M.* (1996); Nardin, J., "Avoiding the Perils of the Muse: H. M., Didactic Literature, and Eighteenth-Century Criticism," *PLL* 36 (Fall 2000): 377–91

LYNN McDONIE

MORE, [Sir] Thomas
b. 7 February 1477, London; d. 6 July 1535, London

British man of letters, statesman, and Chancellor of England (1529–32), M. was one the leading humanists in northern Europe, including among his friends Desiderius ERASMUS and John COLET. He was also an early sponsor of the painter Hans Holbein the Younger. Falling from office because of his opposition to HENRY VIII's divorce from Catherine of Aragon, and refusing to accept the repudiation of papal supremacy, M. was imprisoned, and eventually tried and executed. The Roman Catholic Church canonized him on May 19, 1935. The Elizabethan comedy, *Sir Thomas More*, first performed around 1593, celebrated his wit and merriment. Robert BOLT's play *A Man for All Seasons*, and the subsequent film, idealized his character.

At an early stage of his life, M. served as a page in the household of Cardinal John Morton, Archbishop of Canterbury and Lord Chancellor. Torn between a desire to pursue a religious vocation and a need to satisfy his father's ambitions, M. accepted a call to the bar, but also tested his vocation with the Carthusian monks in the Charterhouse of London, lecturing on Augustine's *City of God* and composing poems in English. Thereafter, he entered public life and married, his home becoming an important center for the humanists. Erasmus dedicated *In Praise of Folly* (*Encomium Moriae*) to M.

M.'s writings fall broadly into three phrases, echoing the stages of his life and career. The first phase contains his great humanist works, including his English fabliau, *A Merry Jest*, dating around 1503, Latin translations of the dialogues of Lucian (1506), an English translation of the *Lyfe of Johan Picus Erle of Mirandula* (1510), the *History of King Richard III* (wr. 1513–18), *Utopia* (1516), and his assorted Latin poems, epigrams, and letters. A councilor in the king's service, he wrote *Responsio ad Lutherum* (1523), supporting Henry VIII's *Defence of the Seven Sacraments* against Martin Luther's attack. In the second phase, M. was commissioned in 1528 by Cuthbert Tunstall, Bishop of London, to read and respond to heretical writings in English. Between 1529 and 1533, M. published seven polemical works, the most important of these including *A Dialogue Concerning Heresies* (1529), *Confutation of Tyndale's Answer* (2 vols., 1532–33), *Apology of Sir Thomas More, Knight* (1533), and *Debellation of Salem and Bizance* (1533). As M. recognized his political position was becoming more precarious, he shifted to devotional work, preparing in 1534 *A Treatise on the Passion*. In the final phase, M. produced the so-called Tower Works (wr. 1534–35), *A Dialogue of Comfort against Tribulation* and *De tristitia Christi*, while a prisoner in the Tower of London.

More's *History of King Richard III* is often regarded as the first masterpiece of English historiography. Based on classical models, and drawing on the accounts he gathered in the court of Cardinal Morton, M. created the image of Richard as the crook-backed tyrant that became the basis for William SHAKE-SPEARE's play. Among his later works, the *Dialogue of Comfort* remains a moving contribution to Christian wisdom literature. Set during the siege of Budapest by the Turks, the dialogue is between Vincent and his uncle, Anthony. Tribulation, Anthony explains, is not a punishment, but a divine gift, a spiritual medicine, which focuses men on prayer and spiritual matters.

M.'s masterpiece is *Utopia*. Divided into two parts, it is ostensibly based on a conversation among M., humanist Peter Giles, and the traveler Raphael Hythloday. In the second part, Hythloday, whose name means, "well-learned in nonsense," describes the social, religious, and political institutions of the island kingdom of Utopia, a pagan society based entirely on reason and without Christianity. In the first part, he describes a visit to the court of Cardinal Morton. This centers on a debate over the limited prospects of the humanist scholar in the context of contemporary European courts. In its context, Morton's household becomes the true ideal of the Christian-humanists society, set against the stoic pagan alternative.

Playful and ironic, *Utopia* shares much with Erasmus's *Praise of Folly*. Its elusiveness of tone and wordplay have spawned many contradictory interpretations. Early critics saw it as advocating paganism at the expense of Christianity. More recent readers find a proto-Marxist socialism. Others, looking at the Greek pun in the title—*u-topia* ("no place") and *eu-topia* ("happy place")—note an ironic ambivalence. Like Plato's *Republic*, from which M. draws heavily, the ideal commonwealth is as much a means for criticizing the contemporary state of things, as positing a blueprint for the alternative.

BIBLIOGRAPHY: Ackroyd, P., *The Life of T. M.* (1998); Fox, A., *T. M.* (1982); Marius, R., *T. M.* (1985); Martz, L. L., *T. M.* (1990)

THOMAS L. COOKSEY

MORGAN, Charles [Langbridge]

b. 22 January 1894, Bromley, Kent; d. 6 February 1958, London

M. was a romantic, a philosophic idealist, and something of a mystic. The strong appeal that he made to his English public in the 1930s and early 1940s evaporated in the postwar years, and he rapidly became stranded, the victim of literary fashion. During this period, he continued to exert influence over literary life and his presidency of International PEN, from 1953 to 1958, was a notable success, inspired by his deep knowledge and feeling for Continental culture, and his commitment to international harmony, a theme that runs through many of his writings. His

books were translated into nineteen languages, and his reputation on the Continent, especially in France, was considerably higher than it was at home. He admired what he saw in French thought and literature as the freedom to express ideas, and the French showed their appreciation of his work by making him an officer of the Legion of Honor and a member of the Institute of France, an honor bestowed, at that time, upon only one other British novelist, Rudyard KIPLING.

M. harbored ambitions to become a writer as early as the age of eleven and he entered the navy as a midshipman, with the intention of having a career that would support him and his writing. He started his career in the navy in 1907, at the age of thirteen. His first novel, *The Gunroom* (1919), interleaves his experiences in the navy with a rather soft romance.

Nevertheless, it introduces something of his concerns, particularly in the depiction of the mindless, and largely impersonal, degrading initiation rituals, through which midshipmen were required to pass at that time. The novel went through a series of vicissitudes, including being lost at sea, when a mine sank the ship on which M. was being repatriated to England, during the war. On publication, it is not clear what happened, but it was mysteriously withdrawn from publication, though whether this was due to censorship has never been proved. What is clear is that it contributed to reforms within the navy. M. left the navy in 1913. He intended to enter Brasenose College, Oxford, the next year, but the outbreak of war sent him back into the navy. His active career was even shorter than his previous enlistment as he took part in a disastrous naval attack on Antwerp. Interned in Holland throughout the war, he was billeted as the guest of the de Pallandt family, which was the equivalent of an education in European culture and languages, and inspired his commitment to cultural internationalism. At the end of the war, M. entered Oxford to read history and became president of the Oxford University Dramatic Society. In this capacity, a meeting with A. B. Walkley led to his being appointed to the staff of the *Times,* and, successively, Walkley's deputy and later, principal dramatic critic of the paper. He held this position until 1939. He successfully combined criticism with writing novels, his first major work being *Portrait in a Mirror* (1929), for which he was awarded the Prix Femina/Vie Heureuse. Three years later, *The Fountain* (1932) was the first of his works to achieve best-seller status. The amalgam of a passionate love story, set in 1915, with echoes of the poetry and quietism of 17th-c. mystics, the novel achieved critical as well as popular success and was awarded the Hawthornden Prize for 1933.

M. continued his career with *Sparkenbroke* (1936) and *The Voyage* (1940), for which he was awarded the James Tait Black Memorial Prize. In addition to these two works, he wrote an outstanding book-length essay, *Epitaph on George Moore* (1935), and turned his dramatic faculties to writing a successful play, *The Flashing Stream* (1938; rev. ed., 1948). During World War II, M. rejoined the navy, although his greatest value seems to have been as a propagandist, and in liaison with forces in exile. Articles of his circulated among the French Resistance, he was among the first of the English noncombatants to enter liberated Paris, and his "Ode to France" was read aloud at the reopening of the Comédie Française.

In many ways, M. was a man of his time, reacting and reflecting, rather than acting, upon the events through which he lived, two wars and the rise to power of totalitarian dictatorships. *The Judge's Story* (1947) centers round a conflict between good and evil and *The River Line* (1949), which was later turned into a successful play, is the study of a spiritually minded man set against a background of movement and violence. M. continued to write until his death, including several volumes of essays in which he extended his search for permanent values amid the insecurities and confusions of a troubled and restless time of transition. In the face of what he saw as the materialist threat to individualism and freedom of expression, M. retreated into an almost superhuman singleness of purpose, which crosses the border into mysticism. His detractors saw M.'s work as overliterary and pretentious, especially in its philosophical flights; his "secular mysticism, specious to the point of being persuasive." What cannot be denied is his integrity and the depth of his personal convictions, which were expressed with a high sense of style and conscious craftsmanship. The concerns that were the driving force behind his writing have scarcely diminished. It would be difficult to imagine a sudden revival of critical interest in M.'s literary work, but his essays certainly repay a visit.

BIBLIOGRAPHY: Duffin, H. C., *The Novels and Plays of C. M.* (1959); Lewis, E., ed., *Selected Letters of C. M.* (1967); Morgan, C., *Reflections in a Mirror* (2 vols., 1944–46)

CLIVE BARKER

MORGAN, Edwin [George]
b. 27 April 1920, Glasgow, Scotland

Author of the famous hiccuping comic concrete poem, "The Computer's First Christmas Card" (1963), M. was revered Professor of English at Glasgow University, his alma mater, from 1975 until retirement in 1980. Much of his work is about the impact of new technologies. He has published several volumes of poetry, much of it experimental, many evoking the Scottish urban landscape, as in *Glasgow Sonnets* (1972) and *Sonnets from Scotland* (1984). *The Vision of Cathkin Braes* (1952) was his first col-

lection. There are two volumes of selections: *Poems of Thirty Years* (1982) and *Selected Poems* (1985). Editions of his *Collected Poems* appeared in 1990 and 1996. He has also translated poetry from French, Spanish, German, Hungarian, and Italian originals. A noted literary critic, he has written on a wide range of modern Scottish writers, including Hugh MacDIARMID.

MORGAN, Lady. See OWENSON, Sydney

MORRIS, William
b. 24 March 1834, Walthamstow; d. 3 October 1896, Kelmscott

Poet, designer of textiles and wallpaper, successful businessman, father (often so-called) of the Arts and Crafts movement, radical socialist, writer of prose romances, translator (in collaboration) of the Icelandic sagas and Virgil's *Aeneid* (1875), as well as the *Odyssey* (2 vols., 1887), and inspirer of the revived interest in the book arts at the end of the 19th c., M.'s fate in the modern and postmodern periods has been to be remembered in pieces, if at all. Called a "Renaissance figure" in his own time, and described by his doctor at his death of having died "from doing the work of ten men," his rise and fall as an important 19th-c. figure can almost be used as a gauge for changes in 20th-c. artistic and political culture.

Born in Walthamstow, then a suburb of London, M., the son of a man who had become wealthy (dying when M., one of five children, was twelve), matriculated at Exeter College, Oxford University, in 1853, and there began his friendship with the painter Edward Burne-Jones that was to be central in his life. There, too, he decided (against his mother's intentions) to follow art as a career rather than take Holy Orders; and did the reading and traveling that laid the foundation of much to come. John RUSKIN's *Stones of Venice* and *Edinburgh Lectures,* respectively, encouraged his incipient love of medieval architecture and made him aware of the painters known as the Pre-Raphaelites. Trips to northern France and Belgium, where he saw Bouvais and Rouen Cathedrals, as well as paintings by Memling and van Eyck, furthered the lines of development that reading Ruskin had begun. It was at Oxford that M. began to write poetry.

Articled to the Oxford architect G. E. Street in 1856, the year in which he took his B.A. degree, M. moved to London when Street did, taking rooms with Burne-Jones. By the end of the year, he had also met Dante Gabrial ROSSETTI and, encouraged by Rossetti, abandoned architecture for painting.

His first public success, however, was not as a painter—he was never to succeed as one—but as a poet. *The Defence of Guenevere and Other Poems* was published in 1858 at his own expense and received favorable notice. One critic compared him to Alfred, Lord TENNYSON. But restlessness, variety, and ventures, as well as experiments in new directions, are the keys to M.'s career. Married to the beautiful Jane Burden (daughter of an Oxford stable hand) in 1859, he had his friend Philip Webb build for him and his bride, and he hoped Burne-Jones and his recent bride, Red House, in Upton, Kent. The Burne-Joneses decided against moving in, ending M.'s dream of a "Palace of Art," but Red House proved significant in many ways. Still today regarded as a fine example of imaginative Victorian architecture, it was for M. a new challenge: how to furnish it when he liked nothing being manufactured at the time. Along with his friends, he made and painted furniture and stitched fabrics, and this enterprise led to the formation, in 1861, of Morris, Marshall, Faulkner, and Company, destined to be, under the later name of Morris and Co., a profound influence on Victorian taste in interior decoration and a paradigm for the growing Arts and Crafts movement of the 1880s, itself a preparation for the acceptance of the modern design and painting that Roger FRY introduced in the postimpressionist exhibition of 1910.

In poetry, M., now a busy business man, discovered his true inclination to be the writing of epics, and so began *The Earthly Paradise,* a narrative poem modeled on Geoffrey CHAUCER's *The Canterbury Tales,* another of M.'s early and enduring loves, in which a company of northerners, sailing south to escape the plague, land on a Greek island. There, they and the inhabitants agree to tell two stories a month, the northerners a Nordic tale and the Greeks a classical legend. *The Earthly Paradise,* published in three volumes between 1868 and 1870, extended M.'s reputation as a poet beyond a small circle of critics and admirers.

By 1870, domestic bliss, if it had ever existed, was at an end for M. Jane Morris and Rossetti had become lovers. M.'s two daughters, Jane (Jenny) and Mary (May), were a solace for him, but work was the only real answer. The firm prospered, with M. becoming more and more the chief designer, and in 1876 a new chapter in his life story began. He published *Sigurd the Volsung,* a one-volume EPIC that is one of his finest poetic achievements. He made his first move into politics, becoming the treasurer of Eastern Question Association, a liberal organization devoted to keeping England out of the Russo-Turkish War, no small effort, since Benjamin DISRAELI and the Conservative government thought it essential that Russian expansion into the West be stopped. One year earlier the firm had dissolved, with much bitterness on the part of some, and was renamed Morris and Co. But in 1876, too, M.'s daughter Jenny suffered an epileptic attack, a dark signal that she was to be a semi-invalid the rest of her life, becoming, simultaneously, M.'s

chief worry and the object of his deepest love and devotion.

By 1879, he had helped found the Society for the Protection of Ancient Buildings (SPAB), whose first project was to protest proposed restorations at St. Mark's, Venice. (The implicit cultural imperialism went unnoticed by M.: St. Marks was a possession of all Europe in his eyes.) The creed of the SPAB, taken from Ruskin, was simple. When an ancient building is in need of repairs, do not try to restore it. The building is part of the fabric of history. The 19th-c imagination cannot reconceive and reconstruct the work of an artisan of centuries back: it can only falsify it. Do nothing but stop further deterioration. If a gargoyle has fallen off a medieval cathedral, put a slab of concrete across the exposed surface

But writing poetry, managing the growing business of Morris and Co., as well as designing for it, and forwarding the mission of the SPAB were not enough for M. In 1878, the Russo-Turkish War ended, and the Liberals had succeeded in keeping England out of the conflict. In the next year, M. became treasurer of the National Liberal League, an organization he thought was dedicated to radical social reform at home. But it did not move fast enough for him, and in 1883 he joined H. M. Hyndman's Democratic Federation, the first British socialist group to commit itself to Marx's theory of history and prophecy of a working class revolt. Then began an amazing period of lecturing on behalf of the Democratic Federation— its name soon changed to the Social Democratic Federation—all over England, Scotland, and Ireland. In these many lectures several themes persist. M. is against struggling for change by entering Parliament. Socialists in Parliament do nothing but adopt bourgeois values. A sporadic warning of the danger of revolution permeates the essays from time to time; but the main argument is that there is a need to educate (in Marx's term, "to raise the consciousness of the proletariat") so that it realizes it *is* the working class and that it is engaged in class war with capitalists, the industrialists who own the factories and the mines. M.'s central interest, however, was asking and answering the question, Change society for what purpose? For him, the answer was to liberate the workers to realize themselves as creative, imaginative craftspeople, with enough leisure to take pleasure in their work and with an unfettered imagination at play when they do work. The ideal image is the ordinary individual who helped build the medieval cathedral, hewing out a rough and grotesque gargoyle that expressed the true self of the workman-craftsman: the workman-craftsman who is the protagonist of Ruskin's *Stones of Venice.* The one narrative by M. still most often read today, *News from Nowhere* (1890), is a vision of a future, the 21st c., when, after a revolution along lines prophesied by Marx, the England of the 14th c.

has been restored (not envisioned by Marx) and the inhabitants, who know nothing of money, ugly architecture, or class conflict (there are no classes) devote themselves to making and decorating useful articles, as well as enjoying those made by others, helping to bring in the harvest, and experiencing genuine love and friendship between the sexes—staying married as long as it suits both parties to do so but separating amicably when one or both no longer wants the tie. The story is a dream, encountered by the first-person narrator "Guest," who indeed falls in love with the ideal woman of M./Guest's dreams. Ellen is her name. She is healthy and tanned; working in the fields she is scantily—i.e., sensibly—dressed; she is self-confident, open, merry in spirit; in brief, all that Jane Morris was not for M.

One could go on, detailing M.'s works and achievements, citing the titles of collections of poems, collections of essays, and discussing a series of prose romances he wrote late in his life, notably *A Tale of the House of the Wolfings* (1889), *The Story of the Glittering Plain* (1891), *The Wood beyond the World* (1894), and *The Well at the World's End* (1896). But the one achievement in his later life that carried most forcefully into the 20th c. was the founding of the Kelmscott Press in 1891. Dissatisfied as usual with what the Victorian era had produced, M. became dedicated to reforming what he saw was the deep decline in standards and ideas governing the book arts. He designed his own type, sought out the manufacturers of paper and ink that suited him (he had to go to Germany for the ink), laid down rules for spacing and margins, based on medieval standards, and employed decorative elements, again giving rebirth to the vision of what a book is or should be, which he found in the best medieval manuscripts and early printed books.

Today, many of the books produced by the Kelmscott Press seem to defeat their own purpose—to make the reader unaware of the type while absorbed in reading. But they still succeed in reminding us that there is an important visual dimension to all we read, what Jerome J. McGann calls the "bibliographical codes," and that responding, however subliminally, to type design, spacing, margins, and decorations and illustrations is indeed part of the experience of reading. That the masterpiece of the Kelmscott Press, the *Chaucer,* today brings astronomical sums at auctions, perhaps proves nothing of its intrinsic worth as a book to read. But many people in the book arts regard it, as well as other Kelmscott productions, as inspiring not only the small press movement of the 20th c. but vastly more important, the awareness of the effect of design on the linguistic message, whatever be its context: advertising poster, magazine layout, or, indeed, books. Using the Kelmscott Press as an excuse for indulging himself, M. also built one of the most important 19th-c. collections of medieval manuscripts and early printed books (he needed them as models, he said). Many of the best of them have been kept together and are now in the Pierpont Morgan Library in New York.

Of enormous impact in his own age, as a hero of every movement from poetry to radical politics (the socialist movements in both England and the U.S.—especially England—regarded him as a seminal figure; W. B. YEATS was an early admirer of his poetry; and his fabric designs are still available), as a face that showed up during the 1960s on a lapel button along with others in the series featuring Marx, Engels, Che Guevara, and Mao Zedong, M. to this day inspires a band of loyal devotees. They continue to read him, admire his designs, and base scholarship on his life and works. He has yet to catch fire again in any area with the possible exception of fabric design, but "Renaissance man" that he was, protean figure who left his mark on so many areas of Victorian and early modern culture, he cannot be forgotten. An unpublished novel by the modernist poet H. D., entitled *White Rose and the Red*, has M. as its protagonist. He was in fact a crucial figure to her throughout her life; she never lost her enthusiasm for his poetry and prose romances. And McGann, citing M. as the precursor of the movement in modernist poetry in which typography and design are essential to the substance of a poem (E. E. Cummings, Marianne Moore, and Ezra Pound are examples), has kept M. in the discourse of textual scholarship today. What part of M.'s achievement will be rediscovered next remains to be seen, but it is a good bet that something will—perhaps his socialism, based as much on Ruskin as on Marx, and, at heart, a form of advanced humanism.

BIBLIOGRAPHY: Faulkner, P., ed., *W. M.* (1973); Faulkner, P., and P. Preston, eds., *W. M.* (1999); Kelvin, N., ed., *The Collected Letters of W. M.* (4 vols., 1984–96); MacCarthy, F., *W. M.* (1994); Silver, C., *The Romance of W. M.* (1982); Stansky, P., *Redesigning the World: W. M., the 1880s, and the Arts and Crafts* (1985); Thompson, E. P., *W. M.* (1955)

NORMAN KELVIN

MORTIMER, John [Clifford]
b. 21 April 1923, London

A practicing barrister as well as a prolific and highly regarded author in theater, television, and fiction, M. extends the honorable tradition of the literary lawyer into the 21st c. He has created the most memorable fictional lawyer of the late 20th c. in his short stories and television series about Rumpole of the Bailey, as well as humane comedy in several media.

The son of a prominent barrister and expert in probate and divorce law, M. was educated at the elite public (private) school Harrow and at Oxford University. He emerged from this ruling-class education with a dislike of organized sports and all-male institutions, a disbelief in Christianity, and a progressive outlook on politics and society. After working in the Crown Film Unit during World War II, he followed his father into the law, despite his literary inclinations, qualifying as a barrister in 1948. To support a young family while building up a legal practice, he at first wrote novels, then pragmatically switched to plays in the latter half of the 1950s. This was a time of both expansion and experiment for British dramatists, with new opportunities in radio and television, and the emergence of a critical social realism in the theater. In the law, M. achieved great success in civil liberties trials in the 1960s, defending the young editors of radical publications like *Oz* against charges of obscenity. In the iconoclastic and liberal climate of that decade, his own creativity and legal expertise made him a ready and effective advocate for libertarian issues in Britain and internationally. In 1966, he was instructed by Amnesty International to fly to Nigeria and represent Wole Soyinka, the future recipient of the Nobel Prize for Literature, who was on trial for political offenses. Personal history has become literary subject in some of M.'s most accomplished works, notably his play *A Voyage Round My Father* (perf. 1970; pub. 1971) and his autobiographies, *Clinging to the Wreckage* (1982) and *Murderers and Other Friends* (1992).

His plays of the 1950s offer contemporary vignettes of a residual but threadbare gentility in traditional English institutions and types—the briefless barrister in *The Dock Brief* (1958), the minor public school in *What Shall We Tell Caroline?* (1958), the divorce detective seeking evidence of adultery in a torpid seaside hotel in *I Spy* (1959). These plays were first staged contemporaneously with the early work of John OSBORNE, Harold PINTER, and other "Angry Young Men," fueling the postwar generation's attack on the drawing room dramas and well-made plays of their elders. However, while M. acutely registers the moral torpor and mediocrity of a class and nation in decline, his critique is lightened by adherence to older conventions of comic plotting and dialogue. In *The Dock Brief*, the pathos of the barrister's failure is reversed by an arbitrary but welcome sting in the tail. A similar reversal, though more romantic, concludes *I Spy*. M.'s interest in the forms of comic drama is illustrated in his successful adaptations of Georges Feydeau's French farces, *A Flea in Her Ear* (perf. 1966), *Cat among the Pigeons* (perf. 1969), and *The Lady from Maxim's* (perf. 1977), for the National Theatre, London. The major exception to this predilection for comedy is the play, *The Judge* (1967), in which a criminal court judge returns for the first time to his birthplace, confronting the guilty desires he has repressed in order to function as a punitive judge. While ambitious in theme, this play suffers from a simplistic opposition between law and desire. A much

more sympathetic and nuanced portrait of an authority figure is offered in *A Voyage Round My Father*. Based on his own relationship with his father, this work represents an unsentimental, yet comic, portrait of a blind man demanding attention through the witty and outrageous use of his voice. The vulnerability and understated love of both father and son are complexly developed. The play is notable not only for its verbal expressiveness, but also for its economical and fluid use of space, which enables a number of relationships and milieus to be represented in building this intimate fictional biography. It is generally regarded as M.'s best play.

In the 1970s, M. turned increasingly to television, and found success as the adaptor of literary works such as Robert GRAVES's *I, Claudius* (1972) and Evelyn WAUGH's *Brideshead Revisited* (1981), and with original scripts, notably those presenting the trials of his "Old Bailey hack," Rumpole of the Bailey. LAW AND LITERATURE come together in this doughty, poetry-quoting defender of criminals, who emerges as a practical idealist, tenaciously upholding freedom under the law. With his love of wine and cigars, his forthrightness before judges and colleagues, and his forensic successes, Rumpole is a considerable comic character in the tradition of Charles DICKENS's Sam Weller. Each Rumpole episode raises a significant social issue through his trial, which is doubled in a subplot at home or in his chambers. For example, in "Rumpole and the Golden Thread," the story derived from the defense of Soyinka in 1966, suspicion based on cultural difference is displayed at home and abroad, and important questions about British law and tribal rivalry in a postcolonial society are raised with clarity and economy. At times, facile connections are made, as in "Rumpole and the Genuine Article," which pairs questions of aesthetics raised by a forgery trial of an artist with questions of personal worthiness. Overall, though, Rumpole is an ideal vehicle for M.'s keen comic observations on English society.

In *Paradise Postponed* (1985), simultaneously produced as a novel and television series, the social history implicit in much of M.'s work received full articulation. Through the story of the disputed will of Simeon Simcox, a recently deceased radical clergyman, M. uncovers the hidden relationships and shifting ideological alignments within a traditional English village. The narrative form is reminiscent of Anthony TROLLOPE, with its representative characters, and its acute realization of worldly success and failure. The plot affords a melancholy leftist view of recent British history, as the postwar hope of democratic socialism gives way to Thatcherite economics in the 1980s. While the form is old-fashioned, M. refuses nostalgia in his depiction of mores or in his ending. Leslie Titmuss, the ruthless lower-middle-class boy who embodies Thatcherism, is the subject of a less successful sequel, *Titmuss Regained* (1990). In producing these works for two media, M. found the novel form more congenial, and this genre dominated his writing in the 1990s. *Dunster* (1992) and *Felix in the Underworld* (1998) are in different ways stories of men who in comfortable middle age encounter a radical challenge to their being. In fluent and observant prose, they raise important questions about selfhood in contemporary England.

M. is a comic writer with a materialist philosophy of life. In a universe without the consolation of religious faith, M. registers through comedy the possibilities of experiencing justice, love, luck, and escape from tribulation. As a politically astute writer, his comedy "is on the side of the lonely, the neglected, the unsuccessful." With his power of sympathetic as well as comic characterization, he achieves a tragicomic chiaroscuro in his best work.

BIBLIOGRAPHY: Hayman, R., *British Theatre since 1955* (1979); Taylor, J. R., *The Angry Theatre: New British Drama* (1969); Wellworth, G., *Theatre of Protest and Paradox: Developments in Avant-Garde Drama* (1964)

KIERAN DOLIN

MORTON, Thomas
b. 1764?, Durham; d. 28 March 1838, London

M. is best known for the creation of "Mrs. Grundy," the unseen character from his play *Speed the Plow* (1798) who typified the vigilant and disapproving next-door neighbor. The often repeated "What will Mrs. Grundy say?" produced the term "Grundyism," a form of censorship based on moral respectability. M. was an amateur actor before writing his first play, *Columbus; or, A World Discovered* (1792), and became a popular fixture on the London scene with successful comedies including *The Way to Get Married* (1796), *A Cure for Heartache* (1797), *The School of Reform* (1805), *Town and Country* (1807), *Education* (1813), and *The Slave* (1816).

MOSLEY, Nicholas [Third Baron Ravensdale]
b. 25 June 1923, London

M.'s early novels were in realist mode, his later ones experimental. He went to Eton and Wadham College, Oxford. *Spaces of the Dark* (1951), *The Rainbearers* (1955), and *Corruption* (1957), all relating to World War II, were influenced by Henry JAMES and William Faulkner. *Accident* (1965) was superbly filmed by Joseph Losey (1967), with a screenplay by Harold PINTER, and followed by *Assassins* (1966), *Impossible Object* (1968), and *Natalie, Natalie* (1971). *Catastrophe Practice* (1979) marked a new direction for M.,

being the first of a projected seven-volume sequence, but later reduced to four: *Imago Bird* (1980), *Serpent* (1981), *Judith* (1986), and *Hopeful Monsters* (1990), which received the Whitbread Award. *The Hesperides Tree* (2001) has been praised for its subtlety; but some readers feel that the plot and characters are mere puppets illustrating the philosophical preoccupations of the author. M.'s biographies include a study of Julian Grenfell (1976) and two biographies of his own parents, *Rules of the Game: Sir Oswald and Lady Cynthia Mosley, 1896–1933* (1982) and *Beyond the Pale: Sir Oswald Mosley and Family, 1933–1980* (1983).

MOTION, Andrew
b. 26 October 1952, London

M.'s poetry is meditative, lyrical, and understated. The clarity and directness of his personal and narrative poems make them readily accessible, yet there are intriguing images and a sense of restraint that draw the reader in to the poems and suggest undisclosed undercurrents. In most of his volumes, there is a haunting, elegiac quality, a sense of deep loss, which stems from his mother's death after a prolonged illness. For three of these years, she was in a coma, movingly described in "Anniversaries" from M.'s first volume, *The Pleasure Steamers* (1978). This incident and its aftermath are the theme of many poems and seem to be a part of most others, in which M. explores human relationships and aspects of everyday life with a wistful nostalgia, in many cases.

In *Independence*, a single long narrative poem published in 1981, this sense of loss is evoked through an imaginative inhabiting of another life, that of an English colonial officer in India, who has lost his identity through the loss of position in India after Independence and the loss of his wife through a miscarriage. The poem moves fluidly from stanza to stanza with effective use of enjambment and colloquial language, as the persona speaks to his dead wife, recalling their life together. This experience, of a typical Englishman in the situation and at the time described, reflects the emphasis on England and Englishness that characterizes M.'s poetry. He has written literary studies on Edward THOMAS (1980) and Philip LARKIN (1993), and his work is similar to theirs in terms of the references to English countryside and suburban life respectively. He also follows these poets and others such as A. E. HOUSMAN and Thomas HARDY in his quiet celebration of seasonal change and the reflection in the natural world of human experience and emotion.

In *Secret Narratives* (1983), M. again inhabits other lives and times. Frequently employing the first person narrative form, he presents an outsider's view yet also speaks for the characters themselves, such as Anne Frank in her Amsterdam hideaway; Edward

LEAR staying in a foreign hotel; an unnamed army officer enchanted by a local girl at Glymenopoulo while awaiting orders from his superiors. This is also true of "Dangerous Play," a poem evoking the tensions of English colonial rule in Africa. This was a new poem added to those selected from earlier volumes, in a collection with the same title published in 1986. In the following year, *Natural Causes* was published, a collection containing poems like "The Dancing Hippo," with more sinister undercurrents, emphasizing human domination of animals and hinting again at a sense of guilt regarding England's colonial past, conveyed through the context of a circus act. This poem employs a longer line and a fuller stanza form than many of M.'s poems, which tend to be most frequently composed of unrhymed quatrains.

Love in a Life (1991) has a variety of forms, all carefully constructed to create fluent, controlled insights into more personal incidents and situations. M. nevertheless makes these universal in their appeal, involving the reader and encouraging sympathetic understanding of the trauma of a tube-train bag snatch; the wonder of the sight of unborn children on a monitor screen; a parent's despairing sense of impotence in the face of a child's illness. Illness, loss, and death all recur in this volume, themes that pervade the poetry.

In *The Price of Everything* (1994), the longest section is a fascinating poem, "Lines of Desire," which is much less immediately accessible than others. The form is fragmented, as are the images and scenes depicted. The poet returns to a classroom, in which he learned the poetry of Siegfried SASSOON, and other stanzas play on this relationship between a contemporary poet, who has not faced war firsthand, and a celebrated war poet. M. recalls learning of Sassoon's rejection of his medal, an action that, like his poems, powerfully demonstrated his anger against those in command who seemed to be needlessly extending the First World War and the consequent loss of millions of lives. In contrast, M. particularly emphasizes the detachment of contemporary viewers of war scenes on television news, which they can conveniently turn off at the touch of a button. These sections of the poem are interspersed with depictions of family life and relationships, of the poet and his father linked with his own fatherhood, incidents of killing in sport and play, which contrast with the mass killings of war and yet disturb the poet in their similarity.

There is more experimentation in "Salt Water," the title poem of M.'s 1997 volume, in which he uses a prose description of the history of Orford, a Suffolk coastal town, and extends the succinct prose details in imaginatively developed poetic sequences. There are some sections of rhymed quatrains; others more like prose poems; others a combination of single lines and verses. All explore in different ways the legend of the merman supposedly captured, imprisoned, and tortured in the nearby castle. The images of water and land, sea and sky, are a feature of most of M.'s poetry but perhaps most powerful in this sequence and in "Fresh Water," an elegy for a friend killed when the *Marchioness* was sunk in the river Thames.

In 1999, M. was appointed poet laureate, following the death of Ted HUGHES. He has subsequently written a number of "occasional" poems, as the post demands, and has also mounted a variety of activities and campaigns to bring poetry more into the everyday lives of ordinary people. He has stipulated that the post should be held for only ten years, rather than the rest of the poet's lifetime, as was previously expected. This may well be due to his own respect for other contemporary poets who might have been appointed, like the lesbian poet Carol Ann DUFFY, whose forceful voice is perhaps evidence of the wider social and cultural mix of England today. M. seems more of a representative of "traditional" Englishness, his poetry quiet, calm, and controlled, yet he does face a variety of concerns and controversies created by England's past. His work is not complacent and merely accepting of the status quo: he explores political and personal issues with an imaginative intensity that draws the reader in to the world of a questioning, challenging intelligence.

BIBLIOGRAPHY: Hulse, M., "'I Could Have Outlived Myself There': The Poetry of A. M.," *CritQ* 28 (Autumn 1986): 71–81; Marsack, R. L., "A. M.," in Sherry, V. B., Jr., ed., *Poets of Great Britain and Ireland since 1960*, part 2, *DLB* 40 (1985): 395–400

ROSE ATFIELD

MOTTRAM, R[alph] H[ale]

b. 30 October 1883, Norwich, Norfolk; d. 15 April 1971, King's Lynn, Norfolk

Educated in Norwich and Lausanne, M. authored more than sixty books. John GALSWORTHY encouraged him to write, but M.'s first successful book was *The Spanish Farm* (1924), awarded the Hawthornden Prize, which became the first in a trilogy: the others were *Sixty-four, Ninety-four!* (1925) and *The Crime at Vanderlynden's* (1926). Set on a farm near the front during World War I, it was based on his own experience in France and Flanders and tells the story of the owner and his family and the men they come into contact with. Many of M.'s later novels are set in East Anglia, where he spent most of his life. In 1966, M. was awarded an honorary doctorate of letters by the University of East Anglia at Norwich.

MUIR, Edwin

b. 15 May 1887, Deerness, Orkney Islands, Scotland; d. 3 January 1959, Cambridgeshire

Biography and travel are important elements in both the life and works of M., a poet born on the remote islands of Orkney to the north of Scotland. In his best-known work, his *Autobiography*, published in 1954, M. divides the book into chapters named for the places he has lived, including Wyre (in the Orkneys), Garth (on the Scottish mainland), Glasgow (where his father, mother, and two brothers died), London (where he underwent psychoanalysis), and Prague (where, at the age of thirty-five, he started to write poetry).

As a religious writer, M.'s peripatetic lifestyle is translated in his work into a symbolic quest for truth as a basis for existence. While in Glasgow, seeking solace from the deaths of members of his family and the industrial squalor surrounding him, M. turned to Nietzsche's archetype of the Superman, a mythical being who rises above human frailty and overcomes weakness by the sheer force of individual will. Later, psychoanalysis introduced him to the work of C. G. Jung and his theory of the discovery of universal myth through the unconscious, a myth that all human lives reenact. One of the most important dilemmas facing M. in reconciling this myth to his own life was the inevitable and continual fall of humankind through World War I and II and the advent of the nuclear age, prompting him to ponder how beings who arrived in the world with childhood innocence could grow so belligerent.

M. attempts to resolve this dilemma in his autobiography; his critical writings, notably *The Structure of the Novel* (1928); his novels, such as *The Three Brothers* (1931) and *Poor Tom* (1932); and, in more detailed fashion, in his poetry. Whereas the prose works recollect a dream or reflect on a myth, M.'s poems "re-create the dream and participate in the myth." For example, poems like "The Town Betrayed" depict the fall from innocence as the actual physical destruction of a community through war, a destruction that also finds expression in the classical struggles of Agamemnon against Troy.

The habit of finding a general or universal situation within in a particular one is a vision that M. had already discovered in the work of Franz Kafka. In Kafka, M. also detected a kindred spirit: as a German-speaking Jew in Catholic Czechoslovakia, Kafka was as alien to the surrounding culture as M.'s Orkney origins made him to English culture. M. also saw Kafka perceiving the irreconcilability of the divine with the human, his involvement in a never-ending quest for the right way to exist. In his critical essays, which were a means of participating in the collective imagination of humankind rather than a passing of judgment, M. pinpointed the lack of narrative framework in Kafka's stories, the way that each story becomes solely invention. M. and his wife translated many of Kafka's works into English and were largely responsible for Europe's discovery of this writer.

Finally, like Kafka, M. was not only a religious writer but also a visionary. His most famous poem, "The Horses," forms a congruity between the two seemingly dissimilar realms of the temporal and the eternal world. In describing the spontaneous, magical arrival of horses in a town after a war, M. compares their visit with the evolution of animals during the original act of Creation. He concludes the poem by suggesting that the destruction of war has left mankind with the chance to begin again through reacquainting itself with natural innocence, represented here in the shy and wondering horses.

BIBLIOGRAPHY: Aitchison, J., *The Golden Harvester: The Vision of E. M.* (1988); Butter, P. H., *E. M.* (1966); McCulloch, M., *E. M.* (1993)

                                    SUSAN TETLOW HARRINGTON

MULDOON, Paul

b. 20 June 1951, Portadown, County Armagh, Northern Ireland

M.'s poetry is characterized by a dazzling virtuosity of linguistic play. His wide-ranging themes explore ancient cultures and international history and the intimacy of his rural village birthplace, the Moy. Allusions to rock music, anthropology, and horticulture combine in an intriguing density, fascinating to some, exasperating to others.

M.'s first collection, *New Weather* (1973), was published while he was still a student at Queen's University in Belfast. Already it held evidence of the delighted play on the protean qualities of words: inventive, or indulgent, according to contrasting critical views, but always technically and linguistically skillful. Having been put together during the early years of the latest outbreak of Northern Irish "Troubles," there are references to the bloodshed and turbulence of the time presented in quirky, disconcertingly oblique ways, involving a disturbing black HUMOR.

Mules (1977) reflects its title with a variety of poems exploring juxtapositions and unusual alliances, combinations and disassociations. Themes of mystery and quest are introduced as readers interrogate origins of words and ideas. This puzzle is extended in the title of the third volume, *Why Brownlee Left* (1980). The titular sonnet explores a mysterious disappearance but is left tantalizingly open. Also in this volume is the first of several extended sequences, "Immram," which is another poetic quest, of a medieval legendary character, possibly an ancestor of M., who attempts to take revenge for his dead father's murder. The persona is brought into the 20th c. with references to the Empire State Building, the film *King Kong*, and extraordinary escapades involving meetings with personalities like Howard Hughes, who is presented as reclusive and fixated on ice cream. The divided reactions to this exuberant and absurd fiction were summed up in Alan HOLLINGHURST's comment, "a tour de force which leads nowhere."

M. continues his outlandish language games in *Quoof* (1983). The title is the family name for a hot water bottle and many of the poems examine the shifty and unstable qualities of words, in their personal, political, and historical connotations. Another feature of his poetry, the skillful use of half rhyme, is evident from the earliest collection and underlined in the teasing, often obscurely mischievous, tone of the volume.

The rich and resonant sound qualities of M.'s poems are often enjoyed despite his tendency to include arcane and mystifying references; T. S. ELIOT's dictum that poetry should be enjoyed before it is understood, an instinctive response to the mellifluous power of words, is most appropriate to M. In *Meeting the British* (1987), M. explores the colonial question in the title poem, the imposition of British rule and the raiding of indigenous peoples' culture and possessions, exchanged for nothing but disease and poverty. Although the context seems to be in terms of a native American Indian tribe, the implied consequences could apply equally to Ireland.

Madoc: A Mystery (1990) was published after the poet's move to the U.S., where he teaches at Princeton University. The combination of British and early American sources provides a rich plethora of imagery, "Madoc," a Welsh tribal leader supposedly one of the earliest settlers in the "New World," being a character originally presented in a poem by Robert SOUTHEY. This is linked with M.'s imaginative development of the idea of a "Pantisocracy," envisaged by a group of Romantic poets to be established in America. This long narrative poem is built up on a variety of philosophical and political positions, expressed in the voices of key European thinkers, and balanced in the collection by more concise, pointed lyrics.

American, Irish, and European influences abound in *The Annals of Chile* (1994), which follows a similar pattern of extended sequences and shorter works. The elegy for a close friend, "Incantata," is a reeling, expansive stream of consciousness, packing together almost more tiny incidents and memories than the long-lined, enjambed form will stand, only just kept in control by the typical half rhyme. M.'s mother is directly remembered in this volume, as opposed to his father whom M. frequently recalls and reveres elsewhere.

In the 1998 collection, *Hay*, alongside tricksy forms such as the sestina and villanelle, a rhyme sequence used twice previously in long poems is reworked again, in "The Bangle (Slight Return)," a group of thirty sonnets, the second half of which repeat the rhymes of the first in reverse order. This technical feat is matched by the thematic concern with

parallelism, duality, reflection, and doubleness, explored through images of conjoined twins, different generations of women relatives, repetitive journeys and the seemingly continuous cycle of violence in Northern Ireland. In 2000, M. was appointed Oxford Professor of Poetry and in that same year published a volume of lectures from his first year in office entitled *To Ireland, I.*

BIBLIOGRAPHY: Birkets, S., "About P. M.," *Ploughshares* 26 (Spring 2000): 202–8; Keller, L., "An Interview with P. M.," *ConL* 23 (Spring 1994): 1–29; Kendale, T., *P. M.* (1996)

ROSE ATFIELD

MUNDAY, Anthony

bap. 13 October 1560, London; bur. 9 August 1633, London

Frances MERES in his *Palladis Tamia* refers to M. as "best for comedy" and "our best plotter." M.'s reputation among his fellow writers was less ebullient. He was regularly ridiculed, and his government affiliations won him little but scorn. As late as 1588, M. had been employed to execute the warrants issued by the Archbishop of Canterbury against the Martin Marprelate pamphleteers. Earlier, from 1578 to 1579, he had gone to Rome to gather material for a series of attacks against Jesuits. His *The English Romayne Lyfe* (1582) remains the scholar's best source for the English College at Rome; it is at once an entertaining and rancorous description. In 1581, he joined with Richard Topcliffe, Lord Burghley's unofficial Torturer General, to hunt down recusants.

M.'s literary achievement dates from the time of these endeavors. M. was prolific and his earliest works included popular ballads, translations of Continental romances, and lyrics of some quality. He wrote successfully for the theater in its earliest years, at the same time as John LYLY and George PEELE established themselves. M. has the singular distinction of being the only dramatist of the early period to remain successful after the rise of William SHAKESPEARE and the new style of the mid-1590s. Only three of M.'s unaided dramas survive although Philip Henslowe regularly employed him as writer for the Admiral's Company between 1594 and 1602. A member of the Drapers' Company by virtue of his father's affiliation, M. turned in 1605 to devising civic pageants for the city companies.

M. is almost certainly the target of the ridicule in the anonymous *Histriomastix* (1589) where he is satirized in the character of Posthaste. In the play, Posthaste forms a group of players, calling them "Sir Oliver Owlet's Men" and writes for them for a shilling per page. Posthaste is portrayed as a heavy drinker and an affected courtier who believes that his clean shirt is warrant enough that he is a gentleman. He has no skill at all at extemporizing, as M. had not. M. had early in his career been jeered from the stage and responded by forsaking the profession and writing a tract against playing. Another change of heart led him back into the theater a short time later. Of Posthaste, the players say that it is as dangerous to see his name on a playhouse door as to see a printed bill on a plague house. John MARSTON later added the epithet "goose-quillian" to the character, and that opinion appears to have been shared by the other playwrights who knew M., especially Ben JONSON.

M. wrote a series of romantic chronicle plays that survive. His dramatic reputation rests mainly upon *John a Kent and John a Cumber* (perf. 1594), *The Downfall of Robert, Earl of Huntingdon* (perf. 1598), *The Death of Robert, Earl of Huntingdon* (with Henry CHETTLE, perf. 1598), and *The True and Honorable History of Sir John Oldcastle* (with Michael DRAYTON, Richard Hathway, and Robert Wilson, perf. 1599), all of which were written for Henslowe and the Admiral's Men. He appears to have been particularly interested in the folkloric history genre and wrote two other plays, besides the *Huntingdon* plays, on the Robin Hood legend, now lost, and a probable sequel, also lost, on Richard the Lionheart. He also wrote plays, also lost, on Owen Tudor, Cardinal Wolsey, along with a second part of Sir John Oldcastle. His drama demonstrates appreciation of the popular taste and the haste necessitated by working in the sweat-shop conditions of the Henslowe literary machine. When, for example, Shakespeare's Falstaff suggested a criticism of Oldcastle, M. and company were quick to pen the *Sir John Oldcastle* plays and capitalize on the Chamberlain's Men's misstep.

As deviser of civic pageants, the surviving works that M. created are *The Triumphs of Reunited Britannia* (perf. October 29, 1605), *Chruso-Thriambos* (perf. October 29, 1611), *Himatia Poleos* (perf. October 29, 1614), *Metropolis Coronata* (perf. October 30, 1615), and *Chrysanaleia* (perf. October 29, 1616). Each was a pageant honoring the new Lord Mayor presented by (in order) the Merchant Taylors, Goldsmiths, Drapers (twice), and Fishmongers. He devised a pageant for the Ironmongers in 1618 that included the spectacle of the firing of a real gun. In 1610, he devised the Corporation of London's welcome of Henry, Prince of Wales.

M. has a close link to the mystery surrounding the play of *Sir Thomas More* (wr. ca. 1598). The original of the play is in M.'s hand. However, while the subject matter is characteristic of M.'s interest in English political history, scholars have doubted it was entirely his work even in its original state. It later acquired the collaborative additions of perhaps five other hands, one of which is often argued to be Shakespeare's.

BIBLIOGRAPHY: Eccles, M., "A. M.," in Bennett, J. W., et al., eds., *Studies in the English Renaissance Drama* (1959): 95–106; Turner, J. C., *A. M.* (1928)

BRIAN JAY CORRIGAN

MUNRO, Hector Hugh

(pseud.: Saki) b. 18 December 1870, Akyab, Burma; d. 14 November 1916, Beaumont Hamel, France

M.'s short stories and novels display urbane wit, intricate detail, and a cunning knowledge of human nature. Elements of M.'s eccentric but privileged childhood provide the basis of his characters and settings; his HUMOR and SENTIMENT show the influence of Oscar WILDE. Like George ORWELL, he was stationed in Burma as a young man, but his frail health curtailed his assignment there. M. never acquired the distaste for Imperial Britain cultivated by Orwell, and his criticisms of the political system were based more on his skeptical views of human nature and his upper-class, aloof demeanor. With a pen name plundered from Edward FITZGERALD's *Rubáiyát of Omar Khayyám*, Saki, as he became known, began his publishing career with a series of political satires based on Lewis CARROLL's *Alice in Wonderland*. *The Westminster Alice* (1902), along with a parody of the popular *Rubáiyát*, first appeared serially in the *Westminster Gazette* in the first years of the new century.

M.'s short story collections focus on a unifying series of characters in various social situations. Each story is a compact, crystallized moment of upper-class society, characterized by M.'s sly, sharp humor. The joke is as often on society itself, beyond the vain, shallow figures M. reveals. His awareness of their manner and satire of it is his protest; his subversive message, if any, is only that he may hope, as the author, for human behavior beyond that of his subjects. He does, however, prize cleverness as a virtue, and rewards with the spoils those characters who use their wit to maintain a level of dignity or at least interest.

Reginald and Clovis are the central characters, respectively, of M.'s first three collections: *Reginald* (1904), *Reginald in Russia* (1910), and *The Chronicles of Clovis* (1911). Clovis appears again in *Beasts and Super-Beasts* (1914), its title a satiric response to Bernard SHAW's *Man and Superman*. *The Toys of Peace* maintained M.'s urbane style while addressing issues of the First World War; his final volume of sketches, *The Square Egg*, was published posthumously in 1924.

Stories like "Sredni Vashtar" from *The Chronicles of Clovis*, with its frail hero Conradin, show M.'s ability to draw on autobiographical material for setting and tone, while creating a narrative more like a folk or fairy tale. His interest in Eastern European culture can be seen in this story's mysterious godlike beast, in the power of the rural and wild versus the cultured and sheltered. Other stories demonstrate his use of animals in the folkloric spirit, such as "The Lull" from *Beasts and Super-Beasts*. Most prominent, however, are the short stories depicting the foibles of the wealthy and privileged. M.'s characters reveal their true natures with crisp banter and revealing tirades, either against one another ("The Brogue"), their precocious children ("The Storyteller"), or the servants ("The Byzantine Omelette").

Though it is for his short stories that M. is best known, several novels and plays have been published. *The Unbearable Bassington* (1912) shares the tone of the stories with a more descriptive voice and less banter. *When William Came* (1914) pursues the more cryptic aspects of M.'s work, being a sort of mystery. M.'s only play of significant length, *The Watched Pot* (perf. 1943), coauthored with Charles Maude, displays the civilized repartee in the Wilde tradition that would go on to influence playwrights like Noël COWARD.

BIBLIOHRAPHY: Gillen, C. H., *H. H. M. (Saki)* (1969); Langguth, A. J., *Saki: A Life of H. H. M.* (1981); Spears, G. J., *The Satire of Saki* (1963)

                                    NICOLE SARROCCO

MURDOCH, Iris

b. 15 July 1919, Dublin, Ireland; d. 8 February 1999, Oxford

Although trained as a philosopher, and the author of several highly regarded books of philosophy, M. turned to the novel form precisely because of its ability to create eccentric characters and complicated plots that resist any overarching theories or ideas. The disorderly jumbles and messes to which her characters are rather irreverently subjected by M. deliberately give her novels a shapelessness, even an incoherence, that becomes, ironically, the philosophic ground on which she bases her vision of life. As a result, her novels are not transparent or easily explicable, but instead are full of muddles and confusions, upsetting the ordered lives of characters very like M. herself, that is, well-educated intellectuals and artists of the middle classes living in England in the last half of the 20th c.

Although M.'s plots are filled with comical convolutions, they also always include a sense of the dark side, and as her work developed, M. began to explore even more seriously the nature of evil, coupled with a questioning of God's existence. *The Time of the Angels* (1966), for instance, deals with the idea that the Holocaust and Adolf Hitler ushered in a time without God that has unleashed ambiguous spiritual forces. This novel also features a typical Murdochan "enchanter" figure in the person of Carel Fisher, a demonic priest whose force of personality enthralls a circle of vulnerable friends. Perfectly ordinary people who suddenly come under an enchantment of one kind or another continued to preoccupy M. in her subsequent novels, even as they became longer, deeper, and ever more resonant in mythic rather than rational levels of interpretation. A classic example of this is *The Black Prince* (1973). In this novel, considered one of her best, a boyish young girl unaccountably enthralls a failed novelist named Bradley Pearson, whose helpless fascination for this androgynous "black prince" makes him realize that he can be subject to forces that he can neither control nor understand; this ordeal, however, ultimately leads Bradley down a more mystical path indicated by the presence of the Greek god Apollo, a turn of plot that once again demonstrates that M.'s novels approach the realm of religious fable.

Obsessive love and mystical experience return in M.'s major novel, *The Sea, The Sea* (1978), for which she won the Booker Prize. In this novel, a successful man of the theater, Charles Arrowby, decides to escape his hectic life for a graceful retirement in a strange old house in a remote village next to a rough patch of sea. Instead of rest and reflection, however, Arrowby finds himself overwhelmed by a chance meeting with Mary Hartley Fitch, an unattractive and aging housewife who had once been his childhood sweetheart. Frustrated by Hartley's resistance to his bizarre protestations of love, Arrowby kidnaps her and imprisons her in a windowless, boxlike room in his seaside house. Complicating Charles's demonic attempts to retrieve his lost youth by returning to his first love, is the appearance of his long-lost cousin James, a Buddhist magician. Buddhism also informs not only the character of James but also the theme of this novel, which introduces the concept of karma, a law that exacts retribution for every immoral act or thought committed in a specific lifetime. Further, M. also suggests that Charles is in fact not in retirement, but living in what Buddhists call a "bardo," that is, a kind of purgatory where the soul encounters images of the previous life before assuming a new incarnation.

The Sea, The Sea is an excellent example of the way in which M., a self-described atheist, nevertheless insistently includes mystical and paranormal elements into her work. Along with the Buddhist philosophy in *The Sea, The Sea,* for example, there are also a poltergeist, a sea-monster, and a miraculous rescue from drowning. Miraculous rescues are a recurring motif in M.'s novels—in fact, her last full-length novel, *The Green Knight* (1993), invokes the idiom of Christian Arthurian legend and mysteriously resurrects the title character. Although M.'s characters live in a secular postwar world in which there is little in the way of certain religious belief, M. inevitably places them in situations that always include a great deal of mystical incident—a number of other characters, for instance, are magically rescued from danger or death, and, even more, space aliens make a surprise appearance in *The Nice and the Good* (1968) and flying saucers appear in *The Philosopher's Pupil* (1983). In addition, her work features a number of characters struggling with religious faith, and with problems of good and evil. As M.'s convoluted and mysterious plots play themselves out, modern liberal philosophies and master narratives are sorely tested and generally found wanting when applied to life's actual existential problems. As a result, it has become increasingly clear that M.'s tales of obsessive love and strange enchantments are, beneath their absurd surface, fundamentally serious postmodern parables in which her characters, far from living comfortable and enlightened lives, have in fact lost their way and are, spiritually, in a dark wood with no clear path before them.

BIBLIOGRAPHY: Dipple, E., *I. M.* (1982); Gordon, D. J., *I. M.'s Fables of Unselfing* (1995); Spear, H., *I. M.* (1995)

MARGARET BOE BIRNS

MURPHY, Arthur

b. 27 December 1727, Clooniquin, Ireland; d. 18 June 1805, London

On a marble plaque near M.'s grave in St. Paul's Hammersmith Church, surgeon Jesse Foot summarized his friend's career: "A Barrister at Law of Distinguished Character/A Dramatic Poet of Great Celebrity/A Classicle [*sic*] Scholar of rare Attainments/A Political writer of no Common Consideration[.]" M. laid the foundation for these achievements at the Jesuit school at St. Omer, France (1738–44), where he mastered Latin and Greek and developed what he called "an inordinate Affection for the Drama."

After flirting with commerce, M. in 1752 turned hack writer as a contributor to Henry FIELDING's *Covent Garden Journal*. In 1762, M. produced what would remain for more than a century the standard edition of Fielding's works. Neither M.'s work for Fielding nor his "Gray's-Inn Journal," which appeared first as part of the *New Craftsman* and then independently, proved lucrative. In debt for three hundred pounds, M. turned thespian, debuting as Othello at Covent Garden on October 18, 1754. M. composed the prologue for that performance. M. remained an actor for only two seasons, but his knowledge of the stage is reflected in his farces, comedies, and tragedies.

In the prologue to Robert Jephson's *Braganza* (1775), M. attacked the sentimental comedies of the day: "The comic sister, in hysteric fit,/You'd swear, has lost all memory of wit:/Folly for her, may now exalt on high;/Feathr'd by ridicule no arrows fly,/But

if you are distress'd, she's sure to cry." M. shared with the sentimentalists the desire to use the stage to reform manners, but he chose as his means the Restoration dramatists' wit and ridicule. His first farce, *The Apprentice* (1756), mocks Dick Wingate, an apothecary's apprentice, for his desire to turn actor. *The Englishman from Paris* (perf. 1756)—unpublished until 1969—laughs at Frenchified Englishmen. *The Way to Keep Him* (1760) urges wives to remain amusing and laughs at husbands who fear showing their love. *All in the Wrong* (1761) satirically anatomizes jealousy. Though most of M.'s plays are based on French models, he turned them into English comedies of manners. M.'s genius for comedy exceeded his skill as a tragedian, though *The Grecian Daughter* (1772) held the boards throughout the 18th c.

With *Know Your Own Mind* (perf. 1777; pub. 1778), one of his best works, M. essentially left the theater writing only one more play, the tragedy *The Rival Sisters* (1793), for performance. While pursuing his legal career, he remained devoted to literature. In 1792, he edited the works of his long-time friend Samuel JOHNSON. M.'s translation of Tacitus appeared the following year and his translation of Sallust's *The History of Cataline's Conspiracy, with Four Orations of Cicero* in 1795. M.'s 1798 closet drama *Arminius* attacked the French Revolution, and in 1801 M. published a two-volume biography of actor/playwright David GARRICK.

In his 1786 collected works, M. expressed the hope that no trace remained of his political writings attacking William Pitt the Elder (*The Test*, November 6, 1756-July 9, 1757; *The Auditor*, June 10, 1762-February 8, 1763). His wish has been more than granted. Some two centuries after his death his name is little known. He deserves a better fate. At least two of his comedies, *The Way to Keep Him* and *Know Your Own Mind* contain much HUMOR and compare favorably with the best plays of M.'s contemporaries Oliver GOLDSMITH and Richard Brinsley SHERIDAN.

BIBLIOGRAPHY: Dunbar, H. H., *The Dramatic Career of A. M.* (1946); Emery, J. P., *A. M.* (1946); Spector, R. D., *A. M.* (1979)

JOSEPH ROSENBLUM

MURPHY, Richard

b. 6 August 1927, County Galway, Ireland

M.'s early childhood was spent in Ceylon, but his later education was at Magdalen College, Oxford, and the Sorbonne, Paris. His poetry conveys the landscapes and seascapes of Ireland. Publications include *The Archaeology of Love* (1955), *Sailing to an Island* (1963), which contains his long narrative poem about a fishing tragedy entitled "The Cleggan Disaster," *The Battle of Aughrim* (1968), commissioned by the

BBC, *High Island* (1974), *The Price of Stone* (1985), and *The Mirror Wall* (1989). His *Selected Poems* appeared in 1979 and his *Collected Poems* in 2000. Born to the Protestant ascendancy, he ponders Ireland's tragic history.

MURRAY, [George] Gilbert [Aimé]

b. 2 January 1866, Sydney, Australia; d. 20 May 1957, Oxford

One of the most prominent Greek scholars of the previous century and a half (perhaps even the foremost), M. was many-sided, quite well adapted to succeed in diverse pursuits, and widely acclaimed in his own lifetime, yet ironically, in the final analysis he appears to have been something of a tragic hero on the world's stage. Though it is his literary contribution that is of primary interest here, this may be better understood and appreciated from the broader perspective of what his life was really all about. According to family lore, M. was descended from Irish kings. His parents, living in the Australian bush, were well-to-do landowners—father an Irish Catholic gentleman who had gained knighthood, mother an Anglican who (after her husband died) ran with considerable success a school for young ladies. M.'s home atmosphere was one that encouraged independent thinking and a liberal, humanitarian outlook regarding society (not only human rights but animal rights as well) and the claims of authority—a philosophical perspective that would have staying power with him throughout his life. In 1877, Lady Murray and her son left Australia and settled in England. M. would see again the land of his birth only once, in 1892; Australia was apparently not to his taste. In England began the education and brilliant career of the young man.

M. was educated at Merchant Taylors' School in London, and St. John's College, Oxford. Among the prizes he won for his ability to handle the classical languages was the prize fellowship at New College, Oxford, in 1888. He also completed a novel during his undergraduate years, *Gobi or Shamo* (1889). After he had taken his degree from Oxford in 1889 with first-class honors in Greats and Classical Moderations, at the age of twenty-three he became professor of Greek at Glasgow University. That same year he married Mary Howard, daughter of the enormously wealthy ninth Earl of Carlisle, a scion of one of the prominent aristocratic Whig families influential in the Liberal Party. Lady Mary's father was also a talented artist. Her mother, the Countess of Carlisle, a radical liberal in politics, was intellectual and energetic, and a powerful force within her own family and the circles within which she moved. Lady Mary, however, lacked the force, intellect, and ability to cope that characterized her mother, and this would contribute to the domestic unhappiness of the Murrays and that of their five children.

Between 1899 and 1905, M. was, in the ironic phrase of his biographer Francis West, a "Gentleman of Leisure," ostensibly traveling about and enjoying the benefits of his wife's family's vast estates. Actually, considerable time was devoted to his absorbing current interest, translating Greek drama, particularly the plays of Euripides, for publication and stage production. He also revised his original play *Carlyon Sahib* (perf. 1899; pub. 1900) for the theater, but despite its having the eminent actress Mrs. Patrick Campbell in a major role, the play was a failure. A familiar in London's highest theatrical circles, M. gained further recognition when Bernard SHAW used him, his wife, and his mother-in-law as models for characters in *Major Barbara:* respectively, the professor of Greek, Adolphus Cusins; the heroine, Barbara Undershaft; and her mother, Lady Britomart.

From 1905 to 1908, M. was teaching once again at Oxford, this time as a fellow in New College, yet continuing his work—as translator, editor, and theatrical supervisor—on the plays of Euripides. In addition, he was preparing a series of invitational lectures on Greek poetry, to be delivered at Harvard University in 1907. Those lectures before long constituted half of a more ambitious work, *The Rise of the Greek Epic* (1907), which reappeared later in several revised editions. Here, M. attempted "to demonstrate," according to West, "the thesis that Greek poetry was a force making for the progress of the human race." In 1908, M. was appointed Regius Professor of Greek at Oxford, a post he held until his retirement in 1936. M.'s deep involvement in radical Liberal politics, particularly as it related to his pioneering efforts in helping to create the League of Nations organization after World War I, and his advocacy of the United Nations after World War II, is a complicated matter. However, if an underlying theme might be traced through his political involvement with those two great postwar world peace movements and this lifelong commitment to Greek literature, including his translations of Euripides, Aeschylus, and other dramatists, it would probably be a fear of "barbarians at the gates" and a determination to hold them at bay.

When his long life had nearly run its course, a disillusioned and pessimistic M. wrote to a friend that "civilized powers" had ceased to rule the world, which was now "at the mercy of a mass of little barbarous nations in the United Nations." For all his continuing fame as the foremost Hellenist of the time, M.'s work as translator and interpreter of Greek dramatic verse had not escaped criticism. Bitter domestic quarrels had riven the Murray home over the years, owing to such matters as his long absences from home in order to pursue his scholarly research, his wife's jealousy over his female assistants and colleagues, and parental difficulties with the five Murray children, whose behavior greatly distressed M. and his wife. At the time of M.'s death, only one offspring, Rosalind, had remained close to him; given M.'s aversion to dogmatic religion once he had given up the Roman Catholicism of his earliest years, Rosalind's conversion to that faith was an additional source of unhappiness. However, her husband, the eminent but controversial and unusually biased historian Arnold J. Toynbee (author of the twelve-volume work, *A Study of History*, 1934–61) and M. remained friends and colleagues, for all their temperamental and philosophical differences. But the sadness and dissension of the personal life of this tragic hero, figuratively speaking, was climaxed posthumously, when a controversy (never to be fully resolved) arose over whether M. had become a deathbed convert to his original faith, Roman Catholicism, through the urging of his daughter Rosalind and her priest.

Aside from M.'s celebrated translations and poetic renderings of the Greek dramatists' plays, perhaps his most noteworthy and enduring book for a wider audience is his late version of earlier attempts (dating from 1912 to 1925) to place Greek philosophical and cultural thought in historical perspective, *Five Stages of Greek Religion* (3rd ed., 1951). Among other matters, M. considered certain FOLKLORE themes and story elements in the cultural tradition of Greece and also other ancient cultures in the Near East: the dying and reviving god, for example, and the mother goddess and her savior son. The savior son would be "sacrificed to save his people," and might be "mystically identified with some sacrificial animal" like "a lamb, . . . whose blood has supernatural power"; on the other hand, the savior son might be personified as "a divine or miraculous Babe, for whose birth the whole world has been waiting, who will bring his own Age or Kingdom and 'make all things new.'" M. thus traced Christianity considerably beyond its Jewish roots, and came to a significant conclusion. Christianity's books "are Greek, the philosophical background is Hellenistic."

M.'s studies in comparative religion may in the long run turn out to be his most important contribution, considering the mixed reviews that his Greek translations received over the years (T. S. ELIOT was a particularly harsh critic of M.'s stylistic renderings) and the competition posed by rival translators. The five stages of Greek religion in M.'s schema are: the primal "Age of Innocence"—a period of stupidity, "before Zeus came to trouble men's minds"; the Olympian, classical period—when the powerful gods came into the picture, and "the primitive vagueness [of the first stage] was reduced to a kind of order"; the Great Schools of 4th-c. B.C.E. philosophy: the Cynic and Stoic Schools, and the Epicurean School; the "Failure of Nerve" stage, from Plato, roughly, to St. Paul and earlier Gnostics, a period that included the more popular thought currents of the later Hellenistic Age, when there was a pervasive sense of all-round failure—of belief in the Olympian gods, "of the free city-state" and human government in general, and of Hellenism's great propaganda campaign, that is, Greece's lengthy effort to educate (and civilize) a corrupt, barbaric world; the 4th-c. "Last Protest" stage, when, under the Roman emperor Julian (" the Apostate"), "the old religion . . . roused itself for a last spiritual protest against the all-conquering 'atheism' of the Christians."

BIBLIOGRAPHY: Thomson, J. A. K., and A. J. Toynbee, eds., *Essays in Honour of G. M.* (1936); West, F., *G. M.* (1984)

                                        SAMUEL I. BELLMAN

MURRY, John Middleton

b. 6 August 1889, London; d. 12 March 1957, Bury St. Edmunds, Suffolk

Known primarily as the husband of Katherine MANSFIELD and the friend of D. H. LAWRENCE, M. was in his own right a prolific writer—novelist, poet, playwright, editor, and biographer. He published his first novel, *Still Life*, in 1916, followed by two volumes of lyric poetry in 1918 and 1920, respectively. His oeuvre ranged from religious philosophy—*To the Unknown God* (1924) and *The Life of Jesus* (1926; repub. as *Jesus, Man of Genius*, 1926)—to Marxism, *The Necessity of Communism* (1932)—to political philosophy—*The Necessity of Pacifism* (1937), *The Pledge of Peace* (1938), and *The Defence of Democracy* (1939). M. earned the wrath of many of Mansfield's friends when he initiated the practice of publishing volumes of her work posthumously, including letters and journals that Mansfield intended to be destroyed.

MUSIC AND LITERATURE

The relationship of music and literature, as a specific instance of the relationship of music and language, has its origins in the links between the rhythm and intonation of speech and the rhythmic and pitch patterns of music. Indeed, it was not until the Greeks that music and what we now call poetry began to be distinguished as discrete forms, and the practice of conceiving of the two as unified can be traced up to the early Renaissance. While aestheticians have tended to link music and poetry, as those art forms that rely on, and manipulate, time, the history of musico-literary relations is multifaceted, with each drawing on the resources of the other for different purposes at different times. As such, recent studies in this area have tended to group their findings according to the basic types of relation involved, from music and literature to music as literature.

The sung or accompanied recitation of poetry by amateurs or professionals of the court was common practice during the Middle Ages, a period that was also witness to the importation of the French lyric tradition, with its chansons and troubadours. The influence of this tradition can be found in those works of Geoffrey CHAUCER modeled on the French lyric forms of the ballade and rondeau, and intended for sung performance (although no actual musical settings have been found). Indeed, while he was no musician, Chaucer's works are littered with references to music and performance, from the popular Latin hymn "Angelus ad virginem" sung by Nicholas in "The Miller's Tale" (*The Canterbury Tales*), to representations of the central ceremonial role played by music in activities of court; and from rousing scenes of the popular music of tavern and street, to the extended description of the symbolically contrasting trumpets of Eolus, God of Wind, in *The House of Fame*.

Nevertheless, the primacy of text over music in Chaucer is indicative of what, in the Renaissance, came to be a more clearly delineated separation of literature (or what we now call literature) from music. As such, we can categorize into four groups the variety of their interaction. Beginning with literature and music, we have those musical genres in which words and music coexist—chiefly song, opera, and certain forms of theater. Of particular prominence here are the literature and music of the English Renaissance. The secular meeting of word and music in the early 17th c. came primarily in the form of the madrigal— *The Triumphs of Oriana* (1601), collected in honor of ELIZABETH I by the prime mover of the English madrigal, Thomas Morley, stands as the highpoint— and the more comfortably English lute song. Most notable here is John Dowland, whose widely successful *First Booke of Songes or Ayres* (1597) is a characteristic collection of expressive settings of poems on the joys and sorrows of love. Another English development of French and Italian forms is the masque, primarily a court entertainment—and an allegorical representation of the court—which came to prominence in the first half of the 17th c. An elaborately staged mix of words, music, dance, and pantomime, the masque attracted dramatists such as George CHAPMAN and Thomas MIDDLETON, and the composer brothers William and Henry LAWES. The great partnership in this form, however, was that of dramatist Ben JONSON and architect and designer Inigo Jones, whose allegorical, but nonetheless politically topical, collaborations include *The Masque of Queens* (1609) and *Pleasure Reconcil'd to Virtue* (1618). The latter inspired John MILTON's only masque text, *Comus* (perf. 1634; pub. 1637), a modified masque in which the spoken word takes precedence over pageantry,

dance, and song (music was provided by Milton's friend, Henry Lawes). *Comus* was also inspired by William SHAKESPEARE's most overtly, and variously, musical play, *The Tempest*, in which the influence of the masque is prominent. While very little of the original music used in contemporary performance has survived, *The Tempest* has in turn generated a number of musical works, from the dramatically orchestral— Hector Berlioz's *Fantaisie sur la Tempête* (1830)—to the postmodernistically vocal: Michael Nyman's *Noises, Sounds and Sweet Airs* (1994).

A loose adaptation of *The Tempest* (1674) with words by Thomas SHADWELL and music by Matthew Locke, and others, also served as the first successful example of semi-opera, a peculiarly English response to French developments in music-based theatricals. Musically, the most important semi-operas are those of Henry Purcell. John DRYDEN referred to these as "our English operas," and himself provided the text for several, most notably *King Arthur* (1691). The latter, together with *The Fairy Queen* (1692), an anonymous (and extremely loose) reworking of Shakespeare's *A Midsummer Night's Dream*, is among the most successful examples of the short-lived genre. Of course, the masque and semi-opera can be seen as counterparts to opera itself, which had a troubled entry onto the British stage, the result of a national predilection, in theatrical entertainment, for speech over music and dance. Writing in 1711 on the vexed question of the popularity in London of Italian opera, Joseph ADDISON commented that "If the Italians have a genius for music above the English, the English have a genius for other performances of a much higher nature, and capable of giving the mind a much nobler entertainment." The most famous response to the troublingly foreign spectacle of Italian opera is John GAY's *The Beggar's Opera*, an all-round deflation of the "unnatural" norms of early-18th-c. opera, with folk songs and ballads replacing arias and a fiercely topical cast of London lowlife taking the place of mythical gods and heroes.

Whereas English opera proper—that is, fully sung drama—has a founding work in Purcell's *Dido and Aeneas* (1689), the influence of the British on pre-20th-c. opera is confined almost entirely to the providing of literary source material for librettos. Shakespeare surfaces again, albeit in often very freely adapted form, in major works by Verdi—*Macbeth* (1847), *Otello* (1887), and *Falstaff* (1893)—and minor curios such as Wagner's early opera *Das Liebesverbot* (1836), based on *Measure for Measure*. The novels of Sir Walter SCOTT, second only to Shakespeare in the amount of music they have inspired, lie behind a number of librettos, most famously Gaetano Donizetti's *Lucia di Lammermoor* (1835), loosely adapted from Scott's *The Bride of Lammermoor*. It was not until the 20th c. that British literature and music came together successfully, most notably in the operatic and vocal works of Benjamin Britten. While Shakespeare figures again—*A Midsummer Night's Dream* (1960)—the importance of literature for Britten is demonstrated by the variety of his sources. *Peter Grimes* (1945), the first significant British opera after *Dido and Aeneas*, takes as its source tales from *The Borough* (1810), a poem by the Suffolk poet George CRABBE, while Herman Melville's novella *Billy Budd* (wr. 1891; pub. 1924) was adapted for Britten by E. M. FORSTER and Eric Crozier (*Billy Budd*, 1951). Britten's settings of British literature are many and varied—from John DONNE (*The Holy Sonnets of John Donne*, 1945), to Thomas HARDY (*Winter Words*, 1953), Henry JAMES (*The Turn of the Screw*, 1954), and Wilfred OWEN (*War Requiem*, 1961)—but one prominent literary collaborator is W. H. AUDEN, with whom Britten first worked on the early operetta *Paul Bunyan* (wr. ca. 1940–41). The pair subsequently collaborated on a number of films as well as television and radio broadcasts, and the words of Auden are set by Britten in such works as *Our Hunting Fathers* (1936), *On This Island* (1937), and *Hymn to St. Cecilia* (1942). Working with Chester Kallman, Auden went on to pen librettos for Igor Stravinsky—*The Rake's Progress* (1951)—and Hans Werner Henze— *Elegy for Young Lovers* (1961) and *The Bassarids* (1966)—and the extent of his involvement with music, not least in the appropriation of musical forms in poetry, marks him out as particularly significant in this context.

From at least the 16th c. onward, when declamation and expressiveness came to the fore in vocal music, musical settings of verbal texts have served as readings of those texts, what George STEINER has termed "translations," each a "new whole" in itself. Settings or adaptations of literary works in music fall into the second category of musico-literary interaction, that of literature in music, and while many such works have been mentioned above, it is not only in opera that British literature has had a separate life. Milton, whose father was an amateur composer, served as the prime source for Handel's *L'Allegro, il Penseroso ed il Moderato* (1740) and, in even more modified form, Haydn's oratorio *Die Schöpfung* (1798), which adapts parts of *Paradise Lost*. Notable examples of the use of British literary texts in the 20th c. include a rich seam of British song, exemplified in the many settings of the poetry of A. E. HOUSMAN— the most famous being Ralph Vaughan Williams's *On Wenlock Edge* (1909)—and Stravinsky's settings of T. S. ELIOT and Dylan THOMAS. Of those instrumental compositions that have been explicitly modeled on, or inspired by, British literary works, the most notable composer is Berlioz, whose quintessentially romanticist engagement with Shakespeare produced some key works, including the overture *Le roi Lear* (1840), the

"dramatic symphony" (with voices) *Roméo et Juliette* (1847), and the *Marche funèbre pour la dernière scène d'Hamlet* (1852).

In the case of music in literature, we have not only those literary works that include reference to music and its performance, but also the allusion in literature to more general ideas of musicality: to song and singing, for example. The former is a vast topic indeed, stretching from the influence of Wagner in early-20th-c. works by Forster, Eliot, and D. H. LAWRENCE to the discussion of popular music in the late 20th c., a key sign of allegiances of gender and class in the likes of Nick HORNBY's *High Fidelity*, Irvine WELSH's *Trainspotting*, and Alan Warner's *These Demented Lands* (1997). More particularly, we might single out a musical object prominently displayed in many fictions of the 19th c.: the piano. Domestic music-making was a characteristic bourgeois occupation of the period, and with modest pianism a much touted mark of cultivated femininity, fictional scenes set around, and subplots involving, the piano, came to serve as carefully coded performances. Significant examples occur in Jane AUSTEN's *Emma*, William Makepeace THACKERAY's *Vanity Fair*, and Wilkie COLLINS's *The Woman in White*. In terms of more general allusions to musicality, such gendered scenes of pianistic intrigue are representative of the prominent role assigned to music in 19th-c. fiction, as signifying that which is unspoken (most often romantic inclinations) or unspeakable. Susceptibility to music, while on the one hand a mark of sensibility, can also imply an overly passionate nature, as is the case in George ELIOT's *The Mill on the Floss*, in which music is used to characterize, and foreshadow the fate of, the heroine, Maggie Tulliver—as it is that of the eponymous heroine of Hardy's *Tess of the d'Urbervilles*. (Eliot and Hardy, both amateur musicians, use music extensively in their fiction.) The worrying alliance of music's hypnotic forces with female susceptibility and uncanny foreignness finds ultimate expression in George DU MAURIER's best-selling *Trilby* (1894), in which the singing voice of the eponymous heroine is created by the domineering spell of the German-Polish musician, Svengali, who has become antonomastic.

In the realm of poetry, the 19th c. provides an equally rich store of music in literature, in particular the allusion to music and song in Romantic poetry. Following the revival of interest in national traditions of ballad and song that we find in Robert BURNS and Scott, and, more broadly, the aspiration to balladlike clarity expressed in William WORDSWORTH and Samuel Taylor COLERIDGE's preface to *Lyrical Ballads*, we can trace such a presence in the poetry of the period, and in that of John KEATS and Percy Bysshe SHELLEY in particular. Music functions here as imagery and founding metaphor, carrying associations of the unimpeded voice of nature, of memory, and the passage of time. As such, we are moving here toward ideas of literature as music: not the allusion in literature to musicality, but an aspiration to pass above the word in order to attain the perceived higher plane of music. Such ideas have a long tradition, stretching back to the Pythagorean concept of the music of the spheres, but it was in the aesthetics of the early German Romantics that music, as nonreferential, really came to the fore as a paradigm for art. The influence in British literary circles of such ideas can be seen in Coleridge's philosophical writings, but it was not until the late 19th c. that a sustained attempt on the part of literature to co-opt the perceived abstractions of music was undertaken. Again, rather than a particular style, this is very much music as a generalized ideal, one of which poetry was thought to have lost sight. In line with Walter PATER's famous dictum that all art, "striving to be independent of the mere intelligence," struggles toward the condition of music, modernist literature in general, and symbolism in particular, had music in mind. The two central figures here, Paul Valéry and Stéphane Mallarmé, are French, but music thus perceived figures prominently in the poetry of Eliot. While *The Waste Land* spins a web of allusions to music, Wagner in particular, and was received as a work constructed on musical models, it is in *Four Quartets* that Eliot consciously strove for a musicality of structure and motivic interplay. In the realm of fiction, James JOYCE and Virginia WOOLF are both variously concerned with music, with the "Sirens" episode from Joyce's *Ulysses* offering a striking example of what Aldous HUXLEY—himself a writer who grappled with the question of relations between music and literature—termed "the musicalization of fiction."

The final category of musico-literary interplay—music as literature—brings us full circle, back to a vexed problem: whether, despite the aforementioned strivings toward a literary music, music is really so blissfully detached from the mundane associations of language; whether music is itself not a variety of text, to the extent that we only ever experience music according to a conglomerate of ways and means, of words and their associations, inherited from the world in which we listen. Such an unanswerable question, the latest installment in the ongoing sizing up of literature by music, and vice versa, is neatly encapsulated in novelist Jeanette WINTERSON's *Art and Lies*, in which the final pages reproduce, without comment, the score of the concluding Trio from Richard Strauss and Hugo von Hofmannsthal's opera *Der Rosenkavalier* (1911).

BIBLIOGRAPHY: Brown, C., *Music and Literature* (1948); Burgan, M., "Heroines at the Piano: Women and Music in Nineteenth-Century Fiction," *VS* 30 (1986): 51–76; Gray, B., *George Eliot and Music* (1989); Kirby-Smith, H. T., *The Celestial Twins: Poetry and Music through the Ages* (1999); Kramer, L., *Music and Poetry: The Nineteenth Century and After* (1984); Minahan, J. A., *Word like a Bell: John Keats, Music and the Romantic Poet* (1992); Winn, J. A., *Unsuspected Eloquence: A History of the Relations between Poetry and Music* (1981); Wolf, W., *The Musicalization of Fiction* (1999)

STEPHEN BENSON

MYERS, L[eopold] H[amilton]

b. 6 September 1881, Cambridge; d. 8 April 1944, Marlow-on-Thames, Buckinghamshire

M. was a novelist who explored ethical, philosophical, and spiritual themes in his fiction and was especially concerned with what he saw as the collapse of values in the modern world. His most notable achievement, the tetralogy *The Near and the Far* (1931–43), creates an idealized image of 16th-c. India that functions as an implicit critique of the spiritual emptiness, as M. regarded it, of mid-20th-c. Western life. M. published only fiction, so that reflections which for other writers might have issued in essays and philosophical tracts entered into his novels and turned them into fascinating hybrids that are unusual in an English cultural context that has tended to suspect abstract speculation in the novel.

M. came of an English family of some intellectual achievement, though his father, F. W. H. Myers, ventured into unorthodox territory by becoming one of the founder members of the British Society for Psychical Research. Unorthodoxy also marked M.'s own attitudes. Educated at Eton, one of Britain's most prestigious schools, he rebelled against its ethos; his undergraduate days at Cambridge University were brief; he rejected the BLOOMSBURY GROUP and became a Communist sympathizer. The search for a set of beliefs that would give meaning to modern existence motivated his life and his fiction.

M.'s inherited wealth left him free to pursue his work as a writer without economic pressures. After a false start with a verse play, *Arvat* (1908), which sank with hardly a trace, his first published novel, *The Orissers* (1922), appeared when M. was forty-one. The novel explores the struggle for the ownership of a country estate between the Orissers, who represent a disabling sensitivity and self-consciousness, and the Maynes, who embody a coarse materialism. It is a rather cerebral novel that does not bring characters, incidents, and sensuous experiences vividly before the reader but asks for a more abstract response. *The 'Clio'* (1925), M.'s second novel, is a livelier piece of work: a group of wealthy passengers are stranded aboard a yacht on the bank of the Amazon and are forced to reconsider and in some cases change their lives.

It is, however, in the four novels that comprise *The Near and the Far* that M. finds the most ample means of exploring his preoccupations in fiction. The first three novels—*The Near and the Far* (1929), *Prince Jali* (1931), and *Rajah Amar* (1935)—were originally collected in one volume entitled *The Root and the Flower* (1935), which won both the Femina Vie Heureuse Prize and the James Tait Black Memorial Prize; in 1943, the trilogy turned into a tetralogy when a further novel was added, *The Pool of Vishnu*, and the quartet came out in one volume in that year under the overall title of *The Near and the Far*. This title sums up M.'s key concern: the relationship between the everyday and the transcendent. Though set in the time of Akbar the Great Mogul in 16th-c. India, the tetralogy is not, as M.'s introduction makes clear, an historical novel, and while it draws on Orientalist representations, it does not aim to rival Rudyard KIPLING or E. M. FORSTER in presenting the "reality" of India, a country that M. had never visited. The imaginary India of *The Near and the Far* provides him with the distant vantage point from which the social and ethical problems of the present time might be seen more clearly.

The first volume focuses on the world of ambition and love: the political struggle for succession between Daniyal and Salim, the two sons of the ailing Akbar, and the passions of young men and women such as Hari and Sita. The second volume concerns the quest of the young Prince Jali for self-knowledge and for a deeper understanding of life, while Rajah Amar, the main protagonist of the third volume, is divided between his desire to retreat from the world and his responsibilities as a ruler in the succession crisis. The final volume concentrates on the relationship between Mohan, a Rajah who has renounced political power, and Damayanti, a Rajah's daughter who escapes from a possessive father. With its large cast of characters, its proliferation of situations and incidents, and its range of intertwined themes, *The Near and The Far* is a rich and remarkable exploration of the nature and possibilities of life as M. saw them.

The conflict between the pressures of society and the desire for transcendence, which is a key theme of *The Near and the Far*, is echoed in M.'s one other novel, *Strange Glory* (1936), published in between the third and fourth volumes of the tetralogy. Set in the 20th c., *Strange Glory* portrays a wealthy young woman, Paulina, who is divided between her social obligations and the mystical vision she experiences in a Louisiana swamp. She forms relationships with two men—Stephen, embodying action, and Wentworth, representing mysticism—but both die and she is left, at the end of the novel, preparing to leave the swamp to go and look after Stephen's child. It is questionable, however, whether this commitment will assuage her self-division: *Strange Glory* does not resolve the question of whether it is possible to reconcile life in the world with mystical insight. The novel remains a haunting, evocative exploration of a dilemma that pervades M.'s work.

It is over fifty years since M.'s death by suicide at the age of sixty-three, but in that time, only one book-length critical study, by G. H. Bantock, has so far appeared—and Bantock's approach, derived from the criticism of F. R. LEAVIS, often applies inappropriate criteria and comparisons to M.'s work. In the 21st c., when readers have become used to much broader and more flexible concepts of the novel form, M. should be seen as developing a distinctive kind of fiction that combines philosophy and narrative in a way that is demanding but rewarding; his work provides many of the traditional pleasures of the novel but also prompts the reader to engage in more abstract considerations of key problems of modernity.

BIBLIOGRAPHY: Allen, W., *Tradition and Dream: The English and American Novel from the Twenties to Our Time* (1964); Bantock, G. H., *L. H. M.* (1956); Wilson, C., *Eagle and Earwig* (1965)

NICOLAS TREDELL

MYSTERIES AND MORALITY PLAYS

English medieval drama is today the subject of an enthusiastic scholarly and popular revival. The literary and theatrical qualities of the plays are being newly revealed in academic research and in exciting productions, mounted in physical conditions approximating to the original staging.

Mysteries and morality plays are didactic, religious dramas of the late medieval period. Written in the vernacular, the plays are among the chief glories of English literature from the late 14th to the mid-16th cs. They were conceived as part of a systematic campaign by the church to instruct the laity, in their own language, in the essential features of their faith. The mysteries told, in narrative form, of the relationship between God and mankind as revealed in the Bible. The morality plays told, in allegorical form, of the perpetual struggle between Good and Evil for the possession of the human soul, stressing the inevitability of death and the eternal afterlife in either heaven or hell.

The earliest extant English mysteries and morality plays survive in handwritten manuscripts and in printed books, usually from the 15th and 16th cs. Mostly anonymous, and probably written by members of the clergy, they are clearly the work of educated men, well read in doctrinal literature. They reveal a coherent, theological vision of the Christian universe, of man's place in it, his relationship to God, his fall from grace, and his hope of redemption.

Importantly, however, these are plays written in celebration of God's love and mercy; they were performed at times of holiday festivity and sought to entertain, as well as instruct, their audiences. The responsibility for the staging of the plays was in the hands of the laity, and performances were inventive and imaginative spectacles. The action, frequently juxtaposing the seriousness of the theme with comic and irreverent episodes, was energetic and often included songs, music and dancing, mime and mimicry, tumbling, conjuring, wrestling and fighting; the costumes, masks, properties, and special effects were colorful and ingeniously devised.

The plays are written almost entirely in rhymed verse stanzas, in an English that is archaic and, at first glance, unfamiliar. After the Norman Conquest, three languages were in use in England: Latin—the language of the church; French—the language of the nobility; and English, with its many regional varieties, the language of the majority of the population. The playwrights aimed at compatibility between subject and style, and in the "high style," which characterizes the noble or spiritually enlightened speaker, the vocabulary shows the influence of Latin and French; whereas in the "low style" characteristic of the unenlightened or evil speaker, the vocabulary is a robust, colloquial English. In the "high style," words are woven into elaborate and rhetorically ordered structures, with much use of decorative alliteration; in contrast, the "low style" is down-to-earth, wittily inventive in words of abuse, full of oaths, and sexual or scatological references.

Medieval staging was symbolic rather than realistic, and capable of representing the universe in miniature; the dramatic action moving freely between heaven, earth, and hell. The plays were put on in a variety of venues, indoor and outdoor, in city streets, in or in front of churches, in playing fields, marketplaces, or in the great halls of royal, noble, or collegiate households. Mystery plays were performed in the open air, either processionally on pageant wagons in the streets of towns or cities, or in the type of fixed staging known as "place-and-scaffold," which could be either a sizeable arena out in the countryside or merely two or three booth stages erected in a market place or churchyard. Morality plays were performed either indoors in great halls or outside on place-and-scaffold stages.

Mysteries and morality plays were written to be seen, not read, and it is known from a variety of sources that their staging was elaborate and expensive. Current research is largely devoted to the collection of documentary evidence concerning their production, and much of the newly available data is bewildering in its implications.

The terms "mystery play," "mystery cycle," and "mysteries" have been the cause of some confusion. "Mystery" in this context derives from the Latin word "ministerium," meaning a craft or trade, and is traditionally used to describe those cycles of biblical plays that encompassed the whole spiritual history of man-

kind from God's creation of the world to its end, and whose central theme was Christ's sacrifice and the redemption of man. These plays evolved over a long period and were the work of many hands; the productions were financed and staged by the craft guilds and the plays acted by their members. Four of these great mystery cycles have survived virtually complete, three from the north of England, and the fourth from East Anglia. It is these four cycles that are generally known as the "mysteries," but other manuscripts also exist of numerous isolated plays and incomplete fragments.

The mysteries are also often known as the "Corpus Christi" plays because their origin is closely linked to the medieval church's Festival of Corpus Christi, established by the Pope early in the 14th c. and soon afterward widely observed in Britain and Europe. The purpose of this festival was to celebrate the Mystery of the Blessed Sacrament, and to give thanks for its redemptive power. At the feast, which occurred in early summer, the Eucharist was carried in procession from the principal church through the streets of the town, followed by the clergy and members of the craft guilds. As the processions became more elaborate, the guilds vied with each other in the provision of a series of religious tableaux that, mounted on floats, accompanied the parade. While scholars agree that it is impossible to date the precise beginning of the Corpus Christi plays, it is probable that the tableaux gradually developed some action and dialogue, and evolved into short scenes enacting episodes from the Bible.

The four cycles that have survived are those of York (forty-eight plays), Chester (twenty-four plays), Wakefield—also known as the Towneley cycle—(thirty-two plays), and the N-Town cycle—previously attributed to Coventry and now known to be from East Anglia—(forty-two plays). The plays in each may be grouped in order thematically: those telling of the Creation of the world and the Fall of man; those that prophesy the Redemption of man; plays of the nativity; plays of the Passion; and lastly, plays celebrating the triumph of Christ and ending at doomsday.

The length of the cycles is astonishing; documentary evidence reveals that at York, where the cycle was performed on Corpus Christi day, the actors assembled before dawn and performances continued throughout the day and into the night; at other places, performances were spread over two or three days. The civic records of York and Chester show that their plays were performed processionally on pageant wagons. Each guild was responsible for the presentation of a separate pageant, or episode, in the story, on a wagon that was drawn from one "station," or prearranged acting place, to another through the town. Although no contemporary picture of a pageant wagon exists, it is known that they were expensive to build and ingenious in their effects. Several plays require an upper level to represent heaven, others need two simultaneous "sets," and some require a gaping hell-mouth from which terrifying devils could emerge to drag the damned down into the eternal flames. Similar dramatic effects would have been achieved in those cycles, like the N-Town, which were arranged for static performance on raised booth stages.

Determined by the central importance of the Passion of Christ and man's hope of Redemption, the grouping of biblical episodes and the selection of characters is specific. Plays dramatizing the fall of Lucifer, Adam, and Cain highlight man's fallen state, while vivid characterizations of figures such as Herod, Pilate, and Judas illustrate the corruption of man's nature. Many ordinary men, women and children—shepherds, soldiers, servants, wives, and mothers—are witnesses to and participants in the unfolding drama, and events such as the Massacre of the Innocents and the Crucifixion are portrayed with an unflinching realism. Old Testament stories are clearly seen as prefiguring events in the New Testament, and many Old Testament figures, for example Adam, Noah, and Isaac are seen as "types" who prefigure Christ. In a similar way, the tree of knowledge in the Garden of Eden has an emblematic correspondence with the cross on Calvary. Prophecy and "typology" are recurring devices in the plays, and are of didactic and dramatic importance. Another characteristic feature is a bold juxtaposition of sacred and profane images, a technique also found in medieval art and architecture, where frequently the sublime, transcendental, and other-worldly is strikingly set alongside the base, vulgar, and grotesque. The Wakefield cycle play *The Killing of Abel* illustrates the technique; it tells the story of Cain and the first murder, showing how the corruption of sinful mankind intensifies after the fall. Cain, the ploughman, is a rebel, and, in his disobedience to God's commands, he is a "type" of Satan; he is abusive toward his servant, his brother, and God, and refuses to pay his tithes; Abel, the shepherd, is shown in complete visual and verbal contrast—he is obedient to God's command and willingly pays his tithes, and as a good shepherd and sacrificial victim he is presented as a "type" of Christ. The play is grotesquely comic in its opening, with Cain plowing, and swearing obscenely at his horses and his servant; in contrast, his killing of Abel is an almost ritualistic act and God's judgment of him is expressed in powerfully ritualistic language. In another well-known example, the Wakefield *Second Shepherds Play*, the grotesque comedy of Mak, the sheep-stealer, and his wife Gill, is juxtaposed with the nativity of Christ: the sacred image of the Holy Child, symbolized as a lamb, and seen lying in a manger, is in stark contrast with the farcical scene that precedes it, in which Mak hides his stolen sheep in a cradle and persuades his wife to pretend it is a newborn baby when his fellow shep-

herds come in search of it. The mystery cycles were finally suppressed at the time of the Reformation in England, and the last recorded performance of a complete cycle was in 1581.

It is now well established that the "morality"—or moral plays or interludes as they were known in their time—were contemporary with the mystery plays and not, as once thought, a later development. Though similarly dedicated to religious instruction, they are very different. Where the mysteries dramatize a carefully controlled sequence of biblical stories, the moralities are single plays, designed to bring home to each individual in the audience the relevance of faith to daily life. Their message to all mankind was that by following Christ's example everyone could fight off the temptations of the Devil, overcome death, and attain everlasting salvation.

The origin of the morality plays is thought to lie in a dramatic development of the SERMON. During the 14th c., traveling friars made preaching a popular art, making vivid use of "exempla"—characters and illustrative examples of behavior calculated to capture the listeners' attention and enforce the moral point. Other suggested influences on the development of the moralities are the 4th-c. poem the *Psychomachia* of Prudentius, in which vices and virtues battle for the soul of man; and the Paternoster plays, none of which have survived, which were based on the doctrine that within the Lord's Prayer lie the seven "remedies" to the Seven Deadly Sins. In addition to these, there was the grimly powerful visual allegory of the "dance of death."

The typical structure of the plays is an allegorical battle or tournament, with Good and Evil struggling for the soul of man. The protagonist is always a representative Christian, and major characters are the Virtues, among whom are Truth, Justice, Temperance, and Mercy, known as the Four Daughters of God, and Faith, Hope, and Charity, the three Cardinal Virtues; opposed to them are the Vices, among whom are the Seven Deadly Sins: Sloth, Pride, Avarice, Anger, Envy, Gluttony, and Lechery. God, Angels, and the Devil in a variety of guises also appear, as do numerous other personifications of good and evil attributes and qualities, and the stark reminder of man's mortality, the spectral figure of Death.

Most surviving moralities are by unknown playwrights, but among the known authors are Henry Medwall (*Nature,* wr. ca. 1495) and John SKELTON. Three of the best-known English morality plays are the *Castle of Perseverance, Mankind,* and *Everyman;* they well illustrate the diversity and range of the genre. The earliest is the *Castle of Perseverance* (wr. ca. 1405); it was conceived for performance in the open air, and a manuscript of the play contains one of the world's most prized theater drawings, a plan for its staging, showing the circular arena with five platforms set within its circumference, housing the World, the Flesh, the Devil, Avarice, and God; and, at its center, a "castle" on stilts, which housed the soul of mankind, "Humanum Genus"—the play's protagonist. The vigorous action, in the form of a tournament, spans the life of the protagonist from birth to death; there are thirty-five speaking parts and the performance lasts four and a half hours.

Mankind (wr. ca. 1460–70), in contrast, is much shorter, has a cast of only seven and could be staged either indoors or out. The protagonist, Mankind, is an agricultural worker and the specific focus of the play is that honest labor is a remedy for the sin of sloth. With his spade his only prop, Mankind typologically represents the fallen Adam. The play is characterized by its HUMOR, energy, and often bawdy language.

Everyman (wr. ca. 1509–19), which is believed to be a translation of the Dutch *Elkerlife* (wr. ca. 1490), is about holy dying and it is characterized by the awe-inspiring seriousness of its tone; structured on the image of a journey, the solemn, ritualistic action takes place on an unlocalized set; features required are the House of Salvation, possibly resembling a church, where Everyman goes to confession, the grave into which he descends, and an upper level representing heaven to which his soul ascends.

Morality plays were dramatically alive in England until after 1600; and in them lies the foundation of a secular drama. After the religious didacticism of the early moralities was suppressed at the Reformation, playwrights gradually began to create real-life characters in place of personified abstractions. Ben JONSON, Cyril TOURNEUR, Christopher MARLOWE, and William SHAKESPEARE all made frequent allusion in their plays to familiar themes, concepts, and images from the mysteries and moralities.

BIBLIOGRAPHY: Axton, R., *European Drama of the Early Middle Ages* (1974); Beadle, R., ed., *The Cambridge Companion to Medieval English Theatre* (1994); Bevington, D., *From Mankind to Marlowe* (1962); Chambers, E. K., *The Mediaeval Stage* (2 vols., 1903); Kolve, V. A., *The Play Called Corpus Christi* (1966); Potter, R., *The English Morality Play* (1975); Rossiter, A. P., *English Drama from Early Times to the Elizabethans* (1950); Tydeman, W., *Medieval English Theatre, 1400–1500* (1986); Wickham, G., *Early English Stages, 1300–1660* (1959); Woolf, R., *The English Mystery Plays* (1972)

SUSAN MACKLIN

MYTH AND LEGEND

Myth and legend are sometimes distinct, sometimes interwoven, and sometimes blended narrative genres. Often today we regard legend as a form of embroidered or transformed history; that is, its personages and events are considered to have some basis, however sketchy, in actual fact. The "real" King Arthur, for instance, was a 5th-c. cavalry general who won glory by defeating the invading Saxons. Myth, on the other hand, partakes of a more religious, symbolic, or dreamlike order of truth: its origins and elements belong more to the spiritual than to the historical realm. To continue the example, the Holy Grail so fervently sought by Arthur's knights—the chalice holding the blood of the crucified Christ with the power to heal the wounded Fisher King and restore the dying land—yields no discernible trace of historical evidence. And yet it is one of the most central and powerful myths of British literature. The usefulness of the legend/myth distinction is somewhat limited, since many tales mingle the natural with the fantastic, the mundane with the numinous so powerfully that an exact label becomes a moot point.

The original Greek term *mythos,* meaning "speech" or "story," has come to suggest a sacred or archetypal narrative often featuring supernatural beings and events, which may intersect with the lives of humans and the natural world, and which may also be (or have been) associated with certain rituals. Colloquially, we use the word "myth" to denote a fiction or falsehood, and Roland Barthes adopted the term to highlight a cultural construct disguised as natural fact (*Mythologies,* 1973). Both these usages underline myth's relative remove from literal actuality. At the same time, the universality of myths throughout history and around the globe, along with our ardent discussions and continued literary uses of them, confirm the essential and profound value of myths in human life.

As early as the 4th c. B.C.E., Euhemerus hypothesized that the gods of the Greek myths had their origins in human deeds and exploits. "Euhemerism" survived in the efforts of medieval and early modern thinkers to reduce myths to their human and natural sources, to demystify or demythologize the tales. And the 20th c. has seen a host of fresh views of myth. Psychoanalysts Sigmund Freud and C. G. Jung both considered myths as revelations of the contents of the unconscious: to Freud they were evidence of the repressed past, to Jung a germinating or possible future. Anthropologist Claude Lévi-Strauss describes the repeated patterns of myths as reflections of deep structures of the human mind and as paths toward resolution of the internal contradictions inherent in every culture. Philosopher Ernst Cassirer interpreted philosophy's rigorous inquiry as a struggle to liberate the human mind from myth. Other scholars, however, have discerned and defended the presence of myth in modern and postmodern culture, leading some to affirm "the myth of mythlessness." Historian of religion Mircea Eliade captures the enduring power of the mythic when he writes "There is no myth which is not the unveiling of a 'mystery,' the revelation of a primordial event which inaugurated either a constituent structure of reality or a kind of human behavior."

British literature has incorporated myth and legend in a variety of ways and to a variety of effects. A glance at the most readily visible of these strategies will serve to suggest others and to offer avenues of interpretation for works beyond these examples. The first may be called naturalization, a metaphor both of transplanting and new citizenship. The narration of a myth or legend can "naturalize" an imported or outdated tale by transforming it into accessible or literary form, affirming the value of the story and reconstituting it as part of a tradition from which it otherwise might have been omitted or lost. The great OLD ENGLISH EPIC *BEOWULF* blends history, legends, and myths from Sweden and Denmark into a single unified narrative arc portraying a heroic ideal that was meaningful to the 8th, 9th, and 10th cs. The poem infuses the exploits and career of Beowulf with the powerful mnemonic music of Old English alliterative verse. The adopted stories become naturalized to Northumbria, replanted and offered citizenship on the British isle, so to speak, through the alchemy of language and form.

A variant of retelling as naturalization, which we may call valediction, occurs when the literary appropriation is felt to be unsuccessful or impossible. W. B. YEATS opened his first collection, *Crossways,* by announcing the death of the past: "The woods of Arcady are dead,/And over is their antique joy." And by the end of his career, in spite of his efforts in both drama and verse to revive the old heroic tales of Oisin and Cuchulain, he was still mourning "The Circus Animals' Desertion," the fading of the painted stage of the past, the dream from which we have awakened. The longed-for reaffirmation is expressed as a farewell, ironically a kind of *negatio*—an affirmation by ostensible denial. The elegiac beauty of Yeats's great lyric poems captures our need for the inspiration of myth and legend more vividly and memorably even than his verse dramatizations of the legends themselves.

A third role of myth in literature might be called *marriage,* when the myths of two cultures work together harmoniously. In the work of Edmund SPENSER, for instance, the classical and Christian contexts coexist with remarkable smoothness and comfort. Some congruence is felt to be underlying the surface differences, and thus the contrasting contexts enrich rather than contest one another. To take a small but easily visible example, Douglas Bush points out how Spenser's beautiful depiction of the dawn in book 1 of *The Faerie Queene* combines a reference to the sun as the Greek sun-god Phoebus (Apollo) with the image of the sun as a bridegroom borrowed from the nineteenth Psalm.

Another example of the Renaissance marriage of myth with the nonmythic is the intertwining play and playlet in William SHAKESPEARE's *A Midsummer Night's Dream.* The realistic plight of the aristocratic lovers is echoed in the homespuns' farcically enacted mythical tale, with both levels of reality illumined by a third in the interference of the fairies. The amusingly inept dramatization of the tragedy Pyramus and Thisbe is an effective foil to the confusion and increasing desperation of the "real" lovers.

A wholly different effect is created, however, when one mythical system denies or supplants the truth of another. Then the task of the literary work is prioritization. John MILTON makes it very clear in book 1 of *Paradise Lost* that the deities of the ancient pantheons were "fabled" and "erring." His justification of the ways of the Christian God to men takes place through a decentering and disempowering of the old false gods. Milton does not broach explicitly the question, as many have done since, of whether Christianity itself might be yet another myth, and if it is, what this means about religious faith. In a much later prioritization project, D. H. LAWRENCE suggests in *Mornings in Mexico,* published in 1927, that "One man can belong to one great way of consciousness only. He may even change from one way to another. But he cannot go both ways at once." Feeling himself and his civilization to be badly in need of renewal, Lawrence gravitated to myths of ancient Mexico as an answer to the deadened present.

Renewal was a project for 17th-c. writers, too, particularly the metaphysicals, who set about replacing the pagan pantheon with devotion of a "purer" and plainer kind. Indeed, as post-Renaissance enthusiasm for the Greek and Roman myths continued to wear thin, even the classically exuberant 18th c. was not immune to an occasional sense of overexposure. Samuel JOHNSON complained of Nicholas ROWE's *Ulysses* that readers were already so familiar with this hero and his exploits that they were quite uninterested in yet another repetition of the same. In addition (or perhaps therefore), mythical narratives tended more often than before to be reduced to familiar manners of speaking, habits of decorative paraphrase and personification—myth distilled into decorative language. The learned language of allusions was reduced at times to a sort of mythological shorthand, whose deployment was often designed less to enlighten the reader and more to lift the work above that of uneducated scribblers. Bush puts it poetically: "As Milton's influence rolled like a tidal wave up the shores of the 18th c. it deposited everywhere the bleached seaweed of mythology and poetic diction from which the Miltonic life had departed."

Another strategy of distillation or selective incorporation is to make the myth or legend into a narrative scaffold or framework, a sort of armature, for a second, more dominant narrative—myth distilled into structure. Percy Bysshe SHELLEY's *Adonais* is not only or even primarily a retelling of the myth of Adonis and Aphrodite. The poet has adapted the mythical story, sometimes with considerable effort, as a vehicle for his elegy on the tragic death of poet John KEATS, his polemic against certain critics and social attitudes, and his vision of eternal beauty beyond the injustices of this imperfect world. An example of Shelley's adaptation of the myth is his transformation of the shepherd Adonis's flock of sheep into Keats's poetic visions, "The quick Dreams,/The passion-wingèd Ministers of thought,/Who were his flocks." The myth takes on a certain transparency, as its outlines support the thematically dominant narrative.

A similar structural deployment of myth appears almost exactly a century later in James JOYCE's *Ulysses*, in which characters and events of Dublin on June 16, 1904, are patterned on those of Homer's *Odyssey*. In this extraordinarily rich novel, it is not the myth but rather the modern story that takes on a transparency, letting us glimpse behind urban bustle and textures of consciousness the patterns of the ancient tale.

The same Homeric material has been tapped by the Victorian poet Alfred, Lord TENNYSON in "The Lotos-Eaters" and "Ulysses," poems in which we see yet another strategy, namely myth distilled into lyric voice. In the "Choric Song" portion of "The Lotos-Eaters," the voices of Odysseus' mariners relax gradually in lengthening lines and stanzas into the seductions of rest from the labors of life. "Ulysses," too, written shortly after the death of Tennyson's friend Arthur Hallam, adopts from the ancient story the persona of the legendary adventurer and his courage for moving forward into the future. In contrast to these lyrics, Tennyson's late long poem *Idylls of the King* narrates in leisurely detail the whole legend of King Arthur and the myth of the Holy Grail—the poem's task is truly naturalization, an exploration of the contemporary implications of this ancient story.

In contrast with Tennyson's elaborate narration of the Grail myth, we see in T. S. ELIOT's *The Waste Land* a powerful distillation of myth into symbol. Here, the mythic story is assumed rather than told. Glimpses of the Fisher King, the "empty chapel," and the "arid plain" are interwoven with allusions to a wide range of sources that crowd together like fragments of a vast shattered mosaic of civilization in the stunned aftermath of the First World War. And each shard or fragment pulses with intensities of memory, suggestion, and possibilities.

Certainly phenomena as rich as myth and legend will never be exhausted by the most thorough analysis, let alone by a sketchy list such as this one. The inexhaustible and mysterious nature of these tales is one of the great treasures of human culture, a resource that artists and thinkers will surely persist in transfiguring in ever-new ways.

BIBLIOGRAPHY: Bush, D., *Mythology and the Renaissance Tradition in English Poetry* (1932; rev. ed., 1963); Bush, D., *Mythology and the Romantic Tradition in English Poetry* (1937); Cassirer, E., *The Philosophy of Symbolic Forms* (4 vols., 1953–96); Coupe, L., *Myth* (1997); Daniel, G. E., et al., *Myth or Legend?* (1955); Eliade, M., *Myths, Dreams, and Mysteries* (1960); Hungerford, E. B., *Shores of Darkness* (1941); Kirk, G. S., *Myth: Its Meaning and Function in Ancient and Other Cultures* (1970); Scarborough, M., *Myth and Modernity* (1994); Vickery, J. B., *Myths and Texts* (1983)

MARGARET HOLLEY

N

NAIPAUL, [Sir] V[idiadhar] S[urajprasad]
b. 17 August 1932, Chaguanas, Trinidad

Born of East Indian ancestry, N. was educated at Oxford. He began to write after he left the university, and since then has followed no other profession.

N. is a postcolonial writer: that is, whether in Africa, Asia, India, South America, or the West Indies, he investigates the effects of empire. Early books such as *The Mystic Masseur* (1957) and *Miguel Street* (1959) probe the plight of Indians living in the Caribbean. Brought there as a source of labor, they are still denigrated and exploited. He examines similar mistreatment of Indians in *A House for Mr. Biswas* (1961), which describes a man searching for his roots in Trinidad without even knowing exactly where his childhood home stood. Inspired by a visit to that country in 1956, in *A House for Mr. Biswas* N. uses language to dramatize the imposition of outside culture on native peoples: characters use Hindi for emotion and intimacy and English for law and insult, in a country in which all legal proceedings had to be conducted in English, including Hindu marriages, which were not recognized as valid until 1946—even though Indians made up one third of the population. In these and later works, such as *A Flag on the Island* (1967), which discusses the influence of the U.S. on Trinidad, and *The Mimic Men* (1967), focusing on politics in the West Indies, N. emphasizes the problems of individuals trying to maintain their integrity while functioning as members of a collectivized society, which is always unaware of their struggles to survive. Sometimes such characters look to personal relationships to provide solace, but most often these relationships merely reflect existing social tensions.

After 1967, N. turned his attention to the colonialists as well as the colonized. In a book combining short stories and essays entitled *In a Free State* (1971), which won the Booker Prize, Britain's most prestigious literary award, the title story tells of British colonials in a newly independent East African country. In the middle of a political crisis, Bobby, a government servant, and Linda, the wife of a colleague, travel from the capital to the exclusive compound where they live. While neither of them belongs any longer in England, neither do they have much future in Africa. Linda is an elitist, only comfortable in the rarefied atmosphere of the compound, and Bobby is a liberal and a homosexual, rejected by both Linda and the Africans whom he attempts to pick up. Their journey is a modern version of Joseph CONRAD's "Heart of Darkness" in that Bobby and Linda discover their own profound confusion and vulnerability. The story concludes with Bobby being beaten up by African soldiers and insulted by his African houseboy.

Like *Guerillas* (1975), published four years later, other stories in *In a Free State* probe the plight of the colonized, from an even broader perspective than previous works. In such fiction, which always features a collision of cultures, N.'s overall view is that former colonies like Trinidad are too small, too dependent, and too lacking in cohesion to have any future, despite being officially independent. He regards the true enemy as the past—"slavery . . . colonial neglect and a society uneducated from top to bottom." While some critics have found this vision too harsh and deterministic, others have stressed the personal anguish lying behind N.'s determination to alert his audience to the postcolonial predicament. And in 1977, in *India: A Wounded Civilization*, his vision of his own motherland is no more optimistic: he finds contemporary India merely a place of squalor, a lie as compared with long-held images of past grandeur. In his view, Indians have lost touch with any history they might have had and lack the resources to be anything other than "mimic men" of the dominant civilization.

A Bend in the River (1979), however, signals an "extraordinary loosening" of N.'s vision. Although the hero, Salim, is Indian, he is actually rootless, owing nothing to either India or Europe as he struggles to survive as a trader. Salim soon finds himself in love with Yvette, the wife of a Belgian advisor to an African president. He also develops a relationship with Metty, his own servant, and with Ferdinand, a young African from the bush being educated at the lycée. As probably the only examples of productive friendships between those from different cultures in N.'s work, these relationships are abruptly ended when local businesses are nationalized by Africans. But because Salim has opened his house to him, Ferdinand saves Salim's life and he is able to leave town.

N.'s most important recent work is *A Way in the World* (1994). The book consists of a series of illuminated, extended moments in the history of Spanish and British imperialism in the Caribbean, including the last expedition of Sir Walter RALEIGH and Francisco de Miranda's invasion of South America. This book has been received as part of the complex evolution of a writer who, although he writes of the limitations of postcolonial societies, most critics agree is by no means a neocolonialist. Indeed, most regard N.—awarded the 2001 Nobel Prize for Literature—as one of the finest novelists of his generation.

BIBLIOGRAPHY: Hughes, P., *V. S. N.* (1988); Kelly, R., *V. S. N.* (1989); King, B., *V. S. N.* (1993); Naipaul, V. S., *The Overcrowded Barracoon* (1972); Nightingale, P., *Journey through Darkness: The Writing of V. S. N.* (1987); Theroux, P., *V. S. N.* (1972)

SUSAN TETLOW HARRINGTON

NASHE, Thomas

b. November 1567, Lowestoft, Suffolk; d. before December 1601

Pamphleteer, poet, playwright, and wit, N. was omnipresent on the English literary scene in the crucial decade of the 1590s, but was most influential in the development of a vigorous English colloquial prose style. An invariably controversial figure—dismissed by one opponent in the period's various pamphlet wars as a mere "makebate" or creator of strife; praised by his mentor Robert GREENE as "young Juvenal, that biting Satirist"; and celebrated by William SHAKESPEARE as Moth in *Love's Labour's Lost*—N. is best remembered as an enemy of censorship and promoter of subversive pleasures who invested both his life and writing with ferocious energy.

The son of a country parson, N. attended St. John's College, Cambridge, as a sizar (B.A. 1586), after which, rather than taking orders, he migrated with the other so-called University Wits to London to earn his living in the rough and tumble world of the theaters and the nascent sphere of popular journalism. Although no portion of his work for the professional theater survives or can be identified, he is known to have contributed piecemeal to plays, possibly collaborating with Christopher MARLOWE on *Dido, Queen of Car-*

thage (perf. ca. 1586; pub. 1594) and implicated with Ben JONSON in the scandal over *The Isle of Dogs* (perf. 1597).

N. sharpened his writing skills, and first came to the attention of the authorities, in the "Martin Marprelate" controversy. One of several professional writers hired by Archbishop Whitgift to answer a series of anonymous but highly effective Puritan attacks on episcopacy, N. perfected a prose style—what he calls "the extemporal vein"—that was spontaneous, energetic, and occasionally explosive. Relying upon colloquialisms and snatches of popular songs, it was the antithesis of the polished, golden style of John LYLY's *Euphues* then popular among courtiers and evidence of N.'s interest in serving a popular rather than an aristocratic audience. N.'s aggressive, quick-fire wit made his prose style the perfect vehicle for polemical exchanges, his topics shifting so often that it was difficult for an opponent to hold him in sight long enough to fire at him. Literary historians conclude that with *An Almond for a Parrot* (1590) N. decisively settled the Marprelate controversy.

The enormous success of *Pierce Penniless His Supplication to the Devil* (1592)—with five editions within three years—established N. as a figure to note. A SATIRE upon the moral lethargy of the current age, Pierce presents the Seven Deadly Sins in their contemporary guises, scoring hits against numerous highly visible targets. As a complaint against the economics of authorship, the pamphlet is an extraordinary portrait of an evolving literary culture. N. praises poetry (especially that of Sir Philip SIDNEY and Edmund SPENSER), defends the theater, and presents his understanding of his own satiric role as a scourge of vice. Nor does he hesitate to chastise the proliferation of bad poets and of booksellers lacking discrimination. "For who can abide a scurvy peddling poet to pluck a man by the sleeve at every third step in Paul's Churchyard," he asks rhetorically, "and when he comes in to survey his wares, there's nothing but purgations and vomits wrapped up in waste paper. . . . Look to it, you booksellers and stationers, and let not your shops be infected with any such goose giblets or stinking garbage, as the jigs of newsmongers." N.'s irony depends upon the shrewd reader's recognizing that this is exactly how his critics disparaged N.'s own writing.

N.'s popularity grew with *The Unfortunate Traveller; or, The Life of Jack Wilton* (1594), one of the earliest fictional prose narratives in English and a forerunner of the picaresque novel that would be brought to fruition by Daniel DEFOE, Tobias SMOLLETT, and Henry FIELDING a century or more later. Jack Wilton is a page who describes himself as "winnowing my wits to live merrily" among the "chaff" of modern life. However, by attaching him to the Earl of SURREY (who, before Sidney, represented an aristocratic poetic ideal), N. is able to use him to comment further upon Tudor literary culture. Among their adventures, the pair meet the great humanists of an earlier generation, Sir Thomas MORE and Desiderius ERASMUS, and enjoy a demonstration of classical oratory when the magus Cornelius Agrippa conjures up the ghost of Cicero. Although Jack's adventures frequently border on the tragic, a Rabelaisian enjoyment of life dominates the work. As Jack concludes the account of one of his scrapes, "Then was I pitifully whipped for my holiday lie, though they made themselves merry with it many a winter's evening after."

Summers Last Will and Testament, an entertainment performed before Archbishop Whitgift in October 1592, betrays a similar element of Bakhtinian grotesque revelry, as N. plays with the character of Will Summers, the great clown of the Elizabethan stage, and inscribes the work within the cycle of nature. But the entertainment is also a work of high moral seriousness, castigating illiberality as seriously as does Pierce. "What pleasure always lasts? No joy endures," Summers laments. The plague rages outside the doors of the archbishop's country estate, but one must laugh and make merry, maintain hospitality, and refuse to let covetousness further encroach upon communal festivity. That N. can present himself as a scourge, but one with a comic attitude, summarizes the paradox of his work. He is capable of writing works of religious penitence like *Christ's Tears over Jerusalem* (1593), and a lyric like the hauntingly beautiful "Song" from *Summers Last Will:* "Beauty is but a flower,/Which wrinkles will devour,/Brightness falls from the air,/Queens have died young and fair,/Dust hath closed Helen's eye./I am sick, I must die:/Lord, have mercy on us." But it is because he is so conscious of life's invariably tragic end that he can also write works of sexual festivity like *The Choice of Valentines* (date unknown), in which the speaker pays a Valentine's Day visit to his favorite prostitute, only to ejaculate prematurely and leave her to seek satisfaction with a dildo; or his last work, *Nash's Lenten Stuffe* (1599), a festive celebration of red herring. In his oftentimes vitriolic pamphlet war with Cambridge don Gabriel Harvey, which culminated in N.'s *Have with You to Saffron-Walden; or, Gabriel Harvey's Hunt Is Up* (1596), N. found the perfect adversary, Harvey proving as pedantic, self-important, and incapable of festivity as N. was nimble-witted and certain that by taking on Harvey he could expose the Puritan extreme of Elizabethan society.

The date and circumstances of N.'s death remain uncertain. The last record of him to survive dates from early 1599, when he left London, in trouble with the law and hoping to escape a new outbreak of the plague. Although two epitaphs for him circulated in 1601, establishing December of that year as the latest possibility for his death, it is not known how or where he died.

BIBLIOGRAPHY: Hilliard, S. S., *The Singularity of T. N.* (1986); Hutson, L., *T. N. in Context* (1989); Nicholl, C., *A Cup of News: The Life of T. N.* (1984)

RAYMOND-JEAN FRONTAIN

NATURALISM

Literary naturalism began in France around 1865. Its early exponents were Edmond and Jules de Goncourt, who collaborated on *Germinie Lacerteux* (1865), and Émile Zola, who wrote *Thérèse Raquin* (1867), two novels that marked the beginnings of the naturalistic movement in literature. Zola followed his incipient venture into the field with his monumental series of twenty naturalistic novels written between 1871 and 1893 and gathered under the general title *Les Rougon-Macquart*. This group of novels, exemplifying the principles Zola articulated in his seminal essay, *Le Roman expérimental* (1880; *The Experimental Novel*, 1893), served as models for future naturalists.

Zola named the movement, decreeing how ideal naturalists would construct novels. Naturalism moved beyond REALISM, which in England was already flourishing in the novels of Charles DICKENS and William Makepeace THACKERAY. Naturalists applied the techniques of laboratory science to their writing. Zola directed naturalistic authors to apply the exacting rules of laboratory experimentation to their writing. They must observe closely, record with utmost accuracy what they observe, and report their observations dispassionately. Documentation lay at the heart of naturalistic writing. Moralizing and value judgments had no place in pure naturalistic works, although most naturalists found it difficult to remain as detached from their work as Zola commanded.

Naturalists assert that human life is subject to natural laws. The realists had already established the legitimacy of writing about working-class people. The naturalists, usually focusing on working-class people, applied medical and evolutionary theories to their writing, which emphasized the survival of the fittest and the need for people to adapt to their environments. Determinism—social, economic, and genetic—imposes upon individuals situations beyond their control.

Naturalism is well suited to the novel, although a substantial body of naturalistic drama exists as well. Charles DARWIN's ideas in *Origin of Species*, published in 1859, with their emphasis on heredity and survival of the fittest, were wholly compatible with naturalism. Sigmund Freud's psychoanalytical theories, which explained much human behavior in terms of sexual needs and motivations, became influential toward the end of the 19th c. This emphasis on humans as sexual beings added another dimension and considerable momentum to the naturalistic movement. It also caused discomfiture among many readers raised to avoid discussing sex and loath to view humans as mere pawns.

Naturalism flourished in France, Germany, and parts of Scandinavia, where novelists Guy de Maupassant, Alphonse Daudet, and Joris Karl Huysmans, and dramatists Henri Becque, Gerhart Hauptmann, August Strindberg, and Henrik Ibsen produced works consistent with the spirit of Zola's naturalism. In Russia, the movement influenced Leo Tolstoy, who wrote a naturalist play, *Powers of Darkness* (1886), produced in Paris at André Antoine's Théâtre Libre shortly after its opening in 1887. This theater also presented such naturalistic plays as Ibsen's *Ghosts* (1881), Strindberg's *Miss Julie* (1888), and Hauptmann's *The Weavers* (1892).

Beginning shortly before 1900, the naturalistic movement took hold in the U.S. more vigorously than anywhere else in the world. It continued well into the 20th c. Such American novels as Stephen Crane's *Maggie: A Girl of the Streets* (1893), Upton Sinclair's *The Jungle* (1906), Frank Norris's *McTeague* (1899) and *The Octopus* (1901), and Theodore Dreiser's *Sister Carrie* (1900), *The Financer* (1912), and *An American Tragedy* (1925) all reflected the protocols of naturalism, as did Eugene O'Neill's one-act dramas, *The Emperor Jones* (1920) and *The Hairy Ape* (1921), and his longer plays, *Desire under the Elms* (1924) and *Mourning Becomes Electra* (1931).

Naturalism pervaded American literature through much of the 20th c. in the writing of William Faulkner, Sherwood Anderson, John Steinbeck, Tennessee Williams, Clifford Odets, William Inge, and Edward Albee. Despite its popularity on the Continent and in the U.S., the genre was not embraced in Great Britain with nearly the vigor and enthusiasm it met elsewhere.

From 1837 until 1901, Victoria was queen of England. The rising Victorian middle class, often with Noncomformist or Evangelical roots, expected the utmost in propriety and eschewed totally any discussion of the baser human instincts, particularly sex. Censorship flourished in England during Victoria's long reign. Class distinctions were sharply drawn, and although Dickens was able to write realistically about lower-class people, they usually came to bitter ends or, if they were particularly good, were rewarded by discovering they were really members of a higher social class.

The restraints of the period did not encourage naturalism, although it was not unknown in Britain. In drama, Irish playwright John Millington SYNGE's naturalistic one-act play *Riders to the Sea* was well received. It dealt with the economic determinism visited upon a family whose men were fishermen. In this play, a mother over time loses her husband and all her sons to an unforgiving sea. The family's livelihood is fishing, which is all the men of the family know. They realize stoically that the sea may claim them. When the last son is lost, the grief-stricken mother finds comfort in knowing that her son rests in a dry grave.

John GALSWORTHY, who wrote largely from his own privileged background, produced a naturalistic play, *Strife,* which deals with labor unrest and involves a strike and a lockout of workers from their workplace. A compromise is finally struck when both sides abandon their leaders and cooperate. This play, with its overlay of economic and social determinism, was preceded by Galsworthy's *The Silver Box* (perf. 1906; pub. 1909), which, although not wholly naturalistic, reveals naturalistic sentiments in its indictment of society for meting out unequal justice to two men, one rich and one poor, who have committed the same crime but are of different social classes.

George GISSING, familiar with Zola's literary credo concerning naturalism, wrote in that mode. In such novels as *Workers in the Dawn* (3 vols., 1880), *The Unclassed* (3 vols., 1884), *Demos* (3 vols., 1886), and *Thyrza,* however, he diluted the effect of his working-class characters by introducing members of his own class into the novels. Only in *New Grub Street* does he approach anything resembling pure naturalism. In *The Nether World* (3 vols., 1889), produced the following year, he reveals his contempt for vulgar, working-class culture. In most of his naturalistic/realistic writing, Gissing battles his personal inner conflicts regarding heredity and environment.

When George MOORE lived in Paris, he knew Zola, whose work he admired. His novel, *A Mummer's Wife,* was calculatedly naturalistic. His subsequent novels, *A Drama in Muslin, A Mere Accident* (1887), *Confessions of a Young Man* (1888), *Spring Days* (1888), *Mike Fletcher* (1889), and *Vain Fortune* (1891), all contained elements of naturalism but became increasingly psychological novels rather than naturalistic ones. As he moved toward writing his most fully realized novel, *Esther Waters,* he reflected more the aestheticism of Walter PATER and the psychological realism of Ivan Turgenev than Zola's pure naturalism. In *A Mummer's Wife,* Kate Ede, trapped in an uninteresting marriage, becomes intrigued by Dick Lennox, to whom she has rented a room to make ends meet. To the provincial Kate, Dick, an actor who often plays the role of a seducer of virtuous married women, epitomizes romance and excitement. To Dick, Kate represents stability and family cohesion. Ironically, when the two run away together, each is looking for something opposite to what the other wants and needs, so their relationship is doomed. Such ironies pervade naturalistic writing in Britain, particularly that of England's most notable naturalist, Thomas HARDY.

Hardy has been called an antirealist. He is much concerned with what may be viewed as a random determinism, a force lacking in purpose or plan that dictates the outcome of one's life. Hardy uses nature not as a backdrop but as a moving force, almost as a nonhuman character within his work. Egdon Heath in *The Return of the Native* becomes a cruel, punishing— even murderous—force, yet it is impassive. The events it spawns are random occurrences, accidents that change lives. A similar accident alters the entire outcome of Tess's life in *Tess of the D'Urbervilles*, when her confession to Angel is slipped under his door but disappears beneath the carpet, so that he does not receive it. On her wedding night, she tells him the truth and, shocked, he deserts her. It is as though some cruel force is pulling the strings to manipulate the marionettes that Hardy creates as major characters.

Although the impact of naturalism was less great in British literature than in the literatures of France, Germany, Scandinavia, Russia, and the U.S., the movement had sufficient force to be felt and reflected in many ways in Britain. Temperamentally, Britons during the Victorian era were probably unsuited to the emotional demands of thoroughgoing naturalistic writing.

BIBLIOGRAPHY: Baugh, A. C., ed., *A Literary History of England* (2nd ed., 1967); Brosman, C., ed., *Nineteenth-Century French Fiction Writers: Naturalism and Beyond* (1992); Carpenter, R., *Thomas Hardy* (1964); Coustillas, P., ed., *Collected Articles on George Gissing* (1968); Drabble, M., ed., *The Genius of Thomas Hardy* (1976); Olafson, F. A., *Naturalism and the Human Condition* (2001); Powers, L. H., *Henry James and the Naturalist Movement* (1971); Wagner, S. J., and R. Warner, eds., *Naturalism: A Critical Appraisal* (1993)

R. BAIRD SHUMAN

NATURE AND LANDSCAPE

"Nature," Raymond WILLIAMS suggests, "is perhaps the most complex word in the language." He identifies three key areas of meaning for nature: "the essential quality and character *of* something; the inherent force which directs either the world or human beings or both; the material world itself, taken as including or not including human beings." The Oxford English Dictionary notes that landscape was first introduced in the 17th c. as a technical term of painters that was used to describe a picture representing natural inland scenery as opposed to a seascape or some other kind of picture. Landscape can refer either to a representation of the material world (in the form of a painting, drawing, or photograph, as well in speech, writing, or music) or to the material world itself as a product of modifying or shaping processes and agents (whether

natural or human). Therefore, it is perhaps more useful to define landscape as a natural scene that has been mediated by culture.

W. J. T. Mitchell suggests that landscape is itself a medium that encodes cultural meanings and values. The material or natural world can be encoded with these meanings or values both when it is physically transformed by human activity and when it is perceived according to a set of cultural conventions that designate it a "landscape." Significantly, landscapes frequently strive to naturalize their own social and cultural construction. As Mitchell notes, "a landscape is not only a natural scene, and not just a representation of a natural scene, but a *natural* representation of a natural scene, a trace or icon of nature *in* nature itself, as if nature were imprinting and encoding its essential structures on our perceptual apparatus." Landscape thus performs important ideological functions as an instrument of cultural power: "Landscape as a cultural medium . . . has a double role with respect to something like ideology: it naturalizes a cultural and social construction, representing an artificial world as if it were simply given and inevitable, and it also makes that representation operational by interpolating its beholder in some more or less determinate relation to its givenness as sight and site." The ideological implications of landscape have been explored in a variety of ways; however, this discussion will focus on how landscape has worked to naturalize national, class, and gender relations.

Landscape serves an important role in defining relations of power and formulating national identity. The political significance of nature became evident in England at the start of the 18th c. when the landed interest began to be consolidated. Legislative legitimacy was conferred upon the landed interest during this period through their possession of an independent income from heritable property. Views of country estates predominated during this period through landscape gardens, paintings, and descriptions in prose and poetry as the propertied classes employed nature to confirm their political power. Landscapes during this period were often depicted (or were meant to be viewed) from the perspective of a distant prospect. The term "prospect," closely aligned with landscape and perspective, carries the sense of an extensive or commanding sight or view that reflects control over real property. Tim Fulford succinctly explains the ideological significance of the detached prospect view of landscape: "The ability to distinguish and possess shared standards independent of self-interest (standards of aesthetic value or taste) in agreement about the beauty and sublimity of landscape seemed not only a mark of the viewer's gentlemanliness but a criterion for the exercise of legitimate social and political power. And that ability was itself seen to depend upon the capacity of the observer to take a distant, extensive, and detached view of the scene, to be above self-interest." The visual command offered by the prospect view in a literary text is demonstrated in many works from the 18th and 19th cs., perhaps most famously in the topographical passages from James THOMSON's *The Seasons*. These passages of landscape description are distinct from pictorial depictions, however, in that the describing eye is able to roam rather than being restricted to a single elevated vantage point. The landed gentry, freed from the necessity of labor by the fact that they owned land, were ostensibly the only ones able to enjoy the detached prospect-view and thus could legitimize their own exercise of authority by claiming to possess a capacity for disinterested judgment of nature. The prospect-view was not necessarily restricted to the landed classes, however; the single-point perspective of the prospect-view projects a landowner that allows any viewer to vicariously take the place of the owner of the land represented. In an essay in *Prospects for the Nation* (1997), Elizabeth Helsinger suggests that this aspect of the 17th- and 18th-c. landscape form helped create national consciousness by allowing new national subjects from the English middle classes to imagine themselves addressed by landscape views.

By the 19th c., the pastoral landscape of property came to exist in increasing tension with georgic rural scenes that depicted more realistically a countryside inhabited and cultivated by laboring classes. This more actualized view of rural life was characterized as an opportunity to develop a distinctively English landscape tradition that would break from the conventions of classical or European pastoral landscapes. In an essay in Mitchell's *Landscape and Power* (1994), Ann Bermingham suggests that the reform of the picturesque landscape aesthetic was "overdetermined by political events in France," which resulted in a desire to encode liberty differently by valorizing "age, custom, individuality, variety, and rank." At the conclusion of the essay, Bermingham explains how this reordering of representation "ultimately reconfirmed the need for order without seeming to do so." Such portrayals of social order were made to seem natural and organic through the development of rules of decorum governing the depiction of human subjects in landscape paintings. John Barrell notes that the presentation of the rural poor in these more realistic landscapes remained determined by a number of aesthetic constraints. He traces the changes in the portrayal of the rural poor that occurred in the landscape medium from the 18th to the 19th cs.: "The jolly imagery of Merry England, which replaced the frankly artificial imagery of classical Pastoral, was in turn replaced when it had to be by the image of a cheerful, sober, domestic peasantry, more industrious than before; this gave way in turn to a picturesque image of the poor,

whereby their raggedness became of aesthetic interest, and they became the objects of our pity; and when that image would serve no longer, it was in turn replaced by a romantic image of harmony with nature whereby the labourers were merged as far as possible with their surroundings, too far away from us for the questions about how contented or how ragged they were to arise."

One of the most detailed analyses of literary representations of rural life in the 18th and 19th cs. is Williams's *The Country and the City*. Williams examines the changing portrayal of the countryside in relation to the myth of the lost organic community that seems to exist only in the past. The distancing of rural workers that Barrell observes raises many of the concerns about the notion of harmony with nature that characterizes much 18th-c. and Romantic writing. Ironically, true harmony with nature seems to be available only to those who work the land; the observer of the rural scene remains excluded and envious of a condition he or she cannot attain. William WORDSWORTH's narrators, for example, frequently present the plight of the rural poor while at the same time demonstrating their separation from the people and natural environment they are describing.

Landscape involves not only class relations, but also gender relations. Williams notes that nature has been persistently personified as singular Nature: "Nature the goddess, 'nature herself.'" Similarly, feminist critics have noted that landscape is frequently structured as feminine, thus leading to the equation of Woman with Nature. Gillian Rose, for example, suggests that the visual pleasure of gazing upon landscape is inherently masculine pleasure. She suggests that the association of Woman with Nature is especially strong in 19th-c. allegorical landscape paintings, in which nude female figures populate idealized natural landscapes. Because the landscape and the female nude in these paintings were fixed in place while the observer was mobile, she argues that the (male) viewer was allowed both a sense of control and a "kind of sensual pleasure." Her characterization of the masculine gaze can be applied to the visualization of other landscapes. In some senses, the masculine pleasure of the landscape gaze is similar to the visual command offered by the prospect-view: "This masculine gaze sees a feminine body which requires interpreting by the cultured knowledgeable look; something to own, something to give pleasure." Important to this feminist critique is the fact that, for most of its history, the discourse of landscape (not to mention the worlds of art and literature) has been dominated by men. Men possessed the cultured knowledgeable look and were able to cast the gaze of ownership over their property, whether it was land or a woman's body (or both). The argument that landscape evokes masculine pleasure has led to the suggestion by some feminist critics that the shadows and topographical curves of many landscapes resemble the shapes of a woman's body. More recently, critics like Catherine Nash have criticized what they consider to be the ahistorical nature of this feminist characterization of visual pleasure as masculine. The body-landscape metaphor has been freed from any essential equation between nature and femininity. Landscape has certainly been an object of masculine heterosexual desire in the past through an association between nature and femininity, but it is equally possible for it to be an object of female and feminine heterosexual pleasure or even the object of a homoerotic gaze.

Landscapes are produced in order to objectify, rationalize, and naturalize a set of social and cultural relations and values. Indeed, Mitchell asserts that "even the most highly formulaic, conventional, and stylized landscapes tend to represent themselves as 'true' to some sort of nature, to universal structures of 'Ideal' nature, or to codes that are 'wired in' to the visual cortex and deeply instinctual roots of visual pleasure associated with scopophilia [pleasure in looking], voyeurism, and the desire to see without being seen." The history of landscape in England has often been characterized as a movement from the artifice of the landscape of property to a more natural view; however, despite this greater degree of actualization, landscape continues to operate according to a set of conventions whose conventionality has simply been effaced more effectively. The ideological function of landscape—making social relations appear fully natural and timeless—suggests that landscapes are a site (and sight) of struggle, a place for resistance, and a concretization of contest. The production of a landscape can have the effect of staunching such struggles, whether they center on the definition of national identity, class, and gender relations, or other important issues. As social values are naturalized in place, they are historically made concrete. Many critics argue that landscape in the form of the picturesque European tradition is an exhausted medium. It appears evident, however, that English landscapes of the 18th and 19th cs., including both the built environment and its various representations, continue to perform important ideological functions in mass culture as objects of nostalgia.

BIBLIOGRAPHY: Barrell, J., *The Dark Side of the Landscape: The Rural Poor in English Painting, 1730–1840* (1980); Bermingham, A., *Landscape and Ideology: The English Rustic Tradition, 1740–1860* (1986); Fulford, T., *Landscape, Liberty, and Authority: Poetry, Criticism and Politics from Thomson to Wordsworth* (1996); Mitchell, W. J. T., ed., *Landscape and Power* (1994); Rose, G., *Feminism and Geography* (1993); Rosenthal, M., C. Payne, and S. Wilcox, eds., *Prospects for the Nation: Recent Essays in British Landscape, 1750–1880* (1997); Turner, J., *The Politics of Landscape: Rural Scenery and Society in English Poetry 1630–1660* (1979); Williams, R., *Keywords: A Vocabulary of Culture and Society* (1976; rev. ed., 1983); Williams, R., *The Country and the City* (1973)

SEAN BURGESS

NAUGHTON, Bill [William John Francis]
b. 12 June 1910, Ballyhaunis, County Mayo, Ireland; d. 9 January 1992, Ballasalla, Isle of Man

N. was a successful novelist, short story writer, stage, radio, and television dramatist, film writer, children's author, and autobiographer. He is most widely known for *Alfie* (1963), a stage play that became a successful film, but some of his best work is to be found in his short stories, radio plays, and autobiographies. His dialogue and narrative prose demonstrate close attention to the rhythms of language, especially of working-class speech; he can encompass and combine a range of perspectives from comedy to a clear-eyed confrontation with the rigors of life.

Much of the material for N.'s short stories and autobiographies comes from his boyhood in the Lancashire town of Bolton and from his work as a weaver, coal-bagger, and lorry driver. It is shaped, however, by the careful craftsmanship he developed during his difficult apprenticeship as a writer, working full-time during the day and composing his stories at night. He began to publish stories in the 1940s and his first book, *A Roof Over Your Head*, came out in 1945. It was commissioned by the poet and sociologist Charles Madge, one of the founders of the British Mass Observation movement of the 1930s, to which N. himself had belonged. Comprising sketches and diary excerpts, *A Roof Over Your Head* combined the kind of reportage of everyday life that Mass Observation required with the fictional techniques N. had learned from his reading and short story writing. It evokes the effects of economic depression and unemployment in an unsparing way, stirring the heart more strongly because it eschews emotional indulgence. A similar discipline was evident in his novel for boys, *Pony Boy* (1966), and in many of the short stories he continued to publish during the 1950s. A selection of these, *Late Night on Watling Street*, came out in 1959: its title story, based on some experiences of his lorry-driving days, is probably his most accomplished and concentrated work.

N. wrote much for the relatively neglected medium of radio drama and successful work in this field included *Timothy* (1956), *Seeing a Beauty Queen Home* (1960), and *The Mystery* (1973), which earned the Prix Italia. He started to write stage plays in the second half of the 1950s and his first success, produced in 1957, was *My Flesh, My Blood* (1959), which later became *Spring and Port Wine* (perf. 1964; rev. as *Keep It in the Family*, perf. 1967). Turning on the troubles in a Lancashire family sparked off by a father's demand that his teenage daughter should eat a meal of herrings she does not want, it demonstrated N.'s capacity to write solid, popular stage comedy. *Alfie*, about a young womanizer who is finally forced to confront the consequences of his actions, combined comedy with a dramatization of the ethical concerns raised by the widespread changes in the conduct of sexual relationships taking place in the 1960s; the play caught the mood of the time and its eponymous hero was unforgettably incarnated by Michael Caine in the 1970 film scripted by N., who also turned the play into a novel, published in 1966, and tried to sustain the surge of success with a sequel, *Alfie Darling* (1970). This has been judged, however, to be his weakest work.

Further short story collections, children's books and plays followed, but N.'s strongest writing after *Alfie* can be found in his three volumes of AUTOBIOGRAPHY, *On the Pig's Back* (1987), *Saintly Billy* (1988), and the posthumously published *Neither Use Nor Ornament* (1995). *On the Pig's Back* opens with a compelling account of his struggles to become a writer at the age of thirty, turns into an account of his return to his native land when he revisits his birthplace in County Mayo, tells the story of his family's emigration to Bolton in England in hope of better things, and recalls his own early days there during and after World War I. *Saintly Billy* continues the story of his vivid but troubled boyhood in Lancashire; it combines an evocation of key personal experiences—emotional, educational, spiritual, sexual—with the documentary observation that characterized his first book, *A Roof Over Your Head*. *Neither Use Nor Ornament* takes us into the world of manual work that N. entered at fourteen and continues the story of his sexual and religious conflicts. All three volumes of autobiography immediately engage the reader and demonstrate the disciplined directness of N.'s style; they are free of the sentimentality that mars some of his other later work and make a vital contribution to both autobiography and social history.

N. is often categorized as a "working-class" writer in a way that acknowledges the strength of his portrayals of proletarian life but also implies that his scope is limited. There can be no doubt of his humble origins nor of his sustained interest in the working-class life he knew as a boy and young man; but it is also important to recognize his literary sophistication. He was a very well read man who, even in his days of manual labor, made a careful study of literature, and the structure and style of his best work show a concern for the author's craft that entitles him to be seen simply as a writer who made a distinctive contribution to 20th-c. English literature.

BIBLIOGRAPHY: Taylor, J. R., *Anger and After: A Guide to the New British Drama* (1962; rev. ed., 1969); Trewin, J. C., "B. N.," in Weintraub, S., ed., *British Dramatists since World War II*, part 2, *DLB* 13 (1982): 351–54

NICOLAS TREDELL

NENNIUS
fl. 829–30, Bangor, North Wales

N. was a 9th-c. monk of Bangor, North Wales, and supposed author of the *Historia Britonum*, an early Welsh history containing the first apparently historical account of the military exploits of Arthur. Writing in about 830 in response to a perceived negligence among the Britons in the recording and cherishing of their history, N. synthesizes various literary, historical, and oral traditions in his work, colorfully declaring he has "made a heap" of such material and writing up his findings in Latin prose. The earliest complete text survives in a British Library manuscript (Harleian MS 3859), itself a miscellany of items, collecting N.'s *Historia* with the *Annales Cambriae* and a collection of Welsh genealogies.

In a prose periodically reflecting the anti-Saxon bias and pious disposition of the compiler, N. documents the origins of the British, the invasions of the Romans, Picts, and Saxons, the lives of saints Germanus and Patrick, the reign of King Vortigern, and, in chapter 56 of his history, the wars of Arthur. Describing the hero as warrior rather than king, the chapter lists twelve key battles in which the ever victorious Arthur challenges the Saxon dominance of mainland Britain, leading the kings of the Britons on account of his superior military prowess. The impression of historical veracity is heightened by N.'s naming of the specific site of each campaign, knowledge perhaps drawn from a Bardic poem. One is fought at the river Glein, four at the river Dubglas, one at the river Bassas, one at the forest of Celidon, another at the fort of Guinnion, the ninth at the city of the Legion, the tenth at the river Tribuit, the eleventh on the mountain Agned, and the twelfth on Badon Hill.

N. elaborates on two of the battles, describing how at the battle of Fort Guinnion Arthur carried an image of the blessed Virgin Mary on his shield while at the battle of Badon Hill no fewer than 960 men met their deaths at Arthur's hand. If this latter detail reflects N.'s receptivity to more fantastic traditions concerning Arthur, he includes two more such details in his appendix of *Mirabilia* or "Wonders." His account here of two Arthurian marvels establishes that Arthur was already a legendary figure by the early 9th c. First to be described is the Carn Cafal, a stone bearing the paw-print of Arthur's dog, Cafal. N. recounts how the impression was taken when hound and master were embarked on a hunt for the boar Twrch Trwyth and how the stone, if removed, will always mysteriously return to the cairn that Arthur himself assembled. The second marvel concerns the tomb of Amr, Arthur's son. N.'s elliptical reference tells how Amr was killed and buried by Arthur himself and how his tomb mysteriously alters in proportion each time it is measured. The chronicler even attests, "I have tried it myself."

Despite its brevity the text makes a substantial contribution to later Arthurian tradition, forming a principal source for GEOFFREY OF MONMOUTH's *Historia Regum Britanniae* that significantly amplifies N.'s Arthurian material. Details such as Arthur's bearing of an image of the Virgin Mary on his shield and his exaggerated military prowess are developed by Geoffrey and throughout later Arthurian tradition. While N.'s casual blending of myth and history limits the value of his text for those seeking an historical Arthur, it is suggestive that certain of the battle sites listed have been successfully identified while the historicity of the battle of Badon, if not its victor, is confirmed by the mid-6th-c. historian Gildas.

BIBLIOGRAPHY: Barber, R., *King Arthur in Legend and History* (1973); Fletcher, R. H., *The Arthurian Material in the Chronicles* (1906; rev. ed., 1966); Morris J., ed. and trans., *N.: British History and the Welsh Annals* (1980)

ROGER DALRYMPLE

NESBIT, E[dith]
b. 15 or 19 August 1858, London; d. 4 May 1924, Jesson St. Mary's, New Romney, Kent

N., prolific author of essays, stories, poems, and novels, is now remembered as author of the enduringly popular children's books she began in middle age, after nearly twenty years of steady but very moderately rewarding writing. Her writing began as economic necessity. Married to Hubert Bland in 1880, she and her husband found themselves destitute when a business partner looted their small business while Bland recovered from smallpox. Both N. and her husband turned to authorship. Although Bland became a prominent journalist, N. became the chief provider.

The socially conscious Blands were among the founders of the Fabian Society in 1884 and were close friends of H. G. WELLS and Bernard SHAW and Sidney and Beatrice Webb, but their friendships extended far beyond socialist circles. As relaxed, informal bohemian entertainers, they were host to a cross section of late-19th- and early-20th-c. writers, including such diverse figures as G. K. CHESTERTON, Rudyard KIPLING, Laurence HOUSMAN, and Noël COWARD. For all her varied literary and social activities, N. hoped to be known as a poet, but the successes of *Lays and Legends* (1886) and *Lays and Legends: Second Series* (1892) proved temporary.

Her first highly popular work was *The Story of the Treasure Seekers* (1899) in which the six Bastable children search for ways to restore the fortunes of "The House of Bastable." Like most of N.'s fictional children, they are wholesome, intelligent, and highly moral without being saccharine or unbelievable. (They are, perhaps, more believable than many of the benevolent adults they encounter.) Their attempts to dig for treasure, borrow large sums from a money-lender, and sell wine to a minister who opposes the use of alcohol are humorous for adults and entertaining for children. The same family appears in *The Wouldbegoods: Being the Further Adventures of the Treasure Seekers* (1901) and *The New Treasure Seekers* (1904). By 1913, N. had produced over twenty children's books. Afterward, her productivity was hindered by her ill health, by the death of her husband in 1914, and by the trauma of World War I.

Some of her books anticipate the children's fiction of C. S. LEWIS with the introduction of magic and escapes from the present world. The children of *The Enchanted Castle* (1907) encounter bizarre adventures by using a ring that causes invisibility that cannot be reversed at will and grants wishes made casually or carelessly. The children of *The House of Arden* (1908) and *Harding's Luck* (1909) travel in history to become temporarily parts of other families. Unintentionally, they expose the Guy Fawkes plot with casual discussion of what to them is routine 20th-c. knowledge. Dickie Harding, the lame slum child of *Harding's Luck*, finds that he is not lame in other historical periods. He discovers that he is the rightful Lord Arden, kills a Roundhead while defending Arden castle, and magnanimously fakes his death so that a deserving cousin may continue as Lord Arden. Dickie himself will live contentedly in the reign of JAMES I.

These books are entertainment for adults and glorious wish fulfillment for children, but the later ones, with their emphasis on altruism and on high moral conduct, also reflect N.'s Fabian thinking. *Harding's Luck* dwells on the miserable poverty of 20th-c. England and on Lord Arden's plan to convert his estate into a model working-class village. The two boys, Edred Arden and Dickie, are given opportunities of heroic self-sacrifice. Edred rescues Dickie knowing that Dickie (not Edred's father) is the true Lord Arden, only to have Dickie relinquish both his claim and his own 20th-c. life.

Despite its propaganda, N.'s work owes its continued popularity to its understanding of children's wishes and to the willingness of adults to participate in them. Over twenty of her titles now remain in print.

BIBLIOGRAPHY: Briggs, J., *A Woman of Passion: The Life of E. N., 1858–1924* (1987); Streatfeild, N., *Magic and the Magician: E. N. and Her Children's Books* (1958)

DALTON AND MARYJEAN GROSS

NEWBOLT, [Sir] Henry [John]

b. 6 June 1862, Bilston, Staffordshire; d. 19 April 1938, London

N., a prolific writer of novels, verse dramas, legal books (he was a lawyer), and government reports on education and the civil service, is now chiefly remembered as the poet of patriotism and the British Empire. Robert BRIDGES, later to become poet laureate, said to N. on the publication of "Drake's Drum" in 1896 that he wished he could ever have written anything half as good. Other poems are still remembered through anthologies—notably "Admirals All" and "He Fell among Thieves"—and musical settings ("The Old Superb" is one of Stanford's Sea Songs). The refrain of "Vitaï Lampada," in which the qualities required for cricket and for command in warfare are explicitly compared, "Play up, play up, and play the game," acquired near-proverbial status, and is inscribed on a sporting relief sculpture outside Lord's cricket ground in London, headquarters of world cricket. In 1910, N. published his *Collected Poems, 1897–1907*, which was superseded by his *Poems New and Old*, published in 1912. The first volume of his memoirs, *My World as in My Time*, was published in 1932, and the incomplete second volume, *The Later Life and Letters of Sir Henry Newbolt*, was published posthumously in 1942 by his wife, Margaret Newbolt.

MICHAEL GROSVENOR MYER

NEWCASTLE, Margaret Lucas Cavendish, Duchess of

b. 1623, Colchester, Essex; d. 15 December 1673, Welbeck, Nottinghamshire

Known for her originality of dress, her propensity for self-display, and her overwhelming desire for fame, "Mad Madge's" personality long overshadowed her work. Author of twelve published works, N. refused to be restricted by her sex, criticism, or grammar, punctuation, and spelling. She sought out explanations of the world in science, fantasy, and herself. Charles LAMB called her the "somewhat fantastical and original brained, generous Margaret Newcastle."

N.'s first work, *Poems and Fancies* (1653; rev. eds., 1664, 1668), speculated in verse about the squaring of the circle, atomism, and conflict in the world in dialogues between passions, mind and body, even man and oak tree. Her "similizing" such as "The Head of a Man . . . to a Hive of Bees" or death as nature's cook contained bizarrely imaginative, sometimes grotesque conceits. N. continued to write on scientific concepts in *Philosophical Fancies* (1653) and in *Philosophical Letters* (1664) where she argued against leading thinkers such as Thomas HOBBES and Descartes. *The World's Olio* (1655), or "stew" in keeping with N.'s penchant for food imagery, is an eclectic mix of subjects in poems, essays, fragments, and brief sketches. Her preface addressed the inequality of the sexes, blaming it, in part, on women's lack of education, but concluding that nature made most women to be governed by men because they were inferior in body and mind.

Still, N.'s fiction offered unconventional heroines. In *Natures Pictures Drawn by Fancies Pencil to the Life* (1656), Deletia in "The Contract" manipulates perceptions of herself through the spectacle of her dresses until, through her intelligent address to a law court, she is awarded the man she desires. Miseria, in "Assaulted and Pursued Chastity," becomes the boy Travellia to avoid the amorous advances of a prince. The Queen of Amity falls in love with the "boy" who leads her army before her disguise is penetrated and she weds the prince. N.'s *Playes* (1662) and *Plays, Never before Printed* (1668) have been dismissed as long, undramatic, and disjointed. N. referred to them as "dull dead statues"; however, her mixing of gender traits makes for compelling heroines. In "Loves Adventures," Lady Orphant disguises herself as a page and proves such a good soldier s/he is made lieutenant-general; and shy Lady Bashful strikes down a man's sword and threatens to run him through if he does not obey her. Lady Victoria in "Bell in Campo" creates an army of "heroickesses." In the last section of *Orations of Divers Sorts* (1662), a spirited debate among seven female orators shows that woman is not a definable constant.

CCXI Sociable Letters (1664), autobiographical in content and conversational in tone, manifests N.'s paradoxical interiority and sociability as she writes about politics, pregnant women, gender, melancholy, children, shyness, and writing. In "A True Relation of My Birth, Breeding and Life" and her *Life of William Cavendish* (1667), she writes with dignity and honesty about herself, husband, and married life. Her plea is to be remembered in "after ages."

N.'s most fascinating work is the "hermaphrodite" *Observations upon Experimental Philosophy. To which is added, The Description of a New Blazing World* (1666). *Observations* is a scientific treatise, refuting Robert Hooke's *Micrographia* (1665), which praised microscopes and telescopes as the way to truly see the world. N. argued for the application of the mind, not experimentalism. She continued this argument in her "part romancical, philosophical and fantastical" novella in which a woman is carried off to a new world where she weds the emperor and is worshipped by its animal-men. She makes changes in government, religion, and science. Later, she shares an "erotic-Platonic" friendship with the "Duchess of Newcastle's" soul. The "Duchess" is encouraged to make her own world in her mind; and she advises the empress to change the "Blazing World" back to correct her alterations. The second part involves the empress's return to her own world to help her people. Blazoned as a warrior goddess, she appears to walk on the water (in fact, she walks on the backs of fishmen). After saving her country, she returns to the Blazing World but it is not mentioned whether she changes it back to its original. The book is N.'s wish fulfillment: she gains fame and respect; vindicates her husband; overcomes her bashfulness; and is remembered today as "Margaret the First."

BIBLIOGRAPHY: Battigelli, A., *M. C. and the Exiles of the Mind* (1998); Grant, D., *Margaret the First* (1957); Jones, K., *A Glorious Fame: The Life of M. C., Duchess of Newcastle, 1623–1673* (1988)

EARLA WILPUTTE

NEWMAN, John Henry

b. 21 February 1801, London; d. 11 August 1890, Birmingham

N. helped transform the way most Christians in the English-speaking world worship, wrote poems that would remain in the hymnals of various denominations for more than century, and made important contributions to theology, especially in the area of the "development of doctrine." In the prose works for which he is most remembered, he displayed a brilliant style, whether when defending himself or probing the nature of liberal education.

N. attended Trinity College, Oxford, as an evangelical, but during his years as a fellow at Oriel College and especially as vicar of St. Mary's, the University Church (1822–43), he was a central figure in the Oxford movement, which tried to recapture the Church of England's "Catholic" heritage in doctrine, authority, and in liturgy. N. edited and contributed to the "Tracts for the Times," which both gave the movement its second name—"Tractarian"—and helped to draw the suspicions of more "Protestant" Anglicans, who thought N. was slighting the church's Reformation heritage. "Tract 90" (1841), in which N. seemed to assert that the Thirty-Nine Articles, the Church of England's doctrinal statement, were consistent not just with the teachings of the ancient undivided church, but also with those of the modern Catholic Church, brought about a crisis. The Bishop of Oxford asked that the publication of the tracts be suspended, and N. spent almost two years in seclusion with friends at his country parish of Littlemore, where he struggled with the question of whether the Church of England was, as he had argued, part of the ancient Catholic Church. He decided it was not, but he also wrestled with the contrast between the early church and the modern Roman Catholic Church. After coming to see historical development at work in the church, he resolved his doubts. He preached his last Anglican SERMON in 1843 and was received into the Roman Catholic Church in 1845. In that same year, he published the theological fruits of his conversion crisis, *An Essay on the Development of Christian Doctrine.*

While preparing for his reordination as a Roman Catholic priest in Rome, N. wrote a novel that seemed to be a roman à clef about his conversion and a response to other such novels. *Loss and Gain* (1848) seems to many an amateurish novel, but it is an interesting portrait of Oxford in a time of intellectual crisis. N.'s other novel, *Callista: A Sketch of the Third Century* (1856), is also a portrait of conversion. It was in part a response to Charles KINGSLEY's novel *Hypatia.* Both authors set their novels in the early church because the issue between them was whether the modern Catholic and Anglican Churches were genuine continuations of primitive Christianity.

N. founded a community of the Oratory of St. Philip Neri in Birmingham in 1849, but his position in the English Roman Catholic Church was uncomfortable. He was suspected of excessively liberal tendencies by some, especially Cardinal Manning, the Archbishop of Westminster. The one important post he was given was that of rector of the new Catholic university in Dublin. His tenure there was short, but it produced the series of lectures that became *The Idea of a University*, first published in 1852 as *Discourses on the Scope and Nature of University Education,* which remains one of the touchstones in any discussion of liberal education.

In response to an attack on his honesty by Kingsley, N. wrote a series of pamphlets defending himself. Republished as *Apologia pro Vita Sua* (8 parts, 1864) and *History of My Religious Opinions* (1865) and shorn of both their reference to Kingsley and their original indignation, they became one of the great autobiographies in English and restored N. to the place of national prominence he had had before his conversion. In 1870, he published another important work of theology, *A Grammar of Assent.* Despite the hostility of the English hierarchy, he was made a cardinal by Pope Leo XIII in 1879.

Some of N.'s finest works are sermons, including the *Parochial Sermons* (6 vols., 1834–36) and *Sermons Bearing on Subjects of the Day* (1843), or poems, such as the early hymn "Lead Kindly Light" (1833) and the extended poem *The Dream of Gerontius* (1865). But N. was probably most influential in helping to start the movement that led many Protestants, not just Anglicans, to recover parts of the Catholic heritage in their art and liturgy.

BIBLIOGRAPHY: Dessain, C. S., *J. H. N.* (1966); Trevor, M., *N.* (2 vols., 1962); Wolff, R. L., *Gains and Losses: Novels of Faith and Doubt in Victorian England* (1977)

BRIAN ABEL RAGEN

NEW ZEALAND LITERATURE IN ENGLISH

Allen Curnow's "Landfall in Unknown Seas" marks the tercentenary of New Zealand's discovery by Abel Tasman in 1642 with a reminder that the narrative of settlement is not one of triumphant material improvement and civilizing influence. It is "the stain of blood that writes an island story." Curnow was acutely aware of the role of style in nation-making, favoring a stern focus on the reality of life in these islands in place of the frivolous unreality of colonial writing with its decorative flora and appropriated Maori legends. He wanted the descendants of the settlers to accept their transplanted condition; the poet's job was to bring the citizens home by way of adventures in search of the reality that was to hand. Yet the closer the poet looked at the real, the more it retreated. Curnow's poetry begins as a finely tempered verbal exploration of the world at hand and becomes a brilliant mapping of the shifting topographies of the "word-world."

Serious New Zealand literature, in a dominant modernist narrative, begins as a repudiation of the colonial distance between habitation and home, words and things, outmoded literary styles and local ways of saying. Yet colonial writers were merely less adroit negotiators of the tensions the sense of disjunction between word and world has provoked. The inadequacy of literary conventions was frequently the explicit subject rather than the unexamined limitation of colonial writing, as in Jessie Mackay's parody of Alfred, Lord TENNYSON, "The Charge at Parihaka" (1889). The same discrepancy is remarked by the hero of Maurice Duggan's story, "Along Rideout Road That Summer" (1965), caught between "the real and the written."

MODERNISM was latent in the colonial world. Katherine MANSFIELD may have become a high modernist writer after 1915 in Europe, but she did so by reorganizing influences that came to her not only from Oscar WILDE and Anton Chekhov but also from the fractious colonial world in which she grew to young adulthood. An essential element of the modernist style, which Mansfield elaborated after 1915, derived from her response to the world known as "Maoriland," which she found both embarrassing and captivating.

Ursula Bethell and Blanche Baughan rather than the expatriate Mansfield were the acceptable precursors of the modernists, the former for her lucid meditations on her Christchurch garden, a microcosm that might be read as the settled world at last painstakingly being attended to. Baughan, especially in her long poem "The Bush Section" (1908), localizes Walt Whitman's project of giving voice to a raw, new national experience in energetic long lines.

Infected by journalism and FEMINISM, Robin Hyde [Iris Wilkinson] was a problem for the male writers of the 1930s. Yet her writing has enjoyed a more vital afterlife than that of rabid antifeminists like A. R. D. Fairburn. Constrained by the limited kinds of writing at that time believed desirable for women readers, she struggled in her own way against the prevailing sources of "unreality," determining on a direct treatment of social distress, family conflict, and the fraught relations between the sexes.

Less introspective than Curnow, Denis Glover often uses ballad forms and employs a richly observed colloquial voice. In Christchurch in the 1930s, he established the Caxton Press, the center of modern writing in New Zealand for the next three decades. The exemplary editor of Caxton's prestigious literary magazine, *Landfall*, established in 1947, was Charles Brasch. Brasch's poems articulate a bleak but influential understanding of the uneasy relations between settled landscape and settler consciousness.

Together with Curnow, James K. Baxter is New Zealand's most important poet. While the older poet focused in a highly formal style on the details of local reality, Baxter's was from the start a lush, rhetorical voice. He was, moreover, determined to probe not only the avoidances and indecisions of his country in the business of identity-making but also the rich loam of the unconscious in terms of a poetic that did not exclude the metaphysical or the mythical.

In fiction, Frank Sargeson was long considered to be the founder of a serious local writing tradition. His prestige established the preeminence of short story in fiction until the 1970s (in Owen Marshall the form still has a major practitioner). Sargeson's achievement is to have fashioned a colloquial style that claims to represent New Zealandness. Yet the effort to convey the real New Zealander by turning away from suburbia, gentility, and domesticity knows itself to be a fabrication. In the classic stories of down-at-heels blokes he wrote during the 1930s and 1940s, an element of exaggeration signals the artifice; in his later work, the style becomes openly self-conscious, the events surreal.

The fiction of Janet Frame, for all its obvious difference from Sargeson's—its inwardness, the metaphor-packed prose, the sinuous sentences, the surrender to the mirror worlds of language and art—has in common an antagonism to bourgeois life, a suspicion of normality, a division of humanity into the damned many and the saved few. Yet Frame's voice is unconstrained by Sargeson's nationalism or his linguistic puritanism. Frame is the first New Zealand novelist to dissolve the antagonism between local and international readerships by making the material of her own country the stuff of a fiction that is borderless.

Maurice Gee, Vincent O'Sullivan, and C. K. Stead are important transitional figures. Gee fashions a more extensive and historically nuanced REALISM than Sargeson, jettisoning the fable mode in favor of psychologically credible characters. O'Sullivan, a significant novelist and dramatist, humanizes the modernist legacy in his densely imagistic poetry. Stead in a series of critical essays from the 1950s through the 1970s moved beyond the realist and nationalist priorities of his mentors, Curnow and Sargeson, in the process changing the ways in which the older writers could be read. His own poetry, at the outset overly indebted to high modernism, progressively introduces postmodern strategies. Notable for his verbal exactness and stylistic range, Stead is also a major New Zealand novelist, laminating a realist method with metafictional techniques.

From the mid-1960s, Ian Wedde established himself as the foremost voice among a new generation influenced by American poetics and the cultural upheavals of the time. Fluent, lyrical, a poet of sensation, Wedde is also perhaps the finest political poet New Zealand has produced, moving beyond specific causes or occasions to articulate an updated version of Curnow's adventures in search of reality, in which "the real" is located in the ways in which language shapes as well as marks evolving cultural identity.

Hone Tuwhare, the first Maori writer to make a national impact by his poetry of the early 1960s, prepared the ground for the "Renaissance" in Maori writing in the 1970s and 1980s. Seemingly a poet of presence, Tuwhare's voice is deceptively accessible; he is a style-shifter, continually changing gear from demotic speech to more formal kinds of language use. Albert Wendt, born in Samoa, represents the beginnings of multiculturalism in New Zealand writing, yet identifies strongly with the Maori cause and biculturalism. There is an existential edge to his treatment of postcolonial displacement, and his later writing takes an experimental turn that aligns it with POSTMODERNISM.

The Maori Renaissance, which began around 1970 with the stories of Witi Ihimaera and Patricia Grace, gained political urgency in the 1980s. Ihimaera's accusatory EPIC The Matriarch appeared in 1986. By the 1990s, the energies of the movement had dispersed, not in the sense that Maori cultural or political assertiveness had lessened in intensity but in the growing diversity of Maori writing. Alan Duff notoriously adopted a contestatory position toward the values associated with the Maori revival in Once Were Warriors (1990).

The Renaissance was part of a profound shift in New Zealand's cultural orientation over the 1970s and 1980s, as the country adjusted to the trauma of England's economic desertion of her most faithful colony. The old New Zealand—pastoral, patriarchal, Pakeha-centered—died hard. Another strong agency of change was supplied by feminism, and the mid-1970s were marked by the emergence of a group of women writers—Lauris Edmond, Elizabeth Smither, Rachel McAlpine, and Cilla McQueen—whose work would build an audience for writing by women. Keri Hulme's The Bone People in 1983 established how significant this market actually was, especially where it was combined with the new bicultural mood.

In the 1990s, women's writing becomes increasingly difficult to fit into a single compendious category. Edmond became a national icon. McQueen's performance poetry provided an exuberant counterpoint, playful where Edmond is serious. Smither elaborated a variety of metaphysical wit to explore the paradoxes of the human situation.

Throughout the 1970s, the most prominent of the generation born in the late 1940s was Sam Hunt, a bardic entertainer, combining in his persona the romantic outsider and the larrikin. Hunt came to represent "The Poet," much as Baxter had in the 1960s. However, it was Bill Manhire who progressively wrote himself into the most potent narrative of local literary history in the 1980s and 1990s. Indeed, Manhire has cunningly rewritten New Zealand literary history generally.

Manhire has praised the deliberately "unpoetic" quality he finds in New Zealand poetry. Yet Manhire's own writing, for all its understatement, its arch use of clichés, and its ear for curious local usage, is deliberately formal. If there is a "Manhire School," it is evidenced in a habitual underplaying of the use of language in carefully wrought verse: Jenny Bornholdt, Dinah Hawken, James Brown. A poet of the ordinary and the actual, Bornholdt avoids the display of egotism. Her language is spare and precise, her imagery restrained. Yet there is also a surreal edge to her use of language, as she continually discloses the strangeness worked into the familiar world. In Hawken's poetry, there is a meditative preoccupation with the spiritual possibilities of nature and life, yet these inward concerns cohabit with a love of the everyday and a passionate registration of the condition of those marginalized by society. In Brown's "Cashpoint: A Pantoum" (1995), the ordinary interactions of global existence collide with an ancient and elegant poetic form, albeit in the most stilted and mechanical kind of language.

From Victoria University Press come also the fiction writers Elizabeth Knox, Catherine Chidgey, Emily Perkins, and Damien Wilkins. The differences among these younger writers are as apparent as the commonalities. What connects them is a refusal to be limited by the matter of national self-definition, although their work is resonant with the local. Auckland University Press, meanwhile, has consolidated the reputations of a middle generation of poets—notably Murray Edmond and Michele Leggott—more culturally radical than the Wellington writers, more determined to carry forward a postmodern program.

From *Ranolf and Amohia* (1872), the unwieldy cross-cultural epic of Alfred Domett, to Gregory O'Brien's surrealist wordplay, John Newton's dense reworkings of the myths imbricated in the legacy of nationalist poetry, or Chris Orsman's encodings of the personal in family and national narratives, the preoccupying subject of New Zealand writing has been language and its dislocations from place.

The struggle has been not simply to come to terms with a new place, but to attend to all that was here, that which was brought, and to the unexpected results of their collisions. Sometimes the introduced species got away and became pests, yet the pests became part of the landscape, earning their place. As Orsman puts it, even the gorse became "ornamental." So also the words and phrases that were brought with the settlers escaped their owners; they hybridized with the words they found—little by little making a place in language at home with its insecurities.

BIBLIOGRAPHY: Curnow, A., *Look Back Harder: Critical Writings, 1935–1984* (1987); Evans, P., *The Penguin History of New Zealand Literature* (1990); Sturm, T., ed., *The Oxford History of New Zealand Literature in English* (2nd ed., 1998); Williams, M., and M. Leggott, eds., *Opening the Book: New Essays on New Zealand Writing* (1995)

MARK WILLIAMS

NICHOLS, Peter [Richard]
b. 31 July 1927, Bristol

Actor turned playwright and screenwriter, N. began writing for British television in the late 1950s with teleplays such as *Promenade* (perf. 1959; pub. 1960) and *Ben Spray* (1961). In 1966, he coauthored the screenplay for the successful film version of *Georgy Girl*, adapted from the novel by Margaret Forster, and in the following year gained critical recognition with the production of his first stage play, *A Day in the Death of Joe Egg* (repub. as *Joe Egg*). A black comedy that charts the caustic and ultimately destructive relationship between the parents of a spastic child, the play—which received the *Evening Standard* Drama Award—was adapted by N. as a film starring Alan Bates in 1971. His next play, *The National Health* (perf. 1969; pub. 1970), also adapted by N. as a film (1973), was followed by his most popular and successful play, *Forget-Me-Not-Lane* (1971). Other plays include *Chez Nous* (1974), *The Freeway* (perf. 1974; pub. 1975), *Privates on Parade* (1977), *Born in the Gardens* (1979), *Passion Play* (1981), *A Piece of My Mind* (perf. 1987; pub. 1988), and *So Long Life* (pub. 2000; perf. 2001).

NICHOLSON, Norman [Cornthwaite]
b. 8 January 1914, Millom, Cumbria; d. 30 May 1987, Whitehaven, Cumbria

One of the finest regional poets in English, N. was very much aware of William WORDSWORTH, writing about the Lake District and the coastal stretch of Cumbria on its borders, but as a 20th-c. man. He produced novels, criticism, verse plays, and several guides to the Lakes, but his reputation rests on one slim volume, the *Selected Poems* (1943).

He suffered from tuberculosis as a boy and was a semi-invalid, spending his entire life in the same house in Millom. This did not, however, cramp his style, because it enabled him to observe the tiny changes within his community as they happened and because he believed that the town, which had boomed in the 19th c. and then declined, was society writ small. *A Local Habitation* is the name he gave a 1972 collection, and his poetry is firmly rooted in Cumbrian soil. Sea, rock, rivers, mountains are his staple images, but he is also very conscious of the geranium in his window and the bird nesting below the bathroom outflow pipe. He is constantly referring to real places that the reader may not know, but their significance is universal.

His first poems, influenced by W. H. AUDEN and T. S. ELIOT, were published in 1943 together with those of Keith DOUGLAS, and he edited an *Anthology of Religious Verse* in 1942. Christianity was important to him; his late poem "Sea to the West" compares a dazzling sunset to the journey through death. But it also mentions the grimy backyards that are another part of his experience, and the same light-dark imagery appears in "Comprehending It Not," which shows a child waving a Christmas candle in a dreary, postwar world.

Most of his 1940s poems seemed to him not worth collecting, and after *The Pot Geranium* (1954), the poetry books came out at long intervals. His voice, especially in the later, better work, is friendly and informal: "Some people are flower-lovers. I'm a weed-lover," he announced in "Weeds." This suggests his determination to distance himself from the Romantics, who cast a giant shadow over his region. While Wordsworth had described a Lakeland untouched by "sordid industry," N. feared that it might become a tourists' playground and insisted that the industrial belt of Cumbria where he lived was a true part of the Lake District.

Millom—seen against a backcloth of sky and distant fells—is at the center of his interests. "The Seventeenth of the Name" and "The Tune the Old Cow Died Of" relate how his grandparents migrated from country to town, and how the town declined within three generations. "On the Closing of Millom Ironworks" (1968) pinpoints the date when smoke stopped polluting the atmosphere, and men were left without jobs. Gasworks, furnace chimneys, Nonconformist chapels, allotments, and brass bands all get into his poetry, which uses the occasional dialect word and is deeply rooted in ordinary experience. "Nicholson, Suddenly" was inspired by the death of his namesake, an inarticulate man with whom he seems to have had little in common, except that both were victims of serious illnesses caused, perhaps, by their environment. Yet, without any false sentiment, it celebrates the value of this man's life.

Other poems—"Beck," "Shingle," "Cloud on Black Combe"—are not about man at all but the endless natural processes of wind, streams, and sea. Human history is set against the slower movements of glaciers and planets. In a thousand years, the town may be gone, but Scafell Pike will remain; man may destroy the world through the misuse of nuclear power, but it will continue to rotate around the sun. "Windscale," "Comet come," and "Gathering Sticks on Sunday" suggest that we may pay a terrible price for our arrogance; the last ends with an image of a dead earth and moon staring at each other like skulls. "Halley's Comet," perhaps his greatest poem, compares the busy industrial town his father knew in 1910 with the depressed area that the comet will illuminate when it returns.

Yet N.'s tone is not usually depressing. It is often jokey; he refuses to take his poetic persona too seriously and suggests, in "The Bloody Cranesbill," that a fragile flower can, like poetry, flourish in "a lagoon of despoliation." He was a master of free and rhymed verse, who described the human and natural life of his region in what Wordsworth called "the real language of men." His reputation grew steadily in his later years and several distinguished poets paid tribute to him in an anthology, *Between Comets* (1984).

BIBLIOGRAPHY: Gardner, P., *N. N.* (1973); Hunt, I., ed., *N. N.'s Lakeland* (1991); Nicholson, N., *Wednesday Early Closing* (1975); Scammell, W., ed., *Between Comets* (1984)

MERRYN WILLIAMS

NICOLSON, [Sir] Harold [George]
b. 21 November 1886, Tehran, Persia (now Iran); d. 1 May 1968, Sissinghurst

Known primarily as an essayist and biographer, N. was a career diplomat and served as a member of Parliament from 1935 to 1946. His first published work was a biography of Paul Verlaine (1921), followed in that same year with his semiautobiographical novel *Sweet Waters*. His biographies of Alfred, Lord TENNYSON (1923), Lord BYRON (1924), and A. C. SWINBURNE (1926) were followed by the publication in 1927 of *The Development of English Biography*, which established N. as a leading theorist of the genre. Later works include biographies of Benjamin Constant (1949), King George V (1952), and the French poet and critic Charles-Augustin Sainte-Beuve (1957). N.'s unconventional marriage with Vita SACKVILLE-WEST was recounted in *Portrait of a Marriage* (1973), written by their son Nigel Nicolson, who also edited

Vita and Harold: The Letters of Vita Sackville-West and Harold Nicolson (1992).

NORTH, Christopher. See WILSON, John

NORTON, Thomas
b. ca. 1532, Buckhurst, Sussex; d. 10 March 1584

N. was educated at Michaelhouse, Cambridge University, where he matriculated in 1544. By 1550, he was in the service of Edward Seymour, Duke of Somerset. A prominent parliamentarian, N.'s major literary achievement, *Gorboduc; or, Ferrex and Porrex* (perf. 1562; pub. 1565; repub. as *The Tragidie of Ferrex and Porrex,* 1570), the first English blank-verse drama, was prompted by the question of ELIZABETH I's succession. Elizabeth had suffered a nearly fatal bout of smallpox during which time she had failed to name a successor. *Gorboduc*, for which N. wrote the first three acts and Thomas SACKVILLE the final two, sought to explore the danger to the queen of a leaderless England. The play was written as a part of a Christmas pageant for the Inner Temple and was presented later before the queen. It was first published in 1565, but the authorized version was printed in 1570. Sir Philip SIDNEY, in his *Apologie for Poetrie*—some twenty-one years after the play's performance—said of *Gorboduc* that it was "full of stately speeches and well sounding phrases, clymbing to the height of *Seneca* his stile, and full of notable moralitie, which it doth most delightfully teach, and so obtayne the very end of Poesie." Sidney, however, lamented the absence of the Aristotelian principles of unity of both time and place in the play.

NOYES, Alfred
b. 16 September 1880, Wolverhampton; d. 23 June 1958, Isle of Wight

Although N. published at least one book for nearly every year of the first half of the 20th c., spanning the genres of poetry, fiction, CHILDREN'S LITERATURE, drama, criticism, and critical BIOGRAPHY, his reputation survives primarily on the basis of a single poem. "The Highwayman" features N.'s most notable talents of percussive rhythms, intricate alliteration, and compelling narrative. At his best, N. wrote poems of heroic struggles taking place in geographically diverse regions drawn from his own travels and his imagination. These narratives he embellished with rich linguistic technique and challenging formal structures. He wrote extensively in blank verse, attempting to continue an EPIC tradition in English. He dabbled with the difficult hexameter line, borrowed from classical verse. But as the modernist movement emerged, N.'s favorite subject matter—naval battles, exotic locations, fairy stories, and the supernatural—dated him as a throwback to Victorian and imperialist aesthetics.

N. himself held fast to those aesthetics against the rise of MODERNISM, recommending the ban on James JOYCE's *Ulysses* upon its publication. Though out of step with the growing literary trends, N. found an audience among traditionalists longing for another Rudyard KIPLING, from whom he drew influence, along with the Pre-Raphaelites, Edgar Allan Poe, and Henry Wadsworth Longfellow. Critics who might have accepted his nostalgia and love of ornament had he written just a few decades earlier typically find N.'s often book-length narratives overblown, self-indulgent, and even insincere in SENTIMENT. Comparisons with other, modernist, poets exploring similar themes do not flatter N. For instance, Dylan THOMAS made extensive use of heavy alliterative decoration and sentimental themes in his poems. Edwin Arlington Robinson favored anachronistic narrative poems, but with a modernist stance. Even N.'s religious verse, emerging after his conversion to Catholicism in the 1920s, does not hold up in originality against the work of another Catholic modern, Gerard Manley HOPKINS.

"The Highwayman" ranks as N.'s masterwork as much for what it does not articulate as for what it does. The poem begins *in medias res,* with the highwayman galloping toward an unknown yet ominous fate. The echoes, repeated trochees in the broken fourth line of each stanza, help create the sense of doom prevalent in the poem. The death of a beautiful woman follows the dictum of Poe and provides the central tragic moment in a slightly unexpected turn. The highwayman's own abrupt death makes for an almost truncated ending, leaving the reader with more to imagine, unlike the longer N. sagas that leave little mystery. Thus, images of the moon as a "ghostly galleon" and the bunch of lace at the dead highwayman's throat are allowed to retain their power and luxurious beauty, without failing under the weight of sentiment and hyperbole.

Poems such as "A Song of Sherwood" and "The Barrel-Organ" demonstrate N.'s command of rhythm and alliteration and recall A. C. SWINBURNE's technique. His interest in the exotic can be seen in *The Flower of Old Japan* (1903), and even in his poems with American locations. "Old Man Mountain" and "Junipero Finds a Lodging for the Night" have West Coast settings while "The Happy Hunting Ground" represents New England. As a lecturer at Princeton, N. spent much time in the U.S., teaching such future literary figures as Edmund Wilson and F. Scott Fitzgerald. Though his work can seem maudlin, old-fashioned, or windy, N. was a dedicated follower of a dying aesthetic, one he kept alive in works that, at their best, depicted sweeping narrative and poetic glory.

BIBLIOGRAPHY: Jerrold, W., *A. N.* (1930); Lang, D. G., *N.* (1936); Noyes, A., *Two Worlds for Memory* (1953)

NICOLE SARROCCO

NYE, Robert
b. 15 March 1939, London

N. left school at sixteen to become a writer and in the course of a long and prolific career established himself as a poet, novelist, dramatist, editor, and children's author. He published his first collection of poetry, *Juvenilia 1,* in 1961 followed two years later by a second collection, *Juvenilia 2.* His first work for children, *Taliesin,* appeared in 1966 and in the next year he published his first novel, *Doubtfire.* Other novels include *Falstaff* (1976), awarded the *Guardian* Fiction Prize and the Hawthornden Prize, *Merlin* (1979), *Faust* (1980), and *The Voyage of the Destiny* (1982). His *Collected Poems* appeared in 1995 followed in the next year by his edition of the selected poems of Laura Riding. In 1998, he published the novel *The Late Mr. Shakespeare.*

O

O'BRIAN, Patrick

(pseud. of Richard Patrick Russ) b. 12 December 1914, Buckinghamshire; d. 2 January 2000, Dublin, Ireland

After World War II, O. reinvented himself by remarrying, changing his name, and leaving all previous family. O. through a large part of his life lived a bohemian, somewhat reclusive life in the French village of Collioure with his second wife. Later years and success followed by the rediscovery of his work brought him to the wealthier English establishment of clubs and the noble English elite. He did not open his personal life to others and those close to him often did not know of his past. Although born English, he wanted people to believe he was Irish.

O. began writing at a young age having started his first book, *Caesar: The Life Story of a Panda-Leopard* (1930), a story of a fictional panda-leopard, at the age of twelve. In his early work, the HUMOR and wit that make his later works so enjoyable to read are apparent. The bazaars and exotic areas of India are detailed in *Hussein: An Entertainment* (1938) although O. had not been there before writing this story. Both of these books have been reissued after being out of print for some time. His work well received, he continued to write short stories for magazines in Britain and the U.S. right up to the outbreak of the war. He also did translations of numerous works including: memoirs of Simone de Beauvoir and Jean Lacouture's biography of Charles de Gaulle. O. also was a biographer of distinction. He wrote about the lives of Pablo Picasso (1976) and Sir Joseph Banks (1987), the 18th-c. English naturalist who traveled with Captain James Cook in the Pacific. During the war, he drove ambulances and served in intelligence agencies. Surprisingly, O. did not serve in the navy or even in combat, the subject of so much of his later work.

O. came into mainstream popularity after 1999 when W. W. Norton released his twelfth book, *The Letter of the Marque* (1988), in hardcover and reissued *Master and Commander* (1970) and *Post Captain* (1972), the first and second books of this naval series. This series of nautical books is focused during the Napoleonic Wars. The historical fiction stories surround Captain Jack Aubrey and his friend and ship's Doctor Stephen Maturin. Through the some fifteen years these books cover, the two characters travel together through wonderful and thrilling adventures. The novels are said to have derived from the life of Lord Thomas Cochrane, a frigate captain known for his daring and skill. Cochrane was a master of single ship action and was a participant in onshore guerilla raids and, like the Aubrey character, was accused of fraudulent stock trading and had plenty of legal and money issues ashore.

O. has been compared to the Maturin character in the series as both had a high intellect and had worked for the intelligence agencies. They had a strong interest in nature and natural science as well as the intelligence work and were obsessively secretive. Maturin is of slight build much like the author yet still a deadly force in a duel or intelligence plot. The character's biting wit and intelligence are well balanced by Aubrey's skill in handling his ship and crew in battle. The Aubrey-Maturin series cover numerous sea adventures giving the reader an in-depth look at life on the seas and ashore during the 1800s.

O. wrote twenty Aubrey-Maturin novels of the sea beginning with *Master and Commander* and ending with *Blue at the Mizzen* (1999). His work has been touted as some of the best-sustained historical fiction work ever written. The attention to detail and sharp wit have been compared to Jane AUSTEN, and the characters of Aubrey and Maturin to figures of Homer's *Iliad*. The better-known Hornblower series of C. S. FORESTER, although dealing with the same period, lacks the minor character development and daily turmoil that surround Aubrey and Maturin. The details of the 19th-c. navy make the series well worth reading.

The nautical series about Aubrey and Maturin now has a new outcrop of companion books from various other authors relating to the life at sea. These books analyze the masterly and detailed work of O. They range from cookbooks of the meals described aboard the Aubrey ships to the battle diagrams, shiphandling and even 19th-c. medical treatments. The guides open the world of O. even wider to understanding the fine detail found throughout the Aubrey/Maturin series.

BIBLIOGRAPHY: Becker, S., "The Art of Fiction CXLII: P. O.," *PR* 37 (Summer 1995): 110–33; Cunningham, A. E., ed., *P. O.* (1994); King, D., *P. O.* (2000)

GEORGE R. FULLER

O'BRIEN, Edna
b. 15 December 1930, Tuamgraney, County Clare, Ireland

Beginning with her first novel, *The Country Girls* (1960), O.'s controversial female characters have created a stir in her native Ireland and introduced readers abroad to the constricting Irish-Catholic gender politics that create the context for her heroines' struggles with themselves and their men. O.'s more recent novels, most noticeably *House of Splendid Isolation* (1995) and *Wild Decembers* (2000), expand her themes to include contemporary politics and the continuing effects of Irish history. While she is mostly known for her novels and short stories, O has also published a memoir, stage plays, television and screenplays, a collection of folktales for children, and magazine articles.

O. was born in a small town in western Ireland. She evokes rural Ireland, governed by the codes of strict Catholic country morals, in much of her writing, and her indictment of such morals along with her frank treatment of sexuality caused *The Country Girls* and six of the books that followed to be banned in Ireland. *The Country Girls Trilogy—The Country Girls, The Lonely Girl* (1962; repub. as *Girl with Green Eyes*, 1964), and *Girls in Their Married Bliss* (1964)—chronicles the lives of two friends, Kate and Baba, from the women's childhood in the countryside to their marriages that fail in the face of conflicts over sexuality and the women's dependence on men. *Johnny I Hardly Knew You* (1977) returns to O.'s themes of women's sexuality and dependence. Written from the perspective of a woman who has suffocated her younger lover to take revenge against previous careless lovers by whom she feels betrayed, the novel does not indict the woman's crime but illustrates the consequences of obsessive love.

A more relentlessly bleak, and therefore less sympathetic, heroine is Nell Steadman, a former "country girl" from Ireland who has moved to London, and whose failing marriage and complex relationships to her two sons Paddy and Tristan are the subject of the novel *Time and Tide* (1992). The fight for any experience not defined by her overbearing family or her sadistic husband leads into a surreal underworld of drugs and therapy. Nell's self-destructive descent struck O.'s critics as less helpful than her previous novels; the prose, however, is as brilliant and sensuous as that of her earlier works. Along with the early bans of her works in Ireland, this persistent struggle for selfhood O.'s female characters engage in, much of it on the battle fields of love and sexuality, drew feminist critics' attention to O.'s writing, but their responses have been ambivalent: in many ways, O. remains a lush romantic, and her tragic heroines fail to break the fetters the social context of Irish Catholic traditions has put on them.

O.'s second great topic is the complexity of Ireland itself. No matter that she herself left Ireland for London in 1952; her writings retrieve her own past alongside myths and contemporary politics. *House of Splendid Isolation* takes on the conflict over Northern Ireland, "the Troubles," as it intersects the histories of two characters: Josie O'Meara, a widow living alone in the large West Country farmhouse her husband left her after an unpleasant marriage, and McGreevy, an IRA terrorist running from the law. But the hostage story turns redemptive as O'Meara warms to her captor, and the two exchange personal histories that culminate in the realization that a shared bond of humanity connects the two sides of the struggle. O'Meara retains echoes of O.'s earlier women: the appearance of the outsider reminds her of a lost self she now hopes to realize before she dies. In *Wild Decembers*, a classic drama over land ownership and a woman, native Joseph Brennan and newcomer Mick Bugler feud over a mountain in West Ireland and the love of Joseph's sister Breege. The novel's opening, an introduction of a tractor into a farm village grounded in the past, sets up the tension between tradition and modern life. The love between Breege and Bugler is intense but short-lived, and Brennan's unwillingness to compromise becomes his undoing.

O.'s nonfictional treatments of the Irish culture include her collaboration on a book of photos (*Irish Dreams*, 1998) for which she wrote an introduction, as well as her memoir *Mother Ireland* (1976), a collection of autobiographical essays that describe the hardship of the Irish childhood and take the reader from school days in the convent school to the author's marriage and eventual escape to England. As O.'s prolific and varied output positions her in the foreground of contemporary Irish writing, her sense of style and language has prompted comparison to James JOYCE, about whom she published a biographical study in 1999, revisiting the theme she first addressed in the nonfiction work *James and Nora: A Portrait of Joyce's Marriage* (1981). In keeping with the emphasis on women's experiences in O.'s fiction, her 1999 study cites Joyce's mother and wife as important influences. Her treatment of Joyce continues the dual trajectories of her work: a focus on Ireland and on women.

BIBLIOGRAPHY: Carpenter, L., "Tragedies of Remembrance, Comedies of Endurance: The Novels of E. O.," in Bock, H., and A. Werfheim, eds., *Essays on the Contemporary British Novel* (1986): 263–81; Eckley, G., *E. O.* (1974); O'Hara, K., "Love Objects: Love and Obsession in the Stories and E. O.," *SSF* 30 (Summer 1993): 317–25

JULIA F. KLIMEK

O'BRIEN, Flann

(pseud. of Brian O'Nolan or Ó Nualláin) b. 5 October 1911, Strabane, County Tyrone, Northern Ireland; d. 1 April 1966, Dublin, Ireland

O. follows in the footsteps of a long line of Irish satirists—Jonathan SWIFT, Oscar WILDE, John Millington SYNGE, and his near-contemporary James JOYCE, who expressed approval for his first novel, *At Swim-Two-Birds* (1939), famously reading it with the aid of a magnifying glass. O. was educated at Trinity College, Dublin, and served in the Civil Service from 1935 until his retirement in 1953. In a career spanning little more than twenty-five years, he was a novelist, playwright, television scriptwriter, and journalist; renowned in his own time as a columnist, it is for his novels that he is chiefly remembered today.

These two pursuits—columnist and novelist—ran parallel. In 1940 under the pseudonym Myles na gCopaleen ("Myles of the Little Ponies"), O. began writing satirical pieces for the *Irish Times* in a series called "Cruiskeen Lawn" (Little Brimming Jug). These columns ended only with his death, and set the tone for O.'s literary output: satirical and scathing, they targeted pretentiousness, and sentimental, traditionalist views of Ireland. Not for O. the founding myths of a fledgling state that would free Ireland of Britain's (and English's) shadow, nor the "Oirishness" romantically evoked by some Irish writers. O.'s Ireland is comic, often absurd, always offering itself as a parodic corrective to those in authority. If O.'s vision is less bleak than Franz Kafka's, it is none the less equally suspicious of authority.

Despite the critical success of *At Swim-Two-Birds,* O.'s literary career stalled, and was kept going by minor successes on the stage and radio, such as *Faustus Kelly* and *Thirst* respectively (both 1943), whose titles convey something of O.'s playful approach that marks out the novels. Although his only novel written in Irish entitled *An Beal Bocht* was published in 1941, and *Cruiskeen Lawn,* a collection of columns (both under Myles na gCopaleen), two years later, O.'s sec-

ond novel, *The Third Policeman,* written in 1939–40, was rejected by his publisher. Not until the 1960s did the novels appear, O. in the interim relying on newspaper and television writing, which was beginning to take off. *The Hard Life: An Exegesis of Squalor* (1961) was immensely successful, and *The Dalkey Archive* followed in 1964, reprising some of the material of *The Third Policeman,* which finally appeared in 1967. *An Beal Bocht* was translated as *The Poor Mouth* in 1973.

O.'s reputation rests partly on the brilliantly comic writing of the novels and columns, and partly on what some critics identify as a postmodernist tendency. A metafictional interweaving of characters and authors in *At Swim-Two-Birds* produces a novel with three beginnings and three endings, the opening paragraph declaring: "One beginning and one ending for a book was a thing I did not agree with"; *The Third Policeman*'s satirical treatment of scholarship questions whether knowledge is ever attainable. The uncertainty that pervades O.'s/O'Nolan's/na gCopaleen's work is apparent in the disruption of that most fundamental sign of identity: an author's name(s). The plurality of names and problem of identity are part of a very serious postmodern game, which also goes to the heart of a playful examination of how mid-20th-c. Ireland saw itself. It is an achievement that places O. in the first rank of Irish writers.

BIBLIOGRAPHY: Asbee, S., *F. O.* (1991); Booker, M. K., *F. O., Bakhtin, and Menippean Satire* (1995); Clissmann, A., *F. O.* (1975); Clune, A, and T. Hurson, eds., *Conjuring Complexities: Essays on F. O.* (1997); Hopper, K., *F. O.* (1995); Shea, T. F., *F. O.'s Exorbitant Novels* (1992)

MARK HUTCHINGS

O'CASEY, Sean

b. 30 March 1880, Dublin, Ireland; d. 18 September 1964, Torquay

Best known for his "Dublin trilogy," a series of plays set in the city's slums during the violence that led to Irish home rule and produced by the Abbey Theatre in the mid-1920s, O. was also an innovative dramatist who rejected representationalist theater for staging techniques similar to those used by Bertolt Brecht. He also produced a six-volume AUTOBIOGRAPHY, in which he experimented with the use of scenic techniques in the presentation of personal narrative. Throughout a long literary career that also encompassed fiction, poetry, drama criticism, and political polemics, O. remained consistent in his rejection of the institutions that suppressed the rights and ignored the needs of individuals and in his support for organized labor.

Born into the Protestant lower class of Dublin, O. knew the poverty and discomfort that marked the lives of the characters in his Dublin trilogy. He came to drama fairly late in life; he was forty-two years old when the Abbey Theatre produced his first play, *Shadow of a Gunman* (perf. 1923; pub. 1925). Until then, he had worked as a manual laborer and had devoted himself first to Irish nationalism and then—especially when the nationalist movement seemed to be ignoring workers' concerns—to organized labor, an association that influenced his turn toward communism. He began to write polemical articles for nationalist and labor journals in his twenties and published several volumes of socially oriented verse in the 1910s. O. was especially affected by the Great Dublin Lock-Out of 1913, a labor-management confrontation that resulted in considerable suffering for workers in various industries who were attempting to improve their working conditions. Though he supported nationalist action like the Easter Rebellion of 1916, he became more actively involved in organized labor than in the home rule movement after the lock-out. His view that the nationalist movement was ignoring workers influenced the content of his early drama.

Though O. had begun writing plays as early as 1918, the Abbey did not accept one of his works until five years later. *Shadow of a Gunman* reflects contemporary events. It deals with the guerrilla war waged by the Irish Republican Army before a treaty with the British government in 1921 afforded partial self-rule to Ireland. O.'s next play, *Juno and the Paycock* (perf. 1924; pub. 1925), occurs during the civil war that followed the treaty, which some Irish nationalists opposed because it did not extend home rule to all of Ireland. They violently confronted the newly formed Irish Free State, which had agreed to the compromise that left six counties in Ulster as part of the U.K. In 1926, the Abbey produced *The Plough and the Stars,* which takes place during the Easter Rebellion and completes O.'s Dublin trilogy.

The three plays share a common setting: the squalor of Dublin slum life while political conflict is raging outside the walls of the tenements where his characters go about their business. They also demonstrate how the high ideals of nationalists might not correspond to the conditions of individuals such as those characters, whose major concerns involve simply meeting physical and emotional needs on a daily basis. Women characters emerge as more resourceful in coping with their situation, the males in the Dublin trilogy often escaping into alcohol, gambling, and nationalistic idealism. The conflicts in the married life of Jack and Juno Boyle in the second play—as well as the interpersonal conflicts in the other parts of the trilogy—mirror the civil war that is simultaneously occurring, but they also represent what O. regarded as inevitable tensions that arise when such relationships

must exist amid dehumanizing poverty. Pervaded by reminders of that poverty as well as by the specter of violent death from the ongoing political violence, the plays comprising the Dublin trilogy nevertheless provide O. with a forum for mordant HUMOR, rendered in the speech of the Dublin slums—not the same as the Irish peasant English that other early-20th-c. Irish dramatists had used so effectively. This may account for the plays' popularity. All three have been among the most frequently revived in the Abbey Theatre repertoire.

Some stylistic evolution is evident in the three Dublin plays as O. moved from fairly straightforward REALISM in *Shadow of a Gunman* to more experimental approaches in *The Plough and the Stars.* This pattern of development became particularly evident in *The Silver Tassie* (1928), a scathing treatment of the mental and physical effects of World War I on its victims. The language of the play combines the dialects of the Dublin slums and of cockney soldiers behind the lines in Flanders with stylized chant. O. used a variety of approaches to staging and expressionistic techniques in the play's four acts—three of which take place in his familiar Dublin slum locales. While the Abbey Theatre directors, particularly W. B. YEATS, had no problems with the play's subject matter, they perceived it as being more propagandistic than dramatic. That and the play's style resulted in their rejecting it for production. The interchange over the play between O. and Yeats that appeared in several Irish literary journals remains an important series of statements of dramatic philosophy and methodology. Despite the Abbey's rejection, O. remained convinced of the worth of *The Silver Tassie,* and it was produced in London in 1929. O., who remained devoted to Irish culture despite his discomfort with the home rule movement, followed the play to England and lived there the rest of his life. He and Yeats, who had supported the Abbey's production of his early plays, became reconciled when the Dublin-based theater produced *The Silver Tassie* in 1935.

Throughout the 1930s until his death, O. continued to write plays that evinced the expressionistic style that had begun to mark his drama. While some of these plays continued to treat Dublin slum life, his focus broadened to include other subjects, though always his sympathy for individuals caught up by but ignored by movements and institutions was evident. *Within the Gates,* produced in London in 1934, suggested the directions in which O.'s dramatic technique was going. Entirely stylized, this play takes place in a busy urban park, modeled roughly on London's Hyde Park, and gave O. the opportunity to manipulate a large cast of characters. Originally planned as a film script to be directed by Alfred Hitchcock, *Within the Gates* focuses primarily on the attempts of a prostitute to find meaning during the dark days of the Great Depression. As did most of O.'s work following the Dublin trilogy, the play combined elements of REALISM and fantasy presented in verse and prose. Consistent with the Dublin plays, *Within the Gates* sets the concerns of a neglected individual against a sweeping tapestry of events beyond her control and of solutions to political and social problems that ignore her needs.

Other O. plays from the thirties and forties that respond directly to contemporary events include *The Star Turns Red,* which allegorically addresses the rise of fascism by depicting the conflict between workers and the Saffron Shirts, a fascist group supported by the Roman Catholic Church. Produced in 1940, the play is often dismissed as propaganda, as is *Oak Leaves and Lavender,* set during the battle of Britain and produced in 1946. O. was also turning more and more satirical, locating plays in the Ireland where he no longer lived and targeting both state and church in his criticisms. *Purple Dust* (1940), produced in 1943, for example, uses a rural Irish setting to attack the remnants of British imperialism still evident in Irish life. *Red Roses for Me* (1942), first performed the same year, draws upon O.'s own experience of growing up in the Dublin slums to highlight the indifference of organized religion to the needs of the working class. In 1949, the farcical *Cock-a-Doodle Dandy* dramatized the repressive forces of church and state in Irish life, an emphasis that O. sustained through the plays he wrote during the 1950s and 1960s, especially *The Bishop's Bonfire* (1955) and *Behind the Green Curtain* (perf. 1962; pub. 1961). Though there is growing pessimism about the possibilities for individual fulfillment in the face of repressive social structures in these later plays, O. finds hope in the younger characters and suggests a generational conflict between their free-spiritedness and the rigidity of their elders.

In 1939, O. published the first of what eventually became six volumes of autobiography. Like his plays the books became increasingly experimental, though from the first in the series, *I Knock at the Door,* he emphasized a dramatic, detached presentation. Using the third-person to refer to "Sean," he covers about twelve years in each of the six volumes, the last one, *Sunset and Evening Star,* appearing in 1954, a decade before his death. In these autobiographies, O. employs a range of perspectives, prose styles, and structural devices to present a narrative that extends from his childhood in the Dublin slums to literary life in London. His concerns with the ways in which institutions and movements, even those whose ideals he endorsed, might neglect the individual remain central to his autobiography as they had in his plays.

Amazingly prolific, O., who had written verse and social criticism early in his life, published several volumes of essays and reviews after he had become a London-based dramatist. He also published some short fiction during the 1930s.

BIBLIOGRAPHY: Kearney, C., *The Glamour of Grammar: Orality and Politics and the Emergence of S. O.* (2000); Krause, D., *S. O.* (1975); Krause, D., *S. O. and His World* (1976); Krause, D., and R. G. Lowery, eds., *S. O. Centenary Essays* (1981); Mitchell, J., *The Essential O.: A Study of the Twelve Major Plays of S. O.* (1981); Simmons, J., *S. O.* (1990)

WILLIAM M. CLEMENTS

O'CONNOR, Frank

(pseud. of Michael Francis O'Donovan) b. 17 September 1903, Cork, Ireland; d. 10 March 1966, Dublin, Ireland

O., a highly regarded short story writer of the mid-20th c., admired and was influenced by such classic short story writers as Anton Chekhov, Ivan Turgenev, Guy de Maupassant, and Gustave Flaubert. *New Harper's Bazaar* and *Atlantic Monthly* frequently published his works, after which he often revised them and had them published in collections. Although some have criticized him for sentimentality and others for expending a highly developed technique on thin content, many of his works are well worth reading today.

In his book about the short story, *The Lonely Voice* (1962), O. sees the short story as the literature of a "submerged population group," as conveying a "sense of outlawed figures wandering about the fringes of society," and consequently as expressing "an intense awareness of human loneliness." Bonaparte, the young narrator of one of O.'s earliest and most admired story, "Guests of the Nation" (1931), is an Irish rebel guarding two captive English soldiers, Belcher and 'Awkins. Clearly, the captives and their guards have become "chums"; but Bonaparte learns that the English are hostages, and when the English execute Irish prisoners, he is forced to help execute his chums. As he recalls, "I was somehow very small and very lonely," and the closing words of the story tell how his life was changed: "And anything that ever happened me [*sic*] after I never felt the same about again."

O. drew on his war experience as a member of the Irish Republican Army for "Guests of the Nation." He tells of them further in his autobiography, *An Only Child* (1961), and also describes the childhood he drew on throughout most of his writing career for many of his most memorable stories. His father was an ex-soldier, an alcoholic who worked sporadically, and a member of a marching band. His mother, to whom O. was devoted, was reared in a convent orphanage and had more refined taste and expectations than her husband, but need often forced her to work as a maid or cleaning woman.

In "Orpheus and His Lute" (1936), for example, an old man tells the narrator about the dissolution of the Irishtown band, whose thirst for porter overcame their love of music. They pawned their instruments, and when they were unable to redeem them in time to play for St. Patrick's Day, they took instruments from another band by force, played as they had never played before, and then surrendered to the police. Here, as in "Peasants" (1922) and other stories, O. succeeds in his often expressed aim of finding "the right voice," of giving a voice to his people. In the later story "The Cornet Player Who Betrayed Ireland" (1947), the narrator recaptures his perspective as a small boy who witnesses the conflict between his father (an O'Brienite) and the rest of the band (Redmonites) when political feelings overwhelm the band-players' love of music. His obstinate father leaves the band when a fellow member insults him for his political convictions. This story is more sophisticated in structure and more mature in style than "Orpheus and His Lute" and is not comic like the earlier story.

Often the narrator portrays himself as a boy creating a rich interior world and finding disillusionment when he acts on its bases in the real world. In "The Face of Evil" (1954), the boy tries out being a saint and winds up doing more harm than good. In "The Genius" (1957), O.'s alter ego, "Larry Delaney," concludes that being a genius "was a poor, sad, lonesome thing." In "The Study of history" (1957), Larry seeks out one of his father's old girlfriends, shows off before her family, and admires her son, Gussie. When he returns home, this adventure delights his father but upsets his mother. He goes to bed imagining he is Gussie, then panics when he cannot resume his own identity. His mother hears his sobs, comes in to comfort him, they are reconciled, and he is Larry once again, but wiser. O.'s relationship to his parents is also well represented by the parallel relationship in the frequently anthologized story "My Oedipus Complex" (1950).

O.'s mature style has been characterized as lean and clear. His use of dialect contributes to rooting the stories in a particular place—always in Ireland, despite his long sojourns in the U.S. Study of the versions and revisions particular stories went through before and after their various publications leads one to conclude that O. was a careful, conscious craftsman, one in the great tradition of the short story that he so admired.

BIBLIOGRAPHY: Matthews, J., *Voices: A Life of F. O.* (1983); Sheehy, M., ed., *Michael/Frank: Studies on F. O.* (1969); Steinman, M., *F. O. at Work* (1990); Tomory, W. M., *F. O.* (1980)

KENNETH A. ROBB

O'FAOLAIN, Julia

b. 6 June 1932, London

Novelist and short story writer, O. casts a writer's spell upon some central human concerns: the relationship between the sexes, nationalism, and the fading, but still powerful, hold of religion on people's lives. Her fictions frequently depict characters alone and alienated from the friends, families, and faith that ought to sustain them.

The daughter of Irish author Sean O'FAOLAIN and Eileen Gould O'Faolain, O. was educated at home, at a convent school, and University College Dublin. While living in Florence in 1957, she met and married Renaissance historian Lauro Martines. All of O.'s writings are informed by her early experiences: her expansive reading (everything from Russian literature and Irish romances to Catholic devotional literature), her parents' hopes for a Gaelic homeland, and the intensely Catholic environment of Ireland.

The stories in O.'s first collection, *We Might See Sights!* (1968), are about evenly divided between "Irish" and "Italian stories" and set the pattern for future examinations of these two culturally Catholic nations. The Irish stories were republished as *Melancholy Baby and Other Stories* (1978). In the title story of *Man in the Cellar* (1974), the Irish and Italian themes are married. The Irish-born heroine, bullied by her macho Italian husband, takes drastic measures to bring on a divorce: she chains him to a bed in the cellar. Despite the wide-ranging settings of the seven stories in the collection, all the characters, from a 6th-c. nun to a married celibate to an Italian academic in America, are fettered to their own lusts and miseries.

O.'s first novel, *Godded and Codded* (1970), juxtaposes the stories of two Irish compatriots in Paris: Sally, a student, and Fintan, an artist and fugitive from a love affair back home. Sally's sexual awakening, disappointment in love, and dangerous abortion help her escape her own Irishness, with its sexual repression and romanticized view of life. *Women in the Wall* (1975) is a fictionalization of the life of Radegunda, wife of Chlotar I, king of the Franks, who becomes a visionary and finds solace in the arms of a Christ who appears as a handsome young man. Agnes, the abbess of a monastery, has an illicit affair with a poet that produces a child, Ingunda. In expiation, Ingunda immures herself in the convent walls; Agnes follows. These women resolve their conflicts through visions or sex, burying themselves within real or psychological walls.

The title of O.'s *No Country for Young Men* (1980), a finalist for Britain's Booker Prize, replies to "That is no country for old men," a line from W. B. YEATS's "Sailing to Byzantium." Ireland is a country where young men die, and where strong women like Judith Clancy are hidden away in convents or are chained to the female obligations of housekeeping and mothering. In *The Obedient Wife* (1982), though, young mother Carla Verdi survives an affair with a priest and recommits herself to these very female occupations. Her final obedience, however, is not to husband or church, but to her own values—salvation lies, not in religion, but in a secular code that privileges the values of domesticity and family life.

O.'s short story collection *Daughters of Passion* (1982) examines how women deal with sexual, religious, and political obsession. The young woman in "The Nanny and the Antique Dealer" learns that she can only satisfy her lover when she abandons her real self and dresses as his mother. "Mad Marga" and "Daughters of Passion" depict young women who are propelled into violent acts by others: Marga by a radical political group, Maggy by a childhood friend from the convent of the Daughters of Passion. In these disconcerting stories, O. manages to show how dangerous it is to succumb to others' desires.

The Irish Signorina (1984), in contrast, empowers women by upending the conventional tale of the governess in the great house. Anne, visiting the Italian town where her mother had once lived, falls in love with the handsome Guido. She blithely pursues her intention of marrying Guido, even though he is, in fact, her father. Though critics disparaged the plot as clichéd and operatic, the central character serves as an interesting counterpoint to the legions of O.'s beleaguered females.

O.'s novel *The Judas Cloth* (1992) is set in 19th-c. Italy and revolves around the lives of Pope Pius IX and three young men, one of whom experiences a spiritual disillusionment that leads him to renounce the "Judas cloth" of priesthood and Catholicism. This historical novel, a departure from O.'s other works, suffers from its overreliance on documentary detail to the detriment of our interest in the characters.

The people in O.'s works (but especially the women) are often presented with two radical choices: self-containment and moral rectitude on one side; sexual passion and political extremism on the other. For O.'s characters, freedom is possible for those who reject both extremes; all others are fated to life in a formally organized fantasy world.

BIBLIOGRAPHY: Jagodzinski, C. M. "J. O.," in Moseley, M., ed., *British Novelists since 1960*, Fourth Series, *DLB* 231 (2001): 192–99; Weekes, A. O., "J. O.: The Imaginative Crucible," in her *Irish Women Writers* (1990): 174–90

CECILE M. JAGODZINSKI

O'FAOLAIN, Sean

b. 22 February 1900, Cork, Ireland; d. 20 April 1991, Dublin, Ireland

For the greater part of the 20th c., O. confronted the question of what it means to be Irish in almost every form of writing. O. wrote biographies, travel books, journalism, and literary criticism, but his best work is his fiction, his novels and especially the short story, the form with which he began and the only one he employed consistently throughout his career.

O.'s first short story collection, *Midsummer Night Madness* (1932), reflects the period of "the Troubles" and the Irish Civil War and O.'s own experience as a bomb maker and director of publicity for the Irish Republican Army. These stories are highly romantic, but even this early O.'s constant theme of a glorious past giving way to a dismal present begins to take shape. Such characters as Old Henn ("Midsummer Night Madness") and Bella Brown ("The Small Lady") may be enemies of the revolution, but they are also figures of such immense vitality that beside them such venial revolutionaries as Stevey Long dwindle to insignificance. Their removal from Ireland by exile or execution diminishes the life of the country. In the book's final story, "The Patriot," the central character finally abandons political rebellion for life with his wife Norah, a choice O. clearly approves. Despite this hint of disillusion, the stories in *Midsummer Night Madness* are highly romantic both in their content and in their lushly poetic language, a style O. soon repudiated.

The stories in O.'s second collection, *A Purse of Coppers* (1937), emphasize that romantic Ireland is indeed dead and gone, as the romance and poetry of the early stories give way to a more objective treatment of the individual struggling in what O. considered the "dreary Eden" of Eamon de Valera's Ireland. The emphasis now is on loneliness and alienation, best expressed in "A Broken World." In his conversation on a train with a farmer and the narrator, a priest tells the story of his parish, amounting to a history of Ireland that explains what has brought the country to its present condition, and recounts his vision of a once unified world represented by the deserted estates of the rich. The vision is fruitless, however, for the priest has been silenced for urging his parishioners to take over the estates and resurrect the unified world they once represented, the farmer has no understanding of what the priest is saying, and the narrator considers the priest's talk idle philosophizing. There is no communication, and although the narrator ends by hoping for a new dawn we are left with the image, clearly reminiscent of James JOYCE's "The Dead," "under that white shroud covering the whole of Ireland, life was lying broken and hardly breathing."

During this period, O. also explored the theme of past and present in a series of biographies, the glorious past being represented by Daniel O'Connell (*King of the Beggars*, 1938) and Hugh O'Neill (*The Great O'Neill*, 1942), the mediocre present by de Valera (1939). The theme received further fictional treatment in O.'s three novels—*A Nest of Simple Folk* (1933), *Bird Alone* (1936), *Come Back to Erin* (1940)—in each of which a younger character is strongly influenced by an older character representative of Ireland's heroic past. In addition, O. founded and from 1940 to 1946 edited the *Bell*, a magazine for which he provided considerable social and political commentary.

The nature of O.'s short fiction changed after this period of intense activity and involvement. The narrative voice in *The Man Who Invented Sin* (1948) is more detached, the presentation more objective. There is a new emphasis on HUMOR, as in "Teresa," a novice whose idea of being a nun is based entirely on motion pictures, and the past is now viewed not politically but with nostalgia, as in "The Silence of the Valley," in which the death of a cobbler/storyteller marks the end of a whole way of life. The conflict is not the past and the present but innocence and experience, best conveyed in two stories. "The Man Who Invented Sin" recounts how the curate Lispeen, a satanic figure, perverts the future lives of a group of young monks and nuns by making their innocent pleasures seem evil and corrupt. In "Lovers of the Lake," Robert Flannery and his mistress Jenny experience a conflict between conscience and emotion when they attend a pilgrimage at Saint Patrick's Purgatory during which they undergo something of a role reversal, a typical O. plot device, and realize that there is "no solid self that has not a ghost inside it trying to escape," in this case the ghost of a Catholic conscience that will apparently bring their affair to an end. The stories in O.'s next collection, *I Remember! I Remember!* (1961), depart even further from his early work. There is more concern with personality, the conflicts are now primarily internal, and the usual contrast between past and present now leads the characters to insights into themselves, dramatized best by Daniel Cashen in "A Touch of Autumn in the Air," whose memory of one day of his childhood causes him to question the value of his later life as a successful businessman.

These stories are the culmination of O.'s greatest period. O. continued to write stories, but his later work is of a rather different kind. O. gained a much wider audience during the 1960s and 1970s by publishing stories in *Collier's, McCalls, Playboy,* and other popular magazines, but despite their frequent excellence these later stories do not have quite the depth and intensity, and the later collections do not have quite the thematic unity, of O.'s earlier work.

BIBLIOGRAPHY: Bonaccorso, R., *S. O.'s Irish Vision* (1987); Butler, P., *S. O.* (1993); Doyle, P. A., *S. O.* (1968); Harmon, M., *S. O.* (1966)

JOHN ROGERS

O'FLAHERTY, Liam

b. 28 August 1896, Gort na gCapall, Eire, Ireland; d. 7 September 1984, Dublin, Ireland

Several of O.'s most highly regarded novels and many of his short stories are rooted in the daily life of his homeland, Innishmore, the largest of the Aran Islands. He served in World War I, was wounded, shell-shocked, and discharged, then traveled to the Americas, often working as a laborer and becoming attracted to socialism and the Industrial Workers of the World. Returning to Dublin, he led a group of unemployed dockers in seizing the Rotunda and raising the red flag in January 1922; they soon withdrew and O. went to England to write.

Usually considered to be a member of a great generation of Irish storytellers, "the three O.'s," with Sean O'FAOLAIN and Frank O'CONNOR, O. is more naturalistic and forceful in his writing than the others and claimed at times to be unconcerned with style. Most critics have found a handful of his 183 short stories superior to his sixteen novels, but O. preferred the novel form.

Thy Neighbour's Wife (1923) caught the attention of the British publishers' adviser Edward Garnett, who recommended it be published and then became O.'s mentor. Set on an island like Innishmore, *Thy Neighbour's Wife* depicts a young curate's conflict between his religious vocation and his renewed attraction to a former flame, now married to a rich, older man.

Garnett encouraged O. to focus his fiction on life in western Ireland. But O. also drew on his revolutionary experiences. *The Informer* (1925) is probably his best-known novel, partly because the motion picture based on it won several prizes. The protagonist, Gypo Nolan, is physically powerful but rather grotesque and mentally limited. After informing on a friend in "the Organization," he becomes hunted and alienated in the vividly described, sordid Dublin slums. At times, O. succeeds admirably in conveying Gypo's point of view even though it is unlikely that the reader will fully empathize with him.

Many critics prefer *Skerrett* (1932) and *Famine* (1937), both set on the Aran Islands and presenting themes of social and historical change. The former is thematically akin to Thomas HARDY's *The Mayor of Casterbridge*. Skerrett is another of O.'s physically large, forceful protagonists; when he arrives on the island of "Nara" as schoolteacher and attempts to revitalize and preserve the mores of the past, he is opposed and defeated by the parish priest, Father Moclair, whose goal is to modernize Nara. Here, and in *Famine*, O. shows great skill in describing crowds of peasants in rebellion against their oppressors.

In *Famine*, the most tangible oppressors are absentee landlords, their agents, and the English government that protects their rights. But the greatest oppressor is the potato blight that strikes and destroys so many peasants and their way of life, driving the survivors to rebel or emigrate to America. O. portrays these effects by focusing on a fairly typical peasant family, the Kilmartins, but his cast of characters is large and spans spectra of class and political belief. Some critics find that O.'s characters both symbolize class attitude and are well-developed individuals.

O'Connor declared O.'s "The Fairy Goose" (1926) "one of my two favorite stories"; a moral fable, it tells how a goose becomes a village divinity until the priest turns the villagers against her. The interaction of men, animals, and nature is handled more naturalistically and movingly in "Birth" (1926), which tells of a cow bearing its first calf out in the pasture under the watchful eyes of a group of men. In "Spring Sowing" (1924) and "Milking Time" (1925), newlyweds begin the round of chores that will constitute their lives for years to come. "The Parting" (1948), probably autobiographical, movingly depicts the dockside separation of Michael Joyce from his family as the boy leaves for the mainland to continue his schooling; another story depicting great restrained emotion is "Going into Exile" (1924), in which the Feeneys give a farewell party for their children Mary and Michael, who are emigrating to Boston. A late story published in both English and Irish, "The Post Office" (1954), is a wonderfully comic portrayal of a community and its leaders confronted by sophisticated outsiders.

A discussion of O.'s fiction would not be complete without stressing his excellent use of visual detail that particularly enriches such often-praised animal stories as "The Rockfish" (1923), "The Blackbird" (1924), "The Wounded Cormorant" (1925), and, especially, "The Conger Eel" (1924), in which the reader comes to feel the power and grace of the eel in its habitat and the force that drives it to escape the fishermen's net.

BIBLIOGRAPHY: Kelly, A. A., *L. O. the Storyteller* (1976); O'Flaherty, L., *Shame the Devil* (1934); Sheeran, P. F., *The Novels of L. O.* (1976); Zneimer, J., *The Literary Vision of L. O.* (1970)

KENNETH A. ROBB

OKRI, Ben[jamin]

b. 15 March 1959, Minna, Nigeria

Born in Nigeria, O. was reared for part of his childhood in England, where he has lived since 1978. He published his first novel, *Flowers and Shadows,* in 1980, followed in the next year by *The Landscapes Within.* He next published two collections of short stories, *Incidents at the Shrine* and *Stars of the New Curfew,* in 1987 and 1989, respectively. In 1991, O. earned critical acclaim with the publication of *The*

Famished Road, a postmodern novel inspired by magic realism, merging dream and reality, as narrated through the consciousness of an abiku or "spirit-child," born into an endless cycle of death and rebirth. O.'s *Songs of Enchantment* (1993) and *Infinite Riches* (1998) complete the so-called Famished Road trilogy. Other novels include *Astonishing the Gods* (1995) and *Dangerous Love* (1996), a revised version of *The Landscapes Within.* He has also published a volume of poetry, *An African Elegy* (1992), and a collection of essays entitled *A Way of Being Free* (1997). O. is the recipient of numerous international awards, including the Booker Prize for *The Famished Road.*

OLD ENGLISH

Although the development of language, like history, is a continuous process, thus making the assignment of periods a somewhat arbitrary proposition, it is generally agreed that the language written and spoken in England from 450 to 1150 is called Old English. Old English is an Indo-European language of the Western branch of the Germanic triad. It therefore has strong affinities with Scandinavian (North Germanic) languages, including modern-day Swedish, Danish, Norwegian, and Icelandic, and to the (East Germanic) Gothic languages such as Visigothic, Vandalic, and Burgundian, now thought to be extinct. More specifically, along with Old Saxon, Old Low Franconian, and Old Frisian, Old English represents the lowland subgroup of West Germanic, in that it like these shows no impact of the Second, or High German, Sound Shift that took place ca. 600. As a result, despite the many similarities Modern English bears to contemporary High German, our language of today is in fact closer to modern Dutch, Flemish, and "Low" German (Plattdeutsch).

The traditional moment of origin of Old English is 449. In that year, as recorded by the Venerable BEDE in his *Historia Ecclesiatica Gentis Anglorum,* Vortigern, leader of the British Celts, invited a small army from Jutland, on the northern half of the Danish peninsula, to Britain to secure the Scottish border against invading Picts and Scots. Their mission completed, the fiercer Jutes turned on their Celtic hosts and established settlements. These expanded over the course of the next hundred years, attracting other Germanic peoples: according to the *Anglo-Saxon Chronicle* (wr. ca. 890–1154), initially Saxons, from between the Elbe and Ems Rivers, in 477 and 495; Angles, from the lower portion of the Danish peninsula, at the end of the century and in 547; and Frisians (although neither Bede nor the *Chronicle* mentions them), whose territory was along the coast between the Weser River and the Rhine. By ca. 650, settlements had combined variously into seven small kingdoms, known as the Anglo-Saxon Heptarchy. Their names provide modest geographical and tribal information: Northumbria (Anglian, north of the Humber River), Mercia (primarily Anglian, Midlands), East Anglia (eastern territory of the Angles), Kent (Jutish), Essex (territory of the East Saxons), Sussex (territory of the South Saxons), and Wessex (land of the West Saxons).

Old English is thus a combination of the languages spoken by the invading Continental West Germanic tribes, modified over time by contact with each other and, in varying degrees, with the Celtic and Latin spoken by the subjugated Britons. Although the Saxon, Anglian, and Jutish tongues must have been very close, the earliest English written documents (ca. 700) give evidence of four discernible Old English dialects: Northumbrian, Mercian, West Saxon, and Kentish. Of these, Northumbrian and Mercian bear the closest affinity, being in use north of the Thames River in territories settled first by the Angles. Their common features allow them sometimes to be classed together as a single Anglian dialect. Unfortunately, little evidence remains of Northumbrian, Mercian, or Kentish, on which to base detailed study of these dialects. Moreover, what examples there are come from sources of relatively limited variety, including charters, verse fragments, a handful of runic inscriptions, and parts of the Bible with interlinear translations. This contrasts sharply in quantity and quality with examples of West Saxon, the dialect in which almost all known Old English literature is preserved. The disproportionate representation of Old English texts undoubtedly results from the later ascendancy of the West Saxon kingdom, beginning with the rule of Egbert (802–39) and increasing its influence under ALFRED THE GREAT (871–99), whose military and diplomatic successes against the later Danish invaders protected the southwest when the other kingdoms—and their scribal centers—were overrun.

Old English differs from Modern English primarily in four areas: spelling, pronunciation, vocabulary, and grammar. Because of these differences (and despite the ancestral relationship of Old English to contemporary English), a modern reader encountering Old English for the first time might be expected to register Old English as more foreign than present-day Spanish or French. Much strangeness disappears, however, with the recognition of certain basic facts.

The alphabet employed by Old English scribes derived from a combination of Roman and runic characters, the latter employed apparently because Anglo-Saxon writers wished to distinguish sounds not acknowledged as separate by literate Romans. These included two forms of "th": one voiced, represented in Old English as þ, called "thorn"; the other unvoiced, represented as ð, called "eth"; the short sound of "a" represented as æ, called "ash"; and ȝ, called "yogh." Moreover, certain letters and letter combinations common today either did not appear in Old English

("k") or were rare ("z"); and others had different pronunciations.

The primary distinction between Old English and Modern English pronunciation is the result of the Great Vowel Shift of the 15th c., when essentially (and for no clearly understood cause) the so-called long vowels in English began to be spoken from positions higher and more forward in the mouth. Hence, while a short-voweled word like "hand" is identical in spelling, pronunciation, and meaning in Old English and Modern English, other common words such as "stan" ("stone"), "gat" ("goat"), or "hu" ("how") exhibit identical meaning then and now, but clearly indicate with their spelling a change in pronunciation over time. Less importantly, some consonants have also changed, or characters have been added to the Old English alphabet to represent sounds in a new way. Once these differences are accounted for, it is obvious that many Old English words spoken aloud would have sounded less foreign to a modern listener than they initially seem on the page.

That said, however, it is equally obvious that Old English and Modern English are very different. With the exception of a relatively few words borrowed from Celtic (mostly place names) and Latin (the earliest to describe church practices), Old English is a wholly Germanic language. The Norman Conquest brought about the replacement of approximately eighty-five percent of the Old English vocabulary with words derived from French or Latin, and instituted the English habit of borrowing when words were needed, rather than following the Germanic/Old English method of forming new words by compounding old ones. Nonetheless, Old English words remaining in Modern English occur with high frequency—Modern English conjunctions, prepositions, pronouns, and the auxiliary verbs (forms of "to be" and "to have," "will," "shall," etc.) are all nearly "pure" Old English—and/or are basic to the Modern English vocabulary. Old English resembles modern German (and differs from Modern English) in two other important respects; that is, in its reliance on compounds, and on prefixes and suffixes added to the stem, to create new words, rather than on borrowing either words or elements from other languages.

Ultimately it is in their grammars that Old English and Modern English most differ. The evolution of Modern English from Old English has seen the emergence of Modern English as an analytic language— that is, one dependant largely upon word order, and the extensive use of prepositions and auxiliary verbs, to make meaning. Unlike Modern English in this regard (but similar to other Germanic and Indo-European languages), Old English is a synthetic language—that is, the function (and hence the meaning) of words in an Old English sentence is indicated primarily by inflection. While Modern English retains a few select inflections that do important duty ("he," "his," "him," for example), Old English is a fully inflected language and distinguishes four major cases for the noun and adjective in both the plural and the singular; the adjective has separate forms for the three genders; and the verb clearly identifies person, number, tense, and mood. A brief examination of the major parts of speech is necessary by way of illustration.

Nouns are inflected to distinguish number (singular and plural), case, and, to some degree, gender. The four major cases are nominative, genitive, accusative and dative. Old English shows an occasional use of the instrumental, but (unlike many other Indo-European languages) there is no ablative or locative (these having been subsumed into the dative), and the vocative is identical with the nominative. Also noteworthy about Old English nouns is that they exhibit grammatical, not "natural," gender. That is, in Old English and most other Indo-European languages, the gender of a noun for grammatical purposes is established by custom, independent of sex. Hence, in Old English "wif"("wife" or "woman"), "mægden" ("maiden"), and "cild" ("child") are all neuter, but Old English "wifmann" ("woman") is masculine. This "lack of logic" is repaired in Modern English, where things male, female, or sexless are generally sorted accordingly.

Old English follows the general practice of Germanic languages by distinguishing between two declensions of the adjective. The so-called weak form is used when the adjective describes a noun accompanied by a definite article, or a demonstrative or possessive pronoun. "Se goda mann" ("the good man") is an example. The "strong" declension is used when the noun and adjective stand alone; hence, "god mann" ("good man"). The Old English adjective is fully declinable, like the noun, in case, number, and gender.

There are two sorts of pronouns in Old English, the demonstrative and the personal. The demonstrative serves as a relative, as replacement for the personal pronoun, and most importantly as the definite article. As in modern German, it is fully inflected. The personal pronoun distinguishes between all genders, persons, and cases, between singular and plural, and exhibits as well a dual number, indicating two persons or things, a form present in most Indo-European languages at an early stage, but now lost in Modern English.

In Old English, the verb recognizes three moods (indicative, subjunctive, and imperative), two numbers (singular and plural), and three genders; unlike Modern English, there are only two tenses (simple present and simple past), and, with a single exception, no separate form for the passive voice. Old English is typical among Germanic languages in that its verbs

divide into two groups, according to how they form their tenses. So-called strong verbs (often termed "irregular" in Modern English) indicate tense changes by altering the root vowel; "weak" verbs show tense change by adding a dental suffix to the stem (i.e., the way "regular" verbs in Modern English add "-ed"). As in Modern English, weak verbs are more common by far in Old English; only about three hundred strong verbs are known, many of which show tendencies to adopt the weak forms now current.

Literary writing in Old English survives in many examples, both prose and poetry. Although work of stylistic and aesthetic significance was produced in prose by ÆLFRIC, King Alfred, and others, in general the reputation of Old English literature rests upon the power of the poetry. All but a few poems are found in four codices: Vercelli, Exeter, Junius 11, and Cotton Vitellius A.xv. Since at least the late Middle Ages, the *Vercelli Book* has resided in the chapter library of the cathedral of Vercelli, not far from Milan. Along with five minor pieces scattered among homilies, the *Vercelli Book* contains *The Dream of the Rood* (wr. ca. 1000), the finest lyric expression of Christ's dual presence for the Anglo-Saxons, as simultaneously warrior and martyr. By far the largest collection of poetry in Old English is the so-called *Exeter Book*, copied ca. 940, the gift of Leofric, Bishop of Cornwall and Devon, to the cathedral at Exeter. The *Exeter Book* holds many of the best-known shorter poetry, including *Widsith, The Phoenix, The Wanderer, The Seafarer, The Wife's Lament, The Husband's Message, Wulf and Eadwacer, The Ruin,* the much longer three-part *Christ* and the two-part *Guthlac* (A and B), as well as collections of riddles (once attributed to CYNEWULF) and gnomic wisdom, known variously as "Maxims I" or the "Exeter Gnomes." The manuscript cited as Junius 11 (sometimes called the "Cædmon Manuscript," since the work was once believed to be his) bears the name of its first known owner, the antiquary Franciscus Junius, who left his collection of early codices to the Bodleian Library at Oxford University, where the book remains today. First printed in 1655, Junius 11 contains four lengthy poems, all retelling (much embroidered and emended to suit Anglo-Saxon tastes) of Old Testament narratives: *Genesis, Exodus, Daniel,* and *Christ and Satan.* MS Cotton Vitellius A.xv, the BEOWULF manuscript, is in the British Library collection. Once owned by the great collector Sir Robert Cotton, who cataloged his manuscripts by storing them under the marble busts of Roman emperors (hence Vitellius) that ringed his library, contains *Judith* (wr. ca. 930), a poetic version of the Apocryphal Book of Judith, along with *Beowulf,* the greatest known poem in any early Germanic language. Also noteworthy are two other manuscripts, Cotton Tiberius B.i, for its group of wisdom poetry ("Maxims II") and MS Rawlinson B.203, now in the Bodleian, which has the only copy of *The Battle of Maldon* (wr. ca. 1000).

BIBLIOGRAPHY: Brook, G. L., *An Introduction to Old English* (1955); Campbell, A., *Old English Grammar* (1959); Mitchell, B., *On Old English* (1988); Mitchell, B., and F. Robinson, *A Guide to Old English* (6th ed., 2001); Quirk, R., and C. L. Wrenn, *An Old English Grammar* (1955)

R. F. YEAGER

OLDHAM, John
b. 9 August 1653, Shipton Moyne, Gloucestershire;
d. 7 December 1683, Holme Pierrepont, Nottingham

Termed by his contemporaries the "English Juvenal," O. was best known in his lifetime for a collection of poems published as *Satyrs upon the Jesuits* (1681); today, he is remembered as the subject of John DRYDEN's "Upon the Death of Mr. Oldham" (1684), one of the finest elegies in the English language. Born into a clerical family of limited means, O. was educated at home and at Oxford; his early interest in classical forms of poetry emerges in his pindaric ode "To the Memory of Mr. Charles Morwent" (1684), an elegy to an Oxford classmate. This poem, although an apprentice work, shows both depth of feeling and poetic ability. Upon leaving Oxford, O. became an usher at Whitgift School in Croydon, where he attracted the interest of the Earl of ROCHESTER and his circle by circulating in manuscript poems like his "Satyr Against Vertue" (1681), a diatribe against Restoration notions of proper behavior that featured Rochester himself as its speaker. Other works in the same vein include his "Dithyrambique on Drinking" (1681) as well as "Upon the Author of a Play called *Sodom*" and "Sardanapalus," both uncollected until 1987; these poems' crude language and subject matter gained O. a reputation for indecency.

The so-called Popish Plot provided O. with the impetus for his first published collection of poems, *Satyrs upon the Jesuits*. The *Satyrs* consist of four poems: "Garnet's Ghost," in which the writer assumes the persona of the ghost of a Jesuit conspirator who urges his living fellows to commit further atrocities; "Satyr II," in which the speaker of the poem directly attacks the Jesuits, calling for them to be hunted down like rodents; "Loyola's Will," a rant on papal infallibility; and "Ignatius' Image," in which alleged Catholic deceptions are recounted by a wooden statue of Loyola. In all but the second poem, O.'s SATIRE depends on his use of self-condemning narrators, who reduce both themselves and Catholicism to absurdity. These poems gained O. the reputation for rugged verse and harsh satire alluded to in Dryden's elegy; to modern readers, they may appear cruel and forced. Taken in the context of their times,

however, they offer a telling glimpse at the Restoration fear of Catholicism and at the national furor over the plot.

Among O.'s finest works are his "Imitations" of Juvenal, Horace, and Nicolas Boileau. O.'s goal as "imitator" was to bring the work of the other writer into a contemporary English context. His imitation of Horace's "Art of Poetry" (1681) was admired by Alexander POPE; his imitation of Horace's Book I, Satire IX (1681) is a delightful account of the experience of being unable to remove oneself from a bore; Juvenal's Third Satire (1683) becomes a vivid description of the living conditions of Restoration London; and Boileau's Eighth Satire (1683) reveals a writer who has matured in breadth and tone from his earlier harshness. Another fine work from this period, "A Satyr Address'd to a Friend, that is about to leave the University" (1683) details the pitfalls awaiting a young man who is thrust out into the world and forced to choose between penury and a life of dependency on others; this poem offers a clear picture of the life of a Restoration scholar like the poet himself.

When O. died of the smallpox, he was only thirty years old, yet his brief career had produced four volumes of poetry: *Satyrs, Some New Pieces* (1681), *Poems, and Translations* (1683), and *Remains* (1684). As Dryden's elegy attests, O.'s death was mourned by the leading poets of the day. While O.'s poetry pioneered the art of imitation followed by great writers such as Pope and Samuel JOHNSON, his critical reputation has suffered, partly because of the indelicacies of his early satires (which were probably never intended for print) and partly because his most famous work, *Satyrs upon the Jesuits*, is a topical piece that fails to transcend the occasion, lacking the timelessness and majesty of other political poems such as Dryden's "Absalom and Achitophel." Yet O.'s later imitations and satires deserve renewed attention, for the finest of these works evoke life in Restoration London with a striking immediacy and a moving poetic voice.

BIBLIOGRAPHY: Brooks, H. F., ed., *The Poetry of J. O.* (1987); Hammond, P., *J. O. and the Renewal of Classical Culture* (1983); Ziggerell, J., *J. O.* (1983)

JIM OWEN

OLIPHANT, [Mrs.] Margaret
b. Margaret Wilson, 4 April 1828, Wallyford, Scotland; d. 25 June 1897, Windsor

The most prolific of all Victorian novelists, O. injured her reputation by writing an immense number of books and articles, including BIOGRAPHY and criticism. She was a self-supporting author throughout her adult life and reviewed many famous Victorian novels in her chief outlet, *Blackwood's Magazine*. Widowed young, she supported a large and disappointing extended family and outlived all her children.

She was an outsider in two ways, as a Scot living mainly in England and as a woman who did not totally accept Victorian pieties. Her use of irony is very similar to Jane AUSTEN's; characters reveal their flaws unconsciously, in everyday conversation. But as a mother and working woman she had a wider experience of life and was not preoccupied with romantic love. Her "clerical" novels are often compared to Anthony TROLLOPE's, but her style is more elegant and her interest in religion goes much deeper.

She is best known for her "supernatural" stories and for her multivolume *Chronicles of Carlingford* (1863–76). These are set in a provincial town and consider the special problems of the clergy, including Dissenters. The best are *The Doctor's Family* (1863) and *Miss Marjoribanks* (3 vols., 1866), each of which shows a strong woman surrounded by unsatisfactory males. She was cynical about men's ability to cope with problems and her publisher complained of her "hardness of tone." All her best work is antiromantic, depicting selfish and limited people with an unblinking eye and querying clichés about family happiness.

Her experience of bereavement had made her intensely interested in the question of life after death. *A Beleaguered City* (1880) was followed by several *Stories of the Seen and the Unseen*, of which "The Open Door" (1882), "Old Lady Mary" (1884), "The Land of Darkness" (1887), and "The Library Window" (1896) are outstanding. While she took the Christian side in the Victorian debate, these works are not conventionally religious. They are tentative, exploring the possibility that the dead live on in another sphere but aware that the gulf between them and us is unbridgeable.

She also wrote some magnificent late novels, currently out of print. *The Ladies Lindores* (3 vols., 1883) studies cruelty within marriage; there is a shocking scene where a wife rejoices when her husband dies and leaves her free. *A Country Gentleman* (3 vols., 1886) contains a remarkable portrait of an intolerant man who cannot endure the frustrations of living with others. The intrepid Scottish heroine of *Kirsteen* (3 vols., 1890)—probably her masterpiece—runs away from home and makes her family's fortune; most unusually, she remains a spinster. O. had been strongly influenced by the self-sufficient, and often celibate, heroines of Sir Walter SCOTT.

She was brutally disappointed in her husband, brothers, and sons, all of whom relied on her to support them. This is not directly discussed in her fiction, but is a shaping force nonetheless. *The Curate in Charge* (2 vols., 1876) and "Mr. Sandford" (1887) are both about breadwinners, and many other novels feature characters—sometimes priests but, more often, women—who accept a heavy burden of respon-

sibility. Her tone is quite different from other Victorian novelists' in that she does not seem to believe in Providence; the selfless characters are not rewarded and the selfish frequently not punished. As she grew older, she became steadily more sympathetic to FEMINISM. "Queen Eleanor and Fair Rosamond" (1886) is particularly dismissive of men.

Her work was almost forgotten after her death because so many novels were written in haste, with unconvincing plots, one-dimensional characters, and padding. Although she had been compared with her contemporary, George ELIOT, she herself believed that she had sacrificed any hopes of being a great writer for the sake of her family and that most of her books did not deserve to survive. Neither Victorians nor moderns really knew what to make of her. She offended the latter by her attack on Thomas HARDY's *Jude the Obscure* ("The Anti-Marriage League," *Blackwood's*, January 1896), written because the "sex-question" novels of the nineties repelled her; she believed that the world "is round and contains everything, not 'the relations between the sexes' alone." But her contemporaries were disturbed, too, by her often bleak and subversive tone. For many years, her *Autobiography* (1899), which tells the tragic story of her early life with several gaps, was the only book in circulation, but in the later 20th c. many novels were reprinted, critical and biographical studies appeared, and more people began to value her work.

BIBLIOGRAPHY: Gifford, D., and D. McMillan, eds., *A History of Scottish Women's Writing* (1997); Jay, E., ed., *The Autobiography of M. O.* (1990); Trela, D. J., ed., *M. O.* (1995); Williams, M., *M. O.* (1986)

MERRYN WILLIAMS

OLIVER, Douglas

b. 14 September 1937, Southampton; d. 21 April 2000, Paris, France

Known primarily as a poet, O. worked as a journalist before becoming a student and then university lecturer in Britain and Paris before moving to the U.S. Associated with the experimental "Cambridge poets" like J. H. PRYNNE, O. incorporated life experiences into many of his poems, not as a "confessional" device, but as means of grounding his poems in a form of self-revelation and personal moral enquiry so that they might resist didacticism or homily. His early collection *Oppo Hectic* (1969) was followed by *In the Cave of Suicession* (1974). His novella *The Harmless Building* (1973; repub. as *Three Variations on the Theme of Harm*, 1990) was indebted to the French nouveau roman. *The Diagram Poems* (1979) imaginatively combined transcriptions of performance techniques to an account of left-wing rebels in Uruguay, itself based on O.'s journalism. His major poem *The*

Infant and the Pearl (1985) adapted the medieval dream vision and stanzaic form of the *Pearl* poet into a commentary on Thatcherism and is arguably his most inspired work. His collected poems *Kind* (1987) was followed by *Penniless Politics* (1991) and *A Salvo for Africa* (1999), which also examined questions of politics and the public good reflected though personal anecdote. O. wrote an idiosyncratic but civil poetry that attempts to unravel conflicting moral choices.

OPIE, [Mrs.] Amelia

b. 12 November 1769, Norwich; d. 2 December 1853, Norwich

Novelist and poet, O. was the daughter of a radical physician, James Alderson, and married the painter John Opie in 1798. Among their friends were William GODWIN, Mary WOLLSTONECRAFT, actors John and Charles Kemble and their sister Sarah Siddons, Sydney SMITH, Richard Brinsley SHERIDAN, and Madame de Staël. O.'s first novel, *Father and Daughter* (1801), was followed in the next year by a book of verse. Her novel *Adeline Mowbray* (3 vols., 1805) was based on the life of Wollstonecraft. Other fictions were *Simple Tales* (4 vols., 1806), *Temper* (3 vols., 1812), *Tales of Real Life* (3 vols., 1813), *Valentine's Eve* (3 vols., 1816), *Tales of the Heart* (4 vols., 1820), and *Madeline* (2 vols., 1822). Her subjects were domestic, her tone moral and sentimental, and she was satirized in Thomas Love PEACOCK's *Headlong Hall* as "Miss Poppyseed," a loose pun on her name that suggested that her works, like opium, sent readers to sleep. In 1809, she wrote a *Memoir* of her late husband; in 1825, she became a Quaker and gave up writing fiction, becoming active in the Bible Society and the antislavery movement. Her last book of poems, *Lays for the Dead,* appeared in 1834.

OPIE, Iona

b. 13 October 1923, Colchester

OPIE, Peter

b. 25 November 1918, Cairo, Egypt; d. 5 February 1982, West Liss, Hampshire

I. and P. O. spent their joint career researching and collecting the customs, language, and FOLKLORE related to children. Beginning with a small anthology of playground rhymes published modestly during a paper shortage, the Opies went on to establish a standard for a field of folklore that had not previously been explored. Their works from *I Saw Esau* (1947) onward covered rhymes, charms, games, habits, interests, and superstitions of childhood, most of which had flourished through oral transmission only, never appearing before in print. The Opies were the first to

catalogue and thus preserve these first collective literary experiences for their own generation and the generations to follow.

Before marrying Iona Margaret Balfour Archibald in 1943, P. O. published the autobiographical *I Want to Be a Success* (1939). Two more solo works followed, *Having Held the Nettle* (1945) and *The Case of Being a Young Man* (1946). After the birth of their first child, P. O.'s interest in writing prose based on personal experience took the next logical step, addressing the world of children from the adult perspective. Both children of medical professionals, I. and P. O. developed a prescriptive approach to their work involving field research, data collection and analysis, and an organized presentation of their findings in the form of anthologies and analytical works. In the introduction to *The People in the Playground* (1993), a volume published by I. after P.'s death including excerpts from her field notes, I. explains their purpose: "I wanted to recognize that boredom is the bane of humankind, and to exemplify the means children have of keeping it at bay."

After *I Saw Esau*, their first collection of playground and school rhymes, the Opies edited *The Oxford Dictionary of Nursery Rhymes* (1951), annotating the work with the histories of these childhood favorites. *The Oxford Nursery Rhyme Book* followed in 1955, directed more to a juvenile audience. *The Lore and Language of Schoolchildren* (1959) was a blend of literature and cultural anthropology, examining children's behavior in an entirely new, more respectful and serious light. It had enormous impact, and also appeared as a series of broadcasts on the BBC. *The Puffin Book of Nursery Rhymes* (1963) and *Children's Games in Street and Playground* (1969) continued their expanding collection of folklore.

The Oxford Book of Children's Verse (1973) was a new editorial experience for the Opies—unlike the verses of the previous anthologies, all repeated and popularized by children themselves, these rhymes are written by adults for children or on the subject of children. Ranging from Geoffrey CHAUCER and anonymous medieval ballads to 20th-c. classics by Walter DE LA MARE and T. S. ELIOT, the Opies include poems of moral virtue, of instructional merit, and of giddy nonsense. In *The Classic Fairy Tales* (1974), the Opies illuminate the histories of familiar stories, recording their revisions and variants. After P.'s death in 1982, *The Singing Game* (1985) and *Tail Feathers from Mother Goose* (1988) were finished by I., becoming their last collaborative works. In 1992, I. published *A Dictionary of Superstitions* in collaboration with Moira Tatem.

The noted children's illustrator Maurice Sendak seized the opportunity in 1992 to illustrate a new edition of the Opies' first offering, *I Saw Esau*, making the work available to a much wider audience than it had previously seen. *The People of the Playground* shared I.'s field notes, giving insight into the couple's methodology and motivation. The last scene in the published notes describes a class of incoming first year students touring the playground, learning the location of the bathrooms, the rules of behavior. The Opies had a fascination for the transmission of information, the passing of knowledge from one generation to the next, and their preservation of children's lore has assured its permanence in a transitory world.

BIBLIOGRAPHY: Avery, G., and J. Briggs, eds., *Children and Their Books: A Celebration of the Work of I. and P. O.* (1989); Hobb, S., and D. Cornwell, "The Lore and Language of Schoolchildren," *Folklore* 102 (1992): 175–82; Myer, M. G., "The Children's Child," *Folk R* (July 1974): 7–21

NICOLE SARROCCO

ORCZY, Baroness [Emmuska]

b. Emma Magdelena Rosalia Josefa Barbara Orczy, 23 September 1865, Tarna-Eörs, Hungary; d. 12 November 1947, Monte Carlo

Writing in English, a language she learned at age fifteen, O. was a prolific author of historical and detective fiction. *The Scarlet Pimpernel* (1905) introduced her great creation, Sir Percy Blakeney—an effete English gentleman who secretly rescues aristocrats from the guillotine during the Reign of Terror in Paris. O. claimed to see Sir Percy in visions, first at London's Temple underground station and later in her study, where he dictated his adventures. After failing initially to find a publisher, O. and her husband Montagu Barstow adapted *Pimpernel* for the stage in 1903. The play ran for more than two thousand performances, guaranteeing the success of the novel—it has never gone out of print—and its several sequels, including *The Elusive Pimpernel* (1908), *Pimpernel and Rosemary* (1924), *The Way of the Scarlet Pimpernel* (1933). Eschewing the lugubrious model of romancers like OUIDA, O. produced a witty, swashbuckling love story with carefully researched period detail; one novelist who adopted O.'s approach was her friend Rafael Sabatini, creator of Scaramouche and Captain Blood. *The Scarlet Pimpernel* has been frequently filmed, most famously in 1935 with Leslie Howard as Sir Percy.

O.'s influence on detective fiction is considerable. *Royal Magazine* began publishing her "Old Man in the Corner" stories in 1901; the protagonist, designed to be the antithesis of Sherlock Holmes, is arguably the earliest "armchair detective." Most of the thirty-eight Old Man tales are collected in *The Case of Miss Elliott* (1905), *The Old Man in the Corner* (1909), and *Unravelled Knots* (1925). Remarkable attributes of the Old Man are his cynical admiration for successful murderers (the crimes he reviews are officially unsolved) and his anxiety to impress the narrator, a "lady journalist." O. is also credited with the first work of detective fiction featuring a woman detective in *Lady Molly of Scotland Yard* (1920). O.'s forty-five novels include *A Son of the People* (1906), based on the destruction of her father's estates by peasants fearful of a new steam mill, *A True Woman* (1911; repub. as *The Heart of a Woman*, 1911), and *Nicolette* (1922); she also wrote an autobiography, *Links in the Chain of Life* (1947).

BIBLIOGRAPHY: Staples, K., "B. E. O.," in Benstock, B., ed., *British Mystery Writers, 1860–1919*, DLB 70 (1988): 229–34

LISA BERGLUND

ORTON, Joe [John Kingsley]

b. 1 January 1933, Leicester; d. 9 August 1967, London

In reaction against an emotionally and culturally deprived provincial background, O. transformed himself by unremitting effort from a school failure who, according to a teacher, could "hardly string a sentence together" into a well-read literary artist whose witty farces celebrated anarchy. Interviewed on radio in 1964, he said, "the theatre is the Temple of Dionysus, and not Apollo." In his diary he wrote, "my writing is a deliberate satire on bad theatre."

O.'s distinctive contribution is a manipulation of the difference between the spoken and written forms of British English. Unformalized and fluid, these distinctions are operated intuitively by native speakers. O.'s originality was to make several characters speak the written language, so that his dialogue mocks pretentiousness and false refinement to hilarious effect. His satirical targets speak a dialect best described as officialese. Time is eroding this joke, so surprising in the early 1960s, as in the interim the spoken word has been increasingly modified by the jargon of bureaucracy and "management-speak." Manners have coarsened since O.'s day and fewer people aspire to gentility. However, enough of O.'s dialogue, influenced by Oscar WILDE, is anticlimactic and epigrammatic enough still to be funny.

Sir Terence RATTIGAN said, "What Orton had to say about England and society had never been said before." O., a promiscuous homosexual who regularly picked up strangers, was hostile to all authority and in fear of the police. Homosexual acts between consenting adults were not legalized in Britain until the year of his death. At the time, the British police were respected; morality was traditional and family-based. O.'s disaffection and love of the macabre chimed with then inchoate attitudes. The societal changes associated with the 1960s did not have their full diffused effect until the 1980s.

Failing as a writer, the young O. wrote spoof letters to newspapers, using farcical identities. Later, he used his dysfunctional family as material. He and Kenneth Halliwell, his early mentor, whom he met when they were students at the Royal Academy of Dramatic Art, both served prison sentences in 1962 for stealing and defacing library books with startling collages and fake blurbs on blank space on the jackets. They also stole 1,635 plates from art books. Unemployed and poverty-stricken on release, they had to pay compensation. O. declared war on society, then proceeded to charm it with his wit. His vision is amoral, bleak, and nihilistic. His plays could only be performed at the time with the more outrageous improprieties excised by official censorship. The Lord Chamberlain's duty to censor public performances was abolished in 1968 by the Theatres Act.

O.'s first play to be produced, *Entertaining Mr. Sloane* (1964), is about a brother and sister who blackmail their father's murderer into providing them both with sexual services. O. claimed, plausibly, that the play influenced Harold PINTER's *The Homecoming*. Written in 1964, *The Good and Faithful Servant* (perf. 1967; pub. 1976) is a bitter comment on a wasted life as a cog in the industrial machine and on its paltry rewards. In *Loot* (perf. 1965; pub. 1967), a coffin is emptied by the son of the corpse to hide stolen money. After commercial failure and numerous rewrites, *Loot* was voted by the London critics best play of its year. It is memorable for its cynicism: Truscott is a corrupt policeman, created at a time the police enjoyed public confidence; Fay the nurse is no ministering angel but an avaricious woman prepared to commit murder. There is grisly business with a corpse, a coffin, a glass eye, and false teeth. *Funeral Games*, written in 1966, was televised in 1968. It deals with the murder of two women, religious cults, drug addiction, and madness, yet the dialogue sparkles. *The Ruffian on the Stair* (1967), broadcast by the BBC in 1964 and revised for the stage in 1966, takes its title from a poem by W. E. HENLEY: the "ruffian" is death, a theme that preoccupied O.

Televised in 1966, *The Erpingham Camp* (1967) is a dystopic view of Britain as a holiday camp succumbing to destructive forces, a reworking of *The Bacchae* by Euripides, an author who fascinated O. Critical opinion on O.'s posthumous play *What the Butler Saw* (1969) is divided. Many consider it O.'s masterpiece. In addition to O.'s familiar themes of blackmail and abuse of authority, we have an early, brilliant, attack on psychobabble and a plot in which one psychiatrist imposes his own view of reality on another. O. recorded in his diary Halliwell's reaction. Halliwell had pointed out a "Golden Bough subtext . . . castration of Sir Winston CHURCHILL (the father-figure) and the descent of the god at the end—Sergeant Match, drugged and dressed in a woman's

gown . . . something suggestive of leopardskin—this would make it funny when Nick wears it and get the right 'image' for the Euripidean ending when Match wears it." But the play will not bear too heavy a weight of interpretation. Its overelaborate plot makes it ultimately confusing and it has rarely succeeded in the theater.

O.'s very success provoked Halliwell to batter O. to death in a jealous rage before killing himself. John Lahr's biography of O. was filmed in 1987 starring Gary Oldman and Alfred Molina.

BIBLIOGRAPHY: Bigsby, C. W. E., *J. O.* (1982); Charney, M., *J. O.* (1984); Lahr, J., *Prick Up Your Ears: The Biography of J. O.* (1978); Lahr, J., ed., *The O. Diaries* (1986)

VALERIE GROSVENOR MYER

ORWELL, George

(pseud. of Eric Arthur Blair) b. 25 June 1903, Motihari, Bengal; d. 21 January 1950, London

O. is best remembered for his two novels *Animal Farm* (1945) and *Nineteen Eighty-Four* (1949) and for his essays, regarded as 20th-c. masterpieces of the form. However, he also wrote a substantial body of work in the 1930s. Eric Blair adopted the pseudonym George Orwell for his first published work, *Down and Out in Paris and London* (1933). This was a vivid account of life for the poor in the two cities, based on O.'s experiences of living frugally in 1927–29. He had been an assistant superintendent in the Indian Imperial Police, but had resigned, disgusted with imperialism, and determined to become a writer. The book was an immediate success, being recommended by the Book Society, and praised by reviewers.

Burmese Days (1934), a novel, is based in his experiences as a colonial police officer. It tells the story of John Flory, who finds himself isolated in his post in Burma. He feels himself not "at home in the world of the sahibs," but cannot enter into the culture of the Burmese who despise him. A new addition to the English community in the form of a young woman, Elizabeth Lackersteen, seems to promise an end to Flory's despair, but she is horrified by his curiosity about Burmese culture and his disgust at his colleagues' brutal racist superiority. Flory eventually commits suicide. *Burmese Days* is often regarded as the nearest thing to a conventional novel by O., and more successful than most of his fictional writing of the 1930s. It was certainly an accomplished performance for a first novel, giving a strong sense of the underlying hatred of colonial relationships.

A Clergyman's Daughter (1935) is usually seen as less successful. O. said he was ashamed of the book and had written it because he was "half starved" and needed the money. O. criticized what most readers have also found, that the book is "disconnected as a whole." The novel switches between different styles and genres. The third chapter uses Joycean dialogue, derived from *Ulysses,* while other parts handle the first-person narration awkwardly, slipping into documentary observation uncharacteristic of the novel's main character. She is Dorothy Hare, the exploited vicar's daughter, who spends her entire life working for other people's good. Her mind gives way, and losing her memory, she goes missing. Most of the novel is an account of her wandering through Kent and in London, a dislocated person. If the novel as a whole does not always cohere, it contains much of the kind of striking and emblematic depiction of ordinary life for which O. is noted.

Keep the Aspidistra Flying (1936) was equally regretted by O. It does not attempt the modernist experimentation of *A Clergyman's Daughter,* and is in this sense more coherent. But critics have often been bothered by the relationship between the third-person narrator and the protagonist, Gordon Comstock, and by the ending. Gordon rebels against "the money-god" and gives up a "good job" in order to succeed as a writer. Writing—of poetry in particular—is the one role that seems to offer him an escape from the whole "money" system. Giving up his job at the New Albion advertising agency, he works in a second-hand bookshop—allowing the novel to comment on contemporary writing and reading. He then descends further into poverty, from which he is only rescued when his girlfriend Rosemary becomes pregnant, and the two settle down apparently to enjoy domestic bliss, "money-god" notwithstanding. The ending may be a sign of Gordon's defeat, or of his return to the real world. This ambivalence in the novel may well reflect uncertainties in O.'s mind about the relationship between being a writer and being in contact with ordinary "reality."

The Road to Wigan Pier (1937) was a documentary about unemployment in the depressed north of England, commissioned by the publisher Victor Gollancz and published as a Left Book Club edition. It is regarded by some as a classic piece of documentary, by others as deeply flawed by "Orwellian" eccentricities. Gollancz was unhappy about some of its comments about working-class people, and he published it with a critical introduction, distinguishing between its valuable reporting of the real facts and what he argued were distortions. Nevertheless, over 46,000 copies were sold in the 1930s alone.

O.'s next book was also a factual book—an account of his experience of the political situation in Spain, where he had fought for the Republicans with an anarchist group from December 1936 to July 1937. O. was wounded by a rifle bullet that passed through his throat, and then while recovering in Barcelona witnessed the suppression of his anarchist group by their rivals in the Communist Party militias. He returned home to write *Homage to Catalonia* (1938), an account of Spain markedly different from the mainstream leftist line in Britain, which tended to support the Communist faction on the Republican side.

Coming Up for Air (1939) saw a return to the novel form. Though some have seen the first-person narration as marred by slippage into an Orwellian essayistic voice, most regard the novel as highly successful. The protagonist is an everyman figure, the salesman George Bowling, who gives an acute but commonsensical view of the horrors of modern life, and their imminent culmination in war and totalitarianism. George tries to revisit the village where he grew up, as a way of "coming up for air," only to find that, inevitably, modernity has arrived there too. There is no escape. The novel shows O.'s growing command of the novel form and prefigures the treatment of totalitarianism in his two most famous works.

Animal Farm used an allegorical, fabular form that O. had never before attempted. The story uses the farm animals to show how socialism has been corrupted in the Soviet Union, and to show more widely how ruling elites establish themselves. The animals expel the farmer who exploits them and establish a farm run on principles of equality and liberty. The pigs, however, subvert, these principles—sending the exhausted horse Boxer (representing the people) to the knacker's yard. By the end of the narrative, it is impossible to distinguish the pigs from the humans. *Nineteen Eighty-Four* continues to explore how those with power maintain it, again with particular, but not unique, reference to the Soviet Union. The protagonist, Winston Smith, together with Julia, tries to rebel against the state, reading Goldstein's critique of "oligarchical collectivism," but he is defeated—like most Orwellian characters. Even his rebellion, it turns out, has been foreseen and directed from the beginning. There is no escape from the power of Big Brother, and Winston and Julia are broken in Room 101—where everyone meets his or her own worst fear. Eventually, once the state's language "Newspeak" is established, even thoughts of rebellion will be impossible, since there will be no words for it, no words that carry any meaning other than that allowed by the state.

Animal Farm and *Nineteen Eighty-Four* are O.'s major achievements, but his essays are also of note. Among the most famous are "A Hanging" (1931), "Shooting an Elephant" (1936), and "How the Poor Die" (1946). "Good prose is like a window pane," O. wrote. The essays are characterized, like the best of O.'s work, by their commitment to a writing that is exact, resonant, and specific.

BIBLIOGRAPHY: Crick, B., *G. O.* (1980); Davison, P., *G. O.* (1996); Hammond, J. R., *A G. O. Companion* (1982); Meyers, V., *G. O.* (1991); Norris, C., ed., *In-*

side the Myth: O.: Views from the Left (1984); Shelden, M., *O.* (1991); Williams, R., *O.* (1971); Woodcock, G., *The Crystal Spirit: A Study of G. O.* (1967); Zwerdling, A., *O. and the Left* (1974)

CHRIS HOPKINS

OSBORNE, John [James]

b. 12 December 1929, London; d. 24 December 1994, Shropshire

O.'s play *Look Back in Anger* (perf. 1956; pub. 1957) caused a sensation and provided the impetus for a remarkable period of creativity and social relevance from which British drama has yet fully to recover. Caustic, impassioned, and apparently on the side of the have-nots, the play exposed the theater-going public, then habituated to a genteel mode of drama that typically took place in front of French windows, to a bracing new sensibility, one that was to dominate the medium for the next decade and beyond. O. gained immediate notoriety, and exerts a lasting influence, as British theater's original "angry young man," but this singular writer is both more and less than the egalitarian rabble-rouser he at first appeared.

Like Harold PINTER after him, O. graduated to playwriting from life as a jobbing actor in provincial repertory theater, an experience that provided him with both a sure feeling for stagecraft and a lingering sense of underappreciation. Among his earlier plays was *Epitaph for George Dillon* (perf. 1957; pub. 1958), written with Anthony Creighton, its eponymous hero an underappreciated repertory actor and aspiring playwright. A fascinating and accomplished work of the period, the play shares many themes with *Look Back in Anger*, but lacks the rancorous élan of its successor.

The 1956 play that made O.'s name centers around the life and loves of Jimmy Porter, a frustrated rebel of the lower middle classes. Jimmy, bemoaning the absence of any "good, brave causes" for which to fight, instead directs his energies into haranguing his socially superior wife Alison and, when she has finally had enough, her equally refined friend Helena, who becomes his lover. This relationship ends when Alison reappears following the miscarriage of her and Jimmy's baby and the pair are left to find consolation in the simple fact of their affection for one another. Such a synopsis gives some indication of the decided political incorrectness that was to characterize much of O.'s work, but fails to do justice to the splendid verve with which Porter tears into the society he despises, or to the intense human drama played out between Jimmy and Alison, whose silence can, in a good production, match the eloquence of his rhetoric. The play was first staged at London's Royal Court, confirming that theater's position as the chief champion of new writing in postwar British theater, and

was met with outrage, derision, and rapture. Soon it had become a cause célèbre, ticket sales boosted by the televising of an extract and Kenneth Tynan's famous declaration that, "I doubt if I could love anyone who did not wish to see *Look Back in Anger*." Before long, it had been filmed with a smouldering Richard Burton in the starring role, paving the way to future film work including the screenplays for *Tom Jones* (1963), for which O. won an Academy Award, and *The Charge of the Light Brigade* (1968), written with Charles WOOD.

After this dazzling beginning, it would be fair to characterize O.'s subsequent playwriting career as an essentially downward spiral. *The Entertainer* followed in 1957, Laurence Olivier astutely taking the role of Archie Rice, the cynical exponent of an English music hall tradition (comparable to vaudeville) whose decline O. saw as emblematic of the slow death of English society in general. Drawing on Bertolt Brecht and sharing notable stylistic traits with the theater Joan Littlewood was then creating in London's East End, the play expanded O.'s theatrical ground but could not match the intensity of its predecessor. The follow-up marked an early nadir: a musical SATIRE of tabloid journalism and contemporary mores, *The World of Paul Slickey* (1959) is an unfunny and essentially crass piece that for the first time—though not the last—prompted serious doubt that O. would prove more than a one-play wonder. The television play *A Subject of Scandal and Concern* (perf. 1960; pub. 1961) did little to allay such doubts but, in its dramatization of the last British prosecution for blasphemy, it did lay the ground for O.'s next major play, *Luther* (1961). Here, O. once more found his feet, convincingly depicting the historical founder of the Protestant church as a proto-Jimmy Porter obsessed both with theology and with his troubled bowels, but the play's failure to convey dramatically the social consequences of Luther's defiance makes it a qualified success.

O. returned to the present with *Inadmissible Evidence* (perf. 1964; pub. 1965), essentially a character study of Bill Maitland, drunkard, adulterer, and semi-crooked lawyer. The evidence O. presents against his central character is damning, as Maitland digs himself deeper and deeper into a hole of his own creation, but underpinning the play is a characteristic compassion for this wretched but misunderstood individual. The following year, O. attracted further controversy with the historical drama *A Patriot for Me* (perf. 1965; pub. 1966), which showed the downfall of an officer of the Austro-Hungarian army as a result of his homosexuality; the Lord Chamberlain, who until 1968 was charged with ensuring the decency of the British stage, demanded sweeping cuts. Today, in terms of what it shows, *A Patriot for Me* may seem rather tame, but its examination of the interrelation of desire, class, and power in imperial capitalism remains acute.

The late 1960s and 1970s saw O.'s influence and critical standing decline. The poor notices received by his adaptation of Lope de Vega's *La Fianza Satisfecha*, *A Bond Honoured* (1966) led O. to declare to his critics, "after ten years it is now war." *Time Present* and *The Hotel in Amsterdam* (both 1968) trained a doleful but unfocused eye on the creative classes of the time, though the former has the distinction of a female role, that of the lead character Pamela, of equal scope to some of the playwright's greatest parts for men. *West of Suez* (1971) continued this line of attack, this time contrasting the jaded and disinherited English, notably the aging writer Wyatt Gilman, with the empowered and violent inhabitants of the ex-colonial island on which they live. As Michael Billington wrote, O.'s sympathies were with those "left stranded by the tide of history," a theme that pointed to the author's own position: O.'s public library protests, based on an individual sensibility rather than Marxist analysis, had come to seem parochial and even reactionary.

Defiant, O. wrote *A Sense of Detachment* (perf. 1972; pub. 1973), recapturing the urgency of earlier work through the complete abandonment of NATURALISM and narrative. Six generic characters—man, woman, old man, etc.—perform set pieces, lambaste the audience and each other, are kept vaguely in order by a beleaguered Chairman while being subjected to various shades of abuse from characters planted in the auditorium. O. once more courted controversy by having the elderly lady declaim a series of synopses from pornographic film, but it is the passion and eloquence of the closing speeches that really dazzle. The 1970s saw two further plays for the stage, *The End of Me Old Cigar* (1975) and *Watch It Come Down* (1976), the former a surreal comedy in which a feminist coup is thwarted by the simplicity of human love, the latter a somewhat melodramatic piece in which a quick succession of deaths in the closing minutes forces a disillusioned upper-middle-class family to cease its trading of insults.

O.'s name was kept in currency through the 1970s and into the 1980s by a series of television dramas— *The Right Prospectus* (1970), *Very like a Whale* (perf. 1970; pub. 1971), *The Gift of Friendship* (1972), *Ms., or, Jill and Jack* (1974), *Almost a Vision* (perf. 1976), *You're Not Watching Me, Mummy* (perf. 1978; pub. 1980), and *God Rot Tunbridge Wells* (1985)—and adaptations of Henrik Ibsen's *Hedda Gabler* (1972), William SHAKESPEARE's *Coriolanus* (1973), Oscar WILDE's *The Picture of Dorian Gray* (1975), and August Strindberg's *The Father* (1989), the latter being particularly acclaimed. However, it was with the publication of his first volume of AUTOBIOGRAPHY, *A Better Class of Person* (1981), that the playwright really

found his voice once more. O. took to the form with commitment and panache, painting a detailed and memorable picture of the now-departed England of his youth and of the various colorful relatives, notably his be-rouged barmaid mother, who populated it. A television adaptation was followed by a second volume, *Almost a Gentleman* (1991), which cemented his critical rehabilitation and provided further evidence of both the singularity of his vision and the style with which he was capable of conveying it.

In 1991, O.'s first major play for fifteen years surprised many by revisiting the characters of *Look Back in Anger* thirty-five years on. Unfortunately, the all-too aptly titled *Déjà vu*, though by its dabblings in self-referential postmodernity its author showed that he had not wholly lost touch with contemporary cultural developments, emphasized O.'s failings: his once revolutionary characters now seeming isolated, reactionary, and long-winded. His death brought an end to a career of mixed success, but O.'s unrivaled influence on 20th-c. British drama, along with the enduring dramatic power of his best work, ensures that his name will be a significant one for some time to come.

BIBLIOGRAPHY: Gilleman, L., *J. O.* (2002); Hayman, R., *J. O.* (1968); Heilpern, J., *Biography of J. O.* (2002); Hinchcliffe, A. P., *J. O.* (1984); Page, M., ed., *File on O.* (1988); Sulaiman, A., *Rethinking: J. O.'s Look Back in Anger* (1998); Taylor, J. R., *Anger and After* (1962; rev. ed., 1969); Trussler, S., *The Plays of J. O.* (1969)

HARRY DERBYSHIRE

OTWAY, Thomas

b. 3 March 1652, Milland, Sussex; d. 14 April 1685, London

The Restoration began when Charles II landed at Dover on May 25, 1660. Its chief claim to literary fame is the drama. From 1660 to 1700, a tough breed of actors turned playwrights dominated the newly opened theaters that had been closed by the Puritans. These "toughs" included John CROWNE, John DRYDEN, Aphra BEHN, Thomas D'URFEY, Thomas SHADWELL, and Edward Ravenscroft, among others. They produced between them some 150 successful plays. Unlike the dramatic wits of the period, notably Sir John VANBRUGH, Sir George ETHEREGE, and William WYCHERLEY, the former group were first and foremost theater writers. They did not try to elevate the drama or reform the age, despite what they said. They just wanted to earn money, though most ended up poor. The greatest of them, O., ignored by audience, friends, and his king, starved to death.

O. wrote eight plays, two of which, the comedy *The Soldier's* [or *Souldiers*] *Fortune* (1680) and the tragedy *Venice Preserved* (1682), as well as part 2 of *The Soldier's Fortune* entitled *The Atheist* (perf. 1683; pub. 1684), are enduring works. These masterpieces are as alive today as when they were written, primarily because of their language, which is the most brutal, theatrical, and filthiest in English drama: "You whores! you drabs! you fulsome stinking whores! Clusters of poxes on you and no hospital pity you!" (*The Atheist*); "What says the Lady! why she says— she says—odd she had a delicate lip, such a lip, so red, so hard, so plump, so blub; I fancy I am eating cherries every time I think on't—and for her neck and breasts and her—odds live" (*The Soldier's Fortune*).

The language and therefore the characters leap off the page, full of life, lust, and avarice—bullies, crooks, cuckolds, sexual perverts, dirty old men, fanatics, malcontented troublemakers, pimps, bawds, and whores. O. laughs loudly at marriage, virginity, lust, and venereal disease, not because they aren't serious, but because they are also ridiculous. In *The Soldier's Fortune,* he presents a violent sexual intrigue between two dangerous, footloose, young ruffians, Captain Beaugard and Captain Courtine, newly returned from the Dutch wars with two lustful young women, Sylvia and Lady Dunce, whom they are trying to seduce. It is a sport both sides enjoy—the women are as sexually aggressive as the men. Beaugard and Courtine, who have no redeeming features except a certain raffish charm and youth, lust after the women, but they also lust after the money the women can bring them.

O. presents these hard-bitten libertines as heroes while his moralists are to be pitied, if not despised. He achieves his effect by a powerful mixture of farce, burlesque, poetic rhetoric, and satiric comedy. It is always tough-minded and vulgar. The true, underlying situation, as with all good comedy, is brutal. Two soldiers with no prospects, no skills except killing, have to find money, preferably easy money, or else they'll literally starve to death. The situation is too stark and ridiculous for tragedy—the only response is laughter. Amid the savage comedy of *The Soldier's Fortune* is the extraordinary character of Sir Jolly Jumble, a pander and panting voyeur. Sir Jolly almost dies in ecstasy as he imagines two young people having sex: "Hush, hush, hush! . . . All's gone with me, Gentlemen, but my good nature; odd I love to know how matters go, though now and then to see a pretty wench and a young fellow towze and rowze and frouze and mouze; odd I love a young fellow dearly, faith, dearly." This impotent old pander will do anything to satisfy his craving: "I'll pimp for thee dear heart; and shan't I hold the door, shan't I peep hah, shan't I, you devil, you little dog, shan't I?"

Besides the incorrigible, unashamed perversions of Sir Jolly, there is one other monstrous character in *The Soldier's Fortune*, that of Sir Davey Dunce, Lady Dunce's cuckold husband. On the page, he seems just another "straight man" to the comic intrigue. But it is a mark of a good playwright that characters open in all their concealed glory once released from the study and can strut their stuff on stage. In a rare revival of *The Soldier's Fortune* at the Royal Court Theatre, London, a great character comic, Arthur Lowe, made Sir Davey, who is described as an old, greasy, untoward, ill-natured, slovenly, tobacco-taking cuckold, into the dominant figure in the play. In essence, he embodies all the bourgeois characteristics Beaugard and Courtine hate: meanness, thrift, hypocrisy, complacency, avarice, and unsleeping paranoia.

The Soldier's Fortune does have a dramatic structure, however ramshackle. Its sequel *The Atheist* has none. The play has an impenetrable plot, a chaotic narrative, and is really a series of picturesque scenes, vaguely strung together by Beaugard and Courtine— now even more bitter, and longing for the uncomplicated days of war. There is no Davey Dunce or Sir Jolly Jumble. But there is Beaugard's blustering, lecherous old father: "You must have your . . . boney buxom brawny bummel whores." And there is Daredevil—the atheist of the title. He is a would-be assassin. When asked what is his religion, he answers: "The common law religion; I believe in the law, trust in the law, enjoy what I have by the law: for if such a religious gentlemen as you are, get fifty pounds into my debt, I may go to church and pray till my heart aches; but the law must make you pay me at last." In another mood, he says, "A wife! that ever any fellow that has two grains of brains in his skull should give himself trouble to complain of a wife, so long as there is arsenic in the world!" The women are sexy but realistic. Portia tells Courtine, "I never will marry, I have been married already; that is sold." The bawdy comedy of both parts of *The Soldier's Fortune* is driven by sex and money. Whereas *Venice Preserved* and *The Orphan* (perf. ca. 1680; pub. 1680)—a sentimental piece of domestic NATURALISM—held the stage longer than the works of any other English playwright except William SHAKESPEARE, *The Soldier's Fortune* was more or less ignored, until the late 20th c. There have still been scandalously few productions, but it is now, at least, recognized, if not appreciated, as the toughest sex comedy in the repertory.

Venice Preserved has always had its admirers. Even Dryden, a contemporary, had a good word for it, when he usually hadn't a good world for anything he hadn't written himself. It is labeled a tragedy as *The Soldier's Fortune* is labeled a comedy. These simplistic terms are meaningless. *Venice Preserved*— an ironic title as O. implies it is not worth preserving—is streaked with the same savage HUMOR as *The Soldier's Fortune*, just as that play has all the hallmarks of a tragedy, particularly in the depiction of the wasted lives of footloose soldiers, without a war to fight, and the persecution of women, who have only their inheritances to protect them from rape. The story of weak men and women, trapped in a corrupt society, the mingling of the sexual and political, the persistent subtext of black humor is pure Jacobean drama. Its atmosphere is graphically set out by Renault: "A tattered fleet, a murmuring unpaid army,/Bankrupt nobility, a harassed commonality/A factious, giddy, and divided Senate/Is all the strength of Venice." The best men are wrong and the worst triumphant. Made bankrupt because he married Belvidera without her father's consent, Jaffir is desperate for money. He agrees to become involved in a conspiracy to overthrow the corrupt Venetian Senate with his friend Pierre. But Jaffir betrays the conspiracy to the Senate who betray him in turn.

What is fascinating about the play is that all the main characters are open to different interpretations. Pierre could be an idealist or a mercenary opportunist. Jaffir is either a heroic figure or a shifty coward. Belvidera could be a gentle, patient wife or a woman with a will of steel. The characters can be read either way. As in life, we have to judge. It is difficult because there is a chasm between what they say and what they do, what they are and what they appear to be. The play is as much about masochism as betrayal. There is the comedy of masochism embodied in Senator Antonio, pretending to be a dog for his mistress: "Do kick, kick on, now I am under the table, kick again—kick harder—harder yet, bough, waugh, waugh, waugh, bough—'odd I'll have a snap at thy shins—bough, waugh, waugh, waugh, bough—'odd she kicks bravely."

Compare this with the wallowing masochism of Jaffir after Pierre has been sentenced to death: "Tread on me, buffet me, heap wrongs on wrongs/On my poor head." Or the sadomasochism of Jaffir with his wife: "Nay the throats of the whole Senate/Shall bleed, my Belvidera . . . /Whilst thou far off in safety/Smiling, shalt see the wonder of our daring,/And when night comes, with praise and love receive me." The closest parallels to O. in modern drama, with its mixture of tortured sex and pitch black comedy, are Frank Wedekind and August Strindberg.

Among O.'s other work only some poems and a few striking love letters have survived. He had an unhappy life that is reflected in the bitter tang of his plays. His dramatic voice is as hard-edged as the life he lived; once heard, never forgotten. His work was theatrical, poetic and acute, dirty and funny; and finally as bleak as his own end.

BIBLIOGRAPHY: Ghosh, J. C., ed., *The Works of T. O.: Plays, Poems, and Love-Letters* (2 vols., 1932); Taylor, A. M., *Next to Shakespeare* (1950); Warner, K., *T. O.* (1982)

PETER BARNES

OUIDA

(pseud. of Marie Louise de la Ramée) b. 1 January 1839, Bury St. Edmunds, Suffolk; d. 25 January 1908, Viareggio, Italy

During the late 19th c., O. was a financially successful and popular writer whose forty-six books, published between 1863 and 1908, included *Strathmore* (3 vols., 1865), *Under Two Flags* (3 vols., 1867), *A Dog of Flanders and Other Stories* (1872; repub. as *A Leaf in the Storm and Other Stories*, 1872), and *Moths* (3 vols., 1880). O. visited Italy in 1871, where she settled in Florence and remained until her death. In spite of great success, O. died in poverty. Her work is now out of print and not widely known.

O.'s popular romances are often exaggerated, rooted in her belief that life itself is not colorless so neither should literature be: "I do not object to REALISM in fiction; what I object to is the limitation of realism in fiction to what is commonplace, tedious, and bald." O.'s books generally involve fantastic, lavishly detailed stories about beautiful members of the aristocracy, and though she talks about the nobility of the peasants, their role is to serve the genetically superior aristocrats. In the novel *Under Two Flags*, the aristocratic protagonist, Bertie Cecil ("Beauty"), is not only unusually attractive but is impossibly honorable. When accused of a crime committed by his brother, Cecil condemns himself to exile as a member of the French Guard in Algeria rather than dishonor his sibling. The novel, while highly entertaining, is also unbelievable and predictable: the necessity of Cecil's exile is weakly supported, and the spunky female follower of the Guard, Cigarette, sacrifices her life to save Cecil after he and other aristocrats have commented at length about her being doomed to a coarse and unattractive old age.

In spite of her love of honor, O. avoids an attempt to preach morals or other philosophical principles, a failing that during her life led to accusations of immorality. Yet the literary sin of writing glamorous romances peopled with colorful characters may have contributed to her past popularity. *Under Two Flags* went through sixty-three English editions, and her books also sold in France, Italy, America, and Germany.

O.'s best writing involves descriptions of animals, and her most honorable characters are those who are alienated from humans but strongly attached to animals. In *Under Two Flags,* when asked whether he has left a lover in England, Bertie Cecil replies, "No—a horse." Cecil's life is later saved by a poodle. Other stories, such as "The Little Earl" (*Bimbi*, 1882), "A Dog of Flanders," and *Puck* (3 vols., 1870), all employ dog characters emotionally to support humans unable to find empathy among their self-involved peers and family members. O. was an active antivivisectionist whose well-known 1893 article "The New Priesthood" gave its name to the newly emerging field of medical science. At present, O. is primarily known for her antivivisection work.

Though a feisty, independent, unmarried woman, O. was opposed to women's suffrage, and stories such as "A Branch of Lilac" (*A Dog of Flanders*), "A Lemon Tree," and "The Silver Christ" (*The Silver Christ and A Lemon Tree*, 1894) portray good men manipulated by women. Her female characters are often self-involved and less honorable than their male counterparts. Though publicly opposed to the work of the New Women writers, O. was admired by feminists like Sarah GRAND. O.'s work may be presently out of fashion among scholars because of her lack of interest in women's issues and her own political inclinations toward protecting the rights of animals, not women.

BIBLIOGRAPHY: Lansbury, C., *The Old Brown Dog: Women, Workers, and Vivisection in Edwardian England* (1985); Magnum, T., *Married, Middlebrow, and Militant: Sarah Grand and the New Woman Novel* (1998); Stirling, M., *The Fine and the Wicked: The Life and Times of O.* (1958)

LYNNE CROCKETT

OVERBURY, [Sir] Thomas

bap. 18 June 1581, Compton Scorpion, Warwickshire; d. 15 September 1613, London

O. is noteworthy on at least two counts: a notorious intrigue, royal scandal, and mystery; the creation of an array of stereotypic personality profiles, known as "characters," in regard to which another mystery (more modest than the first) is attached. As to the matter involving people in high places, O.'s biographer Beatrice White remarks that he "was one of the few unfortunates who attained the melancholy distinction of dying unofficially in the Tower of London." A product of Queen's College, Oxford, and the Middle Temple, O. developed a friendship with Robert Carr, page to the Earl of Dunbar. With an eye to advancement, O. found his own patron, Sir Robert Cecil, became his servant, and made a trip to the Low Countries, later recording his observations. After learning that Carr was currently the favorite of King JAMES I, O. was able to get himself appointed secretary to the very influential Carr, whose titles would before long come to include Viscount Rochester and Earl of Somerset. O. was knighted in 1608 and was made the king's servitor in ordinary. As O. and Carr, each in his own way, prospered from the very favorable conditions at court, an opinion circulated, according to which Carr was governed by O., and the king was governed by Carr.

O., however, made a serious error in judgment regarding his supposedly fast friend Carr, who clearly outranked him and would resent O.'s intrusion in his private life. Carr had become seriously involved with the Countess of Essex, Frances Howard, a development that may well have been taken by O. as a threat to his future prospects. As a result, O. attempted to admit impediments to any union that might follow from Carr's new amour. He advised Carr against pursuing his campaign to take the countess away from her husband. Moreover, he added to his unflattering opinion of the lady the provocative poem entitled *A Wife,* which was circulated among people of importance who might be particularly responsive to sentiments it contained. Expressed in more modern terms, the third stanza—out of forty stanzas in the poem—reads as follows: "Woman is not Lust's bounds, but Woman-kind;/One is Love's number: who from that doth fall,/Hath lost his hold, and no new rest shall find;/Vice hath no mean, but not to be at all;/A Wife is that enough, Lust cannot find;/For Lust is still with want, or too much, pined."

Results were not slow in coming. Carr's displeasure was evoked, and in the ensuing circumstances this would also be the case with the king himself, and the queen. The family of Howard was able to secure O.'s imprisonment, but a way out of incarceration and ignominy was made available to the hapless O. This came in the form of an overseas post, but O. refused the offer, and he was then transferred to the Tower. The countess, who was bent on getting rid of O., apparently managed to have him slowly poisoned. He died in the Tower, where he was buried. Whether the countess and Carr (commonly referred to in this connection as the Earl of Somerset) were actually complicit in O.'s death has never been satisfactorily determined, and the question mark hovering over O.'s last days remains in place.

In regard to the colorfully drawn characters, or "portraits-in-a-nutshell" of social types, for which O. is best known, the mystery concerns nothing more ominous than authorship. Owing to the contingencies of the publication process at that time, a number of the characters attributed to O. were not written by him. Certain contemporaries of O.'s, such as John DONNE, Thomas DEKKER, John WEBSTER, John Cooke, and Sir Henry WOTTON, contributed to the roster of O. Characters still commonly found in textbooks of 17th-c. English literature. One of the most important characters found in such collections is self-defining and was probably written by O. himself. Thus, "What A Character Is" includes this observation: "It is a quick and soft touch of many strings, all shutting up in one musical close; it is wit's descant on any plain song."

The popularity of the character may be attributed to the publication in 1592 of a Latin translation, by Isaac Casaubon, of the "Characters" of Theophrastus of Lesbos—the prototypal work—which was followed in 1593 by an English version of Casaubon's Latin by John Healey. W. J. Paylor, in his introduction to a reprint edition of "The Overburian Characters" and O.'s poem *A Wife,* indicates that Theophrastus "was the avowed inspiration of Joseph Hall, the first writer of a collection of English Characters, 1608"; Theophrastus also, according to Paylor, probably inspired the short "Character Sketches" Ben JONSON used for his play *Every Man Out of His Humour.* Yet it is strange that despite the general tendency of writers on O. to trace the Overburian characters to Theophrastus, two striking but unremarked examples of the genre occur in the Hebrew Bible, in Proverbs, whose ultimate origins may go back many centuries before the time of Theophrastus. The memorable character of "The Virtuous Woman" is given at the end of Proverbs, 31:10–31. "Who can find a virtuous woman? For her price is far above rubies." The character of "The Fool" is given in scattered form, sometimes in contrast with his opposite number (the wise man, the righteous man), in certain of the verses of chapters, i.e., 18:2, "A fool hath no delight in understanding, but that his heart may discover itself."

The three initial sketches in the 1614 publication of O.'s poem *A Wife,* and the characters of the various authors, were probably written by O., and contrast two basic types of women. "A Good Woman" depicts its model as being "a comfort, like a Man," merely lacking heat. She is decent in dress, sweet in disposition, pure in conduct; she loves knowledge, knows her own mind, marries her husband for love, and is mainly concerned with his welfare. She does "herself kindness upon" her husband. "After his, her chiefest virtue is a good husband," because "She is He." "A Very Very Woman" describes the opposite stereotype. As the archaic wording in the title indicates, a common woman is replete with the (supposed) faults of her sex. Waiting to marry, as soon as she reaches age fourteen, this creature is vain, deceitful, self-serving, and pretentious in innumerable ways. She is a dough-baked (i.e., imperfect) man, or a She intended for a man, but fallen "the two bowes short" in strength and understanding. "Her chief commendation is, she brings a man to repentance." "Her Next Part" adds more details to the selfish, insincere, and immature woman painted in the preceding Character. She is given to traveling about and through this means turns into "a woman of good entertainment," visited by "all the folly in the country," dressed in clean linen. Her religious devotion involves good clothes, which "carry her to Church, express their stuff and fashion, and are silent." The instruments most necessary to her are a chambermaid and a waiting-gentlewoman, whose better gown is what she envies most. She makes each of her husbands, though very modestly dressed, pay for her finery. After many such domestic rounds, she "is delivered to old age and a chair, where

every body leaves her." The character of "A Good Wife," probably written by O., is closely related to "A Good Woman."

BIBLIOGRAPHY: DeFord, M. A., *The O. Affair* (1960); McElwee, W. L., *The Murder of Sir T. O.* (1952); White, B., *Cast of Ravens: The Strange Case of Sir T. O.* (1965)

SAMUEL I. BELLMAN

OWEN, Wilfred [Edward Salter]
b. 18 March 1893, Oswestry, Shropshire; d. 4 November 1918, Ors, France

The greatest poet of World War I, O. was unknown in his lifetime and his reputation grew quite slowly after his death in the last few days of fighting, only taking off in the 1960s. Almost all his major poetry is based on his war experience and he has now become a cult figure; Ted HUGHES acknowledged him as an inspiration and he has appeared in modern novels, poems, plays, and films. Benjamin Britten set his poetry to music in the *War Requiem* (1961), and he is constantly quoted when we talk about war. It seems impossible to discuss 1914–18, in particular, without taking him into account.

He was reared in an obscure lower-middle-class family, longing to become a poet but cut off from any literary circles. He was strongly influenced by his mother's Christian beliefs and spent some time as a church worker; although he ceased to believe in God his social conscience and attraction to Christian ethics remained strong. He eagerly read the older poets while at school, and particularly admired John KEATS and Percy Bysshe SHELLEY. Working in France before the war, he met the Decadent poet Laurent Tailhade and became acquainted with modern French literature.

He joined the army in 1915 and continued to write poetry that is technically accomplished, but uninteresting. In early 1917, he spent three months on the western front and suffered a breakdown, but he still had not found a way to write about what he had seen. But in August he read Siegfried SASSOON's *Old Huntsman* and then met the author in a Liverpool hospital for shell-shocked officers. He had already reread Alfred, Lord TENNYSON and felt contemptuous of his Romantic melancholy, given that he and his generation were experiencing horrors the Romantics never dreamed of. Sassoon, who helped him revise his first important poem, "Anthem for Doomed Youth," showed him that it was possible to write realistically about the war. But although some of his poems ("The Dead-Beat," "The Chances") are written in Sassoon's style, the two men had a very different sensibility.

In certain ways, O. always remained a Romantic. The Sassoon poem he liked best was "The Death-Bed," with its deep sympathy for the dying youth and its purple and scarlet imagery. He loved rhythm, color, sonorous sound, and the type of poetry that loads every rift with ore. But the technical skills that he had honed over the years were now applied to a quite un-Romantic subject matter. His purpose was to make his readers, in an age before the cinecamera, see as far as possible what war was like, and he was offended by the many writers who sentimentalized it. "Dulce et Decorum Est" was inspired by Horace's cliché and dedicated to a scribbler from the *Daily Mail*. This poem, written in an entirely traditional form, has a hideous new subject, poison gas.

Not all his work, however, rhymes in the traditional way. He had learned, probably from Elizabeth Barrett BROWNING, that half-rhyme offered interesting new possibilities, and several of his finest poems are written in this style. "Killed/cold," "silent/salient," "escaped/scooped" are examples from "Insensibility," "Exposure," and "Strange Meeting," and are ways of avoiding tired or predictable rhymes. He was the first English poet to use this method frequently and with complete assurance. He suggested that he was doing in poetry "what the advanced composers are doing in music," and perhaps he needed half-rhyme to distance himself from the tinkling sweetness of conventional verse.

The poems for which he is remembered were all written in his last year of life, before he returned to the front in autumn 1918. There are less than twenty, but all are of superb quality. Sassoon had introduced him to other writers, including Robert GRAVES and Osbert SITWELL, and he planned, if he lived long enough, to publish a collection that would open English people's eyes to the horror of what was happening. His unfinished preface, one of the most famous literary documents of the century, states, "Above all I am not concerned with Poetry. My subject is War, and the pity of War. The Poetry is in the Pity."

"Pity" is the key word. While some poems are angry, satirical pieces, written in the working-class idiom of Sassoon, in most others O. is mourning, in a more elevated and traditional voice, for the loss of young lives. One poem, "Inspection," displays these two styles side by side. He is an impartial observer, looking down "from a vague height" ("The Show") on the tragedy of Europe. He never complained about his own situation but saw himself as a spokesman for the inarticulate men who were being ushered to their deaths by the complacent, and supposedly Christian people at home. His images are of darkness, blood, freezing cold, "the monstrous anger of the guns," anonymous men walking in their sleep or being whirled away by train to an unknown destination. Often they focus on a single, innocent boy-victim who has been sacrificed by his father's generation, like Isaac by Abraham. A young man sits in his wheelchair in a park full of cheerful crowds; another man

commits suicide because no one, least of all his family, realizes what he is enduring. O. was definite that he did not want to write about heroes but to open the wells of compassion.

Two poems seem especially relevant today. "Dulce et Decorum Est" describes the victim of a gas attack in the most ugly words available and then says that if we, the readers, could see what he has seen we would not talk so glibly about war. "Strange Meeting" has the narrator meeting someone in a mysterious dark passage and realizing that this is the man he killed before being killed himself, and that they are in hell. By this time, O. clearly believed that the enemy was war, not people from other nations, and he removed any reference to Germans to give it a wider significance than the war in which he was involved.

"Miners" is the one significant poem that is not overtly about the war, but it too uses images of darkness and the underground. It stresses the great gulf between the victims and the comfortable who are unaware of their sacrifice, and the speed with which men forget.

O.'s generation was the first to experience modern war and some older poets, such as W. B. YEATS and Henry NEWBOLT, disliked him, believing it was better to write about heroism than "passive suffering." Very few of his poems appeared in his lifetime, but Sassoon, the Sitwells, and Edmund BLUNDEN published memorial editions in the fifteen years after the war. His readers, even the earliest, knew that he had been killed and that gave his words added authority. But most people still preferred the idealism of Rupert BROOKE, so he had a limited audience until his own generation was almost gone. As civilians learned more about war, he has become steadily more popular; Dylan THOMAS describing him as "a poet of all times, all places, and all wars."

He admired both the Georgians and the early modernists, writing a few late pieces in their style. His work, which seemed startling at the time, is now very much mainstream. It has been argued that if he, Isaac ROSENBERG, and Edward THOMAS had not been killed, English poetry would have resisted Ezra Pound and T. S. ELIOT's influence and stayed closer to the common reader.

BIBLIOGRAPHY: Hibberd, D., *O. the Poet* (1986); Hibberd, D., *W. O.* (1992); Kerr, D., *W. O.'s Voices* (1993); Owen, H., *Journey from Obscurity* (3 vols., 1963–65); Owen, H., and J. Bell, eds., *W. O.: Collected Letters* (1967); Stallworthy, J., *W. O.* (1974); Williams, M., *W. O.* (1993)

MERRYN WILLIAMS

OWENSON, Sydney [Lady Morgan]

b. 25 December 1776, Dublin, Ireland; d. 14 April 1859, London

Daughter of an actor, O. was acclaimed in Roman Catholic and Liberal circles as "Glorvina," the name of the heroine of the novel that brought her fame, *The Wild Irish Girl* (3 vols., 1806), glorifying Ireland and its history. She knew and understood the Irish poor, but her nationalist views were controversial. Her first novel, *St. Clair* (1803), had already attracted attention, with its ill-judged marriage, doomed love, and passionate nature worship, showing the influence of Goethe and Jean-Jacques Rousseau. *The Lay of an Irish Harp* came out in 1807. In 1812, O. married a surgeon, Charles Morgan, who was later knighted. O. continued to write novels, ten in all: *O'Donnel* (3 vols., 1814) has been considered among her best. Her study of France under the Bourbon Restoration (1817) was accused of Jacobinism, falsehood, licentiousness, and impiety by the ultraconservative *Quarterly.* Her revenge was the novel *Florence Macarthy* (4 vols., 1818), which has a satirical portrait of a *Quarterly* reviewer called Con Crawley. A later novel was *The O'Briens and the O'Flahertys* (4 vols., 1827), also attacked. She published a biography of the painter Salvator Rosa, and travel books on France, Italy, and Belgium, highly successful. *Absenteeism* (1825) was a collection of her articles from the *New Monthly Magazine,* and a series of short pieces came out as *The Book of the Boudoir* (2 vols., 1829). A feminist polemic, *Woman and Her Master,* was published in two volumes in 1840. *Passages from My Autobiography* appeared in 1859, together with some letters.

OXFORD, Edward de Vere, Seventeenth Earl of

b. 2 April 1550, Castle Hedingham, Essex; d. 24 June 1604, Newington, Middlesex

A nephew to Ovid translator Arthur Golding, O. was a prominent figure in ELIZABETH I's court during his minority. O. was an accomplished swordsman, horseman, and tilter. He was also a noted eccentric with a violent temper. Gabriel Harvey ridiculed him as the "Speculum Tuscanismi" for his affected Italianate manner and wardrobe, calling him a "passing singular odd man." O. gave Sir Philip SIDNEY offense by calling him "puppy" and once planned (without success) Sidney's assassination. George PUTTENHAM and Francis MERES hailed O. as "the best for comedy" in his day. But although he was patron of his own group of players, Oxford's Men, none of his dramatic work survives. Several critics tried to claim O. as the true author of William SHAKESPEARE's works based upon questionable internal interpretation, specious cyphers, and revisionist history, but they have largely failed to demonstrate a cogent argument. What does remain of O.'s writing, his poetry, corroborates William WEBBE's opinion of his verse, that he was among the best of the courtier-poets in the early reign of Elizabeth. O., who signed his work "E. O." or "E. of O.," was also patron to the playwright John LYLY and the poet Edmund SPENSER, among others.

PAINTER, William
b. 1540?, London; d. 14 February 1594, London

Educated at St John's College, Cambridge, and later ordained, P. translated stories from Greek, Latin, and Italian, including those of Boccaccio and Matteo Bandello. His collection, *The Palace of Pleasure* (1566; rev. ed., 1575), comprised some sixty tales. A second volume published in the following year contained another thirty-four. In 1575, they were all reprinted, together with another seven. P.'s stories provided plots for dramatists John WEBSTER (*The Duchess of Malfi*), Francis BEAUMONT and John FLETCHER, and James SHIRLEY. William SHAKESPEARE seems to have used P. as a source for his long narrative and philosophical poem, *The Rape of Lucrece*, and probably adapted the story of Giletta of Narbonne for *All's Well That Ends Well*.

PARKS, Tim[othy Harold]
b. 19 December 1954, Manchester

P. is a prolific novelist, short story writer, literary critic, essayist, travel writer, and translator. His first novel, *Tongues of Flame* (1985), is the semiautobiographical story of an adolescent growing up in the household of an Anglican priest. The father becomes involved in the charismatic Christian movement, while the narrator's brother heads in a somewhat opposite direction, indulging in all manner of 1960s rebellions. The novel won both the Betty Trask and Somerset Maugham Awards. P.'s next novel, *Loving Roger* (1986), is a variation on the conventional murder mystery. It opens with the death of Roger at the hands of Anna and proceeds gradually to unravel the motives behind the woman's actions. P. experimented with form in his next novel, *Home Thoughts* (1987), an epistolary novel about an Englishwoman living in Verona. *Destiny* (1999) is considered by several critics to be P.'s best novel to date, a complex, stream of consciousness narrative that follows its protagonist,

Chris Burton, as he and his wife go to bury their son. P.'s other novels include *Family Planning* (1989), *Goodness* (1991), *Shear* (1993), and two novels focusing on the antihero Morris Duckworth: *Cara Massimina* (1990; repub. as *Juggling the Stars*, 1993) and *Mimi's Ghost* (1995), the former published under the pseudonym John MacDowell. P. has published two nonfiction works dealing with life in Italy: *Italian Neighbours* (1992) and *An Italian Education* (1995), and he is also an acclaimed translator. In *Translating Style: The English Modernists and Their Italian Translations* (1998), he undertakes a critical study of the way in which analyzing the particular problems in translation posed by certain authors provides insight into those authors' styles.

PARNELL, Thomas
b. 1679, Dublin, Ireland; d. 24 October 1718, Chester

Minor poet and clergyman, educated at Trinity College, Dublin, P. was early a contributor to the *Spectator* and member of the Scriblerus Club, which included Alexander POPE, Jonathan SWIFT, John GAY, John ARBUTHNOT, William CONGREVE, and Robert HARLEY, first Earl of Oxford. The group invented a fictitious hack writer called Martinus Scriblerus, a vehicle for their SATIRE. Pope, denied a university education because of his Roman Catholicism, was impressed by P.'s knowledge of the classics and P. contributed an "Essay on the Life, Writings and Learning of Homer" as preface to Pope's translation of *The Iliad*, published in 1715. P. published *An Essay on the Different Styles of Poetry* (1713). In 1722, Pope collected P.'s unpublished verse, which anticipates the "graveyard poets" of the mid-18th c. that included Edward YOUNG and Robert BLAIR, among others.

PARR, Katherine [or Catherine]
b. 1513, Kendal Castle, or 1514, London; d. 5 September 1548, Sudeley Castle, Gloucestershire

The eldest child of Maud Green and Sir Thomas Parr, P. was married twice before becoming the sixth wife of HENRY VIII in 1543, and after his death she took Thomas Seymour as her fourth husband. She was reared at court where she was tutored by the humanist scholar Juan Luis Vives. Later, as queen, she helped to propagate humanist ideas by employing scholars at the royal school, and by acting as patron to Nicholas Udall, whose translation of Desiderius ERASMUS's *Paraphrases* on the New Testament she had printed in 1545 at her own expense; she also commissioned Miles Coverdale's translation of the New Testament.

Through her patronage and her own piety, P. served as the first influential female Reformist figure. Initially, she undertook a program of vernacular translations of primarily humanist-inspired religious works. At the suggestion of George Day, Bishop of Chichester, her principal spiritual mentor, she translated from Latin the *Psalms or Prayers taken out of Holy Scripture*, attributed to John Fisher, which had been published in Cologne in 1525. The English publication of this book in 1544 by the king's printer, Thomas Berthelet, was almost certainly the result of P.'s patronage; an indication of this is the inclusion of an English prayer for Henry VIII that was probably composed by P. The English translation of the text was published at the same time without any mention of P.'s involvement as its translator, but the book was repeatedly reprinted in tandem with *Prayers or Meditations*, a work that was undoubtedly hers.

The appearance of *Prayers or Meditations* in 1545 marks the publication of the first original work by an Englishwoman under her own name. The work consists of a series of P.'s own religious exercises, and its import is indicated by its full title: *Prayers, or Meditations, wherein the mynd is stirred, paciently to suffre all afflictions here, to set at nought the vaine prosperitie of this worlde, and always to longe for the everlasting felicitie: collected out of holy woorkes by the most vertuous and gracious Princess Katherine queene of Englaunde, France and Ireland*. P. takes excerpts from the English translation of the third book of Thomas à Kempis's early-14th-c. devotional masterpiece, *The Imitation of Christ*, and rewrites them, covering frequently discussed Christian concepts such as the vanity of worldly things, God's grace, and the individual's unworthiness. To this compilation, she added a set of five original prayers, including "A prayer for the king," and "A prayer for men to say entering into battle," which may have been written during Henry's absence in France.

P. describes her second book, *Lamentacion or Complaynt of a Sinner* (1547), as a "spiritual boke of the crucifix." Here, P. details her personal religious beliefs in a narrative that moves from confession to conversion. It contains highly personalized free-flowing vernacular meditations, and is filled with Protestant assertions concerning justification by faith alone, saving grace, divine election, and predestination.

After this affirmation of the tenets of the Reformist movement, the work concludes with a resounding attack on the Papists. Although the book was not published until after Henry's death, it seems that a first draft was already circulating at court by November 1545, for in that year Bishop Stephen Gardiner denounced it in his correspondence as "this most abominable book." In the following year, a plot against P.'s life emerged, and she was condemned for heresy by Gardiner and the Lord Chancellor, Thomas Wriothesley. It was undoubtedly her involvement in projects related to humanist scholarship and the reformed religion that had antagonized the conservative faction. Both P.'s published works took texts that were essentially Catholic and recast these with a subtle reformist coloring and emphasis. Her works enjoyed considerable popularity at court during her lifetime and were reprinted several times during the 16th c.

BIBLIOGRAPHY: James, S. E., *K. P.* (1999); Martienssen, A., *Queen Katherine Parr* (1973); Mueller, J., "A Tudor Queen Finds Voice: K. P.'s *Lamentation of a Sinner*," in Dubrow, H., and R. Strier, eds., *The Historical Renaissance: New Essays on Tudor and Stuart Literature and Culture* (1988): 15–47

MARGARET CONNOLLY

PATER, Walter [Horatio]
b. 4 August 1839, London; d. 30 July 1894, Oxford

One of the leading influences on the Aesthetic movement of the 1880s, P. was a great exponent of "the desire of beauty, the love of art for art's sake," whose work was tempered by deeply felt ethical concerns and an abiding sense of loss and transience. An essayist, critic, and novelist, P. based his critical approach on Matthew ARNOLD's aim "to see the object as it really is," combined with an insistence on honesty and self-awareness; his involved impressionistic style, the aim of which was always to appreciate rather than to judge, often ignored the details of scholarship in its attempt to convey the essence of a work of art, and he has been criticized for adopting a partisan, nostalgic approach to his subjects. Nevertheless, the integrity of P.'s vision won him many followers among his contemporaries and, through his contribution to modernist aesthetics and importance to writers such as James JOYCE and Virginia WOOLF, he has continued to exert a remarkable influence with an output that consisted of just five complete volumes during his lifetime and two posthumously published works.

P. was a great stylist who, like Marius, the protagonist in his only novel, dispensed with poetry at an early age in favor of what he saw as the more complex discipline of prose. Having contributed articles to the age's rising number of journals, he first gained widespread recognition with *Studies in the History of the*

Renaissance (1873), published when he was a fellow of Brasenose College, Oxford. Part aesthetic criticism, part philosophy, part cultural history, and part fiction, the volume was attacked by some as unscholarly and by others within the university for its "corrupting" elevation of pagan art, but its influence was deep and lasting: Oscar WILDE called it the "holy writ of beauty"; Gerard Manley HOPKINS admired its independence of thought; and W. B. YEATS declared that P.'s writings would remain "permanent in our literature" because of their "revolutionary importance."

At the time of publication, visual arts criticism was a comparatively new genre, introduced to England by John RUSKIN in the 1840s; P.'s book, with its "political indifferentism" and emphasis on mood rather than on the accuracy of the eye, represented an undermining of Ruskin's impassioned teachings. Included in the work were some of the first writings on Botticelli, and essays on Michelangelo, Johann Joachim Winckelmann, and Leonardo da Vinci; in each, P. fused the life and art of his subjects and invested them with his own sympathies, confusing fact with legend to create an aesthetic ROMANCE. P.'s famous evocation of the Mona Lisa, in which he describes her as "older than the rocks among which she sits; like the vampire, she has been dead many times, and learned the secrets of the grave," possesses a unity of vision and liberated use of language rarely found outside the novel. With a self-referential, elaborate style that draws attention to its own medium, the work is now recognized as a modernist text.

Much of P.'s writing, including his study of English boyhood, "The Child in the House," published in *Macmillan's Magazine* (1878), and *Marius the Epicurean* (2 vols., 1885), which many regard as his masterpiece, blurs the boundary between fiction and AUTOBIOGRAPHY. The latter, an eclectic fictional account of a boy growing up in the reign of Marcus Aurelius, Emperor of Rome, is also a revealing depiction of life in late Victorian England. Containing little plot or dialogue, and dominated by a highly polished prose style, *Marius the Epicurean* documents one man's search for a guiding principle among different pagan and Christian philosophies; in many respects, the search was P.'s own and Marius's preoccupations— childhood, death, evolving belief—reflect those of his creator. The autobiographical elements, though, are overshadowed by P.'s developing artistry and the novel is unusual in its fusion of the ancient and the modern mind. Despite being hard to categorize, it was well received on both sides of the Atlantic for its reconciliation of artistic and religious lives, for its author's obvious pleasure in language, and for epitomizing what John BUCHAN called a "searching and beautiful" history of the soul. Significant as the work with which P. turned artist as well as critic, it has survived to be rated by modern critics as an important and sophisticated text.

After *Marius*, P. wrote a number of short fictional works, some of which were published in *Imaginary Portraits* (1887). In 1888, he began to serialize another fictional work, *Gaston de Latour*, which he referred to as "a sort of *Marius* in France," but which remained unfinished at his death. *Appreciations, with an Essay on Style* (1889) contained essays on William SHAKESPEARE and other English writers and confirmed his mastery of prose, and *Plato and Platonism* (1893) collected together his early lectures, blending ancient philosophy with that of his own age. Two works, *Greek Studies* and *Miscellaneous Studies*, were published posthumously in 1895.

BIBLIOGRAPHY: Brake, L., *W. P.* (1994); Evans, L., ed., *Letters of W. P.* (1970); Levey, M., *The Case of W. P.* (1978); Seiler, R. H., *W. P.* (1987)

NICOLA UPSON

PATMORE, Coventry
b. 23 July 1823, Woodford, Essex; d. 26 November 1896, Lymington

P. is an important Victorian poet. His *The Angel in the House* (1858) was one of the most successful poems of the epoch, and his *The Unknown Eros* (1877) is a remarkably powerful and original collection of lyric verse.

P.'s first publication was his *Poems* of 1844. This collection was successful, and such poems as "The Yew-berry," "The River," and "The Falcon" demonstrate how early P. mastered verse technique and found his interest in love as a theme. "The Woodman's Daughter" also appears in this volume. It is a powerful ballad dealing with rustic innocence and romantic betrayal and guilt. It became a favorite of the Pre-Raphaelites and was the inspiration for a major painting by John Everett Millais. P. next published *Tamerton Church-Tower and Other Poems* (1853). The title poem's narrative facility and its treatment of love are remarkable anticipations of *The Angel in the House*.

P.'s marriage in 1847 to Emily Andrews was almost ideally happy, and P.'s joy in his life with Emily inspired *The Angel in the House* and its sequel *The Victories of Love* (1862). These poems formed the basis of P.'s Victorian fame.

The Angel in the House tells of the courtship and marriage of Felix and Honoria Vaughan, characters obviously based on P. and his wife. *The Angel in the House* is a novel in verse and is in many ways a considerable achievement. P.'s poem is realistic and concrete in its basic story, but it treats love as a philosophical and religious universal as well as the center of a specific marriage. For P., love is a mystical force only to be understood within the harmonies and limitations of marriage. Although the poem is fluent in its narrative and almost commonplace in its ordinary setting and characters, it is also witty, urbane, lyrical, and, at times, profound. In gracefully turned tetrameter quatrains, P. alternates and combines narrative and meditative sections that work together to produce a unique combination of love story and philosophical discourse.

The Victories of Love continues the story of Felix and Honoria, but it mainly deals with the less ideal but ultimately happy marriage of Honoria's cousin Frederick Graham and his wife Jane. The poem's story is told in verse letters written in very polished tetrameter couplets, and it too emphasizes the sacred efficacy of marriage as a school for human love.

P.'s later poems are notable for their continuing treatment of love, their increasing mysticism, and their metrical experimentation. P. was converted to Catholicism in 1864, and the poems of *The Unknown Eros* and *Amelia* (1878) reflect the strong influence of Catholic theology and mystical thought. They also reflect P.'s deepening interest in English prosody and the possibilities of the irregular ode as a form. In the major poems of *The Unknown Eros*, P. treats love as a force in nature, human life, national life, and in the soul's longing for God. Instead of the fluency of his earlier verse, these irregular odes on love are difficult, challenging, metaphorically and intellectually complex, and written in a style in which metrical movement and forceful thought become one. Many later critics have admired *The Unknown Eros* as P.'s finest work, but it was little appreciated in its time.

P. has been called the greatest poet of his period, and he has been derided for his allegedly sentimental and conventionally Victorian treatment of women. It seems that P. in the final analysis must be ranked well below Alfred, Lord TENNYSON and Robert BROWNING, but it is also true that his poetry, including *The Angel in the House*, is more interesting and less conventionally Victorian than some commentaries suggest. Taken as a whole, P.'s poetry is the work of a serious, thoughtful, and technically accomplished poet.

BIBLIOGRAPHY: Burdett, O., *The Idea of C. P.* (1921); Oliver, E. J., *C. P.* (1956); Page, F., *C. P.* (1933); Patmore, D., *The Life and Times of C. P.* (1949)

PHILLIP B. ANDERSON

PAULIN, Tom [Thomas Neilson]

b. 25 January 1949, Leeds

P. is a prolific poet and critic, best known for his examination of the political and social issues affecting Northern Ireland. Born in England, P. moved to Belfast at the age of four. He was reared in a Protestant home, and much of his best work reflects on the consciousness of the Protestant role in "the Troubles" of Northern Ireland.

P. learned his social and political consciousness from his reading of Marx, Trotsky, George ORWELL, D. H. LAWRENCE, Joseph CONRAD (especially *Under Western Eyes*), and W. H. AUDEN, among others. In his essay "Political Verse," he defined a political poem as less an ideological statement than an embodiment of "general historical awareness." P. believes that the Protestant tradition in English literature, which produced such rebellious poets as John MILTON, John DRYDEN, Robert BROWNING, and W. B. YEATS, has fostered political poetry by focusing attention on individual conscience. In "Political Verse," P. seems to wrestle with his own contradictory feelings about the role of Protestantism in Northern Ireland's Troubles. Arguing that it is the nature of poetry written in this tradition to be political, P. contends that a Protestant perspective can make its own peculiar contribution to the dialogue about Northern Ireland.

P.'s poetic style is modernist; he seldom uses rhyme or fixed forms. Despite the seriousness of his subject matter, P. uses HUMOR adroitly, often relying on puns or other forms of wordplay. Like other modern Irish poets, Patrick KAVANAGH and Seamus HEANEY most notably, P. frequently gives his poems a local setting, but then moves beyond the local to consider broader, more universal themes. In describing his criticism, P. has noted that he is influenced more by journalism than by literary theory: in the introduction to his volume *Writing to the Moment* (1996), he expresses admiration for journalistic writings of Orwell and Jonathan SWIFT, largely because of the "naked gritty direct plainness of their prose styles." Indeed, P.'s love of what he calls an "apparently formless, iconoclastic mode of composition" is an apt description of his own style in prose and poetry.

While P. writes on a variety of subjects, justice and individual responsibility are his recurring themes. That focus is evident even in the titles of his earliest collections of poetry, such as *A State of Justice* (1977) and *Liberty Tree* (1983). Poems from the former volume often question the nature and legitimacy of a "state." Bernard O'Donoghue has argued that the examination of justice in these volumes extends beyond the condition of Northern Ireland alone, citing resemblances to Eastern European writers like Osip Mandelstam. P. often uses biblical references in his poems to examine ideas of justice, leaving a reader to wonder whether Northern Ireland is existing in an outdated, Old Testament world of retributive justice rather than in the world of mercy provided under the New Covenant. In an essay on James JOYCE, "The British Presence in *Ulysses*," P. recognized Joyce's attempts to establish parallels between Bloom and Moses, and "between Stephen Dedalus, Parnell, and Christ." As P.'s poetry has progressed, he has become increasingly convinced that Northern Ireland cannot, under British rule, escape the vicious cycle of retribution that leads to repeated acts of violence.

In *The Wind Dog* (1999), P.'s sixth volume of poetry, one can see his progress as well as his stubborn allegiance to the themes of politics and justice. "Bournemouth" exemplifies his tendency to root his poetry in a local scene, which then becomes emblematic of larger issues. Here too, P. calls on imagery associated with his Irish Protestant predecessor, Yeats, when he symbolizes Protestantism as a "hard basic tower." And, like William WORDSWORTH, Yeats, and Heaney, P. turns reflection on a place into a personal struggle, in which he comments on his own sins, his betrayals, and the people he has hurt, before stating, "I'm heartsick, lonely, my soul's a void." But the poem concludes with hopeful images of Christ's birth and of the speaker's finding his way to a well-marked path that will lead him out of the wilderness toward home. In "Bournemouth," and in other poems, P. demonstrates that, for all the MODERNISM of his style, he is deeply rooted in the tradition of Protestant ROMANTICISM. His is an intensely reflective poetry, which places great value on memory and connectedness to place.

BIBLIOGRAPHY: Haffenden, J., "T. P.," in his *Viewpoints: Poets in Conversation* (1981): 157–73; O'Donoghue, B., "Involved Imaginings: T. P.," in Corcoran, N., ed., *The Chosen Ground: Essays on Contemporary Poetry of Northern Ireland* (1992): 171–88

DAN ROSS

PEACHAM, Henry

b. 1578, North Mimms, Hertfordshire; d. ca. 1643, London

P., scholar, artist, courtier, and man of letters, is best known as the author of a courtesy book, *The Compleat Gentleman* (1622; rev. eds., 1627, 1634). A staunch royalist, with access to, and devotion for, the Jacobean court, P., while archdeacon at Lincoln (1606) served Prince Henry until the latter's death in 1612. *The Period of Mourning* (1613) is a lament for Henry's passing. During the same period of service, P. translated JAMES I's treatise on government, *Basilicon doron*, into Latin verse in 1610. P.'s *The Duty of All True Subjects to Their King as Also to Their Native Country* (1639) defines his long-term politics and established his conservative views in the face of the coming revolution. *Thalia's Banquet* (1620), a collection of epigrams, advanced P.'s claim as a poet in English, and was begun while P. was master of Wymondham grammar school, Norfolk (ca. 1618).

A visual as well as a literary artist, P.'s earliest publication is *The Art of Drawing with the Pen, and Limning in Water Colours* (1606; rev. as *Graphice*, 1612). A note of pride for P. was that he had sketched the king at dinner, and his translation of James's *Basilicon doron* was illustrated with P.'s original pen-and-ink drawings. The sketcher's eye for detail is apparent in *The Truth of Our Times* (1638), a kind of memoir replete with perceptive observations of London life. It is a source of occasional material of some value (e.g., P.'s recollections of stage performances he witnessed as a schoolboy).

P. was of a good, but not wealthy Hertfordshire family, and took his degree from Trinity College, Cambridge. His term as schoolmaster seems neither to have been lucrative (Wymondham being a free school) nor happy ("whiles that it was free, Myselfe, the Maister, lost my libertie," P. wrote), and despite his early familiarity with the Jacobean court, he was in later life occasionally short of money, as *The Worth of a Peny* (1641; rev. ed., 1664), a "complaint to his purse," attests. Although an outspoken royalist, P. nonetheless was critical of courtly excesses, and (despite disparagement of Puritans in *Thalia's Banquet*) echoed in some regard a Puritan conservatism of lifestyle. Among his friends were the composer John Dowland, architect and stage designer Inigo Jones, and mathematician Edward Wright.

The Compleat Gentleman remains P.'s primary contribution, and its two revised editions attest to its contemporary popularity. It is in most ways representative of its genre, but it goes beyond many other works of its kind produced in the era in its fuller treatment of education, and its broader range of subjects covered (including geometry, cosmography, music, poetry, drawing, painting, and sculpture), which give full play to P.'s interests and humanist learning. *The Compleat Gentleman* remained a reference into the 18th c., as is indicated by Samuel JOHNSON's reliance on the section on heraldry for definitions in his *English Dictionary*.

BIBLIOGRAPHY: Cawley, R., *H. P.* (1971); Heltzel, V. B., ed., *The Complete Gentleman, The Truth of Our Times, and The Art of Living in London* (1962)

R. F. YEAGER

PEACOCK, Thomas Love

b. 18 October 1785, Weymouth; d. 23 January 1866, Lower Halliford, near Chertsey

Self-educated after age thirteen, P. acquired a wide knowledge of Greek, Latin, French, and Italian literature, learning Spanish in old age. In 1812, P. met Percy Bysshe SHELLEY, then aged twenty. Shelley admired P.'s poems, now forgotten. Shelley was amused to read of himself gently teased in P.'s first novel,

Headlong Hall (1816), as Mr. Scythrop, vegetarian and believer in the perfection of society.

In the same novel, Mr. Panscope shares Samuel Taylor COLERIDGE's interest in metaphysics. P.'s novels are debates largely in dialogue form. P.'s learned and topical SATIRE sits uneasily within his framework of conventional plot in *Melincourt* (3 vols., 1817), in which P. attacks Tory principles and those who have recently embraced them. Coleridge appears as Mr. Mystic and Robert SOUTHEY is mocked as Mr. Feathernest. William WORDSWORTH, having accepted a government job distributing postage stamps, is called Mr. Paperstamp. Although in general, P., a Utilitarian and admirer of William COBBETT, believed in laissez-faire, Mr. Forester, like P. himself, refuses to buy rum or sugar, because they are produced by slave labor. *Nightmare Abbey* (1818) reintroduces Scythrop, and two women, representing the deserted Harriet Westbrook Shelley and Shelley's newer love, Mary GODWIN. Shelley declared himself "delighted," adding, "is not the misdirected enthusiasm of Scythrop what J. C. calls 'the salt of the earth'?" Mary, who had just published *Frankenstein,* and disliked P., was irritated by the dismissal of the novel *Mandeville* by her father, William GODWIN, spoken by Mr. Flosky (Coleridge).

Nightmare Abbey is considered the best of P.'s fictions. Others are *Maid Marian* (1822), *The Misfortunes of Elphin* (1829), and *Crotchet Castle* (1831) in which Coleridge reappears as Mr. Skionar, the transcendental poet, and Leigh HUNT is represented by Mr. Eavesdrop. Wordsworth becomes Mr. Wilful Wontsee and Southey Mr. Rumblesack Shantsee, both accused of selling out. Robert Owen appears as Mr. Toogood, Thomas MOORE as Mr. Trillo (formerly O'Trill). Topically, Sir Simon Steeltrap "enclosed commons and woodlands; abolished cottage-gardens; has taken the village cricket ground into his own park, out of pure regard to the sanctity of Sunday; shut up footpaths and alehouses . . . put down fairs and fiddlers." The poor take their revenge by burning hayricks. P.'s last novel was *Gryll Grange* (1860), reflecting a world in which his predictions had largely come true. His targets are new fads, such as "spirit-rapping . . . clairvoyance, table turning," the electric telegraph, and American civilization. For some readers, it is their favorite, as the speakers are more distinctly characterized and there is more plot.

BIBLIOGRAPHY: Burns, B. *The Novels of T. L. P.* (1985); Butler, M., *P. Displayed* (1979); Dawson, C., *T. L. P.* (1968)

PEAKE, Mervyn [Laurence]

b. 9 July 1911, Kuling, Kiang-Hsi province, China; d. 16 November 1968, near Abingdon, Oxfordshire

The creation of the vast, labyrinthine citadel of Gormenghast with its teeming population of grotesques and eccentrics provided P. with an exotic setting against which to enact a drama on a classic tragic scale, shot through with wild and fantastical absurdities. Despite a significant body of work, P. is known almost solely as the author of the trio of novels *Titus Groan* (1946), *Gormenghast* (1950), and *Titus Alone* (1959). Curiously, for a writer of intellect and imagination responsible for a towering creative achievement, P.'s reputation in Britain and Europe is almost exclusively limited to a devotee following while in the U.S. it has scarcely even been established.

A popular misconception has been to couple P.'s Gormenghast novels with J. R. R. TOLKIEN's *The Lord of the Rings* as twin fantasy trilogies of the 20th c. In truth, these works have nothing in common and are not, in either case, genuine trilogies: Tolkien's book being one novel divided, for convenience of publishing, into three volumes and P.'s novels being only the first three books in an ambitious, if unrealized, scheme for an ongoing series.

There are a number of reasons for P.'s writing having failed to receive international recognition as a modern classic: in particular, his elaborate, often extravagant, prose style (that is not to everyone's taste) and the difficulty of finding a suitable categorization with which to pigeonhole his work. Problems with labeling extend to the man himself since P. was a true polymath being a novelist, poet, and playwright as well as a painter and one of the most outstanding and visionary book illustrators of his day. It is impossible to assess P. the writer without reference to his work as an artist since it informed the creation of Gormenghast and much else. The painter's eye is always in evidence in P.'s writing: minute attention to detail; awareness of light and shade as well as the presence (and absence) of color; and a strong sense of scale and the relationship between character and background.

P. first came to public prominence as an illustrator and among the books that he most memorably embellished are the work of authors who undoubtedly contributed to the shaping of P.'s own literary style: such as the freakish folk and logical distortions to be found in Henry FIELDING's *Tom Thumb*, Lewis CARROLL's *Alice in Wonderland*, Robert Louis STEVENSON's *Dr. Jekyll and Mr. Hyde*, and many of the Grimm brothers' *Household Tales*. A diverse quartet of his illustrated books—Carroll's *The Hunting of the Snark* (1941), Samuel Taylor COLERIDGE's *The Rime of the Ancient Mariner* (1943), Stevenson's *Treasure Island* (1949), and Johann David Wyss's *Swiss Family Robinson* (1950)—reflect P.'s fascination with islands and the sensation of being marooned (or, in the case of the Mariner, becalmed) outside the real world: a disease that also infects the lives of Gormenghast's inhabitants.

While some might credit P. with having invented that genre of literature sometimes described as "gormenghastly," it would be truer to say that he excavated and restored the much older edifice of Gothic writing to which he then added various surreal and satiric out-buildings of his own devising. A major theme of the Gormenghast novels is the challenge of change, represented symbolically in the birth of the new earl, the violet-eyed Titus, who at his very christening rips the pages of the sacrosanct book of law, thereby signaling his later noncompliance to the rigidity of Gormenghast's arcane ritual. Simultaneously, below stairs, the kitchen-boy, Steerpike, begins his relentless climb from lowly obscurity to the dizzy heights of power. His rise begins with a fierce, yet commendable, will to survive but eventually corrupts into ruthless ambition and an unyielding quest for bloody insurrection.

The personification of base hatred and blind malignancy, Steerpike is written with such venomous delight that the character's later status as an arch-villain never quite loses the earlier gloss of courageous antiheroism. Indeed, the reader retains an emotional ambiguity toward Steerpike—despite his heinous deeds—to the very moment of his death at Titus's hands.

The cast of characters who revolve around Titus and Steerpike are Dickensian in their bizarre eccentricities, excessive theatricality, and preposterous names: Swelter, Flay, Rottcodd, Sourdust, and Nannie Slagg. There is Gormenghast's melancholy ruler, Lord Sepulchrave, doomed to madness and death at the beaks and claws of owls; the mountainous, red-haired Countess Gertrude, surrounded by a constantly shifting tide of snow-white cats; and Dr. Prunesquallor, the foppish dandy whose braying laugh and garrulous conversation disguise a compassionate heart and a needle-sharp brain.

While the first two volumes form a mounting symphony on the theme of social decay, ruination, and collapse, the third volume (itself written while struggling with the corrosive effects of a protracted and debilitating illness) sees Titus free himself from the world of Gormenghast and venture into a world that more closely resembles our own and yet which is, once again, peopled by a cavalcade of nightmarish beings.

The further volumes about Titus that P. planned to write never progressed beyond a tantalizing list of possible locales, although a disturbing "dream" from Titus's teenage years featured in the novella *Boy in Darkness* (1956), which is a foreshadowing of both P.'s illness and the more phantasmagorical elements in *Titus Alone*.

P.'s remaining work includes several ill-fated plays, most notably *The Wit to Woo* (perf. 1957), a number of striking short stories, and the novel, *Mr.*

Pye (1953). Set on a island that is unequivocally based on the Channel Island of Sark (where, for a while, P. lived and worked), *Mr. Pye* is a fable on the constant conflict between good and evil within the human psyche. In a story that might now be described by the use of the term "magic realism," P.'s title character grapples with surprising manifestations of his alternate piety and sinfulness when he grows first angel wings and then demon horns. For young readers, P. wrote and illustrated books of nonsense rhymes and stories: *Captain Slaughterboard Drops Anchor* (1939), *Rhymes without Reason* (1944), and *Letters from a Lost Uncle* (1948). Owing something of their inspiration to the work of Carroll, Edward LEAR, and Hilaire BELLOC, they are told, quite properly, in a spirit of utter seriousness. His poetry—collected in *Shapes and Sounds* (1941), *The Glassblowers* (1950), *The Rhyme of the Flying Bomb* (1962), *A Reverie of Bone* (1967), and the posthumously published *Selected Poems* (1972)—contains much powerful symbolism and penetrating thought and it is regrettable that (unlike the work of many lesser poets) so little of his verse has remained in print.

Although P.'s extraordinary, often uncomfortable, genius has still to be fully appreciated and acknowledged, the Gormenghast novels remain, in the meantime, as a testament to his unquestioned talents.

BIBLIOGRAPHY: Batchelor, J., *M. P.* (1974); Gilmore, M., *A World Away: A Memoir of M. P.* (1970); Peake, S., *A Child of Bliss* (1989); Watney, J., *M. P.* (1976); Smith, G., *M. P.* (1984); Winnington, G. P., *Vast Alchemies: The Life and Work of M. P.* (2000); Yorke, M., *M. P.* (2000)

BRIAN SIBLEY

PEELE, George
b. July 1556, London; d. 9 November 1596, London

Though P. played an important part in the evolution of Elizabethan drama, his greatest talents were as a poet rather than as a dramatist. Most of his plays are more notable for the quality of the verse they contain than for their author's understanding of dramatic structure, character, or plot. To some extent, this was perhaps the product of P.'s historical situation; he was writing, for the most part, in the early years of the modern drama and did not have the advantage of being able to learn from the successes and failures of a number of predecessors; but the relative dramatic weakness of his plays (most of them) probably also reflects something in P.'s own temperament.

Not all of P.'s work can be dated with anything approaching certainty, making it difficult to be sure of patterns of development in his career. His first play was probably *The Arraignment of Paris* (1584), in which P. makes witty use of the mythological narrative of the Judgment of Paris to pay fulsome tribute to ELIZABETH I. Essentially a pastoral, *The Arraignment* colorfully displays P.'s lyrical prowess in a range of different meters, his gifts as a creator of subtle and memorable verbal music. As so often with P., one is struck both by its old-fashioned qualities (harking back to a range of medieval and classical devices) and its innovations (anticipating later developments in the masque). In the freedom with which it mixes Greek gods and stylized yokels, Jupiter and Hobbinol, as it were, *The Arraignment* typifies that non-Aristotelian heterogeneity that so characterizes much that is best in Elizabethan drama. P.'s next play was perhaps *The Battle of Alcazar* (perf. ca. 1590; pub. 1594, but perhaps wr. as early as 1588). Abounding in incident (much of it presented in dumb show and in the narratives of a Presenter) and in grand and threatening speeches exchanged between its protagonists, the play probably worked well in the theater. P. shows little desire, however, for serious engagement with the moral and historical implications of his material. Using John Poleman's *The Second Part of the Book of Battailes* (1587), P.'s play takes as its subject a battle of 1578 in which both Sebastian of Portugal and the English adventurer Thomas Stukeley had been killed. P. seems to have been responding to theatrical fashions created by Christopher MARLOWE's *Tamburlaine the Great*. The play was also innovative, however, for in the figure of Muly Hamet P. created what was probably the first extended presentation of a Moorish character in English drama. (An incidental interest of the play is that a theatrical "plot" for it survives, recording the props and music needed in performance, cues, etc.)

In *The Old Wives Tale* (perf. ca. 1591–94; pub. 1595), P. offers a very different kind of drama. It, too, provides much spectacle, but of an altogether less bloody kind. It is a unique mixture of motifs from FOLKLORE and ROMANCE, a narrative of magicians and wandering knights, magical wells and speaking heads, all splendidly illogical and strikingly beautiful. Critics have been split on the question of whether the play is to be read as a SATIRE on popular tradition or a celebration of it. What is clear is that P.'s artistry in the play is subtle and sophisticated, albeit unorthodox. The play displays P.'s characteristic metrical variety, some vivacious prose, and a charm that has been much appreciated in a number of modern productions. *King Edward the First, Surnamed Edward Longshanks* (perf. ca. 1590–92; pub. 1593) is only superficially a history play; though many of its characters are historical and though some of the incidents of the play have factual precedents, the predominant mood is romantic. Typically, the work is more a series of set pieces than a coherently designed structure. The comic subplot, especially in the figure of Friar David ap Tuck, is perhaps the most rewarding part of the

play. The "serious" parts of the play again reveal the influence of Marlowe and his "mighty line." Like most of P.'s work, the result is undeniably flawed, but in its mixture of tones and genres this, like other of P.'s plays, anticipates patterns we think of as Shakespearean. *David and Bethsabe* (perf. ca. 1594; pub. 1599), draws on the Bible and on Guillaume de Salluste Du Bartas, and gives us poetry both voluptuous and pathetic. Although P.'s drawing of character (perhaps especially that of Absalon) begins to display a greater sophistication than has generally been evident in his work hitherto, the play is, once again, more a sequence of poetic set pieces than a through-composed whole. Dramatically plausible dialogue is less frequently encountered than metaphorically exuberant, lyrically rhythmical effusions. Yet, despite its evident and real weaknesses, *David and Bethsabe* is a distinctive and striking achievement, a promise of greater things that poverty, illness, and an early death prevented.

In addition to his works for the theater, P. wrote two pageants for the installation of Lord Mayors of London (in 1585 and 1591); a verse epistle to a British expeditionary force under the command of Sir Francis Drake and Sir John Norris (1589); addressed *An Eglogue Gratulatorie* (1589) to the Earl of Essex; and, in *Polhymnia* (1590), *The Honour of the Garter* (1593), and *Anglorum Feriae* (not published until the 19th c.), wrote verses for the chivalric ceremonies fashionable at the court of Elizabeth. All are interesting and competent; at moments, they rise to a much higher level, as in the beautiful lyric "His golden locks Time hath to silver turned" that forms part of *Polyhmnia*. In P.'s plays are other lyrics that are among the finest of their time (itself one of the great ages of the English lyric).

BIBLIOGRAPHY: Braunmuller, A. R., *G. P.* (1983); Hunter, G. K., *Lyly and P.* (1968); Senn, W., *Studies in the Dramatic Construction of Robert Greene and G. P.* (1973)

GLYN PURSGLOVE

PEMBROKE, Mary Herbert, Countess of

b. 27 October 1561, Bewdley, Worcestershire; d. 25 September 1621, London

Although P. was greatly influential in her circle in the 16th and 17th cs., there was little critical mention of her for two hundred years until the first printing of her major work, on the Book of Psalms, in 1823; since then, she has gradually attracted wider attention. Not that her circle was a small one. Sir Philip SIDNEY, her brother, had complained in his *Apologie for Poetrie* about the lamentable state of affairs in England regarding that art; and it would seem that brother and sister, together with their other brother Robert, set about to change the situation. They gathered, at Wilton, the Herbert family home, over twenty years, a coterie of thinkers, writers, and musicians whose influence was widespread into the 17th c. Critics have noted such names as John DONNE, Edmund SPENSER, William SHAKESPEARE, Ben JONSON, and George HERBERT, among others, who came under the Sidney-Herbert influence.

P. was unusually well educated, adept in literature, languages, and music. Her contributions to literature include not only her patronage of other poets, and inspiration (she is mentioned in the poems of several important poets of her time, including William BROWNE's famous epitaph on her grave), but also editing, translating, and composition. She edited Sidney's poems and revised his *Arcadia,* which he had dedicated to her, after his death. She translated from Italian, in terza rima, Petrarch's *Triumph of Death,* and, from French, in quantitative verse, Robert Garnier's tragedy *Antonius* and Philippe de Mornay's *A Discourse of Life and Death,* published together in 1592. Additionally, she circulated a few poems of her own composition, the best known of which is a pastoral dialogue intended as a welcoming present to Queen ELIZABETH I, who was expected as a guest at Wilton.

Falling somewhere between translation and original composition, and much the best known of her writings, possibly as important to her standing as her patronage of other artists, is P.'s redaction of the Psalms. Sidney began this project; after his death, P. took it over. She published it giving the impression that most of the work was his; in fact, most of it was hers. Only forty-three of the 150 psalms are now attributed to Sidney, and these are generally seen as inferior to P.'s. A manifestation of the new Protestant emphasis on the individual encounter with scripture was the plethora of psalm translations in the 16th c. Most of these translations, however, were of little literary merit, aiming merely at ease of understanding and memorization. They took the "fourteener," or hymn stanza, form. P.'s psalms are different. Intended for private reading rather than public recitation, they eschew the hymn stanza in favor of complex forms, and ease of memorization in favor of vivid imagery, intense emotion, and complex syntax. Thus, they are as much original composition as translation, and can easily be seen as "metaphysical" poetry in embryo. The religious poetry of Donne and Herbert in particular shows the influence of P.'s style.

BIBLIOGRAPHY: Brennan, M. G., *Literary Patronage in the English Renaissance* (1988); Rathmell, J. C. A., *The Psalms of Sir Philip Sidney and the Countess of Pembroke* (1963); Waller, G., *Mary Sidney, Countess of Pembroke* (1979)

CECELIA LAMPP LINTON

PEPYS, Samuel

b. 23 February 1633, London; d. 26 May 1703, London

The diary kept by P. from 1660 to 1669 offers an unparalleled example of the diarist's art, combining historical record and observation of human psychology. The language is direct, vivid, and precise, and the picture of public events in the decade that saw the end of the English republican experiment and restoration of the monarchy unsurpassed. The cast of characters is of Shakespearean breadth: servants, shop girls, clerks and children, naval officers, civil servants, politicians, scientists, theater people, courtiers, and royalty crowd its pages. The astonishing frankness of the self-portrait derives from P.'s humanist curiosity about himself, in which he resembles Montaigne; the brilliance of the presentation from his ability to stand aside and observe himself in action, dramatizing the scenes of his private and professional life with the skill of a novelist.

P. was a Londoner, born off Fleet Street, the son of uneducated parents, his father a tailor. His boyhood coincided with the Civil Wars when London backed Parliament against the king, and P. was present, and rejoiced, at the execution of Charles I. His abilities were noticed early, and he attended St. Paul's school and Magdalene College, Cambridge. Here, he wrote a "romance," the first known evidence of his literary ambitions. His health was bad. A kidney stone caused chronic pain that grew worse at Cambridge, and may explain why he did not move straight into a position worthy of his talents after taking his degree. Instead, he did odd jobs for his cousin and patron, Edward Montagu (or Mountagu), soldier, statesman, and friend of Oliver Cromwell.

During this period, in 1655, P. married, for love alone, a fourteen-year-old, Elizabeth de St. Michel, daughter of an improvident Frenchman. She was a beauty, lively and literate, but neither had a penny, and he had no home. He smuggled her into his servant's room at the Montagus' lodgings. Both became ill; they quarreled and she walked out, leaving him humiliated. From this low point, he retrieved himself, getting a second job and undergoing surgery for the stone, a gamble with his life that succeeded. By 1659, he was living with Elizabeth again, in a rented house and with a servant.

His letters to Montagu relating events in London reveal his gifts as a reporter, and from this it was only a step to writing for himself. He had no model, for while others were keeping diaries concerned with politics (Bulstrode Whitelocke), travel and public events (John EVELYN), spiritual progress (many Puritan divines), and family life (Ralph Josselin), none of these were known to P. The opening page of the diary, written in a plain stationer's notebook, announces its double theme, public and private, by alluding within the same paragraph to General Monck and his approaching troops and to Elizabeth's delayed period, as matters of equal importance to the diarist.

He wrote in shorthand, a popular system that had been in use since the 1630s, Thomas Shelton's Tachygraphy. Hardly a day is missed, and when entries were delayed P. kept notes and also shaped his material in his head. The diary runs to 1,250,000 words and fills six fat notebooks that he later had bound in brown leather.

During the last months of the Commonwealth, P. was at the center of events—when Montagu declared for Charles II, P. accompanied him to Holland to fetch the king from exile. P. was then appointed to the Navy Board, becoming a servant of the Crown. The diary shows him learning his profession, conscious of his own intellectual powers, and scathing about colleagues and the king. His family life, with its pleasures of theaters, taverns, and dinners, shopping for books, silver, fabrics, and furniture, commissioning of portraits, musical parties, trouble with servants, trips out of town, and excursions on the river, is laid out in detail. So are his love affairs, shameful, comic, and painful. He offers a classic account of a turbulent marriage. Money is another central theme. Among the great set pieces are descriptions of the Great Plague of 1665 and the Great Fire of 1666.

He closed the diary on the last day of May 1669, believing he was in danger of losing his sight. Giving it up was like a form of death, he wrote, "almost as much as to see myself go into my grave." He was not in fact going blind but suffering from long sight and astigmatism, then untreatable. In November 1669, Elizabeth died of a fever. He acquired a young mistress, Mary Skinner, who remained with him for the rest of his life, but there was no second marriage; and although there were fragmentary diaries later, they are hardly more than jottings.

In 1673, P. entered Parliament and was appointed Secretary to the Admiralty. He established himself as an outstanding administrator, but his position depended on the patronage of the Crown, and he was vulnerable to attacks by its enemies. In 1679, he was driven out, accused of treason; to clear his name, he collected a vast dossier of statements from scores of witnesses, still in manuscript in the Pepys Library in Cambridge. In 1684, his position was restored to him, but in 1688 he fell again when James II was driven into exile.

P. refused the oath of allegiance to William III and was twice imprisoned. He was then allowed a quiet retirement, enlarged his library, entertained, and corresponded with scholars young and old, among them Evelyn. In the last week of his life, in 1703, he arranged for his library to go to his old college with a strict proviso that no book should ever be removed

from it. In this way, he ensured the preservation of the diary, whose six volumes formed part of the collection, and clearly showed his awareness of its value to posterity. It remained in Cambridge unnoticed until 1819, when the publication of Evelyn's diary led to its discovery. The first transcription took three years, and a heavily cut version was published in 1825. It was seen at once to be of great historical interest. Further editions followed, a second transcription was made in the 1870s. P.'s frankness on sexual matters was thought to make a complete edition out of the question, and only after the passing of the Obscene Publications Act in 1959 was a complete text considered possible. Two scholars, Robert Latham and William Matthews, were responsible for the definitive edition, published in eleven volumes (1970–83). Their heroic labors establish beyond any doubt its position as a masterpiece standing beside the works of Geoffrey CHAUCER, William SHAKESPEARE, and Charles DICKENS.

BIBLIOGRAPHY: Bryant, A., *S. P.* (3 vols., 1933); Heath, H. J., *Letters of S. P. and His Family Circle* (1955); Howarth, E. G., *Letters and the Second Diary of S. P.* (1932); Ollard, R., *P.* (1974); Tomalin, C., *S. P.* (2002)

CLAIRE TOMALIN

PERCY, Thomas

b. 24 April 1729, Bridgnorth; d. 30 September 1811, Dromore, Ireland

Though as a young man he wrote a few sonnets addressed to the idealized "Flavia" and a poem, "O Nancy, wilt thou go with me," which Robert BURNS considered the most beautiful of English songs, P. is best remembered today as one of the foremost scholars and editors of late-18th-c. Britain. His body of work included an edition and translation (from a Portuguese version) of a Chinese novel (1761), which he also thoroughly annotated; a brief, but innovative, collection of Icelandic poetry (1763); and an annotated translation of *The Song of Solomon* (1764), which he treated as a pastoral. These were but preludes to his important anthology, *Reliques of Ancient English Poetry* (3 vols., 1765), the most significant product of the enthusiasm for popular balladry that climaxed in the neoclassical period. P.'s *Reliques* also became a major influence on English ROMANTICISM.

According to his own account, P. is supposed to have noticed a weathered manuscript lying on the floor of the parlor in the Staffordshire home where he was visiting. The maids were using pages from it to light the fire. Upon examining the manuscript, P. discovered a collection of popular poetry that was apparently part of a commonplace book in which a minstrel or amateur performer might have written down the words for songs to be recalled for subsequent performance. The pages discovered by P.—which became known as the Percy Folio Manuscript when they were published in their entirety in 1867–68—contained seventeen romances, twenty-four metrical histories, forty-five ballads, and more than a hundred miscellaneous songs.

P. held onto the manuscript for a decade or so before Samuel JOHNSON and others convinced him to publish material from it. The *Reliques,* which appeared in three volumes and went through three subsequent editions during P.'s lifetime, included material from the folio manuscript, from previously published collections of popular poetry like *The Tea-Table Miscellany* (1740), from a Scottish contributor who provided P. with eight previously unpublished ballads, and from some known authors (for example, Michael DRAYTON, Christopher MARLOWE, and Sir Walter RALEIGH). P. wrote introductions to each poem or set of related poems and included four important essays on English literary history, treating English minstrels, alliterative verse, romance literature, and early English drama.

Poetic quality was the principal criterion behind P.'s selection of material for inclusion in the *Reliques,* and he arranged his choices in a rough chronological order. In order to reach his target audience of antiquarians and sophisticated readers, P. edited the material to regularize the meter, to substitute familiar for unfamiliar language, and to fill in lacunae resulting from the damage that had befallen the manuscript. He noted his changes only cursorily. His editorial practice, though motivated by his recognition that popular ballads and lyrics could be serious poetry if judiciously presented to the reading public, drew the criticism of Joseph Ritson, who chided him for altering texts without clearly specifying changes to his readers. Influenced by contemporary questions concerning the poetry attributed to the Scots bard Ossian that had been published at about the same time as the *Reliques,* Ritson even went so far as to accuse P. of having fabricated the folio manuscript. Though he did not feel obligated to display the document, these charges encouraged P. to produce the fourth edition of the *Reliques* (1795), wherein he attempted to be more punctilious in his editing.

Following the success of the *Reliques,* which made P. somewhat of a celebrity in scholarly circles, he turned his attention to what he regarded as more serious matters. Ordained as a priest in 1753, P. had benefited from the sponsorship of several influential patrons and became Bishop of Dromore, Ireland, in 1782. Meanwhile, he had written *A Key to the New Testament* (1766), an instructional work accessible to both clergy and laity. He managed, though, to complement his clerical responsibilities with continued literary scholarship—though at a considerably reduced rate from what he had been doing in the 1760s.

For instance, he translated a French work on Nordic culture as *Northern Antiquities* (1770), a volume that helped to introduce English readers to the FOLKLORE and mythology of Scandinavia. He also composed a long poem in ballad stanzas, *The Hermit of Warkworth* (1771), which—though parodied by the literary establishment—enjoyed considerable popularity among readers. The poem, however, has not stood the test of critical time.

P. must be remembered primarily as the editor of the *Reliques,* whose impact on the ballad revival of the late 18th c. and upon the development of the Romantic movement in England cannot be overestimated. The three volumes included the first printing of some of the best-known folk ballads in English literature (which have come to be called "Child ballads" from their being anthologized by a later editor). William BLAKE and Sir Walter SCOTT were influenced by the popular poetry in the *Reliques,* as were William WORDSWORTH and Samuel Taylor COLERIDGE, who took their famous title, *Lyrical Ballads,* from P.'s work. Their reading of the *Reliques,* a work of scholarship that had repercussions much beyond its scholarly intentions, shaped the ballad imitations that both poets contributed to that volume.

BIBLIOGRAPHY: Davis, B. C., *T. P.* (1981); Fowler, D. C., *A Literary History of the Popular Ballad* (1968); Friedman, A. B., *The Ballad Revival* (1961)

WILLIAM M. CLEMENTS

PHILIPS, John

b. 30 December 1676, Bampton, Oxfordshire; d. 15 February 1708, Hereford

Widely read in his time, P. was influential in the development of early British 18th-c. poetry. Joseph ADDISON in the *Tatler* praised P.'s poem *The Splendid Shilling* (1705), written in imitation of John MILTON, as "the finest burlesque poem in the British language." However, P. was commissioned to write *Blenheim,* published in that same year, a Tory counterblast to Addison's *Campaign.* P.'s *Cyder* (1708), one of the 18th c.'s earliest didactic poems, is modeled on Virgil's *Georgics. Cerealia* (1706), although printed without his name, is generally ascribed to P., whose poems usually contained a eulogy of tobacco.

PHILIPS, Katherine

b. ca. 1 January 1632, London; d. 22 June 1664, London

The first woman to have a play professionally staged in Britain, P. is best known for her learned precocity (she was said to have read the Bible through by the age of four), for her creation of a literary circle, the Society of Friendship, and for her poems, translations, and letters. Both her verse and her virtue were celebrated by such notable contemporaries as Henry VAUGHAN, Jeremy TAYLOR, Abraham COWLEY, John DRYDEN, Anne KILLIGREW, and Anne FINCH, and she was lauded as a modern Sappho, "the Incomparable" and "the matchless Orinda," the latter in reference to her literary sobriquet.

When the sixteen-year-old Katherine Fowler, a royalist, married fifty-four-year-old Parliamentarian James Philips, a relative of her mother's third husband, she settled with him in Wales. There she wrote extensively and circulated her works through her coterie, the Society of Friendship. The exact nature of that group remains controversial. Some argue it may have been similar to a literary salon with members meeting regularly to discuss their writing and intellectual matters. Others suggest P.'s rural isolation precludes this, and members were probably only linked through correspondence and by their royalist values. Great pains, however, have been taken by literary historians to identify members since they assumed fictional code names, such as Antenor (Philips), Lucasia (Anne Owen), Rosania (Mary Aubrey), Silvander (Sir Edward Dering), and Poliarchus (Sir Charles Cotterell).

P.'s verse was often occasional, directed to specific individuals and events, including the deaths of her infant son Hector and of her twelve-year-old stepdaughter. She wrote in a wide range of genres: epithalamia, elegies, epitaphs, philosophical poems, pastoral dialogues, verse letters, poems of parting. Some of her works were set to music, several by the composer Henry LAWES and two by Henry Purcell. Best known for her treatment of the theme of friendship, especially the equality of female friendship, P., while working with modes and conventions typical of male authors, most notably John DONNE, brought to her work a clearly female perspective. Her epithalamia, for example, all focus on the bride. And she appropriates the language of 17th-c. love poetry to present Orinda's relationship to female friends such as Lucasia and Rosania. Influenced by Neoplatonism, P. believed love between women was pure. She is also said to have been influenced by the Précieuse school, a French literary movement made fashionable in England by Queen Henrietta Maria, the French wife of Charles I. P. has numerous political poems that make her royalist sympathies clear—poems written during the Civil Wars, poems celebrating the Restoration, and poems addressed to members of the royal family. Angered by a 1664 pirated edition of seventy-five of her poems, she determined to oversee an authorized edition, a project cut short by her death.

In addition to her poems, she wrote numerous letters to her friends, including Dorothy (Osborne) Temple. Those to her friend and literary mentor, Sir Charles Cotterell, Master of Ceremonies for Charles II, were published posthumously as *Letters from Orinda to Poliarchus* (1705). Cotterell had assisted her in the authorized edition of her poems. P. also translated works from Italian and French. Her translation of Pierre Corneille's *Mort de Pompée* was performed in Dublin in 1663. She was at work on a translation of Corneille's *Horace* when she died of smallpox at thirty-two in 1664. The work was completed by Sir John DENHAM for a 1668 production at court.

Though her life was truncated, she left a significant body of work. Current recognition that early modern writers were not exclusively male has led to a new accessibility of materials by writers like P. as well as burgeoning scholarship about such works. Her poems, letters, and plays are now available in modern editions.

BIBLIOGRAPHY: Andreadis, H., "The Sapphic-Platonics of K. P., 1632–1664," *Signs* 15 (Autumn 1989): 34–60; Hageman, E. H., "K. P.: The Matchless Orinda," in Wilson, K. M., ed., *Women Writers of the Renaissance and Reformation* (1987): 566–608; Souers, P. W., *The Matchless Orinda* (1931); Thomas, P., *K. P. ("Orinda")* (1988)

FRANCES M. MALPEZZI

PHILLIPS, Caryl
b. 13 March 1958, St. Kitts

A prolific writer of many genres, P. is best known as a novelist whose works examine the roots of Western imperialism and illustrate the human consequences of oppressive systems such as slavery, forced migration, and holocaust. P.'s own personal history is one of displacement; born in St. Kitts, he was brought to England as an infant and reared in working-class neighborhoods. P. does not fully identify himself with either location but rather allows himself to be referred to as either a Caribbean or a black British writer.

Though often associated with themes of African diaspora, P. has also gained attention for a narrative technique that emphasizes fragmentation and disruption over resolution and unity. In all but his first two novels, he juxtaposes multiple stories from different time periods, places, and/or perspectives, usually without creating explicit connections between them, to contain and reflect his main subject—people whose lives have been ruptured by monumental historical movements.

In his later novels, P. closely aligns form with content by segmenting his narratives into three or four different stories. *Higher Ground* (1989) combines the unrelated stories of an unnamed African working as a translator at a slave fort, an African American man serving a jail term of indeterminate length in the 1960s, and a Polish Jewess suffering mental disintegration in the xenophobic environment of post–World War II London. Involuntarily exiled from their home communities, they all search for some higher ground from the suffering that threatens to destroy them.

The various stories contained in *Cambridge* (1991) are all situated in the Caribbean of the 19th c., but they differ in perspective. The narrators include an English woman visiting her father's plantation, a freed slave named Cambridge who was recaptured and sold in the Caribbean, and a journalist for a local newspaper. Each gives a different reading of the novel's climatic event: the death of the plantation's overseer. By juxtaposing Cambridge's account with the others, P. exposes the inherent racism of Europeans and calls into question official versions of 19th-c. history. On the other hand, by depicting Cambridge and the English woman as equally educated, articulate, and frustrated by the limitations placed on them, he establishes links between slavery and the 19th-c. practices that confined and silenced women.

Crossing the River (1993)—which won the James Tait Black Memorial Prize (1994)—opens with a prologue by an African man who laments selling his children into slavery. The novel's four narratives feature a freed slave who is sent to Liberia to evangelize, a captain of a slave ship, an African American woman who participates in the settlement of the American west after Emancipation, and a white Englishwomen who is forced to give her son up for adoption when her black GI husband is killed. All these characters, excepting the captain, are engaged in a personal middle passage experience, and by the end of the novel, the African father of the prologue reclaims them all as the children he once abandoned.

P. further complicates his sixth novel, *The Nature of Blood* (1997), by weaving his multiple stories together and by examining the causes and effects of racism and anti-Semitism throughout European history. Two of the stories are set in post-World War II Europe; one describes Eva Stern, a European Jew just liberated from a concentration camp, while the other features the interactions between Eva's uncle and an Ethiopian Jew named Malka who was airlifted out of Ethiopia during the drought of the 1980s. The other two stories take place in Venice during the Renaissance. One brings to life William SHAKESPEARE's Othello, describing his stay in the hostile city and his secret marriage to Desdemona, while the other recounts the tale of three Italian Jews in 1480 who are wrongly accused of ritually sacrificing a Christian boy. The fate of the Italian Jews establishes an historical precedent for Eva's story; similarly, Othello's mistreatment in 17th-c. Italy is paralleled by the poor reception that Malka and the Ethiopian Jews receive in modern-day Israel. Moreover, P. seeks to link the Jewish and the African diasporas by demonstrating that both peoples have been exploited for their usefulness while being ostracized from the people of the societies they inhabit. The numerous parallels in *The Nature of Blood* suggest that the construct of difference is not really about race or creed but is rather the mechanism of power that a dominant group uses arbitrarily to confirm its own sense of identity.

In all of his writing, P. looks at global manifestations of oppression through the lens of individual lives, and he discovers enlightening historical connections in the gaps that exist between the multiple stories of his texts. At the same time, he resists any easy solutions to these historical realities by recognizing that his characters are not all good or all evil but rather inhabit the ambiguous positions that are inherent in oppressive circumstances.

BIBLIOGRAPHY: Okazaki, H., "On Dislocation and Connectedness in C. P.'s Writing," *LCrit* 26, 3 (1991): 34–47; Patteson, R., *Caribbean Passages: A Critical Perspective on New Fiction from the West Indies* (1998)

RENÉE SCHATTEMAN

PHILLIPS, Stephen

b. 28 July 1864, Summertown, Oxfordshire; d. 9 December 1915, London

Greeted in the opening years of the 20th c. as the Great White Hope of the English-speaking theater, the man who would bring living poetry back to the stage, P. died a dozen or so years later penniless and already virtually forgotten. Yet his first two plays had been universally greeted with the most extravagant adulation: the theater reviews teemed with flattering comparisons invoking great and famous names—Ben JONSON, William SHAKESPEARE, even Sophocles.

Curiously, the same phenomenon repeated itself some fifty years later when another poet-playwright burst suddenly on the scene, provoked an initial and immediate stir (again the same great and famous names for comparison), dominated the London theater for a few years, and faded away a decade later leaving scarcely a trace behind. Fickle though the theatergoing public always is, perhaps there is—nevertheless—some reason to suppose that there is a permanent yearning for poetry and fine language in the theater. Perhaps it is not a mere accident that the verse plays of P. and, later, of Christopher FRY reminded their audiences that much the greater number of plays written for the Western theater, from Aeschylus onward, have been written not in prose but in verse and that there may well be sound artistic reasons for this. That having been said, however, it must be admitted that in P.'s case, though the intent was sincere and the effort laudable, the result—seen in retrospect—is uninspired and uninspiring. Even the best of his plays, *Paolo and Francesca* (pub. 1899; perf. 1902), reads very oddly now. Its verse is, with the exception of a line or two here and there, mere exercise stuff—

technically correct but turgid, flat, ordinary, and banal. It is, quite literally, unspeakably dull. It is also pompous and sentimental.

All P.'s plays, eleven in number, are susceptible to these same criticisms and all of them were subject, to their great disadvantage, to the influence of the popular and vulgar taste of the times for what Bernard SHAW called the "splendacious" approach to stage scene design in the late 19th and early 20th cs.: overliteral, overrealistic, and overpraised. The poet and critic Arthur SYMONS, writing an introduction to P.'s posthumously published play, *Harold* (1927), having remarked that "*Harold* is manifestly inferior to the former plays," goes on to say, "Phillip's creatures do but decorate the stage, on which they profess to move and live and have their being. They have said graceful verse with literary intentions, and they have committed violent actions with theatrical intentions; and nothing they have done has moved us, and nothing they have said has moved us, and we can always discuss the acting and the staging."

Discussing, in the same introduction, P.'s volume of verse—simply called *Poems*, published in 1897, before any of the plays were written—Symons refers to it as "poetizing" rather than poetry and says: "Poetizing is like telling lies: however interesting it may be, there is something radically wrong about it." He also comments on the highly imitative nature of P.'s verse: "Verse must be not only good; it must, in some way or other, be new. If you have not something new to say, and a new way of saying it, why say anything at all? P. writes single lines which are really exquisite, startlingly fine lines. But it may be added that he writes fine passages as well as fine lines. Certainly he does this, but he has as yet written no passage that is not molded upon John MILTON, upon Walter Savage LANDOR, upon Robert BROWNING's early work, upon some definite model. Perhaps molded is too definite a word to use. Let us say rather that he plays his own variations but always upon another's air." By 1927, when this was written, it represented a view that was widespread and generally accepted. And even twenty-five years earlier, when the clamor of popular adulation was at its height, there were already dissentient voices urging sterner judgments.

Before publishing *Poems*, the book that first made him famous, P. had briefly been an actor: he was for two years a member of F. R. Benson's Shakespeare Company (Benson was his cousin). This gave him a taste for, and some practical knowledge of, the theater but his interest quickly developed not in the direction of acting, but of playwriting. After one or two false starts, he wrote and published *Paolo and Francesca*. It was almost immediately taken up by George Alexander, the actor-manager, who bought the acting rights to the play in 1900 (though he did not actually produce it until 1902). Meanwhile, P. had obtained two commissions from Herbert Beerbohm Tree, the rival actor-manager, at His Majesty's Theatre. The plays were *Herod* and *Ulysses*. The former opened at His Majesty's on October 31, 1900, and the latter on February 1, 1902. *Paolo and Francesca* followed a month later, on March 6, at the St. James's Theatre. P., overnight, had suddenly become (though somewhat temporarily as it turned out) the most famous playwright in London. Other plays rapidly followed, though the downward curve of fame and approbation was sudden, soon, and steep—*Aylmer's Secret* (perf. 1905; pub. 1921), *Nero* (1906), *Pietro of Siena* (pub. 1910; perf. 1911), and *Everywoman: Her Pilgrimage in Search of Love* (perf. 1912). But that, effectively, was the end.

Between 1912 and his death, P. published four new plays but they were never played. There were no more collections of verse to serve as successors to the two volumes of 1897 and 1908. And after his death, though his old publisher, John Lane, brought out in 1921 a collection of six P. plays, there were no major revivals of any of them in London or New York. Symons, in that devastating introduction, had said: "Then I stated the case for the defense, giving a series of quotations from writers such as [John] Churton Collins, [William] ARCHER, Sidney COLVIN and others, which still seem to me, as they seemed to me then, to contain the most unmerited praise ever given to any writer. And, besides this, famous names were brought for incidental comparison on hardly less than terms of equality, such as Sophocles, Lucretius, Virgil, Dante, Milton, Landor, and in addition to these, [John] WEBSTER."

BIBLIOGRAPHY: Archer, W., *Real Conversations* (1904); Beerbohm, M., *More Theatres* (1979); Thouless, P., *Modern Poetic Drama* (1934)

ERIC SALMON

PHILLPOTTS, Eden

b. 4 November 1862, Mont Aboo, Rajputana, India; d. 29 December 1960, Broad Clyst, Exeter

P. now receives very little scholarly and critical attention, and of his more than two hundred and fifty works only eleven appear in a reprint series now. But in the first three decades of the 20th c., he was popular, well received by critics, and praised by such contemporaries as Arnold BENNETT and William Dean Howells. His phenomenal creative energy became evident early in life. At seventeen, he began work for the Sun Life Insurance Company and after an abortive attempt at acting was soon contributing stories to magazines. By 1890, he could support himself as an author and as assistant editor of the weekly, *Black and White*. P. showed no interest in becoming a public figure. In 1892, he married Emily Topham by whom he had a son and a daughter. By 1899, he and his family had moved to Devonshire, where he remained the rest of his life, never again returning to London. His wife died in 1928, and in 1929 he married Lucy Robina Webb. He lived quietly, continuing to write prolifically well into his nineties.

His first major success, *Lying Prophets* (1897), set in a Cornwall fishing village, develops themes common to the novels that immediately followed. In 1898, P. published *Children of the Mist*, first in a series of twenty Dartmoor novels concluded with *Children of Men* (1923), a series generally regarded as his finest work. With heavy emphasis on the stark, rocky background of Dartmoor, these works are stories of irrational, destructive emotions among the peasantry, including obsessive love, sexual jealousy (justified or unjustified), passion for money, and passion for vengeance.

In *The Secret Woman* (1905), the middle-aged, highly religious Ann Redvers murders Anthony, her adulterous husband, and goes undetected, but feels she must confess. She is held back by her two grown sons, one of whom, Jesse, has an unrequited love for Salome Westaway, a woman he does not realize was his father's mistress. In *Demeter's Daughter* (1911), Alison Cleave remains faithful to her worthless husband Aaron, through poverty, betrayal, and degradation, despite opportunities to leave him.

P.'s reputation has suffered through the comparison of these novels with Thomas HARDY's Wessex novels. It is almost certain that P.'s work is not derivative. He claimed to have discovered his own material years before reading Hardy, and the resemblances between their works are superficial. Both deal with tragedy among the peasantry, but Hardy's peasant culture has a lyrical charm, and P.'s is baldly realistic. Hardy's tragic figures are victims of a malevolent fate. P.'s worldview is Darwinian and agnostic. From an authorial distance, he observes the fates his characters bring on themselves. Yet Hardy's name and P.'s have often been paired to P.'s disadvantage.

His other works include ten volumes of negligible poetry, a series of detective novels, written under the pseudonym of Harrington Hext that were praised by Willard Huntington Wright ("S. S. Van Dine") as among the finest in the language, and numerous plays. His greatest success as a playwright was a comedy, *The Farmer's Wife* (1916), first produced at the Birmingham Repertory Theatre in 1916 and then at the Court Theatre in London in 1924, where it ran for 1,329 performances. Samuel Sweetland, a widowed farmer, sets out with a list of prospective wives whom he offends with a hilarious lack of social intelligence, and then becomes engaged to the housekeeper, Araminta Dench, with whom he first studied his list.

For all its former popularity, this play (like P.'s novels) stirs no current interest. Other factors in addition to the comparison with Hardy have worked against his reputation. He had a habit of self-deprecation and did not seek public attention, and the versatility and quantity of his work raised suspicions about its quality. He is now remembered as a minor figure.

BIBLIOGRAPHY: Girvan, I. W., ed., *E. P.* (1953); Portman, J. "E. P.: A Reassessment Is Long Overdue," *T&T* 42 (January 1961): 33–34

DALTON AND MARYJEAN GROSS

PHILOSOPHY AND LITERATURE

Philosophy and literature have since the Middle Ages each lent their names to wide and historically varying fields of cultural endeavor, with the modern understanding of each being consolidated only in the 19th c. Before this time, the field of philosophy extended beyond logic, ethics, and metaphysics to theology and "natural philosophy" (or the sciences), and at times to such things as alchemy and mysticism, while the term literature was commonly applied to nonfiction writing, including philosophy, as well as to the imaginative works it now principally refers to. In our own time, largely through the influence of poststructuralism, philosophy is again being recognized and critiqued as literature, while conversely imaginative literature is being treated by critics, just as it has been recognized by many of its practitioners throughout history, as offering a range of flexible and subtle discursive practices that can both examine and extend the field of philosophical inquiry.

Geoffrey CHAUCER's Clerk of Oxenford in *The Canterbury Tales* would prefer to have "Twenty bookes, clad in black or reed, / Of Aristotle and his philosophie / Than robes riche." This Oxford graduate's enthusiasm for Aristotle highlights the question of universals, of the origin and status of our ideas and words designating general qualities, which preoccupied intellectuals during the Middle Ages. Aristotle's moderate realism maintains that universals inhere as forms within their particular instances, the form of chair-ness in each and every chair. For the Christian Middle Ages, the relation of universal forms or ideas to God's thought was a crucial question. While the Neoplatonists and St. Thomas Aquinas offered different answers to this question, both schools argued that language was the truthful sign of a real world, a stark contrast to the nominalism of WILLIAM OF OCKHAM, which regards language as an artificial construction and universals as mere names that do not necessarily have an existence outside of the mind. For literature, the art that has language as its medium, there was a great deal at stake in such arguments. Chaucer in particular focuses upon the great philosophical question of literature, namely its relation to reality and truth. While many of the tales in *The Canterbury*

Tales can be seen to represent and explore current philosophical doctrines, as for example the practical consequences of nominalism in "The Clerk's Tale," the subtle and ambiguous possibilities of poetic language, and the "wheel-within-wheel" framing structure of the tales, work to complicate and interrogate the current philosophical debate about language and universals. We, the readers, are positioned with the other characters as listeners to the tales who each have our own story. In this way, the poem presents narrative as a fundamental existential mode of meaning-making, an idea that is entrenched in the postmodern theory and art of our own time. Chaucer also translated Boethius's *Consolation of Philosophy* (ca. early 1380s), which informs his *Troilus and Criseyde* and the "Knight's Tale" in particular and which argues that the apparent contingencies of fortune should be referred to the context of a greater divinely ordained order.

John DONNE's poem "An Anatomy of the World: The First Anniversary" (1611) highlights the transition from medieval to modern thought that occurs during the 16th and 17th cs.: "And new philosophy calls all in doubt," he writes, as the new science of Copernicus, Kepler, and Galileo threaten the stable Christian cosmology of the Middle Ages, which, building upon Ptolemaic system and the biblical account of Genesis, saw the earth to be created by God as the center of the universe and expressly for mankind. The old philosophy was a Christian medieval collection of classical theories of physical and biological nature that by Elizabethan times formed a well-assimilated and integrated package of ideas. For William SHAKE-SPEARE and his contemporaries, they offered a view of the world that was itself aesthetic, drawing all parts of nature into inherently significant relations of correspondence and hierarchy. The world manifested a divinely implanted logic of analogy, which replicated the hierarchical relation of God to Creation in every sphere of the living and social world, with humankind the ruler of nature, the sovereign the ruler of his subjects, the mind the ruler of the body, and so on. The aesthetic symmetry of this cosmology and the authority it gives to analogy makes art the most apt medium for representing the world, and provides a hefty foundation from which Shakespeare not only presents such doctrines but builds his magisterial sequences of parallelisms, where an idea will be illustrated with not one but a series of lyrical analogies. This cosmology also encouraged the seeing of likeness in things that were apparently very different, and so facilitated the audacious metaphors, puns, and other witty conceits found in Donne and the other "metaphysical" poets.

Idealism, the ancient and broad philosophical tradition that locates the truth of things in ideas or forms that the human mind can apprehend, underpins the sort of reasoning by analogy found in medieval and Renaissance literature, and a couple of centuries later in much Romantic and Victorian literature. These forms of holism, of seeing all as integral to an overarching principle of unity, are contested with the rise of modern experimental science and scientific method, which the rationalist Francis BACON first outlines in his *Novum Organum*, the title of which precociously announces that Aristotle's Organum and the medieval scholasticism it informed has been superseded. This is a model of knowledge that begins not with the wholes of ideas but the particulars of experience, a model that finds its literary forms in the aphorisms (or distinct and concise statements of principles) in which the book is written, and in the essay form that Bacon introduced to England, which reflects upon discrete experiences, or "broken knowledges," as he puts it in an early essay, rather than vast cosmologies and systems. With the breakdown of the old order, modern attitudes of doubt and uncertainty and a suspicion of system-making come to permeate English literature and culture. Later, in the 17th c., such rakish Restoration intellectuals as John Wilmot, Earl of ROCHESTER, and John DRYDEN treat current claims to philosophical truth with playfulness and skepticism, while in the next century Jonathan SWIFT's *Gulliver's Travels* satirizes systematizing philosophy as absurdly ambitious jargon, and Samuel JOHNSON's *The History of Rasselas, Prince of Abyssinia*, a philosophical tale about human freedom and the possibility of happiness, ends indecisively with a conclusion "in which nothing is concluded." In the early 19th c., John KEATS formulates his idea of "negative capability," the capacity to live in uncertainty, mystery, and doubt that he considers fundamental to modern life.

While poetry lends itself to the expression of universals, as its analogies bring particulars into relations of unity and universality, prose fiction is suited to recording the particulars of individual experience. The empiricism of Baconian science, the principle that knowledge ultimately comes from sensory experience (rather than ideas), is presupposed by the new 18th-c. form of the novel, which Daniel DEFOE bases upon the form of the AUTOBIOGRAPHY and Samuel RICHARDSON establishes as a form of empirical realism that claims to represent the accidents and passions of everyday life. The preoccupation in the novel of this period with a central individual, who usually gives his or her name to its title, is part of a wider philosophical discussion of selfhood in 18th-c. Britain concerned with questions of the nature of selfhood and consciousness, and the grounds for individual freedom and self-determination. Sense experience is necessarily of matter, which is accordingly the object of knowledge for empiricism. Materialism, which was also promoted by the growing mercantile economy of the time that itself sprang in part from the ethos and success of Baconian science, is entrenched in many novels, from the survivalism of Defoe's *Robinson Crusoe* and *Moll Flanders* to the popular Gothic novels of the second half of the century. As the counterweight to the optimistic enlightenment faith in reason, human nature was seen in these novels to be irredeemably bodily, obsessed by its desires and vulnerability to physical suffering and death. The GOTHIC NOVEL also explores the sublime, the experience of an exhilarating terror that the philosophers Immanuel Kant and Edmund BURKE theorized at this time.

ROMANTICISM in the late 18th and early 19th cs. marks a self-conscious resurgence of interest in idealist philosophy. William BLAKE looks to mystical and Neoplatonic sources to develop a dialectical schema, in which such "contrary" principles as Heaven and Hell, Innocence and Experience, meet in dynamic syntheses. The mature Samuel Taylor COLERIDGE draws upon classical and post-Kantian idealism to establish a sure basis for a faith in the unity of all being and the truth of perception, an abiding struggle for him that is evident from such poems as "The Aeolian Harp" (1795) and "Constancy to an Ideal Object" (1825). William WORDSWORTH also wants to establish an idealist common principle of being and knowing, "A motion and a spirit, that impels/All thinking things, all objects of all thought,/And rolls through all things" ("Tintern Abbey"). Coleridge's efforts to establish this principle is documented in his *Biographia Literaria*, where he accounts for perception, fantasy and the creation of art in his distinction between the primary and secondary imagination.

Forms of philosophical idealism that had become entrenched in poetry through the efforts of the Romantics were subjected to the onslaught of materialistic scientism during the Victorian period. Such poets as Alfred, Lord TENNYSON, Robert BROWNING, Matthew ARNOLD, and Gerard Manley HOPKINS all endeavored to assert versions of Christian natural theology, which sees nature as evidence for the existence and nature of God, and of Romantic idealism against materialism and positivism (the most strict and scientific form of empiricism), and pre-Darwinian and Darwinian forms of biological evolutionism. Writers of prose fiction were much more receptive than the canonical poets to such rapidly ascendant philosophies. George ELIOT embraced Auguste Comte's social philosophy of positivism, which sees human thought to evolve progressively through stages of the religious, the metaphysical, and the scientific, and patterns of gradual evolution in thought and action are depicted through the characters of her novels. The poems and novels of Thomas HARDY exemplify a naturalistic and fatalistic response to Darwinism. In Walter PATER's essays *Studies in the History of the Renaissance* and novel *Marius the Epicurean*, the author moves through the consequences of contemporary materialism and positivism to establish a philosophy that ad-

vocates chaste but intense aesthetic experience as life's goal. Pater's influence can be discerned in Oscar WILDE, who like Pater and Hopkins before him, gained much from his philosophy studies at Oxford. The title of "The Decay of Lying" refers to Plato, the first thinker to describe art as lying, and this work, like "The Critic as Artist," both published in 1891, adopts the literary form of the Platonic dialogue, a form that can be read as fundamental also to Wilde's plays, his novel *The Picture of Dorian Gray*, and the curtailed dialectic of his aphorisms and paradoxes.

Paterian and Wildean aestheticism marks a retreat from the objective world, vouchsafed in earlier centuries by the grand cosmology of the "old philosophy," into individual consciousness. The loss of a consensus about objective reality brought the principle of consciousness to the fore, with such 20th-c. modernists as the imagist poets of the 1910s analyzing it through the intense lyrical images they created for it, while the novelists Virginia WOOLF and James JOYCE similarly explore consciousness as the locus of individual reality and their provisional concepts of selfhood. In philosophy, Friedrich Nietzsche and Ludwig Wittgenstein each argue that there are a range of styles of inquiry, not just a single method for demonstrating truths, as philosophy and science had presupposed. This argument is implicit in the stylistic experimentation of such figures as Joyce, Woolf, T. S. ELIOT, and Mina Loy, all of whom draw upon different registers of language usage to explore the perspectives by which we can come at the world. Such perspectivism is primarily epistemological, concerned with what and how we can know. Joyce's *Ulysses* and *Finnegans Wake* have also been claimed by contemporary POSTMODERNISM for the way that they treat language as the great originator and shaper of both subjective and objective reality, juxtaposing a huge range of historical, literary, philosophical, popular cultural, commercial, and private idioms to generate different ontological registers, a plurality of worlds. Joyce's work, Samuel BECKETT's later novels, and contemporary works by Angela CARTER, Salman RUSHDIE, Tom STOPPARD, and Martin AMIS have all been read as exemplifying what the philosopher and cultural critic Richard Rorty calls "the linguistic turn," which gathers together such different 20th-c. philosophers as Wittgenstein, J. L. Austin, and the poststructuralists, and maintains that there are no facts or reality outside of language, that language mediates all our knowledge and experience, right down to who we are as individuals. This is a position that brings us back to medieval preoccupations with nominalism and rhetoric.

BIBLIOGRAPHY: Anastaplo, G., *The Artist as Thinker: From Shakespeare to Joyce* (1983); Griffiths, A. P., *Philosophy and Literature* (1984); Hordern, P., ed.

The Novelist as Philosopher (1983); Nussbaum, M. C., *Love's Knowledge: Essays on Philosophy and Literature* (1990); Rosenbaum, S. P., ed., *English Literature and British Philosophy* (1971); Shaw, W. D., *The Lucid Veil: Poetic Truth in the Victorian Age* (1987)

DANIEL BROWN

PICKARD, Tom [Thomas]

(pseud of Thomas MacKenna) b. 7 January 1946, Newcastle-upon-Tyne

As a poet, P.—like his contemporary Barry MAC-SWEENEY—emerged from Newcastle in the 1960s on the tide of the young, popular poetry of the decade. Having left school at fourteen, P. formed a friendship with Basil BUNTING who encouraged him to discover American modernist poetry. In turn, P. encouraged him to write again, a debt repaid when Bunting championed his work. As manager of a local bookshop, P. also established a vibrant poetry scene in the city that was visited by American poets. His first collection, *High on the Walls* (1967), revealed the influence of objectivism in its concision, but was set to a resolutely local landscape of industry and youthful frustration. His second collection, *The Order of Chance* (1971), contained the more politically motivated "The Devil's Destroying Angel Exploded" about poverty. These commitments led to his making later documentary programs about labor history, *Jarrow March* (1976) and *We Make Ships* (1989). P. combined vivid imagery with a neo-Romantic mythology of inspiration in such poems as "Dancing Under Fire," and so may have suffered in the turn of poetic fashion against RO-MANTICISM. Later volumes include *Tiepin Eros: New and Selected Poems* (1994), *Fuckwind* (1999; a Renaissance name for a kestrel), and *Hole in the Wall* (2001). He retains a strong commitment to demotic speech and is unafraid to celebrate eroticism in his verse.

PINERO, [Sir] Arthur Wing

b. 24 May 1855, London; d. 23 November 1934, London

Today, P. is best known as the author of very popular "well-made plays" maligned by Bernard SHAW. His most famous play, hugely successful upon its debut, was *The Second Mrs. Tanqueray* (perf. 1893; pub. 1895), a play that Shaw openly lambastes in his response play, *Mrs. Warren's Profession*. Literary history has thus served P. by posing him as Shaw's scarecrow. But P. was one of Britain's most successful playwrights during the late 19th and early 20th cs. Most of his more than fifty plays were hits, and he was respected not only for his craftsmanship, but for his social commentary as well. In particular, he dem-

onstrated an ongoing interest in the issue of gender inequality, and debate about whether his work can truly be considered "feminist" continues to this day. He championed REALISM and natural dialogue, helping to rid the stage of the bombastic traditions of the 19th c. in which he himself was trained while working as a utility actor from 1874 to 1884. While he never created a true dramatic masterpiece, his popular blend of melodrama and "social issue" drama help pave the way for modern drama in Britain.

Son of a solicitor, P. demonstrated an interest in drama at school, and joined an acting troupe soon after finishing his education. He began writing while an actor, crafting sixteen plays, most of which are rarely read or performed today. They exhibit traditional Victorian plots, following a predictable trajectory toward marital bliss, and are thought by critics to be clunky in construction and artificial in dialogue. However, they do show P.'s incipient interest in the "problem" of the intellectually curious, self-actualized woman, and in their numerous and detailed stage directions they hint at an author who wanted control of every aspect of a production, not just the dialogue.

P.'s next group of plays are known collectively as the "Court farces," because they were written for the financially struggling Court Theatre. The first of these, *The Magistrate* (perf. 1885; pub. 1892), proved a tremendous success and ran for more than three hundred performances. Like *The Schoolmistress* (perf. 1886; pub. 1894) and *Dandy Dick* (perf. 1887; pub. 1893), *The Magistrate* focused on a farcical main character whose obsessively correct behavior created great comic effects. P. had found a safe way of lampooning ideals of respectability by creating comic characters who carried those ideals to their illogical extremes. Other farces, *The Hobby-Horse* (perf. 1886; pub. 1892), *The Cabinet Minister* (perf. 1890; pub. 1892) and *The Amazons* (perf. 1893; pub. 1905), were similar in plot structure but somewhat more serious in tone, making them less successful at the box office. While the farces helped the Court survive its financial difficulties, they have generally been considered interesting only insofar as they provided P. with an opportunity to begin honing the skill in stagecraft that would characterize his work. More recent critics have suggested, however, that the Court farces are not only technically masterly in forging an English farcical style, but denounce the Victorian overemphasis on decorum with an almost modernist conception of social roles as masks on top of masks.

The year 1888 saw the production of P.'s top financial success, *Sweet Lavender* (1893). A sentimental comedy tracing the path of an improbably virtuous but poverty-stricken heroine who turns out to be the daughter of a wealthy man, the play is largely scorned by critics today. Other sentimental dramas, *The*

Weaker Sex (perf. 1888; pub. 1894) and *Lady Bountiful* (1891) are similarly dismissed.

P.'s first play of interest to modern critics is usually considered to be *The Profligate* (perf. 1889; pub. 1891). Here, the playwright attacks the Victorian sexual double standard with a daring most critics attribute to the arrival of Henrik Ibsen's problem plays on British stages. Even more successful and controversial was his next play on the same theme, *The Second Mrs. Tanqueray*. The title character of this play is a "woman with a past" who has reformed and made a good marriage. Her attempt at normal life is destroyed, however, when one of her former lovers reappears, engaged to her husband's daughter. Horrified at the pain that her past has caused her new family, she kills herself.

Critics today, following Shaw's attack on the play, are quick to point out that *The Second Mrs. Tanqueray* is not so much a problem play as a "well-made play" based on the French model of polite entertainment pioneered by Victorien Sardou. To modern audiences, the play is certainly formulaic—but no more so than many of Ibsen's problem plays. The play's social critique is attacked as well: while professing to address the double standard, critics argue, P. actually reproduces it by providing the requisite suicide of the "fallen woman." But to say that the play does not go as far as it might is not to say that it goes nowhere at all. Shaw's scathing dismissal of P.'s play has stuck with it for more than a century, obscuring the fact that *The Second Mrs. Tanqueray* was not only a realist play in its audience's eyes, but a well-considered attack on a very real social problem.

P. had hit his stride with social issue dramas. *The Notorious Mrs. Ebbsmith* (1895) follows the course of a freethinking woman who reverses her position, while *The Benefit of a Doubt* (perf. 1895; pub. 1896) concerns another woman with a past. Many critics point to *Iris* (perf. 1901; pub. 1902) as P.'s most successful play in this model: the play follows the career of a flawed but attractive heroine, torn between a wealthy pursuer and the impecunious man she loves. Also successful were *Letty* (perf. 1903; perf. 1904) and *His House in Order* (1906). He returned to the theme of the double standard with *Mid-Channel* (perf. 1909; pub. 1910), a play about a married couple who both stray; the wife can forgive but the husband cannot.

Though it was a successful formula, P. did not restrict himself to social issue dramas. In *The Gay Lord Quex* (perf. 1899; pub. 1900), he wrote a witty comedy of manners, and in *The Beauty Stone* (1898) he tried his hand at opera. He found great success with *Trelawny of the "Wells"* (1898), where he utilized his knowledge of the mid-19th-c. stage to write a charming sentimental comedy that sets a love story between

actors in a theatrical world changing from bombast to realism.

P. was knighted in 1909 and made a fellow of the Royal Society of Literature in 1910. His plays thus far had made him a wealthy man and he moved in the most exalted literary circles. The story told of the remaining twenty-four years of his life is usually one of decline. But P. continued his literary friendships and his prolific activity, writing fourteen more plays including the commercial successes *The "Mind the Paint" Girl* (perf. 1912; pub. 1913) and *The Big Drum* (1915), the absurdist experiments *Playgoers* (1913) and *A Seat in the Park* (1922), and the serious war plays *Mr. Livermore's Dream* (perf. 1917), *Monica's Blue Boy* (perf. 1918), and *The Enchanted Cottage* (1922).

P.'s later plays showed an admirable willingness to experiment, but modernist experimentation could make little use of the vast knowledge of stagecraft that had made him so popular on the 19th-c. stage. Like the poet W. B. YEATS, P. was an author whose literary career spanned the seeming abyss between the peak of Victorian culture and the shattering new world of the 20th c. Unlike Yeats, P. did not entirely make the transition from eminent Victorian to high modernist. At the time of his death, P. was lauded as an eminent playwright. Theater history has since cast him in a more marginal role.

BIBLIOGRAPHY: Dawick, J., *P.* (1993); Fisher, J. L., "The 'Law of the Father': Sexual Politics in the Plays of Henry Arthur Jones and A. W. P.," *EL* 16 (Fall 1989): 203–23; Hendrickx, J. R., "P.'s Court Farces: A Revaluation," *MD* 26 (March 1983): 54–61; Lazenby, W., *A. W. P.* (1972)

GINGER STRAND

PINTER, Harold

b. 10 October 1930, Hackney, London

Born in the East End of London, P. was educated locally—not only at school, but on the streets, where as a Jewish youngster before the war he needed to ward off verbal abuse or worse from intimidating gangs on the fascist fringe. Leaving school at sixteen, he became an actor in provincial and touring companies. From the childhood experience, he began to understand how language can become a form of attack or defense as well as of communication; from the theatrical apprenticeship, he learned how actorly responses and craftsmanship can lend some dignity even to mediocre fare and be trusted with the moments between the words when richer material allows.

P.'s own first play, *The Room* (perf. 1957; pub. 1960), was written at the invitation of his friend Henry Woolf for a production at Bristol University. Its success in his own eyes—he has never been much concerned with reactions from audiences or critics—encouraged him to start work immediately on his first full-length piece, *The Birthday Party* (perf. 1958; pub. 1960), which flopped resoundingly in London in the following year. But with the recent flourishing of new writing for the stage, notably at Joan Littlewood's Theatre Workshop and George Devine's Royal Court, P. was encouraged to persist by commissions from radio and television, and by the inclusion of short, imagist sketches in stage revues. Then, in 1960, *The Caretaker* began its long West End run, ushered in by a London production of *The Room* in a double-bill with *The Dumb Waiter*. P.'s reputation was established—and *The Birthday Party*, revived in 1964 by the Royal Shakespeare Company, belatedly achieved classic status.

From the first, P. was out of sympathy with the neonaturalism practiced by such of his contemporaries as John OSBORNE and Arnold WESKER, as with the more politically directed experiments of John ARDEN and the Workshop school. For better or worse, the influential study by Martin Esslin, *The Theatre of the Absurd* (1962), aligned him in that "movement" with writers such as Samuel BECKETT and Eugène Ionesco. It is true that Beckett is the one stage writer whose influence P. has acknowledged, and that there are certain resemblances in the spare, elliptic, and apparently ambiguous style of his early writing. A recognition of the extremities of human suffering inflicted by Nazism also echoes through the work of both writers. But P.'s voice soon became entirely his own—his choice of ambience always more localized and specific, and his characters closer to the rough surface of life than Beckett's metaphysically agonized or abandoned creations.

P.'s early characters seldom venture beyond their own realistic but claustrophobic four walls, and "comedy of menace" was perhaps an acceptable description of the sense in those plays of an ill-defined external threat—of eviction from the eponymous *Room*, of orders from some unseen but malign force in *The Dumb Waiter*, and from the mysterious new arrivals in a seedy seaside lodging house in *The Birthday Party*. Though no less spatially confined, *The Caretaker* shows a greater concern for the inner life of its characters, as the tramp Davies insinuates himself between two strangely interdependent brothers: the outwardly confident Mick and the fragile, receptive Aston. Davies is perhaps P.'s most psychologically recognizable creation, rendering outwardly the characteristics that disable him from coping with the demands of society. Though canny enough to recognize and try to play on the weaknesses of others, he can neither keep up with the brisk emotional about-turns of Mick nor respond adequately to the gestures toward intimacy offered by Aston. Without compromising its

distinctive vision, *The Caretaker* has remained P.'s most readily accessible and engaging play.

The struggle for domestic dominance played out in *The Caretaker* was taken to an extreme in P.'s next full-length work, *The Homecoming* (1965), set in North London, in which a widowed father living with two of his sons welcomes the return of the third, vacationing from an academic career abroad—with a wife in tow, who is both absorbed by and absorbs the all-male household. She decides to remain, apparently attracted to playing the dual role of willing concubine and dominatrix. Often regarded as the high point of P.'s achievement, the play can also be seen as a transitional piece, marking the final rejection of any "search for verification" by an author as yet uncertain how to render the more impressionistic versions of reality he was soon to produce.

Increasingly, any distinction between "full-length" and "one-act" pieces became irrelevant as P. gained both the dramaturgical confidence and the authority in the theatrical marketplace to let each action determine its proper length, with a marked tendency toward increasing concision. *Landscape* and *Silence* (1969) are thus succinct but self-sufficient explorations of the conflicting ways in which their characters recall shared experiences, as time warps and enwraps memories and emotions in mutually incompatible truths, rendering the past forever uncertain.

What in these plays were delicately textured variations upon the relationship between memory and time appeared coarser-grained, both verbally and structurally, in *Old Times* (1971), in which three recollections of a long-ago triangular affair overlap in the tensile tranquility of a rural drawing room. The disconcerting here-and-nowness of the setting perhaps contributes to the sense that the ideas in *Old Times* are at odds with its dramaturgy. *No Man's Land* (1975) dealt with what may or may not have been a past relationship between Hirst and Spooner, as they renew or perhaps just pursue a relationship after an encounter on Hampstead Heath: though no less of the here-and-now than *Old Times*, the play's anecdotal quality is more congruent with its language and structure, inviting more comfortable performances.

In *Betrayal* (1978), a tentative version of objectivity meshes intriguingly with subjective renderings of events through the device of working backward in time, as two close friends know and do not know that one is having an affair with the wife of the other. The woman remains the most enigmatic character, as so often with P., and as was again to be the case with the women of *Moonlight* (1993)—the wife, mistress, and daughter of the bedridden Andy, who is raging not only against the dying of the light but also, it seems, against his own sense of failure in his emotional dealings with the family who surround him, though whether in time past or time present is often uncertain. The daughter may even be a ghost, so elusively does she flit through the intersecting spaces of this play, her lyrical interludes contrasting with the babbling, almost ritualistic inanities of the sons.

While the play is not one of P.'s most successful, it nonetheless grapples honestly and distinctively with the painful matter of human mortality. But in *Celebration* (2000) the milieu is merely that of one-time yuppies who pass their lives in pointless encounters in expensive restaurants, served by a Waiter who can cap every story with a fantasy encounter of his own. The subject matter is trivial and the encounters are tricked out with "Pinterisms" that lend only a semblance of significance—the Waiter, halfway between a walking symbol and a running gag, being the play's redeeming feature.

P.'s works have always drawn heavily on images, instances, and individuals from his past, although these have never been more than generative moments for larger dramatic worlds. His plays have long ceased to be peopled from the working class into which he was born, their characters now being drawn from the professional and intellectual circles in which he naturally mixes. On occasion, this is of little consequence: it does not much matter that the friends of *Betrayal* are an author and his publisher. It matters more that the inane no-longer-young things of *Celebration* appear to have come from nowhere in particular, and to have nowhere to go beyond the spiritual wasteland of a posh restaurant.

P. has, however, found a new source of creative energy in an unexpected discovery of political commitment—unexpected, since the young writer had been openly contemptuous of the shirtsleeve politics of those of his contemporaries who had been swept into the movements against nuclear weapons and apartheid (often only to sweep out again into middle-aged conservatism). P. first gave dramatic form to his concern for human rights—and for the Western neo-imperialism he saw as often underpinning their denial—in *One for the Road* (1984). Since, his slow-burning anger has also fueled such plays as *Mountain Language* (1988), about a minority group forbidden even to speak in their own tongue, and *The New World Order* (1991), in which torture is discussed as the refined art of which its practitioners believe they are masters.

In its relative brevity, this latter piece is reminiscent of the early, so-called revue sketches, which transcended their ephemeral origins to become vignettes of the streets beyond the rooms of which P. was then writing. Less successful has been P.'s long struggle to reduce Marcel Proust's multivolume novel *In Remembrance of Things Past* first to cinematic and more recently to theatrical viability. But the concern to enhance rather than filter out meaning from such seemingly intractable material is, of course, character-

istic of P.'s lifelong interest in the interaction between memory and time.

A writer who displays supreme self-confidence in his own creations, P. has, however, confessed himself subject to writer's block—a block that one feels he sometimes short-circuits by switching to automatic pilot. Hence, the coinage of the adjective "Pinteresque" to describe those passages that appear self-parodying by reducing his highly distinctive style to a formulaic mix of motifs and mannerisms. The paradox is that P. is so consummately an actors' playwright that even on automatic pilot he can create roles as deceptively riveting for an audience as the P. aglow with renewed creative energy.

BIBLIOGRAPHY: Billington, M., *The Life and Work of H. P.* (1996); Bloom, H., ed., *H. P.* (1987); Esslin, M., *H. P.* (1967); Esslin, M., *The Peopled Wound: The Work of H. P.* (1970); Gale, S. H., ed., *Critical Essays on H. P.* (1990); Hayman, R., *H. P.* (1968); Thompson, D. T., *P.* (1985); Trussler, S., *The Plays of H. P.* (1973)

SIMON TRUSSLER

PIOZZI, Hester Lynch [Salusbury Thrale]

b. 16 January 1741, Pwllheli, Wales; d. 2 May 1821, Clifton Bristol

P. enjoyed a popularity unusual for early modern women writers. Her *Anecdotes of the Late Samuel Johnson, LL.D., During the Last Twenty Years of His Life* sold out its first edition by dinnertime the day it appeared, March 25, 1786, and went into three further editions by the end of that year. Inspired by this success, in 1788 P. produced *Letters to and from the Late Samuel Johnson . . . from the Original MSS. in Her Possession* and a year later published, in two volumes, *Observations and Reflections Made in the Course of a Journey through France, Italy, and Germany*, an account of her travels with her second husband, Gabriel Piozzi. Both works were warmly received by reviewers and by the public.

Though P. was chided for a chatty prose style, her intelligence, wit, and charm, together with continuing interest in Samuel JOHNSON and his circle, ensured an audience for her autobiographical writing. A more ambitious work, however, *British Synonymy; or, An Attempt at Regulating the Choice of Words in Familiar Conversation* (2 vols., 1794) was greeted with censorious rumblings. The first thesaurus in English, *Synonymy* is a usage guide intended for foreigners; P. discriminates 1,180 words in essays that range from a single paragraph to a half-dozen pages. Because it lacks systematic principles for selecting or defining words, some reviewers characterized *Synonymy* as an inadequate trespass upon the territory of the great lexicographer. When universal criticism greeted her abridged history of the world, *Retrospection* (2 vols., 1801), P. published no more.

She remained a public figure, however, thanks to her early enshrinement in literary history as "Dr. Johnson's Mrs. Thrale." Indeed, it was the defining event of her life when P., in 1765 the wife of a prosperous brewer, met Johnson. Johnson soon became an intimate of the household, visiting for weeks at a time and traveling with the Thrales to Wales and to France. By her own account (which James BOSWELL disputes), P. created the domestic tranquility that enabled the notoriously despondent and indolent Johnson to complete his *Lives of the Poets*. The friends also collaborated on casual literary projects: for the 1766 *Miscellanies* of Anna Williams, Johnson wrote the fairy tale "The Fountains," modeling the heroine on P., while P. contributed her often anthologized poem "The Three Warnings." In her diary, *Thraliana* (2 vols., 1942; rev. ed., 1951), edited by Katharine C. Balderston, P. recorded Johnson's conversations and accounts of his childhood, material she later would adapt for *Anecdotes*. Upon Henry Thrale's death, some people thought the widow would marry Johnson (seventy-five years of age and thirty-two years her senior) and even hinted that the shock of her marriage to Piozzi in 1784 hastened Johnson's demise. Unsurprisingly, therefore, *Anecdotes* not only testifies to Johnson's piety and genius but also defends P.'s own conduct in refusing to link her life permanently to his, either as wife or as nurse.

The relative obscurity of *Anecdotes*, despite the persistently strong market for stories about Johnson, may be traced to Boswell, who had an interest in denigrating P.'s work. Imitating the criticism of P. with which the *Life of Johnson* concludes, editors of Boswell and Johnson's modern biographers have valued P. largely as she supplements Boswell's opus, rather than as an independent writer and artist. Editions of the *Life* regularly clarify Boswell's narrative with footnotes derived from *Anecdotes;* P.'s account has been mined for information on the one hand and criticized for insufficiency or inaccuracy on the other. Yet P.'s work should be recognized as more than a footnote to Boswell. P. enjoyed an intimate acquaintance with Johnson, who was disposed to confide in her; the only woman to write an extended portrait of Johnson, from the vantage point of her sex P. supplies insights into Johnson's conduct and character that his male biographers do not. Her eminently readable prose displays a knack for economically vivid description. This ability makes P.'s marginalia memorable and striking. In short, *Anecdotes* is both an engaging and important BIOGRAPHY of a major English literary figure and an intriguing work of personal history.

Describing the limitations attending her record of Johnson's life, limitations that confined most 18th-c. women to domestic circles, P. apologizes in the preface to *Anecdotes* for producing "a mere candlelight picture of his latter days, where everything falls in dark shadow except the face, the index of the mind." The parallel that she draws between *Anecdotes,* the narrative of a man "passing the evening of his life among friends," and the badly illuminated private space to which women were restricted, suggestively anticipates the history of her book as well.

BIBLIOGRAPHY: Clifford, J. L., *H. L. P. (Mrs. Thrale)* (1941; rev. ed., 1968); McCarthy, W., *H. T. P.* (1985); Bloom, E. A., and L. D. Bloom, eds., *The Piozzi Letters: Correspondence of H. L. P., 1784–1821* (5 vols.,1989–)

LISA BERGLUND

PITTER, Ruth

b. 7 November 1897, Ilford, Essex; d. 29 February 1992, Long Crendon, Buckinghamshire

In 1955, P. was the first woman to be awarded the Queen's Gold Medal for Poetry. Though not as widely known as some of her contemporaries, she is one of the most highly regarded female poets of the 20th c. P.'s poetry expresses a connection to the mystic qualities of nature as well as a firm footing in the Christian faith. She writes from a classical discipline, using traditional forms, yet her voice is clearly modern. P. began writing poetry at an early age. She was greatly influenced by her parents who were both assistant teachers in an elementary school. P.'s parents fostered an atmosphere of artistic appreciation in the home, despite their low incomes, and they maintained a small cottage in the Essex forest. It was there that P. discovered her intimate connection to nature that would inform her writing throughout her life. Unable to win a scholarship or pay for her education, P. left school at the beginning of World War I and began working. She rejected the idea of patronage or earning through writing poetry and throughout her life found other means by which to support herself, yet her lack of formal education would often cause her doubts later in life. P. published her first collection of poetry in 1920, but it was not until the publication in 1936 of *A Trophy of Arms* that she received any recognition for her poetry. In 1954, she won the Heinemann Award for *The Ermine* (1953). Later collections include *End of Drought* (1975) and *A Heaven to Find* (1987). Her *Collected Poems* appeared in 1996.

POETRY SINCE 1945

Since 1945, British poetry has moved steadily from what many regard as 20th-c. parochial to a 21st-c. international. In the space of little more than fifty years the insular, clear verse of mainland *English* Britain has changed from being a centralist and predominantly male, seemingly academic, practice to become a multi-hued, postmodern, cultural entertainment, available to all. Some observers see this as a liberating. Others regard it as more of a descent into vernacular sprawl. But, as ever, reality cannot be so readily defined. British poetry here is regarded as writing from Wales, Scotland, Northern Ireland, and England in the English language. Scots Gaelic and Welsh language poetries are excluded as is work from the Irish Republic.

During the late 1940s, the dominance of the prewar modernists like F. S. FLINT and the uncontroversial Georgians such as Walter DE la MARE and W. H. DAVIES who used their verse to depict a vanishing rural and domestic scene was largely overthrown. World War II and the shattering of Europe saw to that. The cerebral surrealists, David GASCOYNE among them, had driven into a blind alley. When the war ended, the new poetry that emerged still bore traces of the measured and uneventful thirties verse that had gone before it. Poets of what became known as the neo-Romantic movement, Vernon WATKINS, W. S. GRAHAM, Patricia Beer, George BARKER, and John HEATH-STUBBS, among others, wrote as if the British world had not changed irrevocably. The influence of prewar founder figures W. B. YEATS, T. S. ELIOT, Edwin MUIR, Louis MacNEICE, W. H. AUDEN, and Robert GRAVES remained strong. The modernists David JONES and Basil BUNTING, with Hugh MacDIARMID in Scotland, stayed outsider forces. In Wales, Dylan THOMAS and R. S. THOMAS made great marks on the map. But the poetry was not yet a true product of its times.

The reaction came in the early 1950s, and by the time Dylan Thomas died in 1953, "The Movement" as the new tendency was called had obtained a coherence. The work of its poets nurtured rationality, was inhospitable to myth, was conversationally pitched (although lacking the speech rhythms of American counterparts like William Carlos Williams) and was deliberately formal and clear. Movement poets opposed MODERNISM and had little involvement with international influences. They regarded themselves as a direct continuation of mainstream English tradition. There were few sparks and much temperate, slow reflection. Members, yoked together somewhat artificially, have not, however, all remained true to their first principles. Thom GUNN and Donald DAVIE went on to encompass the whole gamut of American, open field, and Black Mountain writing with Gunn using syllabic meters and Davie becoming an interpreter of Ezra Pound. But at the center a tight stiff-lipped Englishness glowed in the work of Kingsley AMIS, John WAIN, Philip LARKIN, D. J. ENRIGHT, and Elizabeth JENNINGS. The anthology of the period was Robert CONQUEST's *New Lines*, published in 1956. Dannie ABSE, himself a Movement fellow-traveler, suggests

that "the pitch, tone, strategy, and bias of the Movement poets has predominated, with modifications, to the present day" and as far as mainstream English poetry is concerned he is more or less correct. There has been something about the English suspicion of modernism and insistence on form, often at the expense of content, that has sidelined it on the world stage. While other literatures accommodated mercurial change, mainstream English poetry stuck with decorative, rational discourse. But on the fringes things were different.

The Movement had its significant outsiders. Stevie SMITH was a total original who according to Anthony THWAITE wrote "like William BLAKE rewritten by Ogden Nash." Other poets, less hostile to ROMANTICISM, were also steadily making their mark—Jon Silkin, Sylvia Plath, and two of Britain's greatest 20th-c. poets, Ted HUGHES and Geoffrey HILL, all appeared during the formal English fifties. Hughes, the gritty Yorkshire poet laureate engaged the primordial struggle and won. Hill's dense, formidable, poetry became, for some, the highest achievement of late-20th-c. English verse.

"The Group" was a movement that coalesced around nothing more revolutionary than the desire to discuss. Meeting under the chairmanship of first Philip HOBSBAUM in Cambridge and later Edward LUCIE-SMITH in London, the Group had members who were to form the bedrock from which Michael HOROVITZ's lauded anthology of the period *Children of Albion* would later spring. Working largely in the late 1950s and early 1960s, poets such as Peter PORTER, George MacBETH, Alan BROWNJOHN, Martin Bell, B. S. JOHNSON, and Peter REDGROVE met to discuss how verse was. As with Joan Littlewood's approach to theater where the workshop assumed more significance than the script, so the Group poets honed their work in an atmosphere of trenchant criticism, sobriety, and mutual esteem. The work was largely Movement tradition with side-glances at innovation. MacBeth, in particular, was keen to embrace some of the structural changes he'd seen arrive from Europe.

As the smooth, safe fifties moved into the revolutionary sixties, the critic A. ALVAREZ united what he saw as the new poetry in an anthology of the same name, *The New Poetry* (1962). Here, Group and Movement poets, supplemented by other emerging voices such as Hughes, R. S. Thomas, Michael HAMBURGER, Christopher MIDDLETON, Charles Tomlinson, Ted Walker, Iain Crichton SMITH, and Norman MacCAIG, and others were joined in a spirit of urgency and the poet's "ability and willingness to face the full range of his experience with his full intelligence." Alvarez posited that the New Poetry claimed to be beyond gentility. Looking back on it now the work looks depressingly similar to that which went before—British poetry tracking a gentle English groove.

Alvarez's confessional Americans John Berryman and Robert Lowell had no counterparts, except perhaps that dynamic husband-and-wife duo, Hughes and Plath.

But explosion was around the corner. After a brief dalliance with jazz and stage performances, inspired largely by the Americans Leroi Jones (later Amiri Baraka) and Kenneth Rexroth—Abse, Christopher LOGUE, and Roy FISHER were among British exponents—British poetry took its vital left turn. Across the Western world, cultural values were shifting. The old order, knocked back by two world wars and the fall of empires, was finally teetering. In the U.S., the Beat Generation, who valued spirituality over formality, and freedom over regulation, carried the torch. In England—starting with Horovitz's celebrated Albert Hall poetry reading of 1965—the Underground became, to some, the way on. Valuing open forms and producing an antihierarchical, antiwar protest poetry, the Underground thumbed its nose at centralist values and took its own little mag, alternative route to the people. A poetry built on wild times, popular readings, and independent distribution systems exploded across the U.K. Led by the Liverpool poets—Adrian Henri, Brian Patten, and Roger MCGOUGH—on the back of the Beatles, and aided by Adrian MITCHELL, Jeff Nuttall, Tom PICKARD, and others, Underground poetry became verse's acceptable popular face. Poetry was removing itself from its male-dominated and often academic metropolitan centers.

Not that the Underground was poetry's only route forward. A British dimension to the worldwide concrete poetry movement appeared in the 1960s work of Scottish poets Iain Hamilton FINLAY and Edwin MORGAN, the Dominican monk Dom Sylvester Houedard, artists Tom Phillips and John Furnival, as well as "sound and found" poets such as Bob Cobbing, Peter Mayer, and the London-resident French master Henri Chopin. These "experimental" poets and their followers (Peter Finch, Tom Leonard, Paula Claire) allied themselves with the Underground in their assault on the establishment. The ousting of the mainstream from the august London Poetry Society during the early 1970s was a classic example of the new overwriting the old. *Poetry Review,* the U.K.'s longest-lived poetry journal (founded 1912) and an unstinting supporter of established values, was taken over by Eric Mottram, a fervent supporter of expanded consciousness and alternative verse. In the eastern counties, loosely centered around the magazine *Grosseteste Review,* a group of poets, most of them attached to university English departments and enamored of American models, found themselves constituting what became known as the Cambridge School, poetry united by its non-metropolitan axis and its foregrounding of language over discourse. Andrew Crozier, John James, Veronica Forrest-Thom-

son, Douglas OLIVER, John Riley, Peter Riley, and J. H. PRYNNE were some of the leading practitioners.

Outside these "lunatic fringes," as they were derisively referred to by poets adhering to the traditional center, the English mainstream continued, almost as if nothing else was going on. New poets, many based well away from London, began to add a regional veneer to the U.K.'s Georgian gentility. Tony HARRISON's hard-edged northern realism was supplemented by Douglas DUNN's well-wrought, working-class observations from Hull.

As the seventies turned to the eighties, the experimenters became the neomodernists. Modernism's apparent sterility did not prevent the emergence of a whole new tranche of writers ploughing the furrow initiated by Bunting and Jones. Allen Fisher, Denise Riley, Barry MACSWEENEY, Lee HARWOOD, Chris Torrance, Richard Burns, Peter Didsbury and others, often published by the Ferry and Fulcrum Presses, showed that British poetry was never to fall back on having simply one trick.

In reaction, inevitably, the Empire struck back. In 1982, mainstream neo-Georgian Andrew MOTION (later to become one of Britain's greatest successes as poet laureate, succeeding Ted Hughes in the role in 1998) and Blake Morrison produced the *Penguin Book of Contemporary British Poetry,* an anthology that makes its point more by who it left out than who went in. Pop poetry may have been doing well in the clubs while neomodernists filled the small presses yet here was proof that formalism, structure, traditional meaning, and outright clarity were not qualities that had left these lands. The expected major voices of Seamus HEANEY, Harrison, and Dunn were joined, among others, by Hugo WILLIAMS, Michael LONGLEY, Tom PAULIN, Anne STEVENSON, Fleur ADCOCK, James FENTON, Carol RUMENS, Craig RAINE, and Christopher REID. This final pair also briefly had fame when they invented the Martian school of overblown metaphor. The center once more held, although Larkin could not see what it was that glued them together.

Steady immigration to the U.K. over a long period was by the 1980s affecting its literature. Immigrants like Linton Kwesi JOHNSON drove in new, antiauthoritarian values, made nonstandard orthography acceptable, and, by allying himself with black music, produced a poetry that, in Britain, was pretty much like nothing else. Style and content were matched in importance by delivery. Acceptability by academic institutions came well down the list. British black writing's best-known early exponent, James Berry, edited the first anthology. The movement grew to include many, emerging, second-generation black Britons as well as more who had been resident here for a considerable time. Poets such as Benjamin ZEPHANIAH, John Agard, Grace Nichols, Jackie Kay, Jean "Binta" Breeze, and others readily crossed the racial divide by producing a verse whose values proved utterly beguiling to those, to use Norman Mailer's term, "white Negroes" who disliked prejudice, authority, and the police almost as much as the British Caribbean blacks did. British Asian poetry, extant but minimal, has hitherto fared much worse.

Continued assaults on the citadel of centralist tradition led, by the early 1990s, to somewhat of a poetry boom. The media, whipping the storm, suggested that poetry might be the new rock-'n'-roll. Pop stars began to admit to liking it with the odd one or two to actually writing it. The trend of allying verse with songwriting set by Bob Dylan continued. The new poets of the period ranged from the many-talented and formally experimental Peter Reading to acceptable neotraditionalists such as David CONSTANTINE, Selima Hill, Kit Wright, Bernard O'Donoghue, Sean O'Brien, Michael Donaghy, Michael Hoffman, Carol Ann DUFFY, Simon ARMITAGE, and Don Patterson. The culture was becoming plural. For the first time since the prewar days of Dylan Thomas, the Celtic fringes were on the rise. Since the early 1990s, being an Irish or a Scots poet (yet curiously not a Welsh poet) has carried with it considerable advantage. British culture now values its parts more strongly than its whole. To good postmodernists, the concerns of minorities, linguistic and sexual orientation, origin and gender have all become disproportionately significant. Much of the early nineties mainstream stance is evident in the output of presses such as Carcanet and Bloodaxe and is gathered in the controversial Michael Hulse, David Kennedy, and David Morley anthology *The New Poetry* (1993). Controversial, perhaps, because of its diversity, the anthology has no central thrust other than its multiplicity.

The New Poetry does not, however, contain many examples of Britain's performance poetry. During the past fifteen years, verse has found an increasingly welcome home on the stage of clubs, pubs, and bars. Poetry delivered as entertainment, loud, in your face, and, like much of the rest of our media, instantly appreciable has turned verse from an arcane art into a truly popular one. Building on the strong lead given by the Liverpool poets and their followers in the 1970s, John Cooper Clarke, Attila the Stockbroker, John Hegley, and others have increased public consumption of poetry on a geometric scale. Their work is dynamic, politically apposite and often delivered with considerable HUMOR. Rarely, however, does it also succeed on the page.

The postcolonial cultures of recently politically devolved Scotland, Northern Ireland, and Wales have seen poetry in those countries boom. In Scotland, the influence of MacDiarmid has been strong. Robert Garioch, George Mackay BROWN, Norman MacCaig, Liz Lochead, and others have seen their poetry find acceptance beyond their borders. The same has happened throughout the so-called Troubles in Northern Ireland with the work of Paul MULDOON, Derek MAHON, Longley, Paulin, and others emerging brilliantly alongside the towering presence of Heaney. In Wales, the dominant force, outside her borders, of R. S. Thomas has been followed by those of Gillian CLARKE, Nigel Jenkins, Menna Elfyn, Gwyneth Lewis, Robert Minhinnick, Tony Curtis, and, more recently, Owen Sheers. Only in Scotland have their been significant formal innovators, notably Tom Leonard and W. N. Herbert. Wales and Northern Ireland (with the exception of Muldoon) steer more traditional courses.

By the turn of the millennium, poetry in Britain had reached a multifaceted stand-off. Despite the work of editors such as Armitage and Robert Crawford who have made brave attempts at uniting postmodern, post-Christian, postwar, post-Hiroshima, poststructuralist, postdevolution poetries under one pluralistic banner the many gleaming and disparate parts of British poetry do not like making a coherent whole. In Northern Ireland, Scotland, and Wales, the literatures no longer find themselves overshadowed by an English big brother. The sound coming in from the center can be, and increasingly is, ignored. The argument between form and content remains as strong as ever. It has been raging for a hundred years and there are no winners yet. The counterculture may have changed name and altered its emphasis (from lifestyle to free-form experiment and back) but it remains as strong and has as many adherents as ever. They may say there is no British Language poetry but there are plenty of fellow travelers. The line that runs up from Thomas HARDY, through D. H. LAWRENCE, Larkin, Sir John BETJEMAN, Dunn, Motion, and Armitage continues, although is no longer as central as it once was. Minority writing (ethnic, genre, sexual orientation) has as many proponents and fans as pop writing did in the seventies. Twenty-first century British poetry is no longer precisely *English*. Like the world literature with which it is now firmly allied, it has as many facets as the eye of a fly. Saying exactly what it is remains the problem of the moment.

BIBILIOGRAPHY: Abse, D., ed., *The Hutchinson Book of Post-War British Poets* (1989); Armitage, S., and R. Crawford, *The Penguin Book of Poetry from Britain and Ireland since 1945* (2000); Cobbing, B., and P. Mayer, *Concerning Concrete Poetry* (1978); Hamilton, I., ed., *The Oxford Companion to Twentieth Century Poetry* (1994); Hulse, M., D. Kennedy, and D. Morley, eds., *The New Poetry* (1993); Lucie-Smith, E., ed., *British Poetry since 1945* (1970); Matthias, J., ed., *23 Modern British Poets* (1971); O'Brien, S., *The Deregulated Muse* (1998); Thwaite, A., *Poetry Today* (1996)

PETER FINCH

POLE, Reginald

b. 3 March 1500, Stourton Castle, Staffordshire; d. 17 November 1558, Lambeth

P. was a cousin of HENRY VIII. He was educated at Oxford until 1521 and at Padua (1521–26), and rose to the rank of cardinal. He returned to England after Mary Tudor's accession in 1553, sent as a papal legate with the responsibility of effecting a Catholic restoration. Despite this, P. had a comparatively lenient attitude toward heretics. Under Mary, P. became Archbishop of Canterbury. He was involved in both the English and Italian reformations, and one of the most important international figures of the mid-16th c.

Up to fifty works have been attributed to P., who seems to have been a prolific writer. The most important of his works is undoubtedly *De unitate* (wr. 1536), a mixture of religious faith, political analysis, and literary learning. Usually regarded as a strongly papalist invective, this work condemned Henry VIII's divorce of Catherine of Aragon and presented an evangelical idea of the church that emphasized belief in justification by faith. P. also appealed to the people (that is, the nobility) against the king; he explained what he had meant by this in the subsequent work, *Apologia ad Carolum Quintum* (1539). The latter is an important text in the history of political thought since it constitutes the first sustained attack on Machiavelli. It was also the source of the image of Thomas Cromwell, Henry VIII's chief minister, as an unscrupulous follower of Machiavelli, an opinion that has proved long-lasting.

Other works include *Discorso di pace* (1554), which was written as an address to the emperor Charles V, and *De sacramento* (1555), which lays continued stress on the importance of faith to salvation. *De sacramento* also contains an attack on the perjury of Thomas Cranmer, the imprisoned former Archbishop of Canterbury with whom P. corresponded, and it is possible that P. reworked this text after Cranmer's trial began. P.'s most complex work was *De reformatione ecclesiae,* which was probably written over a period of fifteen years toward the end of his life. *De summo pontifice* was begun during the conclave of Julius III. It offers a charismatic view of papal primacy as founded on the blood of the martyrs rather than institutional and judicial power. Its thesis is that only candidates of Christlike humility were suited for election to the papal office.

P. was secretive about his writing, and many of his works may have been lost. Those that do survive often exist in multiple versions due to the fact that his texts were often reworked by other authors. His archive is scattered across Europe, and the identification of manuscripts of his works is complicated by their large number and dispersed nature. In addition, some of the works formerly attributed to P. are almost certainly spurious.

BIBLIOGRAPHY: Mayer, T. F., *A Reluctant Author: Cardinal Pole and His Manuscripts* (1999); Mayer, T. F., *R. P., Prince and Prophet* (2000); Schenk, W., *R. P., Cardinal of England* (1950)

MARGARET CONNOLLY

POLIAKOFF, Stephen

b. 14 December 1952, London

A graduate of Cambridge University, P. began his playwriting career in the London alternative "fringe" theater. With fellow Cambridge graduate David HARE, who founded the Portable Theatre as an avant-garde group, he and others wrote the collaborative *Lay-By* (perf. 1971; pub. 1972). Centering on the dysfunctional behavior of a consumption-oriented society, it had initial success in London and at the 1971 Edinburgh Festival. At the newly formed pub theater The Bush, under Dominic Dromgoole, P. presented brief satirical and improvisational pieces that attracted audiences from West London with little theater-going experience. Writing for such London new drama venues as the Royal Court, the Little Theatre, Hampstead Theatre, and The Bush, P. developed characters who retreat from the bleak materialism of the 1970s and 1980s into private lives of isolation and spiritual crisis. In 1976, he became a writer in residence of London's National Theatre.

The Bush Theatre production of *Hitting Town* (perf. 1975; pub. 1976) concerns a brother and sister whose sense of personal melancholy and urban desolation propels them into an incestuous relationship. The power of the play lies in its timely theme—the general malaise associated with the disappointment of the more uncertain and grasping 1970s following the exuberance and confidence of the 1960s—but also in the ability to depict an incestuous relationship with sensitivity and meaning. Clare and Ralph inhabit a brutal, self-serving world where defensiveness replaces ideals and urban ugliness inhibits relationships. P.'s 1991 film *Close My Eyes* revisits the theme of sibling incest within an urban environment. The England of the 1990s film presents a more consciously sensitive culture than the 1970s setting of *Hitting Town*. Wealthier, with more beauty and variety, but with no less materialism, its world reveals a sexuality more complex, more threatening in a post-AIDS world, where young urban professionals have it all and yet feel as trapped and estranged as Clare and Ralph.

Brother and sister Richard and Natalie live in the rising world of an expanding national economy that includes a restless underclass and a sophisticated postmodern business elite highly aware of both their social personae and their constructed personal identities. Richard is a young city planner disaffected by the crass material culture of the urban landscape. His new position at the innovative and iconoclastic Urban Alert consulting firm leaves him frustrated and bored, a state he relieves with frequent casual affairs in and out of the office. Natalie's underemployment leaves her resentful of her younger fellow workers, who lack education and awareness. When Richard sees her after a long absence, they feel a mutual attraction that only intensifies with each meeting. Natalie's new husband Sinclair is a status-conscious and ambitious financial advisor for the new British economic boom. The siblings' intensifying relationship develops undercover of the glittering social world of conspicuous consumption and material obsessions. After sleeping with Richard a few times, Natalie tries to distance the relationship, but Richard becomes obsessed with Natalie, just as the emotionally distant Sinclair obsesses over status symbols and personal esteem in his meritocratic world.

At a large going-away party given by Sinclair and Natalie, Richard finally breaks down and drags Natalie away from the party into a nearby urban industrial landscape, where their physical fight finally sobers them. In the final scene, Sinclair joins them as they walk along a bucolic landscape of summer bonfires, where Richard asks Sinclair what will happen to the human race. Sinclair's response is both telling of the characters and the general complacent materialism of the times: "I haven't a clue." The play ends with a nostalgic reference to the quintessential Englishness of the rural bonfires, which draw Sinclair's comment, "I might have begun to miss this." P.'s choice to mollify the disturbing issues raised by the play with a nostalgic ending diminishes the film's effectiveness, but his subtle presentation of forbidden passion and the search for an unnamed lost consciousness amid a postmodern world of highly conscious identity formation accurately depicts late-Thatcher Britain.

Coming in to Land (perf. 1987; pub. 1998), presented at London's National Theatre, explores the elusiveness of personal identity in a globalized world of immigration, terrorism, and displaced populations. Related thematically to P.'s television drama *Caught on a Train* (perf. 1980; pub. 1982), which concerns British isolationism and xenophobia, the play presents the lives of a Polish immigrant woman and a British man who seek marriage for her citizenship. But Halina decides to risk a contrived refugee story rather than marry Neville when she senses their relationship is emotionally dead. While the plot and character motivations are weak—why would Halina bother with the emotional niggardliness of Neville if she seeks only a legalistic marriage to someone she never knew before?—the play resonates with the national mood in its profile of hypocritical self-interest and ethnocentrism.

BIBLIOGRAPHY: Kaufmann, S., "Stanley Kaufmann on Film: Predicaments," *NewR* 206 (February 24, 1992): 42–43; Peacock, D. K., "The Fascination of Fascism: The Plays of S. P.," *MD* 27 (December 1984): 494–505

WILLIAM OVER

POLIDORI, John William

b. 7 September 1795, London; d. 24 August 1821, London

P. is now chiefly remembered as the creator of a character who became the literary ancestor of Bram STOKER's Dracula and as a member of the Geneva group of 1816 that included Lord BYRON, Percy Bysshe SHELLEY, Mary Godwin [SHELLEY], and Claire Clairmont. It was in this milieu that Godwin created *Frankenstein*. P.'s own position in this group partially explains the striking qualities he imparted to his vampire. P. graduated from the medical school of the University of Edinburgh at nineteen and, too young to practice legally in London, accepted an offer to travel as Byron's physician. Dependent, surrounded for the first time by those more talented than himself, P. felt ridiculed, condescended to, and humiliated. He challenged Shelley to a duel and once was about to take poison in his room when Byron appeared consolingly.

When Byron abandoned a story he had begun, P. took it up and created a very Byronic vampire—Byronic, at least, as the general public and apparently P. then thought of Byron. When *The Vampyre* (1819) was first published, it was attributed to Byron, whose habits of self-dramatization made his authorship quite believable. With the help of Byron's angry repudiation, P. was able to lay claim to the work, but he never escaped the unjust imputation that he, rather than the unscrupulous publisher, was responsible for the fraud. In the earliest published versions, the vampire is called Lord Ruthven after the Byron figure in Lady Caroline Lamb's *Glenarvon*. In later versions, he becomes Lord Strongmore.

Strongmore is abnormally pale, with a dead, leaden eye that casts a morbid gloom over everyone who sees him. A hypnotically successful seducer, he reduces innocent women to depravity. He is generous to the corrupt poor, but not to the virtuous. When he gambles, he reduces honest players to poverty, but willingly loses money to known cheats. While he is ostensibly dying, he extorts an oath from the naively idealistic Aubrey to keep the death secret for a year and a day. Strongmore then reappears as Earl of Marsden engaged to Aubrey's sister, planning to marry her exactly one day before the promise expires. Aubrey dies of internal conflict, but at the last moment reveals Strongmore's identity. It is too late. The vampire has drunk Miss Aubrey's blood and disappeared, his cunning sadism now complete.

The Vampyre remains a chilling work. Although it was savaged by anti-Byronic critics, Goethe declared it Byron's finest work, and it went through five "editions" in England in 1819. Most earlier vampires had been like zombies, acting on compulsion. The world of vampires would never be the same. Unfortunately, it was P.'s only major success. *The Diary of Dr. John William Polidori*, edited by William Michael ROSSETTI, did not appear until 1911, when the Geneva experience had made its way with embellishments into Thomas MOORE's *Life of Byron*. P.'s biographer, David Lorne Macdonald, believes that one discussion with Shelley may have inspired Godwin's *Frankenstein*, but her own account does not mention his presence on the crucial occasion.

In 1819, P. published two other works, *Ernestus Berchtold; or, The Modern Oedipus* and *Ximenes, The Wreath, and Other Poems*. The first sold only 199 copies. The second received kind reviews but was generally thought an immature imitation of Byron. A third work, *The Fall of the Angels: A Sacred Poem,* appeared posthumously in 1821 and received only one review. P.'s personal life remained as unfortunate as his writing career. After failing to establish a medical practice in Norwich, he failed to make a living as an author in London; then he studied law. At the time of his death, he had just incurred gambling debts and, almost certainly, poisoned himself.

BIBLIOGRAPHY: Macdonald, D. L., *Poor P.* (1991); Macdonald, D. L., and K. Scherf, eds., *Collected Fiction of J. W. P.* (1994)

DALTON AND MARYJEAN GROSS

POLITICS AND LITERATURE

Cultural debate in Britain has always been dominated by arguments about the relation between politics and literature. From the earliest vernacular writings in English to the texts of the present day, controversy has been generated around three key areas, which might be characterized as the explicit, the theoretical, and the linguistic. Firstly, and most straightforwardly, there are disputes concerning texts that explicitly address political themes, where writers represent political events or state political positions and ideas. Secondly, conflicts have arisen, primarily between critics or theorists, over principle and definition, where the very terms "politics" and "literature" are the primary objects of unease. Thirdly, there are confrontations centered in the English language itself, involving wrangles about the ideological or political history of the national language, highlighting ways in which this medium limits or distorts the voices of certain social groups such as people from former imperial colonies of the British Empire, from the working class, or from provincial regions. There is inevitably much overlap across these areas, and many works and authors fall within all three, but separating them in analysis and

tracing the distinctive historical dynamic of each serve to give initial bearings in this important and powerfully contentious discursive field.

The relation between politics and literature is most immediately and obviously at stake in works that explicitly confront political questions. This is by far the largest category, and shows the extent to which politics and literature are inextricably related in the British cultural context. From William LANGLAND's *Piers Plowman,* an intense meditation on the difficulties of medieval rural life and a brave challenge to many aspects of feudal rule, to Zadie SMITH's *White Teeth,* a narrative of life in postwar London that blends contemporary issues of class, eugenics, immigration, colonialism, and racism, literary works have reflected how we live and are governed, providing both polemical and documentary responses to contemporary and historical conditions. Reviewing centuries of writing, we find that politics is, in this way, ubiquitous at the level of story, statement, and genre. The plots of William SHAKESPEARE's history plays recount the high politics of the reigns of British monarchs—e.g., *Henry V* famously portrays the Agincourt campaign and the wars with France. Andrew MARVELL's poem "An Horatian Ode upon Cromwell's Return from Ireland" offers a dense, ambiguous, and provocative account of the Civil War and the establishment of the Protectorate. In the mid-19th c., many writers engage with what became known as the "condition of England" question. Charles DICKENS has an immense impact on social reform in the Victorian period, demonstrating the popularity of contemporary themes as opposed to the historical and romantic chronicles of authors like Sir Walter SCOTT. Novels like Dickens's *Hard Times* expose and fiercely denounce the terrible conditions in which the new industrial working class live. There is also at this time a current of didactic Chartist novels, describing and encouraging the movement for parliamentary reform: Thomas Martin Wheeler's *Sunshine and Shadow*, serialized 1849–50, and Ernest Jones's *De Brassier: A Democratic Romance*, serialized 1851–52, are typical of the genre. In our time, the polarized political climate of the 1930s and 1940s, which culminates in the Second World War, is epitomized by works of passionate partisanship, such as W. H. AUDEN's poems "Spain" and "September 1, 1939," or the novels of Arthur Koestler (*Darkness at Noon*, 1940) and George ORWELL (*Animal Farm*; *Nineteen Eighty-Four*). Still more recently, compelling works with feminist, gay, or ecological agenda provide evidence of the continuing belief that literature might promote political and social reform. Jeannette WINTERSON's *Oranges Are Not the Only Fruit,* a moving account of a young girl's adolescence in Yorkshire, is a popular success as much for its forthright intervention in contemporary sexual politics as its innovative and challenging appropriation of the techniques of postmodern metafiction.

In many cases, an explicit political challenge is embodied in the genre or form of a literary work. The fantastic allegorical structures of many Renaissance texts, such as Thomas MORE's *Utopia* or Francis BACON's *New Atlantis,* cleverly camouflage their authors' radical political positions. William WORDSWORTH and Samuel Taylor COLERIDGE, galvanized by the French Revolution, conceive their *Lyrical Ballads* as the literary equivalent of that political event, sweeping away the hypertrophied classicism of the Augustan period to inaugurate a new poetic era. Their appropriation and revitalization of the popular ancient tradition of the English ballad draws attention to the ways in which, periodically, some literary forms fall into disuse or disrepute. This is never an innocent process. It is the result of particular choices at the level of publishing, criticism, or promotion, in this case associated with the prejudices of the classically educated, predominantly upper-class taste of the 18th c. Other forms may continue outside this dominant culture, but they are less likely to "stand the test of time" if they are not a part of the conventional mainstream. At other times, nonetheless, new forms do emerge to deal with new experiences and situations. The realist novel evolves during the Victorian era as a response to the need for a mode of narrative that might express something of the unprecedented size and complexity of industrial and metropolitan society. Benjamin DISRAELI's *Sybil* and Elizabeth Cleghorn GASKELL's *North and South* warn of the desperate social and political consequences of a class-ridden society. A statesman and eventual prime minister, Disraeli argues that novels of the period, serialized in magazines with huge readerships and then also distributed through popular circulating libraries, are the best way to influence public opinion: Margaret DRABBLE has called his work "the first truly political novel in English." The particularly close association of this form with political concerns continues in works like Joseph CONRAD's "Heart of Darkness," a concise and haunting account of imperial exploitation and repression in Africa, and *The Secret Agent,* which builds a complex narrative around the spare fact of an anarchist's failed attempt to blow up the Greenwich Observatory. During the 1920s and 1930s, debates about the ideological significance of the realist novel dominate critical discussion, above all within Marxist and communist circles where the development of politically committed writing is a central priority. In recent years, such engagé literature has become unfashionable, with the burden of the most direct political writing being transferred in part to satires like Jonathan COE's *What A Carve Up!,* which in its vivid, hilarious, and moving lampoon of the greed and egotism of the Thatcher years demonstrates, even so, the vitality of the literary tradition of political writing.

The impact of these currents of explicit literary-political engagement is apparent from the range of reactions, often severe, such writing has provoked. From the benign and largely indifferent perspective of today's take-it-or-leave-it mass-market reading public it may seem improbable, but as late as the 1960s literary works are frequently to be found at the heart of political and social turbulence, and even now—one thinks immediately of Salman RUSHDIE and the furor over *The Satanic Verses*—some publications can engender wild political agitation. The very word "publication" evokes a work's entry into the public sphere as the key moment in its genesis. Although most literary critical discussion now takes place in seminar rooms or the pages of newspapers and journals, rather than on the streets, such professional and academic habits are a quite recent phenomenon—English literature as a university subject, as we see below, is essentially a 20th-c. invention. Historically, responses to writers and their work from the state apparatus or the wider public have often been far more extreme, ranging from legal action and censorship, through harassment or suppression, to riot and civil disorder. That literary texts can carry substantial political significance is a commonplace in the medieval and Renaissance periods, when writers such as Geoffrey CHAUCER, Thomas More, Edmund SPENSER, and Sir Philip SIDNEY are also politicians and courtiers. During the Peasants' Revolt of 1381, the insurgents take lines from *Piers Plowman* as their slogans. Spenser's "Letter to Raleigh," explaining his intentions in writing *The Faerie Queene* (appended to the 1590 edition), makes clear the political freight of his "darke conceit." Treatises on history and government, like William BALDWIN's *A Mirror for Magistrates,* consistently address the political implications of poetic, dramatic, and historical writing. Before the Essex uprising of 1601, so many provocative performances of Shakespeare's *Richard II* are staged that ELIZABETH I, sensing the implied identification between herself and Richard II, insists the play be suppressed. During the years of the Civil War and Interregnum (1642 to 1660), theaters are closed entirely. Censorship and suppression have been recurrent responses to literature. Later, published versions of Christopher MARLOWE's *Dr. Faustus* are purged of direct references to God under the terms of the Act to Restrain Abuses of Players (1606). James JOYCE's *Ulysses* is not published in Britain until 1936 because of its alleged obscenity (hundreds of copies being burned by customs officers at Dover). It is only with the famous Chatterley Trial of 1961, which results in the acquittal of Penguin Books from charges of obscenity relating to their edition of D. H. LAWRENCE's *Lady Chatterley's Lover,* that the privileges of the Lord Chamberlain's

Department (responsible for protecting public morals and ensuring order), finally fall into general contempt. In these and many other cases, the act of literature is perceived by the state as an act of actual legal and political consequence.

There is, then, a strong tradition of explicit political engagement in literary works. Literature is a crucial and effective means for the articulation of political opinion. In the preceding paragraphs, the texts cited have all belonged to a recognizable canon, or collection, of works that we now think of as literature, and the issues and events discussed have been, equally conventionally, related to the government and organization of state and society, to what we commonly think of as politics. These assumptions are, however, themselves the problematic products of ongoing disputes, the consideration of which complicates instantly and profoundly any such straightforward account of politics and literature in the British context. This is the theme of the second, "theoretical" area of the topic. Fundamental disagreements over the definition of these words generate passionate antagonisms, exacerbated by the manner in which opinions about the one term have such radical implications for the meaning of the other: to paraphrase the critic David Antin, from the politics you choose, you get the literature you deserve (and vice-versa). This is not simply casual semantics, a fussing over minutiae, although some recent academic debates in this area do betray an exaggerated sense of their own importance. Arguments about this issue have come to define not only the way we talk about literature, but also the object itself.

At one extreme are those who contend that politics belongs to the sphere of public affairs while literature is, or should be, an aspect of the private realm. Politics involves the workings of Parliament, pressure groups and political parties, the turbulence of international affairs and industrial disputes, the confusions of health care and defense policy. Literature, in contrast, is a body of aesthetic objects, subject to discrete formal and technical analyses, providing by turns moral encomium, spiritual uplift, entertainment, or therapy, its workings distinct from the utilitarian partialities and prejudices of daily events. A long tradition of devotional and spiritual writing, for instance, is predicated on separation from the world. Saint Bonaventure's *Meditationes Vitae Christi* (wr. ca. 1250) is the defining text of this ascetic genre, which is at its strongest in the medieval period. Robert Mannyng's *Hanndlyng Synne* (wr. ca. 1300) details ways of removing the self from temptation. In a similar vein, at the onset of the Romantic era in the mid-18th c., poems such as William COLLINS's "Ode on the Poetical Character" and Thomas GRAY's "The Progress of Poesy" argue that the poet should retreat from practical politics, the narrow vicissitudes of public life being inimical to reflection, imagination and creation. At the close of the 19th c., the movement of aestheticism or "art for art's sake" goes still further, celebrating the pure qualities of beauty and form, preaching an exquisite detachment from the cares of the world. Arguably the most sophisticated examples of such work are to be found in Oscar WILDE's clever, paradoxical, and witty effusions, *Lady Windermere's Fan* and *The Importance of Being Earnest*. In the 20th c., this belief in the autonomy of the literary artifact, its removal from the political realm, gains support from a literary critical movement known broadly as formalism. Formalists (also known as New Critics) concentrate their attention on the technical and generic aspects of a text, focusing wholly on "the words on the page." In part, this represents a reaction against the politicization of writing taking place in the 1930s and 1940s, but it is also symptomatic of the need to give substance to the study of English literature at university and school, which became central to the curriculum between the wars. I. A. RICHARDS's *Practical Criticism* is the foundational text for this current in Britain, a rigorous but witty exposure of the inconsequentiality and irrelevance that distorts our proper appreciation of literature.

At the other extreme, there are those for whom politics means the whole system by which we organize our lives, involving not only the apparatus of legislation and rule but also the deep determinants of personality and consciousness. In this case, literature, offering across its myriad forms a representation of all aspects of our common existence, is necessarily an expression, however complexly mediated, of political issues. Much of the impetus for this approach has developed out of Marxist analyses, which emphasize the relation between culture and economics, examining the connections between, for instance, the literary imagination and the economic or political relations into which we are born. The contemporary Marxist critic Fredric Jameson urges us to recognize "that there is nothing that is not social and historical—indeed, that everything is 'in the last analysis' political." From such a perspective, distinctions between public and private spheres, between individual and society, are dissolved, exposed as functions of a specific, and temporary, political ideology. Literature itself is a category determined by particular historical interests and influences. This current of theoretical challenge has potent consequences for our topic. First, it results in a questioning of the parameters of the literary canon, a probing of the criteria and processes by which some works and not others become literature. Second, it focuses critical attention on hitherto less-regarded elements of textuality, exploring a variety of new political implications to be found in representation and form. Third, it has generated sophisticated new techniques of reading, incorporating practices from disciplines such as sociology, history, and philosophy.

The literary canon has become the subject of fierce contestation, with often startling results. The choice of some types of writing as literature, and the exclusion, at different times, of others (such as history, letters, ballads, or diaries), is transformed from an issue of value into an index of prejudice, an intricate guide to political mores. Most often, it is the writing of women, or the popular forms of the lower classes, which are deemed noncanonical. Our understanding of the Romantic poets, for instance, has been changed by the discovery of hitherto forgotten women writers, and by the tracing of their previously anonymous or pseudonymous publications. The work of Joanna BAILLIE, most notably her introduction to *A Series of Plays*, predates Wordsworth and Coleridge's own *Preface to the Lyrical Ballads* and articulates an equally powerful version of the new poetic agenda, but it is rarely given equal notice. Apart from such necessary revisions to our sense of a particular period, these discoveries also expose the presuppositions (historical and contemporary) which have previously shaped our point of view. For critics with a specific political agenda—be it socialist or conservative, feminist, postcolonial, or pragmatic—it makes possible radical challenges to received opinion. Much of the momentum for such work in this area comes from professional literary criticism and the academic discipline of English literature. As the French critic Roland Barthes wryly observes, nowadays literature is simply what gets taught. Politics, we might add, is how it gets taught. This broadened sense of political significance also has implications for texts formerly considered largely apolitical, which are transformed by a welter of new perspectives and new critical techniques. Scott's *Waverley* and *Ivanhoe*, as we saw earlier, make no reference to contemporary affairs, but recent studies of the political significance of these texts, considering such elements as the nature of the characters' consciousnesses (looking at what can be thought within the confines of the ideological moment); the representation of social and sexual roles (discovering how identity is determined and restricted); the course and resolution of plots and subplots (assessing the horizons of imaginative/ideological possibility); and even the things that are not in the text (studying the nature of self-censorship or the limits of literary imagination); have resulted in original and provocative reinterpretations.

The final key area of debate in our topic concerns the English language itself, which bears in its very etymology and structure whole histories of conflict and accommodation. Its form is a testament not only to the earliest struggles of the indigenous peoples with Roman, Viking, and Saxon invaders, but also to centuries of complex interaction with the Celtic tribes and with the myriad peoples of the British Empire. What we now think of as English literature originates in the profoundly political decision to compose in the English vernacular taken by such writers as the GAWAIN-POET, Chaucer, and Langland, author of *Piers Plowman*. In a country ruled by a feudal nobility of Norman descent (heirs to William the Conqueror and his allies), where the life of court and government is essentially conducted in French and Latin, such affirmation of the continuing vitality of the native tongue constitutes an open challenge to the dominant class. However, these poets use very different versions of English: as even a glance at their texts will reveal, the vernacular is an unstable and flexible phenomenon. Over the ensuing centuries, the written language becomes codified, materializing around the habits and conventions of the educated and ruling classes, so for subsequent generations of writers from provincial, working-class, or minority communities, the national language begins once again to pose obstacles to self-expression, since the idioms and dialects of specific communities frequently differ markedly in grammar and syntax from this Standard or Proper English. In conforming to normative linguistic expectations, writers therefore find themselves unable properly to represent their thoughts. One solution, as in the case of the Scots writer Robert BURNS, is to write for a smaller audience in the regional dialect, refusing the language of the cultural center or metropolis. His *Poems, Chiefly in the Scottish Dialect*, nonetheless gain wide recognition, and in the energetic "Tam o'Shanter," he manages even to combine Scots with English, though the exceptional (and unparalleled) nature of this work suggests it underlines rather than resolves the linguistic problem. The work of the Yorkshire poet Tony HARRISON addresses many similar difficulties. In *From "The School of Eloquence,"* a sonnet sequence including the wonderfully evocative "On Not Being Milton," he explores the tension between the feelings and language of his home community in Leeds, and the very different language and manners he acquires from university and in literary London. These issues are intensified in the case of the former subjects of the British Empire, who confront predicaments embedded in a language at once native and alien. Writers as diverse as Joyce, Ngugi wa Thiong'o, R. S. THOMAS, and Rushdie struggle with the question as to whether it is even possible to write in the language of the aggressor, the colonizing power, in the medium of ancient oppressions.

Our current senses of the relation between literature and politics contain a long and turbulent history. The vitality of British literature is, in this account, inextricably connected to the countless, controversial ways writing intersects with the nation's political life. The issues are, finally, apparent in miniature in the perfect ambiguity of the word "literate," which embraces the meanings "able to read" and "of polite or humane learning." Such precise etymological and semantic tension, with its implication of the great issues we have traced, suggests something of the perpetually shifting emphases in the relation between politics and literature, and also, perhaps, the inevitability of their association.

BIBLIOGRAPHY: Anderson, P., *English Questions* (1992); Ashcroft, B., G. Griffiths, and H. Tiffin, eds., *The Empire Writes Back: Theory and Practice in Post-Colonial Literatures* (1989); Baldick, C., *The Social Mission of English Criticism, 1848–1932* (1983); Crowley, T., ed., *Proper English? Readings in Language, History, and Cultural Identity* (1991); Davies, D. W., *Presences That Disturb: Models of Romantic Identity in the Literature and Culture of the 1790s* (2002); Dollimore, J., and A. Sinfield, eds., *Political Shakespeare* (1985); Doyle, B., *English and Englishness* (1989); Eagleton, T., *Literary Theory* (1983); Hadfield, A., *Literature, Politics and National Identity: Reformation to Renaissance* (1994); Jameson, F., *The Political Unconscious: Narrative as a Socially Symbolic Act* (1981); Norbrook, D., *Poetry and Politics in the English Renaissance* (1984); Sharpe, K., *Remapping Early Modern England: The Culture of Seventeenth-Century Politics* (2000); Williams, R., *Culture and Society: 1780–1950* (1958)

SEAN MATTHEWS

POPE, Alexander

b. 21 May 1688, London; d. 30 May 1744, Twickenham

P. was the preeminent English poet of the 18th c. His imaginative range, technical virtuosity, and command of language gave a power and point to his poetry unmatched by any of his contemporaries or immediate successors. P. brought a compactness and wit to his chosen form, the heroic couplet, that gainsaid its apparent regularity and gave it a striking variety, liveliness, and penetration. He is particularly celebrated as the fiercest verse satirist in the English language, but his overall poetic achievement greatly surpasses his reputation as a satirist. He was a master craftsman in nearly every kind of poetry written at the time: pastoral, georgic, didactic, elegiac, heroic, EPIC, mock epic, epistolary, ethical, and formal verse SATIRE. He wrote very few lyric poems, but otherwise he wrote acclaimed masterpieces in all the established poetic genres.

What makes this mastery and recognition particularly remarkable was that it was achieved while he belonged to two of the most marginalized groups in English society of the day. P. was a Roman Catholic, at a time when Catholics were persecuted to the extent that a royal edict forbade their living within twenty

miles of London, and he was physically disabled through having contracted Potts disease at about the age of twelve, which left him hump-backed and dwarfed his growth so that he never attained a height greater than four foot six inches. In *An Epistle to Dr. Arbuthnot* (1735), he refers ironically to "this long Disease, my Life," and there was not a single day when he was free of pain.

P. was born of elderly Catholic parents in Lombard Street in the heart of the City of London. His lifelong devotion to his parents, whom he cared for until the time of their respective deaths, is poignantly expressed in the last forty lines of the *Epistle to Dr. Arbuthnot* and is one of the most moving and significant aspects of his life. When he was twelve, the family moved to Binfield, in Berkshire, to comply with legislation prohibiting Catholics from living in London. He was largely self-educated, reading widely in English, French, Italian, Latin, and Greek poetry, "following everywhere as my fancy led me."

His "Pastorals" (1709) were his first published poems. While these were greatly admired by his Tory friends at Will's coffee house, they immediately brought him into conflict with London's rival literary group, Joseph ADDISON's "little Senate" of Whig writers, which met at Button's coffee house. Thus, from the time of his first publication, P. became involved in the party political warfare that was to dominate his literary career. His next publication, *An Essay on Criticism* (1711), was a remarkably precocious poem demonstrating an extraordinarily wide reading in ancient and modern poetry and criticism for a twenty-three-year-old poet. The poem is a kind of guide, or handbook, to neoclassicism synthesizing the best in traditional and modern thought about poetry.

In March 1713, he found himself more strongly drawn into the circle of writers supporting the Tory Government when he published *Windsor-Forest*, celebrating the Treaty of Utrecht, finally ratified by that government on April 11, 1713. This rich, mythological poem showed P. publicly taking up a clear, party-political position. *Windsor-Forest* is a political, patriotic, and visionary poem conceived in strikingly pictorial terms and offering an idealized vision of the golden Augustan Age that the youthful P. briefly hoped was about to begin.

In the following year, P. published the expanded, 5-canto version of the most scintillating of his poems, the mock epic *The Rape of the Lock*. The poem is an attempt "to laugh two feuding Catholic families together," in which P. glowingly evokes the luxurious world of sexual enticement associated with the rituals of 18th-c. English high-society courtship. P.'s imagination was more playfully inventive, exuberant and original, and his language more coruscating in its brilliance in this poem than in any other he wrote.

About this time, P. became friendly with Jonathan SWIFT, John GAY, John ARBUTHNOT, Thomas Parnell, and Robert Harley, Earl of Oxford and leader of the Tory Government. These six persons, who had in common a philosophic belief in conserving the best from the past coupled with a scorn for the leaden weight of much modern learning, met over dinner once a week to joke and talk about literature. They formed the idea of writing the memoirs of a fictional, modern "scribbler," to be called Martinus Scriblerus, which would burlesque the overpedantic works of contemporary scholars. The seeds for many of the later, great, satiric works of the 18th c., such as Swift's *Gulliver's Travels*, Gay's *The Beggar's Opera*, and P.'s *The Dunciad* (1728), were first sown at these meetings.

The death of Queen Anne and accession of George I in 1714 led to the fall of the Tories from power and the end of a position of governmental influence, for P. For the rest of his life, he used his pen to attack the Whig government and particularly Sir Robert Walpole, First Lord of the Treasury. With his loss of political influence, P. turned his attention to translating *The Iliad* (6 vols., 1715–20). He spent six years (1714–20) on this difficult and sometimes tedious work, but the critical reception accorded its publication confirmed him as indisputably the leading English poet of the day. The project to sell the translation by public subscription also demonstrated his financial acumen. This translation, and that of *The Odyssey* (5 vols., 1725–26), which followed, gave him financial independence from political patronage that enabled him to speak out as, and when, he felt: "But (thanks to *Homer*) since I live and thrive,/Indebted to no Prince or Peer alive." P. was the first English author of any kind to be able to live off his writings independently of a patron. He was fiercely proud of this, describing himself in his "Imitation of Horace, Satire II, Part I" (1733) as, "Un-plac'd, un-pension'd, no Man's Heir, or Slave."

After his father's death in 1717, P. and his mother moved to a small villa with five acres of garden, which he leased on the banks of the Thames at Twickenham. Except for occasional expeditions into the surrounding countryside, the last twenty-five years of his life were spent at "Twitnam," as he affectionately called it. The improvements that he wrought to his house, garden, and grotto here became a symbol for those cultural and civilized values—literacy, honesty, generosity, and hospitality—that he profoundly believed in and that he increasingly came to feel were crumbling all about him in Hanoverian England.

After his exertions as a translator, P. turned his attentions to editing. As he wrote to his Catholic friend John Caryll in October 1722, "I am become by due gradation of dullness, from a poet to a translator, and from a translator to a mere editor." Since his heart was not in it, it is hardly surprising that his editorial

work was not of the highest standard. His main editorial project was an edition of William SHAKESPEARE, but when it was published in six volumes in 1725, the leading Shakespearean scholar of the day, Lewis Theobald, published a book demonstrating its many errors. Theobald's accurate, if pedantic, explication of P.'s mistakes was to have consequences for him far more detrimental than he can possibly have imagined.

The Dunciad, in three books, first published in 1728, was P.'s attempt to get even with the many enemies he had collected since the first publication of his *Pastorals* in 1709. Theobald was enthroned as hero, in the name of King Tibbald, as P. set out to annihilate those many "Dunces" who had attacked him over the years. There is undeniably a strong element of personal revenge about *The Dunciad*, but it is important to recognize that the poem grew out of the most profound and deep-rooted of all P.'s feelings about literature. At its base is the firmly held belief that bad literature, indeed bad art generally, is immoral and, if allowed to spread unchecked, will corrupt and eventually destroy civilization.

The Dunciad, in three books, comes to a climax with a vision of the future in which the Goddess of Dulness holds full dominion. By the time of the revised *Dunciad*, in four books, published fifteen years later in 1743, this vision has become reality. Most readers of P. would agree that the revised *Dunciad*, with Colley CIBBER enthroned in place of Theobald, and the fourth book in particular, is his finest sustained piece of satiric poetry. With mounting gravity, the poet builds up to the final apocalyptic vision in which all the accumulating fears of the last decade of his life, concerning cultural and intellectual corruption, are imaginatively realized as Dulness's dread Empire—"Chaos is restor'd; And Universal Darkness buries all."

The period between *The Dunciad*, in three books, and *The Dunciad*, in four books, was filled by satiric and ethical essays, largely in the Horatian mould. *An Essay on Man* (4 vols., 1733–34), the *Moral Essays* (4 vols., 1731–35), the *Imitations of Horace*, published from 1733 to 1738, and the *Prologue* and *Epilogue to the Satires*, published from 1735 to 1738, share a common Horatian ancestry, though the tone and direction of each collection differs. P. was now in his pomp and writing at his ease: poem after poem, in the most urbane and assured manner, flowed from his pen.

An Essay on Man is a compendium of ethical ideas, much as *An Essay on Criticism* had been of critical ones. Despite its prevailing tone of contempt for man and its insistence on cutting humanity down to size, it is finally a very positive poem, offering hope, especially through the possibility of a virtuous life developed in epistle 4, for mankind's spiritual regeneration. The four *Epistles to Several Persons*, gathered together by William Warburton as the *Moral Essays*, were originally intended to be part of a *magnum opus* that was to include *An Essay on Man* and offer a system of ethics in the Horatian way. Although the grand design was never completed, the four individual epistles contain some of P.'s most cutting satire on contemporary standards of taste.

During the five years from 1733 to 1738, P. wrote no fewer than fourteen *Imitations of Horace*. He printed the Latin on the left-hand page with his imitation on the facing page, allowing educated readers to relish the similarities and differences. P. creates a satiric spokesman in these poems who speaks in a seemingly endless variety of voices, ranging from exasperation to composure and from poker-faced irony to genial playfulness. But behind all these voices lies the adopted character of a unified personality who cares deeply about his country's ruin and speaks urgently, when he has to, in the militant tones of a public prosecutor.

P. was, above all else, an ideological and idealistic poet who, if his whole life made him aware of the pains and pressures of everyday reality, nevertheless clung to one particular idea and one great ideal: the idea that the poet has a central role to play in society and the ideal of a well-run society as a reasonable human aspiration. He told his friend Joseph Spence shortly before he died that: "'He has writ in the cause of virtue and done something to mend people's morals' is the only commendation I long for." The strong moral seriousness that imbues his later poetry, even when it is most satirically playful, is directly linked to his conception of the artist's role in 18th-c. society. P. wrote at a time when the artist still held a place at the center of society. He prized his financial and political independence, but he felt no need to isolate himself from the mainstream of life. As Samuel JOHNSON says in his *Life of Pope*, "he did not court the candour, but dared the judgment of his reader."

BIBLIOGRAPHY: Brower, R. A., *A. P.* (1959); Gordon, I. R. F., *A Preface to P.* (1993); Hammond, B. S., *P.* (1986); Johnson, S., *Life of P.* (1781); Mack, M., *A. P.* (1985); Rogers, P., *An Introduction to P.* (1975); Rosslyn, F., *A. P.* (1990)

I. R. F. GORDON

POPULAR SONG AND LYRICS

There is a traditional stereotype of popular song and lyrics that represents them—at least, for most of the 20th c.—as in the grip of the "moon/June" syndrome; a view that they are, almost by definition, likely to be clichéd, bland, and monotonously rhymed. In Britain, a number of composers such as Sir Michael Tippett and Sir Arthur Bliss and literary critics such as F. R. LEAVIS and Richard HOGGART have contrasted the elite classical traditions of music with those of mass culture much to the disadvantage of the latter. Recent developments in popular music have served only to underline such distaste for some observers. But this is to underplay the great diversity of musical material to which words have been matched, and also to ignore the creativity and ingenuity of many "popular" song and lyric writers.

In the first sixty years of the 20th c., writing a popular song lyric developed as a considerable craft. It was seen as a specialist art and not one to be equated with poetry. Vivian Ellis, a highly successful composer and lyricist in the British musical theater, once wrote, "A poem is none the worse for being involved and fanciful, but a lyric to have any chance of popularity, must be both colloquial and concise." Thus, the simplicity of P. G. WODEHOUSE's 1920s lyric for *Showboat*: "He's just my Bill, an ordinary guy,/He hasn't got a thing that I can brag about . . . / . . . and yet . . . I love him, because,/Oh, I don't know,/Because he's just my Bill" is not aiming to be great poetry but complements Jerome Kern's tune perfectly. It has an informality of expression that gives an effective directness and emotion to the sentiments felt. Beyond this, at a very basic level, the lyricists of the 1900s to the 1960s sought to marry the words to the music so that words could suit the singing voice (open vowels for high sustained notes, and the avoidance of excessive tongue-twisting consonants) believing that a song lyric needs "singability" as well as simplicity. What further distinguishes notable examples of the art of this period is the ability to go beyond regular forms of speech and generalized sentiments and find evocative and particular images.

Sometimes it is the potent mixture of tune and words together that creates a successful ambience. Desmond Carter's 1930s lyric "It's the wind in the willows; sadly they sigh/It's the wind in the willows, saying goodbye/For the sound of your laughter vainly I long/Only the trees whisper their song/They are murmuring ever, ever the same/You have vanished forever, gone as you came/Like a dream you have faded, died like a flame/But the wind in the willows whispers your name" has apt imagery and telling economy, but what gives the piece a plangent melancholy is the marriage of the words to Ellis's daring use of Arnold Schoenberg's whole-tone scale in a haunting melody.

Alternatively, it may be the conjuring of particular images that provides the arresting characteristic of the popular song lyric. British poet laureate Sir John BETJEMAN thought that Eric Maschwitz's lyric for "These Foolish Things"—displaying clever rhyming and classical allusions linked to a string of potent images—proved that good song lyricists should be as revered as good poets: "A cigarette that bears a lipstick's traces,/An airline ticket to romantic places/

And still my heart has wings,/These foolish things remind me of you/A tinkling piano in the next apartment/Those stumbling words that told you what my heart meant/A fairground's painted swings/These foolish things remind me of you/You came, you saw, you conquered me/When you did that to me I knew somehow this had to be . . . /The sigh of midnight trains in empty stations/Silk stockings thrown aside, dance invitations,/Oh, how the ghost of you clings!/These foolish things remind me of you." The impeccable, cut-glass, English-voweled diction and emotional phrasing of the West Indian cabaret performer Leslie A. ("Hutch") Hutchinson enhanced the definitive performance of this piece and raised it to classic status. The music was by Jack Strachey. Maschwitz, who spent much of his career working for the BBC, also wrote brilliantly evocative lyrics for many other composers, notably "A Nightingale Sang in Berkeley Square" (music by Manning Sherwin), "Room Five-Hundred-and Four" (music by George Posford), and "He Wears a Pair of Silver Wings" (music by Michael Carr), all songs that came from the 1940s, a rich period musically when British writers used the experience of war to create plaintive and uplifting song lyrics in equal measure. As representative, contrast Moira Heath's heartfelt "I haven't said thanks for that lovely weekend" with Hubert Gregg's jaunty "I'm going to get lit up when the lights go on in London."

The names most frequently quoted in the sphere of popular lyric writing tend to be American—Ira Gershwin, Lorenz Hart, Cole Porter, Dorothy Fields, Oscar Hammerstein II, Johnny Mercer, Hoagy Carmichael, Stephen Sondheim, David Zippel—perhaps because the ebullience of the American musical theater and show-business scene has been so overpowering for many decades. But this is to undervalue the notable contributions of British popular songwriters in the last hundred and fifty years. The distinctive British tradition owes much in origin to the brilliant word-smithery of W. S. GILBERT who provided both romantic and witty lyrics to the music of Sir Arthur Sullivan in a series of late-19th-c. Savoy operettas that have delighted audiences around the world up to the present day. Gilbert delighted in challenging singers to enunciate and inflect clearly, but it is a tribute to his work that his material has been reworked constantly since the expiry of the D'Oyly Carte monopoly on the operettas and that some of the songs remain a yardstick by which the quality of a performer may be judged.

At the turn of the 19th c., the robustness of English music hall provided a stream of memorable working-class lyrics—"My old man said follow the van and don't dilly-dally on the way" (Charles Collins and Fred W. Leigh); "Knocked 'em in the Old Kent Road" and "My Old Dutch" (Albert Chevalier with Charles Ingle), to name but a few—and musical theater also broadened both its style and appeal. Leslie Stuart's

hit song from *Floradora* demonstrated the possibility of a lyric that could be both coy and conversational: "Tell me pretty maiden are there any more at home like you?/There are a few, kind sir, but simple girls—and proper too," and spectacular West End shows such as *The Arcadians* (Arthur Wimperis) and *Chu Chin Chow* (Oscar Asche) provided hit songs for the masses to warble or whistle on their way to work or war.

Noël COWARD and Ivor Novello were two British writers of note who provided musical theater successes of the next three decades and many of their songs spilled over into general popular consciousness. Coward was at his literate best with revue-style material ("Mad Dogs and Englishmen," "Don't Put Your Daughter on the Stage, Mrs. Worthington," "There Are Bad Times Just Around the Corner") though he also penned some durable serious lyrics ("I'll See You Again," "Poor Little Rich Girl," "London Pride"). Novello provided a string of lush romantic songs from his successful musicals ("We'll Gather Lilacs," "Someday My Heart Will Awake," "I Can Give You the Starlight") and won high-profile adoration, but a key part of his success came from working with the poet Christoper Hassall as his lyricist. Hassall was possibly at his best in collaborating with the underrated composer Harry Parr-Davies in a postwar show, *Dear Miss Phoebe*, an adaptation of J. M. BARRIE's *Quality Street* (1913), which featured the elegantly written "I Left My Heart in an English Garden," a light music and concert "standard" for a number of years. The dramatist Christopher FRY was another eminent British literary figure who wrote popular song lyrics in this period, as was the satirist writer A. P. Herbert who mixed an independent parliamentary career with writing book and lyrics for a string of successful postwar musicals with music by Ellis (*Bless the Bride, Big Ben, The Water Gipsies*). Among the more prolific full-time professional writers, Douglas Furber, Jimmy Kennedy, and Ross Parker were eminent, each of them turning out dozens of well-honed lyrics from the 1920s to the 1960s, as dance band and popular music culture found more outlets for expression through the growth of the mass media.

Post–World War II, with the influence of American recordings and musicals now strongly affecting popular tastes, new and more rhythmic music evolved, 4/4 time taking over from 3/4 as a dominant mode. The lyrics of Paddy Roberts ("The Ballad of Barking Creek") Julian More (whose clever "I Want a Man Not a Mouse" was made seductively explosive by film star Diana Dors), and Leslie Bricusse (writing a string of hits for Anthony Newley) preserved the literate British lyric tradition, but in a more modern style. The revival of the British musical in the 1950s and 1960s brought both the music and lyrics of Sandy Wilson (*The Boy Friend, Valmouth*) and Lionel Bart (*Oliver!*,

Blitz, Maggie May) to the fore; Julian Slade (*Salad Days, Free as Air, Follow that Girl*) is the third composer of a famed key trio in this field, but for a whole decade his attractive melodies had disarming words put to them by his lower-profile writing partner, fellow Bristol Old Vic performer, Dorothy Reynolds.

The advent of rock 'n' roll in the late 1950s emphasized the rhythmic beat of popular music, and reduced the opportunity both for subtlety and for length for lyric writers, though Lionel Bart straddled show and pop music worlds in writing big hits for the emerging young British rock stars Tommy Steele and Cliff Richard ("Rock with the Caveman," "Living Doll"). Then, in Britain in the 1960s, four young Liverpool performers, the Beatles, took the music world by storm, writing and performing their own songs. They were so charismatic and phenomenally successful that the somewhat clichéd ideas in their lyrics ("I Want to Hold Your Hand," "Love Me Do") were sometimes disguised by the panache of their performance. Repetitions ("She Loves You, Yeah, Yeah, Yeah," "All You Need Is Love") legitimated platitudes. Enigmatic non sequiturs ("It's Been a Hard Day's Night," "Eight Days a Week") were also a frequent approach in John Lennon and Paul McCartney's oeuvre, sometimes extending to mystifying long passages in published lyrics of hit songs, such as "Let me take you down 'cause I'm going to Strawberry Fields/Nothing is real and nothing to get hung about/Strawberry Fields forever . . . /Always, no, sometimes think it's me/But you know I know when it's a dream/I think I know I mean, er, yes, but it's all wrong/That is, I think I disagree," though they also created some touchingly sensitive and expressive narrative pieces in their repertoire ("Yesterday," "Eleanor Rigby," "She's Leaving Home"). Lennon's later "Imagine" is a faux-naif piece, though sometimes accorded iconic status.

The development of amplification and sophisticated recording technology served to emphasize high decibel levels and performance elements in popular music and thus incidentally diminish the importance of the lyric writer from the 1960s onward, with the notable exception of those working in the show music and folk music genres. With pop groups, those words that were audible were necessarily direct in meaning and frequently nihilistic. The ironic double-negative of the Rolling Stones, "I can't get no satisfaction" (1965) had tremendous sexual energy but was suitably compounded by Pink Floyd's equally popular "We don't want no education" (1979)

The difficulty was that popular tastes fragmented largely on a generational basis from the 1960s onward and that a sophisticated craft notion of lyric writing was challenged by those who sought to raise authenticity and directness of expression as key lyric elements. Radical ideas expressed in song words could

be perceived as profundity or gibberish, depending on the disposition (and age) of the listener. Many post-1960s lyric writers were performers who wrote to express their own feelings and emotions (subsequently enhancing them with elaborate studio effects) rather than, as had happened in the past, to create songs based on character and situation, for widespread distribution and performance by others. "How do they (the 'studio' lyricists) stack up against the likes of Cole Porter and Lorenz Hart? Judged on the basis of how they handled the tools of their trade, the answer has to be: not so good," was Walter Rimler's 1984 judgment, in a book which sought to compare the different eras, but he acknowledged that modern songs could contain individual lines that were memorable or of great beauty.

Some late-20th-c. British singer-songwriters such as Elvis Costello and Van Morrison have produced thoughtful sustained lyrics and some of Bernie Taupin's material repays study; Taupin's "Candle in the Wind," cowritten and performed by Elton John, became the chosen anthem to grace the funeral of Diana, Princess of Wales, in Westminster Abbey in 1997. Working in the Cowardian tradition of revue-style songs, in the 1960s Michael Flanders penned a string of witty lyrics that are quintessentially English in style for his many successful stage appearances with pianist Donald Swann, and the pianist-comedienne Victoria Wood has been prominent in maintaining the quality of that tradition in the later years of the century. Tim Rice's partnership with Andrew Lloyd Webber produced major show musical successes in the 1970s and 1980s; Rice's fluent but informal lyric-writing style suited mold-breaking shows such as *Jesus Christ Superstar* ("I Don't Know How to Love Him") and *Evita* ("Don't Cry for Me, Argentina," "Another Suitcase, Another Hall") before the partnership broke up through a difference about working practices (Rice wanted to give priority to running a cricket team at the weekends). Rice was also disappointed that Lloyd Webber rejected his suggested lyric for the climactic song in Lloyd Webber's musicalization of T. S. ELIOT's *Old Possum's Book of Practical Cats* (1939): all the rest of the lyrics in *Cats* were from Eliot's poems. However, Rice went on to further success working with other composers (the amusing though arcane lyrics for *Blondel* and the better-known material for the Disney production of *The Lion King* being two of his recent achievements). Lloyd Webber turned to the talented parodist Richard Stilgoe for lyrics for *Starlight Express* but found Stilgoe lacked the necessary warmth to provide romantic material for later shows and so chanced his arm by working with the untried young writer Charles Hart for *Phantom of the Opera*. Hart rose to the occasion and produced some poignant and dramatic material ("Think of Me," "The Music of the Night").

Beyond the West End theater, however, at the end of the 20th c., the nature of popular music meant that lyric writing was usually subservient (and sometimes inaudible) in the face of musical innovation, with the exception of the genre of multiculturally inspired "rap." It was perhaps a fitting irony that, as the Millennium turned in Britain, pop groups were unexpectedly elbowed from the top place on the music charts by an aging rock matinee idol, Cliff Richard, who utilized the ancient Scottish folk tune of "Auld Lang Syne" to back a simple and clearly enunciated rendering of words from the Bible, the Lord's Prayer.

The popularity of a lyric has not necessarily indicated its quality throughout the 20th c. but there have been many miniatures of interest and excellence. The English playwright Dennis POTTER produced a brilliant and acclaimed BBC television drama series, *Pennies from Heaven*, in 1978, interweaving the popular songs of the 1930s into dialogue as a tapestry of sound. Writing about the music he had used, he said "You will perhaps find that the skill and the zest of many of these pieces are in themselves enough to divert you. I would not be surprised, though, if you went beyond that into those realms of the imagination where dreams and yearnings and almost inexpressible hungers await the simplest possible release."

BIBLIOGRAPHY: Aldridge, A., ed., *The Beatles Illustrated Lyrics* (1998); Banfield, S., ed., *The Blackwell History of Music in Britain: Twentieth Century*, vol. 6 (1995); Ganzl, K., *The British Musical Theatre* (2 vols., 1986); Kilgarriff, M., *Sing Us One of the Old Songs: A Guide to Popular Song 1860–1920* (1998); Rimler, W., *Not Fade Away: A Comparison of Jazz Age with Rock Era Pop Song Composers* (1984)

REX WALFORD

PORTER, Anna Maria
b. 1780, Durham; d. 21 September 1832, Bristol

PORTER, Jane
b. 3 December 1776, Durham; d. 24 May 1850, Bristol

A. M. P. was popular in her day as a writer of romances, the most successful being *The Hungarian Brothers* (3 vols., 1807), a story set in the French Revolutionary wars. She was less successful, however, than her elder sister, Jane, with whom she published *Tales Round a Winter Hearth* (2 vols., 1826). J. P. published her first novel, the three-volume *The Spirit of the Elbe*, in 1799, followed by *The Two Princes of Persia* (1801). Success came with her historical novel, *Thaddeus of Warsaw* (4 vols., 1803), which was translated into several languages. Her later works include *The Pastor's Fire-Side* (4 vols., 1815), *Duke Christian of Lüneburg* (3 vols., 1824), and *The Field of Forty Footsteps* (1828).

PORTER, Peter [Neville Frederick]
b. 16 February 1929, Brisbane, Australia

Influenced early in his career by W. H. AUDEN, P. is a poet of intellectual depth and intensity, merging intimacy, satiric irony, and pathos. He began publishing his poetry in the 1960s and earned critical recognition with the publication in 1972 of *Preaching to the Converted.* His reputation was further enhanced with the publication of *Living in a Calm Country* and *The Cost of Seriousness,* in 1975 and 1978, respectively. His notable contributions as an editor include Martin Bell's *Complete Poems* (1988) and *The Oxford Book of Modern Australian Verse* (1996). In 2001, P. was awarded the Forward Poetry Prize for *Max Is Missing,* and in the following year he received the Queen's Gold Medal for Poetry.

POSTMODERNISM

The term "postmodernism" has achieved an uncanny double-saturation: ubiquitous in writing on contemporary topics, it is also so overloaded with meanings and associations as to be almost meaningless. Many of the problems in articulating any stable definition become apparent in outlining the word's historical emergence. First employed in the 1930s by the Spanish poet-critic Federico de Onís to attack conservative elements within the local avant-garde, it is shortly afterward appropriated by the British historian Arnold J. Toynbee loosely to identify the period since the Franco-Prussian War. In the early 1950s, American poet Charles Olsen proposes a "post-modern" writing that will refuse the conventions and assumptions of all earlier composition, but later in the decade a group of New York critics (including C. Wright Mills and Irving Howe) uses the same term to designate the complacency and superficiality of postwar fiction. During the 1970s, architects such as Robert Venturi and Charles Jencks begin to celebrate the distinctive built environment of Las Vegas, differentiating its eclectic, exuberant, and excessive style as "postmodern" in explicit opposition to the prevalent "modernist" principles, in urban planning and design, of efficiency and functionalism. At around the same time, the Egyptian academic Ihab Hassan identifies a pattern of contemporary impulses that seem both to extend and refuse the dominant ethos of modernist movements in music, the visual arts, and literature. He is the first to posit the existence of a postmodern sensibility, separated from the seriousness and elitism of MODERNISM by virtue of its playfulness, accessibility, celebration of the ephemeral and fragmentary, and refusal of traditional distinctions between "high" and "low" culture. As the decade closes, Jean-François Lyotard, an expatriate French philosopher, publishes, in Canada, a "Report on Knowledge," which argues similarly that the aggregation of these multiple agitations constitutes *La Condition postmoderne* (1979; *The Postmodern Condition*, 1984). Shortly afterward, his account is radically contested, and modified, by the appearance of *Postmodernism; or, The Cultural Logic of Late Capitalism* (1991), its author Frederic Jameson, a polyglot Marxist literary critic educated in the U.S., France, and Germany. A remarkable, polemical synopsis of art, literature, philosophy, architecture, and cinema in their relation to global currents in economics, politics, and technology, this work (later expanded) still remains the most substantial and provocative assessment of the postmodern world. Through the 1980s and on to the present, a deluge of further work in myriad intellectual contexts and disciplines has taken up the challenge of these initial propositions, demonstrating the continuing force and suggestiveness of this bewildering, controversial notion. The debate around postmodernism has become the primary location—and incitement—for discussion of contemporary life.

Postmodernism is thus first characterized by its range of referents, which all to some extent subsist in common usage despite often appearing incommensurate or contradictory. As with the modernism to which it is so inextricably related (as David Antin wryly remarks, "From the modernism you choose you get the postmodernism you deserve"), postmodernism is at once a period, a movement, and the ex post facto portmanteau term for a vast concatenation of spirits, moods, or styles. There is both overlap and opposition between these different applications, but consideration of each in turn does nonetheless serve to bring something of this infuriating, fissiparous term into focus.

As an historical period the parameters of postmodernity are contested, but the three most suggestive inception dates are as follows: the period from 1939 to 1945; July 15, 1972; and toward the close of the 1970s. Each date gives emphasis to different aspects of the postmodern, and permits the introduction of a different cast of apologists. The period from 1939 to 1945, which encompasses the Second World War, the Holocaust, and the opening of the Atomic Age, represents a final break with the aspirations and assumptions of the Enlightenment, or humanism. The Enlightenment may be characterized succinctly (if perhaps a little reductively) as the period during which the belief prevailed that Reason, in conjunction with human will, would eventually solve all the difficulties of life, such as social turmoil, political conflict, scientific uncertainty, and even personal unhappiness. Enlightenment was, in short, the antidote to those forces of myth, superstition, and irrationality that had previously disrupted human progress. History, in this schema, was synonymous with advancement toward better order, toward the eradication of all forms of

chaos and disorder. Developments in Western democracy, law, science, philosophy, and ethics since the mid-18th c. all derived from this fundamental confidence in the beneficent powers of reason, objectivity, and truth. From the famous proposition of Descartes, "I think, therefore I am," through the immense labors of such thinkers as Immanuel Kant and G. W. F. Hegel, the period became synonymous with the assured exercise of critical reason: human subjects were the stable, knowable and coherent authors of their own higher destiny, sharing timeless and universal qualities. Although such thinkers as Friedrich Nietzsche did begin to question the more complacent aspects of Enlightenment confidence, it was the horrors of two World Wars and the Holocaust that ultimately exhausted any remaining faith in such a worldview. In its place critics begin to identify a postmodern philosophical epoch characterized by profound skepticism about both the foundations and the ends of knowledge. Failures, lacunae, and inadequacies in the Enlightenment project are exposed, its poise and certainty replaced by emphases on contingency and instability, radical indeterminacy, and fragmentation.

In *La Condition postmoderne*, Lyotard argues that this postwar, postmodern intellectual culture evinces "an incredulity towards metanarratives" (or "grand narratives"), that is, a resistance to overarching systems of logic, truth, progress, or civilization. In contrast, all knowledge becomes uncertain, the emphasis is on multiple patterns of micro-narratives; the overwhelming question is how knowledge itself might be legitimated. This process begins when Max Horkheimer and Theodor W. Adorno, in *Dialektik der Aufklärung* (1947; *Dialectic of Enlightenment*, 1972), turn the understanding of the Enlightenment upside down with their proposition that, "Enlightenment is totalitarian": rather than emancipating the human subject, the operation of pure reason generates ever more sophisticated means of enslavement and oppression. Michel Foucault's *Folie et Deraison à l'Age Classique* (1961; *Madness and Civilization,* 1973) presses the case further, exploring how the discourse of reason depends upon the definition and classification of the threat of madness, and thus paradoxically effects the imposition of strict normative limits to behavior and thought. Far from liberating the human subject, reason functions to enslave. In the seminal essay, "La Structure, le signe et le jeu dans le discours des sciences humaines" (1967; "Structure, Sign and Play in the Discourse of the Human Sciences," 1977), Jacques Derrida extends the challenge with new theories of language and discourse, often known collectively as "deconstruction," which expose the inherent instability of language systems, the way meaning is bound up in never-ending processes of signification without foundation or final authentication, without a "transcendental signifier," outside the system of language, which might ultimately confirm or delimit our statements. Derrida argues that the philosophical quest for a foundation to knowledge, a guarantee for its own processes and discourse, is flawed. Instead, he celebrates an intense but playful attention to language, to the endless flow of "dissemination" inherent to thought and expression. Gilles Deleuze and Felix Guattari, in *L'Anti-Oedipe* (1972; *Anti-Oedipus,* 1983), extend these critiques of Enlightenment into the terrain of psychoanalysis, suggesting modern institutions (political, cultural, social) work collectively to repress and distort the powerful energies of human desire, inevitably generating fascist and schizophrenic subjects. In response, Deleuze and Guattari's "schizoanalysis" emphasizes multiple and decentered subject positions, generating new forms of thought and politics. Taken together, these diverse, interwoven interventions constitute what Lyotard calls the "postmodern turn" away from the conventions and convictions of the Enlightenment project that has taken place since the Second World War.

The precise location of the inauguration of postmodernity at 3:32 p.m. on July 15, 1972 has a wholly different symbolic and material force. This moment, the instant of the dynamiting of the Pruitt-Igoe housing development in St. Louis, is isolated by the architecture critic Charles Jencks. Pruitt-Igoe was a prize-winning exemplification of modernist architecture: austere, technocratic, functional, innovative but homogeneous in form, it was the embodiment of Le Corbusier's definition of a building as a "machine for living," the apotheosis of the modernist ambition to engineer a better world through architecture. Jencks identifies Pruitt-Igoe's demise as the terminus of architectural modernism. Henceforth, architectural practice will follow those tendencies most vividly displayed in the spectacular, heterogeneous, playful environment of Las Vegas. In the successive revisions of his *Language of Post-Modern Architecture* (1977; rev. eds., 1978–91), Jencks elaborates a polemical taxonomy of postmodern design, cataloguing as primary characteristics pluralism, tolerance, superabundant choice (deriving from advances in both technical skill and material capability), and a semiotic explosion (in contrast to the austerity of modernism). Postmodern architecture, Jencks maintains, presents a hybrid of contrasting period and regional styles, combining sophisticated classical references with the allusions to popular and commonplace forms, associating "high" architectural syntax with "low" or "mass-production" values. Such designs expose modernism's failure to acknowledge its own modes of communication and connotation, its ornamental and expressive social functions, its historical and local contexts. This attention to the built environment provides the most immediate and conspicuous evidence of Lyotard's postmodern turn, serving as a material index to the stylistic and formal characteristics of postmodernism. At the same time, it should be noted

that controversies within the discourse on architecture also draw upon, and indeed reproduce, the tendencies of the wider repudiation of Enlightenment and modernism.

The final, more indeterminate date for the onset of postmodernity, the later 1970s, points to the period of spreading recognition, in disparate intellectual fields, of a shift in conventional paradigms of understanding, of structuring thought and representation. In literature, the characteristics of the postmodern are first identified by Hassan in *The Dismemberment of Orpheus: Toward a Postmodern Literature* (1971). Hassan's argument is that within the traditions of literary modernism exist tendencies toward what he calls a "literature of silence," typified by minimalism and negation, by a self-reflexive "unmaking" of the artifact from within—the foregrounding, unpicking, and exposure of literary form, as opposed to its perfection and self-sufficiency. Such tendencies are particularly apparent in postmodern writing—in the works of Thomas Pynchon, Kurt Vonnegut, and Salman RUSHDIE, for example—which typically celebrate indeterminacy, play, irony, and difference, the very elements classic modernism labored to contain within its unified, well-wrought forms. Subsequent critics, particularly Brian McHale, in *Postmodernist Fiction* (1987), and Linda Hutcheon, in *A Poetics of Postmodernism: History, Theory, Fiction* (1988), have developed Hassan's case, concentrating on the ways in which postmodern writing explores and accentuates the difficulties of knowing and understanding, of epistemology as opposed to ontology, specifically isolating "metafiction" as the hallmark of postmodern writing. Metafiction is the process by which works of fiction draw attention to their own status as fictions, through self-reflexive techniques such as plurality of narrative voices, plagiarism, unreliable narration, the distortion of chronology, and the systematic disruption of generic conventions, distinctions, and expectations. Frequently, as in Martin AMIS's *Time's Arrow*, such texts represent historical subjects, characters, and events, and demonstrate the interdependency of fiction and history, challenging our assumptions and expectations about both.

Important debates also begin in the late 1970s about the economic, social and political significance of postmodernism. In a series of works, culminating in *Postmodernism; or, The Cultural Logic of Late Capitalism* (1991), Jameson initiates discussion of these issues, giving emphasis to postmodernism "a historical rather than a merely stylistic" phenomenon. He provides, nevertheless, an acute taxonomy of postmodern styles, emphasizing in his account the collapse of generic hierarchies, the prevalence of pastiche (a practice akin to parody, but lacking moral or satirical motive, thus functioning as pure "depthless" mimicry), and the highly mediatized nature of our relation to reality. However, he is primarily concerned to explore the relation between culture and socioeconomic conditions, suggesting that we have entered a distinctive historical phase, a globalized "late capitalism," which determines distinctive cultural practices. As 19th-c. capitalism was in dynamic relation to the realist novel that so dominated literary form of the time, so the new economic and cultural logic of late capitalism is evident in the unique configurations and formal innovations of postmodernism, which represents "a new type of social life and a new economic order—what is often euphemistically called modernization, post-industrial or consumer society, the society of the media or the spectacle, or multinational capitalism."

There is, always, much more to be said about postmodernism. It is an exasperating term, the more so since much of the crucial specificity and force of its initial articulations have now dispersed. Nevertheless, its myriad catchphrases and tag-lines—"nostalgia for the present," "hysterical sublime," "radical indeterminacy," "hyperreality," "society of the spectacle," "an incredulity toward metanarratives"—recur throughout contemporary discourse, revealing the extent to which the postmodern turn has saturated the culture, how this specific critical idiom has both exposed and become the metalanguage of our time. With the opening of the 21st c., and the terrible epochal events of September 11, 2001, however, we may well begin now to assess whether the techniques and preoccupations of postmodernity—as period, movement, or mood—are coming to an end. From the rubble of Manhattan one startling, emblematic coincidence emerges: the architect of the Pruitt-Igoe housing complex, Minoru Yamasaki, was also the designer of the Twin Towers of the World Trade Center. In the curious conjunction of these vastly different, powerfully symbolic events we will perhaps come finally to read, in time, the limits of the postmodern.

BIBLIOGRAPHY: Adorno, T., and M. Horkheimer, *Dialektik der Aufklärung* (1947; *Dialectic of Enlightenment*, 1972); Deleuze, G., and F. Guattari, *L'Anti-Oedipe* (1972; *AntiOedipus*, 1983); Foucault, M., *Folie et Deraison a l'Age Classique* (1961; *Madness and Civilization*, 1973); Hassan, I., *The Dismemberment of Orpheus: Toward a Postmodern Literature* (1971); Hutcheon, L., *A Poetics of Postmodernism: History, Theory, Fiction* (1988); Jameson, F., *Postmodernism; or, The Cultural Logic of Late Capitalism* (1991); Jencks, C., *Language of Post-Modern Architecture* (1977; rev. eds., 1978–91); Lyotard, J.-F., *La Condition Postmoderne* (1979; *The Postmodern Condition*, 1984); McHale, B., *Postmodernist Fiction* (1987)

SEAN MATTHEWS

POTTER, [Helen] Beatrix

b. 28 July 1866, London; d. 22 December 1943, near Sawrey, Lake District

Best known for her creation of *The Tale of Peter Rabbit* and other classic illustrated books for children, P.

was also a gifted watercolor artist of the English countryside and an active benefactor of National Trust lands in England's Lake District. Between 1900 and 1913, she authored and illustrated twenty-one enduringly popular tales featuring animal characters, most of them published as "little books" in a distinctive 4×5-inch format, along with two illustrated collections of nursery rhymes.

Privately educated and often lonely as a child, P. discovered early her passion for drawing and painting especially the flora and fauna where her family spent their summers in Scotland and the Lake District. She and her younger brother doted on a variety of pets including a frog, lizards, mice, a snake, a bat, and their first rabbit, Benjamin, then their second, Peter. Her first book, *The Tale of Peter Rabbit,* began in 1893 as an illustrated letter to five-year-old Noel Moore, son of P.'s former young tutor, Annie Carter Moore. Deciding in 1900 to create a children's book, she borrowed Noel's carefully preserved letter, revised the text, and created a new series of drawings (for her privately printed edition in 1901) and watercolor pictures (for the Frederick Warne & Co. edition in 1902). An instant success—Warne's first printing of 8,000 copies sold out immediately, and 28,000 copies were in print by year's end—this book and its successors have remained favorites around the world for over a century. Moreover, Warne's failure to register the copyright to *Peter Rabbit* in the U.S. opened the way to a flood of editions, adaptations, variations, and related commodities.

The Romantic movement's interest in myths, FOLKLORE, and FAIRY TALES opened the way for such classics in the fantasy genre as Lewis CARROLL's *Alice's Adventures in Wonderland* and *Through the Looking Glass* and Joel Chandler Harris's *Uncle Remus* books. These books, along with William SHAKESPEARE and the Bible, encouraged P. in the development of her own seriocomic tales, which intertwine elements of danger and distress with strands of HUMOR and gentleness. The benign sweetness and magical discoveries of *The Tale of Mrs. Tiggy-Winkle* (1905) may be contrasted with the subtle predatory threats of *The Tale of Jemima Puddle-Duck* (1908), whose naiveté nearly lands her in the stewpot. The dramatic perils of *The Roly-Poly Pudding* (1908; repub. as *The Tale of Samuel Whiskers,* 1926) underline a nearly fatal lesson for mischievous Tom Kitten: Behave or be eaten! The domestic drama is often only one misstep away from the law of the jungle.

Graham GREENE suggested parallels between P.'s tales and her emotional life, and critic Alexander Grinstein has interpreted the stories psychoanalytically, but P. herself vehemently resisted what she called the "Freudian" approach. However, literal biographical links are plentiful. For instance, Mrs. Tiggy-Winkle was the name of P.'s pet hedgehog, and this title character is based on a childhood acquaintance, an old Scottish washerwoman, whose white frilled cap, water-wrinkled hands, and quick little curtsies reappear in the book's depictions of the kindly, if prickly, creature. *The Tailor of Gloucester*—privately printed in 1902 and published by Warne in 1903—was based on an actual series of events that P. heard about during a visit to Gloucestershire, in which an elderly tailor's beautifully embroidered waistcoat was secretly completed by his assistants when the tailor was taken ill. P. adapted the events to a world of humble but enterprising animal heroes. Her illustrations, too, for many of the books are filled with scenes in the Lake District that are clearly recognizable even today.

The style of P.'s books is direct and concise. She noted that she returned to the Bible whenever she felt that her writing needed discipline. Her plain style for children is sparingly but deliberately spiced, at moments of dramatic urgency, with unforgettably apt "big" words. The sparrows witnessing Peter Rabbit's despair at escaping from Farmer McGregor "implored him to exert himself"—a phrase recalled fondly by more than one reminiscing adult.

In 1913, P. married, becoming Mrs. William Heelis and full-time manager of her now considerable lands in the Lake District, purchased with the proceeds of her books. She bred prizewinning Herdwick sheep and kept in touch with her tenants and her now considerably larger family. She died at the age of seventy-seven, leaving behind a treasury of classic tales for children in many lands and languages.

BIBLIOGRAPHY: Greene, G., "B. P.," in his *Collected Essays* (1971): 232–40; Grinstein, A., *The Remarkable B. P.* (1995); Lane, M., *The Tale of B. P.* (1946; rev. ed., 1985); Lane, M., *The Magic Years of B. P.* (1978); Taylor, J., *B. P.* (1986); Taylor, J., et. al., *B. P., 1866–1943: The Artist and Her World* (1987)

MARGARET HOLLEY

POTTER, Dennis [Christopher George]

b. 17 May 1935, Forest of Dean, Gloucestershire; d. 7 June 1994, near Ross-on-Wye, Herefordshire

Playwrights write plays; screenwriters write screenplays; but there is no descriptor for writers of teleplays, perhaps because television, the most massive of the mass media, is deemed inimical, ultimately, to writing as an art form. P.'s career gives the lie to that idea, fairly forcing the invention of some portmanteau term, say, teleplaywright, to acknowledge the seriousness and artistry of his work for the small screen.

Television in the 1960s, especially in Britain, presented a rare opportunity to a young dramatic writer, a field in its first growth, untrampled by centuries of tradition, untilled by great genius, a freehold for an angry young imagination. Prepared as a working-class

youth in a male line of coal miners, a debater at Oxford, a Cold War civil servant, a failed Labour Party politician, a print journalist and commentator for the BBC, and a regularly published television critic, he knew his mind and he knew the medium. A huge preponderance of the stories and words he wrote were for or about television. Of his stage plays, all were adapted from teleplays, except *Sufficient Carbohydrate* (perf. 1983), which was subsequently adapted for television (as *Visitors*, 1987). With early exceptions, his books are collections of his teleplays or writings on television. His screenplays are adaptations of pieces previously aired on television, or are forgotten (except for his adaptation of Martin Cruz Smith's *Gorky Park*, 1983).

In retrospect, however, it appears that the attraction and the fit were the furious desire and futility of promise inherent in both mass-market television and P.'s personality. His stance from the first was a satirist's, and from sketch-writing for *That Was the Week That Was* (1963) to the self-deconstructions of *Karaoke* and *Cold Lazarus* (1996), his work holds its subject, including himself, at arm's length, squeezes tight, and watches close. But not mercilessly and not pitilessly, for he recognizes in his characters and realizes in the dialectical discontinuities of his structures an authentic longing for the triumph of political idealism (*The Nigel Barton Plays*, 1965), religious redemption (*Son of Man*, 1969; *Angels Are So Few*, 1970), romantic love (*Pennies from Heaven*, 1978), childhood innocence (*Blue Remembered Hills*, 1979), redemptive self-knowledge (*The Singing Detective*, 1986), and doomed sexual desire (*Lipstick on My Collar*, 1992).

No longing, though, need fear fulfillment in the face of economic and political corruption, religious fundamentalism, sexual repression, and human weakness, the attendant recurring themes in P.'s dramas. P.'s polished cynicism, which prevails at every turn and return, and his satirist's wit often cast a cold sheen over his work that distances admirers and incenses critics. *Brimstone and Treacle* was produced by the BBC in 1976, then banned by the broadcasters before airing for the unsettling effect and unapologetic tone of its diabolical moral reversals. (It aired in 1987 after several stage productions, 1977 and 1979, and the release of a theatrical film version, 1982.) While conservative moralists decried the blasphemy in P.'s handling of overtly religious themes and imagery, feminists labeled him a misogynist for the exploitative nature of his investigations of female exploitation, especially *Blackeyes* (pub. 1987; perf. 1989). His striving for artistic complexity and moral ambiguity was appreciated in his less successful efforts as cynical manipulation.

P., like Marlow, the eponymous protagonist of his masterpiece, *The Singing Detective*, suffered most of his life from a debilitating case of psoriatic arthropathy. It made the act of writing heroic, though it may be argued that it contributed to the writing's prickly, sometimes impatient tone. P. himself said it was an aid to his art. The pancreatic cancer that killed him can also be seen as an inspiration or an obsession in his final two teleplays, *Karaoke* and *Cold Lazarus*, which he struggled to write while in decline from the disease. Linked narratives, they are also, like all his work, profoundly disjoined; the protagonist of the first appears in the second as a decapitation. The satirist's trope of SCIENCE FICTION revealing current absurdities suffers from comparison to Jonathan SWIFT and George ORWELL, and the disturbing inquiry into the failure of art seems melodramatic. But P. spares neither himself nor his art in his and his protagonist's last harrowing stare before closing his/their eyes.

In a last, remarkable interview, however, given three months before his death, P. is entertaining and enthusiastic, despite the need to stop the interview so he can take painkillers. The sad melodies, striking dissonances, and stirring harmonies of musical performance, pastiche, and collage that recur in his work are not only occasions for Brechtian method, they are a metaphor for his accomplishments. They still echo.

BIBLIOGRAPHY: Carpenter, H., *D. P.* (1998); Creeber, G., *D. P.* (1998); Gilbert, W. S., *Fight and Kick and Bite: The Life and Work of D. P.* (1995)

DENNIS PAOLI

POWELL, Anthony [Dymoke]

b. 21 December 1905, Westminster, London; d. 28 March 2000, Chantry, near Frome, Somerset

P. was the son of an army officer whose ancestry could be traced to Radnorshire in Wales. On his mother's side, P. was descended from the Dymokes of Scrivelsby in Lincolnshire, landed gentry who were hereditary Queen's Champions. During his school and university years, P. was contemporary with such writers as Henry GREEN, Evelyn WAUGH, Cyril CONNOLLY, Graham GREENE, and Peter QUENNELL. In the 1930s, P. worked in publishing and film. P.'s early novels are short and comic, each concentrating on a certain physical and social setting. *Afternoon Men* (1931) concerns the jaded *jeunesse dorée*; *Venusberg* (1932) is set in a country much like Estonia; *From a View to a Death* (1933) centers around hunting; *Agents and Patients* (1936) bohemia and the seedy world of prewar Berlin; and *What's Become of Waring* (1939) publishing and writing. Though P.'s HUMOR is often compared to Charles DICKENS and P. G. WODEHOUSE, and his satire to that of his contemporary Evelyn WAUGH, these early books are remarkably discontinuous with previous British fiction. The single greatest influence on them is probably the early writing of American novelist Ernest Hemingway.

In 1934, P. married Violet Pakenham, of the literary Longford family, who was later herself to publish BIOGRAPHY and memoir. P. served in the Welsh Regiment and in military intelligence during World War II and in 1948 published a biography of John AUBREY. P. became a regular reviewer for the *Daily Telegraph* and was, for a time, literary editor of *Punch*. In 1951, he began what was eventually to become a twelve-novel sequence, *A Dance to the Music of Time,* a volume of which was published every two or three years concluding in 1975. *Dance* includes over four hundred characters and covers a time frame stretching from 1914 to 1971. The sequence features a narrator, Nicholas Jenkins, whose experience is similar to P.'s own. Jenkins, though, for most of the sequence acts as observer and not a traditional protagonist. The sequence begins by focusing on Jenkins's relationship with three contemporaries at a school much like Eton. Charles Stringham is both privileged and burdened by his family connections, Peter Templer is not "cultured" but is filled with an appealing vitality, and Kenneth Widmerpool is an ambitious boy of dubious social origins who at first excites derision with his flabby appearance, thick eyeglasses, and his wearing an inapt overcoat. Jenkins soon finds that his life is mysteriously intertwined with Widmerpool's, as for a time they are interested in the same women, and during World War II Jenkins becomes Widmerpool's subordinate in the Army.

In the 1920s, Widmerpool exudes an unblinking trust in corporate success; in the 1940s, he becomes a zealous fellow-traveler of Stalinism; and in the late 1960s becomes a fan of youth culture and joins a cult. Widmerpool is so complacent in his oily narcissism, so opportunistic in manifesting what is merely a symptomatic relationship to the age in which he lives, that he has become a memorable character. People, especially British politicians, are routinely categorized as "Widmerpools." But Widmerpool is not the only significant character in *Dance*. The interplay of the seemingly disparate spheres of bohemia and high society is figured in the depiction of the painter Ralph Barnby and the composer Hugh Moreland, both of whom, through their romantic relationships and their career ambitions, end up being connected with the hilariously portrayed Sir Magnus Donners, an interwar captain of industry. The onset of war in 1939 causes a fundamental change in the world of the sequence, signaled by the deaths of Stringham, who has struggled with alcoholism only to die as a member of the Mobile Laundry in captured Singapore, and Templer, who dies aiding the resistance in occupied Yugoslavia. The war years see the emergence of Pamela Flitton, Stringham's niece and Templer's lover, who later marries Widmerpool as the latter achieves his social ambition and becomes a member of Parliament and, later, Life Peer and Chancellor of a "plate-glass" university. Jenkins lives to see Widmerpool's eventual downfall; his survival is a kind of triumph, yet the sequence closes on a melancholy, contemplative note.

Dance is filled with allusions to matters great and small and written in a ruminative, Latinate, polished though often eccentric style. P. was often accused of only writing about the upper classes. This is untrue, in that many of the characters in *Dance*, especially in the war volumes, are not upper class. In addition, one of the themes of the sequence is the permeable nature of high society. Jenkins's narrative perspective expresses curiosity about nearly everything it encounters. *Dance* observes life's events in all their complex detail, yet never neglects their ultimate significance. It can be read with profit by those looking for a subjective yet empirical sense of 20th-c. Britain and by more abstrusely minded readers in search of elaborate narrative patterns.

O, How the Wheel Becomes It! (1983) and *The Fisher King* (1986) are two late nonsequence novels and are masterful technical treatments of, respectively, memory and narrative perspective.

P.'s memoirs, published between 1976 and 1982 as *To Keep The Ball Rolling*, lack a traditional autobiographical structure but, perhaps for that reason, are skillfully executed and provide valuable background. His *Journals*, published between 1995 and 1997, are more immediately accessible. The journals are all the more remarkable for being written between the ages of seventy-six and eighty-seven. They rank with the diaries of Virginia WOOLF in terms of quality and interest.

P. was acclaimed during his lifetime, yet was always underrated in certain corners of the literary world. The generous treatment he received in obituaries on both sides of the Atlantic may herald a heightening of his reputation in the 21st c.

BIBLIOGRAPHY: Bader, R., *A. P.'s "Music of Time" as a Cyclic Novel of Generations* (1980); Birns, M. B., "A. P.'s Secret Harmonies," *LitR* 25 (Fall 1981): 80–92; Joyau, I., *Investigating P.'s "A Dance to the Music of Time"* (1994); Lilley, G., *A. P.* (1993); Selig, R. L., *Time and A. P.* (1991); Spurling, H., *Invitation to the Dance* (1977)

NICHOLAS BIRNS

POWYS, John Cowper

b. 8 October 1872, Shirley, Devonshire; d. 17 June 1963, Blaenau Ffestiniog, North Wales

P. was one of a large literary family; two of his brothers, T. F. POWYS and Llewelyn POWYS, became famous authors in their own right and many of his other siblings had memorable personalities and were creative in their chosen métiers. P. went to Cambridge, and, after a failed early marriage and some minor volumes

of poetry, decided to make his career in North America as a lecturer on literary topics. P. did not begin to publish novels until his forties and published his most serious work between the ages of fifty-seven and seventy-seven. In 1921, P. met Phyllis Playter, a woman from Kansas City who became his lifelong companion; most of P.'s critics see Playter's influence in the subsequent work.

A typical P. novel is long (over 500 pages), contains a major point-of-view character but also has a far more capacious set of *dramatis personae* than most books, and combines narrative complication with torrents of philosophizing. P.'s major works begin with *Wolf Solent* (1929), in which an unrealized young man returns to his family's original base in Dorset and becomes involved with two women, the preternatural Gerda and the cerebral Christie. P. traverses much of the same topographical and imaginative territory as Thomas HARDY, yet what is notable is how two such kindred, and extraordinary, minds can be so different in their responses to similar material. In *A Glastonbury Romance* (1933), over a thousand pages long and with an overwhelming network of interlocking characters, a salvific apocalypse is postponed, but there is no sense of disappointment or resignation at this. *Glastonbury*, a fantastic book centered around the inner mental life of its characters, was nonetheless sufficiently realistic that its author was sued for libel. *Weymouth Sands* (1934) participates in the modernist topoi of the Punch-and-Judy show and the *commedia dell' arte*, and combines a very specific rendering of a real locality with perhaps P.'s most memorable character, the fiery Jobber Skald. P. had occult and vitalistic interests, but was skeptical about these discourses even as he enunciated them; his expansive, visionary imagination enable his books to open out to various strains of thought but not to profess them ideologically.

P. saw himself as a modernist, and his work can be linked to that of major modernist authors such as James JOYCE, D. H. LAWRENCE, and W. B. YEATS, yet he was not accepted as part of canonical MODERNISM. Part of this may be, as Jerome J. McGann has suggested, that his works retain Victorian elements that give the lie to overly melioristic (or catastrophic) accounts of literary history. Though P.'s long residence in America is only slightly reflected in his fiction, the American landscape (P. spent much time in upstate New York and also traveled extensively across the Midwest and West) helped bring a metaphysical element into P.'s view of nature, and the cultural variety of the U.S., as depicted in *Autobiography* (1934), may have contributed to the polyphonic quality of his fiction.

In 1934, P. returned to Britain; after a troubled period in Dorset, he moved to remote North Wales, first in Corwen and from 1955 in Blaenau Ffestiniog. P., who despite his Welsh name was largely of English ancestry, turned to Welsh history and legend in his next two major novels. *Owen Glendower* (1940) takes on the dangerous mission of tracing a history already covered by William SHAKESPEARE; with the help of the "onlooker's perspective" characteristic of Sir Walter SCOTT, P. achieves an original angle on Glendower's rebellion by constructing his narrative around the education of Rhisiart, a young, Oxford-trained lawyer, about the value of allegiance to a righteous cause and the limitations of all earthly attainments. *Porius* (1951) is an Arthurian story, set (with a nod to Joyce) during a single week in 499. The novel, whose protagonist is a young boy with Roman, Celtic, and archaic ancestry who sets out to visit Arthur's court, is concerned with the different layers of history and ethnicity that underlie modern Britain. *Porius* achieves a vision containing both paganism and Christianity, the chthonic and the speculative (the latter personified by P.'s version of the Merlin-figure, Myrddin Wyllt). In his last years, P. wrote surreal SCIENCE FICTION romances as well as voluminous correspondence with admirers.

P. has had no shortage of prominent backers, which in the 1990s included John Bayley and A. N. WILSON. His fiction inspires a cult following and revivals, in the form of reprints and periodical articles, are intermittently attempted. But the literary world has still not grappled with the seismic implications of P.'s genius.

BIBLIOGRAPHY: Fawkner, H. W., *The Ecstatic World of J. C. P.* (1986); Graves. R. P., *The Brothers P.* (1983); Hopkins, K., *The P. Brothers* (1967); Krissdottir, M., *J. C. P. and the Magical Quest* (1980); Lane, D., *In the Spirit of P.* (1990); Williams, H., *J. C. P.* (1997)

NICHOLAS BIRNS

POWYS, Llewelyn

b. 13 August 1884, Dorchester (Dorset); d. 2 December 1939, Clavadel, Swizerland

The atheist son of a clergyman, a rebel against the upper middle class, P. was, in the words of his wife, Alyse Gregory, a "life-long worshipper of the visible world." P. was twenty-five when he experienced a first shattering experience, consumption. Five years later, he encountered the raw reality of Africa as a stock farmer. There, for the duration of World War I, he accumulated a rich lore of terrifying experiences. This would induce him later to affirm the ultimate supremacy of man and his inborn right to enjoy the wonderful gift of life. His brother John Cowper POWYS defined him as "a poetical materialist, with an unconquerable zest for life—for life on any terms."

P. started writing short stories around 1913, but his literary career really began in the U.S. in 1920 when he was commissioned by the *New York Evening Post* to write articles on Africa. *Ebony and Ivory* (1923), for which Theodore Dreiser wrote the introduction, relates the various incidents of his life in Kenya during the Great War. The "demoniac cruelty" of existence is recorded by a seemingly impassive observer in some shockingly violent stories. *Black Laughter* (1924) has again Africa for subject but shows maturity and assurance: its twenty or so stories form a continuous and totally convincing narrative. *Skin for Skin* (1925) established his status as a writer. It is the most directly autobiographical of his works, relating in simple words the two years during which a young man learned to live with the knowledge of his consumption and how it strengthened his character. The seriousness of the subject, its sustained and poetical tone, make a startling contrast with *The Verdict of Bridlegoose* (1926), which followed and which is the unsentimental description of his five years in the U.S., of the life he led, of people he met, such as Dreiser, Edna St. Vincent Millay, and Padraic Colum. It is an entertaining and lively piece of reportage, giving the reader a vivid image of these exhilarating postwar years.

P. then turned his thoughts to religion. A two-months stay in Palestine gave birth to three books, among which the most important is probably *The Cradle of God* (1929) hailed as a tour de force. A paraphrase of the Old Testament and the story of Jesus, in a style that sustains our interest and in which, very respectfully but concisely, he declares his dissent from Christianity, it is the eloquent peroration of a lay preacher urgently pressing young people to "dip [their] hands deep into the salt fresh sea of life." They were present in his mind when he set off to gather his thoughts in what is probably the most important and constructive of his philosophical essays, *Impassioned Clay* (1931). In this work placed under the aegis of Epicurus, P. assesses the place of our little planet in the universe and man's own insignificance, only to reiterate his passionate plea for living to the full our—unique—life: "It is ours, ours this unmatched experience." This lifelong motto he will repeat in *Earth Memories* (1934), a collection of essays: "The past is nothing, the future is nothing, the eternal now alone is of moment. This is understood well enough by every living creature but man."

In his poetical fiction *Love and Death* (1939), an imaginary AUTOBIOGRAPHY, P. expressed for the last time his views on the themes dear to him. The narrator, just before dying, is reminiscing his love for "Dittany Stone" and the moments spent together. The prose, delicate and eloquent, is interspersed with poetry and woven threads of reality and is phrased in a melodious, almost medieval, style.

P. writes a mellow and slightly old-fashioned English, inspired by the 17th-c. poets and nourished by long years of apprenticeship and wide reading, with some influences from Charles LAMB, Walter PATER and Guy de Maupassant. Although by nature a writer, he was not at ease in abstract meditation and always preferred to sift his ideas through true events. His philosophical or literary essays and biographies are written with the supreme eloquence of the propagandist he was. P.'s reputation will probably lie above all upon one admirable book, *Skin for Skin*, and his remarkable essays, and his readers will find great solace in the works of the philosophical poet who in magnificent prose sings the beauties of this life, here and now.

BIBLIOGRAPHY: Elwin, M., *The Life of L. P.* (1946); Foss, P., *A Study of L. P.: His Literary Achievement and Personal Philosophy* (1991); Hopkins, K., *L. P.* (1979)

JACQUELINE PELTIER

POWYS, T[heodore] F[rancis]

b. 20 December 1875, Shirley, Derbyshire; d. 27 November 1953, Mappowder, Dorset

P. is perhaps the most striking of all the Powys brothers although he decided to stop writing early. Except for a pilgrimage around 1900 to visit Rabelais's birthplace in Chinon, France, he deliberately led a very secluded life, devoting himself to writing in spite of his poverty. Unlike his elder brothers, he did not enter Cambridge but was a farmer for a few years. His intimate knowledge of the rural world encompassed in his mind humanity at large. P. is a mystic, obsessed with the problem of evil and of eternity. "God" is always present in the background of his consciousness but he is not interested in dogma, only in the mystery of man in the universe and his wretched destiny. "Man is a collection of atoms through which pass the moods of God."

His first official publication, *The Soliloquy of a Hermit* (1916; repub. as *Soliloquies of a Hermit*, 1918), contains in germ his later philosophy. The next important step was the publication, in 1923, of three short stories under the title *The Left Leg*. The title story is typical of what was to come: the surety of tone, the clarity of plot, the theme of single-minded corruption in a Dorset village, effective dialogue, and the first mention of "Mr. Jar," a supernatural being who will reappear in other books. *Black Bryony*, published that same year, is almost a rural comedy, but here again, through his description of villagers confronted by a drama, P. shows his utter pessimism about human nature.

Mark Only (1924), a compassionate and "Shakespearean" story, and *Mr. Tasker's Gods* (1925), P.'s very dark and gloomy first novel, are but stepping stones to what is considered to be his masterpiece, *Mr. Weston's Good Wine* (1927). A mysterious "Mr.

Weston," wine merchant and salesman, arrives in the village of Folly Down with his young assistant Michael, in a Ford van. He intends to call on a certain number of potential customers. His wines are of two sorts: the light wine of Love, the dark wine of Death. During his visit, all the clocks stop at seven, but life goes on. Many villagers, a medley of good and evil characters, drink or order one or the other vintage, and during his visit, half a dozen dramas reach their climax. Everybody will get his deserts before the mysterious Mr. Weston departs. All the Powysian ingredients are here: HUMOR, wit, compassion, and pessimism, a happy blend of rural but stylized dialogues intertwined with transcendental thoughts, the deliberate and effective use of simple words. All concur to the harmony of this fascinating modern allegory.

The next major publication *Fables* (1929; repub. as *No Painted Plumage*, 1934) is a collection of nineteen stories showing a perfect unity of tone and P.'s most important ideas and philosophy. Like other fables, they offer the gift of speech not only to humans but to a strange medley of beings, a clout, a crumb, a seaweed and a cuckoo clock, a hat, a rabbit. But these fables teach several lessons and provide food for thought.

After *Kindness in a Corner* (1930), P.'s last major work was his novel *Unclay* (1931). The one-word title invented by P. has a typical metaphysical significance: the "hero," John Death, coming to the village of Dodder, carries a paper, signed by God, which enables him to "unclay," that is kill the people named. He loses the paper without which he cannot work, so he takes "a holiday" and makes love to the girls of the village, especially to pretty Susie Dawe, whom he has been charged to "unclay." As he tells her: "We are bound together in the same knot. I could be happy lying with you and one day you will be glad to lie with me." The book includes some unpleasant characters, a few from previous works, and a great many plots, with at its core the eternal duel between the two inescapable realities, love and death. Although *Unclay* does not compare with the perfect roundness of *Mr. Weston's Good Wine*, it is nevertheless a brilliant and challenging novel.

P. then wrote only short stories and after 1937 was content to stop writing and live quietly. But his books will survive him, for as his friend the writer Sylvia Townsend WARNER, wrote, "Mr. Powys is not a writer for everybody, but I am sure that he is a writer for posterity."

BIBLIOGRAPHY: Buning, M., *T. F. P.: A Modern Allegorist*, 1986; Coombes, H., *T. F. P.* (1960); Mitchell, J. L., "The Education of T. F. P.," *PRev* 8, 19 (1986): 3–19; Mitchell, J. L., "'One foot in the furrow': T. F. P. in East Anglia," *PRev* 6, 3 (1989): 3–24

JACQUELINE PELTIER

PRAED, Winthrop Mackworth
b. 26 July 1802, London; d. 15 July 1839, London

P.'s mother belonged to the New England Winthrop family. After Eton, where he founded a magazine, the *Etonian,* P. had a brilliant career at Trinity College, Cambridge, where he studied law, becoming a barrister and member of Parliament. A light poet on topical subjects, he was praised by Austin DOBSON for his "sparkling wit, the clearness and finish of his style, and the flexibility and unflagging vivacity of his rhythm." Like Thomas HOOD, with whom he is often compared, P. sometimes handles grim subjects humorously. His verse appeared chiefly in periodicals, and remained uncollected until 1864.

PRATCHETT, Terry
b 28 April 1948, Beaconsfield

P. is one of the leading living authors in Britain, with each new book reaching a wider audience. Working predominantly in the field of fantasy, a genre notorious despised by critics, P.'s comedies have not received much critical attention, and he is wary of any such attention. P. began publishing in his teens in 1963 with a short story "The Hades Business" in the magazine *Science Fantasy,* and published a handful of stories over the next few years. His work as a journalist limited the amount of time he devoted to writing his own fiction. A meeting with publisher Colin Smythe led to the publication of *The Carpet People* (1971), a fantasy novel with overtones of J. R. R. TOLKIEN's *The Lord of the Rings* set in a carpet. In the next ten years or so, he published two more novels, SCIENCE FICTION pastiches *The Dark Side of the Sun* (1976) and *Strata* (1981). None of these had sold very well, but the latter novel featured a flat world perched on the back of elephants balanced on the back of a turtle, an idea he was to reuse in a comic fantasy *The Colour of Magic* (1983), the first of nearly thirty Discworld novels. P was able to become a full-time writer, with Smythe becoming his agent rather than publisher.

In retrospect *The Colour of Magic* is more of an overture than a fully fledged novel, featuring four novellas about the misadventures of the hopeless wizard Rincewind guiding the naive tourist Twoflower around the city of Ankh-Morpork and its surroundings. Many of the staples of fantasy—barbarian heroes, thieves, dragons—are parodied, with the real world we know occasionally breaking in on it. Rincewind became a popular character with readers, despite the fact that he did little more than run away from danger, and he was to return in a direct sequel, *The Light Fantastic* (1986), *Sourcery* (1988), *Eric* (1990), *Interesting Times* (1994), and *The Last Continent* (1998).

The last two titles illustrate part of P.'s technique, to take what we think we know of a particular phenomenon, parody it, and make fun of our preconceptions. *Interesting Times* draws on Chinese culture, *The Last Continent* on Australian, and *Pyramids* (1989) on Egyptian. In addition, P. has drawn on William SHAKESPEARE (*Wyrd Sisters,* 1988), opera (*Maskerade,* 1995), and rock music (*Soul Music,* 1994). Parallels have been drawn with the Carry On series of films in which a familiar group of characters occur in a variety of specific settings—hospitals, holiday camps and Cleopatra's Egypt.

P.'s protagonists are often children, or child-like, with a naiveté that protects them from the dangers of an often hostile world. In *Mort,* the eponymous character is apprenticed to Death (a character who recurs in all of the Discworld novels) and has to learn the trade of taking people's souls as they pass on. He finds that some deaths are in fact necessary, for the greater good of society, and his meddling in the order of things threatens the stability of reality itself. His lack of awareness of the full enormity of his task protects him from disaster.

P. has a strong female following, and portrays strong female characters in the Discworld novels. In *Equal Rites* (1987), Esk, the natural heir to a wizard turns out to be female, which exposes the sexism of the Unseen University where the wizards live. Initially she is trained by Granny Weatherwax, one of P.'s most powerful and popular characters, who draws power from the Earth but is much more willing to use people's beliefs against them rather than to invoke anything supernatural. From *Wyrd Sisters,* Weatherwax is joined by Nanny Ogg and Magrat Garlick, with the three of them representing stages of womanhood: crone, mother and maiden.

With *Guards! Guards!* (1989), P. introduced Captain Vimes of the City Guard, in part a parody of hard-boiled detectives—cynical, hard-drinking, democratic—but as a further means to explore the notions of power first associated with the witches novels. Anyone who wishes to have power is to be treated with caution, and the novels featuring Vimes usually feature an attempt to restore the ancient monarch of Ankh-Morpork, the last one of which was dispatched by Vimes's ancestor. Vimes has now married into aristocracy and maintains an uneasy balance between law and order and the anarchy of freedom.

For children, P. has written two trilogies: *The Bromeliad* (1989–90), featuring Nomes who have been turned out of their home in a department store and are seeking a new home, and *The Johnny Maxwell Trilogy* (1992–96) about a young man and his encounters with aliens, ghosts, and the Second World War. The former sequence explores issues of leadership in a crisis and how working together can be more effective than individualism. The latter offers a sophisticated exploration of perceptions of the Other, whether through identifying with aliens, or confronting racism and sexism.

P.'s prolific output shows no sign of diminishing, and maintains a remarkable quality. He manages to balance slapstick and more sophisticated comedies with metaphysical and political musings.

BIBLIOGRAPHY: Butler, A., E. James, and F. Mendlesohn, eds. *T. P.* (2000); Butler, A., *The Pocket Essential T. P.* (2001)

ANDREW M. BUTLER

PRIEST, Christopher [McKenzie]
b. 14 July 1943, Cheadle, Cheshire

While P. began as a writer of SCIENCE FICTION, he has resisted being pigeonholed as a genre writer. His novel *The Prestige* (1995) features a pair of battling magicians, who seek to expose each other's tricks. One of them relates a story about a magician who lives his entire life as a weak old man in order to disguise the strength necessary for his tricks. *The Prestige* similarly works by misdirection, an initial present-day narrative about a religious leader who has transported himself across a long distance being forgotten as the historical narratives of the magicians (both unreliable narrators) take center stage.

P.'s first novel, *Indoctrinaire* (1970; rev. ed., 1979), is magic realism masquerading as science fiction, as a scientist working on psychedelic drugs is kidnapped just before a devastating war breaks out and imprisoned in a future Brazil. His experiences may be real or hallucinatory. Similarly, in *Inverted World* (1974) perceptions of reality cannot be trusted. The action appears to be set upon a hyperboloid planet, with the changes in gravity affecting the inhabitants' perceptions; in the end, the planet is rather more close to home than the denizens and the reader anticipate. From the same period dates *Fugue for a Darkening Island* (1972; rep. as *Darkening Island*, 1972), an account of an apocalyptic future dominated by African refugees which owes a lot to the British New Wave of science fiction in the 1960s pioneered by J. G. BALLARD and Brian W. ALDISS and is a rejection of the cozy catastrophe perceived in John WYNDHAM's writings. The novel hovers on the edge of pastiche, as does *The Space Machine* (1976), which continues the narratives of H. G. WELLS's *The Time Machine* and *The War of the Worlds* and features Wells.

P.'s later fiction is more sophisticated, much of it centering on a realm known as the Dream Archipelago, a surreal variant upon England, half submerged under a sea. The Archipelago is explored in the short stories that made up *An Infinite Summer* (1979) and in the novel *The Affirmation* (1981). Sinclair suffers a breakdown in a cottage in the countryside after a messy break-up, and writes an account of his life; Sinclair has won the chance to be made immortal somewhere in the Dream Archipelago and writes an account of his life to try and guarantee that his past will not be forgotten, and to maintain a relationship with his new girlfriend Seri Fulton. From a realist perspective, the Dream Archipelago is clearly the imagined world of a diseased mind, but from a generic perspective it is the real world that is the ravings of a mad man. The novel itself seems to remain agnostic as to what is real, and what is not.

Character names from *The Affirmation* recur in *The Quiet Woman* (1990) in which P.'s narrators are at their most unreliable. In a near-future England, contaminated by radioactive fall-out from power stations, a biographer becomes interested in writing the life of her dead next door neighbor, Eleanor "Seri" Fulton, who was an author and some kind of activist. Her neighbor's son Gordon Sinclair does not wish her to do so, and appears to block publication. Since the son hallucinates bombing raids and the death of his father (Peter Sinclair?) on a big wheel, and may or may not be a member of the secret service, it is impossible to be sure what is real within this narrative. The hallucinations are perhaps too heavy-handed, the echoes of *The Affirmation* perhaps too self-indulgent.

The Extremes (1998) uses virtual reality to explore violence, and was inspired by the Hungerford massacre when a lone gunman shot a number of people at random. An FBI agent, Teresa Simon, grieving from the death of her husband in a random shooting in the U.S., visits a town in England where a shooting occurred on the same day, to discover the two events are somehow linked. No two accounts of the English shooting are alike, and both seem to be traceable to ExEx, Extreme Experience, a shooting simulation program. Teresa becomes aware of how her own investigation has led to the crime, and a realization that (like *The Affirmation*) one person's imagined world is another's real world.

P.'s explorations of twins and doubles and hallucinatory perspectives within an English setting have proved popular with British science fiction audiences, and he has been nominated for a number of awards. The mainstream acceptance he has been presented as wanting, to ensure his liberation from a generic ghetto, has not been forthcoming, although *The Prestige* won the James Tait Black Memorial Award. P.'s characters often embrace their hallucinations and escape into the dreamworlds, just as Ballard's protagonists accept apocalypse. The emphasis is on a singular apocalypse for his characters though, rather than a collective escapism.

BIBLIOGRAPHY: Ruddick, N., *C. P.* (1989); Sawyer, A., "C. P.," in Moseley, M., ed., *British Novelists since 1960*, Third Series, *DLB* 207 (1999): 213–20

ANDREW M. BUTLER

PRIESTLEY, J[ohn] B[oynton]

b. 13 September 1894, Bradford, Yorkshire; d. 14 August 1984, Alveston, Warwickshire

P. was an immensely prolific and popular writer, producing well over twenty novels, nearly forty plays, and a plethora of nonfiction. But his critical reputation always remained insecure. In a sense, he was Britain's last Edwardian writer, not only in terms of theme—his work often returns compulsively to the Edwardian era—but also, and more significantly, in terms of tone and technique; the optimism and accessibility of his work constitute an implicit rejection of the pessimism and difficulty associated with the modernist texts of such writers as James JOYCE and Virginia WOOLF. There is more to P. than this, however; the young man who survived some of the bloodiest fighting in World War I was not innocent of the 20th c., and this shows in his work. Moreover, if he implicitly repudiated MODERNISM in his novels, he did not always shirk formal experimentation in his plays.

P.'s career as a novelist began with *Adam in Moonshine* (1927), but best-selling success came with his fourth novel, *The Good Companions* (1929), a long picaresque tale with a strong underlying structure and a folksy authorial voice that became P.'s trademark. Its three principal characters—Jess Oakroyd, a carpenter, Inigo Jollifant, a schoolmaster, and Elizabeth Trant, a young woman—escape or are ejected from their routine lives and form a traveling theater company, the Good Companions, which undergoes many hardships and adventures until all ends happily. The novel was seen as too sentimental, but its successor, *Angel Pavement* (1930), had a harder thrust, and ranks among P.'s best. *Angel Pavement* explores the public and private lives of the employees of a failing small firm in the City of London in the 1920s that is temporarily revived but finally destroyed by financial chicanery. The novel combines absorbing evocations of the London life of the period with an awareness of postwar dislocation and economic hardship.

P.'s other novels of the 1930s and the early 1940s, while always entertaining, are more lightweight, but *Bright Day* (1946) is a haunting evocation of the Edwardian era, shadowed by the war to come; here, as in his other fiction, P. never tackles the First World War directly but implies its horror obliquely by showing how the prewar world persists as a land of lost promise in the memories of those who survived. A further richly entertaining recreation of the prewar period is the novel *Lost Empires* (1965)—the empires in question being the music halls in which the narrator, Richard Herncastle, worked between November 1913 and August 1914. The deep nostalgia for the past and for a vanished cultural form that P. mines in *Lost Empires* gives way to a sharp engagement with the present and the all too visible cultural forms of what P.

calls "admass"—advertising and the mass media and everything that goes with them—in the two volumes that comprise the satirical novel *The Image Men* (2 vols., 1968–69).

P.'s drama, which started to appear at around the same time as his novels, is driven by two key concerns. Like Henrik Ibsen or Harley GRANVILLE BARKER, he remorselessly sniffs out the scandals lurking behind middle-class facades; and he is peculiarly intrigued by the nature of time. The two concerns come together in an early but highly effective play, *Dangerous Corner* (1932), which, by presenting two alternative sequences of events that start from the same point, demonstrates how a chance remark during a dinner party could either prove innocuous or lead to disaster. The concern with scandal can issue in sharp comedy, as in *Laburnum Grove* (perf. 1933; pub. 1934), where a suburban family man turns out to be a international forger and vigorously defends his behavior. But it takes a much darker turn in *An Inspector Calls* (perf. 1946; pub. 1947), where a mysterious policeman mercilessly lays bare the cruelties and deceits of a prosperous Edwardian family. The concern with time finds its most compelling expression in *Time and the Conways* (1937): the first act shows the Conway family in a state of happiness and expectation in 1919; the second shows them in 1937, beset by financial difficulty and disappointed hopes; when the third act returns to the family in 1919, it is heavily shadowed by irony. Here, P. uses the form of the three act naturalistic play to great effect; but when he came to write *Johnson over Jordan* (1939), in which a dead man looks back over his life, he abandoned such constraints, drawing on REALISM, expressionism, music, dance, and lighting, to create his most experimental drama.

Johnson over Jordan was the culmination of P.'s most creative spell as a stage dramatist, but he did produce more work of quality, especially *The Linden Tree* (perf. 1947; pub. 1948), a play about the different generations of a family. His collaboration with Iris MURDOCH in the 1963 stage adaptation of her novel *A Severed Head* was also notable. The many works of nonfiction that he produced alongside his plays and novels include insightful critical studies such as *George Meredith* (1926); the travelogue *English Journey* (1934), which enjoyed a revival in 1984 when the novelist Beryl BAINBRIDGE made a TV series in which she followed in his footsteps through Margaret Thatcher's England; the autobiographical *Margin Released* (1962); the intriguing *Man and Time* (1964); and the metaphysically speculative *Over the Long High Wall* (1972).

P. is a fertile but flawed writer. His facility often enables him to slide over the artistic and philosophical challenges that modernist writers confronted and can give a sense of the very slickness that he deplored in the "admass" world. The judgment of the most influential English literary critic of the mid-20th c., F. R. LEAVIS, was harsh: life was too short to waste any time on P. A more balanced judgment would be that P. is worth reading—and his plays worth watching—because he is a various and vibrant writer with a sharp edge of social criticism who, at his best, touches deep veins of nostalgia and loss.

BIBLIOGRAPHY: Braine, J., *J. B. P.* (1978); Brome, V., *J. B. P.* (1988); Cook, J., *J. B. P.* (1997); Klein, H., *J. B. P.'s Plays* (1988)

NICOLAS TREDELL

PRIOR, Matthew

b. 21 or 23 September 1664, London; d. 18 September 1721, Wimpole Hall, Cambridgeshire

It is regrettable that many today only know P. through anthologies, because it is necessary to read his work in quantity to acquire an adequate sense of his gifts. The reader who explores his large output will discover a poet of unusual technical versatility, with a varied and yet engaging poetic personality. He attempted songs, epigrams, classical translations, formal satires and epistles, odes, political or satirical ballads, bringing to them all a consistent conscious artistry; but even more striking than the diversity of genres is the range of tone and mood.

P.'s earliest extant poems date from the mid-1680s, and by the turn of the century he had already established a reputation through separate publication of individual poems and by appearances in the miscellanies and literary journals. Two of the finest of his short poems belong to this period: "To the Honourable Charles Montague" (1692) reflects with wry, elusive bitterness upon human aspiration and self-deception; the posthumously published "Written in the Year 1696" (1740), a brief sketch of a holiday moment from his life in Holland as secretary to the English legation, shows a superb control of tone, at once assured and self-deprecating. P. has frequently been credited with carrying the tradition of the late-17th-c. lyric into the 18th c., but his importance here is more than simply historical; in "The Despairing Shepherd" (1704), to take one example, P. succeeds in infusing genuine pathos into the conventions of the Restoration song with its pastoral setting and attenuated Petrarchanism.

P.'s contemporaries admired him especially as a narrative poet and as a humorist in verse. "Henry and Emma" (1709), an extended modernization of the early 16th c. "The Nutbrown Maid," appealed to the incipient sentimentalism of the period. In a different vein are the mildly ribald *fabliaux*, "Hans Carvel" (1701), derived from La Fontaine, and "Paolo Purganti" (1709), which appears to be P.'s own invention.

The former in particular demonstrates the ability for which P. was praised by William COWPER, of being able to reproduce vivid colloquial idiom within the confines of meter.

Some of P.'s longer, more ambitious public poems, such as "Carmen Seculare, For the Year 1700" (1699), addressed to William III, and "An Ode, Humbly Inscrib'd to the Queen" (1706), celebrating Marlborough's victory at Ramillies, now seem at best only coldly impressive. The latter is of some interest in that it is written in a slightly simplified version of the Spenserian stanza, but P. was to use the form much more successfully in "Colin's Mistakes" (1721), a playful complimentary poem addressed to Lady Henrietta Harley. P.'s love of Edmund SPENSER is well attested by his wish to be buried beside the Elizabethan in Westminster Abbey, but he was best able to use Spenser in affectionate parody; and in this he anticipates such later 18th-c. Spenserian imitations as those of James THOMSON, Mark AKENSIDE, and William SHENSTONE.

P. modestly affected to regard his poetry as a diversion from his career as a diplomat, but the latter was brought to an end in 1714 with the Hanoverian succession and the triumph of the Whig party. P., who had left the Whigs for the Tories in 1702, and who had been acting Plenipotentiary during the peace negotiations of the Treaty of Utrecht, was recalled and interrogated in the hope that he might provide evidence against the fallen Tory ministry. Released after a year in custody, P. managed to restore his fortunes by publishing a lavish folio edition of his poetry through subscription, *Poems on Several Occasions* (1718). Two important long poems appeared in this collection. "Alma: or the Progress of the Mind" is a pseudo-scholastic dialogue between P. and a friend named Richard Shelton, written in octosyllabic couplets. Not only is the easily apparent debt to Samuel BUTLER further evidence of P.'s 17th-c. roots, even more than *Hudibras* much of the success of "Alma" depends on its brilliant use of abstruse ideas as a source of comic imagery; it is this which allows it to become a genuinely creative achievement, in spite of the reductive tendencies inherent in the burlesque mode, and indeed makes it one of the most successful burlesque poems in English. Also drawing upon Montaigne's essay "Of Drunkenness," the poem examines satirically both the neo-Aristotelian theory that the mind is coextensive with the entire body, and Descartes's confining it to the brain, and proposes instead that the mind begins in the feet in youth and ends in the head in old age. By contrast "Solomon on the Vanity of the World" is a somber meditation in heroic couplets, adapted from Ecclesiastes, which was traditionally attributed to Solomon himself. In book 1, P.'s Solomon recounts how he sought happiness from knowledge, in book 2 from pleasure, including the love of women, but finds only dissatisfaction; in book 3 he reflects upon the transitory nature of human power and greatness, and concludes that the general human lot is misery: at last finding human reason unable to cope with his religious doubts and scruples, he finds consolation only in a wise resignation to God's will. Because it invites comparison with one of the most poetic books of the Old Testament, "Solomon" is a difficult poem to judge fairly. P. was disappointed that many readers preferred "Alma." Yet modern scholarship has demonstrated that although Alexander POPE and Samuel JOHNSON concurred with the popular judgment, both drew extensively upon "Solomon" in their own ethical writings, Pope in *An Essay on Man,* Johnson in *Rasselas* and in *The Vanity of Human Wishes.* If not a great poem, "Solomon" is an interesting and important one.

Some of P.'s best work remained in manuscript until the publication of A. R. Waller's two-volume Cambridge English Classics edition of 1905–7, and consequently modern readers are in an even better position to appreciate his variety than were his contemporaries. The elegy upon his mistress and housekeeper, or rather mock-elegy since the subject is evidently still alive, entitled by Waller "Jinny the Just," has become one of his best-known poems. It is a tribute to an unaffected woman of simple and spontaneous good nature, at moments affectionately patronizing, but suffused throughout with P.'s characteristic wistful tenderness. Perhaps most interesting of all are four prose "Dialogues of the Dead," between the Emperor Charles V and the grammarian Clenard, between the Vicar of Bray and Sir Thomas MORE, Oliver Cromwell and his deranged porter, and wittiest of all, between Montaigne and John LOCKE. The latter is a salutary reminder that Locke's thought met resistance as well as acceptance, for here he receives a severe drubbing at the hands of the Renaissance sceptic: "Who the Devil did not know all these undoubted truths before you set Pen to Paper, and who ever questioned them since?" P. evidently found Montaigne's Pyrrhonism congenial, for the fragments of the unfinished poem "Predestination" reveal his own religious outlook to have been that of a skeptic who took refuge in fideism.

BIBLIOGRPHY: Legg, L. G. W., *M. P.* (1921); Eves, C. K., *M. P.* (1936); Rippy, F. M., *M. P.* (1986); Wright, H. B., and D. K. Wright, "An Autobiographical Ballad by M. P.," *BLJ* 18 (1992): 163–70

ALEXANDER LINDSAY

PRITCHETT, V[ictor] S[awdon]

b. 16 December 1900, Ipswich; d. 20 March 1997, London

P. (as he was always known), was formed by an erratic lower-middle-class childhood in London and York-shire, described in his autobiography *A Cab at the Door* (1968), sent to work in a leather factory at the age of sixteen, and after selling sketches to the *Christian Science Monitor* lived on his often limited earnings as a professional writer from 1923 until his death. In 1936, when he had already published two novels, a short story collection and a travel book, he offered his first mature story "Sense of Humour" to John LEHMANN's *New Writing*, and from then on steadily established a reputation in a variety of genres which led to his being described on his death as "the last man of letters." Although suggesting an Edwardian outlook of which P. has been accused, the title does justice to the wide-ranging professionalism which he brought to his work over sixty years until 1989, the date of his last collection *A Careless Widow.*

Aside from the short fiction, P. wrote two widely praised volumes of AUTOBIOGRAPHY, five novels—a form he abandoned after the semiautobiographical *Mr. Beluncle* (1951)—and numerous works of travel (Spain was an enduring interest) and criticism. However, it is on his over a hundred short stories that P.'s reputation undoubtedly rests, as he himself wished. Although he acknowledged his admiration for earlier masters of the form, particularly Anton Chekhov, James JOYCE, Sean O'FAOLAIN, Ernest Hemingway, and Isaac Babel, he constantly emphasized the importance of the individual "voice," and his admirers and critics alike recognize a distinctive quality in the P. story which resists periodization.

Some of the earlier stories call to mind those of Hemingway in the reliance on vernacular speech and elliptical narratives in which the main interpretive work must be done by the reader. This is particularly marked in "Sense of Humour," told by Arthur, a salesman, who forms a relationship with an Irish hotel clerk, Muriel, displacing Colin, her former boyfriend. Colin cannot accept the breakup and pursues the couple obsessively, finally dying in a motorcycle accident. The moral ambivalence in Arthur and Muriel's response to the death is dramatized in the final scene where they ride together in front of the hearse, enjoying the respect of passers-by who raise their hats. At the end, the reader feels a characteristically P. sense of resolution combined with unsureness in interpreting what that resolution means.

The key to P.'s results lay at least partly in his methods. He would redraft a story two or three times, reducing its length in the process, he claimed, to a third of the original; and in the redrafting and reduction much explicit signposting was eliminated. As a result, some critics complain that problems vanish, that nothing is ever resolved. While there is no dispute about his skill in constructing narrative and handling irony, or his mastery in evoking his chosen milieus, opinions differ on his aims and on the extent to which his work is marred by lapses into caricature, whimsy, or romanticism. "The Sailor" (1945), one of his best stories, illustrates some of these problems. The narrative (again first-person) of a solitary man who brings home the hopelessly lost ex-sailor Thompson on the basis of a (mis)recognized shared puritanism, it shows their relationship as it develops under the stresses of their responses to temptation presented by a neighbor, the "Colonel's daughter." The narrator, it is implied, has to come to terms with his weaknesses at key points in the narrative; but rather than undergoing a transformation, he is shown at the end parting with Thompson exactly where he found him, with no visible change in anyone except the reader.

"When My Girl Comes Home" (1961), which P. considered his best story, is his longest. Deploying a cast of ten characters, it sets out to describe the difficult postwar readjustment of Londoners through the return of Hilda Johnson. Hilda's family have been searching for her, fearing her dead in a Japanese camp; in fact, Hilda is the widow of a Japanese, interned by the Americans, and has come home as a success story rather than a victim. The disintegration of the extended family which is driven by their reactions to Hilda's story and to the reality of her presence forms the basis for an explicit meditation on the confinement of the war years; but it could also be read as P.'s comment on the multiple readings to which his own stories can give rise, and on their drive to a necessarily fragmented but more complete understanding.

In fact, while many of the stories recall Joyce's "Dubliners," centered as they are in the confinement and frustration of lower-middle-class life, there is no final epiphany to press the point home. It has been claimed accordingly that P., in leaving so much to the reader, is—at least in his best stories—more modern than the moderns. It is doubtful if this was the aim of this dedicated and traditionalist writer.

BIBLIOGRAPHY: Baldwin, D. R., *V. S. P.* (1987); Peden, W., "V. S. P.," in Flora, J. M., ed., *The English Short Story, 1880–1945* (1985): 143–51; Stinson, J. J., *V. S. P.* (1992)

JEAN RADFORD

PROCTER, Bryan Waller

(pseud: Barry Cornwall) b. 21 November 1787, London?; d. 4 October 1874, London

Once well-known and admired, the works of P.—who wrote as "Barry Cornwall"—have fallen on hard times. Few today have read or even heard of them, and those who have almost invariably characterize them as mediocre. Although he also tried his hand at drama and prose, P. made his reputation as a poet. His first collection of verse, *Dramatic Scenes, and Other Poems* (1819; rev. ed., 1857), draws heavily on Re-

naissance and Romantic models. The dramatic scenes of the title, dialogues in blank verse adapted from Boccaccio's *Decameron*, William SHAKESPEARE's tragedies, Italian history, Greek mythology, and Lord BYRON's *Manfred*, were well received; recent critics have attributed their success to the contemporary taste for Elizabethan and Italian material. In *A Sicilian Story, with Diego de Montilla, and Other Poems* (1820), P. shifts his emphasis from dramatic to narrative verse. The title poem adapts a tale from Boccaccio that John KEATS retells in "Isabella; or, The Pot of Basil," though P., unlike Keats, suppresses some of the more graphic details. "Diego de Montilla," an experiment in ottava rima, lacks the vitality of Byron's poems in that meter, which P. apparently was attempting to imitate.

The numerous technical flaws in his next volume, *Marcian Colonna, an Italian Tale; with Three Dramatic Scenes, and Other Poems* (1820), may reflect P.'s rush to publish. They are particularly evident in the lengthy title poem, an original tale of insanity and murder inspired by an account in *Blackwood's Magazine*. The shorter lyrics are more polished; one was mistaken many years later for a passage omitted from Keats's *Endymion*. P.'s fourth collection, *The Flood of Thessaly, The Girl of Provence, and Other Poems* (1823), was his least successful. Critics found the title poem, a retelling of the Greek myth of Deucalion and Pyrrha, anemic and rambling. *Blackwood's*, which had praised P.'s earlier efforts, now placed him regretfully but squarely in the ranks of the Cockney school.

Despite the failure of *The Flood of Thessaly*, the annuals continued to print P.'s lyrics. The positive response to one of these, "The Sea," set to music by Sigismund Neukomm, encouraged P. to publish *English Songs, and Other Small Poems* (1832), his last and most enduring verse collection; its popularity persisted until late in the century. Praise of the sea is a frequent theme in these short lyrics; ironically, P. himself suffered from seasickness. Although marred by sentimentality, the *Songs* have generally been regarded as superior to P.'s earlier work.

Soon after finishing *Marcian Colonna*, P. wrote his only play, *Mirandola: A Tragedy* (1821), another original story with an Italian setting. The Duke of Mirandola's son Guido, falsely reported dead, returns to find his lover, Isidora, married to his father. The Duke, through the machinations of his sister Isabella and the monk Gheraldi, becomes jealous of his son and orders him executed, then dies from grief after discovering Guido's innocence too late to prevent the execution. The play achieved popular success, boasting a sixteen-day run at Covent Garden starring William Macready, who had assisted P. with the plotting.

In his later years, P. turned his attention to prose, eventually collecting his short pieces in *Essays and Tales in Prose* (2 vols., 1853). His friendships with

Edmund Kean and Charles LAMB led to two biographies. *The Life of Edmund Kean* (2 vols., 1835), long on chatty anecdotes but short on serious research, was dismissed by contemporaries as frivolous. In *Charles Lamb: A Memoir* (1866), however, a much older P. approached his subject with more sensitivity, impressing even such readers as Thomas CARLYLE, who had not cared for Lamb.

After P.'s death, Coventry PATMORE edited his unpublished papers as *An Autobiographical Fragment* (1877), an account of P.'s early life and recollections of his many notable acquaintances, including William WORDSWORTH, Samuel Taylor COLERIDGE, Byron, Keats, William HAZLITT, Lamb, Thomas DE QUINCEY, and Sir Walter SCOTT. P.'s own place in literary history is far more modest; his most remarkable quality, in the end, may have been his ability to move easily and without envy among so many whose achievements overshadowed his own.

BIBLIOGRAPHY: Armour, R. W., *Barry Cornwall* (1935); Symons, A., *The Romantic Movement in English Poetry* (1909); Thomas, D. W., "B. W. P.," in Greenfield, J. R., ed., *British Romantic Poets, 1789–1832, DLB* 96 (1990): 288–300

DENISE VULTEE

PRYNNE, J[eremy] H[alvard]
b. 24 June 1936, North Kent

Poet and lecturer in English at Cambridge University, P. is the leading British exponent of an experimental poetry (often generalized as the "Cambridge School") committed to the inheritance of MODERNISM, both in the development of new forms of poetic diction and in its attempt to ground a poetic study of knowledge, often incorporating scientific and economic discourses that has acquired a loyal but small readership amid general public neglect. His reputation was established with his second collection *Kitchen Poems* (1968), *The White Stones* (1969), and *Brass* (1971), containing deliberative poems displaying the influence of the Black Mountain School. Subsequent works such as *The Oval Window* (1983) *Not-You* (1993), and *Pearls That Were* (1999) are more meticulous and concentrated exercises in the exactitude of semantic sense, comparable to the work of Paul Celan. P.'s *Collected Poems* were published in 1998. The difficult artifice of P.'s work should be read as an attempt to register actual phenomenological experience through poetry that rewards the reader with moments of linguistic grace and astonishment.

PURCHAS, Samuel
b. ca. 1577, Thaxted, Essex, England; d. September 1626, London

English clergyman and collector of travel narratives, known chiefly for three works: *Purchas His Pilgrim-age* (1613), which appeared in four editions during his lifetime; *Purchas His Pilgrim. Microcosmus; or, The Historie of Man* (1619); and *Hakluytus Posthumus; or, Purchas His Pilgrimes* (1625). Although he spent his life publishing accounts of far-away places, P., as he tells us, never traveled more than two hundred miles from his birthplace. Born the son of George Purchas, probably a yeoman, P. was educated at St. John's College, Cambridge, where he took B.A. and M.A. degrees in 1597 and 1600. In 1601 he was ordained an Anglican priest. P. served as vicar of Eastwood, Essex, from 1604 to 1614. In 1614 he was appointed chaplain to the Archbishop of Canterbury and rector of St. Martin's, Ludgate. A year later the archbishop awarded P. the title of Bachelor of Divinity, which appears on the title page of *Pilgrimes*. He died, aged forty-nine, leaving his books, globes, and maps to his son Samuel, and copies of the books he authored to his daughter Martha.

P. does not tell us when his interest in geography began, but his biographers speculate that he collected travel narratives during his days in Eastwood, which was a thriving port city, full of voyagers fresh from the seas. Some time before 1614, P. met his most significant influence, Richard HAKLUYT, who died in 1616. Around 1620, in circumstances that remain unclear, P. acquired Hakluyt's unpublished papers, which must have been extensive, since Hakluyt continued collecting for sixteen years after the publication of his *Principal Navigations* in 1600. Much of *Purchas His Pilgrimes*, though how much is uncertain, came from the books and manuscripts P. acquired from Hakluyt's estate.

Purchas His Pilgrim. Microcosmus; or, The Historie of Man is a lesser known but lengthy book, over eight hundred duodecimo pages, which P. started as a Lenten SERMON and expanded after the deaths of four family members. He aimed to produce a full anatomy of all human vanity. Such ambition was characteristic of P., who also planned to publish all significant travel narratives of history. *Pilgrim* includes a survey of many Christian and non-Christian sects and bemoans the fact that so little of the world is (Anglican-Protestant) Christian. He holds particular contempt for the Roman Catholic Church and uses the pope and the Jesuits as examples of vanity throughout the work. Despite *Pilgrim*'s failed euphuistic style and unrelenting pessimism, the book is of antiquarian value, containing motifs found in P.'s other works and, generally, in seventeenth-century culture.

Hakluytus Posthumus; or, Purchas His Pilgrimes, P.'s best-known work, is a massive collection of voyage narratives and related documents that includes stories of travel to virtually every part of the world. *Pilgrimes* is the thematic sequel to P.'s first book, *Purchas His Pilgrimage*, a survey of world religions based on travel narratives (Samuel Taylor COLERIDGE was nodding over *Pilgrimage* when he dreamt of Kubla Khan). That book 1 begins with Old and New Testament journeys, such as King Solomon's expedition to Ophir and the travels of the Apostles, underscores the degree to which Purchas imagined *Pilgrimes* as a work of religious instruction.

Most critics agree that P. lacked Hakluyt's editorial genius. In *Pilgrimes*, P. tells us that he faced a "confused Chaos of printed and written Bookes," and that "these Vast volumes are contracted, and Epitomised, that the nicer Reader might not be cloyed." P.'s detractors charge that he mutilated texts and then lost the originals, that he summarized where he should have let his narrators speak, and that he interjected too much moralizing commentary. P.'s defenders have pointed out that he printed much that would otherwise be lost, and that he shaped the work to educate contemporary readers, not to create an historically accurate archive. Recent scholars, comparing sections of *Pilgrimes* against original documents that are extant, find P.'s editing less arbitrary than has traditionally been assumed.

BIBLIOGRAPHY: Foster, W., "S. P.," in Lynam, E., ed., *Richard Hakluyt and His Successors* (1946): 47–61; Pennington, L. E., ed., *The P. Handbook* (2 vols., 1997)

PATRICK MCHENRY

PUTTENHAM, George
b. 1520?; d. 1591?, London

PUTTENHAM, Richard
b. 1520?; d. 1601?

An important and entertaining critical treatise entitled *The Arte of English Poesie* was published anonymously in 1589; many authorities believe on good evidence that it is the work of G. P., but others attribute it to G.'s brother R. P., still others give credit to John Lumley, Baron Lumley.

The Puttenhams' mother was the sister of the celebrated thinker and writer Sir Thomas ELYOT, and their sister married Sir John Throckmorton. George, married to Lady Elizabeth Windsor (widow of William, Lord Windsor), had received a thorough education in law and the classics. According to family lore, he was estranged from his wife and went abroad in 1563, traveling in Flanders and elsewhere. He enjoyed on-again-off-again relations with the court, and he seems to have been in political trouble more than once. He was imprisoned in 1569 on charges of conspiracy to murder the Bishop of London, and later charged with criticizing Queen ELIZABETH I's counselors. Later, reportedly at the request of the queen herself, he wrote *A Justification of Queen Elizabeth in Relation to the Affair of Mary Queen of Scots*, for which he was awarded the title of a gentleman pensioner.

G. P. was buried at St. Brides, Fleet Street, in January 1591. His will left everything to a servant, Mary Syme. Whoever its author or authors, *The Arte of English Poesie* stands second only to Sir Philip SIDNEY's *Apologie for Poetrie* as a systematic examination of the claims of poetry in society and among the arts of persuasion and pleasing. The first of its three parts sets up definitions of poets and poetry and gives them a high and honorable place among the arts. The second and third parts are more technical, concentrating on hundreds of details of rhetoric and prosody, always with apt examples and lively translations from arid Greek into rambunctious English. The figure of metalepsis, for example, the unusual piling of one metaphor onto another (as in Jack Kerouac's "Walking on water wasn't built in a day"), is farfetched, so P. calls it "the far-fet" (the far-fetcher).

BIBLIOGRAPHY: Doherty, S. J., Jr., ed., *G. P.'s The Arte of English Poesie* (1983); Rollins, H. E., and H. Baker, eds., *The Renaissance in England: Non-Dramatic Prose and Verse of the Sixteenth Century*

WILLIAM HARMON

PYM, Barbara
b. 6 June 1913, Oswestry, Shropshire; d. 11 January 1980, Oxford

Often compared to Jane AUSTEN's, P.'s novels are in the realistic tradition associated with the 19th-c. English novel. But although her novels were deemed old-fashioned and out-of-date when originally published, her work has gradually developed a strong following and increasing critical appreciation. Part of the resistance to P.'s work involves its attention to ordinary life and to "little" characters whose lives are unheroic and, indeed, often unfilled with event. But what distinguishes P. is that her relaxed plots are governed by a detached authorial perspective given validation by her years working for an anthropological society. P.'s astute and sometimes withering perspective, which can occasion comedy as well as darker moments of truth, is what differentiates her work from that of other, similar novels of daily or domestic life. In addition, her skeptical attitude toward love, marriage, and career as a source of fulfillment for women, and her suggestion that friendship and a spiritual life are of greater value, is a considerable departure from the conventional wisdom found in traditional "women's fiction."

P.'s great and essentially autobiographical subject is the situation of unmarried woman living in the second half of the 20th c. A good early example of her witty, compassionate treatment of this subject is *Excellent Women* (1952), whose title indicates its heroine, Mildred Lathbury, a single woman engaged in good works who attempts to live up to high standards of personal morality. A pillar of her local Anglican church, Mildred tries to be a good Christian, but although she is a kind and decent woman, she is also terribly lonely and not particularly well-off. The fact that P.'s "excellent woman" marries in the end, however, only demonstrates that she will now be expected to unselfishly serve the interests of her thoughtless husband. Like many of P.'s novels, *Excellent Women* quietly undermines the suggestion that marriage constitutes a woman's happy ending.

That love and marriage cannot serve as a meaningful center of a woman's life is explored in a number of P.'s novels, perhaps most effectively in *A Glass of Blessings* (1958). Here, P. explores the empty life of Wilmet Forsyth, an elegant married woman who seemingly has everything she desires. With plenty of money, clothes, a beautiful house, Wilmet is pampered by her husband and easily attracts the glances of admiring men. Like the character of Prudence in *Jane and Prudence* (1953) and Leonore in *The Sweet Dove Died* (1978), Wilmet assumes that an exciting, romantic love affair with a handsome man will give her life meaning and value. Wilmet's narcissism is attenuated not through a love affair, however, but through her gradual involvement with a local Anglican church, where she finds genuine friendship and a sense of belonging. The presence of the church in all of P.'s novels, even if accompanied by ineffectual or preposterous clergymen, suggests, as it does here, that religious faith or religious practice are a crucial component to the good life.

The Anglican Church also plays a part in P.'s most respected novel, *Quartet in Autumn* (1977), although the center of the novel is essentially a dark and mordant one. An examination of the problems of aging, this novel is considered P.'s masterpiece, and was shortlisted for the Booker Prize in 1977. This novel explores four office workers whose forced retirements have thrown them into crisis. The most intriguing of these characters is the anorexic and reclusive Marcia Ivory, P.'s greatest and most memorable creation. Suffering from breast cancer and stubbornly resisting the ministrations of a well-meaning social worker, Marcia retreats into complete isolation and dementia. Although seemingly filled with mad trivialities, Marcia's life is, in an inner way, one of considerable passion and interest, and her self-induced death by starvation has about it a tragic grandeur that suggests she has, in spite of everything, remained true to herself.

Marcia's coworker Letty also lives a life whose emptiness belies an inner richness, although without Marcia's heroic level of astonishing eccentricity. Letty is yet another example of the kind of women in whom P. specializes. Understanding that she has been left alone and left behind in a rapidly changing English society, and that her search for love has left her disappointed and uncertain, Letty nevertheless finds that retirement into solitude and utter marginality now has the advantage of allowing her time to think. Through her enforced idleness, Letty develops a heightened and attentive consciousness that allows her to understand herself and those around her in a deeper and wiser way. It is given to her to round off P.'s novel with a surprisingly optimistic conclusion, as she reflects that her life is offering her infinite possibilities for growth and change. The expectation of fulfillment by means of a career and a conventional love affair and marriage is here abandoned in favor of a path that leads instead to friendship and spiritual rewards. This theme is at the heart of all P.'s work, and her witty and insightful depiction of the single soul has attracted a devoted readership.

BIBLIOGRAPHY: Burkhart, C., *The Pleasure of Miss P.* (1987); Holt, H., *A Lot to Ask: A Life of B. P.* (1990); Long, R. E., *B. P.* (1986); Nardin, J., *B. P.* (1985)

MARGARET BOE BIRNS

QUARLES, Francis

b. 1592, Romford; d. 8 September 1644, London

Though his reputation as a poet declined rapidly during the long 18th c., Q. is now regarded positively because of one very popular 17th-c. best-seller. His *Emblemes* (1635) built upon the emblem tradition begun by Alciati and developed by others, but he adapted the near-impenetrable genre for a popular audience.

The son of a gentleman, Q. was educated at Cambridge and Lincoln's Inn; in 1618, he married Ursula Woodgate, who was to author the posthumous biography printed in *Solomon's Recantation* (1645), a paraphrase of Ecclesiastes. After some brief service to the Princess Elizabeth on the Continent, Q. became secretary to scholar and Archbishop James Ussher, living for a time in Ireland. His first published work was *A Feast for Wormes* (1620; rev. ed., 1626), paraphrases and meditative verses on the book of Jonah. This was followed by similar works derived from the books of Esther, Job, Lamentations, and the Song of Solomon. *Argalus and Parthenia* (1629; rev. ed., 1632), Q.'s only truly secular work, was a long poem in couplets based on an incident in Sir Philip SIDNEY's *Arcadia*; eight editions were published in Q.'s lifetime.

Divine Fancies (1632), a collection of four hundred poems, contains some addresses to friends and the king, paraphrases, and satires on both Catholic and Puritan theological positions. These devotional poems are pious, though, rather than truly religious, and lack the psychological and personal intensity of George HERBERT's and John DONNE's devotional verse. The emblematic poems contained in this work, however, provided training for his most significant effort, the *Emblemes*.

Borrowing heavily from two Jesuit emblem books, Q. transformed the nature of the emblem book with the *Emblemes*. Q.'s work copied many of the engravings from his Jesuit models, as well as the pattern of a motto or biblical quotation, devotional poem, sayings from the Fathers of the Church, and an epigram. Traditional emblem books pictured a classical or allegorical symbol, a motto, and epigram. But Q. adapted the verse, transforming the static medieval allegory of the traditional emblem into a dramatic situation (e.g., Emblem I.i is a dialogue between Eve and the serpent). He also rehabilitated the Catholic images for the Protestant reader, his poetry providing a tension between word and image that escaped the earlier emblematists. *Hieroglyphikes of the Life of Man* (1638), Q.'s next venture into the genre, was published together with the *Emblemes* in all later editions of these works. Its latter section depicts the seven ages of man, figured in both poetic text and the slowly burning candle pictured in the emblems. Though not great poetry, the aphoristic style of the epigram suited Q.'s talents; that, and the pictures, attracted the new readers and reading audiences being courted in the 17th c. The work was extremely popular, with twenty-three editions of the combined texts published before 1800; it was reprinted (with new illustrations) frequently through the 19th c.

Q.'s other minor works include elegies for his brother, for Julius Caesar, and various noblemen and women. The *Enchiridion* (1640; rev. ed., 1641), a prose collection of moralistic aphorisms, sold well; a later revision and additions drew heavily from Francis BACON and Machiavelli. Although a sympathizer of the moderate Calvinist wing of the Church of England, Q. was a supporter of Charles I; his political pamphlets, *The Loyal Convert* (1644), *The Whipper Whipt* (1644), and *The New Distemper* (1645), defended Charles's position vis-à-vis the Parliament. The publication of these pamphlets and the subsequent attacks on his character hastened Q.'s death; his wife was left to struggle with publishers about the rights to her husband's remaining writings. Several more religious works were published after his death, including Q.'s one drama, *The Virgin Widow* (1649), a romance that can be read as a political/religious allegory on the Anglican Church of Q.'s day.

No other emblematist achieved the same measure of success as did Q. Though one of the lesser poets, the record of his publication output and the extraordinary success of several of his works shed some light on the tastes and mentality of the 17th-c. reader.

BIBLIOGRAPHY: Freeman, R., *English Emblem Books* (1948); Gilman, E. B., "Word and Image in Q.'s *Emblemes*," *CritI* 6 (1980): 385–410; Horden, J., *F. Q. (1593–1664)* (1953); Roberts, L. M., "F. Q.," in Hester, M. T., ed., *Seventeenth-Century British Nondramatic Poets*, Second Series, *DLB* 126 (1993): 227–38

CECILE M. JAGODZINSKI

QUENNELL, [Sir] Peter
b. 9 March 1905, Bromley, Kent; d. 27 October 1993, London

Q. was educated at Berkhamsted School. While still a schoolboy, he contributed poems in both 1922 and 1923 to the anthology of *Public School Verse,* four of which were reprinted by Edward Marsh in the influential *Georgian Poetry, 1920–1922* (1922). In 1922, he published a slim volume of verse entitled *Masques and Poems,* which was printed by the Golden Cockerel Press. He entered Balliol College, Oxford, in 1923 where he became friendly with many of the prominent literary figures of the day as well as editing, together with Harold Acton, *Oxford Poetry 1924.* He was sent down from Oxford in 1925 for committing "a number of crimes" and in 1926 published a collection of poetry entitled simply *Poems.* Though his poetry was greatly admired—F. T. Prince later described *Poems* as "one of the most unjustly neglected 'slim volumes' of its time"—Q. stopped writing poetry entirely. One of his last acts as a poet was to reply to Virginia WOOLF's pamphlet *A Letter to a Young Poet* by describing the times as unpropitious for poetry and advising the contemporary poet to be patient in the hope that things will change for the better.

Q. turned to BIOGRAPHY. Largely at the suggestion of T. S. ELIOT he wrote *Baudelaire and the Symbolists: Five Essays* (1929) and thus, he said, "I became a biographer; and despite one or two excursions into allied fields, a biographer I have ever since remained." He accepted an appointment to a newly founded chair of English literature at the University of Tokyo, Bunrika Daigaku, primarily a teacher's training college, for which he was entirely unsuitable though he turned his experiences in Japan and the Far East into an unusual travel book, *A Superficial Journey through Tokyo and Peking* (1932). Thereafter, having already published a novel *The Phoenix-Kind* in 1931 and a book of short stories *Sympathy and Other Stories* in 1933, he concentrated largely on discussing, reanimating, and reappraising the work and genius of other writers.

He had already contributed a volume on Lord BYRON to the Great Lives Series published by Duckworth in 1934, but in 1935 he published what he later describe as "my first genuinely adult book," the first part of his life of Byron entitled *Byron: The Years of Fame.* He followed this by publishing the sequel, *Byron in Italy,* in 1941, and together they set entirely new standards in Byron criticism and remain outstanding examples of the biographer's art. Though now superseded by more scholarly works, they are still read for the fascination of the way in which the events of Byron's life are retold, for the excitement of their narrative, their lucidity and the extraordinary quality of Q.'s prose style. He followed this later with an anthology of Byron's poetry and prose and by a two-volume edition of his letters and diaries entitled *Byron: A Self-Portrait, Letters and Diaries, 1798–1824* (1950) in which, apart from brief biographical summaries describing each particular phase of his life, Byron is allowed to speak for himself.

In 1939, Q. published his biography of George II's consort Caroline of Anspach, *Caroline of England: An Augustan Portrait,* which had larger sales than his Byron biography. Though he did not undertake any new research, by relying on his own literary gifts he managed to bring both the queen and the early Hanoverian court amusingly and convincingly to life. His *Four Portraits: Studies of the Eighteenth Century,* published in 1945, showed him to be thoroughly at home in the 18th c., and he writes about James BOSWELL, Edward GIBBON, Laurence STERNE, and John Wilkes with fluency, understanding, and affection. In 1949, he published *John Ruskin: The Portrait of a Prophet,* a study of John RUSKIN's private life that passes over the controversial question of Ruskin's marriage and concentrates on his long drawn out obsession with Rose La Touche. In 1955, Q. returned to the 18th c. with his biography of William Hogarth, *Hogarth's Progress,* that while presenting no new facts about the painter nor even a new interpretation of the known facts was nonetheless, as the *Times Literary Supplement* reviewer commented, "a most readable biography and a rewardingly inquisitive guidebook to eighteenth century London—for which latter, by ingenious posthumous collaboration, Hogarth has provided the illustrations." He followed this in 1968 by his biography, *Alexander Pope: The Education of a Genius 1688–1728* and *Samuel Johnson: His Friends and Enemies* in 1972. In both of these biographies, he addresses the general reader though because he places his subjects within their social settings he manages to combine biography and social history in an elegant, engaging, and authentic manner that also beguiles the scholarly reader.

He published his AUTOBIOGRAPHY in two volumes, *The Marble Foot* (1976) and *The Wanton Chase* (1980). The first volume covers his life to 1938 and is by far the more revealing of the two volumes as it deals with his childhood, his early years, and his experiences in literary and social London, yet both volumes seem to conceal quite as much as they reveal since he is careful to protect his privacy. For the most part, he confines himself to a discussion of his public persona while leaving his private person out of account. He is nonetheless an acute and witty observer of his contemporaries and a convincing painter of the social scene. In addition, he wrote two further volumes, *The Sign of the Fish* (1960) and *Customs and Characters: Contemporary Portraits* (1982), that consist mainly of reminiscences concerning his early friendships and acquaintances. Both mix literary gossip, anecdotes, and personal memories in a rather loose associative way thus lending them the informality of good conversation between informed and civilized people. In his last book, *The Pursuit of Happiness* (1988), he addresses the question of happiness that has, he says, "perplexed and fascinated imaginative artists for the last two thousand years." In this book, Q. renews his enjoyment of life by recounting the ways in which happiness has been captured, lost, and captured again. He looks back with evident pleasure and looks forward with an undimmed appetite to the happiness he is certain is still in store for him. It is a remarkably resilient, assured, and enjoyable performance particularly for an octogenarian.

Apart from being a prolific editor of other people's work—he edited work by, among others, Charles Baudelaire, Henri de Montherlant, Marcel Proust, Vladimir Nabokov, James Pope-Hennessy, and Henry MAYHEW—he edited the *Cornhill Magazine* from 1944 until 1951 when he became coeditor with Alan Hodge of *History Today*. He was honored for his services to history and literature by the award of a CBE in 1973 and a knighthood in 1992.

BIBLIOGRAPHY: Jones, A. R., "P. Q.," in Serafin, S., ed., *Twentieth-Century British Literary Biographers*, DLB 155 (1995): 240–50

A. R. JONES

QUILLER-COUCH, [Sir] Arthur

b. 21 November 1863, Bodmin, Cornwall; d. 12 May 1944, Fowey, Cornwall

Though the passing of several ages of literary taste may have staled his infinite variety, Q.-C. ("a pre-1914 man, really in heart and mind a Victorian," according to his biographer A. L. Rowse) remains a fascinating minor figure in English literature. His long life of service to the public and to the cause of higher learning, combined with his mastery of expressive

English and a deeply felt spirituality that rose above sectarian narrowness, make him all the more interesting as a man and a prolific author. He just might be remembered currently—if at all—for his 1913 essay derived from a Cambridge lecture, "On Jargon" (quite dated, however, and reflecting certain prejudices of its time), and for one of his anthologies, *The Oxford Book of English Verse* (1900; rev. ed., 1939). The first edition of the latter "won recognition as the finest anthology of English verse that had ever been published," according to Q.-C.'s biographer Frederick Brittain.

Q.-C., who would remain attached to his native rural Cornwall all of his life, was awarded a scholarship in 1882 to attend Trinity College, Oxford. After spending five years at Trinity and taking a degree in classics, he remained there for an additional year, having been given the position of lecturer in classics. Within less than a quarter century following his departure from Trinity, Q.-C. had built up a very impressive public reputation for his diversified literary productions, his effective participation on the Cornwall Education Committee, and his service to the Liberal Party in the Government. Accordingly, in 1910, Prime Minister H. H. Asquith honored him by making him a knight bachelor, and not long afterward he was knighted by King George V in St. James's Palace. Two years later, in 1912, Q.-C. received another major appointment when he was named King Edward VII Professor of English Literature at Cambridge, following which he subsequently gained an affiliation with a specific college at Cambridge when he was offered a professorial Fellowship by Jesus College, Cambridge.

In his lifetime, Q.-C. published at least three volumes of verse that underwent reprinting in later editions: *Green Bays* (1893; rev. ed., 1930), *Poems and Ballads* (1896), *The Vigil of Venus and Other Poems* (1912). There were also parodies and odds and ends of verse: the limerick, the clerihew, the special occasion poem. In addition, Q.-C. edited at least five other anthologies besides *The Oxford Book of English Verse*. And Rowse cites the following (which appears in Q.-C.'s essay collection, *From a Cornish Window*, 1906): poetry demands one's belief in something beyond the describable life that one knows and "can reduce to laws and formulas"—that is, it demands a spiritual life within which is "that eternal scheme of things, that universal order, of which the phenomena of this world are but fragments, if indeed they are not mere shadows." Yet Q.-C. himself, for all his versatility, imaginative power, and gift with words, was apparently unable to produce memorable poetry that would place him among the more prominent late Victorian poets or those of the 20th c. Q.-C.'s failure to produce "a great novel," though he published at least twenty-one novels and thirteen story collections, besides completing Robert Louis STEVENSON's unfinished novel, *St. Ives*, has also been noted.

However, a few of Q.-C.'s novels have resonated with his critics and commentators (and, presumably, a number of readers) over the ages. Chief among the books are *Dead Man's Rock* (1887), a spooky adventure story—the title referring to the old Cornish name of Dodman, for the tall rocky mass projecting from a cove off Cornwall's southern shore—evocative of Stevenson's *Treasure Island*; *Hetty Wesley* (1903), a well-documented story about the mistreatment of a talented young woman by her brothers, John and Charles Wesley, founders of Methodism, and their father, Reverend Samuel Wesley; and *The Mayor of Troy* (1905), Troy standing for Q.-C.'s much-loved village of Fowey on Cornwall's south coast, and the Mayor representing a sadly comic figure: a French captive during the Napoleonic Wars, he finds that his eventual release and return home bring him only unhappiness.

One plausible explanation for this preponderance of quantity over quality has been that much of Q.-C.'s time was consumed by his very extensive range of organizational activities and numerous club memberships, in addition to his lifelong career as an academic who was often called on to give special lectures, make public appearances, and write introductions to other writers' books.

Q.-C. was by no means driven to express his deepest emotional responses to life's ups and downs, as many chronically dissatisfied poets and fiction writers are. Rather, he seemed to take great pleasure in his university life away from home—more often than not living a bachelor existence in his rooms at Jesus College, Cambridge (his wife generally remained at home in Fowey), dining at high table in his particularly formal manner, enjoying his alcoholic spirits and his pipe, and concerning himself with all manner of university functions. Finally, a perusal of a bibliography of his many published works—which include three volumes of FAIRY TALES for children, a retelling of William SHAKESPEARE's historical plots, and numerous volumes of literary commentary—makes one thing fairly clear. For all his admirable range of interests and his willingness to embark on seemingly any kind of literary project, in the final analysis, Q.-C. spread himself far too thin.

BIBLIOGRAPHY: Brittain, F., *A. Q.-C.* (1948); Brittain, F., ed., *Q Anthology: A Selection from the Prose and Verse of Sir A. Q.-C.* (1948); Rowse, A. L., *Q. C.* (1988)

SAMUEL I. BELLMAN

QUIN, Ann Marie

b. 17 March 1936, Brighton; d. August? 1973, Brighton

Q. was a writer who never took the novel form for granted; each of her four published novels was a new departure in terms of structure and style. Like a number of other English novelists in the 1960s, such as Alan Burns, Christine BROOKE-ROSE, Eva FIGES, and B. S. JOHNSON, she rejected the model of the traditional realist narrative that was then still dominant in British literary culture and explored, in her own way, a range of alternatives. The constant innovation that characterises her completed novels can be seen as an enactment of their key theme: the quest for identity and relationship in a world in which the self, a fragile, provisional construct, is always threatened with absorption into the desires and discourses of others.

Q.'s first novel, *Berg* (1964), focuses on the most primal affirmation of male identity: killing the father. But while acknowledging the deathly seriousness of the psychoanalytical scenario, Q. gives it a comic turn: Oedipus and Hamlet are refracted through comedian Jerry Lewis. Deserted by his dad when he was a baby, Alistair Berg, now nominally adult, tracks him down to a seaside boarding house, determined to kill him; but his bungling attempts at patricide always hit the wrong target, from a budgerigar to a ventriloquist's dummy. Berg finally moves in with his father's mistress, but his Oedipal triumph is short-lived when he finds that a man resembling his father now has the room next door. It seems that, for Berg, there is no escape from the father, any more than there is from the mother, an absent presence in the novel whose words sound time and again in his head. The structure and style of *Berg* help to draw the reader into its protagonist's tenuous, threatened identity: the novel often blurs or removes conventional narrative signposts, leaving the reader uncertain who is speaking or whether the past or present is being evoked. The uncertainty is enhanced by sudden shifts into metaphor, often signaled by dashes, but not marked by grammatical modulations: "Berg's hand—a mouse—crept over."

Berg won Q. two fellowships—the D. H. Lawrence fellowship from the University of New Mexico in 1964 and the Harkness Fellowship, for the most promising Commonwealth artist under thirty, for the years 1964–67. These enabled her to complete her second novel. *Three* (1966) explores a human triangle. Leonard and Ruth, a prosperous but dissatisfied married couple, project their difficulties and frustrations on to a young female house guest, S, who is recovering from an abortion: S finally disappears, possibly to commit suicide. None of the characters is able to achieve a distinctive identity or form a mutually satisfying relationship. Their difficulties are echoed by the three narrative techniques of the novel, which might be called behaviorist, introspective, and poetic: the behaviorist technique carefully describes the words and actions of Leonard and Ruth but says nothing directly about what is going on inside their heads; the introspective technique provides extracts from S's journal; and the poetic technique consists of transcripts of tape recordings by S that take the form of free verse. But none of these techniques offers the truth about the characters; nor do the techniques fuse together to supply the whole story.

The development of structure and style to explore loss of identity and relationship is taken further in Q.'s third novel, *Passages* (1969). Identity and relationship are now under threat from two forces: the political and the mythical. A man and woman are in a nameless, repressive foreign country; the woman is searching for her vanished brother, who may no longer be alive. The first and third sections of the novel consist of the woman's fragmentary impressions and memories; the second and fourth parts are the man's notes, which are set out in two columns so that they look like a main text with marginal comments. The notes take a variety of forms, from snatches of dialogue to mythological references that often invoke destruction and occasionally imply rebirth. They give a strong sense of the siren lure of the mythical, its fascinating but possibly fatal attraction. The novel ends ambiguously, with the possibility of a journey and a sea crossing, but with no clear sense of destination.

Q.'s final novel, *Tripticks* (1972), is her most fragmented and frenzied. Pursued by, or perhaps pursuing, his former first wife and her lover, the many-faceted narrator's picaresque progress through a caricatured U.S. intermixes with memories of his tortured matrimonial and family relationships and images of the diabolical guru, Nightripper. In this descent into chaos, the desire for identity remains, but it finally seems to entail silence: at the end of *Tripticks*, the narrator is finally unable or unwilling to use words because to do so is to possess their power—a power that he rejects because it is employed to persuade or coerce people to submit to alienating systems.

Q. died by drowning in 1973—the exact date of her death is unknown; it may have been an accident or suicide; she had a history of mental illness. She draws on that history in "The Unmapped Country," a section from a novel in progress that was published posthumously in Giles GORDON's *Beyond the Words*. It is an effective, relatively straightforward account of a young woman, Sandra, recovering from a breakdown in a mental home. The growing difficulty of her novels from *Berg* to *Tripticks* had provoked an increasingly hostile response from reviewers and this may have been one of the reasons for the apparent return to traditional narrative in "The Unmapped Country." Since her death, hostility has turned to neglect; but her work offers rich rewards to the alert reader and critic. Her four novels should stand as demanding but impressive attempts to expand the formal scope of the novel while engaging with one of its constant themes: the quest for identity and relationship.

BIBLIOGRAPHY: Dunn, N., "Ann," in her *Talking to Women* (1965): 126–53; Stevick, P., "Voices in the Head: Style and Consciousness in the Fiction of A. Q.," in Friedman, E. G., and M. Fuchs, eds., *Breaking the Sequence: Women's Experimental Fiction* (1989): 231–39; Tredell, N., "A. Q.," in Moseley, M., ed., *British Novelists since 1960*, Fourth Series, *DLB* 231 (2001): 230–38

NICOLAS TREDELL

RABAN, Jonathan
b. 14 June 1942, Norfolk

R.'s travel books, if read chronologically, follow the progress of a smoking, drinking, bookish, and awkwardly English narrator as he charts his way through middle age with a strong sense of alienation and romance. The first travelogue, *Arabia through the Looking Glass* (1979), takes the unattached author away from a London of uncomfortable immigrants and into a land of homesick expatriates with big ideas. The most recent, *Passage to Juneau: A Sea and its Meanings* (1999), sees R. sailing from his established home in Seattle, Washington, to Juneau, Alaska, and leaving behind a wife and daughter.

Throughout the sequence, the solo traveler's voice is compelling and highly self-conscious—a character in the vein of Paul THEROUX and Bruce CHATWIN. However, while Theroux is a lustful and curmudgeonly train traveler and Chatwin a snobbish self-aggrandizer, R. positions himself as the gangly, balding upshot of a religious childhood (his father was a minister) and a repressed and militaristic schooling. The narrator also has a penchant for quasi-academic literary quotation and analysis; he is a thorough yet casual scholar.

R.'s personal history is woven into all of his books, as is his urge to (physically, at least) leave it behind. For example, *Old Glory: An American Voyage* (1981) opens with an explanation of how, in his asthmatic childhood, R. read Mark Twain as a form of escape; and this explanation is a springboard to his travels down the Mississippi on an unusually small boat wearing self-consciously unusual clothes.

Such unusualness is to be cultivated: there is pleasure in being an eccentric Brit abroad, in wearing pink suits, in trying to order a martini in dry Alabama (*Hunting Mister Heartbreak,* 1990); in being, as R. eventually became in the U.S., an official "Resident Alien"—on the outside looking in. This sense of alienation is at its most focused in *Coasting* (1986),

when R. sails solo around his native Britain, making observations about his tiny, crowded homeland, and detaching himself from the jingoism fueling Margaret Thatcher's Falklands War. The boat serves as a refuge: stocked with choice literature, whisky, and a typewriter, it's an ideal hiding place—a romantic home for one.

This relationship between alienation and romance is perhaps the key to R.'s work. In "Sea Change," for example, a short piece published in *Granta 10* (1984), the narrator becomes tired of his writing life in London and dreams of the sea. He buys an old sextant and eventually a boat. His desire is to float "serenely offshore: half in, half out of the world." Considering this love of ambiguity, R.'s obsession with open water is easy to understand. *Arabia* aside, all of his travelogues involve water voyages of sorts (and most bear evidence of a good deal of foraging into the literature of water voyages). Even *Bad Land: An American Romance* (1996), which follows the trail of early settlers of Montana's barren railroad communities, opens with a description of landscape as ocean. And in 1992, R. edited *The Oxford Book of the Sea*.

If the ocean reflects R.'s alienation, it is also a route to his romantic personal New World: America. In *Hunting Mister Heartbreak*, he sets sail from Liverpool in the footsteps of America's early immigrants and, once he lands, is able to take on a number of personae, including that of John Rayburn, a man with a borrowed dog who lives in Guntersville, Alabama. He is welcomed into the community (being conveniently white and English), yet his mannerisms and his hired Dodge with New York plates mark him out as a privileged Other. This, for the narrator, seems ideal: his cultural baggage gives him an edge without preventing personal reinvention.

By the time of *Bad Land*'s publication, R. has settled in Seattle and switched to American spelling. Indeed, the conclusion of the book sees a comfortable return *home*—to a domestic scene of ironing boards, clutter, and family life. *Passage to Juneau,* however, signals a return to the lone, boat-bound R. of previous form. As he sails from Seattle to Juneau, Alaska, he retraces the voyage of Captain Vancouver. This time, though, the HUMOR of much of his work is overwhelmed by tragedy. He loses his father to cancer and his wife to itchy feet, and writes movingly of both. His return to his father's deathbed foregrounds his awkwardness when faced with the English culture he left behind. Indeed, this theme of the uncomfortable homecoming is the focus of R.'s only novel, *Foreign Land* (1985), in which the protagonist, George Grey, returns to England from Africa after forty years away.

When R.'s wife leaves him, the writer sees something very familiar—and romantic—in her reasons. "America as the land of perpetual reinvention had always been my theme," he writes. "Whenever there had been walking-out to do, I was the one who walked"—or rather, sailed.

BIBLIOGRAPHY: Schramer, J. J., "J. R.," in Brothers, B., and J. M. Gergits, eds., *British Travel Writers, 1940–1997, DLB* 204 (1999): 235–48

NICHOLAS WOOLLEY

RACKHAM, Arthur

b. 19 September 1867, London; d. 6 September 1939, Limpsfield, Surrey

R. is best known for his fantastic illustrations of such subjects as fairies and gnomes pictured among gnarly trees and other strange characters. This extremely imaginative and talented illustrator of both FAIRY TALES and children's classics is considered by many to be the premier illustrator of the early 20th c. Throughout his lifetime, he illustrated more than sixty books. Remaining faithful to the Victorian age in which he was born, he captured a romantic and fantasy filled world in his line drawings and watercolor painting. He worked days in an insurance office for some years, while producing illustrations for newspapers and magazines on the side. Throughout the 1890s, he worked for the *Westminster Budget* depicting the current subjects of the day. This work and his early book illustrations, such as he produced in the *Dolly Dialogues,* were stiff and matter of fact, very different from the style he came to adopt. Perhaps due to the growing popularity of photography over illustration in journals of this period and also likely due to growing recognition, his style changed dramatically to the amusingly odd, whimsically charged characters for which he is known and cherished. His figures were generally drawn from life, using his own quirky form and that of his daughter as models. He also used details from their home and garden in Sussex, with the result of making his creations, while utterly fanciful, also quite believable.

It was with the *Fairy Tales of the Brothers Grimm* (1900) that R. first found success and gained recognition as an artist. His original *Grimm* included ninety-nine of his mainly black and white illustrations, although in a later edition (1909) half of these were turned to color. He became adept at using the new three and four color process to his advantage by his use of muted, earth-tone browns and grays, less affected by the drain of this printing process. Washington Irving's *Rip Van Winkle* (1905) with some fifty illustrations established his reputation in the U.S. and bought him the freedom to be selective in his choice of future works. Authors greatly admired R.'s creative spirit and desired to have him illustrate their books. With his illustration of J. M. BARRIE's *Peter Pan in Kensington Gardens* (1906), R.'s work produced a frenzy of interest, although some critics thought the idea of such luxurious and expensively produced art books going to children was ludicrous. R., however, felt strongly about the value of playful and imaginative pictures in the development of a child. He furthermore believed that children would appreciate the fine artistic details present in such pictures and that they thereby deserved to see the same high quality artwork that adults would expect in their books, regardless of price.

He followed *Peter Pan* with a 1907 edition of Lewis CARROLL's *Alice's Adventures in Wonderland,* which appeared on the market alongside many other *Alice* works after the original copyright lapsed. R. was widely criticized at the time for attempting to supplant Sir John Tenniel's beloved illustrations. Far from doing so however, R.'s work draws from the inspiration of the original illustrations and creates works that further support the classic with details influenced by the Art Nouveau movement. R. went on to publish illustrations in his self-edited *Mother Goose* (1913), Irving's *Legend of Sleepy Hollow* (1928), and Edgar Allan Poe's *Tales of Mystery and Imagination* (1935), ending his illustrious career with a 1940 edition of Kenneth GRAHAME's *The Wind in the Willows.* He had regretted a decision earlier in his career in which he turned down the opportunity to illustrate the first edition, and was thrilled in 1936 when he was again asked to illustrate this work which had become one of his favorite books. R.'s illustration of Rat and Mole loading their boat for a picnic was his last effort before his death, leaving the oars of the boat to be completed by others.

Exaggerated noses and limbs, grotesque and terrifying characters, his creation of so many charming creatures and his sense of HUMOR all contribute to the timeless quality of R.'s art, which was influenced by the works of Albrecht Dürer, the Pre-Raphaelites, and Howard Pyle. With works that stand out for their intricately detailed patterns and textures, as is seen in R.'s depictions of such household accoutrements as fabrics and dishes, his fantasy filled illustrations incorporated the everyday life of late 19th-c. Britain. R.'s life work is now displayed in many of the top galleries in Europe and the U.S., and his art continues to influence the decorative arts and crafts as well as stage design and commercials today.

BIBLIOGRAPHY: Gettings, F., *A. R.* (1975); Hamilton, J., *A. R.* (1990); Hudson, D., *A. R., His Life and Work* (1960); Riall, R., *A New Bibliography of A. R.* (1994)

ANN O'BRIEN FULLER

RADCLIFFE, Ann
b. 9 July 1764, London; d. 7 February 1823, London

R. is the great exemplar of the 18th-c. GOTHIC NOVEL. The best-selling English novelist of the 1790s, her work inspired plays and operas as well as numerous imitations. Her enchanting fictional world influenced some of the greatest literary imaginations of the 19th c., including the Romantic poets—John KEATS named her "mother Radcliffe." Her novels remained popular until the middle years of the Victorian era.

Devalued by early 20th-c. critics because her work influenced but did not conform to a male Gothic tradition, R. was reinstated more recently by feminist critics who highlighted major themes in her work that have resonance with the experiences of contemporary women. All of R.'s major novels figure heroines trapped in patterns of pursuit and imprisonment, persecution and endurance, sexual division and repression, underlined at all times by the absolute necessity of respectability. Criticized for her two-dimensional characters and anachronisms, R.'s success really lay in the psychological reality of her exploration of an inner life behind the contemporary social milieu. She achieved this through a Gothic world of nightmare in which the historical and foreign settings distance the reader from the ordinary daylight world and the characters are overshadowed by scenic intensity.

R.'s first novel, *The Castles of Athlin and Dunbayne: A Highland Story* (1789), is a fast-paced tale of warring clans, influenced by Horace WALPOLE. In *A Sicilian Romance* (2 vols., 1790), R. established the heroine-centered world and familial plot that became typical. The heroine, Julia, goes on a journey of self-discovery, challenging religious and patriarchal authority in an attempt to marry the man of her choice. Ultimately, she has to uncover dark family secrets and rediscover her maternal origins, figured here in the form of Louisa de Mazzini, the ghostly mother, before her new family can be established.

R.'s reputation is based principally on her next three novels, *The Romance of the Forest* (3 vols., 1791), *The Mysteries of Udolpho* (4 vols., 1794), and *The Italian* (3 vols., 1797). For the last two, she was advanced record sums by her publishers. In these, the heroines—sentimental, "accomplished" young lady poets by the names of Adeline, Emily, and Ellena—are plunged into a terrifying and mysterious world as their childhood security disintegrates and they become the victims of unscrupulous villains, evil father figures determined to control them. The hedonistic Marquis de Montalt and the manipulative Montoni are active, ambitious men with much of the old quest hero about them, but R.'s most celebrated villain is the monk Schedoni from *The Italian*, a demonic, powerful embodiment of masculine ferocity. By contrast, the heroes, Theodore, Valancourt, and Vivaldi, are pointedly endowed with qualities more appealing to R.'s female readership—courage and pride, but also a sense of family responsibility, sensitivity, and respect for women.

The keynote of the novels is suspense, which R. creates with technical ingenuity. She is the mistress of suggestion—her settings (dungeons, castles, forests, ruins) are described in detail, yet remain curiously obscure. Elements of the supernatural tantalize the reader (later explained away rather implausibly) and an unreliable narrator adds ambiguity. R. expertly manipulates the plot, supplied with a plentiful combination of short and longer-term mysteries, while the vision of reality is dominated by the heroine's overwrought emotions. As William HAZLITT wrote, "in harrowing up the soul with imaginary horrors, and making the flesh creep, and the nerves thrill with fond hopes and fears, she is unrivaled."

R.'s "narrative of landscape," where scenery is used as an external manifestation of a state of mind or mood, was an important development for the novel. She describes with the eye of a painter. Indeed, R.'s novels are rich in allusions to contemporary aesthetic theories of the sublime and the picturesque, as her characters move against a backdrop of the rugged Appenines, the dark forests of southeastern France, or the lush valleys of Gascony and Savoy. Her characters are measured by their response to landscape, their peak of emotional experience provoked by the pleasurable pain of the Burkean sublime.

R. also published a book of travel writing, *A Journey Made in the Summer of 1794* (1795), which was well received. After *The Italian,* she published no more novels in her lifetime. The reason for this sudden silence remains, like much of her life, a mystery. R. was a private person who did not court the limelight. Her posthumous works include an historical novel, *Gaston de Blondeville* (4 vols., 1826), which was apparently never completed to her satisfaction, owing to ill health.

BIBLIOGRAPHY: Norton, R., *Mistress of Udolpho: The Life of A. R.* (1999); Punter, D., *The Literature of Terror: A History of Gothic Fictions from 1765 to the*

Present Day (1980); Rogers, D. D., *The Critical Response to A. R.* (1994)

REBECCA MORGAN

RAINE, Craig
b. 3 December 1944, Shildon, County Durham

R. was brought up eccentrically, as described in the autobiographical prose section of his third collection of poems, *Rich* (1984). Educated at Barnard Castle School, he read English at Exeter College, Oxford, and became a university lecturer before moving to Faber and Faber as poetry editor. He sees the world freshly, observing unexpected resemblances expressed in unusual metaphors. His first book of verse, *The Onion Memory,* appeared in 1978, followed by *A Martian Sends a Postcard Home* (1979). *History: The Home Movie* (1994) was successful, reaching outside the normal audience for poetry. R. wrote the libretto for an opera by Nigel Osborne, *The Electrification of the Soviet Union* (1986), adapted from a novella by Boris Pasternak. R. has also worked on translations of Pasternak. R.'s *Collected Poems 1978–1998* appeared in 2000. He has also published a version of Jean Racine's *Andromaque* (1990), essays, and literary criticism.

RAINE, Kathleen [Jessie]
b. 14 June 1908, London

Born in the London suburb of Ilford, R. experienced a greater connection to the Northumberland countryside where she spent her youth. Her concern for nature, which is prevalent throughout her creative works, began and was fostered during her time there. While at Girton College, Cambridge, R. studied the natural sciences and received an M.A. in botany and zoology in 1929. It was at Cambridge that her love of poetry was wed with her rational scientific side. Her poetry is ever investigating the human self in connection with its surroundings and nature. Archetype and myth play heavily in this investigation.

R.'s first volume of poetry, *Stone and Flower,* appeared in 1943. This volume displays strong Romantic tendencies and a deep concern with Roman Catholicism. Though the woman's voice is present throughout her volumes, it is more clearly established in *The Pythoness and Other Poems* (1948). Here, she takes leave of the structures of Roman Catholicism and moves toward the natural elements so linked to her childhood in the north of England. R.'s later works continue to incorporate mythic personae whom she uses to explore femininity and the cyclical life of the female and poet. Her volume *The Oracle in the Heart and Other Poems, 1975–1978* (1980) begins a deeper inquiry into the journey of life and choice.

R. is strongly influenced by William BLAKE in her poetry; however, it is her critical work that more predominantly displays her devotion to his works. *Blake and Tradition* (2 vols., 1968) is considered her great critical triumph, displaying years of meticulous examination of anything that may have involved him. In addition to a great number of critical works and over twenty volumes of poetry, R. has written three volumes of AUTOBIOGRAPHY, *Farewell Happy Fields: Memories of Childhood* (1973), *The Land Unknown* (1975), and *The Lion's Mouth* (1977), published together as *Autobiographies* (1992). R.'s *Collected Poems* appeared in 2001.

BIBLIOGRAPHY: Mills, R. J., Jr., *K. R.* (1967); Sellery, J. M., "K. R.," in Stanford, D. E., ed., *British Poets, 1914–1945, DLB* 20 (1983): 288–99

RALEIGH [or RALEGH], [Sir] Walter
b. ca. 1554, Devonshire; d. 29 October 1618, London

Elizabethan courtier, soldier, seafarer, and writer, R. gained the attention of ELIZABETH I after a military command in Ireland in 1580 and received, over the next years, knighthood, several lucrative patents, and the title of Captain of the Guard. As he rose to prominence at court, he came to influence nearly every aspect of public life in England: he sat in Parliament, fought the Spanish, patronized the arts, and sponsored several expeditions to Ireland and North America, including ones sent to establish a colony in Virginia, which R. had named for the queen. R. fell from Elizabeth's graces in 1592 and was banished from court. In part to regain the queen's favor by defying the Spanish, R. sailed to Guiana in 1595. His return to favor was short lived: Elizabeth's death in 1603 and JAMES I's accession to the throne signaled a more conciliatory policy toward Spain, a shift that made R. a liability for the Crown. That same year, R. was tried and convicted of high treason and sentenced to death. R. remained imprisoned in the Tower of London for the next fifteen years, except in 1617 when he conducted an ill-fated second expedition to Guiana. Shortly after R.'s return in 1618, James, under pressure from the Spanish, ordered R.'s beheading.

R. was a central figure in the intellectual life of England. He may not have thought himself a writer in the modern sense, but he produced several volumes of writing as a consequence of an ambitious and eventful life. As a courtier and public figure, R. wrote poetry, political tracts, discourses on war and ships, and a discovery account. As a long-time prisoner of the Tower, R. wrote his longest work, *The History of the World* (1614), which traces the workings of divine providence in events of biblical and classical antiquity. R. encouraged, among other works, Richard HAKLUYT's *Principle Navigations* and Edmund SPENSER's *Faerie*

Queene. R.'s association with Thomas HARRIOT the mathematician, John DEE the occultist, and Christopher MARLOWE the playwright led to persistent rumors of his atheism (a term hurled at any who lacked orthodoxy), but R. expressed no overt heterodoxy in his own writings.

A central issue in the study of R.'s poetry is an uncertain canon. Except for a very few occasional verses, R. did not publish his poems, nor did he supervise any collection. He circulated his verse in manuscript, which makes attribution difficult. Controversial in life, nearly mythical after death, R. had many poems falsely attributed to him, especially as later editors worked to recover what they assumed to be a lost corpus of verse. No definitive edition of R.'s poetry is possible. Among the poems known or generally received as authentic, R. writes in a range of modes. In his poems addressed to the queen, such as "Methought I saw the grave," R.'s narrator plays the Petrarchan lover and loyal servant; in "Ocean to Cynthia," R. creates a series of images that express a lover's penitence and seem to sue for the queen's clemency. Other poems meditate on abstract, often gloomy, themes: "What is our life?," "Even such as Time," and his celebrated "Nymph's Reply to the Shepherd" contemplate the certainty of death and impermanence of love.

The Discoverie of the Large, Rich and Bewtiful Empyre of Guiana is R.'s account of his first expedition to South America and arguably his most important prose work. The expedition itself was unimportant. R.'s fleet sailed from England to Trinidad in 1595; from there, in smaller boats, R. and one hundred men rowed into the Orinoco River delta in search of the golden city the Spanish called El Dorado. After about six weeks, rain and swelling rivers forced R. to turn back, rejoin the fleet, and return to England. In 1596, however, R. turned failure into success by publishing the *Discoverie*, which ran to several editions in his lifetime, many more after his death. It is an engaging narrative, as R. and his crew meet various adversities. He creates an air of erudition by citing previous explorers and using precise terms to describe the landscape and its people; he generates wonder as he ponders the oddities of the New World, such as Amazon women and *Ewaipanoma*—humans with eyes on their shoulders and mouths in their breasts. Modern readers notice R.'s primitivism: his Guiana is an unspoiled Eden whose people are noble, strong, wise—and eager to pledge their loyalty to the queen.

The *Discoverie* invites attention from a variety of disciplines. It is an important document in European and American history, written in the context of hostility between England and Spain at the start of colonization. R.'s goal was to persuade Elizabeth's Privy Council to counter Spanish power by establishing colonies in South America. R.'s description of native peoples, transcriptions of place and tribal names, and accounts of contact between Native Americans and Europeans are of interest to anthropologists and cultural historians. Literary critics have approached the *Discoverie* in countless ways: as a travel narrative, as rhetoric and propaganda, as a performance in which R. fashions a role for himself, and as a narrative that reveals El Dorado to be a projection from R.'s psyche, to mention a few.

R.'s return to Guiana in 1617 occasioned one of his last works, the *Apology*, an able but unsuccessful attempt to justify the disastrous events of the expedition—the deaths of nearly fifty men during the westward crossing, a skirmish with the Spanish in violation of royal policy, his own son Wat's death, his second in command's suicide. A comparison of this pamphlet to the *Discoverie* explains the change in political zeitgeist in England and R.'s precipitous fall.

BIBLIOGRAPHY: Greenblatt, S. J., *Sir W. R.* (1973); May, S. W., *Sir W. R.* (1989); Nicholl, C., *The Creature in the Map* (1995); Rudick, M., ed., *The Poems of Sir W. R.* (1999)

PATRICK MCHENRY

RAMSAY, Allan
b. 1684 or 1685, Lanarkshire, Scotland; d. January 1758, Edinburgh, Scotland

Poet, editor, bookseller, and publisher, R. played a significant role in the 18th-c. revival of Scots poetry and poetic tradition. Following the publication in 1718 of his sequel to the 15th-c. poem *Christ's Kirk on the Green*, R. rejuvenated the use of vernacular Scots first with volumes of comic verse and later in a more serious vein with poems such as *Richy and Sandy* and *Patie and Roger*, published in 1719 and 1720, respectively. Best known for his pastoral drama *The Gentle Shepherd* (1725), R. also compiled a miscellany of Scots songs (1723), a two-volume anthology of Scots poetry (1724), and a collection of Scots proverbs (1737).

RANDOLPH, Thomas
b. June 1605, Newnham-cum-Badby, Northamptonshire; d. March 1635, Blatherwick, Northamptonshire

R.'s reputation with his contemporaries stood very high; many viewed him as Ben JONSON's natural successor. Modern criticism has not ranked R. quite so highly. Encouraged, in part, by knowledge of R.'s death before his thirtieth birthday and of his drinking habits (one early biographer describes R. as "somewhat addicted to libertine indulgences"), the tendency has been to talk of R. in terms of promise unfulfilled rather than actual achievement. There is, of course, some truth in this; had R. lived longer he would doubtless have written more, and perhaps better.

It is important to realize, if we are to judge them fairly, that most of R.'s dramatic works were not written for the public theater. Several were academic entertainments, R. being a student and "minor fellow" of Trinity College, Cambridge. *Aristippus; or, The Jovial Philosopher* (perf. 1625/6; pub. 1630) is a one-act play in which Aristippus (the historical Aristippus, though a disciple of Socrates, was famous for his epicureanism), a philosopher who teaches in a tavern called the Dolphin, wittily propounds the virtues of wine (and its superiority to ale). The play's full subtitle reads "Demonstrativelie prooving, That Quartes, Pintes, and Pottles, Are sometimes necessary Authors in a Scholers Library." *The Drinking Academy* (perf. ca. 1626–32, not published until 1924), in five brief and lively acts, is set in a Jonsonian world of usurers and prodigals, with the tavern again at its center, where Cavalero Whiffe conducts his drinking academy in a witty parody of the academic world R. knew so well. *The Conceited Pedlar* (perf. 1627; pub. 1630) is a an energetic monologue in which the Pedlar, addressing his audience of Cambridge students as "the divine brats of Helicon," displays a good deal of learned wit as he introduces himself and makes many a satirical point as he displays his wares (which include a looking glass, gloves, night-caps, and "a wench made of alabaster"). *Hey for Honesty, Down with Knavery* (1651) was probably a Cambridge production of much the same time. It is a free adaptation of Aristophanes' *Plutus*, full of local and topical color, not least in its satirical treatment of Puritans in the figure of Ananias Goggle. (The surviving text of this play seems to contain interpolations made after R.'s death).

In 1630, *The Muses' Looking Glasse* (originally called *The Entertainment*) was performed by the Children of the Revels at Salisbury Court (there was perhaps an earlier Cambridge performance; it was published in 1638). Two Puritans, Bird and Mistress Flowerdew, described as members of "the sanctified fraternity of Black-friers," who sell their feathers and pins at the theater, but thoroughly disapprove of what goes on there, are given a demonstration by the actor, Roscius, of the moral power of comedy, of its capacity "to vex and cure" the failings of a whole series of characters (with R.'s knowledge of Aristotelean ethical thinking well to the fore). This is one of the more entertaining of the London theater's defenses of itself, and there are some memorable individual scenes, such as the encounter between Colax and Dyscolus. At much the same time, R.'s pastoral drama *Amyntas* was acted, a court performance being recorded in 1631. *Amyntas* is one of the very finest of all English pastoral dramas, the work of a writer who had evidently thought hard about the examples offered by Battista

Guarini and Torquato Tasso. The blank verse is accomplished, the comic scenes are genuinely funny and some of the songs are delightful. It has fewer of the structural weaknesses that generally characterize R.'s work; it was perhaps a more careful piece of work than some others, which can often seem almost improvisatory in their air of spontaneity. R.'s other substantial dramatic work was *The Jealous Lovers* (1632), which offers a rich gallery of pseudo-Jonsonian characters, including Ballio the Pander and Phryne the Courtesan. Its plot, in which brothers unknowingly woo their own sisters, has its moments of absurdity, but these need not be cause for serious complaint. The play was much enjoyed when acted before the king and queen at Cambridge and might well bear revival even now.

R.'s nondramatic verse includes some genuinely witty pieces, such as his lines "On the losse of his finger" and "On Importunate Dunnes," and some love poems that range in tone and attitude from the idealizations of "A Platonick Eligie" ("Love, give me leave to serve thee, and be wise") to the altogether more sensuous sentiments of "A Pastoral Courtship." His translations include a thoroughly Jonsonian version of Horace's Second Epode, several attractive responses to poems by Claudian (R. was himself an accomplished Latin scholar and poet. His translations of his own Latin poems offer an interesting case-study in self-translation). His elegy on Lady Venetia Digby fuses wit and dignity and his "Epithalamium to Mr. F. H." is attractive and assured. His most impressive single poem is perhaps his "Ode to Mr. Anthony Stafford to Hasten Him into the Country," rhythmically adroit in its mixture of long and short lines, using a stanza form probably modeled on Jonson (cf. "Ode to James Earl of Desmond"), intelligently Horatian in its sentiments and full of lively detail.

R.'s work is not, on the whole, innovative. His classical models, his extensive debt to Jonson, are everywhere clear. But he has a scholarly wit of his own and a distinct, warm personality is evident in most of his work. Seemingly very dissimilar poets, such as Henry VAUGHAN and Andrew MARVELL, read (and borrowed from) R. For that reason, as well as for the intrinsic merits of his own best work, R. belongs in any adequate picture of the drama and poetry of the early 17th c.

BIBLIOGRAPHY: Harbage, A., *Cavalier Drama* (1936); Moore-Smith, G. C., "T. R.," *PBA* 13 (1927): 79–121; Mullick, I., *The Poetry of R.* (1974); Summers, C. J., and T.-L. Pebworth, eds., *Classic and Cavalier* (1982)

GLYN PURSGLOVE

RAPHAEL, Frederic [Michael]
b. 14 August 1931, Chicago, Illinois, U.S.A.

R. is a modern man of letters; he writes fiction, reviews, and movies. He is also a man of letters in the more venerable sense; he writes biographies, authors and edits histories of philosophy, and translates classical poetry and drama. In preparation for both limbs of his career, while at Cambridge in the early 1950s he wrote and performed in the famous Footlights Dramatic Club (in a company that included Leslie Bricusse and Jonathan Miller) and read philosophy and classics.

His college days among the brightest and most promising are the core experience of the early novel *The Graduate Wife* (1962), the subsequent *April, June and November* (1972), and *Oxbridge Blues and Other Stories* (1980), and the episodic television play *The Glittering Prizes* (perf. 1976), also adapted as a novel in that same year, perhaps his masterpiece, which explores the compromised talents and ambitions of a shiny Cambridge set as they negotiate life. Screenwriting, from his remarkable stretch of success in the mid-1960s—*Nothing But the Best* (1964), *Darling* (1965, for which he won the Academy Award), and *Two for the Road* (1967)—to his adaptation of Arthur Schnitzler's *Traumnovelle* (1926) for Stanley Kubrick's final film, *Eyes Wide Shut* (1999), has raised his writer's profile. And he has kept his hand in academic publishing with, among other works, his efficient BIOGRAPHY of Lord BYRON (1982) and translations, with Kenneth McLeish, of the poems of Catullus (1978), the plays of Aeschylus (1979, 1991), and Euripides' *Medea* (1994).

Literary fiction, however, is his trade, and his voice is that of the satirist, the objective outsider. Born in Chicago, he moved with his family to London and was soon the American Jew at a British public school. The theme of problematic identity, often Jewish, as in the novel *Lindmann* (1963) and the nonfiction *The Necessity of Anti-Semitism* (1989); female, as in *The Graduate Wife*, *Orchestra and Beginners* (1967), and *Richard's Things* (1973); or a Hollywood writer's, as in *California Time* (1975), *Coast to Coast* (1998), and *All His Sons* (1999), often confronted by assumed privilege, is recurrent in his writing. His feeling for mainland Europe, for the peoples and landscapes of Greece and France in particular, is apparent in the novels *Like Men Betrayed* (1970) and *A Double Life* (1993), stories of identities broken by war, and in his travel writing. R.'s characters fail to resolve their problems of identity or only reach resolution at considerable personal cost, and his authorial sympathies for their struggles are usually rendered ambivalent by his vigilant SATIRE and his keen, cutting dialogue, for which he is especially praised by reviewers. His own criticism is occasion for witticism, and though his critic's tongue can be lashing, it often has to fight its way past his foot to explain what he meant to say. He has fostered controversies throughout his career, most recently over Kubrick's opinion of Steven Spielberg's

film of *Schindler's List* (1994), and author Arthur Koestler's sex life.

Writing for nearly a half-century, R. has built on his early success in fiction to broaden his ambition into the media and the academy, mined his youth, education, and avocations for text and expertise, and honed his craft to a fine edge respected by admirers and enemies alike.

BIBLIOGRAPHY: Kent, J. P., "F. R.," in Halio, J. L., ed., *British Novelists since 1960*, part 2, *DLB* 14 (1983): 614–22

                                    DENNIS PAOLI

RASTELL, John
b. ca. 1475, Coventry; d. July 1536, probably London

Printer, lawyer, author, and member of Parliament, R. was brother-in-law of Sir Thomas MORE. In 1530, R. wrote defending the Roman Catholic doctrine of Purgatory, *A New Boke of Purgatory,* comprising discussion between "a Christian man" and a Turk. This was answered by Cambridge Reformer John Fryth in *A Disputacion of Purgatorie* (1533). R.'s reply was an *Apology against John Fryth,* to which Fryth again replied. According to John FOXE, this converted R. to the opposing view. As a result, R. lost both his legal practice and his printing business and was reduced to poverty. He was imprisoned in 1536, possibly for writing against the payment of tithes, and probably died before release. R.'s best-known work is *The Pastyme of the People, the Chronycles of dyvers Realmys and most specially of the Realme of England* (1529), a chronicle dealing with English history from earliest times until the reign of Richard III. As well as legal works, he is putative author of a morality play (see MYSTERIES AND MORALITY PLAYS), *A New Interlude and a Mery of the Nature of the Four Elements* (ca. 1519).

RATTIGAN, [Sir] Terence [Mervyn]
b. 10 June 1911, London; d. 30 November 1977, Hamilton, Bermuda

It now seems that R. was one of the greatest English playwrights of the 20th c.; and certainly the author of the only English serious play fully to stand comparison in its depth and power to anything being written contemporaneously in the U.S.: *The Deep Blue Sea* (1952). Such was not always the case. After the marked critical acclaim and commercial success of his early career, R.'s reputation suffered a swift decline when the young writers of the English Stage Company at the Royal Court focused on the restraint and tact with which R.'s characters express deep emotion as typical of the middle-class dishonesty which characterized the West End theater. Yet, if there is one theme that courses through R.'s work, it is the conflict of the inarticulate misfit or outsider with middle-class hypocrisy.

R. always stood outside the establishment into which he had been born. Homosexual acts were an imprisonable offense in England until 1967 and R., happily at ease with his sexuality in private life, never felt able to admit or write about his orientation openly. R.'s greatest weakness as a dramatist was that he was unable to write anything but naturalistic dialogue. (Even his comedies have no verbal wit.) Yet such a lack also works to his advantage: just as the rules of the society from which his characters spring prevents them admitting the truth about their lives so, in R.'s prose, the vocabulary of that society prevents them from expressing it. As there is such a gulf between R.'s most mediocre work and his most outstanding, it would be wise to concentrate on those few plays that are now justly considered the finest of their time.

R.'s father, with whom he never got on (a recurring theme of his plays), was a diplomat and his education the best England could then offer: Harrow and Trinity College, Oxford (where, as a modern history scholar, he could have remained as an academic). His second play, *French without Tears* (perf. 1936; pub. 1937), a youthful trifle, albeit a joyous and well-constructed one, ran for over a thousand performances. This was followed by the more serious *After the Dance* (1939), which shows the alcoholic decline that might await the hedonistic young of his earlier plays. During World War II, R. served with distinction in the RAF, an experience that resulted in the serious *Flare Path* (1942) and the comic *While the Sun Shines* (perf. 1943; pub. 1944). But it is *The Winslow Boy* (1946) that places R. at the very top of the first division of dramatists.

Looking back in its form to the Edwardian four-act domestic drama, *The Winslow Boy* is about a naval cadet unjustly accused of stealing a five-shilling postal order. Faultlessly constructed, it champions the liberty of the individual menaced by the new bureaucracy and shows the toll that justice can take on the personal life of the family. A powerful story pitting public events against private causes, it contains a stunning *coup de théâtre* when, at the act 2 curtain, the eminent barrister, against all expectations, decides to take the brief.

The Browning Version (perf. 1948; pub. 1949), one half of a double-bill (whose companion *Harlequinade* is poor stuff), lays claim to be one of the best one-act plays ever written: a deeply moving account of a mediocre and desiccated schoolmaster about to retire—a study of intellectual failure—whose courage and moral worth are restored by the gift of a book from a pupil. Andrew Crocker-Harris's small act of defiance against the headmaster who has tried to rob

him of his right to speak in the customary place at prize-giving seems truly heroic because, although R. writes with great humanity, he keeps situation and emotion on the same small scale.

The Deep Blue Sea is a masterpiece of the first order. A play that was prompted by the suicide of R.'s ex-lover, it is a profound exploration of a potential suicide's psychology. Hester Collyer, a conservative woman in her thirties, has left her husband, a judge, for a young pilot. If she and Sir William Collyer have everything in common except sex, she and Freddie Page have nothing in common but sex, and when that fizzles out, she tries to kill herself, an act that begins the play. All the rest of the action is a discovery of what drove her to that act and whether she is likely to repeat it. Freddie, the ex-Battle of Britain fighter, one of "the Few," a hero at twenty, washed-up and directionless at thirty, with his air force slang and cheery manner disguising mental dimness, is a superb characterization, as is Hester, where an unremarkable exterior conceals turbulent passions of late-discovered sexuality and consequent shame.

Another double-bill *Separate Tables* (perf. 1954; pub. 1955), set in a seaside hotel, tells two unrelated stories, the second of which "Table Number Seven," is about a bogus major exposed to the "respectable" residents as a sexual offender. R. originally intended this offense to be homosexual, but in the first production, this was changed to importuning women in a cinema. The original version is now nearly always performed. At the final curtain, the downtrodden daughter's defiance of her ghastly bigoted mother is a great and moving plea for tolerance: a small triumph in the defeat of ignorance.

Under attack from the Royal Court writers, R. perhaps lost his nerve and certainly his form. He made the mistake of inventing a maiden lady called Aunt Edna, a low-brow "with time on her hands and money to help her spend it" who had existed since the time of Sophocles and whose presence in the audience he said playwrights needed to consider. She appears in the prefaces to the second (1953) and third (1964) volumes of his collected plays. To some young writers, who thought R. took her seriously, she represented everything wrong with the commercial theater, with truth never being told and real issues never tackled. She and they and indeed the whole debate now seem a baffling bore but the "Angry Young Men" used her as a nail in R.'s theatrical coffin.

Of his later plays only *Cause Célèbre* (perf. 1977; pub. 1978) is anywhere near his earlier magnificent standard. The story of a woman whose young lover murders her husband, it is again an indictment of middle-class hypocrisy. Alma may be a slut but she is a life-affirming, loving, and noble one. The censorious woman who finds herself foreman of the jury needs to learn from her—and does—by the end their moral positions are reversed.

Although R. was rightly knighted before his death, he felt he had been dismissed as a serious writer. But that is certainly not the case now and some of his detractors seem pygmies in comparison. As long as anyone is unhappy enough to want to kill themselves, is ashamed of their sexuality, or believes justice for the individual is as important as the conduct of world affairs, R. will be their civilized and dignified spokesman.

BIBLIOGRAPHY: Darlow, M., and G. Hodson, *T. R.* (1979); Duff, C., *The Lost Summer: The Heyday of the West End Theatre* (1995); Wansell, G., *T. R.* (1995); Young, B. A., *The Rattigan Version: Sir T. R. and the Theatre of Character* (1986)

CHARLES DUFF

RAVENHILL, Mark
b. 1966, Haywards Heath, Sussex

Only five years after the opening of his first play, *Shopping and Fucking* (perf. 1996; pub. 1997), R.'s *Mother Clap's Molly House* (2001) was performed at the Royal National Theatre. His rise to prominence invites consideration of critical complaints that his plays merely intend to shock and lack social content, especially since the plays express persistent and explicit social critique. The title *Shopping and Fucking* may be shocking, but it also encapsulates a central argument. These are no longer separate activities but simultaneous and interdependent. Pleasure has become valuable merchandise, and sex a commodity.

Perhaps most troubling to critics, and most definitive of the social critique, is the absence of a preestablished ideal by which to assess characters and action. Settings tend to be defined solely through the actions of the characters. The characters do not compare themselves or others to a preferable or preestablished "norm." Most important, there is an absence of narrative overview: no established story line aids comparative assessment, assists the spectators' expectations or comforts them with a clear perspective or desirable alternative to the present action, or encourages a sense of superiority. Like the characters, the audience is placed in a position of making a viable whole out of sundry available parts.

In its rage against the profit motive as the prime purpose of both individual and social activity and its destruction of values, *Shopping* could be seen as a response to John OSBORNE's early plays (despite R.'s explicit criticism of Osborne's homophobia and his own presentation of homosexual sex onstage). The terms of the argument shed light on the differences between them. Osborne used the music hall to embody the positive personal and community values he sees as endangered by the encroaching profit motive, proposing a preferable alternative and offering the au-

dience an informed choice. In the intervening forty years, alternative structures and values have been bought or abandoned in the wake of wholesale commercialism. Neither the characters in *Shopping* nor their audience are offered such an ideal to aspire to nor one against which behavior might be judged. The question of how the individual can find meaning and value in a world dominated by commerce is asked throughout R.'s plays.

Robbie's reflection in *Shopping* "I think a long time ago there were big stories. Stories so big you could live your whole life in them" recalls Jimmy Porter's "there are no great causes any more." Both bemoan the absence of a signifying context giving meaning to individual life. However, where Jimmy looks to external preexisting "causes" to reflect significance on the individual, Robbie's cry highlights the absence of extended narratives that give pattern and meaning to both society and the individual, not only siting a failure in the external world but expressing the private need to find structure and hence meaning.

The absence of a narrative overview is counteracted by the use of stories illustrating their multiple functions. In the opening scene of *Shopping*, Robbie begs Mark to "to tell the shopping story." Mark relates how he bought Lulu and Robbie at a supermarket. Dramatically, the story's significance is tied to the hitherto undefined setting of the action. If the action takes place in the present, the story must be a fabrication. However, it is conceivable the story is true, thereby setting the action in the near future where humans have become little more than a new form of merchandise. This probability foregrounds the commercialization of our world and its devaluation of individual lives. When Mark retells the story toward the end of the play, its personal relevance is revealed: proof of their "worth" to Mark.

Without external measure, profit is exposed as the sole terms for assessing individual action. People are little more than commodities. Lulu and Robbie sell phone sex that turns the sellers into commodities and depersonalizes the intimacy of sex. Mark offers rent boy Gary a choice between love and money: Gary chooses money. The devaluation of feeling is socially prescribed. Mark's therapist advises him to see relationships as "a transaction . . . if I pay it won't mean anything," but he can't prevent himself becoming emotionally involved. Although the characters are consistently engaged in a day-to-day struggle to acquire enough money to survive, they persist in attempting to find emotional engagement and personal meaning from the meagre material at hand. It is a quest often violent and dangerous; to transcend both the necessities of economic survival and the "virtual" experience of technological offerings demands ever more extreme forms of pain and bodily immolation to achieve genuine feeling. This need for values and pursuit of meaning through interaction creates an undertone of disturbing optimism, and R.'s characters are particularly gifted in expressing moments of deep emotion or dream. Robbie's description of giving away the Es he was supposed to sell creates a resonant image of an unattainable social ideal, a world where individual worth is experienced and valued through the happiness one gives to others.

While *Handbag* (1998), in its discussion of child abuse, intersperses present action with Oscar WILDE's *The Importance of Being Earnest*, questioning moralist calls for the return to "Victorian values," *Some Explicit Polaroids* (perf. 1999; pub. 2001) confronts the argument that former values can arbitrarily be imposed on the present while simultaneously articulating their loss. Nick enters the 1990s after spending fifteen years in prison for torturing a financier. His partner, Helen, is now a local councillor concerned with bus timetables. The political/moral overview that gave him context and meaning is not an alternative but an anachronism. Defeated by the hapless self-interest around him, Nick confines himself to rebuilding his personal relationship with Helen who, ironically, mourns the loss of his "anger."

Contrary to critical protestations, R.'s plays express a strong moral imperative. Despite the absence of an acknowledged signifying overview, the characters strive for engagement, forming small social groups in which they give and receive value, suggesting that social interaction is an endemic human need, despite Margaret Thatcher's famous "there's no such thing as society." The homosexuals in *Mother Clap's Molly House* appear to have achieved this goal. In an 18th c. extoling the virtues of commerce ("God: Enterprise will make you human/Getting, spending-spark divine"), Mrs. Tull turns her brothel into a "Molly House" where gay men meet, engage, and even create simulated families. In the second act, scenes in the Molly House are intercut with a gathering of gay lovers in the present, linking the current public sexual freedom to the pink pound. The glorification of profit and sex as profitable business is spread over the centuries. The inclusion of songs gives the play a celebratory nature, and it ends on a note of almost fantastical optimism. When Mother Clap retires, threatening an end to the Molly House, brothel owner Amelia buys the business and coaxes the Mollies back. Although the expected closing of the House is withheld, the Molly House contains the seeds of its own demise. Born of economic boom and greed, existing primarily for the sake of profit, the community and sexual freedom it has engendered must invariably be at the mercy of economic demands of the market. Warnings for the present day echo as the curtain descends.

BIBLIOGRAPHY: Croall, J., *Inside the Molly House* (2001); Sierz, A., *In-Yer-Face Theatre: British Drama Today* (2001); Wandor, M., *Post-War British Drama: Looking Back in Gender* (2001)

ELAINE TURNER

RAWORTH, Tom [Thomas Moore]
b. 19 July 1938, Bexleyheath, Kent

The poetry of R. challenges the boundaries of Anglo-American poetry, and especially of a prevalent critical orthodoxy that would separate a tradition of English verse from linguistic innovations associated with MODERNISM. R.'s prodigious output of over forty publications, mostly by small presses, is characterized by an abrupt, dense, and paratactic prosody that disrupts syntax and so frustrates the reader's attempt to establish a stable poetic persona and its correlative imagery. Considered "experimental" in comparison with more publicized British poetry, R.'s work has enjoyed greater recognition abroad (including translation) than in the U.K.; significantly, his two volumes of selected poems *Tottering State* (1984) and *Clean and Well Lit* (1996) have received prior publication in the U.S. R. himself, as cofounder of the Golliard Press in 1967, was the first publisher of American poet Charles Olson in the U.K. and has traveled widely in the U.S. and Mexico. A measure of his international reputation came in 1991, when he was the first European in thirty years to be invited to teach at Cape Town University. His work attests to an enduring stream of innovative postwar poetry in Britain despite critical neglect and outright hostility.

R. had left formal education at sixteen to become a jazz musician before he published his first book, *The Relation Ship*, in 1966. His early work reflected the turn from the gentility of "The Movement" poets in that decade to an avowedly younger idiom. The verse of this period used brevity to reduce the identity of a speaker into fragmented states of utterance, as in this mid-stanza of "Collapsible": a jackdaw collecting phrases "it's a chicken!/nothing lonelier than hearing your own pop in another country." Material in *The Big Green Day* (1968), *Lion Lion* (1970), and *Moving* (1971) cultivated a skewed HUMOR through the use of non-sequitur and juxtaposition. This could echo the laconic style of the Beats, yet also shared the exacting detail of the Black Mountain poets (particularly Robert Creeley) and the intelligent enquiry of sensation found in the New York school. As such, he was represented in both Michael HOROVITZ's "counterculture" anthology *Children of Albion* as well as alongside John Ashbery in a Penguin Modern Poets joint introduction to their work. A subsequent backlash against a perceived "Sixties" poetics has arguably stunted this early public recognition of his work.

R.'s work after *Ace* (1974) became an ongoing exploration of narrative possibility within a disjunctive style. Short lines carry successive clusters of descriptive phrases, which entice the reader with the possibility of finding a coherent descriptive thread. R. does not denigrate this desire, but rather respects the polysemy of language to mark its insatiability, as the text outstrips the reader's attempt at closure. The sequence *Sentenced to Death* (1987), *Eternal Sections* (1993), and *Survival* (1994) used a cursory sonnet form to produce vertiginously rapid shifts of syntactical association which evoke particular moments of wonderment—"all seemed strange/ fenced in, isolated from the city/he heard a vast rustling/narcissus petals floating down" (*Eternal Sections*)—and suggest a critique of dominant discourses that would efface that particularity. In the manner of Samuel BECKETT, the poem indicates a continuation of writing that defies (mis) interpretation "it was-eerie/unwilling to believe/in reverent terms/intention the exacting/decomposition of the body/recording all movements/transfixed by it/ signaling survival."

R. may be closer to the Language poets of North America than innovative British contemporaries such as J. H. PRYNNE or Douglas OLIVER who retain an attention to formal closure. Yet such ideas of national diction must remain suspect in this order of writing that emphasises the material abundance of textuality itself.

BIBLIOGRAPHY: Barrell, J., *The Flight of Syntax: Percy Bysshe Shelley and T. R.* (1990); Tuma, K., *Fishing by Obstinate Isles: Modern and Postmodern British Poetry and American Readers* (1988)

J. M. TINK

READ, [Sir] Herbert

b. 4 December 1893, Muscoates Grange, Yorkshire;
d. 12 June 1968, Stonegrave, Yorkshire

R., in all he wrote—minor poetry, important art and literary criticism, admired memoirs, radio plays and lectures, and a novel—was a classic modernist. His poetry is imagist, his memoirs impressionistic, his novel surreal; his criticism was among the earliest to employ psychoanalytic method, drew attention to the avant-garde in the visual arts, and rehabilitated the Romantics in literary history. From his first volume of poetry, *Songs of Chaos* (1915), self-published as he left England to fight in World War I, to his knighthood in 1952 "for services to literature," R.'s career hits the high points and travels the high road of English and Continental MODERNISM.

Reared first on a farm in Yorkshire where he learned to love nature, then in an orphanage in Halifax where he discovered a love for reading, R. had a 19th-c. childhood, and his Romantic's biography persists through his exploits in the war. His maturity, though, is early modernist, complete with leftist politics, a troubled first wife, and the professional frustrations of

a working-class intellectual. In public and private, R. claimed to be a poet. While his verse has been recognized and anthologized as the genuine imagist article, his poetic output has neither the breadth nor ambition of that of his mentor, modernism's model major poet, T. S. ELIOT. Still, in work from the trench poetry of *Naked Warriors* (1919), to the verse play for radio, *Moon's Farm* (1955), and the experimental *Vocal Avowals* (1962), his talent is tenacious, his images wrought from fundamental sensation, focused feeling, and hard-won language.

His novel *The Green Child* (1935), described by critics as a philosophic romance, a fable of frozen innocence, a Utopian allegory, an anti-Utopian parable, a Jungian dream, and a poet's folly, is one of English fiction's oddest one-offs, yet demands and rewards serious reading. His finest writing is in his memoirs of his war experience, *In Retreat* (1925) and "The Raid" (1927), and of his childhood, *The Innocent Eye* (1933). The prose is a poet's, the memories fresh and detailed, starkly yet sensitively recounting his battleground bravery (he was awarded the Military Cross and Distinguished Service Order for heroism in the field) and Yorkshire youth.

The empirical core of his poetics and the psychological bent of his analysis led him to an appreciation of the Romantic poets. Here, R. steps out of Eliot's shadow and stakes his own critical claims, stretching his critical gifts, an apt and ready sensibility and a synthetic taste. His method is biographical, employing Freudian and Jungian analysis to the lives and the works, but his point of view is practical, respecting and responding to the skill of fellow craftsmen. *Wordsworth* (1931), *In Defence of Shelley and Other Essays* (1936), and *Byron* (1951) are persuasive, for the most part, in arguing their subjects' genius and served, with *Reason and Romanticism* (1926) and *The True Voice of Feeling: Studies in English Romantic Poetry* (1953), to help restore ROMANTICISM's literary reputation.

His own reputation as a man of letters was hard earned. He turned his criticism to poets venerable and contemporary in volumes including *Form in Modern Poetry* (1932) and *Poetry and Experience* (1967), was published by Leonard and Virginia WOOLF, edited by Eliot, and he himself edited eminent authors, T. E. HULME and C. G. Jung among them, and anthologies. For over four decades in numerous reviews, essays, commentary, and meditations on art and aesthetics, he championed home-grown English art and emergent movements worldwide, with special interests and expertise in crafts and art education. His political writings, also numerous, marched left over the course of his life, settling comfortably in examinations and rationalizations of anarchy.

The apparent contradictions in his opinions and his oeuvre, his patriotic and anarchist principles, for example, and the inverse proportion of poetic product to his claims for it as his life's work, betray his nature as an authentic, conflicted modern. His final collection of his autobiographical pieces is entitled *The Contrary Experience* (1963).

BIBLIOGRAPHY: King, J., *The Last Modern: A Life of H. R.* (1990); Paoli, D., "H. R.," in Serafin S., ed., *Late Nineteenth- and Early Twentieth-Century British Literary Biographers, DLB* 149 (1995): 197–209; Woodcock, G., *H. R.* (1972)

DENNIS PAOLI

READE, Charles
b. 8 June 1814, Ipsden House, Oxfordshire; d. 11 April 1884, Shepherd's Bush, London

Until fairly recently, R.'s novel of thwarted passion, *The Cloister and the Hearth* (4 vols., 1861), was a much-loved classic, compared with the work of Charles DICKENS. A. C. SWINBURNE placed it among "the very greatest masterpieces" and Henry JAMES called R. a "real master." Walter BESANT preferred R. to Sir Walter SCOTT, then highly valued. Neither medievalism nor "pictorial" novels are in fashion today, but R.'s massively researched picaresque adventure story, set in the 14th c., is entertaining though less admired than it was.

Thanks to family string-pulling, R. was a fellow of Magdalen College, Oxford, which brought him an income for life, but Fellows were forbidden to marry. This plight and its torment underlie the novel. Gerard, tricked by his family into believing his betrothed, Margaret, is dead, becomes a Catholic priest. On his return to Holland from Rome, he learns that the girl is alive and has had his baby. The quiet Dutch landscape (the hearth) is elaborately contrasted with Rome (the cloister). The Dutch family is repressive and its society acquisitive, but its virtues are Protestant uprightness and cleanliness, unlike the dirty beauty of southern Europe, significantly on the other side of the high Alps. Italy can only be reached via a series of dangerous, violent stopping places. Rome was an object of suspicion to Victorians reared in Evangelicalism and hostility to the Oxford movement. Admiration of Dutch "fidelity" in art was an established Low Church attitude and R. elevates the Flemish painters above the Italian: in tune with his period, he prefers "truth to nature" (literal representation) to symbolism. Rome is a trap, confirming Evangelical prejudice: its rule of celibacy imprisons Gerard in Holy Orders. But though Gerard may not touch Margaret, their son will grow up to be Erasmus, spearhead of humanism, who will help save the north from the corruption and superstition of the south.

R.'s enormous output as dramatist and novelist is largely forgotten except for a curious novel, *Griffith*

Gaunt (3 vols., 1866), which again deals with frustrated sexuality and was considered shocking. The protagonist quarrels with his wife about religion and commits bigamy with a working-class girl called Mercy, who bears him a child. The events, including a murder trial, are violent and sensational, but the story ends with Mercy marrying a convenient neighbor and the two women becoming friends. Ostracized, the two couples form a unit against the world. This was R.'s favorite, and some modern critics have agreed with him. Illegitimacy figures in both books, a reminder that sexual love is often at war with the social and economic order.

BIBLIOGRAPHY: Burns, W., *C. R.* (1961); Elwin, M., *C. R.* (1969); Smith, E. E., *C. R.* (1976); Turner, A. M., *The Making of "The Cloister and the Hearth"* (1938)

VALERIE GROSVENOR MYER

REALISM

The 19th c. saw the emergence of the term "realism" as the designation of a mode of writing in European and British literature, particularly the novel, which attempts to create an objectively present social reality and to represent faithfully life and experience as it is.

As a product of the impact of social/political changes and scientific/industrial advances that created the dominant mood of its time, the realist artistic movement lies in direct relational opposition to the idea of life as it should be found in the previous idealistic literary movement of ROMANTICISM. The postrevolutionary period of European history that had encouraged the main tenants of Romanticism to emphasize the state of grace of childhood, the dominance of nature and the supernatural, the role of the poet as the most capable interpreter of experience, the idealization of the working class and the value of the "noble savage" became irrelevant to a new way of life that involved intense industrialization and the mobilization of the middle class. By midcentury, contemporary manners and conventions were under siege and the realist writer provided the reader with a certain degree of "truth telling" or sober factuality about the individual's role in society as the writer eschews the historical remoteness and elitism of Romantic verse for the sincerity and modernity of prose in an effort to describe with accuracy the historical, social and moral moment. Technological advances, like the daguerreotype method of photography in 1839, facilitated and encouraged a more visual imagination and a more exact representation of reality which was to be striven for in fiction.

Broadly speaking, the realist mode denotes an illustrious body of texts that form the core canon of the latter half of 19th-c. literature exemplified in France by Honoré de Balzac, in America by Henry JAMES, and in England by George ELIOT. Realism attempts to create a sincere replica of the social milieu and epoch in which one lives in order to explore human lived experience. Idealization found in the Romantic movement was to be replaced; G. H. LEWES a 19th-c. literary critic and the partner of Eliot, explains that "Art always aims at the *representation* of Reality, i.e. of Truth"; therefore, according to this essential aesthetic criteria, "only *that* literature is effective, and to be prized accordingly, which has *reality for its basis . . . and* [is] *effective in proportion to the depth and breadth of that basis*." Just as Balzac described himself, in the preface to *The Human Comedy* (1842), as a "secretary" to the 19th c., Eliot believed her role as a writer to be "to give a faithful account of men and things as they have mirrored themselves in [her] mind."

The French Realist school of writing in the mid-19th c. produced a manifesto, *Realism* (1857) by Champfleury, which stressed the same inclinations found in English writing of the same era: sincerity of accurate documentation, sociological insight, details of material fact, as well as the conscious avoidance of idealization, poetic language, and exaggeration. Subjects were to be taken from life, preferably from lower- to middle-class life. The intrinsic value of a mirror held up to the reality of everyday life in an increasingly positivist and scientific age was that the reader could see the dramatic effects on society of the political restructuring that was fostered by the spread of literacy, the increasing power of the bourgeois with enfranchisement, the flourishing of the suffrage movement, and the series of parliamentary reform acts that would radically alter the social landscape that both characters and readers necessarily inhabit. Through intensely accurate descriptions of the details or minutiae of everyday life—the ordinary—as well as the representation of complex characters who are rooted in a specific social class and who interact with other characters to create a plot of plausible human life, the realist writer seeks to inquire into the complexity of the relationship between the individual and society within a certain political, conventional and socioeconomic context. The emphasis falls away from melodrama or sensationalism to rest upon intense characterization. Middle-class subjects became both topics and consumers of the realist fiction: characters abound who are extraordinary in their very ordinariness; social types emerge within the dynamics of the fictional worlds to reveal to the reader the lives of governesses, thieves, fallen women, captains of industry, orphans, and society matriarchs.

Vivid pictures of deplorable working-class conditions could be found in texts such as Charles DICKENS's *Hard Times* or Elizabeth Cleghorn GASKELL's *North and South*; frank discussions took place in fiction of the immense implications for workers under the questionable progress of the Industrial Revolution; direct questions are asked in texts such as Eliot's *Middlemarch* about the complex nuances of the new roles of men, women, and children as they begin to see themselves as individuals in society, and the agitation preceding the first Reform Bill (1832) as people begin to adopt a new historical sense that one is a being living in society rather than solely a moral being under religion, resulting in an increased conservatism that gave way later in the century to NATURALISM and decadence.

Unlike the intense theorization of Romanticism by William WORDSWORTH, Samuel Taylor COLERIDGE, and others, aside from the French manifesto, there is no sustained theory by the realist authors themselves; in the absence of such self-definition, realism and its implications remain fruitful areas of exploration as a literary concept for 20th-c. theoreticians. Three crucial types of inquiry have been made. First, the Marxist paradigm sees realism as epistemologically and aesthetically superior to any allegedly antirealist MODERNISM. Second, the structuralist and poststructuralist critique of realism sees it less in terms of substantive representation than as forms that are constructed as real and constructing practices that convert culture into nature. Third, feminist theory has questioned how the representational strategies of realism produce and reproduce the ideological terms of patriarchy. In each case, these approaches move forward from the initial impulses to categorization of realism as a direct or simplistic reporting of truth to an exploration of the many complexities and limitations that are involved in trying to create, in literary form, this representation of real life called realism.

BIBLIOGRAPHY: Auerbach, E., *Mimesis* (1953); Boumelha, P., "Realism and the Ends of Feminism," in Sheridan, S., ed., *Grafts: Feminist Cultural Criticism* (1988): 77–91; Furst, L., ed., *Realism* (1992); James, H., *The Art of Fiction* (1884); Kearns, K., *Nineteenth-Century Literary Realism* (1996); Levine, G., *The Realistic Imagination* (1981); Schor, N., *Breaking the Chain* (1985); Wellek, R., "The Concept of Realism in Literary Scholarship," in his *Concepts of Criticism* (1963): 222–55

SARAH E. MAIER

REDGROVE, Peter [William]
b. 2 January 1932, Kingston-on-Thames, Surrey

For many years resident writer at Falmouth School of Art, Cornwall, P. was educated at Taunton School, Somerset, and Queens' College, Cambridge, where he read natural sciences before becoming a scientific journalist. In 1956, he became a founder member of Philip HOBSBAUM's "The Group" and *The Collector and Other Poems* appeared in 1960. Among other collections, many in small limited editions, are *At the White Monument* (1963), *Sons of My Skin* (1975), *The Weddings at Nether Powers* (1979), *The Apple-Broadcast* (1981), *The Man Named East* (1985), *The Moon Disposes: Poems 1954–1987* (1987), and *The Mudlark Poems and Grand Buveur* (1990). Novels include *In the Country of the Skin* (1972), *The Beekeepers* (1980), and, with Penelope SHUTTLE, *The Terrors of Dr. Treviles* (1974). He and Shuttle collaborated on the famous study of menstruation in its psychological, mythical, and sociological aspects, *The Wise Wound* (1978). P.'s writing is dense and reflects his interest in religion, magic, and mysticism.

REEVE, Clara

b. 23 January 1729, Ipswich; d. 3 December 1807, Ipswich

R.'s novel, *The Champion of Virtue* (1777; repub. as *The Old English Baron*, 1778), was intended as a critique of Horace WALPOLE's groundbreaking *The Castle of Otranto*. Walpole, however, found R.'s tale "insipid." Her hero, the exemplary Edmund, has many adventures of romantic horror before finding his rightful heritage, but the only supernatural element is provided by a ghost. R.'s other novels were *The Two Mentors* (2 vols., 1783), *The Exiles; or, Memoirs of the Count of Cronstadt* (3 vols., 1788), *The School for Widows* (3 vols., 1791), *Memoirs of Sir Roger de Clarendon* (3 vols., 1793), and *Destination* (3 vols., 1799). She also published a critical dialogue, *The Progress of Romance through Times, Countries, and Manners* (2 vols., 1785).

REID, Christopher [John]

b. 13 May 1949, Hong Kong

R. emerged with Craig RAINE in the late 1970s as part of the so-called Martian school of poetry, which promoted an experimental poetry—both playful and innovative—that incorporated techniques of estrangement and disorientation toward creating an imaginative rendering of the contemporary world. Educated at Exeter College, Oxford, R. published his first collection of poetry, *Arcadia*, in 1979—the same year as Raine's *A Martian Sends a Postcard Home*. Subject to mixed critical reception, the controversial work—praised by some and dismissed by others—received both the Somerset Maugham Award and the Hawthornden Prize. Later collections include *Katerina Brac* (1985), *In the Echoey Tunnel* (1991), *Expanded Universes* (1996), and *Mermaids Explained* (2001).

REID, Forrest

b. 24 June 1875 or 1876, Belfast, Ireland; d. 4 January 1947, Belfast, Northern Ireland

At Cambridge University, R. became friends with E. M. FORSTER, who admired his work and wrote an introduction to the trilogy later published as *Tom Barber* (1955), comprising *Uncle Stephen* (1931; rev. ed., 1945), *The Retreat* (1934), and *Young Tom* (1944). R.'s sixteen novels nostalgically contrast the values of childhood with those of Ulster in the early 20th c. and there are hints of the supernatural. Other titles are *The Kingdom of Twilight* (1904), *The Garden God: A Tale of Two Boys* (1905), and *Following Darkness* (1912; rev. ed. pub. as *Peter Waring*, 1936). R.'s sense of the numinous in the natural world of garden and grove is reflected in his volumes of autobiography, *Apostate* (1926) and *Private Road* (1940). R. also wrote critical studies of W. B. YEATS (1915) and of his friend Walter de la MARE (1929).

RELIGION AND LITERATURE

Although most writers in the British tradition have been Christian, that fact only begins to describe the complexity and variety of religious experience in British literature. Many important authors—Geoffrey CHAUCER, possibly William SHAKESPEARE, John DONNE, John DRYDEN, Alexander POPE, John Henry NEWMAN, Gerard Manley HOPKINS, James JOYCE—were Catholic for part or all of their careers, and their religious convictions undoubtedly affected their writings. Yet because of anti-Catholic sentiment, pervasive in Great Britain since the Reformation, the influence of Catholicism on the national literature has been somewhat muted. Thus, considered through its remaining major voices—Edmund SPENSER, John MILTON, Jonathan SWIFT, Samuel RICHARDSON, Henry FIELDING, Samuel JOHNSON, William BLAKE, Jane AUSTEN, the Romantics, Charles DICKENS, Alfred, Lord TENNYSON, Robert BROWNING, W. B. YEATS, T. S. ELIOT, the history of British literature is more Protestant than Catholic.

Although official religious affiliation has had a profound effect on the lives of British authors, it has been less vital to their writings than have knowledge of the Bible and immersion in Christian culture. Christianity, regardless of sectarian differences, is crucial in British literature, even for those writers who challenged or rejected it, because its rich symbolism has provided a deep reservoir of images and literary ideas. To appreciate most works of British literature, a reader need not possess theological sophistication or faith; but fully fathoming even the least Christian writers in the tradition does demand basic knowledge of church matters and some awareness of the history, language, and imagery of Christianity.

Many poems composed before the Norman Conquest, like *BEOWULF*, are of pagan origin and owe their survival to the fact that they were transcribed and preserved by Catholic monks, who often took the liberty of Christianizing them. Due to the church's near monopoly on literacy through the early Middle Ages, most of the Anglo-Saxon writing that survives, like CÆDMON's "Hymn of Creation" or *The Dream of the Rood* (wr. ca. 1000), represents Christian thinking.

Almost all extant MIDDLE ENGLISH literature focuses on Christian themes. Arthurian romance, the roots of which are pagan and Celtic, became progressively Christianized in the Middle Ages. Early English drama consisted of MYSTERIES AND MORALITY PLAYS taken from Bible stories. The anonymous *Sir Gawain and the Green Knight* and William LANGLAND's *Piers Plowman*, two of the most significant poems of the period, are Christian allegories. The greatest British poet of the Middle Ages, Chaucer, an orthodox Catholic, bitterly satirized church abuses. While his writings celebrate life and revel in its sensual variety, beneath the exuberance and worldly joy lie strong moral and religious convictions.

Between Chaucer and Britain's next great poet, Spenser, the Protestant Reformation intervened, and the effects can be seen in the literature. The protagonist of Spenser's *The Faerie Queene*, the Red Cross Knight, functions allegorically as the Anglican Church. Sir Philip SIDNEY's *Apologie for Poetrie*, though penned in reaction to a Puritan attack on poetry, quietly expresses sympathy with some facets of the Puritan antipoetic position while generally defending poetic practice.

The voice of Shakespeare, dominant in British literary history, is ironically one of its most secular ones. But even in Shakespeare's work, the influence of Christianity is incalculable. His career demonstrates that in British literature, even in the work of authors for whom religious questions are not paramount, Christian concerns find expression. The graveyard scene in *Hamlet*, to name a famous example, shows Shakespeare's mind mulling over sacred ground.

From the time of the Authorized Version of the English Bible (1611), virtually all literate men and women in Britain were reared reading the Bible. Many learned it by heart. Even the illiterate knew the stories. No other volume in the history of western literature can claim that depth and breadth of influence.

The first half of the 17th c. witnessed an explosion of excellent devotional verse by such skilled craftsmen as George HERBERT, Donne, and Milton. Ingenious stanza forms and extravagant Christian imagery characterize Herbert's great collection of 160 poems, *The Temple*. Donne, born a Catholic, conformed as an adult to the Established Church and eventually became Dean of St. Paul's. Though much of his poetry exhales a virile worldliness, a marked commitment to Christian principles also finds a voice. Milton, considered by many to be the greatest poet in British literature, was also Latin secretary to the Puritan government during the Interregnum. Idiosyncratic religious thought permeates all his writings. *Paradise Lost*, perhaps Britain's single most influential poem, in its announced intention to "justify the ways of God to man," can be called a Christian EPIC.

The Puritan Interlude made Great Britain wary of religious extremism. The fundamental religious impulses of the century and a half following the career of Oliver Cromwell, leader of the Puritan revolution, were contempt for all things that smacked of religious "enthusiasm" and hatred for "popery." Nevertheless, although the primary literary influences of the period are classical and its major concerns secular, the context for most literary work is still unmistakably Christian. Dryden's *Absalom and Achitophel,* Pope's *Epistles,* and Johnson's *Vanity of Human Wishes*, all clearly demonstrate the rationalized Christian beliefs of their authors.

Although one might think that the Catholicism of Dryden and Pope would be crucial to understanding their work, their Catholic faith did not profoundly affect most of their writings. Dryden, who spent the majority of his career as an Anglican, wrestled conscientiously with his beliefs before finally converting to Catholicism in 1685, at great personal and professional cost; Pope was a Catholic throughout his life: yet the writings of both blend nearly indistinguishably into the secular concerns of the day and express a Christianity broad enough to be spiritually palatable to an Anglican audience. Johnson's religious position as a High-Church Tory is perhaps more readily identifiable in his writings. For example, his strict religious principles led him to criticize Milton's much-admired "Lycidas" for mingling Christian and pagan imagery. Another crucial neoclassical figure, Swift, like Johnson a high churchman, was an ordained clergyman of the Church of England and Dean of St. Patrick's in Dublin. His combination of intellectual intensity, powerful imagination, and stern religious principles gave him formidable moral authority.

The 18th-c. novel seems primarily engaged with secular matters, but a reader should not ignore the influence of Christian language and imagery on the major fiction writers (Daniel DEFOE, Richardson, Fielding, Laurence STERNE, and Austen). Defoe, a dissenter, reveals his Protestant sympathies in *Robinson Crusoe* and *Moll Flanders*, which read like secularized conversion narratives. The fiction of Richardson, whose *Clarissa* is perhaps the most important novel of the period, shows a clear strain of Protestant morality, admired even by Johnson, who had little respect for novelists. Fielding's *Tom Jones*, despite the bluff carnality of its concerns, depicts a broad-church Christian sense of justice. And that unholy cleric Sterne, inclined to mock the church, arrays his fiction with religious trappings, rendering it all but unreadable to those ignorant of Christianity. No author depicts the nearly silent pervasiveness of the church more accurately than Austen, daughter of an Anglican clergyman, whose fictions focus on the worldly concerns of well-to-do country families. In her novels, nearly every character attends church, but even though several of her significant characters are themselves clergymen, rarely does one express an overtly Christian sentiment.

The Romantic poets, often understood to have abandoned traditional Christian beliefs for the tenets of revolutionary politics, still exhibit the effects of their Christian antecedents. Percy Bysshe SHELLEY's avowals of atheism to the contrary, the basic imagery of the Romantics remains that of a transmuted Christianity. Blake hated the Established Church, yet the two deepest influences on his poetry are the biblical prophets and Milton. If William WORDSWORTH and Samuel Taylor COLERIDGE began their careers as revolutionaries, both eventually became orthodox Anglicans. And although the second generation Romantics (Shelley, novelist Mary SHELLEY, Lord BYRON, and John KEATS) lived their relatively short lives as skeptics and produced rebellious works that often look like beautiful but profane transfigurations of neoclassical ideas, the ethos and imagery of their writing maintain a stubbornly Christian cast.

The Victorian period marks a return to straightforward religious concerns. For many reasons, the latter half of the 19th c. witnessed a simultaneous expansion and reduction of faith. Science and secular criticism of the Bible began to erode the faith of the educated public. On the other hand, the Evangelical revival reached its highest point of influence. Among the major novelists, George ELIOT approaches the questions of religion most directly, structuring her didactic fiction around questions of morality. Moreover, in *Daniel Deronda*, she sympathetically examines English Judaism, a subject infrequently explored in the history of British literature. (Shakespeare's *Merchant of Venice* provides a rare early example.) In Charlotte BRONTË's *Jane Eyre*, Evangelical Christianity plays a central role, and in Emily BRONTË's *Wuthering Heights*, where the amoral rascality of Heathcliff and Cathy seems to discard all Christian concerns, a preacher, a SERMON, and a scripture-spouting servant play crucial roles in the story. Moreover, a cynic like Thomas HARDY, who may appear to have rejected all religious consolations, fills his novels and poems with churches, prayers, and spiritual conversions of one kind or another. The fact that *Jude the Obscure*, his last novel, is the one most concerned with religious questions, demonstrates that he remained preoccupied with problems of faith throughout his career.

Dickens, the dominant novelist of the Victorian period, stands as the 19th c.'s most secular major figure, but as with Shakespeare in the Renaissance, the influence of Christianity cannot be denied. It is the cloth from which he worked, even if by the time he's finished with it, the fabric is difficult to identify. For example, he calls the opening section of *Hard Times*, "The One Thing Needful," a biblical phrase. And while, like Blake before him, Dickens thinks nothing of ridiculing much religious activity as hypocritical

and true believers as fanatics (witness Mrs. Jellyby in *Bleak House),* the simple faith of characters like Amy in *Little Dorrit* or Stephen Blackpool in *Hard Times* illustrates his admiration for the basic tenets of the Gospels.

Likewise, most Victorian poetry will remain impenetrable to readers ignorant of the Judeo-Christian tradition. Tennyson's *In Memoriam* is saturated with Christianity. Browning peoples his poems with faithless and tortured church figures, suggesting that their creator was preoccupied with religious questions. And since he sets many of his poems in Catholic Europe, understanding them demands a thorough knowledge of church matters. Matthew ARNOLD's "Stanzas from the Grande Chartreuse" and "Dover Beach," while not exactly expressing profound faith, display nostalgia for a past religious era. And the poems of Hopkins, a Jesuit priest, somewhat anachronistically represent the high water mark for religious poetry of the last three centuries. Poems such as "God's Grandeur" and the book-length *The Wreck of the Deutschland* combine successful poetic innovation and Christian fervor in ways not seen since Milton.

Imperialism, having reached its highest point by midcentury, began introducing to the British literary tradition new religious and cultural influences, witnessed near century's end by such works as Edward FITZGERALD's *Rubáiyát of Omar Khayyám* or even *The Mikado* of W. S. GILBERT and Arthur Sullivan, and at the start of the 20th c. by works like Rudyard KIPLING's *Kim* or E. M. FORSTER's *A Passage to India*. The voices of religions from around the world began to assert increasing influence on literature as Great Britain became more and more international.

The cliché has it that by the turn of the century, the literary influence of Christianity had begun to wane, but the evidence suggests that matters are more complex. The case of Bernard SHAW, legendary socialist doubter, supports the former position. And the works of authors Virginia WOOLF and Lytton STRACHEY clearly mark a rejection of older institutions such as the church. On the other hand, although the brilliant and tragic career of Oscar WILDE would likewise seem to evince a rejection of Christianity, close examination of his work and life demonstrates the critical influence of Christian thought and imagery. Even in the cases of Shaw, Woolf, and Strachey, and other seemingly secular writers like D. H. LAWRENCE, readers ignorant of Christianity would still struggle to comprehend their works.

The poetic output of T. S. Eliot, perhaps the dominant literary intellectual of the early 20th c., certifies the powerfully abiding influence of Christianity. Eliot's final voice is an Anglo-Catholic one, but he composed much of his most influential poetry on the Protestant model of the suffering sinner. Although the career of Yeats can be seen as an attempt to forge a new imagery less reliant on Christianity, poems such as "Byzantium" and "Sailing to Byzantium" display their Judeo-Christian roots. And any reader unschooled in Catholic traditions will find even the early fiction of Joyce bewildering.

In the later 20th c., multicultural and secular influences have enlivened the scene, and the ascendancy of Christianity as a source of literary themes and ideas may be said to have diminished somewhat. The century brought with it an increased commercialism that more than ever competes with religion for the attention of authors and readers. And writers of the former colonies, some of whom have chosen to compose in English, have introduced many new religious influences. Salman RUSHDIE dissects Islamic and Hindu cultural and religious practices in such works as *Midnight's Children* and *The Satanic Verses*. Readers have identified the influence of Buddhist thought in some of the novels of Kazuo ISHIGURO. Yet the tradition of Christian writing still has important adherents. Among influential contemporary novelists who have taken Christian questions seriously are C. S. LEWIS, Evelyn WAUGH, Graham GREENE, Barbara PYM, Muriel SPARK, and David LODGE.

The evidence for Christian influences on British literature does not diminish if one examines its genres. The English drama was born of the Catholic mass, which is structured in the antiphonal form of a dialogue. The lyric derives in part from the psalms and the Song of Solomon. The most celebrated lyric form, the sonnet, was imported from Italy, a Catholic country, but British poets eagerly embraced and adapted the form. English epics, like Blake's *Jerusalem* or Milton's *Paradise Lost*, take the prophetic books of the Bible as significant precursors.

Fictional forms such as the novel and the short story, primarily influenced by the pre-Christian (but eventually Christianized) traditions of EPIC and ROMANCE, derive also in significant ways from the great biblical narratives and Christ's parables. Other religious influences on the novel are various kinds of divine writing, including sermons, and especially spiritual AUTOBIOGRAPHY, the guiding voices of which are St. Augustine and John BUNYAN. Readers have identified the influence of both great predecessors in the first-person narrators of, say, Defoe and Dickens. And the GOTHIC NOVEL, which seems a secular form, relies for some of its horrific effects on deliberately exaggerated Catholic lore.

Moreover, the specifically autobiographical tradition, which finds expression in such varied works as Wordsworth's *Prelude* and Tennyson's *In Memoriam* as well as Newman's *Apologia Pro Vita Sua* and Thomas CARLYLE's *Sartor Resartus*, reflects its divine predecessors even more than does the novel. Carlyle, who has been called a Calvinist without the dogma, preached the gospel of work he borrowed from the

German tradition. Even later works like Eliot's *Four Quartets*, or the complex narratives of Joseph CONRAD, carry with them the faint but still identifiable marks of spiritual autobiography, saints' lives, and conversion testimonies.

Finally, British literature has also produced a tradition of satirical portrayals of Christianity that can be traced from Chaucer through the early Samuel (*Hudibras*) BUTLER, hater of Puritans, and then through Dryden, Swift, Sterne, and Dickens to the later Samuel BUTLER, whose 1903 novel, *The Way of All Flesh*, hilariously satirizes Christian hypocrisy, and to the fiction of Waugh.

BIBLIOGRAPHY: Abrams, M. H., *Natural Supernaturalism* (1971); Bobrick, B., *Wide as the Waters: The Story of the English Bible and the Revolution It Inspired* (2001); Chadwick, O., *The Victorian Church* (1963); DeLaura, D. J., *Hebrew and Hellene in Victorian England* (1969); Houghton, R., *The Victorian Frame of Mind* (1957); Lewalski, B., *Protestant Poetics and the Seventeenth-Century Religious Lyric* (1979); Lewis, C. S., *The Discarded Image* (1964); Lovejoy, A. O., *The Great Chain of Being* (1936); Miller, J. H., *The Disappearance of God* (1963); Tillyard, E. M. W., *The Elizabethan World Picture* (1944); Shell, A., *Catholicism, Controversy, and the English Literary Imagination 1558–1660* (1999); Watt, I., *The Rise of the Novel* (1957)

PAUL H. SCHMIDT

RENAISSANCE DRAMA

The Golden Age of English drama is popularly dated from about 1588 and the production of Thomas KYD's *The Spanish Tragedy* along with the development by Christopher MARLOWE of the dramatic blank verse line. This identification is appealing for several reasons, notably because the thematic Senecanism of the Pembroke school and the prosody of Marlowe's work may be directly linked to the stylistic development of William SHAKESPEARE. The fervor over Shakespeare that has dominated Renaissance dramatic study since the 18th c., however, overlooks the myriad influences and evolutions that mark the English Renaissance drama. Those influences include literary forebears such as, among others, Seneca, chronicle history, native drama, commedia dell'arte, and the Italian innovators Ludovico Ariosto and Torquato Tasso as well as the contemporary world of London drama, which exercised its influence through playhouse architecture, licensing laws, religious and political considerations, and profit motivations.

Interludes, legend plays, and MYSTERIES AND MORALITY PLAYS from early in the Tudor reign exercised an influence upon the evolution of the drama during the reign of ELIZABETH I. The development of popu-

821

lar, amateur street entertainment led to the ultimate development of professional playing and playwriting. It also had an influence upon the moral tone encountered in the early Elizabethan theater. The Pembroke "school" reintroduced classical themes and structures, particularly those found in Seneca. The five-act construction, blood revenge motif, and theatrical ghost may all be traced to the theatrical experiments of Mary, Lady PEMBROKE and her protégés. The so-called University Wits, those young men from Oxford and Cambridge who included Marlowe, Robert GREENE, George PEELE, Thomas NASHE, and Thomas LODGE, introduced and improved dramatic verse forms. Their knowledge of classical patterns and their experimentation with English prosody eventually led to "Marlowe's mighty line," an unaffected verse drama form that allowed for mellifluent character development through unrhymed iambic pentameter.

In addition to the contributions from the universities are the contributions from London's "third university," the Inns of Court. Before there was a permanent theater structure in England, members from the Inner Temple and Gray's Inn were presenting courtly performances of intramural didactic plays. These plays represent the earliest known English attempts at verse structures, genres, and source influence, which are each characteristic of the popular period. *Gorboduc*, written by Thomas SACKVILLE and Thomas NORTON and performed at the Inner Temple Hall, is the first blank-verse play written in English. *Jocasta*, written by George GASCOIGNE and Francis Kinwelmershe and performed at Gray's Inn, continued the tradition; *Jocasta* also represents the first known English adaptation of a Greek play. *The Supposes*, also written by Gascoigne and performed at Gray's Inn in the same year as *Jocasta*, not only represents the first prose comedy written in the English language, it also introduced the use of the prose prologue and supplied the subplot for Shakespeare's *The Taming of the Shrew*. *Gismonde of Salerne* (perf. ca. 1568), a tragedy written by members of the Inner Temple, is the oldest example of an English play based upon an Italian novella. It was later rewritten, "newly revived and polished . . . according to the decorum of these daies," and published as *Tancred and Gismund* (1591). *The Misfortunes of Arthur* (perf. 1588), written by members of Gray's Inn, was contemporaneous with *The Spanish Tragedy* and represents the first English play to treat the Arthurian legend. The continuing interest and involvement of these young lawyers in drama also explains the recurrence of legal terms throughout the popular period.

The Golden Age of drama emerged with the advent of the common poet, the playwright with few or no academic credentials who wrote for a living. The popularity of the "University Wits" was soon eclipsed in the popular mind by the likes of Shakespeare,

Thomas DEKKER, Henry CHETTLE, John HEYWOOD, Anthony MUNDAY, who were shortly joined by George CHAPMAN, Ben JONSON, Sir Francis BEAUMONT, John FLETCHER, and later by Thomas MIDDLETON, John MARSTON, John FORD, and John WEBSTER, among others, for whom play making was a livelihood.

The popularity of the theater can be seen in the rapid expansion of playing places. The first permanent playhouses were built to the east and north: the Red Lion (1567), The Theatre (1576), the first Blackfriars (1576), the Curtain (1577). One playhouse, Newington Butts, was built far to the south of the city in 1576 but seems to have exercised little influence upon the industry. Once the entrepreneurs discovered that their audience lived mostly to the west, however, the theaters began to rise in areas more readily accessible by river or foot. The Rose (1587) on the south bank of the river apparently proved popular enough to require expansion of the house only five years after its erection (1592). It soon found itself crowded by the larger Swan (1595) and Globe (1599), so Philip Henslowe moved his company north, still accessible to the same audience, and established the Fortune (1600) beyond Aldersgate. The Red Bull (1605) opened in the north to offer new competition there. The Boar's Head, a refitted innyard, opened in 1598 in the Whitechapel area to the east of the city. The Hope (1613) opened close to the Rose on the south bank, but the heyday of outdoor amphitheaters had by then run its course.

Indoor theaters afforded less room for crowds, but could offset the potential lost revenue by charging higher admission prices and offset the inconvenience of less space by offering benches to all and both warmer and drier viewing. The indoor, or "coterie," theaters invited more intimate plays and allowed for effects such as darkness and lowered voices unavailable in the amphitheaters. These playhouses sprang up around the Inns of Court to the west. They included the second Blackfriars (1596), St. Paul's (1600), Whitefriars (1605), Porter's Hall (1615), Phoenix/ Cockpit (1617), and Salisbury Court (1629).

Drama in the Renaissance was an ever-evolving enterprise. The influences of traditional styles, innovation, and audience preference kept the literary movement fluid. The early drama of the popular period tended toward the declamatory fustian of Marlow's *Tamburlaine the Great*, parts 1 and 2, the graphic horror of *The Spanish Tragedy*, or the broad comedy of John LYLY's plays. From these early works—most of which remained popular throughout the period—evolved identifiable subgenres. The revenge tragedy, or "the tragedy of blood," adhered to the Senecan model, generally including ghosts, a hero revenger, and graphic death. Shakespeare's *Hamlet* is easily the most famous of this type, but many other plays also explored the territory, such as Marston's

Antonio's Revenge and Middleton's (or Cyril TOUR-NEUR's) *The Revenger's Tragedy* (perf. ca. 1606; pub. 1607). Webster developed the form into the social commentary of *The Duchess of Malfi*, and Middleton went on to refine the form further to produce psychological horror in such plays as *Women Beware Women* and *The Changeling*. In addition to revenge tragedy may be found historical tragedy and classical or Aristotelian tragedy.

The history play probably evolved from the medieval legend play. Treatments of saints' lives gave way to dramatizations of secular heroes and the reigns of monarchs. The chronicle history depended largely upon the printed work of historians. A new art form emerged of creating characters, motivation, and in some cases apologia from often sterile descriptions of incident. The history play could range widely from tragedy, such as Shakespeare's *King Lear*, to romance and comedy, as Greene's *Friar Bacon and Friar Bungay*, which treats its historical context by-the-way, to heroic triumph, like Shakespeare's *Henry V.* History plays also treated Continental and foreign history, as Chapman's French histories or Greene's *The Scottish History of James IV,* performed in 1590. Classical history was also a popular subject, and Roman and Greek themes abound in treatments of the lives of Julius Caesar, Cleopatra, Sejanus, Tiberius, and the Trojan War. Mythological plays, such as Heywood's *Four Ages* plays, should also be included loosely in this category.

Comedy also developed along several lines during the popular period. Besides broad slapstick and farce are the comedies of mistaken identity from the Plautine model, pastoral comedy such as Shakespeare's *As You Like It*, as well as other permutations of the New Comedy tradition. Burlesque was also known, as Beaumont's *The Knight of the Burning Pestle* demonstrates. Perhaps the most remarkable creation was the "city" or citizen comedy. This was a variety of social satire disguised either as intrigue or new comedy and is distinguished by its location, contemporary London. Examples of the subgenre are Dekker and Webster's *Westward Ho, Northward Ho*, and Jonson, Chapman, and Marston's *Eastward Ho*. Middleton was master of the style, illustrated in *Michaelmas Term, A Mad World My Masters*, and *A Chaste Maid in Cheapside*, among others.

Jonson created notable comedies of intrigue while exploring the notion of the "humours" characters—a variety of stock type based upon Renaissance ideas of personality. His comic masterworks include *Volpone, The Alchemist*, and *Bartholomew Fair*. He also modeled tragedies upon the neoclassical ideal by following the neo-Aristotelian unities of time, action, and place.

The last generic innovation of the popular period was the tragicomedy in its guise as the ROMANCE. The invention is usually attributed to Beaumont and Fletcher, who seem in collaboration to have popularized the form although it is more likely to be Fletcher's sole contribution. Tragicomedy, wherein a potentially tragic situation veers from a tragic conclusion at the last moment and ends happily, traces to before the Beaumont and Fletcher collaborations. Marston's *The Malcontent* is probably the best example of the pre-Fletcherian tragicomedy. The romance, probably beginning with Beaumont and Fletcher's *Philaster; or, Love Lies a-Bleeding*, usually features strong passions verging upon the melodramatic, a scene featuring the instant, often undermotivated, conversion of a wicked character, and a last-moment revelation to save an innocent from death. While such elements feature in earlier works, the Fletcherian romance codified the action and set the mode. Even Shakespeare saw profit in the fad and spent his last efforts crafting such Romances after his superincumbent style.

Structure was also fluid, and playwrights experimented freely. Single plots gave rise to double plots. Double plots allowed for a subplot that further explored the themes of the main plot as may be seen in Shakespeare's *King Lear*. Eventually comic subplots were integrated into tragic main plots as in Middleton's *The Changeling*. In *Bartholomew Fair*, Jonson created a comic *coup de théâtre* by intertwining five plot lines into a single play—a feat approached only by Shakespeare in *A Midsummer Night's Dream* (four plot lines) and Middleton in *A Chaste Maid in Cheapside* (four plot lines).

The mainstream of Renaissance drama was a populist exercise. Perhaps the single most noteworthy play from a contemporary perspective, the play that made the greatest impact in its own day, was Middleton's *A Game at Chess*. It was a clever social satire that illegally represented living monarchs on the stage—the kings of England and Spain. The text, though not officially licensed through the Master of the Revels, Herbert's office, was protected by Buckingham, who had political reasons to see the Spanish lampooned. The play opened covertly while JAMES I was out of the city and drew capacity crowds to the Globe Theatre. It became the talk of the town, ran an unprecedented nine consecutive days and closed only after James, responding to official protests from Spain, personally ordered a stop. The King's Men, and presumably the playwright, profited hugely from the production and were reprimanded but lightly.

The history of the Renaissance drama ended abruptly with the Interregnum. Oliver Cromwell's Puritan forces ordered all theaters closed in 1642. Although clandestine performances occurred throughout the period from 1642 to the Restoration in 1660, the industry was destroyed. A few Renaissance playwrights such as James SHIRLEY and Sir William DAVENANT and at least two playhouses, the Red Bull and the Phoenix/Cockpit, survived into the Restoration. But the returning King Charles II brought back with him a Continental taste for Italian-French production values and changed the direction of English drama forever.

BIBLIOGRAPHY: Bentley, G. E., *The Professions of Dramatist and Player in Shakespeare's Time, 1590–1642* (1981); Braunmuller, A. R., and M. Hattaway, eds., *The Cambridge Companion to English Renaissance Drama* (1990); Chambers, E. K., *The Elizabethan Stage* (4 vols., 1923); Corrigan, B., *Playhouse Law in Shakespeare's World* (2002); Gurr, A. J., *Playgoing in Shakespeare's London* (1987); Howarth, R. G., *Literature of the Theatre: Marlowe to Shirley* (1953)

BRIAN JAY CORRIGAN

RENAULT, Mary

(pseud. of Mary Challans) b. 4 September 1905, London; d. 13 December 1983, Cape Town, South Africa

Educated at St. Hugh's, Oxford, R. trained as a nurse and in 1939 published her first novel, *Purposes of Love* (repub. as *Promise of Love*, 1939). During World War II, she continued her nursing career and published *Kind Are Her Answers* (1940) and *The Friendly Young Ladies* (1944; repub. as *The Middle Mist*, 1945). After the war, she traveled extensively throughout Europe and Africa and in 1948 emigrated to South Africa. Her affinity for Greece inspired the publication in 1956 of *The Last of the Wine*, and thereafter R. produced the historical fiction based in classical antiquity for which she is best known: *The King Must Die* (1958), *The Bull from the Sea* (1962), *The Mask of Apollo* (1966), and *The Praise Singer* (1978)—and her major achievement, the fictional portrait of Alexander the Great comprising *Fire from Heaven* (1969), *The Persian Boy* (1972), and *Funeral Games* (1981).

RENDELL, [Baroness] Ruth [Barbara Grasemann]

(pseud.: Barbara Vine) b. 17 February 1930, London

R. is a novelist and short story writer whose reputation for being one of Britain's most prolific crime authors does not jeopardize her status as one of the finest. R. is often linked to P. D. JAMES, but such comparisons should be limited to the quality rather than the nature of her prose. R.'s canon can be divided into three quite separate bodies of work: the Kingsmarkham series—her most structurally orthodox books—set in a fictional mid-Sussex town and featuring Chief Inspector Wexford and his sidekick, Mike Burden; a number of non-series novels that explore violence and abnormal psychology, and are crime-related rather than stories of detection; and a darker, psychological

strain of thrillers, published under the pseudonym Barbara Vine. Television adaptations of all three have contributed significantly to R.'s enormous popularity.

Reginald Wexford made his debut in R.'s first book, *From Doon with Death* (1964); "born at the age of 52," Wexford is a complex and likable figure, who began as an enabler to a story of tragedy and desire but has evolved, in the seventeen subsequent novels to feature him, into an erudite, sensitive, and liberal individual, whose tolerance and very fallibility have made him one of the most popular series characters in contemporary fiction. While R. has been the first to admit that Wexford is not a "realistic" policeman, her sympathetic portrayal of his family—a wife and two grown daughters—render him a deeply credible man; his personal relationships, not least with the more straitlaced and puritanical Burden, form a layer of subplots in R.'s work that are often as engaging as the central murder.

Like many distinguished crime writers, R.'s main interest is in character and social criticism; even her Wexford mysteries should not be classed as inheritances of the Golden Age, but as thoughtful and problematic investigations of personal and collective issues, ranging from a moving exploration of the nature of grief (*No More Dying Then*, 1971) to a repudiation of British militant FEMINISM (*An Unkindness of Ravens*, 1985). Julian SYMONS has insightfully praised R.'s Wexford novels for their unerring depiction of middle-class suburban life and, apart from a tendency to inflict her characters with the most outlandish names, she has an unrivaled eye for detail and ear for dialogue, particularly in *Some Lie and Some Die* (1973), *Shake Hands Forever* (1975), and *Kissing the Gunner's Daughter* (1991). *Simisola* (1994) marked a development in the Wexford novels and is, says R.—a Labour peer and committed socialist—her "state of Britain novel"; here, Kingsmarkham is almost unrecognisable from the earlier books, having become a haven for racism and unemployment. *Road Rage* (1997), peopled with eco-warriors and environmental campaigners; and *Harm Done* (1999), which highlights domestic violence and a community's reaction to the release of a known pedophile, continue this more aggressively political strain. It is a testament to her storytelling ability that she manages to integrate these concerns into the plot without losing control of the suspense.

Despite Wexford's popularity, R. has repeatedly stated a preference for her non-series books, in which characters display neuroses and aberrant personalities and often face personal disaster and humiliation. In these novels, which are much more ambiguous and unsettling, the emphasis is on why rather than who and R. demonstrates a remarkable ability to empathize with the criminal mind: *A Demon in My View* (1976) is a stark portrayal of sexual and psychotic obsession;

and *A Judgement in Stone* (1977), which details the murder of a family by their domestic, is an illuminating insight into the isolation of an illiterate woman. In 1995, she edited *The Reason Why: An Anthology of the Murderous Mind*, which is a literary and cultural investigation of the impetus to kill. R.'s independent novel entitled *Adam and Eve and Pinch Me* (2001) centers on a woman whose fiancé died in the Paddington train crash only to reappear menacingly in her life, and mixes supernatural elements into a classic study of human instincts and failures.

The Barbara Vine novels—*A Dark-Adapted Eye* (1986), *A Fatal Inversion* (1987), *The House of Stairs* (1988), *Gallowglass* (1990), *King Solomon's Carpet* (1991), *Asta's Book* (1993), *No Night Is Too Long* (1994), *The Brimstone Wedding* (1996), *The Chimney Sweeper's Boy* (1998), and *Grasshopper* (2000)—seem to provide R. with a still broader canvas on which to prove her originality, ingenuity, and sheer ability to see a narrative where others would not think to look for one. In *Grasshopper*, she displays a sense of place that is capable of transforming the rooftops of Maida Vale into as legitimate a setting for a novel as any town, street, or village. The mirror image of her subterranean earlier work, *King Solomon's Carpet, Grasshopper* is a complex blend of familiar Vine themes: the hold of the past on the present; lives forever entwined by the smallest of coincidences; buried secrets and deep-seated fears; innocence and the first encounter with true evil; and mystery, carried forward by questions and answers effortlessly woven into the narrative.

Nobody who takes as many stylistic risks as R. can be consistently flawless, but her best work is all the better for that obsession with experimentation and her extensive oeuvre more than justifies the high regard in which she is held by her peers. Over forty years of writing, she has unfailingly reflected the changing moral climate of her time; R.'s books are about the stories within all of us and, in her hands, those stories are beautifully told.

BIBLIOGRAPHY: Rowland, S., *From Agatha Christie to R. R.: British Women Writers in Detective and Crime Fiction* (2001); Symons, J., *Bloody Murder* (1972; rev. eds., 1974, 1985)

NICOLA UPSON

RESTORATION DRAMA

The theaters had been closed in 1642 at the beginning of the English Civil War, and thereafter there had only been some clandestine theatrical presentations. When Charles II regained his throne in 1660, one of his first actions was to establish two acting companies. Thomas KILLIGREW, his semiofficial Court Jester, was given the patent for the King's Company at a small theater

in Vere Street. Sir William DAVENANT was given the patent for the Duke's Company at a converted tennis court in Lincoln's Inn Fields. Their patron was the king's brother, the Duke of York. This swift establishment of the theaters and the ready acceptance of them as a respectable social amenity would not have happened if the restored king had not been actively interested in them. For instance, while in the early 17th c. men had played female characters, the king wished to see plays with actresses as he had during his exile. This led eventually to the appearance of Nell Gwyn, who was only one of several actresses who left the stage for a rich man's bed.

Dramatists before the interregnum had a wider variety of patronage as well as more venues in which to have their work performed. Now, although open to the general public, the theaters were adjuncts of the court. Charles II not only attended both theaters frequently, he called the companies to perform at Whitehall once a week during the season. Both companies were servants to the king or his brother; the actors were Grooms of the Chamber provided with cloth for their liveries, ultimately at the command of their patrons, needing their indulgence, if not their permission, for all they did. This is a subtle yet distinct difference from the position of the players before the Interregnum and from the position of the theater managements dependent on commercial considerations after the accession in 1689 of William and Mary. Moreover the authority of Charles II was based on more than the need to gratify the wishes of a monarch besotted with the theater. Because of his position his wishes, even his suggestions, were royal commands to be obeyed. In 1662, the king wrote to Lord Orrery that he had read his play, liked it, and would have it performed as soon as possible. Not surprisingly Orrery's reply was ecstatic.

Moreover, the king encouraged new plays to be written. He persuaded Sir Samuel Tuke to write his only play *The Adventures of Five Hours* (perf. 1662; pub. 1663) from the Spanish of Pedro Calderón de la Barca. In effect, the dramatists made up a small coterie centered round the court. Of the dozen or so living writers whose work was regularly performed, at least eight were of the nobility and the rest of the gentry, and all were highly educated. Several were related to each other by birth or marriage, most had been concerned with the royalist cause, and most had private means, posts, or patrons and were not dependent on the theater for their livelihood. John DRYDEN was of the circle by virtue of his marriage into the Howard family. Aphra BEHN, while only on the fringes of the inner circle, knew many of the king's intimates.

The upheaval of the Civil War and all that had led up to the regicide in 1649 made the general public wary for a time of any indications of underlying tension in their lives and they were reluctant to involve themselves in such issues again. The older Cavaliers expected the Restoration to be applied not only to the physical return of the monarch but eventually to the political and religious domains. These essentially nostalgic attitudes are reflected in the characters and contents of the plays revived from 1660. The repertoire shows that there was in a sense a retreat to Elizabethan and Jacobean plays. Ben JONSON's comedies were as popular as before the Interregnum. His *Epicoene; or, The Silent Woman*, performed in 1609, believed to have been the first play shown before the king after his return, was played at least seven times in the first six months. *Bartholomew Fair* was seen five times in 1661 and *The Alchemist* three times. The extant prompt copies suggest there were more performances of James SHIRLEY's plays than are recorded, as Dryden's later vilification of him in the satiric poem *Macflecknoe* seems to show. Abraham COWLEY's *The Guardian* was changed to *The Cutter of Coleman Street* and became an anti-Puritan satire. Oddly enough, even then Cowley was rebuked for showing his royalist Colonel Jolly as less than a fair and noble character. Audiences seemed willing only to enjoy political or religious comment in terms of black or white during the early years, while, at the same time accepting that in real life compromise in one form or another was, and had been, inevitable. They preferred to pass their time in more aesthetic interests if not at first the outright debauchery so often offered them. With only two theaters available for presenting plays with the same knowledgeable and articulate audience attending both, the playwrights received direct and immediate responses. Thomas SHADWELL writes of blotting out the main design of *The Humourists* (perf. 1670; pub. 1671) finding it had given offense. There would be a noticeable teleological interaction in such an environment that led to the popularity of comedy while paradoxically the writers thought it an inferior kind of writing.

Restoration comic drama is a very wide category: plays that are labeled comedy on their title page can be very different in content, style, and tone. They encompass the chaste love and honor romances of the earlier years like Robert Howard's *The Surprisal* (perf. 1662; pub. 1665); the coarser city low-life tales that grew out of the comic subplots as in Dryden's *The Wild Gallant*; the sexual intrigues involving disguises, when often the actresses would have an excuse to wear men's clothes and display their legs, as in John Lacy's *The Old Troop* (perf. 1664; pub. 1672); the vehicles for the exchange of witticisms as in Sir George ETHEREGE's *The Man of Mode*, which were a reflection of the types of conversation seen as the epitome of polite society; and the personal, political, or religious satires like *The Rehearsal* by George Villiers, Duke of BUCKINGHAM. Modern academic discussions of the plays have proposed equally diverse theories about the intentions of the writers, the relationships between the plays, common themes, or chronological development. What is clear from the many ideas put forward is that it is not possible to assert any one style to be the quintessence of Restoration comedy when all the plays known to have been written and performed are considered. It is sometimes possible to find one type of play being presented more frequently than another in any one season but the reasons why this should be so can only be conjectured and could depend on such different factors as the availability of particular performers, the topical concerns of the court or the city, or the latest contemporary theory on the nature and function of comedy.

Dryden was disparaging of comedy, seeing it as an inferior kind of writing but he was one of the most prolific writers of the genre although many of the plays he wrote as examples of his theories on language are often disappointingly mundane, fatuously bombastic or, in the case of his later comedies, coarsely indecent. Behn, who wrote nearly as many plays as Dryden, has been reviled for the coarseness of her comedies but modern revivals have shown that they are not the worst of the period. The Restoration sense of HUMOR may well have been rather different from our own. The SATIRE is extraordinarily caustic, although there is a distinction between totally gratuitous insult and sarcastic comment. Such invective appears in the many satirical poems by Dryden, Andrew MARVELL, and John Wilmot, Earl of ROCHESTER and was in a tradition that included Robert GREENE and Thomas NASHE as well as John Eachard. It moves easily from verbal abuse to practical jokes and cruel tricks and is ideally suited to the coarser comic drama. The 17th-c. Hobbesian view of comedy is that it is basically malicious, that we laugh at others because we are not in their predicament ourselves. It is more than laughter at the accidental slip on a banana skin, more than the inevitable workings of fate against hubris. It is laughter at deliberate human contrivance of another's discomfiture or downfall, the killing of the community scapegoat. The dedicatory epistles, the prologues, and epilogues make this extremely clear. The audience did not, at least usually, react against the almost ritualized abuse of such groups as beaux, whores, poets, citizens, and countrymen and such public vilification may paradoxically have been welcomed by the targets as a mode of acknowledgment rather then resented as an affront. The viciousness behind this kind of humor is uncomfortable and disturbing. Perhaps because they better suit modern feelings about appropriate humor, the comedies by William WYCHERLEY, especially *The Country Wife*, and Etherege's *The Man of Mode* are better known today, although they only wrote four and three plays respectively.

The king's response to every play presented would be noted and affect the response of those of influence, or those who hoped for influence, in the audience and thus indirectly effect changes in tone and content of succeeding plays. As the king and his court's behavior became more lax, or perhaps more open, so the sexually explicit plays by Thomas D'URFEY, Edward Ravenscroft, and others began to appear, becoming more and more indecent as time went on. The king discussed *Mr. Limberham* (perf. 1678; pub. 1680), which is more openly obscene than almost any others from the period, with Dryden, and later suggested ideas for *Sir Courtly Nice* to John CROWNE, which he did not live to see carried out.

Tragedy was seen as the epitome of excellence in dramatic literature. All other forms were inferior, not because they lacked anything in theatricality but because they used inferior, in literary terms, styles of language. The Royal Society under the active patronage of Charles II, and to which several of the dramatists belonged, was laying down rules for the use of clear and succinct English. This affected the response to the plays of William SHAKESPEARE, for he was considered inelegant with too extravagant and flamboyant a language. He also departed from the three unities of time, place, and action supposedly laid down by Aristotle that Dryden advocated. Dryden's *All for Love* is his improved version of *Antony and Cleopatra*. Nahum TATE revised *King Lear* to allow Lear and Cordelia to live happily ever after, a version that was more popular for the next hundred years than Shakespeare's tragedy, for audiences preferred what they conceived as poetic justice, or that good should triumph in the end.

Before 1660, scenery and fantastic effects had only been used for the masques at court or for a very occasional play presented privately. But Charles II wanted to see plays against scenery and was responsible for the development of the scenic stage in the public theater. He sent Davenant's actor-manager Thomas Betterton to France several times to discover how to use and improve scenery that led to two purpose-built theaters, Dorset Gardens in 1671 shortly followed by Drury Lane in 1674. Both were designed and fitted out to present spectacular scenery based on painted sliding shutters that could be opened to disclose action behind them or closed together to end one scene while the next continued in front of the shutters. This meant that dramatists could surprise the audience by unexpected discoveries in any play. The scene shutters at first disclosed tableaux of torture scenes reminiscent of Jacobean tragedy as in the ever popular blood and thunder of Dryden's heroic tragedies and others such as Nathaniel LEE's *Caesar Borgia* (perf. 1679; pub. 1680) with three poisonings, five stranglings, and a small boy with his eyes put out, or Thomas OTWAY's *Venice Preserv'd* with attempted rape and a scene on the scaffold. The shutters were as effective in exposing some fool's uncomfortable predicament and the comedies began to include the sudden disclosure of a bedroom scene. Behn's *Sir Patient Fancy* (perf. 1678; pub. 1678) has three although none is as sexually explicit as some modern plays. The possibilities given by the scenic stage meant that from the 1670s spectacular opera style heroic tragedies were being presented with many staging effects. Characters flew on in chariots, scenery rose from under the stage, palaces and gardens appeared as shutters were withdrawn and redrawn across the stage. One of the first of these entertainments was Elkanah Settle's *The Empress of Morocco* (perf. 1673; pub. 1673) shortly followed by Shadwell's *Psyche* (1675). These were put on as an answer to the success of the visiting Italian opera companies. Both *Macbeth* and *The Tempest* by Shakespeare were popular when they were adapted with the resources of the new staging into spectacular musical presentations.

No other monarch has taken such a personal interest in the theater as Charles II. It was not until he was succeeded by James II in 1685 that the core of the royal influence began to change, particularly in a less blatant display of sexuality. Quarrels and financial problems meant the two companies had had to amalgamate in 1682 and few new plays were shown. Moreover, James II was more concerned with religious and political matters for the short time he was on the throne and the resultant upheavals in the country contributed to a lean time for the theaters. William and Mary had little interest in the theater and rarely attended. The audience changed from a majority of influential sycophantic courtiers and their hangers-on to a more commercially based mixture of London merchants and craftsmen, a Protestant bourgeoisie with a more genteel and sentimental taste in drama. George FARQUHAR's plays with middle-class characters set in the provinces satisfied their expectations better, whereas William CONGREVE, although much admired today, was not successful at the time and eventually gave up writing plays. The audience were no longer interested in the witty language and sexual affairs of the nobility and this kind of comedy disappeared until the end of the 1770s when Richard Brinsley SHERIDAN wrote comedies exposing the manners of his society. In addition, Congreve and Sir John VANBRUGH were particularly targeted by Jeremy Collier in his pamphlet *A Short View of the Immorality and Profaneness of the English Stage* (1698) that reviled the stage as irreligious and obscene. Vanbrugh responded by building his own theater for the presentation of opera.

BIBLIOGRAPHY: Holland P., *The Ornament of Action: Text and Performance in Restoration Comedy* (1979); Howe, E., *The First English Actresses, Women and Drama, 1660–1700* (1992); Hume, R. D., *The Development of English Drama in the Late Seventeenth Century* (1976); Love, H., ed., *Restoration Literature:*

Critical Approaches (1972); Malekin, P., *Liberty and Love: English Literature and Society, 1640–88* (1981)

DAWN LEWCOCK

REYNOLDS, John Hamilton

b. 9 September 1796, Shrewsbury, Shropshire; d. 15 November 1852, Newport, Isle of Wight

Friend and correspondent of John KEATS, R. was a minor poet whose true gift was for witty parody, although in 1816 an essay in the *Examiner* placed him alongside Keats and Percy Bysshe SHELLEY. R.'s best serious poetic work is *The Garden of Florence* (1821). Educated at Shrewsbury and St. Paul's School, London, he worked in insurance before taking up law. His first published work, *Safie* (1814), was an Oriental novel after the style of Lord BYRON. R.'s mocking parody of William WORDSWORTH's *Peter Bell,* published in 1819, inspired Shelley's *Peter Bell the Third.* In 1825, R. collaborated with Thomas HOOD in *Odes and Adresses to Great People.*

REYNOLDS, [Sir] Joshua

b. 16 July 1723, Plympton, Devon; d. 23 February 1792, London

Artist and aesthetician, R. was among the foremost British portrait painters of the 18th c. A proponent of the "grand style," he infused Georgian painting with elements that sought to evoke classical values. In turn, his use of color, strong lighting, and paint influenced subsequent painters like Thomas Lawrence, and anticipate artists like Goya. More educated than most artists of the day, R. counted among his friends David GARRICK, Oliver GOLDSMITH, Edmund BURKE, Fanny BURNEY, and especially Samuel JOHNSON. He founded the famous Literary Club to provide Johnson a venue for conversation. Indeed, James BOSWELL dedicated his famous *Life of Johnson* to R. R. was also the first president of the Royal Academy (1768–92), a position from which he worked to raise the status of the visual arts in Britain. While Romantics like William BLAKE dismissed him as "Sir Sploshua," and the Pre-Raphaelites turned to other models of composition, John RUSKIN placed him among the "supreme colourists." In 1905, Roger FRY praised R.'s aesthetics, especially his use of "significant form."

R.'s career as a painter falls into roughly three stages. The first stretches from his apprenticeship through his trip to Italy. The second stretches from his return from Italy until about 1770. The final stage stretches from 1770 until his death. R. was apprenticed to the London portrait painter Thomas Hudson. Thereafter, he set up on his own, producing portraits in a manner that reflected the influence of Godfrey Kneller, Van Dyck, and Rembrandt. Most noteworthy

of this period was the first of a series of portraits of his friend Commodore Augustus Keppel. He visited Italy from 1749 to 1753, absorbing the influence of Michelangelo, Velasquez, Rubens, and the Venetians, especially Titian and Tintoretto. Returning to London, he began producing portraits marked by strong modeling, and bold brushwork, light, and color, developing his mastery of the "Grand Style." During this period, he produced many evocative and literate portraits, such as those of Laurence STERNE, Goldsmith, Burke, and the series of Johnson. In the later part of his career, R. played the role of man of letters. After the death of Allen Ramsay in 1784, he became the principal painter to George III. His masterpiece of this last stage is probably *Mrs. Siddons as the Tragic Muse.* Because of his frequent experimentation with methods and materials, many of R.'s paintings have suffered serious deterioration.

R. founded the Royal Academy in 1768. It originally had forty members, including Benjamin West, Francis Cotes, Paul and Thomas Sandby, Thomas Gainsborough, and Angelica Kauffmann. R.'s addresses to the Academy between 1769 and 1790 became the basis of his *Discourses on Art,* which appeared annually and then biennially. R. wrote in a fluent and flowing style. In the early 1760s, he had contributed several letters to Johnson's *Idler,* including an attack on William Hogarth's equation of beauty with the serpentine line. The fifteen discourses both describe R.'s views on art and artists, and provide an eloquent summary of 18th-c. aesthetics. He posits the Apollo Belvedere and the Portland Vase as the ideals of classical sculpture, and Raphael and Michelangelo as those of Italian painting, though in his late *Journey to Flanders and Holland* (1797), he expresses his admiration for van Eyck and other Dutch and Flemish artists. Nevertheless, while advocating the study of the masters, he rejects slavish copying or the reduction of art to a mechanical application of technique. Central to his aesthetic is that art is a form of intellectual discourse. While the student must learn the grammar of color, composition, and technique, art must go beyond the mechanical. Drawing an analogy with poetry and rhetoric, he argued that the artist must be informed by ideas, aiming for the "general and intellectual."

BIBLIOGRAPHY: Hudson, D., *Sir J. R.* (1958); Penny, N., *R.* (1986); Pointon, M., *Hanging the Head: Portraiture and Social Formation in Eighteenth-Century England* (1993); Waterhouse, E. K., *R.* (1941)

THOMAS L. COOKSEY

RHYS, Jean

b. Ella Gwendoline Rees Williams, 24 August 1890, Roseau, Dominica; d. 14 May 1979, Devon

R. stands second in reputation only to Virginia WOOLF among England's modernist women writers. Between

1927 and 1939, R. published a collection of short stories, written under the mentorship of Ford Maddox FORD, and four novels, after which she seemingly disappeared and her five books went out of print. Those who knew of her strictly by way of her writing assumed she had died. Then in May 1957, the BBC broadcast a dramatized version of her fourth novel, *Good Morning, Midnight* (1939), renewing curiosity about its author and compelling R. to become a writer once again. When *Wide Sargasso Sea* (1966) drew outstanding reviews, R. achieved the critical acclaim that had eluded her for forty years.

R. was born in the West Indies, but at the age of sixteen she was sent to England to pursue an education. Although she aspired to be an actress, she lacked the talent to make a living in the theater. Being young, attractive, and on her own, R. began exploring the underside of Bohemian life in Great Britain and Europe, time and again putting herself into the hands of men who manipulated her. She married three times, gave birth to two children, survived two world wars, and battled both poverty and illness. Her life experiences are reflected in her female characters who make no apologies either for using others or for allowing themselves to be used.

In her early novels, R. writes candidly about the disastrous effects—prostitution, alcoholism, betrayal, exile, alienation—for women of the demimonde who exchange sex for material security. Critics point out that Marya Zella (twenty-eight) of *Postures* (1928; repub. as *Quartet*, 1929), Julia Martin (mid-thirties) of *After Leaving Mr. Mackenzie* (1931), Anna Morgan (eighteen) of *Voyage in the Dark* (1934), and Sasha Jansen (past forty) of *Good Morning, Midnight* form a composite of the R. heroine at various points in her life. Since the age of nineteen, Julia Martin, for instance, has lived on the money that men have given to her. Her emotional baggage includes a failed marriage and a dead son. Having been bought off by her most recent lover, Mr. Mackenzie, Julia drifts aimlessly between Paris and London, visiting family who reject her and asking for money from men with whom she has had previous affairs. Exhausted, finally, she lapses into depression and scarcely recognizes herself as a participant in her own life. R.'s marginalized women have no illusions about themselves or about what life holds for them. They are amoral and submissive because both traits are required of them to survive in relationships in which men wield power and money. When their usefulness or beauty fades, however, they find themselves languishing in cheap hotel rooms that symbolize their self-destructive choices. From among these early works, *Voyage in the Dark* was R.'s only commercial success, leading critics to surmise that she was either ahead of her time or that her subject matter, ultimately, was too sordid for public appeal.

Prior to being rediscovered, R. had been contemplating a novel about Bertha Mason, Edward Rochester's mad Creole wife in Charlotte BRONTË's *Jane Eyre*. "She seemed such a poor ghost," R. once said, "I thought I'd like to write her life." It took R. nine years to complete her prequel to Brontë's Gothic romance, but *Wide Sargasso Sea* is both more stylistically diverse and more psychologically probing than anything R. had attempted before it. *Wide Sargasso Sea* also is R.'s only historical novel, being set in Jamaica and Dominica shortly after the Emancipation Act of 1833 in which Britain abolished slavery throughout its colonies. The novel's plot centers on an arranged marriage between Antoinette (neé Cosway) Mason, a wealthy young plantation heiress who grows up amidst violence and recrimination, and Edward Rochester, a second son who is dispatched to Jamaica to exploit a woman he does not know. Lying between the Azores and the West Indies, the Sargasso Sea geographically separates England from the Caribbean, and clearly Antoinette and Edward belong to different worlds. Whereas she is passive, sensual, and trusting, he is aggressive, cold, and deceitful. Through the figure of Edward Rochester, R. indicts the narrow-mindedness of British culture, patriarchy, and racism. "R.'s great triumph," notes one critic, "resides in her ability to devise a story that combines a personal tragedy with a historical debacle during a time of overwhelming social and gender injustice."

R. followed *Wide Sargasso Sea* with two short story collections, *Tigers Are Better-Looking* (1968) and *Sleep It Off, Lady* (1976), neither of which surpasses her previous achievements. For her contributions to literature, in 1978 R. was made a Commander of the Order of the British Empire. Her novels continue to generate sophisticated interpretations by critics interested in MODERNISM, FEMINISM, and postcolonial theory.

BIBLIOGRAPHY: Maurel, S., *J. R.* (1998); Staley, T. F., *J. R.* (1979); Sternlicht, S., *J. R.* (1997); Thomas, S., *The Worlding of J. R.* (1999)

JOE NORDGREN

RICHARDS, I[vor] A[rmstrong]

b. 26 February 1893, Sandbach, Cheshire; d. 7 September 1979, Cambridge

R.'s reputation will undoubtedly rest on his founding New Criticism and shaping it into one of the most influential schools of literary analysis of the 20th c. Early in his career, R. generated much controversy in his attempt to give literary analysis the rigor of scientific work, with unambiguous methodology and language. Critics often divide his prolific career into several sections. Primarily, R. can be studied as a literary critic and innovator. His second career began with diverse work as a linguist and semantic scholar in England, the U.S., and China. After reaching his sixties, the indefatigable scholar entered into an entirely different career as a poet, and though enthusiasm for his later poetry was not always as strong as it had been for his earlier critical work, he nonetheless achieved general respect and acknowledgment from his peers.

With an eye toward increasing global communication in the wake of World War I, R. and C. K. Ogden collaborated on an instrumental text for semantics, *The Meaning of Meaning* (1923). The ideas of the book would form the basis of R.'s lifelong attempt to develop a better world through communication and education. Shortly thereafter, R. made his individual mark upon the critical world with *Principles of Literary Criticism* (1924). While the book's central thesis of adopting psychology for analyzing literature was not entirely unheard of, R.'s methodology was innovative, and despite disagreements from critics over the validity of his psychological models, the efficiency of his method and insights it provided could hardly be denied.

The publication of *Practical Criticism* (1929), outlining the basic methodology that would become New Criticism, cemented R.'s reputation as a critical giant for the modern period. As with *Principles*, the goal for *Practical Criticism* was to provide clear, unambiguous understanding of works that might otherwise provide stumbling blocks for critics and students. In the decades that followed, R.'s emphasis on analyzing irony, authorial intent, and ambiguity served as critical guideposts for his followers. For the next several decades, he produced a number of critical works continuing the New Critical project. *Coleridge on Imagination* (1934) founded Samuel Taylor COLERIDGE studies for the modern era, while other works such as *The Philosophy of Rhetoric* (1936) and *Interpretation in Teaching* (1938) furthered R.'s general influence. It would take the advent of POSTMODERNISM in the 1960s and 1970s to dislodge New Criticism as the dominant critical method of the late 20th c., but arguably R.'s reliance on context, irony, and reconciling "opposing attitudes" within texts prepared the way for at least partial acceptance of the postmodern emphasis on ambiguity and indeterminism in criticism.

The 1930s were not only spent developing the new literary criticism of the forthcoming decades, however. From the 1930s on, R. spent time in the U.S. (moving to Harvard in 1939) and China, developing and refining Ogden's "Basic English," a simplified version of English with minimal vocabulary and grammar rules intended to promote English speaking and communication. He spent the next several decades helping to direct a language research institute, with an eye to integrating language teaching with any number of growing pictorial or audio-visual technologies of the modern world, using art, film, television,

and any other useful medium for aiding communication and language studies.

Relatively late in life, R. began a third career as a poet. He eventually produced four volumes of poetry, beginning with *Goodbye Earth and Other Poems* (1958), as well as a number of plays. R. used a variety of stanza forms and poetic techniques, though age and reflection upon death are central themes. While his poetry was not nearly as influential as his criticism, reviews were typically respectful, and the depth and intelligence of his work was acknowledged by most readers. In these poems and plays (which often contain sections of verse), R. reveals himself as a scientific as well as poetic thinker, and the influence of his travels in the Far East is also readily apparent. *Playbook: Five Plays for a New Theatre* (1956) contains the work *A Leak in the Universe*, representing scientific theories such as the Heisenberg Uncertainty Principle while simultaneously giving Japanese Buddhism a voice. While circuitry and spaceships can occur as frequent material in both his plays and poems, the works themselves remain particularly human, with personal philosophy and struggles with the basic questions of life remaining always in the forefront.

As a poet, philosopher, critic, and educator, R. exerted a strong influence on the world of literary criticism. His diverse background and willingness to engage in any number of critical enterprises mark him as a particularly valuable member of the intellectual community of the 20th c.

BIBLIOGRAPHY: Brower, R., H. Vendler, and J. Hollander, eds., *I. A. R.* (1973); Russo, J. P., "The Mysterious Mountains: I. A. R. and High Mountaineering," *Shenandoah* 30, 4 (1979): 69–91; Russo, J. P., *I. A. R.* (1989)

STEVEN ZANI

RICHARDSON, Dorothy [Miller]

b. 17 May 1873, Abingdon, Berkshire; d. 17 June 1957, London

Few writers have undergone such changes in fortune as R. Widely emulated during her lifetime as a major force in the development of psychological fiction, R. was a pioneer of the stream of consciousness technique whose first works using that method predate those of both Virginia WOOLF and James JOYCE. Her uncompromisingly experimental writing was later charged with dullness, obscurity and triviality, and she fell into neglect until the wave of feminist criticism in the late 1960s and 1970s created a new interest in her depiction of a female consciousness. While R.'s lifetime output is by no means consistent in its quality, her ambitious objectives and development of a groundbreaking prose style mean that she cannot be ignored in any discussions of MODERNISM or feminist literary tradition.

A novelist, journalist, and translator, R.'s writing career began when she moved to London in 1895 after her mother's suicide and the break up of her family. There, she met many socialist and avant-garde thinkers, including H. G. WELLS, who encouraged her to write, and by 1908 she was contributing regularly to *Crank, Saturday Review, Adelphi,* and *Little Review.* Her journalism, which spanned stories, poems, reviews, essays, and sketches, eventually earned her an income but her lifelong passion, and the work for which she is remembered, is *Pilgrimage,* an EPIC novel published in thirteen volumes: *Pointed Roofs* (1915); *Backwater* (1916); *Honeycomb* (1917); *Interim* (1919); *The Tunnel* (1919); *Deadlock* (1921); *Revolving Lights* (1923); *The Trap* (1925); *Oberland* (1927); *Dawn's Left Hand* (1931); *Clear Horizon* (1935); *Dimple Hill* (1938); and *March Moonlight,* which was published posthumously in 1967.

As the title suggests, *Pilgrimage* chronicles the personal, spiritual, and intellectual journey of Miriam Henderson, R.'s fictional alter ego. Many of the events of Miriam's life run parallel to R.'s own experience: she teaches in a girls' school in Germany (on its publication, *Pointed Roofs* was criticized for its sympathetic attitude toward German culture); becomes a dental assistant; rejects marriage proposals; visits friends; holidays among Quakers in Sussex; and meets "a tall skeleton in tattered garments" who is based on R.'s husband, the painter Alan Odle. The work's main focus, however, is not these external incidents but Miriam's interior life, and R.'s craft as a novelist lies not in the invention of facts but in the shaping of experience.

"The material that moved me would not fit the framework of any novel I had experienced," wrote R., claiming that both realist and romantic fiction left out "certain essentials" and "dramatized life misleadingly." The alternative that she establishes with *Pilgrimage* has much in common with Marcel Proust's extended narration in that it explores an evolving consciousness and shifts values firmly from the public to the private sphere. Rejecting the conventional horizontal portrayal of plot and character, R. set about presenting time as an organic whole rather than a linear progression. Her technique was influenced by two philosophers: William James, who articulated the phrase "stream of thought" or "interior monologue"; and Henri Bergson, whose concept of *la durée* unites past, present, and future in a subjective consciousness. Experience, for Miriam, is impressionistic, made up of recurrent moments of solitude in which time expands and gives a heightened sense of the present moment that simultaneously refers back to the past and looks forward to the future. In *Clear Horizon,* Miriam describes such a moment as "a loop in time, one of

those occasions that bring with peculiar vividness the sense of identity"; R.'s technical achievement in developing a style inseparable from the consciousness of her protagonist, and one that matched her own sense of female experience, is perhaps the most noteworthy aspect of *Pilgrimage,* and gives the work a peculiar intensity, particularly in the later volumes.

R.'s desire "to produce a feminine equivalent of the current masculine REALISM" meant a radical rewriting of the basic sentence: language, so often the province of the male, was, in its current usage, to be distrusted. Believing in "unpunctuated" female prose, she frequently dispensed with full stops to create sentence-long paragraphs and changed the tense or the narrative pronoun within a single phrase; for this, she was credited by Woolf as having invented "the psychological sentence of the feminine gender," a new sentence that is "of a more elastic fibre than the old, capable of stretching to the extreme."

R. has been widely praised for writing one of the earliest and fullest descriptions of a gifted and underprivileged woman forced to make her way in a man's world. She held strong views on women and writing, and these were expressed in the essay "Women in the Arts," published in 1925, four years before Woolf's *A Room of One's Own.* Her FEMINISM, though, lies not in the question of equal rights but in her insistence that a different, and equally valid, reality exists for women. While R. did not share Woolf's ability to distance herself from a work of art, to judge it and to make it flawless, *Pilgrimage,* which occupied her until her death in 1957, is a unique challenge to the traditional restrictions of the novel.

BIBLIOGRAPHY: Fromm, G. G., *D. R.* (1977); Hanscombe, G. E., *The Art of Life: D. R. and the Development of Feminist Consciousness* (1982); Scott, B. K., *The Gender of Modernism* (1990)

NICOLA UPSON

RICHARDSON, Samuel

b. July 1689, Mackworth, Derbyshire; d. 4 July 1761, London

R.'s purpose always was didactic and he was proud of eschewing "romances, monsters and chimeras," though his plots have affinities with fairy tale. His first book, *The Apprentice's Vade Mecum* (1733), was avowedly didactic, as was his own version of *Aesop's Fables.* R. became famous with *Pamela* (2 vols., 1740), a novel in the form of letters and a journal, in which a servant girl resists seduction by her master and is rewarded by marriage. In the sequel (1742), she wins the love of her husband's relatives and friends. This Cinderella story was wildly popular among maidservants and was satirized by Henry FIELDING in *Joseph Andrews* and in the brilliant *Shamela.* Fielding accuses Pamela and R. of hypocrisy: in Fielding's view, Pamela is manipulative, a tease who deliberately inflames. Fielding's view is classbound: in a higher social station, resistance like Pamela's would have been thought virtue, and her offense, in his eyes, is social climbing.

Hester Thrale [PIOZZI] placed R. first among novelists, then Jean-Jacques Rousseau, and "after them, but at an immeasurable distance—Charlotte LENNOX, [Tobias] SMOLLETT and Fielding." She thought that though Fielding and Smollett knew "the husk of life," for "the kernel you must go to either Richardson or Rousseau." Samuel JOHNSON contrasted Fielding's "characters of manners" and R.'s "characters of nature where a man must dive into the recesses of the human heart," also opining that if you read R. for the story, "you would hang yourself": R. was to be read for "the SENTIMENT." All three of his novels are epistolary: he did not invent the form but is its most brilliant exponent. Lacking Fielding's classical education, R.'s mind was soaked in the poetry of William SHAKESPEARE and John MILTON, so that his allusions are still accessible, whereas Fielding's are obscured by time.

R.'s present reputation rests on his masterpiece, *Clarissa* (7 vols., 1747–48). In the 1920s, *Clarissa* was praised for anticipating the stream of consciousness; the novel has been interpreted as commentary on parental oppression, as Christian parable, as exposition of bourgeois social values, as feminist and antifeminist statement. Most recently, critics have noted that the narrative, with its multiple voices, invites deconstruction. There is argument as to which if any, among so many subjective accounts, may be trusted. If the rapist can be accused of sadism, did his victim collude in her fall by unconscious masochism? Some critics have gone so far as to question whether the rape of the heroine "really happened." A coherent though ambiguous interpretation can, however, be reached. Clarissa's account of events is shrewdly challenged by her friend Anna, while Lovelace's corrupt aristocratic morality is eventually corrected by his friend Belford. Clarissa herself is repeatedly described, even by her ravisher Lovelace, as an angel, while he is compared to a devil. Lovelace's dying words are "Thus I EXPIATE!"

Lovelace, deriving, as Belford observed, from Lothario in Nicholas ROWE's *The Fair Penitent*, is one of fiction's great characters, an in-depth psychological portrait of a compulsive seducer, shameless, heartless and witty. Women are prey. So compelling is he that female readers, during serialization, begged R. to let him marry the heroine, instead of punishing her, as he intends, for her resistance, using her degradation to revenge himself on her family for their upstart pride. It is a tribute to R.'s invention that the character who intercepts his "charmer's" letters, forges replies, lies,

cheats, forces her to associate with prostitutes, kidnaps and violates her, should be perceived as attractive by women readers. Lovelace's perverted goal is not sexual pleasure ("a bubble"), but power, the "glory to subdue a girl of family." Clarissa, prompted by Anna, admits she might have loved him had he treated her honorably instead of glorying in his own destructive plots. The heroine is often seen through his gloating, ruthless eyes, whether neat and on her way to church, or disheveled with heaving bosom. R. has been accused of sadism and titillation, despite eventual moral uplift.

D. H. LAWRENCE considered both *Clarissa* and *Pamela* "pornographical." Samuel Taylor COLERIDGE complained that R.'s mind was "vile" and regretted that he was forced to "admire, aye, greatly admire" R.'s work, with its "morbid consciousness of every thought and feeling." As William HAZLITT noted, R. combines the motifs of romance with the "literal minuteness of a common diary." Clarissa is a damsel in distress, her uncle's house is "moated," she is abducted, there is a final duel. Sadness is blended with relief at Clarissa's escape to the next world, "my father's house," as she cryptically expresses it. The dynamic of *Clarissa* is the inescapable human dilemma of flesh and spirit: in the upshot, the spirit wins, but we are never allowed to forget the wanton stings and motions of the sense, the palpable presence of bodies and bodily desires. Clarissa's story has a sexual rhythm, embodying tension, explosion, and release.

R.'s final novel, *The History of Sir Charles Grandison* (7 vols., 1753–54), in which R. set forth his own lower-middle-class idea of what a perfect gentleman should be, was well received, but posterity has generally found it tedious, though Johnson, William BLAKE, Hazlitt, Jane AUSTEN, Thomas Babington MACAULAY, and George ELIOT all liked it and it has found modern defenders. During the composition of his last two novels, R. corresponded with readers, so we know his intentions, in this book arguably unfulfilled. R.'s ignorance of Italy and its culture is damaging and there is no distinction of idiom between English and Italian characters. Despite R.'s avowed intent to keep to everyday life, the plot is romantic and implausible, deriving from conduct books rather than from lived experience. R. published *A Collection of the Moral and Instructive Sentiments, Maxims, Cautions, and Reflections, Contained in the Histories of Pamela, Clarissa, and Sir Charles Grandison, Digested under Proper Heads* (1755). By the end of his century, fashion had turned against him; in the 21st c., criticism is ambivalent, but he remains in the canon.

BIBLIOGRAPHY: Castle, T., *Clarissa's Ciphers* (1982); Doody, M. A., *A Natural Passion: A Study of the Novels of S. R.* (1974); Eagleton, T., *The Rape of Clarissa* (1982); Flynn, C. H., *S. R.: A Man of Letters* (1982);

Keymer, T., *R.'s "Clarissa" and the Eighteenth-Century Reader* (1992); Kinkead-Weekes, M., *S. R.: Dramatic Novelist* (1973); Myer, V. G., ed., *S. R.: Passion and Prudence* (1986); Warner, W. B., *Reading "Clarissa"* (1979); Wendt, A., "Clarissa's Coffin," *PQ* 39 (1960): 481–95; Wilt, J., "He Could Go No Farther: A Modest Proposal about Lovelace," *PMLA* 92, 1 (1977): 9–32

VALERIE GROSVENOR MYER

RICHE, Barnabe
b. ca. 1540; d. 10 November 1617, Ireland

Professional soldier and storyteller, R. was the author of twenty-four books, including some anti-Catholic writings and some on Ireland. R.'s books on military life include *A Right Excellent and Pleasant Dialogue between Mercury and an English Soldier* (1574), *Alarm to England* (1578), and his best-known work, *Riche his Farewell to Militarie Profession conteining verie Pleasaunt discourses fit for a Peaceable tyme* (1581). It offers eight stories, three translated from Italian, the other five, he says, "are forged only for delight, neither credible to be believed, nor hurtful to be perused." "The story of Apolonius and Silla" is one of the sources for William SHAKESPEARE's *Twelfth Night.* Among R.'s other works, influenced by John LYLY's *Euphues,* are *The Strange and Wonderful Adventures of Don Simonides* (1581) and its sequel (1584) and *The Adventures of Brusanus, Prince of Hungaria* (1592).

RICKWORD, [John] Edgell
b. 22 October 1898, Colchester; d. 15 March 1982, London

Poet, editor, and critic, R. was at one time best known as the editor of the *Calendar of Modern Letters* (1925–27) whose column entitled "Scrutinies" inspired the title of F. R. LEAVIS's journal *Scrutiny.* A full-length biography published in 1989 and recent research on MODERNISM and the politics of the 1930s present a complex figure whose poetry has yet to be adequately assessed.

One of the youngest of the First World War trench poets, he wrote his major poetry between 1918 and 1930, emerging alongside T. S. ELIOT, Edith SITWELL, and D. H. LAWRENCE as one of the most promising poets of his generation. His first published collection, *Behind the Eyes* (1921), was followed by *Invocation to Angels and The Happy New Year* (1928) and *Twittingpan and Some Others* (1931). A modernist poet in the 1920s, R. joined the Communist Party in 1934, and while he remained a key figure in the modernist movement, wrote little poetry for the next thirty years. His three later collections, *Collected Poems* (1947), *Fifty Poems* (1970), and *Behind the Eyes: Selected*

Poems and Translations (1976), each contain a selection from his early volumes together with a small amount of new material.

His first volume, *Behind the Eyes,* published when he was twenty-three, contains his major war poetry, including the often anthologized "Winter Warfare," "Trench Poets," and "The Soldier Addresses His Body," which show the influence of Robert GRAVES and Siegfried SASSOON as well as that of the metaphysical poets. (R. like Sassoon was awarded the Military Cross "for conspicuous gallantry and initiative.") As with other survivors, the theme of death remains central to his writing and memories of the war were an important influence on his later political thinking. The volume also contains a number of love poems, lyrics, sonnets, and quatrains that show an impressive poetic talent and technical range.

R. worked as a reviewer for the *Daily Herald,* the *New Statesman,* and the *Times Literary Supplement* and wrote a book on Arthur Rimbaud (1924), before founding the *Calendar of Modern Letters* with Douglas Garman and the Australian poet Bertram Higgins. The monthly (then quarterly) magazine became a beacon for modern literature, carrying fiction and poetry by Lawrence, A. E. COPPARD, Luigi Pirandello, Wyndham LEWIS, Isaac Babel, Dorothy Edwards, Sassoon, Graves, John Crowe Ransom, Allen Tate, and Hart Crane; articles on European and American literature; and a substantial review section. R.'s own critical contributions are both generous and astute, arguing the need for writing which is relevant to the modern world and for the creation of a new idiom in poetry.

His third collection of poems, *Twittingpan,* marks a move into satirical verse, adapting classical models like Horace to address his political and social concerns. A later poem "To the Wife of a Non-Interventionist Statesman," dated 1938, demonstrates this satirical impulse at a weaker point. A political polemic based on conventional sexual politics, it lacks the subtlety of W. H. AUDEN's *Spain* or the personal engagement of John Cornford's Spanish poetry. R.'s poetic silence after 1930 is often attributed to his decision to join the Communist Party in 1934, but according to his biographer, it was a more complex affair. Personal tragedy (the committal of his wife to a mental asylum), the betrayal of the general strike in England and the rise of fascism in Europe led to a mood of nihilism from which he took refuge first in SATIRE, then in silence. His silence as a poet did not however diminish his role in cultural politics. It was R., for example, who found a publisher for Nancy CUNARD's *Negro Anthology,* helped her edit it, and contributed a scholarly article on the 18th-c. slave trade. A prolific essayist and reviewer—a collection of which appeared as *Literature in Society* (1978), R. is remembered primarily as a critic and editor.

BIBLIOGRAPHY: Hobday, C., *E. R.* (1989); Young, A., "E. R.," in Stanford, D. E., ed., *British Poets, 1914–1945, DLB* 20 (1983): 306–11

JEAN RADFORD

RIDLER, Anne [Barbara]
b. 30 July 1912, Rugby, Warwickshire; d. 15 October 2001, Oxford

R. was educated at Downs House School in Berkshire and King's College, University of London, where she received a degree in journalism in 1933. There she was introduced to the Christian apologist Charles Williams, who was to become both mentor and friend. After graduating, R. worked at publisher Faber and Faber as the secretary-assistant to T. S. ELIOT. R.'s first book of poetry, *Poems* (1939), introduces her use of complex metaphors that parallel several images to a single thematic structure within the poem. The bombing of London and the temporary loss of her husband to military service strongly influenced the mood of her second book of poetry, *The Nine Bright Shiners*, published in 1943. In this book, R. loosens the stiff syntax of her first book and writes in a more approachable manner. Published in 1959, *A Matter of Life and Death* includes three poems that are considered to be her finest poems on childhood, "Choosing a Name," "The Gaze," and the title poem. B. is considered to have revived the 17th-c. metaphysical tradition and endowed 20th-c. religious poetry with a new strength. Although known for her poetry, A. wrote plays, translated from the Italian, and worked extensively as an editor.

RILEY, John
b. 10 October 1937, Leeds; d. 27 October 1978, Leeds

R. wrote a unique poetry in postwar Britain: a meditation upon the mysteries of the Russian Orthodox Church through the formal techniques of American MODERNISM, especially Ezra Pound and the projectivist legacy of Charles Olson, as well as in a European tradition of Rainer Maria Rilke and Osip Mandelstahm. In a period of little over a decade, R. produced an erudite and linguistically innovative poetry that, in its restless attempts to transfigure Christian experience into an open-field poetics, remained at a remove from both contemporary devotional verse and the other practitioners of neomodernist verse with whom R. was in contact, like J. H. PRYNNE. R. was born in Leeds and first learned Russian as a conscript in the RAF. In 1968, after working as a schoolteacher, he and Tim Longville set up the *Grosseteste Review*, an influential journal of the so-called Cambridge School of poets influenced by American modernism. A decisive experience in R.'s life was a visit to Istanbul: he was received into the Russian Orthodox Church in 1977.

However, in the following year, R. was murdered by muggers; he was forty-one. A *Collected Works* was published by Grosseteste Press in 1980.

R.'s first collection, *Ancient and Modern* (1967), introduced a pared and precise lyricism that in its exactitude resembled the work of American poet Robert Creeley (whose work R. admired), followed by *What Reason Was* (1970), *Ways of Approaching* (1973), and *That Is Today* (1978). R. could echo traditions of English devotional verse (e.g., "The Shortest Day, Riding Northward") yet also reflect the modernist insistence to place ideas in things, that resulted in attentiveness to natural objects. There was also a prominent theme of yearning in many poems that, given the ambiguity of the addressee, traversed the earthly and the holy: "Let us live barely./In more than a pagan triumph/I have not loved you enough." The relationship of the secular to the theological is an important factor in the reading of R. At their heart is arguably the mystery of Russian Orthodoxy, which considers divinity as immanent in reality: the experience of meditation should recover this presence in the world without rational argument. In R.'s work, this is figured as a sensation of mystery and providence that the poem encounters momentarily through the passage of description. That this is a transient and occasional, rather than magisterial, encounter gives the poetry its fragmentary and unsettled qualities, which are enhanced by the spacious techniques of open-field composition.

R.'s most important poem was the posthumously published long work *Czargrad* (1980), in which his formal and thematic interests found their most sustained expression. Named after the Orthodox title for Constantinople, it imagines a city as the shifting zone of alternating impulses of wonderment and religious conviction. R.'s use of Byzantium in this and other poems (notably "The Poem as Light") recalls W. B. YEATS, but the identification is a fleeting one undercut by the movement of the prosody itself whereby "wisdom hovers, unheld /tangible, almost between sense and idea/the cupped hands/to get to know." The work shares the ambition of T. S. ELIOT's *Four Quartets* and of the Irish poet Brian Coffey's contemporaneous *Advent* (1975). R.'s own work and translations have continued to be published since his death, and although it is not clear what influence his work may have, its formal dexterity and ambition alone deserve attention.

BIBLIOGRAPHY: Longville, T., "J. R.," in Sherry, V. B., Jr., ed., *Poets of Great Britain and Ireland since 1960*, part 2, *DLB* 40 (1985): 491–96; Longville, T., *For J. R.* (1979)

J. M. TINK

RITCHIE, Anne Isabella, [Lady]

b. 9 June 1837, London; d. 26 February 1919, Freshwater, Isle of Wight

R.'s writing spans the time from the Victorian era until World War I. Her father, the novelist William Makepeace THACKERAY, assisted her with her early essays and suggested the ending for her first novel. Her novels, although highly popular in her age, are rarely read today. Yet a few recent articles on R. and the reprinting of her works have helped to make more modern readers aware of her importance. Several of her FAIRY TALES and her essays have been reprinted in collections. In addition, interest in her reminiscences of her father and famous friends has increased in recent years, and in her protofeminist essays on famous women writers. Reared without a mother (her mother was separated from her family following severe postpartum depression in 1840), R. was a companion to her father and a hostess to her father's circle of friends, as well as a devoted friend, mother, wife, and aunt. Virginia WOOLF's tributes to R., her aunt by marriage, include her portrayal of R. as Mrs. Hilbery in *Night and Day*. R. is known for the creation of ordinary heroines who inspire empathy in her readers, for her naturalistic touches, and her sure use of language. Her fiction uses traditional elements of the Victorian marriage novel with hints of the impressionistic depiction of the modern woman.

In her novels, R. confronts both societal mores and deeper psychological issues. Although her heroines search for the right husband, before they marry they must come to understand themselves and their own desires. *The Story of Elizabeth* (1863) tells of a mother's jealousy of her daughter, and the shame brought on the young Elizabeth after she is seen unchaperoned with a man. Part of the fascination of this novel and the next she wrote, *The Village on the Cliff* (1867), comes from their depiction of life among the English expatriates in France, where R. had spent several of her early years. The heroine of *Old Kensington* (1873), Dorothea Vanborough, becomes engaged to the wrong man, someone who wants her to act according to the dictates of society as he interprets them. Her only historical novel, *Miss Angel* (1875), depicts, with fictional touches, the life of the painter Angelica Kauffmann. The novella, *From an Island* (1877), set on the Isle of Wight, portrays characters based on her friends Alfred, Lord TENNYSON and his wife and Julia Margaret and Charles Cameron. The title character of her last novel, *Mrs. Dymond* (1885), marries the wrong man, and only achieves happiness when her husband dies. R. wrote many short stories, among them *To Esther and Other Sketches* (1869), and updated traditional fairy tales in *Five Old Friends and a Young Prince* (1868) and *Bluebeard's Keys and Other Stories* (1874).

Many of R.'s heroines lack the support of a mother or a strong nuclear family and must find their own way in life. This was her own story, and she has recounted it brilliantly in her journals and letters, many of which have been published. R. wrote all her life, and her literary production is varied. She published many essays that have been collected into books including *Toilers and Spinners and Other Essays* (1874), *Blackstick Papers* (1908), and *From the Porch* (1913), as well as introductions to the works of her friends and colleagues, such as Elizabeth Cleghorn GASKELL and Mary Russell MITFORD.

R. composed many tributes to other women. She wrote a BIOGRAPHY of Madame de Sévigné (1881) and a group of women writers in *A Book of Sibyls* (1883). Rather than strict biographies, R.'s works are more impressionistic remembrances and appreciations of her subjects. Her *Records of Tennyson, Ruskin, and Robert and Elizabeth Browning* (1892) and *Chapters from Some Memoirs* (1894) combine AUTOBIOGRAPHY with biography, taking advantage of her unique position in literary society. Through her anecdotal approach, R. was able to present her father as she remembered him in the introductions she wrote to the collections of her father's works (*Biographical Edition* and *Centenary Edition*). R.'s warm and humorous tone, evident in all her works, brings the past into the present, making it live once more.

BIBLIOGRAPHY: Gérin, W., *A. T. R.* (1981); Hill-Miller, K. C., "'The Skies and Trees of the Past': A. T. R. and William Makepeace Thackeray," in Boose, L. E., and B. S. Flowers, eds., *Daughters and Fathers* (1989): 361–83; MacKay, C. H., "Biography as Reflected Autobiography: The Self-Creation of A. T. R.," in Bell, S. G., and M. Yalom, eds., *Revealing Lives: Autobiography, Biography, and Gender* (1990): 65–79

ABIGAIL BURNHAM BLOOM

ROBERTSON, E[ileen] Ar[buth]not

b. 1903, Holmwood, Surrey; d. 1961, London

R.'s first novel, *Cullum* (1928), attracted little attention. *Four Frightened People* (1931) described a trek in the Malayan jungle, which the author had never visited, and displayed a refreshing astringency. Her themes are intellectual and emotional emancipation and changes in women's lives after World War I. Her next novel, *Ordinary Families* (1933), was a bestseller. Set in Suffolk and drawing on the author's wry memories of being taken unwillingly on sailing boats off the English, French, Belgian, and Dutch coasts, and her pleasure in bird watching, it is a story about sex, jealousy, and family friction, sharp and truthful. It describes shrewdly a certain style of middle-class English life between the wars when "words could never be a disinfectant" for the older generation, who preferred to gloss over all unpleasantness. Her principal other works were *Three Came Unarmed* (1929), *The Signpost* (1943), and *Justice of the Heart* (1958). R. was also a successful journalist and broadcaster.

ROBINSON, Henry Crabb
b. 13 March 1775, Bury St. Edmunds; d. 5 February 1867, London

R. was the most important literary diarist of the 19th c. Between 1811 and 1867, R. recorded in his *Diary* (3 vols., 1869) his encounters with and readings of most of the important English writers of his time.

The early sections of R.'s *Diary* are notable for their direct, incisive, and vivid portraits of William WORDSWORTH, Samuel Taylor COLERIDGE, Robert SOUTHEY, Charles LAMB, and William HAZLITT. R.'s accounts of Coleridge and Hazlitt lecturing in London, Lamb's domestic life, Wordsworth's impressive greatness both as a man and a poet, Coleridge's eloquence in private talk, and Hazlitt's combination of literary genius and impossible personality are unforgettable. Another important part of the early *Diary* is R.'s detailed and sensitive account of the grave rift between Wordsworth and Coleridge and their reconciliation in 1812, largely through R.'s diplomatic efforts.

In addition to the figures in R.'s *Diary*, R. gives sharp and often detailed accounts of his astonishingly wide reading in the literature of his day. His devoted and intelligent love of Wordsworth's poetry, his misgivings about Southey's epics, his low opinion of Sir Walter SCOTT's poems, his astonished first experience of *Christabel*, his immediate recognition of John KEATS's promise, and his general dislike of Lord BYRON's poetry are notable among his many responses to verse.

Also important is R.'s almost obsessive reading of novels recorded in the *Diary*. From Scott's *Old Mortality* and Jane AUSTEN's *Emma* to Mary SHELLEY's *Frankenstein* and Thomas Hope's *Anastasius* (3 vols., 1819), R. reads and comments. His enthusiasm for many of Scott's novels and for Austen's *Pride and Prejudice* is expressed with great vigor and discrimination. Among the prose writers of the Romantic age, Lamb, Hazlitt, William Savage LANDOR, and Thomas DE QUINCEY were perhaps R.'s favorites.

Some sections of R.'s *Diary* take on the quality of extended "set pieces" which give more than passing accounts of the authors they treat. Among the best of these are R.'s records of his annual visits to Wordsworth in the Lake District, his travel journals of trips to Switzerland and Italy with Wordsworth, his extended talks with William BLAKE in 1825, and his visit to Landor in Italy in 1830.

R.'s greatest friendships and literary enthusiasms were formed during the Romantic age, and the best of

his *Diary* covers that period. R. lived, however, well into the Victorian epoch, and his *Diary* recounts such things as his mixed response to Thomas CARLYLE, his qualified appreciation of John RUSKIN, his waxing and waning response to Alfred, Lord TENNYSON, and his keen joy in the novels of Charles DICKENS, William Makepeace THACKERAY, and Anthony TROLLOPE. The very last entry in his *Diary* records his sympathetic reading of Matthew ARNOLD's *Essays in Criticism*.

R.'s *Diary* is the work of an intelligent, tolerant, humane, and observant man. R. is keen and generous in his responses to both people and books. He was also able to change his mind. When R. met Percy Bysshe SHELLEY, he thought him arrogant and intolerant, but he continued to read Shelley's poetry and eventually was among the earliest to recognize his true greatness. Similarly, R. often expressed his dislike of Lord Byron's character and the moral tendency of his poetry, but he read Byron extensively and finally declared him to be one of the greatest poets of the age.

R.'s genius was essentially appreciative. In 1858, R. states in his *Diary* that among the things he has been most grateful for in his life have been his travels with Wordsworth, his opportunities to hear Coleridge's eloquence, and his ability to relish the "wit and pathos" of Lamb. R. died five days after the last entry in his *Diary*.

BIBLIOGRAPHY: Baker, J. M., *H. C. R.* (1937); Holmes, R., *Coleridge: Darker Reflections* (1998); Morley, E. J., *The Life and Times of H. C. R.* (1935)

PHILLIP B. ANDERSON

ROBINSON, [Esmé Stuart] Lennox
b. 4 October 1886, Douglas, County Cork, Ireland; d. 14 October 1958, Monkstown, County Dublin, Ireland

Irish all-round man of the theater, actor, playwright, director, and critic, R. worked with the Abbey Theatre, Dublin, for forty years. His first play, *The Clancy Name* (perf. 1908; pub. 1911), was produced there, and he wrote *Ireland's Abbey Theatre* (1951), a memoir, *Curtain Up* (1942), and a collection of lectures entitled *The Irish Theatre* (1939). He also edited, with Donagh MacDonagh, *The Oxford Book of Irish Verse*. Among his plays are *Harvest* (perf. 1910; pub. 1911), *Patriots* (1912), *The Dreamers* (1915), *The Whiteheaded Boy* (perf. 1916; pub. 1920), *Crabbed Youth and Age* (perf. 1922; pub. 1924), *The Big House* (perf. 1926; pub. 1928), *The Far-Off Hills* (perf. 1928; pub. 1931), and *Church Street* (1955).

ROBINSON, Mary
b. 27 November 1758, Bristol; d. 26 December 1800, Surrey

R., one of the most popular figures of her day, combined careers as actress, writer, and celebrity to enormous effect. Painted by Sir Joshua REYNOLDS, George Romney, and Thomas Gainsborough, she was famed for her beauty as well as her scandalous affair with the teenage Prince of Wales (R. herself was in her early twenties). R. fully understood the nature of her public persona as a member of the demi-monde and used it effectively to represent herself as a poet, novelist, and social critic. Her readers saw her as simultaneously a woman of dubious character and a victim of life's vicissitudes.

R. began writing and publishing poetry in the 1770s, ostensibly as a means of making money to pay her husband's debts. *Poems* (1775) and *Captivity, a Poem; and Celadon and Lydia, a Tale* (1777), brought her to the notice of, among others, Georgiana Cavendish, Duchess of Devonshire, and helped to establish R.'s reputation as an innocent brutalized by circumstance. R. used skills honed during her acting days to create an enlarging repertoire of poetic selves; with each new publication she presented herself to a rapt public as a new woman. This was partly achieved through her innovative use of pseudonyms: for instance, as Laura Maria she published sentimental and erotic Della Cruscan poems, while as Tabitha Bramble she wrote satirical narrative poems. Many of her poems were initially published under such pseudonyms in newspapers, another way in which R. maintained her hold on the public imagination. R. was a careful reader of the public mood, and modulated and changed her style in response to changing literary fashions; however, she as often effected those changes as followed them. Her 1791 *Poems*, for example, signaled the end of the Della Cruscan rage, while her 1793 *Poems* included work introducing a recognizably "Romantic" emphasis on introspection and self-reflexivity. In 1793, she also published *Sight, The Cavern of Woe, and Solitude.*

In 1796, R. published *Sappho and Phaon: In a Series of Legitimate Sonnets*, one of the most significant sonnet sequences since William SHAKESPEARE. In it, R. re-creates the story of Sappho, contrasting Sappho's unrequited love for Phaon with her fame as a poet. R., under cover of Sappho, questions the preeminence love is assumed to hold in a woman's life; even as Sappho declares that poetry and love are mutually exclusive, she does so in a complex poetic form. Further, Sappho's laments reveal R.'s conviction of female rationality in an age that saw women as inherently irrational: Sappho pointedly rejects Reason when she decides to pursue Phaon, but welcomes its return at the moment of her death. This poem argues both for the validity of female creativity and the risks attendant on surrendering one's reason to overwhelming emotion. Its politics anticipates those expressed in R.'s pamphlet *Letter to the Women of England on the Cruelties of Mental Subordination* (1799), published initially under the pseudonym Anne Frances Randall but in a second edition (as *Thoughts on the Condition of Women, and On the Injustice of Mental Subordination*) under R.'s own name.

While *Sappho and Phaon* contains a strong political argument filtered through strikingly original poetry, it represents the end of the sonnet revival. Throughout the 1790s, however, R. published a series of short narrative poems primarily in the newspaper the *Morning Post* (of which she was poetry editor from 1799 until her death), collected and published in 1800 under the title *Lyrical Tales*. The title's similarity to the *Lyrical Ballads* of William WORDSWORTH and Samuel Taylor COLERIDGE is not coincidental. R. knew and admired Coleridge (and was in turn admired by him) and found the *Lyrical Ballads* to be "a tribute to genuine nature." R.'s *Tales* pick up on the *Ballads'* attention to natural and rural detail, but delve further into personal characterization and the development of personae. Where Wordsworth maintains a narrative, observational distance, R. allies her authorial personae with her poetic subjects, although as often to expose their inadequacies as to celebrate their individuality. Her facility with meter and stanzaic form, as well as her attention to detailed rhyme schemes, in all her poetry show R. to be a poet deeply concerned with the nature and possibilities of verse.

R. also wrote novels, widely seen by her contemporaries as thinly disguised portraits of high society scandal but read now as exercises in social critique. The first, *Vancenza* (2 vols., 1792), sold out on its day of publication and was immediately reprinted. *The Widow* (2 vols., 1794) and *Angelina* (3 vols., 1796) were followed by *Hubert de Sevrac* (3 vols., 1796), which combined the Gothic with a pro-revolutionary tone that belied its superficial sympathy for its French aristocrat protagonist. *Walsingham* (4 vols., 1797) challenged its readers' preconceptions of gender by focusing on a cross-dressing heroine who lives and loves successfully in her assumed role, and whose true sex is only revealed at the novel's close, while *The False Friend* (4 vols.) and *The Natural Daughter* (2 vols.), both published in 1799, play with the notions of social and personal responsibility. Her posthumous *Memoirs* (4 vols., 1801) purport to tell her life's story but are dressed up with stylistic devices drawn from the Gothic, the romance and novels of sensibility, further emphasizing her flair for literary self-fashioning. One of the most innovative and creative writers of her time, R. is now being recognized as a major voice in early ROMANTICISM.

BIBLIOGRAPHY: Curran, S., "M. R.'s *Lyrical Tales* in Context," in Wilson, C. S., and J. Haefner, eds., *Re-Visioning Romanticism: British Women Writers, 1776–1837* (1994): 17–35; Labbe, J., "Selling One's Sorrows: Charlotte Smith, M. R., and the Marketing of Poetry," *WC* 25 (Spring 1994): 68–71; Pascoe, J., ed., *M. R.: Selected Poems* (2000); Setzer, S.,

"M. R.'s Sylphid Self: The End of Feminine Self-Fashioning," *PQ* 75 (1996): 501–20

JACQUELINE M. LABBE

ROCHESTER, John Wilmot, Second Earl of

b. 1 April 1647, Ditchley, Oxfordshire; d. 26 July 1680, High Lodge, Woodstock Park, Oxfordshire

Traditionally viewed as the occasional output of a highly talented but careless amateur poet who spent most of his short life in dissipation, R.'s poetry is increasingly regarded as the work of a serious artist who invested much time and thought in his writing. In R.'s day, aristocratic gentlemen did not publish under their own names, and most of his poems were copied by scribes and handed round to privileged readers—usually associated with the court of Charles II—before ending up in compilations with which he had nothing to do. For that reason, it remains difficult to determine which of the works attributed to him are actually by R., and the possibility of scribal interpolation must nearly always be considered. Harold Love's landmark edition for the Oxford University Press, *The Works of J. W., Earl of R.* (1999), has fueled fresh debate on the R. "canon."

R. served in various capacities at the court of Charles II and is usually thought of as one of its most notorious rakes, but there is little evidence to the effect that his style of loose living was out of the ordinary. He spent a good deal of time on his and his wife's country estates, and surviving letters suggest that the "wicked Earl" was a loving if faithless husband and an affectionate father to his four legitimate children.

Much of R.'s reputation for recklessness derives from Bishop Gilbert Burnet's *Some Passages of the Life and Death of J. Earl of R.* (1680), by the cleric who oversaw R.'s deathbed reconciliation with the Anglican Church and who thus had a vested interest in portraying the as-yet-unreformed rake in dark colors, and from poems in which drinking and sexual pursuits figure prominently. However, these poems owe a good deal to popular conventions, such as Anacreontic verse, which R. subverted with considerable skill and HUMOR.

Up to the late 1960s, a handful of R.'s poems were banned from publication because of their obscenity, and he has been referred to as a "pornographic" writer. R.'s obscene poems do not titillate, though: on the contrary, they are characteristically concerned with painful aspects of sexual activity. The speaker of "The Imperfect Enjoyment"—in which, again, R. toyed with a popular genre—laments his inability to satisfy his lady after ejaculating prematurely, and the disappointed lover in "A Ramble in St. James's Park" cries out in fury at his mistress's double betrayal: she prefers three witless social climbers to him, and she insults him further by passing on his pillow-talk to them.

R.'s love lyrics—several of which have repeatedly been set to music—are also almost invariably dark in tone: even when the beloved has granted her sexual favors (as in the *Song*s beginning "Absent from thee" and "An Age in her Embraces pas'd," and in "The Fall"), harmony does not ensue. Lasting bliss is kept away by distrust and jealousy, and by the peculiarly Rochesterian dissatisfaction with the good things of this life: the very things that so much of his work holds up as the best that human beings can strive for.

That paradox is not the only one that confronts the reader of R.'s poetry. For instance, his best-known long poem, "A Satyre against Reason and Mankind," attacks reason by ratiocinative means, and the pseudo-argumentation in the eulogy "Upon Nothing" is so cleverly engineered that ultimately the only thing that stands up in it is the addressee. Both these works attack the learned men of the universities, the clergy, and those who rule the state: academics are fools who waste their time (and others') in useless sophistry; the clergy are a hypocritical and rapacious lot who "hunt good Livings, but abhor good Lives" while adding to their offensiveness by lecturing "men of sense"; and as for those who govern, their venality and mendacity are so scandalous and so inescapable that the only way to cope with them is to beat them at their own game.

R. was well read in philosophy, familiar both with the classics and with the leading philosophers of his own time, particularly Thomas HOBBES who is a palpable presence in "A Satyre against Reason and Mankind." Hobbes argued that human beings who are not subjugated under a legitimate authority wage ceaseless war against one another to protect themselves from coming under someone else's tyranny; R.'s "Satyre" claims that humanity is caught up in an endless arms race impelled by fear. R. deviates from Hobbes in maintaining that even ostensibly admirable human behaviour is dictated by fear: when we act bravely and well, it is only because we are too afraid to do anything else.

For such a disillusioned observer of humanity, post-Restoration high society offered plenty of material, and some of R.'s funniest pieces are social satires: "Tunbridge Wells," a set of sharp vignettes portraying the (mis)behavior of guests at a fashionable spa; "Seigneur Dildoe," a hilarious catalogue of prominent court ladies and their sexual predilections; and "Timon," the mock-heroic tale of an abysmal meal with interspersed reflections on contemporary dramatists (Harold Love doubts the authenticity of the last two, though). R. was keenly interested in drama and wrote an extensive adaptation of John FLETCHER's *Valentinian*.

"A Letter from Artemiza in the Towne to Chloe in the Countrey" exhibits the same perspicacity in its handling of social *mores* and bores; but this poem—ostensibly a gossiping letter from one society woman to another—has a more good-humored tone that makes it particularly engaging. Artemiza laments the folly of women who fail to distinguish between true love and silly fashions, betraying both their intelligence and their real inclinations in the pursuit of treacherous glamour. Like some shorter poems with women speakers, among them "The Platonick Lady" and "Song of a Young Lady to her Antient Lover" (with the much-quoted refrain "Antient person of my heart"), it has supplied material for feminist criticism.

Good writing is the subject of one of R.'s most remarkable poems, "An Allusion to Horace." Patterned on Horace's tenth satire in the first book and Nicolas Boileau's *L'Art poétique* (1674), the "Allusion" discusses the leading English writers of R.'s time, complimenting his friends Sir Charles SEDLEY and Charles SACKVILLE while censuring John DRYDEN's "loose slattern Muse." The qualities that a good writer should aim for, according to the "Allusion," are stringency, elegance, and spirit.

Such qualities were, according to R., lacking in his particular enemies Lord Mulgrave and Sir Carr Scroop, and his attacks on them are weighed down by invective. These pieces illustrate R.'s peculiar hatred of stupidity combined with arrogance: folly and pride are bad enough when they manifest themselves separately; together they are unbearable.

Deathbed conversions may be distrusted, but there is reason to believe that R. did turn toward God during his last illness. Few people had seen more of the glories of his time than he, and they never satisfied him. It takes no great effort of the imagination to envisage the tormented sufferer, racked by qualms occasioned by his recollections of a less than exemplary life, taking comfort in Isaiah's words (in chapter 53) on the Man of Sorrow who meekly shoulders the burden of human iniquities. Even so, the lasting impression of R.'s verse is one of radical inquiry into the great existential issues, seasoned by an acrid and irreverent irony that spared nobody, least of all himself.

BIBLIOGRAPHY: Burns, E., ed., *Reading R.* (1995); Farley-Hills, D., *R.'s Poetry* (1978); Fisher, N., ed., *That Second Bottle: Essays on J. W., Earl of R.* (2000); Greer, G., *J. W., Earl of R.* (2000); Griffin, D. H., *Satires against Man: The Poems of R.* (1973); Thormählen, M., *R.: The Poems in Context* (1993); Treglown, J., ed., *Spirit of Wit: Reconsiderations of R.* (1982); Vieth, D. M., ed., *J. W., Earl of R.: Critical Essays* (1988)

MARIANNE THORMÄHLEN

ROGERS, Samuel

b. 30 July 1763, Stoke Newington; d. 18 December 1855, London

At the end of the 18th c. and for several decades thereafter, R. was often regarded as one of the most important poets of his time. Today, he is best remembered as a Regency wit and literary host. R.'s first important publication was *The Pleasures of Memory* (1792). This genteelly discursive poem on memory in animals, mankind, and even angels hit the taste of the day perfectly, and by 1816 more than 23,000 copies had been printed. Intellectually, *The Pleasures of Memory* reflects 18th-c. theories of the picturesque, while the poem's smooth heroic couplets owe much to Oliver GOLDSMITH.

With the triumph of *The Pleasures of Memory*, R. became famous, and he began to establish himself in the social and literary life of London. In 1812, R. consolidated his position as a poet with the publication of his elegantly illustrated *Poems*. This was mainly a collected edition, but it also included the new *Voyage of Columbus*, a short EPIC in heroic couplets.

One of the most important of R.'s literary friendships was with Lord BYRON, and in 1814 the two poets published a joint volume consisting of Byron's *Lara* and R.'s *Jacqueline*. R.'s poem is a quietly sentimental tale dealing with Jacqueline's elopement, her father's disapproval, and their reconciliation. R. added to his reputation in 1819 when he published his *Human Life*. This poem returns to the finely polished manner of *The Pleasures of Memory*, but the interest here is less abstractly philosophical and more concretely human. *Human Life* does little more than survey the general progress of a typical human life from birth to death, but its language and couplets are impressively refined, and at its best the poem is discreetly moving.

Throughout his life, R. was interested in the art and culture of ancient and modern Italy. In 1815 and 1822, he toured Italy, and out of that experience came R.'s most ambitious work, his *Italy* (2 parts, 1822–28). This very long poem, with interpolated prose passages, deals extensively with Swiss and Italian scenery, history, legends, customs, and personalities. If Goldsmith was the model for most of R.'s earlier poetry, Byron is the major influence on *Italy*. R.'s manner in *Italy* is no longer so closely tied to the 18th c., and in surprisingly flexible and resonant blank verse, he approaches his landscapes, narratives, and character sketches with a force, energy, specificity of detail, and even imaginative power not seen in his earlier poetry. Perhaps the most memorable sections of *Italy* are those dealing with the Alps, Venice, Rome, Florence, R.'s meeting with Byron in Bologna, and the tragic history of the Foscari family. Although *Italy* was not notably popular on its first publication, it was reissued in 1830 in a deluxe format with engravings after J. M. W. Turner and enjoyed immense success.

By the end of his long life, R. was better known as a wit, connoisseur, literary host, and patron of the arts than as a poet. Today, he is almost exclusively remembered as a central figure in Regency literary society. Although R.'s poetry is more important than its modern neglect would suggest, R.'s fame as a conversationalist is likely to outlive most of his verse. Happily, in Alexander Dyce's *Recollections of the Table-Talk of Samuel Rogers* (1856) and *Recollections of Samuel Rogers* (1859), edited by R.'s nephew, there is evidence of the wit, charm, and fund of anecdote that once made R. famous.

BIBLIOGRAPHY: Barbier, C. P., ed., *S. R. and William Gilpin* (1959); Marchand, L., *Byron* (1957); Roberts, R. E., *S. R. and His Circle* (1910)

PHILLIP B. ANDERSON

ROLFE, Frederick William

b. 22 July 1860, London; d. 24 October 1913, Venice, Italy

Novelist and short story writer whose fictional and fantasized approach often extended to details of his own "real" life, for one phase of which he extended his name to "Frederick William Serefino Austin Lewis Mary Rolfe" and for another, longer-lasting phase called himself (quite without any official justification) Baron Corvo, under which name some of his books were published. Reared as a Dissenter, he became a Roman Catholic convert and offered himself as a candidate for the priesthood. His extravagances and eccentricities of personality caused this candidacy to be rejected, but in spite of that he often presented himself as "Father Rolfe" or "Father Austin." In short, his fictional life existed both in his writing and in his daily life.

The most extraordinary example of this fusion is the best known and most accomplished of his novels, *Hadrian the Seventh* (1904). Though many readers assume otherwise, it is mistaken to suppose that all fictional writing is, in fact thinly disguised AUTOBIOGRAPHY. But while this assumption is often a gross error it is, in R.'s case, entirely warrantable: *Hadrian the Seventh* is clearly based on facts, dreams, and aspirations drawn from parts of his own life; *Nicholas Crabbe; or, The One and the Many* (1958) adds a second phase of his own disastrous progress and *The Desire and Pursuit of the Whole* (1934) completes the autobiographical picture. Together, they tell, disguised by devices so thin and penetrable as only to make identities clearer and more immediately recognizable, the astonishing story of R.'s own life and experiences. While one could readily speculate on the psychological causes underlying his strange and often

contradictory behavior, the factual causes in themselves are clear and plain. The central issue was the rejection, twice repeated, of his candidacy for entry into the Catholic priesthood. This drove him into extremes of self-pity and acute paranoia and impelled him to flee England and live for some time in Rome and Venice, where he experienced a period of biting penury, partly relieved by a series of petty frauds practiced by him on various friends.

R. returned to England and began to establish a career as a writer but his entire lack of self-discipline, his arrogance, and his delusions of grandeur overwhelmed him and induced him, finally, to return to Italy, there to live a life of intermittent poverty and extravagance characterized by every kind of sexual debauchery and overindulgence. All this he put into his books, along with a feverish dream about an Englishman (clearly himself) who by a series of farcical accidents and coincidences, is elected pope and, so empowered, is able to take his revenge on principalities and powers both civil and ecclesiastical. The prose style of all his work, but especially of the three big autobiographical novels, is astonishingly rich and strange but is distinguished also by an admirable precision and control. Arcane and archaic vocabulary abounds, with fairly frequent new coinages designed to deal with states of experience for which standard verbal practice seemed inadequate; but in the best instances this plunging richness and variety submits to and serves the form and artistic control of the whole work. This is especially true of *Hadrian the Seventh*, which is a novel conceived wholly in poetic terms, many-layered, and with a breath-taking imaginative sweep.

A. J. A. SYMONS, who published in 1934 a remarkably fine biography of R. entitled *The Quest for Corvo*, calls Hadrian VII "one of the most extraordinary achievements in English literature . . . a feat of writing difficult to parallel." W. H. AUDEN, writing a foreword to the 1953 edition of *The Desire and Pursuit of the Whole*, says: "As we read the extraordinary and magnificent twenty-fifth and twenty-sixth chapters of this book . . . we cease to laugh at or pity him and begin to admire." And Frank SWINNERTON, novelist and critic in a letter to the *Times* in December 1924, said: "and I also saw a complete novel which had the title *A Romance of Modern Venice; or The Desire and Pursuit of the Whole*. It was a very beautiful and absorbing story." All this about a book that R. himself could not find a publisher for: it was first published twenty-one years after his death.

R.'s other works are *Stories Toto Told Me* (1898)—a series of short stories, imaginatively conceived and extremely well written, some of which had previously been published in the *Yellow Book; Chronicles of the House of Borgia* (1901; repub. as *A History of the Borgias*, 1931); *Don Tarquinio* (1905);

Don Renato (1909); *The Weird of the Wanderer* (1912); *Hubert's Arthur* (1935); *Three Tales of Venice* (1950); *The Cardinal Prefect of Propaganda and Other Stories* (1957); *Collected Poems* (1972), edited by Cecil Woolf: a collection of twenty-eight items of verse (poems they certainly are not) put together from various scattered sources sixty years after R.'s death.

R.'s novel *Hadrian the Seventh* was taken as the basis of a play devised by Peter Luke in 1967–68 and produced at the Mermaid Theatre in London. Though Luke used R.'s title for his play, the theater program more accurately described the piece as "based on works by Frederick Rolfe." R. himself appears in the piece as a character who has written a novel called "Hadrian the Seventh"; he falls asleep with the manuscript of the novel on his lap and dreams of himself as the central figure of his own novel. The idea is ingenious and the play was, up to a point, theatrically effective but—as is the case of many major novels when adapted for the stage or screen—the depth, subtlety, and poetic sensibility of the original the many-layered quality—was, largely, lost; as was, of course, much of the splendid descriptive language. In exchange, one had to settle for cleverness and ingenuity: R., had he been there to see, would have been ironically amused, no doubt: he was very familiar with seeing his own fastidious artistry roughed up by a blunt-witted world. The central image of the novel is, however, retained in the play and R. himself becomes the figure from his own dream, the man who wrote the bitter and ecstatic book, the Englishman who became Pope and at the end was murdered by Jerry Sant (who appears to be a larger-than-life caricature of Keir Hardie, the founder and first leader of the British Labour Party). Perhaps it is worth noting the distinguished company into which *Hadrian the Seventh* was born: other novels published in London in the same year included G. K. CHESTERTON's *The Napoleon of Notting Hill,* Joseph CONRAD's *Nostromo,* and Henry JAMES's *The Golden Bowl.*

BIBLIOGRAPHY: Parker, P., ed., *The Reader's Companion to the Twentieth-Century Novel* (1994); Symons, A. J. A., *The Quest for Corvo* (1934); Symons, J., *A. J. A. Symons, His Life and Speculations* (1950)

ERIC SALMON

ROLLE, Richard, of Hampole

b. ca. 1300, Thornton, Yorkshire; d. 1349, Hampole, Yorkshire

The mystical writer R. studied at Oxford and (perhaps) in Paris before taking up the life of a hermit. From about 1326, he occupied a cell on the estate of John Dalton, moving four years later to another cell at Ainderby near Northallerton. He later lived at Hampole, near Doncaster, and acted as spiritual guide to a community of Cistercian nuns. His English works were undertaken for the benefit of his female disciples, specifically for Margaret Kirkby and an unnamed nun of Yedingham. In the 15th c., R. was one of the most widely read of all English authors. His works were voluminous, and were written in both Latin and English. R.'s choice of English as a medium was innovative, and he was one of the first religious writers to use the vernacular.

The canon of R.'s works was established in the early 20th c. by Hope Emily Allen, and most subsequent scholars have agreed with her judgment. His works, whether Latin or English, may be classified as scriptural commentaries, original mystical treatises, and lyrical and poetic compositions. The most important of his works are the three great Latin treatises: *De amore Dei contra amatores mundi,* *Incendium amores,* and *Melos Amoris*; and the four Latin and English epistolary tracts: *Emendatio vitae,* the *Form of Living,* the *Commandment,* and the *Ego dormio.* *De amore Dei contra amatores mundi* contrasts the transitory pleasures of the world with the lasting joys of the lover of God; the semiautobiographical *Incendium Amoris* records R.'s experience of spiritual heat, sweetness, and song; and the *Melos Amoris* describes the culmination of R.'s spiritual experience whereby contemplative prayer was transformed into heavenly song. The *Emendatio vitae,* in which R. describes the three stages of love, was R.'s most popular work. It was translated into English several times; one translation was made by the Carmelite Richard Misyn, who also translated the *Form of Living* into Latin. These parallel treatises encourage their readers to reject the world and adopt the contemplative life. The necessity of total submission to God's love is also a theme in the *Commandment* and the *Ego Dormio.*

R.'s other Latin works include: *Canticum Amoris,* an alliterative poem in praise of the Virgin; *Judica Me Deus,* a series of tracts addressed to a friend (who was a priest); the *Office*; and the *Canticles.* R.'s other English prose writings are: *The English Psalter,* which was begun about 1340, and which is the earliest of his English works; a series of commentaries connected with the Psalter; and *Meditations on the Passion,* though the latter is unlike R.'s other works in style and content, and scholars have doubted its authenticity. In addition, there are several short pieces: *The Bee*; *Desyre and Delit*; *Gastly Gladnesse*; *Seven Gifts of the Holy Ghost*; *On the 10 Commandments.*

Criticism of R.'s work has focused on two aspects: his unique set of characteristic themes and his distinctive prose style. Familiar themes in R.'s work include a devotion to the Holy Name of Jesus, and the identification of the effects of spiritual love as *calor, dulcor, canor* (heat, sweetness, and song). A further triad of the grades of love (insuperable, inseparable, and singular) may also be identified, a hierarchy that is essentially dependent upon the philosophy of Richard of St. Victor. R.'s style is highly rhetorical, and makes much use of alliteration. His overall message is basically that it is possible to achieve a personal bond with God by means of contemplation based on love, and that all men and women can attain this. His thinking was enormously influential in terms of pre-Reformation popular piety.

BIBLIOGRAPHY: Allen, H. E., *Writings Ascribed to R. R., Hermit of Hampole, and Materials for His Biography* (1927); Allen, H. E., *English Writings of R. R., Hermit of Hampole* (1931); Watson, N., *R. R. and the Invention of Authority* (1991)

MARGARET CONNOLLY

ROMANCE

The term "romance," which initially merely signified that a work was written in French as opposed to Latin, and which, to a medieval audience, promised tales of great adventure and derring-do, has eventually come to be opposed to REALISM and is now applied to prose fictions that represent characters or events that are more fantastic, picturesque, or heroic than one would actually expect in ordinary life. The term may also encompass works of both highbrow literature and low culture. Thus, at one end of the spectrum the 19th-c. classic novels of Jane AUSTEN and the BRONTË sisters may be classified as romance, whereas at the other end one finds the cheap 20th-c. paperback romances churned out by authors like Barbara Cartland. Further below this still, and barely admitted to the category of "literature," are the formulaic "category romances" that are mass-marketed by the publishers Mills and Boon, and that have done much to ensure that the stigma of triviality has become firmly attached to the genre of popular romance.

The word romance derives from the Old French *roman*, a term that was applied to popular courtly stories in verse whose usual subjects were the adventures and exploits of popular or mythical heroes, such as King Arthur, or the Emperor Charlemagne, or the classical heroes. The genre of romance developed in 12th-c. France and rapidly became a central feature of the European literary tradition, superseding the previously dominant form of EPIC. In England, the romance tradition developed somewhat later; similar stories began to appear from the 13th c., but MIDDLE ENGLISH romances differ from their European cousins, and for a long time because of this they were regarded as critically inferior. While modern romances are primarily love stories, Middle English romances may be more typically defined as adventure stories, and often there will be no love interest whatsoever. This is particularly true of very early examples of the genre, such as the early-13th-c. story of

King Horn, where the main concern of the hero is to defeat heathen invaders and regain his rightful kingdom; Horn's love affair, such as it is, with Rymenhild, is definitely a matter of secondary importance. As this text also shows, the action of romance usually centers on a single figure, and many medieval romances are known by the names of their heroes, such as *Sir Orfeo*, and *Havelok the Dane*, or by the names of their hero and his main adversary, such as *Sir Gawain and the Green Knight*; occasionally the narrative focus is bifurcated, as in the stories of *Floris and Blancheflour* and *Amis and Amiloun*. The subject matter of romance is very varied, but some popular subcategories may be discerned. For example, a significant number focus on the activities of a militant Christian champion, such as *Bevis of Hampton, Guy of Warwick,* and *Richard Coeur de Lyon*. Many others offer variations on the theme of the patient and long-suffering female protagonist—in this regard note, for example, the heroines in *Emare, Octavian, Sir Eglamour of Artois, Sir Torrent of Portyngale,* and *Sir Triamour*. In following such themes, the romance genre covers ground which is shared by the equally popular medieval genre of the saint's life, and one text in which romance and hagiography intersect is the tale of the patient Griselda, told by the Clerk as part of Geoffrey CHAUCER's *Canterbury Tales*.

In romance, the demands of the narrative are more important than those of characterization or description. Typically, the narrative will be action-packed and will progress at a rapid pace, the speed forming part of the pleasure. The narrative is also usually straightforward, with no clever use of flashback, and with little time wasted on description, though occasional lengthy set-piece descriptive passages (perhaps of the hero's monstrous adversary, or the strange new land which he visits), were used to increase suspense and wonder in the audience. Romance usually involves a suspension of normal human circumstances, often by the use of magic, to illustrate a moral point. Thus, in *Sir Orfeo*, a medieval retelling of the classical legend of Orpheus and Eurydice, Heurodis is snatched by the Faerie King and imprisoned, seemingly asleep, in his kingdom for ten years. Her husband renounces his kingdom and lives as a recluse in the wilderness. When they are reunited, they are able to recognize each other without difficulty, despite Orfeo's physical transformation by the ravages of nature; and after Orfeo has regained his bride the couple are able to return instantaneously to their kingdom, be recrowned, and live happily ever after. This brief summary will also demonstrate that the romance genre deals with the improbable adventures of idealized characters in remote or enchanted settings. Romance is supposed to be remote from reality, since realism is the antithesis of romance, but this distance may be achieved with reference either to time or place; thus, romance stories may be set in the past (remote from the present, and directly linked to the "once upon a time" tradition of FAIRY TALES), or in another world, far from the immediate context of the tale-telling (an underworld, fairyland, or even simply in a foreign land). As the Middle English romance genre developed, an increasing stress was placed upon moral values, especially in so-called chivalric romance, and questions about love, loyalty, service, truth, honor, and fidelity, are increasingly brought to the fore. This may be seen especially in the late-14th-c. anonymous alliterative romance, *Sir Gawain and the Green Knight*, where the titular hero must struggle to uphold a complex system of courtly and Christian values, behaving courteously at all times, and yet must resist the amorous advances of his host's wife without giving offense either to her or her husband.

Middle English romances were written in both verse and prose. Initially, verse was the dominant form—of the one hundred and ten medieval romances that survive (excluding the romance stories in the tale collections of Chaucer and John GOWER), ninety were composed in verse. However, by the 15th c., prose is the usual medium, and when Sir Thomas MALORY decided to translate the *Morte D'Arthur* from French he chose prose as his medium. After the 15th c., the romance genre suffered a general decline. This was momentarily arrested by the Elizabethan poet Edmund SPENSER whose work *The Faerie Queene* was deeply influenced by medieval romance. In writing this allegorical work, Spenser invented a completely unique genre, the romance-epic, combining his knowledge of the classical epics of Homer and Virgil, the romantic epics of the contemporary Italian writers Ludovico Ariosto and Torquato Tasso, and the many medieval romances tht would still have been readily available in print in the 16th c. Spenser framed his work around the legendary English figure of Arthur, but followed the later medieval and Renaissance tradition of stressing the moral values of literature; thus, each book of the *Faerie Queene* was intended to tell the story of a particular knight who espoused a particular virtue (for example, in book 1 the action focuses on the Redcrosse knight whose virtue is holiness). By reading the whole of the *Faerie Queene*, the reader would be instructed in the twelve private or moral virtues; it seems that Spenser also intended to write a sequel that would exemplify the twelve public virtues, but in the end he died having completed only six books of his projected scheme. Spenser's work may be seen as the final major flourish of the English medieval romance tradition. William SHAKESPEARE's late plays, the comedies of *Pericles, Cymbeline, The Winter's Tale,* and *The Tempest*, are also late variants of this tradition, making use of romance tropes such as loss and restoration, suffering and redemption, apparent death and rebirth, and relying on magic or

trickery to effect their ultimate happy-ever-after resolutions.

Spenser's contemporary Sir Philip SIDNEY wrote a long and elaborate prose romance called *Arcadia* in the early 1580s; this was subsequently imitated by his niece, Lady Mary WROTH, who published her long prose romance entitled *Urania* in 1621. These works constitute early types of prose fiction, and it is primarily in the realm of fiction that the genre of romance has continued to thrive. From the 18th c. onward, the terms "romance" and "romantic" have been used interchangeably to cover sentimental or Gothic fiction. The elements of adventure and action so typical of medieval romance may be seen to survive in works such as *Oroonoko*, by Aphra BEHN, and the novels of Daniel DEFOE. *Oronooko* is generically complex, but its biographical travel narrative detailing the adventures of the royal slave involves elements of romance, and Behn blurs the line between history and fiction in a way which is similar to Malory's treatment of such concepts. Defoe's novels, such as *Robinson Crusoe* and *Moll Flanders*, are all tales that detail the fictional autobiographies of adventurers or rogues. As the modern novel came into its own in the 1740s, the tendency to focus on the adventures of a single individual, who must overcome adversity and engage in moral struggles, may be seen in works such as Samuel RICHARDSON's *Pamela* and Henry FIELDING's satirical spoof of the latter, *Joseph Andrews*. Romance elements are particularly noticeable in the work that Fielding described as his "comic epic-poem in prose": *The History of Tom Jones, a Foundling*. The titular hero is generous and good-natured, but lacking in prudence, and is repeatedly brought into conflict with cold-hearted and selfish people; again, the emphasis is on virtues and vices, and on the education and development in stature of the individual via chance encounter and adventure. Equally firmly situated in the romance tradition are the picaresque novels of Tobias SMOLLET: *Roderick Random* and *Humphrey Clinker*. The much later rediscovery of, and new interest in, romance by such figures as Sir Walter SCOTT and John KEATS led to the 19th-c. literary movement in which they were so influential being named ROMANTICISM. Scott's novel *Ivanhoe* clearly shows the influence of the medieval tradition of romance, as do works of Gothic fiction such as Ann RADCLIFFE's *The Mysteries of Udolpho*. Novels such as Austen's *Pride and Prejudice* and Charlotte Brontë's *Jane Eyre* established an enduring formula for romance fiction whereby the relationship between the hero and heroine is uneven, disrupted by differences of either status or wealth; in the course of the narrative this gulf is crossed only by the power of true love.

Early-20th-c. authors who have achieved great success in the romance genre include Eleanor Burford Hibbert, who published under various pseudonyms including Jean Plaidy, Victoria Holt, and Philippa Carr; also Georgette HEYER, whose specialty was Regency romance; Dorothy Eden; and the American author Phyllis Whitney. However, the genre of romance in the 20th c. is primarily associated with the name of the prolific author Barbara Cartland, and she was partly responsible for defining the conventions of the genre, especially in decreeing that the heroine should be sexually inexperienced before meeting the hero. The development of American romance is distinguished by its coverage of distinctly American concerns, like life on the frontier. Margaret Mitchell's novel *Gone with the Wind* (1936), set against a backdrop of the American Civil War, is typical of the anti-romance that arose during the 1930s. In this genre, the heroine refuses to conform to the expected stereotype, and the narrative frequently ends without the usual success of a happy marriage. Thus, Mitchell's Scarlett O'Hara is thrice married, including one marriage to the love of her life, though she fails to recognize this; she struggles heroically against deprivation and the destruction of the Southern society in which she was reared, and ends the novel alone. *Gone with the Wind* was made into very successful film starring Clark Gable and Vivien Leigh.

The field of romance has now greatly diversified, and very many different types of novels may be placed in its broad category, including the historical romances of Anya Seton; family sagas such as *Penmarric* and *Cashelmara* by Susan HOWATCH, and Elizabeth Jane Howard's series of novels about the Cazalet family; the uneasy romances that arise in Anne Tyler's novels such as *Dinner at the Homesick Restaurant* (1982) and *The Accidental Tourist* (1985); and the contemporary romances of Danielle Steele. In general, the genre is now mostly dominated by female authors; an exceptional best-selling romance by a male author is Robert James Waller's *The Bridges of Madison County* (1994), which was also made into a successful film starring Clint Eastwood and Meryl Streep.

BIBLIOGRAPHY: Barron, W. R. J., *English Medieval Romance* (1987); Birkhead, E., *The Tale of Terror: A Study of the Gothic Romance* (1921); Duncan, I., *Modern Romance and Transformations of the Novel* (1992); King, A., *The Faerie Queene and Middle English Romance: The Matter of Just Memory* (2000); Mills, M., J. Fellows, and C. Meale, eds., *Romance in Medieval England* (1991); Mussell, K., *Women's Gothic and Romantic Fiction* (1981); Stableford, B., *Scientific Romance in Britain 1890–1950* (1985); Watt, I., *The Rise of the Novel* (1957); Vinson, J., ed., *Twentieth-Century Romance and Gothic Writers* (1982)

MARGARET CONNOLLY

ROMANTICISM

Embracing the historical period from the 1770s to the 1830s or 1840s, Romanticism represents a complex interaction of cultural, political, social, philosophical, and aesthetic responses to the unrest set off by the American Revolution, the French Revolution, the age of Napoleon, and the spirit of nationalism that followed in their aftermath. Economically and socially, it stands at the edge of the Industrial Revolution, the breakdown of the old rural order, and the rise of urbanism. It also stands at a transition in Western colonialism and the formation of worldwide empires. At its most basic level, it points to a response to the epistemic and ontological assumptions of the Enlightenment, and a mistrust of the limits of reason.

Broadly conceived, Romanticism articulates a fundamental shift in Western attitudes toward art, society, history, philosophy, and the notion of what it means to be a human being, and the emergence of the modern consciousness. Romanticism crossed national and linguistic boundaries, including figures such as Foscolo, Manzoni, and Leopardi in Italy; Pushkin and Lermontov in Russia; Adam Mickiewicz in Poland; Goethe, Schiller, the Schlegels, Novalis, Ludwig Tieck, E. T. A. Hoffmann, Frederick Hölderlin, and Georg Büchner in the German-speaking lands; Madame de Staël, Benjamin Constant, Chateaubriand, Alfred de Musset, Victor Hugo, and Georges Sand in France; and somewhat later Ralph Waldo Emerson, James Fenimore Cooper, Henry David Thoreau, Herman Melville, and Walt Whitman in the U.S. It crossed cultural boundaries, finding expression in painting, sculpture, and music in addition to literature, evoking the names of Goya, Friedrich, Géricault, Ingres, Delacroix, Préault, Canova, Overbeck, Beethoven, Schubert, and Berlioz.

British Romanticism is diverse and diffuse, lacking the unity or coherence of a school or movement. British Romanticism is often conventionally dated by modern critics and literary historians as extending from 1798, the date of the first edition of William WORDSWORTH's and Samuel Taylor COLERIDGE's *Lyrical Ballads*, to 1832, the year of the death of Sir Walter SCOTT and the passage of the first parliamentary Reform Bill, signifying the constitutional revolution stimulated by the French Revolution. From the perspective of 20th-c. literary criticism, the first generation of British Romanticism conventionally includes Robert BURNS, William BLAKE, Scott, Coleridge, Charles LAMB, and Thomas DE QUINCEY, and centers most fully on the poetic revolution begun by Wordsworth. The second generation includes William HAZLITT, Percy Bysshe SHELLEY and Mary SHELLEY, John KEATS, and the BRONTËS, and takes its identity from Lord BYRON. More recent expansions of this literary canon have justly recovered important figures such as

John CLARE, Felicia HEMANS, Charlotte SMITH, Anna Laetitia BARBAULD, and Mary Tighe. In the realm of the visual arts, Sir Thomas Lawrence, John Constable, and J. M. W. Turner are significant. In social and political reform, Mary WOLLSTONECRAFT stands as the foremost figure for the rights of women, and William Wilberforce and Hannah MORE for social reform and especially the abolition of the slave trade.

From the perspective of the 20th c., the term can seem arbitrary, often falsifying relationships and combining figures who differed from each other in terms of class, politics, and aesthetics, and would have viewed such linkages with little sympathy. Byron, for instance, would see no connection between himself and the Lake Poets. Keats defined his own aesthetic principles as antithetical to those of Wordsworth. Within the period, critics such as Francis Jeffrey, Sydney SMITH, John Wilson CROKER, and later John Gibson LOCKHART christened several loose configurations, though these often reflected the ideology of their periodicals. Thus, Wordsworth, Robert SOUTHEY, and Coleridge found themselves linked and labeled as the Lake Poets, though each had a separate identity before and after their original affiliation. Byron and Shelley were labeled the "Satanic School of Poetry," and Keats found himself designated a disciple of Leigh HUNT and the "Cockney School." In his satirical roman à clef, *Nightmare Abbey*, Thomas Love PEACOCK saw his contemporaries Coleridge, Byron, and Shelley as different sides of a cultural phenomenon that he juxtaposed against the norm. In 1814, Jeffrey complained that Wordsworth's poetry was contrary to the spirit of British literature. By 1818, Lockhart brought similar charges against the young Keats, citing Wordsworth as the canonical standard. In turn, critics now regard Blake as one of the greatest of the Romantics, though he was largely unknown outside of the circles of a few collectors until the end of the 19th c. By contrast, critics are only now recovering Hemans, who was one of the most widely read writers of her day. At the same time, the term Romanticism distorts chronology. Wordsworth lived until 1850, surviving most of his Romantic contemporaries, and serving as poet laureate to Queen Victoria. Keats, the archetypal Romantic poet, and Thomas CARLYLE, the Victorian Sage, were both born in the year 1795. Croker, who savaged Keats in his infamous review, later savaged Alfred, Lord TENNYSON in similar terms, astutely noting the affinities between the poets.

There is no definitive aesthetic form or expression that joins the Romantics. Both Wordsworth and Coleridge, for instance, aspired to a poetic medium that came closer to the indigenous rhythms and characteristics of English. Wordsworth did this by attempting to find diction closer to natural speech, "a man speaking to men." Coleridge, on the other hand, engaged in a sort of poetic archaeology, reviving various earlier verse forms. Both innovated the classical ode into a form of personal expression, what Coleridge called "conversation poems," or later critics have termed "the greater Romantic lyric." Byron, on the other hand, styled himself after the Restoration wits, and saw himself as the natural inheritor of Alexander POPE. For his masterpiece, *Don Juan*, he domesticated the Italian *ottava rima*. Shelley tended to draw on classical models for his poetry, while Blake drew on Methodist hymnody and Tighe the Spenserian stanza. While Scott was a prolific poet, his enduring contribution rests in the development of the historical novel.

Nor is there a unique political, religious, or ideological center. Wordsworth, Coleridge, and Southey began with a strong sympathy for the French Revolution and what it meant for political reform at home, but drew back after the extremes of the Terror, becoming progressively more conservative. The younger generation, especially Byron, chided them for this change of heart, finding it opportunistic. New Historicist readings of Wordsworth have focused on what seem to be his attempts to revise or even erase his early radicalism. Byron offers analogous paradoxes. An aristocrat, he took pride in his identity as Lord Byron. At the same time, though finding his greatest critical acclaim from the Tory *Quarterly Review*, Byron became the symbol of revolt, dying for the liberation of Greece. More than any other figure, the Byronic persona embodied Romanticism across the Western world. Their religious convictions also run a wide gamut. Burns had a tempestuous relationship with the Kirk of Scotland. Coleridge, always devoutly religious, with sympathies with the Quakers, and preaching as a Unitarian, eventually returned to a Trinitarian orthodoxy. Blake was deeply influenced by Methodism, as well as various millenarian Christian sects. At the opposite extreme, Byron played on the motif of being damned, and Shelley labeled himself an atheist. Given these obvious differences, is there some common denominator that allows for a definition of Romanticism?

In medieval literature the term romantic originally pertained to a work in the vernacular language. Since this was often associated with the courtly tradition, the romance pointed either to something sad and sentimental, or something involving chivalric exploits or the fantastic. In many cases, the medieval ROMANCE combined both. By the 17th c., French marked this distinction with the words *romanesque*, signifying the bizarre or fantastic, and *romantique,* signifying the sad and sentimental. German designated the former *romantisch*. The end of the 18th c. generally defined the terms in opposition to the classical. If the romantic appealed to the imagination and the fantastic, the classical appealed to an idealized vision of Greek and Latin antiquity, taken as a model of civilization and cultural perfection. This sense of the word romantic began to appear in English in the 1820s, and tended to be applied to French and German literature, or to the Gothic. By the middle of the 19th c., a Romantic canon had more or less solidified around Wordsworth, Coleridge, Keats, Shelley, and Byron. Critics like Matthew ARNOLD defined them in terms of their supposed antipathy to the classical and their excessive emotion. Later Nietzsche and T. E. HULME saw in Romanticism a covert tension between religious desire and skepticism, "spilt religion," in Hulme's phrase. Early 20th-c. critics, such as Irving Babbitt and the modernists, dismissed the Romantics as escapist.

Romantic theorists of the day, on the other hand, took a different perspective. Friedrich Schlegel and Ludwig Tieck applied *romantisch* in a literary context to signify works of powerful emotion and imagination, and Madame de Staël, probably echoing Schlegel, applied *romantique* in an analogous fashion. At the same time, they rejected the romantic/classical dichotomy, arguing that all real poetry is by its nature romantic. The poetic is synthetic and creative, while other forms of expression are analytic and descriptive. The term designated not so much a movement, as recognition of the nature of the creative poetic act. While none of the British Romantics used the term "Romantic" to describe themselves, they drew similar distinctions. Looking at the difference between poetry and prose, for instance, Wordsworth articulated a concept of poetry similar to that of Schlegel. Coleridge did the same in his definition of imagination in the *Biographia Literaria,* as well as his notion of the symbol and allegory in *The Statesman's Manual.* Poetic imagination is equivalent to the power of perception to create the world. Hazlitt's concept of "gusto" is also relevant. It is the power or passion in the creation of an object in art. This also applies to Blake's notion of the visionary.

Ever since Arthur O. Lovejoy's famous 1923 address to the Modern Language Association, the definition of Romanticism has itself become a perennial topic of scholarly debate. Lovejoy argued that the various Romanticisms represented a complex and "unstable intellectual compound," concluding that no coherent definition was possible. Since then, critics such as René Wellek, M. H. Abrams, and Northrop Frye respond that Romanticism is not so much a single doctrine as what Frye terms, "an historic center of gravity." Wellek sees this center of gravity as an endeavor among the Romantic writers of Britain, Germany, and France to overcome a split between subject and object, the self and the world, the conscious and the unconscious. Examining Romantic theories of imagination, Abrams draws a similar interpretation. The Romantics, he argues, found in the rationalism and self-consciousness of the Enlightenment, a separation between man and nature. This was manifest variously in a sense of the self in history and a corresponding primitivism, in a search for a more natural, less artificial language, in the discovery of the self in the action of perception and imagination.

Romanticism can also be understood in terms of the construction of the self. That is, the self may be understood as a disposition between the past and the future. Confronted with a present that challenges and threatens to overturn the eternal order, there is a sense of absence or homelessness, a lost innocence or lost Eden. The result is a nostalgia for a time and place closer to the rhythms of nature, or for some lost UTOPIA, whether Edenic, a pastoral state of nature, an ideal medieval realm marked by a unity of science, art, and religion, or a classical republic predicated on sincere values of honor, duty, and virtue. Correspondingly, it posits various possible futures, a return home, a quest for some ideal lost order or a revolutionary struggle for liberty, or an apocalyptic vision of the future, whether a return to a Christian unity or pagan spontaneity. This sense of the self informs Blake's juxtaposition of innocence and experience. It underlies the paradox that Wordsworth articulates in "Intimations of Immortality," in which maturity brings the consolation of a philosophical understanding, but at the cost of the unconscious spontaneity of the child. Similarly, Scott contrasts the lost historical past with the present in his *Waverley Novels*, underlining an awareness of the vulnerability of civilization.

A number of literary and cultural strands anticipate and contribute to Romanticism. Seventeenth and 18th-c. antiquarians created an interest in earlier indigenous cultural artifacts. This encouraged a fashion for folk or primitive literature, resulting in famous compilations such as Thomas PERCY's *Reliques of Ancient English Poetry* or the popular and widely influential Ossian poems, the remains of the supposed Gaelic EPIC collected by James MACPHERSON. It also contributed to the popularity of Burns and other folk poets. These antiquarian interests also contributed to Scott and the development of the historical novel. Corollary to this was the popularity of the Gothic, which cultivated a taste for the mysterious and the fantastic, and explored the darker side of human psychology, stimulating Coleridge, De Quincey, and "Monk" LEWIS. Various 18th-c. aesthetic categories such as natural genius, SENTIMENT, the pastoral, the picturesque, and the sublime also contribute to Romanticism. All of these anticipate an art based on emotion, feelings, or the power of imagination that go beyond the limits of reason. Edmund BURKE's theories of the sublime, much admired by Immanuel Kant, offered Wordsworth and Coleridge a way of perceiving nature aside from the beautiful. The literature of sentiment, made popular by Henry MACKENZIE's novel *The Man of Feeling*, placed an importance on powerful emotions. Thomas CHATTERTON and his Rowley poems contributed to the Romantic myth of the youthful genius.

Works of the so-called graveyard school, including Robert BLAIR's *The Grave*, Edward YOUNG's *Night Thoughts*, both illustrated by Blake, as well as Thomas GRAY's famous "Elegy," anticipate the contemplative character of the "Greater Romantic Lyric." Works by William COWPER, and especially James THOMSON's *The Seasons*, offered Wordsworth both a new and sympathetic vision of nature and a sense of possibilities of blank verse. William COLLINS advanced a conception of poetry as sublime and sacred. At the same time, Continental literature advanced a variety of reciprocal influences from Jean-Jacques Rousseau's focus on the individual in works such as *La Nouvelle Héloïse*, published in 1761 and republished in 1765, and Saint-Just's erotic and apocalyptic epic, *Organt*, published anonymously in 1789, to the ghostly folk ballads of Gottfried Bürger, or the works of the young Goethe, Schiller, and other writers of the German *Sturm und Drang* movement.

While many critics of the last part of the 20th c. have argued that Romanticism is an ideological construction by the critics of the first part of the 20th c., and many continue to debate the precise definition of Romanticism, all agree that this period from around the turn of the 18th and 19th cs. represents a profound turn in the Western mentality, resulting in a rich and significant body of work. While literary fortunes rise and fall, much of the poetry of writers such as Wordsworth, Coleridge, Keats, Burns, and Blake, remains both critically current and widely read in a way that the work of other periods, save that of William SHAKESPEARE, does not. Much in the Romantics anticipates modern sensibilities, and though modernists have deplored their excesses and turned to the metaphysical poets, they were themselves fundamentally bound to the Romantic conception of the poet, sharing more with Wordsworth's search for certitude than with John DONNE's absolute faith. In turn much of our more recent literary theorizing derives directly or indirectly from the examination of language, history, politics, and meaning that shaped the Romantics. To read and study them is to examine the genealogy of our own beliefs. Finally, the contemporary valuation of fantasy and imagination, spirituality and the search for some ideal, a fascination with the rebel artist and individualism, a love of nature, a belief in the primacy of feeling and a mistrust of reason are all mediated by Romanticism. In a very real sense, we are still in the midst of Romanticism.

BIBLIOGRAPHY: Abrams, M. H., *The Mirror and the Lamp* (1956); Berlin, I., *The Roots of Romanticism* (1999); Bloom, H., *The Visionary Company* (1971); Brown, M., *Preromanticism* (1991); Butler, M., *Romantics, Rebels, and Reactionaries* (1981); Chandler, J., *England in 1819: The Politics of Literary Culture and the Case of Romantic Historicism* (1998); Crans-ton, M., *The Romantic Movement* (1994); Frye, N., *A Study of English Romanticism* (1968); Gleckner, R. F., *Romanticism: Points of View* (1970); Magnuson, P., *Reading Public Romanticism* (1998); McGann, J. J., *The Romantic Ideology* (1983); Schenk, H. G., *The Mind of the European Romantics* (1979); Stuart, C., *The Cambridge Companion to British Romanticism* (1993); Weiskel, T. *The Romantic Sublime* (1986); Wu, D., *Romanticism: A Critical Reader* (1995)

THOMAS L. COOKSEY

ROSENBERG, Isaac

b. 25 November 1890, Bristol; d. 31 March or 1 April 1918, Arras, France

R., a major poet of the First World War and a talented painter, was born to Jewish immigrant parents from Latvia living in Bristol. While still a young child, he moved with his family to Stepney in the East End of London. Obliged to leave school at fourteen and earn his living as an apprentice engraver, he snatched what time he could for drawing and writing, meeting friends such as the painters Mark Gertler and David Bomberg, and the poet John Rodker, at the Whitechapel Library and Art Gallery near his home during the evenings. Afterward, they walked the streets discussing art and poetry, pausing under lampposts to read each other's poems.

In 1911, he was noticed copying paintings at the National Gallery by some wealthy Jewish ladies who clubbed together to send him to the Slade School of Fine Art, where most of the interesting painters of the time were trained. As well as his friends Gertler and Bomberg, there were students such as Stanley and Gilbert Spencer, Dora Carrington, and Christopher Wynne Nevinson. All these became well-known artists of the period before and during the First World War. The Slade students were full of the modernist, postimpressionist and cubist ideas flowing across the Channel; R. wrote, "a sharp contour means more than the blending of tone into tone . . . the concise pregnant quality of poetry rather than prose."

After leaving the Slade in 1913, R. visited his sister in South Africa to improve his health and earn some money through painting. It was the last time in his life that he was free to devote himself to his art. War was declared while he was there. In spite of family pressure to stay, he came home and in 1915, without telling even his family, he enlisted as a private soldier, eventually ending up in the regiment of the King's Own Royal Lancasters. He wrote, "I never joined the army from patriotic reasons. Nothing can justify war. I suppose we must all fight to get the trouble over . . . I thought if I'd join there would be the separation allowance for my mother."

R. never committed himself wholly to any cause other than his own pursuit of art and poetry. His pov-

erty, education, and background made him an outsider, yet it was just that experience which equipped
him to cope with the unforeseen horror of war in the
trenches, and make cool and sophisticated use of it as
an artist: "I am determined that this war, with all its
powers for devastation, shall not master my poeting;
that is, if I am lucky enough to come through all right.
I will not leave a corner of my consciousness covered
up, but saturate myself with the strange and extraordinary new conditions of this life, and it will all refine
itself into poetry later on."

He showed characteristic tenacity for one still so
young in producing a substantial body of poetry before the war—much of it naturally unformed and unfinished but also containing much promise and some
fine poems. He is mainly remembered for his war
poems, which now hold a permanent place in the anthologies of the 20th c. They are strikingly different
from those of his fellow poets because of his capacity
to embrace and transmute "the strange and extraordinary conditions" of trench life without the emotional
recoil from the horrors of war with which other major
war poets such as Siegfried SASSOON and Wilfred
OWEN had to deal. For R., the shattering of a Christian
civilization that so affects Owen for example was not
such a shock—as a Jewish immigrant from the East
End of London who had already had to struggle for
his education and the space to exercise his art he had
fewer ideals to lose. He was a private soldier, coping
with the physical squalor as well as the dangers of the
trenches, where virtually all of his fellow poets were
officers—the advantages officer status conferred were
small but significant—pen, paper, and light to write
by for instance. In his last letter home in March 1918,
R. refers to an "inch of candle" he had scrounged,
writing "I must measure my letter by the light."

What is remarkable about his work is its ambition,
its largeness of vision combined with its painterly,
sensuous response to physical detail, splendid and
sordid, as in "Dead Man's Dump": "Burnt black by
strange decay,/Their sinister faces lie/The lid over
each eye,/The grass and coloured clay/More motion
have than they,/Joined to the great sunk silences."

It was astonishing that as a private soldier he managed to write at all, yet he sent home poems scribbled
in pencil on scraps of paper that were among the most
significant produced during the period. R.'s poetic
ability to confront alienation and difficulty, and his
unique artistic gift for turning defeats into victories
have made his life and work increasingly significant
for our own times. He was killed, probably on patrol,
during the night of March 31-April 1, 1918.

BIBLIOGRAPHY: Cohen, J., *Journey to the Trenches:
The Life of I. R., 1890–1918* (1975); Hibberd, D.,
Poetry of the First World War (1981); Liddiard, J.,
I. R. (1975); Parsons, I., ed., *The Collected Works of
I. R.* (1979); Wilson, J. M., *I. R.* (1975)

JEAN P. LIDDIARD

ROSS, Martin. See SOMERVILLE AND ROSS

ROSSETTI, Christina [Georgina]

b. 5 December 1830, London; d. 29 December 1894,
London

One of the finest poets writing during the Victorian
age, arguably the best woman poet of the century and
widely anthologized. "Goblin Market" and "Remember me when I am gone away" are two pieces well
known outside literary circles, the latter being especially familiar as funeral verse. Her oeuvre encompasses lyric, ballad, narrative fantasy, spiritual meditation, children's verse, short fiction, religious
mysticism and devotional studies. In all her work the
language is musical and precise; in the best, the words
spring off the page with irresistible grace and spirit.

Born into a cultured Anglo-Italian family, R. had
a dual linguistic and cultural inheritance. Her father,
Gabriele Rossetti, was a Neapolitan poet and political
exile who devoted his later life to the study of Dante
Alighieri, and her maternal grandfather was a Tuscan
linguist long settled in Britain, while her mother and
aunts followed the Anglican faith and habits of the English side of the family. The youngest child, R. had
one sister, Maria, and two brothers, Dante Gabriel ROS-
SETTI, poet and painter, and William Michael ROSSETTI.

In emulation of her elders, R. began to write at
an early age, and small notebooks of her verses are
preserved, dating from 1842 onward. In 1847, her
proud grandfather printed a selection of her poems
for private circulation, in the custom of the time. The
following year two poems were published in the
Athenaeum, the leading literary weekly, effectively
launching her career—a move complicated by prevailing gender prescriptions that frowned on female
ambition and "display" and by religious promotion
of submissive humility. During her teenage years, R.
was powerfully and permanently influenced by the
Anglo–Catholic movement within the Church of England, always regarding her literary gifts as primarily
devoted to religious ends. This theme is explored in
the juvenile novella *Maude*, composed in 1850 and
published posthumously in 1897.

She was also involved in the cultural excitement
emanating from the artists and writers of the Pre–
Raphaelite Brotherhood that flourished from 1849 to
1852, in which her brothers were major figures. For a
short while she was engaged to painter James Collinson, one of the seven "P.R.B.s," and her own con-

tribution was poems published in the Pre–Raphaelite magazine the *Germ* in 1850. The next few years saw the composition of many accomplished, innovative, urgent, humorous and haunting pieces, in a variety of lyric modes including sonnets and short "songs" of which "When I am dead, my dearest" and "A Birthday" are among the best known. "Echo," "Winter: My Secret," and "My Dream" are other strikingly diverse poems from this period. Further attempts at publication were however unsuccessful until after the composition of "Goblin Market" in 1859. This formed the title poem of her first collection issued in 1862 by Alexander Macmillan, who had previously published the much-quoted "Up-hill."

Deploying a folkloric theme of human encounter with the elf world, "Goblin Market" tells a dramatic tale of the traffic between two young women (Lizzie and Laura) and a troop of seductive, coercive goblins, in a narrative, polyvalent fantasy of 570 lines that was and remains R.'s chef-d'oeuvre. Especially popular in studies of women's literature, it is open to and has provoked a wealth of commentary and interpretation, engaging theoretical perspectives relating to sexuality, psychoanalysis, gender, economics, religion, performance, and visual art. Metrically, it employs daringly varied line lengths and strong but irregular rhymes; together with tumbling syntax and unusual, expressive language that vividly if indirectly evokes erotic arousal, its formal qualities make it a key item in the Victorian canon, linking the work of John KEATS to that of A. C. SWINBURNE and W. B. YEATS. R.'s follow-up poem, "The Prince's Progress," title poem of her second collection in 1866, is less compelling, owing to its slower pace and more overt moral message, although here too are many depths of meaning. It also coincided with the publication of Swinburne's notorious *Poems and Ballads*, and although few poets could be further apart in terms of themes and intent, they share a rhetorical affinity: melody, anaphora, feminine rhymes, and self-sufficiency place R.'s work in the sequence of emerging aestheticism.

Serious illness—debilitating and long-undiagnosed thyroid disease—curtailed poetic output around 1870–72, but in 1870 she published a small collection of short fiction entitled *Commonplace and Other Short Stories*, which has largely been judged a failure, although the subtle wit and observation of her prose deserve acclaim. In 1871 came *Sing-Song*, a collection of enchanting, sometimes unsettling, nursery verses that have been better liked by adults than children and demonstrate R.'s assured command of diction, rhythm and layered meaning. Three years later, a trio of linked stories for children appeared under the title *Speaking Likenesses*; this endeavored to harness narrative devices inspired by Lewis CARROLL's *Alice* books for morally instructional purposes, and is nota-

ble for its oblique self-portrait of the author as an irascible storytelling aunt.

In her middle years, R. became increasingly absorbed with devotional reading that led to devotional writing, despite her observation that "Bishops should write for me, not I for bishops!" *Annus Domini* (1874) is a day-book of original prayers; *Seek and Find* (1879) is a devotional study of the Benedicite; *Called to Be Saints* (1881) explains the minor festivals of the Anglican calendar for young people; *Letter and Spirit* (1883) explores the Commandments; and *The Face of the Deep* (1892) is a long, detailed, spiritual commentary on the Book of Revelation. The context and customs that provided readers for such volumes have now largely vanished, and R.'s texts do not on the whole transcend their contemporary purpose, but they nevertheless belong to a long tradition that besides patristic and medieval literature includes works by English divines and poets such as Lancelot ANDREWES, Robert SOUTHWELL, John DONNE, George HERBERT, and Thomas TRAHERNE.

The most readable of R.'s religious works is *Time Flies* (1885), a "reading diary" of short pieces that include personal and other anecdotes as well as prayers and poems. Close study of Dante and Petrarch informs R.'s third collection of poetry, *A Pageant and Other Poems* (1881), which contains a pair of major sonnet sequences. The fourteen sonnets of *Monna Innominata* take as motif the expression of unfulfilled love from a woman to a man, while the twenty-eight *Sonnets of Later Life* range through a variety of mature and often sobering reflections. Denser in thought and structure than R.'s other ambitious verse, these have yet to receive their due share of critical attention.

R.'s most significant impact on other writers was probably that felt by Gerard Manley HOPKINS, who responded to her poetic expression of faith and fear, and indirectly by Virginia WOOLF, who admired R.'s artistry and wit but deplored her narrow, repressive religion. Although at the time of Alfred, Lord TENNYSON's death in 1892, R. was regarded by many as the finest living English poet, by the 1920s her reputation had declined to a virtually invisible level that was maintained until the 1970s when a recovery began, thanks largely to feminist critics such as Sandra M. Gilbert, Susan Gubar, and Germaine GREER. Lately, R. has been the subject of major critical studies, and her work is in the process of rejoining the main canon of English literature, from which is had been banished to the margins.

BIBLIOGRAPHY: Arseneau, M., A. H. Harrison, and L. J. Kooistra, eds., *The Culture of C. R.* (1999); Chapman, A., *The Afterlife of C. R.* (2000); Crump, R. W., ed., *The Complete Poems of C. R.* (3 vols., 1979–90); Gilbert, S. M., and S. Gubar, *The Madwoman in the Attic: The Woman Writer and the Nine-*

teenth-Century Literary Imagination (1979); Harrison, A. H., ed., *The Letters of C. R.* (4 vols., 1997–); Marsh, J., *C. R.* (1994)

JAN MARSH

ROSSETTI, Dante Gabriel

b. 8 May 1828, London; d. 9 April 1882, Birchington, Kent

The central figure of the Pre-Raphaelite movement in the mid-Victorian era, R. was successful and original both as a poet and a painter—a dual achievement unusual in British culture. In both arts, his reputation declined under modernist criticism, not least because Ezra Pound and T. S. ELIOT repudiated work that powerfully influenced their own poetic beginnings. Latterly, R.'s painting has regained popular and scholarly attention, but with a few signal exceptions his literary works have as yet remained in the critical wilderness. However, both in succession to the ROMANTICISM of John KEATS and early Alfred, Lord TENNYSON, and as a leading element in aestheticism, R.'s writings deserve a significant place in 19th-c. English literature. His verse translations from Italian are also important, as is his role in rescuing William BLAKE's work from oblivion, in contributions to the two-volume biography by Alexander GILCHRIST, published in 1861.

Born into a cultured Anglo-Italian family, R. had a dual linguistic and cultural inheritance, together with a role model in his father, a poet exiled for political reasons who devoted his life in Britain to the study of Dante Alighieri, for whom R. was named. This led to a translation of the *Vita Nuova*, largely completed during the 1840s and published together with other pieces in *Early Italian Poets* (1861), and also to the narrative poem "Dante at Verona," reflecting on the poet's exile and demonstrating the influence of Robert BROWNING, of whose "difficult" poems R. was an early and much appreciated champion. Other youthful enthusiasms included Sir Walter SCOTT, Border Balladry, Gothic romances, and Edgar Allan Poe, as well as the Romantic poets.

In 1848–49, during the excitement surrounding the formation of the Pre-Raphaelite Brotherhood, in which he was a prime mover, R. composed his first published work, including "The Blessed Damozel," a poem blending feminized erotic feeling with sacramental imagery, and "Hand and Soul," the prose tale of a fictional painter from the early Italian period. With half a dozen other pieces, both appeared in the short-lived PRB magazine, the *Germ* (1850), which launched the literary side to the movement. These works attracted attention for their avant-garde qualities, being admired by Robert and Elizabeth Barrett BROWNING, Tennyson, and Coventry PATMORE, and by a younger generation of writers and artists including A. C. SWINBURNE, William MORRIS, and Sir Edward Burne-Jones.

For the next decade, R. concentrated on pictorial art, leaving many poems as, in his own words, "very long beginnings." From 1858, he worked to complete his Italian translations, followed by preparations for a volume of original pieces, whose publication was aborted when in 1862 he consigned the manuscript to the coffin of his wife, Elizabeth Siddal, following her tragic death from an opiate overdose. Seven years later, partly as a result of disturbed vision that threatened his now successful painting career, the poetic impulse revived. For this, he arranged the exhumation of the earlier manuscript—a notorious act that later tended to eclipse all literary claims to fame. The recovered pieces, published in *Poems* (1870), included "Jenny," a dramatic monologue from a young man silently musing beside a sleeping prostitute. Arguably R.'s chef d'oeuvre, this explores contemporary ideas about responsibility for a major social problem, in a judiciously heightened colloquial voice that neatly balances language and imagery, avoiding coarseness, affectation, and moralizing. Other poems included "Dante at Verona," "A Last Confession" (a monologue about a hunted revolutionary in pre-Unification Italy, and the collapse of political idealism), and "Sister Helen," a ballad-inspired tale of betrayed love and sorcery. "Troy Town" and "Eden Bower," the most overtly sexual of the pieces, based respectively on a classical legend of Helen molding a cup to the shape of her breast and the biblical myth of Lilith, can be regarded as poetical correlatives of the sensuous images of fictive women painted by R. during the 1860s. These reflect R.'s close association with Swinburne in this period, as well as his friendship with American painter James McNeill Whistler, and usher into Britain the "art for art's sake" impulse derived from Théophile Gautier and Charles Baudelaire.

In addition, the 1870 volume contained the first fifty sonnets of the "House of Life," a projected sequence, offering a modern variant on the verses in Dante's *Vita Nuova*, treating of love, life, death, fame, and regret in dense and sometimes florid style that strikingly combines particularity with idealized and often abstract conceits. Warmly reviewed by a coterie of friends, the book sold well. Some few months later came a critical assault, under the title "The Fleshly School of Poetry," on the sensuality of selected poems, including the sonnet "Nuptial Sleep," and on the morality of their author, who was privately known to be in love with Jane, wife of William Morris, R.'s close friend and business partner. This poetical and personal attack caused paranoia and nervous collapse, from which R. only partially recovered, with accompanying drug and alcohol abuse that led directly to his premature death.

His second collection, *Ballads and Sonnets* (1881), contained the extended 100-sonnet "House of Life," together with two new long pieces, "The White Ship" and "The King's Tragedy," based on incidents from English and Scottish history, and the grotesque, overlong "Rose Mary," hinging on infidelity. Posthumously, all R.'s poems and fragments were published by his brother William Michael ROSSETTI, in several editions between 1886 and 1911.

Taken together, R.'s life story, paintings, and literary reputation offered a counter-cultural appeal to the next generation, among whom Walter PATER and Oscar WILDE were early adherents of an aesthetic sensibility much indebted to him and Swinburne, as were symbolist and decadent writers both in Britain and continental Europe who valued form and gesture in art above meaning and content. Although a "mystical" reading of R.'s verse continued to flourish well into the 20th c., from 1920 onward its critical reputation fell lower and lower, until his works virtually vanished from the canon of Victorian literature. Christopher Ricks's *Oxford Book of English Verse* (1999) contains only nine, mainly short, items and there is no full scholarly edition.

By contrast, the work of his sister Christina ROSSETTI has regained and redoubled its critical popularity, and it may be that R.'s work will in due course receive a major postmodern revaluation. If so, this will return to the Paterian focus or be largely due to the availability of the online R. Archive, from the University of Virginia, covering all aspects of his literary and pictorial oeuvre.

BIBLIOGRAPHY: D. G. R. Hypermedia Archive at www.iath.virginia.edu/rossetti/fullarch.html.; Harrison, A. H., *The Victorian Poets and Romantic Poems: Intertextuality and Ideology* (1990); Marsh, J., ed., *D. G. R.* (1999); Marsh, J., *D. G. R.* (1999); McGann, J., *D. G. R. and the Game that Must Be Lost* (2000)

JAN MARSH

ROSSETTI, William Michael

b. 25 September 1829, London; d. 5 February 1919, London

Founder-member of the Pre-Raphaelite Brotherhood, R. edited the *Germ*, including some of his own verses, and wrote about the group and later developments in *Ruskin, Rossetti, Praeraphaelitism* [*sic*] (1899) and *Praeraphaelite Diaries and Letters* (1900). He edited the collected works of his elder brother Dante Gabriel ROSSETTI (2 vols., 1890), and the poetry of his sister Christina ROSSETTI (1904). Contributor of countless articles on art and literature to journals, he wrote a life of John KEATS (1887), edited the works of Walt Whitman (1868), Percy Bysshe SHELLEY (2 vols., 1870), and William BLAKE (1874), and translated

Dante's *Inferno* into blank verse. Among his other works were *Lives of Famous Poets* (1878), *Dante Rossetti: His Family Letters with Memoir* (2 vols., 1895), *Some Reminiscences* (2 vols., 1906), and *Democratic Sonnets* (2 vols., 1907).

ROWE, Elizabeth Singer

b. 11 September 1674, Ilchester, Somerset; d. 20 February 1737, Frome, Somerset

R. was probably the most celebrated religious writer of the 18th c. Her poetry was widely reprinted during her lifetime and after her death, and there were eighteen editions of *Friendship in Death: In Twenty Letters from the Dead to the Living* (1728) by 1800. The 20th c. saw a decline of critical interest in R., and it is only recently that critics have begun to rediscover the complexity of her work.

R. was the daughter of a dissenting minister who encouraged her to paint and write. By the early 1690s, R.'s poetry was appearing in London periodicals. In 1696, her *Poems on Several Occasions*, was published, a collection that included amorous verse and a vehement defence of women's right to poetry. In 1710, R. married Thomas Rowe, who was thirteen years her junior. The couple lived together in London until his death in 1715, at the age of twenty-eight. R. was deeply affected by the loss of her husband and retired to rural Somerset, where she devoted the remainder of her life to writing, religious meditation, and educational works.

R.'s approach to devotion was rhapsodic and her poetry is a passionate response to her own religious impulses and her perception of God's presence in the world around her. R.'s main works, *Friendship in Death* and its sequel *Letters Moral and Entertaining* (3 vols., 1728–33), and the biblical verse EPIC *The History of Joseph* (1736), supplemented the collections of poetry that appeared throughout her life. *Friendship in Death* contains letters ostensibly by dead souls in heaven who write in order to dissuade mortal friends and relatives from specific and sensational acts of wrongdoing such as seduction, murder, adultery, incest and revenge. *Letters Moral and Entertaining* was organized similarly, except the letter writers were mortal.

R.'s death was widely mourned, famously in an elegy by the respected scholar Elizabeth CARTER. A response that was less popular with her family was that of the infamous publisher, Edmund Curll, who, exploiting the deathbed popularity of R., published some early poems with her defense of female authorship as *Philomela* in 1737. R.'s family responded to this and other doubtful commemorations with a fervent defense of her reputation as woman and writer. *The Life of Mrs Rowe*, published in 1738, and widely distributed in an edition of R.'s *Miscellaneous Works*

(2 vols., 1739), was part-written and published after her death by Theophilus Rowe, her brother-in-law. The *Life* was a studied representation of R.'s life and work as wholly lacking in passion or interest. Like *Devout Exercises of the Heart* (1738), a collection of heavily edited poetry from R.'s manuscripts that appeared after her death, *The Life of Mrs. Rowe* ignored the fictional letter collections and edited out R.'s penchant for rhapsodic, ecstatic response.

R.'s work is sometimes differentiated into two distinct phases, that of the impetuous Elizabeth Singer and the stolid Mrs. Rowe, but this contradicts the lifelong consistency of R.'s poetic voice. R.'s early poetry is preoccupied with a search for places in which she can reflect without distraction. Her mature work recognizes that only the act of writing itself could furnish the space for meditation that her passionate self so desired.

R. devoted her poetry to the representation of sensual experiences that induce abstract meditation and wrote collections of fictional letters that validated reflection over temporal time or action. Her poetry and prose examine whether enjoyment of the sensual world aids or prevents appreciation of the divine, only to repeatedly solve the conundrum with the fact that the act of writing renders both sensual appreciation and divine meditation valid and socially beneficial.

BIBLIOGRAPHY: Clarke, N., "Soft Passions and Darling Themes: From E. S. R. to Elizabeth Carter," *WW* 7 (2000): 353–70; Richetti, J., "Mrs. E. R.: The Novel as Polemic," *PMLA* 82 (1967): 522–29; Stecher, H., *E. S. R., the Poetess of Frome* (1973)

KATE WILLIAMS

ROWE, Nicholas

bap. 30 June 1674, Little Barford, Bedfordshire; d. 6 December 1718, London

After attending Westminster School, R. entered the Middle Temple to study law, but became rich on his father's death. R.'s first play, *The Ambitious Stepmother* (perf. 1700; pub. 1701), was set in Persepolis and *Tamerlaine* followed in 1702, the hero representing the Protestant King William III. R.'s most famous play is *The Fair Penitent* (1703), adapted from *The Fatal Dowry* by Philip MASSINGER and Nathan FIELD. The character of "the gay Lothario," where "gay" indicates a promiscuous heterosexual, has become proverbial. The virtuous heroine is named Calista, and the play explicitly suggested to Samuel RICHARDSON the names of Clarissa and Lovelace in his novel *Clarissa*. Other plays by R. include *The Biter* (perf. 1704; pub. 1705), *Ulysses* (perf. 1705; pub. 1706), *The Royal Convert* (perf. 1707; pub. 1708), *The Tragedy of Jane Shore* (1714), and *The Tragedy of Lady Jane Grey* (1715). R. called these his "she-tragedies," and

Sarah Siddons starred in them. In 1715, R. succeeded Nahum TATE as poet laureate. R. was the first modern editor of William SHAKESPEARE, despite basing his text (6 vols., 1709) on the unreliable fourth Folio. He collected Shakespearean theatrical traditions from the actor Thomas Betterton and used them in the memoir attached to his edition of the plays. R. was the first to divide the plays into acts and scenes and prefixed a list of characters to each. R.'s three-volume *Works* were first printed in 1728.

ROWLANDS, Samuel

b. ca. 1570, probably London; d. 1630, probably London

Little is known of R.'s life, except that he wrote satirical and sometimes religious verse. His first publication was a sequence of poems entitled *The Betraying of Christ* (1598). Among his satires are *'Tis Merry When Gossips Meet* (1602), *Look to it, for I'll Stab Thee* (1604), and *Hell's Broke Loose* (1605). *A Terrible Battle between the Two Consumers of the Whole World; Time and Death* (1606?) is a dialogue in verse and *The Famous History of Guy, Earl of Warwick* (1607) a comic ballad. A verse monologue, *The Melancholy Knight* (1615), mocks nostalgia for an imaginary romantic past.

ROWLEY, William

b. ca. 1585; d. February 1625 or 1626, London

Nothing is known of R. before his name appeared, with those of William Day and George Wilkins, as the joint author of *The Travels of the Three English Brothers* (1607), a play written for Queen Anne's Company. This episodic romance, which celebrates the exploits of heroic Englishmen abroad, proved typical of R.'s subsequent drama. Collaboratively written on a topical theme for a popular audience, *The Travels* provides many of the pleasures on offer at the Jacobean public theaters: stock characters, patriotic sentiments, conventional morality, and bawdy comedy. Significantly, this play also represents fictionally the historical Will Kemp, the famous English comic actor, noted for his bawdy song and dance routines. Like Kemp, R. became a popular clown, specializing in the role of the simple country fellow, a stock character in the jig tradition. Several contemporary allusions to R.'s corpulence—he was called "the fat foole"—emphasize the physical aspect of his comedy. By 1609, R. was a leading member of the Duke of York's company (later known as Prince Charles's Men), serving for many years as actor, writer, and unofficial representative. By 1623, however, he had joined London's foremost acting company, the King's Men, with whom R. created the part of the Fat Bishop in Thomas

MIDDLETON's notoriously successful *A Game at Chess.*

We cannot know with certainty the extent of R.'s dramatic corpus: much his work may have been uncredited or lost. However, as the joint or sole author of at least eighteen plays in twenty-four years, R. was clearly, like his contemporaries William SHAKESPEARE and Thomas HEYWOOD, a prolific professional playwright. Three plays have been ascribed to R. alone: *A Shoemaker a Gentleman* (perf. 1609; pub. 1638), a neo-miracle play, dramatizing the lives of early British saints; *A New Wonder, a Woman Never Vext* (perf. ca. 1615; pub. 1632), a city comedy in which familial and civic charity triumph over spite and greed; and *All's Lost by Lust* (perf. ca. 1619; pub. 1633), a tragedy, in which R. himself played the role of "a simple clownish Gentleman." Though *All's Lost* has received scant critical praise, it repays attention. In the play's main plot, R. neatly fuses two legendary accounts of the Islamic conquest of Spain. King Rodericke, a lustful tyrant, precipitates the Moorish invasion both through his rape of a nobleman's daughter and his forcible entry into an enchanted castle. With a racism typical of early modern English culture, R. represents the invading Moors as demonic forces, "sooty as the inhabitants of hell," who enact at a national level the violence the king performs privately. Virgin, castle and kingdom are thus linked by an implicit analogy. Although R. shapes this plot in accordance with Jacobean stage conventions, including the familiar opposition between virgin martyr and sexual predator, he gives the traditional conflict a novel twist: his heroine refuses to conform to the pattern of the Roman Lucretia, whose suicide after rape led to her community's liberation from tyranny. Instead Jacinta survives her rape and provokes her father to a rebellion that enslaves rather than frees her country. While Jacinta's behavior—her failure to commit suicide, her virulent anger, her demand for revenge against a legitimate king—may appeal to a modern reader, it would trouble the sympathies of a Jacobean audience. In the subplot, where a wronged woman attempts to have her faithless husband murdered, R. doubles the image of the dangerously vengeful female.

As an author, R. collaborated with some of the best of his fellow playwrights, including Thomas DEKKER, John FORD, John FLETCHER, John WEBSTER, and even, according to the dubious claim on the title page of *The Birth of Merlin* (perf. ca. 1608–19; pub. 1662), Shakespeare. However, R. is now best known for the plays he wrote with Middleton, including *A Faire Quarrel* (perf. ca. 1616; pub. 1617) and *The Changeling* (perf. 1622; pub. 1653), the most critically acclaimed collaborative work of the period. Though Middleton, as the author of the principal scenes between the willful heroine Beatrice-Joanna and the predatory villain DeFlores, has reaped most of the praise for *The Changeling*, R. was responsible for all of the first and last acts, and the subplot. R. thus set up the thematic contrasts (female chastity is lost in the tragic main plot, and preserved in the comic subplot), developed the symbolically powerful madhouse scenes, and drew the plots together in act five. Here, as is *All's Lost*, R. shows himself a skillful dramatic artisan.

R.'s work has been slighted by a critical tradition that ranked sole above collaborative authorship, tragedy above comedy, and the literary above the performative aspects of a dramatic script. As these critical values have been challenged, R. has attracted increased attention.

BIBLIOGRAPHY: Bentley, G. E., *The Profession of Dramatist in Shakespeare's Time, 1590–1642* (1971); Dominik, M., *William Shakespeare and "The Birth of Merlin"* (1985); Mooney, M. E., "'The Common Sight' and Dramatic Form: R.'s Embedded Jig in *A Faire Quarrel*," *SEL* 20 (1980): 306–23

KAREN BAMFORD

ROWLING, J[oanne] K[athleen]

b. 31 July 1965, Chipping Sodbury, near Bristol

R. is a phenomenon. There is surely no other word for one who has single-handedly, and with her first novel, turned a generation of children on to reading, and, even more remarkably, a large number of adults on to reading CHILDREN'S LITERATURE, and done it initially by word of mouth, however cleverly her work has been marketed since. Although the sequence of novels that began with *Harry Potter and the Philosopher's Stone* (1997; repub. as *Harry Potter and the Sorcerer's Stone*, 1998) has its precursors, especially in the work of Diana Wynne Jones, the combination of elements, and especially the progression through time, has its own originality.

It begins with the concept, that alongside ordinary (Muggle) society, there coexists a society of wizards with its own governmental structures, education system, and codes of conduct. There is intermarriage between members of the two societies, and children of such marriages usually inherit the powers of the magic parent, which can be developed by education, such as takes the place at coeducational boarding schools like Hogwarts to which, at the age of eleven, Harry Potter travels from Platform Twentythree and a Half at Kings Cross.

He has lived since infancy with his singularly unpleasant aunt, uncle, and cousin, a Muggle family who were obliged to take him in when his parents were killed. He has been told that they died in a road accident, but they were actually killed by the evil Lord Valdermort; only his Muggle mother's sacrifice saved Harry. Now he is old enough to start in the youngest class at Hogwarts and come into his inheritance as, potentially, a great wizard, beginning a series of adventures in which he regularly finds himself at war with his parents' murderer who, though severely damaged by that first encounter, constantly finds new ways to embody himself and renew his malignant power.

What is the secret of R.'s benignant power? Of course, it is not one single thing. The one most important, however, is that R. knows what most novelists for adults have forgotten: she knows that the desire to be told a story is one of the most profoundly human wishes, and that the narrative book is the storyteller's essential gift; she is brilliant at hooks. She knows to a nicety how much readers need to be told and what they do not need, supplying only the former. Unlike those who sneer at her for writing an old-fashioned school story, she understands that, for young people on the cusp of adolescence, the ideas in such stories to do with loyalty, courage, and deep, painful friendship are powerful and necessary triggers. Well read, she can deploy a rich armory of jokes, allusions and well-chosen names. It may be argued that, in Samuel Taylor COLERIDGE's sense, all this is merely fancy, not imagination, but a healthy literary diet should encompass elements from both these works of the mind. Above all, R. never preaches, but when Harry Potter is assured that he does not belong to the potentially dark House of Slytheryn, although he would have been a success in it, because he did not want to be and "It is our choices . . . that show what we truly are," an essential lesson is quietly slipped under the wire.

That in each volume a mystery is satisfyingly solved, an ally or disguise of Valdermort exposed, gives a strong shape to each. That the projected seven volumes will take the reader right through Harry's secondary schooling reassures young readers that Harry will grow with them, and older ones that the tone is likely to darken appropriately—already in the fourth, *Harry Potter and the Goblet of Fire* (2001), there is a nontrivial death to mar Harry's triumph: perhaps a warning of things to come.

BIBLIOGRAPHY: Bocleshare, J., *A Study of Harry Potter's Novels* (2001); Tucker, N., "The Rise and Rise of Harry Potter," *CLE* 30 (December 1999): 221–34

AUDREY LASKI

RUBENS, Bernice [Ruth]
b. 26 July 1928, Cardiff, Wales

Daughter of Russian Jews, R. read English at the University of Wales and later became a fellow and vice-president of the English Center of International PEN. She has worked in the film industry. Her most famous novel is the 1970 Booker Prize–winning *The Elected*

Member (1969; repub. as *Chosen People*, 1969). Norman, a brilliant barrister, son of a rabbi, is "elected" by his parents to be the family scapegoat, driven to schizophrenia and drug addiction by their exorbitant demands. The story for all its pain has a grim HUMOR. R. has published many books, among them *Madame Sousatzka* (1962), filmed with Shirley Maclaine, directed by John Schlesinger (1988); *Go Tell the Lemming* (1973); *I Sent a Letter to My Love* (1975), filmed subsequently; *The Ponsonby Post* (1977), *A Five Year Sentence* (1978; repub. as *Favours*, 1978), shortlisted for the Booker Prize; *Spring Sonata* (1979); *Birds of Passage* (1981); *Brothers* (1983); *Mr. Wakefield's Crusade* (1985); *Mate in Three* (1989); *Set an Edge* (1989); *Kingdom Come* (1991); *A Solitary Grief* (1991); *Mother Russia* (1992); *Autobiopsy* (1993), *Yesterday in the Back Lane* (1995); and *I , Dreyfus* (2000).

RUDKIN, [James] David
b. 29 June 1936, London

Critics tend to emphasize the intellectual quality of R.'s work. Although the plays clearly reflect scholarly knowledge and rich sources of reference from the Greeks and the Bible to William SHAKESPEARE and philosophy, this approach tends to give the impression that they are unapproachable, neglecting their imaginative and powerful theatricality.

R.'s plays most fully realize the theater proposed by Antoine Artaud: "a serious theater which . . . inspires us with the fiery magnetism of its images and acts upon us like a spiritual therapeutics whose touch can never be forgotten . . . and confronts us with all our possibilities . . . total spectacle . . . addressed to the entire organism." A theater of the imagination, based on myth, constructed through a manipulation of image and language, it reaches to engage the audience through the senses. The enactment of nightmare and dream frees the imagination from the limits of the material world, exposing its construction, confronting fears and proposing fresh possibilities. His manipulation of language reinstates (in Artaud's terms) its incantational, sensual nature, making the familiar unfamiliar and heightening its effect. The arguments take place through image and association creating archetypes elaborating salient issues—the mechanisms of power, the relation of the individual to the social context, individuation, and the manifestation of spirit.

In his first play, *Afore Night Come* (perf. 1962; pub. 1965), two students and an elderly Irish itinerant take on casual work as pear pickers. The technicalities of picking pears and apparently casual conversation among the pickers create a veneer of REALISM. Talk of infertility, the hum of a crop duster, and an impending storm coupled with a focused use of stage and linguistic rhythm create an increasing tension and sense of menace until the ritual murder of the Irishman shatters the fragile surface. The issues raised by the action—the effects of prejudice and superstition, the mass proclivity for scapegoating, salvation through relationship as Johnny Hobnails saves student Larry from implication in the murder—come into focus in reflection, in the aftermath of the growing tension and its horrific release.

The Sons of Light (perf. 1976; pub. 1982) is framed by a familiar formula: a man enters an enclosed world and changes it. The Island of Skaranay is a divided world. Geographically a barren land where natural elements are at odds, it is inhabited by two dissociated groups blind to each other's existence: above ground a religious cult, whose appearance and language suggest puritan throwback, fearfully worship the industrialist Sir Wendell Bain who finances their continuance; below ground, a mine, source of Bain's wealth, where scientist Nebwold dehumanizes the workers using psychology, violence, and a false god. Into this distorted, isolated world, come Pastor Bengry and his three sons, close knit, generously loving in their respect for all of creation and its manifold wonders. Appalled by the islanders' stony hearts, Bengry vows to "turn this painted tabernacle upside down" and breathe the fire of life into this deadened world.

The action is played through a series of macrocosms and microcosms: the divisions of the island reflected in the schizophrenic Child Manatond who both mirrors the process of the island's integration and creates its moral necessity. Biblical references set the action into moral and signifying context, heighten the action by giving it a "mythic" context creating a discernible, archetypal pattern, and invest individual behavior with both social and spiritual content. Thus the action manifests metaphysical considerations to assess the definition and value of human life and consider the relationship of the individual to both society and the natural world. Through the progress of the play, the sons inherit their father's role as central character, as well as his ideals. The younger sons die in the process of revitalising the island, but eventually, John leads the "soldiers" to the surface, bringing his father's vision to fruition. Child Manatond wakes, as if from dream: whole self, bathed in light, completing the realization of an encompassing vision of social and personal transformation.

Triumph of Death (perf. 1981; pub. 1982) takes the form of a medieval pageant moving through time via a series of tableaux vivants in which the Saturnian Papatrix and Mother Manus, embodiment of deathly order, manipulate the language and imagery of Christianity to replace the anarchic and life-giving forces of love with their anal obsession with order and control. In R.'s world, individuals are inherently social, their physicality reflective of the social condition, their individuation achieved through reaching out to others. In *Saxon Shore* (1986), images from history blend with those of horror films to create an experience of social and political strife that echoes in the present. The extremity of the embattled Saxons, squeezed between the native Britons and the departing Romans, is manifested through their transformation into werewolves for night raids on the Britons; their language contributing a justifying context of religion to their guerrilla tactics.

BIBLIOGRAPHY: Brown, D., "D. R.," in Weintraub, S., ed., *British Dramatists since World War II*, part 2, *DLB* 13 (1982): 433–39

ELAINE TURNER

RUMENS, Carol
b. Carol-Ann Lumley, 10 December 1944, London

R. explores human relationships, political situations, European and Russian settings in a wide variety of skillfully crafted poems. Her work particularly emphasizes women's roles and the personal aspect of political circumstances. She has traveled widely and works as a translator, thus her poetry reflects a cosmopolitan background as well as focusing on Belfast, where she has her home.

In her earliest collections, *A Strange Girl in Bright Colours* (1973), *A Necklace of Mirrors* (1978), and *Unplayed Music* (1981), this variety was already evident; the poems are full of colors and sounds, detailed, sensuous descriptions encouraging an unusual or unexpected view of place or situation. The characters R. depicts range from a 17th-c. child commemorated on a cathedral plaque, to a contemporary father trying to make ends meet by mending his children's shoes with pieces from other discarded pairs. She recreates a domestic scene of a mother making a cake and invests it with details of a whole family life; in contrast she depicts the harrowing despair of women in Russia queuing outside a Leningrad jail in fading hope of news of imprisoned loved ones.

The tone of R.'s poetry is often melancholy but there are glimpses of HUMOR and a sense of sympathy is always evident. In the early 1980s, R. published another two volumes, following *Unplayed Music* with *Scenes from the Gingerbread House* (1982) and *Star Whisper* (1983), in which these qualities are extended. She develops a metaphysical quality, combining the everyday and the domestic with philosophical meditation, in poems like "Skins." This is written in one fluent stanza, composed of couplets with both full and half rhymes, creating a musical harmony reflecting the interconnections between human and natural life. A "deal table" is sensuously described "With a silky glissando of dark grain . . . Scrawlings of knife and bottle, child and guest/Have warmed its heart."

In the later 1980s, R. published three further volumes, *Direct Dialling* (1985), *The Greening of Snow Beach* (1988), and *From Berlin to Heaven* (1989). In these volumes, the political elements of the poetry become more universalized by a dislocation created through apparently disjointed fragments, as in "A Blockade Memorial." In this poem, moving descriptions of "graves," "tyre-tracks," the "daily ration" could refer to any place, any people, any time, and the haunting idea of the loss of particular identity in the deprivations and disasters of 20th-c. history is poignantly conveyed. The personal record, R suggests, becomes obsolete in the face of such vast numbers of the dispossessed: "If dry tongues ached against walls and shoe leather—/How could a diary speak?"

In "Leningrad Romance," the details are particularized but the speaker could be any bereft husband and father, "my wife and children—/Perhaps they are just the white ash-fall of night,/Perhaps they are stone." In the second part of the poem, again any woman and any man might be approaching love-making, but R. disturbs the reader with the shock of the description of a bloodied sanitary towel indicating the "safe period." Such detail demonstrates both R.'s resistance to prudishness and euphemism and the ambiguity of language, the phrase describing also a snatched time of comparative peace. In this poem, the skillful repetition of "water" "stone," "burning" and "faded" emphasizes the repetition of violence and destruction of the past century but also offers a tentative hope of nature resurgent. Natural imagery is powerfully employed throughout R.'s work, as illustrated in *Thinking of Skins*, the selected poems published in 1993.

In collections of the later 1990s, *Best China Sky* (1995) and *The Miracle Diet* (1998), R. continues to experiment with a wide variety of form and subject. Her descriptive range moves from the emotional cold of estranged partners in "From a Conversation During Divorce" to the atmospheric cold of "The Stowaway." The form of the former is awkward unrhymed triplets, with frequent repetition of "house" getting "bigger" and "colder," effectively reflecting the awkward strangeness of the former home and dissolved relationship. The latter poem is composed of couplets, with full and half rhymes, long and short lines, complementing contrast in the human and moth relationship explored but also implying, through the title, a sense of concern and empathy for human stowaways caught in an alien environment. In *Best China Sky*, there are also a number of very short, compact poems, one a haiku, which crystallize a particular moment or thought and show yet another aspect of this prolific and always interesting poet.

BIBLIOGRAPHY: Press, J., "C. R.," in Sherry, V. B., Jr., ed., *Poets of Great Britain and Ireland since 1960,* part 2, *DLB* 40 (1985): 497–501; Pykett, L., "Women Poets and 'Women's Poetry': Fleur Adcock, Gillian Clarke, and C. R.," in Day, G., and B. Docherty, eds., *British Poetry from the 1950s to the 1990s* (1997): 253–67

ROSE ATFIELD

RUSHDIE, [Ahmed] Salman
b. 19 June 1947, Bombay, India

There is little question that R. is not only the most renowned contemporary subcontinental novelist writing in English, but that he is also the most famous and successful novelist in England. He has written novels, a SCIENCE FICTION parody, a children's book, and a highly acclaimed collection of short stories. His collection of essays, *Imaginary Homelands* (1991), became a best-seller in both Britain and the U.S. His work combines NATURALISM with all of the best elements of magical realism, HUMOR, and a consistently inventive use of the English language. He is considered by many critics to be one of the most brilliant postmodernist writers in British literature.

Though born in India, R. was educated at one of England's most prestigious public (private) schools, Rugby, and graduated from King's College, Cambridge, in 1968 with honors. Though he moved to Pakistan after his schooling, he returned to England to work in advertising, television, and publishing. His first book, *Grimus* (1975), was a science fiction parody and was, by his own account, a huge commercial failure. Its construction, though, showed R. to be a highly imaginative organizer of disparate materials, particularly in dealing with Asian and Nordic folkloric and mythological materials, a practice that he became even better at in some of his later novels. Critics did praise *Grimus*, though, for its richly humorous use of language.

It was with his first real novel, *Midnight's Children* (1981), that he became, literally, a best-selling author, and the most articulate voice of an emerging contemporary postcolonial literature. The book delighted readers and critics in both India and England; he managed to offend neither audience. It was so critically acclaimed that it won Britain's most prestigious literary award, the Booker Prize, a rare event for an author's first novel. *Midnight's Children* also won the James Tait Black Memorial Prize and "The Booker of Bookers," which was awarded to the best Booker-winning novel of the first twenty-five years of that prize.

The novel's narrator, Saleem Sinai, was born at midnight on August 15, 1947, the date of India's formal declaration of independence from England. Its title refers to the thousand-or-so children born exactly at that hour. R. creates and sustains the narrative history of both Saleem and India from the celebratory atmosphere of their births and throughout both of their turbulent histories, especially during the repressive years of Indira Ghandi's so-called Emergency; that is, the darkest years of her severely authoritarian regime. Her government imprisoned dissidents regularly and even forced certain poor elements of people to be sterilized without their consent. Her propaganda machine brooked no diversion from the party line and forbade any negative comments from the media.

Saleem Sinai is an unreliable narrator primarily because it is virtually impossible to get any kind of honest reporting from either the government or the government-controlled media. Saleem is then thrown back on trusting his own instincts, especially his sense of smell and his inherited sense of telepathy. What emerges, as Saleem awaits execution, is the best he can come up with: imaginative truth. Because he cannot remember what the truth is—he has never experienced it—truth becomes a matter of perspective; illusion becomes as believable, and efficacious, as truth itself. Language formulates Saleem's reality, blending fantasy, memory, and history into a highly entertaining form of POSTMODERNISM.

In R.'s second novel, *Shame* (1983), he continues to use postmodernist techniques to mimic the confusion of modern sensibility. Much of the novel concerns R.'s imaginative recreation of Pakistan, where he lived after graduating from Cambridge. In the novel, R. critically examines those in power in Pakistan, an act which caused the government to ban *Shame* in that country. R. used many fictional techniques which he intertwined with essayistic passages, a mixture that made the work appear to some as a nonfiction novel. The book also addresses the power of language, especially on immigrant populations, and delineates the various ways in which they can become entrapped in the language of their colonizers; the English language becomes one of the major enforcers of imperialism. R. also demonstrates the way shame and humiliation engender violence among immigrant groups; shame becomes for some of them their only method of organizing their lives into some kind of order.

It was R.'s third novel, *The Satanic Verses* (1988), that propelled him into global fame, though detractors of the book would call it infamy. The novel immediately polarized its readers, even though it earned him the prestigious Whitbread Prize in England and the "Author of the Year" award in Germany. Because of certain irreverent references to some of Islam's most sacred tenets, riots broke out in Pakistan, where five Iranians were killed. A Saudi newspaper in London publicly burned copies of the novel in October 1988. And in February 1989, the Ayatollah Khomeini, the religious leader of the Islamic-Iranian revolution, condemned R. to death in a worldwide fatwah; he offered $2.6 million to any Iranian for R.'s assassination, and

$1 million to anyone else. The book was subsequently banned in India, Iran, Bangladesh, Pakistan, and South Africa. The Norwegian publisher of the book was shot in 1993, and the Japanese translator was stabbed to death in 1991.

R.'s most brilliantly organized novel to date, *The Satanic Verses* combines myth, religion, fantasy, and Islamic history in highly imaginative and even humorous ways. The novel begins with the literal fall from grace of two men from an Air India flight, who eventually metamorphose from Gibreel Farishta into the angel Gabriel, and from Saladin Chamcha into Satan. Both characters also become (metamorphosis is a major device throughout the novel) allegorical figures: Gibreel as Everyman looking for spiritual wholeness and Saladin as a divided self torn between East and West. Islamic readers, however, saw R. ridiculing the way a businessman became the Prophet; they regarded the author's satiric treatment of such material as a sacrilegious act. Since many of the characters are English Hindus or Muslims, R. appeared to be satirizing their painful conflicts in trying to preserve their ethnic identity in an alien culture. Fortunately for R., the Iranian government lifted its fatwah in 1998, which allows critics and readers to judge his work on literary rather than political grounds.

The Moor's Last Sigh (1995) was received with much less controversy than *The Satanic Verses*. R. presents the protagonist-narrator, Moraes Zogoiby, in a similar predicament to that of Saleem Sinai of *Midnight's Children*: a death sentence. Zogoiby is given the impossible task of narrating the history of his family, which also parallels the history of Islam. He must accomplish all of this as he sits in his own grave awaiting his execution. Like Scheherazade before him, the longer and more inventive his stories, the longer he is able to delay his death. Zogoiby's own complex cultural diversity mirrors similar conflicts in South India, especially Bombay; and R. takes full advantage of the linguistic possibilities that such a rich mixture of races and languages offers.

The major focus in *The Moor's Last Sigh* is religion, specifically Hindu rather than Islamic fanaticism. But because some Indians believed that R. was mocking certain Hindu political demagogues, the book was initially banned in India when it first appeared. The Moor finds himself trapped between two equally wicked ideologies: materialistic corruption and religious fanaticism. Because human beings have a choice only between two evils, characters begin to fall, literally and symbolically, throughout the novel. But what redeems the dark, fallen world of the Moor is the author's exuberant use of vivid language and colorful metaphors.

In 1999, one of R.'s longest and most critically acclaimed novels appeared, *The Ground beneath Her Feet*. The action of the novel begins on the day that the Ayatollah Khomeini declared the death sentence on R.: Valentine's Day, 1989. The book begins with a literal fall when the heroine is swallowed into an abyss created by an earthquake. It becomes increasingly evident that the author is using the legend of Orpheus and Eurydice on which to build his complex narrative. The atmosphere is surrealistic but the theme is postmodern: the terms of reality are constantly shifting, just as the actual earth does. The mythical Orpheus is embodied in Ormus Cama, a clairvoyant musician of miraculous powers whose genius shares certain characteristics with Bob Dylan, John Lennon, and even Elvis Presley. The mythic Eurydice is Vina Aspara, whose sex goddess attributes resonate with images of Madonna, Princess Diana, and Tina Turner. Most of the novel, after the earthquake, is built on an elaborate flashback of the couple's past lives. R. intertwines complex philosophical discussions with witty anecdotes, all of which are vivified in R.'s typical linguistic virtuosity. Time and apocalypse haunt the novel and create an atmosphere of epistemological and metaphysical destabilization.

While R.'s novel *Fury* (2001) is about half the length of *The Ground beneath Her Feet*, some critics have asserted that *Fury* is his strongest work since *The Moor's Last Sigh*. The narrative focuses on the sudden move of a middle-age professor, Malik Solanka, from England to New York City, the vortex of western capitalism. He virtually abandons his wife and young son and seems to be running away from his all-consuming sense of anger with the world and himself. Confronted with the brutal, self-destructive excesses of a materialistic society, Solanka realizes that if he doesn't conquer his terrifying fury, he will also self-destruct. His inward journey takes him through dangerous love affairs that offer him temporal relief in a soulless society. Neither financial success nor relentless sexual escapades seem to quench his yearning for peace. Solanka discovers that only genuine human connection—open, free, and selfless—might release him from his spiritual demons. R.'s language is as inventive and humorous as his best past work.

Though R. attained global fame—or infamy—only after he was placed under a death sentence, his novels, short stories, and essays have demonstrated that he is unquestionably one of contemporary British literature's most honored and respected writers. Few English novelists have so successfully, or accurately, presented the plight of the marginalized immigrant with such poignancy, care, and humor as he. He has also managed the seemingly impossible task of criticizing the mainstream reading audience in both England and South Asia even though he has also suffered the pain of his own cultural marginalization.

BIBLIOGRAPHY: Appignanesi, L., and S. Maitland, eds., *The R. File* (1990); Brennan, T., *S. R. and the Third World: Myths of the Nation* (1989); Dhawan, R. K., *The Novels of S. R.* (1992); Pipes, D., *The R. Affair: The Novel, the Ayatollah, and the West* (1990)

PATRICK MEANOR

RUSKIN, John

b. 8 February 1819, London; d. 20 January 1900, Coniston, Lancashire [now Cumbria]

R. made his name as a critic of painting and architecture and, despite the limitations of his taste, remains the most powerful writer on visual art in the English language. But art is only one facet of a massive oeuvre of amazing range and complexity. In his lifetime, R. published some 230 titles and the Library Edition of *The Works of John Ruskin* (1903–12) runs to thirty-nine huge quarto volumes. The topics he wrote on include geology, botany and other aspects of natural history, economics, labor and the social ills of his day, literature, religion, anthropology, history, and education. As a master of English prose, he has few rivals, though for modern readers the richness of his writing can make for difficulties. Outside his literary work, he was a striking draughtsman and watercolorist, and the illustrations to his books, whose engraving he oversaw, are works of considerable artistic importance. He was also a connoisseur and art collector, a philanthropist and social reformer, an inspiring drawing-master and professor of fine art. The spread of R.'s influence is as wide as that of his work. His writings crucially affected the Gothic Revival in architecture, though rarely to his satisfaction. He inspired the Pre-Raphaelite painters and the Arts and Crafts movement. He campaigned for the establishment and development of public galleries, libraries, and schools of art and design. His social criticism influenced the British Labour movement and the growth of the Welfare State. A major prophet of conservationism, he opposed the destruction of ancient buildings through what was called "restoration" and the violation of natural beauty by industrial development. Among the great figures who acknowledged him as an influence were Tolstoy, Gandhi, Marcel Proust, William MORRIS, and Bernard SHAW.

R. was the only child of wealthy, middle-aged parents. His father, a successful sherry-merchant and a self-made man, was keen on Romantic art and literature. His mother, a devout Evangelical, was responsible for both the narrowness of his early beliefs and the depth of his biblical knowledge. His parents provided him with his wealth and the substance of his intellectual life, but through their obsessive devotion to him, left him emotionally confused and vulnerable. He was, however, precocious. By the age of twenty-two, he had written and in some cases published a substantial body of poetry, some articles on Alpine geology, a set of essays on vernacular building (later collected as *The Poetry of Architecture*, 1873), and *The King of the Golden River* (1851), a beautiful children's story, which is also the first attempt by a named English writer to imitate the traditional fairy tale. All this early work reflects R.'s love for the Alps and for mountain landscape in general.

That love is also present in his first book, the first of the five volumes of *Modern Painters* (1843–60). This great project began as a defense of R.'s lifelong hero J. M. W. Turner, the paintings of whose old age were increasingly attacked in the periodicals. Over the seventeen years of its composition, it grew into an account of landscape art as the homage paid by humanity to the beauty of God's creation. It therefore repudiates conventionalism in art in favor of "Truth to Nature." But it also deals with much more than modern painting. It deals with the Old Masters, especially those of Renaissance Italy, and it includes analyses of natural forms and structures, evocative descriptions of actual views, reflections on the Bible, and some splendid literary criticism. Above all, it registers the importance for R. of sight: "To see clearly . . .," he writes, "is poetry, prophecy, and religion—all in one."

Like Turner, and like another hero Sir Walter SCOTT, R. had absorbed the Romantic fashion for medieval architecture. While working on 15th-c. painting for the second volume of *Modern Painters* (1846), he began to fear for the medieval heritage, threatened by wholesale and insensitive restoration as well as by the advances of modern life. This concern resulted in a detailed exploration of the value of Romanesque and Gothic building that for some years drew him away from *Modern Painters*. *The Seven Lamps of Architecture* (1849) was followed in 1851 and 1853 by the three volumes of *The Stones of Venice*. His discovery in 1845 of the then-forgotten Venetian painter Jacopo Tintoretto provoked an enquiry into the social roots of art. R.'s childhood love of Venice had been fueled by Turner's paintings of the city and by the poems of Lord BYRON, but his temperament was more than ready to respond to an architecture rich in color and encrusted with gorgeous materials and decorative sculpture. It also responded to the magic of a city in the sea: a great communal artifact intimately connected to the challenges of nature. R. came to the view, however, that the modern decay of Venice had begun with the decline of her medieval faith. The blame lay with Renaissance humanism. The Venetian buildings valued by R. were Gothic and Byzantine, not classical, and their beauty reflected their society's moral health. In other words, the book expresses the modern view of art as historically rooted in particular social formations and codes of belief. It led R. to the conclusion that the failure of his own society to produce what he judged great art was due to a condition of moral sickness. In the central chapter

of volume 2, "The Nature of Gothic," he links the richness of Gothic decoration to the medieval workman's creative freedom and contrasts that with the life in Victorian factories. The greed and inhumanity of capitalist society were at odds with Judaeo-Christian teaching and condemned the great mass of R.'s compatriots to a life devoid of spiritual or aesthetic consolation.

The art critic thus became a social reformer. In 1860, having completed *Modern Painters,* R. began his attempt to account for the malaise of modern life. *Unto this Last* (1862) is the most forcefully condensed of R.'s books and the one he most valued himself: an indictment of capitalist economics and the doctrines of laissez-faire. His standpoint, historically, is that of the agrarian conservative with deep roots in biblical morality, though with his vision of an ordered and interdependent community, he anticipates much in ethical Socialism. His argument reaches its climax with the aphorism "THERE IS NO WEALTH BUT LIFE," which encapsulates his teaching in all his writings. He never succeeded in building on this impassioned critique a convincing account of how the just economy might be organized, though several later books began the attempt: *Munera Pulveris* (six essays, 1862–63), *Time and Tide* (1867), and parts of *Fors Clavigera* (96 letters, 1871–84).

In the course of the 1850s, R. had become a critic of contemporary art who could make or break reputations. In 1851, in a series of letters to the *Times* newspaper, he had defended the young Pre-Raphaelite painters against their detractors in the press and had published a pamphlet on modern art that, acknowledging his hopes for these artists, he called *Pre-Raphaelitism* (1851). Between 1855 and 1859, he issued *Academy Notes*, his annual critiques of new pictures exhibited at the Royal Academy. His enthusiasm for Turner, who had died in 1851, was undiminished. It expressed itself in his work as Turner's executor, in several descriptive catalogues, and in his "illustrative text" to the Turner engravings entitled *The Harbours of England* (1856). R.'s social concerns caused him to offer his services as an unpaid drawing-master to the voluntary Working Men's College in London. Some of his consequent discoveries are recorded in three teaching primers: *The Elements of Drawing* (1857), *The Elements of Perspective* (1859), and later on *The Laws of Fésole* (1879). Other enthusiasms manifest themselves in a Platonic dialogue on crystallography, *The Ethics of the Dust* (1866), and some lectures on Greek religion, *The Queen of the Air* (1869).

In the 1850s and 1860s, R. was in demand as a public lecturer, a role he relished and used to powerful effect. During this period, his religious faith had begun to be shaken, reaching a crisis with what he called his "unconversion" in 1858, but something of his Evangelical background found its way into his lecturing manner as he preached "the religion of humanity." *The Queen of the Air* was the sixth published collection of his lectures. It was preceded by *Lectures on Architecture and Painting* (1854), *The Political Economy of Art* (1857; rev. and repub. as *A Joy Forever*, 1880), *The Two Paths* (1859), *Sesame and Lilies* (1865), and *The Crown of Wild Olive* (1866). R.'s lectures strikingly interweave diverse subject matter, social and aesthetic, one consequence of which is the startling variety of tone.

R.'s appointment in 1870 as first Slade Professor of Fine Art at Oxford University led to some major changes in his work. The first and most obvious result was the Slade lectures. Those published by R. himself are as follows: *Lectures on Art* (1870); *Aratra Pentelici* (1872) on sculpture; *The Eagle's Nest* (1872) on art and science; *The Relation between Michael Angelo and Tintoret* (1872); *Love's Meinie* (3 parts, 1873) on birds; *Val d'Arno* (1874) on Tuscan art; *Ariadne Fiorentina* (1876) on engraving; *The Art of England* (7 parts, 1883–84), and *The Pleasures of England* (4 parts, 1885).

The second effect of the professorship was a number of books designed to back up the lessons he wished to teach with what was supposed to be—but rarely was—solid information. Some of these were guidebooks of a sort, notably *Mornings in Florence* (6 parts, 1875–77) and a new account of Venice, *St. Mark's Rest* (6 parts, 1877–84). Others were books on natural history, written on the understanding that "all great art is the expression of man's delight in God's work, not in *his own*." These were *Proserpina* (10 parts, 1875–86) on flowers and *Deucalion* (6 parts, 1875–79) on geology. Both are connected with two of the lecture volumes: *Love's Meinie* and *The Eagle's Nest*. In spite of their overt subjects, these are personal books, reflecting their author's growing emotional turmoil and raising a challenge to Darwinism.

But the most important effect of R.'s Oxford Chair was *Fors Clavigera*. This huge work consists of ninety-six monthly letters "to the Workmen and Labourers of Great Britain." Conscious of how his academic responsibilities would restrict the range of his attention, R. invented this new genre which enabled him to deal with any matter of any kind that happened to be concerning him. The emphasis, as the dedication suggests, was meant to be social, though few working people can have been sufficiently educated to follow his drift. The book reveals a lonely man at odds with the direction of modern life and on the edge of despair. Even more than the lectures, it startles the reader with its unpredictability. It moves from apocalyptic diatribe to observed physical fact, from vehement SATIRE to vulnerable confession. It is both solemn and funny. As recent critics have argued, the

quotations, the sudden juxtapositions, the conflations of historical time, and the contrasts of register anticipate the methods of MODERNISM, notably in *The Cantos* of Ezra Pound.

Fors is a masterpiece. Nevertheless, most of R.'s writings of the 1870s are disfigured by rant and the loss of a sense of proportion. Almost all of them, moreover, are unfinished. These weaknesses foreshadow a catastrophe. In 1878, he suffered the first of eight mental breakdowns. These shattered the remainder of his life, though he continued to write momentous, if fragmentary, works. In several writings of the early 1880s, he revisited his thoughts on Gothic architecture. The most important of these is *The Bible of Amiens* (5 parts, 1880–85). The last and most apocalyptic of his public lecture series is *The Storm-Cloud of the Nineteenth Century* (2 parts, 1884), overtly a book on meteorology but imbued with the moral force of a Hebrew prophet. During this period, he gathered together his many letters to the press, *Arrows of the Chace* (2 vols., 1880), and several occasional articles and essays, *On the Old Road* (2 vols., 1885). The latter includes "Fiction, Fair and Foul," five essays on the 19th-c. novel.

R.'s last book is his unfinished AUTOBIOGRAPHY, *Praeterita* (28 parts, 1886–89). It is far from flawless. The narrative is episodic, consisting mostly of cameos and epiphanies, and does not reach far beyond the author's thirties. As he admits in his preface, it speaks "of what it gives me joy to remember" and is silent about "things which I have no pleasure in reviewing." Yet as those expressions suggest, it is a great lyrical study of memory and the power of the mind to transcend its circumstances. By turns poetic, witty, and ruminative, *Praeterita* is astonishingly serene for a book written on the verge of madness. The prose, mostly conversational in manner, is as beautiful as any in R.'s oeuvre.

R.'s books are sadly uneven. They are prone to overstatement, dogmatism, and sentimentality—all weaknesses connected with his emotional instability. Yet there is hardly a page in his work that does not contain some insight of startling interest, some uniquely felicitous phrase, or some object closely observed. At his best, moreover, he achieves a balance of acute perception and just emotional force. Of particular value is his ability to earth his ethical and spiritual concerns in the realm of stubborn, intractable matter. It was R. who coined the phrase "pathetic fallacy" for conscious literary solipsism. In describing it sympathetically, he also recorded his admiration for artists who can rise above such devices and render the actual world in all its otherness. He was himself such an artist.

The breakdown that interrupted *Praeterita* ended R.'s creative life. He lived on in silent retirement for ten more years. In the new century, at whose dawn he died, his reputation faded. His invisible influence, however, has never really weakened. It has been at its greatest in the social and environmental spheres. Yet it is also clear that modernists in several of the arts were profoundly affected by him too, though most of them found it politic to dismiss the Victorian patriarch. Proust and Marianne Moore were content to acknowledge the influence. Pound was not, though the presence of R. in his work is inescapable and so has been passed on to subsequent writers. In the 1960s, R.'s reputation began to recover and, by the turn of another century, it had again become possible to talk of him as one of the giants of English thought and literature.

BIBLIOGRAPHY: Birch, D., *R.'s Myths* (1988); Hewison, R., *J. R.* (1976); Hewison, R., I. Warrell, and S. Wildman, *R., Turner and the Pre-Raphaelites* (2000); Hilton, T., *J. R.: The Early Years* (1985); Hilton, T., *J. R.: The Later Years* (2000); Hobson, J. A., *J. R., Social Reformer* (1898); Leon, D., *R. the Great Victorian* (1949); Rosenberg, J. D., *The Darkening Glass: A Portrait of R.'s Genius* (1961); Unrau, J., *R. and St. Mark's* (1984); Wheeler, M., *R.'s God* (1999)

CLIVE WILMER

RUSSELL, Bertrand [Arthur William]

b. 18 May 1872, Trelleck, Monmouthshire, Wales; d. 2 February 1970, Penrhyndeudraeth, Merionethshire, Wales

Awarded the Nobel Prize for Literature in 1950, R. was one of the major intellectual figures of the 20th c. He was a prolific author whose career spanned more than seven decades and produced some one hundred works of fiction, nonfiction, journalism, mathematical and philosophical treatises, and AUTOBIOGRAPHY. At once provocative and controversial, R. was an outspoken critic on diverse social, political, and environmental issues. His widespread notoriety was in part responsible for his status as a best-selling author and contemporary opinion is that R.'s literary and historical reputation has generally declined.

Educated at Cambridge, R. published his first work, *German Social Democracy*, in 1896, followed in the next year by *An Essay on the Foundations of Geometry*. His *Philosophical Essays* (1910; rev. ed., 1966) preceded his most important mathematical work, *Principia Mathematica* (3 vols., 1910–13), written in collaboration with Alfred North WHITEHEAD. Opposed to British involvement in the First World War, R. was dismissed from his lectureship at Trinity College, Cambridge, and later imprisoned for six months as the result of his pacifist activities. During this period, R. established his reputation as a political writer, notably with publications such as *The Philosophy of Pacifism* (1915), *Political Ideals* (1917),

and *Roads to Freedom: Socialism, Anarchism and Syndicalism* (1918; repub. as *Proposed Roads to Freedom: Socialism, Anarchism and Syndicalism*, 1919). In 1920, he published *The Practice and Theory of Bolshevism* (repub. as *Bolshevism: Practice and Theory*, 1920) followed in the next year by *The Analysis of Mind*.

Throughout the 1920s and 1930s, R. continued to publish on a wide variety of topics including international affairs (*The Problem of China*, 1922); science (*The ABC of Relativity*, 1925); religion (*Why I Am Not a Christian*, 1927); philosophy (*The Conquest of Happiness*, 1930); education (*Education and the Social Order*, 1932; repub. as *Education and the Modern World*, 1932); pacifism (*Which Way to Peace?*, 1936); and politics (*Power: A New Social Analysis*, 1938), and in 1945 published his best-known work, *A History of Western Philosophy: Its Connection with Political and Social Circumstances from the Earliest Times to the Present*.

In the early 1950s, R. became increasingly active in global politics, especially the nuclear disarmament movement, and published works of social conscience such as *New Hope for a Changing World* (1951), *The Impact of Science on Society* (1952), *How Near Is War?* (1952), *Human Society in Ethics and Politics* (1954), and *Common Sense and Nuclear Warfare* (1960). During this same time, he also produced two collections of short stories, *Satan in the Suburbs* (1953) and *Nightmares of Eminent Persons* (1954). In 1955, he left England to live in a remote area of northern Wales but remained productive as a writer and committed to social and political activism. Later works include *Fact and Fiction* (1961), *Unarmed Victory* (1963), and *War and Atrocity in Vietnam* (1965). His autobiography appeared in three volumes, published from 1967 to 1969, and in 1972 his *Collected Stories* were published posthumously.

BIBLIOGRAPHY: Clark, R. W., *The Life of B. R.* (1976); Grayling, A. C., *R.* (1996); Moorehead, C., *B. R.* (1992); Ryan, A., *B. R.* (1993); Schoenman, R., ed., *B. R.* (1967)

RUSSELL, George William

(pseud.: Æ) b. 10 April 1867, Lurgan, County Armagh, Ireland; d. 17 July 1935, Bournemouth

Irish poet and mystical painter, R. adopted the pseudonym Æ thanks to a printer's error that confused the scribbled pen name Aeon. An Ulsterman, he was educated at Rathmines School, Dublin, and progressed to the Metropolitan School of Art, where he met W. B. YEATS, with whom he shared an interest in theosophy. In 1902, R.'s poetic drama *Deirdre* was performed with Yeats's *Cathleen Ni Houlihan* by the Irish National Theatre (later the Abbey Theatre, of which R.

was a founder member.) His first collection of poetry, *Homeward: Songs by the Way* (1894), was followed by *The Earth Breath* (1897), *The Divine Vision* (1904), *Voices of the Stones* (1925), *Vale* (1931), and *The House of the Titans* (1934). In addition to publishing poetry, R. joined the Irish Agricultural Organization and organized agriciultural societies. He also worked as a journalist and in 1923 he became editor of the *Irish Statesman.*

RUSSELL, Peter

b. 16 September 1921, Bristol; d. 22 January 2003, San Giovanni Valdarno, Italy

R. has defined his ideal of the "doctus poeta" as "one who draws imaginatively on the heirloom of all our culture from the Paleolithic to the present without the ideological filters of creeds and conventions"; he has written bitterly of "the sort of rootless POSTMODERN-ISM which considers nothing earlier than Marx, Nietzsche and Freud." R.'s own work, like that of Ezra Pound, who he has more than once described as his "master," is certainly rooted in a soil much older and richer than that of postmodernism. Indeed, the range of R.'s reference and quotation, the chronological and linguistic range of the materials on which he draws, and that he transforms in his poetry, can often present the reader with difficulties. His sources and influences range from Plato to Hāfiz, Dante to Blok, and Ficino to Jung (to name but a few). He has translated poetry from all the major European languages, from Persian and Arabic, from Russian—he was the earliest (and remains one of the best) English translator of Osip Mandelshtam. He has written prolifically and the new reader is likely to feel somewhat overwhelmed by the sheer quantity of R.'s work, to be lost as to where to start.

R.'s lyrics provide one relatively easy point of access. The best of the lyrics contained in *The Golden Chain* (1970) are exquisite in their craftsmanship and formal beauty, profoundly resonant in their use of traditional symbols. Poems such as "The Golden Chain" and "Late Winter Spring" remind one that R. is a fitting heir to W. B. YEATS as well as to Pound. The same volume also contains the remarkable nine poems that make up the sequence "Manuela's Poems," a modern dream-vision of compelling power and authenticity. In another branch of the lyric, the sonnet, R. has claims to be regarded as an important modern master. R. has written sonnets throughout his poetic career—a career that began with the collection *Picnic to the Moon* (1944)—and they constitute a fascinating record of the development of his mind. Some of the best were gathered in *Towards an Unknown Life* (1997), but many more remain uncollected. A recent collection, *Sonetti*, was published in a bilingual Italian-English edition in 2000. An earlier bilingual edi-

tion (R. has largely lived in Italy since 1964), *Teorie e altre liriche* (1990) collects a large group of poems in quatrains, including epigrams and ballads, metaphysical arguments, and narratives.

R. has also produced work of the highest quality in some longer contemplative poems, many of which were published together in *Elemental Discourses* (1981) and the nature of which was well described by the poet himself in the long (and brilliant) introduction to that volume as, in intention, "sacred spaces cut out of the chaos of the profane consciousness, spaces in which to consider and observe." The best of the forty poems in *Elemental Discourses*—they include "Missing a Bus," "The Holy Virgin of Mileseva," and "The Act of Love"—are themselves persuasive evidence for R.'s claim, in a lecture delivered in 1996, that "poetry, in its sublimest conception is the language of the Spirit." R.'s finest "contemplative" poem, *Paysages Légendaires*, was first published in 1971; it is a celebration of spirit and landscape (and of their relationship), an affirmation of the re-creative power of memory, beautifully balanced in its interplay of abstract and concrete, image and idea. R. is not, however, only a poet of the loftier areas of the spirit. He is also a satirist and epigrammatist capable of a telling savagery, acerbic in his assault on what he judges to be phony or evil, but also capable of a tolerant amusement at human absurdity. (A substantial selection was published in *Malice Aforethought* in 1981; many later specimens remain uncollected). Both amusement (not always tolerant!) and a moving profundity have characterized R.'s treatment of old age and death in some remarkable poems of recent years (e.g., "My Last Birthday").

One of the most astonishing and fascinating areas of R.'s work as a poet relates to his invention of the late Roman poet Quintilius. In *The Elegies of Quintilius* (1975; rev. ed., 1996) and *From the Apocalypse of Quintilius* (1997), R. "translates" the work of a nomadic Latin poet in search of Truth and Beauty, of knowledge of God and the ideal woman. Quintilius is intimately familiar with pretty well the whole corpus of classical literature and the writings of the Church Fathers; he is an acquaintance of Proclus and a correspondent of Augustine. But "he" also knows the work of Goethe and William SHAKESPEARE, Baudelaire and Giacomo Leopardi. Both comic and profound, remarkably various in form and tone, the Quintilius poems are full of wit and scholarship, of impudent inventiveness and, simultaneously, of spiritual vision and philosophical seriousness. These poems, in their subtle use of pseudo-translation and persona, show how "influence" may be a matter of liberation rather than anxiety; through Quintilius, R. is able to write of one age of cultural decline and confusion (the 5th c. C.E.) and, in doing so, to offer ironic commentary on another such age—our own.

Dana Gioia has described R. as "one of contemporary poetry's few genuine originals." Thomas Fleming has called him "the last of the great modernists." His estrangement from the literary establishment in London, along with the publication of much of his work in relatively fugitive editions, has militated against widespread recognition of his achievement, but the signs are that this is changing.

BIBLIOGRAPHY: Hogg, J., ed., *The Road to Parnassus* (1996); Johnson, A. L., *Studies in the Poetry of P. R.* (1995); Pursglove, G., *A Bibliography of P. R.* (1995); special R. issue, *SwR* 19 (2000)

GLYN PURSGLOVE

RUTHERFORD, Mark

(pseud. of William Hale White) b. 22 December 1831, Bedford; d. 14 March 1913, Groombridge, Sussex

Educated for the Congregational ministry, R. became prey to doubts and in 1854 entered the civil service, supplementing his income by journalism and later working for John Chapman, publisher of the *Westminster Review,* and meeting George ELIOT. R. made his name with three novels "edited" by "His Friend, Reuben Shapcott": *The Autobiography of Mark Rutherford, Dissenting Minister* (1881), a thinly disguised account of his own disillusion with his coreligionists, *Mark Rutherford's Deliverance* (1885), and *The Revolution in Tanner's Lane* (1887), which deals with Dissent, radical politics, and life among the working class. These books nostalgically analyze the decay of the Puritan tradition and the author's journey, characteristic of his era, toward agnosticism. However, intimate knowledge of the Bible and the Puritan habit of self-examination pervade R.'s work. As William Hale White, R. translated Spinoza's *Ethic* (1883; rev. ed., 1894) and *Tractatus de Intellectus Emendatione* (1895). Later books are *Miriam's Schooling and Other Papers* (1890); *Catherine Furze* (2 vols., 1893); *Clara Hopgood* (1896); *Pages from a Journal with Other Papers* (1900), a collection of stories and essays; and under his own name a BIOGRAPHY of John BUNYAN

(1905), for which he was well qualified, having been born in Bunyan's native town and reared as a member of the Bunyan Meeting religious sect. There is also *More Pages from a Journal* (1910) and the posthumous *Last Pages* (1915), edited by his wife, Dorothy V. White.

BIBLIOGRAPHY: Harland, C., "M. R.," in Nadel, I. B., ed., *Victorian Novelists after 1885, DLB* 18 (1983): 258–70; Merton, S., *M. R.* (1967)

RYMER, Thomas

b. 1643, probably in Yafforth, Yorkshire; d. 13 December 1713, London

R. is best probably in remembered, when he is remembered at all, for calling William SHAKESPEARE's *Othello* "a bloody farce" that "First, . . . may be a caution to all Maidens of Quality how, without their Parents consent, they run away with Blackamoors. . . . Secondly, . . . a warning to all good Wives, that they look well to their Linnen. Thirdly, . . . a lesson to Husbands, that before their Jealousie be tragical, the proofs be Mathematical." Yet in the 17th c., he was a critic second in importance only to John DRYDEN. His 1674 translation of René Rapin's *Reflections on Aristotle's Treatise of Poesie* made French neo-Aristotelean theories accessible to English readers. In *The Tragedies of the Last Age Consider'd and Examin'd by the Practice of the Ancients* (1678) he sided with the ancients against the moderns in their literary debate. Although he here claimed to judge plays by common sense, that logic invariably led him to neoclassical rules of decorum. He insisted that tragedies exhibit "poetic justice," a phrase he coined, that they present ideal characters and universal truths. *A Short View of Tragedy* (1693) again praised classical Greek tragedy, briefly traced the history of the genre, and most notoriously condemned *Othello*. In late 1692, R. was appointed historiographer royal. Instructed to collect all English treaties, before his death he had edited fifteen volumes and gathered the material for volume sixteen of these, which were published as *Foedera* (20 vols., 1704–35).

S

SACKVILLE, Charles, Sixth Earl of Dorset

b. 29 January 1643, probably at Copt Hall, Essex; d. 29 January 1706, Bath

S. was a favorite of King Charles II and later served as Lord Chamberlain to King William III. He was patron to John DRYDEN and Matthew PRIOR. John Wilmot, Earl of ROCHESTER, admired S. as satirist. S. was later praised by Alexander POPE as one of the wittiest poets of his day. His reputation now rests on a handful of lyrics, twelve of which were collected in *Poetical Miscellanies* (1704). Most of S.'s verses circulated privately, but in 1665 he wrote a celebrated song, "To All You Ladies Now at Land," composed at sea during the Second Dutch War.

SACKVILLE, Thomas

b. 1536, Buckhurst, Sussex; d. 19 April 1608, London

First Earl of Dorset, Baron Buckhurst, S. was an eloquent and important statesman for ELIZABETH I and during the early reign of JAMES I. He became chancellor of Oxford University. His importance to English letters rests almost entirely upon his contributions to the second edition of *A Mirror for Magistrates* (1563), for which he wrote the induction and the "Complaint of Buckingham," and his participation in the first English blank-verse play, *Gorboduc; or, Ferrex and Porrex* (perf. 1562; pub. 1565; repub. as *The Tragidie of Ferrex and Porrex*, 1570), for which he wrote the final two acts. The play is based on a tale from GEOFFREY OF MONMOUTH's *Historia Regum Britanniae*. Gorboduc and Videna are king and queen in legendary Britain and their sons Ferrex and Porrex quarrel, Porrex killing his brother. Videna kills Porrex and civil war ends with the deaths of king and queen. With characters instead of personifications, the play was an important step in the development of English drama, two years before the birth of William SHAKESPEARE. In the induction to *Mirror*, the most famous part of the work, the poet describes his descent into Hell led by

Sorrow. S. wrote *Gorboduc* in collaboration with Thomas NORTON to address the troubling question of Elizabeth's successor. S.'s writing is stately and controlled and won the praise of Sir Philip SIDNEY in his *Apologie for Poetrie*. It was S. who pronounced the death sentence on Mary Queen of Scots in 1586 and sat to judge the Essex conspiracy trial in 1600.

SACKVILLE-WEST, Vita

b. 9 March 1892, Knole Castle, Sevenoaks, Kent; d. 2 June 1962, Sissinghurst Castle, Cranbrook, Kent

Immortalized by Virginia WOOLF in her fantasy novel *Orlando*, S.-W.—who published as V. Sackville-West—was descended from one of England's most aristocratic families and enjoyed a prolific literary career as a novelist, poet, and biographer. Educated privately at home, she briefly attended a girls' school in London as a teenager. At age twenty, she married Harold NICOLSON and assumed the role of a diplomat's wife while pursuing her own ambition of becoming a writer.

S.-W. published her first collection of poetry, *Poems of East and West*, in 1917, followed in 1919 with the publication of her highly praised novel, *Heritage*. Her reputation, however, was tarnished by her scandalous affair with Violet Keppel (later Trefusis) that informed her romance novel entitled *Challenge* (1923). In the early 1920s, S.-W. was introduced to Woolf and other members of the BLOOMSBURY GROUP; and with Woolf she formed both a personal relationship and lifelong friendship. During this time, she also gained increasing recognition as an author, and the publication in 1926 of her poem *The Land* was awarded the Hawthornden Prize.

In 1930, S.-W. and Nicolson purchased Sissinghurst Castle and began restoring the property and developing the gardens. The publication in that same year of her best-selling novel *The Edwardians* was followed by *All Passion Spent* (1931) and *Family History* (1932). In 1933, she published her *Collected*

Poems, followed in the next year by her novel *The Dark Island*. Her creativity declined in the early 1940s after Woolf's suicide in 1941, but the publication in 1946 of her full-length poem *The Garden* received the Heinemann Award for Literature (1947). In the 1950s, she published another novel, *The Easter Party* (1953), several works on gardening, and a BIOGRAPHY of Anne Marie Louise d'Orleans (1959). In 1961, she published her last novel, *No Signposts in the Sea*.

BIBLIOGRAPHY: Glendinning, V., *Vita: The Life of V. S.-W.* (1983); Nicolson, N., *Portrait of a Marriage* (1973); Stevens, M., *V. S.-W.* (1973); Watson, S. R., *V. S-W.* (1972)

SAKI. See MUNRO, Hector Hugh

SANDYS, George
b. 2 March 1578, Bishopthorpe; d. 4 March 1644, Boxley, near Maidstone, Kent

S. studied at Mary Hall, Oxford, but took no degree. He traveled through France to Venice, Constantinople, Egypt, Palestine, Cyprus, Sicily, Naples, and Rome. His *A Relation of a Journey begun. an. Dom. 1610, in four books, Containing a Description of the Turkish Empire, of Egypt, of the Holy Land, of the Remote Parts of Italy and Islands Adjoining* was published in 1615 and formed a substantial contribution to geography and cultural anthropology. In April 1621, S. sailed to Virginia as colonial treasurer of the Virginia Company, returning in 1631. He had already published an English translation of part of Ovid's *Metamorphoses,* completed in 1626, which formed the basis of his poetic reputation in the 17th and 18th cs. He also began, but did not finish, a version of Virgil's *Aeneid* and in 1636 published his famous *Paraphrase upon the Psalms of David and upon the Hymns Dispersed throughout the Old and New Testaments*; in 1640, he translated *Christ's Passion* from the Latin of Grotius and in 1641 issued a *Paraphrase upon the Song of Solomon.*

SASSOON, Siegfried [Loraine]
b. 8 September 1886, Brenchley, Kent; d. 1 September 1967 Heytesbury, Wiltshire

S. is the most important English poet to survive front-line service in the First World War and is rivaled only by his friend Wilfred OWEN as the most important poetic spokesman of those who fought in the trenches. S.'s war poems began as stirring celebrations of military glory in the vein of his mentor Rupert BROOKE but then became bitter denunciations of the pointless sufferings inflicted on the soldier. That transformation for many symbolized the changing attitude of an entire generation. S. also chronicled the war in two prose narratives, one fictional and one autobiographical, in which he both recalled the idyllic England that existed before the war and chronicled the upheavals that destroyed it.

Although S. was descended from a wealthy Jewish family, he was reared on a country estate as part of the English gentry. His father, who had been disowned by his family on marrying an Anglican, left his wife early in S.'s childhood. S. began writing poetry while at Marlborough School, but his interests were as least as much sporting as academic. He spent two years at Clare College, Cambridge, but left without taking a degree. In the years leading up to the war, he lived at his mother's country house, reading, foxhunting, golfing, and producing ten privately printed books of verse. He enlisted in a cavalry regiment days before war broke out with Germany in 1914.

In 1915, S. sought and received a commission in the Royal Welch Fusiliers, an infantry regiment whose officers included the poet Robert GRAVES. He proved to be a daring soldier and was awarded the Military Cross. During a medical leave in England in 1916, he began associating with pacifists, including Bertrand RUSSELL. He was wounded the next year during the battle of Arras, and while recovering in England, he wrote "A Soldier's Declaration," denouncing the war. S.'s manifesto was published in the *Times* and discussed in the House of Commons. S. envisioned becoming a martyr to the antiwar cause, but Graves intervened to save him. He suggested that S. be treated not as a mutineer but as a victim of shell shock. The War Office found that a diplomatic way of handling the embarrassment of a decorated officer protesting the war, and S. was sent to a military psychiatric hospital, where he was treated by Dr. W. H. R. Rivers. While there, he met Owen, who was also being treated for shell shock, and encouraged him in his poetry. S. came to feel he could not remain in safety while his comrades were still in the trenches and sought to return to active service. Now a company commander, he served in Palestine and again in France, where he was wounded once more in July 1918.

S.'s most famous poems were published during and just after the war in the collections, *The Old Huntsman* (1917), *Counter-Attack* (1918), and *The War Poems of Siegfried Sassoon* (1919). His later verse never matched the popularity or critical esteem of these volumes. S. achieved success again, however, in prose. In 1928, he published *Memoirs of a Fox-Hunting Man*, the first of the three novels that would be collected as *The Complete Memoirs of George Sherston* (1937). That novel and the two that follow it, *Memoirs of an Infantry Officer* (1930) and *Sherston's Progress* (1936), follow S.'s life through the war very closely: Rivers is even presented with his real name.

Perhaps to distance himself from his subject, S. trims all the intellectual interests from the character who represents him and published the first two volumes anonymously in their first editions. The novels show S., despite a postwar flirtation with socialism, yearning for the aristocratic England of his youth.

Soon after finishing his fictionalized autobiography, S. told the story of his life through the war years once again in three memoirs, *The Old Century and Seven More Years* (1938), *The Weald of Youth* (1942), and *Siegfried's Journey, 1916–1920* (1945). He also continued to write poetry, which began to take on a devotional cast. S. became a Roman Catholic late in life. That development was perhaps surprising after the war poems, which seemed to scorn God the Father along with the rest of the "higher-ups" who left men suffering in the trenches.

BIBLIOGRAPHY: Corrigan, F., *S. S.* (1973); Moeyes, P., *S. S.* (1997); Sternlicht, S., *S. S.* (1993); Wilson, J. M., *S. S.* (1997)

BRIAN ABEL RAGEN

SATIRE

Literary satire is a form or mode of writing the principal purpose of which is punitive. As noted by Wyndham LEWIS in his introduction to the 1955 edition of *The Apes of God*, "At the word 'satire' one thinks of institutions and of persons being subjected to punishment of a penal intensity." The satiric composition, whether a poem, play, or prose work, attempts to shame its subject. A work of wit, satire employs such resources as irony and invective, diminution and derision, innuendo and allusion, parody and pastiche in order to expose malpractice and corruption, folly and vice. Some of the funniest works in the language are satires, but HUMOR in true satire is a means to the satirist's end, not the end itself. Critical debate about whether or not a particular writer or composition is satiric or comic often centers on the issue of authorial intention.

English literary satire is usually held to have begun in the Middle Ages. A strong satiric element is present in several forms of medieval literature such as the fabliaux, beast fables, and dream allegories. The works of Geoffrey CHAUCER represent the apogee of urbane ironic satire in the medieval period and reflect the familiar targets of contemporary satirists in this period of literary history: cupidity, corruption and hypocrisy within the church, women, and malpractice in the professions. John SKELTON may be said to have inaugurated an English tradition of satiric colloquial light verse that includes Samuel BUTLER, author of *Hudibras*, Jonathan SWIFT, Lord BYRON, T. S. ELIOT, and W. H. AUDEN. Satire has been written in all periods of British literary history. It is present on the English

Renaissance stage in the plays of Ben JONSON and of William SHAKESPEARE. The Elizabethan and Jacobean period witnessed harsh, rough invective satire in prose and verse. The great period of satire in English is the century between the Restoration of Charles II in 1660 and the accession of George III in 1760, when it was a dominant mode in poetry, prose, and drama. The period witnessed such satirists as Butler, John DRYDEN, John Wilmot, Earl of ROCHESTER, Andrew MARVELL, Alexander POPE, John GAY, and Swift, among many others. The period saw the perfection of the heroic couplet, the octosyllabic couplet, and mock-heroic for the purposes of satire. From the later 18th c., while satire continued to be written, it is no longer a dominant mode in a literature increasingly interested in the self and interiority and in sympathetically exploring rather than imposing judgment on experience. Satire becomes assimilated as an element within the prevailing genre of prose fiction in the 19th and 20th cs.

Satire can hijack any literary vehicle for its purpose. Swift's great misanthropic satire *Gulliver's Travels*, for example, appears in the form of a contemporary travel book and his cold-blooded satiric fantasy *A Modest Proposal*, which ironically proposes a cannibal solution to Ireland's problems, appears in the form of a serious pamphlet in political economy. Satire, however, can also signify a particular literary kind or form as well as a mode of writing that converts other genres to its purposes. The great satiric genre in poetry is the formal verse satire that in English refers to poems based on Roman classical satires by Horace, Persius, and Juvenal. Formal verse satire is characterized by the use of a first-person satiric speaker, the "I" of the poem, who responds to an Adversarius within the poem. The satire is ostensibly reformative; it prosecutes vice but prescribes virtue. Pope's *Epistle to Dr. Arbuthnot*, in which Pope's friend the physician and satirist John Arbuthnot is the Adversarius, is a fine example of formal verse satire and an important apology by a major English satirist for his art. Horace offered satirists a model of informal and urbane satire on follies. Pope self-consciously modeled his satire on Horace, although his *Imitations of Horace*, written during the 1730s, and the end of the fourth book of *The Dunciad* are perhaps closer to Juvenal in their elevated tone of righteous denunciation. Persius provided a model of the satiric moralist in political opposition and was much imitated in the 18th c. Juvenal offered the grandeur of outspoken, righteous indignation at vice. Joseph HALL appears to have inaugurated the Juvenalian satiric mode in English in his book of harsh satires *Virgidemiarum*. Swift, whose famous epitaph speaks of his savage indignation, is often regarded as the English Juvenal, but he in fact rejected the lofty style in his satiric poetry and preferred a more downbeat and familiar style of ridicule and raillery. Samuel JOHNSON wrote Juvenalian satire. His poems *London* and *The Vanity of Human Wishes* are inspired English updates of Juvenal's third and tenth satires respectively.

Although satirical verse continues to be written, formal verse satire declined after the 18th c. and has been pronounced dead. English prose satire, like poetry, has also been described as a form and understood in a generic sense. Menippean or Varronian satire, named after the Greek Cynic philosopher Menippus and his Roman imitator Varro, has signified loosely connected, miscellaneous forms of prose satire. Robert BURTON's *The Anatomy of Melancholy*, published in 1621, is a prose satiric cento. The satirical dialogues of Lucian and the satirical "News from Parnassus" form invented by the Italian prose satirist Traiano Boccalini were among the formal models for English prose satire in the 17th and 18th cs. Prose satire has not stopped, but since the 18th c. it has found a generic home in prose fiction. A satiric dimension is pervasive in the work of many novelists, as in the case of Evelyn WAUGH in the 20th c. Jonathan COE is a contemporary English novelist whose novels have a strong satirical element.

The word "satire" derives from the Latin "satira," a later form of "satura," meaning medley, but in the 16th and 17th cs. a false etymology linked satire with "satyr" and thereby associated satire with the rough and coarse satyrs of the Greek satyr plays. It was also thought that satire derived from the Arabic for "butcher's cleaver." Erroneous etymology aside, satire does have a violent prehistory and a provenance in acts of aggression. Importantly, the roots of satire have been traced to the magical curse in the ancient world. In early Celtic literature satires were thought to do physical harm. The bardic curse had the power to disfigure and kill. The biting satires of the first Greek literary satirist Archilochus are said to have caused the subjects of his satire to hang themselves. The harsh satire produced by Elizabethan and Jacobean satirists such as Hall, John MARSTON, and John DONNE reflects their understanding of satire as a violent instrument. Dryden, in his "Discourse concerning the Original and Progress of Satire," prefixed to *Satires of Juvenal and Persius* (1692), thinks of the butcher's cleaver in relation to satire, but it is butchery as a fine art. He wrote that there is "a vast difference betwixt the slovenly Butchering of a Man, and the fineness of a stroak that separates the Head from the Body, and leaves it standing in its place." The original Archilochan power and the killing curse of satire survive in the violent imaginary of the English satiric tradition. The exterminatory impulse is very evident in Swift's work where there are individual satiric killings and calls to massacre. In a famous mock-astrological literary hoax orchestrated in a sequence of pamphlets in 1708–9, Swift, impersonating an as-

trologer Isaac Bickerstaff, predicted the death of a real London astrologer John Partridge, announced the accomplishment of his prediction, and certified Partridge's death when the astrologer claimed to be alive. Violent personal satire in poems like "Traulus" seems aimed at erasing its subject. In several places, famously in the fourth part of *Gulliver's Travels* where the Houyhnhnms debate whether the humanoid Yahoos "should be exterminated from the Face of the Earth," Swift's punitive fury at an offending humankind expresses itself in echoes of God's words in Genesis 6:7.

Setting up as judges and executioners of their fellow citizens, satirists have of course sought to justify their practice to themselves and to others. They have sought to produce a license to kill in order to prove that they are public hangmen rather than private assassins motivated by personal malice. Declarations of moral purpose and disavowal of personal malice are commonplace in apologies for satire. The apologies are highly suspect and problematic. The actual primacy of satire's aggressive and antisocial impulses seems disclosed even when satire is being defended as a moral art. The claim to be a moralist "is the justification of all Satire," wrote Lewis, "Dryden, for instance, could not fly over the world and drop molten lead upon it otherwise than as a moralist." The seedy late-17th-c. English satirist Tom Brown, in *A Short Essay on English Satire*, published in the 1715 edition of his *Works*, wrote conventionally that "*Satire* is design'd to expose Vice and encourage Vertue," yet he nevertheless described the libertine Earl of Rochester as one of "the greatest *Satirists* of the *English*" acknowledging that "reforming the Age was none of his Province." Swift's satiric practice is defended in his ironic poetic obituary for himself "Verses on the Death of Dr. Swift": "Yet, Malice never was his Aim;/ He lash'd the Vice but spar'd the Name." However, Swift's satire is littered with named victims and this very poem satirizes several individuals by name. The apology for Swift's satire in "Verses on the Death of Dr. Swift" claims that "His Satyr points at no Defect,/ But what all Mortals may correct." Yet a powerful effect of Swiftian satire with its flayed women, dismembered nymphs, and dissected beaux is that the human carcass is radically defective and corrupt and humankind too depraved to save. Swiftian satire administers shock therapy to the body politic of his time but in his great satires *A Tale of a Tub* and *Gulliver's Travels* he also satirizes the satirist who pretends to mend a world that is incapable of correction. The great Romantic satirist Lord Byron, considering the case of Juvenal in the first canto of *Don Juan*, ironically reflects on apologies for satire while amusingly taking the side of society and propriety against the satirist: "I can't help thinking Juvenal was wrong,/ Although no doubt his real intent was good,/For speaking out so plainly in his song,/So much indeed as to be downright rude."

The image of the satirist as physician to the body politic, as a healer rather than a curser or killer, is ubiquitous in the apologetic for satire. Lewis described each character in *The Apes of God* as an "enormously enlarged bacillus" extracted from the social organism and placed on the page and "I handled my hypodermic." As in Lewis's rather alarming use of the traditional trope, the satirist as physician in British literature often seems more interested in the radically invasive procedures than in cures or palliative care for the sick subject. Although the punitive purpose primarily activates satire, since the Middle Ages satire has always had its positive, reformative side. Explicit or implicit reference to some ideal social, moral, or political standard helps to validate or legitimate the punitive satiric project. English satire is often seen as a conservative or even reactionary art positing or appealing to a traditional order and supposed norms as it displays and denounces prevailing contemporary corruption. But satire has been just as important a weapon for antinomian radicals and anti-establishment authors.

While satirists such as Waugh and American author Ambrose Bierce have claimed that satire is dead, it being impossible to produce shame in a modern world that does not recognize vice as a reprehensible quality, satire has continued to be produced. The modern satirical revue, satirical television program, and satirical magazine pioneered in Britain by *Beyond the Fringe*, *That Was The Week That Was*, and *Private Eye* have perhaps revived the original meaning of satire as a medley.

BIBLIOGRAPHY: Carpenter, H., *That Was Satire That Was: The Satire Boom of the 1960s* (2000); Carretta, V., *The Snarling Muse* (1983); Elkin, P. K., *The Augustan Defence of Satire* (1973); Elliott, R. C., *The Power of Satire: Magic, Ritual, Art* (1960); Griffin, D., *Satire: A Critical Reintroduction* (1994); Kernan, A. B., *The Cankered Muse* (1959); Nokes, D., *Raillery and Rage: A Study of Eighteenth Century Satire* (1987); Rawson, C., ed., with J. Mezciems, *English Satire and the Satiric Tradition* (1984); Rawson, C., *God, Gulliver, and Genocide* (2001)

IAN HIGGINS

SAVAGE, Richard
b. 16 January 1697?; d. 1 August 1743, Bristol

S. is probably better known for Samuel JOHNSON's account of his life in the *Lives of the Poets* than he is for any texts of his own. Indeed, S.'s life as variously constructed in many ways overshadows any influence he may have had in the literary culture of early-18th-c. England. S. long claimed to be the illegitimate son

of the fourth Earl Rivers and Lady Macclesfield, a story given full treatment by Johnson. In fact, that story—like the name "Richard Savage" itself—remains unverified yet that persona, one of many S. created, dominates our understanding of S. Leading a very public and in some ways very modern life, S. earned a precarious living as an author, writing political pamphlets, poems, prose satires, and plays. None of his works was particularly successful nor are they widely read or anthologized today. Rather, his notoriety stems from his association with more luminous literary figures of his time—notably Alexander POPE and Johnson—and his unorthodox and at times criminal behavior (he was convicted of murder in 1727). For a while, he was also closely associated with poets such as James THOMSON and Edward YOUNG, and the literary circle surrounding Aaron Hill, which included Eliza HAYWOOD (with whom S. had a personal and literary relationship). Living on the social and literary margins, S. never realized much success, yet some of his poems have an evocative, if limited, power and echo the work of his more notable contemporaries.

His first published poems were Jacobite propaganda, little more than doggerel, published in 1715 contemporaneous with the Jacobite uprising. He quickly turned from poetic (and treasonable) pursuits to the theater and attempted to succeed as a playwright. His first play, *Love in a Veil* (perf. 1718; pub. 1719), was a comedy that was a loose translation from Pedro Calderón de la Barca. He followed it with the more successful *The Tragedy of Sir Thomas Overbury* (perf. 1723; pub. 1724), which took a relatively complex historical situation and reduced it to neoclassical simplicities in verse. Though S. was involved in the theater as both a playwright and (briefly) an actor, his metier was clearly poetry. *The Authors of the Town: A Satire* (1725) directed his wit toward the professional writers who inhabited the print trade of the time. Focusing on poets, critics, and individuals (such as John GAY, Martha Fowke Sansom, and Haywood) with whom he had personal relationships, S. lamented the "trade" of authorship (from which he profited) and the reign of "noxious nonsense." This poem anticipated some of the themes of Pope's *Dunciad*—also echoed in S.'s prose pamphlet *An Author to be Lett* (1729)—causing contemporaries to accuse S. of providing Pope with the detailed information he used.

The Bastard (1728) and *The Wanderer* (1729) are both regarded as his most effective poems. *The Bastard*, dedicated to his alleged mother the Countess of Macclesfield, describes his life as an illegitimate child and the "blessings" that "wait the Bastard's lot." *The Wanderer*, in five cantos, is a meditation on the effects of affliction on the mind as conveyed by a hermit to the wanderer. Containing descriptive passages of NATURE AND LANDSCAPE, the poem's stated subject—"ample Nature"—anticipates the concerns of Pope's

"Essay on Man" and Thomson's *The Seasons*, as well as some of the imagery of the so-called poets of sensibility. *The Wanderer*, like *The Bastard*, also alludes to S.'s claims of his illegitimate birth and the sustained mistreatment by his alleged natural mother.

BIBLIOGRAPHY: Rusche, H., "R. S.," in Sitter, J., ed., *Eighteenth-Century British Poets, First Series, DLB* 95 (1990): 257–67; Tracy, C. R., *The Artificial Bastard: A Biography of R. S.* (1953)

CATHERINE INGRASSIA

SAYERS, Dorothy L[eigh]

b. 13 June 1893, Oxford; d. 17 December 1957, Witham

S. would probably be disappointed, but not greatly surprised, if she could know that nearly half a century after her death she would be chiefly remembered for the novels featuring her aristocratic detective Lord Peter Wimsey, younger brother of the Duke of Denver, rather than for the more serious works of religious drama and verse translation to which she devoted her later years. Penguin Books have superseded her once much-respected translation of Dante in their Penguin Classics series, and it is a long time since the BBC repeated her cycle of plays on the life of Jesus, *The Man Born to Be King* (1943): in their time, during the Second World War, they were felt to be shockingly colloquial but overcame the opposition of traditionalist religious groups to become a triumphant success both for the corporation and for the author, who was a clergy daughter, lifelong religious enthusiast, and Christian apologist.

But the Lord Peter novels run into edition after edition, paperback after paperback, with encomiums from such later luminaries of the genre as Ruth RENDELL and P. D. JAMES on their covers. Lord Peter, with his eyeglass, upper-class manner, epicureanism and expert wine palate, Savile Row wardrobe, first-class Oxford degree and Great War decoration, and elegant but comfortable flat in Picadilly, could easily fall into caricature, a more intellectual version of P. G. WODEHOUSE's Bertram Wooster. The author is aware of this danger, as shown by the frequency with which S. makes Peter enjoin Bunter, his manservant, to "stop talking like Jeeves" whenever he expresses the wish to give satisfaction to his employer. The danger is by no means always avoided. Generally, however, the witty and deceptively facile style, the excellently maintained narrative impetus, and the ingeniously constructed mysteries combine to overcome the reader's possible distaste for the somewhat snobbish manipulation to which he is being subjected. The resultant enjoyment is often enhanced by interesting backgrounds: in *Gaudy Night* (1935), the foreground character is not Lord Peter but Harriet Vane, the detective-novelist whom he had rescued in an earlier novel from a charge of murder. The novel is an informed and fascinating account of life in an Oxford women's college (S. was a first-class Oxford graduate). In *Unnatural Death* (1927; repub. as *The Dawson Pedigree*, 1928), there are strong undertones of lesbianism. *Murder Must Advertise* (1933) deals with the work of an advertising agency, S.'s own livelihood after university. *The Nine Tailors* (1934) depends for its solution on a detailed knowledge of change-ringing on church bells, a topic thoroughly researched.

S.'s approach was always that of a scholar: she delivered a famous lecture at Oxford in 1935 on "Aristotle and the Art of Detective Fiction," arguing that the mystery novel must have strong unity of action, its effectiveness depending on every incident having some relevance to the solution. This did not save her from occasional errors of continuity. In *Have His Carcase* (1932), a character disapproves of his mother's choice of dancing partner, when a few pages earlier he had been arrested and is still in custody; in *The Nine Tailors*, a village school is in session two days after Christmas. In *Gaudy Night,* S.'s alter ego Harriet Vane admits to a friend that she has never avoided at least half a dozen major howlers in any of her stories; nine out of ten readers, she adds, are as confused as the author, so fail to notice; and if the tenth writes to point out the error, she replies with a promise to correct later editions—"But I never do." S. was obviously describing, and perhaps apologizing for, her own practice.

One of the worst errors, Jewish commentators have pointed out, occurs in *Strong Poison* (1930), where she betrays ignorance of Jewish marriage customs and of who may and may not be entitled to marry in the synagogue (as Anthony TROLLOPE had seventy years earlier in *The Way We Live Now*). It should have been a simple matter for the assiduous campanological researcher of *The Nine Tailors* to get it right. S.'s attitude to Jews, who appear obsessively and often irrelevantly in her work, particularly in *Unnatural Death,* and to other ethnic minorities, leaves a disagreeable taste. It could be argued that she was simply displaying attitudes of her class and time, like her contemporary Evelyn WAUGH (most notoriously in *Decline and Fall*). But it is difficult for readers today to suffer with patience the fact that few black or Jewish characters appear without overt hostility, facetiousness, caricature, or patronage from both the author and fellow characters. Oddly, S. was published for many years by Victor Gollancz, the most distinguished British-Jewish publisher of his age. Despite their shortcomings, however, S.'s novels and short stories remain required, and highly enjoyable, reading as exemplars of the elegant murder mysteries of the 1930s, detective fiction's Golden Age.

BIBLIOGRAPHY: Dean, C., ed., *Encounters with Lord Peter* (1991); Hannay, M. P., ed., *As Her Whimsey Took Her* (1979); Ousby, I., *The Crime and Mystery Book* (1997); Reynolds, B., *D. L. S.: Her Life and Soul* (1993; rev. ed., 1998); Scott-Giles, C. W., *The Wimsey Family* (1977)

MICHAEL GROSVENOR MYER

SCHREINER, Olive (Emilie Albertina)

b. 24 March 1855, Wittebergen, Cape Colony; d. 11 December 1920, Cape Town, South Africa

S. was the first South African novelist to gain a reputation abroad and one of the first to emerge from Britain's colonies. She is also an important figure in the history of FEMINISM.

Her novels cannot be separated from her beliefs. She was reared in a lonely colonial outpost, the daughter of missionaries, and was practically self-educated. At an early age, she rejected formal religion, realizing that adults did not genuinely want to follow the teachings of Christ. In 1881, she got herself to London and joined various radical groups that had intense discussions about socialism, religion, and marriage; Havelock ELLIS and Eleanor Marx were among her friends. She would campaign for women's suffrage and against war and would retain the missionary temperament all her life.

The Story of an African Farm (2 vols., 1883) was an instant success, and has remained popular. It does not have a conventional plot—she believed this was unnecessary—but it does have a definite raw power. English audiences were fascinated by her descriptions of the South African landscape, and the time was right for a novel that questioned some key Victorian beliefs. Waldo, the "hero," is tormented by his inability to believe in a loving God. Lyndall, the heroine, is a feminist who refuses to marry the father of her child. "It is only the made-up stories that end nicely," she says, and both these young people die, overwhelmed by the cruelty of their elders and the philistinism of life in South Africa. Both long to get away from the farm and achieve a richer life, but it seems that only the conventional survive, and only the land endures.

Although Lyndall became a cult figure, and S. lived for forty years after writing her first novel, physical and emotional illness made it difficult for her to write more. She published *Dreams*, a book of stories, in 1890, and *Trooper Peter Halket of Mashonaland*, a short novel attacking imperialism, in 1897. Both contain allegories (Christ coming back to earth to denounce the policies of Cecil Rhodes), and neither has much value. A juvenile novel, *Undine*, was published posthumously in 1928. *Woman and Labour* (1911) became a feminist text, and has dated surprisingly little. It argues that modern women cannot be simply housewives and must be admitted to work that is "honoured

and socially useful." S. also believed passionately that once women were equal citizens they would not tolerate seeing their children killed in war. Unable herself to have children or a successful marriage, she brooded constantly about a possible future society where men, women, and children could live in harmony. The waste of potential is a central theme in her novels; so is the suffering of those who cannot accept life as it is.

Her last novel *From Man to Man* is unfinished, was not published until 1926 and then went out of print for half a century. Yet it is a much greater achievement than the *African Farm*, and the lack of a formal ending matters less than one would expect because what she is really doing is to state a problem that has not yet been solved. It is another South African novel in which the Lyndall-figure splits into two sisters who lead almost separate lives, but illustrate two paths that women may take. Both are victims though in different ways; Bertie, like Thomas HARDY's Tess, is a nonintellectual who wants only to live in a happy family but is rejected and sinks into prostitution after being seduced. Rebekah, a "respectable" wife and mother whose husband is unfaithful, channels her unhappiness into creative thinking about women's position in society. She points out that a female William SHAKESPEARE would never have been heard of, yet women's work is not trivial because all life would be extinct without motherhood. Cooking, sewing, and educating children are all positive activities that, like the karroo, had seldom been written about.

S.'s work is dominated by the images of babies, dead and living, and of intensely vulnerable young women and girls. She writes with deep feeling about South Africa, a land that is beautiful but also frightening, and whose future is in doubt because of the attitudes of its people. Women, children, and the nonwhite races are all exploited by the average man whose instincts are to kill, but S. never lost the hope that a better society might be built, and her novels are a passionate protest against cruelty. She was a major influence on other woman writers including Virginia WOOLF and Doris LESSING.

BIBLIOGRAPHY: Cronwright-Schreiner, S. C., *The Life of O. S.* (1924); First, R., and A. Scott, *O. S.* (1980); Monsman, G., *O. S.'s Fiction* (1991)

MERRYN WILLIAMS

SCIENCE AND LITERATURE

In the aftermath of POSTMODERNISM and poststructuralism, "literature and science"—construed as a way of interpreting the two domains as well as the structure of language in relation to diverse texts—has been configured in so many ways that it is impossible to present them here as anything other than lists. The varieties include hovering doubts about the nature of each category: literature and science viewed apart, as modes of thinking embodying distinct types of knowledge; as approaches to reality based on language and representation; as structures of metaphor feeding systems of discourse and ideology; and, not least, as the obvious history of literature and history of science.

Before the 1970s, relations in each of the above categories were primarily guided by two, usually antithetical, concerns: one based on the ultimately optimistic view that science liberates the human imagination by virtue of its fundamental rationality and—when considered collectively within society—leads to human progress and social advance; the other—far more pessimistic and gloomy—forming a critique of science that dwells on the inherent evil in the human condition and the prospect of science's threat to politics and governments.

Historically, each of the views had abundant proponents. Poets, novelists, philosophers, and historians, as well as scientists and politicians, amassed mountains of evidence to prove their case: in the first camp, the view that human history has been perfecting itself over time largely as the result of scientific advancement that improves the quality of human life; in the second, a sustained critique of science on grounds that it feeds man's already irrational nature by enabling him to create all sorts of monsters (nuclear bombs, genomes, and genetic engineering), construct "machines in the garden" (Leo Marx's brilliant phrase intended to capture science's deceptive pastoralism), and tap into man's fundamentally contrary nature. Other, less influential and often more academic, positions about the relations of literature and science have been advanced over the centuries. For example, the view that "literature and science" is a subset of thought about literature and religion because science is "religion" dedicated to another god. But these alternatives are insignificant when compared to the mighty themes of liberation-progress versus the human condition as fundamentally irrational.

While secular views were minimal, progress viewed as improvement was limited, earthly life could only improve in relation to eternity—the afterlife. It was therefore not surprising that medieval science should have focused primarily on "a-concepts"—astrology, astronomy, and alchemy; its interaction with English literature was largely limited to these realms, except for medicine, which has always been in a class of itself because it promised cures down through the ages. But by the time of the European Renaissance, the forms of interaction become more complex, especially through the new importance of medicine within society, as notions of improvement in man's earthy life begin to form themselves apart from his spiritual journey from this life to the next. The drama was the first literary form displaying the

new awareness. Hence, Ben JONSON's characters, especially his most greedy protagonists, are explained not only in terms of their "humors" (the basic physiological model of the time) but also by the way they deal in alchemy and astrology, while Christopher MARLOWE's are presented according to their stars and bodily fluids. Yet even when Thomas MORE had published his *Utopia* charting a better society in the future, secularism was beginning to peep through the clouds of entrenched sects of Christianity. Some years later Francis BACON published the seminal *Advancement of Learning* and *Novum Organun* claiming, for the first time in Europe, that the new science was the most certain route to unlimited progress of the human race, thereby solidifying the first of the two main streams of literature and science. His was not merely the view that science was here to stay and that it permeated every rank of human society, good and bad, but that scientists had a social responsibility.

Bacon's contemporaries held no such developed optimistic views. William SHAKESPEARE, the most eloquent and prolific of the lot, focused on the new physiology and medicine (as in the subtle melancholias of almost all his major figures), but his plays refer abundantly to all the sciences, from anatomy and astronomy, to physiology and zoology, and it would be inaccurate to say that his prolific commentary is a sign of optimism. Indeed the analysis of his protagonists from Hamlet and Lear, to Macbeth and Othello, as well as his clowns and jesters, seems to place him firmly in the second camp—suggesting the inherent malady of the human condition—despite his constant frivolous treatment of the comic side of life. Robert BURTON, an Oxford librarian who spent his life compiling the gargantuan landmark *Anatomy of Melancholy,* published in 1621, dissected the human psyche in each of its temporal states, but his view of man's mind and body was hardly cheerful even if Burton straddled the fence of optimism by suggesting that man's lot forever enables him to learn something about himself. The metaphysical poets, including John DONNE, returned to the three "a's" of the hermetic sciences, suggesting that man's soul was so dark it could only be fathomed through the conceits of an equally obscure alchemy and astrology. Even Sir Thomas BROWNE, a practicing physician who used them effectively in his medical practice and who had profited from Bacon's secular sense of the new science, was lured by the hermeticism of alchemy and astrology in his great anatomy of the world viewed through its religions in *Religio Medici*.

John MILTON resembled Bacon in the encyclopedic breadth of his erudition about science (he had also looked through the new telescopes and seen "worlds without end") and was equally prophetic about the two strains. His cosmology in *Paradise Lost*, especially his dialogue on astronomy in book 8, takes no stand on what can be known about the plurality of worlds. Galileo, Tycho Brahe, Copernicus, Kepler: all speculated about the universe but none could be certain. Man would do better, Milton chided, not to inquire about things beyond our ken. Overreaching Icarian inquiry would push mankind over the precipice and hurl him into disaster, thereby producing the kinds of monsters seen much later in Mary SHELLEY's *Frankenstein*. Even so, Milton could not refrain from using the sciences as structural principles in his literary works; a leap from the restricted uses made of them among (for example) the Elizabethan and Jacobean dramatists. Milton, like Bacon, was remarkable in Renaissance literature for the uses he made of science. If *Paradise Lost* became the premier EPIC poem in the language, it was impossible to read it without recognizing the degree to which the new science was now firmly embedded within the fabric of English literature. No other English author, not even Shakespeare, and certainly not the didactic Bacon whose repertoire was limited to expository prose, had inscribed the sciences into their literary oeuvre as Milton had. It was an embodiment that could not be undone: if science was crucial to the greatest poem in the language, then it must be to the whole firmament of British literature; not merely in forms and metaphors but to the idea of literature as embodying diverse forms of knowledge and constructing universes of reality.

The English Restoration altered Milton's pathway: its creation of a Royal Society for the advancement of science legitimated a new type of scientist, or "virtuoso" as these figures were then called, amateurish and untrained, who dabbled and rambled in specialized areas where they often knew little. If Bacon's call for the responsibility of the scientist was now newly abrogated, so too was Milton's warning about the limits of knowledge in an almost Faustian sense. The new scientists stopped at nothing: fops in the realm of the knowable, they took all learning in their stride without limit. They apotheosized geniuses such as John LOCKE and Isaac Newton, their idolaters worshiping them as gods. British satirists from Samuel BUTLER and John DRYDEN down through Alexander POPE and Charles CHURCHILL feel it incumbent on themselves to debunk this hubris, thereby creating a new universe of English literature based upon it. Jonathan SWIFT's *Gulliver's Travels* fictionalizes an imaginary "Academy of Lagado" where all these corruptions of science are occurring: a sort of modern university perverting the course of the future by assigning scientists the most ridiculous experiments imaginable—all this in the name of progress. When 20th-c. American scholar of literature and science Marjorie Hope Nicolson claimed that "Newton demanded the muse," she epitomized the literature of an epoch commencing at Newton's death in 1727.

Political history intervened yet again, as so often it does, and curbed these activities. Uprisings at home in Britain, wars everywhere abroad, and revolution across the Channel in France, made it clear that human progress might be an illusion without concrete basis. As one social rank after another toppled, the progress of science increasingly appeared to be a chimera of the imagination. William BLAKE, a fierce anti-Newtonian, debunked Newtonian science, as did poets from Christopher SMART (the author of the Blakean poem *Jubilate Agno* or "Rejoice in the Lamb") to W. B. YEATS, who celebrated instead the untrained, or natural human imagination reared in nature, and capable of producing sublime responses among those in its presence.

These dedicated proponents of the pessimistic view were constantly challenged by the optimists. Even William WORDSWORTH, whose Lockeanism and Newtonianism were always curbed, continued to believe that science would liberate the imagination rather than enslave it by permitting poetry to reach its well-deserved place as the star of the tree of knowledge. Science, Wordsworth and his friend and collaborator Samuel Taylor COLERIDGE believed, could not fetter poetry; poetry used science for its own ends and absorbed it into its higher form of certainty. When asked about progress and the responsibility of the scientist, they replied cautiously, hesitatingly, saying that no one could be sure "progress" had occurred and wondering whether scientists (even Lockes and Newtons) could be more responsible than other members of society, thereby indicating how they straddled the fence between the two camps. The Romantics may not have agreed with visionary Blake that modern science inherently produces monsters; yet they could hardly endorse the Baconianism and Newtonianism touting science as the salvation of future worlds.

Late Enlightenment thought stressed that if literature and science were not enemies, science and religion naturally were. Here, the divide—a noncontested border—was sharply polarized: Blake on the side of the spirit, figures like Erasmus DARWIN, grandfather of the great evolutionist Charles, with the optimists. Darwin's poetry celebrates the "loves" of the animal and vegetable kingdom, drawing on the most recent botany and biology as background. The French *philosophes* and German naturalists from Diderot and Voltaire to Goethe to Herder also played a part by siding with the optimists: they could not imagine progress apart from the march of science or without its larger, almost Faustian, context of the fragmentation of the world.

Samuel JOHNSON's contemporaries portrayed him as hostile to science, yet in reality he endorsed whole segments of the Baconian tradition and even thought of writing the "lives of the physicians," as he had the lives of the poets, on grounds it would be instructive. Later on, Percy Bysshe SHELLEY drew on all the sciences, not merely Newtonianism, in his aim to integrate them into one organic view of reality. Like Milton and Darwin before him, Shelley was a modern poetic Prometheus; assimilated all the sciences in such major poems as *Prometheus Unbound*, "Mont Blanc," and *Adonais*. Yet Romantic and Victorian figures were less polarized. Coleridge, already mentioned, and Alfred, Lord TENNYSON in the generation after him, also amalgamated diverse branches of science to construct their best literary works; the former resurrecting whole schools of psychology in the *Biographia Literaria*, the latter geology in *In Memoriam*. Their method could be called the school of eclectic affinities for its process of selection, picking and choosing from the sciences what they needed to do their work. But other Victorians were concerned; Matthew ARNOLD so much so that he mounted a polemical defense of literature in an era he thought dominated by science.

Darwinian evolution established itself by the 1860s as the most controversial theory in the whole history of science; far more so than Galileo's astronomy or Newton's astrophysics. Scientific writers like T. H. Huxley popularized it for the masses, especially in his attack on Arnold in "Science and Culture" (1880), without coming down clearly on one side or the other: Huxley called himself "an ethicist," yet it was not merely Darwin's claims about the descent of man and survival of the fittest that presented the "ethical" problem but also his narrative technique, analogies, and plots. These narrative strategies of the scientific method resembled those of the artists. If Darwin chronicled the "descent of character" in one rhetorical mode, their versions were not so different. George ELIOT was particularly sensitive to Darwin's analogies: like other novelists from Tobias SMOLLETT and Laurence STERNE to William Makespeace THACKERAY and Anthony TROLLOPE, she relied on the medical domain for her major cultural inspiration, constructing the plot of her greatest novel, *Middlemarch*, around Lydgate who epitomizes Victorian society in miniature. Yet Eliot's scientific influences transcended medical realms and reached out beyond Darwin to German science (particularly to Herman von Helmholtz and Ludwig Feuerbach). The most sophisticated philosophical mind among the British novelists of her generation, even she straddled the fence of good and evil in science: if she was no blind optimist about science's potential might (the way it concealed evil in the garden of its discoveries), neither could she abandon the view that science and progress went hand in hand.

By the end of the 19th c., scientific positivism had crescendoed to new heights: the new post-Baconian view was that the only knowledge worth defending was rational, scientific, even mathematical; even more, that knowledge itself was scientifically predetermined. Again, however, as in the Newtonian aftermath, the opposition set in and pessimists such as the two Victorian Thomases—Thomas CARLYLE and Thomas HARDY—voiced their views. Carlyle had immersed himself in the Germans and their supernatural naturalism; Hardy in Darwinian evolution more than the other sciences, as is evident in *Tess of the d'Urbervilles*; neither believed that science had made the world a better place. Evolution rendered Hardy a more sympathetic and compassionate narrator; whether its versions of rationalism improved the world at large, overrun by the poor in squalid, sprawling cities, was doubtful.

Twentieth-century science enlarged this map and produced new antagonisms and stauncher oppositions. Poets such as A. E. HOUSMAN and W. H. AUDEN believed they had more crucial matters to worry about, and even James JOYCE, who was well read in the new theories of time, returned to Renaissance alchemy and astrology for his explanations of the characters in his fictions, while D. H. LAWRENCE found himself in the grip of Freud's theories about sex and the unconscious. Einstein's theories of relativity and Werner Heisenberg's uncertainty principle produced creative responses in Virginia WOOLF and Samuel BECKETT. The 1918 postwar reemergence of SCIENCE FICTION and science fantasy as serious genres became forces for writers to reckon with, together with entropy and the new philosophies of time. Physical time, interior time (stream of consciousness), time in relation to space, all assumed significance as literary motifs: in Yeats (who preferred mythical and allegorical time), T. S. ELIOT (who educated himself on Bradleyan and Bergsonian interior time yet who grappled with relative time as a poetic resource), and Lawrence DURRELL (whose *Alexandria Quartet* is constructed on F. H. Bradley's theories of time and applies Einstein's time-space continuum). Time, far more complex than Marcel Proust had imagined in his interior time and more so than rival hypotheses about gravitation, captivated the imagination of great writers as the Western world was ripped apart by two global wars and a menacing Jewish holocaust.

This enlarged chart of the complex arrangements of literature and science reintroduced pressing concerns about the scientists' social responsibility, making plain that each generation reified in its own terms the antagonism between the two primary views, optimistic and pessimistic. For example, playwright and social philosopher Bernard SHAW was gripped by the new eugenics: what kind of utopian world would it establish? Other utopian writers—notably H. G. WELLS in his *Time Machine* and Aldous HUXLEY in *Brave New World*—predicted a 1984, Big-Brother, nightmarish scenario leaving no doubt about which side of the divide they inhabited. UTOPIA and dystopia, societies good and evil, were literary mirrors of the ancient debate about the role of science in culture. Almost every one of Shaw's plays squarely confronted the utopian dilemma, whether shaped by Darwinian evolution, the new eugenics, medical or vivisectionist practices. Shaw's conclusion (especially in *Man and Superman*) was guardedly bleak: nothing was more menacing than the new science, nor would be in future generations, but you could not remove it from the tip of your imagination. So far as civil societies were concerned, science was here to stay, would become—if it was not already there—the great writer's constant *idée fixe*.

World War II blasted these views. Nagging questions about the moral responsibility or ethical imperative of scientists appeared irrelevant as human cruelty surfaced in ever more brutal forms. What use were these questions when the social conscience of the new technology had been the great villain? Science essentially reduced to theory; could be debated in universities and laboratories; but atom bombs and Hiroshimas were, like Frankenstein's, the monstrous creations of a morally bankrupt technology. If science embodied one type of knowledge, with its own universe of moral responsibility, technology was another altogether, as different from science as was science from religion or poetry. Hence, the old critique of science as rational and logical dissipated under the weight of postwar America and Europe. The Western Alliance prevailed yet remained in tatters: America-the-victor was mired in an oppressive McCarthyism and a new religious Right that was anything but "scientific"; Europe's technological edge economically impoverished. When the "two-cultures controversy" between C. P. SNOW, a scientist who also wrote novels, and F. R. LEAVIS, a Cambridge literary don, broke out in 1962–63, it touched a nerve that proved far more academic—limited to the groves of Academe—than it might have been. It had been anticipated in the 1880s by Arnold and T. H. Huxley. But now Snow claimed in his 1959 Cambridge Reith Lecture that "a gulf of mutual incomprehension" exists between literary and scientific intellectuals, and he proposed remedies to correct this dire state of affairs. Leavis seized upon Snow's arguments and countered that the sciences and non-sciences were fundamentally different types of knowledge. Throughout the fraught decade of the 1960s, academics took sides, bequeathing to the 1970s a sense of the difference by virtue of the persistent debate itself.

The debate also emphasized how the ongoing march of progress in one (science) could not be claimed for the other (non-science). Were there better plays than Shakespeare's, better poems than Milton's? The question about social progress—societies improving or decaying—was too fraught; it was easier

to return to metaphysical debates about two types of knowledge, and this may be why the "two-cultures controversy" polarized intellectuals in the first place. As the breakdown of belief in causality and determinism increased after World War II, it accompanied other developments highlighting how far apart science and the arts had grown. Scientific discovery was marching ahead at such a rapid pace that those interested in the latest developments of science and literature found it hard to stay abreast.

In time, quantum physics surrendered to chaos theory; cybernetics—postulating that machines could incorporate the human brain's neurophysiology—arose; as did virtual reality in Artificial Intelligence and the Internet. Concomitant with these waves were the new global ecology, the rise of science fiction as the supreme fiction of the future, and a new preoccupation with the language of modern science. These developments were predictable: knowledge marches on. Where was socioeconomic progress now? Where humanism after colossal global destruction demonstrating how human cruelty had scaled new heights? Set the chronological dials forward to 1980 or 1990—the historical decade when this essay started in its retrospective glance backward—and the new critics of literature and science were too preoccupied keeping abreast of theoretical science and its social implications to ask. Perhaps it will always be that way.

BIBLIOGRAPHY: Beer, G., *Open Fields: Science in Cultural Encounter* (1996); Beer, G., *Darwin's Plots* (1983); Bruce, D., and A. Purdy, eds., *Literature and Science* (1994); Haynes, R. D., *From Faust to Strangelove: Representations of the Scientist in Western Literature* (1994); Huxley, A., *Literature and Science* (1963); Markley, R., *Fallen Languages: Crises of Representation in Newtonian England, 1660–1740* (1994); Marx, L., *The Machine in the Garden* (1964); Nicolson, M. H., *Newton Demands the Muse* (1946); Nicolson, M. H., *The Breaking of the Circle* (1950); Nicolson, M. H., *Science and Imagination* (1956); Peterfreund, S., ed., *Literature and Science* (1990); Richards, I. A., *Science and Poetry* (1926; rev. ed., 1935); Rousseau, G. S., "Literature and Science: The State of the Field," *Isis* 69 (1978): 583–91; Shaffer, E. S., ed., *The Third Culture* (1998); Sypher, W., *Literature and Technology* (1968); Whitehead, A. N., *Science and the Modern World* (1948)

GEORGE ROUSSEAU

SCIENCE FICTION

In *Ultimate Island: On the Nature of Science Fiction* (1993), Nicholas Ruddick suggests that British science fiction can be seen as a field, U.S. science fiction as a genre. British science fiction shares much of its history with that of the U.S. but is often seen as, in some way, separate. For some, it is cerebral and downbeat, while the American version is brash and optimistic. While there may well be national differences of tone affecting the works of individuals, the significance is more basic: the "industry" and the idea of "science fiction" first crystalized in the U.S. around specialist magazines. In Britain, this niche market was slower to become established. The first British science fiction magazine, *Scoops*, appeared in 1934, eight years after Hugo Gernsback's *Amazing*, and significantly was aimed at children. While Gernsback's "scientifiction" magazines propagandized technological progress, the British "scientific romance" had already appeared in general magazines or as novels but looked for literary models in social SATIRE and utopian fiction instead of the technological adventure story. Nevertheless, British writers were important in the early years of American science fiction, while American writers were and are enormously influential on movements in Britain. It is this creative dialogue with the U.S. that makes sweeping statements about "national characteristics" unfruitful.

Science fiction may well have roots in imaginary voyages such as Jonathan SWIFT's *Gulliver's Travels* or even Thomas MORE's *Utopia*, but Mary SHELLEY's *Frankenstein* is, as Brian W. ALDISS argues in *Billion Year Spree* (1973; rev. as *Trillion Year Spree*, 1986), arguably the most recognizable starting point. As its preface makes clear, we see scientists such as Luigi Galvini and Erasmus DARWIN reflected in Victor Frankenstein. Shelley explores the essential territory of science fiction: not only new scientific development, but its effects on an individual or group. Throughout the 19th c., the industrial revolution and the speculations of Sir Charles Lyell, Charles DARWIN, or Karl Marx changed the world physically and encouraged new thought-experiments about past, present, and future. In 1871, Edward BULWER-LYTTON published his anxious UTOPIA entitled *The Coming Race*, and George Chesney's seminal future-war story *The Battle of Dorking* appeared in *Blackwood's Magazine*. Percy Greg's *Across the Zodiac* (1880) anticipated space travel, William Delisle Hay's *Three Hundred Years Hence* (1881) portrayed a new version of the Victorian apogee, and George Griffith's *The Angel of the Revolution* (1893) saw super-weapons power revolutionary change. By the end of the century, it was clear that utopias (and dystopias) could be created, and the means would be science. It may have been the American Edward Bellamy who wrote *Looking Backward, 2000–1887* (1889), but the Englishman William MORRIS answered with *News from Nowhere*. Even in his pastoral future, powered barges cruise the Thames.

The "scientific romance" crystalized with H. G. WELLS—the towering figure who still influences the subject matter of modern science fiction. From *The Time Machine*, *The Island of Doctor Moreau*, *The War of the Worlds*, and *The First Men in the Moon* (1901) to more explicitly political semi-novels such as *A Modern Utopia* (1905) and *The Shape of Things to Come*, Wells drew upon his scientific training and his political activism to both question and mold the future; though he considered his works fantasies like Apuleius's *The Golden Ass* and Swift's *Gulliver's Travels* rather than "anticipatory inventions" in the manner of Jules Verne. Those British followers or critics of Wells, such as Olaf STAPLEDON (*Last and First Men*) or Sydney Fowler Wright (*Deluge* and *The Island of Captain Sparrow*, both 1928), were also writers whose dialogue was with national and international literatures rather than a named generic tradition of sf—which was hardly, if at all, familiar to many of them. A similar position was held by writers like J. D. Beresford (*The Hampdenshire Wonder*, 1911), while Aldous HUXLEY's *Brave New World*—also written under the shadow of Wells's utopianism—had more modernist literary influence. All however, including such overt cautionary tales as Katharine Burdekin's *Swastika Night* (1937), written as Murray Constantine, and Douglas Brown and Christopher Serpell's *If Hitler Comes* (1940), were as didactic as Gernsback's "instructive" romances. Few of these speculations used specific science fiction tropes such as space travel or aliens—although David Lindsay's *A Voyage to Arcturus* (1920) used a voyage to another world to explore questions of philosophy and ethics—and not all were read by fans of such material. Many, however, were discovered by readers who had followed the Wellsian tradition into the Gernsback magazines, and this contributed to the ironic situation whereby novels such as *Last and First Men* or *Brave New World* "became" science fiction through their adoption by science fiction readers rather than through any intention of writer or publisher.

American magazines, though, directly affected a generation of British fans and writers. The journalist/fan Walter Gillings was at the center of several attempts to found British magazines. John Beynon Harris achieved moderate fame in American pulps. The Oxford don C. S. LEWIS published *Out of the Silent Planet* and also wrote some of the earliest informed science fiction criticism. His love of popular fiction coupled with dislike of "engineer's fiction" and Wellsian scientism, and his religious impulses, turned him to science fiction as criticism of its own aspirations. The visionary fusion of social evolution, galactic vistas, and agnostic spiritual yearnings in *Last and First Men* affected (in somewhat different ways) the young Arthur C. CLARKE and Aldiss, who became the foremost British science fiction writers of their generation. Unlike Clarke and Aldiss, Stapledon was barely aware of the American magazines until introduced to

them by Eric Frank Russell, a writer who himself epitomized the transatlantic ambiguity by fusing a hard-
boiled "Yank" style of writing for *Astounding* with
the kind of insouciant insubordination found in many
who had been through the British military during
World War II. After the war, the main market for writers was still America, with only *New Worlds*, *Science
Fantasy*, *Authentic*, and *Nebula* offering home-grown
markets of stature. However, cheap paperbacks began
to fill the magazines' role, and during the 1950s ambitious and able writers such as Aldiss, Clarke, John
Brunner, and, more slowly, Bob Shaw, emerged to
explore and celebrate space opera and the "sense of
wonder" but also to engage with science fiction's tradition of interrogating its own assumptions.

Postwar British science fiction, as elsewhere, was
marked by anxieties usually set down to the Cold War
and loss of Empire, but also addressed specific concerns about the class system, the early stirrings of the
"generation gap," and Britain's cultural and political
relationship with the U.S. The popular comic-strip
hero Dan Dare of the *Eagle* was the most visible example of science fiction that assumed a British "presence" in space, an assumption that became increasingly more ironic during the postwar decades.
Interestingly, much of the most influential literature
still came from outside the field. George ORWELL's
Nineteen Eighty-Four and William GOLDING's *Lord
of the Flies* were popular "literary" novels in the vein
of Huxley. Virtually every dystopia since has been
compared to Orwell's political masterpiece. Nevil
SHUTE's postnuclear best-seller *On the Beach* was
perhaps less influential on science fiction but took a
straightforward science fiction-like narrative into a
mass audience. From within science fiction, John
Beynon Harris turned toward a more middlebrow audience and, as John WYNDHAM, preached the Wellsian
"logical fantasy." With *The Day of the Triffids*, *The
Chrysalids*, and *The Midwich Cuckoos*, he created
some of the most chillingly effective portrayals of the
English nightmare. Wyndham's invasions of middle-
class complacency sparked off the somewhat misinterpreted "cosy catastrophe" subgenre of which John
Christopher's *The Death of Grass* (1956) is the most
noticeable co-example. Other versions of this story of
change are more eschatological. Clarke's short story
"The Sentinel" (1951) shows us an astronaut on the
moon waiting for the alien contact that will change
history irrevocably: the scenario was to be adapted for
Stanley Kubrick's film *2001: A Space Odyssey*
(1968). Clarke's novels *Childhood's End* and *The
City and the Stars* (an adaptation of an earlier story
published in an American magazine, 1948) are (certainly in the case of the first) rather ambiguous transcendent utopias in his most Stapledonian vein.

The 1950s can be seen to have been a remarkably
fertile period, partly because of the tensions within it.

At the time, however, newer writers—led by Michael
MOORCOCK (who became editor of *New Worlds* in
1964), Aldiss, and J. G. BALLARD—exploded away
from what they saw as the complacency of both science fiction and "literary" establishments, hailing
American writer William Burroughs as a stylistic and
thematic touchstone. The anthology series *New Writings in Sf*, edited by Moorock's predecessor John Car-
nell, did much to introduce young writers, but it was
New Worlds that created a stir. The New Wave (which
meant something different across the Atlantic) was
less an organized movement than an ambitious group
of British (and British-based Americans) united only
by dissatisfaction with the current state of literary affairs. Although *New Worlds* attempted (often successfully) to move to new modes of storytelling and subject matter, its commercial impact was limited and its
literary success controversial. Nevertheless, the
Moorcock, Aldiss, and Ballard "triumvirate" and numerous others were encouraged to find personal
muses rather than imitate conventional models. Ballard, whose early novels such as *The Drowned World*
(1962), *The Drought* (1965), and *The Crystal World*
inverted the "cosy catastrophe," revitalized science
fiction with dream images of inner (rather than outer)
space, and a transformation of anxieties into desires.
More than any other writer of his time, Ballard explored the psychological landscapes of the postnuclear age, and, although with fewer science fiction
trappings, still does so. Inevitably, writers became associated with "New Wave" whether it was appropriate or not and for some it became something of a
millstone. Keith Roberts, whose *Pavane* (1968) became one of the classics of alternate-history, produced a number of fiercely individualistic works such
as *The Chalk Giants* (1974), *Molly Zero* (1980), and
Gráinne (1987) that engaged with the British landscape and an incarnate female muse-figure. Christopher PRIEST brought the "cosy catastrophe" up to date
with his second novel, *Fugue for a Darkening Island*,
explored the concept of perception in *Inverted World*,
and concentrated on his own brand of "visionary realism" in *The Affirmation* and later novels such as *The
Glamour* (1984; rev. eds., 1991, 1996), *The Prestige*,
and *The Extremes*. Like his contemporary M. John
Harrison, Priest (who is almost certainly Britain's
most gifted exponent of a native form of magical realism) remains in an ambiguous relationship with science fiction. It has provided his audience, and the
groundwork for the development of his work, but has
probably blocked his critical reception. John Brunner's "issues" trilogy of the 1960s—*Stand on Zanzibar* (1968), *The Sheep Look Up* (1972), and *The
Shockwave Rider* (1975)—were influenced by the
New Wave in their political engagement and ambitious stylistic experimentation. Brunner, probably
second only to Moorcock among science fiction writ-

ers in being formed by and forming the zeitgeist of the sixties (he was prominent in the Campaign for Nuclear Disarmament) never really returned to the level of those three novels following the breaking of the New Wave on the shores of the more cynical 1970s.

From outside the field—although he made several essays into it—Anthony BURGESS created a horrific future in *A Clockwork Orange*, and Richard Cowper's "Corlay" trilogy—*The Road to Corlay* (1978), *A Dream of Kinship* (1981), and *A Tapestry of Time* (1982)—possibly owed as much to the scientific romance and Sydney Fowler Wright as generic science fiction. Cowper, like Roberts, was another writer to whom a sense of place was important: this concern with locality, rural or urban, can be seen in writers as different as Moorcock (*Mother London*), Robert Holdstock (*Mythago Wood*, 1984), and Jeff Noon (*Vurt*, 1993). Other writers such as Bob Shaw or James White produced work that looked more specifically across the Atlantic for both audience and models, although their Northern Irish background might have nourished the roots of Shaw's sardonic humour (less evident in his novels than in his immensely popular addresses at sf conventions) or the humanitarianism of White's "Sector General" stories and novels set in and about a Galactic hospital station. Ian Watson, since *The Embedding* (1973) has produced astonishing explorations of many of science fiction's central themes, especially those of communications and perception.

Two factors are central to the development of British science fiction in the late 20th c. The first was the foundation of the magazine *Interzone* in 1982, formerly edited by a collective but now published and edited by David Pringle. Without the magazine, writers such as Stephen Baxter or Paul J. McAuley might indeed have been published, but with far greater difficulty. The second was an absorption, remix, and celebration of previous influences, both from within and outside the field.

The Far Eastern setting of Gwyneth Jones's *Divine Endurance* (1984) marks a ferociously original writer. Her "Aleutian trilogy"—*White Queen* (1992), *North Wind* (1994), and *Phoenix Café* (1997)—explores a number of variants of sf's engagement with the alien, including, of course, gender. Brian Stableford, who has been writing since the 1960s and is also one of the field's most active and erudite critics, engages with utopias, fin de siècle styles, and the scientific romance (of which he has written the definitive study). Baxter carries on Stapledon's cosmological speculations, and is widely seen as a successor to Clarke. Cyberpunk and crime-thriller forms influence Michael Marshall Smith, Simon Ings, and Jon Courtenay Grimwood. Mary Gentle fuses Renaissance hereticism, cyberpunk, and alternate history. Expansive neo-space opera has been a feature of fiction by Colin Green-

land, Peter F. Hamilton, and especially Iain M. BANKS, who alternates between science fiction novels from *Consider Phlebas* to *Look to Windward*, often exploring a hedonistic utopia, the "Culture," and novels not designated as science fiction but that often, as his early *The Wasp Factory* and *Walking on Glass*, are recognizably by someone who knows and loves the field. Many of these writers—Banks certainly, and also his fellow-Scot Ken MacLeod—are writers who show political engagement as well as a keen eye for extrapolation and satire.

Nongeneric writers continue to turn to forms of science fiction, either to some extent reinventing the form, or as a mode that they have grown up with. Angela CARTER's *The Passion of New Eve*, Doris LESSING's "Canopus in Argus" series, Alasdair GRAY's *Lanark*, E. P. Thompson's *The Sykaos Papers* (1988), P. D. JAMES's *The Children of Men*, Robert Harris's *Fatherland* (1992), Sanjida O'Connell's *Theory of Mind* (1996), Will SELF's *Great Apes*, and Maggie Gee's *The Ice People* (1998) are only a few recent novels not published as sf—indeed, in at least one case vehemently denied as such—but that science fiction readers have recognized as using plots and motifs central to the mode. Somewhere between specifically "sf" writers and mainstream exponents are writers such as Banks and Noon, who follow the example of Aldiss, himself still triumphantly writing the most nongeneric of recognizable science fiction. Noon, whose *Vurt* won the Arthur C. Clarke Award, is part of a generation of writers for whom generic distinctions are irrelevant. Echoes of Philip K. Dick and cyberpunk can be seen in his work, but the music, clubs, and streets of Manchester are equally visible, and the various strands are united by a surreal HUMOR. It is perhaps no accident that once more location and humor are touchstones. There is an exuberance to much of this writing that has caused some critics to suggest that British science fiction is now closer to a fiction of optimistic transcendence than the bleak and grubby Balkanized futures suggested by writers overinfluenced by William Gibson's cyberpunk novels.

At the beginning of the new millennium, British science fiction stands in a unique situation. Although (apart from Banks and, if he can be called science fiction, Terry PRATCHETT) science fiction writers are rarely if ever seen in the ranks of best-sellers, it is so remarkably creative as to cause some (American) critics to talk about a "renaissance." While overstated, there is truth in this, but also, there are several special circumstances that contribute to the field's health. First, it possesses a living icon—Clarke, knighted and conferred with honorary degrees (including one from Liverpool University to mark the acquisition of the SF Foundation library) and the one living science fiction writer (perhaps the only one since Wells) with a genuinely mass audience. Second, at least two of the field's "founding parents" are inescapably part of the British literary tradition. No science fiction can escape the shadow of Wells, who produced many of the field's thematic "givens," while Mary Shelley created, in Victor Frankenstein, its first icon, the scientist losing control of his creation. Third, British sf occupies a more anomalous place in the literary world than it does in America. It is difficult to think of a major literary figure in the U.S. who writes science fiction and is prepared not just to admit it, but glory in it. In Britain, there is not one, but at least two writing with and for the High Literary Tradition who write what can only be called science fiction. This makes it harder for critics to deny that novels like Lessing's *Memoirs of a Survivor* or Martin AMIS's *Time's Arrow* are science fiction, but it is significantly harder. Finally, satire and humor have been at the heart of British science fiction. Douglas Adams's radio serial *The Hitch-Hiker's Guide to the Galaxy* (1978) resulted in a series of novels. While fantasy in setting, Pratchett's "Discworld" books frequently spoof science and the scientific method; Kim Newman and Eugene Byrne play games with history and popular culture. Increasingly, sf is a somehow natural mode, which can result in some dreadful clichés but which also invigorates the field: two recent examples have been Ben ELTON (*Stark*) and Stephen FRY, whose roots are "comedy" rather than "science fiction." Fry's *Making History* in particular is a time-travel novel as effective as anything published as genre. Meanwhile, numerous British science fiction writers are set fair to carry the field through to the heart of the 21st c., with newer writers such as Adam Roberts, Justina Robson, Roger Levy, Alastair Reynolds, Liz Williams, and China Miéville already producing significant work.

BIBLIOGRAPHY: Aldiss, B. W., and D. Wingrove, *Trillion Year Spree* (1986); Clute, J., and P. Nicholls, eds., *The Encyclopedia of Science Fiction* (1933; rev. ed., 1999); Greenland, C., *The Entropy Exhibition: Michael Moorcock and the British "New Wave" in Science Fiction* (1983); Kincaid, P., *A Very British Genre* (1995); Parrinder, P., ed., *Science Fiction: A Critical Guide* (1979); Ruddick, N., *Ultimate Island: On the Nature of British Science Fiction* (1993); Stableford, B., *The Scientific Romance in Britain 1890–1950* (1985)

ANDY SAWYER

SCOT, Reginald

b. ca. 1538, Kent; d. 9 October 1599, Kent

S. is known primarily for *The Discovery of Witchcraft* (1584), his encyclopedic refutation of what he termed "witch mongering" in 16th-c. England. Written during the height of the European witch craze, this text reflects S.'s disgust with what he saw as extreme superstition (that is, the belief in the real supernatural power of witches), as well as disturbing and widespread abuse of legal procedure to prosecute those suspected of witchcraft. *The Discovery of Witchcraft* is a compelling combination of scientific, rational criticism of what S. saw as illogical and hypocritical means of identifying witches and a theological deconstruction of these beliefs. S.'s main argument against witchcraft is that those who believe in witches are risking heresy by attributing to mortals power that belongs only to God. S.'s theology was too advanced for his contemporaries, it seems. The book was never entered into the Stationer's Register, which suggests that no printer would risk publication of the manuscript; S. had to put forth the money for its printing and distribution himself. JAMES I was reportedly so incensed by the book that he had all copies of it burned in 1603. Though not reprinted again for at least another seventy-five years, *The Discovery of Witchcraft* became more popular and respected as the seventeenth century advanced.

Though S.'s is an autonomous text interesting for its own sake, scholarly work done on *The Discovery of Witchcraft* has focused almost exclusively on its presence in the texts of S.'s contemporaries, particularly dramatists. William SHAKESPEARE, Thomas MIDDLETON, and John LYLY all relied heavily on S.'s portraits of the stereotypical witch in their plays *Macbeth*, *The Witch*, and *Endymion*, respectively. Shakespeare also used S.'s descriptions of nightmares in *The Discovery* for *A Midsummer Night's Dream*. The dramatists who referred to S.'s work, however, tended not to reproduce S.'s skepticism about the reality of sinister old women capable of controlling the weather or killing people via magical charms and bargains with the devil and his minions.

Those scholars who have worked directly on S. have addressed only *The Discovery of Witchcraft*, whereas *A Perfect Platform of a Hop-Garden, and Necessary Instructions for the Making and Maintenance Thereof* (1574), the first known English practical treatise on hop culture, and *Discourse of Devils and Spirits*, which was written later but printed with *The Discovery,* have largely been ignored. Until recently, critics of *The Discovery of Witchcraft* have argued primarily about whether S.'s thesis was more rational than theological or vice versa. Both religionists and rationalists have agreed, however, that S. was well ahead of his time insofar as he was willing to defend innocent old women accused of things of which they could not possibly be capable. New feminist approaches, on the other hand, have seen S.'s insistence on witch mongers' paranoia and the mental instability of old women who believed themselves to be witches as signs of a misogynist fear of women's power, whether supernatural, social, or simply verbal.

While such criticism is a constructive aspect of an overall more gender-sensitive response to Renaissance texts, it tends to ignore the fact that S.'s tract was in some measure successful, at least according to later antiwitch mongering tracts, in decreasing the unfair torture and persecution of women, whether they identified themselves as witches or not.

BIBLIOGRAPHY: Anglo, S., ed., *The Damned Art: Essays in the Literature of Witchcraft* (1977); Purkiss, D., *The Witch in History* (1996); West, R. H., *R. S. and Renaissance Writings on Witchcraft* (1984)

COLLEEN SHEA

SCOTT, Geoffrey
b. 11 June 1884, Hampstead, London; d. 14 August 1929, New York City

Author of one of the most influential works of architectural history in the early 20th c., *The Architecture of Humanism* (1915; rev. ed., 1924), S. is best known for his role in preparing the private papers of James BOSWELL and of his experimental BIOGRAPHY of novelist Isabel de Charrière ("Zélide"). In his *Portrait of Zélide* (1925), S. creates a fragmentary but nonetheless intriguing account of this minor writer and literary figure. In 1927, S. was invited by American collector Lieutenant Colonel Ralph Heyward Isham to edit the Boswell papers acquired from Malahide Castle, near Dublin. Before his death in 1929, S. edited the first six volumes of the eighteen-volume edition (1928–34). The remaining volumes were completed by American scholar Frederick A. Pottle.

SCOTT, Paul [Mark]
b. 25 March 1920, Southgate, London; d. 1 March 1978, London

In 1983, an immensely popular television adaptation of S.'s tetralogy, *The Raj Quartet,* brought about a surge of interest in the writings of an author who had steadily built a substantial popular following over the course of his twenty-five-year literary career. With a few notable exceptions, however, including the award of the Booker Prize in 1977 for his final novel, *Staying On*, S. received relatively little critical recognition of his work during his lifetime. As S.'s novels, particularly those comprising *The Raj Quartet,* were rediscovered following the televised adaptation of that work, his literary reputation has grown, with critics praising his eye for detail, his sophisticated narrative technique, and the way in which that technique contributes to a multifaceted portrayal of India during the late colonial period.

S.'s novels reflect a near-obsession with India. Most of them are set in that country during the period immediately preceding independence in 1947 and are notable for their detailed, richly nuanced descriptions of Indian locales. It is surprising then, that S.'s own experience in India was actually quite limited. He was assigned to India in 1943 as an officer cadet in the air supply wing of the British India Army. In that capacity, he managed to travel extensively throughout the subcontinent, and became enthralled by India's dramatic landscape and complex mix of cultures. S.'s posting to India came shortly after the 1942 confrontation between Indian nationalists and the colonial administration over the British "Quit India" Resolution. This tension between the tottering British raj and the independence movement in India forms the backdrop for much of S.'s work. Following demobilization after the end of World War II, S. left India in 1946 and did not return again until 1964. He made two more brief visits to India in 1969 and 1972.

Beginning with his first novel, *Johnnie Sahib* (1952), S.'s novels were largely centered around two dominant and frequently interrelated themes. The first is the British colonial experience in India and how it affected both ruler and subject. The second primary theme deals with what S. referred to as "his obsession with the relationship between a man and the work he does." These two themes are present even in the two novels S. set in England, *A Male Child* (1956) and *The Bender* (1963). In *A Male Child*, the protagonist, Ian Canning, returns home after serving in the British Indian Army. Suffering from a mysterious disease contracted while overseas—a disease that may well serve as a metaphor for the colonial experience—Canning is too debilitated to "do a proper job and feel he had a stake in the future." Similarly, George Lisle-Spruce, the main character in *The Bender*, is jobless and subsists on an inheritance too meager to really live on but which serves as a disincentive to actually do much about it. Over the course of a forty-eight-hour period, George becomes aware of the insidious effect that the legacy has had on him and reflects on Stendahl's aphorism "Without work the vessel of life has no ballast." In both novels, the lingering and ambivalent effect of the loss of empire forms part of the subtext of the work, with the loss of colonial opportunity set against the moral cost of empire building.

In *The Corrida at San Feliu* (1964), an intricate novel S. considered to be among his finest, he continued to explore the theme of work as a metaphor for life. The novel is presented as the posthumous work of Edward Thornhill, an aging novelist suffering from writer's block. Following the death of Thornhill and his much younger wife, Maya, in an automobile accident in Spain, his editor gathers together the material Thornhill had been working on and publishes it. Although critics were not as positive about the book as S. was, *The Corrida at San Feliu* represents a significant stylistic advance for S., as he made effective use of a technique he perfected in *The Raj Quartet*, that of using multiple viewpoints in order to portray events and characters from differing perspectives.

Prior to *The Jewel in the Crown* (1966), the first of the four novels that comprise *The Raj Quartet*, S. had already written four novels set in the Indian subcontinent in the years shortly before independence. *The Jewel in the Crown* and S.'s subsequent novels show a mastery of theme and narrative technique that typify his later works. Set in 1942, the year of the "Quit India" Resolution and increasing tensions between the British colonial administration and the independence movement, the novel is centered around the rape of a young Englishwoman. Daphne Manners is attacked in the Bibighar Gardens by a gang of Indian assailants while meeting her anglicized Indian lover Hari Kumar. The District Superintendent of Police, Ronald Merrick, arrests Kumar for the crime and Kumar's conviction comes to symbolize the unbridgeable tension between the British and the Indians. In *The Day of the Scorpion* (1968), the depth of Merrick's corruption and complicity in the injustice of the case is explored in more depth, as Hari Kumar finally breaks his silence. Kumar tells his story to a representative of the governor who has renewed the investigation of the incident at the request of Daphne's mother. Kumar is finally released despite Merrick's objections, but Merrick's cold, sadistic "professionalism" distances him both from the colonial administration and from the Indians who see him, merely, as a symbol of the corrupt cruelty of that administration.

In the final two novels of *The Raj Quartet*, *The Towers of Silence* (1971) and *A Division of the Spoils* (1975), S. examines such issues as the English class system in India and the rising tensions between Hindus and Muslims in the waning days of empire. S.'s narrative leaves little doubt that much of the blame for the bloodshed that accompanied independence and partition of the country into India and Pakistan was attributable to the divide and rule policy of the British. Although the featured characters and viewpoints shift throughout the course of the four novels, Police Superintendent Merrick continues to play an increasingly sinister role throughout the cycle up to his violent murder in *A Division of the Spoils*. *Staying On*, which serves as something of a sequel to *The Raj Quartet*, is set in India twenty-five years after independence. S. reintroduces two relatively minor characters from *A Division of the Spoils*, Colonel Tusker Smalley and his wife Lucy, who opted to stay on after independence. S.'s wry take on the "new India" is an ironic one, and his portrayal of the English exiles who stayed on is poignant and perceptive.

While S.'s work has received an increasing, and largely appreciative critical reception in the years since his death, the fact that his work also helped to inaugurate a wave of nostalgia in Britain for the raj has brought its share of criticism as well. Some critics, like Salman RUSHDIE, have claimed that S.'s work is derivative of E. M. FORSTER and insufficiently critical of British imperialism in India despite his rough treatment of many of his British characters—for which he has also been castigated. For the most part, however, S.'s work has received belated critical praise for his skill as a storyteller, for the sophistication of his narrative technique, and for his insightful, multifaceted portrayal of the British colonial experience in India.

BIBLIOGRAPHY: Rao, K. B., *P. S.* (1980); Spurling, H., *P. S.* (1990); Swinden, P., *P. S.* (1980); Weinbaum, F. S., *P. S.* (1992)

DANIEL G. PAYNE

SCOTT, Sarah [Robinson]

b. 21 September 1723, West Layton, Yorkshire; d. 30 November 1795, Catton, Norfolk

Novelist, historian, and letter writer, S. had a literary education, but it was only after the end of her marriage that she started to write in earnest. S. married George Lewis Scott in 1751, but by 1752 the couple had separated. S. moved to Bath to live with her lifelong friend Lady Barbara Montagu and spent the rest of her life in literary endeavor and charitable pursuits.

S.'s first novel, *The History of Cornelia*, appeared in 1750. Cornelia, like Marivaux's *Marianne*, is an orphan alone in the world who is prevented from finding true happiness until the end of the book. The novel, written in the conventional sentimental style, eschewed the growing fashion for psychological immediacy, but was original in its exposition of the benefits of practical charity provided through the initiative of women. Throughout her career, notably in *A Description of Millenium Hall* (1762) and *The History of Sir George Ellison* (2 vols., 1766), S. maintained that women should appropriate corrupt or abused wealth from men for use in plans of supervisory charity toward the poor.

S.'s next work was *Agreeable Ugliness; or, The Trials of the Graces* (1754), a translation of the novel by Pierre-Antoine de La Place, which described the moral and sentimental triumph of a virtuous but ugly woman over the prejudices of society. *A Journey through Every Stage of Life*, S.'s second novel, also published in two volumes in 1754, comprises short tales told by a servant to her royal mistress, who has been imprisoned by her brother lest she claim the throne. S. did not publish again until the biographical *The History of Gustavus Erickson, King of Sweden* (1761) appeared under the pseudonym of Henry Augustus Raymond. This was followed by *The History of Mecklenburgh* (2 vols., 1762), written to gratify public interest in George III's new bride, Charlotte of Mecklenburgh.

In 1762, S. returned to fiction with the famous *A Description of Millenium Hall*, which had reached four editions by 1778. A traveler relates his discovery that a charming estate that he encounters in the countryside houses a community of genteel women united in philanthropic aims. S. intersperses the narrator's description of the Hall with tales told by the inhabitants about their mistreatment at the hands of men. The book concludes with the narrator vowing to reproduce the charitable model in his own estate.

S.'s next novel, *The History of Sir George Ellison*, narrates how Sir George uses the wealth derived from his benevolent slave plantation in Jamaica to create his English estate in the image of Millenium Hall. After the success of these two novels, S. returned to history, with a BIOGRAPHY of the 17th-c. leader of the French Protestants, *The Life of Theodore Agrippa D'Aubigné* (1772). S.'s demonstration of how D'Aubigné's moral constancy contrasts with the maneuvrings of the Medicis, was, like many 18th-c. works of historiography, an indirect comment on contemporary politics, this time on the factions surrounding Lord Chatham. S.'s final work was the epistolary novel, *A Test of Filial Duty* (1772), a narrative of virtue under pressure that ended happily.

S.'s sister, Elizabeth MONTAGU, was celebrated as the "Queen of the Blues," and S.'s writings reflect the Bluestocking circle interest in culture, charity, and the position of women in society. Although profoundly conservative on the subject of class and the social order, S.'s novels are serious examinations of the plight of the single gentlewoman, offering the solution that S. herself employed in her own life. S.'s lone heroines, like herself, busy themselves in establishing schemes of practical charity, and in advertising how this benevolent female agency could be vitally productive to the public sphere.

BIBLIOGRAPHY: Myers, S., *The Bluestocking Circle* (1990); Napier, E. R., "S. S.," in Battestin, M. C., ed., *British Novelists, 1660–1800*, part 2, *DLB* 39 (1985): 413–18

KATE WILLIAMS

SCOTT, [Sir] Walter
b. 15 August 1771, Edinburgh, Scotland; d. 21 September 1832, Abbotsford, Scotland

Poet, novelist, editor, historian, essayist, and collector whose influence pervades European and American 19th-c. literature and historiography, S.'s reputation has undergone remarkable fluctuations. Celebrated during his lifetime for his capacity to confer shape, meaning, and lively interest on Scotland's—and Britain's—national past, known as "the Lion of the North" and "The Great Unknown," S. was created a baronet and his death was a cause for national mourning. Though the influence of his work is embedded in Victorian literature and culture, his critical reputation declined steeply after his death; the lasting importance of S.'s writing began to be recognized in a series of reassessments from the 1930s, when the Marxist critic Georg Lukács identified the revolutionary nature of his historical method.

Born in Edinburgh, reared in the Scottish Borders, S. trained as an advocate in the city, and continued to practice his profession throughout life, but his literary interests dominated from the outset. His first publication included his translations of two German Romantic ballads, *The Chase, and William and Helen* (1796); influenced by Thomas PERCY's *Reliques*, he brought out a substantial collection of Scots ballads, the two-volume *Minstrelsy of the Scottish Border* (1802; rev eds., 1803, 1810), the product of exuberant "raids" or fieldwork in search of oral material; it included some of his own composition, and many older compositions "amended" by his own hand. S. emerged as a poet in his own right with a series of Scottish historical verse epics based on techniques and themes and informed by his omnivorous reading: the first of these, *The Lay of the Last Minstrel* (1805), expanded from an imitation ballad intended for the final volume of the *Minstrelsy* to a framed tale of love, chivalry, and the supernatural with a complex narrative time-scheme that juxtaposed verse epistles to S.'s friends with a vividly realized pageant of medieval Scotland. Its vividness, immediacy, and colorful description won the poem immediate success; 44,000 copies were sold by 1830. *Marmion: A Tale of Flodden Field* (1808) followed, admired for its scenes of battle and its complex English antihero on a fated peacemission to the Scottish court of James IV. Most successful of all, its successor *The Lady of the Lake* (1810) sold more than 20,000 copies in its publication year, and demonstrates S.'s instinctive capacity to grasp and develop the movement of popular interest. Set twenty years after the battle of Flodden, its dramatic love story propelled by disguised identities, idealized heroism, loyalty, and pride of the Scottish Highlanders, celebrated stag-hunt, and descriptions of Loch Katrine and the Trossachs seized the public imagination, and initiated a wave of visitors to the area and fascination with a Romantic vision of Scottishness that S.'s later works contrived to feed. S. meanwhile expanded his literary endeavors as an editor and biographer, bringing out major editions of John DRYDEN (18 vols., 1808) and Jonathan SWIFT (19 vols, 1814).

Effectively trumped as a popular poet by the *éclat* of Lord BYRON's *Childe Harold's Pilgrimage*, S.'s poetic sales began to decline by the time of *Rokeby* (1813), an elaborate historical narrative set in Yorkshire during the English Civil War, in 1813. He responded by turning to prose fiction: the first of the celebrated "Scotch" novels, the three-volume *Waver-*

ley; or, 'Tis Sixty Years Since, appeared anonymously and to great acclaim in 1814. Setting the action during the Jacobite rising against the Hanoverian monarchy in 1745, S. dramatized the enormous pace of change in Scotland during the 18th c. *Waverley* is at once a Bildungsroman, a topographical tour of Great Britain, and an exploration of cultural and political relations. Its eponymous hero is idealistic and naive, a reader of romances who enlists in the English army, and sets off northward from the family estate. In Scotland, he is seduced by a romanticized image of the Highlands, and leaves his troop to explore the region. The strategic importance of his support is seized on by Fergus MacIvor, a heroic but fanatical follower of Charles Edward Stuart, who exploits Waverley's passivity and indecision. Half in love with Fergus's sister Flora, he is maneuvred into transferring his allegiance to the Jacobites, meets Prince Charles ("the Pretender"), and is forced to confront the human consequences of his self-indulgent actions for his troop and fellow English officers. After the battle of Culloden, the Highlanders are routed; Fergus is captured, and Waverley himself is forced into hiding. The effects of Civil War become brutally clear, in the human carnage, wastage of property, and breakdown of relations. Educated into awareness of the realities of rebellion, Waverley escapes the traitor's death imposed on Fergus and retires to marry his true Scottish sweetheart in a symbolic renewal of the political treaty binding England and Scotland in 1707. *Waverley* confronts conflicting interests that continued to be felt by many Scots at the turn of the 19th c.: rational acceptance of the benefits of Union and genuine loyalty to the Hanoverian succession, with strongly local impulses to explore and preserve a past felt to be distinctively Scottish and objectified in atavistic allegiance to the Stuart dynasty. Exploiting this ambivalence, S.'s novels combined his formal training in the Scottish Enlightenment view of the history of all societies as an inevitable progression through stages of development, with antiquarian interest (exhibited in his ballad-collecting activities) in the preservation of aspects of an older way of life in decay and danger of disappearance. Drawing on local memories and earlier experiments in regional REALISM by Maria EDGEWORTH and others, S. developed vivid portrayals of an older Scotland to become one of the major architects of a highly marketable Romantic national tradition that fused a sense of locality, nostalgia, and historical perspective. His invocation of an historical dialectic informs both Hegelian and Marxist theory.

Successive "Waverley" novels, *Guy Mannering* (3 vols., 1815), *The Antiquary* (3 vols., 1816), *Old Mortality* (1816), *Rob Roy* (3 vols., 1818), *The Heart of Midlothian* (1818), *The Bride of Lammermoor* (1819), *Redgauntlet* (3 vols., 1824), and *The Fair Maid of Perth* (3 vols., 1828) all written at speed and—until

failure of his publishers forced bankruptcy and revelation of authorship on S. in 1826—published anonymously, consolidated his fame and brought financial reward unprecedented in publishing history. The novels characteristically display historical process in action through a narrative structure that traces the educational adventures of a young, frequently weak, character through unfamiliar terrain, caught up in major conflicts and encountering their impact on the lives of ordinary people. Without principles of his own, he is taught to understand the motivations of warring factions while arriving at the maturity of moderation and an appreciation of stability over more heroic but less secure modes of being. The EPIC dimensions of historical conflict are juxtaposed on vividly realized scenes of continuing existence embodied in strongly particularized character-portraits: Edie Ochiltree in *The Antiquary*, Cuddie Headrigg in *Old Mortality*, Bailie Nicol Jarvie in *Rob Roy*. These characters possessed an illusion of dramatic solidity that inspired numerous theatrical and operatic adaptations of the novels through the 19th c.

A variant of "wavering hero" structure produced arguably the greatest of the novels. *The Heart of Midlothian* involves an active working-class heroine in the trammels of national and political conflict when she attempts to secure a pardon from the king in England for a sister condemned to death for infanticide. It illuminates a particularly tense moment in Anglo-Scots relations, as Jeanie Deans's personal quest becomes entangled with the consequences of Scottish rebelliousness in the Porteous riots of 1736. Jeanie's "progress" on foot from Edinburgh to London is, like that of John BUNYAN's Pilgrim, also a (partly ironic) allegory of the Christian soul's journey to the Heavenly City, a dramatized debate between law and conscience, and a symbolic narrative of Scotland's rapprochement with England in the years following the Union. The story's emblematic dimensions and a strain of Gothic melodrama that complicates its realism do not eclipse a series of strongly individualized character studies, most notably Jeanie herself, and the crazed guide and inverted double, Madge Wildfire, whose story enacts a tragic version of her sister's fate. Jeanie's compassion cannot save Madge from the consequences of her own guilt, and Madge's death reasserts the power of Calvinist determinism over the ethos of mercy embodied in Jeanie's journey in search of pardon.

Dynamic tension between new and old ways of life, progress and nostalgia, epic action and local color, historic tragedy and daily comedy, continue to structure a series of "Waverley" novels set in England, *Ivanhoe* (1820), *Kenilworth* (1821), *The Fortunes of Nigel* (1822), *Woodstock* (1826), and Europe, *Quentin Durward* (1823), *Anne of Geierstein* (1829). These novels are characteristically set further back in time; the conflicts they document are drawn from written sources unsupplemented (as in the case of the "Scotch novels") by memory and oral testimony. They portray scenes of gratuitous cruelty that focus on the brutality of human motivation; character is reduced to type as individuals appear increasingly to be blown about by violent and deterministic historical forces. The greatest of the novels set in England, *Ivanhoe*, drew again and more extensively on the vogue of medievalism that informed his epic poems in a tale of nation formation that exerted a profound influence on 19th-c. British, European, and American historiography. Here, the factional conflict is between oppressed Saxons and the conqueror race of Normans whose greater organization and initiative will shape the national future. The novel's emotional interest centers on paired heroines, the pale, passive Saxon beauty Rowena whose union with Ivanhoe will seal the historical future at the book's conclusion, and the dark and striking Jewish Rebecca (with her father Isaac the representative of another repressed race), whose decisiveness controls the action and elicits a powerful, and reciprocated, sexual attraction in the hero. The demands of history and politics ensure that Ivanhoe will choose Rowena and abandon Rebecca to the traditional isolation of Judaism; the emotional conviction of the subplot makes clear the sacrifices entailed by destiny. An enormous popular success on publication, *Ivanhoe* was subsequently derided for sham medievalism and "tushery" by critics such as Robert Louis STEVENSON and Mark Twain, and for most of the 20th c. was read as a children's adventure story. More recently, academic criticism has reassessed it as one of the most significantly innovative of the Waverley series.

Following the financial collapse, S. determined to write his way out of bankruptcy and produced novels under increasing pressure of ill health and family bereavement. Readers continued to absorb them, but critical consensus found them hasty, poorly plotted, and lacking the exuberant character interest of the early works. Again, modern critical and textual investigation has begun to recover aspects of unique cultural importance in *Quentin Durward*, *The Monastery* (3 vols., 1820), *The Fair Maid of Perth*, and others. An nine-volume *Life of Napoleon* (1827), and an extensive range of political, historical, and antiquarian works, testify that S. literally wrote himself to death. In his final years, he kept a private journal whose stoicism and resolute refusal of self-pity has led it to be regarded as one of his major and most moving works.

BIBLIOGRAPHY: Anderson, W. E. K., ed., *The Journal of Sir Walter Scott* (1972); Davie, D., *The Heyday of Sir W. S.* (1961); Duncan, I., *Modern Romance and Transformations of the Novel: The Gothic, Scott, Dickens* (1992); Hart, F. R., *Scott's Novels: The Plotting of Historical Survival* (1966); Lukács, G., *The Historical Novel* (1937); Sutherland, J., *The Life of Sir W. S.* (1995); Welsh, A., *The Hero of the Waverley Novels* (1963; rev. ed., 1992)

SUSAN MANNING

SCUPHAM, [John] Peter
b. 24 February 1933, Liverpool

S. read English at Emmanuel College, Cambridge, after attending the Perse School, Cambridge, and St. George's, Harpenden, and subsequently worked as a teacher and owner of the Mandeville Press. He is unusual among contemporary poets in his fastidious preference for traditional patterns, for verse that scans and rhymes: *The Hinterland* (1977) comprises fifteen interlocking sonnets. S. writes about places and heirlooms, meditating on history. *The Snowing Globe* appeared in 1972, followed by *The Gift* (1973), *Prehistories* (1975), *Summer Palaces* (1980), *Winter Quarters* (1983), *Out Late* (1986), *The Air Show* (1988), *Watching the Perseids* (1990), *Selected Poems, 1972–1990* (1990), *The Ark* (1994), and *Night Watch* (1999).

SEDLEY [or SIDLEY], [Sir] Charles
b. March 1639?, Aylesford, Kent; d. August 1701, Southfleet, Kent

In speaking of an age when the practice of literature was regarded by many not as a profession but as a gentlemanly diversion, it is perhaps necessary to look at the "life" before attempting to discuss the "work." S. is a case in point. Twenty or twenty-one years of age at the time of the Restoration of Charles II, and having succeeded to his title four years before on the death of his elder brother, S. quickly became one of the group of select young noblemen and courtiers by which the new king surrounded himself. This group, which included the Earls of ROCHESTER and Dorset, the Duke of BUCKINGHAM, and Sir George ETHEREGE ("the merry gang," Andrew MARVELL called them) quickly acquired a reputation for wit, licentious living, considerable writing skill, and frequently violent behavior. All of them wrote lyrical poetry of varying degrees of aptitude, beauty, and pornographic vulgarity.

The one indisputably great poet among them (and by far the most vulgar) was John Wilmot, Earl of Rochester: Buckingham wrote one play, *The Rehearsal*, which is still occasionally revived (it is a brilliant satire on John DRYDEN's orotund, grandiloquent tragedies): Etherege and S. wrote a handful of plays each, of which the most important is Etherege's *The Man of Mode*. S.'s plays were *The Mulberry Garden* (perf. 1668), *Antony and Cleopatra* (perf. 1677), and *Bellamira* (perf. 1687). All three are more than competent products of their time. *The Mulberry Garden* is loosely based on Molière's *L'Ecole des Maris* (1661) and has echoes, also, of Etherege's *She Would If She Could*; it is written partly in prose and partly in heroic, rhymed couplets; the *Antony and Cleopatra*, completely in heroic couplets, clearly owes a good deal in style to the Dryden tragedies of the late 1660s and early 1670s. (The debt is partly repaid as, it is said, Dryden got the idea of his Antony-and-Cleopatra play—*All for Love; or, The World Well Lost*—which he wrote in 1678, from S.'s piece of the year before.) *Bellamira*, a brilliant but provocatively profane play, was based by S. on the *Eunuchus* of Terence.

S., in his lifetime, was as famous for his oral wit as for his writing, but, by its very nature, much of this is now lost to us. (Though Samuel PEPYS, that snapper-up of unconsidered trifles, has preserved for us a phrase or two.) And his poems, not all of which are negligible, still wear an air of being incidental to the main business of living. Two collections of them were published in 1702, the year after his death, including the exquisite "Phyllis is my Only Joy": the books were called simply, *A Collection of Poems* and *A New Miscellany*. The latter included poems by Lord Buckhurst, Earl of Dorset, as well as those by S. Dorset had been one of "the merry gang" and had also been associated with S. in another way: they appeared together, it was widely conjectured, as Eugenius and Lisideius, two of the four disputants in Dryden's *An Essay in Dramatic Poesie*, S. (Lisideius) being the one who speaks in support of contemporary French theater (the theater of Molière and Racine).

S. settled down in later life as a respectable and respected member of Parliament, taking his responsibilities seriously and carrying them out efficiently. He strongly supported the accession to the throne of William III in 1688–89 as successor to William's father-in-law, James II, who—after a reign of only two years—fled to Ireland.

In retrospect, so far as literature is concerned, S. is chiefly remembered as the author of *The Mulberry Garden*—one of the earlier Restoration plays that, though it is not so immaculate in design as William WYCHERLEY's *The Country Wife* or William CONGREVE's *The Way of the World*, is nevertheless a lively and admirable piece that ought to be better known than it is. Interestingly, in a Restoration comedy, the plot is concerned not with the up-to-the-minute London scene but with the period (1659–60) just before the Restoration. While it has scenes of witty sexual sparring as good as all but the very best of these familiar to us in later Restoration plays and while the play openly admits that such scenes are part of a game and a jest (Wildish, one of the characters, actually says at one point: "Why Madam, I thought that you had understood raillery . . . this is only the way of talking I have got among my companions . . . 'tis held

as a great part of wit to rally women handsomely behind their back, as to flatter 'em to their faces"), it also makes mention several times of the unstable political condition of the country and it weaves into the marital maneuvres considerations of former royalists being deprived of their estates by the Commonwealth government and, contrariwise, the benefits that accrue to noblemen who are loyal to the "Good Old Cause"—that is, to Puritanism. Indeed, the gradual shift of political fortunes is built into the progress of the plot: at the end of act 4 the advice is given: "Let me tell you as a friend, there's like to be a turn suddenly; 'tis thought the general [General George Monck, warily waiting with his army just across the Scottish border] will declare like an honest man—I say no more." By act 5 scene 3, we are told: "the general has this day to some persons of quality declared for the king; all Cavaliers are immediately to have their liberty" and the play ends with a dance and general rejoicing at the prospect of Charles II's return: "I hear the people's voice in joyful cries/Like conquering troops o'er flying enemies;/They seem to teach us in a ruder way/The honour due to this all-healing day." These words are given to Eugenio, one of the young lovers, but they can also legitimately be taken as representing S.'s own sentiments, recalled by him in this play eight years or so after the event.

BIBLIOGRAPHY: Lamb, J., *So Idle a Rogue: The Life and Death of Lord Rochester* (1993); Masters, A., *The Play of Personality in the Restoration Theatre* (1992); Nettleton, G. H., *English Drama of the Restoration and Eighteenth Century* (1914)

ERIC SALMON

SELF, Will[iam Woodward]
b. 26 September 1961, London

S. is widely regarded as one of contemporary British literature's most penetrating satirists of the English middle class. Unlike most of the popular young novelists he is associated with, such as Julian BARNES and Martin AMIS, S.'s best work is his short story collections rather than his two novels. He is considered by many critics as an irreverent but accurate chronicler of the drug culture, having battled drugs himself until the late 1990s. His work is especially popular with the alienated younger generation who applaud his comic debunking of the hypocritical pretensions of the English suburban Home Counties.

Some of his subject matter comes out of his own battles with drug addiction and his own borderline schizophrenic condition diagnosed when he was a teenager. His first collection of short stories, *The Quantity Theory of Insanity* (1991), garnered high praise from writers such as Amis and Doris LESSING. Many of the six stories in the volume dramatize the dubious role of the psychotherapist and drugs in the treatment of mental illness, but they do so in a disturbingly satiric mode. A character that recurs in several of his later works, psychiatrist Dr. Zach Busner, becomes an ironic symbol for one of S.'s favorite themes: sane patients who are being treated by insane doctors. The title story is based upon the perverse theory, created by a team of psychologists, that there is only a limited amount of sanity available in a society at any given time, a crisis that S. uses to theorize on what actually defines insanity and sanity. Several other stories in the collection treat the irrational and its destructive effects on a so-called normal society.

S.'s next work, two novellas entitled *Cock and Bull* (1992), addresses two of the author's pet subjects: sexual identity and masculinity. Relying on elements of fantasy, the woman in *Cock* grows a penis to punish her abusive, alcoholic husband. In *Bull*, a hypermasculine rugby player discovers a vagina has grown behind his left knee. Bull's doctor, in treating his knee, finds that he has become sexually attracted to Bull and they begin an affair. The crisis gets worse when Bull becomes pregnant. S.'s work from this point on deals with disturbing issues of gender identity and masculinity.

Most critics would agree that S.'s first real novel *My Idea of Fun* (1993) has been his most significant work because of the range of its topics. It is a postmodern coming-of-age novel that explores its protagonist Ian Wharton's difficulties with violence, masculinity, psychotic breakdown, therapists, and most crucially, the nature of reality. Because of the power of Wharton's eidetic memory—his ability to create images with utterly realistic details—he is often unable to differentiate between the imagined and the real which, in effect, renders him unable to determine whether he is a victim or a victimizer.

S.'s next short story collection, *Grey Area and Other Stories* (1994), deals with another of S.'s obsessive topics: the pathological ennui of English suburban life. Several stories, "Inclusion" and "Chest," satirize the bureaucratic abstractions of the health care industry, especially mental health professionals. Several other stories are variations on the effects of empty, ritualized repetitive actions and the psychopathology of everyday life in the sterility of London suburbs. Many of the males in these stories are helpless victims of their own libidinous desires, regardless of their social or educational status.

S.'s next work, a novella entitled *The Sweet Smell of Psychosis* (1996), continues his satirical attack on the hypocritical and solipsistic madness of London's media world. The protagonist, Richard Hermes, loses his innocence by becoming addicted to cocaine and thus lives in a nightmarish world of paranoia. S.'s second novel, *Great Apes* (1997), became a best-seller in spite of its strange subject matter. The novel records the painful dilemma of artist Simon Dykes when he awakens one morning to a world in which apes have taken the place of humans as their superiors. S.'s brilliant use of defamiliarization—the exchange of roles—brings the modern world's problems into sharp relief. The psychiatrist Dr. Zach Busner, from an earlier work, reappears to help Dykes adjust his traumatized consciousness to an ape world, or what S. calls "chimpunity."

S. returned to the short-story form in his 1998 collection entitled *Tough, Tough Toys for Tough, Tough Boys*. Again, a number of the stories address issues of masculinity, while others deal with alcoholism, ennui, and the depressive emptiness of London and its suburbs. One of the most entertaining stories is about drugs called "The Rock of Crack as Big as the Ritz," while "Caring Sharing" takes place in a future where the reigning psychiatric establishment assigns each human to a giant humanoid companion called "emoto" whose major function is to nurture emotional health in their clients.

There is little question that S. is one of England's most trenchant social satirists, and he is one of the few who has established his reputation in short stories rather than full-length fiction.

BIBLIOGRAPHY: Middleton, T., "W. S.," in Moseley, M., ed., *British Novelists since 1960*, Third Series, *DLB* 207 (1999): 244–52; Sender, K., "To Have and to Be: Sex, Gender, and the Paradox of Change," *W& Lang* 20 (Spring 1997): 18–23

PATRICK MEANOR

SELVON, Sam

b. 20 May 1923, San Fernando, Trinidad; d. 16 April 1994, Trinidad

S. was a product of the Indian diaspora of 1845–1917 that altered profoundly and permanently Trinidad's economic, social, and cultural complexion. He began his writing career as a journalist at the *Trinidad Guardian* but emigrated to England in 1950 in search of something more substantial than the malaise of Trinidad society.

S.'s years at the *Guardian* were crucial in his development as a writer. His subtle satire and gift for characterization, his sensitivity and compassion, his ability to crystallize a scene in short, trenchant strokes were nurtured at the *Guardian* and are sometimes noticeable in his apprentice work. His early years in London were equally important in his growth as a writer. It was S.'s good fortune to live in London's Balmoral Hostel, for here also lived the displaced colonials—West Indians, Africans, Indians—who would form the matrix from which the eccentric and vivacious characters of his "London fiction" grew.

A Brighter Sun (1952) is an important novel in West Indian literature because of the central character's quest for what has become the most compelling pluralistic society crippled by self-contempt, the psychic scars of slavery, and the dehumanizing Indian indenture system. Tiger, the novel's central intelligence, senses that he and the rest of his society share what V. S. NAIPAUL has called a hobbling "incompleteness." And Tiger's quest for an individuality that transcends racial divisions matches S.'s conception of a united Caribbean free of racial and religious divisiveness, a strong theme in his fiction, essays, and interviews. At the end of the novel, Tiger is regenerated when he affirms his value and the power of the land as the source of an undefined, but certain, inner strength.

S. was the quintessential West Indian. He was reared in an amorphous society that worshiped all things British and American. At the same time, his sensibilities were anchored in the West Indies, so the tension created by amorphousness and the certainty of deeply embedded roots can be found throughout his fiction, especially in *An Island Is a World* (1955) and *I Hear Thunder* (1963). Both novels depict Trinidad in the 1940s and 1950s as a society of petty racism, of men and women lost in the void of colonial neglect who seek some sort of fulfilling wholeness elsewhere. *Turn Again Tiger* (1958), which consolidates the internalizing of Tiger's identity, and *Those Who Eat the Cascadura* (1972) also examine the individual's search for self-definition in a society that tends to ape older, more advanced societies.

The characters of S.'s "London Fiction"—*The Lonely Londoners* (1956), *The Housing Lark* (1965), *Moses Ascending* (1975), *Moses Migrating* (1983)—are also distinctively West Indian in a way that has gone largely unnoticed. Colonialism gave the colonial a spurious security which breaks down under the assault of the rejection and discrimination he encounters in London. S.'s Londoners resemble the feckless, marginalized men of Claude McKay's *Banjo* (1929) who also live on the fly. They have moved to a society largely closed to them, so they come together as a cohesive group defensively; but that cohesiveness is also the result of their psychological need to form a colony with a governor/leader.

Although the decades before the 1950s produced important West Indian writers, a substantial and distinctive body of West Indian literature began to appear only in the fifties and sixties. S.'s work is a major contribution to this literary renaissance. His pioneering work in the use of the Trinidadian dialect not simply as engaging dialogue but as a powerful literary language, his mixture of HUMOR and pathos, and his sensitive treatment of alienated, displaced West Indians, whose follies and deficiencies he is aware of but never ridicules, guarantee him a permanent place in the history of West Indian literature. S.'s subtext is the difficult question: what does it mean to be West Indian? His work is an engaging record of a time and place, of ordinary men and women, most of whom are largely unskilled, living and surviving in a complex, difficult, and rapidly changing world. They survive and grow, supported by their attitudes and humor, above all their resilience, and indeed one of the most important qualities of S.'s work is how skillfully it conveys this resilience and the exhilaration in the lives of these ordinary men and women.

BIBLIOGRAPHY: Barratt, H., "Individual Integrity in S.'s *Turn Again Tiger* and *Those Who Eat the Cascadura*," *TSAR* 5 (Summer 1986): 153–59; Nasta, S., ed., *Critical Perspectives on S. S.* (1988); Ramchand, K., "Song of Innocence, Song of Experience: S. S.'s *The Lonely Londoners* as a Literary Work," *WLWE 21* (Autumn 1982): 644–54

HAROLD BARRATT

SENTIMENT

In modern usage "sentiment" often means "feeling," with a touch of condescension or disapproval through the association with sentimentality. This pejorative association must be distinguished from the literary-historical use of the word although both are affected by its controversial transformations over the last three hundred years. A highly self-conscious cult of sentiment gripped the latter half of the 18th c. as an attempt to base the moral life on feeling and to celebrate benevolent and tender feelings as the mark of true humanity. This new emphasis on feeling promoted social benevolence along with a new importance accorded to the domestic sphere and to the feminine. Yet the significance of the term was not always evident at the time as is apparent in Lady Bradshaigh's 1749 letter to the novelist Samuel RICHARDSON "What . . . is the meaning of the word *sentimental*, so much in vogue among the polite? Everything clever and agreeable is comprehended in that word; but I am convinced a wrong interpretation is given." Her puzzlement is understandable since in retrospect it can be seen that the meaning of the word shifted crucially over the middle decades of the century in a way that reflects a seismic cultural change. It was in effect the change from a theological conception of ethics based on a belief in original sin toward an optimistic Enlightenment myth of the natural goodness of man.

The Enlightenment cult of sentiment, however, is not to be understood in a purely 18th-c. context. It represents the coming into consciousness of longer-term cultural developments in Europe, and its impact, as an "affective turn," has been radical and permanent. Its aftereffects can be seen in the subsequent steep decline of the term "sentimental" from being one of the most honorific terms of the 18th c. to its modern meaning of mawkish emotional indulgence. This semantic decline is far from signifying any simple rejection of the value placed on feeling. On the contrary, in becoming a term of discrimination within the emotional realm, it attests the importance now attached to feeling as such, and therefore to distinguishing true from false feeling. This applies especially in the British context as opposed to continental Europe. In Europe, Jean-Jacques Rousseau was the overwhelmingly significant figure and the developments of sentiment in America, France, and Germany, for example, have different national inflections and time scales. In America, founded at the height of the vogue of sentiment, the question of sentiment has continued to be related to conduct and rhetoric in the public sphere. French culture retains a deep suspicion of feeling as such. In Germany, sensibility is most strikingly transposed into an aesthetic key. Britain was an early influence on all these, however, owing to its early modernization. What follows, therefore, is a brief comment, confined to the British context, on the origins of 18th-c. sentiment; an analysis of the word's usages in the middle of the century; and a brief retrospect on its continuing significance.

Until the 1980s, scholars continued to debate the rival origins of sentimentalism. Protestantism was a prominent source, often in increasingly secularized forms. Puritan examination of conscience is evident in Richardson, while an inclusive emphasis on charity rather than exclusive dogmas of faith, an emphasis associated with the Latitudinarian movement in the established church, can be seen in Henry FIELDING. Contemporary philosophical thought was largely governed by John LOCKE whose psychology of perception and knowledge rested on a bodily sensationalism. Locke's one time pupil, Anthony Ashley Cooper, third Earl of SHAFTESBURY, developed a morally optimistic deism, in explicit opposition to the dark vision of Thomas HOBBES and the disabused economic realism of Bernard MANDEVILLE. Almost contemporaneously with Shaftesbury's influential essays, the *Spectator* papers of Joseph ADDISON and Richard STEELE sought consciously to define and promote a new world of bourgeois sociality. In view of the multiplicity of "sources," later scholars have seen them all as partly independent streams reflecting, and contributing to, the massive cultural change that Lawrence Stone defined as the growth of "affective individualism" between 1600 and 1800. Yet although these developments did not originate in the early 18th c., it was the period in which they became crucially self-conscious and problematic. The fruitful complexity of 18th-c. sentiment is that it encompasses both a naively revealing reflection of a changing culture and sophisticated attempts to understand it.

The crucial significance of the word "sentiment" lay in its elusive linking of thought and feeling, as can be seen in its shifting semantics over the middle of the 18th c. If we were to substitute a modern word for the heavy use of "sentiment" in the period, we would notice that for Richardson, in the 1740s, the word usually meant "principles." When Richardson's characters express their sentiments, they mean the general moral principles by which they seek to conduct their lives. Yet only two decades later, the same experiment conducted on Laurence STERNE would indicate that for him the word means predominantly "feeling." Most importantly, however, neither of these emphases completely effaces the other. It was part of the optimistic Enlightenment myth to accord moral principle the intuitive immediacy of feeling while seeing feeling as intrinsically, almost compellingly, directed toward benevolence and social virtue. Such a conflation of social and moral principle with personal feeling is obviously problematic; it contradicts the traditional awareness that they are too often at odds, a recognition enshrined in the Christian doctrine of original sin. The project was therefore highly vulnerable in its naive forms yet it contained a significant insight. The more enduring intuition underlying the myth of sentiment was that, if "feeling" and "reflection" cannot simply be identified, neither can they be fully separated. In a world increasingly affected by Cartesian dualism, or by what T. S. ELIOT described as a "dissociation of sensibility," a coming apart of thought and feeling, the movement of sentiment represented a significant, if often naive, resistance.

The movement of sentiment, which initially privileged feeling within an assumption of rational control, developed by the latter decades of the century into the excesses of sensibility in which feeling was prized, and given exaggerated public expression, for its own sake. Not surprisingly, these developments had aroused, even by the 1770s, a distinct antisentimentalist reaction from which the modern, critical usage largely derives. In the greater writers and thinkers of sentiment, however, the elusive doubleness of the term reflected, sometimes unwittingly, a sense of inner complexity and ambivalence whose true bearing was not on the general notion of sentiment but on the specific uncertainties of the emotional and moral life. Sterne's *A Sentimental Journey through France and Italy* walks an abyss of ambivalence as it satirizes the very sentiment it celebrates and provokes. Of course, he was almost universally *read* in a sentimental spirit at the time, as was Henry MACKENZIE in *The Man of Feeling*. But Richardson and Sterne enacted an internal dramatic critique of their own versions of sentiment that effectively explored the aspirations and self-deceptions of their characters. In continental Europe, Johann Wolfgang von Goethe produced in *Werther* (1774) a comparably critical yet creative comment on Rousseau's *The New Eloisa* (1761). In effect, the philosophical project of moral sentiment, by its very instability, provided a discourse, and a template, for studying the uncertainties and insincerities of the inner life.

This helps explain why much of the important "thinking" about sentiment was conducted implicitly, unsystematically, and to some extent unwittingly, in imaginative literature. Literature resists the logical clarity and fixity of abstract discriminations. At the same time, literature was charged with a continuous philosophical analysis of the ethical life as necessarily incorporating the aspects of feeling and reflection. At the discursive level, Shaftesbury's *Characteristics of Men, Manners, Opinions, and Times* celebrated the natural benevolence of man although for him such spontaneous feeling is always understood to be socially and aesthetically cultivated rather than simply spontaneous. Within his social culture, he could affirm unproblematically the consonance of feeling, taste, and ethical behavior. Francis Hutcheson, in *An Enquiry into Our Ideas of Beauty and Virtue* (1725), privileged feeling more clearly as a source of the ethical life and thereby put the whole conception under potential strain. David HUME followed Hutcheson in identifying feeling as the irreducible basis of ethical values, but this was part of his radical critique of human reason. The spirit of his claim, in other words, was not sentimental and in his first major treatment of the topic, *A Treatise of Human Nature*, he proposed a notion of sympathy that, rather than being an immediate emotional response to another's distress, depended on an internal act of imaginative reconstruction. This important line of thought was developed fully by Adam SMITH in his *Theory of Moral Sentiments* where sympathy implies the capacity to participate imaginatively in the inner states of others, whether these be happy or painful, good or evil. He developed the idea of the internal, impartial "spectator" who judges all behavior, including one's own, in a spirit of detached participation. Along with Immanuel Kant's *Critique of Judgement* (1790), Smith's was the period's major treatise on ethics and the most summative treatment of the tradition of moral sentiment.

Kant resisted Rousseau's urging of the claims of feeling and wrote in explicit opposition to the British empirical tradition that tended to concern itself with the practical psychology and consequences of behavior as opposed to the awesome mystery of the ethical imperative as such. For Kant, it was necessary to obey the categorical imperative even in circumstances where the effects would be damaging as in the requirement to tell the truth to an intending murderer asking the whereabouts of the victim. Smith took the opposite view. No single principle can govern behaviour in all circumstances and there is no alternative to a holistic assessment of circumstances and the impartial good will symbolized by the figure of the internal "spectator." Smith's model defines the boundary of

what reason can determine in this area and effectively hands the problem over from philosophy to the novel, which was indeed the form in which the next century preeminently developed its sense of social and individual conscience. If by the early 19th c. the term "sentiment" had faded once again into the background to mean morally tinged feeling but without the urgent or grandiose claims of the 18th c., this is partly because the debate had shifted its ground from philosophy to literature.

Since then, the cultural history of sentiment has undergone important further shifts. In a comparative purview, British and American literature of the 19th c. came closest to maintaining the original impulse of sentimentalism. This was often at an undemanding popular level but in the great writers, such as Charles DICKENS and George ELIOT, the irreducible instability of sentiment as learned from its earlier, more literalistic phase, now helped to dramatize the obscurity and self-deceptions of the moral life. The modernist movement of the early 20th c. was in many respects a programmatic attack on the perceived sentimentality of the Victorian era and, since it set much of the agenda for university English studies, it established for many decades the common academic perception. The last two decades of the century, however, saw a cultural, historical, and largely feminist, recuperation of 19th-c. sentiment whereby works like Harriet Beecher Stowe's *Uncle Tom's Cabin* (1852) are newly appreciated for their social impact in which the appeal to popular moral sentiment was of the essence. Some of these critics would give the word "sentimental" a purely descriptive, non-judgmental implication although, apart from the difficulty of legislating linguistic change, this would threaten precisely the internal emotional discrimination which is the great and positive inheritance of the cult of sentiment.

BIBLIOGRAPHY: Barker-Benfield, G. J., *The Culture of Sensibity* (1992); Bell, M., *Sentimentalism, Ethics, and the Culture of Feeling* (2000); Brissenden, R. F., *Virtue in Distress* (1974); Hagstrum, J., *Sex and Sensibility* (1980); McGann, J., *The Poetics of Sensibility* (1996); Mullan, J., *Sentiment and Sociability* (1988); Todd, J., *Sensibility* (1986); Tompkins, J., *Sensational Designs* (1985)

MICHAEL BELL

SERMON

The sermon has long been a part of British literature; many prose sermons have survived from the earliest historical reaches of Christianity in Britain. As remains typical of religious writings, these sermons serve as an interesting study of the historical and social aspects of their day as well as bona fide contributions to the literary landscape. Most authors of sermons were also preachers, although not all were blessed with great oratorical skills.

Most scholarly discussions of the British sermon begin with ÆLFRIC and Wulfstan, Archbishop of York. Consistent with their time in history, both men were Catholic. Their sermons illustrate typical Roman Catholic theology. Ælfric was the abbot of a cloistered monastic order and as such led a life with time for a great deal of study and reflection. He left behind scripture translations, letters, homilies, and stories of the saints' lives. Ælfric had particular agenda points in mind when writing and teaching: he wanted to offer an explanation of canon law to the masses, he wanted to divulge and record church history as accurately as possible, and he wanted to keep the message of the redemptive nature of Christ alive in his work. Ælfric was of the common clerical opinion that the laity could handle only so much information; therefore, he deliberately tempered his writings so that they reflected his perceived level of audience limitations. Ælfric was also, however, interested in writing well and paid close attention to his style, which is still admired in our time.

Wulfstan was an admirer of Ælfric and his work and toiled to live up to the same standards in his own writings. Wulfstan was not cloistered; he had a more casual relationship with the laity. However, he too believed in the limitations of the laity. It was Wulfstan's desire to both reform and renew interest in the church. A common theme in his sermons is the need to strictly follow God's laws. Wulfstan believed that often people had to be coerced into following those laws and was not beyond using his sermons as a method of such coercion. His sermons were not always liturgical; he often focused on topical and occasional themes. Like Ælfric, Wulfstan was also interested in the style of his writing, an interest that has contributed to the continued study of his work.

The MIDDLE ENGLISH sermon writers who followed Ælfric and Wulfstan were mostly clerics intent on following the literary example of their predecessors. The Middle English sermon writers continued to toil at instructing the masses in church law and history as well as at explaining Christian faith in terms the clergy believed could be understood by the laity. There was also some focus on the "problem" of women in the church. Sermons warned of the evils of women, referring to the sins of Eve and the perception of woman as temptress. At the same time, sermons extolled Mary, mother of Christ, as the epitome of womanhood and held up virgins as sanctified beings. Most of the sermons of this period were unsigned and remain anonymous.

A few notable women, like JULIANA OF NORWICH, left behind sermon writings as well. In fact, Juliana's work has been revived and applauded enthusiastically in the past few decades, especially by feminist theologians. Juliana was a mystic; an example of her work is *Revelations of Divine Love*. Of course, Juliana would not have had the opportunity to actually preach.

The Early Reformers of the mid-16th c. were moving away from Catholic influence, as a result of the Protestant Reformation, and instead were influenced by the teachings of Martin Luther. The allegory so often present in earlier sermons virtually disappeared. There was an interest in studying the original languages of the Bible in order to facilitate more accurate translations. Many sermons focused on a simple retelling of the Gospel stories rather than on esoteric intellectual arguments. Sermon writers now urged the laity to read and study the Bible on their own and counted on reader and listener familiarity with the Bible when writing and preaching their sermons. These reformers were also fond of using biblical messages to teach political lessons. One of the more famous sermon writers of the period was Hugh LATIMER.

The latter part of the 16th c. saw the advent of the Elizabethan preachers. William Whitaker, a well-known sermon writer of the period, preached a belief in one true scripture, which was to be found in a literal rather than symbolic interpretation of the Bible. Whitaker held the belief that the Holy Spirit speaks to all believers, not just to those ordained as ministers. Like preachers earlier in the century, Whitaker encouraged the laity to study their Bibles.

There was a distinct Calvinist influence during the Elizabethan period, with a steady rise in Puritanism. Because of political and religious disputes, sermons dealing with theological controversy were not permitted, although of course this does not mean such were not written. Other noted sermon writers of this period were Richard HOOKER, well known for his high level of intelligence and good command of language, Thomas Playfere, known for his style, and John Carpenter.

Anglo-Catholic preachers began the 17th c. Lancelot ANDREWES is considered the father of the Anglo-Catholic church. He is best known for his use of wit in his sermons. John DONNE also falls into this period. Famous for his poetry, Donne was also skillful in the pulpit. His sermons are especially noted for their eloquence and poetry.

Sermons of the 18th and 19th cs. moved more clearly though not exclusively toward Anglican theology. Bishop Reginald Heber is known for both sermons and hymns like the still popular "Holy, Holy, Holy." William Sanday made his mark as both a theologian and a Bible scholar. Henry Parry Liddon, like many other 19th-c. theologians, was an advocate of the High Church. Liddon was a highly influential theologian. *The Divinity of Our Lord and Saviour*, published in 1866, is Liddon's most important collection of sermons. John Henry NEWMAN, a cardinal of the Roman Catholic Church, influenced a large part of the 19th c. with his mastery of prose and his exceptionally clear style.

The 20th c. has not been without its share of sermon writers, including Ramsey of Canterbury, Arthur Michael Ramsey, who served as Archbishop of Canterbury. A true 20th-c. figure, Ramsey was a proponent of the High Church but he was also an enthusiastic advocate of the ecumenical movement, a cause at which many others continue to toil. As always, sermons continue to be written and studied, even as we begin a new century. Ramsey's ideas of ecumenical theology will surely continue to flourish. Most likely, theological debates on social and political issues will also continue in popularity.

BIBLIOGRAPHY: Blake, N. F., *Middle English Religious Prose* (1972); Blench, J. W., *Preaching in England in the Late Fifteenth and Sixteenth Centuries* (1964); Gatch, M. M., *Preaching and Theology in Anglo-Saxon England* (1977); Herr, A. F., *The Elizabethan Sermon* (1969); Mitchell, W. F., *English Pulpit Oratory* (1962)

TERRY D. NOVAK

SEVERN, Joseph
b. 7 December 1793, Hoxton; d. 3 August 1879, Rome, Italy

S. was a painter, and devoted friend and correspondent of John KEATS, of whom he made several portraits and took the deathmask, having accompanied Keats to Italy. Part of the Keats circle that included Leigh HUNT and John Hamilton REYNOLDS, S. lived with his family in England from 1841 to 1860, returning to Italy when he was appointed British Consul in Rome. Retiring in 1872, he remained in Italy until his death. S.'s attempts at fiction were unsuccessful, but in 1863 he published *The Vicissitudes of Keats's Fame.*

SHADWELL, Thomas
b. 1642?, Norfolk; d. 19 November 1692, London

Author of *The Enchanted Island* (1674), an operatic reworking of William SHAKESPEARE's *The Tempest*, S. was educated at Caius College, Cambridge, and the Middle Temple. His first effort was apparently a loose translation of Molière's *Les Fâcheux*, retitled *The Sullen Lovers* and produced in Lincoln's Inn Fields in 1668. His plays comically depict the mores and manners of Restoration London. In his prologue to *The Virtuoso* (1676), he declared his affinity to Ben JONSON when he stated that comedy should blend wit and satire in exposing the humors. His plays *Epsom-Wells* (perf. 1672; pub. 1673) and *Bury-Fair* (1689) are especially demonstrative of his intention. John DRY-

DEN's "MacFlecknoe" arose from a war of words between himself and S. They disagreed bitterly over Dryden's appraisal of Jonson, whom S. held in esteem. A series of satires passed between the two, and their animosity did not ebb. Upon Dryden's dismissal in 1688, S. assumed the office of poet laureate and wrote the history of the revolution. As poet laureate, S. instituted the annual New Year and birthday odes.

SHAFFER, Anthony [Joshua]
b. 15 May 1926, Liverpool; d. 6 November 2001, London

Twin brother of the more famous Peter, S. had a resounding success with his intricately plotted and surprising play, *Sleuth* (1970), which had long runs in London and New York. S. adapted the play for film in 1973 starring Laurence Olivier and Michael Caine. Other work for the theater includes *Murder* (1979), *The Case of the Oily Levantine* (perf. 1979), revised and produced on Broadway as *Whodunnit* (perf. 1982; pub. 1983), *Murderer* (1987), and, with Robin Hardy, *The Wicker Man* (1979). Filmed in 1973 and starring Edward Woodward and Christopher Lee, this British movie about a latter-day human sacrifice has acquired cult status.

SHAFFER, Peter [Levin]
b. 15 May 1926, Liverpool

Frustrated with the realistic theater of the "Angry Young Men" that swept the English stage in the 1950s, dramatist S. borrowed from Antoine Artaud's "Theater of Cruelty," employing music, mime, and other techniques of "total theater" to release within the audience violent emotions presumably repressed since childhood, and in the process return theater to its roots as religious ritual. Aiming less at the discussion of contemporary social problems than at analyzing the religious crisis of modern life, S. proposed the spiritual revitalization of his audience by offering, as Lotte puts it in her toast at the conclusion of *Lettice & Lovage*, "Enlargement for shrunken souls—Enlivenment for dying spirits—Enlightenment for dim, prosaic eyes." A psychological dramatist concerned primarily with the nature of human creativity and the costs that the creative individual pays in contemporary society, S. emerged in the 1960s in the paradoxical guise of the century's last great poet of the numinous who was capable of writing commercially successful plays as well.

Born to a family of Jewish tradesmen, S. attended St. Paul's School, London, with his twin brother Anthony SHAFFER. After serving as a conscript in the coal mines during wartime, he matriculated to Trinity College, Cambridge, graduating with a degree in history in 1950. Moving to New York City, he held down a series of odd jobs while writing music reviews, radio plays, and three murder mystery novels (two in collaboration with his brother). He was nearly thirty when he decided that theater would be his life's profession. His first full-length stage play, *Five Finger Exercise* (1958), was directed by John Gielgud and established S. as one of the most important forces in Anglo-American theater for the next thirty years.

S.'s early plays probe the psyches of young, wounded, creative spirits, but from an invariably laconic perspective that prevents the audience from identifying too closely with the injured innocent even as it is forced to acknowledge society's hypocrisy and capacity for brutal repression. In *Five Finger Exercise*, each member of an upper-middle-class family sacrifices the children's German tutor, who is the only authentic member of the household, to his or her own artistic pretension or romantic self-delusion. Similarly, in *The Battle of Shrivings* (perf. 1970; rev. as *Shrivings*, 1974), an impressionable young man is caught between his father, a realist who has lost the capacity for joy, and his spiritual counselor, an idealist whose seeming equanimity masks painful self-doubt and self-loathing. The conflict between the highly creative but unorthodox person and his/her conformist but hypocritical society is translated into black comedy in the paired plays *The Private Ear and The Public Eye* (1962), in which a maladroit seducer and a screwball private detective try to convince an unaspiring secretary and a sedate businessman, respectively, to look at the world as an occasion for sensual enjoyment so intense that it borders on religious revelation. Through the farcical conceit of turning the stage lights up when the characters' apartment building suffers a power failure, and putting the stage into darkness when the characters are supposedly able to see each other, *Black Comedy* (perf. 1965; pub. 1967)—paired in 1967 with *White Lies* (rev. as *The White Liars and Black Comedy*, 1968)—creates a world of comic misrule in which the facade that people choose to present to each other is rendered meaningless while what they hope to conceal is revealed.

S. is most celebrated, however, for a trio of plays that dramatize the inevitable conflict between a creative person capable of an untraditional religious vision and a representative of society who is repulsed by the chaos of creativity even while hungering for something more spiritually substantial in his own life. In *The Royal Hunt of the Sun* (1964), the explorer Francisco Pizarro not only exposes the emptiness of Christian social values by the way that the Spanish defeat native king Atahuallpa to steal the Incans' gold, but by destroying Incan belief in their king's divinity intensifies his own despair over living without any hope of transcendence. Similarly, in *Equus* (1973), a psychiatrist called upon to treat a teen-aged boy guilty of blinding six horses confronts the stultifying lack of passion in a world governed by the god "Normal." And in *Amadeus* (perf. 1979; pub. 1980), a mediocre but professionally successful court composer confronts the mystery of how the most divine music can emerge with no seeming effort from the obscene adolescent, Wolfgang Amadeus Mozart. All three plays employ highly imaginative techniques of staging that invest the production with an aura of the sacramental and leave the modern audience hungering for a religious and emotional transcendence that can only be accessed through primitive passion. *Yonadab* (perf. 1985; pub. 1989), S.'s final attempt at total theater, draws upon the religious and court rituals of the world of biblical King David to consider sexual intercourse and prayer as related attempts to escape the prison of the self, but the play failed on stage for lack of clear dramatic tension.

S.'s most recent plays continue to focus on the creative power of theater while returning to the mode of black comedy. Lettice Douffet, the title character of *Lettice and Lovage* (perf. 1987; pub. 1988; rev. as *Lettice & Lovage*, 1990), flamboyantly rejects the ugliness of a modern world content with the "mere," and induces Preservation Trust administrator Lotte to do so as well. The play resurrects the female Lord of Misrule that S. first developed in the character of Clea in *Black Comedy*. But, more significantly, by rendering in farcical terms the conflict between the blinders-wearing conformist and the chaotic visionary, S. finally resolves the tension that dominated his three best-known plays, for comedy allows the reconciliation of opposites. In the one-person radio play *Whom Do I Have the Honour of Addressing?* (1989), a middle-aged British typist finds the dreariness of her life momentarily relieved by contact with a sexy young American film actor, only to have to confront the levels of reality that lie behind an actor's mask. *The Gift of the Gorgon* (perf. 1992; pub. 1993), in which a playwright's widow reveals to his alienated son and would-be biographer the secret of his suicide, is a Chinese box in which still another level of playing lies beneath each exposed falseness, and a deeper truth is contained in every lie. With its analysis of theater as "the only religion that can never die," even while challenging the ways in which humans use religion to betray each other and onself, *Gorgon* seems S.'s summary statement of the paradoxical power of theater.

BIBLIOGRAPHY: Gianakaris, C. J., *P. S.* (1992); Mac-Murraugh-Kavanagh, M. K., *P. S.* (1998); Plunka, G. A., *P. S.* (1988); Taylor, J. R., *P. S.* (1974)

RAYMOND-JEAN FRONTAIN

SHAFTESBURY, Anthony Ashley Cooper, Third Earl of

b. 26 February 1671, London; d. 15 February 1713, Chiaia, Italy

S. was tutored by John LOCKE. In 1683, S. went to Winchester School where he was unhappy, and left after three years to travel abroad. In 1698, he published a *Preface to the Sermons of Dr. Whichcote,* a Cambridge Platonist. Product and exemplar of the Age of Reason, S. believed religious fanaticism could be countered with "raillery" (teasing). In 1709, he published *Sensus Communis, an Essay on the Freedom of Wit and Humour* and in the same year *The Moralists, a Philosophical Rhapsody.* S.'s most famous book, *Characteristics of Men, Manners, Opinions, Times* (3 vols., 1711) was, like the others, published anonymously. S. wrote to refute Thomas HOBBES's bleak picture of a life ruled by warring appetites. S. argued, against Locke's rejection of "innate ideas," that mankind had a natural "moral sense," an inbuilt ability to distinguish right from wrong, and that in the words of Alexander POPE "true self-love and social are the same." This sunny doctrine of the intuitive "moral sense" makes no mention of original sin, the Atonement, or the sacraments and implicitly undermines the authority of the church. Pope's *Essay on Man,* especially the First Epistle, is a versification of Locke's and S.'s ideas, though far from the orthodox Catholicism Pope professed and nearer to Deism or "natural religion." S.'s thought was influential on the Continental thinkers of the Enlightenment.

SHAKESPEARE, Nicholas [William Richmond]

b. 3 March 1957, Worcester

S.'s output so far has proven him to be a highly versatile writer, capable in a variety of genres, including fiction, essays, journalism, criticism, and BIOGRAPHY. S.'s first book was *The Men Who Would Be King* (1984), a study of various failed monarchs. This was followed by *Londoners* (1986), a collection of interviews. S.'s first novel, *The Vision of Elena Silves* (1989), grew out of the author's unsuccessful attempts to locate and interview the notorious Peruvian guerrilla leader Abimael Guzman Reynoso. This novel recounts the experiences of a pair of young lovers in revolutionary Peru, and it is notable for its realistic depiction of Peruvian society during the tumultuous years of the Shining Path guerrilla movement. *The Vision of Elena Silves* won both the Somerset Maugham and Betty Trask Awards. *The High Flyer* (1993) tells the story of a British diplomat whose career and marriage are destroyed after he has an affair. He is sent to Abyla, a bizarre country in Spanish North Africa, and the novel describes the colorful characters of this fictional locale. In *The Dancer Upstairs* (1995), S. returns to a Peruvian setting and the world of the Shining Path. This novel is set after the capture of the fictional guerrilla leader El Presidente Ezequiel (also based on the legendary Guzman Reynoso), and focuses on the story of Agustin Rejas, the policeman who captured the rebel leader. In addition to his nov-

els, S. has written film criticism for the *Illustrated London News* and has served on the editorial staff of several London newspapers. S. has also published a well-regarded biography of the writer Bruce CHATWIN (1999).

SHAKESPEARE, William

b. 23? April 1564, Stratford-on-Avon; d. 23 April 1616, Stratford-on-Avon

Seven years after S. died, two fellow-actors, John Heminge and Henry Condell, published a "Collected Works"—something almost without precedent for an author dignified neither by antiquity nor by having written in Latin or Greek, still the *serious* languages of Renaissance Europe. A collection of commendatory verses opens the First Folio, mostly of small merit; but among them is arguably the finest panegyric poem in English, by Ben JONSON, S.'s not uncritical friend and fellow dramatist. There Jonson calls S. the "Swan of Avon": the phrase has since become a cliché for tourist brochures. But when he first said it, it was startling, equating S. with Virgil, traditionally the "Swan of Mantua," and Homer, the "Swan of Maeonia," as the national poet for England, just as Virgil was par excellence the poet of Rome and Homer of Greece.

S. was a man of the late Renaissance, in the peculiar form it took in England. The parameters of his thought—but not the limits—were set by the social expectations and turbulent controversies of his day. The Reformation and Counter-Reformation affected everyone: countries and even families were cruelly divided over theology and the church's authority, and its relation to politics. England was suffering the most profound reshaping of its society, in religion, in politics, and in social structure, that it has ever seen—until now. S. was reared in the religiously conservative town of Stratford-on-Avon, where his father was a substantial citizen. (John Shakespeare remained a lifelong—cautious—Catholic, suffering financial penalties for so doing). A growing body of circumstantial evidence suggests S. himself remained a Catholic, perhaps even having contacts with the Jesuits Edmund Campion and Robert SOUTHWELL (Southwell was his relation through his well-connected mother). S. probably attended the (excellent) Grammar School, but went on to neither Oxford or Cambridge nor to the third "University," the law schools of the London Inns of Court. He is thus unusual among those writers who achieved distinction between 1580 and 1620 in being from outside that educational "Golden Triangle" of Oxford-Cambridge-London, and this may explain some of the resentment at the early success of this talented outsider in established writers like Robert GREENE. But he was soaked in the same sort of books, the same Renaissance humanist culture, as any smart graduate: he was as familiar with Castiglione's *Courtier* as he was with the Bible, with Tacitus and Livy as with Geoffrey CHAUCER and John GOWER.

S. clearly read deeply in Virgil and Horace and, especially, Ovid: their influence, even direct borrowing, is apparent not only in those early poems, *Venus and Adonis* (1593) and *Lucrece* (1594; repub. as *The Rape of Lucrece*, 1616), designed for a cultivated audience—where one might expect such echoes—but also all over plays designed for much more heterogeneous audiences. S., himself alert to classical culture, expected his audiences to be so too. Not only was knowledge of Virgil and Ovid well diffused even among those with no Latin, but the history and politics of Rome, the memory of its Empire, helped form the models on which Renaissance people articulated their understanding of politics. The Christian culture of Europe relied for its educational materials almost entirely on the pagan classical inheritance: an intriguing irony. But it is more than that: for the Christian, with the benefit of revelation, resembles a dwarf sitting on the shoulders of the giants of antiquity. He can see further than they, but could not see at all without their support. And so Ovid, Virgil, Cicero, Livy, Seneca are properly brought into the service of a Christian culture, a Christian worldview, that sees all world history as a narrative that will eventually end with apocalypse. Many writers, thinkers, and rulers in S.'s lifetime—including, perhaps, S. himself—really thought that apocalypse might be very soon, and that in it, England, that "other Eden, demi-Paradise," as S.'s John of Gaunt calls it, would play a special role.

By the late 1580s, S. was in London, connected with the intelligentsia, a world of writing, often for the new theaters (a risky place, given the authorities' dour attitude to theater and players), where fortunes could be made and patrons found. For most aspiring writers, finding an aristocratic (and rich) patron was the first step to security; the commercial world of writing, where sales determine fortunes, is only just being born. Possibly S.'s two "Ovidian" poems, *Venus and Adonis* and *Lucrece*, dedicated to the young, rich Earl of Southampton, both calculated to appeal to young, male, classically educated, rather clever readers, were attempts to secure such a patron. They are the only two works S. ever bothered to see through the press and sign. They certainly replied to fashionable Ovidian poems like, for example, Christopher MARLOWE's *Hero and Leander*—"Anything you can do. . . ." If, as is likely, many of S.'s *Sonnets* (1609) date from this period, we may glimpse in them something of the rivalry for patronage between talented writers, of the deployment of the extremest language of affectionate friendship that attended a relationship with a patron, and something of what Southampton, or any patron, might gain from having

a writer in his circle: a sort of immortality—as S. says of his poems, "So long lives this, and this gives life to thee"—and much kudos. But Southampton did not bite, and S. ended up not as a great man's secretary, but as a dramatist.

By the early 1590s, S. is being noticed, enviously, in that strange new world of theater. Plays and playing had a long history: the theatrical conventions of S.'s generation were formed by the inheritance from the late medieval morality and religious mystery plays—traces are all over S.'s work—which were still played, though less and less frequently. But wholly new in 1580s London were purpose-built theaters that entrepreneurs, often involved in other entertainments such as brothels and bear baiting, erected in the suburbs, outside the jurisdiction of the city's hostile magistrates. John Brayne's Red Lion, in 1567, is the first we know of; James Burbage built "The Theatre" in 1576. These buildings, often designed with much symbolism—the Globe (1599) apparently had as ground plan a cosmic diagram, and the three levels of its stage could represent, as needed, heaven, earth, and hell—were instantly successful with Londoners and even foreign visitors. They were huge: the 1599 Globe could, often did, hold three thousand people—about 2–3 percent of the population of England's largest city. This audience endlessly demanded new plays, and the company in which S. eventually became a major shareholder and chief writer, the Lord Chamberlain's (later King's) Men, might have fifty plays in repertoire in any year. Writers (often themselves actors—S., it is believed, played the Ghost in *Hamlet* and the Archbishop in *Henry V*)—were under pressure to provide new material to win audiences from competitors. And theater, the only mass medium apart from the SERMON, was an important way of influencing public opinion and powerful people could use theater to seek influence. The political controversies of ELIZABETH I's last decade as queen can be seen clearly echoed in S.'s *Richard II* (perf. ca. 1595), *Henry IV,* parts 1 and 2 (perf. ca. 1596–97), and *Henry V* (perf. 1599). Theater was often topical as today's milk, the only space, in that culture, where the unthinkable could be thought by many people at once.

S. is working with some severe, easily overlooked, constraints. He must work with what talent the company has. Its personnel does not change much over the years, so he must write to the strengths, even the personal appearance and habits—John Heminge, who played Polonius and Caesar, stammered—of his company, and avoid their weaknesses. He must keep an eye on the competition, for if you don't fill the theater, you don't eat. He's got to respond alertly to the religious and political controversies of the day, yet not so openly that the theater is closed for sedition or obscenity. His theater has no aids to illusion: no lighting, no scenery. His audience, who have come as much to eat, drink, play cards, and find a whore as to listen to great poetry, is restive, impatient, rude. And all the time colleagues look over his shoulder, thinking they can do better. And he is writing very fast indeed—there is neither time fully to rehearse a new play nor to copy it out so that every player can read it before the first performance. His plays have to be dolt-proof as regards both audience and actors. He also has to design those "roles," the scrolls members of the company get to learn their parts so that no two-word cue—that is all!—on them is repeated elsewhere—otherwise, complete chaos. This is the world, in brief, of S.'s theater. And what he did in it altered forever the English language and with it the way we see ourselves.

Venus and Adonis, Lucrece, and the *Sonnets* ensured that S.'s preeminence as a poet was recognized in his own day. But writing drama had little of the cachet of writing fashionable poetry. He never bothered to see a single one of his plays through the press, and few of the Quartos of single plays before 1600 name him on the title page. Yet his popularity as a dramatist, and the rise in theater's status (which he and Jonson helped make happen), made it profitable for Heminge and Condell to publish the Folio in 1623. S. wrote, in whole or in large part, at least forty plays between the late 1580s and 1613. The First Folio gives him thirty-six; to that list must be added *Sir Thomas More* (perf. ca. 1594–95, wr. in part by S.), *Pericles* (perf. ca. 1606–8; acts 1 and 2 probably by John FLETCHER, the last three by S.), *The Two Noble Kinsmen* (with Fletcher, perf. 1613), and *Edward III*. Legend links S. with a version of part of the *Don Quixote* story, which may be connected with the play *Cardenio* (perf. 1612). Now fossilized as texts like the First Folio, the plays were more likely regarded by S. as working scripts, to be updated as necessary or politic: this clearly happened to *Henry V, Richard II,* and *King Lear* (perf. ca. 1605–6) and S. seems not to have regarded his plays as complete, final books, but as notation for a much more complex, much more ambivalent, and much more unstable creation where no two performances would be exactly alike.

S. uses nearly all the genres, each with its special expectations, recognized in the Renaissance theater. Most of the time, his use is bravura, witty, unexpected—in the strict sense, virtuoso. He pays a sort of homage to the genre of revenge tragedy—an excellent example is Thomas KYD's *The Spanish Tragedy*—in the incomparable *Hamlet* (perf. ca. 1600–1601)—whose subtitle might well be "Not *The Spanish Tragedy.*" He can use the popular chronicle play in *Henry IV,* parts 1 and 2, and brilliantly—unprecedentedly—hybridize it in the Falstaff scenes with a sort of morality. He plays to the growing taste around 1600 for tragedy, with the perfectly formed tragedy of *Richard II,* and its later development in the profundity of *King Lear*—and in both he can reflect on contemporary concerns, for had not Elizabeth said angrily to historian Walter Lambarde in 1594, "I am Richard II, know ye not that?" Had not JAMES I, a mighty hunter who would not stay a jot for dinner, reunited the three parts of Lear's Britain? S. can write a history play of great formal elegance in part 3 of *Henry VI* (perf. ca. 1590–92), culminating in a "tragic," but also blackly comic, "devil" play, *Richard III* (perf. ca. 1591–92): a neat reply to Marlowe's challenge in *The Jew of Malta* and *Tamburlaine the Great,* parts 1 and 2. Later, he can reuse some of those ideas, in *Macbeth* (perf. 1606), returning to the question of the criminal conscience first opened in *Richard III,* and write one of the finest, most shapely of tragedies where we share the mind of a man slipping into very hell. S. can play with Roman comedy, in *The Comedy of Errors* (perf. ca. 1592–94); with stylish court comedy of the type we see in John LYLY's *Campaspe* in *Love's Labour's Lost* (perf. ca. 1594–95); he virtually ignores the sort of "city" comedy Jonson, Thomas DEKKER, and George CHAPMAN wrote, and plays instead with elegant romantic comedy in *Much Ado About Nothing* (perf. ca. 1598–99) or *Twelfth Night* (perf. ca. 1601–2); there are "occasional" plays like, probably, *A Midsummer Night's Dream* (perf. ca. 1595–96), written for a society wedding, that then make it to the public stage; there are a series of plays on Roman themes—where, conveniently, one can without sedition discuss forbidden subjects like republicanism and political assassination. In *Titus Andronicus* (perf. 1594), a far finer play than its reputation suggests, S. asks us to think seriously about the responsibility of power, and how the state is literally dismembered, at last eating up itself, by misrule. Then, as court taste (which inevitably trickles down to public taste) changes with the accession (1603) of a less parsimonious monarch, JAMES I, far fonder of display, S.'s company (now under James's patronage) adapts its style, and S. begins to write plays with much more spectacle and music in them—in *Macbeth* (perf. 1606) we easily forget how long and *spectacular* the pageant of the apparitions and the Banquo-descended kings should be. But just as the fear in the 1590s of what would happen following Elizabeth's death, its preoccupation with questions of succession and power, keeps surfacing in the drama, James's obsession with himself as reconciler of divided peoples supports a new fashion for "what happens after" plays—plays that include tragedy, but also deal with reconciliation, forgiveness, remaking. Tragicomedy was regarded by critics of that decade as a high, noble form, and S.'s tragicomedies, especially *The Winter's Tale* (perf. 1611) and *The Tempest* (perf. 1611), speak powerfully to the hopes of the monarch and his court while recognizing the genuine suffering and loss of the past. In both plays, S. breaks completely new formal ground, and in *The Tempest* writes the finest English Renaissance play fully to obey the critical ideal of the three unities of time, place, and action. In sum, the story of S.'s drama shows us a writer intensely aware of the critical crosscurrents and fashions of his time, ready to adapt to them and shape them to his own ends, and through the fantasy, the make-believe world of plays, address some of the issues that lay perhaps too deep for easy talk: to discuss the undiscussable.

Other S. plays include *The Taming of the Shrew* (perf. 1594), *The Two Gentlemen of Verona* (perf. 1594), *Romeo and Juliet* (perf. ca. 1595–96), *The Merchant of Venice* (perf. ca. 1596–98), *Julius Caesar* (perf. 1599), *As You Like It* (perf. ca. 1599–1600), *All's Well That Ends Well* (perf. ca. 1602–3), *Othello* (perf. 1604), *Antony and Cleopatra* (perf. ca. 1606–7), *Coriolanus* (perf. ca. 1607–8), and *Cymbeline* (perf. 1609).

S., like any Renaissance writer, began with a thorough mastery of rhetoric, that ancient art of persuasion through careful use of words that lies at the heart of writing, poetry—and politics. There are nearly three hundred formal figures of rhetoric, and they form part and parcel of S.'s writing throughout his entire career, the sort of thing an author expects an audience to notice and appreciate. No writer, furthermore, could not take notice of the state of English: a language almost by definition inferior to ancient Greek and Latin, but which must be made—remade—as an adequate expression for a nation casting itself as chosen by God as a vehicle for His reformed Church, with an imperial destiny, and true successor to the grandeur of Rome. And S. is acutely aware, as is abundantly clear in the use of different idiolects and sociolects in *Henry V,* that what makes a nation is not race but language: one speech, Babel reversed. Thomas Mowbray, banished in *Richard II,* is banished from the speech of England as much as the place: the ultimate separation.

Attempts were made, indeed, to force English into the structures of Latin—quantitative meters, for example—but those failed. What did not fail was the remarkable expansion of the vocabulary, so that by 1620 English is the richest language in Europe. Frequently, this is by expansion of vocabulary through developing near-synonyms in the domestication of words from French and especially Latin, thus allowing a whole range of different registers, layers of emphasis, nuances of meaning (particularly when many would know the Latin original of a word). The number of neologisms is a good indicator; it is far higher in S. than anywhere else. S. develops his utterance—our language—by exploiting these resources, providing him with something no other writer enjoys. Instead of giving each character simply the sort of rhetorical level appropriate to his or her status and

situation, S. breaks remarkable new ground in his later drama, where each character has a distinctive idiolect; in these plays, no two people speak quite alike.

Clearly, Renaissance people did not think of the self as we do, and therefore when they wrote plays and poems they did not suddenly invent post-Romantic, post-Freudian characterization. Bascially, it is worth remembering that whereas we tend to work out from the self to the social role, for an earlier age, when life was lived more publicly, it is almost exactly the other way round. Claudio, for example, in *Much Ado About Nothing* sees Hero first with "a soldier's eye" and then, later, adopts the rhetoric and behavior of the lover. Is he in love? Probably not—he asks first about her fortune. But you cannot tell, and he has got a social role to play that everyone understands. Most of S.'s early characters start from that premise, and he never quite loses it. But changes were afoot.

Arguably most important was the effect of post–Reformation spirituality, which forced examination of the self in searching for signs of Grace in the soul. In English, compound words with the element "self-" increase greatly after about 1580: the words mark a shift in perception. This forces attention on the individual as individual, not as social being. Now consider, in S., two closely related characters separated by about fifteen years, Richard III and Macbeth—the latter's play echoes scenes, even lines, of the former's. In each of Richard's appearances, he speaks a different language, playing (self-referentially) a different role. It is brilliant, and grimly funny; but there is no "real" Richard, and we remain ironically distanced from his tragedy. With Macbeth, there is never any doubt about a coherent, articulated self, acutely aware of a private being quite distinct from his public self-presentation. You could make the same point about Hamlet, or Henry V: with them, the world changes: it goes inside. To say, with Harold Bloom, that here S. invents the human is to go too far. But what is certainly arguable is that S. not only, ahead of his rivals, spotted a new idea of the self developing, and a new idea of Englishness, but found a unique language to give both utterance.

Any writer aims to make his audience experience real feelings, that matter, about imaginary things and persons, and however different the world was then, this must be true of S.'s day. We never mistake the actor playing Lear for a real Lear, but our feelings are terrible enough. But one mark of a really great writer is that the issues are never simple: they are always complex, even contradictory. What above all else distinguishes S. from his contemporaries and successors is precisely this capacity: to imagine the other, to perceive the doubleness of things. Macbeth is an appalling regicide, betraying every bond that should bind a man. But he is also heroic, his loss terrible, his self-awareness devastating. In that other world where S.

lived and wrote, Shylock's was always the clown's part, the villain you love to hate: but Shylock, like Caliban, is given a voice that insists that things are not—never were—that simple.

Did, then, the Swan of Avon give England, as the Swan of Mantua gave Rome, a language, a myth of nationhood, an inexhaustible text for the exploration of the puzzle of being human? The consensus of succeeding centuries has been that he did, whether we read him fossilized as a book, or whether we treat his scripts as the infinite, protean, utterance that remakes, reformulates, itself every single time they are performed. Indeed, by the late 1700s, S. had become iconic of Englishness, even for people who never have read a single line: the Stratford Jubilee of 1769 contained not a single performance, but celebrated S. as Englishness personified, the "god of our idolatry." For the Romantics, S. represented the triumph of nature over the repressions of conventional art; for the 19th c., his was a text second in moral authority only to the Bible. To quote S. was to settle the matter—an enormous cultural authority, the anglophone world's definer. And not only in that world. S. has become impossible to ignore anywhere, whether we think of Japan and the startling adaptations of his plays into the idioms, filmic and theatrical, of that country; or Africa; or the Caribbean; or Germany; or Russia.

But such a cultural importance must have those who rebel against it, and latterly, especially in the U.S., there has been a reaction, regarding S.'s works as instruments of a racial and gender and political hegemony. Some, like Nobel laureate Maya Angelou, have tried to appropriate S. to their own cause: "I just *know* S. was a black woman"; others have simply refused all that they think he stands for, and even the idea of any value in his work—or any work. But it is difficult to believe or pretend that the phenomenon never happened, while using the very language it gave us, and the insights to which that language led.

BIBLIOGRAPHY: Bate, J., *S. and Ovid* (1993); Bate, J., *The Genius of S.* (1999); Bloom, H., *S.* (1998); Greenblatt, S., *Renaissance Self-Fashioning* (1980); Greenblatt, S., *Shakespearean Negotiations* (1988); Gurr, A., *The Shakespearean Stage, 1574–1642* (3rd ed., 1992); Gurr, A., *Playgoing in S.'s London* (2nd ed., 1996); Hattaway, M., *Elizabethan Popular Theatre* (1982); Honan, P., *S.* (1999); Kermode, F., *S.'s Language* (2000); Schoenbaum, S., *S.'s Lives* (1991); Thomson, P., *S.'s Professional Career* (1992); Thomson, P., *S.'s Theatre* (1983); Vickers, B., *The Artistry of S.'s Prose* (1968; rev. ed., 1979); Vickers, B., *S.: The Critical Heritage* (6 vols., 1974–81); Vickers, B., *Appropriating S.: Contemporary Critical Quarrels* (1993)

C. W. R. D. MOSELEY

SHARP, William

b. 12 September 1855, Paisley, near Glasgow, Scotland; d. 12 December 1905, Taormina, Sicily, Italy

S. led a double life, as a general man of letters under his own name, but as "Fiona Macleod," a pseudonym maintained with great secrecy and denials, he published stories and sketches that, though in English, contributed to the Gaelic Renaissance. After Glasgow University, S. went to Australia, cruised the Pacific, and settled in London, where he met the Rossetti family, and contributed to various journals. He traveled widely and married his cousin, Elizabeth Amelia Sharp, who collaborated with him in compiling the *Lyra Celtica* (1886). His books of verse were *The Human Inheritance* (1882), *Earth's Voices* (1884), *Romantic Ballads and Poems of Fantasy* (1888), *Sospiri di Roma* (1891), and *Flower o' the Vine* (1892). S. was the general editor of the Canterbury Poets series, and a discriminating anthologist. His *Sonnets of This Century* (1886), with a useful introduction, went to several editions, and was followed by *American Sonnets* (1889). He was biographer of Dante Gabriel ROSSETTI (1882), Percy Bysshe SHELLEY (1887), and Robert BROWNING (1890), edited the memoirs of John KEATS's friend Joseph SEVERN (1892) and published several novels. Meanwhile, from 1894 he was publishing, as Macleod, sketches of the primitive Celtic world and writing letters claiming "she" wrote only under her own name. *Pharais: A Romance of the Isles* was followed by *The Mountain Lovers* (1895), *The Sin-Eater* (1895), and *The Washer of the Ford and Other Legendary Moralities* (1896), among others.

SHARPE, Tom [Thomas Ridley]

b. 30 March 1928, London

Fertile, scabrous, near-anarchic novels of contemporary life have made S. one of the best-known comic novelists of his time. Among his favorite targets for satirical observation are higher education—five of his thirteen novels are academic fictions—and the pretensions of class and power in all aspects of society.

The son of a Unitarian minister, S. was educated in boarding schools, before spending two years as a Royal Marine; then he attended Pembroke College, Cambridge, earning a degree in 1951. Moving to South Africa, he worked as a teacher, a social worker, and a photographer, also writing plays, some of which aroused official displeasure. In 1961, he was deported to England. He became a lecturer at the Cambridgeshire College of Arts and Technology (later Anglia Polytechnic University) in 1963, leaving in 1971 to become a full-time writer.

S.'s first two novels, *Riotous Assembly* (1971) and *Indecent Exposure* (1973), are set in South Africa and, through plots rich in sensational action (one black cook has been buggered to death by a white bishop, for instance) satirize the excesses of the apartheid system, psychiatry, penology, and medicine, including heart transplants, a South African invention. One character comments that there "didn't seem to be any significant difference between life in the mental hospital and life in South Africa as a whole," and this stance—the insanity of ordinary, or official, life—characterizes much of S.'s fiction.

In *Porterhouse Blue* (1974), the scene shifts to England, and an old but intellectually worthless college at Cambridge. Among the events that combine to reveal the dark underside of education are the responses of a reactionary faculty to efforts by a new master, Godber Evans, and his militant wife to modernize the college. Typically, for S., both the modernizers and those who resist them are wrong. At the end, a hoary college tradition leads to a stroke-crippled Skullion, formerly the malign college porter, becoming master. S. continued the Porterhouse story in *Grantchester Grind: A Porterhouse Chronicle* (1995), where the college is threatened by financial disaster and by outsiders such as Karl Kudzuvine, a born-again American television man, and Purefoy Osbert, a misguided criminologist.

In addition to his books about Cambridge University, S. has written three novels about Henry Wilt, a lecturer at a technical college called the Fenland College of Arts and Technology. The college is a reminder of the one where S. taught for eight years and, as for Wilt, the author said, "His teaching routine and his views on it were exactly mine." The three books are *Wilt* (1976), *The Wilt Alternative* (1979), and *Wilt on High* (1984). In each, Henry Wilt responds both to educational problems (sometimes caused by administrative pomposity or stupidity) and farcical complications of his private life. In *Wilt*, for instance, he is arrested for the murder of his dreadful wife Eva after he is seen trying to dispose of a lifesize plastic sex doll in a construction site on campus. In *The Wilt Alternative*, now a department head, reconciled with Eva and the father of quadruplet daughters, Henry proves surprisingly resourceful in rescuing his family from an invasion by international terrorists. The police are no better than the terrorists, and the novel dramatizes an unease with both official power and any sort of ideology. In *Wilt on High*, he is again persecuted by officialdom, this time including the U.S. Air Force, which suspects him of spying. As usual, Eva causes trouble, in this case by administering an aphrodisiac to increase his disappointing sexual abilities.

Blott on the Landscape (1975) revolves around a failed aristocratic marriage and a new motorway and ends with the old aristocrat eaten by his wife's lion and her marriage to Blott, the gardener. In *The Great Pursuit* (1977), S. writes about the world of literature and publishing; it investigates the claims of moral literature, as set out in F. R. LEAVIS's *The Great Tradition*. As in *Blott* and *The Wilt Alternative*, *The Throwback* (1978) includes a siege, violent death by bizarre means, and near-paranoid suspicion of authority. Like *The Throwback*, *Ancestral Vices* (1980) explores the English upper classes, in this case the Petrefact family, and their attempt to conceal a guilty secret from a left-wing American professor who is writing the family history. *Vintage Stuff* (1982) satirizes the excesses of wealth and privilege as well as misguided attempts at education, and includes another siege, this time of an international conference center. S.'s increasingly scatological concerns may culminate in *The Midden* (1996—a midden is a dunghill), a fantastically plotted book with another siege and the violent deaths of at least twenty-three people.

S.'s black comedy is inventive and funny; darker than most SATIRE, it approaches to a dark suspicion of almost all human endeavors, particularly those associated with wealth, any sort of fashionable belief, or political or intellectual authority.

BIBLIOGRAPHY: Dodd, B., *Two Post-1945 British Novelists: Olivia Manning and T. S.* (1985); McCall, R., "The Comic Novels of T. S.," *Critique* 25 (Winter 1984): 57–65; Moseley, M., and S. Edwards, "T. S.," in Moseley, M., ed., *British Novelists since 1960*, Fourth Series, *DLB* 231 (2001): 257–66

MERRITT MOSELEY

SHAW, [George] Bernard

b. 26 July 1856, Dublin, Ireland; d. 2 November 1950, Hertfordshire

No effort to place S. within a specific literary or intellectual movement can be entirely successful. His life straddled the better part of two centuries, and he saw momentous social, political, and technological changes, all of which affected him, provoking both structural and substantial changes in his artistic output. Critic, novelist, dramatist, socialist polemicist, sociopolitical commentator, and screenwriter are but some of the labels one could use to describe him. Winner of the Nobel Prize for Literature in 1925, he is considered to be the most influential playwright in the English language since William SHAKESPEARE.

S. was born in Dublin, Ireland. His mother, Lucinda Elizabeth Gurly, had married for money, but her husband, George Carr Shaw, was a secret drinker and a poor businessman who squandered what little money there was and rather than rescuing his wife condemned her to a life of shabbiness. S. had a lonely childhood. He craved his mother's love and attention, but whatever she had to give she directed at her two musical daughters, Lucy and Elinor.

In 1860, the local music teacher George Vandeleur Lee became acquainted with the Shaw family. It was a fortuitous meeting for both Mrs. Shaw, who looked to Lee as an escape from the disappointment of her marriage, and for her son; the musical society meetings in their home gave S. a good grounding for his future incarnation as Corno Di Bassetto, music critic for the *Star* newspaper in London. Moreover, the triangular relationship between Lee and S.'s parents was to be a template for his romantic life and work. Mrs. Shaw and the girls left Dublin with Lee in 1872. Four years later, S.—like many an ambitious young man from the Protestant middle class—followed them to London, where, without a university education, he set out to conquer the English-speaking world.

S.'s literary reputation was first established as a music, art and drama reviewer for the *Pall Mall Gazette*, the *World,* the *Saturday Review*, and the *Star.* Believing that indifference is the worst insult, he was a formidable critic. From 1885 to 1897, artists, authors, musicians, conductors, and even audiences bore the brunt of his scathing notices. His columns earned him notoriety, but also popularity; he covered a bewildering range of subjects in his reviews, which ensured they were enjoyed by readers who had no interest in art, music, or drama. The reviews are collected in *Music in London 1890–1894* (3 vols., 1931) and *Our Theatres in the Nineties* (3 vols., 1931).

While reviewing kept S. just about solvent, writing was to be his real purpose. He initially devoted himself to the novel and produced five of them between 1879 and 1884. The first was the largely autobiographical *Immaturity* (1930), followed by *The Irrational Knot* (1905), *Love among the Artists* (1900), and *Cashel Byron's Profession* (1886), the eponymous hero of which is a prize-fighter, demonstrating S.'s inclination for unconventional heroes. *An Unsocial Socialist* (1887) is his final attempt in this form. The novels were rejected by most publishing houses on the grounds that, though well written, they dealt with issues that would not be understood by, or be popular with, the general public. However, over the years 1885–88, all but his first novel appeared in print in *To-day*, a progressive political magazine, which serialized *The Irrational Knot, Love among the Artists, Cashel Byron's Profession*, and *An Unsocial Socialist.*

Having devoured Karl Marx's *Das Kapital* in the Reading Room of the British Library, S. joined the newly formed Fabian Society in 1884, a forerunner of the British Labour Party, whose members advocated the spread of socialism through steady, gradual steps. At Fabian and other society meetings, S. began to create the persona of the arrogant but captivating public speaker, a front behind which he hid his shyness and feelings of inadequacy, displacement, and the inescapable conviction that he was an outsider. A series of lectures to the Fabian Society on socialism in contemporary literature was subsequently published as

The Quintessence of Ibsenism (1891; rev. ed., 1913), an analysis of the work of the Norwegian playwright, Henrik Ibsen, whose ideas strongly influenced S. and provided the intellectual foundation for many of his plays. S. was a lonely defender of Ibsen's work, which offered opinions on society similar to his own. He was encouraged by Ibsen's convcition that drama could be an effective channel for the dissemination of ideas.

In 1892, finally taking heed of his friends and critics, S. gave up writing novels and turned to drama. *Widowers' Houses* (1893), his first play, was written for the Independent Theatre, but saw only two stagings in 1892. *The Philanderer* (pub. 1898; perf. 1905) has been universally dubbed his worst play. He fared no better with *Mrs. Warren's Profession* (pub. 1898; perf. 1902), which was banned by the Lord Chamberlain. Undeterred, S. soldiered on and gave *Arms and the Man* (1898) to the Avenue Theatre in 1894 for a modestly successful season backed by Annie Horniman, a wealthy British theater patron.

Anxious to build on the small degree of fame *Arms and the Man* had brought him, S. wrote *Candida* (perf. 1897; pub. 1898) in 1894, with a specific actress in mine. He believed Janet Achurch was sufficiently talented to propel both her and his play into the dizzy realms of popular and commercial success. It did not. An attempt the following year to write a stock West End hit, *You Never Can Tell* (pub. 1898; perf. 1899), proved equally fruitless.

The boost in confidence and personal finances he so badly needed eventually came in 1897 with *The Devil's Disciple* (1901). Set during the American War of Independence, the play was S.'s first attempt at melodrama. Its hero, Dick Dudgeon, is his first spokesperson for the life-force ideology, a concept derived from the writings of Friedrich Nietzsche. Royalties from the play's sell-out run in New York furnished S. with the financial wherewithal to give up theater reviewing, and to propose to Charlotte Payne Townsend, a wealthy Irish heiress, without being thought a gold-digger. *The Devil's Disciple* by no means made him a household name; while his fame was spreading abroad, within Britain S. was still largely unheard of beyond London.

In 1898, S. flouted convention by publishing his plays, even those that had never been staged. *Plays Pleasant and Unpleasant* (1898) grouped together the pleasant plays *Arms and the Man*, *Candida*, and *You Never Can Tell* and the unpleasant *Widowers' Houses*, *The Philanderer*, and *Mrs. Warren's Profession.* *Three Plays for Puritans* (*The Devil's Disciple*, *Caesar and Cleopatra*, and *Captain Brasshound's Conversion*) was published in 1901. These volumes had an important consequence; many people who never went to the theater read his plays. What readers missed in the immediacy and vitality of performance, they gained with another innovation in the business of publishing dramatic works, namely, detailed stage directions and long and informative prefaces.

From 1901 to 1903, S. worked on *Man and Superman* (pub. 1903; perf. 1905). Subtitled "A Comedy, and a Philosophy," the play expounds S.'s theory of creative evolution, a synthesis of religion and science that he hoped would be the religion of the 20th c. The play's famous third act, in which Don Juan debates with the Devil in Hell (the scene is set in the Sierra Nevada), is a move away from the NATURALISM that characterized S.'s earlier work, and is one of his most enduring sequences, often produced independently.

S.'s steady progress as a popular dramatist owed much to his only full-length play about Ireland, *John Bull's Other Island* (perf. 1904; pub. 1907). Here, S. investigates national stereotypes and, in particular, the stage-Irish character. Demonstrating his penchant for paradox, he reverses the stage Irish and stock English characteristics in his protagonists and sends both to Ireland. The comic result shows that it matters not in what country one is born; virtues and faults, in this case, efficiency and inefficiency, can be found in any nationality. Although the Irish were not portrayed in an unequivocally flattering light in *John Bull's Other Island*, S. was proud of his Irishness. Like Oscar WILDE, he knew instinctively that the outsider has a valuable objectivity that, in his hands, became a powerful tool to teach the English about themselves and expose the hypocrisies in their society.

Now that S. had achieved the popular success for which he had slaved since his arrival in London twenty years earlier, he drew little satisfaction from it. Audiences were at his feet, yet he felt a failure. Just as they had appreciated only his comedy and wit in *Arms and the Man*, in *John Bull's Other Island* they had failed again to learn the lessons he had so carefully squeezed into the format of conventional drama. S. resolved at this point to write meaty issue-driven dramas. He could not, however, resist imbuing them with his characteristic sense of irony.

Major Barbara (perf. 1905; pub. 1907) shows the principles of a munitions manufacturer to be more sound than those of the hypocritical volunteers and patrons of the Salvation Army. It is a return to the theme of *Mrs. Warren's Profession*, namely, that capitalism obliges us to make our fortunes where we can, and that success in conventionally unacceptable economic activities, without hypocrisy, beats being poor. In *The Doctor's Dilemma* (perf. 1906; pub. 1911), S.'s target is the medical profession. Not having enough medicine to treat two patients, a group of doctors must decide who is worthy of the cure. The issue is not whether the scientist or the artist is more valuable to society, but how we reach decisions and justify them.

By the early 1900s, S. was living up to his own label of propagandist. In many ways a vain man who relished his celebrity, he had made himself a household name by persistently projecting himself into the public realm. He asked questions, made statements, and allowed his unusually attired image to be captured on film and canvas. His celebrity was reinforced by the Lord Chamberlain, who was responsible for the moral welfare of theatergoers. The Lord Chamberlain banned several of S.'s works (*Mrs. Warren's Profession* for indecency, *The Shewing Up of Blasco Posnet* for blasphemy, *Press Cuttings* as its characters were obviously parodies of politicians of the time), but the press coverage aroused only curiosity and the plays and their author increased in popularity.

Back in the theater, S. supplied a series of disquisitory plays; *Getting Married* (perf. 1908; pub. 1911) and *Misalliance* (perf. 1910; pub. 1914), in which his own experiences of marriage and family life feature. S. launched his next offering, *Fanny's First Play* (perf. 1911; pub. 1914), with the effective publicity coup of not revealing his authorship. *Androcles and the Lion* (perf. 1913; pub. 1916) exemplified S.'s idea of what a children's play should be.

Mainstream success came again with *Pygmalion* (perf. 1914; pub. 1916), S.'s comic masterpiece, and without doubt his most popular play. It was made into an Academy Award–winning film in 1938 and the musical *My Fair Lady* in 1956. It was intended to be a lecture on phonetics but also dealt with love, class, and exploitation in an insightful and entertaining way. It is in the "Preface for Pygmalion" that S. defies the critics who say that great art must never be didactic. He boasts that the success of *Pygmalion* demonstrates art should never be otherwise. S. the socialist was rapidly becoming a very wealthy man. Freed from the economic imperative by a flow of royalties from previous works, S. indulged himself with some wholly uncommercial plays such as a series of five short pieces under the title of *Back to Methuselah* (pub. 1921; perf. 1922).

S.'s reponse to the canonization of Joan of Arc in 1920 was to portray her in *Saint Joan* (perf. 1923; pub. 1924) as a plucky, intelligent girl with enormous self-belief and a healthy disrespect for authority. The challenge was to write a play that would stimulate an audience that already knew the story. He did so by focusing ostensibly on the way we judge people, and by his innovative portrayal of the inquisition scene, in which Joan's casuistical judges are shown to be reasonable men acting according to their own sincere beliefs.

During the First World War, S. had lost favor due to his unorthodox views on the motives of Britain's involvement (*Common Sense about the War*, 1914) and for his defense of Roger Casement, a campaigner for Irish independence who was charged with high treason for smuggling weapons from Germany. *Saint Joan* did much to restore S.'s popular standing, and indeed, by 1925, he was so highly regarded internationally as to be awarded the Nobel Prize for Literature. He accepted the honor, but refused the prize money. By this time, socialism had gained discursive currency in polite society leading S. to begin *The Intelligent Woman's Guide to Socialism and Capitalism* (1928). S. had always been a champion of equal rights for women. His female protagonists, like Joan, were strong and independent models of socialist virtues. The *Guide* preceded by a year the granting of suffrage to women on equal terms with men and may have had some impact on this decision. His plays thereafter tended to reflect an interest in non-Western ways of government and religious expression. They veered toward the allegorical, yet continued to criticize local patterns of political organization—*The Apple Cart* (pub. 1928; perf. 1929), *On the Rocks* (perf. 1933; pub. 1934), *Geneva* (perf. 1938; pub. 1939). Symbolic farce, Aristophanic in style, became his new mode of social critique. His last completed work, *Shakes Versus Shav* (1949), hints, almost seriously, at his canonical centrality alongside the Bard.

Until his death in his ninety-fifth year, S. was firing off letters to newspaper editors and personal friends. His immense correspondence, including love letters to the many women with whom he had romantic relationships, whether mere flirtations or full-blown physical affairs, is brought together in several volumes, *Collected Letters* (4 vols., 1965–88), edited by Dan H. Laurence. Perhaps the most distinguishing feature of S.'s work is that in everything he wrote, there was an underlying didactic thrust. He believed that a visit to the theater that was not an edifying experience was a wasted evening, and this may well explain his early unpopularity. When S. first began playwriting, London audiences were fed on a diet of romance and melodrama, a formula that S. deplored for its creation of a public addicted to innuendo and off-stage sexual intrigue. It was into this climate that he introduced the discussion of moral dilemmas, new political ideologies, and alternative religions, in short a unique combination of philosophy plus life, albeit against the benign backdrop of a conventional three-act play.

While his characters were often thought to lack emotional depth, and indeed they became ever more symbolic as his career progressed, his talent for dialogue was never called into question. His characters duel verbally in an uncontrived way, their utterances never a series of disjointed aphorisms. In many ways, he beat Wilde at his own game. His enduring contribution to drama in English may be his steady conversion of contemporary audiences to the discussion play. Indeed, it was the dependence on sparkling dialogue and the lack of action in his plays that helped spread their popularity; they were perfect for the repertory company, requiring simple sets, ensuring good parts for the whole company, and guaranteeing at least some laughs. In S.'s hand, the pen seduced audi-

ences with comedy, then challenged and unsettled them. Moreover, he applied his audacious intellect to such an immense range of subjects that his contribution to the modern world goes far beyond the theatrical.

BIBLIOGRAPHY: Dervin, D., *B. S.* (1975); Dukore, B. F., *B. S., Playwright* (1973); Holroyd, M., *B. S.* (5 vols., 1988–92); Innes, C., ed., *The Cambridge Companion to G. B. S.* (1998); Kiberd, D., *Inventing Ireland* (1995); Weintraub, R., ed., *Fabian Feminist* (1977); Weintraub, S., *The Unexpected S.* (1982)

EILISH RAFFERTY

SHAW, Robert

b. 9 August 1927, Lancashire; d. 28 August 1978, New Tourmakeady, Ireland

Given his excellence in various cinematic characterizations in the 1960s and 1970s, S. is rarely given much credit for his work as playwright and novelist. What one critic has termed his "crowded life" included regular intellectual forays in the literary world beyond the screen. He recognized, in published interviews, the duality of his public existence: people who saw him in films thought of him as an actor merely; those who knew of him primarily through his three staged plays and five novels expressed surprise that he was also an actor. S. saw no necessary contradictions in his immersion in these two worlds; he was a film actor because the money provided emotional release, solace, and time for his more urgent, solitary explorations of the pragmatics of human existence. Contrary to his perception of himself as a writer whose enjoyment of acting interfered with being taken seriously as a writer, S. received England's prestigious Hawthornden Prize for his second novel, *The Sun Doctor* (1961). His plays, film adaptations, and novels add up to an image of S. as a serious writer without any need of qualification.

Acting was very much a part of S.'s identity: early in his career, he paid his own tuition at the Royal Academy of Dramatic Art after being passed over for a scholarship. He served a difficult apprenticeship, though his experience in (minor) roles while a member of the renowned Shakespeare Memorial Theatre in Stratford-upon-Avon (1948–50) led to many professional introductions. It was here, for example, that S. met Sir Alec Guinness—who was later to star in the film adaptation of S.'s first novel, *The Hiding Place* (1959; American film version: *Situation Hopeless—But Not Serious*, 1965). Guinness was impressed enough by S.'s acting ability to invite him to play opposite him (as Rosencrantz) in Guinness's 1951 production of *Hamlet*. While fighting for a regular place in the acting life, S. starred in the premiere of his first play, *Off the Mainland* (perf. 1956). Set on a prison island in a Communist country, the play details the deteriorating mental condition of a once-humane commandant as he is forced to work in the service of a system that tortures and imprisons political dissidents. Throughout the rest of his life, S. would act and write, perform and pen.

Overall, the combination of political theme and ethical struggle is a recurrent motif in S.'s works. *The Hiding Place* concerns two American soldiers kept imprisoned by a German civilian after World War II has ended. *The Man in the Glass Booth* is probably his best-known work due to its various incarnations: it started as a novel (1967), became a play in that same year that eventually ran on Broadway for over 250 performances (1968), and became an American film (1975; though S. disapproved of the screenplay and had his name removed from the credits). As in so many of his texts, S. refuses simplistic certitudes in favor of indeterminacy. Here, too, S. displays a concern with the way philosophical abstractions work themselves out in the practical exercise of daily existence. *The Man in the Glass Booth* tells the story of wealthy Jewish businessman Arthur Goldman, who pretends to be a brutal Nazi named Adolf Dorf. Goldman/Dorf allows himself to be tried for war crimes to test the concept of "forgiveness" and the sometimes-sanctimonious nature of victim status. For S., circumstance and happenstance easily allow victims to become victimizers. S.'s second novel, *The Sun Doctor*, also develops the relativity of individual actions and ethics. The subject matter of this novel has led many critics to compare S. to Joseph CONRAD, Graham GREENE (especially his *A Burnt-Out Case*), and Saul Bellow (especially his *Henderson, the Rain King*). The plot concerns an Albert Schweitzer-esque doctor who has worked in the Africa jungle for many years. When he returns to London to be knighted for his altruism, the story of the protagonist's murder of an innocent young African woman is related. Especially in the case of *The Man in the Glass Booth*, some critics have taken issue with the moral relativism that they see in S.'s work. On the other hand, his refusal of easy certitude has allowed many other critics to see S. as a writer enmeshed in the increasingly fragmented nature of post-World War II existence. In his third novel, *The Flag* (1965), for example, S. explores the spirituality of the British—or its absence—as he bases his tale of socialism and salvation upon an historical parson, the Reverend Hewlett Johnson, who "raised a red flag" in the 1920s.

His third play, *Cato Street* (perf. 1971; pub. 1972), also marries social issues with individual moral performance. Set against the turbulent period in English history leading up to the passage of the first Reform Bill in 1832, S. presents an historical context—the Peterloo Massacre (1819) of protesting textile workers

and a failed plot to assassinate the British Cabinet in 1820. The tight governmental controls enacted during the Napoleonic era and in the wake of the Congress of Vienna (1815) provide a warning about the possibility of fascism and repression in any society, at any time.

Often, the ideological conflicts in S. work themselves out against a backdrop of captivity, either literally or figuratively. *Off the Mainland*, *The Hiding Place*, and *The Man in the Glass Booth* involve actual physical confinement: allegories for spiritual imprisonment, perhaps. Even his most experimental novel, *A Card from Morocco* (1969) can be read in this way. The story's structure revolves around the conversations of two elderly men in a bar in Madrid who opine, existentially, on the nature of individuality and the "trap" of being human. The more figurative references to captivity in his other works, often involving the "prisons" of cultural expectation, determinism, postcolonial and cultural imperialism, among others, make of S. much more than a memorable character actor who wrote: he works out the problems of moral character in social situations that seldom lend themselves to easy analysis or certitude.

BIBLIOGRAPHY: Carmean, K., and G. Gaston, *R. S.* (1994); French, J., *R. S.* (1993); Page, M., "R. S.," in Halio, J. L., ed., *British Novelists since 1960*, part 2, *DLB* 14 (1983): 654–60

RICHARD E. LEE

SHELLEY, Mary Wollstonecraft

b. 30 August 1797, Somers Town, London; d. 1 February 1851, Chester Square, London

S., daughter of William GODWIN and Mary WOLLSTONECRAFT (who died shortly after giving birth to her), had, by the age of twenty, eloped with Percy Bysshe SHELLEY, journeyed in ravaged post-Napoleonic France, lost a child, given birth to two others, married her lover, and published *Frankenstein; or, The Modern Prometheus* (3 vols., 1818).

Originating in Lord BYRON's proposal that he and his house guests should produce a collection of original ghost stories (1816), *Frankenstein* first appeared anonymously in an edition of only five hundred copies. It attracted abuse for its hideous central idea and praise for its originality; its female authorship was soon discovered. S. with one bound had established herself as a writer to watch, and had unleashed a duo—the mad scientist and his rebellious creation—which, like Quixote, Don Juan, and Dracula, have achieved an ever-proliferating life outside the text.

Frankenstein undoubtedly owes its universal fame to dramatic and film versions. Some have judged it a badly written little shocker that survives by its myth alone. The last twenty-five years, however, have seen a resurgence of *Frankenstein* as text. It is currently the most widely taught novel on U.S. campuses. Critical attention has revealed the same kind of structural complexity and verbal density as are present in Emily BRONTË's *Wuthering Heights* or Charlotte BRONTË's *Jane Eyre*, and has uncovered an astonishing number of sources in S.'s known reading. Additionally, *Frankenstein* has the ability, possessed by all enduring literature, to generate multiple interpretations. It has been called the first SCIENCE FICTION novel, a Faustian-bargain story, an allegory of the French revolution and/or class war, an indictment of the bourgeois family and of the arrogance of male-oriented science. It is said to be about male usurpation of the female role, suppressed female anger, fear of giving birth to a monster, forbidden sexuality, the recovery of S.'s own dead mother. Each interpretation has something in its favor, and none lies outside S.'s possible intentions. Her 1831 introduction to *Frankenstein* declares that her purpose was to speak to "the mysterious fears of our nature" and implicitly acknowledges that books escape from authorial control.

The Shelleys' departure for Italy in 1818, the deaths of their two children, and continual journeying disrupted S.'s plans for another full-length novel. Instead, she wrote the novella *Mathilda* (1819), a study in irrational guilt. Mathilda tells of her father's incestuous passion, his suicide, her consequent sense of pollution, and her imminent death. Unpublished until 1959, *Mathilda* is probably the most frequently read item of S.'s fiction after *Frankenstein*. It has been interpreted as both a fictionalized account of S.'s love-hate relationship with her father and as a dramatic monologue in which S. ironizes Mathilda's self-absorption and self-deception.

Valperga (3 vols., 1823), a well-researched historical romance set in 14th-c. Tuscany, surprised readers by its difference from *Frankenstein*. Undeservedly neglected until the mid-1990s, it is a rare example of the woman-authored 19th-c. political novel. It has longueurs, but is strongly conceived, and contains some of S.'s most beautiful writing. The male protagonist, Castruccio Castracani, an historical character who nearly became overlord of Tuscany, is a type of the Napoleonic empire-builder. Contrasted with him is the invented Euthanasia dei Adimari, Countess of Valperga. An enlightened female rule that seeks to evolve into democracy and eventually into the disappearance of the state (which Godwin had called the "euthanasia of government") opposes male will-to-power and glory.

In 1823, S. returned to England, a penniless widow with a child and a bankrupt father. Her father-in-law gave her a stingy allowance but forbade her to publicize the Shelley name. Her next major work, the multilayered and apocalyptic *The Last Man* (3 vols., 1826), probably the most profound English novel of the 1820s, took over two years to produce. The narrative has been supposedly edited from scattered Sybilline leaves found in 1818, which prophesy humankind's extinction about the year 2100. Set in a future foretold by a prophetess in the remote past, *The Last Man* is at once an elegy for the dead Percy Bysshe Shelley and Byron, a critique of Enlightenment belief in progress, a response to the transcontinental cholera epidemic of the 1820s, and a meditation on "the end of history." Slow to get going, it gathers momentum and closes sublimely with the figure of the solitary human survivor of a universal pandemic. It was badly received; S. was accused of multiplying imaginary horrors. Today, it seems uncannily prescient of millennial anxieties: AIDS, nuclear holocaust, global pollution.

The historical romance *The Adventures of Perkin Warbeck* (3 vols., 1830) had better reviews; it is overlong, but has some engaging passages. Like *Valperga*, it opposes male ambition to female virtue. S. took the minority view that the historical Warbeck, pretender to the English throne, was genuine. (Subsequent research has proved him an imposter.) Like Wollstonecraft, she is a vindicator; vindication of those unjustly treated by historians is a unifying motif in her crowded tapestry.

S.'s last two "domestic" novels are receiving increasing attention. The judgment that *Lodore* (3 vols., 1835), a contemporary story, is a sentimental sell-out has been persuasively challenged. The intellectual Fanny Derham, whose independence is contrasted with the docility of the apparent heroine, Ethel, is one of S.'s most intriguing characters. Family relationships depicted in these late novels are often disturbingly unconventional and a licentious Gothic imagination works subterraneously. This is especially true of *Falkner* (3 vols., 1837), in which the horror of a mother's exhumation is conveyed in a few stark words.

S.'s many literary friends included Leigh HUNT, Washington Irving, Prosper Mérimée, Thomas MOORE, Lady MORGAN, Caroline Norton, and Charles DICKENS, but she belonged to no clearly defined circle. She enjoyed peer-esteem, but was never a bestseller. Between 1823 and 1839, she supplemented her income with short pieces, which, collectively, round out the picture of a multifaceted literary woman. Her reviews for the progressive *Westminster* are graceful, generous, often sharply evaluative. Her tales for the fashionable Christmas annual, the *Keepsake*, edited by a Godwinian disciple, include some well-written stories of psychological depth ("Transformation" and "The Trial of Love," for instance). Her five volumes of short biographies of European writers (1835–39), modeled on both Samuel JOHNSON's *Lives of the Poets* and the popular encyclopedia article, distill the knowledge, taste, and judgment acquired over thirty years by disciplined reading. Ostensibly self-effacing, they afford revealing glimpses into her opinions on literary merit, religious belief, morality, and nationalism. "Machiavelli," "Cervantes," "Pascal," and "Madame de Staël" may be cited here.

The years 1838–39 were punishing ones during which S. published seven volumes of Percy Bysshe Shelley's works. For all their imperfections, they are a landmark of Romantic editing. She now had money to revisit the Continent. Her tours resulted in a highly political travel book, *Rambles in Germany and Italy* (2 vols., 1844), which won plaudits for its elegance and charm and brickbats for its daring to step outside woman's sphere. She had published it to raise money for an Italian revolutionary exile who later proved a blackmailing rogue. A brain tumor ended her writing career.

S.'s reputation has benefited considerably from reclamation work undertaken since the 1970s by feminist literary history, by Gothic studies, and by scholarly editing of her writings. Controversy centers around whether her talent was warped by pressures to achieve respectability. Those disagreeing argue that her career evidences a deliberate wish to experiment rather than to attempt a repetition of her early success; they point to the persistence in her work of peculiarly obsessional themes such as dominant fathers, absent mothers, guilt, pursuit, doubles, and androgyny.

ROMANCE rather than reality is her field. Like Godwin, she frequently sacrifices verisimilitude to achieve intensity of effect, similar to that of expressionist silent cinema or opera. Confessional monologue, not dialogue, is her forte; she analyzes psychology acutely without character drawing. Her personages are both stereotypical and true. Her landscapes are projections of emotions or states of mind. A symbolist, she uses the repetition device—the cave, the mosaic, the Ave Maria—like a musical leitmotif. Episodes are often shaped around an arresting image, as in a history painting or theatrical tableau. Her novels (*Frankenstein* apart) often lack narrative pace, but, like an unnaturally calm sea, are moved by sudden tempests and by undercurrents. Reading her books simply as disguised AUTOBIOGRAPHY is futile, yet there is an irreducible element of self-inscription. For many she is most approachable as a Gothic writer, yet that category does not contain her. Her place in the academic canon is fluid but it looks increasingly unlikely that she will again retrogress to the status of a mere "one book" author.

BIBLIOGRAPHY: Bennett, B. T., *M. W. S.* (1998); Bennett, B. T., and S. Curran, eds., *M. S. in Her Times* (2000); Eberle-Sinatra, M., ed., *M. S.'s Fictions* (2000); Fisch, A. A., A. K. Mellor, and E. H. Schor, eds., *The Other M. S.* (1993); Mellor, A. K., *M. S., Her Life, Her Fictions, Her Monsters* (1988); Seymour, M., *M. S.* (2000); Sunstein, E. W., *M. S.* (1989); Williams, J., *M. S.* (2000)

NORA CROOK

SHELLEY, Percy Bysshe
b. 4 August 1792, Field Place, Horsham, Sussex; d. 8 July 1822, Bay of Spezzia, Italy

S.'s reputation has arguably gone through more revolutions than that of any other major Romantic poet. Widely reviled in his lifetime for disseminating the "detestable principles" of atheism and free love, he was to become an iconic figure, combining at least four powerful stereotypes: Matthew ARNOLD's "beautiful, ineffectual angel," the upper-class rebel and protosocialist, the Romantic egotist, and the prophet with a "passion for reforming the world."

S. was the scion of one of the wealthiest land-owning families in England, heir to a baronetcy, and the eldest brother of adoring sisters, a family pattern that he continually tried to reproduce in later life. At the elite Eton College, "Mad Shelley," as he was called, acquired a fascination with science and was mercilessly bullied. His juvenilia includes two preposterous Gothic novels and a long poem, *The Wandering Jew*. Expelled from Oxford for the pamphlet *The Necessity of Atheism* (1811), he quarreled with his father, hastily married, and engaged in abortive political activity in Ireland, Devon, and Wales.

Early influences were the French intellectual architects of the French Revolution, American republicanism, and William GODWIN's *Political Justice*. S. absorbed Godwin's Necessitarianism, which simultaneously denies free will and asserts the inevitability of progress. Prone to violent anger, he nevertheless adopted Godwin's arguments concerning the unworthiness of revenge and at times advocates a passive resistance resembling Christian pacifism. In later life, he identified himself not only with Cain (society's outcast) but also with Christ (considered as a man and as the misunderstood friend of humanity). The young S. was a materialist, but the later S. was a skeptic with a strong attraction toward Platonism rather than what is generally understood by the term "atheist." For S. "nothing is but as it is perceived."

His first major poem was the innocuously named but inflammatory *Queen Mab* (1813). The Fairy Mab (the first of S.'s inspiring dream women) reveals to Ianthe the wretched state of the world, enslaved to monarchy and religion, bound by custom's chains, and its future transformation into an earthly paradise through the gradual but inevitable workings of Necessity. *Queen Mab*, in later pirated versions, reached a working-class readership and in the 1840s became the "Chartists' Bible." In 1814, S. left his wife Harriet for Godwin's daughter (Mary Wollstonecraft SHELLEY), a decisive act that realized his liberation politics in the domestic sphere, but that came back to haunt him as a perpetual reproach.

With S.'s next major poem *Alastor; or, The Spirit of Solitude* (1816), his characteristic poetic voice emerges. The sensitive Poet, wandering through a surreal landscape of desert, mountain, and forest, consumed by a furious thirst for an ideal woman, appears for the first time. Critical disagreement has centered on whether S. intended a warning against narcissism or a pessimistic recognition of the insufficiency of the material world. The famous Swiss sojourn with Lord BYRON in the summer of 1816 produced "Mont Blanc," a difficult but exhilarating poem in which S. struggles to define the relationship between the human mind and the objects that it contemplates.

Harriet drowned herself in 1816; S. lost custody of his children by her, a factor in his decision to move to Italy in 1818. His major 1817 production was *Laon and Cythna* (*The Revolt of Islam* in its censored version, published in 1818), a twelve-canto EPIC ROMANCE concerning a pair of lovers warring against patriarchal tyranny. It contains a warm tribute to Mary Shelley (by then his wife) and the frankest love scenes in British Romantic poetry. That the lovers were atheistic siblings was the poem's really provocative feature. Incest here is a trope for the revolutionary potential of gender equality; Cythna, with her cry "Can man be free if woman be a Slave?" is S.'s most Wollstonecraftian figure. The suppression of popular uprisings in 1817 prompted his eloquent political pamphlet, *An Address to the People on the Death of the Princess Charlotte*, in which S. pleads that it is the death of British civil liberties that should be mourned, rather than that of a royal princess. His famous sonnet "Ozymandias," in which the downfall of tyranny is symbolized by the Pharoah's massive statue crumbling away into the desert sands, dates from the turn of that year and was collected in *Rosalind and Helen* (1819). The title poem's chief interest lies in its treatment of friendship between women.

S.'s move to Italy in 1818 stimulated his immersion in Greek, Italian, Spanish, and German literature and brought him into closer contact with Byron. A pattern emerges of his using translation to kick-start original composition. These influences hastened his poetic maturity. The year 1819 was his "annus mirabilis." He completed his magnum opus, the lyrical drama *Prometheus Unbound*, a refashioning of the Prometheus myth in which the rebellious Titan is not liberated through compromising with his oppressor, Jupiter (the original resolution). He is freed through his own renunciation of revenge and through the combined agencies of his lover, Asia, and a mysterious being, Demogorgon (who might symbolize Necessity or the power of the people or both, S.'s mature art being polysemous—i.e., working simultaneously on many interpretive levels).

The year 1819 also saw the publication of *The Cenci*, an historical tale of incestuous rape and parricide, probably the most actable verse drama written by any major Romantic. Three major works from that year remained unpublished until more propitious times: *The Mask of Anarchy*, prompted by S.'s fury after the Peterloo Massacre; *Peter Bell the Third*, a satire on William WORDSWORTH; and his longest, most considered political essay, the unfinished "A Philosophical View of Reform." In October 1819, he wrote "Ode to the West Wind," a work asserting the power of words to effect societal change in the same way that the autumnal wind destroys and renovates. The breath-taking changes of pace, the tumultuous images of sea, leaves, clouds, and storm, the arresting last line ("If winter comes, can Spring be far behind?") underpinned by a strict formal organization and a mastery of the difficult Italian terza rima, have given it the status of the quintessential S. lyric.

Between 1820 and 1822, S. lived principally in Pisa, where he gathered around him a circle of British exiles, including Byron. There he published the *Prometheus Unbound* volume (1820), which also contained "The Sensitive-Plant" and "To a Skylark." To this Pisan period also belong *Oedipus Tyrannus; or, Swellfoot the Tyrant* (1820), a caustic burlesque on the antics of the British monarchy, and *Epipsychidion* (1821), a paean to love, in which the speaker's palpable sexual desire for the beautiful addressee, Emily, and his insistence that his love is too unearthly to be understood in any such vulgar sense, are in a state of unresolved tension. His noble elegy for John KEATS, *Adonais* (1821), attacks his critics and has been often interpreted as prophesying his own death. *Hellas* (1822), the last major poem to be published in his lifetime, is a lyrical drama urging the cause of Greek independence. He drowned with the visionary "The Triumph of Life" still unfinished. Apparently a disillusioned fragment about the vanity of the world and the inevitable extinction of youthful idealism, it breaks off at the very point where S. might have reversed its pessimistic trajectory. For many readers, this is his greatest work, despite its cliff-hanging state. Whether S. would have developed it in the direction of despair or of hope or had come to an unbridgeable impasse is irresolvable, yet few readers fail to develop intuitive convictions one way or another.

Attempts by S.'s father's to obliterate the poet's name posthumously were foiled by pirate publishers in Britain, France, and the U.S., by the persistent advocacy of his friends, and by Mary Shelley, through whom were released (1824) other major poems, each testifying to his mastery of a genre. These include: "Julian and Maddalo," a debate over whether the human will can rise above circumstances; "Letter to Maria Gisborne," a testament of friendship; and "The

Witch of Atlas," a playful-serious piece of myth-making.

The years 1870–1914 saw the publication of a peak of S. scholarship and of "Shelley worship." S. became a secular saint (complete with relics of bone fragments), his tomb a shrine. Reaction set in after World War I. The 1920s elevation of the metaphysical poets by T. S. ELIOT and F. R. LEAVIS made S.'s poetry seem diffuse in comparison and generally lacking in tough reasonableness, poise, and a "grasp on the actual," though "The Triumph of Life" and *The Mask of Anarchy* received praise. S.'s characteristic fondness for images of kindling and dwindling, of panting and mingling, for similes that compare an intangible object to something even less tangible—"purple mist" being likened to an "air-dissolved star," for instance—were regarded as exhibiting sloppy diction and unclear thought.

The last forty years have seen another set of major revaluations. Important biographies presented a "crueller and more capable figure" (Richard Holmes), a clever polemicist, and a strenuous intelligence. Nathaniel Brown and Paul Foot effectively argued against a eunuchized S. Historicist approaches have given more accurate maps of his intellectual roots in 18th-c. Enlightenment and the political ferment of the French Revolutionary period and he has received due recognition as a prose writer. The 1990s saw a reaction against treating the Romantics as solitary individualists; instead, S. has been approached as a member of the coterie surrounding Leigh HUNT. Though he was a disciple of Mary WOLLSTONECRAFT and sought the company of women intellectuals, feminist criticism, on the whole, has been less interested in S., regarding him as having had his due share of critical attention. He strikes stronger chords elsewhere. At the fall of the Berlin Wall in 1989, it was remarked that the apparent suddenness of the collapse mirrored the overthrow of Jupiter in *Prometheus Unbound*. S.'s anticapitalism, pacifism, and vegetarianism have obvious relevance to present-day Green Party issues. The poetry has proved strikingly amenable to deconstructionist analysis from the late 1970s onward. Much critical work concerns itself with analyzing the way S.'s poetry enacts his failure to resolve fundamental contradictions in his ideology and personality. He is not so much concerned with representing states of being as states of becoming, in process rather than in outcome.

In paying a renewed attention to his formal artistry, a current trend in S. criticism appears to be taking up the implications of Wordsworth's remark that S. was the best stylist of his generation. The trend has been stimulated by late-20th-c. textual scholarship, which has corrected many errors. S. has been the most inaccurately edited British standard author, partly because of his isolation in Italy and his almost illegible handwriting. Currently, major new editions are proceeding on both sides of the Atlantic, but an up-to-date BIOGRAPHY and editions of his complete prose and letters (not as creative as Keats's, but wonderfully various) are also urgent needs.

The gap between S. as social prophet and S. as consummate artist remains as tantalizingly wide as ever. Concentration on the first tends to lead to a boiling down of his "message," while concentration on the second tends to lead away from society to a transcendent world "Where music and moonlight and feeling/Are one" ("To Jane"). The gap was one that S. himself tried to bridge in *A Defence of Poetry* (wr. 1821; pub. 1840), which passionately argued that the pleasure given by great poetry is inseparable from its capacity to defamiliarize the dead hand of "things as they are" and to stimulate listeners to reimagine society as it could become. His work continues to challenge W. H. AUDEN's dictum "Poetry makes nothing happen."

BIBLIOGRAPHY: Bennett, B. T., and S. Curran, eds., *S: Poet and Legislator of the World* (1996); Brown, N., *Sexuality and Feminism in S.* (1979); Curran, S., *S.'s Annus Mirabilis* (1975); Foot, P., *Red S.* (1980); Gelpi, B. C., *S.'s Goddess: Maternity, Language, Subjectivity* (1992); Holmes, R., *S.* (1974); Keach, W., *S.'s Style* (1984); King-Hele, D., *S., His Thought and Work* (3rd ed., 1984); O'Neill, M., ed., *S.* (1993); Reiman, D. H., *P. B. S.* (1990)

NORA CROOK

SHENSTONE, William

b. 18 November 1714, Halesowen, Shropshire; d. 11 February 1763, Halesowen, Shropshire (now Worcestershire)

Although praised by admirers from Robert BURNS to William HAZLITT, S. is now relegated to a position as a minor 18th-c. poet often writing in imitation of his more talented predecessors such as Edmund SPENSER and Alexander POPE. His first volume of poetry, *Poems upon Various Occasions* (1737), was followed by *The Judgment of Hercules* (1741) and *The School-Mistress* (1742), both printed by London publisher Robert DODSLEY. Owing to his stature at the time, S. figured prominently in Dodsley's influential miscellany *A Collection of Poems*, and his popularity as a poet continued well into the 19th c.

SHERIDAN, Richard Brinsley [Butler]

b. 1751, Dublin, Ireland; d. 7 July 1816, London

Best known as a dramatist, S. became the manager of the Drury Lane Theatre from 1776 to 1809. In the society to which S. aspired, propriety of conduct was essential for both ladies and gentlemen. His first play,

The Rivals (1775), exaggerates the idea of a society in which Mrs. Malaprop is the personification of pretentiousness; where the novels hidden under books of sermons and advice on etiquette can be seen as a metaphor for hiding one's true feelings under masks of SENTIMENT and decorum; where Falkland's agonized indecision exemplifies the refining of one's sentiments taken to the foolish yet logical extreme and Julia's tears express the slightly ridiculous "true" response of a woman of feeling. The audience is made aware of the duplicities that are taking place and they are less concerned with the unraveling of the plot than in watching the reactions of the characters; a technique of dramatic irony used by many dramatists before and after S., but not often by his contemporaries, for focusing attention on the moral fable at the heart of the plot. It is essential that the audience accept with Lydia that she is "myself the dupe at last" when she acknowledges reality when threatened by the danger of the duel. Falkland must also be seen to accept the falsity of excessive sentiment. They must also see that a man of absolute integrity like Sir Anthony can be blind to the pretenses of others and thus fooled by them.

The School for Scandal (perf. 1777; pub. 1780) makes the moral point more bitingly. It shows the corruption of innocence as well as reputation in deliberate, often malicious, slander and denigration, by hypocrisy masquerading as rectitude. Joseph Surface is the tempter, the Vice of the old medieval tradition, and the personification of the vice of hypocrisy while the "school" is made up of various caricatures of the different aspects of slander and gossip. Fashions and behavior at the time had become more extreme and so has S.'s trenchant satire. The function of the problematic picture auction is as a portrayal of appearance versus reality. The slanderers sell reputations as social coinage: Charles is selling representations of shadows but redeems himself when he refuses to sell the true one of his uncle and thus shows himself as a man of feeling. The portraits are visual illustrations of the theme of the play. Reputations can be sold as easily as painted appearances: only if outward appearances accord with inward feelings are reputations safe. Sir Peter's discovery of Lady Teazle behind the screen is the moment when the unmasking of sin is shown most vividly, but it is not the end of the play. This suggests that S. intended the resolution of the characters' behavior to be more important than the comic discomfiting of the Teazles. Although the tidiness of the ending was undoubtedly a concession to sentimental convention, it is not a guarantee of happiness ever after. The Teazles only "intend" to live happily together. Charles refuses to make any promises about reforming. There is more acknowledgment of reality in these responses and in Joseph's equivocal exit than in Julia's sententious speech at the end of *The Rivals.*

Three other plays all comment in one way or another on deceit. The short farce *St. Patrick's Day* (perf. 1775; pub. 1788) shows how a credulous man can be taken in by a false name, lying letters, and seemingly erudite language. In the highly popular musical *The Duenna* (1775), parents are deceived by their children, there is a tilt at the deceptions practiced by priests, and a continuous visual joke in the duping of Isaac about the Duenna's age that ties into Isaac's greedy self-deception. S.'s adaptation of Sir John VANBRUGH's *The Relapse* into *A Trip to Scarborough* (perf. 1777; pub. 1781) is substantially altered from Vanbrugh's play to point the deception of a father by a young man eager to win his daughter and his money. In *The Camp* (perf. 1778; pub. 1795), S. first turns to satirizing national and political matters on the stage. In it are a cheating exciseman, a cheating army contractor, country people who hope to cheat soldiers, and society people using the threats of invasion as an interesting diversion for a day's outing, as fashionable ladies were actually doing. The one honest person is arrested as a spy, even the young girl looking for her lover is in disguise. Far from a bombastic call to arms against France, this is an indictment of national unpreparedness and cupidity in the face of war.

The Critic (perf. 1779; pub. 1781) is often seen today simply as a theatrical burlesque. This tends to ignore the gradually increasing crusading spirit found in S.'s political writings. The country was already at war with France and was soon at war with Spain. There was unease about the ineffectual administration of Lord North and the capacity of the country to defend itself against invasion. The thread of general political comment begins in the opening lines when Dangle is not interested in reality only in the appearance of reality, and Mrs. Dangle looks to actual events solely as sources of amusement. Even so, S. ironically makes her the vehicle for pointing his theme that people should be preparing for invasion: "at the head of one of the Westminster associations" or trailing a volunteer pike in the Artillery ground. The total incomprehensibility and incomprehension of the Italian family is the crux of a carefully structured demonstration of people who both refuse to understand what is being said to them and fail to realize that it is important to understand. Dangle has not understood his wife's allusions to the invasion, nor Sir Fretful the insults to his writing. Part of S.'s case against the government was that it would not listen to advice and criticism. It is supremely ironical that the audience should then watch the characters immerse themselves in watching a rehearsal of an historical invasion. By juxtaposing theatrical burlesque with political satire, the audience is made to feel both privileged and superior, and when the play ends in a patriotic procession they are prepared to indulge themselves in the blatant jingoism, able both to laugh at themselves as a nation that sticks its head in the sand in times of crisis and to understand that this is what S. was warning against.

All through his political life as a member of Parliament, S. attacked not only the shams and hypocrisies of manners and customs but the deeper ills of political maneuvering and the abrogation of principle for personal ambition and gain. These principles are illustrated in *Pizzaro* (perf. 1799), the play S.'s biographers appear unanimous in wishing he had not written, and critics find difficult to assess. It seems that he took some care over it, that he was probably working on it at least six months from December 1798 and may have started in March 1798. It is possible that he was attempting, with heroic language, music, and spectacle, to produce his own version of contemporary tragic style. The theme of corruption inherent in political life would be the ultimate moral question and need to be dignified by the use of a "higher" style than he could use in comic drama. Critics mainly agree *Pizzaro* is a political play but not necessarily on his target. Although generally assumed at the time, it seems unlikely that S. meant Pizzaro to represent Napoleon Bonaparte when the war with France was six years old. S.'s political speeches had been concerned with the plight of Ireland and its current rebellion. If Peru is seen as Ireland and Pizzaro as any of those political opponents S. felt had given up principle for expediency in dealing with the Irish, it would explain why Pizzaro's uptight and honorable but mistaken nature is emphasized for this is how S. regarded his opponents. In this play, S. shows that human motives are dubious, that men can be deceived in themselves about their motives.

S. used the artifices of the stage to demonstrate the masks men use to hide from reality and the consequences of taking the mask for the true face. Paradoxically, he masks his unpalatable truths in such brilliant language and clever technique to make them acceptable to the conventions of his time that we have been far too easily deceived into taking the surface for the whole.

BIBLIOGRAPHY: Auburn, M. S., *S.'s Comedies* (1977); Loftis J., *S. and the Drama of Georgian England* (1976); Morwood, J., *The Life and Works of R. B. S.* (1985); Nicoll, A., *A History of Late Eighteenth Century Drama 1750 to 1800* (1937); Price, C., *The Dramatic Works of R. B. S.* (1973); Price, C., *Theatre in the Age of Garrick* (1973)

DAWN LEWCOCK

SHERRIFF, R[obert] C[edric]

b. 6 June 1896, Surrey; d. 13 November 1975, Kingston-on-Thames

S. is best known for his play *Journey's End* (perf. 1928; pub. 1929), set in the trenches of World War I.

It brought fame to both S. and the first actor to play the lead role of Captain Stanhope, the then unknown Laurence Olivier. According to S., the play broke all the rules: "It was a war play, had no leading lady, takes no unexpected turnings" and was on such a tight budget that Olivier wore S.'s officer's uniform. The play's success lies in S.'s ability to draw the audience into the tense, claustrophobic dug-out where five officers play out the forty-eight-hour wait for a dawn attack. At the center of the drama is the tension between the nerve-strained, embittered, and courageous Captain Stanhope and the keen new officer Raleigh who has known Stanhope in England. In Stanhope, S. redefines heroism as the ability to confront horror to the point of psychological collapse and still carry out one's duty. The larger theme of the play is waiting; each character's inner soul is revealed as he responds to the building tension that moves between moments of comedy and almost unbearable emotional intensity.

Journey's End played to full houses for over two years in London's West End and it was almost inevitable that S.'s next play, *Badger's Green* (1930), would be a flop. However, S. was lured to Hollywood by James Whale, who had been involved in the first production of *Journey's End*, where he wrote screenplays for such notable Hollywood films as *The Invisible Man* (1933), *Goodbye Mr. Chips* (1939), and *Mrs. Miniver* (for which he received an Academy Award, 1942), and coauthored scripts for *The Four Feathers* (1939) and *That Hamilton Woman* (1941). After a long absence from theater, S. had two further critical successes with *Miss Mabel* (perf. 1948; pub. 1949) and *Home at Seven* (1950).

Although best known for his drama, S. also wrote several novels, the most successful of which is *The Fortnight in September* (1931). The apparently slight plot, a lower-middle-class family escaping the drudgery of their everyday working lives for a fortnight's holiday, demonstrates S.'s sympathetic ability to draw his reader into the intense inner life of very ordinary people. A strong sense of physical setting, so important in his plays, is employed in this novel to reveal the nuances of each individual character's awareness of self in relation to place. S.'s classification as a "middlebrow" writer does not do justice to the themes explored in this novel. In particular, the way the subjective individual experience of time is set against an almost obsessive clockwatching routine that orders daily life is close to the modernist preoccupation with the individual consciousness in time and space. In exploring the lives behind "an endless drift of faces," S.'s best writing rescues his apparently mundane characters from contempt, though in his less successful work his characters are too ordinary to sustain interest.

S. had begun writing plays to support his Thames rowing club, and the success of his scriptwriting allowed him to realize a dream of attending Oxford as a mature student to read history and row for Oxford. Although S. never completed his degree, and missed his rowing blue because of injury, his interest in history provided contexts for his writing and allowed him to explore the relationship between ordinary lives and the larger historical theater they inhabit. For S., an intimate knowledge and love of the English countryside was bound up with an awareness of the way the landscape revealed the past, particularly the Roman past. *The Long Sunset* (1955), first dramatized as a radio play, explores the responses of two generations of an ordinary Roman family living in Britain to the collapse of the Roman Empire and the integration of the younger generation into the new Britain.

The understated tone of S.'s autobiography, *No Leading Lady* (1968), presents him as unassuming, leading a life like those of his characters, as an all but invisible insurance agent whose circumstances turn extraordinary when he becomes a rich and famous writer. It provides a detailed account of the genesis and success of *Journey's End* and his later experience as a screenwriter, but offers no introspection or analysis of his inner life.

BIBLIOGRAPHY: Bracco, R. M., *Merchants of Hope; British Middlebrow Writers and the First World War, 1919–1939* (1993); Raby, P., "R. C. S.," in Bull, J., ed., *British and Irish Dramatists* since *World War II, Second Series, DLB* 233 (2001): 266–73

CAROL ACTON

SHIELS, George

b. 24 June 1881, Ballymoney, Ireland; d. 19 September 1949, Dublin?, Ireland

Before turning to playwriting, S. was a contributor to Ulster newspapers. He began writing for the Abbey Theatre, Dublin, in 1921 with *Bedmates* (perf. 1921; pub. 1922) and *Insurance Money* (perf. 1921), followed by the ironical *Paul Twyning* (1922). Among his other plays are *Cartney and Kevney* (perf. 1927; pub. 1930), *Mountain Dew* (perf. 1929; pub. 1930), *The New Gossoon* (perf. 1930; pub. 1936), *The Passing Day* (perf. 1936; pub. 1937), *Give Him a House* (perf. 1939; pub. 1947), *The Rugged Path* (perf. 1940; pub. 1942), *The Summit* (perf. 1941; pub. 1942), *The Fort Field* (perf. 1942; pub. 1947), and *The Caretakers* (1948).

SHIRLEY, James

b. 3 September 1596, London; bur. 29 October 1666, London

S. demands attention both as a dramatist and a poet. He has often been seen as the last of the Elizabethan dramatists, the man whose work brings to a close a great tradition. Beginning with *The School of Compliment* (perf. 1625; pub. 1631; repub. as *Love Tricks,* 1667), S. was the author of some forty plays. They include examples of every available genre and most of them are marked by the professional competence of their author; almost all of them contain rewards for the sympathetic reader and one suspects that many of them would still work well on the stage. Yet none of them quite achieves greatness or, indeed, an absolute individuality of vision or workmanship; most of S.'s work exists in the shadow of what had gone before it, most of it relates to recognizable models (most obviously in William SHAKESPEARE, John FLETCHER, and Ben JONSON, though S. was clearly also an attentive reader of Thomas MIDDLETON and John WEBSTER) drawn on and refashioned with skill and clarity of purpose.

It is perhaps in his comedies that S. is most consistently successful. In plays such as *Hyde Park* (perf. 1632; pub. 1637) and *The Lady of Pleasure* (perf. 1635; pub. 1637), the satire on fashionable London life is well observed and handled (S. has a particular gift for the presentation of gossip), and in the later play's amusing treatment of feminine extravagance and masculine imperceptiveness we are likely to recognize both echoes of the city comedies of Middleton and Philip MASSINGER and anticipations of much in Restoration comedy, not least in its counterpointing of the values of city and country. Those who seek to learn "all the arts of London" generally come to regret their pursuit of such "learning," but S.'s moral disapproval of London highlife cannot hide his fascination with it. S.'s moral purposes (such as they are) are often overtaken by his interest in the comedy of manners. S. is particularly adept at the creation of lively female characters, such as Mistress Carol in *Hyde Park* and Aretina and Celestina in *The Lady of Pleasure.*

S. did much to continue (and imitate) the pattern of tragicomedy that Fletcher had earlier established, and he wrote a good number of plays that belong firmly in that tradition. Indeed, S.'s *The Coronation* (perf. 1635), when first printed in 1640, was described as the work of "John Fletcher, Gent." *The Wedding* (perf. ca. 1626–29) and *The Young Admiral* (perf. 1633; pub. 1637) are among S.'s best works in this genre. S.'s smooth verse rises to considerable heights of rhetorical nobility in *The Young Admiral,* a play that faces its hero with the kind of moral dilemma— his beloved will be killed unless he leads an army against his native Naples, his father will be killed if he does so—one expects from such a play and, since this is a tragicomedy, finds its way to a satisfactory resolution. In *The Wedding* (a play that belongs in that line of narratives of interrupted weddings whose most famous exemplar is Shakespeare's *Much Ado About*

Nothing), the villainous Marwood has a plausible maliciousness and the comic figures of Rawbone ("a thin citizen") and Lodam ("a fat gentleman") speak energetically colloquial prose.

From S.'s work in the tragic genre, two plays stand out—*The Traitor* (perf 1631; pub. 1635) and *The Cardinal* (perf. 1641; pub. 1653). Both display S.'s fluent handling of blank verse at something like its best. In *The Traitor*, the grief of Oriana and Amedia finds expression in limpidly melancholy verse and the rantings of Sciarrha are a match for anything that was to follow in the heroic drama of the Restoration. In *The Cardinal*, the Duchess's suffering is articulated in language of restrained dignity. As is so often the case with S., both plays are full of reminders of their predecessors. Familiar character types, like the Machiavellian villain (Lorenzo in *The Traitor*, the Cardinal in the later play), or much-used dramatic motifs, are met in almost every scene. The reader of *The Cardinal* is inescapably reminded of Webster's *The Duchess of Malfi*. It should also be stressed, however, that S. handles his inherited materials with high competence and that he can rise to moments of memorable stage poetry, as when Lorenzo declares, near the end of *The Traitor*, "Fools start at shadows. I'm in love with night/and her complexion," succinctly crystalizing situation and character.

S. also distinguished himself as a writer of masques and other court entertainments. These included *The Triumph of Peace* (perf. February 3, 1634), *The Contention of Ajax and Ulysses* (perf. ca. 1645), *The Triumph of Beauty* (perf. ca. 1645), and *Cupid and Death* (perf. March 21, 1653). All are, in their different ways, accomplished pieces, several of them fascinating for their subtle observations on a deteriorating political situation. As with a number of his plays, S. the writer of masques displays a particular gift for the inset lyric, as in his justly famous song "The glories of our blood and state" from *The Contention of Ajax and Ulysses* and "Open bless'd Elysium grove" from *Cupid and Death*. S.'s nondramatic verse—most of it collected in *Poems* (1646)—includes his mythological narrative *Narcissus* (which owes an obvious debt to Shakespeare's *Venus and Adonis* but, as is characteristic of its author, is not confined by its indebtedness). For the most part, the contents of *Poems* sit securely within the idioms of the Cavalier tradition; they include some attractive love lyrics (notably "Cupid's Call," "I would the God of Love would die," and "Bid me no more good-night"), some entertaining social verse (e.g., "Two Gentlemen That Broke Their Promise of a Meeting, Made When They Drank Claret") and much intelligent and lucid writing on a range of themes. S.'s "The Garden" invites comparison with Andrew MARVELL, and is strikingly accomplished in its use of the quatrain.

BIBLIOGRAPHY: Forsythe, R. S., *The Relation of S.'s Plays to the Elizabethan Drama* (1914); Lucow, B., *J. S.* (1981); Nason, A. H., *J. S., Dramatist* (1915)

GLYN PURSGLOVE

SHIRLEY, John
b. 1366?; d. 21 October 1456, London

S., best known as a scribe of late-14- and early-15-c. vernacular poetry, was a permanent member of the affinity of Richard de Beauchamp, Earl of Warwick. He was Warwick's secretary, and performed various administrative duties such as writing letters, collecting rents, and carrying monies; in short, he was a trusted household retainer. He also participated, under Warwick, in the campaigns of Henry IV in Wales and Henry V in France.

By the late 1420s, S. was settled in London, and during his later years he copied a number of manuscripts, the most important of which are MSS London, British Library, Additional 16165, Cambridge, Trinity College R.3.20, and Oxford, Bodley Ashmole 59. These three large anthologies contain predominantly English verse and prose, and also some French and Latin texts. Most significantly S. copied the works of Geoffrey CHAUCER and John LYDGATE. His role as a conservator of their poetry was noted by the 16th-c. antiquarian John STOW, who commented that S. had "painefully collected the workes of Geffrey Chaucer, Iohn Lidgate and other learned writers, which workes hee wrote in sundry volumes to remayne for posterity." Some of Chaucer's minor poems like "Adam Scriveyn" have survived only in S.'s hand.

S.'s own compositions consist of his so-called bookplate stanza and his two verse prefaces. The bookplate is a single stanza in rime royal that begins "Yee at desyre in herte and haue plesaunce." It emphasizes S.'s ownership of the two volumes in which it was placed, and reminds borrowers of those books of the obligation to return them. The verse prefaces, each 104 lines long, are written in rhyming couplets, and originally introduced S.'s first two anthologies. The first preface, "If at you list for to entende/Of is booke to here legende," still remains in MS British Library Additional 16165, ff. ii^r–iii^v. The second, "O ye my lordes whan ye be holde/this boke or list it to vnfould," now only exists in MS British Library Additional 29729 ff. 177^v–179^r, a later collection compiled by Stow. The general function of both prefaces is to list the contents of the books that they accompanied, but S. also gives information about the commission of particular texts and their authors, especially Lydgate, and his audience, which was socially mixed. Some of the statements are clearly formulaic, such as the appeal for money (made on Lydgate's behalf), and S.'s self-deprecating remarks about his abilities as an author, made in line with the well-worn humility topos.

S. was also a translator. In 1440, he produced *The Boke of Gode Maners*, an English version of *Le Livre des Bonnes Meurs* by Jacques Legrand. S. also translated another French text, *Le Secret des Secres*, and a Latin chronicle telling of "the dethe and false murdure" of JAMES I OF SCOTLAND, *The Dethe of the Kynge of Scotis*. Since the source-text for the latter is lost, S.'s version represents our only knowledge of this text, which is the earliest contemporary account of the regicide. The three texts are linked in theme and content, each offering moral advice, either directly or by example; collectively, they belong to the "advice-to-princes" genre of instructional literature. In general, S.'s translations are characterized by a willingness to expand and adapt the original text. This practice accords with the medieval doctrine that translators should translate not just word-for-word but sense-for-sense, but S.'s technique is more than usually verbose. The translations survive in MS British Library Additional 5467, a manuscript that is not in S.'s own hand and that was probably produced after his death.

BIBLIOGRAPHY: Connolly, M., *J. S.* (1998); Lerer, S., *Chaucer and His Readers* (1993); Mullally, E., and J. Thompson, eds., *The Court and Cultural Diversity* (1997)

MARGARET CONNOLLY

SHUTE, Nevil

(pseud. of Nevil Shute Norway) b. 17 January 1899, Ealing, Middlesex; d. 12 January 1960, Melbourne, Australia

Engineer and popular novelist, S. was educated at Shrewsbury School and Oxford, and served in both world wars. Later, he became managing director of an aircraft factory. In his most interesting novel, *No Highway* (1948), adapted as a film in 1951, the science of metal fatigue provides the answer to the suspenseful mystery of planes whose tails drop off. S. finally moved to Australia. His 1950 novel about women prisoners of the Japanese in wartime, *A Town like Alice* (meaning Alice Springs, in Australia's Northern Territory), was successfully filmed in 1956. S. is perhaps best known for his novel *On the Beach* (1957), set in Melbourne, Australia, about the last survivors of a nuclear holocaust. The highly successful novel was filmed in 1959 starring Ava Gardner and Gregory Peck. His other novels include *Pastoral* (1944), about a love affair between a man and woman serving in the air force, *The Far Country* (1952), and *Trustee from the Toolroom* (1960).

SHUTTLE, Penelope

b. 12 May 1947, Staines, Middlesex

Poet and novelist, S. explores the mythopoetic dimensions of human drives and relationships. Her first novel, *An Excusable Vengeance* (1967), focuses on two characters, "He" and "She," who flesh out the difficulties of courtship and desire. He is both lovingly seeking a closeness to She and physically repulsed by his licentious desire for her that reveals the sacredness of human sexuality and its possible dangerous and explosive elements. S.'s early collection of poems *Nostalgia Neurosis and Other Poems* (1968) indirectly draws on S.'s earlier bouts with anorexia nervosa, agoraphobia, and a mental breakdown at the age of nineteen, highlighting human distress and healing. In 1969, S. met (and later married) poet Peter REDGROVE with whom she coauthored the critically acclaimed *The Wise Wound* (1978), which seeks to elevate women's menses to a poetic level with the mythical and imaginative implications of its subject matter. More recent collections of her poetry include *An Excusable Vengeance* (1967), *Adventures with My Horse* (1988), *Taxing the Rain* (1992), and *A Leaf Out of His Book* (1999).

SIDNEY, Mary. See PEMBROKE, Mary Herbert, Countess of

SIDNEY, [Sir] Philip

b. 29 November 1554, Penshurst Place, Kent; d. 17 October 1586, Arnhem, The Netherlands

In a short lifetime—he died just before his thirty-second birthday—S. excelled and gained renown as a courtier, politician, diplomat, soldier, philosopher, and most enduringly as a writer and poet. English and European, Protestant and Catholic alike admired him as an exemplar of the chivalrous knight, and for many his death in the defense of Protestantism gave him the additional distinction of being a Christian martyr. This larger-than-life reputation among his contemporaries was furthered by the posthumous publication and widespread influence of his works, which helped make him one of the greatest influences both on the English court and on the English imagination.

S.'s major works are the *Old Arcadia* (wr. 1579), *An Apologie for Poetrie* (wr. ca. 1580–81; pub. 1595), also known as *The Defence of Poetry*, *Astrophel and Stella* (wr. 1582; pub. 1591), and the *New Arcadia*, an incomplete revision of the *Old Arcadia* published in 1590. Other pieces include *The Lady of May* (wr. 1579), an early pastoral entertainment written for Queen ELIZABETH I, and numerous miscellaneous poems, letters, and essays. A great deal may be learned and inferred about S.'s character as well as his steadily growing ability and interests as an artist from the works left unfinished at his death. Chief among these is his translation into English of *The Psalms of David* of which he completed work on only the first forty-three. He also left incomplete the translations he began in 1585 of Philippe Duplessis-Mornay's *De la verité de la religion Chrestienne* and Guillaume de Salluste Du Bartas's *La Semaine ou création du monde*. The former was completed by Arthur Golding and published shortly after S.'s death in 1587. All of S.'s relatively small oeuvre has a secure place among the greatest pieces of 16th-c. literature, while *Astrophel and Stella* and the *Apologie* arguably rank among the greatest pieces of English poetry and prose. Modern criticism increasingly views S.'s writing as lying at the core of the body of works offering the most penetrating understanding of the mind of Elizabethan England.

Both S. himself and his literary achievements become clearer to the modern reader when he is understood not as a man ahead of his time, as one may be tempted to think of him, but rather as the consummate man of his age. In the late 16th c., major forces of European civilization were vying for control of European culture. It was a rare period, a janusian age, which still retained elements of its past even as it advanced—a situation that produces remarkable tensions in personalities and in art. S. and his works exemplify this element of his age by the way in which an older, essentially more medieval, sense of honor and conduct governs, checks, and gives meaning to the individual's appetite for knowledge and power and his growing opportunities to gain them. S.'s personal, professional, and artistic careers are a concerted struggle to reconcile a deeply pious and overarching religious sensibility with the rising flood of humanism both in and around him. Thus, S. becomes very nearly the perfect realization of Castiglione's courtier, equally at ease with ancient and contemporary languages and the sources of art and learning as he is with riding, fencing, or court politics. The great accomplishments of his art arise from his unflagging self-awareness and exploration of the paradoxes and complexities of virtuous living—that is, living by a self-effacing Christian and knightly code of conduct—while seeking to satisfy personal desires and aims.

S. was born at his family's home, Penshurst Place, to Mary Sidney, daughter of John Dudley, Duke of Northumberland, and Sir Henry Sidney, who became one of Elizabeth I's most dedicated servants, holding positions as Lord President of Wales and Lord Deputy of Ireland. S.'s social position straddled peerage and gentry. This position may have contributed to S.'s not marrying Penelope Devereux, the "Stella" of *Astrophel and Stella*. In 1564, along with his lifelong devoted friend and future biographer Fulke GREVILLE, S. enrolled in Shrewsbury School under the austere Calvinist Thomas Ashton. In 1568, he went up to

Christ Church, Oxford, but left early without taking a degree and in 1572 set out on his extensive tour of Europe.

S. was in Paris at the French court—indeed he had just been made a Gentleman of the Chamber—when he witnessed the St. Bartholomew's Day massacre on August 24, 1572. The event deeply affected S., and gave political direction to his Protestantism. Worth considering is the disparity of S.'s experience, on the one hand that of a young favored English aristocrat at the French court, and on the other that of an idealistic Protestant witness to the horrific slaughter of Huguenots. The historical episode highlights the central theme of S.'s literary works: the difficulty of reconciling nobility and virtuous ideals in a world of conflict, compromise, and deadly seriousness.

S. spent the remainder of his tour in Heidelberg, Frankfurt, Vienna, Hungary, and Italy and returned in 1575 by way of Poland and the Netherlands to a promising life at Elizabeth's court. S. possessed every quality to excel as a courtier. He was the rare combination of talent and modest humility. In 1577, at the age of twenty-three, S. was dispatched on a diplomatic mission to Germany to explore a possible alliance of Protestant states against the Pope and Catholic nations, especially Spain. The formation of such a league remained S.'s great political dream, although it never materialized. His involvement in the duplicitous and intrigue-ridden world of the court and politics was terribly trying, and his unflagging support of his Protestant ideals—especially as they related to English involvement in Continental affairs—slowly diminished his appeal at court. In 1579, when Elizabeth was considering marriage to the Catholic Duke of Alençon, S. wrote to her voicing his strong opposition. The letter proved a pivotal act in S.'s political career and highlights what must have been increasingly clear to the capable and scheming Elizabeth: S.'s unwavering adherence to principles made him difficult to manage as a political tool. What made S. an unsuitable—potentially dangerous—presence at court was, in part, what allowed him to accomplish what he did in literature, and as his political career after 1579 became a series of duties at court and (predominantly) self-imposed exile at the house of his sister, Mary, Countess of PEMBROKE, he labored increasingly to realize in writing all that he could not achieve in his public and private life. Mary was immortalized by William BROWNE in his elegy: "Sidney's sister, Pembroke's mother, / Death, ere thou hast slaine another, / Faire, and learn'd, and good as she, / Time shall throw a dart at thee."

All S.'s major and most of his extant writings date from his last seven, remarkably productive, years. In 1579, he completed his first version of *Old Arcadia*, a soaring fantastic blending of pastoral and chivalrous romance intended initially merely to please his sister at whose house he was staying while away from court. The revised *Arcadia,* a prose romance interspersed with eclogues, has been called the first novel in English. It is however, incomplete. In 1593, *The Countess of Pembroke's Arcadia* was published. It brought together the first three revised books of the *New Acadia* and the last two books of the unrevised *Old Arcadia,* thus making a third hybrid version of the text. Read variously as courtesy book, moral treatise, discussion of love, philosophy, and rhetorical handbook, it was influential as a study of character.

By 1581, S. had probably completed his *Apologie.* It is a masterly piece of precisely constructed classical oratory argument, cunningly and powerfully arguing that poetry, more so than either philosophy or history, ought to be seen as man's greatest teacher, for it is uniquely qualified to instruct while delighting its audience. The poet, then, has the gravest artistic, but also social, responsibility to fulfill. As J. A. van Dorsten points out, "This doctrine, ambitious and humble at the same time, is not only crucial to an understanding of [S.'s] life and writings, but also indicates how poetry could cease to be regarded as a mere rhetorical art. In the *Apologie,* the limitless scope of poetry was defined in terms such as no Englishman had ventured to use before."

S. followed his *Apologie* with *Astrophel and Stella,* a Petrarchan sonnet sequence comprising 108 sonnets and eleven songs. The danger in giving a brief description of *Astrophel and Stella* is the temptation to use too many superlatives. Nevertheless, it can be said that the sequence is as pioneering and landmark a work in English poetry as anything else one might point to, important not only for the way in which S. introduces continental sources and themes into English, but for the artistic advances he makes within the sonnet form. Astrophil, or "star lover," pursues his beloved Stella, or "star," through as wide a range of actions and situations as emotions and introspections. Enormous amounts of criticism have taken up the biographical sources for the work, seeing Astrophil as a barely masked S. and Stella as thinly disguised Penelope Devereux, who may well have been S.'s great and unattainable love and who in November 1581 married Lord Rich. Ultimately, however, biographical considerations are secondary to and have often obscured the sublime artistic merits of the sequence.

In 1583, S. was knighted and married Frances, daughter of Sir Francis Walsingham. The following year, he began work both on the *Psalms* and preparations to sail with Sir Francis Drake to the West Indies. Before that journey could begin, however, S.'s political career took a new direction. In 1585, he was appointed Governor of Flushing and the next year traveled to the Netherlands. He was wounded as he led an attack against the Spanish close to Zutphen. The celebrated story of his death records how at Zutphen he gave his own water bottle to another wounded soldier saying, "Thy need is yet greater than mine." Equally memorable, though perhaps less often recalled, were his final words spoken at Arnhem where he died nearly a month later: "Love my memory." S. received a hero's burial at St. Paul's in London on February 16, 1587 amid tremendous outpouring of grief in England and throughout Europe.

BIBLIOGRAPHY: Connell, D., *Sir P. S.* (1977); Duncan-Jones, C., *Sir P. S.* (1991); Hamilton, A. C., *Sir P. S.* (1977); Kay, D., ed., *Sir P. S.* (1987); McCanles, M., *The Text of S.'s Arcadian World* (1989)

JOHN V. GLASS

SILLITOE, Alan
b. 4 March 1928, Nottingham

In a career spanning forty-five years, S. has published more than fifty books in several genres. However, S. remains best known and most respected for his earliest novels and short stories, works that were inspired by S.'s background as a youth reared in Nottingham. These early stories and novels focus on characters who struggle to establish their identities as they deal with alienation, poverty, and class conflict.

Although he enjoyed books and writing, S. left school at age fourteen to work in a factory near his home; by sixteen, he was a lathe operator and a socialist. At seventeen, S. joined the Royal Air Force, and he was sent to Malaya in 1947. In Malaya, S. contracted tuberculosis, and he had to be hospitalized for a year, during which time he began to write seriously.

S.'s reputation rests largely on his early works, particularly the novel *Saturday Night and Sunday Morning* (1958) and the collection of short fiction *The Loneliness of the Long-Distance Runner* (1959), which established S. as one of Britain's "Angry Young Men." Both works were adapted into memorable films (in 1960 and 1962, respectively), and were important in popularizing the new artistic interest in working-class experience, popularly designated "kitchen sink" drama.

Saturday Night and Sunday Morning, S.'s gritty first novel, is his most highly regarded. It is the story of a working-class rogue, Arthur Seaton, a lathe operator in a bicycle factory. Seaton's life is circumscribed by the repetitive labor of his factory job and his hedonistic and chaotic personal life. Seaton is on a voyage of self-discovery in which he grows into maturity and reconciliation with society. By the close of the novel, Seaton has found true love in the character of Doreen, an inexperienced nineteen-year-old, and he has accepted a promotion to foreman in the factory. He has established his own identity, yet he has not shed his working-class heritage.

Critics generally agree that S.'s second book, *The Loneliness of the Long-Distance Runner*, contains some of his most powerful fiction. The title story of this collection, a long story told in the first person by a character named Colin Smith, has received wide critical acclaim. Smith, who commits a petty theft, is assigned a term in a Borstal, a special institution intended to reform youthful transgressors. While at the Borstal, Smith speculates on the relationships between the "in-laws" and the "out-laws," and he becomes an outstanding runner who intentionally loses a race at the end of the story to thwart the Borstal's governor. In doing so, Smith illustrates a theme common to much of S.'s fiction: the individual may never win, but he can fight.

Another impressive story in the collection, "The Fishing-Boat Picture," is S.'s most anthologized work. While the tale is about working-class characters, the focus shifts from class conflict to domestic relationships. Harry, a fifty-two-year-old postal worker, tells the story of his failed marriage, and in doing so, comes to understand himself. Harry finds a job, lets a woman named Kathy pressure him into marriage, and then escapes into a world of travel literature. Kathy leaves the marriage, only to return, destitute, ten years later. Harry befriends her for six more years, yet never attempts to reestablish the marriage. Only after Kathy's death in a traffic accident does Harry come to realize that he has been guilty of a passivity concerning life, a passivity that destroyed not only him but also Kathy and their love for one another.

S. followed these early, well-received works with several collections of short fiction, including *The Ragman's Daughter and Other Stories* (1963), *Guzman, Go Home* (1968), and *Men, Women and Children* (1973), as well as eighteen novels. The most notable of the novels are *The General* (1960), a fable that strays from S.'s working-class settings and themes, a trilogy—*The Death of William Posters* (1965), *A Tree on Fire* (1967), and *The Flame of Life* (1974)—that traces the political evolution of a working-class radical named Frank Dawley, and *The Storyteller* (1979), which examines both the nature of literature and the theme of madness. However, neither these works nor his more recent novels have won the praise and acclaim given to the fiction S. produced in the late 1950s and early 1960s.

BIBLIOGRAPHY: Gerard, D., *A. S.* (1988); Hanson, G. M., *Understanding A. S.* (1999); Penner, A. R., *A. S.* (1972)

DAVE KUHNE

SIMPSON, N[orman] F[rederick]
b. 29 January 1919, London

S. is a highly entertaining playwright who is generally classified as an English practitioner of the Theater of the Absurd. In his seven plays and one novel, there can be no doubt of his keen interest in absurdity. He likes to push logic to the point where it becomes ridiculous; he relishes the juxtaposition of the everyday and the extraordinary. But S.'s is not quite the absurdity of Luigi Pirandello or Samuel BECKETT; he does not fully share their existential anguish, though his plays can convey anger at social stupidity and cruelty. His absurdity is of a very British kind, in a tradition that includes Edward LEAR, Lewis CARROLL, and, on the level of popular culture, the BBC radio shows *Itma* and *The Goons*.

S. first came to public attention with his play *A Resounding Tinkle* (perf. 1957; pub. 1958), which shared the third prize in the 1956 drama competition run by the *Observer* Sunday newspaper. *A Resounding Tinkle* has no sustained plot and is more a series of loosely linked episodes than a traditional well-made play. The common element in all its episodes, however, is the comic but philosophically provocative undermining of conventional expectations of both drama and life. The suburban living room of a married couple called the Paradocks becomes the scene of extraordinary events and verbal exchanges of conversation. In the first act, two comedians pay a visit and, among other things, discuss philosophy and Henri Bergson's theory of HUMOR; in the second act, the Paradocks bicker about the name of an elephant that they have ordered, as they do every year, which is now supposedly in their garden. A theater technician and an author come on stage to deliver long monologues, and in the second act, the author is joined by four critics whose range of verdicts on an imaginary play seems like a preemptive strike at S.'s own potential critics.

S.'s one-act play *The Hole* (perf. 1958; pub. 1964) is more tightly constructed than *A Resounding Tinkle*. The title refers to a hole in the road whose contents are described in widely differing ways by those who peer into it: it may contain an attentive religious congregation, people playing dominoes, boxers, a golfer, an aquarium, a prisoner, a bloodstained knife used in human sacrifice—or a junction box for electricity cables. *The Hole* brilliantly encapsulates the philosophical problem of establishing authoritative knowledge and the psychological process by which interpretations of phenomena are shaped by the desires and interests of their observers.

The play that followed, *One Way Pendulum* (perf. 1959; pub. 1960), combines the structural discipline of *The Hole* with the inventiveness of *A Resounding Tinkle* and adds a strand of satire on the legal system: it is S.'s richest work. Like *A Resounding Tinkle*, it portrays an ordinary household that turns out to be very odd indeed: Kirby Groomkirby is trying, with some difficulty, to teach five hundred Speak Your Weight machines to sing Handel's Hallelujah Chorus while his father builds a replica Old Bailey in the living room from a do-it-yourself kit. Kirby is put on trial in the replica for the forty-three murders he has committed in order to provide himself with a logical pretext for the black clothes that he has been conditioned to wear since he was a baby, and the court uncovers his elaborate plot, in which the weighing machines play a key role, to create a permanent justification for his funereal garb. It is all absurd, of course; but the looking-glass world of *One Way Pendulum* nonetheless seems to provide an uncanny image of our own.

The Cresta Run (perf. 1965; pub. 1966) takes on the subject of spying—S. had himself worked in British Intelligence during the Second World War, but it is Cold War espionage that concerns him in this play. Leonard and Lilian Fawcett are drawn into the world of espionage when an intelligence head called Harker supplies them with a top secret telephone number known only to himself; Harker suffers from Bolgerhausen's Multiple Allegiance Syndrome, a condition that sometimes makes him give away vital information. A highly entertaining series of complications ensue, in which, as so often with S., absurdity arises from pursuing logic too far. The world of espionage provides S. with rich comic pickings but, like the legal system in *One Way Pendulum*, also presents a target for his satire. S.'s next play, *Was He Anyone?* (perf. 1972; pub. 1973), aims at another target—the bureaucracy of the British Welfare State. In National Help You Out Year Week, Mrs. Whitbrace requests help for her husband, Albert, who, after falling from a ship twenty-seven months ago, is still afloat in the sea, buoyed up by his lifejacket but now gradually sinking. S. vividly portrays the way in which bureaucracy generates complications that prevent a simple act of rescue; Albert finally drowns. In *Was He Anyone?* S.'s comedy and absurdity take on a darker tone: the play has a stronger moral dimension than his previous work. This combination of comedy, absurdity, and moral concern also comes through in S.'s one novel, *Harry Bleachbaker* (1976), which was based on the play.

S.'s plays won high praise in the late 1950s from Kenneth Tynan, then one of Britain's most influential theater critics, and S.'s fellow playwright Harold PINTER has commended the precision and resonance of S.'s language. His influence in British culture still needs to be fully traced; Tom STOPPARD's plays, for example *After Magritte,* sometimes call S. to mind, and there were many Simpsonian elements in the television series *Monty Python's Flying Circus*. He remains an undervalued and underperformed playwright who is ripe for theatrical revival and critical study.

BIBLIOGRAPHY: Taylor, J. R., *Anger and After: A Guide to the New British Drama* (1963; rev. ed., 1969); Tynan, K., *Curtains* (1961); Zimmerman, C. D., "N. F. S.," in Weintraub, S., ed., *British Dramatists since World War II*, part 2, *DLB* 13 (1982): 474–81

NICOLAS TREDELL

SINCLAIR, Andrew [Annandale]
b. 21 January 1935, Oxford

Educated at Trinity College, Cambridge, and Harvard and Columbia Universities, S. early in his career earned critical recognition for his first two novels, *The Breaking of Bumbo* and *My Friend Judas*, both published in 1959. His reputation was further enhanced with the publication in 1967 of *Gog*, a complex, experimental novel incorporating fiction, history, and myth as a means to explore the postmodern condition of Britain. A sequel to the novel entitled *Magog* was published in 1972. Noted as well for his social and historical nonfiction, S. is accomplished as a biographer, translator, dramatist, and screenwriter. He has directed several films, including the film version of his screenplay for Dylan THOMAS's *Under Milk Wood*, starring Elizabeth Taylor and Richard Burton.

SINCLAIR, May
b. 23 August 1863, Cheshire; d. 14 November 1946, Stow-on-the-Wold

A critic of Victorian society's limited view of women during the early 20th c., S. earned her literary reputation through her steady output of novels, essays, poems, and short stories. Her position as an author who explored the limited roles of women in pre- and post-World War I made her popular not only in England but in the U.S. as well. However, her literary standing waned several years before her death. Although her views on women's roles in post-Victorian society have generated a renewed critical reappraisal, her experience in and her writing about the First World War should continue to garner critical attention.

S.'s fiction concerns itself primarily with the role of women in society at the beginning of the century. S.'s first critically successful novel was *The Divine Fire* (1904). S. analyzed women as objects of devotion or as objects of commerce. The excellent reviews received by the novel in the U.S. led to the serialization in 1906 of her next novel *The Helpmate* in the *Atlantic Monthly*. S.'s critical view of women who held themselves sexually aloof from their husbands led to mixed reviews for the novel, but ultimately resulted in relaxing standards of decency in American magazines. Suzanne Raitt calls the serialization of the novel "a landmark event in the history of American magazine publishing."

Before the First World War, S. participated in the critical reappraisal of the Victorian era as it pertained to literature. S.'s reputation as a critic of Victorian values, her interest in psychoanalysis, as well as her lifelong interest in Charlotte BRONTË, led her to publish introductions to Charlotte and Emily BRONTË's novels when they were reprinted by Everyman between 1909 and 1921. S.'s belief that the Brontës were ahead of their time in their creation of independent heroines in their fiction contributed to her reputation as a leading figure in Brontë scholarship.

When the First World War began in August 1914, S.—like her male compatriots Wilfred OWEN and Siegfried SASSOON—wanted to participate in the war effort. In 1914, S. served with the Munro Ambulance Corps in Belgium, as well as contributing financially to its creation. Her brief but unhappy experience working as a nurse with the corps inspired several of her novels, poems, and a published journal. In *Tasker Jevons: The Real Story* (1916; repub. as *The Belfry*, 1916), Tasker Jevons, a mature man who is also a famous writer, feels as though he is being used for his position and money. In *Anne Severn and the Fieldings* (1922), Anne Severn faces conflict as she tries to carry out her duties as a field ambulance driver while at the same time battling the jealous manipulations of another woman. S.'s nonfiction account of her time in Belgium, *A Journal of Impressions in Belgium* (1915), was part of the first wave of English women's diaries about the war published during the war.

Although S. cultivated many friendships during her life including those with Richard ALDINGTON, H. D., and Ezra Pound, she spent the remaining years of her life primarily alone. Her literary productivity and popularity waned, and by the 1930s the effects of Parkinson's disease were weakening her considerably. Her death in 1946 caused no resurgence in interest in her writings. Yet her observations of women's roles in post-Victorian society still generates critical interest. Her experience participating in World War I as an ambulance driver in her early fifties will also make her a figure of interest to literary and historical scholars in the future.

BIBLIOGRAPHY: Kaplan, S. J., *Feminine Consciousness in the Modern British Novel* (1975); Raitt, S., *M. S.* (2000); Zegger, H. D., *M. S.* (1976)

KATHLEEN PARRY MOLLICK

SISSON, C[harles] H[ubert]
b. 22 April 1914, Bristol

A graduate of Bristol University, who continued his studies at the Universities of Berlin and Freiberg and the Sorbonne, S. was poet, novelist, essayist, and translator of Heinrich Heine, Catullus, Horace, and Dante. He worked in the Civil Service, of which he has been a sharp critic. An Anglican Christian and classicist, he wrote poetry preoccupied with man's

fallen nature, age, decline, and death. Another theme is Arthurian legend. His first collection entitled *Poems* appeared in 1959. Other collections include *The London Zoo* (1961), *Numbers* (1965), and *The Corridor* (1975). His *Collected Poems* appeared in 1984, followed by collections such as *Antidotes* (1991), *The Pattern* (1993), and *What and Who* (1994).

SITWELL, [Dame] Edith [Louisa]
b. 7 September 1887, Scarborough, Yorkshire; d. 11 December 1964, London

Born into an aristocratic family, S.—the sister of Osbert and Sacheverell SITWELL—was educated at home and in 1914 moved with Helen Rootham, her former governess, to London. In 1915, she published her first collection of poetry, *The Mother and Other Poems*, and from 1916 to 1921 edited *Wheels*, an anthology of contemporary verse published in six volumes. Influenced by MODERNISM and opposed to the limited poetics of the Georgians, S. early in her career developed an interest in spoken poetry and the poems of the innovative *Façade*, published in 1922, were set to music by William Walton and recited in public performance by S. herself.

Following the publication of *Bucolic Comedies* (1923), S. developed a reputation as a poet of social commentary with collections such as *The Sleeping Beauty* (1924) and *Gold Coast Customs* (1929). Simultaneously, she began to fashion her self-created image in dress and appearance as the dramatic and eccentric figure captured in portraits of her and in photographs by Cecil Beaton. In the 1930s, S. turned primarily to prose, publishing biographies of Alexander POPE (1930) and Queen Victoria (1936), a study of nonconformity entitled *The English Eccentrics* (1933; rev. ed., 1957), and her only novel *I Live under a Black Sun* (1937).

The events and aftermath of World War II produced a dark, more surreal tone in S.'s poetry. Many of the poems included in collections such as *Street Songs* (1942), *The Song of the Cold* (1945), and *The Shadow of Cain* (1947) incorporate extensive metaphorical and symbolic use of myth and biblical imagery as a means to explore the magnitude of despair, hope, and redemption. The religious quality of her work serves to illustrate her own spiritual transformation later realized in her conversion to Roman Catholicism.

In 1949, S. published *The Canticle of the Rose: Selected Poems 1920–1947* (rev. ed., 1949), and her *Collected Poems* appeared in 1954 (rev. ed., 1957). In that same year, S. was the first poet to be made Dame Commander of the Order of the British Empire. Her autobiography, *Taken Care Of*, was published posthumously in 1964. S. is both praised and chastised as a poet—more invested in promotion than art—but is generally acknowledged as one of the most significant literary figures of the first half of the 20th c.

BIBLIOGRAPHY: Brophy, J., *E. S.* (1968); Cevasco, G. A., *The Sitwells* (1987); Elborn, G., *E. S.* (1981); Glendinning, V., *E. S.* (1981)

SITWELL, [Sir] [Francis] Osbert [Sacheverell]

b. 6 December 1892, London; d. 4 May 1969, Montegufoni, near Florence, Italy

Heir to a baronetcy to which he succeeded on the death of his father, Sir George Sitwell, S. went to Eton (describing himself as having been "educated in the holidays") and served in World War I, which made him a pacifist. S. published travel books about Europe and the Far East. His most famous novel is *Before the Bombardment* (1926), and he is remembered for his advocacy of MODERNISM in music, art, and dance, and in poetry against the Georgians. S.'s novels are rarely read and his poetry remains a curiosity, but he arranged the biblical words to William Walton's oratorio, *Belshazzar's Feast* (perf. 1931) and his six volumes of AUTOBIOGRAPHY give an unforgettable, if occasionally precious, picture of an ancient family and an age. They are *Left Hand, Right Hand!* (1944), *The Scarlet Tree* (1946), *Great Morning* (1947), *Laughter in the Next Room* (1948), *Noble Essences* (1950), and *Tales my Father Taught Me* (1962). An eccentric aristocrat, Sir George had a mania for building additions to the ancestral home and estate, and was totally self-centered, treating S., his elder son, with contempt and his only daughter, Edith SITWELL, with constant destructive criticism. S. masters this painful material with irony and wit.

SITWELL, [Sir] Sacheverell

b. 15 November 1897, Scarborough; d. 1 October 1988, near Towcester, Northamptonshire

Educated at Eton and Balliol College, Oxford, S. was a diverse and prolific author whose career spanned more than six decades. Cast in the shadow of his more prominent siblings, Edith and Osbert SITWELL, S. was nonetheless an accomplished and gifted poet. His first collection of poetry, *The People's Palace*, appeared in 1918 followed in 1921 with the first canto of his *Doctor Donne and Gargantua*, republished in six cantos in 1930. His *Collected Poems* appeared in 1936, and later collections include *Agamemnon's Tomb* (1972), *Serenade to a Sister* (1977), *Looking for the Gods of Light* (1978), and *An Indian Summer* (1982). Journalist, critic, and editor, S. produced numerous prose works on a wide variety of subjects—art, nature, travel, and history. His AUTOBIOGRAPHY, *For Want of a Golden City*, appeared in 1973, and in 1977

he published *Dodecameron: A Self Portrait in Twelve Poems with an Apologia in Prose.*

SKELTON, John

b. ca. 1460, Yorkshire?; d. 21 June 1529, Westminster

S. is a peculiar mix of religious and social conservatism and literary innovation. He was the first British poet to use short, rhyming lines of verse modeled on the way people actually spoke. So unique is his style that it has been named "Skeltonics." His *Magnyfycence* (perf. 1516; pub. ca. 1530) was the first secular morality play (see MYSTERIES AND MORALITY PLAYS) in the history of British drama. A Roman Catholic cleric, his jocularity in the pulpit made many of his contemporaries question whether he should have been an actor rather than a priest.

In 1490, William CAXTON, in *Eneydos,* praised S.'s early writing. In 1499, Desiderius ERASMUS called S. "the incomparable light and ornament of British letters." In 1489, King Henry VII appointed S. court poet. As such, he advised the king not only on poetry but also on sensitive public and religious issues. Henry VII later employed S. as tutor to his second son, the Duke of York, who, in 1509, became King HENRY VIII.

In 1498, S. advanced from subdeacon to deacon to priest, all in less than one year. He received the benefice at Diss in Norfolk, a choice, privately subsidized ecclesiastical post that he occupied until his death in 1529, although from 1517 until he died, he lived in London. Often referred to as "Skelton Laureate," S. was declared poet laureate by the Universities of Cambridge, Oxford, and Louvain in Belgium (then the Netherlands). This designation implied that he had a degree in rhetoric.

S.'s most celebrated long poem from the time he served in court, *The Bowge of Courte*, printed by Wynken de Worde (ca. 1500), was a SATIRE, written in seven-line (rhyme royal) stanzas, on the abuse of royal favors. The word *bouge*, from which the poem derives its title, refers to free food provided at court for loyal royalists. It was not until after 1500 that S. abandoned conventional meters and developed Skeltonics, for which he is renowned.

S.'s most natural form of expression was satire, an often misunderstood genre. His court poems were mostly in this vein. *Ballad of the Scottisshe Kynge* (1513) was a strenuous attack on the enemies of Henry VIII. S. was a royalist who was openly hostile to the spreading humanism that was afoot in England and to the "New Learning" that was a concomitant of it. Most particularly, he abhorred the growing Lutheran heresy.

In his satirical poetry, S. had three favorite subjects at which he frequently took aim: the mendicant friars, whom he considered hypocrites, who retaliated by letting it be known that S. kept a concubine; William Lily, the grammarian, who retaliated by commenting disparagingly on all of S.'s writing; and, most significantly, the mighty Cardinal Wolsey.

So incensed was Wolsey by *Speke Parrot* (wr. 1521), *Collyn Clout* (wr. 1522), and *Why come ye nat to courte?* (wr. 1522 or 1523), all satirizing both the Cardinal's increasing ecclesiastical and political power and the rise of humanism and the "New Learning," that a warrant was issued in 1523 for S.'s immediate arrest. S. sought refuge in Westminster Abbey, where he was beyond the reach of the law, and remained there for his final six years.

The Tunnyng of Elynour Rummyng (ca. 1522), the S. poem best known by today's readers, offers a bawdy burlesque on a band of drunken country wenches. S. writes in rollicking verses that capture excellently the vernacular and musical speech rhythms of the loud, common women upon whom he focuses.

In his years of sanctuary, S. chose to concentrate on allegorical and lyrical themes. He went so far as to dedicate these later poems to Cardinal Wolsey, which is among his most satirical acts. In an England that became Protestant, S.'s reputation as a poet was obscured by his reputation as a person and as a loyal Catholic. Most of the emerging new poets expressed a cordial dislike for S. and his poetry. Not until the late 20th c. has his true worth as a poet begun to be appreciated. Alexander POPE called him "beastly Skelton."

BIBLIOGRAPHY: Edwards, A., *J. S.* (1996); Sterling, E., *The Movement towards Subversion: The English History Play from S. to Shakespeare* (1996); Walker, G., ed., *J. S.* (1997)

R. BAIRD SHUMAN

SMART, Christopher

b. 11 April 1722, Shipbourne, Kent; d. 22 May 1771, London

For recent generations of readers, the most famous work by S. is one not published until 1939: *Jubilate Agno* (also known as *Rejoice in the Lamb*) remained in manuscript, known to only a few people, until it was made available for publication and edited by William Force Stead. It is known that the manuscript was written while S. was confined to a hospital for mentally disturbed people, with some lines clearly describing events and perceptions he experienced while locked up. For years, the character and genre of the work remained a complete enigma—sequences of lines beginning with "For" and other sequences beginning with "Let," glittering imagery and striking epigrams (some seeming to anticipate the "Proverbs of Hell" in William BLAKE's *Marriage of Heaven and Hell*), extended sequences of names and objects drawn from the Bible, others catalogs of names of S.'s contemporaries, and a now-famous sequence describing the character and behavior of S.'s "cat Jeoffrey."

In 1954, W. H. Bond published a new edition of the work, demonstrating his discovery, while working with the manuscript, that it was composed on antiphonal principles, the "For" lines being responses (as in a church service) to the "Let" lines. While many have struggled to find coherence and even narrative in the work, it remains for most readers a grab-bag of beautiful, often ecstatic, imagery expressing the profound and sometimes troubling religious faith that sustained S. as well as stigmatizing him as an "enthusiast" among his contemporaries; while Samuel JOHNSON is quoted as saying he would "as happily pray with Kit Smart as with any other man," he also shook his head, along with many contemporaries, at the evidence of S.'s mental and emotional distress. Twentieth-century attitudes toward "madness" differ considerably from S.'s time, even to the point of making direct connections between creative artistry and insanity, and so *Jubilate Agno* has moved and inspired modern readers, especially poets who have borrowed, echoed, and praised the work; it seems to fascinate by its sensitivity to the beauty and variety of the natural world along with an extraordinary wealth of arcane and unusual words, phrases, and allusions. Whether S. was "insane during his confinement, or merely hiding out from his creditors" (on the theory that even a madhouse was better than debtor's prison), cannot be known. His behavior at the time—praying aloud in public, declaring himself the agent of a restoration of worship in England, insisting that his role as a poet was comparable to that of King David in his role as psalmist—certainly convinced many that he was "mad," but his religious enthusiasm was out of fashion among his literary peers; such behavior in a different era might have seemed merely eccentric.

The public life of S. was full of contradictions and tensions. He was considered a promising scholar at Pembroke College, Cambridge, but left under a cloud of scandal, secretly married and heavily burdened with gambling and drinking debts. He was well known as a religious poet, having won the Seatonian Prize competition (established by Thomas Seaton for a poem on "the attributes of the Supreme Being") five times. At the same time, he was active in the world of popular entertainment in London, composing and performing humorous and slightly salacious verses for popular musical events, including his own cross-dressed characterization of "Mistress Mary Midnight," based on a pseudonym (Mother Midnight) he used when writing for *The Midwife,* one of the many periodical publications he became involved with. He also wrote fables, somewhat in the popular mode of John GAY, and many comical and flattering verses addressed to friends or potential patrons.

This mixture of lighthearted and lightweight secular writing (presumably for the support of his wife and two daughters) with the substantial and brilliant body of his religious poetry has seemed evidence of his divided self, exacerbated perhaps by his alcoholism. He produced a complete paraphrase of the Psalms, as well as a series of hymns keyed to the liturgical calendar, hoping that his versions might be adopted for the Anglican liturgy. This never happened. As his financial problems led increasingly to legal problems and the threat of imprisonment for debt, he searched for money-making opportunities, including proposing a complete translation of the works of Horace, which he published by subscription in a handsome, four-volume edition in 1757. (Ironically, his earlier prose translation of Horace went through many editions as a convenient crutch for schoolboys, but his great verse translations—among the best into English—were not reprinted until 1996 when Karina Williamson edited them as the fifth of the six volumes of the Oxford edition of the complete poetical works.) S. struggled to resolve his financial problems and reestablish his reputation as a poet after he emerged from the asylum, but his misfortunes continued and he finally died in debtor's prison.

Aside from *Jubilate Agno*, the poem by which S. is best remembered is his masterpiece, "A Song to David." This ecstatic hymn in praise of, and prayer to, the Psalmist, King David, was almost lost. S.'s nephew, Christopher Hunter, who first edited S.'s poetry after his death, included only a part of the eighty-six stanza poem; Hunter explained that it seemed to provide "melancholy evidence" of the mental disturbance of his uncle's later years, and he concluded it would not find favor with readers. Robert BROWNING, however, along with other subsequent poets and readers, considered it the greatest poem of the period, crediting S. with the true poetic fire lacking among his contemporaries. S. will remain a bright, though minor, star among the great lights of 18th-c. British literature; for many, his period and his nationality will be irrelevant to their passionate response to his poetic power.

BIBLIOGRAPHY: Hawes, C., *C. S. and the Enlightenment* (1999); Rizzo, B. W., and R. Mahony, eds., *C. S.* (1984); Sherbo, A., *C. S., Scholar of the University* (1967); Williamson, K., et al., eds., *The Poetical Works of C. S.* (6 vols., 1980–96)

THOMAS F. DILLINGHAM

SMITH, Adam

b. 5 June 1723, Kirkcaldy, Scotland; d. 17 July 1790, Edinburgh, Scotland

Perhaps more so than any other writer, S. has given us the foundation of what we commonly describe as economics. S.'s first work is *The Theory of Moral Sentiments* (1759; rev. eds., 1761, 1767, 1790), but he is most remembered for *The Wealth of Nations* (2 vols., 1776; rev. eds., 1778, 1784), the first clear statement of many basic economic principles, including the balance of supply and demand. It was S. who, for better or worse, popularized the phrase "the invisible hand" to describe the power of free markets to regulate human behavior. Even the most entrenched and bitter opponents of capitalism owe a debt to S.'s lucid insights into its mechanical operations. Like many other defining intellectual projects of the Age of Enlightenment that have become so widely accepted that they now achieve the status of unquestioned fact, the challenge for today's readers has become understanding how S.'s elucidation of the principles of capitalism was at one time a radical set of theories.

The Wealth of Nations is a sprawling nine-hundred page work that is not afraid of prolonged discourse on tangential topics. Part of this is attributable to the fact that, as he was an 18th-c. writer, S.'s interests fell under the more inclusive heading of "moral philosophy" rather than the more restrictive 20th-c. field of economics. Given that he saw his project as a practical guide to charting a national economic policy by explaining the root cause of wealth on a national level, there is simply a lot of ground to cover. It sets up a theoretical view of economic life in pre-Industrial Revolution Britain that has four major forces. The first law of the market mechanism details how self-interest is the moving force behind all human behavior. One can appeal to other interests, like duty, but if we rely on the individual's self-interest in obtaining a profit (on goods and services sold) to motivate him, surely we have found the most trustworthy of all human motivations. So what then checks the forces of self-interest, and keeps the seller of goods and services from charging exorbitant prices? The second law of S.'s marketplace, that of competition, states that people will follow high profits: if one sector of the market experiences increased demand for its products, others will compete by offering the same product or service. This will force prices down. Thus, S. envisions a self-regulating system: creators of goods and services will, in their search for higher profits, continually strive to offer the exact quantity and quality of goods and services that the public demands, guided by the invisible hand of competition. So far, we have the basics of any microeconomics class.

S. goes one step further to complicate this self-governing system. What happens when sellers of goods and services began to accumulate wealth? S.'s Law of Accumulation foresees that wealth begets wealth; once a producer creates wealth, he or she will most likely reinvest in more wealth-producing arrangements. That is to say, once the factory owner can finance another factory from his accumulated profits, he or she will do so. The problem of Accumulation lies in its potential to outstrip the ability of labor to produce. More and more factories will create a greater demand for workers, who will therefore collect higher and higher wages, until the lure of profits for the factory owner are outstripped by labor costs.

Yet the Law of Accumulation is counterbalanced by the fourth market force, or S.'s Law of Population. According to this last law, worker population is also reflexive in relation to wages. If high wages exist, then workers will live comfortably and have additional children who survive into adulthood as a benefit of their parent's overall welfare (childhood mortality rates were stunningly high during S.'s lifetime). In turn, these children will increase the worker population, and drive down wages. In this way, S. retains his reciprocating, self-contained system, with its neat checks and counterbalances: self-interest is offset by competition, accumulation is offset by population.

Explaining these concepts is one-half of the focus of *The Wealth of Nations*; defending them from intervention is the other half. The phrase laissez-faire economics was also popularized by S. Having foreseen the power of the market to regulate human behavior, S. was adamant that government should do little to interfere with its operations. It is important to note that he did not have any particular ideological bent to this advice. Critics of later years have mistakenly attributed a host of conservative philosophies to S.'s economic theories, especially during the Margaret Thatcher or Ronald Reagan years. S. was not insensitive to the needs and welfare of his fellow citizens. Rather, he sincerely believed that, as *The Wealth of Nations* has laid out in detail, an unhindered market system would be the best provider for those needs. Regardless of one's ideological interpretation of economic theory, there is little disagreement that modern economic thought has no greater debt to any single writer than to S.

BIBLIOGRAPHY: Heilbroner, R. L., *The Essential A. S.* (1986); Mizuta, H., ed., *A. S.* (2000); Ross, I. S., *The Life of A. S.* (1995); Wood, J. C., ed., *A. S.* (4 vols., 1984)

ROBERT E. CUMMINGS

SMITH, Alexander

b. 31 December 1830, Kilmarnock, Scotland; d. 5 January 1867, Edinburgh, Scotland

Too poor to go to college, S. followed his father's trade as a lace designer. Early poems appeared in the *Glasgow Citizen*. With P. J. Bailey and Sydney DO-BELL, S. was satirized as one of the "Spasmodic School" in 1854. S. and Dobell collaborated on a book of *War Sonnets* (1855) inspired by the Crimean War. S. also published *City Poems* (1857) and a Nor-

thumbrian EPIC, *Edwin of Deira* (1861). S. was accused of plagiarizing Alfred, Lord TENNYSON in *Edwin,* and turned to prose. *Dreamthorp* (1863) and the posthumous *Last Leaves* (1868) are essay collections. *Alfred Hagart's Household* (1865) is a largely autobiographical novel and *A Summer in Skye* (2 vols., 1865) is a description of the island and its people.

SMITH, Charlotte

b. 4 May 1749, London; d. 28 October 1806, Sussex

Reared in Sussex, a region she came to immortalize in poetry much as William WORDSWORTH did the Lake District, S. was the daughter of a gentleman. Married young to a man who turned out to be neither genteel nor money-wise, she separated from him in 1787 and took on the sole care and responsibility of her nine surviving children (out of twelve). For S., her respectable origins and her status as a mother shaped the personae she chose to present to her reading public; even once her children were grown, she continued to maintain them through her writing. S., as a professional writer, relied on her poetry and novels to support her and her children, and she used her upbringing as a lady as much to justify her entry into a print market as to reassure her reading public of her gentility. S., however, was neither helpless nor shrinking: her writing reveals a woman fully aware of the limitations and restrictions that affected her sex, and suggests her readiness to make use of her audience's preconceptions based on her position as abandoned wife, mother, and genteel lady. One of the most famous and significant women writers of her time, S. is now being recognized as a leading voice in the formation of RO-MANTICISM, and responsible, along with Wordsworth, for establishing many of the most familiar tropes and motifs of its poetry.

Although she wrote poetry from her girlhood, she did not begin publishing until 1784, when her *Elegiac Sonnets* appeared as a money-making venture to free her husband from debtor's prison. They were immediately successful, and between 1784 and 1797 expanded to two volumes and went through six editions. The sonnet had fallen out of literary fashion since the late 17th c., but S.'s edition repopularized this form and led to an explosion in sonnet writing in the 1780s and 1790s. She used the sonnet to establish and explore aspects of the self filtered through an appreciation for and reliance on a nature at once succouring and indifferent. For S., nature is not a nursemaid or a mother, but rather a force both consonant with and opposed to human culture. S. uses her personae to work through issues of exile and alienation; she extends the earlier 18th-c. fashion for graveyard musings, emphasizing bones and decay as much as more esoteric abstracts of evanescence, while also establishing the Romantic mode of self-reflexivity. Her sonnets privilege the "I" as one who dwells on the personal: indeed, by the late 1790s her readers had begun to complain that S. protested too much, an example of a mode losing currency.

S. was an innovative and experimental poet, however, and in 1793 published *The Emigrants*, a two-part blank-verse poem that contrasts the situation of the French emigrant clergy and aristocracy with her own situation as a woman in a repressive English culture. While S. has been misread as a conservative because a poem like *The Emigrants* expresses sympathy for those the revolution had exiled, the poem actually registers not so much antirevolutionary feeling as distaste and contempt for the disintegration of revolutionary ideals into violence and repression. Unlike other writers, however, whose distaste led to a rejection of the revolution altogether, S. maintained the importance and value of overthrowing oppressive regimes; in *The Emigrants*, she comes very close to sedition when she suggests that Britain itself could learn lessons from the French, and further characterizes Britain as a land blighted by sycophancy and cruel class divisions. She carefully places her persona outside and hostile to such a culture, and ends the poem by calling on God to right human wrongs, another instance of her readiness to challenge conventional authority. Her posthumously published masterpiece, *Beachy Head* (1807), continues the theme of exile but pursues as well a new emphasis on the materiality of nature and its formative influence on her art and her life. *Beachy Head* represents a new kind of poetry, more familiar to later readers in the work of Wordsworth, where nature, culture, and the self interweave and multiple voices prevail; interestingly, S. explores aspects of the possibilities of print usually ignored by poets, using footnotes to create a persona antagonistic to that dominating the body of the poem (a device she uses in *The Emigrants* as well but to a much lesser extent). Where the poem's presiding voice is lyrical, imagistic, and adept with metaphor, the footnotes contain a voice concerned with facts, history, geography, and botany: a new kind of female authority underpins a fresh and creative poetical style. In all her poetry, which also includes fables and poems aimed at a juvenile readership, S. rejects the limitations her culture assigned to her sex as well as breaking new ground stylistically.

S. was also a prolific and popular novelist, and as with her poetry she continually set the trend. Her first novel, *Emmeline* (4 vols., 1788), although nominally a work of sensibility, also initiated the use of the castle as emblem of the state of the nation. Her heroine, while displaying all the preternatural accomplishments necessary to the genre, is also unusually independent and resourceful. *Emmeline* is particularly unusual, however, in that a subplot features adultery and

an illegitimate child, the mother of whom is not only allowed to live but who is helped by the virtuous Emmeline and who is rehabilitated through remarriage by the novel's end. Her next novels *Ethelinde* (5 vols., 1789) and *Celestina* (4 vols., 1791) are less remarkable, but it was her fourth novel, *Desmond* (3 vols., 1792), that really challenged her readers' expectations and indeed proved too much for many of them. An overtly pro-revolutionary novel, it also featured adultery and an illegitimate child, fathered by the hero Desmond and adopted by the heroine Geraldine. Plainly, S. was not afraid to deal with taboo subjects in her novels, including politics, as many critics of *Desmond* recognized when they castigated S. for dabbling in concerns not appropriate to a woman. While S. did not back down, her next novel, *The Old Manor House* (4 vols., 1793), considered by many to be her best, did take the precaution of setting its action in the 1770s, so that its critique of British society was somewhat muted and less controversial. This novel features a hero so vacillating that he is more appropriately called an antihero, and allows S. to explore the nature of property ownership and inheritance as well as love crossing class boundaries. *The Wanderings of Warwick* (1794) functions as a sequel.

In all, S. wrote ten novels, three important works of poetry, several works for children, a play, and two translations. Her work challenges stereotypes of gender and genre, and her poetry, especially, shows her to be a formative voice in British Romanticism.

BIBLIOGRAPHY: Curran, S., "Romantic Poetry: The 'I' Altered," in Mellor, A. K., ed., *Romanticism and Feminism* (1988): 185–207; Fletcher, L., *C. S.* (1998); Labbe, J., "Selling One's Sorrows: C. S., Mary Robinson, and the Marketing of Poetry," *WC* 25 (Spring 1994): 68–71

JACQUELINE M. LABBE

SMITH, Dodie [Dorothy Gladys]
b. 3 May 1896, Whitefield, Manchester; d. 24 November 1990, Finchingfield, Essex

It is significant that the four volumes of autobiography S. published in the 1970s take their titles in the form "Look Back, . . ."; it suggests the whimsical, self-deprecating, and slightly malicious HUMOR characteristic of this writer, for it was surely John OSBORNE's play *Look Back in Anger* that virtually destroyed the market, and certainly the critical reputation, of the kind of charming drawing room comedy, or tragicomedy, of which she was the last and probably best exponent.

Initially writing as C. L. Anthony, S. had leapt, almost with Lord BYRON's alacrity, from obscurity to celebrity in 1931 with *Autumn Crocus*, a play she had initially sold as much on the sketches she did of the various scenes as on the play itself, but which made its success on her ability to present a range of amusing characters whose observations of each other formed a good deal of the humor of the piece, and on the wistful, gently unhappy ending that made an audience feel that the comedy that had just entertained them was nevertheless a piece with some serious depth and therefore a proper way to pass an evening. Set in an Alpine hotel with an assortment of mainly English guests, it centered on the doomed romance of the married proprietor and the twenty-seven-year-old spinster traveling with an older woman—without, of course, any of the lesbian overtones that would probably have been implied later in the century. The sense that this would be the heroine's last chance of any sort of fulfillment was what gave the play the necessary element of tragedy and led to the comparisons with Anton Chekhov and Ivan Turgenev which were both a pleasure and a disaster for S., as demanding more than she could really give.

She returned to the spinster's last chance in her most successful play, *Dear Octopus* (1938), which is still revived by amateur companies and occasionally by the BBC, this time permitting her a happy ending, when the son of the family that is the dear octopus of the title realizes that he has been offended by the light flirtations carried on by his mother's companion at the wedding anniversary dance because of his being in love with her, as she has always been with him. As with the first play, the charm of this one depends on a lot of good, amusing lines distributed among a large cast, and on a number of different stories being told or implied: the daughter who has stayed away because she has been embroiled in an affair with a married man, the old friend of the family who has always been in love with the grandfather through her series of marriages, the child whose parents have been killed in an accident and whom nobody quite knows how to help—their problems are rapidly sketched in and, in the comforting way that S. often eschews but here very successfully embraces, resolved.

Between these plays, and after *Dear Octopus* were others, some of which did not work so well. *Service* (perf. 1932; pub. 1937) again deployed a very large cast in the history of a fateful year in the life of a great department store, based on her experiences while working at Heals; she ended this on an optimistic note that comforted some and irritated others at a time when the Great Depression was biting badly. *Touch Wood* (1934) was another play about the attraction of a married man and an unmarried woman, though here the girl is younger and her misery arises from the intensity of her passion rather than a more general sense of life passing her by. In this, as in most of the others, there are important roles for children, which caused some difficulties with the Lord Chamberlain's office; it was thought improper that a young girl should show awareness of her older sister's attempt to seduce a married man, and the problem was, absurdly enough, dealt with by a change of costume that relieved the Lord Chamberlain's mind but actually made the childishness of the character more noticeable.

Much more successful were *Call It a Day* (perf. 1935; pub. 1936), her first work to appear under her own name, and *Bonnet over the Windmill* (1937). Once again, the young woman in love with an older man was featured, and there were many crisp lines that drew laughter from the kind of audience that went to the theater in the 1930s mainly to be amused.

But after the Second World War, which S. spent in the U.S. to protect her pacifist husband from conscription, the brilliant success she had had in the theater began to elude her: as well as the change in critical values implied by the successes of Osborne on the one hand and Samuel BECKETT on the other, there were simple economic factors; theaters could no longer afford the large casts for which S. wrote. She had, anyway, already begun to turn to other forms, beginning, in a way unfortunately, with her best work. *I Capture the Castle* (pub. 1948; perf. 1954) is probably best described as a romance, though, in the tradition of *Autumn Crocus,* it is one without a happy ending for its delightful narrator. Its central narrative is to do with the emotions of two sisters, the young American men who are the landlords of their father's house, and two other people who therefore provide one of those sad chains in which A loves B who loves C, coming back eventually to the wrong person loving A. Entwined with this, however, is the more unusual and deeply interesting account of a possibly great man suffering writer's block, and his second wife, a mysterious artists's model. It is not altogether easy to account for the power of this book, which was republished in 1996 as a Virago Modern Classic; it is partly to do with Cassandra Mortmain's narrative voice—naive, rueful, and funny—partly with the originality and interest of the older characters, partly with the form, supposedly Cassandra's diaries, which pull the reader into a continuous present and sanction her shattering honesty. None of S.'s later novels caught the imagination in the same way, and when the novel was dramatized in 1953 the play version was viciously attacked.

S. turned to other genres, with more and less success. Her children's novel, *The One Hundred and One Dalmatians* (1956), was probably her most commercial venture, especially when it became a Disney animated film in 1961; she wrote in her third volume of autobiography, *Look Back with Astonishment* (1979), about her deep affection for the first of a series of Dalmatians she owned, and clearly it was a joy to her to embark these beloved dogs on fantasy adventures, the first being followed by *The Starlight Barking* (1967). Later came *The Midnight Kittens* (1978).

Other genres did not work so well for her. *The Girl from the Candle-Lit Bath* (1978) was a first attempt at a thriller, again somewhat rooted in her personal life, though with a villain, Cyprian Slepe, almost as over-the-top as Cruella de Vil, but she seems not to have realized how much complexity was needed to make this genre satisfying, so that, though the premise and the title are engaging, and the heroine, despite her silliness, quite attractive, the reader feels that this novel is rather perfunctory, a fatal flaw in a thriller. *The Town in Bloom* ((1965) also drew on her early days, but this romantic novel did not deserve or have the success of *I Capture the Castle*.

The first of her four volumes of autobiography, *Look Back with Love* (1974), was the greatest success of her later years; the spirited account of her childhood charmed the critics, but the subsequent volumes—*Look Back with Mixed Feelings* (1978), *Look Back with Astonishment*, *Look Back with Gratitude* (1985)—had to be touted round different publishers; she could not bear it that her later years were simply less interesting to other people than the days of her childhood, but though her life was long and she had some fascinating friends, most notably Christopher IS-HERWOOD, this was the sad truth, and her final years were full of disappointment.

BIBLIOGRAPHY: Grove, V., *Dear Dodie: The Life of D. S.* (1997); Whelehan, I., "'A Doggy Fairy Tale': The Film Metamorphoses of *The Hundred and One Dalmations*," in Cartmell, D., ed., *Adaptations: From Text to Screen, Screen to Text* (1999): 214–25

AUDREY LASKI

SMITH, Iain Crichton
b. 1 January 1928, Glasgow, Scotland; d. 15 October 1998, Taynuilt, Scotland

S. studied at the Nicholson Institute, Isle of Stornaway, and Aberdeen University and became a teacher until 1977, when he became a prolific full-time writer. He wrote poetry, novels, essays, and short stories in Gaelic and in English, and translated Gaelic poetry written by others. His highly regarded novel *Consider the Lilies* (1968) is a moving account of the Highland Clearances. His work appeared in numerous journals, and he published several separate collections. His first collection, *The Long River,* appeared in 1955, followed by *Thistles and Roses* (1961), *The Law and the Grace* (1965), *From Bourgeois Land* (1969), *Hamlet in Autumn* (1972), *Love Poems and Elegies* (1972), *Orpheus and Other Poems* (1974), *The Permanent Island* (1975), *The Notebooks of Robinson Crusoe* (1975), and *In the Middle* (1977). Editions of his *Se-*

lected Poems appeared in 1970, 1982, 1985, and 1990, and his *Collected Poems* appeared 1992.

SMITH, Ken[neth John]
b. 4 December 1938, East Rudston, Yorkshire

S. read English at Leeds University and taught at Exeter and Dewsbury art colleges. Coeditor with Jon Silkin of the famous but commercially fragile *Stand* poetry magazine, S. left Britain in 1967 for the U.S., returning in 1973. Collections of poetry include *The Pity* (1967), *Work, distances/poems* (1972), *Tristan Craxy* (1978), *Fox Running* (1980), *Abel Baker Charlie Delta Epic Sonnets* (1981), *Burned Books* (1981), *Terra* (1986), and in prose *The Book of Chinese Whispers* (1987). His reputation in Britain was reestablished with the publication in 1982 of *The Poet Reclining: Selected Poems 1962–1980*.

SMITH, Stevie [Florence Margaret]
b. 20 September 1902, Hull; d. 7 March 1971, London

S. inhabits the public imagination as an English eccentric, a dotty spinster who loved cats and chose to spend her entire life with her aunt in the London suburb of Palmers Green. Although she was awarded the Queen's Gold Medal for Poetry in 1969 shortly before her death, she is perceived as a minor poet, whose best-known work is the droll "Not Waving but Drowning." Audiences flocked to her readings in the 1960s, enjoying her unique delivery—she would break into off-key song unexpectedly—but her reputation has not generally risen above that of the comic oddity and amateur depicted in Hugh Whitemore's successful play and film *Stevie* (1977 and 1978, respectively). In her 1988 critical biography, Frances Spalding acknowledged the popularity of S.'s poetry but found it the subject of limited scholarly criticism. Critical attention has tended to offer "an overview rather than an examination in more detail of some aspect of her poetics." Only gradually is this beginning to change.

S.'s reputation as a serious poet has suffered from the constraints of critical expectation. From the start, she was aware that her distinct poetic voice would not be easily absorbed into the poetic tradition. Writing to her friend Naomi MITCHISON in the late 1930s, she complained of publishers that "they can't see what anybody means unless it's said in the accepted voice." Indeed, her first novel, *Novel on Yellow Paper* (1936), was written as the result of her poetry being rejected: on receipt of her poems, Ian Parsons at Chatto & Windus told S. "go away and write a novel and we will then think about the poems." Her first collection of poetry, *A Good Time Was Had By All*, was published subsequently in 1937. The resistance her "unaccepted" voice met with never inspired a movement to conformity however, and the theme of suicide, the questioning of Christian and patriarchal orthodoxies combined with a playful HUMOR, which shape this first collection continued to inform her later work. In a 1961 interview, she stated "I don't think my poems have changed much since I started writing." Apparently preferring to describe a trajectory of poetic development, critics are dismayed by this constancy of style and preoccupations. But S.'s poems are deceptively simple: their apparent artlessness and humor mask anger, despair, and social SATIRE. She reworks legends and FAIRY TALES to explore isolation and alienation from the norms of society. The title poem of her second collection, *Tender Only to One* (1938), uses the child's game of pulling petals from a daisy to reveal an allegiance not to a lover or God but to Death. The chilling denouement of the playful rhyme is characteristic in its congregation of whimsy and stark despair. These contradictions of tone are highlighted in the childlike sketches with which S. accompanied her poems. Although critics have shared Philip LARKIN's view that "her frivolity devalues her seriousness," such juxtapositions often create a profoundly disturbing effect.

S.'s wry humor more often deflates pomposity than it devalues despair. She frequently undermines the mannerisms of the lauded male poetic genius for example. In "Thoughts about the Person from Porlock," S. dares to ask of Samuel Taylor COLERIDGE "why did he hurry to let him in?" and impertinently concludes that "he was already stuck" with his masterpiece. The status of the celebrated poet is subtly diminished by the attribution of characteristics and a family history to the formerly anonymous person from Porlock—"He wasn't much in the social sense/ Though his grandmother was a Warlock." But again this gentle mockery conceals a darker center, while Coleridge cursed the intruder who disrupted his poetic musings, S. longs to be interrupted from her suicidal despair.

Her relationship with her muse is similarly uncomfortable. Although she scorned the label "woman poet" and did not regard herself as a feminist, S. is often critical of stereotypical gender roles, masculinity and femininity. Her rejection of the notion of a graceful muse bestowing inspiration upon a willing male recipient certainly challenges patriarchal convention. Instead, S.'s muse is a neglected figure who "sits forlorn" and "wishes she had not been born," for S. only listens to her when unhappy, "When I am happy I live and despise writing/For my Muse this cannot but be dispiriting." This bittersweet rapport with her muse is emblematic: in her portrayals, S. removes the glamour from human relationships whether they are with lovers, friends, parents, or pets. Instead, she represents them with a reality that is always touching while often mundane—a suitor who is "no

longer passionate" offers conversation instead; a mother sadly reflects that her child's freedoms will be short-lived; in an inverted fairy tale, a woman's cat and dog take care of her in old age.

S. challenged conventional representations and wisdoms throughout her poetry and although a Catholic she was particularly critical of unquestioning adherence to religious or political orthodoxies. She explicitly adapted William BLAKE's simple rhymes to challenge rigid Christian doctrines; sinister children chant "our Bog is dood" and the poet celebrates her independence, from the engulfing seas of doctrine. *Novel on Yellow Paper* and especially *Over the Frontier* (1938) both explore the lure and the dangers of succumbing to concrete and oppressive belief systems. Writing in the late thirties during the rise of popular fascism, she urged a close observance of "the man in Party coloured clothes."

Pompey Casmilus, the narrator of both novels and something of an alter ego for S., describes life during the outbreak of World War II, meditating upon power and cruelty. Her melancholy at her failed reunion with her fiancé, Freddy, is expressed against a background of international menace. While the droll humor and conversational tone of *Novel on Yellow Paper* are initially recalled in *Over the Frontier*, the second half has a nightmarish quality as the threat of imminent war permeates the quotidian and Pompey becomes engaged in espionage. In a chilling exploration of S.'s fear that the "cruelty in the air now" arouses individuals to exchange "death-in-life" for a dehumanized authority, Pompey abandons her sociable life, takes a uniform and—with a punning allusion to nightmare—rides on horseback through the night. Both novels contain meditations on the themes that permeate her poetry, Christianity and politics, and frequently the poems are reproduced within the texts. Like Virginia WOOLF's *Three Guineas*, *Over the Frontier* is punctuated by images of uniforms and haunted by their power to "harden . . . emotional arteries." S. fiercely resists allegiance to "any groupismus whatever" but recognizes instead the ease with which uniforms can be donned, believing "power and cruelty" to form the core that can be aroused from every life.

After her third novel, *The Holiday* (1949), a melancholy tale about the pains of love was initially rejected by publishers, S. turned again to poetry producing a further seven collections including *Harold's Leap* (1950) and *Not Waving but Drowning* (1957). She also compiled a sketchbook of her drawings, *Some Are More Human than Others* (1958), integral to the poems they usually accompanied, and edited a picture book *Cats in Colour* (1959).

BIBLIOGRAPHY: Light, A., "Outside History: S. S., Women Poets and the National Voice," *English* 43 (Autumn 1994): 237–59; Pumphrey, M., "Play, Fantasy and Strange Laughter: S. S.'s Uncomfortable Poetry," *CritQ* 28 (Autumn 1986): 85–96; Spalding, F., *S. S.* (1988)

TORY YOUNG

SMITH, Sydney

b. 3 June 1771, Woodford, Essex; d. 22 February 1845, London

Educated at New College, Oxford, and Edinburgh University, S. was ordained priest in 1796 and became tutor to the local squire's son. His first book, *Six Sermons, preached in Charlotte Chapel, Edinburgh* (1800; repub. as *Sermons*, 2 vols., 1801), was followed by the first number (October 1802) of the famous *Edinburgh Review,* which he founded with Francis Jeffrey and Henry Brougham and for a while edited. The project was to provide an outlet for liberal and Whig opinion as a counterbalance to the high Tory *Quarterly.* Connected by marriage to the influential Lord and Lady Holland, he moved to London and was a welcome visitor to their house. When the Whigs briefly returned to office in 1806, his friends found him a living in Yorkshire, where he reluctantly moved in 1809. He lost his chance of becoming a bishop by his support for Catholic Emancipation. Eventually, he was given two livings in Bristol and a paid post as prebend (member of the chapter, or governing body) of the cathedral. In 1831, S. became a canon of St. Paul's Cathedral. He supported various progressive causes: parliamentary reform, which he rightly considered inevitable, and prison reform, and campaigned against the savage laws against poachers and transportation of criminals. Contemporary letters and journals frequently mention him and he was famous for his extempore wit.

SMITH, Sydney Goodsir

b. 26 October 1915, Wellington, New Zealand; d. 15 January 1975, Edinburgh, Scotland

Son of a celebrated Edinburgh professor of forensic medicine, S. was educated at Edinburgh and Oxford Universities and was in the forefront of the Scottish revival. His first volume of poems, *Skail Wind* (1941), was followed by others, but S.'s reputation as a poet was established by *Under the Eildon Tree* (1948; rev. ed., 1954), which comprises twenty-four elegies on the unhappy loves of poets. He has been called the principal successor to Hugh MacDIARMID. S. authored a patriotic play, *The Wallace* (1960), performed at the Edinburgh Festival, and an ambitious fantasy novel, *Carotid Cornucopius* (1947; rev. ed., 1964). His *Collected Poems* appeared in 1975.

SMITH, William

fl. 1596

Disciple of Edmund SPENSER, S. was a minor Elizabethan writer whose literary ambitions were never fully realized. Little is known about him except that toward the end of the 16th-c. he published a sonnet sequence entitled *Chloris; or, The Complaint of the Passionate Despised Shepheard* (1596): the first two sonnets and the final one are explicitly addressed to Spenser. S. signed his name as "W. Smith" and has sometimes been confused with the topographical writer William Smith and the playwright Wentworth Smith, who collaborated with John DAY, William Haughton, and others.

SMITH, Zadie

b. 27 October 1975, London

S. first appeared on the British literary scene in an explosion of gossip and brilliantly managed public relations. It was rumored that this neophyte writer, aged twenty-one at the time, received an enormous advance for her first novel based solely on an eighty-page excerpt. It was also whispered that S. graduated from Cambridge with a "double first" (a double first-class honors degree) in the same year she began writing the novel. S. refused to confirm either figure or result. *White Teeth* (2000) reflects her apparent precocity as it takes on many of the major concerns of the late 20th c.: race, class, culture, violence, love, war, education, money, and science. Fortunately, it is also good enough to eclipse the gossip surrounding its debut.

A fiercely ambitious book, *White Teeth* traces the histories of two families from their 19th-c. colonial roots to present-day north London. The novel begins with the unlikely friendship of Archie Jones, a meek working-class Englishman incapable of making a decision, and Samad Iqbal, a fiercely proud upper-class Bengali who looks like Omar Sharif. Thrown together in the last days of World War II, they form "a friendship that crosses class and color, a friendship that takes as its basis physical proximity and survives because the Englishman assumes the physical proximity will not continue." When Samad immigrates to London in the 1970s, he and Archie continue their unexpected friendship, linking their wives and families.

The novel is equally concerned with their children, Irie, Millat, and Magid, who grow up between two cultures and dabbling in several others. Irie Jones—born in 1975 to a Jamaican mother and a white British father, as S. herself was—gradually takes over from Archie and Samad as the sympathetic focus of the novel. Irie and Millat develop a close relationship to the Chalfens, a middle-class Jewish family who undertake to "educate" them while simultaneously exoticizing them as "brown strangers." Like their fathers before them, Irie and Millat struggle with the desire for rebellion against their parents, their genes, and their hybrid cultures.

Especially from the 1970s on, S.'s vivid delineation of period fashion and cultural trajectories is impressive, glorying in the details of each diverse time and place—from Archie's mohair suit on his wedding day to Millat's Crew, teens who blend Jamaican patois, Bengali, Gujarati, and English to create their own Raggastani language and style. S. also reveals a remarkable ear for speech patterns, slang, and accents, filling the novel with the complex accents and cadences of north London's linguistic soup. Clara's Jamaican, "Sno prob-lem. If you wan' help: jus' arks farrit"; Millat's adolescent "Tax the window seat, yeah? Nice. I've *blatantly* got to have a fag in here, yeah? I'm fuckin' wired, yeah?"; and the Cockneys ordering "Chicken Jail Fret See wiv Chips, fanks" in Samad's restaurant are resonant, precise, delightful.

Critics almost unanimously note that S.'s quirky narrative techniques and linguistic pyrotechnics owe something to the influence of Salman RUSHDIE, although they differ as to the value of this impact. Some see this as a slightly derivative aspect of S.'s youthful style, which she should abandon as she matures as a writer; others disagree, arguing that her agile and assured storytelling voice eclipses Rushdie's and makes the style all her own. Some readers also chafe at the coy neatness of the novel's last quarter, which links all the novel's disparate subplots. However, it would be ungenerous to claim that the lengthy trail of coincidences leading to the dramatic final set-piece undoes the charm of the bulk of the novel. Indeed, the ending affectionately parodies the rapid happily-ever-after finales of Shakespearean comedies. Above all else, though, S.'s most impressive achievement is the generous, earthy, playful good nature that permeates this sprawling novel and thoroughly charms its readers.

White Teeth, famously characterized by S. as "the literary equivalent of a hyperactive, ginger-haired, tap-dancing 10-year-old," won the 2000 Guardian Fiction Prize, the 2000 Whitbread First Novel Prize, and was shortlisted for the Orange Prize. It was also televised in 2002.

S.'s second novel, *The Autograph Man* (2002), is a meditation on the nature of fame, greed, identity, authenticity, and faith. The title character, Alex-Li Tandem, is a Chinese-Jewish Londoner who trades in celebrity autographs and is himself obsessed with acquiring the autograph of a reclusive film star. While *The Autograph Man* retains the wry wit and fine observational detail of *White Teeth*, reviewers also praise its darker, often sadder, vision of the world and S.'s correspondent evolution as a writer of both pathos and comedy. S. is also the editor of *Piece of Flesh* (2001), a limited-edition collection of erotica.

YING S. LEE

SMOLLETT, Tobias

b. 19 March 1721, Dumbartonshire, Scotland; d. 17 September 1771, Antignano, near Leghorn, Italy

Scottish-born S. occupies an enigmatic position in the prose of 18th-c. Britain. He wrote prolifically, quickly, and on diverse subjects, much of his work drenched in such grotesque color, and morally sharp edged, that he was endeared to generations of future readers as something of an irascible oddity. But he was unable to break into the first rank (Samuel RICHARDSON, Henry FIELDING, Laurence STERNE, Jane AUSTEN) because his literary techniques were unsophisticated and his major characters flat, lacking in genuine psychological complexity. He was as much historian as novelist and his pen was fluent. His writing is uneven in quality, some of it impugned even in his own time. Finally, the lack of one best-seller—a *Robinson Crusoe, Gulliver's Travels, Tristram Shandy, Pride and Prejudice*—hurt him. His greatest books are memorable, but not, perhaps, in the legendary way these have been.

His own age was receptive to his talents, which they found scattered throughout his oeuvre. He began literary life as a playwright. His first play, about Scottish JAMES I and his queen called *The Regicide*, flopped, when it was finally produced (1749). Next he turned to poetry with two Juvenalian satires—*Advice* (1746) and its sequel *Reproof* (1747)—neither of which augured literary success. Then he translated Alain-René Lesage's *Gil Blas* (4 vols., 1749), reflecting the period's obsession with Spanish picaresque literature adapted for English readers. But only in 1748, when he decided to abandon medical practice (he was a qualified surgeon) and had been five years married to Anne Lassells, the daughter of a Jamaica planter, did his career take off. This was in the immediate aftermath of *The Adventures of Roderick Random* (2 vols., 1748), an autobiographical and heavily picaresque novel in the manner of Fielding; the story of a ship's surgeon who falls in love, globe trots in various professions, and eventually returns to blissful pastoral life in Scotland with his bride. The book uniquely fuses adventure, ROMANCE, and SATIRE into its view of life as picaresque, while still reflecting prevailing social conditions.

If S. had produced a steady stream of novels like this, his eminence would have been guaranteed but misfortunes and bad decisions intervened. He took an autumn trip in 1749 to the Low Countries and France, when he could have been working on his second novel. Later that year, he attacked the London theatrical managers as having been prejudiced against him because he was Scottish (they were, and his life was to be riddled with anti-Scottish prejudice). But eventually he settled down and in 1751 published his second novel, the four-volume *Adventures of Peregrine Pickle*, much longer and more ambitious than the more tightly constructed *Roderick Random*. In 1752, he felt compelled to attack Fielding in *The Adventures of Habbakkuk Hilding;* this was followed in that same year by *An Essay on the External Use of Water*, a didactic treatise on cold-water bathing.

A year later he returned to fiction, publishing the two-volume *Adventures of Ferdinand Count Fathom*, which the critics panned and could not understand despite its dedication to himself ("To Doctor *********") and its definition of a novel as "a large picture comprehending the characters of life." Disheartened this time beyond previous discouragement, he returned briefly to his native Scotland for the first time in fifteen years and soon afterward wrote the famous "Apologue" to the fourth edition of *Roderick Random* (1755) proclaiming that human nature is eternally flawed and drawing attention to the analogy between it and brute animal instinct.

This time, however, he wondered whether novel writing was his *métier*, so—now in his thirties—he veered yet again, first translating *Don Quixote* (2 vols., 1755), writing *A Complete History of England* (wr. 1755–57; pub. in 4 vols., 1757–58), then launching with three others a monthly magazine called the *Critical Review* (1756), which he edited and for which influential organ for the shaping of contemporary taste he wrote hundreds of reviews. Then followed another magazine, the *British Magazine*, where his *Adventures of Launcelot Greaves* was serialized in 1760–61; this was republished in two volumes in 1762, as well as his continuation of David HUME's *Complete History of England* (5 vols., 1760–65). Finally, he turned political writer when the Scottish Lord Bute became prime minister and invited him to edit a weekly, the *North Briton*, in support of his countryman.

Just when it seemed that he had refashioned himself as a leading journalist, in 1763 his only child, Elizabeth, died, aged fifteen. This blow was crueler than its predecessors and arrived as his health was deteriorating, perhaps the result of back-breaking work. Broken by grief, now ailing, he and his wife decided to travel abroad to the south of France and Italy. They settled in Nice while he wrote a travel book, *Travels through France and Italy* (2 vols., 1766); like *Roderick Random*, it was well received and prognosticated well for his new life abroad. He returned to England several times, usually after completing a new book. He published *The Present State of All Nations* in 1768 and left for Italy, settling near Leghorn. Here, the couple set up house, and while there S. wrote a political satire on England camouflaged as a travel book about Japan, which he called the *History and Adventures of an Atom* (2 vols., 1769), as well as his last work, *The Expedition of Humphry Clinker* (3 vols., 1771).

This was easily the rival of *Roderick Random*: more innovative, glittering as an epistolary novel composed of five different sets of correspondences, the story of bachelor Matthew Bramble (spiritually benevolent but as prickly as his name) and his family traveling in search of health. They begin at home in Glamorganshire and meander through England—Bath, Bristol, middle England, Yorkshire, Edinburgh—to Bramble's native Scotland, where nostalgia and the pure air regenerate his health and he marries off his heirs. The novel's brilliance extends to commentary on the places and persons they encounter, and amounts to a compendious volume about life and manners in the epoch. But S. never lived to read it, having died before he could see a copy. Every time he was poised for success—whether professional, domestic, personal—life's crises intruded to cut him down. Tragedy and irony combined to temper, as well as energize, one of the major writing talents of the century.

BIBLIOGRAPHY: Basker, J. G., *T. S.* (1988); Boucé, P.-G., *The Novels of T. S.* (1976); Knapp, L. M., *T. S.* (1949); Rousseau, G. S., and P.-G. Boucé, eds., *T. S.* (1971); Rousseau, G. S., *T. S.* (1982)

GEORGE ROUSSEAU

SNOW, C[harles] P[ercy]

b. 15 October 1905, Leicester; d. 1 July 1980, London

S. is best known for *The Two Cultures and the Scientific Revolution* (1959; rev. ed., 1964), which describes the polarization of sciences and the arts, but he was also a novelist, critic, essayist, and playwright. Throughout all his work, S. turns repeatedly to the contrast between the private and public spheres, a concern that reflects S.'s own careers as government administrator, scientist, and writer.

S. initiated his writing career with a mystery, *Death under Sail* (1932), but his major work of fiction is the "Strangers and Brothers" cycle of eleven novels that began in 1940 with *Strangers and Brothers* (repub. as *George Passant*, 1970), and includes *The Light and the Dark* (1947), *Time of Hope* (1949), *The Masters* (1951), *The New Men* (1954), *Homecomings* (1956; repub. as *Homecoming*, 1956), *The Conscience of the Rich* (1958), *The Affair* (1960), *Corridors of Power* (1964), *The Sleep of Reason* (1968), and *Last Things* (1970). The novels are linked by a single narrator, Lewis Eliot, who bears many traits of S. However, there is little about the science in S.'s fiction; the novels focus on the relationship between characters and their search for success. One critic, Robert Gorham Davis, compares S.'s fiction to that of Anthony TROLLOPE's Barsetshire novels, with characters from many social strata, the depiction of political institutions, and dramatic confrontations between characters as the primary motivation for the plot.

Davis's comparison is particularly illuminating, since one of S.'s most accessible and useful works for the modern reader is his 1975 study *Trollope: His Life and Art*, in which S. readily acknowledges Trollope's deficiencies, particularly his difficulty in depicting "a convincing representation of mental existence." For

S., Trollope is not concerned with the present moment per se, but with present experience as it might affect future action; in short, Trollope's interest is in a psychological history leading to a set of moral choices—an interest that concisely defines S.'s own concerns in his novels.

In 1951, S. collaborated with his wife Pamela Hansford JOHNSON on six plays: *The Supper Dance, Family Party, Spare the Rod, To Murder Mrs. Mortimer, Her Best Foot Forward*, and *The Pigeon with the Silver Foot: A Legend of Venice*, but his most important work of the 1950s is *The Two Cultures and the Scientific Revolution*. Delivered as the Rede Lecture at Cambridge in 1958, *The Two Cultures* delineates the dangerous gap S. saw between the scientist and the literary intellectual. As a scientist, administrator, and novelist, S. was uniquely situated to compare the culture of science, which values change and objectivity, with the culture of the literary, which values stability and subjectivity. Divided into four sections, *The Two Cultures* examines the implications of this polarization. S. argues that the greatest event of Western civilization is the scientifically driven industrial revolution, "the biggest transformation in society since the discovery of agriculture." Yet the educational systems of the West are dominated by the literary intellectuals, whom S. calls "natural Luddites," who refuse to come to terms with this revolution. S. proposes the educational system of the then Soviet Union as a model, where both men and women are educated in the sciences; while he concedes (with a nod to the Cold War) that "the Russians have a good deal to learn from us"; "[w]e have a great deal to learn from the Russians, if we are not too proud." In the final section of *The Two Cultures*, S. addresses the gap between the rich industrialized West with the nonindustrialized and poor countries. Technology has made the poor aware of this gap, and S. warns that the gap between the rich and the poor nations will be removed, either peacefully or violently; and implies that it is ultimately to the West's benefit to use its capital and human resources to bridge the gap.

S. was deeply concerned with the social responsibility of the scientist; however much he appreciated and participated in the culture of the literary intellectual, S.'s most powerful writing returns to the role of the scientist in the society. These views are articulated in his 1960 essay, "The Moral Un-Neutrality of Science," and in *The Physicists* (1981), drafted just before his death and that includes the 1960 essay as an appendix. In the essay, S. argues that science differs from every other intellectual activity because of its "built-in moral component": the desire to find the truth. The scientists thus work under a "moral discipline"; the end result of that work, knowledge, itself "contains the spring of moral action," because such knowledge puts "a direct and formal responsibility"

on scientists "to say what they know." *The Physicists*, which sketches the careers of modern particle physicists beginning with Michael Faraday, examines the moral legacy of particle physics: the use of nuclear power for war or for peace. S.'s writing is at its best here; not only does he humanize the physicists but presents their theories in concrete and accessible images: "Schrodinger thought of the electron in its orbit not as a miniature planet, but as a wave—like the wiggles in a rope when you jerk the end up and down."

Throughout all of his work, fiction and nonfiction, S. explores the way individual action impinged on the larger society. In some respects, S.'s work is dated; however, his analyses of the consequences of the scientific revolution on public institutions remain relevant for the modern reader.

BIBLIOGRAPHY: Davis, R. G., *C. P. S.* (1965); De la Mothe, J., *C. P. S. and the Struggle of Modernity* (1992); Halperin, J., *C. P. S.* (1983); Porter, R., "The Two Cultures Revisited," *Boundary 2* 23 (Summer 1996): 1–17

BRIAN ABEL RAGEN

SOMERVILLE and ROSS

SOMERVILLE, Edith [Œnone]
(pseuds.: Geilles Herring, Viva Graham) b. 2 May 1858, Corfu; d. 8 October 1949, Castle Townsend, Ireland

ROSS, Martin
(pseud. of Violet Florence Martin) b. 11 June 1862, Ross House, West Galway, Ireland; d. 21 December 1915, Cork, Ireland

The two women, who were second cousins, met for the first time in 1886 at church in the West Cork village of Castletownshend, where the Somerville residence, Drishane, was situated. They took to each other at once. S. was later to recall the meeting as "the hinge of my life, the place where my fate, and hers, turned over." Both had already tried to earn their own livings independently, S. by graphic art, R. by journalism. Their first joint literary enterprise was a novel, *An Irish Cousin*, published in 1889. They embarked on this work in a spirit of amateurish fun, intending to produce a Gothic thriller on the lines of the popular "'Shilling Shockers" of the period. Somewhat to their surprise, the work was accepted by Richard Bentley & Son, who paid them £25 on publication and a further £25 on sale of five hundred copies. It was during the composition of this first novel that they were vouchsafed a sudden insight into their true vocation as novelists. This came about when S. paid a visit to an elderly relative, who lived in a remote region of County Cork. S., in a moment of genuine epiphany, realized that what she had seen in the old lady's house was "an old stock, isolated from the world at large, wearing itself out in those excesses that are a protest of human nature against unnatural conditions." She realized that her role and R.'s would be to explore their Anglo-Irish, Protestant ascendancy tribe at the crucial historical moment when that hitherto all-powerful group were about to be confronted by an emergent, Catholic nationalist middle class.

Their second novel, *Naboth's Vineyard* (1891), an effective study of village life, rather spoiled by melodramatic plotting, was favorably received and the partners were encouraged to embark on a three-volume novel requested by Richard Bentley. *The Real Charlotte* began its life under the early title, *The Welsh Aunt*, and work began in late 1889. It was then shelved while the partners discharged various journalistic commitments. They returned to the novel in April 1890, but it was not completed until June 1892. It was finally submitted in February 1893. The authors indignantly refused Bentley's offer of £100 and the new book was published in 1894 by Ward & Downey. Critical responses were generally favorable but most of the writers' many relatives ardently disliked the book, claiming to find it depressing and unpleasant. The writers themselves were in no doubt that it was their best work and recent critical opinion supports that view. It is, to use D. H. LAWRENCE's phrase, " a bright book of life," in this case the colorful, privileged life of the Protestant ascendancy gentry of late-19th-c. Anglo-Ireland. The eponymous central character, Charlotte Mullen, is a splendidly realized Machiavel, an ugly, middle-aged manipulator who manages to fulfill all her pecuniary ambitions yet fails to gratify her emotional needs and loses the man she desires. The halcyon heyday of the Anglo-Irish ascendancy is evoked with almost overpowering nostalgia. There are boat trips with handsome British officers, tennis parties, hilarious amateur theatricals, flirtations in sunny arbors, and catty conversations at tea parties. The writers display a new moral authority in their depiction of the malignant central character, their control of an intricate plot structure, and their treatment of the novel's many emotional subtleties.

The partners would achieve international renown with very different work. At the request of the editor of the *Badminton Magazine*, they embarked on a series of short stories that appeared in the magazine at monthly intervals from October 1898 to September 1899. The stories proved so popular that Longmans quickly put them into print as *Some Experiences of an Irish R. M.* in November 1899. This book of twelve comic stories brought the cousins the sort of worldwide acclaim that even their finest novel, published five years earlier, had not earned them. The hilarious adventures of Major Sinclair Yeates (the Resident Magistrate or "R.M." of the title), Flurry Knox, Slip-

per, Mrs. Knox, and many others, offer comic highjinks in an Hibernian world of glib talk, happy accidents, and farcical comic climaxes. Here, S. and R. suspend their awareness of the historical inevitabilities that attend their class and offer instead a comic universe observed with the eye of love. So successful did the formula prove that their literary agent, J. B. Pinker, constantly pressed them for more such stories. As a result, the partners produced two further volumes of the R.M. stories, *Further Experiences of an Irish R.M.* (1908) and *In Mr. Knox's Country* (1915) but never again got around to the kind of serious, lengthy preparation required for the creation of another major novel.

R. died of an inoperable brain tumor in a Cork nursing home in 1915, and S. was so shattered by her loss that, for a long time, she was unable to write. Eventually, inspired by a spiritualistic medium who encouraged her to believe that she was in touch with her dead partner's spirit, S. took up her pen again and, before her death at the age of ninety-one, was to publish a further five novels and a number of interesting reminiscential volumes. The best of the later novels, *Mount Music* (1919) and *The Big House of Inver* (1925), were works on which R. had originally collaborated but which the partners had first set aside because they dealt with such sensitive issues as marriage between Protestant and Catholic at Big House level and the destruction of aristocratic Anglo-Irish dynasties through dissolute irresponsibility of a kind earlier depicted in Maria EDGEWORTH's *Castle Rackrent*. Had R. lived, as S. did, to see the emergence of modern Ireland, they might together have provided in another great novel the sort of searching commentary on the new Ireland that they had achieved on the old in their finest work, *The Real Charlotte*.

BIBLIOGRAPHY: Collis, M., *S. and R.* (1968); Cronin, J., *S. and R.* (1972); Powell, V., *The Irish Cousins* (1970)

JOHN CRONIN

SORLEY, Charles [Hamilton]
b. 19 May 1895, Aberdeen, Scotland; d. 13 October 1915, Loos, France

Though only twenty when he died, S. had a remarkably mature mind and style. His poems were first published in 1916 (his letters followed in 1919), and were modestly successful, making a deep impression on Robert GRAVES who considered him one of the three best poets killed in World War I.

Perhaps his father, a professor of philosophy, gave him his power of seeing all sides of a question, and he relished intellectual argument. S. spent several months in Germany before August 1914, liked the people and culture, and although he joined the army straight away did so without enthusiasm. His sonnet

"To Germany" suggests that the two great powers are blind giants, one perhaps more guilty than the other but with more in common than they think, and that at some time in the future they must come to an understanding. He believed that those who romanticized the war were "indulging in emotional luxuries," and disliked both Thomas HARDY's "Men Who March Away" and the sonnets of Rupert BROOKE.

He had written quite accomplished poetry in the Georgian tradition since childhood, although this was not published outside his school magazine. He also wrote a paper on John MASEFIELD and the 20th-c. "Renaissance" of British poetry. His sensibility was largely formed by cross-country running on the downs around Marlborough, and "The Song of the Ungirt Runners" is an impressive piece, showing a delight in rain, wind, and strenuous physical activity. Like another teenage poem, "The River" (which has echoes of Oscar WILDE's "Ballad of Reading Gaol"), it seems to forecast the fate of his generation.

His war poems do not, like those of Wilfred OWEN, Siegfried SASSOON, and Isaac ROSENBERG, offer detailed descriptions of life on the western front. There is a very high proportion of abstract nouns: "gladness," "regret," "renown," "triumph," "promise," "indignation," "vicissitude," "intelligence," "honour," "woe." They portray the war as an event whose enormity cannot be grasped by an individual; S. and the other men caught up in it are "a hundred thousand million mites." He is philosophical, aware that other generations have perished and that his own generation may as well enjoy its moment of being alive (the theme of "All the hills and vales along"). The 1915 sonnet "Saints have adored the lofty soul of you" has a remarkable sestet in which death is compared to a signpost. This implies that dying is a necessary and perhaps even valuable experience, like exploring unknown hill country in the mist.

It is no accident that the word "millions" keeps recurring. S. refuses to pity himself, knowing that he is only one of many men, from both sides, whose past and future may be blotted out. "Such, such is death" suggests that we sentimentalize those who have died, and although his outlook is religious at times it is never sentimental. His last sonnet, "When you see millions of the mouthless dead," rejects all consolation, insisting that the dead can feel nothing and are not necessarily heroes, and that mourners cannot find the lost loved one in this immense crowd. His coolness and detachment are remarkable in a very young man who was well aware that he might not survive.

This sonnet and "The Song of the Ungirt Runners" are his two best poems. His forms are traditional, since he did not live to be influenced by MODERNISM, and from time to time an archaic expression creeps in. He is one of the most interesting poets of the Great War, and his letters from the front line are extraordinarily intelligent and perceptive.

BIBLIOGRAPHY: Bergonzi, B., *Heroes' Twilight* (1965); Wilson, J. M., *C. H. S.* (1985); Wilson, J. M., ed., *The Collected Letters of C. H. S.* (1990)

MERRYN WILLIAMS

SOUTH AFRICAN LITERATURE IN ENGLISH

Like those of many settler cultures, the history of modern South Africa is multiple, involving the frequently fraught and tragic intersection of colonial cultures, in this case Dutch and British, with the many indigenous cultures over the region that was to become the republic we know today. The political history of South Africa begins with Jan van Riebeeck's founding of the Dutch Cape Colony in 1652, but writing about the region dates back to Luis de Camões's poem, *The Lusiads* (1572), and Sir Thomas Herbert's account of landing on the Cape in *Some Yeares Travaile into Afrique and the Greater Asia* (1627). These narratives of exploration and discovery foreground the danger and wildness inherent in Southern Africa, and such representations of Africa provided by the European explorers have an undoubted impact on the way Southern Africa is perceived and written about to the present day.

South Africa has always been a multicultural and multilingual country, and the 1996 constitution of the republic recognizes no fewer than eleven official languages. Although the literature of indigenous cultures, such as the Xhosa and the Zulu, were traditionally oral, black people who had been educated in missionary schools began to write in both English and their vernacular languages by the mid-19th c. Thomas Mofolo wrote his EPIC, *Chaka* (wr. 1910; pub.1925), in Sotho; Tiyo Soga, the first black man to be ordained a minister in South Africa, translated John BUNYAN's *Pilgrim's Progress* into Xhosa; and Sol T. Plaatje translated William SHAKESPEARE into Setswana and Setswana folktales into English. Also publishing in the late-19th c., F. W. Reitz became the progenitor of Afrikaans literature with his popular volumes of poetry and songs. Even Olive SCHREINER's *The Story of an African Farm*, though considered a classic of English literature, includes Afrikaans-speaking characters and relies frequently on the Afrikaans vernacular in its narrative.

South African literature's relationship to British literature, then, has always been less than congruous, and this has frequently led to the perception that South African literature is itself a sundry assemblage with nothing in common but its geographical origins. Thomas Pringle represents the strongest link between South African poetry and its British counterparts—

Samuel Taylor COLERIDGE writing that he believed Pringle's poem, "Afar in the Desert" (1834), to be one of the "two or three most perfect lyric Poems" in English literature—but Pringle only spent a scant six years in South Africa before returning to England. Although South African authors have enjoyed popularity in Britain and abroad since Pringle—in the cases of Schreiner, Sarah Gertrude Millin, Pauline Smith, Alan Paton, and, more recently, Nadine Gordimer, Bessie Head, J. M. Coetzee, as well as the best-selling popular writer Wilbur Smith—critics have been unable to synthesize these authors into a coherent tradition running parallel to British literary trends and tastes, and have therefore tended to consider South African literature as lacking definition and constituting a tangent to literary history.

As is the case in many settler cultures, however, the literature of South Africa from the 19th c. through to the apartheid era that began in 1948 shared a common sense of alienation from the land the authors are describing. Since van Riebeeck established Cape Town, the settlers of South Africa have been involved in an active struggle for possession of the land and its resources, and so it is not surprising that the literature of white South Africans expresses, in its most recognized examples, a feeling of estrangement from, and a desire to connect with, the South African land. Schreiner's *Story of an African Farm* draws from multiple genres in its composition, demonstrating the inability of the realist genre which dominated contemporaneous British literature to represent the realities of South African life. Smith set her short stories in the Little Karoo region and therefore continued the personification of the South African land as arid, impotent, and unyielding that Schreiner had begun, and in the short fiction of Herman Charles Bosman, the author frequently satirizes the settlers' attempts to bring a reluctant form of civilization to the cantankerous region. The conventions of landscape description that are developed by Schreiner, Smith, and Bosman—portraying South Africa as a harsh and sterile antagonist—continue through to the present day in works like Coetzee's *Disgrace* (1999).

Just as white writers of the early and mid-20th c. were conveying the impenetrable awe they experienced when encountering the African landscape, black writers were recording their feelings of disorientation and loss as a result of colonization and urbanization. The literary protest against colonization dates back to I. W. W. Citashe's 1892 poem, "Your Cattle Is Gone," and continues into the early 20th c. with Sol T. Plaatje's *Native Life in South Africa* (1916), as well as in *Mhudi* (wr. 1920; pub. 1930), the first novel to be published by a black South African. Plaatje's contemporary, R. R. R. Dhlomo, wrote stories in Zulu and English that depicted the degrading force of urbanization on black mine workers, most notably in his

novella, *An African Tragedy* (1928). Peter Abrahams's *Mine Boy* (1946) infuses a Marxist sensibility into his depiction of black miners to demonstrate the economic injustices inherent in South Africa. These early black writers, particularly Plaatje and Abrahams, provide the foundation for black protest writing that would burgeon during the apartheid era.

The polarized attitudes the disparate cultures of South Africa fostered toward one another became increasingly divergent as the 20th c. progressed. The South African War (1899–1902) furthered the animosity between the Dutch-Afrikaans boers and the British colonists and led, eventually, to the rise of the Afrikaans National Party in 1948. At the same time, the regulated segregation of black South Africans from the white population was becoming more stringent, culminating in the advent of the apartheid (literally "apartness") system instituted by the national government in 1948 and maintained until 1994. Although the works of writers like Millin reflected the segregationalist attitude that held popular sway in South Africa, South African literature more often reflected a liberal humanitarian sentiment. Millin's novels, like the internationally acclaimed *God's Stepchildren* (1924), convey a deep-seated pessimism about South African society coupled with a prevailing fear of racial miscegenation. At the same time, Laurens van der Post and Roy CAMPBELL began the literary journal *Voorslag* (Whiplash) in 1926, with the collaborative assistance of William Plomer. The short-lived journal, which presented itself as the foundation of an indigenous South African literature, was also outspoken on issues of racial inequality in their society. Plomer and van der Post attempted to create an empathy in the white reader for black characters in their fiction, and van der Post's first novel, *In a Province* (1934), could be seen as a direct antecedent to Paton's more celebrated oeuvre.

The tradition of liberal white writers questioning public policies on racial segregation became firmly entrenched with the establishment of apartheid. Paton's *Cry, the Beloved Country* (1948) was published in the same year the National Party gained power in South Africa on the apartheid platform. Paton's novel deals extensively with black characters and portrays their plight in the urban setting of Sophiatown as one of continuous demoralization and alienation. Although Paton's portrayal of black Africans as stoic, passive figures has been criticized by critics such as Es'kia (Ezekiel) Mphahlele and Lewis Nkosi for producing a white liberal version of black life, Paton's writing was the first to denounce South African racial policies to an international readership and inspired subsequent novels of social protest, such as Jack Cope's *The Fair House* (1955), Dan JACOBSON's *The Beginners* (1966), and Elsa Joubert's Afrikaans novel *Die Swerfjare van Poppie Nongena* (1978; *Poppie*, 1981).

930

At the same time that Paton was portraying Sophiatown as a den of iniquity and moral dislocation, the vibrant suburb was becoming the site of a renaissance in black African writing. *Drum* magazine, launched in 1950, became a forum for journalistic prose portraits of urban black culture produced by Mphahlele, Nkosi, Can Themba, Bloke Modisane, and Todd Matshikiza. *Drum* magazine offered a portrait of the lively but violent life of shebeen culture and the black tsotsis (gangsters) who frequented them, and the prose was often influenced by the rhythms of shebeen jazz. Writing that consciously mixed journalism and fiction, such as in the prose of Casey Motsisi and Themba, offer a portrait of a thriving, developing, and often hopeful, urban culture that came to a dreary end when the forced removal of the Sophiatown residents began in 1955. The fiction produced at the time, however, offered black writers the possibility of documenting their contemporary urban setting in a style that seemed innovative and organic. Thematically, these narratives primarily focused on the interrelationships of black Africans within the townships rather than on the larger issues of apartheid politics, thus portraying white racism as an encroachment on a self-sustaining community. Mphahlele's famous autobiographical novel, *Down Second Avenue* (1959), spends much of its time describing the interrelationship of family and community, thus making the descriptions of racist encounters all the more discordant. Mphahlele's thematic emphasis influenced writers such as Njabulo Ndebele, who advocated a literary concentration on the dynamics of township life as a means by which the black South African could "rediscover the ordinary," and demonstrated such an exercise in his collection *Fools and Other Stories* (1983).

South African literature became galvanized, even unified, in a way it had never previously accomplished as the repression inherent in the apartheid system became more pronounced and more violent. Certainly, the late apartheid era, extending from the Soweto uprising of 1976 until the democratic elections of 1994, produced a flood of writing, in prose, poetry, and drama, specifically designed to critique and challenge South African racism. This period saw an infusion of black protest fiction such as Miriam Tlali's *Amandla!* (1981), Mongane Wally Serote's *To Every Birth Its Blood* (1981), Mbulelo Mzamane's *The Children of Soweto* (1982), and Nkosi's *Mating Birds* (1986), each of which relies on a naturalist form to portray the profound suffering of black South Africans in the townships. Nadine Gordimer, winner of the 1991 Nobel Prize for Literature, writing in a similarly realist fashion, continues the liberal tradition of white writers like Paton in her prose. Her narratives attempt to reach a broader Western audience by exploring the myriad complexities of white liberal guilt in such novels as *Burger's Daughter* (1979) and *July's People* (1981). The novels of Coetzee and André Brink, on the other hand, resist REALISM in order to convey the absurdity of the apartheid regime. Coetzee's novels, such as *The Life and Times of Michael K* (1983) and *The Age of Iron* (1990), attempt to express the alienation and displacement symptomatic of repression, while Brink foregrounds the subjectivity of his narrators, and therefore the instability of his narrative, in novels such as *'n Droë wit seisoen* (*A Dry White Season*, 1979) and *States of Emergency* (1988).

Poetry, especially by black Africans, became a powerful vehicle for expressions of anger and protest during the late apartheid period. Serote is one of the most prominent of the protest poets, with collections such as *Behold Mama, Flowers* (1978) and *No Baby Must Weep* (1985). Other notable poets of the Black Consciousness movement of the 1970s include James Matthews, Mandlenkosi Langa, Sipho Sepamla, and Modikwe Dikobe. At the same time, lyric poetry by Afrikaans writer Breyten Breytenbach attacked the leaders of the country, using the official language of Afrikaans to subversive ends, while Jeremy Cronin's *Inside* (1983) relays the voices of his fellow prisoners in the Pretoria Maximum Security Prison. The narrative of imprisonment and exile is not particular to Cronin and indeed may be considered a specialized genre of South African literature in itself. Dating back to Bloke Modisane's *Blame Me on History* (1963), which was written in exile in West Germany, and to the prison memoirs of political activists such as Ruth First's *117 Days* (1965) and Albie Sachs's *The Jail Diary of Albie Sachs* (1966), prison and exile writing develops further with Alex La Guma's *The Stone Country* (1967), Dennis Brutus's *Letters to Martha and Other Poems from a South African Prison* (1968), D. M. Zwelonke's *Robben Island* (1973), Arthur Nortje's *Dead Roots* (1973), Breytenbach's *The True Confessions of an Albino Terrorist* (1984), Rian Malan's *My Traitor's Heart* (1990), and Head's *A Woman Alone* (1990). The popularity of the genre continues in South Africa after 1994, with retrospective autobiographies of imprisonment or struggle, such as Mamphela Ramphele's *A Life* (1995) and, most famously, Nelson Mandela's *The Long Walk to Freedom* (1994).

Drama served as an important medium for communicating the struggle and galvanizing the South African community during the apartheid era, and as a result the audiences of the 1970s and 1980s witnessed a surfeit of powerful and innovative performances. Groups such as Athol Fugard's Serpent Players, which produced the controversial *Sizwe Bansi Is Dead* (1973), and Workshop '71, which produced *uNosilimela* (1974), were instrumental in establishing an urban tradition of radical drama. Urban sites such as Johannesburg's innovative Market Theatre complex have sponsored many of these productions, among them Matsemela Manaka's *Egoli* (1980), Zakes Mda's *And the Girls in Their Sunday Dresses* (1988), Gcina Mhlophe's *Have You Seen Zandile?* (1988), and ensemble productions such as *Sophiatown* (1986) and *Tooth and Nail* (1989). Fugard remains the most critically acclaimed dramatist of the apartheid era, producing such politically provocative plays as *The Island* (with John Kani and Winston Ntshona, 1973), and *'Master Harold' . . . and the Boys* (1982).

Even after the first democratic elections of 1994, South African writing has remained predominantly political in its focus. Many postapartheid narratives deal specifically with the apartheid period, not in order to challenge it, but as a way of coming to terms with the tragic past and the South African citizen's role in that society. The political agenda of the "new" South Africa involved eliciting confessions and testimony in order to reveal the extensive atrocities of the apartheid regime and to initiate a climate of forgiveness on which to build a new national community. Such public forums for confession, like the Truth and Reconciliation Commission (TRC) hearings (1994–98), have incited South Africans, especially white South Africans, to contemplate their complicity in the apartheid regime.

It is not surprising, then, that the fiction that emerged from this period is predominately set in the apartheid era, with narratives that both invoke and problematize nostalgia. Both Mark Behr's *The Smell of Apples* (1995) and Etienne van Heerden's *Kikoejoe* (1996; *Kikuyu*, 1998), employ child narrators in order to examine the insidious effects of apartheid ideology on the naive. Zakes Mda's *Ways of Dying* (1995) utilizes a mature but naive protagonist to describe the horror of the violence that raged between Zulu and Xhosa activists in the early 1990s while still attempting to provide a hopeful ending. Marlene van Niekerk's novel, *Triomf* (1994; tran. into English as *Triomf*, 1999) focuses on a family of poor Afrikaners in the days leading up to the 1994 election in order to draw attention to the way the National government dispossessed its own grassroots.

The culture of confession that has established itself in postapartheid South Africa has also become the focus of literary scrutiny. Antjie Krog's controversial memoir, *Country of My Skull* (1998), attempts to personalize the guilt and horror experienced by an Afrikaans journalist who witnesses the testimony presented at the TRC hearings by creating a deliberately unstable narrative intermingling literary genres in order to parallel the author's posttraumatic condition. Novels such as Gordimer's *The House Gun* (1998) and Coetzee's *Disgrace* interrogate the moral imperative of the TRC by presenting protagonists who refuse to confess to their domestic crimes. Postapartheid South African literature, then, focuses on the political

challenges faced by the fledgling republic: how to memorialize the atrocities of the apartheid era while still moving forward into a new era of cultural harmony.

BIBLIOGRAPHY: Attridge, D., and R. Jolly, eds., *Writing South Africa: Literature, Apartheid, and Democracy 1970–1995* (1998); Chapman, M., C. Gardner, and E. Mphahlele, eds., *Perspectives on South African English Literature* (1992); Gray, S., *Southern African Literature* (1979); Klima, V., *South African Prose Writing in English* (1971); Shava, P. V., *A People's Voice: Black South African Writing in the Twentieth Century* (1989); Trump, M., ed., *Rendering Things Visible: Essays on South African Literary Culture* (1990)

MARK LIBIN

SOUTHCOTT, Joanna

b. April 1750, Devonshire; d. 27 December 1814, London

Originally a Methodist, about 1792 S. became convinced she had supernatural gifts and began prophesying in rhyme. She identified herself with the woman mentioned in Revelation, chapter 12, "clothed with the sun and the moon beneath her feet." Invited to London, she "sealed" believers for fees that varied from twelve shillings to a guinea. She wrote over sixty books on religion, including *The Book of Wonders* (5 parts, 1813–14). She attracted a following of over one hundred thousand and even today has a few believers. She left a famous locked box with instructions for it to be opened by the assembled bishops at a time of national crisis: a bishop was present when it was opened in 1928, but nothing interesting was found, though some people still await its revelations. S.'s career may be understood, like that of Margery KEMPE, as self-deceived female assertion, the avenue of religious fanaticism being the only one open to humbly born and uneducated women who craved attention.

SOUTHEY, Robert

b. 12 August 1774, Bristol; d. 21 March 1843, Keswick

History remembers S. first and foremost as the fall-guy of Lord BYRON's comic masterpiece *The Vision of Judgement*. S.'s smugness and lack of charity, coupled with the low quality of much of his versification, give his fate a certain justice, but much of his output remains admirable. Several of his shorter poems, like "After Blenheim," are deservedly well known. His prose is fluent, and his lives of [Viscount] Horatio Nelson (2 vols., 1813) and of John Wesley (2 vols., 1820) are still necessary source-reading. *The Life of Wesley* is especially noteworthy, considering S.'s distaste for religious enthusiasm. S., after becoming poet laureate, was much sought after as a guru, but the quality of his wisdom may be measured by the letter in which he discouraged the young Charlotte BRONTË from trying to make a career as a writer. His own attempts at EPIC writing were unsuccessful, but he was expert on Iberian literature, the first-ever historian of Brazil, and originated the story of "The Three Bears" in a miscellany called *The Doctor, etc.* (7 vols., 1834–47), though the name Goldilocks is a later invention.

S. was handed over by his parents between the ages of two and six to an eccentric spinster aunt, whose bed he shared on condition that, should he wake up before her, he must lie perfectly motionless until she awoke. This is said to account for the stoic frigidity that enabled him to survive many crises, but that made him a burden to his intimates. Educated at Westminster School, he was expelled for his first publication, an essay against flogging written for the school magazine, but eventually went to Oxford University and met Samuel Taylor COLERIDGE, who was visiting. Sharing the revolutionary zeal of the 1790s, they collaborated on a tragedy, *The Fall of Robespierre* (1794), and S. composed another revolutionary historical work, *Wat Tyler* (1817). Their intention was to emigrate to the U.S. and found a new community called the Pantisocracy ("equal government of all"), but the plan petered out for lack of funds. S. and Coleridge cemented their friendship by marrying sisters, Edith and Sara Fricker of Bath. S.'s aunt disapproved and turned him out of doors in the rain.

S. retained his left-wing convictions and wrote his first (anglophobic) epic on the subject of Joan of Arc (1796). In the late 1790s, his relatives tried to persuade him to enter the Anglican ministrty, but he could not accept the Thirty-nine Articles of doctrine necessary for a conscientious priest to believe in. Instead, he accompanied an uncle to Portugal, where he became fluent in Portuguese and Spanish, developing a lifelong love of their literatures. In 1808, he published a translation of the *Chronicle of the Cid*. He edited the works of Thomas CHATTERTON (3 vols., 1803) and Henry Kirke WHITE (3 vols., 1807). His ambition was to write a series of epics that would dignify the cultures they depicted with heroic tales worthy of them, but for which they had, in his opinion, so far lacked writers adequate to the task. He began with a work set in Islam, *Thalaba the Destroyer* (2 vols., 1801), and continued with the theme of Christian-Aztec conflict in *Madoc* (2 vols., 1805), followed by a Hindu fable, *The Curse of Kehama* (1810), and the Hispanic-Christian *Roderick, the Last of the Goths* (1814). A Zoroastrian work was planned, but never materialized. All S.'s epics celebrate chaste and lonely courage pitted victoriously against the wickedness of Napoleonic-style establishments. HUMOR and eroticism are eschewed. S. had a high opinion of *Kehama*, which is uncharacteristically inventive and

tautly plotted. Its well-researched Hindu background makes it enjoyable to read,

S.'s politics changed—as did those of many—as the French Revolution gave way to the Terror and then to the rise of Napoleon. When in 1813 the poet laureate, Henry James Pye, died, the laureateship was offered to Sir Walter SCOTT, who suggested S. instead. S. felt that although he was not a convinced Christian, his belief that religion was a means of uniting society was qualification enough, and accepted. Although conservative, S. was charitably inclined toward the working class and strongly against the evils of the industrial revolution; he was an admirer of Robert Owen and the New Lanark experiment.

In 1814, S. met Byron, who was impressed as much with the noble aquiline head of the poet as with the morality of his poem, *Roderick, the Last of the Goths*. Byron was in a prematrimonial mood of contrition and expiation for previous sins. Once his marriage had failed, however, Byron's evaluation both of *Roderick* and of S. altered for the worse. S.'s political pronouncements (he was a regular contributor to the Tory *Quarterly Review*) had become more and more reactionary, and Byron was delighted when in 1817 someone unearthed S.'s adolescent tragedy, *Wat Tyler*, which showed, in Byron's view, what a turncoat and renegade S. was. Byron's distaste was exacerbated when news reached him that S. had spread rumors of a "League of Incest" among Byron, Percy Bysshe SHELLEY, Mary Godwin [SHELLEY], and Claire Clairmont at Geneva in 1816. Circumstantial evidence suggests that the scandalmongering Byron had heard about was actual, and Byron hit back in a note to his tragedy *The Two Foscari*, but S. had already struck a blow with his preface to *A Vision of Judgement*, published in 1821, in which he referred to a "Satanic School" of poetry, with clear reference to Byron, Shelley, and Thomas MOORE. S.'s *Vision*, a tasteless depiction of the triumphant entry of King George III into heaven, made Byron's blood boil, and the result was Byron's own *The Vision of Judgement,* which makes the king's entry into heaven dependent on the inability of the angels, saints, devils, and damned souls assembled at heaven's gate to listen while S. reads the "spavined dactyls" of his own vision. Everybody flies away, unable to bear the tedium, and King George slips into heaven without anybody noticing.

Edith Southey went mad in 1837, and after her death S. married Caroline Bowles, a poet. Shortly afterward, S.'s own mind began to fail, and he died in a state of dementia.

BIBLIOGRAPHY: Bernhardt-Kabisch, E., *R. S.* (1977); Curry, K., *S.* (1975); Curry, K., *R. S.* (1977); Madden, L., ed., *R. S.* (1972); Simmons, J., *S.* (1945); Storey, M., *R. S.* (1997)

PETER COCHRAN

SOUTHWELL, Robert

b. 1561, Norfolk; d. 21 February 1595, London

Born into a Roman Catholic family in Protestant England, S. was bound for a rocky life that ended in a violent death. In 1578, he was admitted to the Jesuit Order and ordained a Roman Catholic priest in 1584 at Rome. Two years later, he was assigned to the "English Mission," by which priests would infiltrate England surreptitiously in order to minister to the Roman Catholics there. To be caught was to be executed. In 1592, he was ferreted out by the notorious priest-hunter Richard Topcliffe, who took particular delight in catching S. and later watched as the priest was hanged and disembowelled. In spite of his imprisonment, S. was popular for both his prose and poetry, his works selling openly in London. It is his poetry today that remains in print. The poems were written during his imprisonment.

S.'s most famous poem, "The Burning Babe," was praised highly by Ben JONSON who said he would have given up many of his own poems if he could say he had written it. S. writes of seeing a baby on fire, and it turns out to be the Christ child. As the metaphors blend into the details, the poem is a good example of what critics have hailed as S.'s superb anticipation of the metaphysical technique. Some, in fact, have attributed to him a conscious effort to revolutionize the Petrarchan style of writing that was popular in the late Elizabethan period, but S. never concentrated on his poetry with the intention of changing the direction of Renaissance verse. His purpose was purely priestly: he wanted to use his poetry to help people live more religious lives. If in fact he did create a small revolution by writing very fine religious verses at a time when not much religious poetry was written in England, he was an unconscious revolutionary, even though his style leads directly to the work of George HERBERT and Richard CRASHAW.

"The Nativity of Christ" has also been called a significant poem and has been compared to John MILTON's "Nativity Ode," but the two poems have little in common: S.'s poem is quite short (twenty-four lines) and nowhere does S. use mythological references. It is a very simple poem, designed most probably to assist religious people in living their faith, a poem as remarkable as S.'s "Nativity of Christ" is "Saint Peters Complaint," which looks at Christ's Passion from Peter's point of view, in particular his denial of Christ. S.'s most popular poems remain his shorter lyrics. Some are quite theological and seem more catechetical than lyrical. For example, "Of the Blessed Sacrament of the Aulter" labors to explain the Divine presence in even the smallest crumb of consecrated bread.

S., like many of his contemporary recusants, had a particular devotion to Mary Magdalen and captures her spirit in poems such as "Mary Magdalens blush" and "Marie Magdalens complaint at Christs death." Other poems sparkle in their simple evocation of ordinary images and timeless longings: "Seeke flowers of heaven" is an example of a graceful little lyric poem that draws more readers than "Saint Peters Complaint" ever can. Still other poems seem rooted in AUTOBIOGRAPHY: it is impossible to read "Upon the Image of Death" without thinking of the poet himself who wrote the lyric in his prison years between two of the thirteen torture sessions he had to endure while awaiting execution.

BIBLIOGRAPHY: Bouchard, G., "R. S., S.J.: England's First Metaphysical Poet," *ERC* 26 (Summer 2000): 101–19; McDonald, J. H., and N. P. Brown, eds., *The Poems of R. S., S.J.* (1967); Scallon, J. D., *The Poetry of R. S.* (1975)

GEORGE KLAWITTER

SPARK, [Dame] Muriel [Sarah Camberg]

b. 1 February 1918, Edinburgh, Scotland

For over fifty years, S. has written fiction that portrays a violent, amoral, loveless post-World War II British and European society. For example, at the end of her underrated novel *The Takeover* (1976), Hubert Mallindaine strolls through the moonlit woods near Lake Nemi in Italy. He meets his wealthy landlady Maggie, disguised as a gypsy. Over the past year, Maggie has unsuccessfully tried to evict Hubert from one of her villas, while he has relentlessly pilfered everything of value from it. Maggie has also been robbed by an unscrupulous lawyer, whom she has kidnapped and hidden in the nearby caves. She knows that Hubert has betrayed her, but they chat amiably and part cheerfully. S.'s characters have no system of values by which to judge each other or themselves, and they often remain untouched by sex, nature, tragedy, defeat, or betrayal. S. presents their inept or evil actions flatly, without emotional involvement.

Born to a Jewish father and Presbyterian mother, S. spent her school years at the James Gillespie School, the setting for her most famous novel, *The Prime of Miss Jean Brodie* (1961). In 1951, she won the *Observer* short story prize for "The Seraph and the Zambesi," which led Graham GREENE to offer important financial support. She edited *Poetry Review* and recalled this experience in *Loitering with Intent* (1981). During these years, she wrote poetry (collected in 1967 and 1982), criticism, and BIOGRAPHY. Central to S.'s thinking is her conversion to Roman Catholicism in 1954. Though not religious in any conventional sense, her novels are, with Greene's and Evelyn WAUGH's, frequently considered Catholic. She reveals, often through solitary female characters, the frightening problems caused by society's lack of beliefs.

In her first novel, *The Comforters* (1957), S. introduces another career-long concern: how is fiction made and what happens to it when it is read? As she does in most of her novels, Spark focuses on a small group of eccentric characters (a grandmother heads a diamond-smuggling ring). She introduces supernatural events in realistic settings (a character hears mysterious voices dictating the words of the novel she is writing). The narrator speaks with a cool, distanced tone, and S. is developing her unique narrative technique that allows her to reveal plot information while keeping the story unpredictable.

In S.'s third novel, *Memento Mori* (1959), elderly Londoners receive phone calls from another mysterious voice reminding them of their mortality. Typically, the reader never knows what the voice is. Showing a good deal of growth as a novelist, S. is particularly successful in her comic analysis of old age and placement of the supernatural in a realistic setting.

Three novels later, S. published *The Prime of Miss Jean Brodie*, still considered a masterpiece. Originally serialized in the *New Yorker*, it has been a play, a movie, and a television series, as well as a novel. S. is praised for her portrayal of the self-centered manipulative teacher at a girls' school, the novel's complex narrative technique (with flash-forwards and flash-backs), and an authorial omniscience that expertly parallels Brodie's totalitarian personality.

In *The Girls of Slender Means* (1963), a compact comedy of manners, S. reveals the cruelty underneath the camaraderie among a group of young London women after World War II. In *The Mandelbaum Gate* (1965), S.'s eighth novel, which won the James Tait Black Memorial Prize, Barbara Vaughan, like S., is a half-Jewish, half-Protestant Roman Catholic convert. During the Eichmann trials in Israel (which S. reported on), Vaughan makes a dangerous but ultimately liberating pilgrimage into Jordan.

During the 1970s, influenced by her interest in Alain Robbe-Grillet and other French New Novelists, S. wrote several short absurdist novels. In *The Driver's Seat* (1970), the garishly dressed Lise travels to an unnamed southern European city searching for a man who will murder her—by following her instructions. In *Not to Disturb* (1971), the staff of a wealthy aristocratic British family exploits the murder-suicide of the family by planning articles, books, movies, and press releases—before the event. In *The Abbess of Crewe* (1974), a Watergate scandal rocks a convent of nuns—who delete poetry from their transcripts. No one has better portrayed the chilly atmosphere of fearful emptiness that plagues a society without faith.

Her sixteenth novel, *Loitering with Intent*, drew much praise for its mordant wit and ingenious illustra-tion of the thin line between fiction and reality. Fleur Talbot, hired as the secretary of the Autobiographical Association, augments the dry lives of its members with her own fictions. In the meantime, a novel Fleur is writing begins to reflect—or to create?—the life of the association's leader, who steals her novel and encourages her to take care of his elderly mother, Lady Edwina, a vividly created character who willfully urinates on the floor to get her way.

S.'s short stories, collected in 1985 and 1998, contain typically bizarre characters and plots. A young girl is molested by her eye doctor, an infant reports on events during the war, and, in the much-anthologized "Portobello Road," the narrator describes her own murder. In 1992, S. published a matter-of-fact AUTO-BIOGRAPHY of her life until the writing of *The Comforters*. Her restless, far-reaching fertile imagination and unforgiving wit continued to produce spare but many-layered novels through the 1990s. In 2000, she published her twenty-first novel, *Aiding and Abetting*, in which she takes a real contemporary mystery and imagines a fictional outcome.

S.'s prodigious and always interesting writings raise serious questions about reality, art, and faith. She self-consciously uses satire and what she herself calls ridicule to shock her reader. In 1993, she was made a Dame of the Order of the British Empire.

BIBLIOGRAPHY: Bold, A., *M. S.* (1986); Cheyette, B., *M. S.* (2000); Randisi, J., *On Her Way Rejoicing: The Fiction of M. S.* (1991); Richmond, V. B., *M. S.* (1984); Whitaker, R., *The Faith and Fiction of M. S.* (1982)

STEVE FEREBEE

SPEGHT, Rachel
b. ca. 1597, London; d. after 1630

A Mouzell for Melastomus (1617), S.'s concise and convincing rebuttal to Joseph Swetnam's misogynist pamphlet *The Arraignment of Lewd, Idle, Forward, and Unconstant Women* (1615), is the best known of her four extant works. Displaying both her extensive knowledge of the Bible and classical humanist texts, as well as a natural talent for logical refutation, S.'s tract stands in sharp contrast to the usually inflammatory and often irrational contributions to the Jacobean gender debate. As the first Englishwoman to "identify herself, by name, as a polemicist and critic of contemporary gender ideology," S. was probably the only female contributor to the Jacobean pamphlet war. Respondents such as Constantia Munda and Esther Sowernam were most likely pseudonyms disguising male authorship.

Printed with *A Mouzell for Melastomus* but with its own title page, epistle to the reader, and preface was "Certaine Quæres to the Bayter of Women," in which S. attacks specific aspects of Swetnam's tract, primarily his numerous logical self-contradictions and grammatical errors. While *A Mouzell* displays S.'s serious intellectualism and moralism, "Certaine Quæres" reveals a more bitingly sarcastic and playful side to the young author. The narrator of this piece, when addressing Swetnam directly, engages in word-play that makes clear what she thinks of him: his logic is "*wonder-foole,*" and she frequently substitutes "ass" for "as" when addressing his most specious arguments.

Mortalities Memorandum, with A Dreame Prefixed (1621), two separate pieces published together, are S.'s final known works. Both are poems written in six-line iambic pentameter stanzas, but the similarity between the two ends there. "A Dreame" is only three hundred lines in length (in contrast to the 756 lines of "Mortalities Memorandum") and is concerned primarily with what S. sees as women's unfair exclusion from the educational opportunities enjoyed by men. Using more secular imagery than she does in her other works, S. draws upon medieval dream vision poem antecedents (particularly Guillaume de Lorris's portion of *Roman de la Rose*) to critique Renaissance humanists for their failure actually to provide educational opportunities they rhetorically assert should be equally available to both men and women. Constructing her education as a romantic journey with herself as the questing hero, "A Dreame" is S.'s most powerful and potentially subversive work. "Mortalities Memorandum" is a long and fairly conventional Protestant meditation on death and the transience of worldly concerns; however, the connections between it and the prefatory "A Dreame" have yet to be fully explored and could yield interesting new critical readings.

Though S. is often anthologized in collections of Renaissance women's writing, only *A Mouzell for Melastomus* has received significant critical attention. Modern scholars tend to find S.'s protofeminism somewhat limited because she defends only "good women" rather than women generally. S., however, is more concerned with being taken seriously than with being radical. Demonstrating that she is eminently rational is to stand as a living counter-example to raging misogynists like Swetnam and humanists who might argue that women, as the "weaker vessels," are in reality too fragile to handle the same level of education as their male counterparts even if they deserve the same opportunities in theory. Making sweeping and unsupported claims about women's essential goodness in response to Swetnam's assertions of the basic depravity of women would have undermined S.'s conscious attempt to remove herself from a gender debate that tended to deal only in sensational and extremist arguments that made no headway toward legitimizing women's voices.

BIBLIOGRAPHY: Henderson, K. U., and B. F. McManus, eds., *Half Humankind: Contexts and Texts of the Controversy about Women in England, 1540–1640* (1985); Lewalski, B. K., ed., *The Polemics and Poems of R. S.* (1996); Woodbridge, L., *Women and the English Renaissance: Literature and the Nature of Womankind, 1540 to 1620* (1984)

COLLEEN SHEA

SPENDER, [Sir] Stephen [Harold]

b. 28 February 1909, London; d. 16 July 1995, London

Known during the first half of his life primarily as a poet of the political left, in later life S. was better known for his literary criticism than for his poetry, although during 1965 and 1966 he served as the first non-American consultant in poetry for the Library of Congress, a post comparable to that of poet laureate in Great Britain.

Closely associated with such literary figures as W. H. AUDEN, C. DAY-LEWIS, and Christopher ISHERWOOD during the late 1920s and early 1930s, S. established a reputation during the 1930s for his political poems aimed at tweaking the public conscience at a time when Spain was moving toward a catastrophic civil war and Germany and Italy were being caught up in a web of totalitarianism. S. left his studies at University College, Oxford, in 1930 without a degree and went to live in Germany, where he spent considerable time with Isherwood.

Rainer Maria Rilke's poetry, especially the *Duino Elegies*, enchanted S., who also greatly admired the writing of the Spanish poet, Federico García Lorca. His own writing of the early period shows the strong influence of both these poets. During a six-year period, S. turned out three volumes of poetry, *Poems* (1933; rev. ed., 1934), *Vienna* (1934), and *The Still Centre* (1939) as well as a verse play, *Trial of a Judge* (1938), produced in London by the Group Theatre. His poems of this period reflect his compassion, his quest to understand and improve himself, and his conscientious concerns about a world that teetered on the brink of another major war.

As he matured further, S. began to turn from the encompassing political situations that faced him and his world. He became increasingly introspective in his poems. His work veered toward the autobiographical in many of the poems included in such collections as *Ruins and Visions* (1942), *Poems of Dedication* (1947), *The Edge of Being* (1949), *Collected Poems, 1928–1953* (1955), *Inscriptions* (1958), *Selected Poems* (1965), and *The Generous Days* (1969; rev. ed., 1971).

His final collection, *Dolphins* (1994), consists of nineteen poems, some reworkings of earlier poems, and shows S. in a highly reflective mood, similar to that in *Returning to Vienna, 1947: Nine Sketches* (1947), which dwells on what the war did to one of his favorite cities. S. dedicated *Dolphins* to his four closest literary friends, Auden, Day-Lewis, Louis MacNEICE, and Isherwood. Some critics have found S. to be more subtle in his writing than these writers, whom he so much admired. Certainly he was less violent than Auden in his writing about political issues.

During World War II, when S. served in the National Fire Service, he was also closely associated with the literary magazine *Horizon*. From 1953 until 1967, he had a similar close association with *Encounter*. He wrote most perceptive book reviews, some of which are gathered in a collection of his essays, *The Thirties and After* (1978).

S.'s works of literary criticism focused on such individual authors as Percy Bysshe SHELLEY, T. S. ELIOT, and Auden, to each of whom he devoted a full-length consideration, as well as on such broad literary topics as he addressed in *The New Realism* (1939), *Life and the Poet* (1942), *Poetry since 1939* (1946), and *The Making of a Poem* (1955). His perspective not limited to literature, he addressed topics relating to the whole artistic process in *The Creative Element* (1953), *The Imagination in the Modern World* (1962), and *The Struggle of the Modern* (1963). Caught up in America's antiwar demonstrations of the late 1960s, he wrote about them in *The Year of the Young Rebels* (1969) and in *Love-Hate Relations* (1974).

Besides his poetry and criticism, S. wrote one play, *Trial of a Judge*, and did adaptations of four others, *Danton's Death* (1939), *Mary Stuart* (1959), *Rasputin's End* (1963), and *The Oedipus Trilogy* (1985). His novel, *The Backward Son*, was published in 1940. It was preceded by a collection of short stories, *The Burning Cactus* (1936).

Clearly a gifted poet, S.'s potential perhaps was somewhat vitiated by the early concentration in his poems on political matters. S. was a thoroughgoing political idealist but a gentle person who at times lacked the vigor to write as resoundingly as Auden did about similar topics.

BIBLIOGRAPHY: David, H., *S. S.: A Portrait with Background* (1992); Lemming, D., *S. S.* (1999); Sternlicht, S., *S. S.* (1992)

                                    R. BAIRD SHUMAN

SPENSER, Edmund
b. ca. 1552, London; d. 13 January 1599, London

Little is known of S.'s family background or early life. References in his work lead scholars to accept 1552 as the year he was born into a family of moderate means. His father may have been John Spenser, a clothmaker and resident of East Smithfield in London. He attended the newly established Merchant Taylors'

School in London from perhaps as early as 1561, the year the school opened, until at least 1569. There is clear evidence that S. received important financial support from Robert Nowell whose brother, Alexander, was Dean of St. Paul's. This was just the first of the political and social connections S. enjoyed and worked tirelessly to develop all his life. His time at the Merchant Taylors' School is important for the company he was able to keep as well as for the kind of instruction he received. Thomas KYD, Lancelot ANDREWES, and Thomas LODGE were among his classmates. The curriculum under the direction of the noted humanist Richard Mulcaster was steeped in the classics. Students studied Latin and the works and styles of all major Roman authors and orators. Greek and Hebrew were most likely taught as well, along with modern languages. Certainly, it was during this period that S.'s interest in language and his ability as a poet became clear.

In 1569, S. enrolled at Pembroke College, Cambridge. Earlier that year, fourteen of his sonnet translations from French—his earliest known writings—were incorporated into the English edition of Jan van der Noot's *Theatre of Voluptuous Worldlings*. S. took his B.A. degree in 1573, finishing eleventh out of one hundred and twenty-one students, and remained to take his M.A. in 1576 though for this he finished sixty-sixth in a class of seventy. Illness may account for S.'s performance, but the result was that he did not secure a fellowship at Cambridge, as clearly he hoped he might. Nor did he secure a patron for his art despite his being introduced by his good friend Gabriel Harvey to a number of important connections, among them the influential Earl of Leicester. One wonders if this was not a disappointing period for S. By 1578, S. moved to Kent and was working as secretary to John Young, the newly consecrated Bishop of Rochester, whom he had known previously as the master of Pembroke College. This apparent detour, however, proved an important period for S. who continued refining his skills as a poet and took great inspiration from the Kentish countryside for his first major work.

In 1579, S. published *The Shepheardes Calender*, and it was consumed by an audience desperately hungry to satisfy its humanist and neoclassical tastes. Moreover, England had yet to produce any literature to rival what was coming out of Europe, and S.'s readers were in need of something truly British, something to stir a sense of national pride. The *Calender*'s appearance marked a tremendous success both of art and timing, and its influence on the subsequent explosion of English letters should not be underestimated, nor, perhaps, should S.'s estimate of himself or his hopes for his career. S.'s decision to model his first important poem on Virgil's *Eclogues* laid the groundwork for him to become the English heir to the Roman poet.

While it is doubtless true that S. consciously worked to gain such distinction, it is important not to lose sight of the fact that S.'s claim was not based merely on Virgilian imitation or reproduction.

Great poets are great for the way in which they explore new realms of expression and craft a language fitted to those realms. The *Calender* is characteristic of S.'s best works in its fusing of Continental and domestic, and modern and ancient sources. The piece comprises twelve eclogues, modeled on Virgil's, but written in purposefully rustic and archaic language semiderived from medieval English authors, most notably Geoffrey CHAUCER. With wholly original language, S. constructed an astoundingly intricate, entirely unified series of poems displaying virtuosity with meter and musicality that no English poet had yet demonstrated. Arguably because the *Calender* marks such a watershed in English poetry, no English poet has equaled S.'s originality and achievement since. S. surely had some inkling of his accomplishment, and his decision to dedicate the *Calender* to his politically connected acquaintance Sir Philip SIDNEY is suggestive of his constant desire to negotiate any success that might come into something more.

Success was immediate, and S. quickly moved back to London and entered the service of the Earl of Leicester. This new position gave him access to the court and the day's leading political, artistic, and intellectual lights. With, among others, Sidney, Harvey, and Sir Edward DYER, S. formed or joined an informal discussion group called the "Areopagus." S. appeared poised to begin a career as a successful courtier-poet, a position he surely desired, and for which he must have believed himself suited. But though he possessed the poetic talent, S. seems to have lacked some of the courtier's political skill.

Two pieces written during or near S.'s time at Leicester House, though not published for several years, suggest the young poet's difficulties with courtly life may have resulted from his overly idealistic vision of the world and the poet's role in it. S.'s *Fowre Hymns* (1596) were an effort to reconcile Christianity with the Platonic view of beauty as the highest good, but they are largely derivative of contemporary Italian verse and hardly S.'s best work. They establish, however, a position that S. maintained until near the end of his life: that outward beauty is the indication of inner virtue. Around the same time, S. produced another kind of poetry likely to come from a young idealist, an acerbic satire called *Prosopoia; or, Mother Hubbard's Tale*. This Chaucerian allegory of a fox and an ape who rise to rule Britain was intended to expose the threat to England in the proposed marriage of ELIZABETH I to the Catholic Duke of Alençon. Although the piece was not published until 1591 in a collection of somber and comparatively unimpressive poems entitled *Complaints*,

when the poem first appeared Lord Burghley, the primary advocate of Elizabeth's marriage and the fox in S.'s poem, was indignant. The precise details of Burghley's retribution are unknown, but there is little doubt he was partly responsible for S.'s being sent away from London. S. spent the rest of his life trying to regain a place at court.

In 1580, S. moved to Ireland as secretary to the island's newly appointed Lord Governor, Arthur Lord Grey de Wilton, but when Lord Grey left office two years later, S remained in what was to become his adopted country. S.'s relationship to Ireland is difficult to pin down. Ireland and the Irish profoundly inspired S.'s poetry, and it is also true S. lived a full life in Ireland his last twenty years. He was active in politics, gained a sizeable estate, married and had a family, and was awarded a pension from the Crown. Nevertheless, many critics have pointed out S. spent the same twenty years trying in vain to write his way back to London. While still at court S. conceived of what became his great masterpiece. *The Faerie Queene*, an EPIC ROMANCE unique in English in its concept, form, and execution, was to be the great national poem of Britain.

In its scope and design, the *Faerie Queene* is quite simply unlike anything else that has ever been attempted. S.'s intention was to write a national epic, but one that superseded the traditional limitations of that genre. Arthur, England's great mythical ruler from whom the Tudors claimed descent, is S.'s epic hero whose quest is to find and marry Gloriana the Queen of Fairyland. Through Arthur, S. is able indirectly to praise Elizabeth I, Arthur's heir. To do more for his queen, however, S. also makes Elizabeth the model for Gloriana herself, and indeed he invites Elizabeth to see herself represented in varying degrees in all the virtuous heroines in the poem. For another poet, this ambitious outline might have sufficed, but as S. explains in his famous introductory letter that accompanied books 1–3 (1590), the purpose behind the whole work is ultimately "to fashion a gentleman or noble person in vertuous and gentle discipline." To this end, S. devised a secondary plot into which he wove Arthur's adventure. It is this secondary plot that gives form and structure to the overall work. Gloriana sends forth twelve knights each of whom, as S. explains, represents one of "the twelve private moral virtues, as Aristotle hath devised." Overarching unity is achieved by Arthur, who represents the virtue of Magnificence—that virtue which comprises all others—and who appears at intervals to assist the twelve knights on their respective journeys. Thus, S. foresaw the whole work, but in the twenty years he worked on it only six of the twelve books were published. These recount the allegorical journeys of figures representing holiness, temperance, chastity, friendship, justice, and courtesy.

There is little disagreement among scholars that books 1–3 are superior to books 4–6 (1596). As the stories progress, the highly developed, tightly controlled allegory of books 1–3 becomes muddled and S. gradually assumes the mantle of the didactic moralist. Even so, S. remains unequaled, certainly among his contemporaries, in painting with his poetry pictures as vivid, clear, and detailed as any one might find on canvas. His metrical innovations alone would place him among the great English poets, but to these he adds contributions of musicality and rhythms, as well as an ability to weave threads of disparate themes, allusions, and references into a single dazzling tapestry.

S. produced two highly noteworthy sequences about his courtship of and marriage to Elizabeth Boyle in 1594. His *Amoretti*, or "little loves," and his *Epithalamion*, or poem "on the marriage bed," appeared in 1595. Also that year he published *Colin Clout's Come Home Againe*, a sequel to his earlier and still successful *The Shepheardes Calender* (already reprinted in 1581, 1586, and 1591 as it would be again in 1597), and the decidedly less successful *Astrophel*, an allegory of the life of Sidney. Of these, further mention must be made of the *Epithalamion*. It is a unique example in English of poetry written about attained and requited love; it is one of the only departures S. made from allegory writing about his own real wedding day; and it has often been regarded as some of the most beautiful love poetry ever written.

One hopes S. knew the joy in the *Epithalamion*, for in many ways his final years seem fraught with difficulties. As the political situation in Ireland grew increasingly tense, S. must have felt himself caught between his affection for Ireland and his governmental responsibilities in County Cork and at Kilcolman, his estate there. S.'s sympathies are evident in his stirring political tract "A Vewe of the Present State of Ireland" written most likely in late 1597, but not published until well after his death. In October 1598, following the outbreak of Tyrone's Rebellion, Kilcolman was burned and S. and his family fled to Cork. It is possible that books 6–8 of the *Faerie Queene* were destroyed in the attack. S. was shortly thereafter sent to London with letters from Sir Thomas Norris, President of Munster, to the Privy Council. S. arrived in London near the end of the year, and a short time later, on January 13, 1599, died in his rooms on King's Street.

The circumstances of S.'s death remain unclear. Ben JONSON wrote that S. had died "for lake of bread," but how a successful poet and well-connected political figure could die of starvation is uncertain. Three days later, S. was buried with great ceremony in Poet's Corner at Westminster Abbey. The Earl of Essex paid the funeral costs. S.'s grave is suitably next to Chaucer's. The historian William Camden wrote of S.'s funeral and how great numbers of grieving poets threw elegies and the pens with which they wrote them into S.'s open tomb, which bears the inscription "The Prince of Poets of his time."

BIBLIOGRAPHY: Berger, H., Jr., ed., *S.* (1968); Heninger, S. K., Jr., *Sidney and S.* (1989); Hume, A., *E. S.* (1984); King, J. N., *S.'s Poetry and the Reformation Tradition* (1990); Nelson, W., *The Poetry of E. S.* (1963); Waller, G., *E. S.* (1994)

JOHN V. GLASS

STACPOOLE, H[enry] de Vere
b. 9 April 1863, Kingstown, Ireland; d. 12 April 1951, Shanklin, Isle of Wight

Although he was a very popular writer for most of his long life, S. has been largely forgotten during the fifty years since his death. He published more than eighty books—fiction mostly but also poetry, BIOGRAPHY, AUTOBIOGRAPHY, and translation—but is remembered chiefly for one book, *The Blue Lagoon: A Romance* (1908), which was a hit during S.'s lifetime and has been made into movies at least three times, in 1923, 1949 (one of Jean Simmons's youthful roles), and 1980 (starring Brooke Shields). S.'s sequels *The Garden of God* (1923) and *The Gates of Morning* (1925) were also successful, the former being adapted as the film *Return to the Blue Lagoon* in 1991. Somewhat like J. M. BARRIE's play *The Admirable Crichton*, *The Blue Lagoon* speculates on what would happen to civilized people returned to a state of nature on a tropical island; the chief difference is that S.'s central characters are two children. Such works belong in a durable "what-if" category called "Robinsonade," after Daniel DEFOE's *Robinson Crusoe*. The mode continues romantically in the form of the *Blue Lagoon* films, farcically in *Gilligan's Island*, and pessimistically in William GOLDING's *Lord of the Flies*.

STALLWORTHY, Jon [Howie]
b. 18 January 1935, London

S. is perhaps best known as the biographer and editor of Wilfred OWEN. His 1974 BIOGRAPHY of the war poet received the Duff Cooper Memorial Prize (1974) and the W. H. Smith Literary Award (1975), while the American Academy of Arts and Letters honored it with the E. M. Forster Award (1976). *The Complete Poems and Fragments* of Owen were published in two volumes in 1983. S.'s other major poetic biography is *Louis MacNeice* (1995). He is the editor of *The Penguin Book of Love Poetry* (1973; repub. as *A Book of Love Poetry*, 1974), *The Oxford Book of War Poetry* (1984), and *First Lines: Poems Written in Youth from Herbert to Heaney* (1987), as well as the *Collected Poems* of Henry Reed in 1991. A contributing editor of the *Norton Anthology of English Literature* (1993) and the *Norton Anthology of Poetry* (4th ed., 1996), S. is also highly regarded as a literary critic, translator, and professor.

Yet S. sees himself primarily as a poet. He won the Newdigate Prize for Poetry at Oxford in 1958 for *The Earthly Paradise*. His volumes of poetry—from *The Astronomy of Love* (1961) to *The Guest from the Future* (1995)—take as their themes love, family, lineage, and history. His poems have been praised for both their technical skill and the simplicity and directness of their message. Current or political events are not features of S.'s poetry, and he addresses such a deliberate omission head-on in "Letter to a Friend." He prefers to offer a "window" on the world rather than "a looking-glass."

S.'s poems of passionate love are filled with sensual images, simple in themselves and delicately combined, as in "Pour Commencer "and "Breakfast in Bed." His poems of love lost or deferred are equally resonant and evocative. "African Violets" and "You not with me" are particular examples. He writes movingly of his children, especially his first child, a son, born with Down's Syndrome: "The Almond Tree," "Firstborn," and "The Almond Tree Revisited." S. is fascinated by his family history. Born in London the child of third-generation New Zealanders, S. often felt an outsider, something he explores in his 1998 AUTOBIOGRAPHY, *Singing School*. In the volume *Root and Branch* (1969), his parents are tenderly recalled in such poems as "Two Hands" and "The Blackthorn Spray." In *A Familiar Tree* (1978), he studies his lineage in a series of interlinked poems, that trace the lives and relationships of his ancestors as far back as 1738. S. has most recently turned his attention to relationships and conjunctions of others such as Isaiah Berlin and Anna Akhmatova in *The Guest from the Future*. *Rounding the Horn*: *Collected Poems* was published in 1998.

While his poems are largely formal, even "traditional," S. is not averse to experimentation, especially in his later work, and he is attentive to the sound and rhythm of poetry. The poet must have a good ear otherwise a poem runs the risk of degenerating into mere prose. Hence, we can discern in S.'s work the measured lines and rhythms of intentionally controlled verse. Full rhymes and half rhymes are often combined with enjambments so that the reader is unaware of just how measured the lines are: the surface simplicity belies the complexity of structure. For S., the placement of the words on the page and the grouping of sounds are intimately related to the sense or meaning of a poem. Both the eye and the ear must be attuned.

Fascinated by how one becomes a poet, S., in *First Lines,* delineates the ways in which good poets learn their craft, first by imitation of traditional forms, then

by experimentation with forms that suit their individual intentions or voices. In *Singing School*, he explores his own poetic apprenticeship, recalling the moment in 1942, when, as schoolboy, he realized that "what I most wanted to do in the world was to write poems."

BIBLIOGRAPHY: Haberstroh, P. B., "An Interview with J. S.," *ConP* 3, 3 (1978): 1–20; McDowell, M. B., "J. S.," in Sherry, V. B., Jr., ed., *Poets of Great Britain and Ireland since 1960*, part 1, *DLB* 40 (1985): 547–57

JANE POTTER

STANHOPE, Philip Dormer. See CHESTERFIELD, Philip Dormer Stanhope, Fourth Earl of

STANLEY, Thomas
b. September 1625, Cumberlow Green, Hertfordshire; d. 12 April 1678, London

After being privately tutored (his tutor being the son of Edward Fairfax, English translator of Torquato Tasso's *Gerusalemme Liberata*) and study at Pembroke College, Cambridge, the young S. spent some years living in France. He returned to England, perhaps in the mid-1640s, and took up residence in the Middle Temple in London. Inherited wealth allowed him to live a life of some leisure and to act as a patron to other writers. His friends included James SHIRLEY, Edward Sherburne, John Hall, William Hammond, Robert HERRICK, and Richard LOVELACE, putting S. at the center of a network of poets with royalist sympathies. S.'s poems and prose are the product of a privileged life, the work of a scholarly and cultivated gentleman of leisure. Most of S.'s poems were probably written before 1651; he published *Poems and Translations* in 1647/8, reissuing it in revised form as *Poems* in 1651. *Psalterium Carolinum*, paraphrases of the Psalms applied to the events of Charles I's fall and death, was published in 1657, but probably written earlier. After 1651, S. seems to have largely devoted his time to classical scholarship. Between 1655 and 1662, he published the three volumes of his *History of Philosophy: Containing the Lives, Opinions, Actions, and Discourses of the Philosophers of Every Sect*. In 1663, he published an edition of Aeschylus, prepared with the assistance of John Pearson, later Bishop of Chester. S.'s reputation as a scholar had been recognized by his election as a charter member of the Royal Society in 1661.

John Hall described S. as "a severe Critick in Poetry, as well as in Philology, and the Sciences," and everywhere in S.'s work there is a meticulous attention to detail. He was an inveterate reviser, and his fastidious ear for verbal music is evident; his cultivation of musicality is sometimes at the cost of the kind of vigor that distinguishes the very best of Caroline verse. Though clearly an admirer of Ben JONSON, and capable of something of the greater poet's elegance and lucidity, there is much in Jonson that is beyond S.'s range, not least his robustness. The vitality of Jonson—or indeed of Thomas CAREW and Sir John SUCKLING—gives way to a certain bloodlessness in S. This may reflect the extent to which S.'s poems were more the product of his extensive reading than any innate intensity of feeling. Many of S.'s poems are declared to be translations; others are heavily indebted to one or more model (usually Continental, sometimes classical), so much so that the distinction between a translation and an "original" poem is almost meaningless in his work. These comments should not, however, be taken to be damning. S. is the kind of poet whose achievement is open to easy misjudgment by the modern reader. S. and his contemporaries did not place our value on "originality" and were more willing than we often are to appreciate the technical skill with which familiar ideas and images were represented in the work of a poet like S., readier to appreciate the gracefulness and lightness of touch with which he imitates and varies his models.

Among S.'s translations, there are elegant versions of the Anacreontea in lively couplets (though S. characteristically avoids some of the original's less "chaste" moments) and of the pastorals of Bion and Moschus, to represent the Greek poets; his translations from classical Latin include a delightful version of the "Cupid Crucified" by Ausonius and a slightly less convincing attempt at the *Pervigilium Veneris.* Renaissance Latin poetry is represented by versions of some of the *Basia* of Johannes Secundus (some of those omitted were probably too erotic to please S.'s taste in such matters). Some of the finest of S.'s work as a translator comes in his versions from the vernacular poets of the Continental Renaissance. S. was active as a prose translator too; his version of Pico della Mirandola's *Commento sopra una canzone de amore da H. Benivieni* was published, as *A Platonick Discourse upon Love,* in his *Poems* of 1651. It was the first English translation of this important work.

The best of S.'s lyrics—original or translated—are graceful and well-made statements of essentially familiar ideas, love and beauty celebrated (or bemoaned) within the confines of a polite Neoplatonism. "Celia Singing" is a beautifully cadenced contribution to the 17th-c. subgenre of poems celebrating the singing of a beautiful lady; "The Exequies" offers three elegant stanzas of fancifully morbid self-pity. In "The Bracelet," the influence of John DONNE's "The Funeral" is distantly registered, as is that of "A Valediction: forbidding mourning" in "La belle Confidante"; in "The Repulse," affinities with Carew (es-

pecially "A Deposition from Love") are clear. "On a Violet in Her Breast" ventures on a slightly greater sensuousness than S. normally risks and "The Kisse" attractively, and economically, rehearses the Renaissance philosophy of osculation.

BIBLIOGRAPHY: Crump, G. M., *The Poems and Translations of T. S.* (1962); Miner, E., *The Cavalier Mode from Jonson to Cotton* (1971)

GLYN PURSGLOVE

STAPLEDON, [William] Olaf
b. 10 May 1886, Wirral, Cheshire; d. 6 September 1950, Cheshire

S. was educated at Balliol College, Oxford, and took his Ph.D. at Liverpool University, where he lectured on philosophy and psychology. From 1915 to 1919, he served in France with an ambulance unit. He was introduced to speculative fantasy (SCIENCE FICTION) by fellow writer Eric Frank Russell in the late 1930s. S.'s first book in this genre was *Last and First Men* (1930). Notable works that followed were *Odd John* (1935), the story of a superhuman mentality, and in 1944 *Sirius,* about a superhumanly brilliant dog. The great S. opus is *Star Maker* (1937). In 1948, S. told a meeting of the British Interplanetary Society that mankind would probably tamper with the atom until it destroyed itself. But if the species lived long enough it would have a new freedom, the freedom to travel beyond the terrestrial sphere and explore the whole solar system. The S. archive is housed at the Sydney Jones Library at Liverpool University.

STEEL, Flora Annie
b. 2 April 1847, Harrow, Middlesex; d. 12 April 1929, Talgarth, Wales

S.'s novels of colonial life are rightly praised for raising feminist issues in British India. She is critical of English conduct in India, but she accepts the colonial position as a duty in the name of empire, then a dominant ideology. This offends some modern critics, but S. was a woman of her time and such a view was orthodox in her circle. Married in 1867, S. accompanied her husband who worked for the Indian civil service to India, where she became fascinated with Indian customs and FOLKLORE, even teaching herself Punjabi. She is best remembered for her historical novel, *On the Face of the Waters* (1896), for which she was allowed access to the archive of the Indian mutiny at Delhi that serves as a backdrop. Alice Gissing has been noted as being a new kind of independent female character of Anglo-Indian fiction in that she chooses not to associate with the established society and does not exhibit any signs of homesickness. S.'s later works include *A Prince of Dreamers* (1908),

King Errant (1912), *Mistress of Men* (1917), and *The Builder* (1928).

STEELE, [Sir] Richard
b. March 1672, Dublin, Ireland; d. 1 September 1729, Carmarthen, Wales

We think of S. primarily as an essayist and secondarily as a playwright, and it is, indeed, proper that we should, though in his crowded and adventurous life he managed to be at various times a great many other things also—a trooper in the Life Guards, a captain in Lord Lucas's regiment, a courtier in the entourage of Prince George of Denmark, a commissioner of stamps, a member of Parliament, a patentee of Drury Lane Theatre, and a member of the commission appointed to inquire into the estates forfeited by the Jacobite rebels in 1715. For all this welter of community service and good works, he was knighted in 1715. Lady Mary Wortley MONTAGU, in one of her celebrated letters, compares S. with Henry FIELDING, saying: "each of them was so formed for happiness it is a pity he was not immortal." But mortality overtook Fielding when he was forty-seven and S. when he was fifty-seven.

S.'s literary reputation is inextricably entwined with that of Joseph ADDISON because of their joint work on a series of periodicals. This was an entirely new literary form, invented by S. None of them survived for more than a year or two and for some as little as a week or two, but as S.'s indefatigable and restless imagination moved from subject to subject a whole series of these papers developed, covering a period of over ten years and containing some very fine writing, including the famous Sir Roger de Coverley essays (some of them by S, some by Addison) and Addison's eighteen essays on John MILTON's *Paradise Lost* that, along with John DRYDEN's work some forty years earlier, laid the foundations of English literary criticism.

These periodicals appeared two or three times a week (every day in the case of the second series of the *Spectator*). The chief contributors throughout were S. and Addison but from time to time other distinguished writers appeared: Alexander POPE, Laurence Eusden, Ambrose Philips, Montagu, and others. The entire list, for which the organizational credit must go to S., reads as follows: the *Tatler* (1709–11), the *Spectator* (1711–12), the *Guardian* (1713), the *Spectator* (1714), the *Lover* (1714), the *Reader* (1714), the *Tea Table* (1715–16), the *Plebeian* (1719), and the *Theatre* (1720). In his role as editor, S. used the pseudonym "Mr. Bickerstaff," borrowed from Jonathan SWIFT, who had invented it in 1708 for his satirical *Predictions for the Ensuing Year*, a book of mock astrology designed to make fun of John Partridge, a London cobbler turned amateur astrologer. It tickled

S.'s ironic sense of HUMOR to join in the joke. In all, these occasional journal writings contain some of the finest essay writing in the language: belles lettres indeed, in a period before that term acquired a faintly derogatory connotation.

Among all the thunder and fury of a life in literary London in the early years of the 18th c., S. wrote four and three quarter plays between 1701 and 1725. They were: *The Funeral* (perf. 1701; pub. 1702), *The Lying Lover* (perf. 1703; pub. 1704), *The Tender Husband* (1705), *The Conscious Lovers* (perf. 1722), and *The School of Action* (wr. 1723–25)—unfinished: fairly substantial parts of each of four acts completed; *The Gentleman* (date uncertain, but not earlier than 1725)—fragment; only three or four pages completed. All six are designated "comedies" and all six resemble the late-17th-c. comedies of William WYCHERLEY and William CONGREVE in general shape and style, but markedly not in tone: the brilliant wit and the cynical accuracy of observation (both of individual characters and of society as a whole) is replaced by a warmer and more "feeling" sense and by a high-minded moralistic didacticism that would make them unplayable in the modern theater but that had some considerable influence on English playwriting in the 18th and early 19th cs. S., in fact, was following, but with a greater degree of sincerity, the pattern of Colley CIBBER's *Love's Last Shift; or, The Fool in Fashion* and *She Wou'd and She Wou'd Not* and in doing so was contributing to the establishing of the "sentimental comedy" (Diderot's "*comédie larmoyante*") that dominated English playwriting for a hundred years (and was mocked by John Dennis as well as by Oliver GOLDSMITH and Richard Brinsley SHERIDAN). S.'s four completed plays were each immediately produced and published in the years in which they were written and all passed into the standard repertory, being repeated at intervals, *The Funeral* until 1799, *The Lying Lover* until 1746, *The Tender Husband* until 1802, and *The Conscious Lovers* until 1818. This last-named is distinctly superior to the others and has two or three scenes that would still make the play acceptable were it not for the unctuous quality of the rest. But, while *The Conscious Lovers* can be seen to possess some redeeming features, the other three plays—once past their immediate dates of origin—have very rarely been mentioned with anything but scorn. William HAZLITT, for example, described *The Funeral* thus: "as trite, as tedious and full of formal grimace, as a procession of mutes and undertakers."

Certainly, S.'s best writing is not in his plays but in his essays, particularly those in the *Tatler* and the *Spectator* and even there he is frequently outshone by Addison. Nevertheless, there is always something graceful, as well as vigorous and virile, about S.'s writing. One could perhaps say that the key, not only to the writing but to his whole life, was humanitas, human feeling, compassion. In one of his *Spectator* essays (no. 502), he himself says: "I am a Man and cannot help feeling any Sorrow that can arrive at Man." Malcolm Kelsall interestingly suggests, in a paper read to a symposium sponsored by Manchester University Department of Drama in 1971, that the origins of S.'s sentimentalism (which does not mean "sentimentality") probably lie more in Terence—on whose play, *Andria*, S. based *The Conscious Lovers*—and in classical influences generally than in any immediate antipathetic response to the vicious obscenities of Restoration comedy. And in this connection it is also perhaps worth recalling that S.'s very first publication was a pamphlet called *The Christian Hero* (1701).

BIBLIOGRAPHY: Aitken, G. A., *The Life of R. S.* (1889); Blanchard, R., ed., *The Correspondence of R. S.* (1968); Bond, D. F., ed., *The Tatler* (3 vols., 1987); Connely, W., *Sir R. S.* (1934); Kenny, S. S., ed., *The Plays of R. S.* (1971)

ERIC SALMON

STEINER, [Francis] George
b. 23 April 1929, Paris, France

S. is an eloquent and erudite critic whose explorations of the crisis of language and culture in the 20th c. have proved richly provocative. S.'s key concerns, reiterated in a series of influential books and essays, are with the relationship between culture and barbarism; with the fragmentation and near-collapse of classic European humanism in the 20th c.; and with the temptations and trials of translation—S. is himself trilingual in English, French, and German. As a critic, S. sees true criticism as the inevitably inadequate repayment of a debt of love; the critic's task is to convey a sense of the power and achievement of great authors.

S.'s first two books showed his unembarrassed readiness to tackle large themes and provoke controversy. *Tolstoy or Dostoevsky?* (1959) explores the contrast between the two colossi of 19th-c. Russian fiction and also challenges the New Criticism then dominant in the U.S. S. felt that New Criticism was unable adequately to deal with the richness and scale of Leo Tolstoy's and Fyodor Dostoevsky's work. His second book, *The Death of Tragedy* (1961), is a breathtaking sweep through Western tragedy from Aeschylus to Samuel BECKETT, which argues that, with the breakdown of traditional religious and metaphysical frameworks, tragedy is no longer possible. The book provoked Raymond WILLIAMS to produce an implicit riposte in *Modern Tragedy*.

Language and Silence (1967), a collection of essays published between 1958 and 1966, is S.'s most influential book and the best introduction to the key themes of the earlier part of his career. "A Kind of Survivor," for example, is a haunting essay in which S.—who, but for his father's early recognition of the Nazi threat, might himself have been a victim of the concentration camps—tries, but necessarily fails, to grasp the enormity of the Holocaust and its impact upon his imagination. "The Retreat from the Word" and "Silence and the Poet" ask whether language can any longer be adequate to the realities of the modern world, or whether silence is the only possible option. A sheaf of essays explores the relationship between Marxism and literary criticism, at a time when the topic was relatively little discussed, and there are also fascinating commentaries on Franz Kafka, Sylvia Plath, F. R. LEAVIS, and Claude Levi-Strauss. *Language and Silence* testifies to the breadth of S.'s reading and the intensity of his cultural concerns.

In Bluebeard's Castle, the 1971 T. S. Eliot Memorial Lectures at the University of Kent at Canterbury, presents key themes of *Language and Silence* in a more concentrated form and develops S.'s speculations on the nature of what he calls a "post-culture," in which the book and the written word will no longer dominate. *After Babel* (1975) is a rich and substantial study of the act of translation, particularly notable for its close readings of a wide range of texts and for the connections it makes between them; it offers, for example, an illuminating analysis of the ways in which the subgenre of the elegy for a dead poet develops and changes from Thomas CAREW's elegy on John DONNE in the 17th c. to W. H. AUDEN's elegy for W. B. YEATS in the 20th c. *Antigones* (1984) is perhaps S.'s best book, a study of the transformations of an archetypal heroine from Sophocles to Jean Anouilh and beyond.

S.'s later books are less successful. *Real Presences* (1989) is a deeply felt engagement with deconstruction, but its proposed alternative—a reiteration of the belief in the transcendent nature of the text—is asserted rather than argued. *Errata* (1997) is a kind of intellectual AUTOBIOGRAPHY, but its potentially interesting insights into the development of S.'s ideas are overshadowed by the repetition of notions familiar from his earlier work. *The Grammars of Creation* (2001), based on the Gifford Lectures that S. delivered in 1990, elaborates and extends the argument of *Real Presences*, affirming that creation is dependent on the religious sense; but the heady rhetoric of S.'s prose cannot wholly hide a certain hollowness of argument.

S. has produced a number of notable short stories and one outstanding novel, and from the 1980s he is perhaps at his strongest in his fiction rather than in his criticism. In contrast to the flamboyance of his critical style, his fictional prose is pared down and precise. His novel *The Portage to San Cristobal of A. H.* (1981) is a compelling and disturbing thought-experiment that seeks to answer the question: if Adolf Hitler, the "A.H." of the title, had survived the war and later been arrested and brought to trial, what defense of the Holocaust would he have made? S.'s Hitler forcefully argues that anti-Semitism is to be explained as a reaction against the impossible demands that Moses, Jesus, and Karl Marx made upon human beings. This novel was later adapted into a successful play. The aftermath of the attempt to realize the impossible demands of Marx provides the context for S.'s most successful short story, "Proofs" (1992). This focuses on a meticulous master proofreader, who is also a committed Marxist, confronting the loss of his sight and the collapse of Communism. "Proofs" is a restrained and moving elegy for the fading of Utopian hopes.

The note of elegy sounds throughout S.'s work. His deep nostalgia for a cultural tradition that is passing is the source both of his strength and weakness. His writing provides an incomparable introduction to a range of key issues in 20th-c. European thought; his commentaries on a range of writers from Aeschylus to Auden are deeply informed and insightful. But his pessimistic view of recent cultural change has made it difficult for him to appreciate the positive aspects of the "post-culture" of the 21st c.

BIBLIOGRAPHY: Banville, J., "G. S.'s Fiction," in Steiner, G., *The Deeps of the Sea* (1996): vii–xi; Bergonzi, B., *The Myth of Modernism and Twentieth Century Literature* (1986); Tredell, N., "G. S.," in his *Conversations with Critics* (1994): 75–93

NICOLAS TREDELL

STEPHEN, [Sir] Leslie
b. 28 November 1832, London; d. 22 February 1904, London

By the late 1800s, S. was the most important man of letters in England, contributing to history, philosophy, literary criticism, and BIOGRAPHY. He turned literary criticism toward an awareness of the text's relationship with the time of the writer; and, as writer and as editor of the *Dictionary of National Biography* (1885–1901), he considered biography and history as studies of the progress in intellectual development.

In 1850, S. matriculated at Trinity Hall, Cambridge, where he studied mathematics and read widely in philosophy, economics, and literature. John Stuart MILL and August Comte influenced his belief that history and humanity advance through natural laws. In 1862, realizing that he no longer believed in the historical truth of Christianity, S. gave up his position at Cambridge. He left as a radical reformer whose ideas about reform were years ahead of their time. He wrote about his experiences in *Sketches from Cambridge by a Don* (1865).

He visited the U.S. and published his first important work, *The "Times" on the American War: A His-*torical Study (1865), in which he lambasted the London newspaper's failure to present a balanced view of the American Civil War. By the time he collected his articles on religious topics in *Essays on Freethinking and Plainspeaking* (1873), S. was the chief spokesperson for agnosticism. Notable among these essays is "A Bad Five Minutes in the Alps," in which he combines his love of mountain climbing with his skepticism of divine presence in everyday life. Other essays about his beloved mountain climbing appeared in the *Alpine Journal* (1868–72) and *The Playground of Europe* (1871). These essays show not only his ability to write well but also that he was a man who believed that mountain climbing tested character as well as physical stamina.

After leaving Cambridge, S. became a journalist, writing for and editing the most important literary journals of his time. His witty but firm advice to Thomas HARDY about toning down references that might offend typical Victorian readers illustrates the restrictions S. (and Hardy) faced as well as S.'s ability to work with writers. Many of his own *Cornhill Magazine* essays appeared in *Hours in a Library* (3 vols., 1874–79; rev. eds., 1892, 1904). In these essays, S. displays his rational, analytical method of searching for connections between writer, reader, text, and the social conditions that influence all three. S. calls for honesty in biographical portraits. For example, to tell Samuel Taylor COLERIDGE's story without the opium is like the story of Hamlet without the ghost. S.'s work as a journalist established him as a dominant literary force in Victorian letters. George MEREDITH based his character Vernon Whitford in *The Egoist* on this part of S.'s life.

S. also wrote intellectual history. The single most important book he wrote is his powerfully and vividly written *History of English Thought in the Eighteenth Century* (2 vols., 1876). A sequel, *The English Utilitarians* (3 vols., 1900), is not as successful. S. analyzes the revolutionaries David HUME, Adam SMITH, Joseph Butler, and others and sets into historical context the Deist controversy and the utilitarian schools of philosophy. His *History* is a significant contribution to intellectual history and is still considered insightful. Late in his life, S. returned to his favorite century in the Ford Lectures, published as *English Literature and Society in the Eighteenth Century* (1904).

In the year that his daughter Virginia [WOOLF] was born, S. published *The Science of Ethics* (1882), which he told her was his favorite among his books. The book is a study of ethics as an evolutionary science, showing ethics adapting to changes in the environment. But critics fault the book, especially for a lack of empirical evidence and the weakness of his analogy connecting society to smaller organisms in nature.

After reform, journalism, and intellectual history, S. is known for his immense contributions to biography. He wrote four volumes of essays collected in *Studies of a Biographer* (1898–1902); he wrote five contributions to the English Men of Letters series and two other full-length biographies, one of his brother Sir James Fitzjames Stephen (1895); and he edited and wrote 386 entries to all but three of the original sixty-six volumes of the *Dictionary of National Biography*. S. worked himself to death for the *Dictionary*, pushing himself and his contributors to write clear, concise, and accurate portraits of their subjects. Since he saw history as a series of events leading to a discernible outcome, he believed that *Dictionary* articles should follow the development of an individual's life and era to reveal the subject's character and the historical conditions of the time. He says in an essay that biography should reveal the essence of a person's character, "stripped naked." For the *Dictionary*, he wrote on many of the major writers of English literature and letters, including John LOCKE, John MILTON, Alexander POPE, and Jonathan SWIFT (of whom S. remarks that certain readers may think that fire would have been the best editor of some later writings). But S. also wrote on many obscure eccentrics and believed that these portraits accounted for a large part of the *Dictionary*'s value. Twentieth-century biographers like Lytton STRACHEY owe much to S.'s work as a biographer. He was knighted for this work in 1902.

After his second wife died in 1892, S. wrote a memoir of his life with her, referred to by his children and published in 1977 as *Sir Leslie Stephen's Mausoleum Book*. Like his daughter's portrait of him as Mr. Ramsay in *To the Lighthouse*, the memoir shows his dependence on his wife as well as his contrary nature.

In "An Apology for Plainspeaking," the final essay in *Essays on Freethinking and Plainspeaking*, S. urges his readers to think freely and speak plainly about their subjects. Only then can they be assured that they have at least done a little to maintain the truths on which all "moral improvements and happiness" rely. Typical of what was admirable in Victorians, S.'s advice may serve as his epitaph.

BIBLIOGRAPHY: Annan, N., *L. S.* (1984); Maitland, F. W., *The Life and Letters of L. S.* (1906); Von Arx, J. P., *Progress and Pessimism: Religion, Politics, and History in Late Nineteenth-Century Britain* (1985)

STEVE FEREBEE

STEPHENS, James

b. 2 or 9 February 1882, Dublin, Ireland; d. 26 December 1950, London

Poet, playwright, and author, S. was working as a solicitor's clerk in Dublin and educating himself by wide reading when he met Irish mystic and poet Æ (George RUSSELL), who introduced him to the study of theosophy in 1907, and presented him to W. B. YEATS, John Millington SYNGE, and Lady GREGORY, among others, as the best hope for the next generation of the Irish Renaissance. Æ helped to get S.'s first book of poetry, *Insurrections,* published in 1909, and was again instrumental in the publication of a first novel, *The Charwoman's Daughter* (repub. as *Mary, Mary,* 1912), in a periodical in 1911 and as a separate volume in 1912.

In 1912 also came the publication that would solidify S.'s reputation for his own and, apparently, all times: *The Crock of Gold*. In his essay supporting the awarding to S. of the Polignac Prize for *The Crock* of *Gold* in 1913, Yeats appreciates not only S.'s voluptuous language but also his ability to universalize the Irish folk experience so it is comprehensible to those without prior sympathies with fairyland. Another way of stating the same observation is to say that in *The Crock* of *Gold,* S. manages what neither Yeats nor Lady Gregory do in their otherwise admirable fairy tale collections, which is to make the mythology of ancient Ireland feel like legitimate and psychologically sophisticated subject matter for modernist fiction.

The Crock of *Gold* and *The Demi-Gods* (1914) together exemplify an important quality of S.'s fiction, which is that plot is secondary to the spiritual alchemy that ensues when an angry or otherwise befuddled soul finds itself in circumstances (typically the fortuitous appearance of supernatural beings, like the gods of *The Crock of Gold* or the angels of *The Demi-Gods*) requiring transformation of the habitual modes of the characters' perceptions, often to a level of patience or empathy previously incomprehensible. The words "pantheistic" and "mystical" have been applied with justice to S.'s work, though both the milieu and the intention of his writing are a good deal more down-to-earth—even proletarian—than those terms would seem to imply.

S.'s poetry possesses a gentle mysticism and a sympathy for the nonhuman world, and an extreme simplicity (sometimes naiveté) of expression which have caused it, almost reflexively, to be deemed "Blakean," though it is far less muscular and polemical than William BLAKE's works, as well as less programmatic, more a series of thoughtful, incidental observations than a unifying pattern of vision. S.'s poetry—still widely anthologized—has struck commentators as everything from deeply and subtly metaphysical to trivial. At the least, there is no doubting his originality and, given his historical moment, singularity among serious poets.

The Easter Rising of 1916 is chronicled in *The Insurrection in Dublin* (1916), an important piece of historical journalism, as well as a speculative analysis of the metaphysics behind what appeared at the time to be a wasteful and hopeless gesture. It is an interesting experiment to forget for a moment that the 1916 Rising was a real event, and read the book as though it were one of S.'s novels. Narrative of the battle of Sackville Street is interrupted to observe a soldier—otherwise unarmed—chasing enemies away with an umbrella: "It was said that the wonder of the world was not that Ireland was at war, but that after many hours the umbrella was still unbroken." S.'s HUMOR and humanity are unconquerable, even in situations notable for the absence of both.

Other important S. publications include the poetic elegy *Green Branches* (1916), *Reincarnations* (1918), and *Kings of the Moon* (1938), his last volume of poems, as well as the three volumes of fiction he considered his best writing: *Irish Fairy Tales* (1920), *Deirdre* (1923), and *In the Land of Youth* (1924). S.'s poems were collected in 1926, and the volume revised and reissued in 1954.

BIBLIOGRAPHY: Finneman, R. L., ed., *Letters of J. S.* (1974); Manion, J. J., *The Poetry of J. S.* (1986); Martin, A., *J. S.* (1977)

DAVID BRENDAN HOPES

STERN, G[ladys] B[ertha; later changed to Bronwyn]

b. 17 June 1890, London; d. 19 September 1973, Wallingford, Berkshire

W. Somerset MAUGHAM considered S. one of the great novelists of the 20th c. Her successful series of novels about the Jewish Rakonitz family was initiated by *Tents of Israel* (1924; repub. as *The Matriarch*, 1925). The other novels in the series include *A Deputy Was King* (1926), *Shining and Free, a Day in the Life of the Matriarch* (1935), *The Matriarch Chronicles* (1936), and *The Young Matriarch* (1942). She was a friend of novelists May SINCLAIR and Sheila KAYE-SMITH, with the latter of whom she collaborated in *Talking of Jane Austen* (1943; repub. as *Speaking of Jane Austen*, 1944) and *More about Jane Austen* (1949; repub. as *More Talk of Jane Austen*, 1950).

STERNE, Laurence

b. 24 November 1713, Clonmel, Ireland; d. 18 March 1768, London

S.'s two major works, *The Life and Opinions of Tristram Shandy, Gentleman* (9 vols., 1760–67) and *A Sentimental Journey through France and Italy* (2 vols., 1768), are characterized by an emphasis on human feeling and innovative forms that emphasize the acts of narration over the constructions of plot. Ruled by personal idiosyncrasies, S.'s narrators, Tristram and Yorick, tell disordered and episodic stories that are interrupted both by digressions inspired by

personal whimsy and the palimpsestic introduction of additional texts—some by S., some borrowed from other authors. These eccentric narrators often speak in breathless, seemingly spontaneous, sentences barely contained by punctuation, possibly prefiguring the modernist style of "confessional" storytelling; in some ways, they resemble the author himself as self-described in his letters: sincere, garrulous, and charmingly scatterbrained beings trapped in frail bodies. Like S., they are acutely conscious of the passage of time and the inevitability of death; even frivolous moments in S.'s fiction are touched by melancholy. S. focused more on episodic action and the exploration of ideas than conventional plot (unlike his contemporaries, Henry FIELDING and Tobias SMOLLETT) and his tender portrayals of Uncle Toby, the dying Le Fever, and the love-mad Maria contributed to the heightened cultural interest in sensibility toward the end of the century. Comic and erotic aspects of S.'s texts, however, reveal a complex and paradoxical approach toward sensibility.

Born at the army camp in Clonmel, S. spent his early years traveling between England and Ireland with his family. His father, Roger Sterne, was a veteran of England's wars in Ireland (like Uncle Toby) and his mother's father supplied regiments with provisions; S.'s affectionate perspective toward military men in his fiction perhaps developed as the result of the close camaraderie between army families. Before the death of S.'s father in Jamaica in 1731, the generosity of his uncle, Richard, allowed S. to attend school in England. In 1733, he helped S. enter Jesus College, Cambridge, where S. was granted a scholarship instituted by his great-grandfather, who had been master of the College and afterward Archbishop of York. S. was befriended at Cambridge by his Yorkshire neighbor John Hall-Stevenson, with whom he would remain friends for the rest of his life. S. also suffered his first severe attack of consumption at college, a chronic ailment that grew increasingly worse during his lifetime and eventually brought about his death.

S. took orders as an assistant curate near Cambridge in 1737, and, with the assistance of his well-placed uncle Jaques, became vicar of Sutton-on-the-Forest (Yorkshire) in 1738. He would remain there until 1760, living a life typical of an 18th-c. rural English vicar. As the local spiritual leader, S. administered to his congregation and led the cycle of services from one year to the next; he was a popular SERMON giver, and occasionally delivered sermons in the great cathedral of York eight miles away.

S. married Elizabeth Lumley in 1741. Although happy at first, their marriage soon became one more of accommodation than affection, in part, probably, because of S.'s interest in other women. Their only surviving child, Lydia, was born in 1747.

Until 1758, S.'s writing revolved largely around his religious duties. His sermons reveal the conventional content of midcentury Anglicanism, shaped by John Tillotson and including Latitudinarian ideas that encouraged a sympathetic perspective toward others and the toleration of different viewpoints—without challenging orthodox Christian theology. In many ways, Latitudinarianism formed the basis for the idea of SENTIMENT in S.'s fiction, a sentiment far more Christian than secular.

In addition to painting, playing the cello, farming, and occasionally hunting, S.'s diversions included visiting Hall-Stevenson at his ancestral home, Skelton Castle, sometimes in conjunction with other local gentlemen. The group called themselves the "Demoniacs," and enjoyed drinking and joking in the style of Rabelais.

S.'s income and local prestige grew with his involvement in local politics, often in the service of his uncle Jaques; he wrote—for others, and usually under a *nom de guerre*—political pamphlets or items for local newspapers. One credited example is *A Political Romance* (or *The History of a Good Warm Watch-Coat*), a satirical allegory based on local church politics in York in 1758, which S. readied for publication in January 1759; it was immediately suppressed. *A Political Romance* reduces a prerogative quarrel among high officials of the York archdiocese to a parish clerk's struggle to possess an old coat he found in a church.

Although all parties joined to prevent publication of *A Political Romance*, the effort triggered S.'s creative juices; less than a year later, he published the first two volumes of *Tristram Shandy* with a local York printer. Although Robert DODSLEY had rejected his manuscript, S. sent half the copies to London, where they quickly sold out. *Tristram Shandy* became a popular and critical success, due in large part to S.'s canny ability for self-promotion (he once claimed that he wrote "not [to] be *fed*, but to be *famous*"). S. arrived in London in early 1760 already a literary celebrity, and now made arrangements with a contrite Dodsley for a London edition with a sizable advance, and successfully solicited an illustration for it from the famous artist William Hogarth. In spite of his years as a rural parson, S. took immediately to London social life, being befriended by the actor David GARRICK and sitting for a portrait by Joshua REYNOLDS.

Tristram Shandy is a roller coaster ride of narrative idiosyncrasy, vacillating between the comic and the serious, the sacred and the profane. Tristram, struggling to tell the story of his life from the point of conception, is distracted by his own whimsy and tendency to digress by association; he self-consciously veers off the "line" of the story into other tales, discourses, and opinions, reflecting on his own process of composition along the way. Although Tristram re-

veals some adherence to chronological development in the recollection of his life, the work is mainly a series of episodes and digressions tenuously held together by the imperfect attention of its crack-brained narrator. This antistructure finds its roots in the tradition of satiric learned wit (sometimes called "Menippean SATIRE" or, after Northrop Frye, an "anatomy"), which includes the works of Rabelais, Desiderius ERASMUS, Montaigne, Cervantes, Robert BURTON, and Jonathan SWIFT—and behind them, Aristophanes, Petronius, and Lucian.

The first five volumes of *Tristram Shandy* are set in and around Shandy Hall and primarily concern Tristram's birth and his father's attempts to shape his education and destiny. Volume 6 begins the long-promised story of uncle Toby's amours, but volume 7 interrupts this narrative when Tristram flees to France for his health. Volumes 8 and 9 return to complete uncle Toby's affair with widow Wadman. The main figures in the Shandy world are Tristram's occasionally splenetic father, Walter, who is repeatedly defeated in his attempts to systematize the world with logic and learning; uncle Toby, his brother, a kind-hearted veteran who, wounded in the groin at the siege of Namur, pursues his interest in fortifications by replaying sieges on a bowling green adjacent to the house until peace leaves him vulnerable to the widow's sexual desires; and the dedicated Corporal Trim, Toby's servant, who shares his master's military interest, but not his shyness with women. They are joined by Dr. Slop, a rotund "man midwife" who assists in Tristram's delivery, Tristram's subtle mother, the designing widow Wadman, and several imperfect, but affectionately drawn, servants. A brief self-portrait of S. appears as the parson Yorick, doomed by his jesting nature; although he dies in volume I, the erratic chronology allows him to return in every volume as a voice of reason and balance.

Beneath the surface of *Tristram Shandy's* carefully crafted disorder, many ideas lurk that act to unify the text. The idea of "feeling" as an antidote to the excesses of "reason" resurfaces prominently in the contrasting figures of Walter and Toby. The concept of mortality also threads its way through the work: death takes Yorick in volume 1, brother Bobby in volume 5, countless imaginary soldiers in Toby's reenacted battles, and, finally, Tristram as he struggles to finish his story. Perhaps most significantly, though, S. questions the reader's idea of "knowing," by means of textual disorder and the denial of conclusions. In the process, he suggests the impossibility of actually "knowing" the text and challenges the reader's empirical certainty of "knowing" the world, as well. The inability to "know" and find closure is demonstrated by Walter's constantly thwarted attempts to reach and apply authoritative conclusions (about names and breeches, for instance), and Tristram's growing realization of the impossibility of completely telling the story of his life owing to the constraints of time and language.

S.'s interest in John LOCKE's *An Essay Concerning Human Understanding* is reflected (and perhaps parodied) in his manipulation of time (it takes Tristram several chapters to get Walter and Toby down a flight of stairs) as well as in his associative use of language (the word "nose" inevitably comes to mean "penis"). Associations are important in conjunction with the "hobby horses," or ruling passions, of "the characters: for instance, Walter's theory of names, Toby's fortifications, and Tristram's writing all carry their "riders" to ridiculous lengths, proving the strength of irrational over rational processes of thought. Almost every conversation leads Toby to thoughts of military engineering, and he is obsessed with the accuracy and improvement of his model siege towns on the bowling green; Walter's overindulgence in the theoretical makes his learning essentially useless, as evidenced by his book of instructions for raising Tristram, which grows much more slowly than does the child.

S.'s text also includes a black, a marbled, and a blank page, unusual typography, missing chapters, and a ten-page gap, all manifestations of Tristram's self-conscious awareness of textuality. Radically different in structure, composition, and tone from contemporary fictions by Samuel RICHARDSON, Fielding, and Smollett, *Tristram Shandy* was admired for its wit, comedy, and tender sentiment, and criticized for its bawdy and irreverent HUMOR, as well as its formlessness. S. used his instant fame to publish two volumes of sermons (1760) and quickly thereafter two more volumes of *Tristram Shady* (1761). But criticism grew louder, reflecting shock that the suggestive passages and ribald puns in *Tristram Shandy* were written by a clergyman. This belated reaction escalated over the course of *Tristram Shandy's* serial publication. Volumes 5 and 6 appeared in early 1762, after which S. left for Europe for the first of two prolonged stays intended to ease his tubercular illness, aggravated by his busy social life in London. S.'s wife and their daughter relocated to Toulouse. S. returned to England in 1764, finishing volumes 7 and 8 later that year (published 1765). He published two more volumes of sermons in 1766 and in 1767 the lone final volume of *Tristram Shady*, before beginning an account of his travels. During this time, S. was introduced to Elizabeth "Eliza" Draper, with whom he formed a strong emotional attachment, despite her being married and thirty years younger than he. She left for India a few months after they met to rejoin her husband, and for several months thereafter (April–August 1767) S. kept a journal supposedly to be shared with Eliza when she returned. This journal first surfaced in the 19th c. and was published as *Journal to Eliza* in 1904, and most recently in 2002 as *Bram-*

ine's Journal (S.'s title) in the Florida edition of S.'s complete works.

S. returned to London in failing health to see *A Sentimental Journey through France and Italy* through the press in February 1768, which he is reported to have called his "work of redemption." Based in part on his own Continental adventures, the episodic fiction features the somewhat autobiographical figure of Yorick, an English cleric traveling through France. Yorick's interactions with the opposite sex en route—the lady in the remise, the grisette in the glove shop, the *fille de chambre*, and mad Maria—are heavily reliant on spontaneous and unselfish emotional impulses (hence S.'s idea of "sentimental"), but suggest erotic feelings as well. Yorick also engages in more social forms of sentiment, such as his sympathy for beggars and the heartbroken owner of the dead ass. The focus on people in *A Sentimental Journey* is a distinct departure from the conventional travel account of the time, which related visits to monuments and buildings. S.'s francophilic and exquisitely sensitive Yorick is, in fact, directly contrasted with the chauvinistic and splenetic narrator of Smollett's *Travels in France and Italy*, labeled Smelfungus by S. If S.'s health had permitted, *A Sentimental Journey* would probably have been continued, but the two published volumes do convey the idea of a finished work.

Dying in a lodging house in London of complications from his consumption, S. did not live to see the success of *A Sentimental Journey*. Over the next thirty years, the sentimental episodes in the book helped to spawn a culture of sentiment that prized the expression of delicate emotion. The figures of Maria and the monk Lorenzo from *A Sentimental Journey* became cultural icons, appearing in prints and on decorative items, and the sentimental episodes from S.'s works (including the tale of Le Fever in *Tristram Shandy*) were reprinted in collections entitled *The Beauties of Sterne*. Three additional volumes of sermons were published posthumously in 1769.

BIBLIOGRAPHY: Byrd, M., *Tristram Shandy* (1985); Cash, A. H., *L. S.: The Early and Middle Years* (1975); Cash, A. H., *L. S.: The Later Years* (1986); Kraft, E., *L. S. Revisited* (1996); Lamb, J., *S.'s Fiction and the Double Principle* (1989); Mullan, J., *Sentiment and Sociability: The Language of Feeling in the Eighteenth Century* (1988); Myer, V. G., ed., *L. S.: Riddles and Mysteries* (1984); New, M., ed., *Critical Essays on L. S.* (1998); New, M., *Tristram Shandy: A Book for Free Spirits* (1996); Pierce, D., and P. de Voogd, eds., *L. S. in Modernism and Postmodernism* (1996)

W. B. GERARD

STERNHOLD, Thomas

b. Southampton?; d. 23 August 1549, near Blakeney, Gloucestershire

HOPKINS, John

d. October 1570, Awre

S. was a courtier to King HENRY VIII and turned nineteen psalms of the Old Testament of the Bible into metrical English verse in 1547. A second edition of thirty-seven psalms appeared posthumously in 1549. H., a Suffolk clergyman, added a further seven psalms and this third collection appeared in 1557. Although little is known of H.'s life, he was the major contributor to the later complete psalter. *The Whole Book of Psalmes* was added to the Prayer Book in 1562. This enterprise was mocked by John DRYDEN, John Wilmot, Earl of ROCHESTER, and Alexander POPE, who wrote ironically, "Sternhold and Hopkins glad the heart with psalms." Music was supplied in the Geneva edition of 1556 and by 1640 some three hundred editions had been published.

STEVENSON, Anne [Katherine]

b. 3 January 1933, Cambridge

In her poetry, S. explores the tension between the commonplace and the transcendent. She does so through the re-creation of her own experiences as a poet, woman, wife, mother, and grandmother, and also through the evocation of other real or imagined lives. Her work moves flexibly between different voices and eras, and through the varied landscapes and cultures in which she has lived—especially the U.S., England, Scotland, and Wales. Her repertoire of poetic forms is wide, but she works most effectively in two modes: the short lyric that encapsulates concentrated moments of perception, and the verse letter that flexibly accommodates the loose contingency of life.

The well-crafted poems of S.'s first collection, *Living in America* (1965), convey a strong conflict between entrapment and escape. Domestic constraints, the pressure to conform, and the frenzies of city life are contrasted with the promises of travel and of nature that can never be wholly fulfilled. Those unfulfilled promises are explored further in S.'s second volume, *Reversals* (1969), in which modern England proves disappointing to the American migrant, except for those moments when nature provides glimpses of an unattainable transcendence. *Reversals* also explores the ambivalence of motherhood, in which the child is both the mother's triumph and a threat to her freedom. While S. has firmly rejected the feminist label, her poetry does dramatize contradictions that are crucial to modern FEMINISM. Those contradictions are also evident in her third collection, *Travelling be-*

hind Glass (1974). The long title poem uses the image of a woman taking a car journey to consider the conflict between the desire for independence and for involvement, while a much shorter poem, "Generations," provides a compressed genealogy of frustration, tersely tracing the constraints across three generations on a grandmother, a mother, and a daughter.

Correspondences (1974), a family history told mainly through verse letters, develops the genealogy of "Generations." Though partly autobiographical, it is primarily a fictional history that is intended to represent the combination of aspiration and corruption in New England Puritanism. With remarkable resourcefulness, S. finds different styles for each member of the Chandler family that she portrays, from the Reverend Adam Chandler, an immigrant in Vermont in 1829, to Kay Boyd, an American writer living in London in 1968. The recurrent pattern of this history is that of aspiration and failure; attempts to escape repeatedly founder in submission or compromise. *Correspondences* ends with a kind of victory—Kay Boyd has escaped from a stifling marriage and has become a writer—but the ghosts of her thwarted precursors still painfully haunt her.

S.'s fifth volume, *Enough of Green* (1977), explores modes of renunciation that may lead to enhanced insight. "To Be a Poet" affirms that poetry demands isolation, not only from other people, but also from one's own thoughts and feelings; inner silence is the necessary prelude to poetic vision. Other poems in the collection renounce sensory richness, as epitomized by bright colors; green, yellow, and red are rejected in favor of black and brown, the dominant colors of the landscape of the Tay Estuary in Scotland where S. was then living. Color returns, however, in "Green Mountain, Black Mountain," the long central poem of her next collection, *Minute by Glass Minute* (1982); the Green Mountains of Vermont and the Black Mountains of Wales are evoked in the multiple, shifting perspectives of myth, history, and personal memory. Though S. herself has repudiated this poem as affected and impressionistic, it remains rewarding to read. Other key poems in *Minute by Glass Minute*, like "Swifts," take up the recurrent theme of a transcendence that is glimpsed but that stays, necessarily, out of reach.

Mortality is much in evidence in S.'s next collection, *The Fiction Makers* (1985), which includes two elegies for fellow-poets, Elizabeth Bishop and Frances Horovitz. The title poem wryly observes how quickly immediate life events turn into stories, "now" becoming "then" in a way that foreshadows death. The traditional consolations of Christianity are not available to S.; *The Fiction Makers* bears the trace, especially in the fragment "From an Unfinished Poem," of her unsuccessful attempt to find faith at this stage in her life, though more secular affirmations can still be made, for example in the wedding song of "An April Epithalamium."

In 1989, S.'s poetry was overshadowed for a time by the controversy over her biography of Sylvia Plath, *Bitter Fame*, which some critics found unduly hostile. Her next volume of poetry, *The Other House* (1990), included a verse letter to Plath that sought to put her firmly in the past; it is the strongest poem in the book. S. recovered her own identity as a poet in *Four and a Half Dancing Men* (1993), which is especially notable for its "Visits to the Cemetery of the Long Alive," an exploration of the vicissitudes of aging. But after her *Collected Poems* appeared in 1996, S. felt that she would write no more poetry; instead, she published a selection of critical prose, *Between the Iceberg and the Ship* (1998), and *Five Looks at Elizabeth Bishop* (1998), which she saw as a corrective to her 1967 study of the same poet. Poems of her own began to come again, however, and resulted in the collection *Granny Scarecrow* (1999), which extends her exploration of the relationships between the generations, and between past and present in an individual life, and also includes two convincing dramatic monologues. When *Granny Scarecrow* appeared, she told an interviewer that she was already at work on further dramatic monologues.

S.'s considerable body of poetry undoubtedly has its slack moments, but its unobtrusive discipline usually prevails. On the map of English poetry, she inhabits a space somewhere between Plath and Philip LARKIN. Drawn to extremes, she still respects the rich intricacies of the commonplace; often on the move, she knows what it means to come home. At her best, she achieves a poetry of quietly robust wisdom.

BIBLIOGRAPHY: Chamberlin, J. E., "A. S.," in Sherry, V. B., Jr., ed., *Poets of Great Britain and Ireland since 1960*, part 2, *DLB* 40 (1985): 558–65; Malcolm, J., *The Silent Woman: Sylvia Plath and Ted Hughes* (1994); Tredell, N., "A. S.," in Parini, J., ed., *British Writers: Supplement VI* (2001): 253–66

NICOLAS TREDELL

STEVENSON, Robert Louis [Balfour] [a.k.a. Tusitala]

b. 13 November 1850, Edinburgh, Scotland; d. 3 November 1894, Samoa

S. excelled in the historical novel, having a personal and obsessive sense of the past. Through his mother, whose pedigree was traceable back to the early 15th c., he shared a common ancestor with Sir Walter SCOTT, and his father's family could be traced back two hundred years. S.'s paternal grandmother was "remarkable pious," like Ben Gunn's mother in *Treasure Island* (1883). S.'s father was a distinguished marine engineer, a builder of lighthouses, and S. was

expected to follow suit. At Edinburgh University he became president of the Speculative Society, the exclusive debating society, known as the "Spec," and soon abandoned the study of engineering to aspire to a career as a writer. His father insisted that S. should continue at university in order to have a profession to fall back on. He took up law, but the romantic and histrionic aspects appealed to him far more than the tedious office routine, application to detail and the constant necessity for memorising dry facts, though he eventually qualified as an advocate. Short of money as a student, he mixed, in his own words, with "seamen, chimney sweeps and thieves."

Soon after university, a doctor cousin suggested European travel might improve S.'s chest condition. S.'s first two full-length books *An Inland Voyage* (1878) and *Travels with a Donkey in the Cévennes* (1879) resulted. Much of his time was spent in an artists' colony near Fontainebleau, where in 1876 he met his future wife, estranged from her husband and ten years S.'s senior. In 1879, he sailed for the U.S. in an emigrant ship and crossed coast to coast in an emigrant train in order to join her in California. He worked briefly as a reporter on a Monterey newspaper for two dollars a week. He had left Europe with only a brief note to his parents, who were hurt and alarmed. They learned of his whereabouts from his unpaid agent in England, the poet W. E. HENLEY, who had arranged publication of S.'s essays in various journals. His parents immediately provided an adequate allowance and sent blessings on his marriage. His first real success was *The Sea Cook,* a magazine serial published in book form as *Treasure Island.*

His father remained tolerant, but S.'s work shows a preoccupation with troubled father-son relationships, notably in *The Wrecker* (1892), written in collaboration with his stepson, Lloyd Osbourne, and in two of the shorter works of the 1880s, *The Story of a Lie* (1882) and *The Misadventures of John Nicholson* (1887). Even where it is not the main theme, there are hints of it. Both *Treasure Island* and *Kidnapped* (1886) begin with the youthful hero being orphaned and having to find a father-substitute, who in both cases turns out to be unsatisfactory. Long John Silver and David Balfour's Uncle Ebenezer are both treacherous villains and even Alan Breck is not a soothing or useful companion for the young David; however, Dr. Livesey in *Treasure Island* is a suitable mentor for young Jim Hawkins. In *The Master of Ballantrae* (1888), where the theme is fraternal rivalry, the situation is exacerbated by old Lord Durrisdeer's preference for his romantic but villainous elder son over his conscientious but duller brother.

S. disappointed his father in other ways: in typical Victorian fashion, they quarreled about religion when S. was in his early twenties. S.'s freethinking does not seem to have been permanent. One of his later stories,

"The Bottle Imp," concerns a diabolical wish-granting bottle that goes from hand to hand, the catch being that it is a sort of macabre pass-the-parcel, the owner at the time of his death being inevitably condemned to everlasting damnation. It is finally retained voluntarily in an ambivalently "happy" ending: the owner is so corrupt that he considers himself, and is considered by others, to be predestined to damnation anyway. He decides that he might just as well embrace such benefits as the bottle might afford in this life before departing it for the Fiery Pit—a resolution showing more than a trace of Scottish Calvinism. During his last years, when S.'s poor health took him to the South Seas, he instituted regular family prayers in his household of native Samoan servants.

By then, Samoa was no unspoiled Pacific paradise, but a state governed by treaty by a native king "advised" by white officials appointed jointly by Britain, Germany, and the U.S. S. became embroiled in local political tensions. He was indignant at colonial exploitation and his anger surfaces in two novellas, *The Ebb-Tide* (1894), which prefigures Joseph CONRAD's "Heart of Darkness," and *The Beach at Falesá* (1893), which was not published in full until 1984. Both stories undermine the myth of romantic South Sea islands and expose a mercenary European exploitative culture.

The strain of attempting to write historical novels without recourse to a full reference library was considerable, and he was reliant for necessary information on correspondence with friends in England (notably Henley, Henry JAMES, and Sidney COLVIN). He was also in touch with J. M. BARRIE and Rudyard KIPLING by mail, but never met them.

He was improvident and never free of money worries, despite growing fame. In 1886, S. published two of his most successful novels, *Kidnapped* and *The Strange Case of Dr. Jekyll and Mr. Hyde. Kidnapped* is a peculiarly Scots work, based on an historical event following the 1745 rebellion, the murder at Appin of the king's Factor, Campbell of Glenure. In the novel, there is the celebrated tragicomic incident when the hero David Balfour is shipwrecked: unable to understand the Gaelic of the passing fishermen, David almost starves to death on his "desert island," before realizing in the nick of time that it is possible at low tide to wade to the mainland.

Dr. Jekyll and Mr. Hyde was S.'s first runaway best-seller, in Britain and America. However, its very success and, thanks to numerous film treatments, mythic status, have spoiled it for new readers. Its having added a phrase to the language has robbed the mystery of its effect. Objectively read, it is an excellently plotted story: who is the evil, homicidal Hyde and what is the nature of his sinister hold over the respectable Dr. Jekyll? The suspense is maintained until the climax, the final carefully contrived revelation. It doesn't work for us anymore: everyone now knows the solution before starting to read and no element of surprise remains.

However, an important recurrent theme of S.'s fiction gets its most explicit treatment in *Jekyll and Hyde,* that of the contradictions within the human soul, the coexistence of good and evil in the same person. It informs all his most memorable characters, for example Long John Silver, and the Lord Justice-Clerk of his last, unfinished masterpiece, Adam Weir, Lord Hermiston.

Weir of Hermiston (1896) is essentially Scots: setting and atmosphere are entirely of S.'s native land, as are those of *Kidnapped* and its sequel *Catriona* (1893; repub. as *David Balfour*, 1893), *The Misadventures of John Nicholson, The Master of Ballantrae*, and the short "crawlers" (his own name for the supernatural tales), "Thrawn Janet" and "The Body Snatcher." *Weir of Hermiston* is set entirely in Edinburgh and the surrounding countryside. The character of Adam Weir is based on the notoriously severe Scots judge Lord Braxfield, with whose personality and career S. had long been intrigued. As early as 1881, S. had discussed Braxfield's portrait by Sir Henry Raeburn in *Virginibus Puerisque,* a collection of essays. S. confesses to a "sneaking kindness" for Weir: even his faults are in some ways admirable; his work dominates his entire life and mode of thinking. S. always admired what he was temperamentally unable to become, the dedicated professional. The unfinished story prepares us for the projected climax where Lord Hermiston will find himself called upon to be implicated in his son's murder trial, and family feeling must be subordinated to professional duty. It is not clear how the legal difficulty would have been resolved of how to have a judge sitting in judgment on a relative, though S. the lawyer thought of limiting the situation to a first trial where evidence incriminating the son was unexpectedly brought forward. Only a first draft survives, but the book is considered S.'s masterpiece, despite the greater popularity of *Treasure Island.*

Another unfinished novel, *St. Ives,* was completed by Sir Arthur QUILLER-COUCH (1897). S.'s poems are still popular, especially *The Child's Garden of Verses* (1885).

BIBLIOGRAPHY: Hammond, J. R., *A R. L. S. Companion* (1984); Hubbard, T., *Seeking Mr. Hyde: Studies in R. L. S., Symbolism, Myth, and the Pre-Modern* (1995); Maixner, P., ed., *R. L. S.* (1981); Noble, A., *R. L. S.* (1983); Sandison, A., *R. L. S. and the Appearance of Modernism* (1996); Smith, V., *Literary Culture and the Pacific* (1998)

MICHAEL GROSVENOR MYER

STOKER, Bram [Abraham]

b. 8 November 1847, Dublin, Ireland; d. 20 April 1912, London

S. never visited Transylvania, the Rumanian province described in such loving detail in his most celebrated novel. Like Mary SHELLEY's *Frankenstein,* S.'s *Dracula* (1897) has become modern myth. Tourists are nowadays taken to "Dracula's castle," the story having been conflated with the history of the medieval conqueror Vlad Dracul or Vlad the Impaler. At various times a civil servant and a journalist (theater critic) in his native Dublin, S. came to London to be chief personal assistant to the famous actor-manager Sir Henry Irving, whom he was to memorialize in two volumes of *Personal Reminiscences* (1906). S. found time nevertheless for fifteen now forgotten novels; it was not until *Dracula* that his work received significant attention. A few of his short stories of the macabre and supernatural are still read today, notably "Dracula's Guest," in which the eponymous count is an offstage figure controlling the destiny of a hapless traveler caught at night in his forest domains; and "The Squaw," a study of embittered maternal love in which a she-cat wreaks a terrible revenge on a clumsy tourist who has accidentally killed her kitten; and a novel of the supernatural, *The Lair of the White Worm* (1911), is still remembered.

Vampirism, the theme of *Dracula,* was well established as fictional material. Seventy years earlier, *Varney the Vampire*; *or, The Feast of Blood,* had been a runaway best-seller, and S.'s immediate inspiration is often said to be his fellow-Irishman Joseph Sheridan LE FANU's novella *Carmilla.* The vampire superstition has been variously interpreted as allegory of immigration, disease, or other phenomena perceived as insidious threats; or thought to have arisen from observation of such symptoms of porphyria (the disease sometimes blamed for the madness of King George III) as gum-shrinkage and acute sensitivity to daylight. Richard Matheson in *I Am Legend* (1954) offers a SCIENCE FICTION explanation. As with all FOLKLORE, details of the superstition vary: not all vampires fail to cast shadows or reflections, for instance; even within *Dracula* itself there appears to be inconsistency as to whether or not the Count can be up and about in the daytime.

The novel has become an archetypal inspiration for succeeding generations, spawning countless plays, films (two famous actors, Bela Lugosi and Christopher Lee, owe their fame to having been cast as the bloodsucking nobleman), comic strip versions both serious and frivolous, film spoofs such as the 1965 western take-off *Billy the Kid Meets Dracula* (an experience shared by Abbott and Costello in their 1948 spoof) and the "blaxploitation" *Blacula* (1972), the cult teen-television series *Buffy the Vampire Slayer,* even cartoon parodies like the popular kiddie-hour "Duckula." S.'s original tale of the terrible creature that preys on the blood of the living and can be repelled by crucifixes and garlic is at once absurd and powerful. It is told in the form of diaries, letters, and press reports, beginning with the Count's being visited in his castle by a London lawyer whom he consults on the possibility of buying property in England, where, we are gradually made aware, he hopes to spread the poison of his curse. This opening section is by far the most effective. The scene where Dracula is observed from a high window crawling face downward, cloak spread like a huge bat, down the wall of his castle is particularly striking, and the incident of Harker, the lawyer, threatened by moonlight by Dracula's three beautiful female vampire slaves, carries a strong erotic undertone. There are effective later passages, such as Dracula's midnight landing in the form of a wolf on the Yorkshire coast, having driven to suicide the entire crew of a Russian vessel, and the account of his control over a zoophagous madhouse inmate, but in general the English scenes do not compare in power with those set in Transylvania.

BIBLIOGRAPHY: Belford, B., *B. S.* (1996); Carter, M. L., ed., *Dracula: The Vampire and the Critics* (1988); Leatherdale, C., *Dracula: The Novel and the Legend* (1985; rev. ed., 1993); Skal, D. J., *Hollywood Gothic* (1990)

MICHAEL GROSVENOR MYER

STOPPARD, Tom

b. 3 July 1937, Zlín (later Gottwaldov), Czechoslovakia (now Czech Republic)

There is a strong case for naming S. as Britain's outstanding playwright at the turn of the 20th c. With his broad range of subject matter and theatrical flair, he seems set to eclipse the more predictable Harold PINTER. His new plays are eagerly awaited, his old ones are revived around the world, and the best of his canon studied in the schools along with William SHAKESPEARE. Even the Comédie Française relaxed its restriction on foreign plays to produce *Arcadia* in 1998. S.'s stated aim is to wed ideas to farce. Though sometimes classed as a writer for intellectuals because of his focus on ideas, he delights audiences with his dazzling wit, surprising juxtaposition, and stage pyrotechnics. Rocketed to fame by the critic Ronald Bryden's discovery of his clever play *Rozencrantz and Guildenstern Are Dead* (perf. 1966; pub. 1967) at the Edinburgh Festival and its subsequent production in 1967 at London's National Theatre, S. has gone on to create such memorable stage plays as *The Real Inspector Hound* (perf. 1968; pub. 1969), *Jumpers* (1972), *Travesties* (perf. 1974; pub. 1975), *Night and Day* (1978), *The Real Thing* (1982), *Hapgood* (1988),

Arcadia (1993), and *The Invention of Love* (1997). Aside from a number of other plays for the stage, including adaptations of foreign plays by Arthur Schnitzler, Johann Nestroy, Federico García Lorca, and Ferenc Molnár, he has written plays for radio and television, provided film scripts for books such as J. G. BALLARD's *Empire of the Sun* (1987) and Graham GREENE's *The Human Factor* (1980), and coauthored the enormously popular film *Shakespeare in Love* (1999).

Born Tomas Straussler, S. rejects the suggestion that his cerebral plays and precise use of English, sometimes attributed, as in Joseph CONRAD's case, to the educated foreigner, derive from his Continental origin. He regards English as his first language. He was only two when his Jewish family left Czechoslovakia for Singapore in 1939 to escape the Nazis. His father failed to survive the subsequent Japanese invasion of Singapore, but his mother took refuge in India where her two sons were schooled in English. In 1946, his mother married the British army officer, Ken Stoppard, who soon afterward settled his family in Yorkshire. At seventeen, S. became a journalist in Bristol, a city famed for its theater. Productions of Samuel BECKETT's *Waiting for Godot*, John OSBORNE's *Look Back in Anger*, and Pinter's *The Birthday Party* fired his desire to write plays. Yet he expected to make his reputation with his only novel, *Lord Malquist and Mr. Moon* (1966), a bizarre black comedy of ideas, published in the week *Rosencrantz and Guildenstern* opened in Edinburgh. Both works reflect a post-Empire malaise in which man is no longer an initiator of events but an observer. Style becomes paramount, and S. like his Wildean Lord Malquist excels in style.

His first play written in 1960 and televised in 1963, *A Walk on the Water*—later revised as *Enter a Free Man* (1968)—shows S.'s fascination with the odd, marginal character in his creation of the self-deluded George Riley whose grandiose ideas and vulnerability bear a remarkable resemblance to Arthur Miller's Willy Loman in *Death of a Salesman* (1949). Similarly, his fine radio play *Albert's Bridge* (1969) features another dreamer, the university student who devotes himself to painting Clifton Bay Bridge because it gives him perspective, a metaphor for his illusory escape from society.

In *Rosencrantz and Guildenstern*, his best-known play and popularized by S.'s rewrite of it in 1990 for an award-winning film, he appears to take Beckett's existential stance by featuring two courtiers who upon obeying the call to come to Elsinore are doomed, swept along by mysterious forces, implicit in the tossed coin continually coming up heads at the play's opening. S., however, denies having had any knowledge of existentialism or of entertaining any such philosophical outlook himself, though he would admit that such a negative worldview pragmatically serves the ends of his play. What intrigued him about Beckett's *Waiting for Godot,* to which *Rosencrantz and Guildenstern* is so often compared, were the humorous word games, antics, and witty qualifications that Estragon and Vladimir employ to stave off fear and boredom in their fruitless wait. Such witty exercises also serve Elsinore's two visitors well as they battle to maintain their identities in the vortex of Hamlet's world.

Always ready to incorporate another's work to give his plays a starting point or structure, S. makes use of the stock whodunit in *The Real Inspector Hound* (1968), a parody of thrillers like Agatha CHRISTIE's *The Mousetrap* but with the twist of engaging two theater critics in the audience in the action, S. delights in springing such surprises or "ambushes" as he calls them. The whodunit also provides a structure for what he terms his theist play, *Jumpers.* For all its hijinks—a striptease artist on a high wire, a dotty professor trying to prove the existence of God with his pet tortoise and hare for props, a fan-obsessed inspector covering up for the prime murder suspect, Dotty, a musical comedy star—*Jumpers* is an attack on the positivist philosophers, personified by charismatic Archie, the vice-chancellor of the University and his team of acrobats who have spawned an amoral and destructive relativism that cleverly undermines any defender of principles or absolutes. The witty, action-packed spectacle creates enthralling theater, but lost in the farce are the theist arguments of George, the lovable but bumbling moral philosopher who has not the wit to console nerve-shattered Dotty, his wife.

Travesties, another dazzling work, has as its underlying theme the primacy of art. Arguments rage pro and con leading some to think that S. delighted in unresolved debates, but as he maintains, his plays reveal a viewpoint. The play germinated from S.'s discovery that Tristan Tzara, the Dadaist, Lenin, and James JOYCE were all in Zurich in 1917, and that a minor official in the British Consulate, Henry Carr, had sued Joyce for the price of his trousers worn in the writer's production of Oscar WILDE's *The Importance of Being Earnest.* By having the story emerge from the memory of the near senile and garrulous Carr and paralleling the characters with those in Wilde's comedy, S. brilliantly provides a structure for a play full of pronouncements on art, war, and the social economy. Joyce with his limericks seems a lightweight figure, but he gains authority in his guise of Lady Bracknell and reminder to the nihilist Tzara of the immortality of Homer and revelation that he is writing *Ulysses.*

Freedom of expression has always been a passion with S., but the press thought he had suddenly turned political when he wrote two plays about the persecution of dissidents behind the Iron Curtain. *Every Good Boy Deserves Favour* (perf. 1977; pub. 1978), prompted by an invitation from André Previn to write a play incorporating an orchestra, took form after his meeting with Victor Fainberg who had been locked up in a Russian psychiatric prison for his beliefs. In his award-winning television drama on human rights, *Professional Foul* (televised 1977; pub. 1978), S. cleverly plays upon the "fouls" that Anderson, a Cambridge philosophy professor, not only encounters but commits in Communist Prague where he has ostensibly come to read a paper at an academic conference but actually to see a prize football match. Determined to be nonpolitical, Anderson is jolted into a defense of freedom of expression by the secret police's brutal treatment of his former Czech student, Hollar, and the plight of Hollar's little son Sacha. S., the father of four sons, endows little boys appearing in his plays with both innocence and a sense of justice.

S. draws upon his career as a journalist in *The Real Inspector Hound* when he portrays Moon as a second-string theater critic as he himself was for *Scene* magazine in 1962–63. Journalism becomes his subject in *Night and Day*, an uneven play. Set in an African state embroiled in tribal war (though the British and Russians ironically back opposite sides in the name of democracy and communism respectively), it depicts the perils facing journalists and attacks the unions for endangering the freedom of the press by blacking out news—sentiments that branded him as a conservative by left-wing critics, an outlook to which he readily admits.

A professed romantic, S. shows his heart in *The Real Thing*, believed by some critics to be his best play. Henry, a witty playwright like S., is passionate about language: "I don't think writers are sacred, but words are." He is also unconditionally devoted to his actress wife, Annie, despite her affairs. While the audiences warmed to the championship of language and love in *The Real Thing*, they were mainly baffled by his espionage thriller *Hapgood*, in which S. portrays the role of the double agent and the duality of man himself in terms of quantum physics theory. The infinitely more successful *Arcadia*, arguably his best play, places the action in the schoolroom of the Croom family's Derbyshire country house, interweaving the time scheme of 1809 and 1812 with that of the present day as it ranges over subjects as diverse as scientific discoveries, literature, landscape gardening, horticulture, academic rivalry, and even hermits. Again a detective story, much of the hilarity derives from our awareness of what actually happened in the earlier period and the speculations of both the publicity hungry academic Bernard who is sure that Byron has committed a murder on the scene and of the tough professional Hannah who is researching hermits. Central to the narrative is the relationship between the young tutor Septimus and his precocious teenage pupil Thomasina whose discovery of the second law of thermodynamics presages the tragic happenings and contributes to the elegiac strain underlying the play's verbal fireworks and circus entertainment.

An elegiac mood permeates *The Invention of Love*, a portrait of the textual classics scholar and poet A. E. HOUSMAN who never recovered from his unrequited love for his friend and fellow student, Moses Jackson. Incorporated into this amazingly rich play in which S. juxtaposes the Oxford undergraduate Housman and the recently deceased Housman, are a satiric tableau of Victorian Oxford, a championship of knowledge for its own sake, a reverence for the Latin Augustan poets, a potted history of the legislation making homosexuality a criminal act and Wilde's subsequent ruin. The flamboyant Wilde, Housman's foil, seems to have the last word when he tells the classicist in Hades that only his poetry, *The Shropshire Lad*, will live and that love is an invention in the mind of the beholder. Yet Housman who had engaged our sympathies remains the hero of the play.

S.'s greatest but diminishing fault is his desire to entertain at all cost, and hence the spangle, the pun, the joke, the surprise that can distract from the idea that engendered the play. Faultless in this respect is the radio play *In the Native State* (1991), a gem and far superior to the expanded stage version *Indian Ink* (1995). Britain meets India in the play but unlike E. M. FORSTER's Adela who creates havoc in *A Passage to India*, the poet Flora Crewe, notorious for flouting conventions in 1930, confers upon Nirad Das, her deferential Indian, a freedom from his subservience to all things British, including his style of painting. Just how emancipated he became is evident in his portrait of Flora that turns up in contemporary England after her death.

The future presages well for S. as he keeps a tighter rein on his irrepressible wit and allows his humanity to shine through his plays of ideas.

BIBLIOGRAPHY: Billington, M., *S., the Playwright* (1987); Bloom, H., ed., *T. S.* (1986); Delaney, P., ed., *T. S. in Conversation* (1994); Delaney, P., *T. S.: The Moral Vision of the Major Plays* (1990); Jenkins, A., ed., *Critical Essays on T. S.* (1990); Kelly, K. E., *T. S. and the Craft of Comedy* (1991)

TAMIE WATTERS

STOREY, David
b. 13 July 1933, Wakefield, Yorkshire

Unusually, S. has achieved equal distinction as a novelist, his books including *This Sporting Life* (1960) and the Booker Prize–winning *Saville* (1976), and as a dramatist, particularly noted for a series of plays written for the Royal Court Theatre in the late 1960s and early 1970s. His work draws repeatedly on his own experiences to explore the relationship between individual and society in late-20th-c. Britain.

The son of a miner, S. derives many of his themes from the tension between his provincial, working-class roots and the metropolitan, artistic existence his grammar school education facilitated. He supported his London studies in art by playing professional rugby in Leeds, a dual existence that inspired his first published novel, *This Sporting Life*. Its protagonist, Arthur Machin, is a sportsman whose aspirations to personal fulfillment are frustrated by the desensitizing society that pays his wages. Containing echoes of D. H. LAWRENCE's *Sons and Lovers*, and often regarded alongside Alan SILLITOE's *Saturday Night and Sunday Morning* and Keith WATERHOUSE's *Billy Liar* as the literary fruit of postwar education reform, the novel established S.'s reputation. Adapted for film in 1963, *This Sporting Life* also inaugurated a longstanding collaboration with the director Lindsay Anderson, who would later direct many of S.'s plays. Its successor, *Flight into Camden* (1961), follows Margaret, a young woman who flees family constraints for what she hopes will be a freer life with her unmarried lover, while in *Radcliffe* (1963), the conflict is between the innocent, eponymous aristocrat and the antithetical Tolsen. This conflict culminates in a violent confrontation said to have inspired Joe ORTON's murder.

S.'s first theatrical success occurred during a hiatus in his novel-writing career as he wrestled with an ambitious work boasting six main characters. This project, which S. hoped would result in the definitive British postwar novel, remains uncompleted but ongoing at the time of writing. By contrast, one of the most remarkable features of his plays is the speed with which they are written, few occupying more than a week of their author's time. The first, *The Restoration of Arnold Middleton* (perf. 1966; pub. 1967), was based on his experiences as a teacher and introduced two recurrent themes: sexual desire for one's mother-in-law and (in this case consequent) mental breakdown. A succession of plays followed, the first, *In Celebration* (1969), showing three sons returning for their parents' wedding anniversary only to be drawn into the conflicts of class and education explored in S.'s early novels. *Home* (1970) starred John Gielgud and Ralph Richardson in its first production as two amiable old gentlemen whose abode, it gradually becomes apparent, is a mental institution.

Many of S.'s best plays dramatize the experience of work. *The Contractor* (perf. 1969; pub. 1970) shows the erection and dismantling of a marquee; *The Changing Room* (perf. 1971; pub. 1972) the behind-the-scenes activity before, during, and after a rugby match; while *The Farm* (1973) was based on firsthand experience of agrarian labor. *Life Class* (perf. 1974; pub. 1975) drew on S.'s student days, attracting considerable attention by placing a nude model on the stage and exploring that contemporary artistic phenomenon, the "happening." The considerable theatrical impact of these plays lies in their physical transformation of the acting space, and in S.'s unfailing ear for naturalistic dialogue. Among S.'s other plays of the period are the poetic, historical drama *Cromwell* (1973); *Sisters* (perf. 1978; pub. 1980), in which both a glamorous and a domestic sibling have a secret; and *Early Days* (1980), which shows an eminent politician's slippage into senility. *The March on Russia* (1989) was thematically a sequel to *In Celebration* of twenty years earlier and, like other later dramas *Stages* (1992) and *Caring* (1992), concerns tensions and negotiated roles within the family. Revivals in the 1990s of *Home*, *The Changing Room*, *The Contractor*, and *In Celebration* have confirmed S.'s status as one of Britain's most significant postwar playwrights.

The novels *Pasmore* (1972) and *A Temporary Life* (1974) were based on fragments of S.'s ongoing opus, but it was *Saville* that won the Booker Prize. Here, S. traces the life of its titular hero, torn between the expectations of his family and his yearning for self-realization, from birth to eventual flight. S.'s continual revisiting and reworking of his autobiographical themes, the importance he accords even minor events, the precision of his observation and his measured, mesmeric prose all reflect a determination to gain an understanding of life at the deepest level. *A Prodigal Child* (1983) and the political *Present Times* (1984) sustained his fictional output in the 1980s, while *A Serious Man* (1998) won renewed praise for its portrait of Richard Fenchurch, an elderly, divorced writer with a history of mental illness who was previously the protagonist of *Stages*. In seeming acceptance of his decline, Fenchurch gives in to his protective daughter and returns to the North, only to return southward once more at the novel's curiously life-affirming conclusion. Still very much a working writer, S. extended his portfolio with *Storey's Lives* (1992), a substantial volume of sinuous, riddling poetry, and a further novel, *As It Happened* (2002).

BIBLIOGRAPHY: Hutchings, W., *The Plays of D. S.* (1988); Hutchings, W., ed., *D. S.* (1992); Leibman, H., *The Dramatic Art of D. S.* (1996); Taylor, J. R., *D. S.* (1974)

HARRY DERBYSHIRE

STOW, John
b. 1525, London; d. 6 April 1605, London

S., the Elizabethan chronicler and antiquary, appears to have been of humble origins. His father and grandfather were tallow chandlers, but S. himself was apprenticed to a tailor and was admitted to the freedom of the Merchant Taylors' Company in 1547. Nothing is known of his education, and he may have been largely self-taught. He was an avid collector of old manuscripts, charters, and legal documents, and an inveterate borrower of books in his quest for historical knowledge. He made notes from the works he borrowed, sometimes even making complete copies of the books. His predeliction for such materials aroused the suspicions of the authorities, and in 1569 S. was investigated for supposedly favoring the papacy and for possessing "olde phantasticall popishe bokes." Though he was subsequently cleared of these charges by the ecclesiastical commissioners, his love of books was his ruin in a more literal sense, in that his income could barely sustain his passion for collecting. He had various patrons, including Archbishop Matthew Parker and Robert Dudley, Earl of Leicester, and a pension from the Merchant Taylors' Company, but nevertheless he was sometimes reduced to begging.

S.'s interests initially lay in the field of English poetry, and his earliest editorial endeavor may have been an edition of John LYDGATE's *Serpent of Division*. He is more certainly credited with the production of *The Workes of Geoffrey Chaucer* (1561), and his further notes on Geoffrey CHAUCER were published by Thomas Speght in 1598. As S.'s interests matured, they became more historically focused, which is reflected in later publications such as his editions of the works of Matthew Paris (1571), Thomas Walsingham (1574), and the second edition of Raphael HOLINSHED's *Chronicles* (1587).

S.'s own works were also of a more historical nature. In 1565, he published *A Summarie of Englyshe Chronicles*, an annalistic compilation that was frequently reprinted, as was the abridged version of the text that appeared in the following year. S. followed this with *The Chronicles of England* (1580), an uncritical encyclopedia of English history from Brutus down to his own time. A second edition of the work, this time entitled *The Annales of England*, appeared in 1592, and other editions followed in 1601 and 1605. Despite the work's historical format, S. frequently added his own opinions and remarks, and he continued to bring its text up to date until the end of his life. His most famous work, *A Survey of London*, was first published in 1598. This masterpiece of topographical literature again consisted of a mixture of historical fact and personal observation. S. based his work on the evidence of documents he had collected himself, and on his perusal of manuscripts belonging to the city, to which, as a "fee'd chronicler" of the corporation, he was granted access. The vivid picture that he paints of his contemporary London arises in no small part from his own account of the city's physical geography, and the work's retrospective focus is sharpened by the inclusion of the remembrances of old men of S.'s acquaintance. Perhaps unsurprisingly given this heady mix of historical documentation, personal bias, and oral history, *A Survey of London* rapidly became

the foremost authority on the history of the city, with a second edition appearing in 1603, and revised editions continued to be produced in the century after S.'s death.

BIBLIOGRAPHY: Beer, B. L., *Tudor England Observed: The World of J. S.* (1998); Hudson, A., "J. S. (1525?–1605)," in Ruggiers, P. G., ed., *Editing Chaucer: The Great Tradition* (1984): 53–70; Kingsford, C. L., *Chronicles of London* (1905)

MARGARET CONNOLLY

STRACHEY, [Giles] Lytton

b. 1 March 1880, London: d. 21 January 1932, Paris, France

In many important respects the leader of the BLOOMSBURY GROUP, a set of artists and writers who, in the early years of the 20th c., rebelled against the complacency and hypocrisy of the previous generation, S. made his reputation by writing biographies, especially *Eminent Victorians* (1918), a study of four Victorian personalities. S. employed an adept psychological understanding of his subject, a relatively new approach to the writing of BIOGRAPHY.

Educated largely at home by a French governess in his early years, in 1893 S. had a brief but disastrous stay at a school in Derbyshire, where the strenuous work load proved too much for the sickly child, then at Leamington where other boys bullied and ridiculed their tall, emaciated fellow, nicknaming him Scraggs. Later, he attended Liverpool University College, where his misery continued, until finally he entered Trinity College, Cambridge, in 1899. There he found relative peace and happiness in the company of the Cambridge Apostles, many of whom would later become members of Bloomsbury. Thoby Stephen, Virginia [WOOLF] and Vanessa Stephen [BELL], Clive Bell, Leonard WOOLF, G. E. Moore, and John Maynard KEYNES were among those he met while he was at Cambridge, where he finished in 1903.

During his lifetime, S. had several love affairs, with both men and women, including a brief and disastrous one with Virginia Woolf, to whom he proposed marriage. She accepted, but he quickly withdrew the offer, to the relief of them both. His primary sexual interest was in men, and his homosexuality became notorious. During his public trial for conscientious objector status during World War I, he was asked what he would do if he came upon a German soldier raping his sister; his response, "I should try to come between them," aroused an outburst of laughter from the audience who knew of his proclivities.

In 1912, S. published his impressionistic *Landmarks in French Literature*. It includes controversial opinions on Baudelaire, Marivaux, Chénier, Hugo, La Fontaine, Voltaire, Montesquieu, Racine, but omits consideration of Nerval, Mallarmé, and Zola. While this volume sold relatively well, it did not make him rich or famous, and failed to overcome the British reluctance to accept things French. Still, its critical success marked an auspicious start to his career

By 1915, S. had begun working on the portraits that would eventually become *Eminent Victorians* (1918). In this work, comprising four short biographies (of Thomas Arnold, General Gordon, Cardinal Manning, and Florence Nightingale), S. found his characteristic voice, mocking and somewhat irresponsible, disguising its acid critique within seemingly laudatory statements, as in the Cardinal Manning portrait, where he refers to the High Church as "a whole universe of spiritual beings brought into communion with the Eternal by means of wafers." S.'s basic method in this work is to provide a general overview of the lives of his subjects based largely on his own psychological insight into their personalities. The style maintains an aloofness that is set off by the work's total lack of documentation. This procedure allowed S. to employ his adroit ironies without cluttering the prose with evidence and footnotes. Despite these problems, *Eminent Victorians* was immensely successful, its sardonic unmasking of Victorian pretension exactly matching the taste of the post–World War I English reading public.

From about 1921 until the end of his life, S. lived off and on with the painter Dora Carrington, with whom he carried on a kind of platonic love affair, all the while indulging in less platonic relationships with men, including Ralph Partridge, Carrington's husband. Despite these irregularities, Carrington and S. remained devoted to one another. She felt that in S. she had a friend in whom she could always confide without fear of betrayal. On his deathbed, S. said, "If this is death, I don't think much of it." Shortly after his death, Carrington committed suicide.

Even with the success of *Eminent Victorians*, S. began almost immediately working on his next book, *Queen Victoria* (1921), a much more responsible if less memorable book. Readers might have expected another acidulous portrait, but instead S. was relatively careful and scholarly, documenting his claims with footnotes. The portrait of the queen contains HUMOR, but almost totally lacks the malice of the earlier book. Much to the relief of many of his friends (and his mother), and to the disappointment of others, S. treats the queen with respect and even admiration. The closing paragraphs of the work show a kind of loving nostalgia for the reign of Victoria that might astonish a reader of *Eminent Victorians*.

S.'s next and last major work, *Elizabeth and Essex: A Tragic History* (1928), combines the solid scholarship of *Queen Victoria* with the risky psychological insights of *Eminent Victorians*. The most overtly Freudian of S.'s books, his work on ELIZA-BETH I traces her adult conduct to the fact that when she was less than three years old, "her father cut off her mother's head." S. does not shy away from theorizing about what he called the "neurotic condition" of the Virgin Queen's "warped" sexual "postponement." Some critics found his approach disgusting. But at least one important reader approved. Freud himself, whose English translator was S.'s brother, James, and who had read all of S.'s books, especially admired this one, stating in a letter that he felt that S. may have come very close to correctly reconstructing Elizabeth's sexual condition.

S.'s other important works include a collection of critical and biographical essays entitled *Books and Characters: French and English* (1922), a book-length essay on Alexander POPE (1925), and *Portraits in Miniature and Other Essays* (1931).

BIBLIOGRAPHY: Edmonds, M., *L. S.* (1981); Ferns, J., *L. S.* (1988); Holroyd, M., *L. S.* (2 vols., 1967–68; rev. ed., 1994); Sanders, C. R., *L. S.* (1957)

PAUL H. SCHMIDT

STRODE, William

b. ca. 1601, Plympton, Devon; d. 11 March 1645, Oxford

The poems of S. have not received the attention they deserve. S. published no collection during his lifetime and no attempt was made to gather his poems together until 1907. Even now, no satisfactory edition has been published. His contemporaries thought highly of S. Individual poems by him were very popular, as consultation of the manuscript catalogues of the Bodleian Library, Oxford, or the British Library, or browsing through the pages of printed poetical miscellanies of the period, will readily show. Indeed, one of S.'s lyrics, "On Chloris Walking in the Snow," was one of the most popular poems of the century, if we are to trust the evidence of how often it was copied and printed in the verse miscellanies. The poem is a remarkable piece, beautiful in its responsiveness to textures of skin and material, subtle in its use of word-play and aural echo, an intricate (but seemingly simple) fusion of fancy and observation. "On Chloris Walking in the Snow" is perhaps more perfectly realized than all but a few other poems by S., who can sometimes allow a few loosely thought-out lines to mar a fine poem, but it is by no means his only success.

As with other poets of the period, whose work circulated in manuscript, there are problems of attribution involved in any attempt to form a clear idea of S.'s achievement. Among those poems that can be attributed to him with some assurance, there are poems of real quality. His lines "In Commendation of Musick" are a convincing and attractive restatement of Renaissance ideas on music, an affirmation, by statement and enactment, of the proposition that "our souls consist of harmony." The poem's metrical subtlety, most notably in its counterpoint of long and short lines and S.'s characteristic attentiveness (rather akin to Robert HERRICK's) to the exactness of sensations (music's "fallings" are said to be "like snow on wool") make it a minor masterpiece. Very different is the robustness of poems such as the "Chimney-Sweeper's Song" and "A Devonshire Song" where one is reminded, rather, of the ability of poets such as Richard CORBETT and Sir John SUCKLING to capture the idioms and rhythms of popular song in an altogether persuasive fashion.

In topographical pieces such as "On Westwell Down" and "On a Great Hollow Tree," a direct response to the scene is articulated in terms both witty and learned, which yet retain some distinctly colloquial energy of phrase and rhythm. The best of S.'s elegies on friends and dignitaries (mostly of Oxford, where S. made his career) are more rewarding. His poem "On the Death of Mistress Mary Prideaux" displays a convincing tenderness and S. manages to retain the quasi-monumental dignity required of such tributes while also investing his lines with an appropriate degree of personal involvement. At other times, he composed the kind of black-humored, jesting epitaph for which he and his contemporaries had a taste, as in "Epitaph on Mr. Bridgeman." His wit is clear in lighter pieces such as his epigram "On a Butcher Marrying a Tanner's Daughter" and the pointed verses of "A Parallel between Bowling and Preferment." S.'s religious verses are relatively few in number and generally rather disappointing (especially so in the light of the accomplishment evident in his few surviving sermons), though his lines "Of Death & Resurrection" (clearly related to Henry KING's "Sic Vita") have a certain power. His translation of "The Nightingale" from Famiano Strada's *Prolusiones Academicae* (1617) will certainly bear comparison with Richard CRASHAW's more famous version ("Music's Duel").

S.'s solitary dramatic work, *The Floating Island*, was performed before Charles I and his court at Oxford on August 29, 1636, with music by Henry LAWES. Described on its title page as a tragicomedy, it is, in truth, a political allegory making clear reference to a number of contemporary phenomena and individuals. Its island kingdom is ruled by Prudentius, with his councillor Intellectus Agens. They seek to control and direct the excessive and destructive passions of their subjects; these passions seek, in turn, to depose Prudentius. He abdicates, on the advice of Intellectus Agens, and the passions install Fancy as their new queen. She promises to let all do as they wish and in her government to "use as little wisdom

as I can." Soon their quarrels and dissension lead them to "Tumult, Lust, Debate, and Discontent" and they are more than happy to invite Prudentius back to reestablish order, which is represented in a tableau of balancing emotions and we are told that "after the musick ended, the Island appear[ed] Setled." Prudentius and Intellectus Agens are clearly idealized images of Charles I and William Laud (who probably paid the costs of the production), while the disruptive passions represent those opposed to their policies, either as direct attacks on individuals (Melancholico, "a Malcontent turn'd Puritan" clearly represents William Prynne) or as generic types. There is some witty writing, some sharp satire, some ponderous flattery and some moments of tedium.

BIBLIOGRAPHY: Dobell, B., ed., *The Poetical Works of W. S.* (1907); Morris, H., "The Poetry of W. S.," *TSE* 7 (1957): 17–28; Pursglove, G., "W. S.'s 'Faire Chloris' and her Metamorphoses," in Coelsch-Foisner, S., et al., eds., *Trends in English and American Studies* (1996): 111–28

                                          GLYN PURSGLOVE

SUCKLING, [Sir] John
b. February 1609, Twickenham; d. ca. 1641, Paris, France

"Natural, easy Suckling," commented William CONGREVE's Millamant, aptly summarizing S.'s style, as her observation "filthy verses" described much of the content of his poems. Cavalier in res and modo, S. disdained the platonic love posturing of the court of King Charles I and Queen Henrietta Maria and the Petrarchan tradition of love poetry. "She's fair, she's wondrous fair,/But I care not who know it," begins a seemingly conventional lyric. But S.'s next line undercuts the conventional lover's pose: "Ere I'll die for love, I'll fairly forgo it." In S.'s one play produced during his lifetime, *Aglaura* (1638), the anti-Platonic Orsames sings to the platonic ladies Semanthe and Orithie a warning that men will ignore them if they refuse to behave like flesh and blood women. "Upon my Lady Carliles walking in Hampton-Court" is a dialogue between T. C. (Thomas CAREW) and S. Carew initially poses as a Platonic lover, but by the poem's end S. has forced him to confess his libertinage. In Van Dyck's portrait, S. holds a copy of William SHAKESPEARE's plays open to *Hamlet*, suggesting that S. hoped to make his reputation as a dramatist. S.'s three plays, popular in the Restoration, contain some delightful dialogue; but their plots are bewildering. S.'s talent lay in the short poem, of which he is one of the 17th-c masters.

                                          JOSEPH ROSENBLUM

SURREY, Henry Howard, Earl of

b. 1517?, Norfolk, East Anglia; d. 19 January 1547, London

Since his execution, two extraordinary sides of S.'s public life have competed for biographical dominance. On one hand, S. was a Tudor humanist and a spirited and accomplished soldier. By all accounts, S. courted tension and drama because of his tart tongue and fierce political will. On the other hand, S. was a translator of Latin and an innovative poet responsible for popularizing the Shakespearean rhyme scheme in the sonnet form as well as inventing the "short meter" and blank verse, reasons for which Thomas WARTON called S. "the first English classical poet." Despite his poetic accomplishments, his public reputation for pride and his periodic rejection of political diplomacy routinely led to many arrests for fighting. Finally, he was indicted for treason and was beheaded just nine days short of HENRY VIII's own death.

S.'s public life began and ended in Henry VIII's reign. As the son of an English war hero who was the king's uncle, S. was brought to Windsor Castle in 1530 as a companion to Henry's first son. S.'s entrance into royal court life afforded him a rich Renaissance education and wide travel. Because S. lived the life of a nobleman, his family life was marked by political strife. In 1536, his cousin Queen Anne Boleyn was beheaded on charges of incest and adultery, and his other first cousin, Catherine Howard, was executed by Henry VIII in the winter of 1542. In the face of these casualties, S. managed some notable political triumphs: he was knighted in 1541; he was appointed Marshal of the Field in 1543 and returned from France to be the king's aide-de-camp in 1545. At twenty-eight, he achieved the rank of "Lt. General of the king." S.'s powerful public presence amassed some equally powerful rivals and enemies, like the formidable Edward Seymour, the Duke of Somerset. S. was arrested at least four times, and his final arrest on charges of treason led to his imprisonment and execution. Though his combative political life is the material of high drama, his poetic life is composed of high art.

The ingeniousness of S.'s poetic achievements is measured by his bold experiments in a variety of metrical patterns. When S. began his literary career, the social movement of Renaissance humanism was in full growth, and the sonnet emerged as a firm part of England's poetic tradition ever since Geoffrey CHAUCER introduced the Petrarchan sonnet to an English language audience with his own imitations. Although S. was not the first to use the "Shakespearean" rhyme scheme (three quatrains followed by a couplet), his consistent use of and success with this poetic arrangement helped this pattern become the Elizabethan standard. Some scholars note that S.'s invention of blank verse is remarkable for its lack of poetic antecedents and for its lack of clear poetic inspiration. However, when S. traveled to France with Henry VIII, he may have met Luigi Alamanni, the Florentine poet who wrote some poems in unrhymed verse. Though we have no definitive evidence of what sparked his invention of blank verse, this poetic novelty first appeared in English in his translation of books 2 and 4 of Virgil's *Aeneid* (1554).

Overall, S.'s poems speak of love, chivalry, and nature, combining classical allusions with personal experience. His "amatory poems" are frequently composed in short verse but do not shun longer or more elaborate constructions. His ethical and elegiac poems are fewer in number, but he regularly shifted from short verse to sonnets. In varying the form of his poems, S. achieved a rich assortment of poetic structures. He wrote at least three touching elegies for Sir Thomas WYATT. His first elegy, "Wyatt resteth here, that quick could never rest" (1542), spoke of Wyatt's greatness at the expense of his enemies. Although S. was not the first to write a poetic elegy, his efforts further strengthened the Tudor genre of encomiums that praised the accomplishments and virtues of particular noblemen. His highly rhetorical method of writing represents the compatibility with classicism and an emerging English tradition. S.'s poems exude elaborate detail, copious ornamentation, and graceful cadence, all of which reveal S.'s success in compressing a variety of thought into his short verses. For this accomplishment, S. shows exceptional poetic ability. His experiments with poetic convention were bold and unique. The psychological tenor necessary to take such principled poetic risks may have come from the same boldness of attitude with which he approached his political life. The assertiveness of his poetic experiments not only reveals a heightened sensitivity toward language—and a willingness to explore its varied effects—but also illustrates his willingness to explore philosophy, logic, and rhetoric through poetic language, all within the ten short years he had as a professional poet.

BIBLIOGRAPHY: Padelford, F. M., ed., *The Poems of H. H. S.* (1920; rev. ed., 1928); Sessions, W. A., *H. H., the Poet Earl of Surrey* (1999)

DAVID CHRISTOPHER RYAN

SUTRO, Alfred

b. 7 August 1863, London; d. 11 September 1933, Witley, Surrey

As a playwright who wrote over forty plays between 1895 and 1933, S. was a past-master in that style of drama called "the well-made play." He overlapped with and imitated (even, in some cases, improved upon) Arthur Wing PINERO and Henry Arthur JONES.

All three were hugely popular in the London/New York of their day and all three were overtaken and superseded by the sudden innovative vigor of the new British theater of Bernard SHAW, John Millington SYNGE, Harley GRANVILLE BARKER, John MASEFIELD, and John GALSWORTHY, among others. It is noticeable that, by one of those quirks of popularity for which there is no accounting, standard works of literary reference such as the *Oxford Companion to English Literature* and the *Cambridge Guide to Literature in English* have a paragraph or two on Jones and Pinero but nothing on S. Even the *Oxford Companion to the Theatre* takes the same approach: Jones and Pinero in; S. out. But they are really three peas from the same pod.

There is a credible argument to be made that none of them should find a place in a work of literary reference since what they all wrote was not, the argument would say, literature: there can, however, surely be no logical argument in favor of including two of them and leaving out the third. This point gains added potency from the fact that S. has one arrow to his quiver that Jones and Pinero have not: he was responsible, along with William ARCHER, for publishing the first three plays by Maurice Maeterlinck to appear in English translation, thus introducing to English readers and playgoers the plays of one of the most important Continental playwrights of that time. Archer, in fact, led the field with his translation of *Interior* in 1894; S. followed close behind with *The Death of Tintagiles* (1896), *Algavaine and Selysette* (1897), and *Alladine and Palomides* (1899). He added one more in 1911: a play called *Monna Vanna* (perf. 1911). There were, of course, many more Maeterlinck translations to follow in the next thirty years but no more of them are by S. Indeed, the list of those making first translations into English of various Maeterlinck plays is a very interesting one, including Alexander Teixeira de Mattos, who did four; Bernard Miall, who did two; F. M. Atkinson, who did two; and Lawrence Alma-Tadema who translated *Pelleas and Melisande*. But S. can legitimately claim to be among the very first in the field. He also translated three of Maeterlinck's nondramatic works—*The Treasure of the Humble* (1897), *Wisdom and Destiny* (1898), and *The Life of the Bee* (1901).

From 1902 to 1923, first productions of S. plays in London averaged more than one per year (1907 had three—one at the St. James's, one at His Majesty's, and one at the Comedy—and, for good measure, the first production of *A Lonely Life* at the Queen's Theatre, Manchester). It goes without saying that not all of these were very good or very important: who, for instance, ever heard a word of commendation for *Mr. Steinmann's Corner* (pub. 1902; perf. 1907) or *The Romantic Barber* (perf. 1908)? But for the major pieces—*The Walls of Jericho* (perf. 1904; pub. 1906), *Mollentrave on Women* (1905), *The Fascinating Mr.*

Vanderveldt (perf. 1906; pub. 1907), *The Builder of Bridges* (perf. 1908; pub. 1909), *John Glayde's Honour* (perf. 1907; pub. 1908), for example—there was commendation aplenty, at least when the plays first appeared and for a few years thereafter. Among the shrewdest of contemporary commentators on his work was Max BEERBOHM, who was the theater critic for *Saturday Review* from 1898 to 1910 (he succeeded Shaw in that position). Reviewing *Making a Gentleman* in 1909, Beerbohm said: "Mr. Sutro is a highly successful dramatist. But against the ease with which he pleases the public must be set the difficulty he finds in pleasing the critics." But in one respect he dissents from what he regards as the general critical view: "*Making a Gentleman* is possibly not a classic. I daresay posterity will be able to get on quite well without it. But I take it to be, for us, in the autumn of 1909 a very good piece of work. . . . Though evidently his prime aim is to please the public, his play is far more convincing, gives us a far better illusion of reality, than Sir Arthur Pinero's laborious and wholly successful attempt to make us feel ill."

Beerbohm's reference here is to Pinero's play, *Mid-Channel*, which also received its first production in 1909. In his review of the S. play, Beerbohm refers to the Pinero play as "Mid-Gutter" (it is a rather sordid piece about the break-up of a marriage). A little further on in the review Beerbohm again makes comparison of the two dramatists. "One of the several reasons why Sir Arthur [Pinero] fails as a 'photographer' is that he seems to have so little notion of what people say and how they say it. One of Mr. Sutro's chief assets is the keenness of his ear for human speech . . . From first to last, his characters talk as charmingly as concisely. It is a pity that Mr. Sutro, the most literary of our playwrights, does not publish his plays." Beerbohm had made this point at least once before: in May 1906, reviewing *The Fascinating Mr. Vanderveldt*, he had said: "But Mr. Sutro's grace in writing, like his HUMOR, is a thing that comes directly from his inner self. He is, since Oscar WILDE, the most literary of our playwrights—has, more than any other, a fine sense of words and a delicate ear for cadences." Rereading the best of S.'s plays now, almost a hundred years later, one feels that Beerbohm's judgment was sound: S.'s style, at its best, still possesses both charm and vitality.

This stylish vitality and charm of language, however, does not give S.'s plays real originality and profundity. His choice of subject always follows the pattern and stays within the narrow limits of the observed tastes of the time and his plays, therefore, are almost exclusively concerned with the personal peccadilloes and dilemmas of the higher professional and lower aristocratic classes. If anyone lower down the social scale than head gardener manages to sneak into the cast list, you can bet your coronet that they are there either as a joke (if male) or as a temptress (if female). There was an absolute fixation on the topic of adultery, which was treated either as a titillating comic turn or as the world's favorite sin. In the latter case, the matter was always treated solemnly, but never seriously. S. was no worse than Pinero or Jones in this regard; and no better: but, on occasion, he was a bit more clever and a lot more graceful.

He went on writing to within a few months of his death but the plays, from about 1920 onward, became less sprightly and less frequent and more lamentably out of date. The theater, like so much of that overheated, overexcited world to which he had once belonged and over which he had so often momentarily triumphed, had moved on, leaving him behind with scarcely a nod of recognition. He, on the other hand, bade it goodbye in courteously generous terms in a book of memoirs entitled *Celebrities and Simple Souls*, published a few days after his death in 1933.

BIBLIOGRAPHY: Beerbohm, M., *Last Theatres* (1970); Matlaw, M., *Modern World Drama* (1972); Trewin, J. C., *The Theatre since 1900* (1951)

                                                    ERIC SALMON

SWIFT, Graham [Colin]
b. 4 May 1949, London

S., a short story writer and novelist, has won several prestigious awards, including the Booker Prize for *Last Orders* (1996), the Geoffrey Faber Memorial Prize for *Shuttlecock* (1981), and the French Prix du Meilleur Livre Etranger for *Out of This World* (1988). His best-known novel is *Waterland* (1983), shortlisted for the Booker Prize and made into a film in 1992. S. studied at Dulwich College, York University, and Queen's College, Oxford, taking a degree in English literature.

From his first novel, *Shuttlecock,* and stories, *Learning to Swim* (1982), to his *Last Orders* in 1996, S. has dramatized the convergence and divergence of personal and public history, memory and truth, storytelling and history. Along with other writers during the last quarter of the 20th c., S. interrogates and disrupts the "Master Narratives of history" (his phrase from *Waterland*) and so participates in the philosophical currents of contemporary literature. While his fictions are generally first-person narratives, they explore the possibilities of multiple voices and multiple understandings of single events. Individual characters seek to understand their own past and the past of others by creating stories. These characters or voices are generally flawed, often narrating what Leon Higdon sees as confessional stories. As readers, however, we empathize and sympathize with them. Even the central character of *Shuttlecock,* whose sadistic treatment

of animals, children, and his wife appalls, wins some empathy. S.'s own sense of character appears to have changed: the characters of the early short stories are more desperate and despairing and ultimately less attractive than the characters of the later novels.

The voices of the novels, or the narrative forms of the novels, change as well. In *Shuttlecock*, the narrator quotes at some length from his father's memoirs creating a double voice. In *Out of This World*, the two voices are more clearly distinct; the double narration of a father and his daughter counterpoint each other as the father attempts to resolve his relationship to his father and the daughter engages in much the same activity with her psychologist. Tom Crick, the narrator of *Waterland*, regales us and—at times—his classroom with his personal history, the history of eels, the history of the French Revolution, the history of his family, and ultimately the history of history. That is, the voices stem from the same character put in varying rhetorical situations. In *Ever After* (1992), S. weaves together the protagonist's life and that of a 19th-c. surveyor/geologist whose life is shattered by Darwinism. And in *Last Orders*, he creates multiple voices to tell the story of a moving (physically as well as emotionally) wake through the memories and experiences of four narrators. Thus, we can recognize S. as an experimental novelist, interested in exploring the formal possibilities of fiction.

At the same time, S. focuses first on story, what he called in an interview "the heart of the matter"; for him "the meaning is the story." His stories are often of families or individuals dealing with loss and grief, seeking to explain loss by telling stories. In *Waterland*, he aligns that urge with history; history begins when "things go wrong," when we need an explanation. At the center of these experimental fictions lies a quite traditional but not sentimental emotion, love. S. does not appear as detached from or sardonic about his characters as do many contemporary writers: these are characters or stories that elicit fellow-feeling as characters attempt to repair or understand what went wrong in their lives or their relationships.

BIBLIOGRAPHY: Bernard, C., "An Interview of G. S.," *ConL* 38 (Summer 1997): 217–31; Higdon, D. L., "'Unconfessed Confessions': The Narrators of G. S. and Julian Barnes," in Acheson, J., ed., *The British Novel since 1960* (1990): 174–91; Janik, D. I., "History and the 'Here and Now,'" *TCL* 35, 1 (1989): 74–88

                                    MARGUERITE HARKNESS

SWIFT, Jonathan
b. 30 November 1667, Dublin, Ireland; d. 19 October 1745, Dublin, Ireland

Such is the enduring power of S.'s SATIRE that "Swiftian" has entered the English language to distinguish a vein of savage, uncompromising, and powerful moral satire. Admired as the voice of liberty by Alexander POPE, Percy Bysshe SHELLEY, W. B. YEATS, and Ted HUGHES, aspects of his complex and disturbing art continue to capture the imagination. However, frequently his views are identified with causes that his habitual irony questions and where his surprising shifts of judgment dangerously undermine the reader's own preconceptions.

Born in Dublin of Anglo-Irish parentage, S. hoped to succeed in the political world of London but was destined to pursue the duties of an Anglican clergyman in Ireland. For a short period (1710–14), during the reign of Queen Anne, he was an influential political writer in the ministry of Edward Harley, Lord Oxford. But Harley, like Sir William Temple, S.'s previous patron, found it useful to keep him hungry for preferment. While it would have been possible for S. to have combined a clerical position in England with his political work, the collapse of the Tory cause at the accession of George I (1714) removed him from London and from his close English friends to live in Dublin, where he had been made Dean of St. Patrick's Cathedral (1713). He fought for improvement in the conditions of Ireland, downtrodden as a "depending" kingdom by the English Parliament. He often spoke bitterly of this enforced absence as "exile" and "prison" but detested the corruption and license in England so much that when, late in life, the possibility of a living in England was offered he refused, feeling more secure in Dublin as the celebrated "Hibernian patriot." While he rejected this title, he delighted in the recognition of him by the poor among whom he walked as a "freeman among slaves," but at the same time it rankled that he no longer had easy access to persons with political power.

His religious views inform his satire. They were formed in the 17th c., in the aftermath of Puritan excesses of the Cromwellian wars and in the middle of the Roman Catholic plots to gain ascendancy in the restored monarchies of the Stuarts. They emphasize the fallen nature of man and the limitations of reason and accept the mysteries of a revealed religion: "neither did our Saviour think it necessary to explain the nature of God, because, as I suppose, it would be impossible, without bestowing on us other faculties than we possess at present" (*Advice to a Young Clergyman*, 1720). Such religion expresses itself in obedience to Anglican doctrine and the exercise of charitable acts. S.'s particular opinion was that there was more of a threat to this established church from Nonconformists and free-thinking deists than from Roman Catholics. This was a highly political view, directly putting him in opposition to powerful interest groups in the English government.

The political writings of S. argue a case derived from the philosopher John LOCKE: that government is a social contract between people of property and may, as in the English Revolution of 1688, be renegotiated, if necessary by force, when the rulers fail in their obligations. This is shown in his arguments in favor of a peace with France. In his opinion, the wars of 1702–14 no longer served the public good but merely continued to enrich the Duke of Marlborough, commander of the allied forces. Heading the publicity machine of Harley (who was one of the earliest politicians to harness the power of the press), S. wrote a number of brilliant essays in the *Examiner*, culminating in a pamphlet that went into six editions and sold eleven thousand copies: *The Conduct of the Allies* (1711). It stated that this was "a war of the *general* and the *ministry* and not the *prince* or *people*," serving the interests of "that set of people who are called the *monied men*."

Pamphleteering personalized political issues. In *The Conduct of the Allies,* Marlborough is the focus of attention. He is seen filling important positions with family and friends and complaining about "British ingratitude" when the nation awarded him £540,000. S. contrasts this with the cost of a Roman emperor's triumph at £994. Later writings, notably *The Drapier's Letters* (1724), owe much of their vigor to the same simplifying technique of concrete example. An Irish tailor and cloth merchant (S.'s assumed persona) speaks up for his trade and the common people against a profiteering dealer in minting substandard coins for Ireland, James Wood (understood by the readers to stand for an exploitative English Parliament). S.'s personal engagement in the conflict was fearless and even foolhardy in the context of an English-dominated court's powers of summary judgment and imprisonment for sedition. Only his high personal standing and the support of Carteret, Lord Lieutenant of Ireland, saved him from prison but that added spice to the public interest in the contest.

The use of personae to stand for actual figures of politics and religion carries over to the fictive works of S., which were and are eagerly decoded for their hidden implications. *A Tale of a Tub* (1704) is replete with the voices of different narrators, representing the babble of modern pundits and the incipient madness of the press: it includes a bookseller, a fawning dedicator, and the teller of the tale who may also be the pamphleteer who interrupts the tale with digressions, because he is "a most devoted servant of all *modern* forms." The tale itself that manages to get told between these excursive fancies is an allegory of the Christian church, represented by three brothers: Jack (Anglican), Martin (non-conformist), Peter (Roman Catholic) whose misinterpretation of their father's will parodies the different forms of biblical interpretation. The work astonishes with the fertility of its invention: the allegorical aptness, metaphysical wit, metaphoric life, and colloquial energy. S. maintained that he wished to dampen the controversies of religious faction. Nevertheless, the work was also condemned for indecencies and an appearance of tilting at all religion and probably hindered S.'s advancement within the church in England.

Gulliver's Travels (2 vols., 1726), his most famous work, has but one narrator, the sea-going surgeon, Gulliver, but as he is right or wrong to varying degrees, the reader is once again compelled to discriminate and examine the basis of judgments. It has a direct appeal in making actual and attractive the imagined worlds of four voyages: Lilliput, the land of pygmies; Brobdingnag, the land of giants; Laputa, Balnibarbi, Luggnag, Glubbdubdrib, the archipelago of astronomers, mathematicians, impractical scientists, sorcerers, and immortal decrepits; the country of the Houyhnhmns, inhabited by reasoning horses and savage humans (Yahoos). These voyages decode into shifting allegories of political life and the human condition. The range includes church and government, war, colonialism, science, and philosophy. It sums up a lifetime's experience of S.'s observation of the British and Irish world. And it occasionally refers directly to his own part in it. For instance, when Gulliver, a giant in the land of the tiny Lilliputians, urinates to put out the palace fire and is reviled for his indecency, a parallel may be drawn with S.'s publishing *A Tale of a Tub.* Its tone modulates through wit and farce to caustic invective, with a dark undercurrent of the filth and baseness of the world and the fearsomeness of physical decay. His representation of humans (sometimes more specifically the Irish) as the bestial Yahoos has been much debated as showing his misanthropy, promotion of the values of reason or religious self-abasement. He wrote to his friend Thomas Sheridan "Expect no more from man than such an animal is capable of, and you will everyday find my description of Yahoos more resembling. You should think and deal with every man as a villain, without calling him so, or flying from, or valuing him less."

A Modest Proposal (1729) consummately maintains the reasoned voice of a promoter of social improvement who would ameliorate the poverty and hunger in Ireland by the most economic and expedient of means: selling the babies of the poor as food at the markets. The official tone enables S. to quantify and demonstrate the degradation of Ireland, while the pose of a shared "humane" concern entraps the reader as a supposed collaborator in the wicked enterprise.

A considerable volume of verse was written by S. throughout his life, often in an easy and colloquial tetrameter with neat rhyming couplets. Against this he would play knowing half rhymes, intentional metrical stumbles, and dazzling puns. His early verse achieved a polished urbanity in which the specific activities of city life were described in a mock pastoral mode (*A Description of the Morning,* 1709; *A Description of a City Shower,* 1710) and imitations of classical writers drew much of their charm from departures from and consonances with the original and subsequent renderings in translation (e.g., *Baucis and Philemon,* 1709). His more satiric verse ranged from vigorous vituperation (*The Author upon Himself,* 1714) to silky mockery posing as compliment (*On Poetry: A Rhapsody,* 1733). As though exorcizing the fear of death, many of his poems handle the subject in jocular fashion (*Death and Daphne,* 1730; *Verses on the Death of Dr. Swift,* 1731). His fascination in some poems with the scatological, usually satirizing an exquisite fop who cannot bear the idea of excretion, has been variously interpreted in the same manner as his representation of the Yahoos (see above), which has prompted a feminist controversy as to whether this releases the women presented from a male idealizing and belittling sex symbolism or is a vehicle for the author's misogyny. Many of his poems are examples of what he called "raillery," humorous sallies at the expense of the recipients, intended ultimately to compliment them. Language games abound and S. has a keen ear for the dialogue of ordinary people. Much of this appealed to James JOYCE and has been typified as a specially Irish trait. This liveliness and telling observation of life may also be found in his appealing correspondence and the record of his London years in *The Journal to Stella* (wr. 1710–13; pub., 2 vols., 1948).

Given the ferocity of personalized politics, it is not surprising that the reputation of S. suffered in the 18th c. from unsubstantiated accounts of a mean niggardliness with beggars, a deserved madness visited on him in his old age, and a secret marriage whose conditions helped to hasten the death of his beloved Stella (Esther Johnson). S. was in fact thrifty and very charitable, although severe in his morality. His deafness, caused by the early affliction of Ménière's disease, increased with age and combined with the onset of senility to withdraw him from the public. No evidence exists of the marriage and much attests to the mutual esteem of the pair. However, considerable currency was given to the adverse account by Samuel JOHNSON who believed the falsehoods communicated to him by a friend, the Earl of Orrery, and who, it is probable, tried to distance himself, being perturbed by the possibility of identifying himself in much of what S. was and stood for.

BIBLIOGRAPHY: Crook, K., *A Preface to S.* (1998); Downie, J. A., *J. S., Political Writer* (1984); Ehrenpreis, I., *S.* (3 vols., 1962–83); Nokes, D., *J. S., a Hypocrite Reversed* (1985); Rawson, C., *Order from Confusion Sprung* (1985)

KEITH CROOK

SWINBURNE, A[lgernon] C[harles]

b. 5 April 1837, London; d. 10 April 1909, Putney Hill

S. had trouble with critics from the start. He failed to get a publisher for his first book, *Poems and Ballads*, until he tried the plan of writing something else for first publication, and letting the *Poems and Ballads* ride its wake. The strategy worked. *Atalanta in Calydon* (1865), a stately tragedy in the Sophoclean manner, followed soon after in that same year by *Chastelard*, the first of a trilogy of plays on Mary Stuart, won immediate acclaim both from critics and general readers, after which S. was able to publish his *Poems and Ballads* (1866). This work had been refused because of its base subject matter, which publishers feared would shock the reading public. As it turned out, they were right; critics and general readers alike decried the poems as immoral. Few denied, however, that S. was a master of prosody; seldom had the language been worked to an author's purpose with such grace and ease.

In the 20th c., sweeping changes in the world order had such effect on taste and moral codes that S.'s position changed as well. Now, what had been too shocking became acceptable as subject matter for poetry; however, the reading public had lost its taste for formal poems, for measured lines and perfect rhymes such as S. had produced with such facility. Again, critics were hard on S., damning him by faint praise and even sometimes caricature. He has been the target of a distaste that is partly repugnance and partly disdain; the result is that most readers now know him only as the author of a few much-anthologized lines spoken by the chorus in *Atalanta in Calydon*. But S. deserves better.

It is true that the shock to morality in *Poems and Ballads* is more than a shock to proper Victorian manners; many readers even today will find the sadomasochism distasteful at best. One of S.'s most notable poems, for example, is "Anactoria," a dramatic monologue in which Sappho speaks to the object of her desire. Few readers will not flinch as the speaker yearns to inflict a lingering agony of torture and death on the beloved; such delectation of suffering puts one off. Moreover, it is obvious that the delectation is S.'s, not Sappho's; there is nothing of this nature in her extant poems. S. thus demonstrates early his affinity not only for the decadence of the Pre-Raphaelites, who were his friends, but also for Charles Baudelaire and the Marquis de Sade.

But there is more to S. than this. He was, for example, an ardent libertarian and republican, a great admirer of Walter Savage LANDOR and Victor Hugo (to both of whom he wrote tributes) for their republican views, and of those fighting for self-government everywhere. The story is told by Edmund GOSSE that

when S. went to Italy in 1867, shortly after the publication of *Poems and Ballads*, he met Italian patriot Giuseppe Mazzini, who earnestly advised him to write no more erotica, but to devote his talent to the cause of freedom. *A Song of Italy* (1867) soon appeared, the first of S.'s political poems, which proliferated thereafter.

The most famous of S.'s tragedies, *Atalanta in Calydon*, although it falls short of perfection by its message of despair, demonstrates his mastery of the ancient form of tragedy making. *Atalanta* expresses the themes that connect S. with the deterministic writers of the 19th and 20th cs. It tells the story, from Greek mythology, of Meleager, of whom it was prophesied when he was new-born that he would live only as long as the brand then in the fire was alive; when it burnt out, Meleager would die. His mother Althea, hearing the prophecy, snatched the brand out of the fire to preserve her son; eventually, inevitably, she throws it back in, in revenge for his killing of her brothers. In exquisitely beautiful language, the play expresses inevitability, acceptance, and despair.

S. continued to publish for all of his long life. He wrote essays in criticism, political commentary, plays, narrative poetry, and lyrics, drawing adeptly on mythology both classical and medieval. But the thing which critics have found hard to forgive for the last hundred years or so is the very thing that assures him a place among the great Victorian poets: he is unsurpassed at the uses of the English language. In his hands it is powerful, harmonious, and surprising. Even in his decadent erotica, he never goes for the easy shock of the vulgar word, words being possibly the one thing sacred to S.

BIBLIOGRAPHY: Gosse, E., *S.* (1925); Hyder, C. K., ed., *S.* (1970); McCann, J. J., *S.* (1972); Rooksby, R., and N. Shrimpton, eds., *The Whole Music of Passion: New Essays on S.* (1993)

CECELIA LAMPP LINTON

SWINNERTON, Frank

b. 12 August 1884, London; d. 6 November 1982, Cranleigh, Surrey

One of the most prolific British writers of the 20th c., S. enjoyed a successful literary career that spanned nearly seven decades. He published his first novel, *The Merry Heart*, in 1909, followed in the next year by *The Young Idea*, which earned critical recognition both in England and in the U.S. In 1917, S. published the highly acclaimed *Nocturne* and remained popular as a novelist throughout the 1920s and 1930s. His later fiction focused in part on the social and cultural condition of women, notably *A Tigress in Prothero* (1959), *The Grace Divorce* (1960), and *Quadrille* (1965). He also produced numerous works of nonfiction, including *The Georgian Scene: A Literary Panorama* (1934) and *Authors I Never Met* (1956), as well as critical studies of George GISSING (1912), Robert Louis STEVENSON (1914), and Arnold BENNETT (1950 and 1978).

SYLVESTER, Josuah [or Joshuah]
b. 1562 or 1563, Kent; d. 28 September 1618, Middelburg, Zeeland, The Netherlands

Although S. wrote original poetry and translated other works from French and Latin, his reputation has always been tied to that of Guillaume de Salluste Du Bartas, the French Huguenot poet whose works he translated. While both writers were popular in their lifetime, the French poet long ago fell from favor and S. followed suit. The few studies that exist place him in the context of the French influence on English Renaissance literature and the role of divine poetry in that period. Criticism also focuses on his translation of Du Bartas as an allusive source for Edmund SPENSER, William SHAKESPEARE, Michael DRAYTON, John DONNE, Andrew MARVELL, and Alexander POPE.

S.'s most significant endeavor was his translation of Du Bartas's *La Semaine ou Création du monde* (1578) and its sequel, *La Seconde Semaine* (1584), no small project since the work runs to more than twenty thousand lines. *The First Week,* focusing on the days of Creation, provides a compendium of commonplace beliefs about religion, science, and nature as it draws on the hexameral tradition and the medieval encyclopedia. The unfinished *Second Week* was even more ambitiously designed to present the history of man from the Fall through the end of time. Du Bartas, however, had only completed four days before his death.

S. is generally noted for his accuracy in translation, his early grounding in French standing him in good stead. A formative event of his childhood was his enrollment in the Southampton grammar school of Hadrianus Saravia, a Belgian Protestant divine. The school specialized in French-language instruction, and boys who lapsed into English were punished. S. is even faithful to what are often deemed eccentricities of Du Bartas's style, the compound epithet, for instance. He clearly distinguished his own emendations to the text through italics. At the same time, S. particularized his work for his English audience, replacing French references and place names with English ones. He is much more aggressively Protestant than the relatively tolerant Du Bartas, his translation marked with an anti-Catholic fervor absent from the original.

Although the *Divine Weeks,* because of their volume and scope, represent S.'s most significant achievement, he translated other works by Du Bartas. His first publication was a translation of *Cantique de la Victoire* (1590), a poem celebrating the victory of Henry of Navarre at Ivry. In addition, he translated *The Triumph of Faith* (1592), a dream vision, and the EPIC *La Judit,* based on the Apocrypha story of Judith and Holofernes. Although briefer, *L'Uranie* is crucial work in the S. canon because it provides a clear sense of a shared Du Bartasian/Sylvestrian aesthetic. Dramatizing the conversion and education of its poet-protagonist through the intercession of the muse Urania, the poem articulates beliefs about Christian art and the responsibilities of the artist, beliefs that shaped S.'s choice of subject matter throughout his literary career and were shared by many in S.'s society and echoed by later writers.

While Du Bartas's represents S.'s most prominent and extensive efforts in translation, he also translated writings from both French and Latin that would have pleased the Christian muse, including works by Odet de La Noue, Guy du Faur de Pibrac, Pierre Matthieu, and Girolamo Fracastoro.

In addition to his translations, S. also wrote original poetry: *The Woodsmans Bear* (wr. ca. 1595; pub. 1620), an amatory poem regarded by some as autobiographical; *Monodia* (1594), an elegy for Dame Helen Branch; *Lachrimae Lachrimarum* (1612), an elegy for Prince Henry; and *Tobacco Battered* (1617), an antitobacco, antipapist, anti-Spain poem.

Clothier by trade and poet by avocation, S. was once lauded by a range of greats from Gabriel Harvey to Anne Bradstreet. While his popularity has waned, his transformation of Continental material into English works with even stronger Protestant themes should make him a focal point for those concerned with Protestant poetics in England and the continuation of such tradition in early America.

BIBLIOGRAPHY: Lee, S., *The French Renaissance in England* (1910); Simonsen, V. L., "J. S.'s English Translation of Du Bartas' 'La Premiere Sepmaine,'" *OL* 8 (1950): 259–85; Snyder, S., ed., *The Divine Weeks and Works of Guillaume de Saluste Sieur Du Bartas* (2 vols., 1979)

FRANCES M. MALPEZZI

SYMONDS, John Addington
b. 5 October 1840, Bristol; d. 19 April 1893, Rome, Italy

Among the works of the prolific S. were cultural histories, critical studies, biographies, translations, volumes of poetry, travel essays, polemical writings, and memoirs. In the waning years of the Victorian age, S. was probably as well known as contemporaries Walter PATER, John RUSKIN, William MORRIS, and Oscar WILDE. Nowadays, his name is unfamiliar and his books only occasionally read. When he died, S. was perceived mainly as a cultural historian, the author of the daunting *Renaissance in Italy* (7 vols., 1875–86). Today, he is sometimes called the father of the modern gay memoir and regarded as pioneer in the field of homosexual rights.

Educated at Harrow and Oxford, and profoundly influenced by a dominating father, S. was propelled early toward a literary career. In 1872, he published his first important book, a work of literary criticism on Dante. Based on a series of lectures, *An Introduction to the Study of Dante* foreshadowed S.'s later and larger explorations of Italian culture. Other critical analyses by S. included *Studies of the Greek Poets* (2 vols., 1873–76), *Shakespeare's Predecessors in the English Drama* (1884), *Essays Speculative and Suggestive* (2 vols., 1890), and *In the Key of Blue and Other Prose Essays* (1893). Of these works, the Greek poets volumes are the most noteworthy. They reflect S.'s deep-seated love of Greek ideals of beauty, especially masculine beauty, and freedom, especially sexual freedom.

Within the span of about fifteen years, S. wrote biographies of Percy Bysshe SHELLEY (1878), Ben JONSON (1886), Sir Philip SIDNEY (1886), Michelangelo Buonarroti (2 vols., 1893), Walt Whitman (1893), and Giovanni Boccaccio (1895). The most thoroughly researched, most groundbreaking, and most critically acclaimed of these studies is that on Michelangelo. For this project, S. read virtually all prior studies of the master. He carefully examined Michelangelo's artistic works, viewing them either in person or as photographs. Finally, by gaining permission to peruse hitherto suppressed papers in the Casa Buonarroti in Florence, he became the first biographer to disclose evidence of the artist's homosexual inclinations.

A robust biographical subject, Michelangelo was also among the authors whose works S. translated. *The Sonnets of Michelangelo Buonarroti and Tommaso Campanella* was published in 1878. Though this work was well received, it proved far less popular than either of two other translations: *Wine, Women, and Song: Mediaeval Latin Students' Songs* (1884) and *The Life of Benvenuto Cellini* (1888).

Although S. produced various kinds of literary work, he apparently derived his greatest satisfaction from writing poetry. His published poems, consisting largely of sonnets, appeared in such volumes as *Many Moods* (1878), *New and Old* (1880), *Animi Figura* (1882), and *Vagabunduli Libellus* (1884). Not one of these collections attracted favorable notice. On the contrary, critics found S.'s poetry cerebral, self-conscious, labored, cryptic. Along with the poems he made public, S. also wrote a sizable number of verses that he privately printed in pamphlets and circulated only among friends. Typically, these were homoerotic poems, undisguised celebrations of male love.

The monumental *Renaissance in Italy* is probably S.'s major achievement, even though some readers have complained about its florid style, excessive detail, and wayward design. Some things remain unarguable. S. consciously aimed at an ambitious cultural history. He enthusiastically depicted the Italian Renaissance as the fountainhead of modern humanism, the source of liberating learning, art, and scientific inquiry. Wherever possible, he concentrated on vital figures who embodied the spirit of the age. The subtitles of the individual volumes convey a sense of the scope of this massive work: vol. 1: *The Age of the Despots*; vol. 2: *The Revival of Learning*; vol. 3: *The Fine Arts*; vols. 4 and 5: *Italian Literature*; and vols. 6 and 7: *The Catholic Reaction*.

Critics today view S. mainly as a trailblazer in the history of sexual reform. Accordingly, they focus on his polemical writings and memoirs. In his later years, S. became known as an authority on the history and sociology of homosexuality. He believed strongly that homosexual behavior is inborn and fundamentally natural. In strictly limited editions, he printed two treatises outlining his controversial views: *A Problem in Greek Ethics* (1883) and *A Problem in Modern Ethics* (1891). Parts of these works were eventually included, without acknowledgment, in Havelock ELLIS's *Sexual Inversion*.

S.'s memoirs have an unfortunate history. Begun in 1889, his bold confessions were not published in an unabridged and unexpurgated edition until 1984. Consequently, S.'s self-revelations failed to have the explosive impact they doubtless would have had if issued in his own era. Had his life not been cut short by tuberculosis, he undoubtedly would have authored still other works. As it was, his output was prodigious and remains worthy of study.

BIBLIOGRAPHY: Dale, P. A., "Beyond Humanism: J. A. S. and the Replotting of the Renaissance," *CLIO* 17 (Winter 1988): 109–37; Grosskurth, P., *The Woeful Victorian: A Biography of J. A. S.* (1964); Robinson, P., *Gay Lives: Homosexual Autobiography from J. A. S. to Paul Monette* (1999)

DONALD D. KUMMINGS

SYMONS, A[lphonse] J[ames] A[lbert]
b. 16 August 1900, Battersea, London; d. 26 August 1941, Colchester

Known primarily for his experimental BIOGRAPHY of Frederick William ROLFE (or Baron Corvo) entitled *The Quest for Corvo* (1934), S. was the younger brother of writer Julian SYMONS. Prior to the publication of his biography of Rolfe—a minor writer of the late 19th c. and author of the highly eclectic masterpiece *Hadrian the Seventh*—S. published *Emin, the Governor of Equitoria* (1928), *An Anthology of*

"Nineties" Verse (1928), and his first full-length BIOGRAPHY, *H. M. Stanley* (1933), the story of explorer Sir Henry M. Stanley, who discovered Dr. David Livingstone in Africa. In 1950, Julian Symons published a biography of his brother entitled *A. J. A. Symonds: His Life and Speculations*.

SYMONS, Arthur [William]

b. 28 February 1865, Milford Haven, Wales; d. 22 January 1945, Wittersham, Kent

At the age of seventeen, S. embarked on a literary career that by the late 19th c. established him as one of the most prominent men of letters in Britain. His early interest in Robert BROWNING led to the publication in 1886 of his first book, *An Introduction to the Study of Browning* (rev. ed., 1887), when he was twenty-one, and his first collection of poems appeared in 1889. Influenced by French symbolism and the so-called Decadent movement in literature, S. emerged in the 1890s as a leading proponent of the avant-garde—illustrated in his second volume of poetry, *Silhouettes* (1892; rev. ed., 1896), and most notoriously in *London Nights* (1895; rev. ed., 1897)—and a significant figure in the development of MODERNISM. His most important critical work, *The Symbolist Movement in Literature*, appeared in 1900, and in 1907 he published his highly regarded study on William BLAKE. Shortly afterward, S. suffered a mental breakdown from which he never fully recovered and his later work paled in comparison with his early brilliance.

SYMONS, Julian [Gustave]

b. 30 May 1912, London; d. 19 November 1994, Kent

Poet, novelist, editor, and biographer, S. established his critical reputation in the genre of crime fiction. He published his first crime novel, *The Thirty-First of February*, in 1950, followed by numerous others, including *The Narrowing Circle* (1954), *The Colour of Murder* (1957)—which introduced the character of Magnus Newton, who reappears in *The Progress of a Crime* (1960) and *The End of Solomon Grady* (1964)—and *The Players and the Game* (1972). Later in his career, S. also produced fictional representations of actual crimes, *The Blackheath Poisonings* (1978) and *Sweet Adelaide* (1980). As a biographer, S. produced lives of his brother, the noted writer A. J. A. SYMONS (1950), Charles DICKENS (1951), Thomas CARLYLE (1952), and Arthur Conan DOYLE (1979).

SYNGE, John Millington

b. 16 April 1871, Rathfarnham, Ireland; d. 24 March 1909, Dublin, Ireland

Though born into the Protestant upper class and formally educated at Trinity College in Dublin, S. was drawn to the folk culture of western Ireland. A meeting in 1896 with W. B. YEATS, one of the founders of the dramatic movement that produced all but one of S.'s plays, turned his attention to that culture. He spent several weeks during spring 1898 living on the Aran Islands. The most direct literary product of that experience was a series of articles that became his book, *The Aran Islands* (1907). More importantly, the Aran experience—combined with subsequent summers he spent in nearby County Wicklow—provided S. with themes, settings, and characters for his plays and with the dialect of English he would use to good effect in them. S.'s six plays demonstrate the values of freedom over security and show illusion's role in human happiness.

S. began writing plays in 1902. Though his first two attempts survive only in fragments, his second two plays, *In the Shadow of the Glen* (perf. 1903; pub. 1904) and *Riders to the Sea* (perf. 1904; pub. 1905), were both produced by the Irish National Theatre Society, successor to the Irish Literary Theatre founded by Yeats, Lady GREGORY, and Edward MARTYN in 1899. *Shadow* is a comedy set in Wicklow whose plot comes from a story S. records in *The Aran Islands*. Nora is watching over the body of her recently deceased husband, when a tramp takes shelter from the storm in her cottage. Her conversation with the tramp and with a young neighbor, Michael Dara, reveals her distaste for the man now apparently lying dead and by extension the institution of marriage. The husband's death is a sham, and after hearing Michael propose marriage to Nora—more attracted by her property than her person—the "corpse" rises and drives her out into the night where the tramp offers to care for her. Though the play ends with her exile, Nora emerges triumphant to some degree since she has traded a restrictive existence for natural freedom with the tramp. Moreover, the illusion of her husband's demise provides opportunity for her to voice the frustrations that she has repressed throughout their relationship. The play set a pattern for some of S.'s other plays by drawing hostile responses. Some critics believed it cast a slur on Irish women, who would never chafe under their marriage vows nor accept a life away from their husbands.

Riders to the Sea, regarded by many as one of the finest one-act tragedies in English, differs in tone from its contemporary, but still reflects S.'s immersion in the folk culture of western Ireland. Set in the Aran Islands, the play focuses again on Irish women. Unlike Nora, who seeks liberation from the restrictions of her peasant existence, these women await with resignation news that their husbands and sons have drowned in Galway Bay. They identify one drowning victim by examining a bundle of his clothes, counting stitches in the stockings they had knitted for him. The play climaxes when Maurya, the materfamilias, has a vision that foreshadows her last living son's being swept from horseback by the relentless surf. The play opened in Dublin in 1904 and received more favorable responses than had *In the Shadow of the Glen*. Praised for its conciseness and emotional intensity, *Riders to the Sea* is the most unrelentingly tragic of S.'s plays. Some of its power arises from the fatalism and lack of illusion about the riskiness of existence that pervade the perceptions of Maurya and the other Aran women. There are four operatic versions, including Fritz Hart's (wr. 1915; perf. 1997), which used S.'s words unaltered. Hart also wrote an opera based on S.'s *Deirdre of the Sorrows* (1916).

S.'s third play, *The Tinker's Wedding* (1908)—not produced until 1909 and then only in London—returned him to controversy. The action, which covers two acts, deals with a young tinker woman's desire to marry, despite tinkers' customary disregard for such formalities. She arranges with a priest, who agrees to perform the ceremony for a nominal fee and a tin can made by the tinkers. The play's most controversial scene has the priest bound, gagged, and physically threatened—a scene that would have been impossible to stage for Dublin audiences. Though regarded dismissively by most critics and by S. himself, *The Tinker's Wedding* reiterates the playwright's rejection of the restrictive life of convention for the less constrained, more natural existence represented by the tinkers.

In 1905, the Abbey Theatre presented S.'s first three-act play, *The Well of the Saints*. Though based on a medieval French source, the play is set in western Ireland, where a married couple, both blind, are miraculously healed of their infirmity. They discover, though, that the illusions fostered by their blindness had been essential for their happiness, which can be restored only when they again lose their vision at the play's end. The play was received negatively by critics who believed that the characters were too unappealing to be truly Irish and who disapproved of the colorful language. Martin and Mary, the married couple, though, are similar to most of S.'s other characters who live close to nature away from the artifices of Dublin society, and the language—except for some grandiose figures of speech—follows the patterns that S.'s theatrical colleague Lady Gregory had pioneered.

S.'s themes found their fullest expression in *The Playboy of the Western World*, which generated riots when it opened at the Abbey Theatre in 1907. The most direct causes for protests were the play's alleged immorality and violence: an unmarried couple spend a night together (though innocently), a youth achieves hero status for an alleged act of patricide, and the play's protagonist is physically attacked on stage. Set in County Mayo, *Playboy* derives from a story that S. had heard in the Aran Islands about a young man who

had killed his father and sought mercy from some of his relatives. The play's protagonist Christy Mahon, a shy, inexperienced youth, shows up at the cottage of Pegeen Mike, where he admits that he has killed his father by striking him with a spade. The deed impresses Pegeen and others in the neighborhood, and Christy emerges from his naiveté to become a heroic figure, one who has stood up to paternal authority. When the father shows up with bandaged head, though, Christy's admirers reject him. He strikes the old man again, but those who celebrated the deed when they only heard of it are horrified by the act itself. They turn on Christy, and Pegeen, who had accepted Christy's love just before the elder Mahon appeared, burns his leg with a sod from the fire. Christy's father revives once more with newfound recognition of his son's ability. They leave the stage as Pegeen laments what she has lost in Christy.

The celebration of an antiauthority figure and Christy's growing into mature independence in response to the villagers' illusions about his capabilities reinforce S.'s themes. The play suggests that Christy needs someone to believe in him—even if that belief is based on less than the truth—if he is to achieve full personhood. Contemporary audiences, though, did not perceive the play's values, and it provoked the most violent reaction in the history of Irish theater. The strong language in the play joined its alleged immorality and violence in precipitating protests that required police for the play to be staged.

For his final play, S. turned from the oral traditions he had encountered firsthand in western Ireland to the cycle of heroic legends that had survived in medieval manuscripts. The Ulster legend cycle reports that King Conchubar had reared the beautiful Deirdre from a child to be his queen. Not wanting to be tied to an aged husband and in love with the youthful Naisi, Deirdre had run away to Scotland. But Conchubar's obsession with her results in Naisi's murder. Deirdre takes her own life instead of marrying the old king. S. found familiar themes in this story: the pre-birth prediction that Deirdre's beauty would doom her and those she loved recalled the fatalism that pervaded *Riders to the Sea*; her rejection of restrictive conformity for a freer, but riskier, existence found a forerunner in Nora of *In the Shadow of the Glen;* the hopes that she and Naisi build their ill-fated relationship upon are as illusory as the bases for happiness of many of S.'s earlier characters; and the omnipresence of death overshadows most of S.'s other plays. An additional theme that S. incorporates here concerns the permanence of beauty; Deirdre's death in her prime preserves her for eternity from the ravages of aging. Unlike Yeats, who modeled a Deirdre play on classical patterns, S. cast *Deirdre of the Sorrows* (1910) in the peasant mode that he had utilized throughout his career as playwright. The characters speak the dialect, and some have been added that reflect the mordant HUMOR that infuses all of S.'s plays except *Riders to the Sea.*

S. died in 1909—some ten months before the Abbey Theatre produced *Deirdre of the Sorrows.* The play climaxed a career that combined an earthy REAL-ISM, fostered both by his contact with Irish folk culture and by the influences of such dramatists as Henrik Ibsen, with extravagance and idealism about the possibilities for beauty in contexts where it might not usually be sought and about the human potential for dealing with life's inescapable adversities.

BIBLIOGRAPHY: Gerstenberger, D., *J. M. S.* (1990); Gonzalez, A. G., *Assessing the Achievement of J. M. S.* (1996); Grene, N., *S.* (1975); Kopper, E. A., *A J. M. S. Literary Companion* (1988); McCormack, W. J., *Fool of the Family: A Life of J. M. S.* (2001); Skelton, R., *The Writings of J. M. S.* (1971)

WILLIAM M. CLEMENTS

TATE, Nahum

b. 1652, Dublin, Ireland; d. 12 August 1715, Southwark, London

T. graduated from Trinity College, Dublin, in 1672. He wrote a few original plays and many adaptations from William SHAKESPEARE and the Elizabethan dramatists. In his version of *King Lear* (1681), immensely popular in its day, Cordelia survives and marries Edgar. Among T.'s hymns are "As pants the hart for cooling streams" and the Christmas carol, "While Shepherds Watched," both still sung. He collaborated with John DRYDEN on the second part of *Absalom and Achitophel* and succeeded Thomas SHADWELL as poet laureate in 1692. He also translated from Italian and Hebrew and wrote the libretto for Henry Purcell's opera, *Dido and Aeneas* (1689).

TAYLOR, Elizabeth

b. 3 July 1912, Reading, Berkshire; d. 19 November 1975, Penn, Buckinghamshire

Born Elizabeth Coles, T. had a happy and cherished childhood but became all too aware, as she was reared and attended a "good" girls' school, that her family, originally working class, had become middle class only by a whisker. Hence, the continual preoccupation in all her writing with the vagaries, constraints, and absurdities of the English class system, and with concepts of disguise and loss of sense of self. Betty, as she was called until her marriage, was recognized as outstanding by her teachers, and a more securely middle-class girl would, by 1930, have been destined for university. Later, she would claim that the reason she did not go was because she failed mathematics at matriculation; the far more likely reasons were lack of money and parental reluctance for their daughter to go away outside their orbit. It is likely, however, that a university degree—the long-established prerogative of male novelists, and something that had begun to be taken for granted by women writers such as Rosa-mond LEHMANN and Elizabeth JENKINS—might have resulted in T. writing one or two great novels rather than twelve merely outstanding ones. University life might also have given the literary influences and friendships that she sadly lacked.

In 1930, the year she left school, the family moved to a village near High Wycombe and she became a governess (to Oliver Knox, himself a future writer and a first cousin of the novelist Penelope FITZGERALD), an assistant at Boots Lending Library, and a keen participator in amateur dramatic productions; she also got to know artists and intellectuals, some of whom had gravitated to that part of Buckinghamshire because of the artist Eric Gill, and flirted with communism. In 1936, her mother died unexpectedly, this being probably the most traumatic event of T.'s life and one that destroyed part of her equilibrium forever and gives her novels their bleak undertone. In the same year, she married John Taylor, whose father owned a confectionery factory (which he himself later ran); within several years, she had become a well-off new mother in a newly built cottage that backed against the grounds of her in-laws' factory on the edge of High Wycombe. It is not known whether, at this stage, she had any thoughts of writing fiction, although her essays had been highly praised at school and her gift for language had always been recognized; one or two early poems survive.

With the outbreak of World War II, T. became, like so many young wives, very much isolated, and it was now that she began to write short stories, partly because it was more likely that these would be accepted for publication. The first of these was published in 1943 and her first novel, *At Mrs. Lippincote's*, in 1945, in the same autumn that Noël COWARD's *Brief Encounter* was premiered, as well as the film of *National Velvet* starring the young Anglo-American actress Elizabeth Taylor; the fame of the film star was always a disadvantage to the writer and it is a matter for regret that T. did not rapidly reclaim the name of her birth. But naturally all that mattered to the novelist was the almost universal excellence of the reviews of her novel. Now her life settled into the pattern it was to assume for the next thirty years. She worked at home, sitting in an armchair with a notebook on her knee, making a fair copy to be sent to the typist and destroying the original draft (the fair copies have survived). She cooked lunch for her husband, who came home from the factory every day, and apart from that took the bus into Beaconsfield, the town nearest to the village to which she and her husband had moved at the end of the war, to do the shopping—and change her library book; coincidentally, some of the scenes in *Brief Encounter* were filmed there, and the heroine of the film bears many similarities to the heroines of T.'s novels. Her output of novels became steady, as was, from 1949 onward, her output of short stories for the *New Yorker*; it published her for twenty years, and its rejection of first some and then all of her work from 1967 onward greatly shook her self-esteem.

All T.'s novels center on the themes of class, innocence, betrayal, death, deceit, vanity, the absurdity of life, women's friendships, the inability of people ever truly to communicate with one another, men's oppression and women's passivity; all are written with wit, intelligence, intuition, and perception. She was undoubtedly one of the most talented English novelists of the 20th c., but the milieu she wrote about and the small canvas of her themes hindered her from being recognized as such. Themes relating to her own life can be seen in all her novels: for example *At Mrs. Lippincote's*, which is about a young wife isolated in Scarborough while her husband works at the local airforce base; *A View of the Harbour* (1947) is about a fishing village near Scarborough just after the end of the war; later novels have a more "Home Counties" setting; *Angel* (1957), once picked out as one of twenty "Best Novels of Our Time" but which is, in the view of T. devotees, her least characteristic and unappealing novel, is about a popular novelist eaten up with vanity. The novelists she herself most admired were Jane AUSTEN, E. M. FORSTER, Ivy COMPTON-BURNETT, and Elizabeth BOWEN (both of whom she knew) and of course the short story writers Anton Chekhov and Katherine MANSFIELD. Why her work is not better known is one of the mysteries of literary history.

BIBLIOGRAPHY: Leclercq, F., *E. T.* (1985); Liddell, R., *Elizabeth and Ivy* (1986); Stemmler, K. M., "E. T.," in Baldwin, D., ed., *British Short-Fiction Writers, 1945–1980, DLB* 139 (1994): 234–44

NICOLA BEAUMAN

TAYLOR, Jeremy

bap. 15 August 1613, Cambridge; d. 13 August 1667, Lisburn, Ireland

Son of a barber, T. studied at the Perse School, Cambridge, and went on to Gonville and Caius College, Cambridge, as a sizar. Sizars earned their tuition by working as servants to richer students. He was elected a fellow of his college in 1633 and became chaplain to King Charles I. After the Restoration, he became Bishop of Down and Connor in Ireland and later of Dromore, where he is buried in the cathedral. A devotional writer, whose prose combined simplicity with splendor, he did much to shape the Church of England. T.'s best-known works are *The Rule and Exercises of Holy Living* (1650) and *The Rule and Exercises of Holy Dying* (1651).

TAYLOR, John

b. 24 August 1577 or 1578, Gloucester; bur. 5 December 1653, London

T. went to the local grammar school but finding Latin difficult he was apprenticed to a waterman. He served with the Earl of Essex's fleet and was at the siege of Cadiz. Returned to England, he achieved notoriety by making eccentric journeys and writing about them in verse. One such journey took place in a paper boat with dried fish tied to canes for oars; another was described in *A Very Merry, wherry ferry voyage, or Yorke for my money* (1623). His first publication, *The Sculler, Rowing from Tiber to Thames* (1612), was enlarged as *Taylor's Water-Worke* (1614). Sixty-three of T.'s pieces were published in one volume in 1630 as *All the Workes of John Taylor the Water-Poet*.

TENNANT, [the Honourable] Emma [Christina]

b. 20 October 1937, London

T. is a highly prolific writer and has, to date, published twenty-two novels, three volumes of memoirs, and four children's books, as well as editing the literary journal *Bananas* during the 1970s. Her work is difficult to categorize, drawing on SCIENCE FICTION, Gothic, magic realism, and her own unconventional, aristocratic family background in order to create an alternately satirical and poetic style. A concern with feminist politics is evident throughout her fiction, coloring many of her literary rewrites, which reconfigure canonical texts from a contemporary, female perspective. This has led to her association with literary POSTMODERNISM. Her Scottish childhood is also a strong influence on her work, evidenced in both the Highlands setting of *Wild Nights* (1979), a fictionalized representation of the Tennant household, and in her debt to writers such as James HOGG and Robert Louis STEVENSON.

T.'s first novel, *The Colour of Rain* (1964), a scathing account of British upper-class life, was published under the pseudonym Catherine Aydy. However, her career as a novelist was properly established with the publication of *The Time of the Crack* (1973), a speculative novel that takes as its premise the opening of a giant crack in the river Thames, literalizing London's North/South divide and resulting in anarchic farce. The novel is highly fantastic but also satirical in tone, parodying the revolutionary fervor of regressive psychoanalysts, aggressive capitalists, female separatists, and champagne socialists determined to reach the "other side." Other novels from this period, *The Last of the Country House Murders* (1974) and *Hotel de Dream* (1976), share a speculative approach, and are notable for their dark, often macabre HUMOR as well as their use of fantasy. The former is a parody of British detective fiction of the 1930s, in which a totalitarian government stages the murder of aristocratic aesthete Jules Tanner for the entertainment of tourists, and is T.'s first attempt at engaging with the thriller.

The Bad Sister (1978) marked a new direction, feminizing the hitherto largely masculine genre of doppelganger narratives in its adaptation of Hogg's *Confessions of a Justified Sinner*. With a putatively realistic setting, it introduces fantasy and dream sequences further complicated by the precarious psychological state of its heroine, Jane Wild. Hogg's treatment of the covert relationships "between men" is replaced by an examination of those between women, and the psychological splitting women undergo within patriarchy. T. also adapts Hogg's distinctive structure, with an unreliable "confession" sandwiched between the accounts of an equally unreliable "editor." This "found manuscript" technique is one that she frequently reuses elsewhere in order to introduce layers of irony to her texts. She returned to the doppelganger rewrite with *Two Women of London: The Strange Case of Ms. Jekyll and Mrs. Hyde* (1989), reversing Stevenson's narrative by suggesting that the hideous, slatternly single mother, Mrs. Hyde, can metamorphose into an idealized self-image, successful gallery-owner Eliza Jekyll, by means of an Ecstasy-derived compound. The novel critiques the "new Victorian values" of Thatcherism, and suggestively satirizes fashionable postfeminism by suggesting that the oppressed single mother is its repressed secret self.

Wild Nights and *Alice Fell* (1980) demonstrate a more overtly poetic approach, concerned with mythic archetypes rather than politics, and lacking the humor of her earlier works. In the former, the disruptive visits of the magical Aunt Zita to the child-narrator's Scottish family mansion cause a blurring of fantastic and everyday events strongly reminiscent of magic realism. Along with *Queen of Stones* (1982), these texts create an informal trilogy exploring female childhood. *Queen of Stones* is a female version of William GOLDING's *Lord of the Flies* in which a group of girls cut off by fog during an afternoon walk begin to revert not to more "primitive" forms of behavior but to the historical archetypes of Queen ELIZABETH I and Mary Queen of Scots. The novel in the guise of

a fictional editor satirizes psychoanalytic interpretations. Conscious fantasy is shown to be as important as unconscious desires in determining the tragic ending.

The autobiographical content of *Wild Nights* has been much noted, and was resumed in *The Adventures of Robina* (1986), a fictionalized account of T.'s debutante days narrated as a pastiche of Daniel DEFOE. A broader concern with "roots" informs *Black Marina* (1985), in which the mixed-race teenager Mari's search for her father is set against a political backdrop inspired by the invasion of Grenada in 1983. Although clearly inspired by William SHAKESPEARE's *Pericles*, there are also similarities with Jean RHYS's *Wide Sargasso Sea*. Personal and political are shown to be hopelessly intertwined, the politically motivated murder of a black revolutionary sparking family revelations of madness and incest. *The Magic Drum* (1989) also drew on the thriller format, depicting the death of a Sylvia Plath-like poet, Muriel Cole, and its repercussions on succeeding generations. Other novels from this period include *Woman Beware Woman* (1983), *The House of Hospitalities* (1987), *A Wedding of Cousins* (1988), and *Sisters and Strangers* (1990).

In the 1990s, T. turned from postmodern reworkings of earlier narratives to a series of controversial Jane AUSTEN sequels: *Pemberley* (1993), *An Unequal Marriage* (1994), *Elinor and Marianne* (1995), and *Emma in Love* (1996). Austen fans disliked the introduction of 20th-c. themes like lesbianism, but T. defended her work by asserting it was meticulously researched and drew on established academic discussion. T. ended the decade with publication of her memoirs, currently in three volumes. *Strangers* (1998) is a partly fictionalized account of her wealthy, distinguished, and eccentric family; *Girlitude* (1999) describes her high life in upper-class bohemia during the 1950s and 1960s. *Burnt Diaries* (1999), the volume portraying the 1970s, proved controversial for its depiction of T.'s affair with the recently deceased poet Ted HUGHES.

The diversity of T.'s work has possibly enabled her long career, yet the difficulty of pigeonholing her has also perhaps caused her comparative critical neglect. The sense of enigma—inexplicable events, ambiguous endings, unreliable narrators—that characterizes her writing also plays its part. Often, for want of a better label, termed merely a "woman writer," any comprehensive critical assessment of her work is still to come. A novelist of ideas, her achievement lies both in teasing out the delights and horrors of the family romance, and in bringing a timely feminist perspective to canonical texts.

BIBLIOGRAPHY: Anderson, C., "Listening to the Women Talk," in Wallace, G., and R. Stevenson, eds., *The Scottish Novel since the Seventies* (1993): 170–86; Connor, S., "Rewriting Wrong: On the Ethics of Literary Reversion," in D'haen, T., and H. Bertens, eds., *Liminal Postmodernisms* (1994): 79–97; Wesley, M. C., "E. T.: The Secret Lives of Girls," in Werlock, A. H. P., ed., *British Women Writing Fiction* (2000): 175–90

CATHERINE SPOONER

TENNYSON, Alfred, [Lord]

b. 6 August 1809, Somersby, Lincolnshire; d. 6 October 1892, Surrey

T. is perhaps the last poet to achieve fame, fortune, and social standing solely through the practice of his chosen vocation. He was England's poet laureate for forty-two years, the ethical guide and voice of stability for an age that suffered through the crisis of faith associated with Darwinism, the Oxford movement, and the political turbulence occasioned by a variety of political reform movements that threatened the established cultural and social structures that were the foundations of the Empire. At the height of his popularity, no genteel Victorian household was without a copy of his poetry.

T. began writing poetry when he was five years old. At eight, he was sent to school at Louth, where the harsh methods of the master probably helped to determine his lifelong shyness. Later, he was tutored at home by his father, a dark, brooding man of shifting mood. These early experiences undoubtedly contributed to the development of his own intensely self-conscious and shy personality. In 1827, he and his brother Charles had collaborated in *Poems by Two Brothers.* In 1828, he entered Trinity College, Cambridge, but was not a distinguished student and never took a degree. Cambridge, however, played a formative role in his development as a poet, largely through his association with a group of students who identified themselves as the "Twelve Apostles." The Apostles were particularly appreciative of his poetry, and their recognition and influence perhaps helped him in winning the Chancellor's medal for poetry in 1829. One of the Apostles in particular, Arthur Henry Hallam, became his closest friend, and Hallam's untimely death was the occasion for the writing of the great elegy, *In Memoriam.* In 1830, T. published his first volume of poems, but two years later had the misfortune of an extremely harsh review by John Gibson LOCKHART, an influential critic for the *Quarterly Review.* This crushing disappointment, followed soon after by the death of Hallam, threw him into a deep despair, and he published nothing for ten years. During that time, he worked on perfecting the craft of his poetry, receiving indirectly the therapeutic value of coping with the death of his friend through the writing of *In Memoriam.* The publication in 1842 of his two-volume *Poems* was critically acclaimed and T. won the public respect and affection that he was to retain

for the rest of his life. The year 1850 was a time of great personal triumph, filled with personal happiness and professional success. His public recognition as England's preeminent poet was assured with the publication and popular reception of *In Memoriam,* he married his fiancée, Emily Sellwood, to whom he had been engaged for seventeen years, and, upon the death of William WORDSWORTH, he was appointed poet laureate. T. was assured that the post was largely an honorary one, and that he would not have to spend his time writing "laudatory odes to the sovereign;" but he found great satisfaction in the poems he was called upon to write for special occasions, from his "Ode on the Death of the Duke of Wellington" (1852) published on the day of the hero of Waterloo's funeral, to the decidedly jingoistic "Charge of the Light Brigade" (1854). Neither is an example of his finest work, although Robert Louis STEVENSON thought the Wellington ode the finest lyrical poem in the language. Generations of school children, both in England and the U.S., were required to commit to memory and taught to recognize "The Charge of the Light Brigade" not as a classic example of military bungling, but as an admirable testament to unquestioning courage and patriotic duty.

T.'s critical reputation suffered somewhat during the 1920s and 1930s, when there was a generally negative reaction among critics to all things Victorian. He was found to be overly concerned with propriety, excessively sentimental, and given to shallow optimism. Subsequent analysis and evaluation of his work, however, has restored his reputation, and he is today recognized for many qualities, particularly his extraordinary skill with sound and rhythm, and his ability to evoke a dreamlike setting, qualities which combine effectively in poems such as "The Lotos-Eaters," "Ulysses," and "Tithonus" (1842). His ultimate reputation as a great poet rests largely on his masterpiece, *In Memoriam,* and the series of psychologically realistic narratives that inform the poems that make up his *Idylls of the King,* which he began publishing in 1859 and continued to publish until 1885.

In Memoriam is T.'s spiritual AUTOBIOGRAPHY, the recounting of the spiritual struggle initiated with the death of his friend. The central question for the poet was how, in a world ruled by a loving and just God, such a man as Hallam could be cut off at the very beginning of his usefulness. Although T. wrote the poem for himself, it is clear that the problem with which he contends is one which must be faced by all who lose a loved one. In the course of the poem T. faces every crisis of faith that would be evident to the typically Victorian mind, and the ultimate triumph of faith proved an effective and inspirational lesson in an age of anxiety. In the course of his career, T. made no single contribution as original as earlier poets of the

19th c. such as Wordsworth, Samuel Taylor COLE-
RIDGE, Lord BYRON, Percy Bysshe SHELLEY, or John
KEATS, but he had a vastly wider range than any of
them. In a sense he sums up all English poetry, and
in at least one form, the lyric, he is unsurpassed.

BIBLIOGRAPHY: Buckley, J. H., *T.* (1960); Hair, D. S.,
T.'s Language (1991); Priestley, F. E. L., *Language
and Structure in T.'s Poetry* (1973); Sinfield, A., *A. T.*
(1986)

                                    RICHARD KEENAN

TERSON, Peter
(pseud. of Peter Patterson) b. 24 February 1932, Newcastle-upon-Tyne

T.'s first play, *A Night to Make the Angels Weep*
(1967), was performed in 1964. Together with *The
Mighty Reservoy* (perf. 1964), it demonstrated an
original voice and a flair for amusing dialogue, NATU-
RALISM with symbolic weight. *Mooney and His Caravans* was seen on television in 1966 before being
staged in 1968. T. worked in close association with
the Victoria Theatre, Stoke-on-Trent. In 1967, T.'s
Zigger-Zagger (1970), a large-cast work about football (soccer) fans and hooligans, was commissioned
and performed by the National Youth Theatre in London. Other plays are *The Apprentices* (perf. 1968;
pub. 1970), *Rattling the Railings* (perf. 1978; pub.
1979), *The 1861 Whitby Lifeboat Disaster* (perf.
1979), *Spring-Heeled Jack* (1970), *Good Lads at
Heart* (perf. 1971), about young men in a corrective
institution, *The Pied Piper* (perf. 1980; pub. 1982),
Aesop's Fables (perf. 1983; pub. 1986), *Strippers*
(perf. 1984; pub. 1985), and *The Offcuts Voyage*
(1988).

TEY, Josephine. See MACKINTOSH, Elizabeth

THACKERAY, William Makepeace
b. 18 July 1811, Calcutta, India; d. 24 December
1863, London

A major British novelist best known for *Vanity Fair*
(1847–48), first serialized in nineteen monthly parts,
and *The History* of *Henry Esmond, Esq.* (3 vols.,
1852), T. was a contemporary of Charles DICKENS at
a time when the novel was a major social and political
force in Britain. T.'s influence on the writing of Walter
PATER and Anthony TROLLOPE has been widely recognized. The affinity between *Vanity Fair* and American
novelist Margaret Mitchell's *Gone with the Wind*
(1936) is also readily apparent: Amelia Sedley and
Becky Sharp are clearly comparable to Mitchell's
Melanie Hamilton and Scarlett O'Hara.

Although *Vanity Fair* and *Henry Esmond, Esq.*
placed him among the major Victorian novelists, T.
has received neither the critical attention nor the
praise accorded Dickens or George ELIOT. His carefully calculated REALISM at times rivaled that of Dickens, although readers and critics alike have commented on his unaccountable shifts in tone and
frequently bewildering ironies.

Fully cognizant of both the possibilities and pitfalls of the novel, T. embarked upon his writing with
a full sense of the genres of novels he sought to produce. In his early life, having left Cambridge University without a degree and having abandoned the study
of law that he undertook between 1831 and 1833, T.
worked as a journalist. This pursuit enabled him to
gain the fluency he later displayed as the prolific novelist he grew into. Although his journalistic writing
was often published anonymously, T. collected what
he considered his best journalistic pieces and published them in four volumes, entitled *Miscellanies*:
Prose and Verse (1855–57).

T.'s first full-length novel, *The Luck of Barry Lyndon* (1844), was revised and published as *The Memoirs of Barry Lyndon* in 1856. In 1975, *Barry Lyndon*,
fast-moving and successful in its SATIRE, was made
into a successful picaresque film directed by Stanley
Kubrick. *The Book of Snobs* (1848), a collection of
T.'s satirical *Punch* articles, demonstrates his remarkable insights into human nature and his ability to create convincing fictional characters quickly and accurately.

His apprenticeship years in journalism led directly
to the production of T.'s first really mature novel, *Vanity Fair*, which established him as a writer of note. As
was the custom of the day, T. wrote *Vanity Fair* serially over a two-year period. Its segments were published in monthly installments and were consciously
designed, as were most of Dickens's novels, to be
read aloud within families whose members gathered
to read during the long evenings. Serial novelists
quickly developed an ability to pack each segment
with rising action leading to a crucial situation. The
ending of each segment left the reader in a state of
suspense that would be addressed and resolved in the
following installment.

T. set *Vanity Fair* in the second decade of the 19th
c. and consciously sought to write an antiheroic novel,
as the book's subtitle, "A Novel without a Hero,"
clearly implies. In the novel, two dissimilar women,
Amelia Sedley, a passive, refined lady, and Becky
Sharp, a coolly calculating, ambitious, scheming
woman of humble origins, daughter of an impoverished drawing teacher, are sharply juxtaposed to each
other. When Amelia marries, Becky tries to entice
Amelia's husband, George Osborne. George, however, is killed in the battle of Waterloo before he can
fulfill his plan to leave Amelia for Becky. Finally,

974

Rawdon Crawley, Becky's husband, leaves her. Amelia, now widowed, marries Colonel Dobbin, long her devoted admirer. But Dobbin's marriage is a disappointment. It appears, therefore, that goodness triumphs over evil, as is the expectation in proper Victorian novels.

Vanity Fair is considered to be among the greatest novels of its time, notable for its well-drawn characters, its accurate and detailed description, and its clear and direct narrative style. In it, T. emphasizes the incongruities of human nature. Flush from the success of this novel, T. went on to exploit his talent for depicting London society in *The History of Pendennis* (1848–50), an autobiographical serial novel first published in twenty-three monthly parts, in which he consciously set out to create a Bildungsroman, or developmental novel. The protagonist, Arthur Pendennis, is a journalist whose university career and early amatory adventures T. details. Many of his exploits are strikingly similar to those of T. during his university life and his years as a fledgling journalist.

If this novel was, as some 19th-c. critics contended, too loosely structured, T. contrived in his next novel, *Henry Esmond, Esq.*, to create a closely structured and formal plot. Its heroine, Beatrix, is a marvelously complex person whom T. depicts with notable dexterity. As T. painstakingly develops Beatrix's character over a twenty-seven-year period, she emerges as no model of virtue. Henry Esmond, a brave, sensitive soldier of aristocratic background, who has been befriended by Beatrix's parents, Lord and Lady Castlewood, falls in love with her, but finally becomes painfully aware of her limitations. The book shocked Victorian readers because in the end, Henry marries Lady Castlewood, becoming Beatrix's stepfather.

Among T.'s later novels, *The Newcomes* (1853–55), first published in twenty-three monthly parts, depicts upper-middle-class London society with considerable insight, although at times the convoluted plot resembles that of a modern soap opera. *The Virginians* (1857–59), first published in twenty-four monthly parts, set in both America and Britain, considers the lives of two grandsons of Henry Esmond, the brothers George and Henry Warrington. Before he died in 1863, T. produced two more serial novels, *Lovel the Widower* (1860) and *The Adventures of Philip* (3 vols., 1862). He was working on another such novel, *Denis Duval*, published posthumously in 1864, when he died.

T. is remembered for a realism surpassed only by Dickens and for an ability to create convincing, emotionally complex, and consistently memorable characters. His prose is crisp and clear. If his tone is sometimes inconsistent, his ironies occasionally discomfiting, as some critics have suggested, his narra-tive ability is remarkable and his capacity to entrance the audiences of his day is unquestionable.

BIBLIOGRAPHY: Collins, P., ed., *T.: Interviews and Recollections* (1983); Ferris, I., *W. M. T.* (1983); Peters, C., *T.'s Universe* (1987); Ray, G. N., *T.* (2 vols., 1955–58); Stevenson, L., *The Showman of Vanity Fair: The Life of W. M. T.* (1947)

R. BAIRD SHUMAN

THEROUX, Paul [Edward]

b. 10 April 1941, Medford, Massachusetts, U.S.A.

T. was a university lecturer in Uganda with the Peace Corps when he met V. S. NAIPAUL, who introduced T. to his publisher, André Deutsch. T. had already published pieces in African newspapers and magazines, and has now published more than thirty-five books. His first novel, *Waldo,* was published in 1967, but the book that first attracted notice was *The Great Railway Bazaar* (1975) describing a journey across Europe and Russia to Japan; *The Old Patagonian Express* (1979) is about a railway journey down through the Americas. T. admits to being a compulsive traveler. *Riding the Iron Rooster* (1988), which chronicles railway journeys round China, brought T. international fame. He is eminent both as a writer of fiction and as a travel writer, acknowledging as influences Graham GREENE, Bruce CHATWIN, and V. S. PRITCHETT. *Girls at Play* (1969) and *Jungle Lovers* (1971) are about Westerners out of their depth in Africa; *Saint Jack* (1973) deals with a Singapore pimp, and *The Family Arsenal* (1976) is a thriller set in London, where T. has a home to which he returns after wandering the world. His best novel is considered to be *The Mosquito Coast* (1981), set in Honduras, and *O-Zone* (1986) is a futuristic fantasy. *The Consul's File* (1977) and *The London Embassy* (1982) are collections of linked short stories about expatriate communities in Malaya and London reminiscent of Rudyard KIPLING. *Sunrise with Seamonsters: Travels and Discoveries, 1964-1984* appeared in 1985. In 1972, T. published an appreciative introduction to the work of Naipaul, but later quarreled with him and attacked him in print.

THIRKELL, Angela [Margaret]

b. 30 January 1890, Kensington; d. 29 January 1961, Bramley, Surrey

T.'s early life provided excellent experience for the work with which she is most closely identified—a 20th-c. version of Anthony TROLLOPE's Barsetshire and Palliser novels. As her world initially appears, it is secure, comfortable, deeply rooted, and class conscious. Most of her characters are cultivated, and some are learned. With few exceptions, they range in social standing from village gentry to the Duke of Omnium. T. was the granddaughter of Edward Burne-Jones, and her mother was first cousin of Rudyard KIPLING and of Stanley Baldwin. Her father, John William Mackail, held the Chair of Poetry at Oxford before moving to the Ministry of Education.

From 1920 until 1928, T. was removed from this environment. In 1911, she had married John Campbell McInnes, by whom she had three children, two sons and a daughter, who died in infancy. Following her divorce in 1917, she married a Tasmanian, Captain Lancelot Thirkell. In 1920, she moved to Australia where she had a third son, Lancelot George. Unhappy in egalitarian Australia, she honed her literary skills by writing for English and Australian newspapers and magazines, and in 1928 spent a year in England, returning to Australia only to arrange permanent departure from Australia and her husband to her parents' home in Pembroke.

Soon she was writing prolifically and successfully, producing sixteen books between 1931 and 1940. Most of her earlier work was based on personal experience; she first mentioned Barchester in *The Demon in the House* (1934), and from *Summer Half* (1937) on, it became her primary subject. She averaged one Barsetshire novel a year for the rest of her life.

The appeal of these books lies in the cultured tradition, literary allusion, and deft but usually gentle SATIRE. Their plots are slight and usually involve at least one engagement or marriage. In *The Headmistress* (1944), Mr. Oriel discovers that he has an edition of "Flavius Minucius" that he had borrowed forty-one years before from the grandfather of Miss Sparling, elegant headmistress of the Hosiers' Girls' Foundation School. In his embarrassment, he turns his problem over to an Oxford don with the Dickensian name of Sidney Carton. The mutual interest of Mr. Carton and Miss Sparling in Flavius Minucius leads to courtship. In *County Chronicle* (1950), Dr. Crawley, the current Dean of Barchester, is reminded that his grandfather Mr. Crawley, perpetual curate of Hogglestock, once said "Peace, woman," to the voluble and interfering wife of Bishop Proudie (in Trollope's *The Last Chronicle of Barset*).

But for all their playfulness these books are more than escapism. In *Cheerfulness Breaks In* (1940) and *Marling Hall* (1942), for example, one sees the impact of war—financial hardship, necessity of coping with evacuees from London and refugees from the Continent, concern for the fighting men. Willingly, but with distaste, the Barsetshire residents accommodate slum children and Mr. Bissell, socialist headmaster of the Hosiers' Boys' Foundation School. After the war come the shortages of the austerity program and the taxes of the Labour government. The defeat of Labour does not reverse the gentry's declining fortunes. Their financial woes are contrasted with the wealth of newly

rich Sam Adams who employs two thousand men in what was once Mr. Crawley's curacy. He is only an annoyance in *The Headmistress*, but by the time of *County Chronicle* he has become so acclimated that he marries Lucy Marling of Marling Hall.

At the peak of her popularity in the 1940s, T. was an internationally famous best-selling author, asked to speak at Harvard and Yale and invited to the wedding of two of her admirers, Princess Elizabeth and Lieutenant Philip Mountbatten. She was attacked by left-wing critics who disliked her subject matter and her identification with it, and by the 1950s her sales declined somewhat, but today thirty of her titles remain in print. Although she receives little attention from academia, she may come to be recognized as an empathetic observer of the English upper classes in painful transition.

BIBLIOGRAPHY: Fritzer, P., *Ethnicity and Gender in the Barsetshire Novels of A. T.* (1999); McInnes, G., *Humping My Bluey* (1966); Strickland, M., *A. T.* (1977)

DALTON AND MARYJEAN GROSS

THOMAS, D[onald] M[ichael]
b. 27 January 1935, Redruth, Cornwall

Widely known as the author of the highly controversial novel *The White Hotel* (1981), T. has also been critically acclaimed as a prolific poet, translator of Russian writers, biographer, and author of nine other novels. His translations of the poems of Soviet poet Anna Akhmatova won him the Translator's Award of the British Arts Council. He also received the Chomondeley Prize for Poetry in 1978 and a *Guardian*-Gollancz Fantasy Novel Award for *The Flute-Player* in 1979. But it was *The White Hotel* that won him both the Cheltenham Prize and the *Los Angeles Times* Book Award in 1981. That novel was also shortlisted for the Booker Prize in 1981.

It was T.'s training as a Russian translator in the National Service that brought him into contact with the great Russian novelists and poets. His first novel, *The Flute-Player*, took place in Leningrad where the protagonist, Elena, became a victim of totalitarian persecution and where she was raped by those in power. She eventually became the creative muse for her poet-friend, Michael. But it was due to the closure of the college where T. taught for many years that he decided to return to Oxford and earn an additional degree in translation. He also read massively in Sigmund Freud and C. G. Jung. It was his immersion in Freud, however, that became the genesis for *The White Hotel*. One of Freud's case histories tells of a woman named Anna who claimed to be having an affair with Freud's son. T. framed the highly erotic story within the Nazi atrocities at Babi Yar after Anna has been transformed into a famous opera singer. Much of the novel is composed of eroticized fantasy scenes. Many critics were outraged by T.'s use of Holocaust materials, but others praised the imaginative ways in which he combined BIOGRAPHY with case history and actual history. It became a best-seller in England and the U.S.

Because of the financial success of *The White Hotel*, T. was able to explore other genres and began a series of five fantasy novels entitled "Russian Nights." The first two novels, *Ararat* (1983) and *Swallow* (1984), dealt with the theme of improvisation and improvisational competitions, in which storytellers compete for prizes for originality. T. was alternately praised and criticized for these clever studies in intertextuality. The third novel of the series was *Sphinx* (1986), which extends and develops the themes of the two earlier novels. The text becomes even more postmodern as the narrator/writer enters the action to compete with the other writers whom he has created. The work tests the boundaries between fiction and reality. In the fourth and fifth volumes, *Summit* (1987) and *Lying Together* (1990), T. includes thinly veiled but real political figures in both Russia and England. The work traces the role of sex, especially among the wives and daughters of political leaders.

T.'s next novel, *Flying in to Love* (1992), audaciously tests the boundaries between history and fiction in the assassination of President John F. Kennedy; the "Love" of the title alludes to Love Field in Dallas, Texas, where Kennedy arrived on the day of his death. T. creates alternate versions of the events of that day. In some, Kennedy survives the attempt, but in others, he dies and is resurrected. T. hopes in his revisioning the event to make the reader understand what the assassination meant in world politics. It was the publication of *Pictures at an Exhibition* in 1993, though, that caused both the public and the critical community to revive their old charges of transgression and pornography toward T. Once again, T. revisited Holocaust scenes but concentrated on the sexual experimentation that went on at Auschwitz and the spiritual legacy that has remained in spite of the distance of fifty years.

T.'s novel *Eating Pavlova* (1994) portrays a dying Freud whose mind, under the effects of morphine, wanders back to the past where he encounters Charles DARWIN and Isaac Newton but also more recent events such as the trial of Adolf Eichmann and the Vietnam War atrocities. Freud, who does not believe in life after death, realizes that once his daughter Anna dies, he will no longer exist.

T.'s last major work was a critically acclaimed biography of the Russian novelist, Alexander Solzhenitsyn, which St. Martin's Press had asked him to write. He embraced the project because it gave him the opportunity of revisiting the history of the 20th c. in the company of such an important writer.

BIBLIOGRAPHY: Cowart, D., "Being and Seeing, *The White Hotel*," *Novel* 19 (Spring 1986): 216–31; MacInnes, J., "The Case of Anna G.: *The White Hotel* and Acts of Understanding," *Soundings* 77 (Fall-Winter 1994): 253–69

PATRICK MEANOR

THOMAS, Dylan [Marlais]

b. 27 October 1914, Swansea, Wales; d. 9 November 1953, New York City

T. is one of the most written about of 20th-c. poets, author of some celebrated lyrics as well as a notable dramatic piece, *Under Milk Wood* (1954) and an interesting prose work, *Portrait of the Artist as a Young Dog* (1940). However, he also had a reputation as something of a showman, whose poetry places sound effects and verbal patterns above sense. His first published work, *18 Poems* (1934), contained some of the poems on which his reputation is based, including "The Force That through the Green Fuse Drives the Flower." *18 Poems* was published in a modest form rather than by a major publisher (the small volume was sponsored by the *Sunday Referee* newspaper and an independent bookshop). Nevertheless, it came to the notice of some important periodicals, and received reviews that identified T. as having a new poetic voice and much promise. Several also noted a dark, constricted atmosphere and an intricate or tortuous use of language. The *Listener* compared his work with that of John DONNE and the dramatist John WEBSTER. A few reviewers dismissed the poems as nonsensical: "An unconducted tour of bedlam," asserted H. G. Porteus.

"The Force That through the Green Fuse Drives the Flower" is a characteristic poem, both in its themes and technique, and has been seen as representative of T.'s work since its inclusion in the influential *Faber Book of Modern Verse* (1936). As in all T.'s poetry, there are complex and rhetorically impressive patterns of sound, imagery, vocabulary, and syntax. These have an immediate sensuous impact, but also invite the reader to attempts at interpretation. All of T.'s work has inspired detailed explication and commentary, which discovers rich and multiple meanings. T. himself is recorded as already having clear attitudes toward ideas of meaning and interpretation by the early 1930s: "Your meaning is as good as mine," he told a friend who explicated a draft of one of his poems. More aggressively, he wrote in 1934: "I've got to get nearer to the bones of words & to a Matthew ARNOLD's hell with the convention of meaning and sense." As these comments suggest, T. regarded meaning as something to be derived from the poem by individual readers, but also felt that there was an essential structure in his poetry that went beyond conventional ideas of well-formed language. It is clear that "The Force That through the Green Fuse Drives the Flower" relates the forces of nature in the external world to those inside the body and mind of its first-person narrator, and that each of its five sections progresses from spring to "wintry fever." But whatever the stage of the cycle, the speaker of the poem is equally unable to explain it. The words "I am dumb" are repeated in the second part of the first four sections, and in the first part of the final section: "And I am dumb to tell the lover's tomb/How at my sheet goes the crooked worm." Spring and winter, love and death, growth and decay are intertwined in this last couplet as they are throughout the poem.

T.'s highly individual and interpretable poetic, sometimes called neo-Romantic, and his concentration on the lyric and the natural world, were striking in a climate where social relevance was highly rated. W. H. AUDEN and Sir Stephen SPENDER, themselves not long published, were regarded as characteristic of contemporary poetry and had a reputation as leftist poets. T. announced himself as opposed to any such idea of poetry: "They are bogus from skull to navel; finding no subjects for their escapist poetry, they pin on a vague sense of . . . the immediate necessity of a social conscience . . . You can't be true to poetry and party—one must suffer." This was no doubt partly to establish himself as an opposition figure, with his own brand of poetry. But it also reflects his deep-rooted sense that explicit and didactic poetry is nothing of the kind.

Twenty-Five Poems (1936) was regarded by some reviewers as less striking than *18 Poems*, but nevertheless sold quite well after being enthusiastically reviewed by Edith SITWELL. T. was established as a poet, but was perpetually short of funds, and at times feared that his inspiration was fading. Two further volumes of poetry, *The World I Breathe* (1939) and *The Map of Love* (1939), which also contained some short stories, were considered to show a falling off in his gifts, and most of the poems in them are still not thought of highly. However, at this period T. was working in two other veins that were to be significant. He was invited by the BBC to read poetry (not his own) in a radio broadcast in 1937, and was so impressive a reader that he was invited back again in 1938. This time, though, he read his own poetry, together with other prominent poets of the time, including Auden and Spender. In the 1940s and after he did a great deal of radio work and was consistently in demand. In the 1950s, he was able to supplement his earnings in four acclaimed tours of the U.S., in which he read his own work. Secondly, he was writing *The Portrait of the Artist as a Young Dog*. Though it did not then sell well—eclipsed by the outbreak of World

War II—and received mixed reviews, it is now regarded as a sensitive and evocative account of T.'s boyhood, adolescence, and growth as a writer in the Swansea of the 1920s. The book consists of connected short stories—drawing in this respect, as in its portrait of Swansea, and Welsh life, on James JOYCE's *Dubliners* as much as on his *Portrait of the Artist as a Young Man*.

T. was exempted from military service during the war on health grounds, though he constantly feared being directed into factory work. He published *New Poems* (1943), but had a much more notable success with *Deaths and Entrances* (1946). The volume sold some six thousand copies, restoring T.'s reputation to that of his first entrance in 1934, and reassuring his publisher (J. M. Dent). It contained several celebrated poems, including "Fern Hill" and "A Refusal to Mourn the Death, by Fire, of a Child in London." Though still complexly wrought and rich in imagery, rhythm, and sound, the poetry of this period is considered to be clearer and more accessible than earlier work. The themes are still T.'s obsessive concerns with growth and its counterpoint with death. These concerns—particularly through T.'s ability to charge them with high and magnificent emotion—were perhaps more widely shared after experience of war.

In 1952, T. published his *Collected Poems*, preserving the work he considered of value. In May 1953, his play *Under Milk Wood*, conceived for radio, was given its first performances during his third tour to the U.S., in a solo reading by T. sponsored by the Poet's Theatre, in Cambridge, Massachusetts, and then in a reading with a cast of six, including T., at the Poetry Center in New York. The play was a comic masterpiece depicting the strange secret lives of the inhabitants of a small Welsh seaside town, Llareggub (a joke T. was fond of—try reading the word backward). Shortly before his death, on a fourth tour of the U.S., T. gave a solo performance of the final version of *Under Milk Wood*, and then became ill. He had been drinking heavily (even more heavily than usual) and, after medical treatment (some say mistreatment), he fell into a coma and died, perhaps from alcoholic poisoning.

BIBLIOGRAPHY: Ferris, P., *D. T.* (1977); Holbrook, D., *Llareggub Revisited: D. T. and the State of Modern Poetry* (1962); Treece, H., *D. T.* (1949)

CHRIS HOPKINS

THOMAS, [Philip] Edward
b. 3 March 1878, London; d. 9 April 1917, near Arras, France

Poet and prose writer, T. was educated at St. Paul's School and in 1898 was awarded a history scholarship at Lincoln College, Oxford, and graduated in 1900.

Inspired by his early reading of Thomas MALORY, Izaak WALTON, and Richard JEFFERIES and encouraged by James Ashcroft Noble, he combined a love of the countryside with a love of literature and began to publish essays in papers such as the *Speaker* and the *New Age*. Even while at Oxford, he continued to earn money from his journalism. His first book, a collection of essays, *The Woodland Life*, was published in 1897. He married Helen, James Noble's daughter, in 1899 and their first child was born while he was still an undergraduate. On leaving Oxford, he was determined to support himself and his family by his writing and in 1902 he became a literary reviewer on the *Daily Chronicle*. At the same time, he accepted a number of bread and butter commissions to write books on a variety of subjects.

In 1902, T. published *Horae Solitariae*. The following year, he produced an edition of John DYER's poetry and, together with the artist John Fulleylove, a book on Oxford. From then until 1917, he published a book more or less every year, mostly topographical or on a literary figure. These included a BIOGRAPHY of Jefferies (1909), who was such a powerful influence on his own writing, and biographies of Maurice Maeterlinck (1911), Lafcadio Hearn (1912), A. C. SWINBURNE (1912), George Borrow (1912), Walter PATER (1913), John KEATS (1914), and the Duke of Marlborough (1915). Soon after completing his book on Oxford, he was commissioned to write a book on *Beautiful Wales* (1905). As a child, he had spent long holidays with relatives in Wales toward which he felt a strong attachment and in preparation for the writing of his book he took a long walking tour across Wales in search of materials. He walked the length and breadth of England and Wales gathering material for his later topographical books with titles such as *The Heart of England* (1906), *The South Country* (1909), *The Icknield Way* (1913), and *In Pursuit of Spring* (1914). There is no doubt that walking satisfied both his need for solitude and his love of the countryside. Between 1902 and 1917, he produced more than thirty books and numerous articles and reviews and yet in 1914 he was compelled to apply for financial support from the Royal Literary Fund.

The war liberated the poet in T. insofar as he began to write for himself and not the publishers. His friendship with Robert Frost was a turning point in the careers of both poets. T. did everything he could to establish Frost's reputation and Frost, in return, gave T. the confidence he needed to find himself as a poet. In the beginning, Frost encouraged him to base his poems on selected passages taken from his prose though he soon learned to center his poems on a moment of inner perception, truth contained within a formal structure. Between December 1914 and July 1915 when he enlisted in the Artists' Rifles, T. wrote nearly fifty poems including many on which his reputation

now rests, such as "Old Man," "The Other," "Adlestrop," and "The Signpost." Apart from two poems signed Edward Eastaway in *This England* (1915), those published in *Six Poems* (1916) by Edward Eastaway, and the eighteen poems published in *An Annual of New Poetry* (1917), T.'s reputation as a poet is entirely posthumous. He was commissioned into the Royal Artillery in November 1916 and was killed in action on April 9, 1917 at the beginning of the battle of Arras.

The first edition of his poems was published a few months after his death under the pseudonym Edward Eastaway and a further collection, *Last Poems,* was published under his own name in 1918. His *Collected Poems* were published in 1920 and were immediately popular, rapidly going into several editions and numerous reprintings. In the tradition of John CLARE, William BARNES, and Thomas HARDY, and those poets who celebrate the countryside, T. used the language of common speech and traditional poetic forms. Like his friend Frost, he ignored the metropolitan complexities of so many his contemporaries and rooted his poetry in the rural life of England and ordinary experience. Yet while drawing on the richness of the past he nonetheless demonstrated a sensibility that was essentially modern. The rhythms of his poems are the rhythms of speech and the vocabulary is simple, direct, sometimes colloquial, fresh, lucid, and immediately familiar. The themes with which his poems are concerned include the English landscape and the people, birds and animals who make it their home, meditations on the past and the struggle to acknowledge the present, the search for self and the acceptance of death. The tone of the poems is often melancholy, sensitive to the fragile nature of all things and the transient nature of beauty. In many of the poems, such as "As the Team's Head-Brass," "Man and Dog," and "Fifty Faggots," he seems to writing an elegy for the lost world of rural England, a way of life being destroyed by mechanization and commercialism.

His description of the pastoral landscape is accurate and affectionate though his vision is often bleak and the tone melancholy. Yet his poetry is always firmly anchored in the realities of what he sees around him and he manages to achieve an extraordinary intensity of meaning out of quite ordinary experiences. His poems are for the most part characterized by undramatic but precise imagery, speech rhythm that suggests thoughtful meditation, and an unobtrusive subtlety of language in such a way that images, words and phrases take on an intriguing resonance from their context, a combination of simplicity of surface meaning with a profound and disturbing symbolism. Philip LARKIN and "The Movement" poets of the 1950s greatly admired T. and strengthened his reputation.

BIBLIOGRAPHY: Cooke, W., *E. T.* (1970); Marsh, J., *E. T., a Poet for His Country* (1978); Moore, J., *The*

Life and Letters of E. T. (1939); Thomas, R. G., *E. T.* (1985)

A. R. JONES

THOMAS, Gwyn

b. 6 July 1913, Porth, Rhondda Valley, Glamorgan, Wales; d. 13 April 1981, Cardiff, Wales

The youngest of twelve children, T. was educated at Rhondda County Grammar School, Porth, and in 1931 he entered St. Edmund Hall, Oxford. He graduated in modern languages in 1934. After spending six months at the University of Madrid, he returned to South Wales and was employed in a number of teaching posts until 1962 when he decided to live entirely on his writing and broadcasting.

From the 1950s onward, he was a frequent contributor to television and radio programs and broadcast a number of talks, features, documentary programs, and plays that vividly portray his views, particularly of his native Wales. At a time when Welsh nationalism and the Welsh language were being militantly promoted, he did not hesitate to propagate his socialist views and his antinationalist, anti-Welsh language convictions. He became widely known in England and Wales for his brilliant wit, his biting satire, and his sardonic HUMOR that often develops into verbal slapstick. Yet his subject was generally the grim social realities of working-class life in the mining towns of South Wales that he knew so intimately. For many years, he was better known as a broadcaster, television pundit, and raconteur than as a writer.

T. was, though, a fluent and prolific writer. Between 1946 and 1958, he published nine novels: *The Dark Philosophers* (1947); *The Alone to the Alone* (1947); *All Things Betray Thee* (1949); *The World Cannot Hear You* (1951); *Now Lead Us Home* (1952); *A Frost on My Frolic* (1953); *The Stranger at My Side* (1954); *A Point of Order* (1956), and *The Love Man* (1958; repub. as *A Wolf at Dusk,* 1959). A further novel, *Sorrow for Thy Sons*, was published posthumously in 1986. All his novels are concerned with the condition of the working class in the Rhondda, the community in which he lived and grew up and with which he fully identified. He shared their background, their values, and their expectations, sympathized with their poverty and their sufferings, and understood the struggles of their daily lives. His three earliest novels represent his finest achievement as a novelist. They dealt with working-class life in South Wales in the depression, during the Merthyr riots, and in the present. They all side with the common people against authority and are informed by a strong sense of socialist theory reinforced by a nonconformist conscience.

In the novels that followed, he tended to neglect the traditional structures of plot and characterization and relied on an extravagant torrent of comic observation and commentary in language rich in comedy though underpinned by a temperamental melancholy that invited both laughter and regret. The muted anger and bitterness of his earlier naturalistic novels is replaced by a black comedy of manners. The novels are usually written in the first person and the characters whatever their backgrounds or occupations all speak in the accents and idiom of their author. He draws on his experience as a schoolmaster and his knowledge of Spain, but first and foremost he depicts the life and people of urban South Wales, particularly the mining towns of the Rhondda valley where he lived. Since the world of his comic novels is one of absurdity and farce narrated in a stream of outrageous metaphor, simile, and hyperbole, they often threaten to descend into slapstick. He identifies with his subjects, particularly with the deprived and the unemployed, and never patronizes them. He may present them as absurd figures of fun yet somehow he always manages to express his concern and his compassion for those whose lives have been shaped and misshaped by poverty and an inhospitable urban environment. His achievement as a comic novelist especially in *The World Cannot Hear You*, *Now Lead Us Home* and *A Frost on My Frolic* have earned him a respected place among 20th-c. humorists. His work has often been compared with American humorists such as S. J. Perelman and Robert Benchley, who satirized the follies of contemporary life and whose work T. admired.

At the same time, he continued to publish books of short stories: *Where Did I Put My Pity?* (1946); *Gazooka* (1957); *Ring Delirium 123* (1960); and *The Lust Lobby* (1971). In addition, he published two volumes of essays, *A Welsh Eye* (1964) and *A Hatful of Humours* (1965). In 1968, he published his autobiography, *A Few Selected Exits,* an episodic, entertaining though highly selective, narrative of his life from his going to university in Oxford to his journeys to Russia and the U.S. It contains a hilarious account of his time as a schoolmaster, describes his membership of the television Brains Trust forum, and presents a gallery of characters of varying degrees of eccentricity together with memorable portraits of public figures such as Lady Violet Bonham Carter, Dr. Jacob Bronowski, and the director George Devine.

Devine, the director of the English Stage Company Royal, approached T. as he approached other novelists with the suggestion that he should write a play for his company. As a result, he wrote *The Keep* that was first performed at the Royal Court Theatre in 1962. Its popular success encouraged him to write other plays, and for a time he concentrated on the theater, writing *Loud Organs* (perf. 1962), *Jack the Jumper* (perf. 1963), and *The Loot* (perf. 1965) in quick succession. Later plays include *Sap* and *The Breakers,* performed in 1974 and 1976, respectively. The plays he wrote for radio, depending as they did on voices alone, were on the whole more successful since the projection of dramatic characters in action was not a notable feature of either his novels or his plays. Nonetheless, though his work demonstrates his virtuosity as essayist, novelist, and playwright, his virtuosity in his use of the English language, his wit, and verbal originality, characterize every medium in which he chose to express himself.

BIBLIOGRAPHY: Humfrey, B., "G. T.," in Oldsey, B., ed., *British Novelists, 1930–1959*, part 2, *DLB* 15 (1983): 514–19; Michael, I., *G. T.* (1977)

A. R. JONES

THOMAS, R[onald] S[tuart]

b. 29 March 1913, Cardiff, South Glamorgan, Wales;
d. 25 September 2000, Holyhead, Anglesey, Wales

T. is widely considered the finest Welsh poet to have written in the English tongue, not just in the 20th c., but at any time. His only rival in this respect is his namesake Dylan THOMAS. The two, however, could hardly be more different. While Dylan Thomas, always self-consciously precocious, aimed at a sonorous celebration of life, to the extent that his meaning is often obscured by verbal pyrotechnics, the late-developing T. swung pointedly the other way. His work is characteristically lean, hard surfaced, and also hard hearted—a tone and attitude that owed much to his self-perception as a member of a beleaguered minority unable to throw off the historically oppressive yoke of English rule. Yet although T. is variously praised and condemned as a Welsh patriot, his poetry encompasses other weighty themes, sometimes to magically tender effect. He has been called the outstanding religious poet of his age, and the most accomplished nature poet since William WORDSWORTH. While contemporary nonchalance as regards both nature and "God" may devalue such encomiums, they indicate a figure of abiding, albeit lonely, stature.

Perhaps though the measure of T.—referred to by his initials on account of the surfeit of Thomases in Wales—was his dangerous determination to conflate his principal subject matters. God is Welsh and is to be found, if at all, secreted in the barren landscapes of Wales. When the three do converge the poet may, momentarily, find serenity. But militating against such rare epiphanies are the despoliation of the Welsh landscape by the "machine"—Thomas's metaphor for demonic urban modernization—as well as by the careless tourist; the pervasive displacement in Wales of Welsh by the English language; the pusillanimity of the Welsh people in not standing up for their cultural heritage; and, most tellingly of all, the apparent reclusiveness of God himself, as though God, being Welsh, shared the poet's distaste for what can be found.

The resultant anguish is spread across fifty years of verse, and upward of 1,400 poems, with barely a third contained in his *Collected Poems* of 1993. Inevitably, the key to T.'s idiosyncratic mind-set is inlaid in his biography. His professional persona was that of a rural priest. Yet he belonged not to some Welsh Nonconformist sect, but to the Anglican Church in Wales, echoing the bald fact that, with two forgettable exceptions, all his poems were composed in the "alien" tongue, just as they were mainly first published by large London, rather than small Welsh, houses.

T. was born in Cardiff, the only child of a merchant seaman. During World War I, the family lived in English ports—London, Goole, and Liverpool—but in 1918 moved back to Wales, and the rest of the poet's childhood was spent in Holyhead (Anglesey), where his father worked on the "Irish" ferry. He took a poor degree in Latin at the University College of North Wales (Bangor), then enrolled at St. Michael's theological college in Llandaff, Cardiff. Ordained in 1937, he served as a curate first in Chirk, then in Hanmer, before becoming Rector of Manafon, on the Welsh side of the English border, in 1942.

Only at Manafon did T. begin properly learning Welsh; and it was during his time there that he started writing the poetry for which he is known. In all probability, the routine of preaching in an enclosed stone environment had a profound effect on his poetic voice. Habitually, his rigorously chosen words and pithy chiselled statements linger in the air. Henceforward, he regularly published "slim volumes" of verse, over twenty in number, beginning with *The Stones of the Field* (1946), and concluding with *No Truce with the Furies* (1995). His oeuvre also contains, as well as hundreds of fugitive poems, a significant body of prose, increasingly written in Welsh, and including an autobiography (*Neb*, 1985, trans. as *No-one*, 1997) and a nature diary (*Blwyddyn yn Llŷn*, 1990; trans. as *The Year in Llŷn*, 1997).

As T.'s assumed Welshness was scarcely unblemished—some Welsh have difficulty in accepting his choice of wife, the "superior" English artist Mildred E. Eldridge, and the English public school education accorded their son—so his hallmark accidie was in part self-accusatory. Overall, his poetic project may be seen as a quest for a necessarily unobtainable purity very nearly accomplished by a relentless and famous "honesty" that persistently eschews sentimentality.

The early output, which includes many of the pieces most often anthologized (e.g., "A Peasant," "Cynddylan on a Tractor," and "Welsh Landscape"), is the most overtly polemical, reflecting T.'s engagement with the cultural politics of Saunders LEWIS and other nationalists. In his middle period, T. expresses a growing disillusionment with the Welsh cause, or at least with the manner in which it is pursued, and turns increasingly to philosophical speculation. Collections such as *H'm* (1972) and *Laboratories of the Spirit* (1975) are notable for their largely successful exploitation of scientific idiom. Such exploitation however is conducted within the framework of a mainly Christian metaphysic, and in its final phase T.'s work becomes overtly religious, *Destinations* (1985), *Experimenting with an Amen* (1986), and *Mass for Hard Times* (1992) speaking for themselves as volume titles.

Yet T. avoids mere religiosity. Instead, he sustains a skepticism present from his first collections, so that even his late poetry may appeal to the agnostic reader. Nor are his chosen themes pursued in a mutually exclusive manner. Just as there are manifestly religious poems in the first collections, so there are manifestly "Welsh" poems in the last. Having once alighted upon an idea or motif, T. never wholly lets it go; likewise, his prosody. Although across his fifty years T. rings stylistic changes, his voice remains consistent. Jettisoning the established props of fixed meter and rhyme, T. instead relies on alliteration, assonance, and patterned phrasing. While therefore his verse may look free, in reality, steeped in both English and Welsh prosodic traditions, it is anything but.

BIBLIOGRAPHY: Thomas, M. W., ed., *The Page's Drift: R. S. T. at Eighty* (1993); Thomas, R. S., *Autobiographies* (1997); Ward, J. P., *The Poetry of R. S. T.* (1987); Wintle, J., *Furious Interiors: Wales, R. S. T., and God* (1996)

JUSTIN WINTLE

THOMPSON, Francis [Joseph]

b. 16 December 1859, Preston; d. 13 November 1907, London

"Had he written nothing else but 'The Hound of Heaven' and 'The Kingdom of God,' Francis Joseph Thompson would probably still be the most well known representative of the late Victorian revival of creative literary activity among English Catholics." This statement is made by Paul van Kuykendall Thomson at the beginning of his preface to his biography of T. published in 1961. Whether or not one feels that the poetic preferences of a particular religious sect is a matter of supreme importance, the fact remains that, judged by purely artistic criteria and not as religious propaganda, these two poems are far and away the most important poems that T. ever wrote and one of them, "The Kingdom of God" is almost perfect of its kind. Unlike much of his earlier work, this poem is completely free of stultifying affectation and willfully obscure diction. Its imagery is fresh, powerful, and coherent. Its unity of artistic purpose is perfect: nothing of it is incidental, gratuitous, or irrele-

vant. Even to the ear of a devout Christian unbeliever there is a strange thrill and chill about some of its lines: "But (when so sad thou canst not sadder)/Cry—and upon thy so sore loss/Shall shine the traffic of Jacob's ladder/Pitched betwixt Heaven and Charing Cross . . . /Yet in the night, my Soul, my daughter/Cry—clinging Heaven by the hems/And lo, Christ walking upon the water/Not of Gennesareth, but Thames."

Judeo-Christian mythology is used in the same general and genuine way in which a poet might use images drawn from Greek or Norse myth. Incidentally, this poem's title was given to it not by T. himself but by his editor and friend of long standing, Wilfrid Meynell. It was one of the unpublished poems that Meynell found after T.'s death. T. had called the poem "In No Strange Land"; Meynell superimposed "The Kingdom of God," printed above the author's title, and published the poem in his definitive three-volume edition of T.'s *Works* (1913). Yet despite early praise for T. as a poet, W. B. YEATS in his early "Celtic Twilight" phase is infinitely more important and better known; and Ernest DOWSON, Lionel JOHNSON, and Arthur SYMONS are still remembered (if no longer actually read). A. E. HOUSMAN, who was born in the same year as T., and whose *A Shropshire Lad* was published in 1896, is still well remembered and is still read and frequently quoted. T., on the other hand, has—apart from the two important poems already mentioned—already faded from the memory of all but specialist scholars and critics. Andrew Sanders, for example, in *The Short Oxford History of English Literature* (1994), refers to him as "The once-influential Catholic apologist." Peter Conrad's *Everyman History of English Literature* (1985) does not even mention T., nor does Michael Schmidt in his *Lives of the Poets* (1998).

The almost complete critical neglect of T. is, however, a mistake. He is a minor figure but that does not make him negligible. In addition to three volumes of verse, published in 1893, 1895, and 1897, he wrote a good deal of admirable literary criticism for *Academy* and *Athenaeum*, the two most distinguished literary journals of the day. In 1909, his *Shelley: An Essay* was published and in 1910 the still very readable *A Renegade Poet and Other Essays*. Since his death, some of his occasional pieces have been collected and published by Terence L. Connolly, S.J. They are contained in *Literary Criticisms by F. T.* (1948) and *Minor Poets: Criticisms by F. T.* (1949). Thomson, discussing T.'s progress as a poet, remarks that "some of the poetry in 'Love in Dian's Lap' has a luxuriance which is ample evidence that in 1890 he had still not outgrown the notion that to produce rich imagery is to create poetry." The comment is a valid one, but it is only fair to add that some of his later poems—not a great many, but enough to make the point—do demonstrate that he did at last learn this most difficult lesson, though whether he was ever wholly conscious of it, or whether—on the other hand—he apprehended it only instinctively, is impossible to say. Certainly it informs most tellingly some of his later works and speaks with a true poetic tongue. Then, quite suddenly apparently, it was gone: after 1897, he wrote no more verse. His older contemporary, A. C. SWINBURNE (a far greater poet than T., of course) suffered the same fate but reacted in the opposite way: long after the Promethean fire had faded he continued to pour out verse, but he wrote very little more poetry; *Atalanta in Calydon* was long ago in the past. The tongueless vigil and all the pain were over, smothered in the suburban safety of Putney.

But though, in the case of T., the authentic poetic voice died before the man did, the mind of the discerning critic yet remained. In his essay entitled *Shelley*, he shrewdly summed up his *intellectual* understanding of a poet's position: "A poet must to some extent be a chameleon and feed on air. But it need not be the musty breath of the multitude." And every now and again, even in the lesser poems, one comes upon an image that startles as in "Ode to Easter": "Spring is come home with her world-wandering feet/And all the things are made young with young desires."

BIBLIOGRAPHY: Connolly, T. L., *Poems of F. T.* (1932; rev. ed., 1941); Meynell, E., *The Life of F. T.* (1913); Reid, J. C., *F. T., Man and Poet* (1960); Thomson, P. van K., *F. T.* (1961)

ERIC SALMON

THOMSON, James

b. 11 September 1700, Ednam; d. 27 August 1748, Richmond

T. was the most popular nature poet of the 18th c.; his topographical poetry contributed greatly to the development of descriptive poetry, particularly the picturesque aesthetic. His childhood in the Scottish border country of Roxburghshire influenced his later literary landscapes. The son of a Presbyterian minister, T. went to Edinburgh University at fifteen to study divinity, but during his years there he demonstrated some promise as a poet and was attracted to the city's literary life. When he arrived in London in early 1725, T.'s professed intention was to complete his religious education; however, he supported himself as a tutor and began to compose the earliest version of *Winter* (1726) with the encouragement of his friend David Mallet.

Winter soon became popular for its sublime blank-verse depictions of seasonal storms and human suffering. *Summer* (1727) describes the process of a summer's day; its georgic descriptions culminate in a panegyric to Great Britain. *Spring* (1728) describes the

effects of the season on the natural world, ascending from inanimate matter to humankind, and concludes with a passage praising nuptial love over its unregulated counterpart. The much revised and expanded seasonal cycle was completed with *The Seasons* (1730; rev. eds., 1744, 1746), which included *Autumn*, a description of harvest-time and condemnation of hunting that concludes with a panegyric on the "Philosophic Country Life" and a *Hymn to the Seasons*. T. continued to expand and revise the poem over the next sixteen years. The poem remained remarkably popular: it was printed fifty times between 1730 and 1800.

T.'s Grand Tour of France and Italy as a tutor to the son of the solicitor-general resulted in the long patriotic poem *Liberty* (4 vols., 1735–36) in which Liberty narrates her progress through the ages in Greece, Rome, and Britain. The political observations that resulted from contrasting contemporary Italy and contemporary England on the one hand with the ancient classical world on the other were commonplaces of the day. T. traces the catastrophic effects of luxury upon Greece and Rome as cautionary examples, but he implies that there is still hope for Britain because of its potential patriots and its government, which balances monarchy, aristocracy, and democracy.

Although he is best known as a poet, T. was also a dramatist. He produced a series of tragedies, including *Sophonisba* (perf. 1730), *Agamemnon* (1738), and *Edward and Eleanora* (1739). Two more tragedies, an adaptation from Alain-René Lesage's *Gil Blas* (4 vols., 1715–35) called *Tancred and Sigismunda* (pub. 1745; perf. 1752), and *Coriolanus* (perf. 1749), were produced after his death. The patriotic masque *Alfred* (perf. 1740) was written with Mallet and the composer Thomas Arne on the subject of the Saxon king. The masque's climactic ode "Rule, Britannia" became an alternative national anthem. T. wrote several patriotic poems, including *Britannia* (1729), *Liberty*, and parts of *The Seasons*, but this ode stands as his most enduring celebration of the British empire.

Four months before his death, T. published *The Castle of Indolence* (1748), a deeply autobiographical work in Spenserian stanzas. The poem allegorizes his own romantic propensity toward imaginative idleness and his anxiety that it becomes self-indulgent and self-absorbed when it is not linked with reason and selfless activity. In the first canto, the wizard Indolence lures weary pilgrims into his castle, where they succumb to torpor and are imprisoned in a dungeon. The second canto describes the conquest of the castle by the knight of Art and Industry.

Samuel JOHNSON criticized *The Seasons* for its "want of method"; however, the comprehensiveness of its vision was an important factor in the poem's success. T. kept nature at the center of his scrutiny, but used his close observations of the physical world to meditate upon many of his other preoccupations: Whig politics, imperial expansion, ancient history, Christian faith, and modern science. The poem links and navigates all these topics not so much by "method" as by the restless motion of the poet's mind.

T.'s predominantly visual descriptions of external nature are characterized by great particularity and exactness. However, his depictions are not always or wholly naturalistic: his landscapes are frequently populated by personified abstractions, and he often presents objects and events (both physical and metaphysical) that cannot be seen with the corporeal eye. Critics have noted that his influential topographical passages are often written from a "bird's-eye" view or elevated prospect that asserts visual control over the landscape. Others have suggested that his encyclopedic connections and juxtapositions anticipate later environmental writing.

BIBLIOGRAPHY: Grant, D., *J. T.* (1951); Sambrook, J., *J. T. (1700–1748)* (1991); Terry, R., ed., *J. T.* (2000)

SEAN BURGESS

THRALE, Hester Lynch. See PIOZZI, Hester Lynch

THUBRON, Colin [Gerald Dryden]
b. 14 June 1939, London

Educated at Eton, T. is the son of a soldier-diplomat and a collateral descendant of John DRYDEN. T. is known as a author of six novels but even better known as author of nine best-selling travel books. He has made television programs and worked in publishing, and traveled in the Middle East, Russia, Siberia, and China. He felt he had to face what he was afraid of: "The Russian bear and the Yellow Peril." He writes in longhand in notebooks. His 1989 novel *Falling* won the Silver Pen Award and his travelogue *The Lost Heart of Asia* (1994) won the Thomas Cook Award. Among his novels are *The God in the Mountain* (1977), *A Cruel Madness* (1984), and *Distance* (1996). He notes that his fiction, unlike his other books, is often set in enclosed spaces. Travel and history books include *Mirror to Damascus* (1967), *Jerusalem* (1969), *The Hills of Adonis: A Journey in Lebanon* (1969), *Journey into Cyprus* (1975), *Istanbul* (1978), *The Venetians* (1980), *Among the Russians* (1983; repub. as *Where Nights Are Longest* 1984), *Behind the Wall: A Journey through China* (1987), *The Silk Road China* (1989), and *In Siberia* (1999).

THWAITE, Anthony [Simon]
b. 23 June 1930, Chester

T. was educated at Kingswood School, Bath, and Christ Church, Oxford. He has been influential as editor and lecturer and successful as a poet, having published thirty books of poetry, commentary, and translation. A master-craftsman, he uses intricate stanza forms and rhyme schemes. His first collection was *Home Truths* (1957), followed by *The Owl in the Tree* (1963). Later volumes are *The Stones of Emptiness* (1967), *Inscriptions* (1973), *New Confessions* (1974), based on St. Augustine, *A Portion for Foxes* (1977), and *Victorian Voices* (1980), comprising fourteen monologues by marginal Victorian figures. *Poems, 1953–1983* appeared in 1984 , *Selected Poems, 1956–1996* in 1997, and *A Different Country* in 2000. T. has edited the letters of Philip LARKIN (1999) and a collection of essays, *Larkin at Sixty* (1982). He has also edited Larkin's poems (1988) and the poems of R. S. THOMAS (1996). Formerly literary editor of the *Listener* and the *New Statesman,* and co-editor of *Encounter,* T. has lectured in Japan and in Libya, and traveled extensively for the British Council. T.'s *Poetry Today: A Critical Guide to British Poetry 1960–1995* appeared in 1996.

TILNEY, Edmund
b. ca. 1536; d. 20 August 1610, Leatherhead, Surrey

T. was Master of the Revels from 1579 until his death. Although his authority began as little more than procurer of entertainments for the Crown, as the office had done since about 1494, his scope expanded after his official commission in 1581. By the end of the century, T. had under his control all of the adult acting companies and theaters, and the authority to enroll actors for the Queen's Men. In 1607, he officially acquired the plenary power to censor, license, and otherwise approve all plays written either for publication or performance. An author in his own right, T. had earlier annoyed the queen with his prose tract, *The Flower of Friendship* (1568), which encouraged her to marry. Nevertheless, his greatest impact upon literature was in his office as licenser and de facto censor of English RENAISSANCE DRAMA.

T.'s role in Renaissance drama was a consequence of the growing popularity of the form in the mid-1570s. An abortive attempt in 1567 to create a permanent theater, the Red Lion, in the Whitechapel district prefigured the building of the Newington Butts playhouse, the Theatre in Shoreditch and the first Blackfriars Theatre, all in 1576. The enterprise was popular enough to see another theater, the Curtain, built the next year. Two years later, T. became Master of the Revels. Though his official duties initially extended no further than supplying all entertainment for the court, T. rapidly moved to bring the burgeoning theater industry under the control of his office. His original allowance was £35 (£20 for a house and £15 for the revels office and wardrobe). By the end of his career, and certainly after 1607, he was earning many times that sum through licensing fees.

T.'s office soon evolved. It changed in character from providing entertainment for the queen and began to censor public drama in compliance with governmental policy. By 1589, T. can be found siding with the Lord Mayor and calling for an outright ban on performance within the city of London. His position could have been a reaction to the "Martin Marprelate" controversy, which involved dramatists. But it is also possible that the removal of playing spaces from the city Inns such as the Bell, the Bull, the Cross Keys, and the Bel Savage worked as an additional advantage for the office of the Master of the Revels. Moving theaters into the suburbs removed a layer of administrative control and left the plenary and unquestioned authority to license and approve plays, playhouses, and playing companies in the hands of the office of the Master of the Revels.

By the mid-1590s, the office of the Master of the Revels devoted most of its energies to rooting out politically sensitive and potentially seditious dramatic expression. T.'s job, as he saw it, included not only reviewing plays for licensing but also suggesting changes to questionable passages and requiring the exclusion of whole scenes from plays deemed otherwise acceptable. T. apparently took his office seriously. Instances of expurgated plays are not uncommon, and examples of T.'s modifications are not difficult to find. Once a play was licensed, it could not be modified for performance without risking reprisals extending from fines to closure of the theater and loss of a company's license to play. Players apparently did have the right to shorten approved plays for time. Minor alterations in performance to allow for comic extemporizing and lapses in an actor's memory were also admitted without penalty. However, an approved text could not be substantially altered through revision or extension without undergoing an additional licensing procedure.

In 1603, T. began investing more authority in his nephew and deputy, George Buc. The grooming of Buc began about 1597 much to the chagrin of John LYLY, who had been promised the office from as early as 1585. Buc continued to extend the authority of the office. By March 30, 1622, Buc had "gone mad." His successor, Sir John Astley, almost immediately sold the office to Sir Henry Herbert in 1623.

BIBLIOGRAPHY: Chambers, E. K., "The Revels Office," in his *The Elizabethan Stage* (1923), vol. 1: 71–105; Eccles, M., "Sir George Buc, Master of the Revels," in Sisson, C. J., ed., *Thomas Lodge and Other Elizabethans* (1966): 409–506; Streitberger, W. R., *E. T.* (1986)

BRIAN JAY CORRIGAN

TÓIBÍN, Colm

b. 1955, Enniscorthy, Wexford, Ireland

T. is a novelist, travel writer, and journalist whose prose—both fiction and nonfiction—is characterized by a sparse, understated poetry and compassionate sensitivity. One of the finest of a new generation of Irish writers, T. has received considerable attention from critics who have praised his skillful rendering of time and place and his ear for language, and who have compared his deceptively simple style to the work of Graham GREENE and John McGahern. What distinguishes T. most among his contemporaries, however, is the wisdom that pervades his writing; through four novels and several volumes of journalism, he places emotional and spiritual truths quietly at the heart of political and personal identity to give an intense but lasting picture of an unsettled Ireland, an unsettled Europe.

The high regard for T.'s work began with the publication of his debut novel, *The South* (1990), which won the *Irish Times*–Aer Lingus prize for a first work of fiction. With a painterly eye and a confidence rarely to be found so early in an author's career, he tells a moving story of an artist who leaves behind her failed marriage in southern Ireland to find fulfillment in a new life in Spain. Amid the violence of Franco's regime, art and politics fuse until the marks on a canvas become synonymous with the difficulties and pain involved in changing the course of one's life. The novel's carefully honed, episodic narrative, with a casual dropping of significant information that is redolent of Virginia WOOLF's *To the Lighthouse*, is interspersed with intense emotional confessionals, emphasizing the pain of escaping—and eventually returning to—Ireland and the family.

T.'s next novel, *The Heather Blazing* (1992), delivered all that *The South* promised and underlined his place at the forefront of contemporary fiction. The absorbing story of Eamon Redmond, a High Court judge in Dublin who returns each summer to the southeast coast of Ireland where he was reared, is as affecting in its beautiful portrayal of the little moments of everyday life as it is in its dealings with the bigger questions of sexual awakening, loss, and grief. Akin to James JOYCE's *Dubliners* in its treatment of childhood, adolescence, and maturity, *The Heather Blazing* is a complex exploration of the way in which the past commands the present, eating away at the heart of Redmond just as the sea erodes his native coastline.

Set in Buenos Aires in the 1980s, *The Story of the Night* (1996) follows the progress of a lonely young man trying to live openly with his homosexuality. This haunting, troubled novel, at once erotic and brutal, sensuous and intelligent, juxtaposes its protagonist's coming out with Argentina's emergence from repressive rule to tentative hope, and gives a memorable new context to the conventional tale of forbidden love against the backdrop of war.

In his Booker Prize–nominated novel, *The Blackwater Lightship* (1999), T. pulls together his recurrent concerns—love, loss, morality, and personal responsibility—and gives them a new intensity. Set in Ireland in the 1990s, the book tells the story of three generations of women, full of memory and recrimination, who are forced to an uneasy peace with each other when they discover that their young brother/son/grandson is dying from an AIDS-related illness. A domestic novel about tolerance, which manages to resist empty polemic, *The Blackwater Lightship* epitomizes T.'s ability to penetrate straight to the heart of his characters' lives, and to highlight the fragility of human experiences against a powerful and indifferent nature. It is a testament to the profound beauty of T.'s writing that a novel so palpably about death can at once speak so strongly for life.

The clarity and empathy that grace T.'s fiction are also present in his journalism, all of which focuses in some way on national, religious, and sexual politics: *The Sign of the Cross* (1994) explores the complications and contradictions of the Catholic Church and their influence on a country's sense of nationalism; *Homage to Barcelona* (1990) is a personal and carefully researched account of the city; and *Walking along the Border* (1987; repub. as *Bad Blood: A Walk along the Irish Border*, 1994) is an account of his travels along the Irish border soon after the Anglo-Irish agreement, and an insight into the fear and anger that has imprinted itself on to the landscape and its inhabitants. T.'s criticism includes an insightful essay on the future of Irish fiction, in which he foresees a waning of national themes in the wake of the Anglo-Irish Agreement and European Union. His nonfiction work, *Love in a Dark Time* (2002), is an illuminating discussion of the relationship between artists and their homosexuality; its subjects range from Oscar WILDE to filmmaker Pedro Almodóvar.

BIBLIOGRAPHY: Herron, T., "ContamiNation: Patrick McCabe and C. T.'s Pathographies of the Republic," in Harte, L., and M. Parker, eds., *Contemporary Irish Fiction* (2000): 168–91; Tillman, L., "C. T.," *BOMB* 38 (Winter 1992): 22–23

NICOLA UPSON

TOLKIEN, J[ohn] R[onald] R[euel]

b. 3 January 1892, Bloemfontein, South Africa; d. 2 September 1973, Bournemouth

When T.'s *The Lord of the Rings* (3 vols., 1954–55) headed a poll for the book of the century run by a British chain of bookstores, it was felt that the result had been rigged by obsessive fans, determined to see their favorite volume triumph. Whatever the truth of the story, it indicates two things: first that there is a dismissive attitude toward T. and his readership, and that it is a work that cast a shadow over the century, being the benchmark for better or worse for how fantasy is judged.

Although T. is best known for *The Lord of the Rings* and its precursor, *The Hobbit* (1937), he had actually been working on the materials that would eventually produce these works during the First World War. T. was a philologist, and had worked on the *Oxford English Dictionary*, and his interest in languages led him to invent his own. But language does not exist meaningfully in the abstract: it needs to be part of a society with a series of myths underlying that society. The struggle was to find a means of telling a story to which his mythos could act as background. The posthumous early volumes of the "History of Middle-Earth," especially *The Book of Lost Tales I* (1983) and *II* (1984), edited by T.'s son Christopher, demonstrate a number of attempts at this, and different versions of the same story. In contrast the earlier, but still posthumously published, *The Silmarillion* (1977), in its editing together of the mythos as continuous text, shows how indigestible such an endeavor could be.

The Hobbit had been the breakthrough text, the narrative of a rather lazy, bourgeois hobbit, Bilbo Baggins, who is tricked by his old friend the wizard Gandalf into going on an adventure to kill a dragon and restore the kingdom to the dwarfs who had been driven out. As the characters undergo their quest, individual episodes allowed T. to reveal the history of this world, both in terms of backstories for characters met en route and in the stories and songs the characters tell each other.

As *The Hobbit* was an unexpected success with both children and adults, there was a demand for a sequel. *The Lord of the Rings* was conceived on a vaster scale, and is a much richer text as a result. A ring of invisibility that Bilbo had found on his travels turns out to be a ring of rare power, on which the fate of the world depends. The power of the evil Sauron is rising in the east and he is seeking for the ring; the only chance of salvation is to destroy the ring in the furnace which had forged it. The quest is here to get rid of something rather than to find it, but is told against a political context: the relations between "dwarves" and elves, the battle over who will be king of men, and the reactions of various other kingdoms to the battle between good and evil. As the book was drafted during the Second World War, the temptation is to read a political allegory into the tale, although T. himself denied it. What is clearly working on the level of allegory is the account of the destruction of the Shire, the realm of the hobbits, which echoes the industrialization of the English countryside.

The novel, split initially into three volumes with appendices, set the tone for much EPIC fantasy, as did T.'s friend and colleague C. S. LEWIS in the Narnia books. Quests would be set for various male heroes (there are very few female characters in T.) across a huge imagined landscape, with the narrative covering as much of the map of the invented world as possible.

Some critics have viewed the novel as being too conservative, too comfortable and middle class. Others have delved for Jungian archetypes or Freudian symbolism.

T. wrote a number of novellas located in other rural settings, such as *Farmer Giles of Ham* (1949) and *Smith of Wootton Major* (1967). His critical work is also of significance, from his groundbreaking work on the epic BEOWULF, "The Monsters and the Critics," to his essay defending the imagining of self-contained imagined worlds, "On Fairy Tales." He also worked with E. V. Gordon on a critical edition of *Sir Gawain and the Green Knight* (1925) and produced a translation into modern English of that and other poems by the so-called GAWAIN-POET.

However, from 1960s counterculture phenomenon to contemporary publishing industry, it is the works set in Middle Earth that dominate. With numerous editions of the novels, some with T.'s original illustrations, some with works by later artists, in print at any time, it is difficult for people to evaluate the work as literature rather than as a publishing category. Recent filmed versions, *The Lord of the Rings: The Fellowship of the Ring* (2001) and *The Lord of the Rings: The Two Towers* (2002), only add to this sense.

BIBLIOGRAPHY: Carpenter, H., *J. R. R. T* (1977); Crabbe, K. W., *J. R. R. T.* (1988); Flieger, V., and C. F. Hostetter, eds., *T.'s Legendarium: Essays on The History of Middle-Earth* (2000)

ANDREW M. BUTLER

TOMALIN, Claire
b. 20 June 1933, London

T. had a French father and an English mother, the composer Muriel Herbert, parents who separated when she was a child. Educated at the Lycée Français de Londres, Hitchin Girls' Grammar School, and Dartington Hall, she graduated from Newnham College, Cambridge, with first-class honors in English literature in 1954. In the following year, she married the charismatic, renowned journalist Nicholas Tomalin, who was killed reporting the Yom Kippur war in Israel in 1973, leaving her with four children.

In 1974, T. became literary editor of the *New Statesman* and in that same year published *The Life and Death of Mary Wollstonecraft,* which won the Whitbread First Book Award. From 1979 to 1986, T. was the literary editor of the *Sunday Times*. In 1980, she published *Shelley and His World*, which was followed by *Katherine Mansfield: A Secret Life* (1987). The facts formed the background of T.'s play, *The Winter Wife* (1991). *The Invisible Woman* (1990), T.'s BIOGRAPHY of actress Ellen Ternan, young mistress of the aging Charles DICKENS, exposed another secret life and revealed the existence of an illegitimate child. The book, part social history of the 19th-c. theater,

part detective story, won the Hawthornden Prize, the James Tait Black Memorial Prize, and the NCR Book Award.

T.'s next book was also concerned with the theater: *Mrs. Jordan's Profession: The Story of a Great Actress and a Future King* (1994; repub. as *Mrs. Jordan's Profession: The Actress and the Prince*, 1995) was originally intended as a general study of actresses working in 18th- and 19th.-c Britain, but developed into the story of the actress Dorothy (Dora) Jordan, who bore the Duke of Clarence ten children before his marriage to a German princess and his accession to the throne as King William IV. Six hundred of Mrs. Jordan's letters in the Henry Huntingdon Library in California had previously attracted only one editor, who omitted without explanation a crucial letter that accompanied the return of all the Duke's letters to her; this letter exonerates Mrs. Jordan from the accusation of blackmail. T. combs through these and other scattered sources to produce a fluid and entertaining narrative filled with anecdote and insight.

Jane Austen: A Life (1997) is generally agreed to be the best of the numerous lives of this author. T.'s work is distinguished by exhaustive historical research, empathy, and elegant prose, aptly illustrated in T.'s Whitbread Award–winning *Samuel Pepys: The Unequalled Self* (2002). Married to playwright Michael FRAYN, T. is a frequent broadcaster on television and radio.

BIBLIOGRAPHY: King, J., "C. T.," in Serafin, S., ed., *Twentieth-Century British Literary Biographers, DLB* 155 (1995): 305–9

TORRINGTON, Jeff
b. 1935, Glasgow, Scotland

Published in 1992, *Swing Hammer Swing!*, T.'s acclaimed novel about a down-and-out and would-be writer, was the result of decades of work and economic hardship. Though less prolific and well known than contemporary novelists James KELMAN and Irvine WELSH, T. is among the pivotal authors in something of a popular renaissance of Scottish fiction. The desire and struggle to articulate oneself, so vibrant in his characters, reflects T.'s own struggle with Parkinson's disease and his affinities with marginalized working-class people.

Set in the Gorbals in the late 1960s, *Swing Hammer Swing!* is a raucous, robust book that won the Whitbread Award in 1992. Tom Clay, the wisecracking narrator of his own picaresque, stumbles through atheism and chronic unemployment toward imminent fatherhood and a dire sort of respectability. In episodic misadventures featuring various mistaken identities and missing persons, Tom contends with the contradictions of liberty and responsibility, wondering in his course "how human hope came to flower in its strangling clays." The novel is as comic as it is philosophical, and the two qualities intersect in the emphasis on the Glaswegian vernacular and the potential for multiplicity in words.

The Devil's Carousel (1996) is an assembly line of a book, a regulated stream of interwoven stories about the workers, operators, and union stewards at the Centaur Car Plant. Strangely ornate for their plainness, the colloquially told anecdotes such as "Boag's Gallery" and "Twitcher Haskins Gets the Bird!" display a central predilection for nicknames, unusual contractions, and puns. T.'s characters either show resilient wit or else they perish. Between the stories are issues of KIKBAK, a roughly typed anarchist broadsheet of articles and rhymes that offer barely disguised commentary on the plant's ongoing labor-management aggravations. Eventually, and perhaps predictably, the plant is shut down and the workers laid off, left without even a target for their frustrations.

T.'s language play at its best approaches Joycean heights and his comic sensibility's rough edges stay unsmoothed and unsentimental. That so little criticism has thus far been written of his work signals only a slow reaction to fast wit.

TIM CONLEY

TOTTEL, Richard
b. ca. 1535, Exeter; d. 1594

Best known as the printer and possibly editor of the first printed anthology of poetry in England, *Songes and Sonettes*, published June 5, 1557, and curiously revised thoroughly eight weeks later in a second edition, July 31, 1557, which became the standard text for at least ten Elizabethan editions and a resource for lyric genres and thematic topoi for later 16th-c. poets. He was one of the founding members of the Company of Stationers, which received its royal charter in 1556, and later served several terms as warden and master. In 1553, he received a royal patent to print law books that he maintained through Mary Tudor's reign and well into the Elizabethan period. Part of his prosperity came from the theological markets created when Protestant printers were put out of business after Mary Tudor ascended the throne.

The patent and lack of significant competition in the printing business ensured enough financial security to venture into the realm of publishing literary texts besides the anthology, such as Richard Smith's *A Bouclier of the Catholic Faith* (1554), dedicated to Mary Tudor, John LYDGATE's *The Fall of Princes*, and Stephen HAWES's *The Pastime of Pleasure*, two works previously printed by Protestant printers. In 1557, he coproduced the Catholic Thomas MORE's *Works*, a massive project of 1458 leaves, all of which, except the first quire, which was produced by the printer John Cawood, were printed by T. In the same year, he published *Songes and Sonettes*, between the first and second editions of which he published Henry Howard,

the Earl of SURREY's translations of Virgil's *Aeneid*, books 2 and 4, in blank verse. On ELIZABETH I's accession in 1558, T. quickly published *The Passage of Most Drad Soveraigne Lady Quene Elyzabeth through the Citie of London to Westminster the Day before Her Coronation*. He was one of the few printers in the late 1550s who negotiated a successful career by shifting affiliation between church and state. In total, there are over seven hundred entries of T. cited in the *Short Title Catalogue* that by the standards of the day indicates a very busy career. His influence as a printer was to improve the standards of law texts; to make more intelligible to the student and practicing lawyer those manuscripts often written in Latin or French, with an abundance of marginalia, revisions, and obscure legalese. He was known to employ legal professionals to assist him in decoding these works, which added to the cost, but improved the product enormously. His compositors were an impressive lot, and at the height of his career, he owned three printing houses and employed four apprentices. He became a wealthy man in the trade that he eventually all but devoted to the legal profession, and from which he himself withdrew after failing health in 1586.

In literary circles, T. is best known for his publication of *Songes and Sonettes* whose "small parcelles" of poems, he claims in the preface, prove that English could be as "well written" as Latin or Italian. By reading the poems one would become more skillful in speech, T. claims, for the "statelinesse of stile" would purge the "swinelike grosseness" of the common ear, which prevents one from tasting the "swete [marjoram]" of English verse. Though traditionally thought a miscellany of poems in no particular order, on closer analysis the text is educative on another level: in the first edition but more so in the second, the arrangement of the verses provides a narrative trajectory that begins with descriptions of the Petrarchan lover, but evolves to more didactic poems whose purpose is to instruct the reader in the complex nature of virtuous action.

BIBLIOGRAPHY: Knott, C. A., "R. T.," in Bracken, J. K., and J. Silver, eds., *The British Literary Book Trade, 1475–1700*, DLB 170 (1996): 308–13; Marquis, P. A., "Recent Studies in R. T.'s *Songes and Sonettes*," ELR 28 (Spring 1998): 299–313; Marquis, P. A., "Politics and Print: The Curious Revisions to T.'s *Songes and Sonettes*," SP 97 (Spring 2000): 145–64

PAUL A. MARQUIS

TOURNEUR, Cyril
b. ca. 1575–80, possibly in Essex; d. 28 February 1626, Kinsale, Ireland

The work upon which T.'s posthumous reputation was most firmly established, *The Revenger's Tragedy* (perf. 1606; pub. 1607), is now generally agreed to have been written by another playwright, probably Thomas MIDDLETON. T.'s dramatic reputation now rests upon his one surviving play, *The Atheist's Tragedy* (perf. ca. 1610–11; pub. as *The Atheist's Tragedie; or, The Honest Man's Revenge,* 1611), and to a far lesser extent upon John FLETCHER's *The Honest Man's Fortune,* in which T.'s hand has been suggested, mainly on the strength of the title, but never authenticated. We know of two other T. plays, *The Nobleman* (perf. 1612) and *The Great Man* (possibly the same play as *The Nobleman*), both lost, and one other collaboration, *The Arraignment of London* (perf. 1613, with Robert Daborne), which is also lost. T. wrote an earlier satiric poem, "The Transformed Metamorphosis" (1600), and an elegy on the death of Prince Henry (1613). From 1613 until his death, T. would appear to have left writing entirely.

T.'s undisputed work, *The Atheist's Tragedy,* though dramatically flawed, is nevertheless a sincere attempt to dramatize his view of morality in the popular mode. And while the flaws are to be found in the insistent didactic tone of the play, the play is more than mere polemic. If many of the sequences are overwrought, at least they are not entirely moralistic. Obvious as their moral vision may be, they are also demonstrably spectacular and dramatic with a reasonable grasp of literary intent. The play presents a bifurcated supernatural world: one of nature, which D'Amville espouses, and the other of religious faith, feigned by Snuff but dear to the hero, Charlemont.

The play is anomalous in the canon of RENAISSANCE DRAMA in being a non-revenge tragedy of revenge. The wronged characters achieve their revenge by standing by, patient in their innocence, and allowing evil to burn itself out. The underlying message is to leave vengeance to God. And, in an incident worthy of notice to Renaissance scholars, Rousard has the distinction of being one of the extremely few characters in Renaissance tragedy to die a natural death during the course of his play.

The Atheist's Tragedy has long been thought a companion work for the earlier *Revenger's Tragedy* mainly on the strength of a misascription of authorship in 1656. Critics have sought to demonstrate the counterpoint of the two plays, blood revenge followed by bloodless revenge, and suggest that T., as author of both works, intentionally explored the extremes of the genre. Despite the appeal of such a suggestion, internal and external evidence as well as questions of style militate strongly against the suggestion that *The Revenger's Tragedy* could even possibly be T.'s. We are left therefore with the conclusion that T. enjoyed a brief and creditable flirtation with the popular theater before returning to government service. He was employed in foreign service to the Low Countries, moving at last to Cadiz where he assumed the responsibilities of secretary to the council of war under Sir Edward Cecil. Wounded during the raid on Cadiz, he was disembarked with other wounded men in Ireland where he died.

BIBLIOGRAPHY: Forker, C. R., "C. T.," in Logan, T. P., and D. S. Smith, eds., *The New Intellectuals* (1977): 248–80; Schuman, S., *C. T.* (1977)

BRIAN JAY CORRIGAN

TOWNSHEND, Aurelian
b. ca. 1583, possibly in Norfolk; d. ca. 1651

T. has generally had a rather bad press. Sir John SUCKLING, considering the candidates for the post of poet laureate in his 1637 poem "A Sessions of the Poets," mentions T. as one of those "wits of the town" he condescends to name, but doesn't judge worthy of discussion. A document of the early 1640s, written by Philip, Earl of Pembroke, Lord Chamberlain to Charles I, refers to T. as "a poore & pocky Poett" and Pembroke was evidently more impressed by the beauty of his "fine and fayer daughter" than by any of the productions of his pen. In the 20th c., T. S. ELIOT wrote, in passing, of the "faint, pleasing tinkle" of T.'s work. Compared to the grander music of John DONNE, Ben JONSON, or John MILTON, T.'s poetry is not unjustly described as a "faint . . . tinkle"; but we ought also to give some weight to the second of Eliot's adjectives, for it also deserves the epithet "pleasing."

We have, unfortunately, little to go on in forming an estimate of T. What survives (and can be attributed to him with reasonable confidence) amounts to no more than some twenty-five poems, two masques, and fragments of a third. The two complete masques, *Albion's Triumph* and *Tempe Restored* were produced at court within a few weeks of one another in 1632. He later supplied a masque (which survives only in incomplete form) to follow a court performance of the French pastoral *Florimene* in 1635. *Albion's Triumph* was produced under the patronage of the king in January 1632. It celebrates the triumph of Albanactus Caesar (a type of Charles I) over excessive passion and vice (Albanactus has a "mind . . . armed with so many moral virtues that he daily conquers a world of vices"), closing with personifications of Concord, Religion, Justice, and Affection to the Country, eager to be associated with the government of king and queen's "virtuous minds." *Tempe Restored* was a kind of reciprocal offering, produced under the patronage of the queen. It celebrates another triumph, in which the destructive charms of Circe are superseded by those of Divine Beauty (the queen), assisted by the power of Heroic Virtue (the king). It may be that *Tempe Restored* saw the first appearance of female actresses (Madame Coniack and Mrs. Shepherd are named in the text) on an English stage, and another performer was Nicholas Lanier the composer. Though in no way memorable, the words of T.'s two masques are attractive and offer evidence of a sharp intelligence.

T.'s nondramatic verse survives in a variety of manuscript and printed miscellanies. His work, naturally enough, registers the influence of greater poets than himself. "Hide Not Thy Love" and "A Paradox" show his familiarity with Donne (though both poems might have benefited from slightly greater attention to Donne's economy of language). "In praise of his Mistress" ("Thou Shepheard, whose intentive eye") is unmistakably related to Robert HERRICK's "Mistresse Elizabeth Wheeler, under the name of the lost Shepardesse." T.'s best poems have, however, a more individual quality. "Let not thy beauty make thee proud" is composed of five beautiful and lucid stanzas of moral advice on the proper use of beauty. It was perhaps addressed to his "fayer" daughter (an unlikely but rewarding comparison might be made with W. B. YEATS's "A Prayer for My Daughter"). The poem's argument is for the avoidance of extremes in the use of beauty's power—and one suspects that T. was well aware that his poem was capable of a political reading too. In "Victorious Beauty," the conventional flattery that the poem hints at, and leads its reader to anticipate, takes a surprising turn that gives an attractively human qualification to the absoluteness of the praise originally offered by the poem. In "Youth and Beauty" ("Thou art so fair, and yong withall"), there is an exactness of mythological wit that is impressively effective; his "Elegy on the death of the King of Sweden: sent to Thomas Carew" (which elicited the more famous response from Thomas CAREW, "Why dost thou sound, my dear Aurelian") displays a shrewd political intelligence and some well-judged rhetoric. Others of T.'s elegies are rather more banal, though that on Venetia Digby has some striking passages. Carew, indeed, praised T. for his "sweetly-flowing numbers" and his "rich fancy" in *Tempe Restored*, a work that, according to Carew, dispensed "knowledge and pleasure to the soul and sense."

BIBLIOGRAPHY: Brooks, C., *Historical Evidence and the Reading of Seventeenth-Century Poetry* (1991); Brown, C. C., *Poems and Masques of A. T.* (1983); Sharpe, K., *Criticism and Compliment* (1987)

GLYN PURSGLOVE

TRACY, Honor [Lilibush Wingfield]

b. 19 October 1913, Bury St. Edmunds, Suffolk; d. 13 June 1989, Oxford

T.'s writing career was both diverse and prolific. Educated in England, Germany, and France, T. lived in

Japan and Ireland, traveling extensively. Her global mind-set is reflected in all of the genres in which she wrote. A freelance writer from 1937 to 1939, T. enlisted in the British Women's Auxiliary Air Force, Intelligence Division, from 1939 to 1941, and earned the rank of sergeant. In 1941, she became a specialist in political warfare for the Ministry of Information. She held this position until 1945, during which time she was sent to Japan to report on the American occupation. In 1946, T. became an assistant editor of the Dublin literary magazine, the *Bell*; she went to work as the Dublin correspondent for London's *Sunday Times* in 1950. Additionally T. was a correspondent and contributor of features for the BBC's "Third Programme." During this period, T. formed an association with an Irish literary review edited by Sean O'FAOLAIN; she contributed short stories and articles to both English and American periodicals.

T.'s earliest works are nonfiction. *Kakemono: A Sketch Book of Post-War Japan* (1950) critically examined General Douglas MacArthur and the American occupation of Japan, and is considered to be a striking analysis of postwar Japan. It was followed by *Mind You, I've Said Nothing!: Forays in the Irish Republic* (1953), a collection of essays from her life in Ireland as a correspondent, including reference to a libel suit filed against her by a local priest that will later show up as a part of the plot in her novel *The Straight and Narrow Path* (1956). Other nonfiction works include *Silk Hats and No Breakfast: Notes on a Spanish Journey* (1957), *Spanish Leaves* (1964), and *Winter in Castille* (1973), all of which relate to T.'s visits to Spain. T.'s nonfiction reflects her interest in travel and appreciation of diverse cultures, and is highly regarded by critics for her honest description.

T. is best known for her humorous novels, incorporating wit and satire, beginning with *The Straight and Narrow Path*, her most popular work. Set in Ireland, it concerns an Englishman who confronts the oddities of Irish life with hilarious results, much like T.'s own experiences related in *Mind You, I've Said Nothing!* T.'s actual experience with a libel suit is crafted into the novel as a lawsuit against Andrew Butler, the main character, an English anthropologist on leave in Ireland, who writes an article about nuns who he believes have been involved in fertility rites. The groundwork for the HUMOR is developed by the contrast between the rational Englishman and the nonrational, emotional Irish.

The structure of a logical central character caught in illogical surroundings is repeated in much of T.'s fiction. Other common themes in her work include satire of the English Establishment and contempt for newspapers, whose purpose (according to T.) appears to be to distort the truth to serve their own needs.

Later novels relating to the Irish are *The Prospects Are Pleasing* (1958), *The First Day of Friday* (1963),

The Quiet End of Evening (1972), *In a Year of Grace* (1975), *The Man from Next Door* (1977), and *The Battle of Castle Reef* (1979). Other novels include *A Number of Things* (1960), set in Trinidad; *A Season of Mists* (1961), set in England; *Men at Work* (1966); *The Beauty of the World* (1967; repub. as *Settled in Chambers*, 1967); and *The Butterflies of the Province* (1970), set in Spain.

T.'s fiction and nonfiction have been translated into a number of languages. In 1968, T. received an award for the best feature script of the year from the British Writers Guild for her radio piece, "Sorrows of Ireland."

BIBLIOGRAPHY: Boylan, V., "H. T.," in Oldsay, B., ed., *British Novelists, 1930–1959*, part 2, *DLB* 15 (1983): 531–38; Gindin, J. J., *Postwar British Fiction: New Accents and Attitudes* (1962)

REBECCA FABER

TRAHERNE, Thomas

b. 1637 or 1638, Hereford; d. October 1674, Middlesex

Fame came late to T. since a substantial body of his literary output was a discovery by 20th-c. scholarship. As a result, little is known of his life. Probably the son of a shoemaker, he and his brother Philip were orphaned early and probably adopted by a relative. T. attended Oxford, took holy orders, and served as rector in a country parish and as chaplain to Sir Orlando Bridgeman, Lord Keeper of the Great Seal.

Only one of T.'s books, *Roman Forgeries* (1673), was published during his lifetime. Possibly a thesis for an academic degree and published anonymously, this anti-Catholic polemic argued for the purity of the early church and attacked doctrines such as transubstantiation and purgatory. Three other works were published posthumously in the late 17th and early 18th cs.: *Christian Ethics* (1675), *A Serious and Pathetical Contemplation of the Mercies of God* (1699), containing a group of poems now known as *Thanksgivings,* and in 1717 the hexameral *Meditations on the Six Days of the Creation.*

Nearly two hundred years elapsed before more of T.'s work came to light. In 1896–97, William T. Brooke picked up two anonymous manuscripts at a London bookstall. He gave these to Alexander B. Grosart, who believed them to be the work of Henry VAUGHAN and prepared to bring out an edition. When Grosart died in 1899, the material fell to Bertram Dobell who ultimately identified the author as T.

The first manuscript was the *Centuries of Meditations*, published in 1908, a collection of prose meditations interspersed with poetry. There are four centuries with one hundred pieces and a fifth section containing only ten. Their stated purpose was to instruct and encourage a friend, probably Mrs. Susanna Hopton, in Felicity, an important concept in T. that involves rejoicing and delighting in God. The *Centuries* have received praise for their individuality and complexity in their development through incantatory repetition of words and phrases.

The second manuscript contains a group of poems and miscellaneous items, including reading notes and expense accounts. The poems were edited and published by Dobell in 1902. Another collection, "Poems of Felicity," edited by Philip Traherne, had been acquired by the British Museum in 1818, then forgotten until the appearance of Dobell's edition. Published in 1910, the poems had been extensively edited by the poet's brother, but the work does contain thirty-nine poems not in the Dobell manuscript.

After H. M. Margoliouth's 1958 two-volume edition of *Centuries, Poems, and Thanksgivings*, T. received serious critical attention, and his reputation was established. In 1964, another manuscript, *Commentaries of Heaven,* was discovered on a burning rubbish heap and in 1982 identified as T.'s. Poems from this manuscript were published in 1989. The manuscript contains other material, including an alphabetical encyclopedia designed to reveal the mysteries of Felicity.

In the past, T.'s prose was valued above his poetry, but critics now take the latter more seriously. Because of his emphasis on childhood, he is often compared to Vaughan and to William WORDSWORTH, while his style has caused him to be seen as a precursor of William BLAKE and Walt Whitman. Certain themes link both his prose and poetry. Felicity is a unifying factor as is his emphasis on the biblical, mystical, and symbolic dimensions of childhood. He is said to have provided the first convincing depictions of childhood experience in English literature. Identifying himself as a Christian epicurean, he takes joy in nature, sees the presence of God therein, and argues the need for the adult to regain the wonder of the child in viewing the natural world. Influenced by scripture, Neoplatonism, hermeticism, and the new science, T. is regarded by some as a philosopher, by others as a mystic. Yet because a significant portion of the T. canon remains unpublished, definitive pronouncements about his work are problematic.

BIBLIOGRAPHY: Clements, A. L., *The Mystical Poetry of T. T.* (1969); Day, M., *T. T.* (1982); Martz, L. L., *The Paradise Within: Studies in Vaughan, T., and Milton* (1964); Stewart, S., *The Expanded Voice: The Art of T. T.* (1970)

FRANCES M. MALPEZZI

TRAVEL AND LITERATURE

Although travel guides, sea voyage narratives, itineraries, picturesque tour descriptions, and other types of travel writing have never constituted more than minor genres, travel itself—as topic, as allegorical mode, or as metaphor—always has been central to British literature. Epics typically describe dangerous journeys, as do quest narratives. The picaresque novel involves a real or figurative journey. The novel of learning (the Bildungsroman) and the novel of artistic development (the Künstlerroman) often do as well. Utopian literature generally requires a voyage to reach UTOPIA. Pastoral idyllic literature frequently includes travel, as does locodescriptive writing.

While nearly all literature can be described through travel metaphors (with references to moving narratives, topoi, and so on), even the purest forms of travel writing combine with other forms of writing and do more than describe the factual circumstances of places that a writer encounters. Topographical poetry lends itself to travel description, for example, though it also often includes what Samuel JOHNSON calls "historical retrospection or incidental meditation." The many forms and purposes involved in travel writing have led some to view it as a hybrid literary type and a few to deny that it is a useful category at all.

An important and controversial distinction is often made between nonfictional and fictional travel accounts (or alternatively nonliterary and literary accounts). The distinction would seem at first glance to be absolute. Nonfictional travel accounts may be most valuable for the factual, authentic, objective information that they appear to convey. Fictional accounts may elide the factual in favor of imaginative, aesthetic, and other concerns. A closer look, though, blurs the distinction. The most enduring nonfictional travel accounts also often tell a good story and aestheticize objects of description. The most enduring fictional travel accounts often establish their plausibility and power by relating to the world as it is known.

Moreover, nonfictional as well as fictional travel narratives come from cultural and ideological perspectives that tell readers as much about the circumstances of individual writers as they do about the locations described. A British travel narrative describing Katmandu is also inevitably about Britain and a British subjectivity. It is about the British subject's own past and about the ways that other writers whom the writer has read and whose path the writer is following have written about Katmandu. Historically, writers have long recognized the relation between exterior worlds and the self, though the recognition has manifested itself variously in their texts. Medieval and Renaissance poets often use descriptions of external landscapes in travel narratives to develop allegories of human experience. During the 18th c., there is an increasing literary concern with the way the internal, subjective self creates and is created by the external world, resulting in romantic travel narratives that involve corresponding psychological and spiritual quests. Postmodern travel writers often use their explicit awareness of the limits of their perspective to develop cultural explorations and critiques.

As a sampling of the extensive body of travel literature shows, the purposes behind writing travel accounts are extremely varied. Two of the most famous OLD ENGLISH elegies, *The Seafarer* and *The Wanderer*, use travel as a means of examining the human condition. While there are early examples of nonfictional travel narratives, guides, and itineraries—such as a text (often considered the first English travel book) by a Heidenheim nun, which describes the travels of Willibald who voyaged with his family to Rome around 718—the form becomes popular only with *The Travels of Sir John Mandeville* (1357), a highly imaginative guide (describing the discovery of a fountain of youth and encounters with Cyclopses, for example) for pilgrims to Jerusalem and travelers to Egypt, Turkey, India, China, and beyond. Mandeville's *Travels* influenced another fictional late-14th-c. pilgrimage account: Geoffrey CHAUCER's *Canterbury Tales*.

As the British traveled overseas in the 15th and 16th cs., accounts of exploration such as Thomas HARRIOT's *A Brief and True Report of the New Found Land of Virginia* and Walter RALEIGH's *Discoverie of the Large, Rich and Bewtiful Empyre of Guiana* increasingly appeared. At the end of the 16th c., the geographer Richard HAKLUYT published *Principal Navigations, Voyages, and Discoveries of the English Nation*, a compilation of sea voyage narratives. Hakluyt's publication participated in a growing vogue for exploration narratives that extended through the 17th c. and included works ranging from *The Travels of John Sanderson in the Levant* (1584–1602) and George SANDYS's *A Relation of a Journey*, both of which contributed to early British Orientalist ideas, to William Dampier's *New Voyage round the World* (1697), *Voyages and Descriptions* (1698), and *A Voyage to New Holland* (1699).

Dampier's texts were widely read and marked the beginning of the golden age of British travel literature, the 18th c. Travel at this time increasingly became an activity of leisure and self-education—that is, tourism—as well as of exploration and business. Along with exploration narratives and descriptions of the natural resources and the products of foreign lands came accounts of the aesthetics of landscape and amusing anecdotes. Many texts, both nonfiction and fiction, emerged from the increasingly fashionable Grand Tour. The Grand Tour took travelers, usually young men of the upper and (by midcentury) middle classes, through Europe, generally for two or three years. Travelers on the Grand Tour studied classical history, refined their social and aesthetic tastes, and admired natural scenery. The path of the Tour, and the tourists' practices on it, became conventional and helped determine how writers—and readers—of travel accounts related to the world beyond Britain.

At the same time, travel within Britain (including the Home Tour) became more common with the improvement of roads and the increase in leisure time among the middle classes. Aesthetic theories of the picturesque, promoted most famously by William Gilpin, and of the sublime and beautiful, discussed influentially by Edmund BURKE, could be applied as easily to the mountains of the English Lake District as to the French Alps.

Literary writers, journalists, and nonprofessional writers alike published accounts of their travels at this time, and a sample of their texts demonstrates the growing variety of functions of travel writing. Joseph ADDISON's *Remarks on Several Parts of Italy* influenced the way many early-18th-c. travelers understood Italy on the Grand Tour. Daniel DEFOE's three-volume *A Tour through the Whole Island of Great Britain* is a guidebook written after Defoe's extensive British travels. Lady Mary Wortley MONTAGU's *Letters of the Right Honourable Lady M—y W—y M—e Written, during her travels in Europe, Asia and Africa* (3 vols., 1763) covers territories rarely traveled in by other 18th-c. British women and introduced the smallpox inoculation to Britain.

Henry FIELDING's *Journal of a Voyage to Lisbon* concerns a voyage he took in unfulfilled hopes of regaining failing health, an increasingly common motive for foreign travels, which earlier had been thought dangerous to health and well-being. Oliver GOLDSMITH's topographical poem *The Traveller* uses European locodescription as a means of social critique. Tobias SMOLLETT's *Travels through France and Italy*, deriding the French and Italians, led Laurence STERNE to call Smollett "the learned Smelfungus" in his own *Sentimental Journey through France and Italy*.

James BOSWELL describes a 1773 trip with Johnson to Scotland and the Hebrides in *The Journal of a Tour to the Hebrides*, Johnson already having published his own account in *A Journey to the Western Islands of Scotland*. The slave narrative *The Interesting Narrative of the Life of Olaudah Equiano* (2 vols., 1789) details Equiano's travels from when he was taken captive in Africa to when he worked as a shipboard slave in Britain and the British colonies to when he eventually settled in England as a free man. Arthur Young's *Travels in France* (1792) records Young's French travels from 1787 to 1790, taking him through the French Revolution. *An Account of a Voyage Round the World* (1773), *A Voyage towards the South Pole* (1777), and *A Voyage to the Pacific Ocean* (1784) describe the explorations of Captain James Cook.

Travel writing continued to proliferate in the 19th c. William WORDSWORTH's *Guide through the Lakes* (1810) exemplified a growing vogue for travel in Brit-

ain, especially in the Lake District, a vogue encouraged by picturesque tour writers and illustrators such as Gilpin and Thomas West and reflected in works by Ann RADCLIFFE and Jane AUSTEN. Wordsworth also wrote tour poems such as "Descriptive Sketches," about a European tour, and "An Evening Walk," about a walk in the Lake District, as well as sonnet sequences about tours through Scotland and Europe. William COBBETT's *Rural Rides* describes the harsh conditions of agrarian life as Cobbett witnessed them on horseback rides through England and criticizes the people and policies he considered responsible for those conditions, while also appreciating occasional beauty. Lord BYRON's *Childe Harold's Pilgrimage* and *Don Juan* recount the wide wanderings of their heroes. The writings of Wordsworth, Cobbett, and Byron, as well as many other British Romantic authors such as Percy Bysshe and Mary Wollstonecraft SHELLEY, are inseparable from the travels that gave the texts locations and, frequently, driving force.

Much travel writing at this time provides insights into a changing social and aesthetic ethos within Britain and into a changing worldview as the British increased their colonial incursions. British interest in world travel at this time, especially concerning places that showed potential as colonies, is clear from the publication of works such as Laurence Oliphant's *A Journey to Khatmandu* (1852); Sir Richard BURTON's *Personal Narrative of a Pilgrimage to El-Medinah and Mecca*, *The Lake Regions of Central Africa* (2 vols., 1860), and *Unexplored Syria* (2 vols., 1872), not to mention his unexpurgated editions of *The Kama Sutra* and *Arabian Nights*; David Livingstone's *Missionary Travels and Researches in South Africa* (1857) and *Narrative of an Expedition to the Zambesi and Its Tributaries* (1865); Sir Henry M. Stanley's *How I Found Livingstone* (1872); Mary H. Kingsley's *Travels in West Africa* (1897); and ultimately the novella "Heart of Darkness" by Joseph CONRAD, a prolific writer of fiction that involves travel. These texts often are oriented toward readers concerned with the social sciences, though one of the most famous 19th-c. travel books was written by an explorer interested in the natural sciences: Charles DARWIN's *Voyage of the Beagle*, first published in 1839, describes the journey that provided him the data he used when writing *On the Origin of Species*.

In the 20th c., especially after the First World War, much travel writing is characterized by an ironic viewpoint that contributes to a critique of Western culture and, in the last decades of the century, by an awareness of the traveler's limitations of perspective. Important 20th-c. travel texts include Aldous HUXLEY's *Jesting Pilate* (1926) and *Beyond the Mexique Bay* (1934), T. E. Lawrence's *The Seven Pillars of Wisdom* (1922; rev. ed., 1926), Graham GREENE's

Lawless Roads and *Journey without Maps* (1936), Rebecca WEST's *Black Lamb and Grey Falcon: A Journey through Yugoslavia*, Evelyn WAUGH's *Remote People* (1931; repub. as *They Were Still Dancing*, 1932) and *Ninety-Two Days* (1934), V. S. PRITCHETT's *The Spanish Temper* (1954), and Bruce CHATWIN's *In Patagonia* and *The Songlines*.

The ethical problems of a British subject's experience of travel in colonized or less powerful lands also inflect much, though certainly not all, 20th-c. travel writing. In one of the most interesting developments, increasing numbers of English-language writers born into current or former British colonies write about travels to colonial or postcolonial places or, occasionally, to the British Isles, complicating the Anglo-centric viewpoints that preceded them. While this phenomenon is not new (Equiano wrote of his mid-18th-c. travels from the perspective of a man born in Benin, Africa, and shaped in the West Indies and the American colonies), works such as V. S. NAIPAUL's *The Middle Passage* (1962) on the Caribbean, *An Area of Darkness* (1964) on India, and *Among the Believers* (1981) on the Islamic East, Vikram Seth's *From Heaven Lake* (1983) on Sinkiang and Tibet, and Salman RUSHDIE's *The Jaguar Smile* (1987) on Nicaragua contribute to a multifaceting of travel literature.

BIBLIOGRAPHY: Buzard, J., *The Beaten Track: European Tourism, Literature, and the Ways to Culture, 1800–1918* (1993); Cocker, M., *Loneliness and Time: The Story of British Travel Writing* (1992); Cox, E. G., *A Reference Guide to the Literature of Travel* (3 vols., 1935–49); Korte, B., *English Travel Writing from Pilgrimages to Postcolonial Explorations*, trans. by C. Matthias (2000); Pratt, M. L., *Imperial Eyes: Travel Writing and Transculturation* (1992)

MICHAEL WILEY

TRAVERS, Ben[jamin]

b. 12 November 1886, Hendon, Middlesex; d. 18 December 1980, London

Author of custom-made farces for the Aldwych Company under the supervision of Tom Walls, T. was one of the most successful British playwrights of the 1920s and 1930s. The best of his plays include *A Cuckoo in the Nest* (perf. 1925; pub. 1938) and *Rookery Nook* (perf. 1926; pub. 1930), both adapted from novels published in 1922, *Thark* (1927), and *Plunder* (perf. 1928; pub. 1931), and *A Cup of Kindness* (perf. 1929; pub. 1934). T. continued to write intermittently through the late 1950s and his later comedy *The Bed before Yesterday* (1975) was successfully produced in his ninetieth year.

TRELAWNY, Edward John

b. 13 November 1792, Cornwall?; d. 13 August 1881, Sompting, Surrey

Throughout his long life, which spanned the Romantic and much of the Victorian periods, T. was his own most fascinating creation. He is known primarily as the man who rescued Percy Bysshe SHELLEY's heart from the funeral pyre and as the author of two ostensibly autobiographical prose works: *Adventures of a Younger Son* (3 vols., 1831) and *Recollections of the Last Days of Shelley and Byron* (1858), later revised as *Records of Shelley, Byron and the Author* (1878). So artfully did T. fashion his own image that when the *Adventures* appeared, seven years after Lord BYRON's death, readers assumed that its author and Byronic hero had served as the model for Byron's *Corsair* rather than the other way around. But T. had not met Byron or the Shelleys until early in 1822, when he joined them in Italy and regaled them with tales of his purported exploits as a renegade Royal Navy captain and privateer in the Indian Ocean—tales that he would eventually publish in the *Adventures.*

T.'s fictionalized account of his life begins with his childhood under the tyranny of his strict and miserly father, a retired lieutenant-colonel. He valorizes his protagonist's acts of rebellion—killing his father's pet raven, setting fire to a room at boarding school—as evidence of a wild and indomitable spirit. At age twelve, T. joined the Royal Navy, and from that point in his narrative fact yields increasingly to fiction. As T. tells it, after nearly killing his lieutenant in a barroom brawl in Bombay, he deserted from the navy and joined a French privateer, de Ruyter, a character T. apparently invented on the model of the infamous French corsair Robert Surcouf and Byron's Conrad in *The Corsair.* T.'s protagonist survives a series of violent adventures in the Indian Ocean, acquiring along the way a beautiful young Arab wife, Zela (who meets a tragic death), and returning to England after de Ruyter is killed. Mary SHELLEY oversaw publication of the book and persuaded T. to omit a number of passages she considered offensive.

Nearly three decades passed before T. published *Recollections of the Last Days of Shelley and Byron*, an inaccurate but vivid account of his acquaintance with the Shelley circle at Pisa and his adventures in Greece with Byron and, after Byron's death, in the company of the mercenary Odysseus Androutsos. The book was highly popular, although many readers balked at such lapses in taste as the voyeuristic scene in which T. succumbs to an impulse to remove Byron's shroud in order to satisfy his curiosity about the dead poet's club foot.

Twenty years later, with the assistance of William Michael ROSSETTI, T. published a revised version of the *Recollections* under the new title *Records of Shelley, Byron, and the Author* (2 vols., 1878). Its most notable departures from the earlier edition are T.'s unflattering descriptions of Mary Shelley, whom he characterizes as hypocritical and unworthy of her late husband, and of Byron, whose character and physical prowess he belittles. In T.'s final assessment of the Shelley circle, only Percy Bysshe Shelley himself emerges untarnished. If the episode with Byron's corpse had offended his earlier readers, this later perceived betrayal of one-time friends redoubled T.'s reputation as an ill-bred ingrate.

Although T. embellished the story of his life with adventures he had never had and "friends" (like John KEATS) whom he had never met, his accounts were so vividly realized that they fully persuaded his Victorian audience. More recently, research has revealed that T.'s naval career was far tamer than the one he describes in the *Adventures* (he left the Royal Navy as a midshipman in 1811 because of illness), and critics have sought psychological explanations for the violence and misogyny of his narratives.

BIBLIOGRAPHY: Crane, D., *Lord Byron's Jackal* (1999); Miller, J., *T. with Shelley and Byron* (1922); St. Clair, W., *T.* (1977)

DENISE VULTEE

TREMAIN, Rose
b. 2 August 1943, London

T.'s most successful books are the historical novels *Restoration* (1989) and *Music and Silence* (1999), but she has also written short stories, popular history, radio and television plays, and novels set in contemporary times. Her fiction is distinguished by vivid characterization and great variety in setting and theme. A feminist whose first book was the nonfiction work *The Fight for Freedom for Women* (1973), T. often writes from the male point of view, and traces fictional lives as various as those of a young transsexual and a 17th-c. royal consort. T. has "strenuously resisted categorization as a 'woman's writer,'" declaring her intention to take risks with form and "express ideas through characters absolutely unlike myself." Not as experimental as Angela CARTER or Jeannette WINTERSON, T. works largely within a realist tradition, although her subjects are sometimes unusual and discomfiting.

The *Times Literary Supplement* in 1981 wrote that "when it comes to depicting psychological injuries she has few rivals." Born Rose Thomson, T. experienced early the suffering she writes about. When she was ten, her parents separated and her father, a minor playwright, stated his wish to have nothing to do with the family. T. attended boarding school and later the Sorbonne, which awarded her a diploma in literature in 1963. Her fiction often features divisions between parent and child and, more generally, lovelessness. Two early marriages ended in divorce (Tremain is the surname of her first husband). In the 1990s, she met biographer Richard Holmes; they make a home together in Norfolk.

T. studied under Sir Angus WILSON at the University of East Anglia, where she later taught creative writing. On receiving her B.A. in English in 1967, she worked as a teacher and editor before publishing two nonfiction books, including a BIOGRAPHY of Joseph Stalin (1975). Her first three novels, *Sadler's Birthday* (1976), *Letter to Sister Benedicta* (1978), and *The Cupboard* (1981), were praised for T.'s ability to inhabit the lives of diverse characters—a lonely butler, a neglected middle-aged wife, and an elderly novelist planning her own death. Although some critics have made claims for T.'s sympathy and good HUMOR, her world can be a harsh one, marked by isolation, thwarted desire, and the presence of death.

In 1983, T. was named one of the "Twenty Best Young British Novelists," along with writers such as Martin AMIS and Salman RUSHDIE. *The Swimming Pool Season* (1985), her fourth novel, is set in France, where Larry Kendal worries about his marriage and builds an elaborate pool. The novel features a large, interconnected cast of characters representing various classes and nationalities. This chorus of voices appears in several subsequent works, including *Sacred Country* (1992) and *Music and Silence*, as well as short stories like "Trade Wind over Nashville," one of several enthusiastic but unconvincing attempts to capture American working-class life.

T.'s first major success arrived with *Restoration: A Novel of Seventeenth-Century England*, nominated for the Booker Prize. *Restoration* was T.'s most ambitious novel to that time, admired for its historic specificity and the bold choice of unheroic protagonist Robert Merivel, dissolute physician and professional cuckold for King Charles II. Commentators noted the parallel between the hedonism of the Restoration era and the mood in England under Margaret Thatcher. One of the key images of *Restoration* is a visible, beating human heart that Merivel is allowed to touch. He discovers it is "utterly without feeling." The problem of the heart—betrayed, pained, or numbed—recurs in T.'s fiction, for example in "The Candle Maker," in which a jilted peasant woman fashions a heart of wax to inflict magical harm on an old lover. In *Restoration*, Merivel eventually allows his own heart to be touched, figuratively, by his Quaker friend, Pearce, who insists that Merivel use his medical talent in a mental asylum. Merivel falls into his old ways and seduces a madwoman, Katherine, who dies in childbirth. Their daughter, Margaret, is a hazy indicator of hope at the novel's dreamlike conclusion. The title refers in part to Merivel's journey from fool and coward to compassionate healer and father.

Sacred Country is T.'s boldest exploration of the troubled ground of gender and identity. Mary Ward, hated by her father, is convinced that she is really Martin, and the story follows her quest, through painful surgery and hormone treatments, for a male body. Mary's determination to alter her identity is only the most drastic evidence of restlessness felt among all the characters. Like Merivel in *Restoration,* Sadler in *Sadler's Birthday*, and Erica in *The Cupboard*, Mary is not, on the whole, a likable personality. While T. may have intended a criticism of masculine violence in the scene where Mary/Martin assaults beloved friend Pearl, the effect is disturbing. T.'s determination to avoid sentimentality can result in this unsettling distance from her characters.

In 1997, *The Way I Found Her* featured Lewis Little, a precocious Devon schoolboy who spends a melodramatic summer in Paris, falling in love with Russian novelist Valentina Gavrilovich and investigating her sudden disappearance. Although T.'s ability to present Lewis's point of view was praised, reviewers were hesitant about the unlikely plot, which features drug money and kidnapping. T.'s graphic descriptions of the boy's sexual practices highlight another distinctive feature of her fiction. Her people are filled with longings often more painful than tender, and their sexual desires frequently leave them ashamed and unsatisfied.

With *Music and Silence,* T. returned to the historical novel, this one set in the court of Danish King Christian IV, where music is admired but musicians must play in a dark cellar. Lacking the subtly anachronistic postmodern style of *Restoration, Music and Silence* provides a happier and more conventional depiction of love than any of her previous novels. Although lutenist Peter Claire and his lover Emilia Tilsen seem colorless in comparison with the vulnerable, unhappy king and his lascivious consort Kirsten Munk, the satisfaction of seeing the honorable Peter and Emilia rewarded at the novel's end clearly pleased readers, and the novel won the Whitbread Prize. One of the intriguing aspects of *Music and Silence* is T.'s complex portrait of monarchy. Both Charles II in *Restoration* and Christian IV in *Music and Silence* are flawed individuals, yet they seem to possess more imagination and compassion than T.'s characters typically exhibit. Charles II is also given Godlike qualities, including his ability to see into the souls of his subjects and inspire their adoration. T.'s exploration of the positive power of kings sits oddly beside her more expected liberal feminist criticisms of organized religion, class antagonism, and the limitations of marriage.

Three books of short stories, *The Colonel's Daughter* (1984), *The Garden of the Villa Mollini* (1987), and *Evangelista's Fan* (1994), were published as T.'s *Collected Short Stories* in 1996. T.'s use of stratagems such as dialect or changing point of view has become more assured, so that recent stories like "The Unoccupied Room" achieve a fearful gripping quality that earlier stories lacked. In "Over," an old man's defining memory—shooting a bird in view of his young son—is presented with particular and savage sharpness. In some respects, T.'s preoccupation with despair and longing has lessened in recent years, but her fiction continues to emphasize the harsh realities that separate characters from fulfillment and from each other.

BIBLIOGRAPHY: Graff, E. J., "Delusions of Gender," *WRB* 10 (July 1993): 25–26; Fendler, S., and R. Wittlinger, "R. T.'s *Restoration* and Thatcherism," *CC* 3 (Winter 2000): 29–50

SUE SORENSEN

TRESSELL, Robert

(pseud. of Robert Noonan) b. ca. 1870, Ireland; d. 3 February 1911, Liverpool

Little is known about T.'s life, except that he was probably reared in Dublin, spent time in South Africa, and was for many years a skilled house painter in Hastings (Mugsborough). He had no literary contacts, and his one novel, *The Ragged Trousered Philanthropists*, was published posthumously and almost by accident in 1914. This edition was savagely mangled, and the complete novel, of about 250,000 words, did not appear until 1955. T. is still unrecognized by academics, but his book had a vast readership among working-class people and is the best-loved novel of the British labor movement.

The title, like much else, is ironic—"All through the summer the crowd of ragged-trousered philanthropists continued to toil and sweat at their noble and unselfish task of making money for Mr. Rushton." The central characters are building workers slaving for a bad employer, whose name means "rush-it-on." Other names are heavily symbolic, as in *Pilgrim's Progress*—Sweater, Grinder, Starvem, Crass, Slyme. T. described the book as "the story of twelve months in Hell, told by one of the damned." He obviously knew the Bible and William SHAKESPEARE quite well but comes over as a man without formal education, writing in the plain unpretentious language of George ORWELL (who called it "a wonderful book"). Just as his style is utterly different from that of most published novelists, so is his subject matter. He has no time for romance and melodrama and goes back to the fathers of the English novel, Daniel DEFOE and John BUNYAN, concentrating on the day-to-day struggle to survive and the war between the forces of good and evil for control of an individual's soul.

The builders have a miserable existence, underpaid, overworked, and in ever-present danger of unemployment. Nothing happens which is not fairly normal; a man is sacked for being old, loses his home and eventually dies in the workhouse; another man is killed in an accident; all of them are bullied by the overseer (Hunter); there is constant petty thieving. Most of the action occurs in the workplace, but we also follow the men home and see their wives attempting to feed the family and to keep out of debt. They are all semi-starved and have absolutely nothing to look forward to. The characters are vivid, though not complex, and their stories are told with a wealth of detail—"everyday experience," Orwell said, "but which simply had not been noticed before." T. insisted that whatever one thought of his politics, his picture of life in "Mugsborough" was essentially true.

Yet life does not have to be like this. The workers are constructing a house that they could never afford to live in and are forced to skimp the work to save money when they would prefer to do it well. Work ought to be fulfilling, life ought to be pleasant for everyone, but the system makes it impossible. Socialism for T. is like the Eternal City for Bunyan, the shining goal that offers the only hope in darkness.

There are several formal arguments in which Owen, the socialist sign painter dying of tuberculosis, tries to convince his mates that the world can be changed. They do not believe him, and this makes T. extremely bitter; he can never really understand why the majority allow themselves to be exploited. He is particularly scathing about the churches (mostly Nonconformist), which he accuses of preying on the poor. Several of his working men behave cruelly and stupidly, especially to women, and very few are prepared to think seriously about their situation. Owen is mad, we are told sardonically, because he is trying to reason with people who are incapable of logical thought.

Yet the novel ends on a note of hope, and is always readable, often savagely funny. Some believe it is merely a fascinating document from a vanished age. Manual workers in the West are no longer very poor, nor are they deferential to their "betters," and organized religion has lost its power. But the profit motive, with its indifference to morality, is still much as he describes it; so is the trivial and philistine nature of popular culture. The men who blame foreigners for their problems and object to paying tax for the general good, the women and boys who stuff their heads with cheap romances and horror comics, all have their parallels a hundred years on. *The Ragged-Trousered Philanthropists* is a book of extraordinary power that has been gravely underestimated.

BIBLIOGRAPHY: Alfred, D., ed., *The R. T. Lectures, 1981–1988* (1988); Ball, F. C., *T. of Mugsborough* (1951); Mitchell, J., *R. T. and the Ragged Trousered Philanthropists* (1969)

MERRYN WILLIAMS

TREVELYAN, [Sir] George Otto
b. 20 July 1838, London; d. 17 August 1928, Wallington, Northumberland

The nephew of Thomas Babington MACAULAY (Lord Macaulay), T. was educated at Trinity College, Cambridge, and much like his uncle established a distinguished career as both stateman and man of letters. T.

was a member of Parliament from 1865 to 1897, and he served at various times in the cabinet of William Ewart Gladstone. In 1876, T. published his two-volume *Life and Letters of Lord Macaulay*, praised for providing an insightful portrait of the private man behind the public persona. In the following year, T. edited a selection of his uncle's writings, and from 1880 to 1914 produced his fourteen-volume history *The American Revolution*.

TREVOR, William
b. 24 May 1928, Mitchelstown, County Cork, Ireland

Beginning his literary career at the age of thirty, T. is now regarded as one of the finest and most honored short story writers in the English language. He relocated permanently to England in 1960. This prolific writer's output includes not only short stories, but also novels and dramas. Noted for his skillful characterizations of those who exist on the fringe of society, T. explores their psychological make-ups, invoking a sense of pathos with the comic. While many of his earlier works are set in England, T.'s more recent works are set in his native Ireland. His short stories, in particular, exhibit the influence of James JOYCE, with whom he is often favorably compared.

Although T.'s first novel, *A Standard of Balance*, appeared in 1958, it was *The Old Boys* (1964) that attracted considerable attention, launching his literary career. The book focuses on the members of the Old Boys' Association of an English public school who reunite to elect the next president. Underneath an air of affected formality, the aging men scheme against one another, rekindling rivalries and hostilities of distant school days.

In *The Boarding House* (1965), suggesting comparison to Joyce's story of the same title from *The Dubliners*, T. offers a macabre view of a distorted world. The novel focuses on a small, strange group of boarders taken in by William Wagner Bird because they are the type that society would never miss. *The Love Department* (1966) uses a suburban setting in which Edward Blakeston-Smith leaves the protection of a monastery to find employment in the "Love Department" of a national magazine, supervised by Lady Dolores Bourhardie. At the direction of Bourhardie, Edward's mission is to hunt down the seductive pervert and home-wrecker, Septimus Taum.

Using comic British characters, T. creates the tale of Miss Gomez, a convert to the church of the Brethren of the Way in *Miss Gomez and the Brethren* (1971). Convinced a sex crime is soon to be committed, Gomez cannot find a receptive audience until Prudence Tuke disappears, the police arrive, and the newspapers proclaim a "Sex Crime Prophecy."

Fools of Fortune (1983) centers on Willie Quinton and is set in Ireland during the Anglo-Irish War. An ordered family life is shattered by the War, and, seeking revenge for the murder of his family, Quinton kills the British soldier responsible for their deaths. Consumed by guilt, he flees to Italy, where he is hounded by past memories. Receiving generally favorable reviews, *Fools of Fortune* examines the tragic results of violence and vengeance. Set in 1931 on a small island off the coast of Cork, *The Silence in the Garden* (1988) explores the Rollestons, a once vital Anglo-Irish family that has slipped into hopelessness. Although criticized for lacking a certain vitality, the novel managed to win the *Yorkshire Post* Book of the Year Award.

Published as two paired novellas, *Two Lives: Reading Turgenev; My House in Umbria* (1991) contains two narratives that mirror one another. "Reading Turgenev" explores the world of a young Irish girl, Mary Louise Dallon, who uses reading as a means of escape from her unhappy marriage, while "My House in Umbria" focuses on Mrs. Delahunty, a former madam turned romance novelist. *Two Lives* met with mixed reviews, being criticized for its somewhat labored quality.

Felicia's Journey (1994) and *Death in Summer* (1999) focus on young women with little education. *Felicia's Journey* is a combination quest novel and psychological thriller in which the central character, a young Irish woman, becomes pregnant and sets off to find Johnny Lysaght, the father of her child. Along the way, she encounters Mr. Hilditch, a seemingly kind older gentleman. Hilditch, however, steals Felicia's money, manipulating her into accepting his hospitality. Told from the viewpoints of both Felicia and Hilditch, T. compellingly underscores both the loss of innocence and corruption. In *Death in Summer*, T. explores human vulnerability. Creating a suspenseful mystery focusing on Pettie, an orphanage runaway who obtains a position as nanny, and Thaddeus Davenant, the head of the household, T. shifts between viewpoints of the two.

Although T. has achieved substantial success as a novelist, he considers himself primarily a short story writer. *The Day We Got Drunk on Cake* (1967) was T.'s first collection to appear in print. *The Ballroom of Romance*, which centers on feminine characters whose desires are frustrated by brutish men, appeared in 1972, followed by *Angels at the Ritz and Other Stories* in 1975. It was *Angels at the Ritz* that won T. a solid reputation as a short story writer.

Most of the twelve stories included in *After Rain* (1997) first appeared in the *New Yorker* and other magazines. The collection generally explores unhappiness, particularly as caused by marriage. Critically, T. was praised for the specificity and REALISM exhibited in the collection. Avoiding the sentimental, T.'s *The Hill Bachelors* (2000) concentrates on characters caught in conflict between human desire and circumstance. Dealing with a wide range of characters, from English elitists to Irish farmers, the twelve stories have been praised for their realistic, hopeful comment on being human.

Throughout his prolific and distinguished career, T. has received numerous awards, including the Hawthornden Prize (1964), the Allied Irish Banks' Prize (1976), and the Whitbread Award (1976, 1983, 1994).

BIBLIOGRAPHY: Glitzen, J., "The Truth-Tellers of W. T.," *Crit* 21 (1979): 59–72; MacKenna, D., *W. T.* (1999); Mortimer, M., "W. T. in Dublin," *EI* 4 (1975): 77–85; Paulson, S. M., *W. T.* (1993)

                                        SAMUEL GAUSTAD

TROLLOPE, Anthony

b. 24 April 1815, London; d. 6 December 1882, Harting Grange, near Petersfield, Sussex

T. took the precaution of laying down the outlines of his own life in his *An Autobiography*, written from 1875 onward, published posthumously in 1883. Despite a barrage of biographical attention at the end of the 20th c., his own account of Anthony Trollope stands, more or less intact. The Trollopes were, famously, a novel-writing family. Frances Milton Trollope—the redoubtable "Mrs. Trollope"—had produced a dozen best-selling works of fiction before her youngest son (Anthony) made his debut in 1847; T.'s elder brother Thomas Adolphus wrote twenty novels during an otherwise full and busy life. Thomas's wife (also called Frances) wrote eleven. Even T.'s sister, Cecilia, produced a novel before expiring, prematurely, at the age of thirty-one. The most productive member of the Trollopes (less a family than a fiction-producing collective) was, of course, T. with a lifetime score of forty-seven—and, as he proudly records in *An Autobiography,* some £90,000 in earnings.

Like other great Victorian novelists, T. initially wanted to do something else (something "worthier") with his life than scribbling fiction. That he turned to literature was, in a sense, an admission of failure. According to his own version (it has, one may note, been questioned by some modern investigators), his childhood was unusually wretched. His father, a failed barrister, failed farmer, failed husband and—by implication—sadly failed paterfamilias obliged the redoubtable Mrs. Trollope to put bread on the table with the fluent earnings of her pen. Meanwhile her brood of consumptive children died around her—only two of her offspring survived their mother. Mrs. Trollope's indomitable spirit was something that she passed on to T. (never, as he bitterly felt, her favorite child). T., his father's son (at least in his early life), failed utterly at school.

Unlike other males in his family, T. did not go to university (he would, doubtless, have failed there as well). He even failed as a lowly post office clerk. Those wanting to plumb the depth of his youthful despair and humiliation should read, in addition to the *Autobiography*, his autobiographical novel, *The Three Clerks* (3 vols., 1858). The hero, Charley Tudor, comes close to ruining himself with dissipation and marriage to a barmaid—Norah Geraghty (she has, it later emerges, a heart of gold: slightly tarnished). Like Charley, T. finally made good when, after some spectacular mishap in the London office, he was posted to Ireland in 1841. Here, he found a wife, success in his primary profession (he rose high in the post office, before retiring in 1867), and a second profession as a novelist (in which he again rose high—although judgment has traditionally placed him as "the lesser Thackeray").

T.'s first effort in fiction was an Irish novel, *The Macdermots of Ballycloran* (3 vols., 1847). Irish fiction, as popularized by Charles Lever and Samuel Lover, was traditionally merry. T.'s effort was a notably glum saga of seduction, bastardy, murder, alcoholism, and madness among a degraded Hibernian gentry. The work was published by a second-rate house, only through his mother's good offices and failed abysmally. The period of the Famine was not a propitious time for Irish wares. T. followed up with two other Irish novels—*The Kellys and the O'Kellys* (3 vols., 1848) and *Castle Richmond* (3 vols., 1860)—neither of which was well received. Neither was an historical novel, *La Vendée* (3 vols., 1850). But T. (whose motto was, like Josiah Crawley's, "it's dogged as does it") carried on in what must have seemed, at times, a very hard furrow.

In 1851, T. was posted back to England, with a roving commission to visit rural post offices. It was now he discovered what was to be his main line of fiction: the institutional comedy. The first work in this genre was *The Warden* (1855). This story of ecclesiastical infighting enjoyed more success. It is, essentially, a battle between Anglican frogs and mice revolving around two issues which are big in Lilliput-Barchester: who will get the wardenship of Hiram's Hospital (an almshouse, containing a dozen Bedesmen); and will John Bold marry Eleanor Harding? It was William Makepeace THACKERAY, drawing on the example of Sir Walter SCOTT and Honoré de Balzac, who pioneered the sequence novel. *The Warden* supplied the foundation for what is known as the "Barsetshire novels." They are ecclesiastical—that is, about the institution of the church—not "religious." T. studiously avoids issues of doctrine although it is clear that his sympathies tend to be with the High rather than the Low Church party. Other novels in the sequence are *Barchester Towers* (3 vols., 1857), in which a new-broom bishop arrives at the cathedral;

Doctor Thorne (3 vols., 1858), like all T.'s fictions, is a "Who will she marry?" tale, she in this case being Mary Thorne, a girl of mysterious parentage adopted by the doctor of the title; *Framley Parsonage* (3 vols., 1861), a novel about the embarrassment of debt—another perennial Trollopian theme; this was T.'s first serial novel, published in the newly launched *Cornhill Magazine*; it was also the work with which he achieved his first notable fame; *The Small House at Allington* (2 vols., 1864), a story tinged with the dark hues of T.'s later period, centered around a jilted, and fragrant heroine, Lily Dale—jilted maidens are another staple of Trollopian fiction; *The Last Chronicle of Barset* (32 parts, 1867), dark verging on black—the novel in which T. "killed" the redoubtable Mrs. Proudie. The hero is the insanely rectitudinous Josiah Crawley who is falsely accused of theft, while poor Lily is left, poignantly, to wither on the shelf of spinsterhood having rejected the addresses of her true love, Johnny Eames.

The Barsetshire novels represent a huge and majestic achievement in Victorian fiction. It is partnered by another, equally vast, Trollopian structure—the Palliser novels. These are, by contrast, metropolitan (not rural) and parliamentary (not ecclesiastical). The principal character, Plantagenet Palliser (later Duke of Omnium and prime minister of England), is introduced as hero in the first of the series *Can You Forgive Her* (20 parts, 1865) in which his union with the plucky and admirable Scottish heiress, Glencora MacCluskie, is forged (she rejects, for the stiff—but inherently noble—"Planty Pall" a dashing rival suitor, Burgo Fitzgerald; T.'s most ambitious moral claim for his fiction was that it would instruct young ladies in how to choose their husbands). The Palliser series moves from the parliamentary to the more generally political with *Phineas Finn* (2 vols., 1869), a novel that articulates Finn's complex "Liberal Conservatism" and that clearly coincides with the author's own ambition to get into parliament—"the highest object of ambition" for any Englishman, as T. declared. T.'s abject failure to get a seat in Westminster (following a spectacularly dirty campaign at Beverley, in Yorkshire) is recorded in *Ralph the Heir* (19 parts, 1871).

The Eustace Diamonds (1872), the third of the Palliser sequence, is interesting as T.'s sole experiment in writing "sensational," plot-driven fiction, of the kind Wilkie COLLINS had made fashionable in the 1860s. The plot of *The Eustace Diamonds* revolves (as the title suggests) around jewelry theft and introduces T.'s version of Thackeray's criminal adventuress, Becky Sharp, in the person of Lizzie Eustace. The fourth of the Palliser novels, and by some judgments the finest, is *Phineas Redux* (2 vols., 1874) in which the engaging Irish hero of the earlier novel finds himself falsely accused of murder—only to be rescued by the most enigmatic of T.'s heroines, Madame Max Goesler. In

The Prime Minister (8 parts, 1876) Plantagenet arrives, finally, at the top of Disraeli's "slippery pole"—only to find that the achievement has no savor. His role, ironically, is to do nothing—merely keep the ship of state intact until a more dynamic helmsman takes over. The sequence winds up with *The Duke's Children* (3 vols., 1880), which recycles the themes of *Can You Forgive Her?* a generation on. The darkness of the previous novels has mellowed. Ideally, the Palliser sequence (like the Barsetshire novels) should be taken whole, and—literally—in sequence: exhausting as that reading task is. They represent, between them, twin peaks of Victorian literature. No one who has not scaled them can claim to know the genre.

There are many other achievements to be mentioned in T.'s record. He was not (one must insist, against the author's own pertinacious insistence) a "mechanical" novelist who got up at crack of dawn every day to write the same novel, over and over again, before breakfast and the real business of life. Among his many other achievements are *Miss Mackenzie* (2 vols., 1865) in which he consciously attempted something un-Trollopian with a story based on a thirty-five-year-old spinster who, unexpectedly, finds herself an heiress in a small way (and consequently a target for fortune hunters). The novel has a rare delicacy of touch. *The Claverings* (1867) is notable as the most successful portrayal of a stock Trollopian hero, the "hobbledehoy." That is, the young man who seems destined for failure but who, against all the odds, comes good in the end. In this novel, the hobbledehoy hero is Harry Clavering. Others of the genus are Johnny Eames and Ralph Newton, in *Ralph the Heir*.

T. prided himself on his heroines, especially the maidens—although he is also good on battleaxes. Both varieties appear in his inheritance melodrama (based, transparently, on the Tichborne heir controversy of the period) *Is He Popenjoy?* (3 vols., 1878). Mary Germain (née Lovelace) is the most attractive of his defiant-submissive young wives (part Beatrice, part patient Grizzel) and, elsewhere in the narrative's comic subplot territory, we are introduced to the magnificent protofeminist, the Baroness Banmann, with her rousing slogan "Ze manifest infairiority of ze tyrant sex" (T. had little time for the emergent woman's movement and lost no opportunity to satirize it in his fiction and magazine writing). T.'s most pathetic jilted maiden (Lily Dale apart) is found in a short, late novella: *An Eye for an Eye* (2 vols., 1879) that climaxes with the most melodramatic episode in his fiction (a literal cliff-hanger).

In his later career, T. also cultivated a line in the older man's disappointments in affairs of the heart. *An Old Man's Love*, published posthumously in 1883, stands out. A much traveled man, T. wrote a fine Aus-

tralian novel, *John Caldigate* (3 vols., 1879), and introduced foreign settings into many of his novels and—particularly—his short stories (these small pieces of fiction fill two volumes in his collected works). The work of T.'s that has found most favor among today's readers is his bitter, Juvenalian satire on British commercial morals, *The Way We Live Now* (20 parts, 1875). On his return from a trip to America, T. discovered in England an all-pervading "dishonesty"—particularly in business and political life. In this novel he creates the magnificently corrupt tycoon, Augustus Melmotte, who "buys" English society and a seat in Parliament, with his wholly spurious riches. When the bubble bursts, Melmotte kills himself (like Charles DICKENS's Merdle—a clear inspiration, although T. always denied it). If only one work of T.'s is read, it should be *The Way We Live Now*. The novel is only slightly marred by the author's anti-Semitism (although Melmotte, in the final analysis, is revealed to be Irish-American). T. is less an author than a library of Victorian writing. In addition to the mountainous quantity of his fiction there is much interesting nonfictional prose and some of the best travel books produced in the period.

His critical reputation has been uneven. After his death (partly as a result of the *Autobiography's* revelations about his working methods), he was downgraded as a mere "novel-writing machine." Rehabilitation came with the pioneering biographical, critical, and bibliographic work of Michael Sadleir, in the 1920s and 1930s. During the Second World War, a boom in popularity was sparked off by radio serialization of his Barchester novels. Reading T. became something of a cult (the revelation that he was Harold Macmillan's favorite writer helped in the 1950s). Television miniseries based on the Palliser and Barchester series in the 1970s propelled T. into the first rank of Victorian novelists. By the end of the 20th c., all of his novels were available in cheap editions in the U.K. and U.S. (many of them in competing editions). His popularity was sustained with a big-budget BBC miniseries of *The Way We Live Now* in 2001.

BIBLIOGRAPHY: Glendinning, V., *T.* (1992); Hall, N. J., *The Letters of A. T.* (2 vols., 1983); Hall, N. J., *T.* (1991); Mullen, R., *A. T.* (1990), Sadleir, M., *T.* (1927); Snow, C. P., *T.* (1975)

JOHN SUTHERLAND

TROLLOPE, Joanna

b. 9 December 1943, Gloucestershire

T. began her writing career in the late 1970s by authoring historical novels (under the name Caroline Harvey). She turned to modern-day fiction in 1987, and has written sixteen novels in as many years. T., a distant relation to Anthony TROLLOPE, is known for her complex relationship dramas. Stylistically, she has been compared to American novelist Laurie Colwin and to Mary WESLEY. Her work is characterized as realist, escapist fiction elevated to literary heights.

A Village Affair (1989) illustrates the range of T.'s interests: dissatisfaction in marriage, children, small village life, and friendship. T.'s protagonist, Alice, is deeply unhappy after the birth of her third child. To rouse her out of her depression, her husband buys a house in a small village. Alice remains unhappy until she meets another woman with whom she begins an affair. This contemporary novel brings home the intricate and complex problems of a confused and disillusioned woman. *The Rector's Wife* (1991) addresses similar problems, though through very different circumstances. Anne Bouverie, her protagonist, is the rector's wife. She scrimps and saves, to no avail. As money becomes more and more problematic, Anne is forced to make difficult decisions. T.'s treatment of domestic strife is witty, bright, and affirming. Her vision of existence in small town England, peopled with thwarted expectations, was met with acclaim by both readers and reviewers. The novel rose quickly to the best-seller list and was adapted by T. for television.

In *The Best of Friends* (1995), T. looks at platonic friendship as well as marriage. Gina and Lawrence are childhood friends who have sustained a friendship throughout their adult lives. Both are married, and the four share a close relationship. When one of the couples separates, the fabric of their friendship is torn and mended in unexpected ways. The novel analyzes the nature of romantic love, marriage, and shifts in relationships. Alterations in the family structure are the focus of many of T.'s novels, including *Other People's Children* (1998). Moving with the times, she explores the almost unbearable difficulties inherent in stepfamilies. One of T.'s strengths is the sympathetic depiction of character. Her empathy with each character, child and adult, makes it possible to identify and care for them, despite the sometimes vile behavior they engage in.

The theme of disenchantment with marriage and the rediscovery of love is one that runs through many of T.'s novels. *Marrying the Mistress* (2000) continues T.'s exploration of domestic strife, though in this novel she reaches further in her definition of family. When Guy Stockdale decides to leave his wife for his mistress of eight years, his family must put their lives back together. Like many of T.'s earlier novels, *Marrying the Mistress* focuses on the aftermath of marital breakdown. While T.'s work has been described as "cozy" and "light," her treatment of the contemporary family and its hardships is straightforward. She takes an unwavering look at the realities and difficulties of marriage, divorce, and discontent. The female characters in her novels often find and utilize strengths they didn't realize they had, and rise to all occasions.

BIBLIOGRAPHY: Taylor, H. C., "J. T.," in Moseley, M., ed., *British Novelists since 1960*, Third Series, *DLB* 207 (1999): 294–300

MARIKA BRUSSEL

TURNBULL, Gael [Lundin]
b. 7 April 1928, Edinburgh, Scotland

Scottish-born poet, T. trained as a doctor and has lived in Canada, England, and the U.S. Introduced to the poetry of the Black Mountain School while in the U.S., T. later founded the literary magazine *Migrant* that was among the first to publish their work in Britain. Influenced by the sparseness of Robert Creeley, his work was so detached from the British poetry mainstream that as an American resident he was nearly published as part of Donald M. Allen's *The New American Poetry* (1960). At the same time, however, he made connections with Basil BUNTING and Roy FISHER as fellow dissident poets in Britain. Beginning to write in the 1950s, his early work was collected in *A Trampoline* (1968) and *Scantlings* (1970). These combined pared minimalist lyrics with longer collage pieces like *Twenty Words, Twenty Days* (1966), an attempt to record a diary by responding to randomly chosen words, which coincided with the assassination of President John F. Kennedy. Subsequent work has diversified as T. enjoys the scope of many styles ranging from ballads and songs to satires, as exemplified in *A Gathering of Poems* in 1983. An underrated and accessible poet, he has been overlooked in recent decades.

TYNAN, Katharine
b. 23 January 1861, Dublin, Ireland; d. 2 April 1931, London

In a career that spanned fifty years, T. produced over 150 titles, including works of poetry, fiction, and nonfiction; she also contributed frequently to the popular press. She created work in keeping with the earliest years of the Celtic Twilight and the Irish Literary Renaissance and also addressed the disillusioned climate of Europe after the end of World War I. Her earliest successes encouraged a generation of Irish writers to pursue their native traditions. As George RUSSELL wrote in his introduction to his edition of her *Collected Poems* (1930), "Katharine Tynan was the earliest singer in that awakening of our imagination which has been spoken of as the Irish Renaissance. I think she had as much natural sunlight in her as the movement ever attained." Unfortunately, T. was overshadowed by her friend and fellow poet W. B. YEATS and other leaders of the movement she fostered in its early days. In addition to her involvement with the revival of Irish literature, T. in her light romantic fiction and journalism captured the sentiments of her readers as times changed and was able to support herself in a literary establishment dominated by men. While she was always able to make a living with her work, she is little read today in part because of her sentimentality and attention to the mechanics of verse, in part because she devoted so much time to the creation of minor prose fiction. The early death of her husband forced her to use her writing as a source of income, and she acknowledged her novels were for "boiling the pot." Her view of her work as part of a "Holy War, the struggle to keep the fire on the hearth for the children, and the securities and sanctities of home about them" suggests both the strength and weakness of T.'s career. While her work centers on concerns that may be considered the purview of polite women, readers should understand the daring example she set as she made a name for herself as a writer.

T. had little formal education after the age of fourteen. Although she read widely, she read indiscriminately; thus, her form of expression is direct and genuine with only a vague hint of influence from any given author or movement. T. began her career as a published author in 1885 with a volume entitled *Louise de la Vallière and Other Poems*. Although her father financed the publication, the book went on to become a financial and critical success and set the themes and tone of her poetry for the rest of her career. She began and stayed within a rather narrow range of subjects, which included close observation and description of nature, religious poems that emphasized the beautiful and spiritual elements of the earthly world and a simple faith, and poems that emphasized the beauty of Ireland and drew on the legend and lore. After her marriage in 1893, T. added the subject of married love and finally the joyful relation between mothers and children to her list of subjects. Over the course of her career, T. produced a number of autobiographical volumes, including *Twenty-Five Years* (1913), *The Middle Years* (1916), *The Years of the Shadow* (1919), *The Wandering Years* (1922), and *Life in the Occupied Area* (1925), which create a rich image of her life and times and exhibit her easy facility with prose. They tend to emphasize her love of her homeland, her father, and the joys of her life as a writer and a family woman. Despite the direct and personal tone of the volumes, she rarely dwells on tragedies like the early death of her husband and her own near blindness. She has left a detailed record of an extraordinary life that avoids both self-pity and self-aggrandizement.

In addition to these images of her own life, T. produced over a hundred volumes of fiction, including volumes of sketches, light romantic fiction, and increasingly realistic novels. She began by concentrating on sketches of Irish life and set her first novel, *The Way of a Maid* (1895), in Ireland. From first to last, she wrote formulaic novels with worthy women, strong heroes and happy endings. Even after the end of World War I, when she tried to concentrate on the effects of the war on a generation of men and women, she continued to find ways to solve their problems to make sure that everything turned out well in the end. Almost all critics agree that there is little to distinguish any of T.'s novels. They pleased a reading public by never offending anyone's sensibilities, at the same time that they showed a certain skill in dealing with the details of daily life in an accomplished prose style.

While T. made a living as a novelist, she hoped to be remembered for poetry as a form of writing she kept "pure and undefiled." She took great pride in the praise she received from other poets such as Yeats and Russell, who felt she "had something which is rather rarer among poets than most people imagine, a natural gift for song." Critics have seen traces of Alfred, Lord TENNYSON, Robert BROWNING, and the ROSSETTIS in her verse. The poem "The Purblind Praises the Lord," from the 1922 volume *Evensong* best summarizes T.'s spirit and her talent. The simple quatrains of the poem suggest that T.'s lifelong struggle with her sight, instead of being a burden or a curse, has only enhanced her sense of the physical and spiritual beauty of the earth.

Despite her persistent optimism, T. was not naive or unfamiliar with sorrow and the realities of modern life. Just as she turned in her novels to a greater realism during and after the Great War, in her poetry, including works like "The Vestal," she addresses the tragedy of a generation of men and women deprived by the war of the happiness of innocent and easy relationships. Still, it is for her happiest poems that she is best remembered. *A Lover's Breast-Knot* (1896), for example, her first volume of poems written after her marriage, uses images from nature to intensify her depiction of her love for her husband. In poems such as "Any Woman," "Any Wife," and "The Meeting," T. sums up the joy of her life as wife and mother with great sensuality and directness. While her simplicity of faith and close observation of nature were the hallmark of her talent, she tended to return too often to the same subjects and themes, so that while there are a few memorable poems, no one work or volume stands out as her best. Moreover, because she devoted so much time to the business of writing prose, she rarely experimented with her verse forms. The result was a simple and natural lyric that never seemed to grow or change, a predictable and ultimately unexciting kind of verse that sold well but creates no lasting impression.

While T. will probably never be regarded as more than a minor poet, she should be viewed as someone who was able to make a living writing, who helped to foster one of the most important literary movements of the early 20th c., and who wrote with sincerity and passion about the beauties of ordinary life.

BIBLIOGRAPHY: Fallon, A. C., *K. T.* (1979); Rose, M. G., *K. T.* (1974); Yeats, W. B., *Letters to K. T.,* ed. by R. MacHugh (1953)

                                    CATHERINE FRANK

TYNDALE, William

b. 1494, Gloucestershire; d. 6 October 1536, Vilvorde

T. is distinguished as the translator of the first English Bible. As a humanist scholar and Protestant reformer, T. was driven by a profound will to facilitate among the common people a personal understanding of the Holy Scripture absent from the influence of Roman Catholic Church doctrine. As the basis for all English text Bibles, the enduring strength and vitality of T.'s translations is often credited as an inspiration in the development of the modern English language.

Educated at Oxford and Cambridge, T. is believed to have studied under the renowned Greek editor Desiderius ERASMUS where he mastered Greek as well as Hebrew, Latin, Italian, Spanish, and French. Throughout his education, T. kept the company of humanist scholars with whom he closely associated and came to believe deeply in the words of the Holy Scripture. Embracing the Reformation ideals that had taken firm hold in Europe, T. was animated by a profound conviction that the Bible, not the centralized Roman authority, should dictate church doctrine and practice. The Latin Vulgate, translated from Hebrew and Greek text more than one thousand years earlier and firmly upheld by the church, had long remained the standard Bible. T., however, reasoned that even "the boy that driveth the plough" should be afforded personal study of the Scriptures and undertook to produce an English translation.

Though previously charged with heresy by the Gloucestershire diocese for an earlier translation of Erasmus's "Handbook of the Christian Soldier" (1503), T. sought permission for his endeavor in London but was sharply rebuked by the bishop. For King HENRY VIII and the church who bestowed upon him the title of "Defender of the Faith," the potentially destabilizing nature of a Bible in the vernacular caused great concern and though no reasons were afforded, its translation was forbidden. As the persecution of Reformers in England intensified, T. sought the shelter of Martin Luther's growing Reform movement on the Continent to pursue his work and in 1525, he completed his first translation of the New Testament. Before its printing, however, word of T.'s endeavors had reached church authorities in London and production in Cologne was halted. T. escaped with his manuscripts to Worms where a second printing was completed and by February 1526, the first translated Bibles were smuggled into England.

T.'s Bible was met with bitter hostility by the Church who denounced his heretical defiance of Cath-

olic authority and attacked his translation as a distortion of the text. In his *Dialogue Concerning Heresies*, (1530), Sir Thomas MORE sharply criticized the decentralized nature of T.'s interpretations, taking issue with his replacement of words such as "church" with "congregation" and "penance" with "repentance." church authorities made a frequent spectacle of publicly burning T.'s Bible and under the charge of heresy ordered his arrest.

While taking refuge among the Continental Reformers, T. continued his revision of the New Testament and began translation of the Pentateuch. He also composed a series of polemical works whose successively bold undercurrents fundamentally challenged and confronted church doctrine. In his *The Obedience of a Christian Man* (1528), T. audaciously reasoned that to disobey formal church doctrine was to obey God. When his Bible was criticized by More, he cited the Greek texts of Erasmus to justify the basis of his translations in *An Answere unto Sir Thomas Mores Dialoge* (1531) and extolled the importance of faith over custom. In his most defiant work, *The Practyse of Prelates* (1530), T. indicted the grounds upon which Henry VIII sought to divorce Catherine of Aragon, a provocation that could not be ignored by the king or church authorities.

As the scholarship surrounding T.'s work indicates, his translation of the first English Bible holds implications far beyond the Reformation or the literacy in England it encouraged. Through his intimate understanding of Greek and Hebrew, T. derived a lyrical, but accurate, pattern and nuance in his translation that allowed him to achieve a common, familiar appeal. His style and grammatical construct thus set the standard from which future English translations would be rendered. The Matthew's Bible, the first "authorized" English text, was based entirely on T.'s translation. Consequently, as much as eighty percent of the King James Bible is cited as T.'s original text.

In striving to transcend the formal obscurity of Church interpretations of the Latin Vulgate, T. employed vivid, simple expressions with powerful and lasting resonance. Such frequently recurring aphorisms as "Let there be light" (Genesis 1), "The truth shall make you free" (John 8), and "The spirit is willing but the flesh is weak," (Matthew 26), not only endured subsequent translations but also served to inspire the use and style of future English phraseology.

Imprisoned in the Netherlands in 1535, T. was charged with heresy and committed to Protestant martyrdom, burning at the stake in 1536.

BIBLIOGRAPHY: Campbell, W., *Erasmus, T., and More* (1949); Daniel, D., *W. T.* (1994); Thomas, A., *The Life and Martyrdom of W. T.* (1936); Williams, C. H., *W. T.* (1969)

                                    JACK BRODERICK

U

UNSWORTH, Barry [Forster]
b. 10 August 1930, Durham

The historical and geographical range of U.'s fiction is wide, from 14th-c. Britain in *Morality Play* (1995) to late 20th-c. Italy in *After Hannibal* (1996). But his remarkable capacity to evoke different times and places is combined with a consistent concern: the ways in which human beings try to possess and oppress each other, through sexuality and violence, and also, more ambiguously, through art. Artifacts like statues, and other kinds of material artifact, play a significant role in his fiction, as objects of desire and exchange, and as symbols of character, relationships, and the nature of human existence.

U.'s first three novels demonstrate his craftsmanship and signal some of his enduring concerns. *The Partnership* (1966) focuses on a business association between two male art dealers, Moss and Foley, that breaks up due to the stirrings of Moss's sexual desire for Foley. Brian Kennedy in *The Greeks Have a Word for It* (1967) is a kind of confidence trickster working as a teacher in Greece, whose fate becomes intertwined with that of Mitsos, a bitter man seeking vengeance for his mother's rape and father's murder. Rape also figures in *The Hide* (1970), where the quasi-artistic acts of voyeurism perpetrated by one of its characters, Simon, lead into sexual violence.

With *Mooncranker's Gift* (1973), U. moved into a new phase characterized by an increasingly effective use of symbolism. This novel, which won the Heinemann Fiction Award, is centered on an artifact: a swaddled sausage-meat effigy of Christ that the middle-aged Mr. Mooncranker gives to the thirteen-year-old Charles Farnaby and that appalls Charles when it starts to go rotten. The bulk of the novel concerns Farnaby's partial recovery, in his young adulthood in Turkey, from this early encounter with corruption. U.'s next novel, *The Big Day* (1976), was a relatively lightweight satire on higher education, but its successor, *Pascali's Island* (1980; repub. as *The Idol Hunter*,

1980), is one of his best books. Set on an Aegean island in the twilight of the Ottoman Empire in 1908, its narrative takes the form of a report by an informer, Pascali, to the Ottoman sultan. Like *Mooncranker's Gift*, it centers on an artifact: an ancient bronze statue, which becomes the object of an attempted theft that has lethal consequences. After a powerful but less focused novel set in the same period, *The Rage of the Vulture* (1982), U. produced another effective artifact-centered novel, *Stone Virgin* (1985), in which a sculptured Madonna links three men from different centuries: its 15th-c. creator, Girolamo; an 18th-c. rake, Ziani; and Simon Raikes, an unsuccessful sculptor turned restorer. The novel explores both the way in which objects may become invested with human desires and the way in which human desires may turn other people into objects.

This phenomenon is the crucial concern of U.'s next two novels, *Sugar and Rum* (1988) and *Sacred Hunger* (1992). Both novels address one notorious but still underacknowledged aspect of English history: Britain's involvement in the slave trade. The difficulty of approaching such a topic is dramatized in *Sugar and Rum*, which focuses on a novelist, Clive Benson, who finds that he is unable to begin his projected novel about the Liverpool slave trade. *Sacred Hunger*, which might be seen as U.'s mammoth realization of Benson's project, is structured around two cousins: Matthew Price, who becomes a ship's surgeon and sees the workings of the slave trade at first hand; and Erasmus Kemp, who becomes a ruthless merchant embodying the sanctified greed epitomized in the novel's title. A powerful if sometimes melodramatic work, rich in character and incident, *Sacred Hunger* was joint winner of Britain's 1992 Booker Prize.

U.'s next novel, *Morality Play*, is a compelling mystery tale with philosophical overtones, sometimes calling to mind Italian author Umberto Eco's *The Name of the Rose* (1980). Three interlinked desires—for truth, for a scapegoat, for representation—mix in this novel, in which a traveling company of actors, wishing to win a bigger audience, replay the murder of a boy while the supposed culprit is awaiting the gallows—and thus raise doubts about the culprit's guilt. *Morality Play* shows how the appeal of representation may work against the urge for a scapegoat and reawaken the desire for truth. *After Hannibal* returns to U.'s concern with the way in which artifacts can be invested with human desires. In this case, the artifacts are the houses in Umbria, in modern Italy, bought by foreigners in order to try to realize their dreams: in the novel, the dreams and the houses flounder as the traces of violence from the recent and ancient past resurface in the present. Traces of past violence are also crucial to U.'s next novel, *Losing Nelson* (1999), where the desire for possession is directed not toward objects, but toward an historical hero, Horatio Nelson, the victor of the battle of Trafalgar (1805). Charles Cleasby has worshiped Lord Nelson from childhood and is now writing a biography of Britain's greatest naval hero, but he urgently needs to find an honorable explanation of the great man's apparent betrayal of the Neapolitan Jacobin rebels in 1799. He descends into crisis as the challenge of the existing evidence is compounded by the increasingly informed questions posed by Miss Lily, the erotically disturbing young woman whom he hires as his typist. *Losing Nelson* is U. at his most compelling.

U. has now produced a powerful body of work that provides a multifaceted fictional analysis of the drive to possession and oppression. His prose, at its best, is precise and evocative, his use of symbolism is disciplined and resonant, and his most successful novels are strongly structured. His fiction succeeds both in making the reader think about the issues it addresses and in vividly re-creating the texture of human life in a variety of historical and contemporary situations.

BIBLIOGRAPHY: Naufftus, W. M., "B. U.," in Moseley, M., ed., *British Novelists since 1960*, Second Series, *DLB* 124 (1998): 270–78

NICOLAS TREDELL

UPWARD, Allen

b. 1863, Worcester; d. 12 November 1926, London

Although praised by Ezra Pound as a neglected genius, U. was nonetheless a minor writer who remains a curiosity in English letters primarily for his two major polemics, *The New Word* (1908) and *The Divine Mystery* (1913). Trained as a barrister, U. pursued a wide range of interests and at various times was a journalist, politician, adventurer, and publisher. Determined to establish a literary reputation, U. experimented in a variety of genres. In 1888, he published a collection of poetry, which was followed in the next decade by a series of romance novels, plays, popular works of fiction, and nonfiction. He gained some measure of

success as a novelist, but his esoteric polemical works met with mixed reaction. Late in his career, U. became increasingly despondent about his failure to achieve the critical recognition he felt he deserved and at age sixty-three committed suicide.

URQUHART, Fred[erick Burrows]

b. 12 July 1912, Edinburgh, Scotland; d. 2 December 1995, Edinburgh, Scotland

One of the preeminent Scottish writers of short fiction in the second half of the 20th c., U. blended precise narrative detail and brillant use of dialogue, especially Scots dialect, to create a realistic and uncompromising portrayal of both urban and rural life in contemporary Scotland. Leaving school at age fifteen, U. worked in a secondhand bookstore while pursuing a career as a writer. He first gained critical attention with the publication in 1938 of his novel *Time Will Knit*, a vivid portrait of a working-class Edinburgh family, followed by his first collection of stories, *I Fell for a Sailor* (1940). In 1944, U. left Scotland for England, where he remained for the greater part of his adult life. Working as a freelance writer, script reader, and editor, U. produced a steady stream of stories for more than five decades. His later collections include *The Last Sister* (1950), *Proud Lady in a Cage* (1980), *A Diver in China Seas* (1980), and *Full Score* (1989).

URQUHART [or URCHARD], [Sir] Thomas

b. ca. 1611, Scotland; d. ca. 1660, Scotland

U. was educated at King's College, Aberdeen, and in 1641, having left Scotland for London, was knighted for his military exploits against the Covenanters. In the English Civil War, U. fought on the losing royalist side in the battle of Worcester and was imprisoned in the Tower of London for two years. Returning to Scotland, he began the famous translation from the French of François Rabelais's *Gargantua and Pantagruel*. The first two books appeared in 1653 and a third book was completed by Peter Anthony Motteux in 1694. This was the translation, known as Urquhart-Motteux, familiar to Laurence STERNE. U. also published books on mathematics and language under Greek titles, among them *Ekskubalauron* (1651), familiarly known as *The Jewel*, which includes the story of the "Admirable" James Crichton, Scottish athlete, Latin poet, and polymath. Sir J. M. BARRIE wrote a play using the phrase, which had become proverbial, *The Admirable Crichton*, as the title.

UTOPIA

Most discussions of utopia in British literature center around Sir Thomas MORE's *Utopia*, published in 1516, the tale of a traveler, Raphael Hythloday, and his journey to an island that represents More's idea of an ideal society governed by good sense and high principles. The literal meaning of the word "utopia" is "nowhere" or "no place," but utopian literature does not deal with despair or improbability of discovery as the translation might suggest. Instead, it tends to deal with an ideal, a place that is nowhere in existence but one that the author sincerely wishes were available for habitation. Two types of utopia merge from the canon of utopian literature: eutopia, or a good place, and dystopia, or a bad place. "Utopia" and "eutopia" have grown to mean the same thing, a moving toward good. Dystopia has become a natural outgrowth of utopian ideas and literature and has therefore become embraced under the larger umbrella of utopian literature, even though one might at first view these two ideas as opposing points.

Throughout the centuries, utopian literature has melded with many other genres. One can find utopian ideas in travel and adventure literature, such as More's *Utopia* and Jonathan SWIFT's *Gulliver's Travels*. The ever-popular SCIENCE FICTION is also considered utopian literature, although this has been debated by scholars. Of course, a good deal of dystopia is found in works of science fiction, with its authors striving to show the ills that may come from unbridled social advances or scientific inquiry. Feminist literature also often leans into utopian ideals, as do social and political SATIRE. In many ways, the idea of utopia and utopian literature leads to natural ambiguities. Nevertheless, a certain canon of utopian literature is solidly in place in British literature; this canon includes essays, poetry, and drama but is most often studied in terms of utopian fiction.

After More opened utopian literature possibilities in British literature in the 16th c., his work was followed by that of numerous other writers. The 17th c. gave way to utopian works by authors such as Francis BACON and Margaret CAVENDISH. Bacon's *New Atlantis* couples utopia with Christianity, as do many other utopian works. *New Atlantis* presents a conservative view of ideal life by using what we would call today "traditional family values." It also presents a scientific version of utopia. Bacon's scientific ideas in the novel led to the founding of the Royal Society in 1660. Cavendish also brings religion into her utopian work, *The Description of a New Blazing World*. Like many traditional FAIRY TALES and allegories, *Blazing World* features animal characters who take on human qualities. Cavendish also includes a system of monarchy in her work, although this system works with far fewer laws than one would find in a realistic monarchy.

Perhaps, given the Christian tradition that looks forward to the Second Coming and Christ's kingdom upon earth, it is not surprising that there should be less overtly utopian literature than dystopian. Alexander POPE took the view that "Hope springs eternal in the human breast; Man never is, but always to be, blest." His friend Swift, at a time when the idea of the "noble savage" was gaining currency, warned against taking an over-romantic view of the alternative societies his Gulliver goes bumbling through. Islands occur often in utopian literature, isolated and virgin, offering opportunities for a fresh start. Making imaginative use of the microscope and the telescope, Swift peoples the flying island of Laputa with archetypal mad scientists. Undercutting the pretensions of experimental science, Swift has as agenda not the creation of an ideal society but a reiteration of the age-old question: what does it mean to be human?

The utopian works of Swift and Daniel DEFOE have much in common, in that the ideal world is viewed as one in which the individual must overcome physical and spiritual weaknesses in order to rise to hitherto unimagined heights. Both works are also social satires and commentaries. Swift's work in particular lends itself to political and social analysis, something often seen in utopian literature beyond the 18th c.

The fourth and final part of *Gulliver's Travels* takes Gulliver to the Houyhnhnm society, a land ruled by horses with the best of human characteristics where humans themselves have the worst of human characteristics. Gulliver becomes enthralled with this society, which he views as far superior to his native land. In fact, when he must return to England, Gulliver becomes despondent and never fully recovers from his regret at having to leave the Houyhnhnms. In the end, Gulliver has gone mad (he cannot bear the stink of his wife and children, who appear to him as mere Yahoos) and it is clear that the horses offer no role models for humanity. Stoic apathy is no defense against the pain of self-consciousness. Samuel JOHNSON's novella *Rasselas,* which is about the impossibility of utopias, is paralleled by his poem "The Vanity of Human Wishes," in being equally expressive of Johnson's Christian pessimism. The Romantic attitude at the turn of the 18th c. was more optimistic: Samuel Taylor COLERIDGE and Robert SOUTHEY dreamed of setting up a utopian commune on the banks of the Susquehanna, but got no further than naming it the "Pantisocracy." Percy Bysshe SHELLEY hoped that scattering his words like dead leaves through the universe would bring about the desired changes in society. Early hopes that the French Revolution, with its ideals of Liberty, Equality, and Fraternity, was harbinger of social justice had, however, died with the shock of the Terror as the guillotine fell on neck after neck. William WORDSWORTH, who had thought it bliss in that dawn to be alive, moved, as did Coleridge, increasingly toward political conservatism.

The 19th c. continued to see an abundance of utopian literature, with authors and readers alike caught up in a fascination with idealism versus reality and the possibilities of a scientific and social reality gone wrong. In *The Coming Race*, Edward BULWER-LYTTON brings the reader to the center of the Earth and presents a utopia contingent on the use of reason as the means to existing in an ideal society. Charles KINGSLEY's midcentury novel *Alton Locke* has an oppressed first-person narrator, a self-educated working man, who longs for the perfection of society through Chartism. He has to be reeducated by the author, who makes him die on his way to the imagined island paradise in the South Seas, thus teaching the antiutopian lesson that perfection is not to be found in this life, only in the next. Kingsley's commitment to Christian socialism was more religious than political. Samuel BUTLER's classic *Erewhon* continues with the style of social and political satire as fodder for utopian literature. Butler paints a picture of a society that reaches its ideals because it acts in almost direct opposition to the realistic English society of which Butler was a part.

H. G. WELLS contributed greatly to utopian literature in both the 19th and 20th cs. His famous *The Time Machine* pairs class issues with the desire for an ideal society, illustrating the uselessness of class structure in a true utopia. Wells continued with several other utopian tales, including *A Modern Utopia* (1905), a novel that treats all that is purely ideal in the utopian philosophy.

Continuing into the 20th c., C. S. LEWIS, best known for his texts on Christianity and for his fantasy novels, produced a utopian trilogy—the Space Trilogy—over a period of seven years. *Out of the Silent Planet* introduces space traveler Ransom, who is held captive on the planet Mars and fights for his escape. *Perelandra*, perhaps the most critical work in the trilogy, engages the hero Ransom in a battle with the Devil himself, fighting for ultimate control over the soul of the planet Venus's Green Woman, a parallel to the legend of Eve. Ransom is victorious in the battle and saves the inhabitants of the planet Venus from the fate of Earth—the spiritual Fall of humankind and all of the consequences resulting from that fall. The final

book, *That Hideous Strength*, brings Ransom back to Earth where he engages in a fight against the madness of government rule. In this utopian trilogy, Lewis brings together Christian principles, science fiction and fantasy, and social and political commentary, all popular elements of utopian literature, though the reader does not usually find all these elements working at once.

William GOLDING's classic *The Lord of the Flies* also has a place in the canon of utopian literature, although by strict definition this novel deals with a dystopia rather than a utopia. There are certainly elements of the search for a perfect society in the novel, as the boys set about trying to make some sort of order for themselves, but the reader finds that human nature gets in the way of a search for perfection, and the worst of human nature comes out in the end. Still, *The Lord of the Flies* contains the elements of utopian literature and certainly evokes philosophical discussion of good versus evil.

Numerous other utopian works have been produced in the 20th c., with many using the subgenres of dystopia and science fiction. George ORWELL's famous *Animal Farm* examines society gone awry; his *Nineteen Eighty-Four* tells of a not-so-futuristic society that revolves around loss of individual freedom. Aldous HUXLEY also reveals a less-than-perfect future in *Brave New World*. Daphne DU MAURIER presents an American dystopia in *Rule Britannia*, published in 1972. There continues to be a fascination with depicting the perfect world as well as with offering social and political warnings of gravely imperfect worlds and their horrid consequences. As we move further away from More's *Utopia* in time, our literature tends to move more toward dystopia than utopia.

BIBLIOGRAPHY: Johnson, J. W., ed., *Utopian Literature* (1968); Kamenka, E., ed., *Utopias* (1987); Nelson, W., ed., *Twentieth Century Interpretations of Utopia* (1968); Sargent, L. T., *British and American Utopian Literature* (1979); Walsh, C., *From Utopia to Nightmare* (1962)

TERRY D. NOVAK

VANBRUGH, [Sir] John
b. ca. 21 January 1664, London; d. 26 March 1726,
London

As an architect, V. was responsible for designing an
earlier Haymarket Theatre (the current Haymarket
dating only from 1821) and Blenheim Palace. His
plays, which include *The Relapse; or, Virtue in Danger* (perf. 1696; pub. 1697), *The Confederacy* (1705),
and both *The Provok'd Wife* (1697) and *The Provok'd
Husband* (completed by Colley CIBBER and produced
in 1728), are marked by composition that is brisk, vigorous, and believable. His characters speak with an
extemporaneous air, almost without thought or construction. They are drawn, as are William CONGREVE's
characters, from the upper classes, but unlike Congreve, V. creates brutes in fine dress, high-born persons with thinly veiled, low-born sensibilities. Wife
beaters, cheats, usurers, and libertines (repentant and
unrepentant) figure in many of his plays. It is an historical irony that V.'s first play, *The Relapse*, was a
continuation of Cibber's *Love's Last Shift* and that his
last play, *The Provok'd Husband*, was completed by
Cibber.

VAUGHAN, Henry
b. 1621 or 1622, Llansantffraed, Wales; d. 23 April
1695, Llansantffraed, Wales

For the first half of the 20th c., scholars loosely referred to a certain coterie of Renaissance poets as the
"metaphysicals" of which V. was a chief member.
Even though Rosalie Colie helped to dispel the shortcomings of genre-based literary theory during the
early 1960s, it was not until the 1980s that New Historicists began to dispel the notion of a strictly metaphysical brand of poetry. The term metaphysical was
first coined somewhat derisively by Samuel JOHNSON
in his *Lives of the Poets* as he attacked these Renaissance poets for saturating their works with excessive
learning. Nonetheless, T. S. ELIOT and his disciples

came to employ the notion of metaphysical poetry in
a more pragmatic sense as a catch-all phrase attempting to deal with multivalent types of verse that grew
from the highly syncretic well of learning informed
by the visual arts, music, science, etc. Science to the
Renaissance scholar involved a knowledge of plants,
nature, astrology, alchemy, angelology, etc., much of
which is displayed in the work of V. Even though V.
has long been referred to as an emulator of George
HERBERT's verse, V.'s often idiosyncratic and passionate poetry has played a singular and important role in
the growth of English poetry.

However, the comparison of V. to Herbert is not
without substance regarding their styles, content, and
theologies. The recurring theme of death, the downward plummeting of the soul, and subsequent rebirth
through the redemption by Christ's Passion declared
by Herbert is found in many of V.'s poems. For example, in the final octet of V.'s "The Storm," the narrator
asks the Lord to send storm clouds, "And wind and
water to thy use . . . and wing my soul." V.'s utiliza-
tion of "wing" is obviously a conscious appropriation
of Herbert's most famous emblem, "Easter Wings."
But as any careful reader of V. should notice, his borrowing from other poets is in part an act of homage
and often he explicitly states so as in his "To the most
Excellently accomplish'd Mrs. K. [Katherine] PHIL-
IPS, the 'Matchless Orinda.'"

V. expressed an admiration for the "Sons of Ben,"
and like Ben JONSON V. had a great love of the neoclassical form, devoting a fair amount of his work to
composing Latinate poetry and doing translations.
One of V.'s earliest publications was Juvenal's *Tenth
Satire Translated* (1646). V. worked in the classic
prosody of the time and achieved some notable results
in following scanned meter while sometimes approaching the liberty that John MILTON took in opening English verse to a more free assimilation of normal speech patterns.

The core of V.'s work is contained in parts 1 and 2
of *Silex Scintillans* (1650). In the *Scintillans* series,

there is a definite sequence and contiguity prevalent that we see in few poets of the time. One of the central aspects of part 1 is V.'s attempts to reckon with a deep mourning and depression most likely caused by the deaths of his younger brother William in 1648 and his wife Catherine in 1650, the year of part 1's publication. Part 1 signals V.'s emergence from his own figurative death or dark night of the soul into the realm of the spiritually reborn. The cycle of life, death, and rebirth is central to the Rosicrucian mysteries that V.'s brother Thomas VAUGHAN was instrumental in disseminating. Moreover, Thomas produced some worthwhile poetry in his own right, besides his alchemical texts, and it is probable that the two brothers had a reciprocal influence on each other's written work.

V.'s love of nature seemed to act as a counterbalance to his Christian beliefs. His collection *Olor Iscanus* (1651) was composed in honor of the Iscanus, the Latinate title of the river Usk. Here, V. is referred to as Henry Vaughan "Silurist," or one who is from the Welsh territory inhabited by the ancient tribe of the Silures as opposed to assuming a British voice solely. In *Silex* part 2 we see V. embracing the regenerative and perennial life-force in nature after the mourning and dejection that weighs on the poetry of *Silex* part 1 so heavily. For example, in "The Bird," V. discloses his account of the divine signature or God's impression left in all things, popularized by the German mystic Jacob Boehme in the 16th c. In "The Bird," V. states succinctly "For each inclosed Spirit is a star/ Inlightning his own little sphaere." Furthermore, V. relays various alchemical principles and symbols through his reference to creatures like "The Crow" whose blackness typified the stage of nigredo or first stage of the alchemical process where the base elements are reduced and decompose. V. was a staunch loyalist all of his life and with the execution of Charles I, V.'s poetic commentaries on the state of the Empire showed that he viewed England's condition as being in that same state of nigredo or putrifaction.

V. was not just a proficient poet but a practicing physician. Although there are no records of his having ever taken a medical degree, we do know he successfully treated a local Welsh magistrate for a severe illness. V.'s lifelong pursuits were as poetic and as varied in content as his verse. And undoubtedly, his poetry will continue to challenge and stimulate students not only of British poetry but of interdisciplinary studies for years to come.

BIBLIOGRPHY: Calhoun, T. O., *H. V., the Achievement of Silex Scintillans* (1981); Holmes, E., *H. V. and the Hermetic Philosophy* (1932); Hutchinson, F. E., *H. V.* (1947)

BOB PODGURSKI

VAUGHAN, Thomas

b. 1621 or 1622, Llansantffread, Wales; d. 27 February 1666, Llansantffread, Wales

Although his elder twin brother, Henry VAUGHAN, is better known for his contributions to English literature, V.'s prose and poems form an essential metaphysical and occult backbone of popular Renaissance thought. In fact, the San Francisco poet and essayist Kenneth Rexroth suggested that V. was "the leading 'Spiritual Alchemist' of the entire literature." V. worked extensively on the transmutation or perfection of base metals, and in early physical chemistry to develop a rudimentary understanding of vegetable, animal, and mineral properties. In fact, V.'s writing was studied and amassed by notable figures such as Sir Isaac Newton, Robert Boyle, and other early scientific pioneers of the late 17th c.

One of V.'s greatest influences on Western literature was exerted through his publishing the primary manifestoes of Rosicrucianism: "The Fame and Confession of the Rosicrucian Fraternatis," or the "*Fama and Confessio*" as they are most commonly called. With the exception of the appearance in 1616 of Johann Valentine Andrea's *The Chemical Wedding of Christian Rosencreutze*, the first Rosicrucian text published on the Continent, V.'s publications are primarily responsible for bringing Rosicrucianism to the light of day. Andrea's text apparently served as a manifesto for the Rosicrucians wherein the main character's—Christian Rosencreutze (literally Rosecross)—magical quest to wed and subsequent ordeals served as a model allegory of the alchemical union of the opposites culminating in the elixir or philosopher's stone. In the "Fame and Confession," V. affords a lengthy and discursive account of the magical tradition in the West discussing the philosophy of Hermes Trismegistus as the founder of Hermeticism. When V. finally broaches the topic of the Rosicrucians, he describes their cosmology and account of creation as an alchemical allegory. The alchemical philosophy was basically hypostatic or a triadic foundation of Mercury (spirit), Sulfur (soul), and Salt (earth or physical body). The rose was taken to represent the soul of Christ or of men in general: sacrificed upon the cross and seen as a thing of beauty in its death or blossoming. This flowering or transformation of the soul depicts the glory of the rebirth or resurrection, thus forming the basis for much alchemical thought of the time.

Overall, V was not very prolific; the entire gamut of his occult views and alchemical thought is contained within six works, each averaging from ten to sixty pages in length. In his *Magica Adamica; or, The Antiquity of Magic* (1650), V. traces the magical and occult philosophy beginning with Adam, the first true Cabalist, who understood the language of nature. V.

describes Adam's magical heirs spanning Moses, Hermes Trismegistus, Raymond Lull, etc. In his *Anima Magica Abscondita; or, A Discourse on the Universal Spirit of Nature* (1650), V. reflects upon the hypostasis or triplicities that occur throughout nature, which he describes as the animating soul, spirit of the universe, and universal water or universal matrix. The "Coelom Terrae"—subtitled "The Magician's Heavenly Chaos"—is not about chaos in our modern sense at all but about the "prima materia" or primal uncontrollable component of all things. V.'s *Aula Lucis; or, The House of Light* (1652) is a text composed in the long line of Cabalistic and Hermetic texts that treat the "Light" or Lux Fiat as the source without a source, and tell how the elements as well as knowledge are emanations of this light.

Lumen De Lumine (1651) forms V.'s magnum opus. In this text, he discloses his initiation, as it were, into the temple of nature. The piece begins with a description of the muse Thalia, and how she guided him through the temple. This book is a description of V.'s ascent into the light and the illuminations he received on the Sophic Fire, the Ether, etc. At the end of the text, V. appended his "Magical Aphorisms" beginning with the "first truth": "The point came forth before all things." V.'s notion of the monad here bears a strong resemblance to the first two theorems of John DEE's *Monas Hieroglyphica*.

Interspersed throughout V.'s essays are Latinate poems bearing a great resemblance to his brother Henry's work. V. touches on many of same topics as his brother Henry, such as the river Usk, death, and mourning, as well as a plethora of alchemical formulae and topics. Outside of poetry, V.'s use of alchemical and Rosicrucian allegory in his texts was to have a long-lasting impact on writers such as Arthur Llewellyn MACHEN, Lord DUNSANY, Edward BULWER-LYTTON, and other authors of supernatural fiction. And as certain factions within modern science move toward resolving theological and scientific issues, V.'s work may take on a greater relevance than many would have ever speculated. This would be fitting for the work of this unique Renaissance thinker.

BIBLIOGRAPHY: Hutchinson, F. E., *H. V.* (1947); Rudrum, A., ed., *The Works of T. V.* (1984); Yates, F. A., *The Rosicrucian Enlightenment* (1972)

BOB PODGURSKI

VERGIL, Polydore

b. ca. 1470, Urbino, Italy; d. 18 April 1555, Urbino, Italy

V. is best known for authoring the *Anglica Historia* (1534; rev. eds., 1546, 1555), a twenty-seven book English history written in Latin. Today, V. is justly celebrated for his methodology, which resembles that of a modern historian: in sharp contrast to the clerics who composed most of the histories in the medieval period, V. weighed the authorities against one another in order to create the most accurate account possible, and he approached the various legends and traditions of Britain with a skeptical attitude. The *Anglica Historia* thus represents a significant advance in the development of the English history. The grandson of a doctor of philosophy at the University of Paris, V. received a humanist education at Padua and at Bologna. After serving as secretary to Guidobaldo da Montefeltro, the powerful Duke of Urbino, and as chamberlain to Pope Alexander VI, he was sent to England in 1502 to work as a deputy collector for Rome. In England, he served as archdeacon of Wells and befriended such prominent humanists as Sir Thomas MORE, John COLET, William LILY, Richard Pace, and Sir Thomas LINACRE. For nine months in 1515, V.'s bitter enemy Thomas Wolsey had him imprisoned in the Tower of London on charges of conspiracy. V. spent the rest of his life moving between England and Italy, doing his best to stay out of the religious and political controversies of the day.

Before he began work on his English history, V. composed two popular and influential Latin works, the *Proverbiorum libellus* (1498) and the *De Inventoribus Rerum* (1499; rev. ed., 1521). The *Proverbiorum libellus*, which went through twenty editions before 1550, collects 306 proverbs from classical sources (the 1519 edition adds 431 biblical proverbs). It is the first collection of its kind, predating Desiderius ERASMUS's famous collection by almost two years. V. offers brief commentary on each of the proverbs, occasionally seizing the opportunity to attack contemporary evils. The *De Inventoribus Rerum* is the first book dedicated to listing inventors. It was even more popular than Erasmus's *Adages*: in the 16th and 17th cs., 110 editions were published in seven different languages. By modern standards, the *De Inventoribus Rerum* is hardly a scientific study. In the book, V. attempts to establish a Jewish origin for the invention of all good things. Moreover, for V., there is no evolution; things are simply invented in their full form and then imitated.

At the behest of Henry VII, V. began working on the *Anglica Historia* in 1506. The first eight books deal with the period up to 1066; subsequent books are organized around the reign of a particular king. V. despised GEOFFREY OF MONMOUTH's *Historia Regum Britanniae*, the 12th-c. chronicle in which Brutus and King Arthur first appear. Finding no historical evidence for the existence of either Brutus or Arthur, V. judges them to be mythical. In the final books, V. seeks to legitimize the rule of his patrons, the Tudors. Thus, V. portrays Richard III as an evil despot and his defeat by Henry Tudor as divinely ordained; in V.'s narrative, the Tudors are England's saviors. To avoid controversy, V. waited until 1555 to publish the twenty-seventh book, which deals with the reign of HENRY VIII. This book is perhaps most famous for V.'s vilification of his old enemy Wolsey. Throughout the *Anglica Historia*, V. sees human beings as frail and human glory as fleeting; a mysterious but ultimately just God frequently punishes kings for their crimes. The work was widely scorned in early modern England, largely because V. rejected the historicity of Brutus and Arthur and because he was a Catholic European with little sympathy for Protestantism. Nevertheless, the 16th-c. English chroniclers who followed him drew heavily upon his history. The portion of *Anglica Historia* on the 15th and early 16th cs. served as the basis for Edward HALL's *The Union of the Two Noble and Illustre Families of Lancaster and York*, one of the principal sources for William SHAKESPEARE's history plays.

BIBLIOGRAPHY: Galdieri, L. V., "P. V.," in Richardson, D. A., ed., *Sixteenth-Century British Nondramatic Writers*, First Series, *DLB* 132 (1993): 316–21; Hay, D., *P. V.* (1952)

T. D. DRAKE

VICTORIAN WOMEN POETS

In a now famous letter of 1845 Elizabeth Barrett BROWNING lamented the seeming lack of a tradition of English women poets that she could look back to and engage with. "England has had many learned women," she argued, "and yet where are the poetesses? . . . I look everywhere for grandmothers and see none." Ironically, the disappearance of women poets from literary history that this quotation suggests was also to affect Browning herself, for by the beginning of the 20th c. the woman who had once been internationally renowned for her outspoken political and polemical poetry, and who had once been seriously considered for the post of poet laureate, had been all but erased from anthologies and critical studies of 19th-c. literature. As Virginia WOOLF humorously yet astutely expressed it in 1932, MODERNISM had relegated Browning to the "servants' quarters" of the house of English literature, where she "bangs the crockery around and eats vast handfuls of peas on the point of her knife." What had replaced her was the mythologized image of the sofa-bound Romantic heroine of Rudolph Besier's play *The Barretts of Wimpole Street* (1930), wasting away until Robert [BROWNING] sweeps in to whisk her off to marriage and health in Italy. Nor was this marginalization and mythologization process limited to Browning alone, for Christina ROSSETTI too was to suffer, demoted from her position as the highly regarded writer of some of the most widely read and influential poetry of the second half of the 19th c. and reconfigured into

an emblem of pious, unquestioning religious faith or a neurotic recluse figure occupying the shadowy hinterlands of the (male) Pre-Raphaelite circle. Many other Victorian women poets, despite their successes in their own day, failed to even make it this far, being simply erased altogether through the machinations of literary history and "canonization."

One of the most exciting and energetic developments in Victorian studies in recent decades, however, has been the recovery and rereading of these "lost" women poets. From the early days of 1970s FEMINISM, the "Big Three" of Browning, Rossetti, and Emily BRONTË have been reinterpreted and revaluated, so that each is now regularly anthologized and their critical status has been—or at least, is in the process of being—transformed. Subsequently, a second wave of critical attention in the 1990s started to bring to light the host of other women writing poetry in the Victorian period—women such as Mathilde Blind, Mary COLERIDGE, Dora Greenwell, Jean Ingelow, Amy LEVY, Alice MEYNELL, Constance Naden, Adelaide Proctor, and Augusta Webster, whose names, let alone their works, have remained unknown since the 19th c. What this recovery work has done, therefore, is to establish a clear tradition of Victorian women poets (or possibly, rather, traditions), highlighting continuities, differences, and developments between one generation and the next and helping, on a wider scale, to bring about a reconfiguration of our conceptual thinking concerning Victorian poetry and the role of the Victorian poet in general. As our own poetic "grandmothers" resurface one by one, then, the variety, dynamism, power, and artistry of the contributions made by women poets during the 19th c. is increasingly evident.

Victorian women's poetry does not emerge independently, of course, but rather develops out of, and in reaction to, the dominant models of women's poetry circulating in the preceding decades. As Angela Leighton has mapped out in her groundbreaking work *Victorian Women Poets: Writing against the Heart* (1992), two of the most important precursors of major 19th-c. poets such as Browning and Rossetti were Felicia HEMANS and Letitia Elizabeth LANDON, both of whom remained popular for decades after their deaths and who far outstripped succeeding generations in terms of sales. Between them, however, they also established a number of disabling assumptions about women poets and their appropriate subject matter that were subsequently difficult to dislodge. Hemans in particular focuses on issues of domesticity and the importance of the family unit, sometimes set with a patriotic framework (her most famous poem is "Casabianca" that begins "The boy stood on the burning deck") and often with an underlying conservative agenda (i.e., "Homes of England"). Even such an energetic poem as "Corinne at the Capitol," inspired by Madame de Staël's hugely influential and scandalous 1807 novel, celebrates for five stanzas Corrine's power as an independent creative artist before concluding with the reactionary reassertion of the superior joys of housewifery—"Happier, happier far than thou/With the laurel on thy brow,/She that makes the humblest hearth/Lovely but to one on earth." Mid-1990s feminist criticism started to reread Hemans's work, questioning the degree of conservatism in her work and highlighting, for example, her emphasis on female rather than male heroism in *Records of Women*, but for many Victorian women poets, including Browning, Hemans was often associated with a sentimentality and conservatism that they aimed to move beyond.

Landon similarly left a problematic legacy that many later women poets had to negotiate. As with Hemans, Landon had to write to support herself, a situation that helped ascribe a professionalism to the work of women poets but that could also lead to such rapid production that overall quality was lessened. Certainly, in her catering to public taste in order to maximize income, Landon helped establish what would come to be considered as the acceptable parameters of subject matter for women poets: forsaken or unrequited love (Browning would pointedly critique Landon's insistent inscribing of "love and love" in her elegy "L. E. L.'s Last Question"), death and grieving, nature, and devout religion. Moreover, Landon's highly popular poem *The Improvisatrice*, which focuses on a female poet who bursts into song at a moment's notice, was to construct an idea of the woman poet composing spontaneous and therefore seemingly artless pieces that was surprisingly resilient throughout the century. Indeed, even as late as 1904, William Michael ROSSETTI could write in his "Memoir" of his sister Christina that her compositions were "entirely of the casual and spontaneous kind," despite the detailed reworkings and revisions that are recorded in R. W. Crump's variorum edition.

Overall, then, the early to mid-Victorian woman poet inherited a legacy of disabling assumptions and preoccupations that left her caught within the seemingly private and "womanly" worlds of heart and hearth, piety, and melancholy. If she attempted to leave these prescribed bounds and engage with more public issues head on, then she was likely to incur the condemnation of the literary establishment, as Browning constantly discovered. Indeed, as Margaret Homans has demonstrated, the inhibiting and reactionary Romantic idea that women were meant to inspire poetry (as muse, wife, or sister) rather than write it was still current in many quarters, as was the equally problematic concept that poetry, higher up the literary hierarchy than the novel, was still a predominantly male area of endeavor.

In the year following Browning's lamentation for the lack of grandmothers, however, a new poetic voice appeared in *Poems by Currer, Ellis and Acton Bell*. Although only two copies of this small volume by the emerging BRONTË sisters were sold at the time, the poems by Ellis (Emily) were consistently singled out in the press for their originality and after Emily's death they received far wider critical attention and became influential on many succeeding women poets, including A. Mary F. Robinson and Charlotte MEW. With their absolutist and iconoclastic themes, Brontë's poems stand near the head of a line of Victorian women's lyric writing that articulates a struggle to escape from psychological and physical entrapment and a striving for liberty, autonomy, and unity of self. The power of such poems as "High Waving Heather," "To Imagination," "Stars," "The Philosopher's Conclusion," and the shocking "No Coward Soul" certainly justified Charlotte BRONTË's assertion that these were "not at all like the poetry women generally write."

Probably the most influential and radical voice in the history of Victorian women's poetry, however, was that of Browning. Extensively self-educated in classics, languages, literature, history, and philosophy, Browning, in parallel with her heroine Aurora Leigh, was dedicated to the vocation of poet from a remarkably early age, her first volume being privately printed when she was fourteen. While this in itself was not unusual for Victorian women poets—both Hemans and Rossetti also published in their teens—Browning's subject certainly was, *The Battle of Marathon* being a pseudo-epic based on the defining moment of the emergence of Greek political democracy. Throughout her career, Browning would continually write on political and social issues, focusing in particular on the idea of the freedom of the individual that was a fundamental principle of her Whig beliefs, and continually championing and giving a voice to oppressed groups, whether women, children, the working class, factory "hands," slaves, or whole countries such as Greece and Italy trying to achieve independence. The power of the poems on heroism and nationalism (seen in the early "Death of Lord Byron" and "Riga's Last Song" as well as the later *Casa Guidi Windows* and *Poems before Congress*), of the poems on female independence (e.g., "The Romaunt of the Page" and the sonnets to George Sand), and of the cutting social critiques (e.g., "The Cry of the Children" and "The Runaway Slave at Pilgrim's Point") still resonates today and during the Victorian period made Browning into a formidable literary voice who was far more widely regarded than her husband. A major experimenter in form as well as subject (she used epics, verse essays, and dramatic monologues as well as ballads, lyrics, and sonnet sequences), she was dedicated to representing contemporary life, as she said in *Aurora Leigh*, "unflinchingly." *Aurora Leigh* was the work that brought Browning her greatest fame as well as her greater degree of notoriety, a nine-book epic-like Kunstlerroman that depicts the development of the eponymous heroine into a successful woman poet and which was shocking to its mid-Victorian audience in many respects. Browning incorporates into it discussion and often sharp attacks on received opinion to do with a range of contemporary social issues—the nature of useful work for women, female education, sexuality, prostitution, economic exploitation, the limits of religion, and the slums and new urban environments—often expressed with startling and violent imagery (contemporary critics were particularly horrified at the frequent use of "gynocentric" figures drawn from the female body, childbirth, breastfeeding, and menstruation).

At the center of the text, however, is Aurora's struggle to become a professional poet as she fights against ingrained prejudices ("Women as you are, mere women," argues her utilitarian socialist cousin Romney in book 2, "We get no Christ from you—and verily/We shall not get a poet, in my mind"). The text belies this, however, as Aurora proves herself highly capable of achieving her desired vocation, her final union with Romney indicating the coming together of poetic art and a socialist/humanitarian agenda that, the logic of the poem suggests, marks a way forward for women's art. By 1873, Aurora Leigh had gone through thirteen editions and in many ways it functioned as a poetic manifesto for succeeding women poets, advocating professionalism and voicing the important contributions women could make in the world of letters. Certainly, through Aurora Leigh, Browning was to become one of the poetic forebears whose absence she had previously lamented.

If Browning was to be considered the foremost woman poet of the 1840s and 1850s, it was Rossetti who was to occupy that position during the 1860s and 1870s. In the year following Browning's death in 1861, Rossetti published her first and arguably her most successful volume, Goblin Market and Other Poems, thereby effectively inheriting her predecessor's laurels. Rossetti was a great admirer of Browning, but she attempted to mark out her different compass when she argued that—"It is not in me, and therefore it will never come out of me, to turn to politics or philanthropy with Mrs. Browning." While it is true that Rossetti was never overtly engaged in politics in the same way as Browning, recent feminist criticism has demonstrated how her often deceptively simple surfaces cover critiques of social institutions and the assigned role of the middle-class woman that are certainly just as cutting as Browning's own. The exuberant "Goblin Market," for example, with its depictions of uncanny, threatening male figures, sexual temptation, and female heroism and solidarity, has, like Aurora Leigh, recently been recovered as some-

thing of a feminist "classic" in recent rereadings, while many of Rossetti's other poems are also being fruitfully discussed in terms of their challenging gender politics. Poems such as "Love from the North," The Prince's Progress (1866), "Cousin Kate," and the startling sonnet "A Triad" (which had to be withdrawn after publication) attack in varying ways the notion of romantic love and heterosexual relations, while many others depict female figures as marginalized and either locked out or entrapped (e.g., "Shut Out," "The Poor Ghost," and "At Home," and "In an Artist's Studio"). Rossetti is equally known, however, as an accomplished religious poet, with poems such as "Uphill," "A Better Resurrection," "A Birthday," and "An Old-World Thicket" being frequently anthologized in the Victorian period. Hers is not the simple unquestioning faith it is often thought to be, though, but a site of anxiety and constant doubt as is clearly revealed in poems like "Despised and Rejected." Indeed, in both Goblin Market and From House to Home (1858) there is a significant reconfiguration of Christ as a female figure, and Rossetti's questioning of received doctrine is also evident in her empathetic poem "Eve." Not always the serious figure she has been made out to be either, Rossetti also has a strand of grotesquerie and whimsy running through her work that is to be found in such poems as "My Dream," "Freaks of Fashion," and the playful "Winter: My Secret," where HUMOR is used, as it was by other women poets, as a strategy for undercutting established norms and societal expectations.

Later women poets working in the fin de siècle drew on Browning and Rossetti as models in both subject and style, some paying explicit tribute to their predecessors in poems that help to affirm a self-conscious tradition. Many of the New Women poets emerging during this period, like the New Women novelists, were concerned with articulating the problems of continued oppression in poems of either strident REALISM or unnerving Gothic—contrast, for example, E. NESBIT's "The Wife of All Ages" with Coleridge's "The Other Side of a Mirror" or Rosamund Marriot Watson's "Ballad of the Were-Wolf"). Simultaneously, however, a new sense of possibilities for liberation began to find expression with Mary Coleridge, for example, celebrating the widening female access to education ("A Clever Woman") and the aunt and niece collaboration "Michael Field" (Katharine Bradley and Edith Cooper) relished their commitment to lesbian sexuality and a paganlike sensuality (e.g., "A Girl," "Unbosoming," and "Constancy"). A number of fin de siècle women poets also drew upon the new scientific discourses of Darwinism, often using them to critique heterosexual relations and to suggest a scientific basis for the idea of gender equality (e.g., Blind's *The Ascent of Man* [1889; rev. ed., 1890] and Naden's "Scientific Wooing" and "Natural Selection"), and in the wake of Browning and the new emphasis on women's public voices, many continued to address major political and social issues. Blind critiques the clearing of the crofter communities in the Scottish Highlands in *The Heather on Fire* (1886), for example, while Greenwell attacks practices of vivisection in "Fidelity Rewarded" and Nesbit tackles the perennial 19th-c. theme of the urban wasteland in "A Great Industrial Centre."

By the close of the century, then, women poets had made great advances. They had all but completely shaken off the disabling images and subjects associated with women's poetry in the late-Romantic period and claimed increasing strength and authority in their writings. Indeed, as feminist and historicist critical practices continue to show, the tradition of Victorian women's poetry was strong, varied, challenging, and engaging.

BIBLIOGRAPHY: Armstrong, I., and V. Blain, eds., *Women's Poetry: Late Romantic to Late Victorian* (1998); Armstrong, I., and J. Bristow, eds., *Nineteenth Century Women Poets* (1996); Breen, J., ed., *Victorian Women Poets, 1830–1901* (1994); Bristow, J., ed., *Victorian Women Poets* (1995); Coslett, T., ed., *Victorian Women Poets* (1996); Gilbert, S. M., and S. Gubar, *The Madwoman in the Attic* (1979); Gilbert, S. M., and S. Gubar, *Shakespeare's Sisters* (1979); Homans, M., *Women Writers and Poetic Identity* (1980); Leighton, A., *Victorian Women Poets: Writing against the Heart* (1992); Leighton, A., and M. Reynolds, eds., *Victorian Women Poets* (1995); Leighton, A., ed., *Victorian Women Poets: A Critical Reader* (1996)

SIMON AVERY

WADE, Thomas

b. 1805, Walworth; d. 19 September 1875, St. Helier, Jersey

W. is little known, but he is important in the history of English poetry as one of the most distinctively Romantic voices between the death of Lord BYRON and the rise of Alfred, Lord TENNYSON as a major poet in 1842. W.'s beginnings are obscure, but he developed quickly as a poet. His *Tasso and the Sisters* (1825) was published when he was still a minor, and it met with some success. It shows the strong influence of Percy Bysshe SHELLEY, John KEATS, Byron, and Leigh HUNT, but it also shows metrical invention and imaginative power. Especially notable are the ambitious mythological poems "The Nuptials of Juno" and "The Spirits of Ocean."

In 1828, W. turned to the stage, and his *Woman's Love* (1829) and *The Phrenologists* (1830) were popular. *Woman's Love* deals with a heroic wife's patience in the face of her husband's tormenting cruelty, while *The Phrenologists* is a farcical mockery of false science. W.'s career as a dramatist was badly damaged later in 1830 with the production of his *The Jew of Arragon*. This tragedy treated its two central Jewish characters as noble victims of Christian persecution, and despite the considerable merits of the drama, the London audience was outraged, and the play closed after a single performance.

In 1835, W. returned to poetry with a large volume of verse entitled *Mundi et Cordis Carmina*. This contains a good deal of impressive poetry, but it was both a critical and commercial failure. W. was so frustrated that he published a broadside sonnet "To Certain Critics" (1835), in which he rebuked his attackers for their deafness to true poetry.

Despite its initial failure, *Mundi et Cordis Carmina* is a significant contribution to Romantic poetry. It deals with almost every major Romantic theme, often with power and originality. The first poem in the collection, "To Poesy," expresses a profoundly Romantic conception of poetry. "The Coming of Night" and "The Winter Shore" are blank-verse descriptions of nature and are among W.'s best poetry. "The Copse" and "Corfe Castle Ruins" are interesting philosophical meditations on nature and the nature of reality. *Mundi et Cordis Carmina* is also notable for its several tributes to Shelley and its series of experimental sonnets on an unusual mixture of personal and philosophical subjects.

The failure of *Mundi et Cordis Carmina* was a great disappointment to W., but he continued his efforts to establish himself as a poet. In the late 1830s, he published a series of poems in pamphlet form that include much of his best work. The first of these poems was *The Contention of Death and Love* (1837). This poem is written in tetrameter lines with alternating rhyme, and it debates somewhat doubtfully the question of whether poetry can really be a means of redemptive transcendence. *Helena* (1837), perhaps the best of these poems, is a symbolic narrative in a complex seven-line stanza that deals with a wide range of Romantic symbols in its overall concern with the uncertainties and dangers of Romantic love. *The Shadow-Seeker* (1837) is a strangely haunting poem on the puzzling relationship between the real and the ideal, while *Prothanasia* (1839) is a Romantic narrative in blank verse that raises serious questions about both Romantic beauty and transcendence.

These poems were published in tiny editions, and they had little success, but they are all serious and interesting works that combine intense ROMANTICISM and intense skepticism. Other than fugitive poems in various periodicals, W. issued no poetry after *Prothanasia*. His later life was largely devoted to journalism. His last significant work was the critical essay "What Does *Hamlet* Mean?" published as a pamphlet in 1844. This shows W. to have been a competent Shakespearean critic in the Romantic manner.

BIBLIOGRAPHY: Bloom, H., *The Visionary Company* (1971); Bush, D., *Mythology and the Romantic Tradi-*

tion in English Poetry (1937); McLean, J. L., ed., *The Poems and Plays of T. W.* (1997); Nicoll, W. R., and T. J. Wise, eds., *Literary Anecdotes of the Nineteenth Century* (2 vols., 1895–96)

PHILLIP B. ANDERSON

WAIN, John [Barrington]

b. 14 March 1925, Stoke-on-Trent, Staffordshire; d. 24 May 1994, Oxford

W. wrote scornfully about academics and journalists, yet he was himself both academic and working journalist. Educated at St. John's College, Oxford, he lectured at Reading University, and was Professor of Poetry at Oxford (1973–78). He was labeled an "Angry Young Man" when his first novel, *Hurry on Down*, appeared in 1953. Slight in retrospect, it chimed with fashion in having a graduate hero of lower-middle-class origins who has chosen menial work. Other novels are *The Contenders* (1958), *A Travelling Woman* (1959), *Strike the Father Dead* (1962), *The Young Visitors* (1965), *The Pardoner's Tale* (1978), and *Young Shoulders* (1982; repub. as *The Free Zone Starts Here*, 1982), rarely read now. As a poet, W. was associated with "The Movement" and published several volumes of verse, collected in *Poems 1949–1979* (1981); he also wrote an AUTOBIOGRAPHY, *Sprightly Running* (1962). However, he has lasted best as critic and essayist, with an admirable BIOGRAPHY of Samuel JOHNSON (1974; rev. ed., 1988) and the excellent *The Living World of Shakespeare* (1964).

WALEY, Arthur [David]

b. Arthur David Schloss, 19 August 1889, London; d. 27 June 1966, London

W. occupies a special place not just in British but in world literature. A celebrated Orientalist, he reconciled distant and seemingly mutually incomprehensible cultures through a flow of scholarly but eminently readable translations of Chinese and Japanese classics, minor as well as major, into English at a time when few had more than an inkling that the East possessed as great a literary tradition as the West. But if W. set the standard for such subsequent translators and exegetists as Ivan Morris, Donald Keene, Edward Seidensticker, and Jonathan Spence, contemporaneously he was regarded as a considerable poet, gaining the prestigious Queen's Medal for Poetry in 1953. During a half-century of East-West conflict, sometimes manifested militarily, he helped foster a more civilized interhemispheric dialogue.

In Japan, particularly, W.'s contribution to the still-unfolding global *éclaircissement* between cultures is held in high regard. Yet W. never once set foot beyond Istanbul. His entire professional life was centered on the British Museum and its environs, making him at the least an honorary member of the BLOOMSBURY GROUP, several of whom were known to him. Something of an eccentric, he became a byword for concentrated application in his chosen fields. Travel to China or Japan, he feared, would merely cause an unnecessary distraction to his work.

W. was educated first at Rugby, then at King's College, Cambridge, where he read classics. In 1913, he was appointed assistant keeper at the British Museum's Department of Prints and Drawings, a post he retained until 1929. Thereafter, he depended for his livelihood on lecture fees, principally from London University's School of Oriental and African Studies, where he also ran seminars, and on his writings. Eschewing full-time academic employment as another potential distraction, he nonetheless continued living close to both the museum and the university.

His primary genius was linguistic. As well as fluency in the main European languages, he achieved familiarity with Sanskrit, Syriac, Mongolian, and Ainu. Yet his published output was restricted, almost exclusively, to Chinese and Japanese, which he taught himself from 1913 onward, at a time when the modern glut of primers, dictionaries, and other prompts was simply unavailable.

W. excelled at deciphering the older forms of both languages. His largest undertaking was a six-volume translation of *The Tale of Genji* (1925–33), the vast and complex medieval Japanese novel written by Lady Murasaki in the early 11th c. Equally impressive are his verse translations of Chinese poetry, spread across several decades, though it is the single volume, *A Hundred and Seventy Chinese Poems* (1918), for which he is best known.

W. was equally at home in the keenly differentiated idioms of the Han, Tang, Qing, and other Chinese dynasties. From the preimperial archaic period, he also translated *The Book of Songs* (1937). But what counts quite as much as such linguistic virtuosity is the style of his translation. Never one to insist upon or abide by a strict one-to-one correspondence to the text-in-hand, W., as he revealed in a BBC interview with Roy Fuller, regarded its intrinsic *feeling*, intellectual and/ or emotional, as the translator's true starting point.

Because of this, and his fine ear for nuance, he was able to deploy English idiom in his translations, especially of prose works. When it came to rendering verse, however, an even greater imaginative leap was required, and it was here W. came closest to self-realization. Rather than attempt to replicate Chinese verse forms, he evolved a stress-based *vers libre* that neatly avoided both stifling exactitude and the cloying rigmaroles of fixed-meter rhyming English prosody.

Sometimes but unhelpfully compared to Gerard Manley HOPKINS's "sprung rhythm," W.'s idiosyncratic response to the problems of verse translation contributed to the progressive liberalization of English prosody itself. He also published a string of enduringly important studies, among them biographies of the poets Po Chü-i (1949), Li Po (1950), and Yuan Mei (1956), and an overview of the wellsprings of Chinese culture, *Three Ways of Thought in Ancient China* (1939), covering Confucianism, Daoism, and Buddhism.

In retrospect, W.'s choice of texts to be translated embodied a faintly elitist aversion for the modern. His is a world of exquisite sensibilities.

BIBLIOGRAPHY: Johns, F. A., *A Bibliography of A. W.* (1968); Morris, I., ed., *Madly Singing in the Mountains: An Appreciation and Anthology of A. W.* (1970); Waley, A., *A Half of Two Lives* (1982)

JUSTIN WINTLE

WALLACE, [Richard Horatio] Edgar

b. 1 April 1875, London; d. 10 February 1932, Hollywood, California, U.S.A.

Crime novelist and thriller writer, W. was at work on the screenplay of the absurd but powerful *King Kong* when he died—the film was subsequently produced in 1933. Born in the slums, W. did various menial jobs until he became a correspondent for Reuters and the *Daily Mail* during the Boer War. His first novel was *The Four Just Men* (1905; rev. ed., 1906) and his published works included nearly a hundred thrillers, fifty volumes of short stories, almost thirty plays and screenplays, four volumes of verse, and a ten-volume history of World War I. His autobiography originally entitled *People* (1926) was republished in 1929 as *Edgar Wallace: A Short Autobiography.*

WALLER, Edmund

b. 3 March 1606, Coleshill, Hertfordshire (now in Buckinghamshire); d. 21 October 1687, Coleshill, Hertfordshire (now in Buckinghamshire)

Best known for his widely anthologized lyric "Go, lovely Rose," W.'s poems—love lyrics, public panegyrics, and occasional verses—were greatly admired by his contemporaries for their grace, charm, and "smoothness." He was highly praised by his successors, including John DRYDEN and Alexander POPE, for refining the language and developing the rhetorical rhythms of the heroic couplet that was to become the staple and glory of Augustan poetry.

The year of the poet's birth is sometimes listed as 1605 because of the local practice of beginning the new year on March 25. He was educated at Eton and at King's College, Cambridge, which he left early to enter Parliament. W. may have first gained recognition as a poet during the 1630s for a series of sixteen love lyrics addressed to "Sacharissa." The object of his

attentions in these poems was Lady Dorothy Sidney, grandniece of the great Renaissance poet Sir Philip SIDNEY, whose presence imbues several of the verses. The poems are quietly enraptured in tone, balanced, and flowing in their movement. "The Story of Phoebus and Daphne, Applied" shows W.'s skillful deployment of mythological parallels and his pleasure at turning his unsuccessful courtship of the lady into his success as a poet. The well-known "Go, lovely Rose" of some years later, with its 3-, 4-, 2-, 4-, and 4-beat lines in alternating rhyme, is a particularly engaging and musical unfolding of a trope that was taken up by countless classical and English poets from Martial to Edmund SPENSER, Robert HERRICK, and Pope. It has often been praised as the perfect Cavalier lyric.

W. lived and wrote during one of the most dramatic periods of English history—the civil war of 1642–48, the Protectorate, and the Restoration. Throughout these changes, W. used his verses to celebrate the leaders and lords of the land and to commemorate significant public occasions. "To the King, on his navy" and "Upon His Majesty's Repairing of St. Paul's" both marshal mythological and biblical motifs in praise of Charles I's piety as the source of his worldly power. They exemplify W.'s political as well as aesthetic championing of traditional values, peace, and moderation. Surprisingly then, through an effort to organize resistance to arbitrary taxation, the poet became embroiled in what is now known as Waller's Plot, for which he was arrested in 1643 and exiled from England in 1644. Permitted by the new regime to return in 1652, W. promptly composed one of his finest political poems, "A Panegyrick to My Lord Protector . . . ," a warm-hearted appreciation of Oliver Cromwell, a cousin of his mother by marriage. In forty-seven quatrains composed of paired heroic couplets, W. details with considerable energy and ingenuity the virtues of the new ruler of England. His panegyric for Charles II just a few years later in 1660, "To the King, upon His Majesties happy return," was received even by the monarch himself as a noticeably lesser production, to which W. has been quoted as replying deftly, "Poets, Sire, succeed better in fiction than in truth."

After the Restoration, W. returned to the House of Commons, where he was valued for his good-hearted wit and moderation. Throughout his career—early in "To Mr. Henry Lawes" and later in "Upon the Earl of Roscommon's Translation of Horace"—W. espoused the neoclassical view that poetry's sounds add persuasive charm to its fundamental task of teaching and elevating. He lived to present two panegyrics to James II but not to welcome the Glorious Revolution of 1688. A small group of final verses have a sustained religious focus. The six cantos comprising "Of

Divine Love" are thought to be as skilled, if not as lively as his earlier work.

The intellectual changes overtaking Western Europe during W.'s lifetime are evident in two of his early lyrics. "On a Girdle" ends with the image of the sun moving around the earth, whereas on the other side of the Copernican revolution the song "Stay, Phoebus! stay" speaks of "the error of those antique books" and closes with the movement of "the rolling earth." Today, with his once exalted reputation long gone, only W.'s precise stature as a minor poet and notable transitional figure continues to be discussed by critics, all of whom agree that he set high standards of grace and polish for the great poets who were to follow him.

BIBLIOGRAPHY: Cherniak, W. L., *The Poetry of Limitation: A Study of E. W.* (1968); Donnelly, M. L., "E. W.," in Hester, M. T., ed., *Seventeenth Century British Nondramatic Poets, DLB* 126 (1993): 264–85; Gilbert J. G., *E. W.* (1979); Thorn Drury, G., ed., *The Poems of E. W.* (2 vols., 1904)

MARGARET HOLLEY

WALPOLE, Horace, Fourth Earl of Oxford

b. 24 September 1717, London; d. 2 March 1797, London

W. remains an intriguing figure in literary history. The youngest son of the prime minister, he enjoyed the privileges of an affluent life: preparation at Eton (1727–34), education at King's College, Cambridge (1735–38), the Grand Tour (1739) with poet Thomas GRAY, member of Parliament (1741–68). W.'s intellectual life at university was highlighted by his formation of the Quadruple Alliance with Gray, Richard West, and Thomas Ashton.

W.'s humanistic interests included extensive letter writing, garden theory and design, architecture, art history, fiction, and publishing. The extent of his endeavors makes him an important figure in 18th-c. studies. For example, his *Works* (5 vols., 1798) runs to two thousand pages; at his death, he left four thousand unpublished letters, memoirs, and journals totaling approximately three million words. The magnificent Yale edition of his works runs to forty-eight volumes.

It is a curiosity of the 18th c. that W.'s architecture and literature were clearly intertwined. In 1747, W. purchased a small Twickenham estate that he renamed Strawberry Hill. Here, he began his career as gardener and then, by 1750, architect. W. shocked even some of his contemporaries when he chose the Gothic style for his new home. This ornate style had, however, already begun to enjoy a resurgence in popularity among both preservationists and the ministry. As W. moved into Gothic architecture, he was about to immortalize himself as author of the first English GOTHIC NOVEL. When the first phase of Strawberry

Hill was complete, the house became a tourist attraction well known for its towers, turrets, cloisters, long corridors, etc. Near his estate, W. founded the Strawberry Hill Press, which published his four-volume *Anecdotes of Painting in England* (1762–80). The history was based on the notebooks of engraver George Vertue purchased from Vertue's estate. The final volume of *Anecdotes* included W.'s "Essay on Modern Gardening."

The 18th c. was a century of letter writing, and W. is one of its major epistolary authors. Nostalgic and anecdotal in nature, W.'s letters record his impressions of the dashing highwayman M'Lean, the beautiful Countess of Coventry, the trials and deaths of Jacobite lords, and the funeral of George II. W. apparently chose his major correspondents Sir Horace Mann in Florence and George Montagu and William Cole in England for their respective knowledge of politics, social affairs, and antiquities.

W. stated in the second preface to *Castle of Otranto* that he originally sought to meld the ancient with the modern in his 1765 ROMANCE. It was his wish to revive, in briefer form, the French romance and yet avoid using the commonplace in his fiction. What W. hybridized typifies the revolt against the rationalistic creed of Samuel RICHARDSON and Henry FIELDING and may well have begun the Romantic revival in England. W.'s knowledge of medieval architecture greatly enriched the terror he created in the romance. Underground passages, courtyards, long hallways, etc. added a nightmare maze to the stagecraft of the narrative. The tension in the Gothic is, more often than not, between past and present, with the novel opening in Naples in 1095 and running to ca. 1243. Strawberry Hill and Trinity College, Cambridge, are the inspiration for the architectural centerpiece in the novel.

W. fabricated memorable if ludicrous Gothic terrors in *Otranto*: huge swords, mysterious giant helmets falling from the sky, bleeding statues, etc. It is, however, the natural rather than the supernatural devices in the novel that are most effective: the cloisters, the breathlessness of pursuit, and the light and dark play of sunshine and shadow. Characterization in the novel is stereotypical, since all characters are based upon 18th-c. costume types. Manfred is the usurping prince, his wife Hippolita is the subservient wife, Mathilda is the helpless damsel in distress, Isabella is the innocent young maiden, and Theodore is the handsome oaf. The incest motif in the romance has drawn significant recent interest. Manfred's lust for his son's fiancée Isabella is interpreted as a manifestation of Manfred's desire for other men, thus linking heterosexual incest and homosexuality. W.'s *The Mysterious Mother* (1768) also explores the theme of incest. In that work, set in the early Renaissance, the Countess of Narbonne takes the place of the woman her son was about to seduce. Sixteen years later, the son very nearly marries his own daughter, marking what some have referred to as a theme of double incest.

To historians, W. remains linked to the creation and evolution of the English Gothic romance, to studies in art and architecture, and to epistolary writing. As an 18th-c. gentleman, he is a major exponent of the cultivated humanism that produced him.

BIBLIOGRAPHY: Fothergill, B., *The Strawberry Hill Set: H. W. and His Circle* (1983); Ketton-Cramer, R. W., *H. W.* (3rd ed., 1966); Lewis, W. S., *Rescuing H. W.* (1978); Smith, W. H., ed., *H. W.* (1967)

GEORGE C. LONGEST

WALTON, Izaak

b. 9 August 1593, Stafford; d. 15 December 1683, Winchester

W.'s fame has largely depended on the enduring popularity of his delightful prose-pastoral *The Compleat Angler*. First published in 1653, this was much enlarged and revised on its republication two years later. When it reached a fifth edition in 1676, it contained further new material and a second part by Charles COTTON. The book has been much reprinted ever since. Most of its readers have not themselves been anglers, and they have not been reading it for what it has to say about "the nature and breeding, and seasons, and catching of fish" (to quote W.'s "Epistle to the Reader" from the fifth edition). What has continued to attract readers has, rather, been its picture of the author's mind and its vision of an idealized English countryside. The work, it should be noted was published at the height of Puritan dominance in the governance of church and state.

The Compleat Angler is a work of withdrawal, simultaneously a politico-religious statement and a prose restatement of that motif of the Happy Man ("beatus ille") familiar to many of W.'s original readers from Horace's second epode or Virgil's *Georgics*. We need to remember that W. was a royalist, that is to say a supporter of the losing side in the Civil War and admirer of the recently executed king; that he was an Episcopalian at a time when the Church and its hierarchy were being violently dismantled. His "Discourse" is a literary re-creation of a lost paradise. W. tells the reader "I have made myself a recreation of a recreation" and we should give full etymological weight to that word re-creation. In the pages of his treatise, and the life it represents, W. can find companionship of precisely the kind he wants, telling us that most anglers are, like "the primitive Christians . . . quiet men, and followers of peace"; he can find the poetry he admires, much better, he feels, than the sort "now in fashion in this critical age." Above all, he can, in nature and silence, find the means to prayer

and contemplation, for the pursuit of a particular kind of Anglican quietude. And, of course, he can find the day's dinner, whether it be an eel ("a most dainty fish: the Romans have esteemed her the Helena of their feasts") or a pike, cooked with oysters, herbs, and wine ("This dish of meat is too good for any but anglers, or very honest men"). The seeming straightforwardness of W.'s manner (not least in his prose style) and attitudes has sometimes led to his being thought of as a naive figure; the facts of W.'s background, his relative lack of education, his time as apprentice to a sempstress in London and the like, have perhaps encouraged this perception of him. To make such a judgment is, however, to be deceived by the art with which W. has concealed his art. Though there is little that is ostentatious in *The Compleat Angler*, there is much that is sophisticated.

Calculated artistry, often concealed behind a similar mask of simplicity, underlies the series of five biographies that W. composed, four of which were published together in 1670 (and in a revised form in 1675). The earliest of these was *The Life of John Donne* (1640; rev. ed., 1658); it was succeeded by *The Life of Mr. Richard Hooker* (1665; rev. ed., 1666), *The Life of Sir Henry Wotton* (1651; rev. ed., 1654), and *The Life of Mr. George Herbert* (1670). In 1678, appeared *The Life of Dr. Robert Sanderson*, of which a revised edition was published in 1681. In his *Lives*, W.'s essential purpose was to provide accounts of individuals he took to be exemplary figures, models for the imitation of well-intentioned members of the Anglican Church. His *Lives* served as definite a purpose as his treatise of *Love and Truth: in two modest and peacable letters, concerning the distempers of the present times. Written from a quiet and conformable Citizen of London, to two busie and factious Shopkeepers in Coventry* (1680). Written in response to the demands of the Nonconformists, *Love and Truth* is characteristic of W. in its adoption of a "modest and peacable" persona, in its stress on the values of "quiet" and being "conformable."

More explicitly than other of W.'s works, the *Lives* are offered as a response to "the distempers of the present time." Though they don't declare it on their title pages, *The Compleat Angler* and the *Lives* might just as readily be seen as other such responses. Inaccuracies and omissions, simplifications and diplomatic silences, in the *Lives* are largely the product of conscious religio-political purpose, rather than of naiveté or ignorance on W.'s part. His life of John DONNE offers a figure of largely uncomplicated piety; there is no serious attempt to do justice to the poetry. The *Life of Hooker* was a contribution to disputes that followed the Restoration, and W. seems more interested in making use of Richard HOOKER's life and work to support one side of this particular argument than in undertaking a serious study of the man himself. In writing of Sir Henry WOTTON, W. largely concentrates on his subject's last years, avoiding some of the details of Wotton's more worldly early years, details that might have blurred his picture of retired and contemplative piety. His picture of George HERBERT, too, involves a certain slanting of the facts so as to enforce, uncluttered by complexity, a striking lesson—here was a man of great family who chose a relatively humble life in the service of the (Anglican) Church. The skill with which W. molds his exempla of retirement, of the turning away from worldly ambition and by implication creates the model of that church that he (and his powerful friends such as Bishop Morley) were seeking to further is assured and purposeful. These *Lives* may fail to meet many of the demands we now make of BIOGRAPHY; to complain of this is to apply historically inappropriate standards. The task that W. set himself, to write persuasive and readable accounts that would serve a specific didactic (or propagandist if one prefers the term) purposes, he carried out to something like perfection.

BIBLIOGRAPHY: Chadwick, O., *The Fisherman and His God* (1984); Cooper, J. R., *The Art of the Compleat Angler* (1968); Novarr, D., *The Making of W.'s Lives* (1958); Stanwood, P. G., *I. W.* (1998)

GLYN PURSGLOVE

WAR AND LITERATURE

The transformative experience of war has always been fertile ground for the literary imagination. World War I particularly inspired working soldiers to create an epistolary and autobiographical tradition that continued into later conflicts. Poets and novelists wrote works of vivid REALISM that extolled the virtues of heroism yet challenged the romantic preconceptions of noncombatants at home. Many of them died at the height of their powers, leaving succeeding generations of writers and critics lamenting the incalculable loss of works never written. Historically, the contradictions and ironies of rationalized violence have attracted the attention of authors who never experienced war directly. Pacifists and militarists alike have found themselves captivated by circumstances that inspire the extremes of human behavior. The daily experience of combat alters the sinews of the psyche, challenging and often destroying the human capacity for hope and belief, sometimes rendering impotent the impulse to love. War strikes violently at the heart of the human experience. From the early accounts of Norse and Anglo-Saxon forebears to the Arthurian renderings of ancient conflicts, from the Hundred Years' War to the mechanized carnage of the 20th c., war has served as source material for many stark, vivid, and beautiful works of literature.

In England, the literature of war originates perhaps with the first acknowledged masterwork of the Anglo-Saxon period, the EPIC poem *BEOWULF*. A poem of 3,182 lines deriving historical sources from the 6th c., it survives in a 10th-c. manuscript and tells of major events in the life of a Geatish hero and warrior king. This material is legendary and fantastic, the conflicts centering around bloody battles with dragons and monsters rather than with human combatants. But in its realistic treatment of violence and in its explorations of the extent and limits of heroism, *Beowulf* prefigures the war literature that will follow. A more historically centered and realistic rendering of the subject appears during the English Renaissance in the works of William SHAKESPEARE. The history plays of the Hundred Years' War, *Henry IV*, parts 1 and 2, and *Henry V*, establish two perspectives on the issue of heroism that will influence the perspectives of the war poets and war writers in later centuries. Bernard Bergonzi argues that in *Henry IV*, part 1, Hotspur exemplifies "the moral virtues of heroism and single-minded pursuit of honour" while Falstaff embodies "the biological virtue of cowardice" together with the "human burden of consciousness." Bergonzi further argues that Shakespeare represents these as extremes, endorsing neither, but seeing them as polar responses to the experience of war. Hotspur's perspective certainly would have commanded the moral and nationalist sentiments of the Renaissance, as can be seen in the idealized sculpture of the condottiere Bartolomeo Colleoni by Verrocchio in Venice or in the heroic figures of the stage: Bussy D'Ambois, Coriolanus, and Tamburlaine. But eventually Falstaff emerged as the realist, the man who sees things clearly, who weighs the human cost of war against the false ideals that often precipitate it. For him, honor in the face of violence "hath no skill in surgery" and reveals itself finally as "mere scutcheon."

This same conflict appears in the contrasting romanticisms of Sir Walter SCOTT and Lord BYRON. In romances such as *The Heart of Midlothian*, *Ivanhoe*, and *Rob Roy*, Scott reconstitutes the epic poem in the novel form, using the romance-novel to create affirmative myths of nationalism and cultural identity centering around the heroic virtues of warfare and violence. In *Don Juan*, however, Byron undercuts expressions of heroism and the valorization of "honour," savagely criticizing the mindless pursuit of glory for its own sake. Although he died himself in a military conflict, Byron anticipates the ironic skepticism of later poets and writers who experienced the realities of war and came to question the "virtues" that give war its impetus.

In the English tradition, the largest concentration of literature directly concerned with war was written in the 20th c., much of it emerging out of the shocking experience of World War I. Military historians sometimes debate whether the American Civil War or World War I represent the first example of "modern war." Certainly, there can be no discounting the human carnage experienced on the otherwise pastoral landscapes of Virginia, Pennsylvania, and Tennessee, at battles such as the Wilderness, Gettysburg, and Shiloh. There is no doubt that the horrific accumulation of blood and death in these places was owing to new battlefield technologies, particularly modern artillery and the rifled musket. But the American Civil War also involved the strategic movement of vast armies and the tactical genius of great generals, while the patterns of conflict were consciously constructed based upon a Napoleonic model. Although modern tactics were apparent in Ulysses S. Grant's siege of Vicksburg and William Tecumseh Sherman's violent sweep across the civilian South, the true experience of mechanized warfare, in which the machine and logistics and attrition rendered the human combatant less than consequential, did not occur until the Great War of 1914–18. The literature of this period was precipitated by a number of works that provided both literary and historical reference. With the exception of the Crimean War and the Boer War, Great Britain had not experienced a war of consequence for over one hundred years. Aside from "The Charge of the Light Brigade," a commemoration of the charge at Balaclava written by Alfred, Lord TENNYSON, little significant war literature was produced for some time. There was, however, much written in the Victorian era about wars elsewhere in the world. Rudyard KIPLING's *Barrack-Room Ballads* collection of 1892 contains many poems about the wars being fought in India and North Africa during the period, and his short story collections such as *Plain Tales from the Hills, Wee Willie Winkie,* and particularly *Soldiers Three* contain many stories with an Indian army setting; even the school stories in *Stalky and Co* are set in a school specializing in the education of future army officers. H. Rider HAGGARD's novels deal with wars among the Zulus and other South African tribes. It was also a great period of novels and poems reliving past triumphs and "battles long ago," by such writers as G. A. Henty, W. Harrison Ainsworth, Thomas Babington MACAULEY, Robert Louis STEVENSON, Frederick MARRYAT, Charles KINGSLEY, Henry NEWBOLT, and Stanley J. Weyman, a tradition continued into our own day by C. S. FORESTER, Patrick O'BRIAN, J. G. Farrell, and George MacDonald FRASER.

The literary figures of the Great War were prolific and multigeneric. They were poets, novelists, autobiographers, diarists, and masters of epistolary correspondence. For the most part, they were products of their age—intelligent, reflective, educated, and erudite young men whose sensibilities reflected the historical tensions of the time. They were motivated by a devotion to their nation and culture and driven by a sense of duty and commitment. At the same time, they were sensitive enough in perspective to see the ironies and inconsistencies that distinguished the mythologies of war from the realities of their own experience. They included such figures as Rupert BROOKE, A. E. HOUSMAN, Siegfried SASSOON, Ford Madox FORD, Ivor GURNEY, Isaac ROSENBERG, Robert GRAVES, and Wilfred OWEN. German and American authors included such notable figures as Erich Maria Remarque, author of *All Quiet on the Western Front* (1929); and Ernest Hemingway, author of *In Our Time* (1925), *The Sun Also Rises* (1926), and *A Farewell to Arms* (1929). The experiences portrayed in their various works emerge from an historically distinctive and horrific set of circumstances. A trench system was established in France and Belgium along a four hundred mile line that ran from the Swiss border in the south to the North Sea. The conditions of modern warfare were manifest in a conflict of attrition and stalemate, and battles were lost and won by machine guns, poison gas, artillery, influenza, factories, and the stubborn ability of statesmen and industrialists to demand that others wait and die.

In a poem written in 1964, Philip LARKIN reflects upon the experience of the Great War, concluding his verse with the ambivalent tonality of loss: "Never such innocence again." This sense of disillusionment together with sense of commitment and duty is reflected in the fiction emerging from the war, most notably Ford's *The Good Soldier* and *Parade's End.* Ford explores not only the experience of violence but the effects of the Great War on the structure and social patterns of English life. The experience of battle appears in the work of poets such as Brooke, Housman, Graves, Sassoon, and Owen. Although Brooke died of blood poisoning on the eve of real battle, in sonnets such as "Peace" and "The Soldier," he combines personal reflection on the possibility of love and death with the mythic linkage of the individual to the embattled nation. In "Epitaph on an Army of Mercenaries," Housman extols the heroic virtues of the English professional soldier, inspiring the angry response of Hugh MACDIARMID in "Another Epitaph on an Army of Mercenaries." MacDiarmid sees the mercenaries as self-serving antiheroes who "took/Their blood money and impious risks and died." This emphasis on the darker aspects of war appears in the works of perhaps the two greatest poets of World War I: Sassoon and Owen. In *The Old Huntsman* and *Counter-Attack,* Sassoon renders the realities of war in vivid and realistic terms, and both collections attracted the attention of critics at home and soldiers in the trenches because of their fidelity to detail and satiric power. Poems like "Blighters" especially level a satiric thrust at the propagandists at home. Sassoon's transition from enthusiastic combatant to pacifist was a remarkable one, appearing in his poetry and explored with greater intellectual exactitude in his diaries and in his *Memoirs of an Infantry Officer* and *Siegfried's Journey*. Sassoon began as a brave and sometimes ferocious soldier, referred to as "Mad Jack" by members of his company. Graves recalls an initial encounter with Sassoon, the latter showing the yet inexperienced young man a copy of his collection of poems portraying the realities of war. Betraying initially his Georgian idealism, Sassoon argued that the war should not be portrayed realistically and unheroically. But as the conflict continued, and as he witnessed the carnage, Sassoon began to question the motivations of leaders at home and argued for a negotiated settlement. He finally refused further participation in the war, was nearly court-martialed, and ended up being temporarily held in a mental ward in Edinburgh where he met the younger Owen.

Owen is by many considered the greatest poet of the war. Sassoon acknowledged this, saying "It was Owen who revealed how, out of realistic horror and scorn, poetry might be made." An officer of middle-class background and education, Owen's principal influences were John KEATS and Percy Bysshe SHELLEY, but after experiencing the war firsthand, he became the realistic portrayer of the antiheroic mode prefigured in Byron and Stendhal. Together with Sassoon, Owen undermines the mythic treatment of war that had received continual currency in epic poetry and historical ROMANCE, reflecting a modern shift in sensibility brought on by the horrors of mechanized war. Death by poison gas or machine gun or mortar fire was substantively different from death by sword in a gallant Napoleonic charge. Owen captures this change with unyielding clarity. In "Dulce Et Decorum Est," he speaks directly to an older generation at home who cling to Hotspurian notions of patriotism and valor and who see war as a glorious endeavor, "If you could hear, at every jolt, the blood/Come gargling from froth-corrupted lungs,/Obscene as cancer. . . . My friend, you would not tell with such high zest/To children ardent for some desperate glory,/the old Lie: Dulce et Decorum Est/Pro patria mori." These same sentiments appear in poems such as "Insensibility" and "Anthem for Doomed Youth." But it must be remembered that this voice of protest emerged from experience than from distanced consideration. Owen was a winner of the Military Cross, and a week before the Armistice he led his men on yet another attack on the western front. In that final conflict, he was machine-gunned to death.

Although the Great War shocked the Western world, ushering in the cataclysmic effects of the modern machine, no event in human history can compare with the devastation of World War II. Over seventy-eight million people were killed or wounded, more than half of them civilians. More than fifty million men and women served in the military. To the writers and poets of the period, the apocalyptic scope of the war tended to shock them into silence, and the Second World War resulted in significantly less literary output than the war preceding it. Although popular propaganda was nationalistic and affirmative, the literature of the period was a literature of irony, disillusionment, angst, and despair. The poet/writer/combatant of the Second World War was weary from the start. The first war promised world peace but precipitated yet another more bloody conflict, and the carnage of war was exactly that—carnage: senseless and without purpose. The British literature of World War II appeared in the works of figures such as Herbert READ, Alun LEWIS, Henry Reed, John Pudney, Keith DOUGLAS, among many others. Poets such as Read, Lewis, and Reed emphasized the antiheroic and dehumanizing aspects of the soldier's experience. In "To a Conscript of 1940," Read reflects upon the human cost of both wars, and is aghast at seeing the conflict renewed on a larger scale. In "All Day It Has Rained," Lewis uses natural imagery and vivid description to create a context for the soldier and his experience. The individual is absorbed in a whirl of naturalistic forces, both subjective and objective, and the rain suggests a conflict too large and omnipresent to yield to singular heroic action. In "Naming of Parts" (1946), one of a suite of three poems entitled *Lessons of the War* (1970), Reed uses a rifle as a metaphor for the modern machine, creating an ironic contrast between the destructive potential of modern mechanized war and the unifying power of benign nature. Poets, novelists, writers of memoirs and autobiographies of World War II explore the realities of modern war, attempting to comprehend the scope of the carnage. For the most part, they find meaning only by portraying it truly, in recognizing the irony inherent in the motives informing it, and in portraying the tragedy that attends it.

Thus, in Great Britain the literature of war emerges over time as a literature of internal as well as external conflict. The militarism of empire is reflected in the mythologies of the medieval period and continues into the Renaissance. Shakespeare establishes a contrast in perspective that serves to define the treatment of war from the late 16th c. through the world conflicts of the 20th c. The poets and writers of the modern period attempt to redefine valor in the context of mechanized war. Heroism and antiheroism, militarism and pacifism, idealism and realism, become the ideological and aesthetic tensions that inform and enrich the literature of war. If any small compensation may be drawn from the carnage and bloodshed of military history, it may be that the tragedy and violence of war are yet again a powerful impetus for human expression.

BIBLIOGRAPHY: Banerjee, A., *Spirit above Wars: A Study of the English Poetry of the Two World Wars* (1975); Bergonzi, B., *Heroes' Twilight: A Study of the Literature of the Great War* (1965); Cross, T., ed., *The*

Lost Voices of World War I: An International Anthology of Writers, Poets and Playwrights (1989); Fussell, P., *The Great War and Modern Memory* (1975); Fussell, P., ed., *The Norton Book of Modern War* (1991); Fussell, P., *Wartime: Understanding and Behavior in the Second World War* (1989); Harvey, A. D., *A Muse of Fire: Literature, Art and War* (1998); Knowles, S. D. G., *A Purgatorial Flame: Seven British Writers and the Second World War* (1990)

STEVEN FRYE

WARD, Mary Augusta

b. 11 June 1851, Hobart, Tazmania; d. 24 March 1920, London

W., better known as Mrs. Humphry Ward, was well connected and a self-educated scholar, attuned to the intellectual currents of her day. Her novel *Robert Elsmere* (3 vols., 1888), the one of her twenty-five novels on which her present reputation rests, brilliantly dissects the religious and social turmoil of the 19th c. About a marriage under strain because of doctrinal differences, it tells the story of her own parents' troubled relationship, softening only the violence of their quarrels. It may also be the first fictional account of postnatal depression. The book was published when doubt was causing havoc among the clergy, and was an instant success, translated into dozens of languages. Its strength lies in its topical relevance and power of cultural analysis.

It includes the famous line, "in my youth people talked about [John] Ruskin; now they talk about drains." The issue of "sanitary reform," popularized by Charles KINGSLEY's *Yeast,* stimulated by the "condition of England" novels of Benjamin DISRAELI, Elizabeth Cleghorn GASKELL, and Charles DICKENS, was an essential ingredient of the movement for social and consequent, it was hoped, moral reform. The clergy and their wives, in *Robert Elsmere* as in real life, nursed the poor through water-borne diseases, supplying coals and blankets. To W., religious controversy was the most absorbing of issues. She observed shrewdly in her introduction to *Robert Elsmere*, "The main Darwinian battle had been won long before 1870 . . . it was in literature, history and theology that evolutionary conceptions were most visibly . . . at work."

The heroine struggles to do her duty as her clergyman husband abandons Christian orthodoxy and evolves into theistic humanism, allied to practical social work. This pragmatic stance was the author's own hard-won solution to the anguish caused by her own father's oscillation between the churches of England and Rome, which wrecked his career. W. was granddaughter of Thomas Arnold, famous headmaster of Rugby school, and niece of Matthew ARNOLD. Her father, Thomas Arnold, was the original of Philip in Arthur Hugh CLOUGH's poem, *The Bothie of Toper-*

na-fuosich, who "rounded the sphere to New Zealand." After failing at farming, Thomas moved to Tasmania. In 1856, he converted to Roman Catholicism. In 1865, he returned to the Church of England and became a lecturer at Oxford, but in 1876 reentered the Church of Rome, throwing away the chance of an Oxford Chair.

W. was at the center of Anglican intellectual ferment. She peopled her novel with characters drawn from life. *Robert Elsmere* is a roman à clef to 19th-c. Oxford. W. understands the history of her century and the influence of background on character. When her husband drifts away from the church, the heroine, Catherine, warped by her training in submissiveness, is tempted to suicide. She is contrasted with her healthier sister, the rebellious Rose. Like her heroine, W. had been reared in Evangelical piety and taught to be submissive. *Robert Elsmere* was her revenge, although Rose, the sister who represents nature and instinct, is shunted off at the end into marriage, her aspiration to study music frustrated. Henry JAMES deplored this outcome, and complained that Rose's devotion to art should have been more serious. W. knew that women in her society were forced to compromise.

BIBLIOGRAPHY: Jones, E. H., *Mrs. Humphry Ward* (1973); Peterson, W. S., *Victorian Heretic* (1976); Trevelyan, J. P., *The Life of Mrs. Humphry Ward* (1923)

VALERIE GROSVENOR MYER

WARNER, Marina [Sarah]

b. 9 November 1946, London

W. is a novelist and cultural historian whose work combines strong ethical and political concerns, formidable erudition, a keen pleasure in the use of language, and a capacity to range widely across cultures. Born of an Italian mother and an English father, educated as a Catholic in Protestant England, fluent in French and Italian, her life and work exemplify that *métissage*, that biological and cultural interbreeding, that she values highly and that has become increasingly significant in her writing. Her fiction and nonfiction often complement each other and explore similar themes: the pressure of religion, especially of Roman Catholicism; the representation of women, particularly in iconic form; the significance of myth and fairy tale; the relationship of the past to the present; and the meeting and mixing of cultures.

W.'s nonfiction is well researched, lucid, penetrating, and provocative; her fiction is carefully and intricately structured and is particularly marked by parallels, echoes, and mirrorings across times and cultures. Her first two books—*The Dragon Empress* (1972) and *Alone of All Her Sex: The Myth and Cult of the Virgin Mary* (1976)—were analyses of female icons. W. has said herself, of the second, more substantial work, that she would have been much happier if it had been a novel but that it would have seemed frivolous to explore her love-hate relationship with Roman Catholicism through fiction. Once she had proved her seriousness with *Alone of All Her Sex*, however, she felt able to move on to a fictional exploration of the complexities of the religious life. Her first novel, *In a Dark Wood* (1977), focuses on a 20th-c. Jesuit priest, Gabriel Namier, and his 17th-c. counterpart, Andrew de Rocha, whose biography Namier is writing: the lives of the two men echo each other through their sojourns in China, the divisions of the church of which they are members, and their possible homosexuality. The novel builds up to a somber conclusion. A study of a further female icon, *Joan of Arc* (1981), was followed by her second novel, *The Skating Party* (1982). Here, the focus at first seems to narrow to a single day in which a group of family and friends slide down a frozen English river; but the past soon breaks through the ice. Thoroughly modern in its rendering of middle-class social and sexual manners in 1970s Britain, the novel also evokes practices and artifacts from other cultures and times that resonate with its central situation: a witch-exorcism ceremony on a Pacific island, which relates, obliquely, to W.'s book on Joan of Arc; a set of rediscovered Renaissance frescos that mirror the relationships of its characters.

After *Monuments and Maidens* (1985), a fourth study of female icons that ranges from Minerva to Margaret Thatcher, W. turned in her next novel to a woman's quest for a patriarch. *The Lost Father* (1988) combines a variety of narrative modes in its story of an English woman who is drawing on a range of sources, from newspaper articles to personal recollections, to write a novel based on the life of her Italian grandfather. Postmodernist in its skepticism about narrative truth, *The Lost Father* nonetheless provides a richly persuasive portrayal of a Southern Italian village community. The mixing of narrative modes is taken further in W.'s next novel, *Indigo; or, Mapping the Waters* (1992), which combines REALISM, ROMANCE, adventure, fantasy and fairy tale and moves back and forth between the 17th and the 20th cs., shuffling images of the precolonial, the colonial, and the postcolonial. *Indigo* dramatizes the long involvement of the Everard family with the exploitation of a Caribbean island whose original inhabitants recall Sycorax, Caliban and Ariel in William SHAKESPEARE's *The Tempest*. The fraught, complex relationships of the present-day Everards provide a concentrated image of the perplexities—and possibilities—of postcolonialism: W.'s 20th-c. Miranda finally marries a Caliban, not a Ferdinand, and their baby symbolizes the positive outcome of *métissage*.

W. has acknowledged that *Indigo* has a fairy tale ending, and she pursued her interest in FAIRY TALES, legends, and myths in her nonfiction of the 1990s—*Managing Monsters* (1994; repub. as *Six Myths of Our*

Time, 1994), which looks at modern myths, *From the Beast to the Blonde* (1994), which traces the history of fairy tales, and *No Go the Bogeyman* (1998), which considers the ways in which stories can frighten, comfort, and mock. Myths and fairy tales also feature in her short story collection *Mermaids in the Basement* (1993), which demonstrates, on a smaller scale, the stylistic versatility increasingly evident in her later novels. It was not until the new millennium, however, that she produced her fifth novel, *The Leto Bundle* (2001).

The "bundle" of the title consists of a mummy and a collection of associated objects and documents that make it possible to piece together the tale of Leto, a partly real, partly mythical, woman whose life stretches from the ancient world to the present, passing through the medieval era and 19th-c. Europe. Characteristically for W., history and past myth are mobilized both for their own intrinsic interest and in order to provide deeper perspectives on key aspects of the postmodern world: *The Leto Bundle* is her imaginative challenge to the fear and hate-filled modern myths that have gathered around migration, *métissage*, displacement, and asylum-seeking, not least in present-day Britain. The novel is notable for its evocations of the past and its engagement with the present, for its narrative complexity, and for the variety of styles that it employs, from pastiche translations of ancient papyri to the patois of modern emails.

The Leto Bundle demonstrates the assurance that W. has now attained as a novelist, her ability to encompass the remarkable range of her concerns in sophisticated, compelling, and challenging fiction. While her novels can certainly stand alone, they yield even more when read alongside her nonfiction. The whole body of her work is perhaps best seen as an ongoing project, rather like Simone de Beauvoir's, in which imagination, emotion, and reason all contribute to a deeply engaged exploration of human existence.

BIBLIOGRAPHY: McBride, K. B., "M. W.," in Moseley, M., ed., *British Novelists since 1960*, Second Series, *DLB* 194 (1998): 279–87; Tredell, N., "M. W.," in his *Conversations with Critics* (1994): 234–54

NICOLAS TREDELL

WARNER, Sylvia Townsend

b. 6 December 1893, Harrow-on-the-Hill, London; d. 1 May 1978, Maiden Newton, Dorset

W. was one of the generation of modernists who began learning their sexual, social, and literary politics during the First World War. Between 1925 and 1978, she published seven novels, ten collections of short stories, seven volumes of poetry, a prize-winning BIOGRAPHY, two translations, and numerous essays, articles, and political fables in periodicals ranging from the *Countryman* to *New Masses*. The apparent accessibility of W.'s novels and poetry may be a cause of her exclusion from the experimental British modernist canon; in the absence of free verse or stream of consciousness narrative, most critics have failed to value W.'s complexity—her emphasis on the marginalities of class, race, gender, and sexuality; her learned but apparently off-hand allusions to literature and history; her lesbian, feminist, communist, anarchist SATIRE, and her delight in the comic and the absurd. In the U.S., feminist and queer criticism has centered on *Lolly Willowes; or, The Loving Huntsman* (1926) and *Summer Will Show* (1936), but W. is still chiefly remembered as the author of short stories published for forty years in the *New Yorker*.

Satire of imperialist ideology—degeneration theory, primitivism, eugenics—informs W.'s three 1920s novels, *Lolly Willowes, Mr. Fortune's Maggot* (1927), and *The True Heart* (1929). Their plots are fantastic: Laura (Aunt Lolly) Willowes escapes her lot as a middle-class old maid by transforming into a witch: Mr. Fortune loses his missionary faith and recognizes his homosexual love on the Polynesian island of Fanua; in *The True Heart*'s retelling of the myth of Cupid and Psyche, Sukey Bond (Psyche), an orphan maid-of-all-work, is personally empowered by Queen Victoria (Persephone) to marry the beautiful, middle-class "idiot," Eric (Eros). But these books already reflect W.'s deepening criticism of imperialism, war, and the class and sex/gender systems.

An episode of the class war forms the climax of each of W.'s historical novels of the 1930s and 1940s. *Summer Will Show* provides the most overt, positive fictional representation of lesbianism published in Britain between the 1928 censorship of Radclyffe HALL's *The Well of Loneliness* and the 1960s. W.'s book concludes, however, with the massacres of the working class in Paris at the end of the 1848 Revolution. A deadly skirmish between peasants and soldiers ends *After the Death of Don Juan* (1938), a political fable set in the 18th c. but about the Spanish Civil War. *The Corner That Held Them* (1948) chronicles thirty-three years in the life of a nunnery, from the Black Death until the 1381 suppression of the angry, hopeful journey of the people to the young king in London—the "Peasants' Revolt." W.'s seventh novel, *The Flint Anchor* (1954; repub. as *The Barnards of Loseby*, 1974), is a study of the Victorian hypocrisy that dominates the Barnard family, extinguishing both love and rage and producing instead drunkenness, fear, depression, heartlessness, and despair. The satire is sometimes hilarious but unremittingly dark; the joy and generosity that are driven from the Barnard household are embodied and expressed by the bisexual fisherman, Crusoe.

The bleak poverty of English country life is the subject of many of W.'s early short stories and of the poems published in *The Espalier* (1925) and *Time Importuned* (1928), culminating in *Opus 7* (1931), a bitterly ironic rhymed narrative satire depicting the rural gloom that followed the cannibalistic prosperity of the war years. W.'s joint publication with her lover, Valentine Ackland, of *Whether a Dove or Seagull* (1933) was a leftist "experiment in presentation," aimed at compulsory heterosexuality and the literary canon; the volume does not attribute individual poems to either woman whose names appear on the joint title page. The intricate harmony of "After my marriage-night, she said" and "Go the long way, the long way home" points forward to such W. masterpieces as "Anne Donne" and "Gloriana Dying," published in *King Duffus and Other Poems* (1968) and *Twelve Poems* (1980).

W.'s short stories range from terse realist sketches such as "Step This Way," in which a mother, her daughter, and a midwife discuss abortion (*The Museum of Cheats*, 1947), through her prize-winning "A Love Match" (*A Stranger with a Bag*, 1966, and *Selected Stories*, 1988) to the worldly, earthbound tales of the seemingly supernatural in her last book, *The Kingdoms of Elfin* (1977). In its sexual radicalism, its challenge to conventional repression and hypocrisy, its social comedy and political seriousness, "A Love Match" represents the best of W.'s writing. She deserves to be widely read.

BIBLIOGRAPHY: Harman, C., *S. T. W.* (1989); Marcus, J., "S. T. W.," in Scott, B. K., ed., *The Gender of Modernism* (1990): 531–38; Mulford, W., *This Narrow Place: S. T. W. and Valentine Ackland* (1988); Wachman, G., *Lesbian Empire: Radical Crosswriting in the Twenties* (2001)

GAY WACHMAN

WARNER, William

b. 1558, London; d. 9 March 1609, Great Amwell, Hertfordshire

Cambridge-educated, W. became a London attorney. *Pan His Syrinx; or, Pipe, Compact of Seven Reedes* (1584; repub. as *Syrinx*, 1597) is a book of prose tales and W. translated Plautus's *Menaechmi* (1595). W.'s chief work is a verse history of England (4 vols., 1586), from Noah to the Normans. Later editions bring the story up to Queen ELIZABETH I (1589 and 1592). It was further enlarged and the 1612 version reaches the reign of King JAMES I. Although praised in his time by notables such as Frances MERES, Thomas NASHE, and Michael DRAYTON, W. is all but forgotten by modern readers.

WARTON, Joseph

b. April 1722, Dunsfold, Surrey; d. 23 February 1800, Wickham, Hampshire

Both as a poet and a critic, W. was a significant figure in the long process by which Augustan neoclassicism gave way to the values of ROMANTICISM. In 1744, W. graduated from Oxford and published his first significant work, *The Enthusiast*. This substantial contemplative poem in Miltonic blank verse was a striking expression of anti-neoclassical feeling, and it stands as one of the seminal poems of the mid-18th c. In *The Enthusiast*, W. celebrates the simple beauties and sublimities of nature at the expense of neoclassical architecture, gardens, and art. He also dismisses the correctness of the neoclassical Joseph ADDISON in favor of the natural power of William SHAKESPEARE. Finally, W. embraces the life of primitive mankind while rejecting the corruption of "civilized" humanity, and, in the last lines of the poem, expresses his longing to escape modern Britain and find a refuge in the unspoiled wilds of America. In its Miltonic blank verse, its passion for nature, its attack on Augustan values, and its pervasive primitivism, *The Enthusiast* is one of the central expressions of what is sometimes called the "school of sensibility."

The values of *The Enthusiast* are also to be found in W.'s *Odes on Various Subjects* (1746). In the "Advertisement" for this volume, W. states that didactic poetry and verse essays on morality have replaced true poetry, which is based on invention and imagination, and that he hopes to "bring Poetry into its right channel." Of the odes in this collection, the most important is W.'s "Ode to Fancy." This ode, written in Miltonic tetrameter couplets, invokes Fancy as a creative power associated with wild nature, intense passion, poetic energy, and inspiration. W. calls upon Fancy to give to some modern poet the power she once gave Shakespeare and, in so doing, redeem English poetry from "The rhyming throng." Another interesting ode from W.'s 1746 collection is his "Ode to Solitude." Here, W. shows the influence of John MILTON's "Il Penseroso" as he calls upon "Solitude" to allow him access to her retired world of congenial gloom from which he may meditate on the corruptions of the "folly-fetter'd world" of mirth and business.

Three years after his *Odes*, W. published separately his "Ode to Evening" (1749). Evening was a favorite subject among the poets of sensibility, and W.'s quatrains in praise of Evening's serenity and peace invite comparison with William COLLINS's "Ode to Evening" and Thomas GRAY's "Elegy." Much of W.'s poetry shows a strong element of primitivism, and in several of his poems he refers to America. Among these, the best is "The Dying Indian" (1755). In this blank-verse dramatic monologue, an Inca warrior speaks eloquently of his faithfulness to the ways of his people and of his outraged contempt for the invading Europeans and their religion.

W.'s later works are mainly literary criticism. Of these, by far the most important is his *Essay on Pope* (1756; rev. eds., 1762, 1772, 1782). In this book-length essay, W. expresses admiration for Alexander POPE as a satiric and didactic poet. W. goes on to say, however, that the greatest poetry, unlike Pope's, is based on the transcendently sublime and pathetic. Finally, W. places Pope in the second class of English poets and ranks him below the "sublime and pathetic" Shakespeare, Milton, and Edmund SPENSER.

Although critics have long debated the exact degree of both W.'s originality and influence, the entire thrust and character of W.'s poetry and criticism give him a central place in the school of sensibility and among those who furthered the spread of essentially Romantic values and ideas.

BIBLIOGRAPHY: MacClintock, W. D., *J. W.'s Essay on Pope* (1933); Pittock, J., *The Ascendancy of Taste: The Achievement of Joseph and Thomas Warton* (1973); Sitter, J., *Literary Loneliness in Mid-Eighteenth-Century England* (1982)

PHILLIP B. ANDERSON

WARTON, Thomas

b. 9 January 1728, Basingstoke; d. 21 May 1790, Oxford

W. is a crucial figure in the history of 18th-c. English literature. W.'s poetry and his criticism occupy a virtually unique place in the long struggle between neoclassical literary values and those values that would eventually produce ROMANTICISM.

W.'s first important work was his *The Pleasures of Melancholy* (1747). This poem is indebted to earlier poets from John MILTON to Mark AKENSIDE in its celebration of the gloomy delights of melancholy contemplation, but W.'s handling of blank verse, the distinctive sensuousness of his approach to sadness, and the pointed force with which he rejects the classical in favor of the Gothic and the visionary mark this poem as a crucial expression of mid-18th-c. sensibility.

W.'s next significant work, *Observations on the Faerie Queene of Spenser* (1754), established him as a major critic and literary historian. In the *Observations*, W. uses a genuinely historical approach and insists that Edmund SPENSER cannot be judged by neoclassical standards of which he never heard. This methodology, coupled with W.'s obvious love of the medieval ROMANCE tradition, represented a serious challenge to neoclassical literary theory.

In the years following his *Observations*, W. published a number of minor works, but his next notable publication was his *Poems* (1777). This volume shows W.'s mature powers as a poet, and it is also important in literary history for its role in the revival of the sonnet. Between Milton and W., the sonnet as an English poetic form largely disappeared, and when W. produced his sonnets, he was ridiculed by Samuel JOHNSON and others. Nevertheless, W.'s sonnets are effective, and they influenced others to revive the form between 1780 and 1820. W.'s sonnets show Milton's influence, but they achieve their own eloquence in their treatments of nature, the pleasures of antiquarianism, and their celebration of the poetic imagination. Among the best of them are "Written in a Blank Leaf of Dugdale's Monasticon," "Written at Stonehenge," and "To Mr. Gray." In addition to his sonnets, the *Poems* of 1777 contains several poems that demonstrate W.'s ability to recapture imaginatively the Middle Ages, and such poems as "The Crusade" and, especially, "The Grave of King Arthur" are a strong anticipation of Sir Walter SCOTT and other Romantic medievalists.

W.'s later years were mainly devoted to literary scholarship. His great achievement in this area was his immense *The History of English Poetry* (4 vols., 1774–81). Although W.'s *History* is incomplete and often inaccurate in detail, it combines scholarship, sound criticism, and a genuinely historical approach in such a way as to make this work the true beginning of literary historiography in English. W.'s powers as a literary historian are also evident in his *An Enquiry into the Authenticity of the Poems Attributed to Thomas Rowley* (1782). In this *Enquiry*, W. demonstrates effectively that the poems written by Thomas CHATTERTON but attributed to a supposed medieval monk could not possibly have been written in the Middle Ages.

W.'s last important work was *Verses on Sir Joshua Reynolds's Painted Window at New College* (1782), in which he dramatizes the conflict between neoclassical and Gothic values and his own ambivalence about that conflict. W. was named poet laureate in 1785.

BIBLIOGRAPHY: Pittock, J., *The Ascendancy of Taste: The Achievement of Joseph and Thomas Warton* (1973); Rinaker, C., *T. W.* (1916); Sitter, J., *Literary Loneliness in Mid-Eighteenth-Century England* (1982); Wellek, R., *The Rise of English Literary History* (1966)

PHILLIP B. ANDERSON

WATERHOUSE, Andrew
b. 27 November 1958, Gainsborough, Lincolnshire; d. 20 October 2001, near Longframlington, Northumberland

One of the most promising poets of his generation, W. first gained critical recognition in the mid-1990s and received the Forward Prize for best first poetry collection in 2000 for *In*. A passionate environmentalist and accomplished musician, W. studied agriculture at Newcastle University and later earned an M.Sc. degree from Wye College. In 1996, he received an M.A. in creative writing from Northumbria University and for many years lectured at Kirkley Hall College, near Morpeth in Northumberland. With the success of his first collection, W. seemed to have finally come of age as a poet, but suffering from severe depression and ill health he ended his own life at age forty-two. His was a poetry at once vibrant and intimate that traveled "inner and outer territories" and shifted between "the bleak and the playful." He once said of his work, "I can only be aware and do my best."

WATERHOUSE, Keith [Spencer]
b. 6 February 1929, Hunslet, Leeds

W. is one of Britain's most prolific and versatile writers in the second half of the 20th c. Probably best known as a novelist, though his many plays have given him an important status as man of the theater, he has also written television dramas, children's books, two volumes of engaging AUTOBIOGRAPHY, books on style, and a medley of classic HUMOR. His work is, seen as a whole, that of a comic writer, though he is capable of vivid social realism and stark psychological insight.

Born into a working-class family, W. left school at fifteen and studied at Leeds College of Commerce, then, after National Service in the Royal Air Force, became a journalist—first in Yorkshire, then in London—which he has been ever since. He has lived in London since 1951 and has been married and divorced twice.

W.'s novelistic career began with *There Is a Happy Land* (1957), a study of childhood in Yorkshire; his next book, *Billy Liar* (1959), established his success, leading to a play, a film, and a sequel, *Billy Liar on the Moon* (1975). Among his fourteen additional novels, among the most notable are *Jubb* (1963), *Office Life* (1978), and *Maggie Muggins* (1981), all of them focusing on the displacements and derangements of urban life. *Jubb* is a splendid study of increasing mania, *Maggie Muggins* (W.'s favorite among his novels) of the life lived by a female transient in Earl's Court. *Thinks* (1984) chooses an unusual technique to render the interior life of a man whose life, the reader comes to realize, is collapsing. *Our Song* (1988) is a vivid portrayal of a desperate advertising executive's desperate love for an undeserving woman.

Among his more lighthearted fictions, several strike a nostalgic note. *In the Mood* (1983), for instance, is about three Yorkshire boys who scheme to get to London for the Festival of Britain in 1951: the mood they are in is one of sexual readiness. *Soho* (2001) is a tribute to Soho as it was when W. first came to London; its protagonist is a northern naif, from Leeds, come south to find his girl and discovering instead, or in addition, a rich feast of London experiences and characters.

Another strain is of SATIRE, usually fairly good-humored, as in *Unsweet Charity* (1992), an exaggerated look at the English middle-class propensity for fund-raising, *Good Grief* (1997), about the whole array of services surrounding death and its aftermath, and *Bimbo* (1990), the pretended autobiography of Debra Chase, a famous topless model for tabloid newspapers. Debra is reminiscent of Sharon and Tracy, two frequent topics for his newspaper columns, collected in *Sharon & Tracy & the Rest* (1992), the best of his columns.

W. was taken by George and Weedon GROSSMITH's classic comic novel, *The Diary of a Nobody;* around it he has built *Mr. and Mrs. Nobody* (a play, 1992), *Mrs. Pooter's Diary* (comic diary, 1983), and *The Collected Letters of a Nobody* (1986). Another of his plays built on an adaptation is *Jeffrey Bernard Is Unwell* (1989), an extremely popular work based on Bernard's weekly column about his difficult life.

W. has had a long successful career as a playwright, which began with the adaptation of *Billy Liar* for the stage, in 1961, in partnership with his childhood friend and, from that time forward, longtime collaborator Willis Hall. So prolific that for a time they were called "The Writing Factory," W. and Hall followed the first play with *Celebration* (1961), *All Things Bright and Beautiful* (1963), *Come Laughing Home* (1966)—all on working-class Leeds themes—and a great many more successful plays. They include some very adept and funny farces, such as *Say Who You Are* (perf. 1965; pub. 1966), *Who's Who* (perf. 1968; pub. 1974), *Whoops-a-Daisy* (perf. 1968; pub. 1978), and *Children's Day* (perf. 1969; pub. 1975), as well as *England, Our England* (1964), a revue obviously inspired in part by the success of *Beyond the Fringe.*

W.'s continuous newspaper work has produced *W. at Large* (1985), another collection of his work, and two books on writing style, one of which began as an attempt to update the stylebook for the *Daily Mail.* Recently, he has written two volumes of memoirs: *City Lights: A Street Life* (1994) and *Streets Ahead: Life after City Lights* (1995), both finely evocative and informative accounts of his career.

W. is clearly a sort of virtuoso. His critical reception has been mixed. The very fecundity of his output; the fact that he usually writes humor; and a quality that seems to make him a man's writer whom women sometimes find irritating: all have qualified his critical esteem. Thus, Julie Burchill sums him up as a "grumbling old geezer" with stodgy and misogynist attitudes. Critic Auberon WAUGH, on the other hand, regularly named him the best living English writer.

BIBLIOGRAPHY: Gray, N., *The Silent Majority: A Study of the Working Class in Post-War British Fiction* (1973); Schlueter P., "K. W.," in Oldsey, B., ed., *British Novelists, 1930–1959*, part 2, *DLB* 15 (1983): 559–69

MERRITT MOSELEY

WATERMAN, Andrew [John]
b. 28 May 1940, London

W. left home at seventeen and did various clerical and manual jobs before reading English at Leicester University. He taught at the New University of Ulster, Coleraine. His first collection of poems, *Living Room* (1974), reflected on his journey from London to Ulster. *From the Other Country* (1977) was followed by *Over the Wall* (1980). *Out for the Elements* (1981) was a verse AUTOBIOGRAPHY in 178 rhymed stanzas borrowed from Alexander Pushkin, in deliberately ordinary language, a partial homage to William WORDSWORTH. His *Selected Poems* appeared in 1986 and *Collected Poems, 1959–1998* in 2000. In 1981, W. edited, with an introduction, *The Poetry of Chess.*

WATKINS, Vernon [Phillips]
b. 27 June 1906, Maesteg, South Wales; d. 8 October 1967, Seattle, Washington, U.S.A.

W. has been described by the poet Roland MATHIAS as "the most vaguely lauded and the least understood" of the 20th-c. Welsh poets in the English language. Despite the commendations of, among others, T. S. ELIOT, Kathleen RAINE, and Philip LARKIN, he remained throughout much of his career in the shadow of his friend and fellow-poet Dylan THOMAS. An Anglican Christian, who had been idyllically happy at his English public school, and a family man who followed his father into Lloyd's Bank and pursued a quiet career in a Swansea branch, W. was very different from the more flamboyant Thomas, except in the devotion they shared to the art and craft of poetry.

During his lifetime, W. published six collections of poetry—*Ballad of the Mari Lwyd* (1941), *The Lamp and the Veil* (1945), *The Lady with the Unicorn* (1948), *The Death Bell* (1954), *Cypress and Acacia* (1959), and *Affinities* (1962)—and another, *Fidelities* (1968), appeared posthumously. Dedicated to achieving and proclaiming the conquest of time and the eternal value of our transient lives, W. envisioned his poetry as a personal search for "metaphysical truth." William BLAKE, the Romantic poets, and W. B. YEATS were all influences on W., who was widely read too in the literature of other European languages, ancient and modern. The Neoplatonist idea of the replica, the perfect ideal form twinned with each earthly form, was to merge in W.'s poetry with the view of Christ as the ultimate conqueror of time and its depredations.

In proclaiming his main theme, W. used subsidiary ones, above all the paradoxical interdependence of opposites (i.e., white and black, in his "Music of Colours" poems). The emphasis that has understandably been laid on the philosophical and religious content of W.'s work should not obscure his gift of expressing human feeling and the beauty of this world. Often his poetry rejects a cerebral approach in favor of artistic perception—truth lives in the "glittering drops/caught on a thread of glass/two frosty branches bear/in trance like air." In the poem "Waterfalls," W. evokes a valley of his boyhood where there is always "the voice/ Of waters falling," and voices of memory. Likewise, the rural elegies "Loiterers," "A Man with a Field," and "The Scythe" are all the more moving for their specific visual detail. In "Taliesen in Gower," for example, W. evokes in long pulsing lines the "prodigious" coast and seascapes of the Welsh peninsula. In addition, there are poems for W.'s children, and a light-hearted "Poem for Conrad," about the joy and laughter of the poet's own childhood. In his philosophical poems, W. makes much use of symbols. A recurrent one is the sycamore, that long-lived tree whose great fertility is shown in its hundreds of seedbearing keys. There are numerous images in which water is eternally passing: "The fountain gathers, in a single jet,/Fidelities where beams together run,/ thrives upon loss, enriches us with debt."

W.'s long lines and some of his stanza forms are much influenced by those he encountered in his study of the classics. He was a meticulous craftsman, whose poems went through draft after draft. Those in classical form and meter achieve some of his grandest effects; one of his finest is the visionary winter poem "Great Nights Returning." But he wrote also many poems in a minimal verse form, apt for aphorism. It may be that his strong, simple ballads, such as "Ballad of Culver Hole" and "Ballad of the Trial of Sodom," with its thumping ominous refrains, have attracted readers who later tried his richer and more difficult poems.

When W.'s inspiration weakens, the poems usually keep a cold perfection of technique; but when he writes at his best, there is a passion in the music. Some poems have a lapidary quality, a feeling of absolute, inevitable rightness. Such a poem is "The Heron": "Calamity about him cries,/ But he has fixed his golden eyes/ On water's crooked tablet,/ On light's reflected word." He also has wonderful endings, as in "Gravestones"—"Break, buried dawn,/ For the dead live, and I am of their kind." Another poem, "Fidelities," ends with lines that seem a fit epitaph for a man of integrity and a dedicated poet: "For me neglect and world wide fame were one./I was concerned with those the world forgot,/In the tale's ending saw its life begun;/And I was with them still when time was not."

BIBLIOGRAPHY: Mathias, R., *V. W.* (1974); Norris, L., ed., *V. W. 1906–1967* (1970); Polk, D., *V. W. and the Spring of Vision* (1977); Watkins, G., *V. W. and the Elegiac Muse* (1973)

RUTH BIDGOOD

WAUGH, Alec [Alexander Raban]

b. 8 July 1898, London; d. 3 September 1981, Tampa, Florida, U.S.A.

W. was the elder brother of Evelyn WAUGH. *The Loom of Youth* (1917), W.'s precocious novel of life in a public school, shocked the public because of its hints of homosexuality but was a considerable commercial success. It seems very tame today. W. remained a successful writer of novels, including *Love in These Days* (1926), *Nor Many Waters* (1928; repub. as *Portrait of a Celibate*, 1929), and *So Lovers Dream* (1931; repub. as *That American Woman*, 1932). *Island in the Sun* (1956) was filmed 1957 with an all-star cast, including Harry Belafonte. His last novel, *Married to a Spy*, was published in 1976. W. wrote several volumes of AUTOBIOGRAPHY, including *The Early Years of Alec Waugh* (1962) and *My Brother Evelyn and Other Profiles* (1967).

WAUGH, Auberon [Alexander]

b. 17 November 1939, Dulverton, Somerset; d. 16 January 2001, Taunton

During a tour of duty with the Royal Horse Guards in Cyprus, W., son of British author Evelyn WAUGH, was grievously wounded when he accidentally shot himself in the chest. This absurd and darkly comic incident in his own life would not seem out of place in W.'s novels, which portray members of British society as, at best, ineffectual bumblers and, at worst, malicious schemers. These novels, as well as his essays and his fictional "Diary," established W. as a major 20th-c. British humorist.

W.'s first two novels, *The Foxglove Saga* (1960) and *Path of Dalliance* (1963), are both set largely within academic milieus. In the first, the upper-class Martin Foxglove and the less well-off Kenneth Stoat attend a Catholic boarding school together, and the novel, inspired largely by W.'s own experiences in school and the military, follows the characters through national service and hospital stays. *Path of Dalliance* again focuses on a pair of protagonists, Jamey Sligger and Frazer Robinson, this time at Oxford University. Although none of his characters is sympathetic, W. seems most critical, particularly in *Path of Dalliance,* of the lower classes and of ostensibly liberal student radicals, whose plans for the liberation of the world's oppressed are depicted as so much empty rhetoric and hypocrisy. The uselessness and hypocrisy of supposedly altruistic people is also a theme in *Who Are the Violets Now?* (1965). In this episodic tale, freelance writer Arthur Friendship devotes great energy to the cause of world peace, but his cohort includes an opportunistic lecher, a shallow dilettante, a hypocritical black radical poet, and a Nazi war criminal. Arthur's ineffectuality is illustrated by his one "heroic" act: he rushes into a burning building to rescue a baby and is horribly disfigured as a result. Unbeknownst to Arthur, however, the "baby" he rescues is merely a lump of dirty laundry, the real child presumably perishing in the blaze. *Consider the Lilies* (1968) is W.'s strongest novel, perhaps because the first-person narration allows the reader a greater sense of identification with another essentially unlikable protagonist. Nicholas Trumpeter, an Anglican priest, is not only completely apathetic toward religion, but he is so devoid of conventional priestly virtues that he conducts an affair with his patron's young daughter, contemplates murdering his wife, and gradually loses his mind over the question of whether the modern world suffers from a Freudian "anal obsession."

W. stopped writing novels after *A Bed of Flowers; or, As You Like It* (1972). This novel dealt with the Nigerian Civil War, a subject W. had also broached in *Biafra: Britain's Shame* (with Suzanne Cronje, 1969). For the remainder of his career, W. was a prolific columnist and reviewer for such publications as *Private Eye*, *Daily Telegraph*, the *Spectator*, and the *New Statesman*, among others. From 1972 to 1986, W. published his "Diary" in *Private Eye,* and it is for this that he may be most remembered. Neither a true diary nor conventional fiction, these sketches provide satirical looks at various facets of contemporary British life. The highly conservative, always cantankerous W. displays a true gift for humorous observation in these short pieces, many of which are collected in *Four Crowded Years: The Diaries of A. W., 1972–1976* (1976) and *A Turbulent Decade: The Diaries of A. W., 1976–1985* (1985). W. also produced collections of essays and an AUTOBIOGRAPHY, *Will This Do? The First Fifty Years of A. W.* (1991).

BIBLIOGRAPHY: Moseley, M., "A. W.," in Moseley, M., ed., *British Novelists since 1960*, Second Series, *DLB* 194 (1998): 288–96; Sutherland, J. A., *Fiction and the Fiction Industry* (1978)

JASON BERNER

WAUGH, Evelyn [Arthur St. John]

b. 28 October 1903, London; d. 10 April 1966, Combe Florey, Somerset

W. is the finest satirical novelist of the 20th c. His novels fall into two periods, the first running from *Decline and Fall* (1928) to *Put Out More Flags* (1942). The frequent darkness of these frenetic novels foreshadows W.'s later pessimism. War separates the early comedy from the nostalgia of *Brideshead Revisited* (1945) and the disillusion of the war trilogy.

W.'s satires exploit absurdity. Characters endure an antic world where the follies of a hedonistic, graceless society produce sequences of events like slippery slopes; lost footing is rarely regained. The ironies and outrageous coincidences of a nonsensical universe replace cause and effect. One of W.'s seedy young men remarks to his girlfriend that he could eat her. "You will," she replies; unwittingly he does, at a cannibal feast later in the novel *Black Mischief* (1932). Trivial events randomly produce calamity. Little Lord Tangent's heel is slightly grazed by a bullet fired by an intoxicated schoolmaster in *Decline and Fall*. At irregular intervals, bulletins inform us of the little boy's unpredictable decline into death. His mother, Lady Circumference, is greatly upset that her absence from the hero's wedding will be attributed to her son's death instead of her social disapproval of the bride, revealing the ferocious snobbery of her class.

Decline and Fall is W.'s first and best novel. Paul Pennyfeather, a theology student, is sent down from Oxford, ostensibly for indecent exposure, but really for his social insignificance, and the fact that his tie is too easily mistaken for that of the Bollinger Club, with whose annual orgy he becomes accidentally involved. Outraged members of the Bollinger debag him for wearing their tie. Paul's adventures are paradigmatic of W.'s grotesque universe. Advised that those expelled for indecency generally become teachers, Paul becomes a master at Llanabba Castle, an upmarket Dotheboys Hall, run by shady Dr. Augustus Fagan, Ph.D. Among Paul's colleagues is Captain Grimes, a pederast, who rarely sees the end of a term, but who, as a public-school man, always finds employment in his chosen profession. Margot Beste-Chetwynde, mother of one of Paul's pupils, whisks him off to high society and offers marriage. Innocently, Paul becomes involved in Margot's business (ownership of a chain of brothels) and is arrested on his wedding day for white slavery, while Margot paradoxically receives the universal sympathy. Paul finds prison reassuring, like his public school, or Oxford before his fall. Margot arranges Paul's escape. Fleeing the world, Paul retreats to his old college, and becomes the theologian whom we met in the first chapter.

Paul escapes, but Adam Fenwick-Symes, in *Vile Bodies* (1930), only glimpses a vanishing, pastoral England in Doubting Hall ("Doubting 'All" to the locals). But its bankrupt owner leases the hall to a sleazy movie company as the setting for its debased version of English history. *Vile Bodies* is populated by the "bright young people," a generation without past or future, trapped in a round of parties ending in exhaustion or death. Bright young Agatha Runcible spins out of control, drunk in charge of a racing car. She dies partying madly at the nursing home where she is recovering. The novel ends in the biggest battle-field of the biggest war ever.

W.'s least attractive (but most seductive) young man is Basil Seal, the cynical hero of *Black Mischief*, who inadvertently devours his mistress. Set in the African kingdom of Azania, the novel satirizes the attempted "modernization" of Azania by the predatory Basil. In *A Handful of Dust* (1934), Tony Last owns a neo-Gothic country house in constant need of expensive repair. The house, Tony's obsession, imprisons his wife. She escapes to adultery and a glitzy London apartment. Lost in Amazonia, condemned to read Charles DICKENS aloud to a crazy planter, Tony becomes prisoner of another's obsession. *Scoop* (1938) fictionalizes W.'s journalistic experience in Abyssinia. *Put Out More Flags* grows from W.'s vain hope that World War II would redeem the England of Grimes, Fagan, and Margot Beste-Chetwynde.

Brideshead Revisited expresses both nostalgia for the lost Eden of a prewar England, and W.'s Roman Catholicism (he converted in 1930). The rich evocation of Oxford and Brideshead, with the finely realized charm of Sebastian Flyte, are the best elements of the novel and account for the usual view that this is W.'s finest, a view reinforced by the lushness of the television production. SATIRE is muted by the pathos of Sebastian's decline, the looming fate of the great house, and a new seriousness of characterization. Nonetheless, *Brideshead* is a *partial* success. The Catholicism does not persuade, even in Lord Marchmain's deathbed scene, or in Ryder's humility before the religion he had mocked. That the Flytes will be providentially recalled to their faith is asserted, not realized fictively. The novel's strength is the glorious realization of loss and longing for return.

Men at Arms (1952), *Officers and Gentlemen* (1955), and *Unconditional Surrender* (1961; repub. as *The End of the Battle*, 1961)—the Sword of Honour trilogy—recount the decline into disillusion of Guy Crouchback, scion of an old Catholic family, and initially idealistic volunteer for military service. The first recounts Crouchback's training. The hilarity, however, is overdone. Revelation of the absurdities of military life involves a labored cloacal joke. Brigadier Ritchie-Hook's decline into a pantomime character sits uneasily with an oversolemn reverence for military life. Crouchback suffers through the Cretan disaster in *Officers and Gentlemen*. *Unconditional Surrender* sees Crouchback finally disillusioned by the contorted partisan politics of wartime Yugoslavia. The simple faith of Crouchback's father is intended to outweigh the pessimism evoked by the modern world in arms, but the religious element is not persuasive.

W.'s reputation rests on the early novels and *Brideshead*. His biographies, other fiction, and travel writing have weathered unevenly.

BIBLIOGRAPHY: Amory, M., ed., *The Letters of E. W.* (1980); Davie, M., ed., *The Diaries of E. W.* (1976); Stannard, M., *E. W.: The Early Years 1903–1939* (1986); Stannard, M., *E. W.: The Later Years 1939–1966* (1992)

ANGUS SOMERVILLE

WEBB, Mary

b. Mary Gladys Meredith, 25 March 1881, Leighton, Shropshire; d. 8 October 1927, St. Leonards-on-Sea, Sussex

During her brief career, W. published poetry, short stories, essays, and journalism, but is remembered mainly for her six novels, the most enduring of which are *Gone to Earth* (1917) and *Precious Bane* (1924). Her work reflects her passionate and mystical love of the Shropshire countryside and its people: for the most part ignoring the present in favor of a rural past, it is characterized by themes of love, violence, cruelty, and beauty, and by the unfathomable power of nature. Although W. received little regard during her lifetime, praise from the prime minister, Stanley Baldwin, brought her posthumous fame. Her work has always sharply divided critics: her ardent prose was mercilessly parodied by Stella Gibbons in *Cold Comfort Farm* (1932), but admired by John BUCHAN, who praised her "rare beauty, and simplicity," and by Rebecca WEST, who called her a genius.

W. began to write in her first period of convalescence from Graves' disease, an affliction accompanied by a physical disfigurement that would influence her later work. *The Spring of Joy*, a collection of verse written before her first novel but not published until 1917, is stifled by an adherence to the fashionable vocabulary and structures of the day, and it was in her novels that her individuality, with all its passion and HUMOR, most fully emerged. From the outset, her books are well plotted and peopled with sympathetic characters, and adopt a symmetry and symbolism more often found in poetry. *The Golden Arrow* (1916) is a semiautobiographical work that explores unorthodox religious experience. Shropshire FOLKLORE is shown as an integral part of human existence and, although the novel does not quite work as a unified whole, it contains many memorable scenes; as in Thomas HARDY's work, the landscape acts as a character in its own right, heightening the emotional force of the book.

Gone to Earth is a tale of passion, seduction, and tragedy in which the struggle of two men for one woman is mirrored by the conflict between nature and man—a subject that strongly preoccupied W. after the advent of World War I. Containing less narrative comment and more drama, and displaying a Dickensian eccentricity in its characterization, *Gone to Earth* is far more successful than its predecessor. Here, W. displays an intuitive understanding of natural phenomena and an ability to convey that elemental power: love of nature was, for her, a first step toward the extremes of human love and a comprehension of divinity.

By contrast, her next novel, *The House in Dormer Forest* (1920), moved away from the external force of nature to the internal workings of the mind. Although the suffocating atmosphere of malevolence within the house is well described, action is lost to mood and introspection; the narrative is more forced, the characters less richly realized, and the overall effect is fragmented and disappointing. The same loose structure is to be found in *Seven for a Secret: A Love Story* (1922), another Gothic and sinister tale in which a character must decide between two suitors, one physically attractive and the other a poet-mystic.

With *Precious Bane*, however, which takes its title from the first book of John MILTON's *Paradise Lost*, W. created her masterpiece. The story of Prue Sarn, the heroine with a harelip that was the fictional counterpart of W.'s own afflictions, won the Femina-Vie Heureuse Prize in 1926 for "the best imaginative work in prose or verse descriptive of English life by an author who has not gained sufficient recognition." Baldwin wrote a preface to the 1928 reprint, praising W.'s "blending of human passion with the trees and skies," and the book's many qualities—its lyrical intensity, perceptive and sensitive narrator, and brilliant evocation of the landscape and the slow, contained lives of the men and women who inhabit it—continue to make it popular today, despite the author's brave decision to use a West Midlands dialect throughout.

W. never again achieved that perfect fusion of plot, imagery, and characterization. *Armour Wherein He Trusted* (1929), an historical novel set in the Middle Ages, remained unfinished on the author's death in 1927 and the cold critical response to its dense and monotonous pages reflected W.'s own feelings about the book, which she had tried to burn. *Fifty-One Poems*, published posthumously in 1946, have something of the melancholy of A. E. HOUSMAN, and have also been compared to the work of Christina ROSSETTI and Walter DE LA MARE.

W. had no desire to challenge literary forms through her prose or poetry, and her work is often flawed by a fervor that borders on naiveté and a sadness that strays into the morbid. Nevertheless, her ability to depict the complexities of a female response to the world and the atmospheric power of her finest prose have a lasting importance, as Buchan noted: "Mary Webb need fear no comparison with any writer who has attempted to capture the soul of Nature in words."

BIBLIOGRAPHY: Barale, M. A., *Daughters and Lovers: The Life and Writing of M. W.* (1986); Coles, G. M., *The Flower of Light: A Biography of M. W.* (1978)

NICOLA UPSON

WEBBE, William
d. 1591

W. was the author of *A Discourse of English Poetry, Together with the Author's Judgment Touching the Reformation of Our English Verse,* written and published in 1586, the first extensive treatment of English poetry to appear in print. Little is known of W.'s life other than he graduated from Cambridge and apparently earned his living by teaching. Late in life, W. befriended clergyman Robert Wilmot and wrote a complimentary letter "To his friend R. W." attached to Wilmot's play entitled *Tancred and Gismund,* published in 1591.

WEBSTER, John
b. ca. 1579, London; d. ca. 1634, probably London

On the basis of two plays, W. is generally considered to be the greatest playwright of the early 17th c., excepting only William SHAKESPEARE. Sometimes criticized for his violent and confusing plots, he was rediscovered in the 19th c. by the Romantic poets, and again in the 20th by T. S. ELIOT, all of whom admired his powerful poetry and dark, uncompromising vision.

Although recent scholarship has established that W. was the son of a London carriage maker, little is known about his family background and youth. He probably attended the respected Merchant Taylors' School, as his father belonged to this guild, but no solid evidence of this exists. He may even have studied law—a John Webster was admitted to study law at the Middle Temple in 1598—but again this is a matter of speculation. Evidence from his plays suggests he had an interest in and familiarity with the law. The first sure historical record of W. is when he appears in theater manager Philip Henslowe's diary as one of a group of authors being paid in advance for a play called *Caesar's Fall,* later referred to as *Two Shapes.* Sadly, the play is lost, for W.'s collaborators included some of the age's most respected playwrights: Anthony MUNDAY, Michael DRAYTON, Thomas MIDDLETON, and Thomas DEKKER.

W. continued to work collaboratively for years with a variety of authors, including Henry CHETTLE and Thomas HEYWOOD. The most important of these collaborative works was a scurrilous satire written with Dekker titled *Westward Ho* (perf. 1604; pub. 1607). After a group of playwrights including George CHAPMAN and Ben JONSON replied with the comedy *Eastward Ho,* Dekker and W. produced *Northward Ho* (perf. 1605; pub. 1607). Confusingly plotted and full of satirical allusions, these plays have recently garnered critical interest for their clever SATIRE and self-conscious theatricality.

Except for an induction to John MARSTON's play *The Malcontent*, W.'s next known work is *The White Devil* (1612), which made his name. The play traces the paths of a variety of ambiguous characters, centering on Flamineo, secretary to the Duke of Brachiano. When Brachiano conceives an adulterous lust for Flamineo's sister Vittoria, Flamineo helps him to seduce her. But Vittoria, in a clever speech couched as a dream, insists that her husband, Camillo, and the Duke's adoring wife, Isabella, must be killed before she will yield. Brachiano arranges their murders, enacted in dumb show, bringing upon himself the vengeance not only of Isabella's brother, Francisco, Duke of Florence, but also of Cardinal Monticelso, cousin to Camillo, who later becomes Pope.

The play unfolds as a series of complex plots and subplots as characters form and reform alliances and loyalties. Everyone in the play, excepting the hapless victims and Vittoria's mother Cornelia, is morally ambiguous. Vittoria is condemned to a convent for reformed whores—later she is sprung by Brachiano—but in her trial she defends herself in impressively eloquent terms, causing many readers and critics to see her as a heroine. Meanwhile, the ostensible hero Francisco succeeds in killing Brachiano, but only because he is wilier, not because his motives are purer. And the villain Flamineo vacillates at the end of the play, expressing regret for his misdeeds even while defending himself in strongly commercial terms. No one, in short, seems to have the means—moral, religious, or spiritual—to resist the lures of passion, power, and wealth. W. draws a portrait of a world—displaced onto Italy—severely decentered by its lack of strong moral leaders. Vittoria's dying words are typically eloquent as they damn her entire milieu: "Oh, happy they that never saw the court/Nor ever knew great men but by report!"

The White Devil shares many features with a favored dramatic form of the late 16th and early 17th c.: the "revenge tragedy." Based on the model of Senecan tragedy, revenge tragedies found their apex in Shakespeare's *Hamlet*. Typically, a revenge tragedy centered on a hero's search for vengeance, usually spurred on by the victim's ghost. Other common elements include poisonings and other devious forms of murder, unnatural acts involving adulterous or incestuous passions, graveyard scenes and meditations on death, and metatheatrical devices such as pretended madness, disguises, and the play-within-a-play. W.'s play utilizes many of these devices to good effect, but his hero is less heroic than most, making the end result more powerfully disturbing and destabilizing.

W.'s second independent play, *The Duchess of Malfi* (perf. 1614; pub. 1623), is generally considered a better play than *The White Devil*. Here, W. has created a more straightforward plot, based on a true story from Italy, and a truly heroic central figure in the

Duchess. The plot is simple: after being widowed, the Duchess is told not to remarry by her brothers, Ferdinand the Duke of Calabria and the Cardinal. While the Cardinal is drawn as evil and scheming, the play's language hints that Ferdinand's motives are driven at least in part by incestuous love for his sister. In defiance of their demands, the Duchess falls in love with and secretly marries her noble but low-born steward, Antonio. Even though she gives birth to two children, the marriage is only discovered years later, when Ferdinand's spy Bosola reports her. Attempting to flee, she is captured and tortured, and finally killed along with her two small children. Here, the play continues into a fifth act that many critics have found superfluous. All the malefactors are dealt evil ends: Bosola, remorseful, kills the Cardinal; Ferdinand kills Bosola then goes mad himself, believing himself to be a wolf. The play descends to the lurid as Ferdinand is found returning from a graveyard with a human leg in his possession.

As in *The While Devil*, W. creates in *The Duchess of Malfi* a world that has gone deeply wrong, and characters at a loss for moral signposts in a sea of avarice, lust and sin. Bosola, like Flamineo, is ambivalent, wavering between sadistic HUMOR, unadulterated greed and more noble impulses. Betrayed by the Cardinal in the past, Bosola is painted as a character who has despaired of the world, believing it to be corrupt, brutal and loathsome. W.'s peculiar and affecting talent is to have painted the world for his audience through his character's embittered eyes.

After *The Duchess of Malfi*, W.'s independent writing career fades away. He is believed to have contributed thirty-two "characters"—short, witty poetic sketches of personality types—to a popular collection by Sir Thomas OVERBURY called *New and Choice Characters, of Several Authors* (1615). He also seems to have written a lost play referred to as *Guise* by scholars. His next known play, *The Devil's Law Case* (perf. ca. 1619; pub. 1623), is generally considered to be almost incoherent, though critics have periodically made arguments for various types of unity in it.

In 1624, a member of the Merchant Taylors' guild, to which W. belonged, was made Lord Mayor of London. W. devised the pageant produced by the guild, a very public role. Several more plays were subsequently printed with W.'s name among the collaborators, with varying degrees of likelihood attending his authorship. Plays in which he is believed to have had a hand include *The Late Murder of the Son upon a Mother* with John FORD (perf. 1624, now lost), *Appius and Virginia* with Heywood (perf. 1634; pub. 1654), and *A Cure for a Cuckhold* with William ROWLEY (perf. ca. 1624–25; pub. 1661), along with a few others less confidently attributed. But W.'s reputation has always rested upon his two independent plays.

That reputation has consistently been in dispute. Praised for his poetry, particularly by the Romantics, W. has always had detractors who objected to his extreme violence and lack of a clear moral purpose. Eliot famously championed his cause, arguing that his was "a very great literary and dramatic genius directed towards chaos," citing "Webster was much possessed by death / And saw the skull beneath the skin." Other critics, especially in the wake of poststructuralism, have attempted to delineate an ordering consciousness behind the powerful emotion of the plays, some finding it optimistic about human nature, others declaring the opposite. In either case, his position in the canon is assured.

BIBLIOGRAPHY: Berry, R. T., *The Art of J. W.* (1972); Bliss, L., *The World's Perspective: J. W. and the Jacobean Drama* (1983); Bradbook, M. C., *J. W., Citizen and Dramatist* (1980); Brooke, R., *J. W. and the Elizabethan Drama* (1916); Forker, C. R., *Skull beneath the Skin: The Achievement of J. W.* (1986); Moore, D. D., *J. W. and His Critics, 1617–1964* (1966); Person, J., *Tragedy and Tragicomedy in the Plays of J. W.* (1980)

GINGER STRAND

WELDON, Fay
b. 22 September 1931, Alvechurch, Worcestershire

It is with a clamorous and caustic chuckle that W. motions the discovery of female identity through her eccentric design of action and character development in which her women first recognize and then challenge the atrophied images of self. In her novels, short stories, television scripts, and plays, W. maps the great divide between women and men, particularly in what it is that women need but, as she sardonically makes evident, cannot get from their male counterparts and, on a more inclusive platform, from their culture, whose regulating principles have trickled into their streams of consciousness. W. does, however, bequeath to her pent-up and disillusioned women the will and certainly the imagination to redirect their lives and fight the good fight, which is, in her tales, marked by anger and revenge at deceivers, male or female. She is not preoccupied with handing over to her women a clearly cut feminist epiphany, and her female protagonists, such as Chloe in *Female Friends* (1975), the title character of *Praxis* (1978), and Angelica in *Splitting* (1995), tread in murky waters. However, W. is fixated on transformation, and while her women might not always attain a holistic metamorphosis, they do take over the steerage of their own lives.

W. was born Franklin Birkenshaw—a name she has preferred to veil; several years into her early life, her family relocated to New Zealand. There, when she

was six, her father, Frank Thornton Birkenshaw, a doctor, and her mother, Margaret Jepson Birkenshaw, who had seen two novels published in the 1930s under the pen name Pearl Bellairs, divorced. When W. was fourteen, her mother returned with her two children to London, where, in Belsize Park, they found a single room that would soon receive a fourth woman, W.'s grandmother. W.'s childhood and adolescence paved, as she has attested, the bumpy walk upon which her female protagonists journey. Women at home and school (she attended a convent high school in London) surrounded W.; men were simply an absence during those formative years.

In 1949, on a scholarship, W. began her studies in economics and psychology at St. Andrew's University in Scotland, where she was eventually awarded an M.A. In her twenties with a son from a quickly dissolved first marriage, W. began her writing life, but her novels, at this early stage, were rejected and instead her time was invested in making a living, as, for one example, a propaganda writer for the British Foreign Office. In the early 1960s, she remarried, gave birth to three more boys, and found success, for a number of years, in her work as an advertising copywriter. She moved on to television, theater, and radio scripts, and in 1967 wrote her first novel, *The Fat Woman's Joke* (originally produced as a television play in 1966), which, while not being deemed a consequential work, did establish W.'s thematic as well as stylistic idiosyncrasies of revengeful women and the application of a biting sense of HUMOR.

Throughout the 1970s, in books such as *Down among the Women* (1971), *Female Friends, Remember Me* (1976), *Words of Advice* (1977), and *Praxis,* W. successively wrote of the as yet to be emancipated women, undervalued by the men in their lives and, in a reciprocal fashion, by themselves. In *Female Friends,* W. was critically received as a writer whose rhetorical dexterity is as playful and snappy as, beneath its chatty like veneer, insightful. By the late 1970s, W.'s growing corpus of fiction attracted readers, critics, and some feminists to her hilarious accounts of women's—predominately white, middle class—everyday struggles within a late-20th-c. milieu. *Praxis* is considered to be one of her most defining achievements as in it W. amply develops her leading lady, maintaining her satiric carriage while layering her into the complex folds of reality.

If middle-class Western culture carries—along with its other traits—an impotence to interact authentically with others, and individual ways of being in the world that are severed from inner truths, then W.'s fictive universe is deliberately situated within this consciousness. It is in such a space that Ruth operates, in W.'s eleventh novel, *The Life and Loves of a She-Devil* (1983)—revised for television in 1986 into a four-episode production and later brought to film in the American version, featuring Meryl Streep. Ruth's anger at the world and her individual situation orbits her out of the realm of the ordinary—after all she is a She-Devil. On her journey, she leaves her children and convinces Vickie, a young single mother, that liberation is more important than motherhood (Ruth wants her to sell her children in this cause), and although W. risks making Ruth into a misguided evil avenger, she does create out of her character a wildly inventive and potent female force.

W.'s work tends toward action rather than internal illumination, and she has been criticized for creating one-dimensional characters. But they are palpable, sometimes downright roguish in their defiance of convention. Joanna May in *The Cloning of Joanna May* (1990) finds that her former husband has cloned her and, not having any children of her own—she is in her early sixties—her desire is to bring them on home; Eleanor in *Darcy's Utopia* (1991) creates a new religion; *Affliction* (1993) is a terrifying study of the power of therapists over patients' lives. She has been criticized for arbitrary plotting, but her construction in *Worst Fears* (1996) is masterly. The novel, unfashionably lucid and consequential in its narrative, offers a chain of exploding plot surprises and shifting perceptions. The octogenarian Felicity in *Rhode Island Blues* (2000) revisits love in a retirement home in Rhode Island while her granddaughter tries to recover the ability to love in the shadow of her mother's mental illness and later suicide.

W. continues to provoke her audience, and her recent novel, *The Bulgari Connection* (2001), certainly provides the bait for a good argument. W. transgressed the more explicit division between art and commerce by allowing this book to be commissioned and, at least initially, privately printed by none other than its namesake Bulgari—a corporate jewelry giant, perhaps in the cause of bringing the issue of to shop or not to shop out of the feminist closet. W. always has a sense of humor even if it sometimes comes to a good laugh at herself.

BIBLIOGRAPHY: Barreca, R., ed., *F. W.'s Wicked Fictions* (1994); Sage, L., *Women in the House of Fiction: Post-War Women Novelists* (1992); Waugh, P., "Contemporary Women Writers Challenging Postmodernist Aesthetics," in her *Feminine Fictions: Revisiting the Postmodern* (1989): 168–217

LISA TOLHURST

WELLS, H[erbert] G[eorge]

b. 21 September 1866, Bromley, Kent; d. 13 August 1946, London

W. holds an ambiguous position in contemporary critical esteem, being seen by many SCIENCE FICTION scholars as the founder and master of that genre while being considered a second-rate author by critics of the novel. While W.'s late Victorian scientific romances and Edwardian social comedies do receive some critical attention, his many short stories of the 1880s and 1890s and indeed all of his fictional output between 1909 and 1945 are badly neglected by literary critics today. Such neglect is also apparent when one considers W.'s nonfictional writing, though in the last few years there has been some acknowledgment of the influence of W.'s human rights activities of the 1930s and 1940s on the development of international law and especially such creations as the United Nations Declaration of Human Rights (1948), the Japanese Constitution (1948), and the U.K.'s recently passed Human Rights Act (2000).

W. was born to servants-turned-shopkeepers, and his rise from lower-middle-class poverty in the 1880s to successful author by 1895, with the publication of *The Time Machine*—a reputation further enhanced with the masterly *The War of the Worlds* (1898)—had a profound impact on his writing. His early comedies, such as *The Wheels of Chance* (1896), *Kipps* (1905), and *The History of Mr. Polly* (1910), all depict the struggles of the "little man" trying to succeed in a hostile environment, with class divisions and inadequate education acting as barriers to social advancement.

Although, as part of his successful rise, W. benefited from university science instruction under T. H. Huxley, his first fictional works (his "scientific romances" to use W.'s phrase) demonstrated the dangers of misapplied science in a world where technological advance appeared to be outpacing humanity's ability to control what it created. Hence, in *The Island of Doctor Moreau* (1896), *The Invisible Man* (1897), and *The Food of the Gods, and How It Came to Earth* (1904), the reader comes to understand how the perversion of science can serve greedy ends.

In addition to using his lower-middle-class upbringing and his science education under Huxley as material for his stories, W. used his relationships with women, especially his failed first marriage to Isabel Wells and his relatively more successful second marriage to Amy Catherine Robbins, as themes for his late Victorian and Edwardian writings. In a series of novels between 1900 and 1914, W. investigates male-female relations and clearly edges toward a feminist position on relationships by the time of *The Wife of Sir Isaac Harman* (1914). The first novel in the series, *Love and Mr. Lewisham* (1900), portrays an ambitious young science student thwarted in his attempt to become a full-time researcher by the demands of a dissatisfied wife. Through the next few novels, *Ann Veronica* (1909), *The New Machiavelli* (1910), *Marriage* (1912), and *The Passionate Friends* (1913), W. depicts struggles for liberation by both partners followed by conventionality in marriage and (usually) childbirth. Only with *The Wife of Sir Isaac Harman* does W. consider that marriage and childbirth may not be the only ends in a male-female relationship, but instead portrays the ending of a marriage in favor of unwed bliss between two mutually attracted persons.

With the outbreak of World War I in 1914, W.'s fiction shifted focus for a time, concentrating more on international events than on individual lives. *The Research Magnificent* (1915) introduces two important themes that W. was to return to in the interwar period—the open conspiracy and the world encyclopedia. That novel discusses humanity's need to control its emotions and work toward cooperative solutions to global problems, politically through an "open conspiracy" of like-minded people acting for the good of the species, and educationally, through the creation of a "world encyclopedia" that would provide all the people of the world with access to all the knowledge required to live a full life and to participate as much or as little in government affairs as each individual desired. *Mr. Britling Sees It Through* (1916) was a hugely successful novel throughout the world, portraying life on the British home front and discussing dispassionately the future of Europe after the war, a future based on British-Franco-German reconciliation and the end to nationalist oppression and colonial empires. Finally, *Joan and Peter* (1918) presents the education of a "sample" couple from birth, through school and university, to war and marriage. The novel was intended as a clarion call to the younger generation, which W. hoped would inherit the political field after the war, to reform education, moving away from narrowly nationalist schooling to cosmopolitan education based upon international friendship and the transfer of knowledge throughout the world.

The end of the Great War left W. bitterly disappointed and for a time he turned away from fictional writing to concentrate on political and educational works and unofficial international statesmanship, visiting Lenin (1920), Franklin D. Roosevelt (1933), Joseph Stalin (1934), and other world leaders, and producing the best-selling *The Outline of History* (1920), *The Science of Life* (3 vols., 1930), and *The Work, Wealth and Happiness of Mankind* (2 vols., 1931). His return to fiction reflected his mood at the time, with *The Shape of Things to Come* (1933), *The Croquet Player* (1936), and *The Holy Terror* (1939) being warnings and prophecies of what the future might hold for humankind if it did not plan common economical, educational, and political strategies.

Following a lifetime of extramarital affairs, the late 1930s saw W. return to the writing of novels about male-female relations. He produced the heavily autobiographical *Brynhild* (1937) and *Apropos of Dolores* (1938), which used Jungian psychological apparatus to discuss the nature of love and hate in relationships and the way sexual drives determine human behavior in extrasexual matters.

The outbreak of World War II in 1939 again deflected W. from purely "literary" pursuits. His final three novels, *Babes in the Darkling Wood* (1940), *All Aboard for Ararat* (1940), and *You Can't Be Too Careful* (1941), again turned to questions of the future of the human race, the first being a rewrite of the Great War's *Joan and Peter* and the last considering the global political consequences of the cynicism and carefree attitude of the average person in the face of potentially world-destroying phenomena, particularly global war. W. remained intellectually active until 1945, initiating a war-aims debate and advancing his own human rights charter, *The Rights of Man* (1940), as a legal protection against the rise of extremist political organizations in the future. His last published work of fiction was *The Happy Turning* (1945), an allegory on the misunderstanding of good men, including a dream-discussion with Jesus Christ in which the latter explains his downfall and condemns the flagrant abuse of his message made by future generations of "so-called Christians."

BIBLIOGRAPHY: Murray, B., *H. G. W.* (1990); Parrinder, P., *Shadows of the Future: H. G. W., Science Fiction and Prophecy* (1995); Smith, D. C., *H. G. W.* (1986); Wagar, W. W., *H. G. W. and the World State* (1961); West, G., *H. G. W.* (1930)

JOHN S. PARTINGTON

WELLS, Robert

b. 17 August 1947, Oxford

W. read English and classics at King's College, Cambridge. Poet and translator, he worked for many years as a forester, and his poetry combines sensitivity to the natural environment with classical elegance. He has taught in Italy and Iran and translated Virgil's *Georgics* (1981) and the *Idylls* (1988) of Theocritus. His poetry appeared in a Cambridge anthology *Shade Mariners* (1970) with that of Dick DAVIS and Clive WILMER and in Michael Schmidt's *Ten English Poets* (1976). His collections include *The Winter's Task* (1977), *Selected Poems* (1986), and *Lusus* (1999).

WELSH, Irvine

b. 1958, Edinburgh, Scotland

W. is a prolific writer whose work is noted for its black HUMOR, distinctive voice, heavy Scots dialect, and relentless profanity. His fictional field is the disenfranchised; the generally white, lower-class Edinburgh youth. W.'s writing brings humanity and empathy to his unsentimental characters—those who tend toward violence, alcoholism, and drugs. In both theme and voice, W. has been compared to compatriot James KELMAN. A best-selling author, W. has quickly risen to cult status while also earning the respect of critics and reviewers.

W.'s first book, *Trainspotting* (1993), offers a close look at Edinburgh's junkie class. This collection of loosely connected stories centers around a group of heroin users in the Leith neighborhood of Edinburgh in the mid-1980s. W.'s debut looks closely at life in and around the "schemes" (Scotland's housing projects), AIDS, addiction, and life on the dole. *Trainspotting* was extremely well received by both readers and critics, and was shortlisted for the Booker Prize in 1993. The film version of the book was greeted with enormous media attention in 1996, which earned W. cult status. *The Acid House* (1994), W.'s second collection of stories, was published close to six months after *Trainspotting*, and came out with much media attention. Like his first book, *The Acid House* is set in the underworld of addicts and thieves. Critics touted the book as imaginative, original, and bleakly funny.

W.'s third book, *Marabou Stork Nightmares* (1995), is his first attempt at a more traditional novel. The book introduces football (soccer) thug Roy Strang. As the story opens, he is unconscious in the hospital suffering from bad acid and a suicide attempt. This continuous narrative recollects Strang's life and struggles up until his hospital stay. Stylistically, W. furthers his literary reach, using flashbacks, character shifts, and different typefaces to illustrate Strang's changing consciousness. *Marabou Stork Nightmares* was greeted by reviewers as ambitious and commanding.

Ecstasy: Three Tales of Chemical Romance (1996) was not met with satisfactory acclaim. Although W. himself voiced disappointment with the collection of novellas ("Lorraine Goes to Livingston: A Rave and Regency Romance," "Fortune's Always Hiding: A Corporate Drug Romance," and "The Undefeated: An Acid House Romance"), it nonetheless reached best-seller status in Scotland (along with his first three books). "Lorraine" is the story of an author of Regency Romances and a student nurse who become friends and take revenge on the romance author's husband. "Fortune's Always Hiding" is also about revenge, this time with a hooligan helping a deformed woman take revenge on the drug company who marketed the drug that deformed her. "The Undefeated" tells the tale of an unhappy housewife who discovers the drug Ecstasy and the world that opens before her as a result.

With *Filth* (1998), W. reestablished himself in the literary world. In *Filth*, W. shows his compassion for his characters and their sordid lives. Sergeant Bruce Robertson, a callous and despicable character, discovers that his genital sore has been caused by an enormous tapeworm living in his stomach. The worm turns out to be the voice of his conscience. Again, W. provides reasons for his characters' behavior, making them understandable and therefore less hateful. *Filth* quickly became a best-seller, though critics were divided.

In 2001, W. published the novel *Glue*. The title refers to the bonds that connect four boys reared in "the scheme." In this gritty Bildungsroman, W. returns to earlier themes of AIDS, drugs, redemption, loyalty, and betrayal. The novel moves forward in decades, tracing the boys' growth, adventures, and losses. *Glue* was followed by the publication in 2002 of *Porno,* a sequel to the highly acclaimed *Trainspotting.*

BIBLIOGRAPHY: Freeman, A., "Ghosts in Sunny Leith: I. W.'s *Trainspotting,*" in Hageann, S., ed., *Studies in Scottish Fiction: 1945 to the Present* (1996): 251–62; Oliver, F., "The Self-Debasement of Scotland's Postcolonial Bodies," *SPAN* 42–43 (October 1996): 114–21

MARIKA BRUSSEL

WERTENBAKER, Timberlake
b. 1951, U.S.A.

Born in the U.S. in the decade British drama's modern renaissance began, W. was reared in France and came to prominence in London alongside a new generation of politically committed dramatists in the 1980s. Closely associated with the Royal Court, the theater that nurtured radical playwrights in the 1960s, W.'s plays are at once politically inflected, chiefly by a feminist-leftist sensibility, and alert to the theatrical, and often metatheatrical, properties and possibilities of performance. In yoking these political and formal elements together in *Our Country's Good* (perf. 1988; pub. 1989), her best-known play, W. taps into a longstanding theatrical tradition of self-referentiality, but more importantly insists, like her forebears of the 1960s, that past is prologue: exploring history is a means of understanding the present.

Like fellow Royal Court writer Caryl CHURCHILL, W. is concerned with the often conflictive relationship between gender and class: how, broadly, leftist thinking has not always embraced FEMINISM but has instead continued to reinforce patriarchal values. In *Case to Answer* (perf. 1980), it is patriarchal language governing a marriage that allows the male to colonize and control the female body. Like Churchill's *Top Girls,* W.'s play asks if it is possible for women to escape male dominance and find their own voice, or whether they are doomed to replicate their oppressor's; in *Abel's Sister* (perf. 1983), the quest for a UTOPIA is frustrated because characters are unable or unwilling to put theory into practice. While this might appear to suggest political defeatism, it leads to a more interrogative form of theater—drama with questions rather than answers.

W. shares with contemporary dramatists an interest in revisiting earlier drama as well as incorporating it into her own work, adapting it for radio and television as well as theater. In addition to translation work—Marivaux's *False Admissions* (perf. 1983), *Successful Strategies* (perf. 1983), and *La Dispute* (perf. 1987), Jean Anouilh's *Léocadia* (perf. 1985), Maurice Maeterlinck's *Pelleas and Melisande*, Ariane Mnouchkine's *Mephisto* (perf. 1986), Sophocles' *The Theban Plays* (perf. 1991), and Euripides' *Hecuba* (perf. 1995; pub. 1996)—and *Dianeira* (perf. 1999), her version of Sophocles' *Women of Trachis*, which she codirected, W. has set several of her major plays in the past. In *New Anatomies* (perf. 1981; pub. 1984), the action takes place in Europe and Algeria at the beginning of the 20th c.; *The Grace of Mary Traverse* (1985) is set in 18th-c. England; *Our Country's Good*, drawing on Thomas Keneally's novel *The Playmaker* (1987), dramatizes the life of transported convicts in late-18th-c. Australia; and *The Love of the Nightingale* (perf. 1988; pub. 1989) reprises the Philomel myth and draws on Ovid's *Metamorphoses*.

This pattern of reading the present through the past (though never passively) moves a stage further in *After Darwin* (perf. 1998), where past (South America, 1831) and present collide in a metadramatic juxtaposition. W. had earlier treated theatrical disguise and cross-dressing in *New Anatomies*. In *Our Country's Good*, she brilliantly explored the possibilities of a formal framing of content, focusing on the question of identity by depicting a convict production of George FARQUHAR's play *The Recruiting Officer*. *After Darwin* dramatizes a theatrical production that addresses the philosophical implications of evolution through the familiar device of the play-within-a-play.

Given her background, it is perhaps not surprising that the politics of exile is a recurring theme. This is particularly so in her most recent work, at a time when the issues of racial integration and asylum seekers are high on the agenda of right-wing commentators. *The Love of a Nightingale* treated the subject of intolerance experienced by minority groups. Her reworking of a fairy-tale *Cinderella* entitled *The Ash Girl* (2000) features an exiled Asian prince whose isolation and unhappiness are evident to the young spectators. The issue is addressed more directly, and to a different audience, in *Credible Witness* (2001), which reiterates a question central to W.: how much does history matter? Politically, the playwright is clearly on the side of the asylum seekers, but dramatically, and indeed psychologically, the issue is less clear cut. Those who seek assimilation do so at some cost: they lose their history, and, perhaps, their identity. Those forced to prove their plight is genuine must perform their history to the satisfaction of immigration officers; one character proves her story by revealing her history—the credibility of the title—written on her body in cigarette burns.

In the two decades since she emerged, W. has consistently addressed political and philosophical issues; but rather than treat these subjects didactically she uses theater as a self-consciously interrogating device. The staging of the critically acclaimed *Our Country's Good*, itself in part inspired by an acting performance by inmates of Wormwood Scrubs prison, in various prisons illustrates a metatheatrical strain running through her work, but more importantly it exemplifies her belief that drama is primarily a creative and ultimately liberating process.

BIBLIOGRAPHY: Carlson, S., "Language and Identity in T. W.'s Plays," in Aston, E., and J. Reinelt, eds., *The Cambridge Companion to Modern British Women Playwrights* (2000): 134–49; Rabey, D. I., "Defining Difference: T. W.'s Drama of Language, Dispossession and Discovery," *MD* 33 (December 1990): 518–28

MARK HUTCHINGS

WESKER, Arnold

b. 24 May 1932, London

One of the original "Angry Young Men," a label he denies, W.'s substantial contribution to the explosion of new British playwriting in the late 1950s earned him lasting international renown. A prolific and earnest dramatist whose best work demonstrates both his passion for social justice and compassion for humanity in general, W. has remained active in the face of declining interest in his work, at least in the U.K.

W.'s working-class Jewish upbringing in London's East End informs many of his plays' depictions of tight-knit communities. With his first play, *The Kitchen* (perf. 1959; pub. 1960), W. drew on his own experience as a pastry chef, placing the world of work on stage with thrilling theatricality and treating his characters as professional, social beings rather than isolated individuals. W.'s next three works are known collectively as *The Wesker Trilogy*, would prove his best known. The first part, *Chicken Soup with Barley* (perf. 1958; pub. 1959), grippingly evoked clashes between the Jewish working class and Oswald Mosley's fascist movement in 1930s London. The second, *Roots* (1959), showed Beatie, a country girl, struggling first to communicate, then to overcome, the influence of her intellectual, city-dwelling boyfriend, its final scene in which she at last finds her own voice being among the period's most memorable. *I'm Talking about Jerusalem* (1960) concludes the trilogy with a philosophical exploration of defeated idealism.

W.'s next play, *Chips with Everything* (1962), brought his greatest commercial success, its presentation of the transformation of conscripted civilians into well-drilled airmen providing a theatrical counterpoint to the play's critique of military dehumanization. By contrast, *The Four Seasons* (1965) tracks the arc of a love affair over the course of a year, while *Their Very Own and Golden City* (1966) is a study of idealistic young architects that flashes forward to reveal the compromises they will go on to make.

In the late 1960s, W.'s career began to lose impetus. *The Friends*, written in 1967, did not receive a British production until 1970, though its confrontation of the reality of death makes for a brave, unsettling work. Written in 1971, *The Journalists* (1975) is a return to the work-based drama of *The Kitchen* commissioned but not performed by the Royal Shakespeare Company, due to the cast's extraordinary refusal to play it. *The Old Ones* (perf. 1972; pub. 1980) examined the fears and rewards of old age with a compassionate eye, though without much narrative drive.

W. returned to form with *The Wedding Feast* (perf. 1977; pub. 1980), a comic but telling fable of labor relations, and *The Merchant*, later renamed *Shylock* (perf. 1977; pub. 1980). In this important work, W. reworks William SHAKESPEARE's original sources for *The Merchant of Venice* to redress what he sees as the slander of Shylock propagated by the latter play. Unfortunately, *The Merchant*'s chances of Broadway success were scuppered by the death of its star, an experience later recounted in the memoir *The Birth of Shylock and the Death of Zero Mostel* (1997).

In succeeding decades, W.'s output has not slackened, and he has moved into new areas with the compassionate study of Christian self-sacrifice *Caritas* (1981), the bawdy comedy *One More Ride on the Merry Go Round* (perf. 1985; pub. 1990), and the cross-race sexual romance *Lady Othello* (1990). He has achieved some success with a series of one-woman plays, notably *Annie Wobbler* (perf. 1985; pub. 1989) and *Whatever Happened to Betty Lemon?* (perf. 1987; pub. 1989), and performances of later plays such as *Blood Libel* (perf. 1996; pub. 1994) and *When God Wanted a Son* (perf. 1997; pub. 1990) have complemented successful revivals of earlier works at the Royal Court and National Theatre. His recently staged piece *Denial* (perf. 2000) confronts the emotive issue of "recovered memory syndrome" and the effects of accusations of child abuse on the family unit. W. has also published volumes of essays (*Fears of Fragmentation*, 1973, and *Distinctions*, 1985), short stories (*Love Letters on Blue Paper*, 1974, and *Said the Old Man to the Young Man*, 1978) and writings for young people (*Fatlips*, 1978).

W. has made no secret of his frustration that much of his later work has not been professionally staged in Britain, documenting with apparent bewilderment and increasing bitterness a series of professional setbacks that a more circumspect writer might have left undisclosed. In his later years, volumes such as his bemusedly received collection of fairy-tale erotica (*The King's Daughters*, 1998) and his unremittingly and

uncomfortably candid autobiography (*As Much as I Dare*, 1994) have done little to revive his fortunes. His contribution to British theater, however, is a substantial one, and the international interest shown in his work both old and new indicates that there is a lasting demand for his brave and committed drama.

BIBLIOGRAPHY: Dornon, R. W., ed., *A. W.* (1998); Leeming, G., ed., *W. on File* (1985); Wilcher, R., *Understanding A. W.* (1991)

                                        HARRY DERBYSHIRE

WESLEY, Charles
b. 18 December 1707, Epworth, Lincolnshire; d. 29 March 1788, London

W. is usually thought of as one of the founders of Methodism. He himself, however, was a priest of the Church of England, and while he formed part of the Methodist movement within the church, he was appalled when his brother John's appointment of ministers for the American colonies—essentially, the ordination of the ministers who claimed to be able to do all that Church of England priests could—led to the schism that created a new denomination. All the same, his hymns—and most of the hymns published under the names of both brothers are, in fact W.'s—became first part of the characteristic hymnody of the Methodists and then an important part of the common heritage of all English-speaking Christians, from evangelicals to Roman Catholics.

W. was the youngest son of parents who were people of profound learning, and his mother also inspired her children in deep piety. W. excelled academically at Westminster School and then at Christ Church, Oxford. He also became the first person to be given the name "Methodist" because of his methodical study and fasting and his weekly reception of the sacrament. With other students he formed "The Holy Club," whose members tried to live lives that included fastidious study, strict observance of the services in the Book of Common Prayer, and practical charity, like visiting prisoners in jails.

W. followed his brother's lead in seeking holy orders in 1735 and followed him when he went to Georgia as a missionary. W. served for a time as secretary to James Oglethorpe, the philanthropist who founded that colony as a utopian experiment in providing new lives for prisoners, debtors, and persecuted Protestants from continental Europe. The last group included Moravians, whose spirituality influenced W. profoundly. The hardships of missionary work drove W. back to England, but during his time in America he and John prepared their first collection of hymns.

In 1738, W. underwent a conversion experience, after which he felt "at peace with God" and became still more dedicated to spreading the gospel and sharing with others his joyful feeling of the divine presence. He traveled throughout Britain, preaching and writing hymns, which were sung by the growing Methodist Societies at revivals. Hymns were not then sung in Church of England services, which were devoted to the chanting of the psalms and other appointed texts. The revival moved great masses of people on both sides of the Atlantic. It offered them not a new theology, but a new sort of religious feeling, something more emotional than the spirituality then offered by the established church. This very emotionalism created hostility among many, who saw it as a dangerous example of "enthusiasm," or religious fanaticism. The sermons and hymns of both Wesleys helped shape the new movement, though it extended beyond their Arminian version of Anglicanism to include Calvinists and Dissenters.

W.'s hymns set forth in verse the doctrines he and his brother championed, such as the free availability of grace to all and the need for personal conversion. They are at once personal and topical. While some are primarily devotional and doctrinal, others, including those in collections like *Hymns on the Expected Invasion* (2 vols., 1759), dealt directly with Christian life in a period of world crisis. Many of W.'s hymns, such as those on the loss of children, grew directly from personal experience; some on marriage are adapted directly from a poem addressed to Sarah Gwynne, whom he married in 1749. W. was widely popular and astonishingly prolific, publishing thousands of hymns and leaving almost as many in manuscript. Musicians including Handel wrote music specifically for his words. W. could also work in forms beyond the hymn, such as the verse epistle in heroic couplets, as his irenic letter to his Calvinist fellow evangelist George Whitefield shows.

While W. was less active in the Methodist movement in his later years, he left behind in *A Collection of Hymns, for the Use of the People Called Methodists* (1780), which John edited, one of the greatest collections of devotional poetry in English.

BIBLIOGRAPHY: Baker, F., *C. W.'s Verse* (1964); Davie, D., "The Classicism of C. W.," in his *Purity of Diction in English Verse* (1952): 70–81; Gill, F. G., *C. W.* (1964)

BRIAN ABEL RAGEN

WESLEY, Mary

b. Mary Aline Mynors Farmar, 24 June 1912, Englefield Green, Surrey; d. 30 December 2002, Totnes, Devon

Although W. published two books early in her career, *The Sixth Seal* (1969; rev. ed., 1984) and *Speaking Terms* (1969), it was not until she was in her seventies that her career took off. W. was divorced from her first husband in the early 1940s, which was an unconventional move for the times. She lived with her second husband for several years before their marriage, an act

that disinherited her and left her poverty-stricken. As W.'s books became popular in the 1990s, she regained the wealth she had been stripped of earlier in her life. She produced novels at an amazing rate: ten books in as many years, many of which became best-sellers. W.'s characters often include a female character who resembles her own younger self: alienated and shy, surrounded by independent and strong women. Her work offers a humorous and tender portrait of love and sex in the British middle and upper classes.

W.'s first major novel *Jumping the Queue* (1983) portrays a recently widowed woman who is planning to commit suicide, but whose designs get thwarted at every turn. Through the character's struggle, she rediscovers her true self, a recurring theme in W.'s fiction. After the novel's publication, W. published numerous books including *The Camomile Lawn* (1984), which was subsequently adapted for television, and *Harnessing Peacocks* (1985).

In *Harnessing Peacocks,* a young, unmarried mother turns to prostitution to support her son's education. W.'s own experience as a single mother, and a woman choosing an individualistic life, come into play in the novel. *The Vacillations of Poppy Carew* (1986), a more humorous novel, also looks at individualism and the choices women make. When Poppy's husband leaves her for a richer woman, she cannot decide whether she hates him or not, whether to have an affair, or, eventually, whether or not to marry the lower-class man who really loves her. W. has been lauded by critics as a first-rate purveyor of social comedy.

While her novels all deal with the difficulties and joys of being a woman, the plot lines W. chooses all stand alone. *Second Fiddle* (1988) features a middle-aged woman having an affair with a much younger man, while in *A Sensible Life* (1990), a shy and introverted ten-year-old girl decides to live a "sensible life," one without the confusion and messiness of love, a decision that is challenged when she is in her forties. Like *A Sensible Life,* many of W.'s stories follow her characters on a trajectory that spans several decades. *A Dubious Legacy* (1992) begins in 1954, when two intended marriage proposals spark a drama that unfolds over the next forty years. With wit and style, W. writes about the outcast experience, the rediscovery of self, and the promise of romantic love in all of life's stages.

BIBLIOGRAPHY: Short, S., "M. W.," in Moseley, M., ed., *British Novelists since 1960*, Fourth Series, *DLB* (2000): 283–91

MARIKA BRUSSEL

WEST, [Dame] Rebecca

(pseud. of Cicily Isabel Fairfield) b. 21 December 1892, County Kerry, Ireland; d. 15 March 1983, London

W. was sometimes described as the "Bernard Shaw in Petticoats," and in 1916 Bernard SHAW himself wrote that the young Rebecca could "handle a pen as brilliantly as ever I could and much more savagely." W.—who took the name Rebecca West after the strong-minded heroine of Henrik Ibsen's play *Rosmersholm* in which she had acted in 1912—established her reputation as a journalist, critic, and reviewer at a very early age. She wrote with verve, passion, and outspoken honesty in left-wing and feminist papers, first in the short-lived pioneering feminist periodical, the *Freewoman*, then in Robert Blatchford's socialist weekly, the *Clarion*, and later in the American journal, the *New Republic*, and also in the *New Statesman* where she was a columnist writing her regular "Notes on Novels" in the 1920s. Converted to the cause of votes for women while still at school, her early writings reflected the strong feminist conviction that led George E. G. Catlin to dedicate his edition of *The Rights of Woman and The Subjection of Woman* (1929) "To Rebecca West who stands, in this generation, for that tradition which Mary WOLLSTONECRAFT and Mill have handed down." Virginia WOOLF used W. as an example of the spirited feminist writer in *A Room of One's Own*.

Although W.'s politics moved to the right as she grew older, and she became preoccupied with the meaning of treason and virulently anticommunist in later life, she remained an inspirational figure for many women. This was not only due to her brilliance as a social commentator and feminist polemicist but also because of her sustained interest in the friction, tension, and misunderstandings between the two sexes and in the question of marital incompatibility. The problem of ill-matched partners had interested her since her review of H. G. WELLS's novel *Marriage* that had first brought her into contact with Wells, the father of her illegitimate child, Anthony, born in 1914. Marital unhappiness is a leitmotif in much of her fiction, as for example in *The Return of the Soldier* (1918), a terse and economical antiwar novella depicting a triangle of love in which a plain, motherly, lower-class woman is able to provide the redemptive love for a shell-shocked soldier that his own unhappy marriage lacks, or in *The Thinking Reed* (1936), a biting SATIRE on the lives of the monied classes in which W. depicts a woman's marriage placed in jeopardy by a combination of her husband's inveterate gambling and the corrosive effect of her miscarriage on their already fragile relationship.

Critics continually comment on the weakness of W.'s male characters. It is the women characters who dominate and they often do so through their sexuality. W. creates women who are sexually exciting but also exceedingly plucky and resourceful when things go wrong. Her women learn very early in life that life can be hard, especially for their sex. In *The Judge* (1922), W.'s feminist and Freudian influenced revisioning of the Oedipal triangle, a young, unmarried, pregnant woman is cruelly stoned in the streets. The

genteel, impoverished matriarch in *The Fountain Overflows* (1956) determinedly nurtures the musical talents of two of her daughters although her own career as a professional pianist ends when her feckless husband deserts his family. This was deservedly W.'s most popular novel as well as being a critical success doing much to revive her reputation that had declined in the twenty years since the publication of *The Thinking Reed*. Interest in W. waned again but was rekindled in the 1980s by the reissuing of some of her novels by the feminist publishing house Virago and the republication of her essays and journalism from the period 1911–17 as *The Young Rebecca* (1982).

W.'s fiction reflects the influence of MODERNISM, experimentation, and psychoanalysis, particularly in her London fantasy, *Harriet Hume* (1929). However, she made use of diverse fictive techniques and her novels are also marked by the solid characterization and careful scene setting in *The Judge* of the traditional 19th-c. realist novel. Her writing spans a number of literary and nonliterary modes and genres including fiction, travel writing, journalism, literary criticism, BIOGRAPHY, and trial reporting, which make her a difficult writer to categorize. In his critical introduction to *The Essential Rebecca*, Samuel Hynes identifies the "wide interstices between her work" as a problem for W.'s reputation and notes that "Dame Rebecca's work has not fused in the minds of the critics."

W. has had a significant readership and critical recognition in the U.S. in which she traveled extensively. *The Strange Necessity* (1928) is an early collection of critical essays expressing her conviction of the moral necessity of art, most of which were originally written for the *New York Herald Tribune*, and bring together her ideas on literature after many years as a book reviewer. Another collection, *The Harsh Voice* (1935), comprises four short novels, three of which had been published in *Saturday Evening Post* and *Woman's Home Companion* in the U.S.

W.'s widely admired travelogue, *Black Lamb and Grey Falcon: A Journey through Yugoslavia* (2 vols., 1941), excavates the past and the present in Yugoslavia to understand the ethnic tensions in the region and how and why Europe had arrived at the verge of the Second World War. *The Meaning of Treason* (1947; rev. ed., 1952; repub. as *The New Meaning of Treason*, 1964) arose from W.'s reporting of the trial of William Joyce (Lord Haw-Haw). Later editions were expanded to deal with the traitors Guy Burgess and Donald Maclean. Her interest in intrigue, duplicity, and personal betrayal is apparent in her densely plotted political novel *The Birds Fall Down* (1966) set among expatriate Russians before the Russian Revolution. *Family Memories* (1987) imaginatively depicts W.'s maternal genealogy. *This Real Night* (1984) and *Cousin Rosamond* (1985), both published posthumously, complete the trilogy that began with *The Fountain Overflows*.

The posthumous works did little to help W.'s reputation, which has fluctuated since her death. Most critics have followed her biographer Victoria Glendinning in attaching greater importance to the work of W.'s early years. There is also general agreement that W.'s artistic vision in which the forces of good and evil, life and death, relentlessly clash is greater than the achievement of individual novels in which she sometimes fails to do herself justice. The magisterial *Black Lamb and Grey Falcon* has stood the test of time well. Now regarded as a classic, it is frequently cited in debates about the break-up of the old Yugoslovia. Much of the curiosity about W. in literary circles has centered on the nature of her relationship with Wells and with her son, the author Anthony West, often at the expense of critical engagement with her writing. Anthony, with whom she had a very troubled relationship, wrote many autobiographical pieces about his unhappy childhood highly critical of his mother's role in his upbringing. More recently, W has benefited from the revival of academic interest in women's writing of the interwar period and has been bracketed with Elizabeth BOWEN, Rosamond LEHMANN, Storm JAMESON, Sylvia Townsend WARNER, Naomi MITCHISON, and Woolf as one of the most significant British woman writers of the 1920s and 1930s.

BIBLIOGRAPHY: Deakin, M. F., *R. W.* (1980); Glendinning, V., *R. W.* (1987); Hammond, J. R., *H. G. Wells and R. W.* (1991); Hynes, S., *The Essential R. W.* (1977); Marcus, J., ed., *The Young Rebecca: Writings of R. W., 1911–1917* (1982); Rollyson, C., *R. W.* (1995)

MARY JOANNOU

WEYMAN, Stanley J[ohn]
b. 7 August 1855, Ludlow Shropshire; d. 10 April 1928, Ruthin, Wales

Described by Hugh Walpole as "the finest English historical novelist since [Sir Walter] SCOTT," W. was educated at Shrewsbury School and Christ Church, Oxford. He became a history teacher then read for the bar in 1877, giving up the law in 1891. He began by writing short stories for magazines, but *The House of the Wolf* (1890) launched his career. *A Gentleman of France* (3 vols., 1893), set in the period of Henry of Navarre, was praised by Robert Louis STEVENSON. *Under the Red Robe* (1894), about Cardinal Richelieu, was successfully dramatized in 1896 and filmed in 1937, starring Conrad Veidt and Raymond Massey. Other novels include *The Red Cockade* (1895), *The Castle Inn* (1898), *Count Hannibal* (1901), about the St. Bartholomew's Day massacre, and *Chippinge*

(1906; repub. as *Chippinge Borough*, 1906), set in England at the time of the Reform Bill of 1832.

WHETSTONE, George
b. 1550, London; d. September 1587, Bergen op Zoom

Soldier, dramatist, and poet, W. collected stories, mainly from Italian sources, in his *The Rock of Regard* (1576). His rhyming verse play *Promos and Cassandra* (1578) is based on a prose romance by Giraldi Cinthio called *Hecatommithii* (1565). *Promos and Cassandra* was never performed, but the basic plot was used by William SHAKESPEARE in *Measure for Measure*. After visiting Italy in 1580, W. tried to import Italian social graces into England with his *Heptameron of Civill Discourses* (1582). He became a patriotic reformer using foreign materials in his *Mirour for Magestrates of Cyties* and *Touchstone for the Time*, published together in 1584. In *The English Myrror* (1586), he strove to unite the English against their enemies. W.'s *The Censure of a Loyall Subject* (1587) tells of the execution for high treason of the six conspirators who planned to assassinate Protestant Queen ELIZABETH I and replace her with Roman Catholic Mary Queen of Scots. Led by Anthony Babington, who was in correspondence, if not in direct collusion, with Mary, the conspiracy is known as the Babington plot. Among W.'s other works are a verse elegy upon George GASCOGINE (1577) and a verse BIOGRAPHY of Sir Philip SIDNEY (1587), among others. W. fought at the battle of Zutphen when Sidney was killed in 1586. W. died in a duel.

WHITE, Antonia
b. Eirene Adelaide Botting, 31 March 1899, West Kensington, London; d. 10 April 1980, Danehill, Sussex

W.'s four novels—*Frost in May* (1933), *The Lost Traveller* (1950), *The Sugar House* (1952), and *Beyond the Glass* (1954)—are strongly autobiographical and deal with the pressures on a young Catholic girl in the early 20th c., struggling to reconcile her religion with her wish for freedom. They are also concerned with the creative impulse and the experience of going mad.

W. was taken into the Catholic Church at the age of seven by her father who dominated her youth; he and her mother are very vividly portrayed in her books. She was educated in a convent, which expelled her for writing a "scandalous" novel, did some clerical jobs, had an unconsummated marriage followed by an intense love affair, and went mad for nine months when she was twenty-three. These experiences form the raw material of her work.

She is one of the few novelists who can write about her own life with artistic detachment; indeed, she was not able to write convincingly about anything else. *The Lost Traveller* is the weakest of the quartet because it centers on a melodramatic event that never happened. Her experience in the newspaper world made it easy for her to write clear, accessible "women's" fiction, and her heroine is always conscious of herself as a writer. Her childhood conflicts with the nuns are played out in terms of books, and when Clara in the later novels begins to disintegrate she is still able to produce frothy advertisements.

Frost in May, her most famous novel, is about the effect on a young mind of a rigorous Catholic education. W. had lapsed when she wrote it, and for most of the time her attitude to the church appears hostile. It has much in common with James JOYCE's *Portrait of the Artist*, but it is written in a simpler style and the protagonist is a girl, not a boy. The child Nanda, who is herself, feels it is almost impossible to please the nuns who educate her because she is not a "cradle Catholic" and will never fully understand the rules. Her real problem is that she wants to preserve an inner core of self untouched by religion; this is called spiritual pride, and is connected with her wish to write. Her juvenile novel, which she thinks harmless, seems wicked to her teachers and her frightening father, and she is expelled. But whereas Joyce's Stephen Dedalus totally rejects the church, Nanda cannot do this and will try all her life to reconcile her Catholicism with her instinctive desires.

The other three novels were written years afterward, when W. had gone back to the church (this is described in *The Hound and the Falcon*, 1965) and had two more broken marriages and a return of mental illness, which she kept at bay by going into Freudian analysis. They continue the story of her life up to her release from Bedlam in 1923. Nanda has become a young woman, named Clara. She lives in a sophisticated postwar world where religion has lost its power, the actors and artists she mixes with do not understand her Catholicism and she has difficulty finding satisfying work or relationships. *The Lost Traveller* is flawed but *The Sugar House* is much better, using Freudian imagery to suggest that Clara is being destroyed by her sexless marriage and her wish to please her father by behaving "well." In *Beyond the Glass*, a very powerful novel, her repressions collapse and she becomes a raving animal, recovering only to find that her lover is married. But her religion enables her to cope and there is a suggestion, as at the end of *Frost in May*, that God is asking her to suffer so that another person can be received into the church.

So W.'s attitude to Catholicism is ambivalent. She is well aware that it is out of step with modern life, and even suggests in her letters that it may not be literally true. Yet she felt the attraction of a creed that demands total sacrifice, and believed it helped her to control the dark forces of the unconscious, which, however, must not be denied. She suffered from serious writer's block and was never able to get any further with Clara's story, although she wrote two children's books about her cats, Minka and Curdy, and a fine collection of short stories, *Strangers* (1954). Her novels went out of print for years but were reissued as Virago Modern Classics in the 1970s and are now greatly admired.

BIBLIOGRAPHY: Chitty, S., ed., *As Once in May: The Early Autobiography of A. W. and Other Writings* (1983); Dunn, J., *A. W.* (1998); Williams, M., *Six Women Novelists* (1987)

MERRYN WILLIAMS

WHITE, Gilbert

b. 18 July 1720, Selborne, Hampshire; d. 26 June 1793, Selborne

On graduating from Oriel College, Oxford, W. was elected to a fellowship and was ordained in 1747. In 1761, he became curate of his beloved native parish. W.'s four brothers were all interested in science, and W. corresponded with the chief botanists and antiquarians of his time. The famous *Natural History and Antiquities of Selborne* appeared in 1789. W. kept a nature diary and his careful recording of temperatures and the progress of his garden, his observation of plants and creatures, with anecdotes of conflict between rich and poor, make fascinating reading. W. was read with pleasure by Charles DARWIN. *The Life and Letters of Gilbert White of Selborne*, by W.'s great-grand-nephew, Rashleigh Holt-White, appeared in 1901.

WHITE, Henry Kirke

b. 21 March 1785, Nottingham; d. 19 October 1806, Cambridge

As a trainee lawyer with Evangelical Christian convictions, W. published *Clifton Grove, a Sketch in Verse, with Other Poems* (1803), dedicated to Georgiana, Duchess of Devonshire, hoping to raise funds for ordination. He was violently attacked in the *Monthly Review* (February 1804), but received a kind letter from Robert SOUTHEY. Influential friends secured him a place at St. John's College, Cambridge, in 1805 as a sizar. Sizars paid their way by acting as servants to other students, but W. was already consumptive and he died at age twenty-one. Lord BYRON had a high opinion of W.'s talent. Southey edited W.'s *Remains* (3 vols., 1807–22), with letters and an account of W.'s life. W. was also the author of the well-known hymn, "Oft in danger, oft in woe."

WHITE, William Hale. See RUTHERFORD, Mark

WHITEHEAD, Alfred North

b. 15 February 1861, Ramsgate, Isle of Thanet, Kent; d. 30 December 1947, Cambridge, Massachusetts, U.S.A.

One of the major intellectual figures of the first half of the 20th c., W. incorporated into his work a broad spectrum of knowledge on religion, science, education, literature, and the history of Western culture. Educated at Trinity College, Cambridge, he first gained recognition as a mathematician, collaborating with Bertrand RUSSELL on *Principia Mathematica* (3 vols., 1910–13). In the early 1920s, he established himself primarily as a philosopher with *The Concept of Nature* (1920), *The Principle of Relativity, with Applications to Physical Science* (1922), and his best-known work, *Science and the Modern World* (1925), a comprehensive survey of the historical development of scientific theory and practice. His later works include *Nature and Life* (1934), *Modes of Thought* (1938), and *Essays in Science and Philosophy* (1947). Throughout his career, W. was highly regarded as a university lecturer and held academic appointments at Trinity College, Cambridge (1885–1910), University College, London (1911–14), Imperial College, London (1914–24), and Harvard University (1924–36).

WHITEHEAD, William

bap. 12 February 1715, Cambridge; d. 14 April 1785, London

W. attended Winchester College and Clare Hall, Cambridge, being made a fellow in 1742. In the previous year, he had published a verse epistle, "The Danger of Writing Verse," a warning to aspirant poets of the miseries of a literary career. However, in 1757 he was successful enough as a playwright to be appointed poet laureate in succession to Colley CIBBER. W.'s most successful play was *The School for Lovers* (1762), performed at the Theatre Royal in Drury Lane. Samuel JOHNSON found W.'s "grand nonsense . . . insupportable," and W. was mocked in verse by Charles CHURCHILL. His two-volume *Plays and Poems* appeared in 1774 and a third volume in 1788.

WHITING, John [Robert]

b. 15 November 1917, Salisbury, Wiltshire; d. 16 June 1963, London

Regarded by many as the most promising British playwright of the early 1950s, W. sought to challenge where many of his contemporaries preferred to reas-

sure. Never quite in fashion, his potential cannot be said to have been fulfilled by the time of his early death, but his ambitious and challenging drama fascinatingly reflects the times in which he wrote.

W.'s experiences as an actor, working extensively in repertory theater, and as a soldier, serving in the Royal Artillery between 1939 and 1944, gave him a well-developed sense of stagecraft and a will to grapple with the disturbing questions raised by the Second World War and its aftermath. His earliest plays, *No More A-Roving* and *Conditions of Agreement*, written in the late 1940s, give an indication of the individuality, if not the quality, of his later work, the former a distinctly postwar romantic comedy, the latter, more ambitious and less successful, a tragicomedy of grudges.

A Penny for a Song (perf. 1951; pub. 1957), his first play to be staged, is a comic examination of the follies of the English at war. Set during the Napoleonic Wars in a rural England beset by rumors and awash with unlikely schemes to repel putative invaders, the play proved too whimsical for contemporary critics, though it was twice revived in the 1990s. In 1962, a revised version added criticisms of revolution and revolutionaries thought by many to refer to the "angry" playwrights of the Royal Court whose work had, by then, eclipsed that of W.

Written earlier but performed a few months after *A Penny for a Song*, *Saint's Day* (perf. 1951; pub. 1957) came to public attention when it won the Festival of Britain Prize in 1951. The play's intensity and opacity made it a controversial choice, and the critics were again hostile, but it is nonetheless a remarkable work. Set in the remote house of reclusive poet Paul Southman, the play begins relatively conventionally, but becomes steadily more sinister as three escaped soldiers and the death of a dog ignite simmering tensions between Southman and the inhabitants of a nearby village. The accidental shooting of Southman's daughter begins a chain of events that leads to the destruction of the village by fire and the execution by hanging of the poet and his son-in-law. Though at times somewhat wordy, the piece's vertiginous momentum and chilling atmosphere form a link between the drama of T. S. ELIOT, whose influence is plain, and that of Harold PINTER. Just as W.'s dialogue, though written in prose, achieves the effect of poetry, so the story holds together in naturalistic terms while referring on a more symbolic level to the Holocaust, nuclear warfare, and the consequences of lost faith.

Marching Song (1954), which W. himself regarded as his most important play, is more fully realized but less dramatically engaging. Set in an unspecified European capital, the play's central figure is Rupert Foster, an ex-general who must stand trial for the nation's military failures or, as he is strongly advised, commit suicide. In the course of the play, and through interaction with his abandoned lover Catherine, the city girl

Dido, and the defeated liberal Harry, he moves from resignation to reengagement with life and back again. W. himself thought of the play as "anti-theatrical" in its unwavering thematic focus, but the corollary to this is a lack of dramatic action that renders the piece lengthy and austere, though fascinating in its exploration of what it means to be a man and, specifically, a man of war. W. returned to comedy, though of a crueler kind than before, with *The Gates of Summer* (perf. 1956; pub. 1969), which provides a counterpoint to *Marching Song* by portraying life, and all the anguish of the previous play, as futile and absurd.

W. wrote a number of minor works for radio, television, and film, some short stage works including *No Why* (perf. 1964; pub. 1961) and *The Nomads* (perf. 1965; pub. 1969), and numerous critical essays and reviews, later published as *At Ease in a Bright Red Tie* (1999). His final completed play was *The Devils* (1961), based on Aldous HUXLEY's historical work *The Devils of Loudon*. The play tells the story of Urbain Grandier, a driven but unconventional priest in 17th-c. France who falls prey to false accusations of devilry from a group of nuns acting either from hysteria or malice. A companion to American dramatist Arthur Miller's earlier *The Crucible* and John OSBORNE's contemporaneous *Luther* in its study of the interaction of religious conviction and politics, the play's EPIC structure sits uncomfortably with its focus on Grandier's spiritual struggles, but, as always with W., it contains some striking dramatic writing. *The Devils*, produced by the Royal Shakespeare Company and later filmed by Ken Russell, was the author's greatest critical and commercial success, ending his often luckless career on a high note.

BIBLIOGRAPHY: Hayman, R., *J. W.* (1969); Robinson, G., *A Private Mythology: The Manuscripts and Plays of J. W.* (1989); Salmon, E., *The Dark Journey: J. W. as Dramatist* (1979); Trussler, S. *The Plays of J. W.* (1972)

HARRY DERBYSHIRE

WILDE, Oscar [Fingall O'Flahertie Wills]
b. 16 October 1854, Dublin, Ireland; d. 30 November 1900, Paris, France

When asked about his ambitions as a young man, W. responded: "God knows! I won't be a dried-up Oxford don, anyhow. I'll be a poet, a writer, a dramatist. Somehow or other I'll be famous, and if not famous I'll be notorious." W. fashioned himself into one of the preeminent figures of the Aesthetic movement, a dandy who was revered by those of a like temperament and vilified by many who were not. At the crest of his popularity, W. said that he had put his genius into his life and merely his talent into his work. But his talent was considerable. Poet, short story writer, editor, reviewer, novelist, critic, and playwright: no

one of his day aspired to be more versatile than did W., nor more intent on living his art.

A student of the classics, W. won a demyship to Magdalen College, Oxford, in 1874, where he encountered John RUSKIN and Walter PATER. Whereas Ruskin influenced W.'s social conscience and guided him toward probing the connections between life and art, Pater inspired his eclectic individualism by advising that success in life required one "to burn always with this hard, gemlike flame." Albeit from different perspectives, Ruskin and Pater encouraged young people to rebel against the aesthetic standards of late 19th c., and W. eagerly took up the crusade of "art for art's sake" while debunking Victorian prudery. In addition to his scholarly achievements—a first in Moderations and a first in Greats—W. won Oxford's prestigious Newdigate Prize for his poem *Ravenna* (1878).

After Oxford, W. set out to dazzle London, and he soon endeared himself to a select group of artists and celebrities. As a consequence of his flamboyant dress and manners, he was lampooned by *Punch* and caricatured by W. S. GILBERT and Arthur Sullivan in their operetta *Patience* (perf. 1881). W. exploited this publicity to bring out *Poems* (1881) at his own expense, one thousand copies of which sold largely because of his reputation. Reviewers quickly dismissed the book as an assembly of gaudy imitations modeled upon the works of Lord BYRON, John KEATS, Dante Gabriel ROSSETTI, and A. C. SWINBURNE. Undeterred by this blow to his vanity, in 1882 W. embarked on a tour of the U.S. and Canada, where he was billed as "The Great Aesthete" and promoted his worship of beautiful things from Boston to San Francisco. Living on the profits from his tour, W. settled briefly in Paris and completed *The Duchess of Padua* (perf. 1891), a revenge drama that eventually was rejected by the American actress Mary Anderson who had advanced W. a thousand dollars to write a "first class tragedy." When W.'s money ran out in Paris, he arranged to sell himself to audiences throughout Ireland and Great Britain. By the middle of 1884, W. had married, settled in London, and transformed his residence at No. 16 Tite Street into a monument of good taste.

W.'s literary reputation rests upon the works he generated between 1888 and 1895. His three collections *The Happy Prince and Other Tales* (1888), *Lord Arthur Savile's Crime and Other Stories* (1891), and *A House of Pomegranates* (1891) introduce by way of style, subject, and theme much of what he would refine throughout his career. During this same period, he also completed his two famous critical dialogues, "The Decay of Lying" (1889) and "The Critic as Artist" (1890), which remain of greater significance to his oeuvre. Although W.'s disputants verge upon sophistry, they also present his central ideas about life imitating art and about the critic's necessary vocation of interpreting himself through the creative work that is before him.

Next, W. allegorically postulated his artistic views in *The Picture of Dorian Gray* (1891). Faust and Narcissus figure prominently in this fin de siècle "decadent novel" involving Basil Hallward (artist), Lord Henry Wotton (dandy aesthete and corrupter of youth), and Dorian Gray (subject). When twenty-year-old Dorian Gray becomes obsessed by his own beauty in the portrait that Basil Hallward has painted of him, he exchanges his soul for eternal youth. Soon thereafter, Dorian comes under the influence of Lord Henry Wotton, who convinces him not to squander his golden years by pandering to the "false ideals" of his age. As time passes, Dorian develops a fetish for the subjective feelings elicited by new experiences, regardless of how grotesque those experiences might be. Through eighteen years of pleasure and crime, Dorian retains his youthful beauty while his portrait becomes increasingly hideous. In the climactic scene when Dorian stabs the sinister picture, his portrait mysteriously recaptures its exquisite youth while he crashes to floor, a withered man with a knife in his heart. Ostensibly indifferent to W.'s stated theme that "all excess brings its own punishment," reviewers censured the novel for being impious. The *Daily Chronicle*, in fact, described it as "A poisonous book, the atmosphere of which is heavy with the mephitic odours of moral and spiritual putrefaction." *Salome* (perf. 1896; pub. 1894), W.'s brilliant symbolist drama, was dealt with even more harshly, given that the Lord Chamberlain refused to license the play in 1892 because it included biblical characters. When *Salome* was published in London two years later, W. stood accused of transforming the sacred into the morbid. Richard Ellmann, W.'s authoritative biographer, opened the door for new interdisciplinary interpretations of the play when he discussed it as a type of psychodrama: the Ruskin of W.'s imagination (Jokanaan, the untouchable moral prophet) pitted against his Pater (Salome, the sensualist yearning to kiss forbidden lips).

W. found his true creative mark when he began writing "Society comedies." Although *Lady Windemere's Fan* (perf. 1892; pub. 1893), *A Woman of No Importance* (perf. 1893; pub. 1894), and *An Ideal Husband* (perf. 1895; pub. 1899) made W. remarkably popular, *The Importance of Being Earnest* (perf. 1895; pub 1899) stands as his defining triumph and continues to be a staple in international repertories. Farcical comedy provided W. with the conventions for his assault on Victorian earnestness. By intent, the play's four main characters are extraordinarily superficial; they dress and speak impeccably, but they are all style and very little substance. Jack Worthing and Algernon Moncrief, dandies par excellence, have elevated lying to a fine art: in order to escape from his country manor house and his dreadfully serious responsibilities as guardian for Miss Cecily Cardew, Jack pretends to have a wicked younger brother named Ernest who lives in London and needs rescuing from numerous scrapes. Conversely, in order to escape from London and the boring social obligations imposed upon him by his mercenary aunt, Lady Bracknell, Algernon pretends to have an invalid friend named Bunbury who lives in the country and requires constant attention. Jack poses as Ernest in the city and hopes to marry Gwendolen Fairfax, Algernon's cousin; Algernon poses as Jack's fictional brother Ernest in the country and hopes to marry Cecily Cardew. For their parts, Cecily and Gwendolen claim as their highest ideal the love for the proper name Ernest, compelling Jack and Algernon to go scurrying after Canon Chasuble in order to be christened. W. unties these knots in the most outlandishly trivial denouement in the history of the English theater. Jack, a foundling, discovers not only that he and Algernon are brothers, but also that his true given name is Ernest, thus clearing the way for a laughably contrived happy ending. W. utilizes paradox to make the serious concerns of the upper-class seem absurdly trivial and its trivial concerns seem absurdly serious. In so doing, his epigrammatic witticisms are designed to mock without alienating the affluent West End audiences he had hoped to captivate.

W.'s personal life became his undoing. In 1891, he met Lord Alfred Douglas, the third son of Lord Queensberry. W. and Douglas's father became bitter enemies, and when the Marquess accused him of "posing as a Somdomite [*sic*]," W. foolishly sued for libel; consequently, his personal affairs were made public in court. W. was convicted of homosexual activity and sentenced to two years hard labor. While in prison, he wrote *De Profundis* (wr. 1897; pub. 1905), and evidence suggests that he intended for it to be both a personal letter to Douglas and an autobiographical account of his discovery that sorrow is essential for artistic development. Upon his release in 1897, W. vowed never to return to England, and months later during a trip to Italy, he wrote his last and finest poem, *The Ballad of Reading Gaol* (1898), which conveys directly the psychological experience of institutional cruelty.

W. extended himself in many directions to prove that life and literature were his supreme arts. Along the way he satirized and subverted conventional notions about religion, morality, family, class, money, and prestige. Ideas were his casualties. Most notably, after a fallow century dating back to Richard Brinsley SHERIDAN's *The School for Scandal*, W. ushered in a new age of comedy. In the one hundred years since his death, W.'s literary reputation has become fixed, for critics uniformly rank him and Bernard SHAW as the only major playwrights to emerge from the late Victorian era.

BIBLIOGRAPHY: Cohen, P. K., *The Moral Vision of O. W.* (1978); Ellmann, R., *O. W.* (1987); Hyde, H. M., *O. W.* (1976); Jullian, P., *O. W.* (1969); Kohl, N., *O. W.* (1988); Pearson, H., *The Life of O. W.* (1946); Raby, P., *O. W.* (1988); Roditi, E., *O. W.* (1947); San Juan, E., Jr., *The Art of O. W.* (1967); Woodcock, G., *O. W.* (1988)

JOE NORDGREN

WILLIAM OF OCKHAM [also Occam]
b. 1285, Ockham, Surrey?; d. ca. 1347–49, Munich, Bavaria

W., along with Thomas Aquinas and John Duns Scotus, is one of the major philosophers of the High Middle Ages. A Franciscan philosopher, theologian, and political theorist, he is often associated with the doctrines of nominalism. His rigorous command of logic earned him the epithets *Venerabilis inceptor* and *Doctor invincibilis*, as well as the wrath of two popes.

The facts about W.'s early life before his 1306 ordination are largely conjecture. He probably received his early philosophical training at the Greyfriars in London. Between 1317 and 1319, W. lectured at Oxford on the *Magister Sententiarum,* or Master of the Sentences, of Peter Lombard, written 1145–50, the standard work of medieval theology. His commentaries survive in the *Reportatio* (wr. 1317–18) on books 2–4 of the *Sentences* and the *Ordinatio* on book 1. Entering into one of the most productive periods of his life, W. was appointed in 1321 a lecturer in philosophy, at a Franciscan school, producing work on logic, natural philosophy, and theology. These include the *Expositio aurea, Expositio super libros Elenchorum*, and *Expositio in libros Physicorum Aristotelis*. He also wrote his *Summa logicae* and five of his *Quodlibeta septum*. At this time, he also composed his treatises on the sacraments and the Eucharist, *De quantitate, De corpore Christi,* and *De sacramento altaris.*

Much of W.'s philosophy derives from his identity as a Franciscan theologian, deeply influenced by, if not always agreeing with, John Duns Scotus. God is understood as totally transcendent. As such, God is the only absolute necessity; everything else is contingent. Divine decrees represent one willed and realized possibility out of others. The result is that God holds within a natural and spiritual order, as a function of divine will, and is manifest in the natural order of the world. This underlies the "rule of parsimony," sometimes termed "Ockham's Razor," that entities should not be multiplied beyond necessity; in other words, given a range of possibilities, one should select the simplest proposition. His views of logic anticipate much in modern analytic philosophy.

Central to W.'s nominalism is that individual qualities are physical realities in human experience. Contrary to Aristotle, he argued that universal concepts like those we use to make propositional statements do not come from some shared nature. Ontologically, the idea of universals is an inference derived from the experience of individual things. Epistemologically, this lays the groundwork for a scientific empiricism that posits an intuitive cognition between the knowing mind and the existing object.

W. traveled to Avignon to defend himself against charges of heresy. There he became embroiled in the ongoing debate between the Franciscans and the papacy over the Franciscan doctrine of poverty, that is, since Christ and the Apostles had renounced property, should not the church? Instructed by Michael of Cesena, minister general of the order, W. analyzed the documents, concluding that Pope John XXII was a heretic and should be removed from office. W. and Michael fled Avignon in 1328, joining the entourage of the Holy Roman Emperor, Ludwig IV of Bavaria. Excommunicated by the Pope, W. followed the emperor to Munich, where he spent the rest of his life. During this last period, he was active in polemics, writing a number of political and ethical works, including the *Opus nonagrinta dierum* (wr. 1332–34), *Tractatus contra Ioannem* (wr. 1335), and the *Dialogus* (wr. 1335, 1338–46). The latter is the most important, presented in the form of a dialogue between a master and pupils on matters of heresy, papal authority, and government. Like his contemporary Marsilius of Padua, W. argues for the authority of the emperor in secular matters. But where Marsilius advocated a unitary principle of government and the primacy of the emperor, W. contended that pope and emperor represented two different realms of authority, the one derived from Peter, and the other from the people.

Critical of scholasticism and emphasizing the role of logic and the empirical method, Ockhamism was the last great school of medieval philosophy. Its followers included Pierre d'Ailly, Jean Buridan, Gregory of Rimini, and Jean Gerson.

BIBLIOGRAPHY: Adams, M. M., *W. O.* (2 vols., 1989); Freppert, L., *The Basis of Morality According to W. of O.* (1988); McGrade, A. S., *The Political Thought of W. of O.* (1974); Spade, P. V., ed., *The Cambridge Companion to O.* (1999)

THOMAS L. COOKSEY

WILLIAMS, [George] Emlyn
b. 26 November 1905, Mostyn, Flintshire, Wales; d. 25 September 1987, London

Widely known as an actor and playwright, W.'s most popular work remains *The Corn Is Green* (1938). A ubiquitous figure in London's theatrical world of the 1930s and 1940s, W. also worked as director, screenwriter of film and television scripts, and novelist. As a playwright, W. often focused on the macbre, the supernatural, and the theatrical, helping to establish the popularity of the psychological thriller.

W.'s earliest play, *Virgil* (perf. 1925), is a one-act drama focusing on Issaiah, a farm boy who plans his cruel master's murder, foreshadowing W.'s fascination with murder and the mysterious. His first full-length play, *Full Moon* (perf. 1927), deals with the central conflict between an overly possessive father and a young girl in love with his son. In *Glamour* (perf. 1928), W.'s drew on his Welsh background for the setting, one he would use repeatedly throughout his career.

A Murder Has Been Arranged (1930), W.'s first important play, combined murder with the supernatural and theatrical, and is set on a supposedly haunted stage. The central conflict is between Sir Charles Jasper, a wealthy eccentric, and his nephew, Maurice Mullins. Celebrating his birthday with a costume ball held on the haunted stage, Jasper stands to inherit two million pounds if he is still alive at eleven p.m. If not, the money goes to Mullins. During a re-creation of the murder responsible for the theater's haunting, Mullins murders Jasper, making it look like a suicide. The ghost of the dead man, however, returns, forcing Mullins to confess. Although favored critically, *A Murder Has Been Arranged* was a commercial failure.

The suspenseful thriller *Night Must Fall* (1935) secured W.'s popularity as both playwright and actor. He played the role of the central character, Dan, in the original production. Extremely self-centered and selfish, Dan has murdered a guest of the hotel at which he is a bellhop, carrying her severed head around in a hatbox. He manipulates his way into the life of Mrs. Bramson, the invalid destined to become Dan's next victim. Olivia, Mrs. Bramson's niece, discovers Dan's identity but does not divulge this information about the psychopathic killer. *Night Must Fall* sustained a run of 435 performances at the Duchess Theatre in London, followed by a favorable run at the Ethel Barrymore Theater in New York. Ultimately, the play was successfully adapted for film in 1937 and again, albeit less successfully, in 1964.

Set in a Welsh mining town at the turn of the 20th c., W.'s next major success was *The Corn Is Green*, his best-known work. Compared to earlier works, *The Corn Is Green* uses a relatively realistic setting and situation and generally more sympathetic characters. Drawing on his experience of growing up in Wales, this semiautobiographical drama focuses on the relationship between Miss Moffat, an outspoken, brusque schoolteacher and her intelligent and spirited student, Morgan Evans. Using a conventional plot structure, W. deals with the shifting, often conflicting, aspects of their relationship. As a complication, W. introduces Bessie, a young slut with whom Evans becomes involved and who ultimately bears his child. Although Williams often adapted characters to plot, the plot of *The Corn Is Green* is determined more by character. The ending, often criticized for its artificiality, leaves Moffat deciding to rear the child, freeing Evans to pursue his education. After a two-year run, the play was adapted for the successful 1945 film version. In 1974, a musical adaptation appeared unsuccessfully as *Miss Moffat*

As an actor, W. achieved international success with his one-man shows based on the writings of Charles DICKENS (formed in 1951) and Dylan THOMAS, *Dylan Thomas Growing Up* (formed in 1955). W. wrote two autobiographical volumes, *George: An Early Autobiography* (1961), dealing with his childhood and youth, and *Emlyn: An Early Autobiography: 1927–1935* (1973), continuing his story to *Night Must Fall*. An account of the "moors murders" of 1963–64 appeared as the nonfiction novel, *Beyond Belief: A Chronicle of Murder and Its Detection* (1967), and W.'s first novel, *Headlong* (1980), concerned English royalty in the 1930s.

Although now often criticized for the structural artificiality of his plays, W.'s work retains a certain entertaining quality and always a solid sense of the theatrical. In recognition of his substantial and distinguished career as an actor and playwright, W. was named a Commander of the Order of the British Empire in 1962. He will be remembered best for the psychological thriller *Night Must Fall* and the more realistic and sympathetic *The Corn Is Green*.

BIBLIOGRAPHY: Dale-Jones, D., *E. W.* (1979); Findlater, R., *E. W.* (1956); Harding, J., *E. W.* (1993); Stephens, J. R., *E. W.* (2000)

SAMUEL GAUSTAD

WILLIAMS, Hugo [Hugh Mordaunt Vyner]
b. 20 February 1942, Windsor, Berkshire

W. is a minor lyric poet with a reserved, self-deprecating, quintessentially English voice. He is usually included in post-1945 anthologies, but excluded from those for the whole century. His work has provoked no major studies; the critical debate is conducted in reviews and book-length general surveys.

He comes from a family of actors. His father, Hugh Williams, is remembered as Hindley opposite Laurence Olivier's Heathcliff in the 1938 film version of *Wuthering Heights* and his brother Simon as Captain Bellamy in the ITV's *Upstairs Downstairs*; while his actress mother, Margaret Vyner, gained postwar fame for the drawing room comedies she cowrote with her husband ("Four Plays by Hugh and Margaret Williams"). W. himself wanted to be an actor until his father diverted him toward poetry ("A Start in Life"), so instead consoled himself with the inferior part of actor-poet. Acutely aware of public image, he initially presented himself as a spaced-out hippy and more recently as the dandy on motorbike; in between, he has posed as the only old Etonian to prefer bohemian poverty to running the country (he has largely supported himself as assistant editor, television, theater, and film critic of various small magazines; his charmingly inconsequential *Times Literary Supplement* columns have been collected as *Freelancing,* 1995). His poetry, written to be spoken, though not declaimed, has the elegance of the best comedy-of-manners dialogue. He does indeed regard poems as urbane entertainments, designed to please, in which small, recognizable scenes are simply enacted. Though the poet typically plays himself, he sometimes dons a mask for a dramatic monologue—most particularly, that of Sonny Jim, his subversive alter ego. His minidramas tend to represent life as a theatrical or—since his French wife, Hermine, has been a high-wire artist—circus performance. They exhibit an extreme awareness of the impression the speaker is making; he is forever looking in mirrors to adjust tie, collar, or smile and assessing relationships according to the effect they have on the cut of his clothes or hair.

W. first gained notice as a stalwart of the Oxford-based *Review* (1962–72), which provided support for A. ALVAREZ's campaign on behalf of confessional poetry. Typical *Review* poems by Ian HAMILTON, David HARSENT, or Colin Falck read like anglicized Robert Lowell, the American poet—seemingly autobiographical life studies, depicting fraught domestic situations—but what distinguished them was a parallel adherence to the imagist tradition of short, radically concentrated, visual poems, in which nondiscursive images were bound tightly into free-verse lines by powerful cadences. The confessional element precluded imagist objectivity, but the poems did try to preserve the image as an intellectual and emotional complex where a tense, intricate depth of implication lay beneath a clear lyric surface.

W.'s *Review* poems dramatize those issues that have divided reviewers ever since. One could emphasize their Poundian prose virtues: exactly rendered sense notations, real situations presented without rhetoric, a cool tone, a limpid conversational style, and a free verse without inversion or archaism. However, one could equally point to their formlessness: the absence of both synthesizing intensity of thought and feeling, and cohesive cadences, as well as the arbitrary relation between syntax and stanza shape. One could further argue the free verse is only placed in traditional forms to disguise the flat rhythms and general amorphousness.

W.'s earliest work (1956–62), published as *First Poems* (1985), is untypical of the later style with its blank verse, rhymes, formal diction, and pastoral themes. Similarly, *Symptoms of Loss* (1965) assumes Thom GUNN's "Movement" manner of tough, confident poses, small riddling allegories and argumentative rigor in a way that was never repeated. However, *Sugar Daddy* (1970) provides intimations of the mature mode with its mildly confessional, intermittent narrative, progressing from bachelorhood, marriage, and fatherhood to separation, its melancholic irony beneath a charmingly simple, cool surface, and mixture of gritty metropolitan and exotic foreign subjects. W.'s travels have also produced two prose works: *All the Time in the World* (1966) and *No Particular Place to Go* (1981). Thereafter, while the manner remains constant, the subject matter slowly evolves. *Some Sweet Day* (1975) continues themes of marital disharmony and tense bonding with his daughter Murphy, the volume's dedicatee, but introduces the antiheroic persona, Sonny Jim, and rueful memories of boarding school.

Love-Life (1979), though given a new dimension by Jessica Gwynne's drawings, ultimately disappoints in its unimaginative recycling of the narrative of marital estrangement and separation. However, *Writing Home* (1985), dealing with a son's painful inability to relate to either his father as famous actor, desert warrior, and postwar bankrupt, or his boarding school, is such a recovery of form some critics have hailed it as a minor masterpiece. *Always and Always: Wartime Letters of Hugh and Margaret Williams* (1995), edited by Kate Dunn, confirms with what artistry W. adapted his father's correspondence. While *Self-Portrait with a Slide* (1990) revisits the subject of dysfunctional marriage, the development of Sonny Jim and a sharper sense of failure allow a passionate surreal note to enter. However, a certain tiredness is suggested by the number of metapoems about the business of writing and selling poetry. *Dock Leaves* (1995), dedicated to his mother, fails to do for her what *Writing Home* did for his father, but does include "Message Not Left on an Answerphone (for C)," the genesis of his most confessional collection, *Billy's Rain* (1999). This volume, which presents snapshots from a ten-year affair with an art student younger than his daughter, expertly controls narrative sympathy by showing only the deserted man's suffering until the penultimate poem reveals he is married, but has refused to leave his wife for "Carolyn." Its title, referring to film sound effects' fake rain, warns the reader W. is playing with notions of confessional authenticity in a witty postmodernist manner.

BIBLIOGRAPHY: Corcoran, N., *English Poetry since 1940* (1993); Herbert, W. N., and M. Hollis, eds., *Strong Words* (2000); Hulse, M., "H. W.," in Sherry,

V. B., Jr., ed., *Poets of Great Britain and Ireland since 1960*, part 2, *DLB* 40 (1985): 633–37

DAVID FULTON

WILLIAMS, Raymond [Henry]

b. 31 August 1921, Llanfihangel Crocorney, Monmouthshire, Wales; d. 26 January 1988, London

A literary theorist, novelist, and social critic, W. is among the most prolific and influential thinkers of his age. He wrote over three dozen books including *The Long Revolution* (1961), *The English Novel from Dickens to Lawrence* (1970), *The Country and the City* (1973), and *Towards 2000* (1982; repub. as *The Year 2000*, 1984). Born in Monmouthshire, Wales, and reared in a working-class neighborhood, W. served as a captain in the British army during World War II, participating in the landings at Normandy. In 1946, he broke social barriers to attend Trinity College, Cambridge, on scholarship, earning an M.A. and, later, a doctorate of literature. As a student at Trinity, W. became acutely conscious of the role of class in daily life. In his subsequent work, he insisted on interpreting culture in relation to the economic system of its production. W.'s particular obsession throughout his career would be to discover the ways in which people made that connection for themselves, in their own way, in their own words.

Most recognized for his involvement with the Centre for Contemporary Cultural Studies at the University of Birmingham, W. was a leading figure, along with E. P. Thompson and Richard HOGGART, of Britain's postwar New Left movement. It is from this Centre that the influential intellectual movement of the 1980s and 1990s, Cultural Studies, draws its name. His written work, spanning a range of disciplines and genres from literary criticism and novels to political essays and sociological treatises, bears the stamp of his socialist convictions.

W. departed radically from classically inspired standards of taste, which considered artistic creations to belong in a rarified sphere outside of the political and the quotidian. W. termed his more anthropological perspective "cultural materialism." He explains in *The Sociology of Culture* (1982), published originally as *Culture* (1981), that in order to understand the social significance of a work of art—or any cultural production such as television and popular music—critics must reveal the process behind the production of that art, as well as engage with art as a product. Such a mode of analysis places cultural artifacts within the context of their creation and their reception. One goal of cultural materialism, then, was to reduce the focus on the genius of the individual creator, and emphasize instead, the coherent expression of a collective worldview.

In *Culture and Society, 1780–1950* (1958), W. observes that "I feel myself committed to the study of actual language, that is to say, to the words and sequences of words which particular men and women have used in trying to give meaning to their experience." Indeed, he structures the text around the etymological variations surrounding the word culture, and a handful of others, in Great Britain from the Industrial Revolution to his own day. W. argues that better understanding the meaning of the term culture, we can better understand our response to the growth of industrial society and democracy.

This interest in words and their use would continue to fascinate W. throughout his career. *Marxism and Literature* (1977) clarifies such terms as "hegemony" that refers to political dominance; "base" that corresponds roughly to material elements of society; and "superstructure" that describes the dominant ideas and laws in a society. His analysis seeks both to sharpen the use of theoretical and literary terms and to unearth their ideological underpinnings. Less intellectually rigid than other European Marxists, W. also developed new terminology in order to better explain subtle cultural phenomena. Such a term as "structure of feeling," which describes a common mode of perception characteristic of certain classes and groups within society, allowed W. the intellectual room to fine-tune the overused concept of ideology without provoking conceptual turf wars.

W.'s creative fusions of sociological, political, and materialist discourse with the literary, aesthetic and anthropological, help to establish a vocabulary for Cultural Studies, and influenced scholars in communication studies, history, linguistics, literature, and sociology. The subtitle to his widely read work, *Keywords* (1976), most clearly articulates his legacy; for many, he did indeed provide "A Vocabulary of Culture and Society."

Beyond his work as a Marxist literary critic, W. was also a public intellectual, committed to understanding and participating in contemporary society. He appeared in numerous television interviews throughout the 1960s and 1970s, and wrote a weekly column on television for the BBC magazine, the *Listener*. In addition to producing literary, sociological, and popular culture criticism, W. wrote seven novels and a number of screenplays. His most successful novel was *Border Country* (1960), an autobiographical story about a London professor named Matthew Price who returns to the small, Welsh town in which he had been born, to tend to his ill father. W.'s own father was a railway worker, and railways, literally and symbolically a means of communication, were an important theme in his fiction and in his lectures at Cambridge University in the 1960s. In 1979, the Welsh Arts Council awarded W. the prize for fiction, for *The Fight for Manod*, in which Matthew Price returns, and is drawn into a scandal involving a corporations and an unscrupulous development project in rural Wales.

BIBLIOGRAPHY: Eagleton, T., *R. W.* (1989); Inglis, F., *R. W.* (1995); Prendergast, C., *Cultural Materialism: On R. W.* (1995); Wallace, J., *R. W. Now: Knowledge, Limits, and the Future* (1997)

JOSEPH McNICHOLAS

WILMER, Clive

b. 10 February 1945, Harrogate, Yorkshire

W.'s work from the early 1970s onward, as poet, translator, editor, critic, and anthologist, has been applauded for its unfailing probity, craftsmanship, and scholarship. An insistence upon continuities in the language of poetry, a sense of tradition that involves an interdependence between poems and poets of different ages (Dante, Ezra Pound, Donald DAVIE, and John Peck, for example) underpins his belief in art's redemptive power. His work eschews fashions for confessional outpouring, "accessibility" or limiting ironies; he holds fast to the etymological root of "poet" as "maker." Integrity in the relationship between artist and material is central to W.'s poetics and is very often his subject matter; thus, the kinship of previous fellow artistic "labourers" is especially important, and here John RUSKIN is a particular mentor. Some of W.'s best poetry is "Ruskinian" in its evocation of the spiritual world to be glimpsed by a close and faithful artistic record of physical detail. W.'s brand of MODERNISM might then best be understood as a form of "radical conservation."

In *The Dwelling-Place* (1977), his first collection, W. ponders questions of endurance; his nostalgic and elegiac kinship with other cultures (Victorian Gothic, Arthurian myth, the pre-Romanesque) is stayed in lucid and chaste diction—as illustrated in his introduction to an edition of Dante Gabriel ROSSETTI's *Selected Poems and Translations* (1991). A finely tuned mastery of inherited meter, syntax, and rhyme embodies the struggles and triumphs of other "makers" (goldsmiths, architects, musicians, artists); the dominant mood is somber yet celebratory, the affinities realized in understatement, implication, and containment. Many poems resemble well-built places of refuge. Davie's example is evident in many poems including W.'s ars poetica "Saxon Buckle," the collection's final poem. Here, W. renders in language the talismanic workmanship of the buckle as it simultaneously captures and fends off forces of destruction. The poem's stilled "unrest" epitomizes a keynote of heroic resistance in W.'s work: threatened territories finding sanctity and illumination in the "keep" of the poetic "architecture."

In *Devotions* (1982), W. plants personal concerns (addresses to his family, for example) into the broader tradition of devotional poetry: the result is remarkable for its spiritually resonant secular "prayers"; many of the poems are, in the deepest sense, preservation acts. Yearnings for a home and an awareness of exile, the perilous state of "civilization" or "reason," apprehensions of the natural world: these are central themes explored in individual poems and movements through and across them in a larger "polyphonic" pattern. The formal restraint and control of poems such as "A Peaceable Kingdom" and "The Parable of the Sower" is complemented by more experimental verse forms (as in "Air and Earth") that owe much to Thom GUNN's example.

William MORRIS's utopian socialism, romantic medievalism, and lectures on work are shadowing influences on W.'s next, and possibly finest, collection *Of Earthly Paradise* (1992); two sequences, "The Infinite Variety" and "A Catalogue of Flowers" are typical of a sacramental view of the natural world in the face of environmental neglect. The historical and religious resonance to W.'s seeks to manifest the spiritual liberation that is latent in careful and respectful observation of physical detail. His *Selected Poems* (1995) includes new and uncollected poems (homages, anthems, verse letters) as well as traces of major works of cotranslation, with George Gömöri, of the Hungarian poets Miklós Radnóti—*Forced March: Selected Poems* (1979) and *The Life and Poetry of Miklós Radnóti: Essays* (1999)—and György Petri—*Night Song of the Personal Shadow: Selected Poems* (1991) and *Eternal Monday: New and Selected Poems* (1999). W. reveals in the former a model of classical restraint in the face of tryranny, and in the latter a dark lyricism and acerbic political SATIRE. His work from 1989 to 1992 as interviewer of twenty-one contemporary poets is collected as *Poets Talking: The "Poet of the Month" Interviews from BBC Radio 3* (1994); the transcripts reveal W.'s sympathy, knowledge, and the high esteem of his fellow writers.

The Falls (2000) is W.'s most technically adventurous collection to date, arranged along musical lines: the groupings of elegies, homages, and epiphanies ponder the interanimations of body and spirit, man and nature, flow and constraint. In the title poem, a celebration of a waterfall's "eternal power," "Vision," and "The Holy of Holies" the keynote is awe: the possibilites of other worlds are suggested by subtle juxtapositions and historical "intersections" in rhythm and diction, (remarkable furtherances of modernist examples, particularly that of Pound): "the same pattern, never/the same water."

BIBLIOGRAPHY: Jackson, K., "C. W. in Conversation," *PN Review* 22 (January-February 1996): 39–42; Middleton, D. E., "C. W.," in Sherry, V. B., Jr., ed., *Poets of Great Britain and Ireland since 1960*, part 2, *DLB* 40 (1985): 637–48

PETER CARPENTER

WILSON, A[ndrew] N[orman]
b. 27 October 1950, Stone, Staffordshire

W. is a productive and often provocative novelist, biographer, and controversialist. His fiction is often very funny, but it is also seriously engaged with moral and spiritual questions, and has grown darker in tone over the years. As a novelist, he moves confidently over ground that has already been well mapped in English fiction—the Anglican Church, the Oxbridge and London intelligentsia, the Westminster political scene—and he draws on a tradition of comedy and SATIRE that includes novelists such as Ronald FIRBANK, Barbara PYM, and Evelyn WAUGH. But W. applies this tradition to a society in the throes of unprecedented crisis and change, and demonstrates that the ground the English once took for granted is now giving way under their feet.

The Sweets of Pimlico (1977), his first novel, explores the complex relationships between Evelyn Tradescant, a young teacher, her brother Jeremy, with whom she has an incestuous relationship, a strange older man, Theo Gormann, and a confectionery manufacturer, "Pimlico" Price, who is one of Jeremy's lovers. The sense of a sexual cauldron boiling beneath the polite lid of English life is characteristic of W.'s fiction and provides him with opportunities for social criticism and comedy that sometimes lead into farce. The farcical tendency is indulged freely in his next two novels, *Unguarded Hours* (1978) and *Kindly Light* (1979), which feature Norman Shotover, an idle but privileged innocent whose excursion into and finally out of the priesthood involves him in a range of grotesque situations. A more serious note is sounded in the novel that followed, *The Healing Art* (1980): this turns on an inadvertent exchange of X-rays that leads one woman, Pamela, to be wrongly diagnosed as suffering from terminal cancer, and another, Dorothy, to be wrongly assured that she is all right: W. traces the consequences for each woman of this error and their eventual discovery of the truth. *Who Was Oswald Fish?* (1981) reopens a broader vein of satire in its account of a network of people who discover their common descent from a Victorian architect and womanizer, Oswald Fish, but the serious note returns and sounds more deeply in *Wise Virgin* (1982). This novel features a twice widowed, aging scholar of medieval texts who is losing his sight and who falls more deeply into loneliness and failure as a result of the rejection of his work, his refusal to marry his young female assistant, and the departure of his daughter for a younger man. Closely observed,

fraught with ironies, balancing sympathy and detachment, *Wise Virgin* is one of W.'s best books.

Scandal; or, Priscilla's Kindness (1983) is a much cruder though often entertaining work, a satire on a recurrent real-life situation in postwar British politics, in which a politician goes to criminal extremes to prevent public exposure of his sexual transgressions. In this case, Derek Blore tries to perpetrate murder and treason in a futile attempt to conceal his sadomasochism. *Gentlemen in England* (1985) has greater depth, returning to Victorian Britain to dramatize, through the conflicts in and around the Nettleby family, the religious, intellectual, and erotic tensions of the era. W. comes back to modern times in *Love Unknown* (1986), a more schematic novel in which three women who once shared a flat find, twenty years on, that they are implicated in untruths.

During the 1980s, W. had also produced three challenging biographies of writers deeply involved with religion: *Hilaire Belloc* (1984), *Tolstoy* (1988), and *C. S. Lewis* (1990). W. himself had moved from the Christian commitment of his book-length essay *How Can We Know?* (1985) to a rejection of faith in his polemical pamphlet *Against Religion* (1992), and had caused controversy with his books *Jesus* (1992) and *Paul* (1997). In view of his concern with religious questions in his nonfiction, it is not surprising that he makes the collapse of belief central to the protagonist of his novel *The Vicar of Sorrows* (1993). Like W.'s second and third novels, this focuses on a clergyman in crisis, but in a way that comes closer to tragedy than to farce. Francis Kreer loses his faith, falls for a young woman, leaves his wife, suffers exclusion and condemnation, and ends close to madness after he learns of his daughter's rape. The violation of the vulnerable at the end of *The Vicar of Sorrows* becomes a vital strand in the disturbing *Dream Children* (1998), which turns on the revelation that a failed philosopher, Oliver Gold, has taken sexual advantage of a trusting ten-year-old girl. The novel is an uncompromising anatomy of corruption that nonetheless solicits sympathy for its predatory protagonist.

W. has also produced the quintet of novels that make up "The Lampitt Chronicles": *Incline Our Hearts* (1989), *A Bottle in the Smoke* (1990), *Daughters of Albion* (1991), *Hearing Voices* (1995), and *A Watch in the Night* (1996). Moving from the 1930s to the year 2000 and beyond, passing through London, New York, Venice, and Italy, and taking in a wide range of characters, these novels follow the search of their narrator, Julian Ramsay, for the facts about the life and mysterious death of an Edwardian man of letters, James Petworth Lampitt. They have been compared to the novels of Anthony POWELL's sequence *A Dance to the Music of Time,* but they are much less focused.

W. has now amassed an ample body of work. While he sometimes sacrifices structure to the pressure of material, his best books show considerable structural skill; although he does not take pains with his style, his prose, like good conversation, compensates for its occasional lapses by its frequent moments of HUMOR, precision, and insight. His novels constitute a panorama of key sectors of upper-middle-class British life in the later 20th c. and provide a series of urbane, often pained, and at times lacerating observations of the embarrassments and agonies of living in an old country in the late modern era.

BIBLIOGRAPHY: Greer, R., "A. N. W.," in Moseley, M., ed., *British Novelists since 1960*, Second Series, *DLB* 194 (1998): 317–24; Pritchard, W. H., "A. N. W.," in Parini, J., ed., *British Writers: Supplement VI* (2001): 297–310

NICOLAS TREDELL

WILSON, [Sir] Angus [Frank Johnstone]
b. 11 August 1913, Bexhill, Sussex; d. 31 May 1991, Hawstead, Suffolk

W. was the liveliest new talent in British fiction to emerge in the years immediately following World War II. His first book, a collection of short stories entitled *The Wrong Set*, published in 1949, was a success with critics and public alike for the mixed sharpness and sympathy, and the sheer vivacity, with which it presented the English social milieu of the 1930s and 1940s. W.'s eye, and ear, for telling details of dress, speech, and behavior, especially in situations involving falsity, pretentiousness, and precariousness, seemed impeccable, and a wide range of readers felt a shock of recognition at seeing their world presented with such liberating frankness. A second short story collection, *Such Darling Dodos*, followed in 1950, quickly adding to W.'s reputation as an acute semicomic observer of human behavior, who among other things conveyed the weakness, as well as the strength, of prewar liberal humanism. The English social structure seemed to be dissolving, and for the moment W. was its most penetrating witness.

W.'s own background gave him much of his material, and accounted for the mixed feelings with which he presented it. Born in the genteel seaside resort of Bexhill to a Scottish *rentier* father and a South African mother, W. was the youngest of six brothers, and spent part of his childhood in Durban, Natal, part of it at a preparatory school in Seaford, Sussex, run by his second-eldest brother, and a later part of it, when not attending Westminster School as a day boy, in a succession of small hotels in the Kensington area of London affordable by middle-class people with social pretensions greater than their diminishing capital. In one of these hotels, in 1929, W.'s mother died at the

age of sixty. Money inherited from her enabled W. to go to Merton College, Oxford, in 1932, and study medieval history; but his enjoyment of this, and of the decade, was tempered by increasing political uncertainties, by the not very congenial work he obtained in 1936 as a cataloger at the British Museum, and by the declining health and death in 1938 of his father, to whom, after his mother's death, he had become very close. W.'s mother and father, exemplars respectively of bourgeois "pluck" and raffish, though often charming, irresponsibility, occur in various guises in much of his fiction, as objects of affection and sympathy, as well as fascinated aversion. Also recurrent is W.'s sensitivity to different lifestyles, to the clashes that occur as the upwardly mobile encounter the socially sinking; to the coexistence of liberal values and imagination with brutality (powerfully illustrated in W.'s first short story of 1946, "Raspberry Jam"), and of solid institutions (school, university, cultural establishments of all kinds) with an "underworld," separated from them by only thin ice or crusted lava, of nonrespectability, crime, and moral evil—the literary manifestations of which were the subject of W.'s Northcliffe Lectures at London University in 1961, "Evil in the English Novel."

It had become clear to W. in the 1930s that he was homosexual, and thus, by the standards of the time, in an inherently precarious position. The difficulty of retaining balance in human relationships, and the balance of one's mind, became further evident when W. suffered a nervous breakdown while doing his war service at the Foreign Office's code-breaking Intelligence unit at Bletchley Park. It was this event that led to W.'s beginning to write fiction, not immediately but in 1946, one short story at a time. His startling literary debut at the age of thirty-six, which prompted Edmund Wilson in 1950 to nominate him as the heir of Evelyn WAUGH, had, therefore, a weight of by no means commonplace experience behind it, as well as the formidable strength and skill that gave W. the air of springing on the world fully formed.

In the 1950s, W. produced one further, less successful, collection of short stories, *A Bit Off the Map* (1957), and his only play, *The Mulberry Bush*, set in a liberal-humanist academic milieu, enjoyed a moderate success when it was performed by the Bristol Old Vic Company in 1955 and at the Royal Court Theatre, London, in 1956. But between 1950 and 1980, it was to the novel that W. devoted his creative energies, in a life increasingly to be taken up by critical writing (*Emile Zola*, 1952; *The World of Charles Dickens*, 1970; *The Strange Ride of Rudyard Kipling*, 1977), invited lecturing at many American universities, and his part-time professorship (1966–73) at the University of East Anglia, where he was a founding teacher in the creative writing program. In his 1960 Ewing Lectures at UCLA (published in 1963 as *The Wild*

Garden), W. spoke of the relation, in his own habits and psyche, of a wish for rootedness and a need to travel, a need for order and an awareness of chaos; these conflicting impulses may be said to be also represented by W. the official "public man" and W. the private, free imaginer. But essentially the two sides are complementary, mutually fructifying.

W.'s first novel, *Hemlock and After* (1952), is also his shortest, written during a month's leave of absence from the British Museum, where he had become deputy superintendent of the Reading Room. The novel, dense in texture and with many interlacing characters and episodes, essentially presents the predicament of a distinguished liberal-agnostic man of letters, Bernard Sands, whose success and security are gradually undermined by an increasing sense of evil in the world and a streak of cruelty in himself, and by his own homosexual nature—laying him open to blackmail—which has largely superseded his "normal" feelings for his wife and grown-up children. Hamlet-like, Bernard becomes almost incapable of action, and after his death—of poison, like Socrates, but accidentally—it is his wife, recovered from a nervous breakdown, who deals in her own much brisker way with the various human problems that have weighed on Bernard's mind. The novel—ironic, compassionate, groundbreakingly honest about sexual matters—shocked some readers but won the admiration of many more as an acute portrayal of the crosscurrents of British society in 1951, the year of the Festival of Britain.

W.'s two other novels of the 1950s, after his retirement from the British Museum in 1955 to become a full-time writer, living in the Suffolk countryside not far from Bury St. Edmunds, were less fierce than *Hemlock* but much longer, both in size and time span. *Anglo-Saxon Attitudes* (1956), loosely based on the story of the "Piltdown man" hoax of 1912, exposed in 1953, is an elaborate combination, rendered partly in flashback, of detective story and detailed character-analysis, centered on Gerald Middleton, a rich professor who needs to face various truths about himself—professional, emotional, familial—before he can regain self-respect and the ability to act with the decision expected of the most distinguished living medieval historian. W.'s skill in pacing his elaborate story and handling a large and varied cast of characters, and his ability to analyze the academic milieu, were greatly admired: the novel prompted comparison with Charles DICKENS, and was a Book Society Choice. *The Middle Age of Mrs. Eliot* (1958), though it won the James Tait Black Memorial Prize, had a more mixed reception, some finding very impressive the detailed conscientiousness with which W. presents the adaptation of an upper-middle-class barrister's wife to abrupt widowhood and straitened means, others feeling that both she and her quietist brother David, with whom she stays while recovering her im-

petus, were simply not interesting enough to deserve such extended treatment. Nevertheless, W. was generally praised for his insight into his female protagonist, and her London milieu.

The three novels that Wilson published in the 1960s expanded his range in various ways, and confirmed W.'s position as one of the most interesting novelists writing. Unique in his work, *The Old Men at the Zoo* (1961) employs a first-person narrator, thirty-five-year-old Simon Carter, administrative secretary of the London Zoo, and is set ten years into the future, when the clashing policies of successive Zoo directors (themselves representing different attitudes to the treatment of animals) are overtaken by political changes that lead England away from the U.S. (and Russia) and into a neofascist "Uni-European" alliance that is grotesque and horrifying, but mercifully short. The multilayered ethical dilemmas presented in the novel through Carter's consciousness are given an extra bite by one's own awareness, stimulated from time to time by allusions in W.'s text, of how close England came, through the "old men" appeasers of the 1930s, to an accommodation with monsters. W.'s fears for the future were, essentially, a memory of the dangers of the past, with the organization of an imagined London Zoo standing in for the British Museum and the establishment at Bletchley Park.

A postwar organizational phenomenon, the "new town"—purpose-built satellite towns set up around London to house relocated city-dwellers and provide sites for light industry—provided the setting for *Late Call* (1964). W.'s left-wing political views lay behind his interest in such places (lower on his social scale than usual), but the example he creates, Carshall, is seen very much through the innocently accusing eyes of Sylvia Calvert, aged about sixty, a countrywoman by birth, whose own progress from self-effacement to self-worth provides the novel's more deeply engaging material. Quiet, occasionally dull, yet curiously haunting, *Late Call* was followed in 1967 by *No Laughing Matter*, a panoramic novel and W.'s longest, covering over five decades of the 20th c. from 1912 onward through the experiences of six children called Matthews and their upper-middle-class parents. The family is loosely based on W.'s own, and the novel is essentially a family saga, analogous to John GALSWORTHY's *The Forsyte Saga;* but the presentation is varied by sections in play form (whose models range from Bernard SHAW to Samuel BECKETT) and by interior monologues recalling James JOYCE and Virginia WOOLF, who had also used six main characters in *The Waves. No Laughing Matter* is at once W.'s most densely packed historico-imaginative fiction and his most virtuoso intertextual performance as one who was by now reviewer, critic, and professor of creative writing as well as novelist. Deservedly, it was greeted with almost universal praise, though W. once pronounced *The Old Men at the Zoo* his best book, and for many who started to read W. in the 1950s *Anglo-Saxon Attitudes* has continued to seem his most satisfying novel.

A stream of honors came to W. from about this time: Companion of the Order of the British Empire in 1968, Companion of Literature (the highest honor awarded by the Royal Society of Literature) in 1972, and in 1980 a knighthood. His last two novels, however, were less successful than their predecessors. *As If By Magic* (1973), an ambitious novel set variously in London, Morocco, Goa, Borneo, and Japan, seems in part the product of a sixty-year-old who, like W. B. YEATS, envies "the young in one another's arms" but, unlike him, cannot yet be reconciled to being a golden bird in Byzantium. Its intercutting of the travels of the homosexual plant-geneticist Hamo Langmuir (of W.'s generation) and his goddaughter Alexandra Grant (a student at a "new University" like East Anglia), and its attempts to blend searches for the "ideal youth," and Eastern religious panaceas, with a pervasive sense of Third World poverty and unease produce much of interest by the way but end up artistically incoherent. *Setting the World on Fire* (1980) is Apollonian rather than Dionysiac, aristocratic not hippie, tracing two brothers, Piers and Tom Mosson, through lives that seem an idealized version of W.'s own at Westminster School and Oxford. W. creates a heroic world of splendid architecture and operatic music against which he sets the forces of anarchy embodied in an Italian woman in love with the excitement of chaos and a disaffected retainer who plans, à la the Gunpowder Plot, to blow up the Houses of Parliament. Collecting many motifs from W.'s earlier work and life, the novel has considerable power, but of an unusual kind—a defense of the nobility of the artistic impulse that to some critics seemed out of keeping with egalitarian values and to others out of step with the commercial ruthlessness of Margaret Thatcher's Britain.

Taken together, W.'s literary output is of remarkable distinction. He published little that was significant after 1980, but his achievement won him, from 1982 to 1988, the presidency of the Royal Society of Literature. He spent three years of the later 1980s living in St. Remy de Provence, but when he died it was not far from his longtime home at Felsham Woodside in Suffolk.

BIBLIOGRAPHY: Drabble, M., *A. W.* (1995); Faulkner, P., *A. W.* (1980); Gardner, A., *A. W.* (1987); Gransden, K. W., *A. W.* (1969); Halio, J. L., *A. W.* (1964); McDowell, F. P. W., "An Interview with A. W.," *IowaR* 3 (Fall 1972): 77–105

AVERIL GARDNER

WILSON, Colin [Henry]
b. 26 June 1931, Leicester

W.'s fame began with the publication in 1956 of *The Outsider*. The book became a classic examination of the spiritual, psychological, and social alienation in postwar Britain. It was a philosophical exploration of what W. called "the new existentialism." It was also the first of over one hundred books that W. has written and/or edited on such diverse topics as literature, philosophy, sexuality, violence—especially murder—and the occult. His many novels range from REALISM to fantasy, police procedural, mystery, and SCIENCE FICTION. But his most frequent recurring theme in both his fiction and nonfiction is the belief that human beings can achieve a condition of higher consciousness by sheer will power and dogged effort, and that artists—especially writers—should create the imaginative structure that will allow the emergence of such an evolutionary high consciousness.

Though active in many different genres of discourse, W. believes that the novel most effectively transforms peoples' minds and enables them to move beyond their limited conditioning. W. came from a working-class family and dropped out of school at the age of sixteen, but he educated himself with voracious regimes of reading. He worked in factories, hospitals, and business offices, but always managed to gather as much information as he could from whatever seemingly menial jobs he took.

His first book, *The Outsider,* was published when he was twenty-four-years old; it was a collection of nonfiction meditations on the emptiness of an industrialized civilization and its dehumanizing aspects. Though it became an immediate best-seller, critics were outraged by W.'s attacks on William SHAKESPEARE as an overrated dramatist and his admiration for English fascist Oswald Mosley. Several powerful critics praised the book for its youthful audacity and it became a veritable handbook of existentialism for the disaffected youth of both England and the U.S. But is was his second nonfiction book, *Religion and the Rebel* (1957), that brought down the wrath of both the academic and religious establishment for his vicious attack on Christianity.

His first novel, *Ritual in the Dark* (1960), however, restored his reputation to some degree. The protagonist, Gerard Sorme, a writer, befriends a mass-murderer and a variety of other "outsiders," an experience that enables Sorme to accept the inevitable complexity of life and to realize that there are no easy answers to most problems. Critics were pleased that W. proved himself a compelling storyteller. *Adrift in Soho* (1961) presents the picaresque adventurers of Harry Preston, who is learning to live by his wits from the drifters and bohemians he associates with in Soho. Though he learns much about writing, he also realizes that he is hopelessly middle class.

It was the publication, though, of W.'s third novel, *Man without a Shadow: The Diary of an Existentialist* (1963), that critics began to appreciate W.'s insight as a perceptive social psychologist. The diaristic novel—its American title was *The Sex Diary of Gerard*

Sorme—documents Sorme's pursuit of sexual experience as a method of expanding and intensifying consciousness. That theme pervades much of W.'s later novels and essays.

W. continues his examination of the connection between sex and violence in *Necessary Doubt* (1964) and *The Glass Cage* (1966). But it was his first science fiction novel, *The Mind Parasites* (1967), that became a best-seller and was praised by most commentators for its creative novelistic techniques. The novel's postmodern form consisted of the papers, conversations, and recordings of archeologist Gilbert Austin, warning nations that their citizens were being infested with parasites that were draining energy from them. Such activity was impeding evolutionary progress. His next science fiction novel, *The Philosopher's Stone* (1969), expands some of the themes of *The Mind Parasites* and focuses on cultivating higher consciousness as a way of moving human beings into higher evolutionary levels. Humanity is continually threatened, however, with the self-destructive impulses of the unconscious.

W.'s lifelong obsession with death found its clearest expression in his nonfiction novel entitled *The Killer* (1970). Though based on composite portraits of serial killers, W.'s protagonist, Dr. Samuel Kahn, becomes fascinated with a killer, Arthur Lingard, who, with proper guidance, could have become a major artist. Dr. Kahn ponders what forces caused him to become a serial rapist-killer instead. The protagonist of two earlier novels, Gerard Sorme reappears as the main character of *The God of the Labyrinth* (1970; repub. as *The Hedonists*, 1971). Sex, rather than violence, is the topic of the novel. Sorme becomes so engrossed in the sexual adventures of an 18th-c. Irish lecher that Sorme becomes convinced that their minds and desires are merging.

In *The Black Room* (1971), W. demonstrates his ability as a deft creator of spy fiction that focuses on experiments with sense deprivation. Though the protagonist finds ways of overcoming long-term sense deprivation, the novel becomes a metaphor for human ways of combating and surviving the darkness of the existential abyss. W. also produced several well-wrought police procedural novels in the 1970s and 1980s; recent works include *The Personality Surgeon* (1985) and *The Magician from Siberia* (1988); the first is about a Faustian pact between a doctor and an evil tycoon and the second is a nonfiction novel about the life of Rasputin.

W.'s more recent accomplishments are in the area of science fiction in his *Spider World* series (1987–92); they present the protagonist Niall's battle with an army of giant spiders that is trying to occupy the earth. Few authors can boast the publication of over one hundred books or of literary occupations ranging through novelist, detective writer, fantasy and science fiction novelist, historian and social scientist.

BIBLIOGRAPHY: Dossor, H. F., *C. W.* (1990); Tredel, N., *The Novels of C. W.* (1982); Weigel, J. A., *C. W.* (1975); Wilson, C., *Voyage to a Beginning: An Intellectual Autobiography* (1969)

PATRICK MEANOR

WILSON, John

(pseud: Christopher North) b. 18 May 1785, Paisley, Scotland; d. 3 April 1854, Edinburgh, Scotland

W. published numerous articles in *Blackwood's Magazine* under the pseudonym "Christopher North." Educated at Magdalen College, Oxford, where he won the Newdigate Prize for poetry, W. inherited an estate and an income aged twenty-two, but lost his fortune in 1815. In 1812, he had published *The Isle of Palms,* a volume of poetry, followed by *The City of the Plague* (1816). He read law and was called to the Scottish bar, beginning to write and edit for *Blackwood's* in 1817. A confirmed Tory, he was in 1820 elected to the chair of moral philosophy at Edinburgh University, which left him ample leisure, since he commissioned a friend to write his lectures for him. In 1834, he contributed over fifty articles to the magazine. He wrote three novels, *Lights and Shadows of Scottish Life* (1822), *The Trials of Margaret Lyndsay* (1823), and *The Foresters* (1825), described by William WORDSWORTH as "mawkish." The three-volume *Recreations of Christopher North* appeared in 1842.

WILSON, Thomas

b. 1525, Lincolnshire; d. 16 June 1581, London

An uncompromising Protestant who served ELIZABETH I as chief interrogator of insurgents, as ambassador to the Netherlands, and finally as Secretary of State, the Cambridge-educated W. wrote the most important rhetorical manual of the 16th c., *The Arte of Rhetorique* (1553). W.'s treatise is justly celebrated for its comprehensiveness. There had been two English rhetorical manuals published in the early 16th c., but *The Arte of Rhetorique* is the first to examine all five parts of Ciceronian rhetoric: invention, disposition, style, memory, and utterance. Moreover, whereas the earlier manuals were intended primarily for Latin students, W. wrote for any reader of English who could benefit from instruction in writing and speaking. The precepts that W. lays out are drawn almost entirely from Aristotle, Cicero, and Quintilian. In his section on invention, which takes up two-thirds of the treatise, W. departs from most rhetoricians since Cicero by expanding his discussion of rhetorical proofs to include a consideration of ethical, aesthetic, and pathetic proofs. In his discussion of style, W. famously condemns grossly inflated diction, the "inkhorn terms" that obscure rather than clarify the writer's meaning. W. is especially critical of the use of foreign idioms and phrases in English contexts. For W., the effective communicator must strive to be neither "overfine" nor "overcareless." Much of the section on style consists of an exhaustive analysis of tropes, rhetorical schemes, and exempla.

W., who firmly believed that verbal persuasion makes civilization possible, had considerable success in his self-appointed task of bringing classical rhetoric to England. Expanded by W. in 1560, *The Arte of Rhetorique* was reprinted eight times before the end of the 16th c. It became standard reading in the universities, and it enjoyed great popularity at the royal court. Scholars generally agree that the treatise played a significant role in the development of English literature. W.'s call for the use of common vernacular words was particularly influential in the late 16th and early 17th cs.

W. wrote several other major works. *The Rule of Reason* (1551; rev. eds., 1552, 1553) is the first manual of logic in English. Printed seven times in the last half of the 16th c., it is a distinctly humanist work that for the most part rejects the scholastic approach to logic that had prevailed in universities during the High Middle Ages. In his role as one of Elizabeth's main counselors, W. strongly supported English intervention in the Netherlands on behalf of the Protestants who were battling Philip II of Spain. In an attempt to persuade the queen that joining the conflict was necessary for England's survival, W. produced a fine translation from the Greek of the *Orations of Demosthenes* (1570)—orations in which the Athenian statesman pleads with his fellow Athenians to assist the Olynthians against Philip II of Macedonia, who he felt threatened Greek independence. *A Discourse upon Usurye* (1572) presents a dialogue between a merchant, a lawyer, a civilian, and a preacher. After lengthy and at times highly technical arguments addressing both sides of the issue, the preacher wins over the lawyer and the merchant to his position that usury is unequivocally evil.

Like his fellow humanists Thomas ELYOT and Roger Ascham, W. championed the English language. He wrote all of his works in English, and, in the preface to the *Rule of Reason*, he harshly criticizes those who would have learning "hidden" in Greek and Latin. The most abstruse concepts, he asserts, can be expressed gracefully in English. W.'s prose style is, above all, clear and concise, free of the affectation and pedantry that he so passionately denounced in his most famous work.

BIBLIOGRAPHY: Howell, W. S., *Logic and Rhetoric in England 1500–1700* (1956); Medine, P. E., *T. W.* (1986); Mueller, J., *The Native Tongue and the Word: Developments in English Prose Style 1380–1580* (1984); Vos, A., "Humanistic Standards of Diction in the Inkhorn Controversy," *SP* 73 (1976): 376–96

T. D. DRAKE

WINCHILSEA, Anne Finch, Countess of

b. Anne Kingsmill, April 1661, Sidmonton; d. 5 August 1720, London

The literary reputation of W. was established during her lifetime. Her admirers included Matthew PRIOR, Nicholas ROWE, Alexander POPE, and Jonathan SWIFT. After her death, her fame gradually declined until she was rediscovered by William WORDSWORTH, who appreciated her nature imagery and anthologized some of her verse. After the Romantic period, her reputation once more waned, but she has again received attention with the upsurge of interest in early women writers.

Born into a well-to-do royalist family, W. lost both parents during her childhood. Little is known about succeeding circumstances, except that her father left instructions providing for a good education for her. At twenty-one, she became maid of honor to Mary of Modena, wife of James, Duke of York (later James II). Mary, fluent in several languages and concerned with art, music, and literature, encouraged the education and literary endeavors of her attendants. In Mary's court, W. became friends with two other maids of honor who would eventually publish—Sarah Churchill and Anne Killigrew. She also met and eventually married Heneage Finch, gentleman of the bedchamber of the Duke of York. Many of her poems testify to the happiness of this marital union.

Sympathetic to the Stuart court, the couple supported James after his accession and after his deposition refused to take the oath of allegiance to William and Mary. Severing themselves from court, they eventually settled at a family estate in Kent where they found not only a refuge from political strife but a pastoral setting conducive to W.'s writing and a coterie of friends who encouraged and supported her work.

W. wrote in a wide range of genres on a variety of subjects. Her speaker, Ardelia, signals the literary influence wielded by the earlier poet, Katharine PHILIPS, since it is the name of a figure in Philips's Society of Friends. Like Phillips, W. had a circle of literary supporters and wrote of friendship, of her relationship to other women and women writers. Poems like W.'s "Friendship between Ephelia and Ardelia" make clear the way Phillips set a literary precedent. In addition to dealing with personal relationships, W.'s poetry takes on social issues relevant to women. She laments society's concern for the superficial to the exclusion of women's intellectual accomplishments and their relegation to domestic affairs. She not only delineates the criticism and obstacles faced by women authors who are disdained as presumptuous intruders upon a male domain but also lauds female role models from the past, like the biblical Deborah.

W. also wrote about melancholy, a condition from which she suffered. "Ardelia to Melancholy" deals with futile attempts to banish depression through mirth and music, through friendship, and through writing, finally concluding that only heaven can set her free. One of her best-known poems, the Pindaric ode *The Spleen* (1709), describes the mood swings and insomnia of the afflicted melancholic. Because many of W.'s poems focus on nature, she has been viewed as a precursor of the Romantic movement. "A Nocturnal Reverie" with its detailed observations of the pastoral world or "The Petition for an Absolute Retreat" make understandable Wordsworth's later appreciation of her.

In addition to Scriptural paraphrases and numerous adaptations of fables from Aesop and La Fontaine, W. also wrote two blank-verse dramas, *Triumphs of Love and Innocence*, about two sets of lovers, and the heroic tragedy *Aristomenes; or, The Royal Shepherd*, published in 1713. In her dramas, W. readily acknowledged the influence of Philips, the first woman to have a play professionally staged in Britain.

The substantial body of her work, the formal and topical range of her material, her link through Philips to a previous generation and through Wordsworth to a later literary period, her noteworthy subjects, especially her concern with issues regarding women in general and women writers in particular attest to the importance of her inclusion in the literary canon.

BIBLIOGRAPHY: Hinnant, C. H., *The Poetry of A. F.* (1994); McGovern, B., *A. F. and Her Poetry* (1992)

FRANCES M. MALPEZZI

WINSTANLEY, Gerrard

b. October? 1609, Wigan, Lancashire; d. September? 1676, London

The significance of W. derives from the brief period of 1648–51 when, during the high point of the Puritan Revolution against Charles I, he attempted to establish an agrarian commune in Surrey with an association named the Diggers, and published a number of visionary and radical pamphlets in support of this campaign. While much of his life is undocumented and his writing was neglected for centuries, he has since been reclaimed as a writer in a tradition of radical Protestant dissent including John BUNYAN and George Fox and also a precursor of communist political thought.

W. was baptised in Wigan, Lancashire, in 1609; the son of a mercer. He began an apprenticeship under Sarah Gater of the Merchant Taylors' Company, who also possessed an extensive library that W. may have used. Tellingly, apprenticeship was one social institu-

tion he would later support in print. By 1643, he had sworn the solemn League and Covenant in support of Parliament and been bankrupted as a merchant. According to his later testimony *The Saints Paradice* (1648?), the mid-1640s was a period of spiritual crisis. W. emerged in print in 1648 producing five pamphlets of "experimental" Christianity and millenarian typology, similar to other radical Puritan writing of the period. In April 1649, W. and his comrades published *The True Levellers' Standard Advanced*, a defense of a commune started on common land at St. George's Hill: Diggers were called "true" Levellers as a radicalizing of the existing Leveller group in the parliamentary army. The next seven pamphlets, including *A Declaration from the Poor Oppressed People of England* (1649), were rapidly written defenses of the commune presented to the army and Parliament as it struggled against local opposition and was forced to move to Cobham. *Fire in the Bush* (1650) was a return to religious meditation. W.'s last work, *The Law of Freedom in Platform*, dated October 1651 and dedicated to Oliver Cromwell, is a more systematic economic program for a model commonwealth after the final disintegration of the communal experiment. W.'s radicalism had ebbed by the end of the decade and he returned to the Church of England and respectability after the Restoration.

Although W.'s texts are ostensibly addressing specific institutional readerships, and some of the typological arguments attest to a popular religious context that is now remote, they also use a plain prose style with a powerful symbolic framework. Earthly, kingly power associated with Adam and the clergy is a usurpation of an original right reason and liberty founded upon revelation. According to W., "England is a prison . . . the lawyers are jailors, and the poor men are the prisoners." In opposition to this "The work of digging, being freedom or the appearance of Christ in the earth, hath tried the priests and professors to the uttermost." W. advocates a commonwealth where the earth's resources are enjoyed as a common treasury and scholastic knowledge is replaced by technical artisanship where the people "work together, eat bread together."

The Digger movement was unsuccessful and left no immediate legacy in Britain. W.'s reputation has instead been a project of modernity's rereading of the Civil War period since the 19th c. For some, W.'s communism prefigured an implicitly secular precursor of modern socialism in its celebration of revolutionary liberty. Other critics would stress the essentially Puritan and eschatological dimension of his writing and its authoritarian potential, especially in the disciplinary proposals of his last work. In this regard, W. is bound up with ongoing debates about the ideological basis of the English Revolution: topics that should be addressed in a forthcoming scholarly edition of his works. He endures as one of the most evocative radical prose writers of the period.

BIBLIOGRAPHY: Bradstock, A., *W. and the Diggers 1649–1999* (2000); Rogers, J., *The Matter of Revolution: Science, Poetry, and Politics in the Age of Milton* (1996); Sabine, G. H., ed., *The Works of G. W.* (1941)

J. M. TINK

WINTERSON, Jeanette

b. 27 August 1959, Manchester

W. is a novelist and essayist who, over the course of her fictional works, has sharply divided critics between those who admire her unconventional narrative style and imaginative audacity, and those who view her ruthless stylistic experimentation as self-indulgent rhetoric. A writer who self-consciously explores objective reality, W. has always had a high media profile and recent years have seen an increasing academic interest in her work. Her novels interrogate history, explore issues of truth and representation, and show a postmodern concern with the relationship between the text and the reader; many feature outsider characters who succeed against the odds; all have at their heart the timeless emotional themes of love, loss, desire, and estrangement.

W.'s debut, *Oranges Are Not the Only Fruit* (1985), won the Whitbread Award for a first novel and was successfully adapted by her for television. Drawing on her evangelistic upbringing and the realization of her lesbian identity, the book is often read as AUTOBIOGRAPHY, but it would be truer to say, perhaps, that the author reinvented herself as a fictional character, and that W.'s authorial voice can be heard as strongly in each of her works. Despite its themes of religious obsession, sex, and exile, and its vivid depiction of a world in which everything is "a symbol of the Great Struggle between good and evil," there are a sympathy and light-heartedness about *Oranges Are Not the Only Fruit* that make it all the more moving. W.'s particular sense of fun and literary playfulness was further developed in her next book, *Boating for Beginners* (1985), a comic fable based on the story of Noah. Although W. subsequently claimed to regret publishing it, this surreal rewriting of the Book of Genesis is an intriguing exploration of the power of myth.

W.'s own evangelism is geared toward the importance of love. In her next two novels, she uses history as a means of creating a world in which to explore it—a world free of the conventional assumptions of time and narratorial identity, in which language flourishes and words are living things. *The Passion* (1987) is a bawdy historical fantasy that centers on Henri, a French peasant who worships Napoleon, becomes his chicken chef, and falls in love with a bisexual Vene-

tian girl with webbed feet; it is a beautiful meditation on the "unfulfillable condition of humanity," and it possesses a genuine feeling for magic and mystery, not least the mysteries of a love that is viewed as destiny rather than choice. The novel's refrain—"I'm telling you stories. Trust me."—encapsulates W.'s general premise that history and storytelling are not always separable, that fact and fiction share a common ground as discourse: for her, fiction is where truth and lies meet.

Similarly, *Sexing the Cherry* (1989) is a Gothic farce that explores the tenuousness of reality in an impressively confident retelling of the fairy tale of the twelve dancing princesses. Dazzling in its exuberance, the book is set predominantly in the 17th c. and bears poetic witness to the strange and the fabulous, from the first banana to the Civil War and the execution of Charles I. Its central characters, the Dog Woman and her adopted son Jordan, fished from the Thames as a baby, are quite brilliantly imagined.

In *Written on the Body* (1992), W. turned her attention to the dynamics of a triangular relationship in a radical, contemporary love story, told by a subversive Lothario whose gender remains undeclared. The book is a highly individual expression of a universal emotion that reassesses power relations between the sexes and dissects the clichés that too often cloud what she was to refer to in a later novel as "the strange story of you and I"; intense and erotic, it shows the extent to which W. is capable of delivering prose that is deceptively simple and searingly truthful, which strips love and passion down to the bare bones and which has an inclusive humanity about it.

That directness is evident, too, in *Art and Lies* (1994), but here it blends with W. at her excessive worst. Three separate voices, Handel, Picasso, and Sappho, separately flee a London of the near future and find themselves on the same train, drawn to one another through the curious agency of a book. Stories within stories take the reader into a world of lyrical beauty that is, alas, marred by frequently impenetrable prose: paragraphs of Latin, German, and French; fragments of opera; and linguistic twists that feel uncharacteristically contrived.

When W. is at her best, very few novelists can match her ability to manipulate language and metaphysical conceit. *Gut Symmetries* (1997), arguably her finest work, is a funny and eclectic celebration of love, set in New York, Liverpool, and on board the QE2. Its heroine is a physicist, and the principles of quantum physics provide W. with a vibrant metaphor for the instability of identity once a "rogue element" like desire enters the equation. In *The. PowerBook* (2000), it is the turn of the computer to act as a vehicle for exploring what we mean when we talk about love; chapters like "Open Hard Drive" unfold the life of an e-mail writer who supplies interactive stories to customers, offering them freedom for just one night through the power of the imagination. In this balancing of truth and fantasy, in the notion that one life is never enough, there are echoes of that ultimate transformational text, Virginia WOOLF's *Orlando;* however, because its narrative is forced and restless, because it confuses fiction with polemic, *The. Power-Book* is almost a parody of W.'s earlier books in which magical realism becomes a rehashing of myths and legends, sex becomes a clinical coupling of DNA, and love becomes an obsession with the emotion itself.

In addition to her novels, W. has published a screenplay, *Great Moments in Aviation* (1994), and an eloquent and inspiring volume of literary and cultural criticism, *Art Objects: Essays on Ecstasy and Effrontery* (1995). She is a subversive writer, whose complex, multilayered narratives provoke deeply felt and divergent reactions; undeniably, though, she is a generous and thoughtful novelist whose greatest achievement is, perhaps, to bring emotional substance to the novel of ideas.

BIBLIOGRAPHY: Grice, H., and T. Woods, eds., *'I'm Telling You Stories': J. W. and the Politics of Reading* (1998); Harris, A. L., *Other Sexes: Rewriting Difference from Woolf to W.* (2000)

NICOLA UPSON

WITHER, George

b. 1588, Bentworth, Hampshire; d. 2 May 1667, London

The career of W. presents a peculiar problem to the literary historian. Protestant belief that all God's people are prophets was used in the early Reformation to justify the liberty of nonestablishment clergy to speak out on religious matters without episcopal approval or threat of prosecution. Thus, William Perkins's *Art of Prophecying,* translated from Latin in 1607, not only instructs preachers how to deliver sermons with the enthusiasm that allows the congregation to feel the presence of the Holy Spirit, but proves an early, highly qualified argument in favor of freedom of speech. Parliament's check upon episcopal power in the events leading up to, and during, the Civil War, however, raised a different issue regarding inspiration. W. is one of a generation of nonclerical writers who give every evidence of believing themselves to be divinely inspired and of expecting both government and citizenry to heed their pronouncements. W. is possibly the only poet in English tradition who believed himself to be literally inspired by God rather than metaphorically inspired by a muse. The uneven quality of his poetry, and several scandals attached to his personal life, however, made it unlikely that he would receive from either his contemporaries or posterity the respect that he felt he deserved.

Although educated at Magdalen College and subsequently at Lincoln's Inn, W. left Oxford without taking a degree and never seriously practiced law. His early publications were Spenserian pastorals and panegyrics for the royal family, which suggests that initially he looked to follow the traditional path of poetic preferment. With *Abuses Stript and Whipt* (1613), however, W. identified himself as a prophet compelled by "the Voice" to speak out on national affairs (he attributed a plague that ravaged London, for example, to divine displeasure with Charles's reliance upon the unpopular Buckingham), a role that he would continue in such works as *Britain's Remembrancer* (1628), *Furor-Poeticus (i.e.) Propheticus* (1660), *Ecchoes from the Sixth Trumpet* (1666), and *Fragmenta Prophetica* (1669). Holding that "A sacred *Fury* hath possest my braines," W. recognized that others might mistake his "raptures" as the utterances of a "Madman or Phanatick" (as, indeed, his governing metaphor of "fury" allowed them to do), and that there was danger in speaking out on public affairs (he was twice imprisoned for his comments). Even while repeatedly imploring "th'Almighties ayd" for the courage needed to speak "with boldness" and assure the "Countries welfare," he resigned himself that a prophet is never appreciated in his own time and place.

Although not a few of his readers found W.'s foretellings justified by subsequent events, W.'s litigious nature, coupled with possibly apocryphal scandals attached to his name, suggest how difficult most of his contemporaries found it to take him seriously. He unsuccessfully sued the Stationers' Company to enforce a patent ordering that his metrical psalms be bound with every copy of the popular Thomas STERNHOLD and John HOPKINS. For a number of years, he daily petitioned Parliament for the sequestered land of royalist supporters, particularly those of Sir John DENHAM, who—in an earlier reversal of fortune such as marked the Civil War—reportedly spared W.'s life to ensure that the title of worst living poet did not devolve upon him. And whether the story of his clowning in the royal coronation robes after the capture and trial of Charles I is true or not, it suggests how weak people believed his judgment to be. He died in straitened circumstances without help from the restored Stuarts, whose praise he had begun his career by singing, or any of the parliamentary survivors whose cause he had so ardently advanced.

W. should be remembered as a strong example of the biblical ethos that emerged in 17th-c. popular culture. His *A Preparation to the Psalter* (1619) is a well-argued appreciation of the poetic qualities of the Psalms, which he hopes would function as the model for all poetic effort. He provided metrical paraphrases of the Psalms himself, as well as volumes of hymns. And with Francis QUARLES, he helped institute the vogue in emblem poetry that asked the reader to sharpen his or her spiritual vision and hone one's interpretation of written and visual texts. Most importantly, he advanced a biblically founded authority for the poet to speak out on political affairs, developing the idea of the poet as the conscience of his society.

BIBLIOGRAPHY: Hensley, C. S., *The Later Career of G. W.* (1969); Norbrook, D., "Leveling Poetry: G. W. and the English Revolution," *ELR* 21 (Spring 1991): 217–56; Pritchard, A., "G. W.: The Poet as Prophet," *SP* 59 (April 1962): 211–30

RAYMOND-JEAN FRONTAIN

WODEHOUSE, [Sir] P[elham] G[renville]

b. 15 October 1881, London; d. 14 February 1975, Southhampton, New York, U.S.A.

One of the most prolific of 20th-c. writers, W. produced a never-ending stream of comic novels, short stories, books and lyrics for musicals, translations of Central European plays, and poems for humorous magazines. Caught in France, and then in Germany, at the beginning of World War II, W. was tempted to write and broadcast to the then neutral U.S. a series of light-hearted essays on his predicament, naively failing to realize how this would be taken in wartime Britain. So astonished, distressed, and indeed terrified was he by the British reaction (there were vicious press campaigns and even threats of prosecution for High Treason, a capital offense in British law) that he spent almost the whole of his many remaining years in America—which had, in fact, been his adoptive second home since early in the century. Most of his celebrated stories of English middle- and upper-class life first appeared in the *Saturday Evening Post,* and he collaborated on musicals with composers of the caliber of Jerome Kern (whom he had first met in London); the lyrics of the famous song "Bill" in Kern and Oscar Hammerstein II's *Show Boat* are W.'s work.

W. is best remembered for his novels and short stories, told in a misleadingly bland and matter-of-fact tone that pulls off the difficult feat of being able to time a joke in print, of a sort of Never-Never-England: a country where a young man whose innocent politeness may have been mistaken for a proposal is honor-bound to proceed to marriage unless he can find means to induce the young woman to break off the supposed engagement, and where a magistrate is supposedly entitled to convene his court wherever he happens to be and sentence anyone around to imprisonment or fine. This world is chronicled in several linked series of novels and short stories: the golfing stories concerning the Oldest Member of the club; tales of Mr. Mulliner, tale-teller of the Angler's Rest public house about his nephew who is a Hollywood scriptwriter (an opportunity for W. to work off some

animus regarding one of the least-enjoyed periods of his own career); the aspirations and misfortunes of con-man cum entrepreneur Stanley Featherstonehaugh Ukridge; the attempts of the Earl of Emsworth of Blandings Castle to evade the henpecking of his sister Lady Constance, the misplaced gallantries of his society-loving younger brother The Honourable Galahad Threepwood, the frequent financial and amatory disasters of his feckless son Freddie and the officious attentions of his secretary the Efficient Baxter and his dour Scottish gardener McAllister, in order to attend to the true business and delight of his life, the raising and preparation for competition of his prize-winning pig the Empress of Blandings.

Probably the most popular sequence is that comprising the unreliable narrations of Bertram Wooster, wealthy but foolish cadet of a noble family, and his impeccable and indispensable manservant Jeeves, whose intelligence and resource are constantly called upon to rescue his master from many a disastrous scrape. Bertram is surrounded also by numbers of exigent aunts, most prominent among whom are Mrs. Dahlia Travers, a "good egg" who shares many of her nephew's tastes and interests but has a habit of landing him with distasteful tasks of a social nature, and the contrasting Aunt Agatha who, according to her nephew's suspicions, chews broken bottles and sacrifices babies at dark of the moon. Although the background to the stories alters with contemporary events (the Wooster stories, for instance, continued uninterrupted from the First World War to well after the Second), the characters never age or change. The story-cycles, those already mentioned and others concerning Uncle Fred (an ingenious peer of the realm whose good-natured machinations on his inept nephew's behalf are narrated by the young man himself), and Psmith whose success dated from the time he adopted this spelling to lend distinction to an otherwise over-familiar name, are largely self-contained and exclusive, though Bertram does once mention having met Gally Threepwood, brother of Lord Emsworth of the Blandings stories, at his favorite haunt, the Drones Club.

Honored with a knighthood by the queen shortly before his death, former controversies and misunderstandings forgotten or forgiven, W. remarked with typical self-deprecatory wit that, now he was Sir Pelham and his waxwork was in Madame Tussaud's famous exhibition, he had nothing more to wish for.

BIBLIOGRAPHY: Dold, B. E., *Edwardian Fall-Out: The Ironic School* (1972); Edwards, O. D., *P. G. W.* (1977); Thompson, K., *Wooster Proposes, Jeeves Disposes* (1992); Usborne, R., *W. at Work to the End* (1977); Usborne, R., *A W. Companion* (1981); Wind, H. W., *The World of P. G. W.* (1981)

MICHAEL GROSVENOR MYER

WOLCOT, John

(pseud: Peter Pindar) bap. 9 May 1738, Dodbrooke; d. 14 January 1819, London

So successful were W.'s satires at the end of the 18th c. that in the winter of 1793–94 the publishers Robinson, Goulding, and Walker bought W.'s copyrights for an annual pension of £250. Written under the name Peter Pindar, his verses addressed whatever was in the news of the moment. This topicality guaranteed popularity in W.'s day and oblivion thereafter.

W.'s first book, *Persian Love Elegies* (1773), imitated William COLLINS's *Persian Eclogues*. But W. soon turned to satire with *The Noble Criketers* and *A Poetical, Supplicating, Modest and Affecting Epistle to Those Literary Colossuses, the Reviewers* (both 1778). In 1781, W. moved from Truro to London with his protege, painter John Opie. Himself a talented amateur painter, W. published a series of genial satires prompted by the annual exhibitions at the Royal Academy: *Lyric Odes to the Royal Academicians* (1782–85), published in three volumes, and a fourth volume entitled *Farewell Odes* (1786). W. apportioned praise and blame, urging artists to follow the bent of their genius.

James BOSWELL's *Journal of a Tour to the Hebrides* provoked from W. a mock-encomium (*A Poetical and Congratulatory Epistle to James Boswell, Esq.*, 1786), and when Hester Thrale [PIOZZI] published her *Anecdotes of the Late Doctor Johnson* W. poked fun at both biographers in *Bozzy and Piozzi* (1786), a clever pastiche of Johnsonian anecdote that is one of W.'s best pieces. In *A Complimentary Epistle to James Bruce, Esq.* (1790), W. again used a mock encomium to question the veracity of Bruce's *Travels to Discover the Source of the Nile* (1790).

W. mocked artists, writers, publishers, and scientists like Sir Joseph Banks, president of the Royal Society from 1778 to 1820, but his chief targets were George III and his long-time prime minister William Pitt the Younger. Any act, however trivial, could provide the pretext for a poem. Indeed, the more trivial the behavior, the more likely W. was to pounce on it. W.'s best-known work *The Lousiad* (5 vols., 1785–95) is a mock heroic poem in five cantos inspired by George III's discovering a louse on his dinner plate and consequently ordering that all members of the kitchen staff have their heads shaved.

W.'s attacks on king and minister did not reflect sympathy with the revolutionary or reformist tendencies of the period. W. criticized Thomas Paine (*Odes to Mr. Paine*, 1791) and the French Revolution (*The Remonstrance*, 1791) with equal vigor. Rather, W. consistently advocated the neoclassical values of reason, moderation, decorum, and common sense, pointing out violations wherever he saw them.

A master caricaturist, he captured in his witty lines the follies of the day. There they remain, like flies in amber, for anyone seeking a humorous glimpse of England in the later 18th and early 19th cs.

BIBLIOGRAPHY: Girtin, T., *Doctor with Two Aunts: A Biography of Peter Pindar* (1959); Vales, R. L., *Peter Pindar (J. W.)* (1973)

JOSEPH ROSENBLUM

WOLLSTONECRAFT, Mary [Godwin]

b. 27 April 1759, London; d. 10 September 1797, London

Recognized today as England's first major feminist writer, W. has suffered from vicissitudes in her reputation since her death over two hundred years ago. Celebrated in her own day as a powerful advocate of freedom both for mankind in general and for women in particular, she was reviled by the conservative press after she died, when the scandalous events of her life became public knowledge. The resulting collapse of her reputation meant that it was almost a century before feminists felt able cautiously to acknowledge the contribution of her ideas to their developing ideology. Even in the first half of the 20th c., her admirers found it necessary to apologize for the unconventionality of her lifestyle. It was only in the 1960s, with the emergence of feminist literary studies, that the importance of her work was fully acknowledged.

Born into a moderately wealthy middle-class family, W. spent her early years in London. As her father increasingly squandered his inheritance, the family became rootless, moving between various rented homes around the country. No money was available for schooling the daughters of the family, and W. was forced to educate herself through reading. At the age of nineteen, she left home and spent several unhappy years in a variety of occupations: lady's companion, schoolteacher, seamstress, and governess. She also tried her hand at writing, and her first book, *Thoughts on the Education of Daughters* (1787), brought her into contact with the radical London publisher Joseph Johnson, who offered her work as a translator and editor. Through Johnson, W. entered the circle of radical intellectuals that included the philosopher William GODWIN and the political writer Thomas Paine. By 1793, having written two successful political works, and suffering from the effects of an unrequited passion, she moved to revolutionary Paris, where she entered into a relationship with Gilbert Imlay, an American businessman. After the birth of their daughter, Imlay became increasingly distant and, after following him to London, W. twice attempted suicide. She regained happiness and stability through a new relationship, with Godwin, whom she married when she discovered herself to be pregnant. Complications followed the birth of her daughter Mary (later to marry the poet Percy Bysshe SHELLEY), and W. died of a puerperal infection ten days later at the age of thirty-eight.

It was in the wake of the French Revolution that W., who until then had been learning her craft by experimenting in a variety of genres from adult fiction to didactic educational works, first found her own distinctive voice. Her *Vindication of the Rights of Men* (1790), one of a number of replies to an antirevolutionary pamphlet by the politician Edmund BURKE, placed her firmly on the radical side of contemporary political thought. The success of this publication led her on to what has become her most celebrated work, *A Vindication of the Rights of Woman* (1792). Taking as her starting point the revolutionary rhetoric of the day, which asserted the "natural rights" of all mankind, she took the argument a stage further and applied it to that half of the human race, women, who, she rightly pointed out, had been deprived of any legal, political, or moral rights since the beginning of history. One of her most controversial points was the fundamental premise that, so far as the ability to reason was concerned, men and women were equal. Femininity, which her society equated with weakness and ignorance, was in her view a social construct, and one for which she blamed a faulty educational system. While men were educated to make their own way in the world, the sole purpose of female education was, she said, to make girls attractive to the opposite sex. She pleaded for a reformed system, one that would enable women to think independently, and suggested that they could be trained for professions such as medicine and business.

During her stay in Paris, W. wrote *An Historical and Moral View of the Origin and Progress of the French Revolution* (1794), which, as the title suggests, combined a history of recent events with her own commentary. The work is notable for its demonstration of her difficulty in maintaining her optimistic view of the Revolution in the light of the Reign of Terror that was sweeping through France even as she was writing. Her next book, *Letters Written During a Short Residence in Sweden, Norway, and Denmark* (1796), has been much admired. Based on an actual journey undertaken on Imlay's behalf, the work combines social observation with reflection and AUTOBIOGRAPHY, and touchingly reveals W.'s deep unhappiness as she struggled to come to terms with her lover's desertion. In the last year of her life, she began a novel, *Maria; or, The Wrongs of Woman*. A highly politicized work, it set out to demonstrate in fictional form the many legal and social injustices imposed on women by a male-dominated society. The novel remained unfinished at W.'s death, and was published by her widower as part of a four-volume edition of her *Posthumous Works* in 1798.

A pioneering writer, notable for the way in which she based her intellectual arguments firmly in her own personal experience, W. undeniably made an important contribution to the history of ideas of her period.

BIBLIOGRAPHY: Butler, M., and J. Todd, eds., *The Works of M. W.* (7 vols, 1989); Jump, H. D., *M. W.* (1994); Todd, J., *M. W.* (2000); Tomalin, C., *The Life and Death of M. W.* (1974; rev. ed., 1992)

HARRIET DEVINE JUMP

WOOD, Anthony [or Anthony à Wood]

b. 17 December 1632, Oxford; d. 28 November 1695, Oxford

W.'s schooling was interrupted by the Civil War, but he entered Merton College, Oxford, in 1647. In 1655, he took his master's degree and published a volume of sermons by his late elder brother, Edward. Stimulated by Sir William Dugdale's *The Antiquities of Warwickshire* (1656), W. began systematically to copy monumental inscriptions and to search for antiquities in the neighborhood of Oxford. Much damage had been done during the war. W. went through the Christ Church registers and later steadily investigated the records of all the colleges, then the registers of the whole university and in 1674 published *Historia et Antiquitates Universitatis Oxoniensis* (*The History and Antiquities of the University of Oxford*) in two volumes, the first devoted to the university in general, the second to individual colleges. W. received much unacknowledged help from John AUBREY. In 1667, W. went to London to look at the Cottonian library and the Tower of London documents. W.'s great work was *Athenae Oxoniensis: an Exact History of all the Writers and Bishops who have had their Education in the University of Oxford from 1500 to 1690, to which are added the Fasti, or Annals for the said time* (2 vols., 1691–92). Henry Hyde objected to a libel on his father, the first Earl of CLARENDON, and W. was expelled from the university in 1693. W. left a diary for the years 1657–95 (5 vols., 1891–1900) and an AUTOBIOGRAPHY. He bequeathed his library to the Ashmolean Museum, Oxford.

WOOD, Charles [Gerald]

b. 6 August 1932, St. Peter Port, Guernsey, Channel Islands

W.'s parents were professional actors in his grandfather's touring company. Educated at Chesterfield Grammar School and King Charles I School, Kidderminster, where his parents ran a theater, and where W. worked as a child actor, W. took a keen interest in the technics and design. This led him to Birmingham College of Art. From 1950 to 1955, W. was a professional soldier and then worked for two years in a factory. In 1957, he became a stage manager and designer, working with Joan Littlewood's Theatre Workshop.

W.'s experiences have molded his plays and his antiauthoritarianism. His first trilogy, *Cockade* (perf. 1963; pub. 1965) satirized the army at its worst and was followed by *Don't Make Me Laugh* (perf. 1965), showing a soldier at home. The farcical fantasy *Meals on Wheels* was performed the same year. Another triple bill, *Welfare* (perf. 1971), included a shortened version of *Meals,* together with *Labour* and *Tie Up the Ballcock.* This title referred to the official advice on how to modify the plumbing in the event of a nuclear attack. W. has authored some fifty plays, of which among the most interesting are *Fill the Stage with Happy Hours* (perf. 1966; pub. 1967), a tragicomedy set in a small provincial theater, and *Dingo* (perf. 1967; pub. 1969), set in a North African prisoner of war camp, and which debunked the popular heroes of World War II in stylized language and absurdist mode. *H: being, Monologues at Front of Burning Cities* (perf. 1969; pub. 1970) explored General Havelock's conflicts at the time of the relief of Lucknow in the Indian Mutiny: both *Dingo* and *H.* are antiwar tirades. *Veterans; or, Hairs in the Gates of the Hellespont* (1972) was about two actors waiting to be called on to a film set in Turkey. Based on W.'s experience of collaborating with John OSBORNE on *The Charge of the Light Brigade* (1968) and starring the late Sir John Gielgud, it was written partly in verse, and was interpreted as homage to Gielgud. W., however, has written that it is about the loneliness of stardom. *Has "Washington" Legs?* (1978) is also about filmmaking and attacks the dominance of the director. *Red Star* (perf. 1984) is about a Russian actor tempted by stardom and corruption.

W. has written several film scripts, including those for *The Knack* (1965), *Help!* (with Mark Behm, 1965), *How I Won the War* (1967), *The Charge of the Light Brigade, The Long Day's Dying* (1968), and *Wagner* (1983). His television plays include *Prisoner and Escort* (seen originally in *Cockade*), *Drill Pig, Do As I Say*, and *Love Lies Bleeding,* a series called *Don't Forget to Write*, and *Puccini.*

BIBLIOGRAPHY: King, K., "C. W.," in Weintraub, S., ed., *British Dramatists since World War II,* part 2, *DLB* 13 (1982): 571–76; Taylor, J. R., "C. W.," in his *The Second Wave: British Drama for the Seventies* (1971): 59–76

WOOD, Mrs. Henry
b. Ellen Price, 17 January 1814, Worcester; d. 10 February 1887, London

Daughter of a wealthy glove manufacturer, W. was a semi-invalid who married a merchant and banker and moved to France. In 1860, her first novel, *Danesbury House,* won a prize offered for "temperance" (anti-

alcohol) literature, and in 1861 she published in three volumes *East Lynne,* which sold in millions and earned her worldwide fame. The heroine, divorced then deserted by her paramour, disfigured in a railway accident, becomes governess to her own children. Successfully dramatized, the play (though not the novel) contains the poignant line, "Dead, dead and never called me mother!" *Mrs. Halliburton's Troubles* (3 vols., 1862) portrayed W.'s father as the glovemaker Mr. Ashley; the minutiae of the glovemaking industry are solidly and interestingly described. Jane Halliburton is a struggling widow who knows Latin and supports her sons by teaching it. They imbibe her gospel of work and qualify for professions. The setting is Worcester ("Hestonleigh" in several of her novels). *The Channings* (3 vols., 1862) has as backdrop the cathedral and its school. In 1867, W. bought the journal *Argosy,* which had suffered scandal by publishing Charles READE's controversial novel *Griffith Gaunt.* W. used *Argosy* to publish her own work. She deals with Victorian industrial and professional life, often set in her native Worcestershire, forty novels in all, with a Christian bias.

WOODFORDE, James
b. 27 June 1740, Ansford, Somerset; d. 1 January 1803, Weston Longeville, Norfolk

Son of a clergyman, educated at Winchester College and New College, Oxford, W. was a bachelor country parson whose *Diary,* from age eighteen to sixty-two, provides a uniquely detailed picture of English life when most of the population lived in villages. W. describes enormous meals, gossip, folk remedies, charities, hare coursing, cricket matches, and the minutiae of daily life, in unpretentious language. Like many others in that part of the world, he profited by smuggling, untroubled by conscience. Its very triviality is what gives the diary value and interest. Unpublished during his lifetime, the manuscript held in the Bodleian Library, Oxford, has been published in several 20th-c. editions under various titles, including *The Ansford Diary of James Woodforde* and *The Diary of a Country Parson.*

WOOLF, Leonard [Sidney]
b. 25 November 1880, London; d. 14 August 1969, Rodmell, Sussex

A well-rounded man of letters, W. was preeminently a publisher and political figure. Essentially his contributions to literature are in the form of a five-volume AUTOBIOGRAPHY and, indirectly, through the publishing house, Hogarth Press, that he and his wife, novelist Virginia WOOLF, established in 1917. Their press provided an outlet for the early writing of T. S. ELIOT and E. M. FORSTER.

W. was an internationalist and a political liberal. His internationalism was reflected in his political work and writing that underlay elements of the official policy of the League of Nations following World War I and the United Nations following World War II. *After the Deluge: A Study in Communal Psychology* (2 vols., 1931, 1939) and *Quack, Quack!* (1935) are essentially studies of the sort of mob psychology that made Adolf Hitler's Germany possible. In both *Barbarians at the Gate* (1939; repub. as *Barbarians Within and Without*, 1939) and *In Savage Times* (1973), W. warned about the dangers of a divided world. In *The Intelligent Man's Way to Prevent War* (1933), which he edited, W. and other notable internationalists argued the case for international bodies like the League of Nations. *Letters of Leonard Woolf,* published in 1989, contains many items that reveal W.'s dedicated internationalism.

The first three volumes of his autobiography, *Sowing* (1960), *Growing* (1961), and *Beginning Again* (1964), examine W.'s life up to 1918. These early volumes, especially *Sowing*, reflect what it is like to grow up as a politically liberal Jew. W. denied being victimized by anti-Semitism, but in veiled ways contradicts his denials. In both *Sowing* and *Growing,* W. presents interesting information about his education, his intellectually charged years at Cambridge University. W. was also the author of a moving autobiographical novel entitled *The Wise Virgins* (1914).

After graduation, W. was a civil servant in Ceylon from 1904 until 1911. Living in Ceylon made him staunchly anti-imperialist and resulted in his producing his *Stories of the East* (1921) and *Diaries in Ceylon, 1908–1911* (1962). His Ceylon experience also helped to inform W.'s anti-imperialist study, *Empire and Commerce in Africa: A Study in Economic Imperialism* (1920).

Beginning Again relates how, on a one-year leave in England in 1911–12, W. renewed his brief, earlier friendship with Virginia Stephen and her sister Vanessa, with whom W. had fallen in love. Vanessa, however, was soon to marry Clive Bell. As the time approached for W. to return to Ceylon, where he was on the fast track to become governor, he grew increasingly attached to Virginia. Finally, when his request for an extension of his leave was denied, he resigned his post and continued his courtship of Virginia, whom he married in September 1912. W. was keenly aware of Virginia's fragile mental state but learned how to comfort her and lend her strength.

This third volume of the autobiography details the literary contacts the Woolfs formed in Bloomsbury during the war years. It tells how they collaborated in establishing the Hogarth Press as the war was reaching its climax. Despite this global conflict, the two lived much of their lives within the relatively insulated atmosphere of their sheltered literary world.

The last two autobiographical volumes, *Downhill All the Way* (1967) and *The Journey Not the Arrival Matters* (1969), both written after Virginia Woolf's suicide in 1941, reflect a sensitive, idealistic man discouraged by the course the world and his life have taken. In *The War for Peace* (1940), W. had accepted Britain's need to enter World War II but was disillusioned that world conflicts could not be settled by more civilized means than combat.

W. is remembered for his work toward establishing worldwide organizations to resolve national conflicts and prevent wars. In his later years, he was not sanguine that such an outcome could occur.

BIBLIOGRAPHY: Marder, H., *The Measure Of Life: Virginia Woolf's Last Years* (2000); Rosenfeld, N., *Outsiders Together: Virginia and L. W.* (2000); Wilson, D., *L. W.* (1978)

R. BAIRD SHUMAN

WOOLF, [Adeline] Virginia

b. 25 January 1882, London; d. 28 March 1941, Sussex

W. is not only one of the most innovative writers of the 20th c., she has become a cultural and feminist icon. Early critics read her innovation in largely stylistic terms, concentrating on her use of stream of consciousness, but the growth of feminist criticism from the 1970s onward meant a shift in focus to W.'s constant engagement with the political and sociocultural environment of her day. This has continued to be a concern of recent criticism, superseding earlier portraits of her as apolitical, concerned only with aesthetics. It now appears that her greatest innovation as a modernist writer lay in the way in which her technical experimentation arose out of and gave voice to her feminist, pacifist, socialist, and anti-imperialist politics.

Born into an upper-middle-class London family, daughter of the editor and writer Sir Leslie STEPHEN, W. was denied a formal education, teaching herself, instead, using the contents of her father's library. Unlike some of her modernist contemporaries who rejected their Victorian heritage, W. remained ambivalent toward her predecessors. She retained, in particular, an interest in the realist novel, and its representation of cultural and social change. Throughout her career, she combined a materialist grounding with experiments of form, narrative, and image. This experimentation included a wide-ranging use of genre (novel, short story, essay, review, letter, memoir, BIOGRAPHY, diary, play), and a frequent interrogation of such categories themselves through hybrid texts, like the fictionalized book-length essay *A Room of One's Own* (1929).

Again, unlike other modernists such as T. S. ELIOT or Ezra Pound, who were antipathetic to the mass, W. was very interested in the "common reader" as her eponymous essay collections (1925 and 1932) suggest, as does her support of adult education through the Workers' Educational Association and Morley College. The image of Mrs. Brown, an ordinary woman in a railway carriage, found in W.'s important essay "Mr. Bennett and Mrs. Brown" (1924) is crucial to her desire to reclaim hidden or forgotten lives, those "lives of the obscure" left out of official narratives. Readings of W. as elitist, only concerned with her own social milieu (such as those by her contemporaries F. R. and Q. D. LEAVIS), miss her complex and hesitant wish to represent positions other than her own. An outsider due to her career as a woman writer and her increasingly outspoken feminist politics, she returned continually to the outsider's view. Her use of narrative techniques such as stream of consciousness or free indirect speech cannot be separated from her desire to represent the lives and thoughts of women: women as subject rather than object.

W.'s essays, short stories, diaries, and letters form as significant a part of her oeuvre as her novels. She began her writing career as a journalist in 1905, after the death of her father, in 1904 and her move from the Kensington of her childhood to Bloomsbury. This unchaperoned life in a bohemian area of London, full of single, working women, as well as the friendship and support of the emergent BLOOMSBURY GROUP, proved influential in her early career. The group's interdisciplinary nature, including painters Roger FRY (whose biography she wrote in 1940) and Duncan Grant, her sister, artist Vanessa BELL, art critic Clive Bell, economist John Maynard KEYNES, influenced much of her thinking, particularly the crossover between visual and verbal representation. Her marriage to ex-colonial administrator, Leonard WOOLF, in 1912, his socialism and anti-imperialism, gave support to her own involvement in the Labour Party and the Women's Co-operative Guild. The Woolfs' founding of the Hogarth Press in 1917 had a major impact on W.'s work, offering her freedoms of content and production. The Press's authors included Eliot, Katherine MANSFIELD, and Sigmund Freud.

Her first novel, *The Voyage Out* (1915), follows its heroine, Rachel Vinrace, on a journey to South America, traces her engagement to Terence Hewet and subsequent death of fever. This novel explores female sexuality and independence and connections between patriarchy and imperialism that will reappear later in W.'s writing. In *Night and Day* (1919), Katherine Hilbery, a woman whose work on a biography of her deceased, poet grandfather stifles her own interest in mathematics, is contrasted with Mary Datchet, a single woman who works for a suffragist organization in Russell Square. W. looks at the options open to women in the context of prewar, urban modernity.

Jacob's Room (1922) begins a period of increased technical experimentation, here used to investigate masculinity and war. Jacob Flanders, as his name suggests, represents the multitude of young men killed in World War I. Jacob, however, consistently resists definition, the female narrator's lack of omniscience emphasizing her exclusion, along with the other women in his life, from his privileged male world at Cambridge. In *Mrs. Dalloway* (1925), W. continues her focus on the war. Set on a June day in 1923, the novel follows shell-shocked veteran Septimus Smith and Clarissa Dalloway, a woman frustrated by her choice of a conventional marriage to a Conservative member of Parliament. Septimus's suicide, his refusal to conform to conventional notions of normality and masculinity, acts as a foil to Clarissa's existence as Mrs. Dalloway, the society wife. Alone in London, however, her thoughts find freedom and expression. This text is at the heart of W.'s fascination with urban culture. She focuses on the outsider's view of London, looking in particular at the freedoms that the city offers women such as Clarissa, as well as its enactment of patriarchal and imperial power.

As Clarissa's daughter, Elizabeth, signals change as she symbolically invades the male province of London on a double-decker bus, so to does Lily in *To the Lighthouse* (1927), the novel that is also in part an elegy to W.'s own parents. Mr. and Mrs. Ramsay represent the conventional, 19th-c marriage, he the head of the family, demanding and petulant, she, self-sacrificing, caring for her husband and children, and various house guests. One such guest, Lily Briscoe, a single woman artist, fights against Mrs. Ramsay's desire that she marry and become an "angel in the house." But, like W., Lily's position is ambivalent. She both adores and resists Mrs. Ramsay. The text culminates with the completion of her painting: Lily's nonfigurative art is simultaneously a new way of seeing and a memorialization of Mrs. Ramsay. The novel depicts the changes wrought by modernity and war, celebrating, in the "Time Passes" section, women's work during the war, as seen in character of Mrs. McNab, the cleaning woman who brings the Ramsay home back from ruin.

W.'s most stylistically experimental text, *The Waves* (1931) consists of a series of dramatic soliloquies from six protagonists, three male (Neville, Bernard, and Louis), three female (Jinny, Susan, and Rhoda). Here, W. abandons her favored narrative technique, free indirect speech, for first-person narration, in order to explore the formation of identity. Essentially plotless, the text charts the periodic reunions of the group of friends and their lives from childhood to old age. The characters rewrite themselves, identities merging and fluctuating, refusing summation.

In the posthumously published *Between the Acts* (1941) set on the eve of World War II, a small village prepares for its annual pageant. The novel interrogates British national identity and the place of art and the artist in the face of war. The pageant form represents national identity and tradition, but its director, Miss LaTrobe, an outsider as a lesbian artist, offers a new Britishness in her unconventional version of the nation's history. The audience become performers as mirrors are turned on them at the close of the pageant, just as the novel exposes fascism at home, most notably in the figure of Giles Oliver.

In 1929, W. published *A Room of One's Own*, one of the most influential feminist texts of the 20th c. Originally given as talks at Newnham and Girton, Cambridge's women's colleges, the text discusses women both as writers and as written. The text calls women to write, but also to "think back through their mothers" to establish a tradition of women writers. Her focus is materialist: William SHAKESPEARE's sister could not overcome the social obstacles put upon her. The woman writer needs space of her own and £500 a year for the independence necessary for freedom of expression.

In 1931, W. conceived of a sequel to *A Room of One's Own* to focus on the sexual life of women. This became *The Pargiters,* an essay-novel, which, never published itself, turned into her novel *The Years* (1937) and her pacifist, antifascist, feminist polemic *Three Guineas* (1938). All through the 1930s, as fascism grew both at home and abroad, W.'s politics became more urgent. She supported various antifascist organizations, and she collected notebooks full of cuttings concerning her growing dismay at the role of women. Reactions to *Three Guineas* were hostile, unsurprisingly given the radical argument W. was expounding: the connections between fascism, militarism, and misogyny. Public tyrannies, she argued, are linked to private ones. The dictator is not only abroad, he is in the private homes of Britain. *The Years* expresses such ideas in fictional form, focusing on the female members of the Pargiter family from 1880 to the "Present Day," and their exclusion from education and employment. Although W. never wrote a conventional AUTOBIOGRAPHY (her memoir "A Sketch of the Past" was the closest she came), she experimented with various forms of life writing. In 1928, she published a mock biography, *Orlando,* a testament to her love affair with Vita SACKVILLE-WEST, as well as a deconstruction of the rigidities of biography, Orlando living through four centuries and changing gender along the way. In *Flush* (1933), W.'s biography of Elizabeth Barrett BROWNING's spaniel, she makes literal the underdog position: the footnote becomes the text. Often overlooked by critics, and viewed merely

as a Woolfian joke, this text is crucial to W.'s 1930s interest in the dictator in the home, and her ongoing resistance to hierarchies of class, gender, location, and pedigree.

On March 28, 1941, W. drowned herself in the river Ouse. She was ill again, an illness that had recurred periodically throughout her life, and her fear of a German invasion had become both obsessive and destructive. She knew too well the implications of Leonard's Jewishness: the Woolfs had planned a joint suicide in the event of invasion. They were indeed on the Gestapo's "Black List." Hers was not the death of an insular aesthete, but the act of one who had written all her life against forms of tyranny and refused to live without the freedom to do so. W. is one of the foremost feminist thinkers and political novelists of the 20th c. In the decades following her death, she gained little critical recognition, but in the 1970s this changed dramatically, particularly in the U.S. Her critical and general readership continues to rise, as new contexts for her work and new editions of her writing appear.

BIBLIOGRAPHY: Beer, G., *V. W.* (1996); Bowlby, R., *Feminist Destinations and Further Essays on V. W.* (1997); Hussey, M., ed., *V. W. and War* (1991); Lee, H., *V. W.* (1996); Marcus, J., *V. W. and the Languages of Patriarchy* (1987); Peach, L., *V. W.* (2000); Roe, S., and S. Sellers, eds., *The Cambridge Companion to V. W.* (2000); Silver, B. R., *V. W. Icon* (1999); Snaith, A., *V. W.* (2000); Zwerdling, A., *V. W. and the Real World* (1986)

ANNA SNAITH

WORDSWORTH, Dorothy

b. 25 December 1771, Cockermouth; d. 25 January 1855, Rydal Mount

Orphaned early and reared separately, William WORDSWORTH and his sister Dorothy were deeply attached. After living with various relatives, she made her home with William in 1795 and after his marriage in 1802 she lived with him and his wife. "She gave me eyes, she gave me ears," said the poet. She began her journal on January 20, 1798, the year of *Lyrical Ballads*, and in September of that year she left for Germany with William and Samuel Taylor COLERIDGE, a partial account of which journey was published in 1897. On May 14, 1800, she began the "Grasmere Journal" for William, who was away from home. She abandoned it at the end of the year and resumed on January 1, 1802, closing on January 11, 1803. Coleridge described her as "simple, ardent, expressive," as William's "exquisite sister . . . her eye watchful in minutest observation of nature." W. in her diaries intersperses with accounts of humdrum activities such as laundry, mending clothes, and growing vegetables, precise and delicate observations of people, some speaking the local dialect, scenery, birds, and flowers. She mentions copying out Italian poems, studying German, reading Geoffrey CHAUCER and Edmund SPENSER aloud, ironing, breadmaking, and cooking giblet pie, walks lasting four and five hours, and hearing "dearest" Coleridge ("Great Boils upon his neck") read "Christabel." We hear the charming prattle of Coleridge's small son Hartley [COLERIDGE].

On Friday, October 3, 1800, W. and William on a walk met an old man, "bent almost double," with an "interesting" face, dark eyes, and a long nose, wearing a coat thrown over his shoulders, an apron and nightcap and carrying a bundle. The old man had formerly been a leech-gatherer, but now leeches were scarce because of the dry season was reduced to begging and selling "a few godly books." His wife and ten children were all dead. This encounter was the germ of William's famous poem, "Resolution and Independence," which meditates on not only leech-gathering but poetry as a life's work. Here, we have W.'s description of a figure who was to become iconic. On March 13, 1802, she noted that William wrote "the Poem of the Beggar woman taken from a Woman whom I had seen in May—(now nearly two years ago)."

It was she who first noticed the daffodils, used by her brother for his most anthologized poem. In her words (Thursday, April 15, 1802), the flowers "a long belt of them beside the shore . . . tossed and reeled and danced and seemed as if they verily laughed with the wind that blew upon them over the lake, they looked so gay ever glancing ever changing."

In 1803, W. composed *Recollections of a Tour Made in Scotland*, published in 1874. In 1805, she journalized a walking tour of the Lake District, and in 1820 she recorded a journey in Europe, but refused to publish. *The Journal of a Tour on the Continent*—the most complete edition published in 1941—is remarkable for its intense response to the magnificence of Swiss scenery and its account of her brother in middle age. Among her many trips was a return to Scotland with Joanna Hutchinson, and she kept accounts of them all, but they were unpublished until much later. Her lively accounts of *An Excursion on the Banks of Ullwater* (1805) and *An Excursion to Scafell Pike* (1818) were used by William in his *Guide to the Lakes* (1825). In 1829, she had a severe nervous breakdown and never recovered.

BIBLIOGRAPHY: Gittings, R., and J. Manton, *D. W.* (1985); Hill, A. G., M. Moorman, and C. L. Shaver, eds., *The Letters of William and D. W.* (6 vols., 1967–82); Levin, S. M., *D. W. and Romanticism* (1987)

WORDSWORTH, William

b. 7 April 1770, Cockermouth, Cumberland; d. 23 April 1850, Cumberland

W. has always been regarded as the keystone in the arch of English Romantic poetry. His influence has been extensive and was powerful on his contemporaries, including Samuel Taylor COLERIDGE, Lord BYRON, Percy Bysshe SHELLEY, and John KEATS. He eventually became poet laureate, a figure of national stature much visited and celebrated. W. was born in northwestern England on the edge of the Lake District, educated at a local grammar school and at Cambridge University. He became active in politics and lived in France for a time at the height of the revolutionary period. He had a daughter out of wedlock by a French girl in Orleans, returning to England to devote himself to the profession of poetry. His early book-length poems such as *Descriptive Sketches* and *An Evening Walk,* both published in 1793, are derivative but accomplished and "Descriptive Sketches," in particular, attracted the attention of Coleridge, his younger by two years, leading to a meeting, subsequent friendship, and then a creative partnership. W. returned to live in the Lake District, married Mary Hutchinson in 1802, and shared his various homes with his devoted sister and inspirational muse figure, Dorothy WORDSWORTH. After his death, his reputation continued to grow, his poetry of nature providing consolation in an age of increasing religious skepticism. In the 20th c., however, his work, although still acknowledged as seminal, seemed to speak to fewer as the reputations of Byron and Shelley correspondingly increased, making an appeal to the young and to members of the political left. In many respects, this has been unjust to W. and in the latter years of the century he has reemerged, for example, as the "green" W., whose poetry is perceived to be of central significance for ecological issues and the welfare of the planet.

W.'s well-documented youthful rebelliousness would bear fruit in his collaborative effort with Coleridge to transform the nature and direction of English poetry. This was the collection of twenty-three poems (nineteen by W.) published anonymously in Bristol in 1798 as *Lyrical Ballads.* At the beginning, W. placed an "Advertisement" that announced that the poems were experiments, drawing attention to their unexpected language and subject matter, and attempting to preempt criticism by asking for a readership's informed judgment to be brought to them and its consent to be pleased in spite of preestablished tastes. Many of the poems in *Lyrical Ballads* were not, in fact, unduly challenging. The subject matter of some, on rural themes involving marginal suffering or displaced individuals, had currency in near-contemporary magazine literature, and other poems like "Tintern Abbey" had precedents in much loco-topographical poetry of the time. However, the cumulative effect of the publication, bringing "polite" literature within the same orbit as folk idiom and popular forms like the ballad caused unease, not only within literary but also wider political circles, in that its democratic purpose and sentiments were considered inflammatory in a decade in which England was perceived to be under threat from revolution in France and radical sympathizers at home.

Although there is a preponderance of narrative verse in *Lyrical Ballads,* many of them are not, strictly speaking, ballads at all. W. said that their emphasis was to be on the whole one of feeling that would give importance to the action of a poem, rather than action giving importance to feeling. In this sense, the title, *Lyrical,* is appropriate as often the story line of a poem peters out or is simply abandoned and the reader has to bring his or her own judgment and feelings to the interpretation of the meaning or significance of an event or sequence of events. Such is the case, for example, with "Simon Lee," "The Idiot Boy," "Anecdote for Fathers," "We Are Seven," and "The Thorn." To the last, W. appended an important note in which he defended its apparently tautological language as expressive of great beauty, comparable to the sublime repetitiveness of biblical constructions and reflecting contemporary interest in cultural primitivism and in the Bible itself as the product of Hebrew poets at the dawn of history.

Critical reception of the work was mixed, however. In order both to defend and explain his own and Coleridge's intentions, W. added to the supplemented 1800 edition, published only under his own name, a preface that has subsequently become a form of Romantic manifesto. His purpose, he said, was to reeducate his readers' sensibilities. Dull occupations and uniformity in city life had produced an unhealthy craving for excitement, pandered to by sensational contemporary poetry, fiction, and theater. Anticipating later 19th-c. writers and polemicists such as Thomas CARLYLE, Karl Marx, Charles DICKENS, John RUSKIN, and William MORRIS, W. was already identifying the consequences of man's alienation from his work and environment through urban and industrial expansion.

To examine the 1800 preface is to become aware of how influential many of its precepts have since become in the formulation of a Romantic aesthetic. Poetry, for example, becomes the "spontaneous overflow of powerful feelings." It should avoid tutored diction and be true both to outward nature and to the inner emotions. That which communicates both what the "eye and ear . . . half create/And what perceive" ("Tintern Abbey") can be said to indicate the greatest strength of W., his matter-of-factness, on the one hand, and the authenticity he gives to recondite modes of consciousness on the other, grappling with their complexity and struggling to achieve their expression. In an 1802 addendum, W. asked "What is a Poet?" Poets, somewhat like the child of his own "We Are Seven," are "affected more than other men by absent things as if they were present," thus pointing to the power and relevance of the formative vision and sensibilities of childhood for his own poetry in particular.

Lyrical Ballads established W.'s position as a significant new voice in the pantheon, though his reputation was slow to make its way and he had to endure continuing criticism and opposition to his principles for poetry from some of the prominent reviewers of the time. Nevertheless, W. would insist in his "Essay Supplementary to the Preface" to his collected poems of 1815 that a poet must himself create the taste by which he was to be enjoyed, and his career is characterized by a sense of conviction and purposive single-mindedness.

W.'s next published collection was *Poems in Two Volumes* (1807), which contained a variety of poetic forms, ranging through odes, lyrics, and sonnets on public and personal themes, as well as narrative poems reminiscent of the earlier *Lyrical Ballads.* The collection represents the strengths of W. in his greatest creative period and contains many of the poems on which his reputation is based. Among them might be mentioned "Resolution and Independence" and "The Solitary Reaper," in one sense straightforward narratives but with, nevertheless, a complexity and inward significance for the mind of the poet himself. The "Ode: Intimations of Immortality" regrets the loss of childhood vision and its subjection to the dead hand of custom, while the sonorous "Elegiac Stanzas Suggested by a Picture of Peele Castle in a Storm" is an elegy on the death of W.'s favorite brother, John, in a shipwreck (1805), becoming a defining moment in the history of the poet's career, turning him away from the lonely communings of his previous work to a realization that to what he would call the "self-sufficing power of solitude" must be added relationship and human-heartedness. *Poems in Two Volumes* contains perhaps W.'s most enduring lyric, "I wandered lonely as a cloud," which, despite its overfamiliarity, yields up profundities central to his beliefs. It portrays the poet's evolution from an initial sense of exclusion and loneliness to the "bliss" of full communion with an active universe in a heightened Coleridgean apprehension of the "one life." Equally, it demonstrates W.'s assertion in the preface that poetry takes its origin from "emotion recollected in tranquillity," one of his more famous speculations on the processes of poetical composition.

Throughout this productive decade, W., in common with many of his contemporaries, had become disillusioned by what he perceived as France's imperialistic aggression and betrayal of revolutionary principles. W. was by temperament a reflective individual whose best instincts were solitary communings on his own intense relationship with the natural world. Coleridge, in fact, had always thought of W. as primarily a philosopher and had urged him to write an EPIC involving an examination of man's moral self within a narrative describing some kind of fall and redemptive process. This notional work in three parts, to be entitled "The Recluse," preoccupied W. for the rest of his life and now exists only as one of the more significant Romantic fragment poems. By far the most important part has become *The Prelude; or, Growth of a Poet's Mind* (1850, not W.'s title), which he began as early as 1798 and had completed by 1805. This work, in Miltonic blank verse and consciously sharing John MILTON's own process of close self-scrutiny preparatory to the writing of a proposed epic, traces W.'s history from early childhood, through university and city life, describing his hopes while resident in revolutionary France and his subsequent disillusionment, and draws to a conclusion by showing how true revolution can be achieved only through the transforming powers of imagination.

The Prelude was revised many times and not published until after W.'s death. The final 1850 version differs from that of 1805 in being in some respects tidier and more orthodox, perhaps even less true to the experiences of his younger self. But as a poem it was innovatory and the most successful Romantic epic to confront the great legacy of Milton's *Paradise Lost* taking it further. It combines passages of an intense, visionary quality with others of moral commentary and didactic purpose. Since its publication, readers have been tempted to skip the latter, preferring the great set pieces that represent the peculiar power that has contributed the adjective "Wordsworthian" to the English language. However, W. was a meticulous craftsman and *The Prelude* requires to be read as a continuous whole, its meaning, in fact, depending on a reader's close attention to the positioning of its verse-paragraphs. The completed poem that W. himself regarded as no more than a kind of "ante-chapel" to the "Gothic cathedral" of his proposed work has now come to be regarded as his greatest achievement and the most successful of all Romantic long poems. In some respects, *The Prelude* had been anticipated in "Tintern Abbey," published in *Lyrical Ballads,* where he had traced his response to the natural world through episodes of his history, asserting that nature, providential on man's behalf, has a moral and redemptive power. *The Prelude,* however, expands and develops this theme into a program for social reform.

W. had always thought of himself as a teacher, and his most cherished principles are contained in his "Prospectus" to *The Recluse* in which he speaks as a poet in direct line of descent from Milton, and in prophetic but nevertheless secular terms, of how the mind of man, the "main region" of his song, contains its own potential for the creation of happiness in this world. The "Prospectus," a key passage, was finally placed at the head of *The Excursion,* part 2 of *The Recluse,* in 1814. "The Excursion," which met with mixed reviews and which many have seen, perhaps mistakenly, as representing W.'s diminishing powers as a poet, had a long period of gestation and is consequently an uneven performance. Its earlier books are

true to W.'s belief in the creative power of the imagination, but its later ones on contemporary society anticipating the themes of the "condition of England" writers of the later 19th c., often reflect the ageing poet's increasing conservatism and orthodox recourse to a higher "Providence."

W. continued to write prolifically to the end of his life, still capable of producing works that evince the elemental power and the pressure of intelligence to be found in his earlier output. Much of the material of the later years has been neglected but now shows signs, as it is critically revisited, of yielding up new and often surprising relevance.

BIBLIOGRAPHY: Barker, J., *W.* (2000); Bate, J., *Romantic Ecology*: *W. and the Environmental Tradition* (1991); Bromwich, D., *Disowned by Memory* (1998); Gill, S., *W. W.* (1989); Hartman, G. H., *W.'s Poetry, 1787–1814* (1964); Jacobus, M., *Tradition and Experiment in W.'s "Lyrical Ballads"* (1976); Jones, J., *The Egotistical Sublime*: *A History of W.'s Imagination* (1954); Roe, N., *W. and Coleridge: The Radical Years* (1988)

JOHN GILROY

WOTTON, [Sir] Henry

b. 30 March 1568, Boughton Malherbe, Kent; d. 5 December 1639, Eton

English diplomat, scholar, poet, and traveler, W. is known for *Reliquaie Wottonianae,* a collection of his tracts, letters, and poetry published posthumously in 1651 with a *Life* by W.'s close friend and fishing companion, Izaak WALTON. Born into a prominent family, W. was educated at Winchester School, New College, and Queen's College, Oxford. Sent abroad in 1586 or 1587, evidently to prepare him for a diplomatic career, W. spent seven years on the Continent, traveling through Bavaria, Austria, Italy, Switzerland, and France. His family connections served him well: in Germany he met Edward, Lord Zouche and began a correspondence (1590–93) on politics and current events that formed the basis of the *Reliquaie;* in Geneva, W. stayed in the house of the scholar Isaac Casaubon.

Returning to England in 1594, W. entered the Middle Temple in 1595, and the service as well of Robert Devereux, second Earl of Essex, having provided information to the earl while abroad, and continuing to do so regarding events in Transylvania, Poland, Italy, and Germany until Devereux's downfall in 1601. Not implicated in the affair, W. nonetheless fled to France and Italy; in Florence in 1602, W. was sent to Scotland by the Duke of Tuscany (with Italian antidotes for poisons) to prevent a plot against the life of JAMES VI, who, upon his ascension to the English throne, knighted W. and sent him to Venice as ambassador, a post W. held for nearly twenty years. On leave in England in 1612, W. was forced to defend his loyalty (once publicly and again in private audience with James I), following the publication in a scurrilous attack on the king of W.'s now most famous remark, that an ambassador is "an honest man sent to lie abroad for the good of his country." Eventually cleared, W. was sent to The Hague in 1614, and returned to his post in Venice in 1616. In 1620, he was dispatched to the court of Ferdinand II in Vienna, to assist Elizabeth, queen of Bohemia and daughter to James I. (For her, W. apparently developed a true attachment, captured in perhaps his finest poem, "On His Mistress, the Queen of Bohemia.") Following renewed service at Venice, in 1624 W. returned to England to become provost at Eton, a position he occupied until his death. W. was granted a pension by the Crown of £200 in 1627, which was raised to £500 three years later, in anticipation of a "historie of England" that never apparently materialized.

Although W. published only two works during his lifetime, *The Elements of Architecture* (1624), closely following Marcus Vitruvius Pollio, and an address to James I in Latin (1633), his firsthand involvement with significant events, his wide acquaintance, and correspondence, with courtiers, scholars, and literary figures, all find their way into *Reliquaie Wottonianae,* and establish it—and W.'s—importance. In addition to Walton (with whom W. regularly fished the Thames), W. was on close terms with Albericus Gentilis and John DONNE at Oxford; his letter to John MILTON on *Comus* is justly famous. Of the fifteen poems by W. in *Reliquaie,* two—"On His Mistress," and "The Character of a Happy Life"—exhibit notable skill and grace.

BIBLIOGRAPHY: Pebworth, T.-L., "Sir H. W.," in Hester, M. T., ed., *Seventeeth-Century Nondramatic Poets, DLB* 121 (1992): 286–95; Smith, L. P., *The Life and Letters of Sir H. W.* (2 vols., 1907)

R. F. YEAGER

WREN, P[ercival] C[hristopher]

b. 1 November 1875, Deptford; d. 22 November 1941, Amberley, near Stroud

W. was a prolific writer of fiction and nonfiction whose work is largely forgotten except for the popular success of his adventure novel *Beau Geste* (1924), the tale of brothers enlisted in the French Foreign Legion whose courage and perseverance is tested under the tyranny of the maniacal Sergeant-Major Lejaune. Filmed in 1926, 1929, and 1966, *Beau Geste* is often compared to A. E. W. Mason's *The Four Feathers* (1902), also adapted into a successful film. Sequels to the novel, *Beau Sabreur* and *Beau Ideal*, published in 1926 and 1928, respectively, were inferior to the orig-

inal and failed to produce a Geste series. W.'s later novels, set for the most part in England, include *Cardboard Castle* (1938) and *Paper Prison* (1939).

WROTH, Lady [Mary]

b. probably 18 October 1587, Penshurst Place, Kent; d. 1651

W., author and patroness, is the first Englishwoman of the Renaissance to have written a pastoral drama, a prose ROMANCE, and a sequence of sonnets. Born the daughter of Sir Robert Sidney, brother to Sir Philip SIDNEY, and named for her aunt, Mary [Sidney] Herbert, Countess of PEMBROKE, W.'s literary lineage was both illustrious and influential, providing W. not only with models of authorship to emulate, but also with material to incorporate directly into her work.

W.'s drama, *Love's Victory* (wr. ca. 1620), romance, *The Countesse of Montgomeries Urania* (1621), and sonnet sequence, *Pamphilia to Amphilanthus* (wr. 1621) all became public within a year, and arguably reflect the most emotionally intense period of W.'s life. Married at seventeen to Sir Robert Wroth, with whom she had little in common (he preferring hunting in the country, she life at court), W. was drawn to her cousin, the handsome, witty, and amoral William Herbert. Upon the deaths of her husband and only legitimate son in 1616, W. and the married Herbert became open lovers, their scandalous, extended union producing two children—and W.'s banishment from court.

W.'s work is highly biographical, fictitious names and places only lightly veiling real people and events. W. and Herbert appear as heroine and hero, respectively, in all her works: as Pamphilia ("all-loving") and Amphilantus ("lover of two") in *Urania* and the sonnet sequence, as Musella (W.) and Philisses (Herbert) in *Love's Victory*. W.'s husband, Robert Wroth, is visible as "Rustic(k)" in *Urania* and *Love's Victory*. Others of her family and acquaintance appear variously. The technique afforded enduring interest, and occasional difficulty: As late as 1651, W. was asked by the Earl of Rutland to unmask characters in *Urania*, of which the first half alone was published, only to be withdrawn and the second half suppressed—it has yet to see print—notably to appease the anger of Lord Denny, who recognized himself portrayed there as "a bladder blown with wind."

W.'s writing demonstrates both wide reading, especially in the genres she adopts as her own, and close intertextual relations with works of the Sidney family. Thus, W.'s *The Countesse of Montgomeries Urania* seemingly echoes in its title her uncle Philip Sidney's earlier prose romance, *The Countess of Pembroke's Arcadia;* her sonnet sequence *Pamphilia and Amphilantus* recalls the sequence *Astrophel and Stella,* again by her uncle; *Love's Victory,* while offering the least obvious connection, may derive nonetheless from Petrarch's *Triumph of Love,* companion work to his *Triumph of Death,* translated by Mary [Sidney] Herbert in 1600. Moreover, W.'s characters and events often seem based on those found in works of her family members (e.g., Pamphilia shares much with Stella of *Astrophel and Stella,* Amphilantus with Astrophil)—characters and events that are themselves autobiographical (e.g., Stella is Penelope Rich, Astrophil is Philip Sidney)—thus producing a highly complex interreferentiality.

It remains unclear how influential W.'s work may have been during her lifetime. Only *Urania,* and that only in part, appeared in print, and was shortly withdrawn. The sonnets perhaps circulated among her friends, but to unknown extent, or result. *Love's Victory* was never performed, although there is indication in the better of two extant manuscripts that W. was preparing it for production, undoubtedly at one of the Sidney houses where private showings were regularly staged. W. had some theatrical experience, having taken part in Ben JONSON's *The Masque of Blackness* (1604), and perhaps in his now-lost *The May Lord.* Her greatest contemporary influence may have been as a patron, for she contributed support for many writers and men of letters, including Jonson, who praises her in *Underwood* (1640).

BIBLIOGRAPHY: Lewalski, B. K., *Writing Women in Jacobean England* (1993); Roberts, J. A., ed., *The Poems of Lady M. W.* (1983); Waller, G., *The Sidney Family Romance: M. W., William Herbert, and the Early Modern Construction of Gender* (1993)

R. F. YEAGER

WYATT, [Sir] Thomas
b. ca. 1503, Allington Castle, Kent; d. 11 October 1542, Sherborne, Dorset

Diplomat, courtier, and purported lover of HENRY VIII's second queen Anne Boleyn, W. originated the vogue for Italian literature that powered the English poetic Renaissance. Upon his return from a diplomatic mission to Italy in 1527, W. began experimenting with the love sonnet, ultimately translating and adapting thirty of Petrarch's sonnets and canzoni into English. In addition, he initiated the epistolary SATIRE in England by imitating those of Luigi Alamanni, and in 1549 freely adapted Pietro Aretino's *Penitential Psalms* as the fictive framework for his own rendering of the poems. Although W. wrote for a coterie audience, his poems circulating in manuscript copies among members of the court, the popularity of *Songes and Sonetts* (1557), more popularly known as TOTTEL's *Miscellany,* established W. posthumously as the most important poetic voice of the early Tudor Renaissance.

W.'s adaptations of Petrarch paradoxically reinvented the love sonnet as a potentially anti-Petrarchan genre. Petrarch's great *Canzonieri* is a poetic narrative running from the moment that the speaker first saw his beloved Laura, through her subsequent death and his learning to transcend the agony of unrequited desire, each poem capturing like a snapshot a specific moment in the history of the relationship, recording by stages the male speaker's evolving consciousness. In W.'s poems, however, the beloved woman is anything but a transcendent ideal who is as close to heaven as the speaker can come on earth. In "Whoso list to hunt," she is rendered as a deer whom the speaker hunts at his own cost, for—as she herself warns him—she is "wild for to hold though I seem tame." W. presents a troublingly unidealized view of courtship as an exhausting chase. The desired woman is not a saint or angel, but a wild animal; rather than eventually leading the male to heaven, she is an ever present danger to his peace of mind, the arduous pursuit resulting only in further grief once she's captured. There is nothing transcendent to such a love. Indeed, that the poem opens with a general address to any other man who enjoys the chase suggests that, rather than jealously guarding his lady's identity, the speaker is so disgusted by her nature that he puts hardier, less discerning, men on her scent. That W. did not write a narrative of a love relationship (as Edmund SPENSER, Sir Philip SIDNEY, William SHAKESPEARE, and a host of others would later do), but instead produced a number of isolated poems that the reader cannot be certain pertain to the same woman, suggests how disruptive and fragmentizing an experience love was for W.

Similarly, whereas in the Petrarchan scheme the lover's consciousness of his unworthiness is emphasized by the perfection of his beloved, allowing him finally to forswear sexual desire, any renunciation of love in W. is motivated by sexual disgust rather than by the speaker's growth to transcendence. In "Farewell Love, and all thy laws for ever!," the speaker renounces love as something on which only the young have time and energy to waste; he hopes to give himself over to reading Seneca and Plato. The poem appears a gracious renunciation until the reader reaches the final couplet: "For hitherto though I have lost all my time,/Me lusteth no longer rotten boughs to climb." The speaker imagines the danger of his aspiring to gratify his passion in terms of a tree limb that gives way, causing him to fall. But the image also suggests his disgust at having desired a woman whose limbs ("boughs") are now rotting from venereal infection. Sex is a sullying, contaminating force in W.'s world.

The speaker's desire to commit himself to the Stoic philosophy of Seneca or to Plato's philosophy of ideal forms and disembodied ideas posits reason as the antithesis of love. Rather than illuminate the mind, love darkens it; and rather than provide guidance, it causes the speaker to become lost. "My galley charged with forgetfulness" adapts the Petrarchan conceit of the beloved woman as the North Star by which the male speaker sails, any disruption in their relationship proving to be like clouds that obscure the North Star and placing the speaker in danger of becoming lost at sea. But whereas in the Petrarchan tradition the speaker and his beloved are invariably reconciled, saving him from painful loss, W. presents the woman as his enemy, and can imagine no redemption by the end of the poem: "The stars be hid that led me to this pain,/Drowned is reason that should me comfort,/And I remain despairing of the port." It is the loss of reason's guidance that seems to concern the speaker most; philosophy has been subverted by passion and is unavailable to console the speaker when he most needs it.

Not surprisingly, the first of W.'s works that can be dated with certainty is his translation of Plutarch's *De tranquillitate et securitate animi* as *The Quyete of Mynde* (1528). W.'s poems might best be described as a troubled man's search for a mind at "ease" with itself, for it is not simply love that proves changeable and disruptive. Love, rather, figures the condition of an uncertain world. In the powerful sonnet, "The pillar perished is whereto I leant," the speaker laments the loss of "the strongest stay of mine unquiet mind." That "pillar" is never identified, but the speaker can only spend the remainder of his life in complaint. Similarly, the epistle "Mine own John Poyntz" is dark satire on a courtly world in which hypocrisy is the only mode of advancement. And it is in this context as well that W.'s reworking of the *Penitential Psalms,* his most important sustained poetic achievement, must be viewed. The sequence is most often viewed as evidence of an emerging Protestant or Reformist poetics in England, but biblical David's search to ease his troubled mind after a sullying sexual experience is pure W.

W.'s poems circulated during his lifetime in manuscript among a coterie audience. Fifty love poems were included with thirty others in "Tottel's Miscellany," where they had enormous popularity. Difficulties establishing his canon attendant upon manuscript circulation, coupled with a longstanding misunderstanding of his metrics, however, caused literary historians to give pride of place to his younger contemporary, Henry Howard, Earl of SURREY. W. is now accepted as the most important poetic voice of the early Tudor Renaissance, the progenitor of the line of plain-speaking poets noted for their "rough masculine force" that includes John DONNE and, with qualifications, John Wilmot, second Earl of ROCHESTER and W. H. AUDEN.

BIBLIOGRAPHY: Ferry, A., *The "Inward" Language: Sonnets of W., Sidney, Shakespeare, Donne* (1983); Foley, S. M., *Sir T. W.* (1990); Heale, E. M., *W., Surrey, and Early Tudor Poetry* (1998); Muir K., *Life and Letters of Sir T. W.* (1963)

RAYMOND-JEAN FRONTAIN

WYCHERLEY, William

b. 1640, Clive near Shrewsbury, Shropshire; d. 1 January 1716, London

The year after W.'s birth, Parliament closed the theaters of Britain, and they remained dark for eighteen years (1642–60). When King Charles II was restored to power, he reopened them. At first, they offered plays by William SHAKESPEARE, Ben JONSON, and Francis BEAUMONT and John FLETCHER. The time was ripe, however, for new drama to emerge.

Born in Shropshire, W. was sent to school in France in 1655. While there he converted to Roman Catholicism, but on his return to attend Oxford in 1660, the year in which the theaters were reopened, he became a Protestant and remained one until his reconversion to Roman Catholicism in 1685. W. left Oxford without a degree and studied law at the Inner Temple. He was, however, more interested in the pleasures that London offered, particularly theater, than he was in studying law. Theater became his passion.

W.'s first play, *Love in a Wood* (1672), was produced in March 1671 and enjoyed considerable success. The attention it brought him led to his having an affair with the Duchess of Cleveland, who was also having an affair with King Charles II, and provided W. with an entree to the court. His second play, *The Gentleman Dancing-Master* (perf. 1672; pub. 1673), did not meet with the success of his first venture into drama. Both of these early plays had exceptionally witty farcical moments. W. was skillful at presenting ostentatious characters and holding them up to ridicule in exceptionally amusing ways.

If his second play disappointed, W. redeemed himself with *The Country Wife* (1675), which opened on January 12, 1675, at the new Theatre Royal in Drury Lane. This drama is W.'s best and most enduring play. The play holds up the manners and society of the time to scrutiny, but it does so with a bawdy wit that has enticed audiences for over three hundred years. His last drama, *The Plain-Dealer* (perf. 1676; pub. 1677), is a stinging but witty SATIRE about greed. The play makes its points crudely and sometimes rudely, but the satire is direct and consistently hits its mark.

A severe illness brought on by his debauched life immobilized W. in 1678. King Charles sent him to France to recover. Upon his return to England the following year, he secretly married a rigidly puritanical widow, Laetitia-Isabella, Countess of Drogheda, who dominated him and presumably discouraged his writing. This marriage caused W. to lose favor at court.

The countess died one year after their marriage, willing her substantial fortune to her husband. The will, however, was contested, and W. spent considerable time and all his money fighting in the courts to receive his due. It was at this time that he wrote his *Epistles to the King and Duke* (1683) pleading his case in poetic form. So severely did he deplete his financial resources that in 1682 he landed in debtors' prison, remaining there for seven years before Charles II's successor, James II, rescued him, paid his debts, and awarded him a small pension.

W. decided in the early 1690s, as a means of restoring his literary reputation, to publish a collection of his poems to be sold by subscription, a common means of financing such publications. The collection was complete by 1693, but it still remained unpublished in 1696, when Samuel Briscoe agreed to publish it. When the collection remained unpublished in 1700, W. sued Briscoe and retrieved his manuscript. *Miscellany Poems* finally appeared in 1704.

W. had little talent for verse. Even the verse he wrote for the prologue of *The Plain-Dealer* is technically weak, occasionally jarring, and sometimes grating to the ear. The intellectual content of W.'s poems is mediocre and the work overall lacks the vigor and enthusiasm of his plays. Their popularity is suggested by the publication following his death in 1714 of two collections of his work, Lewis Theobald's edition (1728) and Alexander POPE's edition (1729).

BIBLIOGRAPHY: Marshall, W. G., *A Great Stage of Fools: Theatricality and Madness in the Plays of W. W.* (1993); McCarthy, B. E., *W. W.* (1979); Rogers, K. M., *W. W.* (1972); Vance, J. A., *W. W. and the Comedy of Fear* (2000)

R. BAIRD SHUMAN

WYNDHAM, John

(pseuds: John Beynon, John Beynon Harris, Lucas Parkes, and others) b. John Wyndham Parkes Lucas Beynon Harris, 10 July 1903, Birminghan, d. 11 March 1969, Petersfield, Hampshire

W.'s reputation rests upon a quartet of novels published during the 1950s. He became known for the cosy catastrophe in which some crisis hits London, leading to the surviving population being scattered across the southeast of England, and the action focusing upon a small band of survivors rebuilding society, taking their pick of what has been left behind. Such narratives clearly owe a debt to H. G. WELLS's *The War of the Worlds,* but it is another theme from Wells—evolution—that W. makes his own and has caused that cosy label to be questioned of late. The doctrine of the survival of the fittest, with the uncomfortable truth about what happens to the weak, underlies much of his fiction.

W.'s career appears to have started with *The Curse of the Burdens* (1927), as by John B. Harris, a mystery novel, and W. wrote more crime before SCIENCE FICTION came to dominate his writing. *The Secret People* (1935) took as its narrative the flooding of the Sahara desert, which threatens a lost society with drowning. A more alien race is encountered in *Planet Plane* (1936; repub. in abridged form as *Stowaway to Mars,* 1953) when a series of Mars missions from Earth encounter a dying race of Martians.

Throughout the decade, W. sold to American pulp magazines devoted to science fiction. He was uncomfortable with the genre title and his postwar fiction was not published as such when printed by Penguin. His breakthrough novel, *The Day of the Triffids* (1951; repub. as *Revolt of the Triffids,* 1952), was serialized in the slick magazine *Colliers.* This is an account of the breakdown of society when faced with ambulant, carnivorous plants, a situation out of control because almost all of the population has been blinded by strange lights in the sky. The narrative is a familiar one; the protagonist has been in hospital, his eyes bandaged up after an accident with a triffid, and thus avoids the blinding lights. He makes his way through a devastated London, and survives on his wits before joining an isolated community. In the context of the aftermath of the Second World War, it is easy to see how fragile society is, and how the regeneration could fail at any point. Humanity can only survive through intelligence, and its position as most evolved species is under threat. The scenes of despair of some of the survivors seem very far from cosy. The origin of the lights in the sky is kept carefully ambiguous—with speculation as to whether they are meteors or Russian or American satellites breaking up.

An early Cold War context also informs *The Kraken Wakes* (1953; repub. as *Out of the Deeps,* 1953), which begins with strange meteors crashing into the sea and then a series of attacks on shipping, blamed initially on Western or Communist bloc actions. An alien intelligence is at work, and begins to rework Earth to suit its needs; the ice caps are partially melted and the sea level rises, flooding London. Humanity seems helpless when faced with the changing environment, and barely able to adapt. Mike Watson, the journalist hero who has watched the crisis from the start, is resourceful, but not as resourceful as his wife Phyllis, who has thought to stock their west country retreat with a cellar full of food. Phyllis, one of many strong female characters in the mature fiction of W., is thought to be based on W.'s long-time lover Grace Wilson.

W.'s next few novels featured invasions from within rather than from elsewhere; *Re-Birth* (1955; repub. as *The Chrysalids,* 1955) being the most disturbing. In post–nuclear holocaust Labrador, genetic impurities are not tolerated. David and a handful of friends must keep their telepathic abilities secret or face certain execution. This is made impossible with the birth of Sophie, a telepath so strong that she locates a telepath colony in New Zealand. We follow the group through a period of demanding human rights to demanding equality with nontelepathic humans, before many of their tribe are wiped out in their move to a separate (and separatist) society. It is made clear that when a new species evolves, it has to wipe out its rivals, but the genocide makes uncomfortable reading. In *The Midwich Cuckoos* (1957), all the women in an English country village become pregnant on the same night. Whereas *Re-Birth* had told the story from the point of view of the new species, this tells the story of the usurped. The film version of *The Midwich Cuckoos* appeared in 1960 as *Village of the Damned* and its sequel was released in 1963 as *Children of the Damned*.

W.'s inclusion on school syllabi has led to the critical assumption that he is a cosy writer; most critics recently have tended to note a disturbing edge to his work in relation to its social Darwinism.

BIBLIOGRAPHY: Clareson, T. D., and A. S. Clareson, "The Neglected Fiction of J. W.," in Garnett, R., and R. J. Ellis, eds., *Science Fiction Roots and Branches* (1990): 88–103; Wymer, R., "How 'Safe' is J. W.," *Foundation* 55 (Summer 1992): 25–36

ANDREW M. BUTLER

YEARSLEY, Ann

bap. 15 July 1753, Clifton, Bristol; d. 8 May 1806, Wiltshire

The story of the brief rise to fame and subsequent descent back to obscurity of Y., known in her own day as "Lactilla" or "The Milkwoman of Bristol," exemplifies the fate of many laboring-class poets of her era. Talented, intelligent, and increasingly politically aware, she was also difficult, proud, and defensive. Always fiercely conscious of her own plebeian origins, she was increasingly drawn, as her later poetry shows, into a bourgeois subject position. Taken up, patronized, and praised, she seems to have made a deliberate decision to retire from literary life and to choose to end her days in rural seclusion.

It was in 1785 that Y., a hard-working, self-educated milkwoman, was discovered by the poet and social-reformer Hannah MORE. More's class-specific expectations were rather comically confounded when she discovered that her protégée's favorite poets included Virgil, John MILTON, and Edward YOUNG; later, Y. revealed that she had taken some of her classical allusions from "little ordinary prints which hung in a shop window." Together with another female writer, Elizabeth MONTAGU, More arranged for the publication of Y.'s first volume, *Poems, on Several Occasions* (1785), a work that was enthusiastically received by the critics. However, although the poet expressed her gratitude to her patrons in this work, the relationship quickly turned sour when More and Montagu refused to let Y. handle her own finances, believing that the possession of money would give her ideas above her station. A bitter wrangle ensued. Having extricated herself from this unhappy situation, Y. found herself another patron, the Earl of Bristol, under whose aegis she brought out her second volume, *Poems on Various Subjects* (1787). The earl also helped to secure an apprenticeship for one of her sons, and to provide her with a less menial occupation by setting her up in a circulating library near Bristol Hot-

wells. Her next few years were productive and successful. Her *Poem on the Inhumanity of the Slave-Trade* (1788) made her something of a civic heroine, and her play, *Earl Goodwin: A Tragedy* (perf. 1789; pub. 1791) was produced in Bath and Bristol. In 1796, she published her final volume of poetry, *The Rural Lyre*, and the final two volumes of an historical novel, *The Royal Captives* (4 vols., 1795–96). Her health had by now begun to fail, and she moved to the Wiltshire countryside to live near one of her sons for the remaining ten years of her life.

Especially in her early poetry, Y. tended to emphasize her "rough soul"; in her supposedly uncultured mind, she writes, "rude ideas strove/Awhile for vent, but found it not, and died" ("To Stella," 1785). However, what strikes a reader today is the remarkable skill with that she handles the complexities of blank verse, a medium that she evidently preferred, and the many moments in which her poetry aspires to a pre-Wordsworthian sublimity. Like William WORDSWORTH (whose visionary poetry would not begin to appear for almost a decade), she celebrates nature as the source of "beauteous imagery" that "awak'd/My ravish'd soul to extacy untaught,/To all the transport the rapt sense can bear" ("To Mrs. Montagu," 1785).

Like many of her literary contemporaries, Y. greeted the early stages of the French Revolution with optimism: her play *Earl Goodwin* celebrates the triumph of an oppressed peasantry over their tyrannical rulers. Her radicalism retreated somewhat, however, in the face of the Terror and the executions of Louis XVI and Marie Antoinette. Her *Reflections on the Death of Louis XVI*, which appeared in early 1793 within weeks of that event, while condemning the "barbed dart/Of hot Oppression," deplores the indignities suffered by the deposed king: "'Tis vile!/So wantonly to loose the wolves of law/ On that defenceless frame." In her powerful sonnet "Anarchy," the speaker is Anarchy itself, personified to represent the sanguinary tendencies of the Terror in France: "Furies! Why sleep amid the carnage?—rise!/Bring up my wolves of war, my pointed spears,/Daggers, yet reeking, banners filled with sighs, /And paint your cheeks with gore, and lave your locks in tears."

Y.'s last volume, *The Rural Lyre* (1796), contains her most mature and accomplished poetry. The most ambitious poem in the collection is her 523-line "Brutus: A Fragment," which celebrates "native" British liberty through the narrative of Brutus's discovery of Britain. The poem also has an erotic subtext, ending with the tragic but passionate love between Brutus and Hermia, an "untutor'd" British woman. Y.'s interest in the classics is further demonstrated in this volume by a series of epistles that undertake to imitate "the simplicity of the ancients." Another impressive poem in the collection is "To Mira, On the Care of her Infant." Opposing the male-dominated world of war to the female one of domesticity and child care, Y. recommends a warm, natural maternal upbringing that, it is argued, will produce balance and harmony in the coming generations. An interesting feature of the poem is the passage that deplores the harshness of an ill-educated and "artful" wet nurse, whose "coarse" viciousness seems to be result of her lower-class origins, origins that differ little, the reader may notice, from those of the poet herself.

Y.'s reasons for choosing a self-imposed silence after the publication of this volume are not entirely clear, although health problems may well have had a bearing on her decision. More or less forgotten for many years, her poems are increasingly recognized today not only as important documents in the history of the articulation of class and gender but also as having a literary importance in their own right.

BIBLIOGRAPHY: Ferguson, M., "Resistance and Power in the Life and Writings of A. Y.," *ECent* 27 (Fall 1986): 247–68; Landry, D., *The Muses of Resistance: Labouring-Class Women's Poetry in Britain, 1739–1796* (1990)

HARRIET DEVINE JUMP

YEATS, Jack B[utler]

b. 29 August 1871, London; d. 28 March 1957, Dublin, Ireland

Artist, illustrator, novelist, and playwright, Y. was the youngest child of celebrated artist John Butler Yeats. In 1894, he married Mary Cottenham White ("Cottie"), an artist in a more art nouveau style than Y.'s own.

Almost without question Ireland's most renowned painter, Y. started out as a commercial artist and cartoonist for periodicals such as *Punch* and the *Manchester Guardian.* After a brief stint at the Westminster School of Art, Y. developed, in apparent isolation, into a deeply nationalistic painter and a modernist of profound and unique vision. Nearly fifty years after

his death, Y. is still the greatest local influence on Irish visual art, inspiring some to emulation, others to reaction, in the manner of all towering figures.

Personal and epistolary relationships with James JOYCE, Samuel BECKETT, and especially, John Millington SYNGE make his probable development as a writer more transparent, if somewhat less well known. Though the intensely private Y. was not forthcoming about influences and motivations, the assumption is made that growing up with his yeomanly Pollexfen grandparents in still-rural Sligo was the formative element of his youth, contrasting with the more cosmopolitan upbringing of his older brother, W. B. YEATS, with their father in London and Dublin. Later literary works, such as *Sailing, Sailing Swiftly* (1933), *The Amaranthers* (1936), and *The Charmed Life* (1938), directly address the issue of the gracious life, of achieving balance somewhere between the grasping practicality of the up-and-coming Pollexfens, and the lovely, if perhaps self-delighted, artistic sensibility of the Yeatses.

Y. seems to have veered deliberately away from his brother's course whenever possible, choosing to portray homespun, rural, sporting, or grittily proletarian elements of Irish life, in contrast to W. B. Yeats's grander or more mythological perspective, though the brothers—and their two sisters, too—did collaborate on projects for the Cuala Press, and Y. often did designs for his brother's books.

Y.'s work is characterized by a playfulness—full of puns, skew observation, wit, a love of the gently grotesque—and informed by a sense of technical experimentation different from that of his brother. Though it would be difficult to find a passage in which W. B. Yeats is actually humorous—at least without some labor—good HUMOR and sweetness of attitude light every line of Y.'s work, a sunny and humane laughter complementary to his great Irish counterparts, Jonathan SWIFT and Beckett, whose visions one may find to be, however, considerably harder and darker. One would not necessarily call Y. a comic writer, but rather one whose cadences customarily lift, whose characters drink from cups which they themselves believe to be half full.

Y.'s literary efforts begin with plays written for a toy theater, and theater is never fully absent from his concern. Even works usually characterized as novels, *Sligo* (1930), *Ah Well* (1942), *And to You Also* (1944), for example, take the form of monologues, and could be—perhaps have been—delivered as theatrical works.

The speaking voice, the unabashed "I" of direct witness is the unifying principle of Y.'s literary output. A book such as *Sligo* illustrates the degree to which visionary subjectivity lends itself to the technique of stream of consciousness. Those who have settled on the "Big Three" of this important modernist technique—Joyce, Virginia WOOLF, William Faulkner—

might do well to add Y. as a fourth. Furthermore, Y.'s efforts in stream of consciousness writing are, perhaps, less self-dramatizing and more organic, feeling like the natural overflow of the talk of some brilliant, half-inebriate village genius delivered from a Sligo barstool. One might find *Sligo* as rewarding a book in its way as *Ulysses,* or at least one that demands, page by page, less homage from and offers more welcome to its readers.

Y.'s present obscurity as a writer may be relative to his eminence as a painter, and the difficulty—partially overcome in rare figures such as William BLAKE or Dante Gabriel ROSSETTI—of scholarship in dealing with accomplishments in unrelated arts. Perhaps it is related to his brother's singular position in the hierarchy of letters, beside which it may be difficult to locate a sibling with obvious but different talents. The immediate and material cause, however, is surely simple availability: most of Y.'s works are out of print and obtainable only from rare books stores or online.

BIBLIOGRAPHY: Arnold, B., *J. Y.* (1988); McGuinness, N. A., *The Literary Universe of J. B. Y.* (1992); Purser, J. W., *The Literary Works of J. B. Y.* (1991)

DAVID BRENDAN HOPES

YEATS, W[illiam] B[utler]

b. 13 June 1865, Sandymount, near Dublin, Ireland; d. 28 January 1939, Cap Martin, France

The eldest child of noted Irish portraitist John Butler Yeats, Y. was the elder brother of painter and writer Jack B. YEATS. He is one of a tiny international handful who may justly vie for the title "Greatest Poet of the Twentieth Century," and certainly his image in his own nation—however complicated it might have been during his lifetime—has become sacred, a touchstone of passionate Irishness, without rival and without foreseeable diminishment of influence.

Part of Y.'s power was his ability to tool the events of his life into occasions for his art. Belying several "truisms" about poets and poetry, Y.'s best work was not done in his youth, nor was he enslaved to a small and much-repeated cluster of ideas, but he reinvented himself almost decade by decade, in response to the demands of a turbulent age and a perpetually questing intellect.

After a dreamy and unfocused youth, Y. met the poet George RUSSELL (Æ) in 1884, and an interest in the occult was sparked that would remain with him his entire life. The following year he met John O'Leary, who added a love for Irish legendary history and, at a somewhat pastoral remove, contemporary Irish politics to the mix. These two influences may be seen in *Crossways* (1889), with its Pre-Raphaelite interplay of Hinduism and Irishry. Even in this very early selection appear works, such as "Down by the Salley Gardens" and "The Stolen Child," so in tune

with the Irish spirit that they seem like folk songs, and have attained the status in Ireland of cherished public property.

In 1889, Y. met Maud Gonne, actress and social activist, whose great beauty and strength of character would haunt Y. to the end of his days, and inspire some of his greatest and some of his bitterest verse. Examples may be found in *The Rose* (1893), a selection presided over by a sense of languid defeat at the hands of love.

Gonne's preference for the "Man of Action" (which would lead her to marry Major John Mac-Bride, the "drunken, vainglorious lout" of Y.'s "Easter 1916") encouraged Y. to exchange the dreamy ROMANTICISM of *The Celtic Twilight* (1893; rev. ed., 1902) for a more active posture. *The Wind among the Reeds* (1899) successfully mingles Irish mythology with the immediate—and occasionally retributive—sensations of love. Again, Y.'s skill with the folk idiom creates works such as "The Hosting of the Sidhe" and "The Fiddler of Dooney," without which the Irish Renaissance, as it has come to be known, would be unthinkable.

In 1896, Y. met Lady [Augusta] GREGORY, who would be his patron, mentor, and friend throughout her life, and whose house at Coole Park would provide Y. with a vision of gracious domestic life, one that would become darker and wilder as it began to relocate to the wind-swept stone tower at Thoor Ballylee. Lady Gregory, Y., Edward MARTYN, and later Annie Horniman began to conceive of the idea of an Irish National Theatre, which was founded in 1902 with Y. as its president, and which later became the Abbey Theatre, still one of the great national theaters of the world.

In 1902, Y. wrote *Cathleen ni Houlihan* (with Gonne in the title role), a play of such unassailable patriotic credentials that it saved Y.'s nationalist reputation on several later occasions. In 1907, the Abbey produced John Millington SYNGE's *The Playboy of the Western World,* the ignorant reception of which by the Dublin audience set Y. permanently at odds with "Biddy and Paudeen," the pious Catholic peasantry—whether urban or rural—which seemed to Y. to oppose every effort to establish the beautiful and the heroic.

Y.'s meeting in 1912 with American poet Ezra Pound set his poetry on yet another course, this time toward greater directness and modernity, a trend that can be seen in the great and often austere poems of *Responsibilities* (1914) and *The Wild Swans at Coole* (1917; rev. ed., 1919)—the latter work in part an extended tribute to his generous friend, Lady Gregory.

The Easter Rising of 1916 and the Anglo-Irish War (1917–20) were the occasions of some of Y.'s greatest work, including "Easter 1916," "The Second Coming," and "Prayer for My Daughter." Y. was at the height of his powers when he produced *The Tower* in

1928, one of the most vibrant, impassioned, and fully achieved works of 20th-c. art, nor was there evident diminishment in *The Winding Stair and Other Poems* (1933). Both *The Tower* and *The Winding Stair* derive their central images from Thoor Ballylee, the 16th-c. "castle" Y. restored and inhabited after his marriage to Georgie Hyde-Lees in 1917.

His marriage seems to be one of the few events of his life that did not affect Y.'s poetry much, though, beginning on their honeymoon journey, Y. did exhibit a talent for automatic writing under the spell of various powerful spirits, which led to the publication of *A Vision* in 1925, and its revision in 1937. Though the worldly might say that Y.'s wife had to find something with which to compete with the looming and undiminished specter of Gonne, both the poet and their son, Michael Yeats, were convinced that, whatever else they might have been, the automatic writings were absolutely genuine.

Y. received the Nobel Prize for Literature in 1923, and published *Autobiographies* in 1926, an effort to control the details of his own life that was at least in part successful because the work seems to be at once honest, so far as recollection allows, and personally unsparing. (Y.'s *Autobiography*, published in 1938, was revised and expanded in 1955, also published as *Autobiographies*.) Y. was appointed a senator in the Irish Free State, but later resigned the honor due to failing health, and, one suspects, disappointment with the direction the Free State government was taking at the time, one of retribution against rather than integration of the Protestant Ascendancy that Y. believed—with some justification—to be the cultural backbone of Irish society.

Y.'s final glory was that his amazing productivity continued into extreme old age, and the best sources assert he finished the play *The Death of Cuchulain,* (1939) and his last poems just days before his death. What is certain is that the posthumously published *Last Poems and Two Plays* (1939) contain among his greatest—and in some cases, least characteristic—poetical works.

Though Y.'s wish to be buried in Drumcliffe Churchyard, County Sligo, Ireland, under the shadow of Ben Bulben, could not be honored because of World War II, his remains were reinterred there in 1948, where they have become a pilgrimage site, sometimes for people who only have a vague idea of the work of the man beneath the stone, but an acute sense of lasting celebrity.

BIBLIOGRAPHY: Adams, J., *Y. and the Masks of Syntax* (1984); Archibald, D., *Y.* (1983); Donoghue, D., *W. B. Y.* (1971); Ellmann, R., *Y.* (1976); Finneran, R. J., *The Prose Fiction of W. B. Y.* (1973); Harper, G. M., ed., *Y. and the Occult* (1975); Marcus, P. L., *Y. and Artistic Power* (1992)

DAVID BRENDAN HOPES

YONGE, Charlotte M[ary]

b. 11 August 1823, Otterbourne, Hampshire; d. 24 March 1901, Otterbourne, Hampshire

Y. was broadly contemporaneous with Anthony TROLLOPE, and it is perhaps not wholly fanciful to see them sharing the parentage of a narrative form that became, in both serious and popular modes, an important one in the 20th c.. The Palliser novels of Trollope fathered the *roman-fleuve;* Y.'s novels of contemporary life were surely mother to the soap opera, and especially the very English form exemplified by the radio soap *The Archers,* where the fourth generation of the families involved are, in 2001, of an age to begin embarking on love affairs.

What makes Y.'s device so remarkable is that she not only writes long and thick novel after novel after children's story about the same family, but that she then does it again with a different family, and then brings these families together, and does that repeatedly, so that the Mays of *The Daisy Chain* (2 vols., 1856), the Merrifields of *The Stokesley Secret* (1861), the Caergwents of *Countess Kate* (1862), the Underwoods of *The Pillars of the House* (4 vols., 1873), and the Mohuns of the very early *Scenes and Characters* (1847; repub. as *Beechcroft*, 1956) and the much later *The Two Sides of the Shield* (1885) keep meeting and intermarrying. There is considerable courage, and evidence of the skill that should have made her a serious novelist of repute, in her choosing to do this, for a lesser writer would not have been able to do it without deadly resemblances destroying all verisimilitude and interest.

This is especially so because each of her large families has certain emblematic purposes. Devoted daughter of a clergyman and intense follower of the Oxford movement, Y. was as much writing an allegory as was Edmund SPENSER when she set some of these families out on the journey of their lives often with some shattering disaster, in *The Daisy Chain* the accident that widows Dr. May and paralyzes Margaret, the oldest daughter, and in *The Pillars of the House* the fall on the stairs that cripples Geraldine, and leads to Mrs. Underwood's premature senility and the mental deficiency of Baby Theodore: each member will come to represent some aspect of the temptations and triumphs of the Christian life. Thus, with a less gifted writer, one would expect that, as well as family resemblances among the Mays, there would be similar resemblances between them and the Underwoods. However, Ethel, the clever, ugly, great-hearted spinster May could not be more different from Geraldine, the talented, neurotic spinster Underwood: alike in their asexual devotion, Ethel's to her father and Geraldine's to her brother Felix, they are utterly different in their emotional tone, as well as in their abilities. Similarly, there are strong and subtle differences between the worldliness that entraps Flora May and its bad consequences, and those affecting Alda Underwood.

But this lively differentiation and the skill with which chapter openings hook the reader with the spirited language of genuine-sounding young people have not secured a lasting readership for Y. and the chief reason lies in the impulse that drove her to write at all: her commitment to the High Church Anglo-Catholic version of Christianity taught by John Keble. John KEATS said, "We hate poetry that has a palpable design upon us," and Y.'s design is palpable in the extreme. But this is not the whole story. If it were all, there could be a similar hostility to *The Pilgrim's Progress*. Y.'s difficulty is that, with this purpose in mind, she sets out to write a realistic story of contemporary life, or a similarly realistic historical novel, and so gives herself two contradictory aims. Her need to show the guiding hand of God in everything is fatal to the verisimilitude she seeks, and her lack of the poetic force that entitles Charles DICKENS to the operatic coincidences that fill his pages, robs her of the right to them.

When Oliver Twist is set to burgle the very house that shelters his own young aunt, the powerful engine of the writing carries the reader past the awkward moment and leads to acceptance of a sense of universal justice at work; when, in *The Trial* (2 vols., 1864), Tom May happens to be in a Paris hospital at the very moment when the dying villain Sam Axworthy is brought in clutching the document that will resolve the plot, or when, in *The Pillars of the House,* Fernan, who has been trying for years to trace Edgar Underwood, is enabled by chance, not his researches, to be present at his deathbed, Y.'s language, serviceable as it is, is too mundane to make the reader willing to accept her vision of her God as a tidy-minded puppet-master, especially as He had earlier placed Fernan in a City of London street at exactly the right moment to demonstrate his Christian forgiveness by saving the life of his deadly rival, Sir Adrian. And yet, the portrait of that scoundrelly aristocrat is so neatly drawn, as he slithers in and out of the story, that the reader can only regret the way Y. falls between the poetic mastery of Dickens and the narrative restraint of George ELIOT.

These interlinked soaps were, of course, not the whole of Y.'s enormous oeuvre—some 160 volumes, many of them nonfiction like *John Keble's Parishes* (1898), as well as the editorship of *Aunt Judy's Magazine,* a publication for girls. Her most famous novel, *The Heir of Redclyffe* (1853), notable for being the book Jo March is reading in the early pages of Louisa May Alcott's *Little Women* (2 parts, 1868–69), stands alone, though it is, like the others, a tale of sacrifice and the hollowness of worldly success; so do many of her other novels of contemporary life designed for

adults or young adults, such as *The Clever Woman of the Family* (2 vols., 1865), *The Three Brides* (2 vols., 1876), and *Hopes and Fears* (2 vols., 1860). Although without the connections to other novels, these still remind the reader of the modern soap opera in the way they punctuate comfortable narratives of everyday life with occasional outbreaks of high drama or at least melodrama; where Raymond Chandler recommends bringing in a man with a gun when a thriller plot is flagging, Y. in such a difficulty introduces a violent accident or a ghastly epidemic illness.

As well as all these, however, and her nonfiction histories and essays, there are the historical novels and children's stories, which demonstrate a thoroughness worthy of Robert SOUTHEY in her historical research, though there is a depressing primness in her attempts at period language, where she loses the quality of vibrancy and immediacy that make the conversations of her contemporary young people so attractive. She ranged widely, sometimes going back as far as the 10th c., though her favorite period seems to have been that of the Tudors; probably her best historical novel takes place in Germany in the 15th c.: *The Dove in the Eagle's Nest* (2 vols., 1866) tells a tale that recurs in her contemporary novels, like *Heartsease; or, The Brother's Wife* (2 vols., 1854), of a serious, simple Christian soul acting as a catalyst on all around her, to bring them to the one true faith. As with those contemporary stories, her ability to create suspense and to develop engaging characters, which she scarcely believed in herself, enables her to push the implicit sermon forward. Even for a modern reader too disgusted by those preachings, and by her powerful anti-feminist politics, to enjoy them as literature, the contemporary novels still provide a detailed enough picture of a certain kind of Victorian middle-class life to make them a valuable study today.

BIBLIOGRAPHY: Battiscombe G., and M. Laski, eds., *A Chaplet for C. Y.* (1965); Dennis, B., *C. Y.* (1992); Hayter, A., *C. Y.* (1996); Mare, M., and A. C. Percival, *Victorian Best-Seller: The World of C. M. Y.* (1947)

AUDREY LASKI

YOUNG ADULT FICTION

There is a considerable problem with the concept of literature for young adults. What is a young adult, and when does he or she become simply an adult? Clearly, the answer is likely to differ from person to person; there are plenty of thirteen-year-olds reading what adults regard as adult fiction, and always have been in households where adult fiction is not locked away. More to the point, perhaps, many thirteen-year-olds who like to read will today read anything, shooting ahead to Beryl BAINBRIDGE and back to Enid Blyton, with Terry PRATCHETT's Discworld series providing the middle ground. Meanwhile, the Discworld and the Harry Potter series are also being read by bright ten-year-olds and happy forty and seventy-year-olds.

At one time, the differentiation would have been almost entirely to do with sex; the novel for young adults would be one in which falling in love might happen, but it would find no expression except a distant dream of marriage, thought of entirely in terms of a wedding, and possibly the family life that would follow, but never of the wedding night. In the 19th c., the power of Mrs. Grundy—the censorious character from Thomas MORTON's play *Speed the Plow*—and Dr. Thomas Bowdler, expressed through the censorship of the circulating libraries, was such that there was little problem with young people reading adult fiction, since, as William Makepeace THACKERAY bitterly complained, novelists dared not show a man's sexuality, and the arrival of babies, though obscurely connected with marriage in happy cases and with an obscure fall in dire ones like Hetty Sorrel's in George ELIOT's *Adam Bede*, seemed to be mysterious enough to validate the gooseberry bush theory. Particularly directed at young people, however, might be seen those novels of family life, like Charlotte M. YONGE's, where there were always a crop of adolescents enduring such growing pains as were then recognized. Here, a secret engagement was sufficiently heinous an offense against parental authority to provide all the darkness needed.

However, when the adult novel began to be bolder about sex, a greater differentiation began to be needed, and with the growth of literacy following the Education Acts of the latter part of the 19th c., there was a proliferation of adventure stories that, by keeping its young heroes too busy killing wild beasts and thwarting evil foreigners to think of sex, provided boys at least with material seen as appropriate to their ages. This was not yet officially young adult fiction; the readers of H. Rider HAGGARD and G. A. Henty would again have ranged from ten-year-olds to forty-year-olds. In the first half of the 20th c., the existence of a wide range of genre fiction, originally intended for adults but sexually modest and substituting thrills and confirmed expectations for any serious considerations, made a specific young adult category seem unnecessary; readers moved easily from children's books to detective stories, spy thrillers, SCIENCE FICTION, and ROMANCE without their presumed innocence being disturbed.

After World War II, however, there were new developments. The Penguin publishers saw a market niche between their adult fiction and the excellent Puffin category of children's books and began to publish what were then called Peacocks. The first few of these were in fact titles that had begun in the adult market, such as Georgette HEYER's *Devil's Cub* and Dodie SMITH's *I Capture the Castle*, but they soon added novels written deliberately with the older adolescent in mind. Other publishers of course followed suit. Meanwhile, the American children's book market led the way into books written for adolescents that boldly addressed issues like sexuality, initially entirely in terms of problems, and for a while the market on both sides of the Atlantic was flooded with very weak novels whose main purpose seemed to be to mention as many dangers of modern life as could be crammed into a single volume: date rape, pregnancy, drugs, suicide, parental divorce, grandparental dementia, and anything else the author happened to have read about in the morning papers.

Gradually, however, writers of real quality began to address the perceived need of adolescents for novels that, while tending to novella length and revolving round people of their own age and thus differing from novels intended for adults, had the courage to look seriously at important issues and to address them in rich, perhaps difficult language. A pioneer of such complexity was Alan Garner, who moved from fantasy for children to darker and more demanding writing for young adults with *The Owl Service* (1967), in which a disastrous love affair first told in the Mabinogion is played out again in modern Wales, and *Red Shift* (1973), a text as challenging as a French nouveau roman. What has been particularly satisfying about these developments is that, although anxiety concerning issues to do with sex was obviously what most disturbed adults about adolescents' reading, and this is manifest in Garner's work, the best young adult fiction has also approached many other topics of real importance.

For example, another of the earliest writers who have made the last thirty years rich for adolescent readers is James Watson, whose novels are powerful challenges to do with the state of the world. Sometimes they deal with past, though not distant history: *The Freedom Tree* (1976), for example, is about the Spanish Civil War. But he also writes of more recent conflicts, and with few inhibitions; *Justice of the Dagger* (1998), set in the recent conflict in East Timor, makes no bones about the appropriate retaliation a brave girl inflicts on a rapist army officer. Sex is relevant here, but the real theme is oppression and response, and a powerful rebuttal of the idea that the young are too young to fight back. Areas of conflict provide him with settings in which he makes, again and again, the point that the courage of the young may not triumph, but it will not be destroyed. Such engagement of the young in political and revolutionary activity has also been well written about by Peter Dickinson in such novels as *AK* (1990).

More demanding even than these is a single novel from Aidan Chambers, *Postcards from No Man's Land* (1999), which runs in parallel the growing pains of an adolescent boy visiting Holland for a ceremony in the Second World War cemetery where his grandfather is buried and a narrative about the love affair of a young Dutch girl and the Allied airman her family sheltered during that war. The boldness and integrity with which this novel confronts homosexuality, bisexuality, and euthanasia make it powerfully different from those feeble novels referred to earlier that tried to cram in as many "issues" as possible: the issues here involve the real feelings of well-imagined people, and demand serious ethical choices from them, and the movement of the novel brings them in naturally, not artificially.

This is not, of course, to suggest that everything being published for young adults is of this level of seriousness or that political engagement is the only important issue that arises in literature for adolescents. The excellent writing that has made the last decades of the 20th and the first of the 21st c. so rich for teenage readers covers every possibility. There is, for example, serious romance: Diana Wynne Jones, who usually writes for younger children, in *Fire and Hemlock* (1984) picks up the old ballad of Tam Lin and makes an intensely emotional narrative of the heroine's attempt to rescue her demon lover. There is also frivolous romance: Louise Rennison has produced a series of adolescent versions of the voguish first-person narrative of a young woman's anxieties about her sex life and her shape, like *Knocked Out by My Nunga-Nungas* (2001). Similarly, as well as the general run of horror stories that young adult readers have eagerly picked up from the U.S. Point Horror publishers, there are really dark, complex, and, again, emotionally satisfying stories like John Gordon's *The Flesh Eater* (1997), where the flesh-creeping properties of the narrative are counterbalanced by the reality of the hero's attempts to ground his life in feelings he is only beginning to understand.

The use of genres like horror to give a narrative focus to stories with deeper issues to deal with is common, and science fiction provides one of the most powerful of these. Three outstanding very recent novels start from such a basis to develop the kind of depth of which science fiction, as well as young people's literature, is not supposed to be capable. Different kinds of science fiction idea are used in each. *The Sterkarm Handshake* (1998), by Susan Price, uses the notion of controlled time travel: a modern multinational business has been able to set up a time tunnel that gives access to the Scottish/English Borders in the days when they were the center of wild thieving and revenges, and send a young woman anthropologist to live with a band of reivers with whom they believe they can do useful business; appalled and fascinated, she falls in love with the son of the chief and it is hard to describe the outcome other than as tragedy. Jan Mark's *Eclipse of the Century* (1999) brings together a number of different peoples, some of whom do not seem to belong to this planet, in a millennial confrontation in Central Asia that again has an ambiguous but almost certainly tragic outcome. Lesley Howarth's *Ultraviolet* (2001) looks forward to a near future in which the power of the sun has become so destructive that people live underground most of the year, and only the rich can afford the protective plastic that the heroine's father's firm is producing in deliberately controlled quantities to maximize its profits; by involving Violet in a virtual reality computer game, the novelist makes it extraordinarily difficult for the reader to know whether what is happening is real or her fantasy, or, rather, at what stage what is happening shifts from real to fantasy and back. Looking at each of these novels, it is hard to see how they could have been deepened, darkened, or made a more challenging read if they had been designed for an adult rather than young adult readership, or indeed if they had been "serious" rather than science fiction.

There is certainly plenty of serious material; the novel of feelings for the adolescent is very strong, though usually linked to some specific social cause; for example, novels grounded in the experience of refugees, asylum seekers, and illegal immigrants have become important, beginning, perhaps, with Annie Campling's *Smiling for Strangers* (1998), and climaxing recently with the award-winning *The Other Side of Truth* (2000) by Beverley Naidoo. The strength of such fictions causes some skepticism about Melvin Burgess's implied claim to be the only writer dealing with the realities of young people's lives today; his prize-winning *Junk* (1997), about heroin addiction, and his recent *Lady: My Life as a Bitch* (2001) about promiscuity certainly deal powerfully with some of the outer edges of such realities, but are no more typical of the lives of the majority of young people than is *Kerosene* (1999) by Chris Wooding, a strong and disturbing novel about a young arsonist and the social and emotional forces that drive him, and in which all his friends and enemies smoke, and some actually deal in, marijuana. The truth is that fiction for young adults today has become a remarkably wide-ranging and stimulating field of literature, which perhaps suffers from being included with children's fiction in the market for prizes; it would certainly be timely for it to be taken more seriously; that its bibliography is coterminous with that for CHILDREN'S LITERATURE is sad evidence of the lack of proper attention.

BIBLIOGRAPHY: Carpenter, H., and M. Prichard, *The Oxford Companion to Children's Literature* (1984); Feehan, P. E., and P. P. Barron, eds., *Writers on Writing for Young Adults* (1991); Hunt, P., ed., *The International Companion Encyclopedia of Children's Literature* (1996); MacRae, C. D., *Presenting Young Adult Fantasy Fiction* (1998)

AUDREY LASKI

YOUNG, Edward

bap. 3 July 1683, Upham, near Winchester; d. 5 April 1765, Welwyn

Recalled primarily for his introspective observations on death and spirituality, Y. is traditionally associated with the graveyard school of the Augustan Age. As a poet and dramatist, Y. demonstrated a diversity of interests and motivations. Although his poetic achievements are significant, his substantive and stylistic inconsistencies have historically invited contrasting criticisms.

Born to privileged class at the twilight of the Restoration, Y. was afforded the educational and social advantages that such fortune implied. The son of the Dean of Salisbury, Y. was educated at Oxford and recognized as a young poet amid the political upheaval that prefaced the Hanoverian succession. He soon found a place among the influential literary circles of London and his personal associations with Joseph ADDISON, Richard STEELE, Alexander POPE, and Jonathan SWIFT served as a vital foundation of influence for his work throughout his life.

Y.'s earliest recognition followed the success of his first dramatic works. Emblematic of the contemporary tragedy, his first play, *Busiris, King of Egypt* (1719), possessed a balance of complexity, violence, and surprise that earned its acclaim at Drury Lane. Likewise, the traitorous themes and keen, simple plot of his second tragedy, *The Revenge* (1721), earned him the esteem of the London theater community and an annuity from the Duke of Wharton to whom Y. had dedicated both works.

Like his dramatic works, Y.'s first poetic achievements were a conventional reflection of the Augustan ethos. His satirical multiyear series, *The Universal Passion* (7 vols., 1725–28), employed the rhythm of heroic couplet and entertained the popular preoccupation with the vices of vanity and pretense. Though thoughtfully conceived and widely read, the more celebrated titles of the genre by Pope readily eclipsed his work, a dynamic that proved a life-long frustration for Y.

Having taken holy orders and a royal pension as chaplain to King George I, Y.'s poetic focus was frequently predicated on the attraction of influential political figures to ensure future gains. Although this motivation was common for the era, Y. received criticism for his unabashed flattery and unmemorable form. His extensive treatises and dedications to royalty that included *A Vindication of Providence; or, A True Estimate of Human Life* (1728), *Ocean: An Ode* (1728), and *Imperium Pelagi* (1730) would be regarded for their substance, but harshly criticized for their weak lyrical composition.

Moved by the successive deaths of his wife, stepdaughter, and close friend, Y.'s *The Complaint; or, Night-Thoughts on Life, Death, and Immortality* (6 vols., 1741–45), published in separate "Nights," marked a profound departure from any of his previous work. Regarded as his most significant and best-known work, the series was produced over a period of five years and divided into nine individual poems containing his moral reflections on life, death, human nature, and the ultimate acceptance of Christianity. A dramatic dialogue of blank verse comprising more than 10,000 lines, a feature uncommon in the period, the work drew criticism for its ineffectiveness and moral bombast, but praise for its strength and emotional resonance. The mournfully expressive undercurrents of "Nights" ultimately categorized it as a feature of the graveyard school of James THOMSON and Thomas GRAY.

While the emotion of "Nights" had already suggested a personal transformation from the neoclassical conventions of sensibility, Y.'s later prose, *Conjectures on Original Composition* (1759) gave way to a more Romantic disposition. His letter to Samuel RICHARDSON employed natural imagery and metaphors to impress the necessity of originality and self-expression. For such themes that plainly anticipated the literary evolution to come, Y. is regarded as among the precursors to early Romantic thought.

Review of Y.'s character and composition is often grounded in the unavoidable dichotomy that is presented by dogged morality, placed against the backdrop of seemingly blatant adulation. Thus, criticism of Y. has historically underscored his lyrical inability and rejected his motivation, perhaps unfairly, as insincere contrivance. In recent decades, however, criticism has sought to assess his approach in the context of Augustan social conventions and more importantly as a transformational element to the Romantic movement. Y. continued to serve as rector of Welwyn and publish smaller works until his death in April 1765. Though his name would remain in the shadow of more prominent Augustans, his recognition as a preface to ROMANTICISM is of genuine consequence.

BIBLIOGRAPHY: Bliss, I. St. J., *E. Y.* (1969); Foster, H., *E. Y.* (1986); Wicker, C. V., *E. Y. and the Fear of Death* (1952)

JACK BRODERICK

Z

ZANGWILL, Israel

b. 21 January 1864, London; d. 1 August 1926, Midhurst, Sussex

Between 1892—the year of publication in three volumes of *Children of the Ghetto*—and his death, Z. occupied a central position in the Jewish community, first as a writer in Britain, and after 1900 increasingly as a political thinker and activist internationally. At the same time, it was his consistent aim to write for a wider audience, whether by leaving the Jewish milieu altogether or by developing his vision of Judaism to have that universal appeal that he admired in his model Spinoza. Aside from one novel, he is now virtually unread, and his wayward contributions to the founding of Zionism tend to be disregarded by his successors. However, his writer's concern for the detail of Jewish life, on the problems of immigration, tradition, innovation, and assimilation are as much a part of fin de siècle Jewish thought as the works of Max Nordau and Theodor Herzl, and in the range of his concerns he was unmatched.

Z. began his career as a writer of short stories and occasional pieces, as a journalist both for the London Jewish press and for Jerome K. JEROME's popular "New Humor" collections. An essay entitled "English Judaism," contributed to the *Jewish Quarterly Review* in 1889, attracted widespread attention, and led to Mayer Sulzberger's proposal that Z. should write a Jewish version of Mrs. Humphry WARD's *Robert Elsmere,* a novel that would point a religious way forward. Despite initial doubts, Z. immersed himself in the project, and the result—which predictably bears little resemblance to its prescribed model—was the widely acclaimed *Children of the Ghetto.* In this novel, Z. draws on his journalistic experience to draw a realistic picture of the different estates within English Jewry, concentrating first on the poverty-stricken East European immigrants and sweatshops of the East End, and then on the wealthy and self-satisfied Anglo-Jewry whom Amy LEVY had recently satirized in *Reuben Sachs.* These two centers correspond to the two parts of the novel, in which a loosely woven plot meditated on generational conflict and problems of tradition and modernity; characteristically, at the end of each part, escape to America is presented as the solution to the problems of assimilation with which English society faces Jews, rich or poor. Throughout the novel, which is rich in SATIRE and Meredithian dialogue, there is a productive tension between Z.'s overt identification with the rising generation—the grandchildren of the ghetto—and their wider aspirations, and his insistence on the values of the older immigrants, however limited and repressive they may appear.

The 1890s marked Z.'s peak as a writer, with the publication of some fine short stories, notably "Satan Mekatrig" and the novella "The King of Schnorrers." His most ambitious work, *Dreamers of the Ghetto* (1898), branches out into a new genre—a collection of fictionalized stories of Jewish figures, mainly historical, who Z. saw as carrying the essential Judaism of the rebel and the heterodox. They include Spinoza, the pseudo-Messiah Sabbatai Zevi, Heinrich Heine, Ferdinand Lassalle, and even the delegates to the First Zionist Congress; and these stories are interspersed with meditations on the tortured relationship of Judaism and Christianity, on persecution and emancipation, on festivals, the Law, and the meaning of the Holy Land. Initially welcomed by Jews and non-Jews alike as showing a unique understanding of modern Judaism, *Dreamers of the Ghetto* is now virtually forgotten.

For twenty years after 1900, the "dreamer" Z. was to be a fiercely polemical activist in different factions of the Zionist movement. At the same time, he continued to write novels, no longer on Jewish themes, and plays of which the best known is *The Melting Pot* (1909). Here, the "American solution" seen in *Children of the Ghetto* is used to bring together a pair of lovers, a Russian-Jewish composer and the daughter of a Russian anti-Semite; the "melting-pot" of

America and the recognition that they share beliefs that transcend racial particularity unites them at the end. In contrast to his stories, Z.'s efforts at drama were generally judged to be unsuccessful, didactic, and wordy.

It could be said that Z. has suffered the fate of many pioneers. Among the first to diagnose the problems of emancipated Jewry, and the conflict between traditional values and universal ones, he lived to see his various suggested solutions become irrelevant in the cataclysm of the First World War and its aftermath. Since then, the larger disasters of Europe, of Jews and Arabs, some of which he had foreseen, have made his ideas of a transcendent reconciliation that somehow preserved Jewish specificity still more remote. Yet in his refusal to deny the value either of traditional Judaism or of the generation who impatiently rejected it—the children and grandchildren of the ghetto—he remained, in his best work, a committed and complex writer.

BIBLIOGRAPHY: Adams, E. B., *I. Z.* (1971); Leftwich, J., *I. Z.* (1957); Udelson, J. H., *Dreamer of the Ghetto: The Life and Works of I. Z.* (1990)

JEAN RADFORD

ZEPHANIAH, Benjamin [Obadiah Iqbal]
b. 15 April 1958, Handsworth, Birmingham

Born in England, Z. was reared both in Jamaica and Handsworth in Birmingham. This heavy doubling of cultural roots produced at first the allegedly uncontrollable individual who spent much of his teens in approved schools and later had a taste of prison life, convicted of burglary. Whether the prison experience made him a poet or not is debatable but certainly after this time Z. rehabilitated himself via music and poetry. He learned to read at the age of twenty-one and his abilities as an impersonator and a reggae DJ in and around Birmingham all fed directly into the totality of his performances. He cites Martin Luther King, Malcolm X, Michael X, Angela Davis, Marcus Garvey, and the reggae musician Big Youth as influences upon his work and thought.

Z. has been categorized variously as a Rasta poet, a reggae poet, a dub poet, a performance poet, a pub poet, a rap poet, and a black poet. While remaining unoffended by these labels, he prefers the title of oral poet, thus aligning himself with ancient traditions in poetry, and especially recalling African roots and implicitly casting some suspicion upon Western manipulations of printed text. Watching Z. in action, one can see at once the importance to him of the direct link between poet and audience, and the play made between audience reactions and performance. Z. dislikes the way that the West tries to categorize what he does and enjoys the wide-ranging scope of the oral experi-

ence. Like the Caribbean calypso singer or African griot, he attempts the mixing of several career styles—newscaster, political commentator, poet, agitator, comedian, actor, and teller of stories.

The British literary establishment seems in some ways to want to retain Z.'s own distinction between performance poetry and "literature," and frequently the attitude is one of reaction, or simply to overlook his work altogether. This underscores his relationship to the fragile oral traditions globally, where in more violent and politicized regimes, whole cultural spectra are being obliterated.

Z. began as a performer in a church in 1968 and generated a following in his hometown by the age of fifteen, but he found the local horizons too small. The dub poet Linton Kwesi JOHNSON was instrumental in paving the way for Z. and other poets with his groundbreaking *Dread Beat and Blood,* and when Z. moved to London his *Pen Rhythm* (1980) ran into three editions. Z.'s poetic career in the 1980s was given a boost by his enormously popular output as a dub poet, initially with *Dub Ranting* (1982) and *Rasta* (1983) featuring The Wailers, which famously led to his meeting with Nelson Mandela. Z. continued his output with several other compilations such as *Us An Dem* (1990) and *Belly of De Beast* (1996). Subjects covered in these productions include especially social and political polemic, foregrounding the "street politics" that are central to his work, on his quest to take poetry to all the corners of the globe using all kinds of media, to change the "dead, white and boring image of poetry." In 1991, he realized this global ambition, performing to audiences on every continent during a twenty-two day stint, lending a new modern meaning to the idea of oral poetry.

In 1992, *City Psalms* was published by Bloodaxe. This seminal volume succinctly displays Z.'s exceptional abilities in rhythm, couplet rhyme, alliterative effects, irony, and subtle variations of line length and cadence. The broad subject area of this volume covers male behavior, the arms industry, money, injustice, police brutality, the freedoms of pen and voice, Cold Wars, being African, ideas of God, black life in the so-called Mother Country, the example of Royalty, righteous brawling against the National Front, green issues, the underprivileged, not playing cricket, domestic violence, boxing, and tabloid newspapers.

The poem "Rapid Rapping" list Z.'s peers in performance poetry "bringing poetry alive." Z.'s poem "Dis Poetry" sets out firstly the condition of being a practicing oral poet, and secondly serves as his poetic manifesto, showing a poetry that despite being "Verbal Riddim" is "not afraid of going ina book." The stunning variety of line length and layout arrangements on the pages of this volume is a tribute to this poet's skill in his medium. The volume *Propa Propaganda* (1996) is another exceptional book of poems in the same vein, mingling ironic HUMOR in "White Comedy" with subjects that horrify in their brutality, like "The Death of Joy Gardner." Z. has also published a series of radical plays including the bittersweet radio play *Hurricane Dub* (1989), *Streetwise* (1990), and *Mickey Tekka* (1991).

Despite his initial fears about diluting poetry into categories or age groups, Z. is also a very successful and inspirational writer for children. His writings in this field include *Talking Turkeys* (1994) and *Funky Chickens* (1996), which boldly cover "adult" subjects, real issues, and supply a need for young people to have a literature of their own and to enjoy the accessibility he promotes. His 1999 novel for the younger audience entitled *Face* explores the fate of a white kid who loses his face in a joyriding accident and is brought into a revelatory understanding of discrimination.

To some extent, Z. remains a thorn in the side of the British academic establishment whose reactions to his narrowly defeated short-listing for a fellowship in Trinity College, Cambridge, in 1987 and his nomination for Oxford Professor of Poetry, elicited predictable anxieties and outrages. His work however continues to flourish. He is a wonderfully entertaining and stimulating stage presence, and a radical voice addressing the "downpressor" in every walk of life.

BIBLIOGRAPHY: Donnell, A., and S. L. Welsh, *The Routledge Reader in Caribbean Literature* (1996); Middleton. D. J., "Chanting Down Babylon: Three Rastafarian Dub Poets," in Nelson, A. M. S., ed., *"This Is How We Flow": Rhythm in Black Culture* (1999): 74–86

CHRISTOPHER J. P. SMITH

Monarchs of Great Britain

Monarchs of England

House of Wessex
Egbert (802–39)
Æthelwulf (839–55)
Æthelbald (855–60)
Æthelbert (860–6)
Æthelred (866–71)
Alfred the Great (871–99)
Edward the Elder (899–925)
Athelstan (925–40)
Edmund the Magnificent (940–6)
Eadred (946–55)
Eadwig (Edwy) All-Fair (955–59)
Edgar the Peaceable (959–75)
Edward the Martyr (975–78)
Aethelred the Unready (978–1016)
Edmund Ironside (1016)

Danish Line
Svein Forkbeard (1014)
Canute the Great (1016–35)
Harald Harefoot (1035–40)
Hardicanute (1040–42)

House of Wessex, Restored
Edward the Confessor (1042–66)
Harold II (1066)

Norman Line
William I the Conqueror (1066–87)
William II Rufus (1087–1100)
Henry I Beauclerc (1100–35)
Stephen (1135–54)
Empress Matilda (1141)

Plantagenet, Angevin Line
Henry II Curtmantle (1154–89)
Richard I the Lionheart (1189–99)
John Lackland (1199–1216)
Henry III (1216–72)
Edward I Longshanks (1272–1307)

Edward II (1307–27)
Edward III (1327–77)
Richard II (1377–99)

Plantagenet, Lancastrian Line
Henry IV Bolingbroke (1399–1413)
Henry V (1413–22)
Henry VI (1422–61, 1470–1)

Plantagenet, Yorkist Line
Edward IV (1461–70, 1471–83)
Edward V (1483)
Richard III (1483–85)

House of Tudor
Henry VII Tudor (1485–1509)
Henry VIII (1509–47)
Edward VI (1547–53)
Lady Jane Grey (1553)
Mary I Tudor (1553–58)
Elizabeth I (1558–1603)

Monarchs of Great Britain

House of Stuart
James I (1603–25)
Charles I (1625–49)

The Commonwealth
Oliver Cromwell (1649–58)
Richard Cromwell (1658–59)

House of Stuart, Restored
Charles II (1660–85)
James II (1685–88)

House of Orange and Stuart
William III, Mary II (1689–1702)

House of Stuart
Anne (1702–14)

House of Brunswick, Hanover Line
George I (1714–27)
George II (1727–60)

George III (1760–1820)
George IV (1820–30)
William IV (1830–37)
Victoria (1837–1901)

House of Saxe-Coburg-Gotha
Edward VII (1901–10)

House of Windsor
George V (1910–36)
Edward VIII (1936)
George VI (1936–52)
Elizabeth II (1952–present)

Monarchs of Scotland

Kenneth I (843–58)
Donald I (858–62)
Constantine I (863–77)
Aed (877–78)
Giric (878–89) and Echaid (878–89)
Donald II (889–900)
Constantine II (900–943)
Malcolm I (943–54)
Indulf (954–62)
Dubh (962–67)
Culen (967–71)
Kenneth II (971–95)
Constantine III (995–97)
Kenneth III (997–1005)
Malcolm II (1005–34)
Duncan I (1034–40)
Macbeth (1040–57)
Lulach (1057–58)
Malcolm III (1058–93)
Donald III (1093–94)
Duncan II (1094)
Duncan III, Restored (1094–97)
Edgar (1097–1107)
Alexander I (1107–24)
David I (1124–53)
Malcolm IV (1153–65)
William I (1165–1214)
Alexander II (1214–49)
Alexander III (1249–86)
Margaret (1286–90)
Interregnum (competition for Crown)
John (1292–96)
Interregnum
Robert I (1306–29)
David II (1329–71)
Robert II (1371–90)
Robert III (1390–1406)
James I (1406–37)
James II (1437–60)
James III (1460–88)

James IV (1488–1513)
James V (1513–42)
Mary Queen of Scots (1542–67)
James VI (1567–1625)
Charles I (1625–49)
Charles II (1649–85)
James VII (1685–89)
William II (1689–1702) and Mary II (1689–94)
Anne (1702–7)

Monarchs of Wales

Gwynedd
Rhodri Mawr (Rhodri the Great) (844–78)
Anarawad ap Rhodri (878–916)
Idwal the Bald (916–42)
Hywel Dda (Hywel the Good) (942–50)
Ieuaf ap Idwal (950–69) and Igao ap Idwal
    (950–79)
Hywel ap Ieuaf (979–85)
Cadwallon ap Ieuaf (985–86)
Maredudd ap Owain (986–99)
Cynan ap Hywel (999–1005)
Llywelyn ap Seisyll (1005–23)
Iago ap Idwal ap Meurig (1023–39)
Gruffydd ap Llywelyn (1039–63)
Rhiwallon ap Cynfyn (1063–70) and Bleddyn ap
    Cynfyn (1063–75)
Trahaern ap Caradog (1075–81)
Gruffydd ap Cynan (1081–1137)
Owain Gwynedd (1137–70)

East Gwynedd
Dafydd ab Owain (1170–95)

West Gwynedd
Rhodri ab Owain (1170–90)

Gwynedd, Restored
Llywelyn ap Iorwerth (1195–1240)
Dafydd ap Llywelyn (1240–46)
Owain Goch (1246–55) and Llywelyn ap Gruffydd
    (1246–82)
Dafydd ap Gruffydd (1282–83)

Deheubarth
Hywel Dda (Hywel the Good) (920–950)
Interregnum
Owain ap Hywel (954–86)
Maredudd ap Owain (986–99)
Cynan ap Hywel (999–1005)
Edwin and Cadell ap Einion (1005–18)
Llywelyn ap Seisyll (1018–23)
Rhydderch ab Iestyn (1023–33)
Hywel ap Edwin (1033–44)
Interregnum
Gruffydd ap Rhydderch (1047–55)

Gruffydd ap Llywelyn (1055–63)
Maredudd ap Owain (1063–72)
Rhys ap Owain (1072–78)
Rhys ap Tewdwr (1078–93)
Interregum (Norman possession)
Gruffydd ap Rhys (1116–36)
Anarawd ap Gruffydd (1136–43)
Cadell ap Gruffydd (1143–51)
Maredudd ap Gruffydd (1151–55)
Rhys ap Gruffydd (1155–97)
Gruffydd ap Rhys (1197–1201)

Powys
Bleddyn ap Cynfyn (1063–75)

Maredudd ap Bleddyn (1116–32)
Madog ap Maredudd (1132–60)

Southern Powys
Owain Cyfeiliog (1160–95)
Gwenwynwyn (1195–1216)
Gruffydd ap Gwenwynwyn (1240–57; restored
     1263–74; restored 1277–86)

Northern Powys
Gruffudd Maelor I (1160–91)
Madog ap Gruffudd (1191–1236)
Gruffydd Maelor II (1236–69)

Historical-Literary Timeline

ca. 5000–ca. 2500 B.C.E	Neolithic Period	
ca. 2500–ca. 750	Bronze Age; henge monuments erected; warrior class emerges (ca. 1200–ca. 1000)	
ca. 659–C.E. 43	Iron Age; period of invasion and immigration; spread of Celtic influence (ca. 500–100)	
43–410	Roman conquest and occupation	
ca. 440–50	Civil war and famine	
450–650	Anglo-Saxon Britain (ca. 450–650); Old English language and literature (ca. 450–1150)	
597	St. Augustine introduces Roman Christianity in England; becomes Archbishop of Canterbury (602)	
600		Aneirin, *Y Gododdin; Widsith* (wr. ca. 600)
604	St. Paul's Cathedral in London founded	
670		Cædmon, "Hymn of Creation" (wr. ca. 670)
700		*Lindisfarne Gospels* (wr. ca. 700); *Beowulf* (wr. ca. 700–750); *The Ruin, The Wanderer, The Seafarer, The Wife's Lament, The Husband's Message* (wr. ca. 700–1000)
731		Bede, *Historia Ecclesiastica Gentis Anglorum* (comp.)
787	Viking raids begin; invasion and settlement continue through 11th c.	
800	Charlemagne crowned Holy Roman Emperor	*Book of Kells* (wr. ca. 800)
802	Accession of Egbert and the House of Wessex	
830		Nennius, *Historia Britonum* (wr. ca. 830)

843	Kenneth MacAlpin becomes Kenneth I of Scotland	
844	Rhodri ap Merfyn becomes king of Gwynedd	
871	Death of Æthelred; succeeded by Alfred (later "The Great")	
890		*Anglo-Saxon Chronicle* (wr. 890–1154)
899	Death of Alfred; succeeded by Edward (later "the Elder")	
930		*Judith* (wr. ca. 930)
970		*Annales Cambriae* (wr. 970)
990		Ælfric, *Catholic Homilies* (wr. 990–92)
1000		*The Battle of Maldon; The Dream of the Rood* (wr. ca. 1000)
1014–42	Danish line of kings	
1018	Death of Malcolm II of Scotland; succeeded by Duncan I	
1039	Gruffydd ap Llywelyn becomes king of Gwynedd	
1040	Duncan I of Scotland murdered; succeeded by Macbeth	
1042	Edward (later "the Confessor") becomes king; founds Westminster Abbey (1052)	
1066	Death of Edward; succeeded by Harold II; Norman Conquest begins; William (later "the Conqueror") becomes king	
1086	Domesday Book (comp.)	
1095	First Crusade begins; Jerusalem captured (1099)	
1100	Middle English language and literature (ca. 1100–ca. 1500)	
1124	Death of Alexander I of Scotland; succeeded by David I	
1136		Geoffrey of Monmouth, *Historia Regum Britanniae* (wr. ca. 1136)
1154	Death of Stephen; Henry Plantagenet becomes Henry II	
1155		Robert "Maistre" Wace, *Roman de Brut* (wr. ca. 1155)
1162	Thomas Becket becomes Archbishop of Canterbury; Constitutions of Clarendon (1164); Becket murdered in Canterbury Cathedral (1170)	
1174	Treaty of Falaise	

1175		*Poema Morale* (wr. ca. 1175)
1189	Death of Henry II; succeeded by Richard I (later "the Lionheart")	
1190		"Katherine Group" (wr. ca. 1190–1225)
1196	Llywelyn ap Iorwerth becomes king of Gwynedd	
1199	Death of Richard I; succeeded by John	
1200		*The Owl and the Nightingale* (wr. ca. 1200)
1205		Layamon, *Brut* (wr. ca. 1205)
1214	Death of William II; Alexander II becomes king of Scotland	
1215	Magna Carta signed	
1216	Death of John; succeeded by Henry III	
1218	Treaty of Worcester	
1225		*King Horn* (wr. ca. 1225)
1230		*Ancrene Wisse* (wr. ca. 1230)
1235		Matthew Paris, *Chronica Majora* (wr. ca. 1235–59)
1237	Treaty of York	
1249	Death of Alexander II; succeeded by Alexander III; University College, Oxford, founded	
1250		*Llyfr Du Caerfyrddin* (Black Book of Carmarthen); *Mabinogion* (comp. ca. 1250); Towneley Plays (perf. ca. 1250–ca. 1450)
1264	Merton College, Oxford, founded	
1267	Treaty of Montgomery	Roger Bacon, *Opus Maius; Opus minus; Opus tertium* (wr.)
1272	Death of Henry III; succeeded by Edward I	
1283	Annexation of Wales to England	
1284	Statue of Rhuddlan; Peterhouse College, Cambridge, founded	
1290		*Horn Childe* (wr. ca. 1290–1340)
1295	Model Parliament	
1297	Scottish rebellion; Robert Bruce becomes Robert I of Scotland (1306)	
1300	Early Scots language and literature (ca. 1300-ca. 1450)	*Cursor Mundi; Guy of Warwick* (wr. ca. 1300)
1314	Battle of Bannockburn	

1325		*Llyfr Gwyn Rhydderch* (White Book of Rhydderch, comp. ca. 1325)
1328	Treaty of Northampton	
1337	Hundred Years' War begins (1337–1453)	
1338	Treaty of Koblenz	
1348	Black Death (bubonic plague) reaches England	
1360		William Langland, *Piers Plowman* (A-text; wr. ca. 1360)
1368		Geoffrey Chaucer, *The Book of the Duchess* (wr. ca. 1368)
1375	Truce of Bruges	*Sir Gawain and the Green Knight* (wr. ca. 1375); York Plays (perf. ca. 1375–ca. 1569)
1376		John Barbour, *The Bruce* (wr.); John Gower, *Mirour de l'Omme* (wr.)
1377	Death of Edward III; succeeded by Richard II	Langland, *Piers Plowman* (B-text; comp.)
1380		English New Testament (comp.)
1381	Peasants' Revolt	
1382		Chaucer, *The Parliament of Fowls* (wr. ca. 1382)
1385		Chaucer, *Troilus and Criseyde* (wr. ca. 1358)
1386		Chaucer, *The Canterbury Tales* (wr. ca. 1386)
1390		Gower, *Confessio Amantis* (wr. ca. 1390–92)
1399	Death of John of Gaunt; Richard II deposed and murdered (1400); Henry of Bolingbroke becomes Henry IV	
1400		*Llyfr Coch Hergest* (Red Book of Hergest, comp. ca. 1400)
1411	St. Andrew's University founded	John Hoccleve, *The Regiment of Princes* (wr. 1411–12)
1412		John Lydgate, *Troy Book* (wr. ca. 1412–20)
1413	Death of Henry IV; succeeded by Henry V	
1420		Andrew of Wyntoun, *Oryngynale Cronykil* (wr. ca. 1420); Lydgate, *The Siege of Thebes* (wr. ca. 1420–22)
1422	Death of Henry V; succeeded by Henry VI	
1431		Lydgate, *Fall of Princes* (wr. ca. 1431–39)
1436		Margery Kempe, *The Book of Margery Kempe* (wr. ca. 1436–38)

1440		N-Town Plays (perf. ca. 1440–ca. 1500)
1441	King's College, Cambridge, founded	
1445	Johannes Gutenberg, in Germany, develops first printing press with movable type	
1450	Golden Age of Scottish poetry begins (1450–1568); Middle Scots language and literature (ca. 1450–ca. 1620)	
1451	University of Glasgow founded	
1454	War of the Roses begins	
1458	Magdalen College, Oxford, founded	
1460	Battle of Northampton; Henry VI captured; Edward of York becomes Edward IV (1461)	*Mankind* (wr. ca. 1460–70)
1470	Henry VI restored to the throne; death of Henry VI (1471); Edward IV restored to the throne	
1476	William Caxton establishes printing press at Westminster	
1483	Death of Edward IV; Edward V and his brother are murdered in the Tower of London; Richard III becomes king	
1485	Battle of Bosworth Field: Henry Tudor defeats and kills Richard III; becomes Henry VII and marries Elizabeth of York, uniting houses of York and Lancaster	Thomas Malory, *Le Morte d'Arthur*
1492	Christopher Columbus discovers the West Indies	
1495	King's College (later University of Aberdeen) founded	Henry Medwall, *Nature* (wr. ca. 1495)
1500		Chester Plays (perf. ca. 1500–ca. 1575)
1501		Desiderius Erasmus, *Enchiridion*
1506		John Colet, *A Rightful Fruitful Meditation*
1509	Death of Henry VII; succeeded by Henry VIII	*Everyman* (wr. ca. 1509–19); Alexander Barclay, *The Ship of Fools* (tr.); Stephen Hawes, *The Pastime of Pleasure*
1511		Erasmus, *Encomium Moriae; In Praise of Folly*
1512	St. Paul's School founded	
1513	Battle of Flodden Field; death of James IV	John Skelton *Ballade of the Scottisshe Kynge;* Barclay, *Eclogues* (wr. 1513–14)
1516		Erasmus, *The Novum Instrumentum;* Thomas More, *Utopia;* Skelton, *Magnyfycence* (perf.)
1517	Protestant Reformation begins in Germany	

1521		Henry VIII of England, *Assertio septem sacramentorum adversus Martinum Lutherum*
1522		Skelton, *The Tunnyng of Elynour Rummyng* (ca. 1522)
1525		William Tyndale, New Testament (tr.)
1529	Sir Thomas More appointed Lord Chancellor	
1530		John Rastell, *A New Boke of Purgatory* (wr.); Tyndale, *The Practyse of Prelates*
1531		Thomas Elyot, *The Boke Named the Governour*
1533	Henry VIII marries Anne Boleyn; excommunicated by Pope Clement VII	Elyot, *Pasquil the Playne;* John Heywood, *The Play of the Wether;* T. More, *Apology of Sir Thomas More*
1534	Act of Supremacy	Elyot, *The Castel of Helth;* Polydore Vergil, *Anglica Historia*
1535	Sir Thomas More executed	English Bible (comp.)
1536		Robert Copland, *The High Way to the Spyttell House* (ca. 1536); Reginald Pole, *De unitate* (wr.)
1538		Elyot, *Dictionary* (Latin/English)
1542	Mary Stuart becomes queen of Scotland	
1545		Roger Ascham, *Toxophilus;* Elyot, *A Preservative agaynste Deth;* Katherine Parr, *Prayers or Meditations*
1546	Trinity College, Cambridge, founded	*Yn y Lhyvyr Hwnn;* J. Heywood, *A Dialogue Conteinying the Number in Effect of All the Proverbs in the Englishe Tongue, Compacte in a Matter Concernying Two Maner of Mariages*
1547	Death of Henry VIII; succeeded by Edward VI	William Baldwin, *A Treatise of Moral Philosophy*
1548		Edward Hall, *The Union of the Two Noble and Illustre Families of Lancaster and York* (2nd ed.)
1549		*The Book of Common Prayer*
1551	Censorship of the theater begins; continues through mid-20th c.	Thomas Wilson, *The Rule of Reason*
1553	Death of Edward VI; Protestant Lady Jane Grey proclaimed queen; reigned nine days, was beheaded; Catholic Mary Tudor becomes Mary I	Nicholas Udall, *Ralph Roister Doister* (perf. 1553; pub. ca. 1556)
1554		John Foxe, *Commentarii rerum in ecclesia gestarum*
1555	Roman Catholicism restored	Andrew Boorde, *The Fyrste Book of the Introduction of Knowledge*

1556		*Gammer Gurton's Needle* (perf.); J. Heywood, *The Spider and the Flie*
1557		Foxe, *Christus Triumphans;* Richard Tottel, *Songes and Sonettes*
1558	Death of Mary I; succeeded by Elizabeth I	John Knox, *The First Blast of the Trumpet against the Monstrous Regiment of Women*
1559		*A Mirror for Magistrates*
1560	Treaty of Edinburgh	
1562		Thomas Norton and Thomas Sackville, *Gorboduc* (perf.)
1563	Thirty-Nine Articles; Church of England established	Foxe, *Actes and Monuments;* Barnabe Googe, *Eclogues, Epitaphs and Sonnets*
1564	Peace of Troyes	Richard Edwards, *Damon and Pythias* (perf.)
1566		George Gascoigne, *Jocasta* (perf.); *The Supposes* (perf.); William Painter, *The Palace of Pleasure*
1567		Geoffrey Fenton, *Certaine Tragicall Discourses written oute of Frenche and Latin*
1568		Edmund Tilney, *The Flower of Friendship*
1570		Baldwin, *Beware the Cat*
1571	Jesus College, Oxford, founded	
1572	St. Bartholomew's Day massacre	
1576		Edwards, *The Paradyse of Dainty Devises;* George Whetstone, *The Rock of Regard*
1577	Sir Francis Drake circumnavigates the globe; James Burbage opens first theater in London	Raphael Holinshed, *The Chronicles of England, Scotland, and Ireland*
1578		John Lyly, *Euphues, the Anatomy of Wit*
1579		Edmund Spenser, *The Shepheardes Calender*
1580		John Stow, *The Chronicles of England*
1581	Merchant Taylors' School founded	Sir Philip Sidney, *Old Arcadia* (comp.)
1582	University of Edinburgh founded	Richard Hakluyt, *Diverse Voyages Touching the Discovery of America*
1584	Roanoke Island, North Carolina, founded	Hakluyt, *A Discourse of Western Planting* (wr.); James VI of Scotland, *Essayes of a Prentise in the Divine Art of Poesie;* George Peele, *The Arraignment of Paris;* Reginald Scot, *The Discovery of Witch-craft*
1586		William Camden, *Britannia;* William Webbe, *A Discourse of English Poetry*

1587	Mary Stuart (Mary Queen of Scots) beheaded	Knox, *Historie of the Reformation of Religioun within the Realme of Scotland;* Christopher Marlowe, *Tamburlaine the Great* (perf. 1587–88)
1588	Defeat of the Spanish Armada	Thomas Harriot, *A Brief and True Report of the New Found Land of Virginia;* Lyly, *Endimion* (perf.)
1589		Robert Greene, *Menaphon Camillas Alarum to Slumbering Euphues;* Hakluyt, *Principal Navigations, Voyages, and Discoveries of the English Nation;* Thomas Lodge, *Scillaes Metamorphosis;* Lyly, *Midas* (perf. ca. 1589); George or Richard Puttenham, *The Arte of English Poesie*
1590		R. Greene, *Greenes Mourning Garment;* T. Lodge, *Rosalynde;* Marlowe, *The Jew of Malta* (perf. ca. 1590); Peele, *King Edward the First* (perf. ca. 1590–92); P. Sidney, *New Arcadia;* Spenser, *The Faerie Queene* (bks. 1–3)
1591	Trinity College, Dublin, founded	R. Greene, *Greenes Farwell to Folly;* James VI of Scotland, *His Maiesties Poeticall Exercises at vacant houres;* Peele, *The Old Wives Tale* (perf. ca. 1591–94); William Shakespeare, *Richard III* (perf. ca. 1591–92); P. Sidney, *Astrophel and Stella*
1592	Presbyterian Church in Scotland established	*Arden of Feversham;* Henry Constable, *Diana;* R. Greene, *Greenes Groats-Worth of Wit;* Thomas Kyd, *The Spanish Tragedy;* Thomas Nashe, *Pierce Pennilesse His Supplication to the Devil;* Shakespeare, *The Comedy of Errors* (perf. ca. 1592–94)
1593		Barnabe Barnes, *Parthenopil and Parthenophe;* Michael Drayton, *Idea, the Shepheards Garland;* Richard Hooker, *Of the Laws of Ecclesiastical Polity* (bks. 1–4); Nashe, *Christ's Tears over Jerusalem;* Shakespeare, *Venus and Adonis*
1594	Irish rebellion against English rule	Richard Barnfield, *The Affectionate Shepheard;* Drayton, *Peirs Gaveston;* Marlowe, *Dr. Faustus* (perf.); Nashe, *The Unfortunate Traveller;* Shakespeare, *Lucrece; Love's Labour's Lost* (perf. ca. 1594–95)
1595		*Catalogue of English Printed Books* (pts. 1–2); Drayton, *Endimion and Phoebe;* Shakespeare, *Richard II* (perf. ca. 1595); *A Midsummer Night's Dream* (perf. ca. 1595–96); *Romeo and Juliet* (perf. ca. 1595–96); P. Sidney, *An Apologie for Poetrie*

1596		Sir John Davies, *Orchestra;* Nashe, *Have with You to Saffron-Walden;* Shakespeare, *Henry IV* (pts. 1–2, perf. ca. 1596–97); *The Merchant of Venice* (perf. ca. 1596–98); William Smith, *Chloris;* Spenser, *The Faerie Queene* (bks. 4–6)
1597		Francis Bacon, *Essays* (1st ed.); Joseph Hall, *Virgidemiarum;* Hooker, *Of the Laws of Ecclesiastical Polity* (bk. 5); James VI of Scotland, *Dæmonologie*
1598		Ben Jonson, *Every Man in His Humour* (perf.); Shakespeare, *Much Ado About Nothing* (perf. ca. 1598–99); Stow, *A Survey of London*
1599		Sir John Davies, *Nosce Teipsum;* Thomas Dekker, *The Shoemaker's Holiday* (perf.); James VI of Scotland, *Basilikon Doron;* Nashe, *Nash's Lenten Stuffe;* Shakespeare, *Henry V* (perf.); *Julius Caesar* (perf.)
1600	East India Company founded	John Marston, *Antonio and Melinda; Antonio's Revenge* (perf.); Shakespeare, *Hamlet* (perf. ca. 1600–1601)
1601		Dekker and Marston, *Satiromastix* (perf.); Shakespeare, *Twelfth Night* (perf. ca. 1601–2)
1602		Thomas Campion, *Observations in the Art of English Poesie;* Marston, *The Malcontent* (perf. ca. 1602–3); Shakespeare, *Troilus and Cressida* (perf. ca. 1602); *All's Well That Ends Well* (perf. ca. 1602–3)
1603	Death of Elizabeth I; union of England and Scotland; James VI of Scotland becomes James I of England	Samuel Daniel, *A Defence of Ryme;* John Davies of Hereford, *Microcosmus;* Thomas Heywood, *A Woman Killed with Kindness* (perf.)
1604		George Chapman, *Bussy D'Ambois* (perf.); Shakespeare, *Othello* (perf. ca. 1604); *Measure for Measure* (perf. ca. 1604)
1605	Gunpowder Plot	F. Bacon, *The Advancement of Learning;* Shakespeare, *King Lear* (perf. ca. 1605–6)
1606		J. Hall, *The Art of Divine Meditation;* Jonson, *Volpone* (perf.); Thomas Middleton, *A Mad World, My Masters* (perf. ca. 1606); Shakespeare, *Macbeth* (perf); Cyril Tourneur (or Middleton), *The Revenger's Tragedy* (perf.)
1607	Jamestown, Virginia, founded	Francis Beaumont, *The Knight of the Burning Pestle* (perf. ca. 1607)
1608		T. Heywood, *The Rape of Lucrece* (perf. ca. 1608)

1609	Henry Hudson explores the Delaware and Hudson Rivers	Beaumont and John Fletcher, *Philaster* (perf. ca. 1609); Dekker, *The Guls Horne-book;* Jonson, *Epicoene* (perf.)
1610	Episcopal Church in Scotland established	John Donne, *Pseudo-Martyr;* Jonson, *The Alchemist* (perf.); Tourneur, *The Atheist's Tragedy* (perf. ca. 1610–11)
1611	English and Scottish Protestant colonists settle in Ulster; authorized (King James) version of the Bible (comp.)	Beaumont and J. Fletcher, *The Maid's Tragedy* (perf. ca. 1611); Chapman, *The Iliads of Homer* (tr.); Thomas Coryate, *Coryate's Crudities;* Shakespeare, *The Tempest* (perf.); *The Winter's Tale* (perf.)
1612		F. Bacon, *Essays* (2nd ed.); Drayton, *Poly-Olbion* (pt. 1); J. Fletcher and Shakespeare, *Cardenio* (perf.); John Taylor, *The Sculler;* John Webster, *The White Devil*
1613		William Brown of Tavistock, *Britannia's Pastorals;* Campion, *Songs of Mourning;* Elizabeth Cary, Lady Falkland, *The Tragedy of Mariam, the Fair Queen of Jewry;* J. Fletcher and Shakespeare, *Henry VIII* (perf.); *The Two Noble Kinsmen* (perf.); T. Middleton, *A Chaste Maid in Cheapside* (perf. ca. 1613); Samuel Purchas, *Purchas his Pilgrimage;* George Wither, *Abuses Stript and Whipt*
1614		Jonson, *Bartholomew Fair* (perf.); Walter Raleigh, *The History of the World;* J. Webster, *The Duchess of Malfi* (perf.)
1616	Ben Jonson becomes first (unofficial) poet laureate	Jonson, *The Devil Is an Ass*
1617		Rachel Speght, *A Mouzell for Melastomus*
1618	The Thirty Years' War begins	
1619		Purchas, *Microcosmus*
1620	Plymouth, New England, founded	F. Bacon, *Novum Organum*
1621		John Barclay, *Argenis;* Lady (Mary) Wroth, *The Countesse of Montgomeries Urania*
1622	*Weekly News* begins publication	Drayton, *Poly-Olbion* (pt. 2); Henry Peacham, *The Compleat Gentleman*
1624		Donne, *Devotions upon Emergent Occasions;* Edward Herbert, *De Veritate*
1625	Death of James I; succeeded by Charles I; Carolean Age (1625–49)	F. Bacon, *Essays or Counsels, Civill and Morell;* Philip Massinger, *A New Way to Pay Old Debts* (perf.); Purchas, *Hakluytus Posthumus*
1628	Petition of Right	John Earle, *Micro-cosmographie*
1629	Charles I dissolves Parliament	
1630		John Ford, *'Tis Pity She's a Whore; The Broken Heart* (perf. ca. 1630–33)

1632	Galileo summoned before Inquisition; forced to recant	Massinger, *The City Madam* (perf.)
1633		Phineas Fletcher, *The Purple Island;* Fulke Greville, *A Treatie of Humane Learning;* George Herbert, *The Temple*
1634		William Habington, *Castara;* John Milton, *Comus* (perf.)
1635		Francis Quarles, *Emblemes;* James Shirley, *The Lady of Pleasure* (perf.)
1636		John Hales, *A Tract Concerning Schism and Schismatic* (wr. ca. 1636); William Strode, *The Floating Island* (perf.)
1638	William Davenant becomes poet laureate	Richard Brathwait, *Barnabee's Journal;* Milton, "Lycidas"; John Suckling, *Aglaura*
1639	Act of Toleration	Thomas Fuller, *Historie of the Holy Warre*
1640		James Howell, *Dendrologia*
1642	English Civil War begins (1642–46); theaters closed by Puritans	Thomas Browne, *Religio Medici;* Fuller, *The Holy State*
1643	Licensing Act	
1644		Milton, *Areopagitica*
1645		Howell, *Epistolae Ho-Elianae* (1645–55)
1646		T. Browne, *Pseudodoxia Epidemica;* Richard Crashaw, *Steps to the Temple*
1648	Treaty of Westphalia	Robert Herrick, *Hesperides;* Hooker, *Of the Laws of Ecclesiastical Polity* (bks. 6, 8)
1649	Charles I beheaded; Commonwealth established; Charles II proclaimed King of Scots and England in Scotland	E. Herbert, *The Life and Raigne of King Henry the Eighth;* Richard Lovelace, *Lucasta;* Milton, *The Tenure of Kings and Magistrates;* Gerrard Winstanley, *A Declaration from the Poor Oppressed People of England*
1650		Jeremy Taylor, *The Rule and Exercises of Holy Living;* Henry Vaughan, *Silex Scintillans*
1651	Battle of Worcester; Charles II escapes to France	William Davenant, *Gondibert;* Thomas Hobbes, *Leviathan;* Henry King, *The Psalmes of David;* Jeremy Taylor, *The Rule and Exercises of Holy Dying;* Thomas Vaughan, *Lumen De Lumine*
1653	Oliver Cromwell becomes Lord Protector	Izaak Walton, *The Compleat Angler*
1656		Abraham Cowley, *Poems;* Davenant, *The Siege of Rhodes* (pt. 1, perf.)
1658	Death of Oliver Cromwell; succeeded by Richard Cromwell	T. Browne, *Hydriotaphia*

1660	Protectorate is overthrown; restoration of monarchy; theaters reopened	
1662	Act of Uniformity	Samuel Bulter, *Hudibras* (pt. 1); Fuller, *History of the Worthies of England;* Hooker, *Of the Laws of Ecclesiastical Polity* (bk. 7)
1663		Butler, *Hudibras* (pt. 2); John Dryden, *The Rival Ladies* (perf.); *The Wild Gallant* (perf.)
1665	Great Plague of London; *Oxford Gazette* (later the *London Gazette*) founded	
1666	Great Fire of London	John Bunyan, *Grace Abounding*
1667		Dryden, *Annus Mirabilis; An Essay in Dramatick Poesie;* Milton, *Paradise Lost*
1668	John Dryden becomes first official poet laureate; *Mercurius Librarius* founded	George Etherege, *She Would If She Could;* Charles Sedley, *The Mulberry Garden* (perf.)
1670	Treaty of Dover	
1671		Dryden, *Marriage à la Mode* (perf.); Milton, *Paradise Regain'd;* George Villiers, Second Duke of Buckingham, *The Rehearsal* (perf.)
1673		Thomas Traherne, *Roman Forgeries*
1674	Treaty of Westminster	Milton, *Paradise Lost* (rev. ed.); Thomas Shadwell, *The Enchanted Island*
1675		Traherne, *Christian Ethics;* William Wycherley, *The Country Wife*
1676		Etherege, *The Man of Mode;* Wycherley, *The Plain Dealer* (perf.)
1677		Aphra Behn, *The Rover;* Butler, *Hudibras* (pt. 3)
1678		Bunyan, *Pilgrim's Progress* (pt. 1)
1680		Bunyan, *The Life and Death of Mr. Badman;* Robert Filmer, *Patriarcha;* Thomas Otway, *The Soldier's Fortune*
1681		Dryden, *Absalom and Achitophel;* Andrew Marvell, *Miscellaneous Poems;* John Oldham, *Satyrs upon the Jesuits*
1682	Library of Advocates (later National Library of Scotland) founded	Bunyan, *The Holy War;* Dryden, *Mac Flecknoe;* Otway, *Venice Preserved*
1684		Bunyan, *Pilgrim's Progress* (pt. 2)
1685	Death of Charles II; succeeded by James II	John Crowne, *Sir Courtly Nice*
1687	Declaration of Indulgence	Dryden, *The Hind and the Panther;* Isaac Newton, *Philosophiae naturalis principia mathematica*

1688	"Glorious Revolution"; James II deposed; succeeded by William of Orange and Mary II, reigning jointly	Behn, *Oroonoko*
1689	Bill of Rights; Thomas Shadwell becomes poet laureate	
1690	Battle of the Boyne	John Locke, *Essay Concerning Human Understanding; Two Treatises on Government*
1691	*Gentleman's Journal* begins publication	Richard Bentley, *Epistola ad Millium;* Anthony Wood, *Athenae Oxoniensis* (1691–92)
1692	Nahum Tate becomes poet laureate	William Congreve, *Incognita; The Old Batchelour* (perf.)
1693		Congreve, *The Double Dealer* (perf.)
1694	Death of Queen Mary; Bank of England founded	Dryden, *Love Triumphant*
1695	Licensing Act lifted; Bank of Scotland founded	Richard Blackmore, *Prince Arthur;* Congreve, *Love for Love*
1696		John Vanbrugh, *The Relapse* (perf.)
1697		Vanbrugh, *The Provok'd Wife*
1699		George Farquhar, *Love and a Bottle; The Constant Couple* (perf.)
1700		Congreve, *The Way of the World*
1701	Act of Settlement	
1702	Death of William III; succeeded by Anne; *Daily Courant* begins publication	Colley Cibber, *She Wou'd and She Wou'd Not* (perf.); Edward Hyde Clarendon, *History of the Rebellion* (1702–4); Farquhar, *The Twin-Rivals* (perf.)
1704	Battle of Blenheim; Britain gains control of Gibraltar	Cibber, *The Careless Husband* (perf.); Newton, *Opticks;* Charles Sackville, *Poetical Miscellanies;* Jonathan Swift, *A Tale of a Tub*
1705		R. Blackmore, *Eliza;* John Philips, *The Splendid Shilling*
1706	*Evening Post* begins publication	Farquhar, *The Recruiting Officer*
1707	Act of Union between England and Scotland	Joseph Addison, *Rosamond;* Farquhar, *The Beaux Stratagem;* Newton, *Arithmetica universalis*
1708	First Jacobite rebellion in Scotland	
1709	*Tatler* founded	George Berkeley, *New Theory of Vision;* Earl of Shaftesbury, *Sensus Communis;* Anne Finch, Countess of Winchilsea, *The Spleen*
1710	*Examiner* founded	Berkeley, *A Treatise Concerning the Principles of Human Knowledge*

1711	*Spectator* founded; South Sea Company established	Alexander Pope, *An Essay on Criticism*; Shaftesbury, *Characteristics of Men, Manners, Opinions, Times*
1712	Toleration Act	
1713	Treaty of Utrecht; *Guardian* founded	Addison, *Cato*; Berkeley, *Three Dialogues between Hylas and Philonous*; Pope, *Windsor-Forest*
1714	Death of Anne; George of Hanover becomes George I	Pope, *The Rape of the Lock* (enl. ed.); J. Swift, *The Author upon Himself*
1715	Second Jacobite rebellion; Nicholas Rowe becomes poet laureate	
1716		Addison, *The Drummer*; John Gay, *Trivia*
1718	Laurence Eusden becomes poet laureate	Matthew Prior, *Poems on Several Occasions*
1719		Daniel Defoe, *The Life and Strange Surprising Adventures of Robinson Crusoe*; Eliza Fowler Haywood, *Love in Excess* (1719–20)
1721		Defoe, *The Fortunes and Misfortunes of the Famous Moll Flanders*; Edward Young, *The Revenge*
1722		Penelope Aubin, *The Noble Slaves*; R. Blackmore, *Redemption*; Defoe, *A Journal of the Plague Year*
1723		R. Blackmore, *Alfred*
1724		Defoe, *Roxana*; *A Tour through the Whole Island of Great Britain* (1724–27)
1725	Treaty of Hanover (1725–26)	Allan Ramsay, *The Gentle Shepherd*; Young, *The Universal Passion* (1725–28)
1726	*Craftsman* founded	Aubin, *The Life and Adventures of the Lady Lucy*; J. Swift, *Gulliver's Travels*; James Thomson, *Winter*
1727	Death of George I; succeeded by George II	John Dyer, "Grongar Hill"; Thomson, *Summer*
1728		Gay, *The Beggar's Opera*; Pope, *The Dunciad*; Elizabeth Singer Rowe, *Friendship in Death*; Richard Savage, *The Bastard*; Thomson, *Spring*; Young, *A Vindication of Providence*
1729		Savage, *The Wanderer*; J. Swift, *A Modest Proposal*
1730	Irish famine; First Great Awakening begins (1730–70); Colley Cibber becomes poet laureate	Henry Fielding, *The Author's Farce*; *Tom Thumb*; Thomson, *The Seasons*
1731	*Gentleman's Magazine* founded	
1732	*London Magazine* founded (1832–85)	Berkeley, *Alciphron*
1733		Pope, *An Essay on Man* (1733–34)

1735		Berkeley, *The Querist* (1735–37); Viscount Henry St. John Bolingbroke, *A Dissertation upon Parties;* Pope, *An Epistle to Dr. Arbuthnot*
1736		H. Fielding, *Pasquin*
1737	Licensing Act	H. Fielding, *The Historical Register for the Year 1736;* William Shenstone, *Poems upon Various Occasions*
1738		Samuel Johnson, *London*
1739		Bolingbroke, *The Idea of a Patriot King* (wr. 1739); Mary Collier, *The Woman's Labor;* David Hume, *A Treatise of Human Nature* (1739–40)
1740		J. Dyer, *The Ruins of Rome;* Samuel Richardson, *Pamela*
1741		John Arbuthnot, *Memoirs of Martin Scriblerus;* H. Fielding, *An Apology for the Life of Mrs. Shamela Andrews;* Shenstone, *The Judgment of Hercules;* Young, *The Complaint* (1741–45)
1742		William Collins, *Persian Eclogues;* H. Fielding, *The History and Adventures of Joseph Andrews;* Shenstone, *The School-Mistress*
1743	Battle of Dettingen	Robert Blair, *The Grave;* H. Fielding, *Miscellanies;* Pope, *The Dunciad* (rev. and enl. ed.)
1744	Sotheby's founded	Mark Akenside, *The Pleasures of Imagination;* Sarah Fielding, *The Adventures of David Simple;* Haywood, *The Fortunate Foundlings;* S. Johnson, *Life of Richard Savage;* Joseph Warton, *The Enthusiast*
1745	Jacobite rebellion in Scotland begins (1745–46)	
1746	Battle of Culloden	William Collins, *Odes on Several Descriptive and Allegorical Subjects;* J. Warton, *Odes on Various Subjects*
1747		S. Richardson, *Clarissa* (1747–48); Thomas Warton, *The Pleasures of Melancholy*
1748		John Cleland, *Memoirs of a Woman of Pleasure* (1748–49); Hume, *Philosophical Essays Concerning Human Understanding;* Tobias Smollett, *The Adventures of Roderick Random;* Thomson, *The Castle of Indolence*
1749	*Monthly Review* founded	H. Fielding, *The History of Tom Jones;* S. Johnson, *The Vanity of Human Wishes*

1750	*Rambler* founded	John Hill, *Lucine since concubitu;* Charlotte Lennox, *The Life of Harriot Stuart*
1751		Francis Coventry, *The History of Pompey the Little;* H. Fielding, *Amelia;* Thomas Gray, "Elegy Written in a Country Churchyard"; Haywood, *Miss Betsy Thoughtless;* Hume, *An Enquiry Concerning the Principles of Morals;* Smollett, *The Adventures of Peregrine Pickle*
1752	Gregorian calendar adopted in England and Scotland	Lennox, *The Female Quixote*
1753	Jewish Naturalization Bill; British Museum, *World* founded	S. Richardson, *The History of Sir Charles Grandison* (1753–54); Smollett, *The Adventures of Ferdinand Count Fathom*
1754	Anglo-French war in North America begins	Hume, *History of England* (1754–62)
1755		S. Johnson, *A Dictionary of the English Language*
1756	*Literary Magazine; Critical Review* founded; Seven Years' War begins (1756–63)	J. Warton, *Essay on Pope*
1757	Battle of Plassey; British East India Company gains control of India; William Whitehead becomes poet laureate	Edmund Burke, *A Philosophical Enquiry into the Origin of Our Ideas of the Sublime and Beautiful;* Elizabeth and Richard Griffith, *A Series of Genuine Letters between Henry and Frances* (1757–70); Smollet, *A Complete History of England* (1757–58)
1758	*Annual Register* founded	
1759	*British Magazine* founded	S. Fielding, *The Countess of Dellwyn;* S. Johnson, *The Prince of Abyssinia;* Laurence Sterne, *A Political Romance;* Charles Wesley, *Hymns on the Expected Invasion;* Young, *Conjectures on Original Composition*
1760	Death of George II; succeeded by George III; Industrial Revolution begins (ca. 1760–ca. 1790)	James Macpherson, *Fragments of Ancient Poetry;* Sterne, *The Life and Opinions of Tristram Shandy, Gentleman* (1760–67)
1761		Charles Churchill, *The Rosciad; The Apology*
1762	*North Briton* founded	Oliver Goldsmith, *The Citizen of the World;* Macpherson, *Fingal;* Sarah Scott, *A Description of Millennium Hall;* Smollett, *The Adventures of Sir Launcelot Greaves;* William Whitehead, *The School for Lovers*
1763	Treaty of Paris	Macpherson, *Temora*

1764	Gothic literature flourishes (1764–ca. 1820)	Charles Churchill, *Gotham;* Goldsmith, *The Traveller*
1765		Thomas Percy, *Reliques of Ancient English Poetry;* Horace Walpole, *Castle of Otranto*
1766	Townshend Acts (1766–70)	Goldsmith, *The Vicar of Wakefield;* Smollett, *Travels through France and Italy*
1768		*Encyclopædia Britannica* (1st. ed., 1768–71); James Boswell, *An Account of Corsica;* Cleland, *The Woman of Honour;* Goldsmith, *The Good Natured Man;* S. Johnson, *The History of Rasselas, Prince of Abyssinia;* Sterne, *A Sentimental Journey through France and Italy;* Walpole, *The Mysterious Mother*
1769	*Morning Chronicle* founded; Captain James Cook explores the Pacific (1769–70); claims Australia for Great Britain	Thomas Chatterton, *Aella* (wr.)
1770	Boston Massacre (U.S.)	Goldsmith, *The Deserted Village;* Percy, *Northern Antiquities*
1771		Smollett, *The Expedition of Humphrey Clinker*
1772	*Morning Post* founded	Anna Laetitia Barbauld, *Poems;* William Jones, *Poems*
1773	Tea Act; Boston Tea Party (U.S.)	Hester Chapone, *Letters on the Improvement of the Mind;* Goldsmith, *She Stoops to Conquer;* Richard Graves, *The Spiritual Quixote*
1774		T. Warton, *The History of English Poetry* (1774–81)
1775	Battles of Lexington and Concord (U.S.); American War of Independence begins	S. Johnson, *A Journey to the Western Isles of Scotland;* Richard Brinsley Sheridan, *The Rivals*
1776	Declaration of Independence (U.S.)	Edward Gibbon, *The History of the Decline and Fall of the Roman Empire* (1776–88); John Hawkins, *A General History of the Science and Practice of Music;* Adam Smith, *The Wealth of Nations*
1777		Hugh Blair, *Sermons* (1777–1801); S. Johnson, *Lives of the English Poets* (1777–81); Clara Reeve, *The Champion of Virtue;* Sheridan, *The School for Scandal* (perf.)
1778		Fanny Burney, *Evelina;* Sheridan, *The Camp* (perf.)
1779		Richard Graves, *Columella;* Hume, *Dialogues Concerning Natural Religion;* Sheridan, *The Critic* (perf.)

1780	*Morning Herald and Public Adviser* founded; English Reform movement begins	
1781		Barbauld, *Hymns in Prose for Children;* George Crabbe, *The Library*
1782		Robert Bage, *Mount Henneth;* Burney, *Cecilia;* William Cowper, *Poems*
1783	Treaty of Paris	William Beckford, *Dreams, Waking Thoughts and Incidents;* William Blake, *Poetical Sketches;* Crabbe, *The Village;* Sophia Lee, *The Recess* (1783–85)
1784	East India Act	Bage, *Barham Downs;* William Hayley, *The Two Connoisseurs;* Charlotte Smith, *Elegiac Sonnets*
1785	*Daily Universal Register* founded; becomes *The Times;* Thomas Warton becomes poet laureate	Boswell, *The Journal of a Tour to the Hebrides;* Cowper, *The Task;* Richard Graves, *Eugenius;* John Wolcot, *The Lousiad* (1785–95); Ann Yearsley, *Poems, on Several Occasions*
1786		Beckford, *Vathek;* Robert Burns, *Poems, Chiefly in the Scottish Dialect;* Hester Lynch Piozzi, *Anecdotes of the Late Samuel Johnson, LL.D.*
1787		Bage, *The Fair Syrian;* Mary Wollstonecraft, *Thoughts on the Education of Daughters;* Yearsley, *Poems on Various Subjects*
1788	*Analytical Review* founded	Bage, *James Wallace*
1789	French Revolution begins (1789–95); Utilitarianism flourishes (1789–1874)	Blake, *Songs of Innocence; The Book of Thel;* Ann Radcliffe, *The Castles of Athlin and Dunbayne;* Yearsley, *Earl Goodwin* (perf.)
1790	Henry James Pye becomes poet laureate	Burke, *Reflections on the Revolution in France and on the Proceedings in Certain Societies in London Relative to That Event;* Hayley, *Eudora* (perf.); Lennox, *Euphemia;* Radcliffe, *A Sicilian Romance;* Wollstonecraft, *A Vindication of the Rights of Men*
1791	*Observer* founded	Boswell, *The Life of Samuel Johnson, LL.D.;* Radcliffe, *The Romance of the Forest*
1792		Bage, *Man As He Is;* Hayley, *Zelma; or, The Will O' Th' Wisp* (perf.); Samuel Rogers, *The Pleasures of Memory;* Wollstonecraft, *A Vindication of the Rights of Woman*
1793	Reign of Terror in France begins; Louis XVI and Marie Antoinette beheaded	Blake, *America a Prophecy;* Burns, "Tam o'Shanter"; William Godwin, *An Enquiry Concerning Political Justice, and*

		Its Influence on General Virtue and Happiness; C. Smith, *The Old Manor House*
1794	*Morning Adviser* founded	Blake, *Songs of Innocence and of Experience;* Godwin, *Things As They Are;* Radcliffe, *The Mysteries of Udolpho*
1795		Robert Anderson, *Life of Samuel Johnson, LL.D.;* Blake, *The Book of Los; The Book of Ahania; The Song of Los*
1796	*Monthly Magazine* founded; Napoleonic Wars begin (1796–1815)	Bage, *Hermsprong;* Burney, *Camilla;* William Cobbett, *Life and Adventures of Peter Porcupine;* Mary Hays, *Memoirs of Emma Courtney;* Elizabeth Inchbald, *Nature and Art;* M. G. Lewis, *The Monk;* Mary Robinson, *Sappho and Phaon;* Yearsley, *The Rural Lyre*
1797		Radcliffe, *The Italian*
1798	Irish rebellion; Romanticism flourishes (ca. 1798–ca. 1832)	Joanna Baillie, *A Series of Plays* (1798–1812); Walter Savage Landor, *Gebir;* Thomas Malthus, *An Essay on the Principle of Population;* William Wordsworth and Samuel Taylor Coleridge, *Lyrical Ballads*
1799		Thomas Campbell, *The Pleasures of Hope*
1800	Act of Union between England and Ireland	Robert Bloomfield, "The Farmer's Boy"; Maria Edgeworth, *Castle Rackrent;* Sydney Smith, *Six Sermons*
1801		Edgeworth, *Belinda;* Robert Southey, *Thalaba the Destroyer*
1802	Treaty of Amiens; *Edinburgh Review* founded; Society for the Supression of Vice founded	Charles Lamb, *John Woodvil;* Walter Scott, *Minstrelsy of the Scottish Border*
1803		Erasmus Darwin, *The Temple of Nature;* Jane Porter, *Thaddeus of Warsaw*
1804	Napoleon becomes Emperor of France	Blake, *Milton* (wr. 1804–8); *Jerusalem* (wr. 1804–20)
1805	Battle of Trafalgar	William Hazlitt, *An Essay on the Principles of Human Action;* Amelia Opie, *Adeline Mowbray;* W. Scott, *The Lay of the Last Minstrel;* Southey, *Madoc*
1806		Bloomfield, *Wild Flowers;* Lord Byron, *Fugitive Pieces;* Landor, *Simonidea;* Sydney Owenson, *The Wild Irish Girl*
1807	Slave trade abolished in Great Britain	Byron, *Poems on Various Occasions; Hours of Idleness;* George Crabbe, *Poems;* Charles and Mary Lamb, *Tales from Shakespeare;* Thomas Moore, *Irish Melodies;* Anna Maria Porter, *The Hungarian Brothers*
1808	*Examiner* founded	W. Scott, *Marmion*

1809	*Quarterly Review* founded	Byron, *English Bards, and Scotch Reviewers;* T. Campbell, *Gertrude of Wyoming*
1810		Crabbe, *The Borough;* W. Scott, *The Lady of the Lake*
1811	Prince of Wales (later George IV) becomes Regent; Luddite riots (1811–12)	Jane Austen, *Sense and Sensibility;* Bloomfield, *The Banks of the Wye;* Percy Bysshe Shelley, *The Necessity of Atheism*
1812	War of 1812 begins (1812–14)	Barbauld, *Eighteen Hundred and Eleven;* Byron, *Childe Harold's Pilgrimage,* (cantos 1–2); Landor, *Count Julian*
1813		Austen, *Pride and Prejudice;* Byron, *The Bride of Abydos; The Giaour;* James Hogg, *The Queen's Wake;* P. B. Shelley, *Queen Mab;* Joanna Southcott, *The Book of Wonders* (1813–14); Southey, *Life of Nelson*
1814	Napoleon abdicates; exiled to Elba; Treaty of Ghent; *New Monthly Magazine* founded	Austen, *Mansfield Park;* Burney, *The Wanderer;* Byron, *The Corsair; Lara;* W. Scott, *Waverley;* Southey, *Roderick, the Last of the Goths*
1815	Battle of Waterloo; Congress of Vienna	W. Scott, *Guy Mannering; The Lord of the Isles; The Field of Waterloo*
1816		Austen, *Emma;* Byron, *The Prisoner of Chillon; Childe Harold* (canto 3); *The Siege of Corinth; Parisina;* S. T. Coleridge, *Christabel;* "Kubla Khan, a Vision"; Leigh Hunt, *The Story of Rimini;* P. B. Shelley, *Alastor;* John Wilson, *The City of the Plague*
1817	*Literary Gazette; Edinburgh Monthly Magazine* (later *Blackwood's Edinburgh Magazine*) founded; becomes *Blackwood's Magazine* (1906)	Byron, *Manfred;* S. T. Coleridge, *Biographia Literaria;* John Keats, *Poems;* T. Moore, *Lalla Rookh;* Thomas Love Peacock, *Melincourt;* Southey, *Wat Tyler*
1818		Lucy Aikin, *Memoirs of the Court of Queen Elizabeth;* Austen, *Northanger Abbey; Persuasion;* Byron, *Childe Harold* (canto 4); Susan Ferrier, *Marriage;* Hazlitt, *Lectures on the English Poets;* Keats, *Endymion;* Peacock, *Nightmare Abbey;* W. Scott, *Rob Roy;* Mary Wollstonecraft Shelley, *Frankenstein*
1819	*Indicator* founded	Byron, *Don Juan* (cantos 1–2); T. Campbell, *Specimens of the British Poets;* Crabbe, *Tales of the Hall;* John William Polidori, *The Vampyre;* John Hamilton Reynolds, *Peter Bell;* W. Scott, *The Bride of Lammermoor;* M. W. Shelley, *Mathilda;* P. B. Shelley, *The Cenci; Rosalind and Helen*

1820	Death of George III; succeeded by George IV; *London Magazine* founded (1820–29)	John Clare, *Poems Descriptive of Rural Life;* Keats, *Lamia, Isabella, The Eve of St. Agnes, and Other Poems;* W. Scott, *The Monastery; Ivanhoe;* P. B. Shelley, *Prometheus Unbound;* Southey, *The Life of John Wesley*
1821	*Manchester Guardian* founded; famine in Ireland (1821–23)	Thomas Lovell Beddoes, *The Improvisatore;* Byron, *Don Juan* (cantos 3–5); *Marino Faliero; Sardanapalus;* Clare, *The Village Minstrel;* Hazlitt, *Table-Talk;* P. B. Shelley, *Adonais;* Southey, *A Vision of Judgement*
1822	Royal Academy of Music; *Liberal* founded	Aikin, *Memoirs of the Court of King James the First;* Alan Cunningham, *Sir Marmaduke Maxwell*
1823	Royal Academy of Music established	Byron, *Werner; The Age of Bronze*
1824	National Gallery established; *Westminster Review* founded	Ferrier, *The Inheritance;* Hogg, *The Private Memoirs and Confessions of a Justified Sinner;* Landor, *Imaginary Conversations*
1825		Hazlitt, *The Spirit of the Age*
1826	University College, London, founded	Barbauld, *A Legacy for Young Ladies;* Thomas Hood, *Whims and Oddities;* M. W. Shelley, *The Last Man*
1827		Jeremy Bentham, *Rationale of Judicial Evidence;* Hood, *The Plea of the Midsummer Fairies*
1828	*Athenaeum* (later *Nation and Athenaeum*) founded	Aikin, *Memoirs of the Court of King Charles the First;* Felicia Hemans, *Records of Woman;* John Gibson Lockhart, *Life of Robert Burns*
1830	Death of George IV; succeeded by William IV; *Fraser's Magazine* founded	Cobbett, *Rural Rides*
1831	*Englishman's Magazine; Garrick Club* founded	Anna Brownell Jameson, *Memoirs of Celebrated Female Sovereigns;* Letitia Elizabeth Landon, *Romance and Reality;* Peacock, *Crotchet Castle;* Edward John Trelawny, *Adventures of a Younger Son*
1832	First Reform Act; Great Britain occupies the Falkland Islands; *Chambers's Edinburgh Journal* (later *Chambers's Journal*) founded	Edward Bulwer-Lytton, *Eugene Aram;* Benjamin Disraeli, *Contarini Fleming;* A. B. Jameson, *Characteristics of Women, Moral, Poetical and Historical*
1833	Slavery abolished throughout the British Empire; Oxford movement flourishes (1833–64)	Robert Browning, *Pauline;* Hartley Coleridge, *Poems;* C. Lamb, *Last Essays of Elia;* Frederick Marryat, *Peter Simple*
1834	Poor Law Act	Bulwer-Lytton, *The Last Days of Pompeii;* Southey, *The Doctor* (1834–47)
1835		R. Browning, *Paracelsus;* Bulwer-Lytton, *Rienzi;* Samuel Egerton Brydges, *The Life of John Milton;* M. W.

		Shelley, *Lodore;* Thomas Wade, *Mundi et Cordis Carmina*
1836		Thomas Carlyle, *Sartor Resartus;* Charles Dickens, *Sketches by Boz* (1st. series); *The Posthumous Papers of the Pickwick Club* (1836–37); Landor, *Pericles and Aspasia*
1837	Death of William IV; succeeded by Victoria; *Bentley's Miscellany* founded	Bulwer-Lytton, *Ernest Maltravers;* Charlotte Campbell Bury, *The Divorced;* T. Carlyle, *The French Revolution;* C. Dickens, *Sketches by Boz* (2nd series); Disraeli, *Henrietta Temple; Venetia;* Landor, *The Pentameron and Pentalogia;* Lockhart, *Memoirs of the Life of Sir Walter Scott* (1837–38)
1838	Chartist movement flourishes (1837–49)	Elizabeth Barrett Browning, *The Seraphim;* C. Dickens, *Oliver Twist; The Life and Adventures of Nicholas Nickleby* (1838–39); A. B. Jameson, *Winter Studies and Summer Rambles in Canada*
1839	Opium War in China (1839–42); Spasmodic school flourishes (1838–58)	Marryat, *The Phantom Ship*
1840	London Library founded	R. H. Barham, *The Ingoldsby Legends;* R. Browning, *Sordello;* P. B. Shelley, *A Defence of Poetry*
1841	*Punch* founded	C. Dickens, *The Old Curiosity Shop*
1842	Treaty of Nanking; Hong Kong becomes a British possession; Philological Society founded	Bulwer-Lytton, *Zanoni;* T. Campbell, *The Pilgrim of Glencoe and other Poems;* Thomas Babington Macaualay, *Lays of Ancient Rome;* Alfred, Lord Tennyson, *Poems*
1843	*Economist* founded	T. Carlyle, *Past and Present;* John Stuart Mill, *System of Logic;* John Ruskin, *Modern Painters* (1843–60)
1844		William Barnes, *Poems of Rural Life, in the Dorset Dialect;* E. B. Browning, *Poems;* Disraeli, *Coningsby;* William Makepeace Thackeray, *The Luck of Barry Lyndon*
1845	Anglo-Sikh War in India (1845–46); Potato Famine in Ireland (1845–49); *Daily News* founded	A. B. Jameson, *Sacred and Legendary Art* (1845–64); Edward Lear, *A Book of Nonsense*
1846		Anne Brontë, Emily Brontë, and Charlotte Brontë, *Poems by Currer, Ellis and Acton Bell*
1847	Factory Act	A. Brontë, *Agnes Grey;* C. Brontë, *Jane Eyre;* E. Brontë, *Wuthering Heights;* Disraeli, *Tancred;* Thackeray, *Vanity Fair* (1847–48); Anthony Trollope, *The Macdermots of Ballycloran*

1848	Karl Marx and Friedrich Engels, *The Communist Manifesto;* Pre-Raphaelite movement flourishes (1848–50s)	A. Brontë, *The Tenant of Wildfell Hall;* Arthur Hugh Clough, *The Bothie of Toper-na-fuosich;* Elizabeth Cleghorn Gaskell, *Mary Barton;* T. B. Macaulay, *The History of England from the Accession of James II* (1848–61); J. S. Mill, *Principles of Political Economy*
1849	*Notes and Queries* founded	Matthew Arnold, *The Strayed Reveller and Other Poems;* C. Brontë, *Shirley;* Bulwer-Lytton, *The Caxtons;* C. Dickens, *David Copperfield* (1849–50); Ruskin, *The Seven Lamps of Architecture*
1850	*Germ* founded	Beddoes, *Death's Jest-Book;* E. B. Browning, *Sonnets from the Portuguese;* Wilkie Collins, *Antonina;* Charles Kingsley, *Alton Locke;* Tennyson, *In Memoriam;* Wordsworth, *The Prelude*
1851		E. B. Browning, *Casa Guidi Windows;* Gaskell, *Cranford;* George Meredith, *Poems*
1852		Arnold, *Empedocles on Etna and Other Poems;* C. Dickens, *Bleak House* (1852–53); Peter Mark Roget, *The Thesaurus of English Words and Phrases;* Thackeray, *The History of Henry Esmond, Esq.*
1853	Crimean War begins (1853–56)	C. Brontë, *Villette;* Gaskell, *Ruth;* Benjamin Robert Haydon, *Autobiography and Journals;* Charlotte M. Yonge, *The Heir of Redclyffe*
1854		Wilkie Collins, *Hide and Seek;* C. Dickens, *Hard Times*
1855	*Daily Telegraph* founded	R. Browning, *Men and Women;* C. Dickens, *Little Dorrit* (1855–57); Gaskell, *North and South;* Kingsley, *Westward Ho!;* A. Trollope, *The Warden*
1856	Anglo-Chinese War (1856–60)	Dinah Maria Craik, *John Halifax, Gentleman;* Kingsley, *The Heroes;*
1857	Peace of Paris; Obscene Publications Act; Indian Mutiny erupts	C. Brontë, *The Professor;* E. B. Browning, *Aurora Leigh;* Gaskell, *Life of Charlotte Brontë;* Thomas Hughes, *Tom Brown's Schooldays;* A. Trollope, *Barchester Towers*
1858	Second Opium War	R. M. Ballantyne, *The Coral Island;* Clough, *Amours de Voyage;* George Eliot, *Scenes of Clerical Life;* Coventry Patmore, *The Angel in the House;* Trelawny, *Recollections of the Last Days of Shelley and Byron;* A. Trollope, *Doctor Thorne; The Three Clerks*
1859	*Macmillan's Magazine* founded	Charles Darwin, *On the Origin of Species by Means of Natural Selection;* C. Dickens,

		A Tale of Two Cities; G. Eliot, *Adam Bede;* Edward Fitzgerald, *Rubáiyát of Omar Khayyám;* Meredith, *The Ordeal of Richard Feverel;* J. S. Mill, *On Liberty;* Tennyson, *Idylls of the King* (1859–85)
1860	*Cornhill Magazine* founded	Wilkie Collins, *The Woman in White;* G. Eliot, *The Mill on the Floss;* Thackeray, *Lovel the Widower;* A. Trollope, *Castle Richmond*
1861	War between the States (American Civil War, 1861–65)	C. Dickens, *Great Expectations;* G. Eliot, *Silas Marner;* Charles Reade, *The Cloister and the Hearth;* A. Trollope, *Framley Parsonage;* Mrs. Henry Wood, *East Lynne*
1862		Mary Elizabeth Braddon, *Lady Audley's Secret;* R. H. Gronow, *Recollections and Reminiscences* (1862–66); Meredith, *Modern Love;* Christina Rossetti, *Goblin Market and Other Poems*
1863		G. Eliot, *Romola;* Gaskell, *Sylvia's Lovers;* Alexander Gilchrist, *Life of William Blake, "Pictor Ignotus";* Kingsley, *The Water Babies;* Sheridan Le Fanu, *The House by the Churchyard;* Margaret Oliphant, *Chronicles of Carlingford* (1863–76)
1864		Le Fanu, *Uncle Silas; Wylder's Hand;* A. Trollope, *The Small House at Allington*
1865	*Argosy; Fortnightly Review; Pall Mall Gazette* founded	Lewis Carroll, *Alice's Adventures in Wonderland;* A. C. Swinburne, *Atalanta in Calydon*
1866	*Contemporary Review* founded	Wilkie Collins, *Armadale;* Gaskell, *Wives and Daughters;* Reade, *Griffith Gaunt;* Swinburne, *Poems and Ballads*
1867	Second Reform Act, dominion of Canada founded	Ouida, *Under Two Flags;* Swinburne, *A Song of Italy;* A. Trollope, *The Last Chronicle of Barset; The Claverings*
1868		R. Browning, *The Ring and the Book* (1868–69); Wilkie Collins, *The Moonstone;* William Morris, *The Earthly Paradise* (1868–70)
1869	Suez Canal opens; *Academy* founded	Arnold, *Culture and Anarchy;* R. D. Blackmore, *Lorna Doone;* J. S. Mill, *The Subjection of Women;* Henry Crabb Robinson, *Diary*
1870	Third Republic proclaimed in France	Wilkie Collins, *Man and Wife;* C. Dickens, *The Mystery of Edwin Drood;* Disraeli, *Lothair;* Anne Burrows Gilchrist, "A Woman's Estimate of Walt Whitman"; Lear, *Nonsense Songs, Stories, Botany and Alphabets;* Dante Gabriel Rossetti, *Poems*

1871		Arnold, *Friendship's Garland;* C. Darwin, *The Descent of Man;* G. Eliot, *Middlemarch* (1871–72); Thomas Hardy, *Desperate Remedies*
1872	*Isis* founded	Samuel Butler, *Erewhon;* Carroll, *Through the Looking-Glass;* Hardy, *Under the Greenwood Tree;* A. Trollope, *The Eustace Diamonds*
1873		Arnold, *Literature and Dogma;* Walter Pater, *Studies in the History of the Renaissance;* Yonge, *The Pillars of the House*
1874		Hardy, *Far from the Madding Crowd*
1875		Wilkie Collins, *The Law and the Lady;* W. E. Henley, *In Hospital;* Gerard Manley Hopkins, *The Wreck of the Deutschland* (wr.); John Addington Symonds, *Renaissance in Italy* (1875–86); A. Trollope, *The Way We Live Now*
1876	Newnham College, Cambridge; *Mind* founded	Carroll, *The Hunting of the Snark;* G. Eliot, *Daniel Deronda;* Hardy, *The Hand of Ethelberta;* Henry James, *Roderick Hudson;* Meredith, *Beauchamp's Career;* George Otto Trevelyan, *Life and Letters of Lord Macaulay*
1877	*Nineteenth Century* founded	H. James, *The American;* Lear, *Laughable Lyrics;* Patmore, *The Unknown Eros*
1878	Congress of Berlin	W. S. Gilbert and Arthur Sullivan, *H. M. S. Pinafore;* Hardy, *The Return of the Native;* H. James, *The Europeans*
1879	Zulu War in South Africa; *Cambridge Review* founded	Gilbert and Sullivan, *Pirates of Penzance* (perf.); H. James, *Hawthorne;* Meredith, *The Egoist*
1880	Naturalism flourishes (ca. 1880–ca. 1920)	Sabine Baring-Gould, *Mehalah;* Disraeli, *Endymion;* Henley, *Deacon Brodie;* Vernon Lee, *Studies of the Eighteenth Century in Italy;* A. Trollope, *The Duke's Children*
1881	Irish Land and Coercion Acts; first Boer War; *Tit-Bits* founded	Gilbert and Sullivan, *Patience;* Hardy, *A Laodicean;* H. James, *The Portrait of a Lady; Washington Square;* Amy Levy, *Xantippe;* D. G. Rossetti, *Ballads and Sonnets;* Robert Louis Stevenson, *Virginibus Puerisque;* Oscar Wilde, *Poems*
1882	*Longman's Magazine* founded; Egypt comes under British control	F. Anstey, *Vice Versa;* J. A. Froude, *Thomas Carlyle;* Gilbert and Sullivan, *Iolanthe;* Hardy, *Two on a Tower;* Richard Jefferies, *Bevis*
1883		Edward Carpenter, *Towards Democracy;* A. B. Gilchrist, *Mary Lamb;* Olive Schreiner, *The Story of an African Farm;*

		R. L. Stevenson, *Treasure Island;* A. Trollope, *An Autobiography*
1884	Fabian Society founded	
1885	Irish Literary Renaissance flourishes	*Dictionary of National Biography* (1885–1901); Gilbert and Sullivan, *The Mikado;* H. Rider Haggard, *King Solomon's Mines;* Meredith, *Diana of the Crossways;* Pater, *Marius the Epicurean;* Arthur Wing Pinero, *The Magistrate* (perf.); R. L. Stevenson, *The Child's Garden of Verses*
1886	Indian National Congress established	Walter Besant, *Children of Gibeon;* Frances Hodgson Burnett, *Little Lord Fauntleroy;* Marie Corelli, *A Romance of Two Worlds;* Hardy, *The Mayor of Casterbridge;* H. James, *The Bostonians; The Princess Casamassima;* Bernard Shaw, *Cashel Byron's Profession;* R. L. Stevenson, *Kidnapped; The Strange Case of Dr. Jekyll and Mr. Hyde*
1887	Queen Victoria's Golden Jubilee; British East Africa Company chartered	R. D. Blackmore, *Springhaven;* Arthur Conan Doyle, *A Study in Scarlet;* George Gissing, *Thyrza;* Hardy, *The Woodlanders;* Pater, *Imaginary Portraits*
1888		H. James, *The Aspern Papers;* Rudyard Kipling, *Plain Tales from the Hills;* Mary Augusta Ward, *Robert Elsmere;* Oscar Wilde, *The Happy Prince and Other Tales*
1889	*New Review; Library* founded	Jerome Jerome, *Three Men in a Boat (To Say Nothing of the Dog)*
1890	Literature of "Decadence" flourishes (ca. 1890–ca. 1899)	James Frazer, *The Golden Bough;* Kipling, *The Light That Failed*
1891	*Bookman* founded	Gissing, *New Grub Street;* Hardy, *Tess of the D'Urbervilles;* Wilde, *The Picture of Dorian Gray*
1892		A. C. Doyle, *The Adventures of Sherlock Holmes;* George and Weedon Grossmith, *The Diary of a Nobody;* Wilde, *Lady Windermere's Fan* (perf.); Israel Zangwill, *Children of the Ghetto*
1893	Zulu rebellion in South Africa	E. F. Benson, *Dodo;* Sarah Grand, *The Heavenly Twins;* Beatrice Harraden, *Ships That Pass in the Night;* Kipling, *Many Inventions;* Pinero, *The Second Mrs. Tanqueray* (perf.); Beatrix Potter, *The Tale of Peter Rabbit;* R. L. Stevenson, *Catriona;* Wilde, *A Woman of No Importance* (perf.); W. B. Yeats, *The Celtic Twillight*
1894	*Yellow Book* founded; Alfred Dreyfus affair; Sino-Japanese War (1894–95)	R. D. Blackmore, *Perlycross;* A. C. Doyle, *The Memoirs of Sherlock Holmes;*

		George Du Maurier, *Trilby;* Anthony Hope, *The Prisoner of Zenda;* Kipling, *Jungle Books* (1894–95); George Moore, *Esther Waters*
1895	National Trust established	Joseph Conrad, *Almayer's Folly;* Corelli, *The Sorrows of Satan;* Victoria Cross, *The Woman Who Didn't;* Hardy, *Jude the Obscure;* Lear, *Nonsense Songs and Stories;* Meredith, *The Amazing Marriage;* Arthur Symons, *London Nights;* H. G. Wells, *The Time Machine;* Wilde, *An Ideal Husband* (perf.); *The Importance of Being Earnest* (perf.)
1896	Queen Victoria's Diamond Jubilee; Nobel Prizes established	Hilaire Belloc, *The Bad Child's Book of Beasts;* A. E. Housman, *A Shropshire Lad;* Arthur Quiller-Couch, *Poems and Ballads;* Flora Annie Steel, *On the Face of the Waters;* H. G. Wells, *The Island of Doctor Moreau*
1897		Conrad, *The Nigger of the "Narcissus";* Kipling, *"Captains Courageous";* Meredith, *An Essay on Comedy;* B. Shaw, *Candida* (perf.); Bram Stoker, *Dracula;* H. G. Wells, *The Invisible Man*
1898		John Meade Falkner, *Moonfleet;* Hardy, *Wessex Poems;* Kipling, *The Day's Work;* Eden Phillpotts, *Children of the Mist;* B. Shaw, *Mrs. Warren's Profession;* H. G. Wells, *The War of the Worlds;* Wilde, *The Ballad of Reading Gaol*
1899	Irish Literary Theatre founded; Second Boer War (1889–1902)	H. James, *The Awkward Age;* Stephen Phillips, *Paolo and Francesca;* Edith Somerville and Martin Ross, *Some Experiences of an Irish R. M.;* W. B. Yeats, *The Wind among the Reeds*
1900	*Monthly Review* founded; Boxer Rebellion in China (1900–1901); symbolism flourishes (ca. 1900–ca. 1940)	*The Oxford Book of English Verse* F. Anstey, *The Brass Bottle;* J. M. Barrie, *Tommy and Grizel;* Conrad, *Lord Jim;* H. G. Wells, *Love and Mr. Lewisham*
1901	Commonwealth of Australia founded	Samuel Butler, *Erewhon Revisited;* E. M. Forster, *A Room with a View* (wr.); Kipling, *Kim;* B. Shaw, *The Devil's Disciple*
1902	British Academy; *Times Literary Supplement* founded	Barrie, *The Admirable Crichton* (perf.); Arnold Bennett, *The Grand Babylon Hotel; Anna of the Five Towns;* Conrad, *Typhoon;* A. C. Doyle, *The Hound of the Baskervilles;* Augusta Gregory, *Cuchulain of Muirthemne;* H. James, *The Wings of the Dove;* Kipling, *Just So Stories for Little Children;* Arthur Llewellyn Machen, *Hieroglyphics;* W. B. Yeats, *Cathleen ni Houlihan*

1903	Women's Social and Political Union founded	Samuel Butler, *The Way of All Flesh;* Erskine Childers, *The Riddle of the Sands;* Falkner, *The Nebuly Coat;* Gissing, *The Private Papers of Henry Ryecroft;* H. James, *The Ambassadors;* B. Shaw, *Man and Superman*
1904	Abbey Theatre, Dublin, opened; Royal Academy of Dramatic Art; Leeds University founded; Bloomsbury Group flourishes (1904–14)	Barrie, *Peter Pan* (perf.); G. K. Chesterton, *The Napoleon of Notting Hill;* Conrad, *Nostromo;* Walter de la Mare, *Henry Brocken;* Hardy, *The Dynasts* (1904–8); H. James, *The Golden Bowl;* M. R. James, *Ghost Stories of an Antiquary;* Kipling, *Traffics and Discoveries;* Frederick William Rolfe, *Hadrian the Seventh;* B. Shaw, *John Bull's Other Island* (perf.); May Sinclair, *The Divine Fire;* John Millington Synge, *Riders to the Sea* (perf.)
1905		Chesterton, *Heretics;* A. C. Doyle, *The Return of Sherlock Holmes;* E. M. Forster, *Where Angels Fear to Tread;* St. John Hankin, *The Return of the Prodigal* (perf); Baroness Emmuska Orczy, *The Scarlet Pimpernel;* B. Shaw, *Major Barbara* (perf.); Edgar Wallace, *The Four Just Men;* Wilde, *De Profundis*
1906	Labour Party formed; English Association founded	Barrie, *Peter Pan in Kensington Gardens;* Algernon Blackwood, *The Empty House and Other Ghost Stories;* John Galsworthy, *The Man of Property;* Kipling, *Puck of Pook's Hill*
1907	Rudyard Kipling receives Nobel Prize for Literature; Imperial College, London, founded	Conrad, *The Secret Agent;* E. M. Forster, *The Longest Journey;* Elinor Glyn, *Three Weeks;* Edmund Gosse, *Father and Son;* Hankin, *The Two Mr. Wetherbys;* Machen, *The Hill of Dreams;* Synge, *The Playboy of the Western World* (perf.)
1908	*English Review* founded	Lascelles Abercrombie, *Interludes and Poems;* Arnold Bennett, *The Old Wives' Tale;* Chesterton, *Orthodoxy;* W. H. Davies, *The Autobiography of a Super-Tramp;* Kenneth Grahame, *The Wind in the Willows;* E. V. Lucas, *Over Bemerton's;* Somerville and Ross, *Further Experiences of an Irish R. M.;* H. de Vere Stacpoole, *The Blue Lagoon*
1909	Poetry Society founded; Italian futurism flourishes (1909–44)	Kipling, *Actions and Reactions;* Percy Lubbock, *Samuel Pepys;* Zangwill, *The Melting Pot*
1910	Expressionism flourishes (ca. 1910–ca. 1918); Union of South Africa formed; Georgian era (1910–36)	Arnold Bennett, *Clayhanger;* John Buchan, *Prester John;* E. M. Forster, *Howards End;* Wilfrid Wilson Gibson, *Daily Bread;* Harley Granville Barker,

		The Madras House; Kipling, *Rewards and Fairies;* Hector Hugh Munro, *Reginald in Russia;* H. G. Wells, *The History of Mr Polly*
1911	Republic of China established	Max Beerbohm, *Zuleika Dobson;* Arnold Bennett, *Hilda Lessways;* Rupert Brooke, *Poems;* F. H. Burnett, *The Secret Garden;* Chesterton, *The Innocence of Father Brown;* Conrad, *Under Western Eyes;* Munro, *Chronicles of Clovis*
1912	*Poetry Review* founded; Vorticism flourishes (1912–18)	Belloc, *The Servile State;* William Hope Hodgson, *The Night Land;* Stanley Houghton, *Hindle Wakes;* Ada Leverson, *Tenterhooks;* Munro, *The Unbearable Bassington;* James Stephens, *The Crock of Gold*
1913	*New Statesman* founded; modernism flourishes (ca. 1913–39)	E. C. Bentley, *Trent's Last Case;* de la Mare, *Peacock Pie;* St. John Ervine, *Jane Clegg* (perf.); James Elroy Flecker, *The Golden Journey to Samarkand;* D. H. Lawrence, *Sons and Lovers;* Marie Belloc Lowndes, *The Lodger;* Compton Mackenzie, *Sinister Street* (1913–14); Allen Upward, *The Divine Mystery*
1914	World War I begins (1914–18); Irish Home Rule Act; *New Freewoman* (later the *Egoist*) founded	Chesterton, *The Flying Inn; The Wisdom of Father Brown;* James Joyce, *Dubliners;* B. Shaw, *Pygmalion* (perf.); Leonard Woolf, *The Wise Virgins;* W. B. Yeats, *Responsibilities*
1915	Albert Einstein's Theory of Relativity formulated	Richard Aldington, *Images 1910–15;* Harold Brighouse, *Hobson's Choice;* Brooke, *1914 and Other Poems;* Buchan, *The Thirty-Nine Steps;* Conrad, *Victory;* Ervine, *John Ferguson;* F. S. Flint, *Cadences;* Ford Madox Ford, *The Good Soldier;* D. H. Lawrence, *The Rainbow;* C. Mackenzie, *Guy and Pauline;* W. Somerset Maugham, *Of Human Bondage;* Dorothy Richardson, *Pilgrimage* (1915–67); Somerville and Ross, *In Mr. Knox's Country;* Virginia Woolf, *The Voyage Out*
1916	Battle of Verdun; Easter Uprising in Ireland; Dadaism founded	Arnold Bennett, *These Twain;* Blackwood, *Julius Le Vallon;* Buchan, *Greenmantle;* Robert Graves, *Over the Brazier;* Maurice Hewlett, *The Song of the Plow;* Joyce, *A Portrait of the Artist as a Young Man;* Sheila Kaye-Smith, *Sussex Grose;* Lucas, *The Vermilion Box;* G. Moore, *The Brook Kerith;* Phillpotts, *The Farmer's Wife;* H. G. Wells, *Mr. Britling Sees It Through*
1917	Russian Revolution begins	Conrad, *The Shadow-Line;* T. S. Eliot, *Prufrock and Other Observations;*

		Siegfried Sassoon, *The Old Huntsman;* Alec Waugh, *The Loom of Youth;* Mary Webb, *Gone to Earth;* W. B. Yeats, *The Wild Swans at Coole*
1918		Gerard Manley Hopkins, *Poems;* Lytton Strachey, *Eminent Victorians*
1919	Treaty of Versailles; *London Mercury* founded; Jazz Age (U.S., 1919–29)	Beerbohm, *Seven Men;* Buchan, *Mr. Standfast;* Maugham, *The Moon and Sixpence;* Sassoon, *War Poems;* V. Woolf, *Night and Day*
1920	League of Nations; *Time and Tide* founded	E. F. Benson, *Queen Lucia;* Agatha Christie, *The Mysterious Affair at Styles;* T. S. Eliot, *The Sacred Wood;* Flint, *Otherworld;* Galsworthy, *In Chancery;* D. H. Lawrence, *Women in Love;* Wilfred Owen, *Poems;* Edward Thomas, *Collected Poems;* H. G. Wells, *The Outline of History*
1921	British Broadcasting Corporation (BBC); *Now and Then* founded	Gordon Bottomley, *Gruach;* Clemence Dane, *A Bill of Divorcement;* de la Mare, *Memoirs of a Midget;* Galsworthy, *To Let;* Aldous Huxley, *Chrome Yellow;* Lubbock, *The Craft of Fiction;* Rose Macaulay, *Dangerous Ages;* B. Shaw, *Back to Methuselah*
1922	Irish Free State founded; Union of Soviet Republics (USSR) formed; *Criterion* founded; Hartlem Renaissance (U.S., 1922–29); surrealism flourishes (1922–40)	T. S. Eliot, *The Waste Land;* David Garnett, *Lady into Fox;* William Gerhardie, *Futility;* Granville Barker, *The Exemplary Theatre;* Joyce, *Ulysses;* D. H. Lawrence, *Aaron's Rod;* Katherine Mansfield, *The Garden Party and Other Stories;* Edith Sitwell, *Façade;* V. Woolf, *Jacob's Room*
1923	Adolf Hitler's Beer Hall Putsch; W. B. Yeats receives Nobel Prize for Literature	Arnold Bennett, *Riceyman Steps;* Conrad, *The Rover;* Ronald Firbank, *The Flower beneath the Foot;* A. Huxley, *Antic Hay;* D.H. Lawrence, *Kangaroo;* Mansfield, *The Doves' Nest and Other Stories;* John Masefield, *Collected Poems;* Sean O'Casey, *Shadow of a Gunman* (perf.); Dorothy L. Sayers, *Whose Body?;* B. Shaw, *Saint Joan* (perf.)
1924	Hitler begins *Mein Kampf; Transatlantic Review* founded	Abercrombie, *The Theory of Poetry;* Michael Arlen, *The Green Hat;* F. M. Ford, *Parade's End* (1924–28); E. M. Forster, *A Passage to India;* T. E. Hulme, *Speculations;* Margaret Kennedy, *The Constant Nymph;* Masefield, *Sard Harker;* A. A. Milne, *When We Were Very Young;* O'Casey, *Juno and the Paycock* (perf.); I. A. Richards, *Principles of Literary Criticism;* G. B. Stern, *Tents of Israel;* Webb, *Precious Bane;* P. C. Wren, *Beau Geste*

1925	Bernard Shaw receives Nobel Prize for Literature; Scopes trial (U.S.); National Book League founded	Chesterton, *The Everlasting Man;* Ivy Compton-Burnett, *Pastors and Masters;* Noël Coward, *Hay Fever;* C. Day-Lewis, *Beechen Vigil;* A. Huxley, *Those Barren Leaves;* Frederick Lonsdale, *The Last of Mrs. Cheyney;* Liam O'Flaherty, *The Informer;* Geoffrey Scott, *Portrait of Zélide;* Stern, *The Matriarch;* Ben Travers, *A Cuckoo in the Nest* (perf.); Arthur Waley, *The Tale of Genji* (tr. 1925–33); Alfred North Whitehead, *Science and the Modern World;* V. Woolf, *Mrs. Dalloway;* W. B. Yeats, *A Vision*
1926		Christie, *The Murder of Roger Ackroyd;* Dane, *Granite;* Kipling, *Debits and Credits;* D. H. Lawrence, *The Plumed Serpent;* T. E. Lawrence, *The Seven Pillars of Wisdom;* Hugh MacDiarmid, *A Drunk Man Looks at the Thistle;* Milne, *Winnie-the-Pooh;* O'Casey, *The Plough and the Stars* (perf.); Vita Sackville-West, *The Land;* Osbert Sitwell, *Before the Bombardment;* Travers, *Rookery Nook* (perf.); Sylvia Townsend Warner, *Lolly Willowes*
1927	Charles Lindbergh makes solo flight across the Atlantic	E. M. Forster, *Aspects of the Novel;* Granville Barker, *Prefaces to Shakespeare* (1927–47); A. P. Herbert, *Misleading Cases in the Common Law;* Rosamond Lehmann, *Dusty Answer;* Milne, *Now We Are Six;* Harold Nicolson, *The Development of English Biography;* T. F. Powys, *Mr. Weston's Good Wine;* Sayers, *Unnatural Death;* V. Woolf, *To the Lighthouse*
1928	All women gain right to vote in Britain; first television broadcast aired	Edmund Blunden, *Undertones of War;* E. M. Forster, *The Eternal Moment;* Galsworthy, *Swan Song;* Radclyffe Hall, *The Well of Loneliness;* A. Huxley, *Point Counter Point;* Milne, *The House at Pooh Corner;* O'Casey, *The Silver Tassie;* Jean Rhys, *Postures;* Sassoon, *Memoirs of a Fox-Hunting Man;* R. C. Sherriff, *Journey's End* (perf.); Evelyn Waugh, *Decline and Fall;* V. Woolf, *Orlando;* W. B. Yeats, *The Tower*
1929	*Listener* founded; Great Depression (1929–41)	Aldington, *Death of a Hero;* Robert Bridges, *The Testament of Beauty;* David Cecil, *The Stricken Deer;* Robert Graves, *Good-Bye to All That;* Graham Greene, *The Man Within;* Richard Hughes, *A High Wind in Jamaica;* Elizabeth Mackintosh, *Kif;* T. F. Powys, *Fables;* J. B. Priestley, *The Good Companions;* Richards, *Practical*

		Criticism; Rebecca West, *Harriet Hume;* V. Woolf, *A Room of One's Own*
1930	Rise of Nazism in Germany	W. H. Auden, *Poems;* Samuel Beckett, *Whoroscope;* Coward, *Private Lives;* Elizabeth Daryush, *Verses;* E. M. Delafield, *The Diary of a Provincial Lady;* William Empson, *Seven Types of Ambiguity;* Wyndham Lewis, *The Apes of God;* Maugham, *Cakes and Ale;* Priestley, *Angel Pavement;* Olaf Stapledon, *Last and First Men;* Katharine Tynan, *Collected Poems;* E. Waugh, *Vile Bodies;* Jack B. Yeats, *Sligo*
1931		Rodney Ackland, *Strange Orchestra* (perf.); Beckett, *Proust;* E. F. Benson, *Mapp and Lucia;* John Betjeman, *Mount Zion;* L. H. Myers, *The Near and the Far* (1931–43); V. Woolf, *The Waves*
1932	*Scrutiny* founded; John Galsworthy receives Nobel Prize for Literature	Auden, *The Orators;* G. Greene, *Stamboul Train;* J. B. S. Haldane, *The Causes of Evolution;* Georgette Heyer, *Devil's Cub;* A. Huxley, *Brave New World;* Christopher Isherwood, *The Memorial;* D. H. Lawrence, *Lady Chatterley's Lover* (expurgated); F. R. Leavis, *New Bearings in English Poetry;* Q. D. Leavis, *Fiction and the Reading Public;* Anthony Powell, *Venusberg;* E. Waugh, *Black Mischief*
1933	Hitler appointed German Chancellor; *New Verse* founded	Walter Greenwood, *Love on the Dole;* Mackintosh, *Richard of Bordeaux;* John Cowper Powys, *A Glastonbury Romance;* E. Arnot Robertson, *Ordinary Families;* Antonia White, *Frost in May*
1934		Margery Allingham; *Death of a Ghost;* Christie, *Murder on the Orient Express;* Robert Graves, *I, Claudius; Claudius the God;* Storm Jameson, *Company Parade* (*Mirror in Darkness Trilogy,* bk. 1); Mackintosh, *The Laughing Woman; Queen of Scots;* Sayers, *The Nine Tailors;* A. J. A. Symons, *The Quest for Corvo;* Angela Thirkell, *The Demon in the House;* E. Waugh, *A Handful of Dust*
1935	Holocaust takes place in Europe (1935–45)	Auden and Christopher Isherwood, *The Dog beneath the Skin;* Enid Bagnold, *National Velvet;* T. S. Eliot, *Murder in the Cathedral;* Empson, *Some Versions of Pastoral;* Laurence Housman, *Victoria Regina;* Isherwood, *Mr. Norris Changes Trains;* S. Jameson, *Love in Winter* (*Mirror in Darkness Trilogy,* bk. 2); Gwyn Jones, *Richard Savage;* Emlyn Williams, *Night Must Fall*

1936	Death of George V; succeeded by Edward VIII; Rome-Berlin Axis; Penguin Books established; Spanish Civil War (1936–39)	Auden and Isherwood, *The Ascent of F6;* E. M. Forster, *Abinger Harvest;* Winifred Holtby, *South Riding;* A. Huxley, *Eyeless in Gaza;* S. Jameson, *None Turn Back* (*Mirror in Darkness Trilogy*, bk. 3); John Maynard Keynes, *The General Theory of Employment, Interest, and Money;* C. S. Lewis, *The Allegory of Love;* George Orwell, *Keep the Aspidistra Flying;* Sassoon, *Sherston's Progress;* Sacheverell Sitwell, *Collected Poems;* Stevie Smith, *Novel on Yellow Paper;* S. T. Warner, *Summer Will Show*
1937	Edward VIII abdicates; Duke of York becomes George VI	Ackland, *The Dark River;* Eric Ambler, *Uncommon Danger;* Auden and MacNeice, *Letters from Iceland;* Compton-Burnett, *Daughters and Sons;* Oliver St. John Gogarty, *As I Was Going Down Sackville Street;* David Jones, *In Parenthesis;* Orwell, *The Road to Wigan Pier;* Priestley, *Time and the Conways;* J. R. R. Tolkien, *The Hobbit;* V. Woolf, *The Years*
1938	Munich Conference	Kenneth Allott, *Poems;* Beckett, *Murphy;* Elizabeth Bowen, *The Death of the Heart;* Cyril Connolly, *Enemies of Promise;* Daphne du Maurier, *Rebecca;* Orwell, *Homage to Catalonia;* E. Waugh, *Scoop;* E. Williams, *The Corn Is Green;* V. Woolf, *Three Guineas*
1939	World War II (1939–45)	Ambler, *The Mask of Dimitrios;* Compton-Burnett, *A Family and a Fortune;* T. S. Eliot, *The Family Reunion; Old Possum's Book of Practical Cats;* Gavin Ewart, *Poems and Songs;* G. Greene, *The Confidential Agent;* A. Huxley, *After Many a Summer;* Elspeth Huxley, *Red Strangers;* Isherwood, *Goodbye to Berlin;* Joyce, *Finnegan's Wake;* Louis MacNeice, *Autumn Journal;* Flann O'Brien, *At Swim-Two-Birds;* Orwell, *Coming Up for Air;* Llewelyn Powys, *Love and Death;* Rhys, *Good Morning, Midnight;* Christopher Smart, *Jubilate Agno;* L. Woolf, *Barbarians at the Gate;* W. B. Yeats, *Last Poems and Two Plays*
1940	Germany invades France; bombing blitz begins; Winston Churchill becomes Prime Minister; *Horizon* founded	Betjeman, *Old Lights for New Chancels;* G. Greene, *The Power and the Glory;* C. S. Lewis, *The Problem of Pain;* Dylan Thomas, *Portrait of the Artist as a Young Dog;* Fred Urquhart, *I Fell for a Sailor*
1941	Pearl Harbor (U.S.); Germany invades Russia; Manhattan Project (U.S.)	Auden, *The Double Man;* Compton-Burnett, *Parents and Children;* Coward,

		Blithe Spirit; C. Mackenzie, *The Monarch of the Glen;* Vernon Watkins, *Ballad of the Mari Lwyd*
1942		Cyril Hare, *Tragedy at Law;* Patrick Kavanagh, *The Great Hunger;* Alun Lewis, *Raiders' Dawn;* C. S. Lewis, *The Screwtape Letters;* Stephen Spender, *Ruins and Visions;* E. Waugh, *Put Out More Flags*
1943	Benito Mussolini in Italy deposed; Warsaw Ghetto	Bagnold, *Lottie Dundas;* Coward, *Present Laughter;* T. S. Eliot, *Four Quartets;* David Gascoyne, *Poems 1937–1942*
1944	D day invasion of Normandy; V-2 rocket designed; Battle of the Bulge	Auden, *For the Time Being;* H. E. Bates, *Fair Stood the Wind for France;* Joyce Cary, *The Horse's Mouth;* Compton-Burnett, *Elders and Betters;* Eleanor Farjeon, *The Glass Slipper* (perf.); Maugham, *The Razor's Edge*
1945	Atomic bomb dropped on Hiroshima and Nagasaki; World War II ends; United Nations founded; Nuremberg War Crimes Tribunal begins	Betjeman, *New Bats in Old Belfries;* E. Bowen, *The Demon Lover;* Henry Green, *Loving;* Gwyn Jones, *The Buttercup Field;* A. Lewis, *Ha! Ha! Among the Trumpets;* Nancy Mitford, *The Pursuit of Love;* Orwell, *Animal Farm;* Bertrand Russell, *A History of Western Philosophy;* E. Waugh, *Brideshead Revisited*
1946	First electronic supercomputer developed; civil war in China (1946–49)	Roy Campbell, *Taking Bronco;* L. P. Hartley, *The Sixth Heaven;* Mervyn Peake, *Titus Groan;* Priestley, *An Inspector Calls* (perf.); Terence Rattigan, *The Winslow Boy*
1947	India granted independence by Great Britain	Auden, *The Age of Anxiety;* Compton-Burnett, *Manservant and Maidservant;* Hartley, *Eustace and Hilda;* Philip Larkin, *A Girl in Winter;* Malcolm Lowry, *Under the Volcano;* Lubbock, *Portrait of Edith Wharton;* C. Mackenzie, *Whisky Galore;* MacNeice, *The Dark Tower;* Priestley, *The Linden Tree* (perf.); C. P. Snow, *The Light and the Dark;* Spender, *Poems of Dedication*
1948	State of Israel created; Mohandas Gandhi assassinated; British Citizenship Act; T. S. Eliot receives Nobel Prize for Literature	A. L. Barker, *Innocents;* Winston Churchill, *The Second World War* (1948–53); Christopher Fry, *The Lady's Not for Burning* (perf.); G. Greene, *The Heart of the Matter;* Hamish Henderson, *Elegies for the Dead in Cyrenaica;* Gwyn Jones, *The Still Waters;* F. R. Leavis, *The Great Tradition;* Kathleen Raine, *The Pythoness and Other Poems;* Rattigan, *The Browning Version* (perf.); Sydney Goodsir Smith, *Under the Eildon Tree*

1949		E. Bowen, *The Heat of the Day;* T. S. Eliot, *The Cocktail Party* (perf.); Farjeon, *The Silver Curlew* (perf.); Marghanita Laski, *Little Boy Lost;* N. Mitford, *Love in a Cold Climate;* Orwell, *Nineteen Eighty-Four;* Edith Sitwell, *The Canticle of the Rose;* Snow, *Time of Hope*
1950	Korean War (1950–53); Theater of the Absurd flourishes (ca. 1950–ca. 1963); Bertrand Russell receives Nobel Prize for Literature	Wynyard Browne, *The Holly and the Ivy;* William Cooper, *Scenes from Provincial Life;* G. Greene, *The Third Man;* C. S. Lewis, *The Lion, the Witch and the Wardrobe;* Peake, *Gormenghast;* Julian Symons, *The Thirty-First of February;* A. White, *The Lost Traveller;* Angus Wilson, *Such Darling Dodos*
1951	*Essays in Criticism* founded	E. M. Forster, *Two Cheers for Democracy;* G. Greene, *The End of the Affair;* John Hewitt, *The Arts in Ulster;* N. C. Hunter, *Waters of the Moon;* C. S. Lewis, *Prince Caspian;* Nicholas Monsarrat, *The Cruel Sea;* Powell, *A Dance to the Music of Time* (1951–75); Snow, *The Masters;* Gwyn Thomas, *The World Cannot Hear You;* John Wyndham, *The Day of the Triffids*
1952	Death of George VI; succeeded by Elizabeth II; Bonn Convention	Allingham, *The Tiger in the Smoke;* Beckett, *Waiting for Godot* (pub. in Fr.); Donald Davie, *Purity of Diction in English Verse;* D. Jones, *The Anathemata;* F. R. Leavis, *The Common Pursuit;* Doris Lessing, *Martha Quest;* C. S. Lewis, *The Voyage of the Dawn Treader;* Rattigan, *The Deep Blue Sea;* D. Thomas, *Collected Poems;* E. Waugh, *Men at Arms;* A. White, *The Sugar House;* A. Wilson, *Hemlock and After*
1953	DNA structure discovered; Sir Winston Churchill receives Nobel Prize for Literature; *Encounter* founded	Brigid Brophy, *Hackenfeller's Ape;* T. S. Eliot, *The Confidential Clerk* (perf.); Ian Fleming, *Casino Royale;* G. S. Fraser, *The Modern Writer and His World;* L. P. Hartley, *The Go-Between;* Gwyn Jones, *Shepherd's Hey;* R. Lehmann, *The Echoing Grove;* C. S. Lewis, *The Silver Chair;* Ruth Pitter, *The Ermine;* John Wain, *Hurry On Down*
1954	*London Magazine* founded	Kingsley Amis, *Lucky Jim;* Brendan Behan, *The Quare Fellow* (perf.); Betjeman, *A Few Late Chrysanthemums;* Christy Brown, *My Left Foot;* William Golding, *Lord of the Flies;* Thom Gunn, *Fighting Terms;* Lessing, *A Proper Marriage;* C. S. Lewis, *The Horse and His Boy;* Rattigan, *Separate Tables* (perf.); Snow, *The New Men;* D. Thomas, *Under Milk Wood;* Tolkien, *The Fellowship of the*

		Ring; The Two Towers (*The Lord of the Rings,* pts. 1–2); A. White, *Beyond the Glass;* John Whiting, *Marching Song*
1955		K. Amis, *That Uncertain Feeling;* Bagnold, *The Chalk Garden* (perf.); Compton-Burnett, *Mother and Son;* Golding, *The Inheritors;* W. S. Graham, *The Nightfishing;* G. Greene, *The Quiet American;* Robin Jenkins, *The Cone-Gatherers;* Ruth Prawer Jhabvala, *To Whom She Will;* Larkin, *The Less Deceived;* C. S. Lewis, *Surprised by Joy; The Magician's Nephew;* Forrest Reid, *Tom Barber;* Tolkien, *The Return of the King* (*The Lord of the Rings,* pt. 3)
1956	Suez Canal crisis	W. Churchill, *A History of the English-Speaking Peoples* (1956–58); James Kirkup, *The True Mistery of the Nativity;* C. S. Lewis, *The Last Battle;* R. Macaulay, *The Towers of Trebizond;* John Osborne, *Look Back in Anger* (perf.); Sam Selvon, *The Lonely Londoners;* Dodie Smith, *The One Hundred and One Dalmatians;* Snow, *Homecomings;* Honor Tracy, *The Straight and Narrow Path;* West, *The Fountain Overflows;* A. Wilson, *Anglo-Saxon Attitudes;* Colin Wilson, *The Outsider*
1957		Beckett, *Endgame* (pub. in Fr.); John Braine, *Room at the Top;* Christine Brooke-Rose, *The Languages of Love;* Lawrence Durrell, *Justine* (*Alexandria Quartet,* bk. 1); Fleming, *From Russia, with Love;* Richard Hoggart, *The Uses of Literacy;* Ted Hughes, *The Hawk in the Rain;* E. Huxley, *The Flame Trees of Thika;* Colin MacInnes, *City of Spades;* J. Osborne, *The Entertainer;* Harold Pinter, *The Room* (perf.); Nevil Shute, *On the Beach;* Stevie Smith, *Not Waving but Drowning;* Elizabeth Taylor, *Angel;* Wyndham, *The Midwich Cuckoos*
1958	First satellite launched; space race begins	K. Amis, *I Like It Here;* Bates, *The Darling Buds of May;* Beckett, *Krapp's Last Tape* (perf.); Behan, *Borstal Boy;* Betjeman, *Collected Poems;* Shelagh Delaney, *A Taste of Honey* (perf.); Durrell, *Balthazar; Mountolive* (*Alexandria Quartet,* bks. 2–3); T. S. Eliot, *The Elder Statesman* (perf.); G. Greene, *Our Man in Havana;* Lessing, *A Ripple from the Storm;* Pinter, *The Birthday Party* (perf.); Mary Renault, *The King Must Die;* Peter Shaffer, *Five Finger Exercise;* Alan Sillitoe, *Saturday Night and Sunday Morning;* Snow, *The*

		Conscience of the Rich; Spender, *Inscriptions;* Arnold Wesker, *Chicken Soup with Barley* (perf.); A. Wilson, *The Middle Age of Mrs. Eliot*
1959	Obscene Publications Act; *Critical Quarterly* founded	John Arden, *Serjeant Musgrave's Dance* (perf.); Malcolm Bradbury, *Eating People Is Wrong;* David Caute, *At Fever Pitch;* Fleming, *Goldfinger;* Geoffrey Hill, *For the Unfallen;* Laurie Lee, *Cider With Rosie;* MacInnes, *Absolute Beginners;* Peake, *Titus Alone;* Anne Ridler, *A Matter of Life and Death;* Sillitoe, *The Loneliness of the Long-Distance Runner;* Snow, *The Two Cultures and the Scientific Revolution;* Muriel Spark, *Memento Mori;* Keith Waterhouse, *Billy Liar;* Wesker, *The Kitchen* (perf.); *Roots*
1960	Sharpeville Massacre in South Africa	K. Amis, *Take a Girl like You;* Stan Barstow, *A Kind of Loving;* Alan Bennett, et al., *Beyond the Fringe* (perf.); Betjeman, *Summoned by Bells;* Robert Bolt, *A Man for all Seasons;* Durrell, *Clea* (*Alexandria Quartet,* bk. 4); Ted Hughes, *Lupercal;* D. H. Lawrence, *Lady Chatterley's Lover* (full text); Peter Levi, *The Gravel Ponds;* MacInnes, *Mr. Love and Justice;* Olivia Manning, *The Great Fortune* (*The Balkan Trilogy,* bk. 1); Brian Moore, *The Luck of Ginger Coffey;* Edna O'Brien, *The Country Girls;* Pinter, *The Caretaker;* Snow, *The Affair;* David Storey, *This Sporting Life*
1961	John F. Kennedy becomes president (U.S.); Amnesty International founded; Berlin Wall constructed	Compton-Burnett, *The Mighty and Their Fall;* Roy Fisher, *City;* Winston Graham, *Marnie;* Gunn, *My Sad Captains;* Jim Hunter, *The Sun in the Morning;* John le Carré, *Call for the Dead;* MacNeice, *Solstices;* V. S. Naipaul, *A House for Mr. Biswas;* Spark, *The Prime of Miss Jean Brodie;* George Steiner, *The Death of Tragedy;* E. Waugh, *Unconditional Surrender;* Whiting, *The Devils;* A. Wilson, *The Old Men at the Zoo*
1962	Cuban Missile Crisis	Dannie Abse, *Poems, Golders Green;* Ambler, *The Light of Day;* Auden, *The Dyer's Hand;* Beckett, *Happy Days* (pub. in Fr.); Bolt, *Lawrence of Arabia;* Edward Bond, *The Pope's Wedding* (perf.); Brophy, *Flesh;* Anthony Burgess, *A Clockwork Orange;* Giles Cooper, *Everything in the Garden* (perf.); Dick Francis, *Dead Cert;* P. D. James, *Cover Her Face;* le Carré, *A Murder of Quality;* Lessing, *The Golden Notebook;* Manning, *The Spoilt City* (*The Balkan Trilogy,* bk. 2); E. O'Brien, *The Lonely Girl*

1963	Kennedy assassinated (U.S.); Beatlemania begins	Burgess, *Inside Mr Enderby;* Margaret Drabble, *A Summer Bird-Cage;* John Fowles, *The Collector;* B. S. Johnson, *Travelling People;* le Carré, *The Spy Who Came in from the Cold;* Hugh Leonard, *The Poker Session* (perf.); MacNeice, *The Burning Perch;* Bill Naughton, *Alfie;* Spark, *The Girls of Slender Means*
1964	*Sun* founded	Arden, *Armstrong's Last Goodnight* (perf.); Brooke-Rose, *Out;* Brophy, *The Snow Ball;* Roald Dahl, *Charlie and the Chocolate Factory;* Fleming, *Chitty-Chitty-Bang-Bang* (1964–65); Golding, *The Spire;* Frank Harris, *My Life and Loves;* Gwyn Jones, *The Norse Atlantic Saga;* Larkin, *The Whitsun Weddings;* Henry Livings, *Eh?* (perf.); E. O'Brien, *Girls in Their Married Bliss;* Joe Orton, *Entertaining Mr. Sloane;* J. Osborne, *Inadmissible Evidence* (perf.); P. Shaffer, *The Royal Hunt of the Sun;* Snow, *Corridors of Power;* William Trevor, *The Old Boys;* A. Wilson, *Late Call*
1965		Fowles, *The Magus;* le Carré, *The Looking-Glass War;* Lessing, *Landlocked;* Manning, *Friends and Heroes* (*The Balkan Trilogy*, bk. 3); Frank Marcus, *The Killing of Sister George;* Orton, *Loot* (perf.); Pinter, *The Homecoming;* Spark, *The Mandelbaum Gate*
1966		Brian W. Aldiss, *The Saliva Tree;* John Bowen, *After the Rain* (perf.); G. Cooper, *Happy Family* (perf.); Ewart, *Londoners; Pleasures of the Flesh;* G. Greene, *The Comedians;* Seamus Heaney, *Death of a Naturalist;* David Lodge, *Language of Fiction;* Rhys, *Wide Sargasso Sea;* Paul Scott, *The Jewel in the Crown;* Tom Stoppard, *Rozencrantz and Guildenstern are Dead* (perf.)
1967	Six Day War in Middle East	Angela Carter, *The Magic Toyshop;* Drabble, *Jerusalem the Golden;* Eva Figes, *Winter Journey;* Christopher Hampton, *When Did You Last See My Mother?;* Michael Holroyd, *Lytton Strachey* (1967–68); P. J. Kavanagh, *The Perfect Stranger;* Peter Nichols, *A Day in the Death of Joe Egg;* Robert Shaw, *The Man in the Glass Booth;* Steiner, *Language and Silence;* A. Wilson, *No Laughing Matter;* C. Wilson, *The Mind Parasites*
1968	Theatres Act; Martin Luther King, Jr. assassinated; protests against American military involvement in Vietnam begin; "Prague Spring" movement in	K. Amis, *I Want It Now;* Peter Barnes, *The Ruling Class* (perf.); E. Bowen, *Eva Trout;* Burgess, *Enderby Outside;* Carter, *Several Perceptions;* Hampton, *Total*

	Czechoslovakia; Cecil Day-Lewis becomes poet laureate	*Eclipse* (perf.); Lee Harwood, *The White Room;* Thomas Kinsella, *Night Walker and Other Poems;* Barry MacSweeney, *The Boy from the Green Cabaret Tells of His Mother;* J. H. Prynne, *Kitchen Poems;* P. Scott, *The Day of the Scorpion;* Snow, *The Sleep of Reason;* Stoppard, *The Real Inspector Hound* (perf.)
1969	Northern Ireland disturbances begin; Samuel Beckett receives Nobel Prize for Literature	K. Amis, *The Green Man;* A. L. Barker, *John Brown's Body;* Douglas Dunn, *Terry Street;* Fowles, *The French Lieutenant's Woman;* George MacDonald Fraser, *Flashman;* G. Greene, *Travels With My Aunt;* David Harsent, *A Violent Country;* L. Harwood, *Landscapes;* Holroyd, *A Dog's Life;* Kinsella, *The Tain* (tr.); L. Lee, *As I Walked Out One Midsummer Morning;* Lessing, *The Four-Gated City;* Nichols, *The National Health* (perf.); Orton, *What the Butler Saw;* Ann Marie Quin, *Passages;* Bernice Rubens, *The Elected Member;* Anne Stevenson, *Reversals*
1970		Caute, *The Demonstration;* Elaine Feinstein, *The Circle;* Giles Gordon, *Pictures from an Exhibition;* Germaine Greer, *The Female Eunuch;* Hampton, *The Philanthropist;* David Hare, *Slag* (perf.); L. Harwood, *The Sinking Colony;* Susan Hill, *I'm the King of the Castle;* Ted Hughes, *Crow;* John Mortimer, *A Voyage Round My Father* (perf.); Patrick O'Brian, *Master and Commander;* Anthony Shaffer, *Sleuth;* Snow, *Last Things;* Storey, *Home*
1971	Open University established	A. Alvarez, *The Savage God;* K. Amis, *Girl, 20;* Alan Bennett, *Getting On;* Bond, *Lear* (perf.); E. M. Forster, *Maurice;* Frederick Forsyth, *The Day of the Jackal;* Jane Gardam, *A Long Way from Verona;* Simon Gray, *Butley;* Susan Howatch, *Penmarric;* P. D. James, *Shroud for a Nightingale;* Naipaul, *In a Free State;* Tom Pickard, *The Order of Chance;* Terry Pratchett, *The Carpet People;* P. Scott, *The Towers of Silence;* Storey, *The Changing Room* (perf.)
1972		Alan Ayckbourn, *Absurd Person Singular* (perf.); Beryl Bainbridge, *Harriet Said;* Quentin Bell, *Virginia Woolf;* John Berger, *G;* E. M. Forster, *The Life to Come;* Forsyth, *The Odessa File;* Heaney, *Wintering Out;* John Heath-Stubbs, *Artorius;* Kinsella, *Butcher's Dozen;* Renault, *The Persian Boy;* Stoppard, *Jumpers*

1973	Yom Kippur War	Martin Amis, *The Rachel Papers;* Auden, *Forewords and Afterwords;* Ayckbourn, *The Norman Conquests* (perf.); Bainbridge, *The Dressmaker;* J. G. Ballard, *Crash;* Nina Bawden, *Carrie's War;* Bond, *Bingo* (perf.); Bradbury, *Possibilities;* D. J. Enright, *The Terrible Shears;* Leonard, *Da* (perf.); Lessing, *The Summer before the Dark;* Penelope Lively, *The Ghost of Thomas Kempe;* Iris Murdoch, *The Black Prince;* P. Shaffer, *Equus;* Barry Unsworth, *Mooncranker's Gift;* Raymond Williams, *The Country and the City*
1974		K. Amis, *Ending Up;* M. Amis, *Dead Babies;* Auden, *Thank You, Fog;* Ayckbourn, *Absent Friends;* Bainbridge, *The Bottle Factory Outing;* Burgess, *The Clockwork Testament;* Forsyth, *The Dogs of War;* S. Hill, *In the Springtime of the Year;* Larkin, *High Windows;* Audrey Laski, *Night Music;* le Carré, *Tinker, Tailor, Soldier, Spy;* Lessing, *Memoirs of a Survivor;* Spark, *The Abbess of Crewe;* Claire Tomalin, *The Life and Death of Mary Wollstonecraft*
1975		Steven Berkoff, *East* (perf.); Bradbury, *The History Man;* Drabble, *The Realms of Gold;* Michael Frayn, *Alphabetical Order* (perf.); Trevor Griffiths, *Comedians* (perf.); D. Hare, *Fanshen* (perf.); Heaney, *North;* Jhabvala, *Heat and Dust;* Linton Kwesi Johnson, *Dread Beat an' Blood;* Lodge, *Changing Places;* Ian McEwan, *First Love, Last Rites;* Stephen Poliakoff, *Hitting Town* (perf.); Peter Russell, *The Elegies of Quintilius;* P. Scott, *A Division of the Spoils;* Selvon, *Moses Ascending;* Iain Crichton Smith, *The Permanent Island;* Paul Theroux, *The Great Railway Bazaar;* Fay Weldon, *Female Friends*
1976	National Theatre opens	Keith Alldritt, *The Good Pit Man;* John Banville, *Doctor Copernicus;* Bawden, *Afternoon of a Good Woman;* Elspeth Davie, *The High Tide Talker;* David Edgar, *Destiny;* Frayn, *Donkeys' Years* (perf.); Gunn, *Jack Straw's Castle;* Robert Nye, *Falstaff;* Frederic Raphael, *The Glittering Prizes;* Storey, *Saville*
1977	Queen Elizabeth's Silver Jubilee	Bruce Chatwin, *In Patagonia;* Fowles, *Daniel Martin;* Pam Gems, *Queen Christina* (perf.); Lively, *The Road to Lichfield;* Manning, *The Danger Tree* (*The*

		Levant Trilogy, bk. 1); Barbara Pym, *Quartet in Autumn;* P. Scott, *Staying On;* Stoppard, *Professional Foul* (perf.); Theroux, *The Consul's File;* R. Williams, *Marxism and Literature;* A. N. Wilson, *The Sweets of Pimlico*
1978	First test-tube baby born, in England	K. Amis, *Jake's Thing;* M. Amis, *Success;* Bainbridge, *Young Adolf;* A. S. Byatt, *The Virgin in the Garden;* Penelope Fitzgerald, *The Bookshop;* Gordon, *Enemies: A Novel about Friendship;* G. Greene, *The Human Factor;* D. Hare, *Plenty;* Tony Harrison, *From "The School of Eloquence";* Manning, *The Battle Lost and Won* (*The Levant Trilogy,* bk. 2); McEwan, *The Cement Garden;* Timothy Mo, *The Monkey King;* J. Mortimer, *Rumpole of the Bailey;* Murdoch, *The Sea, The Sea;* Craig Raine, *The Onion Memory;* Renault, *The Praise Singer;* Weldon, *Praxis*
1979	*London Review of Books* founded; Margaret Thatcher becomes first female prime minister (1979–90)	Fleur Adcock, *The Inner Harbour;* Berger, *Pig Earth;* A. Carter, *The Bloody Chamber and Other Stories;* Caryl Churchill, *Cloud Nine;* Zoë Fairbairns, *Benefits;* P. Fitzgerald, *Offshore;* Golding, *Darkness Visible;* Heaney, *Field Work;* Naipaul, *A Bend in the River;* C. Raine, *A Martian Sends a Postcard Home;* Christopher Reid, *Arcadia;* P. Shaffer, *Amadeus* (perf.); Emma Tennant, *Wild Nights*
1980		Julian Barnes, *Metroland;* Eavan Boland, *In Her Own Image;* Howard Brenton, *The Romans in Britain* (perf.); Burgess, *Earthly Powers;* Isabel Colegate, *The Shooting Party;* Drabble, *The Middle Ground;* Edgar, *The Life and Adventures of Nicholas Nickleby* (perf.); Ewart, *The Collected Ewart, 1933–1980;* Golding, *Rites of Passage;* Ronald Harwood, *The Dresser;* Heaney, *Preoccupations;* Tom Kempinski, *Duet for One* (perf.); le Carré, *Smiley's People;* Manning, *The Sum of Things* (*The Levant Trilogy,* bk. 3); Paul Muldoon, *Why Brownlee Left;* Julia O'Faolain, *No Country for Young Men;* John Riley, *Czargrad;* Unsworth, *Pascali's Island;* A. N. Wilson, *The Healing Art;* Benjamin Zephaniah, *Pen Rhythm*
1981	Anwar Sadat (Egypt) assassinated	M. Amis, *Other People;* Banville, *Kepler;* William Boyd, *On the Yankee Station;* Alison Brackenbury, *Dreams of Power;* Maureen Duffy, *Gor Saga;* Figes,

		Waking; Alasdair Gray, *Lanark;* Griffiths, *Country;* Christopher Logue, *War Music;* Andrew Motion, *Independence;* Christopher Priest, *The Affirmation;* Jonathan Raban, *Old Glory;* Salman Rushdie, *Midnight's Children;* Spark, *Loitering with Intent;* Steiner, *The Portage to San Cristobal of A. H.;* Theroux, *The Mosquito Coast;* D. M. Thomas, *The White Hotel*
1982	Falklands War	Peter Ackroyd, *The Great Fire of London;* Aldiss, *Helliconia Spring;* Boyd, *An Ice-Cream War;* Caryl Churchill, *Top Girls;* James Fenton, *The Memory of War;* Frayn, *Noises Off;* Ivor Gurney, *Collected Poems;* Kazuo Ishiguro, *A Pale View of Hills;* Kempinski, *Dreyfus* (perf.); Stoppard, *The Real Thing;* Theroux, *The Mosquito Coast;* A. N. Wilson, *Wise Virgin*
1983	William Golding receives Nobel Prize for Literature	Ackroyd, *The Last Testament of Oscar Wilde;* Howard Barker, *Victory;* Edgar, *Maydays;* J. Fenton, *Children in Exile;* S. Hill, *The Woman in Black;* Pratchett, *The Colour of Magic;* Rushdie, *Shame;* Trevor, *Fools of Fortune;* Weldon, *The Life and Loves of a She-Devil;* Mary Wesley, *Jumping the Queue*
1984	AIDS virus identified; Indira Gandhi (India) assassinated	K. Amis, *Stanley and the Women;* M. Amis, *Money;* John Ash, *The Branching Stairs;* Ballard, *Empire of the Sun;* Iain Banks, *The Wasp Factory;* J. Barnes, *Flaubert's Parrot;* Anita Brookner, *Hotel du Lac;* Burgess, *Enderby's Dark Lady;* Carter, *Nights at the Circus;* Michael Hastings, *Tom and Viv* (perf.); Heaney, *Station Island;* C. Raine, *Rich;* Tom Raworth, *Tottering State*
1985		Ackroyd, *Hawksmoor;* H. Barker, *The Castle;* P. Barnes, *Red Noses;* D. Dunn, *Elegies;* J. Mortimer, *Paradise Postponed;* Douglas Oliver, *The Infant and the Pearl;* Tim Parks, *Tongues of Flame;* Caryl Phillips, *The Final Passage;* Rose Tremain, *The Swimming Pool Season;* Jeanette Winterson, *Oranges Are Not the Only Fruit*
1986	Chernobyl nuclear accident	K. Amis, *The Old Devils;* Simon Armitage, *Human Geography;* Banks, *The Bridge;* Banville, *Mefisto;* Brooke-Rose, *Xorandor;* Brookner, *A Misalliance;* Wendy Cope, *Making Cocoa for Kingsley Amis;* Sarah Daniels, *Neaptide;* Fisher, *A Furnace;* Ishiguro, *An Artist of the Floating World*

1987		Ackroyd, *Chatterton;* M. Amis, *Einstein's Monsters;* Ash, *Disbelief;* Banks, *Consider Phlebas;* Bawden, *Circles of Deceit;* Boyd, *The New Confessions;* George Mackay Brown, *The Golden Bird;* Chatwin, *The Songlines;* Caryl Churchill, *Serious Money;* Drabble, *The Radiant Way;* Heaney, *The Haw Lantern;* Kempinski, *Separation* (perf.); Lively, *Moon Tiger;* Adam Mars-Jones, *Darker Proof;* McEwan, *The Child in Time*
1988		K. Amis, *Difficulties with Girls;* H. Barker, *The Possibilities;* Chatwin, *Utz;* Heaney, *The Government of the Tongue;* Heath-Stubbs, *Collected Poems;* Alan Hollinghurst, *The Swimming Pool Library;* Lessing, *The Fifth Child;* D. Lodge, *Nice Work;* Hilary Mantel, *Eight Months on Ghazza Street;* Rushdie, *The Satanic Verses;* Graham Swift, *Out of This World;* Trevor, *The Silence in the Garden;* Timberlake Wertenbaker, *Our Country's Good* (perf.)
1989	"Velvet Revolution" in Czechoslovakia; Berlin Wall comes down	M. Amis, *London Fields;* Armitage, *Zoom!;* Bainbridge, *An Awfully Big Adventure;* Banville, *The Book of Evidence;* J. Barnes, *A History of the World in 10½ Chapters;* Humphrey Carpenter, *The Brideshead Generation;* Lindsay Clarke, *The Chymical Wedding;* Janice Galloway, *The Trick Is to Keep Breathing;* Hampton, *Dangerous Liaisons;* Ishiguro, *The Remains of the Day;* C. Phillips, *Higher Ground;* Nicholas Shakespeare, *The Vision of Elena Silves;* A. Stevenson, *Bitter Fame;* Colin Thubron, *Falling;* Tremain, *Restoration;* K. Waterhouse, *Jeffrey Bernard is Unwell;* Winterson, *Sexing the Cherry*
1990	Reunification of Germany	Boyd, *Brazzaville Beach;* Byatt, *Possession;* Edgar, *The Shape of the Table;* Alice Thomas Ellis, *The Inn at the Edge of the World;* P. Fitzgerald, *The Gate of Angels;* D. Hare, *Racing Demon;* Hanif Kureishi, *The Buddha of Suburbia;* J. Mortimer, *Titmuss Regained;* Muldoon, *Madoc;* Colm Tóibín, *The South*
1991	Gulf War; Union of Soviet Socialist Republics dissolves	M. Amis, *Time's Arrow;* Ballard, *The Kindness of Women;* J. Barnes, *Talking It Over;* Carter, *Wise Children;* A. T. Ellis, *The Summerhouse Trilogy;* Gardam, *The Queen of the Tambourine;* D. Hare, *Murmuring Judges;* Heaney, *Seeing Things;* D. Lodge, *Paradise News;* Michael Longley, *Gorse Fires;* Ben Okri,

			The Famished Road; Ruth Rendell, *King Solomon's Carpet*
1992			Ackroyd, *English Music;* Armitage, *Xanadu;* Bradbury, *Dr Criminale;* Byatt, *Angels and Insects;* Tibor Fischer, *Under the Frog: A Black Comedy;* Esther Freud, *Hideous Kinky;* A. Gray, *Poor Things;* Gunn, *The Man with the Night Sweats;* Harrison, *The Gaze of the Gorgon;* McEwan, *Black Dogs;* Nick Hornby, *Fever Pitch;* Dennis Potter, *Lipstick on My Collar;* Jeff Torrington, *Swing Hammer Swing!;* Unsworth, *Sacred Hunger;* Marina Warner, *Indigo;* Clive Wilmer, *Of Earthly Paradise;* Zephaniah, *City Psalms*
1993			Banville, *Ghosts;* Boyd, *The Blue Afternoon;* Burgess, *A Dead Man in Deptford;* Roddy Doyle, *Paddy Clark Ha Ha Ha;* Sebastian Faulks, *Birdsong;* Fenton, *Out of Danger;* D. Hare, *The Absence of War;* Le Carré, *The Night Manager;* C. Phillips, *Crossing the River;* Will Self, *My Idea of Fun;* Stoppard, *Arcadia;* R. S. Thomas, *Collected Poems;* Irvine Welsh, *Trainspotting;* A. N. Wilson, *The Vicar of Sorrows*
1994	Nelson Mandela elected president of South Africa		Ackroyd, *Dan Leno and the Limehouse Golem;* Gilbert Adair, *A Void* (tr.); K. Amis, *You Can't Do Both;* Ballard, *Rushing to Paradise;* Boland, *In a Time of Violence;* Brookner, *A Private View;* Jonathan Coe, *What a Carve Up!;* Edgar, *Pentecost;* Hollinghurst, *The Folding Star;* James Kelman, *How late it was, how late;* MacDiarmid, *Complete Poems;* Mantel, *A Change of Climate;* Muldoon, *The Annals of Chile;* C. Raine, *History: The Home Movie;* Trevor, *Felicia's Journey*
1995	Seamus Heaney receives Nobel Prize for Literature		M. Amis, *The Information;* Kate Atkinson, *Behind the Scenes at the Museum;* P. Fitzgerald, *The Blue Flower;* Francis, *Come to Grief;* Heaney, *The Redress of Poetry;* Hornby, *High Fidelity;* Ishiguro, *The Unconsoled;* Sarah Kane, *Blasted* (perf.); Lessing, *Under My Skin;* Priest, *The Prestige;* Joanna Trollope, *The Best of Friends*
1996	"Stone of Destiny," Scotland's Coronation Stone, returned From London to Edinburgh Castle		Ballard, *A User's Guide to the Millennium;* J. Barnes, *Cross Channel;* Ben Elton, *Popcorn;* Mark Ravenhill, *Shopping and Fucking* (perf.); G. Swift, *Last Orders;* Unsworth, *After Hannibal*
1997			Armitage, *CloudCuckooLand;* Atkinson, *Human Croquet;* Gillian Clarke, *Collected*

		Poems; J. K. Rowling, *Harry Potter and the Philospher's Stone;* Stoppard, *The Invention of Love;* Tomalin, *Jane Austen*
1998		Armitage, *All Points North;* Banks, *Inversions;* Boland, *The Lost Land;* Caute, *Fatima's Scarf;* Frayn, *Copenhagen;* Ted Hughes, *Birthday Letters;* McEwan, *Amsterdam;* Muldoon, *Hay;* Okri, *Infinite Riches;* Welsh, *Filth;* A. N. Wilson, *Dream Children*
1999	Scotish Parliament reinstated	Atkinson, *Emotionally Weird;* P. Barnes, *Dreaming;* Jim Crace, *Being Dead;* Parks, *Destiny;* Tom Paulin, *The Wind Dog;* Tóibín, *The Blackwater Lightship;* Tremain, *Music and Silence*
2000	Human Rights Act; World Trade Center attack	Ackroyd, *London;* Banville, *Eclipse;* Brackenbury, *After Beethoven;* Longley, *The Weather in Japan;* E. O'Brien, *Wild Decembers;* Pinter, *Celebration;* Zadie Smith, *White Teeth;* Anthony Thwaite, *A Different Country;* J. Trollope, *Marrying the Mistress;* Wertenbaker, *The Ash Girl;* Winterson, *The.PowerBook*
2001	V. S. Naipaul receives Nobel Prize for Literature	P. Barnes, *Jubilee;* Coe, *The Rotters' Club;* Crace, *The Devil's Larder;* Heaney, *Electric Light;* Kevin Crossley-Holland, *Selected Poems;* Edgar, *The Prisoner's Dilemma;* Hornby, *How to Be Good;* Ravenhill, *Mother Clap's Molly House;* Rushdie, *Fury;* M. Warner, *The Leto Bundle;* Weldon, *The Bulgari Connection;* Welsh, *Glue;* Wertenbaker, *Credible Witness*
2002		Abse, *The Strange Case of Dr. Simmonds and Dr. Glas;* Banville, *Shroud;* Boyd, *Any Human Heart;* Brookner, *The Next Big Thing;* Frayn, *Spies;* Self, *Dorian;* Z. Smith, *The Autograph Man;* Tóibín, *Love in a Dark Time;* Tomalin, *Samuel Pepys;* Trevor, *The Story of Lucy Gault;* Sarah Waters, *Fingersmith*

Poets Laureate

1619–37	Ben Jonson*	1813–43	Robert Southey
1638–68	William Davenant	1843–50	William Wordsworth
1668–89	John Dryden**	1850–92	Alfred, Lord Tennyson
1689–92	Thomas Shadwell	1896–1913	Alfred Austin
1692–1715	Nahum Tate	1913–30	Robert Bridges
1715–18	Nicholas Rowe	1930–67	John Masefield
1718–30	Laurence Eusden	1967–72	Cecil Day-Lewis
1730–57	Colley Cibber	1972–84	Sir John Betjeman
1757–85	William Whitehead	1984–98	Ted Hughes
1785–90	Thomas Warton	1999–	Andrew Motion
1790–1813	Henry James Pye		

*Generally regarded as first poet laureate, though Geoffrey Chaucer and Edmund Spenser sometimes considered to have filled the role
**First official poet laureate

Literary Awards and Prizes

Hans Christian Andersen Award

Writing

1956	Eleanor Farjeon
1958	Astrid Lindgren
1960	Erich Kästner
1962	Meindert DeJong
1964	René Guillot
1966	Tove Jansson
1968	James Krüss
	José Maria Sanchez-Silva
1970	Gianni Rodari
1972	Scott O'Dell
1974	Maria Gripe
1976	Cecil Bødker
1978	Paula Fox
1980	Bohumil Riha
1982	Lygia Bojunga Nunes
1984	Christine Nöstlinger
1986	Patricia Wrightson
1988	Annie M. G. Schmidt
1990	Tormod Haugen
1992	Virginia Hamilton
1994	Michio Mado
1996	Uri Orlev
1998	Katherine Paterson
2000	Ana Maria Machado
2002	Aidan Chambers

Illustration

1966	Alois Carigiet
1968	Jirí Trnka
1970	Maurice Sendak
1972	Ib Spang Olsen
1974	Farshid Mesghali
1976	Tatjana Mawrina
1978	Svend Otto S.
1980	Suekichi Akaba
1982	Zbigniew Rychlickı
1984	Mitsumasa Anno
1986	Robert Ingpen

1988	Dusan Kállay
1990	Lisbeth Zwerger
1992	Kveta Pacovská
1994	Jörg Müller
1996	Klaus Ensikat
1998	Tomi Ungerer
2000	Anthony Browne
2002	Quentin Blake

James Tait Black Memorial Prize

Fiction

1919	Hugh Walpole, *The Secret City*
1920	D. H. Lawrence, *The Lost Girl*
1921	Walter de la Mare, *Memoirs of a Midget*
1922	David Garnett, *Lady into Fox*
1923	Arnold Bennett, *Riceyman Steps*
1924	E. M. Forster, *A Passage to India*
1925	Liam O'Flaherty, *The Informer*
1926	Radclyffe Hall, *Adam's Breed*
1927	Francis Brett Young, *Portrait of Clare*
1928	Siegfried Sassoon, *Memoirs of a Fox-Hunting Man*
1929	J. B. Priestley, *The Good Companions*
1930	E. H. Young, *Miss Mole*
1931	Kate O'Brien, *Without My Cloak*
1932	Helen Simpson, *Boomerang*
1933	A. G. Macdonell, *England, Their England*
1934	Robert Graves, *I, Claudius* and *Claudius the God*
1935	L. H. Myers, *The Root and the Flower*
1936	Winifred Holtby, *South Riding*
1937	Neil M. Gunn, *Highland River*
1938	C. S. Forester, *A Ship of the Line* and *Flying Colours*
1939	Aldous Huxley, *After Many a Summer Dies the Swan*
1940	Charles Morgan, *The Voyage*
1941	Joyce Cary, *A House of Children*
1942	Arthur Waley, *Monkey by Wu Ch'eng-en*
1943	Mary Lavin, *Tales from Bectine Bridge*
1944	Forrest Reid, *Young Tom*

1945	L. A. G. Strong, *Travellers*
1946	G. Oliver Onions, *Poor Man's Tapestry*
1947	L. P. Hartley, *Eustace and Hilda*
1948	Graham Greene, *The Heart of the Matter*
1949	Emma Smith, *The Far Cry*
1950	Robert Henriquez, *Along the Valley*
1951	W. C. Chapman-Mortimer, *Father Goose*
1952	Evelyn Waugh, *Men at Arms*
1953	Margaret Kennedy, *Troy Chimneys*
1954	C. P. Snow, *The New Men* and *The Masters*
1955	Ivy Compton-Burnett, *Mother and Son*
1956	Rose Macaulay, *The Towers of Trebizond*
1957	Anthony Powell, *At Lady Molly's*
1958	Angus Wilson, *The Middle Age Of Mrs. Eliot*
1959	Morris West, *The Devil's Advocate*
1960	Rex Warner, *Imperial Caesar*
1961	Jennifer Dawson, *The Ha-Ha*
1962	Ronald Hardy, *Act of Destruction*
1963	Gerda Charles, *A Slanting Light*
1964	Frank Tuohy, *The Ice Saints*
1965	Muriel Spark, *The Mandelbaum Gate*
1966	Christine Brooke-Rose, *Langrishe*
	Aidan Higgins, *Go Down*
1967	Margaret Drabble, *Jerusalem the Golden*
1968	Maggie Ross, *The Gasteropod*
1969	Elizabeth Bowen, *Eva Trout*
1970	Lily Powell, *The Bird of Paradise*
1971	Nadine Gordimer, *A Guest of Honour*
1972	John Berger, *G*
1973	Iris Murdoch, *The Black Prince*
1974	Lawrence Durrell, *Monsieur; or, The Prince of Darkness*
1975	Brian Moore, *The Great Victorian Collection*
1976	John Banville, *Doctor Copernicus*
1977	John le Carré, *The Honourable Schoolboy*
1978	Maurice Gee, *Plumb*
1979	William Golding, *Darkness Visible*
1980	J. M. Coetzee, *Waiting for the Barbarians*
1981	Salman Rushdie, *Midnight's Children*
	Paul Theroux, *The Mosquito Coast*
1982	Bruce Chatwin, *On the Black Hill*
1983	Jonathan Keates, *Allegro Postillions*
1984	J. G. Ballard, *Empire of the Sun*
	Angela Carter, *Nights at the Circus*
1985	Robert Edric, *Winter Garden*
1986	Jenny Joseph, *Persephone*
1987	George Mackay Brown, *The Golden Bird: Two Orkney Stories*
1988	Piers Paul Read, *A Season in the West*
1989	James Kelman, *A Disaffection*
1990	William Boyd, *Brazzaville Beach*
1991	Iain Sinclair, *Downriver*
1992	Rose Tremain, *Sacred Country*
1993	Caryl Phillips, *Crossing the River*
1994	Alan Hollinghurst, *The Folding Star*

1995	Christopher Priest, *The Prestige*
1996	Graham Swift, *Last Orders*
	Alice Thompson, *Justine*
1997	Andrew Miller, *Ingenious Pain*
1998	Beryl Bainbridge, *Master Georgie*
1999	Timothy Mo, *Renegade or Halo²*
2000	Zadie Smith, *White Teeth*
2001	Sid Smith, *Something Like a House*

Biography

1919	Henry Festing Jones, *Samuel Butler, Author of Erewhon (1835–1902)*
1920	G. M. Trevelyan, *Lord Grey of the Reform Bill*
1921	Lytton Strachey, *Queen Victoria*
1922	Percy Lubbock, *Earlham*
1923	Sir Ronald Ross, *Memoirs, Etc.*
1924	Rev. William Wilson, *The House of Airlie*
1925	Geoffrey Scott, *The Portrait of Zélide*
1926	Rev. Dr. H. B. Workman, *John Wyclif: A Study of the English Medieval Church*
1927	H. A. L. Fisher, *James Bryce, Viscount Bryce of Dechmont, O.M.*
1928	John Buchan, *Montrose*
1929	Lord David Cecil, *The Stricken Deer; or, The Life of Cowper*
1930	Francis Yeats Brown, *Lives of a Bengal Lancer*
1931	J. Y. R. Greig, *David Hume*
1932	Stephen Gwynn, *The Life of Mary Kingsley*
1933	Violet Clifton, *The Book of Talbot*
1934	J. E. Neale, *Queen Elizabeth*
1935	R. W. Chambers, *Thomas More*
1936	Edward Sackville-West, *A Flame in Sunlight: The Life and Work of Thomas de Quincey*
1937	Lord Eustace Percy, *John Knox*
1938	Sir Edmund Chambers, *Samuel Taylor Coleridge*
1939	David C. Douglas, *English Scholars*
1940	Hilda F. M. Prescott, *Spanish Tudor*
1941	John Gore, *King George V*
1942	Lord Ponsonby of Shulbrede, *Henry Ponsonby: Queen Victoria's Private Secretary*
1943	G. G. Coulton, *Fourscore Years*
1944	C. V. Wedgwood, *William the Silent*
1945	D. S. MacColl, *Philip Wilson Steer*
1946	Richard Aldington, *Wellington*
1947	Rev. C. C. E. Raven, *English Naturalists from Neckham to Ray*
1948	Percy A. Scholes, *The Great Dr. Burney*
1949	John Connell, *W. E. Henley*
1950	Cecil Woodham-Smith, *Florence Nightingale*
1951	Noel G. Annan, *Leslie Stephen*

1952	G. M. Young, *Stanley Baldwin*
1953	Carola Oman, *Sir John Moore*
1954	Keith Feiling, *Warren Hastings*
1955	R. W. Ketton-Cremer, *Thomas Gray*
1956	St John Greer Ervine, *George Bernard Shaw*
1957	Maurice Cranston, *Life of John Locke*
1958	Joyce Hemlow, *The History of Fanny Burney*
1959	Christopher Hassall, *Edward Marsh*
1960	Canon Adam Fox, *The Life of Dean Inge*
1961	M. K. Ashby, *Joseph Ashby of Tysoe*
1962	Meriol Trevor, *Newman: The Pillar of the Cloud* and *Newman: Light in Winter*
1963	Georgina Battiscome, *John Keble: A Study in Limitations*
1964	Elizabeth Longford, *Victoria R.I.*
1965	Mary Moorman, *William Wordsworth*
1966	Geoffrey Keynes, *The Life of William Harvey Such*
1967	Winifred Gérin, *Charlotte Brontë: The Evolution of Genius*
1968	Gordon S. Haight, *George Eliot*
1969	Antonia Fraser, *Mary Queen of Scots*
1970	Jasper Ridley, *Lord Palmerston*
1971	Julia Namier, *Lewis Namier*
1972	Quentin Bell, *Virginia Woolf*
1973	Robin Lane Fox, *Alexander the Great*
1974	John Wain, *Samuel Johnson*
1975	Karl Miller, *Cockburn's Millennium*
1976	Ronald Hingley, *A New Life of Chekhov*
1977	George Painter, *Chateaubriand: The Longed-For Tempests*
1978	Robert Gittings, *The Older Hardy*
1979	Brian Finney, *Christopher Isherwood: A Critical Biography*
1980	Robert B. Martin, *Tennyson: The Unquiet Heart*
1981	Victoria Glendinning, *Edith Sitwell: Unicorn among Lions*
1982	Richard Ellmann, *James Joyce*
1983	Alan Walker, *Franz Liszt: The Virtuoso Years*
1984	Lyndall Gordon, *Virginia Woolf: A Writer's Life*
1985	David Nokes, *Jonathan Swift: A Hypocrite Reversed*
1986	D. Felicitas Corrigan, *Helen Waddell*
1987	Ruth Dudley Edwards, *Victor Gollancz: A Biography*
1988	Brian McGuinness, *Wittgenstein: A Life—Young Ludwig (1889–1921)*
1989	Ian Gibson, *Federico García Lorca: A Life*
1990	Claire Tomalin, *The Invisible Woman: The Story of Nelly Ternan and Charles Dickens*

1991	Adrian Desmond and James Moore, *Darwin*
1992	Charles Nicoll, *The Reckoning: The Murder of Christopher Marlowe*
1993	Richard Holmes, *Dr. Johnson and Mr. Savage*
1994	Doris Lessing, *Under My Skin*
1995	Gitta Sereny, *Albert Speer: His Battle with the Truth*
1996	Diarmaid MacCulloch, *Thomas Cranmer: A Life*
1997	R. F. Foster, *W. B. Yeats: A Life—The Apprentice Mage 1865–1914*
1998	Peter Ackroyd, *The Life of Thomas More*
1999	Kathryn Hughes, *George Eliot: The Last Victorian*
2000	Martin Amis, *Experience*
2001	Robert Skidelsky, *John Maynard Keynes: Fighting for Britain 1936–1946*

Booker Prize*

1969	P. H. Newby, *Something to Answer For*
1970	Bernice Rubens, *The Elected Member*
1971	V. S. Naipaul, *In a Free State*
1972	John Berger, *G*
1973	J. G. Farrell, *The Siege of Krishnapur*
1974	Stanley Middleton, *Holiday*
	Nadine Gordimer, *The Conservationist*
1975	Ruth Prawer Jhabvala, *Heat and Dust*
1976	David Storey, *Saville*
1977	Paul Scott, *Staying On*
1978	Iris Murdoch, *The Sea, the Sea*
1979	Penelope Fitzgerald, *Offshore*
1980	William Golding, *Rites of Passage*
1981	Salman Rushdie, *Midnight's Children*
1982	Thomas Keneally, *Schindler's Ark*
1983	J. M. Coetzee, *Life and Times of Michael K*
1984	Anita Brookner, *Hotel du Lac*
1985	Keri Hulme, *The Bone People*
1986	Kingsley Amis, *The Old Devils*
1987	Penelope Lively, *Moon Tiger*
1988	Peter Carey, *Oscar and Lucinda*
1989	Kazuo Ishiguro, *The Remains of the Day*
1990	A. S. Byatt, *Possession*
1991	Ben Okri, *The Famished Road*
1992	Michael Ondaatje, *The English Patient*
	Barry Unsworth, *Sacred Hunger*
1993	Roddy Doyle, *Paddy Clarke Ha Ha Ha*

Special Prize for Best of the Past 25 Years, Salman Rushdie, *Midnight's Children*

1994	James Kelman, *How late it was, how late*
1995	Pat Barker, *The Ghost Road*

*Renamed the Man Booker Prize in 2002

1996	Graham Swift, *Last Orders*
1997	Arundhati Roy, *The God of Small Things*
1998	Ian McEwan, *Amsterdam*
1999	J. M. Coetzee, *Disgrace*
2000	Margaret Atwood, *The Blind Assassin*
2001	Peter Carey, *True History of the Kelly Gang*
2002	Yann Martel, *Life of Pi*

Carnegie Medal

1936	Arthur Ransome, *Pigeon Post*
1937	Eve Garnett, *The Family from One End Street*
1938	Noel Streatfeild, *The Circus Is Coming*
1939	Eleanor Doorly, *Radium Woman*
1940	Kitty Barne, *Visitors from London*
1941	Mary Treadgold, *We Couldn't Leave Dinah*
1942	"BB" (D. J. Watkins-Pitchford) *The Little Grey Men*
1943	No award
1944	Eric Linklater, *The Wind on the Moon*
1945	No award
1946	Elizabeth Goudge, *The Little White Horse*
1947	Walter de la Mare, *Collected Stories for Children*
1948	Richard Armstrong, *Sea Change*
1949	Agnes Allen, *The Story of Your Home*
1950	Elfrida Vipont Foulds, *The Lark on the Wing*
1951	Cynthia Harnett, *The Woolpack*
1952	Mary Norton, *The Borrowers*
1953	Edward Osmond, *A Valley Grows Up*
1954	Ronald Welch (Felton Ronald Oliver), *Knight Crusader*
1955	Eleanor Farjeon, *The Little Bookroom*
1956	C. S. Lewis, *The Last Battle*
1957	William Mayne, *A Grass Rope*
1958	Philippa Pearce, *Tom's Midnight Garden*
1959	Rosemary Sutcliff, *The Lantern Bearers*
1960	Dr. I. W. Cornwell, *The Making of Man*
1961	Lucy M. Boston, *A Stranger at Green Knowe*
1962	Pauline Clarke, *The Twelve and the Genii*
1963	Hester Burton, *Time of Trial*
1964	Sheena Porter, *Nordy Bank*
1965	Philip Turner, *The Grange at High Force*
1966	No award
1967	Alan Garner, *The Owl Service*
1968	Rosemary Harris, *The Moon in the Cloud*
1969	Kathleen Peyton, *The Edge of the Cloud*
1970	Leon Garfield and Edward Blishen, *The God beneath the Sea*
1971	Ivan Southall, *Josh*
1972	Richard Adams, *Watership Down*

1973	Penelope Lively, *The Ghost of Thomas Kempe*
1974	Mollie Hunter, *The Stronghold*
1975	Robert Westall, *The Machine Gunners*
1976	Jan Mark, *Thunder and Lightnings*
1977	Gene Kemp, *The Turbulent Term of Tyke Tiler*
1978	David Rees, *The Exeter Blitz*
1979	Peter Dickinson, *Tulku*
1980	Peter Dickinson, *City of Gold*
1981	Robert Westall, *The Scarecrows*
1982	Margaret Mahy, *The Haunting*
1983	Jan Mark, *Handles*
1984	Margaret Mahy, *The Changeover*
1985	Kevin Crossley-Holland, *Storm*
1986	Berlie Doherty, *Granny Was a Buffer Girl*
1987	Susan Price, *The Ghost Drum*
1988	Geraldine McCaughrean, *A Pack of Lies*
1989	Anne Fine, *Goggle-Eyes*
1990	Gillian Cross, *Wolf*
1991	Berlie Doherty, *Dear Nobody*
1992	Anne Fine, *Flour Babies*
1993	Robert Swindells, *Stone Gold*
1994	Theresa Breslin, *Whispers in the Graveyard*
1995	Philip Pullman, *His Dark Materials: Northern Lights*
1996	Melvin Burgess, *Junk*
1997	Tim Bowler, *River Boy*
1998	David Almond, *Skellig*
1999	Aidan Chambers, *Postcards from No Man's Land*
2000	Beverley Naidoo, *The Other Side of Truth*
2001	Terry Pratchett, *The Amazing Maurice and His Educated Rodents*

Arthur C. Clarke Award

1987	Margaret Atwood, *The Handmaid's Tale*
1988	George Turner, *The Sea and Summer*
1989	Rachel Pollack, *Unquenchable Fire*
1990	Geoff Ryman, *The Child Garden*
1991	Colin Greenland, *Take Back Plenty*
1992	Pat Cadigan, *Synners*
1993	Marge Piercy, *Body of Glass*
1994	Jeff Noon, *Vurt*
1995	Pat Cadigan, *Fools*
1996	Paul J. McAuley, *Fairyland*
1997	Amitav Ghosh, *The Calcutta Chromosome*
1998	Mary Doria Russell, *The Sparrow*
1999	Tricia Sullivan, *Dreaming in Smoke*
2000	Bruce Sterling, *Distraction*
2001	China Miéville, *Perdido Street Station*
2002	Gwyneth Jones, *Bold as Love*

David Cohen Prize

1993	V. S. Naipaul
1995	Harold Pinter
1997	Muriel Spark
1999	William Trevor
2001	Doris Lessing

Commonwealth Writers Prize

Best Book

1987	Olive Senior, *Summer Lightning*
1988	Festus Iyayi, *Heroes*
1989	Janet Frame, *The Carpathians*
1990	Mordecai Richler, *Solomon Gursky Was Here*
1991	David Malouf, *The Great World*
1992	Rohinton Mistry, *Such a Long Journey*
1993	Alex Miller, *The Ancestor Game*
1994	Vikram Seth, *A Suitable Boy*
1995	Louis de Bernières, *Captain Corelli's Mandolin*
1996	Rohinton Mistry, *A Fine Balance*
1997	Earl Lovelace, *Salt*
1998	Peter Carey, *Jack Maggs*
1999	Murray Bail, *Eucalyptus*
2000	J. M. Coetzee, *Disgrace*
2001	Peter Carey, *True History of the Kelly Gang*
2002	Richard Flanagan, *Gould's Book of Fish*

Best First Book

1987	Witi Ihimaera, *The Matriarch*
1988	George Turner, *The Sea and Summer*
1989	Bonnie Burnard, *Women of Influence*
1990	John Cranna, *Visitors*
1991	Pauline Melville, *Shape-Shifter*
1992	Robert Antoni, *Divina Trace*
1993	Githa Hariharan, *The Thousand Faces of Night*
1994	Keith Oatley, *The Case of Emily V*
1995	Adib Khan, *Seasonal Adjustments*
1996	Vikram Chandra, *Red Earth and Pouring Rain*
1997	Ann-Marie MacDonald, *Fall on Your Knees*
1998	Tim Wynveen, *Angel Falls*
1999	Kerri Sakamoto, *The Electrical Field*
2000	Jeffrey Moore, *Prisoner in a Red-Rose Chain*
2001	Zadie Smith, *White Teeth*
2002	Manu Herbstein, *Ama: A Story of the Atlantic Slave Trade*

T. S. Eliot Prize

1993	Ciaran Carson, *First Language*
1994	Paul Muldoon, *The Annals of Chile*
1995	Mark Doty, *My Alexandria*
1996	Les Murray, *Subhuman Redneck Poems*
1997	Don Paterson, *God's Gift to Women*
1998	Ted Hughes, *Birthday Letters*
1999	Hugo Williams, *Billy's Rain*
2000	Michael Longley, *The Weather in Japan*
2001	Anne Carson, *The Beauty of the Husband*
2002	Alice Oswald, *Dart*

Forward Poetry Prize

1992	Thom Gunn, *The Man with Night Sweats*
1993	Carol Ann Duffy, *Mean Time*
1994	Alan Jenkins, *Harm*
1995	Sean O'Brien, *Ghost Train*
1996	John Fuller, *Stones and Fires*
1997	Jamie McKendrick, *The Marble Fly*
1998	Ted Hughes, *Birthday Letters*
1999	Jo Shapcott, *My Life Asleep*
2000	Michael Donaghy, *Conjure*
2001	Sean O'Brien, *Downriver*
2002	Peter Porter, *Max Is Missing*

Guardian Fiction Prize

1965	Clive Barry, *Crumb Borne*
1966	Archie Hind, *The Dear Green Place*
1967	Eva Figes, *Winter Journey*
1968	P. J. Kavanagh, *A Song and a Dance*
1969	Maurice Leitch, *Poor Lazarus*
1970	Margaret Blount, *Where Did You Last See Your Father?*
1971	Thomas Kilroy, *The Big Chapel*
1972	John Berger, *G*
1973	Peter Redgrove, *In the Country of the Skin*
1974	Beryl Bainbridge, *The Bottle Factory Outing*
1975	Sylvia Clayton, *Friends and Romans*
1976	Robert Nye, *Falstaff*
1977	Michael Moorcock, *The Condition of Muzak*
1978	Neil Jordan, *Night in Tunisia*
1979	Dambudzo Marechera, *The House of Hunger*
1980	J. L. Carr, *A Month in the Country*
1981	John Banville, *Kepler*
1982	Glyn Hughes, *Where I Used to Play on the Green*
1983	Graham, Swift, *Waterland*
1984	J. G. Ballard, *Empire of the Sun*
1985	Peter Ackroyd, *Hawksmoor*
1986	Jim Crace, *Continent*
1987	Peter Benson, *The Levels*
1988	Lucy Ellman, *Sweet Desserts*

1989	Carol Lake, *Rosehill: Portrait from a Midlands City*
1990	Pauline Melville, *Shape-Shifter*
1991	Alan Judd, *The Devil's Own Work*
1992	Alasdair Gray, *Poor Things*
1993	Pat Barker, *The Eye in the Door*
1994	Candia McWilliam, *Debatable Land*
1995	James Buchan, *Heart's Journey in Winter*
1996	Seamus Deane, *Reading in the Dark*
1997	Anne Michaels, *Fugitive Pieces*
1998	Jackie Kay, *Trumpet*

Guardian First Book Award*

1999	Philip Gourevitch, *We Wish to Inform You That Tomorrow We Will Be Killed with Our Families*
2000	Zadie Smith, *White Teeth*
2001	Chris Ware, *Jimmy Corrigan: The Smartest Kid on Earth*
2002	Jonathan Safran, *Everything Is Illuminated*

Hawthornden Prize

1919	Edward Shanks, *The Queen of China*
1920	John Freeman, *Poems Old and New*
1921	Romer Wilson, *The Death of Society*
1922	Edmund Blunden, *The Shepherd*
1923	David Garnett, *Lady into Fox*
1924	Ralph Hale Mottram, *This Spanish Farm*
1925	Sean O'Casey, *Juno and the Paycock*
1926	Vita Sackville-West, *The Land*
1927	Henry Williamson, *Tarka the Otter*
1928	Siegfried Sassoon, *Memoirs of a Fox-Hunting Man*
1929	Lord David Cecil, *The Stricken Deer*
1930	Geoffrey Dennis, *The End of the World*
1931	Kate O'Brien, *Without My Cloak*
1932	Charles Morgan, *The Fountain*
1933	Vita Sackville-West, *Collected Poems*
1934	James Hilton, *Lost Horizon*
1935	Robert Graves, *I, Claudius*
1936	Evelyn Waugh, *Edmund Campion*
1937	Ruth Pitter, *A Trophy of Arms*
1938	David Jones, *In Parenthesis*
1939	Christopher Hassall, *Penthesperon*
1940	James Pope-Hennessy, *London Fabric*
1941	Graham Greene, *The Power and the Glory*
1942	John Llewllyn Rhys, *England Is My Village*
1943	Sidney Keyes, *The Cruel Solstice* and *The Iron Laurel*
1944	Martyn Skinner, *Letters to Malaya*
1945–57	No awards

1958	Dom Moraes, *A Beginning*
1959	No award
1960	Alan Sillitoe, *The Loneliness of the Long Distance Runner*
1961	Ted Hughes, *Lupercal*
1962	Robert Shaw, *The Sun Doctor*
1963	Alistair Horne, *The Price of Glory: Verdun 1916*
1964	V. S. Naipaul, *Mr. Stone and the Knights Companions*
1965	William Trevor, *The Old Boys*
1966	No award
1967	Michael Frayn, *The Russian Interpreter*
1968	Michael Levey, *Early Renaissance*
1969	Geoffrey Hill, *King Log*
1970	Piers Paul Read, *Monk Dawson*
1971–73	No awards
1974	Oliver Sacks, *Awakenings*
1975	David Lodge, *Changing Places*
1976	Robert Nye, *Falstaff*
1977	Bruce Chatwin, *In Patagonia*
1978	David Cook, *Walter*
1979	P. S. Rushforth, *Kindergarten*
1980	Christopher Reid, *Arcadia*
1981	Douglas Dunn, *St. Kilda's Parliament*
1982	Timothy Mo, *Sour Sweet*
1983	Jonathan Keates, *Allegro Postillions*
1984–87	No awards
1988	Colin Thubron, *Behind the Wall*
1989	Alan Bennett, *Talking Heads*
1990	Kit Wright, *Short Afternoons*
1991	Claire Tomalin, *The Invisible Woman*
1992	Ferdinand Mount, *Of Love and Asthma*
1993	Andrew Barrow, *The Tap Dancer*
1994	Tim Pears, *In the Place of Fallen Leaves*
1995	James Michie, *The Collected Poems*
1996	Hilary Mantel, *An Experiment in Love*
1997	John Lanchester, *The Debt to Pleasure*
1998	Charles Nicholl, *Somebody Else*
1999	Antony Beevor, *Stalingrad*
2000	Michael Longley, *The Weather in Japan*
2001	Helen Simpson, *Hey Yeah Right Get a Life*
2002	Eamon Duffy, *The Voices of Morebath*

Hugo Award for Best Science Fiction Novel

1953	Alfred Bester, *The Demolished Man*
1954	No award
1955	Mark Clifton and Frank Riley, *They'd Rather Be Right*
1956	Robert A. Heinlein, *Double Star*
1957	No award
1958	Fritz Leiber, *The Big Time*
1959	James Blish, *A Case of Conscience*
1960	Robert A. Heinlein, *Starship Troopers*

*Renamed in 1999

1961	Walter M. Miller, Jr., *A Canticle for Leibowitz*
1962	Robert A. Heinlein, *Stranger in a Strange Land*
1963	Philip K. Dick, *The Man in the High Castle*
1964	Clifford D. Simak, *Way Station*
1965	Fritz Leiber, *The Wanderer*
1966	Frank Herbert, *Dune*
1966	Roger Zelazny, . . . *And Call Me Conrad; or, This Immortal*
1967	Robert A. Heinlein, *The Moon Is a Harsh Mistress*
1968	Roger Zelazny, *Lord of Light*
1969	John Brunner, *Stand on Zanzibar*
1970	Ursula K. Le Guin, *The Left Hand of Darkness*
1971	Larry Niven, *Ringworld*
1972	Philip Jose Farmer, *To Your Scattered Bodies Go*
1973	Isaac Asimov, *The Gods Themselves*
1974	Arthur C. Clarke, *Rendezvous with Rama*
1975	Ursula K. Le Guin, *The Dispossessed*
1976	Joe Haldeman, *The Forever War*
1977	Kate Wilhelm, *Where Late the Sweet Birds Sang*
1978	Frederik Pohl, *Gateway*
1979	Vonda McIntyre, *Dreamsnake*
1980	Arthur C. Clarke, *The Foundations of Paradise*
1981	Joan D. Vinge, *Snow Queen*
1982	C. J. Cherryh, *Downbelow Station*
1983	Isaac Asimov, *Foundation's Edge*
1984	David Brin, *Startide Rising*
1985	William Gibson, *Neuromancer*
1986	Orson Scott Card, *Ender's Game*
1987	Orson Scott Card, *Speaker for the Dead*
1988	David Brin, *The Uplift War*
1989	C. J. Cherryh, *Cyteen*
1990	Dan Simmons, *Hyperion*
1991	Lois McMaster Bujold, *The Vor Game*
1992	Lois McMaster Bujold, *Barryar*
1993	Vernor Vinge, *A Fire upon the Deep*
1994	Kim Stanley Robinson, *Green Mars*
1995	Lois McMaster Bujold, *Mirror Dance*
1996	Neal Stephenson, *The Diamond Age*
1997	Kin Stanley Robinson, *Blue Mars*
1998	Joe Haldeman, *Forever Peace*
1999	Connie Willis, *To Say Nothing of the Dog*
2000	Vernor Vinge, *A Deepness in the Sky*
2001	J. K. Rowling, *Harry Potter and the Goblet of Fire*
2002	Neil Gaiman, *American Gods*

International IMPAC Dublin Literary Award

1996	David Malouf, *Remembering Babylon*

1997	Javier Marias, *A Heart So White*
1998	Herta Müller, *The Land of Green Plums*
1999	Andrew Miller, *Ingenious Pain*
2000	Nicola Barker, *Wide Open*
2001	Alistair MacLeod, *No Great Mischief*
2002	Michel Houellebecq, *Atomised* (also pub. as *The Elementary Particles*)

Irish Times Literature Prizes

Irish Literature Prizes

1989	Fiction, Frank Ronan, *The Man Who Loved Evelyn Cotton*
1990	Fiction, John McGahern, *Amongst Women*
	Poetry, Ciaran Carson, *Belfast Confetti*
1991	Nonfiction, J. J. Lee, *Ireland 1912–1985*
	First Book, Colm Tóibín, *The South*
1992	Fiction, Patrick McCabe, *The Butcher Boy*
	Poetry, Derek Mahon, *Selected Poems*
1993	Nonfiction, Brian Keenan, *An Evil Cradling*
	First Book, John MacKenna, *The Fallen and Other Stories*
1995	Fiction, Kathleen Ferguson, *A Maid's Tale*
	Nonfiction, Paddy Devlin, *Straight Left*
	Poetry, Robert Greacen, *Collected Poems*
1997	Fiction, Seamus Deane, *Reading in the Dark*
	Nonfiction, Declan Kiberd, *Inventing Ireland*
	Poetry, Paul Muldoon, *New Selected Poems*
1999	Fiction, Antonia Logue, *Shadow-Box*
	Nonfiction, Neil Belton, *The Good Listener: Helen Bamber—A Life against Cruelty*
	Poetry, Seamus Heaney, *Opened Ground: Selected Poems 1966–1996*

International Fiction Prize

1989	Don DeLillo, *Libra*
1990	A. S. Byatt, *Possession*
1991	Louis Begley, *Wartime Lies*
1992	Norman Rush, *Mating*
1993	E. Annie Proulx, *The Shipping News*
1995	J. M. Coetzee, *The Master of Petersburg*
1997	Seamus Deane, *Reading in the Dark*
1999	Lorrie Moore, *Birds of America*

Samuel Johnson Prize for Nonfiction

1999	Antony Beevor, *Stalingrad*
2000	David Cairns, *Berlioz: Servitude and Greatness*
2001	Michael Burleigh, *The Third Reich*

2002   Margaret Macmillan, *Peacemakers: The Paris Peace Conference of 1919 and Its Attempt to End War*

Somerset Maugham Award

1947   A. L. Barker, *Innocents*
1948   P. H. Newby, *Journey to the Interior*
1949   Hamish Henderson, *Elegies for the Dead in Cyrenaica*
1950   Nigel Kneale, *Tomato Cain and Other Stories*
1951   Roland Camberton, *Scamp*
1952   Francis King, *The Dividing Stream*
1953   Emyr Humphreys, *Hear and Forgive*
1954   Doris Lessing, *Five Short Novels*
1955   Kingsley Amis, *Lucky Jim*
1956   Elizabeth Jennings, *A Way of Looking*
1957   George Lamming, *In the Castle of My Skin*
1959   Thom Gunn, *A Sense of Movement*
1960   Ted Hughes, *The Hawk in the Rain*
1961   V. S. Naipaul, *Miguel Street*
1962   Hugh Thomas, *The Spanish Civil War*
1963   David Storey, *Flight into Camden*
1964   Dan Jacobson, *Time of Arrival*
      John le Carré, *The Spy Who Came in from the Cold*
1965   Peter Everett, *Negatives*
1966   Michael Frayn, *The Tin Men*
      Julian Mitchell, *The White Father*
1967   B. S. Johnson, *Trawl*
      Andrew Sinclair, *The Better Half*
1968   Paul Bailey, *At the Jerusalem*
      Seamus Heaney, *Death of a Naturalist*
1969   Angela Carter, *Several Perceptions*
1970   Jane Gaskell, *A Sweet Sweet Summer*
      Piers Paul Read, *Monk Dawson*
1971   Susan Hill, *I'm the King of the Castle*
      Richard Barber, *The Knight and Chivalry*
      Michael Hastings, *Tussy Is Me*
1972   Douglas Dunn, *Terry Street*
      Gillian Tindall, *Fly Away Home*
1973   Peter Prine, *Play Things*
      Paul Strathern, *A Season in Abyssinia*
      Jonathan Street, *Prudence Dictates*
1974   Martin Amis, *The Rachel Papers*
1975   No award
1976   Dominic Cooper, *The Dead of Winter*
      Ian McEwan, *First Love, Last Rites*
1977   Richard Holmes, *Shelley: The Pursuit*
1978   Tom Paulin, *A State of Justice*
      Nigel Williams, *My Life Closed Twice*
1979   Helen Hodgman, *Jack and Jill*
      Sara Maitland, *Daughter of Jerusalem*
1980   Max Hastings, *Bomber Command*

      Christopher Reid, *Arcadia*
      Humphrey Carpenter, *The Inklings*
1981   Julian Barnes, *Metroland*
      Clive Sinclair, *Hearts of Gold*
      A. N. Wilson, *The Healing Art*
1982   William Boyd, *A Good Man in Africa*
      Adam Mars-Jones, *Lantern Lecture*
1983   Lisa St. Aubin de Teran, *Keepers of the House*
1984   Peter Ackroyd, *The Last Testament of Oscar Wilde*
      Timothy Garton Ash, *The Polish Revolution: Solidarity*
      Sean O'Brien, *The Indoor Park*
1985   Blake Morrison, *Dark Glasses*
      Jeremy Reed, *By the Fisheries*
      Jane Rogers, *Her Living Image*
1986   Patricia Ferguson, *Family Myths and Legends*
      Adam Nicolson, *Frontiers*
      Tim Parks, *Tongues of Flame*
1987   Stephen Gregory, *The Cormorant*
      Janni Howker, *Isaac Campion*
      Andrew Motion, *The Lamberts*
1988   Jimmy Burns, *The Land That Lost Its Heroes*
      Carol Ann Duffy, *Selling Manhattan*
      Matthew Kneale, *Whore Banquets*
1989   Rupert Christiansen, *Romantic Affinities*
      Alan Hollingshurst, *The Swimming Pool Library*
      Deirdre Madden, *The Birds of the Innocent Wood*
1990   Mark Hudson, *Our Grandmother's Drums*
      Sam North, *The Automatic Man*
      Nicholas Shakespeare, *The Vision of Elena Silves*
1991   Peter Benson, *The Other Occupant*
      Lesley Glaister, *Honour Thy Father*
      Helen Simpson, *Four Bare Legs in a Bed*
1992   Geoff Dyer, *But Beautiful*
      Lawrence Norfolk, *Lempriere's Dictionary*
      Gerard Woodward, *Householder*
1993   Dea Birket, *Jella*
      Duncan McLean, *Bucket of Tongues*
      Glyn Maxwell, *Out of the Rain*
1994   Jackie Kay, *Other Lovers*
      A. L. Kenndy, *Looking for the Possible Dance*
      Philip Marsden, *Crossing Place*
1995   Patrick French, *Younghusband*
      Simon Garfield, *The End of Innocence*
      Kathleen Jamie, *The Queen of Sheba*
      Laura Thompson, *The Dogs*
1996   Katherine Pierpoint, *Truffle Beds*
      Alan Warner, *Morvern Callar*

1997	Rhidian Brook, *The Testimony of Taliesin Jones*
	Kate Clanchy, *Slattern*
	Philip Hensher, *Kitchen Venom*
	Francis Spufford, *I May Be Some Time*
1998	Rachel Cusk, *The Country Life*
	Jonathan Rendall, *The Bloody Mary Is the Last Thing I Own*
	Kate Summerscale, *The Queen of Whale Cay*
	Robert Twigger, *Angry White Pyjamas*
1999	Andrea Ashworth, *Once in a House on Fire*
	Paul Farley, *The Boy from the Chemist Is Here to See You*
	Giles Foden, *The Last King of Scotland*
	Jonathan Freedland, *Bring Home the Revolution*
2000	Bella Bathurst, *The Lighthouse Sevensons*
	Sarah Waters, *Affinity*
2001	Edward Platt, *Leadville*
	Ben Rice, *Pobby and Dingan*
2002	Charlotte Hobson, *Black Earth City*
	Marcel Theroux, *The Paperchase*

Nobel Prize for Literature

1901	René-François-Armand-Sully Prudhomme
1902	Theodor Mommsen
1903	Bjørnstjerne Bjørnson
1904	José Echegara
	Frédéric Mistral
1905	Henryk Sienkiewicz
1906	Giosué Carducci
1907	Rudyard Kipling
1908	Rudolf Eucken
1909	Selma Lagerlöf
1910	Paul Heyse
1911	Maurice Maeterlinck
1912	Gerhart Hauptmann
1913	Rabindranath Tagore
1914	No award
1915	Romain Rolland
1916	Verner von Heidenstam
1917	Karl Kjellerup
	Henrik Pontoppidan
1918	No award
1919	Carl Spitteler
1920	Knut Hamsun
1921	Anatole France
1922	Jacinto Benavente y Martínez
1923	W. B. Yeats
1924	Wladyslaw Reymont
1925	Bernard Shaw
1926	Grazia Deledda
1927	Henri Bergson

1928	Sigrid Undset
1929	Thomas Mann
1930	Sinclair Lewis
1931	Erik Axel Karlfeldt
1932	John Galsworthy
1933	Ivan Bunin
1934	Luigi Pirandello
1935	No award
1936	Eugene O'Neill
1937	Roger Martin du Gard
1938	Pearl S. Buck
1939	F. E. Sillianpää
1940–43	No awards
1944	Johannes V. Jensen
1945	Gabriela Mistral
1946	Herman Hesse
1947	André Gide
1948	T. S. Eliot
1949	William Faulkner
1950	Bertrand Russell
1951	Pär Lagerkvist
1952	François Mauriac
1953	Winston S. Churchill
1954	Ernest Hemingway
1955	Halldór Laxness
1956	Juan Ramón Jiménez
1957	Albert Camus
1958	Boris Pasternak
1959	Salvatore Quasimodo
1960	Saint-John Perse
1961	Ivo Andrić
1962	John Steinbeck
1963	George Seferis
1964	Jean-Paul Sartre
1965	Mikhail Sholokhov
1966	S. Y. Agnon
	Nelly Sachs
1967	Miguel Ángel Asturias
1968	Yasunari Kawabata
1969	Samuel Beckett
1970	Alexander Solzhenitsyn
1971	Pablo Neruda
1972	Heinrich Böll
1973	Patrick White
1974	Eyvind Johnson
	Harry Martinson
1975	Eugenio Montale
1976	Saul Bellow
1977	Vincente Aleixandre
1978	Isaac Bashevis Singer
1979	Odysseus Elytis
1980	Czesław Miłosz
1981	Elias Canetti
1982	Gabriel García Márquez
1983	William Golding
1984	Jaroslav Seifert
1985	Claude Simon

1986	Wole Soyinka		1981	D. J. Enright
1987	Joseph Brodsky		1986	Norman MacCaig
1988	Najíb Mahfúz		1988	Derek Walcott
1989	Camilo José Cela		1989	Allen Curnow
1990	Octavio Paz		1990	Sorley Maclean
1991	Nadine Gordimer		1991	Judith Wright
1992	Derek Walcott		1992	Kathleen Raine
1993	Toni Morrison		1996	Peter Redgrove
1994	Kenzaburō Ōe		1998	Les Murray
1995	Seamus Heaney		2000	Edwin Morgan
1996	Wisława Szymborska		2001	Michael Longley
1997	Dario Fo		2002	Peter Porter
1998	José Saramago			
1999	Günter Grass			
2000	Gao Xingjian			
2001	V. S. Naipaul			
2002	Imre Kertész			

Orange Prize for Fiction

1996	Helen Dunmore, *A Spell of Winter*
1997	Anne Michaels, *Fugitive Pieces*
1998	Carol Shields, *Larry's Party*
1999	Suzanne Berne, *A Crime in the Neighborhood*
2000	Linda Grant, *When I Lived in Modern Times*
2001	Kate Grenville, *The Idea of Perfection*
2002	Ann Patchett, *Bel Canto*

Queen's Gold Medal for Poetry

1934	Laurence Whistler
1936	W. H. Auden
1940	Michael Thwaites
1952	Andrew Young
1953	Arthur Waley
1954	Ralph Hodgson
1955	Ruth Pitter
1956	Edmund Blunden
1957	Siegfried Sassoon
1959	Francis Cornford
1960	John Betjeman
1962	Christopher Fry
1963	William Plomer
1964	R. S. Thomas
1965	Philip Larkin
1967	Charles Causley
1968	Robert Graves
1969	Stevie Smith
1970	Roy Fuller
1971	Sir Stephen Spender
1973	John Heath-Stubbs
1974	Ted Hughes
1977	Norman Nicholson

John Llewellyn Rhys Prize

1942	Michael Richey, *Sunk by a Mine*
1943	Morwenna Donelly, *Beauty for Ashes*
1944	Alun Lewis, *The Last Inspection*
1945	James Aldridge, *The Sea Eagle*
1946	Oriel Malet, *My Bird Sings*
1947	Anne-Marie Walters, *Moondrop to Gascony*
1948	Richard Mason, *The Wind Cannot Read*
1949	Emma Smith, *Maiden's Trip*
1950	Kenneth Allsop, *Adventure Lit Their Star*
1951	Elizabeth Jane Howard, *The Beautiful Visit*
1952	No award
1953	Rachel Trickett, *The Return Home*
1954	Tom Stacey, *The Hostile Sun*
1955	John Wiles, *The Moon to Play With*
1956	John Hearne, *Voice under the Window*
1957	Ruskin Bond, *The Room on the Roof*
1958	V. S. Naipaul, *The Mystic Masseur*
1959	Dan Jacobson, *A Long Way from London*
1960	David Caute, *At Fever Pitch*
1961	David Storey, *Flight into Camden*
1962	Robert Rhodes James, *An Introduction to the House of Commons*
	Edward Lucie-Smith, *A Tropical Childhood and Other Poems*
1963	Peter Marshall, *Two Lives*
1964	Nell Dunn, *Up the Junction*
1965	Julian Mitchell, *The White Father*
1966	Margaret Drabble, *The Millstone*
1967	Anthony Masters, *The Seahorse*
1968	Angela Carter, *The Magic Toyshop*
1969	Melvyn Bragg, *Without a City Wall*
1970	Angus Calder, *The People's War*
1971	Shiva Naipaul, *Fireflies*
1972	Susan Hill, *The Albatross*
1973	Peter Smalley, *A Warm Gun*
1974	Hugh Fleetwood, *The Girl Who Passed for Normal*
1975	David Hare, *Knuckle*
	Tim Jeal, *Cushing's Crusade*

1976	No award
1977	Richard Cork, *Vorticism and Abstract Art in the First Machine Age*
1978	A. N. Wilson, *The Sweets of Pimlico*
1979	Peter Boardman, *The Shining Mountain*
1980	Desmond Hogan, *The Diamonds at the Bottom of the Sea*
1981	A. N. Wilson, *The Laird of Abbotsford*
1982	William Boyd, *An Ice-Cream War*
1983	Lisa St Aubin de Teran, *The Slow Train to Milan*
1984	Andrew Motion, *Dangerous Play*
1985	John Milne, *Out of the Blue*
1986	Tim Parks, *Loving Roger*
1987	Jeanette Winterson, *The Passion*
1988	Matthew Yorke, *The March Fence*
1989	Claire Harman, *Sylvia Townsend Warner*
1990	Ray Monk, *Ludwig Wittgenstein: The Duty of Genius*
1991	A. L. Kennedy, *Night Geometry and the Garscadden Trains*
1992	Matthew Kneale, *Sweet Thames*
1993	Jason Goodwin, *On Foot to the Golden Horn: A Walk to Istanbul*
1994	Jonathan Coe, *What a Carve Up!*
1995	Melanie McGrath, *Motel Nirvana*
1996	Nicola Barker, *Heading Inland*
1997	Phil Whitaker, *Eclipse of the Sun*
1998	Peter Ho, *The Ugliest House in the World*
1999	David Mitchell, *Ghostwritten*
2000	Edward Platt, *Leadville*
2001	Susanna Jones, *The Earthquake Bird*

W. H. Smith Book Awards

Literary Award

1959	Patrick White, *Voss*
1960	Laurie Lee, *Cider with Rosie*
1961	Nadine Gordimer, *Fridays's Footprint*
1962	J. R. Ackerley, *We Think the World of You*
1963	Gabriel Fielding, *The Birthday King*
1964	Ernst H. Gombrich, *Meditations on a Hobby-Horse*
1965	Leonard Woolf, *Beginning Again*
1966	R. C. Hutchinson, *A Child Possessed*
1967	Jean Rhys, *Wide Sargasso Sea*
1968	V. S. Naipaul, *The Mimic Men*
1969	Robert Gittings, *John Keats*
1970	John Fowles, *The French Lieutenant's Woman*
1971	Nan Fairbrother, *New Lives, New Landscapes*
1972	Kathleen Raine, *The Lost Country*
1973	Brian Moore, *Catholics*
1974	Anthony Powell, *Temporary Kings*
1975	Jon Stallworthy, *Wilfred Owen*

1976	Seamus Heaney, *North*
1977	Ronald Lewin, *Slim: The Standardbearer*
1978	Patrick Leigh Fermor, *A Time of Gifts*
1979	Mark Girouard, *Life in the English Country House*
1980	Thom Gunn, *Selected Poems 1950–1975*
1981	Isabel Colegate, *The Shooting Party*
1982	George Clare, *Last Waltz in Vienna: The Destruction of a Family 1842–1942*
1983	A. N. Wilson, *Wise Virgin*
1984	Philip Larkin, *Required Writing*
1985	David Hughes, *The Pork Butcher*
1986	Doris Lessing, *The Good Terrorist*
1987	Elizabeth Jennings, *Collected Poems, 1953–1985*
1988	Robert Hughes, *The Fatal Shore: A History of the Transportation of Convicts to Australia, 1787–1868*
1989	Christopher Hill, *A Turbulent, Seditious and Factious People: John Bunyan and His Church, 1628–1688*
1990	V. S. Pritchett, *A Careless Widow and Other Stories*
1991	Derek Walcott, *Omeros*
1992	Thomas Pakenham, *The Scramble for Africa*
1993	Michèle Roberts, *Daughters of the House*
1994	Vikram Seth, *A Suitable Boy*
1995	Alice Munro, *Open Secrets*
1996	Simon Schama, *Landscape and Memory*
1997	Orlando Figes, *A People's Tragedy: The Russian Revlution 1891–1924*
1998	Ted Hughes, *Tales from Ovid*
1999	Beryl Bainbridge, *Master Georgie*
2000	Melvyn Bragg, *The Soldier's Return*
2001	Philip Roth, *The Human Stain*
2002	Ian McEwan, *Atonement*

Betty Trask Prize

1985	Ronald Frame, *Winter Journey*
1986	Susan Kay, *Legacy*
1987	Tim Parks, *Tongues of Flame*
1988	Helen Flint, *Return Journey*
	Peter Benson, *The Levels*
1988	Alex Martin, *The General Interruptor*
	Candia McWilliam, *A Case of Knives*
1989	Nigel Watts, *The Life Game*
1990	Robern McLiam Wilson, *Ripley Bogle*
1991	Amit Chaudhuri, *A Strange and Sublime Address*
1992	Liane Jones, *The Dreamstone*
1993	Mark Blackaby, *You'll Never Be Here Again*
1994	Colin Bateman, *Divorcing Jack*
1995	Robert Newman, *Dependence Day*

1996   John Lanchester, *The Debt of Pleasure*
1997   Alex Garland, *The Beach*
1998   Kiran Desai, *Hullaballoo in the Guava Orchard*
1999   Elliot Perlman, *Three Dollars*
2000   Jonathan Tulloch, *The Season Ticket*
2001   Zadie Smith, *White Teeth*
2002   Hari Kunzru, *The Impressionist*

Whitbread Award

Biography
1971   Michael Meyer, *Henrik Ibsen*
1972   James Pope-Hennessey, *Trollope*
1973   John Wilson, *CB: A Life of Sir Henry Campbell-Bannerman*
1974   Andrew Boyle, *Poor Dear Brendan*
1975   Helen Corke, *In Our Infancy*
1976   Winifred Gérin, *Elizabeth Gaskell*
1977   Nigel Nicolson, *Mary Curzon*
1978   John Grigg, *Lloyd George: The People's Champion*
1979   Penelope Mortimer, *About Time*
1980   David Newsome, *On the Edge of Paradise: A. C. Benson the Diarist*
1981   Nigel Hamilton, *Monty: The Making of a General*
1982   Edward Crankshaw, *Bismarck*
1983   Victoria Glendinning, *Vita*
1983   Kenneth Rose, *King George V*
1984   Peter Ackroyd, *T. S. Eliot*
1985   Ben Pimlott, *Hugh Dalton*
1986   Richard Mabey, *Gilbert White*
1987   Christopher Nolan, *Under the Eye of the Clock*
1988   A. N. Wilson, *Tolstoy*
1989   Richard Holmes, *Coleridge: Early Visions*
1990   Ann Thwaite, *A. A. Milne: His Life*
1991   John Richardson, *A Life of Picasso*
1992   Victoria Glendinning, *Trollope*
1993   Andrew Motion, *Philip Larkin: A Writer's Life*
1994   Brenda Maddox, *The Married Man: A Life of D. J. Lawrence*
1995   Roy Jenkins, *Gladstone*
1996   Diarmaid MacCulloch, *Thomas Cranmer: A Life*
1997   Graham Robb, *Victor Hugo*
1998   Amanda Foreman, *Georgiana, Duchess of Devonshire*
1999   David Cairns, *Berlioz*
2000   Lorna Sage, *Bad Blood: A Memoir*
2001   Diana Souhami, *Selkirk's Island*
2002   Claire Tomalin, *Samuel Pepys: The Unequalled Self*

Book of the Year
1994   William Trevor, *Felicia's Journey*
1995   Kate Atkinson, *Behind the Scenes at the Museum*
1996   John Lanchester, *A Debt to Pleasure*
1997   Pauline Melville, *The Ventriloquist's Tale*
1998   Ted Hughes, *Birthday Letters*
1999   Seamus Heaney, *Beowulf*
2000   Matthew Kneale, *English Passengers*
2001   Philip Pullman, *The Amber Spyglass*
2002   Claire Tomalin, *Samuel Pepys: The Unequalled Self*

Children's Book of the Year Award
1971   No award
1972   Rumer Gooden, *The Diddakoi*
1973   Alan Aldridge and William Plomer, *The Butterfly Ball and the Grasshopper's Feast*
1974   Russell Hoban and Quentin Blake, *How Tom Beat Captain Najork and His Hired Sportsmen*
        Jill Paton Walsh, *The Emperor's Winding Sheet*
1975   No award
1976   Penelope Lively, *A Stitch in Time*
1977   Shelagh Macdonald, *No End to Yesterday*
1978   Philippa Pearce, *The Battle of Bubble and Squeak*
1979   Peter Dickinson, *Tulku*
1980   Leon Garfield, *John Diamond*
1981   Jane Gardam, *The Hollow Land*
1982   W. J. Corbett, *The Song of Pentecost*
1983   Roald Dahl, *The Witches*
1984   Barbara Willard, *The Queen of the Pharisees' Children*
1985   Janni Howker, *The Nature of the Beast*
1986   Andrew Taylor, *The Coal House*
1987   Geraldine McCaughrean, *A Little Lower than the Angels*
1988   Judy Allen, *Awaiting Developments*
1989   Hugh Scott, *Why Weeps the Brogan?*
1990   Peter Dickinson, *AK*
1991   Diana Hendry, *Harvey Angell*
1992   Gillian Cross, *The Great Elephant Chase*
1993   Anna Fine, *Flour Babies*
1994   Geraldine McCaughrean, *Gold Dust*
1995   Michael Morpurgo, *The Wreck of the Zanzibar*
1996   Anna Fine, *The Tulip Touch*
1997   Andrew Norriss, *Aquila*
1998   David Almond, *Skellig*
1999   J. K. Rowling, *Harry Potter and the Prisoner of Azkaban*
2000   Jamila Gavin, *Coram Boy*
2001   Philip Pullman, *The Amber Spyglass*
2002   Hilary McKay, *Saffy's Angel*

Novel

1971	Gerda Charles, *The Destiny Waltz*
1972	Susan Hill, *The Bird of Night*
1973	Shiva Naipaul, *The Chip-Chip Gatherers*
1974	Iris Murdoch, *The Sacred and Profane Love Machine*
1975	William McIlvanney, *Docherty*
1976	William Trevor, *The Children of Dynmouth*
1977	Beryl Bainbridge, *Injury Time*
1978	Paul Theroux, *Picture Palace*
1979	Jennifer Johnston, *The Old Jest*
1980	Novel and Book of the Year, David Lodge, *How Far Can You Go?*
1981	Maurice Leitch, *Silver's City*
1982	John Wain, *Young Shoulders*
1983	William Trevor, *Fools of Fortune*
1984	Christopher Hope, *Kruger's Alp*
1985	Peter Ackroyd, *Hawksmoor*
1986	Novel and Grand Prize, Kazuo Ishiguro, *An Artist of the Floating World*
1987	Ian McEwan, *The Child in Time*
1988	Salman Rushdie, *Satanic Verses*
1989	Lindsay Clarke, *The Chymical Wedding*
1990	Nicholas Mosley, *Hopeful Monsters*
1991	Jane Gardam, *The Queen of the Tambourine*
1992	Alasdair Gray, *Poor Things*
1993	Novel and Grand Prize, Joan Brady, *Theory of War*
1994	Novel and Book of the Year, William Trevor, *Felicia's Journey*
1995	Salman Rushdie, *The Moor's Last Sigh*
1996	Beryl Bainbridge, *Every Man for Himself*
1997	Jim Crace, *Quarantine*
1998	Justin Cartwright, *Leading the Cheers*
1999	Rose Tremain, *Music and Silence*
2000	Matthew Kneale, *English Passengers*
2001	Patrick Neate, *Twelve Bar Blues*
2002	Michael Frayn, *Spies*

First Novel

1981	William Boyd, *A Good Man in Africa*
1982	Bruce Chatwin, *On the Black Hill*

1983	John Fuller, *Flying to Nowhere*
1984	James Buchan, *A Parish of Rich Women*
1985	Jeanette Winterson, *Oranges Are Not the Only Fruit*
1986	Jim Crace, *Continent*
1987	Francis Wyndham, *The Other Garden*
1988	Paul Sayer, *The Comforts of Madness*
1989	James Hamilton-Paterson, *Gerontius*
1990	Hanif Kureishi, *The Buddha of Suburbia*
1991	Gordon Burn, *Alma Cogan*
1992	Jeff Torrington, *Swing Hammer Swing!*
1993	Rachel Cusk, *Saving Agnes*
1994	Fred D'Aguiar, *The Longest Memory*
1995	Kate Atkinson, *Behind the Scenes at the Museum*
1996	John Lanchester, *A Debt to Pleasure*
1997	Pauline Melville, *The Ventriloquist's Tale*
1998	Giles Foden, *The Last King of Scotland*
1999	Tim Lott, *White City Blue*
2000	Zadie Smith, *White Teeth*
2001	Sid Smith, *Something Like a House*
2002	Norman Lebrecht, *The Song of Names*

Poetry

1985	Douglas Dunn, *Elegies*
1986	Peter Reading, *Stet*
1987	Seamus Heaney, *The Haw Lantern*
1988	Peter Porter, *The Automatic Oracle*
1989	Michael Donaghy, *Shibboleth*
1990	Paul Durcan, *Daddy, Daddy*
1991	Michael Longley, *Gorse Fires*
1992	Tony Harrison, *The Gaze of the Gorgon*
1993	Carol Ann Duffy, *Mean Time*
1994	James Fenton, *Out of Danger*
1995	Bernard O'Donoghue, *Gunpowder*
1996	Seamus Heaney, *The Spirit Level*
1997	Ted Hughes, *Tales from Ovid*
1998	Ted Hughes, *Birthday Letters*
1999	Seamus Heaney, *Beowulf*
2000	John Burnside, *The Asylum Dance*
2001	Selma Hill, *Bunny*
2002	Paul Farley, *The Ice Age*

Contributors

Carol Acton, St. Jerome's University; Rick Allen, Anglia Polytechnic University; Phillip B. Anderson, University of Central Arkansas; Lana Asfour, London, England; Elaine Aston, Lancaster University; Rose Atfield, Brunel University; Simon Avery, University of Hertfordshire; Paige Bailey, Tulane University; Chris Baldick, Goldsmiths College, University of London; E. Lindsey Balkan, Community College of Baltimore County; Karen Bamford, Mount Allison University; Clive Barker, Rugby, England; Peter Barnes, London, England; Harold Barratt, Windsor, Ontario; Nicola Beauman, London, England; Michael Bell, University of Warwick; Sandra Bell, University of New Brunswick; Samuel I. Bellman, California State University, Pomona; Joe Bennett, Christchurch, New Zealand; Stephen Benson, Brunel University; Lisa Berglund, Buffalo State College; Jason Berner, Contra Costa College; Jacques Berthoud, University of York; Ruth Bidgood, Powys, Wales; Margaret Boe Birns, New School University; Nicholas Birns, New School University; Andrew Biswell, Aberdeen University; Abigail Burnham Bloom, New York City; Howard J. Booth, University of Manchester; Janet Bottoms, Cambridge University; S. K. Brehe, North Georgia College and State University; Derek Brewer, Emmanuel College, Cambridge; Jack Broderick, Alexandria, Virgina; Daniel Brown, University of Western Australia; Marika Brussel, Santa Fe, New Mexico; Sean Burgess, Queen's University, Kingston, Ontario; Miriam Elizabeth Burstein, State University of New York, College at Brockport; Andrew M. Butler, Buckinghamshire Chilterns University College; Tanya Butler, Queen's University, Kingston, Ontario; Sandie Byrne, Balliol College, Oxford; Peter Carpenter, Kent, England; Julie Chappell, Tarleton State University; Subarno Chattarji, New Delhi, India; William M. Clements, Arkansas State University; Peter Cochran, Cambridge, England; Tim Conley, Queen's University, Kingston, Ontario; Margaret Connolly, University College Cork; Thomas L.

Cooksey, Armstrong Atlantic University; Brian Jay Corrigan, North Georgia State University; Lynne Crockett, State University of New York at New Paltz; John Cronin, Queen's University of Belfast; Keith Crook, Cambridge, England; Nora Crook, Anglia Polytechnic University; Robert E. Cummings, University of Georgia; Roger Dalrymple, St. Hugh's College, Oxford; Harry Derbyshire, King's College London; Thomas F. Dillingham, Stephens College; Kieran Dolin, University of Western Australia; T. D. Drake, Queen's College, Kingston, Ontario; Charles Duff, London, England; Vicki Eng, Santa Fe, New Mexico; Rebecca Faber, University of Nebraska–Lincoln; Lynette Felber, Indiana University–Purdue University Fort Wayne; Rachel Falconer, University of Sheffield; Steve Ferebee, North Carolina Wesleyan College; Peter Finch, Cardiff, Wales; Joseph M. Flora, University of North Carolina at Chapel Hill; Martin K. Foys, Florida State University; Catherine Frank, University of North Carolina at Chapel Hill; Raymond-Jean Frontain, University of Central Arkansas; Steven Frye, California State University, Bakersfield; Ann O'Brien Fuller, Savannah, Georgia; George R. Fuller, Savannah, Georgia; David Fulton, Brunel University; Judith E. Funston, State University of New York at Potsdam; Averil Gardner, Memorial University of Newfoundland; Philip Gardner, Memorial University of Newfoundland; Samuel Gaustad, Phillips Community College; W. B. Gerard, Auburn University Montgomery; Bryan A. Giemza, University of North Carolina at Chapel Hill; John Gilroy, Anglia Polytechnic University; John V. Glass, Atlanta, Georgia; Esther Godfrey, London, England; Philip Gooden, Bath, England; I. R. F. Gordon, Anglia Polytechnic University; Desmond Graham, University of Newcastle-upon-Tyne; Dalton and MaryJean Gross, Southwest Texas State University; Mary Grover, Sheffield, England; Bonnie J. Gunzenhauser, Millikin University; Keith Hale, McAllen, Texas; Margaret Hamer, Cambridge, England; Marguerite Harkness, Virgina

Commonwealth University; **William Harmon**, University of North Carolina at Chapel Hill; **Susan Tetlow Harrington**, University of South Florida; **Stephen J. Harris**, University of Massachusetts, Amherst; **Stuart Harris**, University of Sheffield; **Dominic Hibberd**, Oxford, England; **Pilar Hidalgo**, Málaga University; **Ian Higgins**, Australian National University; **Pam Hirsch**, Cambridge University; **Margaret Holley**, Weizmann Institute of Science; **David Brendan Hopes**, University of North Carolina at Asheville; **Chris Hopkins**, Sheffield Hallam University **Lisa Hopkins**, Sheffield Hallam University; **Hayley Horvat**, Hunter College, City University of New York; **Mark Hutchings**, University of Reading; **Catherine Ingrassia**, Virginia Commonwealth University; **Cecile M. Jagodzinski**, Indiana University; **Mary Joannou**, Anglia Polytechnic University; **Judith Johnston**, University of Western Australia; **A. R. Jones**, University of Wales; **Harriet Devine Jump**, Edge Hill College; **Richard Keenan**, University of Maryland Eastern Shore; **Norman Kelvin**, Graduate Center, City University of New York; **David Kirby**, Florida State University; **George Klawitter**, St. Edward's University; **Julia F. Klimek**, Coker College; **Neil ten Kortenaar**, University of Toronto at Scarborough; **Dave Kuhne**, Texas Christian University; **Donald D. Kummings**, University of Wisconsin–Parkside; **Jacqueline M. Labbe**, University of Warwick; **Audrey Laski**, London, England; **John Laski**, London, England; **Richard E. Lee**, State University of New York, Oneonta; **Ying S. Lee**, Queen's University, Kingston, Ontario; **Dawn Lewcock**, Cambridge University; **Mark Libin**, University of British Columbia; **Jean P. Liddiard**, London, England; **Alexander Lindsay**, Cambridge, England; **Cecelia Lampp Linton**, Manassas, Virginia; **Max Loges**, Lamar University; **George C. Longest**, Virginia Commonwealth University; **Susan Macklin**, Milhars, France; **Ian MacKillop**, University of Sheffield; **Sarah E. Maier**, University of New Brunswick; **Frances M. Malpezzi**, Arkansas State University; **Susan Manning**, University of Edinburgh; **Fred Marchant**, Suffolk University; **Jayne E. Marek**, Franklin College; **Paul A. Marquis**, St. Francis Xavier University; **Jan Marsh**, London, England; **Sean Matthews**, University of Wales; **Colleen McCutcheon**, Hunter College, City University of New York; **Lynn McDonie**, Antelope Valley Community College; **Patrick McHenry**, Columbus State University; **Joseph McNicholas**, California State University, San Bernardino; **Patrick Meanor**, State University of New York, College at Oneonta; **Chris Megson**, University of London; **Kathleen Parry Mollick**, Tarleton State University; **Rebecca Morgan**, Worcestershire, England; **C. W. R. D. Moseley**, Cambridge University; **Merritt Moseley**, University of North Carolina at Asheville; **Brian Murray**, Loyola College; **Michael Grosvenor Myer**, Cambridge, England; **Valerie Grosvenor Myer**, Cambridge University; **W. H. New**, University of British Columbia; **Joe Nordgren**, Lamar University; **Terry D. Novak**, Johnson and Wales University; **Ian Ousby**, Cambridge, England; **William Over**, St. John's University; **Jim Owen**, Columbus State University; **Dennis Paoli**, Hunter College, City University of New York; **John S. Partington**, University of Reading; **Daniel G. Payne**, State University of New York, College at Oneonta; **Jacqueline Peltier**, Lannion, France; **Bob Podgurski**, Gastonia, North Carolina; **Jane Potter**, Oxford, England; **Glyn Pursglove**, University of Wales; **Jean Radford**, Ilmington, Shipston-on-Stour; **Eilish Rafferty**, Dublin, Ireland; **Brian Abel Ragen**, Southern Illinois University, Edwardsville; **Paul Ranger**, Oxford University; **Jennifer A. Rich**, Hunter College, City University of New York; **Kenneth A. Robb**, Bowling Green, Ohio; **John Rogers**, Vincennes University; **Joseph Rosenblum**, University of North Carolina at Greensboro; **Dan Ross**, Columbus State University; **George Rousseau**, Magdalen College, Oxford; **Susanna Roxman**, Lund, Swenden; **Herbert K. Russell**, John A. Logan College; **Richard Rankin Russell**, Baylor University; **David Christopher Ryan**, Texas Christian University; **Eric Salmon**, East Sussex, England; **Nicole Sarrocco**, University of North Carolina at Chapel Hill; **Andy Sawyer**, University of Liverpool; **Renée Schatteman**, Georgia State University; **Paul H. Schmidt**, Georgia State University; **Steven R. Serafin**, Hunter College, City University of New York; **Colleen Shea**, Queen's University, Kingston, Ontario; **R. Baird Shuman**, University of Illinois at Urbana-Champaign; **Brian Sibley**, London, England; **Christopher J. P. Smith**, Neath College; **Monica Smith**, University of Georgia; **Anna Snaith**, Anglia Polytechnic University; **Angus Somerville**, Brock University; **Sue Sorensen**, University of Winnipeg; **Catherine Spooner**, Falmouth College of Arts; **Jordan Stouck**, Queen's University, Kingston, Ontario; **Ginger Strand**, Gallatin School, New York University; **John Sutherland**, University College, London; **Marcy Tanter**, Tarleton State University; **Andrew Taylor**, University College Dublin; **Marianne Thormählen**, Lund University; **J. M. Tink**, University of Sussex; **Lisa Tolhurst**, Hunter College, City University of New York; **Claire Tomalin**, Newnham College, Cambridge; **Nicolas Tredell**, University of Sussex; **Elizabeth Trelenberg**, Florida State University; **Simon Trussler**, London, England; **Elaine Turner**, Brunel University; **Claire M. Tylee**, Brunel University; **Nicola Upson**, Cambridge, England; **K. D. Verma**, University of Pittsburgh at Johnstown; **Denise Vultee**, University of Missouri; **Gay Wachman**, State University of New York, College at Old Westbury; **Rex Walford**, Cambridge University; **Tamie Watters**, Mapledurham Village, England; **Patricia M. Wharton**, Gosport, England; **R. S. White**, University of Western Australia; **Michael Wiley**, University of North Florida; **Albert Wilhelm**, Tennessee Technological University; **Kate Williams**, Somerville College, Oxford; **Mark Williams**, Victoria University of Wellington; **Merryn Williams**, Open University **Clive Wilmer**, Cambridge, England; **Earla Wil-** putte, St. Francis Xavier University; **Justin Wintle**, London, England; **Nicholas Woolley**, Kingston, Ontario; **R. F. Yeager**, University of North Carolina at Asheville; **Tory Young**, Anglia Polytechnic University; **Steven Zani**, Lamar University

Index